After a quarter century of remarkable usefulness globally, Wayne Grudem's *Systematic Theology*, in its second edition, remains remarkable for its extraordinary juxtapositions. It is penetrating but not confusing; forthright and unequivocal but not reckless or overstated; readable and clear but not superficial; biblically grounded, even biblically saturated, but not textually careless or glib; devout and reverent but not uncritical or naive; practical but not trendy or sentimental; comprehensive but not majoring on minors; a book for the church but not parochial or sectarian. I thank God for this precious gift to Christ's people worldwide.

—**John Piper**, founder and teacher, Desiring God, chancellor, Bethlehem College and Seminary

Wayne Grudem's second edition of *Systematic Theology* displays all the virtues of the first. He shows and explains how the doctrines discussed stem from the biblical text. Even if readers disagree here or there, they understand why Grudem argues as he does since he makes his case from the Scriptures. The book stands out for its clarity and accessibility. Academics, immersed in technical study for years, are prone to forget that most people have never read a systematic theology before. The lucidity and simplicity of Grudem makes his work an ideal textbook. This is not to say that scholars cannot profit from his work as well since he lays out arguments cogently. The pastoral tone of the work shines through as well. The hymns and songs concluding the chapters remind us that theology isn't a matter of abstract teaching but should lead us to praise and worship of the Lord.

—**Thomas R. Schreiner**, James Buchanan Harrison Professor of New Testament Interpretation and Professor Of Biblical Theology, Southern Baptist Theological Seminary

Wayne Grudem studied with me in the early 1970s, and both of us have endorsed one another's systematic theologies. That is perhaps unusual. Our two books look at theology from somewhat different "perspectives," as I like to say, and so they appeal to somewhat different readers. But Grudem's book has sold a lot more copies, and deservedly so. I couldn't be happier. I wish that all Christian writers could be as thankful for God's ministry through friendly "rivals," authors who bless the church through biblical, clear, and winsome teaching. Scripture is so rich that we need to look at it from many angles. We need more systematic theologies, not fewer. But for now, Wayne's work is the best.

—**John Frame**, professor of systematic theology and philosophy emeritus, Reformed Theological Seminary

It is impossible to estimate the benefit that Wayne Grudem's *Systematic Theology* has had for countless individuals, churches, Bible colleges, and seminaries over the past twenty-five-plus years. I've gladly used it as my main text in teaching theology to thousands of students whom I've had the privilege to teach at Trinity Evangelical Divinity School and Southern Seminary. And oh how my students have loved the clarity, comprehensiveness, worshipfulness, and biblical fidelity of this textbook. But now we have, due to Dr. Grudem's painstaking work, an even better, more complete, updated version of this excellent theology book. Praise be to God, and deep thanks to Wayne Grudem, for extending the life of this work and making it even better for another generation of theological students of God's Word.

—**Bruce A. Ware**, T. Rupert and Lucille Coleman Professor of Christian Theology, Southern Baptist Theological Seminary, Louisville, Kentucky

*Systematic Theology* by Wayne Grudem stands squarely in the stream of broadly Reformed tradition on the main issues of theology, including the doctrine of Scripture, the doctrine of God, and the doctrine of salvation. Perhaps the strongest feature of the book is its accessibility. Grudem does not water down the meat of theology. But by minimizing technical terminology and by including hymns, questions, and indications of application, he makes systematic theology much more accessible and life-invigorating for a large range of Christian readers. In this second edition he has made further improvements by including new material and by modifying his views on a few difficult issues.

—**Vern Poythress**, distinguished professor of New Testament,
biblical interpretation, and systematic theology,
Westminster Theological Seminary

I can neither quantify nor qualify all the ways in which Wayne Grudem's *Systematic Theology* has assisted me over the past twenty-five years. I've turned to it innumerable times and for innumerable reasons, and it has invariably proven a trusted and steady guide. It was there when I was first exploring Christian doctrine and there when I was ready to dive deeper. I can say truly that few books have been more meaningful or had more influence. With the arrival of this long-awaited second edition, it is fitting that the book that has so guided me and my generation can be refreshed in such a way that it can equally impact my children and theirs. I have every confidence that it will.

—**Tim Challies**, author of *Epic: An Around-the-World
Journey through Christian History*

I used to tell people that Grudem's *Systematic Theology* was the best single volume theology available. After using it for a quarter of a century, I now believe it is the best of all the systematic theologies in print, single or multivolume. It is one of those rare works that can challenge the scholar and instruct the beginner. This new edition addresses the most important changes in the theological landscape since 1994, and it has completely updated bibliographies. It is simply indispensable.

—**Dr. Jack Deere**, author and Old Testament scholar

Our current generation is seeing a resurgence in Reformed theology and practice, fueled by the likes of John Piper, R. C. Sproul, John MacArthur, the Gospel Coalition, and the Southern Baptist Theological Seminary. At the heart of this renaissance is a textbook read by over 750,000 students, pastors, Christian leaders, and lay people in churches. Defining and explaining scores of doctrines, connecting them to the Bible, providing interpretations of key supporting passages, defending a Reformed theological understanding of the doctrines, and offering concrete applications of them, Wayne Grudem's *Systematic Theology: An Introduction to Biblical Doctrine* has provided an essential foundation for this Reformed resurgence. This second edition, updated and expanded, will undoubtedly continue to energize this reawakening!

—**Gregg R. Allison**, professor of Christian theology,
Southern Baptist Theological Seminary, author,
*Historical Theology: An Introduction to Christian Doctrine*

How does one improve on a classic? You can't, say some. But I beg to differ. In this second and expanded edition of *Systematic Theology*, Wayne Grudem has made his classic work even better, more insightful, significantly more detailed, and an even greater resource for the Christian and the local church. When I'm asked to recommend a good and comprehensive volume on Christian doctrine and practice, I never hesitate. My encouragement is precise and to the point: "Get Grudem!"

—**Sam Storms, PhD,** lead pastor for preaching and vision,
Bridgeway Church, Oklahoma City

If you were hoping to find a student's textbook of theology that seeks your spiritual no less than your intellectual formation, rejoice. Wayne Grudem has written exactly what you wanted, and he has done so very competently indeed. [endorsement for the first edition]

—**J. I. Packer†,** Regent College

As a theology professor at Biola University, where I have taught for over twenty years, I feel like I coteach all my classes with Wayne Grudem. Our students are taught the basic doctrine of the Christian faith in three semesters of required courses. Grudem's *Systematic Theology* provides the core content for my classes and many of the other undergraduate theology courses at the university. Grudem wrote this book to strengthen the church, and it excels in its clarity, readability, and biblically based approach that seeks to get theology into real life. *Systematic Theology* consistently accomplishes Grudem's goal—to lead the reader to greater knowledge and worship of the God of the Bible.

—**Erik Thoennes, PhD,** professor of and chair of theology, Talbot School of Theology
and Biola University, pastor, Grace Evangelical Free Church of La Mirada

Grudem's *Systematic Theology* is well organized, easy to understand, usually persuasive, and devotional. Grudem does not merely inform you; he stirs your affections to love and worship the triune God. Grudem is not attempting to write a cutting-edge contemporary theology that plays theological ping-pong with trendy nonevangelical theologians. Nor is he attempting to write a historical theology that exhaustively explains what significant Bible interpreters and theologians have believed. Rather, he is serving the church by helping Christians who are not experts in theology better understand what the whole Bible says about God, God's Word, man, Christ, the Holy Spirit, angels and demons, salvation, the church, and the end times.

—**Andy Naselli,** associate professor of systematic theology and New Testament,
Bethlehem College and Seminary, Minneapolis, pastor, Bethlehem Baptist Church

The whole church is indebted to Wayne Grudem for a fresh presentation of evangelical Christianity. . . . Even those who do not share his . . . positions on certain issues will be enriched by Grudem's clear statement of basic evangelical theology and his helpful cross-references to other major theological positions. Of particular value is his constant eye to the application of doctrine to personal life, ministry, and the church. For Grudem, intellectual understanding cannot be separated from heart experience.

—**Allan Coppedge,** former Beeson Professor of Christian
Theology, Asbury Theological Seminary

I warmly welcome the second edition of *Systematic Theology*. There is nothing like it. Here is an introduction to biblical doctrine that every believer can read and understand. As we read we are not only informed but edified and led to worship. And when we disagree or simply want to dig deeper, we are pointed to other resources in the Christian tradition. Just as the first edition was widely used, so I trust this new edition will do much good.

—**Bill James,** principal, London Seminary, UK

Wayne Grudem's *Systematic Theology* can help any Christian who is thinking through the great questions of our faith—the questions we all inevitably ask. The answers offered here are biblical, insightful, and clearly written. I have turned here many times through the years, and I have *always* been helped and enriched.

—**Ray Ortlund,** Immanuel Church, Nashville

My favorite systematic theology by my favorite systematic theologian just got even better. *Systematic Theology* is simple but not simplistic, thorough but not tedious, decided in its positions but not dogmatic on debatable matters, and it provides ready explanations for even the thorniest theological questions. Best of all, Wayne's writing is warm, devotional, and Christ-exalting. There are good reasons to own other systematic theologies, but there is not a good reason to not own this one!

—**C. J. Mahaney,** senior pastor,
Sovereign Grace Church of Louisville

"I think the best place to start is the chapter in Grudem's *Systematic Theology*." I must have said that dozens of times over the last quarter century or so to Cambridge University undergraduate and graduate students (as well as many others) when they have asked me for a good resource on a particular question about theology. And I have frequently reached for it myself. In 1995 it was the best new systematic theology in decades. Since then it has done more for theological literacy in the UK than almost any other book. This new edition will extend its preeminence and usefulness. The commitment to Scripture and to the gospel of Christ remain as strong as ever. The learning is, if anything, deeper and more considered. When I do find something I disagree with, I am always helped by reading Wayne's arguments. The tone is fair-minded, loving, and doxological. Its very special quality is its atmosphere of worship: the book breathes Christ. With Wayne in person, you are never far from a smile and a prayer; this new edition (in addition to all its other qualities) retains that fragrance.

—**Julian Hardyman,** senior pastor,
Eden Baptist Church, Cambridge, UK

I know of no other systematic theology that has had such an impact on so many believers. I have personally benefited from it and widely recommended it. Both its accessibility and its thoroughness have served to draw many thousands of believers into serious Bible study. I am delighted to recommend this new edition with its additional material.

—**Terry Virgo,** founder, Newfrontiers family of churches

For more years than I can remember, "Grudem" (as I and most of my friends refer to it now) has been the go-to reference book in my songwriting, as it invariably brings clarity, balance, and profound insight in exploring the central themes of the Christian faith. And I'm delighted that this updated edition includes much-needed discussion on some hot topics of the moment, including penal substitution and the creation debate. This is a must-have addition to the libraries not only of pastors and teachers but also of worship songwriters who take their lyric writing seriously. I highly recommend it.

—**Stuart Townend**, hymn writer of "In Christ Alone"
and "How Deep the Father's Love"

Since the first edition was published in 1994, Wayne Grudem's introduction to biblical doctrine has equipped a generation of students, church members, church leaders, and pastors around the world with a robustly biblical systematic theology. This updated second edition will ensure that a new generation is helped in the same way. The great strength of Grudem's work is that it is unashamedly biblical in approach, reflecting in its methodology his deep convictions about the inerrancy, sufficiency, and clarity of Scripture. It is accessible and well structured and is written with an irenic spirit that evaluates different opinions amongst evangelicals without being afraid to draw firm conclusions. In this new edition Grudem clarifies and affirms his commitment to divine impassibility, the eternal generation of the Son, and the ontological equality of the Father and the Son within the Trinity. He adds helpful and succinct critiques of the "new perspective" on Paul, Roman Catholicism, and Mormonism. The inclusion of questions for personal application, traditional hymns, and contemporary worships songs ensures that the truths explained never remain abstract or purely intellectual, and he helpfully highlights the implications of theology for contemporary church life and ministry. These revisions and updates will ensure that this work remains unsurpassed as a one-volume introduction to biblical doctrine, and my prayer is that it will help foster a love of contemporary Reformed evangelical theology in the coming generation, just as the first edition did in mine.

—**John Stevens**, national director, Fellowship of Independent
Evangelical Churches, United Kingdom

I have been thankful to God for Wayne Grudem's *Systematic Theology* for many reasons, but here are the top three. First, it is a means of making theology accessible and clear for every Christian. I have commended this work to many and ensured that our children had it as part of their "essential Christian library" before leaving home. Second, Wayne Grudem is rightly convinced that theology should be lived and prayed and sung. The study of God and his Word compels holy awe, joyful worship, and willing obedience. Third, this book has an absolute commitment to the authority and infallibility of Scripture, alongside the recognition that believers who submit to the authority of the Word differ on the interpretation of numerous issues. Each section provides a comprehensive listing of alternative works. I am delighted that this updated edition is now available for a new generation.

—**Dr. Sharon James,** social policy analyst,
the Christian Institute, UK, author and speaker

# Systematic Theology

SECOND EDITION

# Systematic Theology

An Introduction to Biblical Doctrine

SECOND EDITION

# WAYNE GRUDEM

ZONDERVAN
ACADEMIC

ZONDERVAN ACADEMIC

*Systematic Theology, Second Edition*
Copyright © 1994, 2020 by Wayne Grudem

Published in Grand Rapids, Michigan, by Zondervan. Zondervan is a registered trademark of The Zondervan Corporation, L.L.C., a wholly owned subsidiary of HarperCollins Christian Publishing, Inc.

Requests for information should be addressed to customercare@harpercollins.com.

Zondervan titles may be purchased in bulk for educational, business, fundraising, or sales promotional use. For information, please email SpecialMarkets@Zondervan.com.

ISBN 978-0-310-51797-9 (hardcover)
ISBN 978-0-310-51799-3 (ebook)
ISBN 978-0-310-12002-5 (audio Part 1)
ISBN 978-0-310-12010-0 (audio Part 2)

This book is published jointly with Inter-Varsity Press, 36 Causton St, London SW1P 4ST, Great Britain.
ISBN 978-1-78974-208-4 (hardcover)

*Cover design: Brand Navigation*
*Cover photos: © Brandon Bourdages / 123RF*
*Interior design: Kait Lamphere*

*Printed in the United States of America*

24 25 26 27 28 29 30 31 32 33 34 35 /TRM/ 20 19 18 17 16 15 14 13 12 11 10

*This book is dedicated to eight people*
*whom God sovereignly brought into my life:*
*Arden and Jean Grudem, my parents,*
*who taught me to believe the Bible,*
*to trust in God,*
*and to speak and write clearly;*
*A. Kenneth Ham, my Baptist pastor,*
*who awakened in me a love for systematic theology*
*by teaching a class on Christian doctrine*
*when I was thirteen years old,*
*and who taught me by example to believe*
*every word of Scripture;*
*Edmund Clowney, John Frame, and Vern Poythress,*
*Westminster Seminary professors and friends,*
*who influenced my theological understanding*
*more than anyone else,*
*and who taught me Reformed theology in*
*humble submission to every word of Scripture;*
*and Harald Bredesen and John Wimber,*
*pastors and friends,*
*who, more than anyone else,*
*taught me about the power and work*
*of the Holy Spirit.*

# Contents

## PART 3: The Doctrine of Man in the Image of God

## PART 4: The Doctrines of Christ and the Holy Spirit

## PART 5: The Doctrine of the Application of Redemption

## PART 6: The Doctrine of the Church

## PART 7: The Doctrine of the Future

# Abbreviations

| | |
|---|---|
| BAGD | *A Greek-English Lexicon of the New Testament and Other Early Christian Literature.* Edited by Walter Bauer. Revised and translated by Wm. Arndt, F. W. Gingrich, and F. Danker. Chicago: University of Chicago Press, 1979. |
| BDAG | *A Greek-English Lexicon of the New Testament and Other Early Christian Literature*, 3rd ed. Edited by Walter Bauer. Revised and translated by Frederick W. Danker, Wm. Arndt, and F. W. Gingrich. Chicago: University of Chicago Press, 2000. |
| BDB | *A Hebrew and English Lexicon of the Old Testament.* By F. Brown, S. R. Driver, and C. Briggs. 1907. Reprint, Oxford: Clarendon, 1968. |
| BTDB | *Baker's Evangelical Dictionary of Biblical Theology.* Edited by Walter A. Elwell. Grand Rapids: Baker, 1996. |
| *BETS* | *Bulletin of the Evangelical Theological Society* |
| *BibSac* | *Bibliotheca Sacra* |
| cf. | compare |
| *CRSQ* | *Creation Research Society Quarterly* |
| *CT* | *Christianity Today* |
| *CThRev* | *Criswell Theological Review* |
| *DPCM* | *Dictionary of Pentecostal and Charismatic Movements.* Edited by Stanley M. Burgess and Gary B. McGee. Grand Rapids: Zondervan, 1988. |
| *EBC* | *Expositor's Bible Commentary.* Edited by Frank E. Gaebelein. Grand Rapids: Zondervan, 1976. |
| ed. | edited by, *or* edition |
| *EDT1* | *Evangelical Dictionary of Theology.* Edited by Walter Elwell. Grand Rapids: Baker, 1984. |
| *EDT3* | *Evangelical Dictionary of Theology.* Edited by Daniel J. Treier and Walter A. Elwell. Grand Rapids: Baker, 2017. |
| et al. | and others |
| *IBD* | *The Illustrated Bible Dictionary.* Edited by J. D. Douglas et al. 3 vols. Leicester: Inter-Varsity Press; Wheaton, IL: Tyndale, 1980. |

| | |
|---|---|
| *ISBE* | *International Standard Bible Encyclopedia.* Rev. ed. Edited by G. W. Bromiley. Grand Rapids: Eerdmans, 1982. |
| *JAMA* | *Journal of the American Medical Association* |
| *JBL* | *Journal of Biblical Literature* |
| *JETS* | *Journal of the Evangelical Theological Society* |
| *JSOT* | *Journal for the Study of the Old Testament* |
| *LSJ* | *A Greek-English Lexicon.* 9th ed. Edited by Henry Liddell, Robert Scott, H. S. Jones, R. McKenzie. Oxford: Clarendon Press, 1940. |
| LXX | Septuagint |
| mg. | margin or marginal notes |
| n.d. | no date of publication given |
| n.p. | no place of publication given |
| *NDT1* | *New Dictionary of Theology.* Edited by S. B. Ferguson, D. F. Wright, and J. I. Packer. Leicester: Inter-Varsity Press; Downers Grove, IL: Inter-Varsity Press, 1988. |
| *NDT2* | *New Dictionary of Theology.* Edited by M. Davie, T. Grass, S. R. Holmes, J. McDowell, and T. A. Noble. London: Inter-Varsity Press; Downers Grove, IL: InterVarsity Press, 2016. |
| *NIDCC* | *New International Dictionary of the Christian Church.* Edited by J. D. Douglas et al. Grand Rapids: Zondervan, 1974. |
| *NIDNTT* | *The New International Dictionary of New Testament Theology.* 3 vols. Edited by Colin Brown. Grand Rapids: Zondervan, 1975–78. |
| NIGTC | New International Greek Testament Commentaries |
| *NTS* | *New Testament Studies* |
| *ODCC* | *Oxford Dictionary of the Christian Church.* Edited by F. L. Cross. London and New York: Oxford University Press, 1977. |
| rev. | revised |
| *TB* | *Tyndale Bulletin* |
| *TDNT* | *Theological Dictionary of the New Testament.* 10 vols. Edited by G. Kittel and G. Friedrich. Translated by G. W. Bromiley. Grand Rapids: Eerdmans, 1964–76. |
| TNTC | Tyndale New Testament Commentaries |
| TOTC | Tyndale Old Testament Commentaries |
| trans. | translated by |
| *TrinJ* | *Trinity Journal* |
| vol. | volume |
| WBC | Word Biblical Commentary |
| *WTJ* | *Westminster Theological Journal* |

# Preface to the Second Edition

I am grateful to God that he has allowed the first edition of this book to have such widespread use. People have often told me that reading this book strengthened their spiritual life and walk with God, deepened their faith, and significantly increased their understanding of the teachings of the Bible.

The changes in this edition mainly consist of additional material:

1. completely updated bibliographies
2. all Scripture quotations changed from RSV to ESV
3. new sections on the differences between evangelical Protestant theology and Protestant theological liberalism (additional note to chapter 4), Mormonism (additional note to chapter 14), and Roman Catholicism (additional note to chapter 45, with extensive quotations from the 1997 edition of *Catechism of the Catholic Church*)
4. additional discussion of specific "problem verses" for biblical inerrancy (chapter 5)
5. a completely revised, stronger chapter on the clarity of Scripture (chapter 6)
6. updated sections on God's atemporal eternity (chapter 11), the relationship of the Son to the Father in the Trinity (chapter 14), seeker-sensitive churches (chapter 44), the role of women in the church (chapter 47), contemporary worship music (chapter 51), and miraculous gifts of the Holy Spirit (chapters 52 and 53)
7. a more extensive critique of open theism (chapter 12)
8. a completely revised, stronger chapter on creation and evolution, including recent evidence for intelligent design, a longer critique of theistic evolution, and a summary of recent evidence regarding the age of the earth (chapter 15)
9. a new discussion and critique of middle knowledge (or Molinism) (chapter 16)
10. a reply to recent criticisms of the penal substitutionary view of the atonement (chapter 27)
11. an extensive discussion of "Free Grace" theology (chapter 35)
12. a critique of the "new perspective on Paul" and its view of justification (chapter 36)

13. a critique of the preterist view that Christ has already returned in AD 70 (chapter 54)

14. a contemporary worship song added at the end of each chapter (while retaining the traditional hymns as well)

15. indexing of topics covered in twenty-one new systematic theology texts (including new translations of older texts by Turretin and Vos) that have been published since 1993

16. numerous smaller modifications that have been prompted by letters and emails from people around the world and by interaction with the many wonderful, insightful students as I have taught through this material over the last twenty-six years both at Trinity Evangelical Divinity School and at Phoenix Seminary

As a result of this added material, this second edition is about 16 percent longer than the first edition.

"Did you change your mind about anything?" is the question people often ask me about this second edition.

The short answer is, "Very little," but there are a few changes: (1) I now affirm the doctrine of God's impassibility in the sense of "incapable of suffering harm," a meaning that I had mistakenly failed to consider in the first edition (chapter 11). (2) Because of substantial new evidence about the meaning of the Greek word *monogenēs*, I now think that this word should be translated as "only begotten" rather than simply "only" in John 3:16 (and elsewhere), and I now endorse the doctrine of the eternal generation of the Son by the Father (chapter 14). (3) I now think that the scientific evidence in favor of an old earth (4.5 billion years) and an old universe (13.8 billion years) has become overwhelming, with the result that I now advocate an old earth position, though I still believe that both old earth and young earth viewpoints are valid for Christian leaders to hold today (chapter 15).

There has been an explosion of systematic theology texts (along with some shorter surveys of theological topics) in the evangelical Protestant world since the publication of the first edition of this book in 1994. These new books have come from various traditions, including Anglican (Packer, Bird, Bray), Baptist (Akin, Erickson's 3rd edition), dispensational (Geisler, MacArthur and Mayhue), charismatic/Pentecostal (Stanley Horton, Menzies and Horton, Duffield and Van Cleave), and especially Reformed (Reymond, Van Genderen and Velema, Michael Horton, Culver, Frame, Allen and Swain, Barrett, and Letham, as well as new translations of Vos, Turretin, and Bavinck). I view these books as a wonderful indication that the study of systematic theology is alive and well in the evangelical world. I have added cross-references to these twenty-one additional books at the end of each chapter, indicating the pages on which each book treats the topic discussed in that chapter. I hope this will be a useful resource for students seeking to compare different authors and different viewpoints on a particular theological topic.

Many people have helped me in preparing this revised edition, including first of all the students in my seminary classes, and also many members of my Christian Essentials class for adults at Scottsdale Bible Church. In addition, faculty colleagues at Phoenix Seminary, including Brian Arnold, Darryl DelHousaye, John DelHousaye, Peter Gurry, Malcolm Hartnell, Bing Hunter, Jonathan Logan, John Meade, Justin Smith, and Steve Tracy have helped me at various times with advice about areas in which they had specialized knowledge. Mitch Miller, the remarkably knowledgeable reference and acquisitions librarian at Phoenix Seminary, compiled substantial additions to the bibliographies at the end of the chapters. Yvonne Gonzales printed the entire manuscript showing in color every change from the first edition.

Chris Herrington, the worship leader at Illuminate Church in Scottsdale, compiled an entire list of fifty-seven contemporary worship songs that fit the themes of the fifty-seven chapters (I have added these to the ends of the chapters, but in a few cases I substituted some of my favorite contemporary worship songs). Casey Sandberg sent me many additional bibliography suggestions. Trent Poling once again saved me from some difficult computer problems at a crucial time when the book manuscript was nearing completion.

Hugh Ross, Ken Wolgemuth, Günter Bechly, and John Wiester helped me with research on the age of the earth. Ann Gauger helped me understand evolutionary views about human origins. Titus Vogt, who translated this book into German, sent me a long list of small editing corrections (such as exact Bible verse references in the Septuagint and vowel transliterations in Hebrew words) that no one else had noticed (or at least mentioned to me) in twenty-six years. And my long-time friends Gregg Allison, Ray Ortlund, John Piper, Vern Poythress, Tom Schreiner, Sam Storms, Erik Thoennes, and Bruce Ware have provided helpful interaction about theological topics at various times over the past twenty-six years.

Stan Gundry at Zondervan, Sam Richardson at SPCK, and Brian Wilson at IVP-UK had valuable conversations with me regarding the scope and contents of this revised edition. Editors Madison Trammel (Zondervan), Philip Duce (IVP-UK), and especially the primary editor Matt Estel (Zondervan) gave me excellent editorial input at many points. Also at Zondervan, Jesse Hillman has been very helpful regarding cover design and marketing plans.

I am grateful to several excellent student assistants at Phoenix Seminary who have helped me over the last five years: Josh McCoy and Jason Miller completed the massive task of converting every Scripture quotation from the RSV to the ESV. Jason Miller also helped me with computer problems on a number of occasions. Phil Hoshiwara, Eric Wildgen, Ryan Carpenter, Jesse Bustamante, and Brett Gray provided significant help in proofreading, verifying footnotes, adding to the bibliographies for each chapter, and completing other detailed tasks in manuscript preparation. Brett Gray also updated the glossary and patiently coaxed numerous music publishers to accept a very reasonable fee in exchange for permission to quote the lyrics of the fifty-seven contemporary worship songs that have been added to the ends of the chapters. I am also grateful to the music publishers who granted permission to reprint the lyrics to the fifty-seven contemporary worship songs found at the ends of the chapters, and especially to Capitol Music Group (CMG) who granted permission for thiry-nine of those songs.

Many people have prayed for me as I worked on this second edition, including some friends whom I call my "prayer partners," and the special friends who are members of the small group that Margaret and I have met with for Bible study and prayer for the past nine years. I am thankful to all of you for your prayers.

Finally, I am grateful to my remarkable, wonderful wife Margaret, who celebrated with me in June our fiftieth anniversary, and who regularly prays for me, encourages me, brings meals to my study when I am writing, and simply brings joy and laughter into my life again and again.

When I was diagnosed with Parkinson's disease in December 2015, I wrote in an online article,

> Parkinson's usually does not shorten a person's life expectancy very much, but in any case, I'm happy to live as long as the Lord wills that I live, and to keep on being productive for as long as he enables me to do so. "In your book were written, every one of them, the days that were formed for me, when as yet there was none of them" (Ps. 139:16).
>
> But I would like, if God allows, to finish my current major writing projects:
>
> 1. a textbook on Christian ethics, which I hope will take me about one more year to finish after the first draft is done—or until January 2017
> 2. a revised edition of my book *Systematic Theology*, which should take from 2017 to 2019.[1]

God has been exceptionally kind to me in the nearly four years since I wrote that. My Parkinson's symptoms are still very mild, and my doctor says that the disease is progressing "very slowly." The first book that I mentioned, *Christian Ethics*, was published in 2018, and now this second project is finally coming to an end. I plan to continue to teach (half-time) at Phoenix Seminary, and I have committed to preparing a revised edition of a commentary on 1 Peter that I published in 1988, but beyond that I do not know what else the Lord has in mind for me to do. I feel well, and I am thankful for good health at seventy-one years of age.

---

1. Wayne Grudem, "I Have Parkinson's and I Am at Peace," *Desiring God*, December 22, 2015, https://www.desiringgod .org/articles/i-have-parkinsons-and-i-am-at-peace.

I am grateful to God for the widespread ministry of the first edition of this book (1994). The book so far has been translated into nineteen languages, with more translations in process.[2] In addition, Jeff Purswell prepared a 528-page condensation of this book, *Bible Doctrine*,[3] and my son Elliot further condensed that into a 159-page book, *Christian Beliefs*.[4] Finally, Erik Thoennes prepared a further condensation for a 6-page laminated study guide.[5] With God's blessing, these shorter publications have also proved helpful to many people and churches.

Two other volumes have directly supplemented the material in this book. I have found immensely helpful the chapter-by-chapter historical surveys for these same doctrines that are found in Gregg Allison's *Historical Theology: An Introduction to Christian Doctrine; A Companion to Wayne Grudem's* Systematic Theology.[6] And Erik Thoennes and Brianna Smith have compiled a new companion volume, *Systematic Theology Workbook*,[7] which contains study questions and practical exercises to help in learning the material in each chapter.

I commit this second edition into the Lord's hands, asking that he may use it to inform and strengthen the faith of those who read it and to deepen their personal relationship with him.

"Not to us, O Lord, not to us, but to your name give glory" (Ps. 115:1).

WAYNE GRUDEM
Phoenix Seminary

2. Albanian, Amharic, Arabic, Burmese, Chinese (traditional script), Chinese (simplified script), French, German, Italian, Jinghpaw-Kachin, Korean, Nepali, Portuguese, Romanian, Russian, Singhalese, Spanish, Tajik, and Tamil. In cases where publication information is available to me, I have posted on my website waynegrudem.com.

3. Wayne Grudem, *Bible Doctrine*, ed. Jeff Purswell (Grand Rapids: Zondervan; Leicester: Inter-Varsity Press, 1999).

4. Wayne Grudem, *Christian Beliefs*, ed. Elliot Grudem (Grand Rapids: Zondervan; Nottingham: Inter-Varsity Press, 2005).

5. Wayne Grudem and Erik Thoennes, *Systematic Theology Laminated Sheet* (Grand Rapids: Zondervan; Nottingham: Inter-Varsity Press, 2008).

6. Gregg Allison, *Historical Theology: An Introduction to Christian Doctrine; A Companion to Wayne Grudem's* Systematic Theology (Grand Rapids: Zondervan, 2011).

7. Wayne Grudem, Erik Thoennes, and Brianna Smith, *Systematic Theology Workbook: Study Questions and Practical Exercises for Learning Biblical Doctrine* (Grand Rapids: Zondervan, 2020).

# Preface to the First Edition

I have not written this book for other teachers of theology (though I hope many of them will read it). I have written it for students—and not only for students, but also for every Christian who has a hunger to know the central doctrines of the Bible in greater depth.

This is why I have called the book *An Introduction to Biblical Doctrine*. I have tried to make it understandable even for Christians who have never studied theology before. I have avoided using technical terms without first explaining them. And most of the chapters can be read on their own, so that someone can begin at any chapter and grasp it without having read the earlier material.

Introductory studies do not have to be shallow or simplistic. I am convinced that most Christians are able to understand the doctrinal teachings of the Bible in considerable depth, provided that they are presented clearly and without the use of highly technical language. Therefore I have not hesitated to treat theological disputes in some detail where it seemed necessary.

Yet this book, despite its size, is still an *introduction* to systematic theology. Entire books have been written about the topics covered in each chapter of this book, and entire articles have been written about many of the verses quoted in this book. Therefore each chapter is capable of opening out into additional study in more breadth or more depth for those who are interested. The bibliographies at the end of each chapter give some help in that direction.

The following six distinctive features of this book grow out of my convictions about what systematic theology is and how it should be taught.

**1. A Clear Biblical Basis for Doctrines.** Because I believe that theology should be explicitly based on the teachings of Scripture, in each chapter I have attempted to show where the Bible gives support for the doctrines under consideration. In fact, because I believe that the words of Scripture themselves have power and authority greater than any human words, I have not just given Bible references; I have frequently quoted Bible passages at length so that readers can easily examine for themselves the scriptural evidence and in that way be like the noble Bereans, who were "examining the Scriptures daily to see if these things were so" (Acts 17:11). This conviction about the unique nature of the Bible as God's words has also led to the inclusion of a Scripture memory passage at the end of each chapter.

**2. Clarity in the Explanation of Doctrines.** I do not believe that God intended the study of theology to result in confusion and frustration. A student who comes out of a course in theology filled only with doctrinal uncertainty and a thousand unanswered questions is hardly "able to give instruction in sound doctrine and also to rebuke those who contradict it" (Titus 1:9). Therefore I have tried to state the doctrinal positions of this book clearly and to show where in Scripture I find convincing evidence for those positions. I do not expect that everyone reading this book will agree with me at every point of doctrine; I do think that every reader will understand the positions I am arguing for and where Scripture can be found to support those positions.

I think it is only fair to readers of this book to say at the beginning what my own convictions are regarding certain points that are disputed within evangelical Christianity. I hold to a conservative view of biblical inerrancy, very much in agreement with the "Chicago Statement" of the International Council on Biblical Inerrancy (chapter 5 and appendix 1), and a traditional Reformed position with regard to questions of God's sovereignty and man's responsibility (chapter 16), the extent of the atonement (chapter 27), and the question of predestination (chapter 32). Consistent with the Reformed view, I hold that those who are truly born again will never lose their salvation (chapter 40). With regard to male-female relationships, I argue for a view that is neither traditional nor feminist, but "complementarian"—namely, that God created man and woman equal in value and personhood, and equal in bearing his image, but that both creation and redemption indicate some distinct roles for men and women in marriage (chapter 22) and in the church (chapter 47). On church government, I advocate a modified congregational form of government, with plural elders in governing positions (chapter 47). I argue for a baptistic view of baptism, namely, that those who give a believable profession of personal faith should be baptized (chapter 49). I hold that "baptism in the Holy Spirit" is a phrase best applied to conversion, and subsequent experiences are better called "being filled with the Holy Spirit" (chapter 39); moreover, that all the gifts of the Holy Spirit mentioned in the New Testament are still valid for today, but that "apostle" is an office, not a gift, and that office does not continue today (chapters 52, 53). I believe that Christ's second coming could occur any day, that it will be premillennial—that is, that it will mark the beginning of his thousand-year reign of perfect peace on the earth—but that it will be posttribulational—that is, that many Christians will go through the great tribulation (chapters 54, 55).

This does not mean that I ignore other views. Where there are doctrinal differences within evangelical Christianity I have tried to represent other positions fairly, to explain why I disagree with them, and to give references to the best available defenses of the opposing positions. In fact, I have made it easy for students to find a conservative evangelical statement on each topic from within their own theological traditions, because each chapter contains an index to treatments of that chapter's subject in thirty-four other theology texts classified by denominational background. (If I have failed to represent an opposing view accurately I would appreciate a letter from anyone who holds that view, and I will attempt to make corrections if a subsequent edition of this book is published.)

**3. Application to Life.** I do not believe that God intended the study of theology to be dry and boring. Theology is the study of God and all his works! Theology is meant to be lived and prayed and sung! All of the great doctrinal writings of the Bible (such as Paul's epistle to the Romans) are full of praise to God and personal application to life. For this reason I have incorporated notes on application from time to time in the text, and have added "Questions for Personal Application" at the end of each chapter, as well as a hymn related to the topic of the chapter. True theology is "teaching that accords with godliness" (1 Tim. 6:3), and theology when studied rightly will lead to growth in our Christian lives, and to worship.

**4. Focus on the Evangelical World.** I do not think that a true system of theology can be constructed from within what we may call the "liberal" theological tradition— that is, by people who deny the absolute truthfulness of the Bible, or who do not think the words of the Bible to be God's very words (see chapter 4, on the authority of Scripture). For this reason, the other writers I interact with in this book are mostly within what is today called the larger "conservative evangelical" tradition—from the great Reformers John Calvin and Martin Luther, down to the writings of evangelical scholars today. I write as an evangelical and for evangelicals. This does not mean that those in the liberal tradition have nothing valuable to say; it simply means that differences with them almost always boil down to differences over the nature of the Bible and its authority. The amount of doctrinal agreement that can be reached by people with widely divergent bases of authority is quite limited. I am thankful for my evangelical friends who write extensive critiques of liberal theology, but I do not think that everyone is called to do that, or that an extensive analysis of liberal views is the most helpful way to build a positive system of theology based on the total truthfulness of the whole Bible. In fact, somewhat like the boy in Hans Christian Andersen's tale who shouted, "The Emperor has no clothes!" I think someone needs to say that it is doubtful that liberal theologians have given us any significant insights into the doctrinal teachings of Scripture that are not already to be found in evangelical writers.

It is not always appreciated that the world of conservative evangelical scholarship is so rich and diverse that it affords ample opportunity for exploration of different viewpoints and insights into Scripture. I think that ultimately we will attain much more depth of understanding of Scripture when we are able to study it in the company of a great number of scholars who all begin with the conviction that the Bible is completely true and absolutely authoritative. The cross-references to thirty-four other evangelical systematic theologies that I have put at the end of each chapter reflect this conviction: though they are broken down into seven broad theological traditions (Anglican/Episcopalian, Arminian/Wesleyan/Methodist, Baptist, Dispensational, Lutheran, Reformed/Presbyterian, and Renewal/Charismatic/ Pentecostal), they all would hold to the inerrancy of the Bible and would belong to what would be called a conservative evangelical position today. (In addition to these thirty-four conservative evangelical works, I have also added to each chapter a section of cross-references to two representative Roman Catholic theologies, because Roman Catholicism continues to exercise such a significant influence worldwide.)

**5. Hope for Progress in Doctrinal Unity in the Church.** I believe that there is still much hope for the church to attain deeper and purer doctrinal understanding, and to overcome old barriers, even those that have persisted for centuries. Jesus is at work perfecting his church "so that he might present the church to himself in splendor, without spot or wrinkle or any such thing, that she might be holy and without blemish" (Eph. 5:27), and he has given gifts to equip the church "until we all attain to the unity of the faith and of the knowledge of the Son of God" (Eph. 4:13). Though the past history of the church may discourage us, these Scriptures remain true, and we should not abandon hope of greater agreement. In fact, in this century we have already seen much greater understanding and some greater doctrinal agreement between Covenant and Dispensational theologians, and between charismatics and noncharismatics; moreover, I think the church's understanding of biblical inerrancy and of spiritual gifts has also increased significantly in the last few decades. I believe that the current debate over appropriate roles for men and women in marriage and the church will eventually result in much greater understanding of the teaching of Scripture as well, painful though the controversy may be at the present time. Therefore, in this book I have not hesitated to raise again some of the old differences (over baptism, the Lord's Supper, church government, the millennium and the tribulation, and predestination, for example) in the hope that, in some cases at least, a fresh look at Scripture may provoke a new examination of these doctrines and may perhaps prompt some movement not just toward greater understanding and tolerance of other viewpoints, but even toward greater doctrinal consensus in the church.

**6. A Sense of the Urgent Need for Greater Doctrinal Understanding in the Whole Church.** I am convinced that there is an urgent need in the church today for much greater understanding of Christian doctrine, or systematic theology. Not only pastors and teachers need to understand theology in greater depth—the whole church does as well. One day by God's grace we may have churches full of Christians who can discuss, apply, and live the doctrinal teachings of the Bible as readily as they can discuss the details of their own jobs or hobbies—or the fortunes of their favorite sports team or television program. It is not that Christians lack the ability to understand doctrine; it is just that they must have access to it in an understandable form. Once that happens, I think that many Christians will find that understanding (and living) the doctrines of Scripture is one of their greatest joys.

Many people have helped me in the writing of this book. First I should mention my students, past and present, both at Bethel College in St. Paul, Minnesota (1977–81), and then at Trinity Evangelical Divinity School (1981–present). Their thoughtful, insightful contributions during classroom discussions have influenced every chapter of this book.

God has blessed me with help from some excellent typists. The typing of the manuscript was started by Sherry Kull several years ago. Later, Mary Morris, Ron Tilley, Kathryn Sheehan, Shelly Mills, Rebecca Heidenreich, Jenny Hart, and Carol Pederson typed several portions. Then the largest part of the manuscript was typed with great skill and care by Tammy Thomas, who also helped with some editing. Andi Ledesma and Joyce Leong cheerfully helped with photocopying many times. Finally, Kim Pennington faithfully and accurately typed in the many corrections and changes that came during the editorial process. I am grateful to all of them for their help.

John O. Stevenson did excellent work in compiling the bibliographies, and Don Rothwell completed a significant portion of the cross-references to other theology texts. H. Scott Baldwin, Tom Provenzola, and Mark Rapinchuk were a great help in proofreading and in library research. Mark Rapinchuk also compiled the indexes of authors and Scripture references. Beth Manley provided excellent help in proofreading. George Knight III, Robert Reymond, Harold Hoehner, Robert Saucy, Doug Moo, Tom Nettles, Tom McComiskey, Doug Halsne, Steve Nicholson, Doug Brandt, Steve Figard, Gregg Allison, Ellyn Clark, and Terry Mortenson provided detailed comments on different portions. Raymond Dillard kindly provided me with a computerized text of the Westminster Confession of Faith. Bruce Shauger solved my computer problems several times, and Tim McLaughlin repaired my computer at a crucial time. My long-time friend John Hughes gave me needed advice on computers and manuscript publication several times. My sons also helped me when deadlines approached: Elliot with library research, and Oliver and Alexander (and Alexander's friend Matt Tooley) with compiling and correcting the indexes.

One person has had greater influence on the final form of this book than any other: David Kingdon, theological books editor at Inter-Varsity Press, England, has been helpful far beyond my expectations in his work as an astute, conscientious, and wise editor. He has worked through every chapter with great care, suggesting corrections, additions, and deletions, and interacting with my arguments in extensive memos. His wide-ranging knowledge of theology, biblical studies, and the history of doctrine has been of immense value to me, and the book is much better as a result of his work. Moreover, Frank Entwistle of Inter-Varsity Press and Stan Gundry, Jim Ruark, and Laura Weller of Zondervan have been gracious and patient with me about many details regarding publication of the book.

I could not have completed this work without the generous provision of sabbaticals from Trinity Evangelical Divinity School in the fall of 1983, the fall of 1985, the winter of 1989, and the fall of 1991, and I am grateful to Trinity's board of directors for allowing me this time to write. I am also very thankful for the support of my parents, Arden and Jean Grudem, who generously provided financial help that enabled me to write during these and other times, and who have also been a constant encouragement to me along the way, both in their prayers and in their unwavering belief that a book like this—written in nontechnical language so that they and thousands of Christians like them could understand it—would be valuable for the church.

I think that almost everyone who knew me was praying for this project at some time or other—especially my student advisees over several years at Trinity, and many friends in my church. I have frequently been aware of the Lord's help in response to those prayers, giving me health and strength, freedom from interruptions, and an unwavering desire to complete the book.

Most of all, I am thankful for the support of my wife, Margaret, and my sons, Elliot, Oliver, and Alexander. They have been patient and encouraging, have prayed for me and loved me, and continue to be a great source of joy in my life, for which I thank God.

I am sure that this book, like all merely human books, has mistakes and oversights, and probably some faulty arguments as well. If I knew where they were, I would try to correct them! Therefore I would be grateful if any interested readers would send me suggestions for changes and corrections. I do not guarantee that I can acknowledge every letter, but I will give consideration to the material in every letter and make corrections where I can.

"O give thanks to the LORD, for he is good; for his steadfast love endures forever!" (Ps. 118:29).

"Not to us, O LORD, not to us, but to your name give glory" (Ps. 115:1).

WAYNE GRUDEM
Trinity Evangelical Divinity School

# CHAPTER 1

# Introduction to Systematic Theology

*What is systematic theology?*
*Why should Christians study it?*
*How should we study it?*

## EXPLANATION AND SCRIPTURAL BASIS

### A. DEFINITION OF SYSTEMATIC THEOLOGY

What is systematic theology? Many different definitions have been given, but for the purposes of this book the following definition will be used: *systematic theology is any study that answers the question, "What does the whole Bible teach us today?" about any given topic.*[1]

This definition indicates that systematic theology involves collecting and understanding all the relevant passages in the Bible on various topics and then summarizing their teachings clearly so that we know what to believe about each topic. However, it is important to state at once that the study of *church history* (including the great creeds of the church and the writings of major theologians in church history) and the study of *philosophy* can often be of great benefit in helping us understand what the whole Bible in fact does teach about various topics. But they do not contain any authority greater than or equal to the authority of Scripture.

### 1. Relationship to Other Disciplines

As my definition indicates, the emphasis of this book will not be on *historical theology*[2] (a historical study of how Christians in different periods have understood various

---

1. This definition of systematic theology is taken from Professor John Frame, now emeritus professor at Reformed Theological Seminary of Orlando, Florida, under whom I was privileged to study in 1971–73 (at Westminster Theological Seminary, Philadelphia). Though it is impossible to acknowledge my indebtedness to him at every point, it is appropriate to express gratitude to him at this point, and to say that he has probably influenced my theological thinking more than anyone else, especially in the crucial areas of the nature of systematic theology and the doctrine of the Word of God. Many of his

former students will recognize echoes of his teaching in the following pages, especially in those two areas.

2. Gregg Allison, *Historical Theology: An Introduction to Christian Doctrine; A Companion to Wayne Grudem's* Systematic Theology (Grand Rapids: Zondervan, 2011), provides an excellent survey of church history from the end of the New Testament to the present day for each of the topics discussed in this book. I am grateful to Gregg, a former student and now a life-long friend, for the remarkable amount of work that was required in writing this excellent book.

theological topics) or *philosophical theology* (studying theological topics largely without use of the Bible, but using the tools and methods of philosophical reasoning and what can be known about God from observing the universe) or *apologetics* (providing a defense of the truthfulness of the Christian faith for the purpose of convincing unbelievers). These three subjects, which are worthwhile subjects for Christians to pursue, are sometimes also included in a broader definition of the term *systematic theology*. In fact, some consideration of historical, philosophical, and apologetic matters will be found at points throughout this book. This is because historical study informs us of the insights gained and the mistakes made by others previously in understanding Scripture; philosophical study helps us understand right and wrong thought forms common in our culture and others; and apologetic study helps us bring the teachings of Scripture to bear on the objections raised by unbelievers. But these areas of study are not the focus of this volume, which rather interacts directly with the biblical text in order to understand what the Bible itself says to us about various theological subjects.

If someone prefers to use the term *systematic theology* in the broader sense (including especially historical theology and philosophy, as well as apologetics) instead of the narrow sense that has been defined above, it will not make much difference. Those who use the narrower definition will agree that these other areas of study definitely contribute in a positive way to our understanding of systematic theology, and those who use the broader definition will certainly agree that historical theology, philosophical theology, and apologetics can be distinguished from the process of collecting and synthesizing all the relevant Scripture passages for various topics. Moreover, even though historical and philosophical studies do contribute to our understanding of theological questions, only Scripture has the final authority to define what we are to believe,[3] and it is therefore appropriate to spend some time focusing on the process of analyzing the teaching of Scripture itself.

Systematic theology, as we have defined it, also differs from *Old Testament theology*, *New Testament theology*, and *biblical theology*. These three disciplines organize their topics historically and in the order the topics are presented in the Bible. Therefore, in Old Testament theology, one might ask, "What does Deuteronomy teach about prayer?" or "What do the Psalms teach about prayer?" or "What does Isaiah teach about prayer?" or even, "What does the whole Old Testament teach about prayer, and how is that teaching developed over the history of the Old Testament?" In New Testament theology one might ask, "What does John's gospel teach about prayer?" or "What does

---

3. Charles Hodge says, "The Scriptures Contain All the Facts of Theology" (section heading in *Systematic Theology*, 1:15). He argues that ideas gained from intuition or observation or experience are valid in theology only if they are supported by the teaching of Scripture. Similarly, Lutheran theologian Francis Pieper (1852–1931) says, "We can obtain the whole body of the Christian doctrine only by taking each doctrine from those passages—considered of course in their context—which treat of that specific doctrine. . . . The Church has no doctrine of its own, no doctrine alongside and without Christ's Word." Pieper, *Christian Dogmatics*, 4 vol. (St. Louis: Concordia, 1950), 1:202.

Paul teach about prayer?" or even "What does the New Testament teach about prayer and what is the historical development of that teaching as it progresses through the New Testament?"

*Biblical theology* has a technical meaning in theological studies. It is the larger category that contains both Old Testament theology and New Testament theology as we have defined them above. Biblical theology gives special attention to the teachings of *individual authors and sections* of Scripture and to the place of each teaching in the *historical development* of Scripture.[4] So one might ask, "What is the historical development of the teaching about prayer as it is seen throughout the history of the Old Testament and then of the New Testament?" Of course, this question comes very close to the question, "What does the whole Bible teach us today about prayer?" (which would be *systematic theology* by our definition). It then becomes evident that the boundary lines between these various disciplines often overlap at the edges, and parts of one study blend into the next. Yet there is still a difference, for biblical theology traces the *historical development* of a doctrine and the way one's place in that historical development affects one's understanding and application of that particular doctrine. Biblical theology also focuses on the understanding of each doctrine that the individual biblical authors and their original hearers or readers possessed.

Systematic theology, on the other hand, makes use of the material of biblical theology and often builds on the results of biblical theology. At some points, especially where great detail and care is needed in the development of a doctrine, systematic theology will even use a biblical-theological method, analyzing the development of each doctrine through the historical development of Scripture. But the focus of systematic theology remains different: its focus is on the collection and then the summary of the teaching of all the biblical passages on a particular subject. Thus systematic theology asks, for example, "What does the whole Bible teach us today about prayer?" It attempts to summarize the teaching of Scripture in a brief, understandable, and very carefully formulated statement.

## 2. Application to Life

Furthermore, systematic theology focuses on summarizing each doctrine as it should be understood by present-day Christians. This will sometimes involve the use of terms and even concepts that were not used by any individual biblical author but that are the proper result of combining the teachings of two or more biblical authors on a particular subject. The terms *Trinity*, *incarnation*, and *deity of Christ*, for example, are not found in the Bible, but they usefully summarize biblical concepts.

---

4. The term *biblical theology* might seem to be a natural and appropriate one for the process I have called systematic theology. However, its usage in theological studies to refer to tracing the historical development of doctrines throughout the Bible is too well established, so that starting now to use the term biblical theology to refer to what I have called systematic theology would only result in confusion.

Defining systematic theology to include "what the whole Bible *teaches us* today" implies that application to life is a necessary part of the proper pursuit of systematic theology. Thus a doctrine under consideration is seen in terms of its practical value for living the Christian life. Nowhere in Scripture do we find doctrine studied for its own sake or isolated from life. The biblical writers consistently apply their teaching to life. Even those books of the Bible that have the most doctrinal content (such as Romans, Ephesians, and Hebrews) contain much material that is also directly applicable to the Christian life. Therefore, any Christian reading this book should find his or her Christian life enriched and deepened during this study; indeed, if personal spiritual growth does not occur, then the book has not been written properly by the author or the material has not been rightly studied by the reader.

### 3. Systematic Theology and Disorganized Theology: The Key Differences

If we use this definition of systematic theology, it will be seen that most Christians actually do systematic theology (or at least make systematic-theological statements) many times a week. For example: "The Bible says that everyone who believes in Jesus Christ will be saved." "The Bible says that Jesus Christ is the only way to God." "The Bible says that Jesus is coming again." These are all summaries of what Scripture says, and as such, they are systematic-theological statements. In fact, every time a Christian says something about what the whole Bible says, he or she is in a sense doing systematic theology—according to our definition—by thinking about various topics and answering the question, "What does the whole Bible teach us today?"[5]

How then does this book differ from the "systematic theology" that most Christians do? First, it treats biblical topics in a *carefully organized way* to guarantee that all important topics will receive thorough consideration. This organization also provides one sort of check against inaccurate analysis of individual topics, for it means that all other doctrines that are treated can be compared with each topic for consistency in methodology and absence of contradictions in the relationships between the doctrines. This also helps to ensure balanced consideration of complementary doctrines: Christ's deity and humanity are studied together, for example, as are God's sovereignty and man's responsibility, so that wrong conclusions will not be drawn from an imbalanced emphasis on only one aspect of the full biblical presentation.

In fact, the adjective *systematic* in systematic theology should be understood to mean something like "carefully organized by topics," with the understanding that the topics

---

5. Robert L. Reymond, "The Justification of Theology with a Special Application to Contemporary Christology," in *The Challenge of Evangelical Theology: Essays in Approach and Method*, ed. Nigel M. Cameron (Edinburgh: Rutherford, 1987), 82–104, cites several examples from the New Testament of this kind of searching through all of Scripture to demonstrate doctrinal conclusions: Jesus in Luke 24:25–27 (and elsewhere), Apollos in Acts 18:28, the Jerusalem Council in Acts 15, and Paul in Acts 17:2–3; 20:27, and all of Romans. To this list could be added Heb. 1 (on Christ's divine Sonship), Heb. 11 (on the nature of true faith), and many other passages from the Epistles.

studied will be seen to fit together in a consistent way, and will include all the major doctrinal topics of the Bible. Thus *systematic* should be thought of as the opposite of "randomly arranged" or "disorganized." In systematic theology topics are treated in an orderly or "systematic" way.

A second difference between this book and the way most Christians do systematic theology is that it treats topics in *much more detail* than most Christians do. For example, as a result of regular reading of the Bible an ordinary Christian may make the theological statement, "The Bible says that everyone who believes in Jesus Christ will be saved." That is a perfectly true summary of a major biblical teaching. However, in this book we devote several pages to elaborating more precisely what it means to "believe in Jesus Christ,"[6] and twelve chapters (chapters 32–43) are devoted to explaining what it means to "be saved" in all of the many implications of that term.

Third, a formal study of systematic theology will make it possible to formulate summaries of biblical teachings with *much more accuracy* than Christians would normally arrive at without such a study. In systematic theology, summaries of biblical teachings must be worded precisely to guard against misunderstandings and to exclude false teachings.

Fourth, a good theological analysis must find and treat fairly *all the relevant Bible passages* for each particular topic, not just some or a few of the relevant passages. This often means that it must depend on the results of careful exegesis (or interpretation) of Scripture as generally agreed upon by evangelical interpreters, or when there are significant differences of interpretation, systematic theology will include detailed exegesis.

## 4. Beliefs Must Be Based on Scripture, Not Human Authorities or Traditions

Because of the large number of topics covered in a study of systematic theology and because of the great detail with which these topics are analyzed, it is inevitable that someone studying a systematic theology text or taking a course in systematic theology for the first time will have many of his or her personal beliefs challenged or modified, refined or enriched. It is of utmost importance therefore that each person beginning such a course firmly resolve to abandon as false any idea found to be clearly contradicted by the teaching of Scripture. But it is also very important for each person to resolve not to believe any individual doctrine simply because this textbook or any other textbook or teacher says that it is true, unless this book or the instructor in a course can convince the student from the text of Scripture itself. It is Scripture alone and not "conservative evangelical tradition" or any other human authority that must function as the normative authority for what we should believe.

---

6. See chapter 35, pp. 861–79, on saving faith.

### 5. What Are Doctrines?

In this book, the word *doctrine* will be understood in the following way: *a doctrine is what the whole Bible teaches us today about some particular topic.* This definition is directly related to our earlier definition of systematic theology, since it shows that a "doctrine" is simply the result of the process of doing systematic theology with regard to one particular topic. Understood in this way, doctrines can be very broad or very narrow. We can speak of "the doctrine of God" as a major doctrinal category, including a summary of all that the Bible teaches us today about God. Such a doctrine would be exceptionally large. On the other hand, we may also speak more narrowly of the doctrine of God's eternity or the doctrine of the Trinity or the doctrine of God's justice.[7]

The book is divided into seven major sections according to seven major doctrines:

Part 1:   The Doctrine of the Word of God
Part 2:   The Doctrine of God
Part 3:   The Doctrine of Man in the Image of God
Part 4:   The Doctrines of Christ and the Holy Spirit
Part 5:   The Doctrine of the Application of Redemption
Part 6:   The Doctrine of the Church
Part 7:   The Doctrine of the Future

Within each of these major doctrinal categories many more specific teachings have been selected as appropriate for inclusion. Generally these meet at least one of the following three criteria: (1) they are doctrines that are most emphasized in Scripture; (2) they are doctrines that have been most significant throughout the history of the church and have been important for all Christians at all times; (3) they are doctrines that have become important for Christians in the present situation in the history of the church (even though some of these doctrines may not have been of such great interest earlier in church history). Some examples of doctrines in the third category would be the doctrine of the inerrancy of Scripture, the doctrine of baptism in the Holy Spirit, the doctrine of Satan and demons with particular reference to spiritual warfare, the doctrine of spiritual gifts in the New Testament age, and the doctrine of the creation of man as male and female in relation to the understanding of roles appropriate to men and women today. Because of their relevance to the contemporary situation, doctrines such as these have received greater emphasis in the present volume than in other systematic theology textbooks.

---

7. The word *dogma* is an approximate synonym for *doctrine*, but I have not used it in this book. *Dogma* is a term more often used by Roman Catholic and Lutheran theologians, and the term frequently refers to doctrines that have official church endorsement. *Dogmatic theology* is another term for *systematic theology.*

## 6. The Difference between Systematic Theology and Christian Ethics

Although there is inevitably some overlap between the study of theology and the study of ethics, I have tried to maintain a distinction in emphasis. The emphasis of systematic theology is on what God wants us to *believe* and to *know*, while the emphasis in Christian ethics is on what God wants us to *do* and what *attitudes* he wants us to have. Such a distinction is reflected in the following definition: *Christian ethics is any study that answers the question, "What does the whole Bible teach us about which acts, attitudes, and personal character traits receive God's approval, and which do not?"*[8] Thus theology tells us what we should *believe* while ethics tells us how we should *live*. There is some overlap in topics between theology and ethics (for example, marriage could be treated in both), but in general terms, theology focuses on beliefs while ethics focuses on situations in life.

A textbook on ethics, for example, would discuss topics such as marriage and divorce, lying and telling the truth, stealing and ownership of property, abortion, birth control, homosexuality, the role of civil government, discipline of children, capital punishment, war, care for the poor, racial discrimination, and so forth. Of course there is some overlap: theology must be applied to life (therefore it is often ethical to some degree). And ethics must be based on proper ideas of God and his world (therefore it is theological to some degree).

This book will emphasize systematic theology, though it will not hesitate to apply theology to life where such application comes readily. Still, for a thorough treatment of Christian ethics, see my companion book, *Christian Ethics: An Introduction to Biblical Moral Reasoning.*

## B. INITIAL ASSUMPTIONS OF THIS BOOK

We begin with two assumptions or presuppositions: (1) the Bible is true and is, in fact, our only absolute standard of truth, and (2) the God who is spoken of in the Bible exists, and he is who the Bible says he is—the Creator of heaven and earth and all things in them. These two presuppositions, of course, are always open to adjustment or modification or deeper confirmation, but at this point, these two assumptions form the point at which we begin.

## C. WHY SHOULD CHRISTIANS STUDY THEOLOGY?

Why should Christians study systematic theology? That is, why should we engage in the process of collecting and summarizing the teachings of many individual Bible passages on particular topics? Why is it not sufficient simply to continue reading the Bible regularly every day of our lives?

---

8. This definition of Christian ethics is found in my book *Christian Ethics: an Introduction to Biblical Moral Reasoning* (Wheaton, IL: Crossway, 2018), 37. I have adapted the definition from John Frame, *The Doctrine of the Christian Life* (Phillipsburg, NJ: P&R, 2008), 10.

## 1. The Basic Reason

Many answers have been given to this question, but too often they leave the impression that systematic theology somehow can "improve" on the Bible by doing a better job of organizing its teachings or explaining them more clearly than the Bible itself has done. Thus we may begin implicitly to deny the clarity of Scripture (see chapter 6) or the sufficiency of Scripture (see chapter 8).

However, in the Great Commission, Jesus commanded his disciples and now commands us also to *teach* believers to observe all that he commanded: "Go therefore and make disciples of all nations, baptizing them in the name of the Father and of the Son and of the Holy Spirit, *teaching them* to observe all that I have commanded you. And behold, I am with you always, to the end of the age" (Matt. 28:19–20).[9] Now to teach all that Jesus commanded, in a narrow sense, is simply to teach the content of the oral teaching of Jesus as it is recorded in the gospel narratives. However, in a broader sense, "all that Jesus commanded" includes the interpretation and application of his life and teachings, because in the book of Acts it is implied that it contains a narrative of what Jesus *continued* to do and teach through the apostles after his resurrection (note that Acts 1:1 speaks of "all that Jesus *began* to do and teach"). "All that Jesus commanded" can also include the Epistles, since they were written under the supervision of the Holy Spirit and were also considered to be a "command of the Lord" (1 Cor. 14:37; see also John 14:26; 16:13; 1 Thess. 4:15; 2 Peter 3:2; and Rev. 1:1–3). Thus in a larger sense, "all that Jesus commanded" includes all of the New Testament.

Furthermore, when we consider that the New Testament writings endorse the absolute confidence Jesus had in the authority and reliability of the Old Testament Scriptures as God's words (see chapter 4), and when we realize that the New Testament Epistles also endorse this view of the Old Testament as absolutely authoritative words of God, then it becomes evident that we cannot teach "all that Jesus commanded" without including all of the Old Testament (rightly understood in the various ways in which it applies to the new covenant age in the history of redemption) as well.

The task of fulfilling the Great Commission includes therefore not only evangelism but also *teaching.* And the task of teaching all that Jesus commanded us is, in a broad sense, the task of teaching what the whole Bible says to us today. To effectively teach ourselves and to teach others what the whole Bible says, it is necessary to *collect* and *summarize* all the Scripture passages on a particular subject.

For example, if someone asks me, "What does the Bible teach about Christ's return?" I could say, "Just keep reading your Bible and you'll find out." But if the questioner begins reading at Genesis 1:1, it will be a long time before he or she finds the answer to that question. By that time many other questions will have needed answers, and the list of

---

9. Every instance of italics in biblical passages has been added by the author.

unanswered questions will begin to grow very long indeed. What does the Bible teach about the work of the Holy Spirit? What does the Bible teach about prayer? What does the Bible teach about sin? There simply is not time in our lifetimes to read through the entire Bible looking for an answer for ourselves every time a doctrinal question arises. Therefore, for us to learn what the Bible says, it is very helpful to have the benefit of the work of others who have searched through Scripture and found answers to these various topics.

We can teach others most effectively if we can direct them to the most relevant passages and suggest an appropriate summary of the teachings of those passages. Then the person who questions us can inspect those passages quickly for himself or herself and learn much more rapidly what the teaching of the Bible is on a particular subject. Thus the necessity of systematic theology for teaching what the Bible says comes about primarily because we are finite in our memory and in the amount of time at our disposal.

The basic reason for studying systematic theology, then, is that it enables us to teach ourselves and others what the whole Bible says, thus fulfilling the "teaching" part of the Great Commission.

## 2. The Benefits to Our Lives

Although the basic reason for studying systematic theology is that it is a means of obedience to our Lord's command, there are some additional specific benefits that come from such study.

First, studying theology helps us *overcome our wrong ideas*. If there were no sin in our hearts, we could read the Bible from cover to cover, and although we would not immediately learn everything in the Bible, we would most likely learn only true things about God and his creation. Every time we read it we would learn more true things, and we would not rebel or refuse to accept anything we found written there. But with sin in our hearts and with false beliefs rampant in our cultures, we retain some rebelliousness against God. At various points there are—for all of us—biblical teachings that for one reason or another we do not want to accept. The study of systematic theology is of help in overcoming those rebellious ideas.

For example, suppose there is someone who does not want to believe that Jesus is personally coming back to earth again. Perhaps we could show this person one or two verses that speak of Jesus' return to earth, but the person might still find a way to evade the force of those verses or read a different meaning into them. But if we collect twenty-five or thirty verses that say that Jesus is coming back to earth personally and write them all out on paper, our friend who hesitated to believe in Christ's return is much more likely to be persuaded by the breadth and diversity of biblical evidence for this doctrine. Of course, we all have areas like that, areas where our understanding of the Bible's teaching is inadequate. In these areas, it is helpful for us to be confronted with the *total weight of the teaching of Scripture* on that subject, so that we will more readily be persuaded even against our initial wrongful inclinations.

Second, studying systematic theology helps us to be *able to make better decisions later* on new questions of doctrine that may arise. We cannot know what new doctrinal controversies will arise in the churches in which we will live and minister ten, twenty, or thirty years from now, if the Lord does not return before then. These new doctrinal controversies will sometimes include questions that no one has faced very carefully before. Christians will be asking, "What does the whole Bible say about this subject?" (The precise nature of biblical inerrancy and the appropriate understanding of biblical teaching on gifts of the Holy Spirit are two examples of questions that have arisen in the past fifty years with much more forcefulness than ever before in the history of the church.)

Whatever the new doctrinal controversies are in future years, those who have learned systematic theology well will be much better able to answer the new questions that arise. The reason for this is that everything the Bible says is somehow related to everything else the Bible says (for it all fits together in a consistent way, at least within God's own understanding of reality, and in the nature of God and creation as they really are). Thus the new question will be related to much that has already been learned from Scripture. The more thoroughly that earlier material has been learned, the better able we will be to deal with those new questions.

This benefit extends even more broadly. We face problems of applying Scripture to life in many more contexts than formal doctrinal discussions. What does the Bible teach about husband-wife relationships? About raising children? About witnessing to a friend at work? What principles does Scripture give us for studying psychology or economics or the natural sciences? How does it guide us in spending money or in saving or in tithing? In every area of inquiry certain theological principles will come to bear, and those who have learned well the theological teachings of the Bible will be much better able to make decisions that are pleasing to God.

A helpful analogy at this point is that of a jigsaw puzzle. If the puzzle represents "what the whole Bible teaches us today about everything," then a course in systematic theology would be like filling in the border and some of the major items pictured in the puzzle. But we will never know everything that the Bible teaches about everything, so our jigsaw puzzle will have many gaps, many pieces that remain to be put in. Solving a new real-life problem is analogous to filling in another section of the jigsaw puzzle: the more pieces one has in place correctly, the easier it is to fit new pieces in, and the less apt one is to make mistakes. In this book the goal is to enable Christians to put into their "theological jigsaw puzzle" as many pieces with as much accuracy as possible, and to encourage Christians to go on putting in more and more correct pieces for the rest of their lives. The Christian doctrines studied here will act as guidelines to help in the filling in of all other areas, areas that pertain to all aspects of truth in all aspects of life.

Third, studying systematic theology will *help us grow as Christians*. The more we know about God, about his Word, about his relationships to the world and humankind, the better we will trust him, the more fully we will praise him, and the more readily we will obey him. Studying systematic theology rightly will make us more mature Christians. If it does not do this, we are not studying it in the way God intends.

In fact, the Bible often connects sound doctrine with maturity in Christian living: Paul speaks of *"the teaching that accords with godliness"* (1 Tim. 6:3) and says that his work as an apostle is "for the sake of the faith of God's elect and their knowledge of *the truth which accords with godliness*" (Titus 1:1). By contrast, he indicates that all kinds of disobedience and immorality are "contrary to sound doctrine" (1 Tim. 1:10).

### 3. What Is the Difference between "Major" and "Minor" Doctrines?

It is appropriate to ask what the difference is between a "major doctrine" and a "minor doctrine." Christians often say they want to seek agreement in the church on major doctrines but also to allow for differences on minor doctrines. I have found the following guideline useful:

> A major doctrine is one that has a significant impact on our thinking about other doctrines, or that has a significant impact on how we live the Christian life. A minor doctrine is one that has very little impact on how we think about other doctrines, and very little impact on how we live the Christian life.

By this standard doctrines such as the authority of the Bible (chapter 4), the Trinity (chapter 14), the deity of Christ (chapter 26), justification by faith (chapter 36), and many others would rightly be considered major doctrines. People who disagree with the historic evangelical understanding of any of these doctrines will have wide areas of difference with evangelical Christians who affirm these doctrines. By contrast, it seems to me that differences over forms of church government (chapter 47) or some details about the Lord's Supper (chapter 50) or the timing of the great tribulation (chapter 55) concern minor doctrines. Christians who differ over these things can agree on perhaps every other area of doctrine, can live Christian lives that differ in no important way, and can have genuine fellowship with one another.

Of course, we may find doctrines that fall somewhere between "major" and "minor" according to this standard. For example, Christians may differ over the degree of significance that should attach to the doctrine of baptism (chapter 49) or the millennium (chapter 55) or the extent of the atonement (chapter 27). That is only natural, because many doctrines have *some* influence on other doctrines or on life, but we may differ over whether we think it to be a "significant" influence. We could even recognize that there will be a range of significance here and just say that the more influence a doctrine has on other doctrines and on life, the more "major" it becomes. This amount of influence may even vary according to the historical circumstances and needs of the church at any given time. In such cases, Christians will need to ask God to give them mature wisdom and sound judgment as they try to determine to what extent a doctrine should be considered "major" in their particular circumstances.

## D. A Note on Three Objections to the Study of Systematic Theology
### 1. "The Conclusions Are 'Too Neat' to Be True"

Some scholars look with suspicion at systematic theology when—or even because—its teachings fit together in a noncontradictory way. They object that the results are "too neat" and that systematic theologians must therefore be squeezing the Bible's teachings into an artificial mold, distorting the true meaning of Scripture to get an orderly set of beliefs.

To this objection two responses can be made. (1) We must first ask the people making the objection to tell us at what specific points Scripture has been misinterpreted, and then we must deal with the understanding of those passages. Perhaps mistakes have been made, and in that case there should be corrections.

Yet it is also possible that the objector will have no specific passages in mind, or no clearly erroneous interpretations to point to in the works of the most responsible evangelical theologians. Of course, incompetent exegesis can be found in the writings of the less competent scholars in *any* field of biblical studies, not just in systematic theology, but those "bad examples" constitute an objection not against the scholar's field but against the incompetent scholar himself.

It is very important that the objector be specific at this point because this objection is sometimes made by those who—perhaps unconsciously—have adopted from our culture a skeptical view of the possibility of finding universally true conclusions about anything, even about God from his Word. This kind of skepticism regarding theological truth is especially common in the modern university world where systematic theology—if it is studied at all—is studied only from the perspectives of philosophical theology and historical theology (including perhaps a historical study of the various ideas that were believed by the early Christians who wrote the New Testament and by other Christians at that time and throughout church history). In this kind of intellectual climate the study of "systematic theology" as defined in this chapter would be considered impossible because the Bible would be assumed to be merely the work of many human authors who wrote out of diverse cultures and experiences over the course of more than one thousand years; trying to find "what the whole Bible teaches" about any subject would be nearly as hopeless as trying to find "what all philosophers teach" about some question, for the answer in both cases would include not one view but many diverse and often conflicting views. This skeptical viewpoint must be rejected by evangelicals who see Scripture as the product of human *and* divine authorship and therefore as a collection of writings that teach noncontradictory truths about God and about the universe he created.

(2) Second, it must be answered that in God's own mind, and in the nature of reality itself, *true* facts and ideas are all consistent with one another. Therefore if we have accurately understood the teachings of God in Scripture we should expect our conclusions to "fit together" and be mutually consistent. Internal consistency, then, is an argument for, not against, any individual results of systematic theology.

## 2. "The Choice of Topics Dictates the Conclusions"

Another general objection to systematic theology concerns the choice and arrangement of topics, and even the fact that such topically arranged study of Scripture, using categories sometimes different from those found in Scripture itself, is done at all. Why are *these* theological topics treated rather than just the topics emphasized by the biblical authors, and why are the topics *arranged in this way* rather than in some other way? Perhaps—this objection would say—our traditions and our cultures have determined the topics we treat and the arrangement of topics so that the results of this systematic-theological study of Scripture, though acceptable in our own theological tradition, will in fact be untrue to Scripture itself.

A variant of this objection is the statement that our starting point often determines our conclusions on controversial topics: if we decide to start with an emphasis on the divine authorship of Scripture, for example, we will end up believing in biblical inerrancy, but if we start with an emphasis on the human authorship of Scripture, we will end up believing there are some errors in the Bible. Similarly, if we start with an emphasis on God's sovereignty, we will end up as Calvinists, but if we start with an emphasis on man's ability to make free choices, we will end up as Arminians,[10] and so forth. This objection makes it sound as if the most important theological questions could probably be decided by flipping a coin to decide where to start, since *different* and *equally valid* conclusions will inevitably be reached from the different starting points.

Those who make such an objection often suggest that the best way to avoid this problem is not to study or teach systematic theology at all, but to limit our topical studies to the field of biblical theology, treating only the topics and themes the biblical authors themselves emphasize and describing the historical development of these biblical themes through the Bible.

In response to this objection, much of the discussion in this chapter about the necessity to teach Scripture will be relevant. Our choice of topics need not be restricted to the main concerns of the biblical authors, for our goal is to find out what God requires of us in all areas of concern to us today.

For example, it was not the *main* concern of any New Testament author to explain such topics as "baptism in the Holy Spirit," women's roles in the church, or the doctrine of the Trinity, but these are valid areas of concern for us today, and we must look at all the places in Scripture that have relevance for those topics (whether those specific terms are mentioned or not, and whether those themes are of primary concern to each passage we examine or not) if we are going to be able to understand and explain to others "what the whole Bible teaches" about them.

The only alternative—for we *will* think *something* about those subjects—is to form

---

10. See chapter 16, pp. 420, 445–64, for a discussion of the terms *Calvinist* and *Arminian*.

our opinions haphazardly from a general impression of what we feel to be a "biblical" position on each subject or perhaps to buttress our positions with careful analysis of one or two relevant texts with no guarantee that those texts present a balanced view of "the whole counsel of God" (Acts 20:27) on the subject being considered. In fact this approach—one all too common in evangelical circles today—could, I suppose, be called "unsystematic theology" or even "disorderly and random theology"! Such an alternative is too subjective and too subject to cultural pressures. It tends toward doctrinal fragmentation and widespread doctrinal uncertainty, leaving the church theologically immature, like "children, tossed to and fro by the waves and carried about by every wind of doctrine" (Eph. 4:14).

Concerning the objection about the choice and sequence of topics, there is nothing to prevent us from going to Scripture to look for answers to *any* doctrinal questions, considered in *any sequence*. The sequence of topics in this book is a very common one and has been adopted because it is orderly and lends itself well to learning and teaching. But the chapters could be read in any sequence one wanted and the conclusions should not be different, nor should the persuasiveness of the arguments—if they are rightly derived from Scripture—be significantly diminished. In fact, I suspect that most readers of this book will not read it through from chapter 1 to chapter 57 but will begin with the chapters of most interest to them and read others later. That does not really matter because I have tried to write the chapters so that they can be read as independent units, and I have added cross-references to sections in other chapters where relevant. Whether one reads the chapter on the new heavens and new earth (chapter 57) first or last or somewhere in between, the arguments will be the same, the Scripture passages quoted for support will be the same, and the conclusions should be the same.

## 3. "You Can't Just Get Doctrine Directly from the Pages of Scripture"

This third objection is not about systematic theology in general but about my particular approach in this book. Although many of the reviews of the first edition of this book were very positive, one criticism concerned the method I used in constructing the book. Why did I think I could go directly to Scripture, quote a number of verses, and then conclude that we should believe x or y or z, on the basis of those verses? Did I not realize that doctrines needed to be developed through interaction with the writings of the great theologians in the history of the church and also with the writings of contemporary theologians who were famous in the academic world?

Coming from evangelical faculty members who teach and write in university contexts where they often seek to influence other scholars who hold a more liberal theological position, such an objection is understandable. I have studied in such contexts myself (at Harvard and Cambridge), and I would not write a book like this one—in which I assume the understandability and the complete truthfulness, authority, and internal consistency of Scripture—for the purpose of persuading other faculty members in such contexts. That is because most or all of the nonevangelicals in that context would not share my belief that the words of the Bible are the very words of God and come with his authority. The basis of shared assumptions would be much narrower for such an audience.

For most theologians who are outside the evangelical world, the words of the Bible are *merely human words* expressing human ideas about God.[11] And the writings of the great theologians in the history of the church are, similarly, human ideas expressed in merely human words. Therefore, from their perspective, as we attempt to construct the doctrines that we should believe, all we have to work with are the human ideas about God that have been expressed both in the Bible and in Christian theological writings since the Bible was completed.

That is why, today, evangelical students are still able to study the writings of theologians such as Augustine, Calvin, or Luther on an equal footing with liberal students and faculty members who also study those writings. They all agree that these are merely human writings, and so there is no fundamental disagreement on the question of authority, or whether these writers might at times have been wrong.

But in such university contexts, evangelical students would not find shared assumptions if they were to base their research and writing on the assumption that the entire Bible is the word of God and therefore absolutely truthful and absolutely authoritative. In fact, upon receiving a copy of the first edition of this book in 1994, my always-gracious doctoral supervisor at Cambridge, Professor C. F. D. Moule (1908–2007), wrote to thank me as follows (note what he appreciates and what he does not appreciate):

> I am writing . . . to thank you for your extremely generous gift of your *maximum opus*. . . . I am filled with admiration—as I always have been—for your exceptional capacity for hard and accurate work. . . . And Zondervan have done a very nice job, haven't they? . . . I know you wouldn't expect me to agree with you doctrinally! We are poles apart in our understanding of authority, which is the basis of so much; but we can rejoice to have the same Lord and to be fellow-members in the body."[12]

But I did not write this book to gain his approval. I wrote it for evangelical Christians who believe the Bible to be the very words of God, written by ordinary human beings under the guidance of the Holy Spirit (see chapters 2, 3, 4, and 5).

In addition, I could never have written a book like this if I had tried to do it as a brand-new believer, apart from the previous work of many theologians in the history of the church. My understanding of the doctrine of Scripture was the result of reading

---

11. I should add the qualification that many Roman Catholic scholars would not consider themselves to be "evangelicals," but they would also agree that the words of the Bible are words of God.

12. Personal letter to Wayne Grudem from C. F. D. Moule, December 19, 1994. I had received my PhD from Cambridge in 1979, but Professor Moule regularly kept in touch with his former students.

the works of B. B. Warfield, J. Gresham Machen, and E. J. Young, and learning from Westminster Seminary professors John Frame, Edmund Clowney, Richard Gaffin, and others including my life-long friend Vern Poythress. My understanding of other areas of theology had been heavily influenced by the writings of John Calvin, John Murray, Louis Berkhof, Herman Bavinck, Charles Hodge, and the Westminster Confession of Faith. And all of those theologians had learned from the work of many who had gone before them, and they in turn had learned from others before them, going all the way back to the beginning of the church in the first century. At times in this book I cite one or another of these authors, but even where I do not (for this is an introductory textbook), those who are familiar with their writings will recognize their influence. (However, in the chapters where I deal with current differences of viewpoint among evangelical authors, I do cite and interact with the arguments of numerous other writers.)

In the end, however, I accepted or rejected various parts of all of their writings depending on whether, in my judgment, their viewpoints represented faithfully the teachings of the Bible itself, which I had been reading every day of my life for thirty-nine years when the first edition of this book was published in 1994. So yes, while taking into account those valuable influences, I do think it is possible to build a system of doctrine directly from the pages of Scripture. But I would also say that this cannot be done well without an awareness of the theological convictions of other Christian writers throughout the history of the church.

## E. How Should Christians Study Systematic Theology?

How then should we study systematic theology? The Bible provides some guidelines for answering this question.

### 1. We Should Study Systematic Theology with Prayer

If studying systematic theology is simply a certain way of studying the Bible, then the passages in Scripture that talk about the way in which we should study God's Word give guidance to us in this task. Just as the psalmist prays in Psalm 119:18, "Open my eyes, that I may behold wondrous things out of your law," so we should pray and seek God's help in understanding his Word. Paul tells us in 1 Corinthians 2:14 that "the natural person does not accept the things of the Spirit of God, for they are folly to him, and he is not able to understand them because they are spiritually discerned." Studying theology is therefore a spiritual activity in which we need the help of the Holy Spirit.

No matter how intelligent a student might be, if the student does not continue to pray for God to give him or her an understanding mind and a believing and humble heart, and the student does not maintain a personal walk with the Lord, then the teachings of Scripture will be misunderstood and disbelieved, doctrinal error will result, and the mind and heart of the student will not be changed for the better but for the worse. "Keep your heart with all vigilance, for from it flow the springs of life" (Prov. 4:23). Students of systematic theology should resolve at the beginning to keep their lives free from any disobedience to God or any known sin that would disrupt their relationship with him. They should resolve to maintain with great regularity their own personal devotional lives. They should continually pray for wisdom and understanding of Scripture.

Charles Hodge, recognized as one of America's greatest theologians, taught at Princeton Seminary from 1820 to 1878 (Princeton was at that time conservative in its view of the authority of Scripture). But for two years (1826–28) he studied in Germany. When he returned to Princeton in 1828, he asked, in an address to students, how it was that, in the former great centers of Protestantism—especially Germany—Christianity had ceased to be even a nominal religion. Hodge answered that the reason was the decline of what he called "vital religion":

> Holiness is essential to the correct knowledge of divine things and the great security from error. . . . Wherever you find vital piety, there you find the doctrines of the fall, of depravity, of regeneration, of atonement, and of the deity of Jesus Christ. . . . Keep your hearts with all diligence, for out of them are the issues of life. . . . Holiness is essential to correct knowledge of divine things, and the great security from error. . . . When men lose the life of religion, they can believe the most monstrous doctrines, and glory in them.[13]

Since it is the Holy Spirit who gives us the ability rightly to understand Scripture, we need to realize that the proper thing to do, particularly when we are unable to understand some passage or some doctrine of Scripture, is to pray for God's help. Often what we need is not more data but more insight into the data we already have available. This insight is given only by the Holy Spirit (cf. 1 Cor. 2:14; Eph. 1:17–19).

## 2. We Should Study Systematic Theology with Humility

Peter tells us, "Clothe yourselves, all of you, with humility toward one another, for 'God opposes the proud, but gives grace to the humble'" (1 Peter 5:5). Those who study systematic theology will learn many things about the teachings of Scripture that are perhaps not known or not known well by other Christians in their churches or by relatives who are older in the Lord than they are. They may also find that they understand things about Scripture that some of their church officers do not understand and that even their pastor has perhaps forgotten or never learned well.

In all of these situations it would be very easy to adopt an attitude of pride or superiority toward others who have not made such a study. But how ugly it would be if anyone were to use this knowledge of God's Word simply to win arguments or to put down a

---

13. David B. Calhoun, *Princeton Seminary*, vol.1, *Faith and Learning, 1812–1868* (Edinburgh and Carlisle, PA: Banner of Truth, 1994), 123.

fellow Christian in conversation or to make another believer feel insignificant in the Lord's work. James's counsel is good for us at this point: "Let every person be quick to hear, slow to speak, slow to anger; for the anger of man does not produce the righteousness of God" (James 1:19–20). He tells us that one's understanding of Scripture is to be imparted in humility and love:

> Who is wise and understanding among you? By his good conduct let him show his works in the meekness of wisdom. . . . But the wisdom from above is first pure, then peaceable, gentle, open to reason, full of mercy and good fruits, impartial and sincere. And a harvest of righteousness is sown in peace by those who make peace. (James 3:13, 17–18)

Systematic theology rightly studied will not lead to the knowledge that "puffs up" (1 Cor. 8:1) but to humility and love for others.

## 3. We Should Study Systematic Theology with Reason

First, it is right for us to reason from Scripture. We find in the New Testament that Jesus and the New Testament authors often quote a verse of Scripture and then draw logical conclusions from it. They reason from Scripture. It is therefore not wrong to use human understanding, human logic, and human reason to draw conclusions from the statements of Scripture. Nevertheless, when we reason and draw what we think to be correct logical deductions from Scripture, we sometimes make mistakes. The deductions we draw from the statements of Scripture are not equal to the statements of Scripture in certainty or authority, for our ability to reason and draw conclusions is not the ultimate standard of truth—only Scripture is.

What then are the limits on our use of our reasoning abilities to draw deductions from the statements of Scripture? The fact that reasoning to conclusions that go beyond the mere statements of Scripture is appropriate and even necessary for studying Scripture, and the fact that Scripture itself is the ultimate standard of truth, combine to indicate to us that *we are free to use our reasoning abilities to draw deductions from any passage of Scripture so long as these deductions do not contradict the clear teaching of some other passage of Scripture.*[14]

This principle safeguards against our misguided or incorrect logical deductions from Scripture. Our supposedly logical deductions may be erroneous, but Scripture is not erroneous. Thus, for example, we may read Scripture and find that God the Father is called God (1 Cor. 1:3), that God the Son is called God (John 20:28; Titus 2:13), and that God the Holy Spirit is called God (Acts 5:3–4). We might deduce from this that there are

---

14. This guideline is also adopted from Professor John Frame of Reformed Theological Seminary (see p. 1).

three Gods! But then we find the Bible explicitly teaching us that God is one (Deut. 6:4; James 2:19). Thus we conclude that what we *thought* to be a valid logical deduction about three Gods was wrong and that Scripture teaches both (a) that there are three separate persons (Father, Son, and Holy Spirit), each of whom is fully God, and (b) that there is one God. But how can this be? In our human experience, we understand what it means to know three separate persons—three friends, for example. But these three friends are three separate beings. How can God be three persons and yet one being?

Second, Christian theology can tolerate a paradox, but God never asks us to believe a contradiction. We cannot understand exactly how these two statements about God can both be true, so together they constitute a *paradox* ("a seemingly contradictory statement that may nonetheless be true").[15] We can tolerate a paradox (such as "God is three persons and one God") because we have confidence that ultimately God knows fully the truth about himself and about the nature of reality and that in his understanding the different elements of a paradox are fully reconciled,[16] even though at this point God's thoughts are higher than our thoughts (Isa. 55:8–9). But a true contradiction (such as, "God is three persons and God is not three persons") would imply ultimate contradiction in God's understanding of himself or of reality, and this cannot be.

When the psalmist says, "The sum of your word is truth, and every one of your righteous rules endures forever" (Ps. 119:160), he implies that God's words are not only true individually but also viewed together as a whole. Viewed collectively, their "sum" is also "truth." Ultimately, there is no internal contradiction either in Scripture or in God's own thoughts.

---

15. *The American Heritage Dictionary of the English Language*, ed. William Morris (Boston: Houghton-Mifflin, 1980), s.v. paradox, p. 950 (first definition). Essentially the same meaning is adopted by *Oxford English Dictionary* (1913 ed.), 7:450; *Concise Oxford Dictionary* (1981 ed.), 742; *Random House College Dictionary* (1979 ed.), 964; and *Chambers Twentieth Century Dictionary*, 780, though all note that *paradox* can also mean "contradiction" (though less commonly); cf. *Encyclopedia of Philosophy*, ed. Paul Edwards (New York: Macmillan; Free, 1967), 5:45, and the entire article "Logical Paradoxes" by John van Heijenoort on pp. 45–51 of the same volume, which proposes solutions to many of the classical paradoxes in the history of philosophy. (If *paradox* meant "contradiction," such solutions would be impossible.)

When I use the word *paradox* in the primary sense defined by these dictionaries today, I realize that I am differing somewhat with the article "Paradox" by K. S. Kantzer in the *EDT*, ed. Walter Elwell, 826–27 (which takes *paradox* to mean essentially "contradiction"). However, I am using *paradox* in an ordinary English sense and one also familiar in philosophy. There seems to me to be available no better word than *paradox* to refer to an apparent but not real contradiction.

There is, however, some lack of uniformity in the use of the term *paradox* and a related term, *antinomy*, in contemporary evangelical discussion. The word *antinomy* has sometimes been used to apply to what I here call *paradox*, that is, "seemingly

contradictory statements that may nonetheless both be true" (see, e.g., John Jefferson Davis, *Theology Primer* [Grand Rapids: Baker, 1981], 18). Such a sense for *antinomy* gained support in a widely read book, *Evangelism and the Sovereignty of God*, by J. I. Packer (London: Inter-Varsity Press, 1961). On pp. 18–22 Packer defines *antinomy* as "an appearance of contradiction" (but admits on p. 18 that his definition differs with the *Shorter Oxford Dictionary*). My problem with using *antinomy* in this sense is that the word is so unfamiliar in ordinary English that it just increases the stock of technical terms Christians have to learn in order to understand theologians, and moreover such a sense is unsupported by any of the dictionaries cited above, all of which define *antinomy* to mean "contradiction" (e.g., *Oxford English Dictionary*, 1:371). The problem is not serious, but it would help communication if evangelicals could agree on uniform senses for these terms.

A paradox is certainly acceptable in systematic theology, and paradoxes are in fact inevitable so long as we have finite understanding of any theological topic. However, it is important to recognize that Christian theology should never affirm a *contradiction* (a set of two statements, one of which denies the other). A contradiction would be "God is three persons and God is not three persons" (where the term *persons* has the same sense in both halves of the sentence).

16. Another way of saying that we can tolerate a paradox is to say that we can tolerate a mystery in Christian theology.

## 4. We Should Study Systematic Theology with Help from Others

We need to be thankful that God has put teachers in the church ("God has appointed in the church first apostles, second prophets, third *teachers* . . ." [1 Cor. 12:28]). We should allow those with gifts of teaching to help us understand Scripture. This means that we should make use of systematic theologies and other books written by some of the teachers God has given to the church over the course of its history. It also means that our study of theology should include *talking with other Christians* about the things we study. Among those with whom we talk will often be some with gifts of teaching who can explain biblical teachings clearly and help us to understand more easily. In fact, some of the most effective learning in systematic theology courses in colleges and seminaries often occurs outside the classroom in informal conversations among students who are attempting to understand Bible doctrines for themselves.

## 5. We Should Study Systematic Theology by Collecting and Understanding All the Relevant Passages of Scripture on Any Topic

This point was mentioned in our definition of systematic theology at the beginning of the chapter, but the actual process needs to be described here. How does one go about making a doctrinal summary of what all the passages of Scripture teach on a certain topic?

For topics covered in this book, many people will find that studying the relevant chapters in this book (and other systematic theology books) and reading the Bible verses noted in those chapters is enough. But some people will want to do further study of Scripture on a particular topic or study some new topic not covered here. How could a student go about using the Bible to research its teachings on some new subject, perhaps one not discussed explicitly in any of his or her systematic theology textbooks?

The process would look like this: (1) Find all the relevant verses. The best help in this step is a good concordance or Bible search program, which enables one to look up key words and find the verses in which the subject is treated. For example, in studying what it means that man is created in the image and likeness of God, one needs to find all the verses in which *image* and *likeness* and *create* occur. (The words *man* and *God* occur too often to be useful for a concordance search.) In studying the doctrine of prayer, many words could be looked up (*pray, prayer, intercede, petition, supplication, confess, confession, praise, thanks, thanksgiving,* etc.)—and perhaps the list of verses would grow too long to be manageable, so that the student would have to skim the concordance entries or search results without looking up the verses, or the search would probably have to be divided into sections or limited in some other way. Verses can also be found by thinking through the overall history of the Bible and then turning to sections where there would be information on the topic at hand. For example, a student studying prayer would want to read passages like the one about Hannah's prayer for a son (1 Sam. 1), Solomon's prayer at the dedication of the temple (1 Kings 8), Jesus' prayer in the Garden of Gethsemane

(Matt. 26 and parallels), and so forth. Then in addition to using a concordance or a search program and reading other passages that one can find on the subject, checking the relevant sections in some systematic theology books will often bring to light other verses that had been missed, sometimes because none of the key words used for the concordance were in those verses.[17]

(2) The second step is to read, take notes, and summarize the points made in the relevant verses. Sometimes a theme will be repeated often and the summary of the various verses will be relatively easy. At other times, there will be verses difficult to understand, and the student will need to take some time to study a verse in depth (just by reading rather the verse in context over and over or by using specialized tools such as commentaries and dictionaries) until a satisfactory understanding is reached.

(3) Finally, the teachings of the various verses should be summarized into one or more points that the Bible affirms about that subject. The summary does not have to take the exact form of anyone else's conclusions on the subject, because we each may see things in Scripture that others have missed, or we may organize the subject differently or emphasize different things.

On the other hand, at this point it is also helpful to read related sections, if any can be found, in several systematic theology books. This provides a useful check against error and oversight, and often makes one aware of alternative perspectives and arguments that may cause us to modify or strengthen our position. If a student finds that others have argued for strongly differing conclusions, then these other views need to be stated fairly and then answered. Sometimes other theology books will alert us to historical or philosophical considerations that have been raised before in the history of the church, and these will provide additional insight or warnings against error.

The process outlined above is possible for any Christian who can read his or her Bible and can look up words in a concordance or use a Bible search program. Of course people will become faster and more accurate in this process with time and experience and Christian maturity, but it would be a tremendous help to the church if Christians generally would give much more time to searching out topics in Scripture for themselves and drawing conclusions in the way outlined above. The joy of discovery of biblical themes would be richly rewarding. Especially pastors and those who lead Bible studies would find added freshness in their understanding of Scripture and in their teaching.

## 6. We Should Study Systematic Theology with Rejoicing and Praise

The study of theology is not merely a theoretical exercise of the intellect. It is a study of the living God and of the wonders of all his works in creation and redemption.

---

17. I have read a number of student papers telling me that John's gospel says nothing about how Christians should pray, for example, because they looked at a concordance and found that the word *prayer* was not in John, and the word *pray* only occurs four times in reference to Jesus praying in John 14, 16, and 17. They overlooked the fact that John contains several important verses where the word *ask* rather than the word *pray* is used (John 14:13–14; 15:7, 16, et al.).

We cannot study this subject dispassionately! We must love all that God is, all that he says and all that he does. "You shall love the LORD your God with all your heart" (Deut. 6:5). Our response to the study of the theology of Scripture should be that of the psalmist who said, "How precious to me are your thoughts, O God!" (Ps. 139:17). In the study of the teachings of God's Word, it should not surprise us if we often find our hearts spontaneously breaking forth in expressions of praise and delight like those of the psalmist:

> The precepts of the LORD are right,
>> rejoicing the heart. (Ps. 19:8)

> In the way of your testimonies I delight
>> as much as in all riches. (Ps. 119:14)

> How sweet are your words to my taste,
>> sweeter than honey to my mouth! (Ps. 119:103)

> Your testimonies are my heritage forever,
>> for they are the joy of my heart. (Ps. 119:111)

> I rejoice at your word
>> like one who finds great spoil. (Ps. 119:162)

Often in the study of theology the response of the Christian should be similar to that of Paul in reflecting on the long theological argument that he has just completed at the end of Romans 11:32. He breaks forth into joyful praise at the richness of the doctrine which God has enabled him to express:

> Oh, the depth of the riches and wisdom and knowledge of God! How unsearchable are his judgments and how inscrutable his ways!

> "For who has known the mind of the Lord,
>> or who has been his counselor?"
> "Or who has given a gift to him
>> that he might be repaid?"

> For from him and through him and to him are all things. To him be glory forever. Amen. (Rom. 11:33–36)

# QUESTIONS FOR PERSONAL APPLICATION

These questions at the end of each chapter focus on application to life. Because I think doctrine is to be felt at the emotional level as well as understood at the intellectual level, in many chapters I have included some questions about how a reader *feels* regarding a point of doctrine. I think these questions will prove quite valuable for those who take the time to reflect on them.

1. In what ways (if any) has this chapter changed your understanding of what systematic theology is? What was your attitude toward the study of systematic theology before reading this chapter? What is your attitude now?
2. What is likely to happen to a church or denomination that gives up learning systematic theology for a generation or longer? Has that been true of your church?
3. Are there any doctrines listed on the table of contents for which a fuller understanding would help to solve a personal difficulty in your life at the present time? What are the spiritual and emotional dangers that you personally need to be aware of in studying systematic theology?
4. Pray for God to make this study of basic Christian doctrines a time of spiritual growth and deeper fellowship with him, and a time in which you understand and apply the teachings of Scripture rightly.

## Special Terms

*apologetics*
*biblical theology*
*Christian ethics*
*contradiction*
*doctrine*
*dogmatic theology*
*historical theology*
*major doctrine*
*minor doctrine*
*New Testament theology*
*Old Testament theology*
*paradox*
*philosophical theology*
*presupposition*
*systematic theology*

# BIBLIOGRAPHY

In these bibliographies I have usually listed only works written from what would today be called a conservative evangelical position. This is because the purpose of this section is to give the student ready access to other treatments of each topic by theologians who share with this book the same general convictions about the nature of Scripture—that all of it is totally truthful and that it is God's unique and absolutely authoritative Word to us. Once we step outside of that conviction, the variety of theological positions becomes amazingly large, and sufficient bibliographies are easily found in the more recent works cited below. (However, I have also included two representative Roman Catholic works because of the great influence of the Roman Catholic Church in almost every society in the world.)

Writers are grouped according to broad denominational categories, and the writers within the groups are arranged chronologically. Of course, the categories below are not airtight, for there is often overlap—many Anglicans and many Baptists are theologically Reformed, while others in those groups are theologically Arminian; many Dispensationalists are also Baptists, while others are Presbyterians, and so forth. Yet the categories are fairly representative of distinguishable theological traditions within evangelicalism.

Dates given are the dates of publication of the final edition of each author's systematic theology or major theological writing. Where no single major theological work was published, the dates represent the years during which the author was actively teaching and writing about systematic theology. Complete bibliographical data may be found on pp. 1489–96.

## SECTIONS IN EVANGELICAL SYSTEMATIC THEOLOGIES

### 1. Anglican (Episcopalian)
1882–92 . . . . . Litton, 1–8
1930 . . . . . . . . Thomas, xvii–xxviii, 146–52
2001 . . . . . . . . Packer, xi–xiii
2013 . . . . . . . . Bird, 19–86
2014 . . . . . . . . Bray, 27–68

### 2. Arminian (Wesleyan or Methodist)
1875–76 . . . . . Pope, 1:3–32, 42–46
1892–94 . . . . . Miley, 1:2–54
1940 . . . . . . . . Wiley, 1:13–123
1960 . . . . . . . . Purkiser, 19–38
1983 . . . . . . . . Carter, 1:19–101
1992 . . . . . . . . Oden, 1:11–14, 375–406
2002 . . . . . . . . Cottrell, 9–36

### 3. Baptist
1767 . . . . . . . . Gill, 1:vii–xxx
1887 . . . . . . . . Boyce, 1–8
1907 . . . . . . . . Strong, 1–51
1976–83 . . . . . Henry, 1:13–411; 6:7–34
1987–94 . . . . Lewis and Demarest,
                1:13–123
1990–95 . . . . . Garrett, 1–48
2007 . . . . . . . . Akin, 2–71
2013 . . . . . . . . Erickson, xi–117

### 4. Dispensational
1947 . . . . . . . . Chafer, 1:3–17
1949 . . . . . . . . Thiessen, 1–20
1986 . . . . . . . . Ryrie, 9–22
2002–2005 . . Geisler, 1:15–226
2017 . . . . . . . . MacArthur and Mayhue,
                33–68

### 5. Lutheran
1917–24 . . . . . Pieper, 1:3–190
1934 . . . . . . . . Mueller, 1–89

### 6. Reformed (or Presbyterian)
1559 . . . . . . . . Calvin, 1:3–33, 35–43
                (prefaces and 1.1–2)
1679–85 . . . . . Turretin, *IET,* 1:1–54
1724–58 . . . . . Edwards, 2:157–63
1871–73 . . . . . Hodge, 1:1–150
1878 . . . . . . . . Dabney, 133–44
1887–1921 . . . Warfield, *SSW,* 2:207–320
1894 . . . . . . . . Shedd, 43–84
1910 . . . . . . . . Vos, 1:vii–x
1937–66 . . . . . Murray, *CW,* 1:3–8, 169–73;
                *CW,* 4:1–21
1938 . . . . . . . . Berkhof, *Intro.,* 15–128,
                170–86
1998 . . . . . . . . Reymond, xxv–xxxvi

2008 . . . . . . . . Van Genderen and Velema,
1–19
2011 . . . . . . . . Horton, 13–34
2013 . . . . . . . . Culver, 1–18
2013 . . . . . . . . Frame, 3–52
2016 . . . . . . . . Allen and Swain, 1–6
2017 . . . . . . . . Barrett, 43–66
2019 . . . . . . . . Letham, 33–38

### 7. Renewal (or charismatic/Pentecostal)

1988–92 . . . . . Williams, 1:11–28
1993 . . . . . . . . Menzies and Horton, 9–13
1995 . . . . . . . . Horton, 7–60
2008 . . . . . . . . Duffield and Van Cleave, 5–6

## SECTIONS IN REPRESENTATIVE ROMAN CATHOLIC SYSTEMATIC THEOLOGIES

### 1. Roman Catholic: Traditional

1955 . . . . . . . . Ott, 1–10

### 2. Roman Catholic: Post–Vatican II

1980 . . . . . . . . McBrien, 1:3–78, 183–200
2012 . . . . . . . . *CCC*, pp. 1–16, paragraphs
1–25

## OTHER WORKS

Baker, D. L. "Biblical Theology." In *NDT1*, 671.

Berkhof, Louis. *Introduction to Systematic Theology*. Grand Rapids: Eerdmans, 1982, 15–75.

Bray, Gerald L., ed. *Contours of Christian Theology*. Downers Grove, IL: InterVarsity Press, 1993.

———. "Systematic Theology, History of." In *NDT1*, 671–72.

Cameron, Nigel M., ed. *The Challenge of Evangelical Theology: Essays in Approach and Method*. Edinburgh: Rutherford House, 1987.

Carson, D. A. "Systematic Theology and Biblical Theology." In *NDBT*, 89–104.

———. "Unity and Diversity in the New Testament: The Possibility of Systematic Theology." In *Scripture and Truth*, edited by D. A. Carson and John Woodbridge, 65–95. Grand Rapids: Zondervan, 1983.

Clark, David K. *To Know and Love God: Method for Theology*. Wheaton, IL: Crossway, 2003.

Davis, John Jefferson. *Foundations of Evangelical Theology*. Grand Rapids: Baker, 1984.

———. *The Necessity of Systematic Theology*. Grand Rapids: Baker, 1980.

———. *Theology Primer: Resources for the Theological Student*. Grand Rapids: Baker, 1981.

Demarest, Bruce. "Systematic Theology." In *EDT1*, 1064–66.

Enns, Paul. "Introduction to Systematic Theology." In *The Moody Handbook of Theology*, Revised and Expanded Edition, 149–53. Chicago: Moody Publishers, 2008.

Erickson, Millard J. *Concise Dictionary of Christian Theology*. Grand Rapids: Baker, 1986.

Erickson, Millard J., and L. Arnold Hustad. *Introducing Christian Doctrine*, 3rd ed. Grand Rapids: Baker Academic, 2015.

Frame, John. *Salvation Belongs to the Lord: An Introduction to Systematic Theology*. Phillipsburg, NJ: P&R, 2006.

———. *Van Til the Theologian*. Phillipsburg, NJ: Pilgrim, 1976.

Geehan, E. R., ed. *Jerusalem and Athens*. Nutley, NJ: Craig, 1971.

Grenz, Stanley J. *Revisioning Evangelical Theology: A Fresh Agenda for the 21st Century*. Downers Grove, IL: InterVarsity Press, 1993.

Horton, Michael Scott. *Pilgrim Theology: Core Doctrines for Christian Disciples*. Grand Rapids: Zondervan, 2011.

House, H. Wayne. *Charts of Christian Theology and Doctrine*. Grand Rapids: Zondervan, 1992.

———. *Charts on Systematic Theology*. Grand Rapids: Kregel, 2006.

Kuyper, Abraham. *Principles of Sacred Theology*. Translated by J. H. DeVries. Grand Rapids: Eerdmans, 1968 (reprint; first published as *Encyclopedia of Sacred Theology* in 1898).

Machen, J. Gresham. *Christianity and Liberalism*. Grand Rapids: Eerdmans, 1923. (This 180-page book is, in my opinion, one of the most significant theological studies ever written. It gives a clear overview of major biblical doctrines and shows the vital differences with Protestant liberal theology at every point, differences that still confront us today. It is required reading in all my introductory theology classes.)

Morrow, T. W. "Systematic Theology." In *NDT1*, 671.

Poythress, Vern. *Symphonic Theology: The Validity of Multiple Perspectives in Theology*. Grand Rapids: Zondervan, 1987.

Preus, Robert D. *The Theology of Post-Reformation Lutheranism: A Study of Theological Prolegomena*. 2 vols. St. Louis: Concordia, 1970.

Thornbury, Gregory Alan. "Prologomena: Introduction to the Task of Theology." In *A Theology for the Church*, edited by Daniel L. Akin et al., rev. ed., 3–70. Nashville: B&H, 2007.

Treier, D. J. "Systematic Theology." In *EDT3*, 853–55.

Vanhoozer, K. J. "Systematic Theology." In *NDT2*, 885–86.

Van Til, Cornelius. *In Defense of the Faith*, vol. 5, *An Introduction to Systematic Theology*. Philadelphia: Presbyterian and Reformed, 1976, 1–61, 253–62.

———. *The Defense of the Faith*. Philadelphia: Presbyterian and Reformed, 1955.

———. *Introduction to Systematic Theology: Prolegomena and the Doctrines of Revelation, Scripture, and God*. 2nd ed. Edited by William Edgar. Phillipsburg, NJ: P&R, 2007.

Vos, Geerhardus. "The Idea of Biblical Theology as a Science and as a Theological Discipline." In *Redemptive History and Biblical Interpretation*, ed. Richard Gaffin, 3–24. Phillipsburg, NJ: Presbyterian and Reformed, 1980 (article first published 1894).

Warfield, B. B. "The Indispensableness of Systematic Theology to the Preacher." In *Selected Shorter Writings of Benjamin B. Warfield*, ed. John E. Meeter, 2:280–88. Nutley, NJ: Presbyterian and Reformed, 1973 (article first published 1897).

———. "The Right of Systematic Theology." In *Selected Shorter Writings of Benjamin B. Warfield*, ed. John E. Meeter, 2:21–279. Nutley, NJ: Presbyterian and Reformed, 1973 (article first published 1896).

Wells, David. *No Place for Truth: Or Whatever Happened to Evangelical Theology?* Grand Rapids: Eerdmans, 1993.

Woodbridge, John D., and Thomas E. McComiskey, eds. *Doing Theology in Today's World: Essays in Honor of Kenneth S. Kantzer*. Grand Rapids: Zondervan, 1991.

Yarnell, M. B. "Systematic Theology, History of." In *NDT2*, 886–89.

## SCRIPTURE MEMORY PASSAGE

Students have repeatedly mentioned that one of the most valuable parts of any of their courses in college or seminary has been the Scripture passages they were required to memorize. "I have stored up your word in my heart, that I might not sin against you" (Ps. 119:11). In each chapter, therefore, I have included an appropriate memory passage so that instructors may incorporate Scripture memory into the course requirements wherever possible.

**Matthew 28:18–20:** And Jesus came and said to them, "All authority in heaven and on earth has been given to me. Go therefore and make disciples of all nations, baptizing them in the name of the Father and of the Son and of the Holy Spirit, teaching them to observe all that I have commanded you. And behold, I am with you always, to the end of the age."

# HYMN

Systematic theology at its best will result in praise. It is appropriate therefore at the end of each chapter to include a hymn related to the subject of that chapter. In a classroom setting, the hymn can be sung together at the beginning or end of class. Alternatively, an individual reader can sing it privately or simply meditate quietly on the words.

For almost every chapter the words of the hymns were found in *Trinity Hymnal*,[18] the hymnal of the Presbyterian Church in America and the Orthodox Presbyterian Church, but most of them are found in many other common hymnals. Unless otherwise noted,[19] the words of these hymns are now in public domain and no longer subject to copyright restrictions: therefore they may be freely copied for PowerPoint use or photocopied.

Why have I used so many old hymns? The great hymns of the church have a doctrinal richness and breadth that is still unequaled. But many contemporary worship songs also have beauty and rich content, so for this second edition of *Systematic Theology*, I have added (with much help from Chris Herrington) a contemporary worship song at the end of each chapter as well.

For this chapter, however, I found no hymn ancient or modern that thanked God for the privilege of studying systematic theology from the pages of Scripture. Therefore I have selected a hymn of general praise, which is always appropriate.

## "O for a Thousand Tongues to Sing"

This hymn by Charles Wesley (1707–88) begins by wishing for "a thousand tongues" to sing God's praise. Verse 2 is a prayer that God would "assist me" in singing his praise throughout the earth. The remaining verses give praise to Jesus (vv. 3–6) and to God the Father (v. 7).

*O for a thousand tongues to sing*
*My great Redeemer's praise,*
*The glories of my God and King,*
*The triumphs of His grace.*

*My gracious Master and my God,*
*Assist me to proclaim,*
*To spread through all the earth abroad,*
*The honors of Thy name.*

*Jesus! the name that charms our fears,*
*That bids our sorrows cease;*
*'Tis music in the sinner's ears,*
*'Tis life and health and peace.*

*He breaks the pow'r of reigning sin,*
*He sets the prisoner free;*
*His blood can make the foulest clean;*
*His blood availed for me.*

---

18. *Trinity Hymnal* (Philadelphia: Great Commission, 1990). This hymn book is completely revised from a similar hymnal of the same title published by the Orthodox Presbyterian Church in 1961.

19. Copyright restrictions still apply to the hymns in chapters 21, 37, and 5, and these may not be reproduced without permission from the owner of the copyright.

He speaks and, list'ning to His voice,
New life the dead receive;
The mournful, broken hearts rejoice;
The humble poor believe.

Hear him, ye deaf; his praise, ye dumb,
Your loosened tongues employ,
Ye blind, behold your Savior come;
And leap, ye lame, for joy.

Glory to God and praise and love
Be ever, ever giv'n
By saints below and saints above—
The church in earth and heav'n.

Author: Charles Wesley, 1739, alt.

## CONTEMPORARY WORSHIP SONG

### "O Praise The Name" (Anástasis)

I cast my mind to Calvary,
Where Jesus bled and died for me.
I see His wounds His hands His feet,
My Savior on that cursed tree.
His body bound and drenched in tears.
They laid Him down in Joseph's tomb.
The entrance sealed by heavy stone,
Messiah still and all alone.

*Chorus*
O praise the Name of the Lord our God,
O praise His Name forevermore!
For endless days we will sing Your praise,
Oh Lord, oh Lord our God!

Then on the third, at break of dawn,
The Son of heaven rose again.
O trampled death, where is your sting?
The angels roar for Christ the King!
He shall return in robes of white.
The blazing sun shall pierce the night,
And I will rise among the saints,
My gaze transfixed on Jesus' face.

Words by Benjamin Hastings, Dean
Ussher, and Marty Sampson[20]

# PART 1

# The Doctrine of the Word of God

# CHAPTER 2

# The Word of God

*What are the different forms of the Word of God?*

## EXPLANATION AND SCRIPTURAL BASIS

What is meant by the phrase "the Word of God"? Actually, there are several different meanings taken by this phrase in the Bible. It is helpful to distinguish these different senses clearly at the beginning of this study.

### A. "THE WORD OF GOD" AS A PERSON: JESUS CHRIST

Sometimes the Bible refers to the Son of God as "the Word of God." In Revelation 19:13, John sees the risen Lord Jesus in heaven and says, "The name by which he is called is The Word of God." Similarly, in the beginning of John's gospel we read, "In the beginning was the Word, and the Word was with God, and the Word was God" (John 1:1). It is clear that John is speaking of the Son of God here because in verse 14 he says, "And the Word became flesh and dwelt among us, and we have seen his glory, glory as of the only Son from the Father, full of grace and truth." These verses (and perhaps 1 John 1:1) are the only instances where the Bible refers to God the Son as "the Word" or "the Word of God," so this usage is not common. But it does indicate that among the members of the Trinity it is especially God the Son who, in his person as well as in his words, has the role of communicating the character of God to us and of expressing the will of God for us.

### B. "THE WORD OF GOD" AS SPEECH BY GOD

### 1. God's Decrees

Sometimes God's words take the form of powerful decrees that cause events to happen or even cause things to come into being. "And God said, 'Let there be light,' and there was light" (Gen. 1:3). God even created the animal world by speaking his powerful word: "And God said, 'Let the earth bring forth living creatures according to their kinds—livestock and creeping things and beasts of the earth according to their kinds.' And it was so" (Gen. 1:24). Thus, the psalmist can say, *"By the word of the LORD* the heavens were made, and by the breath of his mouth all their host" (Ps. 33:6).

These powerful, creative words from God are often called God's decrees.[1] A *decree* of

---

1. I am grateful to Professor John Frame for first making me aware of the four categories in this section and how the full authority of God applies to all four of them.

31

God is a word of God that causes something to happen. These decrees of God include not only the events of the original creation but also the continuing existence of all things, for Hebrews 1:3 tells us that Christ continually "upholds the universe by the word of his power."

## 2. God's Words of Personal Address

God sometimes communicates with people on earth by speaking directly to them. These can be called instances of God's Word of *personal address*. Examples are found throughout Scripture. At the very beginning of creation God speaks to Adam: "The LORD God commanded the man, saying, 'You may surely eat of every tree of the garden; but of the tree of the knowledge of good and evil you shall not eat, for in the day that you eat of it you shall surely die'" (Gen. 2:16–17). After the sin of Adam and Eve, God still comes and speaks directly and personally to them in the words of the curse (Gen. 3:16–19). Another prominent example of God's direct personal address to people on earth is found in the giving of the Ten Commandments: "*God spoke all these words*, saying, 'I am the LORD your God, who brought you out of the land of Egypt, out of the house of slavery. You shall have no other gods before me'" (Ex. 20:1–3). In the New Testament, at Jesus' baptism, God the Father spoke with a voice from heaven, saying, "This is my beloved Son, with whom I am well pleased" (Matt. 3:17).

In these and several other instances where God spoke words of personal address to individual people it was clear to the hearers that these were the actual words of God: they were hearing God's very voice, and they were therefore hearing words that had absolute divine authority and that were absolutely trustworthy. To disbelieve or disobey any of these words would have been to disbelieve or disobey God and therefore would have been sin.

Though the words of God's personal address are always seen in Scripture to be the actual words of God, they are *also "human" words* in that they are spoken in ordinary human language that is immediately understandable. The fact that these words are spoken in human language does not limit their divine character or authority in any way: they are still entirely the words of God, spoken by the voice of God himself.

Some theologians have argued that since human language is always in some sense "imperfect," any message that God addresses to us in human language must also be limited in its authority or truthfulness. But these passages and many others that record instances of God's words of personal address to individuals give no indication of any limitation of the authority or truthfulness of God's words when they are spoken in human language. Quite the contrary is true, for the words always place an absolute obligation on the hearers to believe them and to obey them fully. To disbelieve or disobey any part of them is to disbelieve or disobey God himself.

## 3. God's Words as Speech Through Human Lips

Frequently in Scripture God raises up prophets through whom he speaks. Once again, it is evident that although these are human words, spoken in ordinary human language by ordinary human beings, the authority and truthfulness of these words is in no way diminished: they are still completely God's words as well.

In Deuteronomy 18, God says to Moses:

> I will raise up for them a prophet like you from among their brothers. *And I will put my words in his mouth*, and he shall speak to them all that I command him. And whoever will not listen to my words that he shall speak in my name, I myself will require it of him. But the prophet who presumes to speak a word in my name that I have not commanded him to speak, or who speaks in the name of other gods, that same prophet shall die. (Deut. 18:18–20)

God made a similar statement to Jeremiah: "Then the LORD put out his hand and touched my mouth. And the LORD said to me, '*Behold, I have put my words in your mouth*'" (Jer. 1:9). God tells Jeremiah, "Whatever I command you, you shall speak" (Jer. 1:7; see also Ex. 4:12; Num. 22:38; 1 Sam. 15:3, 18, 23; 1 Kings 20:36; 2 Chron. 20:20; 25:15–16; Isa. 30:12–14; Jer. 6:10–12; 36:29–31, et al.). Anyone who claimed to be speaking for the Lord but who had not received a message from him was severely punished (Ezek. 13:1–7; Deut. 18:20–22).

Thus God's words spoken through human lips were considered to be just as authoritative and just as true as God's words of personal address. *There was no diminishing of the authority of these words* when they were spoken through human lips. To disbelieve or disobey any of them was to disbelieve or disobey God himself.

## 4. God's Words in Written Form (the Bible)

In addition to God's words of decree, God's words of personal address, and God's words spoken through the lips of human beings, we also find in Scripture several instances where God's words were put in *written form*. The first of these is found in the narrative of the giving of the two tablets of stone on which were written the Ten Commandments: "He gave to Moses, when he had finished speaking with him on Mount Sinai, the two tablets of the testimony, tablets of stone, written with the finger of God" (Ex. 31:18). "The tablets were the work of God, and the writing was the writing of God, engraved on the tablets" (Ex. 32:16; 34:1, 28).

Further writing was done by Moses:

> Then Moses wrote this law and gave it to the priests, the sons of Levi, who carried the ark of the covenant of the LORD, and to all the elders of Israel. And Moses commanded them, "At the end of every seven years . . . you shall read this law before all Israel in their hearing . . . that they may hear and learn to fear the LORD your God, and be careful to do all the words of this law, and that their children, who have not known it, may hear and learn to fear the LORD your God." (Deut. 31:9–13)

This book, which Moses wrote, was then deposited by the side of the ark of the covenant: "When Moses had finished *writing the words of this law in a book* to the very end, Moses commanded the Levites who carried the ark of the covenant of the LORD, 'Take this Book of the Law and put it by the side of the ark of the covenant of the LORD your God, that it may be there for a witness against you'" (Deut. 31:24–26).

Further additions were made to this book of God's words. "*Joshua wrote these words* in the Book of the Law of God" (Josh. 24:26). God commanded Isaiah, "Now, go, *write it before them on a tablet and inscribe it in a book*, that it may be for the time to come as a witness forever" (Isa. 30:8). Once again, God said to Jeremiah, "*Write in a book* all the words that I have spoken to you" (Jer. 30:2; cf. Jer. 36:2–4, 27–31; 51:60). In the New Testament, Jesus promises his disciples that the Holy Spirit would bring to their remembrance the words which he, Jesus, had spoken (John 14:26; cf. 16:12–13). Paul can say that the very words he writes to the Corinthians are "a command of the Lord" (1 Cor. 14:37; cf. 2 Peter 3:2).

Once again it must be noted that these words are still considered to be God's own words, even though they are written down mostly by human beings and always in human language. Still, they are absolutely authoritative and absolutely true: to disobey them or disbelieve them is a serious sin and brings judgment from God (1 Cor. 14:37; Jer. 36:29–31).

Several benefits come from the writing down of God's words. First, there is a much *more accurate preservation* of God's words for subsequent generations. To depend on memory and the repeating of oral tradition is a less reliable method of preserving these words throughout history than is their recording in writing (cf. Deut. 31:12–13). Second, the *opportunity for repeated inspection* of words that are written down permits careful study and discussion, which leads to better understanding and more complete obedience. Third, God's words in writing are *accessible to many more people* than they are when preserved merely through memory and oral repetition. They can be inspected at any time by any person and are not limited in accessibility to those who have memorized them or those who are able to be present when they are recited orally. Thus the reliability, permanence, and accessibility of the form in which God's words are preserved are all greatly enhanced when they are written down. Yet there is no indication that their authority or truthfulness is diminished.

## C. The Focus of Our Study

Of all the forms of the Word of God,[2] the focus of our study in systematic theology is God's Word in written form, that is, the Bible. This is the form of God's Word that

---

2. In addition to the forms of God's Word mentioned above, God communicates to people through different types of "general revelation"—that is, revelation that is given not just to certain people but to all people generally. General revelation includes both the revelation of God that comes through nature (see Ps. 19:1–6; Acts 14:17) and the revelation of God that comes through the inner awareness of God's existence and inner sense of right and wrong in every person's heart (Rom. 2:15). These kinds of revelation are nonverbal in form, and I have not included them in the list of various forms of the Word of God discussed in this chapter. (See chapter 7, pp. 143–47, for further discussion of general revelation.)

is available for study, for public inspection, for repeated examination, and as a basis for mutual discussion. It tells us about and points us to the Word of God as a person, namely Jesus Christ, whom we do not now have present in bodily form on earth. Thus we are no longer able to observe and imitate his life and teachings firsthand.

The other forms of the Word of God are not suitable as the primary basis for the study of theology. We do not hear God's words of decree and thus cannot study them directly but only through observation of their effects. God's words of personal address are uncommon, even in Scripture. Furthermore, even if we did hear some words of personal address from God to ourselves today, we would not have certainty that our understanding of it, our memory of it, and our subsequent report of it was wholly accurate. Nor would we be readily able to convey to others the certainty that the communication was from God, even if it was. God's words as spoken through human lips ceased to be given when the New Testament canon was completed.[3] Thus, these other forms of God's words are inadequate as a primary basis for study in theology.

It is most profitable for us to study God's words as written in the Bible. It is God's written Word that he commands us to study. The man is "blessed" who "meditates" on God's law "day and night" (Ps. 1:1–2). God's words to Joshua are also applicable to us: "This Book of the Law shall not depart from your mouth, but *you shall meditate on it day and night*, so that you may be careful to do according to all that is written in it. For then you will make your way prosperous, and then you will have good success" (Josh. 1:8). It is the Word of God in the form of written Scripture that is "breathed out by God" and is "profitable for teaching, for reproof, for correction, and for training in righteousness" (2 Tim. 3:16).

## QUESTIONS FOR PERSONAL APPLICATION

1. Do you think you would pay more attention if God spoke to you from heaven or through the voice of a living prophet than if he spoke to you from the written words of Scripture? Would you believe or obey such words more readily than you do Scripture? Do you think your present level of response to the written words of Scripture is an appropriate one? What positive steps can you take to make your attitude toward Scripture more like the kind of attitude God wants you to have?

2. When you think about the many ways in which God speaks and the frequency with which God communicates with his creatures through these means, what conclusions might you draw concerning the nature of God and the things that bring delight to him?

---

3. See chapter 3, pp. 47–57, on the canon of Scripture. For a discussion of the nature of contemporary Christian prophecy, see chapter 53, pp. 1303–13.

# BIBLIOGRAPHY

(For an explanation of this bibliography see the note on the bibliography to chapter 1, pp. 23–24. Complete bibliographical data may be found on pp. 1489–96.) The subject of this chapter has not been treated explicitly in many systematic theologies, but similar material is often covered in the section on the authority of the Word of God; see the bibliography at the end of chapter 4 for that subject.

## SECTIONS IN EVANGELICAL SYSTEMATIC THEOLOGIES

### 1. Anglican (Episcopalian)
1882–92 . . . . . Litton, 9–10
2001 . . . . . . . . Packer, 3–6
2013 . . . . . . . . Bird, 62–70
2017 . . . . . . . . Bray, 137–48

### 2. Arminian (Wesleyan or Methodist)
1940 . . . . . . . . Wiley, 1:124–65
1992 . . . . . . . . Oden, 1:330–35, 345–51,
            379–82
2002 . . . . . . . . Cottrell, 23–28

### 3. Baptist
1990–95 . . . . . Garrett, 1:105–212
2007 . . . . . . . . Akin, 118–175
2013 . . . . . . . . Erickson, 121–42, 143–67,
            168–87, 210–29

### 4. Dispensational
2002–2005 . . Geisler, 1:229–43
2017 . . . . . . . . MacArthur and Mayhue,
            69–142

### 5. Lutheran
(no explicit treatment)

### 6. Reformed (or Presbyterian)
1679–85 . . . . . Turretin, *IET*, 1:55–61
1894 . . . . . . . . Shedd, 85–124
1906–11 . . . . Bavinck, *RD*, 1:283–300,
            301–22, 323–51, 401–2
1998 . . . . . . . . Reymond, 3–24
2008 . . . . . . . . Van Genderen and Velema,
            58–116
2011 . . . . . . . . Horton, 151–219
2013 . . . . . . . . Culver, xvi–xvii
2013 . . . . . . . . Frame, 519–693
2016 . . . . . . . . Allen and Swain, 30–56
2017 . . . . . . . . Barrett, 145–88
2019 . . . . . . . . Letham, 41–65

### 7. Renewal (or charismatic/Pentecostal)
1993 . . . . . . . . Menzies and Horton, 15–40
1995 . . . . . . . . Horton, 61–116
2008 . . . . . . . . Duffield and Van Cleave, 5–8

## SECTIONS IN REPRESENTATIVE ROMAN CATHOLIC SYSTEMATIC THEOLOGIES

### 1. Roman Catholic: Traditional
1955 . . . . . . . . Ott (no explicit treatment)

### 2. Roman Catholic: Post-Vatican II
2012 . . . . . . . . *CCC*, paragraphs 101–41

## OTHER WORKS

Cameron, Nigel M. de S. "Bible, Authority of the." In *BTDB*, 55–58.

Carson, D. A., ed. *The Enduring Authority of the Christian Scriptures*. Grand Rapids: Eerdmans, 2016.

Fanning, B. M. "Word." In *NDBT*, 848–53.

———. "Bible, Inspiration of the." In *BTDB*, 60–61.

———. "Revelation, Idea of." In *BTDB*, 679–682.

Frame, John M. *The Doctrine of the Word of God.* Vol. 4. Phillipsburg, NJ: P&R, 2010.

Holmes, S. R. "Revelation." In *NDT2*, 770–73.

Kline, Meredith. *The Structure of Biblical Authority.* Grand Rapids: Eerdmans, 1972.

Kuyper, Abraham. *Principles of Sacred Theology.* Translated by J. H. de Vries. Grand Rapids: Eerdmans, 1968, 405–12 (originally published as *Encyclopedia of Sacred Theology* in 1898).

Lillback, Peter A., and Richard B. Gaffin, eds. *Thy Word Is Still Truth: Essential Writings on the Doctrine of Scripture from the Reformation to Today.* Phillipsburg, NJ: P&R, 2013.

McDonald, H. D. *Theories of Revelation: An Historical Study, 1860–1960.* Grand Rapids: Baker, 1979.

———. "Word, Word of God, Word of the Lord." In *EDT3*, 945–47.

McKim, D. K., and P. S. Chung. "Revelation and Scripture." In *GDT*, 758–67.

McRay, John. "Bible, Canon of the." In *BTDB*, 58–60.

Meadors, Gary T. "Scripture, Unity and Diversity of." In *BTDB*, 715–18.

Meadowcroft, T. J. *The Message of the Word of God: The Glory of God Made Known.* Downers Grove, IL: InterVarsity Press, 2011.

Packer, J. I. "Scripture." In *NDT2*, 821–25.

Pinnock, C. H. "Revelation." In *NDT1*, 585–87.

Pyne, Robert A. *Humanity & Sin: The Creation, Fall, and Redemption of Humanity.* Nashville: Word, 1999.

Vos, Geerhardus. *Biblical Theology: Old and New Testaments.* Grand Rapids: Eerdmans, 1948, 28–55, 321–27.

Ward, Timothy. *Words of Life: Scripture As the Living and Active Word of God.* Downers Grove, IL: IVP Academic, 2009.

Witmer, John Albert. *Immanuel: Jesus Christ, Cornerstone of our Faith.* Nashville: Word, 1998.

## SCRIPTURE MEMORY PASSAGE

**Psalm 1:1–2:**

*Blessed is the man*
*who walks not in the counsel of the wicked,*
*nor stands in the way of sinners,*

*nor sits in the seat of scoffers;*
*but his delight is in the law of the LORD,*
*and on his law he meditates day and night.*

## HYMN

**"Break Thou the Bread of Life"**

This hymn is a prayer asking the Lord to give us not physical bread but spiritual nourishment from the "bread of life," a metaphor referring both to the written Word of God ("the sacred page," v. 1) and to Christ himself, the "Living Word" (see vv. 1, 3).

*Break thou the bread of life, dear Lord, to me,*
*As thou didst break the loaves beside the sea;*
*Throughout the sacred page I seek thee, Lord,*
*My spirit pants for thee, O Living Word.*

*Bless thou the truth, dear Lord, to me, to me,*
*As thou didst bless the bread by Galilee;*
*Then shall all bondage cease, all fetters fall;*
*And I shall find my peace, my all in all.*

Thou art the bread of life, O Lord, to me,
Thy holy Word the truth that saveth me;
Give me to eat and live with thee above;
Teach me to love thy truth, for thou art love.

O send thy Spirit, Lord, now unto me,
That he may touch mine eyes, and make me see:
Show me the truth concealed within thy Word,
And in thy Book revealed I see the Lord.

Author: Mary A. Lathbury, 1877

## CONTEMPORARY WORSHIP SONG

### "Thy Word"

*Chorus*
*Thy Word is a lamp unto my feet,*
*And a light unto my path.*
*Thy Word is a lamp unto my feet,*
*And a light unto my path.*

*When I feel afraid,*
*And I think I've lost my way,*
*Still You're there right beside me.*
*Nothing will I fear*

*As long as You are near.*
*Please be near me to the end.*

*I will not forget,*
*Your love for me, and yet,*
*My heart forever is wandering.*
*Jesus be my guide*
*And hold me to Your side.*
*I will love You to the end.*

Words by Amy Grant, Music
by Michael W. Smith[4]

# CHAPTER 3

# The Canon of Scripture

*What belongs in the Bible and what does not belong?*

## EXPLANATION AND SCRIPTURAL BASIS

The previous chapter concluded that it is especially the written words of God in the Bible to which we are to give our attention. Before we can do this, however, we must know which writings belong in the Bible and which do not. This is the question of the canon of Scripture, which may be defined as follows: *the canon of Scripture is the list of all the books that belong in the Bible.*

We must not underestimate the importance of this question. The words of Scripture are the words by which we nourish our spiritual lives. Thus we can reaffirm the comment of Moses to the people of Israel in reference to the words of God's law: "For it is no empty word for you, *but your very life*, and by this word you shall live long in the land that you are going over the Jordan to possess" (Deut. 32:47).

To add to or subtract from God's words would be to prevent God's people from obeying him fully, for commands that were subtracted would not be known to the people, and words that were added might require extra things of the people which God had not commanded. Thus Moses warned the people of Israel, "You shall not *add to the word* that I command you, *nor take from it*, that you may keep the commandments of the LORD your God that I command you" (Deut. 4:2).

The precise determination of the extent of the canon of Scripture is therefore of the utmost importance. If we are to trust and obey God absolutely, we must have a collection of words that we are certain are God's own words to us. If there are any sections of Scripture about which we have doubts whether they are God's words or not, we will not consider them to have absolute divine authority, and we will not trust them as much as we would trust God himself.

### A. THE OLD TESTAMENT CANON

Where did the idea of a canon begin—the idea that the people of Israel should preserve a collection of written words from God? Scripture itself bears witness to the historical development of the canon. The earliest collection of written words of God was the Ten Commandments. The Ten Commandments thus form the beginning of the biblical canon. God himself wrote on two tablets of stone the words which he commanded his people: "He gave to Moses, when he had finished speaking with him on Mount Sinai, the two tablets of the testimony, tablets of stone, *written with the finger of God*" (Ex. 31:18). Again we read, "The tablets were the work of God, and *the writing was the writing of God*, engraved on the tablets" (Ex. 32:16; cf. Deut. 4:13; 10:4). The tablets were deposited in the ark of the covenant (Deut. 10:5) and constituted the terms of the covenant between God and his people.[1]

This collection of absolutely authoritative words from God grew in size throughout the time of Israel's history. Moses himself wrote additional words to be deposited beside the ark of the covenant (Deut. 31:24–26). The immediate reference is apparently to the book of Deuteronomy, but other references to writing by Moses indicate that the first four books of the Old Testament were written by him as well (see Ex. 17:14; 24:4; 34:27; Num. 33:2; Deut. 31:22). After the death of Moses, Joshua also added to the collection of written words of God: "Joshua wrote these words in the Book of the Law of God" (Josh. 24:26). This is especially surprising in light of the command not to add to or take away from the words which God gave the people through Moses: "You shall not add to the word that I command you, nor take from it" (Deut. 4:2; cf. 12:32). In order to have disobeyed such a specific command, Joshua must have been convinced that he was not taking it upon himself to add to the written words of God, but that God himself had authorized such additional writing.

Later, others in Israel, usually those who fulfilled the office of prophet, wrote additional words from God:

> Samuel told the people the rights and duties of the kingship, and he wrote them in a book and laid it up before the LORD. (1 Sam. 10:25)

> The acts of King David, from first to last, are written in the Chronicles of Samuel the seer, and in the Chronicles of Nathan the prophet, and in the Chronicles of Gad the seer. (1 Chron. 29:29)

> Now the rest of the acts of Jehoshaphat, from first to last, are written in the chronicles of Jehu the son of Hanani, which are recorded in the Book of the Kings of Israel. (2 Chron. 20:34; cf. 1 Kings 16:7 where Jehu the son of Hanani is called a prophet)

> Now the rest of the acts of Uzziah, from first to last, Isaiah the prophet the son of Amoz wrote. (2 Chron. 26:22)

---

1. See Meredith Kline, *The Structure of Biblical Authority* (Grand Rapids: Eerdmans, 1972), esp. 48–53 and 113–30.

> Now the rest of the acts of Hezekiah and his good deeds, behold, they are written in the vision of Isaiah the prophet, the son of Amoz, in the Book of the Kings of Judah and Israel. (2 Chron. 32:32)

> Thus says the LORD, the God of Israel: Write in a book all the words that I have spoken to you.[2] (Jer. 30:2)

The content of the Old Testament canon continued to grow until the time of the end of the writing process. If we date Haggai to 520 BC, Zechariah to 520–518 BC (with perhaps more material added after 480 BC), and Malachi around 435 BC, then we have an idea of the approximate dates of the last Old Testament *prophets*. Roughly coinciding with this period are the last books of Old Testament *history*—Ezra, Nehemiah, and Esther. Ezra went to Jerusalem in 458 BC, and Nehemiah was in Jerusalem from 445–433 BC.[3] Esther was written sometime after the death of Xerxes I (a.k.a. Ahasuerus) in 465 BC, and a date during the reign of Artaxerxes I (464–423 BC) is probable. Thus, after approximately 435 BC there were no further additions to the Old Testament canon. The subsequent history of the Jewish people was recorded in other writings, such as the books of the Maccabees, but these writings were not thought worthy to be included with the collections of God's words from earlier years.

When we turn to Jewish literature outside the Old Testament, we see that the belief that divinely authoritative words from God had ceased is clearly attested in several different strands of extrabiblical Jewish literature. In 1 Maccabees (about 100 BC) the author writes of the defiled altar, "So they tore down the altar and stored the stones in a convenient place on the temple hill until there should come a prophet to tell what to do with them" (1 Macc. 4:45–46 RSV). They apparently knew of no one who could speak with the authority of God as the Old Testament prophets had done. The memory of an authoritative prophet among the people was one that belonged to the distant past, for the author could speak of a great distress "such as had not been since the time that prophets ceased to appear among them" (1 Macc. 9:27 RSV; cf. 14:41).

Josephus (born c. AD 37/38) explained, "From Artaxerxes to our own times a complete history has been written, but has not been deemed worthy of equal credit with the earlier records, because of the failure of the exact succession of the prophets" (*Against Apion* 1.41; he identifies Artaxerxes as the Ahasuerus from the book of Esther in his *Jewish Antiquities* 11.184). This statement by the greatest Jewish historian of the first century AD shows that he knew of the later writings now considered part of the "Apocrypha," but that he (and many of his contemporaries) considered these other writings "not . . . worthy of equal credit" with what we now know as the Old

---

2. For other passages that illustrate the growth in the collection of written words from God see 2 Chron. 9:29; 12:15; 13:22; Isa. 30:8; Jer. 29:1; 36:1–32; 45:1; 51:60; Ezek. 43:11;

Dan. 7:1; Hab. 2:2. Additions to it were usually through the agency of a prophet.

3. See "Chronology of the Old Testament," in *IBD*, 1:277.

Testament Scriptures. There had been, in Josephus's view, no more "words of God" added to Scripture after about 435 BC.

In this same context, Josephus (writing in about AD 95) also indicated that there was a fixed number of books that the Jewish people counted as "Scripture," and that this number of books had been fixed for "long ages." He wrote,

> We do not possess myriads of inconsistent books, conflicting with each other. Our books, those which are justly accredited, are but two and twenty, and contain the record of all time.
>
> Of these, *five* are the books of Moses, comprising the laws and the traditional history from the birth of man down to the death of the lawgiver. This period falls only a little short of three thousand years. From the death of Moses until Artaxerxes, who succeeded Xerxes as king of Persia, the prophets subsequent to Moses wrote the history of the events of their own times in *thirteen* books. The remaining *four* books contain hymns to God and precepts for the conduct of human life.
>
> From Artaxerxes to our own time the complete history has been written, but has not been deemed worthy of equal credit with the earlier records, because of the failure of the exact succession of the prophets.
>
> We have given practical proof of our reverence for our own Scriptures. For, although *such long ages have now passed*, no one has ventured either to add, or to remove, or to alter a syllable; and it is an instinct with every Jew, from the day of his birth, to regard them as the decrees of God, to abide by them, and, if need be, cheerfully to die for them. (*Against Apion* 1:38–42).

But if our Old Testament today has thirty-nine books, why does Josephus only have twenty-two (five + thirteen + four)? The answer is that according to Jewish reckoning at that time, several books were combined and counted as one book, probably according to the following pattern:[4]

### Five books of Moses:
1. Genesis
2. Exodus
3. Leviticus
4. Numbers
5. Deuteronomy

---

4. I have taken this enumeration of Old Testament books from Henry St. John Thackeray, trans., *Josephus: The Life; Against Apion*, Loeb Classical Library (Cambridge, MA: Harvard University Press, 1926), 179. For a discussion of various explanations of the number of twenty-two canonical books given by Josephus, see Edmon L. Gallagher and John D. Meade, *The Biblical Canon Lists from Early Christianity: Text and Analysis* (Oxford: Oxford University press, 2017), 60n12 and 62n27.

***Thirteen historical books:***
1. Joshua
2. Judges-Ruth
3. 1–2 Samuel
4. 1–2 Kings
5. 1–2 Chronicles
6. Ezra-Nehemiah
7. Esther
8. Job
9. Isaiah
10. Jeremiah-Lamentations
11. Ezekiel
12. Daniel
13. The Twelve Minor Prophets (Hosea, Joel, Amos, Obadiah, Jonah, Micah, Nahum, Habakkuk, Zephaniah, Haggai, Zechariah, Malachi)

***Hymns and precepts for conduct:***
1. Psalms
2. Song of Solomon
3. Proverbs
4. Ecclesiastes

This is a significant statement regarding the extent of the canon as understood by Jewish leaders in the first century. Writing in approximately AD 95, Josephus said that no Jew has dared to alter a syllable of this fixed collection of books of "Scripture" for "long ages," by which in this context means the time of Esther ("Artaxerxes" = Ahasuerus, Est. 1:1). Josephus implied that the canon of Scripture acknowledged by the Jews was completed at the time of the book of Esther and had not changed since that day.

Rabbinic literature reflects a similar conviction in its repeated statement that the Holy Spirit (in the Spirit's function of inspiring prophecy) departed from Israel. "After the latter prophets Haggai, Zechariah, and Malachi had died, the Holy Spirit departed from Israel, but they still availed themselves of the *bath qôl*" (*Babylonian Talmud*, Yomah 9b, repeated in Sota 48b, Sanhedrin 11a, and Midrash Rabbah on Song of Songs, 8.9.3).[5]

The Qumran community (the Jewish sect that left behind the Dead Sea Scrolls) also awaited a prophet whose words would have authority to supersede any existing regulations (see 1 QS 9.11), and other similar statements are found elsewhere in ancient Jewish

---

5. That "the Holy Spirit" is primarily a reference to divinely authoritative prophecy is clear both from the fact that the *bath qôl* (a voice from heaven) is seen as a substitute for it, and from the very frequent use of "the Holy Spirit" to refer to prophecy elsewhere in Rabbinic literature.

literature (see 2 Baruch 85.3; Prayer of Azariah 15). Thus writings subsequent to about 435 BC were not accepted by the Jewish people generally as having equal authority with the rest of Scripture.

Both Jesus and the earliest generations of New Testament Christians accepted all the books found in the Hebrew Bible, no more and no less, as their "Old Testament" (see Paul's reference to the "old covenant" in 2 Cor. 3:14). One bit of evidence in support of this is that in the New Testament we have no record of any dispute between Jesus and the Jews over the extent of the canon. Apparently there was full agreement between Jesus and his disciples, on the one hand, and the Jewish leaders or Jewish people, on the other hand, that additions to the Old Testament canon had ceased after the time of Ezra, Nehemiah, Esther, Haggai, Zechariah, and Malachi. This fact is confirmed by the quotations of Jesus and the New Testament authors from the Old Testament. According to one count, Jesus and the New Testament authors quote various parts of the Old Testament Scriptures as divinely authoritative over 295 times,[6] but not once do they cite any statement from the books of the Apocrypha or any other writings as having divine authority.[7] The absence of any such reference to other literature as divinely authoritative, and the extremely frequent reference to hundreds of places in the Old Testament as divinely authoritative, gives strong confirmation to the fact that the New Testament authors agreed that the established Old Testament canon, no more and no less, was to be taken as God's very words.

What then shall be said about the Apocrypha, the collection of books included in the canon by the Roman Catholic Church but excluded from the canon by Protestantism?[8] These books were never accepted by the Jews as Scripture, but throughout the early history of the church there was a divided opinion on whether they should be part of Scripture or not. In fact, the earliest Christian evidence is decidedly against viewing the Apocrypha as Scripture, but the use of the Apocrypha gradually increased in some parts of the church until the time of the Reformation.[9] The fact that these books were included by Jerome in his Latin Vulgate translation of the Bible (completed in AD 404)

---

6. See Roger Nicole, "New Testament Use of the Old Testament," in *Revelation and the Bible*, ed. Carl F. H. Henry (London: Tyndale, 1959), 137–41.

7. Jude 14–15 does cite 1 Enoch 60.8 and 1.9, and Paul at least twice quotes pagan Greek authors (see Acts 17:28; Titus 1:12), but these citations are more for purposes of illustration than proof. Never are the works introduced with a phrase like "God says" or "Scripture says" or "it is written," a phrase that would imply the attribution of divine authority to the words cited. (It should be noted that neither 1 Enoch nor the authors cited by Paul are part of the Apocrypha.) No book of the Apocrypha is even mentioned in the New Testament, nor is any statement from the Apocrypha ever cited as authoritative Scripture.

8. The Apocrypha includes the following writings: 1 and 2 Esdras, Tobit, Judith, the Rest of Esther, the Wisdom of Solomon, Ecclesiasticus, Baruch (including the Epistle of Jeremiah), the Song of the Three Holy Children, Susanna, Bel and the Dragon, the Prayer of Manasseh, and 1 and 2 Maccabees. These writings are not found in the Hebrew Bible, but they were included with the Septuagint (the translation of the Old Testament into Greek, which was used by many Greek-speaking Jews at the time of Christ). A good modern translation is *The Oxford Annotated Apocrypha* (RSV), ed. Bruce M. Metzger (New York: Oxford University Press, 1965). Metzger includes brief introductions and helpful annotations to the books.

9. A detailed historical survey of the differing views of Christians regarding the Apocrypha is found in F. F. Bruce, *The Canon of Scripture* (Downers Grove, IL: InterVarsity Press, 1988), 68–97. An even more detailed study is found in Roger Beckwith, *The Old Testament Canon of the New Testament Church and Its Background in Early Judaism* (repr., Eugene,

gave support to their inclusion, even though Jerome himself said they were not "books of the canon" but merely "books of the church" that were helpful and useful for believers. The wide use of the Latin Vulgate translation in subsequent centuries guaranteed their continued accessibility, but the lack of any known Hebrew text behind most of them, and their exclusion from the Jewish canon, as well as the lack of their citation in the New Testament, led many to view them with suspicion or to reject their authority. For instance, the earliest Christian list of Old Testament books that exists today is by Melito, bishop of Sardis, writing about AD 170:[10]

> When I came to the east and reached the place where these things were preached and done, and learnt accurately the books of the Old Testament, I set down the facts and sent them to you. These are their names: five books of Moses, Genesis, Exodus, Numbers, Leviticus, Deuteronomy, Joshua the son of Nun, Judges, Ruth, four books of Kingdoms,[11] two books of Chronicles, the Psalms of David, the Proverbs of Solomon and his Wisdom,[12] Ecclesiastes, the Song of Songs, Job, the prophets Isaiah, Jeremiah, the Twelve in a single book, Daniel, Ezekiel, Ezra.[13]

It is noteworthy here that Melito names none of the books of the Apocrypha, but he includes all of our present Old Testament books except Esther.[14] The church historian Eusebius, writing in AD 325, also quotes Origen (who died AD 254) as affirming most of the books of our present Old Testament canon (including Esther), but no book of the Apocrypha is affirmed as canonical, and the books of Maccabees are explicitly said to be "outside of these [canonical books]."[15] Similarly, in AD 367, when the great church leader Athanasius, bishop of Alexandria, wrote his Paschal Letter, he listed all the books

---

OR: Wipf & Stock, 2008), esp. 338–433. Beckwith's book has established itself as the definitive evangelical work on the Old Testament canon. At the conclusion of his study Beckwith says, "The inclusion of various Apocrypha and Pseudepigrapha in the canon of the early Christians was not done in any agreed way or at the earliest period, but occurred in Gentile Christianity, after the church's breach with the synagogue, among those whose knowledge of the primitive Christian canon was becoming blurred." He concludes, "On the question of the canonicity of the Apocrypha and Pseudepigrapha the truly primitive Christian evidence is negative" (436–37).

10. From Eusebius, *Ecclesiastical History* 4.26.14. Eusebius, writing in AD 325, was the first great church historian. This quotation is from the translation by Kirsopp Lake, *Eusebius: The Ecclesiastical History*, 2 vols. (London: Heinemann; Cambridge, MA: Harvard, 1975), 1:393.

11. That is, 1 Samuel, 2 Samuel, 1 Kings, and 2 Kings.

12. This does not refer to the apocryphal book called the Wisdom of Solomon but is simply a fuller description of Proverbs. Eusebius notes in 4.22.9 that Proverbs was commonly called Wisdom by ancient writers.

13. Ezra would include both Ezra and Nehemiah, according to a common Hebrew way of referring to the combined books.

14. For some reason there was doubt about the canonicity of Esther in some parts of the early church (in the East but not in the West), but the doubts were eventually resolved, and Christian usage eventually became uniform with the Jewish view, which had always counted Esther as part of the canon, although it had been opposed by certain rabbis for their own reasons. (See the discussion of the Jewish view in Beckwith, *Canon*, 288–97.)

15. Eusebius, *Ecclesiastical History* 6.15.2. Origen died about AD 254. Origen names all the books of the present Old Testament canon except the twelve minor prophets (which would be counted as one book), but this leaves his list of "twenty-two books" incomplete at twenty-one, so apparently Eusebius's citation is incomplete, at least in the form we have it today. Eusebius himself elsewhere repeats the statement of the Jewish historian Josephus that the Scriptures contain twenty-two books, but nothing since the time of Artaxerxes (3.10.1–5), and this would exclude all of the Apocrypha.

of our present New Testament canon and all the books of our present Old Testament canon except Esther. He also mentioned some books of the Apocrypha such as the Wisdom of Solomon, the Wisdom of Sirach, Judith, and Tobit, and said these are "not indeed included in the Canon, but appointed by the Fathers to be read by those who newly join us, and who wish for instruction in the word of godliness."[16] However, other early church leaders did quote several of these books as Scripture.[17]

There are doctrinal and historical inconsistencies found in a number of books of the Apocrypha. E. J. Young notes:

> There are no marks in these books which would attest a divine origin. . . . Both Judith and Tobit contain historical, chronological and geographical errors. The books justify falsehood and deception and make salvation to depend upon works of merit. . . . Ecclesiasticus and the Wisdom of Solomon inculcate a morality based upon expediency. Wisdom teaches the creation of the world out of pre-existent matter (11:17). Ecclesiasticus teaches that the giving of alms makes atonement for sin (3:30). In Baruch it is said that God hears the prayers of the dead (3:4), and in I Maccabees there are historical and geographical errors.[18]

It is true that the Apocrypha was acknowledged as Scripture in three North African church councils, the Council of Hippo (393), and the Council of Carthage (397 and 419),[19] but these were regional councils, not ecumenical councils of all the churches like Nicaea or Chalcedon. However, these councils do indicate that the books of the Apocrypha were increasingly counted as part of Scripture. Gregg Allison points out that this was due to the immense influence of Jerome's *Latin Vulgate* translation of the Bible, which included the Apocrypha. Allison says, "As the Vulgate became the new Bible of the church, however, the Apocrypha was regarded as part of canonical Scripture."[20]

Still, it was not until 1546, at the Council of Trent, that the Roman Catholic Church officially declared the Apocrypha to be part of the canon (with the exception of 1 and 2 Esdras and the Prayer of Manasseh). It is significant that the Council of Trent was the response of the Roman Catholic Church to the teachings of Martin Luther and the rapidly spreading Protestant Reformation, and the books of the Apocrypha contain support for the Catholic teaching of prayers for the dead and justification by faith plus works, not by faith alone. In affirming the Apocrypha as within the canon, Roman Catholics would hold that the church has the authority to constitute a literary work

---

16. Athanasius, *Letter 39*, in *Nicene and Post Nicene Fathers*, 2nd ser., vol. 4, *Athanasius*, ed. Philip Schaff and Henry Wace (Grand Rapids: Eerdmans, 1978), 551–52.

17. See Metzger, *Apocrypha*, xii–xiii. Metzger notes that none of the early Latin and Greek church fathers who quoted from the Apocrypha as Scripture knew any Hebrew. Beckwith, *Canon*, 386–89, argues that the evidence of Christian writers

quoting the Apocrypha as Scripture is considerably less extensive and less significant than scholars often claim it to be.

18. E. J. Young, "The Canon of the Old Testament," in *Revelation and the Bible*, 167–68.

19. See Gregg Allison, *Historical Theology* (Grand Rapids: Zondervan, 2011), 50.

20. Ibid.

as "Scripture," while Protestants have held that the church cannot make something to be Scripture, but can only recognize what God has already caused to be written as his own words.[21] (One analogy here would be to say that a police investigator can recognize counterfeit money as counterfeit and can recognize genuine money as genuine, but he cannot make counterfeit money to be genuine, nor can any declaration by any number of officers make counterfeit money to be something it is not. Only the official treasury of a nation can make money that is real money; similarly, only God can make words to be his very words and worthy of inclusion in Scripture.)

Thus the writings of the Apocrypha should not be regarded as part of Scripture: (1) they do not claim for themselves the same kind of authority as the Old Testament writings; (2) they were not regarded as God's words by the Jewish people from whom they originated; (3) they were not considered to be Scripture by Jesus or the New Testament authors; and (4) they contain teachings inconsistent with the rest of the Bible. We must conclude that they are merely human words, not God-breathed words like the words of Scripture. They do have value for historical and linguistic research, and they contain a number of helpful stories about the courage and faith of many Jews during the period after the Old Testament ends, but they have never been part of the Old Testament canon, and they should not be thought of as part of the Bible. Therefore, they have no binding authority for the thought or life of Christians today.

In conclusion, with regard to the canon of the Old Testament, Christians today should have no worry that anything needed has been left out or that anything that is not God's words has been included.

## B. The New Testament Canon

The development of the New Testament canon begins with the writings of the apostles. It should be remembered that the writing of Scripture primarily occurs in connection with God's great acts in redemptive history. The Old Testament records and interprets for us the creation of the world, the calling of Abraham and the lives of his descendants, the exodus from Egypt and the wilderness wanderings, the establishment of God's people in the land of Canaan, the establishment of the monarchy, and the Exile and return from captivity. Each of these great acts of God in history is interpreted for us in God's own words in Scripture. The Old Testament closes with the expectation of the Messiah to come (Mal. 3:1–4; 4:1–6). The next stage in redemptive history is the coming of the Messiah, and it is not surprising that no further Scripture would be written until this next and greatest event in the history of redemption occurred.

---

21. It should be noted that Roman Catholics use the term *deuterocanonical* rather than *apocryphal* to refer to these books. They understand this to mean "later added to the canon" (the prefix *deutero-* means "second").

This is why the New Testament consists of the writings of the apostles.[22] It is primarily the apostles who are given the ability from the Holy Spirit to recall accurately the words and deeds of Jesus and to interpret them rightly for subsequent generations.

Jesus promised this empowering to his disciples (who were called apostles after the resurrection) in John 14:26: "But the Helper, the Holy Spirit, whom the Father will send in my name, he will teach you all things and bring to your remembrance all that I have said to you." Similarly, Jesus promised further revelation of truth from the Holy Spirit when he told his disciples, "When the Spirit of truth comes, he will guide you into all the truth, for he will not speak on his own authority, but whatever he hears he will speak, and he will declare to you the things that are to come. He will glorify me, for he will take what is mine and declare it to you" (John 16:13–14). In these verses the disciples are promised amazing gifts to enable them to write Scripture: the Holy Spirit would teach them "all things," would cause them to remember "all" that Jesus had said, and would guide them into "all the truth."

Furthermore, those who have the office of apostle in the early church are seen to claim an authority equal to that of the Old Testament prophets, an authority to speak and write words that are God's very words. Peter encourages his readers to remember "the commandment of the Lord and Savior through your apostles" (2 Peter 3:2). To lie to the apostles (Acts 5:2) is equivalent to lying to the Holy Spirit (Acts 5:3) and lying to God (Acts 5:4).

This claim to be able to speak words that were the words of God himself is especially frequent in the writings of the apostle Paul. He claims not only that the Holy Spirit has revealed to him "what no eye has seen, nor ear heard, nor the heart of man imagined" (1 Cor. 2:9) but also that when he declares this revelation, he speaks it "in words not taught by human wisdom but taught by the Spirit, interpreting Spiritual things in Spiritual words" (1 Cor. 2:13, author's translation).[23]

Similarly, Paul tells the Corinthians, "If anyone thinks that he is a prophet, or spiritual, he should acknowledge that the things I am writing to you are a command of the Lord" (1 Cor. 14:37). Thus Paul claims that his directives to the church at Corinth are not merely his own but a command of the Lord. Later, in defending his apostolic office, Paul says that he will give the Corinthians "proof that Christ is speaking in me" (2 Cor. 13:3). Other similar verses could be mentioned (for example, Rom. 2:16; Gal. 1:8–9; 1 Thess. 2:13; 4:8, 15; 5:27; 2 Thess. 3:6, 14).

The apostles, then, have authority to write words that are God's own words, equal in truth status and authority to the words of the Old Testament Scriptures. They do this to

---

22. A few New Testament books (Mark, Luke, Acts, Hebrews, and Jude) were not written by apostles but by others closely associated with them and apparently authorized by them; see the discussion below, pp. 48–52.

23. This is my translation of the last phrase of 1 Cor. 2:13; see Wayne Grudem, "Scripture's Self-Attestation," in *Scripture and Truth*, ed. D. A. Carson and John Woodbridge

(Grand Rapids: Zondervan, 1983), 365n61. The ESV margin has "interpreting spiritual truths in spiritual language," and the NIV says, "explaining spiritual realities with Spirit-taught words." But the translation of the last phrase is not crucial to the main point: namely, that Paul speaks words taught by the Holy Spirit, a point that is affirmed in the first part of the verse, no matter how the second half is translated.

record, interpret, and apply to the lives of believers the great truths about the life, death, and resurrection of Christ.

It would not be surprising therefore to find some of the New Testament writings being placed with the Old Testament Scriptures as part of the canon of Scripture. In fact, this is what we find in at least two instances. In 2 Peter 3:16, Peter shows not only an awareness of the existence of written epistles from Paul but also a clear willingness to classify "all of his [Paul's] epistles" with "the other Scriptures." Peter says, "Just as our beloved brother Paul also wrote to you according to the wisdom given him, as he does in all his letters when he speaks in them of these matters. There are some things in them that are hard to understand, which the ignorant and unstable twist to their own destruction, *as they do the other Scriptures*" (2 Peter 3:15–16). The word translated "Scriptures" here is *graphē*, a word that occurs fifty-one times in the New Testament and that refers to the Old Testament Scriptures in every one of those occurrences. Thus the word *Scripture* was a technical term for the New Testament authors, and it was used only of those writings that were thought to be God's words and therefore part of the canon of Scripture. But in this verse, Peter classifies Paul's writings with the "other Scriptures" (meaning the Old Testament Scriptures). Paul's writings are therefore considered by Peter also to be worthy of the title "Scripture" and thus worthy of inclusion in the canon.

A second instance is found in 1 Timothy 5:17–18. Paul says, "Let the elders who rule well be considered worthy of double honor, especially those who labor in preaching and teaching. *For the Scripture says*, 'You shall not muzzle an ox when it treads out the grain,' and, 'The laborer deserves his wages.'" The first quotation from "Scripture" is found in Deuteronomy 25:4, but the second quotation, "The laborer deserves his wages," is found nowhere in the Old Testament. It does occur, however, in Luke 10:7 (with exactly the same words in the Greek text). So here we have Paul apparently quoting a portion of Luke's gospel[24] and calling it "Scripture," that is, something that is to be considered part of the canon.[25] In both of these passages (2 Peter 3:16 and 1 Tim. 5:17–18) we see evidence that very early in the history of the church the writings of the New Testament began to be accepted as part of the canon.

Because the apostles, by virtue of their apostolic office, had authority to write words of Scripture, the authentic written teachings of the apostles were accepted by the early church as part of the canon of Scripture. If we accept the arguments for the traditional views of authorship of the New Testament writings,[26] then we have most of the New

---

24. Someone might object that Paul could be quoting an oral tradition of Jesus' words rather than Luke's gospel, but it is doubtful that Paul would call any oral tradition "Scripture," since the word (Gk. *graphē*, "writing") is always in New Testament usage applied to written texts, and since Paul's close association with Luke makes it very possible that he would quote Luke's written gospel.

25. Luke himself was not an apostle, but his gospel is here accorded authority equal with that of the apostolic writings.

Apparently this was due to his very close association with the apostles, especially Paul, and the endorsement of his gospel by an apostle.

26. For a defense of traditional views of authorship of the New Testament writings, see D. A. Carson and Douglas Moo, *An Introduction to the New Testament*, 2nd ed. (Grand Rapids: Zondervan, 2005); also Donald Guthrie, *New Testament Introduction*, 4th ed. (Downers Grove, IL: InterVarsity Press, 1990).

Testament in the canon because of direct authorship by the apostles. This would include Matthew; John; Romans to Philemon (all of the Pauline Epistles); James;[27] 1 and 2 Peter; 1, 2, and 3 John; and Revelation.

This leaves five books, Mark, Luke, Acts, Hebrews, and Jude, which were not written by apostles. The details of the historical process by which these books came to be counted as part of Scripture by the early church are scarce, but Mark, Luke, and Acts were commonly acknowledged very early, probably because of the close association of Mark with the apostle Peter, and of Luke (the author of Luke-Acts) with the apostle Paul. Similarly, Jude apparently was accepted by virtue of the author's connection with James (see Jude 1) and the fact that he was the brother of Jesus.[28]

It is also very likely that the living apostles themselves gave guidance to the churches concerning which works they intended to be preserved and used as Scripture in the churches (see Col. 4:16; 2 Thess. 3:14; 2 Peter 3:16). There were apparently some writings that had absolute divine authority but that the apostles did not decide to preserve as "Scripture" for the churches (such as Paul's "previous letter" to the Corinthians [see 1 Cor. 5:9] and the letter that Paul apparently wrote to the Laodiceans [see Col. 4:16]). Moreover, the apostles did much more oral teaching, which had divine authority (see 2 Thess. 2:15) but was not written down and preserved as Scripture. Thus, in addition to apostolic authorship, preservation by the church under the direction of the apostles was necessary for a work to be included in the canon.

The acceptance of Hebrews as canonical was urged by many in the church on the basis of an assumed Pauline authorship. But from very early times there were others who rejected Pauline authorship in favor of one or another of several different suggestions. Origen, who died about AD 254, mentions various theories of authorship and concludes, "But who actually wrote the epistle, only God knows."[29] Thus the acceptance of Hebrews as canonical was not entirely due to a belief in Pauline authorship.[30] Rather, the intrinsic qualities of the book itself must have finally convinced early readers, as they continue to convince believers today, that whoever its human author may have been, its ultimate author can only have been God himself. The majestic glory of Christ shines forth from the pages of the epistle to the Hebrews so brightly that no believer who reads it seriously should ever want to question its place in the canon.

This brings us to the heart of the question of canonicity. For a book to belong in the canon, it is absolutely necessary that the book have divine authorship. If the words of the book are God's words (through human authors), and if the early church, under the

---

27. James seems to be considered an apostle in 1 Cor. 15:7 and Gal. 1:19. He also fulfills functions appropriate to an apostle in Acts 12:17; 15:13; 21:18; Gal. 2:9, 12; see p. 56 below.

28. The acceptance of Jude in the canon was slow, primarily because of doubts concerning his quotation of the noncanonical book of 1 Enoch.

29. Origen's statement is quoted in Eusebius, *Ecclesiastical History*, 6.25.14.

30. Even those who doubted Pauline authorship of Hebrews would have recognized it's connection to the circle of Paul's traveling companions because of the mention of "our brother Timothy" in Hebrews 13:23.

direction of the apostles, preserved the book as part of Scripture, then the book belongs in the canon. But if the words of the book are not God's words, it does not belong in the canon. The question of authorship by an apostle is important because it was primarily the apostles to whom Christ gave the ability to write words with absolute divine authority. If a writing can be shown to be by an apostle, then its absolute divine authority is automatically established.[31] Thus the early church automatically accepted as part of the canon the written teachings of the apostles which the apostles wanted preserved as Scripture.

But the existence of some New Testament writings that were not authored directly by apostles shows that there were others in the early church to whom Christ also gave the ability, through the work of the Holy Spirit, to write words that were God's own words and also therefore intended to be part of the canon. In these cases, the early church had the task of recognizing which writings had the characteristic of being God's own words (through human authors).

For some books (at least Mark, Luke, and Acts, and perhaps Hebrews and Jude as well), the church had, at least in some areas, the personal testimony of some living apostles to affirm the absolute divine authority of these books. For example, Paul would have affirmed the authenticity of Luke and Acts (and perhaps Hebrews), and Peter would have affirmed the authenticity of Mark as containing the gospel which he himself preached. In other cases, and in some geographical areas, the church simply had to decide whether it heard the voice of God speaking in the words of these writings. In these cases, the words of these books would have been *self-attesting*—that is, the words would have borne witness to their own divine authorship as Christians read them. This could well have been the case with Hebrews.

It should not surprise us that the early church was able to recognize Hebrews and other writings not written by apostles as God's very words. Had not Jesus said, "My sheep hear my voice" (John 10:27)? It should not be thought impossible or unlikely, therefore, that the early church would be able to use a combination of factors, including apostolic endorsement, consistency with the rest of Scripture, and the perception of a writing as "God-breathed" on the part of an overwhelming majority of believers, to decide that a writing was in fact God's words (through a human author) and therefore worthy of inclusion in the canon. Nor should it be thought unlikely that the church would be able to use this process over a period of time—as writings were circulated to various parts of the early church—and finally to come to a completely correct decision, without excluding any writings that were in fact "God-breathed" and without including any that were not.[32]

---

31. Of course, this does not mean that everything an apostle wrote, including even grocery lists and receipts for business transactions, would be considered Scripture. We are speaking here of writings done when acting in the role of an apostle and giving apostolic instructions to churches and to individual Christians (such as Timothy or Philemon).

32. I am not discussing at this point the question of textual variants (that is, differences in individual words and phrases that are to be found among the many ancient copies of Scripture that still exist). This question is treated in chapter 5, pp. 92–93.

The process of copying the New Testament books by hand, circulating them throughout hundreds of churches, and confirming their authenticity while rejecting spurious books that were circulating occurred slowly by modern standards, but eventually the churches throughout the ancient world reached agreement on the extent of the canon.[33] In AD 367 the Thirty-Ninth Paschal Letter of Athanasius contained an exact list of the twenty-seven New Testament books we have today. This was the list of books accepted by the churches in the eastern part of the Mediterranean world. Thirty years later, in AD 397, the Council of Carthage, representing the churches in the western part of the Mediterranean world, agreed with the eastern churches on the same list. These are the earliest final lists of our present-day canon.

Should we expect any more writings to be added to the canon? The opening sentence in Hebrews puts this question in the proper historical perspective, the perspective of the history of redemption: "*Long ago*, at many times and in many ways, God spoke to our fathers by the prophets, but *in these last days* he has spoken to us by his Son, whom he appointed the heir of all things, through whom also he created the world" (Heb. 1:1–2).

The contrast between the former speaking by the prophets and the recent speaking "in these last days" suggests that God's speech to us by his Son is the culmination of his speaking to mankind and is his greatest and final revelation to humankind in this period of redemptive history. The exceptional greatness of the revelation that comes through the Son, far exceeding any revelation in the old covenant, is emphasized again and again throughout chapters 1 and 2 of Hebrews. These facts all indicate that there is a finality to the revelation of God in Christ and that no more is to be expected once this revelation has been completed.

But where do we learn about this revelation through Christ? The New Testament writings contain the final, authoritative, and sufficient interpretation of Christ's work of redemption. The apostles and their close companions report Christ's words and deeds and interpret them with absolute divine authority. When they have finished their writing, there is no more to be added with the same absolute divine authority. Thus, once the writings of the New Testament apostles and their authorized companions are completed, we have in written form the final record of everything that God wants us to know about the life, death, and resurrection of Christ, and its meaning for the lives of believers for all time. Since this is God's greatest revelation for mankind, no more is to be expected once this is complete. In this way, then, Hebrews 1:1–2 shows us why no more writings can be added to the Bible after God's greatest revelation, his revelation in his only Son, a revelation which is recorded and explained in the books that make up the New Testament. Therefore the canon is now closed.

---

33. An excellent discussion of the details of this process in early church history is found in Allison, *Historical Theology*, 37–58.

A similar kind of consideration may be drawn from Revelation 22:18–19:

> I warn everyone who hears the words of the prophecy of this book: if anyone adds to them, God will add to him the plagues described in this book, and if anyone takes away from the words of the book of this prophecy, God will take away his share in the tree of life and in the holy city, which are described in this book.

The primary reference of these verses is clearly to the book of Revelation itself, for John refers to his writing as "the words of the prophecy of this book" in verses 7 and 10 of this chapter (and the entire book is called a prophecy in Rev. 1:3). Furthermore, the reference to "the tree of life and . . . the holy city, which are described in this book" indicates that the book of Revelation itself is intended.

It is, however, not accidental that this statement comes at the end of the last chapter of Revelation, and that Revelation is the last book in the New Testament. In fact, Revelation has to be placed last in the canon. For many books, their placement in the assembling of the canon is of little consequence. But just as Genesis must be placed first (for it tells us of creation), so Revelation must be placed last (for its focus is to tell us of the future and God's new creation). The events described in Revelation are historically subsequent to the events described in the rest of the New Testament and require that Revelation be placed where it is. Thus, it is not inappropriate for us to understand this exceptionally strong warning at the end of Revelation as applying in a secondary way to the whole of Scripture. Placed here, where it must be placed, the warning forms an appropriate conclusion to the entire canon of Scripture. Along with Hebrews 1:1–2 and the history-of-redemption perspective implicit in those verses, this broader application of Revelation 22:18–19 also suggests to us that we should expect no more Scripture to be added beyond what we already have.

How do we know, then, that we have the right books in the canon of Scripture we now possess? The question can be answered in two different ways. First, if we are asking upon what we should base our confidence, the answer must ultimately be that our confidence is based on the faithfulness of God. We know that God loves his people, and it is supremely important that God's people have his own words, for they are our life (Deut. 32:47; Matt. 4:4). They are more precious, more important to us than anything else in this world. We also know that God our Father is in control of all history, and he is not the kind of Father who will trick us or fail to be faithful to us or keep from us something we absolutely need.

The severity of the punishments in Revelation 22:18–19 that come to those who add to or take from God's words also confirms the importance for God's people of having a correct canon. There could be no greater punishments than these, for they are the punishments of eternal judgment. This shows that God himself places supreme value on our having a correct collection of God-breathed writings, no more and no less. In the light of this fact, could it be right for us to believe that God our Father, who controls all history, would allow all of his church for almost two thousand years to be deprived of something he himself values so highly and is so necessary for our spiritual lives?[34]

The preservation and correct assembling of the canon of Scripture should ultimately be seen by believers, then, not as part of church history subsequent to God's great central acts of redemption for his people, but as an integral part of the history of redemption itself. Just as God was at work in creation, in the calling of his people Israel, in the life, death, and resurrection of Christ, and in the early work and writings of the apostles, so too was God at work in the preservation and assembling together of the books of Scripture for the benefit of his people for the entire church age. Ultimately, then, we base our confidence in the correctness of our present canon on the faithfulness of God.

The question of how we know that we have the right books can, secondly, be answered in a somewhat different way. We might wish to focus on *the process by which we become persuaded* that the books we have now in the canon are the right ones. In this process two factors are at work: the activity of the Holy Spirit convincing us as we read Scripture for ourselves, and the historical data that we have available for our consideration.

As we read Scripture the Holy Spirit works to convince us that the books we have in Scripture are all from God and are his words to us. It has been the testimony of Christians throughout the ages that as they read the books of the Bible, the words of Scripture speak to their hearts as no other books do. Day after day, year after year, Christians find that the words of the Bible are indeed the words of God speaking to them with an authority, power, and persuasiveness that no other writings possess. Truly the Word of God is "living and active, sharper than any two-edged sword, piercing to the division of soul and of spirit, of joints and of marrow, and discerning the thoughts and intentions of the heart" (Heb. 4:12).

Yet the process by which we become persuaded that the present canon is right is also helped by historical data. Of course, if the assembling of the canon was one part of God's central acts in the history of redemption (as was stated above), then Christians today should not presume to take it upon themselves to attempt to add to or subtract from the books of the canon: the process was completed long ago. Nevertheless, a thorough investigation of the historical circumstances surrounding the assembling of the canon is helpful in confirming our conviction that the decisions made by the early church

---

34. This is of course not to affirm the impossible notion that God providentially preserves *every word* in *every copy* of every text, no matter how careless the copyist may be. In fact, we find that among the various ancient Hebrew and Greek manuscripts of the Bible (many of which are copies of copies of copies), there are numerous small differences in wording due to copyists mistakes. These differences are called "textual variants," and the academic study of these variants is called "textual criticism." For our purposes at this point, it is important to state that in God's good providence there is no significantly attested textual variant that would change any point of Christian doctrine or ethics, so faithfully has the text been transmitted and preserved. However, we must also say clearly that there are a number of differing words in the different ancient manuscripts of the Bible that are preserved today. The question of textual variants within the surviving manuscripts of the books that belong in the canon is discussed in chapter 5, pp. 92–93.

were correct decisions. Some of this historical data has been mentioned in the preceding pages. More detailed data is available for those who wish to pursue more specialized investigations.[35]

Yet one further historical fact should be mentioned. Today there exist no strong candidates for addition to the canon and no strong objections to any book presently in the canon. Of those writings that some in the early church wanted to include in the canon, it is safe to say that there are none that present-day evangelicals would want to include. Some of the very early writers distinguished themselves quite clearly from the apostles and their writings from the writings of the apostles, showing that they knew that their own writings did not belong in the New Testament. Ignatius, for example, about AD 110, said, "I do not order you as did Peter and Paul; *they were apostles,* I am a convict; they were free, I am even until now a slave" (Ignatius, *To the Romans,* 4.3; compare the attitude toward the apostles in 1 Clement 42:1, 2; 44:1–2 [AD 95]; Ignatius, *To the Magnesians,* 7:1; 13:1–2, et al.).

Even those writings that were for a time thought by some to be worthy of inclusion in the canon contain doctrinal teaching that is contradictory to the rest of Scripture. "The Shepherd" of Hermas, for example, teaches "the necessity of penance" and "the possibility of the forgiveness of sins at least once after baptism. . . . The author seems to identify the Holy Spirit with the Son of God before the Incarnation, and to hold that the Trinity came into existence only after the humanity of Christ had been taken up into heaven."[36]

The *Gospel of Thomas,* which for a time was held by some to belong to the canon, ends with the following absurd statement (par. 114):

> Simon Peter said to them: "Let Mary go away from us, for women are not worthy of life." Jesus said: "Lo, I shall lead her, so that I may make her a male, that she too may become a living spirit, resembling you males. For every woman who makes herself a male will enter the kingdom of heaven."[37]

All other existing documents that had in the early church any possibility of inclusion in the canon are similar to these in that they either contain explicit disclaimers of canonical status or include some doctrinal aberrations that clearly make them unworthy

35. A helpful recent survey of this field is David Dunbar, "The Biblical Canon," in *Hermeneutics, Authority, and Canon,* ed. D. A. Carson and John Woodbridge (Grand Rapids: Zondervan, 1986), 295–360. In addition, here are some excellent longer studies: Roger Beckwith, *The Old Testament Canon of the New Testament Church and Its Background in Early Judaism* (London: SPCK, 1985; Grand Rapids: Eerdmans, 1986; repr., Wipf & Stock, 2008); Bruce Metzger, *The Canon of the New Testament: Its Origin, Development, and Significance* (Oxford: Clarendon; New York: Oxford University Press, 1987); F. F. Bruce, *The Canon of Scripture* (Downers Grove, IL: InterVarsity Press, 1988); Michael Kruger, *Canon Revisited: Establishing the Origins and Authority of the New Testament Books* (Wheaton, IL: Crossway, 2012); Kruger, *The Question of Canon: Challenging the Status Quo in the New Testament Debate* (Downers Grove, IL: IVP Academic, 2013).

36. *ODCC,* 764.

37. This document was not written by Thomas the apostle. Current scholarly opinion attributes it to an unknown author in the second century AD who used Thomas's name.

of inclusion in the Bible. Even if these early writings come from a very early date (such as the *Didache*), that alone does not prove that they were authorized by the apostles, that they should be used as a source of doctrine or practice today, or that they have the God-breathed quality of the genuine books of the New Testament.[38]

On the other hand, there are no strong objections to any book currently in the canon. In the case of several New Testament books that were slow to gain approval by the whole church (books such as 2 Peter or 2 and 3 John), much of the early hesitancy over their inclusion can be attributed to the fact that they were not initially circulated very widely and that full knowledge of the contents of all the New Testament writings spread through the church rather slowly. (Martin Luther's hesitancies concerning James are quite understandable in view of the doctrinal controversy in which he was engaged, but such hesitancy was certainly not necessary. The apparent doctrinal conflict with Paul's teaching is easily resolved once it is recognized that James is using three key terms, *justification*, *faith*, and *works* in senses different from those with which Paul used them.)[39]

There is therefore historical confirmation for the correctness of the current canon. Yet it must be remembered in connection with any historical investigation that the work of the early church was not to *bestow* divine authority or even ecclesiastical authority upon some merely human writings but rather to *recognize* the divinely authored characteristic of writings that already had such a quality. This is because the ultimate criterion of canonicity is divine authorship, not human or ecclesiastical approval.

At this point someone may ask a hypothetical question about what we should do if another one of Paul's epistles were discovered, for example. Would we add it to Scripture? This is a difficult question because two conflicting considerations are involved. On the one hand, if a great majority of believers were convinced that this was indeed an authentic Pauline epistle, written in the course of Paul's fulfillment of his apostolic office, then the nature of Paul's apostolic authority would guarantee that the writing

---

38. It is appropriate here to say a word about the writing called the *Didache*. Although this document was not considered for inclusion in the canon during the early history of the church, many scholars have thought it to be a very early document and some today quote it as if it were an authority on the teaching of the early church on the same level as the New Testament writings. I think this is a mistake. The *Didache* was first discovered in 1875 at a library in Constantinople but probably dates from the first or second century AD. Yet it contradicts or adds to the commands of the New Testament at many points. For example, Christians are told to let alms sweat in their hands until they know to whom they are giving (1.6); food offered to idols is forbidden (6.3); people are required to fast before baptism, and baptism must be done in running water (7.1–4); fasting is required on Wednesdays and Fridays but prohibited on Mondays and Thursdays (8.1); Christians are required to pray the Lord's Prayer three times a day (8.3); unbaptized persons are excluded from the Lord's Supper, and prayers unknown in

the New Testament are given as a pattern for celebrating the Lord's Supper (9.1–5); apostles are prohibited from staying in a city more than two days (11.5; but note that Paul stayed a year and a half in Corinth and three years in Ephesus!); prophets who speak in the Spirit cannot be tested or examined (11.7, in contradiction to 1 Cor. 14:29 and 1 Thess. 5:20–21); salvation requires perfection at the last time (16.2). Such a document, of unknown authorship, is hardly a reliable guide for the teachings and practices that were upheld by the apostles in the early church.

39. See R. V. G. Tasker, *The General Epistle of James*, TNTC (London: Tyndale, 1956), 67–71. Although Luther placed James near the end of his German translation of the New Testament, he did not exclude it from the canon, and he cited over half of the verses in James as authoritative in various parts of his writings. See Douglas Moo, *The Letter of James*, TNTC (Leicester: Inter-Varsity Press; Downers Grove, IL: InterVarsity Press, 1985), 18; see also pp. 100–117 on faith and works in James.

would be God's very words (as well as Paul's) and that its teachings would be consistent with the rest of Scripture. On the other hand, the fact that it was not preserved as part of the canon would indicate that it was not among the writings the apostles wanted the church to preserve as part of Scripture. Moreover, it must immediately be said that such a hypothetical question is just that: hypothetical. It is exceptionally difficult to imagine what kind of historical data might be discovered that could convincingly demonstrate to the church as a whole that a letter lost for over 1,900 years was genuinely authored by Paul, and it is more difficult still to understand how our sovereign God could have faithfully cared for his people for over 1,900 years and still allowed them to be continually deprived of something he intended them to have as part of his final revelation of himself in Jesus Christ. These considerations make it so highly improbable that any such manuscript would be discovered at some time in the future, that such a hypothetical question really does not merit further serious consideration.

In conclusion, are there any books in our present canon that should not be there? No. We can rest our confidence in this fact in the faithfulness of God our Father, who would not lead all his people for nearly two thousand years to trust as his Word something that is not. And we find our confidence repeatedly confirmed both by historical investigation and by the work of the Holy Spirit in enabling us to hear God's voice in a unique way as we read from every one of the sixty-six books in our present canon of Scripture.

But are there any missing books, books that should have been included in Scripture but were not? The answer must be no. In all known literature there are no candidates that even come close to Scripture when consideration is given both to their doctrinal consistency with the rest of Scripture and to the type of authority they claim for themselves (as well as the way those claims of authority have been received by other believers). Once again, God's faithfulness to his people convinces us that there is nothing missing from Scripture that God thinks we need to know for obeying him and trusting him fully. The canon of Scripture today is exactly what God wanted it to be, and it will stay that way until Christ returns.

## QUESTIONS FOR PERSONAL APPLICATION

1. Why is it important to your Christian life to know which writings are God's words and which are not? How would your relationship with God be different if you had to look for his words that were scattered among all the writings of Christians throughout church history? How would your Christian life be different if God's words were contained not only in the Bible but also in the official declarations of the church throughout history?

2. Have you had doubts or questions about the canonicity of any of the books of the Bible? What caused those questions? What should one do to resolve them?

3. Mormons and Jehovah's Witnesses, among others, have claimed present-day revelations from God that they count equal to the Bible in authority. What reasons can you give

## Special Terms

*Apocrypha*
*apostle*
*canon*
*canonical*
*covenant*
*God-breathed*
*history of
redemption*
*self-attesting*

to indicate the falsity of those claims? In practice, do these people treat the Bible as an authority equal to these other "revelations"?

4. If you have never read any parts of the Old Testament Apocrypha, perhaps you would want to read some sections.[40] Do you feel you can trust these writings in the same way you trust Scripture? Compare the effect these writings have on you with the effect Scripture has on you. You might want to make a similar comparison with some writings from a collection of books called the New Testament Apocrypha,[41] or perhaps with the *Book of Mormon* or the *Qur'an*. Is the spiritual effect of these writings on your life positive or negative? How does it compare with the spiritual effect the Bible has on your life?

## BIBLIOGRAPHY

(For an explanation of this bibliography see the note on the bibliography to chapter 1, pp. 23–24. Complete bibliographical data may be found on pp. 1489–96.)

In the "Other Works" section of this chapter's bibliography I have included some works written from a nonevangelical perspective because of their importance for investigating the historical data relevant to the question of canon.

### SECTIONS IN EVANGELICAL SYSTEMATIC THEOLOGIES

*1. Anglican (Episcopalian)*

1882–92 . . . . . Litton, 10–18

1930 . . . . . . . . Thomas, 101–15
2013 . . . . . . . . Bray, 137–48

*2. Arminian (Wesleyan or Methodist)*

1875–76 . . . . . Pope, 1:193–230
1940 . . . . . . . . Wiley, 1:185–214
1983 . . . . . . . . Carter, 1:291–94
1992 . . . . . . . . Oden, 1:331, 335–39

*3. Baptist*

1907 . . . . . . . . Strong, 145–72; 236–40
1976–83 . . . . . Henry, 2:69–76; 4:405–75
1987–94 . . . . . Lewis and Demarest, 1:147–48
1990–95 . . . . . Garrett, 1:137–52
2007 . . . . . . . . Akin, 164–71

---

40. See *The Oxford Annotated Apocrypha* (RSV). There is also a collection of nonbiblical writings from the time of the New Testament called "New Testament apocrypha" (see next note), but these are much less commonly read. When people speak of "the Apocrypha" without further specification, they are referring only to the Old Testament Apocrypha.

41. E. Hennecke, *New Testament Apocrypha*, ed. W. Schneemelcher; trans. and ed. R. McL. Wilson, 2 vols. (London: SCM, 1965). It should also be noted that some other, more

orthodox literature from the early church can be found conveniently in a collection of writings referred to as the "Apostolic Fathers." A good translation is found in Kirsopp Lake, trans., *The Apostolic Fathers*, Loeb Classical Library, 2 vols. (Cambridge, MA: Harvard University Press, 1912, 1913), but other useful translations are also available, including Michael W. Holmes, ed., *The Apostolic Fathers: Greek Texts and English Translations*, 3rd ed. (Grand Rapids: Baker, 2007).

## 4. *Dispensational*

1947 . . . . . . . . Chafer, 1:95–102, 124–28

1949 . . . . . . . . Thiessen, 50–61

1986 . . . . . . . . Ryrie, 105–9

2017 . . . . . . . . MacArthur and Mayhue,
119–26

2002–2005 . . Geisler, 1:514–40

## 5. *Lutheran*

1917–24 . . . . . Pieper, 1:330–48

## 6. *Reformed (or Presbyterian)*

1679–85 . . . . . Turretin, *IET*, 1:95–106,
112–16

1871–73 . . . . . Hodge, 1:152–53

1887–1921 . . . Warfield, *IAB*, 411–18

1894 . . . . . . . . Shedd, 146–52

1906–11 . . . . . Bavinck, *RD*, 1:393–401

1938 . . . . . . . . Berkhof, *Intro.*, 116–43

1998 . . . . . . . . Reymond, 60–70

2008 . . . . . . . . Van Genderen and Velema,
63–69

2011 . . . . . . . . Horton, 151–55

2013 . . . . . . . . Frame, 585–90

2016 . . . . . . . . Allen and Swain, 30–56

2017 . . . . . . . . Barrett, 145–88

2019 . . . . . . . . Letham, 186–90

## 7. *Renewal (or charismatic/Pentecostal)*

1993 . . . . . . . . Menzies and Horton, 28–40

1995 . . . . . . . . Horton, 78–81, 107–09

2008 . . . . . . . . Duffield and Van Cleave,
9–15

## SECTIONS IN REPRESENTATIVE ROMAN CATHOLIC SYSTEMATIC THEOLOGIES

## 1. *Roman Catholic: Traditional*

1955 . . . . . . . . Ott (no explicit treatment)

## 2. *Roman Catholic: Post–Vatican II*

1980 . . . . . . . . McBrien, 1:50–62, 201–43;
2:817–42

2012 . . . . . . . . *CCC*, paragraph 120

## OTHER WORKS

Allert, Craig D. *A High View of Scripture? The Authority of the Bible and the Formation of the New Testament Canon*. Grand Rapids: Baker Academic, 2007.

Allison, Gregg R. *Historical Theology: An Introduction to Christian Doctrine; A Companion to Wayne Grudem's* Systematic Theology. Grand Rapids: Zondervan, 2011, 37–58.

Beckwith, R. T. "The Canon of Scripture." In *NDBT*, 27–34.

———. "Canon of the Old Testament." In *IBD*, 1:235–38.

Beckwith, Roger. *The Old Testament Canon of the New Testament Church and Its Background in Early Judaism*. Grand Rapids: Eerdmans, 1985.

Bird, M. F. "Canon of Scripture" In *EDT3*, 156–58.

Birdsall, J. N. "Apocrypha." In *IBD*, 1:75–77.

———. "Canon of the New Testament." In *IBD*, 1:240–45.

Bruce, F. F. "*Canon*." In *DJG*, 93–100.

———. *The Canon of Scripture*. Downers Grove, IL: InterVarsity Press, 1988.

Carson, D. A., ed. *The Enduring Authority of the Christian Scriptures*. Grand Rapids: Eerdmans, 2016.

Carson, D. A., and John Woodbridge, eds. *Hermeneutics, Authority, and Canon*. Grand Rapids: Zondervan, 1986.

Dunbar, David G. "The Biblical Canon." In *Hermeneutics, Authority, and Canon*, edited by D. A. Carson and John Woodbridge. Grand Rapids: Zondervan, 1986.

Dockery, David S., and David P. Nelson. "Special Revelation." In *A Theology for the Church*, edited by Daniel L. Akin et al., 164–69. Nashville: B&H, 2007.

Evans, Craig A., and Emanuel Tov, eds. *Exploring the Origins of the Bible: Canon Formation in*

*Historical, Literary, and Theological Perspective.* Grand Rapids: Baker Academic, 2008.

Feinberg, John S. *Light in a Dark Place: The Doctrine of Scripture.* Foundations of Evangelical Theology Series. Wheaton, IL: Crossway, 2018.

Gallagher, Edmon L., and John D. Meade. *The Biblical Canon Lists from Early Christianity: Texts and Analysis.* New York: Oxford University Press, 2017.

Geisler, Norman L., and William E. Nix. *A General Introduction to the Bible.* Rev. ed. Chicago: Moody Publishers, 1986, 203–317.

Green, William Henry. *General Introduction to the Old Testament: The Canon.* New York: Scribner's, 1898.

Harris, R. Laird. "Chronicles and the Canon in New Testament Times." *JETS* 33, no. 1 (March 1990): 75–84.

———. *Inspiration and Canonicity of the Bible: An Historical and Exegetical Study.* Grand Rapids: Zondervan, 1989.

Hill, Charles E. *Who Chose the Gospels? Probing the Great Gospel Conspiracy.* Oxford: Oxford University Press, 2012.

Hixson, Elijah, and Peter J. Gurry, eds. *Myths and Mistakes in New Testament Textual Criticism.* Downers Grove, IL: IVP Academic, 2019.

Kline, Meredith G. *The Structure of Biblical Authority.* Grand Rapids: Eerdmans, 1972.

Kruger, Michael J. *Canon Revisited: Establishing the Origins and Authority of the New Testament Books.* Wheaton, IL: Crossway, 2012.

Leiman, S. Z. *The Canonization of Hebrew Scripture: The Talmudic and Midrashic Evidence.* Hamden, CT: Archon, 1976.

McDonald, Lee Martin. *The Biblical Canon: Its Origin, Transmission, and Authority.* 3rd ed. Peabody, MA: Hendrickson, 2007.

———. "Canon." In *DLNT*, 134–44.

———. *The Formation of the Biblical Canon.* 2 vols. London; New York: Bloomsbury T&T Clark, 2017.

McRay, John R. "Bible, Canon of the." In *BTDB*, 58–60.

Metzger, Bruce M. *The Canon of the New Testament: Its Origin, Development, and Significance.* Oxford: Clarendon; New York: Oxford University Press, 1987.

Packer, J. I. "Scripture." *NDT2*, 821–25.

Patzia, Arthur G. "Canon." In *DPL*, 85–92.

———. *The Making of the New Testament: Origin, Collection, Text & Canon.* Downers Grove, IL: InterVarsity Press, 1995.

Ridderbos, Herman N. *Redemptive History and the New Testament Scriptures.* Formerly, *The Authority of the New Testament Scriptures,* translated by H. D. Jongste, revised by Richard B. Gaffin Jr., 2nd ed. Phillipsburg, NJ: Presbyterian and Reformed, 1988.

Trafton, Joseph L. "Apocrypha." In *BTDB*, 30–32.

Trebolle Barrera, Julio C. *The Jewish Bible and the Christian Bible: An Introduction to the History of the Bible.* Leiden: Brill; Grand Rapids: Eerdmans, 1998.

Wegner, Paul D. *The Journey from Texts to Translations: The Origin and Development of the Bible.* Grand Rapids: Baker Academic, 2004.

Westcott, Brooke Foss. *The Bible in the Church: A Popular Account of the Collection and Reception of the Holy Scriptures in the Christian Churches.* First ed. with alterations. London: Macmillan, 1901.

Zahn, Theodor. *Geschichte des Neutestamentlichen Kanons.* 2 vols. Erlangen: Deichert, 1888–90. Reprint, Hildesheim and New York: Olms, 1975.

## SCRIPTURE MEMORY PASSAGE

**Hebrews 1:1–2:** Long ago, at many times and in many ways, God spoke to our fathers by the prophets, but in these last days he has spoken to us by his Son, whom he appointed the heir of all things, through whom also he created the world.

## HYMN

### "O Word of God Incarnate"

*O Word of God incarnate, O wisdom from on high,*
*O truth unchanged, unchanging, O light of our*
*    dark sky;*
*We praise thee for the radiance that from the*
*    hallowed page,*
*A lantern to our footsteps, shines on from age to age.*

*The church from her dear Master received the*
*    gift divine,*
*And still that light she lifteth o'er all the earth to*
*    shine.*
*It is the golden casket, where gems of truth are stored;*
*It is the heav'n-drawn picture of Christ, the*
*    Living Word.*

*It floateth like a banner before God's host unfurled;*
*It shineth like a beacon above the darkling world.*
*It is the chart and compass that o'er life's*
*    surging sea,*
*'Mid mists and rocks and quicksands, still guides,*
*    O Christ, to thee.*

*O make thy church, dear Savior, a lamp of*
*    purest gold,*
*To bear before the nations thy true light, as of old.*
*O teach thy wand'ring pilgrims by this their path*
*    to trace,*
*Till, clouds and darkness ended, they see thee face*
*    to face.*

Author: William Walsham How, 1867

## CONTEMPORARY WORSHIP SONG

### "I Exalt Thee"

*For Thou, O Lord, art high above all the earth.*
*Thou art exalted far above all gods.*
*For Thou, O Lord, art high above all the earth.*
*Thou art exalted far above all gods.*

*I exalt Thee, I exalt Thee,*
*I exalt Thee, O Lord.*
*I exalt Thee, I exalt Thee,*
*I exalt Thee, O Lord.*

*For Thou, O Lord, art high above all the earth.*
*Thou art exalted far above all gods.*

*For Thou, O Lord, art high above all the earth.*
*Thou art exalted far above all gods.*

*I exalt Thee, I exalt Thee,*
*I exalt Thee, O Lord.*
*I exalt Thee, I exalt Thee,*
*I exalt Thee, O Lord.*

*We exalt Thee, we exalt Thee,*
*We exalt Thee, O Lord.*
*We exalt Thee, we exalt Thee,*
*We exalt Thee, O Lord.*

Author: Pete Sanchez[42]

42. © 1977 Pete Sanchez Jr., Admin. by Gabriel Music Inc., PO Box 840999 Houston, TX 77284-0999. Used by permission.

# CHAPTER 4

# The Four Characteristics of Scripture: (1) Authority

*How do we know that the Bible is God's Word?*

In the previous chapter our goal was to determine which writings belong in the Bible and which writings do not. But once we have determined what the Bible is, our next step is to ask what the Bible is like—what are its characteristics? What does the whole Bible teach us about itself?

The major teachings of the Bible about itself can be classified into four characteristics (sometimes termed attributes): (1) the authority of Scripture; (2) the clarity of Scripture; (3) the necessity of Scripture; and (4) the sufficiency of Scripture.

With regard to the first characteristic, most Christians would agree that the Bible is our authority in some sense. But in exactly what sense does the Bible claim to be our authority? And how do we become persuaded that the claims of Scripture to be God's Word are true? These are the questions addressed in this chapter.

## EXPLANATION AND SCRIPTURAL BASIS

*The authority of Scripture means that all the words in Scripture are God's words in such a way that to disbelieve or disobey any word of Scripture is to disbelieve or disobey God.*

This definition may now be examined in its various parts.

### A. The Bible Claims that All Its Words Are God's Words
### 1. Hundreds of Verses Claim that the Bible's Words Are God's Words

Whether or not someone begins with a conviction that the Bible's words are God's words to us, every interested reader should at least acknowledge that the Bible frequently *claims* that its words are God's very words (as well as words that were written down by human authors).[1] Such claims are clearly evident from the text, whether a person first approaches the Bible believing those claims or not.

---

1. Of course, I do not mean to say that every word in Scripture was *audibly spoken* by God himself, since the Bible records the words of hundreds of different people, such as King David and Peter and even Satan himself. But I do mean that even the quotations of other people are *God's* reports of what they said, and, rightly interpreted in their contexts, they come to us with God's authority.

In the Old Testament, this is frequently seen in the introductory phrase, "Thus says the LORD," which appears hundreds of times (it is found 417 times in the ESV text of the Old Testament). In the world of the Old Testament, this phrase would have been recognized as identical in form to the phrase "Thus says king . . . ," which was used to preface the edict of a king to his subjects, an edict that could not be challenged or questioned but that simply had to be obeyed.[2] Therefore, when the prophets say, "Thus says the Lord," they are claiming to be messengers from the sovereign King of Israel, namely, God himself, and they are claiming that their words are the absolutely authoritative words of God. When a prophet spoke in God's name in this way, every word he spoke had to come from God, or he would be a false prophet (cf. Num. 22:38; Deut. 18:18–20; Jer. 1:9; 14:14; 23:16–22; 29:31–32; Ezek. 2:7; 13:1–16).

Furthermore, there are several verses where God is said to speak "through" the prophet (1 Kings 14:18; 16:12, 34; 2 Kings 9:36; 14:25; Jer. 37:2; Zech. 7:7, 12). What the prophet says in God's name, God says (1 Kings 13:26 with v. 21; 1 Kings 21:19 with 2 Kings 9:25–26; Hag. 1:12; cf. 1 Sam. 15:3, 18). In these and other instances in the Old Testament, words that the prophets spoke can equally be referred to as words that God himself spoke. To disbelieve or disobey anything a prophet says is to disbelieve or disobey God himself (Deut. 18:19; 1 Sam. 10:8; 13:13–14; 15:3, 19, 23; 1 Kings 20:35, 36).

These specific verses of course do not claim that *all* the words in the Old Testament are God's words, for these verses themselves are referring only to specific sections of spoken or written words in the Old Testament. But the cumulative force of these passages, including the hundreds of passages that begin "Thus says the Lord," is to demonstrate that *within the Old Testament we have written records of words that are claimed to be God's own words.* These words when written down constitute large sections of the Old Testament.

In the New Testament, a number of passages indicate that all of the Old Testament writings are thought of as God's words. As 2 Timothy 3:16 says, "All Scripture is breathed out by God and profitable for teaching, for reproof, for correction, and for training in righteousness."[3] Here "Scripture" (*graphē*) must refer to the Old Testament, for that is what the word *graphē* refers to in every one of its fifty-one occurrences in the New Testament.[4] Furthermore, the "sacred writings" of the Old Testament are what Paul[5] has just referred to in verse 15.

---

2. See Wayne Grudem, *The Gift of Prophecy in 1 Corinthians* (Lanham, MD: University Press of America, 1982), 12–13; also Wayne Grudem, "Scripture's Self-Attestation and the Problem of Formulating a Doctrine of Scripture," in *Scripture and Truth*, ed. D. A. Carson and J. Woodbridge (Grand Rapids: Zondervan, 1983), 21–22.

3. Some have suggested an alternative translation, namely, "Every God-breathed Scripture is also profitable for teaching." However, this translation is highly unlikely because it makes the *kai* ("also") extremely awkward in the Greek sentence. In coherent speech, one must say that something has one characteristic

before saying that it *also* has another characteristic. The *also* must indicate an addition to something that has previously been predicated. Thus *theopneustos* ("God-breathed") and *ōphelimos* ("profitable") are both best understood as predicate adjectives, and the best translation is, "All Scripture is God-breathed and is profitable for teaching."

4. In at least two cases, 1 Tim. 5:18 and 2 Peter 3:16, *graphē* also includes some of the New Testament writings along with the Old Testament writings that it is referring to (see discussion below).

5. I assume Pauline authorship of 1 and 2 Timothy and Titus throughout this book. For arguments defending Pauline

Paul here affirms that all of the Old Testament writings are *theopneustos*, "breathed out by God." Since it is *writings* that are said to be "breathed out," this breathing must be understood as a metaphor for speaking the words of Scripture. This verse thus states in brief form what was evident in many passages in the Old Testament: Paul is claiming that the Old Testament writings are God's Word in written form. For every word of the Old Testament, God is the one who spoke (and still speaks) it, although God used human agents to write these words down.[6]

A similar indication of the character of all Old Testament writings as God's words is found in 2 Peter 1:21. Speaking of the prophecies of Scripture (v. 20), which means at least the Old Testament Scriptures to which Peter encourages his readers to give careful attention (v. 19), Peter says that no Old Testament prophecy was ever "produced by the will of man," but that "men spoke from God as they were carried along by the Holy Spirit." It is not Peter's intention to deny completely human volition or personality in the writing of Scripture (he says that the men "spoke"). Instead, he claims that the ultimate source of every prophecy was never a man's decision about what he wanted to write but rather the Holy Spirit's action in the prophet's life, carried out in ways unspecified here (or, in fact, elsewhere in Scripture). Therefore, Peter is also saying that all of the Old Testament prophecies (and in light of vv. 19–20 this probably includes all of the written Scripture of the Old Testament) are spoken "from God"—that is, they are God's words.

Many other New Testament passages speak in similar ways about sections of the Old Testament. In Matthew 1:22, Isaiah's words in Isaiah 7:14 are cited as "what *the Lord had spoken* by the prophet." In Matthew 4:4 Jesus says to the devil, "Man shall not live by bread alone, but by *every word that comes from the mouth of God*." In the context of Jesus' repeated citations from Deuteronomy to answer every temptation, Jesus is saying that the words that proceed "from the mouth of God" are the written Scriptures of the Old Testament.

In Matthew 19:5, Jesus quotes the words of Genesis 2:24 as words that God "said." This is important because nothing in Genesis 2:24 explicitly claims that the words are God's words—they are just words of the unnamed narrator of these events in the garden of Eden. But Jesus affirms that God both "made them male and female" (Matt. 19:4)

---

authorship see George W. Knight III, *The Pastoral Epistles*, NIGTC (Grand Rapids: Eerdmans; Carlisle: Paternoster, 1992), 4–54; William Mounce, *Pastoral Epistles*, WBC (Nashville: Nelson, 2000), lxxxiii–cxxx; D. A. Carson and Douglas Moo, *An Introduction to the New Testament* (Grand Rapids: Zondervan, 2005), 554–68.

6. Older systematic theologies used the words *inspired* and *inspiration* to speak of the fact that the words of Scripture are spoken by God. This terminology was based especially on an older translation of 2 Tim. 3:16, which said, "All scripture is given by inspiration of God" (KJV). However, the word *inspiration* has such a weak sense in ordinary usage today (every poet or songwriter claims to be "inspired" to write, and even athletes are said to give "inspired" performances) that I have not used it in this text. The ESV translation "breathed out by God" is preferable (the NIV rendering "God-breathed" is similar). The older phrase *"plenary* inspiration" meant that *all* the words of Scripture are God's words (the word *plenary* means "full"), a fact that I affirm in this chapter without using the actual phrase.

*"and said"* (Matt. 19:5) the words of Genesis 2:24. This suggests that Jesus could quote any passage from anywhere in the Old Testament and claim that "God said" the words of that passage, whether or not the Old Testament passage contain the words "thus says the Lord" or any similar claim.

In Mark 7:9–13, the same Old Testament passage can be called interchangeably "the commandment of God," or what "Moses said," or "the word of God." In Acts 1:16, the words of Psalms 69 and 109 are said to be words that *"the Holy Spirit spoke* beforehand by the mouth of David." Words of Scripture are thus said to be *spoken* by the Holy Spirit. In Acts 2:16–17, in quoting "what was uttered through the prophet Joel" in Joel 2:28–32, Peter inserts *"God declares,"* thus attributing to God words written by Joel and claiming that God is presently saying them.

Many other passages could be cited (see Luke 1:70; 24:25; John 5:45–47; Acts 3:18, 21; 4:25; 13:47; 28:25; Rom. 1:2; 3:2; 9:17; 1 Cor. 9:8–10; Heb. 1:1–2, 6–7), but the pattern of attributing to God the words of Old Testament Scripture should be very clear. Moreover, in several places it is *all* of the words of the prophets or the words of the Old Testament Scriptures that are said to compel belief or to be from God (see Luke 24:25, 27, 44; Acts 3:18; 24:14; Rom. 15:4).

But if Paul meant only the Old Testament writings when he spoke of "Scripture" in 2 Timothy 3:16, how can this verse apply to the New Testament writings as well? Does it say anything about the character of the New Testament writings? To answer that question, we must realize that the Greek word *graphē* ("Scripture") was a technical term for the New Testament writers and had a very specialized meaning. Even though it is used fifty-one times in the New Testament, every one of those instances uses it to refer to the Old Testament writings, not to any other words or writings outside the canon of Scripture. Thus everything that belonged in the category "Scripture" had the character of being "God-breathed": its words were God's very words.

But at two places in the New Testament we see New Testament writings also being called "Scripture" along with the Old Testament writings. As we noted in chapter 3, in 2 Peter 3:16, Peter shows not only an awareness of the existence of written epistles from Paul but also a clear willingness to classify "all of his [Paul's] epistles" with "the other Scriptures." This is an indication that very early in the history of the church, while many of the apostles were still living, all of Paul's epistles were considered to be God's written words in the same sense as the Old Testament texts were. Similarly, in 1 Timothy 5:18, Paul quotes Jesus' words as found in Luke 10:7 and calls them "Scripture."[7]

These two passages taken together indicate that during the time of the writing of the New Testament documents there was an awareness that *additions* were being made

---

7. See chapter 3, p. 49, for discussion of 2 Peter 3:16 and 1 Tim. 5:17–18.

to this special category of writings called "Scripture," writings that had the character of being God's very words. Once we establish that a New Testament writing belongs to the special category "Scripture," then we are correct in applying 2 Timothy 3:16 to that writing as well and saying that that writing also has the characteristic Paul attributes to "all Scripture": it is "God-breathed," and all its words are the very words of God.

Is there further evidence that the New Testament writers thought of their own writings (not just the Old Testament) as being words of God? In some cases there is. In 1 Corinthians 14:37, Paul says, "If anyone thinks that he is a prophet, or spiritual, he should acknowledge that *the things I am writing to you are a command of the Lord*." Paul has here instituted a number of rules for church worship at Corinth and has claimed for them the status of "commands of the Lord."

One objection to seeing the words of New Testament writers as words of God is sometimes brought from 1 Corinthians 7:12 where Paul distinguishes his words from words of the Lord: "To the rest I say (I, not the Lord)." A proper understanding of this passage is gained from verses 25 and 40, however. In verse 25 Paul says he has no command of the Lord concerning the unmarried but will give his opinion. This must mean that he had possession of *no earthly word that Jesus had spoken on this subject* and probably also that he had received no subsequent revelation about it from Jesus. This is unlike the situation in verses 10 and 11 where he could simply repeat the content of Jesus' earthly teaching, "the wife should not separate from her husband" and "the husband should not divorce his wife." Thus verse 12 must mean that Paul has *no record of any earthly teaching of Jesus* on the subject of a believer who is married to an unbelieving spouse. Therefore, Paul gives his own instructions: "To the rest *I say (I, not the Lord)* that if any brother has a wife who is an unbeliever, and she consents to live with him, he should not divorce her" (1 Cor. 7:12).

It is remarkable therefore that Paul can go on in verses 12–15 to give several specific ethical standards for the Corinthians. What gave him the right to make such moral commands? He said that he spoke as one "who by the Lord's mercy is trustworthy" (1 Cor. 7:25). He seems to imply here that his considered judgments were able to be placed on the same authoritative level as the words of Jesus. Thus 1 Corinthians 7:12, "To the rest I say (I, not the Lord)," is an amazingly strong affirmation of Paul's authority: if he did not have any record of earthly words of Jesus to apply to a situation, he would simply use his own words, for his own words had just as much authority as the words of Jesus!

Indications of a similar view of the New Testament writings are found in John 14:26 and 16:13, where Jesus promised that the Holy Spirit would bring all that he had said to the disciples' remembrance and would guide them into all the truth. This indicates a special superintending work of the Holy Spirit whereby the disciples would be able to remember and record without error all that Jesus had said. Similar indications are also found in 2 Peter 3:2; 1 Corinthians 2:13; 1 Thessalonians 4:15; and Revelation 22:18–19.

## 2. We Are Convinced of the Bible's Claims to Be God's Words as We Read the Bible

It is one thing to affirm that the Bible *claims* to be the words of God. It is another thing to be convinced that those claims are true. Our ultimate conviction that the words of the Bible are God's words comes only when the Holy Spirit speaks *in* and *through* the words of the Bible to our hearts and gives us an inner assurance that these are the words of our Creator speaking to us. Just after Paul has explained that his apostolic speech consists of words taught by the Holy Spirit (1 Cor. 2:13), he says, "The natural person does not accept the things of the Spirit of God, for they are folly to him, and he is not able to understand them because they are spiritually discerned" (1 Cor. 2:14). Apart from the work of the Spirit of God, a person will not receive spiritual truths and in particular will not receive or accept the truth that the words of Scripture are in fact the words of God.

But for those in whom God's Spirit is working there is a recognition that the words of the Bible are the words of God. This process is closely analogous to that by which those who believed in Jesus knew that his words were true. He said, "My sheep hear my voice, and I know them, and they follow me" (John 10:27). Those who are Christ's sheep hear the words of their great Shepherd as they read the words of Scripture, and they are convinced that these words are in fact the words of their Lord.

It is important to remember that this conviction that the words of Scripture are the words of God does *not* come *apart from* the words of Scripture or *in addition to* the words of Scripture. It is not as if the Holy Spirit one day whispers in our ear, "Do you see that Bible sitting on your desk? I want you to know that the words of that Bible are God's words." It is rather *as people are reading Scripture* that they hear their Creator's voice speaking to them in the words of Scripture and realize that the book they are reading is unlike any other book, that it is indeed a book of God's own words speaking to their hearts.

## 3. Other Evidence Is Useful but Not Finally Convincing

The previous section is not meant to deny the validity of other kinds of arguments that may be used to support the claim that the Bible is God's words. It is helpful for us to learn that the Bible is historically accurate, that it is internally consistent, that it contains prophecies that have been fulfilled hundreds of years later, that it has influenced the course of human history more than any other book, that it has continued changing the lives of millions of individuals throughout its history, that through it people come to find salvation, that it has a majestic beauty and a profound depth of teaching unmatched by any other book, and that it claims hundreds of times over to be God's very words. All of these arguments and others are useful to us and remove obstacles that might otherwise come in the way of our believing Scripture. But all of these arguments taken individually or together cannot finally be convincing. As the Westminster Confession of Faith said in 1643–46,

We may be moved and induced by the testimony of the Church to an high and reverent esteem of the Holy Scripture. And the heavenliness of the matter, the efficacy of the doctrine, the majesty of the style, the consent of all the parts, the scope of the whole (which is, to give all glory to God), the full discovery it makes of the only way of man's salvation, the many other incomparable excellencies, and the entire perfection thereof, are arguments whereby it doth abundantly evidence itself to be the Word of God: yet notwithstanding, our full persuasion and assurance of the infallible truth and divine authority thereof, is from the inward work of the Holy Spirit bearing witness by and with the Word in our hearts. (chap. 1, para. 5)

## 4. The Words of Scripture Are Self-Attesting

The fact that we are convinced that the words of Scripture are the words of God *as we are reading the Bible* means that the words of Scripture are "self-attesting." They cannot be "proved" to be God's words by appeal to any higher authority. For if an appeal to some higher authority (say, historical accuracy or logical consistency) were used to prove that the Bible is God's Word, then the Bible itself would not be our highest or absolute authority: it would be subordinate in authority to the thing to which we appealed to prove it to be God's Word. If we ultimately appeal to human reason, logic, historical accuracy, or scientific truth as the authority by which Scripture is shown to be God's words, then we have assumed the thing to which we appealed to be a higher authority than God's words and one that is more true or more reliable.

## 5. Objection: This Is a Circular Argument

Someone may object that to say Scripture proves itself to be God's words is to use a circular argument: we believe that Scripture is God's Word because it claims to be that. And we believe its claims because Scripture is God's Word. And we believe that it is God's Word because it claims to be that, and so forth.

It should be admitted that this is a kind of circular argument. However, that does not make its use invalid, for all arguments for an absolute authority must ultimately appeal to that authority for proof; otherwise the authority would not be an absolute or highest authority. This problem is not unique to the Christian who is arguing for the authority of the Bible. Everyone either implicitly or explicitly uses some kind of circular argument when defending his or her ultimate authority for belief.

Although these circular arguments are not always made explicit and are sometimes hidden beneath lengthy discussions or are simply assumed without proof, arguments for an ultimate authority in their most basic form take on a similar circular appeal to that authority itself, as some of the following examples show:

- "My reason is my ultimate authority because it seems reasonable to me to make it so."
- "Logical consistency is my ultimate authority because it is logical to make it so."

- "The findings of human sensory experiences are the ultimate authority for discovering what is real and what is not, because our human senses have never discovered anything else: thus, human sense experience tells me that my principle is true."
- "I know there can be no ultimate authority because I do not know of any such ultimate authority."

In all of these arguments for an ultimate standard of truth, an absolute authority for what to believe, there is an element of circularity involved.[8]

How then does a Christian, or anyone else, choose among the various claims for absolute authorities? Ultimately the truthfulness of the Bible will commend itself as being far more persuasive than other religious books (such as the *Book of Mormon* or the *Qur'an*) or than any other intellectual constructions of the human mind (such as logic, human reason, sense experience, scientific methodology, etc.). It will be more persuasive because in the actual experience of life, all of these other candidates for ultimate authority are seen to be inconsistent or to have shortcomings that *disqualify* them, while the Bible will be seen to be fully in accord with all that we know about the world around us, about ourselves, and about God.

The Bible will commend itself as being persuasive in this way, that is, if we are thinking rightly about the nature of reality, our perception of it and of ourselves, and our perception of God. The trouble is that because of sin our perception and analysis of God and creation is faulty. Sin is ultimately irrational, and sin makes us think incorrectly about God and about creation. In a world free from sin, the Bible would commend itself convincingly to all people as God's Word. But because sin distorts people's perception of reality, they do not recognize Scripture for what it really is. Therefore it requires the work of the Holy Spirit, overcoming the effects of sin, to enable us to be persuaded that the Bible is indeed the Word of God and that the claims it makes for itself are true.

Thus, in another sense, the argument for the Bible as God's Word and our ultimate authority is *not* a typical circular argument. The process of persuasion is perhaps better likened to a spiral in which increasing knowledge of Scripture and increasingly correct understanding of God and creation tend to supplement one another in a harmonious way, each tending to confirm the accuracy of the other. This is not to say that our knowledge of the world around us serves as a higher authority than Scripture, but rather that such knowledge, if it is correct knowledge, continues to give greater and greater assurance and deeper conviction that the Bible is the only truly ultimate authority and that other competing claims for ultimate authority are false.

---

8. This point has been made well by John M. Frame, "God and Biblical Language: Transcendence and Immanence," in *God's Inerrant Word*, ed. John Warwick Montgomery (Minneapolis: Bethany Fellowship, 1974), 159–77. See also J. P. Moreland, "The Rationality of Belief in Inerrancy," *TrinJ* 7, no. 1 (1986): 75–86, for a helpful discussion of the way we reach convictions about issues of major significance in our lives.

## 6. The Divine Authorship of the Bible Does Not Imply Dictation from God as the Sole Means of Communication

The entire preceding part of this chapter has argued that all the words of the Bible are God's words. At this point a word of caution is necessary. The fact that all the words of Scripture are God's words should not lead us to think that God dictated every word of Scripture to the human authors.

When we say that all the words of the Bible are God's words, we are talking about the *result* of the process of bringing Scripture into existence. To raise the question of dictation is to ask about the *process* that led to that result or the manner by which God acted in order to ensure the result that he intended.[9] It must be emphasized that the Bible does not speak of only one type of process or one manner by which God communicated to the biblical authors what he wanted to be said. In fact, there is indication of *a wide variety of processes* God used to bring about the desired result.

Yes, a few scattered instances of dictation are explicitly mentioned in Scripture. When the apostle John saw the risen Lord in a vision on the island of Patmos, Jesus spoke to him as follows: "To the angel of the church in Ephesus *write* . . ." (Rev. 2:1); "And to the angel of the church in Smyrna *write* . . ." (Rev. 2:8); "And to the angel of the church in Pergamum *write* . . ." (Rev. 2:12). These are examples of dictation pure and simple. The risen Lord tells John what to write, and John writes the words he hears from Jesus.

Something akin to this process is probably also seen occasionally in the Old Testament prophets. We read in Isaiah, "Then the word of the Lord came to Isaiah: 'Go and say to Hezekiah, Thus says the Lord, the God of David your father: I have heard your prayer; I have seen your tears. Behold, I will add fifteen years to your life. I will deliver you and this city out of the hand of the king of Assyria, and will defend this city'" (Isa. 38:4–6). The picture given us in this narrative is that Isaiah heard (whether with his physical ear or with a very forceful impression made upon his mind is difficult to say) the words God wanted him to say to Hezekiah, and Isaiah, acting as God's messenger, then took those words and *spoke* them as he had been instructed.

But in many other sections of Scripture such direct dictation from God is certainly not the manner by which the words of Scripture were caused to come into being. The author of Hebrews says that God spoke to our fathers by the prophets "at many times and *in many ways*" (Heb. 1:1). On the opposite end of the spectrum from dictation we have, for instance, Luke's ordinary historical research for writing his gospel. He says,

> Inasmuch as many have undertaken to compile a narrative of the things that have been accomplished among us, just as those who from the beginning were eye-witnesses and ministers of the word have delivered them to us, it seemed good to me

---

9. In some systematic theologies, this process by which God used human authors to write his very words is called "the mode of inspiration." I have not used this terminology in this book, since it does not seem to be a readily understandable phrase today.

also, having followed all things closely for some time past, to write an orderly account for you, most excellent Theophilus. (Luke 1:1–3)

This is clearly not a process of dictation. Luke used ordinary processes of speaking to eyewitnesses and gathering historical data in order that he might write an accurate account of the life and teachings of Jesus. He did his historical research thoroughly, listening to the reports of many eyewitnesses and evaluating his evidence carefully. The gospel he wrote emphasizes what he thought important to emphasize and reflects his own characteristic style of writing.

In between these two extremes of dictation pure and simple on the one hand and ordinary historical research on the other hand, we have many indications of various ways by which God communicated with the human authors of Scripture. In some cases Scripture hints at these various processes: it speaks of dreams, of visions, of hearing the Lord's voice or standing in the council of the Lord, of people who were with Jesus and observed his life and listened to his teaching, of people whose memories of these words and deeds was made completely accurate by the working of the Holy Spirit as he brought things to their remembrance (John 14:26). Yet in many other cases the manner used by God to bring about the result that the words of Scripture were his words is simply not disclosed to us. Apparently many different methods were used, but it is not important that we discover precisely what these were in each case.

In cases where the ordinary human personality and writing style of the author were prominently involved, as seems the case with most of Scripture, all that we are able to say is that God's providential oversight and direction of the life of each author was such that their personalities, their backgrounds and training, their abilities to evaluate events in the world around them, their access to historical data, their judgment with regard to the accuracy of information, and their individual circumstances when they wrote[10] were all exactly what God wanted them to be, so that when they actually came to the point of putting pen to paper, the words were fully their own words but also fully the words that God wanted them to write, words that God would also claim as his own.

## B. To Disbelieve or Disobey Any Word of Scripture Is to Disbelieve or Disobey God

The preceding section has argued that all the words in Scripture are God's words. Consequently, to disbelieve or disobey any word of Scripture is to disbelieve or disobey God. Thus Jesus can rebuke his disciples for not believing the Old Testament Scriptures (Luke 24:25). Believers are to keep or obey the disciples' words (John 15:20: "If they kept my word, they will also keep yours"). Christians are encouraged to remember "the

---

10. This would also include even the influence of a secretary (technically called an amanuensis) on the wording of a book; see the greeting from Tertius in Rom. 16:22.

commandment of the Lord and Savior through your apostles" (2 Peter 3:2). To disobey Paul's writings was to make oneself liable to church discipline, such as excommunication (2 Thess. 3:14) and spiritual punishment (2 Cor. 13:2–3), including punishment from God (this is the apparent sense of the passive verb "he is not recognized" in 1 Cor. 14:38). By contrast, God delights in everyone who "trembles" at his word (Isa. 66:2).

Throughout the history of the church the greatest preachers have been those who recognized that their primary task was to bring the powerful words of God in Scripture to bear on the hearts and minds of the hearers. They have recognized that *the actual words of Scripture* have more spiritual power than any merely human words or human wisdom, and therefore their sermons have focused on explaining the text and then relating real-life stories not merely to entertain but rather to illustrate how the text has made a difference in their own lives and the lives of other believers. In this way, week after week, the people who hear such preaching regularly experience how "the word of God is living and active, sharper than any two-edged sword, piercing to the division of soul and of spirit, of joints and of marrow, and discerning the thoughts and intentions of the heart" (Heb. 4:12). It is "like a hammer that breaks the rock in pieces" (Jer. 23:29). It is the very word of God, which, God says, "shall not return to me empty, but it shall accomplish that which I purpose, and shall succeed in the thing for which I sent it" (Isa. 55:11).

## C. The Truthfulness of Scripture
### 1. God Cannot Lie or Speak Falsely

The essence of the authority of Scripture is its ability to compel us to believe and to obey it and to make such belief and obedience equivalent to believing and obeying God himself. Because this is so, it is necessary to consider the truthfulness of Scripture, since to believe all the words of Scripture implies confidence in the complete truthfulness of the Scripture that we believe. Although this issue will be dealt with more fully when we consider the inerrancy of Scripture (see chapter 5), a brief treatment is given here.

Since the biblical writers repeatedly affirm that the words of the Bible, though human, are God's own words, it is appropriate to look at biblical texts that talk about *the character of God's words* and to apply these to the character of the words of Scripture. Specifically, there are a number of biblical passages that talk about the truthfulness of God's speech. Titus 1:2 speaks of "God, who never lies," or (more literally translated) "the unlying God." Because God is a God who cannot "lie," his words can always be trusted. Since all of Scripture is spoken by God, all of Scripture must be "unlying," just as God himself is: there can be no untruthfulness in Scripture.[11]

---

11. Some scholars object that it is "too simplistic" to argue as follows: "The Bible is God's words. God never lies. Therefore the Bible never lies." Yet it is precisely that kind of argument that Paul uses in Titus 1:2. He refers to the promises of eternal life made "before the ages began" in Scripture and says the promises were made by God "who never lies." He thus calls on the truthfulness of God's own speech to prove the truthfulness of the words of Scripture. A "simple" argument this may be, but it is scriptural, and it is true. We should therefore not hesitate to accept it and use it.

Hebrews 6:18 mentions two unchangeable things (God's oath and his promise) "in which *it is impossible for God to lie.*" Here the author says not merely that God does not lie but that it is *not possible* for him to lie. Although the immediate reference is only to oaths and promises, if it is impossible for God to lie in these utterances, then certainly it is impossible for him ever to lie (for Jesus harshly rebukes those who tell the truth only when under oath: Matt. 5:33–37; 23:16–22). Similarly, David says to God, "You are God, and *your words are true*" (2 Sam. 7:28).

## 2. Therefore, All the Words in Scripture Are Completely True and without Error in Any Part

Since the words of the Bible are God's words, and since God cannot lie or speak falsely, it is correct to conclude that there is no untruthfulness or error in any part of the words of Scripture. We find this affirmed several places in the Bible. "The words of the LORD are *pure words*, like silver refined in a furnace on the ground, purified seven times" (Ps. 12:6). Here the psalmist uses vivid imagery to speak of the undiluted purity of God's words: they are like silver that has been through a fiery purifying process "seven times" (and seven is the number of perfection in Scripture). Therefore there is no imperfection in these words of God. In Proverbs 30:5 we read, "*Every word of God proves true*; he is a shield to those who take refuge in him." It is not just some of the words of Scripture that are true, but every word. In fact, God's Word is fixed in heaven for all eternity: "Forever, O LORD, *your word is firmly fixed in the heavens*" (Ps. 119:89). Jesus can speak of the eternal nature of his words: "Heaven and earth will pass away, but my words will not pass away" (Matt. 24:35). God's speech is placed in marked contrast to all human speech, for "God is not man, that he should lie, or a son of man, that he should change his mind" (Num. 23:19). These verses affirm explicitly what was implicit in the requirement that we believe all of the words of Scripture, namely, that there is no untruthfulness or falsehood affirmed in any of the statements of the Bible.

## 3. God's Words Are the Ultimate Standard of Truth

In John 17 Jesus prays to the Father, "Sanctify them in the truth; *your word is truth*" (John 17:17). This verse is interesting because Jesus does not use the adjectives *alēthinos* or *alēthēs* ("true"), which we might have expected, to say, "Your word is true." Rather, he uses a noun, *alētheia* ("truth"), to say that God's Word is not simply "true," but it is truth itself.

The difference is significant, for this statement encourages us to think of the Bible not simply as being "true" in the sense that it conforms to some higher standard of truth but rather to think of the Bible as being itself the final standard of truth. The Bible is God's Word, and God's Word is the ultimate definition of what is true and what is not true: God's Word is itself *truth*. Thus we are to think of the Bible as the ultimate standard of truth, the reference point by which every other claim to truthfulness is to be measured. Those assertions that conform with Scripture are "true" while those that do not conform with Scripture are not true.

What then is truth? Truth is what God says, and we have what God says (accurately but not exhaustively) in the Bible.

## 4. Might Some New Fact Ever Contradict the Bible?

Will any new scientific or historical fact ever be discovered that will contradict the Bible? Here we can say with confidence that this will never happen—it is in fact impossible. If any supposed "fact" is ever discovered that is said to contradict Scripture, then (if we have understood Scripture rightly) that "fact" must be false, because God, the author of Scripture, knows all true facts (past, present, and future). No fact will ever turn up that God did not know about ages ago and take into account when he caused Scripture to be written. Every true fact is something that God has known already from all eternity and is something that therefore cannot contradict God's speech in Scripture.

Nevertheless, it must be remembered that scientific or historical study (as well as other kinds of study of creation) can cause us to reexamine Scripture to see if it really teaches what we thought it taught. The Bible certainly does not teach that the earth was created in the year 4004 BC, as some once thought (for the genealogical lists in Scripture have gaps in them).[12] Yet it was in part historical, archaeological, astronomical, and geological study that caused Christians to reexamine Scripture to see if it really taught such a recent origin for the earth. Careful analysis of the biblical text showed that it did not teach this.

Similarly, the Bible does not teach that the sun goes around the earth, for it only uses descriptions of phenomena as we see them from our vantage point and does not purport to be describing the workings of the universe from some arbitrary "fixed" point somewhere out in space. Yet until the study of astronomy advanced enough to demonstrate the rotation of the earth on its axis, people *assumed* that the Bible taught that the sun goes around the earth. Then the study of scientific data prompted a reexamination of the appropriate biblical texts. Thus, whenever confronted with some "fact" that is said to contradict Scripture, we must not only examine the data adduced to demonstrate the fact in question; we must also reexamine the appropriate biblical texts to see if the Bible really teaches what we thought it does.

We should never fear but always welcome any new facts that may be discovered in any legitimate area of human research or study. For example, discoveries by archaeologists working in Syria have brought to light the Ebla Tablets. These extensive written records from the period around 2000 BC have significant potential to increase our understanding of the world of the patriarchs and the events connected with the lives of

---

12. See chapter 15, pp. 385–413, for discussion of the age of the earth, and pp. 385–88 for discussion of gaps in the genealogies.

Abraham, Isaac, and Jacob. Should Christians entertain any lingering apprehension that the ongoing publication and analysis of such data will prove some fact in Genesis to be incorrect? Certainly not! We should eagerly anticipate the publication of all such data with the absolute confidence that if it is correctly understood it will all be consistent with Scripture and will all confirm the accuracy of Scripture. No true fact will ever contradict the words of the God who knows all facts and who never lies.

## D. OUR FINAL AUTHORITY IS WRITTEN SCRIPTURE, NOT ACADEMIC SPECULATIONS ABOUT BACKGROUND TOPICS

It is important to realize that the final form in which Scripture remains authoritative is its *written* form. It was the words of God *written* on the tablets of stone that Moses deposited in the ark of the covenant. Later, God commanded Moses and subsequent prophets to write their words in a book. And it was *written* Scripture (*graphē*) that Paul said was "breathed out by God" (2 Tim. 3:16). Similarly, it is Paul's *writings* that are "a command of the Lord" (1 Cor. 14:37) and that could be classified with "the other Scriptures" (2 Peter 3:16).

This is important because people sometimes (intentionally or unintentionally) attempt to substitute some other final standard than the written words of Scripture. For example, people will sometimes refer to "what Jesus really said" and claim that when we translate the Greek words of the Gospels back into the Aramaic language that Jesus spoke, we can gain a better understanding of Jesus' words than was given by the writers of the Gospels. In fact, it is sometimes said that this work of reconstructing Jesus' words in Aramaic enables us to correct the erroneous translations made by the gospel authors.

In other cases, people have claimed to know "what Paul really thought" even when that is different from the meaning of the words he wrote. Or they have spoken of "what Paul should have said if he had been consistent with the rest of his theology." Similarly, others have spoken of "the church situation to which Matthew was writing" and have attempted to give normative force either to that situation or to the solution they think Matthew was attempting to bring about in that situation.

Another mistaken view of the authority of Scripture is seen when critics of the Bible bring up some wrong ideas that people in the ancient world believed, and then criticize those ideas rather than criticizing *what the Bible actually says*. For example, Peter Enns claims that a common worldview in the ancient Near East held that the world was a flat disk with a solid dome above it that held back huge amounts of water and that the author of Genesis shared that worldview. He says, "Genesis—as other stories of the ancient world—thus portrays the world as a flat disk with a dome above."[13] But this argument by Enns directly undermines people's belief in the authority of Scripture

---

13. Peter Enns, *Inspiration and Incarnation: Evangelicals and the Problem of the Old Testament* (Grand Rapids: Baker, 2005), 54. On that same page, Enns illustrates this worldview with a diagram which he labels "Biblical and ancient Near-eastern worldview."

because obviously today we do not believe that the world is a flat disk with a solid dome above it that holds back water. My response to such a claim is that we are required to believe God's words in Scripture, not some speculations about ancient ideas that Moses or other biblical authors might or might not have held. (No passage of Scripture actually teaches that the earth is a flat disk or that the sky is a solid dome holding back water.)[14] It does not really matter whether Moses believed that the earth was a flat disk, a round sphere, or something else. What matters is *what he wrote in Scripture*. The authority of Scripture requires us to believe what the text of Scripture affirms as true. We are not required to believe someone's speculation about what Moses or any other biblical author might or might not have believed.

In all of these instances we must admit, of course, that asking about the words or situations that lie "behind" the text of Scripture may at times be helpful to us in understanding what the text means. Nevertheless, our *speculations* about the original Aramaic words, the thoughts that were in Paul's mind, or the various church situations can never replace or compete with *the words of Scripture itself* as the final authority, nor should we ever allow them to contradict or call into question the accuracy of any of the words of Scripture. And if the Greek words written by Matthew, Mark, Luke, and John are in fact the very words of God, then those very words are the best and most accurate translation of anything Jesus originally said in Aramaic. We must continually remember that we have *in the written words of the Bible* God's very words, and we must not try to "improve" them in some way, for this cannot be done. Rather, we should seek to understand them, trust them, and obey them with our whole heart.

## E. Liberal Protestant Theology Understands the Bible to Be Merely Human Words, Not God's Words

One of the primary features that distinguishes liberal Protestantism from evangelical Protestantism is its understanding of the Bible. Those who hold to what is called a "liberal" theological position do not agree with the viewpoint that I have advocated in this chapter, namely, that the words of the Bible are not only human words but also the very words of God. This conviction is essential to conservative or "evangelical" Protestant beliefs, and it has been the dominant view by far throughout the history of the Christian church.

By contrast, liberal Protestants understand the writings of the Bible to be merely human writings, "a fallible human record of religious thought and experience."[15] Therefore, according to liberalism, the Bible contains historical inaccuracies, internal inconsistencies, and, most importantly, outdated theological and ethical teachings that

---

14. Gen. 7:11 says, "The windows of the heavens were opened," but that expression is easily understood as poetic imagery rather than teaching that there were literal windows in the heavens.

15. J. I. Packer, "Liberalism and Conservatism in Theology," in *NDT*, 385.

we must reject as unacceptable in today's world. This is the dominant view, and in most cases the exclusive view, advocated in courses about the Bible or religion in most secular universities today.

Of course, if a liberal theologian is convinced that there can be no such thing as a Bible that is truly God's revelation to us, then it follows that evangelicals are deceiving themselves when they claim that the words of the Bible are the words of God. They are inventing their own theological ideas and claiming that these ideas came from God himself—an immodest and in fact dangerous procedure. This is why Harvard Divinity School professor Gordon D. Kaufman could write, "Theology is in every respect a human work. . . . Liberal Christian theologians have recognized this clearly; and they have often, therefore, denounced the claims of traditional theologians to be speaking with divine authorization . . . as a presumptuous and insidious form of self-idolatry," and could also say that such claims reflect "authoritarian pomposity" and "demonic authoritarianism."[16]

But if the Bible is in fact God's revelation to us, and if its words are in fact the very words of God, then to claim that Scripture speaks to us with divine authority is not arrogant at all; rather, it reflects an appropriate humility when confronted with our Creator's words to us. And that is the kind of authority that, hundreds of times, the Bible claims for itself. Far different from the claims of Protestant liberalism is the bold assertion of the apostle Paul: "For I would have you know, brothers, that the gospel that was preached by me *is not man's gospel*. For I did not receive it from any man, nor was I taught it, but I received it through a revelation of Jesus Christ" (Gal. 1:11–12).

## ADDITIONAL NOTE: CHRISTIANITY AND THEOLOGICAL LIBERALISM

Nearly 100 years ago, J. Gresham Machen, a New Testament professor at Princeton Seminary, published *Christianity and Liberalism*,[17] a book that has become a recognized classic in Christian theology because of its clear explanation of the differences between Christianity as taught in the New Testament and theological liberalism, which was rapidly infiltrating many churches and seminaries in Machen's day. (Because of the conflict between Christianity and liberalism, Machen left Princeton to help found Westminster Seminary in 1929.)

I found the book wonderfully helpful when I read it in 1969 as an undergraduate student. It helped me understand specific biblical reasons why I had instinctively distrusted

---

16. Gordon D. Kaufman, "Doing Theology from a Liberal Christian Point of View, in *Doing Theology in Today's World: Essays in Honor of Kenneth S. Kantzer*, ed. John Woodbridge and Thomas McComiskey (Grand Rapids: Zondervan, 1991), 408, 414.

17. J. Gresham Machen, *Christianity and Liberalism* (Grand Rapids: Eerdmans, 1923; repr., 2009).

the liberal approach to the Bible that was being taught in religion classes and in the weekly chapel services held at my (very secular) university.

For many years now, I have assigned the book as required reading every time I teach the class on introduction to theology and the doctrine of the Word of God. Students who have grown up in a liberal Protestant church or who have taken classes in the Bible at a secular university regularly report their surprise at discovering that many of the ideas Machen criticized a century ago are still being promoted today.

Because one of the foundational commitments of theological liberalism is viewing the Bible as a merely human book, it is appropriate to include this additional note at the end of this chapter on the authority of the Bible. In the chart below, I have summarized Machen's arguments (with a few minor clarifications in my own words), and have given the relevant page numbers in Machen's book for those who wish to pursue the topic further.

| Doctrine | Liberalism | Christianity | Relevant Scripture Passages | Pages in Machen, *Christianity and Liberalism* |
|---|---|---|---|---|
| Basic worldview | Naturalism (the natural world is all we can know) | Supernaturalism (we can also know supernatural events that God reveals to us) | Gen. 1:1; 1 Cor. 2:1–16; Heb. 11:6 | 2, 98–116 |
| The Bible | A merely human book | Both human and divine | 2 Tim. 3:16; 2 Peter 1:21 | 72–79 |
| | Not God's words | God's very words | 2 Tim. 3:16; Exod. 20:1 | 72–79 |
| | A human record of people's religious experiences and ideas | A divine revelation from God | John 16:13; 1 Cor. 2:9–10; 2 Tim. 3:16 | 69–79 |
| | Reports of supernatural events are myths | Reports of supernatural events are true | Prov. 30:5; 2 Peter 1:16–18 | 98–116 |
| Doctrine | Doctrine is not important. People's experiences should be the test of truth. | Doctrine is a statement of historical facts with their meaning. Without true doctrine, there is no Christian faith. | 1 Tim. 3:15; Titus 1:9; Jude 3 | 18–32, 78–79 |
| God | God loves all people no matter what they do | God holds all people accountable for their actions, and he calls all people to repent of their sins | Acts 17:30–31; Rom. 1:18–32; 1 Peter 4:4–5 | 58–68, 157–58 |
| | God is the Father of all people; all religions worship the same God | The only way to know God is through Jesus Christ | John 14:6; Acts 4:11–12; 1 Tim. 2:5 | 59–62, 122–24 |

| Doctrine | Liberalism | Christianity | Relevant Scripture Passages | Pages in Machen, *Christianity and Liberalism* |
|---|---|---|---|---|
| Human beings | Human beings are inherently good | All human beings are sinners in need of God's forgiveness | Rom. 3:23; 6:23 | 68 |
| Jesus Christ | Jesus was a great moral teacher, a remarkable human being | Jesus is both God and man | John 1:1–3, 14; Col. 2:9; Heb. 1:1–4 | 80–116 |
| | Jesus is an example whose life we should imitate | Jesus is the Savior who died for our sins, and in whom we trust | Mark 10:45; John 11:25–26; Rom. 5:8; 1 Cor. 15:3–4 | 80–116, 125–56 |
| | The idea of the virgin birth of Christ is scientifically impossible | Jesus was miraculously born to the virgin Mary | Isa. 7:14; Matt. 1:23–25; Luke 1:34–35; 3:23 | 98–109 |
| Salvation | Salvation comes through human self-improvement and improvement of society | Salvation comes through trusting in Christ for forgiveness of our sins | John 1:12; Rom. 10:5–17; 1 Cor. 15:3–4 | 65, 117–56 |
| | The idea that God poured out his wrath on Christ contradicts the truth of the love of God | Jesus bore the wrath of God against sin that we deserved | Isa. 53:4–12; Rom. 3:25; Heb. 2:17 | 117–40 |
| The church | The church is an association for human self-improvement | The church was created by Jesus Christ to be a fellowship of redeemed people | Matt. 16:18; Eph. 5:25, 29; 1 Tim. 3:15 | 65, 157–59, 180 |
| | The purpose of the church is to renew society, not to evangelize individual people | The purpose of the church is to worship God, build up believers, and proclaim the gospel to unbelievers | Isa. 43:6–7; Eph. 1:12–14; 1 Cor. 14:12; Matt. 28:19–20 | 157–59, 178–80 |
| | The church should not have doctrinal boundaries for its leadership | Pastors must believe and teach sound Christian doctrine | 1 Tim. 3:15; Titus 1:9; Jude 3 | 159–66 |
| Conclusion | Liberalism is not Christianity. It is another religion altogether. | | | 6–8, 52, 160, 172–78 |

# QUESTIONS FOR PERSONAL APPLICATION

1. If you want to persuade someone that the Bible is God's Word, what do you want that person to read more than any other piece of literature?

2. Who would try to make people want to disbelieve something in Scripture? To disobey something in Scripture? Is there anything in the Bible that you do not want to believe? To obey? If your answers to either of the preceding two questions were positive, what is the best way to approach and to deal with the desires you have in this area?

3. Do you know of any proven fact in all of history that has shown something in the Bible to be false? Can the same be said about other religious writings such as the *Book of Mormon* or the *Qur'an*? If you have read in other books such as these, can you describe the spiritual effect they had on you? Compare that with the spiritual effect that reading the Bible has on you. Can you say that when you read the Bible you hear the voice of your Creator speaking to you in a way that is true of no other book?

4. Do you ever find yourself believing something not because you have external evidence for it but simply because it is written in Scripture? Is that proper faith according to Hebrews 11:1? If you do believe things simply because Scripture says them, what do you think Christ will say to you about this habit when you stand before his judgment seat? Do you think that trusting and obeying everything that Scripture affirms will ever lead you into sin or away from God's blessing in your life?

5. Have you interacted with someone with a theologically liberal view of the Bible? After reading this chapter, how would you discuss the authority of Scripture differently with him or her?

**Special Terms**

*absolute authority*
*authority of Scripture*
*circular argument*
*dictation*
*God-breathed*
*inspiration*
*liberalism*
*plenary inspiration*
*Scripture*
*self-attesting*

# BIBLIOGRAPHY

(For an explanation of this bibliography see the note on the bibliography to chapter 1, pp. 23–24. Complete bibliographical data may be found on pp. 1489–96.)

**SECTIONS IN EVANGELICAL SYSTEMATIC THEOLOGIES**

*1. Anglican (Episcopalian)*
    1882–92 . . . . . Litton, 18–40

1930........Thomas, 115–20, 123–33,
           141–45
2001........Packer, 16–18
2013........Bird, 63
2013........Bray, 137–48

**2. *Arminian (Wesleyan or Methodist)***
1875–76 .....Pope, 1:92–99, 156–92
1892–94 .....Miley, 2:481–89
1940........Wiley, 1:166–84
1960........Purkiser, 60–80
1983........Carter, 1:287–330
1992........Oden, 1:335–404
2002........Cottrell, 64–66

**3. *Baptist***
1767........Gill, 1:15–37
1907........Strong, 111–242
1976–83 .....Henry, 2:247–334; 3:28–47,
           203–488; 4:7–271, 470–93
1987–94 .....Lewis and Demarest,
           1:93–171
1990–1995...Garrett, 1:193–212
2007........Akin, 162–63
2013........Erickson, 210–29

**4. *Dispensational***
1947........Chafer, 1:21–104, 120–23
1949........Thiessen, 43–49, 62–74
1986........Ryrie, 20–22, 63–76
2002–2005 ..Geisler, 1:239–241, 246, 495
2017........MacArthur and Mayhue,
           100–107

**5. *Lutheran***
1917–24 .....Pieper, 1:193–317, 349–59
1934........Mueller, 90–136

**6. *Reformed (or Presbyterian)***
1559 ........Calvin, 1:7–8, 74–93
1679–85 .....Turretin, *IET*, 1:62–69,
           85–94, 116–27, 154–62
1871–73 .....Hodge, 1:153–82
1887–1921 ...Warfield, *IAB*, 3–410,
           419–42; *SSW*, 2:537–638
1906–11 .....Bavinck, *RD*, 1:449–74
1937–66 .....Murray, *CW*, 3:256–62; *CW*,
           4:30–57
1938........Berkhof, *Intro.*, 144–65,
           182–86
1998........Reymond, 73–78
2008........Van Genderen and Velema,
           84–96
2011........Horton, 194, 197–98
2013........Frame, 581, 610–11
2016........Allen and Swain, 30–56
2017........Barrett, 145–88
2019........Letham, 188–99

**7. *Renewal (or charismatic/Pentecostal)***
1988–92 .....Williams, 1:22–25
1993........Menzies and Horton, 17–20
1995........Horton, 81–89

## SECTIONS IN REPRESENTATIVE ROMAN CATHOLIC SYSTEMATIC THEOLOGIES

**1. *Roman Catholic: Traditional***
1955........Ott (no explicit treatment)

**2. *Roman Catholic: Post–Vatican II***
1980........McBrien, 1:62–77, 201–44
2012........*CCC*, paragraphs 75–83

## OTHER WORKS

Allison, Gregg R. *Historical Theology: An
    Introduction to Christian Doctrine; A Companion*

*to Wayne Grudem's* Systematic Theology. Grand Rapids: Zondervan, 2011, 79–98.

Belt, H. van den. *The Authority of Scripture in Reformed Theology: Truth and Trust*. Leiden: Brill, 2008.

Cameron, Nigel M. de S. "Bible, Authority of the." In *BTDB*, 55–58.

———. "Bible, Inspiration of the." In *BTDB*, 60–61.

Carson, D. A., ed. *The Enduring Authority of the Christian Scriptures*. Grand Rapids: Eerdmans, 2016.

Carson, D. A., and John Woodbridge, eds. *Hermeneutics, Authority, and Canon*. Grand Rapids: Zondervan, 1986.

———. *Scripture and Truth*. Grand Rapids: Zondervan, 1983.

Dockery, David S. *Christian Scripture: An Evangelical Perspective on Inspiration, Authority, and Interpretation*. Nashville: B&H, 1995.

Dockery, David S. and David P. Nelson. "Special Revelation." In *A Theology for the Church*, ed. Daniel L. Akin et al., 162–63. Nashville: B&H, 2014.

Feinberg, John S. *Light in a Dark Place: The Doctrine of Scripture*. Foundations of Evangelical Theology Series. Wheaton, IL: Crossway, 2018.

Feinberg, P. D. "Bible, Inerrancy and Infallibility of." In *EDT3*, 124–27.

Frame, John M. *The Doctrine of the Word of God*. Vol. 4. Phillipsburg, NJ: P&R, 2010.

Geisler, Norman L., ed. *Inerrancy*. Grand Rapids: Zondervan, 1980.

Grudem, Wayne A. *The Gift of Prophecy in 1 Corinthians*. Washington, DC: University Press of America, 1982, 1–54.

Helm, Paul. *The Divine Revelation: The Basic Issues*. Westchester, IL: Crossway, 1982.

Henry, Carl F. H. "Bible, Inspiration of." In *EDT3*, 127–29.

Hoffmeier, James Karl, and Dennis Robert Magary, eds. *Do Historical Matters Matter to Faith? A Critical Appraisal of Modern and Postmodern Approaches to Scripture*. Wheaton, IL: Crossway, 2012.

King, David T., and William Webster. *Holy Scripture: The Ground and Pillar of Our Faith*. 3 vols. Battle Ground, WA: Christian Resources, 2001.

Kuyper, Abraham. *Principles of Sacred Theology*. Translated by J. H. de Vries. Reprint, Grand

Rapids: Eerdmans, 1968, 413–563 (first published as *Encyclopedia of Sacred Theology* in 1898).

Marshall, I. H. "Infallibility and Inerrancy of the Bible." In *NDT2*, 453–55.

McKim, D. K., and P. S. Chung. "Revelation and Scripture." In *GDT*, 758–67.

Montgomery, John W., ed. *God's Inerrant Word*. Minneapolis: Bethany Fellowship, 1974.

Nash, Ronald H. *The Word of God and the Mind of Man*. Grand Rapids: Zondervan, 1982.

Packer, J. I. *"Fundamentalism" and the Word of God*. London: Inter-Varsity Press, 1958.

———. "Infallibility and Inerrancy of the Bible." In *NDT1*, 337–39.

———. "Scripture." In *NDT2*, 821–25.

Pinnock, Clark. *Biblical Revelation*. Chicago: Moody Publishers, 1971.

Radmacher, Earl D., and Robert D. Preus, eds. *Hermeneutics, Inerrancy, and the Bible*. Grand Rapids: Zondervan, 1984.

Tatlock, Mark, ed. *The Implications of Inerrancy for the Global Church: The Truthfulness of God's Word Defended, Explained, and Extolled by Authors from Seventeen Countries across the Globe*. Maitland, FL: Xulon, 2015.

Van Til, Cornelius. *In Defense of the Faith*. Vol. 1, *The Doctrine of Scripture*. Ripon, CA: den Dulk Christian Foundation, 1967.

———. *In Defense of the Faith*. Vol. 5, *An Introduction to Systematic Theology*. Phillipsburg, NJ: Presbyterian and Reformed, 1976, 110–58.

Warfield, B. B. *Limited Inspiration*. Philadelphia: Presbyterian and Reformed, 1962.

Wells, Paul. *James Barr and the Bible: Critique of a New Liberalism*. Phillipsburg, NJ: Presbyterian and Reformed, 1980.

Wenham, John W. *Christ and the Bible*. London: Tyndale, 1972.

Woodbridge, John. *Biblical Authority: A Critique of the Rogers/McKim Proposal*. Grand Rapids: Zondervan, 1982.

Westminster Seminary Faculty. *The Infallible Word*. 3rd ed. Philadelphia: Presbyterian and Reformed, 1967.

Young, Edward J. *Thy Word Is Truth*. Grand Rapids: Eerdmans, 1957.

### WORKS FROM A NONINERRANCY PERSPECTIVE

Baillie, John. *The Idea of Revelation in Recent Thought.* New York: Columbia University Press, 1956.

Barr, James. *Fundamentalism.* London: SCM, 1977.

Barton, John. *People of the Book? The Authority of the Bible in Christianity.* Louisville: Westminster John Knox, 1988.

Beegle, Dewey M. *Scripture, Tradition, and Infallibility.* Grand Rapids: Eerdmans, 1973.

Berkouwer, G. C. *Holy Scripture.* Translation by Jack B. Rogers. Grand Rapids: Eerdmans, 1975.

Burtchaell, James Tunstead. *Catholic Theories of Biblical Inspiration Since 1810: A Review and Critique.* Cambridge: University Press, 1969.

Davis, Stephen T. *The Debate about the Bible.* Philadelphia: Westminster, 1977.

McKim, Donald K., ed. *The Authoritative Word: Essays on the Nature of Scripture.* Grand Rapids: Eerdmans, 1983.

Pinnock, Clark. *The Scripture Principle.* San Francisco: Harper and Row, 1984.

Rogers, Jack, ed. *Biblical Authority.* Waco, TX: Word, 1977.

Rogers, Jack, and Donald K. McKim. *The Authority and Interpretation of the Bible: An Historical Approach.* San Francisco: Harper and Row: 1979.

Vawter, Bruce. *Biblical Inspiration.* Philadelphia: Westminster, 1972 (a recent Roman Catholic work).

## SCRIPTURE MEMORY PASSAGE

**2 Timothy 3:16:** All Scripture is breathed out by God and profitable for teaching, for reproof, for correction, and for training in righteousness.

## HYMN

**"Standing on the Promises"**

This hymn speaks of the promises of God's Word as the eternally firm and unchanging foundation on which we can rest our faith. In the midst of doubt and fear these promises "cannot fail." By standing firm on them we will be able to sing "Glory in the highest!" for eternity. Yet the hymn speaks not merely of the promises of God's Word, but of all the contents of Scripture: the Bible is "the living Word of God" by which we "prevail" in the midst of adversity (v. 2), and it is the "Spirit's sword" by which we may be "overcoming daily" (v. 3). There is no other sure foundation on which to rest our faith than on the very words and promises of God. "I am standing on the promises of God!" is the joyful exclamation of a heart filled with faith, and it shall be our song throughout eternity.

*Standing on the promises of Christ my King,*
*Through eternal ages let his praises ring!*
*Glory in the highest I will shout and sing*
*Standing on the promises of God!*

*Chorus*
*Standing, standing, standing on the promises of*
*    God my Savior;*
*Standing, standing, I'm standing on the promises*
*    of God.*

*Standing on the promises that cannot fail*
*When the howling storms of doubt and*
      *fear assail;*
*By the living Word of God I shall prevail*
*Standing on the promises of God!*

*Standing on the promises of Christ the Lord,*
*Bound to him eternally by love's strong cord,*
*Overcoming daily with the Spirit's sword*
*Standing on the promises of God!*

*Standing on the promises I cannot fall,*
*List'ning every moment to the Spirit's call,*
*Resting in my Savior as my all in all*
*Standing on the promises of God!*

Author: R. Kelso Carter, 1886

## CONTEMPORARY WORSHIP SONG

### "Here I Am To Worship"

*Light of the world,*
*You stepped down into darkness,*
*Opened my eyes, let me see,*
*Beauty that made*
*This heart adore You,*
*Hope of a life spent with You.*

*Chorus*
*So here I am to worship,*
*Here I am to bow down,*
*Here I am to say that You're my God,*
*And You're altogether lovely,*
*Altogether worthy,*
*Altogether wonderful to me.*

*King of all days,*
*Oh so highly exalted,*
*Glorious in heaven above,*
*Humbly You came*
*To the earth You created,*
*All for love's sake became poor.*

*Bridge*
*And I'll never know how much it cost*
*To see my sin upon that cross.*
*And I'll never know how much it cost*
*To see my sin upon that cross.*

Words by Tim Hughes[18]

## CHAPTER 5

# The Inerrancy of Scripture

*Are there any errors in the Bible?*

Most books on systematic theology have not included a separate chapter on the inerrancy of the Bible. The subject has usually been dealt with under the heading of the authority of Scripture, and no further treatment has been considered necessary. However, this issue of inerrancy is of such concern in the evangelical world today that it warrants a separate chapter following our treatment of the authority of the Word of God.

## EXPLANATION AND SCRIPTURAL BASIS

### A. The Meaning of Inerrancy

We will not at this point repeat the arguments concerning the authority of Scripture that were given in chapter 4. There it was argued that all the words in the Bible are God's words, and that therefore to disbelieve or disobey any word in Scripture is to disbelieve or disobey God. It was argued further that the Bible clearly teaches that God cannot lie or speak falsely (2 Sam. 7:28; Titus 1:2; Heb. 6:18). Therefore, all the words in Scripture are claimed to be completely true and without error in any part (Num. 23:19; Pss. 12:6; 119:89, 96; Prov. 30:5; Matt. 24:35). God's words are, in fact, the ultimate standard of truth (John 17:17).

Especially relevant at this point are those Scripture texts that indicate the total truthfulness and reliability of God's words. *"The words of the LORD are pure words*, like silver refined in a furnace on the ground, purified seven times" (Ps. 12:6) indicates the absolute reliability and purity of Scripture. Similarly, *"Every word of God proves true*; he is a shield to those who take refuge in him" (Prov. 30:5) indicates the truthfulness of every word that God has spoken. Though error and at least partial falsehood may characterize the speech of every human being from time to time, it is the characteristic of God's speech even when spoken through sinful human beings that it is never false and that it never affirms error. "God is not man, that he should lie, or a son of man, that he should change his mind" (Num. 23:19) was spoken by sinful Balaam specifically about the prophetic words that God had spoken through his own lips.

With evidence such as this we are now in a position to define biblical inerrancy: *the inerrancy of Scripture means that Scripture in the original manuscripts does not affirm anything that is contrary to fact.*

85

This definition focuses on the question of truthfulness and falsehood in the language of Scripture. The definition in simple terms just means that *the Bible always tells the truth*, and that it always tells the truth *concerning everything it talks about*. This definition does not mean that the Bible tells us every fact there is to know about any one subject, but it affirms that what it does say about any subject is *true*.

It is important to realize at the outset of this discussion that the focus of this controversy is on the question of truthfulness in speech. It must be recognized that absolute truthfulness in speech is consistent with some other types of statements, such as the following:

## 1. The Bible Can Be Inerrant and Still Speak in the Ordinary Language of Everyday Speech

This is especially true in "scientific" or "historical" descriptions of facts or events. The Bible can speak of the sun rising (Ps. 113:3; James 1:11) and the rain falling (Isa. 55:10; Matt. 7:25) because from the perspective of the speaker this is exactly what happens. From the standpoint of an observer standing on the sun (were that possible) or on some hypothetical "fixed" point in space, the earth rotates and brings the sun into view, and rain does not fall downward but upward or sideways or whatever direction necessary for it to be drawn by gravity toward the surface of the earth. But such explanations are hopelessly pedantic and would make ordinary communication impossible. From the standpoint of the speaker, the sun *does* rise and the rain *does* fall, and these are perfectly true descriptions of the natural phenomena the speaker observes.

A similar consideration applies to numbers when used in measuring or in counting. A reporter can say that 8,000 men were killed in a certain battle without thereby implying that he has counted everyone and that there are not 7,999 or 8,001 dead soldiers. If roughly 8,000 died, it would of course be false to say that 16,000 died, but it would not be false in most contexts for a reporter to say that 8,000 men died when in fact 7,823 or 8,242 had died: the limits of truthfulness would depend on the degree of precision implied by the speaker and expected by his original hearers.

This is also true for measurements. Whether someone says, "I don't live far from my office," or "I live a little over a mile from my office," or "I live one mile from my office," or "I live 1.287 miles from my office," all four statements are still approximations to some degree of accuracy. Further degrees of accuracy might be obtained with more precise scientific instruments, but these would still be approximations to a certain degree of accuracy. Thus measurements also, in order to be true, should conform to the degree of precision implied by the speaker and expected by the hearers in the original context. It should not trouble us, then, to affirm both that the Bible is absolutely truthful in everything it says and that it uses ordinary language to describe natural phenomena or to give approximations or round numbers when those are appropriate in the context.

We should also note that language can make vague or imprecise statements without being untrue. Someone can say, "I live a little over a mile from my office," which is a vague and imprecise statement, but it is also inerrant: there is nothing untrue about it. It does not affirm anything that is contrary to fact. In a similar way, biblical statements can be imprecise and still be totally true. Inerrancy has to do with *truthfulness*, not with the degree of precision with which events are reported.

## 2. The Bible Can Be Inerrant and Still Include Loose or Free Quotations

The method by which one person quotes the words of another person is a procedure that in large part varies from culture to culture. In contemporary American and British culture, we are used to quoting a person's exact words when we enclose the statement in quotation marks (this is called direct quotation). But when we use indirect quotation (with no quotation marks) we only expect an accurate report of the substance of a statement. Consider this sentence: "Elliot said that he would return home for supper right away." The sentence does not quote Elliot directly, but it is an acceptable and truthful report of Elliot's actual statement to his father, "I will come to the house to eat in two minutes," even though the indirect quotation included none of the speaker's original words.

Written Greek at the time of the New Testament had no quotation marks or equivalent kinds of punctuation, and an accurate citation of another person needed to include only a correct representation of the *content* of what the person said (rather like our indirect quotations): it was not expected to cite each word exactly. Thus inerrancy is consistent with loose or free quotations of the Old Testament or of the words of Jesus, for example, so long as the *content* is not false to what was originally stated. The original writer did not ordinarily imply that he was using the exact words of the speaker and only those, nor did the original hearers expect verbatim quotation in such reporting.

## 3. It Is Consistent with Inerrancy to Have Unusual or Uncommon Grammatical Constructions in the Bible

If it were left up to us to imagine what an inerrant Bible would be like, we might say that it would have a consistently elegant, magnificent literary style throughout with no misspelled (or irregularly spelled) words and no deviations from accepted grammatical rules. But the Bible nowhere claims to be "perfect" in things such as style, grammar, or spelling. What it claims is that its statements are truthful (see the verses cited above). In fact, what we find in the Bible is a wide variety of writing styles. Some of the language is elegant and stylistically excellent. Other scriptural writings contain the rough-hewn language of ordinary people. At times this includes a failure to follow the commonly accepted "rules" of grammatical expression (such as the use of a plural verb where grammatical rules would require a singular verb, the use of a feminine adjective where a masculine one would be expected, or different spelling for a word than the one commonly used, etc.).

These stylistically or grammatically irregular statements (which are especially found in the book of Revelation) should not trouble us, for they do not affect the *truthfulness* of the statements under consideration: a statement can be ungrammatical or include misspellings but still be entirely true. For example, an uneducated backwoodsman in a rural area may be the most trusted man in the county even though his grammar is poor, because he has earned a reputation for never telling a lie. Or I could be typing quickly and send an email that says, "I teech theology at Phoenix Seminaary," a statement that is completely truthful even though two words are misspelled. Similarly, there are a few statements in Scripture (in the original languages) that are ungrammatical (according to current standards of proper grammar at that time) or contain irregular spellings of words, but these statements are still *inerrant* because they are completely true. The issue with the doctrine of inerrancy is *truthfulness* in speech.

## B. Some Current Challenges to Inerrancy

In this section we examine the major objections that are commonly made against the concept of inerrancy.

### 1. Objection: The Bible Is Only Authoritative for Matters of "Faith and Practice"

One of the most frequent objections to inerrancy is raised by those who say that the purpose of Scripture is to teach us in areas that concern "faith and practice" only; that is, in areas that directly relate to our religious beliefs ("faith") or to the ethical conduct of our lives ("practice"). This position would allow for the possibility of false statements in Scripture, for example, in *other* areas such as in minor historical details or scientific facts—these areas, it is said, do not concern the purpose of the Bible, which is to instruct us in what we should believe and how we are to live.[1] Since about the mid-1960s, the advocates of this view have been willing to say that the Bible is "*infallible*," but they have hesitated to use the word *inerrant*.[2]

The response to this objection can be stated as follows: the Bible repeatedly affirms that *all* of Scripture is profitable for us (2 Tim. 3:16) and that *all* of it is "God-breathed." Thus it is completely pure (Ps. 12:6), perfect (Ps. 119:96), and true (Prov. 30:5). The Bible itself does not make any restriction on the kinds of subjects to which it speaks truthfully.

The New Testament contains further affirmations of the reliability of all parts of Scripture: in Acts 24:14, Paul says that he worships God, "*believing everything*

---

1. A good defense of this position can be found in a collection of essays edited by Jack Rogers, *Biblical Authority* (Waco, TX: Word, 1977); and, more extensively, in Jack B. Rogers and Donald McKim, *The Authority and Interpretation of the Bible: An Historical Approach* (San Francisco: Harper and Row, 1979).

2. Until about 1960 or 1965 the word *infallible* was used interchangeably with the word *inerrant*. But in recent years, at least in the United States, the word *infallible* has been used in a weaker sense to mean that the Bible will not lead us astray just in matters of faith and practice.

laid down by the Law and written in the Prophets." In Luke 24:25, Jesus says that the disciples are "foolish ones" because they are "slow of heart to believe *all* that the prophets have spoken." In Romans 15:4, Paul says that "*whatever* was written" in the Old Testament was "written for our instruction." These texts give no indication that there is any part of Scripture that is not to be trusted or relied on completely. Similarly, in 1 Corinthians 10:11, Paul can refer even to minor historical details in the Old Testament (sitting down to eat and drink, rising up to play; v. 7) and can say both that they "*happened*" (thus implying historical reliability) and "were written down for our instruction."

If we begin to examine the way the New Testament authors trust the smallest historical details of the Old Testament narrative, we see no intention to separate out matters of "faith and practice," to say that this is somehow a recognizable category of affirmations, or to imply that statements not in that category need not be trusted or thought to be inerrant. Rather, it seems that the New Testament authors are willing to cite and affirm as true *every detail* of the Old Testament.

In the following list are some examples of these historical details cited by New Testament authors. If all of these are matters of "faith and practice," then *every* historical detail of the Old Testament is a matter of "faith and practice," and this objection ceases to be an objection to inerrancy. On the other hand, if so many details can be affirmed, then it seems that all of the historical details in the Old Testament can be affirmed as true, and we should not speak of restricting the necessary truthfulness of Scripture to some category of "faith and practice" that would exclude certain minor details. There are no types of details left that could not be affirmed as true.

The New Testament gives us the following data: David ate the bread of the Presence (Matt. 12:3–4); Jonah was in the whale (Matt. 12:40); the men of Nineveh repented (Matt. 12:41); the queen of the South came to hear Solomon (Matt. 12:42); Elijah was sent to the widow of Zarephath (Luke 4:25–26); Naaman the Syrian was cleansed of leprosy (Luke 4:27); on the day Lot left Sodom fire and brimstone rained from heaven (Luke 17:29; cf. v. 32 with its reference to Lot's wife who turned to salt); Moses lifted up the serpent in the wilderness (John 3:14); Jacob gave a field to Joseph (John 4:5); many details of the history of Israel occurred (Acts 13:17–23); Abraham believed and received the promise before he was circumcised (Rom. 4:10); Abraham was about one hundred years old (Rom. 4:19); God told Rebekah before her children were born that the elder child would serve the younger (Rom. 9:10–12); Elijah spoke with God (Rom. 11:2–4); the people of Israel passed through the sea, ate and drank spiritual food and drink, desired evil, sat down to drink, rose up to dance, indulged in immorality, grumbled, and were destroyed (1 Cor. 10: 1–11); Abraham gave a tenth of everything to Melchizedek (Heb. 7:1–2); the Old Testament tabernacle had a specific and detailed design (Heb. 9:1–5); Moses sprinkled the people and the tabernacle vessels with blood and water, using scarlet wool and hyssop (Heb. 9:19–21); the world was created by the Word of God

(Heb. 11:3);[3] many details of the lives of Abel, Enoch, Noah, Abraham, Moses, Rahab, and others actually happened (Heb. 11, passim); Esau sold his birthright for a single meal and later sought it back with tears (Heb. 12:16–17); Rahab received the spies and sent them out another way (James 2:25); eight persons were saved in the ark (1 Peter 3:20; 2 Peter 2:5); God turned Sodom and Gomorrah to ashes but saved Lot (2 Peter 2:6–7); Balaam's donkey spoke (2 Peter 2:16).

This list indicates that the New Testament writers were willing to rely on the truthfulness of any part of the historical narratives of the Old Testament. No detail was too insignificant to be used for the instruction of New Testament Christians. There is no indication that they thought of a certain category of scriptural statements that were unreliable and untrustworthy (such as "historical and scientific" statements as opposed to doctrinal and moral passages). It seems clear that the Bible itself does not support any restriction on the kinds of subjects to which it speaks with absolute authority and truth; indeed, many passages in Scripture actually exclude the validity of this kind of restriction.

A second response to those who limit the necessary truthfulness of Scripture to matters of "faith and practice" is to note that this position mistakes the *major* purpose of Scripture for the *total* purpose of Scripture. To say that the major purpose of Scripture is to teach us in matters of "faith and practice" is to make a useful and correct summary of God's purpose in giving us the Bible. But as a *summary* it includes only the most prominent purpose of God in giving us Scripture. It is not, however, legitimate to use this summary to deny that it is *part* of the purpose of Scripture to tell us about minor historical details or about some aspects of astronomy or geography, and so forth. A summary cannot properly be used to deny one of the things it is summarizing! To use it this way would simply show that the summary is not detailed enough to specify all of the items in question.

It is better to say that the *whole purpose* of Scripture is to say everything it does say, on whatever subject. Every one of God's words in Scripture was deemed by him to be important for us. Thus God issues severe warnings to anyone who would take away even one word from what he has said to us (Deut. 4:2; 12:32; Rev. 22:18–19): we cannot add to God's words or take from them, for all are part of his larger purpose in speaking to us. *Everything* stated in Scripture is there because God intended it to be there. God does not say anything unintentionally! So this first objection to inerrancy makes a wrong use of a summary and thereby incorrectly attempts to impose artificial limits on the kinds of things about which God can speak to us.

---

3. This is not a minor detail, but it is useful as an example of a "scientific" fact that is affirmed in the Old Testament and one about which the author says that we have knowledge "by faith"; thus, faith here is explicitly said to involve trust in the truthfulness of a scientific and historical fact recorded in the Old Testament.

## 2. Objection: The Term *Inerrancy* Is a Poor Term

People who make this second objection say that the term *inerrancy* is too precise and that it denotes a kind of absolute scientific precision that we do not want to claim for Scripture, since it contains the everyday speech of ordinary people, round numbers, and free quotations. Furthermore, those who make this objection note that the term *inerrancy* is not used in the Bible itself. Therefore, it is probably an inappropriate term for us to insist upon.

The response to this objection may be stated as follows: first, the scholars who have used the term *inerrancy* have defined it clearly for over a hundred years, and they have always allowed for the "limitations" that attach to speech in ordinary language. In no case has the term been used to denote a kind of absolute, modern scientific precision by any responsible representative of the inerrancy position. Therefore those who raise this objection to the term are not giving careful enough attention to the way in which it has been used in theological discussions for more than a century.

Second, it must be noted that we often use nonbiblical terms to summarize a biblical teaching. The word *Trinity* does not occur in Scripture, nor does the word *incarnation*. Yet both of these terms are helpful because they allow us to summarize in one word a true biblical concept, and they are therefore helpful in enabling us to discuss a biblical teaching more easily.

It should also be noted that no other single word has been proposed which says as clearly what we want to affirm when we wish to talk about total truthfulness in language. The word *inerrancy* does this quite well, and there seems no reason not to continue to use it for that purpose.

Finally, in the church today we seem to be unable to carry on the discussion around this topic without the use of this term. People may object to this term if they wish, but like it or not, this is the term about which the discussion has focused and almost certainly will continue to focus in the next several decades. When the International Council on Biblical Inerrancy (ICBI) in 1977 began a ten-year campaign to promote and defend the idea of biblical inerrancy, it became inevitable that this word would continue to be the one about which discussion would proceed. The "Chicago Statement on Biblical Inerrancy," which was drafted and published in 1978 under ICBI sponsorship (see appendix 1), defined what most evangelicals mean by inerrancy, perhaps not perfectly, but quite well, and further objections to such a widely used and well-defined term seem to be unnecessary and unhelpful for the church.[4]

---

4. Another indication of the permanence of the term *inerrancy* in theological discussion is the fact that the over 4,000 member Evangelical Theological Society, the largest professional society for evangelical scholars engaged in biblical and theological research, includes this as part of its doctrinal basis: "The Bible alone, and the Bible in its entirety, is the Word of God written and is therefore inerrant in the autographs," and then the bylaws give this further explanation of the word *inerrant*: "For the purpose of advising members regarding the intent and meaning of the reference to biblical inerrancy in the ETS Doctrinal Basis, the Society refers members to the Chicago Statement on Biblical Inerrancy (1978)." Cited from http://www.etsjets.org/about/bylaws.

### 3. Objection: We Have No Inerrant Manuscripts; Therefore, Talk About an Inerrant Bible Is Misleading

Those who make this objection point to the fact that inerrancy has always been claimed for the first or *original copies of the biblical documents*.[5] Yet none of these survive. We have only copies of copies of what Moses or Paul or Peter wrote. What is the benefit, then, of placing such great importance on a doctrine that applies only to manuscripts no one has?

In reply to this objection, it may first be stated that for over 99 percent of the words of the Bible, we *know* what the original manuscript said. Even for many of the verses where there are textual variants (that is, different words in different ancient copies of the same verse), the correct decision is clear, and there are very few places where the textual variant is both difficult to evaluate and significant in determining the meaning. In the small percentage of cases where there is significant uncertainty about what the original text said, the general sense of the sentence is usually quite clear from the context. (In addition, someone does not have to be a Hebrew or Greek scholar to identify these significant variants because all modern English translations indicate them in marginal notes with words such as "some ancient manuscripts read" or "other ancient authorities add.")

This is not to say that the study of such textual variants is unimportant, but it is to say that the study of textual variants has not left us in confusion about what the original manuscripts said.[6] It has rather brought us extremely close to the content of those original manuscripts. For most practical purposes, then, the *current published scholarly texts* of the Hebrew Old Testament and Greek New Testament *are the same as the original manuscripts*. Thus, when we say that the original manuscripts were inerrant, we are also implying that over 99 percent of the words in our present manuscripts are also inerrant, for they are exact copies of the originals. Furthermore, we *know* where the uncertain readings are (for where there are no textual variants we have no reason to expect faulty copying of the original).[7] Thus, our present manuscripts are for most purposes the same

---

5. In theological terms, these original copies are called the "autographs," using the prefix *auto-*, meaning "self," and the root *graph*, meaning "writing," to refer to a manuscript written by the original author.

6. For a discussion of the work of studying textual variants in the extant manuscripts of the Old and New Testaments, see Paul D. Wegner, *A Student's Guide to Textual Criticism of the Bible* (Downers Grove, IL: IVP Academic, 2006); see also Bruce M. Metzger and Bart Ehrman, *The Text of the New Testament: Its Transmission, Corruption, and Restoration*, 4th ed. (Oxford: Oxford University Press, 2005). For a recent defense of the accuracy of the Greek texts that are published today, see Elijah Hixson and Peter J. Gurry, eds., *Myths and Mistakes in New Testament Textual Criticism* (Downers Grove, IL: IVP Academic, 2019).

7. Of course the theoretical possibility exists that there was a copying error in the very first copy made of one of Paul's epistles, for instance, and that this error has been reproduced in all remaining copies. But this must be thought unlikely because (1) it would require that only one copy was made of the original, or that only one copy was the basis for all other extant copies, and (2) our earlier argument about the faithfulness of God in preserving the canon (see chapter 3, p. 54) would seem to imply that if such a mistake did occur, it would not be one that would materially affect our understanding of Scripture. The existence of such a copying error cannot be either proven or disproven, but further speculation about it apart from hard evidence does not appear to be profitable.

as the original manuscripts, and the doctrine of inerrancy therefore directly concerns our present manuscripts as well.

A modern analogy may help to illustrate this principle. The original copy of the United States Constitution is housed in the National Archives Building in Washington, DC. Now suppose that a massive tornado or earthquake or hurricane hit that building (God forbid!) and the original copy of the Constitution was lost. Would we be able to determine the exact words of the original Constitution? Of course we would. There are thousands of accurate copies, and we could compare them, and where they agreed, we would have confidence that we know what the original said. In a similar way, though we don't have the original copy of the book of Romans, we do know with a high degree of confidence what the original copy said.

It is extremely important to affirm the inerrancy of the original documents, for the subsequent copies were made by human beings with no claim or guarantee by God that these copies would be perfect. But the original manuscripts are those to which the claims to be God's very words apply. If we have mistakes in the copies (as we do), then these are only *human mistakes*. But if we have mistakes in the *original manuscripts*, then we are forced to say not only that human beings made mistakes but also that *God* made a mistake and spoke falsely. This we cannot do.

## 4. Objection: The Biblical Writers "Accommodated" Their Messages in Minor Details to the False Ideas Current in Their Day and Affirmed or Taught Those Ideas in an Incidental Way

This objection to inerrancy is slightly different from the one that would restrict the inerrancy of Scripture to matters of faith and practice, but it is related to it. Those who hold this position argue that it would have been very difficult for the biblical writers to communicate with the people of their time if they had tried to correct all the false historical and scientific information believed by their contemporaries. Therefore, they claim, when the biblical writers were attempting to make a larger point, they sometimes incidentally affirmed some false ideas (such as scientific ideas) that were believed by the people of their time.

Daniel P. Fuller represented this view in a famous and controversial 1968 article. He proposed that God "deliberately accommodated his language in nonrevelational matters to the way the original readers viewed the world about them, so as to enhance the communication of revelational truth." For example, although Jesus said that the mustard seed "is the smallest of all seeds" (Matt. 13:32), Fuller said that "the mustard seed is not really the smallest of all seeds, yet Jesus referred to it as such because to the Jewish mind of Jesus' day . . . the mustard seed denoted the smallest thing the eye could detect. Were Jesus not to have accommodated himself thus to the Jewish mind but to have drawn instead upon his omniscience to state what was indeed the smallest seed, what he said would then have failed to enhance communication with his hearers about the all-important revelational matters of faith and the kingdom of God."[8]

To this objection to inerrancy it can be replied, first, that God is Lord of human language and can use human language to communicate perfectly without having to affirm any false ideas that may have been held by people during the time of the writing of Scripture. This objection to inerrancy essentially denies God's effective lordship over human language.

Second, we must respond that such "accommodation" by God to our misunderstandings would imply that God had acted contrary to his character as the God who "never lies" (Titus 1:2; cf. Num. 23:19; Heb. 6:18). It is not helpful to divert attention from this difficulty by repeated emphasis on the gracious condescension of God to speak on our level. Yes, God does condescend to speak our language, the language of human beings. But no passage of Scripture teaches that he "condescends" so as to act contrary to his moral character as the God who cannot lie. He is never said to be able to condescend so as to affirm—even incidentally—something that is false. If God were to "accommodate" himself in this way, he would cease to be the God who "never lies." He would cease to be the God the Bible represents him to be. Such activity would not in any way show God's greatness, for God does not manifest his greatness by acting in a way that contradicts his character. This objection to inerrancy misunderstands the purity and unity of God as they affect all of his words and deeds.

It is not necessary to agree with Daniel Fuller that Jesus affirmed a falsehood when he said that the mustard seed "is the smallest of all seeds" (Matt. 13:32). An important principle of biblical interpretation is that we should understand words to mean what the original hearers and readers would have taken them to mean at that time and in that culture. In this case, Fuller has misunderstood what the word *seed* would have meant to an agrarian people living in first century Palestine. When Jesus spoke of *seeds*, they would not have understood him to be speaking about all the hundreds of thousands of kinds of botanical seeds that might someday be found in all the plants on the earth. They would rather have understood him to be speaking about *agricultural seeds*, seeds which they would plant in the earth to grow crops. This is what the Greek term *sperma* ("seed") refers to four other times in Matthew's gospel (Matt. 13:24, 27, 37, 38). And in that sense of *seed*, Jesus is not telling a lie about mustard seeds, but is affirming something that is completely truthful.[9]

Third, Fuller's attempt to separate "revelational" matters (truthful) from other matters (not always truthful) in Scripture is contradicted by the passages cited at the beginning of this chapter claiming that *every word* of God is true, not just words that

8. An explanation of this view can be found in Daniel P. Fuller, "Benjamin B. Warfield's View of Faith and History," *BETS* 11 (1968): 75–83.

9. The 1984 edition of the NIV in fact gave this sense with the translation, "it is the smallest of all your seeds" (Matt. 13:32), but there is nothing in the Greek text that would explicitly justify the pronoun "your," and the 2011 NIV adopted the more literal translation, "it is the smallest of all seeds."

God speaks about certain "religious" topics. (See also the discussion above showing that it is wrong to restrict Scripture's truthfulness just to matters of "faith and practice.")

Fourth, this "accommodation to ancient falsehoods" theory would be terribly destructive to our confidence in the Bible. Soon we would begin to see passage after passage where we would wonder, "Is this another part of Scripture that affirms an ancient falsehood that we should not believe today?" Once the doors open to this kind of possibility, hundreds and perhaps thousands of passages of Scripture would be thrown into question.

Finally, if Scripture contained such kinds of "accommodations" that *affirmed things that were false* simply to communicate better, this would create a serious moral problem for us. We are to be imitators of God's moral character (Lev. 11:44; Luke 6:36; Eph. 5:1; 1 Peter 5:1, et al.). We are to imitate God's truthfulness in our speech (see Eph. 4:24–25). However, if the accommodation theory is correct, then God *intentionally* made incidental affirmations of falsehood in order to enhance communication. Therefore, would it not also be right for us *intentionally* to make incidental affirmations of falsehood whenever it would enhance communication? Yet this would be tantamount to saying that a minor falsehood told for a good purpose (a "white lie") is not wrong. Such a position, contradicted by the Scripture passages cited above concerning God's total truthfulness in speech, cannot be held to be valid.

## 5. Objection: Inerrancy Overemphasizes the Divine Aspect of Scripture and Neglects the Human Aspect

This more general objection is made by those who claim that people who advocate inerrancy so emphasize the divine aspect of Scripture that they downplay its human aspect.

I agree that Scripture has both a human and a divine aspect and that we must give adequate attention to both. However, those who make this objection almost invariably go on to insist that the truly "human" aspects of Scripture *must* include the presence of some errors in Scripture. We can respond that though the Bible is fully human in that it was written by human beings using their own language, the activity of God in overseeing the writing of Scripture and causing it to be also his words means that it is different from much other human writing in precisely this aspect: it does not include error. That is exactly the point made even by sinful, greedy, disobedient Balaam in Numbers 23:19: God's speech through sinful human beings is different from the ordinary speech of men because "God is not man that he should lie." Moreover, it is simply not true that all human speech and writing contains error, for we make dozens of statements each day that are completely true. For example: "My name is Wayne Grudem." "I have three children." "I ate breakfast this morning."

## 6. Objection: There Are Some Clear Errors in the Bible

This final objection, that there are clear errors in the Bible, is either stated or implied by most of those who deny inerrancy, and for many of them the conviction that there are some actual errors in Scripture is a major factor in persuading them to challenge the doctrine of inerrancy.

In every case, the first answer that should be made to this objection is to ask where such errors are. In which specific verse or verses do these errors occur? It is surprising how frequently one finds that this objection is made by people who have little or no idea where the specific errors are but who believe there are errors because others have told them so.

In other cases, however, people will mention one or more specific passages where, they claim, there is a false statement in Scripture. In these cases, it is important that we look at the biblical text itself, and look at it very closely. If we believe that the Bible is indeed inerrant, we should be eager and certainly not afraid to inspect these texts in minute detail. In fact, our expectation will be that close inspection will show there to be no error at all. Once again it is surprising how often it turns out that a careful reading just of the English text of the passage in question will bring to light one or more possible solutions to the difficulty.

In a few passages, no solution to the difficulty may be immediately apparent from reading the English text. At that point it is helpful to consult some commentaries on the text. Both Augustine (AD 354–430) and John Calvin (1509–64), along with many more recent commentators, have taken time to deal with most of the alleged "problem texts" and to suggest plausible solutions to them. Furthermore some writers have made collections of all the most difficult texts and have provided suggested answers for them.[10]

There are a few texts where a knowledge of Hebrew or Greek may be necessary to find a solution, and those who do not have firsthand access to these languages may have to find answers either from a more technical commentary or by asking someone who does have this training. Of course, our understanding of Scripture is never perfect, and this means that there may be cases where we will be unable to find a solution to a difficult passage at the present time. This may be because the linguistic, historical, or contextual evidence we need to understand the passage correctly is presently unknown to us. This should not trouble us in a small number of passages so long as the overall pattern of our investigation of these passages has shown that there is, in fact, no error where one has been alleged.[11]

---

10. The interested reader may consult, for example, Gleason L. Archer, *Encyclopedia of Bible Difficulties* (Grand Rapids: Zondervan, 1982); William Arndt, *Does the Bible Contradict Itself?* (St. Louis: Concordia, 1955); Arndt, *Bible Difficulties* (St. Louis: Concordia, 1932); and John W. Haley, *Alleged Discrepancies of the Bible* (1874; repr., Grand Rapids: Baker, 1977); Norman L. Geisler and Thomas A. Howe, *When Critics Ask: A Popular Handbook On Bible Difficulties* (Grand Rapids, MI: Baker, 1997). Almost all of the difficult texts have reasonable proposed solutions in the notes to the *ESV Study Bible* (Wheaton, IL: Crossway, 2008) and in D A. Carson, ed., *NIV Zondervan Study Bible* (Grand Rapids: Zondervan, 2015).

11. J. P. Moreland, "The Rationality of Belief in Inerrancy," in *TrinJ* 7, no. 1 (1986): 75–86, argues convincingly that Christians should not abandon the doctrine of inerrancy simply because of a small number of "problem texts" for which they presently have no clear solution.

But while we must allow the *possibility* of being unable to solve a particular problem, it should also be stated that there are many evangelical Bible scholars today who will say that they do not presently know of any problem texts for which there is no satisfactory solution. It is possible, of course, that some such texts could be called to their attention in the future, but during the past fifty years or so of controversy over biblical inerrancy, no such "unsolved" text has been brought to their attention.[12]

Finally, a historical perspective on this question is helpful. There are no really "new" problems in Scripture. The Bible in its entirety is over 1,900 years old, and the alleged "problem texts" have been there all along. Yet throughout the history of the church there has been a firm belief in the inerrancy of Scripture in the sense in which it is defined in this chapter. Moreover, for these hundreds of years highly competent biblical scholars have read and studied those problem texts and still have found no difficulty in holding to inerrancy. This should give us confidence that the solutions to these problems are available and that belief in inerrancy is entirely consistent with a lifetime of detailed attention to the text of Scripture.[13]

## C. Examples of Some Difficult Texts

At this point it will be useful to examine three specific passages where people have thought there might be an historical error in Scripture (in addition to the "mustard seed" passage which I discussed above). The first example is rather simple, and I include it merely to illustrate how I would think through different possible explanations, but the other two are among the most challenging difficulties that have been raised against the doctrine of inerrancy.

### 1. The Order of Jesus' Temptations (Matt. 4:3–8; Luke 4:3–9).

In Matthew, the order of temptations is (1) bread, (2) temple, (3) worship:

> And the tempter came and said to him, "If you are the Son of God, command these *stones* to become loaves of *bread*." ...
>
> Then the devil ... set him on the pinnacle of the *temple* and said to him, "If you are the Son of God, *throw yourself down* ..."
>
> Again, the devil ... showed him all the kingdoms of the world. ... And he said to him, "All these I will give you, if you will *fall down and worship me*." (Matt. 4:3–9)

But in Luke, the order of temptations is (1) bread, (2) worship, (3) temple:

---

12. Speaking from my own experience, I can affirm that during the last forty-eight years (since I entered a seminary MDiv program in 1970), I have examined dozens of these "problem texts" that have been brought to my attention in the context of the inerrancy debate. In every one of those cases, upon close inspection of the text a plausible solution has become evident.

13. On the history of inerrancy in the church, see the essays by Philip Hughes, Geoffrey W. Bromiley, W. Robert Godfrey, and John D. Woodbridge and Randall H. Balmer in *Scripture and Truth*. See also the more extensive study by John D. Woodbridge, *Biblical Authority: A Critique of the Rogers and McKim Proposal* (Grand Rapids: Zondervan, 1982).

The devil said to him, "If you are the Son of God, command this *stone* to become *bread*." . . .

And the devil . . . showed him all the kingdoms of the world . . . and said . . . If you, then, will *worship me*, it will all be yours." . . .

And he took him to Jerusalem and set him on the pinnacle of the *temple* and said to him, "If you are the Son of God, *throw yourself down* from here." (Luke 4:3–9)

Which gospel tells us the order in which the events actually occurred? It is difficult to be certain. Our first impression is that Luke has arranged the events for a thematic purpose and does not intend to tell us the order in which they occurred because he just joins the events with "and" (Greek *kai* in v. 5 and *de* in v. 9) without indicating a sequence. By contrast, Matthew seems to suggest a chronological sequence with "then" (Greek *tote*) in verse 5 and "again" (Greek *palin*) in verse 8. But further study of these adverbs shows that they need not always signal chronological sequence, and Matthew elsewhere tends to arrange events for topical purposes without implying strict chronological order, so there are also some arguments that Matthew is the one who has arranged the events for a thematic purpose, not chronologically. In any case, this is not a serious challenge to inerrancy because at least one of the authors has simply used a thematic arrangement of the temptations and has not claimed otherwise.

## 2. The Order of Theudas and Judas (Acts 5:34–39)

Some readers have thought that Luke (the author of Luke-Acts) made a historical error in reporting a speech by Gamaliel:

But a Pharisee in the council named Gamaliel, . . . stood up . . . And he said to them, "Men of Israel, take care what you are about to do with these men. For before these days *Theudas rose up*, claiming to be somebody, and a number of men, about four hundred, joined him. He was killed, and all who followed him were dispersed and came to nothing. *After him Judas the Galilean rose up* in the days of the census and drew away some of the people after him. He too perished, and all who followed him were scattered. So in the present case I tell you, keep away from these men and let them alone, for if this plan or this undertaking is of man, it will fail; but if it is of God, you will not be able to overthrow them. You might even be found opposing God!" (Acts 5:34–39)

In this case, Luke clearly specifies a chronological sequence with the words "after him" (Greek *meta touton*, "after this one"). The difficulty with this passage is that it seems to conflict with the Jewish historian Josephus, writing in AD 95, who also talks about the Jewish revolutionaries Theudas and Judas, but he puts Judas first and Theudas second, opposite the order in Acts:

> But a certain *Judas* . . . from a city named Gamala . . . threw himself into the cause of rebellion. (*Jewish Antiquities* 18.4; he is called a Galilean in *Jewish War* 2.118)

Then recounting a later period, Josephus writes,

> During the period when Fadus was procurator of Judea, a certain imposter named *Theudas* persuaded the majority of the masses to take up their possessions and to follow him to the Jordan River. . . . Fadus, however . . . sent against them a squadron of cavalry. . . . Theudas himself was captured, whereupon they cut off his head and brought it to Jerusalem. (*Jewish Antiquities* 20.97–98)

So Josephus says that Theudas came *after* Judas the Galilean, but Acts 5:34–37 says Theudas came *before* Judas. Does this indicate a historical error in the Bible?

One suggestion (mentioned by students when I discuss this passage in class) is that Gamaliel himself is the one who got the names mixed up and Luke simply quoted Gamaliel's mistake accurately. But Gamaliel was a prominent Jewish leader at the time of these rebellions, so it is highly unlikely that he got these names mixed up.

Another suggestion (which I heard long ago in a public lecture by a prominent New Testament professor) is that Luke mistakenly switched the order of the names, *but that does not matter,* because what is important is the "punchline" of the episode, which is Gamaliel's statement, "If this plan or this undertaking is of man, it will fail; but if it is of God, you will not be able to overthrow them" (Acts 5:38–39). I cannot accept that explanation, however, because it would require me to agree that Scripture is not truthful in some of the historical details that it reports, and that would mean that I no longer hold to biblical inerrancy in historical details. It would require me to agree that God's Word does not always speak the truth.

Some have suggested that Josephus made the mistake and erroneously placed the rebellion of Theudas during the time when Fadus was procurator of Judea. Eckhard Schnabel says, "Josephus may be wrong about dating Theudas to the governorship of Fadus."[14] Such a mistake would not be impossible, for Fadus was procurator AD 44–46, and Josephus was writing fifty years later, about AD 95.

However, a better solution, it seems to me, is that Gamaliel in Acts 5 and Josephus are speaking about two different men, both of whom have the name of Theudas. Schnabel writes, "Theudas is a name that is not as infrequent as some have supposed. Since the name is not uncommon, it is possible, in theory, that there was an earlier Theudas" (than the one mentioned by Josephus).[15]

This then would be the sequence of events (with approximate dates):

---

14. Eckhard Schnabel, *Acts*, ZECNT (Grand Rapids: Zondervan, 2012), 315, with reference to an extensive study of other problems in Josephus's accounts.

15. Schnabel, *Acts*, 316, with reference to other evidence.

Before AD 6:  Rebellion by the first Theudas (Acts 5:36)

AD 6:  Rebellion by Judas the Galilean from Gamala (Acts 5:37 and Josephus, *Antiquities* 18.4)

AD 33–34:  Gamaliel speaks in defense of the apostles, mentioning the first Theudas and Judas the Galilean (Acts 5:34–39)

AD 44–46:  Rebellion by the second Theudas (Gamaliel could not have mentioned this rebellion ten years before it happened)

AD 62:  Luke wrote Acts

AD 93–95:  Josephus published *Jewish Antiquities*, mentioning rebellions by Judas the Galilean and the second Theudas

The main objection to this solution is that there is no other historical record of a rebellion by a first Theudas before AD 6. But our record of many of the events in first century Judea is incomplete, and therefore that is not a decisive objection.[16]

In conclusion, this passage presents one of the most difficult challenges for inerrancy, and yet there are at least two reasonable solutions. It seems to me far easier to accept one of these solutions (especially the second one) than to agree that there are untruthful historical statements in the Bible.

### 3. Take Sandals and a Staff or Don't Take Sandals or a Staff? (Matt. 10:9–10; Mark 6:8–9; Luke 9:3)

Upon first reading the parallel accounts in Matthew, Mark, and Luke, it appears that the accounts conflict with each other. In Matthew, Jesus says *not* to take sandals or staff, but in Mark, he says they *should* take a staff and wear sandals. Then Luke says *not* to take a staff:

Acquire (Greek *ktaomai*, "acquire, procure for oneself") no gold or silver or copper for your belts, no bag for your journey, or two tunics *or sandals or a staff*, for the laborer deserves his food. (Matt. 10:9–10)

He charged them to take (Greek *airō*) nothing for their journey except a staff—no bread, no bag, no money in their belts—*but to wear sandals* and not put on two tunics. (Mark 6:8–9)

---

16. Other commentators also think it likely that Gamaliel is mentioning an earlier Theudas, and that Luke records Gamaliel's speech accurately. See I. Howard Marshall, *The Acts of the Apostles*, TNTC (Leicester: Inter-varsity, 1980), 122; David G. Peterson, *The Acts of the Apostles*, PNTC (Grand Rapids: Eerdmans, 2009), 225; and Darrell Bock, *Acts*, BECNT (Grand Rapids: Baker, 2007), 250. F. F. Bruce explains why this solution is most likely: "Luke's Theudas has been identified with Josephus's Theudas by some who find Luke guilty of a double blunder: *(a)* making Gamaliel refer to a rising which took place well after his present speech purports to have been delivered.... [and] *(b)* making an event of AD 44 take place before the rising under Judas of Galilee, which is firmly dated in AD 6/7" (Bruce, *The Book of the Acts*, rev. ed., NICNT [Grand Rapids: Eerdmans, 1988], 116n57).

> And he said to them, "Take (Greek *airō*) nothing for your journey, *no staff*, nor bag, nor bread, nor money; and do not have two tunics." (Luke 9:3)

If we only had the accounts in Matthew and Mark, there would be a rather simple solution. In Matthew, Jesus tells his disciples not to "acquire" (that is, not to go out and purchase) an extra pair of sandals and an extra staff, "for the laborer deserves his food" (v. 10). This last clause explains that as they travel and preach, people will provide for their needs, so there is no need to bring extra sandals and an extra staff. Then in Mark, another part of the same conversation seems to be recorded, where Jesus clarifies that, of course, he expected them to *take along the staffs they had* and to *wear sandals* on the journey (it is highly unlikely that Jesus commanded them to travel barefoot on the rocky roads in first century Palestine, which would have made travel terribly painful and slow).

But can the statement in Luke be reconciled with this solution? It is certainly possible that Luke 9:3 has a similar meaning to Matthew 10:9–10. In both passages, Jesus is telling them not to take along *extra* supplies (such as "bread" or "money" or "two tunics," Luke 9:3), because people will provide for their needs. Therefore, in Luke as in Matthew, Jesus tells the disciples not to take along an extra staff.[17]

One objection to this interpretation is that Luke uses the same Greek verb (*airō*) as Mark, and therefore we should conclude that there is a direct contradiction: Mark says to "take" a staff and Luke says not to "take" a staff. However, this objection is not persuasive because the verb *airō* ("take") is not a technical term with only one specialized usage in the New Testament, for it is a very common verb (it occurs 101 times in the New Testament). There is no reason that the same verb could not be used to say "take the staff you have" (Mark) and "take no extra staff" (Luke), if that is a suitable meaning in the two contexts.[18] (Later, Luke 10:4 says not to "carry" sandals–presumably an extra pair— which is also similar in meaning to the prohibition of acquiring sandals in Matt. 10:10.)

Another objection is that it would be unlikely for someone to carry an extra staff on a journey. My reply is that we really don't know how likely or unlikely this would be. Already in the early church a number of scribes who copied the gospel of Matthew, and who were more familiar with ancient travel customs than we are, apparently thought that Jesus was prohibiting bringing along more than one staff, because quite a few ancient manuscripts have the plural word "staffs" (Greek *rhabdous*, plural) in Matthew 10:10,[19] and that is the wording followed in the KJV ("staves") and NKJV ("staffs") still today.[20]

---

17. This is the solution preferred by Darrell Bock, *Luke 1:1–9:50*, BECNT (Grand Rapids: Baker, 1994), 816. Bock also lists and rejects six other proposed solutions (p. 815).

18. D. A. Carson notes that *airō* "has a semantic range large enough" to mean "procure" in Luke 9:3 ("Matthew," *EBC* 8 [Grand Rapids: Zondervan, 1984], 247), thus making Luke 9:3 similar in meaning to Matthew 10:9–10.

19. The plural *rhabdous* rather than the singular *rhabdon*

is found in the following manuscripts: C, L, W, *f*¹³, M , a, ff¹, k, μ, syʰ, boᵐˢ.

20. Another solution is proposed by Grant Osborne: that Matthew and Luke are reporting "a different set of instructions given on another occasion" (*Matthew*, ZECNT [Grand Rapids: Zondervan, 2010], 379). However, I think that solution unlikely because the circumstances given in the surrounding contexts in each gospel seem to be so similar.

In conclusion, a reasonable solution is that in Mark Jesus tells the disciples that they can wear sandals and carry a staff, but in Matthew and Luke he tells them not to acquire extra sandals or an extra staff.

At this point, readers should ask themselves if they find these solutions to these last two difficult problems for inerrancy to be reasonably possible solutions. If so, I do not think that they will encounter any other passages that present more difficult challenges to inerrancy than these. There are several other passages that interpreters have used to claim that there are historical errors or contradictions in Scripture, but to my knowledge, all of them have reasonable solutions that are readily available in the academic commentaries.[21]

## D. Problems with Denying Inerrancy

The problems that come with a denial of biblical inerrancy are not insignificant, and when we understand the magnitude of these problems it gives us further encouragement not only to affirm inerrancy but also to affirm its importance for the church. Some of the more serious problems are listed here.

With respect to the previous section where I discussed some challenges to inerrancy, I could add that the difficulty of thinking that Gamaliel was referring to an earlier revolutionary named Theudas in Acts 5:36, or the difficulty of thinking that Jesus was telling his disciples not to take along an extra staff in Luke 9:3, seem to me to pale into insignificance when compared with the difficulty of saying that some of God's words in Scripture are not completely truthful.

### 1. If We Deny Inerrancy, a Serious Moral Problem Confronts Us: May We Imitate God and Intentionally Lie in Small Matters Also?

This is similar to the point made in response to objection #4, above, but here it applies not only to those who espouse objection #4 but also more broadly to all who deny inerrancy. Ephesians 5:1 tells us to be imitators of God. But a denial of inerrancy that still claims that the words of Scripture are God-breathed words necessarily implies that God intentionally spoke falsely to us in some of the less central affirmations of Scripture. But if this is right for God to do, how can it be wrong for us? Such a line of reasoning would, if we believed it, exert strong pressure on us to begin to speak untruthfully in situations where that might seem to help us communicate better, and so forth. This position would be a slippery slope with ever-increasing negative results in our own lives.

---

21. In addition, the *ESV Study Bible*, for which I served as general editor, includes in its notes proposed solutions to most or all of the more difficult passages for inerrancy (see note 10 above, which also includes a reference to the *NIV Zondervan Study Bible*, another book that includes many proposed solutions).

## 2. If Inerrancy Is Denied, We Begin to Wonder If We Can Really Trust God in Anything He Says

Once we become convinced that God has spoken falsely to us in some minor matters in Scripture, then we realize that God is *capable* of speaking falsely to us. This will have a detrimental effect on our ability to take God at his word and trust him completely or obey him fully in the rest of Scripture. We will begin to disobey initially those sections of Scripture that we least wish to obey, and to distrust initially those sections that we are least inclined to trust. But such a procedure will eventually increase, to the great detriment of our spiritual lives. Of course, such a decline in trust and obedience to Scripture may not necessarily follow in the life of every individual who denies inerrancy, but this will certainly be the general pattern, and it will be the pattern exhibited over the course of a generation that is taught to deny inerrancy.

## 3. If We Deny Inerrancy, We Essentially Make Our Own Human Minds a Higher Standard of Truth Than God's Word Itself

We use our minds to pass judgment on some sections of God's Word and pronounce them to be in error. But this is in effect to say that we know truth more certainly and more accurately than God's Word does (or than God does), at least in these areas. Such a procedure, making our own minds to be a higher standard of truth than God's Word, is the root of all intellectual sin.[22]

## 4. If We Deny Inerrancy, Then We Must Also Say That the Bible Is Wrong Not Only in Minor Details but in Some of Its Doctrines as Well

A denial of inerrancy means that we say that the Bible's teaching about the *nature of Scripture* and about the *truthfulness and reliability of God's words* is also false. These are not minor details but are major doctrinal concerns in Scripture.[23]

# QUESTIONS FOR PERSONAL APPLICATION

1. Why do you think the debate about inerrancy has become such a large issue in this century? Why do people on both sides of the question think it to be important?
2. If you thought there were some small errors affirmed by Scripture, how do you think that would affect the way you read Scripture? Would it affect your concern for truthfulness in everyday conversation?

---

22. See chapter 4, pp. 73–74, for a discussion of the Bible as our absolute standard of truth.

23. Although the undesirable positions listed above are logically related to a denial of inerrancy, a word of caution is in order: not all who deny inerrancy will also adopt the undesirable conclusions just listed. Some people (probably inconsistently) will deny inerrancy but not take these next logical steps. In debates over inerrancy, as in other theological discussions, it is important that we criticize people on the basis of views they actually hold, and distinguish those views clearly from positions we think they would hold if they were consistent with their stated views.

3. Do you know of any Scripture texts that seem to contain errors? What are they? Have you tried to resolve the difficulties in those texts? If you have not found a solution to some text, what further steps might you try?

4. As Christians go through life learning to know their Bibles better and growing in Christian maturity, do they tend to trust the Bible more or less? In heaven, do you think you will believe the Bible is inerrant? If so, will you believe it more firmly or less firmly than you do now?

5. If you are convinced that the Bible teaches the doctrine of inerrancy, how do you feel about it? Are you glad that such a teaching is there, or do you feel it to be something of a burden which you would rather not have to defend?

6. Does belief in inerrancy guarantee sound doctrine and a sound Christian life? How can Jehovah's Witnesses say that the Bible is inerrant while they themselves have so many false teachings?

7. If you agree with inerrancy, do you think belief in inerrancy should be a requirement for church membership? For teaching a Sunday school class? For holding a church office such as elder or deacon? For being ordained as a pastor? For teaching at a theological seminary? Why or why not?

8. When there is a doctrinal controversy in the church, what are the personal dangers facing those whose position is more consistent with Scripture? In particular, how could pride in correct doctrine become a problem? What is the solution? Do you think inerrancy is an important issue for the future of the church? Why or why not? How do you think it will be resolved?

**Special Terms**

*autograph*
*faith and practice*
*ICBI*
*inerrancy*
*infallible*
*textual variant*

# BIBLIOGRAPHY

(For an explanation of this bibliography see the note on the bibliography to chapter 1, pp. 23–24. Complete bibliographical data may be found on pp. 1489–96.)

## SECTIONS IN EVANGELICAL SYSTEMATIC THEOLOGIES

(In this section, when referring to some significant older works that do not include a specific discussion of inerrancy, I have listed instead the pages where they discuss biblical authority generally. In those cases the pages here duplicate the listings for chapter 4 on the authority of Scripture.)

*1. Anglican (Episcopalian)*
1882–92 . . . . . Litton, 18–40
1930 . . . . . . . . Thomas, 500–501

2001.........Packer, 16–18
2013.........Bird, 63
2013.........Bray, 137–48

2. *Arminian (Wesleyan or Methodist)*
1875–76 .....Pope, 1:36–192
1892–94 ....Miley, 2:41–49
1940.........Wiley, 1:166–84
1960.........Purkiser, 66–80
1992.........Oden, 1:335–404
2002.........Cottrell, 64–66

3. *Baptist*
1767.........Gill, 11–18
1907.........Strong, 222–42
1976–83 .....Henry, 3:248–487; 4:129–
                255, 353–404
1990–95 .....Garrett (Vol 1), 193–212
2007.........Akin, 154–62
1987–94 .....Lewis and Demarest, 1:93–171
2013.........Erickson, 188–209

4. *Dispensational*
1947.........Chafer, 1:63–88
1949.........Thiessen, 105–15
1986.........Ryrie, 77–104
2002–2005 ..Geisler, 1:248–49, 293–94,
                299–300, 410–11, 499–513
2017.........MacArthur and Mayhue,
                100–107

5. *Lutheran*
1917–24 .....Pieper, 1:232–65, 338–49
1934.........Mueller, 101–37

6. *Reformed (or Presbyterian)*
1559 .........Calvin, 1:74–92
1679–85 .....Turretin, *IET,* 1:70–85, 106–12

1871–73 .....Hodge, 1:163–82
1878.........Dabney, *DET,* 1:282–313,
                466–81
1887–1921 ...Warfield, *IAB,* passim
1937–66 .....Murray, *CW,* 1:9–15; *CW,*
                4:22–29
1938.........Berkhof, *Intro,* 144–65, 182–86
1998.........Reymond, 73–78
2011.........Horton, 194, 197–98
2013.........Frame, 597–606
2016.........Allen and Swain, 30–56
2017.........Barrett, 145–88
2019.........Letham, 190–94

7. *Renewal (or charismatic/Pentecostal)*
1988–92 .....Williams, 1:36–43
1993.........Menzies and Horton, 17–20
1995.........Horton, 81–89

## SECTIONS IN REPRESENTATIVE ROMAN CATHOLIC SYSTEMATIC THEOLOGIES

1. *Roman Catholic: Traditional*
1955.........Ott (no explicit treatment)

2. *Roman Catholic: Post–Vatican II*
1980.........McBrien, 1:64
2012.........*CCC,* paragraphs 75–83

## OTHER WORKS

(See also the bibliography for chapter 4, "Authority," much of which is also relevant here, but only part of which has been listed again.)

Allison, Gregg R. *Historical Theology: An Introduction to Christian Doctrine; A Companion to Wayne Grudem's* Systematic Theology. Grand Rapids: Zondervan, 2011, 99–119.

Archer, Gleason. *Encyclopedia of Bible Difficulties.* Grand Rapids: Zondervan, 1982.

Arndt, William. *Bible Difficulties.* St. Louis: Concordia, 1932.

———. *Does the Bible Contradict Itself?* St. Louis: Concordia, 1955.

Beale, G. K. *The Erosion of Inerrancy in Evangelicalism: Responding to New Challenges to Biblical Authority.* Wheaton, IL: Crossway, 2008.

Boice, James, ed. *The Foundation of Biblical Authority.* Grand Rapids: Zondervan, 1978.

Carson, D. A., ed. *The Enduring Authority of the Christian Scriptures.* Grand Rapids: Eerdmans, 2016.

———. *Scripture and Truth.* Grand Rapids: Zondervan, 1983.

Carson, D. A., and John Woodbridge, eds. *Hermeneutics, Authority, and Canon.* Grand Rapids: Zondervan, 1986.

Dockery, David S. and David P. Nelson. "Special Revelation." In *A Theology for the Church,* edited by Daniel L. Akin et al., 156–62. Nashville: B&H, 2014.

Feinberg, P. D. "Bible, Inerrancy and Infallibility of." In *EDT3,* 124–27.

Geisler, Norman, ed. *Biblical Errancy: An Analysis of Its Philosophical Roots.* Grand Rapids: Zondervan, 1981.

———, ed. *Inerrancy.* Grand Rapids: Zondervan, 1979 (papers from the October 1978 Chicago Conference of the ICBI).

Geisler, Norman, and William C. Roach. *Defending Inerrancy: Affirming the Accuracy of Scripture for a New Generation.* Grand Rapids: Baker, 2011.

Gundry, Stanley N., Stephen M. Garrett, and James R. A. Merrick, eds. *Five Views on Biblical Inerrancy.* Grand Rapids: Zondervan, 2013.

Haley, John W. *Alleged Discrepancies of the Bible.* Grand Rapids: Baker, 1977 (first published 1874).

Hixson, Elijah, and Peter J. Gurry, eds. *Myths and Mistakes in New Testament Textual Criticism.* Downers Grove, IL: IVP Academic, 2019.

Lewis, Gordon R., and Bruce A. Demarest. *Challenges to Inerrancy: A Theological Response.* Chicago: Moody Publishers, 1984.

Lindsell, Harold. *The Battle for the Bible.* Grand Rapids: Zondervan, 1976.

———. *The Bible in the Balance.* Grand Rapids: Zondervan, 1979.

Montgomery, John W., ed. *God's Inerrant Word.* Minneapolis: Bethany Fellowship, 1974.

Moo, Douglas J., ed. *Biblical Authority and Conservative Perspectives.* Grand Rapids: Kregel, 1997.

Murray, John. "Infallibility of Scripture." In *Thy Word Is Still Truth: Essential Writings on the Doctrine of Scripture from the Reformation to Today,* edited by Peter A. Lillback and Richard B. Gaffin. Phillipsburg, NJ: P&R, 2013.

Packer, J. I. "Scripture." In *NDT2,* 821–25.

———. "Infallibility and Inerrancy of the Bible." In *NDT,* 337–39.

Poythress, Vern Sheridan. *Inerrancy and the Gospels: A God-Centered Approach to the Challenges of Harmonization.* Wheaton, IL: Crossway, 2012.

Schaeffer, Francis. *No Final Conflict: The Bible without Error in All That It Affirms.* Downers Grove, IL: InterVarsity Press, 1975.

Tatlock, Mark, ed. *The Implications of Inerrancy for the Global Church: The Truthfulness of God's Word Defended, Explained, and Extolled by Authors from Seventeen Countries across the Globe.* Maitland, FL: Xulon, 2015.

Warfield, B. B. *Limited Inspiration.* Philadelphia: Presbyterian and Reformed, 1962.

White, James R. *Scripture Alone.* Minneapolis: Bethany House, 2004.

Woodbridge, John. *Biblical Authority: A Critique of the Rogers/McKim Proposal.* Grand Rapids: Zondervan, 1982.

Young, Edward J. *Thy Word Is Truth.* Grand Rapids: Eerdmans, 1957.

## WORKS FROM A NONINERRANCY PERSPECTIVE

See also the bibliography for chapter 4.

Barr, James. *Fundamentalism.* London: SCM, 1977.

Barton, John. *People of the Book? The Authority of the Bible in Christianity.* Louisville: Westminster John Knox, 1988.

Beegle, Dewey M. *Scripture, Tradition, and Infallibility.* Grand Rapids: Eerdmans, 1973.

Davis, Stephen T. *The Debate about the Bible.* Philadelphia: Westminster, 1977.

McKim, Donald K., ed. *The Authoritative Word: Essays on the Nature of Scripture*. Grand Rapids: Eerdmans, 1983.

Pregeant, Russell. *Reading the Bible for All the Wrong Reasons*. Minneapolis: Fortress, 2011.

Rogers, Jack, ed. *Biblical Authority*. Waco, TX: Word, 1977.

Rogers, Jack B., and Donald K. McKim. *The Authority and Interpretation of the Bible: An Historical Approach*. San Francisco: Harper and Row, 1979.

Stewart, Robert B. *The Reliability of the New Testament: Bart Ehrman and Daniel B. Wallace in Dialogue*. Minneapolis: Fortress, 2011.

## SCRIPTURE MEMORY PASSAGE

**Psalm 12:6:**
*The words of the LORD are pure words,*
*like silver refined in a furnace on the ground,*
*purified seven times.*

## HYMN

**"The Law of the Lord is Perfect"**

This modern setting of Psalm 19:7–11 expresses the perfection of God's Word in several different ways and shows various aspects of its application to our lives.

*The law of the Lord is perfect,*
*converting the soul.*
*The testimony of the Lord is sure,*
*making wise the simple.*

*Refrain*
*More to be desired are they than gold,*
*yea than much fine gold.*
*Sweeter also than honey*
*and the honeycomb.*

*The statutes of the Lord are right,*
*rejoicing the heart.*
*The commandments of the Lord are pure,*
*enlight'ning the eyes.*

*The fear of the Lord is clean,*
*enduring forever.*
*The judgments of the Lord are true,*
*and righteous altogether.*

Author: Anonymous (from Ps. 19:7–11)

## CONTEMPORARY WORSHIP SONG

**"Speak, O Lord"**

*Speak, O Lord, as we come to You*
*To receive the food of your holy word.*

*Take Your truth, plant it deep in us;*
*Shape and fashion us in Your likeness,*

*That the light of Christ might be seen today*
*In our acts of love and our deeds of faith.*
*Speak, O Lord, and fulfil in us*
*All Your purposes, for Your glory.*

*Teach us Lord full obedience,*
*Holy reverence, true humility.*
*Test our thoughts and our attitudes*
*In the radiance of Your purity.*
*Cause our faith to rise*
*Cause our eyes to see,*
*Your majestic love and authority.*
*Words of power that can never fail;*
*Let their truth prevail over unbelief.*

*Speak, O Lord, and renew our minds;*
*Help us grasp the heights of Your plans for us.*
*Truths unchanged from the dawn of time,*
*That will echo down through eternity.*
*And by grace we'll stand on Your promises;*
*And by faith we'll walk as You walk with us.*
*Speak, O Lord, 'til your church is built*
*And the earth is filled with Your glory.*

Words by Keith Getty and Stuart Townend[24]

24. Copyright © 2006 Thankyou Music (PRS) (adm. worldwide at CapitolCMGPublishing.com excluding Europe which is adm. by Integrity Music, part of the David C Cook family. Songs@integritymusic.com). All rights reserved. Used by permission.

# CHAPTER 6

# The Four Characteristics of Scripture: (2) Clarity

*Is it possible for us to understand the Bible rightly?*

## EXPLANATION AND SCRIPTURAL BASIS

Anyone who has begun to read the Bible seriously will realize that some parts can be understood very easily while other parts seem puzzling.[1] In fact, Peter reminded his readers very early in the history of the church that some parts of Paul's epistles were difficult to understand: "Just as our beloved brother Paul also wrote to you according to the wisdom given him, as he does in all his letters when he speaks in them of these matters. There are some things in them that are *hard to understand*, which the ignorant and unstable twist to their own destruction, as they do the other Scriptures" (2 Peter 3:15–16). We must admit therefore that not all parts of Scripture are able to be understood easily.

But it would be a mistake to think that most of Scripture or Scripture in general is difficult to understand. In fact, the Old Testament and New Testament frequently affirm that Scripture is written in such a way that its teachings are able to be understood by ordinary believers. Even in Peter's statement just quoted, the context is an appeal to the teachings of Paul's letter, which Peter's readers had read and understood (2 Peter 3:15). In fact, Peter assigns some moral blame to those who twist these passages "to their own destruction." And he does not say that there are things *impossible* to understand, but only *difficult* to understand.

We may define the clarity of Scripture as follows: *the clarity of Scripture means that the Bible is written in such a way that it is able to be understood, but right understanding requires time, effort, the use of ordinary means, a willingness to obey, and the help of the Holy Spirit; and our understanding will remain imperfect in this lifetime.*[2]

---

1. This chapter has been substantially revised from the first edition of this book. Much of this chapter in its present form was first given as the John Wenham Lecture at a meeting of the Tyndale Fellowship on July 8, 2009, in Cambridge, England, and was subsequently published as Grudem, "The Perspicuity of Scripture" in *Themelios* 34, no. 3 (2009): 288–308.

2. The old term for the clarity of Scripture was *perspicuity*, a term that simply means "clarity." That term itself is not very clear to people today, and I have not used it in this book.

## A. The Bible Frequently Affirms Its Own Clarity

## 1. Old Testament Affirmations of Clarity

Several Old Testament passages affirm an expectation that the words of Scripture are able to be understood. For example, "These words that I command you today shall be on your heart. *You shall teach them diligently to your children*, and shall talk of them when you sit in your house, and when you walk by the way, and when you lie down, and when you rise" (Deut. 6:6–7). But surely talking of God's words "when you walk by the way" was not limited to only one verse about marriage or relationships with neighbors or worship of God. Children naturally seek not partial discussions but the "bottom line," the final result of all that the words of God say about a topic. They seek teaching that they can follow that very day. They seek direct answers for what to believe and how to live. They seek, in simple form, systematic theology and "whole Bible" ethical teaching. Thus the command to teach children assumes an ability to summarize and make plain, at some level, "the whole counsel of God" (Acts 20:27) regarding many different topics.

Other passages in the Old Testament also assume that God's words are able to be understood by his people:

> For this commandment that I command you today *is not too hard for you*, neither is it far off. It is not in heaven, that you should say, "Who will ascend to heaven for us and bring it to us, that we may hear it and do it?" Neither is it beyond the sea, that you should say, "Who will go over the sea for us and bring it to us, that we may hear it and do it?" But the word is very near you. It is in your mouth and in your heart, so that you can do it. (Deut. 30:11–14)

> The law of the LORD is perfect,
>     reviving the soul;
> the testimony of the LORD is sure,
>     *making wise the simple*. (Ps. 19:7)

The idea here seems to be that God's testimonies make *even simple people* to be wise, and if they make wise the simple, then surely they make everyone else wise as well. A similar idea is found in Psalm 119:

> The unfolding of your words gives light;
>     it imparts understanding to the simple. (v. 130)

Elsewhere in the same Psalm, the metaphor of a lamp conveys the idea of imparting understanding—in this case, understanding how to live in the ordinary events on the "path" of life:

> Your word is a *lamp* to my feet
>     and a *light* to my path. (Ps. 119:105)

The apostle Peter expressed a similar view of the Old Testament writings:

> And we have *the prophetic word* more fully confirmed, to which you will do well to pay attention as to a *lamp* shining in a dark place, until the day dawns and the morning star rises in your hearts. (2 Peter 1:19)

## 2. New Testament Affirmations of Clarity

There is a similar emphasis in the New Testament. Jesus himself, in his teachings, his conversations, and his disputes, never responds to any questions with a hint of blaming the Old Testament Scriptures for being unclear. Even while speaking to first century people who were removed from David by about 1,000 years and from Abraham by about 2,000 years, Jesus still *assumes* that such people are able to read and to understand rightly the Old Testament Scriptures.

In a day when it is common for people to tell us how hard it is to interpret Scripture rightly, we would do well to remember that not once in the gospels do we ever hear Jesus saying anything like this: "I sympathize with your frustration—the Scriptures relevant to this topic contain unusually complex interpretative difficulties that have puzzled scholars for many years."

Instead, whether he is speaking to scholars or untrained common people, Jesus *blames the misunderstandings* not on the Scriptures themselves but *on those who misunderstand or fail to accept them*. Again and again he answers questions with statements like these:

"have you not read what David did . . ." (Matt. 12:3),
"have you not read in the Law" (Matt. 12:5),
"have you not read" (Matt. 19:4),
"have you never read in the Scriptures . . ." (Matt. 21:42),
"have you not read what was said to you by God" (Matt. 22:31),
"go and learn what this means, 'I desire mercy, and not sacrifice'" (Matt. 9:13),
"are you the teacher of Israel and yet you do not understand these things?" (John 3:10),
    and even,
"you are wrong, because you know neither the Scriptures nor the power of God"
    (Matt. 22:29).

On the road to Emmaus Jesus rebuked two disciples, "O foolish ones, and slow of heart to believe all that the prophets have spoken!" (Luke 24:25). The blame for failing to understand is always on the reader, never on the Scriptures themselves.

Similarly, most of the New Testament Epistles are written not to church leaders but to entire congregations. Paul writes,

> "to the church of God that is in Corinth" (1 Cor. 1:2),
> "to the churches of Galatia" (Gal. 1:2), and
> "to all the saints in Christ Jesus who are at Philippi, with the overseers and deacons" (Phil. 1:1).

Paul assumes that his hearers will understand what he writes, and he encourages the sharing of his letters with other churches: "When this letter has been read among you, have it read also in the church of the Laodiceans; and see that you also read the letter from Laodicea" (Col. 4:16).

The exhortations to read Scripture *publicly* also affirm an expectation that ordinary believers in ordinary congregations could understand the Scriptures: "Until I come, devote yourself to the public reading of Scripture, to exhortation, to teaching" (1 Tim. 4:13; cf. John 20:30–31; 2 Cor. 1:13; Eph. 3:4; 1 Tim. 4:13; James 1:1, 22–25; 1 Peter 1:1; 2:2; 2 Peter 1:19; 1 John 5:13). There are even some sections that assume that *children* are in the audience, listening to Paul's letters as they are read and understanding at least part of what is written, for Paul writes, "*Children*, obey your parents in the Lord, for this is right. 'Honor your father and mother' (this is the first commandment with a promise), 'that it may go well with you and that you may live long in the land'" (Eph. 6:1–3).

Whenever the New Testament authors quote the Old Testament (about 300 times), they assume that they have understood the Old Testament rightly and that their readers will realize that they are understanding it rightly—or at least that there is a right interpretation that the New Testament authors can appeal to. This is true not only for individual verses but also for collections of verses that they compile to prove a certain theme, such as the universal sinfulness of mankind (Rom. 3:9–20), the majesty and deity of Christ (Heb. 1), or the nature of faith (Heb. 11).

Should we define the clarity of Scripture merely to say that Scripture was able to be understood *only by its original readers* and not necessarily by readers today? No, I am not willing to add such a qualification because Jesus repeatedly held his hearers responsible for understanding the Old Testament writings, many of which were written more than 1,000 years prior and because the New Testament authors similarly expected their readers to know and to be able to understand the Old Testament rightly. Therefore, I think that the clarity of Scripture requires us to believe that it is still able to be understood rightly by readers today.

The appropriate conclusion from these passages is that Scripture repeatedly affirms that it is *able* to be understood. Not only certain verses or statements but the meaning of the whole of Scripture on many topics is able to be understood by God's people. These affirmations are not limited to understanding the basic way of salvation, only major themes, or certain topics or parts.[3] These are affirmations about the nature of Scripture in any part,[4] apparently grounded in a deep assumption that the Scriptures are communication from a God who is able to communicate clearly to his people.

And such a quality of Scripture seems necessary if God is going to hold us morally accountable for obeying his Word. If he has given us commands that are confusing or that most people cannot understand, then we might wonder how he can rightly hold us accountable for obeying them.

## B. Requirements for Understanding Scripture Rightly

However, we must add some necessary qualifications, or we will certainly misunderstand this doctrine as it has been understood by thoughtful writers throughout the history of the church. (Qualifications like these are not new, but they have been emphasized in responsible treatments of this doctrine at least since the time of the Reformation, as demonstrated clearly by Mark Thompson's 2006 book, *A Clear and Present Word*.[5]) These qualifications remind us that Scripture does not conform to whatever concept of clarity we might bring to the text. Rather, we need to give careful attention to the text of Scripture and allow it to define in what sense we should understand its clarity.

### 1. Time

This first requirement reminds us that understanding Scripture is a *process* that does not happen all at once. The biblical commands to *meditate* on God's law assume that further study will lead to further understanding:

> This Book of the Law shall not depart from your mouth, but you shall *meditate* on it day and night, so that you may be careful to do according to all that is written in it. For then you will make your way prosperous, and then you will have good success. (Josh. 1:8)

> But his delight is in the law of the LORD,
>     and *on his law he meditates day and night.* (Ps. 1:2; see also Ps. 119:15, 23, 48, 78)

The frequent prayers for understanding in Psalm 119 also indicate that fuller understanding comes with further study, such as:

---

3. The Westminster Confession of Faith affirms the clarity of Scripture with respect to those things "which are necessary to be known, believed, and observed for salvation" (WCF 1.7). The inclusion of "observed" makes me think that "salvation" is intended in a broader sense ("the entire experience of the blessings of salvation throughout our lives") rather than a narrow sense ("initial saving faith"). In any case, I do not see in the Scripture passages just mentioned any warrant for restricting the clarity of Scripture to certain topics or certain types of passages.

4. But see the discussion below under qualification (3), "The Use of Ordinary Means," about the need for translation into the reader's own language and the recognition that there are still today a few words that we are not sure how to translate.

5. Mark D. Thompson, *A Clear and Present Word: The Clarity of Scripture*, New Studies in Biblical Theology (Nottingham: Apollos; Downers Grove, IL: InterVarsity Press, 2006).

> Teach me, O LORD, the way of your statutes;
> and I will keep it to the end. (Ps. 119:33)

Even the apostles gradually came to a fuller understanding of the application of Old Testament laws to gentile believers, for the Jerusalem Council in Acts 15 was the culmination of a process of seeking consensus in understanding this issue. And once the leaders gathered in Jerusalem, resolution took some time:

> *And after there had been much debate*, Peter stood up and said to them, "Brothers, you know that in the early days God made a choice among you, that by my mouth the Gentiles should hear the word of the gospel and believe." (Acts 15:7)

Afterward, Barnabas and Paul spoke, then James spoke, and then they wrote a letter:

> It has seemed good to us, *having come to one accord*, to choose men and send them to you with our beloved Barnabas and Paul. (Acts 15:25)

> For *it has seemed good to the Holy Spirit and to us* to lay on you no greater burden than these requirements. (Acts 15:28)

Paul speaks of a process of gaining fuller understanding when he says, "For we are not writing to you anything other than what you read and understand and I hope you will fully understand" (2 Cor. 1:13). And deeper understanding is given to those who are more mature in their faith:

> Yet *among the mature* we do impart wisdom, although it is not a wisdom of this age or of the rulers of this age, who are doomed to pass away. But we impart a secret and hidden wisdom of God, which God decreed before the ages for our glory. (1 Cor. 2:6–7)

> But *solid food is for the mature*, for those who have their powers of discernment trained by constant practice to distinguish good from evil. (Heb. 5:14)

Scripture affirms that it is able to be understood, *but not all at once*: growth in understanding is a lifelong process. *Clarity is a property of Scripture*, not a property of its readers, who vary widely in their understanding.[6]

---

6. I am grateful to Gregg Allison for first emphasizing to me how the focus of this doctrine must be on the nature of Scripture, not the misunderstandings of its various readers. See Gregg Allison, "The Protestant Doctrine of the Perspicuity of Scripture: A Reformulation on the Basis of Biblical Teaching" (PhD diss., Trinity Evangelical Divinity School, 1995).

## 2. Effort

The same verses above on meditation affirm that *effort* is involved, just as "Ezra had set his heart to *study* the Law of the LORD, and to do it and to teach his statutes and rules in Israel." (Ezra 7:10). Ezra presumably already knew the Law of the Lord, but he studied in order to understand it more fully.

And the clarity of Scripture does not mean that it is all *easy* to understand! Some parts are more difficult than others, as even Peter acknowledges:

> And count the patience of our Lord as salvation, just as our beloved brother Paul also wrote to you according to the wisdom given him, as he does in all his letters when he speaks in them of these matters. *There are some things in them that are hard to understand*, which the ignorant and unstable twist to their own destruction, as they do the other Scriptures. (2 Peter 3:15–16)

The things that are hard to understand in Scripture will take more effort on our part.

## 3. The Use of Ordinary Means

The Westminster Confession of Faith says that "in a due use of the ordinary means" even "the unlearned" may "attain unto a sufficient understanding" of those things in Scripture "which are necessary to be known, believed, and observed for salvation" (WCF 1.7).

What are such "ordinary means"? I am going to suggest several, perhaps a longer list than would commonly come to mind:

A. Using a *translation of the Bible in one's own language,* for people cannot understand a text if they do not know the language in which the text is written (see 1 Cor. 14:10–11, 16).[7] This need of a translation has led Christians to translate the Bible, or parts of the Bible, into more than 3,000 languages.

The need for a translation brings up one specific difficulty: there are some places in Scripture where we still are not sure what a certain Hebrew or Aramaic or Greek word means. One example is *selāh* in the Psalms (it occurs seventy-one times in Psalms and three times in Habakkuk).[8] Most modern translations just print it as a transliterated word "Selah" and add a footnote saying that the meaning is uncertain, but it probably is a musical or liturgical term.[9] Does this kind of problem modify or correct the doctrine of the clarity of Scripture?

---

7. I am grateful for a thoughtful email from David Instone-Brewer that prompted me to add translation to this list of means of interpretation.

8. I am grateful to Daniel Hill for bringing up the difficulty of unknown words such as *selāh* and for discussing it with me at some length.

9. Most translations indicate that it probably is some kind of musical or liturgical direction. The lexicons are uncertain whether it means "pause" or "interlude" or "lift up" (that is, lift up the volume or pitch of singing) or something else.

I certainly am not claiming that the meaning of a word is "clear" when we don't know what the word means! Therefore we might say, with additional precision regarding this requirement, "Scripture affirms that it is able to be understood, but understanding requires the use of ordinary means, *including translation into the reader's own language*," and that qualification implies, in the specific details where we have a yet-unknown word, that we *probably* do not know the meaning. Yet I say "probably" because context is a great help, and context makes it likely that the word indicated some kind of pause in reading or singing—we have a general sense of the word from its placement, as well as from cognate terms. And we still know that the surrounding verses contain praises, prayers, or words of lament, and *selāh* does not substantially change those meanings. To take another example, we are uncertain of the precise identity of some of the precious stones listed in Exodus 28:17–20, but we know many of them, and we know that the uncertain words refer to other precious stones.

Therefore, I would say that Scripture is able to be understood *everywhere where we are able to translate it accurately*, that the yet-unknown words are relatively few in comparison to the whole scope of Scripture, and that even where the meaning of a *word* is unknown, the sense of the *passage* as a whole is usually quite understandable.

B. Listening to *teachers* of the Word, for God has given the gift of teaching to the church (1 Cor. 12:28).[10]

C. Reading of *commentaries* where available, for these are merely the written form of what is taught by teachers in the church.[11]

D. Being aware of the wisdom contained in the *history of interpretation* of the church (even if this only comes not firsthand but through reading commentaries that reflect some knowledge of that tradition).

E. Seeking understanding in *fellowship with others*, as in small group Bible studies (or at academic conferences).[12]

F. Using modern *tools* such as concordances, Hebrew and Greek lexicons, grammars, and sources of historical background information, which help modern readers understand more precisely the sense of the original language and the historical context in which a passage was written.[13]

---

10. I am grateful to David Reimer and Gordon Wenham for helping me to realize that this category of "teachers" may be quite broad, including not only the officially recognized pastors and teachers in a church but also fathers and mothers who impart a biblical worldview to children and more mature believers who serve as spiritual "fathers" and "mothers" to a new Christian.

11. Points (a), (b), (c), and (f) in this list all reflect the value of advanced academic work of the type done at evangelical seminaries around the world and also at specialized research libraries, such as the Tyndale House Library in Cambridge.

12. This is one reason why I have been an active member of the Evangelical Theological Society (ETS) in the United States for over thirty years. I encourage evangelical scholars to participate regularly in ETS meetings and in similar other societies and to read papers, for which there is always valuable and sometimes intense interaction!

13. Gregg Allison draws attention to a process of explaining the meaning of foreign words that is found in Scripture itself (these verses come from a detailed teaching outline on perspicuity which was sent to me by Gregg Allison): "'Behold, the virgin shall conceive and bear a son, and they shall call his

Readers who begin to use such tools to help interpret Scripture will often encounter two specialized terms: *hermeneutics* and *exegesis*. The word *hermeneutics* (from the Greek word *hermēneuō*, "to interpret") refers to *the study of correct methods of interpretation* (especially interpretation of Scripture).[14]

The word *exegesis* refers more to the actual practice of interpreting Scripture, not to theories and principles about how it should be done: *exegesis is the process of interpreting a text of Scripture.* Consequently, when one studies principles of interpretation, that is hermeneutics, but when one applies those principles and begins actually explaining a biblical text, he or she is doing exegesis.

In the use of ordinary means for understanding Scripture, do we ever need more historical information than what is found in the Bible itself? For example, do we ever need more information from archaeology or from ancient literature outside the Bible in order to understand a passage rightly?

My reply is that background information from historical sources is *often helpful* for giving us a more vivid and more precise understanding of a passage, but I doubt that it is ever necessary for understanding the general sense of a passage,[15] and I do not think that historical background information can ever properly be used to nullify or overturn something the biblical text actually says. For example, a translation will tell me that Ezra journeyed from Babylon to Jerusalem (see Ezra 7:9), and background information will tell me that it was a journey of about 900 miles (1,448 km.), and will tell me what the terrain was like. Other background information might tell me that a man like Ezra would average twenty or twenty-five miles per day when walking on a journey like this, and so the journey might have taken Ezra forty or forty-five days. This does not change my understanding of the passage (which still means that Ezra traveled to Jerusalem). But it does give me a more vivid sense of the journey.

---

name Immanuel' (which means, God with us)" (Matt. 1:23); "Taking her by the hand he said to her, 'Talitha cumi,' which means, 'Little girl, I say to you, arise'" (Mark 5:41); "Thus Joseph, who was also called by the apostles Barnabas (which means son of encouragement), a Levite, a native of Cyprus" (Acts 4:36). There is also some explanation of possibly unfamiliar customs: "Now this was the custom in former times in Israel concerning redeeming and exchanging: to confirm a transaction, the one drew off his sandal and gave it to the other, and this was the manner of attesting in Israel. So when the redeemer said to Boaz, 'Buy it for yourself,' he drew off his sandal" (Ruth 4:7–8).

14. For a thorough discussion of the various means used in interpretation see Grant R. Osborne, *The Hermeneutical Spiral* (Downers Grove, IL: InterVarsity, 1991). For an extensive analysis of modern (especially postmodern) theories of meaning, see Kevin J. Vanhoozer, *Is There a Meaning in this Text?* (Grand Rapids: Zondervan, 1998).

15. Andrew Naselli, in his excellent book, *How To Under-*

*stand and Apply the New Testament* (Phillipsburg, NJ: P&R, 2017), 165–67, suggests that information about the historical-cultural context is necessary to understand rightly passages such as 1 Corinthians 11:2–16 (head coverings for women) and Revelation 3:15–16 (hot, cold, and lukewarm water). I agree that the historical-cultural information he refers to does make our understanding of these passages much more precise and detailed. But I also recall that, before I was aware of any such information, I still understood the *general sense* of 1 Corinthians 11:2–16 to indicate that there should be some differences between men and women in the way they dress in church and that women's head covering at that time must have indicated an acceptance of God-ordained differences in roles for men and women. And when reading Revelation 3:15–16, I understood, from common human experience, that people would rather have hot water for bathing and cold water for drinking, but lukewarm water for neither. So perhaps we just differ on how broadly we would understand the "general sense" of the passage.

## 4. A Willingness to Obey

A *willingness to obey* should also be considered necessary to the right understanding of Scripture:

> Be *doers* of the word, and *not hearers only, deceiving yourselves.* For if anyone is a hearer of the word and not a doer, he is like a man who looks intently at his natural face in a mirror. For he looks at himself and goes away and at once forgets what he was like. But the one who looks into the perfect law, the law of liberty, and perseveres, being no hearer who forgets but a doer who acts, he will be blessed in his doing. (James 1:22–25)

And Psalm 119 connects a prayer for understanding with a desire to obey what is understood: "Give me understanding, that I may keep your law and observe it with my whole heart" (Ps. 119:34).

By contrast, Jesus spoke of some of his Jewish opponents' unwillingness to receive what he was teaching: "Why do you not understand what I say? It is because you cannot bear to hear my word." (John 8:43).[16]

Paul implies that the moral and spiritual immaturity of the Corinthian church prevented him from imparting deeper wisdom ("solid food" and not "milk" to them):

> But I, brothers, could not address you as spiritual people, but as people of the flesh, as infants in Christ. *I fed you with milk, not solid food*, for you were not ready for it. And even now you are not yet ready, for you are still of the flesh. For while there is jealousy and strife among you, are you not of the flesh and behaving only in a human way? (1 Cor. 3:1–3).

The practical implication of this qualification is that Christians who begin to practice willful, repeated sin (and even—or especially—pastors and scholars who begin to practice willful, repeated sin!) will likely soon begin to lose sound judgment in interpretation and will become less and less able to understand Scripture rightly.

## 5. The Help of the Holy Spirit

In Psalm 119, the frequent prayers for understanding imply a need for God's help:

> *Open my eyes*, that I may behold
> wondrous things out of your law. (Ps. 119:18)

---

16. The words "bear to hear" translate the Greek verb *akouō*, which means "hear" in the sense of "hear and receive," "hear and respond appropriately." The NET says, "It is because you cannot accept my teaching."

> *Make me understand* the way of your precepts,
>     and I will meditate on your wondrous works. (Ps. 119:27)

> *Give me understanding*, that I may keep your law
>     and observe it with my whole heart. (Ps. 119:34)

> Your hands have made and fashioned me;
>     *give me understanding* that I may learn your commandments. (Ps. 119:73)

The New Testament expresses a similar perspective on the need for divine help in understanding:

> Then he said to them, "These are my words that I spoke to you while I was still with you, that everything written about me in the Law of Moses and the Prophets and the Psalms must be fulfilled." *Then he opened their minds to understand the Scriptures.* (Luke 24:44–45)

> The *natural person* does not accept the things of the Spirit of God, for they are folly to him, and he is not able to understand them because they are *spiritually discerned.* (1 Cor. 2:14)

> But *their minds were hardened.* For to this day, when they read the old covenant, that same veil remains unlifted, because only through Christ is it taken away. Yes, to this day whenever Moses is read *a veil lies over their hearts.* But when one turns to the Lord, the veil is removed. (2 Cor. 3:14–16)

> And even if our gospel is veiled, it is veiled to those who are perishing. In their case *the god of this world has blinded the minds of the unbelievers*, to keep them from seeing the light of the gospel of the glory of Christ, who is the image of God. (2 Cor. 4:3–4)

But why do we affirm that it is specifically a work of the Holy Spirit to help us in understanding? Probably because of the emphasis on the Holy Spirit as a teacher:

> But the Helper, the Holy Spirit, whom the Father will send in my name, he will teach you all things and bring to your remembrance all that I have said to you. (John 14:26)

> Now we have received not the spirit of the world, but the Spirit who is from God, that we might understand the things freely given us by God. (1 Cor. 2:12)

## 6. A Humble Recognition That Our Understanding Is Imperfect

Clarity is *a property of Scripture*, not a property of its readers. The clarity of Scripture affirms that Scripture is *able* to be understood rightly, not that it *will always* be understood rightly.

Every believer in this age retains some measure of sin, which distorts our understanding. Moreover, our understanding is partial because we are finite. For both of these reasons, we are liable to some misunderstanding.

The disciples failed to understand some of Jesus' teachings:

"Let these words sink into your ears: The Son of Man is about to be delivered into the hands of men." But *they did not understand this saying*, and it was concealed from them, so that they might not perceive it. And they were afraid to ask him about this saying. (Luke 9:44–45)

So they took branches of palm trees and went out to meet him, crying out, "Hosanna! Blessed is he who comes in the name of the Lord, even the King of Israel!" And Jesus found a young donkey and sat on it, just as it is written, "Fear not, daughter of Zion; behold, your king is coming, sitting on a donkey's colt!" *His disciples did not understand these things at first*, but when Jesus was glorified, then they remembered that these things had been written about him and had been done to him. (John 12:13–16)

Then the other disciple, who had reached the tomb first, also went in, and he saw and believed; for *as yet they did not understand the Scripture*, that he must rise from the dead. (John 20:8–9)

In addition, there will always be in the church some who willfully misunderstand and distort what Scripture says: "There are some things in them that are hard to understand, *which the ignorant and unstable twist to their own destruction*, as they do the other Scriptures" (2 Peter 3:16; cf. 3:3–6)"

The clarity of Scripture guarantees, then, that it is *capable* of being understood rightly, not that all believers will understand it rightly. The clarity of Scripture is a doctrine about its *understandability*, not about how various people actually understand it.

In fact, much of the work of evangelical scholars indirectly bears witness to a deep confidence in Scripture's ultimate understandability. We write articles and commentaries even about those passages that seem most puzzling, and this indicates some expectation that the passages can eventually be understood rightly.

If all of God's people are to be like the "blessed man" of Psalm 1 and "meditate" on God's law day and night, then this implies that we will *always* be able to learn more from it. The other encouragements to God's people to meditate on Scripture (see section B.1 above) similarly imply this.

There is an *initial* level of understanding available to first readers of the Bible and available to some extent to children, and there are *deeper* levels of understanding that come with further reading and growth in Christian maturity.[17] "But solid food is for the mature, for those who have their powers of discernment trained by constant practice to distinguish good from evil" (Heb. 5:14).

A real-life example of how there is always more to be learned from Scripture happened to me during the year I spent writing a commentary on 1 Peter (1985–86).[18] There are only 105 verses in 1 Peter, and someone might think that a year would be more than enough time to understand it fully. But at the end of the year, when I completed the commentary, I realized that there was still much more that I could learn from 1 Peter if I only had more time.

Why is there always more that we can learn from Scripture? One reason is because it is the product of the infinite wisdom of God. Another reason is because understanding Scripture rightly is not merely a matter of understanding the individual sentences and paragraphs, but it is also a matter of understanding how *each verse* of Scripture relates to every other verse of Scripture, how *each combination of several verses* relates to each combination of several other verses or teachings, and how all of these relate to every situation of life, for all of history.

Following David, we too might say of comprehensive knowledge of God's Word: "Such knowledge is too wonderful for me; it is high; I cannot attain it" (Ps. 139:6). And Isaiah writes, "For my thoughts are not your thoughts, neither are your ways my ways, declares the LORD. For as the heavens are higher than the earth, so are my ways higher than your ways and my thoughts than your thoughts" (Isa. 55:8–9).

We might say, then, that *we do understand Scripture* because it is able to be understood, and *we are always seeking to understand Scripture more fully* because it is always able to be understood more fully. Both are implications of its clarity.

These six requirements for right understanding should not be surprising. These are sensible requirements appropriate to understanding an intricate and complex book. They are far different from saying (i) that Scripture is internally contradictory, so no clear message can be understood or taught, or (ii) that in the final analysis Scripture is baffling, like the sayings of the Delphic Oracle, or simply nonsense, like the writings of a lunatic that make no sense at all.

---

17. Grant Osborne recognizes that there are levels of understanding Scripture, as implied even in the title of his book, *The Hermeneutical Spiral*. He writes, "The average person is again justified in asking whether biblical understanding is increasingly being reserved for the academic elite. I would argue that it is not. First, there are many levels of understanding. . . . Each level has its own validity and its own process. Furthermore, those who wish to learn the hermeneutical principles that pertain to these various levels may do so. They are not restricted to any "elite" but are available to all who have the interest and energy to learn them. Basic hermeneutics can and should be taught at the level of the local church" (*The Hermeneutical Spiral*, 10).

18. Wayne Grudem, *The First Epistle of Peter*, TNTC (Leicester: Inter-Varsity; Grand Rapids: Eerdmans, 1988).

## 7. The Reasons for These Requirements

We might ask why God did not give us something simpler, something where our understanding would be instantaneous and automatic? Perhaps for several reasons:

1. **The Complexity of the Subject Matter.** God communicated to human beings in Scripture with the purpose of guiding the entire belief system and the lifelong conduct of billions of different people in hundreds of cultures throughout centuries of history. Communication sufficient for this task must necessarily be quite extensive and intricate. An infinite God is telling us about himself and his purposes in all creation! The subject matter is vast.
2. **The Value of Relationship.** God delights to teach us in relationship with himself. The prayers for understanding that are found in Scripture (see section B.5 above) indicate an awareness that Scripture is rightly understood *only in personal relationship with God*, only in a context of *prayer* for his presence and his help in right understanding.
3. **The Value of a Lifelong Process.** God causes us to delight in the *process* of growing in likeness to him. Growth in understanding Scripture is merely part of the larger process of growth in sanctification, and God in his wisdom has ordained that sanctification is a process, a lifelong journey.

God seems to delight in process, for he delights in gradually disclosing his glory over time. He took delight in creating the world not in one day but in six. He took delight in promising that the seed of the woman would bruise the head of the serpent and then in preparing the way for thousands of years so that "when the fullness of time had come, God sent forth his Son, born of woman, born under the law" (Gal. 4:4). He has taken delight in building and purifying his church for the past two thousand years.

And he takes delight when we continually increase in the knowledge of himself and his ways through his Word:

> And so, from the day we heard, we have not ceased to pray for you, asking that you may be filled with the knowledge of his will in all spiritual wisdom and understanding, so as to walk in a manner worthy of the Lord, fully pleasing to him, bearing fruit in every good work and *increasing in the knowledge of God*. (Col. 1:9–10)

The process of understanding more of Scripture and more of God is one that will never end in this life. I expect that it will never end even in the age to come. We are finite and we can rejoice in the unending and delightful process of learning more about our infinite Creator.

## C. God's Character Provides the Basis for Scripture's Clarity

The theological reason for affirming the clarity of Scripture is found in the nature of God. He is the omnipotent God who created the marvelous gift of human language so that he could use it to communicate clearly with us. He is the infinitely wise God who knows the most effective way to communicate with us. He is the infinitely loving God who cares for his people and desires to communicate clearly with us. He is the truly personal God who delights in interpersonal communication. He is the omnipresent God who remains ever near us.

As Mark Thompson says,

> While the doctrine always remained the clarity of *Scripture* . . . it is richly theological in the sense that it speaks about God and his activity amongst us. Even if we were to move forward into the seventeenth century . . . a commitment to the relevance of God's *presence*, his sovereign *power* and his rich *benevolence* remains.[19]

## D. Objections to the Clarity of Scripture

It is appropriate to mention briefly three major categories of objections to this doctrine.

### 1. Theological Liberalism

In classic Protestant liberal theology, the Bible is not thought to be the words of God as well as man but rather a collection of merely human witnesses to the work of God in people's lives. J. I. Packer writes that, in most liberal theological thinking, one finds "a view of the Bible as a fallible human record of religious thought and experience rather than a divine revelation of truth and reality."[20]

According to this view, it is only natural to expect to find that Scripture contains *numerous conflicting meanings* because it was written by *numerous human authors* who lived in widely differing Hebrew, Greek, and Roman cultures and who had widely differing ideas of God. While this viewpoint may affirm that specific individual writings are relatively clear, it would not affirm clarity as a characteristic of Scripture as a whole or as a result of divine authorship by a God who communicates to us in the words of Scripture. (This understanding of the Bible as a merely human book is the dominant viewpoint in the intellectual atmosphere in all secular universities today, and it is the assumed viewpoint from which any secular university classes about the Bible will be taught.)

---

19. Thompson, *A Clear and Present Word*, 157, emphasis added.

20. J. I. Packer, "Liberalism and Conservatism in Theology," in *NDT*, 385.

**Response:** This viewpoint is based on a fundamental difference in how we understand the nature of Scripture. I have addressed the question of the simultaneous human and divine authorship of Scripture at some length in chapters 3–5 above.[21] Such differing views of the nature of Scripture will understandably lead to differing views of the clarity of Scripture. Therefore, a confidence that the message of Scripture can actually be known with regard to many doctrines can often indicate someone's confidence in the divine authorship of Scripture as well. Belief in the clarity of Scripture as a whole is usually a telltale indicator of a prior belief in the divine authorship of Scripture.

### 2. Postmodern Hermeneutics

According to much postmodern hermeneutics, there is no absolute truth, nor is there any single meaning in a text—meaning depends on the assumptions and purposes that an interpreter brings to a text. Therefore, *claims* to know what Scripture means on a topic are just disguised attempts to exert power over others. Mark Thompson notes that postmodernism has developed the suspicion stated in the nineteenth century by Friedrich Nietzsche (1844–1900), "that all claims to know what is true are in reality covert attempts to manipulate people."[22]

Thompson gives a much more detailed explanation of this position than I can provide here,[23] but by way of brief response, I agree with Thompson that such a denial that the meaning of Scripture can be known is ultimately an attack on the character of God—his goodness, his power, and his ability to communicate clearly to his people. It is inconsistent with the assumption of the understandability of Scripture that is found in Deuteronomy's instructions to parents, in the Psalmist's exhortations to meditate daily on Scripture, in Jesus' repeated expectations that his hearers should know and understand Scripture, and in the willingness of Paul and Peter to address entire congregations with the expectation of being rightly understood. Postmodern insistence on indeterminate meaning stands in sharp contrast to the views the biblical authors themselves urge upon us page after page.

In addition, Scriptural authors frequently base an argument on the idea that a text means one thing and not another. For example,

> We say that faith was counted to Abraham as righteousness. How then was it counted to him? Was it before or after he had been circumcised? It was *not* after, but before he was circumcised. (Rom. 4:9–10)

---

21. See also Wayne Grudem, "Scripture's Self-Attestation and the Problem of Formulating a Doctrine of Scripture," in *Scripture and Truth*, ed. D. A. Carson and John Woodbridge (Grand Rapids: Zondervan, 1983), 19–59.

22. Thompson, *A Clear and Present Word*, 33.
23. Ibid., 30–47.

That is why his faith was "counted to him as righteousness." But the words "it was counted to him" were *not* written for his sake alone, but for ours also. It will be counted to us who believe in him who raised from the dead Jesus our Lord. (Rom. 4:22–24)

For it was not to angels that God subjected the world to come, of which we are speaking. It has been testified somewhere, "What is man, that you are mindful of him, or the son of man, that you care for him?" (Heb. 2:5–6)

For if Joshua had given them rest, God would not have spoken of another day later on. (Heb. 4:8)

By faith we understand that the world was created by the word of God, so that what is seen was not made out of things that are visible. (Heb. 11:3)

## 3. Roman Catholic Teaching

The Catechism of the Catholic Church explains that the correct interpretation of Scripture must come from the teaching officers of the church:

The task of giving an authentic interpretation of the Word of God, whether in its written form or in the form of Tradition, has been entrusted to the living, teaching office of the Church alone. Its authority in this matter is exercised in the name of Jesus Christ. This means that *the task of interpretation has been entrusted to the bishops in communion with the successor of Peter, the Bishop of Rome.*[24]

But neither the teachings of Jesus nor the New Testament Epistles give any hint that believing readers of Scripture need an authoritative interpreter such as the Bishop of Rome. Not even in the first century did the apostles suggest that ordinary believers needed an authoritative interpreter in order to understand Scripture rightly. The Scripture remains clear enough that it is able to be understood, now as in all previous ages, by ordinary believers who will take the needed time and effort, who employ ordinary means, and who are willing to obey it and rely on the Holy Spirit's help.

## E. THE ROLE OF SCHOLARS

Is there any role then for Bible scholars or for those with specialized knowledge of Hebrew (for the Old Testament) and Greek (for the New Testament)? Certainly there is a role for them in at least four areas:

24. *Catechism of the Catholic Church* (San Francisco: Ignatius, 1994), 27 (section 85), emphasis added.

1. Scholars in biblical studies can *teach* Scripture clearly, communicating its content to those who are preparing to become pastors and others in full-time ministry, thus fulfilling the office of "teacher" mentioned in the New Testament (1 Cor. 12:28; Eph. 4:11).

2. Scholars in biblical studies can *explore* new areas of understanding the teachings of Scripture. This exploration will seldom (if ever) involve denial of the main teachings the church has held throughout its centuries, but it will often involve the application of Scripture to new areas of life, the answering of difficult questions that have been raised by both believers and unbelievers at each new period in history, and the continual activity of refining and making more precise the church's understanding of detailed points of interpretation of individual verses or matters of doctrine or ethics. Though the Bible may not seem large in comparison with the vast amount of literature in the world, it is a rich treasure-house of wisdom from God that surpasses in value all the other books that have ever been written. The process of relating its various teachings to one another, synthesizing them, and applying them to each new generation is a greatly rewarding task that will never be completed in this age. Every scholar who deeply loves God's Word will soon realize that there is much more in Scripture than can be learned in any one lifetime!

3. Scholars in biblical studies can *defend* the teachings of the Bible against attacks by other scholars or those with specialized technical training. The role of teaching God's Word also at times involves correcting false teachings. One must be able not only "to give instruction in sound doctrine" but also "to rebuke those who contradict it" (Titus 1:9; cf. 2 Tim. 2:25, "correcting his opponents with gentleness"; and Titus 2:7–8). Sometimes those who attack biblical teachings have specialized training and technical knowledge in historical, linguistic, or philosophical study, and they use that training to mount rather sophisticated attacks against the teaching of Scripture. In such cases, believers with similar specialized skills can use their training to understand and respond to such attacks. Such training is also very useful in responding to the false teachings of cults and sects. This is not to say that believers without specialized training are incapable of responding to false teaching (for most false teaching can be clearly refuted by a believer who prays and has a good knowledge of the Bible) but rather that technical points in arguments can only be answered by those with skills in the technical areas appealed to.

4. Scholars in biblical studies can *supplement* the study of Scripture for the benefit of the church. Bible scholars often have training that will enable them to relate the teachings of Scripture to the rich history of the church and to make the interpretation of Scripture more precise and its meaning more vivid with a greater knowledge of the languages and cultures in which the Bible was written.

These four functions benefit the church as a whole, and all believers should be thankful for those who perform them. However, these functions do *not* include the right to decide for the church as a whole what is true and false doctrine or what is proper conduct in a difficult situation. If such a right were reserved for formally trained Bible scholars, then they would become a governing elite in the church, and the ordinary functioning of the government of the church as described in the New Testament would cease. The church's decision-making process must be left to the officers of the church, whether they are scholars or not (and in a congregational form of church government not only to the officers but also to the people of the church as a whole).[25]

## F. IMPLICATIONS OF THE DOCTRINE OF THE CLARITY OF SCRIPTURE

The implications of this doctrine are numerous and immensely valuable.

## 1. The Meaning of Scripture Can Be Known

The clarity of Scripture implies, first, that various texts of Scripture, and Scripture as a whole, have a meaning that can be known.

A. Therefore, the clarity of Scripture assures us that we can proclaim the gospel message with confidence, for we can know what it says and what it means.
B. Therefore, the clarity of Scripture reminds us that we as Christians should all be reading Scripture daily for our entire lives.
C. Therefore, the clarity of Scripture encourages us that we can teach *biblical doctrine* to our churches. We need not limit ourselves, for example, to teaching "Pauline theology" or "Old Testament theology" (both of which are valuable in their own right), but we should be able to teach "whole Bible theology," and so should every pastor in every church.
D. Therefore, the clarity of Scripture encourages us that we can teach *biblical ethics* to our churches—not just "Pauline ethics," "Mosaic ethics," or "Old Testament ethics" (all of which are valuable in their own right), but "whole Bible ethics" with clear application to people's lives today.

These two points (c. and d. above) show why the *clarity* of Scripture is absolutely essential to any effectual authority of Scripture in people's lives. Without the clarity of Scripture someone could say, "I believe fully in the absolute divine authority of Scripture—but I have no idea what it requires me to believe or how it requires me to live." In this way, if Scripture has no clarity, its authority is effectively nullified in real life.

---

25. See the discussion of various forms of church government in chapter 47, pp. 1135–50.

E. Therefore, scholars with advanced training in Old Testament or New Testament studies should use some of their research and writing to help the church learn what the *whole Bible* teaches about some of the important issues of the day, especially the ethical issues. I say this because there can be a temptation to speak and write only to the wider, nonevangelical academic community that does not share a belief that the whole of Scripture speaks clearly to doctrinal or ethical topics, and thus there is a temptation never to publish anything that claims to explain what the entire Bible teaches the church today about some topic. But should this be the case? Should it be that *the more people know* about how to interpret the Bible with academic precision, *the less willing they are* to explain to the church what the whole Bible says? Who then is supposed to do this? Only the pastors, with less training than the professional bible scholars? Or only the lay people, with less training than the pastors? Is that really what God intended for us? If the teaching of Scripture is able to be understood, not only in part but also in whole, then shouldn't those with the most training give the church examples of how to understand the whole?

If evangelical scholars do not do this, I'm afraid that the clarity of Scripture—and much of its message—may be covered up and hidden in our generation, not by a priesthood that keeps the Bible in a Latin language that nobody else can read, but by a new scholarly "priesthood" that by its actions implies nobody today is sufficiently well trained to teach the church what the whole Bible says about anything. The loss to the church would be immense.

## 2. Translations Should Be Encouraged

The second implication of the clarity of Scripture is that the church should be constantly giving people the Bible in their own language (that is, in translation).

In contrast to the Qur'an, which Islam teaches cannot be properly translated, the Bible contains the justification for its own translation, because the New Testament authors frequently quote directly from the Septuagint, a Greek *translation* of the Old Testament, and use it as the word of God. By this process they justify the work of translation of Scripture into other languages.

And so the conviction that people should be able to have a *translated* Bible in their own language is based in large measure on this very doctrine, the clarity of Scripture. If Scripture is *able to be understood* by ordinary believers (not perfectly, but quite well), and if Scripture is *able to be translated* and gives warrant for its own translation, then the church should eagerly translate Scripture into the languages that people speak and understand today.

This conviction has actually changed history. A conviction about the clarity of Scripture led John Wycliffe and William Tyndale and others to risk their lives in order to translate the Bible into English. A conviction about the clarity of Scripture led Martin Luther to risk his life and spend nearly a year in hiding in order to translate the New

Testament into German, and later the Old Testament as well. A conviction about the clarity of Scripture has led thousands of Wycliffe Bible translators, and many others, to devote their entire lives to the translation of Scripture into thousands of other languages.

### 3. Bible Reading Should Be Encouraged

The third implication of the clarity of Scripture is that churches should strongly encourage personal Bible reading by every believer and regular small group Bible studies.

In addition, in every nation on earth the church should be in the forefront of advocating universal literacy. In fact, in northern Europe, one of the great consequences of the Reformation was a great emphasis on universal literacy. Both boys and girls were taught to read because parents wanted their children to be able to read the Bible and to teach it to their children. The doctrine of the clarity of Scripture, where it is believed, leads directly to universal literacy in a nation.

### 4. When Christians Disagree, the Fault Is Not with the Bible

The existence of many disagreements about the meaning of Scripture throughout history reminds us that the doctrine of the clarity of Scripture does not imply or suggest that all believers will agree on all the teachings of Scripture. Nevertheless, it does tell us something very important—that the problem always lies not with Scripture but with ourselves. The situation is in fact similar to that of the authority of Scripture. Whereas we affirm that the words of Scripture have all the authority of God himself, we also realize that many people do not acknowledge that authority or submit themselves to it. Similarly, we affirm that all the teachings of Scripture are clear and able to be understood, but we also recognize that people often (through their own shortcomings) misunderstand what is clearly written in Scripture.

The doctrine of the clarity of Scripture therefore has a very important, and ultimately very encouraging, practical implication. It tells us that where there are areas of doctrinal or ethical disagreement (for example, over baptism or predestination or church government), there are only two possible causes for these disagreements: (1) On the one hand, it may be that we are *seeking to make affirmations where Scripture itself is silent.* In such cases we should be more ready to admit that God has not given us the answer to our quest and to allow for differences of viewpoint within the church. (This will often be the case with very practical questions, such as methods of evangelism or styles of Bible teaching or appropriate church size.) (2) On the other hand, it is possible that we have made *mistakes in our interpretation* of Scripture. This could have happened because the data we used to decide a question of interpretation were inaccurate or incomplete. Or it could be because there is some personal inadequacy on our part, whether it be, for example, personal pride, greed, lack of faith, selfishness, giving too much credence to non-Christian convictions in the surrounding culture, or even failing to devote enough time to prayerfully reading and studying Scripture.

But in no case are we free to say that the teaching of the Bible on any subject is confusing or incapable of being understood correctly. In no case should we think that persistent disagreements on some subject through the history of the church mean that we will be unable to come to a correct conclusion on that subject ourselves. Rather, if a genuine concern about some such subject arises in our lives, we should sincerely ask God's help and then go to Scripture, searching it with all our ability, believing that God will enable us to understand rightly. [26]

Furthermore, even though we admit that there have been many doctrinal disagreements in the history of the church, we must not forget that there has been an amazing amount of doctrinal agreement on the most central truths of Scripture throughout the history of the church. Indeed, those who have had opportunities for fellowship with Christians in other parts of the world have discovered the remarkable fact that wherever we find a group of vital Christians, almost immediately a vast amount of agreement on all the central doctrines of the Christian faith becomes apparent. Why is this true, no matter what the society, or culture, or denominational affiliation? It is because they all have been reading and believing the same Bible, and its primary teachings have been clear.

## 5. A Personal Note: The Profound Effect of This Doctrine on My Life

The doctrine of the clarity of Scripture has had a pervasive effect in my own life. Long before I had ever heard of this doctrine, the clarity of Scripture was implicit in my assumption, as a young boy of about seven or eight, that I could begin to read the King James Version of the Bible with some understanding of its message. I simply sounded out the hard words and plowed forward, no doubt with some nourishment to my soul. I simply *assumed* that God had given us a Bible that could be understood!

Then in my first teaching position at Bethel College in St. Paul, Minnesota, and later when I taught at Trinity Evangelical Divinity School and at Phoenix Seminary, a conviction about the clarity of Scripture led me to think that *I could actually use the Bible as the basis for teaching theology* to students. I would reason and argue with students from Scripture, trying to persuade them that the Bible *actually taught* certain doctrines and *contradicted* others—just as Paul in Thessalonica went into the synagogue "as was his custom, and on three Sabbath days he *reasoned* with them from the Scriptures" (Acts 17:2). Such reasoning from Scripture assumes that there is a meaning that can be understood, and that other proposed meanings are incorrect.

During my first few years of teaching theology, I used as my primary text Louis Berkhof's book *Systematic Theology*[27]—a remarkably erudite and valuable book,

---

26. I do not mean to suggest that the activity of interpreting Scripture should be an individualistic one: God will often use the writings of others or the personal advice of others to enable us to understand his Word rightly. The main point is that by whatever means, and primarily through the means of reading Scripture for themselves, Christians should expect that they will be enabled by God to understand the teachings of Scripture rightly.

27. Louis Berkhof, *Systematic Theology* (Grand Rapids: Eerdmans, 1941).

wonderfully useful for all who can read untranslated Hebrew, Greek, Latin, French, German, and of course Dutch, as well as dozens of technical theological terms that are *presumably* part of the English language—but in actuality these terms are known only to those in the academic guild. Students found Berkhof difficult.

Then I reflected on the situation. Neither Jesus nor Paul nor the writer to the Hebrews felt compelled to make their teaching of doctrine *so inaccessible* to ordinary Christians, and I wondered if it might be possible to imitate the clarity of Scripture rather than the opacity of Berkhof in writing about theology. The result was that I wrote the first edition of this book, *Systematic Theology*[28] with an attempt to combine responsible understanding and exegesis of Scripture with an explanation of its doctrines that did not assume prior technical training in academic theology. The clarity of Scripture tells me that its doctrines can be taught in a way that ordinary people are able to understand.

But more importantly, the doctrine of the clarity of Scripture convinced me that I could write such a book as *Systematic Theology* at all. Some evangelical scholars might object (and some did!) that no one should assume that he can just discover and prove points of Christian doctrine by referring to various passages of Scripture as I did in this book—what about all the alternative interpretations of all those verses found in all the commentaries? What about the thousands of pages on every one of those doctrines that were written by philosophers and theologians throughout the 2,000-year history of the church? How can you think you can use Scripture (someone might say) to support any doctrine until you have done original research in all of that material, in all the primary scholarly languages?

After pondering this objection, I concluded that to do such original research thoroughly for all the topics in theology would take several lifetimes. And yet I did not believe that God would require several lifetimes of work just to learn (or to teach) what he wanted us to believe. So I went forward with the training that I had at age thirty-seven and just started to write—not perfectly, and no doubt with many shortcomings, but for the most part reflecting the mainstream evangelical (and largely Reformed) position that seemed to me (from seminary training, from doctoral work, and from several more years of reading and teaching) to be most faithful to Scripture as a whole. I wrote this book because I believed it was *possible* for Christians today to know what Scripture taught about the great doctrines of the faith and that God wanted his people to be able to learn what it taught in clear and understandable English words.

This same conviction—that God wanted his people to be able to discover what his Word as a whole taught about various topics, and that Scripture was clear enough to make this possible—was a major factor leading me to write other books, books that attempted to explain the teaching of the entire Bible on appropriate roles for men and

28. Wayne Grudem, *Systematic Theology: An Introduction to Biblical Doctrine* (Leicester: Inter-Varsity Press; Grand Rapids: Zondervan, 1994).

women in marriage and in the church,[29] on business,[30] on politics and government,[31] on economic development,[32] and on dozens of other specific ethical issues.[33] In short, the doctrine of the clarity of Scripture has profoundly affected my entire life.

## G. Conclusion

The clarity (or perspicuity) of Scripture is no minor doctrine. It provides the basis for giving us the Bible in our own language. It provides the basis for thinking we can read the Bible and understand it. It provides the basis for thinking that we even have a Gospel message to proclaim. It provides the basis for thinking that we can know what God wants us to believe and how he wants us to live. It provides the basis for thinking that detailed study of Scripture, even extensive academic study of Scripture, has great value because it will eventually yield even fuller understanding of a Bible that is an infinite storehouse of wisdom and knowledge. It assures us that our infinite Creator, whom we seek to know and to worship, has loved us enough to speak to us in words that we can understand, not only with our minds but with our hearts. Through these words of God, we know and follow him. And thus we experience in our lives what Jesus tells us will happen: "My sheep hear my voice, and I know them, and they follow me" (John 10:27).

## QUESTIONS FOR PERSONAL APPLICATION

1. If the doctrine of the clarity of Scripture is true, why does there seem to be so much disagreement among Christians about the teaching of the Bible? Observing the diversity of interpretations of Scripture, some conclude, "People can make the Bible say anything they want." How do you think Jesus would respond to this statement?

2. What would happen to the church if most believers gave up reading the Bible for themselves and only listened to Bible teachers or read books about the Bible? If you thought that only expert scholars could understand the Bible rightly, what would happen to your personal reading of Scripture? Has this already happened to some extent in your life or in the lives of those you know?

3. Do you think that there are right and wrong interpretations of most or all passages of Scripture? If you thought the Bible was generally unclear, how would your answer change? Will a conviction about the clarity of Scripture affect the care you use when studying a text of Scripture? Will it affect the way you approach Scripture when trying to gain a biblical answer to some difficult doctrinal or moral problem?

---

29. John Piper and Wayne Grudem, eds., *Recovering Biblical Manhood and Womanhood: A Response to Evangelical Feminism* (Wheaton, IL: Crossway, 1991); also Wayne A. Grudem, *Evangelical Feminism and Biblical Truth: An Analysis of More Than One Hundred Disputed Questions* (Sisters, OR: Multnomah, 2004).

30. Wayne A. Grudem, *Business for the Glory of God: The Bible's Teaching On the Moral Goodness of Business* (Wheaton, IL: Crossway, 2003).

31. Wayne A. Grudem, *Politics according to the Bible: A Comprehensive Resource for Understanding Modern Political Issues in Light of Scripture* (Grand Rapids: Zondervan, 2010).

32. Wayne Grudem and Barry Asmus, *The Poverty of Nations: A Sustainable Solution* (Wheaton, IL: Crossway, 2013).

33. Wayne Grudem, *Christian Ethics: An Introduction to Biblical Moral Reasoning* (Wheaton, IL: Crossway, 2018).

4. If even seminary professors disagree about some Bible teaching, can other Christians ever hope to come to a correct decision on that teaching? (Give reasons for your answer.) Do you think ordinary people among the Jews at the time of Jesus had a hard time deciding whether to believe Jesus or the scholarly experts who disagreed with him? Did Jesus expect them to be able to decide?

5. How can a pastor preach biblically based sermons each Sunday without giving the impression that only people with seminary training (like himself) are able to interpret Scripture rightly? Do you think it should ever be necessary, in a doctrinal or ethical controversy, for a Bible scholar to speak in a church and base his main arguments on special meanings of Greek or Hebrew words that the church members themselves are unable to evaluate or take issue with personally? Is there an appropriate way for a scholar to use such technical knowledge in popular writing or speaking?

6. Church leaders at the time of Martin Luther said they wanted to keep the Bible in Latin to prevent the common people from reading it and then misinterpreting it. Evaluate this argument. Why do you think Martin Luther was so anxious to translate the Bible into German? Why do you think church leaders in previous centuries have persecuted and even killed men—like William Tyndale in England—who were translating the Bible into the language of the people? Why is the task of Bible translation into other languages so important a part of the work of missions?

7. Does the doctrine of the clarity of Scripture mean that the New Testament can be fully understood by people who do not have access to an Old Testament?

**Special Terms**
*clarity of Scripture*
*exegesis*
*hermeneutics*
*ordinary means*
*perspicuity*

# BIBLIOGRAPHY

(For an explanation of this bibliography see the note on the bibliography to chapter 1, pp. 23–24. Complete bibliographical data may be found on pp. 1489–96.)

## SECTIONS IN EVANGELICAL SYSTEMATIC THEOLOGIES

1. *Anglican (Episcopalian)*
   2001 . . . . . . . . Packer, 6–8
   2013 . . . . . . . . Bird, 62
   2013 . . . . . . . . Bray, 137–148

2. *Arminian (Wesleyan or Methodist)*
   1875–76 . . . . . Pope, 1:223–30
   1983 . . . . . . . . Carter, 2:747–67

3. *Baptist*
   1767 . . . . . . . . Gill, 30–32
   1976–83 . . . . . Henry, 4:272–367
   1990–95 . . . . . Garrett, 153–178
   2007 . . . . . . . . Akin, 163–64
   2013 . . . . . . . . Erickson, 222–25

### 4. Dispensational

1947 . . . . . . . . Chafer, 1:105–19
1986 . . . . . . . . Ryrie, 110–18
2002–2005 . . Geisler, 3:92
2017 . . . . . . . . MacArthur and Mayhue, 26

### 5. Lutheran

1917–24 . . . . . Pieper, 1:319–30, 359–70
1934 . . . . . . . . Mueller, 138–41

### 6. Reformed (or Presbyterian)

1679–85 . . . . . Turretin, *IET*, 1:143–47,
                   148–49
1871–73 . . . . . Hodge, 1:183–90
1906–11 . . . . . Bavinck, *RD*, 1:475–81
1938 . . . . . . . . Berkhof, *Intro.*, 167
1998 . . . . . . . . Reymond, 87–88
2008 . . . . . . . . Van Genderen and Velema,
                   96–101
2011 . . . . . . . . Horton, 197
2013 . . . . . . . . Frame, 606–612
2016 . . . . . . . . Allen and Swain, 30–56
2017 . . . . . . . . Barrett, 145–88
2019 . . . . . . . . Letham, 206–8

### 7. Renewal (or charismatic/Pentecostal)

1995 . . . . . . . . Horton, 46

## SECTIONS IN REPRESENTATIVE ROMAN CATHOLIC SYSTEMATIC THEOLOGIES

(no explicit treatment)

## OTHER WORKS

In this section I have listed several works on developing greater skill in biblical interpretation, including three helpful works by nonevangelical authors (one by Barr and two by Hirsch).

Allison, Gregg R. *Historical Theology: An Introduction to Christian Doctrine; A Companion to Wayne Grudem's* Systematic Theology. Grand Rapids: Zondervan, 2011, 120–41.

Barr, James. *The Semantics of Biblical Language.* London: Oxford University Press, 1961.

Berkhof, Louis. *Principles of Biblical Interpretation.* Grand Rapids: Baker, 1950.

Callahan, James Patrick. *The Clarity of Scripture: History, Theology and Contemporary Literary Studies.* Downers Grove, IL: InterVarsity Press, 2001.

Carson, D. A., ed. *The Enduring Authority of the Christian Scriptures.* Grand Rapids: Eerdmans, 2016.

———. *Exegetical Fallacies*, 2nd ed. Grand Rapids: Baker, 1996.

Dockery, David S. *Biblical Interpretation Then and Now: Contemporary Hermeneutics in the Light of the Early Church.* Grand Rapids: Baker, 1992.

Dockery, David S. and David P. Nelson. "Special Revelation." In *A Theology for the Church*, edited by Daniel L. Akin et al., 163–64. Nashville: B&H, 2014.

Fee, Gordon D., and Douglas Stuart. *How to Read the Bible for All Its Worth.* 4th ed. Grand Rapids: Zondervan, 2014.

Feinberg, John S. *Light in a Dark Place: The Doctrine of Scripture.* Foundations of Evangelical Theology Series. Wheaton, IL: Crossway, 2018.

Frame, John M. *The Doctrine of the Word of God.* Vol. 4. Phillipsburg, NJ: P&R, 2010.

Hirsch, E. D., Jr. *The Aims of Interpretation.* Chicago: University of Chicago Press, 1976.

———. *Validity in Interpretation.* New Haven and London: Yale University Press, 1967.

Hubbard, Robert L., William W. Klein, and Craig L. Blomberg. *Introduction to Biblical Interpretation.* 2nd ed. Nashville: Nelson, 2004.

Inch, Morris A., and C. Hassell Bullock, eds. *The Literature and Meaning of Scripture.* Grand Rapids: Baker, 1981.

King, David T., and William Webster. *Holy Scripture: The Ground and Pillar of Our Faith.* 3 vols. Battle Ground, WA: Christian Resources, 2001.

Kaiser, Walter C., Jr. *Toward an Exegetical Theology.* Grand Rapids: Baker, 1982.

MacArthur, John. "Perspicuity of Scripture: The Emergent Approach." *The Master's Seminary Journal* 17, no. 2 (Fall 2006): 141–58.

Marshall, I. Howard, ed. *New Testament Interpretation: Essays on Principles and Methods*. Grand Rapids: Eerdmans, 1977.

McCown, Wayne, and James Earl Massey, eds. *Interpreting God's Word for Today: An Inquiry Into Hermeneutics From a Biblical Theological Perspective*. Wesleyan Theological Perspectives 2. Anderson, IN: Warner, 1982.

McKnight, Scot, ed. *Introducing New Testament Interpretation*. Grand Rapids: Baker, 1990.

———. *Interpreting the Synoptic Gospels*. Grand Rapids: Baker, 1988.

Mickelsen, A. Berkeley. *Interpreting the Bible*. Grand Rapids: Eerdmans, 1963.

Osborne, Grant R. *The Hermeneutical Spiral: A Comprehensive Introduction to Biblical Interpretation*. 2nd ed. Downers Grove, IL: InterVarsity Press, 2006.

Packer, J. I. "Infallible Scripture and the Role of Hermeneutics." In *Scripture and Truth*, edited by D. A. Carson and John Woodbridge, 325–56. Grand Rapids: Zondervan, 1983.

———. "Scripture." In *NDT2*, 821–25.

Pettegrew, Larry Dean. "The Perspicuity of Scripture." *The Master's Seminary Journal* 15, no. 2 (Fall 2004): 209–25.

Ramm, Bernard. *Protestant Biblical Interpretation*. 3rd ed. Grand Rapids: Baker, 1970.

Schultz, Samuel J., and Morris A. Inch, eds. *Interpreting the Word of God: Festschrift in Honor of Steven Barabas*. Chicago: Moody Publishers, 1976.

Silva, Moises. *Biblical Words and Their Meanings*. Grand Rapids: Zondervan, 1983.

———. *Has the Church Misread the Bible? The History of Interpretation in the Light of Contemporary Issues*. Grand Rapids: Zondervan, 1987.

Sire, James. *Scripture Twisting: Twenty Ways the Cults Misread the Bible*. Downers Grove, IL: InterVarsity Press, 1980.

Sproul, R. C. *Knowing Scripture*. Downers Grove, IL: InterVarsity Press, 1977.

Thiselton, Anthony C. *New Horizons in Hermeneutics: The Theory and Practice of Transforming Biblical Reading*. Grand Rapids: Zondervan, 1992.

———. *The Two Horizons: New Testament Hermeneutics and Philosophical Description*. Grand Rapids: Eerdmans, 1980.

Thompson, Mark. *A Clear and Present Word: The Clarity of Scripture*. Downers Grove, IL: InterVarsity Press, 2006.

Ward, Timothy. *Words of Life: Scripture As the Living and Active Word of God*. Downers Grove, IL: IVP Academic, 2009.

Webster, John. "Biblical Theology and the Clarity of Scripture." In *Out of Egypt: Biblical Theology and Biblical Interpretation*, ed. Craig Bartholomew et al., 352–84. Grand Rapids: Zondervan, 2004.

## SCRIPTURE MEMORY PASSAGE

**Deuteronomy 6:6–7:** And these words that I command you today shall be on your heart. You shall teach them diligently to your children, and shall talk of them when you sit in your house, and when you walk by the way, and when you lie down, and when you rise.

## HYMN

### "Jehovah's Perfect Law"

This section of Psalm 19 set to music reminds us of many excellent qualities of Scripture, among them the fact that it is written clearly: "The testimony of the LORD is sure, making wise the simple" (v. 7). (To the tune of "We Come, O Christ, to You.")

*Jehovah's perfect law restores the soul again;*
*His testimony sure gives wisdom unto men;*
*The precepts of the LORD are right,*
*And fill the heart with great delight.*

*The LORD's commands are pure; they light and*
*    joy restore;*
*Jehovah's fear is clean, enduring evermore;*
*His statutes, let the world confess,*
*Are wholly truth and righteousness.*

*They are to be desired above the finest gold;*
*Than honey from the comb more sweetness far*
*    they hold;*
*With warnings they your servant guard,*
*In keeping them is great reward.*

*His errors who can know? Cleanse me from*
*    hidden stain;*
*Keep me from willful sins, nor let them o'er*
*    me reign;*
*And then I upright shall appear*
*And be from great transgressions clear.*

*Whene'er you search my life, may all my thoughts*
*    within*
*And all the words I speak your full approval win.*
*O Lord, you are a rock to me,*
*And my Redeemer you shall be.*

From: *The Psalter*, 1912 (taken from Ps. 19:7–14)

## CONTEMPORARY WORSHIP SONG

### "Ancient Words"

*Holy words long preserved,*
*For our walk in this world;*
*They resound with God's own heart.*
*Oh, let the ancient words impart.*

*Words of life, words of hope,*
*Give us strength, help us cope.*
*In this world, where'er we roam,*
*Ancient words will guide us home.*

*Chorus*
*Ancient words, ever true,*
*Changing me, changing you.*
*We have come with open hearts;*
*O let the ancient words impart.*

*Holy words of our faith,*
*Handed down to this age,*
*Came to us through sacrifice.*
*O heed the faithful words of Christ.*

*Martyr's blood stains each page;*
*They have died for this faith.*
*Hear them cry through the years,*
*Heed these words, and hold them dear.*

Words by Lynn DeShazo[34]

# CHAPTER 7

# The Four Characteristics of Scripture: (3) Necessity

*For what purposes is the Bible necessary?*
*How much can people know about God without the Bible?*

D o we need to have a Bible, or do we need at least to learn about what the Bible says in order to know that God exists? Or that we are sinners needing to be saved? Or to know how to find salvation? Or to know God's will for our lives? These are the kinds of questions which an investigation of the necessity of Scripture is intended to answer.

## EXPLANATION AND SCRIPTURAL BASIS

The necessity of Scripture may be defined as follows: *the necessity of Scripture means that the Bible is necessary for knowing the gospel, for maintaining spiritual life, and for knowing God's will, but it is not necessary for knowing that God exists or for knowing something about God's character and moral laws.*

As I explain below, when this definition says that the Bible is necessary for certain things, I do not mean to imply that an actual printed copy of the Bible is necessary for every person because sometimes people hear the Bible read aloud or hear others tell them some of the contents of the Bible. But even these oral communications of the contents of the Bible are based on the existence of written copies of the Bible to which other people have access.

That definition may now be explained in its various parts.

### A. The Bible Is Necessary for Knowledge of the Gospel
### 1. Several Passages Emphasize That Salvation Only Comes through Faith in Jesus Christ

In Romans 10:13–17 Paul says:

> For "everyone who calls on the name of the Lord will be saved." How then will they call on him in whom they have not believed? And *how are they to believe in him of whom they have never heard?* And how are they to hear without someone preaching? . . . So *faith comes from hearing*, and hearing through the word of Christ.

This statement indicates the following line of reasoning: (1) It first assumes that one must call upon the name of the Lord to be saved. (In Pauline usage generally as well as in this specific context [see v. 9], "the Lord" refers to the Lord Jesus Christ.) (2) People can only call upon the name of Christ if they believe in him (that is, that he is a Savior worthy of calling upon and one who will answer those who call). (3) People cannot believe in Christ unless they have heard of him. (4) They cannot hear of Christ unless there is someone to tell them about Christ ("someone preaching"). (5) The conclusion is that saving faith comes from *hearing* the gospel message, and this hearing of the gospel message comes about through the word of Christ (that is, the preaching about Christ). The implication seems to be that without hearing the preaching of the gospel of Christ, no one can be saved.[1]

This passage is one of several that show that eternal salvation comes only through belief in Jesus Christ and no other way. Speaking of Christ, John 3:18 says, "Whoever believes in him is not condemned, *but whoever does not believe is condemned already, because he has not believed in the name of the only Son of God.*" Similarly, in John 14:6 Jesus says, "I am the way, and the truth, and the life. *No one comes to the Father except through me.*"

Peter, on trial before the Sanhedrin, says, "*There is salvation in no one else,* for there is *no other name* under heaven given among men by which we must be saved" (Acts 4:12). Of course, the exclusiveness of salvation through Christ is because Jesus is the only one who died for our sins and who could have done so. Paul says, "For there is one God, and *there is one mediator between God and men, the man Christ Jesus, who gave himself as a ransom for all*" (1 Tim. 2:5–6). There is no other way to be reconciled to God than through Christ, for there is no other way of dealing with the guilt of our sin before a holy God.[2]

But if people can be saved only through faith in Christ, someone might ask how believers under the old covenant could have been saved. The answer must be that those who were saved under the old covenant were also saved through trusting in Christ, even though their faith was a forward-looking faith based on God's word of promise that a Messiah or a Redeemer would come. Speaking of Old Testament believers such as Abel, Enoch, Noah, Abraham, and Sarah, the author of Hebrews says, "*These all died in faith,* not having received the things promised, but *having seen them and*

---

1. Someone might object that the following verse, Rom. 10:18, in its quotation of Ps. 19:4, "Their voice has gone out to all the earth, and their words to the ends of the world," implies that all people everywhere have already heard the gospel message or the message of Christ. But in the context of Ps. 19, verse 4 only speaks of the fact that the natural creation, especially the heavens above, proclaim God's glory and the greatness of his creative activity, not of the saving work of Christ. There is no thought here of the proclamation of salvation through Christ. The idea that all people everywhere have heard the gospel of Christ through natural revelation would also be contrary to Paul's missionary activities.

2. On the question of whether it is fair of God to condemn people who have never heard of Christ, see the discussion in chapter 19, pp. 521–23, and chapter 32, pp. 831–32.

*greeted them from afar*" (Heb. 11:13). The same chapter goes on to say that Moses "considered the reproach *of Christ* (or the Messiah) greater wealth than the treasures of Egypt, for he was looking to the reward" (Heb. 11:26). And Jesus can say of Abraham, "Your father Abraham rejoiced that he would see my day. *He saw it* and was glad" (John 8:56). This again apparently refers to Abraham's joy in looking forward to the day of the promised Messiah. Therefore, even Old Testament believers had saving faith in Christ, to whom they looked forward, not with exact knowledge of the historical details of Christ's life, but with great faith in the absolute reliability of God's word of promise.

The Bible is necessary for salvation, then, in this sense: one must either read the gospel message in the Bible for oneself or hear it from another person. Even those believers who came to salvation in the old covenant did so by trusting in God's words that promised a Savior to come.

In fact, these repeated instances of people trusting in God's *words* of promise, together with the verses above that affirm the necessity of hearing about and believing in Christ, seem to indicate that sinful people need more on which to rest their faith than just an intuitive guess that God might provide a means of salvation. It seems that the only foundation firm enough to rest one's faith on is the *word* of God itself (whether spoken or written). This in the earliest times came in very brief form, but from the very beginning we have evidence of *words* of God promising a salvation yet to come, words that were trusted by those people whom God called to himself.

For example, even in the lifetime of Adam and Eve there are words of God that point toward a future salvation. In Genesis 3:15 the curse on the serpent includes a promise that the seed of the woman (one of her descendants) would bruise the head of the serpent but would himself be hurt in the process—a promise ultimately fulfilled in Christ. The fact that the first two children of Adam and Eve, Cain and Abel, offered sacrifices to the LORD (Gen. 4:3–4) indicates their consciousness of a need to make some kind of payment for the guilt of their sin, and of God's promise of acceptance of sacrifices offered in the right way. Genesis 4:7, "If you do well, will you not be accepted?" indicates again in the very briefest form a word from God that offered the provision of some kind of salvation through trusting in the promise of God offered in that word. As the history of the Old Testament progressed, God's words of promise became more and more specific, and the forward-looking faith of God's people accordingly became more and more definite. Yet it seems always to have been a faith resting specifically on the *words* of God himself.

Although it will be argued below that people can know that God *exists* and can know something of his *laws* apart from Scripture, it seems that there is no possibility of coming to *saving faith* apart from specific knowledge of God's words of promise. (See pp. 629–31 regarding the salvation of infants who die.)

## 2. Different Views of How People Can Be Saved

In addition to the view presented above, several other views have been advocated. Here are the most common ones:

A. *Universalism*: All people who ever lived will be saved (because God loves everyone and won't judge anyone).

B. *Religious pluralism*: All sincere religious people from all religions will be saved (because all religions are different paths to the same God).

C. *Inclusivism*: People can only be saved through the redeeming work of Christ, but all people who ever lived will still be saved, because after people die they will find out that they were saved by Christ's work (they were "included"), even people who had never heard of him or believed in him.

D. *Annihilationism*: People who have not believed in Christ will not be saved, but after they die they will not be punished (or not for very long) because they will be annihilated and cease to exist.

E. *Postmortem evangelism*: After unbelievers die, they will be given another opportunity (or a first opportunity) to trust in Christ, and most or all of them will be saved in this way.

F. *Exclusivism*: Only those who have heard of Christ and trusted in him will be saved.

The viewpoint that I have advocated above falls in the last category, "exclusivism" (though the term has a somewhat pejorative connotation and I would not have chosen it myself, but it is the term that is generally used). I hold this position because, as I explained above, it seems so clearly taught in several explicit passages of Scripture.

But is there any possibility that those who have never heard of Christ will be saved? It is understandable that our love for others would lead us to hope that some people who have not heard of Christ might be saved in other ways, such as through the testimony of angels, or through Jesus appearing to them in dreams. I acknowledge the possibility that there are aspects of this issue that God has not told us about, but it still seems to me that the Bible does not encourage us to have confidence in such a hope or to think that such ways of salvation, if they exist at all, are frequent or normal in the way God interacts with the world. What the New Testament clearly emphasizes is that salvation comes to people when Christians proclaim to them the good news about Jesus Christ. In addition, we must remember that if people hear about Christ through angels or dreams, these would not be alternative paths of salvation apart from trusting in Christ but would be additional means of making the gospel of Jesus Christ known so that people could come to trust in Christ for salvation, and so they would still fall in the category of "exclusivism." Still, the emphasis of the New Testament is on the proclamation of the gospel of Christ by human beings, Christians who eagerly travel to the ends of the earth to spread the gospel (see Rom. 10:14; 15:20–21). This has been the motivation for Christian missionary work throughout the history of the church.

And the actual situation of most people in distant, unreached villages, for example, is that they are devoted to idol worship and practices that are contrary to God's moral laws (which is Paul's argument in Romans 1–3). Furthermore, we must remember that God is always just, and his judgment will be appropriate to what people knew and how they responded to the knowledge they had (even though Romans 1–3 shows that no one fully lives up to that knowledge).

The idea that no one in the world can be saved apart from personal trust in Jesus Christ, though it has been almost universally held by Bible-believing Christians throughout church history, is a deeply unpopular idea in nearly all secular cultures today. It is thought to be "arrogant" and "intolerant of other viewpoints" by people who do not believe that there is one true God who has created everything and has spoken to us authoritatively in the Bible. Therefore, whether or not a person is willing to unashamedly affirm that eternal salvation comes only through personal faith in Jesus Christ is usually a good indication of whether that person has submitted to the absolute authority of the Bible as the Word of God or still holds the values of secular culture as a higher authority.

## B. The Bible Is Necessary for Maintaining Spiritual Life

Jesus says in Matthew 4:4 (quoting Deut. 8:3), "Man shall not live by bread alone, but by every word that comes from the mouth of God." Here Jesus indicates that our spiritual life is maintained by daily nourishment with the Word of God, just as our physical lives are maintained by daily nourishment with physical food. To neglect regular reading of God's Word is as detrimental to the health of our souls as the neglect of physical food is detrimental to the health of our bodies.

Similarly, Moses tells the people of Israel of the importance of God's words for their lives: "For it is no empty word for you, but *your very life*, and by this word you shall live long in the land that you are going over the Jordan to possess" (Deut. 32:47). And Peter encourages the Christians to whom he writes, "Like newborn infants, long for the pure spiritual milk, that by it you may grow up into salvation" (1 Peter 2:2). The "pure spiritual milk" in this context must refer to the Word of God about which Peter has been speaking (see 1 Peter 1:23–25). The Bible, then, is necessary for maintaining spiritual life and for growth in the Christian life.

## C. The Bible Is Necessary for Certain Knowledge of God's Will

I will argue below that all people ever born have *some* knowledge of God's will through their consciences. But this knowledge is often indistinct and cannot give certainty. In fact, if there were *no* written Word of God, we *could not* gain certainty about God's will through other means such as conscience, advice from others, an internal witness of the Holy Spirit, changed circumstances, and the use of sanctified reasoning and common sense. These all might give an approximation of God's will in more or less reliable ways, but from these means alone no certainty about God's will could ever be attained—at least in a fallen world where sin distorts our perception of right and wrong, brings faulty reasoning into our thinking processes, and causes us to suppress from time to time the testimony of our consciences (cf. Jer. 17:9; Rom. 2:14–15; 1 Cor. 8:10; Heb. 5:14; 10:22; also 1 Tim. 4:2; Titus 1:15).

In the Bible, however, we have clear and definite statements about God's will. God has not revealed all things to us, but he has revealed enough for us to know his will: "The secret things belong to the LORD our God, but *the things that are revealed belong to us and to our children forever*, that we may do all the words of this law" (Deut. 29:29). As it was in the time of Moses, so it is now with us: God has revealed his words to us that we might obey his laws and thereby do his will. To be "blameless" in God's sight is to "walk in the law of the LORD" (Ps. 119:1). The "blessed" man is one who does not follow the will of wicked people (Ps. 1:1), but delights "*in the law of the* LORD," and meditates on God's law "day and night" (Ps. 1:2). To love God (and thereby to act in a way that is pleasing to him) is to "keep his commandments" (1 John 5:3). If we are to have a certain knowledge of God's will, then, we must attain it through the study of Scripture.

In fact, in one sense it can be argued that the Bible is necessary for certain knowledge about anything. A philosopher might argue as follows: The fact that we do not know *everything* requires us to be somewhat uncertain about everything we do claim to know. This is because some fact unknown to us may yet turn out to prove that what we thought to be true was actually false. For example, we think we know our date of birth, our name, our age, and so forth. But we must admit that it is possible that some day we could find that our parents had given us false information, and our "certain" knowledge would then turn out to be incorrect. Regarding events that we personally have experienced, we all realize how it is possible for us to "remember" words or events incorrectly and find ourselves later corrected by more accurate information. We can usually be more certain about the events of our present experience, so long as it remains present (but even that, someone might argue, could be a dream, and we will only discover this fact when we wake up!). At any rate, it is difficult to answer the philosopher's question: If we do not know *all* the facts in the universe, past, present, and future, then how can we ever attain *certainty* that we have correct information about any one fact?

Ultimately, there are only two possible solutions to this problem. (1) We must learn all the facts of the universe in order to be sure that no subsequently discovered fact will prove our present ideas to be false; or (2) someone who *does* know all the facts in the universe, and who never lies, could tell us some true facts that we can then be sure will never be contradicted.

This second solution is in fact what we have when we have God's words in Scripture. God knows all facts that ever have been or ever will be. And this God who is omniscient (all-knowing) has absolutely certain knowledge: there can never be any fact that he does not already know; thus, there can never be any fact that would prove that something God thinks is actually false. Now it is from this infinite storehouse of certain knowledge that God, who never lies, has spoken to us in Scripture, in which he has told us many true things about himself, about ourselves, and about the universe that he has made. No fact can ever turn up to contradict the truth spoken by this one who is omniscient.

Thus, it is appropriate for us to be *more certain* about the truths we read in Scripture than about any other knowledge we have. If we are to talk about degrees of certainty of knowledge we have, then the knowledge we attain from Scripture would have the highest degree of certainty: if the word *certain* can be applied to any kind of human knowledge, it can be applied to this knowledge.[3]

This concept of the certainty of knowledge that we attain from Scripture then gives us a reasonable basis for affirming the correctness of much of the other knowledge that we have. We read Scripture and find that its view of the world around us, of human nature, and of ourselves corresponds closely to the information we have gained from our own sense-experiences of the world around us. Thus we are encouraged to trust our sense experiences of the world around us: our observations correspond with the absolute truth of Scripture; therefore, our observations are also true and, by and large, reliable. Such confidence in the general reliability of observations made with our eyes and ears is further confirmed by the fact that it is God who has made these faculties and who in Scripture frequently encourages us to use them (cf. Prov. 20:12: "The hearing ear and the seeing eye, the LORD has made them both").

In this way the Christian who takes the Bible as God's Word escapes from philosophical skepticism about the possibility of attaining certain knowledge with our finite minds. In this sense, then, it is correct to say that, for people who are not omniscient, the Bible is necessary for certain knowledge about anything.

This fact is important for the following discussion where we affirm that unbelievers *can* know something about God from the general revelation that is seen in the world

---

3. This statement assumes that we have become convinced that Scripture is indeed the very words of God and that we have understood at least some portions of Scripture correctly. Yet at this point the doctrine of the clarity of Scripture discussed in the previous chapter assures us that we will be able to understand the teachings of Scripture correctly, and the overwhelming testimony of Scripture to its own divine authorship (discussed in the chapters above concerning different forms of the Word of God and concerning the authority of Scripture), made persuasive to us by the work of the Holy Spirit, convinces us of the divine authorship of Scripture. In this sense the argument becomes not so much circular as something like a spiral where each section of the doctrine of Scripture reinforces the other and deepens our persuasion of the truthfulness of other sections of the doctrine of Scripture. By this process, our persuasion that Scripture is God's Word, that it is truth, that it is clear, and that knowledge which we attain from it is certain, becomes stronger and stronger the more we study and reflect on it.

We can of course speak of degrees of certainty that we might have concerning the fact that the Bible is God's Word, and degrees of certainty that our interpretation of any one teaching in Scripture is correct. Then from the standpoint of individual personal experience, we could say that our certainty of the correctness of knowledge that we have from Scripture becomes greater in proportion to our certainty about the God-breathed character and clarity of Scripture.

Yet from a theological standpoint, if we begin with an agreement that Scripture is God-breathed and that we do understand its teachings (at least its major teachings) correctly, then it is appropriate to say that the knowledge we attain from Scripture is more certain than any other knowledge we have.

around them. Although this is true, we must recognize that in a fallen world knowledge gained by observation of the world is always imperfect and always liable to error or misinterpretation. Therefore, the knowledge of God and creation gained from Scripture must be used to interpret correctly the creation around us. Using the theological terms that we will define below, we can say that we need special revelation to interpret general revelation rightly.[4]

### D. But the Bible Is Not Necessary for Knowing That God Exists

What about people who do not read the Bible? Can they obtain *any* knowledge of God? Can they know anything about his laws? Yes, without the Bible some knowledge of God is possible, even if it is not absolutely certain knowledge.

People can obtain knowledge *that God exists* and knowledge of *some of his attributes* simply from observing themselves and the world around them. David says, "*The heavens declare the glory of God*, and the sky above proclaims his handiwork" (Ps. 19:1). To look at the sky is to see evidence of the infinite power, wisdom, and even beauty of God; it is to observe a majestic witness to the glory of God. Similarly, Barnabas and Paul tell the Greek inhabitants of Lystra about the living God, who made the heavens and the earth: "In past generations he allowed all the nations to walk in their own ways. Yet *he did not leave himself without witness*, for he did good by giving you rains from heaven and fruitful seasons, satisfying your hearts with food and gladness" (Acts 14:16–17). Rains and fruitful seasons, the food produced from the earth that we see every day in a local grocery store, and frequent gladness that we see in people's hearts all bear witness to the fact that our Creator is a God of mercy, of love, and even of joy. These evidences of God are all around us in creation to be seen by those who are willing to see them.

Even those who by their wickedness suppress the truth cannot avoid the evidences of God's existence and nature in the created order:

> For *what can be known about God is plain to them*, because God has shown it to them. *For his invisible attributes*, namely, his eternal power and divine nature, *have been clearly perceived*, ever since the creation of the world, *in the things that have been made*. So they are without excuse. For *although they knew God*, they did not honor him as God or give thanks to him, but they became futile in their thinking, and their foolish hearts were darkened. (Rom. 1:19–21)

Here Paul says not only that creation gives evidence of God's existence and character but also that even wicked people recognize that evidence. What can be known about God is "plain to them" and in fact "they knew God" (apparently, they knew who he was), but

---

4. See p. 146 for definitions of general revelation and special revelation.

"they did not honor him as God or give thanks to him." This passage allows us to say that all persons, even the most wicked, have some internal knowledge or perception that God exists and that he is a powerful Creator. This knowledge is seen "in the things that have been made," a phrase that refers to all creation. Yet it is probably in seeing humankind created in the image of God—that is, in seeing both themselves and other people—that even wicked persons see the greatest evidence of God's existence and nature.[5]

Even without the Bible, all persons who have ever lived have had evidence in creation that God exists, that he is the Creator, and that they are his creatures, as well as some evidence of his character. As a result, they have known something about God from this evidence (even though this is never said to be a knowledge that is able to bring them to salvation).

## E. THE BIBLE IS NOT NECESSARY FOR KNOWING SOMETHING ABOUT GOD'S CHARACTER AND MORAL LAWS

Paul goes on in Romans 1 to show that even unbelievers who have no written record of God's laws still have in their consciences some understanding of God's moral demands. Speaking of a long list of sins ("envy, murder, strife, deceit"), Paul says of wicked people who practice them, "Though *they know God's righteous decree that those who practice such things deserve to die*, they not only do them but give approval to those who practice them" (Rom. 1:32). Wicked people know that their sin is wrong, at least in large measure.

Paul then talks about the activity of conscience in gentiles, who do not have the written law:

> For when Gentiles, who do not have the law, by nature do what the law requires, they are a law to themselves, even though they do not have the law. They show that *the work of the law is written on their hearts*, while their conscience also bears witness, and their conflicting thoughts accuse or even excuse them." (Rom. 2:14–15)

The consciences of unbelievers bear witness to God's moral standards, but at times this evidence of God's law on the hearts of unbelievers is distorted or suppressed.[6] Sometimes

---

5. The Swiss theologian Karl Barth (1886–1968) denied that natural man can know anything of God through the general revelation found in nature and insisted that knowledge of God can only come through a knowledge of God's grace in Christ. His radical rejection of natural revelation has not gained wide acceptance; it rests upon the unlikely view that Rom. 1:21 refers to a knowledge of God in theory but not in fact.

6. The consciences of unbelievers will be suppressed or hardened in various areas of morality, depending on cultural influences and personal circumstances. A cannibalistic society, for example, will have many members whose consciences are hardened and insensitive with regard to the evil of murder, while modern American society, for example, exhibits very little sensitivity of conscience with regard to the evil of falsehood in speech, or disrespect for parental authority, or sexual immorality. Moreover, individuals who repeatedly commit a certain sin will often find the pangs of conscience diminishing after time: a thief may feel very guilty after his first or second robbery but feel little guilt after his twentieth. The witness of conscience is still there in each case, but it is suppressed through repeated wickedness (Paul speaks of people "whose consciences are seared" in 1 Tim. 4:2).

their thoughts "accuse" them and sometimes their thoughts "excuse" them, Paul says. The knowledge of God's laws derived from such sources is never perfect, but it is enough to give an awareness of God's moral demands to all mankind. (And it is on this basis that Paul argues that all humanity is held guilty before God for sin, even those who do not have the written laws of God in Scripture.)

The knowledge of God's existence, character, and moral law, which comes through creation to all humanity, is often called *general revelation* (because it comes to all people generally).[7] General revelation comes through observing nature, through seeing God's directing influence in history, and through an inner sense of God's existence and his laws that he has placed inside every person. General revelation is distinct from *special revelation*, which refers to God's words addressed to specific people, such as the words of the Bible, the words of the Old Testament prophets and New Testament apostles, and the words of God spoken in personal address, such as at Mount Sinai or at the baptism of Jesus.[8]

Special revelation includes all the words of Scripture but is not limited to the words of Scripture, for it also includes, for example, many words of Jesus that were not recorded in Scripture, and probably there were many divinely authoritative words spoken by Old Testament prophets and New Testament apostles that were not recorded in Scripture either.

The fact that all people know something of God's moral laws is a great blessing for society, for unless they did, there would be no societal restraint on the evil that people would do and no restraint from their consciences. Because there is some common knowledge of right and wrong, Christians can often find much consensus with non-Christians in matters of civil law, community standards, basic ethics for business and professional activity, and acceptable patterns of conduct in ordinary life. Moreover, we can appeal to the sense of rightness within people's hearts (Rom. 2:14) when attempting to enact better laws or overturn bad laws or to right some other injustices in society around us. The knowledge of God's existence and character also provides a basis of information that enables the gospel to make sense to a non-Christian's heart and mind: unbelievers know that God exists and that they have broken his standards, so the news that Christ died to pay for their sins should truly come as *good news* to them.

However, it must be emphasized that Scripture nowhere indicates that people can know the gospel or the way of salvation through such general revelation. They may know that God exists, that he is their Creator, that they owe him obedience, and that

---

7. For an extensive discussion of the history of the doctrine of general revelation and its basis in Scripture, see Bruce Demarest, *General Revelation* (Grand Rapids: Zondervan, 1982); see also the excellent treatment of this doctrine in Gordon R. Lewis and Bruce A. Demarest, *Integrative Theology* (Grand Rapids: Zondervan, 1987–94), 1:59–91.

8. See chapter 2, pp. 32–34, for a discussion of God's words of personal address, God's words spoken through the lips of human beings, and God's words in Scripture, all of which fall in the category of special revelation.

they have sinned against him. The existence of systems of sacrifice in primitive religions throughout history attests to the fact that these things can be clearly known by people apart from the Bible. The repeated occurrences of the "rain and fruitful seasons" mentioned in Acts 14:17 may even lead some people to reason that God is not only holy and righteous but also loving and forgiving. But how the *holiness and justice* of God can ever be reconciled with his *willingness to forgive sins* is a mystery that has never been solved by any religion apart from the Bible. Nor does the Bible give us any hope that it ever can be discovered apart from specific revelation from God. It is the great wonder of our redemption that God himself has provided the way of salvation by sending his own Son, who is both God and man, to be our representative and bear the penalty for our sins, thus combining the justice and love of God in one infinitely wise and amazingly gracious act. This fact, which seems commonplace to the Christian ear, should not lose its wonder for us: it could never have been conceived by man alone apart from God's special, verbal revelation.

Furthermore, even if an adherent of a primitive religion could think that God somehow *must have* himself paid the penalty for our sins, such a thought would only be an extraordinary speculation. It could never be held with enough certainty to be the ground on which to rest saving faith unless God himself confirmed such speculation with his own words, namely, the words of the gospel proclaiming either that this indeed was going to happen (if the revelation came in the time before Christ) or that it indeed has happened (if the revelation came in the time after Christ). The Bible never views human speculation apart from the Word of God as a sufficient basis on which *to rest saving faith*: such saving faith, according to Scripture, is always confidence or trust in God that rests on the truthfulness of God's own words.[9]

## QUESTIONS FOR PERSONAL APPLICATION

1. When you are witnessing to an unbeliever, what is the one thing above all others that you should want him or her to read? Do you know of anyone who ever became a Christian without either reading the Bible or hearing someone tell him or her what the Bible said? What then is the primary task of an evangelistic missionary? How should the necessity of Scripture affect our missionary orientation?
2. Do you nourish your soul on the spiritual food of the Word as carefully and diligently as you nourish your body on physical food? What makes us so spiritually insensitive that we feel physical hunger much more acutely than spiritual hunger? What is the remedy?

---

9. In the New Testament, we should also note that it is specifically the Word of God that is said to be the agent that God uses in giving people spiritual life (James 1:18; 1 Peter 1:23).

3. When we are actively seeking to know God's will, where should we spend most of our time and effort? In practice, where do you spend most of your time and effort when seeking to find God's will? Do God's principles in Scripture and the apparent guidance we receive from feelings, conscience, advice, circumstances, human reasoning, or society ever seem to conflict? How should we seek to resolve the conflict?

4. Is it a hopeless task to work for civil legislation based on standards that accord with God's moral principles in Scripture? Why is there good reason to hope that we will finally be able to persuade a great majority of our society to adopt laws consistent with scriptural norms? What would hinder this effort?

**Special Terms**
*general revelation*
*natural revelation*
*necessity of Scripture*
*special revelation*

# BIBLIOGRAPHY

(For an explanation of this bibliography see the note on the bibliography to chapter 1, pp. 23–24. Complete bibliographical data may be found on pp. 1489–96.)

## SECTIONS IN EVANGELICAL SYSTEMATIC THEOLOGIES

1. *Anglican (Episcopalian)*
   1882–92 . . . . . Litton (no explicit treatment)
   1930 . . . . . . . . Thomas, 258–60
   2013 . . . . . . . . Bird, 63
   2013 . . . . . . . . Bray, 137–148

2. *Arminian (Wesleyan or Methodist)*
   1983 . . . . . . . . Carter, 1:288–89

3. *Baptist*
   1767 . . . . . . . . Gill, 1:32–36
   1976–83 . . . . . Henry, 1:17–29; 2:91–123;
               4:494–522; 6:360–69
   2013 . . . . . . . . Erickson, 144–67

   1987–94 . . . . . Lewis and Demarest, 1:59–92
   2007 . . . . . . . . Akin, 155–56

4. *Dispensational*
   1947 . . . . . . . . Chafer, 1:48–60
   2002–2005 . . Geisler, 1:65–80, 153–54, 496

5. *Lutheran*
   1934 . . . . . . . . Mueller, 90–98

6. *Reformed (or Presbyterian)*
   1559 . . . . . . . . Calvin, 1:69–74, 838–49
               (1.6; 3.19.6–16)
   1679–85 . . . . . Turretin, *IET*, 1:55–61
   1724–58 . . . . . Edwards, 2:479–85
   1861 . . . . . . . . Heppe, 31–33
   1871–73 . . . . . Hodge, 1:18–60, 364–65
   1878 . . . . . . . . Dabney, 64–78
   1906–11 . . . . . Bavinck, *RD*, 1:465–69
   1938 . . . . . . . . Berkhof, *Intro.*, 128–33;
               165–66

1998........Reymond, 56–58

2008........Van Genderen and Velema, 106–07

2013........Frame, 612–15

2016........Allen and Swain, 30–56

2017........Barrett, 145–188

2019........Letham, 52–65, 186

### 7. Renewal (or charismatic/Pentecostal)

1988–92.....Williams, 33–36, 239–41

1995........Horton, 375–76

## SECTIONS IN REPRESENTATIVE ROMAN CATHOLIC SYSTEMATIC THEOLOGIES

### 1. Roman Catholic: Traditional

1955........Ott (no explicit treatment)

### 2. Roman Catholic: Post–Vatican II

1980........McBrien, 1:151–61; 245–81

2012........*CCC*, paragraphs 131–33

## OTHER WORKS

Allison, Gregg. *Historical Theology: An Introduction to Christian Doctrine; A Companion to Wayne Grudem's* Systematic Theology. Grand Rapids: Zondervan, 2011, 142–61.

Barrick, William D. "The Necessity of Scripture." *Master's Seminary Journal* 15, no. 2 (Fall 2004): 151–164.

Berkouwer, G. C. *General Revelation*. Grand Rapids: Eerdmans, 1955.

Carson, D. A., ed. *The Enduring Authority of the Christian Scriptures*. Grand Rapids: Eerdmans, 2016.

Demarest, Bruce A. *General Revelation*. Grand Rapids: Zondervan, 1982.

———. "Revelation, General." In *EDT1*, 944–45.

Frame, John M. *The Doctrine of the Word of God*. Vol. 4. Phillipsburg, NJ: P&R, 2010.

Gundry, Stanley N., Dennis L. Okholm and Timothy R. Phillips, eds. *Four Views on Salvation in a Pluralistic World*. Grand Rapids: Zondervan, 1996.

Henry, Carl F. H. "Revelation, Special." In *EDT*, 945–48.

Jensen, P. F. "Revelation." In *EDT3*, 747–48.

Jensen, Peter. *The Revelation of God*. Downers Grove, IL: InterVarsity Press, 2002.

Kuyper, Abraham. *Principles of Sacred Theology*. Translated by J. H. de Vries. Grand Rapids: Eerdmans, 1968, 341–405 (originally published as *Encyclopedia of Sacred Theology* in 1898).

Lillback, Peter A., and Richard B. Gaffin, eds. *Thy Word Is Still Truth: Essential Writings on the Doctrine of Scripture from the Reformation to Today*. Phillipsburg, NJ: P&R, 2013.

McKim, D. K., and P. S. Chung. "Revelation and Scripture." In *GDT*, 758–67.

Moore, Russell D. "Natural Revelation." In *A Theology for the Church*, edited by Daniel L. Akin et al., 71–117. Nashville: B&H, 2014.

Packer, J. I. "Scripture." In *NDT1*, 821–25.

Van Til, Cornelius. *Common Grace and the Gospel*. Nutley, NJ: Presbyterian and Reformed, 1973.

———. *In Defense of the Faith*. Vol. 1, *The Doctrine of Scripture*. Ripon, CA: den Dulk Christian Foundation, 1967, 1–15.

———. *In Defense of the Faith*. Vol. 5, *An Introduction to Systematic Theology*. Phillipsburg, NJ: Presbyterian and Reformed, 1976, 62–109.

Ward, Timothy. *Words of Life: Scripture As the Living and Active Word of God*. Downers Grove, IL: IVP Academic, 2009.

# SCRIPTURE MEMORY PASSAGE

**Matthew 4:4:** But he answered, "It is written, 'Man shall not live by bread alone, but by every word that comes from the mouth of God.'"

# HYMN

## "Teach Me, O Lord, Your Way of Truth"

*(Use the familiar tune of "Jesus Shall Reign.")*

Teach me, O Lord, your way of truth,
   And from it I will not depart;
That I may steadfastly obey,
   Give me an understanding heart.

In your commandments make me walk,
   For in your law my joy shall be;
Give me a heart that loves your will,
   From discontent and envy free.

Turn now my eyes from vanity,
   And cause me in your ways to tread;
O let your servant prove your Word
   and thus to godly fear be led.

Turn away my reproach and fear;
   Your righteous judgments I confess;
To know your precepts I desire;
   Revive me in your righteousness.

From: *The Psalter*, 1912 (taken
from Ps. 119:33–40)

An alternative hymn for this chapter is a modern Scripture song, "Seek Ye First the Kingdom of God." The second verse of this song ("Man shall not live on bread alone . . .") is a quotation of Matthew 4:4 and expresses the necessity of Scripture for maintaining our spiritual life: we live on every word that proceeds from the mouth of God. The other verses of the song do not speak directly of the doctrine of the necessity of Scripture but do contain the words of gospel invitation (vv. 1, 4, 5). All verses in the song are direct quotations of Scripture and, as such, will be spiritually nourishing for us to sing and meditate on.

# CONTEMPORARY WORSHIP SONG

## "In Christ Alone"

In Christ alone my hope is found,
He is my light, my strength, my song;
This Cornerstone, this solid Ground,
Firm through the fiercest drought and storm.
What heights of love, what depths of peace,
When fears are stilled, when strivings cease!
My Comforter, my All in All,
Here in the love of Christ I stand.

In Christ alone!—who took on flesh,
Fullness of God in helpless babe.
This gift of love and righteousness,
Scorned by the ones He came to save:
Till on that cross as Jesus died,
The wrath of God was satisfied –
For every sin on Him was laid;
Here in the death of Christ I live.

*There in the ground His body lay,*
*Light of the world by darkness slain:*
*Then bursting forth in glorious day*
*Up from the grave He rose again!*
*And as He stands in victory*
*Sin's curse has lost its grip on me,*
*For I am His and He is mine –*
*Bought with the precious blood of Christ.*

*No guilt in life no fear in death,*
*This is the power of Christ in me;*
*From life's first cry to final breath,*
*Jesus commands my destiny.*
*No power of hell, no scheme of man,*
*Can ever pluck me from His hand:*
*Till He returns or calls me home,*
*Here in the power of Christ I'll stand.*

Words by Keith Getty and
Stuart Townend[10]

# CHAPTER 8

# The Four Characteristics of Scripture: (4) Sufficiency

*Is the Bible enough for knowing what God wants us to think or do?*

## EXPLANATION AND SCRIPTURAL BASIS

Are we to look for other words from God in addition to those we have in Scripture? The doctrine of the sufficiency of Scripture addresses this question.

### A. DEFINITION OF THE SUFFICIENCY OF SCRIPTURE

We can define the sufficiency of Scripture as follows: *the sufficiency of Scripture means that Scripture contains all the words of God we need for salvation, for trusting him perfectly, and for obeying him perfectly.*

This definition emphasizes that it is in Scripture alone that we are to search for God's words to us.[1] It also reminds us that God considers what he has told us in the Bible to be enough for us and that we should rejoice in the great revelation he has given us and be content with it.

Significant scriptural support and explanation of this doctrine is found in Paul's words to Timothy: "From childhood you have been acquainted with the sacred writings, which are *able to make you wise for salvation* through faith in Christ Jesus" (2 Tim. 3:15). The context shows that "sacred writings" here means the written words of Scripture (2 Tim. 3:16). This is an indication that the words of God that we have in Scripture are all the words of God we need in order to be saved: these words are able to make us wise "for salvation." This is confirmed by other passages that talk about the words of Scripture as the powerful means God uses to bring us to salvation (James 1:18; 1 Peter 1:23).

Other passages indicate that the Bible is sufficient to equip us for living the Christian life. Once again Paul writes to Timothy, "All Scripture is breathed out by God and profitable for teaching, for reproof, for correction, and for training in righteousness, *that the man of God may be complete, equipped for every good work*" (2 Tim. 3:16–17).

---

1. I understand subjective impressions of guidance by the Holy Spirit and the use of the gift of prophecy to be in a different category from the unique, absolutely authoritative words of God that we have Scripture alone. See further discussion below and also in chapter 53.

Here Paul indicates that one purpose for which God caused Scripture to be written is to train us that we might be "equipped for every good work." If there is any "good work" that God wants a Christian to do, this passage indicates that God has made provision in his Word for training the Christian in it. Thus there is no "good work" that God wants us to do other than those that are taught somewhere in Scripture: it can equip us for *every* good work.

A similar teaching is found in Psalm 119:1: "Blessed are those whose way is *blameless*, who *walk in the law of the* LORD!" This verse shows an equivalence between being "blameless" and "walking in the law of the LORD": those who are blameless are those who walk in the law of the Lord. Here again is an indication that all God requires of us is recorded in his written Word: simply to do all that the Bible commands us is to be blameless in God's sight.

To be morally perfect in God's sight, then, what must we do in addition to what God commands us in Scripture? Nothing! Nothing at all! If we simply keep the words of Scripture, we will be "blameless," and we will be doing "every good work" that God expects of us.

## B. We Can Find All That God Has Said on Particular Topics, and We Can Find Answers to Our Questions

Of course, we realize that we will never perfectly obey all of Scripture in this life (see James 3:2; 1 John 1:8–10; and chapter 24, below). So it may not at first seem very significant to say that all we have to do is what God commands us in the Bible, since we will never be able to obey it all in this life anyway. But the truth of the sufficiency of Scripture is of great significance for our Christian lives, for it enables us to *focus* our search for God's words to us on the Bible alone and saves us from the endless task of searching through all the writings of Christians throughout history, all the teachings of the church, or all the subjective feelings and impressions that come to our minds from day to day[2] in order to find what God requires of us. In a very practical sense,

---

2. This is not meant to imply that subjective impressions of God's will are useless or that they should be ignored. That would suggest almost a deistic view of God's (non)involvement in the lives of his children and a rather mechanical, impersonal view of guidance. God can and indeed does use subjective impressions of his will to remind and encourage us and often to prompt our thoughts in the right direction in many rapid decisions that we make throughout the day—and it is Scripture itself that tells us about these subjective factors in guidance (see Acts 16:6–7; Rom. 8:9, 14, 16; Gal. 5:16–18, 25). Yet these verses on the sufficiency of Scripture teach us that such subjective impressions can only remind us of moral commands that are already in Scripture or bring to mind facts that we (in theory at least) could have known or did know otherwise or give wise guidance regarding a specific situation; they can never add to the commands of Scripture that are for all of God's people for

all time or replace Scripture in defining with absolute divine authority what God's will is or equal Scripture in authority in our lives. See also Wayne Grudem, *Christian Ethics: An Introduction to Biblical Moral Reasoning* (Wheaton, IL: Crossway, 2018), chapter 6, on knowing God's will.

Because people from all kinds of Christian traditions have made serious mistakes when they felt confident that God was "leading them" to make a particular decision, it is important to remember that, except where an explicit text of Scripture applies directly to a situation, we can never have 100 percent certainty in this life that we know what God's will is in a situation. We can only have varying degrees of confidence in different situations. Though our ability to discern God's will should increase as we grow in Christian maturity, we will inevitably make some mistakes. In this regard, I have found helpful a sentence from Edmund Clowney: "The degree of certainty we have it means that we are able to come to clear conclusions on many teachings of Scripture. For example, though it requires some work, it is possible to find all the biblical passages that are directly relevant to the matters of marriage and divorce, the responsibilities of parents to children, or the relationship between a Christian and civil government.

This doctrine means, moreover, that it is possible to collect all the passages that directly relate to doctrinal issues such as the atonement, the person of Christ, or the work of the Holy Spirit in the believer's life today. In these and hundreds of other moral and doctrinal questions, the biblical teaching about the sufficiency of Scripture gives us confidence that *we will be able to find* what God requires us to think or to do in these areas. In many of these areas we can attain confidence that we, together with the vast majority of the church throughout history, have found and correctly formulated what God wants us to think or to do. Simply stated, the doctrine of the sufficiency of Scripture tells us that it is possible to study systematic theology and ethics and find answers to our questions.

At this point we differ from Roman Catholic theologians, who would say that we have not found all that God says to us about any particular subject until we have also listened to the official teaching of the church throughout its history. The *Catechism of the Catholic Church* says, "The Church . . . to whom the transmission and interpretation of Revelation is entrusted, 'does not derive her certainty about all revealed truths from the holy Scriptures alone. *Both Scripture and Tradition must be accepted and honored with equal sentiments of devotion and reverence.*'"[3]

We would respond that although the history of the church may help us to *understand* what God says to us in the Bible, never in church history has God *added* to the teachings or commands of Scripture. Nowhere in church history outside of Scripture has God *added* anything that he requires us to believe or to do. Scripture is sufficient to equip us for "every good work" and to walk in its ways is to be "blameless" in God's sight. This is the Reformation doctrine of *sola Scriptura* ("Scripture alone").

At this point we also differ from nonevangelical theologians who are not convinced that the Bible is God's Word in any unique or absolutely authoritative sense and who would therefore search not only the Bible but also many other early Christian writings in an attempt to find not so much *what God said* to mankind but rather *what many early Christians experienced* in their relationship with God. They would not expect to arrive at a single, unified conclusion about what God wants us to think or do with regard to any particular question but to discover a variety of opinions and viewpoints collected around some major unifying ideas. All of the viewpoints held by early Christians in any

---

with regard to God's will in a situation is directly proportional to the degree of clarity we have as to how the Word of God applies to the situation" (from a personal conversation, November 1992). I probably would have modified this slightly to say it is "*ordinarily* directly proportional."

3. *Catechism of the Catholic Church*, 2nd ed. (New York: Doubleday, 1997), paragraph 82 (p. 31), italics added.

of the early churches would then be potentially valid viewpoints for Christians to hold today as well. To this we would reply that our search for answers to theological and ethical questions is not a search to find what various believers have thought in the history of the church but a quest to find and understand what God himself says to us in his own words, which are found in Scripture and only in Scripture.

## C. The Amount of Scripture Given Was Sufficient at Each Stage of Redemptive History

The doctrine of the sufficiency of Scripture does not imply that *God* cannot add any more words to those he has already spoken to his people at any point in redemptive history, or that God had to give all of Scripture all at one time, for in fact he gave Scripture "at many times and in many ways" (Heb. 1:1) over a period of about 1,500 years. This doctrine rather implies that *no human author* can add any words to those that God has already spoken. Furthermore, it implies that in fact *God has not spoken* to mankind any more words which he requires us to believe or obey other than those which we have now in the Bible.

This point is important, for it helps us to understand how God could tell his people that his words to them were sufficient at many different points in the history of redemption and how he could nevertheless add to those words later. For example, in Deuteronomy 29:29 Moses says, "The secret things belong to the Lord our God, but the things that are revealed belong to us and to our children forever, that we may do all the words of this law."

This verse reminds us that God has always taken the initiative in revealing things to us. He has decided what to reveal and what not to reveal. At each stage in redemptive history, the things that God had revealed were for his people for that time, and they were to study, believe, and obey those things. With further progress in the history of redemption, more of God's words were added, recording and interpreting that history (see chapter 3 regarding the development of the canon).

At the time of the death of Moses, the first five books of our Old Testament were sufficient for God's people. But God directed later authors to add more so that Scripture would be sufficient for believers in subsequent times. For Christians today, the words from God that we have in the Old and New Testaments together are sufficient for us during the church age. After the death, resurrection, and ascension of Christ, the founding of the early church as recorded in the New Testament, and the assembling of the books of the New Testament canon, no further central redemptive acts of God in history (acts that have direct relevance for all God's people for all subsequent time) have occurred, and thus no further words of God have been given to record and interpret those acts for us.

This means that we can cite Scripture texts from throughout the canon to show that the principle of the sufficiency of God's revelation to his people at each particular time has remained the same. In this sense, these verses that talk about the sufficiency of Scripture in earlier periods are directly applicable to us as well, even though the extent of the Bible to which they refer in our situation is greater than the extent of the Scripture to which they referred in their original setting. The following texts from Scripture thus apply to us also in that sense:

> *You shall not add to the word that I command you*, nor take from it, that you may keep the commandments of the LORD your God that I command you. (Deut. 4:2)

> Everything that I command you, you shall be careful to do. *You shall not add to it or take from it.* (Deut. 12:32)

> Every word of God proves true;
>   he is a shield to those who take refuge in him.
> *Do not add to his words*,
>   lest he rebuke you and you be found a liar. (Prov. 30:5–6)

> I warn everyone who hears the words of the prophecy of this book: *if anyone adds to them*, God will add to him the plagues described in this book, and if anyone takes away from the words of the book of this prophecy, God will take away his share in the tree of life and in the holy city, which are described in this book. (Rev. 22:18–19)[4]

## D. Practical Applications of the Sufficiency of Scripture

The doctrine of the sufficiency of Scripture has several practical applications to our Christian lives. The following list is intended to be helpful but not exhaustive.

### 1. We Can Teach Theology and Ethics

The sufficiency of Scripture should encourage us as we try to discover what God would have us to *think* (about a particular doctrinal issue) or to *do* (in a particular situation). We should be encouraged that *everything* God wants to tell us about that question is to be found in Scripture. This does not mean that the Bible answers all the questions that we might think up, for "The secret things belong to the LORD our God" (Deut. 29:29). But it does mean that when we are facing a problem of genuine importance to our Christian life, we can approach Scripture with the confidence that from it God will provide us with guidance for that problem.

There will of course be some times when the answer we find is that Scripture does not speak directly to our question. (This would be the case, for example, if we tried to

---

4. The primary reference of this verse is of course to the book of Revelation itself, but its placement here at the very end of the only book that could come last in the New Testament canon can hardly be accidental. Thus a secondary application of this verse to the entire canon does not seem inappropriate (see the discussion in chapter 3, pp. 53–57).

find from Scripture what "order of worship" to follow on Sunday mornings, whether it is better to kneel or perhaps to stand when we pray, or at what time we should eat our meals during the day, etc.) In those cases, we may conclude that God has not required us to think or to act in any certain way with regard to that question (except, perhaps, in terms of more general principles regarding our attitudes and goals). But in many other cases we will find direct and clear guidance from the Lord to equip us for "every good work" (2 Tim. 3:17).

As we go through life, frequent practice in searching Scripture for guidance will result in an increasing ability to find accurate, carefully formulated answers to our problems and questions. Lifelong growth in understanding Scripture will thus include growth in the skill of rightly understanding the Bible's teachings and applying them to specific questions.

## 2. We Should Add No Other Writings to Scripture or Alongside Scripture

The sufficiency of Scripture reminds us that *we are to add nothing to Scripture* and that *we are to consider no other writings of equal value to Scripture*. This principle is violated by almost all sects that are deviant offshoots of Christianity. Mormons, for example, claim to believe the Bible, but they also claim divine authority for the *Book of Mormon*, which in practice functions as a higher authority (they also say that many errors have come into the Bible through faulty transmission and translation). Christian Scientists similarly claim to believe the Bible, but in practice they hold the book *Science and Health with a Key to the Scriptures* by Mary Baker Eddy above Scripture in authority. Since these claims violate God's commands not to add to his words, we should not think that any additional words from God to us would be found in these writings. Even in Christian churches, a similar error is sometimes made when people go beyond what Scripture says and assert with great confidence new ideas about God or heaven, basing their teachings not on Scripture but on speculation or even on claimed experiences of dying and coming back to life.

This same principle should also put our minds at ease that we need not search through other ancient literature in the hopes of finding more words from God or more words that Jesus or the apostles spoke while on earth. During the early centuries of the Christian church, a number of other writings were composed that claimed to be authentic "gospels," for example, but they were all eventually rejected by the living apostles or those who came after them and followed their teaching. These include documents such as the Gospel of Peter, the Gospel of Thomas, the Gospel of Philip, and Gospel According to Mary, and many others.[5] It is, of course, possible that some of the

---

5. Interested readers may find English translations of these and other documents in E. Hennecke, *New Testament Apocrypha*, vol. 1, *Gospels and Related Writings*, rev. ed. (London: SCM, 2012); and Wilhelm Schneemelcher and R. Mcl. Wilson, eds., *New Testament Apocrypha*, rev. ed., vol. 2, *Writings Relating to the Apostles, Apocalypses and Related Subjects* (Louisville: Westminster John Knox, 1992); or in other editions of the New Testament apocryphal books.

"sayings of Jesus" found in these writings are accurate records of things Jesus actually said (though it is now impossible for us to determine with any high degree of probability which sayings those are). But it would not matter for our Christian lives if we never read any of those sayings, for God has caused to be recorded in Scripture everything that we need to know about Jesus' words and deeds in order to trust and obey him perfectly. Though these collections of sayings do have limited value in linguistic research and perhaps in the study of the history of the church, they are of no direct value whatever for us in learning what we should believe about the life and teachings of Christ or in formulating our doctrinal and ethical convictions.

It should also be noted at this point that whenever challenges to the sufficiency of Scripture have come in the form of other documents to be placed alongside Scripture (whether from extrabiblical Christian literature of the first century or from the accumulated teachings of the Roman Catholic Church, or from the books of various cults such as the *Book of Mormon*), the result has always been (1) to deemphasize the teachings of the Bible itself and (2) to begin to teach some things that are contrary to Scripture. This is a danger of which the church must constantly be aware.

### 3. We Should Consider No Modern Revelations from God to Be Equal to Scripture in Authority

At various times throughout the history of the church, and particularly in the modern charismatic movement, people have claimed that God has given revelations through them for the benefit of the church. However we may evaluate such claims,[6] we must be careful never to allow (in theory or in practice) the placing of such revelations on a level equal to Scripture.[7] We must insist that God does not require us to believe anything about himself or his work in the world that is contained in these revelations but not in Scripture. And we must insist that God does not require us to obey any moral directives that come to us through such means but that are not confirmed by Scripture. The Bible contains all the words of God we need for trusting and obeying him perfectly.[8]

With respect to subjective perceptions that we may have of being "guided" by the Holy Spirit, I believe that these can be a valid part of a Christian's everyday life (see Acts 16:6–7; Rom. 8:9, 14, 16; Gal. 5:16–18, 25), but we must remember that the Holy Spirit will never lead us to disobey any command of Scripture, nor should our sense

---

6. See chapter 52, pp. 1280–84, on the possibility of some kinds of revelation from God continuing today when the canon is closed, and especially chapter 53, pp. 1293–1313, on the gift of prophecy.

7. In fact, the more responsible spokesmen for the modern charismatic movement seem generally to agree with this caution; see Wayne Grudem, *The Gift of Prophecy in the New Testament and Today* (Eastbourne, UK: Kingsway; Westchester, IL: Crossway, 1988), 110–12; 245–50.

8. I do not wish to imply at this point that I am adopting a "cessationist" view of spiritual gifts (that is, a view that holds that certain gifts, such as prophecy and speaking in tongues, ceased when the apostles died). I only wish at this point to state that there is a danger in explicitly or even implicitly giving these gifts a status that effectively challenges the authority or the sufficiency of Scripture in Christians' lives. More detailed discussion of these gifts is given in chapter 53 below and in Grudem, *The Gift of Prophecy in the New Testament and Today* (see n4 above).

of the Holy Spirit's individual guidance ever carry the same weight as Scripture in our thinking. One additional word of caution concerns a limitation to individual applicability: while I believe that God may guide me individually to take a certain action (such as, for example, fasting on Thursdays or deciding to cancel my subscription to the Sunday newspaper), I should never try to force that decision on all the Christians in my church (by saying that everyone should fast on Thursdays or cancel their subscriptions to the Sunday paper). Only the commands of the Bible have universal applicability to all Christians (see Rom. 14:1–12).

### 4. We Should Consider Nothing to Be Sin That Is Not Forbidden by Scripture (Either Explicitly or by Implication)

In every generation, there is a temptation to add to the list of sins that are already forbidden by Scripture. But the sufficiency of Scripture reminds us that *nothing is sin that is not forbidden by Scripture either explicitly or by implication.* To walk in the law of the Lord is to be "blameless" (Ps. 119:1). Therefore, we are not to add prohibitions to those already stated in Scripture.

Some Christian leaders and some churches in previous generations required people to follow specific rules such as not attending movie theaters, not dancing, or not using playing cards.[9] Today few if any churches promote these specific taboos, but we still need to be careful not to begin, even implicitly, to impose new rules in different areas of life where (in my opinion) Christians should be willing to allow a variety of personal preferences within fairly broad outer limits. These might include things such as food preferences (organic? vegetarian?), babies (when to have them, how many to have, how many to adopt), schools (homeschooling, Christian schooling, public schools), health (how much a person exercises or weighs), holidays (how people celebrate Halloween, Christmas, Easter, Lent), time (how much time spent with family, with sports activities, with church activities, on one's job), music preferences, shaving styles, and so forth. I agree that there are wise decisions and foolish mistakes that can be made in each of these categories, but unless Scripture clearly requires or prohibits something, Christians would do well to allow for a considerable variety of personal preferences and individual choices.[10]

---

9. When Margaret and I moved to England for my PhD studies in 1973, we became friends with many wonderful Christians, but we were surprised to find that many of them saw nothing wrong with drinking wine (which was forbidden at the Wisconsin church I grew up in), but they did think it wrong for women to wear makeup or for Christians to buy the Sunday newspaper.

10. Of course, human societies such as nations, churches, and families can make rules for the conduct of their own affairs (such as "Children in this family may not watch television on weeknights"). No such rule can be found in Scripture, nor is it likely that such a rule could be demonstrated by implication

from the principles of Scripture. Yet obedience to these rules is required by God because Scripture tells us to be subject to governing authorities, including parents (Rom. 13:1–7; Col. 3:20; 1 Peter 2:13–3:6, et al.). This is similar to the case of subjective guidance discussed above. A denial of the sufficiency of Scripture would occur only if someone attempted to give the rule a generalized application outside of the situation in which it should appropriately function ("No member of our church should watch TV on weeknights," or "No Christian should watch TV on weeknights"). In such a case it has become not a rule for conduct in one specific situation but a moral command apparently intended to apply to all Christians no matter what

Furthermore, whenever we add to the list of sins that are prohibited by Scripture itself, there will be harm to the church and to the lives of individual believers. The Holy Spirit will not empower obedience to rules that do not have God's approval from Scripture, nor will believers generally find delight in obedience to commands that do not accord with the laws of God written on their hearts. In some cases, Christians may repeatedly and earnestly plead with God for "victory" over supposed sins that are in fact no sins at all, yet no "victory" will be given, for the attitude or action in question is in fact not a sin and is not displeasing to God. Great discouragement in prayer and frustration in the Christian life generally may be the outcome.

In other cases, continued or even increasing disobedience to these new "sins" will result, together with a false sense of guilt and a resulting alienation from God. Often there arises an increasingly uncompromising and legalistic insistence on these new rules on the part of those who *do* follow them, and genuine fellowship among believers in the church will fade away. Evangelism will often be stifled, for the silent proclamation of the gospel that comes from the lives of believers will at least *seem* (to outsiders) to include the additional requirement that one must fit this uniform pattern of life in order to become a member of the body of Christ.

One clear example of such an addition to the commands of Scripture is found in the opposition of the Roman Catholic Church to "artificial" methods of birth control, a policy that finds no valid support in Scripture. Widespread disobedience, alienation, and false guilt have been the result. Yet such is the propensity of human nature to make such rules that other examples can probably be found in the written or unwritten traditions of almost every denomination.

## 5. We Should Consider Nothing to Be Required of Us That Is Not Commanded in Scripture (Either Explicitly or by Implication)

This reminds us that the focus of our search for God's will ought to be on what Scripture teaches rather than on seeking guidance through prayer for changed circumstances or altered feelings or direct guidance from the Holy Spirit apart from Scripture. It also means that if someone *claims* to have a message from God telling us what we ought to do, we need never assume that it is sin to disobey such a message unless it can be confirmed by the application of Scripture itself to our situation.

The discovery of this great truth could bring tremendous joy and peace to the lives of thousands of Christians who, spending countless hours seeking God's will outside of Scripture, are often uncertain about whether they have found it. In fact, many Christians today have very little confidence in their ability to discover God's will with any degree of

---

their situation. We are not free to add such rules to Scripture and to attempt to impose them on all the believers over whom we have influence, nor can the church as a whole attempt to do this. (Here again, Roman Catholics would differ and would say that God gives to the church the authority to impose moral rules in addition to Scripture on all the members of the church.)

certainty. Thus there is little striving to do God's will (for who can know it?) and little growth in holiness before God.[11]

The opposite ought to be true. Christians who are convinced of the sufficiency of Scripture should begin eagerly to seek and find God's will in Scripture. They should be eagerly and regularly growing in obedience to God, knowing great freedom and peace in the Christian life. Then they would be able to say with the psalmist:

> I will keep your law continually,
>     forever and ever,
> and I shall walk in a wide place,
>     for I have sought your precepts. . . .
> Great peace have those who love your law;
>     nothing can make them stumble. (Ps. 119:44–45, 165)

## 6. We Should Emphasize What Scripture Emphasizes and Be Content with the Scripture That God Has Given

There are some subjects about which God has told us little or nothing in the Bible. We must remember that "the secret things belong to the LORD our God" (Deut. 29:29) and that God has revealed to us in Scripture exactly what he deemed right for us. We must accept this and not think that Scripture is something less than it should be, nor should we begin to wish that God had given us much more information about subjects on which there are very few scriptural references. Of course, there will be some situations where we are confronted with a particular problem that requires a great deal of attention, far greater than the emphasis that it receives in the teaching of Scripture. But those situations should be relatively infrequent and should not be representative of the general course of our lives or ministries.

Many unorthodox Christian sects emphasize obscure portions or teachings of Scripture (one thinks of the Mormon emphasis on baptism for the dead, a subject that is mentioned in only one verse in the Bible [1 Cor. 15:29], in a phrase whose exact meaning is apparently impossible to determine with certainty now). But a similar error was made by an entire generation of liberal New Testament scholars in the earlier part of this century, who devoted most of their scholarly lives to a futile search for the sources "behind" our present gospel narratives or for what they were willing to consider as the "authentic" sayings of Jesus.

Unfortunately, a similar pattern has too often occurred among evangelicals within various denominations. The doctrinal matters that have divided evangelical Protestant denominations from one another have almost uniformly been matters on which the Bible places relatively little emphasis and matters in which our conclusions must be drawn from

---

11. See my extensive discussion of knowing God's will in Grudem, *Christian Ethics*, chapter 6.

skillful inference much more than from direct biblical statements. For example, abiding denominational differences have occurred or have been maintained over the "proper" form of church government, the exact nature of Christ's presence in the Lord's Supper, the exact sequence of the events surrounding Christ's return, the categories of persons who should be admitted to the Lord's Supper, the way God planned that the merits of Christ's death would be applied to believers and not applied to unbelievers, the proper subjects for baptism, the correct understanding of the "baptism in the Holy Spirit," and so forth.

We should not say that these issues are all unimportant, nor should we say that Scripture gives no solution to any of them (indeed, with respect to many of them, a specific solution will be defended in subsequent chapters of this book). However, since all of these topics receive *relatively little direct emphasis in Scripture*, it is ironic and tragic that denominational leaders will so often give much of their lives to defending precisely the minor doctrinal points that make their denominations different from others. Is such effort really motivated by a desire to bring unity of understanding to the church, or might it stem in some measure from human pride, a desire to retain power over others, and an attempt at self-justification, which is displeasing to God and ultimately unedifying to the church?

## QUESTIONS FOR PERSONAL APPLICATION

1. In the process of growing in the Christian life and deepening your relationship with God, approximately how much emphasis have you placed on reading the Bible itself and how much on reading other Christian books? In seeking to know God's will for your daily life, what is the relative emphasis you have put on reading Scripture itself and on reading other Christian books? Do you think the doctrine of the sufficiency of Scripture will cause you to place more emphasis on reading Scripture itself?

2. What are some of the doctrinal or moral questions you are wondering about? Has this chapter increased your confidence in the ability of Scripture to provide a clear answer for some of those questions?

3. Have you ever wished that the Bible would say more than it does about a certain subject? Or less? What do you think motivated that wish? After reading this chapter, how would you approach someone who expressed such a wish today? How is God's wisdom shown in the fact that he chose not to make the Bible a great deal longer or a great deal shorter than it actually is?

4. If the Bible contains everything we need God to tell us for obeying him perfectly, what roles do the following sources have in helping us find God's will: advice from others; sermons or Bible classes; our consciences; our feelings; the leading of the Holy Spirit as we sense him prompting our inward desires and subjective

impressions; changes in circumstances; the gift of prophecy (if you think it can function today)?

5. In the light of this chapter, how would you find God's "perfect" will for your life? Is it possible that there would be more than one "perfect" choice in many decisions we make? (Consider Ps. 1:3 and 1 Cor. 7:39 in seeking an answer.)

6. Have there been times when you have understood the principles of Scripture well enough with regard to a specific situation but have not known the facts of the situation well enough to know how to apply those scriptural principles correctly? In seeking to know God's will, can there be any other things we need to know except (a) the teaching of Scripture and (b) the facts of the situation in question, together with (c) skill in applying (a) to (b) correctly? What then is the role of prayer in seeking guidance? What should we pray for?

**Special Terms**

*blameless*
*sufficiency of Scripture*

# BIBLIOGRAPHY

(For an explanation of this bibliography see the note on the bibliography to chapter 1, pp. 23–24. Complete bibliographical data may be found on pp. 1489–96.)

### SECTIONS IN EVANGELICAL SYSTEMATIC THEOLOGIES

1. *Anglican (Episcopalian)*
   1930 . . . . . . . . Thomas, 120–23
   2013 . . . . . . . . Bird, 63
   2013 . . . . . . . . Bray, 137–48

2. *Arminian (Wesleyan or Methodist)*
   1875–76 . . . . . Pope, 1:206–9
   1983 . . . . . . . . Carter, 1:290–91

3. *Baptist*
   1767 . . . . . . . . Gill, 1:25–30
   2013 . . . . . . . . Erickson, 225–29

   2007 . . . . . . . . Akin, 163–64

4. *Dispensational*
   1947 . . . . . . . . Chafer, 1:60
   2002–2005 . . Geisler, 1:64–65, 69–70, 153, 496

5. *Lutheran*
   1917–24 . . . . . Pieper, 1:317–19
   1934 . . . . . . . . Mueller, 137–38

6. *Reformed (or Presbyterian)*
   1559 . . . . . . . . Calvin, 1:93–96 (1.9)
   1679–85 . . . . . Turretin, *IET*, 1:13, 38, 134–43
   1871–73 . . . . . Hodge, 1:182–83
   1906–11 . . . . . Bavinck, *RD*, 1:481–94
   1937–66 . . . . . Murray, *CW*, 1:16–22; *PC*, 11–26

1938 . . . . . . . . Berkhof, *Intro.*, 167–69

1998 . . . . . . . . Reymond, 83–86

2008 . . . . . . . . Van Genderen, 102–06

2011 . . . . . . . . Horton, 198–201

2013 . . . . . . . . Frame, 618–29, 679–80

2016 . . . . . . . . Allen and Swain, 30–56

2017 . . . . . . . . Barrett, 145–88

2019 . . . . . . . . Letham, 200–206

7. *Renewal (or charismatic/Pentecostal)*

1988–92 . . . . . Williams, 1:43–44

## SECTIONS IN REPRESENTATIVE ROMAN CATHOLIC SYSTEMATIC THEOLOGIES

### 1. *Roman Catholic: Traditional*

1955 . . . . . . . . Ott (no explicit treatment)

### 2. *Roman Catholic: Post-Vatican II*

1980 . . . . . . . . McBrien, 1:62–77

2012 . . . . . . . . *CCC*, paragraphs 75–83

## OTHER WORKS

Allison, Gregg. *Historical Theology: An Introduction to Christian Doctrine; A Companion to Wayne Grudem's* Systematic Theology. Grand Rapids: Zondervan, 2011, 142–61.

Barrett, Matthew. *God's Word Alone: The Authority of Scripture; What the Reformers Taught . . . and Why It Still Matters.* Grand Rapids: Zondervan, 2016.

Blomberg, C. L. "The Unity and Diversity of Scripture." In *NDBT*, 64–72.

Carson, D. A., ed. *The Enduring Authority of the Christian Scriptures.* Grand Rapids: Eerdmans, 2016.

Dockery, David S. and David P. Nelson. "Special Revelation." In *A Theology for the Church*, edited by Daniel L. Akin et al., 163–64. Nashville: B&H, 2014.

Duncan, J. Ligon. "The Sufficient Word of God." In *Solid Ground: The Inerrant Word of God in an Errant World.* Phillipsburg, NJ: P&R, 2012.

Feinberg, John S. *Light in a Dark Place: The Doctrine of Scripture. Foundations of Evangelical Theology Series.* Wheaton, IL: Crossway, 2018.

Friesen, Garry, and J. Robin Maxson. *Decision Making and the Will of God, 25th anniversary ed., rev. and updated.* Sisters, OR: Multnomah, 2004.

King, David T., and William Webster. *Holy Scripture: The Ground and Pillar of Our Faith*, 3 vols. Battle Ground, WA: Christian Resources, 2001.

MacArthur, John, Richard Mayhue, and John A. Hughes, eds. *Think Biblically! Recovering a Christian Worldview.* Wheaton, IL: Crossway, 2003.

Packer, J. I. "Scripture." In *NDT2*, 821–25.

Ward, Timothy. "The Diversity and Sufficiency of Scripture." In *The Trustworthiness of God: Perspectives on the Nature of Scripture.* Grand Rapids: Eerdmans, 2002, 192–218.

———. *Word and Supplement: Speech Acts, Biblical Texts, and the Sufficiency of Scripture.* Oxford: Oxford University Press, 2002.

———. *Words of Life: Scripture As the Living and Active Word of God.* Downers Grove, IL: IVP Academic, 2009.

Weeks, Noel. *The Sufficiency of Scripture.* Edinburgh and Carlisle, PA: Banner of Truth, 1988.

# SCRIPTURE MEMORY PASSAGE

**Psalm 119:1:**

*Blessed are those whose way is blameless,*
*who walk in the law of the LORD!*

# HYMN

**"How Firm a Foundation"**

Few if any hymns deal specifically with the sufficiency of Scripture, perhaps because Christians have failed to realize the great comfort and peace that this doctrine brings to the Christian life. But the first verse of the following hymn contains a statement of this doctrine. It begins by telling us that God has laid a firm foundation for our faith in his Word. Then it says, "What more can he say than to you he hath said . . . ?" The rich and full promises of God throughout Scripture are sufficient for our every need in every circumstance. This should be great cause for rejoicing! The subsequent verses contain quotations, paraphrases, and allusions to promises of God that are scattered throughout Scripture, many of them from Isaiah. Verses 2–6 are all written as sentences that are spoken by God to us, and when we sing them we should think of ourselves singing the words of God's promises to others in the congregation for their comfort and encouragement.

*How firm a foundation, ye saints of the Lord,*
  *Is laid for your faith in his excellent Word!*
*What more can he say than to you he hath said,*
  *You who unto Jesus for refuge have fled?*
  *You who unto Jesus for refuge have fled?*

*"Fear not, I am with thee, O be not dismayed;*
  *I, I am thy God, and will still give thee aid;*
*I'll strengthen thee, help thee, and cause thee*
    *to stand,*
  *Upheld by my righteous, omnipotent hand,*
  *Upheld by my righteous, omnipotent hand.*

*"When through the deep waters I call thee to go,*
  *The rivers of woe shall not thee overflow;*
*For I will be with thee thy troubles to bless,*
  *And sanctify to thee thy deepest distress,*
  *And sanctify to thee thy deepest distress.*

*"When through fiery trials thy pathway shall lie,*
  *My grace, all sufficient, shall be thy supply;*
*The flame shall not hurt thee; I only design*
  *Thy dross to consume, and thy gold to refine,*
  *Thy dross to consume, and thy gold to refine.*

*"E'en down to old age all my people shall prove*
  *My sovereign, eternal, unchangeable love;*
*And when hoary hairs shall their temples adorn,*
  *Like lambs they shall still in my bosom*
    *be borne,*
  *Like lambs they shall still in my bosom*
    *be borne.*

*"The soul that on Jesus hath leaned for repose,*
  *I will not, I will not desert to his foes;*
*That soul, though all hell should endeavor*
    *to shake,*
  *I'll never, no, never, no, never forsake,*
  *I'll never, no, never, no, never forsake."*

From: Rippon's Selection of Hymns, 1787

# CONTEMPORARY WORSHIP SONG

### "Jesus, Son of God"

*You came down from Heaven's throne.*
*This earth You formed was not Your home.*
*A love like this the world had never known.*
*A crown of thorns to mock Your name.*
*Forgiveness fell upon Your face.*
*A love like this the world had never known.*

*Chorus*
*On the altar of our praise*
*Let there be no higher name,*
*Jesus, Son of God.*
*You laid down Your perfect life,*
*You are the sacrifice,*
*Jesus, Son of God*
*You are Jesus, Son of God.*

*You took our sin, You bore our shame,*
*You rose to life, You defeated the grave,*
*And a love like this the world has never known.*
*'Cause You took our sin, You bore our shame,*
*You rose to life, You defeated the grave,*
*A love like this the world has never known.*

*Bridge*
*Be lifted higher than all You've overcome.*
*Your name be louder than any other song.*
*There is no power that can come against Your love.*
*The cross was enough.*
*The cross was enough.*

Words by Chris Tomlin, Matt
Maher, and Jason Ingram[12]

---

# PART 2

# The Doctrine of God

# CHAPTER 9

# The Existence of God

*How do we know that God exists?*

## EXPLANATION AND SCRIPTURAL BASIS

How do we know that God exists? The answer can be given in two parts: First, all people have an inner sense of God. Second, we believe the evidence that is found in Scripture and in nature.

### A. HUMANITY'S INNER SENSE OF GOD

All persons everywhere have a deep, inner sense that God exists, that they are his creatures, and that he is their Creator. Paul says that even gentile unbelievers "knew God" but did not honor him as God or give thanks to him (Rom. 1:21). He says that wicked unbelievers have "exchanged the truth about God for a lie" (Rom. 1:25), implying that they actively or willfully rejected some truth about God's existence and character that they knew. Paul says that "what can be known about God is plain to them" and adds that this is "because God has shown it to them" (Rom. 1:19).

Yet Scripture also recognizes that some people deny this inner sense of God and even deny that God exists. It is the "fool" who says in his heart, "There is no God" (Ps. 14:1; 53:1). It is the wicked person who first "curses and renounces the LORD" and then in pride repeatedly thinks "there is no God" (Ps. 10:3–4). These passages indicate both that sin leads people to think irrationally and to deny God's existence, and that it is someone who is thinking irrationally or who has been deceived who will say, "There is no God."

Paul also recognizes that sin will cause people to deny their knowledge of God: he speaks of those who "by their unrighteousness *suppress the truth*" (Rom. 1:18) and says that those who do this are "without excuse" for this denial of God (Rom. 1:20). A series of active verbs indicates that this is a willful suppression of the truth (Rom. 1:23, 25, 28, 32).[1]

In the life of a Christian this inner awareness of God becomes stronger and more distinct. We begin to know God as our loving Father in heaven (Rom. 8:15), the Holy Spirit bears witness with our spirits that we are children of God (Rom. 8:16), and we

---

1. Some people deny that they have an inner sense of God. But their awareness of God will often make itself evident in a time of personal crisis, when deep-seated convictions of the heart show themselves in outward words and deeds. Several years ago I was a passenger in a car with several friends, including a young woman who in conversation was firmly denying that she had any inner awareness of God's existence. Shortly thereafter the car hit a patch of ice and spun around in a complete circle at high speed. Before the car came to rest in a large snow bank (with no serious damage) this same woman could be heard distinctly calling out, "Lord Jesus, please help us!" The rest of us looked at her in amazement when we realized that her agnosticism had been disproved by words from her own mouth.

come to know Jesus Christ living within our hearts (Eph. 3:17; Phil. 3:8, 10; Col. 1:27; John 14:23). The intensity of this awareness for a Christian is such that though we have not seen our Lord Jesus Christ, we indeed love him (1 Peter 1:8).

## B. Believing the Evidence in Scripture and Nature

In addition to people's inner awareness of God that bears clear witness to the fact that God exists, clear evidence of his existence is to be seen in Scripture and in nature.

The evidence that God exists is of course found throughout the Bible. In fact, the Bible everywhere assumes that God exists. The first verse of Genesis does not present evidence for the existence of God but begins immediately to tell us what he has done: "In the beginning, God created the heavens and the earth." If we are convinced that the Bible is true, then we know from the Bible not only that God exists but also very much about his nature and his acts.

The world also gives abundant evidence of God's existence. Paul says that God's eternal nature and deity have been "clearly perceived . . . in the things that have been made" (Rom. 1:20). This broad reference to "the things that have been made" suggests that in some sense every created thing gives evidence of God's character. Nevertheless, it is human beings, created in the image of God, who most abundantly bears witness to the existence of God: whenever we meet another human being, we should (if our minds are thinking correctly) realize that such an incredibly intricate, skillful, communicative living creature could only have been created by an infinite, all-wise Creator.

In addition to the evidence seen in the existence of living human beings, there is further excellent evidence in nature. The "rains and fruitful seasons" as well as the "food and gladness" that all people experience and benefit from are also said by Barnabas and Paul to be witnesses to God (Acts 14:17). David tells us of the witness of the heavens:

> *The heavens declare the glory of God,*
> *and the sky above proclaims his handiwork.*
> *Day to day pours out speech,*
> *and night to night reveals knowledge.* (Ps. 19:1–2)

To look upward into the sky by day or by night is to see sun, moon, stars, sky, and clouds, all continually declaring by their existence and beauty and greatness that a powerful and wise Creator has made them and sustains them in their order.

This wide variety of testimonies to God's existence from various parts of the created world suggests to us that in one sense *everything that exists* gives evidence of God's existence. For those who have eyes to see and evaluate the evidence correctly, every leaf on every tree, every blade of grass, every star in the sky, and every other part of creation all cry out continuously, "God made me! God made me! God made me!" If our hearts and minds were not so blinded by sin, it would be impossible for us to look closely at the complexity of a leaf from any tree and say, "No one created this: it just happened." The beauty of a snowflake, the majestic power of a thunderstorm, the skill of a honeybee, the refreshing taste of cold water, the incredible abilities of the human hand—all these and thousands of other aspects of creation simply could not have come into existence apart from the activity of an all-powerful and all-wise Creator.[2]

For those who are correctly evaluating the evidence, *everything* in Scripture and *everything* in nature proves clearly that God exists and that he is the powerful and wise Creator that Scripture describes him to be. Therefore, when we believe that God exists, we are basing our belief *not* on some blind hope apart from any evidence but on *an overwhelming amount of reliable evidence from God's words and God's works*. It is a characteristic of true faith that it is a confidence based on reliable evidence, and faith in the existence of God shares this characteristic.

Furthermore, these evidences can all be seen as valid proofs for the existence of God, even though some people reject them. This does not mean that the evidence is invalid in itself, only that those who reject the evidence are evaluating it wrongly.

## C. Traditional "Proofs" for the Existence of God

The traditional "proofs" for the existence of God that have been constructed by Christian (and some non-Christian) philosophers at various points in history are in fact attempts to analyze the evidence, especially the evidence from nature, in extremely careful and logically precise ways, in order to persuade people that it is not rational to reject the idea of God's existence. If it is true that sin causes people to think *irrationally*, then these proofs are attempts to cause people to think *rationally* or correctly about the evidence for God's existence, in spite of the irrational tendencies caused by sin.

Most of the traditional proofs for the existence of God can be classified in four major types of argument.

1. The *cosmological argument* considers the fact that every known thing in the universe has a cause. Therefore, it reasons, the universe itself must also have a cause, and the cause of such a great universe can only be God.

2. The *teleological argument* is really a subcategory of the cosmological argument. It focuses on the evidence of harmony, order, and design in the universe, and argues that its design gives evidence of an intelligent purpose (the Greek word *telos* means "end" or "goal" or "purpose"). Since the universe appears to be designed with a purpose, there must be an intelligent and purposeful God who created it to function this way.

---

2. Much of secular culture today assumes that a neo-Darwinian theory of evolution can explain the existence of all living things, but that explanation has become increasingly unconvincing in light of multiple recent critiques. For extensive scientific, philosophical, and biblical answers to that claim, see *Theistic Evolution: A Scientific, Philosophical, and Theological Critique*, ed. J. P. Moreland, Stephen C. Meyer, Christopher Shaw, Ann K. Gauger, and Wayne Grudem (Wheaton, IL: Crossway, 2017). See also chapter 15 for further discussion.

3. The *ontological argument* begins with the idea of God, who is defined as a being "greater than which nothing can be imagined." It then argues that the characteristic of existence must belong to such a being, since it is greater to exist than not to exist.[3]

4. The *moral argument* begins from man's sense of right and wrong, and of the need for justice to be done, and argues that there must be a God who is the source of right and wrong and who will someday mete out justice to all people.

Because all of these arguments are based on facts about the creation that are indeed true facts, we may say that all of these proofs (when carefully constructed) are, in an objective sense, valid proofs. They are valid in that they correctly evaluate the evidence and correctly reason to a true conclusion—in fact, the universe *does* have God as its cause, and it *does* show evidence of purposeful design, and God *does* exist as a being greater than which nothing can be imagined, and God *has* given us a sense of right and wrong and a sense that his judgment is coming someday. The *actual facts* referred to in these proofs, therefore, are *true*, and in that sense the proofs are valid, even though not all people are persuaded by them.

But in another sense, if *valid* means "able to compel agreement even from those who begin with false assumptions," then of course none of the proofs is valid because not one of them is able to *compel agreement* from *everyone who considers them*. Yet this is because many unbelievers either begin with invalid assumptions or do not reason correctly from the evidence. It is not because the proofs are invalid in themselves.

The value of these proofs, then, lies chiefly in overcoming some of the intellectual objections of unbelievers. They cannot bring unbelievers to saving faith, for that comes about through belief in the testimony of Scripture when the Holy Spirit awakens in a person the ability to believe God's words. But such proofs can help overcome objections from unbelievers, and for believers they can provide further intellectual evidence for something they have already been persuaded of from their own inner sense of God and from the testimony of Scripture.

## D. ONLY GOD CAN OVERCOME OUR SIN AND ENABLE US TO BE PERSUADED OF HIS EXISTENCE

Finally, it must be remembered that in this sinful world *God must enable us to be persuaded* or we would never believe in him. We read that "the god of this world has *blinded the minds of the unbelievers*, to keep them from seeing the light of the gospel of the glory of Christ" (2 Cor. 4:4). Furthermore, Paul says that "since, in the wisdom of God, the world did not know God through wisdom, it pleased God through the folly of what we preach to save those who believe" (1 Cor. 1:21). In this sinful world, human wisdom is inadequate for coming to know God. Thus Paul's preaching came "in demonstration of the Spirit and of power, *so that your faith might not rest in the wisdom of men but in the*

---

3. The stem *ont-* in "ontological" is derived from a Greek word that means "being."

*power of God*" (1 Cor. 2:4–5). We are dependent upon God to remove the blindness and irrationality caused by sin and to enable us to evaluate the evidence rightly, believe what Scripture says, and come to saving faith in Christ.

## QUESTIONS FOR PERSONAL APPLICATION

1. When the seraphim around God's throne cry out, "Holy, holy, holy is the LORD of hosts; *the whole earth is full of his glory*" (Isa. 6:3), do you think they are seeing the earth from a somewhat different perspective than ours? In what ways? How can we begin to see the world more from this perspective?

2. When is your inner sense of God's existence strongest? Weakest? Why? In which of these situations are you in a condition more like the one you will have in heaven? In which of these types of situations are your judgments more reliable?

3. Look at your hand. Is it more or less complex than a wristwatch or a cell phone? Is it logical to think that either one of them just came about by an accidental combination of elements?

4. Do most people today believe in the existence of God? Has this been true throughout history? If they believe that God exists, why have they not worshiped him rightly?

5. Why do some people deny the existence of God? Does Romans 1:18 suggest there is often a moral factor influencing their intellectual denial of God's existence (cf. Ps. 14:1–3)? What is the best way to approach someone who denies the existence of God?

**Special Terms**

*cosmological argument*
*inner sense of God*
*moral argument*
*ontological argument*
*teleological argument*

## BIBLIOGRAPHY

(For an explanation of this bibliography see the note on the bibliography to chapter 1, pp. 23–24. Complete bibliographical data may be found on pp. 1489–96.)

**SECTIONS IN EVANGELICAL SYSTEMATIC THEOLOGIES**

*1. Anglican (Episcopalian)*
1882–92 . . . . . Litton, 42–58
1930 . . . . . . . . Thomas, 3–14
2001 . . . . . . . . Packer, 9–10, 23–25

2013 . . . . . . . . Bird, 89–91
2013 . . . . . . . . Bray, 121–132

*2. Arminian (Wesleyan or Methodist)*
1875–76 . . . . . Pope, 1:233–48
1892–94 . . . . . Miley, 1:57–136
1940 . . . . . . . . Wiley, 1:217–40
1960 . . . . . . . . Purkiser, 39–59
1983 . . . . . . . . Carter, 1:107–11
1992 . . . . . . . . Oden, 1:17–52
2002 . . . . . . . . Cottrell, 37–43

### 3. Baptist

1767 . . . . . . . . Gill, 1:1–15
1887 . . . . . . . . Boyce, 8–46
1907 . . . . . . . . Strong, 52–110
1990–95 . . . . . Garrett, 1:213–222
2007 . . . . . . . . Akin, 179–82, 214–16
2013 . . . . . . . . Erickson, 16–17, 129–42,
            241–43

### 4. Dispensational

1947 . . . . . . . . Chafer, 1:129–78
1949 . . . . . . . . Thiessen, 21–42
1986 . . . . . . . . Ryrie, 25–34
2002–2005 . . Geisler, 1:18–41, 171, 565–84
2017 . . . . . . . . MacArthur and Mayhue,
            143–45

### 5. Lutheran

1917–24 . . . . . Pieper, 1:371–74
1934 . . . . . . . . Mueller, 143–47

### 6. Reformed (or Presbyterian)

1559 . . . . . . . . Calvin, 1:43–69 (1.3–5)
1679–85 . . . . . Turretin, *IET*, 1:169–77
1871–73 . . . . . Hodge, 1:191–334
1878 . . . . . . . . Dabney, 5–26
1887–1921 . . . Warfield, *SSW*, 1:34–40
1894 . . . . . . . . Shedd, 201–18
1906–11 . . . . . Bavinck, *RD*, 2:77–91
1938 . . . . . . . . Berkhof, 19–28
1998 . . . . . . . . Reymond, 131–152
2008 . . . . . . . . Van Genderen and Velema,
            20–41
2011 . . . . . . . . Horton, 210–11
2013 . . . . . . . . Frame, 612–15
2013 . . . . . . . . Culver, 29–43
2016 . . . . . . . . Allen and Swain, 7–29
2017 . . . . . . . . Barrett, 218–22

2019 . . . . . . . . Letham, 42–52

### 7. Renewal (charismatic/Pentecostal)

1993 . . . . . . . . Menzies and Horton, 46–48
1995 . . . . . . . . Horton, 117–144
2008 . . . . . . . . Duffield and Van Cleave, 53–57

## SECTIONS IN REPRESENTATIVE ROMAN CATHOLIC SYSTEMATIC THEOLOGIES

### 1. Roman Catholic: Traditional

1955 . . . . . . . . Ott, 13–17

### 2. Roman Catholic: Post–Vatican II

1980 . . . . . . . . McBrien (no explicit treatment)
2012 . . . . . . . . *CCC*, paragraphs 198–231

## OTHER WORKS

Allison, Gregg. *Historical Theology: An Introduction to Christian Doctrine; A Companion to Wayne Grudem's* Systematic Theology. Grand Rapids: Zondervan, 2011, 187–209.

Boa, Kenneth, and Robert M. Bowman. *20 Compelling Evidences That God Exists: Discover Why Believing in God Makes so Much Sense.* Tulsa, OK: RiverOak, 2002.

Brown, Colin. *Philosophy and the Christian Faith.* Downers Grove, IL: InterVarsity Press, 1968.

Bullock, C. Hassell. "God." In *BTDB*, 288–95.

Charnock, Stephen. *The Existence and Attributes of God.* 1655–80; Reprint, Evansville, IN: Sovereign Grace Book Club, n.d., 11–67.

Clark, Gordon H. *Religion, Reason, and Revelation.* Nutley, NJ: Craig, 1961.

Craig, William Lane. *The Existence of God and the Beginning of the Universe.* San Bernardino, CA: Here's Life, 1979.

Davis, Stephen T. *God, Reason, and Theistic Proofs.* Grand Rapids: Eerdmans, 1997.

Dembski, William A. *The Design Revolution: Answering the Toughest Questions about Intelligent Design.* Downers Grove, IL: InterVarsity Press, 2004.

France, R. T. *The Living God.* Downers Grove, IL: InterVarsity Press, 1970.

Ganssle, Gregory E. *Thinking about God: First Steps in Philosophy*. Downers Grove, IL: InterVarsity Press, 2004.

Geisler, Norman. *Christian Apologetics*. Grand Rapids: Baker, 1976.

Geisler, Norman, and Paul Feinberg. *Introduction to Philosophy: A Christian Perspective*. Grand Rapids: Baker, 1980.

George, Timothy. "The Nature of God: Being, Attributes, and Acts." In *A Theology for the Church*, ed. Daniel L. Akin et al., 214–216. Nashville: B&H, 2014.

Guthrie, Donald and R. P. Martin. "God." In *DPL*, 354–69.

Hackett, Stuart. *The Resurrection of Theism*. Chicago: Moody Publishers, 1957.

Holmes, S. R. "God." In *NDT2*, 369–73.

Hoover, A. J. "God, Arguments for the Existence of." In *EDT*, 447–51.

Jastrow, Robert. *God and the Astronomers*. 2nd ed. New York: Norton, 1992.

Kärkkäinen, Veli-Matti. "God, Doctrine of." In *GDT*, 349–56.

Lewis, Gordon R. *Testing Christianity's Truth Claims*. Chicago: Moody Publishers, 1976.

Mavrodes, George I. *Belief in God*. New York: Random House, 1970.

McDowell, Josh. *Evidence That Demands a Verdict*. San Bernardino, CA: Here's Life, 1972.

Moreland, J. P., and William Lane Craig. *Philosophical Foundations for a Christian Worldview*. Downers Grove, IL: InterVarsity Press, 2003.

Newman, C. C. "God." In *DLNT*, 412–31.

Packer, J. I. "God." In *NDT1*, 274–77.

Sire, James. *The Universe Next Door: A Basic World View Catalog*. 5th ed. Downers Grove, IL: InterVarsity Press, 2009.

Swinburne, Richard. *The Existence of God*. Oxford: Clarendon, 1979.

———. *Is There a God?* Oxford: Oxford University Press, 1996.

Van Til, Cornelius. *The Defense of the Faith*. Philadelphia: Presbyterian and Reformed, 1955.

Yandell, Keith. *Christianity and Philosophy*. Studies in a Christian World View. Grand Rapids: Eerdmans; Leicester: Inter-Varsity Press, 1984.

## SCRIPTURE MEMORY PASSAGE

**Romans 1:18–20:** For the wrath of God is revealed from heaven against all ungodliness and unrighteousness of men, who by their unrighteousness suppress the truth. For what can be known about God is plain to them, because God has shown it to them. For his invisible attributes, namely, his eternal power and divine nature, have been clearly perceived, ever since the creation of the world, in the things that have been made. So they are without excuse.

## HYMN

### "The Spacious Firmament on High"

This hymn, based on Psalm 19:1–4, speaks of the testimony of the sun, moon, and stars to their Creator. The word *firmament* in the first verse refers to the expanse or open space that is visible to us as we look upward from earth; it is the place in which the sun, moon, and stars exist, and might be translated "sky" or "heavens." The third verse reminds us that though these heavenly bodies make no sounds that can be heard by our physical ears, they nonetheless proclaim, to all who think rightly about them, "The hand that made us is divine."

The spacious firmament on high,
  With all the blue ethereal sky,
And spangled heav'ns, a shining frame,
  Their great original proclaim.
Th' unwearied sun, from day to day,
  Does his Creator's pow'r display,
And publishes to every land
  The work of an Almighty hand.

Soon as the evening shades prevail,
  The moon takes up the wondrous tale,
And nightly to the list'ning earth
  Repeats the story of her birth;

Whilst all the stars that round her burn,
  And all the planets in their turn,
Confirm the tidings as they roll,
  And spread the truth from pole to pole.

What though in solemn silence all
  Move round this dark terrestrial ball?
What though nor real voice nor sound
  Amidst their radiant orbs be found?
In reason's ear they all rejoice,
  And utter forth a glorious voice;
For ever singing, as they shine,
  "The hand that made us is divine."

Author: Joseph Addison, 1712

Alternative hymns: "I Sing th' Almighty Power of God"; "This Is My Father's World"; or "Day Is Dying in the West"

## CONTEMPORARY WORSHIP SONG

### "Psalm 23"

The Lord's my Shepherd; I'll not want.
He makes me lie in pastures green.
He leads me by the still, still waters.
His goodness restores my soul.

*Chorus*
And I will trust in You alone,
And I will trust in You alone,
For Your endless mercy follows me.
Your goodness will lead me home.

He guides my ways in righteousness,
And He anoints my head with oil,
And my cup it overflows with joy.
I feast on His pure delights.

And though I walk the darkest path,
I will not fear the evil one,
For You are with me,
And Your rod and staff
Are the comfort I need to know.

Words by Stuart Townend[4]

---

# CHAPTER 10

# The Knowability of God

*Can we really know God?*
*How much of God can we know?*

## EXPLANATION AND SCRIPTURAL BASIS

### A. The Necessity for God to Reveal Himself to Us

If we are to know God at all, it is necessary that he reveal himself to us. Even when discussing the revelation of God that comes through nature, Paul says that what can be known about God is plain to people "because *God has shown it to them*" (Rom. 1:19). The natural creation reveals God because he chose to have himself revealed in this way.

With regard to the personal knowledge of God that comes in salvation, this idea is even more explicit. Jesus says, "No one knows the Son except the Father, and no one knows the Father except the Son and *anyone to whom the Son chooses to reveal him*" (Matt. 11:27). This kind of knowledge of God is not found through human effort or wisdom: "in the wisdom of God, *the world did not know God through wisdom*" (1 Cor. 1:21; cf. 1 Cor. 2:14; 2 Cor. 4:3–4; John 1:18).

The necessity for God to reveal himself to us also is seen in the fact that sinful people misinterpret the revelation about God found in nature. Those who "by their unrighteousness suppress the truth" are those who "became futile in their thinking, and their foolish hearts were darkened. . . . They exchanged the truth about God for a lie" (Rom. 1:18, 21, 25). Therefore, we need Scripture if we are to interpret natural revelation rightly. Hundreds of false religions in the world are evidence of the way sinful people, without guidance from Scripture, will always misunderstand and distort the revelation about God found in nature. But the Bible alone tells us *how to understand the testimony about God from nature.* Therefore, we depend on God's active communication to us in Scripture for our true knowledge of God.

### B. We Can Never Fully Understand God

Because God is infinite and we are finite or limited, we can never fully understand God. In this sense God is said to be *incomprehensible*, where the term *incomprehensible* is used with an older and less common sense, "unable to be *fully* understood." This sense must be clearly distinguished from the more common meaning, "unable to be understood." It is not true to say that God is unable to be understood, but it is true to say that he cannot be understood fully or exhaustively.

Psalm 145 says, "Great is the LORD, and greatly to be praised, and *his greatness is unsearchable*" (Ps. 145:3). God's greatness is beyond searching out or discovering; it is too great ever to be fully known. Regarding God's understanding, Psalm 147 says, "Great is our LORD, and abundant in power; *his understanding is beyond measure*" (Ps. 147:5). We will never be able to measure or fully know the understanding of God; it is far too great for us to equal or to understand. Similarly, when thinking of God's knowledge of all his ways, David says, "*Such knowledge is too wonderful for me*; it is high; I cannot attain it" (Ps. 139:6; cf. v. 17).

Paul implies this incomprehensibility of God when he says that "the Spirit searches everything, even the depths of God" and then goes on to say that "no one comprehends the things[1] of God except the Spirit of God" (1 Cor. 2:10–12). At the end of a long discussion on the history of God's great plan of redemption, Paul breaks forth into praise: "Oh, the depth of the riches and wisdom and knowledge of God! How unsearchable are his judgments and how inscrutable his ways!" (Rom. 11:33).

These verses allow us to take our understanding of the incomprehensibility of God one step further. It is not only true that we can never fully understand God; it is also true that *we can never fully understand any single thing about God*. His greatness (Ps. 145:3), his understanding (Ps. 147:5), his knowledge (Ps. 139:6), his riches, wisdom, judgments, and ways (Rom. 11:33) are *all* beyond our ability to understand fully. Other verses also support this idea: as the heavens are higher than the earth, so are God's ways higher than our ways and his thoughts than our thoughts (Isa. 55:9). Job says that God's great acts in creating and sustaining the earth are "but the outskirts of his ways," and Job exclaims, "how small a whisper do we hear of him! But the thunder of his power who can understand?" (Job 26:14; cf. 11:7–9; 37:5).

Thus we may know *something* about God's love, power, wisdom, and so forth, both from nature and (more accurately) from Scripture. But we can never know his love completely or *exhaustively*. We can never know his power exhaustively. We can never know his wisdom exhaustively, and so forth. In order to know any single thing about God exhaustively, we would have to know it as he himself knows it. That is, we would have to know it in its relationship to everything else about God and in its relationship to everything else about creation throughout all eternity! We can only exclaim with David, "Such knowledge is too wonderful for me; it is high; I cannot attain it" (Ps. 139:6).

This doctrine of God's incomprehensibility has much positive application for our own lives. It means that we will never be able to know "too much" about God, for we will never run out of things to learn about him, and we will thus never tire in delighting in the discovery of more and more of his excellence and of the greatness of his works.

---

1. The ESV, RSV, NIV, and NASB all supply the word *thoughts* because the parallel expression in v. 11, *ta tou anthrōpou* ("the things of the man"), seems to require that we supply the word *thoughts* as necessary to the context. But the Greek phrase in verse 10 is *ta tou theou*, which simply means, more literally, "the things of God" (so KJV). Paul's mention of "the depths of God" in v. 10 suggests that not only God's thoughts but all of God's being is referred to in both v. 10 and v. 12.

Even in the age to come, when we are freed from the presence of sin, we will never be able fully to understand God or any one thing about him. This is seen from the fact that the passages cited above attribute God's incomprehensibility not to our sinfulness but to his infinite greatness. It is because we are finite and God is infinite that we will never be able to understand him fully.[2] For all eternity we will be able to go on increasing in our knowledge of God and delighting ourselves more and more in him, saying with David as we learn more and more of God's own thoughts,

> How precious to me are your thoughts, O God!
>     How vast is the sum of them!
> If I would count them,
>     they are more than the sand. (Ps. 139:17–18)

But if this is so in eternity future, then it certainly must be so in this life. In fact, Paul tells us that if we are to lead a life "worthy of the Lord, fully pleasing to him," it must be one in which we are continually "*increasing in the knowledge of God*" (Col. 1:10). We should be growing in our knowledge of God through our entire lives.

If we ever wished to make ourselves equal to God in knowledge, or if we wished to derive satisfaction from the sin of intellectual pride, the fact that we will never stop growing in knowledge of God would be a discouraging thing for us—we might become frustrated that God is a subject of study that we will never master! But if we rather delight in the fact that God alone is God, that he is always infinitely greater than we are, that we are his creatures who owe him worship and adoration, then this will be a very encouraging idea. Even though we spend time in Bible study and fellowship with God every day of our lives, there will always be more to learn about God and his relationships to us and the world, and thus there will always be more that we can be thankful for and for which we can give him praise. When we realize this, the prospect of a lifelong habit of regular Bible study, and even the prospect of a lifetime of study of theology (if it is theology that is solidly grounded in God's Word), should be a very exciting prospect to us. To study and to teach God's Word in both formal and informal ways will always be a great privilege and joy.

## C. YET WE CAN KNOW GOD TRULY

Even though we cannot know God exhaustively, we can know *true* things about God. In fact, *all that Scripture tells us* about God is true. It is true to say that God is love

---

2. This is not contradicted by 1 Cor. 13:12, "Now I know in part; then I shall know fully, even as I have been fully known." The phrase "know fully" is simply an attempt to translate the word *epiginōskō*, which suggests deeper or more accurate knowledge (or perhaps, in contrast with present partial knowledge, knowledge free from error or falsehood) but does not imply omniscience. Paul never says anything like, "Then I shall know all things," which would have been very easy to say in Greek (*tote epignōsomai ta panta*) if he had wished to do so.

(1 John 4:8), that God is light (1 John 1:5), that God is spirit (John 4:24), that God is just or righteous (Rom. 3:26), and so forth. To say this, does not imply or require that we know everything about God or about his love or his righteousness or any other attribute. When I say that I have three sons, that statement is entirely true, even though I do not know everything about my sons, nor even about myself. So it is in our knowledge of God: we have true knowledge of God from Scripture, even though we do not have exhaustive knowledge. We can know some of God's thoughts—even many of them—from Scripture, and when we know them, we, like David, find them to be "precious" (Ps. 139:17).

Even more significantly, we know *God himself*, not simply facts about him or actions he takes. We make a distinction between knowing *facts* and knowing *persons* in our ordinary use of English. It would be true for most any citizen of the United States to say that he knows many *facts about* the president of the United States, but it would not be true for that citizen to say that he knows *him*. To say that he knows him would imply that he had met him and talked with him, and that he had developed at least to some degree a personal relationship with him.

Now some people say that we cannot know God himself but that we can only know facts about him or know what he does. Others have said that we cannot know God as he is in himself, but we can only know him as he relates to us (and there is an implication that these two are somehow different). But Scripture does not speak that way. Several passages speak of our *knowing God himself.* We read God's words in Jeremiah:

> Let not the wise man boast in his wisdom, let not the mighty man boast in his might, let not the rich man boast in his riches, but let him who boasts boast in this, that he understands and *knows me*, that I am the LORD who practices steadfast love, justice, and righteousness in the earth. For in these things I delight, declares the LORD. (Jer. 9:23–24)

Here God says that the source of our joy and sense of importance ought to come not from our own abilities or possessions but from the fact that we know him. Similarly, in praying to his Father, Jesus could say, "And this is eternal life, that *they know you*, the only true God, and Jesus Christ whom you have sent" (John 17:3). The promise of the new covenant is that all shall know God, "from the least of them to the greatest" (Heb. 8:11), and John's first epistle tells us that the Son of God has come and given us understanding to "*know him* who is true" (1 John 5:20; see also Gal. 4:9; Phil. 3:10; 1 John 2:3; 4:8). John can say, "I write to you, children, because *you know the Father*" (1 John 2:13).

The fact that we do know God himself is further demonstrated by the realization that the richness of the Christian life includes a personal relationship with God. As these passages imply, we have a far greater privilege than mere knowledge of facts *about* God. We *speak* to God in prayer, and he speaks to us through his Word and draws near to us in personal interaction and relationship: "Draw near to God, and he will draw near to you" (James 4:8). We commune with him in his presence, we sing his praise, and we are aware that he personally dwells among us and within us to bless us, for Jesus promised, "If anyone loves me, he will keep my word, and my Father will love him, and *we will come to him and make our home with him*" (John 14:23). And surely a personal relationship with Jesus—analogous to welcoming a guest into your own home—is implied by this promise: "Behold, I stand at the door and knock. If anyone hears my voice and opens the door, I will come in to him and eat with him, and he with me" (Rev. 3:20).

Indeed, truly *knowing God himself*, which is what happens in this *personal relationship* with God the Father, with God the Son, and with God the Holy Spirit, may be said to be the greatest of all the blessings of the Christian life.

## QUESTIONS FOR PERSONAL APPLICATION

1. Sometimes people say that heaven sounds boring. How does the fact that God is incomprehensible yet knowable help to answer that objection?
2. How can we be sure that when we reach heaven God will not tell us that most of what we had learned about him was wrong and that we would have to forget what we had learned and begin to learn different things about him?
3. Do you want to go on knowing God more and more deeply for all eternity? Why or why not? Would you like sometime to be able to know God exhaustively? Why or why not?
4. Why do you think God decided to reveal himself to us? Do you learn more about God from his revelation in nature or his revelation in Scripture? Why do you think it is that God's thoughts are "precious" to us (Ps. 139:17)? Would you call your present relationship to God a personal relationship? How is it similar to your relationships with other people, and how is it different? What would make your relationship with God better?

**Special Terms**
*incomprehensible*
*knowable*

## BIBLIOGRAPHY

(For an explanation of this bibliography see the note on the bibliography to chapter 1, pp. 23–24. Complete bibliographical data may be found on pp. 1489–96.)

**SECTIONS IN EVANGELICAL SYSTEMATIC THEOLOGIES**

*1. Anglican (Episcopalian)*
   2001 . . . . . . . . Packer, 19–20

2013 . . . . . . . . Bird, 167–71
2013 . . . . . . . . Bray, 99–112

## 2. Arminian (Wesleyan or Methodist)

1875–76 . . . . . Pope, 1:242–48
1892–94 . . . . . Miley, 1:137–58
1992 . . . . . . . . Oden, 117–52
2002 . . . . . . . . Cottrell, 44–49

## 3. Baptist

1767 . . . . . . . . Gill, 2:352–64
1887 . . . . . . . . Boyce, 8–54
1976–83 . . . . . Henry, 2:17–167, 247–334;
   5:375–409
1990–95 . . . . . Garrett, 1:223–38
2007 . . . . . . . . Akin, 180–81
2013 . . . . . . . . Erickson, 109, 146–49,
   165–67, 239–41

## 4. Dispensational

1947 . . . . . . . . Chafer, 1:179–86
1986 . . . . . . . . Ryrie, 25–34
2017 . . . . . . . . MacArthur and Mayhue,
   145–54

## 5. Lutheran

1917–24 . . . . . Pieper, 1:375–81

## 6. Reformed (or Presbyterian)

1559 . . . . . . . . Calvin, 1:33–43 (1.1–2)
1679–85 . . . . . Turretin, *IET*, 1:183–87
1871–73 . . . . . Hodge, 1:191–202, 335–65
1894 . . . . . . . . Shedd, 185–200
1906–11 . . . . . Bavinck, *RD*, 2:27–31
1910 . . . . . . . . Vos, 1:1–2
1938 . . . . . . . . Berkhof, 29–40
1998 . . . . . . . . Reymond, 96–102

2008 . . . . . . . . Van Genderen and Velema,
   117–31
2011 . . . . . . . . Horton, 47–57
2013 . . . . . . . . Frame, 304–6, 697–716
2013 . . . . . . . . Culver, 44–52
2016 . . . . . . . . Allen and Swain, 7–29
2017 . . . . . . . . Barrett, 218–22
2019 . . . . . . . . Letham, 62–63, 162

## 7. Renewal (or charismatic/Pentecostal)

1988–92 . . . . . Williams, 1:29–46
1993 . . . . . . . . Menzies and Horton, 20, 263
1995 . . . . . . . . Horton, 121–22
2008 . . . . . . . . Duffield and Van Cleave, 52–53

## SECTIONS IN REPRESENTATIVE ROMAN CATHOLIC SYSTEMATIC THEOLOGIES

### 1. Roman Catholic: Traditional

1955 . . . . . . . . Ott, 17–24

### 2. Roman Catholic: Post–Vatican II

1980 . . . . . . . . McBrien (no explicit
   treatment)
2012 . . . . . . . . *CCC*, paragraphs 199–204

## OTHER WORKS

Allison, Gregg. *Historical Theology: An Introduction to Christian Doctrine; A Companion to Wayne Grudem's* Systematic Theology. Grand Rapids: Zondervan, 2011, 187–209.

Blackaby, Henry T. *Experiencing God: Knowing and Doing the Will of God.* Nashville: B&H, 1994.

Bray, Gerald L. *The Doctrine of God.* Downers Grove, IL: InterVarsity Press, 1993.

———. "God." In *NDBT*, 511–21.

Charnock, Stephen. *The Knowledge of God. The Complete Works of Stephen Charnock.* Vol. 4. Edinburgh: James Nichol, 1865; Reprint, Edinburgh: Banner of Truth, 1985, esp. 3–164.

Dowey, Edward A, Jr. *The Knowledge of God in Calvin's Theology*. Grand Rapids: Eerdmans, 1994.

Frame, John M. *The Doctrine of the Knowledge of God*. Phillipsburg, NJ: Presbyterian and Reformed, 1987.

France, R. T. *The Living God*. Downers Grove, IL: InterVarsity Press, 1970.

Geivett, R. D. "Knowledge." In *EDT3*, 469–71.

Goldsworthy, Graeme. *Prayer and the Knowledge of God: What the Whole Bible Teaches*. Leicester: Inter-Varsity Press, 2003.

Holmes, S. R. "God." In *NDT2*, 369–73.

Issler, Klaus Dieter. *Wasting Time with God: A Christian Spirituality of Friendship with God*. Downers Grove, IL: InterVarsity Press, 2001.

Needham, David C. *Close to His Majesty: An Invitation to Walk with God*. Portland, OR: Multnomah, 1987.

Packer, J. I. "God." In *NDT1*, 274–77.

———. *Knowing God*. London: Inter-Varsity Press, 1973, 13–37.

Parker, T. H. L. *Calvin's Doctrine of the Knowledge of God*. Grand Rapids: Eerdmans, 1959.

Phillips, Timothy R. "Knowledge of God." In *BTDB*, 458–459.

Piper, John. *Desiring God*. Portland, OR: Multnomah, 2003.

Tozer, A. W. *The Knowledge of the Holy*. New York: Harper and Row, 1961.

Van Til, Cornelius. *In Defense of the Faith*. Vol. 5, *An Introduction to Systematic Theology*. Phillipsburg, NJ: Presbyterian and Reformed, 1976, 159–99.

Wakefield, Norm. *Living in God's Presence*. Loveland, CO: Walking Carnival, 2013.

Wright, Christopher J. H. *Knowing God the Father through the Old Testament*. Downers Grove, IL: IVP Academic, 2007.

## SCRIPTURE MEMORY PASSAGE

(Verse 3 of this passage tells us that God can never be fully known, but the fact that David is praising God and speaking to him shows also that he does know true things about God and does have a personal relationship to him.)

**Psalm 145:1–3:**
*I will extol you, my God and King,*
*    and bless your name forever and ever.*
*Every day I will bless you*
*and praise your name forever and ever.*
*Great is the LORD, and greatly to be praised,*
*    and his greatness is unsearchable.*

## HYMN

### "I Will Thee Praise, My God, O King"

Throughout the history of the church Christians have enjoyed rearranging the words of psalms to fit some poetic meter and then setting these psalms to music for personal or group worship. This is an old metrical arrangement of the words to Psalm 145, set to the familiar melody of the hymn, "Jesus Shall Reign Where'er the Sun." Stanza 2 speaks of God's incomprehensibility ("The Lord is great; he praise exceeds; his greatness fully search can none"), and many of the other stanzas speak of various attributes of God that we know from Scripture. It should give us joy to sing this song, knowing both that we are singing absolutely true things about God, and that his greatness far exceeds any praise we will ever be able to sing to him.

*I will thee praise, my God, O King,*
    *And I will ever bless thy name;*
*I will extol thee every day*
    *And evermore thy praise proclaim.*

*The Lord is great; he praise exceeds;*
    *His greatness fully search can none;*
*Race shall to race extol thy deeds*
    *And tell thy mighty acts each one.*

*Upon thy glorious majesty*
    *And wondrous works my mind shall dwell;*
*Men shall recount thy dreadful acts,*
    *And of thy greatness I will tell.*

*They utter shall abundantly*
    *The mem'ry of thy goodness great,*
*And shall sing praises cheerfully*
    *While they thy righteousness relate.*

*Jehovah very gracious is;*
    *In him compassions also flow;*
*In lovingkindness he is great,*
    *And unto anger he is slow.*

*O'er all his works his mercies are;*
    *The Lord is good to all that live.*
*Praise, Lord, to thee thy works afford;*
    *Thy saints to thee shall praises give.*

From: *The Book of Psalms with Music*
(Pittsburgh: Reformed Presbyterian Church of
North America, 1973), Psalm 145 (pp. 350–51)

Alternative hymn: "O Worship the King" (see this hymn at the end of chapter 12)

# CONTEMPORARY WORSHIP SONG

### "Knowing You (All I Once Held Dear)"

*All I once held dear, built my life upon.*
*All this world reveres, and wars to own.*
*All I once thought gain I have counted loss,*
*Spent and worthless now, compared to this.*

*Chorus*
*Knowing you, Jesus.*
*Knowing you, there is no greater thing.*
*You're my all, you're the best,*
*You're my joy, my righteousness,*
*And I love you, Lord.*

*Now my heart's desire is to know you more,*
*To be found in you and known as yours,*
*To possess by faith what I could not earn,*
*All-surpassing gift of righteousness.*

*Oh, to know the power of your risen life,*
*And to know You in Your sufferings,*
*To become like you in your death, my Lord,*
*So with you to live and never die.*

Words by Graham Kendrick[3]

---

3. © 1994 Make Way Music (admin. by Music Services in the Western Hemisphere). All Rights Reserved. ASCAP.

# CHAPTER 11

# The Character of God: "Incommunicable" Attributes

*How is God different from us?*

## EXPLANATION AND SCRIPTURAL BASIS

### A. INTRODUCTION TO THE STUDY OF GOD'S CHARACTER

### 1. Classifying God's Attributes

When we come to talk about the character of God, we realize that we cannot say everything the Bible teaches us about God's character at once. We need some way to decide which aspect of God's character to discuss first, which aspect to discuss second, and so forth. In other words, we need some way to categorize the attributes of God. This question is not as unimportant as it may seem. There is the possibility that we would adopt a misleading order of attributes or that we would emphasize some attributes so much that others would not be presented properly.

Several different methods of classifying God's attributes have been used. In this chapter we will adopt probably the most commonly used classification: the *incommunicable attributes* of God (that is, those attributes that God does not share or "communicate" to others) and the *communicable attributes* of God (those God shares or "communicates" with us).

Examples of the incommunicable attributes would be God's eternity (God has existed for all eternity, but we have not), unchangeableness (God does not change, but we do), or omnipresence (God is everywhere present, but we are present only in one place at one time). Examples of the communicable attributes would be love (God is love, and we are able to love as well), knowledge (God has knowledge, and we are able to have knowledge as well), mercy (God is merciful, and we are able to be merciful too), or justice (God is just, and we too are able to be just). This classification of God's attributes into two major categories is helpful, and most people have an initial sense of which specific attributes should be called incommunicable and which should be called communicable. Thus it makes sense to say that God's love is communicable but his omnipresence is not.

However, upon further reflection we realize that this distinction, although helpful, is not perfect. That is because there is no attribute of God that is *completely* communicable, and there is no attribute of God that is *completely* incommunicable! This will be evident if we think for a moment about some things we already know about God.

For example, God's *wisdom* would usually be called a communicable attribute because we also can be wise. But we will never be infinitely wise as God is. His wisdom is *to some extent* shared with us, but it is never *fully* shared with us. Similarly, we can share God's *knowledge* in part, yet we shall never share it fully, for God's thoughts are higher than ours "as the heavens are higher than the earth" (Isa. 55:9). We can imitate God's love and share in that attribute to some degree, but we will never be infinitely loving as God is. So it is with all the attributes that are normally called "communicable attributes": God does indeed share them with us *to some degree,* but none of these attributes is completely communicable. It is better to say that those attributes we call "communicable" are those that are *more shared* with us.

Those attributes we call "incommunicable" are better defined by saying that they are attributes of God that are *less shared* by us. Not one of the incommunicable attributes of God is completely without some likeness in the character of human beings. For example, God is unchangeable, while we change. But we do not change completely, for there are some aspects of our characters that remain largely unchanged: our individual identities, many of our personality traits, and some of our long-term purposes remain substantially unchanged over many years (and will remain largely unchanged once we are set free from sin and begin to live in God's presence forever).

Similarly, God is eternal, and we are subject to the limitations of time. However, we see *some* reflection of God's eternity in the fact that we will live with him forever and enjoy eternal life, as well as in the fact that we have the ability to remember the past and to have a strong sense of awareness of the future (unlike much of God's creation; cf. Eccl. 3:11). God's attributes of independence and omnipresence are perhaps those that are least easy to see reflected in our own natures, but even these can be seen to be faintly reflected in us when we compare ourselves with much of the rest of God's creation. As we grow to adulthood we attain some degree of independence from others for our existence. And though we cannot be at more than one place at one time, we have the ability to act in ways that have effects in many different places at once, such as through prayer, telephone, email, and video conferencing (this again sets us apart from most of the rest of creation; see also 1 Cor. 5:3).

We will use the two categories of "incommunicable" and "communicable" attributes then, while realizing that they are not entirely precise classifications, and that there is in reality much overlap between the categories.

## 2. The Names of God in Scripture

In the Bible a person's name is a description of his or her character. Likewise, the names of God in Scripture are various descriptions of his character. In a broad sense, then, God's "name" is equal to all that the Bible and creation tell us about God. When we pray, "hallowed be your *name*," as part of the Lord's Prayer (Matt. 6:9), we are praying that people would speak about God in a way that is honoring to him and that accurately reflects his character. This honoring of God's name can be done with actions as well as words, for our actions reflect the character of the Creator whom we serve (Matt. 5:16). To honor God's name is therefore to honor him. The command "You shall not take the *name* of the Lord your God in vain" (Ex. 20:7) is a command that we not dishonor God's reputation either by words that speak of him in a foolish or misleading way or by actions that do not reflect his true character.

Now the Bible does give many individual names to God, all of which reflect some true aspect of his character. Many of these names are taken from human experience or emotions in order to describe parts of God's character, while many other names are taken from the rest of the natural creation. In a sense, all of these expressions of God's character that speak in terms of things found in the universe are "names" of God because they tell us something true about him.

Herman Bavinck, in *The Doctrine of God*,[1] gives a long list of such descriptions of God taken from creation: God is compared to a lion (Isa. 31:4), an eagle (Deut. 32:11), a lamb (Isa. 53:7), a hen (Matt. 23:37), the sun (Ps. 84:11), the morning star (Rev. 22:16), a light (Ps. 27:1), a torch (Rev. 21:23), a fire (Heb. 12:29), a fountain (Ps. 36:9), a rock (Deut. 32:4), a hiding place (Ps. 119:114), a tower (Prov. 18:10), a moth (Ps. 39:11), a shadow (Ps. 91:1), a shield (Ps. 84:11), a temple (Rev. 21:22), and so forth.

Taken from human experience, Bavinck finds an even more extensive list, which is reproduced here only in part: God is called bridegroom (Isa. 61:10), husband (Isa. 54:5), father (Deut. 32:6), judge and king (Isa. 33:22), man of war (Ex. 15:3), builder and maker (Heb. 11:10), shepherd (Ps. 23:1), physician (Ex. 15:26), and so forth. Furthermore, God is spoken of in terms of human actions such as knowing (Gen. 18:21), remembering (Gen. 8:1; Ex. 2:24), seeing (Gen. 1:10), hearing (Ex. 2:24), smelling (Gen. 8:21), testing (Ps. 11:5), sitting (Ps. 9:7), rising (Ps. 68:1), walking (Lev. 26:12), wiping away tears (Isa. 25:8), and so forth. Human emotions are attributed to God, such as joy (Isa. 62:5), grief (Ps. 78:40; Isa. 63:10), anger (Jer. 7:18–19), love (John 3:16), hatred (Deut. 16:22), wrath (Ps. 2:5), and so forth.

Even though God does not have a physical body,[2] Scripture uses various parts of the human body to describe God's activities in a metaphorical way. Scripture can speak of God's face or countenance (Ex. 33:20, 23; Isa. 63:9; Ps. 16:11; Rev. 22:4), eyes (Ps. 11:4; Heb. 4:13), eyelids (Ps. 11:4), ears (Ps. 55:1; Isa. 59:1), nose (Deut. 33:10), mouth

---

1. Herman Bavinck, *The Doctrine of God*, trans. and ed. William Hendriksen (Grand Rapids: Eerdmans, 1951), 86–89.

2. Although Jesus Christ now has a physical body as God-man, the Father and Holy Spirit do not, nor did the Son before he was conceived in Mary's womb. (In the Old Testament "theophanies," in which God appeared in human form, these human bodies were only temporary appearances and did not involve the permanent uniting, in one divine-human person, of a full human nature with the divine nature of the Son, as happened in the incarnation of Christ. See chapter 26.)

(Deut. 8:3), lips (Job 11:5), tongue (Isa. 30:27), neck (Jer. 18:17), arms (Ex. 15:16), hand (Num. 11:23), finger (Ex. 8:19), heart (Gen. 6:6), foot (Isa. 66:1), and so forth. Even terms describing personal characteristics, such as good, merciful, gracious, righteous, holy, just, and many more, are terms whose meaning is familiar to us through an experience of these qualities in other human beings. And even those terms that seem least related to creation, such as eternity or unchangeableness, are understood by us not intuitively but by negating concepts that we know from our experience (eternity is not being limited by time and unchangeableness is not changing).

The point of collecting all these passages is to show, first, that in one sense or another *all of creation reveals something about God to us* and that the higher creation—especially human beings, who are made in God's image—reveals him more fully.

The second reason for mentioning this long list is to show that all that we know about God from Scripture comes to us in terms that we understand because they describe events or things common to human experience. Using a more technical term, we can say that *all that Scripture says about God uses anthropomorphic language—that is, language that speaks of God in human terms.*[3] Sometimes people have been troubled by the fact that there is anthropomorphic language in Scripture. But this should not be troubling to us, for, if God is going to teach us about things we do not know by direct experience (such as his attributes), he has to teach us in terms of what we do know. This is why all that Scripture says about God is "anthropomorphic" in a broad sense (speaking of God either in human terms or in terms of the creation that we know). This fact does not mean that Scripture gives us wrong or misleading ideas about God, for this is the way that God has chosen to reveal himself to us truly and accurately. Nonetheless, it should caution us not to take any one of these descriptions by itself and isolate it from its immediate context or from the rest of what Scripture says about God.[4] If we did that, we would run the risk of misunderstanding or of having an imbalanced or inadequate picture of who God is. Each description of one of God's attributes must be understood in the light of everything else that Scripture tells us about God. If we fail to remember this, we will inevitably understand God's character wrongly.

For example, we have an *idea* of love from human experience. That helps us to understand what Scripture means when it says that God is love, but our understanding of the meaning of *love* when applied to God is not identical with our experience of love in human relationships. So we must learn from observing how God acts in all of Scripture and from the other attributes of God that are given in Scripture, as well as from our real-life experiences of God's love, if we are to refine our idea of God's love in an appropriate

---

3. *Anthropomorphic* comes from two Greek words, *anthrō-pos*, "man," and *morphē*, "form." An anthropomorphic description of God describes God in human forms or human terms.

4. This mistake would be made, for example, by people who argue that God has a human body because Scripture talks about his eyes, ears, mouth, and so forth. By the same reasoning

they should say that God also looks like a lion, a lamb, an eagle, a fire, a rock, a hen, a fountain, the sun, a shield, a shadow, and a temple—all at once! The mistake is to fail to recognize that these are all metaphors that tell us about God's character. God himself is "spirit" (John 4:24) and has no material body.

way and avoid misunderstanding. Thus anthropomorphic language about God is *true* when it occurs in Scripture, but it can be understood rightly only when we consistently read Scripture in order to understand this language in the context of the entirety of Scripture.

There is yet a third reason for pointing out the great diversity of descriptions about God taken from human experience and from the natural world. This language should remind us that *God made the universe so that it would show forth the excellence of his character*, that is, that it would show forth his glory. God is worthy to receive glory because he created all things (Rev. 4:11); therefore, all things should honor him.

Psalm 148 is an example of all creation being summoned to give praise to God:

> Praise him, sun and moon,
>     praise him, all you shining stars! . . .
> Praise the LORD from the earth,
>     you great sea creatures and all deeps,
> fire and hail, snow and mist,
>     stormy wind fulfilling his word!
> Mountains and all hills,
>     fruit trees and all cedars! . . .
> Kings of the earth and all peoples . . .
> Let them praise the name of the Lord,
>     for his name alone is exalted;
>     his majesty is above earth and heaven. (Ps. 148:3, 7–11, 13)

As we learn about God's character from Scripture, it should open our eyes and enable us to interpret creation rightly. As a result, we will be able to see reflections of the excellence of God's character everywhere in creation: "The whole earth is full of his glory" (Isa. 6:3).

It must be remembered that although all that Scripture tells us about God is true, what it communicates is not exhaustive. Scripture does not tell us everything about God's character. We will never know God's *full or complete "name"* in the sense that we will never understand God's character exhaustively. We will never know all there is to know about God. For this reason theologians have sometimes said, "God has many names, yet God has no name." God has many names in that we know many true descriptions of his character from Scripture, but God has no name in that we will never be able to describe or understand all of his character.

## 3. Balanced Definitions of God's Incommunicable Attributes

The incommunicable attributes of God are perhaps the most easily misunderstood, probably because they represent aspects of God's character that are least familiar to our experience. In this chapter, therefore, each of the incommunicable attributes of God is defined with a two-part sentence. The first part defines the attribute under discussion, and the second part guards against misunderstanding the attribute by stating a balancing or opposite aspect that relates to that attribute. For example, God's unchangeableness is defined as follows: "God is unchanging in his being, perfections, purposes, and promises, *yet* God does act, and he acts differently in response to different situations." The second half of the sentence guards against the idea that unchangeableness means inability to act at all. Some people do understand unchangeableness in this way, but such an understanding is inconsistent with the biblical presentation of God's unchangeableness.

## B. The Incommunicable Attributes of God

### 1. Independence

God's independence is defined as follows: *God does not need us or the rest of creation for anything, yet we and the rest of creation can glorify him and bring him joy.* This attribute of God is sometimes called his self-existence or his *aseity* (from the Latin words *a se*, which mean "from himself").

Scripture in several places teaches that God does not need any part of creation in order to exist or for any other reason. God is absolutely independent and self-sufficient. Paul proclaims to the men of Athens, "The God who made the world and everything in it, being Lord of heaven and earth, does not live in temples made by man, *nor is he served by human hands, as though he needed anything*, since he himself gives to all mankind life and breath and everything" (Acts 17:24–25). The implication is that God does not need anything from mankind.

God asks Job, "Who has first given to me, that I should repay him? *Whatever is under the whole heaven is mine*" (Job 41:11). No one has ever contributed to God anything that did not first come from God who created all things. Similarly, we read God's word in Psalm 50:

> For every beast of the forest is mine,
>     the cattle on a thousand hills.
> I know all the birds of the hills,
>     and all that moves in the field is mine.
> If I were hungry, I would not tell you;
>     for *the world and its fullness are mine*. (Ps. 50:10–12)

People have sometimes thought that God created human beings because he was lonely and needed fellowship with other persons. If this were true, it would mean that God is not completely independent of creation. It would mean that God *needed* to create persons in order to be completely happy or completely fulfilled in his personal existence.

Yet there are some specific indications in Jesus' words that show this idea to be inaccurate. In John 17:5, Jesus prays, "Father, glorify me in your own presence with *the glory that I had with you before the world existed.*" Here is an indication that there was a sharing of glory between the Father and the Son before creation. Then in John 17:24, Jesus speaks to the Father of "my glory that you have given me *because you loved me before the foundation of the world.*" There was love and communication between the Father and the Son before creation.

These passages indicate explicitly what we can learn elsewhere from the doctrine of the Trinity, namely, that among the persons of the Trinity there has been perfect love and fellowship and communication for all eternity. The fact that God is three persons yet one God means that there was no loneliness or lack of personal fellowship on God's part before creation. In fact, the love and interpersonal fellowship, as well as the sharing of glory, have always been and will always be far more perfect than any communion we as finite human beings will ever have with God. And as the second verse quoted above speaks of the glory the Father gave to the Son, we should also realize that there is a giving of glory by the members of the Trinity to one another that far surpasses any bestowal of glory that could ever be given to God by all creation.

With regard to God's existence, this doctrine also reminds us that only God exists by virtue of his very nature and that he was never created and never came into being. He always was. This is seen from the fact that all things that exist were made by him ("For you created *all things*, and by your will they existed and were created" [Rev. 4:11]; this is also affirmed in John 1:3; Rom. 11:35–36; 1 Cor. 8:6). Moses tells us that God existed before there was any creation: "*Before* the mountains were brought forth, or ever you had formed the earth and the world, from everlasting to everlasting *you are God*" (Ps. 90:2). God's independence is also seen in his self-designation in Exodus 3:14: "God said to Moses, 'I AM WHO I AM.'" It is also possible to translate this statement "I will be what I will be," but in both cases the implication is that God's existence and character are determined by himself alone and are not dependent on anyone or anything else. This means that God's being has always been and will always be exactly what it is. God is not dependent upon any part of creation for his existence or his nature. Without creation, God would still be infinitely loving, infinitely just, eternal, omniscient, Trinitarian, and so forth.

God's being is also something totally unique. It is not just that God *does not* need the creation for anything; God *could not* need the creation for anything. The difference between the creature and the Creator is immense, for God exists in a fundamentally different order of being. It is not just that we exist and God has always existed; it is also that God *necessarily* exists in an infinitely better, stronger, more excellent way. The difference between God's being and ours is more than the difference between the sun and a candle, more than the difference between the ocean and a raindrop, more than the difference between the arctic ice cap and a snowflake, more than the difference between the universe and the room we are sitting in: God's being is *qualitatively different*. No limitation or imperfection in creation should be projected onto our thought of God. He is the Creator; all else is creaturely. All else can pass away in an instant; he *necessarily exists* forever.

The balancing consideration with respect to this doctrine is the fact that *we and the rest of creation can glorify God and bring him joy.* This must be stated in order to guard against any idea that God's independence makes us meaningless. Someone might wonder, if God does not need us for anything, then are we important at all? Is there any significance to our existence or to the existence of the rest of creation? In response it must be said that we are in fact very meaningful because God has created us and has determined that we would be *meaningful to him.* That is the final definition of genuine significance.

God speaks of his sons and daughters from the ends of the earth as "everyone who is called by my name, whom I created *for my glory,* whom I formed and made" (Isa. 43:7). Although God did not have to create us, he chose to do so in a totally free choice. He decided that he would create us to glorify him (cf. Eph. 1:11–12; Rev. 4:11).

It is also true that we are able to bring real joy and delight to God. It is one of the most amazing facts in Scripture that God actually delights in his people and rejoices over them. Isaiah prophesies about the restoration of God's people:

> You shall be a crown of beauty in the hand of the LORD,
>     and a royal diadem in the hand of your God.
> You shall no more be termed Forsaken
>     and your land shall no more be termed Desolate,
> but you shall be called My Delight Is in Her,
>     and your land Married;
> for the LORD delights in you
>     and your land shall be married. . . .
> as the bridegroom rejoices over the bride,
>     so shall your God rejoice over you. (Isa. 62:3–5)

Similarly, Zephaniah prophesies that the Lord "will rejoice over you with gladness; he will quiet you by his love; *he will exult over you with loud singing*" (Zeph. 3:17–18). God does not need us for anything, yet it is the amazing fact of our existence that he chooses to delight in us and to allow us to bring joy to his heart. This is the basis for personal significance in the lives of all God's people: to be significant to God is to be significant in the most ultimate sense. No greater personal significance can be imagined.

## 2. Unchangeableness

We can define the unchangeableness of God as follows: *God is unchanging in his being, perfections, purposes, and promises, yet God does act and feel emotions, and he acts and feels differently in response to different situations.*[5] This attribute of God is also called God's *immutability.*

**a. Evidence in Scripture.** In Psalm 102 we find a contrast between things that we may think to be permanent such as the earth or the heavens, on the one hand, and God, on the other hand. The psalmist says,

> Of old you laid the foundation of the earth,
>> and the heavens are the work of your hands.
> They will perish, but you will remain;
>> they will all wear out like a garment.
> You will change them like a robe, and they will pass away,
>> but you are the same, and your years have no end. (Ps. 102:25–27)[6]

God existed before the heavens and earth were made, and he will exist long after they are permanently changed (see chapter 57). God causes the universe to change, but in contrast to this change he is "the same."

Referring to his own qualities of patience, long-suffering, and mercy, God says, "For *I the* Lord *do not change*; therefore you, O children of Jacob, are not consumed" (Mal. 3:6). Here God uses a general statement of his unchangeableness to refer to some specific ways in which he does not change.

James reminds his readers that all good gifts come ultimately from God *"with whom there is no variation or shadow due to change"* (James 1:17). His argument is that since good gifts have always come from God, we can be confident that only good gifts will come from him in the future, because his character never changes in the slightest degree.

The definition given above specifies that God is unchanging—not in every way that we might imagine, but only in ways that Scripture itself affirms. The Scripture passages already cited refer either to God's own being or to some attribute of his character. From these we can conclude that God is unchanging, at least with respect to his *"being"* and with respect to his *"perfections"* (that is, his attributes or the various aspects of his character).

The great Dutch theologian Herman Bavinck notes that the fact that God is unchanging in his being is of the utmost importance for maintaining the Creator-creature distinction and for our worship of God:

> The doctrine of God's immutability is of the highest significance for religion. The contrast between being and becoming marks the difference between the Creator

---

5. The four key words (*being, perfections, purposes, promises*) used as a summary of the ways in which God is unchanging are taken from Louis Berkhof, *Systematic Theology* (Grand Rapids: Eerdmans, 1941), 58.

6. It is significant that this passage is quoted in Heb. 1:11–12 and applied to Jesus Christ. Heb. 13:8 also applies the attribute of unchangeableness to Christ: "Jesus Christ is the same yesterday and today and forever." Thus God the Son shares fully in this divine attribute.

and the creature. Every creature is continually becoming. It is changeable, constantly striving, seeks rest and satisfaction, and finds this rest in God, in him alone, for only he is pure being and no becoming. Hence, in Scripture God is often called the Rock.[7]

The definition given above also affirms God's unchangeableness or immutability with respect to his *purposes*. "The counsel of the Lord stands forever, the plans of his heart to all generations" (Ps. 33:11). This general statement about God's counsel is supported by several specific verses that talk about individual plans or purposes of God that he has had for all eternity (Matt. 13:35; 25:34; Eph. 1:4, 11; 3:9, 11; 2 Tim. 2:19; 1 Peter 1:20; Rev. 13:8). Once God has determined that he will assuredly bring something about, his purpose is unchanging, and it will be achieved. In fact, God claims through Isaiah that no one else is like him in this regard:

> I am God, and there is none like me,
> declaring the end from the beginning
>     and from ancient times things not yet done,
> saying, "My counsel shall stand,
>     and I will accomplish all my purpose" . . .
> I have spoken, and I will bring it to pass;
>     I have purposed, and I will do it. (Isa. 46:9–11)

Furthermore, God is unchanging in his *promises*. Once he has promised something, he will not be unfaithful to that promise: "God is not man, that he should lie, or a son of man, that he should change his mind. Has he said, and will he not do it? Or has he spoken, and will he not fulfill it?" (Num. 23:19; cf. 1 Sam. 15:29).

**b. Does God Sometimes Change His Mind?** Yet when we talk about God being unchanging in his purposes, we may wonder about places in Scripture where God said he would judge his people and then because of prayer or the people's repentance (or both) God relented and did not bring judgment as he had said he would. Examples of such withdrawing from threatened judgment include the successful intervention of Moses in prayer to prevent the destruction of the people of Israel (Ex. 32:9–14), the adding of another fifteen years to the life of Hezekiah (Isa. 38:1–6), or the failure to bring promised judgment upon Nineveh when the people repented (Jonah 3:4, 10). Are these not cases where God's purposes in fact did change? Then there are other passages where God is said to be sorry that he had carried out some previous action. One thinks of the time before the flood, where "the Lord *regretted* that he had made man on the earth, and it grieved him to his heart" (Gen. 6:6), or the time when God told Samuel, "I *regret* that I have made Saul king, for he has turned back from following me" (1 Sam. 15:11). Did not God's purposes change in these cases?

---

7. Bavinck, *The Doctrine of God*, 149.

These instances should all be understood as true expressions of God's *present* attitude or intention *with respect to the situation as it exists at that moment*. If the situation changes, then of course God's attitude or expression of intention will also change. This is just saying that *God responds differently to different situations*. The example of Jonah preaching to Nineveh is helpful here. God sees the wickedness of Nineveh and sends Jonah to proclaim, "Yet forty days, and Nineveh shall be overthrown!" (Jonah 3:4). The possibility that God would withhold judgment if the people repented is not explicitly mentioned in Jonah's proclamation as recorded in Scripture, but it is of course *implicit* in that warning: the *purpose* for proclaiming a warning is to bring about repentance. Once the people repented, the situation was different, and God responded differently to that changed situation: "*When God saw what they did*, how they turned from their evil way, *God relented of the disaster that he had said he would do to them*, and he did not do it" (Jonah 3:10).

The situations with Hezekiah and with the intercession of Moses are similar, but in these cases the important change was that someone prayed. God had said that he would send judgment, and that was a true declaration, *provided that the situation remained the same*. But then the situation changed. Someone started to pray earnestly (Moses in one case and Hezekiah in the other). Here *prayer itself was part of the new situation* and was in fact what changed in the situation. God responded to that changed situation by answering the prayer and withholding judgment.

In the cases of God regretting that he had made man or that he had made Saul king, these should be understood to mean that (a) God felt sorrow when considering the sinful results that had come after his earlier actions, but this is still consistent with the idea that (b) God knew that these events that caused him grief would still fulfill his long-term purpose of showing his justice and holiness when he brought judgment on sinful behavior. These verses should not be understood to mean that God thought he had made a mistake or that if he could start again and act differently, he would in fact not create man or not make Saul king. The verses should be understood as *expressions of God's present displeasure* toward the sinfulness of man. God's previous actions led to events that, in the short term, caused him sorrow but that nonetheless, in the long term, would achieve his good purposes. This is somewhat analogous to a human father who allows his child to embark on a course he knows will bring much sorrow, both to the parent and to the child, but who allows it nonetheless because he knows that greater long-term good will come from it.

Does God then change his mind? It depends on what we mean by that. When a situation changes (such as when people repent or pray or both) God often in Scripture changes his *present attitude* toward the specific situation. But God's *long-term purposes* never change.

**c. The Question of God's Impassibility.** Sometimes in discussions of God's attributes theologians have spoken of another attribute, namely, the *impassibility* of God.

This should not be understood to mean that God does not have passions or emotions, for God certainly does feel emotions: God rejoices (Isa. 62:5). He is grieved (Ps. 78:40; Eph. 4:30). His wrath burns hot against his enemies (Ex. 32:10). He pities his children (Ps. 103:13). He loves with everlasting love (Isa. 54:8; Ps. 103:17). If we understand *impassible* to mean "incapable of feeling emotions," then it is not correct to say that God is impassible.

However, there is another sense of impassible. (I mistakenly failed to consider this other sense in the first edition of this book.) Impassible can mean, "immunity to suffering," or "incapable of suffering harm." God's being cannot be changed or harmed by anything outside of himself.[8] When God does feel grief or sorrow over the sinfulness of people he created, this sorrow does not surprise him, nor is it forced on him by external circumstances somehow outside his control, but it is his genuine response to events that he ordained would come to pass. In this sense, God is impassible.

**d. The Challenge from Process Theology.** God's unchangeableness has been denied frequently in recent years by the advocates of *process theology*, a theological position that says process and change are essential aspects of genuine existence, and therefore God must be changing over time also, just like everything else that exists. In fact, Charles Hartshorne, the father of process theology, would say that God is continually adding to himself all the experiences that happen anywhere in the universe, and thus God is continually changing.[9] The real appeal of process theology comes from the fact that all people have a deep longing to mean something, to feel significant in the universe. Process theologians dislike the doctrine of God's immutability because they think it implies that nothing we do can really matter to God. If God is really unchangeable, process theologians will say, then nothing we do—in fact, nothing that happens in the universe—has any real effect on God because God can never change. So what difference do we make? How can we have any ultimate meaning? In response to this question process theologians reject the doctrine of God's immutability and tell us that our actions are so significant that they have an influence on the very being of God himself! As we act, and as the universe changes, God is *truly* affected by these actions and the being of God changes—God *becomes* something other than what he was.[10]

---

8. See the helpful discussions in John Frame, *Systematic Theology* (Phillipsburg NJ: P&R, 2013), 412–19; and Michael Bird, *Evangelical Theology* (Grand Rapids: Zondervan, 2013), 130–31. See also Michael Horton, *The Christian Faith: A Systematic Theology for Pilgrims on the Way* (Grand Rapids: Zondervan, 2011), 242–53.

9. Charles Hartshorne (1897–2000) taught at the University of Chicago, Emory University, and the University of Texas. An introduction to process theology by two of its advocates is *Process Theology: An Introductory Exposition* by John B. Cobb Jr. and David R. Griffin (Philadelphia: Westminster, 1976). Detailed evangelical analyses may be found in Carl F. H. Henry, "The Resurgence of Process Philosophy," in *God, Revelation,*

*and Authority* (Waco, TX: Word, 1983), 6:52–75, and Royce Gruenler, *The Inexhaustible God: Biblical Faith and the Challenge of Process Theism* (Grand Rapids: Baker, 1983).

Two excellent articles from an evangelical perspective have been written by Bruce A. Ware: "An Exposition and Critique of the Process Doctrines of Divine Mutability and Immutability," *WTJ* 47 (1985): 175–96 (a critique of process theology), and "An Evangelical Reformulation of the Doctrine of the Immutability of God," *JETS* 29 (1986): 431–46 (a positive restatement of an orthodox view of God's immutability).

10. See Ware's revealing discussion of Hartshorne's idea that we contribute value to God that he would otherwise lack: "Exposition and Critique," 183–85.

Advocates of process theology often mistakenly accuse evangelical Christians (or the biblical writers themselves) of believing in a God who does not act in the world or who cannot respond differently to different situations (errors we have discussed above). With regard to the idea that we must be able to influence the very being of God in order to be significant, we must respond that this is an *incorrect assumption* imported into the discussion, and that it is not consistent with Scripture. Scripture is clear that our ultimate significance comes not from being able to change the being of God, but from the fact that God has created us for his glory and that *he* counts us as significant.[11] God alone gives the ultimate definition of what is significant and what is not significant in the universe, and if he counts us significant, then we are!

The other fundamental error in process theology is in assuming that God must be changeable like the universe he created. This is what Scripture explicitly denies:

> You, Lord, laid the foundation of the earth in the beginning,
>> and the heavens are the work of your hands;
> they will perish, but you remain;
>> they will all wear out like a garment. . . .
>> *They will be changed.*
> *But you are the same,*
>> and your years will have no end. (Heb. 1:10–12, quoting Ps. 102:25–27)

**e. God Is Both Infinite and Personal.** Our discussion of process theology illustrates a common difference between biblical Christianity and all other systems of theology. In the teaching of the Bible, God is both *infinite* and *personal*. He is infinite in that he is not subject to any of the limitations of humanity or of creation in general. He is far greater than everything he has made, far greater than anything else that exists. But he is also personal. He interacts with us as a person, and we can relate to him as persons. We can pray to him, worship him, obey him, and love him, and he can speak to us, rejoice in us, and love us.

Apart from the true religion found in the Bible, no system of religion has a God who is both infinite and personal.[12] For example, the gods of ancient Greek and Roman mythology were *personal* (they interacted frequently with people), but they were not infinite; they had weaknesses and frequent moral failures, even petty rivalries. On the other hand, deism portrays a God who is *infinite* but far too removed from the world to be personally involved in it. Similarly, pantheism holds that God is infinite (since the whole universe is thought to be God), but such a God can certainly not be personal or relate to us as persons.

---

11. See chapter 21, pp. 565–67, on the reasons for the creation of man.

12. Technically speaking we must recognize that Judaism, so far as it is based on what we call the Old Testament, also has a view of God that shows him to be both infinite and personal, although Judaism has never recognized the indications of God's Trinitarian nature that are present even in the Old Testament (see chapter 14, pp. 269–72).

The error of process theology fits this general pattern. Its advocates are convinced that a God who is unchanging in his being is so different from the rest of creation—so infinite, so unlimited by the change that characterizes all of our existence—that he *cannot* also be personal in a way that we make a difference to him. So in order to gain a God who is personal, they think they have to give up a God who is infinite for a God who is continually in process of change. This kind of reasoning is typical of many (perhaps all) objections to the kind of God presented in the Bible. People say that if God is infinite, he cannot be personal, or they say that if God is personal, he cannot be infinite. The Bible teaches that God is both infinite and personal. We must affirm both that God is infinite (or unlimited) with respect to change that occurs in the universe (nothing will change God's being, perfections, purposes, or promises), that God is *also* personal, and that he relates to us personally and counts us valuable.

**f. The Importance of God's Unchangeableness.** At first it may not seem very important to us to affirm God's unchangeableness. The idea is so abstract that we may not immediately realize its significance. But if we stop for a moment to imagine what it would be like if God *could* change, the importance of this doctrine becomes more clear. For example, if God *could* change (in his being, perfections, purposes, or promises), then any change would be either for the better or for the worse. But if God changed for the better, then he was not the best possible being when we first trusted him. And how could we be sure that he is the best possible being now? But if God could change for the worse (in his very *being*), then what kind of God might he become? Might he become, for instance, a little bit evil rather than wholly good? And if he could become a little bit evil, then how do we know he could not change to become largely evil—or *wholly* evil? And there would be not one thing we could do about it, for he is so much more powerful than we are. The idea that God could change leads to the horrible possibility that thousands of years from now we might come to live forever in a universe dominated by a wholly evil, omnipotent God. It is hard to imagine any thought more terrifying. How could we ever trust such a God who could change? How could we ever commit our lives to him?

Moreover, if God could change with regard to his *purposes*, then even though when the Bible was written he promised that Jesus would come back to rule over a new heaven and new earth, he has perhaps abandoned that plan now, and thus our hope in Jesus' return is in vain. Or if God could change in regard to his *promises*, then how could we trust him completely for eternal life? Or for anything else the Bible says? Maybe when the Bible was written he promised forgiveness of sins and eternal life to those who trust in Christ, but (if God can change) perhaps he has changed his mind on those promises now—how could we be sure? Or perhaps his omnipotence will change someday, so that even though he wants to keep his promises, he will no longer be able to do so.

A little reflection like this shows how absolutely important the doctrine of God's unchangeableness is. If God is not unchanging, then the whole basis of our faith begins to fall apart, and our understanding of the universe begins to unravel. This is because our faith and hope and knowledge all ultimately depend on a *person* who is *infinitely worthy of trust*—because he is *absolutely* and *eternally* unchanging in his being, perfections, purposes, and promises.

## 3. Eternity

God's eternity may be defined as follows: *God has no beginning, end, or succession of moments in his own being, and he sees all time equally vividly, yet God sees events in time, and he acts in time.*

Sometimes this doctrine is called the doctrine of God's infinity with respect to time. To be infinite is to be unlimited, and this doctrine teaches that time does not limit God.

This doctrine is also related to God's unchangeableness. If it is true that God does not change, then we must say that *time* does not change God; it has no effect on his being, perfections, purposes, or promises. But that means that time has no effect on God's knowledge, for instance. God never learns new things or forgets things, for that would mean a change in his perfect knowledge. This implies also that the passing of time does not add to or detract from God's knowledge. He knows all things past, present, and future and knows them all equally vividly.

**a. God Is Timeless in His Own Being.** The fact that God has no beginning or end is seen in Psalm 90:2: "Before the mountains were brought forth, or ever you had formed the earth and the world, *from everlasting to everlasting you are God.*" Similarly, in Job 36:26, Elihu says of God, "the number of his years is unsearchable."

God's eternity is also suggested by passages that talk about the fact that God always is or always exists. "'I am the Alpha and the Omega,' says the Lord God, 'who is and who was and who is to come, the Almighty'" (Rev. 1:8; cf. 4:8).[13]

It is also indicated in Jesus' bold use of a present tense verb that implies continuing present existence when he replied to his Jewish adversaries, "Before Abraham was, *I am*" (John 8:58). Jesus is saying that over 2,000 years ago (before Abraham existed), he was already existing. But he affirms more than that. He does not simply say, "Before Abraham was, I was already alive" (that would be shocking enough). He says, "Before Abraham was, *I am*." This placement of a present tense verb in a statement referring to the distant past suggests that Jesus has a kind of "presentness" at all stages of past history.

Jesus' statement here is itself an explicit claiming of the name of God, "I AM WHO I AM," from Exodus 3:14, a name that also suggests a continual present existence: God is the eternal "I AM," the one who eternally exists. In addition, God says through Isaiah, "For thus says the One who is high and lifted up, *who inhabits eternity*" (Isa. 57:15).

(1) God created time. The fact that God never began to exist can also be concluded from the fact that God created all things, and that he himself is an immaterial spirit.

---

13. Alpha and omega are the first and last letters of the Greek alphabet, so when God says that he is the Alpha and the Omega, he implies that he is before everything else and after everything else; he is the beginning of everything and will always be the end (or goal) of everything.

Before God made the universe, there was no matter, but then he created all things (Gen. 1:1; John 1:3; 1 Cor. 8:6; Col. 1:16; Heb. 1:2). The study of physics tells us that matter and time and space must all occur together: if there is no matter, there can be no space or time either. This would mean that, before God created the universe, there was no "time," at least not in the sense of a succession of moments one after another. Therefore, when God created the universe, he also created time. "In the beginning" (Gen. 1:1) then points not just to the time when God created the universe, but also to the beginning of time—what we might truly call "The Beginning." When God began to create the universe, time began, and there began to be a succession of moments and events one after another. But we need not reach this conclusion only on the basis of modern physics because even before the advent of modern physics respected interpreters of Scripture understood the first words of the Bible, "In the beginning," to refer to the very beginning of time itself.[14]

Before there was a universe, and *before there was time, God always existed*, without beginning, and without being influenced by time. And time, therefore, does not have existence in itself, but, like the rest of creation, depends on God's eternal being and power to keep it existing.

(2) Scripture speaks of events "before time." Does it make sense to talk about something "before time"? William Lane Craig, a prominent Christian philosopher and also a long-time friend, has objected that it is contradictory to talk about God existing "before time began," because the word "before" implies that one event happens after another, and therefore the word "before" is inconsistent with a state of timelessness.[15]

My response is to say that the Bible itself uses this kind of language to tell us things that were true of God "before" creation and even before time. Jude writes, "To the only God, our Savior, through Jesus Christ our Lord, be glory, majesty, dominion, and authority, *before all time* and now and forever" (Jude 25). Jude ascribes glory to God "before all time."[16] Similarly, Paul speaks of the grace that God "gave us in Christ Jesus *before the ages began*" (2 Tim. 1:9).[17] The same Greek expression is used elsewhere to say that God promised eternal life "before the ages began" (Titus 1:2). Therefore, following the biblical pattern, it seems appropriate and not contradictory to speak of God existing "before time."

---

14. Keil and Delitzsch say that "In the beginning" refers to "the very first beginning . . . when time itself began" (C. F. Keil and F. Delitzsch, *Keil and Delitzsch Commentary On the Old Testament Pentateuch*, vol. 1 [1866–91; repr., Peabody, MA: Hendrickson, 2006], 29). Herman Bavinck says, "If there were no creatures, there would be no time. . . . time began 'with the creature'," (*The Doctrine of God*, 155).

15. See William L. Craig, "A Critique of Grudem's Formulation & Defense of the Doctrine of Eternity," *Philosophia Christi* 19, no. 1 (Spring 1996): 33–38. I responded in a subsequent article: "The Nature of Divine Eternity: A Response to William Craig," *Philosophia Christi* 20, no. 1 (Spring 1997): 55–70.

16. The KJV and NKJV do not have this expression because the Greek words are missing from the Textus Receptus, the Greek manuscript tradition on which those translations are based. But these words are so well attested in more reliable manuscripts that their omission is not even mentioned as a variant in the UBS⁴ Greek text.

17. The Greek phrase is *pro chronōn aiōniōn*, which is more literally "before times eternal" or "before unending time." This expression is fully consistent with the view I am supporting in this chapter, namely, that God existed *before* time began, that God created time, and now that time exists, it will never end. (The NET and CSB translations render the expression, "before time began," and the NIV says, "before the beginning of time.")

In fact, while it is possible for us to think of the idea of time beginning and then going forward forever, the idea of time extending infinitely far into the past seems impossible—for if past time is infinite, then it would be impossible to ever reach the present moment.[18]

The foregoing Scripture passages and the fact that God always existed before there was any time combine to indicate to us that God's own being does not have a succession of moments or any progress from one state of existence to another. To God himself, all of his existence is always somehow "present,"[19] though admittedly that idea is difficult for us to understand, for it is a kind of existence different from that which we experience.

**b. God Sees All Time Equally Vividly.** It is somewhat easier for us to understand that God sees all time equally vividly. We read in Psalm 90:4, "For a *thousand years* in your sight are but as *yesterday* when it is past, or as a *watch* in the night." It is sometimes difficult for us to remember events that occurred several weeks ago, several months ago, or several years ago. We remember recent events more vividly, and the clarity of our memory fades with the passing of time. Even if it were possible for us to live "a thousand years," we would remember very few events from hundreds of years earlier, and the clarity of that memory would be very low. But here Scripture tells us that God views a thousand years "as yesterday." He can remember all the detailed events of a thousand years at least as clearly as we can remember the events of "yesterday." In fact, to him a thousand years is "as a watch in the night," a three-or four-hour period during which a guard would stand watch. Such a short period of time would pass quickly and all the events would be easily recalled. Yet this is how a thousand years seems to God.

It is important to pay attention to the precise wording in Psalm 90:4. When the text says that a thousand years are "as *yesterday* when it is past," it still indicates that God sees past events in human history *as past events*, not as events that are presently happening. It does not say, "a thousand years in your sight are but as *today* when it is happening," but rather, "a thousand years in your sight are but as *yesterday* when it is past." God still sees the past in human history as past.

When we realize that the phrase "a thousand years" does not imply that God forgets things after 1,100 or 1,200 years but instead expresses as long a time as one might imagine, it becomes evident that *all of the past* is viewed by God with great clarity and vividness; all of time since the creation is as vivid in God's mind as if it just happened.

---

18. The alternative to saying that time began when God created the universe is to say that time never began, but there has *always* been a succession of moments one after another, extending infinitely far back into the past, but never having a starting point. But to have time without a beginning seems to many people to be absurd and is probably impossible. Bavinck says, "Eternal time in the sense of time without beginning is inconceivable" (*The Doctrine of God*, 157). This objection is one form of saying that an actual infinite cannot exist, a philosophical conception that is explained skillfully by William Lane Craig in *The Existence of God and the Beginning of the Universe* (San Bernardino, CA: Here's Life, 1979), 35–53; and, with fuller reference to philosophical responses to this argument, by J. P. Moreland, *Scaling the Secular City: A Defense of Christianity* (Grand Rapids: Baker, 1987), 15–34.

19. As we shall see below, this does not mean that all events of history look to God as if they were present, for God sees events *in time* and acts *in time*.

And it will always remain just that clear in his consciousness, throughout millions of years of eternity future.

But there is more. In the New Testament, Peter tells us, "With the Lord *one day is as a thousand years*, and a thousand years as one day" (2 Peter 3:8). The second half of this statement had already been made in Psalm 90, but the first half introduces an additional consideration, "One day is as a thousand years." That is, any one day from God's perspective seems to last for "a thousand years"; it is as if that day never ends, but somehow is always being experienced. Again, since "a thousand years" is a figurative expression for "as long a time as we can imagine" or "all history," we can say from this verse that the events of each day in human history remain vivid in God's consciousness forever.

This does not mean that God is unaware of the passage of time within human history, for Scripture frequently tells how God reminds his people of what he has done in the past and repeatedly demonstrates that he alone is able to predict the future (see below). But it does at least mean that God's experience of time is far different from ours. In God's perspective, any extremely long period of time is as if it just happened. And any very short period of time (such as one day) seems to God to last forever: it never ceases to be visible to his mind. Thus God sees and knows all events past, present, and future with equal vividness.

However, this should never cause us to think that God does not see events *in time* and act *in time*, but just the opposite: God is the eternal Lord and Sovereign over time and over history, and he sees it more clearly and acts in it more decisively than any other. But once we have said that, we still must affirm that these verses speak of God's relationship to time in a way that we do not and cannot experience. God's experience of time is not just a patient endurance through eons of endless duration, but he has a *qualitatively different* experience of time than we do. This is consistent with the idea that in his own being, God is timeless; he does not experience a succession of moments. Before God created the world, there was no passage of time, but God timelessly existed. God's timeless eternity has been the dominant view of Christian orthodoxy throughout the history of the church,[20] though it has been frequently challenged.

One substantial challenge to the idea that God is timeless in his own being is found in the massive volume on the doctrine of God, *No One Like Him*, by my friend and former teaching colleague John Feinberg.[21] He writes, "I believe that the best way to understand God's relation to time is to see God as atemporal."[22] He offers four objections to the idea of divine timelessness (what he calls "atemporal eternity"): (1) *Puzzling idea*: "It is hard to make sense of the notion of atemporal eternity.... anything that endures seems to do so through time." (2) *No new thoughts*: "If [God] is temporal, he cannot think anything

20. Carl F. H. Henry argues for God's timeless eternity as the historic position of Christian orthodoxy in *God, Revelation, and Authority*, 5:235–67, and gives a detailed analysis of current challenges from both nonevangelical and evangelical theologians. A thorough philosophical defense of God's timeless eternity is Paul Helm, *Eternal God: A Study of God without Time* (Oxford: Clarendon, 1988).

21. See John Feinberg, *No One Like Him: The Doctrine of God* (Wheaton, IL: Crossway, 2001), 375–436.

22. Ibid., 428.

new or in a new way, because that would be a change," but "Always thinking the same thought . . . is surely not the way Scripture depicts God." (3) *No interpersonal fellowship*: "In addition, with atemporalism how can we speak of fellowship within the Godhead," and "Scripture also portrays God as having fellowship with and interacting with human beings at various times in their lives. How is this possible for a God who has no sequence in his mental life?" (4) *Can timeless acts happen in time?* "Atemporalist claims about God acting timelessly and having the effects occur at the right time are hard to understand."[23]

In response, I agree that the idea of God's timelessness is "hard to understand" (1 and 4). But to admit that *we do not understand* how a timelessly eternal God can act in time does not prove that God *cannot* be timeless in his own being and still create time and act in time. Surely here, when talking about the relationship between God and time, it would be folly to say that what we cannot understand must be impossible—especially when several passages of Scripture affirm that God existed and acted "before" time.

I also agree with Feinberg that (2) Scripture frequently portrays God as having different thoughts at different times regarding events in human history (for example, in the time of the Old Testament he knew that the Messiah had not yet come in human history, but since the earthly ministry of Jesus, he knows that the Messiah has come). And I agree that (3) God eternally experiences interpersonal fellowship among the members of the Trinity, and personally interacts with human beings throughout history. But once again, since God is Lord over time, I maintain that he is able *to act in time* in different ways while (in a way that we do not understand) remaining timeless in his own being.[24]

An analogy with the incarnation of Christ may be helpful here. When God the Son took to himself a human nature, this act of uniting with part of creation did not give to the divine nature of the Son any properties of the creation, but as the Chalcedonian Creed affirmed, the incarnation happened with "the property of each nature being preserved" (see discussion in chapter 26). God's divine nature remained unchanged. By analogy, the timeless eternity of God's own being was not changed when he created the world, created time, and interacted repeatedly with human beings.

Because there is such a vast difference between the Creator and the creature, there are several things that Scripture teaches about God that are impossible for us to

---

23. Ibid., 428–30.

24. Stephen Davis also objects that God cannot be "timelessly eternal" in the sense described above because the moment he creates something, he is acting in time and therefore he must exist in time. (See, e.g., Stephen T. Davis, *Logic and the Nature of God* [Grand Rapids: Eerdmans, 1983], 11–24.) Davis says that we have no coherent notion of "causation in which an eternal cause produces a temporal effect" (21), but that can be explained by recognizing that all of our life experiences have occurred in this time-bound creation, and therefore it is not surprising that we cannot understand how a timeless God can create time and act in time.

Davis also falls into another form of the "if God is infinite, he cannot be personal" mistake mentioned above (see note 12). He says, "A timeless being cannot be the personal, caring, involved God we read about in the Bible" (p. 14). But to prove this he just talks about God's actions in time, without ever showing why God cannot *both* act in time (be personally involved) and be timeless in his own being (be infinite or unlimited with respect to time). Finally, while he mentions the possibility that time was created but will sometime cease to exist (23), he fails to consider the alternative that seems much more likely in view of the Bible's promises of eternal life, namely, that time was once created but will never cease to exist in the future.

understand. We cannot understand how God can be three persons yet only one God. We cannot understand how Jesus can be fully God and fully man yet one person. We cannot understand how God can be present at every point of space with his whole being, yet he is unable to be contained in any space. It should not be surprising that we cannot understand how God can be timeless in his own being and yet act in time.

We can picture God's relationship to time as in figure 11.1. This diagram is meant to show that God created time and is Lord over time. Therefore he can see all events in time equally vividly, yet he also can see events in time and act in time.

The diagram also anticipates the following discussion, since it indicates that God knows events in the future, even the infinitely long eternal future. With regard to the future, God frequently claims through the Old Testament prophets that *he alone is the one who knows and can declare future events*:

> For I am God, and there is no other;
>> I am God, and *there is none like me*,
> declaring the end from the beginning
>> and from ancient times things not yet done,
> saying, "My counsel shall stand,
>> and I will accomplish all my purpose." (Isa. 46:9–10; cf. 41:23, 26; 42:9; 44:7–8; 24–28; 48:3–5)

Thus God somehow stands above time and is able to see it all plainly in his consciousness. Although the analogy is not perfect, we might think of the moment we finish reading a long novel. Before putting it back on the shelf we might flip quickly through the pages once more, calling to mind the many events that had occurred in that novel. For a brief moment, things that transpired over a long period of time all seem to be "present" to our minds. Perhaps this is faintly analogous to God's experience of seeing all of history as equally present in his consciousness.

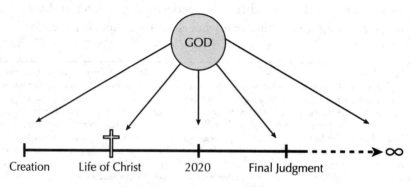

**The Relationship of God to Time**
*Figure 11.1*

**c. God Sees Events in Time, and He Acts in Time.** Yet once all this has been said it is necessary to guard against misunderstanding by completing the definition of God's eternity: "God sees events in time and acts in time." Paul writes, *"When the fullness of time had come, God sent forth his Son*, born of woman, born under the law, to redeem those who were under the law" (Gal. 4:4–5). God observed clearly and knew exactly what was happening with events in his creation as they occurred over time. We might say that God watched the progress of time as various events occurred within his creation. Then at the right time, "when the time had fully come," God sent forth his Son into the world.

It is evident throughout Scripture that God acts within time and acts differently at different points in time. For example, Paul tells the men of Athens, "The times of ignorance God overlooked, but *now* he commands all people everywhere to repent, because *he has fixed a day on which he will judge the world* in righteousness by a man whom he has appointed" (Acts 17:30–31). This statement includes a description of a previous way in which God acted, God's present way of acting, and a future activity that he will carry out, all in time.

Indeed, the repeated emphasis on God's ability to predict the future in the Old Testament prophets requires us to realize that God predicts his actions at one point in time and then carries out his actions at a later point in time. And on a larger scale, the entire Bible from Genesis to Revelation is God's record of the way he has acted over time to bring redemption to his people.

We must therefore affirm both that God has no succession of moments in his own being and sees all history equally vividly and that in his creation he sees the progress of events over time and acts differently at different points in time. In short, he is the Lord who created time and who rules over it and uses it for his own purposes. God can act in time *because* he is Lord of time. He uses it to display his glory. In fact, it is often God's good pleasure to fulfill his promises and carry out his works of redemption over a period of time so that we might more readily see and appreciate his great wisdom, his patience, his faithfulness, his lordship over all events, and even his unchangeableness and eternity.

**d. We Will Always Exist in Time.** Will we ever share in God's eternity? Specifically, in the new heaven and new earth which are yet to come, will time still exist? Some have thought that it would not. In fact, there is a hymn that begins, "When the trumpet of the Lord shall sound, and time shall be no more." And we read in Scripture, "The city has no need of sun or moon to shine on it, for the glory of God gives it light, and its lamp is the Lamb . . . and there will be no night there" (Rev. 21:23, 25; cf. 22:5).

Nevertheless, it is not true to say that heaven will be "timeless," or without the presence of time or the passage of time. As long as we are finite creatures we will necessarily experience events one after another. Even the passage that talks about no night being in heaven also mentions the fact that the kings of the earth will bring into the heavenly city "the glory and the honor of the nations" (Rev. 21:26). We are told concerning the light of the heavenly city, "By its light will the nations walk" (Rev. 21:24). These activities of bringing things into the heavenly city and walking by the light of the heavenly city imply that events are done one after another. Something is outside the heavenly city, and then later, this thing is part of the glory and honor of the nations that are brought into the heavenly city. To cast one's crown before the throne of God (Rev. 4:10) requires that at one moment the person has a crown and that at a later moment that crown is cast before the throne. To sing a new song of praise before God in heaven requires that one word be sung after another. In fact, the "tree of life" in the heavenly city is said to be *yielding its fruit each month* (Rev. 22:2), which implies a regular passage of time and the occurrence of events in time.[25]

Therefore, there will still be a succession of moments one after another and things happening one after another in heaven. We will experience eternal life not in an exact duplication of God's attribute of eternity but rather in a duration of time that will never end. We, as God's people, will experience fullness of joy in God's presence for all eternity—not in the sense that we will no longer experience time, but in the sense that our lives with him will go on forever: "And night will be no more. They will need no light of lamp or sun, for the Lord God will be their light, *and they will reign forever and ever*" (Rev. 22:5).

## 4. Omnipresence

Just as God is unlimited or infinite with respect to time, so God is unlimited with respect to space. This characteristic of God's nature is called God's omnipresence (the Latin prefix *omni-* means "all"). God's omnipresence may be defined as follows: *God does not have size or spatial dimensions and is present at every point of space with his whole being, yet God acts differently in different places.*

The fact that God is Lord of space and cannot be limited by space is evident first from the fact that he created it, for the creation of the material world (Gen. 1:1) implies the creation of space as well. Moses reminded the people of God's lordship over space: "Behold, to the LORD your God belong heaven and the heaven of heavens, the earth with all that is in it" (Deut. 10:14).

**a. God Is Present Everywhere.** There are specific passages that speak of God's presence in every part of space. We read in Jeremiah, "Am I a God at hand, declares the LORD, and not a God far away? Can a man hide himself in secret places so that I cannot see him? declares the LORD. *Do I not fill heaven and earth?* declares the LORD" (Jer. 23:23–24). Here God is rebuking the prophets who think their words or thoughts are hidden from God. He is everywhere and fills heaven and earth.

---

25. Rev. 10:6 in the KJV reads, "that there should be time no longer," but "delay" is a better translation for the Greek term *chronos* in this context (as in the ESV, RSV, NRSV, NASB, NET, NIV, NLT, and NKJV). In fact, the next verse assumes the continuation of time, for it talks of events to be fulfilled "in the days of the trumpet call to be sounded by the seventh angel" (Rev. 10:7).

God's omnipresence is beautifully expressed by David:

> Where shall I go from your Spirit?
>     Or where shall I flee from your presence?
> If I ascend to heaven, you are there!
>     If I make my bed in Sheol, you are there!
> If I take the wings of the morning
>     and dwell in the uttermost parts of the sea,
> even there your hand shall lead me,
>     and your right hand shall hold me. (Ps. 139:7–10)

There is nowhere in the entire universe, on land or sea, in heaven or in hell, where one can flee from God's presence.

We should note also that there is no indication that simply a *part* of God is in one place and a part of him in another. It is *God himself* who is present wherever David might go. We cannot say that some of God or just part of God is present, for that would be to think of his being in spatial terms, as if he were limited somehow by space. It seems more appropriate to say that God is present *with his whole being* in every part of space (cf. Acts 17:28, where Paul affirms the correctness of the words, "In him we live and move and have our being"; and Col. 1:17, which says of Christ, "In him all things hold together").

**b. God Does Not Have Spatial Dimensions.** While it seems necessary for us to say that God's whole being is present in every part of space or at every point in space, it is also necessary to say that *God cannot be contained by any space*, no matter how large. Solomon says in his prayer to God, "But will God indeed dwell on the earth? Behold, *heaven and the highest heaven cannot contain you*; how much less this house that I have built!" (1 Kings 8:27). Heaven and the highest heaven cannot contain God; indeed, he cannot be contained by the largest space imaginable (cf. Isa. 66:1–2; Acts 7:48). While the thought that God is everywhere present with his whole being ought to encourage us greatly in prayer no matter where we are, the fact that no one place can be said to contain God should also discourage us from thinking that there is some special place of worship that gives people special access to God. He cannot be contained in any one place.

We should guard against thinking that God extends infinitely far in all directions so that he himself exists in a sort of infinite, unending space. Nor should we think that God is somehow a "bigger space" or bigger area surrounding the space of the universe as we know it. All of these ideas continue to think of God's being in spatial terms, as if he were simply an extremely large being. Instead, we should try to avoid thinking of God in terms of size or spatial dimensions. God is a being who exists *without* size or dimensions in space. In fact, before God created the universe, there was no matter or material so there was no space either. Yet God still existed. Where was God? He was not in a place that we could call a "where," for there was no "where" or space. But God still was!

This fact makes us realize that God relates to space in a far different way than we do or than any created thing does. He exists as a kind of being that is far different and far greater than we can imagine.

We must also be careful not to think that God himself is equivalent to any part of creation or to all of it. A pantheist believes that everything is God or that God is everything that exists. The biblical perspective is rather that God is *present* everywhere in his creation but also distinct from his creation. How can this be? The analogy of a sponge filled with water is not perfect, but it is helpful. Water is present everywhere in the sponge, but the water is still completely distinct from the sponge. Now this analogy breaks down at very small points within the sponge, where we could say that there is sponge at one point and not water, or water and not sponge. Yet this is because the analogy is dealing with two materials that have spatial characteristics and dimensions, while God does not.

**c. God Can Be Present to Punish, to Sustain, or to Bless.** The idea of God's omnipresence has sometimes troubled people who wonder how God can be present, for example, in hell. In fact, isn't hell the opposite of God's presence, or the absence of God? For example, Paul says that unbelievers "will suffer the punishment of eternal destruction, *away from the presence of the Lord* and from the glory of his might" (2 Thess. 1:9; cf. Is. 59:2; Matt. 25:41). How then can God be everywhere?

This difficulty can be resolved by realizing that *God is present in different ways in different places* or that God acts differently in different places in his creation. Sometimes God is *present to punish*. A terrifying passage in Amos vividly portrays this presence of God in judgment:[26]

> Not one of them shall flee away,
>     not one of them shall escape.
> If they dig into Sheol,
>     from there shall my hand take them;
> if they climb up to heaven,
>     from there I will bring them down.
> If they hide themselves on the top of Carmel,
>     from there I will search them out and take them;
> and if they hide from my sight at the bottom of the sea,
>     there I will command the serpent, and it shall bite them.
> And if they go into captivity before their enemies,
>     there I will command the sword, and it shall kill them;
> and I will fix my eyes upon them for evil and not for good. (Amos 9:1–4)

---

26. See also Rev. 14:9–10, where those who worship the beast and its image "will be tormented with fire and sulfur in the presence of the holy angels and *in the presence of the Lamb*."

At other times God is present neither to punish nor to bless but merely *present to sustain*, to keep the universe existing and functioning in the way he intended it to function. In this sense the divine nature of Christ is everywhere present: "He is before all things, and in him all things hold together" (Col. 1:17). The author of Hebrews says of God the Son that he (continually) "upholds the universe by his word of power" (Heb. 1:3).[27]

Yet at other times or in other places God is *present to bless*. David says, "*In your presence* there is fullness of joy, at your right hand are pleasures forevermore" (Ps. 16:11). Here David is speaking not of God's presence to punish or merely to sustain but of God's presence to bless.

In fact, *most of the time that the Bible talks about God's presence, it is referring to God's presence to bless.* For example, it is in this way that we should understand God's presence above the ark of the covenant in the Old Testament. We read of "the ark of the covenant of the LORD of hosts, who is *enthroned on the cherubim*" (1 Sam. 4:4; cf. Ex. 25:22), a reference to the fact that God made his presence known and acted in a special way to bring blessing and protection to his people at the location he had designated as his throne, namely, the place above the two golden figures of heavenly beings ("cherubim") that were over the top of the ark of the covenant. It is not that God was not present elsewhere but rather that here he especially made his presence known and here he especially manifested his character and brought blessing to his people.

In the new covenant, there is no one place on earth that God has chosen as his particular dwelling place, for we can worship him anywhere (see John 4:20). But now and for all eternity God has chosen the place the Bible calls "heaven" to be the focus of the manifestation of his character and the presence of his blessing and glory. So when the new Jerusalem comes down out of heaven from God, John in his vision hears a loud voice from God's throne saying, "Behold, the dwelling place of God is with man. He will dwell with them, and they will be his people, and God himself will be with them as their God" (Rev. 21:3). We might find it misleading to say that God is "more present" in heaven than anywhere else, but it would not be misleading to say that God is present in a special way in heaven, present especially there to bless and to show forth his glory. We could also say that God manifests his presence more fully in heaven than elsewhere.

In this way also Paul's statement about Christ can be understood: "In him the whole fullness of deity dwells bodily" (Col. 2:9). In one sense of course we could say that God's whole being is present at every point in space and therefore at every point in every person, not only in Christ. But there are two difficulties with speaking this way: (1) The Bible never speaks about God's presence in unbelievers in a direct way, probably to avoid any connection between God and the responsibility or blame for evil deeds, and

---

27. The present participle *pherōn*, "carrying along," in Heb. 1:3 implies that Christ's activity of "carrying along all things" (that is, keeping all things in the universe existing and functioning regularly) is a continual activity, one that never ceases.

probably also to avoid any suggestion of God's presence to bless, since it is only a presence to sustain. (2) Furthermore, this sense of "present to sustain" is not the sense Paul has in mind in Colossians 2:9. In fact, there Paul does not even seem to mean simply "present to bless" in the same sense in which God is present to bless in the lives of all believers. Rather, Paul seems to mean that in Christ God's own nature is present to bless and to manifest his character in the fullest and most complete way possible.

Our difficulty in understanding how to express the way in which God is present in unbelievers, for example, leads us to realize that although the Bible *can* speak of God as being present everywhere, when the Bible says that God is "present," it *usually* means "present to bless." That is, although there are a few references to God's presence to sustain or presence to punish, the vast majority of biblical references to God's presence are simply more brief ways of stating that he is *present to bless.* When we become more and more familiar with this biblical pattern of speech, it becomes more and more difficult to speak of God's presence in any other way. And perhaps it is even misleading to do so unless a clear explanation of our meaning can be given.

Some examples of the usual biblical means of expression are as follows: 2 Corinthians 3:17: "Where the Spirit of the Lord is, there is freedom"; Romans 8:9–10: "You ... are ... in the Spirit, if in fact the Spirit of God dwells in you. ... If Christ is in you ... the Spirit is life"; John 14:23: "If anyone loves me, he will keep my word, and my Father will love him, and we will come to him and make our home with him," and so forth. All of these verses talk about God's presence and assume that we understand that they mean God's presence *to bless.*

In a parallel expression, when the Bible talks about God being "far away," it usually means he is "not present to bless." For example, Isaiah 59:2 says, "Your iniquities have made a separation between you and your God," and Proverbs 15:29 declares, "The LORD is far from the wicked, but he hears the prayer of the righteous."

In summary, God is present in every part of space with his whole being, yet God acts differently in different places. Furthermore, when the Bible speaks of God's presence, it usually means his presence to bless, and it is only normal for our speech to conform to this biblical usage.

Herman Bavinck, in *The Doctrine of God*, quotes a beautiful paragraph illustrating the practical application of the doctrine of God's omnipresence:

> When you wish to do something evil, you retire from the public into your house where no enemy may see you; from those places of your house which are open and visible to the eyes of men you remove yourself into your room; even in your room you fear some witness from another quarter; you retire into your heart, there you meditate: he is more inward than your heart. Wherever, therefore, you shall have fled, there he is. From yourself, whither will you flee? Will you not follow yourself wherever you shall flee? But since there is One more inward even than yourself, there

is no place where you may flee from God angry but to God reconciled. There is no place at all whither you may flee. Will you flee from him? Flee unto him.[28]

## 5. Unity

The unity of God may be defined as follows: *God is not divided into parts, yet we see different attributes of God emphasized at different times*. This attribute of God has also been called *God's simplicity*, using *simple* in the less common sense of "not complex" or "not composed of parts." But since the word *simple* today has the more common sense of "easy to understand" and "unintelligent or foolish," it is more helpful now to speak of God's "unity" rather than his "simplicity."[29]

**a. Each Attribute Characterizes the Whole Being of God.** When Scripture speaks about God's attributes it never singles out one attribute of God as more important than all the rest. There is an assumption that every attribute is completely true of God and is true of all of God's character. For example, John can say that "God is light" (1 John 1:5) and then a little later say also that "God is love" (1 John 4:8). There is no suggestion that part of God is light and part of God is love or that God is partly light and partly love. Nor should we think that God is more light than love or more love than light. Rather it is *God himself* who is light, and it is *God himself* who is also love.

The same is true of other descriptions of God's character, such as that in Exodus 34:6–7:

> The LORD passed before him and proclaimed, "The LORD, the LORD, a God merciful and gracious, slow to anger, and abounding in steadfast love and faithfulness, keeping steadfast love for thousands, forgiving iniquity and transgression and sin, but who will by no means clear the guilty, visiting the iniquity of the fathers on the children and the children's children, to the third and the fourth generation."

We would not want to say that these attributes are only characteristic of some part of God but rather that they are characteristic of God himself and therefore characteristic of all of God.

These considerations indicate that we should not think of God as some kind of collection of various attributes added together as in figure 11.2.

---

28. Bavinck, *The Doctrine of God*, 164. The citation is reproduced in the book with no indication of its source.

29. Systematic theologians have often distinguished another aspect of God's unity at this point, namely the "unity" found in the fact that God is one God, not many gods. This fact has been called the "unity of singularity," whereas what I have here called God's unity has then been called the "unity of simplicity."

While I agree that God is one God, it can be confusing to speak of two different kinds of unity in God. Therefore, I have not used the term *unity of singularity* or discussed the concept here. Rather, I have treated the question in chapter 14, on the Trinity.

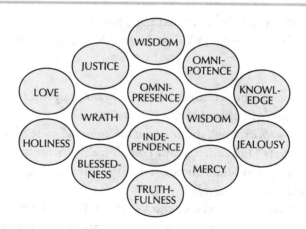

**God's Being Is Not a Collection of Attributes Added Together**
*Figure 11.2*

Nor should we think of the attributes of God as something external from God's real being or real self, something added on to who God really is, after the analogy of figure 11.3.

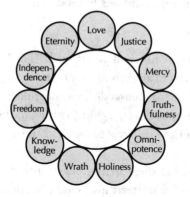

**God's Attributes Are Not Additions to His Real Being**
*Figure 11.3*

Rather, we must remember that God's *whole being* includes all of his attributes: he is *entirely* loving, *entirely* merciful, *entirely* just, and so forth. Every attribute of God that we find in Scripture is true of *all* of God's being, and we therefore can say that *every attribute of God also qualifies every other attribute.*

Figure 11.4 may be helpful in understanding this doctrine of God's unity. In the diagram, let us assume that the horizontal lines represent the attribute of love, and that the vertical lines represent the aspect of God's justice.

**God's Love and Justice**
*Figure 11.4*

Furthermore, let us understand the diagonal lines going from upper left to lower right as representing God's holiness and the diagonal lines going from upper right to lower left as representing God's wisdom, as in figure 11.5.

**God's Love, Justice, Holiness, and Widsom**
*Figure 11.5*

We could of course go on with different sorts of lines for each of the different attributes of God. But it should be clear that each attribute is simply a way of describing one aspect of God's total character or being. God himself is a *unity*, a unified and completely integrated whole person who is infinitely perfect in *all* of these attributes.

Why then does Scripture speak of these different attributes of God? It is probably because we are unable to grasp all of God's character at one time, and we need to learn of it from different perspectives over a period of time. Yet these perspectives should never be set in opposition to one another, for they are just different ways of looking at the totality of God's character.

**b. God Is the Same God Always.** In terms of practical application, this means that we should never think, for example, that God is a loving God at one point in history and a just or wrathful God at another point in history. He is the same God always, and everything he says or does is fully consistent with all his attributes. It is not accurate to say, as some have said, that God is a God of justice in the Old Testament and a God of love in the New Testament. God is and always has been infinitely just and infinitely loving as well, and everything he does in the Old Testament as well as the New Testament is completely consistent with both of those attributes.

Now it is true that some actions of God show certain of his attributes more prominently. Creation demonstrates his power and wisdom, the atonement demonstrates his love and justice, and the radiance of heaven demonstrates his glory and beauty. But all of these in some way or other *also* demonstrate his knowledge and holiness and mercy and truthfulness and patience and sovereignty and so forth. It would be difficult indeed to find some attribute of God that is not reflected at least to some degree in any one of his acts of redemption. This is due to the fact mentioned above: God is a unity and everything he does is an act of the whole person of God.

**c. No One Attribute of God Is Most Important.** Moreover, the doctrine of the unity of God should caution us against attempting to single out any one attribute of God as more important than all the others. At various times people have attempted to see God's holiness, love, self-existence, righteousness, or some other attribute as the most important attribute of his being. But all such attempts seem to misconceive of God as a combination of various parts, with some parts being somehow larger or more influential than others. Furthermore, it is hard to understand exactly what "most important" might mean. Does it mean that there are some actions of God that are not fully consistent with some of his other attributes? That there are some attributes that God somehow sets aside at times in order to act in ways slightly contrary to those attributes? Certainly we cannot maintain either of these views, for that would mean that God is inconsistent with his own character or that he changes and becomes something different from what he was previously. Rather, when we see all the attributes as merely various aspects of the total character of God, then such a question becomes quite unnecessary and we discover that there is no attribute that can be singled out as more important. It is *God himself in his whole being* who is supremely important, and it is God himself in his whole being whom we are to seek to know and to love.

## QUESTIONS FOR PERSONAL APPLICATION

1. As you think of God's independence, unchangeableness, eternity, omnipresence, and unity, can you see some faint reflections of these five incommunicable attributes in yourself as God created you to be? What would it mean to strive to become more like God in these areas? At what point would it be wrong to even want to be like God in each of these areas because it would be attempting to usurp his unique role as Creator and Lord?

2. Using each of these five incommunicable attributes, explain how we will be more like God in heaven than we are now, and also how we will for all eternity be unlike God in each of these five areas.

3. Explain how each aspect of the doctrine of God's independence makes you feel emotionally. Does this doctrine have a positive or negative effect on your spiritual life? Explain why.

4. Explain how the doctrine of God's immutability or unchangeableness helps to answer the following questions: Will we be able to do a good job of bringing up

children in such an evil world as we have today? Is it possible to have the same close fellowship with God that people had during biblical times? What can we think or do to make Bible stories seem more real and less removed from our present life? Do you think that God is less willing to answer prayer today than he was in Bible times?

5. If you sin against God today, when would it start bringing sorrow to God's heart? When would it stop bringing sorrow to God's heart? Does this reflection help you understand why God's character requires that he punish sin? Why did God have to send his Son to bear the punishment for sin instead of simply forgetting about sin and welcoming sinners into heaven without having given the punishment for sin to anyone? Does God now think of your sins as forgiven or as unforgiven sins?

6. If you sing praise to God today, when will the sound of that praise cease being present in God's consciousness and bringing delight to his heart? Do songs of praise to God have any ultimate meaning? What about trusting in him hour by hour or obeying him throughout each day?

7. Is control over the use of your time a struggle in your own life? As we grow toward maturity in the Christian life and toward conformity to the image of Christ, will we become more like God in our mastery over time? In what ways?

8. Explain how each of the five incommunicable attributes of God discussed in this chapter can be a help in your own prayer life.

**Special Terms**

anthropomorphic language
aseity
atemporal eternity
communicable attributes
eternity
immutability
impassibility
incommunicable attributes
independence
infinite
infinity with respect to space
infinity with respect to time
names of God
omnipresence
self-existence
simplicity
unchangeableness
unity

# BIBLIOGRAPHY

(For an explanation of this bibliography see the note on the bibliography to chapter 1, pp. 23–24. Complete bibliographical data may be found on pp. 1489–96.)

Note: For this chapter on God's incommunicable attributes, it should be noted that some systematic theologies classify and discuss God's attributes in categories other than communicable and incommunicable, so an exact cross-reference to parallel sections is not always possible. A fuller list of the sections in systematic theology texts that discuss the attributes of God in general will be found in the bibliography at the end of chapter 13.

## SECTIONS IN EVANGELICAL SYSTEMATIC THEOLOGIES

### 1. Anglican (Episcopalian)
1882–92 . . . . . Litton, 58–67
2001 . . . . . . . . Packer, 26–53
2013 . . . . . . . . Bird, 126–139
2013 . . . . . . . . Bray, 112–14

### 2. Arminian (Wesleyan or Methodist)
1875–76 . . . . . Pope, 1:248–55, 287–325
1892–94 . . . . . Miley, 1:159–80, 214–22
1940 . . . . . . . . Wiley, 1:241–393
1960 . . . . . . . . Purkiser, 127–44
1992 . . . . . . . . Oden, 1:53–130
2002 . . . . . . . . Cottrell, 67–99

### 3. Baptist
1767 . . . . . . . . Gill, 25–31, 33–50, 119–22
1887 . . . . . . . . Boyce, 1:125–35, 183–90
1907 . . . . . . . . Strong, 243–303
1987–94 . . . . . Lewis and Demarest, 1:175–248
1990–95 . . . . . Garrett, 1:223–304
2007 . . . . . . . . Akin, 221–38
2013 . . . . . . . . Erickson, 233–53

### 4. Dispensational
1947 . . . . . . . . Chafer, 1:179–191, 212–24, 260–71
1949 . . . . . . . . Thiessen, 118–28
2002–2005 . . Geisler, 2:1–312, 338–55, 385–419, 518–95
2017 . . . . . . . . MacArthur and Mayhue, 168–78

### 5. Lutheran
1917–24 . . . . . Pieper, 1:427–47
1934 . . . . . . . . Mueller, 160–67

### 6. Reformed (or Presbyterian)
1559 . . . . . . . . Calvin, 1:96–120
1679–85 . . . . . Turretin, IET, 1:189–91
1871–73 . . . . . Hodge, 1:366–93
1878 . . . . . . . . Dabney, ST, 38–45, 144–54
1887–1921 . . . Warfield, SSW, 1:69–87; ST, 109–14
1894 . . . . . . . . Shedd, 274–310
1906–11 . . . . . Bavinck, RD, 2:131–32, 134–36, 148–77
1910 . . . . . . . . Vos, 1:3–37
1938 . . . . . . . . Berkhof, 47–63
1998 . . . . . . . . Reymond, 163–204
2008 . . . . . . . . Van Genderen, 164–192
2011 . . . . . . . . Horton, 223–258
2013 . . . . . . . . Frame, 307–27, 335–419
2013 . . . . . . . . Culver, 60–92, 216–226
2016 . . . . . . . . Allen and Swain, 57–77
2017 . . . . . . . . Barrett, 217–40
2019 . . . . . . . . Letham, 158–60

### 7. Renewal (or charismatic/Pentecostal)
1988–92 . . . . . Williams, 55–59, 77–79
1993 . . . . . . . . Menzies and Horton, 48–53
1995 . . . . . . . . Horton, 120–131
2008 . . . . . . . . Duffield and Van Cleave, 58–61, 70–76

## SECTIONS IN REPRESENTATIVE ROMAN CATHOLIC SYSTEMATIC THEOLOGIES

### 1. Roman Catholic: Traditional
1955 . . . . . . . . Ott, 24–38

### 2. Roman Catholic: Post-Vatican II
1980 . . . . . . . . McBrien, 1:238–341
2012 . . . . . . . . CCC, 214–21

### OTHER WORKS

Allison, Gregg. *Historical Theology: An Introduction to Christian Doctrine; A Companion to Wayne Grudem's* Systematic Theology. Grand Rapids: Zondervan, 2011, 210–30.

Bray, G. L. "God." In *NDBT*, 511–21.

Bromiley, G. W. "God." In *ISBE*, 2:493–503.

Bullock, C. Hassell. "God." In *BTDB*, 288–95.

Charnock, Stephen. *The Existence and Attributes of God.* 1665–80; Reprint, Evansville, IN: Sovereign Grace Book Club, n.d., 69–180.

Diehl, D. W. "Process Theology." In *EDT1*, 880–85.

Dillard, Raymond B. "Name of God." In *BTDB*, 295–97.

Dolezal, James E. *God without Parts: Divine Simplicity and the Metaphysics of God's Absoluteness.* Eugene, OR: Pickwick, 2011.

Duby, Steven. *Divine Simplicity: A Dogmatic Account.* London: T&T Clark 2016.

Enns, Paul. "Theology Proper: Doctrine of God." In *The Moody Handbook of Theology.* Rev. ed., 191–200. Chicago: Moody Publishers, 2008.

Feinberg, John S. *No One Like Him: The Doctrine of God.* Wheaton, IL: Crossway, 2006.

George, Timothy. "The Nature of God: Being, Attributes, and Acts." In *A Theology for the Church*, edited by Daniel L. Akin et al., 176–241. Nashville: B&H, 2014.

Helm, Paul. *Eternal God: A Study of God without Time.* Oxford: Clarendon, 1988.

Hinlicky, Paul R. *Divine Simplicity: Christ the Crisis of Metaphysics.* Grand Rapids: Baker Academic, 2016.

Hoggard-Creegan, N. "Process Theology." In *EDT3*, 700–701.

Horton, M. "God." In *EDT3*, 343–48.

Kaiser, Christopher B. *The Doctrine of God.* Westchester, IL: Good News, 1982.

Lewis, Gordon R. "God, Attributes of." In *EDT1*, 451–59.

Lister, Rob. *God Is Impassible and Impassioned: Toward a Theology of Divine Emotion.* Wheaton, IL: Crossway, 2013.

Martens, Elmer. "Names of God." In *BTDB*, 297–300.

McComiskey, T. E. "God, Names of." In *EDT3*, 349–52.

Newman, C. C. "God." In *DLNT*, 412–31.

Packer, J. I. *Knowing God.* London: Hodder and Stoughton, 1973, 67–79.

Saucy, R. H. "God, Doctrine of." In *EDT1*, 459–64.

Tozer, A. W. *The Knowledge of the Holy.* New York: Harper and Row, 1961.

## SCRIPTURE MEMORY PASSAGE

**Psalm 102:25–27:**
*Of old you laid the foundation of the earth,*
*    and the heavens are the work of your hands.*
*They will perish, but you will remain;*
*    they will all wear out like a garment.*

*You change them like a robe, and they will*
*    pass away,*
*    but you are the same, and your years have*
*    no end.*

## HYMN

**"Immortal, Invisible, God Only Wise"**

In several lines of this hymn the various attributes of God are mentioned in such rapid succession that it is impossible for us to reflect on each one individually as we sing. That is not entirely a disadvantage of the hymn, however, for it makes us realize that when we finally see God in all his glory in heaven, the wonder of beholding him and all his perfections at once will overwhelm us far more completely than does this hymn, and we will find ourselves lost in praise.

*Immortal, invisible, God only wise,*
  *In light inaccessible hid from our eyes,*
*Most blessed, most glorious, the Ancient of Days,*
  *Almighty, victorious, thy great name*
    *we praise.*

*Unresting, unhasting, and silent as light,*
  *Nor wanting, nor wasting, thou rulest*
    *in might;*

*Thy justice like mountains high soaring above*
  *Thy clouds which are fountains of goodness*
    *and love.*

*Great Father of glory, pure Father of light,*
  *Thine angels adore thee, all veiling their sight;*
*All praise we would render; O help us to see*
  *'Tis only the splendor of light hideth thee!*

Author: Walter Chalmers Smith, 1867

Alternative hymn: "Have You Not Known, Have You Not Heard?"

# CONTEMPORARY WORSHIP SONG

## "How Great Is Our God"

*The splendor of the King*
*Clothed in majesty,*
*Let all the earth rejoice,*
*All the earth rejoice.*
*He wraps Himself in light,*
*And darkness tries to hide,*
*And trembles at His voice,*
*And trembles at His voice.*

**Chorus**
*How great is our God!*
*Sing with me,*
*How great is our God!*
*And all will see how great,*
*How great is our God!*

*And age to age He stands,*
*And time is in His hands,*
*Beginning and the End,*
*Beginning and the End.*
*The Godhead three in one,*
*Father, Spirit, Son,*
*The Lion and the Lamb,*
*The Lion and the Lamb.*

**Bridge**
*Name above all names,*
*Worthy of all praise!*
*My heart will sing*
*How great is our God!*

Words by Chris Tomlin, Jesse
Reeves, and Ed Cash[30]

# CHAPTER 12

# The Character of God: "Communicable" Attributes (Part 1)

*How is God like us in his being and in mental and moral attributes?*

## EXPLANATION AND SCRIPTURAL BASIS

In this chapter we consider the attributes of God that are "communicable," or more shared with us than those mentioned in the previous chapter. It must be remembered that this division into "incommunicable" and "communicable" is not an absolute division and there is some room for difference of opinion concerning which attributes should fit into which categories.[1] The list of attributes here put in the category "communicable" is a common one, but understanding the definition of each attribute is more important than being able to categorize them in exactly the way presented in this book.

Furthermore, any list of God's attributes must be based on some understanding of how finely one wishes to make distinctions between various aspects of God's character. Are God's goodness and love two attributes or one? What about knowledge and wisdom, or spirituality and invisibility? In this chapter, each of these attributes is treated separately, and the result is a rather long list of various attributes. Yet in several cases it would not make much difference if someone were to treat these pairs as various aspects of the same attribute. If we remember that it is the entire and wholly integrated person of God about whom we are talking, it will be apparent that the division into various attributes is not a matter of great doctrinal significance but is something that must be based on one's judgment concerning the most effective way to present the biblical material.

This chapter divides God's "communicable" attributes into five major categories, with individual attributes listed under each category as follows:

---

1. See discussion of communicable and incommunicable attributes in chapter 11, pp. 185–86.

  A. Attributes Describing God's Being
    1. Spirituality
    2. Invisibility
  B. Mental Attributes
    3. Knowledge (or Omniscience)
    4. Wisdom
    5. Truthfulness (and Faithfulness)
  C. Moral Attributes
    6. Goodness
    7. Love
    8. Mercy (Grace, Patience)
    9. Holiness
    10. Peace (or Order)
    11. Righteousness (or Justice)
    12. Jealousy
    13. Wrath
  D. Attributes of Purpose
    14. Will
    15. Freedom
    16. Omnipotence (or Power, and Sovereignty)
  E. "Summary" Attributes
    17. Perfection
    18. Blessedness
    19. Beauty
    20. Glory

Because God's communicable attributes are to be imitated in our lives,[2] each of these sections will include a short explanation of the way in which the attribute in question is to be imitated by us.

## A. ATTRIBUTES DESCRIBING GOD'S BEING

### 1. Spirituality

People have often wondered, what is God made of? Is he made of flesh and blood like ourselves? Certainly not. What then is the material that forms his being? Is God made of matter at all? Or is God pure energy? Or is he in some sense pure thought?

The answer of Scripture is that God is none of these. Rather, we read that "God is *spirit*" (John 4:24). This statement is spoken by Jesus in the context of a discussion with

---

2. Note that Eph. 5:1 tells us to "be imitators of God, as beloved children." See also the discussion of the fact that God created us to reflect his character in our lives, in chapter 21, pp. 571–75.

the woman at the well in Samaria. The discussion is about the *location* where people should worship God, and Jesus is telling her that true worship of God does not require that one be *present* either in Jerusalem or in Samaria (John 4:21), for true worship has to do not with physical location but with one's inner spiritual condition. This is because "God is spirit," and this apparently signifies that God is in no way limited to a spatial location.

Thus we should *not* think of God as having *size* or *dimensions*, even infinite ones (see the discussion on God's omnipresence in the previous chapter). We should not think of God's existence as spirit as meaning that God is infinitely large, for example, for it is not *part* of God but *all* of God that is in every point of space (see Ps. 139:7–10). Nor should we think that God's existence as spirit means that God is infinitely small, for no place in the universe can surround him or contain him (see 1 Kings 8:27). Thus God's being cannot be rightly thought of in terms of space, however we understand his existence as "spirit."

We also find that God forbids his people to think of *his very being* as similar to *anything* else in the physical creation. We read in the Ten Commandments:

> You shall not make for yourself a carved image, or *any likeness of anything* that is in heaven above, or that is in the earth beneath, or that is in the water under the earth. You shall not bow down to them or serve them; *for I the* LORD *your God am a jealous God*, visiting the iniquity of the fathers on the children to the third and the fourth generation of those who hate me, but showing steadfast love to thousands of those who love me and keep my commandments. (Ex. 20:4–6)

The creation language in this commandment ("heaven above, or . . . earth beneath, or . . . water under the earth") is a reminder that God's *being*, his essential mode of existence, is different from everything that he has created. To think of his being in terms of anything else in the created universe is to misrepresent him, to limit him, to think of him as less than he really is. To make a carved image of God as a golden calf, for example, may have been an attempt to portray God as a God who is strong and full of life (like a calf), but to say that God was like a calf was a horribly false statement about God's knowledge, wisdom, love, mercy, omnipresence, eternity, independence, holiness, righteousness, justice, and so forth. Indeed, while we must say that God has made all creation so that each part of it reflects something of his own character, we must also now affirm that to picture God as *existing* in a form or *mode of being* that is like anything else in creation is to think of God in a horribly misleading and dishonoring way.

This is why God's jealousy is given as the reason for the prohibition against making images of him: "For I the LORD your God am a jealous God" (Ex. 20:5). God is jealous to protect his own honor. He eagerly seeks for people to think of him as he is and to worship him for all his excellence, and he is angered when his glory is diminished or his character is falsely represented (cf. Deut. 4:23–24, where God's intense jealousy for his own honor is again given as the reason for a prohibition against making any images of him).

Thus God does not have a physical body, nor is he made of any kind of matter like much of the rest of creation. Furthermore, God is not merely energy or thought or some other element of creation. He is also not like vapor or steam or air or space, all of which are created things: *God's being* is not like any of these. God's being is not even exactly like our own spirits, for these are created things that apparently are able to exist only in one place in one time.

Instead of all these ideas of God, we must say that God is *spirit*. Whatever this means, it is a kind of existence that is unlike anything else in creation. It is a kind of existence that is far superior to all our material existence. We might say that God is "pure being" or "the fullness or essence of being." Furthermore, this kind of existence is not less real or less desirable than our own existence. Rather, it is more real and more desirable than the material and immaterial existence of all creation. Before there was any creation, God existed as spirit. His own being is so very real that it was able to cause everything else to come into existence!

At this point we can define God's spirituality: *God's spirituality means that God exists as a being that is not made of any matter, has no parts or dimensions, is unable to be perceived by our bodily senses, and is more excellent than any other kind of existence.*

We may ask why God's being is this way. Why is God spirit? All that we can say is that this is the greatest, most excellent way to be! This is a form of existence far superior to anything we know. It is amazing to meditate on this fact.

These considerations make us wonder if God's spirituality should perhaps be called an "incommunicable" attribute. To do so would indeed be appropriate in some ways, since God's being is so different from ours. Nevertheless, the fact remains that God has given us spirits in which we worship him (John 4:24; 1 Cor. 14:14; Phil. 3:3), in which we are united with the Lord's spirit (1 Cor. 6:17), with which the Holy Spirit joins to bear witness to our adoption in God's family (Rom. 8:16), and in which we pass into the Lord's presence when we die (Luke 23:46; Eccl. 12:7; Heb. 12:23; cf. Phil. 1:23–24). Therefore there is clearly some communication from God to us of a spiritual nature that is something like his own nature, though certainly not in all respects. For this reason it also seems appropriate to think of God's spirituality as a communicable attribute.

## 2. Invisibility

Related to God's spirituality is the fact that God is invisible. Yet we also must speak of the visible ways in which God manifests himself. God's invisibility can be defined as follows: *God's invisibility means that God's total essence, all of his spiritual being, will never be able to be seen by us, yet God still shows himself to us partially in this age and more fully in the age to come.*

Many passages speak of the fact that God is not able to be seen. "No one has ever seen

God" (John 1:18). Jesus says, "Not that anyone has seen the Father except he who is from God; he has seen the Father" (John 6:46). Paul gives the following words of praise: "To the King of ages, immortal, *invisible*, the only God, be honor and glory forever and ever. Amen" (1 Tim. 1:17). He speaks of God as one "who alone has immortality, who dwells in unapproachable light, *whom no one has ever seen or can see*" (1 Tim. 6:16). John says, "No one has ever seen God" (1 John 4:12).

In addition, there is the fact that we do not see God today with our physical eyes. We may perhaps wonder why God has decided to remain invisible to us in this age, but we should realize at least two benefits: (1) God's invisibility means that God himself decides to whom he will reveal himself: "No one knows the Father except the Son and anyone to whom the Son chooses to reveal him" (Matt. 11:27). (2) God's invisibility means that we must daily, intentionally seek after fellowship with him and not take it for granted: "You will seek me and find me, when you seek me with all your heart" (Jer. 29:13).

We must remember that these passages were all written after events in Scripture where people saw some outward manifestation of God. For example, very early in Scripture we read, "Thus the LORD used to speak to Moses face to face, as a man speaks to his friend" (Ex. 33:11). Yet God told Moses, "You cannot see my face, for man shall not see me and live" (Ex. 33:20). Nevertheless, God caused his glory to pass by Moses while he hid Moses in a cleft of the rock, and then God let Moses see his back after he had passed by, but said, "my face shall not be seen" (Ex. 33:21–23). This sequence of verses and others like it in the Old Testament indicate that there was some sense in which God could not be seen at all, but that there was also some outward form or manifestation of God which at least in part was able to be seen by man.

It is right, therefore, to say that although God's *total essence* will never be able to be seen by us, nevertheless, God still shows something of himself to us through visible, created things. This happens in a variety of ways.

If we are to *think* of God, we must think of him somehow. God understands this and gives us hundreds of different analogies taken from our human lives or from the created world.[3] This huge diversity of analogies from all parts of creation reminds us that we should not focus overly much on any one of these analogies. Yet if we do not focus exclusively on any one of these analogies, all of them help to reveal God to us in a somewhat "visible" way (cf. Gen. 1:27; Ps. 19:1; Rom. 1:20).

The Old Testament also records a number of theophanies. A *theophany* is "an appearance of God." In these theophanies God took on various visible forms to show himself to people. God appeared to Abraham (Gen. 18:1–33), Jacob (Gen. 32:28–30), the people of Israel (as a pillar of cloud by day and fire by night: Ex. 13:21–22), the elders of Israel (Ex. 24:9–11), Manoah and his wife (Judg. 13:21–22), Isaiah (Isa. 6:1), and others.

---

3. See the discussion of the names of God taken from creation in chapter 11, p. 187.

A much greater visible manifestation of God than these Old Testament theophanies was found in the person of Jesus Christ himself. He could say, "Whoever has seen me has seen the Father" (John 14:9). And John contrasts the fact that no one has ever seen God with the fact that God's only Son has made him known to us: "No one has ever seen God; the only begotten God,[4] who is in the bosom of the Father, he has made him known" (John 1:18, author's translation). Furthermore, Jesus is "the image of the invisible God" (Col. 1:15), and is "the bright radiance of the glory of God" and is "the exact representation of his nature" (Heb. 1:3 author's translation). In the person of Jesus we have a unique visible manifestation of God in the New Testament that was not available to believers who saw theophanies in the Old Testament.

But how will we see God in heaven? We will never be able to see or know all of God, for "his greatness is unsearchable" (Ps. 145:3; cf. John 6:46; 1 Tim. 1:17; 6:16; 1 John 4:12, which were mentioned above). Nevertheless, Scripture says that we will see God himself. Jesus says, "Blessed are the pure in heart, for *they shall see God*" (Matt. 5:8). We will be able to see the human nature of Jesus, of course (Rev. 1:7). But it is not clear in exactly what sense we will be able to "see" the Father, the Holy Spirit, and the divine nature of God the Son (cf. Rev. 1:4; 4:2–3, 5; 5:6). Perhaps the nature of this "seeing" will not be known to us until we reach heaven.

Although what we see will not be an exhaustive vision of God (who is infinite, while we are finite), it will be a completely true and clear and real vision of God. We shall see "face to face" (1 Cor. 13:12), and "we shall see him as he is" (1 John 3:2). The most remarkable description of the open, close fellowship with God that we shall experience is seen in the fact that in the heavenly city "the throne of God and of the Lamb will be in it, and his servants will worship him; *they will see his face*, and his name will be on their foreheads" (Rev. 22:3–4).

When we realize that God is the perfection of all that we long for or desire, that he is the summation of everything beautiful or desirable, then we realize that the greatest joy of the life to come will be that we "shall see his face" and experience the close interpersonal fellowship that this implies. This seeing of God "face to face" has been called the *beatific vision*, meaning "the vision that makes us blessed or happy" ("beatific" is from two Latin words: *beatus*, "blessed," and *facere*, "to make"). To look at God changes us and makes us like him: "We shall be like him, because *we shall see him as he is*" (1 John 3:2; cf. 2 Cor. 3:18). This vision of God will be the consummation of our knowing God and will give us full delight and joy for all eternity: "In your presence there is fullness of joy; at your right hand are pleasures forevermore" (Ps. 16:11).

---

4. There is a textual variant at this point, but "the only begotten God" (*monogenēs theos*) is better attested than "the only begotten Son," and this reading is not foreign to the context; see Leon Morris, *The Gospel according to John* (Grand Rapids: Eerdmans, 1971), 113–14.

## B. MENTAL ATTRIBUTES

## 3. Knowledge (Omniscience)

God's knowledge may be defined as follows: *God fully knows himself and all things actual and possible in one simple and eternal act.*

Elihu says that God is the one "who is *perfect in knowledge*" (Job 37:16), and John says that God "*knows everything*" (1 John 3:20). The quality of knowing everything is called omniscience, and because God knows everything, he is said to be omniscient (that is, "all-knowing").

**a. God Knows Himself.** The definition given above explains omniscience in more detail. It says first that God fully knows himself. This is an amazing fact since God's own being is infinite or unlimited. Of course, only he who is infinite can fully know himself in every detail. This fact is implied by Paul when he says, "For the Spirit searches everything, even the depths of God. For who knows a person's thoughts except the spirit of that person, which is in him? So also no one comprehends the thoughts of God except the Spirit of God" (1 Cor. 2:10–11).

This idea is also suggested by John's statement that "God is light and in him is no darkness at all" (1 John 1:5). In this context "light" has a suggestion of both moral purity and full knowledge or awareness. If there is "no darkness at all" in God, but he is entirely "light," then God is himself both entirely holy and also entirely filled with self-knowledge.

**b. God Knows All Things Actual.** The definition also says that God knows "all things *actual*." This means all things that exist and all things that happen. This applies to creation, for God is the one before whom "no creature is hidden from his sight, but all are naked and exposed to the eyes of him to whom we must give account" (Heb. 4:13; cf. 2 Chron. 16:9; Job 28:24; Matt. 10:29–30). God also knows the future, for he is the one who can say, "I am God, and there is none like me, declaring the end from the beginning and from ancient times things not yet done" (Isa. 46:9–10; cf. 42:8–9 and frequent passages in the Old Testament prophets). He knows the tiny details of every one of our lives, for Jesus tells us, "Your Father knows what you need before you ask him" (Matt. 6:8), and "Even the hairs of your head are all numbered" (Matt. 10:30).

In Psalm 139 David reflects on the amazing detail of God's knowledge of our lives. He knows our actions and thoughts: "O LORD, you have searched me and known me! You know when I sit down and when I rise up; you discern my thoughts from afar" (Ps. 139:1–2). He knows the words we will say before they are spoken: "Even before a word is on my tongue, behold, O LORD, you know it altogether" (Ps. 139:4). And he knows all the days of our lives even before we are born: "Your eyes saw my unformed substance; in your book were written, every one of them, the days that were formed for me, when as yet there was none of them" (Ps. 139:16).

**c. God Knows All Things Possible.** The definition of God's knowledge given above also specifies that God knows "all things *possible*." This is because there are some instances in Scripture where God gives information about events that might happen but that do not actually come to pass. For example, when David was fleeing from Saul he rescued the city of Keilah from the Philistines and then stayed for a time at Keilah. He decided to ask God whether Saul would come to Keilah to attack him and, if Saul came, whether the men of Keilah would surrender him into Saul's hand. David said,

> "Will Saul come down, as your servant has heard? O LORD, the God of Israel, please tell your servant." And the LORD said, "He will come down." Then David said, "Will the men of Keilah surrender me and my men into the hand of Saul?" And the LORD said, "They will surrender you." Then David and his men, who were about six hundred, arose and departed from Keilah, and they went wherever they could go. When Saul was told that David had escaped from Keilah, he gave up the expedition. (1 Sam. 23:11–13)

Similarly, Jesus could state that Tyre and Sidon *would have* repented if Jesus' own miracles had been done there in former days: "Woe to you, Chorazin! Woe to you, Bethsaida! For if the mighty works done in you had been done in Tyre and Sidon, they would have repented long ago in sackcloth and ashes" (Matt. 11:21). Similarly, he says, "And you, Capernaum, will you be exalted to heaven? You will be brought down to Hades. For if the mighty works done in you had been done in Sodom, it would have remained until this day" (Matt. 11:23; cf. 2 Kings 13:19, where Elisha tells what would have happened if King Joash had struck the ground five or six times with the arrows).

The fact that God knows all things possible can also be deduced from God's full knowledge of himself. If God fully knows himself, he knows everything he is able to do, which includes all things that are possible. This fact is indeed amazing. God has made an incredibly complex and varied universe—as is evident, for example, when we observe the remarkable variety of animals in a zoo or fish in an aquarium. But there are thousands upon thousands of other variations or kinds of animals and fish and other things that God *could have created* but did not. God's infinite knowledge includes detailed knowledge of what each of those other possible creations would have been like and what would have happened in each of them! "Such knowledge is too wonderful for me; it is high; I cannot attain it" (Ps. 139:6). "For as the heavens are higher than the earth, so are my ways higher than your ways and my thoughts than your thoughts" (Isa. 55:9).[5]

**d. God Is Always Aware of Everything.** Our definition of God's knowledge speaks of God knowing everything in one "simple act." Here again the word *simple* is used in the sense "not divided into parts." This means that God is always fully aware of everything. If he should wish to tell us the number of grains of sand on the seashore or the number of stars in the sky, he would not have to count them all quickly like some kind of giant computer,

---

5. For a discussion of the view called "middle knowledge" or Molinism, see chapter 16, pp. 456–62.

nor would he have to call the number to mind because it was something he had not thought about for a time. Rather, he always knows all things at once. All of these facts and all other things that he knows are always fully present in his consciousness. He does not have to reason to conclusions or ponder carefully before he answers, for he knows the end from the beginning, and he never learns and never forgets anything (cf. Ps. 90:4; 2 Peter 3:8; and the verses cited above on God's perfect knowledge). Every bit of God's knowledge is always fully present in his consciousness; it never grows dim or fades into his nonconscious memory. Finally, the definition talks about God's knowledge as not only a simple act but also an "eternal act." This means that God's knowledge never changes or grows. If he were ever to learn something new, he would not have been omniscient beforehand. From all eternity God has known all things that would happen and all things that he would do.

Someone may object that God promises to forget our sins. For example, he says, "I will not remember your sins" (Isa. 43:25). Yet passages like this can certainly be understood to mean that God will never again let the knowledge of these sins play any part in the way he relates to us: he will "forget" them in his relationship to us. Another objection to the biblical teaching about God's omniscience has been brought from Jeremiah 7:31; 19:5; and 31:35, where God refers to the horrible practices of parents who burn to death their own children in the sacrificial fires of the pagan god Baal, and says, "which I did not command, *nor did it come into my mind*" (Jer. 7:31). Does this mean that before the time of Jeremiah God had never *thought* of the possibility that parents would sacrifice their own children? Certainly not, for that very practice had occurred a century earlier in the reigns of Ahaz (2 Kings 16:3) and Hoshea (2 Kings 17:17), and God himself had forbidden the practice eight hundred years earlier under Moses (Lev. 18:21). The verses in Jeremiah are probably better translated quite literally, "nor did it enter into my *heart*" (KJV),[6] giving the sense, "nor did I wish for it, desire it, think of it in a positive way."[7]

### e. The Challenge of Open Theism: Does God Know Future Human Choices?

Another difficulty that arises in connection with God's omniscience is the question of the relationship between God's knowledge of everything that will happen in the future and the reality and degree of freedom we have in our actions. If God knows everything that will happen, how can our choices be at all "free"?

This difficulty has loomed so large that some theologians have concluded that God does not know all of the future, and they have adopted a view known as "open theism." They have said that God does not know things that cannot (in their opinion) be known, such as the free acts of people that have not yet occurred (sometimes the phrase used is the "contingent acts of free moral agents," where *contingent* means "possible but not certain"). Therefore the future is not fixed or certain but "open," even to God.

---

6. The KJV has "heart" in Jer. 7:31, as does the NASB margin. The Hebrew word is *lēb*, most frequently translated "heart."

7. The same phrase ("to have a thought enter into the heart") seems to have the sense "desire, wish for, long for" in all five of its occurrences in the Hebrew Old Testament: Isa. 65:17; Jer. 3:16 (where it cannot mean simply "have a factual knowledge of"); 7:31; 19:5; 32:35; as well as in the equivalent Greek phrase *anebē epi tēn kardian* in Acts 7:23.

Richard Rice takes this position.[8] Rice says, "God knows a great deal about what will happen. . . . All that God does not know is the content of future free decisions, and this is because decisions are not there to know until they occur."[9] In order to take this position and maintain God's omniscience, Rice redefines omniscience: "An omniscient being knows everything logically knowable,"[10] and then he defines "logically knowable" to exclude future human choices. On this basis, Rice argues that God does not know the results of future free decisions of human beings, since these are not logically knowable.

Clark Pinnock also explains how he came to this position: "I knew the Calvinist argument that exhaustive foreknowledge was tantamount to predestination because it implies the fixity of all things from 'eternity past,' and I could not shake off its logical force."[11] He rejected exhaustive foreknowledge and decided that *"God knows everything that can be known,* but that free choices would not be something that can be known even by God because they are not yet settled in reality. Decisions not yet made do not exist anywhere to be known even by God. . . . God too moves into a future not wholly known because not yet fixed."[12]

But such a position is unsatisfactory because it ultimately means that God is ignorant of *all future human choices,* which is clearly contrary to much of the Bible. Open theism would mean that God does not even know what the stock market will do tomorrow, who will be elected as the next president of the United States, who will be converted to Christ, or what you will have for lunch tomorrow. Such a God is not truly omniscient, for he learns many billions of new facts every day, as he watches to find out what human beings will choose to do.

On this view, what event of human history *could* God know with certainty in advance? None of them. Every human event that happens is the result of at least one and often dozens of human choices. This idea stands contrary to the multiple of examples of unfailing predictive prophecy in Scripture, the fulfillment of which demonstrates that God is the true God.

Bruce Ware has provided an extensive and compelling critique of open theism in his book *God's Lesser Glory.*[13] He demonstrates that, particularly in Isaiah 40–48, "the true God knows and declares the future (including future free human actions) before it

---

8. Richard Rice, "Divine Foreknowledge and Free-Will Theism," in *The Grace of God, The Will of Man: A Case for Arminianism,* ed. Clark H. Pinnock (Grand Rapids: Zondervan, 1989), 121–39 (esp. 129, 134–37). Other defenses of open theism include Greg Boyd, *God of the Possible: A Biblical Introduction to the Open View of God* (Grand Rapids: Baker, 2000); Clark H. Pinnock, *Most Moved Mover: A Theology of God's Openness* (Grand Rapids: Baker, 2001); Clark H. Pinnock et al., *The Openness of God: A Biblical Challenge to the Traditional Understanding of God* (Downers Grove, IL: InterVarsity, 1994); John Sanders, *The God Who Risks: A Theology of Providence* (Downers Grove, IL: InterVarsity, 1998).

9. Rice, "Divine Foreknowledge and Free-Will Theism," 134.
10. Ibid., 128.
11. Clark H. Pinnock, "From Augustine to Arminius: A Pilgrimage in Theology," in *The Grace of God, the Will of Man,* 25.
12. Ibid., 25–26, emphasis mine.
13. Bruce Ware, *God's Lesser Glory: The Diminished God of Open Theism* (Wheaton, IL: Crossway, 2000). Ware argues that open theism is contrary to Scripture, internally contradictory, destructive to our Christian lives, and ultimately portrays a different God than the God of the Bible. For another extensive critique of open theism see John M. Frame, *No Other God: A Response to Open Theism* (Phillipsburg, NJ: P&R, 2001).

occurs, while those imposter rivals neither know nor declare any such thing."[14] Here are some of the Isaiah texts highlighted by Ware:

> *Tell us what is to come hereafter,*
>     *that we may know that you are gods....*
> Who declared it from the beginning, that we might know,
>     and beforehand, that we might say, "He is right"?
> *There was none who declared it*, none who proclaimed....
> Behold, they are all a delusion;
>     their works are nothing
>     their metal images are empty wind. (Isa. 41:23, 26, 29)

> I am the LORD; that is my name;
>     my glory I give to no other,
>     nor my praise to carved idols.
> Behold, the former things have come to pass,
>     *and new things I now declare;*
> *before they spring forth*
>     *I tell you of them.* (Isa. 42:8–9)

> Thus says the LORD, the King of Israel
>     and his Redeemer, the LORD of hosts:
> "I am the first and I am the last;
>     besides me there is no god.
> *Who is like me? Let him proclaim it.*
>     Let him declare and set it before me,
> since I appointed an ancient people.
>     *Let them declare what is to come, and what will happen.* (Isa. 44:6–7)

> Thus says the LORD, your Redeemer,
>     who formed you from the womb:
> "I am the LORD, who made all things ...
> *who frustrates the signs of liars*
>     *and makes fools of diviners ...*
> who confirms the word of his servant
>     and fulfills the counsel of his messengers,
> who says of Jerusalem, 'She shall be inhabited,'
>     and of the cities of Judah, 'They shall be built,

---

14. Ware, *God's Lesser Glory*, 102.

and I will raise up their ruins' . . .
who says of Cyrus, 'He is my shepherd,
    and he shall fulfill all my purpose';
saying of Jerusalem, 'She shall be built,'
    and of the temple, 'Your foundation shall be laid.'" (Isa. 44:24–26, 28)[15]

remember the former things of old;
for I am God, and there is no other;
    I am God, and there is none like me,
*declaring the end from the beginning*
    *and from ancient times things not yet done,*
saying, "My counsel shall stand,
    and I will accomplish all my purpose." (Isa. 46:9–10)

Ware concludes, "How utterly impertinent and presumptuous to deny of God divine foreknowledge and so deny the very basis by which God himself has declared that his claim to deity shall be vindicated and made known."[16]

And there are many hundreds of other prophecies of human actions in Scripture. Steven C. Roy has compiled a list of 4,017 biblical prophecies, of which 2,323 relate to free human decisions.[17] Scripture does not view such prophecies as God's opinion of "what will most likely occur" (as open theism would claim) but as God's firm declarations of what will certainly occur. There is strong evidence throughout Scripture that God's omniscience includes knowledge of all future free human decisions and actions and therefore that open theism is not a viewpoint that is faithful to Scripture.

**f. If God Knows Our Future Choices, How Can They Be Free?** How then are we to resolve this difficulty? Although this question will be treated in much more detail in chapter 16 on God's providence, it may be helpful at this point to note the suggestion of Augustine, who said that God has given us "reasonable self-determination." There is some advantage in the fact that his statement does not involve the terms *free* or *freedom*, for these terms often have different meanings to different people. But this statement

---

15. This remarkable prophecy (including further details in Isa. 45:1–7), given by Isaiah around 700 BC, predicts by name Cyrus the Great, king of Persia (ruled 559–530 BC and conquered Babylon in 539 BC) and foretells that he will be God's "shepherd" to fulfil God's purpose that the Jewish people would return from exile to "Jerusalem" and to "the cities of Judah" (44:26). The decree of Cyrus that the Jews should return to Jerusalem is recorded in Ezra 1:1–4 and took place in 538 BC—about 160 years after Isaiah's prophecy (Isaiah wrote when Babylon, not Persia, was the dominant empire).

16. Ware, *God's Lesser Glory*, 104.

17. See his list at http://evangelicalarminians.org/wp-content/uploads/2015/12/Roy.-Predictive-Prophecies-Involving-Future-Free-Human-Choices.pdf. At the beginning of this list he says, of the larger list of 4,017, there are "128 prophecies about what God will do in and through nature; 1,893 prophecies about what God will do in and to and through human beings; 1,474 prophecies about what believers will do or have happen to them (without God explicitly being said to do these things); and 522 prophecies about what unbelievers will do or have happen to them." He adds, "I have not included any prophetic statements that are explicitly conditional in grammatical form." See also his perceptive analysis of open theism in Steven C. Roy, *How Much Does God Foreknow? A Comprehensive Biblical Study* (Downers Grove, IL: IVP Academic, 2006).

does affirm what is important to us and what we sense to be true in our own experience, that our choices and decisions are "reasonable." That is, we think about what to do, consciously decide what we will do, and then we follow the course of action that we have chosen.

Augustine's statement also says that we have "self-determination." This is simply affirming that our choices really do determine what will happen. It is not as if events occur *regardless* of what we decide or do, but rather that they occur *because of* what we decide and do. Whether or not we reach a satisfactory understanding of the way in which our choices are "free," that is not the really important issue; for us, it is important that we think, choose, and act, and that these thoughts, choices, and actions are real and actually have eternal significance. If God knows all our thoughts, words, and actions long before they occur, then there must be some sense in which our choices are not absolutely free.

If we wish to use the expression "free will," it is fair to say that our choices are "free" in the way that Bruce Ware defines "freedom of inclination": "We are free when we choose according to our strongest inclination or deepest desire. In short, we are free when we do what we most want to do."[18] But further discussion of this issue is better left until it can be treated more fully in chapter 16.

## 4. Wisdom

*God's wisdom means that God always chooses the best goals and the best means to those goals.* This definition goes beyond the idea of God knowing all things and specifies that God's decisions about what he will do are always wise decisions: that is, they always will bring about the best results (from God's ultimate perspective), and they will bring about those results through the best possible means.

Scripture affirms God's wisdom in general in several places. He is called "the only wise God" (Rom. 16:27). Job says that God "is wise in heart" (Job 9:4), and "With God are wisdom and might; he has counsel and understanding" (Job 12:13). God's wisdom is seen specifically in creation. The psalmist exclaims, "O LORD, how manifold are your works! In wisdom have you made them all; the earth is full of your creatures" (Ps. 104:24). As God created the universe, it was perfectly suited to bring him glory, both in its day-by-day processes and in the goals for which he created it. Even now, while we still see the effects of sin and the curse on the natural world, we should be amazed at how harmonious and intricate God's creation is.

God's wisdom is also seen in his great plan of redemption. Christ is "the wisdom of God" to those who are called (1 Cor. 1:24, 30), even though the word of the cross is "foolishness" to those who reject it and think themselves to be wise in this world (1 Cor.

---

18. Bruce A. Ware, *God's Greater Glory: The Exalted God of Scripture and the Christian Faith* (Wheaton, IL: Crossway, 2004), 114. He distinguishes this sense of free will from "libertarian free will," which he defines as, "The ability, all things being just what they are, to choose differently" (112). See the further discussion of human free will in chapter 16.

1:18–20). Yet even this is a reflection of God's wise plan: "For since, in the wisdom of God, the world did not know God through wisdom, it pleased God through the folly of what we preach to save those who believe. . . . God chose what is foolish in the world to shame the wise . . . so that no human being might boast in the presence of God" (1 Cor. 1:21, 27, 29).

Paul knows that what we now think of as the "simple" gospel message, understandable even to the very young, reflects an amazing plan of God, which in its depths of wisdom surpasses anything man could ever have imagined. At the end of eleven chapters of reflection on the wisdom of God's plan of redemption, Paul bursts forth into spontaneous praise: "Oh, the depth of the riches and wisdom and knowledge of God! How unsearchable are his judgments and how inscrutable his ways!" (Rom. 11:33).

When Paul preaches the gospel both to Jews and to gentiles, and they become unified in the one body of Christ (Eph. 3:6), the incredible "mystery" that was "hidden for ages in God who created all things" (Eph. 3:9) is plain for all to see, namely, that in Christ such totally diverse people become united. When groups so different racially and culturally become members of the one body of Christ, then God's purpose is fulfilled, "that through the church the manifold *wisdom of God* might now be made known to the rulers and authorities in the heavenly places" (Eph. 3:10).

Today this means that God's wisdom is shown even to angels and demons ("rulers and authorities") when people from different racial and cultural and social class backgrounds are united in Christ in the church. If the Christian church is faithful to God's wise plan, it will be always in the forefront in breaking down racial and social and social class barriers in societies around the world and will thus be a visible manifestation of God's amazingly wise plan to bring great unity out of great diversity and thereby to cause all creation to honor him.

God's wisdom is also shown in our individual lives. "And we know that for those who love God all things work together for good, for those who are called according to his purpose" (Rom. 8:28). Here Paul affirms that God does work wisely in all the things that come into our lives, and that through all these things he advances us toward the goal of conformity to the image of Christ (Rom. 8:29). It should be our great confidence and a source of peace day by day to know that God causes all things to move us toward his ultimate goal for our lives, namely, that we might be like Christ and thereby bring glory to him. Such confidence enabled Paul to accept his thorn in the flesh (2 Cor. 12:7) as something that, though painful, God in his wisdom had chosen not to remove (2 Cor. 12:8–10).

Every day of our lives, we may quiet our discouragement with the comfort that comes from the knowledge of God's infinite wisdom: if we are his children, we can know that he is working wisely in our lives, even today, to bring us into greater conformity into the image of Christ.

God's wisdom is, of course, in part communicable to us. We can ask God confidently for wisdom when we need it, for he promises in his Word, "If any of you lacks wisdom, let him ask God, who gives generously to all without reproach, and it will be given him" (James 1:5). This wisdom, or skill in living a life pleasing to God, comes primarily from reading and obeying his Word: "The testimony of the LORD is sure, *making wise the simple*" (Ps. 19:7; cf. Deut. 4:6–8).

"The fear of the LORD is the beginning of wisdom" (Ps. 111:10; Prov. 9:10; cf. Prov. 1:7), because if we fear dishonoring God or displeasing him, and if we fear his fatherly discipline, then we will have the motivation that makes us want to follow his ways and live according to his wise commands. Furthermore, the possession of wisdom from God will result not in pride but in humility (Prov. 11:2; James 3:13), not in arrogance but in a gentle and peaceful spirit (James 3:14–18). The person who is wise according to God's standards will continually walk in dependence on the Lord and with a desire to exalt him.

Yet we must also remember that God's wisdom is not entirely communicable: we can never fully share God's wisdom (Rom. 11:33). In practical terms, this means that there will frequently be times in this life when we will not be able to understand why God allowed something to happen. Then we have simply to trust him and go on obeying his wise commands for our lives: "Therefore let those who suffer according to God's will entrust their souls to a faithful Creator while doing good" (1 Peter 4:19; cf. Deut. 29:29; Prov. 3:5–6). God is infinitely wise and we are not, and it pleases him when we have faith to trust his wisdom even when we do not understand what he is doing.

## 5. Truthfulness (and Faithfulness)

*God's truthfulness means that he is the true God, and all his knowledge and words are both true and the final standard of truth.*

The term *veracity*, which means "truthfulness" or "reliability," has sometimes been used as a synonym for God's truthfulness.

The first part of this definition indicates that the God revealed in Scripture is the true or real God and that all other so-called gods are idols. "The LORD is the true God; he is the living God and the everlasting King. . . . The gods who did not make the heavens and the earth shall perish from the earth and from under the heavens" (Jer. 10:10–11). Jesus says to his Father, "And this is eternal life, that they know you *the only true God*, and Jesus Christ whom you have sent" (John 17:3; cf. 1 John 5:20).

We might ask what it means to be the true God as opposed to other beings who are not God. It must mean that God in his own being or character is the one who fully conforms to the idea of what God should be: namely, a being who is infinitely perfect in power, in wisdom, in goodness, in lordship over time and space, and so forth. But we may further ask, *whose* idea of God is this? What idea of God must one conform to in order to be the true God?

At this point our train of thought becomes somewhat circular, for we must not say that a being must conform to *our* idea of what God should be like in order to be the true God! We are mere creatures! We cannot define what the true God must be like! So we must say that it is *God himself* who has the only perfect idea of what the true God should be like. And he himself is the true God because in his being and character he perfectly conforms to his own idea of what the true God should be. In addition, he has implanted in our minds a reflection of his idea of what the true God must be, and this enables us to recognize him as God.

The definition given above also affirms that all of God's *knowledge* is true and is the final standard of truth. Job tells us that God is "perfect in knowledge" (Job 37:16; see also the verses cited above under the discussion of God's omniscience). To say that God knows all things and that his knowledge is perfect is to say that he is never mistaken in his perception or understanding of the world. All that he knows and thinks is true and is a correct understanding of the nature of reality. In fact, since God knows all things infinitely well, we can say that the standard of true knowledge is conformity to God's knowledge. If we think the same thing God thinks about anything in the universe, we are thinking truthfully about it.

Our definition also affirms that God's words are both *true* and the *final standard of truth*. This means that God is reliable and faithful in his words. With respect to his promises, God always does what he promises to do, and we can depend on him never to be unfaithful to his promises. Thus he is "a God of faithfulness" (Deut. 32:4).

In fact, this specific aspect of God's truthfulness is sometimes viewed as a distinct attribute: God's faithfulness means that *God will always do what he has said and fulfill what he has promised* (Num. 23:19; cf. 2 Sam. 7:28; Ps. 141:6, et al.). He can be relied upon, and he will never prove unfaithful to those who trust what he has said. Indeed, the essence of true faith is taking God at his word and relying on him to do as he has promised.

In addition to the fact that God is faithful to his promises, we must also affirm that all of God's *words* about himself and about his creation completely correspond to reality. That is, God always speaks truth when he speaks. He is the God "who never lies" (Titus 1:2), the God for whom it is impossible to lie (Heb. 6:18), the God whose every word is perfectly "pure" (Ps. 12:6), the one of whom it can be said, "*Every word* of God proves true" (Prov. 30:5). God's words are not simply true in the sense that they conform to some standard of truthfulness outside of God. Rather, they are truth itself; they are the final standard and definition of truth. So Jesus can say to the Father, "Your word is *truth*" (John 17:17). What was said about the truthfulness of God's knowledge can also be said about God's words, for they are based on his perfect knowledge and accurately reflect that perfect knowledge. God's words are "truth" in the sense that they are the final standard by which truthfulness is to be judged; whatever conforms to God's own words is also true, and what fails to conform to his words is not true.

The truthfulness of God is communicable in that we can imitate it by striving to have true knowledge about God and about his world. In fact, as we begin to think true thoughts about God and creation, thoughts that we learn from Scripture and from allowing Scripture to guide us in our observation and interpretation of the natural world, we begin to think God's own thoughts after him! We can exclaim with the psalmist, "How precious to me are your thoughts, O God! How vast is the sum of them!" (Ps. 139:17).

This realization should encourage us in the pursuit of knowledge in all areas of the natural and social sciences and the humanities. Whatever the area of our investigation, when we discover more truth about the nature of reality, we discover more of the truth that God already knows. In this sense we can affirm that "all truth is God's truth"[19] and rejoice whenever the learning or discovery of this truth is used in ways pleasing to God. Growth in knowledge is part of the process of becoming more like God or becoming creatures who are more fully in God's image. Paul tells us that we have put on the "new self," which, he says, "is being *renewed in knowledge* after the image of its creator" (Col. 3:10).

In a society that is exceedingly careless with the truthfulness of spoken words, we as God's children are to imitate our Creator and take great care to be sure that our words are always truthful. "*Do not lie to one another,* seeing that you have put off the old self with its practices and have put on the new self" (Col. 3:9–10). Again Paul admonishes, "Therefore, having put away falsehood, let each one of you *speak the truth* with his neighbor" (Eph. 4:25). In his own ministry, Paul says that he sought to practice absolute truthfulness: "But we have renounced disgraceful, underhanded ways. We refuse to practice cunning or to tamper with God's word, but *by the open statement of the truth* we would commend ourselves to everyone's conscience in the sight of God" (2 Cor. 4:2). God is pleased when his people put "devious talk" far from them (Prov. 4:24) and speak with words that are acceptable not only in the sight of people but also in the sight of the Lord himself (Ps. 19:14).

Furthermore, we should imitate God's truthfulness in our own reaction to truth and falsehood. Like God, we should *love* truth and *hate* falsehood. The commandment not to bear false witness against our neighbor (Ex. 20:16), like the other commandments, requires not merely outward conformity but also conformity in heart attitude. One who is pleasing to God "speaks truth in his heart" (Ps. 15:2) and strives to be like the righteous man who "hates falsehood" (Prov. 13:5). God commands his people through Zechariah, "Do not devise evil in your hearts against one another, and love no false oath, for all these things I hate, declares the LORD" (Zech. 8:17).

These commands are given because God himself loves truth and hates falsehood: "Lying lips are an abomination to the LORD, but those who act faithfully are his delight" (Prov. 12:22; cf. Isa. 59:3–4). Falsehood and lying come not from God but from Satan, who delights in falsehood: "When he lies, he speaks out of his own character, for he is a liar and the father of lies" (John 8:44). It is appropriate then that with "the cowardly, the faithless, the detestable" and the "murderers, the sexually immoral, sorcerers, [and] idolaters" who are found in "the lake that burns with fire and sulfur" far from the heavenly city, are found also "all *liars*" (Rev. 21:8).

Thus Scripture teaches us that lying is wrong not only because of the great harm that comes from it (and much more harm comes from lying than we often realize) but also for

---

19. See Arthur Holmes, *All Truth Is God's Truth* (Grand Rapids: Eerdmans, 1977).

an even deeper and more profound reason: when we lie we dishonor God and diminish his glory, for we, as those created in God's image and created for the purpose of reflecting God's glory in our lives, are acting in a way that is contrary to God's own character.[20]

## C. Moral Attributes
### 6. Goodness

*The goodness of God means that God is the final standard of good, and all that God is and does is worthy of approval.*

In this definition we find a situation similar to the one we faced in defining God as the true God. Here, *good* can be understood to mean "worthy of approval," but we have not answered the question, approval by whom? In one sense, we can say that anything that is truly good should be worthy of approval by us. But in a more ultimate sense, we are not free to decide by ourselves what is worthy of approval and what is not. Ultimately, therefore, God's being and actions are perfectly worthy of his own approval. He is therefore the final standard of good. Jesus implies this when he says, "No one is good except God alone" (Luke 18:19). The Psalms frequently affirm that "the Lord is good" (Ps. 100:5) or exclaim, "Oh give thanks to the Lord, for he is good" (Pss. 106:1; 107:1, et al.). David encourages us, "Oh, taste and see that the Lord is good!" (Ps. 34:8).

But if God is himself good and therefore the ultimate standard of good, then we have a definition of the meaning of *good* that will greatly help us in the study of ethics and aesthetics. What is *good*? Good is what God approves. We may ask then, why is what God approves good? We must answer, "Because he approves it." That is to say, there is no higher standard of goodness than God's own character and his approval of whatever is consistent with that character. Nonetheless, God has given us some reflection of his own sense of goodness, so that when we evaluate things in the way God created us to evaluate them, we will also approve what God approves and delight in things in which he delights.

Our definition also states that all that God *does* is worthy of approval. We see evidence of this in the creation narrative: "God saw everything that he had made, and behold, it was *very good*" (Gen. 1:31). The psalmist connects the goodness of God with the goodness of his actions: "You are good and do *good*; teach me your statutes" (Ps. 119:68). Psalm 104 is an excellent example of praise to God for his goodness in creation, while many psalms, such as Psalms 106 and 107, give thanks to God for his goodness in all his actions toward his people. And Paul encourages us to discover in practice how God's will for our lives is "*good* and acceptable and perfect" (Rom. 12:2).

Scripture also tells us that God is the source of all good in the world. "Every good gift

---

20. For a more extensive defense of the idea that it is never right to lie (in the sense of affirming something that you know is false), see Wayne Grudem, *Christian Ethics: An Introduction* to *Biblical Moral Reasoning* (Wheaton, IL: Crossway, 2018), chapter 12.

and every perfect gift is from above, coming down from the Father of lights with whom there is no variation or shadow due to change" (James 1:17; cf. Ps. 145:9; Acts 14:17). Moreover, God does only good things for his children. We read, "No good thing does he withhold from those who walk uprightly" (Ps. 84:11). And in the same context in which Paul assures us that "for those who love God all things work together for good" (Rom. 8:28), he also says, "He who did not spare his own Son but gave him up for us all, how will he not also with him graciously give us all things?" (Rom. 8:32). Much more than an earthly father, our heavenly Father will "give good things to those who ask him" (Matt. 7:11), and even his fatherly discipline is a manifestation of his love and is for our good (Heb. 12:10). This knowledge of God's great goodness should encourage us to "give thanks in all circumstances" (1 Thess. 5:18).

In imitation of this communicable attribute, we should ourselves do good (that is, we should do what God approves) and thereby imitate the goodness of our heavenly Father. Paul writes, "So then, as we have opportunity, let us do good to everyone, and especially to those who are of the household of faith" (Gal. 6:10; cf. Luke 6:27, 33–35; 2 Tim. 3:17). Moreover, when we realize that God is the definition and source of all good, we will realize that God himself is the ultimate good that we seek. We will say with the psalmist, "Whom have I in heaven but you? And there is nothing on earth that I desire besides you. My flesh and my heart may fail, but God is the strength of my heart and my portion forever" (Ps. 73:25–26; cf. 16:11; 42:1–2).

God's goodness is closely related to several other characteristics of his nature, among them love, mercy, patience, and grace. Sometimes these are considered separate attributes and are treated individually. At other times these are considered part of God's goodness and are treated as various aspects of God's goodness. In this chapter we will treat love as a separate attribute since it is so prominent in Scripture. The other three characteristics (mercy, patience, and grace), while also prominent in Scripture, will be treated together as aspects of God's goodness to individuals in specific situations (see below, section C.8, on mercy, patience, and grace).

## 7. Love

*God's love means that God eternally gives of himself to others.*

This definition understands love as self-giving for the benefit of others. This attribute of God shows that it is part of his nature to give of himself in order to bring about blessing or good for others.

John tells us that "God is love" (1 John 4:8). We see evidence that this attribute of God was active even before creation among the members of the Trinity. Jesus speaks to his Father of "my glory that you have given me *because you loved me before the foundation of the world*" (John 17:24), thus indicating that there was love and a giving of honor from the Father to the Son from all eternity. It continues at the present time, for we read, "The Father loves the Son and has given all things into his hand" (John 3:35).

This love is also reciprocal, for Jesus says, "I do as the Father has commanded me, so that the world may know that I love the Father" (John 14:31). The love between the Father and the Son also presumably characterizes their relationship with the Holy Spirit, even though it is not explicitly mentioned. This eternal love of the Father for the Son, the Son for the Father, and of both for the Holy Spirit makes heaven a world of love and joy because each person of the Trinity seeks to bring joy and happiness to the other two.

The self-giving that characterizes the Trinity finds clear expression in God's relationship to humanity, and especially to sinful human beings. "In this is love, not that we have loved God but that he loved us and sent his Son to be the propitiation for our sins" (1 John 4:10). Paul writes, "God shows his love for us in that while we were still sinners, Christ died for us" (Rom. 5:8). John also writes, "For God so loved the world, that he gave his only Son, that whoever believes in him should not perish but have eternal life" (John 3:16). Paul also speaks of "the Son of God, who *loved me* and gave himself for me" (Gal. 2:20), thus showing an awareness of the directly personal application of Christ's love to individual sinners. It should cause us great joy to know that it is the purpose of God the Father, Son, and Holy Spirit to give of themselves to us to bring us true joy and happiness. It is God's nature to act that way toward those upon whom he has set his love, and he will continue to act that way toward us for all eternity.

We imitate this communicable attribute of God, first by loving God in return, and second by loving others in imitation of the way God loves them. All our obligations to God can be summarized in this: "You shall love the Lord your God with all your heart and with all your soul and with all your mind. . . . You shall love your neighbor as yourself" (Matt. 22:37, 39). If we love God, we will obey his commandments (1 John 5:3) and thus do what is pleasing to him. We will love God, not the world (1 John 2:15), and we will do all this because he first loved us (1 John 4:19).

It is one of the most amazing facts in all Scripture that just as God's love involves his giving of himself to make us happy, so we can in return give of ourselves and actually bring joy to God's heart. Isaiah promises God's people, "As the bridegroom rejoices over the bride, so *shall your God rejoice over you*" (Isa. 62:5), and Zephaniah tells God's people, "The LORD your God is in your midst. . . . He will rejoice over you with gladness; he will quiet you by his love; he will exult over you with loud singing" (Zeph. 3:17).

Our imitation of God's love is also seen in our love for others. John makes this explicit: "Beloved, if God so loved us, we also ought to love one another" (1 John 4:11). In fact, our love for others within the fellowship of believers is so evidently an imitation of Christ that by it the world recognizes us as his: "By this all people will know that you are my disciples, if you have love for one another" (John 13:35; cf. 15:13; Rom. 13:10; 1 Cor. 13:4–7; Heb. 10:24). God himself gives us his love to enable us to love each other (John 17:26; Rom. 5:5). Moreover, our love for our enemies especially reflects God's love (Matt. 5:43–48).

## 8. Mercy, Grace, Patience

God's mercy, grace, and patience may be seen as three separate attributes or as specific aspects of God's goodness. The definitions given here show these attributes as special examples of God's goodness when it is used for the benefit of specific classes of people.

God's *mercy* means God's goodness toward those in misery and distress.

God's *grace* means God's goodness toward those who deserve only punishment.

God's *patience* means God's goodness in withholding of punishment toward those who sin over a period of time.

These three characteristics of God's nature are often mentioned together, especially in the Old Testament. When God declared his name to Moses, he proclaimed, "The LORD, the LORD, a God *merciful and gracious, slow to anger,* and abounding in steadfast love and faithfulness" (Ex. 34:6). David says in Psalm 103:8, "The LORD is *merciful and gracious, slow to anger* and abounding in steadfast love."

Because these characteristics of God are often mentioned together, it may seem difficult to distinguish among them. Yet the characteristic of mercy is often emphasized where people are *in misery or distress.* David says, for example, "I am in great distress. Let us fall into the hand of the LORD, for his *mercy* is great" (2 Sam. 24:14). The two blind men who wish Jesus to see their plight and heal them cry, "Have *mercy* on us, Son of David" (Matt. 9:27). When Paul speaks of the fact that God comforts us in affliction, he calls God the "Father of *mercies* and God of all comfort" (2 Cor. 1:3).[21] The author of Hebrews tells us that we should "draw near to the throne of grace" so that "we may receive mercy and find grace to help *in time of need*" (Heb. 4:16; cf. 2:17; James 5:11). We are to imitate God's mercy in our conduct toward others: "Blessed are *the merciful,* for they shall receive mercy" (Matt. 5:7; cf. 2 Cor. 1:3–4).

With respect to the attribute of *grace,* we find that Scripture emphasizes that God's grace, or his favor toward those who deserve no favor but only punishment, is never obligated but is always freely given on God's part. God says, "I will be gracious to whom I will be gracious, and will show mercy on whom I will show mercy" (Ex. 33:19; quoted in Rom. 9:15). Yet God is regularly gracious toward his people: "Turn to me and be *gracious* to me, *as is your way* with those who love your name" (Ps. 119:132). In fact, Peter can call God "the God of all grace" (1 Peter 5:10).

Grace as God's goodness especially shown to those who do not deserve it is seen frequently in Paul's writings. He emphasizes that salvation by grace is the opposite of salvation by human effort, for grace is a freely given gift. "For all have sinned and fall short of the glory of God, and are justified by his *grace* as a gift, through the redemption that is in Christ Jesus" (Rom. 3:23–24). The distinction between grace and a salvation earned by works that merit a reward is also seen in Romans 11:6: "But if it is by grace,

---

21. This verse uses *oiktirmos,* "compassion, mercy," rather than *eleos,* "mercy," but the terms are closely related in meaning and both refer to compassion or goodness toward those in distress.

it is no longer on the basis of works; otherwise grace would no longer be grace." Grace, then, is God's favor freely given to those who do not deserve this favor.

Paul also sees that if grace is unmerited, then there is only one human attitude appropriate as an instrument for receiving such grace, namely, faith: "That is why it depends on faith, in order that the promise may rest on grace" (Rom. 4:16). Faith is the one human attitude that is the opposite of depending on oneself, for it involves trust in or dependence upon another. It is devoid of self-reliance or any attempt to gain righteousness by human effort. If God's favor is to come to us apart from our own merit, then it must come when we depend not on our own merit but on the merits of another, and that is precisely when we have faith.

In the New Testament, and especially in Paul, not only the forgiveness of sins but also *the entire living of the Christian life* can be seen to result from God's continuous bestowal of grace. Paul can say, "By the grace of God I am what I am" (1 Cor. 15:10). Luke speaks of Antioch as the place where Paul and Barnabas "had been commended to the grace of God for the work that they had fulfilled" (Acts 14:26), indicating that the church there, in sending out Paul and Barnabas, saw the success of their ministry as dependent upon God's continuing grace. Furthermore, the blessing of "grace" upon Paul's readers is the most frequent apostolic blessing in his letters (see, e.g., Rom. 1:7; 16:20; 1 Cor. 1:3; 16:23; 2 Cor. 1:2; 13:14; Gal. 1:3; 6:18).

God's *patience*, similarly, was mentioned in some of the verses cited above in connection with God's mercy. The Old Testament frequently speaks of God as *"slow to anger"* (Ex. 34:6; Num. 14:18; Ps. 86:15; 103:8; 145:8; Jonah 4:2; Nah. 1:3, et al.). In the New Testament, Paul speaks about God's "kindness and forbearance and *patience*" (Rom. 2:4), and says that Jesus Christ displayed his "perfect patience" toward Paul himself as an example for others (1 Tim. 1:16; cf. Rom. 9:22; 1 Peter 3:20).

We are also to imitate God's patience and be "slow to anger" (James 1:19), and be patient in suffering as Christ was (1 Peter 2:20). We are to lead a life "with patience" (Eph. 4:2), and "patience" is listed among the fruit of the Spirit in Galatians 5:22 (see also Rom. 8:25; 1 Cor. 13:4; Col. 1:11; 3:12; 2 Tim. 3:10; 4:2; James 5:7–8; Rev. 2:2–3, et al.). As with most of the attributes of God that we are to imitate in our lives, patience requires a moment-by-moment trust in God to fulfill his promises and purposes in our lives at his chosen time, which is the best time (though we easily become impatient). If we renew our confidence that the Lord will fulfill his purposes at the best time for our good (Rom. 8:28) and his glory, this will enable us to be patient. James makes this connection when he says, "You also, be patient. Establish your hearts, for the coming of the Lord is at hand" (James 5:8).

## 9. Holiness

*God's holiness means that he is separated from sin and devoted to seeking his own honor.*
This definition contains both a relational quality (separation from) and a moral quality

(the separation is from sin or evil, and the devotion is to the good of God's own honor or glory). The idea of holiness as including both separation from evil and devotion to God's glory is found in a number of Old Testament passages. The word *holy* is used to describe both parts of the tabernacle, for example. The tabernacle itself was a place separate from the evil and sin of the world, and the first room in it was called the "holy place." It was set apart and dedicated to God's service. But then God commanded that there be a veil, "And the veil shall separate for you the Holy Place from the Most Holy" (Ex. 26:33). The most holy place, where the ark of the covenant was kept, was the place most separated from evil and sin and most fully devoted to God's service.

The place where God himself dwelt was itself holy: "Who shall ascend the hill of the LORD? And who shall stand in his *holy* place?" (Ps. 24:3). The element of dedication to God's service is seen in the holiness of the Sabbath day: "The LORD blessed the Sabbath day and made it holy [or 'hallowed it']" (Ex. 20:11; cf. Gen. 2:3).[22] The Sabbath day was made holy because it was set apart from the ordinary activities of the world and dedicated to God's service. In the same way the tabernacle and the altar, as well as Aaron and his sons, were to be "made holy" (Ex. 29:44), that is, set apart from ordinary tasks and from the evil and sin of the world and dedicated to God's service (cf. Ex. 30:25–33).

God himself is the Most Holy One. He is called the "Holy One of Israel" (Pss. 71:22; 78:41; 89:18; Isa. 1:4; 5:19, 24, et al.). The seraphim around God's throne cry, "Holy, holy, holy is the LORD of hosts; the whole earth is full of his glory!" (Isa. 6:3). "The LORD our God is holy!" exclaims the psalmist (Ps. 99:9; cf. 99:3, 5; 22:3).

God's holiness provides the pattern for his people to imitate. He commands them, *"You shall be holy,* for I the LORD your God am holy" (Lev. 19:2; cf. 11:44–45; 20:26; 1 Peter 1:16). When God called his people out of Egypt and brought them to himself and commanded them to obey his voice, then he said, "You shall be to me a kingdom of priests and a *holy nation*" (Ex. 19:6). In this case the idea of separation from evil and sin (which here included in a very striking way separation from life in Egypt) and the idea of devotion to God (in serving him and in obeying his statutes) are both seen in the example of a "holy nation."

New covenant believers are also to "strive . . . for the *holiness* without which no one will see the Lord" (Heb. 12:14) and to know that God's discipline is given to us "that we may *share his holiness*" (Heb. 12:10). Paul encourages Christians to be separate from the dominating influence that comes from close association with unbelievers (2 Cor. 6:14–18) and then encourages them, "Let us cleanse ourselves from every defilement of body and spirit, *bringing holiness to completion in the fear of God*" (2 Cor. 7:1; cf. Rom. 12:1). The church itself is intended by God to grow "into a holy temple in the Lord" (Eph. 2:21), and Christ's present work for the church is "that he might sanctify her . . .

---

22. The verb is a Piel form of *qādash* and means "to make holy."

that he might present the church to himself in splendor . . . that she might be *holy* and without blemish" (Eph. 5:26–27). Not only individuals but also the church itself must grow in holiness!

Zechariah prophesies a day when everything on earth will be "holy to the LORD." He says,

> And on that day there shall be inscribed on the bells of the horses, "*Holy to the* LORD." And the pots in the house of the LORD shall be as the bowls before the altar. And every pot in Jerusalem and Judah shall be holy to the LORD of hosts. (Zech. 14:20–21)

At that time, everything on earth will be separated from evil, purified from sin, and devoted to the service of God in true moral purity.

## 10. Peace (or Order)

In 1 Corinthians 14:33 Paul says, "God is not a God of confusion but of *peace*." Although "peace" and "order" have not traditionally been classified as attributes of God, Paul here indicates another quality that we could think of as a distinct attribute of God. Paul says that God's actions are characterized by "peace" and not by "disorder" (Gk. *akatastasia*, a word meaning "disorder, confusion, unrest" and translated as "riots" in 2 Cor. 6:5). God himself is "the God of *peace*" (Rom. 15:33; 16:20; Phil. 4:9; 1 Thess. 5:23; Heb. 13:20; cf. Eph. 2:14; 2 Thess. 3:16). In the Old Testament, the peace that God gives is described with the rich and full concept of the Hebrew term *shalôm*, meaning "peace" with an overall sense of well-being in all situations and relationships. "May the LORD bless his people with peace!" (Ps. 29:11). However, those who walk in wickedness do not have peace: "'There is no peace,' says the LORD, 'for the wicked'" (Isa. 48:22; 57:21; cf. 59:8).

When God looks with compassion upon the people whom he loves, he sometimes sees them as "afflicted . . . storm-tossed (LXX, *akatastatos*, "in disorder, in confusion"), and not comforted" (Isa. 54:11), and promises to establish their foundations with precious stones (Isa. 54:11–12) and lead them forth in "peace" (Isa. 55:12). The proclamation of God's plan of redemption contains the promise of peace to God's people (Pss. 29:11; 85:8; 119:165; Prov. 3:17; Isa. 9:6–7; 26:3; 57:19; John 14:27; Rom. 8:6; 2 Thess. 3:16, et al.). In fact, the third element that Paul lists as part of the fruit of the Spirit is "peace" (Gal. 5:22).

This peace certainly does not imply inactivity, for it was at a time of intense growth and activity that Luke could say that "the church throughout all Judea and Galilee and Samaria *had peace* and was being built up" (Acts 9:31). Furthermore, although God is a God of peace, he is also the one who "will neither slumber nor sleep" (Ps. 121:4). He is the God who is continually working (John 5:17). And even though heaven is a place of peace, it is a place also of continual praise to God and service for him.

Thus God's peace can be defined as follows: *God's peace means that in God's being and in his actions he is separate from all confusion and disorder, yet he is continually active in innumerable well-ordered, fully controlled, simultaneous actions.*

This definition indicates that God's peace does not have to do with inactivity but with ordered and controlled activity. To engage in infinite activity of this sort, of course, requires God's infinite wisdom, knowledge, and power.

When we understand God's peace in this way, we can see an imitation of this attribute of God not only in "peace" as part of the fruit of the Spirit in Galatians 5:22–23 but also in the last-mentioned element in the fruit of the Spirit, namely, "self-control" (Gal. 5:23). When we as God's people walk in his ways, we come to know more and more fully by experience that the kingdom of God is indeed "righteousness and *peace* and joy in the Holy Spirit" (Rom. 14:17), and we can say of the path of God's wisdom, "Her ways are ways of pleasantness, and all her paths are *peace*" (Prov. 3:17).

## 11. Righteousness, Justice

In English the terms *righteousness* and *justice* are different words, but in both the Hebrew Old Testament and the Greek New Testament there is only one word group behind these two English terms. (In the Old Testament the terms primarily translate forms of the *tsedek* word group, and the New Testament members of the *dikaios* word group.) Therefore, these two terms will be considered together as speaking of one attribute of God.[23]

*God's righteousness means that God always acts in accordance with what is right and is himself the final standard of what is right.*

Speaking of God, Moses says, "All his ways are *justice*. A God of faithfulness and without iniquity, *just* and *upright* is he" (Deut. 32:4). Abraham successfully appeals to God's own character of righteousness when he says, "Shall not the Judge of all the earth do what is *just*?" (Gen. 18:25). God also speaks and commands what is right: "The precepts of the LORD are *right*, rejoicing the heart" (Ps. 19:8). And God says of himself, "I the LORD speak the truth; I declare what is *right*" (Isa. 45:19). As a result of God's righteousness (or justice), it is necessary that he treat people *according to what they deserve*. Thus it is necessary that God punish sin, for it does not deserve reward; it is wrong and deserves punishment.

When God does not punish sin, it seems to indicate that he is unrighteous, unless some other means of punishing sin can be seen. This is why Paul says that when God sent Christ as a sacrifice to bear the punishment for sin, it "was to show God's righteousness, because in his divine forbearance he had passed over former sins. It was to show

---

23. However, I would not object if someone wanted to consider righteousness and justice as two different attributes by distinguishing the English word *righteousness* in the sense of personal conformity to God's moral law from the English word *justice* in the sense of dispensing rewards and punishments *to* others in conformity to God's moral law. See, for example, Millard Erickson, *Christian Theology*, 3rd ed. (Grand Rapids: Baker, 2013), 258–60.

his righteousness at the present time, so that he might be just and the justifier of the one who has faith in Jesus" (Rom. 3:25–26). When Christ died to pay the penalty for our sins, it showed that God was truly righteous because he did give appropriate punishment to sin, even though he did forgive his people their sins.

With respect to the definition of righteousness given above, we may ask, what is "right"? In other words, what *ought* to happen and what *ought* to be? Here we must respond that *whatever conforms to God's moral character is right*. But why is whatever conforms to God's moral character right? It is right because it conforms to his moral character! If indeed God is the final standard of righteousness, then there can be no standard outside of God by which we measure righteousness or justice. He himself is the final standard. (This is similar to the situation we encountered with respect to truth and God being the ultimate standard of truth.) Whenever Scripture confronts the question of whether God himself is righteous or not, the ultimate answer is always that we as God's creatures have no right to say that God is unrighteous or unjust. The creature cannot say that of the Creator. Paul responds to a very difficult question about God's righteousness by saying, "But who are you, O man, to answer back to God? Will what is molded say to its molder, 'Why have you made me like this?' Has the potter no right over the clay, to make out of the same lump one vessel for honorable use and another for dishonorable use?" (Rom. 9:20–21).

In answer to Job's questioning about whether God has been righteous in his dealings with him, God answers Job, "Shall a faultfinder contend with the Almighty? . . . Will you even put me in the wrong? Will you condemn me that you may be in the right?" (Job 40:2, 8). Then God answers *not* in terms of an explanation that would allow Job to *understand* why God's actions were right but rather in terms of a statement of God's own majesty and power! God does not need to explain the rightness of his actions to Job, for God is the Creator and Job is the creature. "Have you an arm like God, and can you thunder with a voice like his?" (Job 40:9). "Have you commanded the morning since your days began, and caused the dawn to know its place . . . ?" (Job 38:12). "Can you lift up your voice to the clouds, that a flood of waters may cover you? Can you send forth lightnings, that they may go and say to you, 'Here we are'?" (Job 38:34–35). "Do you give the horse his might?" (Job 39:19). "Is it by your understanding that the hawk soars and spreads his wings toward the south?" (Job 39:26). Job answers, "Behold, I am of small account; what shall I answer you? I lay my hand on my mouth" (Job 40:4).

Nevertheless, it should be a cause for thanksgiving and gratitude when we realize that righteousness and omnipotence are both possessed by God. If he were a God of perfect righteousness without power to carry out that righteousness, he would not be worthy of worship and we would have no guarantee that justice will ultimately prevail in the universe. But if he were a God of unlimited power, yet without righteousness in his character, how unthinkably horrible the universe would be! There would be unrighteousness at the center of all existence and there would be nothing anyone could do to change it. Existence would become meaningless, and we would be driven to the most utter despair. We ought therefore continually to thank and praise God for who he is, "for *all his ways are justice. A God of faithfulness and without iniquity, just and upright is he*" (Deut. 32:4).

## 12. Jealousy

Although the word *jealous* is frequently used in a negative sense in English, it also takes a positive sense at times. For example, Paul says to the Corinthians, "I feel a divine jealousy for you" (2 Cor. 11:2). Here the sense is "earnestly protective or watchful." It has the meaning of being deeply committed to seeking the honor or welfare of someone, whether oneself or someone else.

Scripture represents God as being jealous in this way. He continually and earnestly seeks to protect his honor. He commands his people not to bow down to idols or serve them, saying, "for I the LORD your God am a *jealous* God" (Ex. 20:5). He desires that worship be given to himself and not to false gods. Therefore, he commands the people of Israel to tear down the altars of pagan gods in the land of Canaan, giving the following reason: "For you shall worship no other god, for the LORD, whose name is Jealous, is a jealous God" (Ex. 34:14; cf. Deut. 4:24; 5:9).

Thus, God's jealousy may be defined as follows: *God's jealousy means that God continually seeks to protect his own honor.*

People sometimes have trouble thinking that jealousy is a desirable attribute in God. This is because jealousy for our own honor as human beings is almost always wrong. We are not to be proud, but humble (James 4:6; 1 Peter 5:5–6). Yet we must realize that pride is wrong for a theological reason: we do not deserve the honor that belongs to God alone (cf. 1 Cor. 4:7; Rev. 4:11).

It is not wrong for God to seek his own honor, however, for he deserves it fully. God freely admits that his actions in creation and redemption are done for his own honor. Speaking of his decision to withhold judgment from his people, God says, "For my own sake, for my own sake, I do it. . . . *My glory I will not give to another*" (Isa. 48:11). It is healthy for us spiritually when we settle in our hearts the fact that God deserves all honor and glory from his creation, and that it is right for him to seek this honor. He alone is infinitely worthy of being praised. To realize this fact and to delight in it is to find the secret of true worship.

## 13. Wrath

It may surprise us to find how frequently the Bible talks about the wrath of God. Yet if God loves all that is right and good and all that conforms to his moral character, then it should not be surprising that he would hate everything that is opposed to his moral character. God's wrath directed against sin is therefore closely related to God's holiness and justice. God's wrath may be defined as follows: *God's wrath means that he intensely hates all sin.*

Descriptions of God's wrath are found frequently in the narrative passages of

Scripture, especially when God's people sin greatly against him. God sees the idolatry of the people of Israel and says to Moses, "I have seen this people. . . . Now therefore let me alone, that my *wrath* may burn hot against them and I may consume them" (Ex. 32:9–10). Later Moses tells the people, "Remember and do not forget how you provoked the LORD your God to *wrath* in the wilderness. . . . Even at Horeb you provoked the LORD to *wrath*, and the LORD was so angry with you that he was ready to destroy you" (Deut. 9:7–8; cf. 29:23; 2 Kings 22:13).

The doctrine of the wrath of God in Scripture is not limited to the Old Testament, however, as some have falsely imagined. We read in John 3:36, "Whoever believes in the Son has eternal life; whoever does not obey the Son shall not see life, but *the wrath of God remains on him.*" Paul says, "For the *wrath of God* is revealed from heaven against all ungodliness and unrighteousness of men" (Rom. 1:18; cf. 2:5, 8; 5:9; 9:22; Col. 3:6; 1 Thess. 1:10; 2:16; 5:9; Heb. 3:11; Rev. 6:16–17; 19:15). Many more New Testament verses also indicate God's wrath against sin.

As with the other attributes of God, this is an attribute for which we should thank and praise God. It may not immediately appear to us how this can be done, since wrath seems to be such a negative concept. Viewed alone, it would arouse only fear and dread. Yet it is helpful for us to ask what God would be like if he were a God that did not hate sin. He would then be a God who either delighted in sin or at least was not troubled by it. Such a God would not be worthy of our worship, for sin is hateful and it is *worthy* of being hated. Sin ought not to be. It is in fact a virtue to hate evil and sin (cf. Heb. 1:9; Zech. 8:17, et al.), and we rightly imitate this attribute of God when we feel hatred against great evil, injustice, and sin.[24]

Furthermore, we should feel no fear of God's wrath as Christians, for although we "were by nature children of wrath, like the rest of mankind" (Eph. 2:3), we now have trusted in Jesus, "who delivers us from the wrath to come" (1 Thess. 1:10; cf. Rom. 5:10). When we meditate on the wrath of God, we will be amazed to think that our Lord Jesus Christ bore the wrath of God that was due to our sin, in order that we might be saved (Rom. 3:25–26).[25]

Moreover, in thinking about God's wrath we must also bear in mind his patience. Both patience and wrath are mentioned together in Psalm 103: "The LORD is . . . *slow to anger* [patience] and abounding in steadfast love. He will not always chide, nor will he keep his anger [wrath] forever" (Ps. 103:8–9). In fact, the delay of the execution of God's wrath upon evil is for the purpose of leading people to repentance (see Rom. 2:4).

Thus, when we think of God's wrath to come, we should simultaneously be thankful for his patience in waiting to execute that wrath in order that yet more people may be saved: "The Lord is not slow to fulfill his promise as some count slowness, but is patient toward you, not wishing that any should perish, *but that all should reach repentance*. But

---

24. It is appropriate for us in this regard to "hate the sin but love the sinner," as a popular slogan puts it.

25. See the discussion of Christ's bearing of the wrath of God in chapter 27, pp. 712–17.

the day of the Lord will come like a thief, and then the heavens will pass away with a roar" (2 Peter 3:9–10). God's wrath should motivate us to evangelism and should also cause us to be thankful that God finally will punish all wrongdoing and will reign over new heavens and a new earth in which there will be no unrighteousness.

## QUESTIONS FOR PERSONAL APPLICATION

### SPIRITUALITY

1. Why is God so strongly displeased at carved idols, even those that are intended to represent him? How then shall we picture God or think of God in our minds when we pray to him?

2. What is it about our culture or our way of thinking today that makes us think of the physical world as more real and more permanent than the spiritual world? What can we do to change our intuitive perspective on the reality of the spiritual world?

### KNOWLEDGE

3. When should we try to hide our thoughts and deeds from God? How is your answer to this question a blessing for your life?

4. With regard to the circumstances of your life, will God ever make a mistake, or fail to plan ahead, or fail to take into account all the eventualities that occur? How is the answer to this question a blessing in your life?

5. When did God learn that you would be at the location you are now in, reading this sentence, at this time on this day? How is the realization of your answer to this question a blessing to your life?

### WISDOM

6. Do you really believe that God is working wisely today in your life? In the world? If you find this difficult to believe at times, what might you do to change your attitude?

### TRUTHFULNESS

7. Why are people in our society, sometimes even Christians, quite careless with regard to truthfulness in speech? Why do we not very often realize that the greatest harm of all that comes from lying is the fact that God himself is dishonored? Do you need to ask God's help to more fully reflect his truthfulness in speech in any of the following areas: promising to pray for someone; saying that you will be some place at a certain time; exaggerating events to make a more exciting story; taking care to remember and then be faithful to what you have said in business commitments; reporting what other people have said or what you think someone else is thinking; fairly representing your opponent's viewpoint in an argument?

## GOODNESS

8. Remembering that every good and perfect gift is from God (James 1:17), see how many good gifts from God you can list on a piece of paper in five minutes. When you have finished, ask yourself how often you have an attitude of thankfulness to God for most of these gifts. Why do you think we tend to forget that these blessings come from God? What can we do to remember more frequently?

## LOVE

9. Is it appropriate to define love as "self-giving" with respect to our own interpersonal relationships? In what ways could you imitate God's love specifically today?

10. Is it possible to decide to love someone and then to act on that decision, or does love between human beings simply depend on spontaneous emotional feelings?

## MERCY

11. If you were to reflect God's mercy more fully, for whom among those you know would you show special care during the next week?

## HOLINESS

12. Are there activities or relationships in your present pattern of life that are hindering your growth in holiness because they make it difficult for you to be separated from sin and devoted to seeking God's honor?

## PEACE

13. As you think about reflecting God's peace in your own life, think first about your own emotional, mental, and spiritual state. Can you say that by and large you have God's peace in the sense that your inner life is separate from confusion and disorder, and is frequently or continually active in well-ordered and well-controlled actions that further God's glory? Then ask the same questions concerning what may be called the "external circumstances" of your life, that is, your family relationships, your relationships with neighbors, your activities in studying or at your job, and your relationships in church activities. What about the overall picture of your life, viewed as a whole? Does it exhibit God's peace? What might you do to reflect God's peace more fully?

## RIGHTEOUSNESS

14. Do you ever find yourself wishing that some of God's laws were different than they are? If so, does such a wish reflect a dislike for some aspect of God's moral character? What passages of Scripture might you read to convince yourself more fully that God's character and his laws are right in these areas?

## JEALOUSY

15. Do you reflect God's jealousy for his own honor instinctively when you hear him dishonored in conversation or on television or in other contexts? What can we do to deepen our jealousy for God's honor?

## WRATH

16. Should we love the fact that God is a God of wrath who hates sin? In what ways is it right for us to imitate this wrath, and in what ways is it wrong for us to do so?

# BIBLIOGRAPHY

Since chapters 12 and 13 are so closely related in subject matter, the bibliographic material for both is at the end of chapter 13.

# SCRIPTURE MEMORY PASSAGE

**Exodus 34:6–7:** The LORD passed before him and proclaimed, "The LORD, the LORD, a God merciful and gracious, slow to anger, and abounding in steadfast love and faithfulness, keeping steadfast love for thousands, forgiving iniquity and transgression and sin, but who will by no means clear the guilty, visiting the iniquity of the fathers on the children and the children's children, to the third and the fourth generation."

Note: The last section of this passage speaks of God "visiting the iniquity of the fathers on the children and the children's children." Some might want to stop short of this part in memorizing the passage, but we should remember that this too is Scripture and is written for our edification. This statement shows the horrible nature of sin in the way it has effects far beyond the individual sinner, also harming those around the sinner and harming future generations as well. We see this in tragic ways in ordinary life, where the children of alcoholics often become alcoholics and the children of abusive parents often become abusive parents.

Christians who are forgiven by Christ should not think of these phrases as applying to them, however, for they are in the other category of people mentioned just before

## Special Terms

*attributes of being*
*beatific vision*
*communicable attributes*
*faithfulness*
*good*
*goodness*
*grace*
*holiness*
*impassible*
*invisibility*
*jealousy*
*justice*
*knowledge*
*love*
*mental attributes*
*mercy*
*moral attributes*
*omniscience*
*one simple and eternal act*
*open theism*
*order*
*patience*
*peace*
*reasonable self-determination*
*righteousness*
*spirituality*
*theophany*
*truthfulness*
*veracity*
*wisdom*
*wrath*

this section on "the guilty": they are among the "thousands" to whom God continually shows "steadfast love" and continually is "forgiving iniquity and transgression and sin" (v. 7). When someone comes to Christ, the chain of sin is broken. Here it is important to remember Peter's words: "*You were ransomed from the futile ways inherited from your forefathers*, not with perishable things such as silver or gold, but with the precious blood of Christ" (1 Peter 1:18–19).

# HYMN

### "O Worship the King"

Almost the entire hymnbook could be used to sing of one aspect or another of God's character. Literally hundreds of hymns would be appropriate. Yet this hymn contains a listing of many of God's attributes and combines them in such a way that the hymn is worthy of being sung again and again. Verse 1 speaks of God's glory, power, love; verse 2 speaks of his might, grace, wrath; and so forth. In verse 6, *ineffable* means "incapable of being expressed fully." The hymn is written as an encouragement for Christians to sing to one another, exhorting each other to "worship the King all-glorious above." Yet in the process of such exhortation the song itself also contains much high praise.

*O worship the King all-glorious above,*
*O gratefully sing his pow'r and his love;*
*Our shield and defender, the Ancient of Days,*
*Pavilioned in splendor, and girded with praise.*

*O tell of his might, O sing of his grace,*
*Whose robe is the light, whose canopy space.*
*His chariots of wrath the deep thunder-*
*        clouds form,*
*And dark is his path on the wings of the storm.*

*The earth with its store of wonders untold,*
*Almighty, your power has founded of old;*
*Has 'stablished it fast by a changeless decree,*
*And round it has cast, like a mantle, the sea.*

*Your bountiful care what tongue can recite?*
*It breathes in the air; it shines in the light;*
*It streams from the hills; it descends to the plain;*
*And sweetly distills in the dew and the rain.*

*Frail children of dust, and feeble as frail,*
*In you do we trust, nor find you to fail;*
*Your mercies how tender, how firm to the end,*
*Our maker, defender, redeemer, and friend!*

*O measureless might! Ineffable love!*
*While angels delight to hymn you above,*
*The humbler creation, though feeble their ways,*
*With true adoration shall lisp to your praise.*

Author: Sir Robert Grant, 1833
(based on Psalm 104)

Alternative hymn: "Round the Lord in Glory Seated"

# CONTEMPORARY WORSHIP SONG

## "Rejoice"

Come and stand before your maker
Full of wonder full of fear;
Come behold his power and glory
Yet with confidence draw near,
For the one who holds the heavens
And commands the stars above
Is the God who bends to bless us
With an unrelenting love.

### Chorus 1
Rejoice!
Come and lift your hands and raise your voice;
He is worthy of all praise,
Rejoice!
Sing the mercies of your King
And with trembling, rejoice.

We are children of the promise,
The beloved of the Lord.
Won with everlasting kindness,
Bought with sacrificial blood.
Bringing reconciliation
To a world that longs to know
The affections of a father
Who will never let them go.

All our sickness, all our sorrows
Jesus carried up the hill.
He has walked this path before us,
He is walking with us still;
Turning tragedy to triumph,
Turning agony to praise,
There is blessing in the battle
So take heart and stand amazed.

### Chorus 2
Rejoice!
When you cry to him he hears your voice,
He will wipe away your tears.
Rejoice!
In the midst of suffering
He will help you sing.

Words by Dustin Kensrue and Stuart Townend[26]

# CHAPTER 13

# The Character of God: "Communicable" Attributes (Part 2)

*How is God like us in attributes of will and in attributes that summarize his excellence?*

## EXPLANATION AND SCRIPTURAL BASIS

In the previous chapter we discussed the attributes of God that described his *being* (spirituality, invisibility), his *mental* attributes (knowledge, wisdom, and truthfulness), and his *moral* attributes (goodness, love, mercy, grace, patience, holiness, peace, righteousness, jealousy, and wrath). In this chapter we will examine God's attributes of *purpose*, that is, attributes that have to do with making and carrying out decisions (will, freedom, and omnipotence) and his *summary* attributes (perfection, blessedness, beauty, and glory).

### D. ATTRIBUTES OF PURPOSE

In this category of attributes we will discuss first God's will in general, then the freedom of God's will, and finally the omnipotence (or infinite power) of God's will.

### 14. Will

*God's will is that attribute of God whereby he approves and determines to bring about every action necessary for the existence and activity of himself and all creation.*

This definition indicates that God's will has to do with deciding and approving the things that God is and does. It concerns God's choices of what to do and what not to do.

**a. God's Will in General.** Scripture frequently indicates God's will as the final or most ultimate reason for everything that happens. Paul refers to God as the one "who works all things *according to the counsel of his will*" (Eph. 1:11). The phrase here translated "all things" (*ta panta*) is used frequently by Paul to refer to everything that exists or everything in creation (see, for example, Eph. 1:10, 23; 3:9; 4:10; Col. 1:16 [twice],

17; Rom. 11:36; 1 Cor. 8:6 [twice]; 15:27–28 [twice]).[1] The word translated "works" (*energeō*, "works, works out, brings about, produces") is a present participle and suggests continual activity. The phrase might more explicitly be translated, "who continually brings about everything in the universe according to the counsel of his will."

More specifically, all things were created by God's will: "For you created all things, and *by your will they existed and were created*" (Rev. 4:11). Both Old and New Testaments speak of human government as coming about according to God's will: the voice from heaven tells Nebuchadnezzar that he is to learn "that the Most High rules the kingdom of men and gives it to whom he will" (Dan. 4:32), and Paul says that "there is no authority except from God, and those that exist have been instituted by God" (Rom. 13:1).

The church at Jerusalem believed that all the events connected with the death of Christ were according to God's will, for in their prayer they said, "Truly in this city there were gathered together against your holy servant Jesus, whom you anointed, both Herod and Pontius Pilate, along with the Gentiles and the peoples of Israel, to do *whatever your hand and your plan had predestined to take place*" (Acts 4:27–28). The specific mention of the various parties involved at different stages of the crucifixion, together with the indefiniteness of the plural relative pronoun "whatever" (Gk. *hosa*, "the things which") implies that not simply the fact of Jesus' death but all the detailed events connected with it are comprehended in this statement: God's hand and will had predestined that all those things would come about.

Sometimes it is God's will that Christians suffer, as is seen in 1 Peter 3:17, for example: "For it is better to suffer for doing good, *if that should be God's will*, than for doing evil." Then in the next chapter Peter says, "Therefore let those who suffer *according to God's will* entrust their souls to a faithful Creator while doing good" (1 Peter 4:19). In this verse, the phrase "according to God's will" cannot refer to the manner in which Christians endure suffering, for then it would make the verse say essentially, "Let those who suffer *while doing right, do right* and entrust their souls." This would make the phrase "according to God's will" redundant. Rather, the phrase "according to God's will" must refer to the fact that these Christians are suffering, just as "God's will" referred to suffering in the previous chapter (1 Peter 3:17).

James encourages us to see all the events of our lives as subject to God's will. To those who say, "Today or tomorrow we will go into such and such a town and spend a year there and trade and make a profit," James says, "you do not know what tomorrow will bring. . . . Instead you ought to say, '*If the Lord wills*, we will live and do this or that'" (James 4:13–15). To attribute so many events, even evil events, to the will of God often causes misunderstanding and difficulty for Christians. Some of the difficulties

---

1. The phrase does not always carry that meaning (cf. Rom. 11:32; 1 Cor. 12:6; 2 Cor. 12:19), but in contexts where the scope of Paul's thought is cosmic or universal in nature (as in this passage), the phrase does seem quite clearly to refer to everything in creation.

connected with this subject will be treated here and others will be dealt with in chapter 16 on God's providence.

**b. Distinctions in Aspects of God's Will.** Some distinctions made in the past may help us understand various aspects of God's will. Just as we can will or choose something eagerly or reluctantly, happily or with regret, secretly or publicly, so also God in the infinite greatness of his personality is able to will different things in different ways.

(1) One helpful distinction applied to aspects of God's will is the distinction between God's *necessary will* and God's *free will*. God's necessary will includes everything that he must will according to his own nature. What does God will necessarily? He wills himself. God eternally wills to be, or wants to be, who he is and what he is. He says, "I AM WHO I AM," or "I will be what I will be" (Ex. 3:14). God *cannot* choose to be different than he is or to cease to exist.

God's *free will* includes all things that God decided to will but had no necessity to will according to his nature. Here we must put God's decision to create the universe and all the decisions relating to the details of that creation. Here we must also place all God's acts of redemption. There was nothing in God's nature that required him to decide to create the universe or to redeem out of sinful mankind a people for himself (see the discussion above concerning God's independence). However, God did decide to create and to redeem, and these were totally free choices on his part. Though within the members of the Trinity love and fellowship and glory exist in infinite measure for all eternity (see John 17:5, 24), nonetheless God decided to create the universe and to redeem us for his own glory (cf. Isa. 43:7; 48:9–11; Rom. 11:36; 1 Cor. 8:6; Eph. 1:12; Rev. 4:11). It would be wrong for us ever to try to find a necessary cause for creation or redemption in the being of God himself, for that would rob God of his total independence. It would be to say that without us God could not truly be God. God's decisions to create and to redeem were totally free decisions.

(2) A second helpful distinction applied to different aspects of God's will is the distinction between God's *secret will* and his *revealed will*. Even in our experience we know that we are able to will some things secretly and then only later make this will known to others. Sometimes we tell others before the thing that we have willed comes about, and at other times we do not reveal our secret will until the event we willed has happened.

Surely a distinction between different aspects of God's will is evident in many passages of Scripture. According to Moses, "The *secret things* belong to the LORD our God, but the *things that are revealed* belong to us and to our children forever, that we may do all the words of this law" (Deut. 29:29). Those things that God has revealed are given to us for the purpose of obeying God's will: "that we may *do* all the words of this law." There were many other aspects of his plan, however, that he had not revealed to them: many details about future events, specific details of hardship or of blessing in their lives, and so forth. With regard to these matters, they were simply to trust him.

Because God's revealed will usually contains his commands or "precepts" for our moral conduct, God's revealed will is sometimes also called God's *will of precept* or will of command. This revealed will of God is God's declared will concerning *what we should do* or what God *commands* us to do.

On the other hand, God's secret will includes most of his hidden decrees by which he governs the universe and determines everything that will happen. He does not ordinarily reveal these decrees to us (except in prophecies of the future), so these decrees really are God's "secret" will. We find out what God has decreed when events actually happen. Because this secret will of God has to do with his decreeing of events in the world, this aspect of God's will is sometimes also called God's *will of decree*.[2]

There are several instances where Scripture mentions God's revealed will. In the Lord's Prayer, the petition "*Your will be done*, on earth as it is in heaven" (Matt. 6:10, meaning "May your will be done," as expressed in NET and NLT) is a prayer that people would obey God's *revealed* will, his commands, on earth *just as they do in heaven* (that is, fully and completely). This could not be a prayer that God's secret will (that is, his decrees for events that he has planned) would in fact be fulfilled, for what God has decreed in his secret will shall certainly come to pass. To ask God to bring about what he has already decreed to happen would simply be to pray, "May what is going to happen happen." That would be a hollow prayer indeed, for it would not be asking for anything at all. Furthermore, since we do not know God's secret will regarding the future, the person praying a prayer for God's secret will to be done would never know for what he or she was praying. It would be a prayer without understandable content and without effect. Rather, the prayer "*Your will* be done" must be understood as an appeal for the *revealed* will of God to be followed on earth.

If the phrase is understood in this way, it provides a pattern for us to pray on the basis of God's commands in Scripture. In this sense, Jesus provides us with a guide for an exceedingly broad range of prayer requests. This teaching encourages us to pray, for example, that people would repent of their sins and trust in Christ as Savior (John 1:12; Acts 16:31; 17:30). But praying "Your will be done" also means it is right to pray, for example, that specific people whom we know would honor their father and mother (Ex. 20:12), not murder (Ex. 20:13), not commit adultery (Ex. 20:14), not steal (Ex. 20:15), not bear false witness (Ex. 20:16), and not covet (Ex. 20:17). To pray these things is to pray that God's *revealed will* would be done "on earth as it is in heaven." For the same reason, it is also right to pray that society would not excuse or glorify such sins (as much of society does today). If we understand "your will be done" to refer to God's revealed will, then *all the moral teachings of Scripture* provide guidelines for teaching us how to pray.

A little later, Jesus says, "Not everyone who says to me, 'Lord, Lord,' will enter

---

2. See the discussion of God's decrees in chapter 16, pp. 440–42.

the kingdom of heaven, but the one who does the *will* of my Father who is in heaven" (Matt. 7:21). Once again, the reference cannot be to God's secret will or will of decree (for everyone follows this, even if unknowingly), but to God's *revealed* will, namely, the moral law of God that Christ's followers are to obey (cf. Matt. 12:50; probably also 18:14). When Paul commands the Ephesians to "understand *what the will of the Lord is*" (Eph. 5:17; cf. Rom. 2:18), he again is speaking of God's revealed will. So also is John when he says, "If we ask anything *according to his will* he hears us" (1 John 5:14).

It is probably best to put 1 Timothy 2:4 and 2 Peter 3:9 in this category as well. Paul says that God "*desires* [or 'wills, wishes,' Gk. *theleō*] all people to be saved and to come to the knowledge of the truth" (1 Tim. 2:4). Peter says that the Lord "is not slow to fulfill his promise as some count slowness, but is patient toward you, *not wishing* that any should perish, but that all should reach repentance" (2 Peter 3:9). In neither of these verses can God's will be understood to be his secret will, his decree concerning what will certainly occur. This is because the New Testament is clear that there will be a final judgment and not all will be saved. It is best therefore to understand these references as speaking of God's *revealed will*, his commands for mankind to obey and his declaration to us of what is pleasing in his sight.

On the other hand, many passages speak of God's secret will. When James tells us to say, "*If the Lord wills*, we will live and do this or that" (James 4:15), he cannot be talking about God's revealed will or will of precept, for with regard to many of our actions we *know* that it is according to God's command that we do one or another activity that we have planned. Rather, to trust in the secret will of God overcomes pride and expresses humble dependence on God's sovereign control over the events of our lives.

Another instance is found in Genesis 50:20. Joseph says to his brothers, "As for you, you meant evil against me, but *God meant it for good*, to bring it about that many people should be kept alive, as they are today." Here God's *revealed* will to Joseph's brothers was that they should love him and not steal from him or sell him into slavery or make plans to murder him. But God's *secret* will was that in the disobedience of Joseph's brothers a greater good would be done when Joseph, having been sold into slavery into Egypt, gained authority over the land and was able to save his family.

When Paul says to the Corinthians, "I will come to you soon, *if the Lord wills*" (1 Cor. 4:19), he is not speaking of God's revealed will, for Paul has already determined, in obedience to God and in fulfillment of his apostolic office, to come to visit the Corinthians. He is speaking rather of God's secret will, his hidden plan for the future, which is unknown to Paul and which will be known only as it comes to pass (cf. Acts 21:14; Rom. 1:10; 15:32; Eph. 1:11; 1 Peter 3:17; 4:19).[3]

Both the revealing of the good news of the gospel to some and its hiding from others

---

3. In Eph. 1:9–10 Paul says that God is "making known to us the mystery of his will ... to unite all things in him." Here he tells us that part of God's secret will has become God's revealed will because God made it known to the apostles and then to the church.

are said to be according to God's will. Jesus says, "I thank you, Father, Lord of heaven and earth, that you have hidden these things from the wise and understanding and revealed them to little children; yes, Father, *for such was your gracious will*" (Matt. 11:25–26). This again must refer to God's secret will, for his revealed will is that all come to salvation. Indeed, only two verses later, Jesus commands everyone, "Come to me, all who labor and are heavy laden, and I will give you rest" (Matt. 11:28). And both Paul and Peter tell us that God wills all people to be saved (see 1 Tim. 2:4; 2 Peter 3:9). Thus the fact that some are not saved and some have the gospel hidden from them must be understood as happening according to God's secret will, unknown to us and inappropriate for us to seek to pry into. In the same way we must understand the mention of God's will in Romans 9:18 ("He has mercy on whomever he wills, and he hardens whomever he wills") and Acts 4:28 ("to do whatever your hand and your plan had predestined to take place") as references to God's secret will.

There is danger in speaking about evil events as happening according to the will of God, even though we sometimes see Scripture speaking of them in this way. One danger is that we might begin to think that God takes pleasure in evil, which he does not do (see Ezek. 33:11), though he can use it for his good purposes (see chapter 16 for further discussion). Another danger is that we might begin to blame God rather than ourselves for sin or to think that we are not responsible for our evil actions. Scripture, however, does not hesitate to couple statements of God's sovereign will with statements of human responsibility for evil. Peter could say in the same sentence that Jesus was "delivered up according to the definite plan and foreknowledge of God," and also that "this Jesus . . . *you crucified and killed* by the hands of *lawless men*" (Acts 2:23). Both God's hidden will of decree and the culpable wickedness of "lawless men" in carrying it out are affirmed in the same statement. However we understand the secret workings of God's hidden will, we must never understand it to imply that we are freed from responsibility for evil or that God is ever to be blamed for sin. Scripture never speaks that way, and we may not either, even though how this can be so may remain a mystery for us in this age.[4]

## 15. Freedom

*God's freedom is that attribute of God whereby he does whatever he pleases.* This definition implies that nothing in all creation can hinder God from doing his will. This attribute of God is therefore closely related to his will and his power. Yet this aspect of freedom focuses on the fact that God is not constrained by anything external to himself and that he is free to do whatever he wishes to do. There is no person or force that can ever dictate to God what he should do. He is under no authority or external restraint.

God's freedom is mentioned in Psalm 115, where his great power is contrasted with

---

4. See chapter 16, pp. 428–34 for further discussion of the relationship between the will of God and evil. See also the excellent essay by John Piper, "Are There Two Wills in God? Divine Election and God's Desire for All to Be Saved," in *Still Sovereign*, ed. by Tom Schreiner and Bruce Ware (Grand Rapids: Baker, 2000), 107–32.

the weakness of idols: "Our God is in the heavens; *he does all that he pleases*" (Ps. 115:3). Human rulers are not able to stand against God and effectively oppose his will, for "the king's heart is a stream of water in the hand of the LORD; he turns it wherever he will" (Prov. 21:1). Similarly, Nebuchadnezzar learns in his repentance that it is true to say of God, "*he does according to his will* among the host of heaven and among the inhabitants of the earth; and none can stay his hand or say to him, 'What have you done?'" (Dan. 4:35).

Because God is free, we should not try to seek any more ultimate answer for God's actions in creation than the fact that he willed to do something and that his will has perfect freedom (so long as the actions he takes are consistent with his own moral character). Sometimes people try to discover the reason why God had to do one or another action (such as create the world or save us). It is better simply to say that it was God's totally free will (working in a way consistent with his character) that was the final reason why he chose to create the world and to save sinners.

## 16. Omnipotence (Power, Sovereignty)

*God's omnipotence means that God is able to do all his holy will.* The word *omnipotence* is derived from two Latin words, *omni*, "all," and *potens*, "powerful," and means "all-powerful." Whereas God's freedom referred to the fact that there are no external constraints on God's decisions, God's omnipotence has reference to his own power to do what he decides to do.

This power is frequently mentioned in Scripture. God is "the LORD, *strong and mighty*, the LORD, mighty in battle!" (Ps. 24:8). The rhetorical question, "Is anything too hard for the LORD?" (Gen. 18:14; Jer. 32:27) certainly implies (in the contexts in which it occurs) that nothing is too hard for the LORD. In fact, Jeremiah says to God, "*Nothing* is too hard for you" (Jer. 32:17).

Paul says that God is "able to do far more abundantly than all that we ask or think" (Eph. 3:20), and God is called the "Almighty" (2 Cor. 6:18; Rev. 1:8), a term (Gk. *pantokratōr*) that suggests the possession of all power and authority. Furthermore, the angel Gabriel says to Mary, "Nothing will be impossible with God" (Luke 1:37), and Jesus says, "With God *all things are possible*" (Matt. 19:26).

These passages indicate that God's power is infinite and that he is therefore not limited to doing only what he actually has done. In fact, God is able to do more than he actually does. For example, John the Baptist says in Matthew 3:9, "God is able from these stones to raise up children for Abraham." God is one who "does all that he pleases" (Ps. 115:3); he could have destroyed Israel and raised up a great nation from Moses (cf. Ex. 32:10), but he did not do so.

However, there are some things that God cannot do. God cannot will or do anything that would deny his own character. This is why the definition of omnipotence is stated in terms of God's ability to do "all his holy will." It is not absolutely everything that

God is able to do but everything that is consistent with his character. For example, God cannot lie. In Titus 1:2 he is called (literally) "the unlying God" or the "God who never lies." The author of Hebrews says that in God's oath and promise "it is impossible for God to lie" (Heb. 6:18). Second Timothy 2:13 says of Christ, "He cannot deny himself." Furthermore, James says, "God cannot be tempted with evil, and he himself tempts no one" (James 1:13). Thus God cannot lie, sin, deny himself, or be tempted with evil. He cannot cease to exist, or cease to be God, or act in a way inconsistent with any of his attributes.[5]

This means that it is not entirely accurate to say that God can do anything. Even the Scripture passages quoted above that use phrases similar to this must be understood in their contexts to mean that God can do anything he wills to do or anything that is consistent with his character. Although God's power is infinite, his use of that power is qualified by his other attributes (just as all God's attributes qualify all his actions). This is therefore another instance where misunderstanding would result if one attribute were isolated from the rest of God's character and emphasized in a disproportionate way.

God's exercise of power over his creation is also called God's *sovereignty*. God's sovereignty is his exercise of rule (as "sovereign" or "king") over his creation. This subject will be discussed in more detail in chapter 16, on God's providence.

As we conclude our treatment of God's attributes of purpose, it is appropriate to realize that he has made us in such a way that we show in our lives some faint reflection of each of them. God has made us as creatures with a *will*. We exercise choice and make real decisions regarding the events of our lives. Although our will is not absolutely free in the way God's is, God has nonetheless given us *relative freedom* within our spheres of activity in the universe he has created.

In fact, we have an intuitive sense that it is our ability to exercise our wills and make choices, and to do so in a relatively free way, that is one of the most significant marks of God-likeness in our existence. Of course our desire to exercise our wills and our desire to be free from restraint can show themselves in sinful ways. People can become proud and can desire a kind of freedom that involves rebellion against God's authority and a refusal to obey his will. Nonetheless, when we use our will and our freedom to make choices that are pleasing to God, we reflect his character and bring glory to him. When human beings are deprived of their ability to make free choices by evil governments or by other circumstances, a significant part of their God-likeness is suppressed. It is not surprising that they will pay almost any price to regain their freedom. American revolutionary Patrick Henry's cry, "Give me liberty or give me death!" finds an echo deep within every soul created in the image of God.

---

5. The skeptic's question, "Can God make a rock so big that he can't move it?" should be unashamedly answered with "No." The question is really asking, "Can God do something (make a rock) that contradicts his character (his omnipotence)?" No, he cannot contradict his character. Omnipotence only means that he can do all his holy will—which is all that really matters for our lives and our trust in him.

We do not of course have infinite power or omnipotence any more than we have infinite freedom or any of God's other attributes to an infinite degree. But even though we do not have omnipotence, God has given us *power* to bring about results, both physical power and other kinds of power: mental power, spiritual power, persuasive power, and power in various kinds of authority structures (family, church, civil government, and so forth). In all of these areas, the use of power in ways pleasing to God and consistent with his will is again something that brings him glory as it reflects his character.

## E. "Summary" Attributes

### 17. Perfection

*God's perfection means that God completely possesses all excellent qualities and lacks no part of any qualities that would be desirable for him.*

It is difficult to decide whether this should be listed as a separate attribute or simply be included in the description of the other attributes. Some passages say that God is "perfect" or "complete." Jesus tells us, "You therefore must be perfect, *as your heavenly Father is perfect*" (Matt. 5:48). And David says of God, "His way is *perfect*" (Ps. 18:30; cf. Deut. 32:4). There is some scriptural precedent, therefore, for stating explicitly that God lacks nothing in his excellence: he fully possesses all of his attributes and lacks nothing from any one of those attributes. Furthermore, there is no quality of excellence that it would be desirable for God to have that he does not have. He is "complete" or "perfect" in every way.

This attribute is the first of those classified as a "summary" attribute because it does not fit well into the other categories that have been listed. Even though all the attributes of God modify all the others in some senses, those that fit in this category seem more directly to apply to all the attributes or to describe some aspect of all of the attributes that it is worthwhile to state explicitly.

### 18. Blessedness

To be "blessed" is to be happy in a very full and rich sense. Often Scripture talks about the blessedness of those people who walk in God's ways. Yet in 1 Timothy Paul calls God "the *blessed* and only Sovereign" (1 Tim. 6:15) and speaks of "the gospel of the glory of the *blessed* God" (1 Tim. 1:11). In both instances the word is not *eulogētos* (which is often translated "blessed") but *makarios* (which means "happy").

Thus God's blessedness may be defined as follows: *God's blessedness means that God delights fully in himself and in all that reflects his character.* In this definition the idea of God's happiness or blessedness is connected directly to his own person as the focus of all that is worthy of joy or delight. This definition indicates that God is perfectly happy, that he has fullness of joy in himself.

The definition reflects the fact that God takes pleasure in everything in creation that mirrors his excellence. When he finished his work of creation, he looked at everything that he had made and saw that it was "very good" (Gen. 1:31). This indicates God's delight in and approval of his creation. Then in Isaiah we read a promise of God's future rejoicing over his people: "As the bridegroom rejoices over the bride, so shall your God *rejoice* over you" (Isa. 62:5; cf. Prov. 8:30–31; Zeph. 3:17).

It may at first seem strange or even somewhat disappointing to us that when God rejoices in his creation, or even when he rejoices in us, it is really the reflection of his own excellent qualities in which he is rejoicing. But when we remember that the sum of everything that is desirable or excellent is found in infinite measure in God himself, then we realize that it could not be otherwise: *whatever* excellence there is in the universe, *whatever* is desirable, must ultimately have come from him, for he is the Creator of all and he is the source of all good. "*Every* good gift and *every* perfect gift is from above, coming down from the Father of lights, with whom there is no variation or shadow due to change" (James 1:17).

We ought therefore to say to ourselves, as Paul says to the Corinthians, "What do you have that you did not receive? If then you received it, why do you boast as if you did not receive it?" (1 Cor. 4:7). "For from him and through him and to him are all things. To him be glory forever" (Rom. 11:36).

We imitate God's blessedness when we find delight and happiness in all that is pleasing to God, both those aspects of our own lives that are pleasing to God and the deeds of others. In fact, when we are thankful for and delight in the specific abilities, preferences, and other characteristics with which God has created us as individuals, then we also imitate his attribute of blessedness. Furthermore, we imitate God's blessedness by rejoicing in the creation as it reflects various aspects of his excellent character. And we find our greatest blessedness, our greatest happiness, in delighting in the source of all good qualities, God himself.

## 19. Beauty

*God's beauty is that attribute of God whereby he is the sum of all desirable qualities.* This attribute of God has been implicit in a number of the preceding attributes, and is especially related to God's perfection. However, God's perfection was defined in such a way as to show that he does not *lack* anything that would be desirable for him. This attribute, beauty, is defined in a positive way to show that God actually does possess all desirable qualities: "perfection" means that God doesn't lack anything desirable; "beauty" means that God *has* everything desirable. They are two different ways of affirming the same truth.

Nevertheless, there is value in affirming this positive aspect of God's possession of everything that is desirable. It reminds us that all of our good and righteous desires, all of the desires that really ought to be in us or in any other creature, find their ultimate fulfillment in God and in no one else.

David speaks of the beauty of the LORD in Psalm 27:4: "One thing have I asked of the LORD, that will I seek after: that I may dwell in the house of the LORD all the days of my life, to gaze upon *the beauty of the* LORD and to inquire in his temple." A similar idea is expressed in another psalm: "Whom have I in heaven but you? And there is nothing on earth that I desire besides you" (Ps. 73:25). In both cases, the psalmist recognizes that his desire for God, who is the sum of everything desirable, far surpasses all other desires. This desire culminates in a longing to be near God and to enjoy his presence forevermore. Thus, the greatest blessing of the heavenly city shall be this: "They will see his face" (Rev. 22:4).

Anne R. Cousin certainly had a proper perspective on heaven, for in the last stanza of her hymn "The Sands of Time are Sinking," she wrote:

> The bride eyes not her garment,
>     But her dear bridegroom's face.
> I will not gaze at glory,
>     But on my King of grace;
> Not at the crown he giveth,
>     But on his pierced hand:
> The Lamb is all the glory
>     Of Emmanuel's land.

We reflect God's beauty in our own lives when we exhibit conduct that is pleasing to him. Thus Peter tells wives in the churches to which he writes that their "adorning" (that is, their source of beauty) should be "the hidden person of the heart with the imperishable beauty of a gentle and quiet spirit, which in God's sight is very precious" (1 Peter 3:4). Similarly, Paul instructs servants that by their conduct they should "*adorn the doctrine of God our Savior*" (Titus 2:10).

The beauty of our lives is so important to Christ that his purpose now is to sanctify the entire church "so that he might present the church to himself in splendor, without spot or wrinkle or any such thing, that she might be holy and without blemish" (Eph. 5:27). We individually and corporately reflect God's beauty in every way in which we exhibit his character. When we reflect his character, he delights in us and finds us beautiful in his sight.

But we also delight in God's excellence as we see it manifested in the lives of our brothers and sisters in the Lord. Therefore it is right that we feel joy and delight in the fellowship of one another, and that this joy deepens as our conformity to the life of Christ increases. It is right that we long to be in the fellowship of God's people in which God's character is manifested, for when we delight in the godliness of God's people, we are ultimately delighting in God himself as we see his character evidenced in the lives of his people.

## 20. Glory

In one sense of the word *glory* it simply means "honor" or "excellent reputation." This is the meaning of the term in Isaiah 43:7, where God speaks of his children, "whom I created for my *glory*," or Romans 3:23, which says that all "have sinned and fall short of the *glory* of God." It also has that meaning in John 17:5, where Jesus speaks to the Father of "the *glory* that I had with you before the world existed," and in Hebrews 1:3, which says that the Son "is the radiance of the *glory* of God." In this sense, the glory of God is not exactly an attribute of his being but rather describes the superlative honor that should be given to God by everything in the universe (including, in Heb. 1:3 and John 17:5, the honor that is shared among the members of the Trinity). But that is not the sense of the word *glory* that we are concerned with in this section.

In another sense, God's "glory" means the bright light that surrounds God's presence. Since God is spirit, not energy or matter, this visible light is not part of God's being but is something that was created. We may define it as follows: *God's glory is the created brightness that surrounds God's revelation of himself.*

This "attribute" of God is really not an attribute of God in the sense that the others were, for here we are speaking not of God's character but of the *created* light or brilliance that surrounds God as he manifests himself in his creation. God's glory in this sense is not actually an attribute of God in himself. Nevertheless, God's glory is something that belongs to him alone and is the appropriate outward expression of his own excellence. It seems right therefore to treat it here immediately after the attributes of God.

Scripture often speaks of God's glory. David asks, "Who is this King of glory? The LORD of hosts, *he is the King of glory*!" (Ps. 24:10). We read in Psalm 104:1–2, "O LORD my God, you are very great! You are clothed with splendor and majesty, *covering yourself with light as with a garment*." This glory of God is frequently mentioned in the Old Testament.

It is mentioned again in the New Testament in connection with the annunciation of Jesus' birth to the shepherds: "And an angel of the Lord appeared to them, and *the glory of the Lord shone around them*, and they were filled with great fear" (Luke 2:9). God's glory was also evident at the transfiguration of Christ (cf. Matt. 17:2), and we find in the heavenly city yet to come that "the city has no need of sun or moon to shine on it, for *the glory of God gives it light*, and its lamp is the Lamb" (Rev. 21:23).

It is very appropriate that God's revelation of himself should be accompanied by such splendor and brightness, for this glory of God is the visible manifestation of the excellence of God's character. The greatness of God's being, the perfection of all his attributes, is something that we can never fully comprehend, but before which we can only stand in awe and worship. Thus it is appropriate indeed that the visible manifestation of God be such that we would be unable to gaze fully upon it and that it would be so bright that it would call forth both great delight and deep awe from us when we behold it only in part.

Quite amazingly, God made us to reflect his glory. Paul tells us that even now in our Christian lives we all are being "transformed into the same image from one degree of glory to another" (2 Cor. 3:18; cf. Matt. 5:16; Phil. 2:15). Though we do not now find ourselves surrounded by a visible light, there is often a brightness, a splendor, or a beauty about the manner of life of a person who deeply loves God, and it is often evident to those around such a person. In the life to come, such brightness will be intensified, so that as we reign with Christ, it seems that we also will receive a shining outward appearance that is appropriate to that reign and to our status as image bearers of God and servants of the Lord Jesus Christ (cf. Prov. 4:18; Dan. 12:3; Matt. 13:43; 1 Cor. 15:43).[6]

## QUESTIONS FOR PERSONAL APPLICATION

### WILL, FREEDOM

1. As children grow toward adulthood, what are proper and improper ways for them to show in their own lives greater and greater exercise of individual will and freedom from parental control? Are these to be expected as evidence of our creation in the image of God?

### POWER

2. If God's power is his ability to do what he wills to do, then is power for us the ability to obey God's will and bring about results in the world that are pleasing to him? Name several ways in which we can increase in such power in our lives.

### PERFECTION

3. How does God's attribute of perfection remind us that we can never be satisfied with the reflection of only some of God's character in our own lives? Can you describe some aspects of what it would mean to "be perfect" as our heavenly Father is perfect, with respect to your own life?

### BLESSEDNESS

4. Are you happy with the way God created you—with the physical, emotional, mental, and relational traits he gave you? With the sex he gave you (whether male or female)? With the spiritual gifts he has given you? In what ways is it right to be happy or pleased with our own personalities, physical characteristics, abilities, positions, and so on? In what ways is it wrong to be pleased or happy about these things? Will we ever be fully "blessed" or happy? When will that be and why?

5. Think about the qualities that you admire in other people, both Christians and non-Christians. Which of these are right to admire and which are not? How can you decide? How can we come to delight more frequently and more fully in God himself?

---

6. See the discussion of glorification in chapter 42, pp. 1018–27.

## BEAUTY

6. If we refuse to accept our society's definition of beauty, or even the definitions that we ourselves may have worked with previously, and decide that that which is truly beautiful is the character of God himself, then how will our understanding of beauty be different from the one we previously held? Will we still be able to rightly apply our new idea of beauty to some of the things we previously thought to be beautiful? Why or why not?

7. Can you understand why David's one desire above all others in life was "that I may dwell in the house of the LORD all the days of my life, to gaze upon the beauty of the LORD, and to inquire in his temple" (Ps. 27:4)?

## GLORY

8. When the shepherds near Bethlehem experienced the glory of the Lord shining around them, "they were filled with great fear" (Luke 2:9). Yet when we come to live forever in the heavenly city, we will continually be surrounded by the light of the glory of the Lord (Rev. 21:23). Will we then continually feel this same fear the shepherds felt? Why or why not? Would you like to live in the presence of this glory? Can we experience any of it in this life?

**Special Terms**
*attributes of purpose*
*beauty*
*blessedness*
*freedom*
*free will*
*glory*
*necessary will*
*omnipotence*
*perfection*
*power*
*reasonable self-determination*
*revealed will*
*secret will*
*sovereignty*
*"summary attributes"*
*will*

## BIBLIOGRAPHY

(For an explanation of this bibliography see the note on the bibliography to chapter 1, pp. 23–24. Complete bibliographical data may be found on pp. 1489–96.)

Because systematic theologies have different ways of classifying the attributes of God, some of the sections listed below discuss only the communicable attributes of God, and some discuss all the attributes of God.

### SECTIONS IN EVANGELICAL SYSTEMATIC THEOLOGIES

*1. Anglican (Episcopalian)*
1882–92 . . . . . Litton, 58–74
1930 . . . . . . . . Thomas, 14–20, 495–500
2001 . . . . . . . . Packer, 26–53
2013 . . . . . . . . Bird, 126–139
2013 . . . . . . . . Bray, 112–114

2. *Arminian (Wesleyan or Methodist)*
1875–76 . . . . . Pope, 1:248–55, 287–360
1892–94 . . . . . Miley, 1:159–222
1940 . . . . . . . . Wiley, 1:241–393
1960 . . . . . . . . Purkiser, 127–42
1983 . . . . . . . . Carter, 1:111–27
1992 . . . . . . . . Oden, 1:53–130
2002 . . . . . . . . Cottrell, 67–99

3. *Baptist*
1767 . . . . . . . . Gill, 1:37–187, 359–65
1887 . . . . . . . . Boyce, 54–115
1907 . . . . . . . . Strong, 243–303
1976–83 . . . . . Henry, 2:151–246; 5:9–164,
                214–375; 6:35–89, 251–417
1987–94 . . . . . Lewis and Demarest,
                1:175–248
1990–95 . . . . . Garrett, 1:223–304
2007 . . . . . . . . Akin, 221–238
2013 . . . . . . . . Erickson, 254–66

4. *Dispensational*
1947 . . . . . . . . Chafer, 1:179–224, 260–71
1949 . . . . . . . . Thiessen, 75–88
1986 . . . . . . . . Ryrie, 35–50
2017 . . . . . . . . MacArthur and Mayhue,
                179–88

5. *Lutheran*
1917–24 . . . . . Pieper, 1:405–66
1934 . . . . . . . . Mueller, 160–75

6. *Reformed (or Presbyterian)*
1559 . . . . . . . . Calvin, 1:96–120 (1.10–12)
1679–85 . . . . . Turretin, *IET*, 1:189–91
1871–73 . . . . . Hodge, 1:366–441
1878 . . . . . . . . Dabney, 38–54, 144–74

1887–1921 . . . Warfield, *BTS*, 505–22; *SSW*,
                1:69–81; *ST*, 109–14
1894 . . . . . . . . Shedd, 274–310
1906–11 . . . . Bavinck, *RD*, 2:96–97,
                131–32, 135–36, 178–255
1910 . . . . . . . . . Vos, 1:3–37
1938 . . . . . . . . Berkhof, 41–81
1962 . . . . . . . . Buswell, 1:29–71
1998 . . . . . . . . Reymond, 163–204
2008 . . . . . . . . Van Genderen and Velema,
                164–192
2011 . . . . . . . . Horton, 259–272
2013 . . . . . . . . Frame, 232–279
2013 . . . . . . . . Culver, 60–92, 216–26
2016 . . . . . . . . Allen and Swain, 57–77
2017 . . . . . . . . Barrett, 217–40
2019 . . . . . . . . Letham, 158–59

7. *Renewal (or charismatic/Pentecostal)*
1988–92 . . . . . Williams, 1:47–82
1993 . . . . . . . . Menzies and Horton, 48–53
1995 . . . . . . . . Horton, 120–131
2008 . . . . . . . . Duffield and Van Cleave,
                58–61, 70–76

## SECTIONS IN REPRESENTATIVE ROMAN CATHOLIC SYSTEMATIC THEOLOGIES

1. *Roman Catholic: Traditional*
1955 . . . . . . . . Ott, 24–49

2. *Roman Catholic: Post–Vatican II*
1980 . . . . . . . . McBrien, 1:283–342
2012 . . . . . . . . *CCC*, paragraphs 222–31

## OTHER WORKS

Alcorn, Randy C. *If God Is Good: Faith in the Midst of Suffering and Evil.* Colorado Springs: Multnomah, 2009.

Allison, Gregg. *Historical Theology: An Introduction to Christian Doctrine; A Companion to Wayne Grudem's* Systematic Theology. Grand Rapids: Zondervan, 2011, 210–30.

Bray, Gerald L. *The Doctrine of God.* Downers Grove, IL: InterVarsity Press, 1993.

———. "God." In *NDBT*, 511–21.

Bromiley, G. W. "God." In *ISBE*, 2:493–503.

Charnock, Stephen. *The Existence and Attributes of God.* 1655–80; Reprint, Evansville, IN: Sovereign Grace Book Club, n.d., 181–802.

Duby, Steven J. *God in Himself: Scripture, Metaphysics, and the Task of Christian Theology.* Downers Grove, IL: IVP Academic, 2019.

Feinberg, John S. *No One Like Him: The Doctrine of God.* Wheaton, IL: Crossway, 2006.

Gavrilyuk, Paul L. *The Suffering of the Impassible God: The Dialectics of Patristic Thought.* Oxford: Oxford University Press, 2004.

Holmes, S. R. "God." In *NDT2*, 369–73.

House, H. Wayne, and Max Herrera. *Charts on Open Theism and Orthodoxy.* Grand Rapids: Kregel, 2003.

Kaiser, Christopher B. *The Doctrine of God.* Westchester, IL: Good News, 1982.

Keating, James, and Thomas Joseph White. *Divine Impassibility and the Mystery of Human Suffering.* Grand Rapids: Eerdmans, 2009.

Laney, J. Carl. *God: Who He Is, What He Does, How to Know Him Better.* Nashville: Word, 1999.

Lewis, Gordon R. "God, Attributes of." In *EDT1*, 451–59.

———. "Impassibility of God." In *EDT3*, 422–23.

Packer, J. I. "God." In *NDT1*, 274–77.

———. *Knowing God.* London: Inter-Varsity Press, 1973, 80–254.

Piper, John. *Desiring God.* Sisters, OR: Multnomah, 2003.

———. *The Pleasures of God.* Sisters, OR: Multnomah, 2000.

Saucy, R. L. "God, Doctrine of." In *EDT1*, 459–64.

Tozer, A. W. *The Knowledge of the Holy.* New York: Harper and Row, 1961.

Van Til, Cornelius. *In Defense of the Faith.* Vol. 5, *An Introduction to Systematic Theology.* Phillipsburg, NJ: Presbyterian and Reformed, 1976, 200–252.

Wenham, John W. *The Goodness of God.* London: Inter-Varsity Press, 1974.

## SCRIPTURE MEMORY PASSAGE

**Psalm 73:25–26:**
*Whom have I in heaven but you?*
*And there is nothing on earth that I desire besides you.*

*My flesh and my heart may fail,*
*but God is the strength of my heart and my portion forever.*

## HYMN

**"If Thou but Suffer God to Guide Thee"**

This is undoubtedly one of the most beautiful hymns ever written that expresses trust in God for his sovereignty.

*If thou but suffer God to guide thee,*
*And hope in him through all thy ways,*
*He'll give thee strength, whate'er betide thee,*

*And bear thee through the evil days:*
*Who trusts in God's unchanging love*
*Builds on the rock that naught can move.*

What can these anxious cares avail thee,
    These never-ceasing moans and sighs?
What can it help, if thou bewail thee
    O'er each dark moment as it flies?
Our cross and trials do but press
    The heavier for our bitterness.

Only be still, and wait his leisure
    In cheerful hope, with heart content
To take whate'er thy Father's pleasure
    And all-deserving love hath sent;
Nor doubt our inmost wants are known
    To him who chose us for his own.

All are alike before the highest;
    'Tis easy to our God, we know,
To raise thee up though low thou liest,
    To make the rich man poor and low;
True wonders still by him are wrought
    Who setteth up and brings to naught.

Sing, pray, and keep his ways unswerving,
    So do thine own part faithfully,
And trust his Word, though undeserving,
    Thou yet shalt find it true for thee;
God never yet forsook at need
    The soul that trusted him indeed.

Author: Georg Neumark, 1641

Alternative hymns: "God Moves in a Mysterious Way" (printed at the end of chapter 16); "Crown Him With Many Crowns"

## CONTEMPORARY WORSHIP SONG

**"Your Name"**

As morning dawns and evening fades,
You inspire songs of praise
That rise from earth to touch Your heart
And glorify Your Name.

*Chorus*
Your Name is a strong and mighty tower.
Your Name is a shelter like no other.
Your Name let the nations sing it louder
'Cause nothing has the power to save
But Your Name.

Jesus in Your Name we pray,
    Come and fill our hearts today.
Lord give us strength to live for You
And glorify Your Name.

Words by Glenn Packiam and Paul Baloche[7]

# CHAPTER 14

# God in Three Persons: The Trinity

***How can God be three persons yet one God?***

The preceding chapters have discussed many attributes of God. But if we understood only those attributes, we would not rightly understand God at all, for we would not understand that God, in his very being, has always existed as more than one person. In fact, God exists as three persons, yet he is one God.

It is important to remember the doctrine of the Trinity in connection with the study of God's attributes. When we think of God as eternal, omnipresent, omnipotent, and so forth, we may have a tendency to think only of God the Father in connection with these attributes. But the biblical teaching on the Trinity tells us that all of God's attributes are true of all three persons, for each is fully God. God the Son and God the Holy Spirit are also eternal, omnipresent, omnipotent, infinitely wise, infinitely holy, infinitely loving, omniscient, and so forth.

The doctrine of the Trinity is one of the most important doctrines of the Christian faith. To study the Bible's teachings on the Trinity gives us great insight into the question that is at the center of all of our seeking after God: What is God like in himself? Here we learn that in himself, in his very being, God exists in the persons of Father, Son, and Holy Spirit, yet he is one God.

## EXPLANATION AND SCRIPTURAL BASIS

We may define the doctrine of the Trinity as follows: *God eternally exists as three persons, Father, Son, and Holy Spirit, and each person is fully God, and there is one God.*

### A. THE DOCTRINE OF THE TRINITY IS PROGRESSIVELY REVEALED IN SCRIPTURE

### 1. Partial Revelation in the Old Testament

The word *trinity* is never found in the Bible, though the idea represented by the word is taught in many places. The word *trinity* means "tri-unity" or "three-in-oneness." It is used to summarize the teaching of Scripture that God is three persons yet one God.

Sometimes people think the doctrine of the Trinity is found only in the New Testament, not in the Old. If God has eternally existed as three persons, it would be surprising to find no indications of that in the Old Testament. Although the doctrine of the Trinity is not explicitly found in the Old Testament, several passages suggest or even imply that God exists as more than one person.

For instance, according to Genesis 1:26, God said, "Let *us* make man in *our* image, after *our* likeness." What do the plural verb ("let us") and the plural pronoun ("our") mean? Some have suggested they are plurals of majesty, a form of speech a king would use in saying, for example, "We are pleased to grant your request."[1] However, in Old Testament Hebrew there are no other examples of a monarch using plural verbs or plural pronouns of himself in such a "plural of majesty," so this suggestion has no evidence to support it.[2] Another suggestion is that God is here speaking to angels. But angels did not participate in the creation of man, nor was man created in the image and likeness of angels, so this suggestion is not convincing. The best explanation is that already in the first chapter of Genesis we have an indication of a plurality of persons in God himself.[3] We are not told how many persons, and we have nothing approaching a complete doctrine of the Trinity, but it is implied that more than one person is involved. The same can be said of Genesis 3:22 ("Behold, the man has become like one of *us* in knowing good and evil"), Genesis 11:7 ("Come, let *us* go down and there confuse their language"), and Isaiah 6:8 ("Whom shall I send, and who will go for *us*?"). (Note the combination of singular and plural in the same sentence in the last passage.)

Moreover, there are passages where one person is called "God" or "the Lord" and is distinguished from another person who is also said to be God. In Psalm 45:6–7, the psalmist says,

> Your throne, O God, is forever and ever. . . .
>> You have loved righteousness and hated wickedness.
> Therefore God, your God, has anointed you
>> with the oil of gladness beyond your companions.

Here the psalm passes beyond describing anything that could be true of an earthly king and calls the king "God" (v. 6), whose throne will last "forever and ever." But then, still speaking to the person called "God," the author says that "God, your God, has anointed

---

1. Both Alexander the Great (in 152 BC) and King Demetrius (about 145 BC) refer to themselves in this way, for example, in the Septuagint text of 1 Macc. 10:19 and 11:31, but this is in Greek, not Hebrew, and it was written long after Genesis 1.

2. See E. Kautzsch, ed., *Gesenius' Hebrew Grammar*, 2nd ed. (Oxford: Clarendon, 1910), Section 124g, n2, with reference to the suggestion of a plural of majesty: "The plural used by God in Genesis 1:26, 11:7, Isaiah 6:8 has been incorrectly explained in this way." They understand Gen. 1:26 as "a plural of self-deliberation." My own extensive search of subsequent Jewish interpretation in the Babylonian Talmud, the targumim,

and the midrashim showed only that later Rabbinic interpreters were unable to reach agreement on any satisfactory interpretation of this passage, although the "plural of majesty" and "God speaking to angels" interpretations were commonly suggested.

3. "The plural 'We' was regarded by the fathers and earlier theologians almost unanimously as indicative of the Trinity" (Keil and Delitzsch, *Old Testament Commentaries* [Grand Rapids: Associated Publishers and Authors, n.d.], 1:48, with objections to other positions and an affirmation that Gen. 1:26 contains "the truth that lies at the foundation of the Trinitarian view").

you with the oil of gladness" (v. 7). So two separate persons are called "God" (Heb. *'Elōhîm*). In the New Testament, the author of Hebrews quotes this passage and applies it to Christ: "Your throne, O God, is forever and ever" (Heb. 1:8).

Similarly, in Psalm 110:1, David says, "The LORD says to my Lord: 'Sit at my right hand, until I make your enemies your footstool.'" Jesus rightly understands that David is referring to two separate persons as "Lord" (Matt. 22:41–46), but who is David's "Lord" if not God himself? And who could be saying to God, "Sit at my right hand" except someone else who is also fully God? From a New Testament perspective, we can paraphrase this verse: "God the Father said to God the Son, 'Sit at my right hand.'" But even without the New Testament teaching on the Trinity, it seems clear that David was aware of a plurality of persons in one God. Jesus, of course, understood this, but when he asked the Pharisees for an explanation of this passage, "no one was able to answer him a word, nor from that day did anyone dare to ask him any more questions" (Matt. 22:46). Unless they are willing to admit a plurality of persons in one God, Jewish interpreters of Scripture to this day will have no more satisfactory explanation of Psalm 110:1 (or of Gen. 1:26, or of the other passages just discussed) than they did in Jesus' day.

Isaiah 63:10 says that God's people "rebelled and grieved his Holy Spirit," apparently suggesting both that the Holy Spirit is distinct from God himself (it is "his Holy Spirit"), and that this Holy Spirit can be "grieved," thus suggesting emotional capabilities characteristic of a distinct person. (Isa. 61:1 also distinguishes "The Spirit of the Lord GOD" from "the LORD," even though no personal qualities are attributed to the Spirit of the Lord in that verse.)

Similar evidence is found in Malachi, when the Lord says, "The Lord whom you seek will suddenly come to his temple; and the messenger of the covenant in whom you delight, behold, he is coming, says the LORD of hosts. But who can endure the day of his coming, and who can stand when he appears?" (Mal. 3:1–2). Here again the one speaking ("the LORD of hosts") distinguishes himself from "the Lord whom you seek," suggesting two separate persons, both of whom can be called "Lord."

In Hosea 1:7, the Lord says of the house of Judah, "I will save them by the LORD their God," once again suggesting that more than one person can be called "Lord" (Heb. *Yahweh*) and "God" (*'Elōhîm*).

And in Isaiah 48:16, the speaker (apparently the servant of the Lord) says, "Now the Lord GOD has sent me and his Spirit."[4] Here the Spirit of the Lord, like the servant of the Lord, has been "sent" by the Lord GOD on a particular mission. The parallel between the two objects of sending ("me" and "his Spirit") would be consistent with seeing them both as distinct persons: it seems to mean more than simply "the Lord has sent me and

---

4. This ESV translation of Isa. 48:16 accurately reproduces both the literal sense of the Hebrew words and the word order in the Hebrew text.

his power."[5] In fact, from a full New Testament perspective (which recognizes Jesus the Messiah to be the true servant of the Lord predicted in Isaiah's prophecies), Isaiah 48:16 has Trinitarian implications: "Now the Lord GOD has sent me and his Spirit," if spoken by Jesus the Son of God, refers to all three persons of the Trinity.

Furthermore, several Old Testament passages about "the angel of the LORD" suggest a plurality of persons in God. The word translated "angel" (Heb. *mal'āk*) means simply "messenger." If this angel of the LORD is a "messenger" of the LORD, he is then distinct from the LORD himself. Yet at some points the angel of the LORD is called "God" or "the LORD" (see Gen. 16:13; Ex. 3:2–6; 23:20–22 [note "my name is in him" in v. 21]; Num. 22:35 with 38; Judg. 2:1–2; 6:11 with 14). At other points in the Old Testament "the angel of the LORD" simply refers to a created angel, but at least in these texts the special angel (or "messenger") of the LORD seems to be a distinct person who is fully divine.

## 2. More Complete Revelation of the Trinity in the New Testament

When the New Testament opens, we enter into the history of the coming of the Son of God to earth. It is to be expected that this great event would be accompanied by more explicit teaching about the Trinitarian nature of God, and that is in fact what we find. Before looking at this in detail, we can simply list several passages where all three persons of the Trinity are named together.

When Jesus was baptized, "the heavens were opened to him, and he saw the Spirit of God descending like a dove and coming to rest on him; and behold, a voice from heaven said, 'This is my beloved Son, with whom I am well pleased'" (Matt. 3:16–17). Here at one moment we have three members of the Trinity performing three distinct activities. God the Father is speaking from heaven, God the Son is being baptized and is then spoken to from heaven by God the Father, and God the Holy Spirit is descending from heaven to rest upon and empower Jesus for his ministry.

At the end of Jesus' earthly ministry, he tells the disciples that they should go "and make disciples of all nations, baptizing them in the name of the Father and of the Son and of the Holy Spirit" (Matt. 28:19). The very names "Father" and "Son," drawn as they are from the family, the most familiar of human institutions, indicate very strongly the distinct personhood of both the Father and the Son. When the "Holy Spirit" is put in the same expression and on the same level as the other two persons, it is hard to avoid the conclusion that the Holy Spirit is also viewed as a person and of equal standing with the Father and the Son.

When we realize that the New Testament authors generally use the name "God" (Gk. *theos*) to refer to God the Father and the name "Lord" (Gk. *kyrios*) to refer to God the Son, then it is clear that there is another Trinitarian expression in 1 Corinthians

---

5. The NIV translation, "endowed with his Spirit," is not required by the Hebrew text and tends to obscure the parallel thoughts of the Lord sending "me" and "his Spirit." The expression "endowed with" in the NIV is the translators'

interpretation of the Hebrew conjunction *w* which most commonly means simply "and." The common Hebrew word for "with" (*'im*) is not in the text, and there is no separate word in the Hebrew text that means "endowed."

12:4–6: "Now there are varieties of gifts, but the same *Spirit*; and there are varieties of service, but the same *Lord*; and there are varieties of activities, but it is the same *God* who empowers them all in everyone."

Similarly, the last verse of 2 Corinthians is Trinitarian in its expression: "The grace of the *Lord Jesus Christ* and the love of *God* and the fellowship of the *Holy Spirit* be with you all" (2 Cor. 13:14). We see the three persons mentioned separately in Ephesians 4:4–6 as well: "There is one body and one *Spirit*—just as you were called to the one hope that belongs to your call—one *Lord*, one faith, one baptism, one *God and Father* of all, who is over all and through all and in all."

All three persons of the Trinity are mentioned together in the opening sentence of 1 Peter: "According to the foreknowledge of God the Father, in the sanctification of the Spirit, for obedience to Jesus Christ and for sprinkling with his blood" (1 Peter 1:2). And in Jude 20–21, we read: "But you, beloved, building yourselves up in your most holy faith and praying in the Holy Spirit, keep yourselves in the love of God, waiting for the mercy of our Lord Jesus Christ that leads to eternal life."

However, the KJV translation of 1 John 5:7 should not be used in this connection. It reads, "For there are three that bear record in heaven, the Father, the Word, and the Holy Ghost: and these three are one." The problem with this translation is that it is based on a very small number of unreliable Greek manuscripts, the earliest of which comes from the fourteenth century AD. No modern translation (except the NKJV) includes this KJV reading, but all omit it, as do the vast majority of Greek manuscripts from all major text traditions, including several very reliable manuscripts from the fourth and fifth century AD, and also including quotations by church fathers such as Irenaeus (d. ca. AD 202), Clement of Alexandria (d. ca. AD 212), Tertullian (d. after AD 220), and the great defender of the Trinity, Athanasius (d. AD 373).

## B. THREE STATEMENTS SUMMARIZE THE BIBLICAL TEACHING

In one sense the doctrine of the Trinity is a mystery that we will never be able to understand fully. However, we can understand something of its truth by summarizing the teaching of Scripture in three statements:

1. God is three persons.
2. Each person is fully God.
3. There is one God.

The following section will develop each of these statements in more detail.

## 1. God Is Three Persons

The fact that God is three persons means that the Father is not the Son; they are distinct persons. It also means that the Father is not the Holy Spirit, but that they are distinct persons. And it means that the Son is not the Holy Spirit. These distinctions are seen in a number of the passages quoted in the earlier section as well as in many additional New Testament passages.

John 1:1–2 tells us: "In the beginning was the Word, and the Word was with God, and the Word was God. He was in the beginning with God." The fact that the Word (who is seen to be Christ in vv. 9–18) is "with" God shows distinction from God the Father. In John 17:24, Jesus speaks to God the Father about "my glory that you have given me because you loved me before the foundation of the world," thus showing distinction of persons, sharing of glory, and a relationship of love between the Father and the Son before the world was created.

We are told that Jesus continues as our High Priest and Advocate before God the Father: "If anyone does sin, we have an advocate with the Father, Jesus Christ the righteous" (1 John 2:1). Christ is the one who "is able to save to the utmost those who draw near to God through him, since he always lives to make intercession for them" (Heb. 7:25). Yet in order to intercede for us before God the Father, it is necessary that Christ be a person distinct from the Father.

Moreover, the Father is not the Holy Spirit, and the Son is not the Holy Spirit. They are distinguished in several verses. Jesus says, "But the Helper, the Holy Spirit, whom the Father will send in my name, he will teach you all things and bring to your remembrance all that I have said to you" (John 14:26). The Holy Spirit also prays or "intercedes" for us (Rom. 8:27), indicating a distinction between the Holy Spirit and God the Father to whom the intercession is made.

Finally, the fact that the Son is not the Holy Spirit is also indicated in the several Trinitarian passages mentioned earlier, such as the Great Commission (Matt. 28:19), and in passages that indicate that Christ went back to heaven and then sent the Holy Spirit to the church. Jesus said, "It is to your advantage that I go away, for if I do not go away, the Helper will not come to you. But if I go, I will send him to you" (John 16:7).

Some have questioned whether the Holy Spirit is indeed a distinct person rather than just the "power" or "force" of God at work in the world. But the New Testament evidence is quite clear and strong.[6] First are the several verses mentioned earlier where the Holy Spirit is put in a coordinate relationship with the Father and the Son (Matt. 28:19; 1 Cor. 12:4–6; 2 Cor. 13:14; Eph. 4:4–6; 1 Peter 1:2): since the Father and Son are both persons, the coordinate expression strongly intimates that the Holy Spirit is a person also. Moreover, the names *helper, counselor,* and *comforter* (Gk. *paraklētos*) are terms commonly used to speak of a person who helps or gives comfort or counsel to another person or persons and are used of the Holy Spirit in John's gospel (14:16, 26; 15:26; 16:7).[7]

---

6. The following section on the distinct personality of the Holy Spirit follows quite closely the excellent material in Louis Berkhof, *Systematic Theology* (Grand Rapids: Eerdmans, 1941), 96.

7. Some writers (including me in the previous edition of *Systematic Theology*) have argued that the masculine pronoun *he* (Gk. *ekeinos*) in John 14:26; 15:26; and 16:13–14 also argues for the personhood of the Holy Spirit, since one would not expect a masculine pronoun from the rules of Greek grammar,

Other personal activities are ascribed to the Holy Spirit, such as teaching (John 14:26), bearing witness (John 15:26; Rom. 8:16), interceding or praying on behalf of others (Rom. 8:26–27), searching the depths of God (1 Cor. 2:10), knowing the thoughts of God (1 Cor. 2:11), willing to distribute some gifts to some and other gifts to others (1 Cor. 12:11), forbidding or not allowing certain activities (Acts 16:6–7), speaking (Acts 8:29; 13:2; and many times in both Old and New Testaments), evaluating and approving a wise course of action (Acts 15:28), and being grieved by sin in the lives of Christians (Eph. 4:30).

Finally, if the Holy Spirit is understood simply to be the power of God rather than a distinct person, then a number of passages would simply not make sense, because in them the Holy Spirit and his power or the power of God are both mentioned. For example, Luke 4:14, "Jesus returned in the power of the Spirit to Galilee," would have to mean, "Jesus returned in the power of the power of God to Galilee." In Acts 10:38, "God anointed Jesus of Nazareth with the Holy Spirit and with power," would mean, "God anointed Jesus with the power of God and with power" (see also Rom. 15:13; 1 Cor. 2:4).

Although so many passages clearly distinguish the Holy Spirit from the other members of the Trinity, one puzzling verse has been 2 Corinthians 3:17: "Now the Lord is the Spirit, and where the Spirit of the Lord is, there is freedom." Interpreters often assume that "the Lord" here must mean Christ because Paul frequently uses "the Lord" to refer to Christ. But that is probably not the case here, for a good argument can be made from grammar and context to say that this verse is better translated with the Holy Spirit as subject, "Now the Spirit is the Lord."[8] In this case, Paul would be saying that the Holy Spirit is also "Yahweh" (or "Jehovah"), the Lord of the Old Testament (note the clear Old Testament background of this context, beginning at v. 7). Theologically this would be quite acceptable, for it could truly be said that just as God the Father is "Lord" and God the Son is "Lord" (in the full Old Testament sense of "Lord" as a name for God), so also the Holy Spirit is the one called "Lord" in the Old Testament—and it is the Holy Spirit who especially manifests the presence of the Lord to us in the new covenant age.[9]

---

for the word *spirit* (Gk. *pneuma*) is neuter, not masculine. But this is not a correct argument, for a closer examination of those verses shows that the antecedent for *ekeinos* ("he") in those verses is the masculine noun *paraklētos* ("Helper"), not *pneuma* ("Spirit"). This is true even in John 16:13, where the order of phrases in the Greek text shows that *ekeinos* restates the *ekeinos* in v. 8, which has *paraklētos* in v. 7 as its antecedent. See the careful discussion in Andrew Naselli and Philip Gons, "Proof-texting the Personality of the Holy Spirit: An Analysis of the Masculine Demonstrative Pronouns in John 14:26, 15:26, and 16:13–14," *Detroit Baptist Seminary Journal* 16 (2011): 65–89. (The noun *paraklētos* still refers to a masculine *person*, so the verses still refer to the Holy Spirit as a person.)

8. Grammatically both "the Spirit" (*to pneuma*) and "the Lord" (*ho kyrios*) are in the nominative case, which is the case taken both by the subject and by the predicate noun in a sentence

with the verb "to be." And word order does not indicate the subject in Greek as it does in English. The definite article (*ho*, "the") before "Lord" here is probably anaphoric (that is, it refers back to the previous mention of "Lord" in v. 16 and says that the Spirit is "the Lord" who was just mentioned in the previous sentence). (See Murray Harris, "2 Corinthians," *EBC*, 10:338–39.)

9. Another possible interpretation is to say that this is speaking of the function of Christ and the function of the Holy Spirit as so closely related in the New Testament age that they can be spoken of as one in purpose. The verse would then mean something like "The Lord Jesus is in this age seen and known through the activity of the Holy Spirit, for the Holy Spirit's function is to glorify Christ." But this is a less persuasive interpretation, since it seems unlikely that Paul would speak of an identity of function in such an obscure way, or even that Paul would want to say that the work of Christ and the work of the Spirit are identical.

## 2. Each Person Is Fully God

In addition to the fact that all three persons are distinct, the abundant testimony of Scripture is that each person is fully God as well.

First, *God the Father is clearly God.* This is evident from the first verse of the Bible, where God created the heaven and the earth. It is evident through the Old and New Testaments, where God the Father is clearly viewed as sovereign Lord over all and where Jesus prays to his Father in heaven.

Next, *the Son is fully God.* Although this point will be developed in greater detail in chapter 26, "The Person of Christ," we can briefly note several explicit passages at this point. John 1:1–4 clearly affirms the full deity of Christ:

> In the beginning was the Word, and the Word was with God, and the Word was God. He was in the beginning with God. All things were made through him, and without him was not any thing made that was made. In him was life, and the life was the light of men.

Here Christ is referred to as "the Word," and John says both that he was "with God" and that he "was God." The Greek text echoes the opening words of Genesis 1:1 ("In the beginning") and reminds us that John is talking about something that was true before the world was made. God the Son was always fully God.

The translation "the Word was God" has been challenged by the Jehovah's Witnesses, who translate it "the Word was *a god*," implying that the Word was simply a heavenly being but not fully divine. They justify this translation by pointing to the fact that the definite article (Gk. *ho*, "the") does not occur before the Greek word *theos* ("God"). They say therefore that *theos* should be translated "a god." However, their interpretation has been followed by no recognized Greek scholar anywhere, for it is commonly known that the sentence follows a regular rule of Greek grammar, and the absence of the definite article merely indicates that "God" is the predicate rather than the subject of the sentence.[10] (A recent publication by the Jehovah's Witnesses now

---

10. This rule (called "Colwell's rule") is covered as early as chapter 6 of a standard introductory Greek grammar. See John Wenham, *The Elements of New Testament Greek* (Cambridge: Cambridge University Press, 1965), 35; also, *BDF*, 273. The rule is simply that in sentences with the linking verb "to be" (such as Gk. *eimi*), a definite predicate noun will usually drop the definite article when it precedes the verb, but the subject of the sentence, if definite, will retain the definite article. So if John had wanted to say, "The Word was God," John 1:1 is exactly the way he would have said it. (Recent grammatical study has confirmed and even strengthened Colwell's original rule; see Lane C. McGaughy, *Toward a Descriptive Analysis of EINAI as a Linking Verb in the New Testament*, SBLDS 6 [Missoula, MT: SBL, 1972], esp. pp. 49–53, 73–77; and the

important review of this book by E. V. N. Goetchius in *JBL* 95 [1976]: 147–49.)

Of course, if John had wanted to say, "The Word was a god" (with an indefinite predicate, "a god"), it would also have been written this way, since there would have been no definite article to drop in the first place. But if that were the case, there would have to be some clues in the context that John was using the word *theos* to speak of a heavenly being that was not fully divine. So the question becomes, what kind of God (or "god") is John talking about in this context? Is he speaking of the one true God who created the heavens and the earth? In that case, *theos* was definite and dropped the definite article to show that it was the predicate noun. Or is he speaking about some other kind of heavenly being ("a god") who is not the one acknowledges the relevant grammatical rule but continues to affirm their position on John 1:1 nonetheless.)[11]

The inconsistency of the Jehovah's Witnesses' position can further be seen in their translation of the rest of the chapter. For various other grammatical reasons the word *theos* also lacks the definite article at other places in this chapter, such as verse 6 ("There was a man sent from God"), verse 12 ("the right to become children of God"), verse 13 ("but of God"), and verse 18 ("No one has ever seen God"). If the Jehovah's Witnesses were consistent with their argument about the absence of the definite article, they would have to translate all of these with the phrase "a god," but they translate "God" in every case.

John 20:28 in its context is also a strong proof for the deity of Christ. Thomas had doubted the reports of the other disciples that they had seen Jesus raised from the dead, and he said he would not believe unless he could see the nail prints in Jesus' hands and place his hand in his wounded side (John 20:25). Then Jesus appeared to the disciples when Thomas was with them. He said to Thomas, "Put your finger here, and see my hands; and put out your hand, and place it in my side. Do not disbelieve, but believe" (John 20:27). In response to this, we read, "Thomas answered him, 'My Lord and my God!'" (John 20:28). Here Thomas calls Jesus "my God." The narrative shows that both John in writing his gospel and Jesus himself approve of what Thomas has said and encourage everyone who hears about Thomas to believe the same things that Thomas did. Jesus immediately responds to Thomas, "Have you believed because you have seen me? Blessed are those who have not seen and yet have believed" (John 20:29). As far as John is concerned, this is the dramatic high point of the gospel, for he immediately tells the reader—in the very next verse—that this was the reason he wrote it:

---

true God? In that case, *theos* was indefinite and never had a definite article in the first place.

The context decides this question clearly. From the other uses of the word *theos* to mean "God" in vv. 1, 2, 6, 12, 13, et al., and from the opening words that recall Gen. 1:1 ("In the beginning"), it is clear that John is speaking of the one true God who created the heavens and the earth. That means that *theos* in v. 2 must be understood to refer to that same God as well.

11. The argument is found in a detailed, rather extensive attack on the doctrine of the Trinity: *Should You Believe in the Trinity?*, by anonymous (Brooklyn, NY: Watchtower Bible and Tract Society, 1989). This group apparently deems this booklet a significant statement of their position, for page 2 states, "First printing in English: 5,000,000 copies." The booklet first advances the traditional argument that John 1:1 should be translated "a god" because of the absence on the definite article (p. 27). But then it later acknowledges that Colwell's rule is relevant for John 1:1 (p. 28) and there admits that the context, not the absence of the definite article, determines whether we should translate "the Word was God" (definite) or "the Word was a god" (indefinite). Then it argues as follows: "when the context requires it, translators may insert an indefinite article in front of the noun in this type of sentence structure. Does the context require an indefinite article at John 1:1? Yes, for the testimony of the entire Bible is that Jesus is not Almighty God" (p. 28).

We should note carefully the weakness of this argument: They admit that context is decisive, but then they quote not one shred of evidence from the context of John 1:1. Rather, they simply assert again their conclusion about "the entire Bible." If they agree that this context is decisive, but they can find nothing in this context that supports their view, they have simply lost the argument. Therefore, having acknowledged Colwell's rule, they still hold their view on John 1:1, but with no supporting evidence. To hold a view with no evidence to support it is simply irrationality.

The booklet as a whole will give an appearance of scholarly work to laypersons, since it quotes dozens of theologians and academic reference works (always without adequate documentation). However, many quotations are taken out of context and made to say something the authors never intended, and others are from liberal Catholic or Protestant scholars who themselves are questioning both the doctrine of the Trinity and the truthfulness of the Bible.

Now Jesus did many other signs in the presence of the disciples, which are not written in this book; but these are written so that you may believe that Jesus is the Christ, the Son of God, and that by believing you may have life in his name. (John 20:30–31)

Jesus speaks of those who will not see him and will yet believe, and John immediately tells the reader that he recorded the events written in his gospel in order that they may believe in just this way, imitating Thomas in his confession of faith. In other words, the entire gospel is written to persuade people to imitate Thomas, who sincerely called Jesus "My Lord and my God." Because this is set out by John as the purpose of his gospel, the sentence takes on added force.[12]

Other passages speaking of Jesus as fully divine include Hebrews 1:3, where the author says that Christ is the "exact imprint" (Gk. *charaktēr*, "exact duplicate") of the nature or being (Gk. *hypostasis*) of God—meaning that God the Son exactly duplicates the being or nature of God the Father in every way: whatever attributes or power God the Father has, God the Son has them as well. The author goes on to refer to the Son as "God" in verse 8 ("But of the Son he says, 'Your throne, O God, is forever and ever'"), and he attributes the creation of the heavens to Christ when he says of him, "You, Lord, laid the foundation of the earth in the beginning, and the heavens are the work of your hands" (Heb. 1:10, quoting Ps. 102:25). Titus 2:13 refers to "our great *God* and Savior Jesus Christ," and 2 Peter 1:1 speaks of "the righteousness of our *God* and Savior Jesus Christ."[13] Romans 9:5, speaking of the Jewish people, says, "To them belong the

---

12. The Jehovah's Witnesses' booklet *Should You Believe in the Trinity?* offers two explanations for John 20:28: (1) "To Thomas, Jesus was like 'a god,' especially in the miraculous circumstances that prompted his exclamation" (p. 29). But this explanation is unconvincing, because Thomas did not say, "You are like a god," but rather called Jesus "my God." The Greek text has the definite article (it cannot be translated "a god") and is explicit: *ho theos mou* is not "a god of mine" but "my God."

(2) The second explanation offered is that "Thomas may simply have made an emotional exclamation of astonishment, spoken to Jesus but directed to God" (ibid.). The second part of this sentence, "spoken to Jesus but directed to God," is simply incoherent: it seems to mean, "spoken to Jesus but not spoken to Jesus," which is not only self-contradictory, but also impossible: if Thomas is speaking to Jesus he is also directing his words to Jesus. The first part of this sentence, the claim that Thomas is really not calling Jesus "God," but is merely swearing or uttering some involuntary words of exclamation, is without merit, for the verse makes it clear that Thomas was not speaking into the blue but was speaking directly to Jesus: "Thomas answered and said *to Him*, 'My Lord and my God!'" (John 20:28 NASB). And immediately both Jesus and John in his writing commend Thomas, certainly not for swearing but for believing in Jesus as his Lord and his God.

13. Both Titus 2:13 and 2 Peter 1:1 have marginal readings in the RSV whereby Jesus is referred to as a different person than "God" and therefore is not called God: "the great God and our Savior Jesus Christ" (Titus 2:13 mg.) and "our God and the Savior Jesus Christ" (2 Peter 1:1 mg.). These alternative translations are possible grammatically but are unlikely. Both verses have the same Greek construction, in which one definite article governs two nouns joined by the Greek word for *and* (*kai*). In all cases where this construction is found the two nouns are viewed as unified in some way, and often they are two separate names for the same person or thing. Especially significant is 2 Peter 1:1, for exactly the same construction is used by Peter three other times in this book to speak of "Our Lord and Savior Jesus Christ" (2 Peter 1:11; 2:20; 3:18). In these three other verses, the Greek wording is exactly the same in every detail except that the word *Lord* (*kyrios*) is used instead of the word *God* (*theos*). If these other three instances are all translated "Our *Lord* and Savior Jesus Christ," as they are in all major translations, then consistency in translation would seem to require the translation of 2 Peter 1:1 as "Our *God* and Savior Jesus Christ," again referring to Christ as God. In Titus 2:13 Paul is writing about the hope of Christ's second coming, which the New Testament writers consistently speak of in terms that emphasize the manifestation of Jesus Christ in his glory, not in terms that emphasize the glory of the Father.

patriarchs, and from their race, according to the flesh, is the Christ, who is God over all, blessed forever. Amen."[14]

In the Old Testament, Isaiah 9:6 predicts,

> For to us a child is born,
>     to us a son is given;
> and the government shall be upon his shoulder,
>     and his name shall be called
> "Wonderful Counselor, Mighty God."

As this prophecy is applied to Christ, it refers to him as "Mighty God." Note the similar application of the titles "LORD" and "God" in the prophecy of the coming of the Messiah in Isaiah 40:3, "In the wilderness prepare the way of the LORD, make straight in the desert a highway for our God," quoted by John the Baptist in preparation for the coming of Christ in Matthew 3:3.

Many other passages will be discussed in chapter 26 below, but these should be sufficient to demonstrate that the New Testament clearly refers to Christ as fully God. As Paul says in Colossians 2:9, "In him the whole fullness of deity dwells bodily."

Next, *the Holy Spirit is also fully God*. Once we understand God the Father and God the Son to be fully God, then the Trinitarian expressions in verses like Matthew 28:19 ("baptizing them in the name of the Father and of the Son and of the Holy Spirit") assume significance for the doctrine of the Holy Spirit because they show that the Holy Spirit is classified on an equal level with the Father and the Son. This can be seen if we recognize how unthinkable it would have been for Jesus to say something like, "baptizing them in the name of the Father and of the Son and of the archangel Michael"—this would give to a created being a status entirely inappropriate even to an archangel. Believers throughout all ages can only be baptized into the name (and thus into a taking on of the character) of God himself.[15] (Note also the

---

14. The marginal reading in the NIV is similar to the reading in the main text of the RSV, which is, "and of their race, according to the flesh, is the Christ. God who is over all be blessed for ever. Amen" (Rom. 9:5 RSV). But this translation is far less likely on grammatical and contextual grounds and is justified primarily by arguing that Paul would not have referred to Christ as "God." The NIV translation, which refers to Christ as "God over all," is preferable because (1) Paul's normal pattern is to declare a word of blessing concerning the person about whom he has just been speaking, who in this case is Christ; (2) the Greek participle *ōn*, "being," which makes the phrase say literally, "who, being God over all is blessed forever," would be redundant if Paul were starting a new sentence as the RSV has it; (3) when Paul elsewhere begins a new sentence with a word

of blessing to God, the word "blessed" comes first in the Greek sentence (see 2 Cor. 1:3; Eph. 1:3; cf. Peter's pattern in 1 Peter 1:3), but here the expression does not follow that pattern, making the RSV translation unlikely. See Donald Guthrie, *New Testament Theology* (Leicester: Inter-Varsity Press, 1981), 339–40. For a definitive treatment of all the New Testament texts that refer to Jesus as "God," see Murray Harris, *Jesus as God* (Grand Rapids: Baker, 1992).

15. 1 Tim. 5:21 should not be seen as a counterexample to this claim, for there Paul is simply warning Timothy in the presence of a host of heavenly witnesses, both divine and angelic, who he knows are watching Timothy's conduct. This is similar to the mention of God and Christ and the angels of heaven and the "spirits of the righteous made perfect" in Heb. 12:22–24,

other Trinitarian passages mentioned above: 1 Cor. 12:4–6; 2 Cor. 13:14; Eph. 4:4–6; 1 Peter 1:2; Jude 20–21.)

In Acts 5:3–4, Peter asks Ananias, "Why has Satan filled your heart to lie to the Holy Spirit . . . ? You have not lied to man but *to God.*" According to Peter's words, to lie to the Holy Spirit is to lie to God. Paul says in 1 Corinthians 3:16, "Do you not know that you are God's temple and that God's Spirit dwells in you?" God's temple is the place where God himself dwells, which Paul explains by the fact that "God's Spirit" dwells in it, thus apparently equating God's Spirit with God himself.

David asks in Psalm 139:7–8, "Where shall I go from your Spirit? Or where shall I flee from your presence? If I ascend to heaven, you are there!" This passage attributes the divine characteristic of omnipresence to the Holy Spirit, something that is not true of any of God's creatures. It seems that David is equating God's Spirit with God's presence. To go from God's Spirit is to go from his presence, but if there is nowhere that David can flee from God's Spirit, then he knows that wherever he goes he will have to say, "You are there."

Paul attributes the divine characteristic of omniscience to the Holy Spirit in 1 Corinthians 2:10–11: "For the Spirit searches everything, even the depths of God. For who knows a person's thoughts except the spirit of that person, which is in him? So also no one comprehends the thoughts of God [Gk. literally 'the things of God'] except the Spirit of God."

Moreover, the activity of giving new birth to everyone who is born again is the work of the Holy Spirit. Jesus said, "unless one is born of water and the Spirit, he cannot enter the kingdom of God. That which is born of the flesh is flesh, and that which is born of the Spirit is spirit. Do not marvel that I said to you, 'You must be born again'" (John 3:5–7). But the work of giving new spiritual life to people when they become Christians is something that only God can do (cf. 1 John 3:9, "born of God"). This passage therefore gives another indication that the Holy Spirit is fully God.

Up to this point we have two conclusions, both abundantly taught throughout Scripture:

1. God is three persons.
2. Each person is fully God.

If the Bible taught only these two facts, there would be no logical problem at all in fitting them together, for the obvious solution would be that there are three Gods. The Father is fully God, the Son is fully God, and the Holy Spirit is fully God. We would have a system where there are three equally divine beings. Such a system of belief would

---

where a great heavenly assembly is mentioned. 1 Tim. 5:21 should therefore be seen as significantly different from the Trinitarian passages mentioned above, since those passages speak of uniquely divine activities, such as distributing gifts to every Christian (1 Cor. 12:4–6) or having the name into which all believers are baptized (Matt. 28:19).

be called "polytheism"—or more specifically "tritheism," belief in three Gods. But that is far from what the Bible teaches.

## 3. There Is One God

Scripture is abundantly clear that there is one and only one God. Not only are the three different persons of the Trinity one in purpose and in agreement on what they think, but they are also one in essence, one in their essential nature. In other words, God is only one being. There are not three Gods. There is only one God.

One of the most familiar passages of the Old Testament is Deuteronomy 6:4–5: "Hear, O Israel: The LORD our God, the LORD is one. You shall love the LORD your God with all your heart and with all your soul and with all your might."

When Moses sings,

> Who is like you, O LORD, among the gods?
> > Who is like you, majestic in holiness,
> > Awesome in glorious deeds, doing wonders? (Ex. 15:11)

the answer obviously is "No one." God is unique. There is no one like him and there can be no one like him. In fact, Solomon prays "that all the peoples of the earth may know that the LORD is God; there is no other" (1 Kings 8:60).

When God speaks, he repeatedly makes it clear that he is the only true God; the idea that there are three Gods to be worshiped rather than one would be unthinkable in the light of these extremely strong statements. God alone is the one true God and there is no one like him. When he speaks, he alone is speaking—he is not speaking as one God among three who are to be worshiped. He says,

> I am the LORD, and there is no other,
> > besides me there is no God;
> > I equip you, though you do not know me,
> that people may know, from the rising of the sun
> > and from the west, that there is none besides me;
> > I am the LORD, and there is no other. (Isa. 45:5–6)

Similarly, he calls everyone on earth to turn to him:

> And there is no other god besides me,
> a righteous God and a Savior;
> > there is none besides me.
> Turn to me and be saved,

all the ends of the earth!
For I am God, and there is no other. (Isa. 45:21–22; cf. 44:6–8)

The New Testament also affirms that there is one God. Paul writes, "For *there is one God*, and there is one mediator between God and men, the man Christ Jesus" (1 Tim. 2:5). Paul affirms that "God is one" (Rom. 3:30) and that "there is one God, the Father, from whom are all things and for whom we exist" (1 Cor. 8:6).[16] Finally, James acknowledges that even demons recognize that there is one God, even though their intellectual assent to that fact is not enough to save them: "You believe that God is one; you do well. Even the demons believe—and shudder!" (James 2:19). But clearly James affirms that one "does well" to believe that "God is one."

## 4. All Analogies Have Shortcomings

Sometimes people have used several analogies drawn from nature or human experience to attempt to explain this doctrine. Although these analogies are helpful at an elementary level of understanding, they all turn out to be inadequate or misleading on further reflection. To say, for example, that God is like a three-leaf clover, which has three parts yet remains one clover, fails because each leaf is only part of the clover, and any one leaf cannot be said to be the whole clover. But in the Trinity, each of the persons is not just a separate part of God, each person is fully God. Moreover, the leaf of a clover is impersonal and does not have distinct and complex personality in the way each person of the Trinity does.

Others have used the analogy of a tree with three parts: the roots, trunk, and branches all constitute one tree. But a similar problem arises, for these are only parts of a tree, and none of the parts can be said to be the whole tree. Moreover, in this analogy the parts have different properties, unlike the persons of the Trinity, all of whom possess all of the attributes of God in equal measure. And the lack of personality in each part is a deficiency as well.

The analogy of the three forms of water (steam, water, and ice) is also inadequate because (a) no single molecule of water is ever all three of these at the same time,[17] (b) they have different properties or characteristics, (c) the analogy has nothing that corresponds to the fact that there is only one God (there is no such thing as "one water" or "all the water in the universe"), and (d) the element of intelligent personality is lacking.

Other analogies have been drawn from human experience. It might be said that the Trinity is something like a man who is both a farmer, the mayor of his town, and

---

16. 1 Cor. 8:6 does not deny that God the Son and God the Holy Spirit are also "God," but here Paul says that God the Father is identified as this "one God." Elsewhere, as we have seen, he can speak of God the Son and God the Holy Spirit as also "God." Moreover, in this same verse, he goes on to speak of "one Lord, Jesus Christ, through whom are all things and through whom we exist." He is here using the word *Lord* in its full Old Testament sense of "Yahweh" as a name for God, and saying that this is the person through whom all things were created, thus affirming the full deity of Christ as well, but with a different name. Thus this verse affirms both the unity of God and the diversity of persons in God.

17. There is a certain atmospheric condition (called the "triple point" by chemists) at which steam, liquid water, and ice can all exist simultaneously, but even then the molecules of water that are steam are not ice or liquid; the molecules that are liquid are not steam or ice, etc.

an elder in his church. He functions in different roles at different times, but he is one man. However, this analogy is very deficient because there is only one person doing these three activities at different times, and the analogy cannot deal with the personal interaction among the members of the Trinity. (In fact, this analogy simply teaches the heresy called modalism, discussed below.)

Another analogy taken from human life is the union of the intellect, the emotions, and the will in one human person. While these are parts of a personality, however, no one factor constitutes the entire person. And the parts are not identical in characteristics but have different abilities.

So what analogy shall we use to teach the Trinity? Although the Bible uses many analogies from nature and life to teach us various aspects of God's character (God is like a rock in his faithfulness, he is like a shepherd in his care, etc.), it is interesting that Scripture nowhere uses any analogies to teach the doctrine of the Trinity. The closest we come to an analogy is found in the titles "Father" and "Son" themselves, titles that clearly speak of distinct persons and of the close relationship that exists between them in a human family. But on the human level, of course, we have two entirely separate human beings, not one being comprised of three distinct persons. It is best to conclude that no analogy adequately teaches about the Trinity, and, on deeper reflection, we see that all are ultimately misleading in significant ways.

## 5. God Eternally and Necessarily Exists as the Trinity

When the universe was created God the Father spoke the powerful creative words that brought it into being, God the Son was the divine agent who carried out these words (John 1:3; 1 Cor. 8:6; Col. 1:16; Heb. 1:2), and God the Holy Spirit was active "hovering over the face of the waters" (Gen. 1:2). So it is as we would expect: if all three members of the Trinity are equally and fully divine, then they have all three existed for all eternity, and God has eternally existed as a Trinity (cf. also John 17:5, 24). Moreover, God cannot be other than he is, for he is unchanging (see chapter 11 above). Therefore, it seems right to conclude that God necessarily exists as a Trinity—he cannot be other than he is.

## C. ERRORS HAVE COME BY DENYING ANY ONE OF THE THREE STATEMENTS SUMMARIZING THE BIBLICAL TEACHING

In the previous section we saw how the Bible requires that we affirm the following three statements:

1. God is three persons.
2. Each person is fully God.
3. There is one God.

Before we discuss further the differences between the Father, Son, and Holy Spirit and the way they relate to one another, it is important that we recall some of the doctrinal errors about the Trinity that have been made in the history of the church. In this historical survey we will see some of the mistakes that we ourselves should avoid in any further thinking about this doctrine. In fact, the major Trinitarian errors that have arisen have come through a denial of one or another of these three primary statements.[18]

## 1. Modalism (or Sabellianism) Claims That There Is One Person Who Appears to Us in Three Different Forms (or "Modes")

At various times people have taught that God is not really three distinct persons but only one person who appears in different "modes" at different times. For example, in the Old Testament God appeared as "Father." Throughout the Gospels, this same divine person appeared as "the Son" as seen in the human life and ministry of Jesus. After Pentecost, this same person then revealed himself as the "Spirit" active in the church.

This teaching is also referred to by two other names. Sometimes it is called Sabellianism, after a teacher named Sabellius who lived in Rome in the early third century AD. Another term for modalism is "modalistic monarchianism" because this teaching says not only that God revealed himself in different "modes" but also that there is only one supreme ruler ("monarch") in the universe, God himself, who consists of only one person.

Modalism gains its attractiveness from the desire to emphasize clearly the fact that there is only one God. It may claim support not only from the passages talking about one God but also from passages such as John 10:30 ("I and the Father are one") and John 14:9 ("Whoever has seen me has seen the Father"). However, the last passage can simply mean that Jesus fully reveals the character of God the Father, and the former passage (John 10:30), in a context in which Jesus affirms that he will accomplish all that the Father has given him to do and save all whom the Father has given to him, seems to mean that Jesus and the Father are one in purpose (though it may also imply oneness of essence).

As with many other doctrinal errors, modalism is an attempt to make the Trinity easy to understand. Modalism makes God similar to a human being who plays different roles at different times, such as a man (for example) who sometimes works as a *farmer*, at other times acts as a *mayor* of his own town, and at other times serves as an *elder* in his church. The *same person* is a farmer, a mayor, and an elder. And if we say God is one person with different roles like that, there is no mystery in the Trinity, nothing difficult to understand.

The fatal shortcoming of modalism is the fact that it must deny that the three persons of the Trinity are *distinct individuals*, and it must deny the interpersonal relationships within the Trinity that appear frequently in Scripture (or it must affirm that these

---

18. An excellent discussion of the history and theological implications of the Trinitarian heresies discussed in this section is found in Harold O. J. Brown, *Heresies: The Image of Christ* in the *Mirror of Heresy and Orthodoxy from the Apostles to the Present* (Garden City, NY: Doubleday, 1984), 95–157.

were simply an illusion and not real). Thus it must deny three separate persons at the baptism of Jesus, when the Father speaks from heaven, the Son is being baptized, and the Spirit descends on Jesus like a dove (Matt. 3:16–17). And modalism must say that all those instances where Jesus is praying to the Father (Matt. 11:25; 26:39; John 11:41–42; 12:28; 14:16) are an illusion or a charade. The idea of the Son or the Holy Spirit interceding for us before God the Father (Rom. 8:26–27, 34) is lost. Finally, modalism ultimately loses the heart of the doctrine of the atonement—that is, the idea that God sent his Son (John 3:16) as a substitutionary sacrifice, that the Son bore the wrath of God in our place, and that the Father, representing the interests of the Trinity, saw the suffering of Christ and was satisfied (Isa. 53:11; Rom. 3:25).

Moreover, modalism denies the independence of God, for if God is only one person, then he has no ability to love and to communicate without other persons in his creation. Therefore it was necessary for God to create the world, and God would no longer be independent of creation (see chapter 12, above, on God's independence). It is no wonder that modalism has been decisively rejected throughout the history of the Christian church.

One present denomination within Protestantism (broadly defined), the United Pentecostal Church, is modalistic in its doctrinal position.[19]

## 2. Arianism and Other Ancient Heresies Deny the Full Deity of the Son and the Holy Spirit

### a. The Arian Controversy

The term *Arianism* is derived from Arius (d. 336), a presbyter (elder) of the church in Alexandria whose views were condemned at the Council of Nicaea in AD 325. Arius taught that God the Son was at one point *created by God the Father*, and that before that time the Son did not exist, nor did the Holy Spirit, but the Father only. Thus, though the Son is a heavenly being who existed before the rest of creation and who is far greater than all the rest of creation, he is still not equal to the Father in all his attributes—he may even be said to be "like the Father" or "similar to the Father" in his nature, but he cannot be said to be "of the same nature" as the Father, according to Arian teaching.

**1. Scripture Verses Used by Arians.** The Arians depended heavily on texts that called Christ God's *"only begotten"* Son (see John 1:14; 3:16, 18; 1 John 4:9 in NASB, NKJV, or KJV).[20] If Christ were "begotten" by God the Father, they reasoned, it must mean that he was brought into existence by God the Father (for the word *beget* in ordinary human experience refers to the father's role in conceiving a child). Further support

---

19. Some of the leaders who formed this group had earlier been forced out of the Assemblies of God when the Assemblies decided to insist on a Trinitarian statement of faith for its ministers in 1916. The United Pentecostal Church is sometimes identified with the slogan "Jesus only," and it insists that people should be baptized in the name of Jesus, not in the name of the Father, Son, and Holy Spirit. Because of its denial of the three distinct persons in God, the denomination should not be considered to be evangelical.

20. For a discussion of the Greek term *monogenēs*, which these translations render as "only begotten" but other translations render as "only" or "one and only," see pp. 293–98.

for the Arian view was found in Colossians 1:15, "He is the image of the invisible God, *the firstborn of all creation*." Does not *firstborn* here imply that the Son was at some point brought into existence by the Father? And if this is true of the Son, it must necessarily be true of the Holy Spirit as well.

Proverbs 8:22 was also used by the Arians. One possible way to translate the verse is, "The LORD *created me* at the beginning of his work, the first of his acts of old" (Prov. 8:22 RSV). Arians claimed that "Wisdom," who was speaking in this chapter, was in fact the Son of God, and verse 22 taught that he was "created." The Septuagint (which was for the ancient church their commonly used Greek translation of the Old Testament) helped the Arians, for it explicitly said, "The LORD *created me*" (Gk. *kyrios ektisen me*, using the verb *ktizō*, "create").[21]

**2. Answers to Arian Interpretations.** In response to Arianism, church leaders who defended the full deity of the Son concluded that whatever "only begotten" means in John 3:16 and elsewhere, it cannot mean "created" but must refer to something in the eternal relationship between the Father and the Son. This view found expression in the Nicene Creed in the words, "the only-begotten Son of God, begotten of the Father *before all ages . . .* begotten, *not made*" (see discussion below).

Colossians 1:15, which calls Christ "the firstborn of all creation," is better understood to mean that Christ has the rights or privileges of the "firstborn"—that is, according to biblical usage and custom, the right of leadership or authority in the family for one's generation. (Note Heb. 12:16 where Esau is said to have sold his "firstborn status" or "birthright"—the Greek word *prototokia* is cognate to the term *prototokos*, "firstborn" in Col. 1:15.) So Colossians 1:15 means that Christ has the privileges of authority and rule, the privileges belonging to the "firstborn," but with respect to the whole creation. The NIV makes this sense explicit: "the firstborn *over all creation*" (also the NKJV, NLT, and NET).

Proverbs 8:22 is best understood not to be speaking about the Son of God but about Wisdom, personified as a woman calling out in the street for people to follow her: "To you, O men, I call. . . . O simple ones, learn prudence" (Prov. 8:4–5). Wisdom in Proverbs 8:1–9:12 is set in contrast to "Folly," also personified as a woman calling out in the streets in Proverbs 9:13–18: "The woman Folly is loud; she is seductive and knows nothing. She sits at the door of her house . . . calling to those who pass by . . . 'Whoever is

---

21. The Jehovah's Witnesses, who are modern-day Arians, also point to Rev. 3:14, where Jesus calls himself "the *beginning* of God's creation," and take it to mean that "Jesus was created by God as the beginning of God's invisible creations" (anonymous, *Should You Believe in the Trinity?* [Brooklyn, NY: Watch Tower Bible and Tract Society, 1989], 14). But this verse does not mean that Jesus was the first being that God created but rather that Christ was the origin or first cause of God's creation, as it says in Col. 1:16, "by him all things were created."

Significantly, in that same context (Col. 1:18), Christ is also called "the beginning," using the same Greek term (Gk. *archē*) as in Rev. 3:14. The Jewish historian Josephus uses this same word to call God the "beginning (*archē*)" of "all things," but certainly he does not think that God himself was created; see *Against Apion* 2.190.

Another possibility is that in Rev. 3:14 the word *archē* means "ruler" (so NIV; see BDAG, 138, meaning 6; see the same meaning in Luke 12:11; Titus 3:1).

simple, let him turn in here!'" (9:13–16). So 8:22 is speaking about Wisdom, not about the Son of God.[22]

**3. The Nicene Creed.** As I mentioned above, the texts that say that Christ was God's "only begotten Son" were understood by early church leaders to refer to an eternal relationship between the Father and the Son. But the many texts affirming Christ's deity were so strong that the early church concluded that whatever "only begotten" meant, it did not mean "created." Therefore, the Nicene Creed in AD 325 affirmed that Christ was "begotten, not made":

> We believe in one God, the Father Almighty, Maker of all things visible and invisible. And in one Lord Jesus Christ, the Son of God, begotten of the Father, the only-begotten; that is, of the essence of the Father, God of God, Light of Light, very God of very God, *begotten, not made*, being of one substance (*homoousion*) with the Father.[23]

This same phrase was reaffirmed at the Council of Constantinople in 381. In addition, the phrase "before all ages" was added after "begotten of the Father," to show that this begetting was eternal. This begetting never began to happen but has been true of the relationship between the Father and the Son eternally. However, the nature of begetting has never been defined very clearly, other than to say that it has to do with the relationship between the Father and the Son, and that in some sense the Father has eternally had a primacy in that relationship.[24]

In further repudiation of the teaching of Arius, the Nicene Creed insisted that Christ was "of the *same substance* (or same nature) as the Father." The dispute with Arius concerned two words that have become famous in the history of Christian doctrine, *homoousios* ("of the same nature") and *homoiousios* ("of a similar nature").[25] The difference depends on the different meaning of two Greek prefixes, *homo-*, meaning "same," and *homoi-*, meaning "similar." Arius was happy to say that Christ was a supernatural heavenly being, that he was created by God before the creation of the rest of the universe, and even that he was "similar" to God in his nature. Arius would agree to the word *homoiousios*.

But the Council of Nicaea in 325 and the Council of Constantinople in 381 realized

---

22. In addition, I do not think Prov. 8:22 should be understood to mean that the Lord "created" wisdom, but rather that he "possessed" it: "The LORD possessed me at the beginning of his work, the first of his acts of old" (Prov. 8:22 ESV; NASB, KJV, NKJV also have "possessed"). The meaning is that the Lord took possession of wisdom and began to work with wisdom as he created. The Hebrew word that commonly means "create" (*bārā'*) is not used in verse 22; rather the word is *qānāh*, which occurs eighty-four times in the Old Testament and almost always means "to get, acquire." (Note this sense of the word in Gen. 39:1; Ex. 21:2; Prov. 4:5, 7; 23:23; Eccl. 2:7; Isa. 1:3 ["owner"].)

23. This is the original form of the Nicene Creed, but it was later modified at the Council of Constantinople in 381 and there took the form that is commonly called the "Nicene Creed" by churches today. This text is taken from Philip Schaff, *Creeds of Christendom*, 3 vols. (1931; repr., Grand Rapids: Baker, 1983), 1:28–29.

24. See the further discussion of "only begotten" (Gk. *monogenēs*) at pp. 293–98.

25. Older translations of *homoousios* sometimes use the term *consubstantial*, an uncommon English word simply meaning "of the same substance or nature."

that this did not go far enough, for if Christ is not of exactly the *same nature* as the Father, then he is not fully God. So both councils insisted that orthodox Christians confess Jesus to be *homoousios*, of the *same* nature as God the Father. The difference between the two words was only one letter, the Greek letter iota, and some have criticized the church for allowing a doctrinal dispute over a single letter (!) to consume so much attention for most of the fourth century AD. Some have wondered, "Could anything be more foolish than arguing over a single letter in a word?" But the difference between the two words was profound, and the presence or absence of the iota really did mark the difference between biblical Christianity, with a true doctrine of the Trinity, and a heresy that did not accept the full deity of Christ and therefore was non-Trinitarian and ultimately destructive to the whole Christian faith.

### b. Subordinationism

In affirming that the Son was of the *same nature* as the Father, the early church also excluded a related false doctrine, subordinationism. While Arianism held that the Son was created and was not divine, subordinationism held that the Son was eternal (not created) and divine but still not equal to the Father in being or attributes—the Son was inferior or "subordinate" in being and attributes to God the Father.[26] The early church father Origen (c. 185–c. AD 254) advocated a form of subordinationism by holding that the Son was inferior to the Father in being and that the Son eternally derives his being from the Father. Origen was attempting to protect the distinction of persons and was writing before the doctrine of the Trinity was clearly formulated in the church. The rest of the church did not follow him but clearly rejected his teaching at the Council of Nicaea.

Although many early church leaders contributed to the gradual formulation of a correct doctrine of the Trinity, the most influential by far was Athanasius. He was only twenty-nine years old when he came to the Council of Nicaea in AD 325, not as an official member but as secretary to Alexander, the Bishop of Alexandria. Yet his keen mind and writing ability allowed him to have an important influence on the outcome of the Council, and he himself became Bishop of Alexandria in 328. Though the Arians had been condemned at Nicaea, they refused to stop teaching their views and used their considerable political power throughout the church to prolong the controversy for most of the rest of the fourth century. Athanasius became the focal point of Arian attack, and he devoted his entire life to writing and teaching against the Arian heresy. "He was hounded through five exiles embracing seventeen years of flight and hiding," but, by his untiring efforts, "almost single-handedly Athanasius saved the Church from pagan intellectualism."[27] The "Athanasian Creed" that bears his name is not today thought to stem from Athanasius himself, but it is a very clear affirmation of Trinitarian doctrine

---

26. The heresy of subordination*ism*, which holds that the Son is inferior in being to the Father, should be clearly distinguished from the orthodox doctrine that the Son is subordinate to the Father in role or function. (See section D below on the differences between the Father, Son, and Holy Spirit.)

27. S. J. Mikolaski, "Athanasius," *NIDCC*, 81.

that gained increasing use in the church from about AD 400 onward and is still used in Protestant and Catholic churches today. (See appendix 1.)

### c. Adoptionism

Before we leave the discussion of Arianism, one related false teaching needs to be mentioned. "Adoptionism" is the view that Jesus lived as an ordinary man until his baptism, but then God "adopted" Jesus as his "Son" and conferred on him supernatural powers. Adoptionists would not hold that Christ existed before he was born as a man; therefore, they would not think of Christ as eternal, nor would they think of him as the exalted, supernatural being created by God that the Arians held him to be. Even after Jesus' "adoption" as the "Son" of God, they would not think of him as divine in nature, but only as an exalted man whom God called his "Son" in a unique sense.

Adoptionism never gained the force of a movement in the way Arianism did, but there were people who held adoptionist views from time to time in the early church, though their views were never accepted as orthodox. Many modern people who think of Jesus as a great man and someone especially empowered by God but not really divine would fall into the adoptionist category. We have placed it here in relation to Arianism because it too denies the deity of the Son (and similarly the deity of the Holy Spirit).

The controversy over Arianism was drawn to a close by the Council of Constantinople in AD 381. This council reaffirmed the Nicene statements and added a statement on the deity of the Holy Spirit, which had come under attack in the period since Nicaea. After the phrase, "And in the Holy Spirit," Constantinople added, "the Lord and Giver of Life; who proceeds from the Father; who with the Father and the Son together is worshiped and glorified; who spake by the Prophets." The version of the creed that includes the additions at Constantinople is what is commonly known as the Nicene Creed today. (See pp. 1438–39 for the text of the Nicene Creed.)

### d. The Filioque Clause

In connection with the Nicene Creed, one unfortunate chapter in the history of the church should be briefly noted, namely the controversy over the insertion of the *filioque* clause into the Nicene Creed, an insertion that eventually led to the split between Western (Roman Catholic) Christianity and Eastern Christianity (consisting today of various branches of eastern orthodox Christianity, such as the Greek Orthodox Church, the Russian Orthodox Church, etc.) in AD 1054.

The word *filioque* is a Latin term that means "and from the Son." It was not included in the Nicene Creed in either the first version of AD 325 or the second version of AD 381. Those versions simply said that the Holy Spirit "proceeds from the Father." But in AD 589, at a regional church council in Toledo (in what is now Spain), the phrase "and the Son" was added, so that the creed then said that the Holy Spirit "proceeds from the Father *and the Son (filioque)*." In the light of John 15:26 and 16:7, where Jesus said that he would send the Holy Spirit into the world, it seems there could be no objection to such a statement if it referred to the Holy Spirit proceeding from the Father and the Son at a point in time (particularly at Pentecost). But this was a statement about the nature of the Trinity, and the phrase was understood to speak of the *eternal* relationship between the Holy Spirit and the Son, something Scripture never explicitly discusses.[28] The form of the Nicene Creed that had this additional phrase gradually gained in general use and received an official endorsement in AD 1017. The entire controversy was complicated by ecclesiastical politics and struggles for power, and this apparently very insignificant doctrinal point was the main doctrinal issue in the split between Eastern and Western Christianity in AD 1054. (The underlying political issue, however, was the relation of the Eastern church to the authority of the Pope.) The doctrinal controversy and the split between the two branches of Christianity have not been resolved to this day.

Is there a correct position on this question? The weight of evidence (slim though it is) seems clearly to favor the Western church. In spite of the fact that John 15:26 says that the Spirit of truth "proceeds from the Father," this does not deny that he proceeds also from the Son (just as John 14:26 says that the Father will send the Holy Spirit, but John 16:7 says that the Son will send the Holy Spirit). In fact, in the same sentence in John 15:26 Jesus speaks of the Holy Spirit as one "whom I shall send to you from the Father." And if the Son together with the Father sends the Spirit into the world, by analogy it would seem appropriate to say that this reflects an *eternal* ordering of their relationships. This is not something that we can clearly insist on based on any specific verse, but much of our understanding of the *eternal* relationships among the Father, Son, and Holy Spirit comes by analogy from what Scripture tells us about the way they relate to the creation *in time*.

Moreover, the Eastern formulation (without the addition of *filioque*) runs the danger of suggesting an unnatural distance between the Son and the Holy Spirit, leading to the possibility that even in personal worship an emphasis on more mystical, Spirit-inspired experience might be pursued to the neglect of an accompanying rationally understandable adoration of Christ as Lord. Nevertheless, the controversy was ultimately over such an obscure point of doctrine (essentially, the relationship between the Son and Spirit before creation) that it certainly did not warrant division in the church. In reality, the controversy was probably due more to underlying differences about church government (especially the power of the Pope), with the *filioque* clause as more of a pretext for the division than the real reason for it.

## 3. Tritheism Denies That There Is Only One God

A final possible way to attempt an easy reconciliation of the biblical teaching about the Trinity would be to deny that there is only one God. The result is to say that God is

28. The word *proceeds* was not understood to refer to a creating of the Holy Spirit or any deriving of his being from the Father and Son but instead to indicate the way the Holy Spirit eternally relates to the Father and Son.

three persons and each person is fully God. Therefore, there are three Gods. Technically this view would be called "tritheism."

Few persons have held this view in the history of the church. It has similarities to many ancient pagan religions that held to a multiplicity of gods. This view would result in confusion in the minds of believers. There would be no absolute worship or loyalty or devotion to one true God. We would wonder to which God we should give our ultimate allegiance. And at a deeper level, this view would destroy any sense of ultimate unity in the universe: even in the very being of God there would be plurality but no unity.

Although no modern groups advocate tritheism, perhaps many evangelicals today unintentionally tend toward tritheistic views of the Trinity, recognizing the distinct personhood of the Father, the Son, and the Holy Spirit, but seldom being aware of the unity of God as one undivided being.

## 4. The Importance of the Doctrine of the Trinity

Why was the church so concerned about the doctrine of the Trinity? Is it really essential to hold to the full deity of the Son and the Holy Spirit? Yes it is, for this teaching has implications for the very heart of the Christian faith. First, the atonement is at stake. If Jesus is merely a created being and not fully God, then it is hard to see how he, a creature, could bear the full wrath of God against all of our sins. Could any creature, no matter how great, really save us? Second, justification by faith alone is threatened if we deny the full deity of the Son. (This is seen today in the teaching of the Jehovah's Witnesses, who do not believe in justification by faith alone.) If Jesus is not fully God, we would rightly doubt whether we can really trust him to save us completely. Could we really depend fully on any *creature* for our salvation?

Third, if Jesus is not infinite God, should we pray to him or worship him? Who but an infinite, omniscient God could hear and respond to all the prayers of all God's people? And who but God himself is worthy of worship? Indeed, if Jesus is merely a creature, no matter how great, it would be idolatry to worship him—yet the New Testament commands us to do so (Phil. 2:9–11; Rev. 5:12–14). Fourth, if someone teaches that Christ was a created being but nonetheless one who saved us, then this teaching wrongly begins to attribute credit for salvation to a creature and not to God himself. But this wrongfully exalts the creature rather than the Creator, something Scripture never allows us to do. Fifth, the independence and personal nature of God are at stake: If there is no Trinity, then there were no interpersonal relationships within the being of God before creation, and without personal relationships, it is difficult to see how God could be genuinely personal or be without the need for a creation to relate to. Sixth, the unity of the universe is at stake: if there is not perfect plurality and perfect unity in God himself, then we have no basis for thinking there can be any ultimate unity among the diverse elements of the universe either. Clearly, in the doctrine of the Trinity, the heart of the Christian faith is at stake. Herman Bavinck says that "Athanasius understood better than any of his contemporaries that Christianity stands or falls with the confession of the deity of Christ and of the Trinity."[29] He adds, "In the confession of the Trinity throbs the heart of the Christian religion: every error results from, or upon deeper reflection may be traced to, a wrong view of this doctrine."[30]

## D. What Are the Distinctions between the Father, the Son, and the Holy Spirit?

After completing this survey of errors concerning the Trinity, we may now go on to ask if anything more can be said about the distinctions between the Father, Son, and Holy Spirit. If we say that each member of the Trinity is fully God, and that each person fully shares in all the attributes of God, then *is there any difference at all among the persons?* We cannot say, for example, that the Father is more powerful or wiser than the Son, that the Father and Son are wiser than the Holy Spirit, or that the Father existed before the Son and Holy Spirit existed, for to say anything like that would be to deny the full deity of all three members of the Trinity. But what then are the distinctions between the persons?

### 1. The Persons of the Trinity Have Different Primary Functions in Relating to the World

When Scripture discusses the way in which God relates to the world, both in creation and in redemption, the persons of the Trinity are said to have different functions or primary activities. Sometimes this has been called the "economy of the Trinity," using *economy* in an old sense meaning "ordering of activities." (In this sense, people used to speak of the "economy of a household" or "home economics," meaning not just the financial affairs of a household but all of the "ordering of activities" within the household.) The "economy of the Trinity" means the different ways the three persons act as they relate to the world and (as we shall see in the next section) to each other for all eternity.

We see these different functions in the work of creation. God the Father spoke the creative words to bring the universe into being. But it was God the Son, the eternal Word of God, who carried out these creative decrees. "All things were made through him, and without him was not any thing made that was made" (John 1:3). Moreover, "By him all things were created, in heaven and on earth, visible and invisible, whether thrones or dominions or rulers or authorities—all things were created through him and for him" (Col. 1:16; see also Ps. 33:6, 9; 1 Cor. 8:6; Heb. 1:2). The Holy Spirit was active as well in a different way, in "moving" or "hovering" over the face of the waters (Gen. 1:2), apparently sustaining and manifesting God's immediate presence in his creation (cf. Ps. 33:6, where "breath" should perhaps be translated "Spirit"; see also Ps. 139:7).

---

29. Herman Bavinck, *The Doctrine of God*, trans. and ed. William Hendriksen (Grand Rapids: Eerdmans, 1951), 281.

30. Ibid., 285.

In the work of redemption there are also distinct functions. God the Father planned redemption and sent his Son into the world (John 3:16; Gal. 4:4; Eph. 1:9–10). The Son obeyed the Father and accomplished redemption for us (John 6:38; Heb. 10:5–7, et al.). God the Father did not come and die for our sins, nor did God the Holy Spirit. That was the particular work of the Son. Then, after Jesus ascended back into heaven, the Holy Spirit was sent by the Father and the Son to apply redemption to us. Jesus speaks of "the Holy Spirit, whom the Father will send in my name" (John 14:26), but Jesus also says that he himself will send the Holy Spirit, for he says, "If I go, I will send him to you" (John 16:7), and he speaks of a time "when the Helper comes, whom I will send to you from the Father, the Spirit of truth" (John 15:26). It is especially the role of the Holy Spirit to give us regeneration or new spiritual life (John 3:5–8), to sanctify us (Rom. 8:13; 15:16; 1 Peter 1:2), and to empower us for service (Acts 1:8; 1 Cor. 12:7–11). In general, the work of the Holy Spirit seems to be to bring to completion the work that has been planned by God the Father and begun by God the Son. (See chapter 30, on the work of the Holy Spirit.)

So we may say that the role of the Father in creation and redemption has been to plan and direct and send the Son and Holy Spirit. This is not surprising, for it shows that the Father and the Son relate to one another as a father and son relate to one another in a human family: the father directs and has authority over the son, and the son obeys and is responsive to the directions of the father. The Holy Spirit is obedient to the directives of both the Father and the Son.

Thus, while the persons of the Trinity are equal in all their attributes, they nonetheless differ in their relationships to the creation. The Son and Holy Spirit are completely equal in deity to God the Father, but they are subordinate in their roles.

Moreover, these differences in role are not temporary but will last forever: Paul tells us that even after the final judgment, when the "last enemy," that is, death, is destroyed and when all things are put under Christ's feet, "then the Son himself will also be subjected to him who put all things in subjection under him, that God may be all in all" (1 Cor. 15:28).

## 2. The Meaning of *Monogenēs*: Is Jesus God's "Only Begotten" Son?

In John 3:16, Jesus is said to be God's "only begotten Son" in three Bible translations: "For God so loved the world, that He gave His *only begotten Son*, that whoever believes in Him shall not perish, but have eternal life" (John 3:16 NASB; KJV and NKJV also have "only begotten").

But most modern translations do not say "only begotten Son." All of the other widely used English translations simply say "only Son" or "one and only Son," with no notion of begetting: "For God so loved the world, that he gave his *only Son*, that whoever believes in him should not perish but have eternal life" (John 3:16 ESV; similarly, RSV and NRSV, while CSB, NET, NIV, and NLT all have "one and only Son"). The difference in translation is due to different understandings of the underlying Greek word *monogenēs*, which refers to Christ here and in four other verses.[31] Historically, the word was understood to mean "only begotten," with *mono* meaning "only" and *genēs* as an adjective related to the verb *gennaō*, "to beget, to bear," a verb commonly used to refer to the father's (or less commonly the mother's) role in the birth of a child.

However, beginning in 1886, various New Testament scholars challenged the meaning "only begotten," arguing that the word carries no suggestion of "begetting" and that it should instead be understood to mean "only, unique, one of a kind." They argued that the second half of the word is not closely related to the verb *gennaō* ("beget," "bear"; spelled with two *n*'s) but rather to the term *genos* ("class," "kind"; spelled with one *n*). Thus the verse refers not to the "only begotten" Son but to the "one-of-a-kind" or "unique" Son.[32] These arguments have seemed persuasive to most Bible translation committees. I too adopted the translation "only" because it was favored by the Bauer-Danker-Arndt-Gingrich *Greek-English Lexicon*,[33] several translations, and a large majority of commentaries. I also added an appendix defending the translation "only" to the first edition of this book.[34] I recommended that it would be better not to speak of the "eternal begetting (or generation) of the Son."[35]

But then, in 2017, substantial new evidence came to light.[36] Charles Lee Irons published a significant essay, "A Lexical Defense of the Johannine 'Only Begotten.'"[37] Irons reported that he had found many hundreds of examples of *monogenēs* in the early church fathers who wrote in Greek. He then pointed to B. F. Westcott's 1886 commentary on the epistles of John as the earliest support for the meaning "unique" rather than "only begotten."[38] Westcott was followed by other publications, and eventually the meaning "only" appeared in these five verses in the RSV in 1946, and other Bible translations followed.

In response to the '"only, unique" view, Irons argues that the difference between single and double *n* in *genos* and *gennaō* has no significance since both words ultimately share the same root and the doubling of *n* is a common spelling variation in Greek.

---

31. The other four verses with *monogenēs* are also in John's writings: "And the Word became flesh, and dwelt among us, and we saw His glory, glory as of the *only begotten* from the Father, full of grace and truth" (John 1:14 NASB). "No one has seen God at any time; the *only begotten* God who is in the bosom of the Father, He has explained *Him*" (John 1:18 NASB). "He who believes in Him is not judged; he who does not believe has been judged already, because he has not believed in the name of the *only begotten* Son of God" (John 3:18 NASB). "By this the love of God was manifested in us, that God has sent His *only begotten* Son into the world so that we might live through Him" (1 John 4:9 NASB).

32. See Dale Moody, "The Translation of John 3:16 in the Revised Standard Version," *JBL* 72 (1953): 213–19. See also the standard New Testament Greek lexicon, BDAG, 658.

33. Ibid.

34. Grudem, "The *Monogenēs* Controversy: 'Only' or 'Only Begotten'?," appendix 6 in *Systematic Theology*, 1st ed. (Grand Rapids: Zondervan, 2000), 1233–34. (This appendix was not included in earlier printings of the book from 1994–2000 but was included in the book beginning with a newly typeset printing of the first edition in 2000.)

35. Grudem, *Systematic Theology*, 1st ed., 1233.

36. I had access to this material in November 2016 thanks to the kindness of Dr. Irons, and I was able to incorporate it into my presentation on the Trinity that month at the Evangelical Theological Society.

37. Charles Lee Irons, "A Lexical Defense of the Johannine 'Only Begotten,'" in *Retrieving Eternal Generation*, ed. Fred Sanders and Scott Swain (Grand Rapids: Zondervan, 2017), 98–116.

38. Ibid., 100.

Significantly, Irons found "at least 145" words in ancient Greek that are built upon the *-genēs* stem. By far the largest number of them have the idea of being born or produced. These include *thalassogenēs* ("sea-born"), *neogenēs* ("newborn"), *patrogenēs* ("begotten of the father"), *proterēgenēs* ("born sooner, older") , and *purigenēs* ("born in or from fire").[39] He says, "Fewer than 12 of the 145—*genēs* words involve meetings related to 'kind'."

Irons does not claim that *monogenēs* always means "only begotten," because there are numerous clear examples where it does mean simply "only, unique, one-of-a-kind." But Irons is claiming that many hundreds of examples prove that it certainly *can* mean "only begotten," and that "*monogenēs* is used most basically and frequently in reference to an only child begotten by a parent, with the implication of not having any siblings."[40]

He adds another argument:

> If the word meant "only," then we would expect to find it used to modify many other nouns that do not involve the concept of being begotten or being an offspring, for example, "only wife," "only brother," "only friend," "only slave". . . . "only garment," "only house," "only sword," and so on. But such collocations are completely absent in extrabiblical Greek. This suggests that the literal meaning . . . is the straightforward biological meaning: "only begotten," that is, "without siblings."[41]

Irons then explains that "this basic meaning gets gradually extended in ever new non-literal, metaphorical directions," including the meaning "only legitimate child or heir" (applied to Isaac in Heb. 11:17) and eventually the meaning "only one of its kind."[42]

Finally, Irons considers the meaning of *monogenēs* in the New Testament. John 1:14 is especially significant: "The Word became flesh and dwelt among us, and we have seen his glory, glory as of *the only Son* from the Father, full of grace and truth" (John 1:14). The problem is that the word *son* (Gk. *huios*) is not in the Greek text, which just says *doxan hōs monogenous para patros*. If we translate *monogenēs* as "only," we end up with the nonsense phrase, "glory as of *the only* from the Father." When Bible translations such as the ESV and NIV have to insert the word "Son," Irons says, they show that *monogenēs* cannot mean simply "only" in this case but that the notion of being a child or being begotten was part of the meaning signified by the word *monogenēs* itself. By contrast, the translation "glory as of *the only begotten* of the Father" is a coherent idea.[43]

In addition, the view that Christ was eternally begotten by the Father is explicitly affirmed in the Nicene Creed, which has been widely used by Christians since it was first written in AD 325 (and revised in AD 381). It begins this way:

---

39. Irons, "Lexical Defense," 104.
40. Irons, "Lexical Defense," 106.
41. Ibid., 106–7.
42. Ibid., 107–13.
43. Irons also adds that in John 1:18 "the only begotten

God, who is at the Father's side" (the translation recommended by Irons) is much more consistent with New Testament teaching than the ESV's "the only God, who is at the Father's side" (ibid., 113–15).

> I believe in one God the Father Almighty; Maker of heaven and earth, and of all things visible and invisible.
>
> And in one Lord Jesus Christ, the *only begotten* [Gk. *monogenēs*] Son of God, *begotten of the Father* before all ages, God of God, Light of Light, very God of very God, *begotten, not made*, being of one substance with the Father; by whom all things were made.

Clearly, the authors of the Nicene Creed understand *monogenēs* to mean "only begotten," not just "only, unique," because they use the verb *gennaō* ("beget") twice to explain what *monogenēs* means: (1) it is an eternal begetting that never had a beginning because Christ was "begotten (*gennēthenta*) of the Father *before all ages*," and (2) it does not mean that the Son was created, for the Son was "begotten, *not made*" (*gennēthenta, ou poiēthenta*).

The evidence and arguments produced by Irons have convinced me that *monogenēs* when used of God the Son in the New Testament means "only begotten." As a result, I have removed appendix 6 (where I had argued against "only begotten") from this edition of *Systematic Theology*. In addition, I am now willing to affirm the doctrine of the eternal generation of the Son (also called the eternal begetting of the Son).

## 3. The Meaning of the Eternal Generation of the Son

As indicated in the previous section, I now think the following verses (and John 3:18; 1 John 4:9) should be translated to reflect the meaning "only begotten" for the Greek word *monogenēs*:

> And the Word became flesh and dwelt among us, and we have seen his glory, glory as of *the only begotten* from the Father, full of grace and truth. (John 1:14)

> No one has ever seen God; *the only begotten* God, who is at the Father's side, he has made him known. (John 1:18)[44]

> For God so loved the world, that he gave his *only begotten* Son, that whoever believes in him should not perish but have eternal life. (John 3:16)

But what can it mean that Christ is God's "only begotten Son"? Because so many other passages affirm the full deity of Christ (see section B.2 above, and chapter 26), and because God has existed eternally, we must stay away from any idea that the Son was somehow created by the Father in the distant past. In this respect the analogy with human begetting breaks down and does not apply.

---

44. In a personal email to me on August 18, 2018, my friend Bruce Ware helpfully noted that the fact that John says "God" rather than "Son" in John 1:18 "indicates a begetting that relates to the Son in his divine personage, not in the incarnation, *per se*."

On the other hand, the examples in the previous section show that compound words using *-genēs* tend to carry an implication of some kind of origin. And there are other verses that speak of the Son as existing in some sense "from" the Father: Christ is "the *radiance* of the glory of God and the *exact imprint* of his nature" (Heb. 1:3). The word *radiance* (Gk. *apaugasma*) gives the sense of bright light shining from a source of light, and *exact imprint* (Gk. *charaktēr*) is a word elsewhere used for an exact duplicate of an original pattern (such as a coin stamped out at a mint). Both words indicate that the Son, while not created, is in some sense "from" the Father. Similarly, the Son is said to be the "Word" of God (John 1:1–2), and a word is something that is spoken outward from a person. And John quotes Jesus as saying, "For as the Father has life in himself, so he has granted the Son also to have life in himself" (John 5:26).

Bruce Ware, I think rightly, adds the following argument for eternal generation: "Since the Father is *really* Father, as opposed to being Father nominally (i.e., in name only), and since the Father is eternal Father, then it follows that he must *really* have a Son, who is genuinely from Him (otherwise He isn't *really* Father), and that this Son from Him must likewise be *eternally* from Him (otherwise He isn't *eternal* Father)."[45]

What, then, does the eternal generation of the Son mean? It means that the Son is in some sense "from" the Father. But beyond that, it is easier to define what it does not mean than to clearly explain what it does mean. Eternal generation is not something that ever began, but it is eternal. It does not mean that the Son was created by the Father. And it does not mean that the Father possesses any of the attributes of God in a greater measure than the Son.

Speaking positively, we can say that the eternal generation of the Son implies that (1) the Son is of the *same nature* as the Father (for a father begets a son like himself), (2) the Son is a *distinct person* from the Father (for the Son is begotten and the Father is unbegotten), and (3) there is a specific *order* in the relationship between Father and Son (the biblical pattern is always *from* the Father *through* the Son, as in 1 Cor. 8:6). But all three of these points can be established from the clear testimony of many passages of Scripture without any need for a doctrine of eternal generation (as is evident, for example, from the fact that I affirmed all three of these points in the first edition of this book while denying eternal generation). Still, the idea of the eternal generation of the Son implies all three of these points at once, while otherwise they would have to be established by a combination of the teachings of several different verses.[46]

Can we explain anything more about what happens in this eternal generation? What kind of generation is this? There have been at least two common explanations that do not clearly contradict any text of Scripture or any essential element in the doctrine of the Trinity:

---

45. Personal email from Bruce Ware to me, August 18, 2018.

46. This is the point made by Scott Swain, "The Radiance of the Father's Glory: Eternal Generation, the Divine Names, and Biblical Interpretation," in Sanders and Swain, *Retrieving Eternal Generation*, 29–43.

A. Eternal generation means that *the Father eternally communicates to the Son the divine essence*, so that the Son fully shares in every attribute of the Father. John 5:26 can be understood to support this idea: "For as the Father has life in himself, so he has granted the Son also to have life in himself." This does not mean that the Father is greater than the Son in any attribute, for the Father's communication of the divine essence is so complete that the Son is the "exact imprint" (or exact duplicate) of the Father (Heb. 1:3). And because this generation is *eternal*, the Son was not created but eternally existed as "the only begotten Son." This has been the most common view through the history of the church.[47]

B. Eternal generation means that *the Father is the source of the personal distinctions* between Father and Son (and, by implication, the Holy Spirit), but he is not the source of their divine essence (or being). This was the view of John Calvin,[48] who was concerned that the first option (saying that the Father communicates the divine essence to the Son) seems to imply that the Son and Spirit are lesser deities, that they somehow do not fully have all the attributes of the Father.

I find it difficult to decide between these two options, but option (a) seems to be a more natural conclusion from the meaning of "only begotten" (John 1:14, 18; 3:16), from the very names Father and Son, and from the verses that speak of the Son as the *Word* of God (John 1:1–2), "the *radiance* of the glory of God and the *exact imprint* of his nature" (Heb. 1:3), and the one whom the Father has granted to "have life in himself" (John 5:26).

However, I am not convinced that God has revealed enough information in Scripture for us to affirm or deny either option (a) or (b) with confidence. The actual meaning of the eternal generation of the Son might in fact be option (c), an explanation that we do not now understand or even know about. What we do have is five verses that say that Christ is the "only begotten" Son of the Father, and we have other verses that teach that God is eternal.[49] Therefore, we can affirm with confidence the eternal generation of the Son. But we are dealing here with a topic of great mystery,[50] and it seems wise to admit that much of this topic remains among the "secret things" that "belong to the Lord our God" (Deut. 29:29).

---

47. See Chad Van Dixhoorn, "Post-Reformation Trinitarian Perspectives," in Sanders and Swain, *Retrieving Eternal Generation*, 185, 207; Josh Malone, "Eternal Generation: Pro-Nicene Pattern, Dogmatic Function, and Created Effects," in Sanders and Swain, *Retrieving Eternal Generation*, 275.

48. See Van Dixhoorn, "Perspectives," 185–87; also Richard Muller, *Post-Reformation Reformed Dogmatics* (Grand Rapids: Baker, 2003), 4:324–32.

49. See chapter 11, pp. 199–206.

50. Augustine believed that "the generation of the Son is beyond human comprehension," according to Keith Johnson, "Eternal Generation in the Trinitarian Theology of Augustine," in Sanders and Swain, *Retrieving Eternal Generation*, 166.

## 4. The Different Functions (or Roles) of Father, Son, and Holy Spirit Are Appropriate to Their Distinct Identities

We might wonder why the persons of the Trinity take different roles in relating to creation. Was it accidental or arbitrary? Could God the Father have come instead of God the Son to die for our sins? Could the Holy Spirit have sent God the Father to die for our sins and then sent God the Son to apply redemption to us?

No, it does not seem that these things could have happened, for the role of initiating, directing, and sending is appropriate to the position of the Father, who is first in the regular ordering of persons in the Trinity (from the Father, through the Son, in the Spirit) and the one after whom all human fatherhood is patterned (Eph. 3:14–15). And the role of responding to the Father's initiatives, obeying his directions, going as the Father sends, and revealing God to us is appropriate to the role of the Son, who is also called the Word of God (cf. John 1:1–5, 14, 18; 17:4; Phil. 2:5–11). These roles could not have been reversed or the Father would have ceased to be the Father and the Son would have ceased to be the Son. And by analogy from that relationship, we may conclude that the role of the Holy Spirit is similarly one that was appropriate to the relationship he had with the Father and the Son before the world was created.

But it is possible to say even more. Before the Son came to earth, and even before the world was created, for all eternity the Father has been the Father, the Son has been the Son, and the Holy Spirit has been the Holy Spirit. These identities and their respective relationships are eternal, not something that occurred only in time. We may conclude this first from the unchangeableness of God (see chapter 11): if God now exists as Father, Son, and Holy Spirit, then he has always existed as Father, Son, and Holy Spirit. We may also conclude that the relationships are eternal from other verses in Scripture that speak of the relationships the members of the Trinity had to one another before the creation of the world. For instance, when Scripture speaks of God's work of election (see chapter 32) before the creation of the world, it speaks of the Father choosing us "in" the Son: "Blessed be the God and Father of our Lord Jesus Christ. . . . *He chose us in him before the foundation of the world*, that we should be holy and blameless before him" (Eph. 1:3–4). The initiatory act of choosing is attributed to God the Father, who regards us as united to Christ or "in Christ" before we ever existed. Similarly, of God the Father, it is said that "those whom he foreknew he also predestined to be conformed to the image of his Son" (Rom. 8:29). We also read of the "foreknowledge of God the Father" in distinction from particular functions of the other two members of the Trinity (1 Peter 1:2; cf. 1:20).[51] Even the fact that the Father "gave his only Son" (John 3:16) and sent the Son into the world (John 3:17) indicates that there was a Father-Son relationship before

---

51. Another passage that may suggest such a distinction in function is John 17:5: When Jesus asks the Father, "glorify me in your own presence with the glory that I had with you before the world existed" (John 17:5), he suggests that it is the Father's right to give glory to whom he will and that this glory had been given to the Son by the Father because the Father loved the Son before the foundation of the world.

Christ came into the world. The Son did not become the Son when the Father sent him into the world. Rather, the great love of God is shown in the fact that the one who was *always* Father gave the one who was *always* his only Son: "For God so loved the world, that he gave his only Son" (John 3:16). "But when the fullness of time had come, God sent forth his Son" (Gal. 4:4).

When Scripture speaks of creation, once again it speaks of the Father creating *through* the Son, indicating a relationship prior to when creation began (see John 1:3; 1 Cor. 8:6; Heb. 1:2; also Prov. 8:22–31). But nowhere does it say that the Son or Holy Spirit created through the Father. These passages again imply that there was a relationship of Father (as originator) and Son (as active agent) before creation and that their relationship made it appropriate for the different persons of the Trinity to fulfill the roles they actually did fulfill.

Therefore, the different functions that we see the Father, Son, and Holy Spirit performing are simply the appropriate outworkings of an eternal relationship between the three persons, one that has always existed and will exist for eternity. God has always existed as three distinct persons: Father, Son, and Holy Spirit. These distinct personal identities are essential to the very nature of God himself, and they could not be otherwise.

Yet we must also reaffirm that there are no differences in deity, attributes, or essential nature between the Father, Son, and Holy Spirit. Each person is fully God and has all the attributes of God. *The distinctions between the members of the Trinity are in the ways they relate to each other and to the creation.* In those relationships they carry out roles that are appropriate to each person.

This truth about the Trinity can be summarized in the phrase "ontological equality but relational differences," where the word *ontological* means "being." Both parts of this expression are necessary to a true doctrine of the Trinity: if we do not have ontological equality, then not all the persons are fully God, but if we do not have relational differences (historically called subordination in function),[52] then there is no inherent difference in the way the three persons relate to one another, and consequently we do not have the three distinct persons eternally relating in distinctive ways as Father, Son, and Holy Spirit.

Some recent evangelical writings, primarily from authors who hold an evangelical feminist view of male-female relationships but also from others more recently, have denied an eternal subordination in role among the members of the Trinity,[53] but it has

52. Economic subordination should be carefully distinguished from the error of "subordinationism," which holds that the Son or Holy Spirit are inferior in being to the Father (see section C.2 above, pp. 285–90.)

53. See, for example, Gilbert Bilezikian, *Community 101: Reclaiming the Church as a Community of Oneness* (Grand Rapids: Zondervan, 1997), 190–91; Rebecca Merrill Groothuis,

*Good News for Women: A Biblical Picture of Gender Equality* (Grand Rapids: Baker, 1997), 57; Kevin Giles, *The Trinity and Subordinationism: The Doctrine of God and the Contemporary Gender Debate* (Downers Grove, IL: InterVarsity, 2002); Kevin Giles, *Jesus and the Father: Modern Evangelicals Reinvent the Doctrine of the Trinity* (Grand Rapids: Zondervan, 2006); Millard Erickson, *Who's Tampering with the Trinity? An Assessment* clearly been part of the church's doctrine of the Trinity (in Catholic, Protestant, and Orthodox expressions), at least since Nicaea (AD 325). So Charles Hodge says,

> The Nicene doctrine includes, (1) the principle of the subordination of the Son to the Father, and of the Spirit to the Father and the Son. But this subordination does not imply inferiority. . . . The subordination intended is only that which concerns the mode of subsistence and operation. . . .
>
> The creeds are nothing more than a well-ordered arrangement of the facts of Scripture which concern the doctrine of the Trinity. They assert the distinct personality of the Father, Son, and Spirit . . . and their consequent perfect equality; and the subordination of the Son to the Father, and of the Spirit to the Father and the Son, as to the mode of subsistence and operation. These are scriptural facts, to which the creeds in question add nothing; *and it is in this sense they have been accepted by the Church universal.*[54]

Similarly, A. H. Strong says,

> Father, Son, and Holy Spirit, while equal in essence and dignity, stand to each other in an order of personality, office, and operation. . . .
>
> The subordination of the *person* of the Son to the *person* of the Father, or in other words an order of personality, office, and operation which permits the Father to be officially first, the Son second, and the Spirit third, is perfectly consistent with equality. Priority is not necessarily superiority. . . . *We frankly recognize an eternal subordination of Christ to the Father*, but we maintain at the same time that this subordination is a subordination of order, office, and operation, not a subordination of essence.[55]

## 5. Does the Son Eternally Submit to the Authority of the Father?

I have argued elsewhere that Scripture indicates a consistent pattern in which the Son always submits to the authority of the Father and that this aspect of the Father-Son relationship in the Trinity has existed eternally.[56] I will first summarize that argument

---

*of the Subordination Debate* (Grand Rapids: Kregel, 2009). Robert Letham ("The Man-Woman Debate: Theological Comment," *WTJ* 52, no. 1 [Spring 1990]: 65–78) sees this tendency in recent evangelical writings as the outworking of an evangelical feminist claim that a subordinate role necessarily implies lesser importance or lesser personhood. Of course, if this is not true among members of the Trinity, then it is not necessarily true between husband and wife either.

54. Hodge, *Systematic Theology*, 3 vols. (1871–73; repr., Grand Rapids: Eerdmans, 1970), 1:460–62 (italics mine).

55. Strong, *Systematic Theology* (Valley Forge, PA: Judson, 1907), 342 (third italics mine).

56. Wayne Grudem, "Biblical Evidence for the Eternal Submission of the Son to the Father," in *The New Evangelical Subordinationism? Perspectives on the Equality of God the Father and God the Son*, ed. Dennis W. Jowers and H. Wayne House (Eugene, OR: Wipf & Stock, 2012), 223–61; Grudem, "Doctrinal Deviations in Evangelical Feminist Arguments about the Trinity," in *One God in Three Persons: Unity of Essence, Distinction of Persons, Implications for Life*, ed. Bruce Ware and John Starke (Wheaton, IL: Crossway, 2015), 17–45.

here and then consider various recent objections, including the objections that *authority* and *submission* are inappropriate terms, that there can only be one will in God, that this submission is only for the purposes of the incarnation, and that this submission only applies to God's voluntary activities outside of himself.

**a. The Father Acts as the Leader before Creation and after Final Judgment.** There are several reasons to think that the pattern of the Son's submission to the Father while on earth was a reflection of the fact that the Son has been subject to the authority of the Father before creation, and therefore eternally.

(1) The eternal names Father and Son indicate differences in the relationship. In the biblical world, the father in a family had a leadership role, an authority, that a son did not have even as an adult, and the authors and original readers of Scripture would have naturally associated such a relationship with the names Father and Son. (2) The Father chose us in the Son "before the foundation of the world" (Eph. 1:4; cf. Rom. 8:29; 2 Tim. 1:9; Rev. 13:8), indicating an eternal action in which the Father is the person who initiates or leads in choosing who will be saved. (3) The Father "created the world" (Heb. 1:2) through the Son, for "all things were made *through* him" (John 1:3). This is not an eternal act, of course, but it does show that the Father's primary role in the relationship existed long before the incarnation (that is, when the Son came to earth as a man; see chapter 26). (4) The Father "gave his only Son" (John 3:16) and "sent forth his Son" into the world (Gal. 4:4), which means that *before* Christ took on a human nature he willingly obeyed the direction of the Father, who sent him into the world. (5) The doctrine of the eternal generation of the Son (see previous section, pp. 296–98) indicates that the Son is eternally "from" the Father, which indicates that the Father has always had some kind of priority in the relationship. More specifically, the Son's submission to the Father's authority is appropriate to and flows from the eternal generation of the Son by the Father.

This pattern in the Father-Son relationship continues through the time of Jesus' earthly ministry and after he ascended into heaven. (6) While Jesus was on earth, he said, "I have come down from heaven, not to do my own will but the will of him who sent me" (John 6:38), and "I always do the things that are pleasing to him" (John 8:29). (7) Shortly before his crucifixion, Jesus said, "You heard me say to you, 'I am going away, and I will come to you.' If you loved me, you would have rejoiced, because I am going to the Father, for *the Father is greater than I*" (John 14:28).[57] D. A. Carson observes that, although the verse assumes "the distinction between the Father in his glory and the Son in his incarnation, nevertheless this verse also attests to the pattern of functional subordination of the son to the Father . . . that extends backward into eternity past."[58]

---

57. Hongyi Yang, *A Development, Not a Departure: The Lacunae in the Debate of the Doctrine of the Trinity and Gender Roles* (Phillipsburg, NJ: P&R, 2018), 288–99, notes that John 14:28 has not received adequate attention from supporters of the eternal functional submission of the Son. She also drew my attention to the interpretation by D. A. Carson that I have quoted here.

58. D. A. Carson, *The Gospel According to John* (Grand Rapids: Eerdmans, 1991), 508.

(8) Now that Jesus has ascended into heaven, he "is interceding for us" (Rom. 8:34; cf. Heb. 7:25), which means he is bringing requests before the Father on our behalf. (9) After Christ's ascension, he received authority from the Father to pour out the Holy Spirit on the church (Acts 2:32–33). (10) Jesus received revelation from the Father to give to John the predictions of the future in the book of Revelation: The book begins, "The revelation of Jesus Christ, which God gave him to show to his servants the things that must soon take place" (Rev. 1:1). (11) He now sits "at the right hand of the Majesty on high" (Heb. 1:3), and being seated at the right hand is a position of secondary authority, subordinate to the king.[59] (12) He has received from the Father the authority to execute final judgment (John 5:26–27; cf. Acts 10:42). (13) After the final judgment, he will deliver the kingdom to God the Father, and then for all eternity "the Son himself will also be subjected to him who put all things in subjection under him, that God may be all in all" (1 Cor. 15:28).

(14) D. A. Carson, in a later article, notes that a parallel pattern in the sending of the Spirit by the Father and the Son:

> What is worth pondering in the case of the Spirit, however, is that the obedience of the Spirit cannot be cast in terms of his human nature since he has no human nature.... Yet there is demonstrable *taxis* [order] with the Father (and the Son) sending or giving the Spirit and the Spirit going and being given.... The least that must be inferred is that within the Trinity, being at the "receiving" end of a relationship— the end that receives commands and obeys, the end that is commissioned to go and proceeds, the end that is sent, the end that is "shown" what the Father does and does the same thing—cannot be said to betray any sort of inferiority.[60]

**b. This Pattern Is Never Reversed.** This priority of the Father (or leadership role, or authority, of the Father) with respect to the Son is a consistent pattern in Scripture that is true prior to creation (in the eternal predestining of believers and in the names Father and Son) and continues far into the future, beyond the final judgment. The pattern is never reversed. The Son does not eternally beget the Father. The Son does not predestine us in the Father in the eternal councils of the Trinity. The Son does not create through the Father. The Son does not send the Father into the world. We never read that the Son so loved the world that he gave his only Father. Never does the Father pray to the Son or intercede for us before the Son. The Father does not receive authority from the Son to pour out the Holy Spirit. The Father did not receive revelation from the Son to give to the church in the book of Revelation. Never does the Father sit at the right hand of the Son. Never does the Son give the Father authority to execute final judgment.

---

59. See these examples where sitting at the right hand of a ruler implies an authority second only to the ruler himself: Ps. 45:9; 110:1; Matt. 20:20-21.

60. D. A. Carson, "John 5:26: *Crux Interpretum* for Eternal Generation," in Sanders and Swain, *Retrieving Eternal Generation*, 95.

Never is it said that the Father will after the final judgment be subjected to the Son who put all things under him. This pattern of Father-Son interaction in Scripture is one-directional, *from* the Father and *through* the Son.

To deny these unidirectional relationships between Father and Son is to fail to speak the way the Scripture speaks about the eternal relationship between the Father and the Son. No single text or biblical teaching anywhere in Scripture suggests or teaches that the Father is ever, in any instance, under the authority of the Son or carries out any single action or set of actions in obedience to the Son. Every biblical text on this question shows the Father in the position of preeminence in authority, and the Son always and only carrying out the will of the Father.

Therefore, the consistent testimony of Scripture is that the Father, by virtue of being Father, eternally has authority to plan, initiate, lead, direct, command, and send, and this is a kind of authority that the Son and Holy Spirit do not have with respect to the Father. The Son, by virtue of being Son, eternally submits, joyfully and with great delight, to the authority of his Father.

It is only in a sinful world deeply marred by hostility toward authority and overly focused on status and power that we would fail to see that submission to the authority of the Father is one aspect of the great glory of the Son. Both *authority* and *submission to authority* are wonderful parts of the great glory of the Father and the Son, and this will be their glory for all eternity.

**c. Are *Authority* and *Submission* the Right Terms to Use?** I have used the terms *authority* and *submission* to describe this pattern in the Father-Son relationship throughout Scripture, while specifying that the Father and the Son have always been in full agreement. Others have told me that the terms *authority* and *submission* are inappropriate because they suggest or even imply that there was some disagreement by the Son that had to be overcome by the greater authority of the Father. I do not think the terms imply even a potential disagreement between Father and Son, and I suggest that they better express the fulness of the Scriptural witness than alternative terms.

I would caution those who object to the terms *authority* and *submission* to realize that we live in an age where unbelievers deeply despise any kind of authority, even the legitimate authority of parents or governments—and most of all the authority of God. I wonder how much of the resistance people have to the idea of authority is due to accepting some of the assumptions of modern culture. Surely in the age to come, we will willingly and joyfully submit to the greater authority of God, even though with sinless hearts we will never disagree with his directions. And among the sinless angels there seem to be positions of greater and lesser authority, since there are angels and archangels (1 Thess. 4:16; Jude 9). Therefore, *authority* and *submission* seem to be positive qualities that we should delight in and affirm (while recognizing, of course, that they can be wrongfully used by sinful human beings).

But this authority/submission terminology is not the primary issue. For those who are still uncomfortable with the terms *authority* and *submission*, several other pairs of terms could also be used to describe this consistent pattern of action that we see throughout Scripture. We could say that there is an unchanging "order" (Greek *taxis*) of Father-Son-Holy Spirit within the Trinity and that this order is reflected in the works of God in creation and redemption. Or we could use other pairs of terms such as saying that the Father always "initiates" and the Son always "responds." Or that the Father always "leads" and the Son always "follows" that leadership, or that the Father "directs" and the Son "obeys." We could also say that, in the works of God, the Father is always "first" and the Son is always "second," or that the Father is always "primary" and the Son is always "secondary."

No matter which terms we use, it is a mistake to insist that the Father-Son relationship in Scripture is always perfectly symmetrical. It would be unfaithful to the consistent pattern of Scriptural language to deny any primacy to the role of the Father. Yet that is what some egalitarian authors have recently done. (This is a significant part of their argument that there should be no leadership role that belongs to the husband in a marriage, but the husband-wife relationship should be entirely a relationship of "mutual submission." Just as there is no inherently appropriate leadership role for any member of the Trinity, so there is no leadership role that automatically falls to the husband in a marriage.)[61]

However, if in the Trinity the Son is always subject to the authority of the Father yet also equal to the Father in deity and in honor, then it is understandable that, in various kinds of relationships between persons, the existence of authority and submission within the relationship is compatible with both persons being equal in importance and honor. This has important implications for authority and submission relationships among human beings, such as the submission of citizens to the authority of governments (Rom. 13:1), of employees to employers (cf. Eph. 6:5), of children to parents (Eph. 6:1), of students to teachers and school administrators, of church members to elders(1 Peter 5:5), and of wives to husbands (Eph. 5:22; see chapter 22). In these relationships, the person who submits to a rightful authority should not think that submission implies lesser importance, nor should the person in authority think that this authority implies greater importance, and the example that proves this is the submission of the Son to the authority of the Father.

**d. A Serious Misrepresentation of This Teaching.** Unfortunately, in the midst of some thoughtful recent discussions about the eternal relationship between the Father and the Son, one writer seriously misrepresents the position that I am advocating here.

61. This is the argument made by several evangelical feminist authors, such as those I mentioned on p. 300n53 above. They all have denied that the Son is eternally subject to the authority of the Father within the Trinity. See also the following essays in Dennis Jowers and H. Wayne House, *The New Evangelical Subordinationism? Perspectives on the Equality of God the Father* *and God the Son* (Eugene, OR: Pickwick, 2012): Phillip Cary, "The New Evangelical Subordinationism: Reading Inequality into the Trinity," 1–12; Linda Belleville, "'Son' Christology in the New Testament," 59–81; Kevin Giles, "The Trinity without Tiers," 262–87; and Dennis Jowers, "The Inconceivability of Subordination within a Simple God," 375–410.

Aimee Byrd, in *Recovering from Biblical Manhood and Womanhood*,[62] falsely claims that Bruce Ware and I, in advocating the doctrine of "eternal relations of authority and submission," are making a serious doctrinal error because "this doctrine teaches that the Son, the second person of the Trinity, is subordinate to the Father, not only in the economy of salvation but *in his essence*,"[63] and we are therefore "unorthodox teachers that are not in line with Nicene Trinitarian doctrine."[64]

I consider this criticism to be an exceptionally serious misrepresentation of my position (and the position of Bruce Ware) because it is an accusation that I have deviated from orthodox teaching in such a central doctrine as the doctrine of the Trinity. And it is completely false.

In the first edition of *Systematic Theology*, as well as in this second edition, and in subsequent writings on the doctrine of the Trinity, I have repeatedly and explicitly affirmed that the Son and Father are of the *same* essence or *same* being (*homoousios*), that the Son is fully God, and that the Father, Son, and Holy Spirit share in ontological equality (see above, sections C.2 and D.4). I also described in detail the early church's rejection of the idea that the Son is a lesser being than the Father, a teaching that I also strongly rejected (see section C.2.b above). I wrote, "In affirming that the Son was of the same nature as the Father, the early church also excluded a related false doctrine, subordinationism. . . . Subordinationism held that the Son was eternal (not created) and divine but still not equal to the Father in being or attributes—the Son was inferior or 'subordinate' in being to God the Father."[65] I did not affirm but rejected "the heresy of subordinationism, which holds that the Son is inferior in being to the Father." (In these sentences, I used the word *being* as a synonym for *essence*.) I also repeatedly denied inferiority or subordination in essence (though I more often used the word *being*) in *Evangelical Feminism and Biblical Truth*.[66] On the very page that Byrd quotes, I say that the doctrine of the Trinity that has been accepted throughout the church "includes a subordination in role, but not in essence or being" and that "the orthodox doctrine has always been that there is equality in essence and subordination in role, and these that these two are consistent with each other."[67]

And since November 2016, when I read a paper on the Trinity at the Evangelical Theological Society annual meeting, I have been happy to affirm the eternal generation of the Son as well (as I explained in section D.2 above). I wholeheartedly affirm the

62. Byrd, *Recovering from Biblical Manhood and Womanhood* (Grand Rapids: Zondervan, 2020).

63. Ibid., 101.

64. Ibid., 173.

65. Grudem, *Systematic Theology*, 1st ed., 244–45. On page 301 above, I quote with approval the words of A. H. Strong, who says, "We maintain at the same time that this subordination is a subordination of order, office, and operation, *not a subordination of essence.*"

66. Wayne Grudem, *Evangelical Feminism and Biblical Truth* (Wheaton, IL: Crossway, 2012), 415, 421, 428, and in the boldfaced heading on 441.

67. John Piper and Wayne Grudem, eds., *Recovering Biblical Manhood and Womanhood* (Wheaton, IL: Crossway, 1991), 457. Byrd's citation of this page is found on page 103n13.

Nicene Creed as a faithful representation of the doctrines taught in Scripture. For Byrd to claim that I (and Bruce Ware) are "not in line with Nicene Trinitarian doctrine" is, in my view, not merely a harmless mistake in her citation of our publications, and not merely a legitimate difference of opinion, but a serious accusation that clearly misrepresents what we have explicitly written and taught for many years.

**e. The Unified Will of God and the Three Distinctive Expressions of That Will.** The attributes of God are not divided into parts (see chapter 11 on God's unity), and so in speaking about the will of God as an attribute of his nature, there is one will. In addition, we must insist, of course, that there has never been a disagreement between the Father, the Son, and the Holy Spirit. They have always been in complete agreement. In that sense also, there is one will in God. Jesus says, "He who sent me is with me. He has not left me alone, for I always do the things that are pleasing to him" (John 8:29). Paul indicates such complete agreement when he writes, "The Spirit intercedes for the saints according to the will of God" (Rom. 8:27).

On the other hand, within the one unified will of God, we must say that there have been three *distinctive expressions* of that will by the Father, the Son, and the Holy Spirit. Otherwise, it is difficult to see how we can do justice to statements such as John 6:38: "For I have come down from heaven, *not to do my own will* but *the will of him who sent me*." The "I" in this verse cannot be the human nature of Christ, for the human nature of Christ did not "come down from heaven," but rather the divine nature of the Son did this. And yet he distinguishes "my own will" from "the will of him who sent me," which must imply that there are different expressions of the unified will of God among the three persons of the Trinity.[68]

The same argument can be made from John 8:42: "I came from God and I am here. *I came not of my own accord*, but he sent me." The Father willed to send the Son, and the Son willed to be sent. These are not the same, because the Son did not will to send the Father, and the Father did not will to be sent. There are several other verses like this, especially in John's gospel. Whether we call these three *distinctive expressions* of the unified will of God or use some other description, we need some terminology to do justice to verses such as these. I see no reason why the one will in God's nature could not will that the *person* of the Father would will to send the *person* of the Son into the world to gain our redemption and also will that the person of the Son would will to come to earth in response to that sending by the Father.

A similar observation can be made about Philippians 2:6, "Who, though he was in the form of God, did not count equality with God a thing to be grasped." This must

---

68. Someone might object that the verse means, "I [in my divine nature] have come down from heaven, not to do my own [human] will, but the will of him [the Father] who sent me [in my divine nature]." But this requires the doubtful interpretative step of saying that the word "my" refers to something different than "I" and "me" that occur before and after it in the same sentence.

refer to the divine nature of the Son *before* the incarnation (for it was this "not counting" that resulted in the incarnation), and this "not counting" is a or distinctive expression of God's will. If it were not referring to a decision of the divine nature of the Son, it could not count as an illustration of humility, which is Paul's point in this context.[69]

Puritan theologian John Owen (1616–1683) explained how God could have one unified will and also exercise three different expressions of that will:

> It is true that the will of God the Father, Son, and Holy Ghost, is but one. It is a natural property, and where there is but one nature there is but one will: but in respect of their distinct personal actings, this will is appropriated to them respectively, so that the will of the Father and the will of the Son may be considered [distinctly] in this business; which though essentially one and the same, yet in their distinct personality it is distinctly considered, as the will of the Father and the will of the Son. Notwithstanding the unity of essence that is between the Father and the Son, yet is the work distinctly carried on by them; so that the same God judges and becomes surety, satisfieth and is satisfied, in these distinct persons.
>
> Thus, though this covenant be eternal, and the object of it be that which might not have been, and so it hath the nature of the residue of God's decrees in these regards, yet because of this distinct acting of the will of the Father and the will of the Son with regard to each other, it is more than a decree, and hath the proper nature of a *covenant* or compact. Hence, from the moment of it (I speak not of time), there is a new habitude of will in the Father and Son towards each other that is not in them essentially; I call it new, as being in God freely, not naturally. And hence was the salvation of men before the incarnation, by the undertaking, mediation, and death of Christ.[70]

Scott Swain quotes a similar statement from Owen and concludes, "Because the Son eternally proceeds from the Father in his personal manner of subsisting, so too does his personal manner of willing proceed from the Father."[71]

---

69. This is the point made by Michael Ovey, *Your Will Be Done: Exploring Eternal Subordination, Divine Monarchy, and Divine Humility* (London: Latimer Trust, 2016), 105. See also Denny Burk, "Christ's Functional Subordination in Philippians 2:6: A Grammatical Note with Trinitarian Implications," in *The New Evangelical Subordinationism? Perspectives on the Equality of God the Father and God the Son*, ed. Dennis W. Jowers and H. Wayne House (Eugene, OR: Pickwick, 2012), 82–107.

70. John Owen, *The Works of John Owen*, 16 vols. (London: Banner of Truth, 1967), 12:497. I am grateful to Denny Burk for pointing me to this statement from John Owen and for pointing me to the perceptive analysis of Owen on this topic

by Matthew Barrett. See Burk, "The Will of the Father and the Will of the Son in the Covenant of Redemption," DennyBurk.com, August 13, 2019, https://www.dennyburk.com/the-will-of-the-father-and-the-will-of-the-son-in-the-covenant-of-redemption/; and Barrett, "Better Late Than Never: The Covenant of Redemption and the Trinity Debates," *Credo*, June 16, 2016, http://www.credomag.com/2016/06/16/better-late-than-never-the-covenant-of-redemption-and-the-trinity-debates-matthew-barrett/.

71. Scott Swain, "Covenant of Redemption," in *Christian Dogmatics: Reformed Theology for the Church Catholic*, ed. Michael Allen and Scott R Swain (Grand Rapids: Baker, 2016), 122.

**f. Recent Objections to the Eternal Submission of the Son.**[72] A healthy and (for the most part) respectful discussion of this topic has occurred in the evangelical world within the last several years, and a number of respected writers have differed with the position I represented in the first edition of this book. For example, readers may wish to consider the thoughtful essays by Matthew Emerson and Luke Stamps in the 2019 book *Trinitarian Theology*.[73] They object that "if the persons are distinguished in terms of authority and submission, does this not require distinct wills in the Godhead?"[74] But that is a problem, they say, because "the traditional doctrine of the Trinity has maintained that the three persons share one divine will."[75] Emerson and Stamps do not claim that it is contrary to the wording of the Nicene Creed to claim that the Son is eternally subject to the Father, but they claim it is contrary to the viewpoint of many early church fathers who supported the understanding of the Trinity that is found in the Nicene Creed. For example, they cite Gregory of Nazianzus (ca. AD 329–390) and Gregory of Nyssa (ca. AD 335–395) in support and add that "there are many more that we could cite to make the same point: God is one in every way (the relations of origin excepted), including in his volitional faculty."[76]

Another writer, D. Glenn Butner Jr., objected to the idea that the Son eternally submits to the authority of the Father because, he claimed, that would require that the Son has his own will, distinct from the will of the Father. But Butner claims that would mean that the wills belong to each *person* in the Trinity and not to the nature of God. He believes that would contradict the Sixth Ecumenical Council at Constantinople (AD 680–681), which decided, *with respect to the person of Christ*, that the wills belong to each nature (human will for the human nature and divine will for the divine nature) and not to the person. But by the same reasoning, Butner argues, the will of God must belong to the *nature* of God (which is one), not to the individual *persons*. Therefore there can only be one will in God. But authority and submission implies two different wills, and so we cannot have authority and submission within the Trinity.[77]

With respect to the numerous verses in Scripture that show the Son being subject to the Father, obeying the Father, being sent by the Father, carrying out the Father's will, and so forth, Butner's response is to say (1) the doctrine of the "inseparability of actions" among the members of the Trinity shows that all three persons of the Trinity

---

72. A detailed overview and careful analysis of this controversy is Hongyi Yang, *A Development Not a Departure: The Lacunae in the Debate of the Doctrine of the Trinity and Gender Roles* (Phillipsburg, NJ: P&R, 2018). Yang largely favors the position I have advocated here.

73. Matthew Emerson and Luke Stamps, "On Trinitarian Theological Method" and "Response to Bruce A. Ware and Matthew B. Yarnell III," in *Trinitarian Theology: Theological Models and Doctrinal Application*, ed. Keith Whitfield (Nashville: B&H, 2019), 95–128 and 157–73. See also Michael Bird and Scott Harrower, eds., *Trinity without Hierarchy:*

*Reclaiming Nicene Orthodoxy in Evangelical Theology* (Grand Rapids: Kregel, 2019).

74. Emerson and Stamps, "Method," 118.

75. Ibid., 119.

76. Ibid., 121.

77. See D. Glenn Butner Jr., "Eternal Functional Subordination and the Problem of the Divine Will," *JETS* 58, no. 1 (2015): 131–49. He expanded his argument in *The Son Who Learned Obedience: A Theological Case Against the Eternal Submission of the Son* (Eugene, OR: Pickwick, 2018).

were involved in every action done by any one of them,[78] and (2) many of these verses are speaking only about the human nature of the Son, not about his divine nature, or else they are speaking about the Son in connection with the incarnation, which is a special case that is different from an eternal relationship of authority and submission.[79]

**g. Reply to Objections.** My response to Emerson and Stamps includes several points.

(1) Their objections are based not directly on Scripture or even on major creeds but on several writers, such as Gregory of Nyssa and Gregory of Nazianzus, who defended the doctrine of the Trinity in the fourth century AD. While Emerson and Stamps affirm that we should have "a rigorous engagement with individual passages of Scripture in our doctrinal formulations,"[80] the heart of their objection here is not that *Scripture* denies that the Son is eternally subject to the Father, but that "the *pro-Nicene theologians* consistently affirmed that there is in God one will, one wisdom, one power, and one authority," and to prove that statement Emerson and Stamps appeal not to any Scripture passages but to the writings of various fourth century theologians who supported the Nicene Creed.[81] I point this out not to disagree with these fourth century theologians (for I agree with them that there is one will in the nature of God) but to note that disagreements on this issue are not direct disagreements with specific verses in Scripture, nor even disagreements with the secondary authority of the formulation of the doctrine of the Trinity in the Nicene Creed (with which I fully agree), nor disagreements with the third-level consideration of the writings of respected fourth century theologians (for I agree there is one will in God), but are instead disagreements with the fourth-level inference that the one will in God requires that there cannot be *different expressions* of that one will among the different persons in the Trinity. But this is an inference that is not drawn by any fourth century theologian (to my knowledge) but drawn instead by twenty-first-century writers.

In addition, it is important to remember that the writings of the early church fathers do not come to us with the same authority as Scripture or even the same authority as the early creeds. Charles Hodge says, "There is, therefore, a distinction between the speculations of the Nicene fathers, and the decisions of the Nicene Council. The latter have been accepted by the church universal, but not the former."[82]

I would say that, even if we affirm the existence of one divine will, that does not rule out the idea that each person in the Trinity can have different actualizations or different expressions of that will (see the previous section on the unified will of God, pp. 307–8).

Surely there must be some kinds of distinction in the one will of God because there is a difference between the Father's willing to send and the Son's willing to be sent. There is a

78. Butner, *The Son Who Learned Obedience*, 35–48 and 49–57.

79. Ibid., 62–121; brief summaries are found on 91, 95–97, and 197.

80. Emerson and Stamps, "Method," 100.
81. Ibid, 111–13, 119–21.
82. Hodge, *Systematic Theology*, 1:471.

difference between the Father's willing to pour out divine wrath against sin and the Son's willing to bear that wrath for our sake. There is a difference between the Father's will to say "You are my beloved son; with you I am well pleased" (Mark 1:11) and the Son's will to receive such approval as the beloved Son. There is a difference between the Son bringing requests before the Father (Heb. 7:25) and the Father hearing those requests.

(2) Emerson and Stamps rely on only part of the evidence from the early church Fathers. Michael Ovey has produced significant evidence from Athanasius, Hillary, Augustine, and others showing that they believed in both the full deity of the Son *and also* the obedience or submission of the Son to the Father. He quotes one of the most influential advocates of the Trinity, Hilary of Poitiers (ca. AD 310–367), as follows:[83]

> That the Son is not on a level with the Father and is not equal to Him is chiefly shown in the fact that *He was subjected to Him to render obedience,* . . . in that He then sat down at the right hand of God . . . ; in that He is sent, in that He receives, in that He submits in all things to the will of Him who sent Him. But the subordination of filial love is not a diminution of essence. . . . God is nevertheless One, and the subjection and dignity of the Son are both taught in that by being called Son. . . . He is subject to the Father both in service and name; yet in such a way that the subordination of His name bears witness to the true character of His natural and exactly similar essence.[83]

Ovey also quotes Augustine (354–430) referring to the divine nature of the Son: "Hence, if true reasoning admits that the equal Son obeys his equal Father, we do not deny the obedience, but if you want to believe that he is inferior in nature by reason of this obedience, we forbid it."[84]

Chrysostom (c. 347–407) writes about the Son's obedience as follows (commenting on 1 Cor. 11:3): "The Son also, though he did become obedient to the Father, it was as the Son of God, it was as God. For as the obedience of the Son to the Father is greater than we find in men towards the authors of their being, so also His liberty is greater."[85]

These citations from Augustine and Chrysostom are examples of a repeated claim by fourth and fifth century defenders of the Trinity who argued that, yes, the Son was obedient to the Father, but this did not mean that he had an inferior nature to the Father, for the fact that he was a true Son demonstrates that he had the *same nature* as the Father. In this way they responded to the Arian claim that submission to the Father was evidence that he was a lesser being. Michael Ovey says that a "key premise" of the Arians was that "relational subordination rules out ontological equality."[86]

---

83. De Synodis ("On the Councils"), 51. (NPNF, 2nd series, vol. 9, p. 18.)

84. Ovey, *Your Will*, 74, citing Augustine, *Answer to Maximus the Arian II*, 18.3.

85. Chrysostom, *Homilies on First Corinthians*, Homily 26 (NPNF, 1st series, 12:150).

86. Ovey, *Your Will*, 125.

(3) Emerson and Stamps are perhaps overly confident in their ability to be sure that something cannot be true about the relationship between the three persons and the one nature of God. In dealing with the doctrine of the Trinity, we should be cautious about relying too much on arguments that take the form of "if there is one, there cannot be three" or "if there are three, there cannot be one." Louis Berkhof wisely says, "It is especially when we reflect on the relation of the three persons to the divine essence that all analogies fail us and we become deeply conscious of the fact that the Trinity is a mystery far beyond our comprehension. It is the incomprehensible glory of the Godhead."[87]

I realize that Emerson and Stamps might reply that I am similarly overconfident in my conclusion that the Son is eternally subject to the authority of the Father, but there is a difference because my conclusion is consistent with the overwhelming testimony of Scripture that the Son obeys the Father in every aspect of his relationship to the world.

(4) Butner's argument is different because he begins with the two natures and therefore two wills (human and divine) of Christ (with which I agree; see chapter 26), and he reasons that the attribute of will is a property of the nature, not the person, and therefore there cannot be three wills in the one divine nature of the Trinity. However, Butner's reasoning is fatally flawed, for it takes the analysis that churches in the seventh century made regarding *one topic* (the God-man Jesus Christ) and improperly applies some of its categories to *another topic* (the Trinity). But there are monumental differences because with Christ we are talking about only one person, but with the Trinity we are talking about three persons.

The Sixth Ecumenical Council at Constantinople (AD 680–81; also called the Third Council of Constantinople) declared that there can be two wills within the *one person* of Christ, *thus implying that one person could have two wills*. The council declared nothing about how many different expressions of one will there could be with *three persons*, nor did they deny that the divine nature could have three distinctive expressions of the one will, all working in unity.

It is significant that Butner at this point appeals not to the official declarations of the Sixth Ecumenical Council but rather to the writings of two rather obscure figures from church history, Maximus the Confessor (c. 580–662)[88] and Pope Agatho (who was pope 678–81).[89] Their speculations regarding the doctrine of the Trinity may be interesting, but to look to them as infallible authorities on the Trinity is a procedure that is far removed from the direct authority of the teachings of Scripture.

If we deny that there is *any sense* in which there can be three distinctive expressions of one will among the three persons of the Trinity, it is difficult to understand how we really have three persons. Michael J. Ovey rightly observes, "Eternal subordination involves a distinction of 'wills' between Father and Son at the level of personal relation and not a distinction at the level of nature."[90]

87. Berkhof, *Systematic Theology*, 88.
88. Ibid, 69–80.
89. Ibid., 95.
90. Ovey, *Your Will*, 105.

Butner also appeals to a doctrine of "inseparability of actions" among the members of the Trinity. If this doctrine means that, by virtue of the one nature or essence in God, all three persons of the Trinity are in some way involved in every action of any one of the persons, then I am happy to affirm this doctrine. But if it is taken to mean that all three persons in the Trinity act *in exactly the same way* in every action (so that the Son does not submit to the Father any more than the Father submits to the Son), then it is contrary to many of the passages of Scripture cited above.

Butner's objection that many passages that speak of the Son's obedience can be explained with reference to his human nature only is not persuasive for a number of verses. For example, God did not create the world "through" the human nature of the Son but through his divine nature (Heb. 1:2). The Father "chose us" in the Son "before the foundation of the world" (Eph. 1:4), which must refer to the divine Son (for the human nature did not exist at that time). When God "so loved the world that he gave his only Son" (John 3:16), it was not the human nature but the divine person of the Son whom the Father gave for our salvation. When God "did not spare his own Son but gave him up for us all" (Rom. 8:32), it was the divine Son, not just Christ's human nature, whom God did not spare. When Christ in heaven "is interceding for us" before the Father (Rom. 8:34; cf. Heb. 7:25), he is praying for the specific situations of millions of people around the world at the same time, something that only an infinite, divine person could do.

Hebrews 5:8 does say, "Although he was a son, he learned obedience through what he suffered," but this does not mean that he had never been obedient to the Father before his time on earth. It can readily mean " although he was eternally God the Son, while he lived for more than thirty years on earth as both God and man, he learned for the first time what it was to be obedient even when obedience included the price of suffering as a human being suffers." He had been eternally obedient to the Father, but now he was newly obedient as God-man.

And even if someone were to claim that the obedience of the Son to the Father is only seen in the incarnation of Christ as God-man, we still have the simultaneous presence of equality in nature and importance (both Son and Father are fully divine) and a difference in role (for the Son submits to the authority of the Father).

(5) No creed or confession of faith known to me in the history of the church has ever said that the view that the Son is eternally subject to the Father is an unorthodox doctrine. There is certainly a difference of opinion today between theologians who affirm the eternal submission of the Son to the Father and those who deny it, but it would be good to be thankful that theologians on both sides of this question today wholeheartedly affirm the doctrine of the Trinity as expressed in the Nicene Creed and the doctrine of the two natures in one person of Christ as expressed in the Chalcedonian Creed (or the Chalcedonian definition). We are dealing here with a matter of great complexity and substantial mystery, and advocates on both sides are sincerely seeking to faithfully

represent the teachings of Scripture about a topic that we can never fully understand in this lifetime, and probably not even in the age to come. Accusations that those we disagree with are "anti-Nicene" or "non-Trinitarian" or outside the bounds of orthodoxy simply will not help to advance the discussion.

(6) The idea that the Son is eternally subject to the authority of the Father is not a new idea, but has been affirmed and reaffirmed over the centuries by a veritable Who's Who of evangelical theologians. I have listed several of them in the next section.

### h. Evangelical Theologians Who Affirm the Eternal Obedience or Submission of the Son to the Authority of the Father.

I have included in this section a repetition of statements on this topic by two renowned American theologians from previous generations (Hodge and Strong) that I quoted earlier in this chapter but that are useful to repeat at this point.

Charles Hodge (1871–73):

> The Nicene doctrine includes, (1) the principle of the subordination of the Son to the Father, and of the Spirit to the Father and the Son. But this subordination does not imply inferiority.... The subordination intended is only that which concerns the mode of subsistence and operation....
>
> The creeds are nothing more than a well-ordered arrangement of the facts of Scripture which concern the doctrine of the Trinity. They assert the distinct personality of the Father, Son, and Spirit ... and their consequent perfect equality; and the subordination of the Son to the Father, and of the Spirit to the Father and the Son, as to the mode of subsistence and operation. These are scriptural facts, to which the creeds in question add nothing; *and it is in this sense they have been accepted by the Church universal.*[91]

Herman Bavinck (1895-1901):

> For as Mediator, the Son is subordinate to the Father, calls him God ..., is his servant ... who receives a reward ... for the obedience accomplished.... Still, this relation between Father and Son, though most clearly manifest during Christ's sojourn on earth, was not first initiated at the time of the incarnation, for the incarnation itself is already included in the execution of the work assigned to this the Son, but occurs in eternity and therefore also existed already during the time of the Old Testament.[92]

---

91. Hodge, *Systematic Theology*, 3 vols. (1871–73; repr., Grand Rapids: Eerdmans, 1970), 1:460–62 (italics mine).
92. Herman Bavinck, *Reformed Dogmatics*, ed. John Bolt, trans. John Vriend, vol. 3, Sin and Salvation in Christ (Grand Rapids: Baker, 2006), 214.

Augustus H. Strong (1907):

In the God in whose image man is made, there is diversity in unity, and *a triple consciousness and will* are consistent with, and even find their perfection in, a single essence.[93]

Father, Son, and Holy Spirit, while equal in essence and dignity, stand to each other in an order of personality, office, and operation. . . . The subordination of the *person* of the Son to the *person* of the Father, or in other words an order of personality, office, and operation which permits the Father to be officially first, the Son second, and the Spirit third, is perfectly consistent with equality. Priority is not necessarily superiority. . . . We frankly recognize an eternal subordination of Christ to the Father, but we maintain at the same time that this subordination is a subordination of order, office, and operation, not a subordination of essence.[94]

Louis Berkhof (1939):

The only subordination of which we can speak, is a subordination in respect to order and relationship. . . . Generation and procession take place within the Divine Being, and imply a certain subordination as to the manner of personal subsistence, but not subordination as far as the possession of the divine essence is concerned. This ontological Trinity and its inherent order is the metaphysical basis of the economical Trinity.[95]

J. I. Packer (1973):

Thus the obedience of the God-man to the Father while He was on earth was not a new relationship occasioned by the incarnation, but the continuation in time of the eternal relationship between the Son and the Father in heaven.[96]

Carl F. H. Henry (1982):

The creeds speak of the subordination, distinction and union of the three persons without implying an inferiority of any; since all three persons have a common divine essence they affirm the Son's subordination to the Father, and the Spirit's subordination to the Father and the Son. This subordination pertains to mode of subsistence and to mode of operations.[97]

---

93. Strong, *Systematic Theology*, 1:332.
94. Strong, *Systematic Theology*, 342.
95. Berkhof, *Systematic Theology*, 88–89.
96. J. I. Packer, *Knowing God* (Downers Grove, IL: Inter-Varsity Press, 1973), 54–55.

97. Carl F. H. Henry, *God, Revelation and Authority*, 6 vols. (Waco, TX: Word, 1976–83), 5:205.

Thomas Oden (1987, 1989, 1992):

The obedience of the Son to the Father (John 15:10) does not imply that the son is inferior to the Father. The Son did not become less than the father by becoming eternally obedient to the father's will (Philippians 2:5–11).[98]

John Feinberg (2001):

Even as Father, Son, and Holy Spirit deeply love one another, work together to accomplish their goals in our universe, and when needed, *submit their individual will to the wishes and plans of the other member of the Godhead* (e.g., Matt 26:39, where Jesus says not his will but the Father's), we find our model for interpersonal relations."[99]

John Frame (2002):

The persons of the Trinity voluntarily subordinate themselves to one another in the roles they perform in respect to creation. As we have seen, the Father sends the Son into the world, and *the Son joyfully obeys his Father's will.* . . . The Son and the Spirit are voluntarily subordinate to the commands of the Father, because that kind of subordination is appropriate to their eternal nature as persons.[100]

Robert Letham (2004):

The Son's submission to the Father is compatible with his full and unabbreviated deity. Therefore, we may rightly say that the Son submits in eternity to the Father, without in any way breaking his indissoluble oneness with the Father or the Holy Spirit, and without in any way jeopardizing his equality.[101]

Bruce Ware (2019):

Within the relations and rules of the Father, the Son, and the Spirit, one finds a prevailing authority and submission structure that flows from the eternal relations of origin and gives order and direction to the ways the three Trinitarian persons relate and function. This claim finds wide and uniform biblical support."[102]

98. Thomas Oden, *Classic Christianity: A Systematic Theology*, 3 vols. in 1 (New York: HarperOne, 1992), 109.

99. John S. Feinberg, *No One Like Him: The Doctrine of God* (Wheaton, IL: Crossway, 2001), 441–42.

100. John M. Frame, *The Doctrine of God* (Phillipsburg, NJ: P&R, 2002), 719–20.

101. Robert Letham, *The Holy Trinity* (Phillipsburg, NJ: 2004), 402.

102. Bruce Ware, "Unity and Distinction of the Trinitarian Persons," in *Trinitarian Theology: Theological Models and Doctrinal Application*, ed. by Keith Whitfield (Nashville: B&H, 2019), 60.

Michael Horton (2011):

> Furthermore, biblical revelation identified each of these persons as a think-
> ing, *willing*, and active agent. Nothing exhibits this fact more than the covenant
> of redemption (*pactum salutis*) made between the divine persons in eternity. . . .
> Although all three persons are mutually active in every external work of the
> Godhead, they are active differently."[103]

In light of these statements, it is surprising to find some opponents of the eternal
submission of the Son claiming that this belief is inconsistent with an orthodox understanding of the doctrine of the Trinity. This implies the remarkable claim that such
widely influential and highly respected theologians as Charles Hodge, A. H. Strong,
Louis Berkhof, J. I. Packer, Carl F. H. Henry, Thomas Oden, and John Frame are all
wrong about one of the central doctrines of the Christian faith.

Moreover, the opponents of the idea of the Son's eternal submission have a glaring
weakness in the arguments: where is even one quotation from any significant theologian
in the history of the church (prior to about 1980) saying that it is contrary to Scripture
to say that the Son has eternally been obedient to the Father or subject to the authority
of the Father? I have seen no such statement quoted in any of their objections. So are
these objections actually an innovation in the history of Christian doctrine?

**i. Should We Say That the Submission of the Son to the Father Is Eternal but
Not Necessary?** Is this authority/submission relationship between Father and Son only
found in the works of God outside of himself (such as creation and redemption), the
works that theologians have called the *opera ad extra* ("works to the outside")? Or does
this relationship also belong to the necessary activity of God within the Trinity, what
theologians have called the *opera ad intra* ("works to the inside")? We must be cautious
here because the eternal relationships among the three members of the Trinity are
largely a matter of mystery, with little explicit testimony from Scripture.

I think we can say at least that (1) the names Father and Son (and Spirit) are *eternal*
names and suggest some kind of priority for the Father in the relationship; (2) all of
God's works outside himself (his *opera ad extra*) are voluntary, not necessary (see the
discussion of God's free will in chapter 13, p. 254), and therefore all the works of God
in creation and redemption that show a pattern of the Son's submission to the Father
were entirely voluntary, not necessary; (3) what Scripture reveals to us about God's
works in creation and redemption is the primary way we have of knowing what God is
like in himself (that is, the economic Trinity reflects the ontological Trinity); (4) the
eternal generation of the Son is necessary to the very nature of God and this suggests the

---

103. Michael Scott Horton, *The Christian Faith: A Systematic Theology for Pilgrims on the Way* (Grand Rapids:
Zondervan, 2011), 303.

appropriateness of some kind of internal ordering of the relationship;[104] and (5) many of those who deny an eternal relationship of authority and submission end up supporting a kind of egalitarian relationship among the members of the Trinity for which there is no explicit support in Scripture while also claiming that everything revealed in Scripture about the Father-Son relationship does not really tell us who God is in himself.[105]

Although the nearly 400-year-old wording is somewhat difficult, the comments of Jonathan Edwards (1703–1758) are helpful:

> Though a subordination of the persons of the Trinity in their actings be not from any proper natural subjection one to another, and so must be conceived of as in some respect established by mutual free agreement . . . yet this agreement establishing this economy is not to be looked upon as merely arbitrary. . . . But there is a natural decency or fitness in that order and economy that is established. 'Tis fit that the order of the acting of the persons of the Trinity should be agreeable to the order of their subsisting: that as the Father is first in the order of subsisting, so he should be first in the order of acting. . . . therefore the persons of the Trinity all consent to this order, and establish it by agreement, as they all naturally delight in what is in itself fit, suitable and beautiful. Therefore. . . . This order [or] economy of the persons of the Trinity with respect to their actions ad extra is to be conceived of as prior to the covenant of redemption. . . .
>
> That the economy of the persons of the Trinity, establishing that order of their acting that is agreeable to the order of their subsisting, is entirely diverse from the covenant of redemption, and prior to it, not only appears from the nature of things, but appears evidently from the Scripture.[106]

**j. Should We See an Analogy between the Father-Son Relationship in the Trinity and the Husband-Wife Relationship in Marriage?** Since "God created man in his own image . . . male and female he created them" (Gen. 1:27), there are numerous ways in which we see analogies to the Trinitarian God in our human lives. Essential to any analogy is the fact that the things compared are similar in some ways and different in other ways, and so it is here. Yes, Scripture does point to an analogy between marriage and the relationship between Christ and the church (Eph. 5:22–33), but elsewhere it also points to an analogy between marriage and the relationship of Christ and the Father (1 Cor. 11:3),[107] and there should be no objection to our using this analogy and

---

104. Scott Swain and Michael Allen say that "the obedience of the Son is the economic extension of his eternal generation to a Spirit-enabled, creaturely life of obedience" (Scott Swain and Michael Allen, "The Obedience of the Eternal Son," *International Journal of Systematic Theology* 15, no. 2 [April 2013]: 117).

105. I am grateful to my friend Bruce Ware for this fourth

point and for helpful interaction on this entire section on the Father-Son relationship in the Trinity.

106. Jonathan Edwards, "Miscellanies," in *Works of Jonathan Edwards*, vol. 20, no. 1062 (New Haven, CT: Yale University Press, 1957–), 431.

107. When Paul says, "The head of every man is Christ, the head of a wife is her husband, and the head of Christ is God"

pointing out both the similarities and the differences. One important similarity is that just as Christ is equal to the Father in his deity and also subject to the Father in their relationship, so a wife is equal to her husband in her humanity and importance and also subject to his leadership in the relationship.

## 6. What Is the Relationship between the Three Persons and the Being of God?

After the preceding discussion, one question remains unresolved: What is the difference between "person" and "being" in this discussion? How can we say that God is one undivided being yet that in this one being there are three persons?

First, it is important to affirm that each person is completely and fully God; that is, that each person has the whole fullness of God's being in himself. The Son is not partly God or just one-third of God, but the Son is wholly and fully God, and so is the Father and the Holy Spirit. Thus it would not be right to think of the Trinity according to figure 14.1, with each person representing only one-third of God's being.

Rather, we must say that the person of the Father possesses the *whole being* of God in himself. Similarly, the Son possesses the *whole being* of God in himself, and the Holy Spirit possesses the *whole being* of God in himself. When we speak of the Father, Son, and Holy Spirit together we are not speaking of any greater being than when we speak of the Father alone, or the Son alone, or the Holy Spirit alone. The Father is *all* of God's being. The Son also is *all* of God's being. And the Holy Spirit is *all* of God's being.

**God's Being Is Not Divided into Three Equal Parts
Belonging to the Three Members of the Trinity**
*Figure 14.1*

This is what the Athanasian Creed affirmed in the following sentences:

And the Catholic Faith is this: That we worship one God in Trinity, and Trinity in Unity; Neither confounding the Persons: nor dividing the Substance [Essence].
For there is one Person of the Father: another of the Son: and another of the Holy

(1 Cor. 11:3), his first use of the word "Christ" must refer to the incarnate Christ as God-man, and so the second use of "Christ" in that verse must also refer to Christ as the God-man. But the fact remains that he is still fully divine, and therefore he is still equal to the Father in all his divine attributes, yet he is also subject to the authority of the Father who is his "head" in this verse.

Spirit. But the Godhead of the Father, of the Son, and of the Holy Spirit, is all one: the Glory equal, the Majesty coeternal. Such as the Father is: such is the Son: and such is the Holy Spirit. . . . For like as we are compelled by the Christian verity: to acknowledge every Person by himself to be God and Lord: So are we forbidden by the Catholic Religion: to say, There be [are] three Gods, or three Lords.

But if each person is fully God and has all of God's being, then we also should not think that the personal distinctions are any kind of additional attributes added on to the being of God, something after the pattern of figure 14.2.

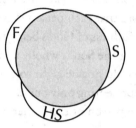

**The Personal Distinctions in the Trinity Are Not
Something Added onto God's Real Being**
*Figure 14.2*

Rather, each person of the Trinity has all of the attributes of God, and no one person has any attributes that are not possessed by the others.

On the other hand, we must say that the persons are real, that they are not just different ways of looking at the one being of God. (This would be modalism or Sabellianism, as discussed above.) So figure 14.3 would not be appropriate.

Rather, we need to think of the Trinity in such a way that the reality of the three persons is maintained, and each person is seen as relating to the others as an "I" (a first person) and a "you" (a second person) and a "he" (a third person).

The only way it seems possible to do this is to say that the distinction between the persons is not a difference in "being" but a difference in "relationships." This is something far removed from our human experience, where every different human "person" is a different being as well. Somehow God's being is so much greater than ours that within his one undivided being there can be an unfolding into interpersonal relationships, so that there can be three distinct persons.

What then are the differences between Father, Son, and Holy Spirit? There is no difference in attributes at all. The only difference between them is the way they relate to each other and to the creation. The unique quality of the Father is the way he *relates as Father* to the Son and Holy Spirit. The unique quality of the Son is the way he *relates as Son*. And the unique quality of the Holy Spirit is the way he *relates as Spirit*.

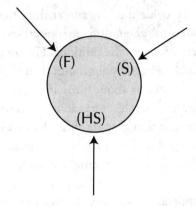

**The Persons of the Trinity Are Not Just Three Different
Ways of Looking at the One Being God**
*Figure 14.3*

While the three diagrams given above represented erroneous ideas to be avoided, the following diagram may be helpful in thinking about the existence of three persons in the one undivided being of God.

In figure 14.4, the Father is represented as the section of the circle designated by F, and also the rest of the circle, moving around clockwise from the letter F; the Son is represented as the section of the circle designated by S, and also the rest of the circle, moving around clockwise from the letter S; and the Holy Spirit is represented as the section of the circle marked HS and also the rest of the circle, moving around clockwise from the HS. Thus there are three distinct persons, but each person is fully and wholly God. Of course the representation is imperfect, for it cannot represent God's infinity or personality—or indeed any of his attributes. It also requires looking at the circle in more than one way in order to understand it: the dotted lines must be understood to indicate personal relationship, not any division in the one being of God. Thus the circle itself represents God's being while the dotted lines represent a form of personal existence other than a difference in being. But the diagram may nonetheless help guard against some misunderstanding.

**There Are Three Distinct Persons, and the Being of
Each Person Is Equal to the Whole Being of God**
*Figure 14.4*

Our human personalities provide another faint analogy that might help in thinking about the Trinity. A man can think about different objects outside of himself, and when he does this, he is the subject who does the thinking. He can also think about himself, and then he is the object who is being thought about; then he is both subject and object. Moreover, he can reflect on his ideas about himself as a third thing, neither subject nor object, but *thoughts* that he as a subject has about himself as an object. When this happens, the subject, object, and thoughts are three distinct things. Yet each thing in a way includes his whole being. All of the man is the subject, and all of the man is the object, and the thoughts (though in a lesser sense) are thoughts about all of himself as a person.[108]

But if the unfolding of human personality allows this kind of complexity, then the unfolding of God's personality must allow for far greater complexity than this. Within the one being of God, the "unfolding" of personality must allow for the existence of three distinct persons, while each person still has the whole of God's being in himself. The difference in persons must be one of relationship, not one of being, and yet each person must really exist. This tripersonal form of being is far beyond our ability to comprehend. *It is a kind of existence far different from anything we have experienced* and far different from anything else in the universe.

Because the existence of three persons in one God is something beyond our understanding, Christian theology has come to use the word *person* to speak of these differences in relationship, not because we fully understand what is meant by the word *person* when referring to the Trinity, but rather so that we might say something instead of saying nothing at all. Augustine wrote,

> Yet, when the question is asked, What three? human language labors altogether under great poverty of speech. The answer, however, is given, three "persons," not that it might be [completely] spoken, but that it might not be left [holy] unspoken.[109]

## 7. Can We Understand the Doctrine of the Trinity?

We should be warned by the errors that have been made in the past. They have all come about through attempts to *simplify* the doctrine of the Trinity and make it completely understandable, removing all mystery from it. This we can never do. However, it is not correct to say that we cannot understand the doctrine of the Trinity at all. Certainly we can understand and know that God is three persons, and that each person is fully God, and that there is one God. We can know these things because the

---

108. We said above that no analogy teaches the Trinity perfectly, and this one has several shortcomings as well: this man remains as one person; he is not three persons. And his "thoughts" do not equal all of him as a person. But the analogy is helpful in hinting at something of the complexity even of human personality and suggesting that the complexity of divine personality is something far greater than this.

109. Augustine, *On the Trinity* 5.9, in *Nicene and Post-Nicene Fathers*, series 1, vol. 3, ed. Philip Schaff (repr., Grand Rapids: Eerdmans, 1993), 92.

Bible teaches them. Moreover, we can know some things about the way the persons relate to each other (see the section above). But what we cannot understand fully is how to fit together those distinct biblical teachings. We wonder how there can be three distinct persons, and each person have the whole being of God in himself, and yet God is only one undivided being. This we are unable to understand. In fact, it is spiritually healthy for us to acknowledge openly that God's very being is far greater than we can ever comprehend. This humbles us before God and draws us to worship him without reservation.

But it should also be said that Scripture does not ask us to believe in a contradiction. A contradiction would be "There is one God and there is not one God," or "God is three persons and God is not three persons," or even (which is similar to the previous statement) "God is three persons and God is one person." But to say that "God is three persons and there is one God" is not a contradiction. It is something we do not understand, and it is therefore a mystery or a paradox, but that should not trouble us as long as the different aspects of the mystery are clearly taught by Scripture, for as long as we are finite creatures and not omniscient deity, there will always (for all eternity) be things that we do not fully understand. Louis Berkhof wisely says,

> The Trinity is a mystery . . . man cannot comprehend it and make it intelligible. It
> is intelligible in some of its relations and modes of manifestation, but unintelligible
> in its essential nature. . . . The real difficulty lies in the relation in which the persons
> in the Godhead stand to the divine essence and to one another; and this is a difficulty
> which the Church cannot remove, but only try to reduce to its proper proportion by a
> proper definition of terms. It has never tried to explain the mystery of the Trinity but
> only sought to formulate the doctrine of the Trinity in such a manner that the errors
> which endangered it were warded off.[110]

Berkhof also says, "It is especially when we reflect on the relation of the three persons to the divine essence that all analogies fail us and we become deeply conscious of the fact that the Trinity is a mystery far beyond our comprehension. It is the incomprehensible glory of the Godhead."[111]

## E. APPLICATION

Because God in himself has both unity and diversity, it is not surprising that unity and diversity are also reflected in the human relationships he has established. We see this first in marriage. When God created man in his image, he did not create merely isolated individuals, but Scripture tells us, "male and female he created them" (Gen. 1:27). And in the unity of marriage (see Gen. 2:24) we see not a triunity as with God

---

110. Berkhof, *Systematic Theology*, 89.          111. Ibid., 88.

but a remarkable unity of two persons, persons who remain distinct individuals yet also become one in body, mind, and spirit (cf. 1 Cor. 6:16–20; Eph. 5:31). In fact, in the relationship between man and woman in marriage we see also a picture of the relationship between the Father and Son in the Trinity. Paul says, "But I want you to understand that the head of every man is Christ, the head of a wife is her husband, and the head of Christ is God" (1 Cor. 11:3). Here, just as the Father has a leadership role with respect to the Son in the Trinity, so the husband has a leadership role with respect to his wife in marriage. The husband's role is parallel to that of God the Father and the wife's role is parallel to that of God the Son. Moreover, just as Father and Son are equal in deity and importance and personhood, so the husband and wife are equal in humanity and importance and personhood. And although it is not explicitly mentioned in Scripture, the gift of children within marriage, coming from both the father and the mother, and subject to the authority of both father and mother, is analogous to the relationship of the Holy Spirit to the Father and Son in the Trinity.

But the human family is not the only way in which God has ordained that there would be both diversity and unity in the world that reflect something of his own excellence. In the church we have "many members" yet "one body" (1 Cor. 12:12). Paul reflects on the great diversity among members of the human body (1 Cor. 12:14–26) and says that the church is like that. We have many different members in our churches with different gifts and interests, and we depend on and help each other, thereby demonstrating great diversity and great unity at the same time. When we see different people doing many different things in the life of a church, we ought to thank God that this allows us to glorify him by reflecting something of the unity and diversity of the Trinity.

We should also notice that God's purpose in the history of the universe has frequently been to display unity in diversity—and thus to display his glory. We see this not only in the diversity of gifts in the church (1 Cor. 12:12–26) but also in the unity of Jews and gentiles, so that all people, diverse as they are, are united in Christ (Eph. 2:16; 3:8–10; see also Rev. 7:9). Paul is amazed that God's plans for the history of redemption have been like a great symphony so that his wisdom is beyond finding out (Rom. 11:33–36). Even in the mysterious unity between Christ and the church, in which we are called the bride of Christ (Eph. 5:31–32), we see unity beyond what we ever would have imagined, unity with the Son of God himself. Yet in all this we never lose our individual identity but remain distinct persons always able to worship and serve God as unique individuals.

Eventually the entire universe will partake of this unity of purpose with every diverse part contributing to the worship of God the Father, Son, and Holy Spirit, for one day, at the name of Jesus, every knee will bow "in heaven and on earth and under the earth, and every tongue confess that Jesus Christ is Lord, to the glory of God the Father" (Phil. 2:10–11).

On a more everyday level, there are many activities that we carry out as human beings (in the labor force, in social organizations, in musical performances, and in athletic teams, for example) in which many distinct individuals contribute to a unity of purpose or activity. As we see in these activities a reflection of the wisdom of God in allowing us both unity and diversity, we can see a faint reflection of the glory of God in his Trinitarian existence. Though we will never fully comprehend the mystery of the Trinity, we can worship God for who he is both in our songs of praise and in our words and actions as they reflect something of his excellent character.

## ADDITIONAL NOTE: CHRISTIANITY AND MORMONISM

At the end of these chapters on the attributes of God and the doctrine of the Trinity, it is appropriate to say something about the differences between Christianity and Mormonism, because Mormons teach a vastly different understanding of who God is.

The ten main points in this additional note are taken from the brief, remarkably insightful book by Ron Rhodes, *The 10 Most Important Things You Can Say to a Mormon*.[112] After each point I have added some comments of my own, taken both from the discussion of Mormonism by Rhodes and from my own understanding of Christian theology. (For those who are interested, Rhodes has also published a much more extensively documented book on Mormonism, *Reasoning from the Scriptures with the Mormons*.)[113]

I could also add a personal note. I have known a number of Mormon friends in my life, and they have consistently been kind, thoughtful, friendly, and gracious persons. In addition, we often find that we have moral convictions about human conduct that are very similar. Therefore, I am including these ten points in this book not merely for the sake of being critical but in the genuine hope that many of our Mormon friends might read it and realize that Mormonism is not a different version of the Christian faith but an entirely different religion. And I hope that from that realization will come a desire to enter into a personal relationship with Christ through faith alone, not by works (see point 10 below).

### 1. THE MORMON CHURCH IS NOT THE "RESTORED CHURCH"

In 1820, Joseph Smith, the founder of Mormonism, went into the woods to pray and ask God which church to join. At that point, two personages, the Father and the Son, appeared to him, and the Son told him not to join any church, because "the Personage who addressed me said that all their creeds were an abomination in his sight."[114] This led Smith to found the Mormon church as the "one true church," a "restored church."

It is important to understand the implications of this claim. It means that all the

---

112. Ron Rhodes, *The 10 Most Important Things You Can Say to a Mormon* (Eugene, OR: Harvest House, 2001). Except for the next footnote, all subsequent references to Rhodes in this appendix refer to this book.

113. Ron Rhodes and Marian Bodine, *Reasoning from the Scriptures with the Mormons* (Eugene, OR: Harvest House, 1995).

114. Rhodes, *The 10 Most Important Things*, 9.

majestic, eloquent summaries of the Christian faith that have been preserved in the major creeds throughout the centuries are "an abomination." Consider the Nicene Creed (AD 325, 381):

> I believe in one God the Father Almighty; Maker of heaven and earth, and of all things visible and invisible.
>
> And in one Lord Jesus Christ, the only-begotten Son of God, begotten of the Father before all worlds, God of God, Light of Light, very God of very God, begotten, not made, being of one substance with the Father; by whom all things were made; who, for us men and for our salvation, came down from heaven, and was incarnate by the Holy Spirit of the Virgin Mary, and was made man; and was crucified also for us under Pontius Pilate; he suffered and was buried; and the third day he rose again, according to the Scriptures; and ascended into heaven, and sitteth on the right hand of the Father; and he shall come again, with glory, to judge both the quick and the dead; whose kingdom shall have no end.
>
> And in the Holy Spirit, the Lord and Giver of Life; who proceedeth from the Father and the Son; who with the Father and the Son together is worshiped and glorified; who spake by the Prophets. And one Holy Catholic and Apostolic Church. I acknowledge one Baptism for the remission of sins; and I look for the resurrection of the dead, and the life of the world to come. Amen.

If this creed is an "abomination," then this involves a denial of (1) God as the Creator of heaven and earth, (2) Jesus Christ as the eternal Son of God, (3) the virgin birth of Christ, (4) the crucifixion of Christ for our salvation, (5) the resurrection of Christ on the third day, (6) Christ's second coming, (7) the final judgment at which Christ will be the judge, (8) the deity of the Holy Spirit, (9) our future resurrection, (10) our future eternal life in the world to come. Most of these doctrines and many others are found in numerous other major creeds of the Christian church, including the Apostles Creed, the Chalcedonian Creed, the Formula of Concord, the Westminster Confession of Faith, and many others (see appendix 1, pp. 1438–88).

If creeds such as this are "an abomination," then all the major doctrines of the Christian faith are false, and we no longer have Christianity at all. We are left with a different religion altogether.

Directly related to this idea is the second thing that Mormonism teaches, according to Ron Rhodes: "The Church of Jesus Christ of Latter-Day Saints (Mormons) teaches that total apostasy engulfed the church soon after the death of the last apostle; therefore the 'one true church' needed to be restored."[115] But this claim is simply false, as is clear from an examination of documents from early church history.

---

115. Ibid.

The apostle John, who wrote the book of Revelation, died in AD 90–95. But there were still many Christian leaders and teachers alive who had known John and the other apostles personally before they died. These authors are commonly known as the "Apostolic Fathers," and their writings are easily available in English or in Greek or both.[116] Then for writings of early church leaders immediately after the Apostolic Fathers and until AD 325, there is the frequently reprinted ten-volume set called the *Ante-Nicene Fathers*,[117] all in readily accessible English translations.

Anyone can read these writings and see immediately that, though they are not perfect in their understanding of biblical doctrine, it is simply a falsehood to say that they have committed "total apostasy." Their writings frequently echo and regularly quote passages from both the Old and New Testaments. In fact, merely the *index to scriptural quotations* in these early Christian writers contains fifty-six pages of fine print referring to thousands of quotations from the Bible![118] Far from lapsing into "total apostasy," the early church was repeatedly fighting off false teachers and bringing itself step-by-step into more and more precise and faithful doctrinal summaries of the teachings of Scripture.

Any group that places itself in substantial opposition to the consensus of these early Christian writers, as the Mormon church does, is not a true "restored church," but is itself guilty of complete deviation from the Christian faith as taught in the Bible.

## 2. The Book of Mormon Is Man-Made

The Book of Mormon claims to be "an abridged account of God's dealings with the original inhabitants of the American continent from about 2247 BC to AD 421."[119] Mormons claim that "it was originally engraved on gold plates by ancient prophets in the language of 'Reformed Egyptian,' deposited in a stone box, and buried in the Hill Cumorah in New York.... Smith is said to have 'translated' the Book of Mormon from the gold plates using a 'seer stone.'"[120] In this process, every word and every letter was supposedly given to Joseph Smith by God.

However, "history proves there have been more than 3,913 changes between the original edition of the Book of Mormon published in 1830 and the ones printed and issued through the mid-1970s."[121] If every word and every letter were given directly to Joseph Smith by God, then why would there be a need for nearly 4,000 changes?[122]

116. See Michael W. Holmes, ed., *The Apostolic Fathers in English*, 3rd ed. (Grand Rapids: Baker Academic, 2006); Holmes, *The Apostolic Fathers: Greek Texts and English Translations*, 3rd ed. (Grand Rapids: Baker, 2007).

117. Alexander Roberts and James Donaldson, eds., *The Ante-Nicene Fathers*, 10 Vols. (Edinburgh: T&T Clark, 1867–1873; repr., Grand Rapids: Eerdmans, 1973).

118. Ibid., 9:211–66.

119. Rhodes, *The 10 Most Important Things*, 19.

120. Ibid., 19.

121. Ibid., 21–22.

122. This is far different from what Christians claim about the Bible. Changes to modern Bible translations because of the discovery of more accurate ancient manuscripts is attempting to determine more accurately what the original manuscripts said, not at all an attempt to correct anything in the original manuscripts themselves. But Mormons claim that the Book of Mormon as dictated in English by Joseph Smith was the "original manuscript" in that it contained the words originally given by God directly to Joseph Smith.

In addition, while the accuracy of the Bible has been repeatedly confirmed by thousands of archaeological discoveries in the ancient Mediterranean world,[123] "there is no archaeological support for the Book of Mormon. According to Mormon scriptures, the Nephite and Lamanite nations had huge populations that lived in large, fortified cities. They waged large-scale wars with each other for hundreds of years, culminating in a conflict in which hundreds of thousands of people were killed in AD 385, near Hill Cumorah in present-day New York State. . . . But there is no [archaeological] evidence that it occurred."[124]

The Book of Mormon also contains plagiarism, such as "whole chapters that have been lifted from the book of Isaiah" in the King James Version.[125] But the King James Version was not published until 1611, while Mormons claim the "Reformed Egyptian" tablets that were translated by Joseph Smith were written sometime before AD 421, over 1,000 years before the King James Version. How then could the Book of Mormon, based on AD 421 tablets, just "happen" to have the exact wording of a number of chapters from a 1611 translation of the Bible?

## 3. THE BIBLE IS GOD'S WORD AND IT IS TRUSTWORTHY

Mormons "acknowledge that the original manuscripts penned by biblical authors were the Word of God," but they argue that "what passes as 'the Bible' today is corrupt. It can only be trusted insofar as 'it is translated correctly.'" They also believe that "large portions of the Bible have been lost through the centuries."[126]

However, as I argued extensively in chapter 3 of this book, a study of the canon of Scripture shows that we do have the right books in the Bible today. And as far as the Bible being "translated correctly," there are hundreds of highly trained Bible translation teams throughout the world translating the Bible into hundreds of languages, and there are many English translations produced by experts in Hebrew and Greek, the original languages of the biblical manuscripts. All the major doctrines of the Christian faith could be taught from any of those translations today.

Several thousand ancient manuscripts now stored in research libraries throughout the world confirm the remarkably reliable transmission of the biblical text over many centuries. Everyone recognizes that there are minor differences in spelling and wording among the ancient manuscripts. But in direct contradiction to Mormon claims, there is no historical evidence of any substantial corruption in the copying and transmission of the texts that would change any significant point of Christian teaching today (see chapter 4 for further discussion).

123. Rhodes, *The 10 Most Important Things*, 40–41.

124. Ibid., 25. Rhodes includes references to several academic studies by archaeologists. See also Josh McDowell and Sean McDowell, *Evidence That Demands a Verdict: Life-Changing Truth for a Skeptical World* (Nashville: Nelson, 2017), 414–22; also James Hoffmeier and Dennis Magary, *Do Historical Matters Matter to Faith?* (Wheaton, IL: Crossway, 2012), 427–516; *ESV Archaeology Study Bible* (Wheaton, IL: Crossway, 2016).

125. Rhodes, *The 10 Most Important Things*, 23–24.

126. Ibid., 33.

## 4. The One True God Is an Eternal Spirit Being

Mormons teach "that God the Father was once a mortal man who continually progressed to become a god (an exalted man). . . . Today, then, God, the Eternal Father, our Father in Heaven, is an exalted, perfected, and glorified Personage having a tangible body of flesh and bones."[127]

By contrast, Scripture plainly says that "God is not man" (Num. 23:19; see also Rom.1:23) and that he is "invisible" (Col. 1:15; 1 Tim. 1:17) and eternal (Gen. 1:1; Ps. 90:2; 93:2; Rev. 1:8; 22:13). In chapters 12 and 13 of this book, I have given much more information about the infinite God of the Bible, who is not a limited, finite creature but is eternal, unchanging, omnipresent, and omnipotent. While Mormons say they believe in "God," the God that they describe is not the one true God of the Bible.

## 5. The Trinity Involves Three Persons in One God

Mormonism teaches:

The Father, Son, and Holy Spirit are not three persons in one God, as historic Christianity has taught, but rather that they are three separate gods. . . . There are many other gods as well. . . . In Mormon theology, just as Jesus has a Father, so the Father allegedly has a Father. . . . There is a Father of the Father of the Father of the Father, *ad infinitum*. . . . There is also a heavenly wife (or wives) for each. . . . All of this is part and parcel of the polytheistic world of Mormonism. Mormons believe in numerous gods. . . . And they believe that they, too, will one day become gods.[128]

But Mormon polytheism is far different from the Christian belief in the one true God of the Bible, the Creator of all things in heaven and earth. God says, "I am the Lord, and there is no other, besides me there is no God" (Isa. 45:5). And we read in Deuteronomy, "Hear, O Israel: The Lord our God, the Lord is one" (Deut. 6:4).

As I explained earlier in this chapter, the Christian doctrine of the Trinity, as anchored by many verses of Scripture, is that there are *three persons in one God*, not that there are three gods. This is far different from the polytheism of Mormonism.

## 6. Humans Are Creatures and Never Become Gods

According to Mormon teaching, "the ultimate goal in Mormonism is godhood." Rhodes quotes Mormon leaders as teaching that we were created "to become gods like unto our Father in heaven." He adds, "This exaltation to godhood is known as attaining 'eternal life' to Mormons." In addition, a Mormon teaching manual says, "We can become gods like our heavenly Father. This is exaltation." But in order to reach that

127. Rhodes, *The 10 Most Important Things*, 45.   128. Ibid., 53–54.

status, we must overcome many "physical temptations and trials" during a period of "mortality," which is the Mormon term for our lifetime here on earth.[129]

But the Bible never teaches that we will become gods. We are created "in the image of God" (Gen. 1:26–27), but that simply means that we are like God in various ways and that we represent him. Human beings do not become gods (see chapter 42).

## 7. Jesus Is God, Not the Spirit-Brother of Lucifer

Mormons teach that

> Jesus was begotten as the first Spirit-child of the Father (Elohim) and one of his unnamed wives ("Heavenly Mother"). Jesus was allegedly the first and highest of all the spirit children. . . . Because the heavenly Father and Mother had *many* spirit children, Jesus is often referred to by Mormons as "our elder brother." (Lucifer, too, is the spirit-brother of Jesus.) Jesus progressed by obedience and devotion to the truth in the spirit world until he became God. This allegedly took eons of time. . . . [Mormons] do not worship or pray to Jesus. What this means in terms of Mormon theology is that Jesus is not really unique. . . . When it came time for his mortal birth on earth, Jesus was begotten through sexual relations between a flesh-and-bone heavenly Father and Mary. . . . Jesus "atoned for Adam's sin, leaving us responsible only for our own sins."[130]

In these beliefs about Jesus Christ, Mormonism once again shows itself to be a completely different religion from Christianity. The teaching of the Bible is that Jesus is the Son of God who eternally existed with the Father and Holy Spirit, who was born of the Virgin Mary and lived on this earth as both God and man in one person. Because Christ is fully God, he is worthy of our worship, and he hears our prayers. He paid the penalty for the sins of all who believe in him (see especially chapters 26 and 27). "In the beginning was the Word, and the Word was with God, and the Word was God. He was in the beginning with God. All things were made through him, and without him was not any thing made that was made" (John 1:1–3).

## 8. Salvation Is by Grace through Faith, Not by Works

In Mormon teaching,

> Mormons typically define "sin" as a wrong judgment, a mistake . . . thus removing the moral sting. . . . With this weak view of sin, it is not surprising that Jesus' role in salvation is much reduced. . . . Jesus' atonement basically means He was able to overcome physical death for the human race. . . . Because of what He accomplished,

we will all be *resurrected*. When Mormons talk about "salvation" . . . they essentially mean *resurrection*. . . . Jesus did His part, and now it is up to us to do our part to prove ourselves worthy of exaltation to godhood. Mormons reject the doctrine of justification by faith. . . . Grace is said to be involved in Mormon salvation, but "grace" in "Mormonese" is simply God's enabling power that allows people to lay hold on eternal life and exaltation after they have expended their own best efforts.[131]

These Mormon beliefs on salvation show that, at the heart of the gospel message, Mormonism teaches doctrines that are far different from the New Testament and different from the Christian faith throughout history. Christianity teaches that "Christ died for our sins" (1 Cor. 15:3) and that "we also have believed in Christ Jesus, in order to be *justified by faith in Christ* and not by works of the law, because by works of the law no one will be justified" (Gal. 2:16). See further discussion in chapters 24 (sin), 27 (atonement), 33 (the gospel call), 35 (conversion), and 36 (justification).

## 9. THE AFTERLIFE INVOLVES HEAVEN AND HELL, NOT THREE DEGREES OF GLORY

According to Mormon teaching, after this life people will end up in one of three kingdoms: the "celestial kingdom" which "is inhabited by faithful Mormons. . . . On this level people can attain ultimate exaltation to godhood." The second level is "the terrestrial kingdom," which is reserved for "non-Mormons who live moral lives as well as 'less than valiant' Mormons." The third level is the "telestial kingdom," which is "where the majority of people go."[132]

But Christian teaching, which is faithful to Scripture, teaches that there will be a final judgment, and after that people will end up in either heaven or hell forever (see chapters 56–57).

## 10. JESUS CHANGED MY LIFE FOREVER

After pointing out these nine differences between Mormonism and Christianity, Ron Rhodes emphasizes the importance of personal testimony. He says, "I bring this up because in your personal testimony to a Mormon, a pivotal part of it must be that you are *sure* of going to heaven precisely because you have a *personal relationship with Christ*. You have meaning in your present life not because you obey rules (like the massive list of rules the Mormon must heed during mortality), but because you are Christian. Indeed, you have a *personal relationship with Christ*."[133]

Certainly the idea that we can have an individual, personal relationship with Christ himself is found in many places in the New Testament (see chapter 35), with references

---

131. Ibid., 89–90.
132. Ibid., 103.
133. Ibid., 113, italics in original.

to a number of passages that talk about placing our trust in Christ as a living person. An invitation to such a relationship was beautifully expressed in Jesus' words to the church in Laodicea, words that could also be spoken by Jesus to any of our Mormon friends today: "Behold, I stand at the door and knock. If anyone hears my voice and opens the door, I will come in to him and eat with him, and he with me" (Rev. 3:20). Or this invitation, from Matthew's gospel: "Come to me, all who labor and are heavy laden, and I will give you rest. Take my yoke upon you, and learn from me, for I am gentle and lowly in heart, and you will find rest for your souls. For my yoke is easy, and my burden is light" (Matt. 11:28–30).

## QUESTIONS FOR PERSONAL APPLICATION

1. Why is God pleased when people exhibit faithfulness, love, and harmony within a family? What are some ways in which members of your family reflect the diversity found in the members of the Trinity? How does your family reflect the unity found among members of the Trinity? What are some ways in which your family relationships could reflect the unity of the Trinity more fully? How might the diversity of persons in the Trinity encourage parents to allow their children to develop different interests from each other, and from their parents, without thinking that the unity of the family will be damaged?

2. Have you ever thought that if your church allows new or different kinds of ministries to develop, it might hinder the unity of the church? Or have you thought that encouraging people to use other gifts for ministry than those that have been used in the past might be divisive in the church? How might the fact of unity and diversity in the Trinity help you to approach those questions?

3. Do you think that the Trinitarian nature of God is more fully reflected in a church in which all the members have the same ethnic background or one in which the members come from many different races and ethnicities (see Eph. 3:1–10)?

4. In addition to our relationships within our families, we all exist in other relationships to human authority in government, employment, voluntary societies, educational institutions, and athletics, for example. Sometimes we have authority over others, and sometimes we are subject to the authority of others. Whether in the family or in one of these other areas, give one example of a way in which your use of authority or your response to authority might become more like the pattern of relationships in the Trinity.

5. If we see the Trinitarian existence of God as the fundamental basis for all combinations of unity and diversity in the universe, then what are some other parts of creation that show both unity and diversity (for example, the interdependency of environmental systems on the earth, the fascinating activity of bees in

a hive, or the harmonious working of the various parts of the human body)? Do you think God has made us so that we take spontaneous delight in demonstrations of unity in diversity, such as a musical composition that manifests great unity and yet great diversity of various parts at the same time, or in the skillful execution of some planned strategy by members of an athletic team working together?

6. In the being of God we have infinite unity combined with the preservation of distinct personalities belonging to the members of the Trinity. How can this fact reassure us if we ever begin to fear that becoming more united to Christ as we grow in the Christian life (or becoming more united to one another in the church) might tend to obliterate our individual personalities? In heaven, do you think you will be exactly like everyone else, or will you have a personality that is distinctly your own? How do Eastern religions (such as Buddhism) differ from Christianity in this regard?

## Special Terms

*adoptionism*
*Arianism*
*economic subordination*
*eternal begetting of the Son*
*eternal generation of the Son*
filioque
homoiousios
homoousios
*modalism*
*modalistic monarchianism*
*only-begotten*
*ontological equality*
*Sabellianism*
*subordinationism*
*Trinity*
*tritheism*

## BIBLIOGRAPHY

(For an explanation of this bibliography see the note on the bibliography to chapter 1, pp. 23–24. Complete bibliographical data may be found on pp. 1489–96.)

### SECTIONS IN EVANGELICAL SYSTEMATIC THEOLOGIES

*1. Anglican (Episcopalian)*
   1882–92 . . . . . Litton, 91–108
   1930 . . . . . . . . Thomas, 20–31, 90–99
   2013 . . . . . . . . Bird, 92–125
   2013 . . . . . . . . Bray, 985–1021

*2. Arminian (Wesleyan or Methodist)*
   1875–76 . . . . . Pope, 1:253–87; 2:101–5

   1892–94 . . . . . Miley, 1:223–75
   1940 . . . . . . . . Wiley, 1:394–439
   1960 . . . . . . . . Purkiser, 143–44, 199–203
   1983 . . . . . . . . Carter, 1:127–29, 375–414
   1992 . . . . . . . . Oden, 1:181–224
   2002 . . . . . . . . Cottrell, 70–73

*3. Baptist*
   1767 . . . . . . . . Gill, 1:187–245
   1887 . . . . . . . . Boyce, 125–66
   1907 . . . . . . . . Strong, 304–52
   1917 . . . . . . . . Mullins, 203–13
   1976–83 . . . . . Henry, 5:165–213
   1987–94 . . . . . Lewis and Demarest, 1:251–88

1990–95 . . . . . Garrett, 1:305–38
2007 . . . . . . . . Akin, 182–88
2013 . . . . . . . . Erickson, 291–313

### 4. Dispensational
1947 . . . . . . . . Chafer, 1:272–347; 5:7–38;
        6:7–46
1949 . . . . . . . . Thiessen, 89–99
1986 . . . . . . . . Ryrie, 51–59
2002–2005 . . Geisler, 2:53–54, 278–312
2017 . . . . . . . . MacArthur and Mayhue,
        190–208

### 5. Lutheran
1917–24 . . . . . Pieper, 1:381–404
1934 . . . . . . . . Mueller, 147–60

### 6. Reformed (or Presbyterian)
1559 . . . . . . . . Calvin, 1:120–59 (1.13)
1679–85 . . . . . Turretin, *IET*, 1:253–310
1871–73 . . . . . Hodge, 1:442–534
1878 . . . . . . . . Dabney, 174–211
1887–1921 . . . Warfield, *BTS*, 22–156; *SSW*,
        1:88–92; *BD*, 133–74
1894 . . . . . . . . Shedd, 219–73
1906–11 . . . . . Bavinck, *RD*, 2:256–334
1910 . . . . . . . . Vos, 1:38–76
1937–66 . . . . . Murray, *CW*, 4:58–81
1938 . . . . . . . . Berkhof, 82–99
1998 . . . . . . . . Reymond, 206–342
2008 . . . . . . . . Van Genderen and Velema,
        143–63
2011 . . . . . . . . Horton, 273–308
2013 . . . . . . . . Frame, 39, 421–513
2013 . . . . . . . . Culver, 104–12
2016 . . . . . . . . Allen and Swain, 78–106
2017 . . . . . . . . Barrett, 189–216
2019 . . . . . . . . Letham, 66–154

### 7. Renewal (or charismatic/Pentecostal)
1988–92 . . . . . Williams, 1:83–94
1993 . . . . . . . . Menzies and Horton, 53–58
1995 . . . . . . . . Horton, 145–178
2008 . . . . . . . . Duffield and Van Cleave,
        88–120

## SECTIONS IN REPRESENTATIVE ROMAN CATHOLIC SYSTEMATIC THEOLOGIES

### 1. Roman Catholic: Traditional
1955 . . . . . . . . Ott, 50–75

### 2. Roman Catholic: Post–Vatican II
1980 . . . . . . . . McBrien, 1:343–66
2012 . . . . . . . . *CCC*, paragraphs 232–67

## OTHER WORKS

Allison, Gregg. *Historical Theology: An Introduction to Christian Doctrine; A Companion to Wayne Grudem's* Systematic Theology. Grand Rapids: Zondervan, 2011, 231–53.

Augustine. *On the Trinity.* In *The Nicene and Post-Nicene Fathers,* series 1, vol. 3, edited by Philip Schaff, 1–228. Reprint, Grand Rapids: Eerdmans, 1993. (This is considered the most thorough development of the orthodox doctrine of the Trinity in the history of the church.)

Ayres, Lewis. *Nicaea and Its Legacy: An Approach to Fourth-Century Trinitarian Theology.* Oxford: Oxford University Press, 2004.

Beisner, Calvin. *God in Three Persons.* Wheaton, IL: Tyndale, 1984.

Bickersteth, Edward H. *The Trinity.* Reprint, Grand Rapids: Kregel, 1957.

Bird, Michael F., and Scott D. Harrower, eds. *Trinity without Hierarchy: Reclaiming Nicene Orthodoxy in Evangelical Theology.* Grand Rapids: Kregel, 2019.

Bloesch, Donald G. *The Battle for the Trinity: The Debate Over Inclusive God-Language.* Ann Arbor, MI: Servant, 1985.

Bowman, Robert M., Jr. *Why You Should Believe in the Trinity: An Answer to Jehovah's Witnesses.* Grand Rapids: Baker, 1989.

Bray, G. L. "Trinity." In *NDT2*, 921–24.

———. "Tritheism." In *NDT2*, 924–25.

Bray, Gerald L. *The Doctrine of God*. Downers Grove, IL: InterVarsity Press, 1993.

Brown, Harold O. J. *Heresies: The Image of Christ in the Mirror of Heresy and Orthodoxy From the Apostles to the Present*. Garden City, NY: Doubleday, 1984, 95–157.

Butner, D. Glenn, Jr. *The Son Who Learned Obedience: A Theological Case Against the Eternal Submission of the Son*. Eugene, OR: Wipf & Stock, 2018.

Byrd, Aimee. *Recovering from Biblical Manhood and Womanhood*. Grand Rapids: Zondervan, 2020.

Cole, Graham A. *He Who Gives Life: The Doctrine of the Holy Spirit*. Wheaton, IL: Crossway, 2007.

Coppedge, Allan. *The God Who Is Triune: Revisioning the Christian Doctrine of God*. Downers Grove, IL: IVP Academic, 2007.

Crowe, Brandon D., and Carl R. Trueman, eds. *The Essential Trinity: New Testament Foundations and Practical Relevance*. Phillipsburg, NJ: P&R, 2017.

Davis, Stephen T. *Logic and the Nature of God*. Grand Rapids: Eerdmans, 1983, 132–44.

Edgar, Brian. *The Message of the Trinity: Life in God*. Downers Grove, IL: InterVarsity Press, 2004.

Erickson, Millard J. *God in Three Persons: A Contemporary Interpretation of the Trinity*. Grand Rapids: Baker, 1995.

———. *Making Sense of the Trinity: 3 Crucial Questions*. Grand Rapids: Baker, 2002.

———. *Who's Tampering with the Trinity? An Assessment of the Subordination Debate*. Grand Rapids: Kregel, 2009.

Fairbairn, Donald. *Life in the Trinity: An Introduction to Theology with the Help of the Church Fathers*. Downers Grove, IL: IVP Academic, 2009.

Feinberg, John S. *No One Like Him: The Doctrine of God*. Wheaton, IL: Crossway, 2001.

Frame, John. *The Doctrine of God*. Phillipsburg, NJ: P&R, 2002.

George, Timothy. "The Nature of God: Being, Attributes, and Acts." In *A Theology for the Church*, edited by Daniel L. Akin et al., 182–88. Nashville: B&H, 2014.

Giles, Kevin. *The Trinity and Subordinationism: The Doctrine of God and the Contemporary Gender Debate*. Downers Grove, IL: InterVarsity Press, 2002.

Gruenler, Royce Gordon. *The Trinity in the Gospel of John*. Reprint, Eugene, OR: Wipf & Stock, 2004.

Gundry, Stanley N., and Jason S. Sexton, eds. *Two Views on the Doctrine of the Trinity*. Grand Rapids: Zondervan, 2014.

Gunton, Colin, ed. *Father, Son and the Holy Spirit*. London; New York: T&T Clark, 2003.

Harris, Murray. *Jesus as God*. Grand Rapids: Baker, 1992.

Holmes, S. R. "God." In *NDT2*, 369–73.

Johnson, Keith. *Rethinking the Trinity and Religious Pluralism: An Augustinian Assessment*. Downers Grove, IL: IVP Academic, 2011.

Jowers, Dennis, and H. Wayne House, eds. *The New Evangelical Subordinationism? Perspectives on the Equality of God the Father and God the Son*. Eugene, OR: Pickwick, 2012.

Kaiser, Christopher B. *The Doctrine of God: An Historical Survey*. Westchester, IL: Crossway, 1982, 23–71.

Köstenberger, Andreas J., and Scott R. Swain. *Father, Son, and Spirit: the Trinity and John's Gospel*. Downers Grove, IL: InterVarsity Press, 2008.

Letham, Robert. *The Holy Trinity: In Scripture, History, Theology, and Worship*. 2nd ed. Phillipsburg, NJ: P&R, 2019.

Letham, Robert, and Veli-Matti Kärkkäinen. "Trinity, Triune God." In *GDT*, 901–13.

McCall, Thomas H. *Which Trinity? Whose Monotheism? Philosophical and Systematic Theologians on the Metaphysics of Trinitarian Theology*. Grand Rapids: Eerdmans, 2010.

McGrath, Alister E. *Understanding the Trinity*. Grand Rapids: Zondervan, 1988.

Mikolaski, S. J. "The Triune God." In *Fundamentals of the Faith*, edited by C. F. H. Henry, 59–76. Grand Rapids: Zondervan, 1969.

Ovey, Michael J. *Your Will Be Done: Exploring Eternal Subordination, Divine Monarchy and Divine Humility*. London: Latimer Trust, 2016.

Packer, J. I. "God." *NDT1*, 274–77.

———. *Knowing God*. Downers Grove, IL: InterVarsity Press, 1973, 57–63.

Parvis, S. "Augustine." In *NDT2*, 82–86.

Poythress, Vern S. *Knowing and the Trinity: How Perspectives in Human Knowledge Imitate the Trinity*. Phillipsburg, NJ: P&R, 2018.

Reeves, Michael. *Delighting in the Trinity: An Introduction to the Christian Faith*. Downers Grove, IL: IVP Academic, 2012.

Sanders, Fred. *The Deep Things of God: How the Trinity Changes Everything*. Wheaton, IL: Crossway, 2010.

Sanders, Fred, and Klaus Issler, eds. *Jesus in Trinitarian Perspective: An Introductory Christology*. Nashville: B&H, 2007.

Swain, Scott R., and Fred Sanders, eds. *Retrieving Eternal Generation*. Grand Rapids: Zondervan, 2017.

Ware, Bruce A. *Father, Son, and Holy Spirit: Relationships, Roles and Relevance*. Wheaton, IL: Crossway, 2005.

Ware, Bruce A. and John Starke, eds. *One God in Three Persons: Unity of Essence, Distinction of Persons, Implications for Life*. Wheaton, IL: Crossway, 2015.

Whitfield, Keith S., ed. *Trinitarian Theology: Theological Models and Doctrinal Application*. Nashville: B&H, 2019.

Wright, D. F. "Augustine." In *NDT1*, 58–61.

Yang, Hongyi. *A Development Not a Departure: The Lacunae in the Debate of the Doctrine of the Trinity and Gender Roles*. Phillipsburg, NJ: P&R, 2018.

Yarnell, Malcolm B. *God the Trinity: Biblical Portraits*. Nashville: B&H Academic, 2016.

## SCRIPTURE MEMORY PASSAGE

**Matthew 3:16–17:** And when Jesus was baptized, immediately he went up from the water, and behold, the heavens were opened to him, and he saw the Spirit of God descending like a dove and coming to rest on him; and behold, a voice from heaven said, "This is my beloved Son, with whom I am well pleased."

## HYMN

### "Holy, Holy, Holy"

*Holy, holy, holy, Lord God Almighty!*
  *Early in the morning our song shall rise to thee;*
*Holy, holy, holy! Merciful and mighty!*
  *God in three persons, blessed Trinity!*

*Holy, holy, holy! All the saints adore thee,*
  *Casting down their golden crowns around the glassy sea;*
*Cherubim and seraphim falling down before thee,*
  *Who wert, and art, and evermore shalt be.*

*Holy, holy, holy! Though the darkness hide thee,*
  *Though the eye of sinful man thy glory may not see,*
*Only thou art holy; there is none beside thee*
  *Perfect in pow'r, in love, and purity.*

*Holy, holy, holy! Lord God Almighty!*
  *All thy works shall praise thy name, in earth and sky and sea;*
*Holy, holy, holy! Merciful and mighty!*
  *God in three persons, blessed Trinity!*

Author: Reginald Heber, 1826

# CONTEMPORARY WORSHIP SONG

## "Doxology (Amen)"

*Praise God from whom all blessings flow.*
*Praise Him all creatures here below.*
*Praise Him above you heav'nly host.*
*Praise Father Son and Holy Ghost.*

*Chorus*
*Amen, amen, amen.*
*God we praise You.*
*God we praise You.*

*Praise God for all that He has done.*
*Praise Him for He has overcome.*
*The grave is beaten, love has won.*
*Praise God our Savior Christ the Son.*

*Interlude*
*Oh we're singing.*

*Ending*
*Amen, amen, amen.*
*Amen, amen, amen.*
*We praise You. We praise You.*

Words by Phil Wickham[134]

CHAPTER 15

# Creation

*Why, how, and when did God create the universe?*

## EXPLANATION AND SCRIPTURAL BASIS

How did God create the world?[1] Did he create every different kind of plant and animal directly, or did he use some kind of evolutionary process to guide the development of living things from the simplest to the most complex? And how quickly did God bring about creation? Was it all completed within six twenty-four-hour days, or did he use thousands or perhaps millions of years? How old is the earth, and how old is the human race?

These questions face us when we deal with the doctrine of creation. Unlike most of the earlier material in this book, this chapter treats several questions on which evangelical Christians have differing viewpoints, sometimes very strongly held ones.

This chapter is organized to move from those aspects of creation that are most clearly taught in Scripture, on which almost all evangelicals would agree (creation out of nothing, special creation of Adam and Eve, and the goodness of the universe), to other aspects of creation about which evangelicals have had disagreements (whether God used a process of evolution to bring about much of creation, and how old the earth and the human race are).

We may define the doctrine of creation as follows: *God created the entire universe out of nothing, it was originally very good, and he created it to glorify himself.*

## A. God Created the Universe out of Nothing

### 1. Biblical Evidence for Creation out of Nothing

The Bible clearly requires us to believe that God created the universe out of nothing. (Sometimes the Latin phrase *ex nihilo*, "out of nothing" is used; it is then said that the Bible teaches creation *ex nihilo*.) This means that before God began to create the universe, nothing else existed except God himself.[2]

This is the implication of Genesis 1:1, which says, "In the beginning, God created

---

1. I am grateful for many helpful comments on this chapter made by friends with specialized knowledge about some aspects of it, especially Steve Figard, Doug Brandt, and Terry Mortenson.

2. When we say that the universe was created "out of

nothing," it is important to guard against a possible misunderstanding. The word *nothing* does not imply some kind of existence, as some philosophers have taken it to mean. We mean rather that God did not use any previously existing materials when he created the universe.

the heavens and the earth." The phrase "the heavens and the earth" includes the entire universe. Psalm 33 also tells us,

> By the word of the LORD the heavens were made,
>> and by the breath of his mouth all their host. . . .
> For he spoke, and it came to be;
>> he commanded, and it stood firm. (Ps. 33:6, 9)

In the New Testament, we find a universal statement at the beginning of John's gospel: "*All things* were made through him, and without him was not any thing made that was made" (John 1:3). The phrase "all things" is best taken to refer to the entire universe (cf. Acts 17:24; Heb. 11:3). Paul is quite explicit in Colossians 1 when he specifies all the parts of the universe, both visible and invisible things: "For by him *all things* were created, in heaven and on earth, *visible and invisible*, whether thrones or dominions or rulers or authorities—all things were created through him and for him" (Col. 1:16). The song of the twenty-four elders in heaven likewise affirms this truth:

> "Worthy are you, our Lord and God,
>> to receive glory and honor and power,
> for you created *all things*,
>> and by your will they existed and were created." (Rev. 4:11)

In the last phrase God's will is said to be the reason why things even "existed" at all and why they "were created."

That God created both the heavens and the earth and everything in them is affirmed several other times in the New Testament. For instance, Acts 4:24 speaks of God as the "Sovereign Lord, who made *the heaven and the earth and the sea and everything in them*." One of the first ways of identifying God is to say that he is the one who created all things. Barnabas and Paul explain to the pagan audience at Lystra that they are messengers of "a living God who made the heaven and the earth and the sea and all that is in them" (Acts 14:15). Similarly, when Paul is speaking to pagan Greek philosophers in Athens, he identifies the true God as "The God who made the world and everything in it" and says that this God "gives to all mankind life and breath and everything" (Acts 17:24–25; cf. Isa. 45:18; Rev. 10:6).

Hebrews 11:3 says, "By faith we understand that the universe was created by the word of God, so that what is seen was not made out of things that are visible." This translation (as well as the NASB and NIV) most accurately reflects the Greek text.[3] Though the

---

3. The RSV translation ("so that what is seen was made out of things which do not appear") apparently affirms that God made the universe out of invisible matter of some sort, but the word order of the Greek text (*mē ek phainomenōn*) shows that

text does not quite teach the doctrine of creation out of nothing, it comes close to doing so, since it says that God did not create the universe out of anything that is visible. The somewhat strange idea that the universe might have been created out of something that was invisible is probably not in the author's mind. He is contradicting the idea of creation out of previously existing matter, and for that purpose the verse is quite clear.

Romans 4:17 also implies that God created out of nothing, even if it does not exactly state it. The Greek text literally speaks of God as one who "calls things not existing as existing." The ESV translation, "calls into existence the things that do not exist" (similarly RSV and NASB), is unusual but possible grammatically,[4] and it makes an explicit affirmation of creation out of nothing. Yet even if we translate it so that the Greek word *hōs* takes its common sense "as," the verse says that God "calls the things which do not exist as existing" (NASB mg.). But if God speaks to or calls something that does not exist, as if in fact it did exist, then what is implied? If he calls things that do not exist as though they existed, and if God always speaks truthfully, then it must mean that when God speaks these things immediately exist, irresistibly called into existence by his powerful words.

Because God created the entire universe out of nothing there is no matter in the universe that is eternal. All that we see—the mountains, the oceans, the stars, the earth itself—all came into existence when God created them. There was a time when they did not exist:

> Before the mountains were brought forth,
> or ever you had formed the earth and the world,
> from everlasting to everlasting you are God. (Ps. 90:2)

This reminds us that God rules over all the universe and that nothing in creation is to be worshiped instead of or in addition to God. However, were we to deny creation out of nothing, we would have to say that some matter has always existed and that it is eternal like God. This idea would challenge God's independence, his sovereignty, and the fact that worship is due to him alone: if matter existed apart from God, then what inherent right would God have to rule over it and use it for his glory? And if some parts of it were not created by him, then what confidence could we have that every aspect of the universe will ultimately fulfill God's purposes?

On the positive side, because God created the universe out of nothing, it has meaning and a purpose. God, in his wisdom, created it for something. We should try to

---

the word "not" negates the phrase "out of appearing things." The RSV translation reads as if the word "not" negated the participle "appearing," but it would need to appear immediately before it in order to do that. See discussion in Philip Hughes, *A Commentary on the Epistle to the Hebrews* (Grand Rapids: Eerdmans, 1977), 443–52.

4. See C. E. B. Cranfield, *A Critical and Exegetical Commentary on the Epistle to the Romans*, ICC (Edinburgh: T&T Clark, 1975), 1:244: Greek *hōs* as expressing consequence.

understand that purpose and use creation in ways that fit that purpose, namely, to bring glory to God himself.[5] Moreover, whenever the creation brings us joy (cf. 1 Tim. 6:17), we should give thanks to the God who made it all.

## 2. The Creation of the Spiritual Universe

This creation of the entire universe includes the creation of an unseen, spiritual realm of existence. God created the angels and other kinds of heavenly beings as well as animals and man. He also created heaven as a place where his presence is especially evident. The creation of the spiritual realm is certainly implied in all the verses above that speak of God creating not only the earth but also "heaven and what is in it" (Rev. 10:6; cf. Acts 4:24), but it is also explicitly affirmed in a number of other verses. The prayer of Ezra says very clearly: "You are the LORD, you alone. You have made heaven, the heaven of heavens, with all their host, the earth and all that is on it, the seas and all that is in them; and you preserve all of them; and the host of heaven worships you" (Neh. 9:6). The "host of heaven" in this verse seems to refer to the angels and other heavenly creatures, since Ezra says that they engage in the activity of worshiping God (the same term *host* is used to speak of angels who worship God in Ps. 103:21 and 148:2).[6]

In the New Testament, Paul specifies that in Christ "all things were created, in heaven and on earth, visible *and invisible*, whether thrones or dominions or rulers or authorities—all things were created through him and for him" (Col. 1:16; cf. Ps. 148:2–5). Here the creation of invisible heavenly beings is also explicitly affirmed.

## 3. The Direct Creation of Adam and Eve

The Bible also teaches that God created Adam and Eve in a special, personal way. "The LORD God formed the man of dust from the ground and breathed into his nostrils the breath of life, and the man became a living creature" (Gen. 2:7). After that, God created Eve from Adam's body: "So the LORD God caused a deep sleep to fall upon the man, and while he slept took one of his ribs and closed up its place with flesh. And the rib that the LORD God had taken from the man he made into a woman and brought her to the man" (Gen. 2:21–22). God apparently let Adam know something of what had happened, for Adam said,

> This at last is bone of my bones
>     and flesh of my flesh;
> she shall be called Woman,
>     because she was taken out of Man. (Gen. 2:23)

---

5. See section C below (pp. 347–49) on God's purpose for creation.

6. The word translated "host" (Heb. *tsābā'*) is sometimes used to refer to the planets and stars (Deut. 4:19; Isa. 34:4; 40:26), but none of the examples cited in BDB, 839 (1.c) speak of the stars worshiping God, and most speak of the heavenly bodies as "the host of heaven" who are wrongly worshiped by pagans (Deut. 17:3; 2 Kings 17:16; 21:3; Jer. 8:2, et al.).

These texts are so explicit that it does not seem to me possible to hold to the complete truthfulness of Scripture and still hold that human beings are the result of a long evolutionary process. This is because when Scripture says that the Lord "formed man of dust from the ground" (Gen. 2:7), it does not seem possible to understand that to mean that he did it over a process that took millions of years and employed the random development of thousands of increasingly complex organisms.[7] Even more impossible to reconcile with an evolutionary view is the fact that this narrative clearly portrays Eve as having no female parent: she was created directly from Adam's rib while Adam slept (Gen. 2:21). But on a purely evolutionary view, this would not be possible, for even the very first female "human being" would have had male and female parents who were nearly human but still some higher form of animal. The New Testament reaffirms the historicity of this special creation of Eve from Adam when Paul says, "For man was not made from woman, but *woman from man*. Neither was man created for woman, but woman for man" (1 Cor. 11:8–9).

The special creation of Adam and Eve shows that, though we may be like animals in many respects in our physical bodies, nonetheless we are very different from animals. We are created "in God's image," the pinnacle of God's creation, more like God than any other creature, appointed to rule over the rest of creation. Even the brevity of the Genesis account of creation places a wonderful emphasis on the importance of man in distinction from the rest of the universe. It thus resists modern tendencies to see man as meaningless against the immensity of the universe. Derek Kidner notes that Scripture stands "against every tendency to empty human history of meaning . . . in presenting the tremendous acts of creation as a mere curtain-raiser to the drama that slowly unfolds throughout the length of the Bible. The prologue is over in a page; there are a thousand to follow." By contrast, Kidner notes that the modern scientific account of the universe, true though it may be, "overwhelms us with statistics that reduce our apparent significance to a vanishing-point. Not the prologue, but the human story itself, is now the single page in a thousand, and the whole terrestrial volume is lost among uncatalogued millions."[8] Scripture gives us the perspective on human significance that God intends us to have. (This fact will be discussed in more detail in chapter 21.)

## 4. The Creation of Time

One other aspect of God's creation is the creation of time (the succession of moments one after another). This idea was discussed with respect to God's attribute of eternity in chapter 11,[9] and we need only summarize it here. When we speak of God's existence "before" the creation of the world, we should not think of God as existing in an unending

---

7. But see my discussion of theistic evolution in section 4, below.

8. Derek Kidner, *Genesis: An Introduction and Commentary*, TOTC (Chicago: InterVarsity Press, 1967), 57.

9. See pp. 199–200.

extension of time. Rather, God's eternity means that he has a different kind of existence, an existence without the passage of time, a kind of existence that is difficult for us even to imagine (see Job 36:26; Ps. 90:2, 4; John 8:58; 2 Peter 3:8; Rev. 1:8). The fact that God created time reminds us of his lordship over it and our obligation to use it for his glory.

### 5. The Work of the Son and of the Holy Spirit in Creation

God the Father was the primary agent in initiating the act of creation. But the Son and the Holy Spirit were also active. The Son is often described as the one "through" whom creation came about. "All things were made *through* him, and without him was not any thing made that was made" (John 1:3). Paul says there is "one Lord, Jesus Christ, *through* whom are all things and *through* whom we exist" (1 Cor. 8:6), and "all things were created *through* him and for him" (Col. 1:16). We read also that the Son is the one "through whom" God "created the world" (Heb. 1:2). These passages give a consistent picture of the Son as the active agent carrying out the plans and directions of the Father.

The Holy Spirit was also at work in creation. He is generally pictured as completing, filling, and giving life to God's creation. In Genesis 1:2, "the Spirit of God was hovering over the face of the waters," indicating a preserving, sustaining, governing function. Job says, "The Spirit of God has made me, and the breath of the Almighty gives me life" (Job 33:4). In a number of Old Testament passages, it is important to realize that the same Hebrew word (*rûach*) can mean, in different contexts, "spirit," "breath," or "wind." But in many cases there is not much difference in meaning, for even if one decided to translate some phrases as the "breath of God" or even the "wind of God," it would still seem to be a figurative way of referring to the activity of the Holy Spirit in creation. So the psalmist, in speaking of the great variety of creatures on the earth and in the sea, says, "When you send forth your Spirit, they are created" (Ps. 104:30; note also, on the Holy Spirit's work, Job 26:13; Isa. 40:13; 1 Cor. 2:10). However, the testimony of Scripture to the specific activity of the Holy Spirit in creation is scarce. The work of the Holy Spirit is brought into much greater prominence in connection with the inspiring of the authors of Scripture and the applying of Christ's redemptive work to the people of God.[10]

### B. CREATION IS DISTINCT FROM GOD YET ALWAYS DEPENDENT ON GOD

The teaching of Scripture about the relationship between God and creation is unique among the religions of the world. The Bible teaches that God is distinct from his creation. He is not part of it, for he has made it and rules over it. The term *transcendent* is often used to say that God is much greater than creation. Very simply, this word means that God is far "above" the creation in the sense that he is greater than and independent of creation.

---

10. See chapter 30, pp. 778–96, on the work of the Holy Spirit.

God is also very much involved in creation, for it is continually dependent on him for its existence and its functioning. The technical term used to speak of God's involvement in creation is the word *immanent*, meaning "remaining in" creation. The God of the Bible is no abstract deity removed from and uninterested in his creation. The Bible is the story of God's involvement with his creation—and particularly the people in it. Job affirms that even the animals and plants depend on God: "In his hand is the life of every living thing and the breath of all mankind" (Job 12:10). In the New Testament, Paul affirms that God "gives to all mankind life and breath and everything" and that "in him we live and move and have our being" (Acts 17:25, 28). Indeed, in Christ "all things hold together" (Col. 1:17), and he continually "upholds the universe by the word of his power" (Heb. 1:3). God's transcendence and immanence are both affirmed in a single verse when Paul speaks of "one God and Father of all, who is over all and through all and in all" (Eph. 4:6).

The fact that creation is distinct from God yet always dependent on God, that God is far above creation yet always involved in it (in brief, that God is both transcendent and immanent), may be represented as in figure 15.1.

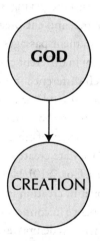

**Creation Is Distinct from God Yet Always Dependent on God**
**(God Is Both Transcendent and Immanent)**
*Figure 15.1*

This is clearly distinct from *materialism*, which is the most common philosophy of unbelievers today, and which denies the existence of God altogether. Materialism would say that the material universe is all there is. It may be represented as in figure 15.2.

Christians today who focus almost the entire effort of their lives on earning more money and acquiring more possessions become "practical" materialists in their activity, since their lives would be not much different if they did not believe in God at all.

**Materialism**
*Figure 15.2*

The scriptural account of God's relation to his creation is also distinct from pantheism. The Greek word *pan* means "all" or "every," and *pantheism* is the idea that everything, the whole universe, is God or is part of God.[11] This can be pictured as in figure 15.3.

**Pantheism**
*Figure 15.3*

Pantheism denies several essential aspects of God's character. If the whole universe is God, then God has no distinct personality. God is no longer unchanging because as the universe changes God also changes. Moreover, God is no longer holy because the evil in the universe is also part of God. Another difficulty is that ultimately most pantheistic systems (such as Buddhism and many other eastern religions) end up denying the importance of individual human personalities: since everything is God, the goal of an individual should be to blend in with the universe and become more and more united with it, thus losing his or her individual distinctiveness. If God himself (or itself) has no distinct personal identity separate from the universe, then we should certainly not strive to have one either. Thus pantheism destroys not only the personal identity of God but also, ultimately, the personal identity of human beings as well.

Any philosophy that sees creation as an "emanation" from God (that is, something that comes out of God but is still part of God and not distinct from him) would be similar to pantheism in most or all of the ways in which aspects of God's character are denied.

The biblical account also rules out *dualism*. This is the idea that both God and the material universe have eternally existed side-by-side. Thus there are two ultimate forces in the universe: God and matter. This may be represented as in figure 15.4.

---

11. Pantheism (everything is God) is different from *panentheism*, which holds that God is *in* everything but God is still distinct from everything else.

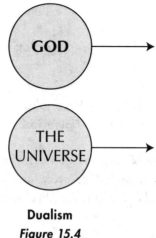

**Dualism**
*Figure 15.4*

The problem with dualism is that it indicates an eternal conflict between God and the evil aspects of the material universe. Will God ultimately triumph over evil in the universe? We cannot be sure because both God and evil have apparently always existed together. This philosophy would deny both God's ultimate lordship over creation and that creation came about because of God's will in order to be used solely for his purposes and to his glory. This viewpoint would also deny that all of the universe was created inherently good (Gen. 1:31) and would encourage people to view material reality as somewhat evil in itself, in contrast with a genuine biblical account of a creation that God made to be good and that he rules over for his purposes.

One example of dualism in modern culture is the series of *Star Wars* movies, which postulate the existence of a universal "Force" that has both a good and an evil side. There is no concept of one holy and transcendent God who rules over all and will certainly triumph over all. When non-Christians today begin to be aware of a spiritual aspect to the universe, they often become dualists, merely acknowledging that there are good and evil aspects to the supernatural or spiritual world. Most "New Age" religion is dualistic. Of course, Satan is delighted to have people think that there is an evil force in the universe that is perhaps equal to God himself.

The Christian view of creation is also distinct from the viewpoint of *deism*. Deism is the view that God is not now directly involved in the creation. It may be represented as in figure 15.5.

Deism generally holds that God created the universe and is far greater than the universe (God is "transcendent"). Some deists also agree that God has moral standards and will ultimately hold people accountable on a day of judgment. But they deny God's present involvement in the world, thus leaving no place for his immanence in the created order. Rather, God is viewed as a divine clock maker who wound up the "clock" of creation at the beginning but then left it to run on its own.

**Deism**
*Figure 15.5*

While deism does affirm God's transcendence in some ways, it denies almost the entire history of the Bible, which is the history of God's active involvement in the world. Many "lukewarm" or nominal Christians today are, in effect, practical deists, since they live lives almost totally devoid of genuine prayer, worship, fear of God, or moment-by-moment trust in God to care for needs that arise.

## C. God Created the Universe to Show His Glory

It is clear that God created his people for his own glory, for he speaks of his sons and daughters as those "whom I created *for my glory*, whom I formed and made" (Isa. 43:7). But it is not only human beings that God created for this purpose. The entire creation is intended to show God's glory. Even the inanimate creation, the stars and sun and moon and sky, testify to God's greatness:

> The heavens declare the glory of God,
>     and the sky above proclaims his handiwork.
> Day to day pours out speech,
>     and night to night reveals knowledge. (Ps. 19:1–2)

The song of heavenly worship in Revelation 4 connects God's creation of all things with the fact that he is worthy to receive glory from them:

> Worthy are you, our Lord and God,
>     to receive glory and honor and power,
> for you created all things,
>     and by your will they existed and were created. (Rev. 4:11)

What does creation show about God? Primarily it shows his great power and wisdom, far above anything that could be imagined by any creature.[12] "It is he who made the earth by his power, who established the world by his wisdom, and by his understanding stretched out the heavens" (Jer. 10:12). In contrast to ignorant men and the "worthless" idols they make, Jeremiah says,

> Not like these is he who is the portion of Jacob
> for he is the one who formed all things. . . .
> The LORD of hosts is his name. (Jer. 10:16)

One glance at the sun or the stars convinces us of God's infinite power. And even a brief inspection of any leaf on a tree, of the wonder of the human hand, or of any one living cell convinces us of God's great wisdom. Who could make all of this? Who could make it out of nothing? Who could sustain it day after day for endless years? Such infinite power, such intricate skill, is completely beyond our comprehension. When we meditate on it, we give glory to God.

When we affirm that God created the universe to show his glory, it is important that we realize that he did not need to create it. We should not think that God needed more glory than he had within the Trinity for all eternity or that he was somehow incomplete without the glory that he would receive from the created universe. This would be to deny God's independence and imply that God needed the universe in order to be fully God.[13] Rather, we must affirm that the creation of the universe was a *totally free act of God*. It was not a necessary act but something that God chose to do. "You created all things, and *by your will* they existed and were created" (Rev. 4:11). God desired to create the universe to demonstrate his excellence. The creation shows his great wisdom and power, and ultimately it shows all of his other attributes as well.[14] It seems that God created the universe, then, to take delight in his creation, for as creation shows forth various aspects of God's character, to that extent he takes delight in it.

This explains why we take spontaneous delight in all sorts of creative activities ourselves. People with artistic or musical or literary skills enjoy creating things and seeing, hearing, or pondering their creative work. God has so made us to enjoy imitating, in a creaturely way, his creative activity. And one of the amazing aspects of humanity—in distinction from the rest of creation—is our ability to create new things. This also explains why we take delight in other kinds of "creative" activity: many people enjoy cooking, decorating their home, working with wood or other materials, producing scientific inventions, or devising new solutions to problems in industrial production. Even children enjoy

---

12. See chapter 7, pp. 141–44, for a discussion of the necessity of Scripture if we are to interpret creation rightly.

13. See the discussion of God's independence in chapter 11, pp. 190–92.

14. See the discussion in chapter 11, pp. 186–89, on the ways in which all of creation reveals various aspects of God's character.

coloring pictures or building houses out of blocks. In all of these activities we reflect in small measure the creative activity of God, and we should delight in it and thank him for it.

## D. THE UNIVERSE GOD CREATED WAS "VERY GOOD"

This point follows from the previous point. If God created the universe to show his glory, then we would expect that the universe would fulfill the purpose for which he created it. In fact, when God finished his work of creation, he did take delight in it. At the end of each stage of creation, God saw that what he had done was "good" (Gen. 1:4, 10, 12, 18, 21, 25). Then at the end of the six days of creation, "God saw everything that he had made, and behold, it was very good" (Gen. 1:31). God delighted in the creation that he had made, just as he had purposed to do.

Even though sin has entered the world, the material creation is still good in God's sight and should be seen as "good" by us as well. This knowledge will free us from a false asceticism that sees the use and enjoyment of the material creation as wrong. Paul says that those who "forbid marriage" and "require abstinence from foods that God created to be received with thanksgiving by those who believe and know the truth" (1 Tim. 4:1–3) are giving heed to "teachings of demons." The apostle takes such a firm line because he understands that "everything created by God is good, and nothing is to be rejected if it is received with thanksgiving, for it is made holy by the word of God and prayer" (1 Tim. 4:4–5). Paul's mention of "the word of God" that consecrates or "sanctifies" the foods and other things we enjoy in the material creation is probably a reference to the blessing of God spoken in Genesis 1:31, "It was very good."

Though the created order can be used in sinful or selfish ways and can turn our affections away from God, nonetheless we must not let the danger of the abuse of God's creation keep us from a positive, thankful, joyful use of it for our own enjoyment and for the good of his kingdom. Shortly after Paul has warned against the desire to be rich and the "love of money" (1 Tim. 6:9–10), he affirms that it is God "who richly provides us with everything to enjoy" (1 Tim. 6:17). This fact gives warrant for Christians to encourage proper industrial and technological development (together with care for the environment), and joyful and thankful use of all the products of the abundant earth that God has created—both by ourselves and by those with whom we are to share generously of our possessions (note 1 Tim. 6:18). Yet in all of this we are to remember that material possessions are only temporary, not eternal. We are to set our hopes on God (see Ps. 62:10; 1 Tim. 6:17) and on receiving a kingdom that cannot be shaken (Col. 3:1–4; Heb. 12:28; 1 Peter 1:4).

## E. THE RELATIONSHIP BETWEEN SCRIPTURE AND THE FINDINGS OF MODERN SCIENCE

In any discussion about the relationship between Scripture and modern science, we must recognize, first of all, that throughout history sincere Christian faith and strong trust in the Bible have frequently led scientists to the discovery of new facts about God's universe, and these discoveries have brought immense benefits to mankind. The lives of Isaac Newton, Galileo Galilei, Johannes Kepler, Blaise Pascal, Robert Boyle, Michael Faraday, James Clerk Maxwell, and many others are examples of this.[15]

On the other hand, there have been times when accepted scientific opinion has been in conflict with people's understanding of what the Bible said. For example, when the Italian astronomer Galileo (1564–1642) began to teach that the earth was not the center of the universe but that the earth and other planets revolved around the sun (thus following the theories of the Polish astronomer Copernicus [1472–1543]), he was criticized, and eventually his writings were condemned by the Roman Catholic Church. This was because many people thought that the Bible taught that the sun revolved around the earth. In fact, the Bible does not teach that at all, but it was Copernican astronomy that made people look again at Scripture to see if it really taught what they thought it taught. In fact, descriptions of the sun rising and setting (Eccl. 1:5 et al.) merely portray events as they appear from the perspective of the human observer, and from that perspective, they give an accurate description. But they imply nothing about the relative motion of the earth and the sun, and nowhere does the Bible explain what makes the sun go "down" in the viewpoint of a human observer. Scripture says nothing at all about whether the earth or the sun or some other body is the "center" of the universe or the solar system—that is not a question Scripture addresses. Yet the lesson of Galileo, who was forced to recant his teachings and who had to live under house arrest for the last few years of his life, should remind us that careful observation of the natural world can cause us to go back to Scripture and reexamine whether Scripture actually teaches what we think it teaches. Sometimes, on closer examination of the text, we may find that our previous interpretations were incorrect.

Scientific investigation has helped Christians reevaluate what earlier generations thought about the age of the earth, for example, so that no evangelical scholar today would hold that the world was created in 4004 BC. Yet that date was once widely believed to be the date of the creation because of the writings of Irish archbishop James Ussher (1581–1656), one of the great scholars of his day, who carefully added together the dates in the genealogies of the Bible to find when Adam was created. Today it is widely acknowledged that the Bible does not tell us the precise date of the creation of the earth or of the human race (see below).

On the other hand, many people in the Christian community have steadfastly refused to agree with the dominant opinion of scientists today regarding evolution. On this matter, thousands of Christians have examined Scripture again and again in great detail, and many have concluded that Scripture is not silent on the process by which

---

15. See August J. Kling, "Men of Science / Men of Faith," *HIS*, May 1976, 26–31, for a brief survey of the life and work of several of these scientists.

living organisms came into being. Moreover, careful observation of the facts of the created universe has produced widespread disagreement regarding theories of evolution (both from scientists who are Christians and from a number of non-Christian scientists as well).[16] So on both biblical and scientific grounds, theories of evolution have been challenged by Christians.

We should also remember that the question of the creation of the universe is unlike many other scientific questions because creation is not something that can be repeated in a laboratory experiment, nor were there any human observers of it. Therefore, pronouncements by scientists about creation and the early history of the earth are at best educated speculation about events long in the past. If we are convinced, however, that the only observer of these events (God himself) has told us about them in the reliable words of the Bible, then we should pay careful attention to the biblical account.

In the following section, we have listed some principles by which the relationship between creation and the findings of modern science can be approached.

## 1. When All the Facts Are Rightly Understood, There Will Be "No Final Conflict" between Scripture and Natural Science

The phrase "no final conflict" is taken from a very helpful book by influential Christian apologist Francis Schaeffer, *No Final Conflict*.[17] Regarding questions about the creation of the universe, Schaeffer lists several areas where, in his judgment, there is room for disagreement among Christians who believe in the total truthfulness of Scripture:

1. There is a possibility that God created a "grown-up" universe.
2. There is a possibility of a break between Genesis 1:1 and 1:2 or between 1:2 and 1:3.
3. There is a possibility of a long day in Genesis 1.
4. There is a possibility that the flood affected the geological data.
5. The use of the word "kinds" in Genesis 1 may be quite broad.
6. There is a possibility of the death of animals before the fall.
7. Where the Hebrew word *bārā'* is not used, there is the possibility of sequence from previously existing things.[18]

Schaeffer makes clear that he is not saying that any of those positions is his own, only that they are theoretically possible. Schaeffer's major point is that in both our understanding of the natural world and our understanding of Scripture, our knowledge is not

---

16. For analysis of the increasingly large body of scientific evidence against evolution, see especially the books by Douglas Axe, Michael Behe, Michael Denton, Phillip E. Johnson, Stephen Meyer, Norman Nevin, Hugh Ross, and Jonathan Wells that are cited in the bibliography to this chapter.

17. Schaeffer, *No Final Conflict* (Downers Grove, IL: InterVarsity Press, 1975).
18. Ibid., 25–33.

perfect. But we can approach both scientific and biblical study with the confidence that when all the facts are correctly understood, and when we have understood Scripture rightly, our findings will never be in conflict with each other: there will be "no final conflict." This is because God, who speaks in Scripture, knows all facts, and he has not spoken in a way that would contradict any true fact in the universe.

This is a very helpful perspective with which the Christian should begin any study of creation and modern science. We should not fear to investigate scientifically the facts of the created world but should do so eagerly and with complete honesty, confident that when facts are rightly understood, they will always turn out to be consistent with God's inerrant words in Scripture. Similarly, we should approach the study of Scripture eagerly and with confidence that, when rightly understood, Scripture will never contradict facts in the natural world.[19]

Someone may object that this whole discussion is inappropriate, for the Bible is given to us to teach religious and ethical matters; it is not intended to teach "science." However, as we noted in chapter 5 above, Scripture places no such restriction on the subjects to which it can speak. Although the Bible is of course not a "textbook" of science in a formal sense, it does nonetheless contain many affirmations about the natural world—its origin, its purposes, its ultimate destiny—and many statements about its day-to-day functions. If we take seriously the idea that it is God himself (as well as the human authors) who speaks all the words of Scripture, then we must take these statements seriously and believe them as well. Indeed, Scripture says that our understanding of some "scientific" facts is a matter of our faith! Hebrews 11:3 tells us, "*By faith* we understand that the universe was created by the word of God, so that what is seen was not made out of things that are visible."

## 2. Purely Secular Theories about Creation Are Clearly Inconsistent with the Teachings of Scripture

Any purely secular theories of the origin of the universe and the origin of life would be unacceptable for those who believe in Scripture. A "secular" theory is any theory of the origin of the universe and the origin of life that does not see an infinite-personal God as responsible for creating the universe by intelligent design. Thus the "big bang" theory (in a secular form in which God is excluded) or theories that suppose matter has always existed would be inconsistent with the teaching of Scripture that God created the universe out of nothing and that he did so for his own glory.

## 3. Scientific Objections to the Darwinian Theory of Evolution

The word *evolution* can be used in different ways. Sometimes it is used to refer to microevolution—small developments within one species, so that we see flies or

---

19. See the discussion in chapter 4, pp. 72–76, on the relationship between Scripture and natural revelation.

mosquitoes becoming immune to insecticides, human beings growing taller, or different colors and varieties of roses being developed. Innumerable examples of such microevolution are evident today, and no one denies that they exist.[20] But that is not the sense in which the word *evolution* is usually used when discussing theories of creation and evolution.

The term *evolution* is more commonly used to refer to macroevolution—that is, the "general theory of evolution," or what is sometimes called neo-Darwinian evolutionary theory. ("Neo-" means "new," so "neo-Darwinian evolution" refers to the modern, more refined form of Darwin's theory of evolution.) Current neo-Darwinian theory is still foundationally similar to Darwin's original position, but with refinements and modifications due to over a hundred years of research. In modern Darwinian evolutionary theory, the history of the development of life began when a mix of chemicals present on the earth spontaneously produced a very simple, probably one-celled life form. This living cell reproduced itself, and eventually there were some mutations or differences in the new cells produced. These mutations led to the development of more complex life forms. A hostile environment meant that many of them would perish, but those that were better suited to their environment would survive and multiply. Thus nature exercised a process of "natural selection" in which the differing organisms most fitted to the environment survived. More and more mutations eventually developed into more and more varieties of living things, so that from the very simplest organism all the complex life forms on earth eventually developed through this process of *random mutation and natural selection.*

In this chapter, when we use the word *evolution*, it is used to refer to macroevolution or the neo-Darwinian general theory of evolution.

In this section, I will explain many of the increasingly persuasive scientific objections to evolution. Then in the following section on theistic evolution (see pp. 366–83), I will explain many biblical objections. Since Charles Darwin first published his *Origin of Species by Means of Natural Selection* in 1859, there have been challenges to his theory by Christians and non-Christians alike. In fact, in the twenty-five years since the first publication of my *Systematic Theology* in 1994 (I am writing this in 2019), a substantial body of new scientific research has presented remarkably strong challenges to modern evolutionary theory. Much of that scientific research has been summarized in the first

---

20. Phillip E. Johnson, *Darwin on Trial* (Downers Grove, IL: InterVarsity Press, 1991), points out that some studies frequently claimed as evidence of evolution are really just temporary population differences with no genetic change. For example, he mentions Kettlewell's observation of "industrial melanism" in the peppered moth, whereby the prevailing color of the moths changed from white to black and back to white again when leaves on trees were light colored, then covered with soot from pollution, then again light colored when the pollution ended. But at every stage, both black and white moths were present, even though in differing proportions (moths that did not match the leaf color were more easily seen and eaten by predators). No evolutionary change occurred at all, for both black and white moths were still industrial moths, just as black and white horses are both still horses. In fact, the moth functioned to preserve its genetic identity in differing circumstances rather than evolving or becoming extinct (see pp. 26–28, 160–61).

17 chapters of a recent book in which I was one of the coeditors, *Theistic Evolution: a Scientific, Philosophical, and Theological Critique*.[21] In the following material, I give an overview of much of that research. (I edited the theological chapters in that book. But in the material that follows here, because I do not have specialized training as a scientist, I use more extensive quotes than I do in the rest of this book.)

**a. Evolution Has No Power to Create New Genetic Information.** Random mutation and natural selection (the two processes essential to Darwinian evolution) do not contain the creative power to generate the new genetic information that is necessary for the creation of new proteins and new forms of life.

Stephen Meyer points to the work of molecular biologist Douglas Axe, who worked as a researcher at Cambridge University from 1990–2003. Axe concluded that "for every DNA sequence that generates a short functional protein fold[22] of just 150 amino acids in length, there are $10^{77}$ *non*functional combinations—$10^{77}$ amino acid arrangements— that will *not* fold into a stable three-dimensional protein structure capable of performing a biological function."[23] Meyer puts the number $10^{77}$ in perspective by pointing out that there are only $10^{65}$ atoms in our entire Milky Way galaxy.

But how many opportunities were there for living things on earth to produce such a new functional protein fold that would be passed on to subsequent generations? Meyer explains,

> Every time an organism reproduces and generates a new organism, an oppor- tunity occurs to generate and pass on a new gene sequence as well. But during the entire three-and-a-half-billion-year history of life on earth, only ten to the fortieth individual organisms have ever lived—meaning that at most only ten to the fortieth power such opportunities have occurred. Yet ten to the fortieth power represents only a small fraction of ten to the seventy-seventh power—only one ten trillion, trillion, trillionth, or $1/10^{37}$ to be exact.[24]

And $1/10^{37}$ is the chance of random mutation producing *only one* fairly simple new protein structure. (The average protein is much more complex, about 300 amino acids in length,[25] which means that the actual chance of producing a new functional protein is far less than these numbers indicate.) Using a common estimate for the entire history of life on earth (3.5 billion years), Meyer concludes that there would be approximately one chance in $10^{37}$ for a new functional protein fold to develop by random means. Then

21. J. P. Moreland, Stephen C. Meyer Christopher Shaw, Ann Gauger, and Wayne Grudem, eds., *Theistic Evolution: A Scientific, Philosophical, and Theological Critique* (Wheaton, IL: Crossway, 2017).

22. A protein fold is a kind of structure that is formed by a protein. More specifically, it is "a distinctive, stable, complex, three-dimensional structure that enables proteins to perform specific biological functions" (Meyer, "Neo-Darwinism and the Origin of Biological Form and Information," in Moreland et al., *Theistic Evolution*, 116).

23. Ibid., 117.
24. Ibid.
25. Ibid., 150.

Meyer adds, "And, of course, the building of new animals would require the creation of many new proteins, not just one."[26]

At this point it is appropriate to recall that, for all living things to have descended from one primitive, simple life form, it would require that random mutation would produce not one but *many thousands* of new proteins that would form the building blocks of all the different life forms on the earth. If the chance of producing just one new functional protein is one in ten with thirty-seven zeros after it, then the chance of this happening successfully *thousands of times* is, for all practical purposes, zero. It is impossible.

**b. Human Intuition Correctly Recognizes That Evolution Is Impossible.** Douglas Axe himself, the molecular biologist mentioned in the previous section, illustrates how human beings intuitively recognize when a claimed sequence of highly unlikely events becomes not just unlikely or improbable but actually impossible:

> My cat used to love walking on my keyboard, but her steps across it never produced anything sensible. How could they? ... What she was doing, pressing keys with her weight, had absolutely no connection to writing, apart from the fact that it made letters appear on my laptop display.
>
> Now, if I had to argue that it's *possible* for a cat's footsteps to compose a sensible paragraph, I know how I'd go about it. I'd break the impossible big outcome—a sensible paragraph—into something much smaller. Paragraphs are written one keystroke at a time, so *that* would be the attainable goal. If you had typed "Novembe," for example, no one would think it impossible for your cat to just *happen* to step on the "r" key, thereby completing the word "November." ... It seems we also have to agree, then, that the cat *could have* stepped on the shift key and then the "N" key to begin with (unlikely, but not impossible). If it did, then we would all agree that stepping on "o" next is well within the realm of possibility. And if *that* were to happen, well ... who would say "v" couldn't be stepped on next?
>
> You get the idea. By continuing the succession of unlikely-but-possible steps, we seem to be forced to conclude that, strictly speaking, it isn't *impossible* for a cat to have written this chapter for me. And yet we all know that, practically speaking, it *is* impossible.
>
> These seemingly contradictory assessments are easily reconciled by distinguishing impossibility in the mathematical sense of $p = 0$ from impossibility in the practical sense of "don't bother waiting for this to happen, because it isn't going to happen." Darwin's explanation of life fails in that practical sense, which is its undoing. ... For accidental causes to have invented life is impossible in the same way that a cat writing an essay is impossible: we can be fully confident that neither *has* ever happened or *will* ever happen.[27]

---

26. Ibid., 118.

27. Axe recognizes that an objection could be raised against his example by saying that evolution has the benefit of natural selection, while the cat does not. His response is that natural selection "cannot possibly rescue evolutionary theory from its fundamental failing. ... [because] it shows up only after the hard work of invention has been done" (99).

**c. Random Mutations Are Overwhelmingly Harmful.** Matti Leisola is professor emeritus of bioprocess engineering at Aalto University in Finland. He writes that actual mutations are very rare and seldom beneficial: "What, then, happens in nature? Average mutation rates are in the order of $10^{-10}$ (how often a certain base in DNA is mutated per cell division). Negative mutations exceed positive ones by a thousand—to a millionfold, according to various estimations."[28] Leisola goes on to summarize the last thirty years of protein and especially enzyme engineering: "Proteins can be modified . . . but only within narrow limits: the changes are not fundamental—basic structures cannot be changed. . . . Even with huge amounts of intellectual input, nothing basically novel has been created."[29]

**d. Nonliving Matter Does Not Contain and Cannot Produce the Information Necessary for Life.** James M. Tour, a synthetic organic chemist, is professor of chemistry, professor of computer science, and professor of materials science and nanoengineering at Rice University. He was named among "The 50 Most Influential Scientists in the World Today" by TheBestSchools.org and was named "Scientist of the Year" by *R&D* magazine in 2013. He writes, "Few biologists have ever synthesized a complex molecule ab initio. My experience with organic synthesis leads me to suggest that chemistry acting on its own simply does not do what it would need to do to generate the biologically relevant macromolecules, let alone the complex nanosystems in a living cell."[30] Tour then paints a picture of an imaginary team of scientists trying to create a living organism:

> The world's best synthetic chemists, biochemists, and evolutionary biologists have combined forces to form a team—a dream team in two quite distinct senses of the word. Money is no object. They have at their disposal the most advanced analytical facilities, the complete scientific literature, synthetic and natural coupling agents, and all the reagents their hearts might desire. Carbohydrates, lipids, amino acids, and nucleic acids are stored in their laboratories in a state of 100 percent enantiomeric purity.
>
> Would the dream team—*please*—assemble a living system?
>
> Take your time, folks, take a few billion years.
>
> Nothing? Well, well, well. . . .

Tour concludes, "We teach our students that, when a mechanism does not support their observations, the mechanism must either be revised to support the facts or entirely discounted. . . . Those who think scientists understand how prebiotic chemical mechanisms produced the first life are wholly misinformed. Nobody understands how this happened. Maybe one day we will. But that day is far from today."[31]

28. Leisola, "Evolution: A Story without a Mechanism," in Moreland et al., *Theistic Evolution*, 142.
29. Ibid., 157–58.
30. Tour, "Are Present Proposals on Chemical Evolutionary Mechanisms Accurately Pointing toward First Life?," in Moreland et al., *Theistic Evolution*, 167.
31. Ibid., 190–91.

Stephen Meyer, director of the Discovery Institute's Center for Science and Culture in Seattle, goes on to explain that nonliving matter does not contain the information necessary to produce life. He says, "Building a living cell in the first place requires assembly instructions stored in DNA or some equivalent molecule." But where did this information come from? Remember, we are not talking about trivial amounts of information. Meyer quotes Bill Gates as saying, "DNA is like a computer program, but far, far more advanced than any software we've ever created."[32]

But could nonliving chemicals, following the laws of nature, generate such information? Meyer responds, "Physical laws do not generate complex sequences. . . . They *describe* highly regular, repetitive, and periodic patterns. . . . According to classical information theory, the amount of information present in a sequence is inversely proportional to the probability of the sequence occurring. Yet the regularities we refer to as laws describe highly deterministic or predictable relationships between conditions and events."[33]

In other words, Meyer is saying that the "laws of nature" predict with near certainty just how nonliving matter will behave in certain circumstances. That means the probability of matter by itself behaving in predictable ways is near to 100 percent. But that means the amount of information present in any arrangement of nonliving matter is essentially zero (the inverse of 100 percent). By contrast, the incredible amount of complex information found in DNA is vast. "The sum total of DNA in ourselves—our genome—can be thought of as a book with 3 billion base pairs of DNA."[34] That means that the probability of DNA information occurring by chance is the inverse of "vast," or essentially zero. Our conclusion must be that it is impossible for the nonliving raw materials found in nature to have created the information necessary for any living organism. The information is so complex and so vast that it must have come from elsewhere, from an intelligent cause of the information.

**e. Creating New Life Forms Would Require More Changes than Just Mutations in DNA.** Popular explanations of evolutionary theory can make it seem as though a few random mutations in an organism's DNA can explain the creation of new life forms. However, molecular biologist Jonathan Wells explains that additional information outside of DNA called "epigenetic information" is necessary for the creation of a new life form. This information directs much embryo development that determines the placement of organs within the body and the overall body form of a living organism. Epigenetic information is apparently contained in cell membranes and in the final folded shape of proteins, but the exact mechanism for this is not yet known.[35] The fact

32. Meyer, "The Difference It Doesn't Make: Why the 'Front-End Loaded' Concept of Design Fails to Explain the Origin of Biological Information," in Moreland et al., *Theistic Evolution*, 224.

33. Ibid., 227.

34. Hössjer, Gauger, and Reeves, "An Alternative Popula-tion Genetics Model," in Moreland et al., *Theistic Evolution*, 505.

35. Jonathan Wells, "Why DNA Mutations Cannot Accomplish What Neo-Darwinism Requires," in Moreland et al., *Theistic Evolution*, 237–56.

that such epigenetic information is necessary means that any attempts by supporters of evolution to explain the creation of life from nonliving matter or the mutation from one life form to another must explain even more than the (supposed) occurrences of beneficial mutations in DNA.

**f. Embryo Development Requires the Coordinated Activity of Thousands of Genes.** The development from an embryo to a fully formed body is an extremely complex process that requires the precise coordination of multiple factors. As a result, "Experiments which generate mutations in genes acting on body plans tend to produce overwhelmingly defective or lethal embryos," according to British developmental biologist Sheena Tyler.[36] One mutation in a gene, or even a handful of small mutations, would not be enough to give an animal a new body form, Tyler explains, because "transformations from one form to another are never 'simple' but require completely integrated transformation of form for all associated structures, and all of these must be functional."[37]

Tyler describes how the development from an embryo to a fully formed body must be carefully "orchestrated," as is evident from an understanding of skeletal development, the nervous system, tooth development, and heart and circulatory system development.[38] For example, an electrical current plays a role in identifying the correct location of a future limb such as an arm or leg, and this electrical current must be produced at the appropriate time and location for the limb, "which implies an underlying prepattern that directs the gene expression itself."[39] Another example is seen in the development of the heart and circulatory system, which requires "the expression of *thousands* of genes at each stage of heart development," and this happens "by interacting with cofactors, and by binding with a constellation of regulatory DNA elements." In addition, "The heart also requires a circulatory system to pump blood into, and it appears that development of both the heart and circulation are simultaneously coordinated."[40] She adds, "Evidences of such orchestration are growing in abundance . . . with secular authors even adding superlatives: it is *exquisitely* orchestrated."[41]

Finally, advocates of Darwinian evolution had previously pointed to similarity in embryo development as evidence of evolution. However, it is now known that significant differences exist very early, when cells first begin to divide. "The spatial arrangement of cells within an embryo as they divide is known as the cleavage pattern. Various animal groups have notable, fundamental differences in these patterns."[42]

36. Sheena Tyler, "Evidence from Embryology Challenges Evolutionary Theory," in Moreland et al., *Theistic Evolution*, 294.

37. Ibid., 295.

38. Ibid., 297–309.

39. Ibid., 299.

40. Ibid., 303–5, italics in original.

41. Ibid., 325, italics in original.

42. Ibid., 313. In that same volume, Casey Luskin and Paul Nelson write, "Embryologists have found considerable differences among vertebrate embryos from the earliest stages onward, contradicting what we are told to expect from common ancestry" (395).

**g. The "Irreducible Complexity" of the Living Cell Defies an Evolutionary Explanation.** The invention and subsequent improvement of the electron microscope in the mid-twentieth century, together with other technological advances, allowed scientists for the first time in history to explore the inner workings of a living cell. Since the end of World War II, an explosion of new research into the cell has shown it to be far more complex than anyone had imagined. In 1996, biology professor Michael Behe published *Darwin's Black Box*,[43] which argued that several parts of the cell contain systems that are "irreducibly complex." He defined this to mean "a single system composed of several well-matched, interacting parts that contribute to the basic function, wherein the removal of any one of the parts causes the system to effectively cease functioning. An irreducibly complex system cannot be produced directly . . . by slight, successive modifications of a precursor system, because any precursor to an irreducibly complex system that is missing a part is by definition nonfunctional."[44]

As an example, Behe explained the cilium, which is a structure that "looks like a hair and beats like a whip," and enables a cell to move around in a liquid, somewhat like a paddle moves a boat. But the cilium will only work if another component within the cell acts like a "motor" to provide energy and still other components act like "connectors" to transmit the energy from the motor to the "paddle." The system is irreducibly complex because the whole system ceases to function if you take away any one part. Behe then argues that evolutionary theory can provide no explanation for this because the individual parts would be useless and would provide no natural advantage to the cell. His book gave worldwide prominence to the scientific arguments for "intelligent design" in living things.

In 2009, Stephen Meyer continued Behe's argument, focusing on DNA, in his book *Signature in the Cell*.[45] Meyer's and Behe's books continue to provide persuasive evidence for the astounding complexity of a living cell and the impossibility that cells have come into existence through a gradual evolutionary process.

**h. The Fossil Record Is Filled with Gaps and Characterized by the Sudden Appearance and Then Continuity of Recognizable Kinds of Animals.** The fossil record was Darwin's greatest problem in 1859, and it has simply become a greater problem since then. In Darwin's time, hundreds of fossils were available showing the existence of many distinct kinds of animals and plants in the distant past. But Darwin was unable to find any fossils from "intermediate types" to fill in the gaps between distinct kinds of animals—fossils showing some characteristics of one animal and a few characteristics of the next developmental type, for example. In fact, many

43. Michael Behe, *Darwin's Black Box: The Biochemical Challenge to Evolution* (New York: Free Press, 2006). The 2006 edition contains an "afterward" in which Behe responds to his critics and says, "The scientific argument for design is stronger than ever. . . . Despite hundreds of probing commentaries . . . the book's argument for design stands. . . . There is very little of the original text that I would change if I wrote it today. There is, however, much I could add" (255–56).

44. Behe, *Darwin's Black Box*, 39.

45. Stephen Meyer, *Signature in the Cell: DNA and the Evidence for Intelligent Design* (New York: HarperCollins, 2009).

ancient fossils exactly resembled present-day animals—showing that (according to the chronological assumptions of his view) numerous animals have persisted for millions of years essentially unchanged. Darwin realized that the absence of "transitional types" in the fossil record weakened his theory, but he thought it was due to the fact that not enough fossils had been discovered. He was confident that further discoveries would unearth many transitional types of animals. However, the subsequent 160 years of intensive archaeological activity has still failed to produce these needed transitional types.[46]

Stephen Meyer and German paleontologist Günter Bechly write,

> In particular, the fossil record also manifests large "morphological gaps" and discontinuities between different groups of organisms, especially at the higher taxonomic levels (of phyla, classes, and orders) representing the major morphological differences between different forms of life. With very few exceptions, the major groups of organisms come into the fossil record abruptly, without discernible connection to earlier (and generally simpler) alleged ancestors in the fossil record.[47]

They add, "We think the most important class of evidence to consider remains the pervasive pattern of discontinuity and the abrupt appearance of major groups of organisms."[48]

**i. Similarities in Structure and Appearance Are Better Understood as Evidence for the Same Designer than as Evidence for the Same Ancestor.** Bechly and Meyer note that advocates of evolution regularly assume that if two organisms share a similar body part or similar molecular structure, that is evidence that both organisms descended from a common ancestor. However, Bechley and Meyer reply,

> The similarity between different genes and proteins in different organisms also might have arisen separately as the result of an intelligent designer choosing to provide similar molecular-level functional capabilities in different organisms. For example, on this view, hemoglobin proteins in chimps and humans should have similar amino acid sequences or structures (as they do) since they perform the same as function in each animal, namely, carrying oxygen in the bloodstream.[49]

Similar comments are made by other contributors to the same book:

---

46. Johnson, *Darwin on Trial*, 73–85, discusses the two examples sometimes claimed out of perhaps 100 million fossils that have been discovered, Archaeopteryx (a bird with some characteristics that resemble reptiles), and some apelike examples thought to be prehuman hominids. Archaeopteryx is still very much a bird, not a near-reptile, and studies of the characteristics of the supposedly prehuman fossils include large amounts of subjective speculation, resulting in strong differences among experts who have examined them.

47. Bechley and Meyer, "The Fossil Record and Universal Common Ancestry," in Moreland et al., *Theistic Evolution*, 339.

48. Ibid., 356.

49. Ibid., 359.

Intelligent agents frequently reuse the same parts in different designs to meet functional requirements, such as reusing wheels on cars and airplanes, or reusing key computer codes in different versions of Microsoft Windows. . . . Thus, common design—the intentional reuse of a common blueprint or components—is a viable explanation for the widespread functional similarities among the biomolecules found in different types of organisms.[50]

**j. Archaeology Points to an Abrupt Appearance of Humans on Earth, Clearly Distinct from Older Apelike Animals.** Although popular journalistic reports can give the impression that human-like creatures have been on earth for two million years, that is not an accurate impression. Casey Luskin writes,

> Known hominins fall into two separate groups: ape-like and human-like, with a distinct gap between them. The genus *Homo* appears in an abrupt, non-Darwinian fashion, without evidence of an evolutionary transition from ape-like hominins. . . . Many researchers have recognized an "explosion" of modern human-like culture in the archaeological record about thirty-five to forty thousand years ago, showing the abrupt appearance of human creativity, technology, art, and even paintings—showing the rapid emergence of self-awareness, group identity, and symbolic thought.[51]

**k. Human Beings Are Vastly Different from Chimpanzees.** There have been widely reported claims that the human genetic code is only 1 percent different from chimpanzees, giving apparent support to the idea that humans and chimps share a common ancestor. But these claims are inaccurate, according to biologist Ann Gauger, Swedish professor of mathematics and statistics Ola Hössjer, and British specialist in mathematical analysis of genetic algorithms Colin Reeves. They write,

> The underlying concept that gives this figure its persistence is common descent. This concept is something that most biologists treat as axiomatic, untouchable, and completely self-evident, which is why the figure of 1% has such staying power. . . . All told, based on current knowledge, there is at least a 5% difference in our DNA, and that does not count rearrangements in the DNA, where segments of the DNA appear flipped end to end in relation to chimp DNA, or where one segment of human DNA is in a different location than in chimpanzees.[52]

---

50. Casey Luskin, "Universal Common Descent: A Comprehensive Critique," in Moreland et al., *Theistic Evolution*, 377–78.

51. Luskin, "Missing Transitions: Human Origins and the Fossil Record," in Moreland et al., *Theistic Evolution*, 472.

(Some readers may differ with Luskin's date range but still recognize the abrupt appearance of human beings on earth.)

52. Gauger, Hössjer, and Reeves, "Evidence for Human Uniqueness," in Moreland et al., *Theistic Evolution*, 476, 481.

They go on to point out many more differences:

> Our brains are larger and continue to develop long after birth. . . . Our muscu-
> lature is weaker, with smaller bone insertion points. Our thyroid hormone metab-
> olism differs. . . . Our immune systems differ. Our diets differ, and our intestines
> reflect that difference. We shed tears; chimpanzees don't. We can swim and have a
> diving reflex, but chimpanzees can't swim. We walk and run upright. Our feet are
> different—ours are designed for walking and chimpanzees' for climbing. . . . Our
> shoulders are designed for throwing, while chimpanzees' are designed for climbing.
> Our pelvis and hips are oriented so as to permit upright walking. . . . Our hands are
> designed for tool use, not knuckle walking. We have greater fine motor control, and
> our thumbs can touch the far side of our hands.
>
> Finally, there are all the cultural and behavioral differences. We plan. We think
> about the past and the future. We make intentional decisions. We can delay gratifi-
> cation for long periods. We engage in long-range trade. Adults play. We dance. We
> make music. We have language and communicate symbolically, and we write novels
> and poetry. We have mathematics and art. We domesticate animals and engage in
> agriculture. We wear clothing. We engage in hospitality. We control fire and we
> measure time. We practice religion and bury the dead. We have empathy for others,
> and altruism on a scale unknown in the animal world. We care for the infirm and
> the elderly. We see nothing like the human scale of behavior in chimpanzees. Our
> culture is exceptional, even unique, by any standard of the animal kingdom. It is
> orders of magnitude more sophisticated than anything chimpanzees do."[53]

Evolutionary theory cannot give a plausible explanation for the origin of these
massive differences. Its defenders have to resort over and over again to implausible
speculations that "events *a*, *b*, and *c* might have happened" and "events *m*, *n*, and *o*
might have happened" and "events *x*, *y*, and *z* might have happened," for all of which
no physical evidence has ever been found, and all of which are highly improbable.
And many of these mutations have to have happened *at the same time*. Gauger and her
colleagues continue,

> But in order for our common descent from an ape-like ancestor by purely natural
> means to be true, many of these features had to arise at the same time in a coordi-
> nated fashion, meaning some number of mutations also had to happen at the same
> time. For example, an enlarged brain would require changes to the jaw and teeth as
> well as to the brain case. This significant and defining anatomical change would have
> needed multiple mutations to occur.[54]

---

53. Ibid., 491–92.                    54. Ibid., 493.

**l. The Genetic Diversity in the Human Race Could Have Arisen from One Original Couple.** Modern evolutionary theory holds that the range of genetic diversity that is present today can only be accounted for by supposing that we have descended from at least 10,000 different individuals, each of whom was a different result of gradual evolution from nearly-human creatures. But Ola Hössjer, Ann Gauger, and Colin Reeves argue that, if we suppose an initial couple who were genetically diverse from each other, we could still get the range of diversity that we see today:

> It is possible, however, that a first founding couple were created with initial diversity, each individual with twenty-two pairs of autosomal chromosomes and either an XX for the female or an XY for the male. Thus there would have been four total copies of each non-sex chromosome (two from each). Those four copies could each have been created unique, giving rise to a very large number of SNPs [genetic differences], all of which were present in the first generation. This could be true for . . . all of the twenty-two sets of four homologous chromosomes. In the same way, the three X-chromosomes copies . . . could have been created with diversity. . . . Since the female carried hundreds of mitochondria that could have been diverse, she may have passed some of that diversity on to her daughters.[55]

**m. The Unproven Assumption behind Evolutionary Theory Is "Methodological Naturalism."** In spite of all the factual evidence against neo-Darwinian evolution mentioned above, it is tragic that the common opinion, perpetuated in many science textbooks today, is that evolution is an established scientific "fact." Behind this viewpoint is one key assumption, the assumption of what is called "methodological naturalism."

> Methodological naturalism asserts that, to qualify as scientific, a theory must explain all phenomena by reference to purely physical or material—that is, non-intelligent—causes or processes.[56]

But that assumption implies a related assumption: living things were *not* created by God, who instantly created living things out of nothing or else changed the natural behavior of matter to form living things. (Or else it assumes that the origin of living things is a topic outside the realm of "science"—but that is an admission most scientists are unwilling to make.)

How can modern scientists, by an unproven assumption, be sure that they have not excluded the one explanation for the origin of living things that is the historical truth, that living things were first made by a special creative act of God? If modern science is

---

55. Hössjer, Gauger, and Reeves, "An Alternative Population Genetics Model," in Moreland et al., *Theistic Evolution*, 511.

56. Stephen C. Meyer and Paul A. Nelson, "Should Theistic Evolution Depend on Methodological Naturalism?," in Moreland et al., *Theistic Evolution*, 564.

defined in a way that excludes such an answer, then several hundred more years, even thousands more years, will never be enough to discover the origin of all living things, for a commitment to methodological naturalism will continually prevent the discovery of the actual truth.[57]

**n. What If Scientists Far in the Future Actually Create Life?** What if, someday, life were actually "created" in the laboratory by scientists? Here it is important to understand what is meant. First, this would not be "creation" in the pure sense of the word, since all laboratory experiments begin with some kinds of previously existing matter. It would not give an explanation of the origin of matter itself, nor would it be the kind of creating that the Bible says God did. Second, most contemporary attempts to "create life" are really just very small steps in the gigantic process of moving from nonliving materials to an independently living organism, even one consisting of only one cell. The construction of a protein molecule or an amino acid nowhere approaches the complexity of a single living cell. But most importantly, what would it demonstrate if the collective work of thousands of the most intelligent scientists in the world, with the most expensive and complex laboratory equipment available, working over the course of several decades, actually did produce a living organism? Would that "prove" that God did not create life? Quite the opposite: it would demonstrate that life simply does not come about by chance but must be intentionally created by an intelligent designer. In theory at least, it is not impossible that human beings, created in the image of God and using their God-given intelligence could someday create a living organism out of nonliving substances (though the complexity of the task far surpasses any technology that exists today). But that would only show that God made us to be "Godlike"—that in biological research as in many other areas of life we in a very small way can imitate God's activity. All such scientific research in this direction really ought to be done out of reverence for God and with gratitude for the scientific capability with which he has endowed us.

**o. Believing Anything but the Bible.** Many unbelieving scientists have been so influenced by the cumulative force of the objections brought against evolution that they have openly advocated novel positions for one part or another of the proposed evolutionary development of living things. Francis Crick, who won the Nobel Prize for helping to discover the structure of DNA molecules, proposed in 1973 that life may have been sent here by a spaceship from a distant planet, a theory that Crick calls "Directed Panspermia."[58] To the present author, it seems ironic that brilliant scientists could advocate so fantastic a theory without one shred of evidence in its favor, all the while rejecting the straightforward explanation given by the one book in the history of the world that has never been proven wrong, that has changed the lives of millions of people, that has

57. Several chapters in Moreland, *Theistic Evolution*, critique in more detail the idea that science should be kept within the bounds of methodological naturalism. See especially chapters 19–20.

58. *Time*, September 10, 1973, 53, summarizing the article F. H. C. Crick and L. E. Orgel, "Directed Panspermia," in *Icarus 19* (1973): 341–46.

been believed completely by many of the most intelligent scholars of every generation, and that has been a greater force for good than any other book in the history of the world.

Why will otherwise intelligent people commit themselves to beliefs that seem so irrational? It seems as though they will believe in anything as long as it is not belief in the personal God of Scripture, who calls us to forsake our pride, humble ourselves before him, ask his forgiveness for failure to obey his moral standards, and submit ourselves to his moral commands for the rest of our lives. To refuse to do this is irrational, but as we shall see in the chapter on sin, all sin is ultimately irrational at its root.

Other challenges to the theory of evolution have been published in the last twenty or thirty years, and no doubt many more will be forthcoming. One only hopes it will not be too long before the scientific community publicly acknowledges the implausibility of evolutionary theory, and textbooks written for high school and college students openly acknowledge that evolution simply is not a satisfactory explanation for the origin of life on the earth.

p. **The Destructive Influences of Evolutionary Theory in Modern Thought.** It is important to understand the incredibly destructive influences that evolutionary theory has had on modern thinking. If in fact life was not created by God, and if human beings in particular are not created by God or responsible to him but are simply the result of random occurrences in the universe, then of what significance is human life? We are merely the product of matter plus time plus chance, and so to think that we have any eternal importance, or really any importance at all in the face of an immense universe, is simply to delude ourselves. Honest reflection on this notion should lead people to a profound sense of despair.

Moreover, if all of life can be explained by evolutionary theory apart from God, and if there is no God who created us (or at least if we cannot know anything about him with certainty), then there is no supreme Judge to hold us morally accountable. Therefore, there are no moral absolutes in human life, and people's moral ideas are only subjective preferences, good for them perhaps but not to be imposed on others. In fact, in such a case the only thing forbidden is to say that one knows that certain things are right and certain things are wrong—a common complaint against Christians today.

There is another ominous consequence of evolutionary theory: If the inevitable processes of natural selection continue to bring about improvement in life forms on earth through the survival of the fittest, then why should we hinder this process by caring for those who are weak or less able to defend themselves? Should we not rather allow them to die without reproducing so that we might move toward a new, higher form of humanity, even a "master race"? In fact, Marx, Nietzsche, and Hitler all justified war on these grounds.[59]

Moreover, if human beings are continually evolving for the better, then the wisdom

---

59. See *NIDCC*, 283.

of earlier generations (and particularly of earlier religious beliefs) is not likely to be as valuable as modern thought. In addition, the effect of Darwinian evolution on many people's opinions of the trustworthiness of Scripture has been a very negative one.

Contemporary sociological and psychological theories that see human beings as simply higher forms of animals are another outcome of evolutionary thought. And the extremes of the modern "animal rights" movement that oppose all killing of animals (for food, leather coats, or medical research, for example) also flow naturally out of evolutionary thought.

### 4. Theistic Evolution Is Inconsistent with the Teachings of Scripture

Ever since the publication of Charles Darwin's book *On the Origin of Species by Means of Natural Selection* (1859), some Christians have proposed that living organisms came about by the process of evolution that Darwin proposed but that *God guided that process* so that the result was just what he wanted it to be. This view is called *theistic evolution* because it advocates belief in God (it is "theistic") and in evolution too.[60]

**a. Definition of Theistic Evolution.** In this section I will interact with the most recent and most prominent advocates of theistic evolution, the Christians who are connected with the BioLogos Institute and who publish on their website BioLogos.org.

More specifically, I will interact with theistic evolution as defined in this way:

> God created matter and after that did not guide or intervene or act directly to cause any empirically detectable change in the natural behavior of matter until all living things had evolved by purely natural processes.

After the publication of the book *Theistic Evolution: A Scientific, Philosophical, and Theological Critique*, from which this definition was taken,[61] some reviews on the BioLogos website objected that this definition misrepresented their position. The primary response was in a thoughtful and gracious review by Deborah Haarsma, president of BioLogos.[62] She proposes an alternative definition of theistic evolution (though she prefers to call it "evolutionary creation"[63]):

60. This section on theistic evolution was adapted and substantially shortened from Wayne Grudem, "Biblical and Theological Introduction: The Incompatibility of Theistic Evolution with the Biblical Account of Creation and with Important Christian Doctrines," and "Theistic Evolution Undermines 12 Creation Events and Several Crucial Christian Doctrines," in *Theistic Evolution: A Scientific, Philosophical, and Theological Critique*, ed. J. P. Moreland, Stephen C. Meyer, Christopher Shaw, Ann Gauger, and Wayne Grudem (Wheaton, IL: Crossway, 2017), 61–77 and 783–838, and is used with permission of the publisher. See those two chapters and pages 839–926 for much more detailed analysis of the topics covered in this

section. Those pages contain detailed replies to the alternative explanations of Genesis 1–3 offered by Wheaton College professor John Walton, which were too lengthy to include in this book.

61. This definition was written by the editors of Moreland et al., *Theistic Evolution* as a concise summary of the view we were opposing (see p. 67).

62. See Deborah Haarsma, "A Flawed Mirror: A Response to the Book 'Theistic Evolution,'" BioLogos, April 18, 2018, https://biologos.org/articles/a-flawed-mirror-a-response-to-the-book-theistic-evolution.

God creates all living things through Christ, including humans in his image, making use of intentionally designed, actively-sustained, natural processes that scientists today study as evolution.

Haarsma adds, "God guided evolution just as much as God guides the formation of a baby from an embryo" (in the previous sentence she had cited Psalm 139:13, which says, "You formed my inward parts; you knitted me together in my mother's womb"). She also says, "Although God in his sovereignty could have chosen to use supernatural action to create new species, evolutionary creationists are convinced by the evidence in the created order that God chose to use natural mechanisms."[64]

But it seems to me that Haarsma's objections only serve to confirm the accuracy of my definition given above.[65] We could modify the definition to *add* more things that she advocates, but the substance of the definition would remain, as in this example:

> God created matter [*with regular properties governed by "natural law"*] and after that [*God continued to sustain matter and preserve its natural properties but he*] did not guide or intervene or act directly to cause any empirically detectable change in the natural behavior of matter until all living things had evolved by purely natural processes [*which God actively sustained but did not change*].

In this modified definition, I have explicitly added the BioLogos belief that God actively upholds and sustains the activity of the entire natural world (as affirmed in Col. 1:17 and Heb. 1:3). I agree with that belief (see chapter 16), so there is no disagreement at that point, and it is consistent with historic Christian doctrine. But the key point in our definition, and the point with which I strongly differ, is the theistic evolutionist claim that God did not *"cause any empirically detectable change* in the natural behavior of matter" until all living things "had evolved by purely natural processes."

---

63. The authors of material on the BioLogos website usually prefer the term *evolutionary creation* to the term *theistic evolution*, but both terms are found in their literature. I have kept the term *theistic evolution* in this book because it has been the standard phrase used to describe this position for a century or more in theological discussion. See, for example, Louis Berkhof, *Systematic Theology* (Grand Rapids: Eerdmans, 1941), 162: "Theistic evolution is not tenable in the light of Scripture." Berkhof also refers to the earlier critique of theistic evolution in the book by Alfred Fairhurst, *Theistic Evolution* (Cincinnati: Standard Publishing, 1919). In addition, the term *evolutionary creation* seems to us to be misleading, because people who support theistic evolution do not believe in "creation" in the ordinary sense that Christians use the term, to refer to God's direct activity in creating specific plants and animals and in creating human beings, but they mean only the initial *creation* of matter with properties that would lead to the evolution of living things. Francis Collins himself had earlier argued against using the word "creation" in connection with theistic evolution "for fear of confusion." Collins, *The Language of God* (New York: Free Press, 2006), 203. (The references and much of the wording in this footnote have been taken from a footnote that I wrote in Moreland et al., *Theistic Evolution*, 65n6.)

64. Haarsma, "A Flawed Mirror."

65. This definition is also consistent with the explanation of prominent theistic evolution advocates Karl Giberson and Francis Collins: "The model for divinely guided evolution that we are proposing here thus requires no 'intrusions from outside' for its account of God's creative process, except for the origins of the natural laws guiding the process." Karl Giberson and Francis Collins, *The Language of Science and Faith* (Downers Grove, IL: InterVarsity, 2011), 115.

Haarsma does not object to this part of our definition, and in fact her proposed definition affirms the same thing: "God creates all living things . . . making use of intentionally designed, actively-sustained natural processes."[66]

**b. Theistic Evolution Confuses Creation with Providence.** The problem with this understanding of creation is that it confuses the Bible's teaching about God's action in *initially creating* the world with the Bible's teaching about God's ongoing action of *providentially sustaining* the world. (Note the present tense verb in their definition of theistic evolution: not "God created" but "God creates.") In another BioLogos review, Jim Stump writes, "Yes, we believe that God guides evolution, the same as we believe God guides photosynthesis."[67]

But this is simply a misleading use of the word *guide*. People ordinarily use the word *guide* to refer to an action that influences the course of an object so that it moves in a particular direction or toward a particular destination.[68] To influence the direction of something implies causing a change in the direction it was going. But the BioLogos explanation shows that they use the word *guide* to mean "does *not* influence the direction of an object but sustains it so that it continues in the direction it otherwise was going." So ordinary English speakers understand *guide* to mean "influence the direction of something," but the BioLogos foundation uses the word *guide* to mean "not influence the direction of something," which is just the opposite. They are using the word *guide* to mean the opposite of what people ordinarily mean by *guide*, and in this way their statement is misleading to ordinary readers.

Regarding the distinction between creation and providence, the narrative of God's creative activity in Genesis 1–2 gives overwhelming evidence that God's work of *creation* was fundamentally different from his *providential* work of preserving creation and maintaining its properties today. This is the reason that theistic evolution cannot be reconciled with any acceptable interpretation of Genesis 1–2, as I will attempt to demonstrate below. In Genesis, after God created man on day six, "God saw *everything that he had made*, and behold, it was very good" (Gen. 1:31), and then God's initial work of creating things was done.

Thus the heavens and the earth were finished, and all the host of them. And on the seventh day God finished his work that he had done, and he rested on the seventh day from all his work that he had done. (Gen. 2:1–2)

**c. Theistic Evolution Claims There Were Not Two but 10,000 Ancestors for the Human Race.** Regarding the origin of the human race, Christians who support theistic

66. See a similar viewpoint in Denis Alexander, *Creation or Evolution: Do We Have To Choose?*, 2nd ed. (Oxford and Grand Rapids: Monarch, 2014), 436.

67. Jim Stump, "Does God Guide Evolution?," BioLogos, April 18, 2018, https://biologos.org/articles/does-god-guide-evolution.

68. *Merriam-Webster*'s online dictionary defines "guide" as "direct in a way or course" or "direct, supervise, or influence usually to a particular end." *Merriam-Webster*, s.v. "guide," accessed April 15, 2020, https://www.merriam-webster.com/dictionary/guide.

evolution differ over whether Adam and Eve actually existed as historical persons. Some do not believe that Adam and Eve ever existed. Denis Lamoureux says bluntly, "Adam never existed,"[69] and "Holy Scripture makes statements about how God created living organisms that in fact never happened," and "Real history in the Bible begins roughly around Genesis 12 with Abraham."[70] Elsewhere on the BioLogos website, Peter Enns argues, "Maybe Israel's history happened first, and the Adam story was written to reflect that history. In other words, the Adam story is really an Israel story placed in primeval time. It is not a story of human origins but of Israel's origins."[71]

Other supporters of theistic evolution believe in a historical Adam and Eve, but even this "historical Adam and Eve" is still not the Adam and Eve of the Bible because these supporters of theistic evolution do not believe that Adam and Eve were the first human beings or that the human race descended from them. Instead, they claim that current genetic studies indicate that the human race today is so diverse that we could not have descended from just two individuals such as an original Adam and Eve.

Francis Collins writes, "Population geneticists . . . conclude that . . . our species . . . descended from a common set of founders, approximately 10,000 in number, who lived about 100,000 to 150,000 years ago."[72] Similarly, Denis Alexander says, "The founder population that was the ancestor of all modern humans . . . was only 9,000–12,500 reproductively active individuals."[73]

Therefore, those Christians who support theistic evolution and also want to retain belief in a historical Adam and Eve propose that God simply *chose* one man and one woman from among the thousands of human beings who were living on the earth and designated the man as "Adam" and the woman as "Eve." He then began to relate to them personally and made them representatives of the entire human race.

What happens, then, to the biblical narratives about Adam and Eve? Denis Alexander explains his view as follows:

> God in his grace chose a couple of Neolithic farmers in the Near East, perhaps around 8,000 years ago, . . . or maybe a community of farmers, to whom he chose to reveal himself in a special way, calling them into fellowship with himself—so that they might know him as a personal God. . . . This first couple, or community, have been termed *Homo divinus*, the divine humans, those who know the one true God,

69. Denis Lamoureux, "No Historical Adam: Evolutionary Creation View," in *Four Views on the Historical Adam*, ed. Matthew Barrett and Ardel Caneday (Grand Rapids: Zondervan, 2013), 58. The same statement by Lamoureux is found in his article, "Was Adam a Real Person?," BioLogos, September 2, 2010, https://biologos.org/articles/was-adam-a-real-person.

70. Lamoureux, "No Historical Adam," 56, 44.

71. Peter Enns, "Adam Is Israel," BioLogos, March 2, 2010, http://biologos.org/blogs/archive/adam-is-israel. In the next paragraph he says that he himself holds this view. Giberson and Collins mention this view of Enns as another possible interpretation of the Adam and Eve story (*Language of Science and Faith*, 211).

72. Collins, *Language of God*, 126; see also 207. Giberson and Collins claim that humans have descended from "several thousand people . . . not just two," in *Language of Science and Faith*, 209.

73. Alexander, *Creation or Evolution*, 265.

corresponding to the Adam and Eve of the Genesis account. . . . Certainly religious beliefs existed before this time, as people sought after God or gods in different parts of the world, offering their own explanations for the meaning of their lives, but *Homo divinus* marked the time at which God chose to reveal himself and his purposes for humankind for the first time. . . . [Adam] is . . . viewed as the federal head of the whole of humanity alive at that time. . . . The world population in Neolithic times is estimated to lie in the range of 1–10 million, genetically just like Adam and Eve, but . . . it was these two farmers out of all those millions to whom God chose to reveal himself.[74]

N. T. Wright proposes a similar explanation:

Perhaps what Genesis is telling us is that God chose one pair from the rest of the early hominids for a special, strange, demanding vocation. This pair (call them Adam and Eve if you like) were to be the representatives of the whole human race.[75]

Karl Giberson and Francis Collins offer a comparable view:

A common synthetic view integrating the biblical and scientific accounts sees human-like creatures evolving as the scientific evidence indicates, steadily becoming more capable of relating to God. At a certain point in history, God entered into a special relationship with those who had developed the necessary characteristics, endowing them with the gift of his image. . . . This view can fit whether the humans in question constituted a group—symbolized by Adam and Eve—or a specific male-female pair.[76]

The difficulty with all of these theistic evolution explanations of "Adam and Eve" arises because they differ significantly from the biblical account in Genesis 1–3, as I explain in the following section.

**d. Theistic Evolution Denies at Least Twelve Events in Genesis 1–3.** *(1) Theistic evolution claims that Adam and Eve were not the first human beings (and perhaps Adam and Eve never existed).* But Genesis 1, which records the initial creation of different parts of the universe, records the creation of the first human beings:

---

74. Alexander, *Creation or Evolution*, 290–91.

75. N. T. Wright, "Excursus on Paul's Use of Adam," in John Walton, *The Lost World of Adam and Eve* (Downers Grove, IL: IVP Academic, 2015), 177. John Walton himself proposes that Adam and Eve can be seen as "elect individuals drawn out of the human population and given a particular representative role in sacred space" ("A Historical Adam: Archetypal Creation View," in *Four Views on the Historical Adam*, ed. Matthew Barrett and Ardel Caneday [Grand Rapids: Zondervan, 2013], 109).

76. Giberson and Collins, *Language of Science and Faith*, 212.

Then God said, "Let us make man in our image, after our likeness. And let them have dominion over the fish of the sea and over the birds of the heavens and over the livestock and over all the earth and over every creeping thing that creeps on the earth." *So God created man in his own image, in the image of God he created him; male and female he created them.* (Gen 1:26–27)

*(2) Theistic evolution claims that Adam and Eve were born from human parents.* Theistic evolution supporters hold that Adam and Eve (if they existed) were ordinary human beings with human parents, but this contradicts the text of Genesis, which affirms that God directly "*formed the man of dust from the ground* and breathed into his nostrils the breath of life, and the man became a living creature" (Gen. 2:7). If this is understood as historical narrative, Adam had no human parents but was formed directly from the earth.

Eve is also portrayed as having no human parents, for we read that she was created from a rib taken from Adam's body: "The rib that the Lord God had taken from the man he made into a woman and brought her to the man" (Gen. 2:22).

*(3) Theistic evolution claims that God did not act directly or specially to create Adam out of dust from the ground.* This point is the counterpart to the previous point about Adam and Eve having no human parents. Theistic evolution requires that "Adam" (if there was an Adam) descended from a long line of previously existing human beings, but the account in Genesis 2 claims that God made the first man from the dust: "Then the Lord God *formed the man of dust from the ground* and breathed into his nostrils the breath of life, and the man became a living creature" (Gen. 2:7). The next chapter of Genesis also affirms Adam's creation directly from the earth: "By the sweat of your face you shall eat bread, till you return to the ground, *for out of it you were taken; for you are dust, and to dust you shall return*" (Gen. 3:19). Then the narrative continues, "Therefore the Lord God sent him out from the garden of Eden to work *the ground from which he was taken*" (Gen. 3:23).

*(4) Theistic evolution claims that God did not directly create Eve from a rib taken from Adam's side.* Theistic evolution requires that "Eve" (if there was an Eve) had human parents, but the narrative in Genesis 2 gives a different explanation of how God created Eve:

So the Lord God caused a deep sleep to fall upon the man, and while he slept *took one of his ribs* and closed up its place with flesh. *And the rib that the Lord God had taken from the man he made into a woman* and brought her to the man. Then the man said, "This at last is bone of my bones and flesh of my flesh; she shall be called Woman, because she was taken out of Man." (Gen. 2:21–23)

*(5) Theistic evolution claims that Adam and Eve were never sinless human beings.* Those who hold to theistic evolution maintain that Adam and Eve were ordinary human

beings, doing morally evil deeds for their entire lives just as all other human beings do. By contrast, the entire story of the creation of Adam and Eve as recorded in Genesis 1–2 indicates only blessing and favor from God, and gives no hint of the existence of any human sin or God's judgment on sin.

God created them, "God blessed them" (Gen. 1:28), and then "God saw everything that he had made, and behold, *it was very good*" (Gen. 1:31). "Very good" in the eyes of a holy God implies the absence of sin in the world.

Where there is no sin or guilt, there also is no shame, and so the picture of a sinless world is confirmed by this statement that closes the narrative in Genesis 2: "And the man and his wife were both naked and were not ashamed" (Gen. 2:25).

*(6) Theistic evolution claims that Adam and Eve did not commit the first human sins, for human beings were doing morally evil things long before Adam and Eve.* This is the counterpart to the previous point about God creating Adam and Eve as sinless people. According to theistic evolution, human beings have always committed morally evil deeds, and therefore human beings were sinning for thousands of years before Adam and Eve.[77]

But Genesis shows that Adam and Eve committed the *first* human sins in a world that was perfect and free from human sin: "So when the woman saw that the tree was good for food, and that it was a delight to the eyes, and that the tree was to be desired to make one wise, she took of its fruit and ate, and she also gave some to her husband who was with her, and he ate" (Gen. 3:6).

*(7) Theistic evolution claims that human death did not begin as a result of Adam's sin, for, in that view, human beings existed long before Adam and Eve, and those pre-Adamic humans were always subject to death.* All living things known to evolutionary science eventually die, including human beings, and therefore theistic evolution requires that human beings have always been subject to death, and that human beings were dying long before Adam and Eve existed.

But according to the biblical narrative, when God first created Adam and Eve, they were not subject to death. The absence of death when Adam and Eve were created is implied by the summary statement at the end of the sixth day of creation: "God saw everything that he had made, and behold, *it was very good*" (Gen. 1:31). In light of later biblical teachings that death is the "last enemy to be destroyed" (1 Cor. 15:26), as well as the prediction that in the age to come, "death shall be no more" (Rev. 21:4), the initial "very good" creation should be understood to imply that Adam and Eve were not subject to death when they were first created.

In the next chapter, God said to Adam, "But of the tree of the knowledge of good and evil you shall not eat, for in the day that you eat of it *you shall surely die*" (Gen. 2:17).

---

77. John Walton says, "Anthropological evidence for violence in the earliest populations deemed human would indicate that there was never a time when sinful (= at least personal evil) behavior was not present" (*The Lost World of Adam and Eve*, 154).

This implies that death would be the *penalty* for disobedience, not something to which they were initially subject. (Nothing is implied in Genesis 2 about animal death, for God's statement directed to Adam implies only human death: "*You* shall surely die.") After Adam sinned, God pronounced the promised judgment, which would be carried out over time through a life filled with painful toil, culminating in death: "By the sweat of your face you shall eat bread, *till you return to the ground*, for out of it you were taken; for you are dust, and to dust you shall return" (Gen. 3:19).

(8) *Theistic evolution claims that not all human beings have descended from Adam and Eve, for there were thousands of other human beings on earth at the time that God chose two of them as Adam and Eve.*

The "Adam and Eve" advocated by theistic evolution were just two individuals among many thousands on the earth at that time, and therefore not all human beings have descended from Adam and Eve. But Genesis portrays Adam and Eve as the first human beings (see section 4.d.1 above), and later in Genesis, "The man called his wife's name Eve, because *she was the mother of all living*" (Gen. 3:20). All human beings have descended from Adam as the male progenitor and from Eve, his wife, as the female progenitor.

By contrast, several theistic evolution authors claim that there must have been many other human beings on the earth at the time of Adam and Eve. The evidence they give is that Cain's wife (Gen. 4:17) had to come from somewhere, and Cain expected that there were other people who would want to kill him (Gen. 4:14). Genesis even says that Cain built a "city," which had to be a place populated by numerous people (Gen. 4:17).

But are we to think that the author of Genesis (whom I believe to be Moses) was unaware of this difficulty? The text of Genesis itself provides an obvious solution to this problem, because it says that Adam lived 930 years, "*and he had other sons and daughters*" (Gen. 5:4–5). How many? The text does not say, but Adam and Eve, created as full-grown adults, could have begun to have children in their very first year. Adam was 130 years old when Seth was born (Gen. 5:3), but he and Eve could well have had many dozens of children both prior to that time and after that time—the text does not tell us.

Yes, this requires that Cain and Seth and others would have married their sisters in the first generation, but that was necessary in order to have the entire human race descend from Adam and Eve, and the prohibitions against incest were not given by God until much later (see Lev. 18:6–18; 20:11–20; Deuteronomy 22:30).

(9) *Theistic evolution claims that God did not directly act in the natural world to create different "kinds" of fish, birds, and land animals.* Theistic evolution claims that God did not cause any empirically detectable change in the natural behavior of matter until all living things had evolved by purely natural processes.

But this proposal is in tension with the picture presented in Genesis, where God carries out *distinct and separate actions* to directly create different specific parts of creation, and then, in further distinct actions, creates specific kinds (or types) of animals.

For example, on day three, "God said, 'Let the earth sprout vegetation'. . . . And it was so" (Gen. 1:11). Then in a separate act on day five, "And God said, 'Let the waters swarm with swarms of living creatures, and let birds fly above the earth across the expanse of the heavens'" (Gen. 1:20). Then on day six there is more creative activity: *"God made the beasts of the earth* according to their kinds *and the livestock* according to their kinds, *and everything that creeps on the ground* according to its kind. And God saw that it was good" (Gen. 1:25).

The Hebrew text includes the direct object marker *'ēth* three times in this verse, showing that there are three distinct direct objects of the verb "made" (Heb. *'āsāh*): the verse says that God specifically made (1) the beasts of the earth, (2) the livestock, and (3) everything that creeps on the ground. In addition, within each of these groups he made creatures "according to their kinds," indicating a number of different specific types of animals within each group (though Scripture gives us no specific definition of the size of each category that is called a "kind"). This verse pictures a direct, active involvement of God in making different kinds of animals, which is far different from the sustaining of matter so that it evolves following its own properties that we find in theistic evolution.

Later, in a separate action on this same day, God said, "Let us *make* [once again, another distinct action designated by Heb. *'āsāh*] man in our image. . . . So God created man in his own image, in the image of God he created him; male and female he created them" (Gen. 1:26–27).

Finally, at the end of the sixth day, "God saw everything *that he had made,* and behold, it was very good" (Gen. 1:31). The scope of "everything that he had made" (once again, Heb. *'āsāh*) must include both the separate kinds of animals (from day six) and also man himself (from day six) which have just been specified as things that God "made."

The picture given in Genesis, therefore, is that God *directly made* various kinds of animals and also made human beings in distinct, separate acts. But theistic evolution says that God did not "make" these things in any sense that the Hebrew reader of these verses would understand from the verb "made" (Heb. *'āsāh*), but only in the sense that inanimate matter that God had created billions of years earlier at the beginning of the universe evolved by virtue of its own properties, with no additional creative action from God, into all these animals and human beings.[78]

None of the original readers of Genesis would have understood these verses to mean

---

78. Theistic evolution advocates frequently affirm that they believe in God's ongoing providential involvement in all of creation, but by this they do not mean that God intervened in or in any way directed the actions of the material universe, but rather that God *sustained* the materials of the universe so that they continually acted according to the physical properties with which they were initially created. Denis Alexander speaks about "the precious materials God has so carefully brought into

being in the dying moments of exploding stars" and says it is wrong to deny that they have the "potentiality to bring about life" (*Creation or Evolution*, 436). But if matter merely acting according to its own created properties can create life, then there would have been no need for God to repeatedly act in the natural world to create different kinds of living things, as Genesis 1 portrays him.

that God originally created nonliving matter and that *this matter then created all living things* over the course of billions of years, without any additional intervention from God. Nor could this have been the intended meaning of any of the authors of these New Testament books. Rather, the intent of the human authors (and of the divine author), as rightly understood by the original readers, would be to affirm that God directly acted in the natural world to create all the different kinds of plants and animals that exist on the earth today.

*(10) Theistic evolution claims that God did not "rest" from his work of creation or stop any special creative activity after plants, animals, and human beings appeared on the earth.* Theistic evolution holds that, after the initial creation of matter, God did not act to change the behavior of matter in the universe to create any living things. Karl Giberson and Francis Collins say, "The model for divinely guided evolution that we are proposing here thus requires no 'intrusions from outside' for its account of God's creative process, except for the origins of the natural laws guiding the process."[79]

But this also means that, according to theistic evolution, there was no special activity of God from which he could have "rested" after the six days of creation recorded in Genesis 1. The biblical record, however, is incompatible with this theistic evolution viewpoint, for after narrating the events of God's six days of creative work, it says,

> Thus the heavens and the earth were finished, and all the host of them. And on the seventh day *God finished his work* that he had done, and *he rested on the seventh day from all his work that he had done.* So God blessed the seventh day and made it holy, because on it *God rested from all his work* that he had done in creation. (Gen 2:1–3)

Yet according to a theistic evolution viewpoint, there was no special kind of work that God did during these six days of creation, because the *providential* work of God in sustaining the materials of the universe while evolution was happening was no different from the ongoing *providential* work of God in sustaining the materials of the universe even today. *There was no particular creative work of God from which he could "rest."* This is another event in the history of the universe that the Bible claims to have happened and that theistic evolution says didn't happen.

*(11) Theistic evolution claims that God originally did not create a "very good" natural world in the sense of a safe environment that was free of thorns, thistles, and similarly harmful things.* Theistic evolution requires that all living plants and animals today resulted from an unbroken line of evolutionary change, and therefore there never was a different kind of natural order from what we know today.

By contrast, for centuries interpreters have understood Genesis 1–2 to speak of an

---

79. Giberson and Collins, *Language of Science and Faith*, 115.

idyllic garden of Eden, an earth with no "thorns and thistles" (Gen. 3:18), no curse on the ground because of sin (Gen. 3:17), and, by implication, no weeds hindering beneficial crops, as well as no natural disasters, such as hurricanes, tornadoes, earthquakes, floods, or droughts. No animals were hostile to human beings because the behavior of animals in this idyllic world was probably similar to their peaceful behavior foretold in the prophetic predictions of God's future restoration of an earth:

> The nursing child shall play over the hole of the cobra,
> > and the weaned child shall put his hand on the adder's den.
> They shall not hurt or destroy
> > in all my holy mountain. (Isa. 11:8–9)

This was understood (I think rightly) to be the kind of earth implied by the summary statement at the end of the sixth day of creation: "It was very good" (Gen. 1:31). Indeed, the kind of earth we have today, with frequent earthquakes, hurricanes, floods, droughts, poisonous snakes, venomous scorpions, malaria-spreading mosquitoes, and man-eating sharks and lions, can hardly be thought to be the best kind of creation that God could make, a creation that would cause God to say, "*It was very good.*"

But theistic evolution cannot affirm such an idyllic creation because it holds that all living things *as they exist today*, including all the things that are hostile to human beings, are the results of a fully natural evolutionary process. Therefore the earth has always been the way it is today. Therefore the picture of an idyllic creation given in Genesis is not a historically reliable narrative.

*(12) Theistic evolution claims that after Adam and Eve sinned, God did not place any curse on the world that changed the working of the natural world and made it more hostile to mankind.*

This belief of theistic evolution advocates is the counterpart of the previous point. They do not believe in an original idyllic creation, and so they also do not believe that God placed a curse on the ground as judgment for Adam's sin or that God altered the operation of nature to make the world more hostile to human beings.

But the biblical text, if understood as a historical record of actual events, shows that God did indeed alter the workings of the natural world when he spoke to Adam in words of judgment:

> And to Adam he said, "Because you have listened to the voice of your wife and have eaten of the tree of which I commanded you, 'You shall not eat of it,' *cursed is the ground because of you*; in pain you shall eat of it all the days of your life; *thorns and thistles* it shall bring forth for you; and you shall eat the plants of the field. By the sweat of your face you shall eat bread, till you return to the ground, for out of it you were taken; for you are dust, and to dust you shall return." (Gen. 3:17–19)

Adam's life would eventually end in death ("to dust you shall return"), but even while he continued alive, his life would consist of painful toil to provide enough food from the ground that had now become hostile ("Cursed is the ground. . . . By the sweat of your face you shall eat bread").

God's statement that the ground would now produce "thorns and thistles" is best understood as a common feature in biblical speech by which two or three concrete examples represent an entire category of things. Taken in this way, God's words of judgment mean that the earth would not only produce thorns and thistles but also harbor insects that would destroy crops (such as locusts, Deut. 28:38; Amos 7:1), diseases that would consume them (see Deut. 28:22), foraging animals that would eat crops, floods and droughts, tornadoes and hurricanes, all of which would make farming difficult and life precarious (see Eccl. 11:4).

Paul affirms in the New Testament that the present operation of the natural world is not the way God originally created it to work, but is a result of God's judgment. He pictures nature as longing to be freed from its bondage in much the same way as we long to be freed from our dying physical bodies and obtain new resurrection bodies:

> For I consider that the sufferings of this present time are not worth comparing with the glory that is to be revealed to us. For *the creation waits with eager longing* for the revealing of the sons of God. For *the creation was subjected to futility*, not willingly, but because of him who subjected it, in hope that *the creation itself will be set free from its bondage to corruption* and obtain the freedom of the glory of the children of God. (Rom 8:18–21).

Paul does not say that the creation will suddenly be raised to a brand-new, wonderful state of operation that it had never known before. Instead, he says that the creation will be "*set free* from its bondage," the bondage to which it was previously "subjected." Surely he is here referring to God's curse on the ground and his alteration of the functioning of nature because of sin in Genesis 3. But theistic evolution requires us to affirm that Paul was also wrong at this point.

**e. Theistic Evolution Denies That Genesis 1–3 Is a Historical Narrative.** Francis Collins says Genesis 1–3 should be understood as "poetry and allegory."[80] But what is the evidence for this? No Bible translation known to me presents the entirety of Genesis 1–3 as poetry, using relatively short lines, one after another, and showing evident parallelism in succeeding sets of balanced lines.

Notice how translation committees present the Psalms, for example:

> The LORD is my shepherd; I shall not want.
> He makes me lie down in green pastures.

---

80. Collins, *Language of God*, 206; also 150, 151, 175, 207.

He leads me beside still waters.
    He restores my soul. (Ps. 23:1–3)

This is poetry. It contains successive short lines that reemphasize similar or related ideas, typical of Hebrew parallelism. But Genesis 1–3 is not written this way, and Genesis 1–3 is not poetry.[81] It is written as a narrative of historical events. John Currid concludes, "If we remove the profoundly historical nature of Genesis 1–3, we will remove the historical foundation on which all the remainder of the Bible rests."[82]

Nor is Genesis 1–3 an extended *allegory*. Essential to allegorical stories is that they have a continuous second level of meaning.[83] For example, in the book of Judges, Jotham told an allegorical story:

> [Jotham] went and stood on top of Mount Gerizim and cried aloud and said to them, "Listen to me, you leaders of Shechem, that God may listen to you. *The trees once went out to anoint a king over them*, and they said to the olive tree, 'Reign over us.' But the olive tree said to them, 'Shall I leave my abundance, by which gods and men are honored, and go hold sway over the trees?' And the trees said to the fig tree, 'You come and reign over us.' But the fig tree said to them, 'Shall I leave my sweetness and my good fruit and go hold sway over the trees?'" (Judg. 9:7–11)

Readers realize at once that this is an allegory, because trees don't actually talk to each other and go out "to anoint a king over them," and because they recognize that the reactions of the different kinds of trees are specific details that carry a continuous second level of meaning that applies to various men who had refused to lead the people.

But Genesis 1–3 is not like this, and it is not an extended allegory. It is not possible to link the details in a coherent second level of meaning, with each part corresponding to something else in the reader's experience, as in Jotham's allegory. To label a narrative passage in a historical book as an allegory when nothing in the context demands that it be taken as an allegory is not proper interpretation; it is "allegorizing." Genesis 1–3 should rather be understood as historical narrative.

In addition, the entire book of Genesis is connected together as a single historical document in two ways. First, the genealogies in later chapters (see Gen. 5; 10; 11) explicitly tie all of the later historical persons and events back to their direct descent

81. There are some poetic verses, such as Genesis 1:27, 2:23, and 3:14–19, but even these recount historical facts using a poetic form of expression, as here: "So God created man in his own image, in the image of God he created him; male and female he created them" (Gen 1:27).

82. See Currid, "Theistic Evolution Is Incompatible with the Teachings of the Old Testament," in Moreland et al., *Theistic Evolution*, 862. Currid points to several additional features in the Hebrew linguistic structure and the interconnectedness of the narrative that demonstrate that these chapters must be taken as historical narrative, not as poetic, figurative, or allegorical literature.

83. I am grateful to my friend Leland Ryken (professor of English emeritus at Wheaton College) for a telephone conversation in which he pointed out to me this characteristic of allegories.

from Adam and Eve in Genesis 1–3, showing that the entire story of Genesis from the beginning is intended to be understood as one historical narrative, reporting people and events that actually happened. Abraham, Isaac, and Jacob are presented as real historical persons who descended from Adam and Eve, and therefore Adam and Eve are also viewed as real historical persons.

Second, the introductory phrase "These are the generations of"[84] (or a similar expression) occurs eleven times in Genesis (2:4; 5:1; 6:9; 10:1; 11:10, 27; 25:12, 19; 36:1, 9; 37:2). This literary device begins with the first link in the chain at Genesis 2:4, "*These are the generations of* the heavens and the earth when they were created." This phrase is the introductory heading for Genesis 2:4 to 4:26, a section that includes the details of the creation of Adam and Eve, the fall, and the stories about Cain, Abel, and Seth. The second link in the chain is Genesis 5:1, "This is the book of the generations of Adam," and it introduces a long list of Adam's descendants including Enoch, Methuselah, and Noah. The third link is Genesis 6:9: "These are the generations of Noah."

The eleventh and last link in this connected literary chain is the story of Jacob and his twelve sons, beginning with the introduction in Genesis 37:2, "These are the generations of Jacob," and ending with the death of Joseph in Genesis 50:26, the end of the book.

Therefore this literary device links together—like an unbroken chain—the story of Adam and Eve with the stories about the lives of Abraham, Isaac, Jacob, and Jacob's twelve sons, stories which are unquestionably intended as factual historical narratives. Therefore, the entire book is intended to be understood as historical narrative.

James Hoffmeier, professor of Old Testament and Near Eastern archaeology at Trinity Evangelical Divinity School, similarly affirms that Genesis 1–11 must be understood as historical:

> Genealogical texts in the ancient Near East, by their very nature, are treated seriously by scholars and not cavalierly dismissed as made-up or fictitious, even if such lists are truncated or selective.... The "family history" structuring of the book [of Genesis] indicates that *the narratives should be understood as historical*, focusing on the origins of Israel back to Adam and Eve, the first human couple and parents of all humanity.... *The narratives are dealing with real events involving historical figures*—and this includes Genesis 1–11.... The author of the narrative goes to great lengths to place Eden within the known geography of the ancient near East, not some made-up mythological, Narnia-like wonderland.[85]

### f. Theistic Evolution Undermines the Historical Trustworthiness of Ten Books of the New Testament. Ten books of the New Testament affirm the historicity of the events recorded in Genesis 1–3.

---

84. Some translations render this as "This is the account of..." (so NASB, NIV, NET, NLT).

85. James Hoffmeier, "Genesis 1–11 as History and Theology," in *Genesis: History, Fiction, or Neither?*, 30, 32; emphasis added.

1. "He who created them from the beginning made them male and female, and said, 'Therefore a man shall leave his father and his mother and hold fast to his wife, and the two shall become one flesh'" (Matt. 19:4–5).

2. "The son of Enos, the son of Seth, *the son of Adam, the son of God*" (Luke 3:38).

3. "The God who made the world *and everything in it*. . . . He made from *one man* every nation of mankind to live on all the face of the earth" (Acts 17:24, 26).

4. "Therefore, just as sin came into the world through one man, and death through sin . . . For if many died through one man's trespass . . . For as by the one man's disobedience the many were made sinners, so by the one man's obedience the many will be made righteous" (Rom. 5:12–19).

5. "For man was not made from woman, *but woman from man*" (1 Cor. 11:8). "For as *by a man came death*, by a man has come also the resurrection of the dead. For as *in Adam all die*, so also in Christ shall all be made alive" (1 Cor. 15:21–22). "Thus it is written, 'The *first man* Adam became a living being'; the last Adam became a life-giving spirit" (1 Cor. 15:45). "The first man was from the earth, *a man of dust*" (1 Cor. 15:47).

6. "But I am afraid that as *the serpent deceived Eve by his cunning*, your thoughts will be led astray from a sincere and pure devotion to Christ" (2 Cor. 11:3).

7. "For by him *all things* were created, in heaven *and on earth*, visible and invisible" (Col. 1:16).

8. "For Adam was formed first, then Eve; and Adam was not deceived, but the woman was deceived and became a transgressor" (1 Tim. 2:13–14).

9. "For he has somewhere spoken of the seventh day in this way: 'And *God rested* on the seventh day from all his works.' . . . For whoever has entered God's rest has also rested from his works as God did from his" (Heb. 4:4, 10).

10. "Worthy are you, our Lord and God, to receive glory and honor and power, for you *created all things*, and by your will they existed and were created" (Rev. 4:11). "Him who lives forever and ever, *who created* heaven and what is in it, *the earth and what is in it*, and *the sea and what is in it*" (Rev. 10:6).

Thus, theistic evolution requires us to believe that both Jesus and the authors of ten New Testament books were wrong in their affirmations of the historical reliability of many details in Genesis 1–3. This is much deeper than a challenge to the historicity of one verse or another. This is a challenge to truthfulness of the three foundational chapters of the entire Bible, and to the truthfulness of ten of the twenty-seven books of the New Testament

**g. Theistic Evolution Denies the Ability of the Bible to Teach Us about Vast Areas of Human Knowledge.** It is important to recognize what is actually happening in the debate about theistic evolution. Proponents of theistic evolution are claiming, in essence, that there are whole areas of human knowledge about which they will not allow the Bible to speak with authority. They will allow the Bible to speak to us about salvation but not about the origin of all living things on the earth, the origin of human beings, the origin of moral evil in the human race, the origin of human death, the origin of natural evil in the world, the perfection of the natural world as God originally created it, and even the nature of Christ's own personal involvement as the Creator of "all things . . . in heaven and on earth, visible and invisible" (Col. 1:16). These are massive areas of human knowledge, affecting our outlook on our entire lives. Yet theistic evolution has decreed that the Bible cannot authoritatively speak to us about these areas of human knowledge.[86] Those topics are seen as the exclusive domain of modern naturalistic science, off-limits for God to speak to us about.

**h. Theistic Evolution Nullifies the Overwhelming Evidence in Nature for God's Existence.** The Bible claims that nature gives abundant evidence of God's existence.[87] Paul writes,

> For what can be known about God is plain to them, because God has shown it to them. For *his invisible attributes,* namely, his eternal power and divine nature, *have been clearly perceived*, ever since the creation of the world, *in the things that have been made.* So they are without excuse. (Rom 1:19–20)

Paul's phrase "the things that have been made" certainly includes plants, animals, and human beings, all of which give clear *evidence* of God's power and other attributes (such as wisdom, knowledge, creativity, love, goodness, and faithfulness). This evidence is so strong that God's attributes are "clearly perceived" in the natural world. Therefore people who rebel against God are *"without excuse." The evidence from creation for God's existence is so overwhelming that God holds people morally accountable for denying it.*

This means that when people ponder the astounding complexity of the human eye, a bird's wing, or a single living cell, the evidence for God's existence is so strong that people have no good excuse for unbelief.

But theistic evolution *takes away that evidence for God completely.* While the Bible says that "the things that have been made" give clear evidence of God's "eternal power and divine nature" (Rom. 1:20), theistic evolution says that the living creatures give no such evidence, for the existence of all living things can be explained solely from the properties of matter itself.[88]

---

86. A supporter of theistic evolution might object that they believe the Bible speaks authoritatively to these issues, but that it does so in poetic or metaphorical language and in a way that does not disagree with modern scientific opinion. But that stance still refuses to allow the Bible to provide us authoritatively with any factual history about the details of creation and, therefore, about these other issues just named. In addition, this viewpoint will not allow the numerous indications of historical narrative within

the text of Genesis 1–3 to inform us that Genesis 1–3 is intended by the author to be understood as historical narrative, representing events that actually happened (see section 4.d above).

87. I wish to thank Casey Luskin of the Discovery Institute for his suggestions that led to a significant strengthening of this section.

88. Some supporters of theistic evolution will say that the fine-tuning of the universe to make it suitable to support

The contrast is clear. While the Bible says that *everything* in nature bears witness to God, theistic evolution says that *no living creature* in nature bears witness to God. When an unbeliever is confronted with the wondrous complexity of living things, theistic evolution allows him just to think that random mutations produce surprising results, and therefore he has no need for any thought of God. Theistic evolution advocates may argue that seemingly random mutations are in fact guided by God, but if an unbeliever sees no empirical evidence for such divine guidance, the evolutionary idea of random mutations without God's guidance provides enough explanation. Evolutionary science has given him (so he thinks) a complete explanation for why life exists. In this way, theistic evolution completely nullifies the evidence for God's existence in living things and therefore significantly hinders evangelism.

**i. Theistic Evolution Undermines Several Other Important Christian Doctrines.** I have explained in detail elsewhere how several Christian doctrines are undermined by a belief in theistic evolution,[89] so I will only list some of them briefly here:

1. *The truthfulness of the Bible:* I have explained this in the previous sections.
2. *The goodness of God:* According to theistic evolution, God is responsible for (somehow) creating a world filled with deadly diseases, dangerous animals, and natural disasters that have brought suffering and destruction to human beings for the entire duration of the human race on the earth. In other words, the earth and its present state is the best kind of earth God could create. By contrast, on a traditional view of Genesis 1–3, the blame for natural evil in the world belongs to Adam and Eve, not God.
3. *The moral justice of God:* According to theistic evolution, the earliest human beings that were somehow "created" by God's use of evolution were sinful human beings, committing morally evil deeds from their earliest existence on earth. But if that is the case, it is hard to escape the conclusion that God himself is responsible for human sin, for he never created sinless human beings who were able to obey him and not to sin.
4. *The atonement:* If we deny that sin came into the world through Adam, and if we deny that all human beings have descended from Adam, then Paul's argument in Romans 5:12 and 5:19 about the unity of the human race as represented by Adam does not work. And then the parallel with the unity of the redeemed who are represented by Christ does not work.

---

human life is evidence of God's existence, and I agree, but that kind of evidence from modern physics and chemistry, evidence which was unknown to ancient readers, would not have been Paul's intention in speaking of "the things that have been made" in Rom. 1:20. He surely would have thought of all living creatures as included in "the things that have been made."

89. See Grudem, "Theistic Evolution Undermines Twelve Creation Events and Several Crucial Christian Doctrines," in Moreland et al., *Theistic Evolution*, 821–37.

5. *The resurrection:* If we deny that death came into the world through Adam, and if we deny the unity of the human race as descending from Adam, then once again the parallel between Adam and Christ in 1 Corinthians 15:21–22 does not work. In this way, theistic evolution undermines the effectiveness of the resurrection to give new life to all who are saved by Christ.

**j. Conclusion.** Theistic evolution, as defined by its most respected defenders today, implies a denial of twelve specific events that are recorded in Genesis 1–3. The placement of these chapters at the beginning of Genesis, the absence of literary markers in these passages signaling to readers that they should be understood in a figurative way, and the matter-of-fact way in which subsequent chapters in Genesis assume that Genesis 1–3 is reliable historical narrative, provide convincing evidence that Genesis 1–3 is intended to be taken as a historical record of events that actually happened. In addition, all of these twelve events are affirmed or implied in various places in ten books in the New Testament.

Because theistic evolution denies the historicity of these twelve events, it also denies or undermines several significant Christian doctrines. In sum, belief in theistic evolution is incompatible with the truthfulness of the Bible and with several crucial doctrines of the Christian faith. It should not be considered a legitimate option that Bible-believing Christians, and especially Christian leaders, may hold today.

## 5. The Theory of a "Gap" between Genesis 1:1 and 1:2 Is Highly Unlikely

Some evangelicals have proposed that there is a gap of millions of years between Genesis 1:1 ("In the beginning, God created the heavens and the earth") and Genesis 1:2 ("The earth was without form and void, and darkness was over the face of the deep"). According to this theory, God made an earlier creation, but there was eventually a rebellion against God (probably in connection with Satan's rebellion), and God judged the earth so that "it became without form and void" (an alternative, but doubtful, translation proposed for Gen. 1:2).[90] What we read in Genesis 1:3–2:3 is really the *second* creation of God, in six literal twenty-four-hour days that occurred only recently (perhaps

---

90. This "gap theory" is given as one possible interpretation of Gen. 1:1–2 in *The New Scofield Reference Bible* (Oxford: Oxford University Press, 1967), in notes to Gen. 1:2 and Isa. 45:18. It also remains commonplace in much popular Bible teaching. An extensive defense of this theory is found in Arthur C. Custance, *Without Form and Void: A Study of the Meaning of Genesis 1:2* (Brockville, Ontario: Doorway Papers, 1970). An extensive critique is in Weston W. Fields, *Unformed and Unfilled* (Nutley, NJ: Presbyterian and Reformed, 1976). A substantial critique of the lexical and grammatical arguments used in the gap theory is also found in Oswald T. Allis, *God Spake by Moses* (Philadelphia: Presbyterian and Reformed, 1951), 153–59.

Some readers may wonder why I have classified this view along with secular views and theistic evolution as a theory that seems "clearly inconsistent with the teachings of Scripture." I should note here that I am doing this only because the arguments for this position seem to me to be based on highly unlikely interpretations of the biblical text, and I do not wish to imply that those who hold to the gap theory are unbelievers, or that they are like many theistic evolutionists who think the Bible cannot teach us about science. On the contrary, advocates of the gap theory have uniformly been believers in the total truthfulness of Scripture on whatever subject it speaks to.

10,000 to 20,000 years ago). The ancient fossils found on the earth, many of which are said to be millions of years old, stem from the *first* creation (4,500,000,000 years ago), which is mentioned only in Genesis 1:1.

The primary biblical argument for this theory is that the words "without form and void" and "darkness" in Genesis 1:2 picture an earth that has suffered the effects of judgment by God: darkness elsewhere in the Old Testament is frequently a sign of God's judgment, and the Hebrew words *tohû* ("without form") and *bohû* ("void, empty") in verses such as Isaiah 34:11 and Jeremiah 4:23 refer to places such as deserts that have suffered the desolating consequences of God's judgment.

But these arguments do not seem strong enough to persuade us that Genesis 1:2 pictures the earth as desolate after God's judgment. If God first forms the earth (v. 1) and later creates light (v. 3), there would have to be darkness over the earth in verse 2—this indicates that creation is in progress, not that any evil is present. In addition, each day has an "evening," and this means there is "darkness" present during the six days of creation (vv. 5, 8, 13, 18–19, et al.), with no suggestion of evil or of God's disapproval (cf. Ps. 104:20). As far as the phrase "without form and void," the sense is just that it is not yet fit for habitation: God's preparatory work has not yet been done. Of course, when God curses a desert, it does become unfit for habitation, but we should not read the cause of that unfitness in one case (God's curse on a desert) into another case, the creation, where the cause of unfitness for habitation is simply that God's work is still in progress; the preparation for man is not yet complete.[91] (It is not proper to read the circumstances that surround a word in one place into the use of that word in another place when the meaning of the word and its use in the second context do not require those same circumstances.)

In addition to the fact that Genesis 1:2 does not give support to this view, two other arguments weigh strongly against the gap theory:

1. There is no verse in Scripture that explicitly talks about this kind of earlier creation. So this theory is lacking even one verse of Scripture to give it explicit support.

2. In Genesis 1:31, when God finished his work of creation, we read, "God saw everything that he had made, and behold, it was very good." According to the gap

---

91. The second word, *bohû*, "void," only occurs two other times in Scripture (Isa. 34:11; Jer. 4:23), both picturing desolate lands that have experienced God's judgment. But the first word, *tohû*, which can mean "formlessness, confusion, unreality, emptiness" (*BDB*, 1062), occurs nineteen other times, sometimes to refer to a desolate place resulting from judgment (Isa. 34:11 and Jer. 4:23, both with *bohû*), and sometimes just to refer to an empty place, with no sense of evil or judgment implied (Job 26:7, of "space" over which God stretches the north, parallel to the "nothingness" in which he hangs the earth; also Deut. 32:10; Job 12:24; Ps. 107:40). The sense "uninhabitable" is especially appropriate in Isa. 45:18, speaking of God's creation of the earth: "He did not create it empty [*tohû*], he formed it to be inhabited." (The fact that God did not create the earth to be "empty" but "formed it to be inhabited" [Isa. 45:18] speaks of God's completed work of creation and does not deny that it was "without form and void" at the earliest stage of creation.)

theory, God would be looking at an earth full of the results of rebellion, conflict, and terrible divine judgment. He would also be looking at all the demonic beings, the hosts of Satan who had rebelled against him, and yet be calling everything "very good." It is difficult to believe that there was so much evil and so many evidences of rebellion and judgment on the earth and that God could still say that creation was very good.

Moreover, while some passages of Scripture do speak of God's judgment on rebellious angels or his judgment on the earth at various times (see Isa. 24:1; Jer. 4:23–26; 2 Peter 2:4), none of the passages places this judgment at a time before the creation narrative in Genesis 1:2–31.

The gap theory does not seem an acceptable alternative for evangelical Christians today.

## F. The Age of the Earth: Some Preliminary Considerations

Up to this point, the discussions in this chapter have advocated conclusions that we hope will find broad assent among evangelical Christians. But now at last we come to a perplexing question about which Bible-believing Christians have differed for many years, sometimes very sharply. The question is simply this: How old is the earth?

It is appropriate to treat this question after all the earlier matters because it is much less important than the doctrines considered above. These earlier matters may be summarized as follows: (1) God created the universe out of nothing; (2) creation is distinct from God, yet always dependent on God; (3) God created the universe to show his glory; (4) the universe God created was very good; (5) there will be no final conflict between Scripture and science; (6) secular theories that deny God as Creator, including Darwinian evolution, are clearly incompatible with belief in the Bible.

The question of the age of the earth is also less important than matters to be treated in subsequent chapters, that is (7) the creation of the angelic world (chapter 19) and (8) the creation of man in the image of God (chapters 21 and 22). It is important to keep these things in mind because there is a danger that Christians will spend too much time arguing over the age of the earth and neglect to focus on much more important and much clearer aspects of the overall teaching of the Bible on creation.

The two options to choose from for a date of the earth are the "old earth" position, which agrees with the consensus of modern science that the earth is 4,500,000,000 years old, and the "young earth" position, which says that the earth is 10,000 or perhaps 20,000 years old, and that secular scientific dating schemes are incorrect. The difference between these two views is enormous: 4,499,990,000 years!

Before considering the specific arguments for both positions, we will examine some preliminary questions about the genealogies in the Bible, differing views on the date of dinosaurs, and the length of the six creation days in Genesis 1.

## 1. There Are Gaps in the Genealogies of the Bible

When one reads the list of names in Scripture together with their ages, it might seem as though we could add together the ages of all the people in the history of redemption from Adam to Christ and come up with an approximate date for the creation of the earth. Certainly this would give a very recent date for creation (such as Archbishop Ussher's date of 4004 BC). But closer inspection of the parallel lists of names in Scripture will show that Scripture itself indicates the fact that the genealogies list only those names the biblical writers thought it important to record for their purposes. In fact, some genealogies include names that are left out by other genealogies in Scripture itself.

For instance, Matthew 1:8–9 tells us that Asaph was "the father of Jehoshaphat, and Jehoshaphat the father of Joram, and Joram the father of Uzziah, and Uzziah the father of Jotham, and Jotham the father of Ahaz." But from 1 Chronicles 3:10–12 (which uses the alternate name Azariah for Uzziah), we learn that three generations have been omitted by Matthew: Joash, Amaziah, and Azariah. So these texts can be compared in the following table:

### Example of Gaps in Genealogies

| 1 Chronicles 3:10–12 | Matthew 1:8–9 |
| --- | --- |
| Asaph | Asaph |
| Jehoshaphat | Jehoshaphat |
| Joram | Joram |
| Ahaziah | |
| Joash | |
| Amaziah | |
| Azariah (Uzziah) | Uzziah |
| Jotham | Jotham |
| Ahaz | Ahaz |
| Hezekiah | Hezekiah |
| (etc.) | (etc.) |

Therefore, when Matthew says that Uzziah was "the father of Jotham," it can mean that he was the father of someone who led to Jotham. Matthew has selected those names that he wants to emphasize for his own purposes.[92] A similar phenomenon is evident in

---

92. See a fuller discussion of the gaps in genealogies in Francis Schaeffer, *No Final Conflict*, 37–43. A similar discussion is found in his *Genesis in Space and Time* (Downers Grove, IL: IVP, 1972), 122–24, 154–56.

Matthew 1:20 where the angel of the Lord speaks to Joseph and calls him, "Joseph, son of David." Now Joseph is not directly the son of David (for David lived around 1000 BC), but Joseph is the descendant of David and is therefore called his "son."

Another example is found in 1 Chronicles 26:24 in a list of officers appointed by King David near the end of his life. We read that "Shebuel the *son of Gershom, son of Moses*, was chief officer in charge of the treasuries" (1 Chron. 26:24). Now we know from Exodus 2:22 that Gershom was the son born to Moses before the exodus, sometime around 1480 BC (or on a late date for the exodus, around 1330 BC). But these officials mentioned in 1 Chronicles 26 were appointed at the time that David made Solomon king over Israel, around 970 BC (see 1 Chron. 23:1). That means that in 1 Chronicles 26:24 Shebuel is said to be "the son of Gershom," who was born 510 (or at least 360) years earlier. Ten or more generations have been omitted in this designation "son of."[93]

But can the genealogies in Genesis 5 and 11 also have gaps? In these chapters, the names of people and their descendants follow a particular pattern such as this: "When Seth had lived 105 years, he fathered Enosh. Seth lived after he fathered Enosh 807 years and had other sons and daughters. Thus all the days of Seth were 912 years, and he died" (Gen. 5:6–8).

In 2018, Andrew Steinmann and Jeremy Sexton debated this question back and forth in the *Journal of the Evangelical Theological Society*.[94] Steinmann argued that the verb translated "fathered" (Hebrew *yālad*), when used in a Hiphil stem, has a causative sense and can mean "caused [someone] to be born." But the direct object of the verb (here, Enosh), though it might refer to someone's son, could also refer to a descendant many generations later. Thus Enosh could in fact be someone who came many generations after Seth. In that case, the large number of years is not meant to give us a chronology that can be added together to get the age of humanity, but rather it is given to show us the health and longevity of someone who could still beget children at more than 100 years old and could even live to 912 years. In fact, in his 1911 article on these genealogies, B. B. Warfield said that the intent of these details is to "make a vivid impression upon us of the vigor and grandeur of humanity in those old days of the world's prime."[95]

In the New Testament, Luke's recounting of the genealogy of Jesus includes "Cainan, the son of Arphaxad," a generation that was skipped in Genesis 11: "the son of Serug, the son of Reu, the son of Peleg, the son of Eber, *the son of Shelah, the son of Cainan, the son of Arphaxad*, the son of Shem, the son of Noah, the son of Lamech" (Luke

---

93. The NIV translates the verse, "Shubael, *a descendant* of Gershom," but this is simply an interpretation, for the Hebrew text simply has the word *ben*, "son." It should not be objected that Gershom may have lived over 500 years, for such long life spans are not found after the flood (note Gen. 6:3); in fact, Abraham was miraculously given a son when he was almost 100 (cf. Rom. 4:19; Heb. 11:12); and Moses, long before David or Solomon, counted man's life as seventy or eighty years:

"The years of our life are seventy, or even by reason of strength eighty" (Ps. 90:10).

94. *JETS* 61, no. 1 (2018): 5–45. Although Sexton raises objections to Steinmann's interpretation, I think Steinmann has the better of the argument.

95. Warfield, "On the Antiquity and Unity of the Human Race," in *Studies in Theology* (New York: Oxford University Press, 1932), 241.

3:35–36). But Genesis 11 omits Cainan's generation between Arphaxad and Shelah: "When Arpachshad had lived 35 years, *he fathered Shelah*" (Gen. 11:12). In this verse "fathered Shelah" must mean "fathered someone who led to Shelah." And so "fathered" could mean this in many other places in Genesis 11 as well.

It seems only fair to conclude that the genealogies of Scripture have some gaps in them and that God only caused to be recorded those names that were important for his purposes. How many gaps there are and how many generations are missing from the Genesis narratives, we do not know. The life of Abraham may be placed at approximately 2000 BC, because the kings and places listed in the stories of Abraham's life can be correlated with archaeological data that can be dated quite reliably (see Gen. 12 and following chapters.),[96] but prior to Abraham the setting of dates is very uncertain. In view of the exceptionally long life spans reported for people prior to the flood, it would not seem unreasonable to think that a few thousand years have been passed over in the narrative. This gives us some flexibility in our thinking about the date that man first appeared on the earth. (It would seem to be quite another thing, however—and quite foreign to the sense of continuity in the narrative—to think that *millions* of years have been omitted and that names and details of the lives of key persons have been remembered and passed down over such a long period of time.)

## 2. The Age of the Human Race

Earlier in this chapter I quoted the following statement by Casey Luskin:

> The genus *Homo* appears in an abrupt, non-Darwinian fashion, without evidence of an evolutionary transition from ape-like hominins. . . . Many researchers have recognized an "explosion" of modern human-like culture in the archaeological record about thirty-five to forty thousand years ago, showing the abrupt appearance of human creativity, technology, art, and even paintings—showing the rapid emergence of self-awareness, group identity, and symbolic thought.[97]

Certainly the existence of creativity, technology, and art such as paintings provides strong evidence for the existence of human beings. If current dating methods are accurate, that would place human beings on the earth 35,000–40,000 years ago. Young earth advocates challenge the dating methods and would claim that human beings appeared on earth no more than 6,000 years ago. My own perspective is that I do not have the technical expertise to assess the dating methods used. A date range of 35,000–50,000 years ago seems a very long time to me, but not impossible if we allow for significant gaps in the genealogies in Genesis. As long ago as 1911, Princeton theology professor B. B.

96. See "Chronology of the Old Testament" in *IBD*, esp. 268–70.
97. Casey Luskin, "Missing Transitions: Human Origins and the Fossil Record," in Moreland et al., *Theistic Evolution*, 472. (Some readers may differ with Luskin's date range but still recognize the abrupt appearance of human beings on earth.)

Warfield wrote, "The question of the antiquity of man has of itself no theological signif-icance. It is to theology, as such, a matter of entire indifference how long man has existed on earth."[98]

## 3. Did Animals Die before the Fall?

For young earth advocates, there is no need to ask whether animals died before the fall, because animals and man were both created on the sixth day, and there may have been only a short time before Adam and Eve sinned. This could have introduced death into the animal kingdom as well, as part of the curse of the fall (Gen. 3:17–19; Rom. 8:20–23).

But for old earth advocates, this is an important question. There are millions of apparently ancient fossils in the earth. Might they have come from animals who lived and died for long ages before Adam and Eve were created? Might God have created an animal kingdom that was subject to death from the moment of creation? This is quite possible.

There was no doubt death in the plant world if Adam and Eve were to eat plants. As for animals, if God had made an original creation in which animals would reproduce and also live forever, the earth would soon be overcrowded with no hope of relief. Even if there were no carnivorous animals eating other animals, it is possible that animals simply grew old and died peacefully.

The warning to Adam in Genesis 2:17 was only that *he* would die if he ate of the forbidden fruit, not that animals would also begin to die. When Paul says, "Sin came into the world through one man and death through sin" (Rom. 5:12a), the following phrase makes clear that he is talking about death for human beings, not for plants and animals, for he immediately adds, "and so death spread *to all men* (Greek *anthrōpos*, human being) because all sinned" (Rom. 5:12b).

From the information we have in Scripture, we cannot now know whether God created animals subject to aging and death from the beginning, but it remains a real possibility.

## 4. What about Dinosaurs?

Current scientific opinion holds that dinosaurs became extinct about sixty-five million years ago, millions of years before human beings appeared on the earth. But those who hold to a young earth and six twenty-four-hour days of creation would say that dinosaurs were among the creatures created by God on the same day he created man (the sixth day). They would therefore say that dinosaurs and human beings lived on the earth at the same time and that dinosaurs subsequently became extinct (perhaps in the

---

98. B. B. Warfield, "On The Antiquity And The Unity Of The Human Race," in *Studies in Theology* (New York: Oxford University Press, 1932; repr., Grand Rapids: Baker, 1991), 235. Originally published in *The Princeton Theological Review* 9 (1911): 1–25.

flood). Young earth advocates of course would differ with the methods used to arrive at such ancient dates for dinosaurs.

Among those who hold to an old earth view, some would say that the sixth day of creation was millions of years long, and that dinosaurs had already become extinct by the time Adam was created and named the animals. In this case, Adam did not name dinosaurs (the Bible does not say that he did), but he only named all the creatures that were living at the time God brought him all the animals to name (Gen. 2:19–20). Of course, this view would require that there was death in the animal world before there was sin (see previous section).

### 5. Are the Six Days of Creation Twenty-Four-Hour Days?

Much of the dispute between "young earth" and "old earth" advocates hinges on the interpretation of the length of "days" in Genesis 1. Many old earth supporters propose that the six "days" of Genesis 1 refer not to periods of twenty-four hours but rather to long periods of time, millions of years, during which God carried out the creative activities described in Genesis 1. This proposal has led to a heated debate with other evangelicals who hold to a young earth and insist that the days in Genesis 1 must be twenty-four-hour days.

**a. The View That the Days Are Long Periods of Time.** In favor of viewing the six days as long periods of time is the fact that the Hebrew word *yôm*, "day," is sometimes used to refer not to a twenty-four-hour literal day but to a longer period of time. We see this when the word is used in Genesis 2:4, for example: "In the *day* that the LORD God made the earth and the heavens," a phrase that refers to the entire creative work of the six days of creation. Other examples of the word *day* to mean a period of time are Job 20:28 ("the *day* of God's wrath"); Psalm 20:1 ("The LORD answer you in the *day* of trouble!"); Proverbs 11:4 ("Riches do not profit in the *day* of wrath"); 21:31 ("The horse is made ready for the *day* of battle"); 24:10 ("If you faint in the *day* of adversity, your strength is small"); 25:13 ("the *time* [*yôm*] of harvest"); Ecclesiastes 7:14 ("In the *day* of prosperity be joyful, and in the *day* of adversity consider: God has made the one as well as the other"); many passages referring to "the *day* of the LORD" (such as Isa. 2:12; 13:6, 9; Joel 1:15; 2:1; Zeph. 1:14); and many other Old Testament passages predicting times of judgment or blessing. A concordance will show that this is a frequent sense for the word *day* in the Old Testament.

An additional argument for a long period of time in these "days" is the fact that the sixth day includes so many events that it must have been longer than twenty-four hours. The sixth day of creation (Gen. 1:24–31) includes the creation of animals and the creation of man and woman both ("male and female he created them," Gen. 1:27). It was also on the sixth day that God blessed Adam and Eve and said to them, "Be fruitful and multiply and fill the earth and subdue it, and have dominion over the fish of the sea and over the birds of the heavens and over every living thing that moves on the earth"

(Gen. 1:28). But that means that the sixth day included God's creation of Adam, God's putting Adam in the garden of Eden to till it and keep it, and giving Adam directions regarding the tree of the knowledge of good and evil (Gen. 2:15–17), his bringing all the animals to man for them to be named (Gen. 2:18–20), finding no helper fit for Adam (Gen. 2:20), and then causing a deep sleep to fall upon Adam and creating Eve from his rib (Gen. 2:21–25). The finite nature of man and the incredibly large number of animals created by God would by itself seem to require that a much longer period of time than part of one day would be needed to include so many events—at least that would be an "ordinary" understanding of the passage for an original reader, a consideration that is not unimportant in a debate that often emphasizes what an ordinary reading of the text by the original readers would lead them to conclude. If the sixth day is shown by contextual considerations to be considerably longer than an ordinary twenty-four-hour day, then does not the context itself favor the sense of *day* as simply a "period of time" of unspecified length?

Related to this is one more consideration. The seventh day, it should be noted, is not concluded with the phrase "and there was evening and there was morning, a seventh day." The text just says that God "rested on the seventh day from all his work that he had done" and that "God blessed the seventh day and made it holy" (Gen. 2:2–3). The possibility, if not the implication, suggested by this is that the seventh day is still continuing. It never ended but is also a "day" that is really a long period of time (see also John 5:17; Heb. 4:4, 9–10).

Some have objected that whenever the word *day* refers to a period of time other than a twenty-four-hour day in the Old Testament, the context makes it clear that this is the case, but since the context does not make this clear in Genesis 1, we must assume that normal days are meant. But to this we may answer that whenever the word *day* means a twenty-four-hour day, the context makes this clear as well. Otherwise, we could not know that a twenty-four-hour day is meant in that context. So this is not a persuasive objection. It simply affirms what everyone agrees to, namely, that the context enables us to determine which sense a word will take when it has various possible meanings.

That brings us back to the original question, namely, what does the word *day* mean in the context of Genesis 1? The fact that the word must refer to a longer period of time just a few verses later in the same narrative (Gen. 2:4) should caution us against making dogmatic statements that the original readers would have certainly known that the author was talking about twenty-four-hour days. In fact, both senses were commonly known meanings in the minds of the original readers of this narrative.[99] Even the very first use of the word "day" in Genesis 1 does not mean a day of twenty-four hours but

---

99. I am assuming here that Moses wrote both Genesis and Exodus and that the original readers were the people of Israel in the wilderness around 1440 BC.

simply the daylight hours: "God called the light *Day*, and the darkness he called Night" (Gen. 1:5).

It is important to realize that those who advocate long periods of time for the six "days" of creation are not saying that the context *requires* that these be understood as periods of time. They are simply saying that the context does not clearly specify for us one meaning of *day* or another, and if convincing scientific data about the age of the earth, drawn from many different disciplines and giving similar answers, convinces us that the earth is billions of years old, then this possible interpretation of *day* as a long period of time may be the best interpretation to adopt.

The situation is something like that faced by those who first held that the earth rotates on its axis and revolves about the sun. They would not say that in their contexts the passages about the sun "rising" or "going down" *require* us to believe in a heliocentric (sun-centered) solar system but that this is a *possible* understanding of the texts, seeing them as only speaking from the standpoint of the observer. Observational evidence taken from science informs us that this is in fact the correct way to interpret those texts.

**b. The View That the Days Are Twenty-Four-Hour Days.** On the other side of this question are the arguments in favor of understanding *day* as a twenty-four-hour day in Genesis 1.

1. It is significant that each of the days of Genesis 1 ends with an expression such as, "And there was evening and there was morning, the first day" (Gen. 1:5). The phrase "And there was evening and there was morning" is repeated in verses 8, 13, 19, 23, and 31. This seems to imply the sequence of events marking a literal twenty-four-hour day and suggests that the readers should understand it in that way.

This is a strong argument from context, and many have found it persuasive. Yet those who hold to a long period of time for these "days" could respond (a) that even evening and morning do not constitute an entire day, but only the end of one day and the beginning of another, so the expression itself may be simply part of the author's way of telling us that the end of the first creative day (that is, long period of time) occurred, and the beginning of the next creative "day" had come;[100] and (b) that the first three creative "days" could not have been marked by evening and morning as caused by the sun shining on the earth, for the sun was not created until the fourth day (Gen. 1:14–19); thus, the very context shows that "evening and morning" in this chapter does not refer to the *ordinary* evening and morning of days as we know them now. So the argument from "evening and morning," though it may give some weight to the twenty-four-hour view, does not seem to tip the balance decisively in its favor.

2. The third day of creation cannot be very long because the sun does not come into being until the fourth day, and plants cannot live long without light. In response to this,

---

100. In fact, the expression "and there was evening and there was morning" is never elsewhere used in the Hebrew Old Testament, so it cannot be said to be a common expression used to designate a normal day.

it might be said that the light that God created on the first day energized the plants for millions of years, or that the sun was created before Day 1, as indicated by the very first verse of Genesis, "In the beginning, God created the heavens and the earth" (Gen. 1:1).

3. It is hard to avoid the conclusion that in the Ten Commandments the word *day* is used to mean a twenty-four-hour day:

> Remember the Sabbath day, to keep it holy. Six *days* you shall labor, and do all your work, but the seventh *day* is a Sabbath to the LORD your God. . . . For in six *days* the LORD made heaven and earth, the sea, and all that is in them, and rested on the seventh day. Therefore the LORD blessed the Sabbath day and made it holy. (Ex. 20:8–11)

Certainly in that text the sabbath day is a twenty-four-hour day. And must we not say that verse 11, which in the same sentence says that the Lord made heaven and earth in "six days," uses "day" in the same sense? This is again a weighty argument. But once again it is not quite conclusive in itself, for one could respond that the readers were ordinary speakers of the Hebrew language who were quite aware that the word *yôm* ("day") could refer in ordinary speech to an unspecified period of time. They would've been aware (from a careful reading of Gen. 1–2) that the days in Genesis 1–2 were unspecified periods of time and that the sabbath commandment merely told God's people that, just as he followed a six-plus-one pattern in creation (six periods of work followed by a period of rest), so they were to follow a six-plus-one pattern in their lives (six days of work followed by a day of rest; also six years of work followed by a sabbath year of rest, as in Ex. 23:10–11). In fact, in the very next sentence of the Ten Commandments, "day" means "a period of time": "Honor your father and your mother, that your days may be long in the land that the LORD your God is giving you" (Ex. 20:12). Certainly here the promise is not for "long" literal days (such as twenty-five- or twenty-six-hour days!) but rather that the period of one's life may be lengthened upon the earth.[101]

4. Those who argue for *day* as a twenty-four-hour day also ask whether anywhere else in the Hebrew Bible the word *days* in the plural, especially when a number is attached (such as "six days"), ever refers to anything but twenty-four-hour days. This argument is not compelling, however, because (a) a plural example of *days* to mean periods of time is found in Exodus 20:12, discussed in the previous paragraph, and (b) if the word clearly takes the sense "period of time" in the singular (which it does, as all admit), then to speak of six such "periods" of time would certainly be understandable to the readers, even if the Old Testament did not elsewhere have examples of such a meaning. The fact

---

101. The Hebrew text does not say "that your days may be *many* (Heb. *rab*)" which is a common Hebrew expression (Gen. 21:34; 37:34; Ex. 2:23; Num. 9:19, et al.), but "that your days may be *long*" (Heb. *'ārak*, "be long," used also as physical length in 1 Kings 8:8; Ps. 129:3; Isa. 54:2 ["lengthen your cords"]; Ezek. 31:5). However, Brett Gray has suggested to me that it may mean "the cumulative number of your days may be long," which I suppose is possible but, it seems to me, not as likely.

that such an expression does not appear elsewhere may mean nothing more than that there was no occasion to use it elsewhere.

5. When Jesus says, "But from the beginning of creation, 'God made them male and female'" (Mark 10:6), he implies that Adam and Eve were not created billions of years after the beginning of creation, but at the beginning of creation. This argument also has some force, but old earth advocates may respond that Jesus is just referring to the whole of Genesis 1–2 as the "beginning of creation," in contrast to the argument from the laws given by Moses that the Pharisees were depending on (v. 4).

I have given an answer to each of the five arguments for a twenty-four-hour day, but these answers may not persuade its advocates. They would respond to the "period of time" position as follows: (1) Of course, it is true that *day* may mean "period of time" in many places in the Old Testament, but that does not demonstrate that *day* must have that meaning in Genesis 1. (2) The sixth day of creation need not have been longer than twenty-four hours, especially if Adam only named major representative kinds of birds and of "every beast of the field" (Gen. 2:20). (3) Though there was no sun to mark the first three days of creation, nonetheless, the earth was still rotating on its axis at a fixed speed, and there was "light" and "darkness" that God created on the first day (Gen. 1:3–4), and he called the light "day" and the darkness "night" (Gen. 3:5). So God in some way caused an alternation between day and night from the very first day of creation, according to Genesis 1:3–5.

**c. Conclusion about the "Days" of Genesis 1.** What shall we conclude about the length of days in Genesis 1? It does not seem at all easy to decide with the information we now have. It is not simply a question of "believing the Bible" or "not believing the Bible," nor is it a question of "giving in to modern science" or "rejecting the clear conclusions of modern science." Even for those who believe in the complete truthfulness of Scripture (such as the present author), the question does not seem to be easy to decide from the text of Genesis 1. The phrase "evening and morning" and the numbering of the days do point toward twenty-four-hour days, but not strongly enough to be decisive.

And there are good arguments on the other side. For the God who lives forever, for whom "one day is as a thousand years, and a thousand years as one day" (2 Peter 3:8), and who delights in gradually working out all his purposes over time, perhaps 13.8 billion years is just the right amount of time to wait for light from vastly distant stars to reach the earth, so that we might be amazed at the greatness of our Creator, who made such an immense universe.

How powerful is God? So powerful that *in a single instant* he created a universe so huge that it takes light itself, traveling at a speed of 186,000 miles per second, 13.8 billion years just to shine across it! Such a distance is beyond our comprehension. To put this in terms of miles, in one year light will travel (in round numbers) 186,000 miles times 31,557,000 seconds, which equals 5,869,602,000,000 miles (over 5.8 trillion miles or 9.4 trillion kilometers). Then multiply that by 13,800,000,000 years—the result is a universe with an unfathomable size of 8,100,050,760,000,000,000,000 miles (over 8 quintillion miles). It would seem appropriate for God to wait 13.8 billion years for light from such distant stars to reach the earth, just so that we could stand in awe of his greatness, his power, his omnipresence, and his eternity.

As for the age of Earth, Hugh Ross sees a significant benefit to billions of years of plants and animals dying before human beings appeared on earth (assuming that Rom. 5:12 refers only to human death resulting from Adam's sin; see page 389). He says, "The 3.8 billion years of plant and animal death and extinction that preceded humanity provided for the needs of civilization. Through that death and decay, God gave humanity enormous biodeposits of sand, limestone, marble, topsoil, coal, oil, and natural gas. . . . Civilization . . . is based on the abundance of these assets. . . . Humans are beneficiaries of the remains of millions of generations of plants and animals that preceded us."[102]

In addition, an earth that is 4.5 billion years old increases our amazement at God's eternity:

> Before the mountains were brought forth,
>> or ever you had formed the earth and the world,
>> from everlasting to everlasting you are God. (Ps. 90:2)

The evidence of incredible antiquity in both the earth and the universe can serve as vivid reminders of the even more amazing nature of God's eternity, just as the incredible size of the universe causes us to wonder at God's even greater omnipresence and omnipotence.

Therefore, with respect to the length of days in Genesis 1, the possibility must be left open that God has chosen not to give us enough information to come to a clear decision on this question, and the real test of faithfulness to him may be the degree to which we can act charitably toward those who in good conscience and full belief in God's Word hold to a different position on this matter.

## 6. Multiple Types of Evidence Indicate That the Earth and the Universe Are Billions of Years Old

The reason that the topic of the age of the earth is vigorously debated today is that (1) Genesis 1–2 seems to many people to be reporting events that happened fairly recently, but (2) different kinds of observational (or scientific) evidence from astronomy and earth sciences seem to indicate that both the earth and the universe are extremely old (13.8 billion years for the universe and 4.5 billion years for the earth).[103] I have discussed

---

102. Hugh Ross, *A Matter of Days: Resolving a Creation Controversy*, 2nd ed. (Covina, CA: RTB, 2015), 95.

103. Terry Mortenson of Answers in Genesis has written a gracious and extensive article disagreeing with my position in the first edition of this book. He argues that only a young earth position is valid for Christians who accept the truthfulness of the entire Bible. I still disagree with him on this matter (he was my student and a faithful teaching assistant many years ago), but readers may wish to consult his arguments. See Terry Mortenson, "Systematic Theology Texts and the Age

the biblical material extensively in the preceding pages, and concluded that both "young earth" and "old earth" viewpoints rest on valid interpretations of Genesis consistent with belief in the complete inerrancy of Scripture. Now it is appropriate to summarize some of the scientific material that seems to indicate a very old earth and even older universe.

In 1994, in the first edition of this book, I made a prediction:

> It is likely that scientific research in the next ten or twenty years will tip the weight of evidence decisively toward either a young earth or an old earth view, and the weight of Christian scholarly opinion (from both biblical scholars and scientists) will begin to shift decisively in one direction or another. This should not cause alarm to advocates of either position, because the truthfulness of Scripture is not threatened (our interpretations of Genesis 1 have enough uncertainty that either position is possible). Both sides need to grow in knowledge of the truth, even if this means abandoning a long-held position.[104]

In fact, twenty-five years have now gone by, and in my opinion, the scientific evidence for an old earth and an old universe has become significantly stronger and more persuasive. I summarize some of that evidence on the following pages. (But out of fairness to the young earth position, I should point out that the website answersingenesis.org presents young earth responses to many of these types of evidence. Readers can evaluate those responses for themselves.)

Much of the following material comes from the Christian astronomer Hugh Ross, in the much-expanded 2015 edition of his book, *A Matter of Days*. A significant feature of this book is that Ross interacts repeatedly and specifically with young earth objections to his arguments.

**1. Expansion rate of the universe.** Astronomers can measure the distance from earth to various stars and galaxies. They can also measure the speed at which they are moving away from us. With those two values, they can "back up" the process to find how long the universe has been expanding. After summarizing three different methods of measuring such expansion, Ross says they show an average age of the universe of "13.79 ± 0.06 billion years," and he adds, "The consistency of the three independent methods is remarkable."[105]

But how do astronomers measure the distance to stars? For many stars, it is a simple matter of geometry. If we select any two points on earth and use the line between them as the base of an isosceles triangle, and then measure the angle from each location to

of the Earth: A Response to the Views of Erickson, Grudem, and Lewis and Demarest," Answers in Genesis, December 16, 2009, https://answersingenesis.org/age-of-the-earth/systematic-theology-texts-and-the-age-of-the-earth.

104. Wayne Grudem, *Systematic Theology* (Leicester: Inter-Varsity Press; Grand Rapids: Zondervan, 1994), 308.
105. Ross, *A Matter of Days*, 147, 150.

the sun (for example), then the sun becomes the third point of the triangle, and we can calculate the distance to the sun.

We might think that the difference in the angles would be too small for such a direct method to be accurate in measuring the distance to stars that are far away. But astronomers have been able to use two points on the entire diameter of the earth's orbit around the sun (186 million miles!) for the base of the isosceles triangle, and this method gives substantially more accurate measurements.

More recently, astronomers have been able to use a base for the isosceles triangle that is "nearly a million times longer" than the diameter of the earth's orbit about the sun. This new, longer base of the triangle is "the diameters of orbits of maser sources about the central black holes of galaxies." (A "maser" is a kind of naturally occurring radiation source found in space.) This is a huge advance because an orbit around the center of an entire galaxy is gigantic compared to an orbit around a single star such as our sun. This method has allowed "direct distance measurements" to the centers of several galaxies, including galaxies at distances of 23 million, 162 million, and 470 million light-years.[106]

In addition to such direct measurements, astronomers have also used other methods (such as "redshift velocities")[107] to measure distances, but these methods are more difficult to understand for nonspecialists (such as the present author).

**2. Starlight from billions of years ago.** Many stars are so far from the earth that it would take millions or even billions of years for their light to reach us. This kind of evidence requires a brief discussion of the speed of light.

The speed of light (in a vacuum) is approximately 186,000 miles per second, and the sun is 92,960,000 miles from the earth. That means it takes just over eight minutes for light from the sun to reach us. Therefore, when we see a sunrise or sunset, we are not seeing the sun as it is at this very moment, but *we are seeing the sun as it was eight minutes ago.*

This principle also applies to light from other stars. When we look through a telescope at Alpha Centauri (the star that is closest to us, after the sun), we are looking at a star that is 4.4 light-years away, which means the light from that star took 4.4 years to reach us. Therefore what we see is Alpha Centauri *as it existed 4.4 years ago.*

Using this process, astronomers are actually looking back into the *past history* of stars and galaxies. When they see galaxies that are immensely far away (billions of light-years away), they are looking at *a very early time in that galaxy's history* (billions of years ago, since it took that long for the light to reach us). This fact alone is another evidence of a universe that is billions of years old.

Young earth supporters may respond that perhaps God created the universe with light rays already in place, so that Adam and Eve would see thousands of stars on the first night after they were created. This of course is possible. Certainly Adam and Eve

106. This information is all from Ross, *A Matter of Days*, 149.        107. See ibid., 146.

themselves had somewhat of an "appearance of age" (God created them as adults, not as infants), as did all the animals that God created as "grown up" animals.

But there are difficulties with this suggestion about creation with light rays in place. First, astronomers can see not only the light from stars but also distinctive variations caused by the light passing through gas clouds and dust in outer space. Why would the light rays look as though they had traveled through gas clouds if in fact they hadn't done this? The second problem with the "appearance of age" view is the existence of white dwarfs, which are formed when stars reach the end of their lifetimes and run out of nuclear fuel.[108] But "a star takes millions of years, minimum, to burn up all of its nuclear fuel and become a white dwarf."[109] If the universe is only 10,000 years old, and if God created stars with light rays in place, why would he also create optical illusions that *look like* material from stars that died billions of years ago, when in fact those stars never even existed?

The same is true for other events that astronomers observe in space, such as the existence of supernovas, which are massive, extremely bright explosions lasting several weeks or months that happen when stars are about to burn out. But according to young earth advocates, as Hugh Ross notes, "The supernova eruption astronomers claim to see in the Large Magellanic Cloud 163,000 light-years away did not occur 163,000 years ago." In fact, it never occurred, since *nothing existed* before 10,000 years ago, according to the young earth view. When astronomers see such supernovas that explode and then quickly die out, these would be just optical illusions placed in outer space to make us *think (wrongly) that supernovas happened* hundreds of thousands of years ago. It would seem contrary to God's character to be so deceptive.[110]

Some young earth advocates have responded that perhaps the speed of light has changed, and perhaps light traveled much faster a few thousand years ago. But the speed of light is one of the most universal constants in physics, and the need to speculate that it might have been vastly different (a million times faster?) seems to me to cast doubt on the entire young earth viewpoint.

**3. Age of white dwarfs.** Ross notes that "by measuring the luminosity and color of the coolest white dwarfs . . . astronomers can ascertain how long the white dwarfs have been cooling. The cool-down time for the oldest white dwarfs exceeds 10 billion years." If we add to that the time needed for the formation and burning of stars to become white dwarfs, this "yields an age for the universe equal to about 13.8 billion years."[111]

**4. Burning cycles of stars.** By looking back in time (through looking at stars that are farther and farther away), astronomers can measure changes in the color and intensity of the light given off by a star during its lifetime. This means that "if astronomers know the

---

108. "White dwarfs are the final state of all stars possessing less than enough mass to become either black holes or neutron stars" (ibid., 156).

109. Ibid.

110. I am glad to see that Answers in Genesis rejects the idea that God created the universe with light rays from stars and the earth already in place; see https://answersingenesis.org/astronomy/starlight/does-distant-starlight-prove-the-universe-is-old/.

111. Ross, *A Matter of Days*, 156–57.

mass of a star, they can determine its age with high precision based on measurements of the star's color and brightness." Using this method, "the latest cosmic age determination based on stellar burning alone is 13.7 ± 0.4 billion years."[112]

**5. The present stability of the sun.** The sun is currently "in an extremely stable state." This is important for advanced life on earth because if the sun were burning erratically, advanced life on earth would alternatively freeze from cold or perish from excessive heat. But the present stability of the sun indicates that it is a "middle-aged" star. This is important because "all stars of approximately the same mass as the Sun manifest unstable luminosities for the first 50 million years and intense x-ray radiation for the first few hundred million years."[113]

**6. Cosmic background radiation temperatures.** The average temperature of outer space is not absolute zero (-459.67° Fahrenheit or -273.15° Celsius) but is 2.72548° Celsius above absolute zero. This is called cosmic microwave background radiation, and it gets hotter as astronomers look at more distant galaxies (that is, as they look farther into the past). Calculating backward to an extremely hot temperature at the beginning of the universe, the most recent calculations "show that the universe was created 13.79 ± 0.06 billion years ago."[114]

**7. Ice layers.** Scientists have drilled deep into the ice layers in the central parts of Antarctica and northern parts of and Greenland. They found that "three ice cores from Antarctica . . . provide a continuous record of the past 800,000, 720,000, and 420,000 years, respectively."[115] A young earth advocate might respond that multiple layers could be laid down within a single year, but Ross notes that "within the layers are dust signatures of known volcanic eruptions," including eruptions of Mount Vesuvius in AD 79, 472, 512, 968, 1037, 1139, 1631, and 1944. "Counting the layers between layers that contain the dust signatures of these eruption events, researchers have confirmed that each layer indeed corresponds to one year."[116]

**8. Coral reef layers.** Ross writes, "The record of coral reef layers extends back 400 million years."[117]

**9. Sediment layers at the bottom of lakes.** Geologists Gregg Davidson and Ken Wolgemuth have written an extensively documented article showing that "finally layered sediments from Lake Suigetsu [in Japan] were deposited annually going back more than 50,000 years." (These sediment layers are called "varves.") They also show that the most recent of these layers of sediment correspond closely with tree rings that go back more than 14,000 years, and that carbon-14 decay rates (measured by various samples taken at various depths of the sediment layers) "have remained unchanged."[118]

---

112. Ibid., 154–55.
113. Ibid., 202.
114. Ibid., 152–54.
115. Ibid., 190.
116. Ibid., 190.

117. Ibid., 193.
118. Gregg Davidson and Ken Wolgemuth, "Testing and Verifying Old Age Evidence: Lake Suigtsu, Varves, Tree Rings, and Carbon-14," *Perspectives on Science and Christian Faith* 70, no. 2 (June 2018): 75–89.

**10. Multiple types of radiometric dating of rocks.** Igneous rocks are rocks that are formed when lava or magma (very hot molten material found beneath the earth) cools and changes from a liquid to a solid. Some igneous rocks consist partly of radioactive material that begins to decay as soon as a rock solidifies, and when it decays it changes into another element. For example, uranium-238 decays and turns into lead-206. But uranium-235 becomes lead-207, and thorium-232 becomes lead-208.[119] For every type of radioactive substance, the rate of such decay can be measured. With that information, geologists can measure the amount of each kind of uranium and thorium isotopes and the amount of each kind of lead isotope in a rock, and with that information they can determine six independent measures of the age of a rock. Since each of the uranium and thorium isotopes decays at a different rate, if a rock sample has all three of the uranium and thorium isotopes and all three isotopes of the resulting lead, the proportion of each kind of uranium, thorium, and lead gives us six different independent measures of the age of the rock. Ross reports that "ratios of different radiometric elements relative to the lead end products and the ratios of the different lead end products relative to one another provide consistent, accurate dates—all saying that the earth is billions of years old."[120]

Different kinds of radiometric substances are more accurate for measuring different ranges of dates. Young earth advocates have pointed out that some kinds of radiometric dating have produced erroneous results, but Ross provides answers to such objections that seem reasonable to me.[121] Other scientists have also given extensive answers to young earth objections to radiometric dating.[122] For example, different types of radiometric dating are only valid for different ranges of years in the past.[123]

Another young earth claim is that radiometric dating techniques are inaccurate because of changes that occurred on the earth at the time of Noah's flood. But geologist Davis Young noted that radiometric dating of rocks from the moon and of meteorites recently fallen to the earth, which could not have been affected by Noah's flood, coincide with many other radiometric evidences from various materials on the earth, and that the results of these tests are "remarkably consistent in pointing to about 4.5–4.7 billion years."[124]

**11. Continental separation.** Fossil-bearing rock fields near the coasts of Africa and South America were apparently previously joined together and then separated by

119. Ibid., 187.
120. Ibid.
121. Ibid., 181–94.
122. For a brief and very clearly written discussion, see Roger Wiens, "So Just How Old Is That Rock?," in *The Grand Canyon: Monument to an Ancient Earth*, ed. Carol Hill, Gregg Davidson, Tim Helble, and Wayne Ranney (Grand Rapids: Kregel, 2016), 89–97. A longer and more detailed discussion is found in Davis A. Young and Ralph F. Stearley, *The Bible, Rocks and Time: Geological Evidence for the Age of the Earth* (Downers Grove, IL: IVP, 2008), 388–443. The book by Young and Stearley is a revised and significantly expanded revision of Davis

A. Young, *Christianity and the Age of the Earth* (Grand Rapids: Zondervan, 1982).
123. Roger Wiens includes a chart showing different types of radiometric dating such as uranium-lead, rubidium-strontium, potassium-argon, argon-argon, uranium series, and carbon-14, and the age ranges covered by each technique (Wiens, "So Just How Old Is That Rock?," 91). He also lists various types of nonradiometric dating techniques.
124. Young, *Christianity and the Age of the Earth*, 63; see also the detailed discussion on 93–116; and *Creation and the Flood: An Alternative to Flood Geology and Theistic Evolution*. Grand Rapids: Baker, 1977., 185–93.

continental drift as the continents gradually moved apart. In fact, anyone who looks at a globe can see that, if the continents of North and South America could be moved eastward and the continents of Europe and Africa could be moved westward, with slight rotation the continental shelves of these continents would fit together. In addition, underneath the Atlantic Ocean there is a large mountain ridge called the Mid-Atlantic Ridge that follows the curved pattern of a line halfway between these continents. All this is evidence of plate tectonics, the scientific study that explains movements of the plates of the earth's crust on which the continents rest.[125]

Now there are two separate methods to determine how long ago the continents separated. Taking samples from the crust of the Atlantic Ocean at the edges of the continents, "maximum ages of about 180 million years for the Atlantic Ocean crust are obtained."[126] This suggests that the continents separated about 180 million years ago, leaving the Atlantic Ocean between them. If we measure the distance from a point on the North American coastline to the corresponding point on the African coastline, the distance is 3,480 miles. If we divide 3,480 miles by 180,000,000 years, it "yields an average rate of 1.2 inches per year."[127] Repeated calculations at different points vary only slightly from 1.1 to 1.7 inches per year.

But are these continents actually moving apart at that rate? Long-term precise satellite "measurements of the relative positions of North America and North Africa document a current spreading rate of approximately 1 inch per year, a value in remarkable agreement with the radiometrically determined rates." This confirms that the continents began to move apart 180,000,000 years ago—but that is impossible if the earth is less than 10,000 years old.

In order to maintain a young earth position, its advocates claim that Noah's flood must have rapidly moved the tectonic plates apart just a few thousand years ago, and then the tectonic plate movement rapidly slowed down to the current rate. Wiens replies, "For this to be true, two entirely unrelated processes—the decay rate of radioactive isotopes and the rate of plate spreading—must have slowed down at exactly the same rate."[128] This is highly unlikely.

**12. No scientists have been persuaded of a young earth by scientific evidence alone.** Hugh Ross, who has frequently interacted with young earth advocates, writes the following:

> John Morris, a geological engineer and current president of the Institute for Creation Research (ICR), once acknowledged in a radio interview that he has never

---

125. I am grateful to retired geology professor John Wiester for calling my attention to the importance of plate tectonics and the Mid-Atlantic Ridge in the age of the earth discussion. I am also grateful to German paleontologist Günter Bechly for an extended phone conversation discussing various evidences for an old earth. Dr. Bechly also called my attention

to this article: Jonathan Baker, "100 Reasons Why the Earth Is Old," Age of Rocks (blog), https://ageofrocks.wordpress.com/100-reasons-the-earth-is-old/.

126. Wiens, "So Just How Old Is That Rock?," 94.

127. Ibid.

128. Ibid.

met (or heard of) a scientist who became convinced on the basis of science alone that the universe or earth is only thousands of years old. Several other prominent young-earth advocates, when asked, have acknowledged the same.[129]

This situation is strikingly different from the arguments about evolution versus creation by intelligent design, because the massive amount of scientific evidence for intelligent design, coming from the incredible complexity and vast amounts of information required for living organisms, has persuaded numerous non-Christian scientists that neo-Darwinian evolutionary theory cannot explain the origin of living things today. The scientific evidence for intelligent design is very powerful, and continues to increase year after year. But that is not the case for scientific arguments for a young earth.

## 7. Both Old Earth and Young Earth Interpretations of the Bible Are Valid Options for Christians Today

After discussing several preliminary considerations regarding the age of the earth, we come finally to the specific arguments from the text of Scripture for old earth and young earth views.

**a. Old Earth Theories of Creation.** In this first category we list four viewpoints held by those who believe in an old earth with an age of about 4.5 billion years and a universe about 13.8 billion years old.

**1. Day-age view (or a "concordist" view).** Many who believe that the earth is many millions of years old maintain that the days of Genesis 1 are extremely long "ages" of time. The arguments given above for long days in Genesis 1 will apply here, and, as we argued above, the words of the Hebrew text do allow for the days to be long periods of time. The evident advantage of this view is that, if the current scientific estimate for an earth 4.5 billion years old is correct, it explains how the Bible is consistent with this fact. Among evangelicals who hold to an old earth view, this is a common position. This view is sometimes called a "concordist" view because it seeks agreement or "concord" between the Bible and scientific conclusions about dating.

The day-age view is certainly possible. A common objection is that the sequence of events in Genesis 1 does not exactly correspond to certain scientific understandings of the stages in the development of life. However, in 2014, astrophysicist Hugh Ross published a persuasive response to this objection, giving a detailed explanation of the different kinds of plant and animal life that are named for each of the six "days" in Genesis 1.[130] Ross argues that the key interpretive step in understanding Genesis 1 is to recognize that the speaker is writing from the vantage point of an observer who is on the surface of the waters that cover the earth,[131] starting with Genesis 1:2: "The Spirit of

---

129. Ross, *A Matter of Days*, 219, with reference to tape recordings of radio interviews.

130. See Hugh Ross, *Navigating Genesis: A Scientist's Journey through Genesis 1–11* (Covina, CA: Reasons to Believe, 2014), 25–67.

131. Ibid., 31.

God was hovering over the face of the waters." In response to the objection that Genesis 1 mistakenly puts vegetation (day three) ahead of sea creatures (day four), Ross cites recent scientific research that claims to have discovered evidence of plant life on earth (day three) far earlier than was previously believed.[132]

Another objection to the day-age view is that it apparently puts the sun, moon, and stars (day four) millions of years *after* the creation of plants and trees (day three). That makes no sense at all according to current scientific opinion, which sees the stars as formed long before the earth or any living creatures on the earth. It also makes no sense in terms of the way the earth now operates, for vegetation does not grow without sunlight. Moreover, how would the waters on the earth keep from freezing for millions of years—or even for a few seconds—without the sun?

In response, those who hold the day-age view say that the sun, moon, and stars were created *before the first day*, when "in the beginning, God created the heavens and the earth" (Gen. 1:1), and that the sun, moon, and stars were only *made visible* or *revealed* on day four, perhaps through the thinning or removal of a haze barrier that had previously been translucent.[133] This fits well with verses 14–15: "God said, 'Let there be lights in the expanse of the heavens to separate the day from the night. And let them be for signs and for seasons, and for days and years, and let them be lights in the expanse of the heavens to give light upon the earth.' And it was so."

The idea that the sun, moon, and stars were simply revealed on day four also fits well with the most likely understanding of Genesis 1:1, namely, that it describes the initial creation of the universe, the stars, and the earth: "In the beginning, God created the heavens and the earth."[134] That means that all the stars including the sun were created before day one.

If this is the correct understanding, then we should understand Genesis 1:16 as providing background information emphasizing that it was God who had created the sun and the moon: "God made the two great lights—the greater light to rule the day and the lesser light to rule the night—and the stars." This cannot refer to something that happened *after* verses 14–15 because in those verses God had already revealed the sun and moon, as is clear from the words "and it was so" (v. 15). And if verse 16 is understood as parenthetical background information,[135] then the verbs in Genesis 1:16 can be taken as perfects, indicating something that God had done before: "God *had made* the two great lights, the greater light to rule the day, and the lesser light to rule

---

132. Ibid., 51.

133. So Ross, *A Matter of Days*, 245.

134. Several grammatical and syntactical arguments in favor of this understanding of the Hebrew text are given by C. John Collins, *Reading Genesis Well: Navigating History, Poetry, Science, and Truth in Genesis 1–11* (Grand Rapids: Zondervan, 2018), 160–63. An even more extensive argument, including interaction with numerous other commentators, is found in

Vern Poythress, "Genesis 1:1 Is the First Event, Not a Summary," in *WTJ* 79 (2017), 97–121; reprinted in Vern Poythress, *Interpreting Eden: A Guide to Faithfully Reading and Understanding Genesis 1–3* (Wheaton, IL: Crossway, 2019), 291–322.

135. So Ross, *A Matter of Days*, 245. Poythress notes that "the phenomena do not exist, are not 'made' by God, until they actually appear in the sky. . . . the focus is on God's making of the appearances" (Poythress, *Interpreting Eden*, 270).

the night—and the stars." Grammatically this is possible (this is how the ESV and NIV both translate the same verb form in 2:8 and 2:19, for example). This option remains as a genuine possibility for the day-age view. With regard to light needed for the plants and warmth needed for the waters, there was already light from the sun shining through the translucent barrier around the earth.

Another answer from the day-age view might be that the fourth day does not exactly represent the historical sequence of events, though an overall outline of progressive work of God is given. Vern Poythress writes, "Genesis 1 does include a sense of progression and a chronological order. . . . But that does not mean that it cannot also, as a sparse account, stick to the main points and group together created objects of one kind for topical simplicity."[136] (Further discussion of disruption in the sequence of days is given in view 3 below.)

**2. The view that there are long periods of time between the twenty-four-hour days.** The idea that the days of Genesis 1 are twenty-four-hour days that are separated by millions of years is a variation of the old earth view. This view was defended by astronomer and theology professor Robert C. Newman in 1977, and I mentioned his view as "possible" in a footnote in the first edition of this book.[137] More recently, Oxford mathematics professor John Lennox has advocated this position.[138] Lennox argues that Genesis 1 speaks of "a sequence of six *creation* days; that is, days of normal length (with evenings and mornings as the text says) in which God acted to create something new, but days that might well have been separated by long periods of time."[139] He also favors the view that the original creation of the heavens and earth in Genesis 1:1–2 may have occurred long before the first "creation day" in Genesis 1:3–5, which would allow for a very old earth and universe.[140] If someone is reluctant to adopt the day-age view, Lennox's position seems quite possible, as it allows for both twenty-four-hour days and an old earth.

**3. "Analogical days" view.** C. John Collins proposed that Genesis 1 is using the ordinary workweek of a Hebrew laborer as an analogy to teach ancient Israelite readers that God (in a way similar to an Israelite laborer) worked to bring about creation. Thus the word *day* implies no specific length of time but only that God carried out his work in a reasonable, orderly way, much like a skilled craftsman. In addition, though "the logic of the presentational sequence makes good sense, at least from the perspective of informal observation," the placement of specific details on each day may or may not be intended in the exact order in which the events occurred because "the sequence serves the literary presentation, which, being analogical, may or may not carry implications about what we might call the 'referential sequence.'"[141]

---

136. Poythress, *Interpreting Eden*, 270.

137. Grudem, *Systematic Theology*, 1st ed. (Grand Rapids: Zondervan, 1994), 298n58. See Robert C. Newman and Herman J. Eckelmann Jr., *Genesis One and the Origin of the Earth* (Downers Grove, IL: InterVarsity Press, 1977).

138. See John C. Lennox, *Seven Days That Divide the World: The Beginning according to Genesis and Science* (Grand

Rapids: Zondervan, 2011), 39–66. He gives a perceptive explanation of various understandings of the days of creation.

139. Ibid., 54, emphasis in original.

140. Ibid., 53.

141. See C. John Collins, *Reading Genesis Well: Navigating History, Poetry, Science, and Truth in Genesis 1–11* (Grand Rapids: Zondervan, 2018), 165. In a personal email on July 22,

**4. Literary framework view.** Another way of interpreting the days of Genesis 1 has gained a significant following among evangelicals. Since it argues that Genesis 1 gives us no information about the age of the earth, it would be compatible with current scientific estimates of a very old earth. This view argues that the six days of Genesis 1 are not intended to indicate a detailed chronological sequence of events but are rather a literary framework that the author uses to teach us about God's creative activity. The framework is skillfully constructed so that the first three days and the second three days correspond to each other.[142]

| Days of forming | Days of filling |
|---|---|
| Day 1:  Light and darkness | Day 4:  Sun, moon, and stars separated (lights in the heaven) |
| Day 2:  Sky and waters separated | Day 5:  Fish and birds |
| Day 3:  Dry land and seas separated, plants and trees | Day 6:  Animals and man |

In this way a parallel construction is seen. On day one God separates light and darkness, while on day four he puts the sun, moon, and stars in the light and in the darkness. On day two he separates the waters and the sky, while on day five he puts the fish in the waters and the birds in the sky. On day three he separates the dry land and the seas and makes plants to grow, while on day six he puts the animals and man on the dry land and gives the plants to them for food.

According to the "framework" view, Genesis 1 should not be read as though the author wanted to inform us about the sequence of days or the order in which things were created, nor did he intend to tell us about the length of time the creation took. The arrangement of six days is a literary device the author uses to teach that God created everything. The six days, which are neither twenty-four-hour days nor long periods of time, give us six different "pictures" of creation, telling us that God made all aspects of the creation, that the pinnacle of his creative activity was man, and that over all creation is God himself, who rested on the seventh day and who calls man therefore to worship him on the sabbath day as well.[143]

---

2019, Collins indicated to me that this view was previously advocated by Herman Bavinck, William G. T. Shedd, and Franz Delitzsch.

142. The following table is adapted from *The NIV Study Bible*, ed. by Kenneth Barker et al. (Grand Rapids: Zondervan, 1985), 6 (note to Gen. 1:11). A forceful defense of the "framework" view is found in Henri Blocher, *In the Beginning: The Opening Chapters of Genesis*, trans. by David G. Preston (Leicester: Inter-Varsity Press, 1984), 49–59. Blocher mentions several other evangelical scholars who hold this position, which he calls the "literary interpretation": N. H. Ridderbos, Bernard Ramm, Meredith G. Kline, D. F. Payne, and J. A. Thompson. This "framework" view is called the "pictorial day" view in Millard Erickson, *Christian Theology*, 3rd ed. (Grand Rapids: Baker, 2013), 381.

143. This framework view is also defended by Ronald Youngblood, *How It All Began* (Ventura, CA: Regal, 1980), 25–33.

In the words of an advocate for this position, "Chronology has no place here."[144] The attractions in favor of this hypothesis are (1) the neat correspondence between the pairs of days as shown in the table above, (2) the fact that it avoids any conflict with modern science over the age of the earth and the age of living creatures (since no detailed chronology is implied), (3) the way it avoids the conflict of sequence between Genesis 1 and 2 in which man (Gen. 2:7) seems to be formed before plants (Gen. 2:8) and animals (Gen. 2:19), a sequence different from Genesis 1, and (4) the fact that Genesis 2:5 shows that the "days" of creation were not literal twenty-four-hour days, for it says that there were no plants on the earth because it had not yet rained, something that would not make sense in a six day creation, since plants can certainly survive three or four days without rain.

Several points may be made against the framework theory.

First, the proposed correspondence between the days of creation is not nearly as exact as its advocates have supposed. The sun, moon, and stars created on the fourth day as "lights in the expanse of the heavens" (Gen. 1:14) are placed not in a space created on day one but in the "expanse" (Heb. *rāqîa'*) that was created on the second day. In fact, the correspondence in language is quite explicit: this "expanse" is not mentioned at all on day one but five times on day two (Gen. 1: 6–8) and three times on day four (Gen. 1:14–19). Of course, day four also has correspondences with day one (in terms of day and night, light and darkness), but if we say that the second three days show the creation of things to fill the forms or spaces created on the first three days, then day four overlaps at least as much with day two as it does with day one.

Moreover, the parallel between days two and five is not exact because in some ways the preparation of a space for the fish, sea mammals, and birds of day five does not come in day two but in day three. It is not until day three that God gathers the waters together and calls them "seas" (Gen. 1:10), and on day five the fish are commanded to "fill the waters in the *seas*" (Gen. 1:22). Again in verses 26 and 28 the fish are called "fish of the *sea*," giving repeated emphasis to the fact that the sphere the fish inhabit was specifically formed on day three. Thus the fish formed on day five seem to belong much more to the place prepared for them on day three than to the widely dispersed waters below the firmament on day two. Establishing a parallel between day two and day five faces further difficulties in that nothing is created on day five to inhabit the "waters above the firmament," and the flying things created on this day (the Hebrew word would include flying insects as well as birds) not only fly in the sky created on day two, but also live and multiply on the "earth" or "dry land" created on day three. (Note God's command on day five: "Let birds multiply on the earth" [Gen. 1:22].) Finally, the parallel between days three and six is not precise, for nothing is created on day six to fill the seas that were gathered together on day three. With all of these points of imprecise correspondence

---

144. Blocher, *In the Beginning*, 52.

and overlapping between places and things created to fill them, the supposed literary "framework," while having an initial appearance of neatness, turns out to be less and less convincing upon closer reading of the text.

Second, since all proposals for understanding Genesis 1 attempt to provide explanations for scientific data about the age of the earth, this is not a unique argument in favor of the framework theory. However, we must recognize that one aspect of the attractiveness of this theory is the fact that it relieves evangelicals of the burden of even trying to reconcile scientific findings with Genesis 1. Yet, in the words of one advocate of this theory, "So great is the advantage, and for some the relief, that it could constitute a temptation." He wisely adds, "We must not espouse the theory on grounds of its convenience but only if the text leads us in that direction."[145]

Third, those who have not adopted the framework theory have seen no conflict in sequence between Genesis 1 and 2, for it has been commonly understood that Genesis 2 implies no description of sequence in the original creation of the animals or plants, but simply recapitulates some of the details of Genesis 1 as important for the specific account of the creation of Adam and Eve in Genesis 2. The NIV avoids the appearance of conflict by translating, "Now the LORD God *had planted* a garden in the East, in Eden" (Gen. 2:8) and "Now the LORD God *had formed out* of the ground all the beasts of the field and all the birds of the air" (Gen. 2:19; the ESV is similar).

Fourth, Genesis 2:5 does not really say that plants were not on the earth because the earth was too dry to support them. If we adopt that reasoning we would also have to say there were no plants because "there was no man to work the ground" (Gen. 2:5), for that is the second half of the comment about no rain coming on the earth. Moreover, the remainder of the sentence says that the earth was the opposite of being too dry to support plants: "and a mist was going up from the land and was watering the whole face of the ground" (Gen. 2:6). The statement in Genesis 2:5 is simply an explanation of the general time frame in which God created man. Genesis 2:4–6 sets the stage, telling us that "no bush of the field was yet in the land and no small plant of the field had yet sprung up— for the LORD God had not caused it to rain on the land, and there was no man to work the ground, and a mist was going up from the land and was watering the whole face of the ground." The statements about lack of rain and no man to till the ground do not give the *physical reason* why there were no plants but only explain that God's work of creation was not complete. This introduction puts us back into the first six days of creation as a general setting—into "the day that the LORD God made the earth and the heavens" (Gen. 2:4). Then in that setting it abruptly introduces the main point of chapter 2: the creation of man. The Hebrew text does not include the word "then" at the beginning of verse 7, but simply begins, "And the LORD God formed man" (Gen. 2:7 KJV).[146]

---

145. Ibid., 50.

146. For further discussion on Gen. 2:5, see Meredith G. Kline, "Because It Had Not Rained," *WTJ* 20 (1957–58):

146–57; and, in response, Derek Kidner, "Genesis 2:5, 6: Wet or Dry?" *TB* 17 (1966): 109–14.

Fifth, the strongest argument against the framework view, and the reason why comparatively few evangelicals have adopted it, is that the whole of Genesis 1 strongly suggests not just a literary framework but a chronological sequence of events. When the narrative proceeds from the less complex aspects of creation (light and darkness, waters, sky, and dry land) to the more complex aspects (fish and birds, animals and man) we see a progressive build-up and an ordered sequence of events that are entirely understandable chronologically. When a sequence of numbers (1–2–3–4–5–6) is attached to a set of days that correspond exactly to the ordinary week human beings experience (days one, two, three, four, five, six, seven, with rest on day seven), the implication of chronological sequence in the narrative is very strong. The sequence of days seems more clearly intended than a literary framework which is nowhere made explicit in the text, and in which many details simply do not fit. As Derek Kidner observes:

> The march of the days is too majestic a progress to carry no implication of ordered sequence; it also seems over-subtle to adopt a view of the passage which discounts one of the primary impressions it makes on the ordinary reader. It is a story, not only a statement.[147]

Sixth, a sequence of days is also implied in God's command to human beings to imitate his pattern of work plus rest: "Remember the Sabbath day, to keep it holy. Six days you shall labor, and do all your work, but the seventh day is a Sabbath to the LORD your God. . . . For in six days the LORD made heaven and earth, the sea, and all that is in them, and rested on the seventh day" (Ex. 20:8–11). But if God did not create the earth by working for six days and resting on the seventh, then the command to imitate him would be misleading or make no sense.

In conclusion, while the "framework" view does not deny the truthfulness of Scripture, it adopts an interpretation of Scripture which, upon closer inspection, seems very unlikely.

**b. "Young Earth" Theories of Creation.** Another group of evangelical interpreters rejects the dating systems that currently give an age of millions of years to the earth and argue instead that the earth is quite young, perhaps less than 10,000 years old. Young earth advocates have produced a number of scientific arguments for a recent creation of the earth.[148] Those who hold to a young earth generally advocate one or both of the following positions:

---

147. Kidner, *Genesis*, 54–55.

148. Several scientific arguments pointing to a young earth (about 10,000–20,000 years old) are given in Henry M. Morris, ed., *Scientific Creationism* (San Diego, CA: Creation-Life, 1974), esp. 131–69; also Kofahl and Segraves, *The Creation Explanation*, 181–213.

A response to most of these arguments, from an "old earth"

perspective, is given by Davis A. Young in *Christianity and the Age of the Earth*, 71–131, and, specifically in response to "flood geology," in *Creation and the Flood*, 171–213. Another book, Howard J. Van Till, Davis A. Young, and Clarence Menninga, *Science Held Hostage: What's Wrong with Creation Science and Evolutionism* (Downers Grove, IL: InterVarsity Press, 1988), 45–125, raises serious objections against the evaluation and

**1. Creation with an appearance of age (mature creationism).** Some who hold to a young earth point out that the original creation must have had some kinds of "appearance of age" even from the first day. (Another term for this view is "mature creationism," since it affirms that God created a mature creation.) The appearance of Adam and Eve as full-grown adults is an obvious example. If someone assumed that they had been born as babies, they appeared as though they had lived for perhaps twenty or twenty-five years, growing up from infancy as human beings normally do, but in fact they were less than a day old. Similarly, they probably saw the stars the first night that they lived, but the light from most stars would take thousands or even millions of years to reach the earth. This suggests that God created the stars with light beams already in place. And full-grown trees would probably have had rings. Following this line of reasoning, might we go further and suppose that many geological formations, when originally created, had a similar appearance to formations that would now take thousands or even millions of years to complete by present "slow" processes? This suggestion has found many supporters, and, initially at least, it seems to be an attractive proposal.

A common objection to this "appearance of age" view is that it "makes God an apparent deceiver,"[149] something that is contrary to his nature. But is God a "deceiver" if he creates a mature man and woman in a day and then tells us explicitly that he did it? Or if he creates mature fish and animals and full-grown trees and tells us that he did it? Or if he allows Adam and Eve to see the stars, which he created in order that people might see them and give glory to him, on the first night that they lived? Rather than manifesting deception, it seems that these actions point to God's infinite wisdom and power. This is particularly so if God explicitly tells us that he created everything in "six days."

But the real problem with the appearance of age view is that there are some things in the universe that it cannot easily account for. Everyone will probably agree that Adam and Eve were created as adults, not newborn infants, and therefore (if we didn't know about their creation) they had an appearance of age. Most who hold to twenty-four-hour days in Genesis 1 would also say there was an appearance of age with plants and trees, with all the animals (the chicken came before the egg!), and probably with light from the stars. But the creation of fossils from long-dead animals presents a real problem, for responsible Christians would not want to suggest that God scattered fossils throughout the earth to give an added appearance of age! This would not be creating something "in process" or in a state of maturity; it would be creating the remains of a dead animal not so the animal could serve Adam and Eve but simply to make people think the earth was older than it

use of scientific research materials by some prominent young earth advocates. A preliminary young earth response to Young's arguments is found in a thirty-four-page pamphlet by Henry M. Morris and John D. Morris, *Science, Scripture, and the Young Earth* (El Cajon, CA: Institute for Creation Research, 1989).

However, for a much more recent (2015) update on these arguments and a vigorous defense of an old earth view point, see Hugh Ross, *A Matter of Days*.

149. Erickson, *Christian Theology*, 352.

really was.[150] Therefore the depositing of fossils in the earth could only be for the purpose of misleading or deceiving human beings regarding the earlier history of the world.

More problematic is that so many different indications of age all seem to point to *the same ages*, namely, a 13.8 billion-year-old universe and a 4.5 billion-year-old earth. It is understandable that Adam, the plants, the animals, and the stars all would have appeared to have *different ages* (because they were created with mature functions in place). But modern astronomical and geological research gives approximately the *same* age estimates from the expansion of the universe, light from distant stars, continental drift, radiometric dating, samples of moon rocks and meteorites, and so on. It is entirely possible that God created an unfathomably immense universe so that we might stand in awe of his omnipresence, and, similarly, that he created human beings to live in an unfathomably old universe so that we might stand in awe of his eternity.

Why would God create so many different indications of a universe that is 13.8 billion years old and an earth (and a moon!) that is 4.5 billion years old if this were not true? Would it not be better to conclude that the earth is 4.5 billion years old, and that God left many indications there to show us this fact rather than in any way imply that he deceived us? So it seems the only credible explanations for the fossil record that Christians can adopt are (1) current dating methods are incorrect by colossal proportions because of flawed assumptions or because of radical changes in the laws and constants of physics brought about by the fall or the flood or (2) current dating methods are approximately correct and the earth is many millions or even billions of years old.

However, those who hold to a young earth view may continue to hold it because they believe that the Bible requires it, and then they can hope that further explanations for these appearances of age will be discovered in the future. Or they can hold to a thoroughgoing, complete appearance of age in which less than 10,000 years ago God created a universe and an earth that simply *appeared* to be billions of years old.

**2. Flood geology.** Another common view among evangelicals is what may be called "flood geology." This is the view that the tremendous natural forces unleashed by the flood at the time of Noah (Gen. 6–9) significantly altered the face of the earth, causing the creation of coal and diamonds, for example, within the space of a year rather than hundreds of millions of years, because of the extremely high pressure exerted by the water on the earth. This view also claims that the flood deposited fossils in layers of incredibly thick sediment all over the earth.[151] The flood geology view is also called "neo-catastrophism" because its advocates attribute most of the present geological status of the earth to the immense catastrophe of the flood.

---

150. Flood geology advocates (see below) will say that no fossils existed at Gen. 1:31, but that they were deposited suddenly by the flood in Gen. 6–9.

151. See Henry M. Morris and John C. Whitcomb, *The Genesis Flood* (Philadelphia: Presbyterian and Reformed, 1961); John C. Whitcomb, *The World That Perished* (Grand Rapids:

Baker, 1988); Stephen A. Austin, *Catastrophes in Earth History* (El Cajon, CA: Institute for Creation Research, 1984). Other studies by flood geology advocates have been published in the *CRSQ*, though by no means all articles in that journal advocate the flood geology perspective, nor do all members of the Creation Research Society hold to flood geology.

The geological arguments put forth by advocates of this view are technical and difficult for the nonspecialist to evaluate. But from what I do understand, I am not persuaded that all of the earth's geological formations were caused by Noah's flood rather than by millions of years of sedimentation, volcanic eruptions, movement of glaciers, continental drift, and so forth.

As I noted above regarding the absence of scientists who have been persuaded on the basis of scientific data alone that the universe and the earth are only 10,000 years old, the controversy over flood geology is also strikingly different from the other areas of dispute regarding creation, for its advocates have persuaded almost no professional geologists, even those who are Bible-believing evangelical Christians. By contrast, the books objecting to evolution that we mentioned above chronicle 160 years of cogent objections to Darwinian evolution that have been raised by a significant number of biologists, biochemists, zoologists, anthropologists, and paleontologists, both Christian and non-Christian, because evolution has so many problems in explaining facts evident from observation of the created world. If present geological formations could only be explained as the result of a flood that covered the whole earth, then would this not be evident even to non-Christians who look at the evidence? Would not the hundreds of Christians who are professional geologists be prepared to acknowledge the evidence if it were there? If the flood geologists are right, we would expect to see more progress in persuading some professional geologists that their case is a plausible one.[152]

## 8. Conclusions on the Age of the Earth: Both Views Are Acceptable

How old is the earth then? Where does this discussion leave us? My strong encouragement to the entire Christian community is that both old earth and young earth viewpoints should be acceptable for leaders in evangelical churches and evangelical parachurch organizations.[153] Dozens or even hundreds of highly trained biblical scholars who believe firmly in full biblical inerrancy can be found on both sides of this question. It is not a question of *believing* the Bible or not believing the Bible. It is not a question of conservative theology versus liberal theology, nor is it a question of believing biblical authority versus believing scientific authority. It is simply a question of *interpreting* the Bible that both sides firmly believe to be entirely true.

As for my own personal view, I can now say that the old earth perspective seems more persuasive to me. The arguments for an old earth that are based on many kinds of scientific data from different disciplines seem (to me at least) to be convincing. This is particularly true of arguments based on the cumulative evidence of various aspects of astronomy and related disciplines, as well as the evidence from fossil-bearing rocks, coral

---

152. The arguments against flood geology have been marshalled by an evangelical who is also a professional geologist; see Young's *Creation and the Flood* and *Christianity and the Age of the Earth*.

153. This is also the position of Theodore Cabal and Peter Rasor II, *Controversy of the Ages: Why Christians Should Not Divide over the Age of the Earth* (Wooster, OH: Weaver, 2017).

reefs, continental drift, and the similarity of results from different kinds of radiometric dating. All of these factors seem to provide convincing evidence of a 13.8-billion-year-old universe and a 4.5-billion-year-old earth.

I realize that young earth advocates will disagree with my assessment of this evidence. They will object that maybe the speed of light was vastly different, maybe the dating of animal fossils should be vastly different, maybe the rate of formation of coral reefs was vastly different, maybe the rate of sediment deposit in lakes was vastly different, maybe the speed of movement of the earth's tectonic plates was vastly different, maybe the rate of decay of radiometric elements in rocks was vastly different, and so forth. Eventually this begins to sound to me like, "If the facts were different, they would support my position." But the facts are not different.

As for the biblical evidence, I think it can be legitimately and honestly understood to allow for either an old earth or a young earth view. I do not think the Bible tells us or intends to tell us the age of the earth or the age of the universe.

## 9. The Way Forward

We must say very clearly that the age of the earth is a matter that is not directly taught in Scripture but is something we can think about only by drawing more or less probable inferences from Scripture. Yet there are continuing debates between old earth and young earth advocates in the evangelical world. Given this situation, it would seem best (1) to admit that God may not allow us to find a definitive solution to this question before Christ returns and (2) to encourage evangelical scientists and theologians who fall in both the young earth and old earth camps to work together with a sense of cooperation in a common purpose, remembering that the wisdom from above is "first pure, then peaceable, gentle, open to reason, full of mercy and good fruits, impartial and sincere," and full of the recognition that "a harvest of righteousness is sown in peace by those who make peace" (James 3:17–18).

As for evangelism and apologetics done in publications designed to be read outside the evangelical world, young earth and old earth proponents could cooperate much more in amassing the extremely strong arguments for creation by intelligent design and in laying aside their differences over the age of the earth. Too often young earth proponents have failed to distinguish scientific arguments for creation by design from scientific arguments for a young earth and have therefore prevented old earth advocates from joining them in persuading the scientific community. Moreover, young earth proponents have sometimes failed to recognize that scientific arguments for a young earth (which seem to them to be very persuasive) are not nearly as strong as the overwhelming scientific arguments for creation by intelligent design. As a result, young earth proponents have too often given the impression that the only true "creationists" are those who believe not only in creation by God but also in a young earth. The result has been unfortunate divisiveness and lack of community among scientists who are Christians—to the delight of Satan and the grieving of God's Holy Spirit.

## G. APPLICATION

The doctrine of creation has many applications for Christians today. It makes us realize that the material universe is good in itself, for God created it good and wants us to use it in ways pleasing to him. Therefore we should seek to be like the early Christians, who "received their food with glad and generous hearts" (Acts 2:46), always with thanksgiving to God and trust in his provisions. A healthy appreciation of creation will keep us from false asceticism that denies the goodness of creation and the blessings that come to us through it. It will also encourage some Christians to do scientific and technological research into the goodness of God's abundant creation, or to support such research.[154] The doctrine of creation will also enable us to recognize more clearly that scientific and technological study glorifies God, for it enables us to discover how incredibly wise, powerful, and skillful God was in his work of creation. "Great are the works of the LORD, studied by all who delight in them" (Ps. 111:2).

The doctrine of creation also reminds us that God is sovereign over the universe he created. He made it all, and he is Lord of all of it. We owe all that we are and have to him, and we may have complete confidence that he will ultimately defeat all his enemies and be manifested as Sovereign King to be worshiped forever. In addition, the incredible size of the universe and the amazing complexity of every created thing will, if our hearts are right, draw us continually to worship and praise him for his greatness.

Finally, as we indicated above, we can wholeheartedly enjoy creative activities (artistic, musical, athletic, domestic, literary, etc.) with an attitude of thanksgiving that our Creator God enables us to imitate him in our creativity.

## QUESTIONS FOR PERSONAL APPLICATION

1. Are there ways in which you could be more thankful to God for the excellence of his creation? Look around you and give some examples of the goodness of the creation that God has allowed you to enjoy. Are there ways you could be a better steward of the parts of God's creation he has entrusted to your care?

2. Might the goodness of all that God created encourage you to try to enjoy different kinds of foods than those you normally prefer? Can children be taught to thank God for variety in the things God has given us to eat? Does the doctrine of creation provide an answer to some strict animal rights advocates who say we should not eat steak or chicken or other meat or wear clothing made from animal

---

154. Frair and Davis, *A Case for Creation*, 135–40, have many specific practical challenges to scientists who believe in creation to do specific kinds of greatly needed research.

skins, since we are simply another form of animal ourselves? (See Gen. 3:21.)

3. In order to understand something of the despair felt by contemporary non-Christians, try to imagine for a moment that you believe that there is no God and that you are just a product of matter plus time plus chance, a spontaneous result of random variation in organisms over millions of years. How would you feel differently about yourself? About other people? About the future? About right and wrong?

4. Why do we feel joy when we are able to "subdue" even a part of the earth and make it useful for serving us—whether it be in growing vegetables, developing a better kind of plastic or metal, or using wool to knit a piece of clothing? Should we feel joy at the accomplishment of these and other tasks? What other attitudes of heart should we feel as we do them?

5. When you think about the immensity of the stars and that God put them in place to show us his power and glory, how does it make you feel about your place in the universe? Is this different from the way a non-Christian would feel?

6. Before reading this chapter, what did you think about the theory of evolution? How has your view changed, if at all?

7. What are some things that Christians can learn about theological discussion in general from observing the current controversy over the age of the earth? What significance do you see in this controversy for your own Christian faith?

# BIBLIOGRAPHY

(For an explanation of this bibliography see the note on the bibliography to chapter 1, pp. 23–24. Complete bibliographical data may be found on pp. 1489–96.)

## SECTIONS IN EVANGELICAL SYSTEMATIC THEOLOGIES

### 1. Anglican (Episcopalian)
1882–92 . . . . . Litton, 74–76

2001 . . . . . . . . Packer, 21–22
2013 . . . . . . . . Bird, 140–63
2013 . . . . . . . . Bray, 77–81

### 2. Arminian (Wesleyan or Methodist)
1875–76 . . . . . Pope, 1:361–420
1892–94 . . . . . Miley, 1:276–310
1940 . . . . . . . . Wiley, 1:440–72
1960 . . . . . . . . Purkiser, 145–48, 149–63

1983.........Carter, 1:130–32, 145–94,
            203–8
1983.........Cottrell, 1:48–191
1992.........Oden, 1:225–69
2002.........Cottrell, 100–26

**3. Baptist**

1767.........Gill, 1:366–75
1887.........Boyce, 166–73
1907.........Strong, 371–410
1917.........Mullins, 251–64
1976–83.....Henry, 6:108–96
1983–85.....Erickson, 365–86
1987–94.....Lewis and Demarest, 2:17–70
1990–95.....Garrett, 1:339–72
2007.........Akin, 242–93

**4. Dispensational**

1947.........Chafer, 7:99–101, 146
1949.........Thiessen, 111–18
1986.........Ryrie, 171–94
2017.........MacArthur and Mayhue,
            213–16

**5. Lutheran**

1917–24.....Pieper, 1:467–82
1934.........Mueller, 179–88

**6. Reformed (or Presbyterian)**

1559.........Calvin, 1:159–83 (1.14)
1724–58.....Edwards, 1:94–121
1871–73.....Hodge, 1:550–574; 2:3–41
1878.........Dabney, 26–38, 247–63
1887–1921...Warfield, *SSW*, 2:132–41
1894.........Shedd, 366–411
1910.........Vos, 1:156–82
1937–66.....Murray, *CW*, 1:325–29; *CW*,
            2:3–13

1938.........Berkhof, 126–40, 150–64
1998.........Reymond, 383–97
2008.........Van Genderen and Velema,
            246–82
2011.........Horton, 324–49
2013.........Culver, 141–63
2016.........Allen and Swain, 126–147
2017.........Barrett, 283–93
2019.........Letham, 271–91

**7. Renewal (or charismatic/Pentecostal)**

1988–92.....Williams, 1:95–116
1993.........Menzies and Horton, 77–81
1995.........Horton, 215–54
2008.........Duffield and Van Cleave,
            121–24

## SECTIONS IN REPRESENTATIVE ROMAN CATHOLIC SYSTEMATIC THEOLOGIES

**1. Roman Catholic: Traditional**

1955.........Ott, 79–86, 92–94, 100

**2. Roman Catholic: Post–Vatican II**

1980.........McBrien, 1:224–28
2012.........*CCC*, paragraphs 279–324

## OTHER WORKS

Alexander, Denis. *Creation or Evolution: Do We Have to Choose?*, 2nd ed. Oxford; Grand Rapids: Monarch, 2014. (favors theistic evolution)

Allison, Gregg. *Historical Theology: An Introduction to Christian Doctrine; A Companion to Wayne Grudem's* Systematic Theology. Grand Rapids: Zondervan, 2011, 254–76.

Axe, Douglas. *Undeniable: How Biology Confirms Our Intuition That Life Is Designed.* New York, New York: HarperOne, 2016.

Barclay, O. R. "Creation." In *NDT1*, 177–79.

Barrett, Matthew. *Four Views on the Historical Adam.* Grand Rapids: Zondervan, 2013.

Behe, Michael J. *Darwin's Black Box: The Biochemical Challenge to Evolution*. 10th ed. New York: Free Press, 2006.

Blocher, Henri. *In the Beginning: The Opening Chapters of Genesis*. Translated by David G. Preston. Leicester: Inter-Varsity Press, 1984.

Brown, Walter T. *In the Beginning: Compelling Evidence for Creation and the Flood*. 7th ed. Phoenix: Center for Scientific Creation, 2001. (young earth view)

Cabal, Theodore, and Peter Rasor II. *Controversy of the Ages: Why Christians Should Not Divide over the Age of the Earth*. Wooster, OH: Weaver, 2017.

Charles, J. Daryl. *Reading Genesis 1-2: An Evangelical Conversation*. Peabody, MA: Hendrickson, 2013.

Collins, Francis S. *The Language of God: A Scientist Presents Evidence for Belief*. New York: Free, 2006. (favors theistic evolution)

Collins, C John. *Did Adam and Eve Really Exist? Who They Were and Why You Should Care*. Wheaton, IL: Crossway, 2011.

———. *Genesis 1-4: A Linguistic, Literary, and Theological Commentary*. Phillipsburg, N.J.: P&R, 2006.

———. *Reading Genesis Well: Navigating History, Poetry, Science, and Truth in Genesis 1–11*. Grand Rapids: Zondervan, 2018.

Coulson, K. P. *Creation Unfolding: A New Perspective on Ex Nihilo*. n.p.: Phaneros, 2020.

Currid, John D. *Against the Gods: The Polemical Theology of the Old Testament*. Wheaton, IL: Crossway, 2013.

Davidson, Gregg R. *When Faith and Science Collide: A Biblical Approach to Evaluating Evolution and the Age of the Earth*. Oxford, MS: Malius Press, 2009.

Dembski, William A. *The Design Revolution: Answering the Toughest Questions about Intelligent Design*. Downers Grove, IL: InterVarsity Press, 2004.

———. *Intelligent Design: The Bridge between Science & Theology*. Downers Grove, IL: InterVarsity Press, 1999.

Dembski, William A., ed. *Darwin's Nemesis: Phillip Johnson and the Intelligent Design Movement*. Downers Grove, IL: IVP Academic, 2006.

———. *Mere Creation: Science, Faith and Intelligent Design*. Downers Grove, IL: InterVarsity Press, 1998.

Denton, Michael. *Evolution: Still A Theory in Crisis*. Seattle: Discovery Institute, 2016. (challenges to evolution from a biologist who is also a medical doctor)

De Young, Donald B. *Astronomy and the Bible: Questions and Answers*. Grand Rapids: Baker, 1989. (young earth view)

Frair, Wayne, and Percival Davis. *A Case for Creation*. Norcross, GA: CRS, 1983.

Giberson, Karl, and Francis S. Collins. *The Language of Science and Faith: Straight Answers to Genuine Questions*. Downers Grove, IL: IVP Books, 2011. (favors theistic evolution)

Gish, D. T. *Evolution: The Challenge of the Fossil Record*. El Cajon, CA: Master, 1985. (young earth view)

Gundry, Stanley N., and Charles Halton, eds. *Genesis: History, Fiction, or Neither? Three Views on the Bible's Earliest Chapters*. Grand Rapids: Zondervan, 2015.

Gundry, Stanley N., J. P. Moreland, and John Mark Reynolds, eds. *Three Views on Creation and Evolution*. Grand Rapids: Zondervan, 1999.

Halton, Charles, ed. *Genesis: History, Fiction, or Neither?* Grand Rapids, Michigan: Zondervan, 2015.

Hiebert, Robert J. V. "Create, Creation." In *BTDB*, 132–36.

Hill, Carol, Gregg Davidson, Tim Helble, and Wayne Ranney, eds. *The Grand Canyon: Monument to an Ancient Earth*. Grand Rapids: Kregel, 2016. (old earth view)

Johnson, Phillip E. *Darwin on Trial*. Downers Grove, IL: InterVarsity Press, 1991.

Kaiser, Christopher B. *Creation and the History of Science*. Grand Rapids: Eerdmans, 1991.

Keathley, Kenneth D., and Mark Rooker. *40 Questions about Creation and Evolution*. Grand Rapids: Kregel Academic, 2014.

Kelly, Douglas F. *Creation and Change: Genesis 1.1–2.4 In the Light of Changing Scientific Paradigms*. Fearn, Ross-shire: Mentor, 2017.

Kerkut, G. A. *Implications of Evolution*. New York: Pergamon, 1960.

Kofahl, Robert E., and Kelly L. Segraves. *The Creation Explanation: A Scientific Alternative to Evolution*. Wheaton, IL: Shaw, 1975. (young earth view)

Lennox, John C. *Seven Days That Divide the World: The Beginning according to Genesis and Science*. Grand Rapids: Zondervan, 2011.

McGrath, Alister E. *A Scientific Theology*. Vol. 1. Grand Rapids: Eerdmans, 2001.

Meyer, Stephen C. *Darwin's Doubt: The Explosive Origin of Animal Life and the Case for Intelligent Design*. New York: HarperOne, 2013.

———. *Signature in the Cell: DNA and the Evidence for Intelligent Design*. New York: HarperOne, 2009.

Moreland, J. P., ed. *The Creation Hypothesis: Scientific Evidence for an Intelligent Designer*. Downers Grove, IL: InterVarsity Press, 1994.

Moreland, J. P., Stephen C. Meyer, Christopher Shaw, Ann K. Gauger, and Wayne Grudem, eds. *Theistic Evolution: A Scientific, Philosophical, and Theological Critique*. Wheaton, IL: Crossway, 2017.

Morris, Henry M., and John D. Morris. *Science, Scripture, and the Young Earth: An Answer to Current Arguments Against the Biblical Doctrine of Recent Creation*. El Cajon, CA: Institute for Creation Research, 1989. (young earth view)

Mortenson, Terry, and Thane H. Ury. *Coming to Grips with Genesis: Biblical Authority and the Age of the Earth*. Green Forest, AR: Master, 2008.

———. *The Great Turning Point: The Church's Catastrophic Mistake On Geology—Before Darwin*. Green Forest, AR: Master, 2004.

Nelson, David P. "The Work of God: Creation and Providence." In *A Theology for the Church*, ed. Daniel L. Akin et al., 242–67. Nashville: B&H, 2007.

Nevin, Norman Cummings, ed. *Should Christians Embrace Evolution? Biblical and Scientific Responses*. Phillipsburg, NJ: P&R, 2011.

Newman, Robert C., and Herman J. Eckelmann. *Genesis One and the Origin of the Earth*. Downers Grove, IL: InterVarsity Press, 1977. (argues against young earth view)

Noble, T. A. "Creation and Evolution." In *NDT2*, 231–32.

Osborn, L. H. "Creation." In *NDBT*, 429–35.

Painter, J. "Creation, Cosmology." In *DLNT*, 250–55.

Pipa, Joseph A., and David W. Hall, eds. *Did God Create in Six Days?* Taylors, SC: Southern Presbyterian Press, 1999. (young earth view)

Pitman, M. *Adam and Evolution*. Grand Rapids: Baker, 1984.

Poythress, Vern S. *Interpreting Eden: A Guide to Faithfully Reading and Understanding Genesis 1–3*. Wheaton, IL: Crossway, 2019.

Richards, Jay, ed. *God and Evolution: Protestants, Catholics, and Jews Explore Darwin's Challenge to Faith*. Seattle: Discovery Institute Press 2010.

Ross, Hugh. *Creation and Time: A Biblical and Scientific Perspective on the Creation-Date Controversy*. Colorado Springs: NavPress, 1994. (an articulate and highly trained scientist who argues against the young earth view on the basis of scientific evidence)

———. *The Genesis Question: Scientific Advances and the Accuracy of Genesis*. 2nd ed. Colorado Springs: NavPress, 2001.

———. *A Matter of Days: Resolving a Creation Controversy*, 2nd ed. Covina, CA: RTB, 2015. (extensive scientific support for old earth view; substantially expanded from first edition)

———. *More Than a Theory: Revealing a Testable Model for Creation*. Grand Rapids: Baker, 2009.

———. *Navigating Genesis: A Scientist's Journey through Genesis 1–11*. Covina, CA: Reasons to Believe, 2014.

Sarfati, Jonathan D. *Refuting Compromise: A Biblical and Scientific Refutation of Progressive Creationism (Billions of Years) as Popularized by Astronomer Hugh Ross*. Green Forest, AR: Master, 2004.

———. *The Genesis Account: A Theological, Historical, and Scientific Commentary On Genesis 1–11*. Powder Springs, GA: Creation Book, 2018.

Schaeffer, Francis. *No Final Conflict*. Downers Grove, IL: InterVarsity Press, 1975.

Stump, J. B., ed. *Four Views on Creation, Evolution, and Intelligent Design*. Grand Rapids: Zondervan, 2017.

Thompson, G. J. "Creation." In *NDT2*, 229–31.

Treier, D. J. "Creation and Evolution." In *EDT3*, 218–21.

Van Till, Howard J., Davis A. Young, and Clarence Menninga. *Science Held Hostage: What's Wrong with Creation Science and Evolutionism?* Downers Grove, IL: InterVarsity Press, 1988. (argues against young earth view)

Walton, John H. *The Lost World of Adam and Eve: Genesis 2–3 and the Human Origins Debate*. Downers Grove, IL: IVP Academic, 2009. (interprets Genesis in a way compatible with theistic evolution)

———. *The Lost World of Genesis One: Ancient Cosmology and the Origins Debate*. Downers Grove, IL: IVP Academic, 2009.

Wells, Jonathan. *The Politically Incorrect Guide to Darwinism and Intelligent Design*. Washington, DC: Regnery, 2006.

Whitcomb, John C. *The World That Perished*. Grand Rapids: Baker, 1988. (young earth view)

Wilder-Smith, A. E. *The Natural Sciences Know Nothing of Evolution*. El Cajon, CA: Master, 1981.

Woodward, Thomas. *Darwin Strikes Back: Defending the Science of Intelligent Design*. Grand Rapids, MI: Baker, 2006.

Young, Davis A. *Christianity and the Age of the Earth*. Grand Rapids: Zondervan, 1982. (argues against young earth view)

———, and Ralph F. Stearley. *The Bible, Rocks, and Time: Geological Evidence for the Age of the Earth*. Downers Grove, IL: IVP Academic, 2008.

## SCRIPTURE MEMORY PASSAGE

**Nehemiah 9:6:** You are the LORD, you alone. You have made heaven, the heaven of heavens, with all their host, the earth and all that is on it, the seas and all that is in them; and you preserve all of them; and the host of heaven worships you.

## HYMN

### "Hallelujah, Praise Jehovah!"

This hymn contains the entire content of Psalm 148 set to music. It summons all creation, including "things visible and things invisible," to worship God our Creator.

*Hallelujah, praise Jehovah, from the heavens*
*    praise his name;*
*    Praise Jehovah in the highest, all his angels,*
*        praise proclaim.*
*All his hosts, together praise him, sun and moon*
*    and stars on high;*
*    Praise him, O ye heav'ns of heavens, and ye*
*        floods above the sky.*

*Refrain*
*Let them praises give Jehovah, for his name alone*
*    is high,*
*    And his glory is exalted, and his glory is*
*        exalted, and his glory is exalted*
*    Far above the earth and sky.*

*Let them praises give Jehovah, they were made at*
*    his command;*
*    Them for ever he established, his decree shall*
*        ever stand.*
*From the earth, O praise Jehovah, all ye seas, ye*
*    monsters all,*
*    Fire and hail and snow and vapors, stormy*
*        winds that hear his call.*

*All ye fruitful trees and cedars, all ye hills and*
*    mountains high,*
*    Creeping things and beasts and cattle, birds*
*        that in the heavens fly,*
*Kings of earth, and all ye people, princes great,*
*    earth's judges all;*
*    Praise his name, young men and maidens,*
*        aged men, and children small.*

Author: William J. Kirkpatrick, 1838–1921

# CONTEMPORARY WORSHIP SONG

## "Indescribable"

*From the highest of heights to the depths of the sea,*
*Creation's revealing Your majesty.*
*From the colors of fall to the fragrance of spring,*
*Every creature unique in the song that it sings.*
*All exclaiming . . .*

*Chorus 1*
*Indescribable, uncontainable,*
*You placed the stars in the sky,*
*And You know them by name.*
*You are amazing God.*
*All powerful, untamable,*
*Awestruck we fall to our knees*
*As we humbly proclaim,*
*You are amazing God.*

*Who has told every lightning bolt where it should go,*
*Or seen heavenly storehouses laden with snow?*
*Who imagined the sun and gives source to its light,*
*Yet conceals it to bring us the coolness of night?*
*None can fathom.*

*Interlude*
*You are amazing God.*

*Chorus 2*
*Indescribable, uncontainable,*
*You placed the stars in the sky,*
*And You know them by name.*
*You are amazing God.*
*Incomparable, unchangeable,*
*You see the depths of my heart,*
*And You love me the same.*
*You are amazing God.*

*You see the depths of my heart,*
*And You love me the same.*
*You are amazing God.*
*You see the depths of our hearts,*
*And You love us the same.*
*You are amazing God.*

Words by Jesse Reeves and Laura Story[155]

---

155. Copyright © 2004 worshiptogether.com Songs (ASCAP) sixsteps Music (ASCAP) Laura Stories (ASCAP) (adm. at CapitolCMGPublishing.com). All rights reserved. Used by permission.

## CHAPTER 16

# God's Providence

*If God controls all things, how can our actions have real meaning?*
*What are the decrees of God?*

## EXPLANATION AND SCRIPTURAL BASIS

Once we understand that God is the all-powerful Creator (see chapter 15), it seems reasonable to conclude that he also preserves and governs everything in the universe as well. Though the term *providence* is not found in Scripture, it has been used traditionally to summarize God's ongoing relationship to his creation. When we accept the biblical doctrine of providence, we avoid four common errors in thinking about God's relationship to creation. The biblical doctrine is neither *deism* (which teaches that God created the world and then essentially abandoned it) nor *pantheism* (which teaches that the creation does not have a real, distinct existence in itself, but is only part of God), but *providence* (which teaches that though God is actively related to and involved in the creation at each moment, creation is distinct from him). Moreover, the biblical doctrine does not teach that events in creation are determined by *chance* (or randomness), nor are they determined by impersonal *fate* (or determinism), but by God, who is the personal yet infinitely powerful Creator and Lord.

We may define God's providence as follows: *God is continually involved with all created things in such a way that he (1) keeps them existing and maintaining the properties with which he created them; (2) cooperates with created things in every action, directing their distinctive properties to cause them to act as they do; and (3) directs them to fulfill his purposes.*

Under the general category of providence, we have three subtopics according to the three elements in the definition above: (1) preservation, (2) concurrence, and (3) government.

We shall examine each of these separately, then consider differing views and objections to the doctrine of providence. It should be noted that this is a doctrine on which there has been substantial disagreement among Christians since the early history of the church, particularly with respect to God's relationship to the willing choices of moral creatures. In this chapter we will first present a summary of the position favored in this textbook (what is commonly called the "Reformed" or "Calvinist" position),[1] then

---

1. Though philosophers may use the term *determinism* (or *soft determinism*) to categorize the position I advocate in

this chapter, I do not use that term because it is too easily misunderstood in everyday English: (1) It suggests a system in consider arguments that have been made from another position (what is commonly called the "Arminian" position).

## A. Preservation

*God keeps all created things existing and maintaining the properties with which he created them.*

Hebrews 1:3 tells us that Christ "upholds the universe by the word of his power." The Greek word translated "upholds" is *pherō*, "carry, bear." This is commonly used in the New Testament for carrying something from one place to another, such as bringing a paralyzed man on a bed to Jesus (Luke 5:18), bringing wine to the steward of the feast (John 2:8), or bringing a cloak and books to Paul (2 Tim. 4:13). It does not mean simply "sustain." It has the sense of active, purposeful control over the thing being carried from one place to another. In Hebrews 1:3, the use of the present participle indicates that Jesus is *"continually* carrying along all things" in the universe by the word of his power. Christ is actively involved in the work of providence.

Similarly, in Colossians 1:17, Paul says of Christ that "in him all things hold together." The phrase "all things" refers to every created thing in the universe (see v. 16), and the verse affirms that Christ keeps all things existing—in him they continue to exist or "endure" (NASB mg.). Both verses indicate that if Christ were to cease his continuing activity of sustaining all things in the universe, then all except the triune God would instantly cease to exist. Such teaching is also affirmed by Paul, "In him we live and move and *have our being*" (Acts 17:28), and by Ezra, "You are the LORD, you alone. You have made heaven, the heaven of heavens, with all their host, the earth and all that is on it, the seas and all that are in them; *and you preserve all of them*; and the host of heaven worships you" (Neh. 9:6). Peter also says that "the heavens and earth that now exist" are "being *kept* until the day of judgment" (2 Peter 3:7).

One aspect of God's providential preservation is the fact that he continues to give us breath each moment. Elihu, in his wisdom, says of God, "If he should set his heart to it and gather to himself his spirit and his breath, all flesh would perish together, and man would return to dust" (Job 34:14–15; cf. Ps. 104:29).

God, in preserving all things he has made, also causes them to maintain the properties with which he created them. God preserves water in such a way that it continues

---

which human choices are not real and make no difference in the outcome of events; and (2) it suggests a system in which the ultimate cause of events is a mechanistic universe rather than a wise and personal God. Moreover, (3) it too easily allows critics to group the biblical view with non-Christian deterministic systems and blur the distinctions between them.

The view advocated in this chapter is also sometimes called "compatibilism," because it holds that absolute divine sovereignty is compatible with human significance and real human choices. I have no objection to the nuances of this term, but I have decided not to use it because (1) I want to avoid the proliferation of technical terms in studying theology, and (2) it seems preferable simply to call my position a traditional Reformed view of God's providence, and thereby to place myself within a widely understood theological tradition represented by John Calvin and the other systematic theologians listed in the "Reformed" category at the end of this chapter.

to act like water. He causes grass to continue to act like grass, with all its distinctive characteristics. He causes the paper on which this sentence is written to continue to act like paper so that it does not spontaneously dissolve into water and float away or change into a living thing and begin to grow! Until this paper is acted on by some other part of creation and thereby its properties are changed (for instance, until it is burned with fire and it becomes ash), it will continue to act like paper so long as God preserves the earth and the creation that he has made.

We should not, however, think of God's preservation as a continuous new creation: he does not continuously create new atoms and molecules for every existing thing every moment. Rather, he *preserves* what has already been created: he "carries along all things" by his word of power (Heb. 1:3, author's translation). We must also appreciate that created things are *real* and that their characteristics are *real*. I do not just imagine that the rock in my hand is hard—it is hard. If I bump it against my head, I do not just imagine that it hurts—it *does* hurt! Because God keeps this rock maintaining the properties with which he created it, the rock has been hard since the day it was formed, and (unless something else in creation interacts with it and changes it) it will be hard until the day God destroys the heavens and the earth (2 Peter 3:7, 10–12).

God's providence provides a basis for science: God has made and continues to sustain a universe that acts in predictable ways. If a scientific experiment gives a certain result today, then we can have confidence that (if all the factors are the same) it will give the same result tomorrow and a hundred years from tomorrow. The doctrine of providence also provides a foundation for technology: I can be confident that gasoline will make my car run today just as it did yesterday, not simply because "it has always worked that way" but because God's providence sustains a universe in which created things maintain the properties with which he created them. The *result* may be similar in the life of an unbeliever and the life of a Christian: we both put gasoline in our cars and drive away. But he will do so without knowing the ultimate reason why it works that way, and I will do so with knowledge of the actual final reason (God's providence) and with thanks to my Creator for the wonderful creation that he has made and preserves.

## B. CONCURRENCE

*God cooperates with created things in every action, directing their distinctive properties to cause them to act as they do.*

This second aspect of providence, *concurrence*, is an expansion of the idea contained in the first aspect, *preservation*. In fact, some theologians (such as John Calvin) treat the fact of concurrence under the category of preservation, but it is helpful to treat it as a distinct category.

In Ephesians 1:11 Paul says that God "works all things according to the counsel of his will." The word translated "works" (*energeō*) indicates that God "brings about" *all things* according to his own will. No event in creation falls outside of his providence. Of course this fact is hidden from our eyes unless we read it in Scripture. Like preservation, God's work of concurrence is not clearly evident from observation of the natural world around us.

In giving scriptural proof for concurrence, we will begin with the inanimate creation, then move to animals, and finally to different kinds of events in the life of human beings.

### 1. Inanimate Creation

There are many things in creation that we think of as merely "natural" occurrences. Yet Scripture says that God causes them to happen. We read of "fire and hail, snow and mist, stormy wind fulfilling his word!" (Ps. 148:8). Similarly,

> For to the snow he says, "Fall on the earth,"
> likewise to the downpour, his mighty downpour. . . .
> By the breath of God *ice* is given,
> and the broad waters are frozen fast.
> He loads the thick cloud with moisture;
> the clouds scatter his *lightning*.
> They turn around and around by his guidance,
> to accomplish all that he commands them
> on the face of the habitable world.
> Whether for correction or for his land
> or for love, he causes it to happen. (Job 37:6, 10–13; cf. 38:22–30)

Again, the psalmist declares that "whatever the LORD pleases, he does, in heaven and on earth, in the seas and all deeps" (Ps. 135:6), and then in the next sentence he illustrates God's doing of his will in the weather: "He it is who makes the clouds rise at the end of the earth, who makes lightnings for the rain and brings forth the wind from his storehouses" (Ps. 135:7; cf. 104:4).

God also causes the grass to grow: "*You cause the grass to grow* for the livestock and plants for man to cultivate, that he may bring forth food from the earth" (Ps. 104:14). God directs the stars in the heavens, asking Job, "Can you bring forth the constellations in their seasons or lead out the Bear with its cubs?" (Job 38:32 NIV; "the Bear" or Ursa Major is commonly called the Big Dipper; v. 31 refers to the constellations Pleiades and Orion). God continually directs the coming of the morning (Job 38:12), a fact Jesus affirmed when he said that God "*makes his sun rise* on the evil and on the good, and *sends rain* on the just and on the unjust" (Matt. 5:45).

## 2. Animals

Scripture affirms that God feeds the wild animals of the field:

> These all look to you,
>> to give them their food in due season.
> When you give it to them, they gather it up;
>> when you open your hand, they are filled with good things.
> When you hide your face, they are dismayed. (Ps. 104:27–29; cf. Job 38:39–41)

Jesus also affirmed this when he said, "Look at the *birds* of the air . . . your heavenly Father *feeds them*" (Matt. 6:26). And he said that not one sparrow "will fall to the ground apart from your Father" (Matt. 10:29).

## 3. Seemingly "Random" or "Chance" Events

From a human perspective, the casting of lots (or modern equivalents such as rolling dice or flipping a coin) is the most typical of random events that occur in the universe. But Scripture affirms that the outcome of such an event is from God: "The lot is cast into the lap, but its every decision is from the LORD" (Prov. 16:33).[2]

## 4. Events Fully Caused by God and Fully Caused by the Creature as Well

For any of these foregoing events (rain and snow, grass growing, sun and stars, the feeding of animals, or casting of lots), we could (at least in theory) give a completely satisfactory "natural" explanation. A botanist can detail the factors that cause grass to grow, such as sun, moisture, temperature, nutrients in the soil, etc. Yet Scripture says that *God* causes the grass to grow. A meteorologist can give a complete explanation of factors that cause rain (humidity, temperature, atmospheric pressure, etc.), and can even produce rain in a weather laboratory. Yet Scripture says that *God* causes the rain. A physicist with accurate information on the force and direction a pair of dice was rolled could fully explain what caused the dice to give the result they did—yet Scripture says that *God* brings about the decision of the lot that is cast.

This shows us that it is incorrect for us to reason that if we know the "natural" cause of something in this world, then God did not cause it. Rather, if it rains, we should thank him. If crops grow, we should thank him. In all of these events, it is not as though the event was partly caused by God and partly by factors in the created world. If that were the case, then we would always be looking for some small feature of an event that

---

2. It is true that Eccl. 9:11 says that "the race is not to the swift, nor the battle to the strong, nor bread to the wise, nor riches to the intelligent, nor favor to those with knowledge, but time and *chance* happen to them all." But Michael Eaton correctly observes, "On the lips of an Israelite 'chance' means what is unexpected, not what is random" (*Ecclesiastes*, TOTC [Leicester: Inter-Varsity Press; Downers Grove, IL: InterVarsity Press, 1983], 70). The rare word here translated "chance" (Heb. *pega'*) occurs only once more in the Bible (1 Kings 5:4[18], of an evil *event*).

we could not explain and attribute that (say 1 percent of the cause) to God. But surely this is not a correct view. Rather, these passages affirm that such events are entirely caused by God. Yet we know that (in another sense) they are entirely caused by factors in the creation as well.

The doctrine of concurrence affirms that God *directs* and *works through* the distinctive properties of each created thing so that these things themselves bring about the results that we see. In this way it is possible to affirm that in one sense events are fully (100 percent) caused by God and fully (100 percent) caused by the creature as well. However, divine and creaturely causes work in different ways. The divine cause of each event works as an invisible, behind-the-scenes, directing cause and therefore could be called the "primary cause" that plans and initiates everything that happens. But the created thing brings about actions in ways consistent with the creature's properties, ways that can often be described by us or by professional scientists who carefully observe the processes. These creaturely factors and properties can therefore be called the "secondary causes" of everything that happens, even though they are the causes that are evident to us by observation.

## 5. The Affairs of Nations

Scripture also speaks of God's providential control of human affairs. We read that God "makes nations great, and he destroys them; he enlarges nations, and leads them away" (Job 12:23). "Kingship belongs to the LORD, and he rules over the nations" (Ps. 22:28). He has determined the time of existence and the place of every nation on the earth, for Paul says, "He made from one man every nation of mankind to live on all the face of the earth, having determined allotted periods and the boundaries of their dwelling place" (Acts 17:26; cf. 14:16). And when Nebuchadnezzar repented, he learned to praise God,

> For his dominion is an everlasting dominion,
>     and his kingdom endures from generation to generation;
> all the inhabitants of the earth are accounted as nothing,
>     and *he does according to his will among the host of heaven*
>     *and among the inhabitants of the earth*;
> and none can stay his hand or say to him,
>     "What have you done?" (Dan. 4:34–35)

## 6. All Aspects of Our Lives

It is amazing to see the extent to which Scripture affirms that God brings about various events in our lives. For example, our dependence on God to give us food each day is affirmed every time we pray, "Give us this day our daily bread" (Matt. 6:11), even though we work for our food and (as far as mere human observation can discern) obtain it through entirely "natural" causes. Similarly, Paul, looking at events with the eye of faith, affirms that "my God will supply every need" of his children (Phil 4:19), even though God may use "ordinary" means (such as other people) to do so.

God plans our days before we are born, for David affirms, "In your book were written, every one of them, the days that were formed for me, when as yet there was none of them" (Ps. 139:16). And Job says that man's "days are determined, and the number of his months is with you, and you have appointed his limits that he cannot pass" (Job 14:5). This can be seen in the life of Paul, who says that God "had set me apart before I was born" (Gal. 1:15), and Jeremiah, to whom God said, "Before I formed you in the womb I knew you, and before you were born I consecrated you; I appointed you a prophet to the nations" (Jer. 1:5).

All our actions are under God's providential care, for "in him we live and *move*" (Acts 17:28). The individual steps we take each day are directed by the Lord. Jeremiah confesses, "I know, O LORD, that the way of man is not in himself, that it is not in man who walks to direct his steps" (Jer. 10:23). We read that "a man's steps are from the LORD" (Prov. 20:24) and that "the heart of man plans his way, but the LORD establishes his steps" (Prov. 16:9). Similarly, Proverbs 16:1 affirms, "The plans of the heart belong to man, but the answer of the tongue is from the LORD."[3]

Success and failure come from God. We read,

> For not from the east or from the west
> and not from the wilderness comes lifting up,
> but it is God who executes judgment,
> putting down one and lifting up another. (Ps. 75:6–7)

So Mary can say, "He has brought down the mighty from their thrones and exalted those of humble estate" (Luke 1:52). The LORD gives children, for "children are a heritage from the LORD, the fruit of the womb a reward" (Ps. 127:3).

All our talents and abilities are from the Lord, for Paul can ask the Corinthians, "What do you have that you did not receive? If then you received it, why do you boast as if you did not receive it?" (1 Cor. 4:7). David knew that to be true regarding his military skill, for, though he must have trained many hours in the use of a bow and arrow, he could say of God, "He trains my hands for war, so that my arms can bend a bow of bronze" (Ps. 18:34).

---

3. David J. A. Clines, "Predestination in the Old Testament," in *Grace Unlimited*, ed. Clark H. Pinnock (Minneapolis: Bethany House, 1975), 116–17, objects that these verses simply affirm that "when it comes to conflict between God and man, undoubtedly it cannot be man who wins the day." He says that these verses do not describe life in general but describe unusual situations where God overcomes man's will in order to bring about his special purposes. Clines denies that these verses mean that God always acts this way or that these verses represent God's control of human conduct generally. Yet no such restriction is seen in these passages (see Prov. 16:1, 9). The verses do not say that God directs a man's steps in rare instances where God needs to intervene to fulfill his purposes; they simply make general statements about the way the world works—God directs man's steps in general, not simply when there is conflict between God and man.

God influences rulers in their decisions, for "the king's heart is a stream of water in the hand of the LORD; he turns it wherever he will" (Prov. 21:1). For example, "the LORD stirred up the spirit of Cyrus king of Persia" (Ezra 1:1) to help the people of Israel, and later the Lord "turned the heart of the king of Assyria" to his people "so that he aided them in the work of the house of God, the God of Israel" (Ezra 6:22). But it is not just the heart of the king that God influences, for he looks down "on all the inhabitants of the earth" and "fashions the hearts of them all" (Ps. 33:14–15). When we realize that the heart in Scripture is the location of our inmost thoughts and desires, this is a significant passage. God especially guides the desires and inclinations of believers, working in us "both *to will* and to work for his good pleasure" (Phil. 2:13).

All of these passages, reporting both general statements about God's work in the lives of all people and specific examples of God's work in the lives of individuals, lead us to conclude that God's providential work of concurrence extends to all aspects of our lives. Our words, our steps, our movements, our hearts, and our abilities are all from the Lord.

But we must guard against misunderstanding. Here also, as with the lower creation, God's providential direction as an unseen, behind-the-scenes "primary cause" should not lead us to deny the reality of our choices and actions. Again and again Scripture affirms we really do *cause* events to happen. We are significant and we are responsible. We *do have choices*, and these real choices bring about real results. Scripture repeatedly affirms these truths as well. Just as a rock is *really hard* because God has made it with the property of hardness, just as water is *really wet* because God has made it with the property of wetness, just as plants are *really alive* because God has made them with the property of life, so our choices are *real choices* with significant effects because God has made us in such a wonderful way that he has endowed us with the property of willing choice.

One approach to these passages about God's concurrence is to say that if our choices are real, they *cannot* be caused by God (see below for further discussion of this viewpoint). But the number of passages that affirm this providential control of God is so considerable, and the difficulties involved in giving them some other interpretation are so formidable, that it does not seem to me that this can be the right approach to them. It seems better to affirm that God causes all things that happen but that he does so in such a way that he somehow upholds our ability to make *willing, responsible choices* that have *real and eternal results* for which we are *held accountable*. Exactly how God combines his providential control with our willing and significant choices, Scripture does not explain to us. But rather than deny one aspect or the other (simply because we cannot explain how both can be true), we should accept both in an attempt to be faithful to the teaching of all of Scripture.

The analogy of an author writing a play may help us to grasp how both aspects can be true. In the Shakespearean play *Macbeth*, the character Macbeth murders King Duncan. Now (if we assume for a moment that this is a fictional account), we may ask, "Who killed King Duncan?" On one level, the correct answer is "Macbeth." Within the play, he carried out the murder and he is rightly to blame for it. But on another level, a correct answer to the question, "Who killed King Duncan?" would be "William Shakespeare caused his death": he wrote the play, he created all the characters in it, and he wrote the part where Macbeth killed King Duncan.

It would not be correct to say that because Macbeth killed King Duncan, William Shakespeare did not (somehow) cause his death. Nor would it be correct to say that because William Shakespeare caused King Duncan's death, Macbeth did not kill him. Both are true. On the level of the characters in the play Macbeth fully (100%) caused King Duncan's death, but on the level of the creator of the play, William Shakespeare fully (100%) caused King Duncan's death. In similar fashion, we can understand that God fully causes things in one way (as Creator), and we fully cause things in another way (as creatures). (One word of caution however: The analogy of an author [= writer, creator] of a play should not lead us to say that God is the "author" [= actor, doer, an older sense of "author"] of sin, for he never does sinful actions, nor does he ever delight in them.)[4]

Of course, characters in a play are not real persons—they are fictional characters. But God is infinitely greater and wiser than we are. While we can only create fictional characters in a play, our almighty God has created us as real persons who make willing choices. To say that God could not make a world in which he (somehow) causes us to make willing choices (as some would argue today; see discussion below) is limiting the power of God. It seems also to deny a large number of passages of Scripture.

## 7. What about Evil?

If God does indeed cause, through his providential activity, everything that comes about in the world, then the question arises, "What is the relationship between God and evil in the world?" Does God actually cause the evil actions that people do? If he does, then is God not responsible for sin?

In approaching this question, it is best first to read the passages of Scripture that most directly address it. We can begin by looking at several passages that affirm that God did, indeed, cause evil events to come about and evil deeds to be done. But we must

---

4. I. Howard Marshall, "Predestination in the New Testament" in Pinnock, *Grace Unlimited*, 132–33, 139, objects to the analogy of an author and a play because the actors "are bound by the characters assigned to them and the lines that they have learned" so that even if the dramatist "makes [the characters] say 'I love my creator' in his drama, this is not mutual love in the real sense." But Marshall limits his analysis to what is possible with human beings acting on a human level. He does not give consideration to the possibility (in fact, the reality!) that God is able to do far more than human beings are able to do and that he can wonderfully create genuine human beings rather than mere characters in a play. A better approach to the analogy of an author and a play would be if Marshall would apply to this question a very helpful statement that he made in another part of the essay: "The basic difficulty is that of attempting to explain the nature of *the relationship between an infinite God and finite creatures*. Our temptation is to think of divine causation in much the same way as human causation, and this produces difficulties as soon as we try to relate divine causation and human freedom. It is beyond our ability to explain how God can cause us to do certain things (or to cause the universe to come into being and to behave as it does)" (137–38). I can agree fully with everything in Marshall's statement at that point and find that to be a very helpful way of approaching this problem.

remember that in all these passages it is very clear that Scripture nowhere shows God as *directly doing anything evil* but rather as bringing about evil deeds through the willing actions of moral creatures. Moreover, *Scripture never blames God for evil or shows God as taking pleasure in evil*, and Scripture never excuses human beings for the wrong they do. However we understand God's relationship to evil, we must *never* come to the point where we think that we are not responsible for the evil that we do or that God takes pleasure in evil or is to be blamed for it. Such a conclusion is clearly contrary to Scripture.

Literally dozens of Scripture passages say that God (indirectly) brought about some kind of evil. I have quoted such an extensive list (in the next few paragraphs) because Christians often are unaware of the extent of this forthright teaching in Scripture. Yet it must be remembered that in all of these examples, the evil is actually done not by God but by people or demons who choose to do it.

A very clear example is found in the story of Joseph. Scripture clearly says that Joseph's brothers were wrongly jealous of him (Gen. 37:11), hated him (Gen. 37:4, 5, 8), wanted to kill him (Gen. 37:20), did wrong when they cast him into a pit (Gen. 37:24), and sold him into slavery in Egypt (Gen. 37:28). Yet later Joseph could say to his brothers, "*God sent me before you* to preserve life" (Gen. 45:5), and "You meant evil against me, but *God meant it for good*, to bring it about that many people should be kept alive, as they are today" (Gen. 50:20).[5] Here we have a combination of evil deeds brought about by sinful men who are rightly held accountable for their sin and the overriding providential control of God whereby God's own purposes were accomplished. Both are clearly affirmed.

The story of the exodus from Egypt repeatedly affirms that God hardened the heart of Pharaoh: God says, "I will harden his heart" (Ex. 4:21), "I will harden Pharaoh's heart" (Ex. 7:3), "the LORD hardened the heart of Pharaoh" (Ex. 9:12), "the LORD hardened Pharaoh's heart" (Ex. 10:20, repeated in 10:27 and again in 11:10), "I will harden Pharaoh's heart" (Ex. 14:4), and "the LORD hardened the heart of Pharaoh king of Egypt" (Ex. 14:8). It is sometimes objected that Scripture also says that Pharaoh hardened his own heart (Ex. 8:15, 32; 9:34), and that God's act of hardening Pharaoh's heart was only in response to the initial rebellion and hardness of heart that Pharaoh himself exhibited of his own free will. But it should be noted that God's promises that he would harden Pharaoh's heart (Ex. 4:21; 7:3) are made long before Scripture tells us that Pharaoh hardened his own heart (we read of this for the first time in Ex. 8:15). Moreover, our analysis of concurrence given above, in which both divine and human agents can cause the same event, should show us that both factors can be true at the same time: even when Pharaoh hardens his own heart, that is not inconsistent with saying that God is causing Pharaoh to do this, and thereby God is hardening the heart of Pharaoh.

---

5. Ps. 105:17 says that God "had sent a man ahead of them, Joseph, who was sold as a slave."

Finally, if someone would object that God is just intensifying the evil desires and choices that were already in Pharaoh's heart, then this kind of action could still in theory at least cover all the evil in the world today, since all people have evil desires in their hearts and all people do in fact make evil choices.

What was God's purpose in this? Paul reflects on Exodus 9:16 and says, "For the Scripture says to Pharaoh, 'For this very purpose I have raised you up, that I might show my power in you, and that my name might be proclaimed in all the earth'" (Rom. 9:17). Then Paul infers a general truth from this specific example: "So then he has mercy on whomever he wills, and he hardens whomever he wills" (Rom. 9:18). In fact, God also hardened the hearts of the Egyptian people so that they pursued Israel into the Red Sea: "I will harden the hearts of the Egyptians so that they shall go in after them, and I will get glory over Pharaoh and all his host, his chariots, and his horsemen" (Ex. 14:17). This theme is repeated in Psalm 105:25: "He turned their hearts to hate his people."

Later in the Old Testament narrative, similar examples are found of the Canaanites who were destroyed in the conquest of Palestine under Joshua. We read, "For it was the LORD's doing to harden their hearts that they should come against Israel in battle, in order that they should be devoted to destruction" (Josh. 11:20; see also Judg. 3:12; 9:23). And Samson's demand to marry an unbelieving Philistine woman "was from the LORD, for he was seeking an opportunity against the Philistines. At that time the Philistines ruled over Israel" (Judg. 14:4). We also read that the sons of Eli, when rebuked for their evil deeds, "would not listen to the voice of their father, for it was the will of the LORD to put them to death" (1 Sam. 2:25). Later, "a harmful spirit from the LORD" tormented King Saul (1 Sam. 16:14).

When David sinned, the LORD said to him through Nathan the prophet, "I will raise up evil against you out of your own house. And I will take your wives before your eyes and give them to your neighbor, and he shall lie with your wives in the sight of this sun. For you did it secretly, but I will do this thing before all Israel and before the sun" (2 Sam. 12:11–12; fulfilled in 16:22). In further punishment for David's sin, "the LORD afflicted the child that Uriah's wife bore to David, and he became sick" and eventually died (2 Sam. 12:15–18). David remained mindful of the fact that God could bring evil against him, because at a later time, when Shimei cursed David and threw stones at him and his servants (2 Sam. 16:5–8), David refused to take vengeance on Shimei but said to his soldiers, "Leave him alone, and let him curse, for the LORD has told him to" (2 Sam. 16:11).

Still later in David's life, the Lord "incited"[6] David to take a census of the people (2 Sam. 24:1), but afterward David recognized this as sin, saying, "I have sinned greatly

---

6. The Hebrew word used when 2 Sam. 24:1 says that the Lord *incited* David against Israel is *sûth*, "to incite, allure, insti-gate" (BDB, 694). It is the same word used in 2 Chron. 21:1 to say that Satan *incited* David to number Israel, in 1 Kings 21:25 to say that Jezebel *incited* Ahab to do evil, in Deut. 13:6(7) to warn against a loved one *enticing* a family member secretly to serve other gods, and in 2 Chron. 18:31 to say that God *moved* the Syrian army to withdraw from Jehoshaphat.

in what I have done" (2 Sam. 24:10), and God sent punishment on the land because of this sin (2 Sam. 24:12–17). However, it is also clear that "the anger of the LORD was kindled against Israel" (2 Sam. 24:1), so God's inciting of David to sin was a means by which he brought about punishment on the people of Israel. Moreover, the means by which God incited David is made clear in 1 Chronicles 21:1: "Then Satan stood against Israel and *incited* David to number Israel." In this one incident the Bible gives us a remarkable insight into the three influences that contributed in different ways to one action: God, in order to bring about his purposes, worked through Satan to incite David to sin, but Scripture regards David as being responsible for that sin. Again, after Solomon turned away from the Lord because of his foreign wives, "the LORD raised up an adversary against Solomon, Hadad the Edomite" (1 Kings 11:14), and "God also raised up as an adversary to him, Rezon the son of Eliada" (1 Kings 11:23). These evil kings were raised up by God.

In the story of Job, though the LORD gave Satan permission to bring harm to Job's possessions and children, and though this harm came through the evil actions of the Sabeans and the Chaldeans, as well as a windstorm (Job 1:12, 15, 17, 19), Job looks beyond those secondary causes and, with the eyes of faith, sees it all as from the hand of the Lord: "The LORD gave, and the LORD has taken away; *blessed be the name of the LORD*" (Job 1:21). The Old Testament author follows Job's statement immediately with the sentence, "In all this Job did not sin or charge God with wrong" (Job 1:22). Job has just been told that evil marauding bands had destroyed his flocks and herds, yet with great faith and patience in adversity, he says, "*The* LORD has taken away." Though Job says that the LORD had done this, he does not blame God for the evil or say that God had done wrong. Job says, "Blessed be the name of the LORD." To *blame* God for evil that he had brought about through secondary agents would have been to sin. Job does not do this, Scripture never does this, and neither should we.

Elsewhere in the Old Testament we read that the Lord "put a lying spirit in the mouth" of Ahab's prophets (1 Kings 22:23) and sent the wicked Assyrians as "the rod of my anger" to punish Israel (Isa. 10:5). He also sent the evil Babylonians, including Nebuchadnezzar, against Israel, saying, "I will bring them against this land and its inhabitants" (Jer. 25:9). Then God promised that later he would punish the Babylonians also: "I will punish the king of Babylon and that nation, the land of the Chaldeans, for their iniquity, declares the LORD, making the land an everlasting waste" (Jer. 25:12). If there is a deceiving prophet who gives a false message, then the Lord says, "if the prophet is deceived and speaks a word, I, the LORD, have deceived that prophet, and I will stretch out my hand against him and will destroy him from the midst of my people Israel" (Ezek. 14:9, in the context of bringing judgment on Israel for their idolatry). As the culmination of a series of rhetorical questions to which the implied answer is always no, Amos asks, "Is a trumpet blown in a city, and the people are not afraid? Does disaster come to a city, unless the LORD has done it?" (Amos 3:6). There follows a series of natural disasters in Amos 4:6–12, where the LORD reminds the people that he gave them hunger, drought, blight and mildew, locusts, pestilence, and death of men and horses, "yet you did not return to me" (Amos 4:6, 8, 9, 10, 11).

In many of the passages mentioned above, God brings evil and destruction on people in judgment upon their sins: they have been disobedient or have strayed into idolatry, and then the LORD uses evil human beings or demonic forces or "natural" disasters to bring judgment on them. (This is not always said to be the case—Joseph and Job come to mind—but it is often so.) Perhaps this idea of judgment on sin can help us to understand, at least in part, how God can righteously bring about evil events. All human beings are sinful. Scripture tells us that "all have sinned and fall short of the glory of God" (Rom. 3:23). None of us deserves God's favor or his mercy, but only eternal condemnation. Therefore, when God brings evil on human beings, whether to discipline his children, or to lead unbelievers to repentance, or to bring a judgment of condemnation and destruction upon hardened sinners, none of us can charge God with doing wrong. Ultimately all will work in God's good purposes to bring glory to him and good to his people. Yet we must realize that in punishing evil in those who are not redeemed (such as Pharaoh, the Canaanites, and the Babylonians), God is also glorified through the demonstration of his justice, holiness, and power (see Ex. 9:16; Rom. 9:14–24).

Through the prophet Isaiah God says, "I form light and create darkness; I make well-being and create calamity; I am the LORD, who does all these things" (Isa. 45:7);[7] the Hebrew word for "create" here is *bārā'*, the same word used in Gen. 1:1. In Lamentations 3:38 we read, "Is it not from the mouth of the Most High that good and bad come?" The people of Israel, in a time of heartfelt repentance, cry out to God and say, "O LORD, why do you make us wander from your ways and harden our heart, so that we fear you not?" (Isa. 63:17).[8]

The life of Jonah is a remarkable illustration of God's concurrence in human activity. The men on board the ship sailing to Tarshish threw Jonah overboard, for Scripture says, "So *they* picked up Jonah and hurled him into the sea, and the sea ceased from its raging" (Jonah 1:15). Yet only five verses later Jonah acknowledges God's providential direction in their act, for he says to God, "*You* cast me into the deep, into the heart of the seas" (Jonah 2:3). Scripture simultaneously affirms that the men threw Jonah into the sea and that God threw him into the sea. The providential direction of God did not force the sailors to do something against their will, nor were they conscious of any divine influence on them—indeed, they cried to the Lord for forgiveness as they threw Jonah

---

7. Other translations render the Hebrew word *rā'*, "calamity," as "disaster" (NIV) or "woe" (RSV) or "calamity" (NASB), and indeed the word can be used to apply to natural disasters such as these words imply. But it may have broader application than natural disasters, for the word is an extremely common word used of evil generally. In any case, Isa. 45:7 does not say that God *does evil* (see discussion below).

8. Another kind of evil is physical infirmity. With regard to this, the Lord says to Moses, "Who has made man's mouth? Who makes him mute, or deaf, or seeing, or blind? Is it not I, the LORD?" (Ex. 4:11).

overboard (Jonah 1:14). What Scripture reveals to us, and what Jonah himself realized, was that God was bringing about his plan through the willing choices of real human beings who were morally accountable for their actions. In a way not understood by us and not revealed to us, God *caused* them to make a *willing choice* to do what they did. They were "free" in the sense that they did what they most wanted to do, taking account of all the circumstances around them.

Similarly, we read both that "Saul took his own sword and fell upon it" (1 Chr. 10:4) and that Saul "did not seek guidance from the LORD. Therefore the LORD put him to death" (1 Chr. 10:14). Both are true, in different senses: Saul killed himself, and the Lord put him to death.

The most evil deed of all history, the crucifixion of Christ, was ordained by God— not just the fact that it would occur but also all the individual actions connected with it. The church at Jerusalem recognized this, for they prayed:

> For truly in this city there were gathered together against your holy servant Jesus, whom you anointed, both Herod and Pontius Pilate, along with the Gentiles and the peoples of Israel, *to do whatever your hand and your plan had predestined to take place.* (Acts 4:27–28)

All the actions of all the participants in the crucifixion of Jesus had been "predestined" by God. Yet the apostles clearly attach no moral blame to God, for the actions resulted from the *willing choices* of sinful people. Peter makes this clear in his sermon at Pentecost: "This Jesus, delivered up according to the definite plan and foreknowledge of God, *you crucified and killed by the hands of lawless men*" (Acts 2:23). In this one sentence, Peter links God's plan and foreknowledge with the moral blame that attaches to the actions of "lawless men." They were not forced by God to act against their wills; rather, God brought about his plan *through their willing choices,* for which they were nevertheless responsible.

In an example similar to the Old Testament account of God sending a lying spirit into the mouth of Ahab's prophets, we read of those who refuse to love the truth: "Therefore God sends them a strong delusion, so that they may believe what is false, in order that all may be condemned who did not believe the truth but had pleasure in unrighteousness" (2 Thess. 2:11–12). And Peter tells his readers that those who oppose them and persecute them, who reject Christ as Messiah, "stumble because they disobey the word, as they were destined to do" (1 Peter 2:8).[9]

---

9. The "destining" in this verse is best taken to refer to both the stumbling and the disobedience. It is incorrect to say that God only destined the fact that those who disobey would stumble, because it is not a fact but persons ("they") who are said to be "destined" in this case. (See discussion in Wayne Grudem, *The First Epistle of Peter,* TNTC [Leicester: InterVarsity Press; Grand Rapids: Eerdmans, 1988], 106–10.)

## 8. Analysis of Verses Relating to God and Evil

After looking at so many verses that speak of God's providential use of the evil actions of men and demons, what can we say by way of analysis?

**a. God Uses All Things to Fulfill His Purposes and Even Uses Evil for His Glory and for Our Good.** Thus, when evil comes into our lives to trouble us, we can have from the doctrine of providence a deeper assurance that "for those who love God all things work together for good, for those who are called according to his purpose" (Rom. 8:28). This kind of conviction enabled Joseph to say to his brothers, "You meant evil against me, but *God meant it for good*" (Gen. 50:20).

We can also realize that God is glorified even in the punishment of evil. Scripture tells us that "the LORD has made everything for its purpose, even the wicked for the day of trouble" (Prov. 16:4).[10] Similarly, the psalmist affirms, "Surely the wrath of man shall praise you" (Ps. 76:10). And the example of Pharaoh (Rom. 9:14–24) is a clear example of the way God uses evil for his glory and for his people's good.

**b. Nevertheless, God Never Does Evil and Is Never to Be Blamed for Evil.** In a statement similar to those cited above from Acts 2:23 and 4:27–28, Jesus also combines God's predestination of the crucifixion with moral blame on those who carry it out: "For the Son of Man goes *as it has been determined*, but woe to that man by whom he is betrayed!" (Luke 22:22; cf. Matt. 26:24; Mark 14:21). And in a more general statement about evil in the world, Jesus says, "Woe to the world for temptations to sin! For it is necessary that temptations come, but woe to the one by whom the temptation comes!" (Matt. 18:7).

James speaks similarly in warning us not to blame God for the evil we do when he says, "Let no one say when he is tempted, 'I am being tempted by God,' for God cannot be tempted with evil, and *he himself tempts no one*. But each person is tempted when he is lured and enticed by his own desire" (James 1:13–14). The verse does not say that God never causes evil to happen; it affirms that we should never think of him as the personal agent who is tempting us or who is to be held accountable for the temptation. We can never blame God for temptation or think that he will approve of us if we give in to it. We are to resist evil and always blame ourselves or others who tempt us, but we must never blame God.

But if God "tempts no one" (James 1:13), why does Jesus tell us to pray, "Lead us not into temptation, but deliver us from evil" (Matt. 6:13)? This makes sense if we carefully distinguish between (1) actively tempting someone and (2) leading someone

---

10. Clines, "Predestination in the Old Testament," 116, retranslates this, "The Lord has made everything with its counterpart, so the wicked will have his day of doom." He does this in order to avoid the conclusion that the Lord has made some wicked people for the day of evil. But his translation is not convincing. The Hebrew word translated "purpose" in the ESV (*ma'aneh*) occurs seventeen times in the Old Testament and usually refers to an "answer" to a question or a statement. So it means something like "appropriate response" or "corresponding purpose." But the preposition *le* is much more accurately translated "for" (not "with"), so in either case the sentence affirms that the Lord has made everything for its appropriate purpose *or* for the response appropriate to it. Therefore, whether we translate "purpose" or "counterpart," the verse affirms that even the wicked have been made by the Lord "for [Heb. *le*] the day of evil."

into a situation where he or she is tempted or tested. God is never the active personal agent who tempts us, but from time to time he may lead us into difficult situations, just as Jesus himself "was led up by the Spirit into the wilderness to be tempted by the devil" (Matt. 4:1).[11]

These verses all make it clear that "secondary causes" (human beings, angels, and demons) are *real* and that human beings do cause evil and are responsible for it. Though God ordained that it would come about, both in general terms and in specific details, yet *God is removed from actually doing evil*, and his bringing it about through "secondary causes" does not impugn his holiness or render him blameworthy. John Calvin wisely says,

> Thieves and murderers and other evildoers are the instruments of divine providence, and the Lord himself uses these to carry out the judgments that he has determined with himself. Yet I deny that they can derive from this any excuse for their evil deeds. Why? Will they either involve God in the same iniquity with themselves, or will they cloak their own depravity with his justice? They can do neither.[12]

A little later, Calvin heads a chapter, "God So Uses the Works of the Ungodly, and So Bends Their Minds to Carry Out His Judgments, That He Remains Pure From Every Stain."[13]

The alternatives to saying that God *uses evil for his purposes*, that *he never does evil*, and that he is *not to be blamed* for it are not desirable ones. If God himself does evil, we would have to conclude that he is not a good and righteous God, and therefore that he is not really God at all. If we maintain that God does not use evil to fulfill his purposes, then we would have to admit that there is evil in the universe that God did not intend, that the universe is not under his control, and that he might not fulfill his purposes. This would make it very difficult for us to affirm that "all things" work together for good for those who love God and are called according to his purpose (Rom. 8:28). If evil came into the world in spite of the fact that God did not intend it and did not want it to be there, then what guarantee do we have that there will not be more and more evil that he does not intend and that he does not want? And what guarantee do we have that he

---

11. On May 22, 2019, Pope Francis officially changed the wording of the Lord's Prayer from "lead us not into temptation" to "do not let us fall into temptation" because, it was claimed, "the original translation implies that God induces temptation. The change, officials said, is closer to the original intent of the prayer" (Caleb Parke, "Pope Francis Made This Big Change to Lord's Prayer," Fox News [online], June 5, 2019, https://www.foxnews.com/world/pope-francis-lords-prayer-our-father-change). But such a change is simply wrong. The Greek verb in Matthew 6:13 is *eispherō*, which means "to bring into an area," or "to cause someone to enter into a certain event or condition,

bring in" (BDAG, 295). It is used in Luke 5:19 to speak about the men who were carrying a paralyzed friend to Jesus, but they found "no way to *bring him in*" to the house where Jesus was teaching, so they dug a hole in the roof. This same verb is also used to say "we *brought* nothing *into* the world" (1 Timothy 6:7). The verb conveys the idea of actively leading or carrying; it does not have the passive meaning "allow someone to fall."

12. John Calvin, *Institutes of the Christian Religion*, ed. John T. McNeill, trans. F. L. Battles, 2 vols., Library of Christian Classics (Philadelphia: Westminster, 1960), 1:217 (1.16.5).

13. Calvin, *Institutes*, 1:228 (1.18.title).

will be able to use it for his purposes—or that he can triumph over it? Surely this is an undesirable alternative position.

**c. God Rightfully Blames and Judges Moral Creatures for the Evil They Do.** Many passages in Scripture affirm this. One is found in Isaiah:

> These have *chosen* their own ways,
>     and their soul *delights in* their abominations;
> I also will choose harsh treatment for them
>     and bring their fears upon them,
> because when I called, no one answered,
>     when I spoke, they did not listen;
> but they did what was evil in my eyes
>     and *chose* that in which I did not delight. (Isa. 66:3–4)

Similarly, we read, "God made man upright, but they have sought out many schemes" (Eccl. 7:29). *The blame for evil is always on the responsible creature*, whether man or demon, who does it, and *the creature who does evil is always worthy of punishment.* Scripture consistently affirms that God is righteous and just to punish us for our sins. And if we object that he should not find fault with us because we cannot resist his will, then we must ponder the apostle Paul's response to that question: "You will say to me then, 'Why does he still find fault? For who can resist his will?' But who are you, O man, to answer back to God? Will what is molded say to its molder, 'Why have you made me like this?'" (Rom. 9:19–20). Whenever we do evil, we know that we *willingly* choose to do it, and we realize that we are rightly to be blamed for it.

**d. Evil Is Real, Not an Illusion, and We Should Never Do Evil, for It Will Always Harm Us and Others.** Scripture consistently teaches that we never have a right to do evil and that we should persistently oppose it in ourselves and in the world. We are to pray, "Deliver us from evil" (Matt. 6:13), and if we see anyone wandering from the truth and doing wrong, we should attempt to bring him back. Scripture says, "If anyone among you wanders from the truth and someone brings him back, let him know that whoever brings back a sinner from his wandering will save his soul from death and will cover a multitude of sins" (James 5:19–20). We should never even *will* evil to be done, for entertaining sinful desires in our minds is to allow them to "wage war" against our souls (1 Peter 2:11) and thereby to do us spiritual harm. If we are ever tempted to say, "Why not do evil that good may come?" as some people were slanderously charging Paul with teaching, we should remember what Paul says about people who teach false doctrine: "Their condemnation is just" (Rom. 3:8).

In thinking about God using evil to fulfill his purposes, we should remember that there are things that are *right* for God to do but *wrong* for us to do: He requires others to worship him, and he accepts worship from them. He seeks glory for himself. He will execute final judgment on wrongdoers. He also uses evil to bring about good purposes, but he does not allow us to do so. Calvin quotes a statement of Augustine with approval: "There is a great difference between what is fitting for man to will and what is fitting for God.... For through the bad wills of evil men God fulfills what he righteously wills."[14] Herman Bavinck uses the analogy of a parent who will himself use a very sharp knife but will not allow his child to use it; likewise, God himself uses evil to bring about good purposes but never allows his children to do so. Though we should imitate God's moral character in many ways (cf. Eph. 5:1), this is one way we are not to imitate him.

**e. We Confess That We Do Not Understand How God Can Ordain That We Carry Out Evil Deeds and Yet Hold Us Accountable for Them and Not be Blamed Himself.** We can affirm that all of these things are true, because Scripture teaches them. But Scripture does *not* tell us exactly *how* God brings this situation about or how it can be that God holds us accountable for what he ordains to come to pass. Here Scripture is silent, and we have to agree with Berkhof that ultimately "the problem of God's relation to sin remains a mystery."[15]

## 9. Are We Free? Do We Have Free Will?

If God exercises providential control over all events, are we in any sense free? The answer depends on what is meant by the word *free*. In some senses of the word *free*, everyone agrees that we are free in our will and in our choices. Even prominent theologians in the Reformed or Calvinistic tradition concur. Both Louis Berkhof in his *Systematic Theology* (103, 173) and John Calvin in his *Institutes of the Christian Religion*[16] are willing to speak *in some sense* of the "free" acts and choices of man. However, Calvin explains that the term is so subject to misunderstanding that he himself tries to avoid using it. This is because "free will is not sufficient to enable man to do good works, unless he be helped by grace."[17] Therefore, Calvin concludes,

> Man will then be spoken of as having this sort of free decision, not because he has free choice equally of good and evil, but because he acts wickedly by will, not by compulsion. Well put, indeed, but what purpose is served by labeling with a proud name such a slight thing?

---

14. Calvin, *Institutes*, 1:234 (1.18.3).

15. Berkhof, *Systematic Theology* (Grand Rapids: Eerdmans, 1941), 175.

16. *Institutes*, 1:296 (2.3.5), quoting St. Bernard with approval: "Among all living beings man alone is free.... For what is voluntary is also free." Later in the same passage he quotes St. Bernard with approval again, where he admits that the will is in bondage to sin and therefore sins of necessity, but then says that "this necessity is as it were voluntary.... Thus the soul ... is at the same time enslaved and free: enslaved because of necessity; free because of will." A little later Calvin himself says

that "man, while he sins of necessity, yet sins no less voluntarily" (1:309 [2.4.1]). Calvin clearly says that Adam, before there was sin in the world, "by free will had the power, if he so willed, to attain eternal life.... Adam could have stood if he wished, seeing that he fell solely by his own will.... His choice of good and evil was free" (1:195 [1.15.8]). So Calvin can use the term *free will* if it means "voluntary, willing," and he can use it of Adam before the fall. Yet he carefully avoids applying the term *free will* to sinful human beings if by it people mean "able to do good in one's own strength" (see text above).

17. *Institutes*, 1:262 (2.2.6).

Calvin continues by explaining how this term is easily misunderstood:

> But how few men are there, I ask, who when they hear free will attributed to man do not immediately conceive him to be master of both his own mind and will, able of his own power to turn himself toward either good or evil. . . . If anyone, then, can use this word without understanding it in a bad sense, I shall not trouble him on this account. . . . I'd prefer not to use it myself, and I should like others, if they seek my advice, to avoid it.[18]

Thus, when we ask whether we have "free will," it is important to be clear as to what is meant by the phrase. Scripture nowhere says that we are "free" in the sense of being outside of God's control[19] or of being able to make decisions that are not caused by anything. (This is the sense in which many people seem to assume we must be free; see discussion below.) Nor does it say we are "free" in the sense of being able to do right on our own apart from God's power.

But we are nonetheless free in the greatest sense that any creature of God could be free—we make *willing* choices, choices that have *real effects*.[20] We are aware of no restraints on our will from God when we make decisions.[21] We must insist that we have the power of *willing* choice; otherwise we will fall into the error of fatalism or determinism and thus conclude that our choices do not matter or that we cannot really make willing choices. On the other hand, the kind of freedom that is demanded by those who deny God's providential control of all things, a freedom to be outside of God's sustaining and controlling activity, would be impossible if Jesus Christ is indeed "continually carrying along all things by his word of power" (Heb. 1:3, author's translation). If this is true, then to be outside of that providential control would simply be not to exist! An absolute "freedom," totally free of God's control, is simply not possible in a world providentially sustained and directed by God.

In academic discussions of human freedom, other terms than the ones I have used in this chapter are often used, and I should mention them. In particular, Bruce Ware has given a brief explanation of two different labels that are commonly used for two different meanings that people have in mind when they speak of "free will." First,

---

18. Ibid., 1:264, 266 (2.2.7–8).

19. In fact, our ability to make willing choices at all is simply a created reflection of God's will and his ability to make willing choices. However, if we were to be *totally* free in our choices, we would be equal to God in our will, and that is something we may never expect either in this life or in the one to come.

20. Arminian theologians dissent from this understanding of free will and argue for a freedom that means our decisions are not caused by anything outside ourselves (see discussion of Jack

Cottrell's objection that freedom must mean more than willing choices on pp. 451–55, below).

21. John Feinberg says, "If the act is according to the agent's *desires*, then even though the act is causally determined, it is free and the agent is morally responsible" ("God Ordains All Things," in *Predestination and Free Will: Four Views of Divine Sovereignty and Human Freedom*, ed. David Basinger and Randall Basinger [Downers Grove, IL: InterVarsity Press, 1986], 37).

1. *Libertarian free will* is "the ability, all things being just what they are, to choose differently."[22]

In this case, the "all things" means that, even taking into account all of a person's surrounding circumstances, and all of God's providential guidance and influence, a person still has the ability to choose either choice A or choice B. Our choices are not determined by God. In contrast to libertarian free will, Ware explains a second type of freedom:

2. *Freedom of inclination* means that "we are free when we choose according to our strongest inclination or deepest desire. In short, we are free when we do what we most want to do."[23]

This understanding of freedom seems to me more consistent with the teachings of Scripture, including many of the verses already mentioned in this chapter. If we have a freedom of inclination, that does not necessarily rule out God's providential direction and his influence in our hearts and minds, and it does not rule out the idea that our choices may ultimately be determined by God in ways invisible to us. It simply says that we are "free" when we choose to do what we most want to do. In this chapter, I have frequently used the expressions "voluntary choices" or "willing choices" to speak of this kind of "freedom of inclination."

## C. GOVERNMENT
## 1. Scriptural Evidence

We have discussed the first two aspects of providence: (1) preservation and (2) concurrence. This third aspect of God's providence indicates that *God has a purpose in all that he does in the world and he providentially governs or directs all things in order that they accomplish his purposes.* We read in the Psalms, "His kingdom rules over all" (Ps. 103:19). Moreover, "he does according to his will among the host of heaven and among the inhabitants of the earth; and none can stay his hand or say to him, 'What have you done?'" (Dan. 4:35). Paul affirms that "from him and through him and to him are all things" (Rom. 11:36) and that "God has put all things in subjection under his feet" (1 Cor. 15:27). God is the one who "works *all things* according to the counsel of his will" (Eph. 1:11), so that ultimately "at the name of Jesus" every knee will bow "in heaven and on earth and under the earth, and every tongue confess that Jesus Christ is Lord, to the glory of God the Father" (Phil. 2:10–11). It is because Paul knows that God is sovereign over all and works his purposes in every event that happens that Paul can declare that "we know that for those who love God all things work together for good, for those who are called according to his purpose" (Rom. 8:28).

---

22. Bruce Ware, *God's Greater Glory* (Wheaton, IL: Crossway, 2004), 112.

23. Ibid., 114. This "freedom of inclination" is also called "compatibilist freedom."

## 2. Distinctions Concerning the Will of God

Though *in God* his will is unified and not divided or contradictory, we cannot begin to understand the depths of God's will, and only in a small part is it revealed to us. For this reason, as we saw in chapter 13,[24] two aspects of God's will appear to us. On the one hand, there is God's *moral will* (sometimes called his "revealed" will). This includes the moral standards of Scripture, such as the Ten Commandments and the moral commands of the New Testament. God's moral commands are given as descriptions of how *we* should conduct ourselves if we would act rightly before him. On the other hand, another aspect of God's will is his *providential government* of all things (sometimes called his "secret will"). This includes all the events of history that God has ordained to come about, for example, the fact that Christ would be crucified by "lawless men" (Acts 2:23). It also includes all the other evil acts that were mentioned in the preceding section.

Some have objected to this distinction between two aspects of the will of God, arguing that it means there is a "self-contradiction" in God.[25] However, even in the realm of human experience, we know that we can will and carry out something painful that we do not desire (such as punishing a disobedient child or getting an inoculation that temporarily makes us ill) in order to bring about a long-term result that we desire more than the avoidance of short-term pain (to bring about the obedience of the child, for example, or to prevent us from getting a more serious illness). And God is infinitely greater and wiser than we are. Certainly it is possible for him to will that his creatures do something that in the short term displeases him in order that in the long term he would receive the greater glory. To say that this is a "self-contradiction" in God is to fail to understand the distinctions that have been made so that this explanation is not contradictory.[26]

## D. THE DECREES OF GOD

The decrees of God are *the eternal plans of God whereby, before the creation of the world, he determined to bring about everything that happens*. This doctrine is similar to the doctrine of providence, but here we are thinking about God's decisions *before the world was created* rather than his providential actions in time. His providential actions are the outworking of the eternal decrees that he made long ago. (See chapter 2, pp. 31–32, for *decree* used in a somewhat different sense.)

David confesses, "In your book were written, every one of them, the days that were formed for me, when as yet there was none of them" (Ps. 139:16; cf. Job 14:5: the days, months, and bounds of man are determined by God). There was also a "definite *plan*

---

24. See pp. 254–57 for a further discussion of God's secret and revealed will.

25. This is the objection of Marshall, "Predestination in the New Testament," 173.

26. John Calvin says of those who object to two senses of the will of God, "Let them tell me, I pray, whether he exercises his judgments willingly or unwillingly.... When we do

not grasp how God wills to take place what he forbids to be done, let us recall our mental incapacity." He also quotes with approval the statement of Augustine: "There is a great difference between what is fitting for man to will and what is fitting for God ... for through the bad wills of evil men God fulfills what he righteously wills" (*Institutes*, 1:233–34 [1.18.3]).

and foreknowledge of God" (Acts 2:23) by which Jesus was put to death, and the actions of those who condemned and crucified him were "predestined" (Acts 4:28) by God. Our salvation was determined long ago because God "chose us in him (Christ) *before the foundation of the world*, that we should be holy and blameless before him" (Eph. 1:4). Our good works as believers are those "which God *prepared beforehand*, that we should walk in them" (Eph. 2:10; cf. Jude 4).

These examples take in many diverse aspects of human activity. It seems appropriate to conclude from these examples that all that God does he has planned before the creation of the world—in fact, these things have been an *eternal plan* with him. The benefit of an emphasis on God's decrees is that it helps us to realize that God does not make up plans suddenly as he goes along. He knows the end from the beginning, and he will accomplish all his good purposes. This should greatly increase our trust in him, especially in difficult circumstances.

## E. THE IMPORTANCE OF OUR HUMAN ACTIONS

We may sometimes forget that God works *through human actions* in his providential management of the world. If we do, then we begin to think that our actions and our choices do not make much difference or do not have much effect on the course of events. To guard against any misunderstanding of God's providence, we make the following points of emphasis.

### 1. We Are Still Responsible for Our Actions

God has made us *responsible* for our actions, which have *real and eternally significant results*. In all his providential acts God will preserve these characteristics of responsibility and significance.

Some analogies from the natural world might help us understand this. God has created a rock with the characteristic of being *hard*, and so it is. God has created water with the characteristic of being *wet*, and so it is. God has created plants and animals with the characteristic of being *alive*, and so they are. Similarly, God has created us with the characteristic of being *responsible for our actions*, and so we are! If we do right and obey God, he will reward us, and things will go well with us both in this age and in eternity. If we do wrong and disobey God, he will discipline and perhaps punish us, and things will go ill with us. The realization of these facts will help us have pastoral wisdom in talking to others and in encouraging them to avoid laziness and disobedience.

The fact that we are responsible for our actions means that we should never begin to think, "God made me do evil, and therefore I am not responsible for it." Significantly, Adam began to make excuses for the very first sin in terms that sounded suspiciously like this: "The woman whom you gave to be with me, she gave me fruit of the tree, and I ate" (Gen. 3:12). Unlike Adam, Scripture *never* blames God for sin. If we ever begin to *think* that God is to blame for sin, we have thought *wrongly* about God's providence, for it is always the creature, not God, who is to be blamed. Now we may object that it is not right for God to hold us responsible if he has in fact ordained all things that happen, but Paul corrects us: "You will say to me then, 'Why does he still find fault? For who can resist his will?' But who are you, O man, to answer back to God?" (Rom. 9:19–20). We must realize and settle in our hearts that it is *right* for God to rebuke and discipline and punish evil. And when we are responsible to do so, it is right for us to rebuke and discipline evil in our families, the church, and even, in some ways, the society around us. We should never say about an evil event, "God willed it and therefore it is good," because we must recognize that some things God's will of decree has planned are not in themselves good, so they should not receive our approval, just as they do not receive God's approval.

## 2. Our Actions Have Real Results and Do Change the Course of Events

In the ordinary working of the world, if I neglect to take care of my health and have poor eating habits, or if I abuse my body through alcohol or tobacco, I am likely to die sooner. God has ordained that our *actions* have effects. God has ordained that *events* will come about *by our causing them*. Of course, we do not know what God has planned even for the rest of this day, to say nothing of next week or next year. But we *do* know that if we trust God and obey him, we will discover that he has planned *good things* to come about through that obedience! We cannot simply disregard others whom we meet, for God brings many people across our paths and gives *us* the responsibility to act toward them in eternally significant ways—whether for good or ill.

Calvin wisely notes that to encourage us to use ordinary caution in life and to plan ahead, "God is pleased to hide all future events from us, in order that we should resist them as doubtful, and not cease to oppose them with ready remedies, until they are either overcome or pass beyond all care. . . . God's providence does not always meet us in its naked form, but God in a sense clothes it with the means employed."[27]

By contrast, if we anticipate that some dangers or evil events may come in the future, and if we do not use reasonable means to avoid them, then we may in fact discover that our lack of action was the means that God used to allow them to come about!

## 3. Prayer Is One Specific Kind of Action That Has Definite Results and That Does Change the Course of Events

God has also ordained that prayer is a very significant means of bringing about results in the world.[28] When we earnestly intercede for a specific person or situation, we will often find that God had ordained that our prayer would be a *means* he would use to bring about the changes in the world. Scripture reminds us of this when it tells

---

27. Calvin, *Institutes*, 1:216 (1.17.4).     28. See chapter 18 for a more extensive discussion of prayer.

us, "You do not have, because you do not ask" (James 4:2). Jesus says, "Until now you have asked nothing in my name. Ask, and you will receive, that your joy may be full" (John 16:24).

## 4. In Conclusion, We Must Act!

The doctrine of providence in no way encourages us to sit back in idleness to await the outcome of certain events. Of course, God may impress on us the need to wait on him before we act and to trust in him rather than in our own abilities—that is certainly not wrong. But simply to say that we are trusting in God *instead of* acting responsibly is sheer laziness and is a distortion of the doctrine of providence.

In practical terms, if one of my sons has school work that must be done the next day, I am right to make him complete that work before he can go out to play. I realize that his grade is in God's hands and that God has long ago determined what it would be, but I do not know what it will be, and neither does my son. What I do know is that if my son studies and does his schoolwork faithfully, he will receive a good grade. If he doesn't, he will not. So Calvin can say,

> Now it is very clear what our duty is: Thus, if the Lord has committed to us the protection of our life, our duty is to protect it; if he offers helps to us, to use them; if he forewarns us of dangers, not to plunge headlong; if he makes remedies available, not to neglect them. But no danger will hurt us, say they, unless it is fatal, and in this case it is beyond remedies. But what if the dangers are not fatal, because the Lord has provided you with remedies for repulsing and overcoming them?[29]

One good example of vigorous activity combined with trust in God is found in 2 Samuel 10:12, where Joab says, "Be of good courage, and let us be courageous for our people, and for the cities of our God" (2 Sam. 10:12), but then adds immediately in the same sentence, "*and may the Lord do what seems good to him.*" Joab will both fight and trust God to do what he thinks to be good.

Similar examples are found in the New Testament. When Paul was in Corinth, in order to keep him from being discouraged about the opposition he had received from the Jews, the Lord appeared to him one night in a vision and said to him, "Do not be afraid, but go on speaking and do not be silent, for I am with you, and no one will attack you to harm you, for *I have many in this city who are my people*" (Acts 18:9–10). If Paul had been a fatalist with an improper understanding of God's providence, he would have listened to God's words, "I have many people in this city," concluded that God had determined to save many of the Corinthians, and decided that, therefore, it did

---

29. Calvin, *Institutes*, 1:216 (1.17.4).

not matter whether Paul stayed: God had already chosen many people to be saved. Paul would have thought that he may as well pack his bags and leave! But Paul does not make that mistake. He rather concludes that if God has chosen many people, then it will probably be through the *means* of Paul's preaching the gospel that those many people would be saved. Therefore Paul makes a wise decision: "*He stayed a year and six months, teaching the word of God among them*" (Acts 18:11).

Paul put this kind of responsible action in the light of God's providence into a single sentence in 2 Timothy 2:10, where he said, "I endure everything *for the sake of the elect, that they also may obtain the salvation that is in Christ Jesus with eternal glory.*" He did not argue from the fact that God had chosen some to be saved that nothing had to be done; rather, he concluded that *much* had to be done in order that God's purposes might come about by the *means* that God had also established. Indeed, Paul was willing to endure "everything," including all kinds of hardship and suffering, that God's eternal plans might come about. A hearty belief in God's providence is not a discouragement but a spur to action.

A related example is found in the story of Paul's journey to Rome. God had clearly revealed to Paul that no one on the ship would die from the long storm they had endured. Indeed, Paul stood before the passengers and crew and told them to take heart,

> for there will be no loss of life among you, but only of the ship. For this very night there stood before me an angel of the God to whom I belong and whom I worship, and he said, "Do not be afraid, Paul; you must stand before Caesar. And behold, God has granted you all those who sail with you." So take heart, men, for I have faith in God that it will be exactly as I have been told. But we must run aground on some island. (Acts 27:22–26)

But shortly after Paul had said this, he noticed that the sailors on board the ship were secretly trying to lower a lifeboat into the sea, "seeking to escape from the ship" (Acts 27:30). They were planning to leave the others helpless with no one who knew how to sail the ship. When Paul saw this, he did not adopt an erroneous, fatalistic attitude, thinking that God would miraculously get the ship to shore. Rather, he immediately went to the centurion who was in charge of the sailors and "Paul said to the centurion and the soldiers, 'Unless these men stay in the ship, you cannot be saved'" (Acts 27:31). Wisely, Paul knew that God's providential oversight and even his clear prediction of what would happen still involved the use of ordinary human *means* to bring it about. He was even so bold to say that those means were *necessary*: "Unless these men stay in the ship, *you cannot be saved*" (Acts 27:31). We would do well to imitate his example, combining complete trust in God's providence with a realization that the use of ordinary means is necessary for things to come out the way God has planned them to come out.

## 5. What If We Cannot Understand This Doctrine Fully?

Every believer who meditates on God's providence will sooner or later come to a point where he or she will have to say, "I cannot understand this doctrine fully." In some ways that must be said about every doctrine since our understanding is finite and God is infinite (see chapter 1, p. 19; cf. pp. 197–208). But particularly is this so with the doctrine of providence: we should believe it because Scripture teaches it even when we do not understand fully how it fits in with other teachings of Scripture. Calvin has some wise advice:

> Let those for whom this seems harsh consider for a little while how bearable their squeamishness is in refusing a thing attested by clear Scriptural proofs because it exceeds their mental capacity, and find fault that things are put forth publicly, which if God had not judged useful for men to know, he would never have bidden his prophets and apostles to teach. For our wisdom ought to be nothing else than to embrace with humble teachableness, and at least without finding fault, whatever is taught in sacred Scripture.[30]

## F. Another Evangelical View: The Arminian Position

There is a major alternative position held by many evangelicals, which for convenience we shall call the "Arminian" view.[31] Among denominations in contemporary evangelicalism, Methodists and Nazarenes tend to be thoroughly Arminian, whereas Presbyterians and the Christian Reformed tend to be thoroughly Reformed (at least by denominational statement of faith). Both views are found among Baptists, Episcopalians (though the Thirty-Nine Articles have a clearly Reformed emphasis), Dispensationalists, Evangelical Free Churches, Lutherans (though Martin Luther was in the Reformed camp on this issue), the Churches of Christ, and most charismatic and Pentecostal groups (though Pentecostal denominations such as the Assemblies of God have been predominantly Arminian).

Those who hold an Arminian position maintain that in order to preserve the *real human freedom* and *real human choices* that are necessary for genuine human personhood, God cannot cause or plan our voluntary choices. Therefore they conclude that God's providential involvement in or control of history must *not* include *every specific*

---

30. Calvin, *Institutes*, 1:237 (1.18.4).

31. The term *Arminianism* was used in the title of a responsible series of essays representing this position; see Clark H. Pinnock, ed., *The Grace of God, The Will of Man: A Case for Arminianism* (Grand Rapids: Zondervan, 1989). In the following section I quote extensively from this book and from an earlier book edited by Pinnock, *Grace Unlimited*. These two books are excellent defenses of the Arminian position.

Jacob Arminius (1560–1609) was a Dutch theologian who differed with the predominant Calvinism of his day. Though he is not personally quoted or referred to very often by Arminians today, his name has become attached to a range of positions that have in common the fact that they differ from the Calvinist position on the question of man's free will, both with respect to God's providence in general (the subject of this chapter) and with respect to predestination or election in specific (the subject of chapter 32).

The term *Arminian* should be distinguished from the term *Armenian*, which refers to people who live in or descend from inhabitants of the ancient country of Armenia in western Asia.

*detail* of every event that happens but that God instead simply *responds* to human choices and actions as they come about and does so in such a way that his purposes are ultimately accomplished in the world.

Those who hold this position argue that God's purposes in the world are more general and could be accomplished through many different kinds of specific events. So God's purpose or plan for the world "is not a blueprint encompassing all future contingencies" but "a dynamic program for the world, the outworking of which depends in part on man."[32] Cottrell says, "God does not have a specific, unconditional purpose for each discrete particle, object, person, and event within the creation."[33] Arminians believe that God achieves his overall goal by responding to and utilizing the free choices of human beings, whatever they may be.[34] Pinnock says that "predestination does not apply to every individual activity, but is rather the comprehensive purpose of God which is *the structural context* in which history moves."[35]

Moreover, advocates of the Arminian position maintain that God's will cannot include evil. Pinnock says, "The fall of man is an eloquent refutation to the theory that God's will is always done."[36] He states that it "is not the case" that God's will "is also accomplished in the lostness of the lost."[37] And I. Howard Marshall quite clearly affirms, "It is not true that everything that happens is what God desires."[38] These statements make it clear that the differences between the Reformed and Arminian positions are not merely differences in terminology: there is a real disagreement in substance. Several arguments are advanced in defense of the Arminian position. I have attempted to summarize them in the four major points that follow.

## 1. The Verses Cited as Examples of God's Providential Control Are Exceptions and Do Not Describe the Way That God Ordinarily Works in Human Activity

In surveying the Old Testament passages referring to God's providential involvement in the world, David J. A. Clines says that God's predictions and statements of his purposes refer to limited or specific events:

32. Clark Pinnock, "Responsible Freedom in the Flow of Biblical History," in *Grace Unlimited*, 18.

33. Jack Cottrell, "The Nature of the Divine Sovereignty," in Pinnock, *The Grace of God, the Will of Man*, 107. Cottrell's essay is, in my view, the most comprehensive and persuasive of the many excellent Arminian essays in this book—the book as a whole is responsibly done and is probably the best modern representation of Arminian thinking. Cottrell does not deny divine omniscience regarding future events as do the essays by Clark Pinnock and Richard Rice in the same volume, and this places him closer to the intuitive Arminianism that seems right to many evangelical laypersons today.

34. I. Howard Marshall claims this at several points in

"Predestination in the New Testament," in Pinnock, *Grace Unlimited*, 127–43. Marshall uses the analogy of a jazz band where individual players can improvise freely but the overall goal and unity of the piece are preserved nonetheless (133). Thus, "the Bible has the picture of a God deciding fresh measures in history and interacting with the wills of men alongside the picture of a God planning things in eternity past, and both pictures are equally valid" (141).

35. Pinnock, "Responsible Freedom," 102.

36. Ibid., 102.

37. Ibid., 106.

38. Marshall, "Predestination in the New Testament," 139.

Almost all of the specific references to God's plans have in view a particular event or a limited series of events, for example, "his purposes against the land of the Chaldeans" (Jer. 50:45). Furthermore, it is not a matter of a *single* divine plan; various passages speak of various intentions, and some references are in fact to God's plans in the plural. . . . [The passages are] an assertion that within history God is working his purposes out.[39]

Jack Cottrell agrees that in some cases God intervenes in the world in an uncommon way, using "subtle manipulation of such [natural] laws and of mental states." But he calls these unusual events "special providence," and says, "It is natural that the Old Testament teems with accounts of special providence. But we have no reason to assume that God was working in Australia and South America in such ways at the same time."[40]

## 2. The Calvinist View Wrongly Makes God Responsible for Sin

Those who hold an Arminian position ask, "How can God be holy if he decrees that we sin?" They affirm that God is not the "author of sin," that "God cannot be tempted with evil, and he himself tempts no one" (James 1:13), that "God is light and in him is no darkness at all" (1 John 1:5), and that "the LORD is upright . . . and there is no unrighteousness in him" (Ps. 92:15).

The view of God's providence advocated above, they would say, makes us into puppets or robots who cannot do anything other than what God causes us to do. But this brings moral reproach on God, for Marshall says, "I am responsible for what my agent does."[41] Pinnock affirms that "it is simply blasphemous to maintain, as this theory does, that man's rebellion against God is *in any sense* the product of God's sovereign will or primary causation."[42]

## 3. Choices Caused by God Cannot Be Real Choices

When the Calvinist claims that God causes us to choose things voluntarily, those who hold an Arminian position would respond that any choices that are ultimately caused by God cannot be real choices and that if God really causes us to make the choices we make, then we are not real persons. Cottrell says that the Calvinist view of God as the primary cause and men as secondary causes really breaks down so there is only one cause, God. If a man uses a lever to move a rock, he argues, "the lever is not a true second cause but is only an instrument of the real cause of the movement. . . . In my

---

39. Clines, "Predestination in the Old Testament," 122; see also 116–17. Similarly, James D. Strauss, "God's Promise and Universal History," in Pinnock, *Grace Unlimited*, 196, says that the example of Jacob and Esau that Paul mentions in Rom. 9:9–13 refers to God's corporate plans for the descendants of Jacob and Esau and should not be taken as an illustration of how God works in people's lives or hearts generally.

40. Cottrell, "The Nature of the Divine Sovereignty," 112–13.
41. Marshall, "Predestination," 136.
42. Pinnock, "Responsible Freedom," 102.

judgment the concept of cause has no real significance when used in this sense. In such a system man contributes only what has been predetermined."[43]

Pinnock writes,

> Personal fellowship of the kind envisioned in the Gospel only exists where consummated in a free decision. If we wish to understand God's grace as personal address to his creatures, we must comprehend it in dynamic, non-manipulative, non-coercive terms, as the Bible does.[44]

He also says,

> If the world were a completely determined structure on which no decision of man's would have any effect, that basic intuition of man's that he is an *actor* and a *free agent* would be nonsensical: There would then be no point to his making plans or exerting efforts intended to transform the world. . . . Human freedom is the precondition of moral and intellectual responsibility.[45]

Why then, in the Arminian view, did the fall and sin come about? Pinnock answers that "they occur because God refuses to mechanize man or to force his will upon him."[46] And Marshall says, with respect to the "possibility of my predetermining a course of action involving myself and another subject," that "on the level of free agents it is impossible."[47] He objects that the analogy of God and world as being like an author and a play is unhelpful because if we ask whether the characters are indeed free, "this is an unreal question."[48]

However, it should be noted that Arminian theologians are certainly willing to allow some kinds of influence by God on human beings. Marshall says, "Prayer also influences men. . . . The wills of men can thus be affected by prayer or else we would not pray for them. *To believe in prayer is thus to believe in some kind of limitation of human freedom, and in some kind of incomprehensible influence upon the wills of men.*"[49]

To drive home their point about the essential freedom of the human will, advocates of an Arminian position draw attention to the frequency of the free offer of the gospel in the New Testament. They would say that these invitations to people to repent and come to Christ for salvation, if *bona fide*, must imply the *ability* to respond to them. Thus, all people without exception have the ability to respond, not just those who have been sovereignly given that ability by God in a special way.

---

43. Cottrell, "The Nature of the Divine Sovereignty," 104–5.
44. Pinnock, *Grace Unlimited*, 15.
45. Pinnock, "Responsible Freedom," 95.
46. Ibid., 108.
47. Marshall, "Predestination," 132. Similarly, he says,

"When we try to think of a person foreordaining the course of a relationship between himself and another person . . . *this concept is logically self-contradictory*" (135).
48. Ibid., 133.
49. Ibid., 139–40 (emphasis in original text).

## 4. The Arminian View Encourages Responsible Christian Living, While the Calvinistic View Encourages a Dangerous Fatalism

Christians who hold an Arminian position argue that the Calvinist view, when thoroughly understood, destroys motives for responsible Christian behavior. Randall Basinger says that the Calvinist view "establishes that what is ought to be and rules out the consideration that things could and/or should have been different."[50] Basinger continues by saying that Christians

> who evoke and act on the basis of God's sovereignty are guilty of an arbitrary, unlivable, and dangerous fatalism. . . . In contrast to this, the Arminian believes that what actually occurs in the world is, to an extent, consequent on the human will; God's exhaustive control over the world is denied. This means that things can occur that God does not will or want; things not only *can* be different but often *should* be different. And from all this follows our responsibility to work with God to bring about a better world.[51]

However, Basinger goes on to make a further point: Calvinists, in practice, often avoid such fatalism and "live and talk like Arminians."[52] Thus, on the one hand, Basinger's challenge is a warning against the practical extremes to which he claims Calvinism should logically drive Christians. On the other hand, his objection claims that when Calvinists live the way they know they must live, in responsible obedience to God, they are either inconsistent with their view of divine sovereignty or else not allowing their view of God's sovereign control to affect their daily lives.

## G. Response to the Arminian Position

Many within the evangelical world will find these four Arminian arguments convincing. They will feel that these arguments represent what they intuitively know about themselves, their own actions, and the way the world functions, and that these arguments best account for the repeated emphasis in Scripture on our responsibility and the real consequences of our choices. However, there are some answers that can be given to the Arminian position.

## 1. Are These Scripture Passages Unusual Examples, or Do They Describe the Way God Works Ordinarily?

In response to the objection that the examples of God's providential control only refer to limited or specific events, it may be said first that the examples are so numerous (see above, pp. 422–33) that they seem to be designed to describe to us the ways in which

---

50. Randall G. Basinger, "Exhaustive Divine Sovereignty: A Practical Critique," in Pinnock, *The Grace of God, the Will of Man*, 94.

51. Ibid., 196.
52. Ibid., 204.

God works all the time. God does not just cause *some* grass to grow; he causes all grass to grow. He does not just send *some* rain; he sends all the rain. He does not just keep *some* sparrows from falling to the ground without his will; he keeps all sparrows from falling to the ground without his will. He does not just know every word on David's tongue before he speaks it; he knows the words on all our tongues before we speak them. He has not just chosen Paul and the Christians in the Ephesian churches to be holy and blameless before him; he has chosen all Christians to be holy and blameless before him. This is why Cottrell's claim, that God was working differently in Australia and South America than in the Old Testament,[53] is so unconvincing: Scripture is given to tell us the ways of God, and when we have dozens of examples throughout Old and New Testaments where there is such clear teaching on this, it is appropriate for us to conclude that this is the way in which God *always* works with human beings. By contrast, there seems to be nothing in Scripture that would indicate that some things are outside God's providential control, or that these ways of God's acting are unusual or unrepresentative of the ways in which he acts generally.

Moreover, many of the verses that speak of God's providence are very general: Christ "continually carries along *all things* by his word of power" (Heb. 1:3, author's translation), and "in him all things hold together" (Col. 1:17). "In him we live and move and have our being" (Acts 17:28). He "works *all things* according to the counsel of his will" (Eph. 1:11).[54] He provides our food (Matt. 6:11), supplies all our needs (Phil. 4:19), directs our steps (Prov. 20:24), and works in us to will and to do his good pleasure (Phil. 2:13). Such Scripture passages have in view more than exceptional examples of an unusual intervention by God in the affairs of human beings; they describe the way God always works in the world.

## 2. Does the Calvinistic Doctrine of God's Providence Make God Responsible for Sin?

Against the Calvinistic view of God's providence (which allows that he decrees to permit sin and evil) Arminians would say that God is not responsible for sin and evil

---

53. Cottrell, "The Nature of the Divine Sovereignty," 113.

54. Cottrell, "The Nature of the Divine Sovereignty," argues that the context of Eph. 1:11 shows that it does not include all things in the universe but is restricted to a specific focus: "This focus is 'the mystery of his will' (1:9), which is the uniting of Jews and Gentiles together into one body, the church (3:6)." Thus, he says, the verse only "refers to 'all things' required for uniting Jews and Gentiles under one Head in one body" (116).

But this argument is not convincing. Cottrell must skip over to Eph. 3:6 to get the contextual restriction he seeks for the "all things" in 1:11. In doing this he ignores the clearly cosmic scope of the context as defined in the immediately preceding verse, a verse that is in the same sentence in the Greek text: "as a plan for the fullness of time, to unite *all things* [*ta panta*]

in him, *things in heaven and things on earth*" (Eph. 1:10). All things in heaven and on earth includes the whole universe. Eph. 1:21–22 further explains that God has exalted Christ "far above all rule and authority and power and dominion . . . And he put *all things* under his feet and gave him as head over *all things* to the church." Once again the scope is universal. The "mystery" of God's will mentioned in Eph. 1:9 is not limited to the uniting of Jews and Gentiles (as in 3:6) but is defined by 1:10 as a plan to unite all things in Christ. The term *mystery* (Gk. *mystērion*) in Paul means something previously hidden but now made known by revelation, and it can refer to different things in different contexts: in Eph. 5:32 it refers to marriage as a symbol of the union between Christ and the church; in 1 Cor. 15:51 it refers to the resurrection body; etc.

*because he did not ordain them or cause them in any way.* This is indeed *one way* of absolving God from responsibility and blame for sin, but is it the biblical way?

The problem is whether the Arminian position can really account for many texts that clearly say that God ordains that some people sin or do evil (see section B.7, pp. 428–33). The death of Christ is the prime example of this, but there are many others in Scripture (Joseph's brothers, Pharaoh, the Egyptians, the Canaanites, Eli's sons, David's census, and the Babylonians, to mention a few). The response could be made that these were unusual events, exceptions to God's ordinary way of acting. But it does not solve the problem, for, on the Arminian view, how can God be holy if he ordains even one sinful act?

The Calvinist position seems preferable: God himself never sins but always brings about his will *through secondary causes*—that is, through personal moral agents who voluntarily, willingly do what God has ordained. These personal moral agents (both human beings and evil angels) are to blame for the evil they do. While the Arminian position objects that, on a human level, people are also responsible for *what they cause others to do*, we can answer that Scripture is not willing to apply such reasoning to God. Rather, Scripture repeatedly gives examples where God in a mysterious way somehow ordains that people do wrong but continually places the blame for that wrong on the individual human who does wrong and never on God himself. The Arminian position seems to have failed to show why God *cannot* work in this way in the world, preserving both his holiness and our individual human responsibility for sin.

### 3. Can Choices Ordained by God Be Real Choices?

In response to the claim that choices ordained by God cannot be real choices, it must be said that this is simply an assumption based once again on human experience and intuition, not on specific texts of Scripture.[55] Yet Scripture does not indicate that we can extrapolate from our human experience when dealing with God's providential control of his creatures, especially human beings. Arminians have simply not answered the question, Where does Scripture say that a choice ordained by God is not a real choice?[56] When we read passages indicating that God works through our will, our power to choose, and our personal volition, on what basis can we say that a choice brought about

---

55. This is the case with Cottrell's analogy of the man who uses a lever to move a rock. He says the lever "is not a true second cause, but only an instrument of the real cause" ("The Nature of the Divine Sovereignty," 104). But here Cottrell makes a common mistake, assuming that analogies from human experience, rather than the testimony of Scripture itself, can determine what is a real cause and what is not. The analogy of a man using a lever to move a rock does not fit, because God is far greater than any man, and we as real persons are far greater than any lever.

56. The lack of scriptural support for this fundamental Arminian idea is evident in Jack Cottrell's discussion of free will. After accurately explaining that Calvinists say we are free only in the sense of making voluntary, willing choices, Cottrell says, "*In my judgment*, however, the mere ability to act in accord with one's desires is not a sufficient criterion of freedom" ("The Nature of the Divine Sovereignty," 103, emphasis mine). He then gives no evidence from Scripture to show why this is his judgment (103–4). I would respond that Cottrell has simply imported into the discussion a nonbiblical *assumption* about the nature of human freedom and then has pronounced Calvinism incapable of meeting his (nonbiblical) criterion.

by God through these means is not a real choice? It seems better to affirm that God *says* that our choices are real and to conclude that therefore they *are real*. Scripture repeatedly affirms that our choices are genuine choices, that they have *real* results, and that those results last for eternity. "Do this, and you will live" (Luke 10:28). "For God so loved the world, that he gave his only Son, that *whoever believes in him* should not perish but have eternal life" (John 3:16).

This causes us to conclude that God has made us in such a way that (1) he ordains all that we do, and (2) we exercise our personal will and make real, voluntary choices. Because we cannot understand this, should we therefore reject it? We cannot understand (in any final sense) how a plant can live, how a bumblebee can fly, or how God can be omnipresent or eternal. Should we therefore reject those facts? Should we not rather simply accept them as true either because we see that plants in fact do live and bumblebees in fact do fly or because Scripture itself teaches that God is omnipresent and eternal?

Calvin several times distinguishes between "necessity" and "compulsion" with regard to our will: unbelievers necessarily sin, but no compulsion forces them to sin against their will.[57] In response to the objection that an act cannot be willing or voluntary if it is a necessary act, Calvin points to both the good deeds of God (who *necessarily* does good) and the evil deeds of the devil (who *necessarily* does evil): "If the fact that he must do good does not hinder God's free will in doing good; if the Devil, who can only do evil, yet sins with his will—who shall say that man therefore sins less willingly because he is subject to the necessity of sinning?"[58]

Who are we to say that choices somehow caused by God *cannot* be real? On what basis can we prove that? God in Scripture tells us that he ordains all that comes to pass. He also tells us that our choices and actions are significant *in his sight*, and that we are responsible *before him* for our actions. We need simply to believe these things and to take comfort in them. After all, *he alone* determines what is significant, what is real, and what is genuine personal responsibility in the universe.

But do our actions have any effect on God? At this point Arminians will object that while Calvinists may *say* that a choice caused by God is a real choice, it is not real in any ultimate sense, because, on a Calvinist view, nothing God does can ever be a response to what we do. Jack Cottrell says,

> Calvinism is still a theology of determinism as long as it declares that nothing God does can be conditioned by man or can be a reaction to something in the world. The idea that a sovereign God must always *act* and never *react* is a point on which almost all Calvinists seem to agree. . . . Reformed theologians agree that the eternal

---

57. See *Institutes*, 1:294–96 (2.3.5).
58. Ibid., 295 (2.3.5).

decree is unconditional or absolute. . . . "Decretal theology" decrees that "God cannot be affected by, nor respond to, anything external to him," says Daane.[59]

But here Cottrell has misunderstood Reformed theology for two reasons. First, he has quoted James Daane, who, though he belongs to the Christian Reformed Church, has written as an opponent, not a defender, of classical Reformed theology, and his statement does not represent a position that most Reformed theologians would endorse. Second, Cottrell has confused God's decrees before creation with God's actions in time. It is true that Calvinists would say that God's eternal decrees were not influenced by any of our actions and cannot be changed by us, since they were made *before creation*.[60] But to conclude from that that Calvinists think God does not react *in time* to anything we do and is not influenced by anything we do is simply false. No Calvinist theologian known to me has ever said that God is not influenced by what we do and does not react to what we do. He is grieved at our sin. He delights in our praise. He answers our prayers. To say that God does not react to our actions is to deny the whole history of the Bible from Genesis to Revelation.

Now a Calvinist would add that God has eternally decreed that he would respond to us as he does. In fact, he has decreed that we would act as we do and how he would respond to our actions. But his responses are still genuine responses, his answers to prayers are still genuine answers to prayer, his delight in our praise is still genuine delight. Cottrell may of course object that a response that God has planned long ago is not a real response, but this is far different from saying that Calvinists believe God does not respond to what we do. Moreover, we return to the same unsupported assumption underlying this objection: on what scriptural basis can Cottrell say that a response God has planned long ago is not a real response?[61]

Here it is helpful for us to realize that there is no other reality in the universe except what God himself has made. Is a thunderstorm caused by God a *real* thunderstorm? Is a king that God establishes on a throne a *real* king? Is a word that God causes me to speak (Ps. 139:4; Prov. 16:1) a *real* word? Of course they are real! There *is* no other reality than that which God brings about! Then is a human choice that God somehow causes to happen a *real* choice? Yes, it is, in the same way that a thunderstorm or a king is real according to their own characteristics and properties. The choice that I make is not a

---

59. Cottrell, "The Nature of the Divine Sovereignty," 102–3. The quotation at the end is from James Daane, *The Freedom of God* (Grand Rapids: Eerdmans, 1973), 160.

60. See above, pp. 440–41, on God's decrees.

61. I am not sure if Cottrell would be able to object that a response planned by God long ago is not a real response because he himself talks about God foreknowing our actions and then planning how he will respond to them. He says, "Even before the creation God foreknew every free-will act. . . . Nothing takes God by surprise. . . . God knew, even before creation, when and how he would have to intervene in his world to accomplish his purposes. . . . God's foreknowledge also enables him to plan his own responses to and uses of human choices even before they are made" ("The Nature of the Divine Sovereignty," 112). But if Cottrell is willing to say that God planned long ago how he would respond to human choices, it is hard to see how he can object to the Calvinist position that God decreed long ago how he would respond when we pray or act.

"forced" or "involuntary" choice—we make choices all the time, and we have absolutely no sense of being forced or compelled to choose one thing rather than another. We have a "freedom of inclination"—that is, we do what we most want to do.

Now some may object that this view makes us mere "puppets" or "robots." But we are not puppets or robots; we are *real persons*. Puppets and robots do not have the power of personal choice or even individual thought. By contrast, we think, decide, and choose. Again the Arminian wrongly takes information from our situation as human beings and then uses that information to place limitations on what God *can* or *cannot* do. All of these analogies from human experience fail to recognize that God is far greater than our limited human abilities. Moreover, we are far more real and complex than any robot or puppet would ever be—we are real persons created by an infinitely powerful and infinitely wise God.

Much of our difficulty in understanding how God can cause us to choose something willingly comes from the finite nature of our creaturely existence. In a hypothetical world where all living things created by God were plants rooted in the ground, we might imagine one plant arguing to another that God *could not* make living creatures who could move about on the earth, for how could they carry their roots with them? And if their roots were not in the ground, how could they receive nourishment? An "Arminian" plant might even argue, "In order for God to create a world with living things, he *had to* create them with roots and with the characteristic of living all their lives in a single place. To say that God *could not* create living things that move about on the earth does not challenge God's omnipotence, for that is simply to say that he cannot do things that logically cannot be done. Therefore, it is impossible that God could create a world where living things also have the capacity of moving about on the earth." The problem with this plant is that it has limited God's power by virtue of its own "plant-like" experience.

On a higher level, we could imagine a creation that had both plants and animals but no human beings. In that creation, we can imagine an argument between a "Calvinist" dog and a "Arminian" dog, where the "Calvinist" dog would argue that it *is* possible for God to create creatures that not only can communicate by barking to one another but also can record their barks in marks on paper and can send them silently to be understood by other creatures many days' journey distant, creatures who have never been seen by the sending creature who first marked his barks down on paper. The "Arminian" dog would reply that God *cannot* do such a thing, because *essential* to the idea of creaturely communication is *hearing* and *seeing* (and usually *smelling*!) the creature from whom one receives the communication. To say that there can be communication without ever hearing or seeing or smelling the other creature is an absurd idea! It is beyond the range of possible occurrences and is logically inconceivable. Therefore, it is impossible to think that God could create a creature with such communicating abilities.

In both cases the "Arminian" plant and the "Arminian" dog are in the wrong because they have incorrectly limited the kind of thing God could create by deriving what was possible for God (in their opinion) from their own finite creaturely existence. But this is very similar to the Arminian theologian who simply asserts (on the basis of his own perception of human experience) that God *cannot* create a creature who makes willing, voluntary, meaningful choices and that those choices are nonetheless ordained by God. Similarly, the Arminian theologian who argues that God *cannot* ordain that evil come about and not yet himself be responsible for evil likewise is limiting God based merely on observation of finite human experience.

## 4. Does a Calvinistic View of Providence Encourage Either a Dangerous Fatalism or a Tendency to "Live Like Arminians"?

The view of providence presented above emphasizes the need for responsible obedience, so it is not correct to say that Calvinism encourages fatalism or a passive attitude toward life that just says that whatever happens is what should happen, and our decisions and actions don't make any difference. Those who accuse Reformed writers of believing this have simply not understood the Reformed doctrine of providence.

But do Calvinists "live like Arminians" anyway? Both Calvinists and Arminians believe that our actions have real results and that they are eternally significant. Both agree that we are responsible for our actions and that we make voluntary, willing choices. Both groups will agree that God answers prayer, that proclaiming the gospel results in people being saved, and that obedience to God results in blessing in life, while disobedience results in lack of God's blessing.

But the differences are very significant. Calvinists when true to their doctrine will live with a far more comprehensive trust in God in all circumstances and a far greater freedom from worry about the future because they are convinced not just that God will somehow cause his major purposes to work out right in the end but that *all things* work together for good for those who love God and are called according to his purpose (Rom. 8:28). They will also be thankful to God for *all* the benefits that come to us from whatever quarter, for the one who believes in providence is assured that the ultimate reason for all things that happen is not some chance occurrence in the universe, nor is it the "free will" of another human being, but it is ultimately the goodness of God himself. They will also have great patience in adversity, knowing that it has not come about because God was unable to prevent it, but because it too is part of his wise plan. So the differences are immense. Calvin says,

> Gratitude of mind for the favorable outcome of things, patience in adversity, and also incredible freedom from worry about the future all necessarily follow upon this knowledge. . . . Ignorance of providence is the ultimate of all miseries; the highest blessedness lies in the knowledge of it.[62]

---

62. Calvin, *Institutes*, 1:219–25 (1.17.7, 11).

## 5. Additional Objections to the Arminian Position

In addition to responding to the four specific Arminian claims mentioned above, some remaining objections to it need to be considered.

**a. On an Arminian View, How Can God Know the Future?** According to the Arminian view, our human choices are not caused by God. They are totally free. But Scripture gives many examples of God predicting the future and of prophecies being fulfilled exactly. How can God predict the future in this way if it is not certain what will happen?

In response to this question, Arminians give three different kinds of answer.

**1. Foreknowledge without foreordination.** The most common Arminian answer is to affirm that God *knows* everything that will happen, but this does not mean that he has *planned* or *caused* what will happen—it simply means that he has the ability to see into the future. (The phrase sometimes used to express this view is "Foreknowledge does not imply foreordination.") This view is ably expressed by Jack Cottrell: "I affirm that God has a true foreknowledge of future free-will choices without himself being the agent that causes them or renders them certain."[63]

The problem with this position is that, even if God did not plan or cause things to happen, the fact that they are foreknown means that they will *certainly come about.* And this means that our decisions are predetermined *by something* (whether fate or the inevitable cause-and-effect mechanism of the universe), and they still are not free in the sense the Arminian wishes them to be free. If our future choices are known, then they are fixed. And if they are fixed, then they are not "free" in the Arminian sense (undetermined or uncaused).

**2. Open theism.** Some Arminians say that God is not able to know what choices individual human beings will make in the future. This view (called "open theism") seems to me to be the most consistent Arminian position, but the result is that, while God may be able to make some fairly accurate predictions based on complete knowledge of the present, these cannot be certain predictions, and they could be wrong. But this is surely not the way the Bible views the predictions that God gives through his prophets.[64]

**3. Middle knowledge (Molinism).** The "middle knowledge" position is often promoted as an attractive alternative to both Calvinism and Arminianism, preserving the important aspects of each of them. But I am classifying it here as a third Arminian viewpoint because, according to middle knowledge, the ultimate factor that determines whether someone is saved is not God's eternal choice of that individual person but the person's own libertarian free will decision to believe in Christ.

This view is sometimes called Molinism, after a Spanish Roman Catholic priest named Luis de Molina (1535–1600), who promoted this view. The most prominent

---

63. Cottrell, "The Nature of the Divine Sovereignty," 111.
64. See the discussion of open theism in chapter 12, pp. 227–30.

contemporary advocate of middle knowledge is William Lane Craig.[65] Others who have recently defended middle knowledge include John Laing and Kirk MacGregor.[66]

According to the middle knowledge view, the future choices of people are not *directly* determined by God, but God knows them anyway, because he knows *how each free creature would respond* in any set of circumstances that might occur, and then he creates a world in which those circumstances will occur.[67] Craig says,

> God's insight into the will of a free creature is of such a surpassing quality that God knows exactly what the free creature would do were God to place him in a certain set of circumstances. . . . By knowing what every possible free creature would do in any possible situation, God can by bringing about that situation know what the creature will freely do. . . . Thus he foreknows with certainty everything that happens in the world.[68]

This view is called middle knowledge because it falls in the middle of the list of three kinds of knowledge that we can distinguish in God:

1. God's *natural* knowledge: Knowledge of all things that God *could* do, including all the different kinds of worlds that he could create and what would happen in those worlds. (God necessarily knows this because he knows himself exhaustively and therefore knows all the possible things he could do.)
2. God's *middle* knowledge: Knowledge of what every one of God's creatures would freely choose, given different sets of circumstances.
3. God's *free* knowledge: Knowledge of what is actually going to happen. (This is called God's free knowledge because it is the result of his free choice to create the kind of world he did create and to influence circumstances in the world the way he actually does influence them.)

Craig quotes Molina in his explanation of middle knowledge:

> In virtue of the most profound and inscrutable comprehension of each free will, He saw in His own essence what each such will [of each creature] would do

65. William Lane Craig, a professor at Talbot School of Theology and Houston Baptist University, has been a personal friend for nearly forty years, and his contributions to Christian apologetics have been immense and have done much good for God's kingdom. I thank God for his ministry, and consider the following material a difference between friends.

66. See John D. Laing, *Middle Knowledge: Human Freedom in Divine Sovereignty* (Grand Rapids: Kregel, 2018); Kirk MacGregor, *Luis de Molina: The Life and Theology of the Founder of Middle Knowledge* (Grand Rapids: Zondervan,

2015); John Laing, Kirk MacGregor, and Greg Welty, eds., *Calvinism and Middle Knowledge: A Conversation* (Eugene, OR: Wipf & Stock, 2019).

67. See William L. Craig, "Middle Knowledge, a Calvinist-Arminian Rapprochement?," in Pinnock, *The Grace of God, the Will of Man*, 141–64. See also Craig, *The Only Wise God: The Compatibility of Divine Foreknowledge and Human Freedom* (Grand Rapids: Baker, 1987).

68. Craig, "Middle Knowledge," 150–51.

with its innate freedom were it to be placed in this or that or, indeed, in infinitely many orders of things—even though it would really be able, if it so willed, to do the opposite.[69]

Craig then gives an example:

> Whereas by his natural knowledge God knows that, say, Peter when placed under a certain set of circumstances *could* either deny Christ or not deny Christ, being free to do either under identical circumstances, by his middle knowledge God knows what Peter *would* do if placed under those circumstances.[70]

He further explains,

> While it is essential to God's nature that he have middle knowledge, the content of that knowledge is contingent because creatures could act differently under identical circumstances. But if their decisions were to be different, then the content of God's middle knowledge would be different.[71]

As for predestination of certain individuals to be saved, Craig says this:

> God in his goodness provides sufficient grace for salvation to all people in the world, and the only reason they are not predestined is that they freely ignore or reject the divine helps that God provides. . . . In Molina's view, we might say that it is up to God whether we find ourselves in a world in which we are predestined, but that it is up to us whether we are predestined in the world in which we find ourselves.[72]

> Given God's immutable determination to create a certain order, those who God knew would respond to his grace are predestined to be saved. It is absolutely certain that they will respond to and persevere in God's grace. . . . They are entirely free to reject God's grace; but were they to do so, then God would have had different middle knowledge than he does and so they would not be predestined. . . . Thus predestination and freedom are entirely compatible.[73]

Craig sees middle knowledge as an excellent way to reconcile Calvinism and Arminianism, because predestination is preserved (making Calvinists happy) and libertarian human freedom is preserved (making Arminians happy). He says, "I am

69. Ibid., 147.
70. Ibid.
71. Ibid., 148.
72. Ibid., 157.

73. Ibid., 158. See also William Lane Craig, "No Other Name: A Middle Knowledge Perspective on the Exclusivity of Salvation through Christ," *Faith and Philosophy* 6, no. 2 (1989).

convinced that a Molinist theory of middle knowledge can go a long way toward reconciling Calvinist and Arminian views."[74] (Craig points out that Molina's purpose was "to avoid the Protestant error of denying genuine human freedom," a problem that Molina claimed was present in the teachings of both Luther and Calvin.)[75]

In response to the theory of middle knowledge, we should be clear that the debate at this point is not about whether God knows how people would respond if various kinds of circumstances came about (I affirmed this in chapter 12, pages 225–31). God does have this kind of knowledge, whether we call it "middle knowledge" or something else. (And John Frame points out that such knowledge is already part of God's necessary knowledge, or what Craig calls natural knowledge.)[76]

Instead, the question is whether this theory of middle knowledge provides a correct understanding of how God's sovereignty relates to human responsibility, and in particular how God's predestination of individuals to be saved relates to human choices to accept Christ or reject him. Regarding that question, several substantial objections can be raised against the middle knowledge position:

First, middle knowledge is a theory foreign to biblical descriptions of predestination. Middle knowledge promotes a theory far different from the way Scripture speaks about God *choosing us as individuals* to be saved (not just choosing to create one of many possible *worlds* and then a specific set of *circumstances* in which we would choose to believe, but choosing *individual persons*):

> Blessed be the God and Father of our Lord Jesus Christ, who has blessed us in Christ with every spiritual blessing in the heavenly places, even as *he chose us in him before the foundation of the world*, that we should be holy and blameless before him. (Eph. 1:3–4)

> For *those whom he foreknew he also predestined to be conformed to the image of his Son*, in order that he might be the firstborn among many brothers. And those whom he predestined he also called, and those whom he called he also justified, and those whom he justified he also glorified. (Rom. 8:29–30)

> When the Gentiles heard this, they began rejoicing and glorifying the word of the Lord, and *as many as were appointed to eternal life believed*. (Acts 13:48)

Second, middle knowledge is a speculative theory devoid of explicit biblical support. Scripture nowhere appeals to the unique features of middle knowledge theory as a solution to the question of how to reconcile God's sovereignty and human choice or

---

74. Craig, "Middle Knowledge," 151.
75. Ibid., 141–44.

76. John Frame, *Systematic Theology* (Phillipsburg, NJ: P&R, 2013), 325.

the question of election and reprobation. I know of no passage in the Bible that says God created the kind of world that he did and arranged the kind of circumstances that happen in the world so that certain people would freely choose to be saved and others not. We already have abundant material in Scripture explaining God's providence (see the previous sections of this chapter), and we do not need an additional theory such as middle knowledge simply in order to make room for an Arminian doctrine of libertarian free will.

Third, God cannot determine a set of circumstances without determining millions of human choices. William Craig says, "By knowing what every possible free creature would do in any possible situation, God can *by bringing about that situation* know what the creature will freely do."[77] Here Craig speaks about God "bringing about that situation." But every situation in which people find themselves is itself the result of thousands, in fact millions, of individual human choices. As I sit at my desk writing this sentence, I am here as a result of my great-grandparents deciding to emigrate from Norway in the 1870s, then meeting and deciding to get married in the United States. I am also here as a result of other ancestors emigrating from Sweden and Ireland. But in another sense, I am here because of the influence of my professors at Westminster Theological Seminary in Philadelphia, and they were there because some conservative faculty members at Princeton Seminary decided to found Westminster in 1929. And that action depended on each of their ancestors deciding to get married, deciding to come to America, deciding (in many cases) to follow Christ and teach their children to follow Christ, and so forth. And I have a job in Arizona because some pastors in Arizona decided to found a seminary here in 1987. In addition, my current "situation" is a result of Moses deciding to obey God and write the first five books of the Bible, and a result of the apostle Paul deciding to write his epistles which have so significantly influenced my thinking. And the lives of Moses and Paul and the other biblical authors were a result of their parents and their grandparents and great-grandparents deciding to get married and to follow God. My current situation is also a result of the Founding Fathers of the United States deciding to declare their independence from Great Britain in 1776, and their lives are the result of—well, such reasoning could go on forever. It would be impossible to list or even be aware of all the human choices that resulted in the exact "situations" in which we find ourselves today. Therefore, in order for God to "bring about a situation," literally millions of prior human choices would have to be decided in a certain way, or else the situation would be different. It is hard to avoid the conclusion that hidden in the phrase that speaks about God "bringing about that situation" is the implied necessity for God not just to create a certain kind of world at the beginning but also to *determine* that millions of human choices would be decided in one way and not in another, in order to bring about the situation he wants at this moment. But such

---

77. Craig, "Middle Knowledge," 151.

a process denies the kind of libertarian free will that middle knowledge advocates are claiming to protect.[78]

Fourth, middle knowledge is inconsistent with the essential claims of both Calvinism and Arminianism. On the one hand, Calvinists cannot agree with the idea that God ordains circumstances but does not choose individual persons for salvation, nor can they agree that God's foreknowledge of human choices is contingent upon what each human being freely chooses (the person could have chosen differently). Nor can Calvinists agree that "it is up to us whether we are predestined," placing the ultimate factor that decides a person's destiny not in God's choice of the person but in the person's decision to choose God. Middle knowledge says that (a) God knows that if person *P* is in a certain set of circumstances, he will trust in Christ, and then (b) God creates the kind of world in which exactly those circumstances will come about, and so predestines person *P* to salvation. But this is just a somewhat complicated variation on the standard Arminian view that predestination is based on God's knowledge of who would freely choose to believe.

Therefore, middle knowledge does not provide a better solution than Calvinism or Arminianism. In fact, the middle knowledge theory is in actuality just a variety of the Arminian position that election is based on God's foreknowledge of our faith. However, it adds the additional details that God, first knowing how individual people *would* respond in certain circumstances, then creates the kind of world and arranges the kind of circumstances in which he knows that a person will "freely" choose to believe, and then he predestines that person to be saved. This is still predestination based on foreknowledge of a person's faith.

On the other hand, Craig's view does not actually result in the kind of human freedom that Arminians want to defend. Craig refers to this freedom as the "possibility of man's choosing in any circumstances other than as he does choose"[79] or the freedom where "creatures could act differently under identical circumstances."[80] (I earlier explained this as "libertarian freedom.") But on Craig's view, God's knowledge of the circumstances and the person's own disposition *guarantee* that a certain choice will be made—otherwise, God could not know what the choice would be. But if God *knows* what the choice will be, then that choice is guaranteed to happen, and then it could not be otherwise.[81]

---

78. John Frame makes a similar point using Craig's example of Peter's denial of Christ. "Once God creates the world (including a world history) that includes Peter's denial, that denial is inevitable. So what room is there in this scenario for libertarian freedom? Once Peter is created, his denial is inevitable: determined, one might say.... How can Peter make a libertarian free choice, when he is part of a world that contains his denial as an event, when the events of his life have been decided before his birth?" (Frame, *Systematic Theology*, 326).

79. Ibid., 144.

80. Ibid., 148.

81. For further discussion of middle knowledge, see Ware, *God's Greater Glory*, 110–30. (Ware has an interesting discussion of the possibility that God, knowing a person's inclinations, could arrange circumstances around that person that God knows would motivate the person to make either a good or evil choice, according to his or her strongest inclination.) See also J. A. Crabtree, "Does Middle Knowledge Solve the Problem of Divine Sovereignty?," in *The Grace of God, the Bondage of the Will*, ed. Thomas Schreiner and Bruce Ware (Grand Rapids: Baker, 1995), 2:429–57; and John Frame, *Systematic Theology* (Phillipsburg, New Jersey: P & R, 2013), 323–26.

In conclusion, Molinism proposes a speculative theory that has no explicit biblical support, that is inconsistent with the biblical descriptions of God choosing individual persons, that is a complicated version of the Arminian view that predestination is based on foreknowledge of a person's faith, that requires that God must determine millions of human choices that lead up to any specific set of circumstances, and that is inconsistent with claims that are essential to both Calvinism and Arminianism.

**b. On an Arminian View, How Can Evil Exist If God Did Not Want It?** Arminians quite clearly say that the entrance of evil into the world was not according to the will of God. Pinnock says, "The fall of man is an eloquent refutation to the theory that God's will is always done."[82] But how can evil exist if God did not want it to exist? If evil happens in spite of the fact that God does not want it to happen, this seems to deny God's omnipotence: he wanted to prevent evil, but he was unable to do so. How then can we believe that this God is omnipotent?

The common Arminian response is to say that God was *able* to prevent evil but he chose to *allow for the possibility* of evil in order to guarantee that angels and humans would have the freedom necessary for meaningful choices. In other words, God *had to* allow for the possibility of sinful choices in order to allow genuine human choices. Cottrell says, "This God-given freedom includes human freedom to rebel and to sin against the Creator himself. By creating a world in which sin was possible, God thereby bound himself to *react* in certain specific ways should sin become a reality."[83]

But this is not a satisfactory response either, for it implies that God will have to allow for the possibility of sinful choices in heaven eternally. On the Arminian position, if any of our choices and actions in heaven are to be genuine and real, then they will *have to* include the possibility of sinful choices. But this implies that even in heaven, for all eternity, we will face the real possibility of choosing evil—and therefore the possibility of rebelling against God and losing our salvation and being cast out of heaven! This is a terrifying thought, but it seems a necessary implication of the Arminian view.

Yet there is an implication that is more troubling: If *real* choices have to allow for the possibility of choosing evil, then (1) God's choices are not real, since he cannot choose evil, or (2) God's choices are real, and there is the genuine possibility that God might someday choose to do evil—perhaps a little, and perhaps a great deal. If we ponder the second implication it becomes terrifying. But it is contrary to the abundant testimony of Scripture.[84] On the other hand, the first implication is clearly false: God is the definition of what is real, and it is clearly an error to say that his choices are not real. Both implications therefore provide good reason for rejecting the Arminian position that real choices must allow the possibility of choosing evil. But this puts us back to the earlier question

---

82. Pinnock, "Responsible Freedom," 102.
83. Cottrell, "The Nature of Divine Sovereignty," 109.
84. See chapter 12, pp. 236–37, 240–42, 243–45, for

scriptural testimony to God's goodness, holiness, and righteousness, and chapter 11, pp. 192–99, on God's unchangeableness.

for which there does not seem to be a satisfactory answer from the Arminian position: How can evil exist if God did not want it to exist?

**c. On an Arminian View, How Can We Know That God Will Triumph over Evil?** If we go back to the Arminian assertion that evil is *not* according to the will of God, another problem arises: if all the evil now in the world came into the world even though God did not want it, how can we be sure that God will triumph over it in the end? Of course, God *says* in Scripture that he will triumph over evil. But if he was unable to keep it out of his universe in the first place and it came in against his will, and if he is unable to predict the outcome of any future events that involve free choices by human, angelic, and demonic agents, how then can we be sure that God's declaration that he will triumph over all evil is in itself true? Perhaps this is just a hopeful prediction of something that (on the Arminian viewpoint) God simply cannot know. Far from the "incredible freedom from worry about the future" that the Calvinist has because he knows that an omnipotent God makes "all things work together for good" (Rom. 8:28), the Arminian position seems logically to drive us to a deep-seated anxiety about the ultimate outcome of history.

Both of these last two objections regarding evil make us realize that, while we may have difficulties in thinking about the Reformed view of evil as ordained by God and completely under the control of God, there are far more serious difficulties with the Arminian view of evil as not ordained or even willed by God and therefore not assuredly under the control of God.

**d. The Difference in the Unanswered Questions.** Since we are finite in our understanding, we inevitably will have some unanswered questions about every biblical doctrine. Yet on this issue the questions that Calvinists and Arminians must leave unanswered are quite different. On the one hand, Calvinists must say that they do not know the answer to the following questions:

1. Exactly how can God not be blamed for evil when he ordains that we do evil willingly?
2. Exactly how can God cause us to choose something willingly?

To both, Calvinists would say that the answer is somehow to be found in an awareness of God's infinite greatness and in the knowledge of the fact that he can do far more than we could ever think possible. So the effect of these unanswered questions is to increase our appreciation of the greatness of God.

On the other hand, Arminians must leave unanswered questions regarding God's knowledge of the future, why he would allow evil when it is against his will, and whether he will certainly triumph over evil. Their failure to resolve these questions tends to diminish the greatness of God—his omniscience, his omnipotence, and the absolute reliability of his promises for the future. And these unanswered questions tend to exalt the greatness of man (his freedom to do what God does not want) and the power of evil (it comes and remains in the universe even though God does not want it). Moreover, by denying that God can make creatures who have real choices that are nevertheless caused by him, the Arminian position diminishes the wisdom and skill of God the Creator.

## H. FURTHER PRACTICAL APPLICATION

Although we have already begun to speak of the practical application of this doctrine, three additional points should be made.

### 1. Do Not Be Afraid, but Trust in God

Jesus emphasizes the fact that our sovereign Lord watches over us and cares for us as his children. He says, "Look at the birds of the air: they neither sow nor reap nor gather into barns, and yet your heavenly Father feeds them. Are you not of more value than they? . . . Therefore do not be anxious, saying, 'What shall we eat?' or 'What shall we drink?' or 'What shall we wear?'" (Matt. 6:26, 31). If God feeds the birds and clothes the grass of the field, he will take care of us. Similarly, Jesus says, "Are not two sparrows sold for a penny? And not one of them will fall to the ground apart from your Father. . . . Fear not, therefore; you are of more value than many sparrows" (Matt. 10:29–31).

David was able to sleep in the midst of his enemies, because he knew that God's providential control made him "dwell in safety," and he could say, "In peace I will both lie down and sleep" (Ps. 4:8). Many of the psalms encourage us to trust God and not to fear, because the LORD keeps and protects his people—for example, Psalm 91 ("He who dwells in the shelter of the Most High") and Psalm 121 ("I lift up my eyes to the hills"). Because of our confidence in God's providential care, we need not fear any evil or harm, even if it does come to us—it can only come by God's will and ultimately for our good. Thus Peter can say that "now for a little while, if necessary, you have been grieved by various trials, so that the tested genuineness of your faith—more precious than gold . . . may be found to result in praise and glory and honor at the revelation of Jesus Christ" (1 Peter 1:6–7). In all of this we need not worry about the future but trust in God's omnipotent care.

### 2. Be Thankful for All Good Things That Happen

If we genuinely believe that all good things are caused by God, then our hearts will indeed be full when we say, "Bless the LORD, O my soul, and forget not all his benefits" (Ps. 103:2). We will thank him for our daily food (cf. Matt. 6:11; 1 Tim. 4:4–5); indeed, we will "give thanks in all circumstances" (1 Thess. 5:18).

### 3. There Is No Such Thing as "Luck" or "Chance"

All things come to pass by God's wise providence. This means that we should adopt a much more "personal" understanding of the universe and the events in it. The universe is not governed by impersonal fate or luck but by a personal God. Nothing "just happens"—we should see God's hand in events throughout the day, causing all things to work together for good for those who love him.

This confidence in God's wise providence certainly does not equal superstition, for it is no belief in impersonal or demonic control, nor is it control by a capricious deity concerned for meaningless ritual rather than obedience and faith. A deepened appreciation for the doctrine of providence will not make us more superstitious; it will make us trust in God more and obey him more fully.

## QUESTIONS FOR PERSONAL APPLICATION

1. Has thinking about the doctrine of providence increased your trust in God? How has it changed the way you think about the future? Are there difficulties or hardships in your life at this time? Give an example of a specific difficulty that you are now facing and explain how the doctrine of providence will help you in the way you think about it.

2. Can you name five good things that have happened to you so far today? Were you thankful to God for any of them?

3. Do you sometimes think of luck or chance as causing events that happen in your life? If you ever feel that way, does it increase or decrease your anxiety about the future? Now think for a moment about some events that you might have attributed to luck in the past. Instead, begin to think about those events as under the control of your wise and loving heavenly Father. How does that make you feel differently about them and about the future generally?

4. Do you ever fall into a pattern of little "superstitious" actions or rituals that you think will bring good luck or prevent bad luck (such as not walking under a ladder, being afraid when a black cat walks across your path, not stepping on cracks on a sidewalk, carrying a certain item "just for good luck," etc.)? Do you think those actions tend to increase or decrease your trust in God during the day and your obedience to him?

5. Explain how a proper understanding of the doctrine of providence should lead a Christian to a more active prayer life.

6. What has been the overall effect of this chapter on how you think and feel about God and the events of your life?

### Special Terms

*Arminian*
*Calvinism*
*concurrence*
*decrees of God*
*free choices*
*free will*
*freedom of voluntary choice*
*freedom of inclination*
*government*
*libertarian free will*
*middle knowledge*
*Molinism*
*preservation*
*primary cause*
*providence*
*Reformed*
*secondary cause*
*voluntary choices*
*willing choices*

# BIBLIOGRAPHY

(For an explanation of this bibliography see the note on the bibliography to chapter 1, pp. 23–24. Complete bibliographical data may be found on pp. 1489–96.)

## SECTIONS IN EVANGELICAL SYSTEMATIC THEOLOGIES

### 1. Anglican (Episcopalian)
1882–92 . . . . . Litton, 76–90
1930 . . . . . . . . Thomas, 176–83
2001 . . . . . . . . Packer, 54–56
2013 . . . . . . . . Bird, 144
2013 . . . . . . . . Bray, 166, 187, 1077–79

### 2. Arminian (Wesleyan or Methodist)
1875–76 . . . . . Pope, 1:437–56; 2:363–67, 386–90
1892–94 . . . . . Miley, 1:211–349; 2:271–308
1940 . . . . . . . . Wiley, 1:478–88
1983 . . . . . . . . Carter, 1:122–24, 130–33, 222–23
1992 . . . . . . . . Oden, 1:270–316
2002 . . . . . . . . Cottrell, 111, 119, 121, 289, 293

### 3. Baptist
1767 . . . . . . . . Gill, 1:246–51, 397–434
1887 . . . . . . . . Boyce, 115–25, 217–30
1907 . . . . . . . . Strong, 353–70, 410–43
1917 . . . . . . . . Mullins, 265–76
1976–83 . . . . . Henry, 5:307–33; 6:455–91
1983–85 . . . . . Erickson, 345–64, 387–432
1987–94 . . . . . Lewis and Demarest, 1:291–335; 2:71–122
1990–95 . . . . . Garrett, 1:373–95
2007 . . . . . . . . Akin, 242–93
2013 . . . . . . . . Erickson, 358–82

### 4. Dispensational
1947 . . . . . . . . Chafer, 1:225–59
1949 . . . . . . . . Thiessen, 100–110, 119–32
2002–2005 . . Geisler, 1:242–43, 411–12, 2:563–95
2017 . . . . . . . . MacArthur and Mayhue, 218–21

### 5. Lutheran
1917–24 . . . . . Pieper, 1:483–97
1934 . . . . . . . . Mueller, 176–78, 189–95, 236–41

### 6. Reformed (or Presbyterian)
1559 . . . . . . . . Calvin, 1:197–237, 309–407 (1.16–18; 2.4–5)
1679–85 . . . . . Turretin, IET, 1:489–538
1724–58 . . . . . Edwards, 1:3–93; 2:107–110, 525–43
1871–73 . . . . . Hodge, 1:535–49, 575–616; 2:280–312
1878 . . . . . . . . Dabney, 120–32, 221–23, 276–91
1887–1921 . . . Warfield, SSW, 1:93–115; SSW, 2:411–47
1894 . . . . . . . . Shedd, 412–15
1906–11 . . . . . Bavinck, RD, 2:374–80, 591–619
1910 . . . . . . . . Vos, 1:183–202
1937–66 . . . . . Murray, CW, 3:161–67, 185–89; CW, 2:60–66
1938 . . . . . . . . Berkhof, 100–108, 165–78
1998 . . . . . . . . Reymond, 398–414
2008 . . . . . . . . Van Genderen and Velema, 283–313
2011 . . . . . . . . Horton, 350–72

2013........Frame, 141–82, 184–203, 282–301
2013........Culver, 191–201
2016........Allen and Swain, 148–64
2017........Barrett, 266–67
2019........Letham, 292–311

*7. Renewal (or charismatic/Pentecostal)*
1988–92.....Williams, 1:117–40, 215–19
1993........Menzies and Horton, 52
2008........Duffield and Van Cleave, 26, 86–88, 376

## SECTIONS IN REPRESENTATIVE ROMAN CATHOLIC SYSTEMATIC THEOLOGIES

*1. Roman Catholic: Traditional*
1955........Ott, 87–91

*2. Roman Catholic: Post–Vatican II*
1980........McBrien (no explicit treatment)
2012........*CCC*, paragraphs 302–24

## OTHER WORKS

Allison, Gregg. *Historical Theology: An Introduction to Christian Doctrine; A Companion to Wayne Grudem's* Systematic Theology. Grand Rapids: Zondervan, 2011, 277–97.

Basinger, David, and Randall Basinger, eds. *Predestination and Free Will: Four Views of Divine Sovereignty and Human Freedom.* Downers Grove, IL: InterVarsity Press, 1986.

Berkouwer, G. C. *The Providence of God.* Translated by Lewis B. Smedes. Grand Rapids: Eerdmans, 1952.

Cameron, N. M. de S. "Providence." In *NDT1,* 177–79.

Carson, D. A. *Divine Sovereignty and Human Responsibility: Biblical Perspectives in Tension.* New Foundations Theological Library. Atlanta: John Knox; London: Marshall, Morgan and

Scott, 1981. Reprint, Eugene, OR: Wipf & Stock, 2002.

———. *How Long, O Lord? Reflections on Suffering and Evil.* Grand Rapids: Baker, and Leicester: Inter-Varsity Press, 1990.

Craig, William Lane. *The Only Wise God: The Compatibility of Divine Foreknowledge and Human Freedom.* Grand Rapids: Baker, 1987.

DiRoberts, Kyle D. *Prayer, Middle Knowledge, and Divine-Human Interaction.* Eugene, OR: Wipf & Stock, 2018.

Elwell, Walter A. "Providence of God." In *BTDB,* 650–53.

Farley, Benjamin Wirt. *The Providence of God.* Grand Rapids: Baker, 1988.

Feinberg, John. *The Many Faces of Evil: Theological Systems and the Problem of Evil.* Rev. ed. Wheaton, IL: Crossway, 2004.

Feinberg, John S. *No One Like Him: the Doctrine of God.* Wheaton, IL: Crossway, 2006.

Flavel, John. *The Mystery of Providence.* 1698. Reprint, Carlisle, PA: Banner of Truth, 1976.

Gundry, Stanley N., and Dennis W. Jowers, eds. *Four Views on Divine Providence.* Grand Rapids: Zondervan, 2011.

Helm, Paul. *The Providence of God.* Leicester: Inter-Varsity Press; Downers Grove, IL: InterVarsity Press, 1994.

———. "Providence." In *NDT2,* 714–15.

Nelson, David P. "The Work of God: Creation and Providence." In *A Theology for the Church,* edited by Daniel L. Akin, et al., 267–92. Nashville: B&H, 2007.

Newman, C. C. "God." In *DLNT,* 412–31.

Parker, T. H. L. "Providence of God." In *EDT3,* 705–6.

Pink, Arthur W. *The Sovereignty of God.* Grand Rapids: Baker, 1930.

Pinnock, Clark H., ed. *The Openness of God: A Biblical Challenge to the Traditional Understanding of God.* Downers Grove, IL: InterVarsity Press, 1994.

Tiessen, Terrance L. *Providence and Prayer: How Does God Work in the World?* Downers Grove, IL: InterVarsity Press, 2000.

Ware, Bruce A. *God's Greater Glory: The Exalted God*

of Scripture and the Christian Faith. Wheaton, IL: Crossway, 2004.

———. God's Lesser Glory: The Diminished God of Open Theism. Wheaton, IL: Crossway, 2000.

Ware, Bruce A., ed. Perspectives on the Doctrine of God: 4 Views. Nashville: B&H Academic, 2008.

Warfield, B. B. Calvin and Calvinism. New York: Oxford University Press, 1931.

Williams, S. N. "Providence." In NDBT, 710–15.

Wood, W. J. "Molinism." In EDT3, 556–57.

## SCRIPTURE MEMORY PASSAGE

**Romans 8:28:** And we know that for those who love God all things work together for good, for those who are called according to his purpose.

## HYMN

### "God Moves in a Mysterious Way"

God moves in a mysterious way
  his wonders to perform;
He plants his footsteps in the sea,
  and rides upon the storm.

Deep in unfathomable mines
  of never-failing skill
He treasures up his bright designs,
  and works his sovereign will.

Ye fearful saints, fresh courage take;
  the clouds ye so much dread
Are big with mercy, and shall break
  in blessings on your head.

Judge not the Lord by feeble sense,
  but trust him for his grace;
Behind a frowning providence
  he hides a smiling face.

His purposes will ripen fast,
  unfolding every hour;
The bud may have a bitter taste,
  but sweet will be the flow'r.

Blind unbelief is sure to err,
  and scan his work in vain;
God is his own interpreter,
  and he will make it plain.

Author: William Cowper, 1774

## CONTEMPORARY WORSHIP SONG

### "The Lord Our God"

Promise maker, promise keeper,
You finish what You begin.
Our provision through the desert,

You see it through till the end.
You see it through till the end.

*Chorus*
The Lord our God is ever faithful,
Never changing through the ages.
From this darkness, You will lead us,
And forever we will say,
You're the Lord our God.

In the silence in the waiting,
Still we can know You are good.
All Your plans are for Your glory.
Yes we can know You are good.
Yes we can know You are good.

*Bridge*
We won't move without You.
We won't move without You.
You're the light of all,
And all that we need.

Words by Kristian Stanfill and Jason Ingram[85]

CHAPTER 17

# Miracles

*What are miracles?*
*Can they happen today?*

## EXPLANATION AND SCRIPTURAL BASIS

A consideration of the subject of miracles is closely connected with God's providence, which was considered in the previous chapter. There we argued that God exercises an extensive, ongoing, sovereign control over all aspects of his creation. This chapter will assume an understanding of that discussion of providence and will build on it in approaching the question of miracles.

### A. DEFINITION

We may define a miracle as follows: *A miracle is a less common kind of God's activity in which he arouses people's awe and wonder and bears witness to himself.*[1] This definition takes into account our previous understanding of God's providence whereby God preserves, controls, and governs all things. If we understand providence in this way, we will naturally avoid some other common explanations or definitions of miracles.

For example, one definition of miracle is "a direct intervention of God in the world." But this definition assumes a deistic view of God's relationship to the world, in which the world continues on its own and God only intervenes in it occasionally. This is certainly not the biblical view, according to which God makes the rain to fall (Matt. 5:45), causes the grass to grow (Ps. 104:14), and continually carries along all things by his word of power (Heb. 1:3). Another definition of miracle is "a more direct activity of God in the world." But to talk about a "more direct" working of God suggests that his *ordinary* providential activity is somehow not "direct" and again hints at a sort of deistic removal of God from the world.

Another definition is "God working in the world without using means to bring about the results he wishes." Yet to speak of God working "without means" leaves us with very few if any miracles in the Bible, for it is hard to think of a miracle that came about with no means at all: in the healing of people, for example, some of the physical properties of the sick person's body were doubtless involved as part of the healing. When

---

1. I have adapted this definition from unpublished lectures given by John Frame, former professor of systematic theology at Westminster Theological Seminary and now professor emeritus at Reformed Theological Seminary, Orlando.

Jesus multiplied the loaves and fishes, he at least used the original five loaves and two fishes that were there. When he changed water to wine, he used water and made it become wine. This definition seems to be inadequate.[2]

Yet another definition of miracle is "an exception to a natural law" or "God acting contrary to the laws of nature." This definition is a little better, but the phrase "laws of nature" in popular understanding implies that there are certain qualities inherent in the things that exist, "laws of nature" that operate independently of God, and that God must intervene or "break" these laws for a miracle to occur.[3] Once again this definition does not adequately account for the biblical teaching on providence.

Another definition of miracle is "an event impossible to explain by natural causes." This definition is inadequate because (1) it does not include God as the one who brings about the miracle; (2) it assumes that God does not use some natural causes when he works in an unusual or amazing way, and thus it assumes again that God only occasionally intervenes in the world; and (3) it will result in a significant minimizing of actual miracles and an increase in skepticism, since many times when God works in answer to prayer, the result is amazing to those who prayed but not absolutely impossible to explain by natural causes, especially for a skeptic who simply refuses to see God's hand at work.

Therefore, the original definition given above, where a miracle is simply a *less common* way of God's working in the world that arouses people's awe and wonder and bears witness to God, seems to be preferable and more consistent with the biblical doctrine of God's providence. This definition does not say that a miracle is a *different* kind of working by God but only that it is a *less common* way of God's working and that it is done so as to arouse people's surprise, awe, or amazement in such a way that God bears witness to himself. (According to this definition, regeneration, or being "born again," can certainly be understood as a miracle, because of the remarkable change that often occurs in people's lives. See chapter 34.)

The biblical terminology for miracles frequently points to this idea of God's power at work to arouse people's wonder and amazement. Primarily three sets of terms are employed: (1) "sign" (Heb. *'ôth*; Gk. *sēmeion*), which means something that points to or indicates something else, especially (with reference to miracles) God's activity and power; (2) "wonder" (Heb. *môpēth*; Gk. *teras*), an event that causes people to be amazed or astonished;[4] and (3) "miracle" or "mighty work" (Heb. *gebûrāh*; Gk. *dynamis*), an

---

2. However, if someone defined a miracle as "a work of God apart from the *ordinary* use of means, to arouse people's awe and wonder," this would be similar in force to the definition I proposed above and would be consistent with the Bible's teaching on God's providence (see Louis Berkhof, *Systematic Theology* [Grand Rapids: Eerdmans, 1941], 176–77).

3. If the phrase "natural law" is understood by Christians simply to refer to the predictable patterns of behavior that God gives to and maintains in each created thing, then this definition is less objectionable because it consciously takes into account God's providence. But the phrase "natural law" is not generally understood that way in English today.

4. The verb *thaumazō*, "to wonder, be amazed," is frequently used in the Gospels to describe people's reaction to miracles.

act displaying great power, especially (with reference to miracles) divine power.[5] Often "signs and wonders" is used as a stock expression to refer to miracles (Ex. 7:3; Deut. 6:22; Ps. 135:9; Acts 4:30; 5:12; Rom. 15:19, et al.), and sometimes all three terms are combined, "mighty works and wonders and signs" (Acts 2:22) or "signs and wonders and mighty works" (2 Cor. 12:12; Heb. 2:4).

In addition to the meanings of the terms used for miracles, another reason supporting our definition is the fact that miracles in Scripture do arouse people's awe and amazement and indicate that God's power is at work. The Bible frequently tells us that God himself is the one who performs "miracles" or "wondrous things." Psalm 136:4 says that God is the one "who alone does great wonders" (cf. Ps. 72:18). The song of Moses declares,

> Who is like you, O LORD, among the gods?
>     Who is like you, majestic in holiness,
>         Awesome in glorious deeds, doing *wonders*? (Ex. 15:11)

Thus the miraculous signs that Moses did when his staff turned into a snake and back again or when his hand became leprous and then clean again (Ex. 4:2–8) were given that Moses might demonstrate to the people of Israel that God had sent him. Similarly, the miraculous signs God did by the hand of Moses and Aaron through the plagues, far surpassing the false miracles or imitation signs done by the magicians in Pharaoh's court (Ex. 7:12; 8:18–19; 9:11), showed that the people of Israel were those who worshiped the one true God. When Elijah confronted the priests of Baal on Mount Carmel (1 Kings 18:17–40), the fire from heaven demonstrated that the LORD was the one true God.

Now if we accept the definition that a miracle is "a less common kind of God's activity in which he arouses people's awe and wonder and bears witness to himself," then we may ask what kinds of things should be considered miracles. Of course, we are right to consider the incarnation of Jesus as God-man and Jesus' resurrection from the dead as the central and most important miracles in all history. The events of the exodus such as the parting of the Red Sea and the fall of Jericho were remarkable miracles. When Jesus healed people and cleansed lepers and cast out demons, those were certainly miracles as well (see Matt. 11:4–5; Luke 4:36–41; John 2:23; 4:54; 6:2; 20:30–31).

But can we consider unusual answers to prayer to be miracles? Apparently so, if they are remarkable enough to arouse people's awe and wonder and cause them to acknowledge God's power at work: the answer to Elijah's prayer that God would send fire from heaven was a miracle (1 Kings 18:24, 36–38), as were the answers to his prayers that the widow's dead son would come back to life (1 Kings 17:21), or that the rain would stop and

---

5. See the extensive discussion of New Testament vocabulary for miracles in W. Mundle, O. Hofius, and C. Brown, "Miracle, Wonder, Sign," *NIDNTT*, 2:620–35.

later start again (1 Kings 17:1; 18:41–45 with James 5:17–18). In the New Testament, the release of Peter from prison in answer to the prayers of the church was certainly a miracle (Acts 12:5–17; note also Paul's prayer for Publius's father in Acts 28:8). But there must have been many miracles not nearly as dramatic as those because Jesus healed many hundreds of people, "*any* who were sick with *various diseases*" (Luke 4:40). Paul healed "the rest of the people on the island who had diseases" (Acts 28:9).

On the other hand, Christians see answers to prayer every day, and we should not water down our definition of miracle so much that every answer to prayer is called a miracle. But when an answer to prayer is so remarkable that people involved with it are amazed and acknowledge God's power at work in an unusual way, then it seems appropriate to call it a miracle.[6] This is consistent with our definition and seems supported by the biblical evidence that works of God that aroused people's awe and wonder were called miracles (Gk. *dynamis*).[7]

But whether we adopt a broad or narrow definition of miracle, all should agree that if God really does work in answer to our prayers, whether in common or uncommon ways, it is important that we recognize this and give thanks to him and that we not ignore it or go to great lengths to devise possible "natural causes" to explain away what God has in fact done in answer to prayer. While we must be careful not to exaggerate in reporting details of answers to prayer, we must also avoid the opposite error of failing to glorify and thank God for what he has done.

## B. Miracles as Characteristic of the New Covenant Age

In the New Testament, Jesus' miraculous signs attested that he had come from God. Nicodemus recognized, "No one can do these signs that you do unless God is with him" (John 3:2). Jesus' changing of water into wine was a "sign" that "manifested his glory. And his disciples believed in him" (John 2:11). According to Peter, Jesus was "a man attested to you by God with *mighty works and wonders and signs* that God did through him in your midst" (Acts 2:22).

Then in the early church, the apostles and others who preached the gospel performed miracles that amazed people and gave confirmation of the gospel that was being preached (Acts 2:43; 3:6–10; 4:30; 8:6–8, 13; 9:40–42, et al.). Even in churches where no apostles were present, miracles occurred. For example, Paul, in writing to several

---

6. Others may prefer to be more restrictive in their definition of miracles, reserving the term (for example) for events that absolutely could not have happened by ordinary means and that are thoroughly witnessed and documented by several impartial observers. In that case, they will see far fewer miracles, especially in a skeptical, anti-supernatural society. But such a definition probably does not encompass all the kinds of things Paul had in mind when he talked about miracles in the churches of Corinth (1 Cor. 12:10, 28–29) and Galatia (Gal. 3:5), and it may prevent people from recognizing a gift of miracles when it

is given to Christians today. (Of course, Christians who hold such a restrictive definition will still readily thank God for many answers to prayer that they would not call miracles.)

7. The appropriateness of such a definition is not lost simply because the same event might be called a miracle by some people and an ordinary event by others, for people's evaluation of an event will vary depending on their nearness to the event, the assumptions of their worldview, and whether they are Christians or not.

churches in the region of Galatia (see Gal. 1:1), assumes this when he asks, "Does he who supplies the Spirit to you and works miracles among you do so by works of the law, or by hearing with faith?" (Gal. 3:5). Similarly, he mentions in the church at Corinth "miracles" (1 Cor. 12:28) and names "the working of miracles" (1 Cor. 12:10) as a gift distributed by the Holy Spirit. These last two verses are especially significant because 1 Corinthians 12:4–31 is not discussing a specific situation at Corinth but the nature of the church in general as the "body of Christ" with many members yet one body.[8]

In fact, it seems to be a characteristic of the New Testament church that miracles occur. B. B. Warfield wrote in 1918, "The Apostolic Church was characteristically a miracle-working church."[9] In the Old Testament, miracles seemed to occur primarily in connection with one prominent leader at a time, such as Moses, Elijah, or Elisha. But in the New Testament, there is a sudden and unprecedented increase in the miracles when Jesus begins his ministry (Luke 4:36–37, 40–41). However, contrary to the pattern of the Old Testament, the authority to work miracles and to cast out demons was not confined to Jesus himself, nor did miracles die out when Jesus returned to heaven. Even during his ministry, Jesus gave authority to heal the sick and to cast out demons not only to the Twelve but also to seventy of his disciples (Luke 10:1, 9, 17–19; cf. Matt. 10:8; Luke 9:49–50). Moreover, the passages noted above from 1 Corinthians and Galatians indicate that performing miracles was not confined to the seventy disciples but was characteristic of the churches of Galatia and the New Testament churches generally. This suggests that the occurrence of miracles is a characteristic of the New Testament church and may be seen as an indication of the powerful new work of the Holy Spirit that began with Pentecost and may be expected to continue through the church age.[10]

---

8. Note, for example, that Paul says that God has appointed in the church, "first apostles . . ." (1 Cor. 12:28). But there were no apostles given specifically to the church at Corinth. Therefore this passage must be talking about the church in general.

B. B. Warfield, *Counterfeit Miracles* (1918; repr., Edinburgh: Banner of Truth, 1972), notes that in the church at Corinth those who took part in the ordinary church worship service "might often have a miraculous gift to exercise." He says that "there is no reason to believe that the infant congregation at Corinth was singular in this. The Apostle does not write as if he were describing a marvelous state of affairs peculiar to that church. . . . The hints in the rest of his letters and in the Book of Acts require us, accordingly, to look upon this beautiful picture of Christian worship as one which would be true to life for any of the numerous congregations planted by the Apostles in the length and breadth of the world visited and preached to by them. . . . We are justified in considering it characteristic of the Apostolic churches that such miraculous gifts should be displayed in them. The exception would be, not a church with, but a church without, such gifts" (4–5).

9. Continuing his argument, Warfield says, "Everywhere, the Apostolic Church was marked out as itself a gift from God, by showing forth the possession of the Spirit in appropriate works of the Spirit—miracles of healing and miracles of power, miracles of knowledge whether in the form of prophecy or of the discerning of spirits, miracles of speech, whether of the gift of tongues or of their interpretation" (*Counterfeit Miracles*, 5).

While I would agree with Warfield's analysis of the New Testament evidence on this question, there is certainly room to disagree with his subsequent point, and the main contention of his book, that the church after the age of the apostles experienced the cessation of miraculous gifts, and that we should not expect such gifts today because God intended them only to confirm the early apostolic message during the time when the apostles were still alive.

10. See further discussion of this question in chapter 52 below, on spiritual gifts and the question of the time of cessation of some gifts.

## C. THE PURPOSES OF MIRACLES

One purpose of miracles is certainly *to authenticate the message of the gospel*. This was evident in Jesus' ministry, as people like Nicodemus acknowledged: "We know that you are a teacher come from God, for no one can do these *signs* that you do unless God is with him" (John 3:2). It also was evident as the gospel was proclaimed by those who heard Jesus, for as they preached, "God also bore witness by *signs and wonders and various miracles* and by gifts of the Holy Spirit distributed according to his will" (Heb. 2:4). Whether this purpose was valid only when the gospel was first preached (before the New Testament was written) or it holds good throughout the church age depends on what we think the miracles are confirming: Are they confirming only the absolute truthfulness of the words of Scripture (as the very words of God), or are miracles given to confirm the truthfulness of the gospel generally, whenever it is preached? In other words, do miracles confirm Scripture or the gospel? As we shall see below, miracles were not limited to those who wrote Scripture or spoke with absolute apostolic authority.[11] This suggests that miracles given in confirmation of the gospel might be expected to continue throughout the church age.

When miracles occur, they give evidence that God is truly at work in connection with the gospel of Christ, and so miracles serve to advance the gospel: the Samaritan woman proclaimed to her village, "Come, see a man who told me all that I ever did" (John 4:29), and many of the Samaritans believed in Christ. This was frequently true in Jesus' ministry, but it was also true in the early church: when Philip went to a city in Samaria,

> the crowds with one accord *paid attention to what was being said by Philip*, when they heard him and saw the *signs* that he did. For unclean spirits, crying out with a loud voice, came out of many who had them, and many who were paralyzed or lame were healed. So there was much joy in that city. (Acts 8:6–8)

When Aeneas the paralytic was healed, "all the residents of Lydda and Sharon saw him, and *they turned to the Lord*" (Acts 9:35). When Tabitha was raised from the dead, "it became known throughout all Joppa, and *many believed in the Lord*" (Acts 9:42). In all of these instances, miracles authenticated the message of the gospel. These verses and others like them repeatedly show the positive value of miracles in bringing people to faith.[12]

---

11. See section D below, pp. 477–85.

12. Some may object that when we say that miracles have value in bearing witness to the gospel this means that we think the gospel message by itself is weak and unable to bring people to faith (see especially James M. Boice, "A Better Way: The Power of Word and Spirit," in *Power Religion*, ed. Michael Scott Horton [Chicago: Moody Publishers, 1992], 119–36). But this is not a valid objection, for Jesus and Paul did not reason that way—both performed miracles in conjunction with their preaching of the gospel, and Jesus commanded his disciples to do this as well (Matt. 10:7–8). We must remember that it is God himself who "bore witness" to the gospel "by signs and wonders and various miracles and by gifts of the Holy Spirit distributed according to his will" (Heb. 2:4), and we cannot say that he has an inappropriate view of the power of the gospel message.

John's gospel is especially instructive in showing the value

A second purpose of miracles in the New Testament is *to show that the kingdom of God has come* and has begun to expand its beneficial results into people's lives, for the results of Jesus' miracles show the characteristics of God's kingdom: Jesus said, "If it is by the Spirit of God that I cast out demons, then the kingdom of God has come upon you" (Matt. 12:28). His triumph over the destructive forces of Satan showed what God's kingdom was like. In this way, every miracle of healing or deliverance from demonic oppression advanced the kingdom and helped fulfill Jesus' ministry, for he came with the Spirit of the Lord on him "to proclaim good news to the poor . . . to proclaim liberty to the captives and recovering of sight to the blind, to set at liberty those who are oppressed" (Luke 4:18).

Similarly, Jesus gave his disciples "power and authority over all demons and to cure diseases, and he sent them out *to proclaim the kingdom of God* and to heal" (Luke 9:1–2). He commanded them, "Proclaim as you go, saying, 'The kingdom of heaven is at hand.' Heal the sick, raise the dead, cleanse lepers, cast out demons" (Matt. 10:7–8; cf. Matt. 4:23; 9:35; Acts 8:6–7, 13).

A third purpose of miracles is *to help those who are in need*. The two blind men near Jericho cried out, "Have mercy on us," and Jesus "in pity" healed them (Matt. 20:30, 34). The miraculous feeding of the 5,000 (Matt. 14:13–21) also falls in this category. Similarly, when Jesus saw a great crowd of people, "he had compassion on them and healed their sick" (Matt. 14:14; see also Luke 7:13). Here miracles give evidence of the compassion of Christ toward those in need.

A fourth purpose of miracles is *to remove hindrances to people's ministries*. As soon as Jesus had healed Peter's mother-in-law, "she rose and began to serve him" (Matt. 8:15). When God had mercy on Epaphroditus and restored his health (whether through miraculous means or not, Paul attributes it to God's mercy in Phil. 2:27), Epaphroditus was then able to minister to Paul and complete his function as a messenger returning to the Philippian church (Phil. 2:25–30). Although the text does not explicitly say that Tabitha (or Dorcas) resumed her "good works and acts of charity" (Acts 9:36) after the Lord through Peter raised her from the dead (Acts 9:40–41), by mentioning her good works and those who bore witness to her selfless care for the needs of others (Acts 9:39), it suggests that she would resume a similar ministry of mercy when she was raised from the dead. Related to this category would be the fact that Paul expects people to be edified (or "built up") when miraculous gifts are used in the church (1 Cor. 12:7; 14:4,

---

of miracles in encouraging people to believe in Christ (see John 2:11, 23; 3:2; 4:53–54; 6:2, 14; 7:31; 9:16; 11:48; 12:11; and, in summary, 20:30–31). This positive emphasis in John stands in contrast to the view of D. A. Carson in "The Purpose of Signs and Wonders in the New Testament," in Horton, *Power Religion*, 100–101, where he admits but minimizes the positive role of miracles in bringing people to faith in John's gospel. Surprisingly, he fails to discuss several of the positive passages mentioned above and sees a depreciation of miracles in passages where no such negative evaluation exists, such as John 2:23–25; 4:48; and 20:29–31. We should not think that when miracles accompany the gospel those who believe will have inferior faith (as Carson suggests, p. 101), for that would lead us to say that those who believed the preaching of Jesus, Peter, and Paul had inferior faith—a conclusion hardly advanced by the New Testament!

12, 26), and removing physical hindrances to people's ministries would certainly serve to build up the church.

Finally, a fifth purpose for miracles (and one to which all the others contribute) is *to bring glory to God*. After Jesus healed a paralytic, the crowds "were afraid, and they glorified God, who had given such authority to men" (Matt. 9:8). Similarly, Jesus said that the man who had been blind from birth was blind "that the works of God might be displayed in him" (John 9:3).

## D. WERE MIRACLES RESTRICTED TO THE APOSTLES?

## 1. An Unusual Concentration of Miracles in the Apostles' Ministry

Some have argued that miracles were restricted to the apostles or to the apostles and those closely connected with them. Before considering their arguments, I want to acknowledge that an unusual concentration of miracles was characteristic of the apostles as special representatives of Christ. For example, God was pleased to allow extraordinary miracles to be done through the apostles, and especially through Peter and Paul:

> Many signs and wonders were regularly done among the people by the hands of *the apostles*. . . . And more than ever believers were added to the Lord, multitudes of both men and women, so that they even carried out the sick into the streets and laid them on cots and mats, that as *Peter* came by at least his shadow might fall on some of them. The people also gathered from the towns around Jerusalem, bringing the sick and those afflicted with unclean spirits, and *they were all healed*. (Acts 5:12–16)

Similarly, when Paul was in Ephesus, "God was doing *extraordinary miracles by the hands of Paul*, so that even handkerchiefs or aprons that had touched his skin were carried away to the sick, and their diseases left them and the evil spirits came out of them" (Acts 19:11–12).[13] Another example is found in the raising of Tabitha: when she had died, the disciples at Joppa sent for Peter to come and pray for her to be raised from the dead (Acts 9:36–42), apparently because they thought that God had given an unusual concentration of miraculous power to Peter (or to the apostles generally). And Paul's ministry generally was characterized by miraculous events because he summarizes his ministry by telling the Romans of the things that Christ had worked through him to win obedience from the gentiles "by the power of *signs and wonders*, by the power of the Spirit of God" (Rom. 15:19).

Nevertheless, the unusual concentration of miracles in the ministries of the apostles does not prove that *no* miracles were performed by others! As we have clearly seen, the

---

13. In neither case should these events be thought of as some kind of "magic" that came automatically through Peter's shadow or handkerchiefs that Paul had touched; rather, the miracles are indications of the fact that the Holy Spirit was pleased to give such a full and remarkable empowering to the ministry of these men that on occasion he extended his work beyond their individual bodily presence even to things that they came near or touched.

"working of miracles" (1 Cor. 12:10) and other miraculous gifts (1 Cor. 12:4–11 mentions several) were part of the ordinary functioning of the Corinthian church, and Paul knows that God "works miracles" in the churches of Galatia as well (Gal. 3:5).

## 2. What Are the "Signs of an Apostle" in 2 Corinthians 12:12?

Why then have some argued that miracles were uniquely the signs that distinguished an apostle? Their case is largely based on 2 Corinthians 12:12, where Paul says, "The *signs of a true apostle* were performed among you with utmost patience, with signs and wonders and mighty works" (2 Cor. 12:12).[14] They say that this implies that others who were not the apostles (or their close companions) did not have that authority or could not work these miraculous signs.[15] They further maintain that the working of the miracles ceased when the apostles and their close associates died. Therefore, they conclude, no further miracles are to be expected today. (Those who hold this position are sometimes known as "*cessationists*" since they hold to the "cessation" (or ceasing) of miracles early in the history of the church.)

The key passage used to establish this point is 2 Corinthians 12:12:

> The signs of a true apostle were performed among you with utmost patience, with signs and wonders and mighty works.

In considering how to interpret this verse, it is crucial to pay attention to the context. When Paul speaks about "the signs of a true apostle," he is *not* attempting to prove that he is an apostle *in distinction from other Christians* who are not apostles. Rather, he is attempting to prove that he is *a true representative of Christ* in distinction from others who are "false apostles" (2 Cor. 11:13), false representatives of Christ, servants of Satan who are disguising themselves as "servants of righteousness" (2 Cor. 11:14–15). In short, the contrast is not between apostles who could work miracles and ordinary Christians who could not but between *genuine Christian apostles* through whom the Holy Spirit worked and *non-Christian pretenders to the apostolic office* through whom the Holy Spirit did not work at all. Therefore, even if we understand the "signs of an apostle" to be miracles, we should recognize that those who use this passage to argue that miracles cannot be done through *Christians* today are taking the phrase "signs of an apostle" out of its context and using it in a way that Paul never intended. Paul is distinguishing himself from non-Christians, whereas they use the passage to distinguish Paul from other Christians.

---

14. The word *true* is not actually in the Greek text, which simply says, "the signs of an apostle." The ESV (quoted here), as well as the NIV, RSV, NRSV, and NASB, has added *true* to give the sense: Paul is contrasting his ministry with that of the false apostles.

15. See Walter J. Chantry, *Signs of the Apostles*, 2nd ed. (Edinburgh: Banner of Truth, 1976), esp. 17–21; B. B. Warfield, *Counterfeit Miracles*; Norman Geisler, *Signs and Wonders* (Wheaton, IL: Tyndale, 1988).

Moreover, a close examination of 2 Corinthians 12:12 shows it to be doubtful that the phrase "signs of an apostle" in this passage means miraculous signs. In this very verse, Paul distinguishes the "signs of a true apostle" from miracles, which he calls "signs and wonders and mighty works," noting that the miracles were done *along with* the signs of an apostle: "The *signs of a true apostle* were performed among you with utmost patience, *with signs and wonders and mighty works*."[16] The latter phrase, *"with* signs and wonders and mighty works," piles up all three terms used for miracles and therefore must refer to miracles (note "signs and wonders" in Acts 4:30; 5:12; 14:3; 15:12; Rom. 15:19; Heb. 2:4, et al.). Therefore the former phrase, "signs of a true apostle," must refer to something different, something that was *accompanied by* (done "with") these signs and wonders.

Although the word *sign* in Greek (*sēmeion*) often refers to miracles, it has a much broader range of meaning than just *miracle. Sēmeion* simply means "something which indicates or refers to something else."[17] In 2 Corinthians 12:12, the "signs" of an apostle are best understood as *everything that characterized Paul's apostolic mission* and showed him to be a true apostle.[18] We need not guess at what these signs were, for elsewhere in 2 Corinthians Paul tells what marked him as a true apostle:

---

16. The grammar of the Greek text forces us to this distinction, since "the signs of an apostle" is in the nominative case, while "signs and wonders and mighty works" is in the dative, and cannot therefore be simply a restatement of "signs of an apostle" in apposition to it, because nouns in apposition in Greek must be in the same case. The preposition *with* is a common meaning for nouns in the dative case (dative of accompaniment). The NIV has an unusual translation, "the marks of a true apostle, *including* signs, wonders and miracles," but there is no word or phrase or grammatical construction in the Greek text that would ordinarily give the sense "including."

17. Many nonmiraculous things are called "signs." For example, Paul's handwritten signature is his "sign" (2 Thess. 3:17); circumcision is a "sign" of Abraham's imputed righteousness (Rom. 4:11); Judas's kiss is a "sign" to the Jewish leaders (Matt. 26:48); the rainbow is a "sign" of the covenant (Gen. 9:12 LXX); eating unleavened bread during Passover every year is a "sign" of the Lord's deliverance (Ex. 13:9 LXX); Rahab's scarlet cord is a "sign" that the spies told her to hang in her window (1 Clem. 12:7).

18. Several commentators understand "signs of a true apostle" to have a much broader meaning than miracles, emphasizing the qualities of Paul's life and the results of his ministry: see Mark Seifrid, *The Second Letter to the Corinthians*, PNTC (Grand Rapids: Eerdmans, 2014), 456–58, who correctly notes that "it is unlikely that Paul at this juncture is introducing a new element into the contention. The expression summarizes the boasting of the 'fool's speech'. . . . The fundamental sign of the apostle is that he does not fail (4:2, 16), despite hardship, affliction, and death itself" (456–57). See also Philip E.

Hughes, *Paul's Second Epistle to the Corinthians*, NIC (Grand Rapids: Eerdmans, 1962), 456–58 (following Chrysostom and Calvin); Ralph P. Martin, *II Corinthians*, WBC (Waco, TX: Word, 1986), 434–38 (with extensive discussion); Alfred Plummer, *A Critical and Exegetical Commentary on the Second Epistle of St. Paul to the Corinthians*, ICC (Edinburgh: T&T Clark, 1915), 359; R. V. G. Tasker, *2 Corinthians*, TNTC (London: Tyndale, 1958), 180; Charles Hodge, *An Exposition of 1 and 2 Corinthians* (repr., Wilmington, DE: Sovereign Grace, 1972), 359–60; John Calvin, *The Second Epistle of Paul the Apostle to the Corinthians . . .*, trans. T. A. Smail, ed. D. W. Torrance and T. F. Torrance (Edinburgh: Oliver and Boyd; Grand Rapids: Eerdmans, 1964), 163–64; see also J. B. Lightfoot, *The Epistle of St. Paul to the Galatians* (Grand Rapids: Zondervan, 1957), 99. Some of these commentators understand the "signs of a true apostle" as accompanied by or including miracles, but none understand the phrase to refer primarily or exclusively to miracles.

However, other commentators understand the "signs of a true apostle" in 2 Cor. 12:12 to be miracles. See Paul Barnett, *The Second Epistle to the Corinthians*, NIC (Grand Rapids: Eerdmans, 1997), 579–81; Colin Kruse, *The Second Epistle of Paul to the Corinthians*, TNTC (Leicester: Inter-Varsity Press; Grand Rapids: Eerdmans, 1987), 209; Jean Héring, *The Second Epistle of Saint Paul to the Corinthians*, trans. A. W. Heathcote and P. J. Allcock (London: Epworth, 1967), 95–96; and Murray Harris, "2 Corinthians," *EBC*, 10:398. Harris, however, notes an alternative view where the "signs" are the changed lives of the Corinthians and the Christlike character of Paul.

1. Spiritual power in conflict with evil (10:3–4, 8–11; 13:2–4, 10)
2. Jealous care for the welfare of the churches (11:1–6)
3. True knowledge of Jesus and his gospel plan (11:6)
4. Self-support (selflessness) (11:7–11)
5. Not taking advantage of churches; not striking people physically (11:20–21)
6. Suffering and hardship endured for Christ (11:23–29)
7. Being caught up into heaven (12:1–6)
8. Contentment and faith to endure a thorn in the flesh (12:7–9)
9. Gaining strength out of weakness (12:10).

The first item may have included miracles, but that is certainly not the primary focus of his reference to the "signs of a true apostle."

Another evidence that the "signs of a true apostle" in 2 Corinthians 12:12 were all these things and not simply miracles is the fact that Paul says, "The signs of a true apostle were performed among you *with utmost patience.*" Now it would make little sense to say that miracles were performed "with utmost patience," for many miracles happen quite quickly, but it would make much sense to say that Paul's Christlike endurance of hardship for the sake of the Corinthians was performed "with utmost patience."

We should note that nowhere in this list does Paul claim miracles to prove his genuine apostleship. In fact, most of the things he mentions would not distinguish him from other true Christians. But these things do distinguish him from servants of Satan, false apostles who are not Christians at all: their lives will be marked not by humility but by pride, not by selflessness but by selfishness, not by generosity but by greed, not by seeking the advantage of others but by taking advantage of others, not by spiritual power in physical weakness but by confidence in their natural strength, not by enduring suffering and hardship but by seeking their own comfort and ease.[19] When Paul acted in a Christlike manner among them, his actions were "signs" that his claim to be an apostle was a true claim: thus, these things were "signs of a true apostle." In this context, the "signs" that mark a true apostle need not be things that showed an absolute difference between him and other Christians but rather things that showed his ministry to be genuine, in distinction from false ministries. He is not here telling the Corinthians how to know who an apostle was in distinction from other Christians (he did that in 1 Cor. 9:1–2; 15:7–11; Gal. 1:1, 11–24, mentioning seeing the risen Christ and being commissioned by him as an apostle), but here he is telling how to recognize what a genuine, Christ-approved ministry was.

Why then does he add that all these signs of a true apostle were done among the Corinthians "with signs and wonders and mighty works"? He is simply adding one additional factor to all the previous marks of his genuine apostleship. Miracles of course had

19. Some interpreters assume that the false apostles were working miracles and claiming revelations from God, so Paul would have to claim greater miracles and revelations. But nothing in 2 Corinthians says that the false apostles claimed miracles or revelations.

a significant function in confirming the truth of Paul's message, and Paul here makes explicit what the Corinthians may or may not have assumed to be included in the phrase "signs of a true apostle." In addition to all these other signs of a true apostle, his ministry showed miraculous demonstrations of God's power as well.[20]

There is yet another very significant reason why miracles did not prove someone to be an apostle. In the larger context of the New Testament, miracles were worked by those who were not apostles, such as Stephen (Acts 6:8), Philip (Acts 8:6–7), Christians in the several churches in Galatia (Gal. 3:5), and those with gifts of "miracles" in the body of Christ generally (1 Cor. 12:10, 28). Miracles cannot then be regarded as exclusively signs of an apostle. In fact, "miracles" and "healers" are actually distinguished from "apostles" in 1 Corinthians 12:28: "God has appointed in the church first *apostles*, second prophets, third teachers, then *miracles*, then gifts of healing."

Similar evidence is seen in Mark 16:17–18. Though there are serious questions about the authenticity of this passage as part of Mark's gospel,[21] the text is nonetheless very early,[22] and even if we do not count it as part of Mark's gospel, at least it bears witness to one strand of tradition within the early church. This text reports Jesus as saying,

> And these signs will accompany those who believe: in my name they will cast out demons; they will speak in new tongues; they will pick up serpents with their hands; and if they drink any deadly poison, it will not hurt them; they will lay their hands on the sick, and they will recover.

Here also the power to work miracles is assumed to be the common possession of Christians. Those who wrote and passed on this early tradition and who thought it represented the genuine teaching of Jesus were certainly not aware of any idea that miracles were to be limited to the apostles and their close associates.[23]

The argument that many other Christians in the New Testament worked miracles is sometimes answered by the claim that it was only the apostles *and those closely associated with them* or those on whom the apostles laid their hands who could work miracles.[24] However, this really proves very little because the story of the New Testament church is the story of what was done through the apostles and those closely associated with them. A similar argument might be made about evangelism or the founding of churches: "In the New Testament, churches were only founded by the apostles or their close

---

20. The following verse also gives confirmation to this interpretation: Paul says, "For in what were you less favored than the rest of the churches...?" (2 Cor. 12:13). The fact that they were not lacking in any of Paul's care and attention would prove to them that the "signs of a true apostle" were performed among them only if these "signs" included all of Paul's ministry to them, but not if the "signs of a true apostle" were only the miracles.

21. The manuscript evidence and considerations of style suggest that these verses were not originally part of the gospel that Mark wrote. (See discussion of textual variants on pp. 92–93.)

22. It is included in several manuscripts of Tatian's Diatessaron (AD 170) and is quoted by Irenaeus (d. AD 202) and Tertullian (d. AD 220).

23. I am grateful to Professor Harold Hoehner of Dallas Theological Seminary for suggesting to me the arguments given here regarding 1 Cor. 12:28 and Mark 16:17–18 (though he may have disagreed with my conclusion in this section).

24. So Chantry, *Signs*, 19–21.

associates; therefore, we should not found churches today," or "In the New Testament, missionary work in other countries was only done by the apostles or their close associates; therefore, we should not do missionary work in other countries today." These analogies show the inadequacy of such an argument. The New Testament primarily shows how the church *should* seek to act, not how it *should not* seek to act.

But if many other Christians throughout the first-century church were working miracles by the power of the Holy Spirit, then the power to work miracles could not be a sign to distinguish the apostles from other Christians.

### 3. Norman Geisler's Restrictive Definition of Miracles

A more recent attempt to deny that miracles occur today has been made by Norman Geisler.[25] Geisler has a much more restrictive definition of *miracle* than that presented in this chapter, and he uses that definition to argue against the possibility of contemporary miracles. Geisler says that "miracles (1) are always successful, (2) are immediate, (3) have no relapses, and (4) give confirmation of God's messenger."[26] He finds support for this thesis largely in the ministry of Jesus, but when he passes beyond the life of Jesus and attempts to show that others who had the power to work miracles were never unsuccessful, his thesis is much less convincing. With regard to the demon-possessed boy whom the disciples could not set free from the demon (Matt. 17:14–21), Geisler says that "the disciples simply forgot for the moment to faithfully exercise the power that Jesus had already given them."[27] But this is an unpersuasive argument: Geisler says that the power to work miracles was always successful, and when the Bible talks about some who were unsuccessful (and who contradict his thesis), he simply says they "forgot."[28] Jesus, however, gives a different reason than Geisler: "Because of your little faith" (Matt. 17:20). Lesser faith resulted in lesser power to work miracles.

With regard to Paul's failure to heal Epaphroditus (Phil. 2:27), Geisler is forced to make the dubious claim that perhaps Paul never attempted to heal Epaphroditus (though he had come to him in prison and was so ill he almost died), or that "Paul no longer possessed the gift of healing at this time."[29] He employs the same claim to explain the fact that Paul "left Trophimus, who was ill, at Miletus" (2 Tim. 4:20). In these instances Geisler goes well beyond the usual cessationist claim that miracles ended with the death of the apostles—he is claiming that miracles ceased in the life of the greatest apostle before his first Roman imprisonment. That is simply an unconvincing argument with respect to the apostle whose ministry was repeatedly characterized "by the power of signs and wonders, by the power of the Spirit of God" (Rom. 15:19) and who could say with triumph in his last epistle, "I have fought the good fight, I have finished the race, I have kept the faith" (2 Tim. 4:7).

Geisler's description of miracles does not fit the case of the blind man upon whom Jesus

---

25. Geisler, *Signs and Wonders.* His definition of miracles is found on pp. 28–32 and 149–55.
26. Ibid., 28–30.
27. Ibid., 150.
28. Ibid.
29. Ibid.

laid his hands, for at first the man did not see clearly but said he saw men who "look like trees, walking." After Jesus laid his hands on him a second time, the man "saw everything clearly" (Mark 8:24–25). Geisler responds that it was Jesus' intention to heal in two stages, to teach the disciples by using an object lesson about the gradual growth of their spiritual lives.[30] Though the text says nothing to this effect, it may have been true, but even so it disproves Geisler's thesis, for if it was Jesus' intention to heal in two stages then, it may also be his intention to heal people in two stages today—or in three or four or more stages. Once Geisler admits that it may be God's intention to work a miracle in stages in order to accomplish his purposes, then his entire claim that miracles must be immediate and complete is lost. Geisler also has much difficulty explaining Mark 5:8 (where Jesus more than once commanded some demons to leave) and Mark 6:5 (where the text says that Jesus was not able to do any miracles in Nazareth because of the unbelief of the people there).[31]

Instead of accepting Geisler's definition, it seems better to conclude that even those whom God gifts with the ability to perform miracles may not be able to perform them whenever they wish, for the Holy Spirit continually is apportioning them to each person "as he wills" (1 Cor. 12:11; the word *apportions* translates a present participle in Greek, indicating a continuing activity of the Holy Spirit). Moreover, there seems no reason to exclude (as Geisler apparently wants to do) unusual or remarkable answers to prayer from the category of "miracle," thus making the definition extremely restrictive. If God answers persistent prayer, for instance, for a physical healing for which there is no known medical explanation and does so only after several months or years of prayer, yet he does so in such a way that it seems quite clearly to be in response to prayer so that people are amazed and glorify God, then there seems no reason to deny that a miracle has occurred simply because the earlier prayers were not answered immediately.

Finally, Geisler fails to recognize that several New Testament texts indicate that spiritual gifts, whether miraculous or nonmiraculous in nature, may vary in strength or degree of intensity.[32]

## 4. Hebrews 2:3–4

Another passage that is used to support the idea that miracles were limited to the apostles and their close associates is Hebrews 2:3–4. There the author says that the message of salvation "was declared at first by the Lord, and it was attested to us by those who heard, while God also bore witness[33] by signs and wonders and various miracles and by gifts of the Holy Spirit distributed according to his will."

Since the miracles here are said to come through those who heard the Lord firsthand

---

30. Ibid., 153–54.
31. Ibid., 149, 152.
32. See discussion in chapter 52, pp. 1262–64, below.
33. The KJV translates, "God also bearing *them* witness, both with signs and wonders." This translation suggests that the miracles bore witness to the people who heard Jesus and first preached. But the word *them* is represented by no word in the Greek text (the KJV puts it in italics to indicate this), and this translation is not followed by the NKJV or other modern versions.

("those who heard"), it is argued that we should not expect them to be done through others who were not firsthand witnesses to the Lord's teaching and ministry.[34]

But this argument also attempts to draw more from the passage than is there. First, the phrase "those who heard" (Heb. 2:3) is certainly not limited to the apostles, for many others heard Jesus as well. But more importantly, this position is claiming something that the text simply does not say. The fact that (1) the gospel message was confirmed by miracles when it was preached by *those who heard Jesus* says nothing at all about (2) whether it would be confirmed by miracles when preached by *others who did not hear Jesus*. Finally, this passage says the message was confirmed not only by "signs and wonders and various miracles" but also by "*gifts of the Holy Spirit.*" If someone argues that this passage limits miracles to the apostles and their companions, then he or she must also argue that gifts of the Holy Spirit are likewise limited to the first-century church. But few would argue that there are no gifts of the Holy Spirit today.[35]

## 5. Conclusion: Were Miracles Restricted to the Apostles?

If ministry in the power and glory of the Holy Spirit is characteristic of the new covenant age (2 Cor. 3:1–4:18), then our expectation would be just the opposite: we would expect that second and third and fourth generation Christians, who also know Christ and the power of his resurrection (Phil. 3:10), who are continually being filled with the Holy Spirit (Eph. 5:17), who are participants in a war that is not a worldly war, but one that is carried on with weapons that have divine power to destroy strongholds (2 Cor. 10:3–4), who have not been given a spirit of timidity but "of power and love and self-control" (2 Tim. 1:7), who are strong in the Lord and in the strength of his might, and who have put on the whole armor of God in order to be able to stand against principalities and powers and spiritual hosts of wickedness in the heavenly places (Eph. 6:10–12), would *also* have the ability to minister the gospel not only in truth and love but also with accompanying miraculous demonstrations of God's power. It is difficult to see, from the pages of the New Testament, any reason why only the preaching of the apostles should come "not in plausible words of wisdom, but *in demonstration of the Spirit and of power*, so that your faith might not rest in the wisdom of men but in the power of God" (1 Cor. 2:4–5).

Though there does seem to have been an unusual concentration of miraculous power in the ministry of the apostles, this is not a reason for thinking that there would be few or no miracles following their deaths. Rather, the apostles were the leaders in a new covenant church whose life and message were characterized by the power of the Holy Spirit

---

34. So Chantry, *Signs of the Apostles*, 18–19: "New Testament miracles are viewed in Scripture itself as God's stamp of approval upon the message of the apostles, which was an inspired record of the things they had seen and heard while with Jesus. Recalling these wonders should deepen our respect for the authority of their words and prompt us to give the more careful heed."

35. Another argument limiting miracles to the first century is based on the claim that some miracles, such as the gift of prophecy, always give new Scripture-quality revelation. That argument is considered in detail in chapters 52–53, pp. 1285–87, 1293–1313.

at work in miraculous ways. They set a pattern that the church throughout its history may well seek to imitate in its own life, insofar as God the Holy Spirit is pleased to work miracles for the edification of the church.[36]

## E. False Miracles

Pharaoh's magicians were able to work some false miracles (Ex. 7:11, 22; 8:7), though they soon had to admit that God's power was greater (Ex. 8:19). Simon the sorcerer in the city of Samaria amazed people with his magic (Acts 8:9–11), but the miracles done through Philip were much greater (Acts 8:13). In Philippi Paul encountered a slave girl "who had a spirit of divination and brought her owners much gain by fortune-telling" (Acts 16:16), but Paul rebuked the spirit and it came out of her (Acts 16:18). Moreover, Paul says that when the man of sin comes, it will be "with all power and false signs and wonders, and with all wicked deception for those who are perishing" (2 Thess. 2:9–10), but those who follow them and are deceived will do so "because they refused to love the truth and so be saved" (2 Thess. 2:10). This indicates that those who work false miracles in the end times by the power of Satan *will not speak the truth but will preach a false gospel.* Finally, Revelation 13 indicates that a second beast will rise "out of the earth," one that has "all the authority of the first beast" and "performs great signs, even making fire come down from heaven to earth in front of people, and by the signs that it is allowed to work in the presence of the beast it deceives those who dwell on earth" (Rev. 13:11–14). But once again a false gospel accompanies these miracles: this power is exercised in connection with the first beast who utters "haughty and blasphemous words. . . . It opened its mouth to utter blasphemies against God, blaspheming his name and his dwelling" (Rev. 13:5–6).

Two conclusions become clear from this brief survey of false miracles in Scripture. (1) *The power of God is greater than the power of Satan* to work miraculous signs, and God's people triumph in confrontations of power with those who work evil. In connection with this, John assures believers that "he who is in you is greater than he who is in the world" (1 John 4:4).[37] (2) The identity of these workers of false miracles *is always known through their denial of the gospel. There is no indication anywhere in Scripture that genuine Christians with the Holy Spirit in them will work false miracles.* In fact, in a city filled with idolatry and demon worship (see 1 Cor. 10:20), Paul could say to the Corinthian believers, many of whom had come out of that kind of pagan background,

---

36. However, Christians should be very cautious and take extreme care to be accurate in their reporting of miracles if they do occur. Much harm can be done to the gospel if Christians exaggerate or distort, even in small ways, the facts of a situation where a miracle has occurred. The power of the Holy Spirit is great enough to work however he wills, and we should never "embellish" the actual facts of the situation simply to make it sound even more exciting than it actually was. God does exactly what he is pleased to do in each situation.

37. Some may object that one exception to this may be

the vision of the end times in Rev. 13:7, where the beast "was allowed to make war on the saints and to conquer them" (Rev. 13:7). But even here there is no indication that the miraculous powers of the beast are greater than the power of the Holy Spirit. This seems to be best understood not as a confrontation of miraculous power but simply as a persecution by military force, for we read later of "those who had been beheaded for the testimony of Jesus and for the word of God, and those who had not worshiped the beast or its image and had not received its mark on their foreheads or their hands" (Rev. 20:4).

that "no one can say 'Jesus is Lord' except in the Holy Spirit" (1 Cor. 12:3). Here he gives them reassurance that those who make a genuine profession of faith in Jesus as Lord do in fact have the Holy Spirit in them. It is significant that he immediately goes on to a discussion of spiritual gifts possessed by "each" true believer (1 Cor. 12:7).

This should reassure us that if we see miracles being worked by those who make a genuine profession of faith (1 Cor. 12:3), who believe in the incarnation and deity of Christ (1 John 4:2), and who show the fruit of the Holy Spirit in their lives and bear fruit in their ministry (Matt. 7:20; cf. John 15:5; Gal. 5:22–23), we should not be suspicious that they are false miracles but should be thankful to God that the Holy Spirit is working, even in those who may not hold exactly the same convictions that we do on every point of doctrine.[38] Indeed, if God waited to work miracles only through those who were perfect in both doctrine and conduct of life, no miracles would be worked until Christ returns.

## F. SHOULD CHRISTIANS SEEK MIRACLES TODAY?

It is one thing to say that miracles might occur today. It is quite another thing to ask God for miracles. Is it right for Christians to ask God to perform miracles today?

The answer depends on the purpose for which miracles are sought. Certainly it is wrong to seek miraculous power to advance one's own power or fame, as Simon the magician did. Peter said to him, "Your heart is not right before God. Repent, therefore, of this wickedness of yours, and pray to the Lord that, if possible, the intent of your heart may be forgiven you" (Acts 8:21–22).

It is also wrong to seek miracles simply to be entertained, as Herod did: "When Herod saw Jesus, he was very glad, for he had long desired to see him, because he had heard about him, and he was hoping to see some sign done by him" (Luke 23:8). But Jesus would not even answer Herod's questions.

It is also wrong for skeptical unbelievers to seek miracles simply to find ground to criticize those who preach the gospel:

And the Pharisees and Sadducees came, and *to test him* they asked him to show them a sign from heaven. He answered them, " . . . An evil and adulterous generation seeks for a sign, but no sign will be given to it except the sign of Jonah." (Matt. 16:1–4)

This rebuke against seeking signs is repeated elsewhere in the Gospels, but it is important to note that rebukes against seeking signs are always directed against hostile unbelievers

---

38. The fact that people who name the name of Christ are able to prophesy and cast out demons and do "many mighty works" in his name (Matt. 7:21–23) does not contradict this because these are non-Christians: Jesus says to them, *"I never knew you*; depart from me, you workers of lawlessness" (Matt. 7:23). Although it is possible that these are false miracles worked by demonic power, it seems more likely that they are operations of common grace (see chapter 31) that God worked through non-Christians, similar to the effectiveness of the gospel that God sometimes allows when it is preached by those who have impure motives and do not know Christ in their hearts (cf. Phil. 1:15–18).

who are seeking a miracle only as an opportunity to criticize Jesus.[39] Never does Jesus rebuke anyone who comes in faith or in need, seeking healing or deliverance or any other kind of miracle, whether for himself or herself or for others.

What shall we say then about 1 Corinthians 1:22–24, where Paul says, "For *Jews demand signs* and Greeks seek wisdom, but we preach Christ crucified, a stumbling block to Jews and folly to Gentiles, but to those who are called, both Jews and Greeks, Christ the power of God and the wisdom of God"? Does Paul mean that he did not work miracles ("signs") at Corinth, or perhaps in his evangelistic work generally?

Here Paul cannot be denying that he performed miracles in connection with the proclamation of the gospel. In fact, in Romans 15:18–19, a passage he wrote while in Corinth, he said,

> For I will not venture to speak of anything except what Christ has accomplished through me to bring the Gentiles to obedience—by word and deed, *by the power of signs and wonders*, by the power of the Spirit of God—so that from Jerusalem and all the way around to Illyricum I have fulfilled the ministry of the gospel of Christ.

And 2 Corinthians 12:12 affirms clearly that Paul did work "signs and wonders and mighty works" among them.

So 1 Corinthians 1:22–24 cannot mean that Paul was denying the validity of *wisdom* or the validity of *signs*, for through Christ he worked signs and taught wisdom. Rather, he is saying that signs and wisdom do not themselves save people; the gospel saves people. Signs and the wisdom that Jews and Greeks were seeking were not the signs and wisdom of Christ but simply signs to entertain or to fuel their hostility and skepticism and wisdom that was the wisdom of the world rather than the wisdom of God.

There is nothing inappropriate in seeking miracles for the proper purposes for which they are given by God: to confirm the truthfulness of the gospel message, to bring help to those in need, to remove hindrances to people's ministries, and to bring glory to God (see section C above). In the Gospels many people came to Jesus seeking miracles, and he healed them for these purposes. Moreover, when he sent his disciples out preaching that the kingdom of heaven was at hand, he told them, "Heal the sick, raise the dead, cleanse lepers,

39. The fact that Jesus only rebukes hostile unbelievers who seek miracles is surprisingly never mentioned by D. A. Carson, "The Purpose of Signs and Wonders in the New Testament," in Horton, *Power Religion*, 89–118, or by James M. Boice, "A Better Way: The Power of Word and Spirit," in Horton, *Power Religion*, 119–36. Both articles use Jesus' rebukes as a means of discouraging believers from seeking miracles today, but to do this they must apply Jesus' statements in a way not justified by the New Testament contexts. (See esp. Boice, who quotes with approval a statement from John Woodhouse, "A desire for further signs and wonders is sinful and unbelieving," p. 126.)

The explicit statement of intent "to test him" is also found in Mark 8:11 and Luke 11:16, parallel contexts where Jesus rebukes an evil generation for seeking a sign from him. The only other context where this rebuke occurs, Matt. 12:38–42, does not include an explicit statement of the intent to test, but Jesus is clearly responding to the "scribes and Pharisees" (v. 38), and the incident follows just after Matt. 12:14, where the Pharisees "went out and conspired against him, how to destroy him," and Matt. 12:24, where the Pharisees say, "It is only by Beelzebul, the prince of demons, that this man casts out demons."

cast out demons" (Matt. 10:7–8). How could they do this without seeking God for miracles everywhere they went? Jesus' command required them to seek for miracles to happen.

After Pentecost, the early church prayed both for boldness to preach the gospel and for God to grant miracles to accompany its preaching. They cried out to God,

> And now, Lord, look upon their threats and grant to your servants to continue to speak your word with all boldness, *while you stretch out your hand to heal*, and *signs and wonders* are performed through the name of your holy servant Jesus. (Acts 4:29–30)

Far from teaching that we should not ask God for miracles, this example of the early church gives us some encouragement to do so. Similarly, the disciples in Lydda sent for Peter to come and pray for Tabitha after she had died, thereby seeking a miraculous intervention by God (Acts 9:38). And James directs that the elders of the church should pray and seek healing for those who are ill (James 5:14). Of course, we should not assume that an obviously miraculous answer to prayer is somehow better than one that comes through ordinary means (such as medical help for sickness), and we must also realize that asking God for a particular need does not guarantee that the prayer will be answered.

On the other hand, our faith that God will work in powerful and even miraculous ways may be far too small. We must beware of being infected by a secular worldview that assumes that God will answer prayer only very seldom, if ever. And we should certainly not be embarrassed to talk about miracles if they occur—or think that a nonmiraculous answer to prayer is better! Miracles are God's work, and he works them to bring glory to himself and to strengthen our faith. When we encounter serious needs in people's lives today, it is right for us to seek God for an answer, and where miraculous intervention seems to be needed, then to ask God if he would be pleased to work in that way.[40] This would seem to be especially appropriate when our motivation is a Christlike compassion for those in need and a burning desire to see Christ's kingdom advance and his name glorified.

## QUESTIONS FOR PERSONAL APPLICATION

1. When you first came to faith in Christ, did the stories of miracles in the Bible have any influence (negative or positive) on your believing the message of Scripture?
2. Before reading this chapter, have you thought of the church at the time of the New Testament as a church with frequent miracles? Have you thought of the

---

40. John Walvoord, the former President of Dallas Theological Seminary, understands the gift of miracles to be "the power to perform miracles at will in the name of Christ." Therefore he holds that the gift of miracles has ceased. But he still argues that we can pray for miracles today: "A Christian can still appeal to God to do wonders, and God does answer prayer. God can still heal and even raise the dead if he chooses, but these miracles are sovereign and individual.... While therefore the gift of miracles is not part of the present program of God, the power of God to perform miracles must be affirmed" (*The Holy Spirit* [Wheaton, IL: Van Kampen, 1954], 179–80).

contemporary church as one with frequent miracles? After reading this chapter, how has your position changed, if at all?

3. If you think that miracles should be characteristic of the church until Christ returns, then why have we not seen very many miracles at many points in the history of the church, and why do we not see many miracles in large sections of the Christian church today?

4. If you hold a "cessationist" position, what kinds of unusual answers to prayer might you still think possible today? (For example, prayer for physical healing, for deliverance from danger, victory over demonic attack through prayer and/or verbal rebuke of an evil spirit, or sudden and unusual insight into a passage of Scripture or a situation in someone's life.) How would you distinguish these things that you might think possible today from "miracles" according to the definition given in this chapter? (You may wish to argue for a different definition of "miracle" as well.)

5. Do miracles have to be large and "remarkable" (such as raising the dead or healing a man blind from birth) to accomplish useful purposes in the church today? What kinds of "small-scale" miracles might also accomplish some of the purposes for miracles listed in this chapter? Have you known of any answers to prayer in your own church (or your own life) that you would characterize as "miraculous" according to the definition given at the beginning of the chapter?

6. Would you like to see more miraculous power of the Holy Spirit (or more unusual answers to prayer) at work in your own church today, or not? If more miracles did occur, what might be the dangers? What might be the benefits?

## Special Terms

*cessationist*
*mighty work*
*miracle*
*natural law*
*sign*
*"signs of a true apostle"*
*wonder*

## BIBLIOGRAPHY

(For an explanation of this bibliography see the note on the bibliography to chapter 1, pp. 23–24. Complete bibliographical data may be found on pp. 1489–96.)

### SECTIONS IN EVANGELICAL SYSTEMATIC THEOLOGIES

1. *Anglican (Episcopalian)*
   2001 . . . . . . . . . Packer, 57–58
   2013 . . . . . . . . . Bray, 993–94

2. *Arminian (Wesleyan or Methodist)*
   1875–76 . . . . . Pope, 1:63–76
   1940 . . . . . . . . Wiley, 1:149, 150, 153, 154
   1992 . . . . . . . . Oden, 1:81
   2002 . . . . . . . . Cottrell, 47, 125, 279, 304

3. *Baptist*
   1907 . . . . . . . . Strong, 117–33
   1987–94 . . . . . Lewis and Demarest, 1:100–109, 115–18

1990–95 . . . . . Garrett, 1:395–412
2007 . . . . . . . . Akin, 673–78, 517–18
2013 . . . . . . . . Erickson, 379–82

4. *Dispensational*
1947 . . . . . . . . Chafer, 7:239
1949 . . . . . . . . Thiessen, 11–13
1986 . . . . . . . . Ryrie, 350–51, 372–73
2002–2005 . . Geisler, 1:43–63, 187–88,
          197–200, 2:608–10, 4:671–79
2017 . . . . . . . . MacArthur and Mayhue,
          216–18

5. *Lutheran*
1917–24 . . . . . Pieper, 1:459–60
1934 . . . . . . . . Mueller, 174

6. *Reformed (or Presbyterian)*
1559 . . . . . . . . Calvin, 1:14–18, 85–88;
          2:1453–1455, 1465–67 (*PA*,
          3; 1.8.5–8; 4.19.6, 18)
1679–85 . . . . . Turretin, *IET*, 1:287–88, 435,
          2:293–94, 3:114–15, 241
1871–73 . . . . . Hodge, 1:617–36
1887–1921 . . . Warfield, *SSW*, 2:167–206
1894 . . . . . . . . Shedd, 416–428
1906–11 . . . . . Bavinck, *RD*, 1:336–39,
          370–76
1910 . . . . . . . . Vos, 1:157, 184, 196–98
1937–66 . . . . . Murray, *CW*, 3:210–14
1938 . . . . . . . . Berkhof, 176–78
1998 . . . . . . . . Reymond, 407–14, 553–59
2008 . . . . . . . . Van Genderen and Velema,
          56, 93, 183, 300, 599
2011 . . . . . . . . Horton, 368–70
2013 . . . . . . . . Frame, 121–38, 141–43, 928–29
2013 . . . . . . . . Culver, 203–13
2019 . . . . . . . . Letham, 302–6

7. *Renewal (or charismatic/Pentecostal)*
1988–92 . . . . . Williams, 1:141–68
1993 . . . . . . . . Menzies and Horton, 113,
          166–67, 178
1995 . . . . . . . . Horton, 12, 58, 466–67
2008 . . . . . . . . Duffield and Van Cleave, 338,
          374, 387, 402, 411–12

## SECTIONS IN REPRESENTATIVE ROMAN CATHOLIC SYSTEMATIC THEOLOGIES

1. *Roman Catholic: Traditional*
1955 . . . . . . . . Ott (no explicit treatment)

2. *Roman Catholic: Post–Vatican II*
1980 . . . . . . . . McBrien, 1:325–28
2012 . . . . . . . . *CCC*, paragraph 156

## OTHER WORKS

Berkouwer, G. C. "Providence and Miracles." In *The Providence of God*, translated by Lewis B. Smedes, 188–231. Grand Rapids: Eerdmans, 1952.

Blackburn, B. L. "Miracles and Miracle Stories." In *DJG*, 549–60.

Blomberg, Craig L. "Miracle." In *BTDB*, 531–34.

Boice, James Montgomery. "A Better Way: The Power of Word and Spirit." In *Power Religion: The Selling Out of the Evangelical Church?*, edited by Michael Scott Horton, 119–35. Chicago: Moody Publishers, 1992.

Bridge, Donald. *Signs and Wonders Today*. Leicester: Inter-Varsity Press, 1985.

Brown, Colin. "Miracle." In *NDT1*, 433–34.

———. *That You May Believe: Miracles and Faith— Then and Now*. Grand Rapids: Eerdmans, 1985.

Carson, D. A. "The Purpose of Signs and Wonders in the New Testament," In *Power Religion: The Selling Out of the Evangelical Church?*, edited by Michael Scott Horton, 89–118. Chicago: Moody Publishers, 1992.

Daunton-Fear, Andrew. *Healing in the Early Church: The Church's Ministry of Healing and Exorcism from the First to the Fifth Century*. Milton Keynes: Paternoster, 2009.

Davids, P. H. "Miracles in Acts." In *DLNT*, 746–52.

Deere, Jack. *Surprised by the Power of the Spirit: A Former Dallas Seminary Professor Discovers That God Still Speaks and Heals Today*. Grand Rapids: Zondervan, 1993.

Geisler, Norman. *Signs and Wonders*. Wheaton, IL: Tyndale, 1988.

———. *Miracles and Modern Thought*. With a response by R. C. Sproul. Grand Rapids: Zondervan; Dallas: Probe Ministries, 1982.

Greig, Gary S., and Kevin N. Springer, eds. *The Kingdom and the Power*. Ventura, CA: Regal, 1993.

Gross, Edward N. *Miracles, Demons, and Spiritual Warfare: An Urgent Call for Discernment*. Grand Rapids: Baker, 1990.

Grudem, Wayne. *Power and Truth: A Response to the Critiques of Vineyard Teaching and Practice by D. A. Carson, James Montgomery Boice, and John H. Armstrong in "Power Religion"*. Anaheim, CA: Association of Vineyard Churches, 1993.

———. "Should Christians Expect Miracles Today? Objections and Answers From the Bible." In *The Kingdom and the Power*, edited by Gary Greig and Kevin Springer, 55–110. Ventura, CA: Regal, 1993.

Hicks, P. A. "Miracle." In *NDT2*, 578–79.

Horton, Michael S., ed. *Power Religion: The Selling Out of the Evangelical Church?* Chicago: Moody Publishers, 1992.

Keener, Craig S. *Miracles: The Credibility of the New Testament Accounts*. 2 Vols. Grand Rapids: Baker Academic, 2011.

Kirk, J. A. "Power." In *NDT1*, 524–25.

Lewis, C. S. *Miracles: A Preliminary Study*. New York: Macmillan, 1947.

Moule, C. F. D., ed. *Miracles*. London: Mowbray, 1965.

Rainey, D. L. "Power." In *NDT2*, 695–96.

Ruthven, J. "Miracle." In *GDT*, 546–50.

Spiceland, J. D. "Miracles." In *EDT3*, 551–52.

Twelftree, Graham H. *Jesus the Miracle Worker: A Historical and Theological Study*. Downers Grove, IL: InterVarsity Press, 1999.

———. *Paul and the Miraculous: A Historical Reconstruction*. Grand Rapids: Baker Academic, 2013.

———. "Signs, Wonders, Miracles." In *DPL*, 875–77.

———. "Signs and Wonders." In *NDBT*, 775–81.

Wenham, David, and Craig Blomberg, eds. *Miracles of Jesus*. Sheffield: JSOT, 1986.

Williams, Don. *Signs, Wonders, and the Kingdom of God: A Biblical Guide for the Skeptic*. Ann Arbor, MI: Servant, 1989.

Wimber, John, with Kevin Springer. *Power Evangelism*. Rev. ed. San Francisco: Harper and Row; London: Hodder and Stoughton, 1992.

## SCRIPTURE MEMORY PASSAGE

**Hebrews 2:3–4:** How shall we escape if we neglect such a great salvation? It was declared at first by the Lord, and it was attested to us by those who heard, while God also bore witness by signs and wonders and various miracles and by gifts of the Holy Spirit distributed according to his will.

## HYMN

### "A Mighty Fortress Is Our God"

*A mighty fortress is our God, a bulwark never failing; Our helper he amid the flood of mortal ills prevailing. For still our ancient foe doth seek to work us woe;*

*His craft and pow'r are great; and, armed with cruel hate, On earth is not his equal.*

Did we in our own strength confide, our striving
   would be losing;
Were not the right man on our side, the man of
   God's own choosing.
Dost ask who that may be? Christ Jesus, it is he,
Lord Sabaoth his name, from age to age the same,
And he must win the battle.

And though this world, with devils filled, should
   threaten to undo us,
We will not fear, for God hath willed his truth to
   triumph through us.

The prince of darkness grim, we tremble not
   for him;
His rage we can endure, for lo! his doom is sure;
One little word shall fell him.

That word above all earthly powers, no thanks to
   them, abideth;
The Spirit and the gifts are ours through him
   who with us sideth;
Let goods and kindred go, this mortal life also;
The body they may kill: God's truth abideth still;
His kingdom is forever.

Author: Martin Luther, 1529

# CONTEMPORARY WORSHIP SONG

## "Our God"

Water You turned into wine,
Opened the eyes of the blind,
There's no one like You,
None like you!
Into the darkness You shine,
Out of the ashes we rise,
There's no one like You,
None like You!

### Chorus
Our God is greater.
Our God is stronger.
God, You are higher than any other.
Our God is healer,
Awesome in power, our God, our God.

### Bridge
And if our God is for us,
Then who could ever stop us?
And if our God is with us,
Then what could stand against?
And if our God is for us,
Then who could ever stop us?
And if our God is with us,
Then what could stand against,
(Then) what could stand against?

Words by Jonas Myrin, Jesse Reeves,
Chris Tomlin, and Matt Redman[41]

---

# CHAPTER 18

# Prayer

*Why does God want us to pray?*
*How can we pray effectively?*

## EXPLANATION AND SCRIPTURAL BASIS

The character of God and his relationship to the world, as discussed in the previous chapters, lead naturally to a consideration of the doctrine of prayer. Prayer may be defined as follows: *prayer is personal communication with God.*

This definition is very broad. What we call "prayer" includes prayers of request for ourselves or for others (sometimes called prayers of petition or intercession), confession of sin, adoration, praise and thanksgiving, and also God communicating to us indications of his response.

### A. Why Does God Want Us to Pray?

Prayer is not made so that God can find out what we need. Jesus tells us, "Your Father knows what you need before you ask him" (Matt. 6:8). God wants us to pray because prayer expresses our trust in God and is a means whereby our trust in him can increase. In fact, perhaps the primary emphasis of the Bible's teaching on prayer is that we are to pray with faith, which means trust or dependence on God. God as our Creator delights in being trusted by us as his creatures, for an attitude of dependence is most appropriate to the Creator-creature relationship. Praying in humble dependence also indicates that we are genuinely convinced of God's wisdom, love, goodness, and power—indeed of all of the attributes that make up his excellent character. When we truly pray, we as persons, in the wholeness of our character, are relating to God as a person, in the wholeness of his character. Thus all that we think or feel about God comes to expression in our prayer. It is only natural that God would delight in such activity and place much emphasis on it in his relationship with us.

The first words of the Lord's Prayer, "Our Father in heaven" (Matt. 6:9), acknowledge our dependence on God as a loving and wise Father and also recognize that he rules over all from his heavenly throne. Scripture many times emphasizes our need to trust God, our good and wise heavenly Father, as we pray. For example, Jesus compares our praying to a son asking his father for a fish or an egg (Luke 11:9–12) and then concludes, "If you then, who are evil, know how to give good gifts to your children, how much more will the heavenly Father give the Holy Spirit to those who ask him!" (Luke 11:13). As children look to their fathers to provide for them, so God expects us to look to him in prayer. Since God is our

Father, we should ask in faith. Jesus says, "Whatever you ask in prayer, you will receive, if you have faith" (Matt. 21:22; cf. Mark 11:24; James 1:6–8; 5:14–15).

But God does not only want us to trust him. He also wants us to love him and have fellowship with him. This, then, is a second reason why God wants us to pray: prayer brings us into deeper fellowship with God, and he loves us and delights in our fellowship with him.

A third reason God wants us to pray is that in prayer God allows us as creatures to be involved in activities that are eternally important. When we pray, the work of the kingdom is advanced. In this way, prayer gives us opportunity to be involved in a significant way in the work of the kingdom and thus gives expression to our greatness as creatures made in God's image.

## B. THE EFFECTIVENESS OF PRAYER

How exactly does prayer work? Does prayer not only do us good but also affect God and the world?

### 1. God Genuinely Responds to Our Prayers by Changing the Way He Acts in the World

James tells us, "You do not have, because you do not ask" (James 4:2). He implies that failure to ask deprives us of what God would otherwise have given to us. We pray, and God responds. Jesus also says, "Ask, and it will be given to you; seek, and you will find; knock, and it will be opened to you. For everyone who asks receives, and the one who seeks finds, and to the one who knocks it will be opened" (Luke 11:9–10). He makes a clear connection between seeking things from God and receiving them. The clear pattern repeated throughout Scripture is that when we ask, God responds.

We see this happening many times in the Old Testament. The Lord declared to Moses that he would destroy the people of Israel for their sin (Ex. 32:9–10): "But Moses implored the LORD his God and said, 'O Lord. . . . Turn from your burning anger and relent from this disaster against your people'" (Ex. 32:11–12). Then we read, "The LORD relented from the disaster that he had spoken of bringing on his people" (Ex. 32:14). When God threatens to punish his people for their sins he declares, "If my people who are called by my name humble themselves, *and pray and seek my face* and turn from their wicked ways, *then I will hear* from heaven and will forgive their sin and heal their land" (2 Chron. 7:14). If and when God's people pray (with humility and repentance), *then* he will hear and forgive them. The prayers of God's people clearly affect how God acts. Similarly, "If we confess our sins, he is faithful and just to forgive us our sins and to cleanse us from all unrighteousness" (1 John 1:9). We confess, and then he forgives.[1]

---

1. Other examples of God answering prayer in Scripture are too numerous to comment on (Gen. 18:22–33; 32:26; Dan. 10:12; Amos 7:1–6; Acts 4:29–31; 10:31; 12:5–11, et al.).

If we were really convinced that God actually does respond to our prayers and change the way he acts, and therefore that God actually does bring about remarkable changes in the world in response to prayer, as Scripture repeatedly teaches that he does, then we would pray much more than we do. If we pray little, it is probably because we do not really believe that prayer accomplishes much at all.

## 2. Effective Prayer Is Made Possible by Our Mediator, Jesus Christ

Because we are sinful and God is holy, we have no right on our own to enter his presence. We need a mediator to come between us and God and to bring us into God's presence. Scripture clearly teaches, "There is one God, and there is one mediator between God and men, the man Christ Jesus" (1 Tim. 2:5).

But if Jesus is the only mediator between God and man, will God hear the prayers of those who do not trust in Jesus? The answer depends on what we mean by "hear." Since God is omniscient, he always "hears" in the sense that he is aware of the prayers made by unbelievers who do not come to him through Christ. God may even, from time to time, answer their prayers out of his mercy and in a desire to bring them to salvation through Christ. However, God has nowhere promised to respond to the prayers of unbelievers. The only prayers that he has promised to "hear" in the sense of listening with a sympathetic ear and undertaking to answer when they are made according to his will, are the prayers of Christians offered through the one mediator, Jesus Christ (cf. John 14:6).

Then what about believers in the Old Testament? How could they come to God through Jesus the mediator? The answer is that the work of Jesus as our mediator was foreshadowed by the sacrificial system and the offerings made by the priests in the temple (Heb. 7:23–28; 8:1–6; 9:1–14, et al.). There was no saving merit inherent in that system of sacrifices (Heb. 10:1–4), however. Through the sacrificial system believers were accepted by God only on the basis of the future work of Christ foreshadowed by that system (Rom. 3:23–26).

Jesus' activity as a mediator is especially seen in his work as a priest: he is our "great high priest who has passed through the heavens," one who "in every respect has been tempted as we are, yet without sin" (Heb. 4:14–15).

As recipients of the new covenant, we do not need to stay "outside the temple," as all believers except the priests were required to do under the old covenant. Nor do we need to stay outside of the "Holy of Holies" (Heb. 9:3), the inner room of the temple where God himself was enthroned above the ark of the covenant and where only the high priest could go, and he but once a year. But now, since Christ has died as our mediational High Priest (Heb. 7:26–27), he has gained for us boldness and access to the very presence of God. Therefore "we have confidence to enter *the holy places* by the blood of Jesus" (Heb. 10:19), that is, into the holy place and into the holy of holies, the very presence of God himself! We enter "by the new and living way" (Heb. 10:20) that Christ opened for us. The author of Hebrews concludes that since these things are true, "and since we have a great priest over the house of God, let us draw near with a true heart in full assurance of faith" (Heb. 10:21–22). In this way, Christ's mediational work gives us confidence to approach God in prayer.

We do not just come into God's presence as strangers, visitors, or laypersons but as priests—as people who belong in the temple and have a right and even a duty to be in the most sacred places in the temple. Using imagery from the ceremony for ordination of priests (see Ex. 29:4, 21), the author of Hebrews pictures all believers as having been ordained as priests to God and thus able to enter into his presence, for he says that we draw near "with our hearts sprinkled clean from an evil conscience and our bodies washed with pure water" (Heb. 10:22; cf. 1 Peter 2:9). Does all this make sense to a modern Christian? No one today goes to Jerusalem to enter the temple and there "draw near" to God. Even if we did go to Jerusalem, we would find no temple standing, since it was destroyed in AD 70. What then does the author of Hebrews mean when he says we enter into the "holy places"? He is talking about a reality in the unseen spiritual realm. With Christ as our Mediator we enter not into the earthly temple in Jerusalem but into the true sanctuary, into "heaven itself," where Christ has gone "to appear in the presence of God on our behalf" (Heb. 9:24).

### 3. What Is Praying "in Jesus' Name"?

Jesus says, "Whatever you ask *in my name*, this I will do, that the Father may be glorified in the Son. If you ask me anything in my name, I will do it" (John 14:13–14). He also says that he chose his disciples "so that whatever you ask the Father *in my name*, he may give it to you" (John 15:16). Similarly, he says, "Truly, truly, I say to you, whatever you ask of the Father in my name, he will give it to you. Until now you have asked nothing *in my name*. Ask, and you will receive, that your joy may be full" (John 16:23–24; cf. Eph. 5:20). But what does this mean?

Clearly it does not simply mean adding the phrase "in Jesus' name" after every prayer, because Jesus did not say, "If you ask anything and add the words 'in Jesus' name' after your prayer, I will do it." Jesus is not merely speaking about adding certain words as if these were a kind of magical formula that would give power to our prayers. In fact, none of the prayers recorded in Scripture have the phrase "in Jesus' name" at the end of them (see Matt. 6:9–13; Acts 1:24–25; 4:24–30;[2] 7:59; 9:13–14; 10:14; Rev. 6:10; 22:20).

To come in the name of someone means that another person has authorized us to come *on his authority*, not on our own. When Peter commands the lame man, "In the name of Jesus Christ of Nazareth, rise up and walk!" (Acts 3:6), he is speaking on the authority of Jesus, not on his own authority. When the Sanhedrin ask the disciples, "By

---

2. In Acts 4:30 the phrase, "through the name of your holy servant Jesus," which appears at the end of a prayer, modifies the main clause immediately preceding it, "and signs and wonders are performed." It is not a general statement about the way in which the whole prayer is made.

what power or *by what name* did you do this?" (Acts 4:7), they are asking, "By whose authority did you do this?" When Paul rebukes an unclean spirit "in the name of Jesus Christ" (Acts 16:18), he makes it clear that he is doing so on Jesus' authority, not his own. When Paul pronounces judgment "in the name of the Lord Jesus" (1 Cor. 5:4) on a church member who is guilty of immorality, he is acting with the authority of the Lord Jesus. *Praying in Jesus' name is therefore prayer made on his authorization.*

But in a broader sense the "name" of a person in the ancient world represented the person himself and therefore all of his character. To have a "good name" (Prov. 22:1; Eccl. 7:1) was to have a good reputation. Thus the name of Jesus represents all that he is, his entire character. This means that praying "in Jesus' name" is not only praying in his authority but *also praying in a way that is consistent with his character,* that truly represents him and reflects his manner of life and his own holy will.[3] In this sense, to pray in Jesus' name comes close to the idea of praying "according to his will" (1 John 5:14–15).[4]

Does this mean that it is wrong to add "in Jesus' name" to the end of our prayers? It is certainly not wrong, as long as we understand what is meant by it, and that it is not necessary to do so. There may be some danger, however, if we add this phrase to every public or private prayer we make, for very soon it will become to people simply a formula to which they attach very little meaning and say without thinking about it. It may even begin to be viewed, at least by younger believers, as a sort of magic formula that makes prayer more effective. To prevent such misunderstanding, it would probably be wise to decide not to use the same words every time and to express the same thought in other words, or simply in the overall attitude and approach we take toward prayer. For example, prayers could begin, "Father, we come to you in the authority of our Lord Jesus, your Son" or "Father, we do not come on our own merits but on the merits of Jesus Christ, who has invited us to come before you" or "Father, we thank you for forgiving our sins and giving us access to your throne by the work of Jesus your Son." At other times even these formal acknowledgments should not be thought necessary, so long as our hearts continually realize that it is our Savior who enables us to pray to the Father at all. Genuine prayer is conversation with a person whom we know well, and who knows us. Genuine conversation between persons who know each other never depends on the use of certain formulas or required words but is instead a matter of sincerity in our speech and in our heart, a matter of right attitudes, and a matter of the condition of our spirit.

---

3. In fact, Paul says that not just our prayers but everything we do is to be done in Jesus' name: "Whatever you do, in word or deed, *do everything in the name of the Lord Jesus,* giving thanks to God the Father through him" (Col. 3:17).

4. Leon Morris says of John 14:13, "This does not mean simply using the name as a formula. It means that prayer is to be in accordance with all that the name stands for. It is prayer proceeding from faith in Christ, prayer that gives expression to a unity with all that Christ stands for, prayer which seeks to set forward Christ himself. And the purpose of it all is the glory of God" (*The Gospel according to John,* 646).

## 4. Should We Pray to Jesus and to the Holy Spirit?

A survey of the prayers of the New Testament indicates that usually they are addressed neither to God the Son nor to the Holy Spirit but to God the Father. Yet a mere count of such prayers may be misleading, for the majority of the prayers we have recorded in the New Testament are those of Jesus himself, who constantly prayed to God the Father but, of course, did not pray to himself as God the Son. Moreover, in the Old Testament, the Trinitarian nature of God was not so clearly revealed, so it is not surprising that we do not find much evidence of prayer addressed directly to God the Son or God the Holy Spirit before the time of Christ.

Though there is a clear pattern of prayer directly to God the Father through the Son (Matt. 6:9; John 16:23; Eph. 5:20), there are indications that prayer spoken directly to Jesus is also appropriate. The fact that it was Jesus himself who appointed all of the other apostles, suggests that the prayer in Acts 1:24 is addressed to him: "You, Lord, who know the hearts of all, show which one of these two you have chosen." The dying Stephen prays, "Lord Jesus, receive my spirit" (Acts 7:59). The conversation between Ananias and "the Lord" in Acts 9:10–16 is with Jesus because in verse 17 Ananias tells Saul, "The Lord Jesus . . . has sent me so that you may regain your sight." The prayer, "Our Lord, come!" (1 Cor. 16:22) is addressed to Jesus, as is the prayer in Revelation 22:20, "Come, Lord Jesus!" And Paul also prayed to "the Lord" in 2 Corinthians 12:8 concerning his thorn in the flesh.[5]

Moreover, the fact that Jesus is "a merciful and faithful high priest" (Heb. 2:17) who is able to "sympathize with our weaknesses" (Heb. 4:15) is viewed as an encouragement to us to come boldly before the "throne of grace" in prayer "that we may receive mercy and find grace to help in time of need" (Heb. 4:16). These verses must give us encouragement to come directly to Jesus in prayer, expecting that he will sympathize with our weaknesses as we pray.

There is therefore clear enough scriptural warrant to encourage us to pray not only to God the Father (which seems to be the primary pattern and certainly follows the example that Jesus taught us in the Lord's Prayer) but also to pray directly to God the Son, our Lord Jesus Christ. Both are correct, and we may pray either to the Father or to the Son.

But should we pray to the Holy Spirit? Though no prayers directly addressed to the Holy Spirit are recorded in the New Testament, there is nothing that would forbid such prayer, for the Holy Spirit, like the Father and the Son, is fully God and is worthy of prayer and is powerful to answer our prayers. (Note also Ezekiel's invitation to the "breath" or "spirit" in Ezek. 37:9, which is possibly a prayer to the Holy Spirit.)

To say that we *cannot* pray to the Holy Spirit is really saying that we cannot talk to him or relate to him personally, which hardly seems right. He also relates to us in

---

5. The name *Lord* (Gk. *kyrios*) is used in Acts and the Epistles primarily to refer to the Lord Jesus Christ.

a personal way since he is a "Helper" or "Counselor" (John 14:16, 26), and surely we should be permitted to talk to someone who is our Helper and Counselor. Other verses say that believers "know him" (John 14:17), and he teaches us (cf. John 14:26), bears witness to us that we are children of God (Rom. 8:16), and can be grieved by our sin (Eph. 4:30). Moreover, the Holy Spirit exercises personal volition in the distribution of spiritual gifts, for he "continually distributes to each one individually as he wills" (1 Cor. 12:11, author's translation). Therefore, it does not seem wrong to pray directly to the Holy Spirit at times, when we are asking him to do something that relates to his special areas of ministry or responsibility.[6]

In fact, through the history of the church several well-used hymns have been prayers to the Holy Spirit (see the end of chapter 30, pp. 799–800; chapter 52, pp. 1291–92; and chapter 53, pp. 1339–40). Another example is the "Doxology" that ends with "Praise Father, Son, and Holy Ghost." And another is, "Spirit of God, Descend upon My Heart." In addition, the Nicene Creed, as revised in AD 381, says, "I believe . . . in the Holy Spirit . . . who with the Father and the Son together is worshiped and glorified" (see appendix 1, pp. 1438–39). If the Holy Spirit is to be worshiped, then certainly prayers to him are also appropriate. But this is not the New Testament pattern, and it should not become the dominant emphasis in our prayer life.

## 5. The Role of the Holy Spirit in Our Praying

In Romans 8:26–27 Paul says,

> Likewise the Spirit helps us in our weakness. For we do not know what to pray for as we ought, but the Spirit himself intercedes for us with groanings too deep for words. And he who searches hearts knows what is the mind of the Spirit, because the Spirit intercedes for the saints according to the will of God.

Interpreters differ on whether the "groanings too deep for words" are (a) the groanings the Holy Spirit himself makes or (b) our own groanings and sighs in prayer, which the Holy Spirit makes into effective prayer before God. It seems more likely that the "sighs" and "groans" here are our groans. When Paul says, "The Spirit *helps* us in our weakness" (v. 26), the word translated "helps" (Gk. *sunantilambanomai*) is the same word used in Luke 10:40, where Martha is working hard serving the meal and wants Mary to come and *help* her. The word does not indicate that the Holy Spirit prays instead of us but that the Holy Spirit takes part with us and makes our weak prayers effective.[7] Such sighing or

---

6. J. I. Packer says, "Is it proper to pray to the Spirit? There is no example of doing this anywhere in Scripture, but since the Spirit is God, it cannot be wrong to invoke and address him if there is good reason to do so" (*Keep in Step with the Spirit* [Old Tappan, NJ: Revell, 1984], 261).

7. Other reasons why these sighs or groans are best understood to be our "groanings" in prayer are (1) v. 23 says that "we ourselves . . . groan," using a verb (*stenazō*) that is cognate to the noun translated "groanings" (*stenagmos*) in v. 26; (2) such "groanings," which seem to imply a degree of distress or

groaning in prayer is best understood to be sighs or groans which we utter, expressing the desires of our heart and spirit, which the Holy Spirit then makes into effective prayer.[8]

Related to this is the question of what it means to pray "in the Spirit." Paul says that we should be "praying at all times in the Spirit, with all prayer and supplication" (Eph. 6:18), and Jude says that we should be "praying in the Holy Spirit" (Jude 20).[9] In order to understand this phrase, we should realize that the New Testament tells us that many different activities can be done "in the Holy Spirit." It is possible just to be "in the Spirit" as John was on the Lord's day (Rev. 1:10; cf. 4:2). And it is possible to rejoice in the Holy Spirit (Luke 10:21), to resolve or decide something in the Holy Spirit (Acts 19:21), to have one's conscience bear witness in the Holy Spirit (Rom. 9:1), to have access to God in the Holy Spirit (Eph. 2:18), and to love in the Holy Spirit (Col. 1:8). As we will explain more fully in chapter 30, below (see pp. 787–88, 793–96), these expressions seem to refer to dwelling consciously in the presence of the Holy Spirit himself, a presence characterized by the Godlike qualities of power, love, joy, truth, holiness, righteousness, and peace. To pray "in the Holy Spirit," then, is to pray with the conscious awareness of God's presence surrounding us and sanctifying both us and our prayers.

## C. Some Important Considerations in Effective Prayer

Scripture indicates a number of considerations that need to be taken into account if we would offer the kind of prayer that God desires from us.

## 1. Praying according to God's Will

John tells us, "This is the confidence that we have toward him, that *if we ask anything according to his will* he hears us. And if we know that he hears us in whatever we ask, we know that we have the requests that we have asked of him" (1 John 5:14–15). Jesus teaches us to pray, "Your will be done" (Matt. 6:10), and he himself gives us an example by praying in the garden of Gethsemane: "Nevertheless, not as I will, but as you will" (Matt. 26:39).

But how do we know what God's will is when we pray? If the matter we are praying about is covered in a passage of Scripture in which God gives us a command or a direct declaration of his will, then the answer to this question is easy: his will is that his Word be obeyed and that his commands be kept. We are to seek for perfect obedience to God's moral will on earth so that God's will may be done "on earth as it is in heaven" (Matt.

---

anguish, are appropriate for creatures (vv. 22, 23) but not for the Creator; and (3) v. 26b, which mentions "groanings too deep for words," explains the first clause in v. 26, which says that the Spirit "helps" us, not that the Spirit replaces our prayers. The phrase "too deep for words" does not necessarily mean "silent or noiseless" but can mean "not able to be put into words."

8. For a further discussion of Rom. 8:26–27, see chapter 53, pp. 1331–32.

9. Some have thought this refers to speaking in tongues, since Paul calls speaking in tongues praying "with the spirit" (1 Cor. 14:15 RSV). But that is not a correct understanding, since in 1 Cor. 14:15 "the spirit" refers not to the Holy Spirit but to Paul's own human spirit: note the contrast between "my spirit" and "my mind" in v. 14. The ESV correctly translates 1 Cor. 14:15 as "my spirit."

6:10). For this reason knowledge of Scripture is a tremendous help in prayer, enabling us to follow the pattern of the first Christians who quoted Scripture when they prayed (see Acts 4:25–26). The regular reading and memorization of Scripture, cultivated over many years of a Christian's life, will increase the depth, power, and wisdom of his or her prayers. Jesus encourages us to have his words within us as we pray, for he says, "If you abide in me, *and my words abide in you*, ask whatever you wish, and it will be done for you" (John 15:7).

This means, for example, that if we are seeking wisdom in the making of an important decision, we do not have to wonder whether it is God's will that we receive wisdom to act rightly. Scripture has already settled that question for us, because there is a promise of Scripture that applies:

> If any of you lacks wisdom, let him ask God, who gives generously to all without reproach, and it will be given him. But let him ask in faith, with no doubting, for the one who doubts is like a wave of the sea that is driven and tossed by the wind. For that person must not suppose that he will receive anything from the Lord; he is a double-minded man, unstable in all his ways. (James 1:5–8)

We should have great confidence that God will answer our prayer when we ask him for something that accords with a specific promise or command of Scripture like this. In such cases, we know what God's will is, because he has told us, and we simply need to pray believing that he will answer.

However, there are many other situations in life where we do not know what God's will is. We may not be sure, because no promise or command of Scripture applies, whether it is God's will that we get the job we have applied for or win an athletic contest in which we are participating (a common prayer among children, especially) or be chosen to hold office in the church, and so on. In all of these cases, we should bring to bear as much of Scripture as we understand, perhaps to give us some general principles within which our prayer can be made. But beyond this, we often must admit that we simply do not know what God's will is. In such cases, we should ask him for deeper understanding and then pray for what seems best to us, giving reasons to the Lord why, in our present understanding of the situation, what we are praying for seems to be best. But it is always right to add, either explicitly or at least in the attitude of our heart, "Nevertheless, if I am wrong in asking this, and if this is not pleasing to you, then do as seems best in your sight," or more simply, "If it is your will." Sometimes God will grant what we have asked. Sometimes he will give us deeper understanding or change our hearts so that we are led to ask for something different. Sometimes he will not grant our request at all but will simply indicate to us that we must submit to his will (see 2 Cor. 12:9–10).

Some Christians object that to add the phrase "if it is your will" to our prayers "destroys our faith." What it actually does is express uncertainty about whether what we pray for is God's will or not. And it is appropriate when we do not really know what God's will is. But at other times this would not be appropriate: to ask God to give us wisdom to make a decision and then say, "If it is your will to give me wisdom here" would be inappropriate, for it would be saying that we do not believe God meant what he said in James 1:5–8 when he told us to ask in faith and he would grant this request.[10]

Even when a command or promise of Scripture applies, there may be nuances of application that we do not at first fully understand. Therefore it is important in our prayer that we not only talk to God but also listen to him. We should frequently bring a request to God and then wait silently before him. In those times of waiting on the Lord (Pss. 27:14; 38:15; 130:5–6), God may change the desires of our heart, give us additional insight into the situation we are praying about, grant us additional insight into his Word, bring a passage of Scripture to mind that would enable us to pray more effectively, impart a sense of assurance of what his will is, or greatly increase our faith so that we are able to pray with much more confidence.

## 2. Praying with Faith

Jesus says, "Therefore I tell you, whatever you ask in prayer, believe that you have received it, and it will be yours" (Mark 11:24). Some translations vary, but the Greek text is best translated, "believe that you *have received it*." Later scribes who copied the Greek manuscripts and some later commentators have taken it to mean "believe that you *will* receive it." However, if we accept the text as it is in the earliest and best manuscripts, the verse says, "believe that you have received it". Jesus is apparently saying that when we ask for something, the kind of faith that will bring results is a settled assurance that when we prayed for something (or perhaps after we had been praying over a period of time), God agreed to grant our specific request. In the personal communion with God that occurs in genuine prayer, this kind of faith on our part could only come *as God gives us a sense of assurance that he has agreed to grant our request*. Of course, we cannot "work up" this kind of genuine faith by any sort of frenzied prayer or great emotional effort to try to make ourselves believe, nor can we force it upon ourselves by saying words we don't think to be true. Only God can give us this assurance, and he may or may not give it each time we pray. This assured faith will often come when we ask God for something and then quietly wait before him for an answer.

In fact, Hebrews 11:1 tells us that "faith is the *assurance* of things hoped for, the conviction of things not seen." Biblical faith is never a kind of wishful thinking or a vague hope that does not have any secure foundation to rest upon. It is rather trust in a person, God himself, based on the fact that we take him at his word and believe what he has said.

---

10. To add, "If it is your will" to a prayer is still very different from not asking at all. If my children come and ask if I will take them to get ice cream, but then (feeling in a cooperative mood) add, "but only if you think it's right, Dad," that is still far removed from not asking me at all. If they had not asked, I would not have considered going to get ice cream. Once they ask, even with the qualification, I will often decide to take them.

This trust or dependence on God, when it has an element of assurance or confidence, is genuine biblical faith.

Several other passages encourage us to exercise faith when we pray. "Whatever you ask in prayer, you will receive, if you have faith," Jesus teaches his disciples (Matt. 21:22). And James tells us we are to "ask in faith, with no doubting" (James 1:6). Prayer is never wishful thinking, for it springs from trust in a personal God who wants us to take him at his word.

## 3. Obedience

Since prayer is a relationship with God as a person, anything in our lives that displeases him will be a hindrance to prayer. The psalmist says, "If I had cherished iniquity in my heart, the Lord would not have listened" (Ps. 66:18). Though "the sacrifice of the wicked is an abomination to the LORD," by contrast, "the prayer of the upright is acceptable to him" (Prov. 15:8). Again we read that "the LORD . . . hears the prayer of the righteous" (Prov. 15:29). But God is not favorably disposed to those who reject his laws: "If one turns away his ear from hearing the law, even his prayer is an abomination" (Prov. 28:9).

The apostle Peter quotes Psalm 34 to affirm that "the eyes of the Lord are on the righteous, and his ears are open to their prayer" (1 Peter 3:12). Since the previous verses encourage good conduct in everyday life, in things such as refraining from speaking evil and turning away from evil and doing right, Peter is saying that God readily hears the prayers of those who live lives of obedience to him. Similarly, Peter warns husbands to live "in an understanding way" with their wives, "so that your prayers may not be hindered" (1 Peter 3:7). Likewise, John reminds us of the need for a clear conscience before God when we pray, for he says, "If our heart does not condemn us, we have confidence before God; and whatever we ask we receive from him, because we keep his commandments and do what pleases him" (1 John 3:21–22).

Now this teaching must not be misunderstood. We do not need to be freed from sin completely before God can be expected to answer our prayers. If God only answered the prayers of sinless people, then no one in the whole Bible except Jesus would have had his or her prayers answered. When we come before God through his grace, we come cleansed by the blood of Christ (Rom. 3:25; 5:9; Eph. 2:13; Heb. 9:14; 1 Peter 1:2). Yet we must not neglect the biblical emphasis on personal holiness of life. Prayer and holy living go together. There is much grace in the Christian life, but growth in personal holiness is also a route to much greater blessing, and that is true with respect to prayer as well. The passages quoted teach that, all other things being equal, more exact obedience will lead to increased effectiveness in prayer (cf. Heb. 12:14; James 4:3–4).

## 4. Confession of Sins

Because our obedience to God is never perfect in this life, we continually depend on his forgiveness for our sins. Confession of sins is necessary in order for God to "forgive us" in the sense of restoring his day-by-day relationship with us (see Matt. 6:12; 1 John 1:9).

It is good when we pray to confess all known sin to the Lord and to ask for his forgiveness. Sometimes when we wait on him, he will bring other sins to mind that we need to confess. With respect to those sins that we do not remember or are unaware of, it is appropriate to pray the general prayer of David, "Declare me innocent from hidden faults" (Ps. 19:12).

Sometimes confessing our sins to other trusted Christians will bring an assurance of forgiveness and encouragement to overcome sin as well. James relates mutual confession to prayer, for in a passage discussing powerful prayer, James encourages us, "Therefore *confess your sins to one another* and pray for one another, that you may be healed" (James 5:16).

## 5. Forgiving Others

Jesus says, "If you forgive others their trespasses, your heavenly Father will also forgive you, but if you do not forgive others their trespasses, neither will your Father forgive your trespasses" (Matt. 6:14–15). Similarly, Jesus says, "Whenever you stand praying, forgive, if you have anything against anyone, so that your Father also who is in heaven may forgive you your trespasses" (Mark 11:25). Our Lord does not have in mind the initial experience of forgiveness we know when we are justified by faith, for that would not belong in a prayer that we pray every day (see Matt. 6:12, 14–15). He refers rather to the *day-by-day relationship with God* that we need to have restored when we have sinned and displeased him. In fact, Jesus commands us to build into our prayers a request that God forgive us in the same way that we have forgiven others who have harmed us (in the same "personal relationship" sense of "forgive"—that is, not holding a grudge or cherishing bitterness against another person or harboring any desire to harm them): "Forgive us our sins, *as we also have forgiven those who sin against us*" (Matt. 6:12, author's translation). If we have not forgiven others when we pray this prayer, then we are asking God *not* to restore a right relationship with us when we sin, just like we have refused to do with others.

Since prayer presumes a relationship with God as a person, this is not surprising. If we have sinned against him and grieved the Holy Spirit (cf. Eph. 4:30), and the sin has not been forgiven, it interrupts our relationship with God (cf. Isa. 59:1–2). Until sin is forgiven and the relationship is restored prayer will, of course, be difficult. Moreover, if we have unforgiveness in our hearts against someone else, then we are not acting in a way that is pleasing to God or helpful to us. So God declares (Matt. 6:12, 14–15) that he will distance himself from us until we forgive others.

## 6. Humility

James tells us, "God opposes the proud, but gives grace to the humble" (James 4:6; also 1 Peter 5:5). Therefore he says, "Humble yourselves before the Lord, and he will exalt you" (James 4:10). Humility is the right attitude to have in praying to God, whereas pride is altogether inappropriate.

Jesus' parable about the Pharisee and the tax collector illustrates this. When the

Pharisee stood to pray, he was boastful: "God, I thank you that I am not like other men, extortioners, unjust, adulterers, or even like this tax collector. I fast twice a week; I give tithes of all that I get" (Luke 18:11–12). By contrast, the humble tax collector "would not even lift up his eyes to heaven, but beat his breast, saying, 'God, be merciful to me, a sinner!'" (Luke 18:13). Jesus said that the tax collector "went down to his house justified," unlike the Pharisee, "for everyone who exalts himself will be humbled, but the one who humbles himself will be exalted" (Luke 18:14). This is why Jesus condemned those who "for a pretense make long prayers" (Luke 20:47) and "love to stand and pray in the synagogues and at the street corners, that they may be seen by others" (Matt. 6:5).

God is rightly jealous for his honor.[11] Therefore he is not pleased to answer the prayers of the proud who take honor to themselves rather than giving it to him. True humility before God, which will also be reflected in genuine humility before others, is necessary for effective prayer.

## 7. Continuing in Prayer over Time

Just as Moses twice stayed on the mountain forty days praying before God for the people of Israel (Deut. 9:25–26; 10:10–11), and just as Jacob said to God, "I will not let you go unless you bless me" (Gen. 32:26), so too we see in Jesus' life a pattern of much time given to prayer. When great multitudes were following Jesus, "he himself was often withdrawing into the wilderness regions and praying" (Luke 5:16, author's translation).[12] At another time, "*all night* he continued in prayer to God" (Luke 6:12).

Sometimes, as in the case of Moses and Jacob, prayer over a long period of time may be prayer for one specific item (cf. Luke 18:1–8). When we earnestly seek God for an answer to a specific prayer, we may repeat the request several times. Paul asked the Lord "three times" (2 Cor. 12:8) that the thorn in his flesh would be taken from him. Jesus himself, when he was in the garden of Gethsemane, asked the Father, "Remove this cup from me. Yet not what I will, but what you will" (Mark 14:36). Then after he came and found the disciples sleeping, Jesus prayed again, making the same request in the same words: "And again he went away and prayed, *saying the same words*" (Mark 14:39). These are instances of earnest repetition in prayer for a deeply felt need. They are not examples of what Jesus forbids—the heaping up of "empty phrases" in the mistaken belief that "many words" will earn a hearing (Matt. 6:7).

There is also an element of a continual fellowship with God in praying over time. Paul calls on us to "pray without ceasing" (1 Thess. 5:17), and he encourages the Colossians to "continue steadfastly in prayer, being watchful in it with thanksgiving" (Col. 4:2). Such continual devotion to prayer even while about daily duties should characterize the life of every believer. The apostles are a telling example. They freed themselves from

---

11. See discussion of God's attribute of jealousy, pp. 245 above.

12. The periphrastic imperfect tense here (Gk. *ēn hypochōrōn*) emphasizes, even more than a simple imperfect would, the repeated or habitual nature of the activity of withdrawing into the wilderness (see *BDF*, 353[1]).

other responsibilities in order to give more time to prayer: "But *we will devote ourselves to prayer* and to the ministry of the word" (Acts 6:4).

## 8. Praying Earnestly

Jesus, who is our model for prayer, prayed earnestly. "In the days of his flesh, Jesus offered up prayers and supplications, with loud cries and tears, to him who was able to save him from death, and he was heard because of his reverence" (Heb. 5:7). In some of the prayers of Scripture, we can almost hear the great intensity with which the saints pour out their hearts before God. Daniel cries out, "O Lord, hear; O Lord, forgive. O Lord, pay attention and act. Delay not, for your own sake, O my God, because your city and your people are called by your name" (Dan. 9:19). When God shows Amos the judgment that he is going to bring on his people, Amos pleads, "O Lord GOD, please forgive! How can Jacob stand? He is so small!" (Amos 7:2).

In personal relationships, if we attempt to fake emotional intensity and put on an outward show of emotion that is not consistent with the feelings of our hearts, others involved will usually sense our hypocrisy at once and be put off by it. How much more is this true of God, who fully knows our hearts. Therefore, intensity and depth of emotional involvement in prayer should never be faked: we cannot fool God. Yet if we truly begin to see situations as God sees them, if we begin to see the needs of a hurting and dying world as they really are, then it will be natural to pray with intense emotional involvement and to expect God, as a merciful Father, to respond to heartfelt prayer. And where such intensely felt prayer finds expression in group prayer meetings, Christians should certainly accept and be thankful for it, for it often indicates a deep work of the Holy Spirit in the heart of the person praying.

## 9. Waiting on the Lord

After crying out to God for help in distress, David says, "*Wait for the* LORD; be strong, and let your heart take courage; wait for the LORD!" (Ps. 27:14). Similarly, he says, "But for you, O LORD, do I wait; it is you, O LORD my God, who will answer" (Ps. 38:15). The psalmist likewise says,

> I wait for the LORD, my soul waits,
>     and in his word I hope;
> my soul waits for the LORD
>     more than watchmen for the morning,
>     more than watchmen for the morning. (Ps. 130:5–6)

An analogy from human experience may help us to appreciate the benefit of waiting before the Lord for a response to prayer. If I wish to invite someone home for dinner, there are various ways I can do so. First, I can issue a vague, general invitation: "It would be nice to have you come to dinner sometime." Almost no one will come to dinner based on that kind of invitation alone. This is rather like the vague, general prayer, "God bless all my aunts and uncles and all the missionaries. Amen." Second, I could make a specific but hurried and impersonal kind of invitation: "Fred, can you come to dinner Friday night at 6:00?"—but as soon as the words are out of my mouth, I rush away leaving Fred with a puzzled expression on his face because I didn't allow him time to respond. This is like many of our prayer requests. We simply speak words to God as if the very act of voicing them, without any heart involvement in what we are saying, will itself bring an answer from God. But this kind of request forgets that prayer is a relationship between two persons, myself and God.

There is a third kind of invitation, one that is heartfelt, personal, and specific. After waiting until I'm sure I have Fred's full attention, I can look him directly in the eye and say, "Fred, Margaret and I would really love to have you come to dinner at our home this Friday at 6:00 p.m. Could you come?"—and then, continuing to look him in the eye, I wait silently and patiently while he decides what to answer. He knows from my facial expression, my tone of voice, my timing, and the setting in which I chose to talk to him that I am putting my whole self into this request and that I am relating to him as a person and as a friend. Waiting patiently for an answer shows my earnestness, my sense of expectancy, and my respect for him as a person. This third kind of request is like that of the earnest Christian who comes before God, gains a sense of being in his presence, earnestly pours out a request to him, and then waits quietly for some sense of assurance of God's answer.

This is not to say that all our requests must be of this nature, or even that the first two kinds of requests are wrong. Indeed, in some situations we pray quickly because we have little time before we need an answer (see Neh. 2:4). And sometimes we do pray generally because we do not have more specific information about a situation, because it is far removed from us, or because of shortness of time. But the material in Scripture on earnest prayer and on waiting for the Lord, as well as the fact that prayer is personal communication between ourselves and God, indicates that prayers such as the third kind of request are much deeper and will undoubtedly bring many more answers from God.

## 10. Praying in Private

Daniel went to his upper chamber and "got down on his knees three times a day and prayed and gave thanks before his God" (Dan. 6:10).[13] Jesus frequently went out into solitary places to be alone to pray (Luke 5:16 et al.). And he teaches us, "When you pray, go into your room and *shut the door* and pray to your Father who is in secret. And your Father who sees in secret will reward you" (Matt. 6:6). This statement is in the context of avoiding the error of the hypocrites who loved to pray at the street corners "that they

---

13. Though Daniel's enemies saw him praying, it was only because they "came by agreement" and apparently spied on him.

may be seen by others" (Matt. 6:5). There is wisdom in Jesus' encouragement to pray in secret, not only that we might avoid hypocrisy but also that we might not be distracted by the presence of other people and therefore modify our prayers to suit what we think they will expect to hear. When we are truly alone with God, in the privacy of a room to which we have "shut the door" (Matt. 6:6), then we can pour out our hearts to him.[14]

The need to pray in private may also have implications for small-group or church prayer meetings: when believers come together to seek the Lord earnestly about a specific matter, it is often helpful if they can be in the privacy of a home where the door is shut so that they can collectively cry out to God. Apparently this was the way the early Christians prayed when they were making earnest supplication to God for the release of Peter from prison (see Acts 12:5, 12–16).

## 11. Praying with Others

Believers find strength in praying together with others. In fact, Jesus teaches us, "Again, I say to you, if two of you agree on earth about anything they ask, it will be done for them by my Father in heaven. For where two or three are gathered in my name, there am I among them" (Matt. 18:19–20).[15]

There are many other examples in Scripture when groups of believers prayed together or when one person led the entire congregation in prayer (note Solomon's prayer "in the presence of all the assembly of Israel" at the dedication of the temple in 1 Kings 8:22–53 or the prayer of the early church in Jerusalem when "they lifted their voices together to God" in Acts 4:24). Even the Lord's Prayer is put in the plural. It does not say, "Give me this day my daily bread" but "Give *us* this day *our* daily bread," "Forgive *us our* sins," and "Lead *us* not into temptation but deliver *us* from evil" (Matt. 6:11–13, author's translation). Praying with others, then, is also right and often increases our faith and the effectiveness of our prayers.

## 12. Fasting

Prayer is often connected with fasting in Scripture. Sometimes these are occasions of intense supplication before God, as when Nehemiah, on hearing of the ruin of Jerusalem, "continued *fasting* and praying before the God of heaven" (Neh. 1:4), or when the Jews learned of the decree of Ahasuerus that they would all be killed, and "there was

---

14. At this point we may also mention that Paul discusses a use of the gift of speaking in tongues during private prayer: "If I pray in a tongue, my spirit prays but my mind is unfruitful. What am I to do? I will pray with my spirit, but I will pray with my mind also; I will sing praise with my spirit, but I will sing with my mind also" (1 Cor. 14:14–15). When Paul says "my spirit prays," he is not referring to the Holy Spirit but to his own human spirit, for the contrast is with "my mind." His own spirit is pouring out requests before God, and those requests are

understood by God and result in personal edification: "The one who speaks in a tongue builds up himself" (1 Cor. 14:4). This gift will be discussed more fully in chapter 53.

15. Although the previous four verses (vv. 15–18) have to do with church discipline, the word "again" at the beginning of v. 19 signals a slight change in subject, and it is not inappropriate to take vv. 19–20 as a broader statement about prayer in general in the context of the church.

great mourning among the Jews, with *fasting* and weeping and lamenting" (Esth. 4:3), or when Daniel sought the Lord "by prayer and pleas for mercy with *fasting* and sackcloth and ashes" (Dan. 9:3). At other times fasting is connected with repentance, for God says to the people who have sinned against him, "'Yet even now,' declares the LORD, 'return to me with all your heart, with *fasting*, with weeping, and with mourning'" (Joel 2:12).

In the New Testament, Anna was "worshiping with *fasting* and prayer night and day" (Luke 2:37) in the temple, and the church at Antioch was "worshiping the Lord and *fasting*" when the Holy Spirit said, "Set apart for me Barnabas and Saul for the work to which I have called them" (Acts 13:2). The church responded with further fasting and prayer before sending Barnabas and Saul on their first missionary journey: "Then after *fasting* and praying they laid their hands on them and sent them off" (Acts 13:3). In fact, fasting was a routine part of seeking the Lord's guidance with regard to church officers, for on Paul's first missionary journey, we read that he and Barnabas, as they traveled back through the churches they had founded, "appointed elders for them in every church, with prayer and fasting" (Acts 14:23).

So fasting appropriately accompanied prayer in many situations: in times of intensive intercession, repentance, worship, and seeking of guidance. In each of these situations, several benefits come from fasting, all of which affect our relationship to God: (1) Fasting increases our sense of humility and dependence on the Lord (for our hunger and physical weakness continually remind us how we are not really strong in ourselves but need the Lord). (2) Fasting allows us to give more attention to prayer (for we are not spending time on eating), and (3) it is a continual reminder that just as we sacrifice some personal comfort to the Lord by not eating, so too we must continually sacrifice all of ourselves to him.[16] Moreover, (4) fasting is a good exercise in self-discipline, for as we refrain from eating food, which we would ordinarily desire, it also strengthens our ability to refrain from sin, to which we might otherwise be tempted to yield. If we train ourselves to accept the small "suffering" of fasting willingly, we will be better able to accept other suffering for the sake of righteousness (cf. Heb. 5:8; 1 Peter 4:1–2). (5) Fasting also heightens spiritual and mental alertness and a sense of God's presence as we focus less on the material things of this world (such as food) and as the energies of our body are freed from digesting and processing food. This enables us to focus on eternal spiritual realities that are much more important.[17] Finally, (6) fasting expresses earnestness and urgency

---

16. Similar reasons (devoting more time to prayer and giving up some personal pleasure) probably explain Paul's permission to married couples to give up sexual relations "by agreement for a limited time, that you may devote yourselves to prayer" (1 Cor. 7:5).

17. In Mark 9:29, when the disciples asked why they could not drive out a certain demon, Jesus replied, "This kind cannot be driven out by anything but prayer." Many early and quite reliable Greek manuscripts and several early manuscripts in other languages read "but prayer *and fasting*." In either case, it cannot mean prayer that is spoken at the time the demon is being cast out, for Jesus simply cast out the demon with a word and did not engage in an extended time of prayer. It must mean rather that the disciples had not previously been spending enough time in prayer and that their spiritual strength was weak. Therefore the "fasting" that is mentioned in many ancient manuscripts fits the pattern of an activity that increases one's spiritual strength and power.

in our prayers: if we continued to fast, eventually we would die. Therefore, in a symbolic way, fasting says to God that we are prepared to lay down our lives that the situation be changed rather than that it continue. In this sense fasting is especially appropriate when the spiritual state of the church is low.

> "Yet even now," declares the LORD,
> "return to me with all your heart,
> with fasting, with weeping, and with mourning;
> and rend your hearts and not your garments." (Joel 2:12–13a)

Though the New Testament does not specifically require that we fast or set special times when we must fast, Jesus certainly assumes that we will fast, for he says to his disciples, *"When* you fast . . ."* (Matt. 6:16). Moreover, Jesus says, "The days will come when the bridegroom is taken away from them, and then they will fast" (Matt. 9:15). He is the bridegroom, we are his disciples, and during this present church age he has been "taken" away from us until the day he returns. Most western Christians do not fast, but if we were willing to fast more regularly—even for one or two meals—we might be surprised how much more spiritual power and strength we would have in our lives and in our churches.

## 13. What about Unanswered Prayer?

We must begin by recognizing that as long as God is God and we are his creatures, there must be some unanswered prayers. This is because God keeps hidden his own wise plans for the future, and even though people pray, many events will not come about until the time that God has decreed. The Jews prayed for centuries for the Messiah to come, and rightly so, but it was not until "the fullness of time had come" that "God sent forth his Son" (Gal. 4:4). The souls of martyrs in heaven, free from sin, cry out for God to judge the earth (Rev. 6:10), but God does not immediately answer; rather he tells them to rest a little longer (Rev. 6:11). It is clear that there can be long periods of delay during which prayers go unanswered, because the people praying do not know God's wise timing.

Prayer will also be unanswered because we do not always know how to pray as we ought (Rom. 8:26), we do not always pray according to God's will (James 4:3), and we do not always ask in faith (James 1:6–8). And sometimes we think that one solution is best, but God has a better plan, even to fulfill his purpose through suffering and hardship. Joseph no doubt prayed earnestly to be rescued from the pit and from being carried off into slavery in Egypt (Gen. 37:23–36), but many years later he found how in all of these events "God meant it for good" (Gen. 50:20).

When we face unanswered prayer, we join the company of Jesus, who prayed, "Father, if you are willing, remove this cup from me. Nevertheless, not my will, but yours, be done" (Luke 22:42). We join also the company of Paul, who asked the Lord "three times" that his thorn in the flesh be removed, but it was not; rather, the Lord told him, "My grace is sufficient for you, for my power is made perfect in weakness" (2 Cor. 12:8–9). We join the company of David, who prayed for his son's life to be saved, but it was not, so he "went into the house of the LORD and worshiped" and said of his son, "I shall go to him, but he will not return to me" (2 Sam. 12:20, 23). We join the company of the martyrs throughout history who prayed for deliverance that did not come, for they "loved not their lives even unto death" (Rev. 12:11).

When prayer remains unanswered we must continue to trust God, knowing that "for those who love God all things work together for good, for those who are called according to his purpose" (Rom. 8:28). We must continue to cast our cares on him, knowing that he continually cares for us (1 Peter 5:7). We must keep remembering that he will give strength sufficient for each day (Deut. 33:25) and that he has promised, "I will never leave you nor forsake you" (Heb. 13:5; cf. Rom. 8:35–39).

We also must continue to pray. Sometimes an answer, long awaited, will suddenly be given, as it was when Hannah after many years bore a child (1 Sam. 1:19–20) and when Simeon saw with his own eyes the long-expected Messiah come to the temple (Luke 2:25–35).

But sometimes prayers will remain unanswered in this life. At times God will answer those prayers after the believer dies. At other times he will not, but even then the faith expressed in those prayers and their heartfelt expressions of love for God and the people he has made will still ascend as a pleasing incense before God's throne (Rev. 5:8; 8:3–4) and will result in "praise and glory and honor at the revelation of Jesus Christ" (1 Peter 1:7).

## D. PRAISE AND THANKSGIVING

Praise and thanksgiving to God, which will be treated more fully in chapter 51, are an essential element of prayer. The model prayer that Jesus left us begins with a word of praise: "hallowed be your name" (Matt. 6:9). And Paul tells the Philippians, "in everything by prayer and supplication *with thanksgiving* let your requests be made known to God" (Phil. 4:6), and the Colossians, "Continue steadfastly in prayer, being watchful in it *with thanksgiving*" (Col. 4:2). Thanksgiving, like every other aspect of prayer, should not be a mechanical mouthing of a "thank you" to God, but the expression of words that reflect the thankfulness of our hearts. Moreover, we should never think that thanking God for the answer to something we ask for can somehow force God to give it to us, for that changes the prayer from a genuine, sincere request to a demand that assumes we can make God do what we want him to do. Such a spirit in our prayers really denies the essential nature of prayer as dependence on God.

By contrast, the kind of thanksgiving that appropriately accompanies prayer must express thankfulness to God for all circumstances, for every event of life that he allows to come to us. When we join our prayers with humble, childlike thanksgiving to God "in all circumstances" (1 Thess. 5:18), they will be acceptable to God.

## QUESTIONS FOR PERSONAL APPLICATION

1. Do you often have difficulty with prayer? What things in this chapter have been helpful to you in this regard?

2. When have you known the most effective times of prayer in your life? What factors contributed to making those times more effective? Which other factors need the most attention in your prayer life? What can you do to strengthen each of these areas?

3. How does it help and encourage you (if it does) when you pray together with other Christians?

4. Have you ever tried waiting quietly before the Lord after making an earnest prayer request? If so, what has been the result?

5. Do you have a regular time each day for private Bible reading and prayer? Are you sometimes easily distracted and turned aside to other activities? If so, how can distractions be overcome?

6. Do you enjoy praying? Why or why not?

### Special Terms
*faith*
*"in Jesus' name"*
*prayer*
*waiting on the Lord*

## BIBLIOGRAPHY

(For an explanation of this bibliography see the note on the bibliography to chapter 1, pp. 23–24. Complete bibliographical data may be found on pp. 1489–96.)

### SECTIONS IN EVANGELICAL SYSTEMATIC THEOLOGIES

*1. Anglican (Episcopalian)*
1882–92 . . . . . Litton, 431–32
2001 . . . . . . . . Packer, 187–89
2013 . . . . . . . . Bird, 122–23, 692

*2. Arminian (Wesleyan or Methodist)*
1940 . . . . . . . . Wiley, 3:40–44, 153
1960 . . . . . . . . Purkiser, 421–24
1992 . . . . . . . . Oden, 1:61, 293, 356

2002 . . . . . . . . Cottrell, 114, 223, 289, 412, 449, 457

*3. Baptist*
1907 . . . . . . . . Strong, 433–39
1990–95 . . . . . Garrett, 429–48
2007 . . . . . . . . Akin, 290–91
2013 . . . . . . . . Erickson, 378–79

*4. Dispensational*
1947 . . . . . . . . Chafer, 5:220–31; 7:252–54
1949 . . . . . . . . Thiessen, 298–301
1986 . . . . . . . . Ryrie, 381–82
2017 . . . . . . . . MacArthur and Mayhue, 136, 641, 779

### 5. Lutheran
1917–24 ..... Pieper, 3:215–19

1934......... Mueller, 428–34, 467–69

### 6. Reformed (or Presbyterian)
1559 ......... Calvin, 2:850–920 (3.20)

1679–85 ..... Turretin, *IET*, 1:319, 328,
　　　　　　2:38–51, 385–90

1724–58 ..... Edwards, 2:74–88, 113–18

1871–73 ..... Hodge, 3:692–709

1878......... Dabney, 713–25

1894......... Shedd, 122, 254, 774

1937–66 ..... Murray, *CW*, 3:168–71

1998......... Reymond, 967–76

2008......... Van Genderen and Velema,
　　　　　　673–74

2011......... Horton, 785–87

2013......... Frame, 931–32, 1053–57

2013......... Culver, 454, 774, 966–67

2016......... Allen and Swain, 23

2017......... Barrett, 74–75, 198

### 7. Renewal (or charismatic/Pentecostal)
1988–92 ..... Williams, 2:295–98, 3:95–98

1995......... Horton, 520–22, 605

2008......... Duffield and Van Cleave, 258,
　　　　　　286–87, 346

## SECTIONS IN REPRESENTATIVE ROMAN CATHOLIC SYSTEMATIC THEOLOGIES

### 1. Roman Catholic: Traditional
1955......... Ott, 91

### 2. Roman Catholic: Post–Vatican II
1980......... McBrien, 1:331–32;
　　　　　　2:1057–99

2012......... *CCC*, paragraphs 2558–97

## OTHER WORKS
Bennett, Arthur, ed. *The Valley of Vision: A Collection of Puritan Prayer and Devotions.* Carlisle, PA: Banner of Truth, 1975.

Bloesch, D. G. "Prayer." In *EDT3*, 690–91.

Bounds, Edward M. *The Complete Works of E. M. Bounds on Prayer.* Grand Rapids: Baker, 1994.

Brother Lawrence. *The Practice of the Presence of God.* New York: Revell, 1895.

Bubeck, Mark I. *Warfare Praying: Biblical Strategies for Overcoming the Adversary.* Chicago: Moody Publishers, 2016.

Carson, D. A., ed. *Teach Us to Pray: Prayer in the Bible and the World.* Grand Rapids: Baker; Exeter: Paternoster, 1990.

Chapell, Bryan. *Praying Backwards: Transform Your Prayer Life by Beginning in Jesus' Name.* Grand Rapids: Baker, 2005.

Clowney, Edmund. *Christian Meditation.* Philadelphia: Presbyterian and Reformed, 1979.

———. "Prayer." In *NDBT*, 691–96.

———. "Prayer, Theology of." In *NDT1*, 526–27.

Dunn, J. D. G. "Prayer." In *DJG*, 617–25.

Forsyth, P. T. *The Soul of Prayer.* Grand Rapids: Eerdmans, 1967 (reprint).

Foster, Richard J. *Celebration of Discipline: The Path to Spiritual Growth.* San Francisco: Harper and Row, 1988.

Hallesby, O. *Prayer.* Translated by Clarence J. Carlsen. Minneapolis: Augsburg, 1959 (reprint).

Hernandez, W. "Prayer." In *GDT*, 701–4.

Houston, James M. *The Transforming Friendship: A Guide to Prayer.* Vancouver: Regent College Publishing, 2010.

Hunter, W. Bingham. *The God Who Hears.* Downers Grove, IL: InterVarsity Press, 1986.

———. "Prayer." In *DPL*, 725–34.

Kelly, Thomas R. *A Testament of Devotion.* New York: Harper, 1941.

Law, William. *A Serious Call to a Devout and Holy Life.* Philadelphia: Westminster, 1948 (reprint).

M'Intyre, D. M. *The Hidden Life of Prayer.* Reprint, Minneapolis: Bethany Fellowship Press, 1962. (The author's name is sometimes spelled McIntyre or MacIntyre in other editions of this book.)

Millar, J. Gary. *Calling on the Name of the Lord*. Downers Grove, IL: InterVarsity Press, 2016.

Murray, Andrew. *The Ministry of Intercessory Prayer*. 1897. Reprint, Minneapolis: Bethany House, 1981 (originally published as *The Ministry of Intercession*).

Noble, T. A. "Prayer, Theology of." In *NDT2*, 697–98.

Okholm, Dennis L. "Prayer." In *BTDB*, 621–26.

Ortlund, Raymond C., Jr. *A Passion for God: Prayers and Meditations on the Book of Romans*. Wheaton, IL: Crossway, 1994.

Packer, J. I. and Carolyn Nystrom, *Praying: Finding Our Way through Duty to Delight*. Downers Grove, IL: InterVarsity, 2006.

Prince, Derek. *Shaping History through Prayer and Fasting*. Old Tappan, NJ: Revell, 1973.

Smith, David R. *Fasting: A Neglected Discipline*. Fort Washington, PA: Christian Literature Crusade, 1969.

Spear, Wayne. *Talking to God: The Theology of Prayer*. Pittsburgh: Crown & Covenant, 2002. Revised edition of *The Theology of Prayer*. Grand Rapids: Baker, 1979.

Thomas à Kempis. *The Imitation of Christ*. Reprint, Grand Rapids: Baker, 1973.

Unknown Christian. *The Kneeling Christian*. Grand Rapids: Zondervan, 1945.

Wallis, Arthur. *God's Chosen Fast: A Spiritual and Practical Guide to Fasting*. Fort Washington, PA: Christian Literature Crusade, 1987.

White, John. *Daring to Draw Near*. Downers Grove, IL: InterVarsity Press, 1977.

Wilkins, M. J. "Prayer." In *DLNT*, 941–48.

Willard, Dallas. *The Spirit of the Disciplines*. San Francisco: Harper and Row, 1988.

## SCRIPTURE MEMORY PASSAGE

**Hebrews 4:14–16:** Since then we have a great high priest who has passed through the heavens, Jesus, the Son of God, let us hold fast our confession. For we do not have a high priest who is unable to sympathize with our weaknesses, but one who in every respect has been tempted as we are, yet without sin. Let us then with confidence draw near to the throne of grace, that we may receive mercy and find grace to help in time of need.

## HYMN

### "From Every Stormy Wind"

From ev'ry stormy wind that blows,
  from ev'ry swelling tide of woes,
There is a calm, a sure retreat;
  'tis found beneath the Mercy Seat.

There is a place where Jesus sheds
  the oil of gladness on our heads,
A place than all besides more sweet;
  it is the blood-stained Mercy Seat.

There is a spot where spirits blend,
  where friend holds fellowship with friend,
Tho' sundered far; by faith they meet
  around the common Mercy Seat.

Ah, whither could we flee for aid,
  when tempted, desolate, dismayed,
Or how the hosts of hell defeat,
  had suff'ring saints no Mercy Seat?

*There, there on eagle wings we soar,*
    *and time and sense seem all no more,*
*And heav'n comes down our souls to greet,*
    *and glory crowns the Mercy Seat.*

*O may my hand forget her skill,*
    *my tongue be silent, cold, and still,*
*This bounding heart forget to beat,*
    *if I forget the Mercy Seat.*

Author: Hugh Stowell, 1828, 1831

## CONTEMPORARY WORSHIP SONG

### "Open the Eyes of My Heart"

*Chorus*
*Open the eyes of my heart, Lord.*
*Open the eyes of my heart.*
*I want to see You.*
*I want to see You.*

*Bridge*
*Holy, holy, holy.*
*Holy, holy, holy.*
*Holy, holy, holy.*
*I want to see You.*

Words by Paul Baloche[18]

*To see You high and lifted up,*
*Shining in the light of Your glory.*
*Pour out Your power and love,*
*As we sing holy, holy, holy.*

# CHAPTER 19

# Angels

*What are angels?*
*Why did God create them?*

## EXPLANATION AND SCRIPTURAL BASIS

### A. What Are Angels?

We may define angels as follows: *angels are created spiritual beings with moral judgment and high intelligence but without physical bodies.*

#### 1. Created Spiritual Beings

Angels have not always existed; they are part of the universe that God created. In a passage that refers to angels as the "host" of heaven (or "armies of heaven"), Ezra says, "You are the LORD, you alone. You have made heaven, the heaven of heavens, *with all their host* . . . and the host of heaven worships you" (Neh. 9:6; cf. Ps. 148:2, 5). Paul tells us that God created all things "visible and invisible" through Christ and for him, and then specifically includes the angelic world with the phrase "whether thrones or dominions or rulers or authorities" (Col. 1:16).

That angels exercise moral judgment is seen in the fact that some of them sinned and fell from their positions (2 Peter 2:4; Jude 6; see chapter 20). Their high intelligence is seen throughout Scripture as they speak to people (Matt. 28:5; Acts 12:6–11, et al.) and sing praise to God (Rev. 4:11; 5:11).

Since angels are "spirits" (Heb. 1:14) or spiritual creatures, they do not ordinarily have physical bodies (Luke 24:39). Therefore they cannot usually be seen by us unless God gives us a special ability to see them (Num. 22:31; 2 Kings 6:17; Luke 2:13). In their ordinary activities of guarding and protecting us (Ps. 34:7; 91:11; Heb. 1:14) and joining with us in worship to God (Heb. 12:22), they are invisible. However, from time to time angels took on a bodily form to appear to various people in Scripture (Matt. 28:5; Heb. 13:2).

#### 2. Other Names for Angels

Scripture sometimes uses other terms for angels, such as "sons of God" (Job 1:6; 2:1), "holy ones" (Ps. 89:5, 7), "spirits" (Heb. 1:14), "watchers" (Dan. 4:13, 17, 23), "thrones," "dominions," "rulers," and "authorities" (Col. 1:16).

### 3. Other Kinds of Heavenly Beings

There are three other specific types of heavenly beings named in Scripture. Whether we think of these as special types of "angels" (in a broad sense of the term), or whether we think of them as heavenly beings distinct from angels, they are nonetheless created spiritual beings who serve and worship God.

**a. The "Cherubim."**[1] The cherubim were given the task of guarding the entrance to the garden of Eden (Gen. 3:24), and God is frequently said to be enthroned on the cherubim or to travel with the cherubim as his chariot (Ps. 18:10; Ezek. 10:1–22). Over the ark of the covenant in the Old Testament were two golden figures of cherubim with their wings stretched out above the ark, and it was there that God promised to come to dwell among his people: "There I will meet with you, and from above the mercy seat, from between the two cherubim that are on the ark of the testimony, I will speak with you about all that I will give you in commandment for the people of Israel" (Ex. 25:22; cf. vv. 18–21).

**b. The "Seraphim."**[2] Another group of heavenly beings, the seraphim, are mentioned only in Isaiah 6:2–7, where they continually worship the Lord and call to one another, "Holy, holy, holy is the LORD of hosts; the whole earth is full of his glory!" (Isa. 6:3).

**c. The Living Creatures.** Both Ezekiel and Revelation tell us of yet other kinds of heavenly beings known as "living creatures" around God's throne (Ezek. 1:5–14; Rev. 4:6–8).[3] With their appearances like a lion, an ox, a man, and an eagle, they are the mightiest representatives of various parts of God's entire creation (wild beasts, domesticated animals, human beings, and birds), and they worship God continually: "Day and night they never cease to say, 'Holy, holy, holy, is the Lord God Almighty, who was and is and is to come!'" (Rev. 4:8).

### 4. Rank and Order among the Angels

Scripture indicates that there is rank and order among the angels. One angel, Michael, is called an "archangel" in Jude 9, a title that indicates rule or authority over other angels. He is called "one of the chief princes" in Daniel 10:13. Michael also appears to be a leader in the angelic army: "Now war arose in heaven, Michael and his angels fighting against the dragon. And the dragon and his angels fought back, but he was defeated" (Rev. 12:7–8). And Paul tells us that the Lord will return from heaven "with the voice of an archangel" (1 Thess. 4:16). Whether this refers to Michael as the only archangel, or whether there are other archangels, Scripture does not tell us.

---

1. In Hebrew, the word *cherub* is singular, while the plural form is *cherubim*.

2. The Hebrew word *seraph* is singular, while *seraphim* is the plural form.

3. The descriptions differ somewhat between Ezekiel and Revelation but also have many similarities. It is difficult to tell whether these are different groups of creatures or whether those in Revelation have been transformed from the form they took in Ezekiel's vision.

### 5. Names of Specific Angels

Only two angels are specifically named in Scripture.[4] Michael is mentioned in Jude 9 and Revelation 12:7–8 as well as in Daniel 10:13, 21, where he is called "Michael, one of the chief princes" (v. 13). The angel Gabriel is mentioned in Daniel 8:16 and 9:21 as a messenger who comes from God to speak to Daniel. Gabriel is also identified as God's messenger to Zechariah and Mary in Luke 1: the angel answers Zechariah, "I am Gabriel. I stand in the presence of God" (Luke 1:19). Then we read, "In the sixth month the angel Gabriel was sent from God to a city of Galilee named Nazareth, to a virgin . . . And the virgin's name was Mary" (Luke 1:26–27).

### 6. Only One Place at One Time

Scripture frequently represents angels as traveling from one place to another, as in the verse mentioned above where Gabriel "was sent from God to a city of Galilee named Nazareth" (Luke 1:26). This is made explicit when an angel comes to Daniel and says:

> I have come because of your words. The prince of the kingdom of Persia withstood me twenty-one days, but Michael, one of the chief princes, came to help me, for I was left there with the kings of Persia, and came to make you understand what is to happen to your people in the latter days. (Dan. 10:12–14)

The idea that an angel can be in only one place at one time is consistent with the fact that angels are created beings. Unlike God, who is omnipresent, they are finite creatures and therefore limited to being in one place at one time, as is everything else that God has created.[5]

### 7. How Many Angels Are There?

Though Scripture does not give us a figure for the number of angels God created, it is apparently a very great number. We read that God on Mount Sinai "came from the *ten thousands of holy ones*, with flaming fire at his right hand" (Deut. 33:2). We also learn that "the chariots of God are twice ten thousand, thousands upon thousands" (Ps. 68:17). When we come to worship we come into the presence of "*innumerable* angels" (Heb. 12:22).[6] Their number is even more strikingly emphasized in Revelation 5:11,

---

4. I have not counted Satan here, who is a fallen angel, and who is sometimes called by other names as well. (See chapter 20, on Satan and demons.)

5. Nevertheless, it seems that a very large number of angels can be in one place at the same time, at least if the example of evil angels or demons is a good indication of this fact. When Jesus asked the demonic forces in the Gadarene demoniac, "What is your name?" he said, "Legion," for "many demons had entered him" (Luke 8:30). Even if we do not understand this literally to mean a number equal to a legion of the Roman army (3,000–6,000 men), and even if we allow that since Satan is the father of lies, the demons in the man could be greatly exaggerating, Luke still says that "many demons had entered him."

6. The Greek term *myrias* ("myriad") is an expression referring to "a very large number, not exactly defined" (BAGD, 529). (See also Jer. 33:22.)

where John says, "I heard around the throne and the living creatures and the elders the voice of many angels, numbering *myriads of myriads* and thousands of thousands." This expression indicates an amazingly large number (from a human standpoint)—an innumerable assembly of angelic beings praising God.

## 8. Do People Have Individual Guardian Angels?

Scripture clearly tells us that God sends angels for our protection:

> For he will command his angels concerning you
> to guard you in all your ways.
> On their hands they will bear you up,
> lest you strike your foot against a stone. (Ps. 91:11–12)

But some people have gone beyond this idea of general protection and wondered if God gives a specific "guardian angel" for each individual in the world, or at least for each Christian. Support for this idea has been found in Jesus' words about little children: "In heaven *their angels* always see the face of my Father who is in heaven" (Matt. 18:10). However, our Lord may simply be saying that angels who are assigned the task of protecting little children have ready access to God's presence. (To use an athletic analogy, the angels may be playing "zone" rather than "man-on-man" defense.)[7] When the disciples in Acts 12:15 say that Peter's "angel" must be knocking at the door, this does not necessarily imply belief in an individual guardian angel. It could be that an angel was guarding or caring for Peter just at that time. There seems to be, therefore, no convincing support for the idea of individual "guardian angels" in the text of Scripture.

---

7. Another possibility is that *angel* in Matt. 18:10 and in Acts 12:15 (where the disciples think that Peter's "angel" is knocking at the gate) means not an angelic being but the "spirit" of the person who has died. For a defense of this view, see B. B. Warfield, "The Angels of Christ's 'Little Ones,'" in *Selected Shorter Writings*, ed. John E. Meeter (Nutley, NJ: Presbyterian and Reformed, 1970), 1:253–66; also D. A. Carson, "Matthew," *EBC*, 8:400–401.

The problem with this interpretation is that not one clear example has been found where the word *angel* (Gk. *angelos*) means "spirit of a person who has died." Warfield (pp. 265–66), followed by Carson, quotes two supposed examples from extrabiblical Jewish literature, 1 Enoch 51:4 and 2 Baruch 51:5, 12. But these texts are not convincing: 1 Enoch 51:4 simply says, "And the faces of [all] the angels in heaven shall be lighted up with joy" (R. H. Charles, *The Apocrypha and Pseudepigrapha of the Old Testament*, 2 vols. [Oxford: Clarendon, 1913], 2:219), but it does not say that people will become angels. And 2 Baruch 51:5 states that the righteous will be transformed "into the splendor of angels" (Charles, 2:508), but this simply means that they will have brightness like the angels, not that they will become angels.

In two related passages, 2 Baruch 51:12 states that the righteous will have excellency "surpassing that in the angels," and 2 Baruch 51:10 says that "they shall be made like unto the angels" (Charles, 2:509), but these texts do not say that people will become angels either. Moreover, since no extant Greek text is available for any of these three passages (1 Enoch is an Ethiopic text with some Greek fragments, and 2 Baruch is a Syriac text), they are not useful for determining the meaning of the Greek word *angelos*.

Warfield also cites *Acts of Paul and Thecla*, ed. Tischendorf, p. 42, para. 5, ad finem, as saying, "Blessed are they that fear God, for they shall become angels of God," but the text dates from the late second century AD (*ODCC*, 1049) and is an unreliable source of information about what the early church believed or what the New Testament teaches.

## 9. Angels Do Not Marry

Jesus taught that in the resurrection people "neither marry nor are given in marriage, but are like angels in heaven" (Matt. 22:30; cf. Luke 20:34–36). This would suggest that angels do not have the kind of family relationships that exist among human beings. Scripture is otherwise silent on this point, so it is wise not to attempt to engage in speculation.[8]

## 10. The Power of Angels

Angels apparently have very great power. They are called "you mighty ones who do his word" (Ps. 103:20) and "powers" (cf. Eph. 1:21) and "dominions" and "authorities" (Col. 1:16). Angels are seemingly "greater in might and power" than rebellious human beings (2 Peter 2:11; cf. Matt. 28:2). At least for the time of their earthly existence, human beings are made "lower than the angels" (Heb. 2:7). Though the power of angels is great, it is certainly not infinite, but it is used to battle against the evil demonic powers under the control of Satan (Dan. 10:13; Rev. 12:7–8; 20:1–3).[9] Nonetheless, when the Lord returns, we will be raised to a position higher than that of angels (1 Cor. 6:3; see section C.1, below).

## 11. Who Is the Angel of the Lord?

Several passages of Scripture, especially in the Old Testament, speak of the angel of the Lord in a way that suggests that he is God himself taking on a human form to appear briefly to various people in the Old Testament.

In some passages *the* angel of the LORD" (not *"an* angel of the LORD") is spoken of as the Lord himself. So "the angel of the LORD" who found Hagar in the wilderness promises her, "I will surely multiply your offspring so that they cannot be numbered for multitude" (Gen. 16:10), and Hagar responds by calling "the name of *the* LORD *who spoke to her,* 'You are a God of seeing'" (Gen. 16:13). Similarly, when Abraham is about to sacrifice his son Isaac, "the angel of the LORD" calls to him from heaven and says, "Now I know that you fear God, seeing you have not withheld your son, your only son, *from me*" (Gen. 22:12). When "the angel of God" appeared to Jacob in a dream, he said, "I am the God of Bethel, where you anointed a pillar and made a vow to me" (Gen. 31:11, 13). Again, when "the angel of the LORD" appeared to Moses in a flame of fire out of the midst of a bush, he then said, *"I am the God of your father,* the God of Abraham, the God of Isaac, and the God of Jacob" (Ex. 3:2, 6). These are clear instances of the angel of the

---

8. We should note that this statement of Jesus is given in answer to the Sadducees' question about a woman who had been married seven times, and Jesus said that their question showed lack of knowledge both of Scripture and of "the power of God" (Matt. 22:29). Jesus' answer, therefore, should comfort us and not trouble us: we should contemplate heaven not with sorrow at the anticipation of diminished interpersonal relationships but with joy at the prospect of enriched relationships. (See chapter 20, p. 535, for a discussion of the "sons of God" in Gen. 6:2, 4.)

9. Whether the angels who sinned lost some of their power when they rebelled against God and became demons, or whether their power is still the same as it was when they were angels, Scripture does not tell us.

Lord or the angel of God appearing as God himself, perhaps more specifically as God the Son taking on a human body for a short time in order to appear to human beings.

At other times the angel of the Lord seems to be distinguished from God (see 2 Sam. 24:16; Ps. 34:7; Zech. 1:11–13), and passages that mention "*an* angel of the Lord" (e.g., Luke 1:11) usually indicate an angel sent by God.

## B. When Were Angels Created?

All the angels must have been created before the seventh day of creation, for we read, "Thus the heavens and the earth were finished, and all the host of them" (Gen. 2:1, understanding "host" to be the heavenly creatures that inhabit God's universe). Even more explicit than this is the statement, "In six days the LORD made heaven and earth, the sea, *and all that is in them,* and rested on the seventh day" (Ex. 20:11). Therefore all the angels were created at least by the sixth day of creation.

But can we be any more specific? There may be a hint at the creation of angelic beings on the first day of creation when we read that "in the beginning God created the heavens and the earth" (Gen. 1:1), and then immediately after we read that "the *earth* was without form and void" (Gen. 1:2), but with no mention of the heavens in this second verse. This may suggest that the uninhabitable state of the earth is contrasted with the heavens where, perhaps, God had already created angelic beings and assigned them various roles and orders. This idea is made more plausible when we read that "the morning stars sang together and all the sons of God shouted for joy" at the time when God laid the "cornerstone" of the earth and sunk its "bases" in the process of forming or founding it (Job 38:6–7). If the angels ("the sons of God") shouted for joy when God was making the earth inhabitable, this could imply that God created the angelic beings early on the first day.

However, since we have only hints in Scripture, we must remain content with the fact that God has not given us much information about the time of the creation of the angels. Further speculation, apart from clear scriptural data, would seem to be useless. "The secret things belong to the LORD our God, but the things that are revealed belong to us and to our children forever, that we may do all the words of this law" (Deut. 29:29).

Sometime before Satan tempted Eve in the garden (Gen. 3:1), a number of angels sinned and rebelled against God (2 Peter 2:4; Jude 6). This event occurred apparently after the sixth day of creation when "God saw everything that he had made, and behold, it was very good" (Gen. 1:31), but beyond this, Scripture gives us no further information.

## C. The Place of Angels in God's Purpose
### 1. Angels Show the Greatness of God's Love and Plan for Us

Human beings and angels (using the term broadly) are the only moral, highly intelligent creatures that God has made. Therefore we can understand much about God's plan and love for us when we compare ourselves with angels.

The first distinction to be noted is that angels are never said to be made "in the image of God," while human beings are several times said to be in God's image (Gen. 1:26–27; 9:6). Since being in the image of God means to be like God,[10] it seems fair to conclude that we are more like God than even the angels are.

This is supported by the fact that God will someday give us authority over angels, to judge them: "Do you not know that *we are to judge angels*?" (1 Cor. 6:3). Though we are "for a little while lower than the angels" (Heb. 2:7), when our salvation is complete we will be exalted above angels and rule over them. In fact, even now, angels already serve us: "Are they not all ministering spirits sent out *to serve* for the sake of those who are to inherit salvation?" (Heb. 1:14).

The ability of human beings to bear children like themselves (Adam "fathered a son in his own likeness, after his image," Gen. 5:3) is another element of our superiority to angels, who apparently cannot bear children (cf. Matt. 22:30; Luke 20:34–36).

Angels also demonstrate the greatness of God's love for us in that, though many angels sinned, none were saved. Peter tells us that "*God did not spare angels when they sinned*, but cast them into hell and committed them to chains of gloomy darkness to be kept until the judgment" (2 Peter 2:4). Jude says that "the angels who did not stay within their own position of authority, but left their proper dwelling, he has kept in eternal chains under gloomy darkness until the judgment of the great day" (Jude 6). And we read in Hebrews, "For surely it is not angels that he helps, but he helps the offspring of Abraham" (Heb. 2:16).

We see, therefore, that God created two groups of intelligent, moral creatures. Among the angels, many sinned, but God decided to redeem none of them. This was perfectly just for God to do, and no angel can ever complain that he has been treated unfairly by God.

Now among the other group of moral creatures, human beings, we also find that a large number (indeed, all) have sinned and turned away from God. As with the angels that sinned, God could have let all of us go on our self-chosen path toward eternal condemnation. Had God decided to save no one out of the entire sinful human race, he would be perfectly just to do so, and no one could complain of unfairness on his part.

But God decided to do much more than merely meet the demands of justice. He decided to save some sinful human beings. If he had decided to save only five human beings out of the entire human race, that would have been much more than justice: it would have been a great demonstration of mercy and grace. If he had decided to save only one hundred out of the whole human race, it would have been an amazing demonstration of mercy and love. But God in fact has chosen to do much more than that. He has decided to redeem out of sinful mankind a great multitude, whom no man can number, "from every tribe and language and people and nation" (Rev. 5:9). This is

---

10. See chapter 21, pp. 567–69.

incalculable mercy and love, far beyond our comprehension. It is all undeserved favor: it is all of grace. The striking contrast with the fate of angels brings this truth home to us.

The fact that we have been saved from a life of rebellion against God means that we are able to sing songs that angels will never be able to sing for all eternity.

> Redeemed, how I love to proclaim it!
> Redeemed by the blood of the lamb;
> Redeemed through his infinite mercy—
> His child, and forever, I am.[11]

This song, and all the great songs proclaiming our redemption in Christ, are ours alone to sing. Unfallen angels see us sing these songs and they rejoice (Luke 15:10), but they will never be able to make them their own.

## 2. Angels Remind Us That the Unseen World Is Real

Just as the Sadducees in Jesus' day said that "there is no resurrection, nor angel, nor spirit" (Acts 23:8), so many in our day deny the reality of anything they cannot see. But the biblical teaching on the existence of angels is a constant reminder to us that there is an unseen world that is very real. It was only when the Lord opened the eyes of Elisha's servant to the reality of this invisible world that the servant saw that "the mountain was full of horses and chariots of fire all around Elisha" (2 Kings 6:17; this was a great angelic army sent to Dothan to protect Elisha from the Syrians). The psalmist too shows an awareness of the unseen world when he encourages the angels, "Praise him, all his angels; praise him, all his hosts!" (Ps. 148:2). The author of Hebrews reminds us that when we worship we come into the heavenly Jerusalem to gather with "innumerable angels in festal gathering" (Heb. 12:22), whom we do not see, but whose presence should fill us with both awe and joy. An unbelieving world may dismiss talk of angels as mere superstition, but Scripture offers it as insight into the state of affairs as they really are.

## 3. Angels Are Examples for Us

In both their obedience and their worship angels provide helpful examples for us to imitate. Jesus teaches us to pray, "Your will be done, on earth as it is in heaven" (Matt. 6:10). In heaven God's will is done by angels, immediately, joyfully, and without question. We are to pray daily that our obedience and the obedience of others would be like that of the angels in heaven. Their delight is to be God's humble servants, each faithfully and joyfully performing their assigned tasks, whether great or small. Our desire and prayer should be that we ourselves and all others on earth would do the same.

---

11. Fanny Jane Crosby, "Redeemed, How I Love to Proclaim It!" (1882).

Angels also serve as our examples in their worship of God. The seraphim before God's throne see God in his holiness and continue to cry out, "Holy, holy, holy is the LORD of hosts; the whole earth is full of his glory" (Isa. 6:3). And John sees around God's throne a great angelic army, "numbering myriads of myriads and thousands of thousands, saying with a loud voice, 'Worthy is the Lamb who was slain, to receive power and wealth and wisdom and might and honor and glory and blessing!'" (Rev. 5:11–12). As angels find it their highest joy to praise God continuously, should we not also delight each day to sing God's praise, counting this as the highest and worthiest use of our time and our greatest joy?

## 4. Angels Carry Out Some of God's Plans

Scripture sees angels as God's servants who carry out some of his plans in the earth. They bring God's messages to people (Luke 1:11–19; Acts 8:26; 10:3–8, 22; 27:23–24). They carry out some of God's judgments, bringing a plague upon Israel (2 Sam. 24:16–17), smiting the leaders of the Assyrian army (2 Chron. 32:21), striking King Herod dead because he did not give God glory (Acts 12:23), or pouring out bowls of God's wrath on the earth (Rev. 16:1). When Christ returns, angels will come with him as a great army accompanying their King and Lord (Matt. 16:27; Luke 9:26; 2 Thess. 1:7).

Angels also patrol the earth as God's representatives (Zech. 1:10–11) and carry out war against demonic forces (Dan. 10:13; Rev. 12:7–8). John in his vision saw an angel coming down from heaven, and he records that the angel "seized the dragon, that ancient serpent, who is the devil and Satan, and bound him for a thousand years, and threw him into the pit" (Rev. 20:1–3). When Christ returns, an archangel will proclaim his coming (1 Thess. 4:16; cf. Rev. 18:1–2, 21; 19:17–18, et al.).

## 5. Angels Directly Glorify God

Angels also serve another function: they minister directly to God by glorifying him. In addition to human beings, there are other intelligent, moral creatures who glorify God in the universe.

Angels glorify God for who he is in himself, for his excellence.

> Bless the LORD, O you his angels,
>> you mighty ones who do his word,
>> obeying the voice of his word! (Ps. 103:20; cf. 148:2)

The seraphim continually praise God for his holiness (Isa. 6:2–3), as do the four living creatures (Rev. 4:8).

Angels also glorify God for his great plan of salvation as they see it unfold. When Christ was born in Bethlehem, a multitude of angels praised God and said, "Glory to God in the highest, and on earth peace among those with whom he is pleased!"

(Luke 2:14; cf. Heb. 1:6). Jesus tells us, "There is joy before the angels of God over one sinner who repents" (Luke 15:10), indicating that angels rejoice every time someone turns from his or her sins and trusts in Christ as Savior.

When Paul proclaims the gospel so that people from diverse racial backgrounds, both Jews and Greeks, are brought into the church, he sees God's wise plan for the church as being displayed before the angels (and demons), for he says that he was called to preach to the gentiles "that through the church the manifold wisdom of God might now be *made known to the rulers and authorities in the heavenly places*" (Eph. 3:10). And Peter tells us that "angels long to look" (1 Peter 1:12) into the glories of the plan of salvation as it works out in the lives of individual believers each day.[12] Paul also notes that Christ was "seen by angels" (1 Tim. 3:16), suggesting that they glorified God for Christ's life of obedience. Moreover, the fact that wives at Corinth were to have head coverings that appropriately signaled that they were married women, "because of the angels" (1 Cor. 11:10), when the church assembled for worship, indicates that angels witness the lives of Christians and glorify God for our worship and obedience. Indeed, Paul reminds Timothy, when he wants to emphasize the seriousness of a command, that our actions are carried out in the presence of angelic witnesses: "In the presence of God and of Christ Jesus *and of the elect angels* I charge you to keep these rules without prejudging, doing nothing from partiality" (1 Tim. 5:21; cf. 1 Cor. 4:9). If Timothy follows Paul's instructions, angels will witness his obedience and glorify God; if he neglects to obey, angels will also see and be grieved.

## D. OUR RELATIONSHIP TO ANGELS

### 1. We Should Be Aware of Angels in Our Daily Lives

Scripture makes it clear, by many verses teaching about angels, that God wants us to be aware of the existence of angels and of the nature of their activity. We should not therefore assume that the Bible's teaching about angels has nothing whatsoever to do with our lives today. Rather, there are several ways in which our Christian lives will be enriched by an awareness of the existence and ministry of angels in the world even today.

When we come before God in worship, we are joining not only with the great company of believers who have died and have come into God's presence in heaven, "the spirits of the righteous made perfect," but also with a great throng of angels, "innumerable angels in festal gathering" (Heb. 12:22–23). Though we do not ordinarily see or hear evidence of this heavenly worship, it certainly enriches our sense of reverence and joy in God's presence if we appreciate the fact that angels join us in the worship of God.

Moreover, we should be aware that angels are watching our obedience or disobedience

---

12. The present tense verb *epithymousin*, "long," gives the sense "are continually longing, even at the present time" to look into these things. This longing includes a holy curiosity to watch and delight in the glories of Christ's kingdom as they find ever fuller realization in the lives of individual Christians throughout the history of the church. (See discussion in Wayne Grudem, *The First Epistle of Peter*, TNTC [Leicester: Inter-Varsity Press; Grand Rapids: Eerdmans, 1988], 73.)

to God through the day. Even if we think our sins are done in secret and bring grief to no one else, we should be sobered by the thought that perhaps even hundreds of angels witness our disobedience and are grieved.[13] On the other hand, when we are discouraged and think that our faithful obedience to God is witnessed by no one and is an encouragement to no one, we can be comforted by the realization that perhaps hundreds of angels witness our lonely struggle, daily "longing to look" at the way Christ's great salvation finds expression in our lives.

As if to make the reality of angelic observation of our service to God more vivid, the author of Hebrews suggests that angels can sometimes take human form, apparently to make "inspection visits," something like the newspaper's restaurant critic who disguises himself and visits a new restaurant. We read, "Do not neglect to show hospitality to strangers, for thereby some have entertained angels unawares" (Heb. 13:2; cf. Gen. 18:2–5; 19:1–3). This should make us eager to minister to the needs of others whom we do not know, all the while wondering if someday we will reach heaven and meet the angel whom we helped when he appeared temporarily as a human being in distress here on earth.

When we are suddenly delivered from a danger or distress, we might suspect that angels have been sent by God to help us, and we should be thankful. An angel shut the mouths of the lions so they would not hurt Daniel (Dan. 6:22), delivered the apostles from prison (Acts 5:19–20), later delivered Peter from prison (Acts 12:7–11), and ministered to Jesus in the wilderness at a time of great weakness, immediately after his temptations had ended (Matt. 4:11).[14]

When a car suddenly swerves from hitting us, when we suddenly find footing to keep from being swept along in a raging river, when we walk unscathed in a dangerous neighborhood, should we not suspect that God has sent his angels to protect us? Does not Scripture promise, "For he will command his angels concerning you to guard you in all your ways. On their hands they will bear you up, lest you strike your foot against a stone" (Ps. 91:11–12)? Should we not therefore thank God for sending angels to protect us at such times? It seems right that we should do so.

## 2. Cautions Regarding Our Relationship to Angels

**a. Beware of Receiving False Doctrine from Angels.** The Bible warns against receiving false doctrine from supposed angels: "But even if we or an angel from heaven should preach to you a gospel contrary to the one we preached to you, let him be accursed" (Gal. 1:8). Paul makes this warning because he knows that there is a possibility

---

13. This is not to deny that the primary deterrent against sinning must be fear of displeasing God himself; it is just to say that as the presence of other human beings serves as an additional deterrent, so the knowledge of the presence of angels should also serve as a deterrent to us.

14. Note also the report in Luke 22:43 that when Jesus was praying in the garden of Gethsemane, "there appeared to him an angel from heaven, strengthening him." This text has substantial ancient attestation.

of deception. He says, "Even Satan disguises himself as an angel of light" (2 Cor. 11:14). Similarly, the lying prophet who deceived the man of God in 1 Kings 13 claimed, *"An angel spoke to me* by the word of the LORD, saying, 'Bring him back with you into your house that he may eat bread and drink water'" (1 Kings 13:18). Yet the text of Scripture immediately adds in the same verse, "But he lied to him."

These are all instances of *false* doctrine or guidance being conveyed by angels. It is interesting that these examples show the clear possibility of satanic deception tempting us to disobey the clear teachings of Scripture or the clear commands of God (cf. 1 Kings 13:9). These warnings should keep any Christians from being fooled by the claims of Mormons, for example, that an angel (Moroni) spoke to Joseph Smith and revealed to him the basis of the Mormon religion. Such "revelation" is contrary to the teachings of Scripture at many points (with respect to such doctrines as the Trinity, the person of Christ, justification by faith alone, and many others), and Christians should be warned against accepting these claims.[15] The closing of the canon of Scripture (see chapter 3) should also warn us that no further revelation of doctrine is to be given by God today, and any claims to have received additional revelation of doctrine from angels today should be immediately rejected as false.

**b. Do Not Worship Angels, Pray to Them, or Seek Them.** "Worship of angels" (Col. 2:18) was one of the false doctrines being taught at Colossae. Moreover, an angel speaking to John in the book of Revelation warns John not to worship him: "You must not do that! I am a fellow servant with you and your brothers who hold to the testimony of Jesus. Worship God" (Rev. 19:10).

Nor should we pray to angels. We are to pray only to God, who alone is omnipotent and thus able to answer prayer and who alone is omniscient and therefore able to hear the prayers of all his people at once. By virtue of omnipotence and omniscience, God the Son and God the Holy Spirit are also worthy of being prayed to, but this is not true of any other being. Paul warns us against thinking that any other "mediator" can come between us and God, "for there is one God, and there is *one mediator* between God and men, the man Christ Jesus" (1 Tim. 2:5). If we were to pray to angels, it would be implicitly attributing to them a status equal to God, which we must not do. There is no example in Scripture of anyone praying to any specific angel or asking angels for help.

Moreover, Scripture gives us no warrant to seek for appearances of angels to us. They manifest themselves unsought. To seek such appearances would seem to indicate an unhealthy curiosity or a desire for some kind of spectacular event rather than a love for God and devotion to him and his work. Though angels did appear to people at various times in Scripture, the people apparently never sought those appearances. Our role is

---

15. Of course, there were times in Scripture when doctrinal truth came through angels (Luke 1:13–20, 30–37; 2:10–14; Acts 1:11; Heb. 2:2). The warning passages mentioned above forbid receiving doctrine contrary to Scripture from angels.

rather to talk to the Lord, who is himself the commander of all angelic forces. However, it would not seem wrong to ask God to fulfill his promise in Psalm 91:11 to send angels to protect us in times of need.

**c. Do Angels Appear to People Today?** In the earliest period of the church's history angels were active. An angel told Philip to travel south on a road that goes from Jerusalem to Gaza (Acts 8:26), instructed Cornelius to send a messenger to get Peter to come from Joppa (Acts 10:3–6), urged Peter to get up and walk out of the prison (Acts 12:6–11), and promised Paul that no one on his ship would be lost and that he himself would stand before Caesar (Acts 27:23–24). Moreover, the author of Hebrews encourages his readers, none of whom are apostles or even first-generation believers associated with the apostles (see Heb. 2:3), that *they* should continue to show hospitality to strangers, apparently with the expectation that they too might sometime entertain angels without realizing it (Heb. 13:2).

There is, therefore, no compelling reason to rule out the possibility of angelic appearances today. Some would dispute this on the grounds that the sufficiency of Scripture (see chapter 8) and the closing of its canon (see chapter 3) rule out the possibility of angelic manifestations now.[16] They would say that we are not to expect God to communicate to us through angels. However, this conclusion does not follow. Though angels would not add to the doctrinal and moral content of Scripture, God *could* communicate information to us through angels as he also does through prophecy[17] or through ordinary communication from other persons, or through our observation of the world. If God can send another human being to warn us of danger or encourage us when we are downcast, there seems to be no reason why he could not occasionally send an angel to do this as well.

However, we should use *extreme caution* in receiving guidance from an angel should such an unusual event happen. (It is perhaps noteworthy that very few instances of such events are recorded today, and many of these involve the communication of antiscriptural doctrine, indicating that they are actually demonic appearances.) The fact that demons can appear as angels of light (see 2 Cor. 11:14) should warn us that the appearance of any angel-like creature does not guarantee that this being speaks truthfully: *Scripture* is our guide, and no angelic creature can give authoritative teaching that is contrary to Scripture (see Gal. 1:8).

An angelic appearance today would be unusual. If one should (apparently) occur, we should evaluate it with caution. But there is no convincing reason for saying that such an event absolutely could not happen, particularly in a time of extreme danger or intense conflict with the forces of evil.

---

16. See the discussion of the cessation of some spiritual gifts in chapter 52, below.

17. See chapter 53, pp. 1293–1313.

## QUESTIONS FOR PERSONAL APPLICATION

1. How might this chapter affect how you think about angels from now on? What difference would it make in your attitude in worship if you consciously thought about being in the presence of angels when you were singing praises to God?
2. Do you think there are angels watching you right now? What attitude or attitudes do you think they have as they watch you? Have you ever experienced a remarkably elevated sense of joy just after praying with someone to receive Christ as personal Savior? Do you think one aspect contributing to that joy might be that angels are also rejoicing with you because a sinner has repented (Luke 15:10)?
3. Have you had a remarkable rescue from physical or other kinds of danger and wondered if angels were involved in helping you at the time?
4. How can the example of angels who joyfully and faithfully perform their assigned tasks, whether great or small, be of help to you in the responsibilities that you face today, whether at work or at home or in the church?
5. How do you think you will feel when God asks you to judge angels (1 Cor. 6:3)? Explain what that fact tells you about the greatness of your humanity as created in the image of God.

**Special Terms**

*angel*
*angel of the Lord*
*archangel*
*cherubim*
*living creatures*
*Michael*
*principalities and powers*
*seraphim*
*sons of God*
*watchers*

## BIBLIOGRAPHY

(For an explanation of this bibliography see the note on the bibliography to chapter 1, pp. 23–24. Complete bibliographical data may be found on pp. 1489–96.)

### SECTIONS IN EVANGELICAL SYSTEMATIC THEOLOGIES

*1. Anglican (Episcopalian)*
1882–92 . . . . . Litton, 125–29
2001 . . . . . . . . Packer, 64–66
2013 . . . . . . . . Bird, 102–3
2013 . . . . . . . . Bray, 803–13

*2. Arminian (Wesleyan or Methodist)*
1892–94 . . . . . Miley, 2:490–96
1940 . . . . . . . . Wiley, 1:472–76
1983 . . . . . . . . Carter, 2:1047–69
1992 . . . . . . . . Oden, 1:240–41
2002 . . . . . . . . Cottrell, 127–33

*3. Baptist*
1767 . . . . . . . . Gill, 1:375–84, 434–35
1887 . . . . . . . . Boyce, 174–81
1907 . . . . . . . . Strong, 443–64
1976–83 . . . . . Henry, 6:229–50

1990–95 . . . . . Garrett, 413–28
2007 . . . . . . . . Akin, 293–339
2013 . . . . . . . . Erickson, 403–15

### 4. *Dispensational*

1947 . . . . . . . . Chafer, 2:3–32
1949 . . . . . . . . Thiessen, 133–50
1986 . . . . . . . . Ryrie, 121–34
2002–2005 . . Geisler, 2:475–99
2017 . . . . . . . . MacArthur and Mayhue, 665–76

### 5. *Lutheran*

1917–24 . . . . . Pieper, 1:498–508
1934 . . . . . . . . Mueller, 196–202

### 6. *Reformed (or Presbyterian)*

1559 . . . . . . . . Calvin, 1:163–72 (1.14.3–12)
1679–85 . . . . . Turretin, *IET*, 1: 335–41, 539–67
1724–58 . . . . . Edwards, 2:604–7, 612–17
1871–73 . . . . . Hodge, 1:637–43
1878 . . . . . . . . Dabney, 264–75
1894 . . . . . . . . Shedd, 44, 57–58, 154, 181
1906–11 . . . . . Bavinck, *RD*, 2: 443–72
1910 . . . . . . . . Vos, 1:4, 39–41, 51
1938 . . . . . . . . Berkhof, 141–48
2008 . . . . . . . . Van Genderen and Velema, 276–82
2011 . . . . . . . . Horton, 406–7
2013 . . . . . . . . Frame, 771–74, 777–79
2013 . . . . . . . . Culver, 164–75
2019 . . . . . . . . Letham, 299

### 7. *Renewal (or charismatic/Pentecostal)*

1988–92 . . . . . Williams, 1:169–96
1993 . . . . . . . . Menzies and Horton, 51, 87, 217, 247

1995 . . . . . . . . Horton, 179–93
2008 . . . . . . . . Duffield and Van Cleave, 471–505

## SECTIONS IN REPRESENTATIVE ROMAN CATHOLIC SYSTEMATIC THEOLOGIES

### 1. *Roman Catholic: Traditional*

1955 . . . . . . . . Ott, 114–21

### 2. *Roman Catholic: Post-Vatican II*

2012 . . . . . . . . *CCC*, paragraphs 328–54

## OTHER WORKS

Allison, Gregg. *Historical Theology: An Introduction to Christian Doctrine; A Companion to Wayne Grudem's* Systematic Theology. Grand Rapids: Zondervan, 2011, 298–320.

Arnold, Clinton E. *Powers of Darkness: Principalities and Powers in Paul's Letters.* Downers Grove, IL: InterVarsity Press, 1992.

Borland, James A. *Christ in the Old Testament.* Chicago: Moody Publishers, 1978.

Bromiley, G. W. "Angels." In *EDT3*, 54–55.

Chisholm, R. B., Jr. "Theophany." In *NDBT*, 815–19.

Cole, Graham A. *Against the Darkness: The Doctrine of Satan, Angels, and Demons.* Wheaton, IL: Crossway, 2019.

Davidson, M. J. "Angels." In *DJG*, 8–11.

Dickason, C. Fred. *Angels, Elect and Evil.* Rev. ed. Chicago: Moody Publishers, 1995.

Garrett, Duane A. *Angels and the New Spirituality.* Nashville: Broadman & Holman, 1995.

Goldberg, Louis. "Angel of the Lord." In *BTDB*, 23.

Graham, Billy. *Angels: God's Secret Agents.* Rev. ed. Waco, TX: Word, 1986.

Harrison, R. K. "Angel." In *BTDB*, 21–23.

Joppie, A. S. *The Ministry of Angels.* Grand Rapids: Baker, 1953.

McComiskey, T. E. "Angel of the Lord." In *EDT3*, 54.

Moyer, J. C. "Theophany." In *EDT3*, 875.

Niehaus, Jeffrey Jay. *God at Sinai: Covenant and Theophany in the Bible and Ancient Near East.* Grand Rapids: Zondervan, 1995.

Nkansah-Obrempong, J. "Angels." In *GDT*, 35–39.

Noll, S. F. "Angels, Heavenly Beings, Angel Christology." In *DLNT*, 44–48.

Noll, Stephen F. *Angels of Light, Powers of Darkness: Thinking Biblically about Angels, Satan, and Principalities.* Downers Grove, IL: InterVarsity Press, 1998.

Piggin, F. S. "Principalities and Powers" In *EDT3*, 698-99.

Reid, D. G. "Angels, Archangels." In *DPL*, 20–23.

Schemm, Peter R. "The Agents of God: Angels." In *A Theology for the Church*, edited by Daniel L. Akin et al., 293–337. Nashville: B&H, 2007.

Twelftree, G. H. "Spiritual Powers." In *NDBT*, 796–802.

Williams, William C. "Theophany." In *BTDB*, 770–71.

## SCRIPTURE MEMORY PASSAGE

**Revelation 5:11–12:** Then I looked, and I heard around the throne and the living creatures and the elders the voice of many angels, numbering myriads of myriads and thousands of thousands, saying with a loud voice, "Worthy is the Lamb who was slain, to receive power and wealth and wisdom and might and honor and glory and blessing!"

## HYMN

### "Angels from the Realms of Glory"

*Angels, from the realms of glory,*
*wing your flight o'er all the earth*
*Ye who sang creation's story,*
*now proclaim Messiah's birth:*
*Come and worship, come and worship,*
*worship Christ the newborn King.*

*Shepherds, in the fields abiding,*
*watching o'er your flocks by night;*
*God with man is now residing,*
*yonder shines the infant light:*
*Come and worship, come and worship,*
*worship Christ the newborn King.*

*Sages, leave your contemplations,*
*brighter visions beam afar;*
*Seek the great desire of nations;*
*ye have seen his natal star:*

*Come and worship, come and worship,*
*worship Christ the newborn King.*

*Saints, before the altar bending,*
*watching long in hope and fear,*
*Suddenly the Lord, descending,*
*in his temple shall appear:*
*Come and worship, come and worship,*
*worship Christ the newborn King.*

*All creation, join in praising*
*God the Father, Spirit, Son;*
*Evermore your voices raising*
*to th' eternal Three in One:*
*Come and worship, come and worship,*
*worship Christ the newborn King.*

Author: James Montgomery, 1816

# CONTEMPORARY WORSHIP SONG

## "Whom Shall I Fear (God of Angel Armies)"

*You hear me when I call.*
*You are my morning song.*
*Though darkness fills the night,*
*It cannot hide the light.*
*Whom shall I fear?*
*You crush the enemy underneath my feet.*
*You are my sword and shield.*
*Though troubles linger still,*
*Whom shall I fear?*

*Chorus*
*I know Who goes before me.*
*I know Who stands behind.*
*The God of angel armies is always by my side.*
*The One who reigns forever,*
*He is a friend of mine.*
*The God of angel armies is always by my side.*

*My strength is in Your name.*
*For You alone can save.*
*You will deliver me.*
*Yours is the victory.*
*Whom shall I fear?*
*Whom shall I fear?*
*(Whom shall I fear?)*

*Bridge*
*(And) nothing formed against me shall stand.*
*You hold the whole world in Your hands.*
*I'm holding on to Your promises.*
*You are faithful.*
*You are faithful.*

Words by Scott Cash, Chris
Tomlin, and Ed Cash[18]

## CHAPTER 20

# Satan and Demons

*How should Christians think of Satan and demons today?*
*How should we understand and practice spiritual warfare?*

## EXPLANATION AND SCRIPTURAL BASIS

The previous chapter leads naturally to a consideration of Satan and demons, since they are evil angels who once were like the good angels but who sinned and lost their privilege of serving God. Like angels, they are also created, spiritual beings with moral judgment and high intelligence but without physical bodies. We may define demons as follows: *demons are evil angels who sinned against God and who now continually work evil in the world.*

### A. THE ORIGIN OF DEMONS

When God created the world, he "saw everything that he had made, and behold, it was very good" (Gen. 1:31). This means that even the angelic world that God had created did not have evil angels or demons in it at that time. But by the time of Genesis 3, we find that Satan, in the form of a serpent, was tempting Eve to sin (Gen. 3:1–5). Therefore, sometime between the events of Genesis 1:31 and Genesis 3:1, there must have been a rebellion in the angelic world with many angels turning against God and becoming evil.

The New Testament speaks of this in two places. Peter tells us, "God did not spare angels *when they sinned*, but cast them into hell and committed them to chains of gloomy darkness to be kept until the judgment" (2 Peter 2:4).[1] Jude also says that "the angels who *did not stay within their own position of authority*, but left their proper dwelling, he has kept in eternal chains under gloomy darkness until the judgment of the great day" (Jude 6). Once again the emphasis is on the fact that they are removed from the glory of God's presence and their activity is restricted (metaphorically, they are in "eternal chains"), but the text does not imply that the influence of demons has been removed from the world or that some demons are kept in a place of punishment apart from the world while

---

1. This does not mean that these sinful angels have no current influence on the world, for in v. 9 Peter says that the Lord also knows how "to keep the unrighteous under punishment until the day of judgment," here referring to sinful human beings who were obviously still having influence in the world and even troubling Peter's readers. 2 Peter 2:4 simply means that the wicked angels have been removed from the presence of God and are kept under some kind of restraining influence until the final judgment, but this does not rule out their continued activity in the world meanwhile.

others are able to influence it.[2] Rather, both 2 Peter and Jude tell us that some angels rebelled against God and became hostile opponents to his Word. Their sin seems to have been pride, a refusal to accept their assigned place, for they "did not stay within their own position of authority, but left their proper dwelling" (Jude 6).

It is also possible that there is a reference to the fall of Satan, the prince of demons, in Isaiah 14. As Isaiah is describing the judgment of God on the king of Babylon (an earthly, human king), he then comes to a section where he begins to use language that seems too strong to refer to any merely human king:

> How you are fallen from heaven,
> > O Day Star,[3] son of Dawn!
> How you are cut down to the ground,
> > you who laid the nations low!
> You said in your heart,
> > "I will ascend to heaven;
> above the stars of God
> > I will set my throne on high;
> I will sit on the mount of assembly
> > in the far reaches of the north;
> I will ascend above the heights of the clouds;
> > I will make myself like the Most High."
> But you are brought down to Sheol,
> > to the far reaches of the pit. (Isa. 14:12–15)

This language of ascending to heaven and setting his throne on high and saying, "I will make myself like the Most High" strongly suggests a rebellion by an angelic creature of great power and dignity. It would not be uncommon for Hebrew prophetic speech to pass from descriptions of human events to descriptions of heavenly events that are parallel to them and that the earthly events picture in a limited way.[4] If this is so, then the sin of Satan is described as one of pride and attempting to be equal to God in status and authority. (Ezek. 28:11–19 also possibly alludes to Satan's fall.)

However, it is unlikely that Genesis 6:2–4 refers to the fall of demons. In these

---

2. Note that 2 Peter 2:4 does not say, "God did not spare *some of* the angels when they sinned," or "God cast *some of* the sinning angels into hell," but it speaks generally of "the angels" when they sinned, implying all of them who sinned. Similarly, Jude 6 speaks of "the angels who did not stay within their own position," implying all who sinned. Therefore, these verses must say something that is true of all demons. Their current home, their dwelling place, is "hell" and "pits of nether gloom," although they can range from there to influence people in the world.

3. The KJV translates "Day Star" as "Lucifer," a name meaning "bearer of light." The name Lucifer does not appear elsewhere in the KJV and does not appear at all in more modern translations of the Bible.

4. See, for example, Ps. 45, which moves from a description of an earthly king to a description of a divine Messiah.

verses, we are told that "the sons of God saw that the daughters of man were attractive. And they took as their wives any they chose. . . . The Nephilim were on the earth in those days, and also afterward, when the sons of God came in to the daughters of man and they bore children to them." Although some have thought that the "sons of God" in this passage are angels who sinned by marrying human women, this is not a likely interpretation.

Angels are nonmaterial beings and according to Jesus do not marry (Matt. 22:30), facts that cast doubt on the idea that "the sons of God" are angels who married human wives. Moreover, nothing in the context of Genesis 6 indicates that the "sons of God" should be understood as angels (this makes this passage unlike Job 1–2, for example, where the context of a heavenly council makes it clear to the reader that angels are being referred to).

It is far more likely that the phrase "sons of God" in Genesis 6:2 (as in Deut. 14:1) refers to people belonging to God and, like God, walking in righteousness (note Gen. 4:26 as an introduction to Gen. 5, marking the beginning of Seth's line at the same time as "people began to call upon the name of the LORD"). In fact, there is an emphasis on sonship as including likeness to one's father in Genesis 5:3. Moreover, the text traces the descendants from God through Adam and Seth to many "sons" in all of chapter 5. The larger purpose of the narrative seems to be to trace the parallel development of the godly (ultimately messianic) line of Seth and the ungodly descendants of the rest of mankind. Therefore, the "sons of God" in Genesis 6:2 are men who are righteous in their imitation of the character of their heavenly Father, and the "daughters of man" are the ungodly wives whom they marry.[5]

## B. Satan as Head of the Demons

"Satan" is the personal name of the head of the demons. This name is mentioned in Job 1:6, where "the sons of God came to present themselves before the LORD, and *Satan* also came among them" (see also Job 1:7–2:7). Here he appears as the enemy of the Lord who brings severe temptations against Job. Similarly, near the end of David's life, "Satan stood against Israel and incited David to number Israel" (1 Chron. 21:1). Moreover, Zechariah saw a vision of "Joshua the high priest standing before the angel of the LORD, and Satan standing at his right hand to accuse him" (Zech. 3:1). The name "Satan" is a Hebrew word (*sātān*) that means "adversary."[6] The New Testament also uses the name "Satan," simply taking it over from the Old Testament. So Jesus, in his temptation in the wilderness, speaks to Satan directly saying, "Be gone, Satan!" (Matt. 4:10), or "I saw Satan fall like lightning from heaven" (Luke 10:18).

---

5. For a more detailed argument see Grudem, *The First Epistle of Peter*, 211–13, which is summarized in the discussion here. Later Jewish interpreters of these verses were about equally divided between those who thought the "sons of God" were angels and those who thought they were human beings.

6. BDB, 966.

The Bible uses other names for Satan as well. He is called "the devil"[7] (only in the New Testament: Matt. 4:1; 13:39; 25:41; Rev. 12:9; 20:2, et al.), "the serpent" (Gen. 3:1, 14; 2 Cor. 11:3; Rev. 12:9; 20:2), "Beelzebul" (Matt. 10:25; 12:24, 27; Luke 11:15), "the ruler of this world" (John 12:31; 14:30; 16:11),[8] "the prince of the power of the air" (Eph. 2:2), or "the evil one" (Matt. 13:19; 1 John 2:13). When Jesus says to Peter, "Get behind me, Satan! You are a hindrance to me. For you are not setting your mind on the things of God, but on the things of man" (Matt. 16:23), he recognizes that Peter's attempt to keep him from suffering and dying on the cross is really an attempt to keep him from obedience to the Father's plan. Jesus realizes that opposition ultimately comes not from Peter, but from Satan himself.

## C. The Activity of Satan and Demons
### 1. Satan Was the Originator of Sin

Satan sinned before any human beings did so, as is evident from the fact that he (in the form of the serpent) tempted Eve (Gen. 3:1–6; 2 Cor. 11:3). The New Testament also informs us that Satan was a "murderer from the beginning" and is "a liar and the father of lies" (John 8:44). It also says that "the devil has been sinning *from the beginning*" (1 John 3:8). In both of these texts, the phrase "from the beginning" does not imply that Satan was evil from the time God began to create the world ("from the beginning of the world") or from the beginning of his existence ("from the beginning of his life") but rather from the "beginning" parts of the history of the world (Genesis 3 and even before). The devil's characteristic has been to originate sin and tempt others to sin.

### 2. Demons Oppose and Try to Destroy Every Work of God

Just as Satan tempted Eve to sin against God (Gen. 3:1–6), so he tried to get Jesus to sin and thus fail in his mission as Messiah (Matt. 4:1–11). The tactics of Satan and his demons are to use lies (John 8:44), deception (Rev. 12:9), murder (Ps. 106:37; John 8:44), and every other kind of destructive activity to attempt to cause people to turn away from God and destroy themselves.[9] Demons will try every tactic to blind people to the gospel (2 Cor. 4:4) and keep them in bondage to things that hinder them from coming to God (Gal. 4:8). They will also try to use temptation, doubt, guilt, fear, confusion, sickness, envy, pride, slander, or any other means possible to hinder a Christian's witness and usefulness.

---

7. The word *devil* is an English translation of Greek *diabolos*, which means "slanderer" (BAGD, 182). In fact, the English word *devil* is ultimately derived from this same Greek word, but the sound of the word changed considerably as the word passed from Greek to Latin to Old English to modern English.

8. John frequently uses "the world" or "this world" to refer to the present evil world system in opposition to God: John 7:7;

8:23; 12:31; 14:17, 30; 15:18, 19; 16:11; 17:14. Scripture does not teach that Satan rules over the entire world, but that he is ruler over the system of sinful opposition to God. Compare Paul's phrase "the god of this world" (2 Cor. 4:4).

9. Cf. John 10:10: "The thief comes only to steal and kill and destroy."

### 3. Yet Demons Are Limited by God's Control and Have Limited Power

The story of Job makes it clear that Satan could only do what God gave him permission to do and nothing more (Job 1:12; 2:6). Demons are kept in "eternal chains" (Jude 6) and can be successfully resisted by Christians through the authority that Christ gives them (James 4:7).

Moreover, the power of demons is limited. After rebelling against God they do not have the power they had when they were angels, for sin is a weakening and destructive influence. The power of demons, though significant, is therefore probably less than the power of angels.

In the area of knowledge, *we should not think that demons can know the future or that they can read our minds or know our thoughts*. In many places in the Old Testament, the Lord shows himself to be the true God in distinction from the false (demonic) gods of the nations by the fact that *he alone can know the future*: "I am God, and there is none like me, declaring the end from the beginning and from ancient times things not yet done" (Isa. 46:9–10).[10]

Even angels do not know the time of Jesus' return (Mark 13:32), and there is no indication in Scripture that they or demons know anything else about the future either.

With respect to knowing our thoughts, the Bible tells us that Jesus knew people's thoughts (Matt. 9:4; 12:25; Mark 2:8; Luke 6:8; 11:17) and that God knows people's thoughts (Gen. 6:5; Ps. 139:2, 4, 23; Isa. 66:18), but there is no indication that angels or demons can know our thoughts. In fact, Daniel told King Nebuchadnezzar that no one speaking by any other power than the God of heaven could tell the king what he had dreamed:

> Daniel answered the king, "*No wise men, enchanters, magicians, or astrologers* can show to the king the mystery that the king has asked, but there is a God in heaven who reveals mysteries, and he has made known to King Nebuchadnezzar what will be in the latter days. Your dream and the visions of your head as you lay in bed are these: . . ." (Dan. 2:27–28)[11]

In addition, God identifies himself as the true God "who forms the mountains and creates the wind, and *declares to man what is his thought*" (Amos 4:13), listing this ability among other things that only God himself can do.

---

10. See the discussion of God's knowledge of the future in chapter 11, pp. 185–86, 199–206.

11. Paul also says, "For who knows a person's thoughts except the spirit of that person, which is in him?" (1 Cor. 2:11), suggesting that there is no other creature who can know a person's thoughts (although admittedly the inclusion of angelic or demonic creatures in Paul's idea is not made explicit in this context as it is in Dan. 2). See also 1 Cor. 14:24–25, where the disclosure of the "secrets" of a visitor's heart is clear evidence that God himself is present, working through the gift of prophecy. This is significant in Corinth, which was filled with demon worship in idol temples (1 Cor. 10:20)—it indicates that demons could not know the secret thoughts in a person's heart. (On Acts 16:16, see the next paragraph.)

But if demons cannot read people's minds, how shall we understand contemporary reports of witch doctors, fortune-tellers, or other people evidently under demonic influence who are able to tell people accurate details of their lives which they thought no one knew, such as (for example) what food they had for breakfast, where they keep some hidden money in their house, and so forth? Most of these things can be explained by realizing that demons can *observe* what goes on in the world and can probably draw some conclusions from those observations. A demon may know what I ate for breakfast simply because it saw me eat breakfast! It may know what I said in a private telephone conversation because it listened to the conversation. Christians should not be led astray if they encounter members of the occult or of other false religions who seem to demonstrate such unusual knowledge from time to time. These results of observation do not prove that demons can read our thoughts, however, and nothing in the Bible would lead us to think they have that power.

## 4. There Have Been Differing Stages of Demonic Activity in the History of Redemption

**a. In the Old Testament.** Because the word *demon* is not often used in the Old Testament, it might at first seem that there is little indication of demonic activity. However, the people of Israel often sinned by serving false gods, and when we realize that these false "gods" were really demonic forces, we see that there is quite a bit of Old Testament material referring to demons. This identification of false gods as demons is made explicit, for example, when Moses says,

> They stirred him [God] to jealousy with strange gods;
>     with abominations they provoked him to anger.
> They sacrificed to demons that were no gods,
>     to gods they had never known. (Deut. 32:16–17)

Moreover, in reflecting on the horrible practice of child sacrifice, which the Israelites imitated from the pagan nations, the psalmist says,

> They mixed with the nations
>     and learned to do as they did.
> They served their idols,
>     which became a snare to them.
> They sacrificed their sons
>     and their daughters *to the demons*. (Ps. 106:35–37)

These references demonstrate that the worship offered to idols in all the nations surrounding Israel was really worship of Satan and his demons. This is why Paul can say of the false religions of the first-century Mediterranean world, "What pagans sacrifice *they offer to demons* and not to God" (1 Cor. 10:20). It is thus fair to conclude that all the nations around Israel that practiced idol worship were engaging in the worship of demons. The battles the Israelites fought against pagan nations were battles against nations who were controlled by demonic forces and thus "in the power of the evil one" (cf. 1 John 5:19). They were as much spiritual battles as physical battles: the people of Israel needed to depend on God's power to help them in the spiritual realm as much as in the physical.

In light of this, it is significant that there is no clear instance of the casting out of demons in the Old Testament. The nearest analogy is the case of David playing the lyre for King Saul: "Whenever the harmful spirit from God was upon Saul, David took the lyre and played it with his hand. So Saul was refreshed and was well, and the harmful spirit departed from him" (1 Sam. 16:23). However, Scripture speaks of this as a recurring event ("whenever"), indicating that the harmful spirit returned after David left Saul. This was not the completely effective triumph over evil spirits that we find in the New Testament.

Consistent with the purpose of Satan to destroy all the good works of God, pagan worship of demonic idols was characterized by destructive practices such as the sacrifice of children (Ps. 106:35–37), inflicting bodily harm on oneself (1 Kings 18:28; cf. Deut. 14:1), and cult prostitution as a part of pagan worship (Deut. 23:17; 1 Kings 14:24; Hos. 4:14).[12] Worship of demons will regularly lead to immoral and self-destructive practices.

**b. During the Ministry of Jesus.** After hundreds of years of inability to have any really effective triumph over demonic forces,[13] when Jesus came casting out demons

---

12. Even today, one distinguishing mark of many non-Christian religions is that their most devoted adherents engage in religious rituals that destroy one or several aspects of humanity, such as their physical health, their mental or emotional stability, or their human sexuality as God intended it to function. Such things clearly fulfill the goals of Satan to destroy everything that God has created good (cf. 1 Tim. 4:1–3). Since Satan is "a liar and the father of lies" (John 8:44), distortion or denial of the truth is always present in false religions as well, particularly when there is strong demonic influence.

13. There were Jewish exorcists in the period between the Old and the New Testaments who attempted to deal with demonic forces, but it is doubtful that they were very effective. Acts 19:13 mentions some "itinerant Jewish exorcists" who attempted to use the name of the Lord Jesus as a new magic formula, though they were not Christians and did not have any spiritual authority from Jesus himself. They met with disastrous results (vv. 15–16). Also when confronting the Pharisees, Jesus said, "If I cast out demons by Beelzebul, by whom do your sons cast them out?" (Matt. 12:27). His statement does not mean that their sons were very successful but only that they were casting out demons, or were trying to, with some limited success. In fact, Jesus' argument works very well if they generally failed: "If my great success in casting out demons is due to Satan, then what is your sons' limited success due to?

Presumably a power less than Satan; certainly not God!" The suggestion is that the Jewish exorcists' limited power was not from God but was from Satan.

Josephus does record an apparently effective example of exorcism by a Jew named Eleazar who used an incantation said to be derived from Solomon (*Antiquities* 8:45–48; cf. a rabbinic story in Numbers Rabbah 19:8; Tobit 8:2–3; and the Testament of Solomon, throughout). It is difficult to know exactly how widespread and how successful such practices were. On the one hand, God himself could have granted some degree of spiritual power over demons to the faithful remnant of Jewish believers in all ages; he certainly did protect the faithful people of Israel in general from the demonic forces of the nations around them. On the other hand, it is not impossible that Satan would work among unbelieving Jews, as well as among many other unbelieving cultures, to give some appearance of limited power to exorcists, witch doctors, and so forth but always with the result of bringing people ultimately into greater spiritual bondage. What is certain is that Jesus came with much more spiritual power over demons than the people had ever seen before, and they were amazed. (An extensive discussion of Jewish exorcism is found in Emil Schürer, *The History of the Jewish people in the Age of Jesus Christ*, rev. ed., ed. G. Vermes et al., 3 vols. in 4 [Edinburgh: T&T Clark, 1973–87], vol. 3.1, pp. 342–61, 376, 440.)

with absolute authority, the people were amazed: "They were all amazed, so that they questioned among themselves, saying, 'What is this? A new teaching with authority! He commands even the unclean spirits, and they obey him'" (Mark 1:27). Such power over demonic forces had never before been seen in the history of the world.

Jesus explains that his power over demons is a distinguishing mark on his ministry to inaugurate the reign of the kingdom of God among mankind in a new and powerful way:

> But if it is by the Spirit of God that I cast out demons, *then the kingdom of God has come upon you.* Or how can someone enter a strong man's house and plunder his goods, unless he first binds the strong man? Then indeed he may plunder his house. (Matt. 12:28–29)

The "strong man" is Satan, and Jesus had bound him, probably at the time of his triumph over him in the temptation in the wilderness (Matt. 4:1–11). During his earthly ministry, Jesus had entered the strong man's "house" (the world of unbelievers who are under the bondage of Satan), and he was plundering his house, that is, freeing people from satanic bondage and bringing them into the joy of the kingdom of God. It was "by the Spirit of God" that Jesus did this; the new power of the Holy Spirit working to triumph over demons was evidence that in the ministry of Jesus "the kingdom of God has come upon you."

**c. During the New Covenant Age.** This authority over demonic powers was not limited to Jesus himself, for he gave similar authority first to the Twelve (Matt. 10:8; Mark 3:15) and then to seventy-two disciples. After a period of ministry, the seventy-two "returned with joy, saying, 'Lord, even the demons are subject to us in your name!'" (Luke 10:17). Then Jesus responded, "I saw Satan fall like lightning from heaven" (Luke 10:18), indicating again a distinctive triumph over Satan's power (once again, this was probably at the time of Jesus' victory in the temptation in the wilderness, but Scripture does not explicitly specify that time).[14] Authority over unclean spirits later extended beyond the seventy-two disciples to those in the early church who ministered in Jesus' name (Acts 8:7; 16:18; James 4:7; 1 Peter 5:8–9), a fact consistent with the idea that ministry in Jesus' name in the new covenant age is characterized by triumph over the powers of the devil (1 John 3:8).

**d. During the Millennium.** During the millennium, the future thousand-year reign of Christ on earth mentioned in Revelation 20,[15] the activity of Satan and demons will be further restricted. Using language that suggests a much greater restriction of Satan's activity than we see today, John describes his vision of the beginning of the millennium as follows:

---

14. Another interpretation says that in the mission of the seventy-two Jesus saw the fall of Satan.

15. See chapter 55 for a discussion of the millennium.

> Then I saw an angel coming down from heaven, holding in his hand the key to the bottomless pit and a great chain. And he seized the dragon, that ancient serpent, who is the devil and Satan, and *bound him for a thousand years, and threw him into the pit, and shut it and sealed it over him, so that he might not deceive the nations any longer,* until the thousand years were ended. After that he must be released for a little while. (Rev. 20:1–3)

Here Satan is described as completely deprived of any ability to influence the earth. During the millennium, however, there will still be sin in the hearts of the unbelievers, which will grow until the end of the thousand years when there will be a large-scale rebellion against Christ, led by Satan who, having been "released from his prison" (Rev. 20:7), will come to lead that rebellion (Rev. 20:8–9). The fact that sin and rebelliousness persist in people's hearts apart from the activity of Satan, even during the thousand-year reign of Christ, shows that we cannot blame all sin in the world on Satan and his demons. Even when Satan is without influence in the world, sin will remain and be a problem in people's hearts.

**e. At the Final Judgment.** At the end of the millennium, when Satan is loosed and gathers the nations for battle, he will be decisively defeated and "thrown into the lake of fire and sulfur" and "tormented day and night forever and ever" (Rev. 20:10). Then the judgment of Satan and his demons will be complete.

## D. Our Relationship to Demons

## 1. Are Demons Active in the World Today?

Some people, influenced by a naturalistic worldview that only admits the reality of what can be seen or touched or heard, deny that demons exist today and maintain that belief in their reality reflects an obsolete worldview taught in the Bible and other ancient cultures. For example, the German New Testament scholar Rudolf Bultmann emphatically denied the existence of a supernatural world of angels and demons. He argued that these were ancient "myths" and that the New Testament message had to be "demythologized" by removing such mythological elements so that the gospel could be received by modern, scientific people. Others have thought that the contemporary equivalent to the (unacceptable) demonic activity mentioned in Scripture is the powerful and sometimes evil influence of organizations and "structures" in our society today—evil governments and powerful corporations that control thousands of people are sometimes said to be "demonic," especially in the writings of more liberal theologians.

However, if Scripture gives us a true account of the world as it really is, then we must take seriously its portrayal of intense demonic involvement in human society. Our failure to perceive that involvement with our five senses simply tells us that we have some deficiencies in our ability to understand the world, not that demons do not exist. In fact, there is no reason to think that there is any less demonic activity in the world today than there was at the time of the New Testament. We are in the same time period in God's overall plan for history (the church age or the new covenant age), and the millennium, when Satan's influence will be removed from the earth, has not yet come. Much of our western secularized society is unwilling to admit the existence of demons and relegates all talk of demonic activity to a category of superstition. But the unwillingness of modern society to recognize the presence of demonic activity today is, from a biblical perspective, simply due to people's blindness to the true nature of reality.

But what kind of activity do demons engage in today? Are there some distinguishing characteristics that enable us to recognize demonic activity when it occurs?

## 2. Not All Evil Is from Satan and Demons, but Some Is

If we consider the overall emphasis of the New Testament Epistles, we will realize that very little space is given to discussing demonic activity in the lives of believers or methods to resist and oppose such activity. The emphasis is on telling believers not to sin but to live lives of righteousness. For example, in 1 Corinthians, when there is a problem of "dissensions," Paul does not tell the church to rebuke a spirit of dissension but simply urges them to "agree" and "be united in the same mind and the same judgment" (1 Cor. 1:10). When there is a problem of incest, he does not tell the Corinthians to rebuke a spirit of incest, but tells them that they ought to be outraged and that they should exercise church discipline until the offender repents (1 Cor. 5:1–5). When there is a problem of Christians going to court to sue other believers, Paul does not command them to cast out a spirit of litigation (or selfishness, or strife), but simply tells them to settle those cases within the church and to be willing to give up their own self-interest (1 Cor. 6:1–8). When there is disorder at the Lord's Supper, he does not command them to cast out a spirit of disorder or gluttony or selfishness but simply tells them that they should "wait for one another" and that each person should "examine himself, then, and so eat of the bread and drink of the cup" (1 Cor. 11:33, 28). These examples could be duplicated many times in the other New Testament Epistles.

With regard to preaching the gospel to unbelievers, the New Testament pattern is the same: although occasionally Jesus or Paul would cast out a demonic spirit that was causing significant hindrance to proclaiming the gospel in a certain area (see Mark 5:1–20 [Gerasene demoniac]; Acts 16:16–18 [soothsaying girl at Philippi]), that is not the usual pattern of ministry presented, where the emphasis is simply on preaching the gospel (Matt. 9:35; Rom. 1:18–19; 1 Cor. 1:17–2:5). Even in the examples above, the opposition was encountered in the process of gospel proclamation.

In marked contrast to the practice of those who today emphasize "strategic level spiritual warfare,"[16] in no instance does anyone in the New Testament (1) *summon a*

---

16. See C. Peter Wagner, *Confronting the Powers: How the New Testament Church Experienced the Power of Strategic-Level Spiritual Warfare* (Ventura, CA: Regal, 1996).

*"territorial spirit"* upon entering an area to preach the gospel (in both examples above the demon was in a person and the demon-influenced person initiated the confrontation), or (2) *demand information from demons about a local demonic hierarchy*, (3) *say that we should believe or teach information derived from demons*, or (4) teach by word or example that certain *"demonic strongholds" over a city have to be broken* before the gospel can be proclaimed with effectiveness. Rather, Christians just preach the gospel, and it comes with power to change lives! (Of course, demonic opposition may arise, or God himself may reveal the nature of certain demonic opposition, which Christians would then pray and battle against, according to 1 Cor. 12:10; 2 Cor. 10:3–6; Eph. 6:12.)

Therefore, though the New Testament clearly recognizes the influence of demonic activity in the world, and even, as we shall see, demonic influence on the lives of believers, its primary focus regarding evangelism and Christian growth is on the choices and actions taken by people themselves (see also Gal. 5:16–26; Eph. 4:1–6:9; Col. 3:1–4:6, et al.). Similarly, this should be the primary focus of our efforts today when we strive to grow in holiness and faith and to overcome the sinful desires and actions that remain in our lives (cf. Rom. 6:1–23) and to overcome the temptations that come against us from an unbelieving world (1 Cor. 10:13).[17] We need to accept our own responsibility to obey the Lord and not to shift blame for our own misdeeds onto some demonic force.

Nevertheless, a number of passages show that the New Testament authors were definitely aware of the presence of demonic influence in the world and in the lives of Christians themselves. Writing to the church at Corinth, which was filled with temples devoted to worship of idols, Paul said that "what pagans sacrifice they offer to demons and not to God" (1 Cor. 10:20), a situation true not only of Corinth but also of most other cities in the ancient Mediterranean world. Paul also warned that in the latter days some would "depart from the faith by devoting themselves to deceitful spirits and teachings of demons" (1 Tim. 4:1) and that this would lead to claims for avoiding marriage and avoiding certain foods (v. 3), both of which God had created as "good" (v. 4). Thus he saw some false doctrine as being demonic in origin. In 2 Timothy, Paul implies that those who oppose sound doctrine have been captured by the devil to do his will: "The Lord's servant must not be quarrelsome but kind to everyone, able to teach, patiently enduring evil, correcting his opponents with gentleness. God may perhaps grant them repentance leading to a knowledge of the truth, and they may come to their senses and *escape from the snare of the devil, after being captured by him to do his will*" (2 Tim. 2:24–26).

Jesus had similarly asserted that the Jews who obstinately opposed him were following their father the devil: "You are of your father the devil, and your will is to do your father's desires. He was a murderer from the beginning, and does not stand in the truth,

---

17. A common way of summarizing the three sources of evil in our lives today is "the world, the flesh, and the devil" (where "flesh" refers to our sinful desires).

because there is no truth in him. When he lies, he speaks out of his own character, for he is a liar and the father of lies" (John 8:44).

Emphasis on the hostile deeds of unbelievers as having demonic influence or sometimes demonic origin is made more explicit in John's first epistle. He makes a general statement that "whoever makes a practice of sinning is *of the devil*" (1 John 3:8) and goes on to say, "By this it is evident who are the children of God, and who are the children of the devil: whoever does not practice righteousness is not of God, nor is the one who does not love his brother" (1 John 3:10). Here John characterizes all those who are not born of God as children of the devil and subject to his influence and desires. So Cain, when he murdered Abel, "was *of the evil one* and murdered his brother" (1 John 3:12), even though there is no mention of influence by Satan in the text of Genesis (Gen. 4:1–16). John also says, "We know that we are from God, and *the whole world lies in the power of the evil one*" (1 John 5:19). Then in Revelation Satan is called "the deceiver of the whole world" (Rev. 12:9). As we noted above, Satan is also called "the ruler of this world" (John 14:30), "the god of this world" (2 Cor. 4:4), and "the spirit that is now at work in the sons of disobedience" (Eph. 2:2).

When we combine all of these statements and see that Satan is thought of as the originator of lies, murder, deception, false teaching, and sin generally, then it seems reasonable to conclude that the New Testament wants us to understand that there is some degree of demonic influence in nearly all wrongdoing and sin that occurs today. Not all sin is caused by Satan or demons, nor is the major influence or cause of sin demonic activity, but demonic activity is probably a factor in almost all sin and almost all destructive activity that opposes the work of God in the world today.

In the lives of Christians, as we noted above, the emphasis of the New Testament is not on the influence of demons but on the sin that remains in the believer's life. Nevertheless, we should recognize that sinning (even by Christians) does give a foothold for some kind of demonic influence in our lives. Thus Paul could say, "Be angry and do not sin; do not let the sun go down on your anger, and *give no opportunity to the devil*" (Eph. 4:26–27). Wrongful anger apparently can give opportunity for the devil (or demons) to exert some kind of negative influence in our lives—perhaps by attacking us through our emotions and perhaps by increasing the wrongful anger that we already feel against others. Similarly, Paul mentions "the breastplate of righteousness" (Eph. 6:14) as part of the armor that we are to use standing against "the schemes of the devil" and in contending "against the rulers, against the authorities, against the cosmic powers over this present darkness, against the spiritual forces of evil in the heavenly places" (Eph. 6:11–12). If we have areas of continuing sin in our lives, then there are weaknesses and holes in our "breastplate of righteousness," and these are areas in which we are vulnerable to demonic attack. By contrast, Jesus, who was perfectly free from sin, could say of Satan, "He has no claim on me" (John 14:30). We may also note the connection between not sinning and not being touched by the evil one in 1 John 5:18: "We know that everyone who has been born of God does not keep on sinning, but he who was born of God protects him, and the evil one does not touch him."

The preceding passages suggest, then, that where there is a pattern of persistent sin in the life of a Christian in one area or another, the primary responsibility for that sin rests with the individual Christian and his or her choices to continue that wrongful pattern (see Rom. 6, esp. vv. 12–16; also Gal. 5:16–26). Nevertheless, there could also be some demonic influence contributing to and intensifying that sinful tendency. For a Christian who has prayed and struggled for years to overcome a bad temper, for example, there might be a spirit of anger that is one factor in that continued pattern of sin. A Christian who has struggled for some time to overcome a sense of depression may have been under attack by a spirit of depression or discouragement, and this could be one factor contributing to the overall situation.[18] A believer who has struggled in other areas, such as unwillingness to submit to rightful authority, or lack of self-control in eating, laziness, bitterness, or envy, among other things, may consider whether a demonic attack or influence could be contributing to this situation and hindering his or her effectiveness for the Lord.

## 3. Can a Christian Be Demon Possessed?

The term *demon possession* is an unfortunate term that has found its way into some English translations of the Bible but is not really reflected in the Greek text. The Greek New Testament can speak of people who "have a demon" (Matt. 11:18; Luke 7:33; 8:27; John 7:20; 8:48, 49, 52; 10:20), or it can speak of people who are suffering from demonic influence (Gk. *daimonizomai*),[19] but it never uses language that suggests that a demon actually "possesses" someone.

The problem with the terms *demon possession* and *demonized* is that they give the nuance of such strong demonic influence that they seem to imply that the person who is under demonic attack has no choice but to succumb to it. They suggest that the person is unable any longer to exercise his or her will and is completely under the domination of the evil spirit. While this may have been true in extreme cases such as that of the

---

18. Not all depression is demonic in origin. Some may be caused by chemical factors that will respond to medical treatment. Other depression may be due to a variety of behavioral patterns or interpersonal relationships that are not being conducted according to biblical standards. But we should not rule out demonic influence as a possible factor. For an analysis of various possible causes, see J. P. Moreland, *Finding Quiet: My Story of Overcoming Anxiety and the Practices That Brought Peace* (Grand Rapids: Zondervan, 2019).

19. This word *diamonizomai*, which may be translated "oppressed by demons" or "under demonic influence" or "demonized," occurs thirteen times in the New Testament, all in the Gospels: Matt. 4:24; 8:16, 28, 33; 9:32; 12:22; 15:22; Mark 1:32; 5:15, 16, 18; Luke 8:36; and John 10:21. All of these instances indicate quite severe demonic influence. I do not recommend using the word *demonized* for most cases, however, because the word *demonized* in English seems to me to suggest extremely strong or pervasive demonic influence or control. (Cf. other similar *-ized* words: pasteurized, homogenized, tyrannized, materialized, nationalized, etc. These words all speak of a total transformation of the object being spoken about, not simply of mild or moderate influence.) But it has become common in some Christian literature today to speak of people under any kind of demonic attack as being "demonized." It would be wiser to reserve the term for more severe cases of demonic influence. (The ESV uses "oppressed by demons" for all but the most severe examples.)

Gerasene demoniac (see Mark 5:1–20; note that after Jesus cast the demons out of him, he was then "in his right mind," v. 15), it is certainly not true with many cases of demonic attack or conflict with demons in many people's lives.

So what should we say to the question, "Can a Christian be demon possessed?" The answer depends on what someone means by "possessed." Since the term *demon possessed* does not reflect any word found in the Greek New Testament, people can define it to mean various things without having clear warrant to anchor it to any verse of Scripture, and it becomes difficult to say that one person's definition is right and another one's wrong. My own preference, for reasons explained above, is not to use the phrase *demon possessed* at all, for any case.

But if people explain clearly what they mean by "demon possessed," then an answer can be given depending on the definition they give. If by "demon possessed" they mean that a person's will is *completely dominated* by a demon so that a person has no power left to choose to do right and obey God, then the answer to whether a Christian could be demon possessed would certainly be no, for Scripture guarantees that sin shall have no dominion over us since we have been raised with Christ (Rom. 6:14, see also vv. 4, 11).

On the other hand, most Christians would agree that there can be *differing degrees of demonic attack* or influence in the lives of believers (see Luke 4:2; 2 Cor. 12:7; Eph. 6:12; James 4:7; 1 Peter 5:8). A believer may come under demonic attack from time to time in a mild or more strong sense.[20] (Note the "daughter of Abraham" whom "Satan bound for eighteen years" so that she "had a disabling spirit" and "was bent over and could not fully straighten herself" [Luke 13:16, 11].) Though Christians after Pentecost have a fuller power of the Holy Spirit working within them to enable them to triumph over demonic attacks,[21] they do not always call upon or even know about the power that is rightfully theirs. So how severe can demonic influence become in the life of a Christian after Pentecost who is indwelt by the Holy Spirit?

Before answering this question, we should note that it is similar to a question about sin: "How much can a genuine Christian let his or her life be dominated by sin and still be a born-again Christian?" It is difficult to answer that question in the abstract, because we realize that when Christians are not living as they ought to live, and when they are not benefiting from regular fellowship with other Christians and from regular Bible study and teaching, they can stray into significant degrees of sin and still can be said to be born-again Christians. But the situation is abnormal; it is not what the Christian life should be and can be. Similarly, if we ask how much demonic influence can come into the life of a genuine Christian, it is hard to give an answer in the abstract.

20. It does not seem very helpful to attempt to define categories or degrees of demonic influence, as has sometimes been done, with words such as "depressed," "oppressed," "obsessed," etc., for Scripture does not define a list of categories like this for us to use, and such categories only tend to make complicated what is a simple truth: that there can be varying degrees of demonic attack or influence in a person's life.

21. See chapter 30, p. 791, and chapter 39, pp. 951–53, for a discussion of the greater power of the Holy Spirit at work in believers' lives after Pentecost.

We are simply asking how abnormal a Christian's life can become, especially if that person does not know about or make use of the weapons of spiritual warfare that are available to Christians, persists in some kinds of sin that give entrance to demonic activity, and is outside the reach of any ministry that is accustomed to giving spiritual help against demonic attack. It would seem that in such cases the degree of demonic attack or influence in a Christian's life could be quite strong. It would not be correct to say there can be no such influence because the person is a Christian. Therefore when someone asks, "Can a Christian be demon possessed?" but really means, "Can a Christian come under quite strong influence or attack by demons?" then the answer would have to be a positive one but with the caution that the word *possessed* is here being used in a confusing way. Since the term *demon possessed* is a misleading one to use in all cases, especially when referring to Christians, I would prefer to avoid it altogether. It seems better simply to recognize that *there can be varying degrees of demonic attack or influence on people, even on Christians,* and to leave it at that. In all cases the remedy will be the same anyway: rebuke the demon in the name of Jesus and command it to leave (see discussion below).

### 4. How Can Demonic Influences Be Recognized?

In severe cases of demonic influence, as reported in the Gospels, the affected person would exhibit bizarre and often violent actions, especially opposition to the preaching of the gospel. When Jesus came into the synagogue in Capernaum, "immediately there was in their synagogue a man with an unclean spirit. And he cried out, 'What have you to do with us, Jesus of Nazareth? Have you come to destroy us? I know who you are—the Holy One of God'" (Mark 1:23–24). The man stood up and interrupted the service by shouting these things (or, more precisely, the demon within the man shouted them).

After Jesus came down from the Mount of Transfiguration, a man brought his son to Jesus saying, "He has a spirit that makes him mute. And wherever it seizes him, it throws him down, and he foams and grinds his teeth and becomes rigid." Then they brought the boy to Jesus, "and when the spirit saw him, immediately it convulsed the boy, and he fell on the ground and rolled about, foaming at the mouth." The father said, "It has often cast him into fire and into water, to destroy him" (Mark 9:17–18, 20, 22). Such violent actions, especially those tending toward destruction of the affected person, were clear indications of demonic activity. Similar actions are seen in the case of the Gerasene demoniac,

> a man with an unclean spirit. He lived among the tombs. And no one could bind him anymore, not even with a chain, for he had often been bound with shackles and chains, but he wrenched the chains apart, and he broke the shackles in pieces. No one had the strength to subdue him. Night and day among the tombs and on the mountains he was always crying out and cutting himself with stones. (Mark 5:2–5)

When Jesus cast out the demons so that they could not destroy the man in whom they had lived, they destroyed the herd of swine into which they immediately entered (Mark 5:13). Satanic or demonic activity always tends toward the ultimate destruction of parts of God's creation and especially of human beings who are made in the image of God (cf. Ps. 106:37, on child sacrifice).

In this regard, it is interesting to note that in one case when Jesus healed an epileptic he did it by casting out a demon (Matt. 17:14–18), but elsewhere epileptics are distinguished from those who are under demonic influence: "They brought him all the sick, those afflicted with various diseases and pains, *those oppressed by demons, those having seizures*, and paralytics, and he healed them" (Matt. 4:24). So it is with other cases of physical sickness: in some cases, Jesus simply prayed for the person or spoke a word and the person was healed. In other cases there are hints or implicit statements of demonic influence in the affliction: a woman who had had "a disabling spirit for eighteen years" (Luke 13:11) was healed by Jesus, and then he explicitly said that she was "a daughter of Abraham *whom Satan bound* for eighteen years" (Luke 13:16). In healing Peter's mother-in-law, Jesus "rebuked the fever, and it left her" (Luke 4:39), suggesting that there was some personal influence (probably therefore demonic) that was capable of receiving a rebuke from Jesus.

In other cases, the Epistles indicate that demonic influence will lead to blatantly false doctrinal statements, such as exclaiming, "Jesus is accursed" (1 Cor. 12:3), or a refusal to confess "that Jesus Christ has come in the flesh" (1 John 4:2–3). In both instances, the context deals with the testing of people who may be "false prophets" and who want to use spiritual gifts to speak in the assembly of the church (1 Cor. 12) or specifically to prophesy (1 John 4:1–6). These passages do not indicate that all false doctrine should be thought to be demonically inspired, but blatantly false doctrinal statements made by those who profess to be speaking by the power of the Holy Spirit would certainly fall into this category. When at Corinth there was active, entrenched opposition to Paul's apostolic authority by those who claimed to be apostles but were not, Paul saw them as servants of Satan disguised as servants of righteousness (2 Cor. 11:13–15).

In addition to these outwardly evident indications, demonic activity was sometimes recognized by a subjective sense of the presence of an evil spiritual influence. In 1 Corinthians 12:10, Paul mentions "the ability to distinguish between spirits" ("discerning of spirits," KJV) as one kind of spiritual gift. This gift would seem to be an ability to sense or discern the difference in the working of the Holy Spirit and the working of evil spirits in a person's life.[22] The gift would apparently include an awareness of demonic influence that would be registered both in terms of objective, observable facts, and also in terms of emotional and/or spiritual uneasiness or perception of the presence of evil.

22. For a detailed analysis of the meaning of the Greek phrase *diakriseis pneumatōn*, "distinguish between spirits," in 1 Cor. 12:10, see W. Grudem, "A Response to Gerhard Dautzenberg on 1 Corinthians 12:10," *Biblische Zeitschrift*, NF, 22, no. 2 (1978): 253–70.

But does this ability to perceive demonic influence have to be limited to those with this special gift? As with all spiritual gifts, it would seem that there are degrees of intensity or strength in the development of this gift as well.[23] Therefore, some may have this gift developed to a very high degree, and others may find it functioning only occasionally. Moreover, in the lives of all believers, there may be something analogous to this gift, some kind of ability to sense in their spirits the presence of the Holy Spirit or to sense demonic influence from time to time in other people.

In fact, Paul speaks of a *positive* kind of spiritual perception that believers have when they encounter him and his coworkers: "For we are the aroma of Christ to God among those who are being saved and among those who are perishing, to one a fragrance from death to death, to the other a fragrance from life to life" (2 Cor. 2:15–16). In the ordinary course of life today, sometimes Christians will have a subjective sense that someone else is a Christian before they have opportunity to find out that that is in fact the case. And it seems likely that an opposite spiritual perception could also occur from time to time, whereby the believer would sense the presence of demonic influence in a person's life before there were other, more objective indications of that fact.

Moreover, sometimes a person who is under spiritual attack from a demonic power will know it or sense it. A mature pastor or a Christian friend, in counseling someone about a difficult problem, may find it wise to ask, "Do you think that an attack by any evil spiritual force could be a factor in this situation?" The person may simply say, "No," but in many instances the person being counseled will have thought of that possibility, or even have been quite clearly aware of it, but afraid to say anything for fear of being thought strange. Such a person will be encouraged that another Christian would consider this as a possible factor.

In all of these attempts to recognize demonic influence, we must remember that no spiritual gift functions perfectly in this age, nor do we have a full knowledge of people's hearts. "We all stumble in many ways," as James recognizes (James 3:2). There are many cases when we are somewhat unsure whether a person is a genuine Christian or when we are somewhat unsure whether a person's motives are sincere. There are also times when we are unclear as to the direction God is leading us in our lives, or we may be uncertain about whether it is appropriate to speak or remain silent about a certain matter. So it should not surprise us that there may be some degree of uncertainty in our perception of the presence of demonic influence as well. This does not mean that we should ignore the possibility of demonic influence, however, and as we grow in spiritual maturity and sensitivity, and as we gain experience in ministering to the needs of others, our ability to recognize demonic influence in various situations will no doubt increase.

---

23. See chapter 52, pp. 1262–64, on the fact that spiritual gifts may vary in strength.

## 5. Jesus Gives All Believers Authority to Rebuke Demons and Command Them to Leave

When Jesus sent the twelve disciples ahead of him to preach the kingdom of God, he "gave them power and authority over all demons" (Luke 9:1). After the seventy-two had preached the kingdom of God in towns and villages, they returned with joy, saying, "Lord, *even the demons are subject to us in your name*!" (Luke 10:17), and Jesus told them, "I have given you authority . . . over all the power of the enemy" (Luke 10:19). When Philip, the evangelist, went down to Samaria to preach the gospel of Christ, "unclean spirits . . . came out of many who had them" (Acts 8:7). And Paul used spiritual authority over demons to say to a spirit of divination in a soothsaying girl: "I command you in the name of Jesus Christ to come out of her" (Acts 16:18).

Paul was aware of the spiritual authority he had, both in face-to-face encounters such as he had in Acts 16 and in his prayer life as well. He said, "For though we walk in the flesh, we are not waging war according to the flesh. For the weapons of our warfare are not of the flesh but have divine power to destroy strongholds" (2 Cor. 10:3–4). Moreover, he spoke at some length of the struggle Christians have against "the schemes of the devil" in his description of conflict "against the spiritual forces of evil in the heavenly places" (see Eph. 6:10–18). James tells all his readers (in many churches) to "*resist the devil*, and he will flee from you" (James 4:7). Similarly, Peter tells his readers in many churches in Asia Minor, "Your adversary the devil prowls around like a roaring lion, seeking someone to devour. *Resist him*, firm in your faith" (1 Peter 5:8–9).[24]

Some may object that Jude 9 teaches that Christians should not command or rebuke evil spirits. It says, "When the archangel Michael, contending with the devil, was disputing about the body of Moses, he did not presume to pronounce a blasphemous judgment, but said, 'The Lord rebuke you.'"

However, in context Jude is not talking about Christians in their encounters with demonic forces but is pointing out the error of immoral and rebellious false teachers who "reject authority" in general and "blaspheme the glorious ones" (Jude 8); on their own authority, apparently, they were foolishly speaking blasphemous words against heavenly beings, whether angelic or demonic. The reference to Michael is simply to show that the greatest angelic creature, no matter how powerful, did not presume to go beyond the limits of the authority that God had given him. The false teachers, however, have far overstepped their bounds, and they show their foolishness when they "blaspheme all that they do not understand" (v. 10). Therefore, the lesson of the verse is simply, "Don't try to go beyond the authority God has given you!" When Jude 9 is viewed in this way, the only question that arises for a Christian from this verse is, "What authority has God given us over demonic forces?" And the rest of the New Testament speaks clearly to that in several

---

24. Of course, our greatest example of dealing with demonic powers by speaking to them directly and commanding them to leave is the example of Jesus himself, who frequently did this in the Gospels, and by example and word he taught the disciples to imitate him.

places. Not only Jesus and his twelve disciples but also the seventy-two disciples, Paul, and Philip (who was not an apostle) are given authority over demons by the Lord Jesus (see verses above). Jude 9 therefore simply cannot mean that it is wrong for human beings to rebuke or command demons or that it is wrong for any but the apostles to do so. In fact, both Peter and James encourage all Christians to "resist" the devil, and Paul encourages believers in general to put on spiritual armor and prepare for spiritual warfare.

Before we examine in more detail how that authority works out in practice, it is important, first, that we recognize that the work of Christ on the cross is the ultimate basis for our authority over demons.[25] Though Christ won a victory over Satan in the wilderness, the Epistles point to the cross as the moment when Satan was decisively defeated. Jesus took on flesh and blood, "that through death he might destroy the one who has the power of death, that is, the devil" (Heb. 2:14). At the cross, God "disarmed the rulers and authorities and put them to open shame, by triumphing over them in him" (Col. 2:15). Therefore Satan hates the cross of Christ because there he was decisively defeated forever. Because the blood of Christ speaks clearly of his death, we read in Revelation of those who overcame Satan by Christ's blood during conflict in this world: "And they have conquered him by the blood of the Lamb and by the word of their testimony" (Rev. 12:11). Because of Christ's death on the cross, our sins are completely forgiven, and Satan has no rightful authority over us.

Second, our membership as children in God's family is the firm spiritual position from which we engage in spiritual warfare. Paul says to every Christian, "For in Christ Jesus you are all sons of God, through faith" (Gal. 3:26). When Satan comes to attack us, he is attacking one of God's children, members of God's family: this truth gives us authority to successfully wage war against him and defeat him.[26]

If we as believers find it appropriate to speak a word of rebuke to a demon, it is important to remember that we need not fear demons. Although Satan and demons have much less power than the power of the Holy Spirit at work within us, one of Satan's tactics is to attempt to cause us to be afraid. Instead of giving in to such fear, Christians should remind themselves of the truths of Scripture, which tell us, "You are from God and have overcome them, for *he who is in you is greater than he who is in the world*" (1 John 4:4), and "God gave us a spirit not of fear but of power and love and self-control" (2 Tim. 1:7). What Paul says about the Philippians in their relationship to human opponents can also be applied when facing demonic opposition to the gospel—Paul tells them to stand firm and to be "*not frightened in anything by your opponents*. This is a clear sign to them of their destruction, but of your salvation, and that from God" (Phil. 1:28). He also tells the Ephesians that in their spiritual warfare they are to use the "shield of faith" with which they can "extinguish all the flaming darts of the evil one" (Eph. 6:16).

---

25. In this paragraph and the following one on adoption I am indebted to the fine work of Timothy M. Warner, *Spiritual Warfare* (Wheaton, IL: Crossway, 1991), 55–63.

26. See chapter 37, pp. 913–19, on adoption.

This is very important, since the opposite of fear is faith in God. He also tells them to be bold in their spiritual conflict, so that, having taken the whole armor of God, they "may be able to withstand in the evil day, and having done all, to stand firm" (Eph. 6:13). In their conflict with hostile spiritual forces, Paul's readers should not run away in retreat or cower in fear but should stand their ground boldly, knowing that their weapons and their armor "have divine power to destroy strongholds" (2 Cor. 10:4; cf. 1 John 5:18).

We may ask, however, why does God want Christians to speak directly to the demon who is troubling someone rather than just praying and asking God to drive away the demon for them? In a way, this is similar to asking why Christians should share the gospel with another person rather than simply praying and asking God to reveal the gospel to that person directly. Or why should we speak words of encouragement to a Christian who is discouraged rather than just praying and asking God himself to encourage that person directly? Why should we speak a word of rebuke or gentle admonition to a Christian whom we see involved in some kind of sin rather than just praying and asking God to take care of the sin in that person's life? The answer to all these questions is that in the world that God has created, he has given us a very *active* role in carrying out his plans, especially his plans for the advancement of the kingdom and the building up of the church. In all of these cases, our *direct involvement* and *activity* is important in addition to our prayers. And so it seems to be in our dealing with demonic forces as well. Like a wise father who does not settle all of his children's disputes for them but sometimes sends them back out to the playground to settle a dispute themselves, so our heavenly Father encourages us to enter directly into conflict with demonic forces in the name of Christ and in the power of the Holy Spirit. Thereby he enables us to gain the joy of participating in eternally significant ministry and the joy of triumphing over the destructive power of Satan and his demons in people's lives. It is not that God could not deal with demonic attacks every time we prayed and asked him to do so, for he certainly could and he no doubt sometimes does. But the New Testament pattern seems to be that God ordinarily expects Christians themselves to speak directly to the unclean spirits.

In practice, this authority to rebuke demons may result in briefly speaking a command to an evil spirit to leave when we suspect the presence of demonic influence in our personal lives or the lives of those around us.[27] We are to "resist the devil" (James 4:7), and he will flee from us.[28] Sometimes a very brief command in the name of Jesus will be enough. At other times it will be helpful to quote Scripture in the process of commanding an evil spirit to leave a situation. Paul speaks of "the sword of the Spirit, which

27. Because Scripture gives no indication that demons can know our thoughts (see above, pp. 415–16), it would seem that the command should be spoken audibly.

28. For example, if we or one of our children wakes up with a frightening dream, in addition to praying to Jesus for comfort and protection, we might also say, "In the name of Jesus, I command any evil spirit causing this frightening dream, be gone!"

Children from a very young age can be taught to say, "In Jesus' name, go away!" to any images of witches, goblins, etc. that may appear in their dreams or in mental images that trouble them at night, and then to pray to Jesus for protection and happy thoughts of him. Such action by those little ones who trust in Christ will often be remarkably effective, for their faith in Jesus is very simple and genuine (see Matt. 18:1–4).

is the word of God" (Eph. 6:17).[29] And Jesus, when he was tempted by Satan in the wilderness, repeatedly quoted Scripture in response to Satan's temptations (Matt. 4:1–11). Appropriate Scriptures may include general statements of the triumph of Jesus over Satan (Matt. 12:28–29; Luke 10:17–19; 2 Cor. 10:3–4; Col. 2:15; Heb. 2:14; James 4:7; 1 Peter 5:8–9; 1 John 3:8; 4:4; 5:18)[30] as well as verses that speak directly to the particular temptation or difficulty at hand.

In our personal lives, if we find sinful emotions that are unusually strong welling up in our minds or hearts (whether they be emotions of irrational fear, anger, hatred, bitterness, lust, or greed), in addition to praying and asking Jesus for help in overcoming them, it would also be appropriate for us to say something like, "Spirit of fear, in Jesus' name, I command you, go away from here and don't return!" Even though we may be unsure whether there is a demonic factor in that particular situation, and even though a demon's presence may be only one factor contributing to the situation, nonetheless, such words of rebuke will sometimes be very effective. Though we do not have in the New Testament a complete record of the personal prayer life of the apostle Paul, he talks openly about wrestling "not . . . against flesh and blood, but . . . against the spiritual forces of evil in the heavenly places" (Eph. 6:12) and about "not waging war according to the flesh" (2 Cor. 10:3). It is reasonable to think that his extensive prayer life included this kind of verbal rebuke of demonic forces as one aspect of his spiritual warfare.

Moreover, such wrestling against "the spiritual forces of evil" may mean that in our private times of intercessory prayer for others we will include an element of verbal rebuke to demonic forces that may be a component in situations for which we are praying. (This kind of spiritual warfare would not be in the presence of the person for whom we are concerned, who in many cases would be confused or frightened unnecessarily.) For example, parents may appropriately include a brief word of rebuke to a spirit of rebelliousness in one child, of laziness in another, or of anger in yet another in addition to praying that the Lord would give victory in those areas and in addition to teaching and disciplining their children.[31]

## 6. Appropriate Use of the Christian's Spiritual Authority in Ministry to Other People

When we pass from the discussion of private spiritual warfare in our lives and perhaps the lives of close family members, we move to the question of direct personal ministry to others who have come under spiritual attack. For example, we may at times

---

29. The Greek word here translated "word" is *rhēma*, which usually refers to spoken words (whether by God or by others). It is sometimes used to speak of the words of Scripture when they are spoken by God or by people quoting Scripture (Matt. 4:4; John 15:7; 17:8; Rom. 10:17; Heb. 6:5; 1 Peter 1:25 [twice]), and that is the sense in which Paul seems to use it in Eph. 6:17: as we speak the words of Scripture they are accompanied by the work of the Holy Spirit and have the power of a spiritual sword.

30. It would be good for Christians to memorize the verses in the list just mentioned so as to be able to speak them from memory when involved in any spiritual warfare.

31. Since Scripture gives no indication that demons can read our minds, such rebukes against demons would have to be spoken audibly, even if softly. By contrast, God of course knows our thoughts, and prayer to him can be in our minds only, without being spoken aloud.

be involved in counseling or prayer with another person when we suspect that demonic activity is a factor in his or her situation. In these cases, some additional considerations must be kept in mind.

First, it is important not to frighten people by talking very glibly about an area that may be familiar to us but quite unfamiliar and somewhat frightening to others. The Holy Spirit is a Spirit of gentleness and peace (see 1 Cor. 14:33). Because of this, it is often considerate simply to ask questions of the person we are helping. We might ask, "Do you think an evil spirit may be attacking you in this situation?" or "Would you mind if I spoke a word of rebuke to any evil spirit that may be a factor in this?" It would also be important to assure the person that if there is a demonic factor involved, it should not be thought of as a negative reflection on the person's spiritual condition but may simply indicate that Satan is trying to attack the person to keep him or her from more effective ministry for the Lord. Each Christian is a soldier in the Lord's spiritual army and therefore subject to attacks from the forces of the enemy.

If the other person gives permission to do so, a brief command should be spoken aloud, telling the evil spirit to leave.[32] Since the person under attack will often have had a sense of a demonic presence, it would be appropriate, after commanding the evil spirit to leave, to ask the person if he or she felt or sensed anything different when those words were spoken. If there really was a demonic influence in the situation, the person may express an immediate feeling of relief or freedom, often with a sense of joy and peace as well.

All of this does not have to be a highly dramatic or emotionally charged procedure. Some contemporary stories tell of long drawn-out battles in which the Christian counselor argues with the demon and shouts at it repeatedly over a period of several hours. But there is no indication in the New Testament that demons are hard of hearing, nor are there examples of such long periods of conflict in order to get a demon to leave. Jesus simply "cast out the spirits with a word" (Matt. 8:16), even though in one case (with the Gerasene demoniac) the evil spirit showed some initial resistance (see Mark 5:8; Luke 8:29). Jesus then asked its name and then cast out many demons at once (Mark 5:9–13; Luke 8:30–33). The power to cast out demons comes not from our strength or the power of our voice but from the Holy Spirit (Matt. 12:28; Luke 11:20). Thus a quiet, confident, authoritative tone of voice should be sufficient.

Second, to avoid being drawn into a long conversation or battle with the demon itself the Christian counselor should focus not on the demon but on the person being ministered to and the truths of the Bible that need to be affirmed and believed. The "belt of truth" (Eph. 6:14) is part of the armor that protects us against Satan, as is the "sword of the Spirit, which is the word of God" (Eph. 6:17). If the person who is receiving ministry

---

32. The verb *exorcise* in English means "to drive out (an evil spirit) by a magic formula or a spoken command." An "exorcism" is defined as the action of driving out an evil spirit in this way. These words do not occur in the Bible (although Acts 19:13 mentions Jewish exorcists). Because these terms are used in pagan as well as Christian contexts throughout history, there is room for Christians to differ over whether it is wise to use them to refer to Christian practices today.

will focus on and believe the truth of Scripture and will renounce sin and thereby put on the "breastplate of righteousness" (Eph. 6:14), then the evil spirit will have no foothold in that person's life. In addition, it is important that the person experiencing demonic oppression genuinely wants the demon to leave, and if the person is clearly under demonic influence, it will be helpful to ask if the person genuinely wants the demon to leave. If the demon refuses to leave in spite of the command given in the name of Jesus, then it may be best to wait until another time after more prayer and personal spiritual preparation on the part of the person being ministered to and the persons who are engaging in this ministry (Matt. 17:19–20; Mark 9:29; see discussions below).[33]

Third, it is important for Christians not to become overly curious in this area of demonic conflict. Though it is a ministry that the Lord gives all Christians authority to engage in, Scripture nonetheless tells us that we are to be "infants in evil" (1 Cor. 14:20). That is, we are not to become overly fascinated with matters of evil and attempt to become "experts" in some kinds of evil just to satisfy our curiosity.[34]

Fourth, if the person being ministered to is not a Christian, it is important that he or she be urged to come to Christ as Savior immediately after the demon is cast out so that the Holy Spirit will reside in the person and protect him or her from future attacks. Otherwise there may be a worse result later.

> When the unclean spirit has gone out of a person, it passes through waterless places seeking rest, but finds none. Then it says, "I will return to my house from which I came." And when it comes, it finds the house empty, swept, and put in order. Then it goes and brings with it seven other spirits more evil than itself, and they enter and dwell there, and the last state of that person is worse than the first. So also will it be with this evil generation. (Matt. 12:43–45)

Fifth, effectiveness in difficult cases of demonic influence may be related to our own spiritual condition. When Jesus had cast a demon out of an epileptic boy, and "the boy was healed instantly," the disciples privately came to Jesus and asked, "Why could we not cast it out?" (Matt. 17:18–19). Jesus said to them, "Because of your little faith" (Matt. 17:20). Mark's gospel reports that Jesus also said in response to the disciples, "This kind cannot be driven out by anything but prayer" (Mark 9:29; several ancient manuscripts add "and fasting"). The disciples apparently were at that time weak in faith; they had not spent enough time in prayer recently and they were not walking fully in the power of the Holy Spirit.[35]

---

33. It would often be wise, in difficult cases, to have help from someone with more maturity and experience in this area.

34. Christians should therefore not be preoccupied with matters concerning the occult or the New Age movement. We should think about things that are "honorable" and "pure" and "worthy of praise" (Phil. 4:8).

35. When Jesus said, "This kind cannot be driven out by anything but prayer" (Mark 9:29), he cannot have meant that it was necessary to pray for a long time about that specific situation before the demon would be cast out, for he did not pray at all but simply spoke a word and cast out the demon at once. He must have meant, rather, that a continual life of prayer and abiding in God will result in a spiritual preparedness and a possession of a spiritual power through the anointing of the Holy Spirit that will be effective in conflict even over very severe demonic attack or influence.

Jesus issues a clear warning that we should not rejoice too much or become proud in our power over demons, but that we should rejoice rather in our great salvation. We must keep this in mind lest we become proud and the Holy Spirit withdraw his power from us. When the seventy-two returned with joy saying, "Lord, even the demons are subject to us in your name!" (Luke 10:17), Jesus told them, "Do not rejoice in this, that the spirits are subject to you, but rejoice that your names are written in heaven" (Luke 10:20).[36]

### 7. We Should Expect the Gospel to Come in Power to Triumph over the Works of the Devil

When Jesus came preaching the gospel in Galilee, "demons also came out of many" (Luke 4:41). When Philip went to Samaria to preach the gospel, "unclean spirits, crying out with a loud voice, came out of many" (Acts 8:7). Jesus commissioned Paul to preach among the gentiles "so that they may turn from darkness to light and from the power of Satan to God, that they may receive forgiveness of sins and a place among those who are sanctified by faith in me" (Acts 26:18). Paul's proclamation of the gospel, he said, was "not in plausible words of wisdom, but in demonstration of the Spirit and of power, so that your faith might not rest in the wisdom of men but in the power of God" (1 Cor. 2:4–5; cf. 2 Cor. 10:3–4). If we really believe the scriptural testimony to the existence and activity of demons, and if we really believe that "the reason the Son of God appeared was *to destroy the works of the devil*" (1 John 3:8), then it would seem appropriate to expect that even today when the gospel is proclaimed to unbelievers, and when prayer is made for believers who have perhaps been unaware of this dimension of spiritual conflict, there will be a genuine and often immediately recognizable triumph over the power of the enemy. We should expect that this would happen, think of it as a normal part of the work of Christ in building up his kingdom, and rejoice in Christ's victory in it.

## QUESTIONS FOR PERSONAL APPLICATION

1. Before reading this chapter, did you think that most demonic activity was confined to the time of the New Testament or to other cultures than your own? After reading this chapter, are there areas in your own society where you think there might be some demonic influence today? Do you feel some fear at the prospect of encountering demonic activity in your own life or the lives of others around you? What does the Bible say that will specifically address that feeling of fear? Do you think that the Lord wants you to feel that fear, if you do?

2. Are there any areas of sin in your own life now that might give a foothold to some demonic activity? If so, what would the Lord have you do with respect to that sin?

---

36. Jesus cannot mean that it is wrong to rejoice when the enemy is vanquished and people are set free from bondage, for that is certainly a good reason for rejoicing. He must rather be putting a relative contrast in absolute terms in telling the disciples that the greatness of their salvation is the primary thing that they should be rejoicing in.

3. Are there cases where you have had victory over some demonic force by speaking to it in the name of Jesus? How can the material in this chapter help you be more effective in this kind of spiritual conflict? What are the dangers of becoming too interested in or too deeply involved in this kind of ministry? How can you safeguard against that excessive emphasis? What do you think Paul's procedure was when he came to preach the gospel in city after city where it had never been heard before and where there was demon worship? How could the church today profit from Paul's example?

# BIBLIOGRAPHY

(For an explanation of this bibliography see the note on the bibliography to chapter 1, pp. 23–24. Complete bibliographical data may be found on pp. 1489–96.)

## SECTIONS IN EVANGELICAL SYSTEMATIC THEOLOGIES

*1. Anglican (Episcopalian)*
1882–92 . . . . . Litton, 129–36
2001 . . . . . . . . Packer, 67–70
2013 . . . . . . . . Bird, 686, 690
2013 . . . . . . . . Bray, 441–45

*2. Arminian (Wesleyan or Methodist)*
1892–94 . . . . . Miley, 1:539–40; 2:497–504
1940 . . . . . . . . Wiley, 1:476–77
1983 . . . . . . . . Carter, 2:1069–97
1992 . . . . . . . . Oden, 3:456–59
2002 . . . . . . . . Cottrell, 170–78

*3. Baptist*
1767 . . . . . . . . Gill, 1:435–40
1887 . . . . . . . . Boyce, 181–89

1907 . . . . . . . . Strong, 450–64
1976–83 . . . . . Henry, 6:229–50
1987–94 . . . . . Lewis and Demarest, 2:257–63
1990–95 . . . . . Garrett, 1:429–50
2007 . . . . . . . . Akin, 303–11
2013 . . . . . . . . Erickson, 415–20

*4. Dispensational*
1947 . . . . . . . . Chafer, 2:33–124
1949 . . . . . . . . Thiessen, 133–50
1986 . . . . . . . . Ryrie, 135–68
2017 . . . . . . . . MacArthur and Mayhue, 676–719
2002–2005 . . Geisler, 2:541–42, 3:174–78

*5. Lutheran*
1917–24 . . . . . Pieper, 1:504–14
1934 . . . . . . . . Mueller, 202–4

*6. Reformed (or Presbyterian)*
1559 . . . . . . . . Calvin, 1:172–79 (1.14.13–19)
1679–85 . . . . . Turretin, *IET*, 1:335–41, 548–49, 601–2, 605–9

1724–58 . . . . . Edwards, 2:607–12

1871–73 . . . . . Hodge, 1:643–48

1894 . . . . . . . . Shedd, 552–53, 701–2, 847, 865, 928, 938

1906–11 . . . . Bavinck, *RD*, 3:146–48, 185–90

1910 . . . . . . . . Vos, 2:41, 43, 49–51, 53, 71, 86, 125–26

1937–66 . . . . . Murray, *CW*, 2:67–70

1938 . . . . . . . . Berkhof, 148–49

1998 . . . . . . . . Reymond, 659–60

2008 . . . . . . . . Van Genderen, 416–17, 484–85

2011 . . . . . . . . Horton, 407, 503

2013 . . . . . . . . Frame, 775–77

2013 . . . . . . . . Culver, 176–90

2016 . . . . . . . . Allen and Swain, 263–64

2017 . . . . . . . . Barrett, 736

**7. Renewal (or charismatic/Pentecostal)**

1988–92 . . . . . Williams, 1:173, 224–36

1993 . . . . . . . . Menzies and Horton, 202–3

1995 . . . . . . . . Horton, 194–214

2008 . . . . . . . . Duffield and Van Cleave, 505–19

## SECTIONS IN REPRESENTATIVE ROMAN CATHOLIC SYSTEMATIC THEOLOGIES

**1. Roman Catholic: Traditional**

1955 . . . . . . . . Ott, 119–24

**2. Roman Catholic: Post–Vatican II**

1980 . . . . . . . . McBrien, 1:329; 2:1105, 1153–54

2012 . . . . . . . . *CCC*, paragraphs 391–95

## OTHER WORKS

Allison, Gregg. *Historical Theology: An Introduction to Christian Doctrine; A Companion to Wayne Grudem's Systematic Theology*. Grand Rapids: Zondervan, 2011, 298–320.

Anderson, Neil. *The Bondage Breaker*. Rev. ed. Eugene, OR: Harvest House, 2000.

———. *The Steps to Freedom in Christ*. 2nd ed. Minneapolis: Bethany House, 2014.

———. *Victory over the Darkness*. 2nd ed. Minneapolis: Bethany House, 2014.

Arnold, Clinton E. *3 Crucial Questions about Spiritual Warfare*. Grand Rapids: Baker, 1997.

———. "Early Church Catechesis and New Christians' Classes in Contemporary Evangelicalism." *JETS* 47, no. 1 (March 2004): 39–54.

———. "Satan, Devil." In *DLNT*, 1077–82.

———. *Powers of Darkness: Principalities & Powers in Paul's Letters*. Downers Grove, IL: InterVarsity Press, 1992.

Beilby, James K. and Paul R. Eddy, eds. *Understanding Spiritual Warfare: Four Views*. Grand Rapids: Baker Academic, 2012.

Buchanan, D. "Satan." In *GDT*, 791–93.

Collins, James Michael. *Exorcism and Deliverance Ministry in the Twentieth Century: An Analysis of the Practice and Theology of Exorcism in Modern Western Christianity*. Eugene, OR: Wipf & Stock, 2009.

Dickason, C. Fred. *Angels, Elect and Evil*. Rev. ed. Chicago: Moody Publishers, 1995.

———. *Demon Possession and the Christian: A New Perspective*. Westchester, IL: Crossway, 1991.

Dunnett, Walter M. "Satan." In *BTDB*, 714–15.

Green, Michael. *I Believe in Satan's Downfall*. Grand Rapids: Eerdmans, 1981.

Kreider, Alan. "Baptism, Catechism, and the Eclipse of Jesus' Teaching in Early Christianity." In *Tyndale Bulletin* 47, no. 2 (November 1996): 315–48.

Lewis, C. S. *The Screwtape Letters*. New York: Macmillan, 1961.

MacMillan, John A. *The Authority of the Believer: A Compilation of "The Authority of the Believer" and "The Authority of the Intercessor."* Harrisburg, PA: Christian Publications, 1980.

McClelland, S. E. "Demon, Demon Possession." In *EDT3*, 236–38.

Mallone, George. *Arming for Spiritual Warfare*. Downers Grove, IL: InterVarsity Press, 1991.

Moreau, A. S. "Satanism." In *EDT3*, 773–74.

Moreau, A. Scott. "Demon." In *BTDB*, 162–65.

Mounce, W. D. "Heavenlies, The" In *EDT3*, 371.

Moreau, A. Scott, ed. *Deliver Us from Evil: An Uneasy Frontier in Christian Mission*. Monrovia, CA. World Vision International, 2002.

Murphy, Edward F. *The Handbook for Spiritual Warfare*. Rev. ed. Nashville: Nelson, 2003.

Nkansah-Obrempong, J. "Angels." In *GDT*, 35–39.

Penn-Lewis, Jessie, with Evan Roberts. *War on the Saints*. Unabridged ed. New York: Lowe, 1973.

Pentecost, Dwight. *Your Adversary, the Devil*. Grand Rapids: Zondervan, 1969.

Powlison, David. *Power Encounters: Reclaiming Spiritual Warfare*. Grand Rapids: Baker, 1995.

Reid, D. G. "Satan, Devil." In *DPL*, 862–67.

Schemm, Peter R. "The Agents of God: Angels." In *A Theology for the Church*, edited by Daniel L. Akin et al., 326–37. Nashville: B&H, 2007.

Twelftree, G. H. "Demon, Devil, Satan." In *DJG*, 163–72.

———. "Devil and Demons." In *NDT1*, 196–98.

———. "Spiritual Powers." In *NDBT*, 796–802.

———. *In the Name of Jesus: Exorcism Among Early Christians*. Grand Rapids: Baker Academic, 2007.

Unger, M. F. "Satan." In *EDT3*, 773.

———. *Demons in the World Today: A Study of Occultism in the Light of God's Word*. Wheaton, IL: Tyndale, 1971.

———. *What Demons Can Do to Saints*. Chicago: Moody Publishers, 1991.

Warner, Timothy M. *Spiritual Warfare: Victory over the Powers of This Dark World*. Wheaton, IL: Crossway, 1991.

Wright, N. G. "Devils and Demons." In *NDT2*, 253–55.

Wright, Nigel. *The Satan Syndrome: Putting the Power of Darkness in Its Place*. Grand Rapids: Zondervan, 1990.

Yong, A. "Discernment, Discerning the Spirits." In *GDT*, 232–35.

## SCRIPTURE MEMORY PASSAGE

**James 4:7–8:** Submit yourselves therefore to God. Resist the devil, and he will flee from you. Draw near to God, and he will draw near to you. Cleanse your hands, you sinners, and purify your hearts, you double-minded.

## HYMN

### "Christian, Dost Thou See Them?"

*Christian, dost thou see them on the holy ground,
  How the pow'rs of darkness rage thy steps around?
Christian, up and smite them, counting gain but loss,
  In the strength that cometh by the holy cross.*

*Christian, dost thou feel them, how they work within,
  Striving, tempting, luring, goading into sin?
Christian, never tremble; never be downcast;
  Gird thee for the battle, watch and pray and fast.*

*Christian, dost thou hear them, how they speak thee fair?
  "Always fast and vigil? Always watch and prayer?"
Christian, answer boldly, "While I breathe I pray!"
  Peace shall follow battle, night shall end in day.*

*Hear the words of Jesus: "O my servant true;*      *But that toil shall make thee some day all mine own,*
*Thou art very weary, I was weary too;*      *And the end of sorrow shall be near my throne."*

Author: John Mason Neale, 1862

Alternative hymns: "Soldiers of Christ Arise"; "Lead On, O King Eternal"; or "Onward, Christian Soldiers."

## CONTEMPORARY WORSHIP SONG

### "Psalm 46 (Lord Of Hosts)"

*O come behold the works of God,*
*The nations at His feet.*
*He breaks the bow and bends the spear*
*And tells the wars to cease.*
*O Mighty One of Israel, You are on our side.*
*We walk by faith*
*In God who burns the chariots with fire.*

*Chorus*
*Lord of hosts, You're with us with us in the fire,*
*With us as a shelter,*
*With us in the storm.*
*You will lead us*
*Through the fiercest battle,*
*Oh where else would we go,*
*But with the Lord of Hosts.*

*O God of Jacob, fierce and great,*
*You lift Your voice to speak.*
*The earth it bows and all*
*the mountains move into the sea.*
*O Lord, You know the hearts of men*
*And still You let them live.*
*O God who makes the mountains melt,*
*Come wrestle us and win.*

*Bridge*
*Though oceans roar, You are the Lord of all,*
*The One who calms the wind and waves*
*And makes my heart be still.*
*Though the earth gives way,*
*The mountains move into the sea,*
*The nations rage,*
*I know my God is in control.*

Words by Jennie Lee Riddle, Josiah Warneking, Josh Miller, and Shane Barnard[37]

# PART 3

# The Doctrine of Man
# in the Image of God

# CHAPTER 21

# The Creation of Man

*Why did God create us?*
*How did God make us like himself?*
*How can we please him in everyday living?*

## EXPLANATION AND SCRIPTURAL BASIS

The previous chapters have discussed the nature of God and his creation of the universe, the spiritual beings that he created, and his relationship to the world in terms of working miracles and answering prayer. In this next section, we focus on the pinnacle of God's creative activity, his creation of human beings, both male and female, to be more like him than anything else he has made. We will consider first God's purpose in creating human beings and the nature of human beings as God created them to be (chapters 21–23). Then we will look at the nature of sin and Adam and Eve's disobedience to God (chapter 24). Finally, we will examine the initiation of God's plan for saving human beings, discussing our relationship to God in the different covenants that God established (chapter 25).

## A. THE USE OF THE WORD *MAN* TO REFER TO THE HUMAN RACE

Before discussing the subject matter of this chapter, it is necessary to consider briefly whether it is appropriate to use the word *man* to refer to the entire human race (as in the title for this chapter). Some people today object to ever using the word *man* to refer to the human race in general (which includes both men and women) because, it is claimed, such usage is insensitive to women. Those who make this objection would prefer that we *only* use "gender neutral" terms such as *humanity, humankind, human beings,* or *persons* to refer to the human race.

After considering this suggestion, I decided to continue to use the word *man* (as well as several of these other terms) to refer to the human race in this book because such usage has divine warrant in Genesis 5 and because I think there is a theological issue at stake. In Genesis 5:1–2 we read, "When God created man, he made him in the likeness of God. Male and female he created them, and he blessed them *and named them Man* when they were created" (cf. Gen. 1:27). The Hebrew term translated "Man" is *'ādām*, the same term used for the name of Adam (Gen. 3:17, 21; 4:1, 25; 5:1). And this was also the same word that had already been used eight times in Genesis 2 to refer to the man in distinction from the woman:

And the rib that the Lord God had taken from the *man* he made into a woman and brought her to the *man*. (Gen. 2:22)

Then the *man* said, "This at last is bone of my bones and flesh of my flesh; she shall be called Woman." (Gen. 2:23)

And the *man* and his wife were both naked and were not ashamed. (Gen. 2:25)

And the *man* and his wife hid themselves from the presence of the Lord God. (Gen. 3:8)

But the Lord God called to the *man* and said to him, "Where are you?" (Gen. 3:9)

The *man* said, "The woman whom you gave to be with me, she gave me fruit of the tree, and I ate." (Gen. 3:12)

The *man* called his wife's name Eve. (Gen. 3:20)

Therefore, the practice of using the same term (1) to refer a male human being and (2) to name the human race generally is a practice that originated with God himself, and we should not find it objectionable or insensitive.

Someone might object that this is just an accidental feature of the Hebrew language, but this argument is not persuasive because Genesis 5:2 specifically describes God's activity of choosing a name that would apply to the human race as a whole.[1]

I am *not* arguing that we must always duplicate biblical patterns of speech *or* that it is wrong to use gender-neutral terms to refer to the human race (as I just did in this sentence), but I am claiming that God's *naming* activity reported in Genesis 5:2 indicates that the use of *man* to refer to the entire race is a good and very appropriate choice, one that we should not avoid.[2]

The theological issue is whether there is a suggestion of male leadership or headship

---

1. A related objection is that we don't know what language Adam and Eve and God were speaking in the garden, and perhaps that language had two different words representing (1) a male human being and (2) the human race. Therefore (it might be said) the use of the same word for both meanings is just a peculiar feature of the Hebrew language, and we should not place too much emphasis on it.

In response, a belief in the full authority and inerrancy of Scripture implies that, even if Adam and Eve and God were speaking a different language than Hebrew, the words of the Hebrew text now in Scripture accurately represent the meaning of that other language. The same principle applies when we say

that, even when Jesus was speaking Aramaic in his teaching, the Gospel records that we have in Greek faithfully and accurately represent the meaning of Jesus' words.

2. However, the question of whether to use *man* to refer to a person indefinitely, as in, "If any *man* would come after me, let him deny himself and take up his cross daily and follow me" (Luke 9:23 RSV), is a different question because the naming of the human race is not in view, and the underlying Greek word (*tis*, "someone, anyone") is not male specific. In such cases, considerateness toward women as well as men, and present-day language patterns, would make it appropriate to use gender-neutral language such as, "If *anyone* would come after me" (ESV).

in the family from the beginning of creation. The fact that God did not choose to call the human race "woman" but "man" probably has some significance for understanding God's original plan for men and women.[3] Of course, this question of the name we use to refer to the race is not the only factor in that discussion, but it is one factor, and our use of language in this regard does have some significance in the discussion of male-female roles today.[4]

## B. Why Was Man Created?

### 1. God Did Not Need to Create Man, Yet He Created Us for His Own Glory

In the discussion of God's independence in chapter 11 (see pp. 190–92), we noted several Scripture passages that teach that God does not need us or the rest of creation for anything, yet we and the rest of creation glorify him and bring him joy. Since there was perfect love and fellowship among members of the Trinity for all eternity (John 17:5, 24), God did not create us because he was lonely or because he needed fellowship with other persons—God did not need us for any reason.

Nevertheless, *God created us for his own glory.* In our treatment of his independence we noted that God speaks of his sons and daughters from the ends of the earth as those "whom I created *for my glory*" (Isa. 43:7; cf. Eph. 1:11–12). Therefore, we are to "do all to the glory of God" (1 Cor. 10:31).

This fact guarantees that our lives are significant. When we first realize that God did not need to create us and does not need us for anything, we could conclude that our lives have no importance at all. But Scripture tells us that we were created to glorify God, indicating that we are important *to God himself.* This is the final definition of genuine importance or significance to our lives: If we are truly important to God for all eternity, then what greater measure of importance or significance could we want?

### 2. What Is Our Purpose in Life?

The fact that God created us for his glory determines the correct answer to the question, "What is our purpose in life?" Our purpose must be to fulfill the reason that God created us: to glorify him. When we are speaking with respect to God, that is a good summary of our purpose. But when we think of our interests, we make the happy discovery that we are to enjoy God and take delight in him and in our relationship to him. Jesus says, "I came that they may have life and have it abundantly" (John 10:10). David tells God, "In your presence there is *fullness of joy*; at your right hand are pleasures

---

3. See chapter 22, p. 589. See also Raymond C. Ortlund Jr., "Male-Female Equality and Male Headship: Genesis 1–3," in *Recovering Biblical Manhood and Womanhood: A Response to Evangelical Feminism,* ed. John Piper and Wayne Grudem (Wheaton, IL: Crossway, 1991), 98. Ortlund writes, "God's naming of the race 'man' whispers male headship" (ibid.).

4. This is probably also recognized by many of those who raise the most objection to the use of *man* to refer to the race (namely, feminists who oppose any unique male headship in the family).

forevermore" (Ps. 16:11). He longs to dwell in the house of the Lord forever, "to gaze upon the beauty of the LORD" (Ps. 27:4). And Asaph cries out,

> Whom have I in heaven but you?
>     And there is nothing on earth that I desire besides you.
> My flesh and my heart may fail,
>     but God is the strength of my heart
>     and my portion forever. (Ps. 73:25–26)

Fullness of joy is found in knowing God and delighting in the excellence of his character. To be in his presence, to enjoy fellowship with him, is a greater blessing than anything that can be imagined.

> How lovely is your dwelling place,
>     O LORD of hosts!
> My soul longs, yes, faints
>     for the courts of the LORD;
> my heart and flesh sing for joy
>     to the living God. . . .
> For a day in your courts is better
>     than a thousand elsewhere. (Ps. 84:1–2, 10)

Therefore, the normal heart attitude of a Christian is rejoicing in the Lord and in the lessons of the life he gives us (Rom. 5:2–3; Phil. 4:4; 1 Thess. 5:16–18; James 1:2; 1 Peter 1:6, 8, et al.).[5]

As we glorify God and enjoy him, Scripture tells us that he rejoices in us. We read, "As the bridegroom rejoices over the bride, *so shall your God rejoice over you*" (Isa. 62:5), and Zephaniah prophesies that the Lord "will rejoice over you with gladness; he will quiet you by his love; he will exult over you with loud singing" (Zeph. 3:17).

This understanding of the doctrine of the creation of man has very practical results. When we realize that God created us to glorify him, and when we start to act in ways that fulfill that purpose, then we begin to experience an intensity of joy in the Lord that we have never before known. When we add to that the realization that God himself is rejoicing in our fellowship with him, our joy becomes inexpressible and filled with heavenly glory (see 1 Peter 1:8).[6]

Someone might object that it is wrong for God to seek glory for himself in creating

---

5. The first question in the Westminster Larger Catechism is "What is the chief and highest end of man?" The answer is, "Man's chief and highest end is to glorify God, and fully to enjoy Him forever."

6. See Grudem, *The First Epistle of Peter*, TNTC (Leicester: Inter-Varsity Press; Grand Rapids: Eerdmans, 1988), 66.

man. Certainly it is wrong for human beings to seek glory for themselves, as we see in the dramatic example of the death of Herod Agrippa I. When he proudly accepted the shout of the crowd, "The voice of a god, and not of man!" (Acts 12:22), "immediately an angel of the Lord struck him down, because he did not give God the glory, and he was eaten by worms and breathed his last" (Acts 12:23). Herod died because he robbed God of glory, glory that God deserved and he did not.

But when God takes glory to himself, from whom is he robbing glory? Is there anyone who deserves glory more than he does? Certainly not! He is the Creator, he made all things, and he *deserves* all glory. He is *worthy* of receiving glory. *Man* may not seek glory for himself, but in this case what is wrong for man is right for God because God is the Creator. It is *right*, not wrong, that he be glorified—in fact, if he did not receive glory from all creatures in the universe, that would be horribly wrong! The twenty-four elders around God's throne continually sing,

> Worthy are you, our Lord and God,
>> to receive glory and honor and power,
> for you created all things,
>> and by your will they existed and were created. (Rev. 4:11)

Paul exclaims, "For from him and through him and to him are all things. To him be glory forever. Amen" (Rom. 11:36). When we begin to appreciate the nature of God as the infinitely perfect Creator who deserves all praise, then our hearts will not rest until we give him glory with all of our "heart . . . soul . . . mind and . . . strength" (Mark 12:30).

## C. Creation in the Image of God
### 1. The Meaning of "Image of God"

Out of all the creatures God made, only one creature, man, is said to be made "in the image of God."[7] What does that mean? We may use the following definition: *the fact that man is in the image of God means that man is like God and represents God.*

I do not mean to suggest that theologians share a general agreement on the meaning of "image of God," for there are a number of different views. In the book *Christian Theology*, Millard Erickson gives a helpful summary of three major views of the image of God in man that have been held throughout the history of the church: (1) the substantive view, which identifies some particular quality of man (such as reason or spirituality) as the image of God in man (Luther, Calvin, many early church writers), (2) relational views, which hold that the image of God has to do with our interpersonal relationships (Emil Brunner; also Karl Barth, who saw the image of God specifically in our being

---

7. The Latin phrase *imago Dei* means "image of God" and is sometimes used in theological discussions in place of the English phrase "image of God." I have not used it elsewhere in this book.

created as male and female), and (3) the functional view, which holds that the image of God has to do with a function we carry out, usually our exercise of dominion over the creation.[8]

The most promising way forward in discovering the meaning of the image of God is, first, gaining a precise understanding of the Hebrew terms used in the Bible to speak about this concept. When God says, "Let us make man in our *image*, after our *likeness*" (Gen. 1:26), the meaning is that God plans to make a creature similar to himself. This is because the Hebrew words for both "image" (*tselem*) and "likeness" (*demût*) refer to something that is *similar* but not identical to the thing it represents or is an "image" of. The word *image* can also be used of something that *represents* something else.[9]

Therefore the Hebrew words that are translated "image" and "likeness" had quite clear meanings to the original readers. These Hebrew words informed the original readers that man was *like* God and would in many ways *represent* God. But this conclusion means that much of the controversy over the meaning of "image of God" is a search for too narrow and too specific a meaning. When Scripture reports that God said, "Let us make man in our image, after our likeness" (Gen. 1:26), it simply would have meant to the original readers, "Let us make man to be *like* us and to *represent* us."

Because image and likeness had these meanings, Scripture does not need to give a more precise explanation of what is meant by the creation of man in the image of God. Such an explanation is unnecessary not only because the terms had clear meanings but also because no such list could do justice to the subject: the text only needs to affirm that man is *like God*, and *the rest of Scripture fills in more details* to explain this. In fact, as we read the rest of Scripture, we realize that a full understanding of man's likeness to God would require a full understanding of *who God is* in his being and in his actions and a full understanding of *who man is* and what he does. The more we know about God and man, the more similarities we will recognize, and the more fully we will understand what Scripture means when it says that man is in the image of God. The expression "image of God" refers to every way in which man is like God. (Therefore there is some truth in the substantive views of the image of God, as well as in relational views and functional views, and we need not choose between them.)

---

8. Millard Erickson, *Christian Theology*, 3rd ed. (Grand Rapids: Baker, 2013), 460–69. A brief survey of various views is found in D. J. A. Clines, "The Image of God in Man," *TB* (1968): 54–61.

9. The word *image* (*tselem*) means an object similar to something else and often representative of it. The word is used to speak of statues or replicas of tumors and of mice (1 Sam. 6:5, 11), of paintings of soldiers on the wall (Ezek. 23:14), and of pagan idols or statues representing deities (Num. 33:42; 2 Kings 11:18; Ezek. 7:20; 16:17, et al.). The word *likeness* (*demût*) also means an object similar to something else, but it tends to be used more frequently in contexts where the idea of similarity is emphasized more than the idea of being a representative or substitute (of a god, for example). King Ahaz's model or drawing of the altar he saw in Damascus is called a "likeness" (2 Kings 16:10), as are the figures of bulls beneath the bronze altar (2 Chron. 4:3–4), and the wall paintings of Babylonian chariot officers (Ezek. 23:15). In Ps. 58:4 (Heb. v. 5) the venom of the wicked is a "likeness" of the venom of a snake: here the idea is that they are very similar in their characteristics, but there is no thought of actual representation or substitution. All of this evidence indicates that the English words *image* and *likeness* are very accurate equivalents for the Hebrew terms they translate.

This understanding of what it means that man is created in the image of God is reinforced by the similarity between Genesis 1:26, where God declares his intention to create man in his image and likeness, and Genesis 5:3: "When Adam had lived 130 years, he fathered a son in his own *likeness* [*demût*], after his *image* [*tselem*], and named him Seth." Seth was not identical to Adam, but he was like him in many ways, as a son is like his father. The text simply means that Seth was like Adam. It does not specify any specific number of ways that Seth was like Adam, and it would be overly restrictive for us to assert that one or another characteristic determined the way in which Seth was in Adam's image and likeness. Was it his brown eyes? Or his curly hair? Perhaps it was his athletic prowess, his serious disposition, or even his quick temper? Of course, such speculation would be useless. It is evident that *every* way in which Seth was like Adam would be a part of his likeness to Adam and thus part of his being "in the image" of Adam. Similarly, *every* way in which man is like God is part of his being in the image and likeness of God.

### 2. The Fall: God's Image Is Distorted but Not Lost

We might wonder whether man could still be thought to be *like God* after he sinned. This question is answered quite early in Genesis when God gives Noah the authority to establish the death penalty for murder among human beings just after the flood. God says "Whoever sheds the blood of man, by man shall his blood be shed, *for God made man in his own image*" (Gen. 9:6). Even though human beings are sinful, there is still enough likeness to God remaining in them that to murder another person (to "shed blood" is an Old Testament expression for taking a human life) is to attack the part of creation that most resembles God, and it betrays an attempt or desire (if one were able) to attack God himself.[10] Man is still in God's image. The New Testament gives confirmation to this when James 3:9 says that people generally, not just believers, "are made in the likeness of God."

However, since man has sinned, he is certainly not as fully like God as he was before. His moral purity has been lost and his sinful character certainly does not reflect God's holiness. His intellect is corrupted by falsehood and misunderstanding; his speech no longer continually glorifies God; his relationships are often governed by selfishness rather than love, and so forth. Though man is still in the image of God, parts of that image have been distorted or lost in every aspect of life. In short, "God made man upright, but they have sought out many schemes" (Eccl. 7:29). After the fall, then, we are still in God's image—we are still like God and still represent God—but the image of God in us is distorted; we are less fully like God than we were before the entrance of sin.

Therefore, it is important that we understand the full meaning of the image of

---

10. For a detailed analysis of this passage, see John Murray, *Principles of Conduct* (Grand Rapids: Eerdmans, 1957), 109–13.

God not simply from observation of human beings as they currently exist but from the biblical indications of the nature of Adam and Eve when God created them and when all that God had made was "very good" (Gen. 1:31). The true nature of man in the image of God was also seen in the earthly life of Christ. The full measure of the excellence of our humanity will not be seen again in life on earth until Christ returns and we have obtained all the benefits of the salvation he earned for us.

### 3. Redemption in Christ: A Progressive Recovering of God's Image

Nonetheless, it is encouraging to turn to the New Testament and see that our redemption in Christ means that we can, even in this life, grow progressively in likeness to God. For example, Paul says that as Christians we have a new nature that is "being renewed in knowledge after the image of its creator" (Col. 3:10). As we gain in true understanding of God, his Word, and his world, we begin to think more and more of the thoughts that God himself thinks. In this way we are "renewed in knowledge" and become more like God in our thinking. This is a description of the ordinary course of the Christian life. So Paul also can say that we "are being transformed into the same image from one degree of glory to another" (2 Cor. 3:18).[11] Throughout this life, as we grow in Christian maturity we grow in greater likeness to God. More particularly, we grow in likeness to Christ in our lives and in our character. In fact, the goal for which God has redeemed us is that we might be "conformed to the image of his Son" (Rom. 8:29) and thus be exactly like Christ in our moral character.

### 4. At Christ's Return: Complete Restoration of God's Image

The amazing promise of the New Testament is that just as we have been like Adam (subject to death and sin), we shall also be like Christ (morally pure, never subject to death again): "Just as we have borne the image of the man of dust, we shall also bear the image of the man of heaven" (1 Cor. 15:49).[12] The full measure of our creation in the image of God is not seen in the life of Adam who sinned, nor is it seen in our lives now, for we are imperfect. But the New Testament emphasizes that God's purpose in creating man in his image was completely realized in the person of Jesus Christ. He "is the image of God" (2 Cor. 4:4). "He is the image of the invisible God" (Col. 1:15). In Jesus we see human likeness to God as it was intended to be, and it should cause us to rejoice that God has predestined us "to be *conformed to the image of his Son*" (Rom. 8:29; cf. 1 Cor. 15:49): "When he appears *we shall be like him*" (1 John 3:2).

---

11. In this verse Paul specifically says that we are being changed into the image of Christ, but then four verses later he says that Christ is the image of God (2 Cor. 4:4; both verses use *eikōn*).

12. The New Testament Greek word for "image" (*eikōn*) has a similar meaning to its Old Testament counterpart (see above). It indicates something that is similar to or very much like the thing it represents. One interesting usage is a reference to the picture of Caesar on a Roman coin. Jesus asked the Pharisees, "Whose likeness [Gk. *eikōn*, "image"] and inscription is this?" They replied, "Caesar's" (Matt. 22:20–21). The image both resembles Caesar and represents him. (The Greek word *homoiōsis*, "likeness," is used in James 3:9 to speak of "people who are made in the *likeness* of God.")

## 5. Specific Aspects of Our Likeness to God

Though we have argued that it would be difficult to define all the ways in which we are like God, we can nevertheless mention several aspects of our existence that show us to be more like God than the rest of creation. Nothing else in God's creation is ever said to be in the image of God.[13]

**a. Moral Aspects.** (1) We are creatures who are morally accountable before God for our actions and this is based on the fact that God requires us to imitate his own moral purity. "You shall be holy, for I am holy" (1 Peter 1:16). Corresponding to that accountability, we have (2) an inner sense of right and wrong that sets us apart from animals (who have little if any innate sense of morality or justice but simply respond from fear of punishment or hope of reward). When we act according to God's moral standards, our likeness to God is reflected in (3) behavior that is holy and righteous before him. By contrast, our *un*likeness to God is reflected whenever we sin.

**b. Spiritual Aspects.** (4) We have not only physical bodies but also immaterial spirits, and we can therefore act in ways that are significant in the immaterial, spiritual realm of existence. This means that we have (5) a spiritual life that enables us to relate to God as persons, to pray and praise him, and to hear him speaking his words to us.[14] No animal will ever spend an hour in intercessory prayer for the salvation of a relative or a friend! But we are in the image of God and we can relate to God, who is spirit (John 4:24). Connected with this spiritual life is the fact that we have (6) immortality; we will not cease to exist but will live forever.

**c. Mental Aspects.** (7) We have an ability to reason and think logically and learn that sets us apart from the animal world, and surely this is part of being in the image of God. Animals sometimes exhibit remarkable behavior in solving mazes or working out problems in the physical world, but they do not engage in abstract reasoning—there is no such thing as the "history of canine philosophy," for example, nor have any animals since creation developed at all in their understanding of ethical problems or use of philosophical concepts. No group of chimpanzees will ever sit around the table arguing about the doctrine of the Trinity or the relative merits of Calvinism or Arminianism! In fact, even in developing physical and technical skills we are far different from animals: beavers still build the same kind of dams they have built for a thousand generations, birds still build the same kind of nests, and bees still build the same kinds of hives. But we continue to develop greater skill and complexity in technology, in agriculture, in science, and in nearly every field of endeavor.

(8) Our use of complex, abstract language sets us far apart from the animals. I could tell my son, when he was four years old, to go and get the big red screwdriver from my

---

13. However, angels also share a significant degree of likeness to God in a number of these aspects.

14. Although it is not a separate aspect of our likeness to God, the fact that we have been redeemed by Christ sets us apart in an absolute way from every other creature God has made. This is a consequence of our being in God's image, and of God's love for us, rather than one part of what it means to be in his image.

workbench in the basement. Even if he had never seen it before, he could easily perform the task because he knew meanings of *go, get, big, red, screwdriver, workbench,* and *basement.* He could have done the same for a small brown hammer, a black bucket beside the workbench, or any of dozens of other items that he perhaps had never seen before but could visualize when I described them in a few brief words. No chimpanzee in all history has been able to perform such a task—a task that has not been learned through repetition with reward but is simply described in words that refer to an item that the hearer has never seen before. Yet four-year-old human beings can do this routinely, and we think nothing of it. Most eight-year-olds can write an understandable letter to their grandparents describing a trip to the zoo or can move to a foreign country and learn any other language in the world, and we think it entirely normal. But no animal will ever write such a letter to its grandparents, give the past, present, and future of one French verb, read and understand a detective story, or understand the meaning of even one verse from the Bible. Human children do all these things quite readily, and in so doing they show themselves so far superior to the whole animal kingdom that we wonder why people have sometimes thought that we are merely another kind of animal.

(9) Another mental difference between humans and animals is that we have an awareness of the distant future, even an inward sense that we will live beyond the time of our physical death, a sense that gives many people a desire to attempt to be right with God before they die (God "has put eternity into man's heart," Eccl. 3:11).

(10) Our creation in the image of God is also seen in our human creativity in areas such as art, music, literature, and scientific and technological inventiveness. We should not think of such creativity as restricted to world-famous musicians or artists—it is also reflected in a delightful way in the play acting or skits put on by children, in the skill reflected in the cooking of a meal or the decorating of a home or the planting of a garden, and in the inventiveness shown by every human being who "fixes" something that just wasn't working correctly.

The foregoing aspects of likeness to God have been ways in which we differ from animals *absolutely*, not merely in degree. But there are other areas where we differ from animals in significant degree, and these also can show our likeness to God.

(11) In the area of emotions, our likeness to God is seen in a large difference in degree and complexity of emotions. Of course, animals do show some emotions (anyone who has owned a dog can remember evident expressions of joy, sadness, fear of punishment when it has done wrong, anger if another animal invades its "turf," contentment, and affection, for example). But in the complexity of emotions that we experience, once again we are far different than the rest of creation. After watching my son's baseball game, I can simultaneously feel sad that his team lost, happy that he played well, proud that he was a good sport, thankful to God for giving me a son and giving me the joy of watching him grow up, joyful because of the song of praise that has been echoing in my mind all afternoon, and anxious because we are going to be late for dinner! It

is very doubtful that an animal experiences anything approaching this complexity of emotional feeling.

**d. Relational Aspects.** In addition to our unique ability to relate to God (discussed above), there are other relational aspects of being in God's image. (12) Although animals no doubt have some sense of community with each other, the depth of interpersonal harmony experienced in human marriage, in a human family when it functions according to God's principles, and in a church when a community of believers is walking in fellowship with the Lord and with each other is much greater than the interpersonal harmony experienced by any animals. In our family relationships and in the church, we are also superior to angels, who do not marry or bear children or live in the company of God's redeemed sons and daughters.

(13) In marriage we reflect the nature of God in the fact that as men and women we have equality in importance but difference in roles from the time that God created us (see discussion in chapter 22).

(14) Man is like God also in his relationship to the rest of creation. Specifically, man has been given the right to rule over the creation and when Christ returns will even be given authority to sit in judgment over angels (1 Cor. 6:3; Gen. 1:26, 28; Ps. 8:6–8).

**e. Physical Aspects.** Is there any sense in which our human bodies are also a part of what it means to be made in the image of God? Certainly we should not think that our physical bodies imply that God himself has a body, for "God is spirit" (John 4:24), and it is sin to think of him or to portray him in any way that would imply that he has a material or a physical body (see Ex. 20:4; Ps. 115:3–8; Rom. 1:23).[15] But even though our physical bodies should in no way be taken to imply that God has a physical body, are there still some ways in which our bodies reflect something of God's own character and thereby constitute part of what it means to be created in the image of God? Certainly this is true in some respects.

For example, our physical bodies give us the ability to see with our eyes. This is a Godlike quality because God sees, and sees far more than we will ever see, although he does not do it with physical eyes like we have. Our ears give us the ability to hear, and this too is a Godlike ability, even though God does not have physical ears. Our mouths give us the ability to speak, reflecting the fact that God is a God who speaks. Our senses of taste and touch and smell give us the ability to understand and enjoy God's creation, reflecting the fact that God himself understands and enjoys his creation, though in a far greater sense than we do.

It is important that we recognize that it is *man* in his entirety who is created in the image of God, not just his spirit or his mind. Certainly our physical bodies are a very important part of our existence, and when they are transformed when Christ returns,

---

15. See also the discussion of God's spirituality in chapter 12, pp. 220–22.

they will continue to be part of our existence for all eternity (see 1 Cor. 15:43–45, 51–55). Our bodies therefore have been created by God as suitable instruments to represent in a physical way our human nature, which has been made to be like God's nature. In fact, almost everything we do is done by means of the use of our physical bodies. Our thinking, our moral judgments, our prayer and praise, our demonstrations of love and concern for each other—all are done using the physical bodies God has given us. Therefore, if we are careful to point out that we are *not* saying that God has a physical body, we may say that (15) our physical bodies in various ways reflect something of God's character as well. Moreover, much physical movement and demonstration of God-given skill comes about through the use of our body. And certainly (16) the God-given physical ability to bear and raise children who are like us (see Gen. 5:3) is a reflection of God's ability to create human beings who are like him.

Especially in the last several points, these differences between human beings and the rest of creation are not *absolute differences* but often differences of very great degree. We mentioned that there is some kind of emotion experienced by animals. There is some experience of authority in relationships where animal communities have leaders whose authority is accepted by the others in the group. Moreover, there is *some* similarity even in those differences we think more absolute: animals are able to reason to some extent and can communicate with each other in various ways that in some primitive sense can be called "language." This should not be surprising: if God made the entire creation so that it reflects his character in various ways, this is what we would expect. In fact, the more complex and highly developed animals are *more* like God than lower forms of animals. Therefore, we should not say that *only* man reflects any likeness to God at all, for in one way or another all of creation reflects some likeness to God.[16] But it is still important to recognize that *only man*, out of all of creation, is so like God that he can be said to be "in the image of God." This scriptural affirmation, together with the scriptural commands that we are to imitate God in our lives (Eph. 5:1; 1 Peter 1:16), and the observable facts that we can recognize in looking at ourselves and the rest of creation, all indicate that we are *much more like God* than all the rest of creation. In some respects the differences are absolute, and in other respects they are relative, but they are all significant.

Finally, our appreciation of the ways in which we are like God can be enhanced by the realization that, unlike the rest of God's creation, we have an ability to grow to become *more like God* throughout our lives. Our moral sense can be more highly developed through study of Scripture and prayer. Our moral behavior can reflect more and more the holiness of God (2 Cor. 7:1; 1 Peter 1:16, et al.). Our spiritual life can be enriched and deepened. Our use of reason and language can become more accurate and truthful and more honoring to God. Our sense of the future can become intensified as we grow

---

16. See discussion of the names of God and the way God's nature is reflected in all of creation in chapter 11, pp. 186–89.

in our hope of living with God forever. Our future existence can be enriched as we lay up treasures in heaven and seek for increased heavenly reward (see Matt. 6:19–21; 1 Cor. 3:10–15; 2 Cor. 5:10). Our ability to rule over the creation can be extended by faithful use of the gifts God has given us; our faithfulness to the God-given purposes for our creation as men and women can be increased as we follow biblical principles in our families; our creativity can be employed in ways that are more and more pleasing to God; our emotions can be more and more conformed to the pattern of Scripture so that we become more like David, a man after God's own heart (1 Sam. 13:14). Our interpersonal harmony in our families and in the church can reflect more and more the unity that exists among the persons in the Trinity. As we consciously seek to grow into greater likeness to God in all these areas, we also demonstrate an ability that itself sets us apart from the rest of creation.

## 6. Our Great Dignity as Bearers of God's Image

It would be good for us to reflect on our likeness to God more often. It will probably amaze us to realize that when the Creator of the universe wanted to create something "in his image," something *more like himself* than all the rest of creation, he made us! This realization will give us a profound sense of dignity and significance as we reflect on the excellence of all the rest of God's creation: the starry universe, the abundant earth, the world of plants and animals, and the angelic kingdoms are remarkable, even magnificent. But we are *more like our Creator* than any of these things. We are the culmination of God's infinitely wise and skillful work of creation. Even though sin has greatly marred that likeness, we nonetheless now reflect much of it and shall even more as we grow in likeness to Christ.

Yet we must remember that even though the manifestations of the image of God have been distorted and diminished because of sin, fallen and sinful man has the *status* of being in God's image (see section C.2 above). Genesis 9:6 affirms that people generally, not just believers, are "in [God's] own image," and James 3:9 says that people in general "are made in the likeness of God." This implies that every single human being, no matter how much the image of God is marred by sin, illness, weakness, age, or any other disability, still has the *status* of being in God's image and therefore must be treated with the dignity and respect that is due to God's image-bearer.

In addition, it is important to emphasize that people from every racial and ethnic background are all "in the image of God" and thus worthy of our respect and care. This has profound implications for our conduct toward others. It means that people of every race and ethnicity deserve equal dignity and rights. It means that elderly people, those seriously ill, the mentally disabled, and children yet unborn, deserve full protection and honor as human beings. If we ever deny our unique status in creation as God's only image bearers, we will soon begin to depreciate the value of human life, will tend to see humans as merely a higher form of animal, and will begin to treat others as such. We will also lose much of our sense of meaning in life.

# QUESTIONS FOR PERSONAL APPLICATION

1. According to Scripture, what should be the major purpose of your life? If you consider the major commitments or goals of your life at the present time (with respect to friendships, marriage, education, job, use of money, church relationships, etc.), are you acting as though your goal were the one that Scripture specifies? Or do you have some other goals that you have acted upon (perhaps without consciously deciding to do so)? As you think about the pattern of most of your days, do you think that God delights in you and rejoices over you?

2. How does it make you feel to think that you, as a human being, are more like God than any other creature in the universe? How does that knowledge make you want to act?

3. Do you think that there are any more intelligent, more Godlike creatures anywhere else in the universe? What does the fact that Jesus became a man rather than some other kind of creature say about the importance of human beings in God's sight?

4. Do you think that God has made us so that we become more happy or less happy when we grow to become more like him? As you look over the list of ways in which we can be more like God, can you name one or two areas in which growth in likeness to God has given you increasing joy in your life? In which areas would you now like to make more progress in likeness to God?

5. Is it only Christians or all people who are in the image of God? How does that make you feel about your relationships to non-Christians?

6. Do you think an understanding of the image of God might change the way you think and act toward people who are racially different or elderly or weak or unattractive to the world?

**Special Terms**
*image of God*
imago Dei
*likeness*

# BIBLIOGRAPHY

(For an explanation of this bibliography see the note on the bibliography to chapter 1, pp. 23–24. Complete bibliographical data may be found on pp. 1489–96.)

## SECTIONS IN EVANGELICAL SYSTEMATIC THEOLOGIES

*1. Anglican (Episcopalian)*
1882–92 . . . . . Litton, 109–22

2001 . . . . . . . . Packer, 71–73
2013 . . . . . . . . Bird, 649–56
2013 . . . . . . . . Bray, 79

*2. Arminian (Wesleyan or Methodist)*
1875–76 . . . . . Pope, 1:430–36
1892–94 . . . . . Miley, 1:355–422, 406–8
1940 . . . . . . . . Wiley, 2:7–50
1960 . . . . . . . . Purkiser, 204–22

1983........Carter, 1:195–236
1992........Oden, 1:23–24
2002........Cottrell, 134–58

3. *Baptist*
1767........Gill, 1:440–51
1887........Boyce, 189–94, 213–17
1907........Strong, 465–83, 514–32
1976–83.....Henry, 2:124–42; 4:494–521
1987–94.....Lewis and Demarest, 2:123–82
1990–95.....Garrett, 1:451–68
2007........Akin, 342–43
2013........Erickson, 423–56, 457–74

4. *Dispensational*
1947........Chafer, 2:125–43, 161–73
1949........Thiessen, 151–57
1986........Ryrie, 189–94
2002–2005..Geisler, 2:449–58; 3:17–79, 552–63
2017........MacArthur and Mayhue, 399–415

5. *Lutheran*
1917–24 .....Pieper, 1:515–27
1934........Mueller, 205–9

6. *Reformed (or Presbyterian)*
1559 ........Calvin, 1:183–96 (1.15)
1679–85.....Turretin, *IET*, 1:451–52, 457–77, 611–13
1871–73.....Hodge, 2:92–116
1878........Dabney, 293–94
1887–1921...Warfield, *BTS*, 238–61
1894........Shedd, 429–93
1906–11.....Bavinck, *RD*, 2:511–29
1937–66.....Murray, *CW*, 2:14–22, 34–46
1938........Berkhof, 181–90, 202–10

1998........Reymond, 415–17
2008........Ven Genderen and Velema, 265–76
2011........Horton, 373–407
2013........Frame, 783–97, 802–6
2013........Culver, 246–47
2016........Allen and Swain, 165–93
2017........Barrett, 293–311
2019........Letham, 315–47

7. *Renewal (or charismatic/Pentecostal)*
1988–92.....Williams, 1:197–220
1993........Menzies and Horton, 77–81
1995........Horton, 215–54
2008........Duffield and Van Cleave, 121–40

### SECTIONS IN REPRESENTATIVE ROMAN CATHOLIC SYSTEMATIC THEOLOGIES

1. *Roman Catholic: Traditional*
1955........Ott, 94–96, 101–6

2. *Roman Catholic: Post–Vatican II*
1980........McBrien, 1:101–78
2012........*CCC*, paragraphs 355–61

### OTHER WORKS

Allison, Gregg. *Historical Theology: An Introduction to Christian Doctrine; A Companion to Wayne Grudem's* Systematic Theology. Grand Rapids: Zondervan, 2011, 321–41.

Baker, William H. *In the Image of God: A Biblical View of Humanity*. Chicago: Moody Press, 1991.

Barclay, O. R. "Creation." In *NDT1*, 177–79.

Berkouwer, G. C. *Man: The Image of God*. Grand Rapids: Eerdmans, 1962.

Blocher, H. A. and W. A. Dyrness. "Anthropology, Theological." In *GDT*, 42–52.

Boston, Thomas. *Human Nature in Its Fourfold State*. 1720. Reprint, London: Banner of Truth, 1964.

Bray, G. L. "Image of God." In *NDBT*, 575–76.

———. "Image of God." In *NDT2*, 438–40.

Cooper, J. W. "Human Being." In *EDT3*, 403–7.

Dearborn, K. L. "Image of God." In *EDT3*, 415–17.

Engel, Mary Potter. *John Calvin's Perspectival Anthropology*. Eugene, OR: Wipf and Stock, 2002.

Ferguson, S. B. "Image of God." In *NDT1*, 328–29.

Grenz, Stanley J. *The Social God and the Relational Self: A Trinitarian Theology of the Imago Dei*. Louisville: Westminster John Knox, 2001.

Hammett, John S. "Human Nature." In *A Theology for the Church*, edited by Daniel L. Akin et al., 340–408. Nashville: B&H, 2007.

Henry, C. F. H. "Image of God." In *EDT1*, 545–48.

Hiebert, Robert J. V. "Create, Creation." In *BTDB*, 132–36.

Hoekema, Anthony A. *Created in God's Image*. Grand Rapids: Eerdmans; Exeter: Paternoster, 1986, 1–111.

Hughes, Philip Edgcumbe. *The True Image: The Origin and Destiny of Man in Christ*. Grand Rapids: Eerdmans; Leicester: Inter-Varsity Press, 1989, 1–70.

Kilner, John Frederic. *Dignity and Destiny: Humanity in the Image of God*. Grand Rapids: Eerdmans, 2015.

Kline, Meredith G. *Images of the Spirit*. Grand Rapids: Baker, 1980.

Laidlaw, John. *The Bible Doctrine of Man*. Edinburgh: T&T Clark, 1905.

Machen, J. Gresham. *The Christian View of Man*. 1937. Reprint, London: Banner of Truth, 1965.

McConville, J. G. *Being Human in God's World: An Old Testament Theology of Humanity*. Grand Rapids: Baker Academic, 2016.

McDonald, H. D. "Man, Doctrine of." In *EDT1*, 676–80.

———. *The Christian View of Man*. Westchester, IL: Crossway, 1981.

Middleton, J. Richard. *The Liberating Image: The Imago Dei in Genesis 1*. Grand Rapids: Brazos, 2005.

Ortlund, Jr., R. C. "Man and Woman." In *NDBT*, 650–54.

Pyne, Robert A. *Humanity and Sin: The Creation, Fall, and Redemption of Humanity*. Nashville: Word, 1999.

Robinson, H. W. *The Christian Doctrine of Man*. 3rd ed. Edinburgh: T. & T. Clark, 1926.

Rosenberg, Stanley, ed. *Finding Ourselves after Darwin: Conversations on the Image of God, Original Sin, and the Problem of Evil*. Grand Rapids: Baker Academic, 2018.

Sherlock, Charles. *The Doctrine of Humanity*. Downers Grove, IL: InterVarsity Press, 1996.

Smail, Thomas Allan. *Like Father, Like Son: The Trinity Imaged in Our Humanity*. Grand Rapids: Eerdmans, 2006.

Thompson, G. J. "Creation." In *NDT2*, 229–31.

## SCRIPTURE MEMORY PASSAGE

**Genesis 1:26–27:** Then God said, "Let us make man in our image, after our likeness. And let them have dominion over the fish of the sea and over the birds of the heavens and over the livestock and over all the earth and over every creeping thing that creeps on the earth." So God created man in his own image, in the image of God he created him; male and female he created them.

## HYMN

### "Love Divine, All Love Excelling"

*Love divine, all love excelling,*
*Joy of heav'n, to earth come down!*
*Fix in us thy humble dwelling;*
*All thy faithful mercies crown.*

*Jesus, thou art all compassion,*
*Pure, unbounded love thou art;*
*Visit us with thy salvation,*
*Enter ev'ry trembling heart.*

*Breathe, O breathe thy loving Spirit*
 *Into ev'ry troubled breast!*
*Let us all in thee inherit,*
 *Let us find the promised rest.*
*Take away the love of sinning;*
 *Alpha and Omega be;*
*End of faith, as its beginning,*
 *Set our hearts at liberty.*

*Come, Almighty to deliver,*
 *Let us all thy life receive;*
*Suddenly return, and never,*
 *Never more thy temples leave.*

*Thee we would be always blessing,*
 *Serve thee as thy hosts above,*
*Pray, and praise thee, without ceasing,*
 *Glory in thy perfect love.*

*Finish, then, thy new creation;*
 *Pure and spotless let us be;*
*Let us see thy great salvation*
 *Perfectly restored in thee:*
*Changed from glory into glory,*
 *Till in heav'n we take our place,*
*Till we cast our crowns before thee,*
 *Lost in wonder, love, and praise.*

Author: Charles Wesley, 1747

## CONTEMPORARY WORSHIP SONG

### "10,000 Reasons (Bless The Lord)"

*Chorus*
*Bless the Lord, O my soul,*
*O my soul.*
*Worship His holy name.*
*Sing like never before,*
*O my soul.*
*I'll worship Your holy name.*

*The sun comes up it's a new day dawning.*
*It's time to sing Your song again.*
*Whatever may pass and whatever lies before me,*
*Let me be singing when the evening comes.*

*You're rich in love, and You're slow to anger.*
*Your name is great, and Your heart is kind.*
*For all Your goodness I will keep on singing,*
*Ten thousand reasons for my heart to find.*

*And on that day when my strength is failing,*
*The end draws near and my time has come,*
*Still my soul will sing Your praise unending,*
*Ten thousand years and then forevermore.*

Words by Matt Redman and Jonas Myrin[17]

# CHAPTER 22

# Man as Male and Female

*Why did God create two sexes?*
*Can men and women be equal and yet have different roles?*

## EXPLANATION AND SCRIPTURAL BASIS

We noted in the previous chapter that one aspect of man's creation in the image of God is his creation as male and female: "So God created man in his own image, in the image of God he created him; *male and female he created them*" (Gen. 1:27). The same connection between creation in the image of God and creation as male and female is made in Genesis 5:1–2, "When God created man, he made him in the likeness of God. *Male and female* he created them, and he blessed them and named them Man when they were created."[1] Although the creation of man as male and female is not the only way in which we are in the image of God, it is a significant enough aspect of our creation in the image of God that Scripture mentions it in the very same verse in which it describes God's initial creation of man. We may summarize the ways in which our creation as male and female represents something of our creation in God's image as follows:

The creation of man as male and female shows God's image in (1) harmonious interpersonal relationships, (2) equality in personhood and importance, and (3) difference in role and authority.[2]

### A. Personal Relationships

God did not create human beings to be isolated persons, but in making us in his image, he made us in such a way that we can attain interpersonal unity of various sorts in all forms of human society. Interpersonal unity can be especially deep in the human family and also in our spiritual family, the church. Between men and women, interpersonal unity comes to its fullest expression in this age in marriage, where husband and wife become, in a sense, two persons in one: "Therefore a man shall leave his father and his mother and hold fast to his wife, and they shall become one flesh" (Gen. 2:24). This

---

1. On the question of whether to use the English word *man* to refer to human beings generally (both male and female), see chapter 21, pp. 563–65.

2. For a more extensive discussion of the theological implications of male-female differentiation in Genesis 1–3, see Raymond C. Ortlund Jr., "Male-Female Equality and Male

Headship: Genesis 1–3," in *Recovering Biblical Manhood and Womanhood: A Response to Evangelical Feminism*, ed. by John Piper and Wayne Grudem (Wheaton, IL: Crossway, 1991), 98. I have depended on Dr. Ortlund's analysis at several points in this chapter.

unity is not only a physical unity; it is also a spiritual and emotional unity of profound dimensions. A husband and wife joined together in marriage are people that "God has joined together" (Matt. 19:6). Sexual union with someone other than one's own wife or husband is an especially offensive kind of sin against one's own body (1 Cor. 6:16, 18–20), and within marriage, husbands and wives no longer have exclusive rule over their own bodies, but share them with their spouses (1 Cor. 7:3–5). Husbands "should love their wives as their own bodies" (Eph. 5:28). The union between husband and wife is not temporary but lifelong (Mal. 2:14–16; Rom. 7:2), and it is not trivial but is a profound relationship created by God in order to picture the relationship between Christ and his church (Eph. 5:23–32).

The fact that God created two distinct persons as male and female, rather than just one man, is part of our being in the image of God because it can be seen to reflect to some degree the plurality of persons within the Trinity. In the verse prior to the one that tells of our creation as male and female, we see the first explicit indication of a plurality of persons within God: "Then God said, 'Let *us* make man in *our* image, after our likeness. And let them have dominion'" (Gen. 1:26). There is some similarity here: just as there was fellowship and communication and sharing of glory among the members of the Trinity before the world was made (see John 17:5, 24; also chapter 14 above on the Trinity), so God made Adam and Eve in such a way that they would share love and communication and mutual giving of honor to one another in their interpersonal relationship. Of course such reflection of the Trinity would come to expression in various ways within human society, but it would certainly exist from the beginning in the close interpersonal unity of marriage.

Someone might object that such a representation of the plurality of persons in God is not really a complete one, for God is three persons in one while God created Adam and Eve as only two persons in one. If God intended us to reflect the plurality of persons in the Trinity, why did he not create three persons rather than two who could reflect the interpersonal unity among the members of the Trinity? First, we must agree that this fact shows the analogy between marriage and the Trinity to be an inexact one. Second, although we cannot be certain of the reasons why God did not do something when Scripture does not explicitly tell us those reasons, we can suggest two possible answers: (1) The fact that God is three in one while Adam and Eve were only two in one may be a reminder that God's own excellence is far greater than ours, that he possesses far greater plurality and far greater unity than we ourselves, as creatures, can possess. (2) Though the unity is not exactly the same, the unity in a family among husband, wife, and children does also reflect to some degree the interpersonal unity yet diversity of persons among the members of the Trinity.

A second objection might be raised from the fact that Jesus himself was unmarried, that Paul was unmarried at the time he was an apostle (and perhaps earlier), and that Paul in 1 Corinthians 7:1, 7–9 seems to say that it is better for Christians not to marry.

If marriage is such an important part of our reflection of the image of God, then why were Paul and Jesus not married, and why did Paul encourage others not to be married?

For Jesus, the situation is unique, for he is both God and man, and sovereign Lord over all creation. Rather than being married to any one individual human being, he has taken the entire church as his bride (see Eph. 5:23–32) and enjoys with each member of his church a spiritual and emotional unity that will last for eternity.

The situation with Paul and his advice to the Corinthian Christians is somewhat different. There Paul does not say that it is wrong to marry (see 1 Cor. 7:28, 36); rather, he views marriage as something good, a right and a privilege that may be given up for the sake of the kingdom of God: "I think that in view of the present distress it is good for a person to remain as he is . . . the appointed time has grown very short. . . . For the present form of this world is passing away" (1 Cor. 7:26, 29, 31). In this way Paul gives up one way he might reflect likeness to God (marriage) in order to further other ways in which he might reflect likeness to God and further God's purposes in the world (namely, in his work for the church). For example, his evangelism and discipleship are thought of as bearing "spiritual children" and nurturing them in the Lord (see 1 Cor. 4:14, where he calls the Corinthians "my beloved children"; also Gal. 4:19; 1 Tim. 1:2; Titus 1:4). Moreover, the entire building up of the church was a process of bringing thousands of people to glorify God as they reflected his character more fully in their lives. In addition, we must realize that marriage is not the only way in which the unity and diversity in the Trinity can be reflected in our lives. It is also reflected in the union of believers in the fellowship of the church—and in genuine church fellowship, single persons (like Paul and Jesus) as well as those who are married can have interpersonal relationships that reflect the nature of the Trinity. Therefore, building the church and increasing its unity and purity also promote the reflection of God's character in the world.

## B. Equality in Personhood and Importance

Just as the members of the Trinity are equal in their importance and in their full existence as distinct persons (see chapter 14, above), so men and women have been created by God to be equal in their importance and personhood. When God created man, he created both "male and female" in his image (Gen. 1:27; 5:1–2). Men and women are made *equally in God's image*, and both men and women reflect God's character in their lives. This means that we should see aspects of God's character reflected in each other's lives. If we lived in a society consisting of only Christian men or a society consisting of only Christian women, we would not gain as full a picture of the character of God as when we see both godly men and godly women in their complementary differences together reflecting the beauty of God's character.

But if we are equally in God's image, then certainly men and women are *equally important* to God and *equally valuable* to him. We have equal worth before him for all eternity. The fact that both men and women are said by Scripture to be "in the image of

God" should exclude all feelings of pride or inferiority and any idea that one sex is "better" or "worse" than the other. In contrast to many non-Christian cultures and religions, no one should feel proud or superior because he is a man, and no one should feel disappointed or inferior because she is a woman.[3] If God thinks us to be equal in value, then that settles the question, for God's evaluation is the true standard of personal value for all eternity.

When in 1 Corinthians 11:7 Paul says, "A man ought not to cover his head, since he is the image and glory of God, but woman is the glory of man," he is not denying that woman was created in the image of God. He is simply saying that there are abiding differences between men and women that should be reflected in the way they dress and act in the assembled congregation. One of those differences is that man in relationship to woman has a particular role of representing God or showing what he is like, and woman in that relationship shows the excellence of the man from whom she was created. Yet in both cases Paul goes on to emphasize their interdependence (see vv. 11–12).

Our equality as persons before God, reflecting the equality of persons in the Trinity, should lead naturally to men and women giving honor to one another. Proverbs 31 is a beautiful picture of the honor given to a godly woman:

> An excellent wife who can find?
> She is far more precious than jewels. . . .
> Her children rise up and call her blessed;
> her husband also, and he praises her:
> "Many women have done excellently,
> but you surpass them all."
> Charm is deceitful, and beauty is vain,
> but a woman who fears the LORD is to be praised. (Prov. 31:10, 28–30)

3. A tragic example of male dominance was reported on the front page of *USA Today: International Edition*, September 6, 1994. "No girls allowed: abortion for sex selection raises moral questions" was the caption on a photo of a doctor performing an ultrasound on a pregnant woman in India. The cover story, "Asians' Desire for Boys Leaves a Deadly Choice," reported that according to Dr. Datta Pai, a Bombay obstetrician, "Ninety-nine percent of those found to be carrying female fetuses aborted their unborn children" (2A). The story explained that "modern technology, the strong cultural desire for boys and pressure to reduce population have joined forces in a deadly combination in India, China and much of Asia to produce a booming business in sex selection. . . . The practice of aborting female fetuses appears common judging by emerging statistics that show lopsided sex ratios throughout Asia and into North Africa. Nor is the practice of sex selection limited to abortion. Female infanticide, the abandonment of baby girls, and the preferential feeding and health care of boys contribute greatly to the imbalanced ratios" (1A–2A). The story goes on to quote Harvard professor Amartya Sen as saying that there are now more than 100 million women "missing" in the population of the world, including 44 million fewer women in China and 37 million fewer in India than should be alive, according to normal sex ratios at birth (2A).

This is a tragedy of unspeakable proportions. In addition to the harm of these lost lives, we must think of the destructive consequences in the lives of those women who survive. From their earliest age, they receive the message from their families and indeed from their whole society that "boys are better than girls" and "I wish you were a boy." The devastation to their own sense of self-worth must be immense. Yet all of this comes about as the result of a failure to realize that men and women, boys and girls, have equal value in God's sight and should have equal value in our sight as well. The first chapter of the Bible corrects this practice, and corrects any lurking sense in our own hearts that boys are more valuable than girls, when it says we are both created in the image of God.

Similarly, Peter tells husbands that they should be "showing honor" to their wives (1 Peter 3:7), and Paul emphasizes, "In the Lord woman is not independent of man nor man of woman; for as woman was made from man, so man is now born of woman" (1 Cor. 11:11, 12). Both men and women are equally important; both depend upon each other; both are worthy of honor.

The equality in personhood with which men and women were created is emphasized in a new way in the new covenant church. At Pentecost we see the fulfillment of Joel's prophecy in which God promises:

> I will pour out my Spirit on all flesh,
> and your *sons* and your *daughters* shall prophesy . . .
> even on my *male servants* and *female servants*
> in those days I will pour out my Spirit, and they shall prophesy.
> (Acts 2:17–18; quoting Joel 2:28–29)

The Holy Spirit is poured out in new power on the church, and men and women *both* are given gifts to minister in remarkable ways. Spiritual gifts are distributed to all men and women, beginning at Pentecost and continuing throughout the history of the church. Paul regards every Christian as a valuable member of the body of Christ, for "to *each* is given the manifestation of the Spirit for the common good" (1 Cor. 12:7). After mentioning several gifts he says, "All these are empowered by one and the same Spirit, who apportions *to each one* individually as he wills," (1 Cor. 12:11). Peter also, in writing to many churches throughout Asia Minor, says, "As *each* has received a gift, use it to serve one another, as good stewards of God's varied grace" (1 Peter 4:10). These texts do not teach that all believers have the same gifts, but they do mean that both men and women will have valuable gifts for the ministry of the church and that we should expect that these gifts will be widely and freely distributed to both men and women.

It seems, therefore, pointless to ask, "Who can pray more effectively, men or women?" or "Who can sing praise to God better, men or women?" or "Who will have more spiritual sensitivity and depth of relationship with God?" To all of these questions, we simply cannot give an answer. Men and women are equal in their ability to receive the new covenant empowerment of the Holy Spirit. There have been both great men and great women of God throughout the history of the church. Both men and women have been mighty warriors in prayer, prevailing over earthly powers and kingdoms and spiritual strongholds in the authority of our Lord Jesus Christ.[4]

---

4. Perhaps the answer to the questions "Who can pray better?" and "Who can praise God better?" should be "both together." Although there is much value in a men's prayer meeting or in a gathering of women for prayer, there is nothing richer and more complete than the whole fellowship of God's people, both men and women, and even their children who are old enough to understand and participate, gathered together before God's throne in prayer: "When the day of Pentecost arrived, they *were all together in one place*" (Acts 2:1). "And when they heard it, they lifted their voices *together* to God"

Equality before God is further emphasized in the new covenant church in the ceremony of baptism. At Pentecost, both men and women who believed were baptized: "Those who received his word were baptized, and there were added that day about three thousand souls" (Acts 2:41). This is significant because in the old covenant, the sign of membership of God's people was circumcision, which was given only to men. The new sign of membership of God's people, the sign of baptism, given to both men and women, is further evidence that both should be seen as fully and equally members of the people of God.

Equality in status among God's people is also emphasized by Paul in Galatians: "For as many of you as were baptized into Christ have put on Christ. There is neither Jew nor Greek, there is neither slave nor free, *there is no male and female*, for you are all one in Christ Jesus" (Gal. 3:27–28). Paul is here underlining the fact that no class of people, such as the Jewish people who had come from Abraham by physical descent or the freedmen who had greater economic and legal power, could claim special status or privilege in the church. Slaves should not think themselves inferior to free men or women, nor should the free think themselves superior to slaves. Jews should not think themselves superior to Greeks, nor should Greeks think themselves inferior to Jews. Similarly, Paul wants to ensure that men will not adopt some of the attitudes of the surrounding culture, or even some of the attitudes of first-century Judaism, and think that they have greater importance than women or are of superior value before God. Nor should women think themselves inferior or less important in the church. Men and women, Jews and Greeks, slaves and free—all are equal in importance and value to God and equal in membership in Christ's body, the church, for all eternity.

In practical terms, we must never think that there are any second-class citizens in the church. Whether someone is a man or woman, employer or employee, Jew or gentile, black or white, rich or poor, young or old, healthy or ill, strong or weak, attractive or unattractive, extremely intelligent or slow to learn, all are equally valuable to God and should be equally valuable to one another as well. This equality is an amazing and wonderful element of the Christian faith and sets Christianity apart from almost all religions and societies and cultures. The true dignity of godly manhood and womanhood can be fully realized only in obedience to God's redeeming wisdom as found in Scripture.

## C. DIFFERENCES IN ROLES

### 1. The Relationship between the Trinity and Male Headship in Marriage

Between the members of the Trinity there has been equality in importance, personhood, and deity throughout all eternity. But there have also been differences in roles

---

(Acts 4:24). Peter "went to the house of Mary, the mother of John whose other name was Mark, where *many were gathered together* and were praying" (Acts 12:12).

between the members of the Trinity.[5] God the Father has always been the Father and has always related to the Son as a Father relates to his Son. Though all three members of the Trinity are equal in power and in all other attributes, the Father has a greater authority. He has a leadership role among all the members of the Trinity that the Son and Holy Spirit do not have. In creation, the Father speaks and initiates, but the work of creation is carried out through the Son and sustained by the continuing presence of the Holy Spirit (Gen. 1:1–2; John 1:1–3; 1 Cor. 8:6; Heb. 1:2). In redemption, the Father sends the Son into the world, and the Son comes and is obedient to the Father and dies to pay for our sins (Luke 22:42; Phil. 2:6–8). After the Son has ascended into heaven, the Holy Spirit comes to equip and empower the church (John 16:7; Acts 1:8; 2:1–36). The Father did not come to die for our sins, nor did the Holy Spirit. The Father was not poured out on the church at Pentecost in new covenant power, nor was the Son. Each member of the Trinity has distinct roles or functions. Differences in roles and authority between the members of the Trinity are thus completely consistent with equal importance, personhood, and deity.

If human beings are to reflect the character of God, then we would expect some similar differences in roles among human beings, even with respect to the most basic of all differences among human beings, the difference between male and female. And this is certainly what we find in the biblical text.

Paul makes this parallel explicit when he says, "I want you to understand that the head of every man is Christ, *the head of a wife is her husband*, and *the head of Christ is God*" (1 Cor. 11:3).[6] Here is a distinction in authority that may be represented as in figure 22.1.

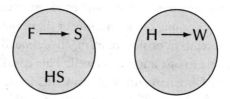

**Equality and Differences in the Trinity Are Reflected
in Equality and Differences in Marriage**
*Figure 22.1*

---

5. See chapter 14, pp. 299–301, on role differences among the members of the Trinity.

6. Some have suggested that the word *head* in 1 Cor. 11:3 means "source" and has nothing to do with authority in marriage. For example, when referring to Paul's use of the word *head* to say that "the head of every man is Christ, the head of a wife is her husband, and the head of Christ is God" (1 Cor. 11:3), Gordon Fee says that "Paul's understanding of the metaphor, therefore, and almost certainly the only one the Corinthians would have grasped, is 'head' as 'source,' especially 'source of life'" (*The First Epistle to the Corinthians*, NIC [Grand Rapids: Eerdmans, 1987], 503).

Similarly, the statement, "Men, Women and Biblical Equality," published as an advertisement in *CT*, April 9, 1990, 36–37, says, "The husband's function as 'head' is to be understood as self-giving love and service within this relationship of

Just as God the Father has authority over the Son, though the two are equal in deity, so in a marriage, the husband has authority over the wife, though they are equal in personhood. In this case, the man's role is like that of God the Father, and the woman's role is parallel to that of God the Son. They are equal in importance, but they have different roles.

## 2. Indications of Distinct Roles Before the Fall

But were these distinctions between male and female roles part of God's original creation, or were they introduced as part of the punishment of the fall? When God told Eve, "Your desire shall be contrary to your husband, but *he shall rule over you*" (Gen. 3:16), was that the time when Eve began to be subject to Adam's authority?

The idea that differences in authority were introduced only after there was sin in the world has been advocated by several writers such as Aida B. Spencer[7] and Gilbert Bilezikian.[8] Bilezikian says, "Because it resulted from the Fall, the rule of Adam over Eve is viewed as satanic in origin, no less than is death itself."[9] However, if we examine the text of the creation narrative in Genesis, we see several indications of *differences in role* between Adam and Eve *even before there was sin in the world.*

**a. Adam Was Created First, Then Eve.** The fact that God first created Adam, then after a period of time created Eve (Gen. 2:7, 18–23), suggests that God saw Adam as having a leadership role in his family. No such two-stage procedure is mentioned for any of the animals God made, but here it seems to have a special purpose. The creation of Adam first is consistent with the Old Testament pattern of "primogeniture," the idea that the firstborn in any generation in a human family has leadership in the family for that generation. The right of primogeniture is assumed throughout the Old Testament text, even when at times because of God's special purposes the birthright is sold or otherwise transferred to a younger person (Gen. 25:27–34; 35:23; 38:27–30; 49:3–4; Deut. 21:15–17; 1 Chron. 5:1–2). The "birthright" belongs to the firstborn son and is his unless special circumstances intervene to change that fact.[10] The fact

---

mutual submission (Eph. 5:21–33; Col. 3:19; 1 Pet. 3:7)" (p. 1, para. 11). Thus they understand "head" to mean "source" (of love and service), not "authority over."

For a response to this interpretation and a discussion of reasons why the word *head* here must mean "authority over" not "source," see (1) Wayne Grudem, *Evangelical Feminism and Biblical Truth: An Analysis of Over 100 Disputed Questions* (Sisters, OR: Multnomah, 2004), 201–11; (2) Grudem, "Does *Kephalē* ('Head') Mean 'Source' or 'Authority Over' in Greek Literature? A Survey of 2,336 Examples," *TrinJ* 6 (Spring 1985): 38–59; (3) Grudem, "The Meaning of *Kephalē* ('Head'): A Response to Recent Studies," *TrinJ* 11 (Spring 1990): 3–72 (repr., *Recovering Biblical Manhood and Womanhood*, 425–68); and especially (4) "The Meaning of *kephalē* ("head"): An Analysis of New Evidence, Real and Alleged," *JETS* 44, no. 1 (March, 2001): 25–65. See also (5) Joseph Fitzmyer, "Another Look at *Kephalē* in 1 Cor. 11:3," *NTS* 35 (1989): 503–11. Over

fifty examples of the word *kephalē* in ancient Greek literature have demonstrated that where person A is called the "head" (*kephalē*) of person(s) B, in every single case, person A is in a position of authority over person B. No counterexamples have ever been found in ancient Greek literature.

7. Spencer, *Beyond the Curse*, 2nd ed. (Nashville: Nelson, 1985), 20–42.

8. Bilezikian, *Beyond Sex Roles* (Grand Rapids: Baker, 1985), 21–58.

9. Ibid., 58.

10. Some object that this would not be appropriate in the Genesis narrative, for animals were created before Adam, and this would give animals the authority to rule over humans (so Bilezikian, *Beyond Sex Roles*, 257n13). But this objection fails to understand that the principle of primogeniture only occurs among human beings and is, in fact, limited to those in the same family. (Bilezikian raises other objections [pp. 255–57]

that we are correct in seeing a purpose of God in creating Adam first, and that this purpose reflects an abiding distinction in the roles God has given to men and women, is supported by 1 Timothy 2:13, where Paul uses the fact that "Adam was formed first, then Eve" as a reason for restricting some distinct governing and teaching roles in the church to men.

**b. Eve Was Created as a Helper for Adam.** Scripture specifies that God made Eve for Adam, not Adam for Eve. God said, "It is not good that the man should be alone; *I will make him a helper fit for him*" (Gen. 2:18). Paul sees this as significant enough to base a requirement for differences between men and women in worship on it. He says, "Neither was man created for woman, but *woman for man*" (1 Cor. 11:9). This should not be taken to imply lesser importance, but it does indicate that there was a difference in roles from the beginning.

Recently some writers have denied that the creation of Eve as a helper fit for Adam signals any difference in role or authority because the word *helper* (Heb. *'ezer*) is often used in the Old Testament of someone who is greater or more powerful than the one who is being helped.[11] In fact, the word *helper* is used in the Old Testament of God himself who helps his people. But the point is that whenever someone "helps" someone else, whether in the Hebrew Old Testament or in our modern-day use of the word *help*, in the specific task in view the person who is helping is occupying a subordinate or inferior position with regard to the person being helped. That is true even when I "help" a young boy in my neighborhood to fix his bicycle—it is his responsibility, and his task, and I am only giving some assistance as needed; it is not my responsibility. David Clines concludes that this is the case throughout the Hebrew Old Testament:

> What I conclude, from viewing all of the occurrences in the Hebrew Bible, is that though superiors may help inferiors, strong may help weak, gods may help humans, in the act of helping they are being "inferior." That is to say, they are subjecting themselves to a secondary, subordinate position. Their help may be necessary or crucial, but they are assisting some task that is someone else's responsibility. They are not actually doing the task themselves, or even in cooperation, for there is different language for that. Being a helper is not a Hebrew way of being an equal.[12]

Another objection is that the Hebrew term translated "fit for" in Genesis 2:18 implies that Eve was actually superior to Adam because the term really means "in front of."[13] But Raymond C. Ortlund correctly points out that the Hebrew term cannot mean "superior

but fails to deal with the New Testament endorsement of this understanding of Gen. 2 in 1 Tim. 2:13.)

11. See Spencer, *Beyond the Curse*, 23–29.

12. David J. A. Clines, "What Does Eve Do to Help? and Other Irredeemably Androcentric Orientations in Genesis 1–3," paper, Society of Biblical Literature annual meeting, December 7, 1987, Boston, Massachusetts.

13. So Spencer, *Beyond the Curse*, 23–26. She says, "The Hebrew text even signifies that the woman is 'in front of' the man or 'over' him!" (p. 26).

to" or Psalm 119:168 would have the psalmist saying to God, "All my ways are *superior* to you"! It simply means "corresponding to."[14]

**c. Adam Named Eve.** The fact that Adam gave names to all the animals (Gen. 2:19–20) indicated Adam's authority over the animal kingdom, because in Old Testament thought the right to name someone implied authority over that person (this is seen both when God gives names to people such as Abraham and Sarah, and when parents give names to their children). Since a Hebrew name designated the character or function of someone, Adam was specifying the characteristics or functions of the animals he named. Therefore when Adam named Eve by saying, "She shall be called Woman, because she was taken out of Man" (Gen. 2:23), it indicated a leadership role on his part as well.[15] This is true before the fall, where Adam names his wife "Woman," and it is true after the fall as well, when "the man called his wife's name Eve, because she was the mother of all living" (Gen. 3:20).[16] Some have objected that Adam doesn't really name Eve before the fall.[17] But certainly calling his wife "Woman" (Gen. 2:23), just as he called all the living creatures by their names (Gen. 2:19–20), is giving her a name. The fact that mothers sometimes give their children names in the Old Testament does not contradict the idea of name-giving as representing authority, since both mothers and fathers have parental authority over their children.

**d. God Named the Human Race "Man," Not "Woman."** The fact that God named the human race "man" rather than "woman" or some gender-neutral term was explained in chapter 21.[18] Genesis 5:2 specifies that "in the day when they were created" (NASB) God *"named them Man."* The naming of the human race with a term that also referred to Adam in particular, or man in distinction from woman, suggests a leadership role belonging to the man. This is similar to the custom of a woman taking the last name of the man when she marries: it subtly signifies his headship in the family.

**e. The Serpent Came to Eve First.** Satan, after he had sinned, was attempting to distort and undermine everything that God had planned and created as good. It is likely that Satan (in the form of a serpent), in approaching Eve first, was attempting to institute a role reversal by tempting Eve to take the leadership in disobeying God (Gen. 3:1). This stands in contrast to the way God approached them, for when God spoke to them, he spoke to Adam first (Gen. 2:15–17; 3:9). Paul seems to have this role reversal in mind when he says, "Adam was not deceived, but the woman was deceived and became a transgressor" (1 Tim. 2:14). This at least suggests that Satan was trying to undermine the pattern of male leadership that God had established in the marriage by going first to the woman.

---

14. Ortlund, "Male-Female Equality," 103–4; cf. BDB, 617, 2a.

15. See the discussion in Ortlund, "Male-Female Equality," 102–3.

16. Gerhard von Rad says, "Let us remind ourselves once more that name-giving in the ancient Orient was primarily an exercise of sovereignty, of command" (*Genesis: A Commentary*, rev. ed. [Philadelphia: Westminster, 1972], 83).

17. See Bilezikian, *Beyond Sex Roles*, 260–61.

18. See pp. 563–65.

**f. God Spoke to Adam First After the Fall.** Just as God spoke to Adam on his own even before Eve was created (Gen. 2:15–17), so, after the fall, even though Eve had sinned first, God *came first to Adam* and called *him* to account for his actions: "But the LORD *God called to the man* and said to *him*, 'Where are you?'" (Gen. 3:9). God thought of Adam as the leader of his family, the one to be called to account first for what had happened in the family. It is significant that though this is after sin has occurred, it is before the statement to Eve, "He shall rule over you" in Genesis 3:16, where some writers today claim male headship in the family began.

**g. Adam, Not Eve, Represented the Human Race.** Even though Eve sinned first (Gen. 3:6), we are counted sinful because of Adam's sin, not because of Eve's sin. The New Testament tells us, *"In Adam* all die" (1 Cor. 15:22; cf. v. 49), and, "Many died through *one man's* trespass" (Rom. 5:15; cf. vv. 12–21). This indicates that God had given Adam headship or leadership with respect to the human race, a role that was not given to Eve.

**h. The Curse Brought a Distortion of Previous Roles, Not the Introduction of New Roles.** In the punishments God gave to Adam and Eve, he did not introduce new roles or functions but simply introduced pain and distortion into the functions they previously had. Thus, Adam would still have primary responsibility for tilling the ground and raising crops, but the ground would bring forth "thorns and thistles" and in the sweat of his face he would eat bread (Gen. 3:18, 19). Similarly, Eve would still have the responsibility of bearing children, but to do so would become painful: "In pain you shall bring forth children" (Gen. 3:16). Then God also introduced conflict and pain into the previously harmonious relationship between Adam and Eve. God said to Eve, "Your *desire* shall be *contrary to your husband*, but he shall rule over you" (Gen. 3:16). Susan Foh has effectively argued that the word translated "desire" (Heb. *teshûqāh*) in this verse implies a hostile disposition so that it means something like "desire to conquer." This indicates Eve would have a wrongful desire to usurp authority over her husband.[19] According to this understanding of the word *desire* (which is now reflected in the 2016 text of the ESV as well as the NLT, NET, and several commentaries), God is introducing

---

19. See Susan T. Foh, "What Is the Woman's Desire?" in *WTJ* 37 (1975): 376–83. Foh notes that this same Hebrew word occurs in a closely parallel statement just a few verses later, when God says to Cain, "Sin is crouching at the door, and its *desire* is contrary to you, but you must master it" (Gen. 4:7). The parallelism in the Hebrew text between the verses is quite remarkable: six words (counting conjunctions and prepositions) are exactly the same, and in the same order. Another four nouns and pronouns are in the same position and have the same function in the sentence, but they differ only because the parties involved are different. But in that sentence the "desire" that sin has for Cain is surely a *desire to overcome or conquer him*, as is evident from the image of an animal "crouching" at the door

waiting for him. The only other biblical example of this Hebrew word is found in Song of Sol. 7:10, where it's the context that indicates a positive sexual desire, not a hostile one. It is unlikely that the word means "sexual desire" in Gen. 3:16, for that did not begin with the fall, nor would it be part of God's curse. Foh does point to some parallels in related Semitic languages to support her argument. See also David Talley, "*teshûqāh*," in NIDOTTE, 4:341–42, who says that the word "emphasizes craving, desire, or urge," with a sexual sense in Song of Sol. 7:10, but "the desire to defeat a foe" in Gen. 4:7 and that a negative usage "seems probable" in Gen. 3:16 (p. 341). See also DCH 8:684 (entry II).

*a conflict into the relationship* between Adam and Eve and a desire on Eve's part to rebel against Adam's authority.

Concerning Adam, God told Eve, "He shall *rule* over you" (Gen. 3:16). Here the word "rule" (Heb. *māshal*) is a strong term usually used of monarchical governments, not generally of authority within a family.[20] The word certainly does not imply any "participatory" government by those who are ruled. Rather, it has nuances of dictatorial or absolute, uncaring use of authority, rather than considerate, thoughtful rule. It suggests harshness rather than kindness. The sense here is that Adam will misuse his authority *by ruling harshly* over his wife, again introducing pain and conflict into a relationship that was previously harmonious. It is not that Adam had no authority before the fall; it is simply that he will misuse it after the fall.

So in both cases, the curse brought a *distortion* of Adam's humble, considerate leadership and Eve's intelligent, willing submission to that leadership which existed before the fall.

**i. Redemption in Christ Reaffirms the Creation Order.** If the previous argument about the distortion of roles introduced at the fall is correct, then what we would expect to find in the New Testament is an undoing of the painful aspects of the relationship that resulted from sin and the curse. We would expect that in Christ, redemption would encourage wives not to rebel against their husbands' authority and would encourage husbands not to use their authority harshly. In fact, that is indeed what we do find: "Wives, *submit to your husbands*, as is fitting in the Lord. Husbands, *love your wives*, and do not be harsh with them" (Col. 3:18–19; cf. Eph. 5:22–33; Titus 2:5; 1 Peter 3:1–7). If it were a sinful pattern for wives to be subject to their husbands' authority, Peter and Paul would not have commanded it to be maintained in Christian marriages! They do not say, for example, "Encourage thorns to grow in your garden" or "Make childbirth as painful as possible" or "Stay alienated from God, cut off from fellowship with him!" The redemption of Christ is aimed at *removing* the results of sin and of the fall in every way: "The reason the Son of God appeared was to destroy the works of the devil" (1 John 3:8). *New Testament commands concerning marriage do not perpetuate any elements of the curse or any sinful behavior patterns*; they rather reaffirm the order and distinction of roles that were there from the beginning of God's good creation.

In terms of practical application, as we grow in maturity in Christ, we will grow to delight in and rejoice in the God-ordained and wisely created differences in roles within the human family. When we understand this biblical teaching, both men and women should be able to say in their hearts, "This is what God has planned, and it is beautiful and right, and I rejoice in the way he has made me and the distinct role he has given me." There is eternal beauty and dignity and rightness in this differentiation in roles both

---

20. See Deut. 15:6, "You shall rule over many nations, but they shall not rule over you"; Prov. 22:7, "The rich rules over the poor"; Judg. 14:4; 15:11 (of the Philistines ruling over Israel); also Gen. 37:8; Prov. 12:24, et al.

within the Trinity and within the human family. With no sense of "better" or "worse," and with no sense of "more important" or "less important," both men and women should be able to rejoice fully in the way they have been made by God.

## 3. Ephesians 5:21–33 and the Frequent Misunderstanding of "Mutual Submission"

In Ephesians 5 we read:

> Wives, submit to your own husbands, as to the Lord. For the husband is the head of the wife even as Christ is the head of the church, his body, and is himself its Savior. Now as the church submits to Christ, so also wives should submit in everything to their husbands. (Eph. 5:22–24)

While on the surface this would seem to confirm what we have argued above about the creation order for marriage, in recent years there has been some debate over the meaning of the verb "submit" (Gk. *hypotassō*) in this passage. Some interpreters have pointed to the preceding verse, "*submitting to one another* out of reverence for Christ" (Eph. 5:21), and claimed that the correct meaning of the entire passage is "mutual submission," meaning that both husband and wife should "submit to one another" by taking into consideration the needs and wants of the other person. Therefore, the point of the text is to say something like, "be thoughtful and considerate; act in love toward one another." If it is understood in this sense, then the text does not teach that a wife has any unique responsibility to submit to her husband's authority, because both husband and wife need to be considerate and loving toward one another. According to this view submission to an authority is not seen in this passage.[21]

However, this "mutual submission" interpretation is incompatible with every established meaning of the term *hypotassō*, which always implies a relationship of *one-directional submission to an authority*.[22] It is used elsewhere in the New Testament of the submission of Jesus to the authority of his parents (Luke 2:51), of demons being

---

21. See, for example, Bilezikian, *Beyond Sex Roles*, 154. See also I. Howard Marshall, "Mutual Love and Submission in Marriage: Colossians 3:18–19 and Ephesians 5:21–33," in *Discovering Biblical Equality*, ed. Ronald Pierce and Rebecca Groothuis (Downers Grove, IL: InterVarsity Press, 2004), 195–98.

22. It is significant that I. Howard Marshall, in arguing for mutual submission in Ephesians 5 and saying that "all believers should place themselves under other believers in this spirit of mutual humility," then admits that he advocates this interpretation "even if this is the only place where the verb *hypotasso-mai [hypotassō]* is so used" (ibid., 197). But this is an admission that no known example of this verb from anywhere in ancient Greek literature is consistent with the mutual submission interpretation. The danger of this process should be clear: once we begin to allow the Greek words in the New Testament to take new meanings for which *no supporting evidence* has ever been found in any of the other uses of the word in any ancient literature, and to do this in passages where a recognized meaning of the word makes sense in the context but we reject every recognized meaning that has been established by hundreds of other examples of the word, then we can make the New Testament say anything whatsoever.

"subject to" the disciples (Luke 10:17—clearly the meaning "act in love, be considerate" cannot fit here), of citizens being "subject to" government authorities (Rom. 13:1, 5; Titus 3:1; 1 Peter 2:13), of the universe being "subject to" Christ (1 Cor. 15:27; Eph. 1:22), of unseen spiritual powers being "subject to" Christ (1 Peter 3:22), of Christ being "subject to" God the Father (1 Cor. 15:28), of church members being "subject to" church leaders (1 Cor. 16:15–16 [see 1 Clem. 42:4]; 1 Peter 5:5), of wives being submissive to their husbands (Col. 3:18; Titus 2:5; 1 Peter 3:5; cf. Eph. 5:22, 24), of the church being "subject to" Christ (Eph. 5:24), of servants being "subject to" their masters (Titus 2:9; 1 Peter 2:18), and of Christians being "subject to" God (Heb. 12:9; James 4:7). *None of these relationships is ever reversed*—that is, husbands are never told to submit or "be subject to" (*hypotassō*) wives, nor the government to citizens, nor masters to servants, nor the disciples to demons, etc. In fact, the term is used outside the New Testament to describe the submission and obedience of soldiers in an army to those of superior rank.[23]

In addition, the following context defines what Paul means by "submitting to one another" in Ephesians 5:21: "submitting to one another" means "submitting *to others in the church who are in positions of authority over you*." This is explained by what follows: (1) wives are to submit to husbands (Eph. 5:22–24), but husbands are never told to submit to wives. In fact, Paul tells wives to "submit to *your own* husbands" (Eph. 5:22), not to everyone in the church or to all husbands. (2) Children are to submit to their parents (to "obey" them; Eph. 6:1–3), but parents are never told to submit to or to obey their children. (3) Servants are to be subject to ("obey") their masters, but not masters to servants.[24] Therefore, the idea of mutual submission (in the sense, "everyone should be submitting to everyone") is not a legitimate understanding of Ephesians 5:21.[25] Similarly, in Colossians 3:18–19 Paul says, "Wives, submit to your husbands, as is fitting in the Lord. Husbands, love your wives, and do not be harsh with them" (see also Titus 2:4–5; 1 Peter 3:1–7).

---

23. See Josephus, *War* 2.566, 578; 5.309; cf. the adverb in 1 Clem. 37:2; also *LSJ*, 1897, which defines *hypotassō* (passive) to mean "be obedient."

24. The misunderstanding of this verse has come about through an assumption that the term *one another* (*allēlous*) must be completely reciprocal (that it must mean "everyone to everyone"). Yet there are many cases where it does not take that sense but rather means "some to others": for example, in Rev. 6:4, "so that people should slay *one another*" means "so that some would kill others"; in Gal. 6:2, "bear *one another's* burdens" means not "everyone should exchange burdens with everyone else," but "some who are more able should help bear the burdens of others who are less able"; 1 Cor. 11:33, "when you come together to eat, wait for *one another*" means "those who are ready early should wait for others who are late"; etc. (cf. Luke 2:15; 21:1; 24:32). Similarly, both the following context and the meaning of *hypotassō* require that in Eph. 5:21 it means, "Those who are under authority should be submitting to others among you who have authority over them." (Regarding the objection that submission in marriage is like submission in slavery, and both are wrong, see chapter 47, p. 1169.)

25. Certainly, all Christians are to love one another and to be considerate of one another. If that is what is meant by "mutual submission," then there should be no objection to it— even though that idea is not taught in Eph. 5:21 but elsewhere in the Bible, using words other than *hypotassō*. But usually the phrase "mutual submission" is used in a different sense than this, a sense that obliterates any unique authority for the husband in a marriage.

## D. Note on Application to Marriage

If our analysis is correct, then there are some practical applications, particularly within marriage, and also with regard to relationships between men and women generally.

When husbands begin to act in selfish, harsh, domineering, or even abusive and cruel ways, they should realize that this is a result of sin, a result of the fall, and is destructive and contrary to God's purposes for them. To act this way will bring great destructiveness in their lives, especially in their marriages. Husbands must rather fulfill the New Testament commands to love their wives, honor them, be considerate of them, and put them first in their interests.

Similarly, when wives feel rebellious, resentful of their husband's leadership in the family, or when they compete with their husbands for leadership in the family, they should realize that this is a result of sin, a result of the fall. They should not act that way because to do so will bring destructive consequences to their marriages as well. A wife desiring to act in accordance with God's pattern should rather be submissive to her husband and agree that he is the leader in their home and rejoice in that.[26]

Once we have said this, we must realize that there are two other, nearly opposite, distortions of the biblical pattern that can occur. If tyranny by the husband and usurpation of authority by the wife are *errors of aggressiveness*, there are two other errors, *errors of passivity* or laziness. For a husband, the other extreme from being a domineering "tyrant" is to be entirely passive and to fail to take initiative in the family—in colloquial terms, to be a "wimp." In this distortion of the biblical pattern, a husband becomes so "considerate" of his wife that he allows her to make all the decisions and even agrees when she urges him to do wrong (note this behavior in Adam, Ahab, and Solomon, among others). Often such a husband is increasingly absent (either physically or emotionally) from the home and occupies his time almost exclusively with other concerns.

The corresponding error on the part of the wife, opposite of attempting to domineer or usurp authority over her husband, is becoming entirely passive, contributing nothing to the decision-making process of the family, and being unwilling to speak words of correction to her husband, even though he is doing wrong. Submission to authority does not mean being entirely passive and agreeing with everything that the person in authority says or suggests—it is certainly not that way when we are submissive to the authority of an employer or of government officials (we can differ with our government and still be subject to it) or even to the authority of the officers in a church (we can be subject to them even though we may disagree with some of their decisions). A wife can certainly be subject to the authority of her husband and still participate fully in the decision-making process of the family.

---

26. See the discussion of what submission means and what it does not mean in Grudem, "Wives Like Sarah, and the Husbands Who Honor Them: 1 Peter 3:1–7," in *Recovering Biblical Manhood and Womanhood*, 194–205.

Husbands, therefore, should aim for loving, considerate, thoughtful leadership in their families. Wives should aim for active, intelligent, joyful submission to their husbands' authority. In avoiding both kinds of mistakes and following a biblical pattern, husbands and wives will discover true biblical manhood and womanhood in all of their noble dignity and joyful complementarity, as God created them to be, and will thus reflect more fully the image of God in their lives.

## QUESTIONS FOR PERSONAL APPLICATION

1. If you are being honest about your feelings, do you think it is better to be a man or a woman? Are you happy with the gender God gave you or would you rather be a member of the opposite sex? How do you think God wants you to feel about that question?

2. Can you honestly say that you think members of the opposite sex are equally valuable in God's sight?

3. Before reading this chapter, have you thought of relationships in the family as reflecting something of the relationships between members of the Trinity? Do you think that is a helpful way of looking at the family? How does that make you feel about your own family relationships? Are there ways in which you might reflect God's character more fully in your own family?

4. How does the teaching of this chapter on differences in roles between men and women compare with some of the attitudes expressed in society today? If there are differences between what much of society is teaching and what Scripture teaches, do you think there will be times when it will be difficult to follow Scripture? What could your church do to help you in those situations?

5. Even apart from the questions of marriage or romantic involvement, do you think God intends us to enjoy times of fellowship with mixed groups of other Christian men and women? Why do you think God puts in our heart the desire to enjoy such fellowship? Does it also reflect something of the plurality of persons in the Trinity, together with the unity of God? Does this help you understand how it is important that unmarried people be included fully in the activities of the church? Do you think that in the past some religious groups have tended to neglect the importance of this or even wrongly to forbid such mixed fellowship among Christians? What are the dangers that should be guarded against in those situations, however?

6. If you are a husband, are you content with the role God has given you in your marriage? If you are a wife, are you content with the role God has given you in your marriage?

**Special Terms**

*difference in role*
*equality in personhood*
*mutual submission*
*primogeniture*

# BIBLIOGRAPHY

(For an explanation of this bibliography see the note on the bibliography to chapter 1, pp. 23–24. Complete bibliographical data may be found on pp. 1489–96.)

## SECTIONS IN EVANGELICAL SYSTEMATIC THEOLOGIES

The topic of this chapter has not commonly been treated as a distinct unit within systematic theologies. Therefore our usual arrangement of listings is abbreviated for this chapter.

*1. Anglican (Episcopalian)*
2001 . . . . . . . . Packer, 74–76

*2. Arminian (Wesleyan or Methodist)*
1983 . . . . . . . . Carter, 1:214–20
2002 . . . . . . . . Cottrell, 134–58
2013 . . . . . . . . Bird, 651–56
2013 . . . . . . . . Bray, 81–88

*3. Baptist*
1990–95 . . . . . Garrett, 1:485–96
2007 . . . . . . . . Akin, 353–61
2013 . . . . . . . . Erickson, 498–501

*4. Dispensational*
1947 . . . . . . . . Chafer, 7:233–34, 310–11
2017 . . . . . . . . MacArthur and Mayhue, 426–33

*5. Lutheran*
1917–24 . . . . . Pieper, 1:523–27
1934 . . . . . . . . Mueller, 209

*6. Reformed*
1679–85 . . . . . Turretin, *IET*, 1:464–65
1894 . . . . . . . . Shedd, 429
1906–11 . . . . Bavinck, *RD*, 2:576–78
2008 . . . . . . . . Van Genderen and Velema, 316, 368–74
2011 . . . . . . . . Horton, 391
2013 . . . . . . . . Frame, 792–97
2013 . . . . . . . . Culver, 240–47
2016 . . . . . . . . Allen and Swain, 165–93
2017 . . . . . . . . Barrett, 293–311
2019 . . . . . . . . Letham, 321–28

*7. Renewal (or charismatic/Pentecostal)*
1988 . . . . . . . . Williams, 1:203–6
1995 . . . . . . . . Horton, 236–38

## SECTIONS IN REPRESENTATIVE ROMAN CATHOLIC SYSTEMATIC THEOLOGIES

*1. Roman Catholic: Traditional*
1955 . . . . . . . . Ott, 460–73 (on matrimony)

*2. Roman Catholic: Post–Vatican II*
1980 . . . . . . . . McBrien, 2:848–54
212 . . . . . . . . . *CCC*, paragraph 369–73

## OTHER WORKS

[Works marked * agree in general with the viewpoint presented in this chapter, while those marked ** disagree.]

Alsford, S. E., and S. Mann. "Feminist Theology." In *NDT2*, 336–41.

Bacchiocchi, Samuele. *Women in the Church: A Biblical Study of the Role of Women in the Church.* Berrien Springs, MI: Biblical Perspectives, 1987.*

Bilezikian, Gilbert. *Beyond Sex Roles: What the Bible Says about a Woman's Place in Church and Family.* 3rd ed. Grand Rapids: Baker, 2006.**

Clark, Stephen B. *Man and Woman in Christ: An Examination of the Roles of Men and Women in Light of Scripture and the Social Sciences.* Ann Arbor, MI: Servant, 1980.*

Clouse, Bonnidell, and Robert G. Clouse, eds. *Women in Ministry: Four Views.* Downers Grove, IL: InterVarsity Press, 1989.

Colwell, J. E. "Anthropology." In *NDT1*, 28–30.

Conn, H. M. "Feminist Theology." In *NDT1*, 255–58.

Cooper, J. W. "Human Being." In *EDT3*, 403–7.

Cottrell, Jack. *Feminism and the Bible: An Introduction to Feminism for Christians.* Joplin, MO: College Press, 1992.*

Creegan, N. H. "Feminist Theology." In *EDT3*, 314–16.**

Creegan, Nicola Hoggard. *Living on the Boundaries: Evangelical Women, Feminism and the Theological Academy.* Downers Grove, IL: InterVarsity Press, 2005.**

Evans, Mary J. *Women in the Bible: An Overview of All the Crucial Passages on Women's Roles.* Downers Grove, IL: InterVarsity Press, 1983.**

Foh, Susan. *Women and the Word of God: A Response to Biblical Feminism.* Phillipsburg, NJ: Presbyterian and Reformed, 1980.*

Grenz, Stanley J., and Denise Muir Kjesbo. *Women in the Church: A Biblical Theology of Women in Ministry.* Downers Grove, IL: InterVarsity Press, 1995.**

Grudem, Wayne. *Evangelical Feminism: A New Path to Liberalism?* Wheaton, IL: Crossway, 2006.*

———. *Evangelical Feminism and Biblical Truth.* Wheaton, IL: Crossway, 2012.*

Grudem, Wayne, ed. *Biblical Foundations for Manhood and Womanhood.* Wheaton, IL: Crossway, 2002.*

Gundry, Patricia. *Heirs Together.* Grand Rapids: Zondervan, 1980.**

———. *Woman Be Free! The Clear Message of Scripture.* Grand Rapids: Zondervan, 1988.**

Hammett, John S. "Human Nature." In *A Theology for the Church*, edited by Daniel L. Akin et al., 353–61, 375–77, 388–93. Nashville: B&H, 2007.

House, H. Wayne. *The Role of Women in Ministry Today.* Nashville: Nelson, 1990.*

Hurley, James. *Man and Woman in Biblical Perspective.* Leicester: Inter-Varsity Press; Grand Rapids: Zondervan, 1981.*

Jepsen, Dee. *Women: Beyond Equal Rights.* Waco, TX: Word, 1984.*

Jewett, Paul K. *Man as Male and Female.* Grand Rapids: Eerdmans, 1975.**

Kassian, Mary A. *Women, Creation and the Fall.* Westchester, IL: Crossway, 1990.*

———. *The Feminist Gospel: The Movement to Unite Feminism with the Church.* Wheaton, IL: Crossway, 1992.*

Keener, C. S. "Man and Woman." In *DPL*, 583–92.**

———. "Woman and Man." In *DLNT*, 1205–15.**

Knight, George W., III. *The Role Relationship of Men and Women: New Testament Teaching.* Chicago: Moody Publishers, 1985.*

Kroeger, C. C. "Women in the Early Church." In *DLNT*, 1215–22.**

Lee-Barnewall, Michelle. *Neither Complementarian nor Egalitarian: A Kingdom Corrective to the Evangelical Gender Debate.* Grand Rapids: Baker Academic, 2016.

Mickelsen, Alvera, ed. *Women, Authority, and the Bible.* Downers Grove, IL: InterVarsity Press, 1986.**

Neuer, Werner. *Man and Woman in Christian Perspective.* Translated by Gordon Wenham. Westchester, IL: Crossway, 1991.*

Noble, T. A. "Anthropology." In *NDT2*, 39–42.

Ortlund, R. C., Jr. "Man and Woman." In *NDBT*, 650–54.*

Payne, Philip B. *Man and Woman, One in Christ: An Exegetical and Theological Study of Paul's Letters.* Grand Rapids: Zondervan, 2009.**

Perriman, Andrew. *Speaking of Women.* Leicester: Inter-Varsity Press, 1998.**

Pierce, Ronald W., and Rebecca Merrill Groothuis, eds. *Discovering Biblical Equality: Complementarity without Hierarchy.* Downers Grove, IL: InterVarsity Press, 2004.**

Piper, John. *What's the Difference? Manhood and Womanhood Defined according to the Bible.* Westchester, IL: Crossway, 1990.*

———, and Wayne Grudem, eds. *Recovering Biblical*

*Manhood and Womanhood: A Response to Evangelical Feminism.* Westchester, IL: Crossway, 1991.*

Spencer, Aída Besançon. *Beyond the Curse: Women Called to Ministry.* Peabody, MA: Hendrickson, 1985.**

————, William Spencer, Steve Tracy, and Celestia Tracy. *Marriage at the Crossroads: Couples in Conversation about Discipleship, Gender Roles, Decision Making, and Intimacy.* Downers Grove, IL: InterVarsity Press, 2009.

Tucker, Ruth A., and Walter Liefeld. *Daughters of the Church: Women in Ministry from New Testament Times to the Present.* Grand Rapids: Zondervan, 1987.**

Van Leeuwen, Mary Stewart. *Gender and Grace: Love, Work and Parenting in a Changing World.* Leicester: Inter-Varsity Press; Downers Grove, IL: InterVarsity Press, 1990.**

Westfall, Cynthia Long. *Paul and Gender: Reclaiming the Apostle's Vision for Men and Women in Christ.* Grand Rapids: Baker Academic, 2016.

Williams, William C. "Sexuality, Human." In *BTDB*, 531–34.

Yang, Hongyi. *A Development Not a Departure: The Lacunae in the Debate of the Doctrine of the Trinity and Gender Roles.* Phillipsburg, NJ: P&R, 2018.*

## SCRIPTURE MEMORY PASSAGE

**Colossians 3:18–19:** Wives, submit to your husbands, as is fitting in the Lord. Husbands, love your wives, and do not be harsh with them.

## HYMN

### "Blest the Man that Fears Jehovah"

This hymn is an older paraphrase of Psalm 128 set to music. It speaks about the blessings of a family that walks in God's ways. (Use the tune of "Jesus Calls Us.")

*Blest the man that fears Jehovah,*
*    walking ever in his ways;*
*By thy toil thou shalt be prospered*
*    and be happy all thy days.*

*In thy wife thou shalt have gladness,*
*    She shall fill thy home with good,*
*Happy in her loving service*
*    and the joys of motherhood.*

*Joyful children, sons and daughters,*
*    shall about thy table meet,*
*Olive plants, in strength and beauty,*
*    full of hope and promise sweet.*

*Lo, on him that fears Jehovah*
*    shall this blessedness attend,*
*For Jehovah out of Zion*
*    shall to thee his blessing send.*

*Thou shalt see God's kingdom prosper*
*    all thy days, till life shall cease,*
*Thou shalt see thy children's children;*
*    on thy people, Lord, be peace.*

From *The Psalter*, 1912, from Psalm 128

# CONTEMPORARY WORSHIP SONG

### "The Lord Is My Salvation"

*The grace of God has reached for me*
*And pulled me from the raging sea,*
*And I am safe on this solid ground.*
*The Lord is my salvation.*

*I will not fear when darkness falls.*
*His strength will help me scale these walls.*
*I'll see the dawn of the rising sun.*
*The Lord is my salvation.*

*Chorus*
*Who is like the Lord our God,*
*Strong to save faithful in love?*
*My debt is paid and the victory won.*
*The Lord is my salvation.*

*My hope is hidden in the Lord.*
*He flow'rs each promise of His Word.*
*When winter fades I know spring will come,*
*The Lord is my salvation.*

*In times of waiting times of need,*
*When I know loss when I am weak,*
*I know His grace will renew these days.*
*The Lord is my salvation.*

*And when I reach the final day,*
*He will not leave me in the grave,*
*But I will rise He will call me home.*
*The Lord is my salvation.*

*Bridge*
*Glory be to God the Father.*
*Glory be to God the Son.*
*Glory be to God the Spirit.*
*The Lord is our salvation.*

Words by Jonas Myrin, Nathan Nockels,
Kristyn Getty, and Keith Getty[27]

# CHAPTER 23

# The Essential Nature of Man

*What does Scripture mean by "soul" and "spirit"?*
*Are they the same thing?*

## EXPLANATION AND SCRIPTURAL BASIS

### A. INTRODUCTION: TRICHOTOMY, DICHOTOMY, AND MONISM

How many parts are there to man?[1] Everyone agrees that we have physical bodies. Many people (both Christians and non-Christians) sense that they also have an immaterial part—a "soul" that will live on after their bodies die.

But here the agreement ends. Some people believe that in addition to "body" and "soul" we have a third part, a "spirit" that most directly relates to God. The view that man is made of three parts (*body, soul, and spirit*) is called *trichotomy*.[2] Though this has been a common view in popular evangelical Bible teaching, there are few scholarly defenses of it today. According to many trichotomists, man's *soul* includes his intellect, his emotions, and his will. They maintain that all people have such a soul, and that the different elements of the soul can either serve God or be yielded to sin. They argue that man's *spirit* is a higher faculty in man that comes alive when a person becomes a Christian. The spirit of a person then would be that part of him or her that most directly worships and prays to God (see John 4:24; Phil. 3:3).

Others have said that "spirit" is not a separate part of man but simply another term for "soul" and that both terms are used interchangeably in Scripture to talk about the immaterial part of man, the part that lives on after our bodies die. The view that man is made up of *two parts* (body and soul/spirit) is called *dichotomy*. Those who hold this view often agree that Scripture uses the word *spirit* (Heb. *rûach*; Gk. *pneuma*) more frequently when referring to our relationship to God, but such usage (they say) is not uniform, and the word *soul* is also used in all the ways that *spirit* can be used.

Primarily outside the realm of evangelical thought we find yet another view, the idea

---

1. See chapter 21, pp. 563–65, for an explanation of why I continue to use the word *man* as one legitimate way to refer to humanity or the human race as a whole, including both male and female persons.

2. For a defense of trichotomy, see Franz Delitzsch, *A System of Biblical Psychology*, trans. R. E. Wallis, 2nd ed. (Grand Rapids: Baker, 1966).

**600**

that man cannot exist at all apart from a physical body, and therefore there can be no separate existence for any "soul" after the body dies (although this view can allow for the resurrection of the whole person at some future time). The view that man is only one element, and that his body is the person, is called *monism*.[3] According to monism, the scriptural terms *soul* and *spirit* are just other expressions for the person himself, or for the person's life. This view has not generally been adopted by evangelical theologians because so many scriptural texts seem clearly to affirm that our souls or spirits live on after our bodies die (see Gen. 35:18: Rachel's "soul was departing (for she was dying)"; Ps. 31:5; Luke 23:43: "today you will be with me in paradise"; Luke 23:46; Acts 7:59: "Lord Jesus, receive my spirit"; Phil. 1:23–24; 2 Cor. 5:8; Heb. 12:23; Rev. 6:9; 20:4; see also chapter 42 on the intermediate state).

But the other two views continue to be held in the Christian world today. Although dichotomy has been held more commonly through the history of the church and is far more common among evangelical scholars today, trichotomy has also had many supporters.[4]

This chapter will support the dichotomist view that man is two parts, body and soul (or spirit), but we shall also examine the arguments for trichotomy.

## B. Biblical Data

Before asking whether Scripture views "soul" and "spirit" as distinct parts of man, we must at the outset make it clear that a frequent emphasis of Scripture is on the overall unity of man as created by God. When God made man, he "breathed into his nostrils the breath of life, and the man became a living creature" (Gen. 2:7). Here Adam is a unified person with body and soul living and acting together. This original harmonious and unified state of man will occur again when Christ returns and we are fully redeemed in our bodies as well as our souls to live with him forever (see 1 Cor. 15:51–54). Moreover, we are to grow in holiness and love for God in every aspect of our lives, in our bodies as well as in our spirits or souls (cf. 1 Cor. 7:34). We are to "cleanse ourselves from every defilement *of body and spirit*, bringing holiness to completion in the fear of God" (2 Cor. 7:1).

But once we have emphasized the fact that God created us to have a unity between body and soul and that every action we take in this life is an act of our whole person, involving to some extent both body and soul, then we can go on to point out that Scripture quite clearly teaches that there is an immaterial part of man's nature. And we can investigate what that part is like.

---

3. For further information, see Millard Erickson, *Christian Theology*, 3rd ed. (Grand Rapids: Baker, 2013), 524–27, and his notes regarding the view of J. A. T. Robinson.

4. See Louis Berkhof, *Systematic Theology* (Grand Rapids: Eerdmans, 1941), 191–92, for a survey of views held in the history of the church.

## 1. Scripture Uses *Soul* and *Spirit* Interchangeably

When we look at the usage of the biblical words translated "soul" (Heb. *nephesh*; Gk. *psychē*) and "spirit" (Heb. *rûach*; Gk. *pneuma*), it appears that they are sometimes used interchangeably. For example, in John 12:27, Jesus says, "Now is my *soul* troubled," whereas in a very similar context in the next chapter John says that Jesus was "troubled in his *spirit*" (John 13:21). Similarly, we read Mary's words in Luke 1:46–47: "My *soul* magnifies the Lord, and my *spirit* rejoices in God my Savior." This seems to be quite an evident example of Hebrew parallelism, the poetic device in which the same idea is repeated using different but synonymous words. This interchangeability of terms also explains why people who have died and gone to heaven or hell can be called either "spirits" (Heb. 12:23, "the *spirits* of the righteous made perfect"; also 1 Peter 3:19, "*spirits* in prison") or "souls" (Rev. 6:9, "the *souls* of those who had been slain for the word of God and for the witness they had borne"; 20:4, "the souls of those who had been beheaded for the testimony of Jesus").

However, there is at least one significant difference in usage between the words for soul and the words for spirit. The words for "soul" (Heb. *nephesh* and Greek *psychē*) can also be used, at times, to refer to the entire person,[5] as in "All the *persons* (Heb. *nephesh*) belonging to Jacob who came into Egypt . . . were 66 *persons* (Heb. *nephesh*) in all" (Gen. 46:26) or "Let every *person* (Gk. psychē) be subject to the governing authorities" (Rom. 13:1). The words for spirit (Heb. *ruach*; Gk. *pneuma*) are not used in this way.

## 2. Scripture Says That Either the Soul or the Spirit Departs at Death

When Rachel died, Scripture says, "Her *soul* was departing (for she was dying)" (Gen. 35:18). Elijah prays that the dead child's "soul" (Heb. *nephesh*) would come into him again (1 Kings 17:21 RSV), and Isaiah says that the Servant of the Lord "poured out his *soul* [Heb. *nephesh*] to death" (Isa. 53:12). In the New Testament God tells the rich fool, "This night your soul [Gk. *psychē*] is required of you" (Luke 12:20). On the other hand, sometimes death is viewed as the returning of the spirit to God. So David can pray, in words later quoted by Jesus on the cross, "Into your hand I commit my *spirit*" (Ps. 31:5; cf. Luke 23:46). At death, "the *spirit* returns to God who gave it" (Eccl. 12:7).[6] In the New Testament, when Jesus was dying, "he bowed his head and gave up his spirit"

---

5. Alan Gomes in fact argues that "soul" in Scripture nearly always refers to the whole person, "a living being in totality," while "spirit" refers not to the whole person but to the nonmaterial part of a person. See Alan Gomes, *40 Questions about Heaven and Hell* (Grand Rapids: Kregel, 2018), 46–50.

6. George Ladd, *A Theology of the New Testament* (Grand Rapids: Eerdmans, 1974), says that in the Old Testament neither soul nor spirit "is conceived of as a part of man capable of surviving the death of *basar* [flesh]" (459). This statement is not accurate in the light of the Old Testament verses just cited in this paragraph. Ladd's analysis in this section is heavily dependent on the work of W. D. Stacey, *The Pauline View of Man* (London: Macmillan, 1956), whom Ladd cites fourteen times on pp. 458–59. Yet Stacey himself thinks that death means extinction for human beings (Ladd, 463). Ladd also notes that Rudolf Bultmann vigorously denied that man has an invisible soul or spirit, but Ladd himself rejects Bultmann's view when dealing with the New Testament data (see pp. 460n17; 464).

(John 19:30), and likewise Stephen before dying prayed, "Lord Jesus, receive my spirit" (Acts 7:59).

In response to these passages, a trichotomist might argue that they are talking about different things, for when a person dies both his soul and his spirit do in fact go to heaven. But it should be noted that Scripture nowhere says that a person's "soul and spirit" departed or went to heaven or were yielded up to God. If soul and spirit were separate and distinct things, we would expect that such language would be affirmed somewhere, if only to assure the reader that no essential part of the person is left behind. Yet we find no such language. The biblical authors do not seem to care whether they say that the soul departs or the spirit departs at death, for both seem to mean the same thing.

We should also note that these Old Testament verses quoted above indicate that it is not correct, as some have claimed, to say that the Old Testament so emphasizes the unity of man that it has no conception of the existence of the soul apart from the body. Certainly several of these Old Testament passages imply that the authors recognize that a person continues to exist after his or her body dies.

### 3. Man Is Said to Be Either "Body and Soul" or "Body and Spirit"

Jesus tells us not to fear those who "kill the body but cannot kill the soul" but to "fear him who can destroy both soul and body in hell" (Matt. 10:28). Here the word *soul* clearly must refer to the part of a person that exists after death. It cannot mean "person" or "life," for it would not make sense to speak of those who "kill the body but cannot kill the person" or who "kill the body but cannot kill the life" unless there is some aspect of the person that lives on after the body is dead. Moreover, when Jesus talks about "soul and body," he seems quite clearly to be talking about the entire person even though he does not mention "spirit" as a separate component. The word *soul* seems to stand for the entire nonphysical part of man.

On the other hand, man is sometimes said to be "body and spirit." Paul wants the Corinthian church to deliver an erring brother to Satan "for the destruction of the flesh, so that his spirit may be saved in the day of the Lord" (1 Cor. 5:5). It is not that Paul has forgotten the salvation of the man's soul as well; he simply uses the word *spirit* to refer to the whole of the person's immaterial existence. Similarly, James says that "the body apart from the spirit is dead" (James 2:26), but he mentions nothing about a separate soul. Moreover, when Paul speaks of growth in personal holiness, he approves the woman who is concerned with "how to be holy in body and spirit" (1 Cor. 7:34) and suggests that this covers the whole of the person's life. Even more explicit is 2 Corinthians 7:1, where he says, "Let us cleanse ourselves from every defilement of body and spirit, bringing holiness to completion in the fear of God." Cleansing ourselves from defilement of the soul or the spirit covers the whole immaterial side of our existence (see also Rom. 8:10; 1 Cor. 5:3; Col. 2:5).

## 4. The Soul or the Spirit Can Sin

Those who hold to trichotomy will usually agree that the soul can sin since they think that the soul includes the intellect, the emotions, and the will. (We see the fact that our souls can sin implied in verses such as 1 Peter 1:22; Rev. 18:14.)

The trichotomist, however, generally thinks of the "spirit" as purer than the soul and, when renewed, as free from sin and responsive to the prompting of the Holy Spirit. This understanding (which sometimes finds its way into popular Christian preaching and writing) is not really supported by the biblical text. When Paul encourages the Corinthians to cleanse themselves "from every defilement of body and *spirit*" (2 Cor. 7:1), he clearly implies that there can be defilement (or sin) in our spirits. Similarly, he speaks of the unmarried woman who is concerned with how to be holy "in body and *spirit*" (1 Cor. 7:34). Other verses speak in similar ways. For example, the Lord hardened the "spirit" of Sihon the king of Heshbon (Deut. 2:30). Psalm 78 speaks of the rebellious people of Israel "whose *spirit* was not faithful to God" (Ps. 78:8). A "haughty *spirit*" goes before a fall (Prov. 16:18), and it is possible for sinful people to be "proud in spirit" (Eccl. 7:8). Isaiah speaks of those "who go astray in spirit" (Isa. 29:24). Nebuchadnezzar's "spirit was hardened so that he dealt proudly" (Dan. 5:20). The fact that "all the ways of a man are pure in his own eyes, but the LORD weighs the spirit" (Prov. 16:2) implies that it is possible for our spirits to be wrong in God's sight. Other verses imply a possibility of sin in our spirits (see Ps. 32:2; 51:10). Finally, the fact that Scripture approves of one "who *rules his spirit*" (Prov. 16:32) implies that our spirits are not simply the spiritually pure parts of our lives that are to be followed in all cases but that they can have sinful desires or directions as well.

## 5. Everything the Soul Is Said to Do, the Spirit Is Also Said to Do, and Vice Versa

Those who advocate trichotomy face a difficult problem defining clearly just what the difference is between the soul and the spirit (from their perspective). If Scripture gave clear support to the idea that our spirit is the part of us that directly relates to God in worship and prayer, while our soul includes our intellect (thinking), our emotions (feeling), and our will (deciding), then trichotomists would have a strong case. However, Scripture appears not to allow such a distinction to be made.

On the one hand, the activities of thinking, feeling, and deciding things are not said to be done by our souls only. Our spirits can also experience emotions, for example, as when Paul's "spirit was provoked within him" (Acts 17:16) or when Jesus was "troubled in his spirit" (John 13:21). It is also possible to have a "crushed spirit," which is the opposite of a "joyful heart" (Prov. 17:22).

Moreover, the functions of knowing, perceiving, and thinking are also said to be done by our spirits. For instance, Mark speaks of Jesus "perceiving [Gk. *epiginōskō*, 'knowing'] in his spirit" (Mark 2:8). When the Holy Spirit "bears witness with our spirit that we are children of God" (Rom. 8:16), our spirits receive and understand that witness, which is certainly a function of knowing something. In fact, our spirits seem to know our thoughts quite deeply, for Paul asks, "who knows a person's thoughts except the spirit of that person, which is in him?" (1 Cor. 2:11). (Cf. Isa. 29:24, speaking of those who now "go astray in spirit" but "will come to understanding.")

The point of these verses is not to say that the spirit rather than the soul feels and thinks things but that *soul* and *spirit* are both terms used of the immaterial side of people generally, and it is difficult to see any real distinction between the use of the terms.

In fact, we should not slip into the mistake of thinking that certain activities (such as thinking, feeling, or deciding things) are done by only one part of us. Rather, these activities are done by the whole person. When we think or feel things, certainly our physical bodies are involved at every point as well. Whenever we think we use the physical brain God has given us. Similarly, our brain and our entire nervous system are involved when we feel emotion, and sometimes those emotions are involved in physical sensations in other parts of our bodies. This is just to reemphasize what was said at the beginning of our discussion, that the overall focus of Scripture is primarily on man as a unity, with our physical bodies and the nonphysical part of our persons continually interacting with each other and functioning together as a unity.

On the other hand, trichotomists claim that our spirit is that element of us that relates most directly to God in worship and in prayer, but that does not seem to be borne out by Scripture. We often read about our *soul* worshiping God and relating to him in other kinds of spiritual activity. "To you, O LORD, I lift up my *soul*" (Ps. 25:1). "For God alone my *soul* waits in silence" (Ps. 62:1). "Bless the LORD, O my *soul*, and all that is within me, bless his holy name!" (Ps. 103:1). "Praise the LORD, O my soul!" (Ps. 146:1). "My soul magnifies the Lord" (Luke 1:46).

These passages indicate that our souls can worship God, praise him, and give thanks to him. Our souls can pray to God, as Hannah implies when she says, "I have been pouring out my soul before the LORD" (1 Sam. 1:15). In fact, the great commandment is to "love the LORD your God with all your heart and with all your soul and with all your might" (Deut. 6:5; cf. Mark 12:30). Our souls can long for God and thirst for him (Ps. 42:1, 2) and can "hope in God" (Ps. 42:5). Our souls can rejoice and delight in God, for David says, "My soul will rejoice in the LORD, exulting in his deliverance" (Ps. 35:9; cf. Isa. 61:10). The psalmist says, "My soul is consumed with longing for your rules at all times" (Ps. 119:20), and, "My soul keeps your testimonies; I love them exceedingly" (Ps. 119:167). There seems to be no area of life or relationship to God in which Scripture says our spirits are active rather than our souls. Both terms are used to speak of all of the aspects of our relationship to God.

However, it would be wrong, in the light of these passages, to suggest that only our souls (or spirits) worship God, for our bodies are involved in worship as well. We are a unity of body and soul/spirit. Our physical brains think about God when we worship and when we love him with all of our "minds" (Mark 12:30). David, longing to be in God's presence, can say, "My flesh faints for you, as in a dry and weary land where there is no water" (Ps. 63:1). Again, we read, "My heart and flesh sing for joy to the living God" (Ps. 84:2). It is obvious that when we pray aloud or sing praise to God, our lips and our vocal cords are involved, and sometimes worship and prayer in Scripture involves clapping of hands (Ps. 47:1) or lifting of hands to God (Pss. 28:2; 63:4; 134:2; 143:6; 1 Tim. 2:8). Moreover, the playing of musical instruments in praise to God is an act that involves our physical bodies as well as the physical materials of which the musical instruments are made (see Ps. 150:3–5). We worship him as whole persons.

In conclusion, Scripture does not seem to support any distinction between soul (when the word refers to the nonphysical part of a person) and spirit. There does not seem to be a satisfactory answer to the questions that we may address to a trichotomist, "What can the spirit do that the soul cannot do? What can the soul do that the spirit cannot do?"

## C. ARGUMENTS FOR TRICHOTOMY

Those who adopt the trichotomist position have appealed to a number of Scripture passages in support of it. We list here the ones that are most commonly used.

1. **1 Thessalonians 5:23.** "Now may the God of peace himself sanctify you completely, and may your whole *spirit and soul and body* be kept blameless at the coming of our Lord Jesus Christ." Does not this verse clearly speak of three parts to man?

2. **Hebrews 4:12.** "For the word of God is living and active, sharper than any two-edged sword, piercing to the *division of soul and of spirit*, of joints and of marrow, and discerning the thoughts and intentions of the heart." If the sword of Scripture divides soul and spirit, then are these not two separate parts of man?

3. **1 Corinthians 2:14–3:4.** This passage speaks of different kinds of people: those who are "of the flesh" (Gk. *sarkinos*, 1 Cor. 3:1), those who are "natural" (Gk. *psychikos*, lit. "soul-ish," 1 Cor. 2:14), and those who are "spiritual" (Gk. *pneumatikos*, 1 Cor. 2:15). Do not these categories suggest that there are different sorts of people, the non-Christians who are "of the flesh," "natural" Christians who follow the desires of their souls, and more mature Christians who follow the desires of their spirits? Would this not suggest that soul and spirit are different elements of our nature?

4. **1 Corinthians 14:14.** When Paul says, "If I pray in a tongue, my spirit prays but my mind is unfruitful" (1 Cor. 14:14), is he not implying that his mind does something different from his spirit, and would not this support the trichotomist's argument that our mind and our thinking are to be assigned to our souls, not to our spirit?

5. **The Argument from Personal Experience.** Many trichotomists say that they have a spiritual perception, a spiritual awareness of God's presence which affects them in a way that they know to be different from their ordinary thinking processes and different from their emotional experiences. They ask, "If I do not have a spirit that is distinct from my thoughts and my emotions, then what exactly is it that I feel that is different from my thoughts and my emotions, something that I can only describe as worshiping God in my spirit and sensing his presence in my spirit? Isn't there something in me that is more than just my intellect and my emotions and my will, and shouldn't this be called my spirit?"

6. **Our Spirit Is What Makes Us Different from Animals.** Some trichotomists argue that both humans and animals have souls, but maintain that it is the presence of a spirit that makes us different from animals.

7. **Our Spirit Is What Comes Alive at Regeneration.** Trichotomists also argue that when we become Christians our spirits come alive: "But if Christ is in you, although the body is dead because of sin, the Spirit is life because of righteousness" (Rom. 8:10).

Now we can consider the seven points given above.

## D. RESPONSES TO ARGUMENTS FOR TRICHOTOMY
## 1. 1 Thessalonians 5:23

The phrase "your whole spirit and soul and body" is by itself inconclusive. Paul could be simply piling up synonyms for emphasis, as is sometimes done elsewhere in Scripture. For example, Jesus says, "You shall love the Lord your God with all your *heart* and with all your *soul* and with all your *mind*" (Matt. 22:37). Does this mean that the soul is different from the mind or from the heart?[7] The problem is even greater in Mark 12:30: "You shall love the Lord your God with all your *heart* and with all your *soul* and with all your *mind* and with all your *strength*." If we go on the principle that such lists of terms tell us about more parts to man, then if we also add spirit to this list (and perhaps body as well), we would have five or six parts to man! But that is certainly a false conclusion. It is far better to understand Jesus as simply piling up roughly synonymous terms for emphasis to demonstrate that we must love God with all of our being.

Likewise, in 1 Thessalonians 5:23 Paul is not saying that soul and spirit are distinct entities, but simply that, whatever our immaterial part is called, he wants God to continue to sanctify us wholly to the day of Christ.

---

7. The "heart" in Scripture is an expression for the deepest, inmost thoughts and feelings of a person (see Gen. 6:5, 6; Lev. 19:17; Pss. 14:1; 15:2; 37:4; 119:10; Prov. 3:5; Acts 2:37; Rom. 2:5; 10:9; 1 Cor. 4:5; 14:25; Heb. 4:12; 1 Peter 3:4; Rev. 2:23, et al.).

## 2. Hebrews 4:12

This verse, which talks about the Word of God "piercing to the division of soul and of spirit, of joints and of marrow," is best understood in a way similar to 1 Thessalonians 5:23. The author is not saying that the Word of God can divide "soul *from* spirit," but he is using a number of terms (soul, spirit, joints, marrow, thoughts and intentions of the heart) that speak of the deep inward parts of our being that are not hidden from the penetrating power of the Word of God. If we wish to call these our "soul," then Scripture pierces into the midst of it and divides it and discovers its inmost intentions. If we wish to call this inmost nonphysical side of our being our "spirit," then Scripture penetrates into the midst of it and divides it and knows its deepest intentions and thoughts. Or if we wish to think metaphorically of our inmost being as hidden in our joints and in the marrow, then we can think of Scripture being like a sword that divides our joints or that pierces deeply into our bones and even divides the marrow in the midst of the bones.[8] In all of these cases the Word of God is so powerful that it will search out and expose all disobedience and lack of submission to God. In any case, soul and spirit are not thought of as separate parts; they are simply additional terms for our inmost being.

## 3. 1 Corinthians 2:14–3:4

Paul certainly distinguishes a person who is "natural" (*psychikos*) from one that is "spiritual" (*pneumatikos*) in 1 Corinthians 2:14–3:4. But in this context *spiritual* seems to mean "influenced by the Holy Spirit," since the entire passage is talking about the work of the Holy Spirit in revealing truth to believers. In this context, *spiritual* might almost be translated "Spiritual." But the passage does not imply that Christians have a spirit whereas non-Christians do not or that the spirit of a Christian is alive while the spirit of a non-Christian is not. Paul is talking not about different parts of man but about coming under the influence of the Holy Spirit.

## 4. 1 Corinthians 14:14

When Paul says, "My *spirit* prays but my mind is unfruitful," he means he does not understand the content of what he is praying. He does imply that there is a nonphysical component to his being, a spirit within him that can pray to God. But nothing in this verse suggests that he regards his spirit as different from his soul. Such a misunderstanding results only if it is assumed that "mind" is part of the soul—a trichotomist claim that, as we noted above, is very difficult to substantiate from Scripture. Paul probably could equally have said, "My soul prays but my mind is unfruitful."[9] The point is simply

---

8. Note that we do not divide joints *from* marrow, for joints are the places where bones meet, not the places where joints meet marrow.

9. However, it is much more characteristic of Paul's terminology to use the word *spirit* to talk about our relationship to

God in worship and in prayer. Paul does not use the word *soul* (Gk. *psychē*) very frequently (fourteen times, compared with 101 occurrences in the New Testament as a whole), and when he does, he often uses it simply to refer to a person's "life," or as a synonym for a person himself, as in Rom. 9:3; 13:1; 16:4;

that there is a nonphysical element to our existence that can at times function apart from our conscious awareness of how it is functioning.

## 5. The Argument From Personal Experience

Christians have a "spiritual perception," an inner awareness of the presence of God experienced in worship and in prayer. At times on this deep inward level, we can feel spiritually troubled or depressed or perhaps have a sense of the presence of hostile demonic forces. Often this perception is distinct from our conscious, rational thought processes. Paul realizes that at times his spirit prays but his mind does not understand (1 Cor. 14:14). But does inward spiritual perception occur in something other than what the Bible calls our "soul"? If we were using the vocabulary of Mary, we would be happy to say, "My soul magnifies the Lord" (Luke 1:46). David would say, "Bless the LORD, O my soul" (Ps. 103:1). Jesus would tell us to love God with all our soul (Mark 12:30). The apostle Paul uses the word *spirit*, but it is simply a difference in terminology and does not point to a different part of man. There is a spirit within us that can perceive things in the spiritual realm (note Rom. 8:16; also Acts 17:16), but we could just as well speak of it as our soul and mean the same thing, for Scripture uses both terms.

## 6. What Makes Us Different from Animals?

We have spiritual abilities that make us different from animals.[10] We are able to relate to God in worship and prayer, and we enjoy spiritual life in fellowship with God who is spirit. But we should not assume that we have a distinct element called "spirit" that allows us to do this, for with our minds we can love God, read and understand his words, and believe his Word to be true. Our souls can worship God and rejoice in him (see above). Our bodies will also be resurrected and live with God forever. Therefore we do not have to say that we have a part distinct from our souls and bodies that makes us different from animals, for our souls and bodies (including our minds) relate to God in ways animals never can. Rather, what makes us different from animals is the spiritual abilities that God has given to both our bodies and souls (or spirits).

The question of whether an animal has a soul depends on how we define *soul*. If we define *soul* to mean "the intellect, emotions, and will," then we will have to conclude that at least the higher animals have a soul. But if we define *soul* as we have in this chapter, to mean the immaterial element of our nature that relates to God (Ps. 103:1; Luke 1:46, et al.) and lives forever (Rev. 6:9), then animals do not have a soul. The fact that the Hebrew word *nephesh*, "soul," is sometimes used of animals (Gen. 1:21; 9:4) shows that the word can sometimes simply mean "life"; it does not mean that animals have the same kind of soul as man.[11]

---

Phil. 2:30. Use of the word *soul* to refer to the nonphysical side of man is more characteristic of the gospels, as well as many passages in the Old Testament.

10. See chapter 21, pp. 571–75, on the numerous differences between human beings and animals.

11. In fact, one passage even speculates about "the spirit of

## 7. Does Our Spirit Come Alive at Regeneration?

The human spirit is not something that is dead in an unbeliever but comes to life when someone trusts in Christ because the Bible talks about unbelievers having a spirit that is obviously alive but is in rebellion against God—whether Sihon, King of Heshbon (Deut. 2:30: the Lord "hardened his spirit"), Nebuchadnezzar (Dan. 5:20: "his spirit was hardened so that he dealt proudly"), or the unfaithful people of Israel (Ps. 78:8: their "spirit was not faithful to God"). Although some translations say, "Your spirits are alive because of righteousness" in Rom. 8:10 (RSV; the NASB and 1984 NIV are similar), this would apparently mean "alive to God," but it does not imply that our spirits were completely dead before, only that they were living out of fellowship with God and were dead in that sense. But most recent translation committees have rendered Romans 8:10 with a meaning similar to the ESV, "the Spirit is life," referring to the Holy Spirit, not our human spirits.[12] In the same way, we as whole persons were "dead" in "trespasses and sins" (Eph. 2:1), but we were made alive to God, and we now must consider ourselves "dead to sin and alive to God" (Rom. 6:11). It is not just that one part of us (called the spirit) has been made alive; we as whole persons are a "new creation" in Christ (2 Cor. 5:17).

## 8. Conclusion

Although the arguments for trichotomy do have some force, none of them provides conclusive evidence that would overcome the wide testimony of Scripture showing that the terms *soul* and *spirit* are frequently interchangeable and are in many cases synonymous.

We might also note the observation of Louis Berkhof on the origin of trichotomy:

> The tripartite conception of man originated in Greek philosophy, which conceived of the relation of the body and the spirit of man to each other after the analogy of the mutual relation between the material universe and God. It was thought that, just as the latter could enter into communion with each other only by means of a third substance or an intermediate being, so the former could enter into mutual vital relationships only by means of a third or intermediate element, namely, the soul.[13]

Some trichotomists today have a tendency to adopt a related error that also was found in Greek philosophy—the idea that the material world, including our bodies, is essentially evil and something to be escaped from. The danger is to say that the realm of the "spirit" is the only thing that is really important, with a resultant depreciation of the

the beast" in contrast with "the spirit of man," (Eccl. 3:21), but the context (vv. 18–22) is one expressing a worldly, cynical perspective that shows the vanity of life and argues that man is but a beast (v. 18): in the overall context of the book it is not clear that this is something the author is encouraging his readers to believe.

12. Several other translations also take this as a reference to

the Holy Spirit; see NRSV, NIV (2011), NET, CSV, NLT, KJV, NKJV. See also the arguments in Douglas Moo, *The Epistle to the Romans*, NIC (Grand Rapids: Eerdmans, 1996), 492; John Murray, *The Epistle to the Romans*, NIC, 2 vols. (Grand Rapids: Eerdmans, 1959, 1965), 1:289–91.

13. Berkhof, *Systematic Theology*, 191.

value of our physical bodies as created by God and "very good" (Gen. 1:31) and therefore as something to be presented to God in service for him (Rom. 12:1).

Trichotomy can also have an anti-intellectual tendency. If we think of the spirit as that element of us that relates most directly to God, and if we think that the spirit is something distinct from our intellect, emotions, and will (all of which belong to the soul, on a trichotomist view), we can easily fall into an anti-intellectual kind of Christianity that thinks that vigorous academic work is somehow "unspiritual"—a view that contradicts Jesus' command to love God with all our "mind" (Mark 12:30) and Paul's desire to "take every thought captive to obey Christ" (2 Cor. 10:5). Such a separation of the realm of the "spirit" from the realm of the intellect can too easily lead to a neglect of sound doctrine or of the need for extensive teaching and knowledge of the Word of God—in contradiction to Paul's goal that he would work among God's people to further both their "faith" and their "knowledge of the truth, which accords with godliness" (Titus 1:1; cf. v. 9). Similarly, if we think of our spirits as a distinct part of us that relates most directly to God, we can easily begin to neglect the role of Bible study and mature wisdom in making decisions, and place too much reliance on "spiritual" discernment in the realm of guidance, an emphasis that has, through the history of the church, led many zealous Christians astray into false teaching and unwise practices. Finally, trichotomy can subtly influence us to think that our emotions are not important or not really spiritual since they are thought to be part of our soul, not part of our spirit.

By contrast, if we hold to a view of dichotomy that upholds the overall unity of man, it will be much easier to avoid the error of depreciating the value of our intellects, emotions, or physical bodies. We will not think of our bodies as inherently evil or unimportant. Such a view of dichotomy within unity will also help us to remember that, in this life, there is a continual interaction between our body and our spirit, and that they affect each other: "A joyful heart is good medicine, but a crushed spirit dries up the bones" (Prov. 17:22).[14]

Moreover, a healthy emphasis on dichotomy within an overall unity reminds us that Christian growth must include all aspects of our lives. We are continually to "cleanse ourselves from every defilement of body and spirit, bringing holiness to completion in the fear of God" (2 Cor. 7:1). We are to be "increasing in the knowledge of God" (Col. 1:10), and our emotions and desires are to conform increasingly to the "desires of the Spirit" (Gal. 5:17), including an increase in godly emotions such as peace, joy, love,[15] and so forth (Gal. 5:22).

---

14. Although many passages of Scripture remind us that our bodies and our spirits do interact with each other and affect one another, Scripture does not tell us very much about how they interact. Berkhof wisely says, "Body and soul are distinct substances, which do interact, though their mode of interaction escapes human scrutiny and remains a mystery for us" (*Systematic Theology*, 195).

15. Some people will object that love is not merely an emotion, because it shows itself in actions and often we can will to perform loving actions toward others even when we do not feel love toward them. I agree with this, but there certainly is an emotional component to love—we can feel love toward others—and we would lose much of the richness of our relationship to God and others if we tried to deny this.

## E. Scripture Does Speak of an Immaterial Part of Man That Can Exist without His Body

A number of non-Christian philosophers have vigorously challenged the idea that man has any immaterial part at all such as a soul or spirit.[16] Perhaps partially in response to such criticism, some evangelical theologians have seemed hesitant to affirm dichotomy in human existence.[17] They have instead affirmed repeatedly that the Bible views man as a unity—which is true but should not be used to deny that Scripture also views man's unified nature as made up of two distinct elements. Of course, philosophers who assume that there is no spiritual realm beyond the reach of our sense perception, and who then proceed from that assumption to argue on the basis of our sense perception that there is no God or heaven or angels or demons will use similar arguments to deny the existence of a distinct soul within human beings. The perception that we have a spirit or soul belongs to the invisible, spiritual realm, and is, even in Christians, generally only a faint, subjective perception. Therefore, our knowledge of the existence of the human soul must be primarily based on Scripture, in which God clearly testifies to the existence of this immaterial aspect of our beings. The fact that this truth about our existence cannot be clearly known apart from the testimony of Scripture should not cause us to shrink from affirming it.

Scripture is very clear that we do have a soul that is distinct from our physical bodies, which not only can function somewhat independently of our ordinary thought processes (1 Cor. 14:14; Rom. 8:16) but also, when we die, is able to go on consciously acting and relating to God apart from our physical bodies. Jesus told the dying thief, "Today you will be with me in paradise" (Luke 23:43), even though, for both of them, their physical bodies were soon to die. When Stephen was dying, he knew he would immediately pass into the presence of the Lord, for he called out, "Lord Jesus, receive my *spirit*" (Acts 7:59). Paul does not fear death, for he says, "My desire is to depart and be with Christ, for that is far better" (Phil. 1:23). He contrasts that with remaining in this life, which he calls "to remain in the flesh" (Phil. 1:24). In fact, he says, "We would rather be *away from the body* and at home with the Lord" (2 Cor. 5:8), indicating a confidence that if he were to die physically his spirit would go into the Lord's presence and there enjoy fellowship with the Lord at once. The book of Revelation reminds us that "the *souls* of those who had been slain for the word of God and for the witness they had borne" (Rev. 6:9) are in heaven and are able to cry out to God to bring justice on the earth (Rev. 6:10; cf. also 20:4).

Therefore, although we must agree that Scripture views us in this life as a unity in which body and spirit act together as one person, there will also be a time between our death and the day Christ returns when our spirits will temporarily exist apart from our physical bodies.[18]

---

16. See the discussion in Erickson, *Christian Theology*, 530–36, with notes to some literature.

17. See, for example, G. C. Berkouwer, *Man: The Image of God*, trans. Dirk W. Jellma (Grand Rapids: Eerdmans, 1962), 194–233.

18. See further discussion of "the intermediate state" between death and Christ's return in chapter 41, pp. 998–1013.

## F. Where Do Our Souls Come From?

What is the origin of our individual souls? Two views have been common in the history of the church.

*Creationism* is the view that God creates a new soul for each person and sends it to that person's body sometime between conception and birth. *Traducianism*, on the other hand, holds that the soul as well as the body of a child are inherited from the baby's mother and father at the time of conception. Both views have had numerous defenders in the history of the church, with creationism eventually becoming the prevailing view in the Roman Catholic Church. Luther was in favor of traducianism, while Calvin favored creationism. On the other hand, there are some later Calvinist theologians such as A. H. Strong who favored traducianism (as do most Lutherans today). Creationism has had many modern evangelical advocates as well.[19]

There is one other popular view called *preexistentianism*, namely, that the souls of people exist in heaven long before their bodies are conceived in the wombs of their mothers and that God then brings the soul to earth to be joined with the baby's body as he or she grows in the womb. But this view is not held by either Roman Catholic or Protestant theologians and is dangerously akin to ideas of reincarnation found in Eastern religions. Moreover, there is no support for this view in Scripture. Before we were conceived in the wombs of our mothers, we simply did not exist. We were not. Of course, God looked forward into the future and knew that we would exist, but that is far removed from saying that we actually did exist at some previous time. Such an idea would tend to make us view this present life as transitional or unimportant and make us think of life in the body as less desirable and the bearing and raising of children as less important.

In favor of traducianism it may be argued that God created man in God's image (Gen. 1:27), and this includes a likeness to God in the amazing ability to "create" other human beings like ourselves. Therefore, just as the rest of the animal and plant world bears descendants "according to their kinds" (Gen. 1:24), so Adam and Eve also were able to bear children who were like themselves, with a spiritual nature as well as a physical body. This would imply that the spirits or souls of Adam and Eve's children were derived from Adam and Eve themselves. Moreover, Scripture sometimes can speak of descendants being somehow present in the body of someone in the previous generation, as when the author of Hebrews says that when Melchizedek met Abraham, "Levi . . . was still in the loins of his ancestor" (Heb. 7:10). Finally, traducianism could explain how the sins of the parents can be passed on to the children without making God directly responsible for the creation of a soul that is sinful or has a disposition that would tend toward sin.

However, the biblical arguments in favor of creationism seem to speak more directly to the issue and give quite strong support for this view. First, Psalm 127 says that

---

19. See, for example, Berkhof, *Systematic Theology*, 196–201.

"children are a heritage from the LORD, the fruit of the womb a reward" (Ps. 127:3). This indicates that not only the soul, but also the entire person of the child, including his or her body, is a gift from God. From this standpoint, it seems strange to think of the mother and father as being responsible by themselves for any aspect of the child's existence. Was it not the Lord who, David says, "knitted me together in my mother's womb" (Ps. 139:13)? Isaiah says that God is the one who "created the heavens," and the one who "spread out the earth," who gives breath (Heb. *nephesh*) to the people on it and spirit to those who walk in it" (Isa. 42:5). Zechariah talks of God as the one who "formed the spirit of man within him" (Zech. 12:1). The author of Hebrews speaks of God as "the Father of spirits" (Heb. 12:9). It is hard to escape the conclusion from these passages that God is the one who creates our spirits or souls.

Yet we must be cautious in drawing conclusions from this data. Our discussion of the doctrine of God's providence in chapter 16 demonstrated that God usually acts through secondary causes. God often brings about the results he seeks through the actions of human beings. Certainly this is so in the conception and bearing of children. Even if we say that God does create individual souls for human beings sometime before they are born, and that he is the one who allows children to be conceived and born, we must also recognize that apart from the physical union of man and woman in the conception of a child, no children are born! So we must not make the mistake of saying that the father and mother have no role in the creation of the child. Even if we say that God is the "Father of spirits" and the Creator of every human soul, just as he is the Maker and Creator of each of us, we must still also affirm that God carries out this creative activity through the amazing process of human procreation. Whether God involves the human mother and father to some degree in the process of the creation of a soul as well as of a physical body, is impossible for us to say. It is something that occurs in the invisible realm of the spirit, which we do not have information about except from Scripture. And on this point Scripture simply does not give us enough information to decide.

However, the arguments listed above in favor of traducianism must be said not to be very compelling ones. The fact that Adam and Eve bear children in their image (see Gen. 5:3) could suggest that children somehow inherit a soul from their parents, but it might also indicate that God gives an individually created soul to the child and that that soul is consistent with the hereditary traits and personality characteristics that God allowed the child to have through its descent from its parents. The idea that Levi was still in the body of Abraham (Heb. 7:10) is best understood in a representative or figurative sense, not a literal sense. Moreover, it is not simply Levi's soul that is talked about but Levi himself, as a whole person, including body and soul—yet Levi's body was certainly not physically present in any meaningful sense in Abraham's body, for there was no distinct combination of genes at that time that could be said to be Levi and no one else. Finally, since God brings about events in the physical world that are consistent with the voluntary activities of human beings, there does not seem to be any real theological difficulty in saying that God gives each child a human soul that has tendencies to sin that are similar to the tendencies found in the parents. In fact, we read in the Ten Commandments of God "visiting the iniquity of the fathers on the children to the third and the fourth generation of those who hate [him]" (Ex. 20:5), and quite apart from the question of the human soul, we know from human experience that children do in fact tend to imitate both the good and bad traits in their parents' lives, not only as a result of imitation but also because of hereditary disposition. For God to give each child a human soul that accords with the imitation of parents that we see in the lives of children would simply be an indication that God, in creating a human soul, acts consistently with the way he acts in relation to the human race in other matters as well.

In conclusion, it seems hard to avoid the testimony of Scripture to the effect that God actively creates each human soul, just as he is active in all the events of his creation. But the degree to which he allows the use of intermediate or secondary causes (that is, inheritance from parents) is simply not explained for us in Scripture. Therefore, it does not seem profitable for us to spend any more time speculating on this question.

## QUESTIONS FOR PERSONAL APPLICATION

1. In your Christian experience, are you aware that you are more than just a physical body, that you have a nonphysical part that might be called a soul or spirit? At what times do you especially become aware of the existence of your spirit? Can you describe what it is like to know the witness of the Holy Spirit with your spirit that you are God's child (Rom. 8:16), to have in your spirit a consciousness of God's presence (John 4:23; Phil. 3:3), to be troubled in your spirit (John 12:27; 13:21; Acts 17:16; 2 Cor. 2:13), to have your spirit worship God (Luke 1:47; Ps. 103:1), or to love God with all your soul (Mark 12:30)? By contrast, are there times when you feel spiritually dull or insensitive? Do you think that one aspect of Christian growth might include an increasing sensitivity to the state of your soul or spirit?

2. Before reading this chapter, did you hold to dichotomy or trichotomy? Now what is your view? If you have changed to an acceptance of dichotomy after reading this chapter, do you think you will have a higher appreciation for the activities of your body, your mind, and your emotions? If you hold to trichotomy, how can you guard against some of the dangers mentioned in this chapter?

3. When you are praying or singing praise to God, is it enough simply to sing or speak words, without being aware of what you are saying? Is it enough to be aware of what you are saying without really meaning it? If you really mean the words with your whole being, then what aspects of your person would be involved in genuine prayer and worship? Do you think you tend to neglect one or another aspect at times?

**Special Terms**

*creationism*

*dichotomy*

*monism*

*soul*

*spirit*

*traducianism*

*trichotomy*

4. Since Scripture encourages us to grow in holiness in our bodies as well as our spirits (2 Cor. 7:1), what specifically would it mean for you to be more obedient to that command?

# BIBLIOGRAPHY

(For an explanation of this bibliography see the note on the bibliography to chapter 1, pp. 23–24. Complete bibliographical data may be found on pp. 1489–96.)

## SECTIONS IN EVANGELICAL SYSTEMATIC THEOLOGIES

1. **Anglican (Episcopalian)**
   1882–92 . . . . . Litton, 113–16, 122–25
   2013 . . . . . . . . Bird, 662–65
   2013 . . . . . . . . Bray, 81–88

2. **Arminian (Wesleyan or Methodist)**
   1875–76 . . . . . Pope, 1:435–36
   1892–94 . . . . . Miley, 1:397–403
   1940 . . . . . . . . Wiley, 2:15–19
   1960 . . . . . . . . Purkiser, 215–20
   2002 . . . . . . . . Cottrell, 134–58

3. **Baptist**
   1887 . . . . . . . . Boyce, 194–212
   1907 . . . . . . . . Strong, 483–513
   1990–95 . . . . . Garrett, 1:469–84, 497–520
   2007 . . . . . . . . Akin, 340–408
   2013 . . . . . . . . Erickson, 475–93

4. **Dispensational**
   1947 . . . . . . . . Chafer, 2:144–99
   1949 . . . . . . . . Thiessen, 158–67
   1986 . . . . . . . . Ryrie, 193–200
   2002–2005 . . Geisler, 3:17–79

2017 . . . . . . . . MacArthur and Mayhue, 416–25

5. **Lutheran**
   1917–24 . . . . . Pieper, 1:94, 476–77
   1934 . . . . . . . . Mueller, 58, 184

6. **Reformed (or Presbyterian)**
   1679–85 . . . . . Turretin, *IET*, 1:477–88
   1871–73 . . . . . Hodge, 2:42–77, 78–91
   1878 . . . . . . . . Dabney, 317–21
   1906–11 . . . . . Bavinck, *RD*, 2:580–88
   1937–66 . . . . . Murray, *CW*, 2:23–33
   1938 . . . . . . . . Berkhof, 191–201
   2011 . . . . . . . . Horton, 379–405
   2013 . . . . . . . . Frame, 797–802
   2013 . . . . . . . . Culver, 258–81
   2016 . . . . . . . . Allen and Swain, 165–93
   2017 . . . . . . . . Barrett, 298–300
   2019 . . . . . . . . Letham, 337–47

7. **Renewal (or charismatic/Pentecostal)**
   1988–92 . . . . . Williams, 1:208–14
   1993 . . . . . . . . Menzies and Horton, 81–85
   1995 . . . . . . . . Horton, 238–53
   2008 . . . . . . . . Duffield and Van Cleave, 129–37

## SECTIONS IN REPRESENTATIVE ROMAN CATHOLIC SYSTEMATIC THEOLOGIES

1. **Roman Catholic: Traditional**
   1955 . . . . . . . . Ott, 96–101

## 2. Roman Catholic: Post–Vatican II

1980.........McBrien (no explicit
　　　　　　treatment)
2012.........*CCC*, paragraphs 362–68

## OTHER WORKS

Note: Several of the books listed in the bibliography for chapter 21, on the creation of man in the image of God, also have sections on the essential nature of man and the origin of the soul.

Allison, Gregg. *Historical Theology: An Introduction to Christian Doctrine; A Companion to Wayne Grudem's* Systematic Theology. Grand Rapids: Zondervan, 2011, 321–41.

Chamblin, J. K. "Psychology." In *DPL*, 765–75.

Colwell, J. E. "Anthropology." In *NDT1*, 28–30.

Cooper, J.W. "Human Being." In *EDT3*, 403–7.

Cooper, John W. *Body, Soul, and Life Everlasting: Biblical Anthropology and the Monism-Dualism Debate.* Grand Rapids: Eerdmans, 1989.

Delitzsch, F. *A System of Biblical Psychology.* Translated by R. E. Wallis. 2nd ed. Grand Rapids: Baker, 1966.

Gundry, Robert H. *Soma in Biblical Theology: With Emphasis on Pauline Anthropology.* Grand Rapids: Zondervan, 1987.

Hammett, John S. "Human Nature." In *A Theology for the Church*, edited by Daniel L. Akin et al., 382–86. Nashville: B&H, 2007.

Heard, J. B. *The Tripartite Nature of Man.* 5th ed. Edinburgh: T&T Clark, 1882.

Hoekema, Anthony A. "The Whole Person." In *Created in God's Image.* Grand Rapids: Eerdmans; Exeter: Paternoster, 1986, 203–26.

Johnston, P. S. "Humanity." In *NDBT*, 564–67.

Ladd, George Eldon. "The Pauline Psychology." In *A Theology of the New Testament*, 457–78. Grand Rapids: Eerdmans, 1974.

Laidlaw, John. *The Bible Doctrine of Man.* 2nd ed. Edinburgh: T&T Clark, 1905.

McDonald, H. D. "Man, Doctrine of." In *EDT1*, 676–80.

Moreland, J. P. *The Soul: How We Know It's Real and Why It Matters.* Chicago: Moody Publishers, 2014.

———, and Scott B. Rae. *Body and Soul: Human Nature and the Crisis in Ethics.* Downers Grove, IL: InterVarsity Press, 2000.

Murphy, Nancey. *Bodies and Souls, or Spirited Bodies?* Cambridge: Cambridge University Press, 2006.

Noble, T. A. "Anthropology." In *NDT2*, 39–42.

Pyne, Robert A. *Humanity and Sin: The Creation, Fall, and Redemption of Humanity.* Nashville: Word, 1999.

Schultz, Carl. "Person, Personhood." In *BTDB*, 602–4.

———. "Soul." In *BTDB*, 743–44.

———. "Spirit." In *BTDB*, 744–45.

Towner, Philip H. "Mind/Reason." In *BTDB*, 527–30.

Travis, S. H. "Psychology." In *DLNT*, 984–88.

Ury, M. William. "Will." In *BTDB*, 818–20.

Waltke, Bruce K. "Heart." In *BTDB*, 331–32.

Ward, W. E. "Dichotomy" In *EDT3*, 245.

———. "Trichotomy" In *EDT3*, 897.

Woodward, John B. *Man as Spirit, Soul, and Body: A Study of Biblical Psychology.* Pigeon Forge, TN: Grace Fellowship International, 2007.

# SCRIPTURE MEMORY PASSAGE

**2 Corinthians 7:1:** Since we have these promises, beloved, let us cleanse ourselves from every defilement of body and spirit, bringing holiness to completion in the fear of God.

# HYMN

## "Be Still, My Soul"

*Be still, my soul: the Lord is on thy side;*
  *Bear patiently the cross of grief or pain;*
*Leave to thy God to order and provide;*
  *In ev'ry change he faithful will remain.*
*Be still, my soul: thy best, thy heav'nly friend*
  *Through thorny ways leads to a joyful end.*

*Be still, my soul: thy God doth undertake*
  *To guide the future as he has the past.*
*Thy hope, thy confidence let nothing shake;*
  *All now mysterious shall be bright at last.*
*Be still, my soul: the waves and winds still know*
  *His voice who ruled them while he dwelt*
  *below.*

*Be still, my soul: when dearest friends depart,*
  *And all is darkened in the vale of tears,*
*Then shalt thou better know his love, his heart,*
  *Who comes to soothe thy sorrow and thy fears.*
*Be still, my soul: thy Jesus can repay*
  *From his own fullness all he takes away.*

*Be still, my soul: the hour is hast'ning on*
  *When we shall be forever with the Lord,*
*When disappointment, grief, and fear are gone,*
  *Sorrow forgot, love's purest joys restored.*
*Be still, my soul: when change and tears are past,*
  *All safe and blessed we shall meet at last.*

Author: Katharina Von Schlegel, 1752

# CONTEMPORARY WORSHIP SONG

## "You Are My All in All"

*You are my strength when I am weak.*
*You are the treasure that I seek.*
*You are my all in all.*

*Seeking You as a precious jewel,*
*Lord to give up I'd be a fool.*
*You are my all in all.*

*Chorus*
*Jesus Lamb of God, worthy is Your name.*
*Jesus Lamb of God, worthy is Your name.*

*Taking my sin my cross my shame,*
*Rising again I bless your name,*
*You are my all in all.*

*When I fall down you pick me up,*
*When I am dry You fill my cup,*
*You are my all in all.*

Words by Dennis Jernigan[20]

---

# CHAPTER 24

# Sin

*What is sin?*
*Where did it come from?*
*Do we inherit a sinful nature from Adam?*
*Do we inherit guilt from Adam?*

## EXPLANATION AND SCRIPTURAL BASIS

### A. THE DEFINITION OF SIN

The history of the human race as presented in Scripture is primarily a history of mankind in a state of sin and rebellion against God and of God's plan of redemption to bring many people back to him. Therefore, it is appropriate now to consider the nature of the sin that separates man from God.

We may define sin as follows: *sin is any failure to conform to the moral law of God in act, attitude, or nature.* Sin is here defined in relation to God and his moral law. Sin includes not only individual *acts*, such as stealing, lying, and committing murder, but also *attitudes* that are contrary to the attitudes God requires of us. We see this already in the Ten Commandments, which not only prohibit sinful actions but also wrong attitudes: "You shall not covet your neighbor's house; you shall not covet your neighbor's wife, or his male servant, or his female servant, or his ox, or his donkey, or anything that is your neighbor's" (Exod. 20:17). Here God specifies that a *desire* to steal or to commit adultery is also sin in his sight. The Sermon on the Mount prohibits sinful attitudes such as anger (Matt. 5:22) or lust (Matt. 5:28). Paul lists attitudes such as jealousy, anger, and selfishness (Gal. 5:20) as works of the flesh opposed to desires of the Spirit (Gal. 5:20). A life that is pleasing to God is one that has moral purity not only in its actions but also in its desires of the heart. In fact, the greatest commandment of all requires that our heart be filled with an attitude of love for God: "You shall love the Lord your God with all your heart and with all your soul and with all your mind and with all your strength" (Mark 12:30).

The definition of sin given above specifies that sin is a failure to conform to God's moral law not only in *action* and in *attitude* but also in our *moral nature*. Our very nature, the internal character that is the essence of who we are as persons, can also be sinful. Before we were redeemed by Christ, not only did we do sinful acts and have sinful attitudes, we were also sinners by nature. So Paul can say that "while *we were still sinners,*

Christ died for us" (Rom. 5:8) and that previously we "were *by nature* children of wrath, like the rest of mankind" (Eph. 2:3). Even asleep, an unbeliever, though not committing sinful actions or actively nurturing sinful attitudes, is still a sinner in God's sight; he or she still has a sinful nature that does not conform to God's moral law.

Other definitions of the essential character of sin have been suggested. Probably the most common definition is to say that the essence of sin is selfishness.[1] However, such a definition is unsatisfactory because (1) Scripture itself does not define sin this way. (2) Much self-interest is good and approved by Scripture, as when Jesus commands us to "lay up for yourselves treasures in heaven" (Matt. 6:20), when we seek to grow in sanctification and Christian maturity (1 Thess. 4:3), and even when we come to God through Christ for salvation. God certainly appeals to the self-interest of sinful people when he says, "Turn back, turn back from your evil ways, for why will you die, O house of Israel?" (Ezek. 33:11). To define the essential character of sin as selfishness will lead many people to think that they should abandon all desire for their own personal benefit, which is certainly contrary to Scripture.[2] (3) Much sin is not selfishness in the ordinary sense of the term—people can show *selfless* devotion to a false religion or to secular and humanistic educational or political goals that are contrary to Scripture, yet these would not be due to "selfishness" in any ordinary sense of the word. Hatred of God, idolatry, and unbelief are not generally due to selfishness, but they are very serious sins. (4) Such a definition could suggest that there was wrongdoing or sinfulness even on God's part, since God's highest goal is to seek his glory (Isa. 42:8; 43:7, 21; Eph. 1:12).[3] But such a conclusion is clearly wrong.

It is far better to define sin in the way Scripture does, in relationship to God's law and his moral character. John tells us that "sin is lawlessness" (1 John 3:4). When Paul seeks to demonstrate the universal sinfulness of mankind, he appeals to the law of God, whether the written law given to the Jew (Rom. 2:17–29) or the unwritten law that operates in the consciences of gentiles who, by their behavior, "show that the work of the

---

1. See, for example, A. H. Strong, *Systematic Theology* (Valley Forge, PA: Judson, 1907), 567–73. However, Strong defines *selfishness* in a very specific way that is different from the ordinary sense of the term—that is, self-interest especially at the expense of other persons. Strong regards *selfishness* as "that choice of self as the supreme end which constitutes the antithesis of supreme love to God" (567) and as "a fundamental and positive choice of preference of self instead of God, as the object of affection and the supreme end of being" (572). By thus defining *selfishness* in relationship to God, specifically as the opposite of love for God, and as the opposite of "love for that which is most characteristic and fundamental in God, namely, his holiness" (567), Strong has actually made *selfishness* approximately equivalent to our definition (lack of conformity to the moral law of God), especially in the area of attitude (which, he explains, results in actions). When Strong defines *selfishness* in this unusual way, his definition is not really inconsistent with

Scripture, for he is just saying that sin is the opposite of the great commandment to love God with all our heart. The problem with this definition, however, is that he uses the word *selfishness* in a way in which it is not commonly understood in English, and therefore his definition of sin is frequently open to misunderstanding. Our discussion in this section is not objecting to sin as selfishness in the unusual sense given by Strong but rather in the way the term *selfishness* is ordinarily understood.

2. Of course, selfishness that seeks our own good at the expense of others is wrong, and that is what is meant when Scripture tells us to "do nothing from selfish ambition or conceit, but in humility count others more significant than yourselves" (Phil. 2:3). Yet the distinction between selfishness in the wrong sense and scripturally enlightened self-interest is unclear in the minds of many people.

3. See discussion of God's jealousy, p. 245.

law is written on their hearts" (Rom. 2:15). In each case their sinfulness is demonstrated by their lack of conformity to the moral law of God.

Finally, we should note that this definition emphasizes the seriousness of sin. We realize from experience that sin is harmful to our lives, that it brings pain and destructive consequences to us and to others affected by it. But to define sin as failure to conform to the moral law of God is to say that sin is more than simply painful and destructive—it is also *wrong* in the deepest sense of the word. Sin is directly opposite to all that is good in the character of God, and just as God necessarily and eternally delights in himself and in all that he is, so God necessarily and eternally hates sin. It is, in essence, the contradiction of the excellence of his moral character. It contradicts his holiness, and he must hate it.

## B. THE ORIGIN OF SIN

Where did sin come from? How did it come into the universe? First, we must clearly affirm that God did not sin. God is not to be blamed for sin. It was human beings who sinned, and it was angels who sinned, and in both cases they did so by willful, voluntary choice. To blame God for sin would be blasphemy against the character of God: "His work is perfect, for all his ways are justice. A God of faithfulness and without iniquity, just and upright is he" (Deut. 32:4). Abraham asks with truth and force in his words, "Shall not the Judge of all the earth do what is just?" (Gen. 18:25). And Elihu rightly says, "Far be it from God that he should do wickedness, and from the Almighty that he should do wrong" (Job 34:10). In fact, it is impossible for God even to desire to do wrong: "God cannot be tempted with evil, and he himself tempts no one" (James 1:13).

Yet we must guard against an opposite error: it would be wrong for us to say there is an eternally existing evil power in the universe similar or equal to God in power. To say this would affirm what is called an ultimate "dualism," the existence of two equally ultimate powers, one good and the other evil.[4] Also, we must never think that sin surprised, challenged, or overcame God in his omnipotent and providential control over the universe. Therefore, even though we must never say that God sinned or that he is to be blamed for sin, we must also affirm that God, who "works all things according to the counsel of his will" (Eph. 1:11), who "does according to his will among the host of heaven and among the inhabitants of the earth; and none can stay his hand or say to him, 'What have you done?'" (Dan. 4:35), ordained that sin would come into the world, even though he does not delight in it and even though he ordained that it would come about through the voluntary choices of moral creatures.[5]

Even before the disobedience of Adam and Eve, sin was present in the angelic world

---

4. See discussion of dualism in chapter 15, pp. 345–46.

5. See chapter 16, pp. 428–37, for further discussion of God's providence in relationship to evil. God is "not a God who delights in wickedness" (Ps. 5:4) but one whose "soul hates the wicked and the one who loves violence" (Ps. 11:5), so that God certainly does not take pleasure in sin; nonetheless, for his own purposes, and in a way that still remains largely a mystery to us, God ordained that sin would come into the world.

with the fall of Satan and demons.[6] But with respect to the human race, the first sin was that of Adam and Eve in the garden of Eden (Gen. 3:1–19). Their eating of the fruit of the tree of the knowledge of good and evil is in many ways typical of sin generally. First, their sin struck at the basis for knowledge, for it gave a different answer to the question, "What is true?" Whereas God had said that Adam and Eve would die if they ate from the tree (Gen. 2:17), the serpent said, "You will not surely die" (Gen. 3:4). Eve decided to doubt the veracity of God's word and conduct an experiment to see whether God spoke truthfully.

Second, their sin struck at the basis for moral standards, for it gave a different answer to the question, "What is right?" God had said that it was morally right for Adam and Eve not to eat from the fruit of that one tree (Gen. 2:17). But the serpent suggested that it would be right to eat of the fruit, and that in eating it Adam and Eve would become "like God" (Gen. 3:5). Eve trusted her own evaluation of what was right and what would be good for her rather than allowing God's words to define right and wrong. She "saw that the tree was good for food, and that it was a delight to the eyes, and that the tree was to be desired to make one wise," and therefore she "took of its fruit and ate" (Gen. 3:6).

Third, their sin gave a different answer to the question, "Who am I?" The correct answer was that Adam and Eve were creatures of God, dependent on him and always to be subordinate to him as their Creator and Lord. But Eve and then Adam succumbed to the temptation to "be like God" (Gen. 3:5), thus attempting to put themselves in the place of God.

It is important to insist on the historical truthfulness of the narrative of the fall of Adam and Eve. Just as the account of the creation of Adam and Eve is tied in with the rest of the historical narrative in the book of Genesis,[7] so also this account of the fall of man, which follows the history of man's creation, is presented by the author as straightforward, narrative history. Moreover, the New Testament authors look back on this account and affirm that "sin came into the world through one man" (Rom. 5:12) and insist that "the judgment following one trespass brought condemnation" (Rom. 5:16) and that "the serpent deceived Eve by his cunning" (2 Cor. 11:3; cf. 1 Tim. 2:14). The serpent was, no doubt, a real, physical serpent that was talking because of the empowerment of Satan speaking through it (cf. Gen. 3:15 with Rom. 16:20; also Num. 22:28–30; Rev. 12:9; 20:2).

Finally, we should note that all sin is ultimately irrational. It really did not make sense for Satan to rebel against God in the expectation of being able to exalt himself above God. Nor did it make sense for Adam and Eve to think that there could be any gain in disobeying the words of their Creator. These were foolish choices. The persistence of Satan in rebelling against God even today is still a foolish choice, as is the decision on the

---

6. See discussion of the sin of angels in chapter 20, esp. pp. 533–35.

7. See also chapter 15, pp. 368–70, on the need to insist on the historicity of Adam and Eve as specific persons.

part of any human being to continue in a state of rebellion against God. It is not the wise man but "the fool" who "says in his heart, 'There is no God'" (Ps. 14:1). It is the "fool" in the book of Proverbs who recklessly indulges in all kinds of sins (see Prov. 10:23; 12:15; 14:7, 16; 15:5; 18:2, et al.). Though people sometimes persuade themselves that they have good reasons for sinning, when examined in the cold light of truth on the last day, it will be seen in every case that sin ultimately just does not make sense.

## C. The Doctrine of Inherited Sin

How does the sin of Adam affect us?[8] Scripture teaches that we inherit sin from Adam in two ways.

### 1. Inherited Guilt: We Are Counted Guilty Because of Adam's Sin

Paul explains the effects of Adam's sin in the following way: "Therefore . . . sin came into the world through one man, and death through sin, and so death spread to all men because *all sinned*" (Rom. 5:12). The context shows that Paul is not talking about actual sins that people commit every day of their lives, for the entire paragraph (Rom. 5:12–21) is taken up with the comparison between Adam and Christ. And when Paul says, "so [Gk. *houtōs*, "thus, in this way"; that is, through Adam's sin] death spread to all men because all sinned," he is saying that through the sin of Adam "all sinned."[9]

This idea, that "all sinned" means that God thought of us all as having sinned *when Adam disobeyed*, is further indicated by the next two verses, where Paul says, "Sin indeed was in the world before the law was given, but sin is not counted where there is no law. Yet death reigned from Adam to Moses, even over those whose sinning was not like the transgression of Adam, who was a type of the one who was to come" (Rom. 5:13–14). Paul points out that from the time of Adam to the time of Moses, people did not have God's written laws. Though their sins were "not counted" (as infractions of the law), they still died. The fact that they died is very good proof that God counted people guilty on the basis of Adam's sin.

The idea that *God counted us guilty because of Adam's sin* is further affirmed in Romans 5:18–19: "Therefore, as one trespass led to condemnation for all men, so one

---

8. I have used the phrase *inherited sin* rather than the more common designation *original sin* because the phrase *original sin* seems so easily to be misunderstood to refer to Adam's first sin rather than to the sin that is ours as a result of Adam's fall (traditionally the technical meaning). *Inherited sin* is much more immediately understandable and less subject to misunderstanding. Some may object that, technically speaking, we do not "inherit" guilt because it is directly imputed to us by God and does not come to us through inheritance from our parents as does the tendency toward sinful actions (traditionally called *original pollution*, and here termed *inherited corruption*). But the fact that our legal guilt is inherited directly from Adam and

not through a line of ancestors does not make it any less inherited: the guilt is ours because it belonged to our first father, Adam, and we inherit it from him.

9. The aorist indicative verb *hēmarton* in the historical narrative indicates a completed past action. Here Paul is saying that something happened and was completed in the past, namely, that "all sinned." But it was not true that all people had actually committed sinful actions at the time that Paul was writing, because some had not even been born yet, and many others had died in infancy before committing any conscious acts of sin. So Paul must be meaning that when Adam sinned, God considered it true that all people sinned in Adam.

act of righteousness leads to justification and life for all men. For as *by the one man's disobedience the many were made sinners*, so by the one man's obedience the many will be made righteous." Paul says explicitly that through the trespass of one man "many were made [Gk. *katestathēsan*, also an aorist indicative, here indicating completed past action] sinners." When Adam sinned, God thought of all who would descend from Adam as sinners. Though we did not yet exist, God, looking into the future and knowing that we would exist, began thinking of us as those who were guilty like Adam. This is also consistent with Paul's statement that "while we were still sinners Christ died for us" (Rom. 5:8). Of course, some of us did not even exist when Christ died. But God nevertheless *regarded us as sinners* in need of salvation.

The conclusion to be drawn from these verses is that all members of the human race were represented by Adam in the time of testing in the garden of Eden. As our representative, Adam sinned, and God counted us guilty as well as Adam. God counted Adam's guilt as belonging to us, and since God is the ultimate judge of all things in the universe, and since his thoughts are always true, Adam's guilt *does in fact belong to us*. (A technical term that is sometimes used in this connection is *impute*, meaning "to think of as belonging to someone, and therefore to cause it to belong to that person." God rightly *imputed* Adam's guilt to us.)

Sometimes the doctrine of inherited sin from Adam is termed the doctrine of "original sin." As explained above,[10] I have not used this expression. If this term is used, it should be remembered that the sin spoken of does not refer to Adam's first sin but to the guilt and tendency to sin with which we are born. It is "original" in that it comes from Adam, and it is also original in that we have it from the beginning of our existence as persons, but *it is still our sin, not Adam's sin, that is meant*. Parallel to the phrase "original sin" is the phrase "original guilt." This is that aspect of inherited sin from Adam that we have been discussing above, namely, the idea that we inherit the guilt from Adam.

When we first confront the idea that we have been counted guilty because of Adam's sin, our tendency is to protest because it seems unfair. We did not actually decide to sin, did we? Then how can we be counted guilty? Is it just for God to act this way?

In response, three things may be said: (1) Everyone who protests that this is unfair has also voluntarily committed many actual sins for which God also holds us guilty. These will constitute the primary basis of our judgment on the last day, for God "will render to each one *according to his works*" (Rom. 2:6), and "the wrongdoer will be paid back *for the wrong he has done*" (Col. 3:25). (2) Moreover, some have argued that if any one of us were in Adam's place, we also would have sinned as he did, and our subsequent rebellion against God demonstrates that. I think this is probably true, but it does not seem to be a conclusive argument, for it assumes too much about what would or would

---

10. See n8.

not happen. Such uncertainty may not help very much to lessen someone's sense of unfairness.

(3) The most persuasive answer to the objection is to point out that if we think it is unfair for us to be represented by Adam, then we should also think it is unfair for us to be represented by Christ and to have his righteousness imputed to us by God. For the procedure that God used was the same, and that is exactly Paul's point in Romans 5:12–21: "As by the one man's disobedience the many were made sinners, so by the one man's obedience the many will be made righteous" (Rom. 5:19). Adam, our first representative sinned—and God counted us guilty. But Christ, the representative of all who believe in him, obeyed God perfectly—and God counted us righteous. That is simply the way in which God set up the human race to work. God regards the human race as an organic whole, a unity, represented by Adam as its head. And God also thinks of the new race of Christians, those who are redeemed by Christ, as an organic whole, a unity represented by Christ as head of his people.

Not all evangelical theologians, however, agree that we are counted guilty because of Adam's sin. Some, especially Arminian theologians, think this to be unfair of God and do not believe that it is taught in Romans 5.[11] However, evangelicals of all persuasions do agree that we receive *a sinful disposition or a tendency to sin* as an inheritance from Adam, a subject we shall now consider.

## 2. Inherited Corruption: We Have a Sinful Nature Because of Adam's Sin

In addition to the legal guilt that God imputes to us because of Adam's sin, we also inherit a sinful nature because of Adam's sin. This inherited sinful nature is sometimes simply called "original sin" and sometimes more precisely called "original pollution." I have used instead the term *inherited corruption* because it seems to express more clearly the specific idea in view.

David says, "Behold, I was brought forth *in iniquity*, and *in sin* did my mother conceive me" (Ps. 51:5). Some have mistakenly thought that the sin of David's mother is in view here, but this is incorrect, for the entire context has nothing to do with David's mother. David is confessing his sin throughout this section. He says,

> Have mercy on *me*, O God . . .
>> blot out *my* transgressions.
> Wash *me* thoroughly from *my* iniquity . . .
>> I know *my* transgressions. . . .
> Against you . . . have *I* sinned. (Ps. 51:1–4)

---

11. See, for example, the thorough discussion in H. Orton Wiley, *Christian Theology*, 3 vols. (Kansas City, MO: Beacon Hill, 1941–49), 3:109–40.

David is so overwhelmed with the consciousness of his sin that as he looks back on his life he realizes that he was sinful from the beginning. As far back as he can remember, he realizes that he has had a sinful nature. Further, when he was born or "brought forth" from his mother's womb, he was "*brought forth* in iniquity" (Ps. 51:5). Even before he was born, he had a sinful disposition: he affirms that at the moment of conception he had a sinful nature, for "in sin did my mother *conceive* me" (Ps. 51:5). Here is a strong statement of the inherent tendency to sin that attaches to our lives from the very beginning. A similar idea is affirmed in Psalm 58:3: "The wicked are estranged from the womb; they go astray from birth, speaking lies."

Therefore, our nature includes a disposition to sin so that Paul can affirm that before we were Christians we "were *by nature* children of wrath, like the rest of mankind" (Eph. 2:3). Anyone who has raised children can give experiential testimony to the fact that we are all born with a tendency to sin. Children do not have to be taught how to do wrong; they discover that by themselves. What we have to do as parents is to teach them how to do right, to "bring them up in the discipline and instruction of the Lord" (Eph. 6:4).

This inherited tendency to sin does not mean that human beings are all as bad as they could be. The constraints of civil law, the expectations of family and society, and the conviction of human conscience (Rom. 2:14–15) all provide restraining influences on the sinful tendencies in our hearts. Therefore, by God's "common grace" (that is, by his undeserved favor that is given to all human beings), people have been able to do much good in the areas of education, scientific and technological progress, the development of civilization, the development of beauty and skill in the arts, the development of just laws, and general acts of human benevolence and kindness to others.[12] In fact, the more Christian influence there is in a society in general, the more clearly the influence of "common grace" will be seen in the lives of unbelievers as well. But in spite of the ability to do good in many senses of that word, our inherited corruption, our tendency to sin, which we received from Adam, means that as far as God is concerned we are not able to do anything that pleases him. This may be seen in two ways.

**a. In Our Natures We Totally Lack Spiritual Good before God.** It is not just that some parts of us are sinful and others are pure. Rather, *every part of our being* is affected by sin—our intellects, our emotions and desires, our hearts (the center of our desires and decision-making processes), our goals and motives, and even our physical bodies. Paul says, "I know that nothing good dwells in me, that is, in my flesh" (Rom. 7:18), and "To the defiled and unbelieving, nothing is pure; but both their minds and their consciences are defiled" (Titus 1:15). Moreover, Jeremiah tells us that "the heart is deceitful above all things, and desperately sick; who can understand it?" (Jer. 17:9). In these passages Scripture is not denying that unbelievers have good thoughts or motives in any sense

---

12. See chapter 31, pp. 803–12, on common grace.

(such as truthfulness, fairness, kindness, courage, mercy, joy, etc.), but it is saying that in God's infinitely holy eyes these thoughts and desires are still tainted by sin and lack a pure devotion to God. No part of our life is completely pure before God.[13]

**b. In Our Actions We Are Totally Unable to Do Spiritual Good before God.** This idea is related to the previous one. Not only do we as sinners lack any spiritual good in ourselves, but we also lack *the ability to do anything* that will in itself please God and *the ability to come to God* in our own strength. Paul says that "those who are in the flesh *cannot please God*" (Rom. 8:8). Moreover, in terms of bearing fruit for God's kingdom and doing what pleases him, Jesus says, "Apart from me you can do nothing" (John 15:5). In fact, unbelievers are not pleasing to God, if for no other reason, simply because their actions do not proceed from faith in God or from love to him, and "without faith it is impossible to please him" (Heb. 11:6). When Paul's readers were unbelievers, he tells them, "You were dead in the trespasses and sins in which you once walked" (Eph. 2:1–2). Unbelievers are in a state of bondage or enslavement to sin because "everyone who practices sin is a slave to sin" (John 8:34). Though from a human standpoint people might be able to do much good, Isaiah affirms that "all our righteous deeds are like a polluted garment" (Isa. 64:6; cf. Rom. 3:9–20). Unbelievers are not even able to understand the things of God correctly, for the "natural person does not accept the things of the Spirit of God, for they are folly to him, and he is not able to understand them because they are spiritually discerned" (1 Cor. 2:14). Nor can we come to God in our own power, for Jesus says, "No one can come to me unless the Father who sent me draws him" (John 6:44).

But if we have a total inability to do any spiritual good in God's sight, then do we still have any freedom of choice? Certainly those who are outside of Christ do still make *voluntary choices*—that is, they decide what they want to do, then they do it. In this sense there is still a kind of "freedom" in the choices that people make.[14] Yet because of their inability to do good and to escape from their fundamental rebellion against God, and because of their fundamental preference for sin, unbelievers do not have freedom in the most important sense of freedom—that is, the freedom to do what is pleasing to God.

The application to our lives is quite evident: if God gives anyone a desire to repent and trust in Christ, he or she should not delay and should not harden his or her heart (cf. Heb. 3:7–8; 12:17). This ability to repent and desire to trust in God is not naturally ours but is given by the prompting of the Holy Spirit, and it will not last forever. "Today, if you hear his voice, do not harden your hearts" (Heb. 3:15).

---

13. This total lack of spiritual good and inability to do good before God has traditionally been called "total depravity," but I will not use the phrase here because it is easily subject to misunderstanding. It can give the impression that no good *in* *any sense* can be done by unbelievers, a meaning that is certainly not intended by that term or by this doctrine.

14. See discussion of the question of free will in chapter 16, pp. 437–39.

## D. Actual Sins in Our Lives

### 1. All People Are Sinful before God

Scripture in many places testifies to the universal sinfulness of mankind. "They have all turned aside; together they have become corrupt; there is none who does good, not even one" (Ps. 14:3). David says, "No one living is righteous before you" (Ps. 143:2). And Solomon says, "There is no one who does not sin" (1 Kings 8:46; cf. Prov. 20:9).

In the New Testament, Paul has an extensive argument in Romans 1:18–3:20 showing that all people, both Jews and Greeks, stand guilty before God. He says, "All, both Jews and Greeks, are under sin, as it is written: 'None is righteous, no, not one'" (Rom. 3:9–10). He is certain that "all have sinned and fall short of the glory of God" (Rom. 3:23). James, the Lord's brother, admits, "We all stumble in many ways" (James 3:2), and if he, as a leader and an apostle[15] in the early church, could admit that he made many mistakes, then we also should be willing to admit that of ourselves. John, the beloved disciple, who was especially close to Jesus, said, "If we say we have no sin, we deceive ourselves, and the truth is not in us. If we confess our sins, he is faithful and just to forgive us our sins and to cleanse us from all unrighteousness. If we say we have not sinned, we make him a liar, and his word is not in us" (1 John 1:8–10).[16]

### 2. Does Our Ability Limit Our Responsibility?

Pelagius, a popular Christian teacher active in Rome about AD 383–410 and then later (until AD 424) in Palestine, taught that God holds man responsible only for those things that man is *able* to do. Since God warns us to do good, therefore, we must have the ability to do the good that God commands. The Pelagian position rejects the doctrine of "inherited sin" (or "original sin") and maintains that sin consists only in separate sinful acts.[17]

---

15. See n27 in chapter 3, p. 50, on whether James the Lord's brother was an apostle.

16. Some popular explanations of this passage deny that v. 8 applies to all Christians. This position is taken in order to say that some Christians can be perfectly free from sin in this life, if they reach the state of perfect sanctification. According to this view, v. 8 ("If we say we have no sin, we deceive ourselves, and the truth is not in us") applies to Christians before they reach the stage of sinless perfection. The next sentence, talking about our confession and God's cleansing us from "all unrighteousness," includes the process of dealing with that past sin and having it forgiven. Then the last sentence (v. 10) does include those who have obtained the state of sinless perfection—they do not any longer need to say that they have sin in the present in their lives but simply have to admit that they had sinned in the past. For them it is true, "If we say we have not sinned, we make him a liar" (1 John 1:10).

But this explanation is not persuasive because John writes the first sentence (v. 8) in the present tense, and it is something

that is true of all Christians at all times. John does not write, "If we say while we are still immature Christians that we have no sin, we deceive ourselves." Nor does he say (as this view would hold), "If we say, before we have reached the state of sinless perfection, that we have no sin, we deceive ourselves." Rather, near the end of his life, writing a general letter to all Christians, including those who have grown in maturity in Christ for decades, John says in no uncertain terms something that he expects to be true of all Christians to whom he writes: "If we say we have no sin, we deceive ourselves, and the truth is not in us." This is a clear statement that applies to all Christians as long as they are in this life. If we say that it does not apply, "we deceive ourselves."

17. Pelagianism was more fundamentally concerned with the question of salvation, holding that man can take the first and the most important steps toward salvation on his own, apart from God's intervening grace. Pelagianism was condemned as a heresy at the Council of Carthage on May 1, AD 418.

However, the idea that we are responsible before God only for what we are able to do is contrary to the testimony of Scripture, which affirms both that we "were *dead* in the trespasses and sins" in which we once walked (Eph. 2:1) and thus unable to do any spiritual good and also that we are all guilty before God. Moreover, if our responsibility before God were limited by our ability, then extremely hardened sinners, who are in great bondage to sin, could be less guilty before God than mature Christians who were striving daily to obey him. And Satan himself, who is eternally able to do only evil, would have no guilt at all—surely an incorrect conclusion.

The true measure of our responsibility and guilt is not our own ability to obey God but the absolute perfection of God's moral law and his own holiness (which is reflected in that law). "You therefore must be perfect, as your heavenly Father is perfect" (Matt. 5:48).

### 3. Are Infants Guilty before They Commit Actual Sins?

Some maintain that Scripture teaches an "age of accountability" before which young children are not held responsible for sin and are not counted guilty before God.[18] However, the passages noted above in section C about "inherited sin" indicate that *even before birth* children have a guilty standing before God and a sinful nature that not only gives them a tendency to sin but also causes God to view them as "sinners." "Behold, I was brought forth in iniquity, and in sin did my mother conceive me" (Ps. 51:5).

Some passages speak of final judgment in terms of actual sinful deeds that people have done (e.g., Rom. 2:6–11). But these verses do not say anything about the basis of judgment *when there have been no individual actions of right or wrong*, as with children dying in early infancy. In such cases we must accept the Scriptures that talk about ourselves as having a sinful nature from before the time of birth. Furthermore, we must realize that a child's sinful nature manifests itself very early, certainly within the first two years of a child's life, as anyone who has raised children can affirm. (David says in Ps. 58:3, "The wicked are estranged *from the womb*; they go astray *from birth*.")

But then what do we say about infants who die before they are old enough to understand and believe the gospel? Can they be saved?

Here we must say that if such infants are saved, it cannot be on their own merits, or on the basis of their own righteousness or innocence, but it must be entirely on the basis of Christ's redemptive work and regeneration by the work of the Holy Spirit within them. "There is one God, and there is one mediator between God and men, the man Christ Jesus" (1 Tim. 2:5). "Unless one is born again, he cannot see the kingdom of God" (John 3:3).

Yet it certainly is possible for God to bring regeneration (that is, new spiritual life)

---

18. This is the position of Millard Erickson, for example, in *Christian Theology*, 639. He uses the term *age of responsibility* rather than *age of accountability*.

to an infant even before he or she is born. This was true of John the Baptist because before John was born the angel Gabriel said, "He will be filled with the Holy Spirit, *even from his mother's womb*" (Luke 1:15). We might say that John the Baptist was "born again" before he was born! In fact, his mother Elizabeth said about him, "the baby in my womb leaped for joy" when Mary, Jesus' mother, arrived and greeted Elizabeth. There is a similar example in Psalm 22:9–10: David speaks about trusting in God even as a tiny infant: "You made me trust you at my mother's breasts. . . . From my mother's womb you have been my God." In addition, the author of Psalm 71 says, "Upon you I have leaned from before my birth" (Ps. 71:6). It is clear, therefore, that God is able to save infants in an unusual way, apart from their hearing and understanding the gospel, by bringing regeneration to them very early, sometimes even before birth. This regeneration is probably also followed at once by a nascent, intuitive awareness of God and trust in him at an extremely early age, but this is something we simply cannot understand.[19]

We must, however, affirm very clearly that this is not the usual way for God to save people. Salvation usually occurs when someone hears and understands the gospel and then places trust in Christ. But in unusual cases like John the Baptist, God brought salvation before this understanding. And this leads us to conclude that it certainly is possible that God would also do this where he knows the infant will die before hearing the gospel.

How many infants does God save in this way? Scripture does not tell us, so we simply cannot know. Where Scripture is silent, it is unwise for us to make definitive pronouncements. However, we should recognize that *it is God's frequent pattern throughout Scripture to save the children of those who believe in him*. We see this in the life of Noah and his children (Gen. 7:1; Heb. 11:7); Rahab's family (Josh. 2:18); Joshua's family (Josh. 24:15); "all" the household of the official whose son Jesus healed from afar (John 4:53); "all" the household of Cornelius the Roman centurion (Acts 11:14); the "entire household" of the Philippian jailer (Acts 16:31); and the "entire household" of Crispus, the ruler of the synagogue in Corinth (Acts 18:8). We are to praise God that his common way of acting is that his righteousness ordinarily extends to "children's children" (Ps. 103:17). It was expected that the children of elders would be believers (Titus 1:6). Other verses indicate similar expectations (see Acts 2:39; 1 Cor. 1:16; 7:14; cf. Matt. 18:10, 14).

These passages do not show that God automatically saves the children of all believers (for we all know of children of godly parents who have grown up and rejected the Lord, and Scripture also gives such examples as Esau and Absalom), but they do indicate that *God's ordinary pattern*, the "normal" or expected way in which he acts, is to bring the children of believers to himself. With regard to believers' children who die very young, we have no reason to think that it would be otherwise.

---

19. However, we all know that infants almost from the moment of birth show an instinctive trust in their mothers and awareness of themselves as persons distinct from their mothers. Thus we should not insist that it is impossible that they would also have an intuitive awareness of God, and if God gives it, an intuitive ability to trust in God as well.

Particularly relevant here is the case of the first child Bathsheba bore to King David. When the infant child had died, David said, "*I shall go to him*, but he will not return to me" (2 Sam. 12:23). David, who through his life had such great confidence that he would live forever in the Lord's presence (see Ps. 23:6, and many of David's psalms), also had confidence that he would see his infant son again when he died. This it is best understood to imply that he would be *with his son in the presence of the Lord forever.*[20] This passage, together with the others mentioned above, should be of similar assurance to all believers who have lost children in their infancy, that they will one day see them again in the glory of the heavenly kingdom.

Regarding the children of unbelievers who die at a very early age Scripture is silent. We simply must leave that matter in the hands of God and trust him to be both just and merciful. If they are saved, it will not be on the basis of any merit of their own or any innocence that we might presume that they have. If they are saved, it will be on the basis of Christ's redeeming work. And their regeneration, like that of John the Baptist before he was born, will be by God's mercy and grace. Salvation is always because of his mercy, not because of our merits (see Rom. 9:14–18). Scripture does not allow us to say more than that.

## 4. Are There Degrees of Sin?

Are some sins worse than others? The question may be answered either yes or no, depending on the sense in which it is intended.

**a. Legal Guilt.** In terms of our legal standing before God, any one sin, even what may seem to be a very small one, makes us legally guilty before God and therefore worthy of eternal punishment. Adam and Eve learned this in the garden of Eden, where God told them that one act of disobedience would result in the penalty of death (Gen. 2:17). And Paul affirms that "the judgment following one trespass brought condemnation" (Rom. 5:16). This one sin made Adam and Eve sinners before God, no longer able to stand in his holy presence.

This truth remains valid through the history of the human race. Paul (quoting Deut. 27:26) affirms it: "Cursed be everyone who does not abide by *all things* written in the Book of the Law, and do them" (Gal. 3:10). And James declares, "Whoever keeps the whole law but fails *in one point* has become guilty of all of it. For he who said, 'Do not commit adultery,' also said, 'Do not murder.' If you do not commit adultery but do murder, you have become a transgressor of the law" (James 2:10–11).[21] Therefore, in terms

---

20. Someone might object that David is only saying that he would go to the state of death just as his son had. But this interpretation does not fit the language of the verse: David does not say, "I shall go *where he is*," but rather, "I shall go *to him*." This is the language of personal reunion, and it indicates David's expectation that he would one day see and be with his son.

21. We may understand this principle more clearly when we realize that the various moral laws of God are simply different aspects of his perfect moral character, to which he expects us to conform. To violate any one part of it is to become unlike him. For example, if I were to steal, I would not only break the commandment against stealing (eighth commandment), but I would also dishonor God's name (third commandment; see Prov. 30:9), dishonor my parents and their good name (fifth

of legal guilt, all sins are equally bad because they make us legally guilty before God and constitute us as sinners.

**b. Results in Life and in Relationship with God.** On the other hand, some sins are worse than others in that they have more harmful consequences in our lives and in the lives of others, and in terms of our personal relationship to God as Father, they arouse his displeasure more and bring more serious disruption to our fellowship with him.

Scripture sometimes speaks of degrees of seriousness of sin. When Jesus stood before Pontius Pilate, he said, "He who delivered me over to you has the *greater sin*" (John 19:11). The reference is apparently to Caiaphas the high priest, the Jewish leader of the plan to deliver Jesus to the Romans in order that they might put him to death (see Matt. 26:3, 57; John 11:49; 18:14). Though Pilate had authority over Jesus by virtue of his governmental office and was wrong to allow an innocent man to be condemned to death, the sin of Caiaphas was far "greater," probably because of the far greater knowledge and malice connected with it.

When God showed Ezekiel visions of sins in the temple of Jerusalem, he first showed Ezekiel certain things, then said, "But you will see *still greater* abominations" (Ezek. 8:6). Next he showed Ezekiel the secret sins of some of the elders of Israel and said, "You will see *still greater* abominations that they commit" (Ezek. 8:13). Then the Lord showed Ezekiel a picture of women weeping for a Babylonian deity and said, "Have you seen this, O son of man? You will see *still greater* abominations than these" (Ezek. 8:15). Finally, he showed Ezekiel twenty-five men in the temple, with their backs to the Lord and worshiping the sun instead. Here clearly we have degrees of increasing sin and hatefulness before God.

In the Sermon of the Mount, when Jesus says, "Whoever relaxes one of *the least of these commandments* and teaches others to do the same will be called least in the kingdom of heaven" (Matt. 5:19), he implies that there are lesser and greater commandments. Similarly, though he agrees that it is appropriate to give a tithe even on the household spices that people use, he pronounces woes on the Pharisees for neglecting "*the weightier matters of the law*: justice and mercy and faithfulness" (Matt. 23:23). In both cases Jesus distinguishes between lesser and greater commandments, implying that some sins are worse than other sins in terms of God's evaluation of their importance.

In general, we may say that some sins have more harmful consequences than other sins if they bring more dishonor to God or if they cause more harm to ourselves, to others, or to the church. Moreover, those sins that are done willfully, repeatedly, and

---

commandment), covet something that does not belong to me (tenth commandment), put some material possession ahead of God himself (first commandment; see Eph. 5:5), and carry out an action that harms another human being and damages his or her life (sixth commandment; cf. Matt. 5:22). With a little

reflection, we can see how almost any sin violates some of the principles embodied in each of the Ten Commandments. This is simply a reflection of the fact that God's laws are a unified whole and reflect the moral purity and perfection of God himself in the integrated oneness of his person.

knowingly with a calloused heart are more displeasing to God than those that are done out of ignorance and are not repeated or those that are done with a mixture of good and impure motives and are followed by remorse and repentance. Thus the laws that God gave to Moses in Leviticus make provisions for cases where people sin "unwittingly" (Lev. 4:2, 13, 22). Unintentional sin is still sin: "If anyone sins, doing any of the things that by the LORD's commandments ought not to be done, though he did not know it, then realizes his guilt, he shall bear his iniquity" (Lev. 5:17). Nonetheless, the penalties required and the degree of God's displeasure that results from the sin are less than in the case of intentional sin.

On the other hand, sins committed with "a high hand," that is, with arrogance and disdain for God's commandments, were viewed very seriously: "But the person who does anything with a high hand, whether he is native or a sojourner, reviles the LORD, and that person shall be cut off from among his people" (Num. 15:30; cf. vv. 27–29).

We can readily see how some sins have much more harmful consequences for ourselves, others, and our relationship with God. If I were to covet my neighbor's car, that would be sin before God. But if my coveting led me to actually steal the car, that would be more serious sin. If in the course of stealing the car I also fought with my neighbor and injured him or recklessly injured someone else as I drove the car, that would be even more serious sin.

Similarly, if a new Christian, who previously had a tendency to lose his temper and get into fights, begins witnessing to his unbelieving friends and, one day, is so provoked he loses his temper and actually strikes someone, that is certainly sin in God's sight. But if a mature pastor or other prominent Christian leader were to lose his temper publicly and strike someone, that would be even more serious in God's sight, both because of the harm that would come to the reputation of the gospel and because those in leadership positions are held to a higher standard of accountability by God: "We who teach will be judged with greater strictness" (James 3:1; cf. Luke 12:48). Our conclusion, then, is that in terms of *results* and in terms of the *degree of God's displeasure*, some sins are certainly worse than others.

However, the distinction between degrees of seriousness of sin does not imply an endorsement of the Roman Catholic teaching that sins can be put into the two categories of "venial" and "mortal."[22] The Roman Catholic Church separates sins into the

---

22. The distinction between mortal and venial sins may seem to be supported by 1 John 5:16–17: "If anyone sees his brother committing a sin not leading to death, he shall ask, and God will give him life—to those who commit sins that do not lead to death. There is sin that leads to death; I do not say that one should pray for that. All wrongdoing is sin, but there is sin that does not lead to death."

In the light of John's concern in this epistle to combat a heresy that did not confess Jesus as God who came in the flesh (see 1 John 4:2–3), it is likely that this sin "unto death" is denying Christ and subsequently failing to obtain salvation through him. In this case, John would simply be saying that we should not pray that God would forgive the sin of rejecting Christ and even teaching seriously heretical doctrine about him. But the fact that John says there is one sin that is "unto death" (rejecting Christ), does not justify establishing a whole category of sins that cannot be forgiven.

categories of "mortal" (such as murder, adultery, or blasphemy) and "venial" (such as "thoughtless chatter or immoderate laughter").[23] In Roman Catholic teaching, a venial sin can be forgiven, but often after punishments in this life or in Purgatory (after death, but before entrance into heaven). A mortal sin is a sin that causes spiritual death and, if it is not repented of before death, cannot be forgiven. Mortal sin excludes people from the kingdom of God.

According to Scripture, however, all sins are "mortal" in that even the smallest sin makes us legally guilty before God and worthy of eternal punishment. Yet even the most serious of sins are forgiven when one comes to Christ for salvation (note the combination of a list of sins that exclude from the kingdom of God and the affirmation that the Corinthians who had committed them have been saved by Christ in 1 Cor. 6:9–11). Thus, in that sense, all sins are "venial."[24] This perspective is preferable to the Catholic view, which can very easily lead either to carelessness with respect to some sins that greatly hinder sanctification and effectiveness in the Lord's work, or, with respect to other sins, to excessive fear, despair, and inability ever to have assurance of forgiveness. And we should realize that the same exact action (such as losing one's temper and striking someone in the example above) can be more or less serious, depending on the person and circumstances involved. It is much better simply to recognize that sins can vary in terms of their results and in terms of the degree to which they disrupt our relationship with God and incur his displeasure, and leave it at that. Then we do not go beyond the general teaching of Scripture on this subject.

The distinction that Scripture makes in degrees of sin does have positive value. First, it helps us know where we should put more effort in our attempts to grow in holiness. Second, it helps us decide when we should simply overlook a minor fault in a friend or family member and when it would be appropriate to talk with an individual about some evident sin (see James 5:19–20). Third, it may help us decide when church discipline is appropriate, and it provides an answer to the objection that is sometimes raised against exercising church discipline, in which it is said that "we are all guilty of sin, so we have no business meddling in anyone else's life." Though we are all indeed guilty of sin, some sins so blatantly harm the church and relationships within the church that they must be dealt with directly. Fourth, this distinction may also help us realize that there is some basis for civil governments to have laws and penalties prohibiting certain kinds of wrongdoing (such as murder or stealing) but not others (such as anger, jealousy, greed, or selfish use of one's possessions). It is not inconsistent to say that some kinds of wrongdoing require civil punishment but not all kinds of wrongdoing require it.

---

23. See *Catechism of the Catholic Church* (1997), 1854–64.

24. On "the unpardonable sin," which is the one exception to this statement, see pp. 637–40, below.

## 5. What Happens When a Christian Sins?

**a. Our Legal Standing Before God Is Unchanged.** Though this subject could be treated later in relation to adoption or sanctification within the Christian life, it is quite appropriate to treat it at this point.

When a Christian sins, his or her legal standing before God is unchanged. He or she is still forgiven, for "there is therefore now no condemnation for those who are in Christ Jesus" (Rom. 8:1). Salvation is not based on our merits but is a free gift of God (Rom. 6:23), and Christ's death certainly paid for all our sins—past, present, and future— Christ died "for our sins" (1 Cor. 15:3), without distinction. In theological terms, we still keep our "justification."[25]

Moreover, we are still children of God and we still retain our membership in God's family. In the same epistle in which John says, "If we say we have no sin, we deceive ourselves, and the truth is not in us" (1 John 1:8), he also reminds his readers, "Beloved, we are God's children now" (1 John 3:2). The fact that we have sin remaining in our lives does not mean that we lose our status as God's children. In theological terms, we keep our "adoption."[26]

**b. Our Fellowship with God Is Disrupted and Our Christian Life Is Damaged.** When we sin, even though God does not cease to love us, *he is displeased with us*. (Even among human beings, it is possible to love someone and be displeased with that person at the same time, as any parent will attest, or any wife, or any husband.) Paul tells us that it is possible for Christians to "grieve the Holy Spirit of God" (Eph. 4:30). When we sin, we cause him sorrow, and he is displeased with us. The author of Hebrews reminds us that "the Lord disciplines the one he loves" (Heb. 12:6, quoting Prov. 3:11–12), and that "the Father of spirits . . . disciplines us for our good, that we may share his holiness" (Heb. 12:9–10). When we sin, God the Father is grieved, much as an earthly father is grieved with his children's disobedience, and he disciplines us. A similar theme is found in Revelation 3, where the risen Christ speaks from heaven to the church of Laodicea, saying, "Those whom I *love*, I *reprove* and *discipline*, so be zealous and repent" (Rev. 3:19). Here again love and reproof of sin are connected in the same statement. Thus the New Testament attests to the displeasure of all three members of the Trinity when Christians sin. (See also Isa. 59:1–2; 1 John 3:21.)

The Westminster Confession of Faith wisely says, concerning Christians, "Although they never can fall from the state of justification, yet they may, by their sins, fall under God's *fatherly displeasure*, and not have the light of His countenance restored unto them, until they humble themselves, confess their sins, beg pardon, and renew their faith and repentance."[27] Hebrews 12, together with many historical examples in Scripture, shows that God's *fatherly displeasure* often leads to discipline in our Christian lives:

---

25. See chapter 36, pp. 884–908, on justification.
26. See chapter 37, pp. 913–19, on adoption.

27. Westminster Confession of Faith 11.5.

"He disciplines us for our good, that we may share his holiness" (Heb. 12:10). Regarding the need for regular confession and repentance of sin, Jesus reminds us that we are to pray each day, "Forgive us our debts, as we also have forgiven our debtors" (Matt. 6:12, using "debt" in the sense of moral obligation from wrongdoing; in other words, sin; cf. Luke 11:4; 1 John 1:9).

When we sin as Christians, it is not only our personal relationship with God that is disrupted. *Our Christian life and fruitfulness in ministry are also damaged.* Jesus warns us, "As the branch cannot bear fruit by itself, unless it abides in the vine, neither can you, unless you abide in me" (John 15:4). When we stray from fellowship with Christ because of sin in our lives, we diminish the degree to which we are abiding in Christ.

The New Testament writers frequently speak of the destructive consequences of sin in the lives of believers. In fact, many sections of the Epistles are taken up with rebuking and discouraging Christians from sin that they are committing. Paul says that if Christians yield themselves to sin, they increasingly become "slaves" of sin (Rom. 6:16), whereas God wants Christians to progress upward on a path of ever-increasing righteousness in life. If our goal is to grow in increasing fullness of life until the day we die and pass into the presence of God in heaven, to sin is to do an about-face and *begin to walk downhill away from the goal of likeness to God*; it is to go in a direction that "leads to death" (Rom. 6:16) and eternal separation from God, the direction from which we were rescued when we became Christians.[28]

Peter says that sinful desires that remain in our hearts *"wage war* against your soul" (1 Peter 2:11)—the military language correctly translates Peter's expression and conveys the imagery that sinful desires within us are like soldiers in a battle and their target is our spiritual well-being. To give in to such sinful desires, to nurture and cherish them in our hearts, is to give food, shelter, and welcome to the enemy's troops. If we yield to the desires that "wage war" against our souls, we will inevitably feel some loss of spiritual strength, some diminution of spiritual power, some loss of effectiveness in the work of God's kingdom.

Moreover, when we sin as Christians we suffer a loss of heavenly reward. A person who has built on the work of the church not with gold, silver, and precious stones, but with "wood, hay, straw" (1 Cor. 3:12) will have his work "burned up" on the day of judgment and "he will suffer loss, though he himself will be saved, but only as through fire" (1 Cor. 3:15). Paul realizes that "we must all appear before the judgment seat of Christ, so that each one may receive what is due for what he has done in the body, whether good

---

28. Paul is not saying in Romans 6:16 that true Christians will ever actually regress to a point at which they fall under eternal condemnation, but he does seem to be saying that when we yield to sin we are (in a spiritual/moral sense) traveling in that direction.

or evil" (2 Cor. 5:10). Paul implies that there are degrees of reward in heaven,[29] and that sin has negative consequences in terms of loss of heavenly reward.

**c. The Danger of "Unconverted Churchgoers."** While a genuine Christian who sins does not lose his or her justification or adoption before God (see above), there needs to be a clear warning that mere association with an evangelical church and outward conformity to accepted "Christian" patterns of behavior does not guarantee salvation. Particularly in societies and cultures where it is easy (or even expected) for people to profess to be Christians, there is a real possibility that some will associate with the church who are not genuinely born again. If such people then become more and more disobedient to Christ in their pattern of life, they should not be lulled into complacency by assurances that they still have justification or adoption in God's family. A consistent pattern of disobedience to Christ coupled with a lack of the elements of the fruit of the Holy Spirit such as love, joy, peace, and so forth (see Gal. 5:22–23) is a warning signal that the person is probably not a true Christian inwardly, that there probably has been no genuine heart-faith from the beginning and no regenerating work of the Holy Spirit. Jesus warns that he will say to some who have prophesied, cast out demons, and done many mighty works in his name, "I never knew you; depart from me, you workers of lawlessness" (Matt. 7:23). And John tells us that "whoever says 'I know him' but does not keep his commandments is a liar, and the truth is not in him" (1 John 2:4; here John speaks of a persistent pattern of life). A long-term pattern of increasing disobedience to Christ should be taken as evidence that the person in question may not really be a Christian at all.

## 6. What Is the Unpardonable Sin?

Several passages of Scripture speak about a sin that will not be forgiven. Jesus says, "Therefore I tell you, every sin and blasphemy will be forgiven people, but the blasphemy against the Spirit will not be forgiven. And whoever speaks a word against the Son of Man will be forgiven, but whoever speaks against the Holy Spirit will not be forgiven, either in this age or in the age to come" (Matt. 12:31–32). A similar statement occurs in Mark 3:29–30, where Jesus says that "whoever blasphemes against the Holy Spirit never has forgiveness" (Mark 3:29; cf. Luke 12:10). Similarly, Hebrews 6 says,

> For it is impossible, in the case of those who have once been enlightened, who have tasted the heavenly gift, and have shared in the Holy Spirit, and have tasted the goodness of the word of God and the powers of the age to come, and then have fallen away, to restore them again to repentance, since they are crucifying once again the Son of God to their own harm and holding him up to contempt. (Heb. 6:4–6; cf. 10:26–27; also the discussion of the sin "that leads to death" in 1 John 5:16–17)

---

29. See chapter 56, pp. 1408–10, on degrees of reward in heaven.

These passages could be talking about the same or different sins; a decision about this will have to be made from an examination of the passages in context.

Several different views of this sin have been taken.[30]

1. Some have thought that it was a sin that could only be committed while Christ was on earth. But Jesus' statement that "every sin and blasphemy will be forgiven people" (Matt. 12:31) is so general that it seems unwarranted to say it is only referring to something that could only happen during his lifetime—the texts in question do not specify such a restriction. Moreover, Hebrews 6:4–6 is speaking of apostasy that has occurred a number of years after Jesus returned to heaven.

2. Some have held that the sin is unbelief that continues until the time of death; therefore, everyone who dies in unbelief (or at least everyone who has heard of Christ and then dies in unbelief) has committed this sin. It is true, of course, that those who persist in unbelief until death will not be forgiven, but the question is whether that fact is what is being discussed in these verses. On close reading of the verses, that explanation does not seem to fit the language of the texts cited, for they do not talk of unbelief in general but specifically of someone who "speaks against the Holy Spirit" (Matt. 12:32), "blasphemes against the Holy Spirit" (Mark 3:29), or has "fallen away" (Heb. 6:6). They have in view a specific sin—willful rejection of the work of the Holy Spirit and speaking evil about it, or willful rejection of the truth of Christ and holding Christ up to "contempt" (Heb. 6:6). Moreover, the idea that this sin is unbelief that persists until death does not fit well with the context of a rebuke to the Pharisees for what they were saying in both Matthew and Mark (see discussion of context below).

3. Some hold that this sin is serious apostasy by genuine believers, and that only those who are truly born again could commit this sin. They base their view on their understanding of the nature of the "apostasy" that is mentioned in Hebrews 6:4–6 (that it is a rejection of Christ and loss of salvation by a true Christian). But that does not seem to be the best understanding of Hebrews 6:4–6.[31] Moreover, though this view could perhaps be sustained with respect to Hebrews 6, it does not explain blasphemy against the Holy Spirit in the gospel passages, in which Jesus is responding to the Pharisees' hard-hearted denial of the work of the Holy Spirit through him.

4. A fourth possibility is that this sin consists of *unusually malicious, willful rejection and slander against the Holy Spirit's work attesting to Christ, and attributing that work to Satan.* A closer look at the context of Jesus' statement in Matthew and Mark shows that Jesus was speaking in response to the accusation of the Pharisees that "it is only by Beelzebul, the prince of demons, that this man casts out demons" (Matt. 12:24). The Pharisees had seen Jesus' works repeatedly. He had just healed a blind and dumb demoniac so that he could see and speak (Matt. 12:22). The people were amazed and were following Jesus in large

---

30. See Louis Berkhof, *Systematic Theology* (Grand Rapids: Eerdmans, 1941), 252–53, for representatives of each position.

31. See the extended discussion of Hebrews 6:4–6 in chapter 40, pp. 979–84.

numbers, and the Pharisees themselves had repeatedly seen clear demonstrations of the amazing power of the Holy Spirit working through Jesus to bring life and health to many people. But the Pharisees, in spite of clear demonstrations of the work of the Holy Spirit in front of their eyes, willfully rejected Jesus' authority and his teaching and attributed it to the devil. Jesus then told them clearly that "no city or house divided against itself will stand. And if Satan casts out Satan, he is divided against himself. How then will his kingdom stand?" (Matt. 12:25–26). So it was irrational and foolish for the Pharisees to attribute Jesus' exorcisms to the power of Satan—it was a classic, willful, malicious lie.

After explaining, "If it is *by the Spirit of God* that I cast out demons, then the kingdom of God has come upon you" (Matt. 12:28), Jesus declares this warning: "Whoever is not with me is against me, and whoever does not gather with me scatters" (Matt. 12:30). He warns that there is no neutrality, and certainly those who, like the Pharisees, oppose his message are against him. Then he immediately adds, "Therefore I tell you, every sin and blasphemy will be forgiven people, but the blasphemy against the Spirit will not be forgiven" (Matt. 12:31). The willful, malicious slander of the work of the Holy Spirit through Jesus, in which the Pharisees attributed it to Satan, would not be forgiven.

The context indicates that Jesus is speaking about a sin that is not simply unbelief or rejection of Christ but a sin that includes (1) a clear knowledge of who Christ is and of the power of the Holy Spirit working through him, (2) a willful rejection of the facts about Christ that his opponents knew to be true, and (3) slanderously attributing the work of the Holy Spirit in Christ to the power of Satan. In such a case the hardness of heart would be so great that any ordinary means of bringing a sinner to repentance would already have been rejected. Persuasion of the truth will not work, for these people have already known the truth and have willfully rejected it. Demonstration of the power of the Holy Spirit to heal and bring life will not work, for they have seen it and rejected it. In this case it is not that the sin itself is so horrible that it could not be covered by Christ's redemptive work, but rather that the sinner's hardened heart puts him or her *beyond the reach of God's ordinary means of bringing forgiveness through repentance and trusting Christ for salvation.* The sin is unpardonable because it cuts off the sinner from repentance and saving faith through belief in the truth.

Berkhof wisely defines this sin in the following way:

> The sin consists in the conscious, malicious, and wilful rejection and slandering, against evidence and conviction, of the testimony of the Holy Spirit respecting the grace of God in Christ, attributing it out of hatred and enmity to the prince of darkness. . . . In committing that sin man wilfully, maliciously, and intentionally attributes what is clearly recognized as the work of God to the influence and operation of Satan.[32]

---

32. Berkhof, *Systematic Theology*, 253.

Berkhof explains that the sin itself consists "not in doubting the truth, nor in a sinful denial of it but in a contradiction of it that goes contrary to the conviction of the mind, to the illumination of the conscience, and even to the verdict of the heart."[33]

The fact that the unpardonable sin involves such extreme hardness of heart and lack of repentance indicates that those who fear they have committed it yet still have sorrow for sin in their heart and desire to seek after God do not fall in the category of those who are guilty of it. Berkhof says that "we may be reasonably sure that those who fear that they have committed it and worry about this, and desire the prayers of others for them, have not committed it."[34]

This understanding of the unpardonable sin also fits well with Hebrews 6:4–6. There the persons who "have fallen away" have had all sorts of knowledge and conviction of the truth: they have "been enlightened" and have "tasted the heavenly gift"; they have participated in some ways in the work of the Holy Spirit and "have tasted the goodness of the word of God and the powers of the age to come," yet they then willfully turn away from Christ and hold "him up to contempt" (Heb. 6:4–6). They too have put themselves beyond the reach of God's ordinary means of bringing people to repentance and faith. Knowing and being convinced of the truth, they willfully reject it.

However, 1 John 5:16–17 seems to fall into another category. That passage does not speak of a sin that can never be forgiven but rather about a sin that, if persisted in, will lead to death. This sin seems to involve the teaching of serious doctrinal error about Christ, a kind of teaching that contradicts the heart of the gospel. In the context of asking in faith according to God's will (1 John 5:14–15) John simply tells us that he does not say that we can pray in faith for God simply to forgive that sin unless the person repents—but he certainly does not prohibit praying that the heretical teachers would turn from their heresy and repent and thereby find forgiveness. Many people who teach serious doctrinal error have still not gone so far as to commit the unpardonable sin and bring on themselves the impossibility of repentance and faith by their own hardness of heart.

## E. THE PUNISHMENT OF SIN

Although God's punishment of sin does serve as a *deterrent* against further sinning and as a *warning* to those who observe it, this is not the primary reason why God punishes sin. The primary reason is that *God's righteousness demands it*, so that he might be glorified in the universe that he has created. He is the Lord who practices "steadfast love, justice, and righteousness in the earth. For in these things I delight, declares the LORD" (Jer. 9:24).

Paul speaks of Christ Jesus, "whom God put forward as a propitiation by his blood, to be received by faith" (Rom. 3:25). Paul then explains why God put forward Jesus as

---

33. Ibid.    34. Ibid., 254.

a "propitiation" (that is, a sacrifice that bears the wrath of God against sin and thereby turns God's wrath into favor): "This was *to show God's righteousness*, because in his divine forbearance he had passed over former sins" (Rom. 3:25). Paul realizes that if Christ had not come to pay the penalty for sins, God could not be shown to be righteous. Because he had passed over sins and not punished them in the past, people could rightly accuse God of unrighteousness, the assumption being that a God who does not punish sins is not a righteous God. Therefore, when God sent Christ to die and pay the penalty for our sins, he showed how he could still be righteous—he had stored up the punishment due to previous sins (those of Old Testament saints), and then, in perfect righteousness, he gave that penalty to Jesus on the cross. The propitiation of Calvary thereby clearly demonstrated that God is perfectly righteous: "It was to show his righteousness at the present time, *so that he might be just* and the justifier of the one who has faith in Jesus" (Rom. 3:26).

In the cross we have a clear demonstration of the reason God punishes sin: if he did not punish sin he would not be a righteous God, and there would be no ultimate justice in the universe. But when sin is punished, God is showing himself to be a righteous judge over all, and justice is being done in his universe.

## QUESTIONS FOR PERSONAL APPLICATION

1. Has reading this chapter increased your awareness of the sin remaining in your life? Are you able to mention any specific ways in which this was true? Did the chapter increase in you any sense of the hatefulness of sin? Why do you not feel more often a deeper sense of the hatefulness of sin? What do you think the overall effect of this chapter will be on your personal relationship with God?

2. Would it ultimately be more comforting to you to think that sin came into the world because God ordained that it would come through secondary agents or because he could not prevent it, even though it was against his will? How would you feel about the universe and your place in it if you thought that evil had always existed and there was an ultimate "dualism" in the universe?

3. Can you name some parallels between the temptation faced by Eve and temptations that you face even now in your Christian life?

4. Do you feel a sense of unfairness that you are counted guilty because of Adam's sin (if you agree that Rom. 5:12–21 teaches this)? How can you deal with this sense of unfairness to keep it from becoming a hindrance in your relationship with God? At a

**Special Terms**

*age of accountability*
*dualism*
*impute*
*inherited corruption*
*inherited guilt*
*inherited sin*
*mortal sin*
*original guilt*
*original pollution*
*original sin*
*Pelagius*
*propitiation*
*sin*
*total depravity*
*total inability*
*unpardonable sin*
*venial sin*

level of deep conviction, do you really think that, before being a Christian, you were totally unable to do any spiritual good before God? Similarly, are you deeply convinced that this is true of all unbelievers, or do you think that this is just a doctrine that may or may not be true, or at least one that you do not find deeply convincing as you look at the lives of the unbelievers whom you know?

5. What kind of freedom of choice do the unbelievers whom you know actually have? Apart from the work of the Holy Spirit, are you convinced that they will not change their fundamental rebellion against God?

6. How can the biblical teaching of degrees of seriousness of sin help your Christian life at this point? Have you known a sense of God's "fatherly displeasure" when you have sinned? What is your response to that sense?

7. Do you think that Christians today have lost sight of the hatefulness of sin to a large extent? Have unbelievers also lost sight of this? Do you think that we as Christians have lost sight of the thoroughgoing pervasiveness of sin in unbelievers, of the truth that the greatest problem of the human race, and of all societies and civilizations, is not lack of education or lack of communication or lack of material well-being, but sin against God?

# BIBLIOGRAPHY

(For an explanation of this bibliography see the note on the bibliography to chapter 1, pp. 23–24. Complete bibliographical data may be found on pp. 1489–96.)

## SECTIONS IN EVANGELICAL SYSTEMATIC THEOLOGIES

### 1. Anglican (Episcopalian)
1882–92 . . . . . Litton, 136–77
1930 . . . . . . . . Thomas, 155–75, 210–14, 234–35, 501–6
2001 . . . . . . . . Packer, 74–86
2013 . . . . . . . . Bird, 666–83
2013 . . . . . . . . Bray, 84–88

### 2. Arminian (Wesleyan or Methodist)
1875–76 . . . . . Pope, 2:1–86
1892–94 . . . . . Miley, 1:423–533; 2:505–24
1940 . . . . . . . . Wiley, 2:51–140
1960 . . . . . . . . Purkiser, 223–42
1983 . . . . . . . . Carter, 1:27–86
2002 . . . . . . . . Cottrell, 159–69

### 3. Baptist
1767 . . . . . . . . Gill, 1:451–90
1887 . . . . . . . . Boyce, 230–47
1907 . . . . . . . . Strong, 533–664
1976–83 . . . . . Henry, 6:229–50, 269–304
1987–94 . . . . . Lewis and Demarest, 2:183–245
1990–95 . . . . . Garrett, 1:521–606
2007 . . . . . . . . Akin, 409–79
2013 . . . . . . . . Erickson, 513–47, 548–64, 565–83, 584–99

**4. *Dispensational***

1947 . . . . . . . . Chafer, 2:200–373

1949 . . . . . . . . Thiessen, 188–98

1986 . . . . . . . . Ryrie, 201–34

2002–2005 . . Geisler, 3:80–178

2017 . . . . . . . . MacArthur and Mayhue, 451–78

**5. *Lutheran***

1917–24 . . . . . Pieper, 1:527–77

1934 . . . . . . . . Mueller, 210–41

**6. *Reformed (or Presbyterian)***

1559 . . . . . . . . Calvin, 1:239–309 (2.1–3)

1679–85 . . . . . Turretin, *IET*, 1: 591–658, 659–85

1724–58 . . . . . Edwards, 1:143–233

1871–73 . . . . . Hodge, 2:122–279

1878 . . . . . . . . Dabney, 36–51

1894 . . . . . . . . Shedd, 535–609

1887–1921 . . . Warfield, *BTS*, 262–69

1906–11 . . . . . Bavinck, *RD*, 3:25–74, 75–125, 126–57, 158–90

1910 . . . . . . . . Vos, 2:21–75

1937–66 . . . . . Murray, *CW*, 2:67–89; *IAS*, 5–95

1938 . . . . . . . . Berkhof, 219–61

1998 . . . . . . . . Reymond, 440–60

2008 . . . . . . . . Van Genderen and Velema, 385–436

2011 . . . . . . . . Horton, 408–45

2013 . . . . . . . . Frame, 845–71

2013 . . . . . . . . Culver, 337–418

2016 . . . . . . . . Allen and Swain, 194–215

2017 . . . . . . . . Barrett, 302–7

2019 . . . . . . . . Letham, 366–400

**7. *Renewal (or charismatic/Pentecostal)***

1988–92 . . . . . Williams, 1:221–74

1993 . . . . . . . . Menzies and Horton, 85–93

1995 . . . . . . . . Horton, 255–90

2008 . . . . . . . . Duffield and Van Cleave, 155–82

## Sections in Representative Roman Catholic Systematic Theologies

**1. *Roman Catholic: Traditional***

1955 . . . . . . . . Ott, 106–14

**2. *Roman Catholic: Post–Vatican II***

1980 . . . . . . . . McBrien, 1:123, 162–68; 2:953–60

2012 . . . . . . . . *CCC*, paragraphs 1846–76

## Other Works

Allison, Gregg. *Historical Theology: An Introduction to Christian Doctrine; A Companion to Wayne Grudem's* Systematic Theology. Grand Rapids: Zondervan, 2011, 342–64.

Berkouwer, G. C. *Sin.* Translated by Philip C. Holtrop. Grand Rapids: Eerdmans, 1971.

Blocher, Henri A. G. "Evil." In *NDBT*, 465–67.

———. "Fall." In *NDT2*, 327–30.

———. *Original Sin: Illuminating the Riddle.* Grand Rapids: Eerdmans, 1999.

———. "Sin." In *NDBT*, 781–88.

Bloesch, D. G. "Sin." In *EDT3*, 808–11.

Brand, Chad Owen, ed. *Perspectives on Our Struggle with Sin: 3 Views of Romans 7.* Nashville: B&H Academic, 2011.

Carson, D. A. *How Long, O Lord? Reflections on Suffering and Evil.* Grand Rapids: Baker, 1990.

Colwell, J. E. "Anthropology." In *NDT1*, 28–30.

———. "Fall." In *NDT*, 249–51.

———. "Sin." In *NDT*, 641–43.

Crisp, O. D., and M. Jenson. "Sin." In *NDT2*, 841–43.

Demarest, B. A. "Fall of Humanity." In *EDT3*, 305–7.

Doriani, Daniel. "Sin." In *BTDB*, 736–39.

Feinberg, J. S. *The Many Faces of Evil: Theological*

*Systems and the Problem of Evil.* Rev. ed.
Wheaton, IL: Crossway, 2004.

———. *Theologies and Evil.* Washington, DC:
University Press of America, 1979.

Geisler, Norman. *The Roots of Evil.* Grand Rapids:
Zondervan, 1978.

Hoekema, Anthony A. *Created in God's Image.*
Grand Rapids: Eerdmans; Exeter: Paternoster,
1986, 112–86.

Hughes, Philip Edgcumbe. *The True Image: The
Origin and Destiny of Man in Christ.* Grand
Rapids: Eerdmans; Leicester: Inter-Varsity Press,
1989, 71–210.

Johnson, D. H. "Flesh." In *DLNT*, 374–76.

Johnson, R. K. "Imputation." In *EDT3*, 423–24.

Lewis, C. S. *The Problem of Pain.* New York:
Macmillan, 1962.

Madueme, Hans and Michael Reeves, eds. *Adam,
The Fall, and Original Sin: Theological, Biblical,
and Scientific Perspectives.* Grand Rapids: Baker
Academic, 2014.

McCall, Thomas H. *Against God and Nature: The
Doctrine of Sin.* Wheaton, IL: Crossway, 2019.

McKnight, Scot. "Blasphemy Against the Holy
Spirit." In *BTDB*, 67–69.

Morgan, Christopher and Robert Peterson, eds.
*Fallen: A Theology of Sin.* Wheaton, IL:
Crossway, 2013.

Morris, Leon. "Sin, Guilt." In *DPL*, 877–81.

Murray, John. *The Imputation of Adam's Sin.* Grand
Rapids: Eerdmans, 1959.

Norman, R. Stanton. "Human Sinfulness." In *A
Theology for the Church*, edited by Daniel L. Akin
et al., 409–78. Nashville: B&H, 2007.

Peters, Ted. *Sin: Radical Evil in Soul and Society.*
Grand Rapids: Eerdmans, 1994.

Peterson, Michael L. *Evil and the Christian God.*
Grand Rapids: Baker, 1982.

Pink, Arthur Walkington. *Gleanings From the
Scriptures: Man's Total Depravity.* Chicago:
Moody Publishers, 1970.

Plantinga, Alvin. *God, Freedom and Evil.* New York:
Harper and Row, 1974.

Porter, S. E. "Sin, Wickedness." In *DLNT*, 1095–98.

Pyne, Robert A. *Humanity & Sin: The Creation,
Fall, and Redemption of Humanity.* Nashville:
Word, 1999.

Ramm, Bernard. *Offense to Reason: The Theology of
Sin.* San Francisco: Harper and Row, 1985.

Reichenbach, B. R. "Evil." In *NDT2*, 316–19.

Ryrie, C. C. "Depravity, Total." In *EDT3*, 240–41.

Shuster, M. and J. Nkansah-Obrempong. "Sin." In
*GDT*, 817–27.

Smith, David L. *With Willful Intent: A Theology of
Sin.* Wheaton, IL: BridgePoint, 1994.

Stenschke, C. W. "Guilt." In *NDBT*, 529–31.

Thomas, R. L. "Sin, Conviction of." In *EDT3*,
811–12.

Turner, David L. "Sin unto Death." In *BTDB*,
739–40.

Vickers, Brian J. *Jesus' Blood and Righteousness: Paul's
Theology of Imputation.* Wheaton, IL: Crossway,
2006.

Wenham, J. W. *The Enigma of Evil: Can We
Believe in the Goodness of God?* Grand Rapids:
Zondervan, 1985.

## SCRIPTURE MEMORY PASSAGE

**Psalm 51:1–4:**
*Have mercy on me, O God,
    according to your steadfast love;
according to your abundant mercy
    blot out my transgressions.
Wash me thoroughly from my iniquity,
    and cleanse me from my sin!*

*For I know my transgressions,
    and my sin is ever before me.
Against you, you only, have I sinned
    and done what is evil in your sight,
so that you may be justified in your words
    and blameless in your judgment.*

# HYMN

## "God, Be Merciful to Me"

This is an excellent example of the words of a psalm set to music. The psalm was originally King David's heartfelt confession of great sin before God, but even today it is an excellent pattern of confession that we ourselves might speak to God.

God, be merciful to me;
   on thy grace I rest my plea;
Plenteous in compassion thou,
   blot out my transgressions now;
Wash me, make me pure within,
   cleanse, O cleanse me from my sin.

My transgressions I confess,
   grief and guilt my soul oppress;
I have sinned against thy grace
   and provoked thee to thy face;
I confess thy judgment just,
   speechless, I thy mercy trust.

I am evil, born in sin;
   thou desirest truth within.
Thou alone my Savior art,
   teach thy wisdom to my heart;
Make me pure, thy grace bestow,
   wash me whiter than the snow.

Broken, humbled to the dust
   by thy wrath and judgment just,
Let my contrite heart rejoice
   and in gladness hear thy voice;
From my sins O hide thy face,
   blot them out in boundless grace.

Gracious God, my heart renew,
   make my spirit right and true;
Cast me not away from thee,
   let thy Spirit dwell in me;
Thy salvation's joy impart,
   steadfast make my willing heart.

Sinners then shall learn from me
   and return, O God, to thee;
Savior, all my guilt remove,
   and my tongue shall sing thy love;
Touch my silent lips, O Lord,
   and my mouth shall praise accord.

From *The Psalter*, 1912, from Psalm 51:1–15

Alternate hymn: "Rock of Ages"

# CONTEMPORARY WORSHIP SONG

## "Lord, I Need You"

Lord, I come, I confess.
Bowing here I find my rest.
And without You I fall apart.
You're the one that guides my heart.

*Chorus*
*Lord, I need You, oh I need You.*
*Every hour I need You.*
*My one defense, my righteousness,*
*Oh God, how I need You.*

*Where sin runs deep Your grace is more.*
*Where grace is found is where You are.*
*And where You are Lord I am free.*
*Holiness is Christ in me.*

*Bridge*
*So teach my song to rise to You*
*When temptation comes my way,*
*And when I cannot stand I'll fall on You.*
*Jesus You're my hope and stay.*

Words by Jesse Reeves, Daniel Carson, Kristian
Stanfill, Christy Nockels, and Matt Maher[35]

# CHAPTER 25

# The Covenants between God and Man

*What principles determine the way God relates to us?*

## EXPLANATION AND SCRIPTURAL BASIS

How does God relate to man? Since the creation of the world, God's relationship to man has been defined by specific requirements and promises. God tells people how he wants them to act and makes promises about how he will act toward them in various circumstances. The Bible contains several summaries of the provisions that define the different relationships between God and human beings that occur in Scripture, and it often calls these summaries "covenants." With respect to covenants between God and man in Scripture, we may give the following definition: *a covenant is an unchangeable, divinely imposed legal agreement between God and man that stipulates the conditions of their relationship.*

Although this definition includes the word *agreement* in order to show that there are two parties, God and man, who must enter into the provisions of the relationship, the phrase "divinely imposed" is also included to show that man can never negotiate with God or change the terms of the covenant: he can only accept the covenant obligations or reject them. Probably for this reason the Greek translators of the Old Testament (who created the Septuagint) and, following them, the New Testament authors did not use the ordinary Greek word for contracts or agreements in which both parties were equal (*synthēkē*) but chose a less common word, *diathēkē*, that emphasized that the provisions of the covenant were laid down by one of the parties only. (In fact, the word *diathēkē* was often used to refer to a "testament" or "will" that a person would leave to assign the distribution of his or her goods after death.)

This definition also notes that covenants are unchangeable. They may be superseded or replaced by a different covenant, but they may not be changed once they are established. Although there have been many additional details specified in the covenants God has made with man throughout the history of Scripture, the essential element at the heart of all of them is the promise, "I will be their God, and they shall be my people" (Jer. 31:33; 2 Cor. 6:16, et al.).

Since the covenant relationship between God and man occurs in various forms throughout Scripture from Genesis to Revelation, a treatment of this subject might be put at several different points in the study of systematic theology. I have put it here at the end of the treatment of man as *created* (in the image of God) and man as *fallen* into sin but before the discussion of the person and work of Christ.

## A. The Covenant of Works

Some have questioned whether it is appropriate to speak of a covenant of works that God had with Adam and Eve in the garden of Eden. The actual word *covenant* is not used in the Genesis narratives. However, the essential parts of the covenant are all present—a clear definition of the parties involved, a legally binding set of provisions that stipulates the conditions of their relationship, the promise of blessings for obedience, and the condition for obtaining those blessings.

Moreover, Hosea, in referring to the sins of Israel, states, "But *like Adam* they transgressed *the covenant*" (Hosea 6:7).[1] This passage views Adam as existing in a covenant relationship that he then transgressed in the garden of Eden. In addition, in Romans 5:12–21 Paul sees both Adam and Christ as heads of a people whom they represent, something that would be entirely consistent with the idea of Adam being in a covenant before the fall.

In the garden of Eden, it seems quite clear that there was a legally binding set of provisions that defined the conditions of the relationship between God and man. The two parties are evident as God speaks to Adam and gives commands to him. The requirements of the relationship are clearly defined in the commands that God gave to Adam and Eve (Gen. 1:28–30; cf. 2:15) and in the direct command to Adam, "You may surely eat of every tree of the garden, but of the tree of the knowledge of good and evil you shall not eat, for in the day that you eat of it you shall surely die" (Gen. 2:16–17).

In this statement to Adam about the tree of the knowledge of good and evil there is a promise of punishment for disobedience—death, most fully understood to mean death in an extensive sense, physical, spiritual, and eternal death and separation from God.[2] In the promise of punishment for disobedience there is implicit a promise of blessing for obedience. This blessing would consist of not receiving death, and the implication is that the blessing would be the opposite of "death." It would involve physical life that would not end and spiritual life in terms of a relationship with God that would go on

---

1. The translation "like Adam" (referring to Adam as a person) is found in ESV, NASB, NLT, and CSB, while the translation "at Adam" is found in NIV, NET, RSV, and NRSV. The *ESV Study Bible* note says, "To whom or to what does 'Adam' refer? Many commentators suggest a geographical locality. The difficulty is that there is no record of covenant breaking at a place called Adam . . . and it requires a questionable taking of the preposition 'like' (Heb. *ke-*) to mean 'at' or 'in'. . . . It is best to understand 'Adam' as the name of the first man" (*ESV Study Bible* [Wheaton, IL: Crossway, 2008], 1631).

2. The punishment of death began to be carried out on the day that Adam and Eve sinned, but it was carried out slowly over time, as their bodies grew old and they eventually died. The promise of spiritual death was put into effect immediately, since they were cut off from fellowship with God. The death of eternal condemnation was rightfully theirs, but the hints of redemption in the text (see Gen. 3:15, 21) suggest that this penalty was ultimately overcome by the redemption that Christ purchased.

forever. The presence of the "tree of life . . . in the midst of the garden" (Gen. 2:9) also signified the promise of eternal life with God if Adam and Eve had met the conditions of a covenant relationship by obeying God completely until he decided that their time of testing was finished. After the fall, God removed Adam and Eve from the garden, partly so that they would not be able to take from the tree of life "and eat, and live forever" (Gen. 3:22).

Another evidence that the covenant relationship with God in the garden included a promise of eternal life if Adam and Eve had perfectly obeyed is the fact that even in the New Testament Paul speaks as though perfect obedience, if it were possible, would actually lead to life. He speaks of a "commandment that promised life" (Rom. 7:10; lit., "the commandment unto life"), and in order to demonstrate that the law does not rest on faith, he quotes Leviticus 18:5 to say about the provisions of the law, "The one who does them shall live by them" (Gal. 3:12; cf. Rom. 10:5).

Other covenants in Scripture generally have an outward "sign" associated with them (such as circumcision, or baptism and the Lord's Supper). No "sign" for the covenant of works is clearly designated as such in Genesis, but if we were to name one, it would probably be the tree of life in the midst of the garden. By partaking of that tree Adam and Eve would be partaking of the promise of eternal life that God would give. The fruit itself did not have magical properties but would be a sign by which God outwardly guaranteed that the inward reality would occur.

Why is it important to speak of the relationship between God and man in the garden as a *covenant* relationship? To do so reminds us of the fact that this relationship, including the commands of obedience and promise of blessing for obedience, was not something that automatically occurred in the relationship between Creator and creature. God did not make any such covenant with the animals that he created, for example.[3] Nor did the nature of man as God created him demand that God have any fellowship with man or that God make any promises concerning his relationship with men or give man any clear directions concerning what he should do. All this was an expression of God's fatherly love for the man and woman he had created. Moreover, when we specify this relationship as a "covenant," it helps us to see the clear parallels between this and the subsequent covenant relationships that God had with his people. If all the elements of a covenant are present (clear stipulation of the parties involved, statement of the conditions of the covenant, and a promise of blessing for obedience and punishment for disobedience), then there seems no reason why we should not refer to it as a covenant, for that is indeed what it was.

Although the covenant that existed before the fall has been referred to by various terms (such as the Adamic Covenant, or the Covenant of Nature), the most helpful

---

3. However, animals were included with human beings in the covenant that God spoke to Noah, promising that he would never again destroy the earth with a flood (Gen. 9:8–17).

designation seems to be "covenant of works," since participation in the blessings of the covenant clearly depended on obedience or "works" on the part of Adam and Eve.

As in all covenants that God makes with man, there is here no negotiating over the provisions. God sovereignly imposes this covenant on Adam and Eve, and they have no opportunity to change the details—their only choice is to keep it or to break it.

Is the covenant of works still in force? In several important senses it is. Paul implies that perfect obedience to God's laws, if it were possible, would lead to life (see Rom. 7:10; 10:5; Gal. 3:12). We should also notice that the punishment for this covenant is still in effect, for "the wages of sin is death" (Rom. 6:23). This implies that the covenant of works is still in force for every human being apart from Christ, even though no sinful human being can fulfill its provisions and gain blessing by it. Finally, we should note that Christ perfectly obeyed the covenant of works for us since he committed no sin (1 Peter 2:22) but completely obeyed God on our behalf (Rom. 5:18–19).

On the other hand, in certain senses, the covenant of works does not remain in force. (1) We no longer are faced with the specific command not to eat of the tree of the knowledge of good and evil. (2) Since we all have a sinful nature (both Christians and non-Christians), we are not able to fulfill the provisions of the covenant of works on our own and receive its benefits—as this covenant applies to people directly, it only brings punishments. (3) For Christians, Christ has fulfilled the provisions of this covenant successfully once for all, and we gain the benefits of it not by actual obedience on our part but by trusting in the merits of Christ's work. In fact, for Christians today to think of themselves as obligated to try to earn God's favor by obedience would be to cut themselves off from the hope of salvation. "All who rely on works of the law are under a curse. . . . Now it is evident that no one is justified before God by the law" (Gal. 3:10–11). Christians have been freed from the covenant of works by virtue of Christ's work and their inclusion in the new covenant, the covenant of grace (see below).

## B. The Covenant of Redemption

Theologians speak of another kind of covenant, a covenant that is not between God and man but is among the members of the Trinity. This covenant they call the "covenant of redemption." It is an agreement among the Father, Son, and Holy Spirit, in which the Son agreed to become a man, be our representative, obey the demands of the covenant of works on our behalf, and pay the penalty for sin, which we deserved. Does Scripture teach its existence? Yes, for it speaks about a specific plan and purpose of God that was agreed upon by the Father, Son, and Holy Spirit in order to gain our redemption.

On the part of the Father, this "covenant of redemption" included an agreement to give to the Son a people whom he would redeem for his own possession (John 17:2, 6), to send the Son to be their representative (John 3:16; Rom. 5:18–19), to prepare a body for the Son to dwell in as a man (Col. 2:9; Heb. 10:5), to accept him as representative of his people whom he had redeemed (Heb. 9:24), and to give him all authority in heaven and on earth (Matt. 28:18), including the authority to pour out the Holy Spirit in power to apply redemption to his people (Acts 1:4; 2:33).

On the part of the Son, there was an agreement that he would come into the world as a man and live as a man under the Mosaic law (Gal. 4:4; Heb. 2:14–18), and that he would be perfectly obedient to all the commands of the Father (Heb. 10:7–9), becoming obedient unto death, even death on a cross (Phil. 2:8). The Son also agreed that he would gather for himself a people in order that none whom the Father had given him would be lost (John 17:12).

The role of the Holy Spirit in the covenant of redemption is sometimes overlooked in discussions of this subject, but certainly it was a unique and essential one. He agreed to do the will of the Father and fill and empower Christ to carry out his ministry on earth (Matt. 3:16; Luke 4:1, 14, 18; John 3:34), and to apply the benefits of Christ's redemptive work to his people after Christ returned to heaven (John 14:16–17, 26; Acts 1:8; 2:17–18, 33).

To refer to the agreement among the members of the Trinity as a "covenant," reminds us that it was something voluntarily undertaken by God, not something that he had to enter into by virtue of his nature. However, this covenant is also different from the covenants between God and man because the parties enter into it as equals, whereas in covenants with man God is the sovereign Creator who imposes the provisions of the covenant by his own decree. On the other hand, it is like the covenants God makes with man in that it has the elements (specifying the parties, conditions, and promised blessings) that make up a covenant.

## C. The Covenant of Grace

### 1. Essential Elements

When man failed to obtain the blessing offered in the covenant of works, it was necessary for God to establish another means, one by which man could be saved. The rest of Scripture after the story of the fall in Genesis 3 is the story of God working out in history the amazing plan of redemption whereby sinful people could come into fellowship with him. Once again, God clearly defines the provisions of a covenant that would specify the relationship between him and those whom he would redeem. In these specifications we find some variation in detail throughout the Old and New Testaments, but the essential elements of a covenant are all there, and the nature of those essential elements remains the same throughout the Old Testament and the New Testament.

The *parties* to this covenant of grace are God and the people whom he will redeem. But in this case Christ fulfills a special role as "mediator" (Heb. 8:6; 9:15; 12:24) in which he fulfills the conditions of the covenant for us and thereby reconciles us to God. (There was no mediator between God and man in the covenant of works.)

The *condition* (or requirement) of participation in the covenant is *faith* in the work of Christ the redeemer (Rom. 1:17; 5:1, et al.). This requirement of faith in the redemptive work of the Messiah was also the condition of obtaining the blessings of the covenant in the Old Testament, as Paul clearly demonstrates through the examples of Abraham and David (Rom. 4:1–15). They, like other Old Testament believers, were saved by looking forward to the work of the Messiah who was to come and putting faith in him.[4]

But while the condition of *beginning* the covenant of grace is always faith in Christ's work alone, the condition of *continuing* in that covenant is said to be obedience to God's commands. Though this obedience did not in the Old Testament and does not in the New Testament earn us any merit with God, nonetheless, if our faith in Christ is genuine, it will produce obedience (see James 2:17), and obedience to Christ is in the New Testament seen as necessary evidence that we are truly believers and members of the new covenant (see 1 John 2:4–6).

The *promise* of blessings in the covenant was a promise of eternal life with God. This promise was repeated frequently throughout the Old and the New Testaments. God promised that he would be their God and that they would be his people. "And I will establish my covenant between me and you and your offspring after you throughout their generations for an everlasting covenant, *to be God to you* and to your offspring after you" (Gen. 17:7). "I will be their God, and they shall be my people" (Jer. 31:33). "And they shall be my people, and I will be their God . . . I will make with them an everlasting covenant" (Jer. 32:38–40; cf. Ezek. 34:30–31; 36:28; 37:26–27). That theme is picked up in the New Testament as well: *"I will be their God, and they shall be my people"* (2 Cor. 6:16; cf. a similar theme in vv. 17–18; also 1 Peter 2:9–10). In speaking of the new covenant, the author of Hebrews quotes Jeremiah 31: "I will be their God, and they shall be my people" (Heb. 8:10). This blessing finds fulfillment in the church, which is the people of God, and it finds its greatest fulfillment in the new heaven and new earth, as John sees in his vision of the age to come: "Behold, the dwelling place of God is with man. He will dwell with them, and *they will be his people, and God himself will be with them as their God*" (Rev. 21:3).

The *sign* of this covenant (the outward, physical symbol of inclusion in the covenant) varies between the Old Testament and the New Testament. In the Old Testament the outward sign of *beginning* the covenant relationship was circumcision. The sign of *continuing* the covenant relationship was continuing to observe all the festivals and ceremonial laws that God gave the people at various times. In the new covenant, the sign of *beginning* a covenant relationship is baptism, while the sign of *continuing* in that relationship is participation in the Lord's Supper.

The reason this covenant is called a "covenant of grace" is that it is entirely based on God's "grace" or unmerited favor toward those whom he redeems.

---

4. See chapter 7, pp. 137–39, for a discussion of the fact that Old Testament believers were saved only by trusting in the Messiah who was to come.

## 2. Various Forms of the Covenant

Although the essential elements of the covenant of grace remain the same throughout the history of God's people, the specific provisions of the covenant vary from time to time. At the time of Adam and Eve, there was only the bare hint of the possibility of a relationship with God found in the promise about the seed of the woman in Genesis 3:15 and in God's gracious provision of clothing for Adam and Eve (Gen. 3:21).

**a. The Noahic Covenant.** The covenant that God made with Noah after the flood (Gen. 9:8–17) is substantially different from the ones that follow, so there is some question whether it should be categorized with the other covenants that follow, that clearly belong in the category "covenant of grace"—but it does also depend on God's grace. However, it was not a covenant that promised all the blessings of eternal life or spiritual fellowship with God. Instead, God promised all mankind and the animal creation that *the earth would no longer be destroyed by a flood.* In this sense the covenant with Noah, although it certainly does depend on God's grace or unmerited favor, appears to be quite different in the parties involved (God and all mankind, not just the redeemed), the condition named (no faith or obedience is required of man), and the blessing that is promised (that the earth will not be destroyed again by flood, certainly a different promise from that of eternal life). The sign of the covenant (the rainbow) is also different in that it requires no active or voluntary participation on man's part.

**b. The Abrahamic Covenant.** Beginning with the covenant with Abraham (Gen. 15:1–21; 17:1–27), the essential elements of the covenant of grace are all present. In fact, Paul can say that "the Scripture . . . preached the gospel beforehand to Abraham" (Gal. 3:8). Moreover, Luke tells us that Zechariah, the father of John the Baptist, prophesied that the coming of John the Baptist to prepare the way for Christ was the beginning of God's working to fulfill the ancient covenant promises to Abraham ("to show the mercy promised to our fathers and *to remember his holy covenant,* the oath that he swore to our father Abraham," Luke 1:72–73). So the covenant promises to Abraham remained in force even as they found fulfillment in Christ (see Rom. 4:1–25; Gal. 3:6–18, 29; Heb. 2:16; 6:13–20).[5]

**c. The Mosaic Covenant.** What then is the "old covenant" in contrast with the "new covenant" in Christ? *It is not the whole of the Old Testament* because the covenants with Abraham and David are never called "old" in the New Testament. Rather, *only the covenant under Moses,* the covenant made at Mount Sinai (Ex. 19–24), is called the "old covenant" (2 Cor. 3:14; cf. Heb. 8:6, 13) to be replaced by the "new covenant" in Christ (Luke 22:20; 1 Cor. 11:25; 2 Cor. 3:6; Heb. 8:8, 13; 9:15; 12:24). The Mosaic covenant

---

5. The covenant promises to Abraham were renewed and further assurances given when God spoke with David (see esp. 2 Sam. 7:5–16; cf. Jer. 33:19–22), giving to David the promise that a Davidic king would reign over the people of God forever. For an excellent discussion of the continuity of God's promises as seen in the covenants made with Abraham and David, and in the new covenant, see Thomas E. McComiskey, *The Covenants of Promise: A Theology of the Old Testament Covenants* (Grand Rapids: Baker, 1985), esp. pp. 59–93.

was an administration[6] of detailed written laws given for a time to restrain the sins of the people and to be a custodian to point people to Christ. Paul says, "Why then the law? It was added because of transgressions, until the offspring should come to whom the promise had been made" (Gal. 3:19), and "The law was our guardian until Christ came" (Gal. 3:24).

We should not assume that there was no grace available to people from Moses until Christ, because the promise of salvation by faith that God had made to Abraham remained in force: "Now the promises were made to Abraham and to his offspring . . . *the law*, which came 430 years afterward, *does not annul a covenant previously ratified by God*, so as to make the promise void. For if the inheritance comes by the law, it no longer comes by promise; but God gave it to Abraham by a promise" (Gal. 3:16–18). Although the sacrificial system of the Mosaic covenant did not really take away sins (Heb. 10:1–4), it foreshadowed the bearing of sin by Christ, the perfect high priest who was also the perfect sacrifice (Heb. 9:11–28). Nevertheless, the Mosaic covenant itself, with all its detailed laws, could not save people. It is not that the laws were wrong in themselves, for they were given by a holy God, but they had no power to give people new life, and the people were not able to obey them perfectly: "Is the law then contrary to the promises of God? Certainly not! For if a law had been given that could give life, then righteousness would indeed be by the law" (Gal. 3:21). Paul realizes that the Holy Spirit working within us can empower us to obey God in a way that the Mosaic law never could, for he says that God "has made us sufficient to be ministers of a new covenant, not of the letter but of the Spirit. For the letter kills, but the Spirit gives life" (2 Cor. 3:6).

**d. The Davidic Covenant.** The covenant that God made with David does not replace the covenant with Abraham or the covenant with Moses but assumes their continuing validity and adds the new promise that the throne of kingship over God's people would belong to David and his descendants forever, with certain conditions regarding the conduct of individual kings. Here are the words the prophet Nathan spoke to David:

> Thus says the LORD of hosts, I took you from the pasture, from following the sheep, that you should be prince over my people Israel. And I have been with you wherever you went and have cut off all your enemies from before you. And I will make for you a great name, like the name of the great ones of the earth. And I will appoint a place for my people Israel and will plant them, so that they may dwell in their own place and be disturbed no more. And violent men shall afflict them no more, as formerly, from the time that I appointed judges over my people Israel. And I will give you rest from all your enemies. Moreover, the LORD declares to you that the LORD will make you a house. When your days are fulfilled and you lie down

---

6. For an excellent discussion of the difference between the overarching covenant of promise and the various "administra-tive covenants" that God used at different times, see McComiskey, *Covenants of Promise*, esp. pp. 139–77, 193–211.

with your fathers, I will raise up your offspring after you, who shall come from your body, and I will establish his kingdom. He shall build a house for my name, and I will establish the throne of his kingdom forever. I will be to him a father, and he shall be to me a son. When he commits iniquity, I will discipline him with the rod of men, with the stripes of the sons of men, but my steadfast love will not depart from him, as I took it from Saul, whom I put away from before you. And your house and your kingdom shall be made sure forever before me. Your throne shall be established forever. (2 Sam. 7:8–16)

This promise of an eternal Davidic kingship was ultimately fulfilled in Jesus Christ, the descendant of David (see Matt. 1:1; Luke 1:32–33; Acts 2:29–32; Rom. 1:3; 2 Tim. 2:8; Rev. 3:7; 5:5; 22:16).

**e. The New Covenant.** The new covenant in Christ is far better because it fulfills the promises of a better covenant that were made long ago in Jeremiah 31:31–34, promises that were later quoted in Hebrews 8:6–13:

But as it is, Christ has obtained a ministry that is as much more excellent than the old as *the covenant he mediates is better*, since it is enacted on better promises. For if that first covenant had been faultless, there would have been no occasion to look for a second.

For he finds fault with them when he says:

"Behold, the days are coming, declares the Lord,
　　when I will establish a new covenant with the house of Israel
　　and with the house of Judah,
　not like the covenant that I made with their fathers
　　on the day when I took them by the hand to bring them out of the
　　　land of Egypt.
For they did not continue in my covenant,
　　and so I showed no concern for them, declares the Lord.
For this is the covenant that I will make with the house of Israel
　　after those days, declares the Lord:
I will put my laws into their minds,
　　and write them on their hearts,
and I will be their God,
　　and they shall be my people.
And they shall not teach, each one his neighbor
　　and each one his brother, saying, 'Know the Lord,'
for they shall all know me,
　　from the least of them to the greatest.

> For I will be merciful toward their iniquities,
>     and I will remember their sins no more."

In speaking of a new covenant, he makes the first one obsolete. And what is becoming obsolete and growing old is ready to vanish away.

In this new covenant, there are far greater blessings, for Jesus the Messiah has come; he has lived, died, and risen among us, atoning once for all for our sins (Heb. 9:24–28); he has revealed God more fully to us (John 1:14; Heb. 1:1–3); he has poured out the Holy Spirit on all his people in new covenant power (Acts 1:8; 1 Cor. 12:13; 2 Cor. 3:4–18); and he has written his laws on our hearts (Heb. 8:10). (I explain the more powerful work of the Holy Spirit in the new covenant in more detail in chapter 39, pp. 951–53.) This new covenant is the "eternal covenant" (Heb. 13:20) in Christ, through which we shall forever have fellowship with God, and he shall be our God, and we shall be his people.

## D. The Relationship between the Covenants

For many decades there have been discussions between the advocates of covenant theology and the advocates of dispensationalism. The overview of the covenants that I presented above is representative of covenant theology, with its emphasis on the continuity between the Old Testament and New Testament (in the covenant of grace). By contrast, dispensationalism emphasizes discontinuity between the ways God related to people during periods of history, or "dispensations." The seven dispensations are (1) innocence (Gen. 1:28–30), (2) conscience (Gen. 3:8–8:22), (3) human government (Gen. 8–11), (4) promise (Gen. 12–Ex. 19:22), (5) law (Ex. 20–Christ's death), (6) grace (Christ's death–second coming), (7) millennial kingdom (Rev. 20:1–10).[7]

Recently, a third alternative, called "progressive covenantalism," has gained influence. This view holds that the Old Testament includes five different covenants (with creation [and renewed with Noah], Abraham, Israel, and David) and that these covenants are fulfilled in Christ. It also holds that covenants in the Bible are both conditional (in one sense—they require a faithful covenant keeper, who is ultimately Christ) and unconditional (in another sense—God will accomplish his purposes).[8]

---

7. A list of these dispensations can be found in many places, but I have taken this from Steve Johnson, "How Does the Bible Fit Together? Three Views," at http://www.ps.edu/bible-fit-together-three-views/.

8. *Ibid*. Extensive explanations of progressive covenantalism can be found in Peter Gentry and Stephen Wellum, *Kingdom through Covenant: A Biblical-Theological Understanding of the Covenants*, second ed. (Wheaton, IL: Crossway, 2018), and Stephen Wellum and Brent Parker, eds., *Progressive Covenantalism: Charting a Course between Dispensational and Covenantal Theologies* (Nashville: B&H, 2016).

# QUESTIONS FOR PERSONAL APPLICATION

1. Before reading this chapter, had you thought of your relationship to God in terms of a "covenant"? Does it give you any added degree of certainty or sense of security in your relationship to God to know that he governs that relationship by a set of promises that he will never change?

2. If you were to think of the relationship between God and yourself personally in terms of a covenant, whereby you and God are the only two parties involved, then what would be the conditions of this covenant between you and God? Are you now fulfilling those conditions? What role does Christ play in the covenant relationship between you and God? What are the blessings God promises to you if you fulfill those conditions? What are the signs of participation in this covenant? Does this understanding of the covenant increase your appreciation of baptism and the Lord's Supper?

**Special Terms**

*covenant*
*covenant of grace*
*covenant of redemption*
*covenant of works*
*new covenant*
*old covenant*
*progressive covenantalism*

# BIBLIOGRAPHY

(For an explanation of this bibliography see the note on the bibliography to chapter 1, pp. 23–24. Complete bibliographical data may be found on pp. 1489–96.)

## SECTIONS IN EVANGELICAL SYSTEMATIC THEOLOGIES

### 1. Anglican (Episcopalian)
1882–92 . . . . . Litton (no explicit treatment)
1930 . . . . . . . . Thomas, 134–41
2001 . . . . . . . . Packer, 87–90
2013 . . . . . . . . Bird, 496–97, 502–06, 508–511
2013 . . . . . . . . Bray, 51–67

### 2. Arminian (Wesleyan or Methodist)
1992 . . . . . . . . Oden, 1: 220
2002 . . . . . . . . Cottrell, 366, 409, 465

1983 . . . . . . . . Carter, 1:476–83

### 3. Baptist
1767 . . . . . . . . Gill, 1:300–359, 491–530
1887 . . . . . . . . Boyce, 247–58
1990–95 . . . . . Garrett, 1:105–15
2007 . . . . . . . . Akin, 199–201

### 4. Dispensational
1947 . . . . . . . . Chafer, 7:96–99
1949 . . . . . . . . Thiessen, 199–205
1986 . . . . . . . . Ryrie, 453–60
2002–2005 . . Geisler, 4:499–546
2017 . . . . . . . . MacArthur and Mayhue, 26, 852, 860, 870–80

### 5. Lutheran
1934 . . . . . . . . Mueller (no explicit treatment)

## 6. Reformed (or Presbyterian)

1679–85 . . . . . Turretin, *IET*, 1:574–78,
                  616–17, 2:169–269, 3:344,
                  472–73
1871–73 . . . . . Hodge, 2:117–22, 354–77
1878 . . . . . . . . Dabney, 292–305, 429–63
1894 . . . . . . . . Shedd, 350, 678–81, 844
1906–11 . . . . . Bavinck, *RD*, 3:193–232
1910 . . . . . . . . Vos, 2:76–138
1937–66 . . . . . Murray, *CW*, 2:47–59,
                  123–31
1938 . . . . . . . . Berkhof, 211–18, 262–301
1962 . . . . . . . . Buswell, 1:307–20
1998 . . . . . . . . Reymond, 404–6
2008 . . . . . . . . Van Genderen and Velema,
                  539–72
2011 . . . . . . . . Horton, 44–47
2013 . . . . . . . . Frame, 17–20, 55–84,
                  248–52
2013 . . . . . . . . Culver, 397–98, 855–56
2016 . . . . . . . . Allen and Swain, 107–25
2017 . . . . . . . . Barrett, 163
2019 . . . . . . . . Letham, 431–67

## 7. Renewal (or charismatic/Pentecostal)

1988–92 . . . . . Williams, 1:275–304
2008 . . . . . . . . Duffield and Van Cleave, 60,
                  68, 221, 379

## SECTIONS IN REPRESENTATIVE ROMAN CATHOLIC SYSTEMATIC THEOLOGIES

### 1. Roman Catholic: Traditional

1955 . . . . . . . . Ott (no explicit treatment)

### 2. Roman Catholic: Post–Vatican II

1980 . . . . . . . . McBrien (no explicit treatment)
2012 . . . . . . . . *CCC*, paragraphs 238, 781,
                  1102, 1612, 2058

## OTHER WORKS

Archer, G. L. "Covenant." In *EDT3*, 214–15.

Bingham, D. Jeffrey and and Glenn R. Kreider, eds. Dispensationalism and The History Of Redemption: A Developing and Diverse Tradition. Chicago: Moody Publishers, 2015.

Blaising, C. A. "Dispensation, Dispensationalism." In *EDT3*, 248–49.

Campbell, W. S. "Covenant and New Covenant." In *DPL*, 179–183.

Collins, G. N. M. "Federal Theology." In *EDT3*, 311–12.

Dumbrell, W. J. *Covenant and Creation*. Nashville: Nelson, 1984.

Fuller, Daniel P. *Gospel and Law: Contrast or Continuum? The Hermeneutics of Dispensationalism and Covenant Theology*. Grand Rapids: Eerdmans, 1980.

Gentry, Peter and Stephen J. Wellum. *Kingdom through Covenant: A Biblical-Theological Understanding of the Covenants*, 2nd ed. Wheaton, IL: Crossway, 2018.

Jocz, Jakob. *The Covenant: A Theology of Human Destiny*. Grand Rapids: Eerdmans, 1968.

Kaiser, Walter C., Jr. *Toward an Old Testament Theology*. Grand Rapids: Zondervan, 1978.

Martens, Elmer. *God's Design: A Focus on Old Testament Theology*. Grand Rapids: Baker, 1981.

McComiskey, Thomas E. *The Covenants of Promise: A Theology of the Old Testament Covenants*. Grand Rapids: Baker, 1985.

Meyer, Jason C. *The End of the Law: Mosaic Covenant in Pauline Theology*. Nashville: B&H Academic, 2009.

Murray, John. *Covenant of Grace*. London: Tyndale, 1954.

Newman, C. C. "Covenant, New Covenant." In *DLNT*, 245–50.

Osterhaven, M. E. "Covenant Theology." In *EDT3*, 215–16.

Pentecost, J. Dwight. *Thy Kingdom Come*. Wheaton, IL: Scripture Press, 1990.

Peters, G. N. H. *The Theocratic Kingdom*. 3 vols. 1884. Reprint, Grand Rapids: Kregel, 1988.

Rayburn, R. S. "Covenant, The New." In *EDT1*, 278–79.

Robertson, O. Palmer. *The Christ of the Covenants*. Grand Rapids: Baker, 1980.

Ryrie, C. C. *Dispensationalism*. Rev. ed. Chicago: Moody Publishers, 2007.

VanGemeren, Willem. *The Progress of Redemption*. Grand Rapids: Zondervan, 1988.

Van Groningen, Gerard. "Covenant." In *BTDB*, 124–32.

Wellum, Stephen, and Brent Parker, eds. *Progressive Covenantalism: Charting a Course between Dispensational and Covenantal Theologies*. Nashville: B&H, 2016.

Williamson, P. R. "Covenant." In *NDBT*, 419–29.

Williamson, Paul R. "The *Pactum Salutis*: A Scriptural Concept or Scholastic Mythology?" *Tyndale Bulletin* 69, no. 2 (2018): 259–81.

## SCRIPTURE MEMORY PASSAGE

**Hebrews 8:10:**

*For this is the covenant that I will make with the house of Israel*
*after those days, declares the Lord:*
*I will put my laws into their minds,*
*and write them on their hearts,*
*and I will be their God,*
*and they shall be my people.*

## HYMN

### "Trust and Obey"

This hymn reminds us that the enjoyment of God's blessings depends on our continuing to fulfill the conditions of faith and obedience as stipulated in the New Testament, which is the written record of the provisions of the new covenant that God has made with us.

*When we walk with the Lord in the light of his Word,*
*What a glory he sheds on our way!*
*While we do his good will, he abides with us still,*
*And with all who will trust and obey.*

*Chorus*
*Trust and obey, for there's no other way*
*To be happy in Jesus, but to trust and obey.*

*Not a shadow can rise, not a cloud in the skies,*
*But his smile quickly drives it away;*
*Not a doubt or a fear, not a sigh nor a tear,*
*Can abide while we trust and obey.*

*Not a burden we bear, not a sorrow we share,*
*But our toil he doth richly repay;*
*Not a grief nor a loss, not a frown or a cross,*
*But is blest if we trust and obey.*

*But we never can prove the delights of his love*
*Until all on the altar we lay;*
*For the favor he shows, and the joy he bestows,*
*Are for them who will trust and obey.*

*Then in fellowship sweet we will sit at his feet,*
*Or we'll walk by his side in the way;*
*What he says we will do, where he sends we will go,*
*Never fear, only trust and obey.*

Author: James H. Sammis, d. 1919

## CONTEMPORARY WORSHIP SONG

**"You Are My King (Amazing Love)"**

*I'm forgiven*
*Because You were forsaken.*
*I'm accepted;*
*You were condemned.*
*I'm alive and well;*
*Your Spirit is within me*
*Because You died*
*And rose again.*

*Chorus*
*Amazing love,*
*How can it be*
*That You my King*
*Would die for me?*
*Amazing love,*
*I know it's true.*
*It's my joy to honor You.*
*In all I do I honor You.*

*Ending*
*You are my King.*
*You are my King.*
*Jesus, You are my King.*
*Jesus, You are my King.*

Words by Billy James Foote[9]

# PART 4

# The Doctrines of Christ
# and the Holy Spirit

# CHAPTER 26

# The Person of Christ

*How is Jesus fully God and fully man, yet one person?*

## EXPLANATION AND SCRIPTURAL BASIS

We may summarize the biblical teaching about the person of Christ as follows: *Jesus Christ was fully God and fully man in one person and will be so forever.*

The scriptural material supporting this definition is extensive. We will discuss first the humanity of Christ, then his deity, and then attempt to show how Jesus' deity and humanity are united in the one person of Christ.

### A. The Humanity of Christ

### 1. Virgin Birth

When we speak of the humanity of Christ it is appropriate to begin with a consideration of the virgin birth of Christ. Scripture clearly asserts that Jesus was conceived in the womb of his mother Mary by a miraculous work of the Holy Spirit and without a human father.

"Now the birth of Jesus Christ took place in this way. When his mother Mary had been betrothed to Joseph, *before they came together* she was found to be with child *from the Holy Spirit*" (Matt. 1:18). Shortly after that, an angel of the Lord said to Joseph, who was engaged to Mary, "Joseph, son of David, do not fear to take Mary as your wife, for *that which is conceived in her is from the Holy Spirit*" (Matt. 1:20). Then we read that Joseph "did as the angel of the Lord commanded him: he took his wife, but knew her not until she had given birth to a son. And he called his name Jesus" (Matt. 1:24–25).

The same fact is affirmed in Luke's gospel, where we read about the appearance of the angel Gabriel to Mary. After the angel had told her that she would bear a son, Mary said, "How will this be, since I am a virgin?" The angel answered,

> The Holy Spirit will come upon you,
>> and the power of the Most High will overshadow you;
> therefore the child to be born will be called holy—
>> the Son of God. (Luke 1:35; cf. 3:23)

The doctrinal importance of the virgin birth is seen in at least three areas.

First, it shows that salvation ultimately must come from the Lord. Just as God had promised that the "seed" of the woman (Gen. 3:15) would ultimately destroy the serpent, so God brought it about by his own power, not through mere human effort. The virgin birth of Christ is an unmistakable reminder that salvation can never come through human effort, but must be the work of God himself. Our salvation only comes about through the supernatural work of God, and that was evident at the very beginning of Jesus' life when "God sent forth his Son, born of woman, born under the law, to redeem those who were under the law, so that we might receive adoption as sons" (Gal. 4:4–5).

Second, the virgin birth made possible the uniting of full deity and full humanity in one person. This was the means God used to send his Son (John 3:16; Gal. 4:4) into the world as a man. If we think for a moment of other possible ways in which Christ might have come to the earth, none of them would so clearly unite humanity and deity in one person. It probably would have been possible for God to create Jesus as a complete human being in heaven and send him to descend from heaven to earth without the benefit of any human parent. But then it would have been very hard for us to see how Jesus could be fully human as we are, nor would he be a part of the human race that physically descended from Adam. On the other hand, it probably would have been possible for God to have Jesus come into the world with two human parents, both a father and a mother, and with his full divine nature miraculously united to his human nature at some point early in his life. But then it would have been hard for us to understand how Jesus was fully God, since his origin was like ours in every way. When we think of these two other possibilities, it helps us to understand how God, in his wisdom, ordained a combination of human and divine influence in the birth of Christ, so that his full humanity would be evident to us from the fact of his ordinary human birth from a human mother, and his full deity would be evident from the fact of his conception in Mary's womb by the powerful work of the Holy Spirit.[1]

Third, the virgin birth also makes possible Christ's true humanity without inherited sin. As we noted in chapter 24, all human beings have inherited legal guilt and a corrupt moral nature from their first father, Adam (this is sometimes called "inherited sin" or "original sin"). But the fact that Jesus did not have a human father means that the line of descent from Adam is partially interrupted. Jesus did not descend from Adam in exactly the same way in which every other human being has descended from Adam. And this helps us to understand why the legal guilt and moral corruption that belongs to all other human beings did not belong to Christ.

This idea seems to be indicated in the statement of the angel Gabriel to Mary, where he says to her,

---

1. This is not to say that it would have been *impossible* for God to bring Christ into the world in any other way, but only to say that God, in his wisdom, decided that this would be the best way to bring it about, and part of that is evident in the fact that the virgin birth does help us understand how Jesus can be fully God and fully man. Whether any other means of bringing Christ into the world would have been "possible" in some absolute sense of "possible," Scripture does not tell us.

The Holy Spirit will come upon you,
  and the power of the Most High will overshadow you;
therefore the child to be born will be called holy—
  the Son of God. (Luke 1:35)

*Because* the Spirit brought about the conception of Jesus in the womb of Mary, the child was to be called "holy."[2] Such a conclusion does not necessarily mean that the transmission of sin in the human race comes only through the father, for Scripture nowhere makes such an assertion. It is enough for us merely to say that *in this case* the unbroken line of descent from Adam was interrupted, and Jesus was conceived by the power of the Holy Spirit. Luke 1:35 connects this conception by the Holy Spirit with the holiness or moral purity of Christ, and reflection on that fact allows us to understand that through the absence of a human father, Jesus was not fully descended from Adam and that this break in the line of descent was the method God used to bring it about that Jesus was fully human yet did not share inherited sin from Adam.

But why did Jesus not inherit a sinful nature from Mary? The Roman Catholic Church answers this question by saying that Mary herself was free from sin, but Scripture nowhere teaches this, and it would not really solve the problem anyway (for why then did Mary not inherit sin from her mother?).[3] A better solution is to say that the work of the Holy Spirit in

---

2. I have quoted here the translation of the ESV, which I think to be correct (so NIV margin). But it is also grammatically possible to translate the words as "so the holy one to be born will be called the Son of God" (NIV; similarly, NASB). The Greek phrase is *dio kai to gennōmenon hagion klēthēsetai, huios theou*. The decision on which translation is correct depends on whether we take *to gennōmenon* as the subject, meaning "the child to be born," or whether we think that the subject is *to hagion*, "the holy one," with the participle *gennōmenon* then functioning as an adjective, giving the sense "the being-born holy one" (this is the way the NIV and NASB understand it).

Recently, more extensive lexical research seems to indicate that the expression *to gennōmenon* was a fairly common expression that was readily understood to mean "the child to be born." Examples of this use can be seen in Plotinus, *Nead*, 3.6.20–24; Plato, *Menexenus*, 237E; *Laws*, 6,775C; Philo, *On the Creation*, 100; *On the Change of Names*, 267; Plutarch, *Moralia*, "Advice to Bride and Groom," 140F; "On Affection for Offspring," 495E. More examples could probably be found with a more extensive computer search, but these should be sufficient to demonstrate that the mere grammatical possibility of translating Luke 1:35 the way the NIV and NASB do is not a strong argument in favor of their translations, because Greek-speaking readers in the first century would ordinarily have understood the two-word expression *to gennōmenon* as a unit meaning "the child to be born." Because of this fact, the ESV represents the sense that first-century readers would have understood from the sentence: "therefore *the child to be born* will be called holy."

(I discovered these examples of *to gennōmenon* by searching the Thesaurus Linguae Graecae data base on the Ibycus computer at Trinity Evangelical Divinity School.)

3. The Roman Catholic Church teaches the doctrine of the *immaculate conception*. This doctrine does not refer to the conception of Jesus in Mary's womb but to the conception of *Mary* in her mother's womb, and it teaches that Mary was free from inherited sin. On December 8, 1854, Pope Pius IX proclaimed, "The most Blessed Virgin Mary was, from the first moment of her conception . . . preserved immune from all stain of original sin" (*Catechism of the Catholic Church*, paragraph 491). The Catholic Church also teaches that "By the grace of God Mary remained free of every personal sin her whole life long" (ibid., paragraph 493).

In response, we must say that the New Testament does highly honor Mary as one who has "found favor with God" (Luke 1:30) and one who is "Blessed . . . among women" (Luke 1:42), but nowhere does the Bible indicate that Mary was free from inherited sin (original sin). The expression, "Greetings, O *favored one*, the Lord is with you!" (Luke 1:28) does not mean that Mary was "full of grace" but simply means that Mary has found much blessing from God; the same word translated "favored" in Luke 1:28 (Gk. *charitoō*) is used to refer to all Christians in Eph. 1:6 (RSV): "his glorious grace which he *freely bestowed* on us in the Beloved." In fact, Ludwig Ott, *Fundamentals of Catholic Dogma*, trans. Patrick Lynch (Rockford: Tan, 1960), says, "The doctrine of the Immaculate Conception of Mary is not explicitly revealed in Scripture" (p. 200), though he thinks it is implicit in Gen. 3:15 and Luke 1:28, 41.

Mary must have prevented not only the transmission of sin from Joseph (for Jesus had no human father) but also, in a miraculous way, the transmission of sin from Mary: "The Holy Spirit will come upon you . . . *therefore* the child to be born will be called *holy*" (Luke 1:35).

It has been common, at least in previous generations, for those who do not accept the complete truthfulness of Scripture to deny the doctrine of the virgin birth of Christ. But if our beliefs are to be governed by the statements of Scripture, then we will certainly not deny this teaching. Whether or not we could discern any aspects of doctrinal importance for this teaching, we should believe it first of all simply because Scripture affirms it. Certainly such a miracle is not too hard for the God who created the universe and everything in it—anyone who affirms that a virgin birth is "impossible" is just confessing his or her own unbelief in the God of the Bible. Yet in addition to the fact that Scripture teaches the virgin birth, we can see that it is doctrinally important, and if we are to understand the biblical teaching on the person of Christ correctly, it is important that we begin with an affirmation of this doctrine.

## 2. Human Weaknesses and Limitations

**a. Jesus Had a Human Body.** The fact that Jesus had a human body just like our human bodies is seen in many passages of Scripture. He was born just as all human babies are born (Luke 2:7). He grew through childhood to adulthood just as other children grow: "And the child *grew and became strong*, filled with wisdom. And the favor of God was upon him" (Luke 2:40). Moreover, Luke tells us that "Jesus increased in wisdom *and in stature* and in favor with God and man" (Luke 2:52).

Jesus became tired just as we do, for we read that "Jesus, *wearied* as he was from his journey, was sitting beside the well" in Samaria (John 4:6). He became thirsty, for when he was on the cross he said, "I *thirst*" (John 19:28). After he had fasted for forty days in the wilderness, we read that "he was *hungry*" (Matt. 4:2). He was at times physically weak, for during his temptation in the wilderness he fasted for forty days (the point at which a human being's physical strength is almost entirely gone and beyond which irreparable physical harm will occur if the fast continues). At that time "angels came and were ministering to him" (Matt. 4:11), apparently to care for him and provide nourishment until he regained enough strength to come out of the wilderness. When Jesus was on his way to be crucified, the soldiers forced Simon of Cyrene to carry his cross (Luke 23:26), most likely because Jesus was so weak following the beating he had received that he did not have strength enough to carry it. The culmination of Jesus' limitations in terms of his human body is seen when he died on the cross (Luke 23:46). His human body ceased to have life in it and ceased to function, just as ours does when we die.

Jesus also rose from the dead in a physical, human body, though one that was made perfect and was no longer subject to weakness, disease, or death. He demonstrates repeatedly to his disciples that he does have a real physical body. He says, "See my hands and my feet, that it is I myself. Touch me, and see. *For a spirit does not have flesh and bones as you see that I have*" (Luke 24:39). He is showing them and teaching them that he has "flesh and bones" and is not merely a "spirit" without a body. Another evidence of this fact is that "they gave him a piece of broiled fish, and he took it and ate before them" (Luke 24:42–43; cf. v. 30; John 20:17, 20, 27; 21:9, 13).

In this same human body (though a resurrection body that was made perfect), Jesus also ascended into heaven. He said before he left, "I am leaving the world and going to the Father" (John 16:28; cf. 17:11). The way in which Jesus ascended up to heaven was calculated to demonstrate the continuity between his existence in a physical body here on earth and his continuing existence in that body in heaven. Just a few verses after Jesus had told them, "A spirit does not have flesh and bones as you see that I have" (Luke 24:39), we read in Luke's gospel that Jesus "led them out as far as Bethany, and lifting up his hands he blessed them. While he blessed them, he parted from them and was carried up into heaven" (Luke 24:50–51). Similarly, we read in Acts, "As they were looking on, he was lifted up, and a cloud took him out of their sight" (Acts 1:9).

All of these verses taken together show that, as far as Jesus' human body is concerned, it was like ours in every respect before his resurrection, and after his resurrection it was still a human body with "flesh and bones" but made perfect, the kind of body that we will have when Christ returns and we are raised from the dead as well.[4] Jesus continues to exist in that human body in heaven, as the ascension is designed to teach.

**b. Jesus Had a Human Mind.** The fact that Jesus "*increased in wisdom*" (Luke 2:52) says that he went through a learning process just as all other children do—he learned how to eat, how to talk, how to read and write, and how to be obedient to his parents (see Heb. 5:8). This ordinary learning process was part of the genuine humanity of Christ.

We also see that Jesus had a human mind like ours when he speaks of the day on which he will return to earth: "But concerning that day or that hour, no one knows, not even the angels in heaven, nor the Son, but only the Father" (Mark 13:32).[5]

**c. Jesus Had a Human Soul and Human Emotions.** We see several indications that Jesus had a human soul (or spirit). Just before his crucifixion, Jesus said, "Now is my soul *troubled*" (John 12:27). John writes just a little later, "After saying these things, Jesus was *troubled* in his spirit" (John 13:21). In both verses the word *troubled* represents the Greek term *tarassō*, a word that is often used of people when they are anxious or suddenly very surprised by danger.[6]

---

4. See chapter 28, pp. 753–54, and chapter 42, pp. 1021–26, on the nature of the resurrection body.

5. See further discussion of this verse below, pp. 698–700.

6. The word *tarassō*, "troubled," is used, for example, to speak of the fact that Herod was "troubled" when he heard that the wise men had come looking for the new king of the Jews (Matt. 2:3); the disciples "were troubled" when they suddenly saw Jesus walking on the sea and thought he was a ghost (Matt. 14:26); Zechariah was "troubled" when he suddenly saw an angel appear in the temple in Jerusalem (Luke 1:12); and the disciples were "troubled" when Jesus suddenly appeared among them after his resurrection (Luke 24:38). But the word is also used in John 14:1, 27, when Jesus says, "Let not your hearts be *troubled*." When Jesus was troubled in his spirit, therefore, we must not think that there was any lack of faith or any sin involved, but it was definitely a strong human emotion that accompanied a time of extreme danger.

Moreover, before Jesus' crucifixion, as he realized the suffering he would face, he said, "My soul is very sorrowful, even to death" (Matt. 26:38). So great was the sorrow he felt that it seemed as though, if it were to become any stronger, it would take his very life.

Jesus had a full range of human emotions. He "marveled" at the faith of the centurion (Matt. 8:10). He wept with sorrow at the death of Lazarus (John 11:35). And he prayed with a heart full of emotion, for "in the days of his flesh, Jesus offered up prayers and supplications, *with loud cries and tears*, to him who was able to save him from death, and he was heard because of his reverence" (Heb. 5:7).

Moreover, the author tells us, "Although he was a son, *he learned obedience* through what he suffered. And being made perfect he became the source of eternal salvation to all who obey him" (Heb. 5:8–9). Yet if Jesus never sinned, how could he "learn obedience"? Apparently as Jesus grew toward maturity he, like all other human children, was able to take on more and more responsibility. The older he became, the more demands his father and mother could place on him in terms of obedience, and the more difficult the tasks that his heavenly Father could assign to him to carry out in the strength of his human nature. With each increasingly difficult task, even when it involved some suffering (as Heb. 5:8 specifies), Jesus' human moral ability, his ability to obey under more and more difficult circumstances, increased. We might say that his "moral backbone" was strengthened by more and more difficult exercise. Yet in all this he never once sinned.

The complete absence of sin in the life of Jesus is all the more remarkable because of the severe temptations he faced, not only in the wilderness but throughout his life. The author of Hebrews affirms that Jesus "*in every respect* has been tempted as we are, yet without sin" (Heb. 4:15). The fact that he faced temptation means that he had a genuine human nature that could be tempted, for Scripture clearly tells us that "God cannot be tempted with evil" (James 1:13).

**d. People Near Jesus Saw Him as Only a Man.** Matthew reports an amazing incident in the middle of Jesus' ministry. Even though Jesus had taught throughout all Galilee, "healing every disease and every affliction among the people" so that "great crowds followed him" (Matt. 4:23–25), when he came to his own village of Nazareth, the people who had known him for many years did not receive him:

> And when Jesus had finished these parables, he went away from there, and coming to his hometown he taught them in their synagogue, so that they were astonished, and said, "*Where did this man get this wisdom and these mighty works?* Is not this the carpenter's son? Is not his mother called Mary? And are not his brothers James and Joseph and Simon and Judas? And are not all his sisters with us? Where then did this man get all these things?" And *they took offense at him.* . . . And he did not do many mighty works there, *because of their unbelief.* (Matt. 13:53–58)

This passage indicates that those people who knew Jesus best, the neighbors with whom he had lived and worked for thirty years, saw him as no more than an ordinary man—a good man, no doubt, fair and kind and truthful, but certainly not a prophet of God who could work miracles and certainly not God himself in the flesh. Although in the following sections we will see how Jesus was fully divine in every way—he was truly God and man in one person—we must still recognize the full force of a passage like this. For the first thirty years of his life Jesus lived a human life that was so ordinary that the people of Nazareth who knew him best were amazed that he could teach with authority and work miracles. They knew him. He was one of them. He was "the carpenter's son" (Matt. 13:55), and he was himself "the carpenter" (Mark 6:3), so ordinary that they could ask, "Where then did this man get all these things?" (Matt. 13:56). And John tells us, "*not even his brothers* believed in him" (John 7:5).

Was Jesus fully human? He was so fully human that even those who lived and worked with him for thirty years, even those brothers who grew up in his own household, did not realize that he was anything more than another very good human being. They apparently had no idea that he was God come in the flesh.

### 3. Sinlessness

Though the New Testament clearly affirms that Jesus was fully human just as we are, it also affirms that Jesus was different in one important respect: he was without sin. Some have objected that if Jesus did not sin, then he was not *truly* human, for all humans sin. But those making that objection simply fail to realize that human beings are now in an *abnormal* situation. God did not create us sinful, but holy and righteous. Adam and Eve in the garden of Eden before they sinned were *truly* human, and we now, though human, do not match the pattern that God intends for us when our full, sinless humanity is restored.

The sinlessness of Jesus is taught frequently in the New Testament. We see suggestions of this early in his life when he was "filled with wisdom" and "the favor of God was upon him" (Luke 2:40). Then we see that Satan was unable to tempt Jesus successfully and failed, after forty days, to persuade him to sin: "When the devil had ended every temptation, he departed from him until an opportune time" (Luke 4:13). We also see in the synoptic gospels (Matthew, Mark, and Luke) no evidence of wrongdoing on Jesus' part. To the Jews who opposed him, Jesus asked, "Which one of you convicts me of sin?" (John 8:46), and he received no answer.

The statements about Jesus' sinlessness are more explicit in John's gospel. Jesus made the amazing proclamation, "I am the light of the world" (John 8:12). If we understand light to represent both truthfulness and moral purity, then Jesus is here claiming to be the source of truth and the source of moral purity and holiness in the world—an astounding claim, and one that could only be made by someone who was free from sin. Moreover, with regard to obedience to his Father in heaven, he said, "I always do the things that are pleasing to him" (John 8:29; the present tense gives the sense of continual activity, "I *am always doing* what is pleasing to him"). At the end of his life, Jesus could say, "I have kept my Father's commandments and abide in his love" (John 15:10). It is significant that when Jesus was put on trial before Pilate, in spite of the accusations of the Jews, Pilate could only conclude, "I find no guilt in him" (John 18:38).

In the book of Acts Jesus is several times called the "Holy One" or the "Righteous One" or is referred to with some similar expression (see Acts 2:27; 3:14; 4:30; 7:52; 13:35). When Paul speaks of Jesus coming to live as a man he is careful not to say that he took on "sinful flesh" but rather says that God sent his own Son "*in the likeness of* sinful flesh and for sin" (Rom. 8:3). And he refers to Jesus as "him . . . who knew no sin" (2 Cor. 5:21).

The author of Hebrews affirms that Jesus was tempted but simultaneously insists that he did not sin: Jesus is "one who in every respect has been tempted as we are, *yet without sin*" (Heb. 4:15). He is a high priest who is "holy, innocent, unstained, separated from sinners, and exalted above the heavens" (Heb. 7:26). Peter speaks of Jesus as "a lamb without blemish or spot" (1 Peter 1:19), using Old Testament imagery to affirm his freedom from any moral defilement. Peter directly states, "*He committed no sin*, neither was deceit found in his mouth" (1 Peter 2:22). When Jesus died, it was "the righteous for the unrighteous, that he might bring us to God" (1 Peter 3:18). And John, in his first epistle, calls him "Jesus Christ the righteous" (1 John 2:1) and says, "In him there is no sin" (1 John 3:5). It is hard to deny, then, that the sinlessness of Christ is taught clearly in all the major sections of the New Testament. He was truly man yet without sin.

In connection with Jesus' sinlessness, we should notice in more detail the nature of his temptations in the wilderness (Matt. 4:1–11; Mark 1:12–13; Luke 4:1–13). The essence of these temptations was an attempt to persuade Jesus to escape from the hard path of obedience and suffering that was appointed for him as the Messiah. Jesus was "led by the Spirit in the wilderness for forty days, being tempted by the devil" (Luke 4:1–2). In many respects this temptation was parallel to the testing that Adam and Eve faced in the garden of Eden, but it was much more difficult. Adam and Eve had fellowship with God and with each other and had an abundance of all kinds of food, for they were only told not to eat from one tree. By contrast, Jesus had no human fellowship and no food to eat, and after he had fasted for forty days he was near the point of physical death. In both cases the kind of obedience required was not obedience to an eternal moral principle rooted in the character of God, but was a test of pure obedience to God's specific directive. With Adam and Eve, God told them not to eat of the tree of the knowledge of good and evil, and the question was whether they would obey simply because God told them. In the case of Jesus, who was "led by the Spirit" for forty days in the wilderness, he apparently realized that it was the Father's will[7] that he eat nothing

---

7. I say "the Father's will" because Jesus' whole life was lived in obedience to his heavenly Father. "He who sent me is with me. . . . I always do the things that are pleasing to him" (John 8:29); "I glorified you on earth, having accomplished the work that you gave me to do" (John 17:4); "Behold, a voice from heaven said, 'This is my beloved Son, with whom I am well pleased'" (Matt. 3:17). Another reason is the parallel with the temptation of Adam and Eve in Gen. 3.

during those days but simply remain there until the Father, through the leading of the Holy Spirit, told him that the temptations were over and he could leave.

We can understand, then, the force of the temptation, "If you are the Son of God, command this stone to become bread" (Luke 4:3). Of course Jesus was the Son of God, and of course he had the power to make any stone into bread instantly. He was the one who would soon change water into wine and multiply the loaves and the fishes. The temptation was intensified by the fact that it seemed as though, if he did not eat soon, his very life would be taken from him. Yet he had come to obey God perfectly in our place, and to do so *as a man*. This meant that he had to obey in his human strength alone. If he had called upon his divine powers to make the temptation easier for himself, then he would not have obeyed God fully *as a man*. The temptation was to use his divine power to "cheat" a bit on the requirements and make obedience somewhat easier. But Jesus, unlike Adam and Eve, refused to eat what appeared to be good and necessary for him, choosing rather to obey the command of his heavenly Father.

The temptation to bow down and worship Satan for a moment and then receive authority over "all the kingdoms of the world" (Luke 4:5) was a temptation to receive power not through the path of lifelong obedience to his heavenly Father but through wrongful submission to the Prince of Darkness. Again, Jesus rejected the apparently easy path and chose the path of obedience that led to the cross.

Similarly, the temptation to throw himself down from the pinnacle of the temple (Luke 4:9–11) was a temptation to "force" God to perform a miracle and rescue him in a spectacular way, thus attracting a large following from the people without pursuing the hard path ahead, the path that included three years of ministering to people's needs, teaching with authority, and exemplifying absolute holiness of life in the midst of harsh opposition. But Jesus again resisted this "easy route" to the fulfillment of his goals as the Messiah (again, a route that would not actually have fulfilled those goals in any case).

These temptations were really the culmination of a lifelong process of moral strengthening and maturing that occurred throughout Jesus' childhood and early adulthood, as he "increased in wisdom . . . and in favor with God" (Luke 2:52) and as he "*learned obedience* through what he suffered" (Heb. 5:8). In these temptations in the wilderness and in the various temptations that faced him through the thirty-three years of his life, Christ obeyed God in our place and as our representative, thus succeeding where Adam had failed, where the people of Israel in the wilderness had failed, and where we had failed (see Rom. 5:18–19).

As difficult as it may be for us to comprehend, Scripture affirms that in these temptations Jesus gained an ability to understand and help us in our temptations. "*Because he himself has suffered when tempted*, he is able to help those who are being tempted" (Heb. 2:18). The author goes on to connect Jesus' ability to sympathize with our weaknesses to the fact that he was tempted as we are: "For we do not have a high priest who is unable to sympathize with our weaknesses, but one who in every respect has been tempted as we are, yet without sin. Let us then [lit., 'therefore'] with confidence draw near to the throne of grace, that we may receive mercy and find grace to help in time of need" (Heb. 4:15–16).

This has practical application for us: in every situation in which we are struggling with temptation, we should reflect on the life of Christ and ask if there were not similar situations that he faced. Usually, after reflecting for a moment or two, we will be able to think of some instances in the life of Christ where he faced temptations that, though they were not the same in every detail, were very similar to the situations that we face every day.[8]

## 4. Could Jesus Have Sinned?

The question is sometimes raised, "Was it possible for Christ to have sinned?" Some people argue for the *impeccability* of Christ, in which the word *impeccable* means "not able to sin."[9] Others object that if Jesus were not able to sin, his temptations could not have been real, for how can a temptation be real if the person being tempted is not able to sin anyway?

In order to answer this question we must distinguish what Scripture clearly affirms, on the one hand, and, on the other hand, what is more in the nature of possible inference on our part. (1) Scripture clearly affirms that Christ never actually sinned (see above). There should be no question in our minds at all on this fact. (2) It also clearly affirms that Jesus was tempted, and that these were real temptations (Luke 4:2). If we believe Scripture, then we must insist that Christ "*in every respect has been tempted as we are, yet without sin*" (Heb. 4:15). If our speculation on the question of whether Christ could have sinned ever leads us to say that he was not truly tempted, then we have reached a wrong conclusion, one that contradicts the clear statements of Scripture.

(3) We also must affirm with Scripture that "God cannot be tempted with evil" (James 1:13). But here the question becomes difficult: if Jesus was fully God as well as fully man (and we shall argue below that Scripture clearly and repeatedly teaches this), then must we not also affirm that (in some sense) Jesus also "could not be tempted with evil"?

---

8. Particularly with respect to family life, it is helpful to remember that Joseph is nowhere mentioned in the Gospels after the incident in the temple when Jesus was twelve years old. It is especially interesting that Joseph is omitted from the verses that list Jesus' mother and other family members, even naming his brothers and sisters (see Matt. 13:55–56; Mark 6:3; cf. Matt. 12:48). It would seem very strange, for example, that "the mother of Jesus" was at the wedding at Cana in Galilee (John 2:1) but not his father, if his father were still living (cf. John 2:12). This suggests that sometime after Jesus was twelve

Joseph had died, and that for a period in his life Jesus grew up in a "single-parent home." This would mean that, as he became older, he assumed more and more of the responsibility of male leadership in that family, earning a living as a "carpenter" (Mark 6:3) and no doubt helping care for his younger brothers and sisters as well. Therefore, although Jesus was never married, he no doubt experienced a wide range of family situations and conflicts similar to those experienced by families today.

9. The Latin word *peccare* means "to sin."

This is as far as we can go in terms of clear and explicit affirmations of Scripture. At this point we are faced with a dilemma similar to a number of other doctrinal dilemmas where Scripture seems to be teaching things that are, if not directly contradictory, at least very difficult to combine together in our understanding. For example, with respect to the doctrine of the Trinity, we affirmed that God exists in three persons, and each is fully God, and there is one God. Although those statements are not contradictory, they are, nonetheless, difficult to understand in connection with each other, and although we can make some progress in understanding how they fit together, we have to admit that there can be no final understanding on our part, in this life at least. Here the situation is somewhat similar. We do not have an actual contradiction. Scripture does not tell us that "Jesus was tempted" and that "Jesus was not tempted" (a contradiction if "Jesus" and "tempted" are used exactly in the same sense in both sentences). The Bible tells us that "Jesus was tempted" and "Jesus was fully man" and "Jesus was fully God" and "God cannot be tempted." This combination of teachings from Scripture leaves open the possibility that as we understand the way Jesus' human nature and divine nature work together, we might understand more of the way in which he could be tempted in one sense and yet, in another sense, not be tempted. (This possibility will be discussed further below.)

At this point, then, we pass beyond the clear affirmations of Scripture and attempt to suggest a solution to the problem of whether Christ could have sinned. But it is important to recognize that the following solution is more in the nature of a suggested means of combining various biblical teachings and is not directly supported by explicit statements of Scripture. With this in mind, it is appropriate for us to say:[10] (1) If Jesus' human nature had existed by itself, independent of his divine nature, then it would have been a human nature just like that which God gave Adam and Eve. It would have been free from sin but nonetheless *able to sin*. Therefore, if Jesus' human nature had existed by itself, there was the abstract or theoretical possibility that Jesus could have sinned, just as Adam and Eve's human natures were able to sin. (2) But Jesus' human nature never existed apart from union with his divine nature. From the moment of his conception, he existed as truly God and truly man as well. Both his human nature and his divine nature existed while united in one person. (3) Although there were some things (such as being hungry or thirsty or weak) that Jesus experienced in his human nature alone and were not experienced in his divine nature (see below), nonetheless, an act of sin would have been a moral act that would apparently have involved the whole person of Christ. Therefore, if he had sinned, it would have involved both his human and divine natures. (4) But if Jesus as a person had sinned, involving both his human and divine natures in sin, then God himself would have sinned, and he would have ceased to be God. Yet that

10. In this discussion I am largely following the conclusions of Geerhardus Vos, *Biblical Theology* (Grand Rapids: Eerdmans, 1948), 339–42.

is clearly impossible because of the infinite holiness of God's nature. (5) Therefore, if we are asking if it was *actually* possible for Jesus to have sinned, it seems that we must conclude that it was not possible. The union of his human and divine natures in one person prevented it.

But the question remains, "How then could Jesus' temptations be real?" The example of the temptation to change the stones into bread is helpful in this regard. Jesus had the ability, by virtue of his divine nature, to perform this miracle, but if he had done it, he would no longer have been obeying in the strength of his human nature alone, he would have failed the test that Adam also failed, and he would not have earned our salvation for us. Therefore, Jesus refused to rely on his divine nature to make obedience easier for him. In like manner, it seems appropriate to conclude that Jesus met every temptation to sin not by his divine power but on the strength of his human nature alone (though, of course, it was not "alone" because Jesus, in exercising the kind of faith that humans should exercise, was perfectly depending on God the Father and the Holy Spirit at every moment). The moral strength of his divine nature was there as a sort of "backstop" that would have prevented him from sinning in any case (and therefore we can say that it was not possible for him to sin), but he did not rely on the strength of his divine nature to make it easier for him to face temptations,[11] and his refusal to turn the stones into bread at the beginning of his ministry is a clear indication of this.

Were the temptations real then? Many theologians have pointed out that only he who successfully resists a temptation to the end most fully feels the force of that temptation. Just as a champion weightlifter who successfully lifts and holds over head the heaviest weight in the contest feels the force of it more fully than one who attempts to lift it and drops it, so any Christian who has successfully faced a temptation to the end knows that that is far more difficult than giving in to it at once. So it was with Jesus: every temptation he faced, he faced to the end, and triumphed over it. The temptations were real, even though he did not give in to them. In fact, they were most real *because* he did not give in to them.

What then do we say about the fact that "God cannot be tempted with evil" (James 1:13)? It seems that this is one of a number of things that we must affirm to be true of Jesus' divine nature but not of his human nature. His divine nature could not be tempted with evil, but his human nature could be tempted and was tempted. How these two natures united in one person in facing temptations, Scripture does not clearly explain to us. But this distinction between what is true of one nature and what is true of another nature is an example of a number of similar statements that Scripture requires us to make (see more on this distinction when we discuss how Jesus could be God and man in one person, pp. 690–700).

---

11. Two other examples can also illustrate this: a swimmer who swims across the English Channel accompanied by a rescue boat but never uses the rescue boat for help, and a tightrope walker who has a safety net below but never falls into it.

## 5. Why Was Jesus' Full Humanity Necessary?

When John wrote his first epistle, a heretical teaching was circulating in the church to the effect that Jesus was not a man. This heresy became known as *docetism*.[12] So serious was this denial of truth about Christ, that John could say it was a doctrine of the antichrist: "By this you know the Spirit of God: every spirit that confesses *that Jesus Christ has come in the flesh* is from God, and every spirit that does not confess Jesus is not from God. This is the spirit of the antichrist" (1 John 4:2–3). The apostle John understood that to deny Jesus' true humanity was to deny something at the very heart of Christianity, so that no one who denied that Jesus had come in the flesh was sent from God.

As we look through the New Testament, we see several reasons why Jesus had to be fully man if he was going to be the Messiah and earn our salvation. We can list seven of those reasons here.

**a. For Representative Obedience.** As we noted in the chapter on the covenants between God and man above,[13] Jesus was our representative and obeyed for us where Adam had failed and disobeyed. We see this in the parallels between Jesus' temptation (Luke 4:1–13) and the time of testing for Adam and Eve in the garden (Gen. 2:15–3:7). It is also clearly reflected in Paul's discussion of the parallels between Adam and Christ, in Adam's disobedience and Christ's obedience: "Therefore, as one trespass led to condemnation for all men, so *one act of righteousness* leads to justification and life for all men. For as by the one man's disobedience the many were made sinners, so *by the one man's obedience* the many will be made righteous" (Rom. 5:18–19). This is why Paul can call Christ "the last Adam" (1 Cor. 15:45) and can call Adam the "first man" and Christ the "second man" (1 Cor. 15:47). Jesus had to be a man in order to be our representative and obey in our place.

**b. To Be a Substitute Sacrifice.** If Jesus had not been a man, he could not have died in our place and paid the penalty that was due to us. The author of Hebrews tells us that "for surely it is not angels that he helps, but he helps the offspring of Abraham. Therefore he *had to* be made like his brothers in every respect, so that he might become a merciful and faithful high priest in the service of God, to make propitiation for the sins of the people" (Heb. 2:16–17; cf. v. 14). Jesus had to become a man, not an angel, because God was concerned with saving men, not with saving angels. But to do this he "had to" be made like us in every way so that he might become "the propitiation" for us, the sacrifice that is an acceptable substitute for us. Though this idea will be discussed more

---

12. The word *docetism* comes from the Greek verb *dokeō*, "to seem, to appear to be." Any theological position that says that Jesus was not really a man, but only appeared to be a man, is called a "docetic" position. Behind docetism is an assumption that the material creation is inherently evil, and therefore the Son of God could not have been united to a true human nature.

No prominent church leader ever advocated docetism, but it was a troublesome heresy that had various supporters in the first four centuries of the church. Modern evangelicals who neglect to teach on the full humanity of Christ can unwittingly support docetic tendencies in their hearers.

13. See chapter 25, pp. 650–51; also chapter 27, pp. 707–9.

fully in chapter 27, on the atonement, it is important here to realize that unless Christ was fully man, he could not have died to pay the penalty for man's sins. He could not have been a substitute sacrifice for us.

**c. To Be the One Mediator between God and Human Beings.** Because we were alienated from God by sin, we needed someone to come between God and us to bring us back to him. We needed a mediator who could represent us to God and who could represent God to us. There is only one person who has ever fulfilled that requirement: "There is one God, and *there is one mediator* between God and men, the man Christ Jesus" (1 Tim. 2:5).[14] In order to fulfill this role of mediator, Jesus had to be fully man as well as fully God.

**d. To Fulfill God's Original Purpose for Man to Rule Over Creation.** As we saw in the discussion of the purpose for which God created man,[15] God put mankind on the earth to subdue it and rule over it as God's representatives. But mankind did not fulfill that purpose but fell into sin. The author of Hebrews realizes that God intended everything to be in subjection to man, but he admits, "At present, we do not yet see everything in subjection to him" (Heb. 2:8). Then when Jesus came as a man, he was able to obey God and thereby have the right to rule over creation *as a man*, thus fulfilling God's original purpose in putting man on the earth. Hebrews recognizes this when it says that now "we see him [Jesus]" in the place of authority over the universe, "crowned with glory and honor" (Heb. 2:9; cf. the same phrase in v. 7). Jesus in fact has been given "all authority in heaven and on earth" (Matt. 28:18), and God has "put all things under his feet and gave him as head over all things to the church" (Eph. 1:22). Indeed, we shall someday reign with him on his throne (Rev. 3:21) and experience, in subjection to Christ our Lord, the fulfillment of God's purpose that we reign over the earth (cf. Luke 19:17, 19; 1 Cor. 6:3). Jesus had to be a man in order to fulfill God's original purpose that man rule over his creation.

**e. To Be Our Example and Pattern in Life.** John tells us, "Whoever says he abides in him ought to walk *in the same way in which he walked*" (1 John 2:6), and reminds us, "when he appears we shall be like him" (1 John 3:2–3). This hope of future conformity to Christ's character even now gives increasing moral purity to our lives. Paul tells us that we are continually being "transformed into the same image" (2 Cor. 3:18), thus moving toward the goal for which God saved us, that we might "be conformed to the image of his Son" (Rom. 8:29). Peter tells us that especially in suffering we have to consider Christ's example: "Christ also suffered for you, *leaving you an example*, so that

---

14. For reasons that I explained in chapter 22 (p. 589), I have continued in this book to use the singular word *man* to refer to the entire human race. But I have not used the plural word *men* to mean "people" or "human beings" generally, except here in discussing 1 Tim. 2:5. I believe the ESV translation (which I have quoted here) is correct when it speaks of "one

mediator between God and *men*, the *man* Christ Jesus," because the combination "men . . . man" faithfully represents the fact that Greek *anthrōpos* ("man, human being") is used twice in this verse, once to refer to human beings generally, and once to refer to Christ.

15. See chapter 15, pp. 347–49, and chapter 21, pp. 565–67.

you might follow in his steps" (1 Peter 2:21). Throughout our Christian life, we are to run the race set before us "looking to Jesus the founder and perfecter of our faith" (Heb. 12:2). If we become discouraged by the hostility and opposition of sinners, we are to "consider him who endured from sinners such hostility against himself" (Heb. 12:3). Jesus is also our example in death. Paul's goal is to become "*like him* in his death" (Phil. 3:10; cf. Acts 7:60; 1 Peter 3:17–18 with 4:1). Our goal should be to be like Christ all our days, up to the point of death, and to die with unfailing obedience to God, with strong trust in him and with love and forgiveness to others. Jesus had to become a man like us to live as our example and pattern.

**f. To Be the Pattern for Our Redeemed Bodies.** Paul tells us that when Jesus rose from the dead, he rose in a new body that was "imperishable . . . raised in glory . . . raised in power . . . raised a spiritual body" (1 Cor. 15:42–44). This new resurrection body that Jesus had when he rose from the dead is the pattern for what our bodies will be like when we are raised from the dead, because Christ is "the firstfruits" (1 Cor. 15:23)—an agricultural metaphor that likens Christ to the first sample of the harvest, showing what the other fruit from that harvest would be like. We now have a physical body like Adam's, but we will have one like Christ's: "Just as we have borne the image of the man of dust, we shall also bear the image of the man of heaven" (1 Cor. 15:49). Jesus had to be raised as a man in order to be the "firstborn from the dead" (Col. 1:18), the pattern for the bodies that we would later have.

**g. To Sympathize as High Priest.** The author of Hebrews reminds us that "because he himself has suffered when tempted, he is able to help those who are being tempted" (Heb. 2:18; cf. 4:15–16). If Jesus had not been a man, he would not have been able to know *by experience* what we go through in our temptations and struggles in this life. But because he has lived as a man, he is able to sympathize more fully with us in our experiences.[16]

## 6. Jesus Will Be a Man Forever

Jesus did not give up his human nature after his death and resurrection, for he appeared to his disciples as a man after the resurrection, even with the scars of the nail prints in his hands (John 20:25–27). He had "flesh and bones" (Luke 24:39) and ate

---

16. This is a difficult concept for us to understand, because we do not want to say that Jesus acquired additional knowledge or information by becoming man: certainly as omniscient God he knew every fact there was to know about the experience of human suffering. But the book of Hebrews does say, "*Because he himself has suffered when tempted, he is able to help those who are being tempted*" (Heb. 2:18), and we must insist that that statement is true—there is a relationship between Jesus' suffering and his ability to sympathize with us and help us in temptation. Apparently the author is speaking not of any additional factual or intellectual knowledge, but of an ability to recall a personal experience that he had himself gone through, an ability he would not have if he had not had that personal experience. Some faint parallel to this might be seen in the fact that a man who is a medical doctor, and has perhaps even written a textbook on obstetrics, might know far more *information* about childbirth than any of his patients. Yet, because he is a man, he will never share in that actual experience. A woman who has herself had a baby (or, to give a closer parallel, a woman physician who first writes a textbook and then has a baby herself) can sympathize much more fully with other women who are having babies.

food (Luke 24:41–42). Later, when he was talking with his disciples, he was taken up into heaven, still in his resurrected human body, and two angels promised that he would return in the same way: "This Jesus, who was taken up from you into heaven, *will come in the same way* as you saw him go into heaven" (Acts 1:11). Still later, Stephen gazed into heaven and saw Jesus as "the Son of Man standing at the right hand of God" (Acts 7:56). Jesus also appeared to Saul on the Damascus Road and said, "I am Jesus, whom you are persecuting" (Acts 9:5)—an appearance that Saul (Paul) later coupled with the resurrection appearances of Jesus to others (1 Cor. 9:1; 15:8). In John's vision in Revelation, Jesus still appears as "one like a son of man" (Rev. 1:13), though he is filled with great glory and power, and his appearance causes John to fall at his feet in awe (Rev. 1:13–17). He promises one day to drink wine again with his disciples in his Father's kingdom (Matt. 26:29) and invites us to a great marriage supper in heaven (Rev. 19:9). Moreover, Jesus will continue forever in his offices as prophet, priest, and king, all of them carried out by virtue of the fact that he is both God and man forever.[17]

All of these texts indicate that Jesus did not *temporarily* become man but that his divine nature was *permanently* united to his human nature. He lives forever not just as the eternal Son of God, the second person of the Trinity, but also as Jesus, the man who was born of Mary, and as Christ, the Messiah and Savior of his people. Jesus will remain fully God and fully man yet one person forever.

## B. The Deity of Christ

To complete the biblical teaching about Jesus Christ, we must affirm not only that he was fully human but also that he was fully divine. Although the word does not explicitly occur in Scripture, the church has used the term *incarnation* to refer to the fact that Jesus was God in human flesh. The incarnation was the act of God the Son whereby he took to himself a human nature.[18] The scriptural proof for the deity of Christ is very extensive in the New Testament. We shall examine it under several categories.[19]

### 1. Direct Scriptural Claims

In this section we examine direct statements of Scripture that Jesus is God or that he is divine.[20]

**a. The Word *God* (*Theos*) Used of Christ.** Although the word *theos*, meaning "God," is usually reserved in the New Testament for God the Father, there are several

---

17. See chapter 29, pp. 767–74, on the offices of Christ.

18. The Latin word *incarnāre* means "to make flesh" and is derived from the prefix *in-* (which has a causative sense, "to cause something to be something") and the stem *caro, carnis-*, "flesh."

19. In the following section I have not distinguished between claims to deity made by Jesus himself and claims made about him by others: while such a distinction is helpful for tracing development in people's understanding of Christ, for our

present purposes both kinds of statements are found in our canonical New Testament Scriptures and are valid sources for building Christian doctrine.

20. An excellent discussion of New Testament evidence for the deity of Christ, drawn especially from the titles of Christ in the New Testament, is found in Donald Guthrie, *New Testament Theology* (Leicester: Inter-Varsity Press; Downers Grove, IL: InterVarsity Press, 1981), 235–365.

passages where it is also used to refer to Jesus Christ. In all of these passages the word *God* is used in the strong sense to refer to the one who is the Creator of heaven and earth, the ruler over all. These passages include John 1:1; 1:18 (in older and better manuscripts); 20:28; Romans 9:5; Titus 2:13; Hebrews 1:8 (quoting Ps. 45:6); and 2 Peter 1:1.[21] I have already discussed these passages in chapter 14, where I argued that each person in the Trinity is fully God, and readers may wish to review those pages briefly at this point.[22] It is enough to note that there are at least these seven passages in the New Testament that clearly and explicitly refer to Jesus as God.

One Old Testament example of the name *God* applied to Christ is seen in a familiar messianic passage: "For to us a child is born, to us a son is given; and the government shall be upon his shoulder, and his name shall be called, 'Wonderful Counselor, *Mighty God*'" (Isa. 9:6).

**b. The Word *Lord* (*Kyrios*) Used of Christ.** Sometimes the word *Lord* (Gk. *kyrios*) is used simply as a polite address to a superior, roughly equivalent to our word *sir* (see Matt. 13:27; 21:30; 27:63; John 4:11). Sometimes it can simply mean "master" of a servant or slave (Matt. 6:24; 21:40).

Yet the same word is also used in the Septuagint (the Greek translation of the Old Testament, which was commonly used at the time of Christ) as a translation for the Hebrew *yhwh*, "Yahweh," or (as it is frequently translated) "the LORD." The word *kyrios* is used to translate the name of the Lord 6,814 times in the Greek Old Testament. Therefore, any Greek-speaking reader at the time of the New Testament who had any knowledge at all of the Greek Old Testament would have recognized that, in contexts where it was appropriate, the word "Lord" was the name of the one who was the Creator and Sustainer of heaven and earth, the omnipotent God.

Now there are many instances in the New Testament where *Lord* is used of Christ in what can only be understood as this strong Old Testament sense, "the Lord" who is Yahweh or God himself. This use of the word *Lord* is quite striking in the word of the angel to the shepherds of Bethlehem: "For unto you is born this day in the city of David a Savior, who is Christ *the Lord*" (Luke 2:11). Though these words are familiar to us from frequent reading of the Christmas story, we should realize how surprising it would be to any first-century Jew to hear that someone born as a baby was the "Christ" (or "Messiah")[23] and, moreover, that this one who was the Messiah was also "the Lord"— that is, the Lord God himself! The amazing force of the angel's statement, which the shepherds could hardly believe, was to say, essentially, "Today in Bethlehem a baby has

---

21. Titus 1:3, in connection with the fact that v. 4 calls Christ Jesus "our Savior" and the fact that it was Jesus Christ who commissioned Paul to preach the gospel, might also be considered another example of the use of the word *God* to refer to Christ.

22. See chapter 14, pp. 276–80, for discussion of passages that refer to Jesus as "God." See also Murray J. Harris, *Jesus as God* (Grand Rapids: Baker, 1992), for the most extensive exegetical treatment ever published dealing with New Testament passages that refer to Jesus as "God."

23. The word *Christ* is the Greek translation of the Hebrew word *Messiah*.

been born who is your Savior and your Messiah, and who is also God himself." It is not surprising that "all who heard it wondered at what the shepherds told them" (Luke 2:18).

When Mary comes to visit Elizabeth several months before Jesus is to be born, Elizabeth says, "Why is this granted to me that the mother of *my Lord* should come to me?" (Luke 1:43). Because Jesus was not even born, Elizabeth could not be using the word *Lord* to mean something like human "master." She must rather be using it in the strong Old Testament sense, giving an amazing sense to the sentence: "Why is this granted me, that the mother of the Lord God himself should come to me?" Though this is a very strong statement, it is difficult to understand the word *Lord* in this context in any weaker sense.

We see another example when Matthew says that John the Baptist is the one who cries out in the wilderness, "Prepare the way of *the Lord*; make his paths straight" (Matt. 3:3). In doing this John is quoting Isaiah 40:3, which speaks about the Lord God himself coming among his people. But the context applies this passage to John's role of preparing the way for Jesus to come. The implication is that when Jesus comes, *the Lord himself* will come.

Jesus also identifies himself as the sovereign Lord of the Old Testament when he asks the Pharisees about Psalm 110:1, "The Lord said to *my Lord*, 'Sit at my right hand, until I put your enemies under your feet'" (Matt. 22:44). The force of this statement is that "God the Father said to God the Son [David's Lord], 'Sit at my right hand.'" The Pharisees know he is talking about himself and identifying himself as one worthy of the Old Testament title *kyrios*, "Lord."

Such usage is seen frequently in the Epistles, where "the Lord" is a common name to refer to Christ. Paul says, "There is one God, the Father, from whom are all things and for whom we exist, and *one Lord*, Jesus Christ, through whom are all things and through whom we exist" (1 Cor. 8:6; cf. 12:3, and many other passages in the Pauline Epistles). Jesus is called "Lord" in this sense that affirms his deity over 400 times in the New Testament.[24]

A particularly clear passage is found in Hebrews 1, where the author quotes Psalm 102, which speaks about the work of the Lord in creation and applies it to Christ:

> You, *Lord*, laid the foundation of the earth in the beginning,
>> and the heavens are the work of your hands;
> they will perish, but you remain;
>> they will all wear out like a garment,
> like a robe you will roll them up,
>> like a garment they will be changed.

---

24. The English word *Lord* occurs 447 times in the ESV text of Acts, the Epistles, and Revelation, and I think 441 of them attribute deity to Christ by calling him *kyrios*, "Lord," in the strong Old Testament sense as the name of God. (*Lord* is used in a weaker sense in Acts 25:26; 2 Cor. 1:24; 1 Peter 3:6; and perhaps Acts 9:5; 22:8; and 26:15, first instance.)

> But you are the same,
>> and your years will have no end. (Heb. 1:10–12)

Here Christ is explicitly spoken of as the eternal Lord of heaven and earth who created all things and will remain the same forever. Such strong usage of the term *Lord* to refer to Christ culminates in Revelation 19:16, where we see Christ returning as conquering King, and "On his robe and on his thigh he has a name written, King of kings and *Lord of lords.*"

**c. Other Strong Claims to Deity.** In addition to the uses of the word *God* and *Lord* to refer to Christ, we have other passages that strongly claim deity for Christ. When Jesus told his Jewish opponents that Abraham had seen his (Christ's) day, they challenged him, "You are not yet fifty years old, and have you seen Abraham?" (John 8:57). Here a sufficient response to prove Jesus' eternity would have been, "Before Abraham was, I was." But Jesus did not say this. Instead, he made a much more startling assertion: "Truly, truly, I say to you, before Abraham was, *I am*" (John 8:58). Jesus combined two assertions whose sequence seemed to make no sense: "Before something in the past happened [Abraham was], something in the present happened [I am]." The Jewish leaders recognized at once that he was not speaking in riddles or uttering nonsense. When he said, "I am," he was repeating the very words God used when he identified himself to Moses as "I AM WHO I AM" (Ex. 3:14). Jesus was claiming for himself the title "I AM," by which God designates himself as the eternal existing One, the God who is the source of his own existence and who always has been and always will be. When the Jews heard this unusual, emphatic, solemn statement, they knew that he was claiming to be God. "So they picked up stones to throw at him, but Jesus hid himself and went out of the temple" (John 8:59).[25]

Another strong claim to deity is Jesus' statement at the end of Revelation, "I am the Alpha and the Omega, the first and the last, the beginning and the end" (Rev. 22:13). When this is combined with the statement of God the Father in Revelation 1:8, "I am the Alpha and the Omega," it also constitutes a strong claim to equal deity with God the Father. Sovereign over all of history and all of creation, Jesus is the beginning and the end.

In John 1:1, John not only calls Jesus "God" but also refers to him as "the Word" (Gk. *logos*). John's readers would have recognized in this term *logos* a dual reference, both to the powerful, creative Word of God in the Old Testament by which the heavens and earth were created (Ps. 33:6) and to the organizing or unifying principle of the universe, the thing that held it together and allowed it to make sense, in Greek thinking.[26] John

---

25. The other "I am" sayings in John's gospel, where Jesus claims to be the bread of life (6:35), the light of the world (8:12), the door of the sheep (10:7), the good shepherd (10:11), the resurrection and the life (11:25), the way, the truth, and the life (14:6), and the true vine (15:1), also contribute to the overall picture of deity that John paints of Christ; see Guthrie, *New Testament Theology*, 330–32.

26. See Guthrie, *New Testament Theology*, esp. p. 326.

is identifying Jesus with both of these ideas and saying that he is not only the powerful, creative Word of God and the organizing or unifying force in the universe but also a man: "The Word became flesh and dwelt among us, and we have seen his glory, glory as of the only Son from the Father, full of grace and truth" (John 1:14). Here is another strong claim to deity coupled with an explicit statement that Jesus also became man and moved among us as a man.

Further evidence of claims to deity can be found in the fact that Jesus calls himself "*the* Son of Man." This title is used eighty-four times in the four gospels but only by Jesus and only to speak of himself (e.g., Matt. 16:13 with Luke 9:18). In the rest of the New Testament, the phrase "*the* Son of Man" (with the definite article *the*) is used only once, in Acts 7:56, where Stephen refers to Christ as the Son of Man. This unique term has as its background the vision in Daniel 7 where Daniel saw one like a "son of man" who "came to the Ancient of Days" and was given "dominion and glory and a kingdom, *that all peoples, nations, and languages should serve him; his dominion is an everlasting dominion,* which shall not pass away" (Dan. 7:13–14). It is striking that this "son of man" came "with the clouds of heaven" (Dan. 7:13). This passage clearly speaks of someone who had heavenly origin and who was given *eternal rule* over the *whole world.* The high priests did not miss the point of this passage when Jesus said, "From now on you will see the Son of Man *seated at the right hand of Power and coming on the clouds of heaven*" (Matt. 26:64). The reference to Daniel 7:13–14 was unmistakable, and the high priest and his council knew that Jesus was claiming to be the eternal world ruler of heavenly origin spoken of in Daniel's vision. Immediately they said, "He has uttered blasphemy. . . . He deserves death" (Matt. 26:65–66). Here Jesus finally made explicit the strong claims to eternal world rule that were earlier hinted at in his frequent use of the title "the Son of Man" to apply to himself.

Though the title "Son of God" can sometimes be used simply to refer to Israel (Matt. 2:15), to man as created by God (Luke 3:38), or to redeemed man generally (Rom. 8:14, 19, 23), there are nevertheless instances in which the phrase "Son of God" refers to Jesus as the heavenly, eternal Son who is equal to God (see Matt. 11:25–30; 17:5; 1 Cor. 15:28; Heb. 1:1–3, 5, 8). This is especially true in John's gospel where Jesus is seen as a unique Son from the Father (John 1:14, 18, 34, 49) who fully reveals the Father (John 8:19; 14:9). As Son he is so great that we can trust in him for eternal life (something that could be said of no created being: John 3:16, 36; 20:31). He is also the one who has all authority from the Father to give life, pronounce eternal judgment, and rule over all (John 3:36; 5:20–22, 25; 10:17; 16:15). As Son he has been sent by the Father, and therefore he existed before he came into the world (John 3:17; 5:23; 10:36).

The first three verses of Hebrews are emphatic in saying that the Son is the one whom God "appointed the heir of all things, through whom also he created the world" (Heb. 1:2). This Son, says the writer, "is the radiance of the glory of God and the exact imprint of his nature, and he upholds the universe by the word of his power" (Heb. 1:3).

Jesus is the exact duplicate of the "nature" (or being, Gk. *hypostasis*) of God, making him exactly equal to God in every attribute. Moreover, he continually upholds the universe "by the word of his power," something that only God could do.

These passages combine to indicate that the title "Son of God" *when applied to Christ* strongly affirms his deity as the eternal Son in the Trinity, one equal to God the Father in all his attributes.

## 2. Evidence That Jesus Possessed Attributes of Deity

In addition to the specific affirmations of Jesus' deity seen in the many passages quoted above, we see many examples of actions in Jesus' lifetime that point to his divine character.

Jesus demonstrated his *omnipotence* when he stilled the storm at sea with a word (Matt. 8:26–27), multiplied the loaves and fish (Matt. 14:19), and changed water into wine (John 2:1–11). Some might object that these miracles just showed the power of the Holy Spirit working through him, just as the Holy Spirit could work through any other human being, and therefore these do not demonstrate Jesus' deity. But the contextual explanations of these events often point not to what they demonstrate about the power of the Holy Spirit but to what they demonstrate about Jesus. For instance, after Jesus turned water into wine, John tells us, "This, the first of his miraculous signs, Jesus did at Cana in Galilee, and *manifested his glory*. And his disciples believed in him" (John 2:11). It was not the glory of the Holy Spirit that was manifested but the glory of Jesus himself, as his divine power worked to change water into wine. Similarly, after Jesus stilled the storm on the Sea of Galilee, the disciples did not say, "How great is the power of the Holy Spirit working through this prophet," but rather, "What sort of man is this, that even winds and sea *obey him*?" (Matt. 8:27). It was the authority of Jesus himself to which the winds and the waves were subject, and this could only be the authority of God who rules over the seas and has power to still the waves (cf. Ps. 65:7; 89:9; 107:29).[27]

Jesus asserts his *eternity* when he says, "Before Abraham was, I am" (John 8:58, see discussion above), and "I am the Alpha and the Omega" (Rev. 22:13).

The *omniscience* of Jesus is demonstrated in his knowing people's thoughts (Mark 2:8), seeing Nathaniel under the fig tree from far away (John 1:48), and knowing "from the beginning who those were who did not believe, and who it was who would betray him" (John 6:64). Of course, the revelation of individual, specific events or facts is something that God could give to anyone who had a gift of prophecy in the Old or New Testaments. But Jesus' knowledge was much more extensive than that. He knew "who those were who did not believe," thus implying that he knew the belief or unbelief that was in the hearts of all people. In fact, John says explicitly that Jesus "needed no one to bear witness

---

27. I recognize that other passages attribute some of Christ's other miracles to the Holy Spirit—see Matt. 12:28; Luke 4:14, 18, 40.

684  The Doctrines of Christ and the Holy Spirit

about man, for he himself *knew what was in man*" (John 2:25). The disciples could later say to him, "Now we know that *you know all things*" (John 16:30). These statements say much more than what could be said of any great prophet or apostle of the Old Testament or New Testament, for they imply omniscience on the part of Jesus.[28]

Finally, after his resurrection, when Jesus asked Peter if he loved him, Peter answered, "Lord, *you know everything*; you know that I love you" (John 21:17). Here Peter is saying much more than that Jesus knows his heart and knows that he loves him. He is rather making a general statement ("You know everything") and from it he is drawing a specific conclusion ("You know that I love you"). Peter is confident that Jesus knows what is in the heart of every person, and therefore he is sure that Jesus knows his own heart.

The divine attribute of *omnipresence* is not directly affirmed to be true of Jesus during his earthly ministry. However, while looking forward to the time that the church would be established, Jesus could say, "Where two or three are gathered in my name, *there am I* among them" (Matt. 18:20). Moreover, before he left the earth, he told his disciples, "I am with you always, to the end of the age" (Matt. 28:20).[29]

That Jesus possessed divine *sovereignty*, a kind of authority possessed by God alone, is seen in the fact that he could forgive sins (Mark 2:5–7). Unlike the Old Testament prophets who declared, "Thus says the LORD," he could preface his statements with the phrase, "But *I say to you*" (Matt. 5:22, 28, 32, 34, 39, 44)—an amazing claim to his own authority. He could speak with the authority of God because he was fully God. He had "all things" delivered into his hands by the Father and the authority to reveal the Father to whomever he chose (Matt. 11:25–27). Such is his authority that the future eternal state of everyone in the universe depends on whether they believe in him or reject him (John 3:36).

Jesus also possessed the divine attribute of *immortality*, the inability to die. We see this indicated near the beginning of John's gospel, when Jesus says to the Jews, "Destroy this temple, and in three days *I will raise it up*" (John 2:19). John explains that he was not speaking about the temple made with stones in Jerusalem, "but he was speaking about the temple of *his body*. When therefore he was raised from the dead, his disciples remembered that he had said this, and they believed the Scripture and the word that Jesus had spoken" (John 2:21–22). We must insist of course that Jesus really did die: this very passage speaks of the time when "he was raised from the dead." But it is also significant that Jesus predicts that he will have an active role in his own resurrection: "*I will raise it up*." Although other Scripture passages tell us that God the Father was active in raising Christ from the dead, here he says that he himself will be active in his resurrection.

---

28. See below, pp. 698–700, on Mark 13:32, and on the question of how omniscience can be consistent with Christ's learning things as a man.

29. I do not mean to imply that these verses show that Jesus' human nature was omnipresent. Jesus' human nature, including his physical body, was never more than one place at one time. It is probably best to understand these verses to refer to Jesus' divine nature (see below, pp. 690–700, for discussion of the distinction between Christ's two natures). See also Matt. 8:13.

Jesus claims the power to lay down his life and take it up again in another passage in John's gospel: "For this reason the Father loves me, because I lay down my life that I may take it up again. No one takes it from me, but I lay it down on my own accord. I have authority to lay it down, and I have authority to take it again. This charge I have received from my Father" (John 10:17–18). Here Jesus speaks of a power no other human being has had—the power to lay down his own life *and* the power to take it up again. Once again, this is an indication that Jesus possessed the divine attribute of immortality. Similarly, the author of Hebrews says that Jesus "has become a priest, not on the basis of a legal requirement concerning bodily descent, but by the power of *an indestructible life*" (Heb. 7:16). (The fact that immortality is a unique characteristic of God alone is seen in 1 Tim. 6:16, which speaks of God as the one "who alone has immortality.")

Another clear attestation to the deity of Christ is the fact that he is counted *worthy to be worshiped*, something that is true of no other being in all creation, including angels (see Rev. 19:10), but only God alone. Yet Scripture says of Christ that "God has highly exalted him and bestowed on him the name that is above every name, so that at the name of Jesus every knee should bow, in heaven and on earth and under the earth, and every tongue confess that Jesus Christ is Lord, to the glory of God the Father" (Phil. 2:9–11). Similarly, God commands the angels to worship Christ, for we read, "When he brings the firstborn into the world, he says, 'Let all God's angels worship him'" (Heb. 1:6).

John is allowed a glimpse of the worship that occurs in heaven, for he sees thousands and thousands of angels and heavenly creatures around God's throne saying, "Worthy is the Lamb who was slain, to receive power and wealth and wisdom and might and honor and glory and blessing!" (Rev. 5:12). Then he hears "*every creature* in heaven and on earth and under the earth and in the sea, and all that is in them, saying, 'To him who sits on the throne *and to the Lamb* be blessing and honor and glory and might forever and ever!'" (Rev. 5:13). Christ is here called "the Lamb who was slain," and he is accorded the universal worship offered to God the Father, thus clearly demonstrating his equality in deity.[30]

## 3. The Kenosis Theory: Did Jesus Give Up Some of His Divine Attributes While on Earth?

Paul writes to the Philippians, "Have this mind among yourselves, which is yours in Christ Jesus, who, though he was in the form of God, did not count equality with God a thing to be grasped, but *emptied himself,* by taking the form of a servant, being born in the likeness of men" (Phil. 2:5–7). Beginning with this text, several theologians in Germany (from about 1860–1880) and in England (from about 1890–1910) advocated a view of the incarnation that had not been advocated before in the history

---

30. See also Matt. 28:17 where Jesus accepted worship from his disciples after his resurrection.

of the church. This new view was called the "kenosis theory," and the overall position it represented was called "kenotic theology." The *kenosis theory* holds that Christ gave up some of his divine attributes while he was on earth as a man. (The word *kenosis* is taken from the Greek verb *kenoō*, which generally means "to empty," and is translated "emptied himself" in Phil. 2:7.) According to the theory Christ "emptied himself" of some of his divine attributes, such as omniscience, omnipresence, and omnipotence, while he was on earth as a man. This was viewed as a voluntary self-limitation on Christ's part, which he carried out in order to fulfill his work of redemption.[31]

But does Philippians 2:7 teach that Christ emptied himself of some of his divine attributes, and does the rest of the New Testament confirm this? The evidence of Scripture points to a negative answer to both questions. We must first realize that no recognized teacher in the first 1,800 years of church history, including those who were native speakers of Greek, thought that "emptied himself" in Philippians 2:7 meant that the Son of God gave up some of his divine attributes. Second, we must recognize that the text does not say that Christ "emptied himself of some powers" or "emptied himself of divine attributes" or anything like that. Third, the text *does* describe what Jesus did in this "emptying": he did it by "taking the form of a servant," that is, by coming to live as a man, and "being found in human form, he humbled himself by becoming obedient to the point of death, even death on a cross" (Phil. 2:8). Thus, the context itself interprets this "emptying" as equivalent to "humbling himself" and taking on a lowly status and position. Thus, the NIV, instead of translating the phrase, "He *emptied* himself," translates it, "*made himself nothing*" (Phil. 2:7 NIV). The emptying includes change of role and status, not essential attributes or nature.

A fourth reason for this interpretation is seen in Paul's purpose in this context. His purpose has been to persuade the Philippians that they should "do nothing from selfish ambition or conceit, but in humility count others more significant than yourselves" (Phil. 2:3), and he continues by telling them, "Let each of you look not only to his own interests, but also to the interests of others" (Phil. 2:4). To persuade them to be humble and to put the interests of others first, he then holds up the example of Christ: "Have this mind among yourselves, which is yours in Christ Jesus, who, though he was in the form of God, did not count equality with God a thing to be grasped, but emptied himself, by taking the form of a servant" (Phil. 2:5–7).

Now in holding up Christ as an example, he wants the Philippians to imitate Christ. But certainly he is not asking the Philippian Christians to "give up" or "lay aside" any of their essential attributes or abilities! He is not asking them to "give up" their intelligence or strength or skill and become a diminished version of what they were. Rather, he is asking them to put the interests of others first: "Let each of you look not only to his own

---

31. A very clear overview of the history of kenotic theology is found in the article "Kenosis, a Kenotic Theology" by S. M. Smith, in *EDT*, 600–602. Surprisingly (for the volume in which his essay appears), Smith ends up endorsing kenotic theology as a valid form of orthodox, biblical faith (p. 602)!

interests, but also to the interests of others" (Phil. 2:4). And because that is his goal, it fits the context to understand that he is using Christ as the supreme example of one who did just that: he put the interests of others first and was willing to give up some of the privilege and status that was his as God.

Therefore, the best understanding of this passage is that it talks about Jesus *giving up the status and privilege that was his in heaven*: he "did not count equality with God a thing to be grasped" (or "clung to for his own advantage") but "emptied himself" or "humbled himself" for our sake and came to live as a man. Jesus speaks elsewhere of the "glory" he had with the Father "before the world existed" (John 17:5), a glory that he had given up and was going to receive again when he returned to heaven. And Paul could speak of Christ who, "though he was rich, yet for your sake he became poor" (2 Cor. 8:9), once again speaking of the privilege and honor that he deserved but temporarily gave up for us.

The fifth and final reason why the "kenosis" view of Philippians 2:7 must be rejected is the larger context of the teaching of the New Testament and the doctrinal teaching of the entire Bible. If it were true that such a momentous event as this happened, that the eternal Son of God ceased for a time to have all the attributes of God—ceased, for a time, to be omniscient, omnipotent, and omnipresent, for example—then we would expect that such an incredible event would be taught clearly and repeatedly in the New Testament, not found in the very doubtful interpretation of one word in one epistle. But we find the opposite of that: we do not find it stated anywhere else that the Son of God ceased to have some of the attributes of God that he had possessed from eternity. In fact, if the kenosis theory were true (and this is a foundational objection against it), then *we could no longer affirm Jesus was fully God while he was here on earth.*[32] The kenosis theory ultimately denies the full deity of Jesus Christ and makes him something less than fully God. S. M. Smith admits, "All forms of classical orthodoxy either explicitly reject or reject in principle kenotic theology."[33]

It is important to realize that the major force persuading people to accept kenotic theory was not that they had discovered a better understanding of Philippians 2:7 or any other passage of the New Testament but rather the increasing discomfort people were feeling with the formulations of the doctrine of Christ in historic, classical orthodoxy. It just seemed too incredible for modern rational and "scientific" people to believe that Jesus Christ could be truly human and fully, absolutely God at the same time.[34]

---

32. Sometimes the word *kenosis* is used in a weaker sense not to apply to the kenosis theory in its full sense but simply to refer to a more orthodox understanding of Phil. 2:7 in which it means simply that Jesus gave up his glory and privilege for a time while he was on earth. (This is essentially the view we have advocated in this text.) But it does not seem at all wise to use the term *kenosis* to refer to such a traditional understanding of Phil. 2:7, for it is too easily confused with the full-blown

kenosis doctrine that essentially denies the full deity of Christ. To take a term that formally applies to a false doctrinal teaching and then use it to apply to a scripturally sound position is just confusing to most people.

33. Smith, "Kenosis, A Kenotic Theology," 601.

34. Smith points out that one of the primary influences leading some to adopt kenotic theology was the growth of modern psychology in the nineteenth century: "The age was

The kenosis theory began to sound more and more like an acceptable way to say that (in some sense) Jesus was God, but a kind of God who had for a time given up some of his Godlike qualities, those that were most difficult for people to accept in the modern world.

## 4. Conclusion: Christ Is Fully Divine

The New Testament, in hundreds of explicit verses that call Jesus "God" and "Lord" and use a number of other titles of deity to refer to him and in many passages that attribute actions or words to him that could only be true of God, affirms again and again the full, absolute deity of Jesus Christ. "In him *all the fullness of God* was pleased to dwell" (Col. 1:19), and "In him the whole fullness of deity dwells bodily" (Col. 2:9). In an earlier section we argued that Jesus is truly and fully man. Now we conclude that he is truly and fully God as well. His name is rightly called "Immanuel," that is, "God with us" (Matt. 1:23).

## 5. Is The Doctrine of the Incarnation "Unintelligible" Today?

Throughout history there have been objections to the New Testament teaching on the full deity of Christ. One attack on this doctrine deserves mention here because it created a large controversy since the contributors to the volume were all recognized church leaders in England. The book was called *The Myth of God Incarnate*, edited by John Hick (London: SCM, 1977). The title gives away the thesis of the book: the idea that Jesus was "God incarnate" or "God come in the flesh" is a "myth"—a helpful story, perhaps, for the faith of earlier generations, but not one that can really be believed by us today.

The argument of the book begins with some foundational assumptions: (1) the Bible does not have absolute divine authority for us today (p. i), and (2) Christianity, like all human life and thought, is evolving and changing over time (p. ii). The basic claims of the book are laid out in the first two chapters. In chapter 1, Maurice Wiles argues that it is possible to have Christianity without the doctrine of the incarnation. The church has given up earlier doctrines, such as the "real presence" of Christ in the Lord's Supper, the

---

learning to think in terms of the categories of psychology. Consciousness was a central category. If at our 'center' is our consciousness, and if Jesus was both omniscient God and limited man, then he had two centers and was thus fundamentally not one of us. Christology was becoming inconceivable for some" (ibid., 600–601). In other words, pressures of modern psychological study were making belief in the combination of full deity and full humanity in the one person of Christ difficult to explain or even intellectually embarrassing: How could someone be so different from us and still be truly a man?

Yet we might respond that modern psychology is inherently limited in that its only object of study is simple human beings. No modern psychologist has ever studied anyone who was perfectly free from sin (as Christ was) and who was both fully God and fully man (as Christ was). If we limit our understanding to what modern psychology tells us is "possible" or "conceivable," then we will have neither a sinless Christ nor a divine Christ. In this as in many other points of doctrine, our understanding of what is "possible" must be determined not by modern empirical study of a finite, fallen world but by the teachings of Scripture itself.

inerrancy of Scripture, and the virgin birth; therefore, it is possible to give up the traditional doctrine of the incarnation and still keep the Christian faith as well (pp. 2–3). Moreover, the doctrine of the incarnation is not directly presented in Scripture but originated in a setting where belief in the supernatural was credible; nevertheless, it has never been a coherent or intelligible doctrine through the history of the church (pp. 3–5).

Regarding the New Testament teaching, Frances Young, in chapter 2, argues that the New Testament contains the writings of many diverse witnesses who tell of their own understanding of Christ, but that no single or unified view of Christ can be gained from the entire New Testament; the early church's understanding of the person of Christ was developing in various directions over time. Young concludes that the situation is similar today: within the Christian church many diverse *personal responses* to the story of Jesus Christ are acceptable for us as well, and that would certainly include the response that sees Christ as a man in whom God was uniquely at work but not by any means a man who was also fully God.[35]

From the standpoint of evangelical theology, it is significant to note, first, that this forthright rejection of Jesus' deity could only be advocated upon a prior assumption that the New Testament is not to be accepted as an absolute divine authority for us, truthful at every point. This question of authority is, in many cases, the great dividing line in conclusions about the person of Christ. Second, much of the criticism of the doctrine of the incarnation focused on the claim that it was not "coherent" or "intelligible." Yet at root this is simply an indication that the authors are unwilling to accept anything that does not appear to fit in with their "scientific" worldview in which the natural universe is a closed system not open to such divine intrusions as miracles and the incarnation. The assertion that "Jesus was fully God and fully man in one person," though not a contradiction, is a paradox that we cannot fully understand in this age and perhaps not for all eternity, but this does not give us the right to label it "incoherent" or "unintelligible." The doctrine of the incarnation as understood by the church throughout history has indeed been coherent and intelligible, though no one maintains that it provides us with an exhaustive explanation of how Jesus is both fully God and fully man. Our proper response is not to reject the clear and central teaching of Scripture about the incarnation but simply to recognize that it will remain a paradox, that this is all that God has chosen to reveal to us about it, and that it is true. If we are to submit ourselves to God and to his words in Scripture, then we must believe it.

---

35. The book was quickly answered by another series of essays, Michael Green, ed., *The Truth of God Incarnate* (Sevenoaks, UK: Hodder and Stoughton; Grand Rapids: Eerdmans, 1977). Later the authors of *The Myth of God Incarnate* and several of their critics published the proceedings of a three-day meeting in a third book: Michael Golder, ed., *Incarnation and Myth: The Debate Continued* (London: SCM, 1979).

## 6. Why Was Jesus' Deity Necessary?

In the previous section we listed several reasons why it was necessary for Jesus to be fully man in order to earn our redemption. Here it is appropriate to recognize that it is crucially important to insist on the full deity of Christ as well, not only because it is clearly taught in Scripture but also because of the following: (1) Only someone who is the infinite God could bear the full penalty for all the sins of all those who would believe in him. Any finite creature would have been incapable of bearing that penalty. (2) "Salvation is from the Lord" (Jonah 2:9 NASB), and the whole message of Scripture is designed to show that no human being, no creature, could ever save man—only God himself could. (3) Only someone who was truly and fully God could be the one mediator between God and man (1 Tim. 2:5), both to bring us back to God and also to reveal God most fully to us (John 14:9).

If Jesus is not fully God, we have no salvation and ultimately no Christianity. It is no accident that throughout history those groups that have given up belief in the full deity of Christ have not remained long within the Christian faith but have soon drifted toward the kind of religion represented by Unitarianism in the United States and elsewhere. "No one who denies the Son has the Father" (1 John 2:23). "Everyone who goes on ahead and does not abide in the teaching of Christ, does not have God. Whoever abides in the teaching has both the Father and the Son" (2 John 9).

## C. The Incarnation: Deity and Humanity in the One Person of Christ

The biblical teaching about the full deity and full humanity of Christ is so extensive that both have been believed from the earliest times in the history of the church. But a precise understanding of how full deity and full humanity could be combined together in one person was formulated only gradually in the church and did not reach the final form until the Chalcedonian Definition in AD 451. Before that point, several inadequate views of the person of Christ were proposed and then rejected. One view, Arianism, which held that Jesus was not fully divine, was discussed above in the chapter on the doctrine of the Trinity.[36] But three other views that were eventually rejected as heretical should be mentioned at this point.

## 1. Three Inadequate Views of the Person of Christ.

a. **Apollinarianism.** Apollinaris, who became bishop in Laodicea about AD 361, taught that the one person of Christ had a human body but not a human mind or spirit and that the mind and spirit of Christ were from the divine nature of the Son of God. This view may be represented as in figure 26.1.

---

36. See the discussion of Arianism in chapter 14, pp. 285–87.

**Apollinarianism**
*Figure 26.1*

But the views of Apollinaris were rejected by the leaders of the church at that time, who realized that it was not just our human body that needed salvation and needed to be represented by Christ in his redemptive work but our human minds and spirits (or souls) as well: Christ had to be fully and truly man if he was to save us (Heb. 2:17). Apollinarianism was rejected by several church councils, from the Council of Alexandria in AD 362 to the Council of Constantinople in AD 381.[37] The leaders of the early church were correct in rejecting this view because it results in a Christ who is truly God but is not truly and fully a man as we are.

**b. Nestorianism.** Nestorianism is the doctrine that there were two separate persons in Christ, a human person and a divine person, a teaching that is distinct from the biblical view that sees Jesus as one person. Nestorianism may be diagramed as in figure 26.2.

**Nestorianism**
*Figure 26.2*

Nestorius was a popular preacher at Antioch, and from AD 428 was bishop of Constantinople. Although Nestorius himself probably never taught the heretical view that goes by his name (the idea that Christ was two persons in one body rather than one person), through a combination of several personal conflicts and a good deal of

---

37. Surprisingly, and I think unfortunately, an Apollinarian view of the person of Christ has recently been advocated by William Lane Craig in a section he wrote for the book *Philosophical Foundations for a Christian Worldview*. J. P. Moreland and William Lane Craig, *Philosophical Foundations for a Christian Worldview* (Downers Grove, IL: IVP Academic, 2003), 608–13.

ecclesiastical politics, he was removed from his office of bishop and his teachings were condemned.[38]

It is important to understand why the church could not accept the view that Christ was two distinct persons. Nowhere in Scripture do we have an indication that the human nature of Christ, for example, is an independent person, deciding to do something contrary to the divine nature of Christ. Nowhere do we have an indication of the human and divine natures talking to each other or struggling within Christ, or any such thing. Rather, we have a consistent picture of a single person acting in wholeness and unity. Jesus always speaks as "I," not as "we,"[39] though he can refer to himself and the Father together as "we" (John 14:23). The Bible always speaks of Jesus as "he," not as "they." And though we can sometimes distinguish actions of his divine nature and actions of his human nature in order to help us understand some of the statements and actions recorded in Scripture, the Bible itself does not say "Jesus' human nature did this" or "Jesus' divine nature did that," as though they were separate persons, but always talks about what the *person* of Christ did. Therefore, the church continued to insist that Jesus was one person, although possessing both a human nature and a divine nature.

**c. Monophysitism (Eutychianism).** A third inadequate view is called *monophysitism*, the view that Christ had one nature only (Gk. *monos*, "one," and *physis*, "nature"). The primary advocate of this view in the early church was Eutyches (c. AD 378–454), who was the leader of a monastery at Constantinople. Eutyches taught the opposite error from Nestorianism, for he denied that the human nature and divine nature in Christ remained fully human and fully divine. He held rather that the human nature of Christ was taken up and absorbed into the divine nature, so that both natures were changed somewhat and *a third kind of nature* resulted.[40] An analogy to Eutychianism can be seen if we put a drop of ink in a glass of water: the mixture resulting is neither pure ink nor pure water, but some kind of third substance, a mixture of the two in which both the ink and the water are changed. Similarly, Eutyches taught that Jesus was a mixture of divine and human elements in which both were somewhat modified to form one new nature. This may be represented as in figure 26.3.

---

38. Harold O. J. Brown says, "Nestorius' incarnate person was a single person, not two as his critics thought, but he could not convince others that it was so. Consequently he has gone down in history as a great heretic although what he actually believed was reaffirmed at Chalcedon" (*Heresies*, 176). Brown's extensive discussion of Nestorianism and related issues on pp. 172–84 is very helpful.

39. There is an unusual usage in John 3:11, where Jesus suddenly shifts to the plural, "Truly, truly, I say to you, *we* speak of what we know, and bear witness to what we have seen." Jesus may have been referring to himself and some disciples with him who are not mentioned, in contrast with the "we" of the Jewish

rulers that Nicodemus alluded to when he opened the conversation: "Rabbi, *we* know that you are a teacher come from God" (John 3:2). Or Jesus may have been speaking of himself together with the witness of the Holy Spirit, whose work is the subject of the conversation (vv. 5–9). In any case, Jesus is not referring to himself as "we," but calls himself "I" in that very sentence. See discussion in Leon Morris, *The Gospel according to John*, 221–22.

40. A variant form of Eutychianism held that the human nature was simply lost in the divine, so that the resulting single nature was the divine nature only.

**Eutychianism**
*Figure 26.3*

Monophysitism also rightly caused great concern in the church because, by this doctrine, Christ was neither truly God nor truly man. If that was so, he could not truly represent us as a man nor could he be true God and able to earn our salvation.

## 2. The Solution to the Controversy: The Chalcedonian Definition of AD 451

In order to attempt to solve the problems raised by the controversies over the person of Christ, a large church council was convened in the city of Chalcedon near Constantinople (modern Istanbul), from October 8 to November 1, AD 451. The resulting statement, called the Chalcedonian Definition, guarded against Apollinarianism, Nestorianism, and Eutychianism. It has been taken as the standard, orthodox definition of the biblical teaching on the person of Christ since that day by Catholic, Protestant, and Orthodox branches of Christianity alike.

The statement is not long, and we may quote it in its entirety:[41]

> We, then, following the holy Fathers, all with one consent, teach men to confess one and the same Son, our Lord Jesus Christ, the same perfect in Godhead and also perfect in manhood; truly God and truly man, of a reasonable [rational] soul and body; *consubstantial [coessential] with the Father according to the Godhead, and consubstantial with us according to the Manhood*; in all things like unto us, without sin; begotten before all ages of the Father according to the Godhead, and in these latter days, for us and for our salvation, born of the Virgin Mary, the Mother of God, according to the Manhood; one and the same Christ, Son, Lord, Only-begotten, to be acknowledged in *two natures, without confusion, without change, without division, without separation*, the distinction of natures being by no means taken away by the union, but rather *the property of each nature being preserved*, and concurring in *one*

---

41. English translation taken from Philip Schaff, *Creeds of Christendom*, 2:62–63, but I have replaced Schaff's words "inconfusedly, unchangeably, indivisibly, inseparably" with the clearer expressions "without confusion, without change, without division, without separation."

*Person* and one Subsistence, not parted or divided into two persons, but one and the same Son, and only begotten, God, the Word, the Lord Jesus Christ, as the prophets from the beginning [have declared] concerning him, and the Lord Jesus Christ himself has taught us, and the Creed of the holy Fathers has been handed down to us.

Against the view of Apollinaris that Christ did not have a human mind or soul, we have the statement that he was *"truly man,* of a *reasonable soul* and body . . . *consubstantial with us* according to the Manhood; in all things like unto us."* (The word *consubstantial* means "having the same nature or substance.")

In opposition to the view of Nestorianism that Christ was two persons united in one body, we have the words *"without division, without separation . . .* concurring in *one Person* and one Subsistence, not parted or divided into two persons."

Against the view of Monophysitism that Christ had only one nature, and that his human nature was lost in the union with the divine nature, we have the words "to be acknowledged in *two natures, without confusion, without change* . . . the distinction of natures being by no means taken away by the union, but rather *the property of each nature being preserved."* The human and the divine natures were not confused or changed when Christ became man, but the human nature remained a truly human nature, and the divine nature remained a truly divine nature.

Figure 26.4 may be helpful in showing this. In contrast to the earlier diagrams, it indicates that the eternal Son of God took to himself a truly human nature, and that Christ's divine and human natures remain distinct and retain their own properties, yet they are eternally and inseparably united together in one person.

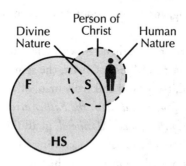

**Chelcedonian Christology**
*Figure 26.4*

Some have said that the Chalcedonian Definition really did not define for us in any positive way what the person of Christ actually *is* but simply told us several things that it *is not.* In this way some have said that it is not a very helpful definition. But such an accusation is misleading and inaccurate. The definition actually did a great deal to help us understand the biblical teaching correctly. It taught that Christ definitely has two natures, a human nature and a divine nature. It taught that his divine nature is exactly the same as that of the Father ("consubstantial with the Father according to the Godhead"). And it maintained that the human nature is exactly like our human nature yet without sin ("consubstantial with us according to the Manhood; in all things like unto us, without sin"). Moreover, it affirmed that in the person of Christ the human nature retains its distinctive characteristics and the divine nature retains its distinctive characteristics ("the distinction of natures being by no means taken away by the union, but rather *the property of each nature being preserved*"). Finally, it affirmed that, whether we can understand it or not, these two natures are united together in the one person of Christ.

When the Chalcedonian Definition says that the two natures of Christ occur together "in one Person and one *Subsistence*," the Greek word translated as "Subsistence" is the word *hypostasis,* "being." Hence the union of Christ's human and divine natures in one person is sometimes called the *hypostatic union.* This phrase simply means the union of Christ's human and divine natures in one being.

### 3. Combining Specific Biblical Texts on Christ's Deity and Humanity

When we examine the New Testament, as we did above in the sections on Jesus' humanity and deity, there are several passages that seem difficult to fit together (How could Jesus be omnipotent and yet weak? How could he leave the world and yet be present everywhere? How could he learn things and yet be omniscient?). As the church struggled to understand these teachings, it finally came up with the Chalcedonian Definition, which spoke of two distinct natures in Christ that retain their own properties yet remain together in one person. This distinction, which helps us in our understanding of the biblical passages mentioned earlier, also seems to be demanded by those passages.

**a. One Nature Does Some Things That the Other Nature Does Not Do.** Evangelical theologians in previous generations have not hesitated to distinguish between things done by Christ's human nature but not by his divine nature or by his divine nature but not by his human nature. It seems that we have to do this if we are willing to affirm the Chalcedonian statement about "the *property of each nature* being preserved." But few recent theologians have been willing to make such distinctions, perhaps because of a hesitancy to affirm something we cannot understand.

When we are talking about Jesus' human nature, we can say that he ascended to heaven and is no longer in the world (John 16:28; 17:11; Acts 1:9–11).[42] But with respect to his divine nature, we can say that Jesus is everywhere present: "Where two or

---

42. Lutheran theologians, following Martin Luther, have sometimes claimed that Jesus' human nature, even his human body, is also everywhere present or "ubiquitous." But this position has not been adopted by any other segment of the Christian church, and it seems to have been a position that Luther himself took mainly in an attempt to justify his view that Christ's body was actually present in the Lord's Supper (not in the elements themselves, but with them).

three are gathered in my name, *there am I* among them" (Matt. 18:20); "I am with you always, to the end of the age" (Matt. 28:20); "If anyone loves me, he will keep my word, and my Father will love him, and *we* will come to him and make our home with him" (John 14:23). So we can say that both things are true about the *person* of Christ—he has returned to heaven, *and* he is also present with us.

Similarly, we can say that Jesus was about thirty years old (Luke 3:23) if we are speaking with respect to his human nature, but we can say that he eternally existed (John 1:1–2; 8:58) if we are speaking of his divine nature.

In his human nature, Jesus was weak and tired (Matt. 4:2; 8:24; Mark 15:21; John 4:6), but in his divine nature he was omnipotent (Matt. 8:26–27; Col. 1:17; Heb. 1:3). Particularly striking is the scene on the Sea of Galilee where Jesus was asleep in the stern of the boat, presumably because he was weary (Matt. 8:24). But he was able to arise from his sleep and calm the wind and sea with a word (Matt. 8:26–27)! Tired yet omnipotent! Here Jesus' weak human nature completely hid his omnipotence until that omnipotence broke forth in a sovereign word from the Lord of heaven and earth.

If someone asks whether Jesus, when he was asleep in the boat, was also "continually carrying along all things by his word of power" (Heb. 1:3, author's translation), and whether all things in the universe were being held together by him at that time (see Col. 1:17), the answer must be yes, for those activities have always been and will always be the particular responsibility of the second person of the Trinity, the eternal Son of God. Those who find the doctrine of the incarnation "inconceivable" have sometimes asked whether Jesus, when he was a baby in the manger at Bethlehem, was also "upholding the universe." To this question the answer must also be yes: Jesus was not just potentially God or someone in whom God uniquely worked but was *truly and fully God*, with all the attributes of God. He was "a Savior, who is Christ *the Lord*" (Luke 2:11). Those who reject this as impossible simply have a different definition of what is possible than God has, as revealed in Scripture.[43] To say that we cannot understand this is appropriate humility. But to say that it is not possible seems more like intellectual arrogance.

In a similar way, we can understand that in his human nature, Jesus died (Luke 23:46;

---

43. A. N. S. Lane explicitly denies the Chalcedonian view of Christ on the ground that it cannot be: "Omniscience and ignorance, omnipotence and impotence cannot coexist. The former swamps the latter" ("Christology Beyond Chalcedon," in *Christ the Lord: Studies in Christology Presented to Donald Guthrie*, ed. Harold H. Rowden [Leicester; Inter-Varsity Press; Downers Grove, IL: InterVarsity Press, 1982], 270). He says that Christ "explicitly denied his omniscience (Mt. 24:36 = Mk. 13:32) but even the clear words of Christ have not sufficed to counter the pull of docetism. . . . The affirmation of the omniscience of the historical Jesus has no biblical basis and indeed runs counter to the clear teaching of the Gospels. . . . It has serious theological implications in that it undermines his true humanity as taught in Scripture" (271).

But (see pp. 697–700, below) Matt. 24:36 and Mark 13:32 are certainly capable of being understood to refer to Jesus' knowledge in his human nature. And when Lane says that omniscience and ignorance "cannot coexist" he is simply pitting one part of a biblical paradox against another and then asserting that one part is impossible. On what grounds are we justified in saying that an omniscient divine nature and a human nature with limited knowledge "cannot coexist"? Or that an omnipotent divine nature and a weak human nature "cannot coexist"? Such assertions fundamentally deny that infinite deity and finite humanity can exist together in the same person—in other words, they deny that Jesus could be *fully* God and *fully* man at the same time. In this way, they deny the essence of the incarnation.

1 Cor. 15:3). But with respect to his divine nature, he did not die but was able to raise himself from the dead (John 2:19; 10:17–18; Heb. 7:16). Yet here we must give a note of caution: it is true that when Jesus died his physical body died and his human soul (or spirit) was separated from his body and passed into the presence of God the Father in heaven (Luke 23:43, 46). In this way he experienced a death that is like the one we as believers experience if we die before Christ returns. And it is not correct to say that Jesus' divine nature died, or could die, if "die" means a cessation of activity, a cessation of consciousness, or a diminution of power. Nevertheless, by virtue of union with Jesus' human nature, his divine nature somehow tasted something of what it was like to go through death. The *person* of Christ experienced death. Moreover, it seems difficult to understand how Jesus' human nature alone could have borne the wrath of God against the sins of millions of people. It seems that Jesus' divine nature had somehow to participate in the bearing of wrath against sin that was due to us (though Scripture nowhere explicitly affirms this). Therefore, even though Jesus' divine nature did not actually die, Jesus went through the experience of death as a whole person, and both human and divine natures somehow shared in that experience. Beyond that, Scripture does not enable us to say more.

The distinction between Jesus' human and divine natures also helps us understand Jesus' temptations. With respect to his human nature, he certainly was tempted in every way as we are, yet without sin (Heb. 4:15). Yet with respect to his divine nature, he was not tempted because God cannot be tempted with evil (James 1:13).

At this point it seems necessary to say that Jesus had two distinct wills, a human will and a divine will, and that the wills belong to the two distinct natures of Christ, not to the person. In fact, there was a position, called the *monothelite* view, which held that Jesus had only "one will," but that was certainly a minority view in the church, and it was rejected as heretical at a church council in Constantinople in AD 681. Since then the view that Christ had two wills (a human will and a divine will) has been generally, but not universally, held through the church. In fact, Charles Hodge says,

> The decision against Nestorius, in which the unity of Christ's person was asserted; that against Eutyches, affirming the distinction of natures; and that against the Monothelites, declaring that the possession of a human nature involves of necessity the possession of a human will, have been received as the true faith by the Church universal, the Greek, Latin, and Protestant.[44]

Hodge explains that the church thought that "to deny Christ a human will, was to deny he had a human nature, or was truly a man. Besides, it precluded the possibility of his having been tempted, and therefore contradicted the Scriptures, and separated

---

44. Charles Hodge, *Systematic Theology*, 3 vols. (1871–73; repr., Grand Rapids: Eerdmans, 1970), 2:405.

him so far from his people he could not sympathize with them in their temptations."[45] Moreover, Hodge notes that along with the idea that Christ had two wills is the related idea that he had two centers of consciousness or intelligence: "As there are two distinct natures, human and divine, there are of necessity two intelligences and two wills, the one fallible and finite, the other immutable and infinite."[46]

This distinction of two wills and two centers of consciousness helps us understand how Jesus could learn things and yet know all things. On the one hand, with respect to his human nature, he had limited knowledge (Mark 13:32; Luke 2:52). On the other hand, Jesus clearly knew all things (John 2:25; 16:30; 21:17). Now this is only understandable if Jesus learned things and had limited knowledge with respect to his human nature but was always omniscient with respect to his divine nature, and therefore he was able any time to "call to mind" whatever information would be needed for his ministry. In this way we can understand Jesus' statement concerning the time of his return: "But concerning that day or that hour, no one knows, not even the angels in heaven, nor the Son, but only the Father" (Mark 13:32). This ignorance of the time of his return was true of Jesus' human nature and human consciousness only, for in his divine nature he was certainly omniscient and certainly knew the time when he would return to the earth.[47]

At this point someone may object that if we say that Jesus had two centers of consciousness and two wills, that *requires* that he was two distinct persons, and we have really fallen into the error of "Nestorianism." But in response, it must simply be affirmed that two wills and two centers of consciousness *do not* require that Jesus be two distinct persons. It is mere assertion without proof to say that they do. If someone responds that he or she *does not understand* how Jesus could have two centers of consciousness and still be one person, then that fact may certainly be admitted by all. But failing to understand something does not mean that it is impossible, only that our understanding is limited. The great majority of the church throughout its history has said that Jesus had two wills and centers of consciousness, yet he remained one person. Such a formulation is not impossible, merely a mystery that we do not now fully understand. To adopt any other solution would create a far greater problem: it would require that we give up either the full deity or the full humanity of Christ, and that we cannot do.[48]

**b. Anything Either Nature Does, the Person of Christ Does.** In the previous section we mentioned a number of things that were done by one nature but not the other in

---

45. Ibid., 2:404–5.

46. Ibid., 2:405.

47. In commenting on Mark 13:32, John Calvin, Anglican commentator H. B. Swete (*The Gospel according to St. Mark* [London: Macmillan, 1913], 316), and Lutheran commentator R. C. H. Lenski (*The Interpretation of St. Mark's Gospel* [repr., Minneapolis: Augsburg, 1961], 590) all attribute this ignorance of Jesus to his human nature only, not to his divine nature.

48. At this point an analogy from our human experience may be somewhat helpful. Anyone who has run in a race knows

that near the end of the race there are conflicting desires within. On the one hand, the runner's lungs and legs and arms seem to be crying out, "Stop! Stop!" There is a clear desire to stop because of the physical pain. On the other hand, something in the runner's mind says, "Go on! Go on! I want to win!" We have all known similar instances of conflicting desires within. Now if we, being ordinary human beings, can have differing or distinct desires within us and yet be one person, how much more possible is that for one who was both man and God at the same time? If we say we do not understand how that could the person of Christ. Now we must affirm that anything that is true of the human or the divine nature is true of the *person* of Christ. Thus Jesus can say, "Before Abraham was, I am" (John 8:58). He does not say, "Before Abraham was, my divine nature existed," because he is free to talk about anything done by his divine nature alone or his human nature alone as something that *he* did.

In the human sphere, this is certainly true of our conversation as well. If I type a letter, even though my feet and toes had nothing to do with typing the letter, I do not tell people, "My fingers typed a letter and my toes had nothing to do with it" (though that is true). Rather, I tell people, "*I* typed a letter." That is true because anything that is done by one part of me is done by *me*.

Thus "*Christ* died for our sins" (1 Cor. 15:3). Even though actually only his human body ceased living and ceased functioning, it was nonetheless *Christ* as a person who died for our sin. This is simply a means of affirming that whatever can be said of one nature or the other can be said of the *person* of Christ.

Therefore, it is correct for Jesus to say, "I am leaving the world" (John 16:28), or "I am no longer in the world" (John 17:11), but at the same time to say, "I am with you always" (Matt. 28:20). Anything that is done by one nature or the other is done by the *person* of Christ.

**c. Titles That Remind Us of One Nature Can Be Used of the Person Even When the Action Is Done By the Other Nature.** The New Testament authors sometimes use titles that remind us of either the human nature or the divine nature in order to speak of the person of Christ, even though the action mentioned may be done only by the other nature than the one we might think of from the title. For example, Paul says that if the rulers of this world had understood the wisdom of God, "they would not have crucified *the Lord of glory*" (1 Cor. 2:8). Now when we see the phrase "the Lord of glory" it reminds us specifically of Jesus' divine nature. But Paul uses this title (probably intentionally to show the horrible evil of the crucifixion) to say that Jesus was "crucified." Even though Jesus' divine nature was not crucified, it was true of Jesus as a *person* that he was crucified, and Paul affirms that about him even though he uses the title "the Lord of glory."

Similarly, when Elizabeth calls Mary "the mother of *my Lord*" (Luke 1:43), the name "my Lord" is a title that reminds us of Christ's divine nature. Yet Mary of course is not the mother of Jesus' divine nature, which has always existed. Mary is simply the mother of the human nature of Christ. Nevertheless, Elizabeth can call her "the mother of my Lord" because she is using the title "Lord" to refer to the person of Christ. A similar expression occurs in Luke 2:11: "For unto you *is born* this day in the city of David a Savior, who is Christ *the Lord*."

In this way, we can understand Mark 13:32, where Jesus says no one knows the time of his return, "not even the angels in heaven, *nor the Son*, but only the Father." Though

be, we simply admit our ignorance of the situation, for none of us has ever experienced what it is like to be both God and man at the same time, nor will we ever have such an experience ourselves. We should not say it is impossible, but if we are convinced that New Testament texts lead us to this conclusion, we should accept it and agree with it.

the term *the Son* specifically reminds us of Jesus' heavenly, eternal sonship with God the Father, it is really used here not to speak specifically of his divine nature, but to speak generally of him as a person, and to affirm something that is in fact true of his human nature only.[49] And it is true that in one important sense (that is, with respect to his human nature) Jesus did not know the time when he would return.

**d. Brief Summary Sentence.** Sometimes in the study of systematic theology, the following sentence has been used to summarize the incarnation: "Remaining what he was, he became what he was not." In other words, while Jesus continued "remaining" what he was (that is, fully divine), he also became what he previously had not been (that is, fully human as well). Jesus did not give up any of his deity when he became man, but he did take on humanity that was not his before.

**e. "Communication" of Attributes.** Once we have decided that Jesus was fully man and fully God, and that his human nature remained *fully* human and his divine nature remained *fully* divine, we can still ask whether there were some qualities or abilities that were given (or "communicated") from one nature to the other. It seems there were.

**Special Terms**

*Apollinarianism*
*Arianism*
*Chalcedonian Definition*
*communication of attributes*
*docetism*
*Eutychianism*
*God*
*hypostatic union*
*impeccability*
*incarnation*
*kenosis theory*
*Logos*
*Lord*
*monophysitism*
*monothelite view*
*Nestorianism*
*Son of God*
*Son of Man*
*virgin birth*

**1. From the divine nature to the human nature.** Although Jesus' human nature did not change its essential character, because it was united with the divine nature in the one person of Christ, Jesus' human nature gained (a) a worthiness to be worshiped and (b) an inability to sin, both of which did not belong to human beings otherwise.[50]

**2. From the human nature to the divine nature.** Jesus' human nature gave him (a) an ability to experience suffering and death; (b) an ability to understand by experience what we are experiencing; and (c) an ability to be our substitute sacrifice, which Jesus as God alone could not have done.

**f. Conclusion.** At the end of this long discussion, it may be easy for us to lose sight of what is actually taught in Scripture. It is by far the most amazing miracle of the entire Bible—far more amazing than the resurrection and more amazing even than the creation of the universe. The fact that the infinite, omnipotent, eternal Son of God could become man and join himself to a human nature forever so that infinite God became one person with finite man—that will remain for eternity the most profound miracle and the most profound mystery in all the universe.

---

49. Similar usage is perhaps seen in John 3:13 and Acts 20:28 (in this latter verse some manuscripts read "with his own blood").

50. See above, p. 695n42, on the Lutheran view that ubiquity was also communicated from the divine nature to the human.

## QUESTIONS FOR PERSONAL APPLICATION

1. After reading this chapter, are there specific ways you now think of Jesus as being more like you than you did before? What are these? How can a clearer understanding of Jesus' humanity help you face temptations? How can it help you to pray? What are the most difficult situations in your life right now? Can you think of any similar situations that Jesus might have faced? Does that encourage you to pray confidently to him? Can you picture what it would have been like if you had been present when Jesus said, "Before Abraham was, I am"? What would you have felt? Honestly, what would your response have been? Now try visualizing yourself as present when Jesus made some of the other "I am" statements recorded in John's gospel.[51]

2. After reading this chapter, is there anything that you understand more fully about the deity of Jesus? Can you describe (and perhaps identify with) what the disciples must have felt as they came to a growing realization of who Jesus actually was? Do you think Jesus is the one person you would be able to trust with your life for all eternity? Will you be happy to join with thousands of others in worshiping around his throne in heaven? Do you delight in worshiping him now?

## BIBLIOGRAPHY

(For an explanation of this bibliography see the note on the bibliography to chapter 1, pp. 23–24. Complete bibliographical data may be found on pp. 1489–96.)

### SECTIONS IN EVANGELICAL SYSTEMATIC THEOLOGIES

*1. Anglican (Episcopalian)*
   1882–92 . . . . . Litton, 178–218
   1930 . . . . . . . . Thomas, 32–49, 223–28
   2001 . . . . . . . . Packer, 104–24
   2013 . . . . . . . . Bird, 343–45
   2013 . . . . . . . . Bray, 211–404

*2. Arminian (Wesleyan or Methodist)*
   1875–76 . . . . . Pope, 2:106–51, 188–96, 254–62
   1892–94 . . . . . Miley, 2:4–62
   1940 . . . . . . . . Wiley, 2:143–86
   1960 . . . . . . . . Purkiser, 164–82
   1983 . . . . . . . . Carter, 1:331–74
   1992 . . . . . . . . Oden, 2:31–196
   2002 . . . . . . . . Cottrell, 224–58

*3. Baptist*
   1767 . . . . . . . . Gill, 1:537–69
   1887 . . . . . . . . Boyce, 258–91
   1907 . . . . . . . . Strong, 669–700
   1976–83 . . . . . Henry, 3:9–215
   1987–94 . . . . . Lewis and Demarest, 2:251–370
   1990–95 . . . . . Garrett, 1: 607–716
   2007 . . . . . . . . Akin, 480–544
   2013 . . . . . . . . Erickson, 603–91

---

51. See the list of "I am" statements at p. 681n25, above.

**4. Dispensational**

1947 . . . . . . . . Chafer, 1:318–96; 5:3–176
1949 . . . . . . . . Thiessen, 206–28
1986 . . . . . . . . Ryrie, 235–53, 260–66
2002–2005 . . Geisler, 2:280–85, 597–631
2017 . . . . . . . . MacArthur and Mayhue,
            235–326

**5. Lutheran**

1917–24 . . . . . Pieper, 2:55–279
1934 . . . . . . . . Mueller, 255–86

**6. Reformed (or Presbyterian)**

1559 . . . . . . . . Calvin, 1:423–94 (2.9–14)
1906–11 . . . . . Turretin, *IET*, 2:271–373
1724–58 . . . . . Edwards, 2:499–510, 949–55
1871–73 . . . . . Hodge, 1:483–521; 2:378–454
1878 . . . . . . . . Dabney, 464–99
1887–1921 . . . Warfield, *BTS*, 157–237;
            *SSW*, 1:139–66; *BD*, 71–100,
            175–212; *PWC*, 4–319; *LG*,
            1–304; *CC*, 3–389, 447–58
1894 . . . . . . . . Shedd, 613–74
1906–11 . . . . . Bavinck, *RD*, 3:233–319
1910 . . . . . . . . Vos, 3:20–84
1937–66 . . . . . Murray, *CW*, 1:29–35,
            340–43; 2:132–41; 4:58–91
1938 . . . . . . . . Berkhof, 305–30
1998 . . . . . . . . Reymond, 545–622
2008 . . . . . . . . Van Genderen and Velema,
            437–61
2011 . . . . . . . . Horton, 446–82
2013 . . . . . . . . Frame, 189, 361, 390–92, 395,
            399, 446–71, 476, 481, 484,
            490–95, 500, 505, 512, 672
2013 . . . . . . . . Culver, 419–638
2016 . . . . . . . . Allen and Swain, 216–42
2017 . . . . . . . . Barrett, 313–46

2019 . . . . . . . . Letham, 471–541

**7. Renewal (or charismatic/Pentecostal)**

1988–92 . . . . . Williams, 1:305–52
1993 . . . . . . . . Menzies and Horton, 59–74
1995 . . . . . . . . Horton, 291–324
2008 . . . . . . . . Duffield and Van Cleave,
            93–108

## SECTIONS IN REPRESENTATIVE ROMAN CATHOLIC SYSTEMATIC THEOLOGIES

**1. Roman Catholic: Traditional**

1955 . . . . . . . . Ott, 125–75

**2. Roman Catholic: Post–Vatican II**

1980 . . . . . . . . McBrien, 1:267–546
2012 . . . . . . . . *CCC*, paragraphs 422–682

## OTHER WORKS

Akin, Daniel L. "The Person of Christ." In *A Theology for the Church*, edited by Daniel L. Akin et al., 480–544. Nashville: B&H, 2007.

Allison, Gregg. *Historical Theology: An Introduction to Christian Doctrine; A Companion to Wayne Grudem's* Systematic Theology. Grand Rapids: Zondervan, 2011, 365–88.

Anselm. "The Incarnation of the Word." In *Anselm of Canterbury*. Vol. 3. Toronto: Mellen, 1976.

———. *Why God Became Man: and The Virgin Conception and Original Sin*. Translated by Joseph M. Colleran. Albany, NY: Magi, 1969.

Athanasius. *On the Incarnation*. Translated by a religious of C.S.M.V. New York: Macmillan, 1946.

Berkouwer, G. C. *The Person of Christ*. Translated by John Vriend. Grand Rapids: Eerdmans, 1954.

Bock, Darrell L., and Robert L. Webb, eds. *Key Events in the Life of the Historical Jesus: A Collaborative Exploration of Context and Coherence*. Grand Rapids: Eerdmans, 2010.

Bowman, Robert M., and J. Ed Komoszewski. *Putting Jesus in His Place: The Case for the Deity of Christ*. Grand Rapids: Kregel, 2007.

Bray, G. L. *Creeds, Councils and Christ*. Leicester: Inter-Varsity Press, 1984.

———. "Christology." In *NDT1*, 137–40.

Brown, Harold O. J. *Heresies: The Image of Christ in the Mirror of Heresy and Orthodoxy From the Apostles to the Present*. Garden City, NY: Doubleday, 1984.

Bruce, F. F. *Jesus: Lord and Savior*. The Jesus Library, edited by Michael Green. Downers Grove, IL: InterVarsity Press, 1986.

Erickson, Millard. *The Word Became Flesh: A Contemporary Incarnational Christology*. Grand Rapids: Baker, 1991.

Green, Joel B., and Max Turner, eds. *Jesus of Nazareth: Lord and Christ: Essays on the Historical Jesus and New Testament Christology*. Eugene, OR: Wipf & Stock, 1999.

Gruenler, Royce Gordon. "Christ, Christology." In *BTDB*, 83–89.

Guthrie, Donald. *Jesus the Messiah*. Grand Rapids: Zondervan, 1972.

———. *New Testament Theology*. Leicester: Inter-Varsity Press; Downers Grove, IL: InterVarsity Press, 1981, 219–365.

Harris, Murray J. *Jesus As God*. Grand Rapids: Baker, 1992.

Higton, M. "Christology." In *NDT2*, 175–79.

House, H. Wayne. *The Jesus Who Never Lived*. Eugene, OR: Harvest House, 2008.

Hughes, Philip Edgcumbe. *The True Image: The Origin and Destiny of Man in Christ*. Grand Rapids: Eerdmans; Leicester: Inter-Varsity Press, 1989, 211–414.

Hurtado, L. W. "Christology." In *DLNT*, 170–84.

Hurtado, Larry W. *Lord Jesus Christ: Devotion to Jesus in Earliest Christianity*. Grand Rapids: Eerdmans, 2003.

Kärkkäinen, V.-M., J. Levison, and P. Pope-Levison. "Christology." In *GDT*, 167–86.

Lincoln, Andrew. *Born of a Virgin? Reconceiving Jesus in the Bible, Tradition, and Theology*. Grand Rapids: Eerdmans, 2013.

Longenecker, Richard. *The Christology of Early Jewish Christianity*. London: SCM, 1970.

Marshall, I. Howard. *I Believe in the Historical Jesus*. Grand Rapids: Eerdmans, 1977.

———. "Jesus Christ." In *NDBT*, 592–602.

McGrath, Alister E. *Understanding Jesus: Who He Is and Why He Matters*. Grand Rapids: Zondervan, 1987.

Moule, C. F. D. *The Origin of Christology*. Cambridge: Cambridge University Press, 1977.

Payne, Philip B. "Jesus' Implicit Claim to Deity in His Parables." *TrinJ* 2, no. 1 (Spring 1981): 3–23.

Reymond, Robert L. *Jesus, Divine Messiah*. Phillipsburg, NJ: Presbyterian and Reformed, 1990.

Runia, Klaas. *The Present-Day Christological Debate*. Leicester: Inter-Varsity Press, 1984.

Sproul, R. C. *The Glory of Christ*. Wheaton, IL: Tyndale, 1990.

Stein, R. H. "Jesus Christ." In *EDT1*, 582–85.

Treier, D. J. "Jesus Christ." In *EDT3*, 442–49.

Wallace, R. S. "Christology." In *EDT1*, 221–27.

Walvoord, John F. *Jesus Christ Our Lord*. Chicago: Moody Publishers, 1969.

Ware, Bruce. *The Man Christ Jesus: Theological Reflections on the Humanity of Christ*. Wheaton, IL: Crossway, 2013.

Wells, David F. *The Person of Christ: A Biblical and Historical Analysis of the Incarnation*. Westchester, IL: Crossway, 1984.

Wellum, Stephen J. *God the Son Incarnate: The Doctrine of Christ*. Wheaton, IL: Crossway, 2016.

Wilkins, Michael J., and J. P. Moreland. *Jesus under Fire: Modern Scholarship Reinvents the Historical Jesus*. Grand Rapids: Zondervan, 1995; Carlisle: Paternoster, 1996.

Witherington, Ben, III. "Christ." In *DLNT*, 152–59.

———. "Christology." In *DPL*, 100–115.

———. *The Christology of Jesus*. Minneapolis: Fortress, 1990.

Witmer, John A. *Immanuel: Jesus Christ, Cornerstone of Our Faith*. Nashville: Word, 1998.

## SCRIPTURE MEMORY PASSAGE

**John 1:14:** And the Word became flesh and dwelt among us, and we have seen his glory, glory as of the only Son from the Father, full of grace and truth.

# HYMN

## "Fairest Lord Jesus"

*Fairest Lord Jesus, ruler of all nature,*
*Son of God and Son of Man!*
*Thee will I cherish, thee will I honor,*
*Thou, my soul's glory, joy, and crown.*

*Fair are the meadows, fair are the woodlands,*
*Robed in the blooming garb of spring:*
*Jesus is fairer, Jesus is purer,*
*Who makes the woeful heart to sing.*

*Fair is the sunshine, fair is the moonlight,*
*And all the twinkling, starry host:*
*Jesus shines brighter, Jesus shines purer*
*Than all the angels heav'n can boast.*

*Beautiful Savior! Lord of the nations!*
*Son of God and Son of Man!*
*Glory and honor, praise, adoration,*
*Now and forever more be thine.*

From *Münster Gesangbuch*, 1677,
translated 1850, 1873

# CONTEMPORARY WORSHIP SONG

## "There Is a Redeemer"

*There is a Redeemer, Jesus, God's own Son,*
*Precious Lamb of God, Messiah, Holy One.*

*Chorus*
*Thank You, O my Father,*
*For giving us Your Son,*
*And leaving Your Spirit*
*Till the work on earth is done.*

*Jesus, my Redeemer, name above all names,*
*Precious Lamb of God, Messiah, o for sinners slain.*

*When I stand in glory, I will see His face.*
*There I'll serve my King forever in that holy place.*

Words by Melody Green[52]

# CHAPTER 27

# The Atonement

*Was it necessary for Christ to die?*
*Did Christ's entire earthly life earn any saving benefits for us?*
*The cause and nature of the atonement.*
*Did Christ descend into hell?*

## EXPLANATION AND SCRIPTURAL BASIS

We may define the atonement as follows: *The atonement is the work Christ did in his life and death to earn our salvation.* This definition indicates that we are using the word *atonement* in a broader sense than it is sometimes used. Sometimes it is used to refer only to Jesus' dying and paying for our sins on the cross. But since saving benefits also come to us from Christ's life, we have included that in our definition as well.[1]

### A. THE CAUSE OF THE ATONEMENT

What was the ultimate cause that led to Christ's coming to earth and dying for our sins? To find this we must trace the question back to something in the character of God himself. And here Scripture points to two things: the *love* and *justice* of God.

The love of God as a cause of the atonement is seen in the most familiar passage in the Bible: "For God *so loved the world*, that he gave his only Son, that whoever believes in him should not perish but have eternal life" (John 3:16). But the justice of God also required that God find a way that the penalty due to us for our sins would be paid (for he could not accept us into fellowship with himself unless the penalty was paid). Paul explains that this was why God sent Christ to be a "propitiation" (that is, a sacrifice that bears God's wrath so that God becomes "propitious" or favorably disposed toward us): it was "*to show God's righteousness*, because in his divine forbearance he had passed over former sins" (Rom. 3:25). Here Paul says that God had been forgiving sins in the Old Testament but no penalty had been paid—a fact that would make people wonder whether God was indeed just and ask how he could forgive sins without a penalty. No God who was truly just could do that, could he? Yet when God sent Christ to die and

---

1. Of course, there are also saving benefits that come to us from Christ's resurrection and ascension, from his continuing high priestly work of intercession for us, and from his second coming. These are discussed as separate topics in subsequent chapters of this book. For the sake of clarity, I have here included under the title "atonement" only those things that Christ did for our salvation during his earthly life and in his death.

pay the penalty for our sins, "it was to show his righteousness at the present time, so that he might be just and the justifier of the one who has faith in Jesus" (Rom. 3:26).

Therefore, both the love and the justice of God were the ultimate cause of the atonement. It is not helpful for us to ask which is more important, however, because without the love of God, he would never have taken any steps to redeem us, yet without the justice of God, the specific requirement that Christ should earn our salvation by dying for our sins would not have been met. Both the love and the justice of God were equally important.

## B. THE NECESSITY OF THE ATONEMENT

Was there any other way for God to save human beings than by sending his Son to die in our place?

Before answering this question, it is important to realize that it was not necessary for God to save any people at all. When we appreciate that "God did not spare angels when they sinned, but cast them into hell and committed them to chains of gloomy darkness to be kept until the judgment" (2 Peter 2:4), then we realize that God could also have chosen with perfect justice to have left us in our sins awaiting judgment: he could have chosen to save no one, just as he did with the sinful angels. So in this sense the atonement was not absolutely necessary.

But once God, in his love, decided to save some human beings, then several passages in Scripture indicate that there was no other way for God to do this than through the death of his Son. The atonement was not absolutely necessary, but as a "consequence" of God's decision to save some human beings, the atonement was absolutely necessary. This is sometimes called the "consequent absolute necessity" view of the atonement.

In the garden of Gethsemane Jesus prays, *"If it be possible*, let this cup pass from me; nevertheless, not as I will, but as you will" (Matt. 26:39). We may be confident that Jesus always prayed according to the will of the Father and that he always prayed with fullness of faith. Thus it seems that this prayer, which Matthew takes pains to record for us, shows that it was *not possible* for Jesus to avoid the death on the cross which was soon to come to him (the "cup" of suffering that he had said would be his). If he was going to accomplish the work that the Father sent him to do, and if people were going to be redeemed for God, then it was necessary for him to die on the cross.

He said something similar after his resurrection, when he was talking with two disciples on the road to Emmaus. They were sad that Jesus had died, but his response was, "O foolish ones, and slow of heart to believe all that the prophets have spoken! Was it not *necessary* that the Christ should suffer these things and enter into his glory?" (Luke 24:25–26). Jesus understood that God's plan of redemption (which he explained for the disciples from many Old Testament Scriptures, Luke 24:27) made it necessary for the Messiah to die for the sins of his people.

As we saw above, Paul in Romans 3 also shows that if God were to be righteous and still save people, he had to send Christ to pay the penalty for sins: "It was to show his righteousness at the present time, so that he might be just and the justifier of the one who has faith in Jesus" (Rom. 3:26). The epistle to the Hebrews emphasizes that Christ had to suffer for our sins: "He *had to* be made like his brothers in every respect, so that he might become a merciful and faithful high priest in the service of God, to make propitiation for the sins of the people" (Heb. 2:17). The author of Hebrews also argues that since "it is impossible for the blood of bulls and goats to take away sins" (Heb. 10:4), a better sacrifice is required (Heb. 9:23). Only the blood of Christ, that is, his death, would be able really to take away sins (Heb. 9:25–26). There was no other way for God to save us than for Christ to die in our place.

## C. The Nature of the Atonement

In this section we consider two aspects of Christ's work: (1) Christ's obedience for us, in which he obeyed the requirements of the law in our place and was perfectly obedient to the will of God the Father as our representative, and (2) Christ's sufferings for us, in which he took the penalty due for our sins and as a result died for our sins.

It is important to notice that in both of these categories the primary emphasis and the primary influence of Christ's work of redemption is not on us but on God the Father. Jesus obeyed the Father in our place and perfectly met the demands of the law. And he suffered in our place, receiving in himself the penalty that God the Father would have visited upon us. In both cases, the atonement is viewed as *objective*, that is, something that has primary influence directly on God. Only secondarily does it have application to us, and this is only because there was *a definite event* in the relationship between God the Father and God the Son that secured our salvation.

## 1. Christ's Obedience for Us (Sometimes Called His "Active Obedience")

If Christ had only earned forgiveness of sins for us, then we would not merit heaven. Our guilt would have been removed, but we would simply be in the position of Adam and Eve before they had done anything good or bad and before they had passed a time of probation successfully. To be established in righteousness forever and to have their fellowship with God made sure forever, Adam and Eve had to obey God perfectly over a period of time. Then God would have looked on their faithful obedience with pleasure and delight, and they would have lived with him in fellowship forever.[2]

For this reason, Christ had to live a life of perfect obedience to God in order to earn righteousness for us. He had to obey the law for his whole life on our behalf so that the positive merits of his perfect obedience would be counted for us. Sometimes this is called Christ's "active obedience," while his suffering and dying for our sins is called his

---

2. See discussion of the covenant of works in chapter 25, pp. 648–50.

"passive obedience."[3] Paul says his goal is that he may be found in Christ, "*not having a righteousness of [his] own* that comes from the law, but *that which comes through faith in Christ*, the righteousness from God that depends on faith" (Phil. 3:9). It is not just moral neutrality that Paul knows he needs from Christ (that is, a clean slate with sins forgiven); Paul needs a positive moral righteousness. And he knows that it cannot come from him or from his effort or work, but it must come through faith in Christ. Similarly, Paul says that Christ has become our "*righteousness*" (1 Cor. 1:30). And he quite explicitly says, "For as by the one man's disobedience the many were made sinners, so by the one man's obedience the many will be *made righteous*" (Rom. 5:19).

This same idea, that Christ's record of perfect righteousness is credited to our account, is seen in 2 Corinthians: "For our sake he made him to be sin who knew no sin, so that in him we might become the righteousness of God" (2 Cor. 5:21). Here Paul says that God made Christ "to be sin," that is, to be thought of as sinful—not on account of his own sin (for he "knew no sin"), but on account of our sin ("For our sake"). And then we "become the righteousness of God." Just as God thought of our sin as belonging to Christ, so he thinks of Christ's righteousness as belonging to us. God thinks of us, regards us, as righteous. How can he do this? Because he thinks of us as being "in him," that is, in Christ—God understands us to be spiritually united to Christ and represented by him, so that Christ's record of perfect righteousness is counted as ours.

Some theologians have not taught that Christ needed to achieve a lifelong record of perfect obedience for us. They have simply emphasized that Christ had to die and thereby pay the penalty for our sins.[4] But such a position does not adequately explain why Christ did more than just die for us; he also became our righteousness before God. Jesus said to John the Baptist, before he was baptized by him, "It is fitting for us *to fulfill all righteousness*" (Matt. 3:15).

It might be argued that Christ had to live a life of perfect righteousness for his own sake, not for ours, before he could be a sinless sacrifice for us. But Jesus had no need to live a life of perfect obedience for his own sake—he had shared love and fellowship with the Father for all eternity and was in his own character eternally worthy of the Father's good pleasure and delight. He rather had to "fulfill all righteousness" for our sake, that is, for the sake of the people whom he was representing as their head. Unless he had

---

3. Some have objected that this "active" and "passive" terminology is not entirely satisfactory, because even in paying for our sins Christ was in one sense actively accepting the suffering given him by the Father and was even active in laying down his own life (John 10:18). Moreover, both aspects of Christ's obedience continued through his whole life: his active obedience included faithful obedience from birth up to and including the point of his death; and his suffering on our behalf, which found its climax in the crucifixion, continued through his whole life (see discussion below). Nevertheless, the distinction between active and passive obedience is still useful because it helps us appreciate the two aspects of Christ's work for us. (See the discussion in John Murray, *Redemption Accomplished and Applied* [Grand Rapids: Eerdmans, 1955], 20–24.) R. L. Reymond prefers the terms *preceptive* (for active) and *penal* (for passive), in his article "Obedience of Christ," *EDT*, 785.

4. For example, I could find no discussion of the active obedience of Christ in the seven-volume *Systematic Theology* by Lewis Sperry Chafer (Dallas: Dallas Seminary Press, 1947–48) or in Millard Erickson's *Christian Theology*, 3rd ed. (Grand Rapids: Baker, 2013), 695–768.

done this for us, we would have no record of obedience by which we would merit God's favor and merit eternal life with him. Moreover, if Jesus had needed only sinlessness and not also a life of perfect obedience, he could have died for us when he was a young child rather than when he was thirty-three years old.

By way of application, we ought to ask ourselves whose lifelong record of obedience we would rather rely on for our standing before God, Christ's or our own? As we think about the life of Christ, we ought to ask ourselves, was it good enough to deserve God's approval? And are we willing to rely on his record of obedience for our eternal destiny?

## 2. Christ's Sufferings for Us (Sometimes Called His "Passive Obedience")

In addition to obeying the law perfectly for his whole life on our behalf, Christ also took on himself the sufferings necessary to pay the penalty for our sins.

**a. Suffering for His Whole Life.** In a broad sense, the penalty Christ bore in paying for our sins was suffering in both his body and soul throughout his life. Though Christ's sufferings culminated in his death on the cross (see below), his whole life in a fallen world involved suffering. For example, Jesus endured tremendous suffering during the temptation in the wilderness (Matt. 4:1–11), when he was assaulted for forty days by the attacks of Satan.[5] He also suffered in growing to maturity, "Although he was a son, he learned obedience through what he *suffered*" (Heb. 5:8). He knew suffering in the intense opposition he faced from Jewish leaders throughout much of his earthly ministry (see Heb. 12:3–4). We may suppose too that he experienced suffering and grief at the death of his earthly father,[6] and certainly he experienced grief at the death of his close friend Lazarus (John 11:35). In predicting the coming of the Messiah, Isaiah said he would be "a *man of sorrows*, and acquainted with grief" (Isa. 53:3).

**b. The Pain of the Cross.** The sufferings of Jesus intensified as he drew near to the cross. He told his disciples something of the agony he was going through when he said, "My soul is very sorrowful, even to death" (Matt. 26:38). It was especially on the cross that Jesus' sufferings for us reached their climax, for it was there that he bore the penalty for our sin and died in our place. Scripture teaches us that there were four different aspects of the pain that Jesus experienced.

**1. Physical pain and death.** We do not need to hold that Jesus suffered more physical pain than any human being has ever suffered, for the Bible nowhere makes such a claim. But we still must not forget that death by crucifixion was one of the most horrible forms of execution ever devised by man.

Many readers of the Gospels in the ancient world would have witnessed crucifixions and thus would have had a painfully vivid mental picture upon reading the simple words

5. In Mark 1:13 the present participle *peirazomenos*, "being tempted," modifies the imperfect main verb of the clause (*ēn*, "was"), indicating that Jesus was continually being tempted throughout the forty days in which he was in the wilderness.

6. Although Scripture does not explicitly say that Joseph died during Jesus' life, we hear nothing of him after Jesus is twelve years old; see discussion in chapter 26, p. 672n8.

"And they crucified him" (Mark 15:24). A criminal who was crucified was essentially forced to inflict upon himself a very slow death by suffocation. When the criminal's arms were outstretched and fastened by nails to the cross, he had to support most of the weight of his body with his arms. The chest cavity would be pulled upward and outward, making it difficult to exhale in order to be able to draw a fresh breath. But when the victim's longing for oxygen became unbearable, he would have to push himself up with his feet, thus giving more natural support to the weight of his body, releasing some of the weight from his arms, and enabling his chest cavity to contract more normally. By pushing himself upward in this way the criminal could fend off suffocation, but it was extremely painful because it required putting the body's weight on the nails holding the feet, and bending the elbows and pulling upward on the nails driven through the wrists.[7] The criminal's back, which had been torn open repeatedly by a previous flogging, would scrape against the wooden cross with each breath. Thus Seneca (first century AD) spoke of a crucified man "drawing the breath of life amid long-drawn-out agony" (Epistle 101, to Lucilius, section 14).

A physician writing in the *Journal of the American Medical Association* in 1986 explained the pain that would have been experienced in death by crucifixion:

> Adequate exhalation required lifting the body by pushing up on the feet and by flexing the elbows. . . . However, this maneuver would place the entire weight of the body on the tarsals and would produce searing pain. Furthermore, flexion of the elbows would cause rotation of the wrists about the iron nails and cause fiery pain along the damaged median nerves. . . . Muscle cramps and paresthesias of the outstretched and uplifted arms would add to the discomfort. As a result, each respiratory effort would become agonizing and tiring and lead eventually to asphyxia.[8]

In some cases, crucified men would survive for several days, nearly suffocating but not quite dying. This was why the executioners would sometimes break the legs of a criminal, so that death would come quickly, as we see in John 19:31–33:

> Since it was the day of Preparation, and so that the bodies would not remain on the cross on the Sabbath (for that Sabbath was a high day), the Jews asked Pilate that their legs might be broken and that they might be taken away. So the soldiers came and broke the legs of the first, and of the other who had been crucified with him. But when they came to Jesus and saw that he was already dead, they did not break his legs.

---

7. The Greek word usually translated "hand" (*cheir*: Luke 24:39–40; John 20:20) can sometimes refer to the arm (BDAG says, "The *arm* may be meant," 1082, at the end of meaning 1; cf. LSJ, 1983, 2). A nail through the hands would not have been able to support the weight of the body, for the hands would have torn.

8. William Edwards, MD, et al., *JAMA* 255, no. 11 (March 21, 1986): 1461.

**2. The pain of bearing sin.** More awful than the pain of physical suffering that Jesus endured was the psychological pain of bearing the guilt for our sin. In our experience as Christians we know something of the anguish we feel when we know we have sinned. The weight of guilt is heavy on our hearts, and there is a bitter sense of separation from all that is right in the universe, an awareness of something that in a very deep sense ought not to be. In fact, the more we grow in holiness as God's children, the more intensely we feel this instinctive revulsion against evil.

Now Jesus was perfectly holy. He hated sin with his entire being. The thought of evil, of sin, contradicted everything in his character. Far more than we do, Jesus instinctively rebelled against evil. Yet in obedience to the Father, and out of love for us, Jesus took on himself all the sins of those who would someday be saved. Taking on himself all the evil against which his soul rebelled created deep revulsion in the center of his being. All that he hated most deeply was poured out fully upon him.

Scripture frequently says that our sins were put on Christ: "The LORD has laid on him the iniquity of us all" (Isa. 53:6), and "He *bore the sin* of many" (Isa. 53:12). John the Baptist calls Jesus "the Lamb of God, who takes away the sin of the world" (John 1:29). Paul declares that God made Christ "*to be sin*" (2 Cor. 5:21) and that Christ became "a curse for us" (Gal. 3:13). The author of Hebrews says that Christ was "offered once to bear the sins of many" (Heb. 9:28). And Peter says, "He himself *bore our sins* in his body on the tree" (1 Peter 2:24).[9]

The passage from 2 Corinthians 5:21 quoted above, together with the verses from Isaiah, indicate that it was God the Father who put our sins on Christ. How could that be? In the same way Adam's sins were imputed to us,[10] God *imputed* our sins to Christ— that is, he *thought of them as belonging to Christ*, and since God is the ultimate judge and definer of what really is in the universe, when God thought of our sins as belonging to Christ, then in fact they actually did belong to Christ. This does not mean that God thought that Christ had himself committed the sins or that Christ himself actually had a sinful nature but rather that the guilt for our sins (that is, the liability to punishment) was thought of by God as belonging to Christ rather than to us.

Some have objected that it was not fair for God to do this, to transfer the guilt of sin from us to an innocent person, Christ. Yet we must remember that Christ voluntarily took on himself the guilt for our sins, so this objection loses much of its force. Moreover, God himself (Father, Son, and Holy Spirit) is the ultimate standard of what is just and

---

9. See Grudem, *1 Peter*, 133–34, for a detailed answer to Deissmann's view that 1 Peter 2:24 means that Christ "carried our sins up to the cross" but did not himself bear the guilt for our sins on the cross. BDAG, 75, 3, following Deissmann, says that, according to 1 Peter 2:24, Christ "brought our sins in his body to the cross" and that the verb *anapherō*, which is used in 1 Peter 2:24, "seems not to take [the] meanings" of "bear" or "take away. But this is incorrect, because Polybius 1.36.3 and Thucydides 3.38.3 provide extrabiblical examples of the meaning "bear," and it certainly has that meaning in the LXX of Isa. 53:4, 11, 12 and in the quotation of Isa. 53:12 in Heb. 9:28; cf. LSJ, 125, 3.

10. See chapter 24, pp. 623–27, for a discussion of the imputation of Adam's sin to us.

fair in the universe, and he decreed that the atonement would take place in this way and that it did in fact satisfy the demands of his righteousness and justice.

**3. Abandonment.** The physical pain of crucifixion and the pain of taking on himself the absolute evil of our sins were aggravated by the fact that Jesus faced this pain alone. In the garden of Gethsemane when Jesus took with him Peter, James, and John, he confided something of his agony to them: "My soul is very sorrowful, even to death. Remain here and watch" (Mark 14:34). This is the kind of confidence one would disclose to a close friend, and it implies a request for support in his hour of greatest trial. Yet as soon as Jesus was arrested, "all the disciples left him and fled" (Matt. 26:56).

Here also there is a very faint analogy in our experience, for we cannot live long without tasting the inward ache of rejection, whether it be rejection by a close friend, by a parent or child, or by a wife or husband. Yet in all those cases there is at least a sense that we could have done something differently, that at least in small part we may be at fault. It was not so with Jesus and the disciples, for "having loved his own who were in the world, he loved them to the end" (John 13:1). He had done nothing but love them; in return, they all abandoned him.

But far worse than desertion by even the closest of human friends was the fact that Jesus was deprived of the closeness to the Father that had been the deepest joy of his heart for all his earthly life. When Jesus cried out "Eli, Eli, lema sabachthani?" that is, "My God, my God, why have you forsaken me?" (Matt. 27:46), he showed that he was finally cut off from the sweet fellowship with his heavenly Father that had been the unfailing source of his inward strength and the element of greatest joy in a life filled with sorrow. As Jesus bore our sins on the cross, he was abandoned by his heavenly Father, who is "of purer eyes than to see evil" (Hab. 1:13). He faced the weight of the guilt of millions of sins alone.

**4. Bearing the wrath of God.** Yet more difficult than these three previous aspects of Jesus' pain was the pain of bearing the wrath of God upon himself. As Jesus bore the guilt of our sins alone, God the Father, the mighty Creator, the Lord of the universe, poured out on Jesus the fury of his wrath: Jesus became the object of the intense hatred of sin and vengeance against sin which God had patiently stored up since the beginning of the world.

Romans 3:25 tells us that God put forward Christ as a propitiation, a word that means "a sacrifice that bears God's wrath to the end and in so doing changes God's wrath toward us into favor." Paul tells us that "This was to show God's righteousness, because in his divine forbearance he had passed over former sins. It was to show his righteousness at the present time, so that he might be just and the justifier of the one who has faith in Jesus" (Rom. 3:25–26). God had not simply forgiven sin and forgotten about the punishment in generations past. He had forgiven sins and stored up his righteous anger against those sins. But at the cross the fury of all that stored-up wrath against sin was unleashed against God's Son.

Many theologians outside the evangelical world have strongly objected to the idea that Jesus bore the wrath of God against sin.[11] Their basic assumption is that since God is a God of love, it would be inconsistent with his character to show wrath against the human beings he has created and for whom he is a loving Father. Sadly, some prominent evangelicals have advocated that position as well.[12]

But evangelical scholars have convincingly argued that the idea of the wrath of God is solidly rooted in both the Old and New Testaments. Australian New Testament scholar Leon Morris writes, "The whole of the argument of the opening part of Romans is that all men, Gentiles and Jews alike, are sinners, and that they come under the wrath and the condemnation of God."[13]

In addition to Romans 3:25, three other crucial passages in the New Testament also refer to Jesus' death as a "propitiation": Hebrews 2:17; 1 John 2:2; and 4:10. The Greek terms used in these passages (the verb *hilaskomai*, "to make propitiation," and the noun *hilasmos*, "a sacrifice of propitiation") have the sense of "a sacrifice that turns away the wrath of God—and thereby makes God propitious (or favorable) toward us."[14] This is the consistent meaning of these words outside the Bible where they were well understood in reference to pagan Greek religions. These verses simply mean that Jesus bore the wrath of God against sin.

Other verses indicating that Christ bore the wrath of God against our sin include 2 Corinthians 5:21, which says that "for our sake" God "made him [Christ] to be sin who knew no sin, so that in him we might become the righteousness of God." This means that God thought of Christ as "sin" and treated him as "sin," which, because of God's justice, would call forth God's wrath upon Christ. This was for our benefit, for just as God counted our sin as belonging to Christ, so he counted Christ's righteousness as belonging to us ("so that in him we might become the righteousness of God"). Similarly, Galatians 3:13 says that "Christ redeemed us from the curse of the law by becoming a

11. See the detailed linguistic argument of C. H. Dodd, *The Bible and the Greeks* (London: Hodder and Stoughton, 1935), 82–95. Dodd argues that the idea of propitiation was common in pagan religions but foreign to the thought of Old Testament and New Testament writers.

12. See the discussion below, pp. 719–22, about three influential evangelicals who have now used this same argument to deny that Christ bore the wrath of God against sin.

13. Leon Morris, "Propitiation," *EDT*, 888 (includes brief bibliography). Morris's own work has represented the best of evangelical scholarship on this question; see Morris, *The Apostolic Preaching of the Cross*, 3rd ed. (London: Tyndale, 1965), 144–213. See also the discussion of the wrath of God in chapter 12, pp. 245–47. A brief but truly excellent presentation of the heart of the atonement as Christ bearing the wrath of God against sin, including a crystal-clear explanation of propitiation, is found in the chapter, "The Heart of the Gospel," in J. I. Packer, *Knowing God* (Downers Grove, IL: InterVarsity, 1973), 161–80.

14. Under the influence of scholars who denied that the idea of propitiation was in the New Testament, the RSV translated *hilasmos* as "expiation," a word that means "an action that cleanses from sin" but includes no concept of appeasing God's wrath. The difference is that in expiation *sin* is affected (it is taken away) while in propitiation *God* is affected (his wrath is turned to favor). The RSV's removal of "propitiation" from Rom. 3:25; Heb. 2:17; and 1 John 2:2 and 4:10 was one of the reasons the RSV never gained widespread acceptance among evangelicals. (C. H. Dodd was a member of the RSV translation committee; see footnote 11.)

The more accurate translation "propitiation" is retained in the ESV, NASB, CSB, NKJV, and KJV, while the NIV has "sacrifice of atonement," a translation that does not specifically speak of a sacrifice that bears God's wrath and changes it to favor.

curse for us"—once again implying that he bore the wrath of God by becoming a "curse" for us. Hebrews 9:28 says that Christ was "offered once to bear the sins of many." And 1 Peter 2:24 says that "he himself bore our sins in his body on the tree," again implying that Christ endured the penalty against sin for us.

The idea of bearing the wrath of God is also represented in the imagery of drinking the cup of God's wrath, thus taking God's wrath into oneself. The image is used in the Old Testament to speak of Jerusalem when it has suffered God's judgment: "O Jerusalem, you have drunk from the hand of the Lord the cup of his wrath" (cf. Ps. 75:8; Isa. 51:22; Jer. 25:15). At the end of the New Testament, the predictions of the coming wrath of God against mankind in the book of Revelation include the judgment on "Babylon the great," whom God will make to "drain the cup of the wine of the fury of his wrath" (Rev. 16:19; see also 14:10). Jesus understands this Old Testament imagery well when he prays in the garden of Gethsemane, "My Father, if it be possible, *let this cup pass from me*; nevertheless, not as I will, but as you will" (Matt. 26:39; cf. John 18:11).

Also in the Old Testament, the remarkably detailed and incredibly accurate predictions of the sufferings of Christ that are found in Isaiah 53 contain several explicit affirmations (in italics below) that Christ bore the punishment from God that was due to us for our sins:

> Surely he has borne our griefs
>     and carried our sorrows;
> yet we esteemed him stricken,
>     *smitten by God*, and afflicted.
> But *he was pierced for our transgressions*;
>     *he was crushed for our iniquities*;
> upon him was the chastisement that brought us peace,
>     and with his wounds we are healed.
> All we like sheep have gone astray;
>     we have turned—every one—to his own way;
> and *the* LORD *has laid on him*
>     *the iniquity of us all.*
>
> He was oppressed, and he was afflicted,
>     yet he opened not his mouth;
> like a lamb that is led to the slaughter,
>     and like a sheep that before its shearers is silent,
>     so he opened not his mouth.
> By oppression and judgment he was taken away;
>     and as for his generation, who considered

that he was cut off out of the land of the living,
    *stricken for the transgression of my people?*
And they made his grave with the wicked
    and with a rich man in his death,
although he had done no violence,
    and there was no deceit in his mouth.

*Yet it was the will of the* LORD *to crush him;*
    *he has put him to grief;*
when his soul makes an offering for guilt,
    he shall see his offspring; he shall prolong his days;
the will of the LORD shall prosper in his hand.
Out of the anguish of his soul *he shall see and be satisfied;*
by his knowledge shall the righteous one, my servant,
    make many to be accounted righteous,
    *and he shall bear their iniquities.*
Therefore I will divide him a portion with the many,
    and he shall divide the spoil with the strong,
because he poured out his soul to death
    and was numbered with the transgressors;
yet he bore the sin of many,
    and makes intercession for the transgressors. (Isa. 53:4–12)

It is important to insist on the fact that Christ bore the wrath of God in our place because it is the heart of the doctrine of the atonement. It means that there is an eternal, unchangeable requirement in the holiness and justice of God that sin be paid for. Furthermore, before the atonement ever could have an effect on our subjective consciousness, it first had an effect on God and his relation to the sinners he planned to redeem. Apart from this central truth, the death of Christ really cannot be adequately understood (see discussion of other views of the atonement below).

Although we must be cautious in suggesting any analogies to the experience Christ went through (for his experience was and always will be without precedent or comparison), nonetheless, all our understanding of Jesus' suffering comes in some sense by way of analogous experiences in our life—for that is how God teaches us in Scripture.[15] Once again our human experience provides a very faint analogy that helps us understand what it means to bear the wrath of God. Perhaps as children we have faced the wrath of a human father when we have done wrong, or perhaps as adults we have known the anger

---

15. See the discussion of anthropomorphic language in Scripture to teach us about God in chapter 11, pp. 188–89.

of an employer because of a mistake we have made. We are inwardly shaken, disturbed by the crashing of another personality, filled with displeasure, into our very selves, and we tremble. We can hardly imagine the personal disintegration that would threaten if the outpouring of wrath came not from some finite human being but from Almighty God. If even the presence of God when he does not manifest wrath arouses fear and trembling in people (cf. Heb. 12:21, 28–29), how terrible it must be to face the presence of a wrathful God (Heb. 10:31).

With this in mind, we are now better able to understand Jesus' cry of desolation, "My God, my God, why have you forsaken me?" (Matt. 27:46). The question does not mean, "Why have you left me forever?" for Jesus knew that he was leaving the world and going to the Father (John 14:28; 16:10, 17). Jesus knew that he would rise again (John 2:19; Luke 18:33; Mark 9:31, et al.). It was "for the joy that was set before him" that Jesus "endured the cross, despising the shame, and is seated at the right hand of the throne of God" (Heb. 12:2). Jesus knew that he could still call God "my God." This cry of desolation is not a cry of total despair. Furthermore, "Why have you forsaken me?" does not imply that Jesus wondered why he was dying. He had said, "The Son of Man came not to be served but to serve, and to give his life as a ransom for many" (Mark 10:45). Jesus knew that he was dying for our sins.

Jesus' cry is a quotation from Psalm 22:1, a psalm in which the psalmist asks why God is so far from helping him, why God delays in rescuing him:

> My God, my God, why have you forsaken me?
>   Why are you so far from saving me, from the words of my groaning?
> O my God, I cry by day, but you do not answer,
>   and by night, but I find no rest. (Ps. 22:1–2)

Yet the psalmist was eventually rescued by God, and his cry of desolation turned into a hymn of praise (vv. 22–31). Jesus, who knew the words of Scripture as his own, knew well the context of Psalm 22. In quoting this psalm, he is quoting a cry of desolation that also has implicit in its context an unremitting faith in the God who will ultimately deliver him. Nevertheless, it remains a very real cry of anguish because the suffering has gone on so long and no release is in sight.

With this context for the quotation, perhaps it is better to understand the question "Why have you forsaken me?" as meaning, "Why have you left me *for so long?*" This is the sense it has in Psalm 22. Jesus, in his human nature, knew he would have to bear our sins, to suffer and to die. But in his human consciousness, he probably did not know how long this suffering would take. Yet to bear the guilt of millions of sins even for a moment would cause the greatest anguish of soul. To face the deep and furious wrath of an infinite God even for an instant would cause the most profound fear. But Jesus' suffering was not over in a minute—or two—or ten. When would it end? Could there be yet more weight of sin? Yet more wrath of God? Hour after hour it went on—the dark weight of sin and the deep wrath of God poured over Jesus in wave after wave. Jesus at last cried out, "My God, my God, why have you forsaken me?" Why must this suffering go on so long? Oh God, my God, will you ever bring it to an end?

Then at last Jesus knew his suffering was nearing completion. He knew he had consciously borne all the wrath of the Father against our sins, for God's anger had abated and the awful heaviness of sin was being removed. He knew that all that remained was to yield up his spirit to his heavenly Father and die. With a shout of victory Jesus cried out, "It is finished!" (John 19:30). Then with a loud voice he once more cried out, "Father, into your hands I commit my spirit!" (Luke 23:46). And then he voluntarily gave up the life that no one could take from him (John 10:17–18), and he died. As Isaiah had predicted, "he poured out his soul to death" and "bore the sin of many" (Isa. 53:12). God the Father saw "the anguish of his soul" and was "satisfied" (Isa. 53:11). And thus the punishment due to us for our sins was fully paid.

### c. Further Understanding of the Death of Christ.

**1. The penalty was inflicted by God the Father.** If we ask, "Who required Christ to pay the penalty for our sins?" the answer given by Scripture is that the penalty was inflicted by God the Father as he represented the interests of the Trinity in redemption. It was God's justice that required that sin be paid for, and among the members of the Trinity, it was God the Father whose role was to require that payment. God the Son voluntarily took upon himself the role of bearing the penalty for sin. Referring to God the Father, Paul says, "For our sake *he made him to be sin* who knew no sin [that is, Christ], so that in him we might become the righteousness of God" (2 Cor. 5:21). Isaiah said, "The LORD has laid on him the iniquity of us all" (Isa. 53:6). He went on to describe the sufferings of Christ: "Yet it was the will of the LORD to crush him; he has put him to grief" (Isa. 53:10).

Herein we see something of the amazing love of both God the Father and God the Son in redemption. Not only did Jesus know that he would bear the incredible pain of the cross, but God the Father also knew that he would have to inflict this pain on his deeply loved Son. "God shows his love for us in that while we were still sinners Christ died for us" (Rom. 5:8).

**2. Not eternal suffering but complete payment.** If we had to pay the penalty for our own sins, we would have to suffer eternally in separation from God.[16] However, Jesus did not suffer eternally. There are two reasons for this difference: (a) If we suffered for our own sins, we would never be able to make ourselves right with God again. There would be no hope because there would be no way to live again and earn perfect righteousness before God, and there would be no way to undo our sinful nature and make it right before God. Moreover, we would continue to exist as sinners who would not suffer

---

16. See chapter 56, pp. 1413–18, on eternal punishment.

with pure hearts of righteousness before God but would suffer with resentment and bitterness against God, thus continually compounding our sin. (b) Jesus was able to bear all the wrath of God against our sin and to bear it to the end. No mere man could ever have done this, but by virtue of the union of divine and human natures in himself, Jesus was able to bear all the wrath of God against sin and bear it to the end. Isaiah predicted: "out of the anguish of his soul [God] shall see *and be satisfied*" (Isa. 53:11). When Jesus knew that he had paid the full penalty for our sin, he said, "*It is finished*" (John 19:30). If Christ had not paid the full penalty, there would still be condemnation left for us. But since he has paid the full penalty that is due to us, "There is therefore now no condemnation for those who are in Christ Jesus" (Rom. 8:1).

It should help us at this point to realize that nothing in the eternal character of God and nothing in the laws God had given for mankind required that there be eternal suffering to pay for man's sins. In fact, if there is eternal suffering, it simply shows that the penalty has never been fully paid, and that the evildoer continues to be a sinner by nature. But when Christ's sufferings at last came to an end on the cross, it showed that he had borne the full measure of God's wrath against sin and there was no penalty left to pay. It also showed that he was himself righteous before God. In this way, the fact that Christ suffered for a limited time rather than eternally shows that his suffering was a sufficient payment for sins. The author of Hebrews repeats this theme again and again, emphasizing the completion and the finality of Christ's redemptive work:

> Nor was it to offer himself repeatedly, as the high priest enters the holy places every year with blood not his own, for then he would have had to suffer repeatedly since the foundation of the world. But as it is, he has appeared once for all at the end of the ages to put away sin by the sacrifice of himself. . . . Christ, having been offered *once* to bear the sins of many, will appear a second time, not to deal with sin but to save those who are eagerly waiting for him. (Heb. 9:25–28)

The New Testament emphasis on the completion and finality of Christ's sacrifice of himself for us has much practical application, because it assures us that there is no more penalty for sin left for us to pay. The penalty has entirely been paid by Christ, and we should have no remaining fear of condemnation or punishment.

**3. The meaning of the blood of Christ.** The New Testament frequently connects the blood of Christ with our redemption. For example, Peter says, "knowing that you were ransomed from the futile ways inherited from your forefathers, not with perishable things such as silver or gold, but with the precious blood of Christ, like that of a lamb without blemish or spot" (1 Peter 1:18–19).

The blood of Christ is the clear outward evidence that his life blood was poured out when he died a sacrificial death to pay for our redemption—"the blood of Christ" means his death in its saving aspects.[17] Although we may think that Christ's blood (as evidence that his life had been given) would have exclusive reference to the removal of our judicial guilt before God—for this is its primary reference—the New Testament authors also attribute to it several other effects. By the blood of Christ our consciences are cleansed (Heb. 9:14), we gain bold access to God in worship and prayer (Heb. 10:19), we are progressively cleansed from remaining sin (1 John 1:7; cf. Rev. 1:5b), we are able to conquer the accuser of the brethren (Rev. 12:10–11), and we are rescued out of a sinful way of life (1 Peter 1:18–19).[18]

Scripture speaks so much about the blood of Christ because its shedding was very clear evidence that his life was being given in judicial execution (that is, he was condemned to death and died paying a penalty imposed both by an earthly human judge and by God himself in heaven). Scripture's emphasis on the blood of Christ also shows the clear connection between Christ's death and the many sacrifices in the Old Testament that involved the pouring out of the life blood of the sacrificial animal. These sacrifices all pointed forward to and prefigured the death of Christ.

**4. Christ's death as penal substitution.** The view of Christ's death presented here has frequently been called the theory of *penal substitution*. Christ's death was "penal" in that he bore a penalty when he died. His death was also a "substitution" in that he was a substitute for us when he died. This has been the orthodox understanding of the atonement held by evangelical theologians, in contrast to other views that attempt to explain the atonement apart from the idea of the wrath of God or payment of the penalty for sin (see below).

This view of the atonement is sometimes called the theory of *vicarious atonement*. A "vicar" is someone who stands in the place of another or who represents another. Christ's death was therefore "vicarious" because he stood in our place and represented us. As our representative, he took the penalty that we deserve.

**5. Some troubling denials of penal substitutionary atonement.** Steve Chalke, a prominent Baptist pastor in London, published a controversial book in 2003, *The Lost Message of Jesus.* In this book he denied that we should understand Christ's death in terms of penal substitution. His main argument was that this view was inconsistent with the love of God—the same argument made by liberal scholars in a previous generation.[19] He wrote, "How then, have we come to believe that at the cross this God of love suddenly decides to vent his anger and wrath on his own Son? The fact is that the cross isn't a form of cosmic child abuse—a vengeful Father punishing his Son for an offense he has not even committed."[20] Chalke said that the penal substitutionary view of the atonement was a "twisted version of events," was "morally dubious," and was "a huge barrier

---

17. So Morris, *The Apostolic Preaching of the Cross*, 112–26.

18. This paragraph has been taken from Wayne Grudem, *The First Epistle of Peter*, TNTC (Leicester: Inter-Varsity Press; Grand Rapids: Eerdmans, 1988), 84.

19. See above, pp. 712–17.

20. Steve Chalke and Alan Mann, *The Lost Message of Jesus* (Grand Rapids: Zondervan, 2003), 182.

to faith." Then he said, "such a concept stands in total contradiction to the statement 'God is love,'" and it "makes a mockery of Jesus' own teaching to love your enemies and to refuse to repay evil with evil."[21]

Chalke does not discuss any of the verses quoted in the section above entitled "Bearing the Wrath of God" (pp. 712–17). He does not mention, much less attempt to answer, the centuries-old, orthodox Protestant view that the atonement had its source not only in the love of God but also in the justice of God.[22] He does not address the question posed by the entire argument of Romans 1–3, that God's justice requires that sin must be punished, for as Paul says, "the wages of sin is death" (Rom. 6:23). He makes the mistake of basing an argument on only one attribute of God, failing to recognize that all of God's actions must be consistent with all of his attributes.[23] His position fails to represent faithfully the teaching of all of Scripture on this topic.

Chalke's book led to significant controversy among evangelicals in the UK[24] and the publication of several responses.[25] Chalke's position seems to indicate that he has moved away from belief in the absolute authority of all of Scripture, for in 2013 he affirmed the legitimacy of monogamous same-sex marriage[26] and stated that he rejects the view that the Bible is infallible or inerrant.[27]

In a 2000 publication, New Testament professor Joel Green and theology professor Mark Baker warn that the view of the cross as penal substitution "has been construed by persons within and outside the church as a form of 'divine child abuse.'"[28] They explain, "The most adamant objections to atonement theology, understood popularly as penal substitution, have come from feminist theologians" because they see it as "the abuse of the one perfect child."[29]

Green and Baker say that "penal substitution . . . is unbiblical" because it "leaves out biblical concepts" and also attempts to serve as "the only correct and needed explanation

21. Ibid., 182–83.

22. See pp. 705–6 above.

23. See chapter 11, pp. 211–14.

24. See Pat Ashworth, "Atonement Row Gets Personal as Evangelical Partnership Splits," *Church Times*, April 26, 2007, https://www.churchtimes.co.uk/articles/2007/27-april/news/uk/atonement-row-gets-personal-as-evangelical-partnership-splits.

25. See especially Steve Jeffery, Michael Ovey, and Andrew Sach, *Pierced for Our Transgressions: Rediscovering the Glory of Penal Substitution* (Nottingham: Inter-Varsity Press; Wheaton, IL: Crossway, 2007); also J. I. Packer and Mark Dever, *In My Place Condemned He Stood: Celebrating the Glory of the Atonement* (Wheaton, IL: Crossway, 2007); Simon Gathercole, *Defending Substitution: An Essay on Atonement in Paul* (Grand Rapids: Baker, 2015). Gathercole wrote that criticisms of penal substitutionary atonement are often "extremely shallow . . . they amount to little more than people saying, 'I don't like this doctrine'" (24).

26. See Ruth Gledhill, "Evangelicals' Leader Backs Gay Marriage," *The Times*, January 15, 2013, https://www.thetimes.co.uk/article/evangelicals-leader-backs-gay-marriage-r9cxk7bv59c.

27. See Derek Flood, "Steve Chalke on Taking the Bible Beyond Fundamentalism and Atheism," HuffPost, April 20, 2014, https://www.huffingtonpost.com/derek-flood/video-steve-chalke-on-tak_b_4799911.html. In an online article, Chalke includes among his "suggested principles" for discussion about understanding the Bible the following: "We do not believe that the Bible is 'inerrant' or 'infallible' in any popular understanding of these terms. . . . The Bible is . . . written by fallible human beings whose work . . . bears the hallmarks of the limitations in preconceptions of the times and the cultures they live in, but also of the transformational experience of their encounters with God." Steve Chalke, Restoring Confidence in the Bible, Kindle edition (Amazon.com services, 2014), loc. 135–42.

28. Joel Green and Mark Baker, *Recovering the Scandal of the Cross: Atonement in New Testament and Contemporary Contexts* (Downers Grove, IL: InterVarsity, 2000), 32 (2nd ed., 49); the "child abuse" objection appears again at 132–33, 181 (2nd ed. 158, 219).

29. Green and Baker, *Recovering the Scandal*, 90–91 (2nd ed., 116), quoting Rita Nakashima Brock in the last phrase.

of the atonement."[30] They also object that this view of the atonement will bring about negative results:

> Where might this imagery lead? Feminist theologians have been quick to observe that atonement theology construed along these lines *legitimates and perpetuates abuse in human relationships*, not least in the home. What is more, locating Jesus, characterized as the willing victim of unjust suffering, at the heart of the Christian faith is for some tantamount to idealizing the values of the victim and *advising the abused to participate in their own victimization.*[31]

They use Princeton theologian Charles Hodge (1797–1878) as the primary representative of the penal substitution view.[32] They claim that Hodge advocated this view because "he roots his model in an individualistic, legal framework borrowed from the world of his day rather than from the Bible. His portrait of God is therefore governed more by concepts of justice among his contemporaries and not by God's revelation of himself in Christ. . . . the Bible does not shape his fundamental conception of the saving work of the cross."[33]

Their objection to Hodge's view of penal substitution fails to engage the numerous detailed, specific arguments from both Old and New Testaments found in the 128 pages of tightly reasoned analysis of the atonement by Hodge,[34] nor do they even attempt to show specifically how his analysis of specific passages of Scripture is incorrect. They merely assert without evidence that Hodge got his view from his contemporary culture instead of the Bible, but Hodge actually has dozens of pages arguing specifically from Scripture. And saying that some feminist opponents of penal substitution *misinterpret it* (to imply divine child abuse) gives us no good reason to reject responsible defenses of that view, such as that of Charles Hodge and others, all of whom would see the idea of child abuse as horribly evil. To reject a view based on an understanding of it that no responsible advocate has ever held is not an effective argument.

Green and Baker published the second edition of their book in 2011.[35] Their basic argument is the same (I have added second edition page numbers to the footnotes for the quotations given above), but they have an additional section arguing that Romans 3:25, in the larger context of Romans 1–3, should be understood *not* in terms of Christ bearing God's wrath against sin *but in other categories* such as "expiation" or wiping away

---

30. Ibid., 148 (2nd ed., 174).

31. Ibid., 92 (2nd ed., 116).

32. Ibid., 142–50 (2nd ed., 170–91).

33. Ibid., 150 (2nd ed., 176).

34. Charles Hodge, *Systematic Theology*, 3 vols. (1872–73. repr., Grand Rapids: Eerdmans, 1970), 2:464–591.

35. Mark Baker and Joel Green, *Recovering the Scandal of the Cross: Atonement in New Testament and Contemporary*

*Contexts*, 2nd ed. (Downers Grove, IL: InterVarsity, 2011). This second edition includes additional material criticizing the penal substitutionary views of I. Howard Marshall, John MacArthur, Martyn Lloyd-Jones, Thomas Schreiner, Watchman Nee, and J. I. Packer (177–84) but expressing appreciation for a defense of penal substitutionary atonement by Kevin Vanhoozer (184–91).

of sin, and forgiveness and the restoration of relationships.[36] However, the fact that the New Testament speaks of *other* things that were accomplished by the atonement (such as the restoration of relationships, the triumph over Satan, the overcoming of shame, and the progressive removal of sin from our lives) does not disprove the central truth supported by multiple passages, that in the atonement Christ actually bore the wrath of God against sin that we deserved.[37] This is the heart of the gospel message, and the gospel message is the primary message of the entire Bible. To attack the idea of penal substitutionary atonement is to attack the central message of the Bible.

**d. New Testament Terms Describing Different Aspects of the Atonement.** The atoning work of Christ is a complex event that has several effects on us. It can therefore be viewed from several different aspects. The New Testament uses different words to describe these; we shall examine four of the more important terms.

The four terms show how Christ's death met the four needs that we have as sinners:

1. We deserve to *die* as the penalty for sin.
2. We deserve to *bear God's wrath* against sin.
3. We are *separated* from God by our sins.
4. We are in *bondage to sin* and to the kingdom of Satan.

These four needs are met by Christ's death in the following ways:

1. Sacrifice. To pay the penalty of death that we deserved because of our sins, Christ died as a sacrifice for us. "He has appeared once for all at the end of the ages to put away sin by the *sacrifice* of himself" (Heb. 9:26).
2. Propitiation. To remove us from the wrath of God that we deserved, Christ died as a propitiation for our sins. "In this is love, not that we have loved God but that he loved us and sent his Son to be the *propitiation* for our sins" (1 John 4:10).
3. Reconciliation. To overcome our separation from God, we needed someone to provide reconciliation and thereby bring us back into fellowship with God. Paul says that God "through Christ *reconciled* us to himself and gave us the ministry of reconciliation; that is, in Christ God was reconciling the world to himself" (2 Cor. 5:18–19).
4. Redemption. Because we as sinners are in bondage to sin and to Satan, we need someone to provide redemption and thereby "redeem" us out of that bondage.

---

36. Ibid., 75 (new section on pp. 72–83).

37. See the section above on "Bearing the Wrath of God," pp. 712–17. For further analysis of Joel Green's view, see Thomas Schreiner, "Penal Substitution Response," in *The Nature of the Atonement: Four Views*, edited by James Beilby and Paul Eddy (Downers Grove, IL: interact to the, 2006), 192–95. Commenting on Green's chapter in that same book, Schreiner observes, "I think he underestimates remarkably the pervasiveness of God's wrath in the biblical story.... It seems to me nothing short of extraordinary that Green asserts that sacrifices are not related to God's anger. Notice that he operates at the level assertion here and not argument.... He actually does not argue for his case exegetically" (194–95).

When we speak of redemption, the idea of a "ransom" comes into view. A ransom is the price paid to redeem someone from bondage or captivity. Jesus said of himself, "For even the Son of Man also came not to be served but to serve, and to give his life *as a ransom for many*" (Mark 10:45).

If we ask to whom the ransom was paid, we realize that the human analogy of a ransom payment does not fit the atonement of Christ in every detail. Though we were in bondage to sin and to Satan, there was no ransom paid either to "sin" or to Satan, for they did not have power to demand such payment, nor was Satan the one whose holiness was offended by sin and who required a penalty to be paid for sin. As we saw earlier, the penalty for sin was paid by Christ and received and accepted by God the Father. But we hesitate to speak of paying a ransom to God the Father because it was not he who held us in bondage but Satan and our sins. Therefore, at this point the idea of a ransom payment cannot be pressed in every detail. It is sufficient to note that a price was paid (the death of Christ) and the result was that we were "redeemed" from bondage.

We were redeemed from bondage to Satan because "the whole world lies in the power of the evil one" (1 John 5:19), and when Christ came he died to "deliver all those who through fear of death were subject to lifelong slavery" (Heb. 2:15). In fact, God the Father "has delivered us from the domain of darkness and transferred us to the kingdom of his beloved Son" (Col. 1:13).

As for deliverance from bondage to sin, Paul says, "So you also must consider yourselves dead to sin and alive to God in Christ Jesus.... For sin will have no dominion over you, since you are not under law but under grace" (Rom. 6:11, 14). We have been delivered from bondage to the guilt of sin and from bondage to its ruling power in our lives.

**e. Other Views of the Atonement.** In contrast to the penal substitution view of the atonement presented in this chapter, several other views have been advocated in the history of the church.

**1. The ransom to Satan theory.** This view was held by Origen (c. AD 185–c. 254), a theologian from Alexandria and later Caesarea and after him by some others in the early history of the church. According to this view, the ransom Christ paid to redeem us was paid to Satan, in whose kingdom all people were by virtue of sin.

This theory finds no direct confirmation in Scripture and has few supporters in the history of the church. It falsely thinks of Satan rather than God as the one who required that a payment be made for sin and thus completely neglects the demands of God's justice with respect to sin. It views Satan as having much more power than he actually does, namely, power to demand whatever he wants from God, rather than as one who has been cast down from heaven and has no right to demand anything of God. Nowhere does Scripture say that we as sinners owe anything to Satan, but it repeatedly says that God requires of us a payment for our sins. This view also fails to deal with the texts that speak of Christ's death as a propitiation offered to God the Father for our sins or with the fact that God the Father represented the Trinity in accepting the payment for sins from Christ (see discussion above).

**2. The moral influence theory.** First advocated by French theologian Peter Abelard (1079–1142), the moral influence theory of the atonement holds that God did not require the payment of a penalty for sin but that Christ's death was simply a way in which *God showed how much he loved human beings by identifying with their sufferings,* even to the point of death. Christ's death therefore becomes a great teaching example that shows God's love to us and draws from us a grateful response, so that in loving him we are forgiven.

The great difficulty with this viewpoint is that it is contrary to so many passages of Scripture that speak of Christ dying for sin, bearing our sin, or dying as a propitiation. Moreover, it robs the atonement of its objective character, because it holds that the atonement had no effect on God himself. Finally, it has no way of dealing with our guilt—if Christ did not die to pay for our sins, we have no right to trust in him for forgiveness of sins.

**3. The example theory.** The example theory of the atonement was taught by the Socinians, the followers of Faustus Socinus (1539–1604), an Italian theologian who settled in Poland in 1578 and attracted a wide following.[38] The example theory, like the moral influence theory, also denies that God's justice requires payment for sin; it says that *Christ's death simply provides us with an example of how we should trust and obey God perfectly,* even if that trust and obedience leads to a horrible death. (Whereas the moral influence theory says that Christ's death teaches us how much God loves us, the example theory says that Christ's death teaches us how we should live.) Support for this view could be found in 1 Peter 2:21, "For to this you have been called, because Christ also suffered for you, leaving you an example, so that you might follow in his steps."

While it is true that Christ is an example for us even in his death, the question is whether this fact is the complete explanation of the atonement. The example theory fails to account for the many Scriptures that focus on Christ's death as a payment for sin, the fact that Christ bore our sins, and the fact that he was the propitiation for our sins. These considerations alone mean that the theory must be rejected. Moreover, this view really ends up arguing that man can save himself by following Christ's example and by trusting and obeying God just as Christ did. Thus it fails to show how the guilt of our sin can be removed because it does not hold that Christ actually paid the penalty for our sins or made provision for our guilt when he died.

**4. The governmental theory.** The governmental theory of the atonement was first taught by Dutch theologian and jurist Hugo Grotius (1583–1645). This theory holds that God did not actually have to require payment for sin. Since he was an omnipotent God,

---

38. The Socinians were anti-Trinitarian since they denied the deity of Christ; their thought led to modern Unitarianism.

he could have set aside that requirement and simply forgiven sins without the payment of a penalty. Then what was the purpose of Christ's death? It was *God's demonstration of the fact that his laws had been broken*, that he is the moral lawgiver and governor of the universe, *and that some kind of penalty would be required* whenever his laws were broken. Thus Christ did not exactly pay the penalty for the actual sins of any people, but simply suffered to show that when God's laws are broken there must be some penalty paid.

The problem with this view, again, is that it fails to account adequately for all the Scriptures that speak of Christ bearing our sins on the cross, of God laying on Christ the iniquity of us all, of Christ dying specifically for our sins, and of Christ being the propitiation for our sins. Moreover, it takes away the objective character of the atonement by making its purpose not the satisfaction of God's justice but simply that of influencing us to realize that God has laws that must be kept. This view also implies that we cannot rightly trust in Christ's completed work for forgiveness of sin because he has not actually made payment for those sins. Moreover, it makes the actual earning of forgiveness for us something that happened in God's mind apart from the death of Christ on the cross—he had already decided to forgive us without requiring any penalty from us and then punished Christ only to demonstrate that he was still the moral governor of the universe. But this means that Christ (in this view) did not actually earn forgiveness or salvation for us, and thus the value of his redemptive work is greatly minimized. Finally, this theory fails to take adequate account of the unchangeableness of God and the infinite purity of his justice. To say that God can forgive sins without requiring any penalty (in spite of the fact that throughout Scripture sin always requires the payment of a penalty) is seriously to underestimate the absolute character of the justice of God.

**f. Did Christ Descend Into Hell?**[39] It is sometimes argued that Christ descended into hell after he died. The phrase "he descended into hell" does not occur in the Bible. But the widely used Apostles' Creed says that Christ "was crucified, died, and was buried; he descended into hell. The third day he rose again from the dead." Does this mean that Christ endured further suffering after his death on the cross? As we shall see below, an examination of the biblical evidence indicates that he did not. But before looking at the relevant biblical texts, it is appropriate to examine the phrase "he descended into hell" in the Apostles' Creed.

**1. The origin of the phrase, "He descended into hell."** A murky background lies behind much of the history of the phrase. Its origins, where they can be found, are far from praiseworthy. The great church historian Philip Schaff has summarized the development of the Apostles' Creed in an extensive chart, part of which is reproduced in part on pages 726–27.[40]

---

39. The following section is taken from Wayne Grudem, "He Did Not Descend Into Hell: A Plea for Following Scripture Instead of the Apostles' Creed," *JETS* vol. 34, no. 1 (March 1991): 103–13.

40. This chart is taken from Philip Schaff, *The Creeds of Christendom*, 3 vols. (1931; repr., Grand Rapids: Baker, 1983), 2:52–55.

| The Gradual Formation of the Apostles' Creed | | | | |
|---|---|---|---|---|
| **CREDO (I believe)** | | | | |
| **Art. III** | | | | |
| Ultimate Text of the Western Creed, Pirminius, AD 750 | Passus | Sub Pontio Pilato | Crucifixus | Mortuus | Et Sepultus |
| English Translation | Suffered | Under Pontius Pilate | Was crucified | Dead | And buried |
| I. St. Irenaeus, AD 200 | καί τὸ πάθος | (SUB PONTIO PILATO) | | | |
| II. Tertullian, AD 220 | CRUCIFIXUM (passum) | sub Pontio Pilato | | (MORTUUM) | (ET SEPULTUM secundum Scripturas) |
| III. St. Cyprian, AD 250 | | | | | |
| IV. Novatian, AD 260 | | | | | |
| V. Marcellus, AD 341 | | τὸν ἐπὶ ποντίου πιλάτου | σταυρωθέντα | | καὶ ταφέντα |
| VI. Rufinus, AD 390 Aquileja | | sub Pontio Pilate | crucifixus | | et sepultus |
| VII. Rufinus, Rome, AD 390 | | sub Pontio Pilate | crucifixus | | et sepultus |
| VIII. St. Augustine, AD 400 | passus | sub Pontio Pilate | crucifixus | | et sepultus |
| IX. St. Nicetas, AD 450 | passus | sub Pontio Pilate | | | |
| X. Eusebius Gallus, AD 550 (?) | | | | mortuus | et sepultus |
| XI. Sacramentarium Gallicanum, AD 650 | passus | sub Pontio Pilate | crucifixus | mortuus | et sepultus |
| **Art. V** | | | | |
| Ultimate Text of the Western Creed, Pirminius, AD 750 | Descendit ad Inferna | Tertia die | Resurrexit | a mortuis | |
| English Translation | He descended into hell | The third day | He rose again | From the dead | |
| I. St. Irenaeus, AD 200 | | | καὶ τὴν ἔγερσιν (et resurgens) | ἐκ νεκρῶν | |
| II. Tertullian, AD 220 | | TERTIA DIE | resuscitatum (a Patre) (resurrexisse) | E MORTUIS | |

| | | | | | |
|---|---|---|---|---|---|
| III. St. Cyprian, AD 250 | | | | | |
| IV. Novatian, AD 260 | | | | | |
| V. Marcellus, AD 341 | | καὶ τῇ τρίτῃ ἡμέρα | ἀναστάντα | ἐκ τῶν νεκρῶν | |
| VI. Rufinus, AD 390 Aquileja | DESCENDIT in INFERNA | tertia die | RESURREXIT | A mortuis | |
| VII. Rufinus, Rome, AD 390 | | tertia die | resurrexit | a mortuis | |
| VIII. St. Augustine, AD 400 | | tertio die | resurrexit | a mortuis | |
| IX. St. Nicetas, AD 450 | | tertio die | resurrexit | vivus a mortuis | |
| X. Eusebius Gallus, AD 550 (?) | | tertia die | resurrexit | a mortuis | |
| XI. Sacramentarium Gallicanum, AD 650 | Descendit AD Inferna | tertia die | resurrexit | a mortuis | |

This chart shows that, unlike the Nicene Creed and the Chalcedonian Definition, the Apostles' Creed was not written or approved by a single church council at one specific time. Rather, it gradually took shape from about AD 200 to 750.

It is surprising to find that the phrase "he descended into hell" was not found in any of the early versions of the Creed (in the versions used in Rome, in the rest of Italy, and in Africa) until it appeared in one of two versions from Rufinus in AD 390. Then it was not included again in any version of the Creed until AD 650. Moreover, Rufinus, the only person who included it before AD 650, did not think that it meant that Christ descended into hell but understood the phrase simply to mean that Christ was "buried."[41] In other words, he took it to mean that Christ "descended into the grave." (The Greek form has *hadēs*, which can just mean "grave," not *geenna*, "hell, place of punishment.") We should also note that the phrase only appears in one of the two versions of the Creed that we have from Rufinus; it was not in the Roman form of the Creed that he preserved.

This means, therefore, that until AD 650 no version of the Creed included this

---

41. See Schaff, *Creeds*, 1:21n6; see also 46n2. Schaff notes that the phrase was found somewhat earlier (around AD 360), but then it was not in any orthodox creeds or any versions of the Apostles' Creed but in some creeds of the Arians—people who denied the full deity of Christ, holding that the Son was created by the Father (see Schaff, *Creeds*, 2:46n2). (Schaff does not give documentation for this reference to Arian creeds.)

It should be noted that Schaff throughout his *Creeds of Christendom* has several editorial comments defending an actual descent of Christ into hell after his death on the cross. Thus, for example, he says that "Rufinus himself, however, misunderstood it by making it to mean the same as buried" (1:21n6)—thus Schaff assumes that to understand the phrase to mean "he descended into the grave" is to *mis*understand it (see also 2:46n2; 3:321n1).

phrase with the intention of saying that Christ "descended into hell"—the only version to include the phrase before AD 650 gives it a different meaning. At this point one wonders if the term *apostolic* can in any sense be applied to this phrase, or if it really has a rightful place in a creed whose title claims for itself descent from the earliest apostles of Christ.

This survey of the historical development of the phrase also raises the possibility that when the phrase first began to be more commonly used, it may have been in other versions (now lost to us) that did not have the expression "and buried." If so, it probably would have meant to others just what it meant to Rufinus: "descended into the grave." But later when the phrase was incorporated into different versions of the Creed that already had the phrase "and buried," some other explanation had to be given to it. This mistaken insertion of the phrase after the words "and buried"—apparently done by someone around AD 650—led to all sorts of attempts to explain "he descended into hell" in some way that did not contradict the rest of Scripture.

Some have taken it to mean that Christ suffered the pains of hell while on the cross. Calvin, for example, says that "Christ's descent into hell" refers to the fact that he not only died a bodily death but that "it was expedient at the same time for him to undergo the severity of God's vengeance, to appease his wrath and satisfy his just judgment."[42]

Similarly, the Heidelberg Catechism, Question 44, asks,

> **Question:** Why is it added: He descended into Hades?
> **Answer:** That in my greatest temptations I may be assured that Christ, my Lord, by his inexpressible anguish, pains, and terrors which he suffered in his soul on the cross and before, has redeemed me from the anguish and torment of hell.[43]

But is this a satisfactory explanation of the phrase, "he descended into hell"? While it is true that Christ suffered the outpouring of God's wrath on the cross, this explanation does not really fit the phrase in the Apostles' Creed—"descended" hardly represents this idea, and the placement of the phrase after "was crucified, dead, and buried" makes this an artificial and unconvincing interpretation.

Others have understood it to mean that Christ continued in the "state of death" until his resurrection. The Westminster Larger Catechism, question 50, says, "Christ's humiliation after his death consisted in his being buried, and continuing in the state of the dead, and under the power of death till the third day; which hath been otherwise expressed in these words, He descended into hell." Though it is true that Christ continued in the state of death until the third day, once again it is a strained and unpersuasive

42. John Calvin, *Institutes of the Christian Religion,* ed. John T. McNeill, trans. F. L. Battles, 2 vols., Library of Christian Classics (Philadelphia: Westminster, 1960), 1.515 (2.16.10).

43. Schaff, *Creeds,* 3.321.

explanation of "he descended into hell," for the placement of the phrase would then give the awkward sense, "he was crucified, dead, and buried; he descended to being dead." This interpretation does not explain what the words first meant in this sequence but is rather an unconvincing attempt to salvage some theologically acceptable sense out of them.

Moreover, the English word *hell* has no such sense as simply "being dead" (though the Greek word *hadēs* can mean this), so this becomes a doubly artificial explanation for English-speaking people.

Finally, some have argued that the phrase means just what it appears to mean on first reading: that Christ actually did descend into hell after his death on the cross. It is easy to understand the Apostles' Creed to mean just this (indeed, that is certainly the natural sense), but then another question arises: Can this idea be supported from Scripture?

**2. Possible biblical support for a descent into hell.** Support for the idea that Christ descended into hell has been found primarily in five passages: Acts 2:27; Romans 10:6–7; Ephesians 4:8–9; 1 Peter 3:18–20; and 1 Peter 4:6. (A few other passages have been appealed to, but less convincingly.)[44] On closer inspection, do any of those passages clearly establish this teaching?

*(a) Acts 2:27.* This is part of Peter's sermon on the Day of Pentecost, where he is quoting Psalm 16:10. In the King James Version the verse reads, "Because thou wilt not *leave my soul in hell*, neither wilt thou suffer thine Holy One to see corruption."

Does this mean that Christ entered hell after he died? Not necessarily, because another sense is certainly possible for these verses. The word *hell* here represents a New Testament Greek term (*hadēs*) and an Old Testament Hebrew term (*shĕ'ōl*, popularly translated as "sheol") that can mean simply "the grave" or "death" (the state of being dead).[45] This sense ("the state of being dead") is preferable to "hell" here because the context emphasizes that Christ's *body* rose from the grave, unlike David's, which remained in the grave. Peter is reasoning that Psalm 16 applies to Christ more than to David because Christ in the flesh rose from the dead, and Psalm 16:9 says, "My flesh also will dwell in hope" (Acts 2:26, quoting from the Septuagint). Peter is using David's psalm to show that Christ's body did not decay—he is therefore unlike David, who "both died and was buried, and his tomb is with us to this day" (Acts 2:29). Therefore, this passage about Christ's resurrection *from the grave* does not convincingly support the idea that Christ descended into hell.

*(b) Romans 10:6–7.* These verses contain two rhetorical questions, again Old Testament quotations (from Deut. 30:13): "Do not say in your heart, 'Who will ascend

---

44. For example, Matt. 12:40, which says that Christ will be three days and nights "in the heart of the earth," simply refers to the fact that he was in the grave between his death and resurrection (cf., in the LXX, Ps. 45:3 [46:2 in English] with Jonah 2:3).

45. The ESV leaves it to the reader to decide which sense of Hades is intended: "You will not abandon my soul to Hades" (Acts 2:27).

into heaven?' (that is, to bring Christ down) or 'Who will descend into the abyss?' (that is, to bring Christ up from the dead)." But this passage hardly teaches that Christ descended into hell. The point of the passage is that Paul is telling people not to ask these questions because Christ is not far away—he is near—and faith in him is as near as confessing with our mouth and believing in our heart (v. 9). These prohibited questions are questions of unbelief, not assertions of what Scripture teaches. However, some may object that Paul would not have anticipated that his readers would ask such questions unless it was widely known that Christ did in fact descend "into the abyss." However, even if this were true, Scripture would not be saying or implying that Christ went into "hell" (in the sense of a place of punishment for the dead, ordinarily expressed by Gk. *geenna*), but rather that he went into "the abyss" (Gk. *abyssos*, a term which often in the LXX is used of the depths of the ocean [Gen. 1:2; 7:11; 8:2; Deut. 8:7; Ps. 106(107):26], but it can also apparently refer just to the realm of the dead [Ps. 70(71):20]).[46]

Paul here uses the word *deep* (*abyssos*) as a contrast to *heaven* in order to give the sense of a place that is unreachable, inaccessible to human beings. The contrast is not, "Who shall go to find Christ in a place of great blessing (heaven) or a place of great punishment (hell)?" but rather, "Who shall go to find Christ in a place that is inaccessibly high (heaven) or in a place that is inaccessibly low (the deep, or the realm of death)?" No clear affirmation or denial of a "descent into hell" can be found in this passage.

*(c) Ephesians 4:8–9.* Here Paul writes, "In saying, 'He ascended,' what does it mean but that he had also descended into the lower regions, the earth?"

Does this mean that Christ "descended" to hell? In the RSV, this verse is translated as "he had also descended into *the lower parts of the earth*," but the ESV (quoted above) gives a better sense, as does the NIV: "What does 'he ascended' mean except that he also descended to the *lower, earthly regions*?" Here the ESV and NIV take "descended" to refer to Christ's coming to earth as a baby (the incarnation). The last phrase ("the lower regions, the earth") is an acceptable understanding of the Greek text, taking the phrase "the lower regions *of* the earth" to mean "lower regions *which are* the earth" (the grammatical form in Greek would then be called a genitive of apposition). We do the same thing in English—for example, in the phrase "the city of Chicago," we mean "the city which is Chicago."

The ESV or NIV rendering is preferable in this context because Paul is saying that the Christ who went up to heaven (in his ascension) is the same one who earlier came down

---

46. 1 Clem. 28:3 uses *abyssos* instead of the Septuagint's *hadēs* to translate Ps. 139:8, "If I make my bed in Sheol, you are there!" In the New Testament, the term is used only in Luke 8:31; Rom. 10:7; and seven times in Revelation (there it refers to the "bottomless pit"). Therefore, although the term can refer to the abode of condemned demons (as in Revelation), this is not its common sense in the LXX or a necessary sense in its New Testament usage. The primary force of the term is a place that is deep, unfathomable to human beings, ordinarily unable to be reached by them. (C. E. B. Cranfield, *A Critical and Exegetical Commentary on the Epistle to the Romans*, ICC (Edinburgh: T&T Clark, 1975), 2.525, notes that *abyssos* is the ordinary LXX translation for Hebrew *tehōm*, and that *tehōm* is used in the Mishnah [Pesahim 7:7; Nazir 9:2] to refer to a grave that had been unknown.)

from heaven (v. 10). That "descent" from heaven occurred, of course, when Christ came to be born as a man. So the verse speaks of the incarnation, not of a descent into hell.[47]

*(d) 1 Peter 3:18–20.* For many people this is the most puzzling passage on this subject. Peter tells us that Christ was "put to death in the flesh but made alive in the spirit, *in which he went and proclaimed to the spirits in prison,* because they formerly did not obey, when God's patience waited in the days of Noah, while the ark was being prepared." There are several different explanations for this passage.

(1) Does this refer to Christ preaching in hell? Some have taken "he went and proclaimed to the spirits in prison" to mean that Christ went into hell and preached to the spirits who were there—either proclaiming the gospel and offering a second chance to repent, or just proclaiming that he had triumphed over them and that they were eternally condemned.

But these interpretations fail to explain adequately either the passage itself or its setting in this context. Peter does not say that Christ preached to spirits generally; instead, he preached only to those "who formerly did not obey . . . *while the ark was being prepared."* Such a limited audience—those who disobeyed during the building of the ark—would be a strange group for Christ to travel to hell and preach to. If Christ proclaimed his triumph, why only to these sinners and not to all? And if he offered a second chance for salvation, why only to these sinners and not to all? Even more difficult for this view is the fact that Scripture elsewhere indicates that there is no opportunity for repentance after death (Luke 16:26; Heb. 10:26–27).

Moreover, the context of 1 Peter 3 makes "preaching in hell" unlikely. Peter is encouraging his readers to witness boldly to hostile unbelievers around them. He had just told them they should always be "prepared to make a defense to anyone who asks you for a reason for the hope that is in you" (1 Peter 3:15). This evangelistic motif would lose its urgency if Peter were teaching a second chance for salvation after death. And it would not fit at all with a "preaching" of condemnation.

(2) Does it refer to Christ preaching to fallen angels? To give a better explanation for these difficulties, several commentators have proposed taking "spirits in prison" to mean demonic spirits, the spirits of fallen angels, and have said that Christ proclaimed condemnation to these demons. This (it is claimed) would comfort Peter's readers by showing them that the demonic forces oppressing them would also be defeated by Christ.

However, Peter's readers would have to go through an incredibly complicated reasoning process to draw this conclusion when Peter does not explicitly teach it. They would have to reason from (a) some demons who sinned long ago were condemned, to (b) other demons are now inciting your human persecutors, to (c) those demons will likewise be

---

47. Referring to Eph. 4:9, H. Bietenhard says, "In modern exposition the reference of this passage to the *descensus* *ad inferos* ("he descended into hell" in the Apostles' Creed) is almost without exception rejected" (*NIDNTT*, 2:210).

condemned someday, to (d) therefore your persecutors will finally be judged as well. Finally Peter's readers would get to Peter's point: (e) don't fear your persecutors.

Those who hold this "preaching to fallen angels" view must assume that Peter's readers would "read between the lines" and conclude all this (points 2–5) from the simple statement that Christ "proclaimed to the spirits in prison, because they formerly did not obey" (1 Peter 3:19–20). But does it not seem too farfetched to say that Peter knew his readers would read all this into the text?

Moreover, Peter emphasizes hostile *persons*, not demons, in the context (1 Peter 3:14, 16). And where would Peter's readers get the idea that angels sinned "while the ark was being prepared"? There is nothing of that in the Genesis story about the building of the ark. And in spite of what some have claimed, if we look at all the traditions of Jewish interpretation of the flood story, we find no mention of angels sinning specifically "while the ark was being prepared."[48] Therefore, the view that Peter is speaking of Christ's proclamation of judgment to fallen angels is really not persuasive either.

(3) Does it refer to Christ's proclaiming release to Old Testament saints? Another explanation is that Christ, after his death, went and proclaimed release to Old Testament believers who had been unable to enter heaven until the completion of Christ's redemptive work.

But again we may question whether this view adequately accounts for what the text actually says. It does not say that Christ preached to those who were believers or faithful to God but to those who "formerly *did not obey*"—the emphasis is on their disobedience. Moreover, Peter does not specify Old Testament believers generally but only those who were disobedient "in the days of Noah, while the ark was being prepared" (1 Peter 3:20).

Finally, Scripture gives us no clear evidence to make us think that full access to the blessings of being in God's presence in heaven were withheld from Old Testament believers when they died—indeed, several passages suggest that believers who died before Christ's death did enter into the presence of God at once because their sins were forgiven by trusting in the Messiah who was to come (Gen. 5:24; 2 Sam. 12:23; Pss. 16:11; 17:15; 23:6; Eccl. 12:7; Matt. 22:31–32; Luke 16:22; Rom. 4:1–8; Heb. 11:5).

(4) Does it refer to Christ preaching through Noah when he was building the ark? The most satisfactory explanation of 1 Peter 3:19–20 seems rather to be one proposed (but not really defended) long ago by Augustine: the passage refers not to something Christ did between his death and resurrection but to what he did "in the spiritual realm of existence" (or "through the Spirit") at the time of Noah. *When Noah was building the ark, Christ "in spirit" was preaching through Noah to the hostile unbelievers around him.*[49]

---

48. For an extensive discussion of Jewish interpretations of the sin of the "sons of God" in Gen. 6:2, 4, and of the identity of those who sinned while the ark was being built, see "Christ Preaching Through Noah: 1 Peter 3:19–20 in the Light of Dominant Themes in Jewish Literature," in Wayne Grudem, *The First Epistle of Peter*, 203–39. (This appendix has a lengthy discussion of 1 Peter 3:19–20, which I have only briefly summarized here.)

49. This section is a brief summary of a more extensive discussion of this passage in Wayne Grudem, *The First Epistle of Peter*, 157–62 and 203–39.

This view gains support from two other statements of Peter. In 1 Peter 1:11, he says that the "Spirit of Christ" was speaking in the Old Testament prophets. This suggests that Peter could readily have thought that the "Spirit of Christ" was speaking through Noah as well. Then in 2 Peter 2:5, he calls Noah a *preacher* of righteousness" (NIV), using the noun (*kēryx*) that comes from the same root as the verb "proclaimed" (*ekēryxen*) in 1 Peter 3:19. So it seems likely that when Christ "proclaimed to the spirits in prison," he did so through Noah in the days before the flood.

The people to whom Christ preached through Noah were unbelievers on the earth at the time of Noah, but Peter calls them "spirits in prison" because they are now in the prison of hell—even though they were not just "spirits" but persons on earth when the preaching was done. (The NASB says Christ preached "to the spirits now in prison.") We can speak the same way in English: "I knew President Bush when he was a college student" is an appropriate statement, even though he was not president when he was in college. The sentence means, "I knew the man who is now President Bush when he was still a student in college." So "Christ preached to the spirits in prison" means "Christ preached to people *who are now spirits in prison* when they were still persons on earth."[50]

This interpretation is very appropriate to the larger context of 1 Peter 3:13–22. The parallel between the situation of Noah and the situation of Peter's readers is clear at several points:

| Noah | Peter's readers |
| --- | --- |
| Righteous minority | Righteous minority |
| Surrounded by hostile unbelievers | Surrounded by hostile unbelievers |
| God's judgment was near | God's judgment may come soon (1 Peter 4:5, 7; 2 Peter 3:10) |
| Noah witnessed boldly (by Christ's power) | They should witness boldly by Christ's power (1 Peter 3:14, 16–17; 3:15; 4:11) |
| Noah was finally saved | They will finally be saved (1 Peter 3:13–14; 4:13; 5:10) |

Such an understanding of the text seems to be by far the most likely solution to a puzzling passage. Yet this means that our fourth possible support for a descent of Christ into hell also turns up negative—the text speaks rather of something Christ did on earth at the time of Noah.

*(e) 1 Peter 4:6.* This fifth and final passage says, "For this is why the gospel was preached even to those who are dead, that though judged in the flesh the way people are,

---

50. My student Tet-Lim Yee has called my attention to another very similar expression elsewhere in Scripture: Naomi speaks of how kindly Ruth and Orpah "have dealt with the dead" (Ruth 1:8), referring to their treatment of their husbands while the husbands were still alive.

they might live in the spirit the way God does." Does this verse mean that Christ went to hell and preached the gospel to those who had died? If so, it would be the only passage in the Bible that taught a "second chance" for salvation after death and would contradict passages such as Luke 16:19–31 and Hebrews 9:27, which clearly seem to deny this possibility. Moreover, the passage does not explicitly say that Christ preached to people after they had died. It could mean that the gospel in general was preached (this verse does not even say that Christ preached) to *people who are now dead*, but it was preached to them while they were still alive on earth.

This is a common explanation, and it seems to fit this verse much better. It finds support in the second word of the verse, "this," which refers back to the final judgment mentioned at the end of verse 5. Peter is saying that it was because of the final judgment that the gospel was preached to the dead.

This would comfort the readers concerning their Christian friends who had already died. They may have wondered, "Did the gospel benefit them, since it didn't save them from death?" Peter answers that the reason the gospel was preached to those who had died was not to save them from physical death (they were "judged in the flesh like men") but to save them from final judgment (they will "live in the spirit like God"). Therefore, the fact that they had died did not indicate that the gospel had failed in its purpose—for they would surely live forever in the spiritual realm.

Thus "the dead" are people who have died and are now dead, even though they were alive and on earth when the gospel was preached to them. (The NIV translates, "For this is the reason the gospel was preached even to *those who are now dead*.") This avoids the doctrinal problem of a "second chance" of salvation after death and fits both the wording and the context of the verse.

We conclude, therefore, that this last passage, when viewed in its context, turns out to provide no convincing support for the doctrine of a descent of Christ into hell.

At this point, people on all sides of the question of whether Christ actually descended into hell should be able to agree at least that the idea of Christ's "descent into hell" is not taught clearly or explicitly in any passage of Scripture. And many people (including the present author) will conclude that this idea is not taught in Scripture at all. But beyond the question of whether any passage positively teaches this idea, we must ask whether it is contrary to any passages of Scripture.

**3. Biblical opposition to a "descent into hell."** In addition to the fact that there is little if any biblical support for a descent of Christ into hell, there are some New Testament texts that argue against the possibility of Christ's going to hell after his death.

Jesus' words to the thief on the cross, "Today you will be with me in paradise" (Luke 23:43), imply that after Jesus died his soul (or spirit) went immediately to the presence of the Father in heaven, even though his body remained on earth and was buried. Some people deny this by arguing that Paradise is a place distinct from heaven, but in both of the other New Testament uses the word clearly means "heaven."

In 2 Corinthians 12:4 it is the place to which Paul was caught up in his revelation of heaven, and in Revelation 2:7 it is the place where we find the tree of life—which is clearly heaven in Revelation 22:2 and 14.[51]

In addition, the cry of Jesus, "It is finished" (John 19:30) strongly suggests that Christ's suffering was finished at that moment and so was his alienation from the Father because of bearing our sin. This implies that he would not descend into hell, but would go at once into the Father's presence.

Finally, the cry, "Father, into your hands I commit my spirit" (Luke 23:46), also suggests that Christ expected (correctly) the immediate end of his suffering and estrangement and the welcoming of his spirit into heaven by God the Father (note Stephen's similar cry in Acts 7:59).

These texts indicate, then, that Christ in his death experienced the same things believers in this present age experience when they die: his dead body remained on earth and was buried (as ours will be), but his spirit (or soul) passed immediately into the presence of God in heaven (just as ours will). Then on the first Easter morning, Christ's spirit was reunited with his body, and he was raised from the dead—just as Christians who have died will (when Christ returns) be reunited to their bodies and raised in their perfect resurrection bodies to new life.[52]

This fact has pastoral encouragement for us: we need not fear death, not only because eternal life lies on the other side, but also because we know that our Savior himself has gone through exactly the same experience we will go through—he has prepared, even sanctified the way, and we follow him with confidence each step of that way. This is much greater comfort regarding death than could ever be given by any view of a descent into hell.

**4. Conclusion regarding the Apostles' Creed and the question of Christ's possible descent into hell.** Does the phrase "he descended into hell" deserve to be retained in the Apostles' Creed alongside the great doctrines of the faith on which all can agree? The single argument in its favor seems to be the fact that it has been around so long. But an old mistake is still a mistake—and as long as it has been around there has been confusion and disagreement over its meaning.

On the other side, there are several compelling reasons against keeping the phrase. It has no clear warrant from Scripture and indeed seems to be contradicted by some

---

51. Further support for this idea is found in the fact that though the word *paradeisos*, "paradise," could simply mean "pleasant garden" (esp. used in the LXX of the garden of Eden), it also frequently meant "heaven" or "a place of blessedness in the presence of God." See Isa. 51:3; Ezek. 28:13; 31:8–9; T. Levi 18:10; 1 Enoch 20:7; 32:3; Sib. Or. 3:48. This was increasingly the sense of the term in intertestamental Jewish literature (for several more references see Joachim Jeremias, *paradeisos*, *TDNT* 5 [1967], 765–73, esp. 767n16–23).

52. John 20:17 ("Do not cling to me, for I have not yet ascended to the Father") is best understood to mean that Jesus in his new resurrected state, with a resurrection body, had not yet ascended back to heaven; therefore, Mary should not try to hold on to Jesus' body. The perfect tense of *anabebēka*, "ascended," gives the sense, "I have not yet ascended and remained in the place where I ascended" or "I am not yet in the ascended state" (the latter phrase is from D. A. Carson, *The Gospel according to John* [Leicester: Inter-Varsity Press; Grand Rapids: Eerdmans, 1991], 644).

passages in Scripture. It has no claim to being "apostolic" and no support (in the sense of a "descent into hell") from the first six centuries of the church. It was not in the earliest versions of the Creed and was only included in it later because of an apparent misunderstanding about its meaning. Unlike every other phrase in the Creed, it represents not some major doctrine on which all Christians agree but rather a statement about which most Christians seem to disagree.[53] It is at best confusing and in most cases misleading for modern Christians. My own judgment is that there would be all gain and no loss if it were dropped from the Creed once and for all.

Concerning the doctrinal question of whether Christ did descend into hell after he died, the answer from several passages of Scripture seems clearly to be no.

## D. The Extent of the Atonement

One of the differences between Reformed theologians and other Catholic and Protestant theologians has been the question of the extent of the atonement. The question may be put this way: when Christ died on the cross, did he pay for the sins of the entire human race or only for the sins of those who he knew would ultimately be saved?

Non-Reformed people argue that the gospel offer in Scripture is repeatedly made to all people, and for this offer to be genuine, the payment for sins must have already been made and must be actually available for all people. They also say that if the people whose sins Christ paid for are limited, then the free offer of the gospel also is limited, and the offer of the gospel cannot be made to all mankind without exception.

On the other hand, Reformed people argue that if Christ's death actually paid for the sins of every person who ever lived, then there is no penalty left for *anyone* to pay, and it necessarily follows that all people will be saved, without exception. For God could not condemn to eternal punishment anyone whose sins are already paid for: that would be demanding double payment, and it would therefore be unjust. In answer to the objection that this compromises the free offer of the gospel to every person, Reformed people answer that we do not know who they are who will come to trust in Christ, for only God knows that. As far as we are concerned, the free offer of the gospel is to be made to everybody without exception. We also know that everyone who repents and believes in Christ will be saved, so all are called to repentance (cf. Acts 17:30). If God foreknew who would be saved, and if he accepted Christ's death as payment for their sins only, that still does not inhibit the free offer of the gospel. Who will respond to it is hidden in the secret counsels of God. That we do not know who will respond no more constitutes a reason for not offering the gospel to all than not knowing the extent of the harvest prevents the farmer from sowing seed in his fields.

---

53. Randall E. Otto adopts a similar recommendation: "To include such a mysterious article in the creed, which is supposed to be a summary of the basic and vital tenets of the faith, seems very unwise" (*Descendit in Inferna*: A Reformed Review of a Doctrinal Conundrum," *WTJ* 52 [1990]: 150).

Finally, Reformed people argue that God's purposes in redemption are agreed upon within the Trinity, and they are certainly accomplished. Those whom God planned to save are the same people for whom Christ also came to die, and to those same people the Holy Spirit will certainly apply the benefits of Christ's redemptive work, even awakening their faith (John 1:12; Phil. 1:29; cf. Eph. 2:2) and calling them to trust in him. What God the Father purposed, God the Son and the Holy Spirit agreed to and surely carried out.[54]

## 1. Scripture Passages Used to Support the Reformed View

Several Scripture passages speak of the fact that Christ died for his people. "The good shepherd lays down his life *for the sheep*" (John 10:11). "I lay down my life for the sheep" (John 10:15). Paul speaks of "the church of God, which he obtained with his own blood" (Acts 20:28). He also says, "He who did not spare his own Son but gave him up for us all, how will he not also with him graciously give us all things?" (Rom. 8:32). This passage indicates a connection between God's purpose in giving up his Son "for us all" and giving us "all things" that pertain to salvation as well. In the next sentence Paul clearly limits the application of this to those who will be saved because he says, "Who shall bring any charge against God's elect?" (Rom. 8:33) and in the next verse mentions Christ's death as a reason why no one shall bring a charge against the elect (8:34). In another passage, Paul says, "Husbands, love your wives, as Christ loved the church and gave himself up *for her*" (Eph. 5:25).

Moreover, Christ during his earthly ministry is aware of a group of people whom the Father has given to him. "All that the Father gives me will come to me, and whoever comes to me I will never cast out . . . this is the will of him who sent me, that I should lose nothing of all that he has given me, but raise it up on the last day" (John 6:37–39). He also says, "I am not praying for the world but for those whom you have given me, for they are yours" (John 17:9). He then goes on from this specific reference to the disciples to say, "I do not ask for these only, but also for those who will believe in me through their word" (John 17:20).

Finally, some passages speak of a definite transaction between the Father and the Son when Christ died, a transaction that had specific reference to those who would believe. For example, Paul says, "God shows his love for us in that while we were still sinners Christ died *for us*" (Rom. 5:8). He adds, "For if while we were enemies *we were reconciled to God by the death of his Son*, much more, now that we are reconciled, shall we be saved by his life" (Rom. 5:10). This reconciliation to God occurred with respect to the specific people who would be saved, and it occurred "while we were enemies." Similarly, Paul says, "*For our sake* he made him to be sin who knew no sin, so that in him we might

---

54. A very extensive recent defense of limited atonement is David Gibson and Jonathan Gibson, eds., *From Heaven He Came and Sought Her: Definite Atonement in Historical,* *Biblical, Theological, and Pastoral Perspective* (Wheaton, IL: Crossway, 2013).

become the righteousness of God" (2 Cor. 5:21; cf. Gal. 1:4; Eph. 1:7). And "Christ redeemed *us* from the curse of the law by becoming a curse *for us*" (Gal. 3:13).

Further support for the Reformed view is found in the consideration that all the blessings of salvation, including faith, repentance, and all of the works of the Holy Spirit in applying redemption, were also secured by Christ's redemptive work specifically for his people. Those for whom he earned forgiveness also have had those other benefits earned for them (cf. Eph. 1:3–4; 2:8; Phil. 1:29).[55]

What I have called "the Reformed view" in this section is commonly referred to as "limited atonement."[56] However, most theologians who hold this position today do not prefer the term *limited atonement* because it is so easily subject to misunderstanding, as if this view somehow held that Christ's atoning work was deficient in some way. The term that is usually preferred is *particular redemption*, since this view holds that Christ died for particular people (specifically, those who would be saved and whom he came to redeem), that he foreknew each one of them individually (cf. Eph. 1:3–5) and had them individually in mind in his atoning work.[57]

The opposite position, that Christ's death actually paid for the sins of all people who ever lived, is called "general redemption" or "unlimited atonement."

## 2. Scripture Passages Used to Support the Non-Reformed View (General Redemption or Unlimited Atonement)

A number of Scripture passages indicate that in some sense Christ died for the whole world. John the Baptist said, "Behold, the Lamb of God, who takes away the sin *of the world*!" (John 1:29). And John 3:16 tells us that "God so loved the world, that he gave his only Son, that whoever believes in him should not perish but have eternal life." Jesus said, "The bread that I will give for the life of the world is my flesh" (John 6:51). Paul says that in Christ "God was reconciling *the world* to himself" (2 Cor. 5:19). We read of Christ that "he is the propitiation for our sins, and not for ours only but also for the sins of *the whole world*" (1 John 2:2). Paul writes that Christ Jesus "gave himself as a

---

55. I am not aware of any Arminians who hold what I have called the "Reformed view," the view that is commonly called "particular redemption" or "limited atonement." But it does not seem logically impossible for someone to hold a traditional Arminian position (that God foreknew who would believe and predestined them on the basis of that foreknowledge) coupled with the belief that Christ's death actually paid the penalty for the sins of those who God knew would believe and not for any others. This is just to say that, while "limited atonement" is necessarily part of a Reformed viewpoint because it logically follows from the overall sovereignty of God in the entire work of redemption, one could (in theory at least) hold to "limited atonement" and not adopt a Reformed position on other points concerning God's sovereignty in life generally or in salvation in particular.

56. Thus, it is the "L" in the acronym "TULIP," which represents the so-called "five points of Calvinism," five doctrinal

positions that distinguish Calvinists or Reformed theologians from many other Protestants. The five points represented by the word are: Total depravity, Unconditional election, Limited atonement, Irresistible grace, and Perseverance of the saints. (This book advocates these five doctrinal points, but it attempts in each case to point out the arguments in favor of an opposing position and to provide an appropriate bibliography representing both views; for the individual points see the following chapters: 24 [T], 32 [U], 27 [L], 34 [I], and 40 [P].)

57. Reformed people argue that it is the other view that really limits the power of the atonement because on that view the atonement does not actually guarantee salvation for God's people but only makes salvation possible for all people. In other words, if the atonement is not limited with respect to the number of people to which it applies, then it must be limited with respect to what it actually accomplishes.

ransom *for all*" (1 Tim. 2:6). And the author of Hebrews says that Jesus was for a little while made lower than the angels "so that by the grace of God he might taste death for everyone" (Heb. 2:9).

Other passages appear to speak of Christ dying for those who will not be saved. Paul says, "By what you eat, do not destroy the one for whom Christ died" (Rom. 14:15). In a similar context he tells the Corinthians not to eat publicly at an idol's temple because they might encourage those who are weak in their faith to violate their consciences and eat food offered to idols. He then says, "And so by your knowledge this weak person is destroyed, the brother *for whom Christ died*" (1 Cor. 8:11). Peter writes about false teachers as follows: "But false prophets also arose among the people, just as there will be false teachers among you, who will secretly bring in destructive heresies, *even denying the Master who bought them*, bringing upon themselves swift destruction" (2 Peter 2:1; cf. Heb. 10:29).

### 3. Some Points of Agreement and Some Conclusions about Disputed Texts

It would be helpful first to list the points on which both sides agree:

1. Not all will be saved.
2. A free offer of the gospel can rightly be made to every person ever born. It is completely true that "whoever will" may come to Christ for salvation, and no one who comes to him will be turned away. This free offer of the gospel is extended in good faith to every person.
3. Christ's death in itself, because he is the infinite Son of God, has infinite merit and is in itself sufficient to pay the penalty of the sins of as many or as few as the Father and the Son decreed. The question is not about the intrinsic merits of Christ's sufferings and death but about the number of people for whom the Father and the Son thought Christ's death to be sufficient payment at the time Christ died.

Beyond these points of agreement, however, a difference remains concerning the following question: "When Christ died, did he *actually pay the penalty* only for the sins of those who would believe in him, or for the sins of every person who ever lived?" On this question it seems that those who hold to particular redemption have stronger arguments on their side. First, an important point that is not generally answered by advocates of the general redemption view is that people who are eternally condemned to hell suffer the penalty for all of their own sins, and therefore their penalty could not have been fully taken by Christ. Those who hold the general redemption view sometimes answer that people suffer in hell because of the sin of rejecting Christ, even though their other sins were paid for. But this is hardly a satisfactory position, for (1) some have never rejected Christ because they have never heard of him, and (2) the emphasis of Scripture when it speaks of eternal punishment is not on the fact that the people suffer because they have rejected Christ, but on the fact that they suffer because of their own sins in this life (see Rom. 5:6–8, 13–16, et al.). This significant point seems to tip the argument decisively in favor of the particular redemption position.

Another significant point in favor of particular redemption is the fact that Christ completely earned our salvation, paying the penalty for all our sins. He did not just redeem us potentially but actually redeemed us as individuals whom he loved. A third weighty point in favor of particular redemption is that there is eternal unity in the counsels and plans of God and in the work of the Father, Son, and Holy Spirit in accomplishing their plans (see Rom. 8:28–30).

With regard to Scripture passages used to support general redemption, the following may be said: Several passages that speak about "the world" simply mean that sinners generally will be saved, without implying that every single person in the world will be saved. So the fact that Christ is the Lamb of God who takes away the sin of the world (John 1:29) does not mean (on anybody's interpretation) that Christ actually removes the sins of every single person in the world, for both sides agree that not all are saved. Similarly, the fact that God was in Christ reconciling the world to himself (2 Cor. 5:19) does not mean that every single person in the world was reconciled to God, but that sinners generally were reconciled to God. Another way of putting these two passages would be to say that Jesus was the Lamb of God who takes away the sin of sinners, or that God was in Christ reconciling sinners to himself. This does not mean that all sinners will be saved or were reconciled but simply that these groups in general, but not necessarily every single person in them, were the objects of God's redeeming work: it essentially means that "God so loved sinners that he gave his only Son . . ." without implying that every sinner in the whole world will be saved.

The passages that speak about Christ dying "for" the whole world are best understood to refer to the free offer of the gospel that is made to all people. When Jesus says, "The bread that I will give *for the life of the world* is my flesh" (John 6:51), it is in the context of speaking of himself as the bread that came down from heaven, which is offered to people and which they may, if they are willing, receive for themselves. Earlier in the same discussion Jesus said that "the bread of God is he who comes down from heaven and gives life to the world" (John 6:33). This may be understood in the sense of bringing redeeming life into the world but not meaning that every single person in the world will have that redeeming life. Jesus then speaks of himself as inviting others to come and take up this living bread: "Whoever comes to me shall not hunger, and whoever believes in me shall never thirst. . . . This is the bread that comes down from heaven, so that one may eat of it and not die. I am the living bread that came down from heaven. If anyone eats of this bread, he will live forever. And the bread that I will give for the life of the world is my flesh" (John 6:35, 50–51). Jesus gives his flesh to bring life into the world and to offer life to the world, but to say that Jesus came to offer eternal life to the world (a point on which both sides agree) is not to say that he actually paid the penalty for the sins of everyone who would ever live, for that is a separate question.

When John says that Christ "is the propitiation for our sins, and not for ours only but also for the sins of the whole world" (1 John 2:2), he may simply be understood to mean that Christ is the atoning sacrifice that the gospel now *makes available for* the sins of everyone in the world. The preposition *for* (Gk. *peri* plus genitive) is ambiguous with respect to the specific sense in which Christ is the propitiation *for* the sins of the world. *Peri* simply means "concerning" or "with respect to" but is not specific enough to define the exact way in which Christ is the sacrifice with respect to the sins of the world. It would be entirely consistent with the language of the verse to think that John is simply saying that Christ is the atoning sacrifice who is available to pay for the sins of anyone in the world.[58] Likewise, when Paul says that Christ "gave himself as a ransom *for all*" (1 Tim. 2:6), we are to understand this to mean a ransom available for all people, without exception.[59]

When the author of Hebrews says that Christ was made lower than the angels "so that by the grace of God he might taste death for everyone" (Heb. 2:9), the passage is best understood to refer to every one of Christ's people, every one who is redeemed. It does not say everyone "in the whole world" or any such expression, and in the immediate context the author is certainly speaking of those who are redeemed (see "bringing many sons to glory" [v. 10]; "those who are sanctified" [v. 11]; and "the children God has given me" [v. 13]). The Greek word *pas*, here translated "every one," is also used in a similar sense to mean "all of God's people" in Hebrews 8:11, "for they shall *all* know me," and in Hebrews 12:8, "If you are left without discipline, in which *all* have participated, then you are illegitimate children and not sons." In both cases the *all* is not explicitly restricted by a specific phrase such as "all of God's people," but this is clearly the sense in the overall context. Of course, in other contexts, the same word *all* can mean "all people without exception," but this must be determined from the individual context in each case.

When Paul speaks in Romans 14:15 and 1 Corinthians 8:11 about the possibility of destroying one for whom Christ died, it seems best here as well to think of the word *for* in the sense that Christ died *"to make salvation available for"* these people or "to bring the free offer of the gospel to" these people who are associated with the fellowship of the church. He does not seem to have in mind the specific question of the inter-Trinitarian

---

58. Compare a similar sense for the phrase "for sins" (Gk. *peri harmartiōn*) in Heb. 10:26 where the author says that if someone continues on sinning deliberately after receiving the knowledge of the truth "there no longer remains a sacrifice for sins." This does not mean that Christ's sacrifice no longer exists, but it is no longer available for that person who has willfully spurned it and put himself beyond the realm of willing repentance. Here "sacrifice for sins" means "a sacrifice available to be claimed for the payment of sins." In the same way 1 John 2:2 can mean "the propitiation *available for* the sins of the whole world [esp. with reference to Gentiles as well as Jews]."

59. When Paul says that God "is the Savior of all people, especially of those who believe" (1 Tim. 4:10), he is referring to God the Father, not to Christ, and probably uses the word "Savior" in the sense of "one who preserves people's lives and rescues them from danger" rather than the sense of "one who forgives their sins," for surely Paul does not mean that every single person will be saved. However, another possible meaning is that God "is the Savior of all sorts of people—that is, of people who believe" (for a defense of this view see George W. Knight III, *The Pastoral Epistles*, NIGTC [Grand Rapids: Eerdmans; Carlisle: Paternoster, 1992], 203–4).

decision regarding whose sins the Father counted Christ's death as a payment for. Rather, he is speaking of those to whom the gospel has been offered. In another passage, when Paul calls the weak man a "brother for whom Christ died" in 1 Corinthians 8:11, he is not necessarily pronouncing on the inward spiritual condition of a person's heart but is probably just speaking according to what is often called the "judgment of charity" by which people who are participating in the fellowship of the church can rightly be referred to as brothers and sisters.[60]

When Peter speaks of false teachers who bring in destructive heresies, "even denying the Master who bought them" (2 Peter 2:1), it is unclear whether the word *Master* (Gk. *despotēs*) refers to Christ (as in Jude 4) or to God the Father (as in Luke 2:29; Acts 4:24; Rev. 6:10). In either case, the Old Testament allusion is probably to Deuteronomy 32:6, where Moses says to the rebellious people who have turned away from God, "Is not he your Father *who has bought you*?" (author's translation).[61] Peter is drawing an analogy between the past false prophets who arose among the Jews and those who will be false teachers within the churches to which he writes: "But false prophets also arose among the people, just as there will be false teachers among you, who will secretly bring in destructive heresies, even denying the Master who bought them" (2 Peter 2:1). In line with this clear reference to false prophets in the Old Testament, Peter also alludes to the fact that the rebellious Jews turned away from God who "bought" them out of Egypt in the exodus. From the time of the exodus onward, any Jewish person would have considered himself or herself one who was "bought" by God in the exodus and therefore a person of God's possession. In this sense, the false teachers arising among the people were denying God their Father, to whom they rightfully belonged.[62] So the text means not that Christ had redeemed these false prophets but simply that they were rebellious Jewish people (or church attenders in the same position as the rebellious Jews) who were rightly owned by God because they had been brought out of the land of Egypt (or their forefathers had), but they were ungrateful to him. Christ's specific redemptive work on the cross is not in view in this verse.[63]

---

60. Another possible interpretation of these two passages is that "destroy" means ruin the ministry or Christian growth of someone who will nonetheless remain a believer but whose principles will be compromised. That sense would certainly fit the context well in both cases, but one argument against it is that the Greek word *apollymi*, "destroy," which is used in both cases, seems a stronger word than would be appropriate if that were Paul's intention. The same word is used often of eternal destruction (see John 3:16; Rom. 2:12; 1 Cor. 1:18; 15:18; 2 Cor. 2:15; 4:3; 2 Peter 3:9). However, the context of 1 Cor. 8:11 may indicate a different sense than these other passages, for this verse does not talk about God "destroying" someone but about other human beings doing something to "destroy" another—which suggests a weaker sense for the term here.

61. Though the Septuagint does not use Peter's term

*agorazō* but rather *kataomai*, the words are synonymous in many cases, and both can mean "buy, purchase"; the Hebrew term in Deut. 32:6 is *qānāh*, which frequently means "purchase, buy" in the Old Testament.

62. This is the view taken by John Gill, *The Cause of God and Truth* (1735; repr. of 1855 ed., Grand Rapids: Baker, 1980), 61. Gill discusses other possible interpretations of the passage, but this seems most persuasive. We should realize that in both of his epistles, Peter very frequently portrays the churches to which he is writing in terms of the rich imagery of the people of God in the Old Testament. See Grudem, *The First Epistle of Peter*, 113.

63. The Greek word *despotēs*, "Master," is elsewhere used of God in contexts that emphasize his role as Creator and Ruler of the world (Acts 4:24; Rev. 6:10).

With regard to the verses that talk of Christ's dying for his sheep, his church, or his people, non-Reformed people may answer that these passages do not deny that he died to pay the penalty for others as well. In response, while it is true that they do not explicitly deny that Christ died for others as well, their frequent reference to his death for his people would at least strongly suggest that this is a correct inference. Even if they do not absolutely imply such a particularizing of redemption, these verses do at least seem to be most naturally interpreted in this way.

In conclusion, it seems to me that the Reformed position of "particular redemption" is most consistent with the overall teaching of Scripture. But once that has been said, several points of caution need to be raised.

## 4. Points of Clarification and Caution Regarding This Doctrine

It is important to state some points of clarification and also some areas in which we can rightly object to the way in which some advocates of particular redemption have expressed their arguments. It is also important to ask what the pastoral implications are for this teaching.

1. It seems to be a mistake to state the question as Berkhof does[64] and focus on the purpose of the Father and the Son rather than on what actually happened in the atonement. If we confine the discussion to the purpose of the atonement, then this is just another form of the larger dispute between Calvinists and Arminians over whether God's purpose is (a) to save all people, a purpose that is frustrated by man's will to rebel—the Arminian position—or whether God's purpose is (b) to save those whom he has chosen—the Calvinist position. This question will not be decided at the narrow point of the question of the extent of the atonement, for the specific scriptural texts on that point are too few and can hardly be said to be conclusive on either side. One's decisions on these passages will tend to be determined by one's view of the larger question as to what Scripture as a whole teaches about the nature of the atonement and about the broader issues of God's providence, sovereignty, and the doctrine of election. Whatever decisions are made on those larger topics will apply specifically to this point, and people will come to their conclusions accordingly.

Rather than focusing on the purpose of the atonement, therefore, the question is rightfully asked about the atonement: Did Christ pay for the sins of all unbelievers who will be eternally condemned, and did he pay for their sins fully and completely on the cross? It seems that we have to answer no to that question.

2. The statements "Christ died for his people only" and "Christ died for all people" are both true in some senses, and too often the argument over this issue has

---

64. Louis Berkhof says, "The question does relate to the design of the atonement. Did the Father in sending Christ, and did Christ in coming into the world, to make atonement for sin, do this with the design or for the purpose of saving only the elect or all men? That is the question, and that only is the question" (*Systematic Theology* [Grand Rapids: Eerdmans, 1941], 394).

been confused because of various senses that can be given to the word "for" in these two statements.

The statement "Christ died for his people only" can be understood to mean that "Christ died to actually pay the penalty for all the sins of his people only." In that sense it is true. But when non-Reformed people hear the sentence "Christ died for his people only," they often hear in it, "Christ died so that he could make the gospel available only to a chosen few," and they are troubled over what they see as a real threat to the free offer of the gospel to every person. Reformed people who hold to particular redemption should recognize the potential for misunderstanding that arises with the sentence "Christ died for his people only," and out of concern for the truth and a pastoral concern to affirm the free offer of the gospel and to avoid misunderstanding in the body of Christ, they should be more precise in saying exactly what they mean. The simple sentence, "Christ died for his people only," while true in the sense explained above, is seldom understood in that way when people unfamiliar with Reformed doctrine hear it, and it therefore is better not to use such an ambiguous sentence at all.

On the other hand, the sentence "Christ died for all people" is true if it means "Christ died to make salvation available to all people" or if it means "Christ died to bring the free offer of the gospel to all people." In fact, this is the kind of language Scripture itself uses in passages like John 6:51; 1 Timothy 2:6; and 1 John 2:2.[65] It really seems to be only nit-picking that creates controversies and useless disputes when Reformed people insist on being such purists in their speech that they object any time someone says that "Christ died for all people." There are certainly acceptable ways of understanding that sentence that are consistent with the speech of the scriptural authors themselves.

Similarly, I do not think we should rush to criticize an evangelist who tells an audience of unbelievers, "Christ died for your sins," if it is made clear in the context that it is necessary to trust in Christ before one can receive the benefits of the gospel offer. In that sense the sentence is simply understood to mean "Christ died to offer you forgiveness for your sins" or "Christ died to make available forgiveness for your sins." The important point here is that sinners realize that salvation is available for everyone and that payment of sins is available for everyone.

At this point some Reformed theologians will object and will warn us that if we say to unbelievers, "Christ died for your sins," the unbelievers will draw the conclusion, "Therefore I am saved no matter what I do." But this does not seem to be a problem in actual fact, for whenever evangelicals (Reformed or non-Reformed) speak about the gospel to unbelievers, they are always very clear on the fact that the death of Christ has no benefit for a person unless that person believes in Christ. Therefore, the problem seems to be more something that Reformed people *think* unbelievers should believe

---

65. Berkhof says that 1 Tim. 2:1 refers to "the revealed will of God that both Jews and Gentiles should be saved" (ibid., 396).

(if they were consistent in reasoning back into the secret counsels of God and the relationship between the Father and Son in the counsels of the Trinity at the point of Christ's propitiatory sacrifice on the cross). But unbelievers simply do not reason that way; they know that they must exercise faith in Christ before they will experience any benefits from his saving work. Moreover, it is far more likely that people will understand the sentence "Christ died for your sins" in the doctrinally correct sense that "Christ died in order to offer you forgiveness for your sins" rather than in the doctrinally incorrect sense, "Christ died and completely paid the penalty already for all your sins."[66]

3. In terms of the practical, pastoral effects of our words, both those who hold to particular redemption and those who hold to general redemption agree at several key points.

First, both sincerely want to avoid implying that people will be saved whether they believe in Christ or not. Non-Reformed people sometimes accuse Reformed people of saying that the elect will be saved irrespective of responding to the gospel, but this is clearly a misrepresentation of the Reformed position. On the other hand, Reformed people think that those who hold to general redemption are in danger of implying that everybody will be saved whether they believe in Christ or not. But this is not a position that non-Reformed people actually hold, and it is always precarious to criticize people for a position that they do not say they hold, just because you think that they should hold that position if they were consistent with their other views.

Second, both sides want to avoid implying that there might be some people who come to Christ for salvation but are turned away because Christ did not die for them. No one wants to say or imply to an unbeliever, "Christ might have died for your sins (and then again he might not have!)." Both sides want to clearly affirm that all who come to Christ for salvation will in fact be saved. "Whoever comes to me I will never cast out" (John 6:37).

Third, both sides want to avoid implying that God is hypocritical or insincere when he makes the free offer of the gospel. It is a genuine offer, and it is always true that all who wish to come to Christ for salvation and who do actually come to him will be saved.

Fourth, we may ask why this matter is so important after all. Although Reformed people have sometimes made belief in particular redemption a test of doctrinal orthodoxy, it would be healthy to realize that Scripture itself never singles this out as a doctrine of major importance, nor does it once make it the subject of any explicit theological discussion. Our knowledge of the issue comes only from incidental references to it in passages whose concern is with other doctrinal or practical matters. In fact, this is really a question that probes into the inner counsels of the Trinity and does so in an area in which there is very little direct scriptural testimony—a fact that should cause us to be cautious. A balanced pastoral perspective would seem to be to say that this teaching

---

66. I am not here arguing that we should be careless in our language; I am arguing that we should not rush to criticize when other Christians unreflectively use ambiguous language without intending to contradict any teaching of Scripture.

of particular redemption *seems* to us to be true, that it gives logical consistency to our theological system, and that it can be helpful in assuring people of Christ's love for them individually and of the completeness of his redemptive work for them—but that it also is a subject that almost inevitably leads to some confusion, some misunderstanding, and often some wrongful argumentativeness and divisiveness among God's people, all of which are negative pastoral considerations. Perhaps that is why the apostles such as John and Peter and Paul, in their wisdom, placed almost no emphasis on this question at all. And perhaps we would do well to ponder their example.

## QUESTIONS FOR PERSONAL APPLICATION

1. In what ways has this chapter enabled you to appreciate Christ's death more than you did before? Has it given you more or less confidence in the fact that your sins have actually been paid for by Christ?

2. If the ultimate cause of the atonement is found in the love and justice of God, then was there anything in you that required God to love you or to take steps to save you (when he looked forward and thought of you as a sinner in rebellion against him)? Does your answer to this question help you to appreciate the character of God's love for you as a person who did not at all deserve that love? How does that realization make you feel in your relationship to God?

3. Do you think that Christ's sufferings were enough to pay for your sins? Are you willing to rely on his work to pay for all your sins? Do you think he is a sufficient Savior, worthy of your trust? When he invites you, "Come to me . . . and I will give you rest" (Matt. 11:28), do you now trust him? Will you now and always rely on him with your whole heart for complete salvation?

4. If Christ bore all the guilt for our sins, all the wrath of God against sin, and all the penalty of the death that we deserved, then will God ever turn his wrath against you as a believer (see Rom. 8:31–39)? Can any of the hardships or sufferings that you experience in life be due to the wrath of God against

### Special Terms

*active obedience*
*atonement*
*blood of Christ*
*consequent absolute necessity*
*example theory*
*general redemption*
*governmental theory*
*impute*
*limited atonement*
*moral influence theory*
*particular redemption*
*passive obedience*
*penal substitution*
*propitiation*
*ransom to Satan theory*
*reconciliation*
*redemption*
*sacrifice*
*unlimited atonement*
*vicarious atonement*

you? If not, then why do we as Christians experience difficulties and sufferings in this life (see Rom. 8:28; Heb. 12:3–11)?

5. Do you think Christ's life was good enough to deserve God's approval? Are you willing to rely on it for your eternal destiny? Is Jesus Christ a reliable enough and good enough Savior for you to trust him? Which would you rather trust in for your eternal standing before God: your own life or Christ's?

6. If Christ has indeed redeemed you from bondage to sin and to the kingdom of Satan, are there areas of your life in which you could more fully realize this to be true? Could this realization give you more encouragement in your Christian life?

7. Do you think it was fair for Christ to be your substitute and to pay your penalty? When you think about him acting as your substitute and dying for you, what attitude and emotion is called forth in your heart?

## BIBLIOGRAPHY

(For an explanation of this bibliography see the note on the bibliography to chapter 1, pp. 23–24. Complete bibliographical data may be found on pp. 1489–96.)

### SECTIONS IN EVANGELICAL SYSTEMATIC THEOLOGIES

1. *Anglican (Episcopalian)*
   1882–92 ..... Litton, 221–36
   1930 ........ Thomas, 49–72, 414–26
   2001 ........ Packer, 131–39
   2013 ........ Bird, 385–434
   2013 ........ Bray, 899–920

2. *Arminian (Wesleyan or Methodist)*
   1875–76 ..... Pope, 2:141–88, 263–316
   1892–94 ..... Miley, 2:65–240
   1940 ........ Wiley, 2:217–300
   1960 ........ Purkiser, 243–68
   1983 ........ Carter, 1:483–505
   1992 ........ Oden, 2:279–450
   2002 ........ Cottrell, 259–83

3. *Baptist*
   1767 ........ Gill, 1:562–83; 2:1–68
   1887 ........ Boyce, 295–341
   1907 ........ Strong, 701–6, 713–75
   1987–94 ..... Lewis and Demarest, 2:371–436
   1990–95 ..... Garrett, 2:3–80
   2007 ........ Akin, 551–71
   2013 ........ Erickson, 713–68

4. *Dispensational*
   1947 ........ Chafer, 3:35–164, 183–205; 5:177–230
   1949 ........ Thiessen, 229–42
   1986 ........ Ryrie, 275–309, 318–23
   2002–2005 .. Geisler, 2:405; 3:202–15, 230–35
   2017 ........ MacArthur and Mayhue, 511–64

5. *Lutheran*
   1917–24 ..... Pieper, 2:280–330, 342–82
   1934 ........ Mueller, 287–95, 305–13

### 6. Reformed (or Presbyterian)

1559 . . . . . . . . Calvin, 1:503–34 (2.16–17)

1679–85 . . . . . Turretin, *IET*, 2:247–57,
    352–56, 438–45

1724–58 . . . . . Edwards, 1:574–80;
    2:565–78

1871–73 . . . . . Hodge, 2:480–591, 610–25

1878 . . . . . . . . Dabney, 485–553

1887–1921 . . . Warfield, *SSW*, 1:167–77;
    *SSW*, 2:308–20; *BD*,
    327–438; *PWC*, 325–530;
    *CC*, 393–444

1894 . . . . . . . . Shedd, 690–760

1906–11 . . . . . Bavinck, *RD*, 3:323–417,
    447–75

1910 . . . . . . . . Vos, 4:173, 175, 179–80

1937–66 . . . . . Murray, *CW*, 1:36–39,
    59–85; 2:142–57; *RAA*, 9–57

1938 . . . . . . . . Berkhof, 331–43, 361–99

1998 . . . . . . . . Reymond, 623–702

2008 . . . . . . . . Van Genderen and Velema,
    462–538

2011 . . . . . . . . Horton, 492–520

2013 . . . . . . . . Frame, 217, 899–920, 969,
    1068

2013 . . . . . . . . Culver, 540–70, 592–600

2016 . . . . . . . . Allen and Swain, 268–90

2017 . . . . . . . . Barrett, 347–92

2019 . . . . . . . . Letham, 376–79, 387–96,
    551–73

### 7. Renewal (or charismatic/Pentecostal)

1988–92 . . . . . Williams, 1:353–80

1993 . . . . . . . . Menzies and Horton, 95–108

1995 . . . . . . . . Horton, 325–74

2008 . . . . . . . . Duffield and Van Cleave,
    183–96

## SECTIONS IN REPRESENTATIVE ROMAN CATHOLIC SYSTEMATIC THEOLOGIES

### 1. Roman Catholic: Traditional

1955 . . . . . . . . Ott, 175–79, 182–92, 211–19

### 2. Roman Catholic: Post–Vatican II

1980 . . . . . . . . McBrien, 1:417–23;
    2:865–901

2012 . . . . . . . . *CCC*, paragraphs 595–623

## OTHER WORKS

Allen, David Lewis. *The Extent of the Atonement: A Historical and Critical Review.* Nashville: B&H Academic, 2016.

Allen, David Lewis, and Steve Lemke. *Whosoever Will: A Biblical-Theological Critique of Five-Point Calvinism.* Nashville: B&H Academic, 2010.

Allison, Gregg. *Historical Theology: An Introduction to Christian Doctrine; A Companion to Wayne Grudem's* Systematic Theology. Grand Rapids: Zondervan, 2011, 389–410.

Baker, Mark D., and Joel B. Green. *Recovering the Scandal of the Cross: Atonement in New Testament and Contemporary Contexts.* 2nd ed. Downers Grove, IL: IVP Academic, 2011.

Bauckham, R. J. "Descent into Hell." In *NDT2*, 251.

Berkouwer, G. C. *The Work of Christ.* Translated by Cornelius Lambregtse. Grand Rapids: Eerdmans, 1965.

Brown, John. *The Sufferings and Glories of the Messiah.* 1852. Reprint, Evanston, IN: Sovereign Grace, 1959.

Campbell, John McLeod. *The Nature of the Atonement.* 6th ed. 1856. Reprint, New York: Macmillan, 1886.

Demarest, B. A. "Amyraldianism." In *EDT3*, 48.

Demarest, Bruce. *The Cross and Salvation: The Doctrine of Salvation.* Wheaton, IL: Crossway, 2006, 27–43.

Eddy, P. R. and J. Beilby. "Atonement." In *GDT*, 84–92.

Elwell, W. A. "Atonement, Extent of the." In *EDT3*, 100–101.

Emerson, Matthew Y. *He Descended to the Dead: An Evangelical Theology of Holy Saturday*. Downers Grove, IL: IVP Academic, 2019.

Gibson, David, and Jonathan Gibson, eds. *From Heaven He Came and Sought Her: Definite Atonement in Historical, Biblical, Theological, and Pastoral Perspective*. Wheaton, IL: Crossway, 2013.

Green, Michael. *The Empty Cross of Jesus*. The Jesus Library, ed. by Michael Green. Downers Grove, IL: InterVarsity Press, 1984.

Grensted, L. W. *A Short History of the Doctrine of the Atonement*. Manchester: University Press; London: Longmans, 1962.

Hodge, Archibald A. *The Atonement*. London: Nelson, 1868.

Kapic, K. M. "Atonement." In *EDT3*, 96–100.

Kendall, R. T. *Calvin and English Calvinism to 1649*. 2nd ed. Eugene, OR: Wipf and Stock, 2011.

Lightner, Robert P. *The Death Christ Died: A Biblical Case for Unlimited Atonement*. 2nd ed. Grand Rapids: Kregel, 1998.

Macleod, Donald. *Christ Crucified: Understanding the Atonement*. Downers Grove, IL: InterVarsity, 2014.

McDonald, H. D. *The Atonement of the Death of Christ*. Grand Rapids: Baker, 1985.

McGrath, Alister E. *Luther's Theology of the Cross: Martin Luther's Theological Breakthrough*. Oxford: Basil Blackwell, 1985.

———. *The Mystery of the Cross*. Grand Rapids: Zondervan, 1988.

———. *What Was God Doing on the Cross?* Grand Rapids: Zondervan, 1993.

Martin, Hugh. *The Atonement: In Its Relations to the Covenant, the Priesthood, the Intercession of Our Lord*. Philadelphia: Smith and English, 1871.

Morey, Robert A. *Studies in the Atonement*. Maitland, FL: Xulon, 2011.

Morris, Leon. *The Apostolic Preaching of the Cross*. 3rd ed. Grand Rapids: Eerdmans, 1965.

———. "Atonement." In *EDT1*, 97.

———. *The Atonement: Its Meaning and Significance*. Leicester: Inter-Varsity Press; Downers Grove, IL: InterVarsity Press, 1983.

———. "Atonement, Theories of the." In *EDT1*, 100–102.

———. *The Cross in the New Testament*. Grand Rapids: Eerdmans, 1965.

———. *The Cross of Jesus*. Grand Rapids: Eerdmans, and Exeter: Paternoster, 1988.

Murray, John. *Redemption Accomplished and Applied*. Grand Rapids: Eerdmans, 1955, 9–78.

Naselli, Andrew David, and Mark A. Snoeberger, eds. *Perspectives on the Extent of the Atonement: 3 Views*. Nashville: B&H Academic, 2015.

Owen, John. *The Death of Death in the Death of Christ*. Reprint, Carlisle, PA: Banner of Truth, 1959 (includes excellent introductory essay by J. I. Packer).

Patterson, Paige. "The Work of Christ." In *A Theology for the Church*, edited by Daniel L. Akin et al., 547–88. Nashville: B&H, 2007.

Reicke, Bo. *The Disobedient Spirits and Christian Baptism: A Study of 1 Pet. III. 19 and Its Context*. Eugene, OR: Wipf & Stock, 2005.

Seifrid, M. A. "Death of Christ." In *DLNT*, 267–86.

Smeaton, George. *The Apostles' Doctrine of the Atonement*. 1870. Reprint, Grand Rapids: Zondervan, 1957.

———. *The Doctrine of the Atonement as Taught by Christ Himself*. 1871. Reprint, Grand Rapids: Zondervan, 1953.

Stott, John R. W. *The Cross of Christ*. Leicester: Inter-Varsity Press; Downers Grove, IL: InterVarsity Press, 1986.

Thomas, G. Michael. *The Extent of the Atonement: A Dilemma for Reformed Theology from Calvin to the Consensus (1536-1675)*. Carlisle: Paternoster, 1997.

Trotter, Andrew H., Jr. "Atonement." In *BTDB*, 42–45.

Turretin, Francis. *The Atonement of Christ*. Translated by James R. Willson. Latin ed. published in 1674. Reprint of 1859 ed., Grand Rapids: Baker, 1978.

Wallace, Ronald S. *The Atoning Death of Christ*. Westchester, IL: Crossway, 1981.

Yarbrough, R. W. "Atonement." In *NDBT*, 389–93.

## SCRIPTURE MEMORY PASSAGE

**Romans 3:23–26:** For all have sinned and fall short of the glory of God, and are justified by his grace as a gift, through the redemption that is in Christ Jesus, whom God put forward as a propitiation by his blood, to be received by faith. This was to show God's righteousness, because in his divine forbearance he had passed over former sins. It was to show his righteousness at the present time, so that he might be just and the justifier of the one who has faith in Jesus.

## HYMN

**"When I Survey the Wondrous Cross"**

*When I survey the wondrous cross*
*    On which the Prince of Glory died,*
*My richest gain I count but loss,*
*    And pour contempt on all my pride.*

*Forbid it, Lord, that I should boast,*
*    Save in the death of Christ my God:*
*All the vain things that charm me most,*
*    I sacrifice them to his blood.*

*See, from his head, his hands, his feet,*
*    Sorrow and love flow mingled down:*

*Did e'er such love and sorrow meet,*
*    Or thorns compose so rich a crown?*

*His dying crimson, like a robe,*
*    Spread o'er his body on the tree;*
*Then am I dead to all the globe,*
*    And all the globe is dead to me.*

*Were the whole realm of nature mine,*
*    That were a present far too small;*
*Love so amazing, so divine,*
*    Demands my soul, my life, my all.*

Author: Isaac Watts, 1707

## CONTEMPORARY WORSHIP SONG

**"The Power of the Cross"** [Oh, to see the dawn]

*Oh, to see the dawn*
*Of the darkest day:*
*Christ on the road to Calvary.*
*Tried by sinful men,*
*Torn and beaten, then*
*Nailed to a cross of wood.*

*Chorus*
*This, the pow'r of the cross:*
*Christ became sin for us;*
*Took the blame, bore the wrath—*
*We stand forgiven at the cross.*

*Oh, to see the pain*
*Written on Your face,*
*Bearing the awesome weight of sin.*
*Ev'ry bitter thought,*
*Ev'ry evil deed*
*Crowning Your bloodstained brow.*

*Now the daylight flees;*
*Now the ground beneath*
*Quakes as its Maker bows His head.*
*Curtain torn in two,*
*Dead are raised to life;*
*"Finished!" the vict'ry cry.*

*Oh, to see my name*
*Written in the wounds,*
*For through Your suffering I am free.*
*Death is crushed to death,*
*Life is mine to live,*
*Won through Your selfless love.*

**Final Chorus**
*This, the pow'r of the cross:*
*Son of God—slain for us.*
*What a love! What a cost!*
*We stand forgiven at the cross.*

Words by Stuart Townend and Keith Getty[67]

# CHAPTER 28

# Resurrection and Ascension

*What was Christ's resurrection body like?*
*What is its significance for us?*
*What happened to Christ when he ascended into heaven?*
*What is meant by the states of Jesus Christ?*

## EXPLANATION AND SCRIPTURAL BASIS

### A. RESURRECTION

### 1. New Testament Evidence

The Gospels contain abundant testimony to the resurrection of Christ (see Matt. 28:1–20; Mark 16:1–8; Luke 24:1–53; John 20:1–21:25). In addition to these detailed narratives in the four gospels, the book of Acts is a story of the apostles' proclamation of the resurrection of Christ and of continued prayer to Christ and trust in him as the one who is alive and reigning in heaven. The Epistles depend entirely on the assumption that Jesus is a living, reigning Savior who is now the exalted head of the church, who is to be trusted, worshiped, and adored, and who will one day return in power and great glory to reign as King over the earth. The book of Revelation repeatedly shows the risen Christ reigning in heaven and predicts his return to conquer his enemies and reign in glory. Thus the entire New Testament bears witness to the resurrection of Christ.

It is appropriate to believe in the resurrection of Christ based on the teachings of the New Testament alone. However, for those who do not accept the authority of the New Testament, there are very substantial historical arguments for the resurrection of Christ, and these arguments have persuaded many skeptics who started to examine the evidence for themselves for the purpose of *disproving* the resurrection.[1]

---

1. One remarkable account of such a change from skepticism to belief is Frank Morison, *Who Moved the Stone?* (London: Faber and Faber, 1930; repr., Grand Rapids: Zondervan, 1987). A widely used booklet summarizing the arguments is J. N. D. Anderson, *The Evidence for the Resurrection* (London; Inter-Varsity Press; Downers Grove, IL: InterVarsity Press, 1966). (Both Morison and Anderson were trained as lawyers.) More recent and detailed presentations are found in William Lane Craig, *The Son Rises: The Historical Evidence for the Resurrection of Jesus* (repr., Eugene, OR: Wipf & Stock, 2000); Gary Habermas and Anthony Flew, *Did Jesus Rise From the Dead? The Resurrection Debate*, ed. Terry L. Miethe (New York: Harper and Row, 1987); Gary Habermas, "Resurrection of Christ," in *EDT*, 938–41; Gary Habermas and Michael Licona, *The Case for the Resurrection of Jesus* (Grand Rapids: Kregel, 2004). An extensive compilation of arguments and quotations from recognized scholars affirming the overwhelming reliability of the evidence for Christ's resurrection is found in Josh McDowell and Sean McDowell, *Evidence that Demands a Verdict*, rev. ed. (Nashville: Nelson, 2017), 232–302.

## 2. The Nature of Christ's Resurrection: A Physical Body Made Perfect

Christ's resurrection was not simply a coming back from the dead, as had been experienced by others before, such as Lazarus (John 11:1–44), for then Jesus would have been subject to weakness and aging and eventually would have died again just as all other human beings die. Rather, when he rose from the dead, Jesus was the "firstfruits"[2] (1 Cor. 15:20, 23) of a new kind of human life, a life in which his body was made perfect, no longer subject to weakness, aging, or death, but able to live eternally.

It is true that two of Jesus' disciples did not recognize him when they walked with him on the road to Emmaus (Luke 24:13–32), but Luke specifically tells us that this was because "their eyes were kept from recognizing him" (Luke 24:16), and later "their eyes were opened, and they recognized him" (Luke 24:31). Mary Magdalene failed to recognize Jesus only for a moment (John 20:14–16), but it may have been still quite dark, and she was not at first looking at him—she had come the first time "while it was still dark" (John 20:1), and she "turned" to speak to Jesus once she recognized him (John 20:16).

On other occasions the disciples seem to have recognized Jesus fairly quickly (Matt. 28:9, 17; John 20:19–20, 26–28; 21:7, 12). When Jesus appeared to the eleven disciples in Jerusalem, they were initially startled and frightened (Luke 24:33, 37), yet when they saw Jesus' hands and his feet and watched him eat a piece of fish, they were convinced that he had risen from the dead. These examples indicate that there was a considerable degree of continuity between the physical appearance of Jesus before his death and after his resurrection. Yet Jesus did not look exactly as he had before he died, for in addition to the initial amazement of the disciples at what they apparently thought could not happen, there was probably sufficient difference in his physical appearance for Jesus not to be immediately recognized. Perhaps that difference in appearance was simply the difference between a man who had lived a life of suffering, hardship, and grief, and one whose body was restored to its full youthful appearance of perfect health. Though Jesus' body was still a physical body, it was raised as a transformed body, never able again to suffer, be weak or ill, or die; it had "put on immortality" (1 Cor. 15:53). Paul says the resurrection body is raised "imperishable . . . in glory . . . in power . . . a spiritual body" (1 Cor. 15:42–44).[3]

The fact that Jesus had a *physical body* that could be touched and handled after the

---

2. See discussion of the term *firstfruits* on p. 757, below.

3. By "spiritual body" Paul does not mean "immaterial" but rather "suited to and responsive to the guidance of the Spirit." In the Pauline Epistles, the word *spiritual* (Gk. *pneumatikos*) seldom means "nonphysical" but rather "consistent with the character and activity of the Holy Spirit" (see, e.g., Rom. 1:11; 7:14; 1 Cor. 2:13, 15; 3:1; 14:37; Gal. 6:1 ["you who are spiritual"]; Eph. 5:19). The RSV translation, "It is sown a *physical* body, it is raised a *spiritual* body," is very misleading, because Paul does not use the word that was available to him if he had meant to speak of a physical body (Gk. *sōmatikos*), but rather uses the word *psychikos*, which means, in this context, "natural" (so ESV, NIV, NASB), that is, a body that is living in its own life and strength and in the characteristics of this present age but is not fully subject to and conforming to the character and will of the Holy Spirit. Therefore, a clearer paraphrase would be, "It is sown a *natural* body subject to the characteristics and desires of this age, and governed by its own sinful will, but it is raised a *spiritual* body, completely subject to the will of the Holy Spirit and responsive to the Holy Spirit's guidance." Such a body is not at all "nonphysical," but it is a physical body raised to the degree of perfection for which God originally intended it.

resurrection is seen in that the disciples "took hold of his feet" (Matt. 28:9), that he appeared to the disciples on the road to Emmaus to be just another traveler on the road (Luke 24:15–18, 28–29), that he took bread and broke it (Luke 24:30), that he ate a piece of broiled fish to demonstrate clearly that he had a physical body and was not just a spirit, that Mary thought him to be a gardener (John 20:15), that "he showed them his hands and his side" (John 20:20), that he invited Thomas to touch his hands and his side (John 20:27), that he prepared breakfast for his disciples (John 21:12–13), and that he explicitly told them, "See my hands and my feet, that it is I myself. Touch me, and see. For *a spirit does not have flesh and bones as you see that I have*" (Luke 24:39). Peter said that the disciples "ate and drank with him after he rose from the dead" (Acts 10:41).

It is true that Jesus apparently was able to appear and disappear out of sight quite suddenly (Luke 24:31, 36; John 20:19, 26). Yet we should be careful not to draw too many conclusions from this fact, for not all the passages affirm that Jesus could suddenly appear or disappear; some just say that Jesus came and stood among the disciples. When Jesus suddenly vanished from the sight of the disciples in Emmaus, this may have been a special miraculous occurrence, such as happened when "the Spirit of the Lord carried Philip away, and the eunuch saw him no more" (Acts 8:39). Nor should we make too much of the fact that Jesus came and stood among the disciples on two occasions when the doors were "locked"[4] (John 20:19, 26), for no text says that Jesus "passed through walls" or anything like that. Indeed, on another occasion in the New Testament where someone needed to pass through a locked door, the door miraculously opened (see Acts 12:10).[5]

### 3. Both the Father and the Son Participated in the Resurrection

Some texts affirm that God the Father specifically raised Christ from the dead (Acts 2:24; Rom. 6:4; 1 Cor. 6:14; Gal. 1:1; Eph. 1:20), but other texts speak of Jesus as participating in his resurrection. Jesus says, "The reason my Father loves me is that I lay down my life—only to take it up again. No one takes it from me, but I lay it down of my own accord. I have authority to lay it down and authority to take it up again. This command I received from my Father" (John 10:17–18 NIV; cf. 2:19–21). It is best to conclude that both the Father and the Son were involved in the resurrection.[6] Indeed, Jesus says, "I am the resurrection and the life" (John 11:25; cf. Heb. 7:16).[7]

---

4. The Greek perfect participle *kekleismenon* may mean either that the doors were "shut" or that they were "locked."

5. I do not wish to argue that it is impossible that Jesus' resurrection body somehow passed through the door or the wall to enter the room, only that no verse in the Bible says that. It is possible, but the possibility does not deserve the status of an assured conclusion that it has reached in much popular preaching and much evangelical scholarship—it is just one possible inference from these verses, among several. Leon Morris says, "Some suggest that Jesus came right through the closed door, or that the door opened of its own accord or the like. But Scripture

says nothing of the mode of Jesus' entry into the room and we do well not to attempt too exact a definition" (*The Gospel according to John* [Grand Rapids: Eerdmans, 1971], 844). The problem with an affirmation that Jesus passed through walls is that it may cause people to think of Jesus' resurrection body as somehow nonmaterial, and this is contrary to the explicit affirmations of material characteristics that we have in several New Testament texts.

6. See the discussion of the participation of the Father and the Son in the resurrection in chapter 26, pp. 684–85.

7. Because the works of God are usually works of the entire

## 4. Doctrinal Significance of the Resurrection

### a. Christ's Resurrection Affirms the Goodness of the Material Creation.
The physical resurrection of Jesus and his eternal possession of a physical resurrection body give clear affirmation of the goodness of the material creation that God originally made: "God saw everything that he had made, and behold, *it was very good*" (Gen. 1:31). We as resurrected men and women will live forever in "new heavens and a new earth in which righteousness dwells" (2 Peter 3:13). We will live in a renewed earth that "will be set free from its bondage to corruption" (Rom. 8:21) and become like a new garden of Eden. There will be a new Jerusalem, and people "will bring into it the glory and the honor of the nations" (Rev. 21:26), and there will be "the river of the water of life, bright as crystal, flowing from the throne of God and of the Lamb through the middle of the street of the city; also, on either side of the river, the tree of life with its twelve kinds of fruit, yielding its fruit each month" (Rev. 22:1–2). In this very material, physical, renewed universe, it seems that we will need to live as human beings with physical bodies, suitable for life in God's renewed physical creation. Specifically, Jesus' physical resurrection body affirms the goodness of God's original creation of man not as a mere spirit like the angels, but as a creature with a physical body that was "very good." We must not fall into the error of thinking that nonmaterial existence is somehow a better form of existence for creatures: when God made us as the pinnacle of his creation, he gave us physical bodies. In a perfected physical body Jesus rose from the dead, now reigns in heaven, and will return to take us to be with himself forever.

### b. Christ's Resurrection Ensures Our Regeneration.
Peter says that "he has caused us to be born again to a living hope *through the resurrection* of Jesus Christ from the dead" (1 Peter 1:3). Here he explicitly connects Jesus' resurrection with our regeneration or new birth. When Jesus rose from the dead he had a new quality of life, a "resurrection life" in a human body and human spirit that were perfectly suited for fellowship and obedience to God forever. In his resurrection, Jesus earned for us a new life just like his. We do not receive all of that new "resurrection life" when we become Christians, for our bodies remain as they were, still subject to weakness, aging, and death. But in our spirits we are made alive with new resurrection power.[8] Thus it is through his resurrection that Christ earned for us the new kind of life we receive when we are "born again." This is why Paul can say that God "made us alive together with Christ—by grace you have been saved—and *raised us up with him*" (Eph. 2:5–6; cf. Col. 3:1). When God raised Christ from the dead he thought of us as somehow being raised "with Christ" and therefore deserving of the merits of Christ's resurrection. Paul says his goal in life is "that I may know him and *the power of his resurrection*" (Phil. 3:10). Paul knew that even in this life the resurrection of Christ gave new power for Christian ministry and obedience to God.

---

Trinity, it is probably true to say that the Holy Spirit also was involved in raising Jesus from the dead, but no text of Scripture affirms that explicitly (but see Rom. 8:11).

8. See chapter 34, pp. 850–56, for a discussion of regeneration.

Paul connects the resurrection of Christ with the spiritual power at work within us when he tells the Ephesians that he is praying that they would know "what is the immeasurable greatness of *his power* toward us who believe, according to the working of his great might that he worked in Christ *when he raised him from the dead* and seated him at his right hand in the heavenly places" (Eph. 1:19–20). Here Paul says that the power by which God raised Christ from the dead is the same power at work within us. Paul further sees us as raised in Christ when he says, "We were buried therefore with him by baptism into death, in order that, just as Christ was raised from the dead by the glory of the Father, we too might walk in newness of life. . . . So you also must consider yourselves dead to sin and alive to God in Christ Jesus" (Rom. 6:4, 11). This new resurrection power in us includes *power to gain more and more victory over remaining sin* in our lives—"Sin will have no dominion over you" (Rom. 6:14; cf. 1 Cor. 15:17)—even though we will never be perfect in this life. This resurrection power also includes *power for ministry in the work of the kingdom*. It was after Jesus' resurrection that he promised his disciples, "You will receive *power* when the Holy Spirit has come upon you, and you will be my witnesses in Jerusalem and in all Judea and Samaria, and to the end of the earth" (Acts 1:8). This new intensified power for proclaiming the gospel and working miracles and triumphing over the opposition of the enemy was given to the disciples after Christ's resurrection from the dead and was part of the new resurrection power that characterized their Christian lives.

**c. Christ's Resurrection Ensures Our Justification.** In only one passage does Paul explicitly connect Christ's resurrection with our justification (or our receiving a declaration that we are not guilty but righteous before God).[9] Paul says that Jesus "was delivered up for our trespasses and *raised for our justification*" (Rom. 4:25). When Christ was raised from the dead, it was God's declaration of approval of Christ's work of redemption. Because Christ "humbled himself by becoming obedient to the point of death, even death on a cross" (Phil. 2:8), "God has highly exalted him" (Phil. 2:9). By raising Christ from the dead, God the Father was in effect saying that he approved of Christ's work of suffering and dying for our sins, that his work was completed, and that Christ no longer had any need to remain dead. There was no penalty left to pay for sin, no more wrath of God to bear, no more guilt or liability to punishment—all had been completely paid for, and no guilt remained. In the resurrection, God was saying to Christ, "I approve of what you have done, and you find favor in my sight."

This explains how Paul can say that Christ was "raised for our justification" (Rom. 4:25). If God "raised us up with him" (Eph. 2:6), then by virtue of our union with Christ, God's declaration of approval of Christ is also his declaration of approval of us. When the Father in essence said to Christ, "All the penalty for sins has been paid and I find you not guilty but righteous in my sight," he was thereby making the declaration

9. See chapter 36, pp. 884–908, on justification.

that would also apply to us once we trusted in Christ for salvation. In this way Christ's resurrection also gave final proof that he had earned our justification.

**d. Christ's Resurrection Ensures That We Will Receive Perfect Resurrection Bodies as Well.** The New Testament several times connects Jesus' resurrection with our final bodily resurrection. "God raised the Lord and will also raise us up by his power" (1 Cor. 6:14). Similarly, "He who raised the Lord Jesus will raise us also with Jesus and bring us with you into his presence" (2 Cor. 4:14). But the most extensive discussion of the connection between Christ's resurrection and our own is found in 1 Corinthians 15:12–58. There Paul says that Christ is the "firstfruits of those who have fallen asleep" (1 Cor. 15:20). In calling Christ the "firstfruits" (Gk. *aparchē*), Paul uses a metaphor from agriculture to indicate that we will be like Christ. Just as the "firstfruits," or the first taste of the ripening crop, show what the rest of the harvest will be like for that crop, so too Christ as the "firstfruits" shows what our resurrection bodies will be like when, in God's final "harvest," he raises us from the dead and brings us into his presence.[10]

After Jesus' resurrection, he still had the nail prints in his hands and feet and the mark from the spear in his side (John 20:27). People sometimes wonder if that indicates that the scars of serious injuries that we have received in this life will also remain on our resurrection bodies. The answer is that we probably will not have any scars from injuries or wounds received in this life, but our bodies will be made perfect, "incorruptible" and raised "in glory." The scars from Jesus' crucifixion are unique because they are an eternal reminder of his sufferings and death for us.[11] The fact that he retains those scars does not mean that we will retain ours. Rather, all will be healed, and all will be made perfect and whole.

## 5. Ethical Significance of the Resurrection

Paul also sees that the resurrection has application to our obedience to God in this life. After a long discussion of the resurrection, Paul concludes by encouraging his readers, "*Therefore*, my beloved brothers, be steadfast, immovable, always abounding in the work of the Lord, knowing that in the Lord your labor is not in vain" (1 Cor. 15:58). Because Christ was raised from the dead, and because we too shall be raised from the dead, we should continue steadfastly in the Lord's work. Everything that we do to bring people into the kingdom and build them up will indeed have eternal significance because we shall all be raised on the day when Christ returns and live with him forever.

Second, Paul encourages us, when we think about the resurrection, to focus on our future heavenly reward as our goal. He sees the resurrection as a time when all the struggles of this life will be repaid. But if Christ has not been raised, and if there is no resurrection, then "your faith is futile and you are still in your sins. Then those also who

---

10. See chapter 42, pp. 1021–26, for a more detailed discussion of the nature of our resurrection bodies.

11. In fact, the evidences of the severe beating and disfigurement that Jesus suffered before his crucifixion were probably all healed, and only the scars in his hands, feet, and side remained as testimony to his death for us: Jesus was raised "in glory" (cf. 1 Cor. 15:43), not in horrible disfigurement just barely brought back to life.

have fallen asleep in Christ have perished. If in Christ we have hope in this life only, we are of all people most to be pitied" (1 Cor. 15:17–19; cf. v. 32). But because Christ has been raised, and because we have been raised with him, we are to seek for a heavenly reward and set our mind on things of heaven:

> If then you have been raised with Christ, *seek the things that are above*, where Christ is, seated at the right hand of God. *Set your minds on things that are above*, not on things that are on earth. For you have died, and your life is hidden with Christ in God. When Christ who is your life appears, then you also will appear with him in glory. (Col. 3:1–4)

A third ethical application of the resurrection is the obligation to stop yielding to sin in our lives. When Paul says we are to consider ourselves "dead to sin and alive to God in Christ Jesus" by virtue of the resurrection of Christ and his resurrection power within us (Rom. 6:11), he then goes on immediately to say, "*Let not sin therefore reign* in your mortal body. . . . Do not present your members to sin" (Rom. 6:12–13). The fact that we have this new resurrection power over the domination of sin in our lives is used by Paul as a reason to exhort us not to sin anymore.

## B. Ascension into Heaven
### 1. Christ Ascended to a Place

After Jesus' resurrection, he was on earth for forty days (Acts 1:3), then he led his disciples out to Bethany, just outside Jerusalem, and "lifting up his hands he blessed them. While he blessed them, he parted from them and was carried up into heaven" (Luke 24:50–51). A similar account is given by Luke in the opening section of Acts:

> And when he had said these things, as they were looking on, he was lifted up, and a cloud took him out of their sight. And while they were gazing into heaven as he went, behold, two men stood by them in white robes, and said, "Men of Galilee, why do you stand looking into heaven? This Jesus, who was taken up from you into heaven, will come in the same way as you saw him go into heaven." (Acts 1:9–11)

These narratives describe an event that is clearly designed to show the disciples that Jesus went *to a place*. He did not suddenly disappear from them, never to be seen by them again. He gradually ascended as they were watching, and then a cloud (apparently the cloud of God's glory) took him from their sight. But the angels immediately said that he would come back *in the same way* in which he had gone into heaven. The fact that Jesus had a resurrection body that was subject to spatial limitations (it could be at only one place at one time) means that Jesus went *somewhere* when he ascended into heaven.

It is surprising that even some evangelical theologians hesitate to affirm that heaven is a place or that Jesus ascended to a definite location somewhere in the space-time universe. Admittedly we cannot now see where Jesus is, but that is not because he passed into some ethereal "state of being" that has no location at all in the space-time universe but rather because our eyes are unable to see the unseen spiritual world that exists all around us. There are angels around us, but we simply cannot see them because our eyes do not have that capacity: Elisha was surrounded by an army of angels and chariots of fire protecting him from the Syrians at Dothan, but Elisha's servant was not able to see those angels until God opened his eyes so that he could see things that existed in that spiritual dimension (2 Kings 6:17). Similarly, when Stephen was dying, God gave him a special ability to see the world that is now hidden from our eyes, for he "gazed into heaven and saw the glory of God, and Jesus standing at the right hand of God. And he said, 'Behold, I see the heavens opened, and the Son of Man standing at the right hand of God'" (Acts 7:55–56). And Jesus himself said, "In my Father's house are many rooms. If it were not so, would I have told you that I go to prepare *a place* for you? And if I go and prepare a place for you, I will come again and take you to myself, that where I am you may be also" (John 14:2–3).

Of course we cannot now say exactly where heaven is. Scripture sometimes pictures people as ascending up into heaven (as Jesus did, and Elijah) or coming down from heaven (as the angels in Jacob's dream, Gen. 28:12), so we are justified in thinking of heaven as somewhere "above" the earth. Admittedly the earth is round and it rotates, so where heaven is we are simply unable to say more precisely—Scripture does not tell us. But the repeated emphasis on the fact that Jesus went *somewhere* (as did Elijah, 2 Kings 2:11), and the fact that the New Jerusalem will come down out of heaven from God (Rev. 21:2), all indicate that there is clearly a localization of heaven in the space-time universe. Those who do not believe in Scripture may scoff at such an idea and wonder how it can be so, just as the first Russian cosmonaut who came back from space and declared that he did not see God or heaven anywhere, but that simply points to the blindness of their eyes toward the unseen spiritual world; it does not indicate that heaven does not exist in a certain place. In fact, the ascension of Jesus into heaven is designed to teach us that heaven does exist as a place in the space-time universe. (See chapter 57 for a further discussion of the nature of heaven.)

## 2. Christ Received Glory and Honor That Had Not Been His Before as the God-Man

When Jesus ascended into heaven, he received glory, honor, and authority that had never been his before as one who was both God and man. Before Jesus died, he prayed, "Father, glorify me in your own presence with the glory that I had with you before the world existed" (John 17:5).[12] In his sermon at Pentecost, Peter said that Jesus was

---

12. This verse shows that the glory Jesus received had been his before as eternal Son of God, but it had not been his before in his incarnate form as God-man.

"exalted at the right hand of God" (Acts 2:33), and Paul declared that "God has highly exalted him" (Phil. 2:9) and that Jesus was "taken up in glory" (1 Tim. 3:16; cf. Heb. 1:4). Christ is now in heaven with the angelic choirs singing praise to him with the words, "Worthy is the Lamb who was slain, to receive power and wealth and wisdom and might and honor and glory and blessing!" (Rev. 5:12).[13]

### 3. Christ Was Seated at God's Right Hand (Christ's Session)

One specific aspect of Christ's ascension into heaven and receiving of honor was the fact that he *sat down* at the right hand of God. This is sometimes called his *session* at God's right hand. (The word *session* formerly meant "the act of sitting down," but it no longer has that meaning in ordinary English usage today.)

The Old Testament predicted that the Messiah would sit at the right hand of God: "The LORD says to my Lord: 'Sit at my right hand, until I make your enemies your footstool'" (Ps. 110:1). When Christ ascended back into heaven he received the fulfillment of that promise: "After making purification for sins, he *sat down* at the right hand of the Majesty on high" (Heb. 1:3). This welcoming into the presence of God and sitting at God's right hand is a dramatic indication of the completion of Christ's work of redemption. Just as a human being will sit down at the completion of a large task to enjoy the satisfaction of having accomplished it, so Jesus sat at the right hand of God, visibly demonstrating that his work of redemption was completed.

In addition to showing the completion of Christ's work of redemption, the act of sitting at God's right hand is an indication that he received authority over the universe. Paul says that God "raised him from the dead and *seated him at his right hand* in the heavenly places, far above all rule and authority and power and dominion, and above every name that is named" (Eph. 1:20–21). Similarly, Peter says that Jesus "has gone into heaven and is *at the right hand of God*, with angels, authorities, and powers having been subjected to him" (1 Peter 3:22). Paul also alludes to Psalm 110:1 when he says that Christ "must reign until he has put all his enemies under his feet" (1 Cor. 15:25).

One additional aspect of the authority that Christ received from the Father when he sat at his right hand was the authority to pour out the Holy Spirit on the church. Peter says on the Day of Pentecost, "Being therefore exalted at the right hand of God, and having *received from the Father the promise of the Holy Spirit*, he has poured out this that you yourselves are seeing and hearing" (Acts 2:33).

The fact that Jesus now sits at the right hand of God in heaven does not mean that he is perpetually "fixed" there or that he is inactive. He is also seen as standing at God's right hand (Acts 7:56) and as walking among the seven golden lampstands in heaven (Rev. 2:1). Just as a human king sits on his royal throne at his accession to the kingship

---

13. Some Lutheran theologians have also said that when Jesus ascended into heaven his human nature became ubiqui- tous (everywhere present); see the discussion in chapter 26, p. 695n42.

but engages in many other activities throughout each day, so too Christ sat at the right hand of God as a dramatic evidence of the completion of his redemptive work and his reception of authority over the universe but is certainly engaged in other activities in heaven as well.

## 4. Christ's Ascension Has Doctrinal Significance for Our Lives

Just as the resurrection has profound implications for our lives, so Christ's ascension has significant implications for us. First, since we are united with Christ in every aspect of his work of redemption,[14] Christ's ascension into heaven *foreshadows our future ascension into heaven with him.* "We who are alive, who are left, will be caught up together with them in the clouds to meet the Lord in the air, and so we will always be with the Lord" (1 Thess. 4:17). The author of Hebrews wants us to run the race of life with the knowledge that we are following in Jesus' steps and will eventually arrive at the blessings of life in heaven that he is now enjoying: "Let us run with endurance the race that is set before us, looking to Jesus the founder and perfecter of our faith, who for the joy that was set before him endured the cross, despising the shame, and is seated at the right hand of the throne of God" (Heb. 12:1–2). And Jesus himself says that he will one day take us to be with him (John 14:3).

Second, Jesus' ascension *gives us assurance that our final home will be in heaven with him.* "In my Father's house are many rooms. If it were not so, would I have told you that I go to prepare a place for you? And if I go and prepare a place for you, I will come again and take you to myself, that where I am you may be also" (John 14:2–3). Jesus was a man like us in every way yet without sin, and he has gone before us so that eventually we might follow him there and live with him forever. The fact that Jesus has already ascended into heaven and achieved the goal set before him gives great assurance to us that we will eventually go there also.

Third, because of our union with Christ in his ascension, *we are able to share now (in part) in Christ's authority* over the universe, and we will later share in it more fully. This is what Paul points to when he says that God "raised us up with him and *seated us with him in the heavenly places* in Christ Jesus" (Eph. 2:6). We are not physically present in heaven, of course, for we remain here on earth at the present time. But if Christ's session at God's right hand refers to his reception of authority, then the fact that God has made us sit with Christ means that we share in some measure in the authority that Christ has, authority to contend against "the spiritual forces of evil in the heavenly places" (Eph. 6:12; cf. vv. 10–18) and to do battle with weapons that "have divine power to destroy strongholds" (2 Cor. 10:4). This sharing in Christ's authority over the universe will be made more fully our possession in the age to come: "Do you not know that we are to

---

14. See the discussion of union with Christ in chapter 43, pp. 1031–39.

judge angels?" (1 Cor. 6:3). Moreover, we will share with Christ in his authority over the creation that God has made (Heb. 2:5–8).[15] Jesus promises, "The one who conquers and who keeps my works until the end, to him I will give authority over the nations, and he will rule them with a rod of iron, as when earthen pots are broken in pieces, even as I myself have received authority from my Father" (Rev. 2:26–27). He also promises, "The one who conquers, I will grant him to sit with me on my throne, as I also conquered and sat down with my Father on his throne" (Rev. 3:21). These are amazing promises of our future sharing in Christ's sitting at the right hand of God, promises that we will not fully understand until the age to come.

### C. States of Jesus Christ

In talking about the life, death, and resurrection of Christ, theologians have sometimes talked about the "states of Jesus Christ." By this they mean the different relationships Jesus had to God's law for mankind, to the possession of authority, and to receiving honor. Generally two states (humiliation and exaltation) are distinguished. Thus the doctrine of "the twofold state of Christ" is the teaching that Christ experienced first the state of humiliation and then the state of exaltation.

Within the humiliation of Christ are included his incarnation, suffering, death, and burial. Sometimes a fifth aspect (descent into hell) is included, but as explained above, the position taken in this book is that that concept is not supported in Scripture.

In the exaltation of Christ, there are also four aspects: his resurrection, ascension into heaven, session at the right hand of God, and return in glory and power. Many systematic theologies use the state of humiliation and the state of exaltation as broad categories to organize their discussion of Jesus' work.[16]

# QUESTIONS FOR PERSONAL APPLICATION

1. As you read this chapter, what aspects of the Bible's teaching about a resurrection body were new to your understanding? Can you think of some characteristics of the resurrection body that you especially look forward to? How does the thought of having such a body make you feel?

2. What things would you like to do now but find yourself unable to do because of the weakness or limitations of your own physical body? Do you think these activities would be appropriate to your life in heaven? Will you be able to do them then?

---

15. See discussion of Heb. 2:5–8 in chapter 26, p. 676; see also p. 349.

16. Although this is a useful method of organization, I have not used it in this book. However, all of the topics included in discussions of these two states have been covered in this and other chapters of this book. For more detailed discussion, see Wayne Grudem, "States of Jesus Christ," *EDT*, 1052–54.

3. When you were born again, you received new spiritual life within. If you think of this new spiritual life as part of the resurrection power of Christ working within you, how does that give you encouragement in living the Christian life and in ministering to people's needs?
4. The Bible says that you are now seated with Christ in the heavenly places (Eph. 2:6). As you meditate on this fact, how will it affect your prayer life and your engaging in spiritual warfare against demonic forces?
5. When you think of Christ now in heaven, does it cause you to focus more attention on things that will have eternal significance? Does it increase your assurance that you will someday be with him in heaven? How do you feel about the prospect of reigning with Christ over the nations and over angels as well?

**Special Terms**

*ascension*
*exaltation of Christ*
*humiliation of Christ*
*incorruptible*
*raised in glory*
*raised in power*
*resurrection*
*session*
*spiritual body*
*states of Jesus Christ*

# BIBLIOGRAPHY

(For an explanation of this bibliography see the note on the bibliography to chapter 1, pp. 23–24. Complete bibliographical data may be found on pp. 1489–96.)

## SECTIONS IN EVANGELICAL SYSTEMATIC THEOLOGIES

*1. Anglican (Episcopalian)*
1882–92 . . . . . Litton, 195–96
2001 . . . . . . . . Packer, 125–28
1930 . . . . . . . . Thomas, 73–87
2013 . . . . . . . . Bird, 435–59

*2. Arminian (Wesleyan or Methodist)*
1875–76 . . . . . Pope, 3:401–6
1992 . . . . . . . . Oden, 2:451–526
2002 . . . . . . . . Cottrell, 12, 27, 42, 272–82

*3. Baptist*
1767 . . . . . . . . Gill, 1:583–602

1907 . . . . . . . . Strong, 706–10, 1015–23
1917 . . . . . . . . Mullins, 44–46, 158–64,
        472–78
1983–85 . . . . . Erickson, 769–79
1987–94 . . . . . Lewis & Demarest, 2:437–96
1990–95 . . . . . Garrett, 2: 81–132
2007 . . . . . . . . Akin, 519–20, 590–96
2013 . . . . . . . . Erickson, 631–33, 709–12

*4. Dispensational*
1947 . . . . . . . . Chafer, 5:231–79
1949 . . . . . . . . Thiessen, 243–50
1986 . . . . . . . . Ryrie, 267–74
2002–2005 . . Geisler, 2:615–28
2017 . . . . . . . . MacArthur and Mayhue,
        565–66

*5. Lutheran*
1917–24 . . . . . Pieper, 2:324–30
1934 . . . . . . . . Mueller, 295–300

### 6. Reformed (or Presbyterian)

1679–85 . . . . . Turretin, *IET*, 1:36, 2:364–69

1861 . . . . . . . . Heppe, 488–509

1871–73 . . . . . Hodge, 2:626–38

1894 . . . . . . . . Shedd, 653

1906–11 . . . . . Bavinck, *RD*, 3:418–47

1910 . . . . . . . . Vos, 3:187

1887–1921 . . . Warfield, *SSW*, 1:178–202; *PWC*, 535–48

1937–66 . . . . . Murray, *CW*, 1:40–43; *CW*, 4:82–91

1938 . . . . . . . . Berkhof, 344–55

1962 . . . . . . . . Buswell, 2:32–40

1998 . . . . . . . . Reymond, 565–582

2008 . . . . . . . . Van Genderen and Velema, 471–486–501

2011 . . . . . . . . Horton, 521–550

2013 . . . . . . . . Frame, 89, 135, 666–67, 908–909

2013 . . . . . . . . Culver, 601–622

2016 . . . . . . . . Allen and Swain, 235–36

2017 . . . . . . . . Barrett, 738–39

2019 . . . . . . . . Letham, 196, 574–86, 862–65

### 7. Renewal (or charismatic/Pentecostal)

1988–92 . . . . . Williams, 1:381–413

1993 . . . . . . . . Menzies and Horton, 69–72

1995 . . . . . . . . Horton, 152–53, 603–04

2008 . . . . . . . . Duffield and Van Cleave, 197–209

## SECTIONS IN REPRESENTATIVE ROMAN CATHOLIC SYSTEMATIC THEOLOGIES

### 1. Roman Catholic: Traditional

1955 . . . . . . . . Ott, 192–96

### 2. Roman Catholic: Post–Vatican II

1980 . . . . . . . . McBrien, 1:405–17

2012 . . . . . . . . *CCC*, paragraphs 638–67

## OTHER WORKS

Adams, Eric W. "Resurrection." In *BTDB*, 676–79.

Allison, Gregg. *Historical Theology: An Introduction to Christian Doctrine; A Companion to Wayne Grudem's* Systematic Theology. Grand Rapids: Zondervan, 2011, 411–29.

Bowald, M. A. "Ascension of Christ." In *EDT3*, 87–88.

Bray, G. L. "Ascension and Heavenly Session of Christ." In *NDT1*, 46–47.

Bryan, David K., and David W. Pao, eds. *Ascent into Heaven in Luke-Acts: New Explorations of Luke's Narrative Hinge*. Minneapolis: Fortress. 2016.

Chester, Tim and Jonny Woodrow. *The Ascension: Humanity in the Presence of God*. Fearn, Ross-shire: Christian Focus, 2013.

Craig, William Lane. *The Son Rises: The Historical Evidence for the Resurrection of Jesus*. Chicago: Moody Publishers, 1981.

Dawson, Gerrit Scott. *Jesus Ascended: The Meaning of Christ's Continuing Incarnation*. Phillipsburg, NJ: P&R, 2004.

Farrow, Douglas. *Ascension and Ecclesia : On the Significance of the Doctrine of the Ascension for Ecclesiology and Christian Cosmology*. Grand Rapids: Eerdmans, 1999.

Fuller, Daniel P. *Easter Faith and History*. Grand Rapids: Eerdmans, 1965.

Gaffin, Richard B., Jr. *Resurrection and Redemption: A Study in Paul's Soteriology*. Formerly, *The Centrality of the Resurrection: A Study in Paul's Soteriology*. Phillipsburg, NJ: Presbyterian and Reformed, 1978.

Giles, K. "Ascension." *In DJG*, 46–50.

Habermas, G. R. "Resurrection of Christ." In *EDT3*, 742–44.

———, and Anthony Flew. *Did Jesus Rise From the Dead? The Resurrection Debate*. Edited by Terry L. Miethe. New York: Harper and Row, 1987.

Harris, Murray J. *From Grave to Glory: Resurrection in the New Testament, Including a Response to Norman L. Geisler*. Grand Rapids: Zondervan, 1990.

———. "Resurrection, General." In *NDT1*, 581–82.

Kreitzer, L. J. "Resurrection." In *DPL*, 805–812.

Ladd, George E. *I Believe in the Resurrection of Jesus*. Grand Rapids: Eerdmans, 1975.

Larkin, W. J., Jr. "Ascension." In *DLNT*, 95–102.

Macleod, D. "Resurrection of Christ." In *NDT1*, 582–85.

McDowell, Josh, and Sean McDowell. *Evidence for the Resurrection: What It Means for Your Relationship with God*. Ventura, CA: Regal, 2009.

Merrick, J. R. A. "Resurrection of Christ." In *NDT2*, 765–69.

Milligan, William. *The Ascension and Heavenly Priesthood of Our Lord*. Eugene, OR: Wipf & Stock, 2006.

Morison, Frank. *Who Moved the Stone?* London: Faber and Faber, 1930; reprint, Grand Rapids: Zondervan, 1958.

O'Donovan, Oliver. *Resurrection and Moral Order*. Leicester: Inter-Varsity Press, 1986.

Orr, Peter C. *Exalted Above the Heavens: The Risen and Ascended Christ*. Downers Grove, IL: InterVarsity Press, 2019.

Osborne, G. R. "Resurrection." In *DJG*, 673–88.

Ovey, M. "Ascension [and Heavenly Session of Christ]." In *NDT2*, 66–68.

Patterson, Paige. "The Work of Christ." In *A Theology for the Church*, edited by Daniel L. Akin et al., 589–596. Nashville: B&H, 2007.

Prime, Derek. *The Shout of a King: The Ascension of Our Lord Jesus Christ and His Continuing Work Today*. Epsom, UK: DayOne, 1999.

Ross, A. "Ascension of Christ." In *EDT*, 86–87.

Stobart, A. J. "Resurrection, General." In *NDT2*, 769–70.

Swete, Henry Barclay. *The Ascended Christ: A Study in the Earliest Christian Teaching*. London: Macmillan, 1910.

Tait, Arthur J. *The Heavenly Session of Our Lord: An Introduction to the History of the Doctrine*. London: Robert Scott, 1912.

Tenney, Merrill C. *The Reality of the Resurrection*. New York: Harper and Row, 1963.

Thomas, Derek. *Taken Up into Heaven: The Ascension of Christ*. Darlington: Evangelical, 1996.

Toon, Peter. *The Ascension of Our Lord*. Nashville: Nelson, 1984.

Torrance, Thomas F. *Space, Time and Resurrection*. Edinburgh: T&T Clark, 2019.

Travis, S. H. "Resurrection." In *DLNT*, 1015–20.

Trotter, Andrew H., Jr. "Ascension of Jesus Christ." In *BTDB*, 38–40.

Wenham, John. *The Easter Enigma*. London: Paternoster, 1984.

## SCRIPTURE MEMORY PASSAGE

**1 Corinthians 15:20–23:** But in fact Christ has been raised from the dead, the firstfruits of those who have fallen asleep. For as by a man came death, by a man has come also the resurrection of the dead. For as in Adam all die, so also in Christ shall all be made alive. But each in his own order: Christ the firstfruits, then at his coming those who belong to Christ.

## HYMN

### "Christ the Lord Is Risen Today"

*"Christ the Lord is risen today," al-le-lu-ia!*
*Sons of men and angels say; al-le-lu-ia!*

*Raise your joys and triumphs high; al-le-lu-ia!*
*Sing, ye heav'ns, and earth reply; al-le-lu-ia!*

*Vain the stone, the watch, the seal; al-le-lu-ia!*
*Christ has burst the gates of hell: al-le-lu-ia!*
*Death in vain forbids him rise; al-le-lu-ia!*
*Christ hath opened paradise. Al-le-lu-ia!*

*Lives again our glorious King; al-le-lu-ia!*
*Where, O death, is now thy sting? Al-le-lu-ia!*
*Once he died, our souls to save; al-le-lu-ia!*
*Where thy victory, O grave? Al-le-lu-ia!*

*Soar we now where Christ has led, al-le-lu-ia!*
*Following our exalted Head; al-le-lu-ia!*
*Made like him, like him we rise; al-le-lu-ia!*
*Ours the cross, the grave, the skies. Al-le-lu-ia!*

*Hail, the Lord of earth and heav'n! Al-le-lu-ia!*
*Praise to thee by both be giv'n; al-le-lu-ia!*
*Thee we greet triumphant now; al-le-lu-ia!*
*Hail, the resurrection thou! Al-le-lu-ia!*

Author: Charles Wesley, 1739

## CONTEMPORARY WORSHIP SONG

### "Christ Is Risen"

*Let no one caught in sin remain*
*Inside the lie of inward shame,*
*But fix our eyes upon the cross,*
*And run to Him who showed great love*
*And bled for us*
*Freely You've bled for us.*

*Chorus*
*Christ is risen from the dead,*
*Trampling over death by death.*
*Come awake, come awake,*
*Come and rise up from the grave.*
*Christ is risen from the dead.*
*We are one with Him again.*
*Come awake, come awake,*
*Come and rise up from the grave.*

*Beneath the weight of all our sin,*
*You bowed to none but heaven's will.*
*No scheme of hell, no scoffer's crown,*
*No burden great can hold You down.*
*In strength You reign.*
*Forever let Your church proclaim.*

*Bridge*
*O death, where is your sting?*
*O hell, where is your victory?*
*O church, come stand in the light.*
*The glory of God has defeated the night.*
*Singing, O death, where is your sting?*
*O hell, where is your victory?*
*O church, come stand in the light.*
*Our God is not dead. He's alive! He's alive!*

Words by Matt Maher and Mia Fieldes[17]

# CHAPTER 29

# The Offices of Christ

*How is Christ prophet, priest, and king?*

## EXPLANATION AND SCRIPTURAL BASIS

There were three major offices among the people of Israel in the Old Testament: the *prophet* (such as Nathan, 2 Sam. 7:2), the *priest* (such as Abiathar, 1 Sam. 30:7), and the *king* (such as King David, 2 Sam. 5:3). These three offices were distinct. The prophet spoke God's words to the people; the priest offered sacrifices, prayers, and praises to God on behalf of the people; and the king ruled over the people as God's representative. These three offices foreshadowed Christ's work in different ways. Therefore, we can look again at Christ's work, now thinking about the perspective of these three offices or categories.[1] Christ fulfills these three offices in the following ways: as *prophet* he reveals God to us and speaks God's words to us, as *priest* he both offers a sacrifice to God on our behalf and is himself the sacrifice that is offered, and as *king* he rules over the church and over the universe as well. We now turn to discuss each of these offices in more detail.

### A. CHRIST AS PROPHET

The Old Testament prophets spoke God's words to the people. Moses was the first major prophet, and he wrote the first five books of the Bible, the Pentateuch. After Moses there was a succession of other prophets who spoke and wrote God's words.[2] But Moses predicted that sometime another prophet like himself would come:

> The LORD your God will raise up for you a *prophet like me* from among you, from your brothers—it is to him you shall listen—just as you desired of the LORD your God. . . . And the LORD said to me . . . "I will raise up for them a prophet like you from among their brothers. And I will put my words in his mouth, and he shall speak to them all that I command him." (Deut. 18:15–18)

However, when we look at the gospels we see that Jesus is not *primarily* viewed as a prophet or as *the* prophet like Moses, though there are occasional references to

---

1. John Calvin (1509–64) was the first major theologian to apply these three categories to the work of Christ (see his *Institutes of the Christian Religion*, book 2, chapter 15). The categories have been adapted by many subsequent theologians as a helpful way of understanding various aspects of Christ's work.

2. See the discussion of the writing of the books in the Old Testament canon in chapter 3, p. 39.

this effect. Often those who call Jesus a "prophet" know very little about him. For instance, various opinions of Jesus were circulating: "Some say John the Baptist, others say Elijah, and others Jeremiah *or one of the prophets*" (Matt. 16:14; cf. Luke 9:8). When Jesus raised the son of the widow of Nain from the dead, the people were afraid and said, "A great *prophet* has arisen among us!" (Luke 7:16). When Jesus told the Samaritan woman at the well something of her past life, she immediately responded, "Sir, I perceive that you are *a prophet*" (John 4:19). But she did not then know very much at all about him. The reaction of the man born blind who was healed in the temple was similar: "He is a prophet" (John 9:17; note that his belief in Jesus' messiahship and deity did not come until v. 37, after a subsequent conversation with Jesus).[3] Therefore, *prophet* is not a primary designation of Jesus or one used frequently by him or about him.

Nevertheless, there was still an expectation that *the* prophet like Moses would come (Deut. 18:15, 18). For instance, after Jesus had multiplied the loaves and fish, some people exclaimed, "This is indeed *the Prophet* who is to come into the world!" (John 6:14; cf. 7:40). Peter also identified Christ as the prophet predicted by Moses (see Acts 3:22–24, quoting Deut. 18:15). So Jesus is indeed the prophet predicted by Moses.

Nevertheless, it is significant that in the Epistles Jesus is never called a prophet or *the* prophet. This is especially significant in the opening chapters of Hebrews because there was a clear opportunity to identify Jesus as a prophet if the author had wished to do so. He begins by saying, "Long ago, at many times and in many ways, God spoke to our fathers *by the prophets*, but in these last days he has spoken to us *by his Son*" (Heb. 1:1–2). Then after discussing the greatness of the Son, in chapters 1–2, the author concludes this section not by saying, "Therefore, consider Jesus, the greatest prophet of all," or something like that, but rather by saying, "Therefore, holy brothers, you who share in a heavenly calling, consider Jesus, *the apostle* and high priest of our confession" (Heb. 3:1).

Why did the New Testament Epistles avoid calling Jesus a prophet? Although Jesus is the prophet whom Moses predicted, he is also far greater than any of the Old Testament prophets in two ways:

1. He is the one *about whom* the prophecies in the Old Testament were made. When Jesus spoke with the two disciples on the road to Emmaus, he took them through the entire Old Testament, showing how the prophecies pointed to him: "Beginning with Moses *and all the Prophets*, he interpreted to them in all the Scriptures the things concerning himself" (Luke 24:27). He told these disciples that they were "slow of heart to believe *all that the prophets had spoken*," showing that it was "necessary that the Christ should suffer these things and enter into his glory" (Luke 24:25–26; cf. 1 Peter 1:11,

---

3. In Luke 24:19 the two travelers on the road to Emmaus also refer to Jesus as a "prophet," thus putting him in a general category of religious leaders sent from God, perhaps for the benefit of the stranger whom they presumed to have little knowledge of the events surrounding Jesus' life.

which says that the Old Testament prophets "predicted the sufferings of Christ and the subsequent glories"). Thus the Old Testament prophets looked *forward* to Christ in what they wrote, and the New Testament apostles looked *back* to Christ and interpreted his life for the benefit of the church.

2. Jesus was not merely a messenger of revelation from God (like all the other prophets) but was himself the *source* of revelation from God. Rather than saying, as all the Old Testament prophets did, "Thus says the Lord," Jesus could begin divinely authoritative teaching with the amazing statement, "But *I say* to you" (Matt. 5:22, et al.). The word of the Lord *came to* the Old Testament prophets, but Jesus spoke on his own authority as the eternal Word of God (John 1:1) who perfectly revealed the Father to us (John 14:9; Heb. 1:1–2).

In the broader sense of *prophet*, meaning one who reveals God to us and speaks to us the words of God, Christ is of course truly and fully a prophet. In fact, he is the one whom all the Old Testament prophets prefigured in their speech and in their actions.

## B. Christ as Priest

In the Old Testament, the priests were appointed by God to offer sacrifices. They also offered prayers and praise to God on behalf of the people. In so doing they "sanctified" the people or made them acceptable to come into God's presence, albeit in a limited way during the Old Testament period. In the New Testament Jesus becomes our great high priest. This theme is developed extensively in the letter to the Hebrews, where we find that Jesus functions as priest in two ways.

### 1. Jesus Offered a Perfect Sacrifice for Sin

The sacrifice that Jesus offered for sins was not the blood of animals such as bulls or goats: "For it is impossible for the blood of bulls and goats to take away sins" (Heb. 10:4). Instead, Jesus offered himself as a perfect sacrifice: "But as it is, he has appeared once for all at the end of the ages to put away sin *by the sacrifice of himself*" (Heb. 9:26). This was a completed and final sacrifice, never to be repeated, a theme frequently emphasized in the book of Hebrews (see 7:27; 9:12, 24–28; 10:1–2, 10, 12, 14; 13:12). Therefore, Jesus fulfilled all the expectations that were prefigured not only in the Old Testament sacrifices but also in the lives and actions of the priests who offered them: he was both the sacrifice and the priest who offered the sacrifice. Jesus is now the "great high priest who has passed through the heavens" (Heb. 4:14) and who has appeared "in the presence of God on our behalf" (Heb. 9:24), since he has offered a sacrifice that ended for all time the need for any further sacrifices.

### 2. Jesus Continually Brings Us Near to God

Not only did the Old Testament priests offer sacrifices, but also in a representative way they came into the presence of God from time to time on behalf of the people. But

Jesus does much more than that. As our perfect high priest, he continually *leads us* into God's presence so that we no longer have need of a Jerusalem temple, or of a special priesthood to stand between us and God. And Jesus does not come into the inner part (the holy of holies) of the earthly temple in Jerusalem, but he has gone into the heavenly equivalent to the holy of holies, the very presence of God himself in heaven (Heb. 9:24). Therefore we have a hope that follows him there: "We have this as a sure and steadfast anchor of the soul, a hope that *enters into the inner place behind the curtain*, where Jesus has gone as a forerunner on our behalf, having become a high priest forever" (Heb. 6:19–20). This means that we have a far greater privilege than those people who lived at the time of the Old Testament temple. They could not even enter into the first room of the temple, the holy place, for only the priests could go there. Then into the inner room of the temple, the holy of holies, only the high priest could go, and he could only enter there once a year (Heb. 9:1–7). But when Jesus offered a perfect sacrifice for sins, the curtain or veil of the temple that closed off the holy of holies was torn in two from top to bottom (Luke 23:45), indicating in a symbolic way on earth that the way of access to God in heaven was opened by Jesus' death. Therefore, the author of Hebrews can make this amazing exhortation to all believers:

> Therefore, brothers, since we have confidence to *enter the holy places* [meaning both the 'holy place' and the 'holy of holies' itself] by the blood of Jesus . . . and since we have a great priest over the house of God, *let us draw near with a true heart in full assurance of faith.* (Heb. 10:19–22)

Jesus has opened for us the way of access to God so that we can continually "draw near" into God's very presence without fear but with "confidence" and in "full assurance of faith."

### 3. Jesus as Priest Continually Prays for Us

One other priestly function in the Old Testament was to pray on behalf of the people. The author of Hebrews tells us that Jesus also fulfills this function: "He is able to save to the uttermost those who draw near to God through him, since he always lives *to make intercession for them*" (Heb. 7:25). Paul affirms the same point when he says Christ Jesus is the one "who indeed *is interceding for us*" (Rom. 8:34).

Some have argued that this work of high priestly intercession is only the act of remaining in the Father's presence as a continual reminder that he himself has paid the penalty for all our sins. According to this view, Jesus does not actually make specific prayers to God the Father about individual needs in our lives; he "intercedes" only in the sense of remaining in God's presence as our high priestly representative.

However, this view does not seem to fit the actual language used in Romans 8:34 and

Hebrews 7:25. In both cases, the word *intercede* translates the Greek term *entygchanō*. This word does not mean merely "to stand as someone's representative before another person" but clearly has the sense of making specific requests or petitions before someone. For example, Festus uses this word to say to King Agrippa, "You see this man about whom the whole Jewish people *petitioned* me" (Acts 25:24). Paul also uses it of Elijah when he "*appeals to* God against Israel" (Rom. 11:2). In both cases the requests are very specific, not just general representations.[4]

We may conclude, then, that both Paul and the author of Hebrews are saying that Jesus continually lives in the presence of God to make specific requests and to bring specific petitions before God on our behalf. This is a role that Jesus, as God-man, is uniquely qualified to fulfill. Although God could care for all our needs in response to direct observation (Matt. 6:8), yet it has pleased God, in his relationship to the human race, to decide to act instead in response to prayer, apparently so that the faith shown through prayer might glorify him. It is especially the prayers of men and women created in his image that are pleasing in God's sight. In Christ, we have a true man, a perfect man, praying and thereby continually glorifying God through prayer. Thus human manhood is raised to a highly exalted position: "There is one God, and there is one mediator between God and men, *the man* Christ Jesus" (1 Tim. 2:5).

Yet in his human nature alone Jesus could not of course be such a great high priest for all his people all over the world. He could not hear the prayers of persons far away, nor could he hear prayers that were only spoken in a person's mind. He could not hear all requests simultaneously (for in the world at any one moment there are millions of people praying to him). Therefore, in order to be the perfect high priest who intercedes for us, he must be God as well as man. He must be one who in his divine nature can both know all things and bring them into the presence of the Father. Yet because he became and continues to be man he has the right to represent us before God and he can express his petitions from the viewpoint of a sympathetic high priest, one who understands by experience what we go through.

Therefore, Jesus is the only person in the whole universe for all eternity who can be such a heavenly high priest, one who is truly God and truly man, exalted forever above the heavens.

The thought that Jesus is continually praying for us should give us great encouragement. He always prays for us according to the Father's will, so we can know that his requests will be granted. Berkhof says,

---

4. Literature outside the New Testament provides further examples of *entygchanō* used to mean "to bring requests or petitions." See, e.g., Wisd. 8:21 ("I *asked* the Lord, and made petition to him"); 1 Macc. 8:32; 3 Macc. 6:37 ("They *requested* the King, that he send them back to their home"); 1 Clem. 56:1; Epistle of Polycarp to the Philippians 4:3; Josephus, *Antiquities* 12:18; 16:170 (the Jews in Cyrene *petition* Marcus Agrippa concerning people in their land who are falsely collecting taxes). More examples could be found as well (cf. also Rom. 8:27, and, using a cognate word, v. 26).

It is a consoling thought that Christ is praying for us, even when we are negligent in our prayer life; that He is presenting to the Father those spiritual needs which were not present to our minds and which we often neglect to include in our prayers; and that He prays for our protection against the dangers of which we are not even conscious, and against the enemies which threaten us, though we do not notice it. He is praying that our faith may not cease, and that we may come out victoriously in the end.[5]

## C. CHRIST AS KING

In the Old Testament the king has authority to rule over the nation of Israel. In the New Testament, Jesus was born to be King of the Jews (Matt. 2:2), but he refused any attempt by people to try to make him an earthly king with earthly military and political power (John 6:15). He told Pilate, "My kingdom is not of this world. If my kingdom were of this world, my servants would have been fighting, that I might not be delivered over to the Jews. But my kingdom is not from the world" (John 18:36).

Nonetheless, Jesus did have a kingdom whose arrival he announced in his preaching. "From that time Jesus began to preach, saying, 'Repent, for *the kingdom of heaven* is at hand'" (Matt. 4:17; cf. 4:23; 12:28, et al.). He is in fact the true king of the new people of God. Thus Jesus refused to rebuke his disciples who cried out at his triumphal entry into Jerusalem, "Blessed is *the King* who comes in the name of the Lord!" (Luke 19:38; cf. vv. 39–40; also Matt. 21:5; John 1:49; Acts 17:7).

After his resurrection, Jesus was given by God the Father far greater authority over the church and over the universe. God raised him up and "seated him at his right hand in the heavenly places, *far above all rule and authority and power and dominion*, and above every name that is named, not only in this age but also in the one to come. And he put all things under his feet and gave him as head over all things to the church" (Eph. 1:20–22; also Matt. 28:18; 1 Cor. 15:25). That authority over the church and over the universe will be more fully recognized by people when Jesus returns to earth in power and great glory to reign (Matt. 26:64; 2 Thess. 1:7–10; Rev. 19:11–16). On that day he will be acknowledged as "*King of kings* and Lord of lords" (Rev. 19:16) and every knee shall bow to him (Phil. 2:10).

## D. OUR ROLES AS PROPHETS, PRIESTS, AND KINGS

If we look back at the situation of Adam before the fall and forward to our future status with Christ in heaven for eternity, we can see that these roles of prophet, priest, and king had parallels in the experience that God originally intended for human beings, and this will be fulfilled in our lives in heaven.

---

5. Louis Berkhof, *Systematic Theology* (Grand Rapids: Eerdmans, 1941), 403.

In the garden of Eden, Adam was a "prophet" in that he had true knowledge of God and always spoke truthfully about God and about his creation. He was a "priest" in that he was able freely and openly to offer prayer and praise to God. There was no need of a sacrifice to pay for sins, but in another sense of sacrifice Adam and Eve's work would have been offered to God in gratitude and thanksgiving, and so would have been a "sacrifice" of another sort (cf. Heb. 13:15). Adam and Eve were also "kings" (or king and queen) in the sense of having been given dominion and rule over the creation (Gen. 1:26–28).

After sin entered into the world, fallen human beings no longer functioned as prophets, for they believed false information about God and spoke falsely about him to others. They no longer had priestly access to God because sin cut them off from his presence. Instead of ruling over the creation as kings, they were subject to the harshness of the creation and tyrannized by flood, drought, and unproductive land, as well as by tyrannical human rulers. The nobility of man as God had created him—to be a true prophet, priest, and king—was lost through sin.

There was a partial recovery of the purity of these three roles in the establishment of the three offices of prophet, priest, and king in the kingdom of Israel. From time to time godly people occupied these offices. But there were also false prophets, dishonest priests, and ungodly kings, and the original purity and holiness with which God intended man to fulfill these offices were never fully realized.

When Christ came, we saw for the first time the fulfillment of these three roles, since he was the perfect prophet, who most fully declared God's words to us, the perfect high priest, who offered the supreme sacrifice for sins and who brought his people near to God, and the true and rightful king of the universe, who will reign forever with a scepter of righteousness over the new heavens and new earth.

But amazingly we as Christians even now begin to imitate Christ in each of these roles, though in a subordinate way. We have a "prophetic" role as we proclaim the gospel to the world and thereby bring God's saving Word to people. In fact, whenever we speak truthfully about God to believers or to unbelievers we are fulfilling a "prophetic" function (using the word *prophetic* in a very broad sense).

We are also priests, because Peter calls us "a royal priesthood" (1 Peter 2:9). He invites us to be built into a spiritual temple and "to be a holy priesthood" as well as "to offer spiritual sacrifices acceptable to God through Jesus Christ" (1 Peter 2:5). The author of Hebrews also views us as priests who are able to enter into the holy of holies (Heb. 10:19, 22) and able to "continually offer up a sacrifice of praise to God, that is, the fruit of lips that acknowledge his name" (Heb. 13:15). He also tells us that our good works are sacrifices pleasing to God: "Do not neglect to do good and to share what you have, for such *sacrifices* are pleasing to God" (Heb. 13:16). Paul also has a priestly role in mind for us when he writes, "I appeal to you therefore, brothers, by the mercies of God, to present your bodies *as a living sacrifice*, holy and acceptable to God, which is your spiritual worship" (Rom. 12:1).

We also share in part now in the kingly reign of Christ, since we have been raised to sit with him in the heavenly places (Eph. 2:6), thus sharing to some degree in his authority over evil spiritual forces that may be arrayed against us (Eph. 6:10–18; James 4:7; 1 Peter 5:9; 1 John 4:4). God has even now committed to us authority over various areas in this world or in the church, giving to some authority over much and to some authority over little. But when the Lord returns those who have been faithful over little will be given authority over much (Matt. 25:14–30).

When Christ returns and rules over the new heavens and new earth, we will once again be true "prophets" because our knowledge will then be perfect and we shall know as we are known (1 Cor. 13:12). Then we will speak only truth about God and about his world, and in us the original prophetic purpose which God had for Adam will be fulfilled. We will be priests forever, for we will eternally worship and offer prayer to God as we behold his face and dwell in his presence (Rev. 22:3–4). We will continually offer ourselves and all that we have and do as sacrifices to our most worthy king.

Yet we shall also, in subjection to God, share in ruling over the universe, for with him we shall "reign forever and ever" (Rev. 22:5). Jesus says, "The one who conquers, I will grant him *to sit with me on my throne*, as I also conquered and sat down with my Father on his throne" (Rev. 3:21). In fact, Paul tells the Corinthians, "Do you not know that *the saints will judge the world*? . . . Do you not know that *we are to judge angels*?" (1 Cor. 6:2–3). Therefore for all eternity, we shall forever function as subordinate prophets, priests, and kings, yet we are always subject to the Lord Jesus, the supreme prophet, priest, and king.

## QUESTIONS FOR PERSONAL APPLICATION

1. Can you see some ways in which an understanding of Christ's role as prophet, priest, and king will help you understand more fully the functions of prophets, priests, and kings in the Old Testament? Read the description of Solomon's kingdom in 1 Kings 4:20–34 and 1 Kings 10:14–29. Do you see in Solomon's kingdom any foreshadowing of the three offices of Christ? Any foreshadowing of Christ's eternal kingdom? Do you think that you have greater or lesser privileges living now as a member of the church in the new covenant age?

2. Can you see any fulfillment of the role of prophet in your life now? Of the role of priest? Of the role of king? How could each of these functions be developed in your life?

**Special Terms**

*intercession*

*king*

*priest*

*prophet*

# BIBLIOGRAPHY

(For an explanation of this bibliography see the note on the bibliography to chapter 1, pp. 23–24. Complete bibliographical data may be found on pp. 1489–96.)

## SECTIONS IN EVANGELICAL SYSTEMATIC THEOLOGIES

### 1. Anglican (Episcopalian)
1882–92 . . . . . Litton, 219–38
2001 . . . . . . . . Packer, 121–22
2013 . . . . . . . . Bird, 359–64
2013 . . . . . . . . Bray, 535–41

### 2. Arminian (Wesleyan or Methodist)
1875–76 . . . . . Pope, 2:197–262
1940 . . . . . . . . Wiley, 2:187–216
1983 . . . . . . . . Carter, 1:363–64
1992 . . . . . . . . Oden, 2:279–316

### 3. Baptist
1767 . . . . . . . . Gill, 1:602–44
1887 . . . . . . . . Boyce, 291–95
1907 . . . . . . . . Strong, 710–76
1990–95 . . . . . Garrett, 1:625–64, 699–710
2007 . . . . . . . . Akin, 546–51
2013 . . . . . . . . Erickson, 695–703

### 4. Dispensational
1947 . . . . . . . . Chafer, 3:17–30
1986 . . . . . . . . Ryrie, 254–59
2017 . . . . . . . . MacArthur and Mayhue, 253–54

### 5. Lutheran
1917–24 . . . . . Pieper, 2:330–96
1934 . . . . . . . . Mueller, 301–18

### 6. Reformed (or Presbyterian)
1559 . . . . . . . . Calvin, 1:494–503 (2.15)
1679–85 . . . . . Turretin, *IET*, 2:303–4, 380–81, 391–94, 397–486
1871–73 . . . . . Hodge, 2:455–90, 592–609
1878 . . . . . . . . Dabney, 475–77, 483–87
1894 . . . . . . . . Shedd, 675–89
1906–11 . . . . . Bavinck, *RD*, 3:244–45, 345, 364–68, 420–21
1910 . . . . . . . . Vos, 3:85–182
1937–66 . . . . . Murray, *CW*, 1:44–58
1938 . . . . . . . . Berkhof, 356–66, 406–12
1998 . . . . . . . . Reymond, 623–24
2008 . . . . . . . . Van Genderen and Velema, 463–68
2011 . . . . . . . . Horton, 483–520
2013 . . . . . . . . Frame, 92, 557–59, 673, 894–96, 900–910
2013 . . . . . . . . Culver, 506–7, 508–9, 629–38, 1103
2016 . . . . . . . . Allen and Swain, 230–31
2017 . . . . . . . . Barrett, 313–46
2019 . . . . . . . . Letham, 545–48, 579–80, 584–94

### 7. Renewal (or charismatic/Pentecostal)
1993 . . . . . . . . Menzies and Horton, 66–68
1995 . . . . . . . . Horton, 297–99

## SECTIONS IN REPRESENTATIVE ROMAN CATHOLIC SYSTEMATIC THEOLOGIES

### 1. Roman Catholic: Traditional
1955 . . . . . . . . Ott, 179–91

### 2. Roman Catholic: Post–Vatican II
1980 . . . . . . . . McBrien (no explicit treatment)

2012 . . . . . . . . *CCC*, paragraph 783

**OTHER WORKS**

Baker, J. P. "Offices of Christ." In *NDT1*, 476–77.

Belcher, Richard P. *Prophet, Priest, and King: The Roles of Christ in the Bible and Our Roles Today.* Phillipsburg, NJ: P&R, 2016.

Boettner, Loraine. "The Offices of Christ." In *Studies in Theology*, 241–59. Phillipsburg, NJ: Presbyterian and Reformed, 1947.

Clowney, Edmund P. *The Unfolding Mystery: Discovering Christ in the Old Testament.* Phillipsburg, NJ: Presbyterian and Reformed, 1988.

Edmondson, Stephen. *Calvin's Christology.* Cambridge; New York: Cambridge University Press, 2004.

Fruchtenbaum, Arnold G. *Messianic Christology: A Study of Old Testament Prophecy Concerning the First Coming of the Messiah.* Tustin, CA: Ariel Ministries, 1998.

Johnson, Dennis E. *Walking with Jesus through His Word: Discovering Christ in All the Scriptures.* Phillipsburg, NJ: P&R, 2015.

Kaiser, Walter C., Jr. "Prophet, Christ as." In *BTDB*, 639–41.

Letham, R. W. A. "Offices of Christ." In *NDT2*, 628–30.

Letham, Robert. *The Work of Christ.* Downers Grove, IL: InterVarsity Press, 1993.

Ortlund, Gavin. "Resurrected as Messiah: The Risen Christ as Prophet, Priest, and King." *JETS* 54, no. 4 (December 2011): 749–66.

Patterson, Paige. "The Work of Christ." In *A Theology for the Church*, edited by Daniel L. Akin et al., 546–51. Nashville: B&H, 2007.

Perrin, Nicholas. *Jesus the Priest.* Grand Rapids: Baker Academic, 2018.

Peterson, Robert A. "Christ's Threefold Office of Prophet, King, and Priest." In *Calvin and the Atonement*, 45–60. Fearn, Ross-shire: Mentor, 1999.

Reymond, R. L. "Offices of Christ." In *EDT3*, 793.

Shoemaker, Melvin H. "King, Christ as." In *BTDB*, 447–49.

———. "Priest, Christ as." In *BTDB*, 631–32.

Wiley, H. Orton. "The Offices and Titles of Christ." In *Man's Need and God's Gift: Readings in Christian Theology*, edited by Millard J. Erickson. Grand Rapids: Baker, 1976.

# SCRIPTURE MEMORY PASSAGE

**1 Peter 2:9–10:** But you are a chosen race, a royal priesthood, a holy nation, a people for his own possession, that you may proclaim the excellencies of him who called you out of darkness into his marvelous light. Once you were not a people, but now you are God's people; once you had not received mercy, but now you have received mercy.

# HYMN

## "Rejoice the Lord Is King"

This powerful hymn encourages us to rejoice at Christ's present and future kingship. (An excellent hymn about Christ's role as priest is "Arise, My Soul, Arise," also by Charles Wesley, and this may be used as an alternative hymn. Another alternative is "How Sweet the Name of Jesus Sounds," by John Newton, esp. v. 4.)

Rejoice, the Lord is King: your Lord and King
  adore;
  Rejoice, give thanks and sing, and triumph
    evermore:
Lift up your heart, lift up your voice;
  Rejoice, again I say, rejoice.

Jesus, the Savior, reigns, the God of truth
  and love;
  When he had purged our stains, he took his
    seat above:
Lift up your heart, lift up your voice;
  Rejoice, again I say, rejoice.

His kingdom cannot fail, he rules o'er earth and
  heav'n;
  The keys of death and hell are to our Jesus
    giv'n:
Lift up your heart, lift up your voice;
  Rejoice, again I say, rejoice.

He sits at God's right hand till all his foes submit,
  And bow to his command, and fall beneath
    his feet:
Lift up your heart, lift up your voice;
  Rejoice, again I say, rejoice.

Author: Charles Wesley, 1746

## CONTEMPORARY WORSHIP SONG

### "Jesus Messiah"

He became sin who knew no sin
That we might become His righteousness.
He humbled Himself and carried the cross.
Love so amazing, love so amazing.

His body the bread, His blood the wine,
Broken and poured out all for love.
The whole earth trembled and the veil was torn.
Love so amazing, love so amazing.

*Chorus*
Jesus Messiah, Name above all names,
Blessed Redeemer, Emmanuel,
The Rescue for sinners,
The Ransom from heaven,
Jesus Messiah, Lord of all.

*Bridge*
All our hope is in You.
All our hope is in You.
All the glory to You God,
The Light of the world.

Words by Jesse Reeves, Daniel Carson,
Ed Cash, and Chris Tomlin[6]

---

## CHAPTER 30

# The Work of the Holy Spirit

*What are the distinctive activities of the Holy Spirit throughout the history of the Bible?*

## EXPLANATION AND SCRIPTURAL BASIS

In the previous chapters we have discussed at some length the person and work of God the Father, and, more recently, the person and work of God the Son, Jesus Christ. We have also examined the biblical evidence for the deity and distinct personality of the Holy Spirit (in connection with the doctrine of the Trinity). It is appropriate now in this chapter that we focus on the distinctive work of the Holy Spirit. Among the different activities of the members of the Trinity, what activities are said to be especially the work of God the Holy Spirit?

We should realize at the outset that other chapters in this book deal more or less directly with certain aspects of the Holy Spirit's work. The chapters on baptism in and filling with the Holy Spirit (39) and the gifts of the Holy Spirit (52–53) deal almost entirely with specific works of the Holy Spirit. Moreover, the chapters on the authority of Scripture (4), prayer (18), the gospel call (33), regeneration (34), sanctification (38), perseverance (40), glorification (42), church discipline (46), the means of grace within the church (48), and worship (51) all treat various aspects of the Holy Spirit's work in the world, and especially in the lives of believers. Nonetheless, in this chapter we will attempt to gain an overview of the teaching of all of Scripture on the work of the Holy Spirit in order to understand more fully what kinds of activities have been especially delegated to the Holy Spirit by God the Father and God the Son.

We may define the work of the Holy Spirit as follows: *the work of the Holy Spirit is to manifest the active presence of God in the world, and especially in the church.* This definition indicates that the Holy Spirit is the member of the Trinity whom the Scripture most often represents as being *present* to do God's work in the world. Although this is true to some extent throughout the Bible, it is particularly true in the new covenant age. In the Old Testament, the presence of God was many times manifested in the glory of God and in theophanies, and in the Gospels Jesus himself manifested the presence of God among men. But after Jesus ascended into heaven, and continuing through the entire church age, the Holy Spirit is now the *primary* manifestation of the presence of the Trinity among us. He is the one who is most prominently *present* with us now.[1]

From the very beginning of creation we have an indication that the Holy Spirit's work is to complete and sustain what God the Father has planned and what God the Son has begun, for in Genesis 1:2, "the *Spirit of God* was hovering over the face of the waters." And at Pentecost, with the beginning of the new creation in Christ, the Holy Spirit comes to grant power to the church (Acts 10:38; 2:4, 17–18). Because the Holy Spirit is the person of the Trinity through whom God particularly manifests his presence in the new covenant age, it is appropriate that Paul should call the Holy Spirit the "firstfruits" (Rom. 8:23) and the "guarantee" (or "down payment," 2 Cor. 1:22; 5:5) of the full manifestation of God's presence that we will know in the new heavens and new earth (cf. Rev. 21:3–4).

Even in the Old Testament, it was predicted that the presence of the Holy Spirit would bring abundant blessings from God: Isaiah predicted a time when the Spirit would bring great renewal.

> For the palace is forsaken, the populous city deserted . . . *until the Spirit is poured upon us from on high*, and the wilderness becomes a fruitful field, and the fruitful field is deemed a forest. Then justice will dwell in the wilderness, and righteousness abide in the fruitful field. And the effect of righteousness will be peace, and the result of righteousness, quietness and trust forever. My people will abide in a peaceful habitation, in secure dwellings, and in quiet resting places. (Isa. 32:14–18)

Similarly, God prophesied through Isaiah to Jacob, "For I will pour water on the thirsty land, and streams on the dry ground; *I will pour my Spirit upon your offspring*, and my blessing on your descendants" (Isa. 44:3).

By contrast, the departure of the Holy Spirit removed the blessing of God from a people: "But they rebelled and *grieved his Holy Spirit*; therefore he turned to be their enemy, and himself fought against them" (Isa. 63:10). Nonetheless, several prophecies in the Old Testament predicted a time when the Holy Spirit would come in greater fullness, a time when God would make a new covenant with his people (Ezek. 36:26–27; 37:14; 39:29; Joel 2:28–29).

In what specific ways does the Holy Spirit bring God's blessing? We may distinguish four aspects of the work of the Holy Spirit to bring evidence of God's presence and to bless: (1) the Holy Spirit *purifies*; (2) the Holy Spirit *unifies*; (3) the Holy Spirit *reveals*;

---

1. In this discussion, when I use the word *present*, I mean "present to bless," as discussed in the section on God's omnipotence in chapter 11. Of course, since he is fully God, the *being* of the Holy Spirit is always present everywhere (he is omnipresent), but he does not always show his presence in activities that bring blessing (see chapter 11, pp. 208–11).

(4) the Holy Spirit *empowers*. We will examine each of these four activities below. Finally, we must recognize that these activities of the Holy Spirit are not to be taken for granted, and they do not just happen automatically among God's people. Rather, the Holy Spirit reflects the pleasure or displeasure of God with the faith and obedience—or unbelief and disobedience—of God's people. Because of this, we need to look at a fifth aspect of the Holy Spirit's activity: (5) the Holy Spirit *shows stronger or weaker evidence* of the presence and blessing of God, according to our response to him.

## A. THE HOLY SPIRIT PURIFIES

Since this member of the Trinity is called the *Holy* Spirit, it is not surprising to find that one of his primary activities is to cleanse us from sin and to "sanctify us" or make us more holy in actual conduct of life. Even in the lives of unbelievers, there is some restraining influence of the Holy Spirit as he convicts the world of sin (John 16:8–11; Acts 7:51). But when people become Christians, the Holy Spirit does an initial cleansing work in them, making a decisive break with the patterns of sin that were in their lives before.[2] Paul says of the Corinthians, "You were washed, *you were sanctified*, you were justified in the name of the Lord Jesus Christ and *by the Spirit of our God*" (1 Cor. 6:11; see also Titus 3:5). This cleansing and purifying work of the Holy Spirit is apparently what is symbolized by the metaphor of fire when John the Baptist says that Jesus will baptize people "with the Holy Spirit and fire" (Matt. 3:11; Luke 3:16).

After the initial break with sin that the Holy Spirit brings about in our lives at conversion, he also produces in us growth in holiness of life. He brings forth the "*fruit of the Spirit*" within us ("love, joy, peace, patience, kindness, goodness, faithfulness, gentleness, self-control," Gal. 5:22–23), those qualities that reflect the character of God. As we continually "are being transformed into the same image from one degree of glory to another," we should be reminded that "this comes from the Lord who is the Spirit" (2 Cor. 3:18). Sanctification comes by the power of the Holy Spirit (2 Thess. 2:13; 1 Peter 1:2; cf. Rom. 8:4, 15–16), so that it is "*by the Spirit*" that we are able to "put to death the deeds of the body" and grow in personal holiness (Rom. 8:13; see 7:6; Phil. 1:19).[3]

Some people today say a purifying (or healing) work of the Holy Spirit occurs when they are "slain in the Spirit," an experience in which they suddenly fall to the ground in a semiconscious state and remain there for minutes or hours. Although the phrase "slaying in the Spirit" is nowhere in Scripture, there are instances when people fell to the ground or fell into a trance in the presence of God.[4] Contemporary experiences should

---

2. See discussion of this in John Murray, "Definitive Sanctification," in *Collected Writings of John Murray* (Edinburgh and Carlisle, PA: Banner of Truth, 1977), 277–84.

3. See chapter 38, pp. 924–37, for a more extensive discussion of sanctification.

4. See Gen. 15:12; Exod. 40:35; 1 Sam. 19:24; 1 Kings 8:11; Ezek. 1:28; 3:23; Dan. 8:27; John 18:6; Acts 9:4; 10:10; Rev. 1:17; 4:10 (compare angelic encounters in Dan. 8:17–18; 10:7–17).

be evaluated according to what lasting results ("fruit") they bear in people's lives (see Matt. 7:15–20; 1 Cor. 14:12, 26c).

## B. The Holy Spirit Unifies

When the Holy Spirit was poured out on the church at Pentecost, Peter proclaimed that the prophecy of Joel 2:28–32 was fulfilled:

> But this is what was uttered through the prophet Joel:
>
> And in the last days it shall be, God declares,
> that I will pour out my Spirit on all flesh,
> and your sons and your daughters shall prophesy,
>     and your young men shall see visions,
>     and your old men shall dream dreams;
> even on my male servants and female servants in those days
>     I will pour out my Spirit, and they shall prophesy. (Acts 2:16–18)

There is an emphasis on the Holy Spirit coming on a community of believers. Not just a leader like Moses or Joshua, but sons and daughters, old men and young men, menservants and maidservants—all will receive the outpouring of the Holy Spirit in this time.[5]

On the day of Pentecost, the Holy Spirit created a new community, the church. The community was marked by unprecedented unity, as Luke reminds us:

> And all who believed were together and had all things in common. And they were selling their possessions and belongings and distributing the proceeds to all, as any had need. And day by day, attending the temple together and breaking bread in their homes, they received their food with glad and generous hearts, praising God and having favor with all the people. (Acts 2:44–47)

Paul blesses the Corinthian church with a blessing that seeks the unifying fellowship of the Holy Spirit for all of them when he says, "The grace of the Lord Jesus Christ and the love of God and the *fellowship of the Holy Spirit* be with you all" (2 Cor. 13:14). In this Trinitarian verse, Paul attributes the deepening of fellowship among believers not to the Father or the Son but to the Holy Spirit, a statement consistent with the overall unifying work of the Spirit in the church.

This unifying function of the Holy Spirit is also evident when Paul tells the Philippians, "So if there is any encouragement in Christ, any comfort from love, *any*

---

5. This was also a fulfillment of Moses' wish that the Lord would put his Spirit on all his people (Num. 11:29), and of the vision of the valley of dry bones revived by the Spirit in Ezek.

37. See also Donald Guthrie, *New Testament Theology* (Leicester: Inter-Varsity Press; Downers Grove, IL: InterVarsity Press, 1981), 512–13, 540, 562.

*participation in the Spirit,* any affection and sympathy, complete my joy by being of the same mind, having the same love, being *in full accord and of one mind*" (Phil. 2:1–2). In a similar way, when he emphasizes the new unity between Jews and gentiles in the church, he says that "through him we both have access *in one Spirit* to the Father" (Eph. 2:18) and that in the Lord they are built into the one new house of God "by the Spirit" (Eph. 2:22). When he wants to remind the church of the unity they should have as Christians, he exhorts them to be "eager to maintain *the unity of the Spirit* in the bond of peace" (Eph. 4:3).

Paul's discussion of spiritual gifts also repeats this theme of the unifying work of the Holy Spirit. Whereas we might think that people who have differing gifts would not readily get along well with each other, Paul's conclusion is just the opposite: differing gifts draw us together because we are forced to depend on each other. "The eye cannot say to the hand, 'I have no need of you,' nor again the head to the feet, 'I have no need of you'" (1 Cor. 12:21). These differing gifts "are empowered by one and the same Spirit, who apportions to each one individually as he wills" (1 Cor. 12:11), so that in the church, "to each is given the *manifestation of the Spirit* for the common good" (1 Cor. 12:7). In fact, "in one Spirit we were all baptized into one body—Jews or Greeks, slaves or free—and all were made to drink of one Spirit" (1 Cor. 12:13).[6]

The idea that the Holy Spirit unifies the church is also evident in the fact that "strife, jealousy . . . rivalries, dissensions, divisions" (Gal. 5:20) are desires of the flesh that are opposed to being "led by the Spirit" (Gal. 5:18; cf. v. 25). The Holy Spirit is the one who produces love in our hearts (Rom. 5:5; Gal. 5:22; Col. 1:8), and this love "binds everything together in perfect harmony" (Col. 3:14). Therefore, when the Holy Spirit is working strongly in a church to manifest God's presence, the church community will be in beautiful harmony and overflowing with love for one another.

## C. The Holy Spirit Reveals

### 1. Revelation to Prophets and Apostles

In chapter 4 we discussed the work of the Holy Spirit in revealing God's words to the Old Testament prophets and New Testament apostles, in many cases so that these words could be put into Scripture (see, for example, Num. 24:2; Ezek. 11:5; Zech. 7:12). The Old Testament Scriptures came about because "men spoke from God as they were carried along *by the Holy Spirit*" (2 Peter 1:21). Several other passages mention the work of the Holy Spirit in Old Testament prophets (see Matt. 22:43; Acts 1:16; 4:25; 28:25; 1 Peter 1:11). The New Testament apostles and others who wrote words of New Testament Scripture were also guided "into all the truth" by the Holy Spirit (John 16:13), who also spoke to the apostles what he heard from the Father and the Son and declared to them

---

6. See the extended discussion of this verse in chapter 39, pp. 946–48.

"the things that are to come" (John 16:13; cf. Eph. 3:5). Others who were filled with the Holy Spirit also spoke or sang words that became part of Scripture, such as Elizabeth (Luke 1:41), Zechariah (Luke 1:67), and Simeon (Luke 2:25).

## 2. He Gives Evidence of God's Presence

Sometimes it has been said that the work of the Holy Spirit is not to call attention to himself but rather to give glory to Jesus and to God the Father. But this seems to be a false dichotomy, not supported by Scripture. Of course the Holy Spirit does glorify Jesus (John 16:14) and bear witness to him (John 15:26; Acts 5:32; 1 Cor. 12:3; 1 John 4:2). But this does not mean that he does not make his actions and words known. The Bible has hundreds of verses *talking about the work of the Holy Spirit*, and the Bible is itself spoken or inspired by the Holy Spirit.

Moreover, *the Holy Spirit frequently made himself known by phenomena that indicated his activity*, both in the Old Testament and New Testament periods. This was true when the Holy Spirit came upon the seventy elders with Moses and they prophesied (Num. 11:25–26), and when the Holy Spirit came upon the judges to enable them to do great works of power (Judg. 14:6, 19; 15:14, et al.). In these instances people could see the effect of the Holy Spirit coming on the Lord's servants. This was also true when the Holy Spirit came mightily upon Saul, and he prophesied with a band of prophets (1 Sam. 10:6, 10), and it was frequently true when God empowered the Old Testament prophets to give public prophecies.

The Holy Spirit also made his presence evident in a visible way when he descended as a dove on Jesus (John 1:32) and when he came as a sound of a rushing wind and with visible tongues of fire on the disciples at Pentecost (Acts 2:2–3). When people had the Holy Spirit poured out on them and began to speak in tongues or praise God in a remarkable and spontaneous way (see Acts 2:4; 10:44–46; 19:6), the Holy Spirit certainly made his presence known as well. And Jesus promised that the Holy Spirit within us would be so powerful he would be like a river of living water flowing out from our inmost beings (see John 7:39)—a simile that suggests that people would be aware of a presence that would somehow be perceptible.

In the lives of individual believers, the Holy Spirit does not entirely conceal his work but makes himself known in various ways. He bears witness with our spirit that we are children of God (Rom. 8:16) and cries, "Abba! Father!" (Gal. 4:6). He provides a guarantee or a down payment of our future fellowship with him in heaven (2 Cor. 1:22; 5:5) and reveals his desires to us so that we can be led by those desires and follow them (Rom. 8:4–16; Gal. 5:16–25). He gives gifts that manifest his presence (1 Cor. 12:7–11). And from time to time, he works miraculous signs and wonders that strongly attest to the presence of God in the preaching of the gospel (Heb. 2:4; cf. 1 Cor. 2:4; Rom. 15:19).

It seems more accurate, therefore, to say that although the Holy Spirit does glorify Jesus, he also frequently calls attention to his work and *gives recognizable evidences that make his presence known*. Indeed, it seems that one of his primary purposes in the new covenant age is *to manifest the presence of God*, to give indications that make the presence of God known. And when the Holy Spirit works in various ways that can be perceived by believers and unbelievers, this encourages people's faith that God is near and that he is working to fulfill his purposes in the church and to bring blessing to his people.

### 3. He Guides and Directs God's People

Scripture gives many examples of direct guidance from the Holy Spirit to various people. In fact, in the Old Testament, God said that it was sin for the people to enter into agreements with others when those agreements were "not of my Spirit" (Isa. 30:1). Apparently the people had been deciding on the basis of their own wisdom and common sense rather than seeking the guidance of God's Holy Spirit before they entered into such agreements. In the New Testament, the Holy Spirit led Jesus into the wilderness for his period of temptation (Matt. 4:1; Luke 4:1); so strong was this leading of the Holy Spirit that Mark can say, "The Spirit immediately drove him out into the wilderness" (Mark 1:12).[7]

In other contexts, the Holy Spirit gave direct words of guidance to people, saying to Philip, for example, "Go over and join this chariot" (Acts 8:29), telling Peter to go with three men who came to him from Cornelius' household (Acts 10:19–20; 11:12), and directing the Christians at Antioch, "Set apart for me Barnabas and Saul for the work to which I have called them" (Acts 13:2).

Also in the category of "giving guidance," but of a much more direct and compelling kind, are several examples where the Holy Spirit actually transported a person from one place to another. This was so when "the Spirit of the Lord carried Philip away; and the eunuch saw him no more. . . . But Philip found himself at Azotus" (Acts 8:39–40)—the guidance in this case could hardly have been clearer! But similar things happened to some Old Testament prophets, for those who knew Elijah seemed to expect that the Spirit of God would snatch him up and transport him somewhere (1 Kings 18:12; 2 Kings 2:16: "It may be that the Spirit of the LORD has caught him up and cast him upon some mountain or into some valley"). Ezekiel says that the Spirit of the Lord "lifted me up" several times, and then the Spirit would take him to one place or another (Ezek. 11:1; 37:1; 43:5), an experience that was also part of John's later visions in Revelation (Rev. 17:3; 21:10).[8]

But in the vast majority of cases, the leading and guiding by the Holy Spirit is not nearly as dramatic. Scripture talks about a day-to-day guidance—being "led" by the Holy Spirit:

---

7. The verb here translated "drove out" is a strong term, *ekballō*, which means "drive out, expel" and more literally can mean "throw out."

8. It is possible that Ezekiel and John are speaking of transportation in a vision (as in Ezek. 8:3 and 11:24) rather than literal physical travel. Paul allows for both possibilities in 2 Cor. 12:2–3.

For all who are *led by the Spirit of God* are sons of God. (Rom. 8:14)

But if you are *led by the Spirit*, you are not under the law. (Gal. 5:18)

How should we understand this "leading"? My friend Garry Friesen, in a very influential book, does not think these verses speak about subjective perceptions of the Holy Spirit's guidance toward specific individual decisions and actions in ordinary life.[9] He says that in these verses the context "is not dealing with daily decision-making in non-commanded areas." Rather, in Romans 8:14, "the leading is guidance into *the moral will of God* to do what is pleasing to Him."[10] And in Galatians 5:18, "this leading is unquestionably related to the moral will of God as revealed in Scripture."[11]

However, I do not think that this interpretation sufficiently accounts for the actual word that Paul uses for "led," which is the Greek verb *agō*, "to lead, bring." This verb is common in the New Testament (sixty-nine times), and it gives a picture of someone specifically leading a person (or even an animal) from one location to another. Here are some examples of this same verb:

> Go into the village in front of you, and immediately you will find a donkey tied, and a colt with her. Untie them and *bring* [*agō*] them to me. (Matt. 21:2)

> And when they *bring* [*agō*] you to trial and deliver you over, do not be anxious beforehand what you are to say, but say whatever is given you in that hour, for it is not you who speak, but the Holy Spirit. (Mark 13:11)

> And Jesus, full of the Holy Spirit, returned from the Jordan and was *led* [*agō*] by the Spirit in the wilderness. (Luke 4:1; this is very close to the wording in Rom. 8:14 and Gal. 5:18, and it means guidance to specific locations in the wilderness. The parallel verse in Matt. 4:1 uses a cognate verb to say that Jesus "was *led up* [*apagō*] by the Spirit into the wilderness.")

> And he *took* [*agō*] him to Jerusalem and set him on the pinnacle of the temple and said to him, "If you are the Son of God, throw yourself down from here." (Luke 4:9)

> He went to him and bound up his wounds, pouring on oil and wine. Then he set him on his own animal and *brought* [*agō*] him to an inn and took care of him. (Luke 10:34)

---

9. The following section interacting with Garry Friesen is adapted from Grudem, *Christian Ethics: An Introduction to Biblical Moral Reasoning* (Wheaton, IL: Crossway, 2018), and is used with permission.

10. Garry Friesen with J. Robin Maxson, *Decision Making and the Will of God*, rev. ed. (1980; repr., Colorado Springs: Multnomah, 2004), 100.

11. Ibid., 102.

He [Andrew] first found his own brother Simon and said to him, "We have found the Messiah" (which means Christ). He *brought* [*agō*] him to Jesus. Jesus looked at him and said, "You are Simon the son of John. You shall be called Cephas" (which means Peter). (John 1:41–42)

Then they *led* [*agō*] Jesus from the house of Caiaphas to the governor's headquarters. (John 18:28)

Luke alone is with me. Get Mark and *bring* [*agō*] him with you, for he is very useful to me for ministry. (2 Tim. 4:11)

There are many similar examples, but the point should be clear. When first century readers (who frequently used the verb *agō* to speak of one person leading or guiding another person from one place to another) saw that Paul used this verb to speak of being "led" by the Holy Spirit, they would have understood it to mean detailed, specific guidance in the various choices and decisions of everyday life. In every New Testament example that uses *agō* to speak of *leading by a personal agent*, as in Romans 8:14 and Galatians 5:18, the leading is to a very specific destination, not simply the imparting of generalized moral concepts.

In fact, in Galatians 5, Paul had just told them to "*walk* by the Spirit" (Gal. 5:16), and a few verses later he said, "if we live by the Spirit, let us also *keep in step* with the Spirit" (Gal. 5:25), two other verses that use the metaphor of walking through life to speak of guidance by the Holy Spirit. The entire passage sustains the image of one's daily conduct as a "walk" that is to be guided by the Holy Spirit. And it is pictured as a regular or continuing activity, for Paul uses present tense verbs in both verses, giving the sense, "all who *are being led* by the Spirit of God, these are the sons of God" (Rom. 8:14 NASB).

I agree with Friesen that the context in both verses shows that those who are led by the Holy Spirit will not live in a pattern of sin against God's moral laws, but that fits well in a context of specific guidance from the Holy Spirit, because Paul is saying that if you are led by the Holy Spirit, you will be following the desires of the Holy Spirit, and those desires will guide you to fulfill God's moral law: "Walk by the Spirit, *and you will not gratify the desires of the flesh*" (Gal. 5:16–17).

This does not mean that the leading of the Holy Spirit is *confined to* teaching us to follow God's moral law in Scripture, but it means that the leading of the Holy Spirit, in whatever detailed path of conduct he chooses, will always be *consistent* with the character of the Holy Spirit, and so will necessarily conform to God's moral law. But the leading of the Holy Spirit is a broader reality than just giving a desire to follow those moral laws—it is an actual *leading* through the path of life.

There are specific examples of the Holy Spirit guiding people directly in the book of Acts. After the decision of the Jerusalem council, the leaders wrote in their letter to the churches, "It has *seemed good to the Holy Spirit* and to us to lay on you no greater burden than these requirements" (Acts 15:28). This verse suggests that the council must have had a sense of the good pleasure of the Holy Spirit in these areas: they knew what "seemed good to the Holy Spirit." On Paul's second missionary journey, Luke writes that they were "forbidden by the Holy Spirit to speak the word in Asia" and then that "they attempted to go into Bithynia, but the Spirit of Jesus did not allow them" (Acts 16:6–7). Of course, no written principle from the Old Testament Scriptures would have led them to conclude that they could not preach in Asia or Bithynia. The Holy Spirit must rather have communicated his direct guidance to them in some specific way, whether through words heard audibly or in the mind or through strong subjective impressions of a lack of the Holy Spirit's presence and blessing as they attempted to travel to these different areas. Later, when Paul is on his way to Jerusalem, he says, "I am going to Jerusalem, *constrained by the Spirit*, not knowing what will happen to me there, except that the Holy Spirit testifies to me in every city that imprisonment and afflictions await me" (Acts 20:22–23). Paul did not think he had another choice—so clearly did the Holy Spirit manifest his presence and desires to him, that Paul could speak of having been "constrained" by the Spirit.[12]

In other cases the Holy Spirit gave guidance to establish people in various ministries or church offices. So the Holy Spirit said to some in the church at Antioch, "Set apart for me Barnabas and Saul for the work to which I have called them" (Acts 13:2). And Paul could say that the Holy Spirit had established the elders of the Ephesian church in their office because he said, "Pay careful attention to yourselves and to all the flock, in which the Holy Spirit has made you overseers" (Acts 20:28). Finally, the Holy Spirit did provide some guidance through the means of spiritual gifts such as prophecy (1 Cor. 14:29–33).[13]

## 4. He Provides a Godlike Atmosphere When He Manifests His Presence

Because the Holy Spirit is fully God and shares all the attributes of God, his influence will be to bring a Godlike character or atmosphere to the situations in which he is active. Because he is the *Holy* Spirit, he will at times bring about a conviction of sin, righteousness, and judgment (John 16:8–11). Because God is love, the Holy Spirit pours God's love into our hearts (Rom. 5:5; 15:30; Col. 1:8), and often the strongly manifested presence of the Holy Spirit will create an atmosphere of love. Because God is "not a

---

12. The word translated "constrained" is a perfect passive participle of *deō*, and signifies an earlier completed event (perhaps a strong conviction from the Holy Spirit that settled Paul's mind on the trip to Jerusalem once for all) that has continuing results in the present, so that Paul remained "constrained" when he spoke (the event still influenced Paul so strongly that he had no other choice but to continue forward toward Jerusalem).

13. However, it is always dangerous to follow spontaneous prophecies alone for guidance in this church age, since we are never to think of any prophecies as inerrant or 100 percent accurate today. Mistakes can especially come in the area of personal guidance. But all that does not allow us to say that there can be no guidance that comes through prophecy. See further discussion about subjective guidance in general and the gift of prophecy in particular in chapter 8, pp. 158–59, and chapter 53, pp. 1310–13.

God of confusion but of peace" (1 Cor. 14:33), the Holy Spirit brings an atmosphere of peace into situations: "The kingdom of God is not a matter of eating and drinking but of righteousness and peace and joy in the Holy Spirit" (Rom. 14:17; cf. Gal. 5:22). This last verse also teaches that the Holy Spirit imparts an atmosphere of joy (see also Acts 13:52; 1 Thess. 1:6). Although the list is not exhaustive, Paul summarized many of these Godlike qualities that the Holy Spirit produces when he listed the various elements of the fruit of the Spirit in Galatians 5:22–23.

Other elements of the atmosphere that the Holy Spirit can impart are truth (John 14:17; 15:26; 16:13; 1 John 5:7), wisdom (Deut. 34:9; Isa. 11:2), comfort (Acts 9:31), freedom (2 Cor. 3:17), righteousness (Rom. 14:17), hope (Rom. 15:13; cf. Gal. 5:5), an awareness of sonship or adoption (Rom. 8:15–16; Gal. 4:5–6), and even glory (2 Cor. 3:8). The Holy Spirit also brings unity (Eph. 4:3) and power (Acts 10:38; 1 Cor. 2:4; 2 Tim. 1:7; cf. Acts 1:8). All of these elements of the Holy Spirit's activity indicate the various aspects of an atmosphere in which he makes his presence—and thereby his character—known.

## 5. He Gives Us Assurance

The Holy Spirit bears witness "with our spirit that we are children of God" (Rom. 8:16) and gives evidence of the work of God within us: "By this we know that he abides in us, by the Spirit whom he has given us" (1 John 3:24). "By this we know that we abide in him and he in us, *because he has given us of his Spirit*" (1 John 4:13). The Holy Spirit not only witnesses to us that we are God's children, but also witnesses that God abides in us and that we are abiding in him. Once again, more than our intellect is involved: the Spirit works to give us assurance at the subjective level of spiritual and emotional perception as well.

## 6. He Teaches and Illumines

Another aspect of the Holy Spirit's revealing work is teaching certain things to God's people and illumining their minds so they can understand. Jesus promised this teaching function especially to his disciples when he said that the Holy Spirit "will *teach* you all things and bring to your remembrance all that I have said to you" (John 14:26) and "will guide you into all the truth" (John 16:13). Moreover, Jesus promised that when his disciples were put on trial because of persecution, the Holy Spirit would teach them at that time what to say (Luke 12:12; cf. Matt. 10:20; Mark 13:11). At other times the Holy Spirit revealed specific information to people—showing Simeon that he would not die until he saw the Messiah, for example (Luke 2:26), revealing to Agabus that a famine would occur (Acts 11:28) or that Paul would be taken captive in Jerusalem (Acts 21:11). In other cases the Holy Spirit revealed to Paul that he would suffer in Jerusalem (Acts 20:23; 21:4), expressly said to Paul things that would happen in the latter days (1 Tim. 4:1), and revealed to him what God has prepared for those who love him (1 Cor. 2:10).

The illuminating work of the Holy Spirit is seen in the fact that he enables us to understand: "We have received not the spirit of the world, but the Spirit who is from God, *that we might understand* the things freely given us by God" (1 Cor. 2:12). Therefore, "the natural person does not accept the things of the Spirit of God," but "the spiritual person judges all things" (1 Cor. 2:14–15). We should pray that the Holy Spirit would give us his illumination and thereby help us understand rightly when we study Scripture or when we ponder situations in our lives. Although he did not mention the Holy Spirit specifically, the psalmist prayed for such illumination when he asked God, "Open my eyes, that I may behold wondrous things out of your law" (Ps. 119:18). Similarly, Paul prayed for the Christians in and around Ephesus,

> that the God of our Lord Jesus Christ, the Father of glory, may give you *the Spirit of wisdom and of revelation* in the knowledge of him, having the eyes of your hearts enlightened, that you may know what is the hope to which he has called you, what are the riches of his glorious inheritance in the saints, and what is the immeasurable greatness of his power toward us who believe, according to the working of his great might. (Eph. 1:17–19)

## D. The Holy Spirit Empowers

## 1. He Gives Life

In the realm of nature it is the role of the Holy Spirit to give life to all animate creatures, whether on the ground or in the sky and sea, for "when you send forth your Spirit, they are created" (Ps. 104:30). Conversely, if God "should set his heart to it and gather to himself his spirit and his breath, all flesh would perish together, and man would return to dust" (Job 34:14–15). Here we see the role of the Spirit in the giving and sustaining of human and animal life.

Parallel with this is the role of the Holy Spirit to give us new life in regeneration.[14] Jesus told Nicodemus, "That which is born of the flesh is flesh, and that which is *born of the Spirit* is spirit. Do not marvel that I said to you, 'You must be born again'" (John 3:6–7; cf. 3:5, 8; 6:63; 2 Cor. 3:6). He also said, "It is *the Spirit who gives life*; the flesh profits nothing" (John 6:63 NASB; cf. 2 Cor. 3:6; Acts 10:44–47; Titus 3:5).[15] Consistent with this life-giving function of the Holy Spirit is the fact that the Spirit conceived Jesus in the womb of Mary, his mother (Matt. 1:18, 20; Luke 1:35). And on the day when Christ returns, the same Holy Spirit will complete this life-giving work by

---

14. See the discussion of regeneration in chapter 34, pp. 850–56. Moreover, as we argue in chapter 39, the phrase "baptism in the Holy Spirit" is used by the New Testament (for example, in 1 Cor. 12:13) to speak of the Holy Spirit's work at the time we become Christians (though many evangelicals today, especially in charismatic and Pentecostal groups, would understand "baptism in the Holy Spirit" to refer to something the Holy Spirit does after conversion).

15. Related to the life-giving work of the Holy Spirit is the fact that he also seals his work to us so that he keeps true believers from falling away from God and losing their salvation (Eph. 1:13).

giving new resurrection life to our mortal bodies: "If the Spirit of him who raised Jesus from the dead dwells in you, he who raised Christ Jesus from the dead will also give life to your mortal bodies *through his Spirit* who dwells in you" (Rom. 8:11).

## 2. He Gives Power for Service

**a. Old Testament.** In the Old Testament, the Holy Spirit frequently empowered people for special service. He empowered Joshua with leadership skills and wisdom (Num. 27:18; Deut. 34:9) and empowered the judges to deliver Israel from their oppressors (note how "the Spirit of the LORD was upon" Othniel in Judg. 3:10, Gideon in 6:34, Jephthah in 11:29, and Samson in 13:25; 14:6, 19; 15:14). The Holy Spirit came mightily upon Saul to arouse him to battle against the enemies of Israel (1 Sam. 11:6), and when David was anointed as king, "the Spirit of the LORD rushed upon David from that day forward" (1 Sam. 16:13), equipping David to fulfill the task of kingship to which God had called him.[16] In a slightly different kind of empowering, the Holy Spirit endowed Bezalel with artistic skills for the construction of the tabernacle and its equipment (Ex. 31:3; 35:31) and with the ability to teach these skills to others (Ex. 35:34).[17]

The Holy Spirit also protected God's people and enabled them to overcome their enemies. For example, God put his Spirit in their midst during the exodus (Isa. 63:11–12) and later, after their return from exile, put his Spirit in their midst to protect them and keep them from fear (Hag. 2:5). When Saul was attempting to capture David by force, the Holy Spirit came upon Saul's messengers (1 Sam. 19:20) and eventually upon Saul himself (v. 23), causing them involuntarily to fall to the ground and to prophesy for hours, thus defeating Saul's purpose and humiliating him in response to his malicious show of force against David and Samuel. In a similar way, while Ezekiel was prophesying judgment by the power of the Holy Spirit against some of the leaders of Israel (Ezek. 11:5), one of the leaders named Pelatiah actually died (Ezek. 11:13). In this way the Holy Spirit brought immediate judgment on him.

Finally, the Old Testament predicted a time when the Holy Spirit would anoint a Servant-Messiah in great fullness and power: "The *Spirit of the* LORD *shall rest upon him,* the Spirit of wisdom and understanding, the Spirit of counsel and might, the Spirit of knowledge and the fear of the LORD. And his delight shall be in the fear of the LORD" (Isa. 11:2–3). Isaiah prophesied that God would say of this coming Servant, "I have put my Spirit upon him" (Isa. 42:1), and he himself would say, "The Spirit of the Lord GOD is upon me, because the LORD has anointed me" (Isa. 61:1; cf. Luke 4:18).

---

16. It is apparently in the sense of equipping for kingship that David asks that the Holy Spirit not be withdrawn from him when he prays, "Cast me not away from your presence, and *take not your Holy Spirit from me*" (Ps. 51:11). Just as the Holy Spirit in his role of anointing Saul for kingship had departed from Saul at the same time as he came upon David (cf. 1 Sam. 16:13 with v. 14), so David, after his sin with Bathsheba (see Ps. 51, title), prayed that the Holy Spirit would not similarly be taken from him.

17. The Holy Spirit also empowered the Old Testament prophets by giving them revelations to speak, but I have included that function under Section C above ("The Holy Spirit Reveals").

Before leaving this discussion of the empowering of the Holy Spirit in the Old Testament, we should note that it sometimes is said that there was no work of the Holy Spirit *within* people in the Old Testament. This idea has mainly been inferred from Jesus' words to the disciples in John 14:17, "He dwells *with* you and will be *in* you." But we should not conclude from this verse that there was no work of the Holy Spirit within people before Pentecost. Although the Old Testament does not frequently speak of people who had the Holy Spirit in them or who were filled with the Holy Spirit, there are a few examples: Joshua is said to have the Holy Spirit *within him*, for he is called "a man in whom is the Spirit" (Num. 27:18; cf. Deut. 34:9). Others in the Old Testament who have the Holy Spirit *within them* are Bezalel (Exod. 31:3), Ezekiel (Ezek. 2:2; 3:24), Daniel (Dan. 4:8–9, 18; 5:11), and Micah (Mic. 3:8).[18] This means that when Jesus says to his disciples that the Holy Spirit "dwells with you and will be in you" (John 14:17), he cannot mean that there was an absolute "within/without" difference between the old and new covenant work of the Holy Spirit. Nor can John 7:39 ("as yet the Spirit had not been given, because Jesus was not yet glorified") mean that there was *no* activity of the Holy Spirit in people's lives before Pentecost. Both of these passages must be different ways of saying that *the more powerful, fuller work of the Holy Spirit that is characteristic of life after Pentecost* had not yet begun in the lives of the disciples. The Holy Spirit had not come within them in the way in which God had promised to put the Holy Spirit within his people when the new covenant would come (see Ezek. 36:26, 27; 37:14), nor had the Holy Spirit been poured out in the great abundance and fullness that would characterize the new covenant age (Joel 2:28–29). In this powerful new covenant sense, the Holy Spirit was not yet at work within the disciples.[19]

**b. New Testament.** The empowering work of the Holy Spirit in the New Testament is seen first and most fully in his anointing and empowering of Jesus as the Messiah. The Holy Spirit descended upon Jesus at his baptism (Matt. 3:16; Mark 1:11; Luke 3:22). John the Baptist said, "I saw the Spirit descend from heaven like a dove, and it remained on him" (John 1:32). Therefore, Jesus entered into the temptation in the wilderness "full of the Holy Spirit" (Luke 4:1), and after his temptation, at the beginning of his ministry, "Jesus returned *in the power of the Spirit* to Galilee" (Luke 4:14). When Jesus came to preach in the synagogue at Nazareth, he declared that Isaiah's prophecy was fulfilled in himself: "The Spirit of the Lord is upon me, because he has anointed me to proclaim good news to the poor. He has sent me to proclaim liberty to the captives and recovering of sight to the blind, to set at liberty those who are oppressed, to proclaim the year of the Lord's favor" (Luke 4:18–19). The power of the Holy Spirit in Jesus' life was then seen in his subsequent miracles, as he cast out demons with a word and healed all who came to him (Luke 4:36, 40–41). The Holy Spirit was pleased to dwell in Jesus and empower

---

18. Before Pentecost occurred in Acts 2 in the New Testament we also find that John the Baptist (Luke 1:15), Elizabeth (Luke 1:41), and Zechariah (Luke 1:67) were all said to be filled with the Holy Spirit. But they were still living under the old covenant.

19. See chapter 39, pp. 950–53, for a fuller discussion of the differences between the work of the Holy Spirit in the old covenant and in the new covenant.

him, for he fully delighted in the absolute moral purity of Jesus' life. In the context of talking about Jesus' ministry and the Father's blessing on that ministry, John says, "He gives the Spirit without measure. The Father loves the Son and has given all things into his hand" (John 3:34–35). Jesus had an anointing of the Holy Spirit without measure, and this anointing "remained on him" (John 1:32; cf. Acts 10:38).

The Holy Spirit empowered Jesus' disciples for various kinds of ministry. Jesus had promised them, "You will *receive power when the Holy Spirit has come upon you*, and you will be my witnesses in Jerusalem and in all Judea and Samaria, and to the end of the earth" (Acts 1:8).[20] There are several specific examples of the Holy Spirit's empowering the early Christians to work *miracles* as they proclaimed the gospel (note Stephen in Acts 6:5, 8; and Paul in Rom. 15:19; 1 Cor. 2:4). But the Holy Spirit also gave great power to the *preaching* of the early church so that when the disciples were filled with the Holy Spirit they proclaimed the Word boldly and with great power (Acts 4:8, 31; 6:10; 1 Thess. 1:5; 1 Peter 1:12). In general, we can say that the Holy Spirit speaks through the gospel message as it is effectively proclaimed to people's hearts. The New Testament ends with an invitation from both the Holy Spirit and the church, who together call people to salvation: "The Spirit and the Bride say, 'Come.' And let the one who hears say, 'Come'" (Rev. 22:17). In fact, not only in the preaching of the gospel message but also in the reading and teaching of Scripture does the Holy Spirit continue to speak to people's hearts each day (see Heb. 3:7 and 10:15, where the author quotes an Old Testament passage and says that the Holy Spirit is now speaking that passage to his readers).

Another aspect of empowering Christians for service is the Holy Spirit's activity of giving *spiritual gifts* to equip Christians for ministry. After listing a variety of spiritual gifts, Paul says, "But *one and the same Spirit works all these things*, distributing to each one individually just as He wills" (1 Cor. 12:11 NASB). Since the Holy Spirit is the one who shows or manifests God's presence in the world, it is not surprising that Paul can call spiritual gifts "manifestations" of the Holy Spirit (1 Cor. 12:7).[21] When spiritual gifts are active, it is another indication of the presence of God the Holy Spirit in the church.[22]

---

20. The word here translated "power" (*dynamis*) occurs nine other times in Acts. In one case (4:33), it is unclear whether this "power" refers to powerful preaching that convicted the hearers or to miraculous signs that accompanied the preaching. But in the other eight examples (2:22; 3:12; 4:7; 6:8; 8:10 [in this verse referring to pagan miracle-working power], 13; 10:38; 19:11) it refers to *power to work miracles*. This meaning of the term *dynamis* is further confirmed by its frequent use in Luke's gospel to refer to miracle-working power. Therefore, when Jesus promised the disciples in Acts 1:8 that they would receive "power" when the Holy Spirit came upon them, it seems likely that they would have understood him to mean at least the power of the Holy Spirit to work miracles that would attest to the truthfulness of the gospel. Because the immediate context of the sentence talks about being witnesses for Jesus, they may

also have understood him to mean that they would receive the power of the Holy Spirit to work through their preaching and bring conviction of sins and awaken faith in people's hearts. This power in their preaching was evident in subsequent events, as when Peter's hearers "were cut to the heart" (Acts 2:37), or when "many of those who had heard the word believed, and the number of the men came to about five thousand" (Acts 4:4).

21. The Greek word translated "manifestation" is *phanerōsis*, which means something that discloses, something that makes publicly evident or clear. The related adjective *phaneros* means "visible, clear, plainly to be seen, open, plain, evident, known" (BAGD, 852).

22. The Holy Spirit also empowers obedience to God during the Christian life (see discussion above on the Holy Spirit's work of purification).

In the prayer lives of individual believers, we find that the Holy Spirit empowers prayer and makes it effective. "We do not know what to pray for as we ought, but the Spirit himself intercedes for us with groanings too deep for words" (Rom. 8:26).[23] And Paul says that we "have access in one Spirit to the Father" (Eph. 2:18). One specific kind of prayer that the New Testament says is empowered by the Holy Spirit is the gift of prayer in tongues (1 Cor. 12:10–11; 14:2, 14–17).[24]

Yet another aspect of the Holy Spirit's work in empowering Christians for service is empowering people to overcome spiritual opposition to the preaching of the gospel and to God's work in people's lives. This power in spiritual warfare was first seen in the life of Jesus, who said, "If it is *by the Spirit of God* that I cast out demons, then the kingdom of God has come upon you" (Matt. 12:28). When Paul came to Cyprus, he encountered opposition from Elymas the magician, but he, "*filled with the Holy Spirit*, looked intently at him and said, 'You son of the devil, you enemy of all righteousness, full of all deceit and villainy, will you not stop making crooked the straight paths of the Lord? And now, behold, the hand of the Lord is upon you, and you will be blind and unable to see the sun for a time.' Immediately mist and darkness fell upon him and he went about seeking people to lead him by the hand" (Acts 13:9–11). The gift of the ability to "distinguish between spirits" (1 Cor. 12:10), given by the Holy Spirit, is also to be a tool in this warfare against the forces of darkness, as is the Word of God, which functions as the "sword of the Spirit" (Eph. 6:17) in spiritual conflict.

## E. The Holy Spirit Shows Stronger or Weaker Evidence of the Presence and Blessing of God according to Our Response to Him

Many examples in both the Old and New Testament indicate that the Holy Spirit will bestow or withdraw blessing according to whether or not he is pleased by the situation he sees. It is noteworthy that Jesus was completely without sin, and the Holy Spirit "remained on him" (John 1:32) and was given to him without measure (John 3:34). In the Old Testament the Holy Spirit came mightily upon Samson several times (Judg. 13:25; 14:6, 19; 15:14) but ultimately left him when he persisted in sin (Judg. 16:20). Similarly, when Saul persisted in disobedience the Holy Spirit departed from him (1 Sam. 16:14). And when the people of Israel rebelled and grieved the Holy Spirit, he turned against them (Isa. 63:10).

Also in the New Testament, the Holy Spirit can be grieved and cease to bring blessing in a situation. Stephen rebuked the Jewish leaders, saying, "You always *resist the Holy Spirit*" (Acts 7:51). Paul warns the Ephesian Christians, "Do not *grieve the Holy Spirit of God*, by whom you were sealed for the day of redemption" (Eph. 4:30), and exhorts the Thessalonian church, "Do not *quench the Spirit*" (1 Thess. 5:19; cf. the metaphor of

---

23. See discussion of Rom. 8:26 in chapter 18, pp. 499–500, and chapter 53, pp. 1331–32.

24. See discussion of speaking in tongues in chapter 53, pp. 1323–32.

delaying to open the door and thereby disappointing one's lover in Song of Sol. 5:3, 6). In a similar vein, Paul gives a serious warning to Christians not to defile their bodies by joining them to a prostitute because the Holy Spirit lives within their bodies: "Do you not know that your body is a temple of the Holy Spirit within you, whom you have from God? You are not your own, for you were bought with a price. So glorify God in your body" (1 Cor. 6:19–20).

Even more serious than grieving or quenching the Holy Spirit is a deeper, more hardened disobedience to him that brings strong judgment. When Peter rebuked Ananias, "Why has Satan filled your heart to lie to the Holy Spirit and to keep back for yourself part of the proceeds of the land?" (Acts 5:3), he fell down dead. Similarly, when Peter said to Ananias's wife Sapphira, "How is it that you have agreed together to test the Spirit of the Lord?" (Acts 5:9), she immediately fell down dead as well. The book of Hebrews warns those who are in danger of falling away that severe punishment is deserved by the one "who has trampled underfoot the Son of God, and has profaned the blood of the covenant by which he was sanctified, and *has outraged the Spirit of grace*" (Heb. 10:29). For such a person there only remains "a fearful expectation of judgment" (Heb. 10:27).[25]

Finally, there remains one more level of offense against the Holy Spirit. This kind of offense is even more serious than grieving him or acting with the hardened disobedience to him that brings discipline or judgment. It is possible so to offend the Holy Spirit that his convicting work will not be brought to bear again in a person's life.

> Every sin and blasphemy will be forgiven people, but the *blasphemy against the Spirit* will not be forgiven. And whoever speaks a word against the Son of Man will be forgiven, but whoever speaks against the Holy Spirit will not be forgiven, either in this age or in the age to come. (Matt. 12:31–32; cf. Mark 3:29; Luke 12:10)

These statements are made in a context in which the Pharisees willfully and maliciously attribute to Satan the powerful work of the Holy Spirit that was evident in the ministry of Jesus. Since the Holy Spirit so clearly manifested the presence of God, those who willfully and maliciously spoke against him and attributed his activity instead to the power of Satan were guilty, Jesus said, "of an eternal sin" (Mark 3:29).[26]

All of these passages indicate that we must be very careful not to grieve or offend the Holy Spirit. He will not force himself on us against our wills (see 1 Cor. 14:32), but if we resist and quench and oppose him, then his empowering will depart and he will remove much of the blessing of God from our lives.

On the other hand, in the life of Christians whose conduct is pleasing to God, the Holy Spirit will be present to bring great blessing. The Holy Spirit was "poured out"

---

25. This passage could also be put in the next category, discussed in the following paragraph.

26. See chapter 24, pp. 637–40, for a fuller discussion of the unpardonable sin.

in fullness at Pentecost (see Acts 2:17–18), and he now dwells within all true believers, making them temples of the living God (1 Cor. 3:16; 6:19–20). We can know close fellowship and partnership with the Holy Spirit in our lives (2 Cor. 3:14; Phil. 2:1). He entrusts gifts (1 Cor. 12:11) and truth (2 Tim. 1:14) and ministries (Acts 20:28) to us. In fact, so full and abundant will be his presence that Jesus could promise that he will flow out of our inmost being like "rivers of living water" (John 7:38–39). Peter promises that his presence especially rests on those who suffer for the sake of Christ: "If you are insulted for the name of Christ, you are blessed, because the Spirit of glory and of God rests upon you" (1 Peter 4:14).

Therefore, it is important that all our ministry be done *in the Holy Spirit*, that is, that we consciously dwell in the Godlike atmosphere created by the Holy Spirit—the atmosphere of power, love, joy, truth, holiness, righteousness, and peace. But greater than these characteristics of the atmosphere created by the Holy Spirit is the sense of the presence of the Holy Spirit himself—*to be in the Holy Spirit is really to be in an atmosphere of God's manifested presence.* This is why people in the New Testament can walk in the comfort of the Holy Spirit (Acts 9:31), and why it is possible just to be "in the Spirit" as John was on the Lord's day (Rev. 1:10; cf. 4:2).

It is surprising how many particular activities are said in the New Testament to be done "in" the Holy Spirit: it is possible to *rejoice* in the Holy Spirit (Luke 10:21), to *resolve* or decide something in the Holy Spirit (Acts 19:21), to have one's *conscience bear witness* in the Holy Spirit (Rom. 9:1), to have *access to God* in the Holy Spirit (Eph. 2:18), to *pray* in the Holy Spirit (Eph. 6:18; Jude 20), and to *love* in the Holy Spirit (Col. 1:8). In the light of these texts, we might ask ourselves, for how many of these activities during each day are we consciously aware of the Holy Spirit's presence and blessing?

It is also possible to be filled with the Holy Spirit (Eph. 5:18; cf. Luke 1:15, 41, 67; 4:1; Acts 2:4; 4:8; 6:3, 5; 7:55; 9:17; 11:24; 13:9). To be filled with the Holy Spirit is to be filled with the immediate presence of God himself, and it therefore will result in feeling what God feels, desiring what God desires, doing what God wants, speaking by God's power, praying and ministering in God's strength, and knowing with the knowledge which God himself gives.[27] In times when the church experiences revival the Holy Spirit produces these results in people's lives in especially powerful ways.

Therefore in our Christian lives it is important to depend on the Holy Spirit's power, recognizing that any significant work is done "not by might, nor by power, *but by my Spirit*, says the LORD of hosts" (Zech. 4:6). Paul is emphatic in telling the Galatians that the Holy Spirit was received by faith in the beginning of their Christian life (Gal. 3:2) and would continue to work according to their faith in their lives subsequent to conversion: "Having begun by the Spirit, are you now being perfected by the flesh? . . .

---

27. See chapter 39, pp. 962–64, for more extensive discussion of being filled with the Holy Spirit.

Does he who supplies the Spirit to you and works miracles among you do so by works of the law, or by hearing with faith?" (Gal. 3:3, 5).

Therefore we are to walk according to the guidance of the Holy Spirit (Rom. 8:12–16; Gal. 5:16–26) and set our minds on the things of the Spirit (Rom. 8:4–6). All our ministry, whatever form it may take, is to be done in the power of the Holy Spirit.

## QUESTIONS FOR PERSONAL APPLICATION

1. In the past, has it been hard for you to think of the Holy Spirit as a person rather than simply as a presence or force? What items (if any) in this chapter have helped you think more readily of the Holy Spirit as a person? Do you think that you have a consciousness of relating to the Holy Spirit as a person who is distinct from God the Father and God the Son? What might help you be more aware of this distinction among the members of the Trinity as they relate to you?

2. Do you perceive any difference in the way the Father, Son, and Holy Spirit relate to you in your Christian life? If so, can you explain what that difference is or how you are aware of it?

3. Have you ever been especially aware of the Holy Spirit's empowering in a specific situation of ministry? (This could have been while doing evangelism or counseling, Bible teaching or preaching, prayer or worship, or in some other ministry situation.) How did you perceive the presence of the Holy Spirit at that time, or what made you aware of his presence?

4. In your own experience, in what ways does the guidance of the Holy Spirit come to you? Is it primarily (or exclusively) through the words of Scripture? If so, are there times when certain Scripture passages seem to come alive or speak with great relevance and forcefulness to you at the moment? How do you know when this is happening? If the Holy Spirit's guidance has come to you in other ways in addition to speaking through the words of Scripture, what have those other ways been?

5. Do you have a sense from time to time of the pleasure or displeasure of the Holy Spirit at some course of action that you are taking? Is there anything in your life right now that is grieving the Holy Spirit? What do you plan to do about it?

6. Did the Holy Spirit immediately leave Samson when he began to sin (see Judg. 13:25; 14:6, 19; 15:14)? Why or why not? Is the presence of spiritual power in someone's ministry a guarantee that the Holy Spirit is pleased with all of that person's life?

## Special Terms

*blasphemy against the Holy Spirit*
*filled with the Holy Spirit*
*Holy Spirit*
*in the Holy Spirit*
*manifestation of God's active presence*

# BIBLIOGRAPHY

(For an explanation of this bibliography see the note on the bibliography to chapter 1, pp. 23–24. Complete bibliographical data may be found on pp. 1489–96.)

## SECTIONS IN EVANGELICAL SYSTEMATIC THEOLOGIES

### 1. Anglican (Episcopalian)
1882–92 . . . . . Litton, 242–47
1930 . . . . . . . . Thomas, 90–99
2001 . . . . . . . . Packer, 143–45
2013 . . . . . . . . Bird, 621–48
2013 . . . . . . . . Bray, 723–984

### 2. Arminian (Wesleyan or Methodist)
1875–76 . . . . . Pope, 2:321–36
1940 . . . . . . . . Wiley, 2:303–33
1960 . . . . . . . . Purkiser, 183–203
1983 . . . . . . . . Carter, 1:415–72
1992 . . . . . . . . Oden, 3:31–78
2002 . . . . . . . . Cottrell, 284–305

### 3. Baptist
1917 . . . . . . . . Mullins, 359–65
1976–83 . . . . . Henry, 4:476–93; 6:370–401
1990–95 . . . . . Garrett, 2:133–240
2007 . . . . . . . . Akin, 604–85
2013 . . . . . . . . Erickson, 771–821

### 4. Dispensational
1947 . . . . . . . . Chafer, 1:397–414; 6:26–298
1949 . . . . . . . . Thiessen, 251–56
1986 . . . . . . . . Ryrie, 341–90
2002–2005 . . Geisler, 2:286–91, 675–78
2017 . . . . . . . . MacArthur and Mayhue, 333–92

### 5. Lutheran
1917–24 . . . . . Pieper (no extensive treatment, but see extensive index entries: 4:391–99)
1934 . . . . . . . . Mueller, 443

### 6. Reformed (or Presbyterian)
1559 . . . . . . . . Calvin, 2:537–42 (3.1)
1679–85 . . . . . Turretin, *IET*, 1:302–10, 2:340–47, 542–58
1887–1921 . . . Warfield, *SSW*, 1:203–22; *BD*, 101–32
1894 . . . . . . . . Shedd, 47, 225, 242–53
1906–11 . . . . . Bavinck, *RD*, 2:182–87, 311–14
1910 . . . . . . . . Vos, 1:53, 66–67
1937–66 . . . . . Murray, *CW*, 1:138–42, 186–92; *CW*, 3:210–14
1938 . . . . . . . . Berkhof, 423–31
1998 . . . . . . . . Reymond, 312–16, 331–37, 391–92
2008 . . . . . . . . Van Genderen and Velema, 753–818
2011 . . . . . . . . Horton, 551–60
2013 . . . . . . . . Frame, 401, 472, 923–27
2013 . . . . . . . . Culver, 574, 707, 758–59, 800
2016 . . . . . . . . Allen and Swain, 101–2
2017 . . . . . . . . Barrett, 393–422
2019 . . . . . . . . Letham, 86–93

### 7. Renewal (or charismatic/Pentecostal)
1988–92 . . . . . Williams, 2:137–207, 237–70
1993 . . . . . . . . Menzies and Horton, 133–44
1995 . . . . . . . . Horton, 375–422
2008 . . . . . . . . Duffield and Van Cleave, 271–87

## SECTIONS IN REPRESENTATIVE ROMAN CATHOLIC SYSTEMATIC THEOLOGIES

### 1. *Roman Catholic: Traditional*
1955 . . . . . . . . Ott (no explicit treatment)

### 2. *Roman Catholic: Post–Vatican II*
1980 . . . . . . . . McBrien (no explicit treatment)

2012 . . . . . . . . *CCC*, paragraphs 687–747

## OTHER WORKS

Allison, Gregg. *Historical Theology: An Introduction to Christian Doctrine; A Companion to Wayne Grudem's* Systematic Theology. Grand Rapids: Zondervan, 2011, 430–52.

Blomberg, Craig L. "Holy Spirit." In *BTDB*, 344–48.

Bruner, Frederick Dale. *A Theology of the Holy Spirit.* Grand Rapids: Eerdmans, 1970.

Burgess, Stanley M. *The Holy Spirit: Ancient Christian Traditions.* Grand Rapids: Baker, 1997.

———. *The Holy Spirit: Eastern Christian Traditions.* Grand Rapids: Baker, 1989.

———. *The Holy Spirit: Medieval Roman Catholic and Reformation Traditions (Sixth–Sixteenth Centuries).* Grand Rapids: Baker, 1997.

Burns, Lanier. *The Nearness of God: His Presence with His People.* Phillipsburg, NJ: P&R, 2009.

Carson, D. A. *Showing the Spirit: A Theological Exposition of 1 Corinthians 12–14.* Grand Rapids: Baker, 1987.

Carter, Charles. *The Person and Ministry of the Holy Spirit.* Grand Rapids: Baker, 1974.

Caulley, T. S. "Holy Spirit." In *EDT1*, 521–27.

Cole, G. A. "Holy Spirit." In *EDT3*, 395–98.

Cole, Graham A. *He Who Gives Life: The Doctrine of the Holy Spirit.* Wheaton, IL: Crossway, 2007.

Duvall, J. Scott. *God's Relational Presence: The Cohesive Center of Biblical Theology.* Grand Rapids: Baker Academic, 2019.

Fee, Gordon D. *God's Empowering Presence: The Holy Spirit in the Letters of Paul.* Peabody, MA: Hendrickson, 1994.

———. *Paul, the Spirit, and the People of God.* Peabody, MA: Hendrickson, 1996.

Gaffin, Richard B., Jr. "The Holy Spirit." *WTJ* 43, no. 1 (Fall 1980): 58–78.

Green, Michael. *I Believe in the Holy Spirit.* Grand Rapids: Eerdmans, 1975.

Gromacki, Robert Glenn. *The Holy Spirit: Who He Is, What He Does.* Nashville: Word, 1999.

Hamilton, James M. *God's Indwelling Presence: The Holy Spirit in the Old & New Testaments.* Nashville: B&H, 2006.

Hawthorne, Gerald F. "Holy Spirit." In *DLNT*, 489–99.

———. *The Presence and the Power: The Significance of the Holy Spirit in the Life and Ministry of Jesus.* Dallas: Word, 1991.

Hildebrandt, Wilf. *An Old Testament Theology of the Spirit of God.* Peabody, MA: Hendrickson, 1995.

Hoekema, Anthony A. "The Role of the Holy Spirit." In *Saved By Grace*, 28–53. Grand Rapids: Eerdmans; Exeter: Paternoster, 1989.

Horton, S. M. *What the Bible Says about the Holy Spirit.* Springfield, MO: Gospel, 1976.

Hughes, Kyle R. *How the Spirit Became God: The Mosaic of Early Christian Pneumatology.* Eugene, OR: Cascade, 2020.

Kärkkäinen, Veli-Matti. "Pneumatology." In *GDT*, 659–69.

Ladd, George E. *The Presence of the Future: The Eschatology of Biblical Realism.* Grand Rapids: Eerdmans, 1974.

Moule, C. F. D. *The Holy Spirit.* Grand Rapids: Eerdmans, 1978.

Pache, Rene. *The Person and Work of the Holy Spirit.* Chicago: Moody Publishers, 1954.

Packer, J. I. "Holy Spirit." In *NDT1*, 316–19.

———. *Keep in Step with the Spirit.* Old Tappan, NJ: Revell, 1984.

Paige, Terence P. "Holy Spirit." In *DPL*, 404–13.

Palmer, Edwin H. *The Person and Ministry of the Holy Spirit.* Grand Rapids: Baker, 1958.

Ryrie, C. C. *The Holy Spirit.* Chicago: Moody Publishers, 1965.

Sawyer, M. James, and Daniel B. Wallace, eds. *Who's Afraid of the Holy Spirit? An Investigation into the Ministry of the Spirit of God Today.* Dallas: Biblical Studies, 2005.

Smail, T. A. "Holy Spirit." In *NDT2*, 421–25.

Smeaton, G. *The Doctrine of the Holy Spirit.* 2nd ed. Edinburgh: T&T Clark, 1889.

Sproul, R. C. *The Mystery of the Holy Spirit.* Wheaton, IL: Tyndale, 1990.

Stott, John R. W. *Baptism and Fullness: The Work of the Holy Spirit Today.* Downers Grove, IL: InterVarsity Press, 1964.

Swete, Henry B. *The Holy Spirit in the New Testament.* 2nd ed. London: Macmillan, 1910.

Turner, M. M. B. "Holy Spirit." In *DJG,* 341–51.

———. "Holy Spirit." In *NDBT,* 551–58.

Walvoord, John F. *The Holy Spirit: A Comprehensive Study of the Person and Work of the Holy Spirit.* Wheaton, IL: Van Kampen, 1954.

White, John. *When the Spirit Comes with Power.* Downers Grove, IL: InterVarsity Press, 1988.

Wood, Leon J. *The Holy Spirit in the Old Testament.* Grand Rapids: Zondervan, 1976.

Yarnell, Malcolm B. "The Person and Work of the Holy Spirit." In *A Theology for the Church,* edited by Daniel L. Akin et al., 604–84. Nashville: B&H, 2007.

## SCRIPTURE MEMORY PASSAGE

**Romans 8:12–14:** So then, brothers, we are debtors, not to the flesh, to live according to the flesh. For if you live according to the flesh you will die, but if by the Spirit you put to death the deeds of the body, you will live. For all who are led by the Spirit of God are sons of God.

## HYMN

### "Come, O Creator Spirit"

This is one of the oldest hymns in any hymnal, written by an anonymous author in the tenth century or earlier. It directly addresses the Holy Spirit and asks him to come and bring blessing in our hearts, filling us with joy and love and praise, and giving us protection from the enemy and peace in our lives.

*Come, O Creator Spirit blest,*
*And in our hearts take up thy rest;*
*Spirit of grace, with heav'nly aid*
*Come to the souls whom thou hast made.*

*Thou art the Comforter, we cry,*
*Sent to the earth from God Most High,*
*Fountain of life and fire of love,*
*And our anointing from above.*

*Bringing from heav'n our sev'n-fold dow'r,*
*Sign of our God's right hand of pow'r,*
*O blessed Spirit, promised long,*
*Thy coming wakes the heart to song.*

*Make our dull minds with rapture glow,*
*Let human hearts with love o'erflow;*
*And, when our feeble flesh would fail,*
*May thine immortal strength prevail.*

*Far from our souls the foe repel,*
*Grant us in peace henceforth to dwell;*
*Ill shall not come, nor harm betide,*
*If only thou wilt be our guide.*

*Show us the Father, Holy One,*
*Help us to know th' eternal Son;*
*Spirit divine, for evermore*
*Thee will we trust and thee adore.*

Anon., tenth century

## CONTEMPORARY WORSHIP MUSIC

### "Holy Spirit"

*Holy Spirit, living Breath of God,*
*Breathe new life into my willing soul.*
*Let the presence of the risen Lord*
*Come renew my heart and make me whole.*
*Cause Your word to come alive in me.*
*Give me faith for what I cannot see.*
*Give me passion for Your purity.*
*Holy Spirit, breathe new life in me.*

*Holy Spirit come abide within.*
*May Your joy be seen in all I do.*
*Love enough to cover ev'ry sin*
*In each thought and deed and attitude.*
*Kindness to the greatest and the least,*
*Gentleness that sows the path of peace,*
*Turn my strivings into works of grace,*
*Breath of God show Christ in all I do.*

*Holy Spirit, from creation's birth*
*Giving life to all that God has made,*
*Show Your power once again on earth.*
*Cause Your church to hunger for Your ways.*
*Let the fragrance of our pray'rs arise.*
*Lead us on the road of sacrifice*
*That in unity the face of Christ*
*May be clear for all the world to see.*

Words by Stuart Townend and Keith Getty[28]

---

# PART 5

# The Doctrine of the Application of Redemption

# CHAPTER 31

# Common Grace

*What are the undeserved blessings that God gives to all people, both believers and unbelievers?*

## EXPLANATION AND SCRIPTURAL BASIS

### A. INTRODUCTION AND DEFINITION

When Adam and Eve sinned, they became worthy of eternal punishment and separation from God (Gen. 2:17). In the same way, when human beings sin today they become liable to the wrath of God and to eternal punishment: "The wages of sin is death" (Rom. 6:23). This means that once people sin, God's justice would require only one thing—that they be eternally separated from God, cut off from experiencing *any* good from him, and that they live forever in hell, receiving only his wrath eternally. In fact, this was what happened to angels who sinned, and it could justly have happened to us as well: *"God did not spare angels when they sinned*, but cast them into hell and committed them to chains of gloomy darkness to be kept until the judgment" (2 Peter 2:4).

But in fact Adam and Eve did not die at once (though the sentence of death *began* to be worked out in their lives on the day they sinned). The full execution of the sentence of death was delayed for many years. Moreover, millions of their descendants even to this day do not die and go to hell as soon as they sin, but they continue to live for many years, enjoying countless blessings in this world. How can this be? *How can God continue to give blessings to sinners who deserve only death*—not only to those who will ultimately be saved but also to millions who will never be saved, whose sins will never be forgiven?

The answer to these questions is that God bestows *common grace*. We may define common grace as follows: *common grace is the grace of God by which he gives people innumerable blessings that are not part of salvation.* The word *common* here indicates something that is common to all people and is not restricted to believers or to the elect only.

In distinction from common grace, the grace of God that brings people to salvation is often called "saving grace." Of course, when we talk about "common grace" and "saving grace," we are not implying that there are two different kinds of grace in God himself but only that God's grace manifests itself in the world in two different ways. Common grace is different from saving grace in its *results* (it does not bring about salvation), in its *recipients* (it is given to believers and unbelievers alike), and in its *source* (it does not directly flow from Christ's atoning work, since Christ's death did not earn any measure of forgiveness for unbelievers, and therefore did not merit the blessings of common grace for them either). However, on this last point it should be said that common grace does flow *indirectly* from Christ's redemptive work because the fact that God did not judge the world at once when sin entered it was primarily or perhaps exclusively due to the fact that he planned eventually to save some sinners through the death of his Son.[1]

## B. Examples of Common Grace

If we look at the world around us and contrast it with the fires of hell that the world deserves, we can immediately see abundant evidence of God's common grace in thousands of examples in everyday life. We can distinguish several specific categories in which this common grace is seen.

## 1. The Physical Realm

Unbelievers continue to live in this world solely because of God's common grace—every breath that people take is of grace, for the wages of sin is death, not life. Moreover, the earth does not produce only thorns and thistles (Gen. 3:18) or remain a parched desert, but by God's common grace it produces food and materials for clothing and shelter, often in great abundance and diversity. Jesus said, "Love your enemies and pray for those who persecute you, so that you may be sons of your Father who is in heaven. For *he makes his sun rise on the evil and on the good, and sends rain on the just and on the unjust*" (Matt. 5:44–45). Here Jesus appeals to God's abundant common grace as an encouragement to his disciples that they too should bestow love and prayer for blessing on unbelievers (cf. Luke 6:35–36). Similarly, Paul told the people of Lystra, "In past generations he allowed all the nations to walk in their own ways. Yet he did not leave himself without witness, for he did good *by giving you rains from heaven and fruitful seasons, satisfying your hearts with food and gladness*" (Acts 14:16–17).

The Old Testament also speaks of the common grace of God that comes to unbelievers as well as to believers. One specific example is Potiphar, the Egyptian captain of the guard who purchased Joseph as a slave: "*The LORD blessed the Egyptian's house* for Joseph's sake; the blessing of the LORD was on all that he had, in house and field" (Gen. 39:5). David speaks in a much more general way about all the creatures God has made: "The LORD is good to all, and his mercy is over all that he has made. . . . The eyes of all look to you, and you give them their food in due season. You open your hand; you satisfy the desire of every living thing" (Ps. 145:9, 15–16).

These verses are another reminder that the goodness that is found in the whole creation is due to God's goodness and compassion.

We even see evidence of God's common grace in the beauty of the natural world. Though nature itself is in "bondage to corruption" and has been "subjected to futility" (Rom. 8:21, 20) because of the curse of the fall (Gen. 3:17–19), much beauty remains

---

1. It should be noted that I have put this chapter on common grace in part 5 of this book, "The Doctrine of the Application of Redemption," not because common grace flows directly from Christ's redemptive work (it does not) but because it has a role of preparing for and assisting in God's work of the application of redemption to believers.

in the natural world. The beauty of multicolored flowers, of grass and woodlands, of rivers and lakes and mountains and ocean shores, remains as a daily testimony to the continuing common grace of God. Unbelievers deserve to enjoy none of this beauty, but by God's grace they can enjoy much of it for their whole lives.

## 2. The Intellectual Realm

Satan is "a liar and the father of lies," and "there is no truth in him" (John 8:44), because he is fully given over to evil and to the irrationality and commitment to false-hood that accompanies radical evil. But human beings in the world today, even unbeliev-ers, are not totally given over to lying, irrationality, and ignorance. All people are able to have some grasp of truth; indeed, some have great intelligence and understanding. This also must be seen as a result of God's grace. John speaks of Jesus as "the true light, *which gives light to everyone*" (John 1:9), for in his role as creator and sustainer of the universe (not particularly in his role as redeemer) the Son of God allows enlightenment and understanding to come to all people in the world.[2]

God's common grace in the intellectual realm is seen in the fact that all people have a knowledge of God: "Although *they knew God*, they did not honor him as God or give thanks to him" (Rom. 1:21). This means that there is a sense of God's existence and often a hunger to know God that he allows to remain in people's hearts, even though it often results in many differing man-made religions. Therefore, even when speaking to people who held to false religions, Paul could find a point of contact regarding knowl-edge of God's existence, as he did when speaking to the Athenian philosophers: "Men of Athens, I perceive that in every way you are very religious. . . . What therefore you worship as unknown, this I proclaim to you" (Acts 17:22–23).

The common grace of God in the intellectual realm also results in an ability to grasp truth and distinguish it from error, and to experience growth in knowledge that can be used in the investigation of the universe and in the task of subduing the earth. This means that *all science and technology carried out by non-Christians is a result of common grace*, allowing them to make incredible discoveries and inventions, to develop the earth's resources into many material goods, to produce and distribute those resources, and to have skill in their productive work. In a practical sense this means that every

---

2. Since the context of John 1 is talking about Christ coming into the world, it is better to take the phrase "was coming into the world" to modify the "true light," Christ (so ESV, RSV, NASB, NIV), rather than "every man" or "everyone" (so KJV, NASB mg., NIV mg.), though both are grammatically possible. In either case, the verse still says that Christ "gives light to" or "enlight-ens" (RSV) every person. Though some have argued that this enlightening is just the shining of the light of Christ's incarnate presence in the world (so D. A. Carson, *The Gospel according to John* [Leicester: Inter-Varsity Press; Grand Rapids: Eerdmans, 1991], 123–24), it is more likely that this enlightening is the light of general revelation that all people receive, the ability to observe and understand many true facts about God and the universe (so Leon Morris, *The Gospel according to John* [Grand Rapids: Eerdmans, 1971], 94–95). This is because (1) when John specifies that Christ "gives light to *everyone*" (rather than "all people" or "the world"), he suggests to us that this enlightening takes place for every individual, which would be true of general knowledge, but not of knowledge of Christ. (2) This sense allows the phrase "gives light to" to speak of an *actual* enlightening, not just a potential one: Christ here is said to enlighten, not just to offer enlightenment. (3) This sense heightens the ironic contrast in vv. 9–10: though Christ gives knowledge to all mankind, and though he created all people, they did not know him or receive him.

time we walk into a grocery store or ride in an automobile or enter a house, we should remember that we are experiencing the results of the abundant common grace of God poured out so richly on all mankind.

### 3. The Moral Realm

God also by common grace restrains people from being as evil as they could be. Once again, the demonic realm, totally devoted to evil and destruction, provides a clear contrast with human society in which evil is clearly restrained. If people persist hard-heartedly and repeatedly in following sin over a course of time, God will eventually "give them up" to greater and greater sin (cf. Ps. 81:12; Rom. 1:24, 26, 28), but in the case of most human beings, they do not fall to the depths to which their sin would otherwise take them because God intervenes and puts restraints on their conduct. One very effective restraint is the force of conscience. Paul says, "When Gentiles, who do not have the law, by nature do what the law requires, they are a law to themselves, even though they do not have the law. They show that *the work of the law is written on their hearts*, while *their conscience also bears witness*, and their conflicting thoughts accuse or even excuse them" (Rom. 2:14–15).

This inward sense of right and wrong that God gives to all people means that they will frequently approve of moral standards that reflect many of the moral standards in Scripture. Even those who are given up to the most base sin, Paul says, "Know God's righteous decree that those who practice such things deserve to die" (Rom. 1:32). In many other cases, this inward sense of conscience leads people to establish laws and customs in society that are, in terms of the outward behavior they approve or prohibit, quite like the moral laws of Scripture: people often establish laws or have customs that respect the sanctity of marriage and the family, protect human life, and prohibit theft and falsehood in speech.[3] Because of this, people will frequently live in ways that are morally upright and outwardly conform to the moral standards found in Scripture. Though their moral behavior cannot earn merit with God (since Scripture clearly says that "no one is justified before God by the law," Gal. 3:11, and that "all have turned aside; together they have become worthless; no one does good, not even one," Rom. 3:12), nevertheless in some sense less than earning God's eternal approval or merit, unbelievers do "do good." Jesus implies this when he says, "If you do good to those *who do good to you*, what benefit is that to you? For *even sinners do the same*" (Luke 6:33; cf. 2 Kings 12:2 and 2 Chron. 24:2, where Joash is said to have done good during his reign as king, with 2 Chron. 24:17–25, where he did such evil as to make it apparent that there was no saving faith in his life). Of course, in areas where the gospel has had great influence and the church is strong, it will have a stronger moral influence on society than in places where the gospel has never reached or where it has little restraining influence (for

---

3. Of course, the operation of conscience is never perfect in sinful people in this life (as Paul realizes in Rom. 2:15), so societies will vary in the degree to which they approve differing aspects of God's moral laws. Nevertheless, significant resemblance to the moral laws of Scripture is found in the laws and customs of every human society.

example, in cannibalistic societies—or even in modern Western society where belief in the gospel and moral absolutes have both been abandoned by the dominant culture).

God also demonstrates his common grace by giving *warnings of final judgment in the operation of the natural world*. God has so ordered the world that living according to his moral standards very often brings rewards in the natural realm, and violating God's standards often brings destruction to people, in both cases indicating the eventual direction of the final judgment: Honesty, hard work, showing love and kindness to others, and faithfulness in marriage and family will (except in the most corrupt societies) bring much more material and emotional reward in this life than dishonesty, laziness, cruelty, marital infidelity, and other wrongs such as drunkenness, drug abuse, theft, and so forth. These normal consequences of sin or righteousness should serve as a warning of judgment to come, and in this way, they are also examples of God's common grace.

## 4. The Creative Realm

God has allowed significant measures of skill in artistic and musical areas, as well as in other spheres in which creativity and skill can be expressed, such as athletics, cooking, writing, and so forth. Moreover, God gives to us an ability to appreciate beauty in many areas of life. And in this area as well as in the physical and intellectual realm, the blessings of common grace are sometimes poured out on unbelievers even more abundantly than on believers. Yet in all cases it is a result of the grace of God.

## 5. The Societal Realm

God's grace is evident in the existence of various organizations and structures in human society. We see this first in the human family, evidenced in the fact that Adam and Eve remained husband and wife after the fall and then had children, both sons and daughters (Gen. 5:4). Adam and Eve's children married and formed families for themselves (Gen. 4:17, 19, 26). The human family persists today—not simply as an institution for believers but for all people.

Human government is also a result of common grace. It was instituted in principle by God after the flood (see Gen. 9:6) and is clearly stated to be given by God in Romans 13:1: "There is no authority except from God, and those that exist have been instituted by God." It is clear that government is a gift from God for mankind generally, for Paul says the ruler is "God's servant for your good" and that he is "the servant of God, an avenger who carries out God's wrath on the wrongdoer" (Rom. 13:4). One of the primary means God uses to restrain evil in the world is human government. Human laws and police forces and judicial systems provide a powerful deterrent to evil actions, and these are necessary, for there is much evil in the world that is irrational and that can only be restrained by force because it will not be deterred by reason or education. Of course, the sinfulness of man can also affect governments so that they become corrupt and actually encourage evil rather than good. This is just to say that human government, like all the other blessings of common grace that God gives, can be used either for good or for evil purposes.

Other organizations in human society include educational institutions, businesses and corporations, voluntary associations (such as many charitable and public service groups), and countless examples of ordinary human friendship. All of these function to bring some measure of good to human beings, and all are expressions of the common grace of God.

### 6. The Religious Realm

Even in the realm of human religion, God's common grace brings some blessings to unbelieving people. Jesus tells us, "Love your enemies and *pray for those who persecute you*" (Matt. 5:44), and since there is no restriction in the context simply to pray for their salvation, and since the command to pray for our persecutors is coupled with a command to love them, it seems reasonable to conclude that God intends to answer our prayers even for our persecutors with regard to many areas of life. In fact, Paul specifically commands that we pray "for kings and all who are in high positions" (1 Tim. 2:1–2). When we seek good for unbelievers, it is consistent with God's practice of granting sunshine and rain "on the just and on the unjust" (Matt. 5:45) and consistent with the practice of Jesus during his earthly ministry when he healed every person who was brought to him (Luke 4:40). There is no indication that he required all of them to believe in him or to agree that he was the Messiah before he granted physical healing to them.

Does God answer the prayers of unbelievers? Although God has not promised to answer the prayers of unbelievers as he has promised to answer the prayers of those who come in Jesus' name, and although he has no obligation to answer the prayers of unbelievers, God may out of his common grace still hear and grant the prayers of unbelievers, thus demonstrating his mercy and goodness in yet another way (cf. Ps. 145:9, 15; Matt. 7:22; Luke 6:35–36). This is apparently the sense of 1 Timothy 4:10, which says that God is "the Savior of all people, especially of those who believe." Here "Savior" cannot be restricted in meaning to "one who forgives sins and gives eternal life" because these things are not given to those who do not believe; "Savior" must have a more general sense here, namely, "one who rescues from distress, one who delivers." In cases of trouble or distress God often does hear the prayers of unbelievers, and graciously delivers them from their trouble. Moreover, even unbelievers often have a sense of gratitude toward God for the goodness of creation, for deliverance from danger, and for the blessings of family, home, friendships, and country. In addition, unbelievers who come in close contact with the church and perhaps associate with it for a time can have some religious experiences that seem very close to the experience of those who are saved (see Heb. 6:4–6; Matt. 7:22–23).[4]

Finally, even the proclamation of the gospel to those who do not ultimately accept it is a clear declaration of the mercy and grace of God, which gives clear witness to the fact that God does not delight in the death or condemnation of any of his creatures (cf. Ezek. 33:11; 1 Tim. 2:4).

---

4. See the extended discussion of Heb. 6:4–6 in chapter 40, pp. 979–84.

## 7. Common Grace and Special Grace Influence Each Other

Common grace, of course, influences and enriches the church, since apart from God's common grace given to carpenters and other kinds of craftsmen, there would be no church buildings; apart from common grace given to printers and typesetters and bookbinders (and even to those who work in paper mills or cut trees from forests to make paper), there would be no Bibles. In countless ways in everyday activities the church benefits from common grace.

On the other hand, the special grace that God gives to those who are saved brings more of the blessings of common grace to unbelievers living in the realm of the church's influence. Unbelievers benefit from the example of Christian lives that they see in society, from the prayers and the acts of mercy that Christians do for the community, from the knowledge of the teachings of Scripture and its wisdom in which they find some intellectual and moral benefit, and from the influence on laws, customs, and beliefs of a society that comes through the social and political activities of Christians. Historically it has often been the powerful presence of those whose lives were changed by the gospel that has resulted in freedom for slaves (in the British colonies and the United States), rights for women, widespread public education, technological and scientific progress, increased productivity in the economy, a high value placed on work and thrift and honesty, and so forth.

## 8. Common Grace Does Not Save People

In spite of all of this, we must realize that common grace is different from saving grace. Common grace does not change the human heart or bring people to genuine repentance and faith—it cannot and does not save people (though in the intellectual and moral sphere it can give some preparation to make people more disposed toward accepting the gospel). Common grace restrains sin but does not change anyone's foundational disposition to sin, nor does it in any significant measure purify fallen human nature.[5]

We must also recognize that the actions of unbelievers performed by virtue of common grace do not in themselves merit God's approval or favor. These actions do not spring from faith ("Whatever does not proceed from faith is sin," Rom. 14:23), nor are they motivated by a love for God (Matt. 22:37) but by love of self in some form. Therefore, although we may readily say that the works of unbelievers that externally conform to the laws of God are "good" in some sense, they nonetheless are not good in terms of meriting God's approval nor of making God obligated to the sinner in any way.

Finally, we should recognize that unbelievers often receive more common grace than

---

5. The viewpoint on common grace presented in this chapter is consistent with the Reformed or Calvinistic perspective of the book as a whole, a perspective that has been argued for more specifically in discussing God's sovereignty (chapter 13, pp. 258–60), God's providence (chapter 16), sin (chapter 24), and election, the gospel call, and regeneration (chapters 32–34). We should note, however, that an Arminian understanding of common grace would be different at this point; an Arminian view would say that common grace gives to every person the *ability* to turn to God in faith and repentance and in fact *influences* the sinner to do this unless he or she specifically resists it. Therefore, on an Arminian understanding, common grace has a function that much more clearly relates to saving grace—in fact, common grace is simply an early expression of the totality of saving grace. This position (that the ability to repent and believe is given to all people) is discussed in chapter 32 on election and chapters 33 and 34 on the gospel call and regeneration.

believers—they may be more skillful, harder working, more intelligent, more creative, or have more of the material benefits of this life to enjoy. This in no way indicates that they are more favored by God in an absolute sense or that they will gain any share in eternal salvation but only that God distributes the blessings of common grace in various ways, often granting very significant blessings to unbelievers. In all of this, they should, of course, acknowledge God's goodness (Acts 14:17), and should recognize that God's revealed will is that "God's kindness" should eventually lead them "to repentance" (Rom. 2:4).

## C. Reasons for Common Grace

Why does God bestow common grace on undeserving sinners who will never come to salvation? We can suggest at least four reasons.

### 1. To Redeem Those Who Will Be Saved

Peter says that the day of judgment and final execution of punishment is being delayed because there are yet more people who will be saved: "The Lord is not slow to fulfill his promise as some count slowness, but is patient toward you, *not wishing that any should perish, but that all should reach repentance.* But the day of the Lord will come like a thief" (2 Peter 3:9–10). In fact, this reason was true from the beginning of human history, for if God wanted to save any people out of the whole mass of sinful humanity, he could not have destroyed all sinners immediately (for then there would be no human race left). He chose rather to allow sinful humans to live for some time, so that they might have an opportunity to repent, and so that they would bear children and enable subsequent generations to live and then hear the gospel and repent.

### 2. To Demonstrate God's Goodness and Mercy

God's goodness and mercy are not only seen in the salvation of believers but also in the blessings he gives to undeserving sinners. When God "is kind to the ungrateful and the evil" (Luke 6:35), his kindness is revealed in the universe, to his glory. David says, "The LORD is *good to all*, and his mercy is over all that he has made" (Ps. 145:9). In the story of Jesus talking with the rich young ruler, we read, "Jesus, looking at him, *loved him*" (Mark 10:21), even though the man was an unbeliever and would in a moment turn away from Jesus because of his great possessions. Berkhof says that God "showers untold blessings upon all men and also clearly indicates that these are the expressions of a favorable disposition in God, which falls short however of the positive volition to pardon their sin, to lift their sentence, and to grant them salvation."[6]

It is not unjust for God to delay the execution of punishment upon sin and to give

---

6. Louis Berkhof, *Systematic Theology* (Grand Rapids: Eerdmans, 1941), 445.

temporary blessings to human beings, because the punishment is not forgotten, just delayed. In delaying punishment, God shows clearly that he has no pleasure in executing final judgment but rather delights in the salvation of men and women. "As I live, declares the LORD God, I have no pleasure in the death of the wicked, but that the wicked turn from his way and live" (Ezek. 33:11). God "desires all people to be saved and to come to the knowledge of the truth" (1 Tim. 2:4). In all of this the delay of punishment gives clear evidence of God's mercy and goodness and love.

### 3. To Demonstrate God's Justice

When God repeatedly invites sinners to come to faith, and when they repeatedly refuse his invitations, the justice of God in condemning them is seen much more clearly. Paul warns that those who persist in unbelief are simply storing up more wrath for themselves: "Because of your hard and impenitent heart you are storing up wrath for yourself on the day of wrath when God's righteous judgment will be revealed" (Rom. 2:5). On the day of judgment "every mouth" will be "stopped" (Rom. 3:19) and no one will be able to object that God has been unjust.

### 4. To Demonstrate God's Glory

Finally, God's glory is shown in many ways by the activities of human beings in all the areas in which common grace is operative. In developing and exercising dominion over the earth, men and women demonstrate and reflect the wisdom of their Creator, demonstrate Godlike qualities of skill and moral virtue and authority over the universe, and so forth. Though all of these activities are tainted by sinful motives, they nonetheless reflect the excellence of our Creator and therefore bring glory to God, not fully or perfectly but nonetheless significantly.

## D. Our Response to the Doctrine of Common Grace

In thinking about the varying kinds of goodness seen in the lives of unbelievers because of God's abundant common grace, we should keep three points in mind.

### 1. Common Grace Does Not Mean That Those Who Receive It Will Be Saved

Even exceptionally large amounts of common grace do not imply that those who receive it will be saved. Even the most skilled, most intelligent, wealthiest, and most powerful people in the world still need the gospel of Jesus Christ, or they will be condemned for eternity! Even our kindest and most moral neighbors need the gospel of Jesus Christ, or they will be condemned for eternity! They may appear outwardly to have no needs, but Scripture still says that unbelievers are "enemies" of God (Rom. 5:10; cf. Col. 1:21; James 4:4) and are "against" Christ (Matt. 12:30). They "walk as enemies of the cross of Christ" and have their "minds set on earthly things" (Phil. 3:18–19) and are "by nature children of wrath, like the rest of mankind" (Eph. 2:3).

### 2. We Must Be Careful Not to Reject the Good
### Things That Unbelievers Do as Totally Evil

By common grace, unbelievers do *some* good, and we should see God's hand in it and be thankful for common grace as it operates in every friendship, every act of kindness, every way in which it brings blessing to others. All of this—though the unbeliever does not know it—is ultimately from God, and he deserves the glory for it.

### 3. The Doctrine of Common Grace Should Stir Our
### Hearts to Much Greater Thankfulness to God

When we walk down a street and see houses and gardens and families dwelling in security, or when we do business in the marketplace and see the abundant results of technological progress, or when we walk through the woods and see the beauty of nature, or when we are protected by government,[7] or when we are educated from the vast storehouse of human knowledge, we should realize not only that God in his sovereignty is ultimately responsible for all of these blessings but also that God has granted them all to sinners who are *totally undeserving* of any of them! These blessings in the world are not only evidence of God's power and wisdom; they are also continually a manifestation of his abundant *grace*. The realization of this fact should cause our hearts to swell with thanksgiving to God in every activity of life.

## QUESTIONS FOR PERSONAL APPLICATION

1. Before you read this chapter, did you have a different viewpoint on whether unbelievers deserved the ordinary benefits of the world around them? How has your perspective changed, if at all?

2. Do you know of examples where God has answered the prayers of unbelievers who were in difficulty, or answered your prayers for the needs of an unbelieving friend? Has it provided an opening for sharing the gospel? Did the unbeliever eventually come to salvation in Christ? Do you think that God often uses the blessings of common grace as a means to prepare people to receive the gospel?

3. In what ways will this doctrine change the way you relate to an unbelieving neighbor or friend? Will it tend to make you thankful for the good that you see in their lives? How do you think this might affect your relationship with that person in a more general sense?

4. As you look around the place where you are at this moment, can you name at least twenty different examples of common grace that you can see? How does that make you feel?

---

7. Paul explicitly directs us to offer to God "thanksgivings" for "kings and all who are in high positions" (1 Tim. 2:1–2).

5. Has this chapter changed the way you view creative activities such as music, art, architecture, or poetry, or (something that is very similar) the creativity expressed in athletic activities?

6. If you are kind to an unbeliever and he or she never comes to accept Christ, has it done any good in God's sight (see Matt. 5:44–45; Luke 6:32–36)? What good has it done? Why do you think that God is good even to those who will never be saved—in what way does it further his purposes for the universe? Do you think we have any obligation to give more effort to showing good to believers than to unbelievers? Can you name any passages of Scripture that help in answering this question?

**Special Terms**
*common grace*
*special grace*

# BIBLIOGRAPHY

(For an explanation of this bibliography see the note on the bibliography to chapter 1, pp. 23–24. Complete bibliographical data may be found on pp. 1489–96.) Note: This subject is not often treated in a separate section in systematic theologies, but see the few sections listed below in the following works:

## SECTIONS IN EVANGELICAL SYSTEMATIC THEOLOGIES

1. *Anglican (Episcopalian)*
   1930 . . . . . . . . Thomas, 210–14
   2001 . . . . . . . . Packer, 9–10

2. *Arminian (Wesleyan or Methodist)*
   1992 . . . . . . . . Oden, 3:83–449
   2002 . . . . . . . . Cottrell, 307

3. *Baptist*
   1990–95 . . . . . Garrett, 1:49–62
   2007 . . . . . . . . Akin, 71–118

4. *Dispensational*
   2002–05 . . . . . Geisler, 3:130–31
   2017 . . . . . . . . MacArthur and Mayhue, 487–89

5. *Lutheran*
   1934 . . . . . . . . Mueller, 242–54

6. *Reformed (or Presbyterian)*
   1679–85 . . . . . Turretin, *IET*, 1:241–44
   1871–73 . . . . . Hodge, 2:654–74
   1894 . . . . . . . . Shedd, 334–35, 758–60
   1906–11 . . . . . Bavinck, *RD*, 2:16–18, 3:216–18, 4:256–57
   1910 . . . . . . . . Vos, 4:10, 12–13, 61
   1937–66 . . . . . Murray, *CW*, 2:93–119
   1938 . . . . . . . . Berkhof, 432–46
   1998 . . . . . . . . Reymond, 402–3
   2008 . . . . . . . . Van Genderen and Velema, 42–57
   2011 . . . . . . . . Horton, 364–68
   2013 . . . . . . . . Frame, 176–77, 242–48
   2013 . . . . . . . . Culver, 415

2017 . . . . . . . . Barrett, 407–8

2019 . . . . . . . . Letham, 355, 443, 649–51

*7. Renewal (or charismatic/Pentecostal)*

2008 . . . . . . . . Duffield and Van Cleave, 147–54

### SECTIONS IN REPRESENTATIVE ROMAN CATHOLIC SYSTEMATIC THEOLOGIES

*1. Roman Catholic: Traditional*

1955 . . . . . . . . Ott, 238–42

*2. Roman Catholic: Post–Vatican II*

2012 . . . . . . . . *CCC*, paragraphs 1996–2005

### OTHER WORKS

Bray, G. L. "Grace." In *NDT2*, 376–78.

Clark, D. Marion, ed. *The Problem of Good: When the World Seems Fine without God*. Phillipsburg, NJ: P&R, 2014.

Green, J. B. "Grace." In *NDBT*, 524–27.

Gundry, Stanley N., Dennis L. Okholm, and Timothy R. Phillips, eds. *Four Views on Salvation in a Pluralistic World*. Grand Rapids: Zondervan, 1996.

Hoekema, Anthony A. "The Restraint of Sin." In *Created in God's Image*, 187–202. Grand Rapids: Eerdmans; Exeter: Paternoster, 1986.

Hughes, P. E. "Grace, Means of." In *EDT3*, 358.

Johnson, Dennis E. "Spiritual Antithesis: Common Grace, and Practical Theology." *WTJ* 64, no. 1 (Spring 2002): 73–94.

Kearsley, R. "Grace." In *NDT*, 280–81.

Kuyper, Abraham. *Common Grace: God's Gifts for A Fallen World*. Collected Works in Public Theology. Bellingham, WA: Lexham, 2016.

Luter, A. B., Jr. "Grace." In *DPL*, 372–74.

Mouw, Richard J. *He Shines in All That's Fair: Culture and Common Grace; The 2000 Stob Lectures*. Grand Rapids: Eerdmans, 2001.

Niehaus, Jeffrey Jay. *Biblical Theology: the Common Grace Covenants*. Vol. 1. Wooster, OH: Weaver, 2014.

Trotter, Andrew H., Jr. "Grace." In *BTDB*, 312–16.

Van Til, Cornelius. *Common Grace and the Gospel*. 2nd ed. Phillipsburg, NJ: P&R, 2015.

Van Til, Cornelius. *In Defense of the Faith*. Vol. 5, *An Introduction to Systematic Theology*. Philadelphia: Presbyterian and Reformed, 1976, 75–99, 253–62.

## SCRIPTURE MEMORY PASSAGE

**Luke 6:35–36:** But love your enemies, and do good, and lend, expecting nothing in return, and your reward will be great, and you will be sons of the Most High, for he is kind to the ungrateful and the evil. Be merciful, even as your Father is merciful.

## HYMN

### "All People That on Earth Do Dwell"

This very old setting of Psalm 100 is a call to all people on earth to praise God because of his abundant goodness.

*All people that on earth do dwell,*
*  Sing to the Lord with cheerful voice;*
*Him serve with fear, his praise forthtell,*
*  Come ye before him and rejoice.*

*The Lord ye know is God indeed;*
*  Without our aid he did us make;*
*We are his folk, he doth us feed,*
*  And for his sheep he doth us take.*

*O enter then his gates with praise,*
*  Approach with joy his courts unto;*
*Praise, laud, and bless his name always,*
*  For it is seemly so to do.*

*For why? The Lord our God is good,*
*  His mercy is forever sure;*
*His truth at all times firmly stood,*
*  And shall from age to age endure.*

Author: William Kethe, 1561

## CONTEMPORARY WORSHIP SONG

### "Unto the King (Now unto the King)"

*Now unto the king eternal,*
*Unto the King immortal,*
*Unto the King invisible,*
*The only wise God,*
*The only wise God—*

*Unto the King be glory and honor,*
*Unto the King forever,*
*Unto the King be glory and honor forever,*
*And ever, Amen, Amen.*

Words by Joey Holder[8]

---

# CHAPTER 32

# Election and Reprobation

*When and why did God choose us?*
*Are some not chosen?*

I n the earlier chapters we talked about the fact that we all have sinned and deserve eternal punishment from God and the fact that Christ died and *earned* salvation for us. But now in this unit (chapters 32–43) we will look at the way God *applies* that salvation to our lives. We begin in this chapter with God's work of election, that is, his decision to choose us to be saved before the foundation of the world. This act of election is, of course, not (strictly speaking) part of the *application* of salvation to us since it came before Christ earned our salvation when he died on the cross. But we treat election at this point because it is chronologically the *beginning* of God's dealing with us in a gracious way. Therefore, it is rightly thought of as the first step in the process of God's bringing salvation to us individually.[1]

Other steps in God's work of applying salvation to our lives include our hearing the gospel call, our being regenerated by the Holy Spirit, our responding in faith and repentance, and God forgiving us and giving us membership in his family, as well as granting us growth in the Christian life and keeping us faithful to himself throughout life. At the end of our life, we die and go into his presence; then when Christ returns, we receive resurrection bodies, and the process of acquiring salvation is complete.

Various theologians have given specific terms to a number of these events, and have often listed them in a specific order in which they believe that they occur in our lives. Such a list of the events in which God applies salvation to us is called the *order of salvation*, and is sometimes referred to by a Latin phrase, *ordo salutis*, which simply means "order of salvation." Before discussing any of these elements in the application of salvation to our lives, we can give a complete list here of the elements that will be treated in the following chapters:

---

1. This chapter could be placed elsewhere in the sequence of topics treated. It could be placed immediately after chapter 16, on God's providence, for example, since election is just one aspect of God's providential control of the world. Or it could be placed in chapter 25, as part of the treatment of the covenant of grace between God and man. Or it could be placed in chapter 40, as part of the discussion of perseverance, especially related to the question of assurance of salvation, since God's choice of us to be saved gives great assurance that he will fulfill his purposes. But I have chosen to place it here at the beginning of the chapters that discuss God's personal dealing with us in grace. (Note the similar ordering of topics by Paul in Rom. 8:29–30.)

*"The Order of Salvation"*

1. Election (God's choice of people to be saved)
2. The gospel call (proclaiming the message of the gospel)
3. Regeneration (being born again)
4. Conversion (faith and repentance)
5. Justification (right legal standing)
6. Adoption (membership in God's family)
7. Sanctification (right conduct of life)
8. Perseverance (remaining a Christian)
9. Death (going to be with the Lord)
10. Glorification (receiving a resurrection body)

We should note here that items 2–6 and part of 7 are all involved in "becoming a Christian." Numbers 7 and 8 work themselves out in this life, number 9 occurs at the end of this life, and number 10 occurs when Christ returns.[2]

We begin our discussion of the order of salvation with the first element, election. In connection with this we will also discuss at the end of this chapter the question of "reprobation," the decision of God to pass over those who will not be saved, and to punish them for their sins. As will be explained below, election and reprobation are different in several important respects, and it is important to distinguish these so that we do not think wrongly about God or his activity.

The term *predestination* is also frequently used in this discussion. In this textbook and in Reformed theology generally, *predestination* is a broader term and includes the two aspects of election (for believers) and reprobation (for unbelievers). However, the term *double predestination* is not a helpful term because it gives the impression that both election and reprobation are carried out in the same way by God and have no essential differences between them, which is certainly not true. Therefore, the term *double predestination* is not generally used by Reformed theologians, though it is sometimes used to refer to Reformed teaching by those who criticize it. The term *double predestination* will not be used in this book to refer to election and reprobation since that term blurs the distinctions between them and does not give an accurate indication of what is actually being taught.

---

2. For a discussion of the order of events in this list, see John Murray, *Redemption Accomplished and Applied* (Grand Rapids: Eerdmans, 1955), 79–87. New approaches to a synthesis of Pauline themes in the order of salvation are found in Vern Poythress, "Using Multiple Thematic Centers in Theological Synthesis: Holiness as a Test Case in Developing a Pauline Theology" (unpublished manuscript available from the Campus Bookstore, Westminster Theological Seminary, P.O. Box 27009, Philadelphia, PA 19118, or at https://www.wtsbooks .com).

## EXPLANATION AND SCRIPTURAL BASIS

We may define election as follows: *election is an act of God before creation in which he chooses some people to be saved, not on account of any foreseen merit in them but only because of his sovereign good pleasure.*

There has been much controversy in the church and much misunderstanding over this doctrine. Many of the controversial questions regarding man's will and responsibility and regarding the justice of God with respect to human choices have been discussed at some length in connection with God's providence (chapter 16). We will focus here only on those additional questions that apply specifically to the question of election.

Our approach in this chapter will be first simply to cite a number of passages from the New Testament that discuss election. Then we will attempt to understand the purpose of God that the New Testament authors see in the doctrine of election. Finally, we will attempt to clarify our understanding of this doctrine and answer some objections, and also to consider the doctrine of reprobation.

### A. Does the New Testament Teach Predestination?

Several passages in the New Testament seem to affirm quite clearly that God ordained beforehand those who would be saved. For example, when Paul and Barnabas began to preach to the gentiles in Antioch in Pisidia, Luke writes, "When the Gentiles heard this, they began rejoicing and glorifying the word of the Lord, and *as many as were appointed to eternal life believed*" (Acts 13:48). It is significant that Luke mentions the fact of election almost in passing. It is as if this were the normal occurrence when the gospel was preached. How many believed? "As many as were appointed to eternal life believed."

In Romans 8:28–30, we read,

And we know that for those who love God all things work together for good, for those who are called according to his purpose. *For those whom he foreknew he also predestined to be conformed to the image of his Son*, in order that he might be the firstborn among many brothers. *And those whom he predestined he also called, and those whom he called he also justified, and those whom he justified he also glorified.*[3]

In the following chapter, when talking about God's choosing Jacob and not Esau, Paul says it was not because of anything that Jacob or Esau had done but simply in order

---

3. Clark Pinnock says that this text does not speak of predestination to salvation but rather to a certain privilege, that of being conformed to Jesus Christ: "There is no predestination to salvation or damnation in the Bible. There is only a predestination for those who are already children of God with respect to certain privileges out ahead of them" (Pinnock, introduction to *Grace Unlimited*, ed. Clark Pinnock [Minneapolis: Bethany Fellowship, 1975], 18). But such a view does not do justice to Rom. 8:29–30, because those who are said to be predestined in this verse are not yet children of God. This is evident from the fact that Paul here speaks of predestination *before* calling or justification. Moreover, the privilege of being conformed to the image of Christ is not just for some Christians but for all.

that God's purpose of election might continue. "Though they were not yet born and had done nothing either good or bad—*in order that God's purpose of election might continue*, not because of works but because of him who calls—she was told, 'The older will serve the younger.' As it is written, 'Jacob I loved, but Esau I hated'" (Rom. 9:11–13).

Regarding the fact that some of the people of Israel were saved, but others were not, Paul says: "Israel failed to obtain what it was seeking. *The elect* obtained it, but the rest were hardened" (Rom. 11:7). Here again Paul indicates two distinct groups within the people of Israel. Those who were "the elect" obtained the salvation that they sought, while those who were not the elect simply "were hardened."

Paul talks explicitly about God's choice of believers before the foundation of the world in the beginning of Ephesians. "*He chose us in him before the foundation of the world*, that we should be holy and blameless before him. *In love he predestined us* for adoption to himself as sons through Jesus Christ, according to the purpose of his will, to the praise of his glorious grace" (Eph. 1:4–6). Here Paul is writing to believers and he specifically says that God "chose us" in Christ, referring to believers generally. In a similar way, several verses later he says, "In him we have obtained an inheritance, having been *predestined . . .* to the praise of his glory" (Eph. 1:11–12).

He writes to the Thessalonians, "For we know, brothers loved by God, that *he has chosen you*, because our gospel came to you not only in word, but also in power and in the Holy Spirit and with full conviction" (1 Thess. 1:4–5). Paul says that the fact that the Thessalonians *believed* the gospel when he preached it ("because our gospel came to you . . . in power . . . and with full conviction") *is the reason he knows that God chose them*. As soon as they came to faith, Paul concluded that long ago God had chosen them, and therefore they had believed when he preached. He later writes to the same church, "But we ought always to give thanks to God for you, brothers beloved by the Lord, because *God chose you as the firstfruits to be saved*, through sanctification by the Spirit and belief in the truth" (2 Thess. 2:13).

Although the next text does not specifically mention the election of human beings, it is interesting at this point also to notice what Paul says about angels. When he gives a solemn command to Timothy, he writes, "In the presence of God and of Christ Jesus and of *the elect angels* I charge you to keep these rules without prejudging" (1 Tim. 5:21). Paul is aware that there are good angels witnessing his command and witnessing Timothy's response to it, and he is so sure that it is God's act of election that has affected every one of those good angels that he can call them "*elect angels*."

When Paul talks about the reason why God saved us and called us to himself, he explicitly denies that it was because of our works but rather points to God's purpose and his unmerited grace in eternity past. He says God is the one "who saved us and called us to a holy calling, not because of our works but because of *his own purpose* and *grace*, *which he gave us in Christ Jesus before the ages began*" (2 Tim. 1:9).

When Peter writes an epistle to hundreds of Christians in many churches in Asia

Minor, he writes, "To those who are *elect* exiles of the Dispersion in Pontus, Galatia, Cappadocia, Asia, and Bithynia" (1 Peter 1:1). He later calls them "a *chosen* race" (1 Peter 2:9).

In John's vision in Revelation, those who do not give in to persecution and begin to worship the beast are persons whose names have been written in the book of life before the foundation of the world: "Authority was given it over every tribe and people and language and nation, and all who dwell on earth will worship it, *everyone whose name has not been written before the foundation of the world in the book of life* of the Lamb who was slain" (Rev. 13:7–8).[4] In a similar way, we read of the beast from the bottomless pit in Revelation 17: "The dwellers on earth *whose names have not been written in the book of life from the foundation of the world* will marvel to see the beast, because it was and is not and is to come" (Rev. 17:8).

## B. How Does the New Testament Present the Teaching of Election?

After reading this list of verses on election, it is important to view this doctrine in the way the New Testament itself views it.

## 1. As a Comfort

The New Testament authors often present the doctrine of election as a comfort to believers. When Paul assures the Romans that "for those who love God all things work together for good, for those who are called according to his purpose" (Rom. 8:28), he gives God's work of predestination as a reason why we can be assured of this truth. He explains in the next verse, "*For* those whom he foreknew he also predestined to be conformed to the image of his Son . . . And those whom he predestined he also called . . . justified . . . glorified" (Rom. 8:29–30). Paul's point is to say that God has *always* acted for the good of those whom he called to himself. If Paul looks into the distant past before the creation of the world, he sees that God foreknew and predestined his people to be conformed to the image of Christ.[5] If he looks at the recent past, he finds that God called and justified his people whom he had predestined. And if he then looks toward the future when Christ returns, he sees that God has determined to give perfect glorified bodies to those who believe in Christ. From eternity to eternity God has acted with the

---

4. Grammatically the phrase "before the foundation of the world" could modify either "whose name has not been written" (as here, in the ESV; also in the NASB and NIV mg.), or "the lamb that was slain" (so KJV, NIV). But the parallel expression in Rev. 17:8, "whose names have not been *written in the book of life from the foundation of the world*," seems decisive, and there only one sense is possible (the parallel wording is striking in the Greek text, since the two verses share eleven identical words in talking about people whose names are written in the book of life). Moreover, the ESV/NASB reading makes much better sense in light of the rest of Scripture: the Bible often talks

about God choosing us before the foundation of the world, but nowhere else does Scripture say that Christ was slain from the foundation of the world—a statement that simply is not true in any literal sense because Christ was not slain until he died on the cross. Therefore, on the NIV/KJV reading, the verse must be interpreted to mean something like, "God *planned* from the foundation of the world that Christ would be slain"—but that is not what the text actually says, on either reading.

5. See the discussion below (pp. 824–25) on the meaning of *foreknow* here.

good of his people in mind. But if God has *always* acted for our good and will in the future act for our good, Paul reasons, then *will he not also in our present circumstances* work every circumstance together for our good as well? In this way predestination is seen as a comfort for believers in the everyday events of life.

## 2. As a Reason to Praise God

Paul says, "He predestined us for adoption to himself as sons through Jesus Christ, according to the purpose of his will, *to the praise of his glorious grace*" (Eph. 1:5–6). Similarly, he says, "In him we have obtained an inheritance, having been predestined . . . so that we who were the first to hope in Christ might be *to the praise of his glory*" (Eph. 1:11–12).

Paul tells the Christians at Thessalonica, "*We give thanks to God* always for all of you. . . . *For we know*, brothers loved by God, *that he has chosen you*" (1 Thess. 1:2, 4). The reason Paul can give thanks to God for the Thessalonian Christians is that he knows God is ultimately responsible for their salvation and has in fact chosen them to be saved. This is made even clearer in 2 Thessalonians 2:13: "But *we ought always to give thanks to God* for you, brothers beloved by the Lord, *because God chose you* as the firstfruits to be saved." Paul was obligated to give thanks to God for the Christians at Thessalonica because he knew that their salvation was ultimately due to God's choice of them. Therefore, it is appropriate for Paul to thank God for them rather than praising them for their own saving faith.

Understood in this way, the doctrine of election does increase praise given to God for our salvation and seriously diminishes any pride that we might feel if we thought that our salvation was due to something good in us or something for which we should receive credit.

## 3. As an Encouragement to Evangelism

Paul says, "I endure everything for the sake of the elect, that they also may obtain the salvation that is in Christ Jesus with eternal glory" (2 Tim. 2:10). He knows that God has chosen some people to be saved, and he sees this as an encouragement to preach the gospel, even if it means enduring great suffering. Election is Paul's guarantee that there will be some success for his evangelism, for he knows that some of the people he speaks to will be the elect, and they will believe the gospel and be saved. It is as if someone invited us to come fishing and said, "I guarantee that you will catch some fish—they are hungry and waiting."

## C. Correcting Misunderstandings of the Doctrine of Election

## 1. Election Is Not Fatalistic or Mechanistic

Sometimes those who object to the doctrine of election say that it is "fatalism" or that it presents a "mechanistic system" for the universe. Two somewhat different objections are involved here. *Fatalism* is a system in which human choices and human decisions really do not make any difference. In fatalism, no matter what we do, things are going to turn out as they have been previously ordained (by an impersonal force called "fate"). Therefore, it is futile to attempt to influence the outcome of events or the outcome of our lives by putting forth any effort or making any significant choices because these will not make any difference anyway. In a true fatalistic system, of course, our humanity is destroyed for our choices really mean nothing, and the motivation for moral accountability is removed.

In a mechanistic system the picture is one of an impersonal universe in which the universe functions in a mechanical way so that human beings are more like machines or robots responding to external stimuli than genuine persons. Here also genuine human personality would be reduced to the level of a machine that simply functions in accordance with predetermined plans and in response to predetermined causes and influences.

By contrast to a fatalistic or mechanistic picture, the New Testament presents the entire outworking of our salvation as something brought about by a *personal* God in relationship with *personal* creatures. "In love he [God] predestined us for adoption to himself as sons through Jesus Christ" (Eph. 1:4–5). God's act of election was neither impersonal nor mechanistic but was permeated with personal love for those whom he chose. Moreover, the personal care of God for his creatures, even those who rebel against him, is seen clearly in God's plea through Ezekiel, "As I live, declares the Lord GOD, *I have no pleasure in the death of the wicked, but that the wicked turn from his way and live*; turn back, turn back from your evil ways, for why will you die, O house of Israel?" (Ezek. 33:11).

When talking about our response to the gospel offer, Scripture continually views us not as mechanistic creatures or robots, but as *genuine persons*, personal creatures who make *willing* choices to accept or reject the gospel.[6] Jesus invites everyone, "*Come to me*, all who labor and are heavy laden, and I will give you rest" (Matt. 11:28). And we read the invitation at the end of Revelation: "The Spirit and the Bride say, 'Come.' And let the one who hears say, 'Come.' And let the one who is thirsty come; let *the one who desires* take the water of life without price" (Rev. 22:17). This invitation and many others like it are addressed to genuine persons who are capable of hearing the invitation and responding to it by a decision of their wills. Regarding those who will not accept him, Jesus clearly emphasizes their hardness of heart and their stubborn refusal to come to him: "Yet you *refuse* to come to me that you may have life" (John 5:40). And Jesus cries out in sorrow to the city that had rejected him, "O Jerusalem, Jerusalem, the city that kills the prophets and stones those who are sent to it! How often would I have gathered your children together as a hen gathers her brood under her wings, *and you were not willing*!" (Matt. 23:37).

In contrast to the charge of fatalism, we also see a much different picture in the New Testament. Not only do we make willing choices as real persons, but these choices are

---

6. See chapter 16, pp. 427–29, 433, 437–39, for a more extensive discussion of how we can be genuine persons and make real choices when God has beforehand ordained what we do.

also *real choices* because they do affect the course of events in the world. They affect our own lives and they affect the lives and destinies of others. "*Whoever believes in him* is not condemned, *but whoever does not believe* is condemned already, because he has not believed in the name of the only Son of God" (John 3:18). Our personal decisions to believe or not believe in Christ have eternal consequences in our lives, and Scripture is quite willing to talk about our decision to believe or not believe as the factor that decides our eternal destiny.

The implication of this is that we certainly must preach the gospel, and people's eternal destiny hinges on whether we proclaim the gospel or not. Therefore, when the Lord one night told Paul, "Do not be afraid, but go on speaking and do not be silent, for I am with you, and no one will attack you to harm you, for *I have many in this city who are my people*" (Acts 18:9–10), Paul did not simply conclude that the "many people" who belong to God would be saved whether he stayed there preaching the gospel or not. Rather, "*he stayed a year and six months*, teaching the word of God among them" (Acts 18:11)—this was longer than Paul stayed in any other city except Ephesus during his three missionary journeys. When Paul was told that God had many elect people in Corinth, he stayed a long time and preached in order that those elect people might be saved! Paul is quite clear about the fact that unless people preach the gospel others will not be saved: "How then will they call on him in whom they have not believed? And how are they to believe in him of whom they have never heard? And how are they to hear without someone preaching? . . . So faith comes from hearing, and hearing through the word of Christ" (Rom. 10:14, 17).

Did Paul know before he went to a city who was elected by God for salvation and who was not? No, he did not. That is something that God does not show to us ahead of time. But once people come to faith in Christ, then we can be confident that God had earlier chosen them for salvation. This is exactly Paul's conclusion regarding the Thessalonians; he says that he knows that God chose them because when he preached to them, the gospel came in power and with full conviction: "For we know, brothers loved by God, that he has chosen you, *because our gospel came to you* not only in word, but also in *power* and in the *Holy Spirit* and *with full conviction*" (1 Thess. 1:4–5). Far from saying that whatever he did made no difference, and that God's elect would be saved whether he preached or not, Paul endured a life of incredible hardship in order to bring the gospel to those whom God had chosen. At the end of a life filled with suffering he said, "Therefore *I endure everything for the sake of the elect, that they also may obtain the salvation* that is in Christ Jesus with eternal glory" (2 Tim. 2:10).

## 2. Election Is Not Based on God's Foreknowledge of Our Faith

Quite commonly people will agree that God predestines some to be saved, but they will say that he does this by looking into the future and seeing who will believe in Christ and who will not. If he sees that a person is going to come to saving faith, then he will predestine that person to be saved, *based on foreknowledge of that person's faith*. If he sees that a person will not come to saving faith, then he does not predestine that person to be saved. In this way, it is thought, the ultimate reason why some are saved and some are not lies *within the people themselves*, not within God. All that God does in his predestining work is to give confirmation to the decision he knows people will make on their own. The verse commonly used to support this view is Romans 8:29: "For those *whom he foreknew* he also predestined to be conformed to the image of his Son."[7]

**a. Foreknowledge of Persons, Not Facts.** But this verse can hardly be used to demonstrate that God based his predestination on foreknowledge of *the fact that a person would believe*. The passage speaks rather of the fact that *God knew persons* ("*those whom* he foreknew"), not that he knew some *fact about them*, such as the fact that they would believe. It is a personal, relational knowledge that is spoken of here: God, looking into the future, thought of certain people in saving relationship to him, and in that sense he "knew them" long ago. This is the sense in which Paul can talk about God's "knowing" someone, for example, in 1 Corinthians 8:3: "But if anyone loves God, he is *known by God*." Similarly, he says, "but now that you have come to know God, or rather *to be known by God*" (Gal. 4:9). When people *know* God in Scripture, or when God *knows* them, it is *personal* knowledge that involves a *saving relationship*. Therefore in Romans 8:29, "those whom he *foreknew*" is best understood to mean, "those whom he long ago *thought of in a saving relationship to himself*." The text actually says nothing about God foreknowing or foreseeing that certain people would believe, nor is that idea mentioned in any other text of Scripture.[8]

Sometimes people say that God elected *groups* of people but not individuals to salvation. In some Arminian views, God just elected the church as a group,[9] while the Swiss theologian Karl Barth (1886–1968) said that God elected Christ, and all people in Christ. But Romans 8:29 talks about *specific people* whom God foreknew ("*those whom* he foreknew"), not just undefined or unfilled groups. And in Ephesians Paul talks about specific people whom God chose, including himself: "He *chose us* in him before the foundation of the world" (Eph. 1:4). To talk about God choosing a group with no people

---

7. The idea that predestination is based on God's foreknowledge of those who would believe is argued in Jack W. Cottrell, "Conditional Election," in *Grace Unlimited*, 51–73. Cottrell says, "Through his foreknowledge God sees who will believe upon Jesus Christ as Savior and Lord, and become united with him in Christian baptism; then even before the creation of the world he predestines these believers to share the glory of the risen Christ" (62).

8. Rom. 11:2 similarly speaks of God's foreknowing *persons*, not facts about people or the fact that they would believe: "God has not rejected his people *whom he foreknew*."

9. In explaining Paul's statement that God "*chose us* in him before the foundation of the world to be holy and blameless in

his sight" (Eph. 1:4), William McDonald says that "us" refers to "the church." He then says, "This is the corporate solidarity or corporate personality concept so easy for patriarchal societies to understand and so alien to the Western tradition of individualism," but nowhere in his article does he say or even raise the question of whether the group he refers to as "the church" had specific individuals in it. He affirms that God chose "the church" but avoids saying that God chose specific, individual people to be in that church. William McDonald, "The Biblical Doctrine of Election," in *The Grace of God, the Will of Man: A Case for Arminianism*, ed. Clark Pinnock (Grand Rapids: Zondervan, 1989), 219–22.

in it is not biblical election at all. Rather, when Scripture talks about God choosing a group of people it means that he chose specific individuals who constituted that group.[10]

**b. Scripture Never Speaks of Our Faith as the Reason God Chose Us.** In addition, when we look beyond these specific passages that speak of foreknowledge and look at verses that talk about the *reason* God chose us, we find that Scripture never speaks of our faith or the fact that we would come to believe in Christ as the reason God chose us. In fact, Paul seems explicitly to exclude the consideration of what people would do in life from his understanding of God's choice of Jacob rather than Esau. Paul says, "Though they were not yet born and had done nothing either good or bad—*in order that God's purpose of election might continue*, not because of works but because of him who calls—she was told, 'The older will serve the younger.' As it is written, 'Jacob I loved, but Esau I hated'" (Rom. 9:11–13). Nothing that Jacob or Esau would do in life influenced God's decision; it was simply in order that his purpose of election might continue.

When discussing the Jewish people who have come to faith in Christ, Paul says, "So too at the present time there is a remnant, *chosen by grace*. But if it is by grace, it is no longer on the basis of works" (Rom. 11:5–6). Here again Paul emphasizes God's grace and the *complete absence of human merit* in the process of election, and therefore this excludes the idea that God would choose people on the basis of knowing that they would choose to trust in Christ.

Someone might reply that faith is not viewed as a "work" in Scripture and therefore God *could* predestine people based on knowing that they would believe, and it would still be true that God's choice of them "is no longer on the basis of *works*." Therefore, Paul could actually mean, "But if it is by grace, it is no longer on the basis of works, *but rather on the basis of whether someone would believe*." However, this proposal does not fit well in this context: Paul is not contrasting human faith and human works; he is contrasting God's sovereign choosing of people with *any* human activity, and he points to God's sovereign will as the ultimate basis for God's choice of the Jews who have come to Christ.

Similarly, when Paul talks about election in Ephesians, there is no mention of any foreknowledge of the fact that we would believe, or any idea that there was anything worthy or meritorious in us (such as a tendency to believe) that was the basis for God's choosing us. Rather, Paul says, "*In love* he predestined us for adoption to himself as sons through Jesus Christ, *according to the purpose of his will*, to the praise of his glorious grace, *with which he has blessed us* in the Beloved" (Eph. 1:4–6). Now if God's grace is to be praised for election, and not any human ability to believe or any decision to believe, then once again it is consistent for Paul to mention nothing about human faith but only to mention God's predestining activity, his purpose and will, and his freely given grace.

---

10. In answer to Barth's view that all are chosen in Christ, see the discussion below on reprobation (the fact that some are not chosen), and chapter 7, pp. 140–41, and chapter 56, pp. 1413–18, on the fact that those who do not believe in Christ will not be saved.

Again in 2 Timothy, Paul says that God "saved us and called us to a holy calling, not because of our works but because *of his own purpose and grace*, which he gave us in Christ Jesus before the ages began" (2 Tim. 1:9). Once again God's sovereign purpose is seen as the ultimate reason for our salvation, and Paul connects this with the fact that God gave us grace in Christ Jesus ages ago—another way of speaking of the truth that God freely gave favor to us when he chose us without reference to any foreseen merit or worthiness on our part.

### c. Election Based on Something Good in Us (Our Faith) Would Be the Beginning of Salvation by Merit.

Yet another kind of objection can be brought against the idea that God chose us because he foreknew that we would come to faith. If the *ultimate* determining factor in whether we will be saved or not is our decision to accept Christ, then we will be more inclined to think that we deserve some credit for the fact that we were saved: in distinction from other people who continue to reject Christ, we were wise enough or good enough in our moral tendencies or perceptive enough in our spiritual capacities to decide to believe in Christ. But once we begin to think this way, we seriously diminish the glory that is to be given to God for our salvation. We become uncomfortable speaking like Paul who says that God "predestined us . . . *according to the purpose of his will*, to the praise of his glorious *grace*" (Eph. 1:5–6), and we begin to think that God "predestined us . . . according to the fact that he knew that we would have enough tendencies toward goodness and faith within us that we would believe." When we think like this we begin to sound very much unlike the New Testament when it talks about election or predestination. By contrast, if election is solely based on God's good pleasure and his sovereign decision to love us in spite of our lack of goodness or merit, then certainly we have a profound sense of appreciation to him for a salvation that is totally undeserved, and we will forever be willing to praise his "glorious grace" (Eph. 1:6).

In the final analysis, the difference between two views of election can be seen in the way they answer a very simple question. Given the fact that in the final analysis some people will choose to accept Christ and some people will not, the question is, "What makes people differ?" That is, what *ultimately* makes the difference between those who believe and those who do not? If our answer is that it is ultimately based on something God does (namely, his sovereign election of those who would be saved), then we see that salvation at its most foundational level is based on *grace alone*. On the other hand, if we answer that the ultimate difference between those who are saved and those who are not is because of *something in man* (that is, a tendency or disposition to believe or not believe), then salvation ultimately depends on a combination of grace plus human ability.[11]

---

11. The fact that the Arminian position ultimately makes something in man the determining factor in whether people are saved or not is seen clearly in the statement of I. Howard Marshall: "The effect of the call of God is to place man in a position where he can say 'yes' or 'no' (which he could not do before God called him; till then he was in a continuous attitude of 'no')" ("Predestination in the New Testament," in Pinnock, *Grace Unlimited*, 140). In this statement of Marshall's we see that the final determinant of whether people are saved or not is whether they say yes or no to God's call, and therefore salvation still ultimately depends on something in man, an ability or tendency within him that persuades him to say yes rather than no.

**d. Predestination Based on Foreknowledge of a Person's Faith Still Does Not Give People Free Choice.** The idea that God's predestination of some to believe is based on foreknowledge of their faith encounters still another problem: upon reflection, this system turns out to give no real freedom to man either. For if God can look into the future and see that person A *will* come to faith in Christ and that person B *will not* come to faith in Christ, then those facts are already *fixed*, they are already *determined* long before these persons were even born. If we assume that God's knowledge of the future is *true* (which it must be), then it is absolutely certain that person A will believe and person B will not. There is no way that their lives could turn out any differently than this. Therefore, it is fair to say that their destinies are still *determined*, for they could not be otherwise: person A could not choose to reject Christ, and person B could not choose to believe in him, or otherwise God's foreknowledge would be proven false.

But *by what* are these destinies determined? If they are determined by God himself, then we no longer have election based ultimately on foreknowledge of faith but rather on God's sovereign will. If these destinies are not determined by God, then who or what determines them? Certainly no Christian would say that there is some powerful being other than God controlling people's destinies. But then what makes it certain that person A will believe and person B will not believe? It seems that the only other possible solution is to say these decisions are determined by some impersonal force, some kind of fate, operative in the universe, making things turn out as they do. But what kind of benefit is this? We have then sacrificed election in love by a personal God for a kind of determinism by an impersonal force, and God is no longer to be given the ultimate credit for our salvation.

**e. Does "Middle Knowledge" Provide a Better Solution than Calvinism or Arminianism?** The doctrine of "middle knowledge" (also called "Molinism") is sometimes proposed as a way to reconcile Calvinism and Arminianism on the question of the relationship between God's sovereignty and man's free will. But in fact, it turns out to be just a complicated variety of the Arminian position that election is based on God's foreknowledge of our faith (it adds the qualification that God creates the kind of world and arranges the kind of circumstances in which he knows that a person will "freely" choose to believe, and then he predestines that person to be saved). I deal with the theory of middle knowledge more fully in chapter 16 (pp. 456–62).

**f. Conclusion: Election Is Unconditional.** It seems best, for the previous four reasons, to reject the idea that election is based on God's foreknowledge of our faith. We conclude instead that the reason for election is simply God's sovereign choice—"In love he predestined us for adoption to himself as sons" (Eph. 1:4–5). God chose us simply because he decided to bestow his love upon us. It was not because of any foreseen faith or foreseen merit in us.

This understanding of election has traditionally been called "unconditional election."[12] It is "unconditional" because it is not *conditioned upon* anything that God sees in us that makes us worthy of his choosing us.[13]

## D. OBJECTIONS TO THE DOCTRINE OF ELECTION

It must be said that the doctrine of election as presented here is by no means universally accepted in the Christian church, either in Catholicism or Protestantism. There is a long history of acceptance of the doctrine as here presented, but many others have objected to it as well. Among current evangelicals, those in more Reformed or Calvinistic circles (conservative Presbyterian denominations, for example) will accept this view, as will many Lutherans and Anglicans (Episcopalians) and a large number of Baptists and people in independent churches. On the other hand, it will be rejected quite decisively by nearly all Methodists, as well as by many others in Baptist, Anglican, and independent churches.[14] While a number of the objections to election are more specific forms of objection to the doctrine of providence presented in chapter 16 and have been answered in more detail there, a few particular objections should be mentioned here.

### 1. Objection: Election Means That We Do Not Have a Choice in Whether We Accept Christ or Not

According to this objection, the doctrine of election denies all the gospel invitations that appeal to the will of man and ask people to make a choice in whether to respond to Christ's invitation or not. In response to this, we must affirm that the doctrine of election is fully able to accommodate the idea that we have a voluntary choice, and we make

---

12. Unconditional election is the *U* in the acronym TULIP, which stands for "the five points of Calvinism." The other letters stand for *T*otal depravity (see chapter 24, pp. 626–27), *L*imited atonement (see chapter 27, pp. 737–38), *I*rresistible grace (see chapter 34, p. 851), and *P*erseverance of the saints (see chapter 40, pp. 970–71). See also p. 851n3.

13. Regarding the doctrine of election, there has been a dispute in Reformed circles (those who hold to election as presented here) between two positions known as *supralapsarianism* and *infralapsarianism*. The difference concerns what happened in God's mind before the foundation of the world. It does not concern something that happened in time, but rather it concerns the *logical* order of God's thoughts. The question is whether, in logical order, (a) God decided first that he would *save some people* and second that he would *allow sin* into the world so that he could save them from it (the supralapsarian position), or whether it was the other way around, so that (b) God first decided that he would *allow sin* into the world and second decided that he would *save some people* from it (the infralapsarian position). The word *supralapsarian* means "before the fall," and the word *infralapsarian* means "after the fall." The discussion is complex and highly speculative because there is very little direct biblical data to help us with it. Good arguments have been advanced in support of each view, and

there is probably some element of truth in each one. But in the last analysis it seems wiser to say that Scripture does not give us enough data to probe into this mystery, and, moreover, it does not seem very edifying to do so.

In fact, I have decided to mention the discussion in this textbook at this point only because the words *supralapsarian* and *infralapsarian* are sometimes used in theological circles as symbols for the most abstract and obscure of theological discussions, and it seemed to me appropriate simply to inform the reader of the nature of this dispute and the meaning of these terms. For those interested, a further discussion is found in Berkhof, *Systematic Theology* (Grand Rapids: Eerdmans, 1941), 118–25.

14. For a full discussion of objections to election, the reader may refer to two excellent recent collections of essays from an Arminian perspective, a perspective that rejects the view of election advocated in this chapter. See Clark H. Pinnock, ed., *Grace Unlimited* (Minneapolis: Bethany Fellowship, 1975), and Pinnock, ed., *The Grace of God, the Will of Man*. In response to these two books, Tom Schreiner and Bruce Ware have edited a substantial collection of essays from Reformed scholars, published as *Still Sovereign: Contemporary Perspectives on Election, Foreknowledge, and Grace* (Grand Rapids: Baker, 2000).

willing decisions in accepting or rejecting Christ. Our choices are voluntary because they are what we want to do and what we decide to do.[15]

It is important at this point that we think very clearly about what we mean by *free will*. Bruce Ware explains a common distinction between two different possible meanings for *free will*:

a. Libertarian free will: "The ability, all things being just what they are, to choose differently."[16] (In the following discussion, I will usually refer to this as "absolutely free will.")

b. Freedom of inclination: "We are free when we choose according to our strongest inclination or deepest desire. In short, we are free when we do what we most want to do."[17] (In the following discussion, I will refer to this as "freedom of inclination," "freedom to choose what we most want," or "freedom of voluntary choice.")

The Reformed understanding of election, which I am arguing for in this chapter, understands the second option, "freedom of inclination" or "freedom of voluntary choice," to be the kind of human free will that is taught in the Bible. In short, we choose to do what we most want to do.

This kind of freedom does not mean that our choices are absolutely free because (as explained in chapter 16) God can work sovereignly and indirectly through our desires so that he guarantees that our choices come about as he has ordained, but choices made in such a system can still be understood as real choices because God has created us and has decided that such choices are real. In short, we can say that, when we come to trust in Christ, God ordains that we will choose Christ voluntarily. The mistaken assumption underlying this objection is that a choice must be absolutely free (that is, "free" in a libertarian sense, and therefore not in any way ordained by God) in order for it to be a genuine human choice.

## 2. Objection: On This Definition of Election, Our Choices Are Not Real Choices

Continuing the discussion in the previous paragraph, someone might object that if a choice is ordained (or somehow indirectly caused) by God, it may appear to us to

---

15. Grant R. Osborne, "Exegetical Notes on Calvinist Texts," in *Grace Unlimited*, ed. Clark Pinnock (Minneapolis: Bethany House, 1975), 167–89, several times points out evidence of human volition or human choice involved in the immediate context of texts that talk about election or predestination. A representative example is seen on p. 175, where Osborne discusses Acts 13:48, "as many as were ordained to eternal life believed." Osborne responds, "While we agree that the basic thrust is divine election, this does not negate the presence of human volition, as seen in the context" (175). Such a

response seems to assume that a Reformed view denies human volition or choice. But it must be answered that the Reformed position as traditionally argued certainly allows for genuine human volition or human will in choices that are made, and simply says that God is so wise and powerful that he *ordains* that we respond *willingly*. Osborne does not directly interact with this position.

16. Bruce Ware, *God's Greater Glory* (Wheaton, IL: Crossway, 2004), 112.

17. Ware, *God's Greater Glory*, 114.

be voluntary and willed by us, but it is nonetheless *not a genuine or real choice* because it is not absolutely free. Once again we must respond by challenging the assumption that a choice must be absolutely free in order to be genuine or valid. If God makes us in a certain way and then tells us that our voluntary choices are real and genuine choices, then we must agree that they are. God is the definition of what is real and genuine in the universe. By contrast, we might ask where Scripture ever says that our choices have to be free from God's influence or providential control in order to be real or genuine choices. It does not seem that Scripture ever speaks in this way.

## 3. Objection: The Doctrine of Election Makes Us Puppets or Robots, Not Real Persons

According to this objection, if God really ordains (or indirectly causes) everything that we choose with regard to salvation, then we are no longer real persons. Once again it must be answered that God has created us and we must allow him to define what genuine personhood is. The analogy of a "puppet" or a "robot" reduces us to a subhuman category of things that have been created by man. But genuine human beings are far greater than puppets or robots because we do have a genuine will and we do make *voluntary* decisions based on our own preferences and wants. We are free to choose whatever we most want to choose. In fact, it is this ability to make *willing choices* that is one thing that distinguishes us from much of the lower creation. We are real people created in God's image, and God has allowed us to make *genuine choices* that have real effects on our lives.

## 4. Objection: The Doctrine of Election Means That Unbelievers Never Had a Chance to Believe

This objection to election says that if God had decreed from eternity that some people would not believe, then there was no genuine chance for them to believe, and the entire system functions unfairly. Two responses can be made to this objection. First, we must note that the Bible does not allow us to say that unbelievers had no chance to believe. When people rejected Jesus, he always put the blame on their willful choice to reject him, not on anything decreed by God the Father. "Why do you not understand what I say? It is because you cannot bear to hear my word. You are of your father the devil, and your *will* is to do your father's desires" (John 8:43–44). He says to Jerusalem, "How often would I have gathered your children together . . . *and you were not willing*!" (Matt. 23:37). He said to the Jews who rejected him, "You *refuse to come to me* that you may have life" (John 5:40). Romans 1 makes it plain that all people are confronted with a revelation from God of such clarity that they are "without excuse" (Rom. 1:20). This is the consistent pattern in Scripture: people who remain in unbelief do so because they are unwilling to come to God, and the blame for such unbelief always lies with the unbelievers themselves, never with God.

At a second level, the answer to this question must simply be Paul's answer to a similar objection: "But who are you, O man, to answer back to God? Will what is molded say to its molder, 'Why have you made me like this?'" (Rom. 9:20).

## 5. Objection: Election Is Unfair

Sometimes people regard the doctrine of election as unfair since it teaches that God chooses some to be saved and passes over others, deciding not to save them. How can this be fair?

Two responses may be given at this point. First, we must remember that *it would be perfectly fair for God not to save anyone*, just as he did with the angels: "God did not spare angels when they sinned, but cast them into hell and committed them to chains of gloomy darkness to be kept until the judgment" (2 Peter 2:4).[18] What would be perfectly fair for God would be to do with human beings as he did with angels, that is, to save none of those who sinned and rebelled against him. But if he does save *some at all*, then this is a demonstration of grace that goes far beyond the requirements of fairness and justice.

But at a deeper level this objection would say that it is not fair for God to create some people who he knew would sin and be eternally condemned and whom he would not redeem. Paul raises this objection in Romans 9. After saying that God "has mercy on whomever he wills, and he hardens whomever he wills" (Rom. 9:18),[19] Paul then raises this precise objection: "You will say to me then, 'Why does he still find fault? For who can resist his will?'" (Rom. 9:19). Here is the heart of the "unfairness" objection against the doctrine of election. If each person's ultimate destiny is determined by God, not by the person himself or herself (that is, even when people make willing choices that determine whether they will be saved or not, if God is actually behind those choices somehow ordaining or indirectly causing them to occur), then how can this be fair?

Paul's response is not one that appeals to our pride, nor does he attempt to give a philosophical explanation of why this is just. He simply calls on God's rights as the omnipotent Creator:

> But who are you, O man, to answer back to God? Will what is molded say to its molder, "Why have you made me like this?" Has the potter no right over the clay, to make out of the same lump one vessel for honorable use and another for dishonorable

---

18. See chapter 19, p. 521–23, for a discussion of the fact that it would be fair for God to save no one.

19. One Arminian view of this verse is given by Jack Cottrell. He argues that Rom. 9:18, "He has mercy on whomever he wills, and he hardens whomever he wills," refers not to God's choice of people for salvation, but to God's choice of people for certain kinds of service: "He chooses whom he pleases for service, not salvation" ("The Nature of the Divine Sovereignty,"

in *The Grace of God, the Will of Man*, ed. Clark Pinnock [Grand Rapids: Zondervan, 1989], 114). This is not a convincing interpretation, however, because the entire context definitely concerns salvation. Paul says, "I have great sorrow and unceasing anguish in my heart," and "I could wish that I myself were accursed and cut off from Christ for the sake of my brothers, my kinsmen according to the flesh" (Rom. 9:2, 3), not because the Jews were not chosen for some particular service, but because

use? What if God, desiring to show his wrath and to make known his power, has endured with much patience vessels of wrath prepared for destruction, in order to make known the riches of his glory for vessels of mercy, which he has prepared beforehand for glory—even us whom he has called, not from the Jews only but also from the Gentiles? (Rom. 9:20–24)[20]

Paul simply says that there is a point beyond which we cannot answer back to God or question his justice. He has done what he has done according to his sovereign will. He is the Creator; we are the creatures, and we ultimately have no basis from which to accuse him of unfairness or injustice.[21] When we read these words of Paul we are confronted with a decision whether or not to accept what God says here, and what he does, simply because he is God and we are not. It is a question that reaches deep into our understanding of ourselves as creatures and of our relationship to God as our Creator.

This objection of unfairness takes a slightly different form when people say that it is *unfair of God to save some people and not to save all*. This objection is based on an idea of justice among human beings that we sense intuitively. We recognize in human affairs that it is right to treat equal people in an equal way. Therefore, it seems intuitively appropriate to us to say that if God is going to save *some* sinners, he ought to save *all* sinners. But in answer to this objection it must be said that we really have no right to impose on God our intuitive sense of what is appropriate among human beings. Whenever Scripture begins to treat this area, it goes back to God's sovereignty as Creator and says he has a right to do with his creation as he wills (see Rom. 9:19–20, quoted above).[22] If God ultimately decided to create some creatures to be saved and others not to be saved, then that was his sovereign choice, and we have no moral or scriptural basis on which we can insist that it was not fair.

---

they were not saved! He speaks in v. 8 not of those who were chosen for service and those who were not, but of those who are "children of God" and those who are not. And he speaks in v. 22 not of some who missed an opportunity for service, but of "vessels of wrath prepared for destruction." Salvation is in view in the entire context.

20. James D. Strauss, "God's Promise and Universal History: The Theology of Romans 9," in Pinnock, *Grace Unlimited*, argues that in Romans 9 "vessels of wrath *made for destruction*" (RSV) should rather be translated "fitted themselves" for wrath (200). But he gives no examples of a genuine reflexive use of the verb *katartizō*, which would be required here. BAGD, 417–18, note that the *passive* can be used intransitively (as here if we translate "made for destruction," as the RSV), but they give no example of an active or middle voice of this verb being used without a direct object. Moreover, Strauss' suggestion, "fitted themselves" for wrath, would not really fit the picture of a potter making vessels of various sorts, for pots do not make themselves, but the potter makes them.

Another objection brought by Strauss is to say that the potter and clay imagery in Rom. 9:20–23 is derived from Old Testament passages that emphasize God's call for people freely to choose repentance and faith. He says that this negates the idea of sovereign predestining on God's part (199). But here Strauss simply misunderstands the Reformed position, which never denies human responsibility or human willingness in making choices.

21. For further discussion, see John Piper, *The Justification of God: An Exegetical and Theological Study of Romans 9:1–23* (Grand Rapids: Baker, 1983).

22. Marshall, "Predestination in the New Testament," 136, specifically says, "I cannot see how it can be just arbitrarily to save one guilty sinner and not another." But that seems to be precisely Paul's point in Rom. 9:18–20: God does save some and decide not to save others, and we have no right, as creatures, to say that this is unjust.

## 6. Objection: The Bible Says That God Wills to Save Everyone

Another objection to the doctrine of election is that it contradicts certain passages of Scripture that say that God wills for all to be saved. Paul writes of God our Savior, *"who desires all people to be saved and to come to the knowledge of the truth"* (1 Tim. 2:4). And Peter says, "The Lord is not slow to fulfill his promise as some count slowness, but is patient toward you, *not wishing that any should perish*, but that all should reach repentance" (2 Peter 3:9). Do not these passages contradict the idea that God has only chosen certain people to be saved?

One common solution to this question (from the Reformed perspective advocated in this book) is to say that these verses speak of God's *revealed will* (telling us what we should do), not his *hidden will* (his eternal plans for what will happen).[23] The verses simply tell us that God invites and commands every person to repent and come to Christ for salvation, but they do not tell us anything about God's secret decrees regarding who will be saved.

The Arminian theologian Clark Pinnock objects to the idea that God has a secret and a revealed will—he calls it "the exceedingly paradoxical notion of two divine wills regarding salvation."[24] But Pinnock never really answers the question of why all are not saved (from an Arminian perspective). Ultimately Arminians *also* must say that God *wills* something more strongly than he wills the salvation of all people, *for in fact all are not saved.* Arminians claim that the reason why all are not saved is that God wills to preserve the absolutely free will of man *more than* he wills to save everyone. But is this not also making a distinction in two aspects of the will of God? On the one hand God wills that all be saved (1 Tim. 2:5–6; 2 Peter 3:9). But on the other hand he wills to preserve man's absolutely free choice. In fact, he wills the second thing *more than* the first. But this means that Arminians also must say that 1 Timothy 2:5–6 and 2 Peter 3:9 do not say that God wills the salvation of everyone in an absolute or unqualified way—they too must say that the verses only refer to one kind or one aspect of God's will.

Here the difference between the Reformed and the Arminian conception of God's will is clearly seen. Both Calvinists and Arminians agree that God's commands in Scripture reveal to us what he wants us to do, and both agree that the commands in Scripture invite us to repent and trust in Christ for salvation. Therefore, in one sense both agree that God wills that we be saved—it is the will that he reveals to us explicitly in the gospel invitation.

But both sides must also say that there is something else that God deems more important than saving everyone. Reformed theologians say that God deems *his own glory* more important than saving everyone and that (according to Rom. 9) God's glory

---

23. For a discussion of the difference between God's revealed will and his secret will, see chapter 13, pp. 254–57; also chapter 16, pp. 440–42. See also John Piper, "Are There

Two Wills in God? Divine Election and God's Desire for All to Be Saved," in Schreiner and Ware, *Still Sovereign*, 107–32.

24. Pinnock, introduction to *Grace Unlimited*, 13.

is also furthered by the fact that some are not saved. Arminian theologians also say that something else is more important to God than the salvation of all people, namely, the preservation of *man's absolutely free will*. So in a Reformed system God's highest value is his own glory, and in an Arminian system God's highest value is the free will of man. These are two distinctly different conceptions of the nature of God, and it seems that the Reformed position has much more explicit biblical support than the Arminian position does on this question.[25]

## E. The Doctrine of Reprobation

When we understand election as God's sovereign choice of some persons to be saved, then there is necessarily another aspect of that choice, namely, God's sovereign decision to pass over others and not to save them. This decision of God in eternity past is called reprobation. *Reprobation is the sovereign decision of God before creation to pass over some persons, in sorrow deciding not to save them, and to punish them for their sins, and thereby to manifest his justice.*

In many ways the doctrine of reprobation is the most difficult of all the teachings of Scripture for us to think about and to accept because it deals with such horrible and eternal consequences for human beings made in the image of God. The love that God gives us for our fellow human beings and the love that he commands us to have toward our neighbor cause us to recoil against this doctrine, and it is right that we feel such dread in contemplating it.[26] It is something that we would not want to believe, and would not believe, unless Scripture clearly taught it.

But are there Scripture passages that speak of such a decision by God? Certainly there are some. Jude speaks of some persons "who *long ago were designated for this condemnation*, ungodly people, who pervert the grace of our God into sensuality and deny our only Master and Lord, Jesus Christ" (Jude 4).

Moreover, Paul, in the passage referred to above, speaks in the same way of Pharaoh and others:

> For the Scripture says to Pharaoh, "For this very purpose I have raised you up, that I might show my power in you, and that my name might be proclaimed in all the earth." So then he has mercy on whomever he wills, and he hardens whomever he wills. . . . What if God, desiring to show his wrath and to make known his

---

25. See chapter 15, pp. 347–49, and chapter 21, pp. 565–67, on the fact that God created us and the whole universe for his own glory. An Arminian may object to putting the difference this way, and may say that God is more glorified when we choose him out of an absolutely free will, but this is simply a doubtful assumption based on intuition or human analogy, and has no specific support from Scripture. Moreover, to be consistent it seems the Arminian would also have to take account of the millions who do not choose God, and would have to say that God is also more glorified by the free choices of the millions who freely decide against God—otherwise, why would God allow them to persist in this free choice of rebellion?

26. John Calvin himself says of reprobation, "The decree is dreadful indeed, I confess." Calvin, *Institutes of the Christian Religion*, ed. John T. McNeill, trans. F. L. Battles, 2 vols., Library of Christian Classics (Philadelphia: Westminster, 1960), 3.23.7 (2:955). But it should be noted that his Latin word, *horribilis*, does not mean "hateful" but rather "fearful, awe-inspiring."

power, has endured with much patience vessels of wrath prepared for destruction? (Rom. 9:17–22)

Regarding the results of the fact that God failed to choose all for salvation, Paul says, "The elect obtained it, but *the rest were hardened*" (Rom. 11:7). And Peter says of those who reject the gospel, "they stumble because they disobey the word, *as they were destined to do*" (1 Peter 2:8).[27]

In spite of the fact that we recoil against this doctrine, we must be careful of our attitude toward God and toward these passages of Scripture. We must never begin to wish that the Bible was written in another way or that it did not contain these verses. Moreover, if we are convinced that these verses teach reprobation, then we are obligated both to believe it and accept it as fair and just of God, even though it still causes us to tremble in horror as we think of it. In this context it may surprise us to see that Jesus can thank God *both* for hiding the knowledge of salvation from some and for revealing it to others: "Jesus declared, 'I thank you, Father, Lord of heaven and earth, that you have hidden these things from the wise and understanding and revealed them to little children; yes, Father, for such was your gracious will'" (Matt. 11:25–26).

Moreover, we must recognize that somehow, in God's wisdom, the fact of reprobation and the eternal condemnation of some will show God's justice and also result in his glory. Paul says, "What if God, *desiring to show his wrath and to make known his power*, has endured with much patience vessels of wrath prepared for destruction" (Rom. 9:22). Paul also notes that the fact of such punishment on the "vessels of wrath" serves to show the greatness of God's mercy toward us: God does this "in order to make known the riches of his glory for vessels of mercy" (Rom. 9:23).

We also must remember that *there are important differences between election and reprobation as they are presented in the Bible.* Election to salvation is viewed as a cause for rejoicing and praise to God, who is worthy of praise and receives all the credit for our salvation (see Eph. 1:3–6; 1 Peter 1:1–3). God is viewed as actively choosing us for salvation and doing so in love and with delight. But reprobation is viewed as something that brings God sorrow, not delight (see Ezek. 33:11), and the blame for the condemnation of sinners is always put on the people or angels who rebel, never on God himself (see John 3:18–19; 5:40). So *in the presentation of Scripture* the cause of election lies in God, and the blame for reprobation lies in the sinner. Another important difference is that the ground of election is God's grace, whereas the ground of reprobation is God's justice. Therefore, "double predestination" is not a helpful or accurate phrase because it neglects these differences between election and reprobation.

---

27. See discussion of this verse in Wayne Grudem, *The First Epistle of Peter*, TNTC (Leicester: Inter-Varsity; Grand Rapids: Eerdmans, 1988), 107–10. The verse does not simply say that God destined the *fact* that those who disobey would stumble but speaks rather of God destining certain *people* to disobey and stumble: "as they were destined to do." (The Greek verb *etethēsan*, "they were destined," requires a plural subject.)

The sorrow of God at the death of the wicked ("I have no pleasure in the death of the wicked, but that the wicked turn from his way and live," Ezek. 33:11) helps us understand how appropriate it was that Paul himself felt great sorrow when he thought about the unbelieving Jews who had rejected Christ. Paul says,

> I am speaking the truth in Christ—I am not lying; my conscience bears me witness in the Holy Spirit—that *I have great sorrow and unceasing anguish in my heart.* For I could wish that I myself were accursed and cut off from Christ for the sake of my brothers, my kinsmen according to the flesh. They are Israelites. (Rom. 9:1–4)

We ought also to feel this great sorrow as well when we think about the fate of unbelievers.

But it might be objected at this point, if God genuinely feels sorrow at the punishment of the wicked, then why does he allow it or even decree that it will come about? The answer must be that God knows that this will ultimately result in greater glory for himself. It will show his power and wrath and justice and mercy in a way that could not otherwise be demonstrated. Certainly in our own human experience it is possible to do something that causes us great sorrow but which we know will result in long-term greater good. And so, after this faint human analogy, we may somewhat understand that God can decree something that causes him sorrow yet ultimately will further his glory.

### F. Practical Application of the Doctrine of Election

In terms of our relationship with God, the doctrine of election does have significant practical application. When we think of the biblical teaching on both election and reprobation, it is appropriate to apply it to our own lives individually. It is right for each Christian to ask of himself or herself, "Why am I a Christian? What is the final reason why God decided to save me?"

The doctrine of election tells us that I am a Christian simply because God in eternity past decided to set his love on me. But why did he decide to set his love on me? Not for anything good in me, but simply because he decided to love me. There is no more ultimate reason than that.

It humbles us before God to think in this way. It makes us realize that we have no claim on God's grace whatsoever. Our salvation is totally due to grace alone. Our only appropriate response is to give God eternal praise.

## QUESTIONS FOR PERSONAL APPLICATION

1. Do you think that God chose you individually to be saved before he created the world? Do you think he did it on the basis of the fact that he knew you would believe in Christ, or was it "unconditional election," not based on anything that

he foresaw in you that made you worthy of his love? No matter how you answered the previous question, explain how your answer makes you feel when you think about yourself in relationship to God.

2. Does the doctrine of election give you any comfort or assurance about your future?

3. After reading this chapter, do you honestly feel that you would like to give thanks or praise to God for choosing you to be saved? Do you sense any unfairness in the fact that God did not decide to save everyone?

4. If you agree with the doctrine of election as presented in this chapter, does it diminish your sense of individual personhood or make you feel somewhat like a robot or a puppet in God's hands? Do you think it should make you feel this way?

5. What effect do you think this chapter will have on your motivation for evangelism? Is this a positive or negative effect? Can you think of ways in which the doctrine of election can be used as a positive encouragement to evangelism (see 1 Thess. 1:4–5; 2 Tim. 2:10)?

6. Whether you adopt a Reformed or Arminian perspective on the question of election, can you think of some positive benefits in the Christian life that those who hold the *opposite* position from yours seem more frequently to experience than you do? Even though you do not agree with the other position, can you list some helpful concerns or practical truths about the Christian life that you might learn from that position? Is there anything that Calvinists and Arminians could do to bring about greater understanding and less division on this question?

## Special Terms

*determinism*
*election*
*fatalism*
*foreknowledge*
*freedom of inclination*
*freedom of voluntary choice*
*predestination*
*reprobation*

## BIBLIOGRAPHY

(For an explanation of this bibliography see the note on the bibliography to chapter 1, pp. 23–24. Complete bibliographical data may be found on pp. 1489–96.)

### SECTIONS IN EVANGELICAL SYSTEMATIC THEOLOGIES

*1. Anglican (Episcopalian)*
  1930 . . . . . . . . Thomas, 236–57

  1882–92 . . . . . Litton, 351–63
  2001 . . . . . . . . Packer, 149–51
  2013 . . . . . . . . Bird, 514–30, 420–34, 586
  2013 . . . . . . . . Bray, 88–96

*2. Arminian (Wesleyan or Methodist)*
  1875–76 . . . . . Pope, 2:363–67
  1892–94 . . . . . Miley, 2:254–308
  1940 . . . . . . . . Wiley, 2:335–57

1992.........Oden, 3:333–34
2002.........Cottrell, 388–99

**3. Baptist**
1767.........Gill, 1:251–88, 300–306
1887.........Boyce, 341–67
1907.........Strong, 779–90
1976–83.....Henry, 6:76–107
1990–95.....Garrett, 2:471–98
2007.........Akin, 707–23
2013.........Erickson, 841–59

**4. Dispensational**
1947.........Chafer, 3:165–82
1949.........Thiessen, 257–63
1986.........Ryrie, 310–18
2002–2005..Geisler, 3:315, 437–41,
            564–68
2017.........MacArthur and Mayhue,
            493–511

**5. Lutheran**
1917–24.....Pieper, 3:473–506
1934.........Mueller, 585–612

**6. Reformed (or Presbyterian)**
1559.........Calvin, 2:920–86 (3.21–24)
1679–85.....Turretin, *IET*, 1:212–18,
            251–52, 311–430, 2:205–16,
            455–82
1871–73.....Hodge, 2:313–53
1878.........Dabney, 223–46
1887–1921...Warfield, *BTS*, 270–333;
            *SSW*, 1:103–11, 285–98; *BD*,
            3–70; *PS*, 13–112
1894.........Shedd, 324–44
1906–11.....Bavinck, *RD*, 2:340–47,

350–52, 362–63, 390–99,
3:228–32
1910.........Vos, 1:54, 97–155
1937–66.....Murray, *CW*, 1:119–23; *CW*,
            2:123–31; *RAA*, 79–87
1938.........Berkhof, 109–25
1998.........Reymond, 465–67
2008.........Van Genderen and Velema,
            198–245
2011.........Horton, 560–75
2013.........Frame, 163–64, 169, 208,
            215–24, 271, 274, 296,
            310–11, 709
2013.........Culver, 671–81
2016.........Allen and Swain, 116–17
2017.........Barrett, 241–82
2019.........Letham, 173–76, 408–27

**7. Renewal (or charismatic/Pentecostal)**
1988–92.....Williams, 2:13–22
1995.........Horton, 355–61
2008.........Duffield and Van Cleave,
            210–13

## SECTIONS IN REPRESENTATIVE ROMAN CATHOLIC SYSTEMATIC THEOLOGIES

**1. Roman Catholic: Traditional**
1955.........Ott, 242–46

**2. Roman Catholic: Post–Vatican II**
1980.........McBrien (no explicit treatment)
2012.........*CCC*, paragraphs 762, 1033,
            1994

## OTHER WORKS

Allison, Gregg. *Historical Theology: An Introduction to Christian Doctrine; A Companion to Wayne*

*Grudem's* Systematic Theology. Grand Rapids: Zondervan, 2011, 453–73.

Basinger, David, and Randall Basinger, eds. *Predestination and Free Will*. Downers Grove, IL: InterVarsity Press, 1985.

Berkouwer, G. C. *Divine Election*. Translated by Hugo Bekker. Grand Rapids: Eerdmans, 1960.

Brand, Chad Owen, ed. *Perspectives on Election: Five Views*. Nashville: B&H, 2006.

Carson, D. A. *Divine Sovereignty and Human Responsibility: Biblical Perspectives in Tension*. Atlanta: John Knox, 1981.

Coppedge, Allan. *John Wesley in Theological Debate*. Wilmore, KY: Wesley Heritage Press, 1987.

Demarest, Bruce. *The Cross and Salvation: The Doctrine of Salvation*. Wheaton, IL: Crossway, 2006, 27–43.

Elwell, Walter A. "Elect, Election." In *BTDB*, 199–201.

———. "Election and Predestination." In *DPL*, 225–29.

Feinberg, John S. "God Ordains All Things." In *Predestination and Free Will: Four Views of Divine Sovereignty and Human Freedom*. David Basinger & Randall Basinger, eds. Downers Grove, IL: InterVarsity Press, 1986.

Godfrey, William R. "Predestination." In *NDT1*, 528–30.

Keathley, Kenneth. "The Work of God: Salvation." In *A Theology for the Church*, edited by Daniel L. Akin et al., 702–23. Nashville: B&H, 2007.

Klein, William W. "Election." In *DLNT*, 317–21.

———. *The New Chosen People: A Corporate View of Election*. Grand Rapids: Zondervan, 1990.

Klooster, F. H. "Elect, Election." In *EDT3*, 267–69.

Nettles, Thomas. *By His Grace and for His Glory: A Historical, Theological and Practical Study of the Doctrines of Grace in Baptist Life*. Grand Rapids: Baker, 1986.

Packer, J. I. "Election." In *IBD*, Vol. 1, 435–38.

Picirilli, Robert E. *Grace, Faith, Free Will: Contrasting Views of Salvation; Calvinism and Arminianism*. Nashville: Randall House, 2002.

Pinnock, Clark H., ed. *Grace Unlimited*. Minneapolis: Bethany House, 1975.

———. *The Grace of God, the Will of Man: A Case for Arminianism*. Grand Rapids: Zondervan, 1989.

Piper, John. *The Justification of God: An Exegetical and Theological Study of Romans 9:1–23*. 2nd ed. Grand Rapids: Baker, 2005.

Poythress, Vern. "Using Multiple Thematic Centers in Theological Synthesis: Holiness as a Test Case in Developing a Pauline Theology." Unpublished manuscript, available from the Campus Bookstore, Westminster Theological Seminary, P.O. Box 27009, Philadelphia, PA 19118, or at https://www.wtsbooks.com. (a study on Pauline themes used to describe the application of redemption).

Reid, W. S. "Reprobation." In *EDT3*, 741.

Russell, S. "Predestination." In *NDT2*, 700–702.

Samson, John. *Twelve What Abouts: Answering Common Objections Concerning God's Sovereignty in Election*. Birmingham, AL: Solid Ground, 2012.

Schreiner, T. "Election." In *NDBT*, 450–54.

Schreiner, Thomas, and Bruce Ware, eds. *Still Sovereign: Contemporary Perspectives on Election, Foreknowledge, and Grace*. Grand Rapids: Baker, 2000.

Shank, R. *Elect in the Son: A Study of the Doctrine of Election*. Springfield, MO: Westcott, 1970.

Sproul, R. C. *Chosen by God*. Wheaton, IL: Tyndale, 1986.

Steele, David N. and Curtis C. Thomas. *The Five Points of Calvinism—Defined, Defended, Documented*. International Library of Philosophy and Theology: Biblical and Theological Studies, edited by J. Marcellus Kik. Phillipsburg, NJ: Presbyterian and Reformed, 1963.

Storms, C. Samuel. *Chosen for Life: An Introductory Guide to the Doctrine of Divine Election*. Grand Rapids: Baker, 1987.

Warfield, B. B. *The Plan of Salvation*. Grand Rapids: Eerdmans, 1942.

———. "Predestination." In *Biblical and Theological Studies*. Philadelphia: Presbyterian and Reformed, 1952.

## SCRIPTURE MEMORY PASSAGE

**Ephesians 1:3–6:** Blessed be the God and Father of our Lord Jesus Christ, who has blessed us in Christ with every spiritual blessing in the heavenly places, even as he chose us in him before the foundation of the world, that we should be holy and blameless before him. In love he predestined us for adoption to himself as sons through Jesus Christ, according to the purpose of his will, to the praise of his glorious grace, with which he has blessed us in the Beloved.

## HYMN

**"When This Passing World Is Done"**

This hymn reminds us that when we are once in heaven and look back on our life we will realize how much more we owe to God's mercy and grace than we ever realized in this life. The last stanza especially emphasizes the fact that our election is not based on anything good in ourselves: "Chosen not for good in me."

*When this passing world is done,*
*  When has sunk yon glaring sun,*
*When we stand with Christ in glory,*
*  Looking o'er life's finished story,*
*Then, Lord, shall I fully know,*
*  Not till then, how much I owe.*

*When I hear the wicked call*
*  On the rocks and hills to fall,*
*When I see them start to shrink*
*  On the fiery deluge brink,*
*Then, Lord, shall I fully know,*
*  Not till then, how much I owe.*

*When I stand before the throne,*
*  Dressed in beauty not my own,*
*When I see thee as thou art,*
*  Love thee with unsinning heart,*
*Then, Lord, shall I fully know,*
*  Not till then, how much I owe.*

*When the praise of heav'n I hear,*
*  Loud as thunders to the ear,*
*Loud as many waters' noise,*
*  Sweet as harp's melodious voice,*
*Then, Lord, shall I fully know,*
*  Not till then, how much I owe.*

*Chosen not for good in me,*
*  Wakened up from wrath to flee,*
*Hidden in the Savior's side,*
*  By the Spirit sanctified,*
*Teach me, Lord, on earth to show,*
*  By my love, how much I owe.*

Author: Robert Murray McCheyne, 1837

# CONTEMPORARY WORSHIP SONG

### "Grace Alone"

*I was an orphan lost at the fall*
*Running away when I'd hear you call,*
*But Father you worked your will.*
*I had no righteousness of my own.*
*I had no right to draw near your throne,*
*But Father you loved me still.*

### Chorus 1

*And in love before you laid the world's*
    *foundation,*
*You predestined to adopt me as your own.*
*You have raised me up so high above my station.*
*I'm a child of God by grace and grace alone.*

*You left your home to seek out the lost.*
*You knew the great and terrible cost,*
*But Jesus your face was set.*
*I worked my fingers down to the bone,*
*But nothing I did could ever atone,*
*But Jesus you paid my debt.*

### Chorus 2

*By Your blood I have redemption and salvation,*
*Lord, you died that I might reap what you*
    *have sown,*
*And you rose that I might be a new creation.*
*I am born again by grace and grace alone.*

### Bridge

*I was in darkness all of my life.*
*I never knew the day from the night,*
*But Spirit you made me see.*
*I swore I knew the way on my own,*
*Head full of rocks a heart made of stone,*
*But Spirit you moved in me.*

### Chorus 3

*And at your touch my sleeping spirit was*
    *awakened.*
*On my darkened heart the light of Christ has*
    *shone.*
*Called into a kingdom that cannot be shaken,*
*Heaven's citizen by grace and grace alone.*

### Ending

*So I'll stand in faith by grace and grace alone.*
*I will run the race by grace and grace alone.*
*I will slay my sin by grace and grace alone.*
*I will reach the end by grace and grace alone.*

Words by Dustin Kensrue[28]

---

# CHAPTER 33

# The Gospel Call and Effective Calling

*What is the gospel message?*
*How does it become effective?*

## EXPLANATION AND SCRIPTURAL BASIS

When Paul talks about the way that God brings salvation into our lives, he says, "Those whom he *predestined* he also *called*, and those whom he called he also *justified*, and those whom he justified he also *glorified*" (Rom. 8:30). Here Paul points to a definite order in which the blessings of salvation come to us. Although long ago, before the world was made, God "predestined" us to be his children and to be conformed to the image of his Son, Paul points to the fact that in the actual outworking of his purpose in our lives God "called" us (here in this context, God the Father is specifically in view). Then Paul immediately lists justification and glorification, showing that these come after calling. Paul indicates that there is a definite order in God's saving purpose (though not every aspect of our salvation is mentioned here). So we will begin our discussion of the different parts of our experience of salvation with the topic of calling.

### A. EFFECTIVE CALLING

When Paul says, "Those whom he predestined *he* also called, and those whom *he* called he also justified" (Rom. 8:30), he indicates that calling is an act of God. In fact, it is specifically an act of God the Father, for he is the one who predestines people "to be conformed to the image of his Son" (Rom. 8:29). Other verses describe more fully what this calling is. When God calls people in this powerful way, he calls them "out of darkness into his marvelous light" (1 Peter 2:9); he calls them "into the fellowship of his Son" (1 Cor. 1:9; cf. Acts 2:39) and "into his own kingdom and glory" (1 Thess. 2:12; cf. 1 Peter 5:10; 2 Peter 1:3). People who have been called by God "belong to Jesus Christ" (Rom. 1:6). They are called to "be saints" (Rom. 1:7; 1 Cor. 1:2) and have come into a realm of peace (1 Cor. 7:15; Col. 3:15), freedom (Gal. 5:13), hope (Eph. 1:18; 4:4), holiness (1 Thess. 4:7), patient endurance of suffering (1 Peter 2:20–21; 3:9), and eternal life (1 Tim. 6:12).

These verses indicate that no powerless, merely human calling is in view. This calling is rather a kind of "summons" from the King of the universe, and it has such power that it brings about the response that it asks for in people's hearts. It is an act of God that *guarantees* a response because, as Paul specifies in Romans 8:30, all who were "called" were also "justified."[1] This calling has the capacity to draw us out of the kingdom of darkness and bring us into God's kingdom so we can join in full fellowship with him: "God is faithful, by whom you were *called into the fellowship of his Son*, Jesus Christ our Lord" (1 Cor. 1:9; cf. 1 Thess. 2:12).

This powerful act of God is often referred to as *effective calling*, to distinguish it from the general gospel invitation that goes to all people and which some people reject. This is not to say that human gospel proclamation is not involved. In fact, God's effective calling comes *through* the human preaching of the gospel, because Paul says, "To this he called you *through our gospel*, so that you may obtain the glory of our Lord Jesus Christ" (2 Thess. 2:14). Of course, there are many who hear the general call of the gospel message—and do not respond—they have only received an *external calling*. But in some cases the gospel call is made so effective by the working of the Holy Spirit in people's hearts that they do respond; we can say that they have received "effective calling."[2]

We may define effective calling as follows: *effective calling is an act of God the Father, speaking through the human proclamation of the gospel, in which he summons people to himself in such a way that they respond in saving faith.*

It is important that we not give the impression that people will be saved by the power of this call *apart from* their own willing response to the gospel (see chapter 35 on the personal faith and repentance that are necessary for conversion). Although it is true that effective calling awakens and brings forth a response from us, we must always insist that this response still has to be a voluntary, willing response in which the individual person puts his or her trust in Christ.

This is why prayer is so important to effective evangelism. Unless God works in peoples' hearts to make the proclamation of the gospel effective, there will be no genuine saving response. Jesus said, "No one can come to me unless the Father who sent me draws him" (John 6:44). An example of the gospel call working effectively is seen in Paul's first visit to Philippi. When Lydia heard the gospel message, "The Lord *opened her heart* to pay attention to what was said by Paul" (Acts 16:14).

In distinction from effective calling, which is entirely an act of God, we may talk about the *gospel call in general* which comes through human speech. This gospel call is offered to all people, even those who do not accept it. Sometimes this gospel call is referred to as *external calling* or *general calling*. (By contrast, the effective calling of God that actually brings about a willing response from the person who hears it is sometimes called *internal calling*.) The broader gospel call is general and external and often rejected,

---

1. See the discussion of justification in chapter 36.
2. The older term used for *effective* calling was *effectual* calling, but the term *effectual* is not as commonly used in English today.

while the effective call is particular, internal, and *always* effective. However, this is not to diminish the importance of the gospel call—it is the means God has appointed through which effective calling will come. Without the gospel call, no one could respond and be saved! "How are they to believe in him of whom they have never heard?" (Rom. 10:14). Therefore, it is important to understand exactly what the gospel call is.

## B. The Elements of the Gospel Call

In human preaching of the gospel, three important elements must be included.

### 1. Explanation of the Facts Concerning Salvation

Anyone who comes to Christ for salvation must have at least a basic understanding of who Christ is and how he meets our needs for salvation. Therefore an explanation of the facts concerning salvation must include at least the following:

1. All people have sinned (Rom. 3:23).
2. The penalty for our sin is death (Rom. 6:23).
3. Jesus Christ died to pay the penalty for our sins (Rom. 5:8), and he rose from the dead and is alive today (1 Cor. 15:3–4).

But understanding those facts and even agreeing that they are true *is not enough for a person to be saved.* There must also be an invitation for a personal response on the part of the individual who will repent of his or her sins and trust personally in Christ.

### 2. Invitation to Respond to Christ Personally in Repentance and Faith

When the New Testament talks about people coming to salvation it speaks in terms of a *personal response* to an invitation from Christ himself. That invitation is beautifully expressed, for example, in the words of Jesus: "Come to me, all who labor and are heavy laden, and I will give you rest. Take my yoke upon you, and learn from me, for I am gentle and lowly in heart, and you will find rest for your souls. For my yoke is easy, and my burden is light" (Matt. 11:28–30).

It is important to make clear that these are not just words spoken a long time ago by a religious leader in the past. Every non-Christian hearing these words should be encouraged to think of them as words that Jesus Christ is *even now*, at *this very moment*, speaking to him or to her individually. Jesus Christ is a Savior who is now alive in heaven, and each non-Christian should think of Jesus as speaking directly to him or her, saying, "*Come to me . . . and I will give you rest*" (Matt. 11:28). This is a genuine *personal* invitation that seeks a personal response from each one who hears it.

John also talks about the need for personal response when he says, "He came to his own, and his own people did not receive him. *But to all who did receive him*, who believed in his name, he gave the right to become children of God" (John 1:11–12). In emphasizing the need to "receive" Christ, John too points to the necessity of an individual response—with an image of welcoming someone into one's own home, but here it is "receiving" Christ into one's life. To those inside a lukewarm church who do not realize their spiritual blindness the Lord Jesus again issues an invitation that calls for personal response: "Behold, I stand at the door and knock. If *anyone* hears my voice and opens the door, I will come in to him and eat with him, and he with me" (Rev. 3:20).

Finally, just five verses from the end of the entire Bible, there is another invitation from the Holy Spirit and the church to come to Christ: "The Spirit and the Bride say, 'Come.' And let the one who hears say, 'Come.' And let the one who is thirsty come; let the one who desires take the water of life without price" (Rev. 22:17).

But what is involved in coming to Christ? Although this will be explained more fully in chapter 35, it is sufficient to note here that if we come to Christ and trust him to save us from our sin, we cannot any longer cling to sin but must willingly renounce it in genuine repentance. In some cases in Scripture both repentance and faith are mentioned together when referring to someone's initial conversion (Paul said that he spent his time "testifying both to Jews and to Greeks of *repentance* toward God and of *faith* in our Lord Jesus Christ," Acts 20:21). But at other times only repentance of sins is named and saving faith is assumed as an accompanying factor ("that *repentance* for the forgiveness of sins should be proclaimed in his name to all nations," Luke 24:47; cf. Acts 2:37–38; 3:19; 5:31; 17:30; Rom. 2:4; 2 Cor. 7:10, et al.). Therefore, any genuine gospel proclamation must include an invitation to make a conscious decision to forsake one's sins and come to Christ in faith, asking Christ for forgiveness of sins. If either the need to repent of sins or the need to trust in Christ for forgiveness is neglected, there is not a full and true proclamation of the gospel.[3]

But what is promised for those who come to Christ? This is the third element of the gospel call.

### 3. A Promise of Forgiveness and Eternal Life

Although the words of personal invitation spoken by Christ do have promises of rest, and power to become children of God, and partaking of the water of life, it is helpful to make explicit just what Christ promises to those who come to him in repentance and faith. The primary thing that is promised in the gospel message is the promise of forgiveness of sins and eternal life with God. "For God so loved the world, that he gave his only Son, that whoever believes in him *should not perish but have eternal life*" (John 3:16). And in Peter's preaching of the gospel he says, "Repent therefore, and turn back, *that your sins may be blotted out*" (Acts 3:19; cf. 2:38).

Coupled with the promise of forgiveness and eternal life should be an assurance that

---

3. See chapter 35, pp. 861–79, for a fuller discussion of the need for both genuine repentance and genuine faith, and a discussion of the question of whether someone can be saved by "accepting Jesus as Savior but not as Lord."

Christ will accept all who come to him in sincere repentance and faith seeking salvation: "Whoever comes to me I will never cast out" (John 6:37).

## C. The Importance of the Gospel Call

The doctrine of the gospel call is important, because if there were no gospel call we could not be saved. "How are they to believe in him of whom they have never heard?" (Rom. 10:14).

The gospel call is important also because through it God addresses us in the fullness of our humanity. He does not save us "automatically" without seeking for a response from us as whole persons. Rather, he addresses the gospel call to our intellects, our emotions, and our wills. He speaks to our intellects by explaining the facts of salvation in his Word. He speaks to our emotions by issuing a heartfelt personal invitation to respond. He speaks to our wills by asking us to hear his invitation and respond willingly in repentance and faith—to decide to turn from our sins and receive Christ as Savior and rest our hearts in him for salvation.

# QUESTIONS FOR PERSONAL APPLICATION

1. Can you remember the first time you heard the gospel and responded to it? Can you describe what it felt like in your heart? Do you think the Holy Spirit was working to make that gospel call effective in your life? Did you resist it at the time?

2. In your explanation of the gospel call to other people, have some elements been missing? If so, what difference would it make if you added those elements to your explanation of the gospel? Do you think those elements are important to add? What is the one thing most needed to make your proclamation of the gospel more effective?

3. Before reading this chapter, had you thought of Jesus in heaven speaking the words of the gospel invitation personally to people even today? If non-Christians do begin to think of Jesus speaking to them in this way, how do you think it will affect their response to the gospel?

4. Do you understand the elements of the gospel call clearly enough to present them to others? Could you easily turn in the Bible to find four or five appropriate verses that would explain the gospel call clearly to people? (Memorizing the elements of the gospel call and the verses that explain it should be one of the first disciplines of anyone's Christian life.)

**Special Terms**

*effective calling*
*external calling*
*gospel call, the*
*internal calling*

# BIBLIOGRAPHY

(For an explanation of this bibliography see the note on the bibliography to chapter 1, pp. 23–24. Complete bibliographical data may be found on pp. 1489–96.)

## SECTIONS IN EVANGELICAL SYSTEMATIC THEOLOGIES

### 1. Anglican (Episcopalian)
1882–92 . . . . . Litton, 239–55
2001 . . . . . . . . Packer, 152–53
2013 . . . . . . . . Bird, 531–532
2013 . . . . . . . . Bray, 509

### 2. Arminian (Wesleyan or Methodist)
1875–76 . . . . . Pope, 336–57
1940 . . . . . . . . Wiley, 2:334–57
1960 . . . . . . . . Purkiser, 269–78
1992 . . . . . . . . Oden, 3:164–169
2002 . . . . . . . . Cottrell, 401

### 3. Baptist
1767 . . . . . . . . Gill, 1:530–37; 2:121–31
1887 . . . . . . . . Boyce, 367–73
1907 . . . . . . . . Strong, 790–93
2007 . . . . . . . . Akin, 723–27
2013 . . . . . . . . Erickson, 860–75

### 4. Dispensational
1947 . . . . . . . . Chafer, 3:210–24, 371–93
1949 . . . . . . . . Thiessen, 257–63
1986 . . . . . . . . Ryrie, 324–25, 335–39
2017 . . . . . . . . MacArthur and Mayhue, 571–76

### 5. Lutheran
1917–24 . . . . . Pieper, 2:423–26, 502; 3:220–52

1934 . . . . . . . . Mueller, 364–65, 470–85

### 6. Reformed (or Presbyterian)
1559 . . . . . . . . Calvin, 1:537–42 (3.1)
1679–85 . . . . . Turretin, *IET*, 2:501–631
1871–73 . . . . . Hodge, 2:639–732
1878 . . . . . . . . Dabney, 553–79
1894 . . . . . . . . Shedd, 810
1906–11 . . . . Bavinck, *RD*, 4: 29–64
1910 . . . . . . . . Vos, 4:35, 37–38, 97
1937–66 . . . . Murray, *CW*, 1:124–34, 143–65; *CW*, 2:161–66; *CW*, 4:113–32; *RAA*, 88–94
1938 . . . . . . . . Berkhof, 454–64
2008 . . . . . . . . Van Genderen and Velema, 578–79
2011 . . . . . . . . Horton, 560–75
2013 . . . . . . . . Frame, 3–4, 166, 923, 937, 939–42
2013 . . . . . . . . Culver, 682–88
2016 . . . . . . . . Allen and Swain, 28–29
2017 . . . . . . . . Barrett, 24
2019 . . . . . . . . Letham, 648–58

### 7. Renewal (or charismatic/Pentecostal)
1988–92 . . . . . Williams, 2:13–33
1993 . . . . . . . . Menzies and Horton, 164
2008 . . . . . . . . Duffield and Van Cleave, 211

## SECTIONS IN REPRESENTATIVE ROMAN CATHOLIC SYSTEMATIC THEOLOGIES

### 1. Roman Catholic: Traditional
1955 . . . . . . . . Ott (no explicit treatment)

### 2. Roman Catholic: Post–Vatican II
1980 . . . . . . . . McBrien (no explicit treatment)

2012.........*CCC*, paragraphs 199–202, 571

### OTHER WORKS

Aldrich, Joseph C. *Life-Style Evangelism: Crossing Traditional Boundaries to Reach the Unbelieving World*. Portland: Multnomah, 1981.

Alleine, Joseph. *Sure Guide to Heaven*. Carlisle, PA: Banner of Truth, 1978. First published in 1672 as *An Alarm to the Unconverted*.

Allison, Gregg. *Historical Theology: An Introduction to Christian Doctrine; A Companion to Wayne Grudem's* Systematic Theology. Grand Rapids: Zondervan, 2011, 474–497.

Barrett, Matthew. *Salvation by Grace: The Case for Effectual Calling and Regeneration*. Phillipsburg, NJ: P&R, 2013.

Baxter, Richard. *A Call to the Unconverted to Turn and Live*. Reprint, Grand Rapids: Zondervan, 1953.

Coleman, Robert E. *The Master Plan of Evangelism*. Old Tappan, NJ: Revell, 1963.

Demarest, Bruce. *The Cross and Salvation: The Doctrine of Salvation*. Wheaton, IL: Crossway, 2006, 27–43.

Hoekema, Anthony A. *Saved by Grace*. Grand Rapids: Eerdmans, and Exeter: Paternoster, 1989, 68–92.

House, H. Wayne. *Charts of Christian Theology and Doctrine*. Grand Rapids: Zondervan, 1992, 102.

Keathley, Kenneth. "The Work of God: Salvation." In *A Theology for the Church*, edited by Daniel L. Akin et al., 723–27. Nashville: B&H, 2007.

Kennedy, D. James. *Evangelism Explosion*. 3rd ed. Wheaton, IL: Tyndale, 1983.

Kevan, Ernest F. *Salvation*. Phillipsburg, NJ: Presbyterian and Reformed, 1973.

Kruse, C. G. "Call, Calling." In *DPL*, 84–85.

Little, Paul. *How to Give Away Your Faith*. Revised by Marie Little. Downers Grove, IL: InterVarsity Press, 1988.

MacArthur, John F., Jr. *The Gospel according to Jesus*. Grand Rapids: Zondervan, 1988.

Motyer, Stephen. "Call, Calling." In *BTDB*, 80–81.

Murray, John. "Effectual Calling." In *Redemption Accomplished and Applied*. Grand Rapids: Eerdmans, 1955, 88–94.

Packer, J. I. "Call, Calling." In *EDT3*, 151–52.

———. *Evangelism and the Sovereignty of God*. Downers Grove, IL: InterVarsity Press, 1961.

Wells, David F. *God the Evangelist: How the Holy Spirit Works to Bring Men and Women to Faith*. Grand Rapids: Eerdmans, 1987.

## SCRIPTURE MEMORY PASSAGE

**Matthew 11:28–30:** Come to me, all who labor and are heavy laden, and I will give you rest. Take my yoke upon you, and learn from me, for I am gentle and lowly in heart, and you will find rest for your souls. For my yoke is easy, and my burden is light.

## HYMN

### "I Heard the Voice of Jesus Say"

*I heard the voice of Jesus say, "Come unto me and rest;*
*Lay down, thou weary one, lay down thy head upon my breast."*

*I came to Jesus as I was, weary and worn and sad,*
*I found in him a resting place, and he has made me glad.*

I heard the voice of Jesus say, "Behold, I freely give
The living water; thirsty one, stoop down and
drink, and live."
I came to Jesus, and I drank of that life-giving
stream;
My thirst was quenched, my soul revived, and
now I live in him.

I heard the voice of Jesus say, "I am this dark
world's light;
Look unto me, thy morn shall rise, and all thy
day be bright."
I looked to Jesus, and I found in him my star,
my sun;
And in that light of life I'll walk, till
trav'lling days are done.

Author: Horatius Bonar, 1846

## CONTEMPORARY WORSHIP SONG

### "I Bow Down"

I bow down before You, Lord.
I bow down before You, Lord.
Holy and faithful, righteous and true,
You are my King.

I bow(kneel) down before You.

I kneel down before You, Lord.
I kneel down before You, Lord.
Redeemer and Healer, Almighty God,
You are my King.

You are Jesus; You're my Savior,
And with all that is within me,

Words by Cindy Rethmeier[4]

4. © 1991 Mercy/Vineyard Publishing (ASCAP). Admin. In
North America By Music Services o/b/o Vineyard Music USA.

## CHAPTER 34

# Regeneration

*What does it mean to be born again?*

## EXPLANATION AND SCRIPTURAL BASIS

We may define regeneration as follows: *regeneration is a secret act of God in which he imparts new spiritual life to us.* This is sometimes called "being born again" (using language from John 3:3–8).

### A. REGENERATION IS TOTALLY A WORK OF GOD

In some of the elements of the application of redemption that are discussed in subsequent chapters, we play an active part (this is true, for example, of conversion, sanctification, and perseverance). But in the work of regeneration we play no active role at all. It is instead totally a work of God. We see this, for example, when John talks about those to whom Christ gave power to become children of God—they "were born, not of blood nor of the will of the flesh nor of the will of man, but of God" (John 1:13). Here John specifies that children of God are those who are "born . . . of God" and our human will ("the will of man") does not bring about this kind of birth.

The fact that we are passive in regeneration is also evident when Scripture refers to it as being "born" or being "born again" (cf. James 1:18; 1 Peter 1:3; John 3:3–8). We did not choose to be made physically alive, and we did not choose to be born—it is something that happened to us; similarly, these analogies in Scripture suggest that we are entirely passive in regeneration.

This sovereign work of God in regeneration was also predicted in the prophecy of Ezekiel. Through him God promised a time in the future when he would give new spiritual life to his people: "And I will give you a *new heart*, and *a new spirit I will put within you*. And I will remove the heart of stone from your flesh and give you a heart of flesh. And I will put my Spirit within you, and cause you to walk in my statutes and be careful to obey my rules" (Ezek. 36:26–27).

Which member of the Trinity causes regeneration? When Jesus speaks of being "born of the Spirit" (John 3:8), he indicates that it is especially the Holy Spirit who produces regeneration. But other verses also indicate the involvement of God the Father in regeneration: Paul specifies that it is God who "made us alive together with Christ" (Eph. 2:5; cf. Col. 2:13). And James says that it is the "Father of lights" who gave us new birth: "Of his own will *he brought us forth* by the word of truth, that we should be a kind of firstfruits of his creatures" (James 1:17–18).[1] Finally, Peter says that God "according to his abundant mercy *has given us new birth* . . . through the resurrection of Jesus Christ from the dead" (1 Peter 1:3, author's translation). We can conclude that both God the Father and God the Holy Spirit bring about regeneration.

What is the connection between effective calling[2] and regeneration? As we will see later in this chapter, Scripture indicates that regeneration must come before we can respond to effective calling with saving faith. Therefore, we can say that regeneration comes before the *result* of effective calling (our faith). But it is more difficult to specify the exact relationship in time between regeneration and the human proclamation of the gospel through which God works in effective calling. At least two passages suggest that God regenerates us at the same time as he speaks to us in effective calling: Peter says, "You have been *born again*, not of perishable seed but of imperishable, *through the living and abiding word of God.* . . . And this word is the good news that was preached to you" (1 Peter 1:23, 25). And James says, "He brought us forth by the word of truth" (James 1:18). As the gospel comes to us through an external calling, God speaks through it to summon us to himself (effective calling) and to give us new spiritual life (regeneration) so that we are enabled to respond in faith. Effective calling is thus God the Father *speaking powerfully to us*, and regeneration is God the Father and God the Holy Spirit *working powerfully in us*, to make us alive. These two things must have happened simultaneously as Peter was preaching the gospel to the household of Cornelius, for while he was still preaching "the Holy Spirit fell on all who heard the word" (Acts 10:44).

Sometimes the term *irresistible grace*[3] is used in this connection. It refers to the fact that God effectively calls people and also gives them regeneration, and both actions guarantee that we will respond in saving faith. The term *irresistible grace* is subject to misunderstanding, however, since it *seems* to imply that people do not make a voluntary, willing choice in responding to the gospel—a wrong idea, and a wrong understanding of the term *irresistible grace*. The term does preserve something valuable, however, because it indicates that God's work reaches into our hearts to bring about a response that is absolutely certain—even though we respond voluntarily.[4]

## B. The Exact Nature of Regeneration Is Mysterious to Us

Exactly what happens in regeneration is mysterious to us. We know that somehow we who were spiritually dead (Eph. 2:1) have been made alive to God and in a very real sense

---

1. When James says that God "brought us forth," he uses language that ordinarily applies to physical birth (being brought forth out of our mothers' wombs, and into the world) and applies it to spiritual birth.

2. See chapter 33, pp. 842–46, on effective calling.

3. This is the *I* in the "five points of Calvinism" represented by the acronym TULIP. The other letters stand for *T*otal depravity (see chapter 24, pp. 626–27), *U*nconditional election (see chapter 32, pp. 827–28), *L*imited atonement (see chapter 27, pp. 737–38), and *P*erseverance of the saints (see chapter 40, pp. 970–71). See also p. 828n12.

4. Some people will object here that God cannot *guarantee* a response that is still willing and voluntary on our part. But this objection simply inserts into the discussion a definition of "voluntary" or "willing" that is not itself supported by Scripture; see discussion in chapter 16, pp. 427–29, 433, 437–39, and chapter 32, pp. 828–30, on God's providence in relation to our voluntary decisions.

we have been "born again" (John 3:3, 7; Eph. 2:5; Col. 2:13). But we don't understand how this happens or what exactly God does to us to give us this new spiritual life. Jesus says, "The wind blows where it wishes, and you hear its sound, but you do not know where it comes from or where it goes. So it is with everyone who is born of the Spirit" (John 3:8).

Scripture views regeneration as something that affects us as whole persons. It is not just that our spirits were dead before—*we* were dead to God in trespasses and sins (see Eph. 2:1). And it is not correct to say that the only thing that happens in regeneration is that our spirits are made alive (as some would teach),[5] for *every part of us* is affected by regeneration: "If anyone is in Christ, *he is a new creation*. The old has passed away; behold, the new has come" (2 Cor. 5:17).

Because regeneration is a work of God within us in which he gives us new life it is right to conclude that it is an *instantaneous event*. It happens only once. At one moment we are spiritually dead, and then at the next moment we have new spiritual life from God. Nevertheless, we do not always know exactly when this instantaneous change occurs. Especially for children growing up in a Christian home or for people who attend an evangelical church or Bible study over a period of time and grow gradually in their understanding of the gospel, there may not be a dramatic crisis with a radical change of behavior from "hardened sinner" to "holy saint," but there will be an instantaneous change nonetheless, when God through the Holy Spirit, in an unseen, invisible way, awakens spiritual life within. The change will *become evident* over time in patterns of behavior and desires that are pleasing to God.

In other cases (in fact, probably most cases when adults become Christians) regeneration takes place at a clearly recognizable time at which the person realizes that previously he or she was separated from God and spiritually dead, but immediately afterward there was clearly new spiritual life within. The results can usually be seen at once—a heartfelt trusting in Christ for salvation, an assurance of sins forgiven, a desire to read the Bible and pray (and a sense that these are meaningful spiritual activities), a delight in worship, a desire for Christian fellowship, a sincere desire to be obedient to God's Word in Scripture, and a desire to tell others about Christ. People may say something like this: "I don't know exactly what happened, but before that moment I did not trust in Christ for salvation. I was still wondering and questioning in my mind. But after that moment I realized that I did trust in Christ and he was my Savior. Something happened in my heart."[6]

---

5. This view of regeneration usually depends on viewing man as trichotomous or consisting of three parts (body, soul, and spirit), a position we discussed in chapter 23 above (pp. 606–7). But if we reject trichotomy and see "soul" and "spirit" as two different but related terms in Scripture that speak in different ways of the immaterial part of our nature, then such an explanation is not persuasive. Even for those who accept trichotomy, the Scriptures that speak of us as a new creation and that say that *we* have been born again (not just our spirits), should be good reason for seeing more in regeneration than merely making our spirits alive.

6. C. S. Lewis tells the story of his own conversion: "I know very well when, but hardly how, the final step was taken. I was driven to Whipsnade one sunny morning. When we set out I did not believe that Jesus Christ is the Son of God, and when we reached the zoo I did. Yet I had not exactly spent the journey in thought. Nor in great emotion" (*Surprised by Joy* [New York: Harcourt, Brace and World, 1955], 237).

Yet even in these cases we are not quite sure exactly what has happened in our hearts. It is just as Jesus said with respect to the wind—we hear its sound and we see the result, but we cannot actually see the wind itself. So it is with the working of the Holy Spirit in our hearts.

## C. In This Sense of Regeneration, It Comes Before Saving Faith

Using the verses quoted above, we have defined regeneration to be the act of God awakening spiritual life within us, bringing us from spiritual *death* to spiritual *life*. On this definition, it is natural to understand that regeneration comes *before* saving faith. It is in fact this work of God that gives us the spiritual *ability* to respond to God in faith. However, when we say that it comes "before" saving faith, it is important to remember that they usually come so close together that it will ordinarily seem to us that they are happening at the same time. As God addresses the effective call of the gospel to us, he regenerates us and we respond in faith and repentance to this call. So *from our perspective* it is hard to tell any difference in time, especially because regeneration is a spiritual work that we cannot perceive with our eyes or even understand with our minds.

Yet there are several passages that tell us that this secret, hidden work of God in our spirits does in fact come before we respond to God in saving faith (though often it may be only seconds before we respond). When talking about regeneration with Nicodemus, Jesus said, "Unless one is born of water and the Spirit, *he cannot enter the kingdom of God*" (John 3:5). Now we enter the kingdom of God when we become Christians at conversion. But Jesus says that we have to be born "of the Spirit" before we can do that.[7] Our inability to come to Christ on our own, without an initial work of God within us, is also emphasized when Jesus says, "No one can come to me unless the Father who sent me draws him" (John 6:44), and "No one can come to me unless it is granted him by the Father" (John 6:65). This inward act of regeneration is described beautifully when

---

7. When Jesus talks about being "born of water" here, the most likely interpretation of this is that he is referring to *spiritual cleansing from sin*, which Ezekiel prophesied when he said, "I will sprinkle clean water on you, and you shall be clean from all your uncleannesses, and from all your idols I will cleanse you. And I will give you a new heart, and a new spirit I will put within you" (Ezek. 36:25–26). Here the water symbolizes spiritual cleansing from sin, just as the new heart and new spirit speak of the new spiritual life that God will give. Ezekiel is prophesying that God will give an internal cleansing from the pollution of sin in the heart at the same time as he awakens new spiritual life within his people. The fact that these two ideas are connected so closely in this well-known prophecy from Ezekiel, and the fact that Jesus assumes that Nicodemus should have understood this truth ("Are you the teacher of Israel and yet you do not understand these things?" [John 3:10]), together with the fact that throughout the conversation Jesus is talking about intensely spiritual concerns, all suggest that this is the most likely understanding of the passage. Another suggestion has been that "born of water" refers to physical birth and the "water" (or amniotic fluid) that accompanies it, but it would hardly be necessary for Jesus to specify that one has to be born in this way when he is talking about spiritual birth, and it is questionable whether first-century Jews would have understood the phrase in this way either. Another interpretation is that Jesus is referring to the water of baptism here, but baptism or any other similar ceremony is not in view in this passage (and it would have been anachronistic for Jesus to speak of Christian baptism here, since that did not begin until Pentecost); moreover, this would make Jesus teach that a physical act of baptism is necessary for salvation, something that would contradict the New Testament emphasis on salvation by faith alone as necessary for salvation, and something which, if it were true, we would certainly expect to find taught much more explicitly in the other New Testament passages that clearly deal with baptism (see chapter 49 on baptism).

Luke says of Lydia, "*The Lord opened her heart* to pay attention to what was said by Paul" (Acts 16:14). First the Lord opened her heart, then she was able to give heed to Paul's preaching and to respond in faith.

By contrast, Paul tells us, "The natural person does not accept the things of the Spirit of God, for they are folly to him, and he is not able to understand them because they are spiritually discerned" (1 Cor. 2:14). He also says of people apart from Christ, "no one understands; no one seeks for God" (Rom. 3:11).

The solution to this spiritual deadness and inability to respond only comes when God gives us new life within. "But God, being rich in mercy, because of the great love with which he loved us, even *when we were dead in our trespasses*, made us alive together with Christ" (Eph. 2:4–5). Paul also says, "You, who were dead in your trespasses and the uncircumcision of your flesh, God made alive together with him, having forgiven us all our trespasses" (Col. 2:13).

The idea that regeneration comes before saving faith is not always understood by evangelicals today. Sometimes people will even say something like, "If you believe in Christ as your Savior, then (after you believe) you will be born again." But Scripture itself never says anything like that. This new birth is viewed by Scripture as something that God does within us in order to *enable us to believe*.

The reason that evangelicals often think that regeneration comes after saving faith is that they *see the results* (love for God and his Word, and turning from sin) *after* people come to faith, and they think that regeneration must therefore have come after saving faith. Yet here we must decide on the basis of what Scripture tells us because regeneration is not something we see or know about directly: "The wind blows where it wishes, and you hear its sound, but you do not know where it comes from or where it goes. So it is with everyone who is born of the Spirit" (John 3:8).

Therefore, it would be best to emphasize that we do not see regeneration but only the results of it in our lives and that faith in Christ for salvation is the first result that we see. In fact, we can never know that we have been regenerated until we come to faith in Christ, for that is the outward evidence of this hidden, inward work of God. Once we do come to saving faith in Christ, we know that we have been born again.

By way of application, we should realize that the explanation of the gospel message in Scripture does not take the form of a command, "Be born again and you will be saved," but rather, "Believe in Jesus Christ and you will be saved."[8] This is the consistent pattern in the preaching of the gospel throughout the book of Acts and in the descriptions of the gospel given in the Epistles.

---

8. It is true that Jesus tells Nicodemus that he needs to be born again (John 3:7: "Do not marvel that I said to you, 'You must be born again'"), but this is not a command to Nicodemus to do something that no one can ever do (that is, give himself new spiritual life). It is an indicative sentence, not an imperative sentence. It is a statement of fact designed to point out to Nicodemus his total spiritual need and lack of ability on his own to enter the kingdom of God. A little later, when Jesus begins to speak about the response that is expected from Nicodemus, he speaks about the personal response of faith as the thing necessary: "So must the Son of Man be lifted up, that *whoever believes in him* may have eternal life" (John 3:14–15).

## D. Genuine Regeneration Must Bring Results in Life

In an earlier section we saw a beautiful example of the first result of regeneration in a person's life: when Paul spoke the gospel message to Lydia, and "the Lord opened her heart to pay attention to what was said by Paul" (Acts 16:14; cf. John 6:44, 65; 1 Peter 1:3). Similarly, John says, "Everyone who believes that Jesus is the Christ *has been born of God*" (1 John 5:1).[9] But there are also other results of regeneration, many of which are specified in John's first epistle. For example, John says, "No one born of God makes a practice of sinning, for God's seed abides in him; and he *cannot keep on sinning*, because he has been born of God" (1 John 3:9). Here John explains that a person who is born again has that spiritual "seed" (that life-generating and growing power) within him, and that this keeps the person living a life free of continual sin. Of course, the person will not have a perfect life, but the pattern of his or her life will not be one of continuing indulgence in sin. When people are asked to characterize a regenerated person's life, the adjective that comes to mind should not be "sinner" but something like "obedient to Christ" or "obedient to Scripture." We should notice that John says this is true of everyone who is truly born again: "*No one* born of God makes a practice of sinning." Another way of looking at this is to say that "everyone who practices righteousness has been born of him" (1 John 2:29).

A genuine Christlike *love* will be one specific result in life: "whoever loves has been born of God and knows God" (1 John 4:7). Another effect of the new birth is *overcoming the world*: "His commandments are not burdensome. For everyone who has been born of God overcomes the world" (1 John 5:3–4). Here John explains that regeneration gives the ability to overcome the pressures and temptations of the world that would otherwise keep us from obeying God's commandments and following his paths. John says that we will overcome these pressures, and therefore it will not be "burdensome" to obey God's commands, but he implies that it will be joyful. He goes on to explain that the process through which we gain victory over the world is continuing in faith: "This is the victory that has overcome the world—our faith" (1 John 5:4).

Finally, John notes that another result of regeneration is *protection from Satan*: "We know that everyone who has been born of God does not keep on sinning, but he who was born of God [that is, Jesus] protects him, *and the evil one does not touch him*" (1 John 5:18). Though there may be attacks from Satan, John reassures his readers that "he who is in you is greater than he who is in the world" (1 John 4:4), and this greater power of the Holy Spirit within us keeps us safe from ultimate spiritual harm by the evil one.

We should realize that John emphasizes these as *necessary* results in the lives of those who are born again. If there is genuine regeneration in a person's life, he or she

---

9. The perfect participle translated here "is born" could more explicitly be translated "has been born and continues in the new life that resulted from that event."

*will* believe that Jesus is the Christ, *will* refrain from a life pattern of continual sin, *will* love his or her neighbor, *will* overcome the temptations of the world, and *will* be kept safe from ultimate harm by the evil one. These passages show that it is impossible for a person to be regenerated and not become truly converted.[10]

Other results of regeneration are listed by Paul where he speaks of the "*fruit of the Spirit,*" that is, the result in life that is produced by the power of the Holy Spirit working within every believer: "The fruit of the Spirit is love, joy, peace, patience, kindness, goodness, faithfulness, gentleness, self-control" (Gal. 5:22–23). If there is true regeneration, then these elements of the fruit of the Spirit will be more and more evident in that person's life. But by contrast, those who are unbelievers, including those who are pretending to be believers but are not, will clearly lack these character traits in their lives. Jesus told his disciples:

> Beware of false prophets, who come to you in sheep's clothing but inwardly are ravenous wolves. *You will recognize them by their fruits.* Are grapes gathered from thornbushes, or figs from thistles? So, every healthy tree bears good fruit, but the diseased tree bears bad fruit. A healthy tree cannot bear bad fruit, nor can a diseased tree bear good fruit. Every tree that does not bear good fruit is cut down and thrown into the fire. Thus you will recognize them by their fruits. (Matt. 7:15–20)

Neither Jesus nor Paul nor John point to activity in the church or miracles as evidence of regeneration. They rather point to character traits in life. In fact, immediately after the verses quoted above Jesus warns that on the day of judgment many will say to him, "Lord, Lord, did we not prophesy in your name, and cast out demons in your name, and do many mighty works in your name?" But he will declare to them, "I *never knew you*; depart from me, you workers of lawlessness" (Matt. 7:22–23). Prophecy, exorcism, and many miracles and mighty works in Jesus' name (to say nothing of other kinds of intensive church activity in the strength of the flesh over perhaps decades of a person's life) do not provide convincing evidence that a person is truly born again. Apparently all these can be produced in the natural man or woman's own strength, or even with the help of the evil one. But genuine love for God and his people, heartfelt obedience to his commands, and the Christlike character traits that Paul calls the fruit of the Spirit, demonstrated consistently over a period of time in a person's life, simply *cannot* be produced by Satan or by the natural man or woman working in his or her own strength. These can only come about by the Spirit of God working within and giving us new life.

---

10. Since we indicated above that a person is first regenerated, and then subsequently comes to saving faith, there will be a brief time in which someone is regenerated and the results (faith, love, etc.) are not yet seen. But John is saying that the results *will* follow; they are inevitable once someone is born again.

## QUESTIONS FOR PERSONAL APPLICATION

1. Have you been born again? Is there evidence of the new birth in your life? Do you remember a specific time when regeneration occurred in your life? Can you describe how you knew that something had happened?

2. If you (or friends who come to you) are not sure whether you have been born again, what would Scripture encourage you to do in order to gain greater assurance (or to be truly born again for the first time)? (Note: further discussion of repentance and saving faith is given in the next chapter.)

3. Have you thought before that regeneration is prior to saving faith? Are you convinced of it now, or is there still some question in your mind?

4. What do you think about the fact that your regeneration was totally a work of God and that you contributed nothing to it? How does it make you feel toward yourself? How does it make you feel toward God? By way of analogy, how do you feel about the fact that when you were born physically you had no choice in the matter?

5. Are there areas where the results of regeneration are not very clearly seen in your life? Do you think it is possible for a person to be regenerated and then stagnate spiritually so that there is little or no growth? What circumstances might a person live in that would lead to such spiritual stagnation and lack of growth (if that is possible), even though the person was truly born again? To what degree does the kind of church one attends, the teaching one receives, the kind of Christian fellowship one has, and the regularity of one's personal time of Bible reading and prayer, affect one's spiritual life and growth?

6. If regeneration is entirely a work of God and human beings can do nothing to bring it about, then what good does it do to preach the gospel to people at all? Is it somewhat absurd or even cruel to preach the gospel and ask for a response from people who cannot respond because they are spiritually dead? How do you resolve this question?

**Special Terms**
*born again*
*born of the Spirit*
*born of water*
*irresistible grace*
*regeneration*

## BIBLIOGRAPHY

(For an explanation of this bibliography see the note on the bibliography to chapter 1, pp. 23–24. Complete bibliographical data may be found on pp. 1489–96.)

**SECTIONS IN EVANGELICAL SYSTEMATIC THEOLOGIES**

1. *Anglican (Episcopalian)*
   1882–92 . . . . . Litton, 320–28

2001 . . . . . . . . Packer, 157–58
2013 . . . . . . . . Bird, 532–37

**2. Arminian (Wesleyan or Methodist)**
1892–94 . . . . . Miley, 2:327–36
1960 . . . . . . . . Purkiser, 292–97
1992 . . . . . . . . Oden, 3:156–77
2002 . . . . . . . . Cottrell, 332–45

**3. Baptist**
1767 . . . . . . . . Gill, 2:107–21
1887 . . . . . . . . Boyce, 373–82
1907 . . . . . . . . Strong, 809–29
1990–95 . . . . . Garrett, 2:178–79, 301–12
2007 . . . . . . . . Akin, 739–45
2013 . . . . . . . . Erickson, 860–64, 872–75

**4. Dispensational**
1947 . . . . . . . . Chafer, 6:104–21
1949 . . . . . . . . Thiessen, 271–76
1986 . . . . . . . . Ryrie, 325–26
2002–2005 . . Geisler, 3:225
2017 . . . . . . . . MacArthur and Mayhue, 576–89

**5. Lutheran**
1917–24 . . . . . Pieper, 2:498–501
1934 . . . . . . . . Mueller, 363–64

**6. Reformed (or Presbyterian)**
1559 . . . . . . . . Calvin, 1:592–621 (3.3)
1679–85 . . . . . Turretin, *IET*, 1:637, 676, 2:532–33, 542–58
1724–58 . . . . . Edwards, 543–65, 849–55
1871–73 . . . . . Hodge, 2:682–732; 3:3–40
1878 . . . . . . . . Dabney, 579–99
1887–1921 . . . Warfield, *BTS*, 351–74; *SSW*, 2:321–24

1894 . . . . . . . . Shedd, 761–86
1906–11 . . . . . Bavinck, *RD*, 4:44–95, 121–26
1910 . . . . . . . . Vos, 4:29–58
1937–66 . . . . . Murray, *CW*, 2:167–201; *RAA*, 95–105
1938 . . . . . . . . Berkhof, 465–79
1998 . . . . . . . . Reymond, 718–21
2008 . . . . . . . . Van Genderen and Velema, 578–88
2011 . . . . . . . . Horton, 572–75
2013 . . . . . . . . Frame, 145, 166–67, 739–41, 937–38, 944–51, 977
2013 . . . . . . . . Culver, 689–88
2017 . . . . . . . . Barrett, 529–31
2019 . . . . . . . . Letham, 658–68, 731–32

**7. Renewal (or charismatic/Pentecostal)**
1988–92 . . . . . Williams, 2:35–59
1993 . . . . . . . . Menzies and Horton, 107, 113, 142
1995 . . . . . . . . Horton, 364–65
2008 . . . . . . . . Duffield and Van Cleave, 233–40

## SECTIONS IN REPRESENTATIVE ROMAN CATHOLIC SYSTEMATIC THEOLOGIES

**1. Roman Catholic: Traditional**
1955 . . . . . . . . Ott, 219–49

**2. Roman Catholic: Post–Vatican II**
1980 . . . . . . . . McBrien, 2:991–1005
2012 . . . . . . . . *CCC*, paragraphs 784, 872, 1213, 1215, 1262

## OTHER WORKS

Allison, Gregg. *Historical Theology: An Introduction to Christian Doctrine; A Companion to Wayne Grudem's* Systematic Theology. Grand Rapids: Zondervan, 2011, 474–97.

Barrett, Matthew. *Salvation by Grace: The Case for Effectual Calling and Regeneration.* Phillipsburg, NJ: P&R, 2013.

Demarest, Bruce. *The Cross and Salvation: The Doctrine of Salvation.* Wheaton, IL: Crossway, 2006, 27–43.

Goldsworthy, G. "Regeneration." In *NDBT*, 720–23.

Hoekema, Anthony A. "Regeneration." In *Saved by Grace.* Grand Rapids: Eerdmans; Exeter: Paternoster, 1989, 93–112.

Keathley, Kenneth. "The Work of God: Salvation." In *A Theology for the Church*, edited by Daniel L. Akin et al., 727–28, 739–45. Nashville: B&H, 2007.

Kevan, E. F. *Salvation.* Phillipsburg, NJ: Presbyterian and Reformed, 1973.

Koch, Carl B., Jr. "New Birth." In *BTDB*, 558–59.

Needham, David C. *Alive for the First Time: A Fresh Look at the New-Birth Miracle.* Sisters, OR: Multnomah, 1995.

Packer, J. I. "Regeneration." In *EDT3*, 734–35.

Showers, Renald E. *The New Nature.* Neptune, NJ: Loizeaux Bros, 1986.

Toon, Peter. *Born Again: A Biblical and Theological Study of Regeneration.* Grand Rapids: Baker, 1987.

Wilkins, M. J. "New Birth." In *DLNT*, 792–95.

## SCRIPTURE MEMORY PASSAGE

**John 3:5–8:** Jesus answered, "Truly, truly, I say to you, unless one is born of water and the Spirit, he cannot enter the kingdom of God. That which is born of the flesh is flesh, and that which is born of the Spirit is spirit. Do not marvel that I said to you, 'You must be born again.' The wind blows where it wishes, and you hear its sound, but you do not know where it comes from or where it goes. So it is with everyone who is born of the Spirit."

## HYMN

### "I Sought the Lord, and Afterward I Knew"

This hymn beautifully expresses thanks to God for the fact that, though we did not know it, he sought us, worked in our hearts in a mysterious way, and enabled us to believe, before we came to trust in him.

*I sought the Lord, and afterward I knew*
*He moved my soul to seek him, seeking me;*
*It was not I that found, O Savior true,*
*No, I was found of thee.*

*Thou didst reach forth thy hand and mine enfold;*
*I walked and sank not on the storm-vexed sea,*
*'Twas not so much that I on thee took hold,*
*As thou, dear Lord, on me.*

*I find, I walk, I love, but, O the whole*
*Of love is but my answer, Lord, to thee;*
*For thou wert long beforehand with my soul,*
*Always thou lovedst me.*

Anon., c. 1904

# CONTEMPORARY WORSHIP SONG

### "Psalm 34 Taste And See"

*I sought the Lord, and He answered me*
*And delivered me from every fear.*
*Those who look on Him are radiant.*
*They'll never be ashamed.*
*They'll never be ashamed.*

*This poor man cried, and the Lord heard me*
*And saved me from my enemies.*
*The Son of God surrounds His saints.*
*He will deliver them.*
*He will deliver them.*

*Chorus*
*Magnify the Lord with me.*
*Come exalt His name together.*
*Glorify the Lord with me.*
*Come exalt His name forever.*

*O taste and see that the Lord is good.*
*O blessed is he who hides in Him.*
*O fear the Lord O all you saints.*
*He'll give you everything.*
*He'll give you everything.*

*Bridge*
*Let us bless the Lord*
*Every day and night,*
*Never ending praise.*
*May our incense rise.*

Words by Joe Rigney and Shane Barnard[11]

# CHAPTER 35

# Conversion (Faith and Repentance)

*What is saving faith?*
*What is true repentance?*
*Is repentance from sin necessary for salvation?*

## EXPLANATION AND SCRIPTURAL BASIS

The last two chapters have explained how God himself (through the human preaching of the Word) issues the gospel call to us and, by the work of the Holy Spirit, regenerates us, imparting new spiritual life within. In this chapter we examine our response to the gospel call. We may define conversion as follows: *conversion is our willing response to the gospel call, in which we sincerely repent of sins and place our trust in Christ for salvation.*

The word *conversion* means "turning"—here it represents a spiritual turn, a turning *from* sin *to* Christ. The turning from sin is called *repentance*, and the turning to Christ is called *faith*. We can look at each of these elements of conversion, and in one sense it does not matter which one we discuss first, for neither one can occur without the other, and they must occur together when true conversion takes place. For the purposes of this chapter, we shall examine saving faith first, and then repentance.

### A. True Saving Faith Includes Knowledge, Approval, and Personal Trust

### 1. Knowledge Alone Is Not Enough

Personal saving faith, in the way Scripture understands it, involves more than mere knowledge. Of course *it is necessary that we have some knowledge of who Christ is and what he has done*, for "how are they to believe in him of whom they have never heard?" (Rom. 10:14). But knowledge about the *facts* of Jesus' life, death, and resurrection for us is not enough, for people can know facts but rebel against them or dislike them. For example, Paul tells us that many people know God's laws but dislike them: "Though they *know* God's righteous decree that those who practice such things deserve to die, they not only do them but give approval to those who practice them" (Rom. 1:32). Even the demons know who God is and know the facts about Jesus' life and saving works, for James says, "You believe that God is one; you do well. Even the demons believe—and shudder!" (James 2:19). But that knowledge certainly does not mean that the demons are saved. Similarly, someone can *know* the historical facts that Jesus died and that he rose from the dead and that the Bible says this was to pay for our sins, but that knowledge alone is not saving faith.

## 2. Knowledge and Approval Are Not Enough

Moreover, merely knowing the facts and *approving* of them or *agreeing* that they are true is not enough. Nicodemus knew that Jesus had come from God, for he said, "Rabbi, we know that you are a teacher come from God, for no one can do these signs that you do unless God is with him" (John 3:2). Nicodemus had evaluated the facts of the situation, including Jesus' teaching and his remarkable miracles, and had drawn a correct conclusion from those facts: Jesus was a teacher come from God. But this alone did not mean that Nicodemus had saving faith, for he still had to put his trust in Christ for salvation; he still had to "believe in him." King Agrippa provides another example of knowledge and approval without saving faith. Paul realized that King Agrippa knew and apparently viewed with approval the Jewish Scriptures (what we now call the Old Testament). When Paul was on trial before Agrippa, he said, "King Agrippa, do you believe the prophets? I know that *you believe*" (Acts 26:27). Yet Agrippa did not have saving faith, for he said to Paul, "In a short time would you persuade me to be a Christian?" (Acts 26:28).

## 3. I Must Decide to Trust Jesus to Save Me Personally

**a. The idea of trusting a person.** In addition to knowledge of the facts of the gospel and approval of those facts, in order to be saved, I must decide to trust or depend on Jesus as a living person to save me. In doing this I move from being an interested observer of the facts of salvation and the teachings of the Bible to being someone who enters into a new relationship with Jesus Christ as a person who is alive, and who even now hears us and sees us and is present with us. We may therefore define saving faith in the following way: *saving faith is trust in Jesus Christ as a living person for forgiveness of sins and for eternal life with God.*

This definition emphasizes that saving faith is not just a belief in facts but *personal trust in Jesus* to save *me*. As we will explain in the following chapters, "salvation" involves much more than simply forgiveness of sins and eternal life. Someone who initially comes to Christ seldom realizes the extent of the blessings of salvation that will come. Moreover, we may rightly summarize the two major concerns of a person who trusts in Christ as "forgiveness of sins" and "eternal life with God." Of course, eternal life with God involves such matters as a declaration of righteousness before God (part of justification, as explained in the next chapter), adoption, sanctification, and glorification, but these things may be understood in detail later. The main thing that concerns an unbeliever who comes to Christ is the fact that sin has separated him or her from the fellowship with God for which we were made, and places him or her in danger of eternal judgment. The unbeliever comes to Christ seeking to have sin and guilt removed and to enter into a genuine relationship with God that will last forever.

The definition emphasizes *personal trust* in Christ, not just belief in facts about Christ. Because saving faith in Scripture involves this personal trust, the word *trust* is a better word to use in contemporary culture than the words *faith* or *belief*. The reason is that we can believe something to be true with no personal commitment or dependence involved in it. I can *believe* that Canberra is the capital of Australia, or that 7 x 6 = 42, but I have no personal commitment or dependence on anyone when I simply believe those facts. The word *faith*, on the other hand, is sometimes used today to refer to an almost irrational commitment to something in spite of strong evidence to the contrary, a sort of irrational decision to believe something that we are quite sure is *not* true! (If your favorite football team continues to lose games, someone might encourage you to "have faith" even though all the facts point the opposite direction.) In these two popular senses, the word *belief* and the word *faith* have a meaning contrary to the biblical sense.

Of course, the words *believe/belief* and *faith* occur frequently in the Bible, and we should not completely give up using them in a proper biblical sense just because our culture sometimes gives them an incorrect sense. My point is simply that when explaining the gospel to an unbeliever, the word *trust* is most likely to convey the biblical sense today.

We are already familiar with trusting persons in everyday life. The more we come to know a person, and the more we see in that person a pattern of life that warrants trust, the more we find ourselves able to place trust in that person to do what he or she promises or to act in ways that we can rely on.

**b. Scripture Passages Emphasizing Trust in Christ as a Living Person.** This sense of personal trust is seen in several passages of Scripture in which initial saving faith is spoken of in very personal terms, often using analogies drawn from personal relationships. John says, "To all who *did receive him*, who believed in his name, he gave the right to become children of God" (John 1:12; cf. Col. 2:6). Much as we would receive a guest into our homes, John speaks of receiving Christ.

John 3:16 tells us that "whoever *believes in him* should not perish but have eternal life." Here John uses a surprising phrase when he does not simply say, "whoever *believes him*" (that is, believes that what he says is true and able to be trusted) but rather, "whoever *believes in him*" (see also John 6:35, 40; 11:25–26). The Greek phrase *pisteuō eis auton* could also be translated "believe *into* him" with the sense of trust or confidence that goes *into* and rests *in* Jesus as a person. Leon Morris can say, "Faith, for John, is an activity which takes men right out of themselves and makes them one with Christ." He understands the Greek phrase *pisteuō eis* to be a significant indication that New

Testament faith is not just intellectual assent but includes a "moral element of personal trust."[1] Such an expression was rare or perhaps nonexistent in the secular Greek found outside the New Testament, but it was well suited to express the personal trust in Christ that is involved in saving faith.

Jesus speaks of "coming to him" in several places. He says, "All that the Father gives me will *come to me*, and whoever comes to me I will never cast out" (John 6:37; cf. 6:35, 44). He also says, "If anyone thirsts, let him *come to me* and drink" (John 7:37). In a similar way, he says, "*Come to me*, all who labor and are heavy laden, and I will give you rest. Take my yoke upon you, and learn from me, for I am gentle and lowly in heart, and you will find rest for your souls. For my yoke is easy, and my burden is light" (Matt. 11:28–30). In these passages we have the idea of coming to Christ and asking for acceptance, for living water to drink, and for rest and instruction. All of these give an intensely personal picture of what is involved in saving faith. The author of Hebrews also asks us to think of Jesus as now alive in heaven, ready to receive us: "He is able to save to the uttermost those who draw near to God through him, since *he always lives* to make intercession for them" (Heb. 7:25). Jesus is pictured here (as many times in the New Testament) as one who is now alive in heaven, always able to help those who come to him.

**C. A Gospel Invitation from John Owen.** Reformed theologian J. I. Packer quotes the following paragraphs from the British Puritan writer John Owen, describing the invitation of Christ to respond in personal faith:

> This is somewhat of the word which he now speaks unto you: Why will ye die? why will ye perish? why will ye not have compassion on your own souls? Can your hearts endure, or can your hands be strong, in the day of wrath that is approaching? . . . Look unto me, and be saved; come unto me, and I will ease you of all sins, sorrows, fears, burdens, and give rest to your souls. Come, I entreat you; lay aside all procrastinations, all delays; put me off no more; eternity lies at the door. . . . Do not so hate me as that you will rather perish than accept of deliverance by me.
>
> These and the like things doth the Lord Christ continually declare, proclaim, plead and urge upon the souls of sinners. . . . He doth it in the preaching of the word, as if he were present with you, stood amongst you, and spake personally to every one of you. . . . He hath appointed the ministers of the gospel to appear before you, and to deal with you in his stead, avowing as his own the invitations which are given you in his name. (2 Cor. 5:19–20)[2]

---

1. Leon Morris, *The Gospel according to John* (Grand Rapids: Eerdmans, 1971), 336, with reference to the longer discussion by C. H. Dodd, *The Interpretation of the Fourth Gospel* (Cambridge: Cambridge University Press, 1953), 179–86, and a note that Dodd finds no parallel to the use of *pisteuō* followed by the preposition *eis*, to refer to trust in a person, in secular Greek. The expression rather is a literal translation of the expression "to believe in" from the Hebrew Old Testament (Num. 14:11; 20:12; 2 Chron. 20:20; Ps. 78:22).

2. J. I. Packer, *Evangelism and the Sovereignty of God* (Downers Grove, IL: InterVarsity Press, 1961), 104.

With this understanding of true New Testament faith, we may now appreciate that when a person comes to trust in Christ, all three elements must be present. There must be some basic knowledge or *understanding* of the facts of the gospel. There must also be *approval* of, or agreement with, these facts. Such agreement includes a conviction that the facts spoken of the gospel are true, especially the fact that I am a sinner in need of salvation and that Christ alone has paid the penalty for my sin and offers salvation to me. It also includes an awareness that I need to trust in Christ for salvation and that he is the only way to God and the only means provided for my salvation. This approval of the facts of the gospel will also involve a desire to be saved through Christ. But all this still does not add up to true saving faith. That comes only when I make a decision of my will to depend on, or put my *trust* in, Christ as *my* Savior. This personal decision to place my trust in Christ is something done with my heart, the central faculty of my entire being by which I make a commitment for myself as a whole person.

## 4. Faith Should Increase as Our Knowledge Increases

Contrary to the current secular understanding of *faith*, true New Testament faith is not something that is made stronger by ignorance or by believing against the evidence. Rather, saving faith is consistent with knowledge and true understanding of facts. Paul says, "Faith comes from hearing, and hearing through the word of Christ" (Rom. 10:17). When people have true information about Christ, they are better able to put their trust in him. Moreover, the more we know about him and about the character of God that is completely revealed in him, the more fully we are able to put our trust in him. Thus faith is not weakened by knowledge but should increase with more true knowledge.

In the case of saving faith in Christ, our knowledge of him comes by believing a reliable testimony about him. Here, the reliable testimony that we believe is the words of Scripture. Since they are God's very words, they are completely reliable, and we gain true knowledge of Christ through them. This is why "faith comes from hearing, and hearing through the word of Christ" (Rom. 10:17). In everyday life, we come to believe many things when we hear testimony from a person that we consider to be reliable or trustworthy. This kind of decision is even more justified in this case, when the actual words of God provide that testimony and we believe it.

## B. Faith and Repentance Must Come Together
## 1. Definition of Repentance

We may define repentance as follows: *repentance is a heartfelt sorrow for sin, a renouncing of it, and a sincere commitment to forsake it and walk in obedience to Christ.*

This definition indicates that repentance is something that can occur at a specific point in time and is not equivalent to a demonstration of change in a person's pattern of life. Repentance, like faith, is an intellectual *understanding* (that sin is wrong), an emotional *approval* of the teachings of Scripture regarding sin (a sorrow for sin and a hatred of it), and a *personal decision* to turn from it (a renouncing of sin and a decision of the will to forsake it and lead a life of obedience to Christ instead). However, we should never say that someone has to actually *live* that changed life over a period of time before repentance can be genuine, or else repentance would be turned into a kind of obedience (a "work") that we could *do* to merit salvation for ourselves, which is contrary to the New Testament teaching that "one is justified by faith apart from works of the law" (Rom. 3:28).

As I will explain below (see pp. 866–70 and 878–79), genuine repentance *will result in a changed life*. In fact, a truly repentant person will begin at once to live a changed life, and we can call that changed life the fruit of repentance. But we should never attempt to require that there be a period of time in which a person actually lives a changed life before we give assurance of forgiveness. Repentance is something that occurs in the heart and involves the whole person in a decision to turn from sin.

It is important to realize that mere sorrow for one's actions, or even deep remorse over one's actions, does not constitute genuine repentance unless it is accompanied by a sincere decision to forsake sin that is being committed against God. Paul preached about "repentance *toward God* and of faith in our Lord Jesus Christ" (Acts 20:21). He says that he rejoiced over the Corinthians, "not because you were grieved, but because you were *grieved into repenting. . . . For godly grief produces a repentance that leads to salvation without regret, whereas worldly grief produces death*" (2 Cor. 7:9–10). A worldly sort of grief may involve great sorrow for one's actions and probably also fear of punishment but no genuine renouncing of sin or commitment to forsake it in one's life. Hebrews 12:17 tells us that Esau wept over the consequences of his actions but did not truly repent. Moreover, as 2 Corinthians 7:9–10 indicates, even true godly grief is just one factor that leads to genuine repentance, but such grief is not itself the sincere decision of the heart in the presence of God that makes genuine repentance.

## 2. Repentance and Faith Occur Together

Scripture puts repentance and faith together as different aspects of the one act of coming to Christ for salvation. It is not that a person first turns from sin and later trusts in Christ or first trusts in Christ and later turns from sin; both occur at the same time. When we turn *to* Christ for salvation from our sins, we are simultaneously turning *away* from the sins that we are asking Christ to save us from. If that were not true, our turning to Christ for salvation from sin could hardly be a genuine turning to him or trusting in him.

The fact that repentance and faith are simply two different sides of the same coin, or two different aspects of the one event of conversion, may be seen in figure 35.1.

In this diagram, the person who genuinely turns to Christ for salvation must at the same time release the sin to which he or she has been clinging and turn away from that sin in order to turn to Christ. Neither repentance nor faith comes first; they must come together. John Murray speaks of "penitent faith" and "believing repentance."[3]

---

3. John Murray, *Redemption Accomplished and Applied* (Grand Rapids: Eerdmans, 1955), 113.

**A Repentance and Turning to Christ in Faith**
*Figure 35.1*

Therefore, it is clearly contrary to the New Testament evidence to speak about the possibility of having true saving faith without having any repentance for sin. It is also contrary to the New Testament to speak about the possibility of someone accepting Christ "as Savior" but not "as Lord" if that means simply depending on him for salvation but not committing oneself to forsake sin and to be obedient to Christ from that point on.

When Jesus invites sinners, "Come to me, all who labor and are heavy laden, and I will give you rest," he immediately adds, "*Take my yoke upon you,* and *learn from me*" (Matt. 11:28–29). To come to him includes taking his yoke upon us, being subject to his direction and guidance, learning from him and being obedient to him. If we are unwilling to make such a commitment, then we have not truly placed our trust in him.

When Scripture speaks of trusting in God or in Christ, it frequently connects such trust with genuine repentance. For example, Isaiah gives an eloquent testimony that is typical of the message of many of the Old Testament prophets:

Seek the LORD while he may be found;    let him return to the LORD, that he may
    call upon him while he is near;        have compassion on him,
let the wicked forsake his way,    and to our God, for he will abundantly
    and the unrighteous man his thoughts;        pardon. (Isa. 55:6–7)

Here both repentance from sin and coming to God for pardon are mentioned.

## 3. Repentance Involves More than a Change of Mind

Some authors claim that *repentance* in the New Testament means just a change of mind without any implication of sorrow for sin or an internal resolve to turn from sin (see discussion of the Free Grace movement in the following section). But the major Greek lexicons (specialized dictionaries) do not support that view. For example, the standard academic dictionary for New Testament Greek, *A Greek-English Lexicon of the New Testament and Other Early Christian Literature* by Bauer, Danker, Arndt, and Gingrich,[4] does give the meaning "change one's mind" as the first possible meaning of the verb *metanoeō* ("to repent"), but it is significant that they do not list any New Testament verse as having that particular meaning. Rather, they put *every* New Testament passage under the second meaning, "feel remorse, repent, be converted (in religio-ethical sense)."[5] They then go on to give many New Testament examples and include this statement: "Since in *metanoeō* the negative impulse of turning away is dominant, it is also used with *apo tinos* [from something]: repent and turn away from something" (examples given include repenting from wickedness, from lawlessness, and with the similar phrase *ek tinos*, repenting of murders, sorceries, sexual immorality, and thefts)."[6] These statements are consistent with the idea that repentance includes a conscious inward resolve to turn from sin.

Other standard reference works make similar statements. The multivolume *Theological Dictionary of the New Testament* says, with reference to "repentance" passages from Acts, Hebrews, 1 Peter, and Revelation, that "it is a turning away from evil . . . and a turning towards God."[7] The more recent *New International Dictionary of New Testament Theology and Exegesis*, says that in later Jewish-Greek writings, "the term has in view the conversion of the whole person." In the synoptic Gospels, "repentance is viewed in terms of commitment to a person; the call to repentance becomes a call to discipleship." In Acts, "the call for repentance" included a call to "conversion," which is "turning from evil . . . to God."[8] The Greek lexicon by Louw and Nida defines *metanoeō* and *metanoia* as "to change one's way of life as the result of a complete change of attitude with regard to sin and righteousness," and they further explain that in the New Testament the emphasis "seems to be more specifically in the total change, both in thought and behavior, with respect to how one should both think and act."[9] Not one of these lexicons says that the New Testament words for repentance (the verb *metanoeō* and the noun *metanoia*) should be translated to indicate merely a "change of one's mind" (a phrase which implies only intellectual agreement and does not include sorrow for sin or any result to turn from sin and turn to Christ).

---

4. *A Greek-English Lexicon of the New Testament and Other Early Christian Literature* by Walter Bauer; translated by Frederick W. Danker, William Arndt, and F. Wilbur Gingrich (Chicago: University of Chicago Press, 1979) (abbreviated BDAG).

5. Ibid., 640.

6. Ibid., 640. They also add, under the cognate noun *metanoia*, "repentance," this explanation: "in our literature with focus on the need of change in view of responsibility to deity" (640). ("Our literature" in BDAG refers to the Greek literature

that is the primary subject of this lexicon, namely, the New Testament and other early Christian literature.)

7. TDNT 4:1004.

8. *New International Dictionary of New Testament Theology and Exegesis*, 5 vols., edited by Moises Silva (Grand Rapids: Zondervan, 2014) 3:29192.

9. Johannes P. Louw and Eugene A. Nida, *A Greek-English Lexicon of the New Testament Based on Semantic Domains*, 2 vols. (New York: United Bible Societies, 1988), 1:510 (section 41.52).

Another significant argument against the definition of *repentance* as a mere "change of mind" is the fact that no widely established Bible translation in English translates the many "repentance" verses in the New Testament as "change your mind." Take, for example, the first instance of *metanoeō* in the New Testament, which reports John the Baptist preaching and saying, "*Repent*, for the kingdom of heaven is at hand" (Matt. 3:2). This verb is translated as "repent" in the following Bible versions: KJV, NKJV, ESV, NASB, NIV, NET, CSB, NLT, RSV, NRSV. I know of no Bible translation that translates this verse as, "*Change your minds*, for the kingdom of heaven is at hand." And for good reason—the English word *repent* does not mean merely "change your mind" but includes nuances of remorse for sin and a resolve to change one's conduct.

### 4. A Call to Repentance Is an Essential Part of Gospel Proclamation

In the New Testament, Paul summarizes his gospel ministry as one of "testifying both to Jews and to Greeks of *repentance* toward God and of *faith* in our Lord Jesus Christ" (Acts 20:21). The author of Hebrews includes as the first two elements in a list of elementary doctrines "*repentance* from dead works" and "*faith* toward God" (Heb. 6:1).

Of course, sometimes faith alone is named as the thing necessary for coming to Christ for salvation (see John 3:16; Acts 16:31; Rom. 10:9; Eph. 2:8–9, et al.). These are familiar passages, and we emphasize them often when explaining the gospel to others. But what we do not often realize is the fact that there are many other passages where *only repentance* is named, for it is simply assumed that true repentance will also involve faith in Christ for forgiveness of sins. The New Testament authors understood so well that genuine repentance and genuine faith had to go together that they often simply mentioned repentance alone with the understanding that faith would also be included, because turning *from* sins in a genuine way is impossible apart from a genuine turning *to* God. Therefore, just before Jesus ascended into heaven, he told his disciples, "Thus it is written, that the Christ should suffer and on the third day rise from the dead, and that *repentance* for the forgiveness of sins should be proclaimed in his name to all nations" (Luke 24:46–47). Saving faith is implied in the phrase "forgiveness of sins," but it is not explicitly named.

The preaching recorded in the book of Acts shows the same pattern. After Peter's sermon at Pentecost, the crowd asked, "Brothers, what shall we do?" Peter replied, "*Repent* and be baptized every one of you in the name of Jesus Christ for the forgiveness of your sins" (Acts 2:37–38).[10] In his second sermon Peter spoke to his hearers in a similar way, saying, "*Repent* therefore, and turn back, that your sins may be blotted out, that times of refreshing may come from the presence of the Lord" (Acts 3:19–20). Later, when the

---

10. See chapter 49, pp. 1202–5, 1211–12, on the question of whether baptism is necessary for salvation.

apostles were on trial before the Sanhedrin, Peter spoke of Christ, saying, "God exalted him at his right hand as Leader and Savior, to give *repentance* to Israel and forgiveness of sins" (Acts 5:31). And when Paul was preaching on the Areopagus in Athens to an assembly of Greek philosophers, he said, "The times of ignorance God overlooked, but now *he commands all people everywhere to repent*" (Acts 17:30). He also says in his epistles, "God's kindness is meant to lead you to repentance" (Rom. 2:4), and he speaks of "a *repentance* that leads to salvation" (2 Cor. 7:10).

We also see that when Jesus encounters people personally, he requires them to turn from their sin before they come to follow him. Whether it be speaking to the rich young ruler and asking that he give up his possessions (Luke 18:18–30), coming to the house of Zacchaeus and declaring that salvation had come to him that day because he had given half his goods to the poor and had repaid fourfold anything that he had stolen (Luke 19:1–10), speaking to the woman at the well and asking her to call her husband (John 4:16), or speaking to Nicodemus and rebuking his rabbinic unbelief and pride in his own knowledge (John 3:1–21), Jesus consistently puts his finger on the area of sin most influential in that person's life. In fact, we may ask whether anyone in the gospels ever came to sincere faith in Christ without repenting of his or her sins.[11]

When we realize that genuine saving faith must be accompanied by genuine repentance for sin, it helps us to understand why some preaching of the gospel has such inadequate results today. If there is no mention of the need for repentance, sometimes the gospel message becomes only, "Believe in Jesus Christ and be saved" without any mention of repentance at all.[12] But this watered-down version of the gospel does not ask for a wholehearted commitment to Christ—commitment *to* Christ, if genuine, must include a commitment to turn *from* sin. Preaching the need for faith without repentance is preaching only half of the gospel. It will result in many people being deceived, thinking that they have heard the Christian gospel and tried it, but nothing has happened. They might even say something like, "I accepted Christ as Savior over and over again, and it never worked." Yet they never really did receive Christ as their Savior, for he comes to us in his majesty and invites us to receive him as he is—the one who deserves to be, and demands to be, absolute Lord of our lives as well.

---

11. The narratives about Jesus' interaction with the woman at the well (John 4) and Nicodemus (John 3) show that John's gospel is not devoid of teaching about repentance, even though the word *repentance* is not used. But John's gospel was written last, and he seems to assume that people are familiar with the contents of Matthew, Mark, and Luke, where repentance is frequently mentioned. In addition, the book of Acts contains many examples of gospel proclamation by the apostles, and repentance is an essential element in several passages, as discussed above. See further discussion in Grudem, *"Free Grace" Theology* (Wheaton, IL: Crossway, 2016), 49–55.

12. It is true that Paul tells the Philippian jailer in Acts 16:31, "Believe in the Lord Jesus, and you will be saved, you and your household." However, even that sentence includes an acknowledgment that Jesus is "Lord," and, moreover, the next sentence makes it clear that Paul said much more to the man than this brief sentence, for we read, "They spoke the word of the Lord to him and to all who were in his house" (Acts 16:32).

## C. The Free Grace Movement

A group of evangelicals in the "Free Grace" movement[13] have disagreed with the view presented here, arguing that a gospel presentation that requires *repentance* (as I have defined it, as an internal resolve to turn from sin) *as well as faith* is really preaching salvation by works. They argue that the view advocated in this chapter, that repentance and faith must go together, is a false gospel of "lordship salvation." They would say that saving faith *only* involves trusting Christ as your Savior, and that submitting to him as your Lord whom you commit to obey is an optional (but commanded and beneficial) later step that is unnecessary for salvation. I interacted extensively with the distinctive Free Grace teachings in a 2016 book, *"Free Grace" Theology: 5 Ways It Diminishes the Gospel*.[14] My friends in the Free Grace movement (and others whom I do not know personally) responded with four of their own books in 2016, 2017, and 2018.[15]

### 1. Saving Faith in Free Grace Teaching

Within the Free Grace movement, some claim that saving faith only requires an *intellectual agreement* with the facts of the gospel. Bob Wilkin, executive director of the Grace Evangelical Society, explains: "Faith in Christ is intellectual assent. Stripped of its pejorative connotation, 'intellectual assent' is a good definition of what faith is."[16] Wilkin explains further:

> For example, do you believe that George Washington was the first President of the United States? If you do, then you know what faith is from a biblical perspective. There is no commitment, no decision of the will, no turning from sins, and no works that are part of faith in Christ. If you are convinced or persuaded that what He promised is true, then you believe in Him.[17]

13. The Free Grace movement is promoted by members of the Free Grace Alliance (freegracealliance.com) and the Grace Evangelical Society (faithalone.org).

14. Wayne Grudem, *"Free Grace" Theology: Five Ways It Diminishes the Gospel* (Wheaton, IL: Crossway, 2016). Several sections in this analysis of the Free Grace movement have been adapted from this book, and are used here with the permission of Crossway Books.

15. See Grant Hawley, editor, *Free Grace Theology: 5 Ways It Magnifies the Gospel* (Allen, TX: Bold Grace Ministries, 2016); Fred Chay, ed., *A Defense of Free Grace Theology: With Respect to Saving Faith, Perseverance, and Assurance* (The Woodlands, TX: Grace Theology Press, 2017); Anthony B. Badger, *Free Grace Theology on Trial: A Refutation of "Historical Protestant" Soteriology* (CreateSpace Independent Publishing Platform, 2017); Robert N. Wilkin and Shawn Lazar, *Grudem Against Grace: Defending Free Grace Theology* (Denton, TX:

Grace Evangelical Society, 2018). None of these books were published by established evangelical publishing houses (such as those that belong to the Evangelical Christian Publishers Association), but all four were self-published by Free Grace advocates or organizations. They also frequently quote other self-published books or articles from Free Grace publications. However, Fred Chay has compiled a long list of authors and publications from 1860 to the present, all of which, in his view, have advocated the main elements of Free Grace theology. See Fred Chay, "The Perennial Problem for Protestants," in Chay, *A Defense*, 21–28.

16. Bob Wilkin, "What Is Free Grace Theology?" *Grace in Focus* 29, no. 5 (September/October 2014): 27.

17. Ibid. On this page, Wilkin goes on to explain that belief in Jesus' promise of eternal life, in order to constitute valid faith, must not include any idea that works are also necessary.

However, others within the Free Grace movement disagree with Wilkin. The Free Grace Alliance says that faith must rest in the person of Christ, not merely in the truth of propositions about him. Their "Covenant" (doctrinal statement) affirms: "The sole means of receiving the free gift of eternal life is *faith in the Lord Jesus Christ*, the Son of God, whose substitutionary death on the cross fully satisfied the requirement for our justification."[18]

I am grateful for this explicit affirmation of the person of Christ as the object of faith. In addition, in response to my 2016 book *"Free Grace" Theology*, several Free Grace authors have strongly affirmed that they agree that there is a need to go beyond mental assent to historical facts about Christ and place one's trust in the person of Christ. David Anderson writes, "He [Grudem] claims that we, as Free Grace theologians, subscribe to the mental assent view of faith: we do not. He invents the accusation that we as Free Grace theologians minimize trust in the person of Christ: we do not."[19]

But here Anderson has not represented me accurately. I do not say that he subscribes to "the mental assent view of faith," for I discuss his viewpoint under the heading, "Other Free Grace advocates say that faith includes trust in the person of Christ."[20] In fact, my entire fourth chapter does not have the title "A *Denial* of Trust in the Person of Christ" but rather "Underemphasis on Trust in the Person of Christ."[21]

Therefore, the difference I have with Free Grace theology at this point is not an absolute difference but one of emphasis. I still do not find in Free Grace literature nearly as much emphasis as we find in the New Testament on *trusting in Christ as a living Savior*, *coming* to him, *receiving* him, and *believing in him* with one's heart.[22] It is certainly not there in *Absolutely Free!*, which is the most influential book published by the foremost advocate of the Free Grace movement, Zane Hodges.[23]

Hodges asks, "But is it *mere* intellectual assent? Of course *not*! To describe faith that way is to demean it as a trivial, academic exercise, when in fact it is no such thing" (italics in original). But then Hodges gives no explanation as to how he intends anything

---

18. "Missions and Beliefs," Free Grace Alliance, https://freegracealliance.com/mission-and-beliefs, accessed February 13, 2020.

19. David Anderson, "The Faith That Saves," in Chay, *A Defense of Free Grace Theology*, 86.

20. Grudem, *"Free Grace" Theology*, 101. This section is clearly placed in contrast to the previous page where I discuss Robert Wilkin under the heading, "Some Free Grace advocates say that faith equals mere intellectual assent" (100). I did not include Anderson or Charles Bing or Joseph Dillow in that category, and I write that Anderson "helpfully emphasizes the fact that saving faith involves personal trust and deep confidence" (103–4).

21. Grudem, *"Free Grace" Theology*, 99. This chapter title is repeated at the top of every odd-numbered page in the chapter.

22. Roger Fankhauser, in responding to my book, *"Free*

*Grace" Theology*, does say that "Free Grace alone keeps an undivided focus on Christ" and "Free Grace genuinely exalts Christ . . . to the greatest degree because it places the entire process of salvation, security, assurance, and motivation for service at the feet of Jesus" (Roger Fankhauser, "Free Grace Exalts Christ and His Work," in Hawley, *Free Grace Theology*, 89, 109). I appreciate these affirmations, but it still seems to me that Free Grace writings place little if any emphasis on the interpersonal nature of *coming* personally to Christ, *receiving* him personally, *welcoming* him personally into one's life, and resting one's trust in Christ as a living person.

23. Zane Hodges, *Absolutely Free! A Biblical Reply to Lordship Salvation* (Grand Rapids: Zondervan, 1989). See his definition of faith on p. 31. (Hodges taught New Testament at Dallas Seminary from 1959–86.)

more than intellectual assent to the truthfulness of propositions. He says that faith "is the inward conviction that what God says to us in the gospel is true." He explains Abraham's faith by saying, "Abraham trusted God's Word to him—he believed what God said."[24] I do not see in this entire chapter on faith any affirmation that includes trust in the *person of Jesus* that goes beyond *agreement with statements about him* in the Bible.

## 2. Misunderstandings about Repentance from Sin in Free Grace Teaching

Free Grace advocates hold two different views of repentance. One group views repentance as merely a "change of mind" regarding the facts of the gospel, so that a person comes to believe these facts are true. This group sees such a change of mind as necessary for salvation but they deny that it requires any decision of the will to forsake sin.[25]

The other group understands repentance to mean "an internal resolve to turn from one's sins" (a definition similar to my own), but they say this is not necessary before saving faith or as a part of saving faith. It is something that is desirable after someone has trusted in Christ for salvation.[26]

In the earlier material in this chapter, I have already discussed my reasons for disagreeing with both of these Free Grace understandings of repentance.

## 3. Good Works Not a Necessary Evidence of Faith in Free Grace Teaching

For those who advocate a Free Grace position, good works and continuing to believe do not necessarily follow from saving faith, and therefore, it is wrong to tell people to consider whether there has been a change in their life ("good works") and whether they are still trusting in Christ as factors that contribute to our assurance of salvation. I discuss this question in chapter 40 (see pp. 989–93).

## 4. The Need for Repentance from Sin and Good Works as Evidence of Faith Have Been Affirmed by All the Main Branches of Protestantism

As I documented elsewhere, all the main denominational branches of historic Protestantism have affirmed that repentance from sin must always accompany genuine

---

24. Hodges, *Absolutely Free!*, 31–32.

25. Charles Bing represents the view that repentance is necessary but requires only a change of mind. See the extensive discussion in Grudem, *"Free Grace" Theology*, 55–66.

26. David Anderson represents the view that repentance is an internal resolve to turn from sin, but is not necessary for saving faith. See the extensive discussion in Grudem, *"Free Grace" Theology*, 66–70. Grant Hawley responds to my criticisms in his chapter, "Free Grace Teaches Us to Turn from Sins," in Hawley, *Free Grace Theology*, 31–53. He does not disagree with my claim that Free Grace theology says repentance is not necessary *for*

*initial saving faith*, but he emphasizes the fact that Free Grace theology gives multiple motives to believers to turn from sin after they have come to initial saving faith, and in that sense he says, "turning from sins is not *optional*, and Free Grace theology does not teach that it is" (52, emphasis in original). See also David Anderson, "The Role of Repentance and Salvation," in Chay, *A Defense of Free Grace Theology*, 98: "For justification we would say that repentance is not optional; it is completely unnecessary. However, for sanctification we would say repentance is *not* optional; it is absolutely *essential*." (emphasis in original).

faith, and that good works and a changed life will necessarily result from genuine faith. This teaching is found in the Reformed theologian John Calvin (1509–1564), the Lutheran *Formula of Concord* (1576), the Anglican/Episcopalian *Thirty-Nine Articles* (1571), the Presbyterian *Westminster Confession of Faith* (1646), the *New Hampshire Baptist Confession* (1833), the writings of John Wesley (1703–1791) the founder of Methodism, and the Assemblies of God *Statement of Fundamental Truths* (1916).[27] Therefore, orthodox Protestant theology has historically disagreed with the distinctive beliefs of the Free Grace movement.

In response to my statement that "the Free Grace movement today is not upholding the Reformation doctrine of *sola fide* or 'justification by faith alone,'"[28] Jeremy Edmondson replies, "We did not get this from the Protestant Reformation, but from the holy Scriptures."[29] His entire chapter[30] argues that the leaders of the Protestant Reformation were mistaken with regard to several doctrines and therefore we need not follow their understanding of justification by faith alone.

### 5. Why It Is Misleading to Call This the "Lordship Salvation" Controversy

The phrase "Lordship Salvation" is a decidedly misleading and unfortunate summary of the central issues involved in this matter.[31] In brief popular terms, the controversy was sometimes summarized as follows:

1. Some people believe that you can accept Jesus *as Savior but not as Lord* (the Free Grace position).
2. Other people believe that you have to accept Jesus *as both Savior and Lord* (this was misleadingly labeled as the "Lordship salvation" position).

The problem is that neither side will ever win or lose the argument when it is framed in those terms. The Free Grace supporters who hold position (1) still affirm strongly that *Jesus is in fact Lord* over the entire universe and over all of our lives, even though we imperfectly submit to his Lordship.[32] And those on the non–Free Grace side, those who hold position (2), all agree that *our submission to Christ's Lordship is imperfect in this life.*[33]

---

27. See the relevant quotations in Grudem, *"Free Grace" Theology*, 28–32, 48.

28. Grudem, *"Free Grace" Theology*, 32.

29. Jeremy Edmondson, "Free Grace Is Returning to Scripture As Our Sole Authority," in Hawley, *Free Grace Theology*, 29.

30. Ibid., 1–29.

31. I was glad to see that John MacArthur said bluntly, "I don't like the term *lordship salvation*. I reject the connotation intended by those who coined the phrase. It insinuates that a submissive heart is extraneous or supplementary to saving faith. Although I have reluctantly used the term to describe my

views, it is a concession to popular usage" (John F. MacArthur Jr., *Faith Works: The Gospel according to the Apostles* [Dallas: Word, 1993], 23).

32. Charles Bing says, "Though both the Lordship Salvation position and the Free Grace position agree that Christ's Lordship is essential for salvation, there is disagreement over how an unsaved person must respond to Christ's Lordship in order to be saved.... Jesus is Lord of all regardless of one's submission to Him" (*Lordship Salvation*, 178–79).

33. John MacArthur says, "I am certain that while some understand more than others, no one who is saved fully

So both sides agree that Jesus is Lord of our lives *in some sense* and is not fully Lord of our lives *in another sense*. Trying to define precisely how much Jesus has to be acknowledged as Lord for genuine saving faith becomes an increasingly muddled task, and it simply does not contribute much clarity to the discussion. Therefore, I do not discuss the Free Grace controversy in terms of the Lordship of Christ. I do not think that is the best way to focus the issue.

In addition, when the Free Grace proponents refer to the position that disagrees with them as the "Lordship salvation" position, they wrongly suggests that this is an unusual or minority view that seeks to add the idea of "Lordship" to the ordinary idea of salvation. But what the Free Grace movement calls the "Lordship Salvation" view has been the mainstream Protestant view since the Reformation. It is not a novel or minority view at all, for it has been held by all the main branches of Protestantism.

## 6. The Relationship between Dispensationalism and the Free Grace Movement

Historically, the initial source of the Free Grace view of the gospel was apparently not Zane Hodges, its primary advocate in the 1980s and 1990s, but Lewis Sperry Chafer, the first president of Dallas Theological Seminary, especially in his *Systematic Theology*, where he says, "The New Testament does not impose repentance upon the unsaved as a condition of salvation."[34] However, Chafer's main concern was to deny that repentance had to include "sorrow and heart-anguish," so that "the way of salvation has thus been made impossible for all who do not experience the required anguish." According to Chafer, because of this mistake, people are led "to measure the validity of their salvation by the intensity of anguish which preceded or accompanied it. It is in this manner that sorrow of heart becomes a more subtle form of meritorious work, and to that extent a contradiction of grace. . . . To imply, as preachers have done so generally, that God must be mollified . . . by human agony is a desperate form of unbelief."[35]

Although my definition of repentance (p. 865) includes "a heartfelt sorrow for sin," I would agree with Chafer that we should not tell people to "measure the validity of their salvation by the intensity of the anguish which preceded or accompanied it." Therefore I

---

understands all the implications of Jesus' lordship at the moment of conversion." But he adds, in distinction from the Free Grace position, "I am, however, equally certain that no one can be saved who is either unwilling to obey Christ or consciously, callously rebellious against His Lordship." MacArthur, *The Gospel according to Jesus*, 2nd ed. (Grand Rapids: Zondervan, 2008), 15.

34. Lewis Sperry Chafer, *Systematic Theology* (1948; repr., Grand Rapids: Kregel, 1976), 3:376. Chafer recognizes that many verses call upon people to repent, but he simply defines repentance as a "change of mind" that does not include sorrow for sin or turning from sin (372–75). Thus he can say,

"Repentance, which is a change of mind, is included in believing" (375). Chafer provides a basis for the view that people must first accept Christ as Savior, and later as Lord, when he says that the preacher has the obligation "of preaching the Lordship of Christ to Christians exclusively, and the Saviorhood of Christ to those who are unsaved" (387).

The Sandemanians were a small group of evangelical churches who taught a view similar to that of Chafer and Zane Hodges in England and the United States from 1725 until they died out around 1900; see R. E. D. Clark, "Sandemanians," in *NIDCC*, 877.

35. Chafer, *Systematic Theology*, 372–73.

have some sympathy with Chafer's opposition to this pastoral mistake, which he apparently thought was too prevalent in his day. But I think he over-corrected the mistake by insisting that repentance only required a change of mind.

Chafer was a leading proponent of dispensationalism (see pp. 656, 1054) and the president of Dallas Theological Seminary from 1924 to 1952, but not all Dallas Seminary faculty or all who advocate Dispensational theology would hold a Free Grace view.[36] A controversy over this point erupted in American evangelicalism in 1988 when John MacArthur, himself a Dispensationalist, published *The Gospel according to Jesus*.[37] This book, which features enthusiastic forewords by J. I. Packer and James Montgomery Boice, strongly criticized the views of writers like Chafer and Zane Hodges on evangelism and the nature of saving faith. MacArthur argued (I think convincingly) from many New Testament passages that one cannot truly accept Christ as Savior without also accepting him as Lord or, in other words, that there can be no true saving faith without genuine repentance in the sense of a commitment to forsake sin and walk in obedience to Christ as well. He said that any other view preaches a cheap gospel that offers unconverted people false security, telling them they are saved simply because they agreed that the facts of the gospel were true or prayed a prayer, but they had no true repentance and no real change of life. MacArthur argued that such unbiblical evangelism has never been the teaching of the church through history and that the weakened gospel heard so often as a result of Free Grace teaching has led to a whole generation of professing Christians whose lives are no different from the surrounding culture and who are really not saved at all. Hodges quickly responded to MacArthur with another book, *Absolutely Free! A Biblical Reply to Lordship Salvation*.

As I have argued in this chapter, it seems clear that MacArthur was right to maintain that true saving faith in New Testament terms is more than mere intellectual assent to facts; it must include a heartfelt coming to Christ in personal dependence on him for salvation, combined with a heartfelt repentance from sin. It is misleading to brand this teaching "Lordship salvation" as if it were some new doctrine or as if there were any other kind of salvation—MacArthur is teaching what has been the historic position of Christian orthodoxy on this matter.[38] This position is not salvation by works but simply states the gospel of *free* grace and salvation by grace through faith in all its biblical fullness. The change of life that will result from genuine conversion does not save us, but it will certainly result if our faith is genuine, for "faith by itself, if it does not have works, is dead" (James 2:17).

---

36. In fact, two prominent faculty members at Dallas seminary, Darrell Bock and Daniel Wallace, wrote endorsements for my book, *"Free Grace" Theology*, which is a critique of the Free Grace movement (see their endorsements on the first two pages inside the front cover).

37. MacArthur, *The Gospel according to Jesus* (1988; rev. ed., Grand Rapids: Zondervan, 1994).
38. Ibid., 221–37.

## 7. Conclusion about the Free Grace Movement

The Free Grace movement preaches a weakened gospel because it avoids any call for people to repent of their sins. This is no minor matter because repentance from sin is such an important part of the gospel in many New Testament summaries and presentations (see above) that it cannot be omitted without grave consequences in the lives of people who hear such a weakened message.

However, I am not willing to say that the Free Grace Gospel is a "false gospel." That is far too strong a category to apply here, and it calls to mind Paul's extremely strong condemnation in Galatians 1:6–10. I think it is certainly possible to distinguish between a *true gospel* that is presented in an incomplete or weakened form (such as with Free Grace teaching) and a *false gospel* that simply proclaims falsehood rather than truth about Jesus Christ and his work of redemption.

The "Covenant" of the Free Grace Alliance says this: "The sole means of receiving the free gift of eternal life is faith in the Lord Jesus Christ, the Son of God, whose substitutionary death on the cross fully satisfied the requirement for our justification."[39] That statement is a wonderful summary of the New Testament gospel message,[40] and it is inconceivable to me that anyone could read that statement and say that people who believe and advocate those truths are preaching a "false gospel." That would just be a slanderous and wrongful accusation.

Another thing that demonstrates that this is not a "false gospel" is the fact that many people who have heard the gospel proclamation as explained by Free Grace advocates have come to genuine saving faith in Christ. Even though the message of the need for repentance from sins was omitted, every unbeliever who comes to Christ comes with a guilty conscience and comes to ask for forgiveness. There is often an instinctive awareness of the need to somehow turn from sin, even though that is not made explicit in the gospel presentation. This is why many such people actually do repent of their sins in their hearts,[41] at least to some extent, and God looks on that heartfelt repentance and sees it as part of genuine faith. Many others start attending a Free Grace church and then repent later, perhaps as they begin reading the Bible, and at that point they first come to genuine saving faith.

Nevertheless, it still seems to me that a deliberate omission of the need to call

---

39. "Missions and Beliefs," Free Grace Alliance, https://freegracealliance.com/mission-and-beliefs, accessed February 13, 2020.

40. However, I would want to specify that "faith" must also include repentance from sin as well as trust in Christ to forgive one's sins.

41. Fred Chay thinks I show "confusion" or "lack of consistent clarity" when I say that (in Dr. Chay's words) "a person can believe the Free Grace message and be saved," but then later I say that "many who believe the same Free Grace message are not saved" ("Perennial Problem," 14). But it is not inconsistent at all to say both (a) that the Free Grace gospel is weakened by its lack of a call to repent from sin and also (b) that *some* who hear the Free Grace message will instinctively repent of their sins anyway because they have an internal sense that such repentance is necessary when they come into the presence of a holy God to seek forgiveness. The tragedy is that many others will not repent because the Free Grace gospel has omitted any call to repentance from sin.

unbelievers to repent of their sins constitutes a significant departure from New Testament patterns, and such a departure cannot be taught and practiced without significant harmful consequences to the church and to many of the people who hear such a gospel.

## D. Should People Pray to Receive Christ?

Finally, what shall we say about the common practice of asking people to *pray* to receive Christ as their personal Savior and Lord? Scripture does talk about "receiving" Christ (see John 1:11–12; Col. 2:6). Since personal faith in Christ must involve an actual decision of the will, it is often very helpful to *express* that decision in spoken words, and this could very naturally take the form of a prayer to Christ in which we tell him of our sorrow for sin, our commitment to forsake it, and our decision actually to put our trust in him. Such a spoken prayer does not in itself save us, but the attitude of heart that it represents does constitute true conversion, and the decision to speak that prayer can often be the point at which a person truly comes to faith in Christ.

## E. Both Faith and Repentance Continue Throughout Life

Although we have been considering initial faith and repentance as the two aspects of conversion at the beginning of the Christian life, it is important to realize that faith and repentance are not confined to the beginning of the Christian life. They are attitudes of the heart that continue throughout our lives as Christians. Jesus tells his disciples to pray daily, "and forgive us our debts, as we also have forgiven our debtors" (Matt. 6:12, using "debts" as a metaphor for sin; see Luke 11:4, which says, "forgive us our sins"). This is a prayer that, if genuine, will certainly involve daily sorrow for sin and genuine repentance. The apostle John writes to Christian believers about regular repentance: "If we confess our sins, he is faithful and just to forgive us our sins and to cleanse us from all unrighteousness" (1 John 1:9). And the risen Christ says to the church in Laodicea, "Those whom I love, I reprove and discipline, so be zealous *and repent*" (Rev. 3:19; cf. 2 Cor. 7:10).

With regard to faith, Paul tells us, "So now faith, hope, and love abide, these three; but the greatest of these is love" (1 Cor. 13:13). He certainly means that these three abide throughout the course of this life, but he probably also means that they abide for all eternity: if faith is trusting God to provide all our needs, then this attitude will never cease, not even in the age to come. But in any case, the point is clearly made that faith continues throughout this life. Paul also says, "The life I now live in the flesh I live *by faith in the Son of God*, who loved me and gave himself for me" (Gal. 2:20).

Therefore, although it is true that *initial* saving faith and *initial* repentance occur only once in our lives, and when they occur they constitute true conversion, nonetheless, the heart attitudes of repentance and faith only begin at conversion. These same attitudes should continue throughout the course of our Christian lives. Each day we should have heartfelt repentance for sins that we have committed and faith in Christ to provide for our needs and to empower us to live the Christian life.

## QUESTIONS FOR PERSONAL APPLICATION

1. Have you come to trust in Christ personally, or are you still at the point of intellectual knowledge and emotional approval of the facts of salvation without having personally put your trust in Christ? If you have not put your trust in Christ yet, what do you think it is that is making you hesitate?

2. Did this chapter help you think of faith in Christ in more personal terms? If so, how might that increase your own level of faith? Do you think that it might be easier for young children than for adults to think of trust in Christ as trust in a real *person* who is alive today? Why or why not? What does this tell you about the way Christian parents should teach their children about Jesus?

3. If your knowledge about God has increased through reading this book, has your faith in God increased along with that knowledge? Why or why not? If your faith has not increased along with your knowledge, what can you do to encourage your faith to grow more than it has?

4. In terms of human relationships, do you trust a person more when you do not know that person very well or after you have come to know him or her quite well (assuming that the person is essentially a trustworthy and reliable person)? What does that fact tell you about how your trust in God might increase? What things might you do during the day to come to know God better, and to come to know Jesus and the Holy Spirit better?

5. Did you feel a sincere sorrow for sin when you first came to Christ? Can you describe what it felt like? Did it lead you to a genuine commitment to forsake sin? How long was it before you noticed a change in your pattern of life?

6. Have you ever truly repented of sin, or do you think you have been taught a watered-down gospel that did not include repentance? Do you think it is possible for someone genuinely to trust in Christ for forgiveness of sins without also sincerely repenting for sins? Do you think that genuine repentance usually involves only a sincere feeling of sorrow for sin in general, or does it involve genuine sorrow for specific sins and turning from those specific sins?

7. Have faith and repentance remained a continuing part of your Christian life, or have those attitudes of heart grown somewhat weak in your life? What has been the result in your Christian life?

### Special Terms

*faith*
*Free Grace theology*
*repentance*
*trust*

# BIBLIOGRAPHY

(For an explanation of this bibliography see the note on the bibliography to chapter 1, pp. 23–24. Complete bibliographical data may be found on pp. 1489–96.)

## SECTIONS IN EVANGELICAL SYSTEMATIC THEOLOGIES

### 1. Anglican (Episcopalian)
1882–92 . . . . . Litton, 288–300
2001 . . . . . . . . Packer, 162–63
2013 . . . . . . . . Bird, 537–40
2013 . . . . . . . . Bray, 513–14

### 2. Arminian (Wesleyan or Methodist)
1875–76 . . . . . Pope, 2:367–85
1940 . . . . . . . . Wiley, 2:357–78
1983 . . . . . . . . Carter, 1:496–99
1992 . . . . . . . . Oden, 3:79–107
2002 . . . . . . . . Cottrell, 292, 333

### 3. Baptist
1767 . . . . . . . . Gill, 2:131–41
1887 . . . . . . . . Boyce, 373–94
1907 . . . . . . . . Strong, 829–49
1990–95 . . . . . Garrett, 2:241–84
2007 . . . . . . . . Akin, 728–732
2013 . . . . . . . . Erickson, 863–66, 875

### 4. Dispensational
1947 . . . . . . . . Chafer, 3:371–93
1949 . . . . . . . . Thiessen, 264–70
1986 . . . . . . . . Ryrie, 324–27
2002–2005 . . Geisler, 3:277–299, 470–551
2017 . . . . . . . . MacArthur and Mayhue, 589–602

### 5. Lutheran
1917–24 . . . . . Pieper, 2:422–503
1934 . . . . . . . . Mueller, 319–66

### 6. Reformed (or Presbyterian)
1559 . . . . . . . . Calvin, 1:340–67, 423–28 (2.6–7, 9; 3.2–5), 542–684
1679–85 . . . . . Turretin, *IET*, 1:414, 2:28, 184–91, 203–204, 558–631, 669–82
1724–58 . . . . . Edwards, 2:578–96
1871–73 . . . . . Hodge, 3:41–113
1878 . . . . . . . . Dabney, 600–612, 651–60
1887–1921 . . . Warfield, *BTS*, 375–403; *SSW*, 1:267–82; *SSW*, 2:655–59; *BD*, 467–510
1894 . . . . . . . . Shedd, 787–92
1906–11 . . . . . Bavinck, *RD*, 4:96–175
1910 . . . . . . . . Vos, 4:58–71
1937–66 . . . . . Murray, *CW*, 2:235–74; *RAA*, 106–16
1938 . . . . . . . . Berkhof, 480–509
1998 . . . . . . . . Reymond, 721–36
2008 . . . . . . . . Van Genderen and Velema, 589–605
2011 . . . . . . . . Horton, 575–86
2013 . . . . . . . . Frame, 164–65, 238–39, 937, 948, 950–55, 958–60, 968–70, 972, 974, 1005–7
2013 . . . . . . . . Culver, 689–713
2016 . . . . . . . . Allen and Swain, 268–83
2017 . . . . . . . . Barrett, 463
2019 . . . . . . . . Letham, 669–77

### 7. Renewal (or charismatic/Pentecostal)
1988–92 . . . . . Williams, 2:28–31

1993 . . . . . . . . Menzies and Horton, 102–6
1995 . . . . . . . . Horton, 361–64
2008 . . . . . . . . Duffield and Van Cleave, 214–24

## SECTIONS IN REPRESENTATIVE ROMAN CATHOLIC SYSTEMATIC THEOLOGIES

### 1. Roman Catholic: Traditional
1955 . . . . . . . . Ott, 252–54

### 2. Roman Catholic: Post–Vatican II
1980 . . . . . . . . McBrien, 1:31–46
2012 . . . . . . . . *CCC*, paragraphs 1427–29

## OTHER WORKS

Allison, Gregg. *Historical Theology: An Introduction to Christian Doctrine; A Companion to Wayne Grudem's* Systematic Theology. Grand Rapids: Zondervan, 2011, 474–497.

Berkouwer, G. C. *Faith and Justification.* Translated by Lewis B. Smedes. Grand Rapids: Eerdmans, 1954.

Boice, James Montgomery. *Christ's Call to Discipleship.* Chicago: Moody Publishers, 1986.

Chantry, Walter. *Today's Gospel: Authentic or Synthetic?* Carlisle, PA: Banner of Truth, 1970.

Chay, Fred, ed. *A Defense of Free Grace Theology: With Respect to Saving Faith, Perseverance, and Assurance.* The Woodlands, TX: Grace Theology Press, 2017.

Chay, Fred W., and John P. Correia. *The Faith That Saves: The Nature of Faith in the New Testament; An Exegetical and Theological Analysis of the Nature of New Testament Faith.* Eugene, OR: Wipf & Stock, 2012.

Clark, Gordon Haddon. *What Is Saving Faith?* Unicoi, TN: Trinity Foundation, 2004.

Davids, P. H. "Faith, Faithfulness." In *DLNT*, 367–70.

Demarest, Bruce. *The Cross and Salvation: The Doctrine of Salvation.* Wheaton, IL: Crossway, 2006, 27–43.

deSilva, D. A. "Repentance, Second Repentance." In *DLNT*, 1011–15.

Dillow, Joseph C. *Final Destiny: The Future Reign of the Servant Kings.* Monument, CO: Paniym, 2012.

Dunnett, Walter M. "Repentance." In *BTDB*, 671–72.

Eastman, B. "Faith, Faithfulness." In *DLNT*, 364–67.

France, R. T. "Faith." In *DJG*, 223–26.

Grudem, Wayne. *"Free Grace" Theology: 5 Ways It Diminishes the Gospel.* Wheaton, IL: Crossway, 2016.

Hawley, Grant, ed. *Free Grace Theology: 5 Ways It Magnifies the Gospel.* Allen, TX: Bold Grace Ministries, 2016.

Hodges, Zane C. *Absolutely Free! A Biblical Reply to Lordship Salvation.* Dallas: Redención Viva; Grand Rapids: Zondervan, 1989.

———. *The Gospel Under Siege: A Study on Faith and Works.* Dallas: Redención Viva, 1981.

———. *Harmony with God: A Fresh Look at Repentance.* Dallas: Redención Viva, 2001.

Hoekema, Anthony A. *Saved by Grace.* Grand Rapids: Eerdmans; Exeter: Paternoster, 1989, 113–51.

Keathley, Kenneth. "The Work of God: Salvation." In *A Theology for the Church*, edited by Daniel L. Akin et al., 728–39. Nashville: B&H, 2007.

Kendall, R T. *Total Forgiveness.* Rev. and updated. Lake Mary, FL: Charisma House, 2007.

Kromminga, C. G. "Repentance." In *EDT3*, 740–41.

Lunde, J. "Repentance." In *DJG*, 669–73.

———. "Repentance." In *NDBT*, 726–27.

MacArthur, John F., Jr. *The Gospel according to Jesus.* Grand Rapids: Zondervan, 1988.

Machen, J. Gresham. *What Is Faith?* Grand Rapids: Eerdmans, 1925.

Morris, Leon. "Faith." In *IBD*. 1:496–98.

———. "Faith." In *DPL*, 285–91.

Murray, John. "Faith and Repentance." In *Redemption Accomplished and Applied*, 106–16. Grand Rapids: Eerdmans, 1955.

———. "Repentance." In *The New Bible Dictionary*. Edited by J. D. Douglas, 1083–84. London: Tyndale Press; Grand Rapids: Eerdmans, 1962.

Packer, J. I. "Evangelicals and the Way of Salvation: New Challenges to the Gospel–Universalism and Justification by Faith." In *Evangelical Affirmations*. Edited by Kenneth S. Kantzer and Carl F. H. Henry, 107–36. Grand Rapids: Zondervan, 1990.

———. *Evangelism and the Sovereignty of God.* London: Inter-Varsity Press, 1961.

———. "Faith." In *EDT3*, 303–5.

Peace, Richard V. *Conversion in the New Testament: Paul and the Twelve.* Grand Rapids: Eerdmans, 2001.

Ryrie, Charles C. *So Great Salvation: What It Means to Believe in Jesus Christ.* Wheaton, IL: Scripture, 1989.

Swartz, Herbert L. "Faith." In *BTDB*, 236–39.

Taylor, S. S. "Faith, Faithfulness." In *NDBT*, 487–93.

Watson, Thomas. *The Doctrine of Repentance.* Carlisle, PA: Banner of Truth, 1987.

Wilkins, M. J. "New Birth." In *DLNT*, 792–95.

## SCRIPTURE MEMORY PASSAGE

**John 3:16:** For God so loved the world, that he gave his only Son, that whoever believes in him should not perish but have eternal life.

## HYMN

**"Just As I Am"**

Just as I am, without one plea
    But that thy blood was shed for me,
And that thou bidd'st me come to thee,
    O Lamb of God, I come, I come.

Just as I am, and waiting not
    To rid my soul of one dark blot,
To thee, whose blood can cleanse each spot,
    O Lamb of God, I come, I come.

Just as I am, though tossed about
    With many a conflict, many a doubt,
Fightings and fears within, without,
    O Lamb of God, I come, I come.

Just as I am, poor, wretched, blind;
    Sight, riches, healing of the mind,
Yea, all I need, in thee to find,
    O Lamb of God, I come, I come.

Just as I am! Thou wilt receive,
    Wilt welcome, pardon, cleanse, relieve;
Because thy promise I believe,
    O Lamb of God, I come, I come.

Just as I am! Thy love unknown
    Has broken ev'ry barrier down;
Now, to be thine, yea, thine alone,
    O Lamb of God, I come, I come.

Author: Charlotte Elliot, 1836

## CONTEMPORARY WORSHIP SONG

**"O Lord My Rock And My Redeemer"**

O Lord, my Rock and my Redeemer,
Greatest treasure of my longing soul,

My God, like You there is no other.
True delight is found in You alone.

*Your grace a well too deep to fathom.*
*Your love exceeds the heavens' reach.*
*Your truth a fount of perfect wisdom.*
*My highest good and my unending need.*

*O Lord, my Rock and my Redeemer,*
*Strong defender of my weary heart,*
*My sword to fight the cruel deceiver,*
*And my shield against his hateful darts.*
*My song when enemies surround me,*
*My hope when tides of sorrow rise,*
*My joy when trials are abounding.*
*Your faithfulness my refuge in the night.*

*O Lord, my Rock and my Redeemer,*
*Gracious Savior of my ruined life,*
*My guilt and cross laid on Your shoulders.*
*In my place You suffered bled and died.*
*You rose the grave and death are conquered.*
*You broke my bonds of sin and shame.*
*O Lord, my Rock and my Redeemer,*
*May all my days bring glory to Your Name.*

Words by Nathan Stiff[42]

---

# CHAPTER 36

# Justification (Right Legal Standing before God)

*How and when do we gain right legal standing before God?*

## EXPLANATION AND SCRIPTURAL BASIS

In the previous chapters we talked about the gospel call (in which God calls us to trust in Christ for salvation), regeneration (in which God imparts new spiritual life to us), and conversion (in which we respond to the gospel call in repentance for sin and faith in Christ for salvation). But *what about the guilt of our sin?* The gospel call invited us to trust in Christ for forgiveness of sins. Regeneration made it possible for us to respond to that invitation. In conversion we did respond, trusting in Christ for forgiveness of sins. Now the next step in the process of applying redemption to us is that God must respond to our faith and do what he promised, that is, actually declare our sins to be forgiven. This must be a *legal declaration* concerning our relationship to God's laws, stating that we are completely forgiven and no longer liable to punishment.

A right understanding of justification is absolutely crucial to the whole Christian faith. Once Martin Luther realized the truth of justification by faith alone, he spiritually became a born-again Christian and overflowed with the new-found joy of the gospel. The primary issue in the Protestant Reformation was a dispute with the Roman Catholic Church over justification. If we are to safeguard the truth of the gospel for future generations, we must understand the truth of justification. Even today, a true view of justification is the dividing line between the biblical gospel of salvation by faith alone and all false gospels of salvation based on good works.

When Paul gives an overview of the process by which God applies salvation to us, he mentions justification explicitly: "Those whom he predestined he also called, and those whom he called he also *justified,* and those whom he justified he also glorified" (Rom. 8:30). As we explained in a previous chapter, the word *called* here refers to the effective calling of the gospel, which includes regeneration and brings forth the response of repentance and faith (or conversion) on our part. After effective calling and the response that it initiates on our part, the next step in the application of redemption is "justification." Here Paul mentions that this is something that God himself does: "Those whom he called *he also justified.*"

Moreover, Paul quite clearly teaches that this justification comes *after* our faith and as *God's response to* our faith. He says that God is "the justifier of the one who *has faith* in Jesus" (Rom. 3:26) and that "one is justified *by faith* apart from works of the law" (Rom. 3:28). He says, "Since we have been justified *by faith*, we have peace with God through our Lord Jesus Christ" (Rom. 5:1). Moreover, "a person is not justified by works of the law but *through faith* in Jesus Christ" (Gal. 2:16).

Just what is justification? We may define it as follows: *justification is an instantaneous legal act of God in which he (1) thinks of our sins as forgiven and Christ's righteousness as belonging to us, and (2) declares us to be righteous in his sight.*

In explaining the elements of this definition, we will look first at the second half of it, the aspect of justification in which God "declares us to be righteous in his sight." The reason for treating these items in reverse order is that the emphasis of the New Testament in the use of the word *justification* and related terms is on the second half of the definition, the legal declaration by God. But there are also passages that show that this declaration is based on the fact that God first thinks of righteousness as belonging to us. So both aspects must be treated, even though the New Testament terms for justification focus on the legal declaration by God.

## A. Justification Includes a Legal Declaration by God

The use of the word *justify* in the Bible indicates that justification is a legal declaration by God. The verb *justify* in the New Testament (Gk. *dikaioō*) has a range of meanings, but a very common sense is "to declare righteous." For example, we read, "When they heard this all the people and the tax collectors *justified* God, having been baptized with the baptism of John" (Luke 7:29 RSV). Of course the people and the tax collectors did not *make* God to be righteous—that would be impossible for anyone to do. Rather they *declared* God to be righteous. This is also the sense of the term in passages where the New Testament talks about us being declared righteous by God (Rom. 3:20, 26, 28; 5:1; 8:30; 10:4, 10; Gal. 2:16; 3:24). This sense is particularly evident, for example, in Romans 4:5: "And to the one who does not work but believes in him who *justifies the ungodly*, his faith is counted as righteousness." Here Paul cannot mean that God "makes the ungodly to be righteous" (by changing them internally and making them morally perfect), for then they would have merit or works of their own to depend on. Rather, he means that God declares the ungodly to be righteous in his sight—not on the basis of their good works but in response to their faith.

The idea that justification is a legal declaration is quite evident also when justification is contrasted with condemnation. Paul says, "Who shall bring any charge against God's elect? It is God who *justifies*. Who is to condemn?" (Rom. 8:33–34). To "condemn" someone is to declare that person guilty. The opposite of condemnation is justification, which, in this context, must mean "to declare someone not guilty." This is also evident from the fact that God's act of justifying is given as Paul's answer to the possibility of someone bringing an accusation or "charge" against God's people: such a declaration of guilt cannot stand in the face of God's declaration of righteousness.

Some Old Testament examples of the word *justify* (Gk. *dikaioō* in the Septuagint, when translating the hiphil of *tsādēk*, "to justify") add support to this understanding. For example, we read of judges who "*justify the righteous* and condemn the wicked" (Deut. 25:1 NASB). Now in this case *justify* must mean "declare to be righteous or not guilty," just as *condemn* means "declare to be guilty." It would make no sense to say that "justify" here means "to make someone to be good internally," for judges simply do not and cannot make people to be good on the inside. Nor does a judge's act of condemning the wicked make that person to be evil on the inside; it simply declares that the person is guilty with respect to the particular crime that has been brought before the court (cf. Ex. 23:7; 1 Kings 8:32; 2 Chron. 6:23). Similarly, Job refuses to say that his comforters were right in what they said: "Far be it from me that I should *declare you right*" (Job 27:5 NASB, using the same Hebrew and Greek terms for "justify"). The same idea is found in Proverbs: "He who *justifies* the wicked and he who condemns the righteous are both alike an abomination to the LORD" (Prov. 17:15). Here the idea of legal declaration is especially strong. Certainly it would not be an abomination to the Lord if *justify* meant "to *make* someone good or righteous inside." In that case, to "justify the wicked" would be a very good thing in God's sight. But if *justify* means "declare to be righteous," then it is perfectly clear why "he who justifies the wicked" is "an abomination to the LORD." Similarly, Isaiah condemns those "who justify the wicked for a bribe" (Isa. 5:23 NASB); again, *justify* must mean "declare to be righteous" (here used in the context of a legal declaration).

In this sense of "*declare* to be righteous" or "*declare* to be not guilty" Paul frequently uses the word to speak of God's justification of us, his declaration that we, though guilty sinners, are nonetheless righteous in his sight. It is important to emphasize that this legal declaration in itself does not change our internal nature or character at all. In this sense of *justify*, God issues a legal declaration about us. This is why theologians have also said that justification is *forensic*, where the word *forensic* means "having to do with legal proceedings."

John Murray makes an important distinction between regeneration and justification:

> Regeneration is an act of God in us; justification is a judgment of God with respect to us. The distinction is like that of the distinction between the act of a surgeon and the act of a judge. The surgeon, when he removes an inward cancer, does something in us. That is not what a judge does—he gives a verdict regarding our judicial status. If we are innocent he declares accordingly.
>
> The purity of the gospel is bound up with the recognition of this distinction. If justification is confused with regeneration or sanctification, then the door is opened for the perversion of the gospel at its center. Justification is still the article of the standing or falling of the Church.[1]

---

1. John Murray, *Redemption Accomplished and Applied* (Grand Rapids: Eerdmans, 1955), 121.

## B. God Declares Us to Be Just in His Sight

In God's legal declaration of justification, he specifically declares that we are just *in his sight*. This declaration involves two aspects. First, it means that he declares we have no penalty to pay for sin, including past, present, and future sins. After a long discussion of justification by faith alone (Rom. 4:1–5:21), as well as a parenthetical discussion on remaining sin in the Christian life, Paul returns to his main argument in the book of Romans and tells what is true of those who have been justified by faith: "There is therefore now *no condemnation* for those who are in Christ Jesus" (Rom. 8:1). In this sense those who are justified have no penalty to pay for sin. This means that we are not subject to any charge of guilt or condemnation: "Who shall bring any charge against God's elect? It is God who *justifies*. Who is to condemn?" (Rom. 8:33–34).

The idea of full forgiveness of sins is prominent when Paul discusses justification by faith alone in Romans 4. Paul quotes David as pronouncing a blessing on one "to whom God counts righteousness apart from works." He then recalls how David said, "Blessed are those *whose lawless deeds are forgiven*, and whose sins are covered; blessed is the man against whom the Lord will not count his sin" (Rom. 4:6–8). This justification therefore clearly involves the forgiveness of sins. David spoke similarly in Psalm 103:12, "As far as the east is from the west, so far does he remove our transgressions from us" (cf. v. 3).

But if God merely declared us to be *forgiven from our sins*, that would not solve our problems entirely, for it would only make us morally neutral before God. We would be in the state that Adam was in before he had done anything right or wrong in God's sight—he was not guilty before God, but neither had he earned a record of righteousness before God. This first aspect of justification, in which God declares that our sins are forgiven, may be represented as in figure 36.1, in which the minus signs represent sins on our account that are completely forgiven when we are justified.

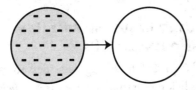

**Forgiveness of Past Sins Is One Part of Justification**
*Figure 36.1*

However, such a movement is not enough to earn us favor with God. We must rather move from a point of moral neutrality to a point of having positive righteousness before God, the righteousness of a life of perfect obedience to him. Our need may therefore be represented as in figure 36.2, in which the plus signs indicate a record of righteousness before God.

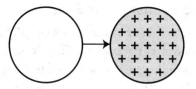

**Imputation of Christ's Righteousness to Us Is the Other Part of Justification**
*Figure 36.2*

Therefore, the second aspect of justification is that God must declare us not merely to be *neutral* in his sight but actually to be *righteous* in his sight. In fact, he must declare us to have the merits of perfect righteousness before him. The Old Testament sometimes speaks of God as giving such righteousness to his people even though they had not earned it themselves. Isaiah says, "He has clothed me with the garments of salvation; *he has covered me with the robe of righteousness*" (Isa. 61:10). But Paul speaks more specifically about this in the New Testament. As a solution to our need for righteousness, Paul tells us that "the righteousness of God has been manifested apart from the law, although the Law and the Prophets bear witness to it—*the righteousness of God through faith in Jesus Christ* for all who believe" (Rom. 3:21–22). He says, "Abraham believed God, and *it was counted to him as righteousness*" (Rom. 4:3, quoting Gen. 15:6). This came about through the obedience of Christ, for Paul says at the end of this extensive discussion of justification by faith that "by the one man's obedience the many will be *made righteous*" (Rom. 5:19). The second aspect of God's declaration in justification, then, is that we have the merits of perfect righteousness before him.

But questions arise: How can God truthfully declare that we have no penalty to pay for sin, and that we have the merits of perfect righteousness, if we are in fact guilty sinners? How can God truthfully declare us to be not guilty but righteous when in fact *we are unrighteous*? These questions lead to our next point.

## C. God Can Declare Us to Be Just Because He Imputes Christ's Righteousness to Us

When we say that God *imputes* Christ's righteousness to us it means that God *thinks of* Christ's righteousness as belonging to us, or regards it *as belonging to* us. He "reckons" it to our account. We read, "Abraham believed God, and *it was counted*[2] *to him as righteousness*" (Rom. 4:3, quoting Gen. 15:6). Paul explains, "To the one who does not work but believes in him who justifies the ungodly, his faith *is counted* as righteousness, just as David also speaks of the blessing of the one to whom *God counts righteousness* apart from

---

2. Gk. *logizomai* in the sense of "reckon, look upon as, consider."

works" (Rom. 4:5–6). In this way, Christ's righteousness became ours. Paul says that we are those who received "the free gift of righteousness" (Rom. 5:17).

This is the third time in studying the doctrines of Scripture that we have encountered the idea of *imputing* guilt or righteousness to someone else. First, when Adam sinned, his guilt was imputed to us; God the Father viewed it as belonging to us, and therefore it did.[3] Second, when Christ suffered and died for our sins, our sin was *imputed* to Christ; God thought of it as belonging to him, and he paid the penalty for it.[4] Now in the doctrine of justification we see imputation for the third time. Christ's righteousness is *imputed* to us, and therefore God *thinks of it* as belonging to us. It is not our righteousness but Christ's righteousness that is freely given to us. So Paul can say that Christ became to us "wisdom from God, *righteousness* and sanctification and redemption" (1 Cor. 1:30). And Paul says that his goal is to be found in Christ, "not having a righteousness of my own that comes from the law, but that which comes through faith in Christ, *the righteousness from God* that depends on faith" (Phil. 3:9). Paul knows that the righteousness he has before God is not anything of his own doing; it is the righteousness of God that comes through Jesus Christ (cf. Rom. 3:21–22).[5]

It is essential to the heart of the gospel to insist that God declares us to be just or righteous *not* on the basis of our actual condition of righteousness or holiness, but rather on the basis of Christ's perfect righteousness, which he thinks of as belonging to us. This was the heart of the difference between Protestantism and Roman Catholicism at the Reformation. Protestantism since the time of Martin Luther has insisted that justification does *not* change us internally, and it is *not* a declaration based in any way on any goodness that we have in ourselves. If justification changed us internally and then declared us to be righteous based on how good we actually were, then (1) we could never be declared perfectly righteous in this life, because there is always sin that remains in our lives, and (2) there would be no provision for forgiveness of past sins (committed before we were changed internally), and therefore we could never have confidence that we are

---

3. See chapter 24, pp. 623–27, on the idea of Adam's sin being imputed to us.

4. See chapter 27, pp. 711–12, on the fact that our guilt was imputed to Christ. Paul says, "God made him who had no sin to be sin for us, so that in him we might become the righteousness of God" (2 Cor. 5:21 NIV).

5. One sometimes hears the popular explanation that *justified* means "just-as-if-I'd-never-sinned." The definition is a clever play on words and contains an element of truth (for the justified person, like the person who has never sinned, has no penalty to pay for sin). But the definition is misleading in two other ways because (1) it mentions nothing about the fact that Christ's righteousness is reckoned to my account when I am justified; to do this it would have to say also "just-as-if-I'd-lived -a-life-of-perfect-righteousness." (2) But more significantly, it cannot adequately represent the fact that I will *never* be in a state that is "just-as-if-I'd-never-sinned," because I will *always*

be conscious of the fact that I *have* sinned and that I am not an innocent person but a guilty person who has been forgiven. This is very different from "just as if I had never sinned"! Moreover, it is different from "just as if I had lived a life of perfect righteousness," because I will forever know that I *have not* lived a life of perfect righteousness, but that Christ's righteousness is given to me by God's grace.

Therefore both in the forgiveness of sins and in the imputation of Christ's righteousness, my situation is far different from what it would be if I had never sinned and had lived a perfectly righteous life. For all eternity I will remember that I am a forgiven *sinner,* and that my righteousness is not based on my own merit, but on the grace of God in the saving work of Jesus Christ. None of that rich teaching at the heart of the gospel will be understood by those who are encouraged to go through their lives thinking "justified" means "just-as-if-I'd-never-sinned."

right before God. We would lose the confidence that Paul has when he says, "Therefore, *since we have been justified by faith*, we have peace with God through our Lord Jesus Christ" (Rom. 5:1). If we thought of justification as based on something that we are internally, we would never have the confidence to say with Paul, "There is therefore now *no condemnation* for those who are in Christ Jesus" (Rom. 8:1). We would have no assurance of forgiveness with God, no confidence to draw near to him "with a true heart in full assurance of faith" (Heb. 10:22). We would not be able to speak of "the *free gift* of righteousness" (Rom. 5:17) or say that "the *free gift* of God is eternal life in Christ Jesus our Lord" (Rom. 6:23).

## D. Differences with the Traditional Roman Catholic View of Justification

The traditional Roman Catholic understanding of justification is very different from this. The Roman Catholic Church understands justification as something that *changes us internally* and makes us more holy within. "According to the teaching of the Council of Trent, justification is 'sanctifying and renewing of the inner man.'"[6] The more recent Catechism of the Catholic Church (1997 update) agrees with this: "Justification includes the remission of sins, sanctification, and the renewal of the inner man. . . . It is granted to us through Baptism."[7] In order for justification to begin, one must first be baptized and then (as an adult) continue to have faith: "The instrumental cause . . . of the first justification is the Sacrament of Baptism."[8] But "the justification of an adult is not possible without Faith. . . . As far as the content of justifying faith is concerned, the so-called fiducial faith does not suffice. What is demanded is theological or dogmatic faith (confessional faith) which consists in the firm acceptance of the Divine truths of Revelation."[9]

Thus baptism is the means by which justification is first obtained, and then faith is necessary if an adult is to receive justification or to continue in the state of justification. Ott explains that "the so-called fiduciary faith" is not enough—meaning that the faith that simply trusts in Christ for forgiveness of sins is not enough. It must be a faith that accepts the content of the teaching of the Catholic Church, "theological or dogmatic faith."

The Roman Catholic view may be said to understand justification as based not on *imputed* righteousness but on *infused* righteousness—that is, righteousness that God actually *puts into us* and that changes us internally and in terms of our actual moral

---

6. Ludwig Ott, *Fundamentals of Catholic Dogma*, trans. Patrick Lynch (Rockford: Tan, 1960), 257; also quoted with approval on p. 250. It should be noted that Ott represents more traditional, pre–Vatican II Roman Catholicism and that many contemporary Roman Catholics have sought an understanding of justification closer to a Protestant view. Although many modern Roman Catholics will affirm that we are "justified by

faith," they are still unable to remain faithful to official Catholic teaching and affirm the Reformation principle of "justification by faith *alone*."

7. *Catechism of the Catholic Church* (New York: Doubleday, 1997), para. 2019–20; cf. 1989.

8. Ibid., 251.

9. Ibid., 252–53.

character. Then he gives us varying measures of justification according to the measure of righteousness that has been infused or placed within us.

The result of this Roman Catholic view of justification is that people cannot be sure if they are in a "state of grace" where they experience God's complete acceptance and favor. The Catholic Church teaches that people cannot be certain that they are in this "state of grace" unless they receive a special revelation from God to this effect. The Council of Trent declared,

> If one considers his own weakness and his defective disposition, he may well be fearful and anxious as to the state of grace, as nobody knows with the certainty of faith, which permits of no error, that he has achieved the grace of God.

To this statement Ott adds the comment,

> The reason for the uncertainty of the state of grace lies in this, that without a special revelation nobody can with certainty of faith know whether or not he has fulfilled all the conditions which are necessary for the achieving of justification. The impossibility of the certainty of faith, however, by no means excludes a high moral certainty supported by the testimony of conscience.[10]

Moreover, since the Roman Catholic Church views justification as including something that God does within us, it follows that people can experience varying degrees of justification. We read, "The degree of justifying grace is not identical in all the just," and "grace can be increased by good works."[11] Ott explains how this Catholic view differs from that of the Protestant Reformers: "As the Reformers wrongly regarded justification as a merely external imputation of Christ's justice, they were obliged also to hold that justification is identical in all men. The Council of Trent, however, declared that the measure of the grace of justification received varies in the individual person who is justified, according to the measure of God's free distribution and to the disposition and the co-operation of the recipient himself."[12]

The logical consequence of this view of justification is that our eternal life with God is based not on God's grace alone but partially on our merit as well: "For the justified eternal life is both a gift of grace promised by God and a reward for his own good works and merits. . . . Salutary works are, at the same time, gifts of God and meritorious acts of man."[13]

To support this view of justification from Scripture, Ott repeatedly mingles passages from the New Testament that talk not only of justification but also of many other

---

10. Ibid., 261–62.
11. Ibid., 262.

12. Ibid., 262.
13. Ibid., 264.

aspects of the Christian life, such as regeneration (which God works in us), sanctification (which is a process in the Christian life and which of course does vary from individual to individual), the possession and use of various spiritual gifts in the Christian life (which differ from individual to individual), and eternal reward (which also varies according to the individual). To classify all of these passages under the category of "justification" only blurs the issue and ultimately makes forgiveness of sins and right legal standing before God a matter of our own merit, not a free gift from God. Therefore, this blurring of distinctions ultimately destroys the heart of the gospel.

That is what Martin Luther so clearly saw, and that is what gave such motivation to the Reformation. When the good news of the gospel truly became the good news of totally free salvation in Jesus Christ, then it spread like wildfire throughout the civilized world. But this was simply a recovery of the original gospel, which declares, "The wages of sin is death, but the *free gift of God* is eternal life in Christ Jesus our Lord" (Rom. 6:23), and insists that "there is therefore now *no condemnation* for those who are in Christ Jesus" (Rom. 8:1).

## E. Justification Comes to Us Entirely by God's Grace, Not on Account of Any Merit in Ourselves

After Paul explains in Romans 1:18–3:20 that no one will ever be able to make himself righteous before God ("For by works of the law no human being will be justified in his sight," Rom. 3:20), he goes on to explain that "all have sinned and fall short of the glory of God, and are justified *by his grace as a gift*, through the redemption that is in Christ Jesus" (Rom. 3:23–24). God's "grace" means his "unmerited favor." Because we are completely unable to earn favor with God, the only way we could be declared righteous is if God freely provides salvation for us by grace, totally apart from our work. Paul explains, "For *by grace* you have been saved through faith. And this is not your own doing; it is the gift of God, not a result of works, so that no one may boast" (Eph. 2:8–9; cf. Titus 3:7). Grace is clearly put in contrast to works or merit as the reason why God is willing to justify us. God did not have any obligation to impute our sin to Christ or to impute Christ's righteousness to us; it was only because of his unmerited favor that he did this.

In distinction from the Roman Catholic teaching that we are justified by God's grace *plus some merit of our own*, as we make ourselves fit to receive the grace of justification and as we grow in this state of grace though our good works, Luther and the other Reformers insisted that justification comes by grace *alone*, not by grace plus some merit on our part.

## F. God Justifies Us through Our Faith in Christ

When we began this chapter, we noted that justification comes after saving faith. Paul makes this sequence clear when he says, "We also have believed in Christ Jesus, *in order to be justified* by faith in Christ and not by works of the law, because by works of the law no one will be justified" (Gal. 2:16). Here Paul indicates that faith comes first, and it does so for the purpose of being justified. He also says that Christ is "to be received by faith" and that God is the "justifier of the one who has *faith* in Jesus" (Rom. 3:25, 26). The entire chapter of Romans 4 is a defense of the fact that we are justified by faith, not by works, just as Abraham and David were. Paul says, "We have been justified *by faith*" (Rom. 5:1).

Scripture never says that we are justified because of the inherent goodness of our faith, as if our faith has merit before God. It never allows us to think that our faith earns favor with God. Rather, Scripture says that we are justified "by means of" our faith, understanding faith to be the instrument through which justification is given to us, not an activity that earns us merit or favor with God. We are justified solely because of the merits of Christ's work (Rom. 5:17–19).[14]

But we may ask why God chose *faith* to be the attitude of heart by which we would obtain justification. Why could God not have decided to give justification to all those who sincerely show love? Or who show joy? Or contentment? Or humility? Or wisdom? Why did God choose *faith* as the means by which we receive justification?

It is apparently because *faith* is the one attitude of heart that is the exact opposite of depending on ourselves. When we come to Christ in faith we essentially say, "I give up! I will not depend on myself or my own good works any longer. I know that I can never make myself righteous before God. Therefore, Jesus, I trust you and depend on you completely to give me a righteous standing before God." In this way, faith is the exact opposite of trusting in ourselves, and therefore it is the attitude that perfectly fits salvation that depends not at all on our own merit but entirely on God's free gift of grace. Paul explains this when he says, "That is why it depends *on faith, in order that the promise may rest on grace* and be guaranteed to all his offspring" (Rom. 4:16). This is why the Reformers from Martin Luther on were so firm in their insistence that justification comes not through faith plus some merit or good work on our part, but only *through faith alone*. "For by grace you have been saved *through faith*. And this[15] is not your own doing; it is the gift of God, not a result of works, so that no one may boast" (Eph. 2:8–9). Paul repeatedly says that "by works of the law no human being will be justified in his sight" (Rom. 3:20); the same idea is repeated in Galatians 2:16; 3:11; 5:4.

---

14. One example from ordinary life might be seen in receiving a paycheck for work that has been done for an employer. The "means" or "instrument" that I use to get this paycheck is the act of reaching out my hand and taking an envelope from my mailbox, then opening it and pulling out the check. But my employer does not pay me for doing any of those actions. The pay is entirely for work that I did prior to that. Actually taking the check did not earn me one cent of the money I received—it was simply the *instrument* or *means* I used to take the payment into my possession. Similarly, faith is the *instrument* we use to receive justification from God, but in itself gains us no merit with God. (The analogy is helpful but not perfect because I had previously worked to earn the money, whereas justification is based on the work of Christ. The analogy would be closer if I had worked and then died, and my wife then picked up the paycheck from my mailbox.)

15. The word translated "this" is the neuter pronoun *touto*, which refers not to "faith" or to "grace" specifically in the previous clause (for they are both feminine nouns in Greek, and would require feminine pronouns), but to the entire idea expressed in the preceding phrase, the idea that you have been saved by grace through faith.

But is this consistent with the epistle of James? What can James mean when he says, "You see that a person is *justified by works* and not by faith alone" (James 2:24). Here we must realize that James is using the word *justified* in a different sense from the way Paul uses it. In the beginning of this chapter we noted that the word *justify* has a range of meanings, and that one significant sense was "declare to be righteous," but we should also notice that the Greek word *dikaioō* can also mean "demonstrate or show to be righteous." For instance, Jesus said to the Pharisees, "You are those who *justify* yourselves before men, but God knows your hearts" (Luke 16:15). The Pharisees were not going around making legal declarations that they were "not guilty" before God, but rather they were always attempting to *show others* that they were righteous by their outward deeds. Jesus knew that the truth was otherwise: "But God knows your hearts" (Luke 16:15). Similarly, the lawyer who put Jesus to a test by asking what he should do to inherit eternal life answered Jesus' first question well. But when Jesus told him, "Do this, and you will live," he was not satisfied. Luke tells us, "But he, *desiring to justify himself,* said to Jesus, 'And who is my neighbor?'" (Luke 10:28–29). Now he was not desiring to give a legal pronouncement about himself that he was not guilty in God's sight; rather, he was desiring to "show himself righteous" before others who were listening. Other examples of the word *justify* meaning "show to be righteous" can be found in Matthew 11:19; Luke 7:35; Romans 3:4.

Our interpretation of James 2 depends not only on the fact that "show to be righteous" is an acceptable sense for the word *justified* but also on the consideration that this sense fits well in the context of James 2. When James says, "Was not Abraham our father *justified by works* when he offered up his son Isaac on the altar?" (v. 21), he is referring to something later in Abraham's life, the story of the sacrifice of Isaac, which occurred in Genesis 22. This is long after the time recorded in Genesis 15:6 where Abraham believed God "and he counted it to him as righteousness." Yet this earlier incident at the beginning of Abraham's covenantal relationship with God is the one that Paul quotes and repeatedly refers to in Romans 4. Paul is talking about the time God justified Abraham once for all, reckoning righteousness to him as a result of his faith in God. But James is talking about something far later, after Abraham had waited many years for the birth of Isaac, and then after Isaac had grown old enough to carry wood up the mountain for a sacrifice. At that point Abraham was "shown to be righteous" by his works, and in that sense James says that Abraham was "justified by works, when he offered his son Isaac upon the altar" (James 2:21).[16]

The larger concern of James in this section also fits this understanding. James is concerned to show that mere intellectual agreement with the gospel is a "faith" that is really no faith at all. He is concerned to argue against those who say they have faith but show no change in their lives. He says, "Show me your faith apart from your works, and I

---

16. James does quote the text, "Abraham believed God, and it was reckoned to him as righteousness" in v. 23, but he says that Scripture "was fulfilled" when Abraham offered his son, apparently meaning that the earlier declaration of righteousness was then worked out and its results were seen to be true in Abraham's life when he offered Isaac on the altar.

will show you my faith by my works" (James 2:18). "For as the body apart from the spirit is dead, so also faith apart from works is dead" (James 2:26). James is simply saying here that "faith" that has no results, or "works," is not real faith at all; it is "dead" faith. He is not denying Paul's clear teaching that justification (in the sense of a declaration of right legal standing before God) is by faith alone apart from works of the law; he is affirming a different truth, namely, that "justification" in the sense of an outward showing that one is righteous only occurs as we see evidence in a person's life. To paraphrase, James is saying that a person is "*shown to be righteous* by his works, and not by his faith alone." This is something with which Paul also would certainly agree (2 Cor. 13:5; Gal. 5:19–24).

The practical implications of the doctrine of justification by faith alone are very significant. First, this doctrine enables us to offer genuine *hope* to unbelievers who know they could never make themselves righteous before God: if salvation is a free gift to be received through faith *alone*, then anyone who hears the gospel may hope that eternal life is freely offered and may be obtained.

Second, this doctrine gives us confidence that God will never make us pay the penalty for sins that have been forgiven on Christ's merits. Of course, we may continue to suffer the ordinary *consequences* of sin (an alcoholic who quits drinking may still have physical weakness for the rest of his or her life, and a thief who is justified may still have to go to jail to pay the penalty for his or her crime). Moreover, God may *discipline* us if we continue to act in ways that are disobedient to him (see Heb. 12:5–11), doing this out of love and for our own good. But God can never nor will ever *take vengeance* on us for past sins or *make us pay the penalty* that is due for them or *punish us out of wrath* and *for the purpose of doing us harm*. "There is therefore now no condemnation for those who are in Christ Jesus" (Rom. 8:1). This fact should give us a great sense of joy and confidence before God that we are accepted by him and that we stand before him as "not guilty" and "righteous" forever.

## F. Good Works Give Evidence of Justification, but They Are Not the Basis of Justification

As I will explain more fully in chapter 40, "good works" (or a pattern of obedience to God's commands) give evidence that we have been justified, though these good works are never the basis for our justification. "Whoever says 'I know him' but does not keep his commandments is a liar, and the truth is not in him, but whoever keeps his word, in him truly the love of God is perfected" (1 John 2:4–5). James says bluntly, "Faith by itself, if it does not have works, is dead" and "I will show you my faith by my works" (James 2:17–18). To put it another way, good works can never earn our justification, but they do give evidence that we have been justified.[17]

---

17. See chapter 40, pp. 986–93, on gaining assurance of salvation.

## G. A Challenge to the Traditional View: the "New Perspective on Paul"

A substantially different understanding of justification has been promoted by advocates of a position broadly known as the "new perspective on Paul." The first major academic work to advocate this viewpoint was the 1977 book *Paul and Palestinian Judaism*[18] by New Testament professor E. P. Sanders, who was then at McMaster University in Hamilton, Ontario, Canada (and later at the University of Oxford and Duke University). Another influential advocate was University of Durham professor James D. G. Dunn in his book *The New Perspective on Paul.*[19]

But the new perspective advocate who has gained the widest hearing is the British New Testament scholar N. T. Wright,[20] who defended his position on justification at some length in his 1997 book *What Saint Paul Really Said*[21] and again in his 2009 book *Justification.*[22] Among new perspective advocates, Wright has had the largest influence in the evangelical world, and it is his position that I will analyze in the following material.

## 1. N. T. Wright's view of justification

**a. Justification.** Wright argues that *justification* does not mean that God declares us legally or morally righteous but instead means that *God declares us to be members of his covenant community* (God's people). Wright says, "'Justification' . . . denotes the verdict of God himself as to who really is a member of his people."[23] He recognizes that much of church history disagrees with him, but his answer is that all those earlier theologians were wrong. He writes, "The discussions of justification in much of the history of the church, certainly since Augustine, got off on the wrong foot . . . and they have stayed there ever since."[24] (Augustine lived AD 354–430.)

**b. The Basis of Justification.** He says that there will be a future justification on the last day, and that "the verdict of the last day will truly reflect what people have actually done."[25] This future justification will be *on the basis of the entire life.*[26] Elsewhere he writes, "Paul has already spoken in Romans 2 about the final justification of God's people, *on the basis of* their whole life. This will take place at the end, when God judges the secrets of all hearts through the Messiah."[27] He also writes, "The whole point about 'justification by faith' is that it is something which happens in the present

18. E. P. Sanders, *Paul and Palestinian Judaism* (London: SCM; Philadelphia: Fortress, 1977).

19. James D. G. Dunn, *The New Perspective on Paul*, rev. ed. (Tübingen: Mohr Siebeck, 2005; Grand Rapids: Eerdmans, 2008).

20. Wright is quick to point out that there are many differences among new perspective advocates, and that he himself has disagreements with Sanders and Dunn; see N. T. Wright, *Justification: God's Plan and Paul's Vision* (Downers Grove, IL: InterVarsity Press, 2009), 28–29.

21. N. T. Wright, *What Saint Paul Really Said* (Grand Rapids: Eerdmans, 1997).

22. Wright, *Justification: God's Plan and Paul's Vision*.

23. Wright, *Justification*, 121; see also *Really Said*, 129.

24. Wright, *Really Said*, 115.

25. Wright, *Justification*, 191.

26. Wright, *Really Said*, 129 (emphasis added).

27. N. T. Wright, *Paul in Fresh Perspective* (Minneapolis: Fortress, 2005), 121 (emphasis added).

time (Romans 3:26) as a proper anticipation of the eventual judgment which will be announced, *on the basis of* the whole life lived, in the future (Romans 2:1–16)."[28]

**c. Imputation.** Wright denies that God imputes Christ's righteousness to us. He writes, "If we use the language of the law court, it makes no sense whatever to say that the judge imputes, imparts, bequeaths, conveys or otherwise transfers his righteousness to either the plaintiff or the defendant.... To imagine the defendant somehow receiving the judge's righteousness is simply a category mistake."[29] Elsewhere he writes, "It is therefore a straightforward category mistake ... to suppose that Jesus 'obeyed the law' and so obtained 'righteousness' which could be reckoned to those who believe in him."[30]

**d. What Is the Gospel?** Wright says that "the gospel" is "not an account of how people get saved. It is ... the proclamation of the Lordship of Jesus Christ."[31]

He explains more fully how this proclamation of the Lordship of Christ has six aspects:

"The gospel" is not, for Paul, a message about "how one gets saved," in an individual ... sense. It is a fourfold announcement about Jesus:

1. In Jesus of Nazareth ... the decisive victory has been won over all the powers of evil....
2. In Jesus' resurrection the New Age has dawned ... when the prophecies would be fulfilled, when Israel's exile would be over....
3. The crucified and risen Jesus was, all along, Israel's Messiah....
4. Jesus was therefore also the Lord, the true King of the world....

It is, moreover, a double and dramatic announcement about God:

1. The God of Israel is the one true God, and the pagan deities are mere idols.
2. The God of Israel is now made known in and through Jesus himself.[32]

Wright then says that "the way in which people appropriate that justification, that redefinition of God's people, is now 'by faith,' by coming to believe in Jesus as Messiah."[33]

**e. Judaism.** Wright claims that Judaism in the first century AD was not a religion of works-righteousness but rather of "covenantal nomism." That is, the Jewish people thought that they were God's people not because they obeyed the Mosaic laws but because of God's election and God's grace. They obeyed the Mosaic laws out of gratitude to God not to *become* the people of God ("to get in") but rather to *show* that they were

28. Wright, *Paul in Fresh Perspective*, 57 (emphasis added); see also 148.

29. Wright, *Really Said*, 98.

30. Wright, *Justification*, 232.

31. Wright, *Really Said*, 133; see also 45, 60 (with fuller explanation), 119, 129, 132.

32. Wright, *Really Said*, 60.

33. Wright, *Justification*, 117.

the people of God ("to stay in"). Wright affirms that E. P. Sanders was largely correct when "Sanders claimed that Judaism in Paul's day, not least rabbinic Judaism, put a priority on keeping Torah not in order to earn membership in God's people but in order to express and maintain it. Judaism, he concludes, was therefore not a religion of 'legalistic works-righteousness' such as generations of scholars, preachers and 'ordinary folk' . . . have imagined."[34]

## 2. Response to Wright's view of justification[35]

**a. An Incorrect Definition of Justification.** Wright says that *justification* refers to God's declaration that we are part of his people. However, in the New Testament, the Greek verb *dikaioō* ("to justify") simply does not take the meaning "to declare someone part of a community." The standard lexicon for New Testament Greek, the Bauer-Danker-Arndt-Gingrich *Greek English Lexicon*, gives us four possible meanings for *dikaioō*: (1) "to take up a legal cause, show justice, do justice . . . ," (2) "to render a favorable verdict" (and, in passive, "be acquitted, be pronounced and treated as righteous"), (3) "to cause someone to be released from personal or institutional claims that are no longer to be considered pertinent or valid, make free/pure," and (4) "to demonstrate to be morally right, prove to be right."[36] There is no definition even close to "declare that someone is a member of a community of people." The same is true for several cognate words, such as the adjective (*dikaios*, "just, righteous, upright"), the noun *dikaiosunē* ("righteousness, justice, fairness"), the noun *dikaiōma* ("righteous deed, right action, requirement"), and the adverb *dikaiōs* ("justly, in an upright manner").[37] All of these terms have to do with *conformity to a moral standard* of goodness or righteousness, and none of them comes anywhere near to the meaning that Wright proposes, "to declare someone a member of a group."

This is highly significant because if Paul's readers were going to understand him, he had to use words with meanings that the readers already knew. If he used a word in an entirely new, unprecedented sense, unrelated to its known meanings, he would simply be speaking unintelligible mysteries to his readers. But that is what Wright implies that Paul is doing, using the verb *dikaioō* ("to justify") to mean something that had never before meant in any other known Greek writings from that time period.

---

34. Wright, *Justification*, 73–74.

35. I have found the following two book-length critiques of N. T. Wright's view of justification very helpful: John Piper, *The Future of Justification: A Response to N. T. Wright* (Wheaton, IL: Crossway, 2007), and Stephen Westerholm, *Justification Reconsidered: Rethinking a Pauline Theme* (Grand Rapids: Eerdmans, 2013). For a shorter analysis that is notably gracious yet still critical, see Thomas R. Schreiner, "Justification: The Saving Righteousness of God in Christ," *JETS* 54, no. 1 (March 2011): 19–34. Another brief yet very insightful critique is Simon Gathercole, "What Did Paul Really Mean?," *Christianity Today*, August 2007, 22–28.

For views about justification held by Christian teachers in the first century after the New Testament, see Brian J. Arnold, *Justification in the Second Century* (Berlin: De Gruyter, 2017; Waco, TX: Baylor University Press, 2018). At this point, I also wish to thank my former student Richard Klaus for sending me materials that helped me understand N. T. Wright more precisely.

36. BDAG, 249.

37. See BDAG, 246–50; see also LSJ, 429.

Stephen Westerholm emphasizes this point: "Paul no doubt had his idiosyncrasies, but using ordinary words in a sense peculiarly his own was not among them. Even when he had fresh ideas to communicate, their successful communication required that he use ordinary words in a recognizable way. . . . He used the language of "righteousness" as others used it, to refer to what one ought to do."[38]

When we realize that *the same Greek verbal root* is behind the verb translated as "to justify" (*dikaioō*) and the noun translated as "righteousness" (*dikaiosunē*), Westerholm's additional statement raises what seems to me to be an insurmountable objection against Wright's view of justification:

> In the Scriptures on which Paul draws both for his essential vocabulary and for texts supporting his doctrine of "justification", the terms for "righteous" and "righteousness" are among the most basic terms in the moral vocabulary: "righteousness" is what one ought to do . . . and the one who does it is "righteous."[39]

Westerholm gives many examples from the Old Testament where *righteousness* does not mean "faithfulness to one's covenant promises" (as N. T. Wright claims with respect to God's righteousness) but means the quality of being morally right or righteous. People who are righteous are said to be "blameless" (Gen. 6:9) or "upright" (Ps. 33:1), and those who are righteous are contrasted with "the wicked," or "those who do evil."[40] People who are called "righteous" are not called by that term because of membership among a group of people, nor are the "righteous" placed in contrast to those who are excluded from some group of people. Westerholm concludes that "'righteousness' does not mean, and by its very nature it *cannot* mean, membership in a covenant. Likewise, it does not mean, and by its very nature *cannot* mean, a status conveyed by the decision of the court. . . . 'Acquitted' and 'righteous' are *not* synonyms, even in a legal setting."[41]

My conclusion is that Wright is promoting a seriously incorrect definition when he says that "'Justification' . . . denotes the verdict of God himself as to who really is a member of his people."[42] The New Testament terminology for justification cannot bear that meaning. But all of Wright's related arguments (see the following discussion) are closely tied to this unconvincing redefinition of justification.

**b. An Incorrect Basis for Justification.** The New Testament never speaks of our good works as the *basis* for our justification. In fact, Paul says just the opposite. After recounting his past life, including the fact that he was "as to righteousness under the law, blameless" (Phil. 3:6), he does not say he depends on that righteousness to be justified before God, but he counts his previous achievements "as rubbish" (Phil. 3:8). He does

---

38. Stephen Westerholm, *Justification Reconsidered: Rethinking a Pauline Theme* (Grand Rapids: Eerdmans, 2013), 65.

39. Ibid., 59.

40. Ibid., 59.

41. Ibid., 63–65.

42. Wright, *Justification*, 121; see also *Really Said*, 129.

not depend on his "whole life lived" to make him right before God but disregards it as worthless "in order that I may gain Christ, and be found in him, *not having a righteousness of my own* that comes from the law, but that which comes through faith in Christ, the *righteousness from God* that depends on faith" (Phil. 3:8–9). Here he places his hope of being "found" (by God as judge) not on the goodness of his "whole life lived" but rather based on being found "in him [Christ]" and *not* based on his own righteousness that "comes from" obeying God's "law" but on Christ's righteousness, "the righteousness from God that depends on faith." Elsewhere he says that it is through being in Christ that we "become the righteousness of God" (2 Cor. 5:21).

This is a crucial point at the heart of the Christian gospel. If our future justification is *based on* the record of how we have lived in our earthly lives, *then our ultimate salvation is based on our works, pure and simple.* This concept stands in direct conflict with the repeated New Testament teaching that our salvation is not based on our good works but on faith in Christ: "For by grace you have been saved through faith. And this is not your own doing; it is the gift of God, *not a result of works*, so that no one may boast" (Eph. 2:8–9).

However, Wright depends strongly on Romans 2:6–11:

> He will render to each one according to his works: to those who by patience in well-doing seek for glory and honor and immortality, he will give eternal life; but for those who are self-seeking and do not obey the truth, but obey unrighteousness, there will be wrath and fury. There will be tribulation and distress for every human being who does evil, the Jew first and also the Greek, but glory and honor and peace for everyone who does good, the Jew first and also the Greek. For God shows no partiality.

It is true that on one interpretation this passage could be understood to speak of a future final judgment *on the basis of* what we have done in this lifetime. But that is not the only possible interpretation. Many commentators understand it in a way that would not contradict the New Testament teaching that we are saved by grace alone through faith alone (Eph. 2:8–9), *on the basis of Christ's redemptive work alone*, and not on the basis of our works.[43] According to this second interpretation, Paul is speaking of good works as the *result* and *evidence* of regeneration and saving faith: those who have been born again and have been justified by faith alone will show evidence of that changed life "by patience in

---

43. Schreiner also says that "Wright's use of the word 'basis' confuses people," but he says that in "subsequent discussion" after a formal panel discussion at the Evangelical Theological Society meeting on November 19, 2010, Wright indicated that he "does not mean that human works are the ultimate basis of one's right standing with God." But Schreiner adds, "It would be clearer if he continued to speak of justification *according to* our works instead of *on the basis of works*" (Schreiner, "Saving Righteousness," 21n8). My analysis in this chapter, however, is based on his published writings, in which his language of final justification "on the basis of works" is so pervasive as to be seriously misleading if that is not what he means.

well-doing" (Rom. 2:7). By contrast, unbelievers will be those who "are self-seeking and do not obey the truth, but obey unrighteousness" (Rom. 2:8).

This is not the only New Testament text that speaks about God's judgment of us. Several other texts, even some in Romans, speak explicitly about the fact that salvation is an entirely *free* gift, not something we can earn by good works done during this lifetime.

> For if Abraham was justified by works, he has something to boast about, but not before God. For what does the Scripture say? "Abraham believed God, and it was counted to him as righteousness." *Now to the one who works, his wages are not counted as a gift but as his due.* And to the one who does not work but believes in him who justifies the ungodly, *his faith is counted as righteousness,* just as David also speaks of the blessing of the one to whom *God counts righteousness apart from works.* (Rom. 4:2–6)

> For the wages of sin is death, but the *free gift* of God is eternal life in Christ Jesus our Lord. (Rom. 6:23)

> Therefore, since we have been *justified by faith,* we have peace with God through our Lord Jesus Christ. (Rom. 5:1)

> What shall we say, then? That Gentiles who did not pursue righteousness have attained it, that is, *a righteousness that is by faith*; but that Israel who pursued a law that would lead to righteousness did not succeed in reaching that law. Why? *Because they did not pursue it by faith, but as if it were based on works.* They have stumbled over the stumbling stone. (Rom. 9:30–32)

> Yet we know that a person is *not justified by works of the law*[44] but through faith in Jesus Christ, so we also have believed in Christ Jesus, in order to be justified by faith in Christ and not by works of the law, because by works of the law no one will be justified. (Gal. 2:16)

> For all who rely on works of the law[45] are under a curse; for it is written, "Cursed be everyone who does not abide by all things written in the Book of the Law, and do them." (Gal. 3:10)

---

44. Wright claims that "works of the law" does not mean obedience to *all* Old Testament moral laws but rather refers more narrowly to actions that mark the Jewish people as distinct, such as circumcision, Sabbath observance, and dietary laws about clean and unclean foods (see *Justification,* 116–17, 147). But that redefinition depends on his incorrect definition of *justification* as God's declaration that people are part of

his covenant community (see above). But if *justification* means God's declaration that we are counted righteous (in a moral sense), then the phrase "works of the law" refers to obedience to all of the Old Testament laws. Paul insists that obedience to these laws is not the basis of our justification.

45. See previous footnote.

There is another objection: If our future justification were based on God's evaluation of our "whole life lived," then no one could be justified, for "all have sinned and fall short of the glory of God" (Rom. 3:23). An ordinary human life that appears to be reasonably moral will never be enough. In fact, Wright himself says, "'Works of the law' will never justify, because what the law does is to reveal sin. Nobody can keep it perfectly."[46]

Finally, Wright's view of this future justification *on the basis of* our works also has implications for justification in our present life, because Wright links present and future justification together. He says our present justification by faith "happens in the present time (Rom. 3:26) *as a proper anticipation of the eventual judgment* which will be announced, *on the basis of* the whole life lived, in the future (Rom. 2:1–16)."[47] But if our *present* justification is understood as an "anticipation" of our *future* judgment, and future judgment is on the basis of our works, this implies that our *present* justification is also, in an indirect sense, based on our good works. This, then, is a denial of the heart of the Christian gospel.

**c. An incorrect denial of imputation.** It is not surprising Wright denies that God imputes Christ's perfect righteousness to us because, if our future justification is to be on the basis of *our* "whole life lived," then what need is there for justification based on the record of *Christ's* perfect life?

Wright objects that, in human courts, the judge does not impute or impart his own righteousness to the plaintiff or the defendant in the courtroom.[48] But God is not constrained to acting only within the limits of one courtroom metaphor to describe his amazing, multi-faceted work of redemption. He is Lord of the entire universe, and he can impute Christ's righteousness to us if he wills to do so. In fact, several passages of the New Testament indicate that he has done exactly that.[49]

> And to the one who does not work but believes in him who justifies the ungodly, *his faith is counted as righteousness.* (Rom. 4:5)

> Just a few verses earlier, Paul had explained what kind of faith this is. He is talking about "the righteousness of God through *faith in Jesus Christ* for all who believe." (Rom. 3:22)

> David also speaks of the blessing of the one to whom *God counts righteousness apart from works.* (Rom. 4:6)

---

46. Wright, *Justification*, 118.

47. Wright, *Paul in Fresh Perspective*, 57 (emphasis added); see also 148.

48. See Wright, *Really Said*, 98; Wright, *Justification*, 232.

49. I have taken this list of verses from John Piper, *The Future of Justification: A Response to N. T. Wright* (Wheaton, IL: Crossway, 2007), 167–80. On those pages, Piper has an excellent discussion of each of these passages.

In Romans 4:6, Paul is speaking about righteousness that does not come from our own effort ("works") but from the fact that God imputes it to us (God "counts" it as ours; Greek *logizomai*, elsewhere used as an accounting term to refer to giving a credit or debit to someone's account).

> You are in Christ Jesus, who became to us wisdom from God, *righteousness* and sanctification and redemption. (1 Cor. 1:30)

> For our sake he made him to be sin who knew no sin, so that in him *we might become the righteousness of God*. (2 Cor. 5:21)

In 2 Corinthians 5:21, we have the imputation of our sin to Christ and the imputation of his righteousness ("the righteousness of God") to us.

> That I may gain Christ and be found in him, not having a righteousness of my own that comes from the law, but that which comes *through faith in Christ*, the *righteousness from God* that depends on faith. (Phil. 3:8–9)

Again Paul emphasizes that he is not depending on his righteousness but on the righteousness that God imparts to him (or imputes to him) through his faith in Christ.

John Piper also points out that if God did not impute Christ's righteousness to us, then God could never truthfully say that we are righteous: "An omniscient, just judge does not say that a defendant has moral righteousness when he is guilty of having no moral righteousness (Rom. 3:10)—unless there is a way that an alien moral righteousness can be counted as his."[50] In other words, *God would be untruthful* if he declared us to be righteous when in fact we were not righteous in ourselves and we did not have Christ's righteousness imputed to us. He would be calling us "righteous" when in fact we were not!

**d. An Incorrect Understanding of the Gospel.** Wright says that "the gospel" is "not an account of how people get saved. It is . . . the proclamation of the Lordship of Jesus Christ."[51]

The Lordship of Christ is clearly *a part* of the New Testament proclamation of the gospel. But Wright is wrong when he says that the gospel is not a message about "how one gets saved." The proclamation of the gospel in Acts certainly includes, again and again, an explanation of "how to get saved," and also—a crucial emphasis not found in *What Saint Paul Really Said*—just *how a person's sins can be forgiven*. How an individual can be "saved" and how a person can have his or her sins forgiven by Christ are themes that repeat again and again in the gospel proclamation found in Acts:

---

50. Piper, *The Future of Justification*, 77.  51. Wright, *Really Said*, 133.

It shall come to pass that everyone who calls upon the name of the Lord *shall be saved*. (Acts 2:21)

Peter said to them, "*Repent* and be baptized every one of you in the name of Jesus Christ *for the forgiveness of your sins*, and you will receive the gift of the Holy Spirit." (Acts 2:38)

The Lord added to their number day by day those who *were being saved*. (Acts 2:47)

*Repent* therefore, and turn back, that your *sins may be blotted out*. (Acts 3:19)

There is *salvation* in no one else, for there is no other name under heaven given among men by which we *must be saved*. (Acts 4:12)

God exalted him at his right hand as Leader and Savior, to give *repentance* to Israel and *forgiveness of sins*. (Acts 5:31)

Send to Joppa and bring Simon who is called Peter; he will declare to you a message by which you *will be saved*, you and all your household. (Acts 11:13–14)

Let it be known to you therefore, brothers, that through this man *forgiveness of sins* is proclaimed to you. (Acts 13:38)

But we believe that we *will be saved* through the grace of the Lord Jesus, just as they will. (Acts 15:11)

Then he brought them out and said, "Sirs, what must I do *to be saved*?" And they said, "Believe in the Lord Jesus, and you *will be saved*, you and your household." (Acts 16:30–31)

The times of ignorance God overlooked, but now he commands all people everywhere to *repent*. (Acts 17:30)

I have appeared to you for this purpose, to appoint you as a servant and witness to the things in which you have seen me and to those in which I will appear to you, delivering you from your people and from the Gentiles—to whom I am sending you to open their eyes, so that they may turn from darkness to light and from the power of Satan to God, that they may receive *forgiveness of sins* and a place among those who are sanctified by faith in me. (Acts 26:16–18)

There are many similar verses in the Epistles as well,[52] but I will quote only one, which is Paul's summary of "the gospel," a statement in which he says the gospel that he preaches is clearly about "how to be saved":

> Now I would remind you, brothers, of *the gospel I preached to you*, which you received, in which you stand, and *by which you are being saved*, if you hold fast to the word I preached to you—unless you believed in vain. (1 Cor. 15:1–2)

Therefore, I conclude that Wright's claim that the gospel is not about "how to be saved" is contradicted by an entire series of New Testament passages.

The tragic result of this misunderstanding is that I can find no clear explanation in Wright's books *What Saint Paul Really Said* and *Justification* of the need for individual sinners to repent of their sins and turn to Christ in faith, asking God to forgive their sins and bring them into a personal relationship with him. Yes, he does say briefly that "the way in which people appropriate that justification, that redefinition of God's people, is now 'by faith,' by coming to believe in Jesus as Messiah,"[53] but even in that mention of faith, there is no hint of the need for repentance from sin or in the need for a personal "receiving" of Christ, trusting in him as a living person. There is no emphasis like "but to all who did *receive him*, who *believed in* his name, he gave the right to become children of God, who were born, not of blood nor of the will of the flesh nor of the will of man, but of God" (John 1:12–13).[54] (See chapter 33, above, on the gospel call.) In fact, Wright goes so far as to say in one place that "*Faith . . . is never and in no way a qualification*, provided from the human side, either *for getting into God's family* or for staying there once in."[55] Really? Faith is in no way a qualification for getting into God's family?

The result is a deeply muddled and unclear gospel message. Piper rightly says, "Following N. T. Wright in his understanding of justification will result in a kind of preaching that will at best be confusing to the church."[56] Piper also rightly observes, "The kind of gospel preaching that will flow from Wright's spring . . . will not deal personally with the human heart of sin with clear declarations of *how* Christ dealt with sin and *how* the fearful heart can find rest in the gospel of grace."[57] By denying that the gospel is about "how people get saved," he leaves his readers of these two influential books in the dark about how to get saved.

---

52. See Rom. 8:24; 10:1, 9–13; 11:26; 1 Cor. 1:18; 3:15; 10:33; 2 Cor. 2:15; Eph. 2:5, 8; 1 Thess. 2:16; 2 Thess. 2:10, 13; 1 Tim. 2:4; 2 Tim. 1:9; Titus 3:5.

53. Wright, *Justification*, 117.

54. I have not searched through more of Wright's numerous books and articles to see if he explains anywhere else what he calls "how to get saved." It is possible that elsewhere in his writings he explains the need not just to acknowledge the fact that Jesus is Lord and the true Messiah, but also the need to personally, individually place one's trust in him as a living Savior.

55. Wright, *Really Said*, 160 (emphasis added). Similarly, he says that faith "is not something one does in order to gain admittance into the covenant people. It is the badge that proclaims that one is already a member" (ibid., 132).

56. Piper, *Future of Justification*, 165.

57. Ibid., 101.

**e. An Incorrect Understanding of First-Century Judaism.**[58] Wright claims that first century Judaism was not a religion of works-righteousness, that is, a religion of seeking to merit God's favor by living a life of obedience to his laws. Instead, they also believed in salvation by God's grace.

Stephen Westerholm replies that there is an important distinction. He quotes E. P. Sanders himself to point out that Judaism did not have a doctrine of the "essential sinfulness" of humankind, and this meant that God's grace could be understood as working *along with* human "works" to produce an acceptable life in God's sight.

But Paul's teaching is significantly different: human beings are "dead" in "trespasses and sins" (Eph. 2:1) and of themselves they "cannot please God" (Rom. 8:8). "None is righteous, no, not one" (Rom. 3:10) Therefore, according to Paul's gospel, salvation must be by *grace alone*, on the basis of *Christ's work alone*. Stephen Westerholm concludes that Paul understood justification "in terms of an exclusive reliance on grace in a way that was foreign to the thinking of contemporary Jews."[59]

Therefore, Wright is incorrect in thinking that first century Judaism and Pauline Christianity were quite similar in their understanding of salvation by grace, for Judaism had no doctrine of salvation by grace alone. In addition, several New Testament passages make clear that first century Judaism was not teaching a message of salvation compatible with the Christian gospel:

> But woe to you, scribes and Pharisees, hypocrites! For *you shut the kingdom of heaven* in people's faces. For *you neither enter yourselves nor allow those who would enter to go in.* Woe to you, scribes and Pharisees, hypocrites! For you travel across sea and land to make a single proselyte, and when he becomes a proselyte, you make him twice as much a child of hell as yourselves. (Matt. 23:13–15)

> Brothers, my heart's desire and prayer to God for them [Paul's fellow Jews] is that they may be saved. For I bear them witness that they have a zeal for God, but not according to knowledge. For, *being ignorant of the righteousness of God, and seeking to establish their own*, they did not submit to God's righteousness. For Christ is the end of the law for righteousness to everyone who believes. (Rom. 10:1–4)

> For we are the circumcision, who worship by the Spirit of God and glory in Christ Jesus and put no confidence in the flesh—though I myself have reason for confidence in the flesh also. If anyone else thinks he has reason for confidence in the flesh, I have

---

58. An extensive critique of new perspective understandings of first century justification is found in *Justification and Variegated Nomism*, ed. D. A. Carson, Peter T. O'Brien, and Mark A. Siefred, 2 vols. (Tübingen: Mohr Siebeck; Grand Rapids: Baker, 2001, 2004).

59. Stephen Westerholm, *Justification Reconsidered: Rethinking a Pauline Theme* (Grand Rapids: Eerdmans, 2013), 33–34.

more: circumcised on the eighth day, *of the people of Israel*, of the tribe of Benjamin, *a Hebrew of Hebrews; as to the law, a Pharisee*; as to zeal, a persecutor of the church; as to righteousness under the law, blameless. But *whatever gain I had, I counted as loss for the sake of Christ*. (Phil. 3:3–7)

Even when speaking of the Jewish people throughout the time of the Old Testament, the New Testament writers do not teach that all Jewish people were saved by election because they belonged to the covenant people of Israel but rather that those who did not have personal faith were not saved:

> For no one is a Jew who is merely one outwardly, nor is circumcision outward and physical. But *a Jew is one inwardly*, and circumcision is a matter of the heart, by the Spirit, not by the letter. His praise is not from man but from God. (Rom. 2:28–29)

> Not all who are descended from Israel belong to Israel. (Rom. 9:6)

> Nevertheless, *with most of them God was not pleased*, for they were overthrown in the wilderness. (1 Cor. 10:5)

> [Speaking of the people of Israel who left Egypt in the exodus:] For who were those who heard and yet rebelled? Was it not all those who left Egypt led by Moses? And with whom was he provoked for forty years? Was it not with those who sinned, whose bodies fell in the wilderness? And to whom did he swear that *they would not enter his rest*, but to those who were disobedient? So we see that *they were unable to enter because of unbelief*. . . . The message they heard did not benefit them, because they were not *united by faith* with those who listened. (Heb. 3:16–4:2)

**f. One Reason for the Attractiveness of Wright's View: Fewer Differences with Judaism and Roman Catholicism.** It is not difficult to understand one reason why Wright's view of justification has gained such an enthusiastic following among many evangelicals, especially in academic circles. It is not always easy to continue to claim that justification (when understood as gaining right legal standing before God) is an essential part of how we become true Christians and that justification is by grace *alone* through faith *alone* in Christ *alone*. This is uncomfortable because it implicitly condemns our Jewish friends who have not placed their trust in Christ and our Roman Catholic friends who believe that justification is a life-long process of internal moral change that comes about through God's grace *plus* the use of the sacraments.

But on Wright's view of justification, these differences are minimized. Wright believes that, if we follow Sanders in understanding the role of grace in first century Judaism, a benefit will be that "Christians should regard Jews with a good deal more respect than in the past." He adds, "Pauline Christians and the successors of first-century Palestinian Judaism should not anathematize each other as they have often been wont to do."[60] In response, I agree that Wright's view of the Christian gospel results in fewer clear differences with Judaism. But his view also minimizes or omits the (supposed) offensiveness of proclaiming the New Testament gospel that people need to repent of their sins and trust in Jesus alone, not in any of their own works, for forgiveness of sins and right standing before God.

Wright's view also minimizes our differences with Roman Catholic friends. We no longer have to maintain that justification happens at the beginning of the Christian life and that it is part of what it means to become a true Christian.[61] That may make the new perspective on justification attractive to some. But it cannot make the view faithful to the New Testament itself.

## QUESTIONS FOR PERSONAL APPLICATION

1. Are you confident that God has declared you "not guilty" forever in his sight? Do you know when that happened in your own life? Did you do or think anything that resulted in God's justifying of you? Did you do anything to deserve justification? If you are not sure that God has justified you fully and for all time, is there something you need to do before that will happen? What would persuade you that God has certainly justified you?

2. If you think of yourself standing before God on the day of judgment, would you think that it is enough simply to have your sins all forgiven, or would you also feel a need to have the righteousness of Christ reckoned to your account?

3. Do you think the difference between the Roman Catholic and Protestant understanding of justification is an important one? Describe how you would feel about your relationship to God if you held the Roman Catholic view of justification. Do modern Roman Catholics you know seem to hold to this traditional Roman Catholic view of justification, or do they have another view?

4. Have you ever wondered if God is still continuing to punish you from time to time for sins you have done in the past, even long ago? How does the doctrine of justification help you deal with those feelings?

### Special Terms

*covenantal nomism*
*forensic*
*impute*
*infused righteousness*
*justification*
*new perspective on Paul*

60. Wright, *Really Said*, 19.    61. Piper, *Future of Justification*, 181–83.

# BIBLIOGRAPHY

(For an explanation of this bibliography see the note on the bibliography to chapter 1, pp. 23–24. Complete bibliographical data may be found on pp. 1489–96.)

## SECTIONS IN EVANGELICAL SYSTEMATIC THEOLOGIES

### 1. Anglican (Episcopalian)
1882–92 .....Litton, 265–320
1930.........Thomas, 184–98, 210–20
2001.........Packer, 164–66
2013.........Bird, 540–41
2013.........Bray, 508–24

### 2. Arminian (Wesleyan or Methodist)
1875–76 .....Pope, 2:358–62, 402–51
1892–94 .....Miley, 2:309–26
1940.........Wiley, 2:379–401
1960.........Purkiser, 287–92
1992.........Oden, 3:108–76
2002.........Cottrell, 318–31

### 3. Baptist
1767.........Gill, 1:291–300; 2:68–93
1887.........Boyce, 394–404
1907.........Strong, 846–68
1990–95 .....Garrett, 2:285–300
2007.........Akin, 745–53
2013.........Erickson, 883–90

### 4. Dispensational
1947.........Chafer, 3:238–46
1949.........Thiessen, 271–76
1986.........Ryrie, 298–300
2002–2005 ..Geisler, 3:227–29, 235–37, 477–78

2017.........MacArthur and Mayhue, 609–23

### 5. Lutheran
1917–24 .....Pieper, 2:3–54, 503–57
1934.........Mueller, 242–54, 367–83

### 6. Reformed (or Presbyterian)
1559.........Calvin, 1:725–833 (3.11–18)
1679–85 .....Turretin, IET, 1:72, 617–19, 2:250, 575–83, 633–88, 3:67
1871–73 .....Hodge, 3:114–212
1878.........Dabney, 618–50
1887–1921 ...Warfield, BTS, 262–68
1894.........Shedd, 793–802
1906–11 .....Bavinck, RD, 4:176–229
1910.........Vos, 4:133–81
1937–66 .....Murray, CW, 2:202–22; RAA, 117–31
1938.........Berkhof, 510–26
1998.........Reymond, 739–56
2008.........Van Genderen and Velema, 606–44
2011.........Horton, 620–47
2013.........Frame, 902, 964–75
2013.........Culver, 733–43
2016.........Allen and Swain, 268–83
2017.........Barrett, 511–45
2019.........Letham, 677–705

### 7. Renewal (or charismatic/Pentecostal)
1988–92 .....Williams, 2:61–82
1993.........Menzies and Horton, 105–06
1995.........Horton, 365–67
2008.........Duffield and Van Cleave, 225–33

## Sections in Representative Roman Catholic Systematic Theologies

### 1. Roman Catholic: Traditional

1955 . . . . . . . . Ott, 250–69

### 2. Roman Catholic: Post–Vatican II

2012 . . . . . . . . CCC, paragraphs 1987–94

## Other Works

Allison, Gregg. *Historical Theology: An Introduction to Christian Doctrine: A Companion to Wayne Grudem's* Systematic Theology. Grand Rapids: Zondervan, 2011, 498–519.

Arnold, Brian J. *Justification in the Second Century.* Berlin: De Gruyter, 2017; Waco, TX: Baylor University Press, 2018.

Berkouwer, G. C. *Faith and Justification.* Translated by Lewis B. Smedes. Grand Rapids: Eerdmans, 1954.

Carson, D. A., ed. *Right with God: Justification in the Bible and the World.* Grand Rapids: Baker, 1992.

Demarest, Bruce. *The Cross and Salvation: The Doctrine of Salvation.* Wheaton, IL: Crossway, 2006, 27–43.

Dunn, James D. G. *The New Perspective on Paul.* Rev. ed. Tübingen: Mohr Siebeck, 2005; Grand Rapids: Eerdmans, 2008.

Hoekema, Anthony A. "Justification." In *Saved by Grace,* 152–91. Grand Rapids: Eerdmans, and Exeter: Paternoster, 1989.

Kärkkäinen, V.-M. "Justification." In *GDT,* 447–52.

Keathley, Kenneth. "The Work of God: Salvation." In *A Theology for the Church,* edited by Daniel L. Akin et al., 745–53. Nashville: B&H, 2007.

Lugioyo, B. "Justification." In *NDT2,* 480–83.

McGrath, Alister E. *Iustitia Dei: A History of the Christian Doctrine of Justification.* 2 vols. Cambridge: Cambridge University Press, 1986.

———. "Justification." In *DPL,* 517–23.

———. *Justification by Faith: An Introduction.* Grand Rapids: Zondervan, 1988.

Morris, Leon. *The Apostolic Preaching of the Cross.* 3rd ed. Grand Rapids: Eerdmans, 1965, 251–98.

———. "Justification." In *BTDB,* 441–43.

Murray, John. "Justification." In *Redemption Accomplished and Applied,* 117–31. Grand Rapids: Eerdmans, 1955.

Packer, J. I. et al. *Here We Stand: Justification by Faith Today.* London: Hodder and Stoughton, 1986.

———. "Justification." In *EDT1,* 593–97.

Pink, A. W. *The Doctrines of Election and Justification.* Grand Rapids: Baker, 1974.

Piper, John. *The Future of Justification: A Response to N. T. Wright.* Wheaton, IL: Crossway, 2007,

Schreiner, Thomas R. "Justification: The Saving Righteousness of God in Christ," *JETS* 54, no. 1 (March 2011): 19–34

Seifrid, M. A. "Righteousness, Justice and Justification." In *NDBT,* 740–45.

Thomas, Matthew T. *Paul's "Works of the Law" in the Perspective of Second-Century Reception.* Downers Grove, IL: IVP Academic, 2020.

Vickers, Brian J. *Jesus' Blood and Righteousness: Paul's Theology of Imputation.* Wheaton, IL: Crossway, 2006.

Westerholm, Stephen. *Justification Reconsidered: Rethinking a Pauline Theme.* Grand Rapids: Eerdmans, 2013.

Wright, N. T. "Justification." In *NDT1,* 359–61.

———. *Justification: God's Plan and Paul's Vision.* Downers Grove, IL: InterVarsity Press, 2009.

———. *What Saint Paul Really Said.* Grand Rapids: Eerdmans, 1997.

Ziesler, J. A. *The Meaning of Righteous in Paul.* Cambridge: Cambridge University, 1972.

# SCRIPTURE MEMORY PASSAGE

**Romans 3:27–28:** Then what becomes of our boasting? It is excluded. By what kind of law? By a law of works? No, but by the law of faith. For we hold that one is justified by faith apart from works of the law.

# HYMN

## "Jesus, Thy Blood and Righteousness"

Jesus, thy blood and righteousness
    My beauty are, my glorious dress;
'Midst flaming worlds, in these arrayed,
    With joy shall I lift up my head.

Bold shall I stand in thy great day;
    For who aught to my charge shall lay?
Fully absolved through these I am
    From sin and fear, from guilt and shame.

When from the dust of death I rise
    To claim my mansion in the skies,
Ev'n then this shall be all my plea,
    Jesus hath lived, hath died, for me.

Jesus, be endless praise to thee,
    Whose boundless mercy hath for me—
For me a full atonement made,
    An everlasting ransom paid.

O let the dead now hear thy voice;
    Now bid thy banished ones rejoice;
Their beauty this, their glorious dress,
    Jesus, thy blood and righteousness.

Author: Count Nikolaus Ludwig Von
Zinzendorf, 1739 (trans. John Wesley, 1740, alt.)

# CONTEMPORARY WORSHIP SONG

## "Before the Throne of God Above"

Before the throne of God above,
I have a strong and perfect plea,
A great High Priest whose name is Love,
Who ever lives and pleads for me.
My name is graven on His hands,
My name is written on His heart.
I know that while in heav'n He stands,
No tongue can bid me thence depart,
No tongue can bid me thence depart.

When Satan tempts me to despair
And tells me of the guilt within,
Upward I look and see Him there,
Who made an end to all my sin.
Because the sinless Savior died,
My sinful soul is counted free;
For God, the Just, is satisfied
To look on Him and pardon me,
To look on Him and pardon me.

*Chorus*
Hallelujah!
My life is found in Jesus Christ.
Hallelujah!
For I am His and He is mine.

*Behold Him there, the risen Lamb,*
*My perfect, spotless righteousness,*
*The great unchangeable I Am,*
*The King of glory and of grace!*
*One with Himself I cannot die.*
*My soul is purchased with His blood!*
*My life is hid with Christ on high,*
*With Christ my Savior and my God,*
*With Christ my Savior and my God.*

*I bow before the cross of Christ,*
*And marvel at this love divine:*
*God's perfect Son was sacrificed*
*To make me righteous in God's eyes.*
*This river's depths I cannot know,*
*But I can glory in its flood.*
*The Lord Most High has bowed down low,*
*And poured on me His glorious love,*
*And poured on me His glorious love.*

Words by Charitie Bancroft and Vicki Cook[62]

# CHAPTER 37

# Adoption (Membership in God's Family)

*What are benefits of being a member of God's family?*

## EXPLANATION AND SCRIPTURAL BASIS

In regeneration God gives us new spiritual life within. In justification God gives us right legal standing before him. But in adoption God makes us members of his family. Therefore, the biblical teaching on adoption focuses much more on the personal relationships that salvation gives us with God and with his people.

### A. Scriptural Evidence for Adoption

We may define adoption as follows: *adoption is an act of God whereby he makes us members of his family.*

John mentions adoption at the beginning of his gospel, where he says, "But to all who did receive him, who believed in his name, he gave the right *to become children of God*" (John 1:12). By contrast, those who do not believe in Christ are not children of God or adopted into his family, but they are "children of wrath" (Eph. 2:3) and "sons of disobedience" (Eph. 2:2; 5:6). Although those Jews who rejected Christ tried to claim that God was their Father (John 8:41), Jesus told them, "If God were your Father, you would love me. . . . You are of your father the devil, and your will is to do your father's desires" (John 8:42–44).

The New Testament Epistles bear repeated testimony to the fact that we are now God's children in a special sense, members of his family. Paul says,

> For all who are led by the Spirit of God are *sons of God*. For you did not receive the spirit of slavery to fall back into fear, but you have received the *Spirit of adoption as sons*, by whom we cry, "Abba! Father!" The Spirit himself bears witness with our spirit that we are *children of God*, and if children, then heirs—heirs of God and fellow heirs with Christ, provided we suffer with him in order that we may also be glorified with him. (Rom. 8:14–17)

But if we are God's children, are we then related to one another as family members? Certainly so. In fact, this adoption into God's family makes us partakers together in *one family* even with the believing Jews of the Old Testament, for Paul says that we are Abraham's children as well: "Not all are children of Abraham because they are his offspring, but 'Through Isaac shall your offspring be named.' This means that it is not the children of the flesh who are the children of God, but the children of the promise are counted as offspring" (Rom. 9:7–8). He further explains in Galatians, "Now you, brothers, like Isaac, are children of promise. . . . We are not children of the slave but of the free woman" (Gal. 4:28, 31; cf. 1 Peter 3:6, where Peter sees believing women as daughters of Sarah in the new covenant).

Paul explains that this status of adoption as God's children was not fully realized in the old covenant. He says that "before faith came, we were held captive under the law . . . the law was our guardian until Christ came, in order that we might be justified by faith. But now that faith has come, we are no longer under a guardian, for *in Christ Jesus you are all sons of God, through faith*" (Gal. 3:23–26). This is not to say that the Old Testament completely omitted talk of God as our Father, for God did call himself the Father of the children of Israel and called them his children in several places (Ps. 103:13; Isa. 43:6–7; Mal. 1:6; 2:10). But even though there was a consciousness of God as Father to the people of Israel, the full benefits and privileges of membership in God's family, and the full realization of that membership, did not come until Christ came and the Spirit of the Son of God was poured into our hearts, bearing witness with our spirit that we were God's children.

What evidence do we see in our lives that we are God's children? Paul sees clear evidence in the fact that the Holy Spirit bears witness in our hearts that we are God's children: "But when the fullness of time had come, God sent forth his Son, born of woman, born under the law, to redeem those who were under the law, so that we might receive adoption as sons. And because *you are sons*, God has sent the Spirit of his Son *into our hearts, crying, 'Abba! Father!'* So you are no longer a slave, but a son, and if a son, then an heir through God" (Gal. 4:4–7).

John's first epistle places much emphasis on our status as children of God: "See what kind of love the Father has given to us, that we should be called *children of God;* and so we are. . . . Beloved, we are God's children now" (1 John 3:1–2; John frequently calls his readers "children" or "little children").[1]

Although Jesus does call us his "brothers" (Heb. 2:12), and he is therefore in one sense our older brother in God's family (cf. Heb. 2:14) and can be called "the firstborn among many brothers" (Rom. 8:29), he is nevertheless careful to make a clear distinction between the way in which God is our heavenly Father and the way in which he relates to God the Father. He says to Mary Magdalene, "I am ascending *to my Father and your Father*, to my God and your God" (John 20:17), thus making a distinction between the far greater and eternal sense in which God is his Father, and the sense in which God is our Father.

---

1. There are several other passages that speak about our status as God's children or our membership in his family (see Matt. 5:48; 7:11; 2 Cor. 6:18; Eph. 5:1; Phil. 2:15; Heb. 2:13–14; 12:5–11; 1 Peter 1:14; 1 John 3:10).

Although the New Testament says that we are *now* God's children (1 John 3:2), we should also note that there is another sense in which our adoption is still future because we will not receive the full benefits and privileges of adoption until Christ returns and we have new resurrection bodies. Paul speaks of this later, fuller sense of adoption when he says, "Not only the creation, but we ourselves, who have the firstfruits of the Spirit, groan inwardly as we wait eagerly for adoption as sons, *the redemption of our bodies*" (Rom. 8:23). Here Paul sees the receiving of new resurrection bodies as the fulfillment of our privileges of adoption, so much so that he can refer to it as our "adoption as sons."

## B. Adoption Follows Conversion and Is an Outcome of Saving Faith

We might initially think that we would become God's children by regeneration, since the imagery of being "born again" in regeneration makes us think of children being born into a human family. But the New Testament never connects adoption with regeneration; indeed, the idea of *adoption* is opposite to the idea of being born into a family!

Rather, the New Testament connects adoption with saving faith and says that in response to our trusting in Christ, God has adopted us into his family. Paul says, "In Christ Jesus you are all *sons of God, through faith*" (Gal. 3:26). And John writes, "But to all who did receive him, who *believed in his name*, he gave the right *to become children of God*" (John 1:12).[2] These two verses make it clear that adoption follows conversion and is God's response to our faith.

One objection to this might be brought from Paul's statement, "*Because you are sons*, God has sent the Spirit of his Son into our hearts, crying, 'Abba! Father!'" (Gal. 4:6). Someone might understand this verse to mean that first God adopted us as sons and then gave us the Holy Spirit to bring regeneration to our hearts. But a few verses earlier Paul had said that we have become sons of God "through faith" (Gal. 3:26). Therefore Paul's statement in Galatians 4:6 is best understood not to refer to the giving of the Holy Spirit in regeneration but rather to an additional activity of the Holy Spirit in which he begins to bear witness with our spirit and to assure us that we are members of God's family. This work of the Holy Spirit gives us *assurance* of our adoption, and it is in this sense that Paul says that, after we have become sons, God causes his Holy Spirit within our hearts to cry, "Abba! Father!" (cf. Rom. 8:15–16).

## C. Adoption Is Distinct from Justification

Although adoption is a privilege that comes to us at the time we become Christians (John 1:12; Gal. 3:26; 1 John 3:1–2), it is nevertheless a privilege that is distinct from justification and distinct from regeneration. In regeneration we are made spiritually

---

2. It is true that in John 1:13 he specifies that these were people who were born "of God," but this is simply giving additional information about them (namely, that they had been regenerated by God). That does not negate the fact that it was to those who "believed in his name" that Christ gave power to become children of God.

alive, able to relate to God in prayer and worship and able to hear his Word with receptive hearts. But it is possible that God could have creatures who are spiritually alive and yet are not members of his family and do not share the special privileges of family members—angels, for example, apparently fall into that category.[3] Therefore, it would have been possible for God to decide to give us regeneration without the great privileges of adoption into his family.

Moreover, God could have given us justification without the privileges of adoption into his family, for he could have forgiven our sins and given us right legal standing before him without making us his children. It is important to realize this because it helps us to recognize how great are our privileges in adoption. Regeneration has to do with our spiritual life within. Justification has to do with our standing before God's law. But adoption has to do with our *relationship* with God as our Father, and in adoption we are given many of the greatest blessings that we will know for eternity. When we begin to realize the excellence of these blessings, and when we appreciate that God has no obligation to give us any of them, then we will be able to exclaim with the apostle John, "See *what kind of love* the Father has given to us, that we should be called children of God; and so we are" (1 John 3:1).

## D. The Privileges of Adoption

The benefits or privileges that accompany adoption are seen, first, in the way God relates to us, and then also in the way we relate to one another as brothers and sisters in God's family.

One of the greatest privileges of our adoption is (1) being able to speak to God and *relate to him as a* good and loving *Father.* We are to pray, "Our Father in heaven" (Matt. 6:9), and we are to realize that we are "no longer a slave, but a son" (Gal. 4:7). Therefore, we now relate to God not as a slave relates to a slave master but as a child relates to his or her father. In fact, God gives us an *internal witness from the Holy Spirit* that causes us instinctively to call God our Father. "The Spirit himself bears witness with our spirit that we are children of God" (Rom. 8:15–16). This relationship to God as our Father is the foundation of many other blessings of the Christian life, and it becomes the primary way we relate to God. Certainly God is our Creator, our judge, our Lord and Master, our teacher, our provider and protector, and the one who by his providential care sustains our existence. But the role that is most intimate and the role that conveys the highest privileges of fellowship with God for eternity is his role as our heavenly Father.

---

3. Although both good and evil angels are in one place in Scripture called "the sons of God" (Job 1:6), this is apparently a reference to the status of sonship that comes by the fact that God created them. It does not seem to indicate that angels generally (especially evil angels) share in any of the family privileges that we receive as God's children. In fact, Heb. 2:14–16 makes a clear distinction between our status as God's children and the status of angels. Moreover, angels are nowhere else referred to as members of God's family or said to have the family privileges that belong to us as God's children. (It is unlikely that Gen. 6:2–4 refers to angels; see Wayne Grudem, *The First Epistle of Peter*, TNTC [Leicester: Inter-Varsity; Grand Rapids: Eerdmans, 1988], 211–15.)

The fact that God relates to us as Father (2) shows very clearly that he *loves us* (1 John 3:1), (3) shows that he *understands us* ("As a father shows compassion to his children, so the LORD shows compassion to those who fear him. For he knows our frame; he remembers that we are dust" [Ps. 103:13–14]), and (4) shows that he *takes care of our needs* ("For the Gentiles seek after all these things, and your heavenly Father knows that you need them all" [Matt. 6:32]). Moreover, in his role as our Father, (5) God *gives us many good gifts*: "If you then, who are evil, know how to give good gifts to your children, how much more will your Father who is in heaven give good things to those who ask him!" (Matt. 7:11). He especially (6) *gives us* the gift of *the Holy Spirit* to comfort us and to empower us for ministry and for living the Christian life (Luke 11:13).[4] In fact, it is not only gifts in this life that God gives to us, but he also (7) gives us a great *inheritance in heaven*, because we have become joint heirs with Christ. Paul says, "You are no longer a slave, but a son, and if a son, then an heir" (Gal. 4:7); we are in fact "heirs of God and fellow heirs with Christ" (Rom. 8:17). As heirs we have the rights to a great eternal "inheritance that is imperishable, undefiled, and unfading, kept in heaven for you" (1 Peter 1:4). All the great privileges and blessings of heaven are laid up for us and put at our disposal because we are children of the King, members of the royal family, princes and princesses who will reign with Christ over the new heavens and new earth (Rev. 2:26–27; 3:21). As a foretaste of this great privilege, (8) angels are even now sent to minister to and serve us (Heb. 1:14).

It is in the context of this relationship with God as our heavenly Father that we are to understand the prayer that Jesus told his disciples to pray daily, "*Our Father* in heaven . . . *forgive us our sins*, as we also have forgiven those who sin against us" (Matt. 6:9–12, author's translation). This daily prayer for forgiveness of sins is not a prayer that God would give us justification again and again throughout our lives, for justification is a one-time event that occurs immediately after we trust in Christ with saving faith. Rather, the prayer for forgiveness of sins each day is a prayer that God's fatherly relationship with us, which has been disrupted by sin that displeased him, be restored, and that he relate to us once again as a Father who delights in his children whom he loves. The prayer, "Forgive us our sins," therefore, is one in which we are relating not to God as eternal judge of the universe but to God as Father. It is a prayer in which we wish to restore the open fellowship with our Father that has been broken because of sin (see also 1 John 1:9; 3:19–22).

The privilege of (9) being *led by the Holy Spirit* is also a benefit of adoption. Paul indicates that this is a benefit whereby the Holy Spirit guides us in daily decisions and puts in us desires to obey God and live according to his will. He says, "All who are *led by*

---

4. In this verse Jesus says, "If you then, who are evil, know how to give good gifts to your children, how much more will the heavenly Father give the Holy Spirit to those who ask him!" Here he seems to mean not the gift of the Holy Spirit dwelling within as he comes at regeneration, but the gift of further empowering for ministry, for gifts to be used in ministry, or for Christian living.

*the Spirit of God* are *sons of God*" (Rom. 8:14), and he gives this as the *reason* Christians should "put to death the deeds of the body" by means of the Holy Spirit working within them (v. 13; note "for" at the beginning of v. 14). He sees the Holy Spirit as leading and guiding God's children in paths of obedience to God.

Another privilege of adoption into God's family, though we do not always recognize it as a privilege, is the fact that (10) God *disciplines us* as his children. "My son, do not regard lightly the discipline of the Lord, nor be weary when reproved by him. For the Lord disciplines the one he loves, and chastises every son whom he receives" (Heb. 12:5–6, quoting Prov. 3:11–12). The author of Hebrews explains, "God is treating you as sons. For what son is there whom his father does not discipline? . . . he disciplines us for our good, that we may share his holiness" (Heb. 12:7, 10). Just as earthly children grow in obedience and righteousness when they are disciplined properly by their earthly fathers, so we grow in righteousness and holiness when we are disciplined by our heavenly Father.

Related to the fatherly discipline of God is the fact that, as children of God and joint heirs with Christ, we have (11) the *privilege of sharing both in his sufferings and in his subsequent glory.* Just as it was "necessary that the Christ should suffer these things and enter into his glory" (Luke 24:26), so God gives us the privilege of walking the same path that Christ walked, enduring sufferings in this life that we may also receive great glory in the life to come: "If children, then heirs—heirs of God and fellow heirs with Christ, *provided we suffer with him* in order that we may also be *glorified with him*" (Rom. 8:17).

In addition to these great privileges that concern our relationship to God and fellowship with him, we also have privileges of adoption that affect the way that we relate to each other and affect our own personal conduct. Because we are God's children, our relationship with each other is far deeper and more intimate than the relationship that angels, for example, have to one another, for (12) we are all *members of one family.* Many times the New Testament refers to Christians as brothers and sisters in Christ (Rom. 1:13; 8:12; 1 Cor. 1:10; 6:8; James 1:2; Matt. 12:50; Rom. 16:1; 1 Cor. 7:15; Philem. 1:2; James 2:15).

We could add here the many verses in which entire churches are referred to as "brothers" (Rom. 1:13; 8:12; 1 Cor. 1:10; 2 Cor. 1:8). These should not be understood to refer to the men in the congregation only but are rather generic references to the whole church and, except where the context explicitly indicates otherwise, should be taken to mean "brothers and sisters in the Lord."[5] The designation "brother" is so common in the Epistles that it seems to be the predominant way in which the New Testament authors refer to the other Christians to whom they are writing. This indicates the strong consciousness they had of the nature of the church as the family of God. In fact,

---

5. A footnote to the word *brothers* in these and many other passages in the ESV explains, "Or *brothers and sisters.* In New Testament usage, depending on the context, the plural Greek word *adelphoi* (translated "brothers") may refer either to brothers or to *brothers and sisters.*"

Paul tells Timothy to relate to the church at Ephesus and to the individuals within the church as he would relate to members of a large family: "Do not rebuke an older man but encourage him as you would a *father*, younger men *as brothers*, older women *as mothers*, younger women *as sisters*, in all purity" (1 Tim. 5:1–2).[6]

This concept of the church as God's family should give us a new perspective on the work of the church; it is "family work," and the various members of the family never should compete with each other or hinder one another in their efforts but should encourage one another and be thankful for whatever good or whatever progress comes to any member of the family, for all are contributing to the good of the family and the honor of God our Father. In fact, just as members of an earthly family often have times of joy and fellowship when they work together on a single project, so our times of working together in building up the church ought to be times of great joy and fellowship with one another. Just as members of an earthly family honor their parents and fulfill the purpose of a family most when they eagerly welcome any brothers or sisters who are newly adopted into that family, so we ought to welcome new members of the family of Christ eagerly and with love.

Another aspect of our membership in God's family is that, as God's children, (13) we are to *imitate our Father* in heaven in all our conduct. Paul says, "Be imitators of God, as beloved children" (Eph. 5:1). Peter echoes this theme when he says, "As obedient children, do not be conformed to the passions of your former ignorance, but as he who called you is holy, you also be holy in all your conduct, since it is written, 'You shall be holy, for I am holy'" (1 Peter 1:14–16). Both Peter and Paul realize that it is natural for children to imitate their earthly fathers. They appeal to this natural sense that children have in order to remind us that we are to imitate our heavenly Father—indeed, this should be something we naturally want to do and delight in. If God our Father in heaven is holy, we should be holy as obedient children.

When we walk in paths of righteous conduct (14) *by our obedience we honor our heavenly Father* and bring glory to him. When we act in a way that is pleasing to God, we are to do so that others "may see your good works and give glory to your Father who is in heaven" (Matt. 5:16). Paul encourages the Philippians to maintain pure conduct before unbelievers "that you may be blameless and innocent, *children of God* without blemish in the midst of a crooked and twisted generation, among whom you shine as lights in the world" (Phil. 2:15). Indeed, a consistent pattern of moral conduct is also evidence that we are truly children of God. John says, "By this it is evident who are the children of God, and who are the children of the devil: whoever does not practice righteousness is not of God, nor is the one who does not love his brother" (1 John 3:10).

---

6. An extensive analysis of the New Testament teaching on the church as a family is found in Vern S. Poythress, "The Church as a Family: Why Male Leadership in the Family Requires Male Leadership in the Church as Well," in *Recovering Biblical Manhood and Womanhood: A Response to Evangelical Feminism*, ed. John Piper and Wayne Grudem (Wheaton, IL: Crossway, 1991), 233–47.

## QUESTIONS FOR PERSONAL APPLICATION

1. Look back over the list of privileges that come with our adoption as God's children. Had you previously thought of these as automatically yours because you had been born again? Can you describe what our eternal life would be like if we had regeneration and justification and many of the other privileges that come with salvation, but no adoption into God's family? Now how do you feel about the fact that God has adopted you into his family compared with the way you felt before reading this chapter?

2. Has your relationship with your own human family become better or more difficult as a result of your becoming a Christian? If your relationship with your earthly family has become more difficult, how have you found Mark 10:29–30 to be true in your life as a Christian?

3. Sometimes people who have had unloving or cruel earthly fathers have found that their background creates difficulty in their thinking about God and relating to him as a heavenly Father. How can Hebrews 12:10; Matthew 7:11; and Luke 11:13, which contrast sinful earthly fathers with our perfect Father in heaven, be of help in that situation? Might 1 Peter 1:18 be helpful in this situation as well? What can a person who has had a cruel and unloving earthly father do to gain a better and better appreciation of who God is and what kind of Father he is? Do you think that any of the people who became Christians in the first century had cruel and unloving fathers, or no living fathers at all? What teachings of the Old Testament would have helped them at this point? Do you think that people who have had evil earthly fathers have a God-given inward sense of what a good father would be like?

4. Think of the people who are members of your church. Has this chapter helped you to think of them more as your brothers and sisters (or if they are older, as those who are like "fathers" and "mothers" to you)? How do you think an added appreciation of this idea of the church as a family would be helpful to your church? How could you encourage a greater appreciation of this idea?

5. Does your church have any sense of competition with other churches that might be overcome by greater appreciation of the doctrine of adoption?

6. In the human family, when one of the children commits a crime and is publicly punished for it, the entire family suffers shame. On the other hand, when a family member is honored for an outstanding achievement, the entire family is proud and rejoices. How does this analogy of events in a human family make you feel about your own personal level of holiness in life, and the way it reflects on the other members of your spiritual family? How does it make you feel about the need for personal holiness among your brothers and sisters in the church? Do you personally have a strong inward desire to imitate your heavenly Father in your conduct (Eph. 5:1; 1 Peter 1:14–16)?

7. Do you sense the Holy Spirit within you bearing witness with your spirit that you are a child of God (Rom. 8:15–16; Gal. 4:6)? Can you describe what that sense is like?

8. Do you sense any discrimination against Christians of other races or other social or economic positions? Can you understand how the doctrine of adoption should obliterate such distinctions in the church (see Gal. 3:26–28)? Can you also see how the doctrine of adoption means that neither men nor women should think of the other sex as more important or less important in the church (see Gal. 3:28)?

**Special Terms**
*adoption*

# BIBLIOGRAPHY

(For an explanation of this bibliography see the note on the bibliography to chapter 1, pp. 23–24. Complete bibliographical data may be found on pp. 1489–96.)

Note: Many systematic theologies do not treat adoption as a separate topic, but include a discussion of the privileges of adoption in a discussion of justification and its results.

## SECTIONS IN EVANGELICAL SYSTEMATIC THEOLOGIES

### 1. Anglican (Episcopalian)
2001........Packer, 167–68
2013........Bird, 571–72

### 2. Arminian (Wesleyan or Methodist)
1875–76.....Pope, 3:1–27
1892–94.....Miley, 2:337–38
1940........Wiley, 2:402–39
1960........Purkiser, 297–98
1992........Oden, 3:47, 83, 127, 158, 193–94, 199

### 3. Baptist
1767........Gill, 1:288–91; 2:93–107
1887........Boyce, 404–9
1990–95.....Garrett, 2:313–34
2007........Akin, 745

2013........Erickson, 891–95

### 4. Dispensational
1947........Chafer, 3:241–43
1949........Thiessen, 278–82
1986........Ryrie, 301–2, 306–7
2002–2005 ..Geisler, 3:226
2017........MacArthur and Mayhue, 624, 31

### 5. Lutheran
1917–24 .....Pieper, 2:408–9

### 6. Reformed (or Presbyterian)
1679–85 .....Turretin, *IET*, 2:231, 656–59, 666–69
1894........Shedd, 715
1906–11 .....Bavinck, *RD*, 4:179, 226–27
1910.........Vos, 4:4, 45, 152, 155–57
1937–66 .....Murray, *CW*, 2:223–34; *RAA*, 132–40
1998........Reymond, 759–62
2008........Van Genderen and Velema, 541, 564, 641
2011........Horton, 620–47
2013........Frame, 975–80
2013........Culver, 744–46
2016........Allen and Swain, 268–83
2017........Barrett, 207–9

2019 . . . . . . . . Letham, 730–33

7. *Renewal (or charismatic/Pentecostal)*
1993 . . . . . . . . Menzies and Horton, 107–8
1995 . . . . . . . . Horton, 367–68
2008 . . . . . . . . Duffield and Van Cleave, 240–42

## SECTIONS IN REPRESENTATIVE ROMAN CATHOLIC SYSTEMATIC THEOLOGIES

1. *Roman Catholic: Traditional*
1955 . . . . . . . . Ott (no explicit treatment)

2. *Roman Catholic: Post–Vatican II*
2012 . . . . . . . . *CCC*, paragraphs 537, 1129, 1197, 1265, 1279

## OTHER WORKS

Brown, William E. "Adoption." In *BTDB*, 11–12.
Burke, Trevor J. *Adopted into God's Family: Exploring a Pauline Metaphor.* Downers Grove, IL: InterVarsity Press, 2006.
———. *Family Matters: A Socio-Historical Study of Kinship Metaphors in 1 Thessalonians.* New York: T&T Clark, 2003.
Ciampa, R. "Adoption." In *NDBT*, 376–78.
Davids, P. H. "Adoption." In *EDT*, 30–31.
Demarest, Bruce. *The Cross and Salvation: The Doctrine of Salvation.* Wheaton, IL: Crossway, 2006, 27–43.
Drane, J. "Sonship, Child, Children." In *DLNT*, 1115–17.
Garner, David B. *Sons in the Son: The Riches and Reach of Adoption in Christ.* Phillipsburg, NJ: P&R, 2016.
Heim, Erin M. *Adoption in Galatians and Romans: Contemporary Metaphor Theories and the Pauline Huiothesia Metaphors.* Leiden; Boston: Brill, 2017.
Kreitzer, L. J. "Adoption, Sonship." In *DPL*, 15–18.
Lewis, Robert Brian. *Paul's "Spirit of Adoption" in Its Roman Imperial Context.* London; New York: T&T Clark, 2016.
Murray, John. "Adoption." In *Redemption Accomplished and Applied.* Grand Rapids: Eerdmans, 1955, 132–40.
Webb, Robert Alexander. *The Reformed Doctrine of Adoption.* Grand Rapids: Eerdmans, 1947.
White, John L. *The Apostle of God: Paul and the Promise of Abraham.* Peabody, MA: Hendrickson, 1999.
Ziegler, Geoffrey M. *Free to Be Sons of God.* Philipsburg, NJ: P&R, 2018.

# SCRIPTURE MEMORY PASSAGE

**Romans 8:14–17:** For all who are led by the Spirit of God are sons of God. For you did not receive the spirit of slavery to fall back into fear, but you have received the Spirit of adoption as sons, by whom we cry, "Abba! Father!" The Spirit himself bears witness with our spirit that we are children of God, and if children, then heirs—heirs of God and fellow heirs with Christ, provided we suffer with him in order that we may also be glorified with him.

# HYMN

## "Children of the Heavenly Father"

*Children of the heav'nly Father
Safely in his bosom gather;*

*Nestling bird nor star in heaven
Such a refuge e'er was given.*

God his own doth tend and nourish,
  In his holy courts they flourish;
From all evil things he spares them,
  In his mighty arms he bears them.

Neither life nor death shall ever
  From the Lord his children sever;
Unto them his grace he showeth,
  And their sorrows all he knoweth.

Praise the Lord in joyful numbers,
  Your Protector never slumbers;
At the will of your Defender
  Every foeman must surrender.

Though he giveth or he taketh,
  God his children ne'er forsaketh;
His the loving purpose solely
  To preserve them pure and holy.

Author: Caroline V. Sandell Berg, c. 1855
(Trans. Ernst W. Olson, 1925)

## CONTEMPORARY WORSHIP SONG

### "All I Have Is Christ"

I once was lost in darkest night
Yet thought I knew the way.
The sin that promised joy and life
Had led me to the grave.
I had no hope that You would own
A rebel to Your will,
And if You had not loved me first
I would refuse You still.

But as I ran my hell-bound race
Indifferent to the cost.
You looked upon my helpless state
And led me to the cross.
And I beheld God's love displayed.
You suffered in my place.
You bore the wrath reserved for me.
Now all I know is grace.

*Chorus*
Hallelujah! All I have is Christ.
Hallelujah! Jesus is my life.

Now, Lord, I would be Yours alone
And live so all might see.
The strength to follow Your commands
Could never come from me.
O Father, use my ransomed life
In any way You choose,
And let my song forever be.
My only boast is You.

Words by Jordan Kauflin[7]

# CHAPTER 38

# Sanctification (Growth in Likeness to Christ)

*How do we grow in Christian maturity?*
*What are the blessings of Christian growth?*

## EXPLANATION AND SCRIPTURAL BASIS

The previous chapters have discussed several acts of God that occur at the beginning of our Christian lives: the gospel call (which God addresses to us), regeneration (by which God imparts new life to us), justification (by which God gives us right legal standing before him), and adoption (in which God makes us members of his family). We have also discussed conversion (in which we repent of sins and trust in Christ for salvation). These events all occur at the beginning of our Christian lives.[1]

But now we come to a part of the application of redemption that is a *progressive* work throughout our earthly lives. It is also a work in which *God and believers cooperate*, each playing distinct roles. This part of the application of redemption is called sanctification: *sanctification is a progressive work of God and believers that makes us more and more free from sin and like Christ in our actual lives.*

### A. Differences between Justification and Sanctification

The following table specifies several differences between justification and sanctification:

| Justification | Sanctification |
|---|---|
| Legal standing | Internal condition |
| Once for all time | Continuous throughout life |
| Entirely God's work | We cooperate |
| Perfect in this life | Not perfect in this life |
| The same in all Christians | Greater in some than in others |

---

1. Although the initial saving faith by which we are justified occurs only at the time of conversion, faith and repentance do continue throughout our lives as well (see chapter 35, p. 878–79). Similarly, although regeneration, justification, and adoption are instantaneous one-time events that occur at the beginning of the Christian life, the results of all of these

924

As this chart indicates, sanctification is something that continues throughout our Christian life. The ordinary course of a Christian's life will involve continual growth in sanctification, and it is something that the New Testament encourages us to give effort and attention to.

## B. THREE STAGES OF SANCTIFICATION

### 1. Sanctification Has a Definite Beginning at Regeneration

A definite moral change occurs in our lives at the point of regeneration, for Paul talks about the "washing of regeneration and renewal of the Holy Spirit" (Titus 3:5). Once we have been born again we cannot continue to sin as a habit or a pattern of life (1 John 3:9) because the power of new spiritual life within us keeps us from yielding to a life of sin.

This initial moral change is the first stage in sanctification. In this sense, there is some overlap between regeneration and sanctification, for this moral change is actually a part of regeneration. But when we view it from the standpoint of moral change within us, we can also see it as the first stage in sanctification. Paul looks back on a completed event when he says to the Corinthians, "But you were washed, *you were sanctified*, you were justified in the name of the Lord Jesus Christ and by the Spirit of our God" (1 Cor. 6:11). Similarly, in Acts 20:32 Paul can refer to Christians as "all those who are sanctified."[2]

This initial step in sanctification involves a definite break from the ruling power and love of sin, so that the believer is no longer ruled or dominated by sin and no longer loves to sin. Paul says, "So you also must *consider yourselves dead to sin* and alive to God in Christ Jesus. . . . For *sin will have no dominion over you*" (Rom. 6:11, 14). Paul says that Christians have been "set free from sin" (Rom. 6:18). In this context, to be dead to sin or to be set free from sin involves the power to overcome acts or patterns of sinful behavior in one's life. Paul tells the Romans not to let sin "reign in your mortal body," and he also says, "Do not present your members to sin as instruments for unrighteousness, but present yourselves to God" (Rom. 6:12–13). To be dead to the ruling power of sin means that we as Christians, by virtue of the power of the Holy Spirit and the resurrection life of Christ working within us, have power to overcome the temptations and enticements of sin. Sin will no longer be our master, as once it was before we became Christians.

In practical terms, this means that we must affirm two things to be true. On the one hand, we will never be able to say, "I am completely free from sin," because our sanctification will never be completed (see below). But on the other hand, a Christian should never say (for example), "This sin has defeated me. I give up. I have had a bad temper for

---

continue throughout life: we continue to have the spiritual life we receive from regeneration, the legal standing we receive from justification, and the membership in God's family we receive from adoption.

2. The Greek expression is *tois hēgiasmenois*, a substantival

perfect passive participle that expresses both a completed past activity (they were sanctified) and a continuing result (they continue to experience the sanctifying influence of that past action).

thirty-seven years, and I will have one until the day I die, and people are just going to have to put up with me the way I am!" To say this is to say that sin has gained dominion. It is to allow sin to reign in our bodies. It is to admit defeat. It is to deny the truth of Scripture, which tells us, "You also must consider yourselves dead to sin and alive to God in Christ Jesus" (Rom. 6:11). It is to deny the truth of Scripture that tells us that "sin will have no dominion over you" (Rom. 6:14).

This initial break with sin, then, involves a reorientation of our desires so that we no longer have a dominant love for sin in our lives. Paul knows that his readers were formerly slaves to sin (as all unbelievers are), but he says that they are enslaved no longer. "You who were once slaves of sin have become obedient from the heart to the standard of teaching to which you were committed, and, having been set free from sin, have become slaves of righteousness" (Rom. 6:17–18). This change of one's primary love and primary desires occurs at the beginning of sanctification.[3]

## 2. Sanctification Increases throughout Life

Even though the New Testament speaks about a definite beginning to sanctification, it also sees it as a process that continues throughout our Christian lives. This is the primary sense in which sanctification is used in systematic theology and in Christian conversation generally today.[4] Although Paul says that his readers have been set free from sin (Rom. 6:18) and that they are "dead to sin and alive to God" (Rom. 6:11), he nonetheless recognizes that sin remains in their lives, so he tells them not to let it reign and not to yield to it (Rom. 6:12–13). Their task, therefore, as Christians is to grow more and more in sanctification, just as they previously grew more and more in sin: "Just as you once presented your members as slaves to impurity and to lawlessness leading to more lawlessness, so now present your members as slaves to righteousness leading to

---

3. Some may wish to add to this section one or more passages from Hebrews that speak about our sanctification as having been completed in the past. For example, the author says that by the will of God "we have been sanctified through the offering of the body of Jesus Christ once for all" (Heb. 10:10). The Greek expression is a periphrastic perfect passive participle, *hēgiasmenoi esmen*, which speaks of a continuing present situation that results from a completed past action: "We are continually in the state of 'having been sanctified' (and we continue to feel the results of that previous act of sanctification)."

But in Hebrews the term *sanctify* (Gk. *hagiazō*) is related more to the Old Testament background of ceremonial purity or holiness as necessary for access to God's presence, and therefore *sanctified* in Hebrews means "made holy and righteous in God's sight and therefore fit to draw near to God in worship." As such, *sanctified* in Hebrews is roughly equivalent to *justified* in Paul's vocabulary. This sense of *sanctified* can be seen in Heb. 9:13; 10:10; 13:12. These passages speak of a ceremonial kind of purification that allows access to God, and, as such, sanctification here applies to the beginning of the Christian life. Nevertheless,

the focus is more on access to God in worship, while the Pauline emphasis is on justification from the penalty of sin that was due under God's law.

4. There is a different usage of the word *sanctified* in the Wesleyan/holiness tradition within Protestantism. In these circles the experience of sanctification is sometimes viewed as a single event subsequent to conversion in which a Christian attains a higher level of holiness, a level sometimes known as "entire sanctification" or "sinless perfection." Within this tradition, sanctification is seen as an experience one seeks for in the Christian life and is sometimes able to attain. (See the systematic theologies listed under the category "Arminian" in the bibliography at the end of this chapter.) Therefore, while most Protestants would say, "I am being sanctified," some within the Wesleyan/Holiness tradition would say, "I *have been* sanctified," referring not to the initial break with sin that comes with conversion, but to a subsequent experience in which they began to know freedom from conscious sin in their lives. The difficulties with this position are outlined in section 4 below, "Sanctification Is Never Completed in This Life."

sanctification" (Rom. 6:19; the words "just as . . . so now" [Gk. *hōsper . . . houtōs*] indicate that Paul wants them to do this in the same way: "just as" they previously yielded to more and more sin, "in just the same way" they are now to yield themselves to more and more righteousness for sanctification).

Paul says that throughout the Christian life "we all . . . are being transformed into the same image from one degree of glory to another" (2 Cor. 3:18). We are progressively becoming more and more like Christ as we go on in the Christian life. Therefore he says, "Forgetting what lies behind and straining forward to what lies ahead, *I press on* toward the goal for the prize of the upward call of God in Christ Jesus" (Phil. 3:13–14)—this is in the context of saying that he is not already perfect but presses on to achieve all of the purposes for which Christ has saved him (vv. 9–12).

Paul tells the Colossians that they should not lie to one another since they have "put on the new self, which is *being renewed* in knowledge after the image of its creator" (Col. 3:10), thus showing that sanctification even involves increasing likeness to God in our thoughts as well as our words and deeds. The author of Hebrews tells his readers to "lay aside every weight, and sin which clings so closely" (Heb. 12:1) and to "*strive for . . . the holiness* without which no one will see the Lord" (Heb. 12:14). James encourages his hearers, "Be doers of the word, and not hearers only" (James 1:22), and Peter tells his readers, "Be holy in all your conduct" (1 Peter 1:15).

It is not necessary to list multiple additional quotations, because much of the New Testament is taken up with instructing believers in various churches on how they should grow in likeness to Christ. All of the moral exhortations and commands in the New Testament Epistles apply here, because they all exhort believers to one aspect or another of greater sanctification in their lives. It is the expectation of all the New Testament authors that our sanctification will increase throughout our Christian lives. (I have written elsewhere at greater length about sanctification.[5])

### 3. Sanctification Is Completed at Death (for Our Souls) and When the Lord Returns (for Our Bodies)

Because there is sin that still remains in our hearts even though we have become Christians (Rom. 6:12–13; 1 John 1:8), our sanctification will never be completed in this life (see below). But once we die and go to be with the Lord, then our sanctification is completed in one sense, for our souls are set free from indwelling sin and are made perfect. The author of Hebrews says that when we come into the presence of God to worship, we come "to the spirits of the righteous *made perfect*" (Heb. 12:23). This is only appropriate because it is in anticipation of the fact that "nothing unclean will ever enter" into the presence of God, the heavenly city (Rev. 21:27).

---

5. See Wayne Grudem, *Christian Ethics: An Introduction to Biblical Moral Reasoning* (Wheaton, IL: Crossway, 2018). The entire book may be understood as a detailed analysis of the process of sanctification as it applies to various areas of moral conduct.

However, when we appreciate that sanctification involves the whole person, including our bodies (see 2 Cor. 7:1; 1 Thess. 5:23), then we realize that sanctification will not be entirely completed until the Lord returns and we receive new resurrection bodies. We await the coming of our Lord Jesus Christ from heaven, and he "will transform our lowly body to be like his glorious body" (Phil. 3:21). "At his coming" (1 Cor. 15:23) we will be made alive with a resurrection body, and then we shall fully "bear the image of the man of heaven" (1 Cor. 15:49).[6]

We may diagram the process of sanctification as in figure 38.1, showing that we are slaves to sin prior to conversion, (1) that there is a definite beginning to sanctification at the point of conversion, (2) that sanctification should increase throughout the Christian life, and (3) that sanctification is made perfect at death. (The completion of sanctification when we receive resurrection bodies is omitted from this chart for the sake of simplicity.)

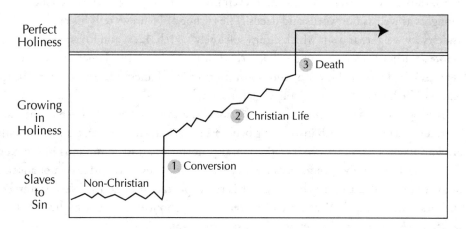

**The Process of Sanctification**
*Figure 38.1*

I have shown the progress of sanctification as a jagged line on this chart, indicating that growth in sanctification is not always one-directional in this life. Progress in sanctification occurs at some times, while at other times we realize that we are regressing. In the extreme case, a believer who makes very little use of the means of sanctification, has bad teaching, lacks good Christian fellowship, pays little attention to God's Word, and neglects prayer may actually go for many years with very little progress in sanctification at all—but this is certainly not the normal or expected pattern of the Christian life. It is, in fact, highly abnormal.

---

6. See chapter 42 on glorification (that is, receiving a resurrection body when Christ returns).

## 4. Sanctification Is Never Completed in This Life

There have always been some in the history of the church who have taken commands such as Matthew 5:48 ("You therefore *must be perfect*, as your heavenly Father is perfect") or 2 Corinthians 7:1 ("let us cleanse ourselves from every defilement of body and spirit, *bringing holiness to completion* in the fear of God") and reasoned that since God gives us these commands, he must also give us the ability to obey them perfectly. Therefore, they have concluded, it is possible for us to attain a state of sinless perfection in this life. Moreover, they point to Paul's prayer for the Thessalonians, "May the God of peace himself sanctify you completely" (1 Thess. 5:23), and infer that Paul's prayer may well have been fulfilled for some of the Thessalonian Christians. In fact, John even says, "No one who abides in him keeps on sinning" (1 John 3:6)! Do these verses not point to the possibility of sinless perfection in the life of some Christians? In this discussion, I will use the term *perfectionism* to refer to this view that sinless perfection is possible in this life.

On closer inspection, these passages do not support the perfectionist position. First, it is simply not taught in Scripture that when God gives a command, he also gives the ability to obey it in every case.[7] God commands all people everywhere to obey all of his moral laws and holds them accountable for failing to obey them, even though unredeemed people are sinners and, as such, dead in trespasses and sins, and thus unable to obey God's commands. When Jesus commands us to be perfect as our Father in heaven is perfect (Matt. 5:48), this simply shows that God's absolute moral purity is the standard toward which we are to aim and the standard for which God holds us accountable. The fact that we are unable to attain that standard does not mean that it will be lowered; rather, it means that we need God's grace and forgiveness to overcome our remaining sin. Similarly, when Paul commands the Corinthians to make holiness perfect in the fear of the Lord (2 Cor. 7:1) or prays that God would sanctify the Thessalonians wholly (1 Thess. 5:23), he is pointing to the goal that he desires them to reach. He does not imply that any reach it but only that this is the high moral standard toward which God wants all believers to aspire.

John's statement that "no one who abides in him keeps on sinning; no one who keeps on sinning has either seen him or known him" (1 John 3:6) does not teach that some of us attain perfection because the present-tense Greek verbs indicate continual or habitual activity (as the ESV makes clear: "keeps on sinning"). This is similar to John's statement a few verses later, "No one born of God *makes a practice of sinning*, for God's seed abides in him; and he cannot *keep on sinning*, because he has been born of God" (1 John 3:9), as well as "Everyone who has been born of God does not *keep on sinning*" (1 John 5:18).

---

7. See chapter 24, pp. 628–29, for a discussion of the fact that God's commands in Scripture do not always imply that we have the ability to obey them.

If these verses were taken to prove sinless perfection, they would have to prove it for all Christians because they talk about what is true of everyone "born of God" and everyone who has seen Christ and known him.

Therefore, there do not seem to be any convincing verses in Scripture that teach that it is possible for anyone to be completely free of sin in this life. On the other hand, there are passages in both the Old and New Testaments that clearly teach that we cannot be morally perfect in this life. In Solomon's prayer at the dedication of the temple, he says, "If they sin against you—for *there is no one who does not sin*" (1 Kings 8:46). Similarly, we read a rhetorical question with an implied negative answer in Proverbs 20:9: "Who can say, 'I have made my heart pure; I am clean from my sin'?" And there is an explicit statement in Ecclesiastes 7:20, "*Surely there is not a righteous man on earth who does good and never sins.*"

In the New Testament, we find Jesus commanding his disciples to pray, "Give us each day our daily bread, and *forgive us our sins,* for we ourselves forgive everyone who is indebted to us" (Luke 11:3–4). Just as the prayer for daily bread provides a model for a prayer that should be repeated each day, so the prayer for the forgiveness of sins is included in the type of prayer that should be made each day in a believer's life.

As we noted above, when Paul talks about the new power over sin that is given to a Christian, he does not say that there will be no sin in the Christian's life, but he simply tells the believers not to let sin "reign" in their bodies nor to "present" their members to sin (Rom. 6:12–13). He does not say that they will not sin but says that sin will not dominate or "have . . . dominion" over them (Rom. 6:14). The very fact that he issues these directions shows his realization that sin will continue to be present in the lives of believers throughout their time on earth. Even James the brother of our Lord could say, "*We all stumble in many ways*" (James 3:2), and if James can say this, then we certainly should be willing to say it as well. Finally, in the same letter in which John declares so frequently that a child of God will not continue in a pattern of sinful behavior, he also says clearly, "If we say we have no sin, we deceive ourselves, and the truth is not in us" (1 John 1:8). Here John explicitly excludes the possibility of being completely free from sin in our lives. In fact, he says that anyone who claims to be free from sin is simply deceiving himself, and the truth is not in him.[8]

But once we have concluded that sanctification will never be completed in this life, we must exercise pastoral wisdom and caution in the way we use this truth. Some may take this fact and use it as an excuse not to strive for holiness or grow in sanctification—a procedure exactly contrary to dozens of New Testament commands. Others may think about the fact that we cannot be perfect in this life and lose hope of making any progress in the Christian life—an attitude that is also contrary to the clear teaching of Romans

---

8. See chapter 24, p. 628n16, for a discussion of the view that 1 John 1:8 does not necessarily apply to all Christians.

6 and other passages about the resurrection power of Christ in our lives enabling us to overcome sin. Therefore, although sanctification will never be completed in this life, we must also emphasize that it should never stop increasing in this life.

Moreover, as Christians grow in maturity, the kinds of sin that remain in their lives are often not so much sins of words or deeds that are outwardly noticeable to others, but inward sins of attitudes and motives of the heart—desires such as pride and selfishness, lack of courage or faith, laziness, lack of zeal in loving God with our whole hearts and our neighbors as ourselves, and failure to fully trust God for all that he promises in every situation. These are real sins! They show how far short we fall of the moral perfection of Christ.

However, recognizing the nature of these sins that will persist even in more mature Christians also helps to guard against misunderstanding when we say that no one will be perfect and free from sin in this life. It is certainly possible that many mature Christians at many times during the day are free from conscious or willful acts of disobedience to God in their words or their deeds. In fact, if Christian leaders are to "set the believers an *example* in speech, in conduct, in love, in faith, in purity" (1 Tim. 4:12), then it will frequently be true that their lives will be free from words or deeds that others will count as blameworthy. But this is far removed from attaining total freedom from sin in our motives and in the thoughts and intents of our hearts.

John Murray notes that when Isaiah the prophet came into the presence of God he could only cry out, "Woe is me! For I am lost; for I am a man of unclean lips, and I dwell in the midst of a people of unclean lips; for my eyes have seen the King, the LORD of hosts!" (Isa. 6:5). And when Job, whose righteousness was earlier commended in the story about his life, came into the presence of almighty God, he could only say, "I had heard of you by the hearing of the ear, but now my eye sees you; therefore I despise myself, and repent in dust and ashes" (Job 42:5–6). Murray concludes from these examples and from the testimony of other saints through the history of the church:

> Indeed, the more sanctified the person is, the more conformed he is to the image of his Savior, the more he must recoil against every lack of conformity to the holiness of God. The deeper his apprehension of the majesty of God, the greater the intensity of his love to God, the more persistent his yearning for the attainment of the prize of the high calling of God in Christ Jesus, the more conscious will he be of the gravity of the sin that remains and the more poignant will be his detestation of it. . . . Was this not the effect in all the people of God as they came into closer proximity to the revelation of God's holiness?[9]

---

9. John Murray, *Redemption Accomplished and Applied* (Grand Rapids: Eerdmans, 1955), 145.

## C. God and Believers Cooperate in Sanctification

Some (such as John Murray)[10] object to saying that God and Christian believers "cooperate" in sanctification, because they want to insist that God's work is primary and our work in sanctification is only a secondary one (see Phil. 2:12–13). However, if we explain the nature of God's role and our role in sanctification clearly, it does not seem inappropriate to say that God and believers cooperate in sanctification. God works in our sanctification and we work as well, and we work for the same purpose. We are not saying that we have equal roles in sanctification or that we both work in the same way but simply that we cooperate with God in ways that are appropriate to our status as God's creatures. And the fact that Scripture emphasizes the role that we play in sanctification (with all the moral commands of the New Testament) makes it appropriate to teach that God calls us to cooperate with him in this activity.[11]

### 1. God's Role in Sanctification

Since sanctification is primarily a work of God, it is appropriate that Paul prays, "May the God of peace himself sanctify you completely" (1 Thess. 5:23). One specific role of God the Father in sanctification is his process of disciplining us as his children (see Heb. 12:5–11). Paul tells the Philippians, "For it is God *who works in you*, both to will and to work for his good pleasure" (Phil. 2:13), thus indicating something of the way in which God sanctifies them—both by causing them to want his will and by giving them power to do it. The author of Hebrews speaks of the role of the Father and the role of the Son in a familiar benediction: "Now may the God of peace . . . *equip you with everything good that you may do his will*, working in us that which is pleasing in his sight, through Jesus Christ, to whom be glory forever and ever" (Heb. 13:20–21).

The role of God the Son, Jesus Christ, in sanctification is, first, that he *earned* our sanctification for us. Paul could say that God made Christ to be "wisdom from God, righteousness and *sanctification* and redemption" (1 Cor. 1:30). Moreover, in the process of sanctification, Jesus is also our *example*, for we are to run the race of life "looking to Jesus the founder and perfecter of our faith" (Heb. 12:2). Peter tells his readers, "Christ also suffered for you, leaving you an example, so that you might follow in his steps" (1 Peter 2:21). And John says, "Whoever says he abides in him ought to walk in the same way in which he walked" (1 John 2:6).

But it is specifically God the Holy Spirit who works within us to change us and sanctify us, giving us greater holiness of life. Peter speaks of the "sanctification of the Spirit" (1 Peter 1:2), and Paul speaks of "sanctification by the Spirit" (2 Thess. 2:13). It is the Holy

---

10. Ibid., 148–49.

11. On the other hand, if we wish to say that sanctification is entirely God's work and that we use the means of sanctification in order to contribute to it (or some similar expression), the meaning is the same. I am simply concerned that if we say sanctification is entirely God's work, we can be misunderstood and encourage an excessively passive role on the part of Christians, who may be led to think that they need to do nothing in the process of sanctification in their lives.

Spirit who produces in us the "fruit of the Spirit" (Gal. 5:22–23), those character traits that are part of greater and greater sanctification. If we grow in sanctification we "walk by the Spirit" and are "led by the Spirit" (Gal. 5:16–18; cf. Rom. 8:14), that is, we are more and more responsive to the desires and promptings of the Holy Spirit in our life and character. The Holy Spirit is the spirit of holiness, and he produces holiness within us.[12]

## 2. Our Role in Sanctification

The role that we play in sanctification is both a *passive* one in which we depend on God to sanctify us and an *active* one in which we strive to obey God and take steps that will increase our sanctification. We can now consider both of these aspects of our role in sanctification.

First, what may be called the "passive" role that we play in sanctification is seen in texts that encourage us to trust God or to pray and ask that he sanctify us. Paul tells his readers, "*Present yourselves to God* as those who have been brought from death to life" (Rom. 6:13; cf. v. 19), and he tells the Roman Christians, "Present your bodies as a living sacrifice, holy and acceptable to God" (Rom. 12:1). Paul realizes that we are dependent on the Holy Spirit's work to grow in sanctification, because he says, "If *by the Spirit* you put to death the deeds of the body, you will live" (Rom. 8:13).

Unfortunately, this "passive" role in sanctification, this idea of yielding to God and trusting him to work in us "to will and to work for his good pleasure" (Phil. 2:13), is sometimes so strongly emphasized that it is the only thing people are told about the path of sanctification. Sometimes the popular phrase "let go and let God" is given as a summary of how to live the Christian life. But this is a tragic distortion of the doctrine of sanctification, for it only speaks of one half of the part we must play and, by itself, will lead Christians to become lazy and to neglect the active role that Scripture commands them to play in their sanctification.

That active role which we are to play is indicated by Romans 8:13, where Paul says, "If by the Spirit *you* put to death the deeds of the body, you will live." Here Paul acknowledges that it is "by the Spirit" that we are able to do this. But he also says we must do it! It is not the Holy Spirit who is commanded to put to death the deeds of the flesh, but Christians! Similarly, Paul tells the Philippians, "Therefore, my beloved, as you have always obeyed, so now, not only as in my presence but much more in my absence, *work out your own salvation* with fear and trembling, for it is God who works in you, both to will and to work for his good pleasure" (Phil. 2:12–13). Paul encourages them to obey even more than they did when he was present. He says that obedience is the way in which they "work out [their] own salvation," meaning that they will "work out" the further realization of the benefits of salvation in their Christian life.[13] The Philippians

---

12. See chapter 30, pp. 780–81, for a further discussion of the work of the Holy Spirit in sanctification.

13. This verse does not use the word *salvation* to refer to initial justification but to the ongoing process of experiencing more and more of the blessings of salvation; here, *salvation* is roughly equivalent to sanctification.

are to work at this growth in sanctification and to do it solemnly and with reverence ("with fear and trembling"), for they are doing it in the presence of God himself. But there is more: the reason why they are to work and to expect that their work will yield positive results is that "God is at work in you"—the prior and foundational work of God in sanctification means that their own work is empowered by God; therefore it will be worthwhile and will bear positive results.

There are many aspects to this active role that we are to play in sanctification. We are to "*Strive . . . for* the *holiness* without which no one will see the Lord" (Heb. 12:14); we are to "*abstain from sexual immorality*" and so obey the will of God, which is our "sanctification" (1 Thess. 4:3). John says that those who hope to be like Christ when he appears will actively work at purification in this life: "Everyone who thus hopes in him *purifies himself* as he is pure" (1 John 3:3). Paul tells the Corinthians to "*flee from sexual immorality*" (1 Cor. 6:18) and not to have partnership with unbelievers (2 Cor. 6:14). He then says, "Let us *cleanse ourselves* from every defilement of body and spirit, bringing holiness to completion in the fear of God" (2 Cor. 7:1). This kind of striving for obedience to God and for holiness may involve great effort on our part, for Peter tells his readers to "*make every effort*" to grow in character traits that accord with godliness (2 Peter 1:5). Many specific passages of the New Testament encourage detailed attention to various aspects of holiness and godliness in life (see Rom. 12:1–13:14; Eph. 4:17–6:20; Phil. 4:4–9; Col. 3:5–4:6; 1 Peter 2:11–5:11, et al.). We are continually to build up patterns and habits of holiness, for one measure of maturity is that mature Christians "have their powers of discernment *trained by constant practice* to distinguish good from evil" (Heb. 5:14).

The New Testament does not suggest any short-cuts by which we can grow in sanctification; it simply encourages us repeatedly to give ourselves to the old-fashioned, time-honored means of Bible reading and meditation (Ps. 1:2; Matt. 4:4; John 17:17), prayer (Eph. 6:18; Phil. 4:6), worship (Eph. 5:18–20), witnessing (Matt. 28:19–20), Christian fellowship (Heb. 10:24–25), and self-discipline or self-control (Gal. 5:23; Titus 1:8).

It is important that we continue to grow both in our passive trust in God to sanctify us and in our active striving for holiness and greater obedience in our lives. If we neglect active striving to obey God, we become passive, lazy Christians. If we neglect the passive role of trusting God and yielding to him, we become proud and overly confident in ourselves. In either case, our sanctification will be greatly deficient. We must maintain faith and diligence to obey at the same time. The old hymn wisely says, "*Trust and obey, for there's no other way, to be happy in Jesus, but to trust and obey.*"[14]

One more point must be added to this discussion of our role in sanctification: sanctification is usually a corporate process in the New Testament. It is something that

---

14. Comparing our life to a tree with two large roots, John Livingstone said, "Satan strikes . . . either at the root of faith or at the root of diligence" (quoted in D. M. M'Intyre, *The Hidden Life of Prayer* [Minneapolis: Bethany Fellowship, 1969], 39).

happens in community. We are admonished, "Let us consider how to *stir up one another to love and good works*, not neglecting to meet together, as is the habit of some, but encouraging one another, and all the more as you see the Day drawing near" (Heb. 10:24–25). Together Christians are "being built up as a spiritual house, to be a holy priesthood" (1 Peter 2:5); together they are "a holy nation" (1 Peter 2:9); together they are to "encourage one another and build one another up" (1 Thess. 5:11). Paul says that "to walk in a manner worthy of the calling to which you have been called" (Eph. 4:1) is to live in a special way in community—"with all humility and gentleness, with patience, bearing with one another in love, eager to maintain the unity of the Spirit in the bond of peace" (Eph. 4:2–3). When that happens, the body of Christ functions as a unified whole, with each part "working properly," so that corporate sanctification occurs as it "makes the body grow so that it builds itself up in love" (Eph. 4:16; cf. 1 Cor. 12:12–26; Gal. 6:1–2). It is significant that the fruit of the Spirit includes many things that build community ("love, joy, peace, patience, kindness, goodness, faithfulness, gentleness, self-control," Gal. 5:22–23), whereas "the works of the flesh" destroy community ("sexual immorality, impurity, sensuality, idolatry, sorcery, enmity, strife, jealousy, fits of anger, rivalries, dissensions, divisions, envy, drunkenness, orgies, and things like these," Gal. 5:19–21).

## D. Sanctification Affects the Whole Person

We see that sanctification affects our *intellect* and our knowledge when Paul says that we have put on the new nature "which is being renewed in *knowledge* after the image of its creator" (Col. 3:10). He prays that the Philippians may see their love "abound more and more, with knowledge and all discernment" (Phil. 1:9). And he urges the Roman Christians to be "transformed by the renewal of your mind" (Rom. 12:2). Although our knowledge of God is more than intellectual knowledge, there is certainly an intellectual component to it, and Paul says that this knowledge of God should keep increasing throughout our lives: a life "worthy of the Lord, fully pleasing to him" is one that is continually "increasing in the knowledge of God" (Col. 1:10). The sanctification of our intellects will involve growth in wisdom and knowledge as we increasingly "take every thought captive to obey Christ" (2 Cor. 10:5) and find that our thoughts are more and more the thoughts that God himself imparts to us in his Word.

Moreover, growth in sanctification will affect our *emotions*. We will see increasingly in our lives emotions such as "love, joy, peace, patience" (Gal. 5:22). We will be able increasingly to obey Peter's command "to abstain from the passions of the flesh, which wage war against your soul" (1 Peter 2:11). We will find it increasingly true that we do not "love the world or the things in the world" (1 John 2:15), but that we, like our Savior, delight to do God's will. In ever-increasing measure we will become "obedient from the heart" (Rom. 6:17), and we will "put away" the negative emotions involved in "bitterness and wrath and anger and clamor and slander" (Eph. 4:31).

Moreover, sanctification will have an effect on our *will*, our decision-making faculty, because God is at work in us, "to *will* and to work for his good pleasure" (Phil. 2:13). As we grow in sanctification, our will will be more and more conformed to the will of our heavenly Father.

Sanctification will also affect our *spirit*, the nonphysical part of our beings. We are to "cleanse ourselves from every defilement of body and *spirit*, bringing holiness to completion in the fear of God" (2 Cor. 7:1), and Paul says that a concern about the affairs of the Lord will mean taking thought for "how to be holy in body and *spirit*" (1 Cor. 7:34).[15]

Finally, sanctification affects our *physical bodies*. Paul says, "May the God of peace himself sanctify you completely, and may your whole spirit and soul *and body* be kept blameless at the coming of our Lord Jesus Christ" (1 Thess. 5:23). Moreover, Paul encourages the Corinthians, "Let us cleanse ourselves from every defilement of *body* and spirit, bringing holiness to completion in the fear of God" (2 Cor. 7:1; cf. 1 Cor. 7:34). As we become more sanctified in our bodies, our bodies become more and more useful servants of God, more and more responsive to the will of God and the desires of the Holy Spirit (cf. 1 Cor. 9:27).[16] We will not let sin reign in our bodies (Rom. 6:12) nor allow our bodies to participate in any way in sexual immorality (1 Cor. 6:13), but we will treat our bodies with care and will recognize that they are the means by which the Holy Spirit works through us in this life. Therefore, our bodies should not be abused or mistreated but should be made useful and able to respond to God's will: "Do you not know that your body is a temple of the Holy Spirit within you, whom you have from God? You are not your own, for you were bought with a price. So glorify God in your body" (1 Cor. 6:19–20).

## E. MOTIVES FOR OBEDIENCE TO GOD IN THE CHRISTIAN LIFE

Christians sometimes fail to recognize the wide range of motives for obedience to God that are found in the New Testament. (1) It is true that a desire to please God and express our love to him is a very important motive for obeying him—Jesus says, "If you love me, you will keep my commandments" (John 14:15), and "Whoever has my commandments and keeps them, he it is who loves me" (John 14:21; cf. 1 John 5:3). But many other motives are also given to us: (2) the need to keep a clear conscience before God (Rom. 13:5; 1 Tim. 1:5, 19; 2 Tim. 1:3; 1 Peter 3:16); (3) the desire to be a "vessel for honorable use" and have increased effectiveness in the work of the kingdom (2 Tim. 2:20–21); (4) the desire to see unbelievers come to Christ through observing

---

15. See chapter 23, pp. 604–6, for a discussion of the fact that *soul* and *spirit* are used roughly synonymously in the Bible.

16. Of course, physical weakness will inevitably come with old age, and sometimes comes earlier due to infirmity, but this can be consistent with increased sanctification as God's power is "made perfect in weakness" (2 Cor. 12:9). Paul clearly teaches

this when he says, "We have this treasure in jars of clay, to show that the surpassing power belongs to God and not to us" (2 Cor. 4:7), and "We do not lose heart. Though our outer self is wasting away, our inner self is being renewed day by day" (2 Cor. 4:16).

our lives (1 Peter 3:1–2, 15–16); (5) the desire to receive present blessings from God on our lives and ministries (1 Peter 3:9–12); (6) the desire to avoid God's displeasure and discipline on our lives (sometimes called "the fear of God") (Acts 5:11; 9:31; 2 Cor. 5:11; 7:1; Eph. 4:30; Phil. 2:12; 1 Tim. 5:20; Heb. 12:3–11; 1 Peter 1:17; 2:17; cf. the state of unbelievers in Rom. 3:18); (7) the desire to seek greater heavenly reward (Matt. 6:19–21; Luke 19:17–19; 1 Cor. 3:12–15; 2 Cor. 5:9–10);[17] (8) the desire for a deeper walk with God (Matt. 5:8; John 14:21; 1 John 1:6; 3:21–22; and, in the Old Testament, Ps. 66:18; Isa. 59:2); (9) the desire that angels would glorify God for our obedience (1 Tim. 5:21; 1 Peter 1:12); (10) the desire for peace (Phil. 4:9) and joy (Heb. 12:1–2) in our lives; and (11) the desire to do what God commands, simply because his commands are right, and we delight in doing what is right (Phil. 4:8; cf. Ps. 40:8).[18]

## F. The Beauty and Joy of Sanctification

It would not be right to end our discussion without noting that sanctification brings great joy to us. The more we grow in likeness to Christ, the more we will personally experience the "joy" and "peace" that are part of the fruit of the Holy Spirit (Gal. 5:22), and the more we will draw near to the kind of life that we will have in heaven. Paul says that as we become more and more obedient to God, "the fruit you get leads to sanctification and its end, eternal life" (Rom. 6:22). He realizes that this is the source of our true joy. "For the kingdom of God is not a matter of eating and drinking but of righteousness and peace and joy in the Holy Spirit" (Rom. 14:17). As we grow in holiness we grow in conformity to the image of Christ, and more and more of the beauty of his character is seen in our own lives. This is the goal of perfect sanctification, which we hope and long for, and which will be ours when Christ returns. "And everyone who thus hopes in him purifies himself as he is pure" (1 John 3:3).

# QUESTIONS FOR PERSONAL APPLICATION

1. Can you remember the definite beginning to sanctification that occurred when you became a Christian? Did you sense a clear break from the ruling power and love of sin in your life? Do you really believe that you are even now dead to the ruling power and love of sin in your life? How can this truth of the Christian life be of help to you in specific areas of your life where you still need to grow in sanctification?

2. As you look back over the last few years of your Christian life, can you see a pattern of growth in sanctification? What are some things that you used to delight in which no longer interest you? What are some things that you used to have no interest in that now hold great interest for you?

---

17. See chapter 56, pp. 1408–10, for a discussion of degrees of reward in heaven.

18. For a fuller discussion of motives for obedience in the Christian life, see Grudem, *Christian Ethics: An Introduction to Biblical Moral Reasoning* (Wheaton, IL: Crossway, 2018), chapter 5.

3. As you have grown to greater maturity and holiness in the Christian life, have you become more conscious of the weight of sin that remains in your heart? If not, why has this not been so? Do you think that it would be helpful if you had a greater consciousness of the sin that remains in your life? If you had this, what difference would it make in your life?

4. How would it affect your life if you thought more about the fact that the Holy Spirit is continually at work in you to increase your sanctification? In living the Christian life, have you maintained a balance between your passive role and your active role in sanctification, or have you tended to emphasize one aspect over the other? Why? What might you do to correct this imbalance, if there is one in your life?

5. Have you thought previously that sanctification affects your intellect and the way you think? What areas of your intellect still need quite a bit of growth in sanctification? With regard to your emotions, in what areas do you know that God still needs to work to bring about greater sanctification? Are there areas or aspects of sanctification that need to be improved with respect to your physical body and its obedience to God's purposes?

6. Are there areas where you have struggled for years to grow in sanctification but with no progress at all in your life? Has this chapter helped you regain hope for progress in those areas? (For Christians who have serious discouragement over lack of progress in sanctification, it is very important to talk personally to a pastor or other mature Christian about this situation rather than letting it go on for a long period of time.)

7. Overall, has this chapter been an encouragement or discouragement to you in your Christian life?

**Special Terms**

*perfectionism*
*sanctification*
*sinless perfection*

# BIBLIOGRAPHY

(For an explanation of this bibliography see the note on the bibliography to chapter 1, pp. 23–24. Complete bibliographical data may be found on pp. 1489–96.)

## SECTIONS IN EVANGELICAL SYSTEMATIC THEOLOGIES

### 1. Anglican (Episcopalian)
1882–92 . . . . . Litton, 330–45

1930 . . . . . . . . Thomas, 199–209, 223–35
2001 . . . . . . . . Packer, 169–171
2013 . . . . . . . . Bird, 541, 631
2013 . . . . . . . . Bray, 848, 884–85

### 2. Arminian (Wesleyan or Methodist)
1875–76 . . . . . Pope, 3:27–100
1892–94 . . . . . Miley, 2:355–84
1940 . . . . . . . . Wiley, 2:440–517; 3:7–102

1960 . . . . . . . . Purkiser, 305–92, 428–41

1983 . . . . . . . . Carter, 1:521–69

1992 . . . . . . . . Oden, 3:236–46

2002 . . . . . . . . Cottrell, 332–345

3. *Baptist*

1767 . . . . . . . . Gill, 2:93–107, 141–51,
364–557

1887 . . . . . . . . Boyce, 409–25

1907 . . . . . . . . Strong, 869–81

1990–95 . . . . . Garrett, 2:387–404

2007 . . . . . . . . Akin, 753–62

2013 . . . . . . . . Erickson, 896–904

4. *Dispensational*

1947 . . . . . . . . Chafer, 3:355–63; 6:162–298

1949 . . . . . . . . Thiessen, 283–89

1986 . . . . . . . . Ryrie, 300–306

2002–2005 . . Geisler, 3:237–40

2017 . . . . . . . . MacArthur and Mayhue,
631–44

5. *Lutheran*

1917–24 . . . . . Pieper, 3:3–86

1934 . . . . . . . . Mueller, 384–435

6. *Reformed (or Presbyterian)*

1679–85 . . . . . Turretin, *IET*, 2:139–40, 143,
250–51, 689–724

1559 . . . . . . . . Calvin, 1:684–725, 833–49
(3.6–10, 19)

1724–58 . . . . . Edwards, 2:173–85

1871–73 . . . . . Hodge, 3:213–465

1878 . . . . . . . . Dabney, 674–87

1887–1921 . . . Warfield, *SSW*, 2:325–28;
Perf., 3–464

1894 . . . . . . . . Shedd, 803–08

1906–11 . . . . . Bavinck, *RD*, 4:230–66

1910 . . . . . . . . Vos, 4:182–226

1937–66 . . . . . Murray, *CW*, 2:277–317;
*RAA*, 141–51

1938 . . . . . . . . Berkhof, 527–44

1998 . . . . . . . . Reymond, 767–81

2008 . . . . . . . . Van Genderen and Velema,
645–66

2011 . . . . . . . . Horton, 648–87

2013 . . . . . . . . Frame, 682, 739–41, 983–95

2013 . . . . . . . . Culver, 755–64

2016 . . . . . . . . Allen and Swain, 284–86,
331–33

2017 . . . . . . . . Barrett, 549–74

2019 . . . . . . . . Letham, 733–42

7. *Renewal (or charismatic/Pentecostal)*

1988–92 . . . . . Williams, 2:83–117, 411–45

1993 . . . . . . . . Menzies and Horton, 145–54

1995 . . . . . . . . Horton, 397–422

2008 . . . . . . . . Duffield and Van Cleave,
242–51

## SECTIONS IN REPRESENTATIVE ROMAN CATHOLIC SYSTEMATIC THEOLOGIES

1. *Roman Catholic: Traditional*

1955 . . . . . . . . . Ott, 254–69

2. *Roman Catholic: Post–Vatican II*

1980 . . . . . . . . McBrien, 2:903–1099

2012 . . . . . . . . *CCC*, paragraphs 767, 1989

## OTHER WORKS

Alexander, Donald L., ed. *Christian Spirituality: Five Views of Sanctification.* Downers Grove, IL: InterVarsity Press, 1988.

Allison, Gregg. *Historical Theology: An Introduction to Christian Doctrine; A Companion to Wayne Grudem's* Systematic Theology. Grand Rapids: Zondervan, 2011, 520–541.

Anderson, Neil T., and Robert L. Saucy. *God's Power at Work in You*. Eugene, OR: Harvest House, 2001.

Berkouwer, G. C. *Faith and Sanctification*. Translated by John Vriend. Grand Rapids: Eerdmans, 1952.

Bockmuehl, Klaus. "Sanctification." In *NDT1*, 613–16.

Chafer, Lewis Sperry. *He That Is Spiritual*. Rev. ed. Grand Rapids: Zondervan, 1967.

Chan, S. "Sanctification." In *GDT*, 789–91.

Cloud, Henry, and John Sims Townsend. *How People Grow: What the Bible Reveals about Personal Growth*. Grand Rapids: Zondervan, 2001.

Coppedge, Allan. *The Biblical Principles of Discipleship*. Grand Rapids: Francis Asbury, 1989.

Downs, Perry G. *Teaching for Spiritual Growth: An Introduction to Christian Education*. Grand Rapids: Zondervan, 1994.

Demarest, Bruce. *The Cross and Salvation: The Doctrine of Salvation*. Wheaton, IL: Crossway, 2006, 27–43.

Gundry, Stanley N., ed. *Five Views on Sanctification*. Grand Rapids: Zondervan, 1996.

Hawthorne, G. F. "Holy, Holiness." In *DLNT*, 485–89.

Hoekema, Anthony A. "Sanctification." In *Saved by Grace*. Grand Rapids: Eerdmans; Exeter: Paternoster, 1989, 192–233.

Holloman, Henry. *The Forgotten Blessing:*

*Rediscovering the Transforming Power of Sanctification*. Nashville: Word, 1999.

Keathley, Kenneth. "The Work of God: Salvation." In *A Theology for the Church*, edited by Daniel L. Akin et al., 753–62. Nashville: B&H, 2007.

Mullen, Bradford A. "Sanctification." In *BTDB*, 708–13.

Murray, John. "Sanctification." In *Redemption Accomplished and Applied*. Grand Rapids: Eerdmans, 1955, 141–50.

Packer, J. I. *Keep in Step with the Spirit*. Old Tappan, NJ: Revell, 1984.

Peterson, D. G. "Holiness." In *NDBT*, 544–50.

Porter, S. E. "Holiness, Sanctification." In *DPL*, 397–402.

Prior, K. *The Way of Holiness*. Downers Grove, IL: InterVarsity Press, 1967.

Ryle, J. C. *Holiness: Its Nature, Hindrances, Difficulties and Roots*. Westwood, NJ: Revell, 1956.

Sheir-Jones, A. "Sanctification." In *NDT2*, 804–8.

White, R. E. O. "Sanctification." In *EDT3*, 770–72.

Willard, Dallas. *The Spirit of the Disciplines: Understanding How God Changes Lives*. San Francisco: Harper and Row, 1988.

Ziesler, J. A. *The Meaning of Righteousness in Paul*. Cambridge: Cambridge University Press, 1972.

## SCRIPTURE MEMORY PASSAGE

**Romans 6:11–14:** So you also must consider yourselves dead to sin and alive to God in Christ Jesus. Let not sin therefore reign in your mortal body, to make you obey its passions. Do not present your members to sin as instruments for unrighteousness, but present yourselves to God as those who have been brought from death to life, and your members to God as instruments for righteousness. For sin will have no dominion over you, since you are not under law but under grace.

## HYMN

### "Take Time to Be Holy"

*Take time to be holy, speak oft with thy Lord;*
*Abide in him always, and feed on his Word.*

*Make friends of God's children; help those who are weak;*
*Forgetting in nothing his blessing to seek.*

Take time to be holy, the world rushes on;
  Spend much time in secret with Jesus alone.
By looking to Jesus, like him thou shalt be;
  Thy friends in thy conduct his likeness
    shall see.

Take time to be holy, let him be thy guide,
  And run not before him, whatever betide;
In joy or in sorrow, still follow thy Lord,
  And, looking to Jesus, still trust in his Word.

Take time to be holy, be calm in thy soul;
  Each thought and each motive beneath
    his control;
Thus led by his Spirit to fountains of love,
  Thou soon shalt be fitted for service above.

Author: William D. Longstaff, 1887

Alternate hymn: "Trust and Obey" (see p. 659)

# CONTEMPORARY WORSHIP SONG

### "Change My Heart, O God"

Change my heart, O God,
Make it ever true;
Change my heart, O God,
May I be like You.
Change my heart, O God,
Make it ever true;
Change my heart, O God,
May I be like You.

You are the Potter,
I am the clay;
Mold me and make me,
This is what I pray.

Change my heart, O God,
Make it ever true;
Change my heart, O God,
May I be like You.

*Chorus*
Jesus, O Jesus, come and fill Your Lambs.
Jesus, O Jesus, come and fill Your Lambs.
O let the Son of God enfold You
With His Spirit and His love.
Let Him fill your heart and satisfy your soul.
O let Him have those things that hold You,
And His Spirit like a dove
Will descend upon your life
And make you whole.

Words by Eddie Espinosa[19]

---

19. © 1982 Mercy/Vineyard Publishing (ASCAP) Admin.
In North America By Music Services o/b/o Vineyard Music
USA.

# CHAPTER 39

# Baptism in and Filling with the Holy Spirit

*Should we seek a "baptism in the Holy Spirit" after conversion?*
*What does it mean to be filled with the Holy Spirit?*

Systematic theology books have not traditionally included a chapter on baptism in the Holy Spirit or filling with the Holy Spirit as part of the study of the "order of salvation," the study of the various steps in which the benefits of salvation are applied to our lives.[1] But with the spread of Pentecostalism that began in 1901, the widespread influence of the charismatic movement in the 1960s and 1970s, and the remarkable growth of Pentecostal and charismatic[2] churches worldwide from 1970 to the present, the question of a "baptism in the Holy Spirit" distinct from regeneration has come into increasing prominence. I have put this chapter at this point in our study of the application of redemption for two reasons: (1) A proper understanding of this question must assume an understanding of regeneration, adoption, and sanctification, all of which have been discussed in previous chapters. (2) All the previous chapters on the application of redemption have discussed events that occur (or in the case of sanctification, that begin) at the point at which a person becomes a Christian. But this question concerns an event that occurs either at the point of conversion (according to one view) or sometime after conversion (according to another view). Moreover, people on both sides of the question agree that some kind of second experience has happened to many people after their conversion, and therefore one very important question is how to understand this experience in the light of Scripture and what scriptural categories properly apply to it.

---

1. See chapter 32, p. 817, for a list of the elements in the order of salvation.

2. I am using the terms *Pentecostal* and *charismatic* in the following way: *Pentecostal* refers to any denomination or group that traces its historical origin back to the Pentecostal revival that began in the United States in 1901 and that holds to the doctrinal positions (a) that baptism in the Holy Spirit is ordinarily an event subsequent to conversion, (b) that baptism in the Holy Spirit is made evident by the sign of speaking in tongues, and (c) that all the spiritual gifts mentioned in the New Testament are to be sought and used today. Pentecostal groups usually have their own distinct denominational structures, the most prominent of which is the Assemblies of God.

*Charismatic* refers to any groups (or people) that trace their historical origin to the charismatic renewal movement of the 1960s and 1970s, seek to practice all the spiritual gifts mentioned in the New Testament (including prophecy, healing, miracles, tongues, interpretation, and distinguishing between spirits) and allow differing viewpoints on whether baptism in the Holy Spirit is subsequent to conversion and whether tongues is a sign of baptism in the Holy Spirit. Charismatics will very often refrain from forming their own denomination but will view themselves as a force for renewal within existing Protestant and Roman Catholic churches. There is no representative charismatic denomination in the United States today, but two influential representatives of the charismatic movement are

# EXPLANATION AND SCRIPTURAL BASIS

## A. THE TRADITIONAL PENTECOSTAL UNDERSTANDING

The topic of this chapter has become important because many Christians say that they have experienced a "baptism in the Holy Spirit" that came after they became Christians and that brought great blessing in their lives. They claim that prayer and Bible study have become much more meaningful and effective, that they have discovered new joy in worship, and often that they have received new spiritual gifts (especially, and most frequently, the gift of speaking in tongues).

This traditional Pentecostal or charismatic position is supported from Scripture in the following way:

(1) Jesus' disciples were born-again believers long before the day of Pentecost, perhaps during Jesus' life and ministry and certainly by the time that Jesus, after his resurrection, "breathed on them and said to them, 'Receive the Holy Spirit'" (John 20:22).

(2) Jesus nevertheless commanded his disciples "not to depart from Jerusalem, but to wait for the promise of the Father" (Acts 1:4), telling them, "you will be *baptized with the Holy Spirit* not many days from now" (Acts 1:5). He told them, "You will receive power when the Holy Spirit has come upon you" (Acts 1:8). The disciples then obeyed Jesus' command and waited in Jerusalem for the Holy Spirit to come upon them so that they would receive new empowering for witness and ministry.

(3) When the disciples had waited for ten days, the day of Pentecost came, tongues of fire rested above their heads, "and they were all filled with the Holy Spirit and began to speak in other tongues as the Spirit gave them utterance" (Acts 2:4). This clearly shows that they received a baptism in (or with)[3] the Holy Spirit. Although the disciples were

---

*Charisma* magazine (edited by Stephen Strang) and Pat Robertson's Christian Broadcasting Network (with the television program "The 700 Club," and Regent University in Virginia Beach, VA).

In the 1980s yet a third renewal movement arose, called the *"third wave"* by missions professor C. Peter Wagner at Fuller Seminary (he referred to the Pentecostal renewal as the first wave of the Holy Spirit's renewing work in the modern church, and the charismatic movement as the second wave). "Third wave" people encourage the equipping of all believers to use New Testament spiritual gifts today and say that the proclamation of the gospel should ordinarily be accompanied by "signs, wonders, and miracles," according to the New Testament pattern. They teach, however, that baptism in the Holy Spirit happens to all Christians at conversion and that subsequent experiences are better called "filling" with the Holy Spirit. The most prominent representative of the "third wave" until his death in 1997 was John Wimber, senior pastor of the Vineyard Christian Fellowship in Anaheim, California, and leader of the Association of Vineyard Churches. Wimber's two most influential books, *Power Evangelism* (San Francisco: Harper and

Row, 1986; rev. ed., 1992) and *Power Healing* (San Francisco: Harper and Row, 1987), both coauthored by Kevin Springer, are widely recognized as representative of distinctive "third wave" emphases.

The definitive reference work for these movements is now Stanley M. Burgess and Gary B. McGee, eds., *Dictionary of Pentecostal and Charismatic Movements* (Grand Rapids: Zondervan, 1988; rev. ed., by Ed van der Maas and Stanley Burgess, 2002).

3. It does not matter much whether we translate the Greek phrase *en pneumati* as "in the Spirit" or "with the Spirit" because both are acceptable translations, and people on all sides of this topic seem to use those two expressions rather interchangeably. I have used "in the Holy Spirit" ordinarily throughout this chapter, but the ESV translation which I quote here generally prefers to use "with the Holy Spirit." I do not make any distinction between these two phrases in the discussion of this chapter. (But see below, pp. 946–48, for a discussion of the frequent claim by Pentecostals that baptism *by* the Holy Spirit [as in 1 Cor. 12:13] is a different event than baptism *in* [or with] the Holy Spirit.)

born again long before Pentecost, at Pentecost they received a "baptism with the Holy Spirit" (Acts 1:5 and 11:16 refer to it this way) that was *subsequent to conversion* and resulted in great empowering for ministry as well as speaking in tongues.[4]

(4) Christians today, like the apostles, should ask Jesus for a "baptism in the Holy Spirit" and thus follow the pattern of the disciples' lives.[5] If we receive this baptism in the Holy Spirit, it will result in much more power for ministry for our own lives, just as it did in the lives of the disciples, and will often (or always, according to some teachers) result in speaking in tongues as well.

(5) Support for this pattern—in which people are first born again and then later are baptized in the Holy Spirit—is seen in several other instances in the book of Acts. In Acts 8, the people of Samaria first became Christians when they "believed Philip as he preached good news about the kingdom of God and the name of Jesus Christ" (Acts 8:12), but only later did they receive the Holy Spirit when the apostles Peter and John came from Jerusalem and prayed for them (Acts 8:14–17). Another example sometimes cited is that of Cornelius in Acts 10. He was a devout man who prayed constantly to God (Acts 10:2), but when Peter came and preached to him and his household, Peter and those with him were amazed "because the gift of the Holy Spirit was poured out even on the Gentiles. For they were hearing them speaking in tongues and extolling God" (Acts 10:45–46).

Yet another example is found in Acts 19, where Paul came and found "some disciples" at Ephesus (Acts 19:1). But "when Paul had laid his hands on them, the Holy Spirit came on them, and they began speaking in tongues and prophesying" (Acts 19:6).

All of these examples (Acts 2, 8, sometimes 10, and 19)[6] are cited by Pentecostals in order to show that a "baptism in the Holy Spirit" subsequent to conversion was a very common occurrence for New Testament Christians. Therefore, they reason, if it was common for Christians in Acts to have this second experience sometime after conversion, should it not be common for us today as well?

We can analyze this issue of the baptism in the Holy Spirit by asking three questions: (1) What does the phrase "baptism in the Holy Spirit" mean in the New Testament?

---

4. Most Pentecostal discussions of baptism in the Holy Spirit include the view that speaking in tongues is a "sign" that one has been baptized in the Holy Spirit, and that this sign will be given to all who have been baptized in the Holy Spirit, even though not all will later have the gift of speaking in tongues as a continuing gift in their lives.

5. I personally heard such teaching on baptism in the Holy Spirit as a first-year university student in 1967, and later privately prayed, as instructed, first repenting of all known sin and once again yielding every area of my life to God, then asking Jesus to baptize me in the Holy Spirit. Though my understanding of that experience has since changed, so that I would explain it in different terms (see below), the result in my life was undoubtedly a positive and lasting one, including a much deeper love for Christ and much greater effectiveness in personal ministry.

6. The case of Paul in Acts 9:17 is sometimes mentioned as well, but it is not as clear-cut since his violent persecution of the church prior to that time indicates that he was not born again before the Damascus Road experience. But some have seen a similar pattern in the distinction between his conversion on the Damascus Road and his receiving the Holy Spirit at the hands of Ananias three days later.

(2) How should we understand the "second experiences" that came to born-again believers in the book of Acts? (3) Are there other biblical expressions, such as "filling with the Holy Spirit," that are better suited to describe an empowering with the Holy Spirit that comes after conversion?

## B. What Does "Baptism in the Holy Spirit" Mean in the New Testament?

### 1. Seven Verses

There are only seven passages in the New Testament where we read of someone being baptized "in" or "with" the Holy Spirit. In these seven verses, while English translations differ, the Greek expression (the verb *baptizō* plus *en pneumati hagiō*) is almost the same in every verse. (The ESV, which is quoted here, uses the word *with* rather than *in*.)[7]

In the first four verses, John the Baptist is speaking of Jesus and predicting that he will baptize people in (or with) the Holy Spirit:

> I baptize you with water for repentance, but he who is coming after me is mightier than I, whose sandals I am not worthy to carry. He will *baptize you with the Holy Spirit* and fire. (Matt. 3:11)

> I have baptized you with water, but he will *baptize you with the Holy Spirit*. (Mark 1:8)

> I baptize you with water, but he who is mightier than I is coming, the strap of whose sandals I am not worthy to untie. He will *baptize you with the Holy Spirit* and fire. (Luke 3:16)

> He who sent me to baptize with water said to me, "He on whom you see the Spirit descend and remain, this is he who *baptizes with the Holy Spirit*." (John 1:33)

It is hard to draw any conclusions from these four passages with respect to what baptism with the Holy Spirit really is. We discover that Jesus is the one who will carry out this baptism and he will baptize his followers. But no further specification of this baptism is given.

The next two passages refer directly to Pentecost:

> [Jesus says,] "John baptized with water, but you will be *baptized with the Holy Spirit* not many days from now." (Acts 1:5)

---

7. See n3 above.

[Referring back to the words of Jesus quoted in the previous verse, Peter says,] "I remembered the word of the Lord, how he said, 'John baptized with water, but you will be *baptized with the Holy Spirit.*'" (Acts 11:16)

These two passages show us that whatever we may understand baptism in the Holy Spirit to be, it certainly happened at the day of Pentecost as recorded in Acts 2, when the Holy Spirit fell in great power on the disciples and those with them, and they spoke in other tongues, and about three thousand people were converted (Acts 2:14).

It is important to realize that all six of these verses use almost exactly the same expression in Greek, with the only differences being some variation in word order or verb tense to fit the sentence, and with one example having the preposition understood rather than expressed explicitly.[8]

The only remaining reference in the New Testament is in 1 Corinthians 12:13.

## 2. 1 Corinthians 12:13

The result of baptism in the Holy Spirit is becoming a part of the body of Christ, the church:

For *in one Spirit* we were all baptized into one body—Jews or Greeks, slaves or free—and all were made to drink of one Spirit. (1 Cor. 12:13)[9]

The question is whether 1 Corinthians 12:13 refers to the same activity as these other six verses above. In many English translations it appears to be something different, for many translations have "*by* one Spirit" instead of "*in* one Spirit":

For *by one Spirit* we were all baptized into one body, whether Jews or Greeks, whether slaves or free, and we were all made to drink of one Spirit. (1 Cor. 12:13 NASB)[10]

Those who support the Pentecostal view of baptism in the Holy Spirit after conversion are quite eager to see this verse as referring to something other than baptism in the Holy Spirit, and they frequently emphasize the difference that comes out in the English translations that say "by one Spirit." In the four Gospel verses mentioned above, Jesus is the one who baptizes people and the Holy Spirit is the "element" (parallel to water in physical baptism) in which or with which Jesus baptizes people. But here in

---

8. The expression used in all six passages is the verb *baptizō* ("baptize") plus the prepositional phrase *en pneumati hagiō* ("in [or with] the Holy Spirit"), except that Mark omits the preposition *en*. Even so, there is no difference in meaning, because the dative noun alone can take the same sense as the preposition *en* plus the dative noun. Matthew and Luke also add "and with fire."

9. The NRSV and NET also have "*in* (the) one Spirit" (also NIV and NASB margins).

10. The NIV, RSV, CSB, NLT, KJV, and NKJV also have "*by* one Spirit."

1 Corinthians 12:13 (so the Pentecostal explanation goes) we have something quite different—here the person doing the baptizing is not Jesus but the Holy Spirit. Therefore, they say, 1 Corinthians 12:13 should not be taken into account when we ask what the New Testament means by "baptism in the Holy Spirit."

This point is important to the Pentecostal position because if we admit that 1 Corinthians 12:13 refers to baptism *in* the Holy Spirit, then it is very hard to maintain that it is an experience that comes after conversion. That is because, in this verse, Paul says that this baptism in/with/by the Holy Spirit made us members of the body of Christ: "In one Spirit we were all baptized *into one body*" (1 Cor. 12:13). But if this really is a "baptism *in* the Holy Spirit," the same as the event that was referred to in the other six verses, then Paul is saying that it happened to all the Corinthians *when they became members of the body of Christ, that is, when they became Christians.* For it was that baptism that resulted in their being members of the body of Christ, the church. Such a conclusion would be very difficult for the Pentecostal position that holds that baptism in the Holy Spirit is something that occurs after conversion, not at the same time.

Is it possible to sustain the Pentecostal view that the other six verses refer to a baptism *by Jesus* in which he baptizes us in (or with) the Holy Spirit and that 1 Corinthians 12:13 refers to something different, to a baptism *by the Holy Spirit*? Although the distinction seems to make sense from some English translations, it really cannot be supported by an examination of the Greek text, for there the expression is almost identical to the expressions we have seen in the other six verses. Paul says *en heni pneumati . . . ebaptisthēmen* ("in one Spirit . . . we were baptized"). Apart from one small difference (he refers to "one Spirit" rather than "the Holy Spirit"),[11] all the other elements are the same: the verb is *baptizō*, and the prepositional phrase contains the same words (*en* plus the dative noun *pneumati*). If we translate this same Greek expression "baptize *in* the Holy Spirit" (or "baptize with the Holy Spirit") in the other six New Testament occurrences where we find it, then it seems only proper that we translate it in the same way in this seventh occurrence. And no matter how we translate, it seems hard to deny that the original readers would have seen this phrase as referring to the same thing as the other six verses, because for them the words were the same.

But why do several modern English translations translate this verse to say, *"By one Spirit* we were all baptized into one body," thus giving apparent support to the Pentecostal interpretation? The reason these translations have chosen the word "by" has apparently been a desire to avoid an appearance of two locations for the baptism in the same sentence. The sentence already says that this baptism was "into one body," and perhaps the translators thought it seemed awkward to say, *"in* one Spirit we were all baptized *into* one body." But this should not be seen as a great difficulty, for Paul says,

---

11. In this context, in which he is talking repeatedly about the Holy Spirit and spiritual gifts, there can be little doubt that he is referring to the Holy Spirit.

referring to the Israelites, "all were baptized *into* Moses *in* the cloud and *in* the sea" (1 Cor. 10:2)—a very closely parallel expression where the cloud and the sea are the "elements" that surrounded or overwhelmed the people of Israel, and "Moses" means the new life of participation in the Mosaic covenant and the fellowship of God's people (led by Moses) that the Israelites found themselves in after they had passed through the cloud and the sea. It is not that there were two locations for the same baptism, but one was the element in which they were baptized (cloud and sea) and the other was the location in which they found themselves after the baptism (they belonged to the Mosaic Covenant people). This is very similar to 1 Corinthians 12:13: the Holy Spirit was the *element* in which they were baptized, and the body of Christ, the church, was the *location* in which they found themselves after that baptism.[12] It thus seems appropriate to conclude that 1 Corinthians 12:13 also refers to baptism "in" or "with" (not "by") the Holy Spirit, and is referring to the same thing as the other six verses mentioned.

But this has a significant implication for us: it means that, as far as the apostle Paul was concerned, *baptism in the Holy Spirit occurred at conversion.* He says that all the Corinthians were baptized in the Holy Spirit and the result was that they became members of the body of Christ: "For in one Spirit we were all baptized *into one body*" (1 Cor. 12:13). "Baptism in the Holy Spirit," therefore, must refer to the activity of the Holy Spirit at the beginning of the Christian life when he gives us new spiritual life (in regeneration) and cleanses us and gives a clear break with the power and love of sin (the initial stage of sanctification). In this way "baptism in the Holy Spirit" refers to all that the Holy Spirit does at the beginning of our Christian lives. But this means that it cannot refer to an experience after conversion, as the Pentecostal interpretation would have it.[13]

12. In addition to the fact that this Greek phrase found in 1 Cor. 12:13 is translated to refer to baptism in (Or with, but not "by") the Holy Spirit in all the other six occurrences, there is a grammatical argument that supports the translation "*in* one Spirit we were all baptized into one body" in 1 Cor. 12:13: if Paul had wanted to say that we were baptized *by* the Holy Spirit, he would have used a different expression. To be baptized "by" someone in the New Testament is always expressed by the preposition *hypo* followed by a genitive noun. This is the way New Testament writers say that people were baptized in the Jordan River "by" John the Baptist (Matt. 3:6; Mark 1:5; Luke 3:7) or that Jesus was baptized "by" John (Matt. 3:13; Mark 1:9), or that the Pharisees had not been baptized "by" John (Luke 7:30), or that John the Baptist told Jesus, "I need to be baptized by you" (Matt. 3:14). Therefore, if Paul had wanted to say that the Corinthians had all been baptized *by* the Holy Spirit he would have used *hypo* plus the genitive, not *en* plus the dative. (It is common in the New Testament for the agent who performs the action expressed by a passive verb to be named using *hypo* plus the genitive.) Further support for the view that 1 Cor. 12:13 means "in (or with) one Spirit" is found in M. J. Harris, "Prepositions and Theology in the Greek New Testament," in *NIDNTT*, 3:1210.

13. Howard M. Ervin, *Conversion-Initiation and the Baptism in the Holy Spirit* (Peabody, MA: Hendrickson, 1984), 98–102, admits that 1 Cor. 12:13, however it is translated, does refer to the beginning of the Christian life (he says it is "initiatory," p. 101), but then he says that the next phrase, "we were made to drink of one Spirit" (his translation) refers to a subsequent empowering for service. He also says that Paul's use of the phrase "baptism in the Holy Spirit" is different from the sense the phrase takes in the other six occurrences in the New Testament. Thus, he apparently grants the non-Pentecostal interpretation of 1 Cor. 12:13 but still says that Paul uses the same phrase with different meaning. Yet this argument does not seem persuasive. It would be very unlikely if Luke, who was Paul's traveling companion throughout much of his missionary activity, and who was probably with Paul in Rome when he wrote the book of Acts (Acts 28:30–31), would use a phrase in a different sense than Paul or that Paul would use this phrase in a different sense than the sense in which it was so prominently used by Matthew, Mark, Luke, and John.

Another attempt to avoid our conclusion on 1 Cor. 12:13 is found in John P. Baker, *Baptized in One Spirit* (Plainfield, NJ: Logos Books, 1970), 18–25, where he argues that 1 Cor. 12:13 does not mean that we were baptized *into* one body, but that

## 3. Pentecost Marked the Beginning of a More Powerful Work of the Holy Spirit in Ordinary Believers

How, then, should we understand the references to baptism in (or with) the Holy Spirit in Acts 1:5 and 11:16, both of which refer to the day of Pentecost? Was Pentecost not an event where the disciples, having *previously* been regenerated by the Holy Spirit, now experienced a *subsequent empowering* from the Holy Spirit that enabled them to minister effectively?

I agree that the disciples were "born again" long before Pentecost, in fact probably long before Jesus breathed on them and told them to receive the Holy Spirit in John 20:22.[14] Jesus had said, "No one can come to me unless the Father who sent me draws him" (John 6:44), but the disciples certainly had come to Jesus and had followed him (even though their understanding of who he was increased gradually over time). Certainly when Peter said to Jesus, "You are the Christ, the Son of the living God" (Matt. 16:16), it was evidence of some kind of regenerating work of the Holy Spirit in his heart. Jesus told him, "Flesh and blood has not revealed this to you, but my Father who is in heaven" (Matt. 16:17). And Jesus had said to the Father regarding his disciples, "I have given them the words that you gave me, and *they have received them* and have come to know in truth that I came from you; and they have believed that you sent me. . . . *I have guarded them*, and *not one of them has been lost* except the son of destruction, that the Scripture might be fulfilled" (John 17:8, 12). The disciples had "little faith" (Matt. 8:26) at times, but they did have faith! Certainly they were regenerated long before the day of Pentecost.[15]

But we must realize that the day of Pentecost is much more than an individual event

---

we were baptized "*for* the one body of Christ" (24). But Baker's argument is not convincing, because the word "for" at the beginning of v. 13 shows that it must be an argument that supports v. 12, where Paul says that we are many members, but one body. Yet in order for v. 13 to show that all Christians are a part of one body, it is necessary for v. 13 to communicate why we are *all* members of one body, and Paul does this by showing that we are all baptized into one body. Baker's view, that this happens only to some "who are already members *of* the body of Christ to enable them to function effectively" (24) is not convincing in view of Paul's statement that "all" Christians were baptized into one body. Moreover, baptism *for the benefit of* one body (which is essentially what Baker takes it to mean) gives a very unusual sense to the preposition *eis*—if Paul had meant this, we would have expected something like *heneka*, "for the sake of," or *hyper* plus the genitive, meaning "in behalf, for the sake of."

14. When Jesus breathed on his disciples and said to them, "Receive the Holy Spirit" (John 20:22), it probably was an acted-out prophecy of what would happen to them at Pentecost. In this same context—in fact, in the verse immediately preceding—Jesus had told them something that would not happen until Pentecost: "As the Father has sent me, *even so I*

am sending you" (John 20:21). But even though he said this before he had ascended into heaven, he did not really send them out to preach the gospel until the Day of Pentecost had come. Therefore, his words were looking forward to what would happen at Pentecost. It is best to understand the words in the next sentence, "Receive the Holy Spirit," in the same way—he was speaking in advance of something that would happen on the Day of Pentecost. On that day they would receive the new covenant fullness and power of the Holy Spirit, a much greater empowering of the Holy Spirit than what they had experienced before.

15. I do not mean to say that believers' experience of regeneration in the old covenant was exactly the same as that of new covenant believers. While considerations listed in the following discussion indicate a less powerful work of the Holy Spirit in the old covenant, defining the nature of the differences is difficult, since Scripture gives us little explicit information about it. But the fact that there was any saving faith at all in old covenant believers requires us to think that there was some kind of regenerating work of the Holy Spirit in them, enabling them to believe. (See the discussion of regeneration in chapter 34, pp. 850–56.)

in the lives of Jesus' disciples and those with them. *The day of Pentecost was the point of transition between the old covenant work and ministry of the Holy Spirit and the new covenant work and ministry of the Holy Spirit.* Of course the Holy Spirit was at work throughout the Old Testament, hovering over the waters of the first day of creation (Gen. 1:2), empowering people for service to God and for leadership and prophecy (Ex. 31:3; 35:31; Deut. 34:9; Judg. 14:6; 1 Sam. 16:13; Ps. 51:11, et al.). But during that time the work of the Holy Spirit in individual lives was, in general, a work of lesser power.

## 4. A Less Powerful Work of the Holy Spirit in the Old Covenant

There are several indications of a less powerful and less extensive work of the Holy Spirit in the old covenant: the Holy Spirit only came to a few people with significant power for ministry (Num. 11:16–17, for example), but Moses longed for the day when the Holy Spirit would be poured out on all of God's people: "Would that all the LORD's people were prophets, that the LORD would put his Spirit on them!" (Num. 11:29). The equipping of the Holy Spirit for special ministries could be lost, as it was in the life of Saul (1 Sam. 16:14), and as David feared that it might be in his life (Ps. 51:11). In terms of spiritual power in the lives of the people of God, there was little power over the dominion of Satan, resulting in very little effective evangelism of the nations around Israel, and no examples of ability to cast out demons.[16] The old covenant work of the Holy Spirit was almost completely confined to the nation of Israel, but in the new covenant there is created a new "dwelling place for God" (Eph. 2:22), the church, which unites both gentiles and Jews in the body of Christ.

Moreover, the Old Testament people of God looked forward to a "new covenant" age when the work of the Holy Spirit would be much more powerful and much more widespread (Num. 11:29; Jer. 31:31–33; Ezek. 36:26–27; Joel 2:28–29).[17]

When the New Testament opens, we see John the Baptist as the last of the Old Testament prophets. Jesus said, "Among those born of women there has arisen no one greater than John the Baptist. Yet the one who is least in the kingdom of heaven is greater than he . . . all the Prophets and the Law prophesied until John, and if you are willing to accept it, he is Elijah who is to come" (Matt. 11:11–14). John knew that he baptized with water, but Jesus would baptize with the Holy Spirit (Luke 3:16). John the Baptist, then, still was living in an "old covenant" experience of the working of the Holy Spirit.

---

16. The closest thing to casting out demons in the Old Testament is the situation where the evil spirit troubling Saul departed from him whenever David played his lyre (1 Sam. 16:23), but this is hardly equivalent to the effective and lasting casting out of demons of which we see in the New Testament age.

17. Of course, there were examples in the Old Testament where certain leaders were remarkably gifted by God and

empowered by the Holy Spirit—Moses, David, Daniel, many of the writing prophets, and even Samson received unusual empowering from the Holy Spirit for specific ministries. But their experiences were not typical of the vast numbers of God's people who were saved by faith as they looked forward to the promised Messiah's coming but who did not have the outpouring of the Holy Spirit in the new covenant power that we experience today.

## 5. A More Powerful Work of the Holy Spirit in the New Covenant

In the life of Jesus, we first see the new covenant power of the Holy Spirit at work. The Holy Spirit descends on him at his baptism (Luke 3:21–22), and after his temptation Jesus "returned *in the power of the Spirit* to Galilee" (Luke 4:14). Then we begin to see what this new covenant power of the Holy Spirit will look like: Jesus casts out demons with a word, heals all who are brought to him, and teaches with authority that people had not heard before (see Luke 4:16–44 et al.).

The disciples, however, do not receive this full new covenant empowering for ministry until the Day of Pentecost, for Jesus tells them to wait in Jerusalem, and promises, "*You will receive power* when the Holy Spirit has come upon you" (Acts 1:8). This was a transition in the lives of the disciples as well (see John 7:39; 14:17; 16:7; Acts 2:16). The promise of Joel that the Holy Spirit would come in new covenant fullness was fulfilled (Acts 2:16) as Jesus returned to heaven and then was given authority to pour out the Holy Spirit in new fullness and power (Acts 2:33).

What was the result in the lives of the disciples? These believers, who had had an old-covenant, less powerful experience of the Holy Spirit in their lives, received on the Day of Pentecost a more powerful, new covenant experience of the Holy Spirit working in their lives.[18] They received much greater "power" (Acts 1:8), power for living the Christian life and for carrying out Christian ministry.

This transition from an old covenant experience of the Holy Spirit to a new covenant experience of the Holy Spirit can be seen in figure 39.1.[19]

In this diagram, the thinner line at the bottom represents the less powerful work of the Holy Spirit in individuals' lives during the old covenant. The thicker line that begins at Pentecost shows the more powerful work of the Holy Spirit in people's lives after that time. The lines for "this age" and "the age to come" overlap now because the powers of the age to come have broken into this present evil age, so that Christians live during an "overlap of the ages." The dotted lines prior to Pentecost indicate that in the life of Jesus the more powerful work of the Holy Spirit had already begun in a way that anticipated (and even surpassed) what would come at Pentecost.[20]

---

18. Ervin, *Conversion-Initiation*, 14, 15–19, objects that the new covenant did not begin at Pentecost but earlier at the time of Jesus' death. This is certainly true, but it misses the point. We are not arguing that the new covenant itself began at the day of Pentecost, but the new covenant experience of the Holy Spirit began at Pentecost, because it was there that Jesus poured out the Holy Spirit in new covenant fullness and power (Acts 2:33; cf. 1:4–5).

Ervin also objects that the disciples at Pentecost received "power-in-mission" from the Holy Spirit, not entrance into the new covenant (17–18). But here Ervin has put forth a false dichotomy. It is not either/or but both/and. At Pentecost the disciples both entered into a new covenant experience of the Holy Spirit and (of course) received a new empowering for ministry with that experience of the Holy Spirit.

19. I have adapted this diagram from George Ladd, *A Theology of the New Testament* (Grand Rapids: Eerdmans, 1974), 68–69.

20. Because of their association with Jesus, the disciples also received some foretaste of the post-Pentecostal power of the Holy Spirit when they healed the sick and cast out demons (cf. Luke 9:1; 10:1, 8, 17–20, and many other verses).

**At Pentecost Believers Experienced a Transition from an Old Covenant Experience of the Holy Spirit to a More Powerful, New Covenant Experience of the Holy Spirit**
*Figure 39.1*

This new covenant power gave the disciples (1) more effectiveness in their witness and their ministry (Acts 1:8; Eph. 4:8, 11–13), (2) greater power for victory over the influence of sin in the lives of all believers (note the emphasis on the power of Christ's resurrection at work within us in Rom. 6:11–14; 8:13–14; Gal. 2:20; Phil. 3:10), and (3) power for victory over Satan and demonic forces that would attack believers (2 Cor. 10:3–4; Eph. 1:19–21; 6:10–18; 1 John 4:4). This new covenant power of the Holy Spirit also resulted in (4) a wide and hitherto unknown distribution of gifts for ministry to all believers (Acts 2:16–18; 1 Cor. 12:7, 11; 1 Peter 4:10; cf. Num. 11:17, 24–29). These gifts also had corporate implications because they were intended not to be used individualistically but for the corporate building up of the body of Christ (1 Cor. 12:7; 14:12). It also meant that (5) the gospel was no longer effectively limited to the Jews only, but all races and all nations would hear the gospel in power and would be united into the church, to the glory of God (Eph. 2:11–3:10).[21] The Day of Pentecost was certainly a remarkable time of transition in the whole history of redemption as recorded in Scripture. It was a remarkable day in the history of the world because on that day the Holy Spirit began to function among God's people with new covenant power.

But this fact helps us understand what happened to the disciples at Pentecost. They received this remarkable new empowering from the Holy Spirit *because they were living at the time of the transition between the old covenant work of the Holy Spirit and the new covenant work of the Holy Spirit.* Though it was a "second experience" of the Holy Spirit, coming as it did long after their conversion, it is not to be taken as a pattern for us, for

---

21. When the Holy Spirit came in power, he ordinarily came to groups of people rather than to isolated individuals (so Acts 2:4; 8:17; 10:44; 19:6; but the conversion of Saul is different: see Acts 9:17–18). A new community, filled with love for one another, was the evident result of the outpouring of the Holy Spirit in this way (see Acts 2:41–47).

we are not living at a time of transition in the work of the Holy Spirit. In their case, believers with an *old covenant empowering* from the Holy Spirit became believers with a *new covenant empowering* from the Holy Spirit.

But we today do not first become believers with a weaker, old covenant work of the Holy Spirit in our hearts and wait until some later time to receive a new covenant work of the Holy Spirit. Rather, we are in the same position as those who became Christians in the church at Corinth: at the moment when we become Christians we are each "*in one Spirit . . . baptized into one body*" (1 Cor. 12:13), just as the Corinthians were and just as were the new believers in many churches who were converted when Paul traveled on his missionary journeys.

In conclusion, the disciples certainly did experience "a baptism in the Holy Spirit" after conversion on the Day of Pentecost, but this happened because they were living at a unique point in history, and this event in their lives is therefore not a pattern that we are to seek to imitate.

What shall we say about the phrase "baptism in the Holy Spirit"? It is a phrase that the New Testament authors use to speak of coming into the new covenant power of the Holy Spirit. It happened at Pentecost for the disciples, but it happened at conversion for the Corinthians and for us.[22] It is not a phrase the New Testament authors would use to speak of any postconversion experience of empowering by the Holy Spirit.

## C. How Should We Understand the Other "Second Experiences" in Acts?

But even if we have correctly understood the experience of the disciples at Pentecost as recorded in Acts 2, are there not other examples of people who had a "second experience" of empowering of the Holy Spirit after conversion, such as those in Acts 8 (at Samaria), Acts 10 (Cornelius' household), and Acts 19 (the Ephesian disciples)?

These are not really convincing examples to prove the Pentecostal doctrine of baptism in the Holy Spirit either. First, the expression "baptism in the Holy Spirit" is not ordinarily used to refer to any of these events,[23] and this should give us some hesitation in applying this phrase to them. But more importantly, a closer look at each case shows more clearly what was happening in these events.

22. My student James Renihan argued (in a lengthy student paper) that baptism in the Holy Spirit, while occurring at the same time as conversion, should nevertheless be considered a distinct element in the "order of salvation" (the list of things that happen to us in experiencing salvation; see chapter 32, p. 817). He notes that baptism in the Holy Spirit is not exactly the same as any of the other elements in the order of salvation (such as regeneration or conversion) and may also be called "receiving the Holy Spirit" (see Acts 8:15–16; 19:2, 6; Rom. 8:9, 11; Gal. 3:2). Renihan's idea is clearly not the charismatic doctrine of a baptism in the Holy Spirit subsequent to conversion (for he would say it always accompanies genuine conversion and always occurs at the same time as conversion). The suggestion is an interesting one and, while I have not presently adopted it in this chapter, I think it deserves further consideration. It would not be inconsistent with my overall argument in this chapter.

23. The only exception is Acts 11:15–17. While this passage does not explicitly call the falling of the Holy Spirit on Cornelius' household a "baptism in the Holy Spirit," when Peter says, "the Holy Spirit fell on them *just as on us at the beginning*," and then recalls Jesus' words about baptism in the Holy Spirit, he clearly implies that the members of Cornelius's household were baptized in the Holy Spirit when he preached to them (see Acts 10:44–48).

## 1. Acts 8: Samaria

In Acts 8:4–25 the Samaritan people "believed Philip as he preached good news about the kingdom of God and the name of Jesus Christ," and "they were baptized, both men and women" (Acts 8:12). Some have argued that this was not genuine saving faith on the part of the Samaritans.[24] However, there is no indication in the text that Philip had a deficient understanding of the gospel (he had been prominent in the Jerusalem church) or that Philip himself thought that their faith in Christ was inadequate, for he allowed them to be baptized (Acts 8:12).

A better understanding of this event would be that God, in his providence, sovereignly waited to give the new covenant empowering of the Holy Spirit to the Samaritans directly through the hands of the apostles (Acts 8:14–17)[25] so that it might be evident to the highest leadership in the Jerusalem church that the Samaritans were not second-class citizens but full members of the church. This was important because of the historical animosity between Jews and Samaritans ("Jews have no dealings with Samaritans," John 4:9) and because Jesus had specified that the spread of the gospel to Samaria would be the next major step after it had been preached in Jerusalem and the region of Judea that surrounded Jerusalem: "You will be my witnesses in Jerusalem and in all Judea *and Samaria*, and to the end of the earth" (Acts 1:8). Thus the event in Acts 8 was a kind of "Samaritan Pentecost," a special outpouring of the Holy Spirit on the people of Samaria, who were a mixed race of Jewish and gentile ancestry, so that it might be evident to all that the full new covenant blessings and power of the Holy Spirit had come to this group of people as well and were not confined to Jews only. Because this is a special event in the history of redemption, as the pattern of Acts 1:8 is worked out in the book of Acts, it is not a pattern for us to repeat today. It is simply part of the transition between the old covenant experience of the Holy Spirit and the new covenant experience of the Holy Spirit.

## 2. Acts 10: Cornelius

The situation in Acts 10 is less complicated, because it is not even clear that Cornelius was a genuine believer before Peter came and preached the gospel to him. Certainly he had not trusted in Christ for salvation. Rather, he is a gentile who was one of the first examples of the way in which the gospel would go "to the end of the earth" (Acts 1:8).[26] Certainly Cornelius had not first believed in Christ's death and resurrection to save him and then later come into a second experience after his conversion.

---

24. This is the argument of James Dunn, *Baptism in the Holy Spirit* (London: SCM, 1970), 55–72.

25. In this section I am largely following the careful discussion of John Stott, *Baptism and Fulness*, 2nd ed. (Leicester: Inter-Varsity Press; Downers Grove, IL: InterVarsity Press, 1976), 31–34.

26. Even if we did regard him as someone who first had a kind of old covenant faith in the Jewish Messiah who was to come, this would only show that he is one more example of someone who first had an old covenant experience of the Holy Spirit and then came into a new covenant experience of the Holy Spirit.

### 3. Acts 19: Ephesus

In Acts 19, once again we encounter a situation of some people who had not really heard the gospel of salvation through Christ. They had been baptized into the baptism of John the Baptist (Acts 19:3), so they were probably people who had heard John the Baptist preach, or had talked to others who had heard John the Baptist preach, and had been baptized "into John's baptism" (Acts 19:3) as a sign that they were repenting of their sins and preparing for the Messiah who was to come. They certainly had not heard of Christ's death and resurrection, for they had not even heard that there was a Holy Spirit (Acts 19:2)—a fact that no one who was present at Pentecost or who had heard the gospel after Pentecost could have failed to know. It is likely that they had not even heard that Jesus had come and lived and died because Paul had to explain to them, "John baptized with the baptism of repentance, telling the people to believe in the one who was to come after him, *that is, Jesus*" (Acts 19:4). Therefore, these "disciples" in Ephesus did not have new covenant understanding or new covenant faith, and they certainly did not have a new covenant empowering of the Holy Spirit—they were "disciples" only in the sense of followers of John the Baptist who were still waiting for the Messiah. When they heard of him, they believed in him and then received the power of the Holy Spirit that was appropriate to the gospel of the risen Lord Jesus Christ.

Because of this, these disciples at Ephesus are not a pattern for us today either, for we do not first have faith in a Messiah that we are waiting for, and then later learn that Jesus has come and lived and died and risen again. We come into an understanding of the gospel of Christ immediately, and we, like the Corinthians, enter immediately into the new covenant experience of the power of the Holy Spirit.[27]

It seems therefore that there are no New Testament texts that encourage us to seek for a second experience of "baptism in the Holy Spirit" that comes after conversion.

## D. What Terms Shall We Use to Refer to an Empowering by the Holy Spirit That Comes after Conversion?

The previous sections have argued that "baptism in the Holy Spirit" is not the term the New Testament authors would use to speak of a postconversion work of the Spirit and that the examples of "second experiences" of receiving the Holy Spirit in the book of Acts are not patterns for us to imitate in our Christian lives. But many questions remain: What is actually happening to the millions of people who claim that they have received this baptism in the Holy Spirit and that it has brought much blessing to their lives?

---

27. Regarding Acts 19:1–7, Ervin, *Conversion-Initiation*, 55–59, objects that these disciples were first baptized and then, when Paul laid his hands on them, they were empowered with the Holy Spirit. We may admit that this is true, but the two events were so closely connected in time that it is hard to make a clear separation between them, and they certainly do not fit the common Pentecostal pattern of instruction and prayer, sometimes weeks or months or years after conversion, seeking a subsequent baptism in the Holy Spirit. If we had asked them later if their baptism in the Holy Spirit was "subsequent" to their conversion, they would probably have said that it was at the same time, so closely connected were these events in the actual historical sequence.

Could it be that this has been a genuine work of the Holy Spirit but that the biblical categories and biblical examples used to illustrate it have been incorrect? Might it be that there are other biblical expressions and biblical teachings that point to this kind of work of the Holy Spirit after conversion and help us understand it more accurately? I think there are, but before we look at these, it is appropriate to comment on the importance of having a correct understanding at this point.

## 1. Harm Comes to the Church From Teaching Two-Class Christianity

At various times in the history of the church Christians have attempted to divide the church into two categories of believers. This is in effect what happens with the Pentecostal doctrine of baptism in the Holy Spirit. It might be pictured as in figure 39.2, which shows the world divided into Christians and non-Christians, and then shows Christians divided into two categories, ordinary believers and Spirit-baptized believers.

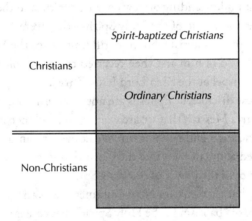

**Christians Divided into Two Categories: Ordinary and Spirit-Baptized**
*Figure 39.2*

But such a division of Christians into two categories is not a unique understanding that is found only in Pentecostal teaching in the twentieth century. In fact, much Pentecostal teaching came out of earlier holiness groups that had taught that Christians could either be ordinary believers or "sanctified" believers. Other groups have divided Christians using different categories, such as ordinary and "Spirit-filled" believers, or ordinary believers and those who are "disciples," or "carnal" and "spiritual" Christians. In fact, the Roman Catholic Church has long had not two but three categories: ordinary believers, priests, and saints. All of these divisions into different categories of Christians can be seen in figure 39.3.[28]

---

28. I have not included in this diagram another division that is sometimes reflected not in any official teaching but in attitude and practice in Reformed circles: the division between ordinary Christians and those who are "truly Reformed."

| | Spirit-filled Christians | Spiritual Christians | "Sanctified" Christians | "Disciples" | Saints |
|---|---|---|---|---|---|
| | | | | | Priests |
| Christians | Ordinary Christians | Carnal Christians | Ordinary Christians | Ordinary Christians | Ordinary Christians |
| Non-Christians | | | | | |

**Other Ways People Have Classified Christians so as to
Divide Them into Two (or Three) Categories**
*Figure 39.3*

Although those who teach the classical Pentecostal view of baptism in the Holy Spirit may deny that they are attempting to divide Christians into two categories, such a division is implicit every time they ask whether someone has been baptized in the Holy Spirit or not. Such a question strongly suggests that there are two groups of Christians, those who have had this experience of "baptism in the Holy Spirit" and those who have not.

What is the problem with viewing Christians as existing in two categories like this? The problem is that it contributes to a "we-they" mentality in churches, which leads to jealousy, pride, and divisiveness. No matter how much these people who have received this special empowering of the Holy Spirit try to be thoughtful and considerate of those who have not, if they genuinely love their fellow brothers and sisters in Christ, and if this has been a very helpful experience in their own Christian lives, they cannot help but give the impression that they would like others to share this experience as well. Even if they are not proud in their hearts (and it seems to me that most are not) with respect to this experience, such a conviction that there is a second category of Christians will inevitably give an impression of pride or spiritual superiority. Yet there will very likely be a sense of jealousy or inferiority on the part of those who have not had such an experience. In this way, a view of two groups within the church is fostered, and the repeated charge of divisiveness that is made against the charismatic movement is given some credibility. In fact, divisions often do occur in churches.

The major objection to this position is that the New Testament teaches no such two-level or two-class Christianity. Nowhere in the Epistles do we read of Paul or Peter telling a church that is having problems, "You all need to be baptized in the Holy Spirit." Nowhere do we hear of the risen Lord Jesus speaking to the troubled and weak churches in Revelation 2–3, "Ask me to baptize you in the Holy Spirit." It is hard to avoid the conclusion that the two-level or two-class view taught by all of these groups throughout history does not have a solid foundation in the New Testament itself.

## 2. There Are Many Degrees of Empowering, Fellowship with God, and Personal Christian Maturity

Is there a better model for understanding the varying degrees of maturity and power and fellowship with God that Christians experience? If we are willing to eliminate the categories that make us think of Christians in one group or another, a better model is possible, as represented in figure 39.4.

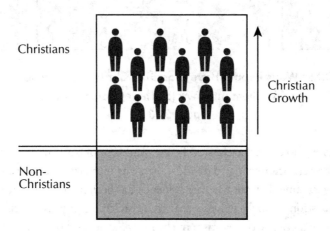

**A Better Picture: Christians Have Experienced Varying Degrees of Growth, but They Should Not Be Divided into Two Distinct Categories**
*Figure 39.4*

This chart shows the world as divided into non-Christians and Christians, but among Christians there are not categories into which we can place believers and divide them into set groups. Rather, Christians occupy all points along a scale of increasing Christian maturity (sanctification), increasing closeness of fellowship in their walk with God (an aspect of adoption), and greater experiences of the power of the Holy Spirit at work in their lives and ministries.

The Christian life should be one of *growth in all of these areas* as we progress throughout life. For many people that growth will be gradual and progressive and will extend over all the years of their lives. We could represent it by the arrow in figure 39.5.[29]

---

29. To be more precise we need to recognize that we can grow in some aspects of the Christian life without growing in others, and a single chart is therefore inadequate to show all of this. For example, Christians can grow in power but not in holiness (as the Corinthian church had done), or people can grow in knowledge but not in power, or knowledge but not in holiness of life (something that tragically happens to some—but certainly not all—students in theological seminaries, and to some pastors who place excessive emphasis on academic pursuits). Or a person can grow in personal fellowship with God but not in knowledge of Scripture (something that happens with an extensive "pietistic" emphasis). Or someone can grow in holiness of life but not in power or use of spiritual gifts. All sorts of combinations like this are possible, but we would need several charts to show them in a schematic way. For the sake of simplicity I have simply represented "Christian growth" in general on this chart.

**For Most Christians Growth Will Be Gradual and Progressive
and Will Extend over Their Whole Lives
Figure 39.5**

**a. How Should We Understand Contemporary Experience?** What then has happened to people who say they have experienced a "baptism in the Holy Spirit" that has brought great blessing to their lives? We must understand first what is commonly taught about the need to prepare for baptism in the Holy Spirit. Very often people will be taught that they should confess all known sins, repent of any remaining sin in their lives, trust Christ to forgive those sins, commit every area of their lives to the Lord's service, yield themselves fully to him, and believe that Christ is going to empower them in a new way and equip them with new gifts for ministry. Then after that preparation, they are encouraged to ask Jesus in prayer to baptize them in the Holy Spirit. But what does this preparation do? It is a guaranteed prescription for significant growth in the Christian life! Such confession, repentance, renewed commitment, and heightened faith and expectation, if they are genuine, can only bring positive results in a person's life. If any Christian is sincere in these steps of preparation to receive baptism in the Holy Spirit, there will certainly be growth in sanctification and deeper fellowship with God. In addition to that, we may expect that at many of these times the Holy Spirit will graciously bring a measure of the additional fullness and empowering that sincere Christians are seeking, even though their theological understanding and vocabulary may be imperfect in the asking. If this happens, they may well realize increased power for ministry and growth in spiritual gifts as well. We could say that a person has moved from point A to point B in figure 39.6 and has made one very large step forward in the Christian life.

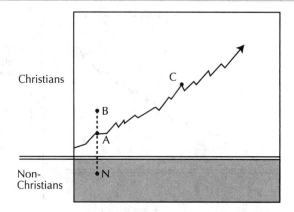

**A Single Experience May Result in a Large Step
of Growth in the Christian Life**
*Figure 39.6*

Of course prayer, Bible study, and worship will seem more meaningful. Of course there will be more fruitfulness in evangelism and other kinds of ministry. But it is important to recognize that someone who moves from point A to point B on the chart is not now in a separate category of Christians, such as those who have been "baptized in the Holy Spirit" and who are therefore different from those who have not had such an experience. There might be another Christian in the same church who has never had such a large step of growth but who has nonetheless been making steady progress for the last forty years of his or her Christian life and has come to point C on the chart above. Though that person has never had a single experience that Pentecostals would call a "baptism in the Holy Spirit," he or she is still much farther along the path of Christian growth than the younger Christian who has recently been "baptized in the Holy Spirit" (according to Pentecostal terminology) and moved from point A to point B. Although the Christian who moved from point A to point B is not farther along in the Christian life than another person who is at point C, the person who moved to point B is certainly farther along *than he or she was before*, and this is certainly a positive result in his or her life. Thus, with this understanding of the Christian life, we have no divisions of Christians into two categories.

Before we leave this chart, one more observation should be made: in many cases the charismatic movement has brought teaching on the baptism of the Holy Spirit into more liberal churches where, for many years, there has not been a clear proclamation of the gospel of salvation by faith in Christ alone, and where people have not been taught that they can believe the Bible completely as God's Word to us. In such cases, many of the people in those churches have never experienced saving faith—they are at point N on the chart above, actually non-Christians and not born again.[30]

---

30. However, in many cases, both in some Protestant churches and in Roman Catholic churches, people have been told that they received Christ and became Christians at their baptism when they were infants.

Now when a representative of a charismatic renewal comes to these churches and tells them that they can experience new vitality in their Christian lives and that the preparation is to repent of all known sins, ask Christ for forgiveness of those sins and trust him to forgive them, and commit their lives totally to Christ as their Lord, they eagerly respond to those directions. Then they pray and ask Jesus to baptize them in the Holy Spirit. The actual result is that they move from point N on the chart to point A or perhaps even point B, because of their sincerity and deep eagerness to draw closer to God. While they think that they have been baptized by the Holy Spirit as a second experience in their Christian lives, what has in fact happened is that they have become Christians for the first time. (They have been "baptized in the Holy Spirit" in the true New Testament sense!) The next day, it is almost impossible to keep them silent—they are so excited. Suddenly, reading the Bible has become meaningful. Suddenly prayer has become real. Suddenly they know the presence of God in their lives. Suddenly worship has become an experience of deep joy, and often they have begun to experience spiritual gifts that they had not known before. It is no wonder that the charismatic renewal has brought such excitement (and often much controversy) to many Roman Catholic parishes and to many mainline, more liberal Protestant denominations. Though we may differ with the way this teaching is actually presented, no one should fault the good results that have come about as a result of it in these churches.

**b. What Terms Should We Use Today?** Now we can understand why our use of terms to describe this experience and the category of understanding we put it in are so important. If we use the traditional Pentecostal terminology of "baptism of the Holy Spirit," then we almost inevitably end up with two-category Christianity, for this is seen as a common experience that *can* and indeed *should* happen to Christians at one point in time and, once it has happened, does not need to be repeated. It is seen as a single experience of empowering for ministry that is distinct from the experience of becoming a Christian, and people either have received that experience or they have not. Especially when the experience is described in terms of what happened to the disciples at Pentecost in Acts 2 (which was clearly a one-time experience for them), the Samaritans in Acts 8, and the Ephesian disciples in Acts 19, it is clearly implied that this is a one-time event that empowers people for ministry but that also puts them in a separate category or group than the one they were in before this experience. The use of the term *baptism in the Holy Spirit* inevitably implies two groups of Christians.

But if we are correct in understanding the experience that has come to millions of people in the charismatic renewal as a large step of growth in their Christian lives, then a different term than "baptism in the Holy Spirit" would seem to be more appropriate. There might be several terms that we could use, so long as they allow for repetition, varying degrees of intensity, and further development beyond that one experience, and so long as they do not suggest that all truly obedient Christians should have the same experience.[31] We have already used one expression, "*a large step of growth* in several aspects of the Christian life." Because this phrase speaks of "*a large step of growth*" it cannot be misunderstood to refer to a single experience that puts Christians in a new category. And because it is referred to as a large step of growth, it clearly implies that others may experience such growth in smaller steps over a longer period of time but reach the same point in the Christian life.[32]

Another term that may be helpful is "a new *empowering for ministry*." It is certainly true that many who have received such a charismatic experience do find new power for ministry in their Christian lives, including the ability to use spiritual gifts that had not been theirs before. However, the problem with this phrase is that it does not say anything about the deepened fellowship with God, the greater effectiveness in prayer and Bible study, and the new joy in worship that often also result from this experience.

**c. What Is "Being Filled with the Spirit"?** Yet an even more commonly used term in the New Testament is "*being filled with the Holy Spirit*." Because of its frequent use in contexts that speak of Christian growth and ministry, *this seems to me to be the best term to use* to describe genuine "second experiences" today (or third or fourth experiences, etc.). Paul tells the Ephesians, "Do not get drunk with wine, for that is debauchery, but *be filled with the Spirit*" (Eph. 5:18). He uses a present tense imperative verb that could more explicitly be translated, "Be continually being filled with the Holy Spirit," thus implying that this is something that should repeatedly be happening to Christians. Such fullness of the Holy Spirit will result in *renewed worship and thanksgiving* (Eph. 5:19–20), and in renewed relationships to others, especially those in authority over us or those under our authority (Eph. 5:21–6:9). In addition, since the Holy Spirit is the Spirit who sanctifies us, such a filling will often result in *increased sanctification*. Furthermore, since the Holy Spirit is the one who empowers us for Christian service and gives us spiritual gifts, such filling will often result in *increased power for ministry* and increased effectiveness and perhaps diversity in the use of *spiritual gifts*.

We see examples of repeated filling with the Holy Spirit in the book of Acts. In Acts 2:4, the disciples and those with them were "all *filled with the Holy Spirit*." Later, when Peter was standing before the Sanhedrin, we read, "Then Peter, *filled with the Holy Spirit*, said to them . . ." (Acts 4:8). But a little later, when Peter and the other apostles had returned to the church to tell what had happened (Acts 4:23) they joined together in prayer. After they had prayed they were again filled with the Holy Spirit, a sequence of events that Luke makes clear: "*When they had prayed*, the place in which they were gathered together was shaken, and *they were all filled with the Holy Spirit* and continued to speak the word of God with boldness" (Acts 4:31). Even though Peter had been filled

---

31. The same criteria could be used to find replacement terms for some of the other "two-category" views mentioned above or else to explain the terms that are used so as to avoid misunderstanding.

32. Paul does say that we "are to grow up *in every way* into him who is the head, into Christ" (Eph. 4:15).

with the Holy Spirit at Pentecost (Acts 2:4) and had later been filled with the Holy Spirit before speaking to the Sanhedrin (Acts 4:8), he was once again filled with the Holy Spirit after the group of Christians he was meeting with had prayed.

Therefore, it is appropriate to understand filling with the Holy Spirit *not as a one-time event* but as *an event that can occur over and over again* in a Christian's life. It may involve a momentary empowering for a specific ministry (such as apparently happened in Acts 4:8; 7:55), but it may also refer to a long-term characteristic of a person's life (see Acts 6:3; 11:24). In either case such filling can occur many times in a person's life: even though Stephen, as an early deacon (or apostolic assistant), was a man "full of the Spirit and of wisdom" (Acts 6:3, 5), when he was being stoned he apparently received a fresh new filling of the Holy Spirit in great power (Acts 7:55).

Someone might object that a person who is already "full" of the Holy Spirit cannot become more full—if a glass is full of water no more water can be put into it. But a water glass is a poor analogy for us as real people, for God is able to cause us to grow and to be able to contain much more of the Holy Spirit's fullness and power. A better analogy might be a balloon, which can be "full" of air even though it has very little air in it. When more air is blown in, the balloon expands and in a sense it is "more full." So it is with us: we can be filled with the Holy Spirit and at the same time be able to receive much more of the Holy Spirit as well. It was only Jesus himself to whom the Father gave the Spirit without measure (John 3:34).

The divisiveness that comes with the term *baptism in the Holy Spirit* could easily be avoided by using any of the alternative terms mentioned in this section. People could be thankful for "being filled with the Holy Spirit" or "a new empowering for ministry" or "a significant step in growth" in some aspect of another Christian's life. There would be no separating into "we" and "they," for we would recognize that we are all part of one body with no separate categories.[33] In fact, many charismatics and even some traditional Pentecostals today are using the term *baptism in the Holy Spirit* far less frequently, preferring to use other terms such as "being filled with the Holy Spirit" instead.[34]

Moreover, many people who have had no single dramatic experience (such as what Pentecostals have called a baptism in the Holy Spirit) have nonetheless begun to experience new freedom and joy in worship (often with the advent of modern worship or praise songs in their churches) and to use a wider variety of spiritual gifts with effectiveness and edification for themselves and their churches (including gifts such as healing, prophecy,

---

33. It is my personal opinion that most of the divisiveness that has come with the influence of charismatic renewal in many churches has not come because of spiritual gifts but because of a misunderstanding of what is happening and the implications of two groups of Christians that come with the term *baptism in the Holy Spirit*.

34. John Wimber, who did not like to identify himself as a Pentecostal or a charismatic, said with much wisdom, "I have discovered that the argument concerning the baptism of the Spirit usually comes down to a question of labels. Good medicine may be incorrectly labeled, which is probably true in this case. The Pentecostals' experience of God is better than their explanation of it" (Wimber with Springer, *Power Evangelism*, 145). In recent years I have noticed in personal conversation with professors at institutions affiliated with the charismatic movement that there is an increasing tendency to talk about filling with the Holy Spirit rather than baptism in the Holy Spirit to represent what has happened to those within the charismatic movement.

working of miracles, discernment of spirits, and the ability to exercise authority over demonic forces with prayer and a word of rebuke spoken directly to the evil spirits). Sometimes the gift of speaking in tongues and the gift of interpretation have been used as well, but in other cases they have not. All of this is to say that the differences between Pentecostals and charismatics on the one hand and more traditional and mainstream evangelical Christians on the other hand seem to be breaking down more and more, and there are fewer and fewer differences between them.

Someone may object that it is specifically the experience of praying for a baptism in the Holy Spirit that catapults people into a new level of power in ministry and effectiveness in use of spiritual gifts. Since this experience has been so helpful in the lives of millions of people, should we so quickly dismiss it? In response, it must be said that if the terminology "baptism in the Holy Spirit" is changed for something more representative of New Testament teaching, there should be no objection at all to speakers coming into churches and encouraging people to prepare their hearts for spiritual renewal by sincere repentance and renewed commitment to Christ and by believing that the Holy Spirit can work much more powerfully in their lives.[35] There is nothing wrong with teaching people to pray and seek this greater infilling of the Holy Spirit, or to expect and ask the Lord for an outpouring of more spiritual gifts in their lives, for the benefit of the body of Christ (see 1 Cor. 12:31; 14:1, 12). In fact, most evangelical Christians in every denomination genuinely long for greater power in ministry, greater joy in worship, and deeper fellowship with God. Many would also welcome increased understanding of spiritual gifts and encouragement to grow in the use of them. If Pentecostal and charismatic Christians would be willing to teach on these things without the additional baggage of two-level Christianity that is implied by the term *baptism in the Holy Spirit*, they might find a new era of greatly increased effectiveness in bringing teaching on these other areas of the Christian life to evangelicals generally.

### 3. Being Filled with the Holy Spirit Does Not Always Result in Speaking in Tongues

One remaining point needs to be made with respect to the experience of being filled with the Holy Spirit. Because there were several cases in Acts where people received the new covenant power of the Holy Spirit and began to speak in tongues at the same time (Acts 2:4; 10:46; 19:6; probably also implied in 8:17–19 because of the parallel with the

---

35. YouTube has a thirty-four-minute video lecture that I gave on how to be filled with the Holy Spirit. See https://www.youtube.com/watch?v=zarT9x4ancA.

My student Jack Mattern, though not himself a charismatic, has told me that in over a decade of working with students on university campuses, he has found a great hunger among Christians to know how they may be filled with the Holy Spirit. He rightly points out that effective teaching on this area must include the need (1) to yield our lives fully to God (Rom. 12:1; Gal. 2:20), (2) to depend fully on God for power to live the Christian life (Rom. 8:13; Gal. 2:20; 3:2–3), and (3) to obey the Lord's commands in our lives (1 John 2:6). These elements are similar to the steps of preparation mentioned above in the discussion of common charismatic teaching. In any case, to these steps could certainly be added a prayer that the Holy Spirit would fill us, in accordance with the will of God as expressed in Eph. 5:18. There should be no objection to teaching Christians to pray daily in accordance with these principles.

experience of the disciples in Acts 2), Pentecostal teaching has commonly maintained that the outward sign of baptism in the Holy Spirit is speaking in tongues (that is, speaking in languages that are not understood by and have not been learned by the person speaking, whether known human languages or other kinds of angelic or heavenly or miraculously given languages).[36]

But it is important to realize that there are many cases where being filled with the Holy Spirit *did not* result in speaking in tongues. When Jesus was filled with the Spirit in Luke 4:1, the result was strength to overcome the temptations of Satan in the wilderness. When the temptations had ended, and Jesus "returned in the power of the Spirit to Galilee" (Luke 4:14), the results were miracles of healing, casting out of demons, and teaching with authority. When Elizabeth was filled with the Holy Spirit, she spoke a word of blessing to Mary (Luke 1:41–45). When Zechariah was filled with the Holy Spirit, he prophesied (Luke 1:67–79). Other results of being filled with the Holy Spirit were powerful preaching of the gospel (Acts 4:31), (perhaps) wisdom and Christian maturity and sound judgment (Acts 6:3), powerful preaching and testimony when on trial (Acts 4:8), a vision of heaven (Acts 7:55), and (apparently) faith and maturity of life (Acts 11:24). Several of these cases may also imply the fullness of the Holy Spirit to empower some kind of ministry, especially in the context of the book of Acts, where the empowering of the Holy Spirit is frequently seen to result in miracles, preaching, and works of great power.[37]

Therefore, while an experience of being filled with the Holy Spirit may result in the gift of speaking in tongues or in the use of some other gifts that had not previously been experienced, it also may come without the gift of speaking in tongues. In fact, many Christians throughout history have experienced powerful infillings of the Holy Spirit that have not been accompanied by speaking in tongues. With regard to this gift as well as all other gifts, we must simply say that the Holy Spirit "apportions to each one individually as he wills" (1 Cor. 12:11).

## QUESTIONS FOR PERSONAL APPLICATION

1. Before reading this chapter, what was your understanding of "baptism in the Holy Spirit"? How has your understanding changed, if at all?
2. Has your own Christian life included one or more events that you could call "a large step of growth" in some area or another in the Christian life? Or has it rather been one of small but continuing steps in sanctification, in fellowship with God, and in use of spiritual gifts and power in ministry?

---

36. See chapter 53, pp. 1323–32, for a discussion of speaking in tongues.

37. Scripture does not specify what result there was in the life of John the Baptist, who was "filled with the Holy Spirit, even from his mother's womb" (Luke 1:15), but "the hand of the Lord was with him" (Luke 1:66), and "the child grew and became strong in spirit" (Luke 1:80).

3. Have you known people who have claimed they received a "baptism in the Holy Spirit" after conversion? In your evaluation, has the result in their lives been mostly positive, mostly negative, or rather mixed? If you have had such an experience yourself, do you think that understanding it as a one-time "baptism in the Holy Spirit" was essential to the experience, or could the same results have come in your Christian life if it had been called "being filled with the Holy Spirit"? Do you think it would be right to seek for an experience of filling with the Holy Spirit in your own life now? How might someone go about doing this?

4. We all realize that it is possible to overemphasize something good in the Christian life to such an extent that our lives become unbalanced and not as effective in ministry as they might be. If we think of the various ways in which we can grow in the Christian life (knowledge of the Word and sound doctrine, prayer, love for God, love for other Christians and for non-Christians, trust in God each day, worship, holiness of life, use of spiritual gifts, effective power of the Holy Spirit in our witness and ministry, daily fellowship with God, etc.), in what areas do you think you need to ask God for more growth in your own life? Would it be appropriate to ask him for a new fullness of the Holy Spirit to accompany growth in those areas?

5. With regard to this topic of baptism in or being filled with the Holy Spirit, do you think that evangelical churches generally have been moving toward more divisiveness or more unity on this issue?

**Special Terms**

*baptism by the Holy Spirit*
*baptism in the Holy Spirit*
*baptism with the Holy Spirit*
*being filled with the Holy Spirit*
*new covenant experience of the Holy Spirit*
*old covenant experience of the Holy Spirit*
*Pentecost*
*two-class Christianity*

# BIBLIOGRAPHY

(For an explanation of this bibliography see the note on the bibliography to chapter 1, pp. 23–24. Complete bibliographical data may be found on pp. 1489–96.) Note: Very few systematic theologies have included explicit treatment of this topic, since it has only become a controversial issue in this century.)

## SECTIONS IN EVANGELICAL SYSTEMATIC THEOLOGIES

*1. Anglican (Episcopalian)*
    2001........Packer, 145
    2013........Bird, 633–37, 766, 772–75
    2013........Bray, 728–35

## 2. *Arminian (Wesleyan or Methodist)*

1983........Carter, 1:435–47

1992........Oden, 3:177–204

2002........Cottrell, 295, 362, 365

## 3. *Baptist*

1990–95.....Garrett, 2:180–182

2007........Akin, 674

2013........Erickson, 799–801

## 4. *Dispensational*

1947........Chafer, 6:138–61

1986........Ryrie, 362–66

2017........MacArthur and Mayhue,
353–58, 372, 925

## 5. *Lutheran*

(no explicit treatment)

## 6. *Reformed (or Presbyterian)*

1679–85.....Turretin, *IET*, 3:28–29

1894........Shedd, 784

1906–11.....Bavinck, *RD*, 496–506

1910........Vos, 4:31, 44–45

1998........Reymond, 764–67

2011........Horton, 555–58

2013........Frame, 926–27

2013........Culver, 112, 667, 740,
873–74, 876, 1110–13

2017........Barrett, 398, 561

2019........Letham, 707–10, 716

## 7. *Renewal (or charismatic/Pentecostal)*

1988–92.....Williams, 2:177–79, 181–207,
271–321

1993........Menzies and Horton, 121–32

1995........Horton, 423–56

2008........Duffield and Van Cleave,
308–28

## SECTIONS IN REPRESENTATIVE ROMAN CATHOLIC SYSTEMATIC THEOLOGIES

### 1. *Roman Catholic: Traditional*

1955........Ott (no explicit treatment)

### 2. *Roman Catholic: Post–Vatican II*

2012........*CCC*, paragraphs 694, 698,
784

## OTHER WORKS

Bennett, Dennis, and Rita Bennet. *The Holy Spirit and You*. Plainfield, NJ: Logos, 1971.

Blomberg, Craig L. "Baptism of the Holy Spirit." In *BTDB*, 49–50.

Brand, Chad Owen, ed. *Perspectives on Spirit Baptism: Five Views*. Nashville: B&H, 2004.

Bruner, Frederick Dale. *A Theology of the Holy Spirit: The Pentecostal Experience and the New Testament Witness*. Grand Rapids: Eerdmans, 1970.

Burgess, Stanley M., and Gary B. McGee. "Williams, John Rodman." In *Dictionary of Pentecostal and Charismatic Movements*, 887–88. Grand Rapids: Zondervan, 1998.

Dunn, James D. G. *Baptism in the Holy Spirit*. London: SCM, 1970.

Ervin, Howard M. *Conversion-Initiation and the Baptism in the Holy Spirit: A Critique of James D. G. Dunn's* Baptism in the Holy Spirit. Peabody, MA: Hendrickson, 1984.

———. *Spirit Baptism*. Peabody, MA: Hendrickson, 1987.

Fee, Gordon D. "Baptism in the Holy Spirit: The Issue of Separability and Subsequence." In *Gospel and Spirit: Issues in New Testament Hermeneutics*. Peabody, MA: Hendrickson, 1994.

Gaffin, Richard. *Perspectives on Pentecost*. Phillipsburg, NJ: Presbyterian and Reformed, 1979.

Green, Michael. *Baptism: Its Purpose, Practice and*

*Power*. Downers Grove, IL: InterVarsity Press, 1987, 127–41.

———. "The Spirit's Baptism." In *I Believe in the Holy Spirit*, 123–47. London: Hodder and Stoughton; Grand Rapids: Eerdmans, 1975.

Hoekema, Anthony A. *Holy Spirit Baptism*. Grand Rapids: Eerdmans, 1972.

Lloyd-Jones, Martyn. *Joy Unspeakable: Power and Renewal in the Holy Spirit*. Edited by Christopher Catherwood. Wheaton, IL: Shaw, 1984.

Macchia, Frank D. *Baptized in the Spirit: A Global Pentecostal Theology*. Grand Rapids: Zondervan, 2006.

McGee, Gary B., ed. *Initial Evidence*. Peabody, MA: Hendrickson, 1991.

Packer, J. I. "Baptism in the Spirit." In *NDT2*, 99–101.

———. *Keep in Step with the Spirit*. Old Tappan, NJ: Revell; Leicester: Inter-Varsity Press, 1984.

Stott, John. *Baptism and Fulness*. Leicester: Inter-Varsity Press; Downers Grove, IL: InterVarsity Press, 1976.

Unger, Merrill F. *The Baptism and Gifts of the Holy Spirit*. Chicago: Moody Publishers, 1974.

White, R. E. O. "Baptism of the Spirit." In *EDT3*, 113–14.

Yun, K. D. "Baptism in the Holy Spirit." In *GDT*, 95–97.

## SCRIPTURE MEMORY PASSAGE

**1 Corinthians 12:12–13:** For just as the body is one and has many members, and all the members of the body, though many, are one body, so it is with Christ. For in one Spirit we were all baptized into one body—Jews or Greeks, slaves or free—and all were made to drink of one Spirit.

## HYMN

### "Spirit of God, Descend Upon My Heart"

*Spirit of God, descend upon my heart;*
*Wean it from earth, through all its pulses move;*
*Stoop to my weakness, mighty as thou art,*
*And make me love thee as I ought to love.*

*Hast thou not bid us love thee, God and King?*
*All, all thine own, soul, heart, and strength and mind.*
*I see thy cross—there teach my heart to cling:*
*O let me seek thee, and O let me find.*

*Teach me to feel that thou art always nigh;*
*Teach me the struggles of the soul to bear,*
*To check the rising doubt, the rebel sigh;*
*Teach me the patience of unanswered prayer.*

*Teach me to love thee as thine angels love,*
*One holy passion filling all my frame;*
*The baptism of the heav'n descended dove*
*My heart an altar, and thy love the flame.*

Author: George Croly, 1854

Alternative hymn: "Spirit of the Living God"

# CONTEMPORARY WORSHIP SONG

### "Let Your Glory Fall"

*Father of creation, unfold Your sovereign plan,*
*Raise up a chosen generation that will march*
*through the land.*
*All of creation is longing for Your unveiling*
*of power*
*Would You release Your anointing? O God,*
*let this be the hour.*

*Ruler of the nations, the world has yet to see*
*The full release of Your promise the church in*
*victory.*
*Turn to us, Lord, and touch us, make us strong in*
*Your might,*
*Overcome our weakness that we could stand up*
*and fight.*

*Chorus*
*Let Your glory fall in this room.*
*Let it go forth from here to the nations.*
*Let Your fragrance rest in this place*
*As we gather to seek Your face.*

*Bridge*
*Let Your kingdom come, let Your kingdom come,*
*Let Your will be done, let Your will be done.*
*Let us see on earth, let us see on earth,*
*The glory of Your Son.*

Words by David Ruis[38]

---

38. © 1993 Mercy/Vineyard Publishing (ASCAP) Admin.
In North America By Music Services o/b/o Vineyard Music
USA.

# CHAPTER 40

# The Perseverance of the Saints (Remaining a Christian)

*Can true Christians lose their salvation?*
*How can we know if we are truly born again?*

## EXPLANATION AND SCRIPTURAL BASIS

Our previous discussion has dealt with many aspects of the full salvation that Christ has earned for us and that the Holy Spirit now applies to us. But how do we know that we shall continue to be Christians throughout our lives? Is there anything that will keep us from falling away from Christ, anything to guarantee that we will remain Christians until we die and that we will in fact live with God in heaven forever? Or might it be that we will turn away from Christ and lose the blessings of our salvation? The topic of the perseverance of the saints speaks to these questions. *The perseverance of the saints means that all those who are truly born again will be kept by God's power and will persevere as Christians until the end of their lives and that only those who persevere until the end have been truly born again.*

This definition has two parts to it. It indicates first that there is assurance to be given to those who are truly born again, for it reminds them that God's power will keep them as Christians until they die, and they will surely live with Christ in heaven forever. On the other hand, the second half of the definition makes it clear that continuing in the Christian life is one of the evidences that a person is truly born again. It is important to keep this aspect of the doctrine in mind as well, lest false assurance be given to people who were never really believers in the first place.

It should be noted that this question is one on which evangelical Christians have long had significant disagreement. Many within the Wesleyan/Arminian tradition have held that it is possible for someone who is truly born again to lose his or her salvation, while Reformed Christians have held that that is not possible for someone who is *truly* born again.[1]

---

1. The doctrine of the perseverance of the saints is represented by "P" in the acronym TULIP, which is often used to summarize the "five points of Calvinism." (See full list at p. 828n12.)

Most Baptists have followed the Reformed tradition at this point; however, they have frequently used the term *eternal security* or *eternal security of the believer* rather than *perseverance of the saints*.

## A. ALL WHO ARE TRULY BORN AGAIN WILL PERSEVERE TO THE END

There are many passages that teach that those who are truly born again, who are genuinely Christians, will continue in the Christian life until death and will then go to be with Christ in heaven. Jesus says,

> I have come down from heaven, not to do my own will but the will of him who sent me. And this is the will of him who sent me, that I should lose nothing of all that he has given me, but raise it up on the last day. For this is the will of my Father, that *everyone who* looks on the Son and *believes in* him should have eternal life, and *I will raise him up on the last day*. (John 6:38–40)

Here Jesus says that everyone who believes in him will have eternal life. He says that he will raise that person up at the last day—which, in this context of believing in the Son and having eternal life, clearly means that Jesus will raise that person up to eternal life with him (not just raise him up to be judged and condemned). It seems hard to avoid the conclusion that everyone who truly believes in Christ will remain a Christian up to the day of final resurrection into the blessings of life in the presence of God.[2] Moreover, this text emphasizes that Jesus does the will of the Father, which is that he should "*lose nothing* of all that he has given me" (John 6:39). Once again, those given to the Son by the Father will not be lost.

Another passage emphasizing this truth is John 10:27–29, in which Jesus says:

> My sheep hear my voice, and I know them, and they follow me. I give them eternal life, and *they will never perish*, and no one will snatch them out of my hand. My Father, who has given them to me, is greater than all, and no one is able to snatch them out of the Father's hand.

---

2. Grant R. Osborne, "Exegetical Notes on Calvinist Texts," in *Grace Unlimited*, ed. Clark Pinnock (Minneapolis: Bethany House, 1975), 170–71, does not give an alternative explanation for Jesus' statement, "I will raise him up at the last day," when he deals with this passage. But he does say that in this context v. 35 emphasizes the fact that eternal life is dependent on the individual person "coming and believing" in Christ (p. 171) and that the present tense verbs used for "believe" in these passages imply not merely an initial decision of faith but rather continuing in that state.

I regret having to differ with my friend and colleague on this question, but there is something to be said in response: while no one would deny that it is necessary for people themselves to believe in Christ for eternal life, and while it is also true that Jesus here speaks not just of initial saving faith but of a faith that continues over time, the verse does not go so far as to specify that "everyone who believes continuously *until his or her death*" will have eternal life," but rather simply says that "he who is *presently in a state of believing* in Christ" will have eternal life and Jesus will raise him up at the last day. The verse speaks about all who presently are in a state of believing in Christ, and it says that all of them will be raised up by Christ at the last day. No further objections to this specific verse are given in Osborne's second essay, "Soteriology in the Gospel of John," in *The Grace of God, the Will of Man* (Grand Rapids: Zondervan, 1989), 248.

Here Jesus says that those who follow him, those who are his sheep, are given eternal life. He further says that "no one will snatch them out of my hand" (v. 28). Now some have objected to this that even though no one else can take Christians out of Christ's hand, we might remove ourselves from Christ's hand. But that seems to be pedantic quibbling over words—does not "no one" also include the person who is in Christ's hand? Moreover, we know that our hearts are far from trustworthy. Therefore, if the possibility remained that we could remove ourselves from Christ's hand, the passage would hardly give the assurance that Jesus intends by it.

But more importantly, the most forceful phrase in the passage is *"they will never perish"* (v. 28). The Greek construction (*ou mē* plus aorist subjunctive) is especially emphatic and might be translated more explicitly, "and they shall certainly not perish forever." This emphasizes that those who are Jesus' "sheep" and who follow him, and to whom he has given eternal life, shall never lose their salvation or be separated from Christ—they shall "never perish."[3]

There are several other passages that say those who believe have "eternal life." One example is John 3:36: "Whoever believes in the Son *has eternal life*" (cf. also John 5:24; 6:47; 10:28; 1 John 5:13). Now if this is truly eternal life that believers have, then it is life that lasts forever with God. It is a gift of God that comes with salvation (it is put in contrast to condemnation and eternal judgment in John 3:16–17, 36; 10:28). Arminians have objected that "eternal life" is simply a quality of life, a type of life in relationship with God, which one can have for a time and then lose. But this objection does not seem to be convincing in view of the clear nuance of unending time involved in the adjective *eternal* (Gk. *aiōnios*, "eternal, without end").[4] Certainly there is a special quality about this life, but the emphasis in the adjective *eternal* is on the fact that it is the opposite of death; it is the opposite of judgment and separation from God; it is life that goes on forever in the presence of God. And he who believes in the Son has this *"eternal* life" (John 3:36).

Evidence in Paul's writings and the other New Testament Epistles also indicates that those who are truly born again will persevere to the end. There remains "no

---

3. The Greek word used here for "perish" is *apollymi*, the same term John uses in John 3:16 to say that "whoever believes in him should not perish but have eternal life."

Grant Osborne, in "Exegetical Notes on Calvinist Texts," 172, says that this verse must not be interpreted apart from the teaching about the vine and the branches in John 15:1–7, but he gives no alternative explanation for the phrase "they shall never perish," and gives no reason why we should fail to understand it to mean that these people will certainly have life with God forever in heaven. In his subsequent article, "Soteriology in the Gospel of John," Osborne again mentions John 10:28, but gives no alternative explanation for it other than to say that this passage emphasizes God's sovereignty, but other passages in John emphasize the faith-response that works together with God's sovereignty.

These articles do not seem to provide a reason why we should not understand these words in an ordinary sense, indicating that one who believes in Christ will certainly never fall away.

Of course, those who believe in the doctrine of the perseverance of the saints (such as myself) would affirm that the *way* God keeps us safe is by causing us to continue to believe in Christ (see discussion below), so to say that Scripture also emphasizes the necessity of continuing in faith is not to object to the doctrine of perseverance of the saints as it has been expressed by Reformed theologians frequently in the history of the church. In other words, there is a way to believe in both sets of texts without concluding that people who are truly born again can lose their salvation.

4. *BAGD*, 28.

condemnation for those who are in Christ Jesus" (Rom. 8:1); therefore, it would be unjust for God to give any kind of eternal punishment to those who are Christians—no condemnation remains for them, for the entire penalty for their sins has been paid.

Then in Romans 8:30, Paul emphasizes the clear connection between God's eternal purposes in predestination and his working out of those purposes in life, together with his final realization of those purposes in "glorifying" or giving final resurrection bodies to those whom he has brought into union with Christ: "Those whom he predestined he also called, and those whom he called he also justified, and those whom he justified he also glorified." Here Paul sees the future event of glorification as such a certainty in God's settled purpose that he can speak of it as if it were already accomplished ("he also glorified"). This is true of all those who are called and justified—that is, all those who truly become Christians.

Further evidence that God keeps those who are born again safe for eternity is the "seal" that God places upon us. This "seal" is the Holy Spirit within us, who also acts as God's "guarantee" that we will receive the inheritance promised to us: "In him you also, when you heard the word of truth, the gospel of your salvation, and believed in him, were *sealed with the promised Holy Spirit*, who is the *guarantee* of our inheritance until we acquire possession of it, to the praise of his glory" (Eph. 1:13–14). The Greek word translated "guarantee" in this passage (*arrabōn*) is a legal and commercial term that means "first installment, deposit, down payment, pledge" and represents "a payment which obligates the contracting party to make further payments."[5] When God gave us the Holy Spirit within, he committed himself to give all the further blessings of eternal life and a great reward in heaven with him. This is why Paul can say that the Holy Spirit is the "*guarantee* of our inheritance until we acquire possession of it" (Eph. 1:14). All who have the Holy Spirit within them, all who are truly born again, have God's unchanging promise and guarantee that the inheritance of eternal life in heaven will certainly be theirs. God's own faithfulness is pledged to bring it about.[6]

Another example of assurance that believers will persevere to the end is found in Paul's statement to the Philippians: "I am sure of this, that he who began a good work in you will bring it to completion at the day of Jesus Christ" (Phil. 1:6). It is true that

---

5. Ibid., 109.

6. Osborne, "Exegetical Notes on Calvinist Texts," 181, answers this verse by saying that Paul also teaches personal responsibility, since "the Christian is warned not to 'grieve' the Spirit (cf. 1 Thess. 4:8)" and "the danger of apostasy is real, and he dare not 'grieve' the Spirit." But once again this objection provides no alternative interpretation to the verse at hand, but simply refers to other verses that teach personal responsibility, a fact that a Reformed theologian would also be eager to affirm.

Arminian theologians frequently assume that if they affirm human responsibility and the need for continuing in faith, they have thereby negated the idea that God's sovereign keeping and protection is absolutely certain and eternal life is guaranteed. But they often do this without providing any other convincing interpretations for the texts cited to demonstrate the doctrine of perseverance of the saints, or any explanation that would show why we should not take these words as absolute guarantees that those who are born again will certainly persevere to the end. Rather than assuming that passages on human responsibility negate the idea of God's sovereign protection, it seems better to adopt the Reformed position that says that God's sovereign protection is consistent with human responsibility, because it works through human responsibility and guarantees that we will respond by maintaining the faith that is necessary to persevere.

the word *you* here is plural (Gk. *hymas*), and thus Paul is referring to Christians in the Philippian church generally, but he is still talking about the specific believers to whom he is writing and saying that God's good work that began in them will continue and will be completed at the day Christ returns.[7] Peter tells his readers that they are those "who *by God's power are being guarded* through faith for a salvation ready to be revealed in the last time" (1 Peter 1:5). The word *guarded* (Gk. *phroureō*) can mean both "kept from escaping" and "protected from attack," and perhaps both kinds of guarding are intended here: God is preserving believers from escaping out of his kingdom, and he is protecting them from external attacks.

The present participle that Peter uses gives the sense "You are continually being guarded."[8] He stresses that this is by God's power. Yet God's power does not work apart from the personal faith of those being guarded, but through their faith. ("Faith," *pistis*, is regularly a personal activity of individual believers in Peter's epistles; see 1 Peter 1:7, 9, 21; 5:9; 2 Peter 1:1, 5; and commonly in the New Testament.) The parallel examples of God working "through" someone or something in Peter's writings (1 Peter 1:3, 23; 2 Peter 1:4; and probably also 1 Peter 1:12; 2:14; 3:1) suggest that the believer's personal faith or trust in God is the means God uses to guard his people. Thus we might give the sense of the verse by saying that "God is continually using his power to guard his people by means of their faith," a statement that seems to imply that God's power in fact energizes and continually sustains individual, personal faith.[9]

This guarding is not for a temporary goal but for a salvation ready to be revealed in the last time. *Salvation* is used here not of past justification or of present sanctification (speaking in theological categories) but of the future full possession of all the blessings of our redemption—of the final, complete fulfillment of our salvation (cf. Rom. 13:11; 1 Peter 2:2). Though already prepared or "ready," it will not be "revealed" by God to mankind generally until the "last time," the time of final judgment.

This last phrase makes it difficult if not impossible to see any end to God's guarding activity. If God's guarding has as its purpose the preservation of believers until they receive their full, heavenly salvation, then it is safe to conclude that God will accomplish that purpose, and they will in fact attain that final salvation. Ultimately their attainment of final salvation depends on God's power. Nevertheless, God's power continually works "through" their faith. Do they wish to know whether God is guarding them?

---

7. Osborne rightly rejects the idea that this refers only to the fact that the church will continue. He says, "Paul does intend that the promise extend to the individual. He will be kept by God with a view to the final salvation, but this does not obviate the need for perseverance" ("Exegetical Notes on Calvinist Texts," 182).

8. The following three paragraphs are taken from Wayne Grudem, *The First Epistle of Peter* (Leicester: Inter-Varsity Press; Grand Rapids: Eerdmans, 1988), 58–59.

9. The translation by J. N. D. Kelly, "as a result of . . . faith," is an extremely unlikely rendering of the very common construction *dia* with the genitive (the few examples of this construction meaning "as a result of," which are suggested in, *BAGD*, 180, IV, are all ambiguous, and Kelly himself gives no examples; see J. N. D. Kelly, *A Commentary on the Epistles of Peter and Jude*, Black's New Testament Commentaries [London: Black, 1969], 52).

If they continue to trust God through Christ, God is working and guarding them, and he should be thanked.

This emphasis on God's guarding in combination with our faith provides a natural transition to the second half of the doctrine of perseverance.

## B. ONLY THOSE WHO PERSEVERE TO THE END HAVE BEEN TRULY BORN AGAIN

While Scripture repeatedly emphasizes that those who are truly born again will persevere to the end and will certainly have eternal life in heaven with God, there are other passages that speak of the necessity of continuing in faith throughout life. They make us realize that what Peter said in 1 Peter 1:5 is true, namely, that God does not guard us *apart from* our faith but only by working *through* our faith so that he enables us to continue to believe in him. In this way, those who continue to trust in Christ gain assurance that God is working in them and guarding them.

One example of this kind of passage is John 8:31–32: "Jesus said to the Jews who had believed him, '*If you abide in my word*, you are truly my disciples, and you will know the truth, and the truth will set you free.'" Jesus is here giving a warning that one evidence of genuine faith is continuing in his word, that is, continuing to believe what he says and living a life of obedience to his commands. Similarly, Jesus says, "*The one who endures to the end* will be saved" (Matt. 10:22), as a means of warning people not to fall away in times of persecution.

Paul says to the Colossian Christians that Christ has reconciled them to God, "in order to present you holy and blameless and above reproach before him, *if indeed you continue in the faith*, stable and steadfast, not shifting from the hope of the gospel that you heard" (Col. 1:22–23). It is only natural that Paul and the other New Testament writers would speak this way, for they are addressing groups of people who profess to be Christians, without being able to know the actual state of every person's heart. There may have been people at Colossae who had joined in the fellowship of the church, and perhaps even professed that they had faith in Christ and had been baptized into membership of the church, but who never had true saving faith. How is Paul to distinguish such people from true believers? How can he avoid giving them false assurance, assurance that they will be saved eternally when in fact they will not, unless they come to true repentance and faith? Paul knows that those whose faith is not real will eventually fall away from participation in the fellowship of the church. Therefore, he tells his readers that they will ultimately be saved "*if indeed you continue in the faith*" (Col. 1:23). Those who continue show thereby that they are genuine believers. But those who do not continue in the faith show that there was no genuine faith in their hearts in the first place.

A similar emphasis is seen in Hebrews 3:14: "For we have come to share in Christ, *if indeed* we hold our original confidence firm to the end." This verse provides an excellent perspective on the doctrine of perseverance. How do we know if "we have come to share in Christ"? How do we know if this being joined to Christ has happened to us at some time in the past?[10] One way in which we know that we have come to genuine faith in Christ is if we continue in faith until the end of our lives.

Attention to the context of Hebrews 3:14 will keep us from using this and other similar passages in a pastorally inappropriate way. We must remember that there are other evidences elsewhere in Scripture that give Christians assurance of salvation,[11] so *we should not think that assurance that we belong to Christ is impossible until we die.* However, continuing in faith is the one means of assurance that is named here by the author of Hebrews. He mentions this to warn his readers that they should not fall away from Christ because he is writing to a situation where such a warning is needed. The beginning of that section, just two verses earlier, said, "Take care, brothers, lest there be in any of you an evil, unbelieving heart, leading you to fall away from the living God" (Heb. 3:12). In fact, in all of the passages where continuing to believe in Christ to the end of our lives is mentioned as one indication of genuine faith, the purpose is never to make those who are presently trusting in Christ worry that sometime in the future they might fall away (and we should never use these passages that way either, for that would be to give wrongful cause for worry in a way that Scripture does not intend). Rather, the purpose is always *to warn those who are thinking of falling away or have fallen away* that if they do this it is a strong indication that they were never saved in the first place. Thus the necessity for continuing in faith should just be used as a warning against falling away, a warning that those who fall away give evidence that their faith was never real.

John clearly states that when people fall away from fellowship with the church and from belief in Christ they thereby show that their faith was not real in the first place and that they were never part of the true body of Christ. Speaking of people who have left the fellowship of believers, John says, "They went out from us, but they were not of us; for *if they had been of us, they would have continued with us.* But they went out, that it might become plain that they all are not of us" (1 John 2:19). John says that those who have departed showed by their actions that they "were not of us"—that they were not truly born again.

## C. Those Who Finally Fall Away May Give Many External Signs of Conversion

### 1. Some Who Regularly Associate with the Church Are Not True Believers

It is not always clear which people in the church have genuine saving faith and which have only an intellectual persuasion of the truth of the gospel but no genuine faith in their hearts. Scripture mentions in several places that *unbelievers* in fellowship with the visible church can give some external signs or indications that make them look or sound like genuine believers. For example, Judas, who betrayed Christ, must have acted almost

---

10. The author uses the perfect tense verb *gegonamen*, "we have become" (at some time in the past, with results that continue into the present).

11. See the list of evidences of salvation given in section D, pp. 986–93, below.

exactly like the other disciples during the three years he was with Jesus. So convincing was his conformity to the behavior pattern of the other disciples, that at the end of three years of Jesus' ministry, when he said that one of his disciples would betray him, they did not all turn and suspect Judas, but they rather "began to say to him one after another, 'Is it I?'" (Matt. 26:22; cf. Mark 14:19; Luke 22:23; John 13:22). However, Jesus himself knew that there was no genuine faith in Judas' heart because Jesus said at one point, "Did I not choose you, the Twelve? And yet one of you is a devil" (John 6:70). John later wrote in his gospel that "Jesus knew from the beginning who those were who did not believe, and who it was who would betray him" (John 6:64). But the disciples themselves did not know.

Paul also speaks of "*false brothers* secretly brought in" (Gal. 2:4) and says that in his journeys he has been in "danger from *false brothers*" (2 Cor. 11:26). He also says that the servants of Satan "*disguise themselves* as servants of righteousness" (2 Cor. 11:15). This does not mean that all unbelievers in the church who nevertheless give some signs of true conversion are servants of Satan secretly undermining the work of the church, for some may be in process of considering the claims of the gospel and moving toward real faith, others may have heard only an inadequate explanation of the gospel message, and others may not have come under genuine conviction of the Holy Spirit yet. But Paul's statements do mean that some unbelievers in the church will be false brothers and sisters sent to disrupt the fellowship, while others will simply be unbelievers who will eventually come to genuine saving faith. In both cases, however, they give several external signs that make them look like genuine believers.

We can see this also in Jesus' statement about what will happen at the last judgment:

> Not everyone who says to me, "Lord, Lord," will enter the kingdom of heaven, but the one who does the will of my Father who is in heaven. On that day many will say to me, "Lord, Lord, did we not prophesy in your name, and cast out demons in your name, and do many mighty works in your name?" And then will I declare to them, "*I never knew you*; depart from me, you workers of lawlessness." (Matt. 7:21–23)

Although these people prophesied, cast out demons, and did "many mighty works" in Jesus' name, the ability to do such works did not guarantee that they were Christians. Jesus says, "I never knew you." He does not say, "I knew you at one time but I no longer know you," nor "I knew you at one time but you strayed away from me," but rather, "I *never* knew you." They never were genuine believers.

A similar teaching is found in the parable of the sower. Jesus says, "Other seed fell on rocky ground, where it did not have much soil, and immediately it sprang up, since it had no depth of soil. And when the sun rose, it was scorched, and since it had no root, it withered away" (Mark 4:5–6). Jesus explains that the seed sown upon rocky ground represents people who "when they hear the word, immediately receive it with joy. And *they have no root in themselves*, but endure for a while; then, when tribulation or persecution arises on account of the word, immediately they fall away" (Mark 4:16–17). The fact that they "have no root in themselves" indicates that there is no source of life within these plants; similarly, the people represented by them have no genuine life of their own within. They have an appearance of conversion, and they apparently have become Christians because they receive the word "with joy," but when difficulty comes, they are nowhere to be found—their apparent conversion was not genuine and there was no real saving faith in their hearts.

### 2. John 15:1–7: The Vine and the Branches

The importance of continuing in faith is also affirmed in the parable of Jesus as the vine, in which Christians are portrayed as branches (John 15:1–7). Jesus says,

> I am the true vine, and my Father is the vinedresser. Every branch in me that does not bear fruit he takes away, and every branch that does bear fruit he prunes, that it may bear more fruit. . . . If anyone does not abide in me he is thrown away like a branch and withers; and the branches are gathered, thrown into the fire, and burned. (John 15:1–2, 6)

Arminians have argued that the branches that do not bear fruit are still true branches on the vine—Jesus refers to "Every branch *in me* that does not bear fruit" (v. 2). Therefore, the branches that are gathered and thrown into the fire and burned must refer to true believers that were once part of the vine but fell away and became subject to eternal judgment. But that is not a necessary implication of Jesus' teaching at this point. The imagery of the vine used in this parable is limited in how much detail it can teach. In fact, if Jesus had wanted to teach that there were true and false believers associated with him, and if he wanted to use the analogy of a vine and branches, then the only way he could refer to people who do not have genuine life in themselves would be to speak of branches that bear no fruit (somewhat after the analogy of the seeds that fell on rocky ground and had "no root in themselves" in Mark 4:17). Here in John 15 the branches that do not bear fruit, though they are in some way connected to Jesus and give an outward appearance of being genuine branches, nonetheless give indication of their true state by the fact that they bear no fruit. This is similarly indicated by the fact that the person "does not abide" in Christ (John 15:6) and is cast off as a branch and withers. If we try to press the analogy any further, by saying, for example, that all branches on a vine really are alive or they would not be there in the first place, then we are simply trying to press the imagery beyond what it is able to teach—and in that case there would be nothing in the analogy that could represent false believers in any case. The point of the imagery is simply that those who bear fruit thereby give evidence that they are abiding in Christ; those who do not, are not abiding in him.

### 3. Hebrews 6:4–8: People Whose Lives Produce Only "Thorns and Thistles"

Finally, there are two passages in Hebrews that also affirm that those who finally fall away may give many external signs of conversion and may look in many ways like Christians. The first of these, Hebrews 6:4–6, has frequently been used by Arminians as proof that believers can lose their salvation. But on closer inspection such an interpretation is not convincing. The author writes,

> For it is impossible, in the case of those who have once been *enlightened*, who have *tasted* the heavenly gift, and have *shared* in the Holy Spirit, and have *tasted* the goodness of the word of God and the powers of the age to come, and then have fallen away, to restore them again to *repentance*, since they are crucifying once again the Son of God to their own harm and holding him up to contempt. (Heb. 6:4–6)

If we are going to understand this passage correctly, it is absolutely crucial that we give close attention to the context, especially the following three verses (Heb. 6:7–9). First, the author gives an example from agriculture:

> For land that has drunk the rain that often falls on it, and produces a crop useful to those for whose sake it is cultivated, receives a blessing from God. But if it bears thorns and thistles, it is worthless and near to being cursed, and its end is to be burned. (Heb. 6:7–8)

In this agricultural metaphor, those who receive final judgment are compared to land that bears no vegetation or useful fruit but rather bears thorns and thistles. When we recall the other metaphors in Scripture where good fruit is a sign of true spiritual life and fruitlessness is a sign of false believers (for example, Matt. 3:8–10; 7:15–20; 12:33–35), we already have an indication that the author is speaking of people whose most trustworthy evidence of their spiritual condition (the fruit they bear) is negative ("thorns and thistles," v. 8), which would indicate that the author is talking about people who are not genuinely Christians.

This metaphor bluntly indicates that those who fall away are like the crop that is brought forth on land that has no worthwhile life growing on it, even though rain "often falls on it" (such land is like a life that receives repeated blessings from God but bears no good fruit). We should notice here that people who commit apostasy are not compared to a field that once bore good fruit and now does not, but that they are like *land that never bore good fruit*, but only thorns and thistles. The land may look good before the crops start to come up, but the fruit gives the genuine evidence, and it is bad.

Then, strong support for this interpretation of Hebrews 6:4–8 is found in verse 9, which is the verse immediately following. Though the author has been speaking harshly about the possibility of falling away, he then returns to speak to the situation of the great majority of the hearers, whom he thinks to be genuine Christians. He says, "Though we speak in this way, *yet in your case*, beloved, *we feel sure of better things—things that belong to salvation*" (Heb. 6:9). The question is, "better things" than what? The plural "*better things*" forms an appropriate contrast to the *good* things that have been mentioned in verses 4–6: the author is convinced that most of his readers have experienced better things than simply the partial and temporary influences of the Holy Spirit and the church talked about in verses 4–6.

In fact, the author talks about these things by saying (literally) that they are "better things, *also belonging to salvation*" (Gk. *kai echomena sōtērias*).[12] These are not only the temporary blessings talked about in verses 4–6, but these are better things, things having not only temporary influence, but "*also* belonging to salvation." In this way the Greek word *kai* ("also") shows that *salvation is something that was not part of the things mentioned in verses 4–6 above*. Therefore, this word *kai* provides a crucial key for understanding the passage. If the author had meant to say that the people mentioned in verses 4–6 were truly saved, then it is very difficult to understand why he would say in verse 9 that he is convinced of *better things* for them, things that belong to salvation, or that have salvation *in addition to* those things mentioned above. He thus shows that he can use a brief phrase to say that people "have salvation" if he wishes to do so (he does not need to pile up many phrases), and he shows, moreover, that the people whom he speaks of in verses 4–6 are not saved.[13]

What exactly are these "better things"? In addition to salvation mentioned in verse 9, they are things that give real evidence of salvation—genuine fruit in their lives (v. 10), full assurance of hope (v. 11), and saving faith of the type exhibited by those who inherit the promises (v. 12). In this way he reassures those who are genuine believers—those who show fruit in their lives and show love for other Christians, who show hope and genuine faith that is continuing at the present time, and who are not about to fall away. He wants to reassure these readers (who are certainly the great majority of the ones to whom he writes) while still issuing a strong warning to those among them who may be in danger of falling away.

After this examination of the immediate context, we are better able to understand the experiences described in verses 4–6. Some have objected that the long description of things that have happened to these people who fall away means that they must have

---

12. *BDAG*, 422, meaning 11, translates the middle participle of *echō* as "hold fast, cling to," and lists Heb. 6:9 as the only New Testament example of this form used "of inner belonging," and thus the ESV rendering says, "things that *belong to* salvation." But even if we translated the middle voice of *echō* in the same way as the active, the phrase would mean, "things also *having* salvation," and my argument in this section would not be affected.

13. Someone might object that the phrase "better things" does not contrast with the temporary blessings in vv. 4–6, but

with the judgment mentioned that is coming to the thorns and thistles who are about to be "burned" in v. 8. But it is unlikely that the author would refer to not being cursed simply as "better things." The comparative "better" (*kreissonkreissōn*) is used thirteen times in Hebrews, and it regularly contrasts something *better* with something *good* (better covenant, better sacrifice, etc.); similarly, here it suggests a comparison with things that are already good (such as the blessings in vv. 4–6), much more than it suggests a contrast with the horrible fate of eternal judgment in v. 8.

been genuinely born again. But that is not a convincing objection when we look at the individual terms used. The author says they have "once been *enlightened*" (Heb. 6:4). But this enlightening simply means that they came to *understand* the truths of the gospel, not that they responded to those truths with genuine saving faith.[14]

Similarly, the word *once* that is used to speak of those who "have once been enlightened" is the Greek term *hapax*, which is used, for example, in Philippians 4:16 of the Philippians' sending Paul a gift "*once* and again" and in Hebrews 9:7 of entrance in the Holy of Holies "*once* a year." Therefore, this word does not mean that something happened "once" and can never be repeated, but simply that it happened once, without specifying whether it will be repeated or not.[15]

The text further says that these people "have *tasted* the heavenly gift" and that they "have *tasted* the goodness of the word of God and the powers of the age to come" (Heb. 6:4–5). Inherent in the idea of tasting is the fact that the tasting is temporary and one might or might not decide to accept the thing that is tasted. For example, the same Greek word (*geuomai*) is used in Matthew 27:34 to say that those crucifying Jesus "offered him wine to drink, mixed with gall, but when he *tasted* it, he would not drink it." The word is also used in a figurative sense meaning "come to know something."[16] If we understand it in this figurative sense, as it must be understood here since the passage is not talking about tasting literal food, then it means that these people have come to understand the heavenly gift (which probably means here that they had experienced some of the power of the Holy Spirit at work, perhaps when Christian friends had prayed for them about specific needs) and to know something of the Word of God and the powers of the age to come. It does not necessarily mean that they had (or did not have) genuine saving faith but may simply mean that they came to understand it and have some experience of spiritual power.[17]

---

14. The word *enlightened* translates the Greek term *phōtizō*, which refers to learning in general, not necessarily a learning that results in salvation—it is used in John 1:9 of "giving light to" everyone that comes into the world, in 1 Cor. 4:5 of the enlightening that comes at the final judgment, and in Eph. 1:18 of the enlightening that accompanies growth in the Christian life. The word is not a "technical term" that means that the people in question were saved.

After completing the following discussion of Hebrews 6:4–6, I wrote a much more extensive study, with additional analysis, supporting data, and interaction with other literature; see Wayne Grudem, "Perseverance of the Saints: A Case Study From Heb. 6:4–6 and the Other Warning Passages of Hebrews," in *Still Sovereign*, ed. Tom Schreiner and Bruce Ware (Grand Rapids: Baker, 2000).

15. This is not the same word as *ephapax*, which is more regularly used in the New Testament of nonrepeatable events (Rom. 6:10; Heb. 7:27; 9:12; 10:10).

16. *BAGD*, 157. They mention other examples of *geuomai* ("taste"), such as Herodotus 6.5, where the people of Miletus had "tasted of freedom," but it was certainly not their own

possession. They also cite Dio Chrysostom, 32.72, where he speaks of the people of Alexandria in a time when they "had a taste of warfare" in an encounter with Roman troops who were simply harassing them and not actually engaging in genuine war. Josephus, *The Jewish War*, 2.158, speaks about the theological views of the Essenes "whereby they irresistibly attract all who have once *tasted* their philosophy." Here again Josephus makes it clear that those who have "once tasted" have not yet made the Essene philosophy their own but are simply very strongly attracted to it. By analogy, in Heb. 6 those who have "tasted" the heavenly gift and the word of God and the powers of the age to come may be strongly attracted to these things, or they may not be, but mere tasting does not mean that they have made it their own—quite the contrary, if all the author can say of them is that they have "tasted" these things, it suggests that they have not fully participated in what they tasted.

17. The word *tasted* is also used in Heb. 2:9 to say that Jesus "tasted death," indicating that he came to know it by experience (but "tasted" is an apt word because he did not remain dead). The same could be true of those who had some experience of heavenly gifts, as can be true even of unbelievers (cf. Matt. 7:22;

The text also further says that these people "have *shared in* the Holy Spirit" (Heb. 6:4). The question here is the exact meaning of the word *metochos*, which is here translated "shared in." It is not always clear to English-speaking readers that this term has a range of meaning and may imply very close participation and attachment or may only imply a loose association with the other person or persons named. For example, the context shows that in Hebrews 3:14 to "share in" Christ means to have a very close participation with him in a saving relationship.[18] On the other hand, *metochos* can also be used in a much looser sense, simply to refer to associates or companions. We read that when the disciples took in a great catch of fish so that their nets were breaking, "they signaled to their *partners* in the other boat to come and help them" (Luke 5:7). Here it simply refers to those who were companions or partners with Peter and the other disciples in their fishing work.[19] Ephesians 5:7 uses a closely related word (*symmetochos*, a compound of *metochos* and the preposition *syn* ["with"]) when Paul warns Christians about the sinful acts of unbelievers and says, "Do not become *partners* with them" (Eph. 5:7). He is not concerned that their total nature will be transformed by the unbelievers but simply that they will associate with them and have their own witness compromised and their own lives influenced to some degree by them.

By analogy, Hebrews 6:4–6 speaks of people who have been "*associated with*" the Holy Spirit and thereby had their lives influenced by him, but it need not imply that they had a redeeming work of the Holy Spirit in their lives or that they were regenerated. By similar analogy with the example of the fishing companions in Luke 5:7, Peter and the disciples could be *associated with* them and even to some degree influenced by them without having a thoroughgoing change of life caused by that association. The very word *metochos* allows for a range of influence from fairly weak to fairly strong, for it only means "one who participates with or shares with or accompanies in some activity." This was apparently what had happened to these people spoken of in Hebrews 6, who had been associated with the church and as such associated with the work of the Holy Spirit, and no doubt had been influenced by him in some ways in their lives.[20]

---

1 Cor. 7:14; 2 Peter 2:20–22). In Heb. 6:4–5 these people's experience of the Holy Spirit's power and of the Word of God was of course a *genuine experience* (just as Jesus *genuinely* died), but that by itself does not show that the people had an experience of regeneration.

18. The same Greek word *metochos* is used in Heb. 3:14, even though the English text of the ESV says "We have come to share in Christ."

19. Heb. 1:9 also uses the same word to speak of "companions" (ESV, NIV, NASB).

20. The other uses of *metochos* in Hebrews (3:1 and 12:8) do suggest closer association or participation, but the small number of examples are not numerous enough to show that the author of Hebrews used this word as a "technical term" that always referred to a saving kind of participation (it did not in

Heb. 1:9 and 12:8). The wide range of meaning *metochos* can take is evident from the Greek literature of the New Testament and in other literature that shares a similar vocabulary with the writers of the New Testament.

The usage of the Septuagint is also instructive with respect to this word, since in several instances it only refers to companionship, not any kind of regenerating or life-changing experience with God or with the Holy Spirit. For instance, in 1 Sam. 20:30, Saul accuses Jonathan of being a "partner" with David. In Ps. 119:63, the psalmist says he is a "companion" of all those who fear God. Eccl. 4:10 says that two are better than one, for if they fall, the one will lift up his "partner." Prov. 28:24, in the translations of Aquila, Symmachus, and Theodotian, uses this word to say that a man who rejects his father or mother is a "companion" of ungodly men. Examples of somewhat stronger

Finally, the text says that it is impossible "to restore again to *repentance*" those who have experienced these things and have then fallen away. Some have argued that if this is a repentance to which they need to be restored again, then it must be genuine repentance. But this is not necessarily the case. First, we must realize that *repentance* (Gk. *metanoia*) does not need to refer to inward heart repentance unto salvation. For example, Hebrews 12:17 uses this word to speak of a change of mind that Esau sought concerning the sale of his birthright and refers to it as repentance (*metanoia*). This would not have been a repentance for salvation, but simply a change of mind and an undoing of the transaction regarding his birthright. (Note also the example of Judas' repentance in Matt. 27:3—howbeit with a different Greek word.)

The cognate verb *to repent* (Gk. *metanoeō*) is sometimes used to refer not to saving repentance but to sorrow for individual offenses in Luke 17:3–4: "If your brother sins, rebuke him, and *if he repents*, forgive him, and if he sins against you seven times in the day, and turns to you seven times, saying, 'I repent,' you must forgive him." We conclude that *repentance* simply means a sorrow for actions that have been done or for sins that have been committed. Whether or not it is a genuine saving repentance, a "repentance unto salvation," may not be always evident right away. The author of Hebrews is not concerned to specify whether it is a genuine repentance or not. He is simply saying that if someone has a sorrow for sin and comes to understand the gospel and experiences these various blessings of the Holy Spirit's work (no doubt in fellowship with the church) and then turns away, it will not be possible to restore such a person again to a place of sorrow for sin. But this does not necessarily imply that the repentance was genuine saving repentance in the first place.

At this point we may ask what kind of person is described by all of these terms. These are no doubt people who have been affiliated closely with the fellowship of the church. They have had some measure of sorrow for sin (repentance). They have understood the gospel (they have been enlightened). They have come to appreciate the attractiveness of the Christian life and the change that comes about in people's lives because of becoming a Christian, and they have probably had answers to prayer in their own lives and felt the power of the Holy Spirit at work, perhaps even using some spiritual gifts in the manner of the unbelievers in Matthew 7:22 (they have become "associated with" the work of the Holy Spirit or have "shared in" the Holy Spirit and have "tasted" the heavenly gift and the powers of the age of come). They have been exposed to the true preaching of the

---

association are seen in Esth. 8:13; Prov. 29:10; Hos. 4:17; 3 Macc. 3:21. The conclusion of this examination of the term *metochos* is that, while it can be used of very close association with saving results in a person's life, it can also be used simply of associating or participating with someone else. Therefore the term itself does not require that the people in Heb. 6:4–6 had saving participation with the Holy Spirit or had been

regenerated. It simply means they had in some ways been associated with and *influenced by the Holy Spirit*.

The people who prophesied and cast out demons and did many mighty works in Jesus' name in Matt. 7:22 are good examples of people who in some way had "shared in" the work of the Holy Spirit but had not been saved: Jesus says, "I never knew you" (Matt. 7:23).

Word and have appreciated much of its teachings (they have "tasted" the goodness of the Word of God).

But then in spite of all this, if they "fall away" and are "crucifying once again the Son of God to their own harm and holding him up to contempt" (Heb. 6:6), then *they are willfully rejecting all of these blessings* and turning decidedly against them. Perhaps all of us have known in our churches people who (sometimes by their profession) have long been affiliated with the fellowship of the church but are not themselves born-again Christians. They have thought about the gospel for years and have continued to resist the wooing of the Holy Spirit in their lives, perhaps through an unwillingness to give up lordship of their lives to Jesus and preferring to cling to it themselves.

Now the author tells us that *if these people willfully turn away from all of these temporary blessings*, then it will be impossible to restore them again to any kind of repentance or sorrow for sin. Their hearts will be hardened and their consciences calloused. What more could be done to bring them to salvation? If we tell them Scripture is true, they will say that they know it but they have decided to reject it. If we tell them God answers prayer and changes lives, they will respond that they know that as well, but they want nothing of it. If we tell them that the Holy Spirit is powerful to work in people's lives and that the gift of eternal life is good beyond description, they will say that they understand that but want nothing of it. Their repeated familiarity with the things of God and their experience of many influences of the Holy Spirit has simply served to harden them against conversion.

Now the author of Hebrews knows that there are some in the community to which he writes who are in danger of falling away in just this way (see Heb. 2:3; 3:8, 12, 14–15; 4:1, 7, 11; 10:26, 29, 35–36, 38–39; 12:3, 15–17). He wants to warn them that, though they have *participated in the fellowship of the church* and *experienced a number of God's blessings* in their lives, yet if they fall away after all that, there is no salvation for them. This does not imply that he thinks that true Christians could fall away—Hebrews 3:14 implies quite the opposite. But he wants them to gain assurance of salvation through their continuing in faith and thereby implies that if they fall away it would show that they were never Christ's people in the first place (see Heb. 3:6: "We are his house, *if indeed* we hold fast our confidence and our boasting in our hope").

Therefore the author wants to give a severe warning to those in danger of slipping away from their Christian profession. He wants to use the strongest language possible to say, "Here is how far a person can come in experiencing *temporary blessings* and still not really be saved." He is warning them to watch out because depending on temporary blessings and experiences is not enough. To do this, he talks not of any true change of heart or any good fruit produced but about the temporary blessings and experiences that have come to these persons and have given them some understanding of Christianity. But their lives had produced only thorns and thistles, and no spiritually good fruit.

## 4. Hebrews 10:26–31: People Who Deliberately Keep on Sinning

A similar teaching is found in Hebrews 10:26–31. There the author says, "If we go on sinning deliberately after receiving the knowledge of the truth, there no longer remains a sacrifice for sins" (Heb. 10:26). Also, a person who rejects Christ's salvation and "has profaned the blood of the covenant by which he was sanctified, and has outraged the Spirit of grace" (Heb. 10:29) deserves eternal punishment. This again is a strong warning against falling away, but it should not be taken as proof that someone who has truly been born again can lose his or her salvation. When the author talks about the blood of the covenant "that sanctified him," the word *sanctified* is used simply to refer to "external sanctification, like that of the ancient Israelites, by outward connection with God's people."[21] The passage does not talk about someone who is genuinely saved, but someone who has received some beneficial moral influence through contact with the church.[22]

## 5. Revelation 3:5: Names in the Book of Life

One other passage in John's writings has been claimed to teach the possibility of loss of salvation. In Revelation 3:5, Jesus says, "The one who conquers will be clothed thus in white garments, and *I will never blot his name out of the book of life.*" Some have claimed that when Jesus says this he implies that it is possible that he would blot out the names of some people from the book of life, people who had already had their names written in it and were thus already saved. But the fact that Jesus emphatically states that he will *not* do something should not be taken as teaching that he will do that same thing in other cases! The same kind of Greek construction[23] is used to give an emphatic negation in John 10:28, where Jesus says, "I give them eternal life, and *they will never perish.*" This does not mean that there are some of Jesus' sheep who do not hear his voice and follow him and who will perish; it is simply affirming that his sheep certainly will not perish. Similarly, when God says, "I will never leave you nor forsake you" (Heb. 13:5), it does not imply that he will leave or forsake others; it just emphatically states that he will not leave nor forsake his people. Or, in even a closer parallel, in Matthew 12:32, Jesus says, "Whoever speaks against the Holy Spirit *will not be forgiven*, either in this age *or in the age to come.*" This does not imply that some sins will be forgiven in the age to come (as Roman Catholics claim in support for the doctrine of purgatory)[24]—that is simply an error in reasoning: to say that something will not happen in the age to come does not

21. A. H. Strong, *Systematic Theology* (Valley Forge, PA: Judson, 1907), 884. Strong mentions an appropriate parallel use of the verb *sanctify* in 1 Cor. 7:14, which speaks about the unbelieving husband being sanctified by the believing wife (1 Cor. 7:14, where the same Greek word, *hagiazō*, is used). Outward ceremonial sanctification is also referred in Heb. 9:13; cf. Matt. 23:17, 19.

22. Ex. 24:7–8 speaks of the blood of the covenant that set apart the people as God's people even though not all were truly born again. In the context of Heb. 10, such imagery, taken from the Old Testament process of sanctifying a people so that they could come before God to worship, is an appropriate background.

23. The construction uses *ou mē* plus the aorist subjunctive to express emphatic negation.

24. See discussion of the doctrine of purgatory in chapter 41, pp. 1006–8.

imply that it might happen in the age to come! In the same way, Revelation 3:5 is just a strong assurance that those who are clad in the white garments and who have remained faithful to Christ will not have their names blotted out of the book of life.[25]

### 6. 1 Samuel 16:14: The Spirit of the Lord Departed from Saul

Finally, one passage from the Old Testament is sometimes used to argue that people can lose their salvation: the story of the Holy Spirit departing from King Saul. But Saul should not be taken as an example of someone who lost his salvation, for when the text says that "the Spirit of the Lord departed from Saul" (1 Sam. 16:14), it reports this immediately after it says that Samuel anointed David king and "the Spirit of the Lord rushed upon David from that day forward" (1 Sam. 16:13). This close connection in the text (the immediately preceding verse) leads us to think that Scripture is not here talking about a total loss of all work of the Holy Spirit in Saul's life but simply about the withdrawing of *the Holy Spirit's function of empowering Saul as king*.[26] But that does not mean that Saul was eternally condemned. It is simply very hard to tell from the pages of the Old Testament whether Saul, throughout his life, was (a) an unregenerate man who had leadership capabilities and was used by God as a demonstration of the fact that someone worthy to be king in the eyes of the world was not thereby suited to be king over the Lord's people or (b) a regenerate man with poor understanding and a life that increasingly strayed from the Lord.

### D. What Can Give a Believer Genuine Assurance?

If it is true, as explained in the previous section, that some people who are unbelievers and who finally fall away may give many external signs of conversion, then what will serve as evidence of genuine conversion? What can give real assurance to a real believer? We can list three categories of questions that a person could ask of himself or herself.

### 1. Do I Have a Present Trust in Christ for Salvation?

Paul tells the Colossians that they will be saved on the last day, "if indeed you *continue in the faith*, stable and steadfast, not shifting from the hope of the gospel that you heard" (Col. 1:23). The author of Hebrews says, "We have come to share in Christ, if indeed we hold our original confidence firm to the end" (Heb. 3:14), and encourages his readers to be imitators of those "who *through faith* and patience inherit the promises" (Heb. 6:12).

---

25. A different kind of book is probably in view in Ex. 32:33, where God says to Moses, "Whoever has sinned against me, I will blot out of my book." Here the New Testament idea of the "book of life" is not mentioned. Rather, the image is one of God keeping a record of those currently dwelling among his people, much as an earthly king would do. To "blot out" someone's name from such a book would imply that the person had died. Using this imagery, Ex. 32:33 is best understood to mean

that God will take the life of anyone who sins against him (see v. 35). Eternal destiny is not in view in this passage.

26. We should give a similar interpretation to David's prayer in Ps. 51:11: "Take not your Holy Spirit from me." David is praying that the Holy Spirit's anointing for kingship would not be removed from him and that the presence and power of God on his life would not depart; he is not praying against a loss of eternal salvation.

In fact, the most famous verse in the entire Bible uses a present tense verb that may be translated, "whoever continues believing in him" may have eternal life (see John 3:16).

Therefore, a person should ask himself or herself, "Do I *today* have trust in Christ to forgive my sins and take me without blame into heaven forever? Do I have confidence in my heart that he has saved me? If I were to die tonight and stand before God's judgment seat, and if he were to ask me why he should let me into heaven, would I begin to think of my good deeds and depend on them, or would I without hesitation say that I am depending on the merits of Christ and am confident that he is a sufficient Savior?"

This emphasis on *present* faith in Christ stands in contrast to the practice of some church "testimonies" where people repeatedly recite details of a conversion experience that may have happened twenty or thirty years ago. If a testimony of saving faith is genuine, it should also be a testimony of faith that is active this very day.

## 2. Is There Current Evidence of a Regenerating Work of the Holy Spirit in My Heart?

The evidence of the work of the Holy Spirit in our hearts comes in many different forms. Although we should not put confidence in the demonstration of miraculous works (Matt. 7:22) or long hours and years of work at some local church (which may simply be building with "wood, hay, straw" [in terms of 1 Cor. 3:12] to further one's ego or power over others or to attempt to earn merit with God), there are many other evidences of a real work of the Holy Spirit in one's heart.

First, there is (1) a subjective testimony of the Holy Spirit within our hearts bearing witness that we are God's children (Rom. 8:15–16; 1 John 4:13). This testimony will usually be accompanied by (2) a sense of being led by the Holy Spirit in paths of obedience to God's will (Rom. 8:14).

In addition, if the Holy Spirit is genuinely at work in our lives, he will be producing the kind of (3) character traits that Paul calls "the fruit of the Spirit" (Gal. 5:22). He lists several attitudes and character traits that are produced by the Holy Spirit: "love, joy, peace, patience, kindness, goodness, faithfulness, gentleness, self-control" (Gal. 5:22–23). Of course, the question is not "Do I perfectly exemplify all of these characteristics in my life?" but rather "Are these things a general characteristic of my life? Do I sense these attitudes in my heart? Do others (especially those closest to me) see these traits exhibited in my life? Have I been growing in them over a period of years?" There is no suggestion in the New Testament that any non-Christian, any unregenerate person, can convincingly fake these character traits, especially for those who know the person most closely.

Related to this kind of fruit is another kind of fruit: (4) the results of one's life and ministry as they have influence on others and on the church. There are some people who profess to be Christians but whose influence on others is to discourage them, to drag them down, to injure their faith, and to provoke controversy and divisiveness. The result of their life and ministry is not to build up others and to build up the church but to tear it down. On the other hand, there are those who seem to edify others in every conversation, every prayer, and every work of ministry they put their hand to. Jesus said, regarding false prophets, "You will recognize them by their fruits. . . . Every healthy tree bears good fruit, but the diseased tree bears bad fruit. . . . Thus you will recognize them by their fruits" (Matt. 7:16–20).

Another evidence of work of the Holy Spirit is (5) continuing to believe and accept the sound teaching of the church. Those who begin to deny major doctrines of the faith give serious negative indications concerning their salvation: "No one who denies the Son has the Father. . . . If what you heard from the beginning abides in you, then you too will abide in the Son and in the Father" (1 John 2:23–24). John also says, "Whoever knows God listens to us; whoever is not from God does not listen to us" (1 John 4:6). Since the New Testament writings are the current replacement for the apostles like John, we might also say that whoever knows God will continue to read and to delight in God's Word and will continue to believe it fully. Those who do not believe and delight in God's Word give evidence that they are not "from God."

Yet another evidence of genuine salvation is (6) a continuing present relationship with Jesus Christ. Jesus says, "Abide in me, and I in you," and "If you abide in me, and my words abide in you, ask whatever you wish, and it will be done for you" (John 15:4, 7). This abiding in Christ will include not only day-by-day trust in him in various situations but also regular fellowship with him in prayer and worship.

Finally, a major area of evidence that we are genuine believers is found in (7) a life of obedience to God's commands. John says, "Whoever says 'I know him' but does not keep his commandments is a liar, and the truth is not in him, but whoever keeps his word, in him truly the love of God is perfected. By this we may know that we are in him: whoever says he abides in him ought to walk in the same way in which he walked" (1 John 2:4–6). A perfect life is not necessary, of course. Instead, John is saying that in general our lives ought to be ones of imitation of Christ and likeness to him in what we do and say. If we have genuine saving faith, there will be clear results in obedience in our lives (see also 1 John 3:9–10, 24; 5:18). Thus James can say, "Faith by itself, if it does not have works, is dead," and "I will show you my faith by my works" (James 2:17–18). One large area of obedience to God includes love for fellow Christians: "Whoever loves his brother abides in the light" (1 John 2:10), and "We know that we have passed out of death into life, because we love the brothers. Whoever does not love abides in death" (1 John 3:14; cf. 3:17; 4:7). One evidence of this love is continuing in Christian fellowship (1 John 2:19), and another is giving to a brother in need (1 John 3:17; cf. Matt. 25:31–46).

## 3. Do I See a Long-Term Pattern of Growth in My Christian Life?

The first two areas of assurance dealt with present faith and present evidence of the Holy Spirit at work in our lives. But Peter gives one more kind of test that we can use to ask whether we are genuinely believers. He tells us that there are some character traits which, if we keep on increasing in them, will guarantee that we will "never fall" (2 Peter 1:10). He tells his readers to add to their faith "virtue . . . knowledge . . . self-control . . . steadfastness . . . godliness . . . brotherly affection . . . love" (2 Peter 1:5–7). Then he says that these things are to belong to his readers and should be "increasing" continually in their lives (2 Peter 1:8). He adds that they are to "be all the more diligent to confirm your calling and election" and says then that "*if you practice these qualities* (the character traits mentioned in vv. 5–7) *you will never fall*" (2 Peter 1:10).

The way that we confirm our call and election, then, is to continue to grow in "these qualities." This implies that our assurance of salvation can be something that increases over time in our lives. Every year that we add to these character traits in our lives, we gain greater and greater assurance of our salvation. Though young believers can have a quite strong confidence in their salvation, that assurance can increase to even deeper certainty over the years in which they grow toward Christian maturity. If they continue to add these qualities, they will confirm their call and election and will "never fall."

The result of these three questions that we can ask ourselves should be to give strong assurance to those who are genuinely believers. In this way the doctrine of the perseverance of the saints will be a tremendously comforting doctrine. No one who has such assurance should wonder, "Will I be able to persevere to the end of my life and therefore be saved?" Everyone who gains assurance through such a self-examination should rather think, "I am truly born again; therefore, I will certainly persevere to the end, because I am being guarded 'by God's power' working through my faith. Therefore, I will never be lost. Jesus will raise me up at the last day and I will enter into his kingdom forever" (see 1 Peter 1:5; John 6:40).

On the other hand, this doctrine of the perseverance of the saints, if rightly understood, should cause genuine worry, and even fear, in the hearts of any who are "backsliding" or straying from Christ. Such persons must clearly be warned that only those who persevere to the end have been truly born again. If they fall away from their profession of faith in Christ and life of obedience to him, they may not really be saved—in fact, the *evidence* that they are giving *is that they are not saved*, and they never really were saved. Once they stop trusting in Christ and obeying him (I am speaking in terms of outward evidence), they have no genuine assurance of salvation, and they should consider themselves unsaved, and turn to Christ in repentance and ask him for forgiveness of their sins.

## 4. How Much Change of Life Is Needed to Have Assurance of Salvation?

As I already mentioned in chapter 35 (see pages 871–78), there is an evangelical Protestant viewpoint called Free Grace theology whose supporters strongly disagree with the perspective on assurance of salvation that I have been presenting here.[27] One of

---

27. The following section has been abbreviated and adapted from Wayne Grudem, *"Free Grace" Theology: 5 Ways It Diminishes the Gospel* (Wheaton, IL: Crossway, 2016), 89–97 and is used with permission of the publisher. See those pages for a much fuller discussion.

its advocates, Joseph Dillow, says that a lack of fruit in a person's life cannot provide a basis for denying the validity of the person's faith: "Just as the presence of fruit cannot prove whether a person is a Christian, *neither can its absence deny it.*"[28]

In order to show that evidence of a change in life should not be used as a basis for assurance, Free Grace advocates sometimes ask, "How many good works does one have to do in order to be assured of salvation?" or "How much evidence of a changed life is necessary for assurance?" For example, David Anderson says that if someone has "a list of ways to test your experience to see if you have the necessary proof to be assured of your salvation," that "such tests only stir up doubt, confusion, or self-deception." He goes on to say,

> If keeping His commandments is the test, then I must ask:
>
> 1. How many do I have to keep?
> 2. How long do I have to keep them?
> 3. Do I have to keep them perfectly?
> 4. Are some more important than others?
> 5. Will He grade on a curve?
>
> The believer quickly becomes disoriented on a sea of subjectivity.[29]

But these questions fail to understand how the Bible talks about assurance. In response to the question, "How many good works does one have to do in order to be assured of salvation?" the proper answer is "Some." To be more specific, *some* change of life gives a basis for *some* measure of assurance, and a greater change of life gives a basis for a stronger assurance. Scripture does not encourage us to demand more specificity than that.

A simple diagram might help to clarify the question of assurance:

| Strong evidence of unbelief | Weak evidence of unbelief | Mixed evidence | Weak evidence of belief | Strong evidence of belief |
|---|---|---|---|---|
|  |  | Unsure about salvation | Weak assurance of salvation | Strong assurance of salvation |
| Unsaved |  |  |  | Saved |

As this diagram indicates, the evidence that a person has actually believed in Christ falls along a spectrum from weak to strong. God alone knows with absolute certainty everyone who is saved and everyone who is lost, for "the Lord knows those who are his"

---

28. Joseph Dillow, *Final Destiny: The Future Reign of The Servant Kings* (Monument, CO: Grace Theology Press, 2018), 684. Emphasis in original.

29. David Anderson, *Free Grace Soteriology* ([Conroe, TX]: Grace Theology Press, 2012), 216.

(2 Tim. 2:19), but we can perceive stronger or weaker outward indications of what is actually in someone's heart, both our hearts and those of others.

In the shaded middle of the spectrum, where people give mixed evidence in their profession of faith and in their conduct of life, we simply have to say that we do not know whether the person is saved or not—the evidence is mixed. One example would be a young man who had understood the gospel clearly and had made a convincing profession of faith in Christ as a teenager but now in his twenties has no affiliation with Christians or with any church. He might say he is unsure if he ever really trusted in Christ, but he gives no strong evidence of unbelief in his personal conduct. A Free Grace supporter would not hesitate to say that this person is clearly saved, based on his earlier profession of faith,[30] but I would say that the New Testament does not allow us to give any assurance of salvation to this person, for we simply do not have adequate evidence to indicate if such a person is a believer or not.

If such a person came to me and asked if I thought he was saved, I would say that I don't know but that he should seriously consider some of the warning passages in the New Testament, such as, "Take care, brothers, lest there be in any of you an evil, unbelieving heart, leading you to fall away from the living God" (Heb. 3:12), and "My brothers, if anyone among you wanders from the truth and someone brings him back, let him know that whoever brings back a sinner from his wandering will save his soul from death and will cover a multitude of sins" (James 5:19–20). His failure to seek any affiliation with other Christians also gives reason to soberly consider this verse: "They went out from us, but they were not of us; for if they had been of us, they would have continued with us. But they went out, that it might become plain that they all are not of us" (1 John 2:19). I would tell him that I do not know if he is truly born again or not, but his present pattern of life gives me no reason to give him assurance of salvation.

But at the right hand side of the spectrum, where people give strong evidence of belief by their personal testimony and by the conduct of their lives, they should have strong assurance that they are truly saved, and we should readily encourage them in that assurance.

---

30. Joseph Dillow quotes this sentence from my 2016 book *"Free Grace" Theology* and then responds, "Personally, after involvement in the so-called 'Free Grace' movement for twenty-six years, I have never met anyone who believes this or would do this" (Joseph Dillow, "Finding Assurance," in *A Defense of Free Grace Theology: With Respect to Saving Faith, Perseverance, and Assurance*, ed. Fred Chay [The Woodlands, TX: Grace Theology Press, 2017], 235–36). But Dillow has not quoted me accurately. The example I gave specified "a young man who had understood the gospel clearly and had made a convincing profession of faith in Christ as a teenager but now in his twenties has no affiliation with Christians or with any church and says he is unsure if he ever really trusted in Christ. But he also gives no strong evidence of unbelief in his personal conduct" (Grudem, *"Free Grace" Theology*, 91). However, Dillow doesn't quote these words but instead summarizes my hypothetical case as follows: "If all a person must do is check a box on a revival card and can then live any kind of life he desires and still go to heaven" (Dillow, "Finding Assurance," 235). Dillow removed the part where I said the man had "understood the gospel clearly and made a convincing profession of faith in Christ," and these are qualifications that, in the eyes of Free Grace supporters, would be sufficient reason for telling the person that he is assured of his salvation. I stand by my statement that, with respect to my specific example, "a Free Grace supporter would not hesitate to say that this person is clearly saved, based on his earlier profession of faith."

Supporters of Free Grace theology would object to a diagram like this. They would say that our assurance of salvation should be *based solely on Scripture*, not on our subjective evaluations of such evidence in our lives. In order to address this objection, it is important to be clear on the question, "Assurance about what?"

The question is not about the truthfulness of Christ's redemptive work. All Protestant theologians would agree that our assurance *that Christ's work has earned salvation for sinners* and *that all who trust in Christ will be saved* should be based fully and entirely on the testimony of God in Scripture and what Scripture teaches us about the finished atoning work of Christ. That is how we are to learn about something that has happened outside of us, long before we ever lived: Christ died and paid the penalty for our sins.

But that is not the question here. The question is not: How do I know that Christ has died for people's sins and that he will save all who believe in him? The question is rather: How do I know *that I have truly believed*?

Reading and agreeing with Bible verses about the atoning work of Christ tells me nothing about *whether I have truly trusted in the person of Christ or not*. Therefore, saying that assurance of my salvation must be based *only* on Scripture and the finished work of Christ is simply a category mistake. It does not address the category of personal belief: How do I know that *I personally have believed in Christ*? The response to this question from some Free Grace advocates has been simply to dismiss it.[31]

Another Free Grace response is to portray saving faith as no different from intellectual agreement with a truthful mathematical equation. Charles Bing writes, "The faith I have in Jesus Christ is the same as the faith I have that 1 + 1 = 2."[32] But saving faith is more than intellectual assent, for it must include a personal trust in the living person of Jesus Christ, not merely assent to statements about his saving work.[33]

The New Testament gives several verses telling me about *various evidences that I have believed*, verses that talk about how I can know that I have come to know God, that I am born of God, that I have faith, that I have passed from death to life, and so forth. (I discussed these verses earlier in this chapter.)

Such evaluation of evidences of salvation can and should lead a person to a solid assurance of his or her salvation. Peter tells his hearers "to *confirm* your calling and election" (2 Peter 1:10), and John says that "if we keep his commandments," then "we *know* that we have come to know him" (1 John 2:3). He also says, "By this we may *know* that we are in him: whoever says he abides in him ought to walk in the same way in which he walked" (1 John 2:5–6).

The Westminster Confession of Faith (1643–46) speaks of believers obtaining an "infallible assurance":

---

31. Zane Hodges refuses to address the question and simply asserts, "People know whether they believe something or not." Rather than explain more deeply what it means to believe in Christ, he dismisses the question as a waste of time: "It is an unproductive waste of time to employ the popular categories—intellect, emotion, or will—as a way of analyzing the mechanics of faith" (Hodges, *Absolutely Free! A Biblical Reply to Lordship Salvation* [Grand Rapids: Zondervan, 1989], 31).

32. Charles C. Bing, "Full Assurance Produces Godly Living," in *Free Grace Theology: 5 Ways It Magnifies the Gospel*, ed. Grant Hawley (Allen, TX: Bold Grace Ministries, 2016), 62.

33. See discussion in chapter 35, pp. 861–79.

> Such as truly believe in the Lord Jesus, and love him in sincerity, endeavoring to walk in all good conscience before him, *may, in this life, be certainly assured that they are in the state of grace.* . . . This certainty is not a bare conjectural and probable persuasion . . . but *an infallible assurance of faith* founded upon the *divine truth* of the promises of salvation, the *inward evidences* of those graces unto which these promises are made, the *testimony of the Spirit* of adoption witnessing with our spirits that we are the children of God. (18:1–2)

By contrast, the Free Grace movement gives false assurance of eternal life to many unsaved people who have never genuinely repented of their sins, who show no evidence of regeneration in their daily lives, and who perhaps even profess to be complete unbelievers. The tragic result of this mistaken Free Grace teaching is that many people who are unsaved for eternity have been wrongly assured they are saved.

## 5. Practical Pastoral Application

At this point, in terms of pastoral care with those who have strayed away from their Christian profession, we should realize that *Calvinists* (those who believe in the perseverance of the saints) and *Arminians* (those who think that Christians can lose their salvation) *will both counsel a "backslider" in the same way.* According to the Arminian, this person was a Christian at one time but is no longer a Christian. According to the Calvinist, such a person never really was a Christian in the first place and is not one now. But in both cases the biblical counsel given would be the same: "You do not appear to be a Christian now—you must repent of your sins and trust in Christ for your salvation!" Though the Calvinist and Arminian would differ on their interpretation of the previous history, they would agree on what should be done in the present.[34]

But here we see why the phrase "eternal security" can be misleading. In some evangelical churches, instead of teaching the full and balanced presentation of the doctrine of the perseverance of the saints, pastors have sometimes taught a watered-down version, which in effect tells people that all who have once made a profession of faith and been baptized are "eternally secure." The result is that some people who are not genuinely converted at all may "come forward" at the end of an evangelistic sermon to profess faith in Christ and may be baptized shortly after that, but then they leave the fellowship of the church and live a life no different from the one they lived before they gained this "eternal security." In this way people are given false assurance and are being cruelly deceived into thinking they are going to heaven when in fact they are not.[35]

---

34. Of course, both the Calvinist and the Arminian would allow for the possibility that the "backslidden" person is truly born again and had just fallen into sin and doubt. But both would agree that it is pastorally wise to assume that the person is not a Christian until some evidence of present faith is forthcoming.

35. Of course, not all who use the phrase *eternal security* make mistakes of this sort, but the phrase is certainly open to such misunderstanding.

# QUESTIONS FOR PERSONAL APPLICATION

1. Do you have assurance that you are truly born again? What evidence do you see in your life to give you that assurance? Do you think that God wants true believers to go throughout life worrying about whether they are really born again or to have firm assurance that they are his people? (See 1 John 5:13.) Have you seen a pattern of growth in your Christian life over time? Are you trusting in your own power to keep on believing in Christ or in God's power to keep your faith active and alive?

2. If you have doubts about whether you are truly born again, what is it in your life that is giving reason for those doubts? What would Scripture encourage you to do to resolve those doubts (see 2 Peter 1:5–11; also Matt. 11:28–30; John 6:37)? Do you think that Jesus now knows about your doubts and understands them? What do you think he would like you to do now to gain greater assurance of salvation?

3. Have you known people, perhaps in your church, whose "fruit" is always destructive or divisive or harmful to the ministry of the church and the faith of others? Do they have very much influence, perhaps even positions of leadership in the church? Do you think that an evaluation of the fruit of one's life and influence on others should be a qualification for church leadership? Is it possible that people would profess agreement with every true Christian doctrine and still not be born again? What are some more reliable evidences of genuine conversion other than intellectual adherence to sound doctrine?

**Special Terms**

*assurance of salvation*
*eternal security*
*perseverance of the saints*

# BIBLIOGRAPHY

(For an explanation of this bibliography see the note on the bibliography to chapter 1, pp. 23–24. Complete bibliographical data may be found on pp. 1489–96.)

## SECTIONS IN EVANGELICAL SYSTEMATIC THEOLOGIES

### 1. Anglican (Episcopalian)
1882–92 . . . . . Litton, 345–51

2001 . . . . . . . . Packer, 241–43
2013 . . . . . . . . Bird, 595–605
2013 . . . . . . . . Bray, 585–603

### 2. Arminian (Wesleyan or Methodist)
1875–76 . . . . . Pope, 3:100–147
1892–94 . . . . . Miley, 2:268–70, 339–54
1960 . . . . . . . . Purkiser, 298–304

1992. . . . . . . . Oden, 3:152, 183, 199–200,
203–4, 236
2002. . . . . . . . Cottrell, 198, 375

**3. Baptist**
1767 . . . . . . . . Gill, 2:151–78
1887 . . . . . . . . Boyce, 425–37
1907 . . . . . . . . Strong, 881–86
1990–95 . . . . . Garrett, 2:357–76
2007 . . . . . . . . Akin, 918–19
2013 . . . . . . . . Erickson, 913–24

**4. Dispensational**
1947 . . . . . . . . Chafer, 3:267–355
1949 . . . . . . . . Thiessen, 290–95
1986 . . . . . . . . Ryrie, 328–34
2002–2005 . . Geisler, 3:300–346
2017 . . . . . . . . MacArthur and Mayhue, 664–53

**5. Lutheran**
1917–24 . . . . . Pieper, 3:89–100
1934 . . . . . . . . Mueller, 436–40

**6. Reformed (or Presbyterian)**
1559 . . . . . . . . Calvin, 2:968–76 (3.24.4–9)
1679–85 . . . . . Turretin, IET, 1:365–72, 392–94, 2:593–616
1724–58 . . . . . Edwards, 596–604
1871–73 . . . . . Hodge, 3:104–13
1878 . . . . . . . . Dabney, 687–713
1894 . . . . . . . . Shedd, 350, 364, 535, 783, 801, 805
1906–11 . . . . . Bavinck, RD, 4:266–70
1910 . . . . . . . . Vos, 4:211, 215–25
1937–66 . . . . . Murray, RAA, 151–60
1938 . . . . . . . . Berkhof, 545–54
1998 . . . . . . . . Reymond, 764–67

2008. . . . . . . . Van Genderen and Velema, 667–76
2011 . . . . . . . . Horton, 648–87
2013 . . . . . . . . Frame, 178–79, 665–70, 998–1007
2013 . . . . . . . . Culver, 765–71
2016 . . . . . . . . Allen and Swain, 370–75
2017 . . . . . . . . Barrett, 582
2019 . . . . . . . . Letham, 673–74, 724–30, 742–49

**7. Renewal (or charismatic/Pentecostal)**
1988–92 . . . . . Williams, 2:119–36
1995 . . . . . . . . Horton, 368–73
2008. . . . . . . . Duffield and Van Cleave, 259–70

## SECTIONS IN REPRESENTATIVE ROMAN CATHOLIC SYSTEMATIC THEOLOGIES

**1. Roman Catholic: Traditional**
1955 . . . . . . . . Ott (no explicit treatment)

**2. Roman Catholic: Post–Vatican II**
2012. . . . . . . . CCC, paragraphs 162, 2016

## OTHER WORKS

Allison, Gregg. Historical Theology: An Introduction to Christian Doctrine; A Companion to Wayne Grudem's Systematic Theology. Grand Rapids: Zondervan, 2011, 542–64.
Baker, W. R. "Endurance, Perseverance." In DLNT, 326–30.
Barnett, P. W. "Apostasy." In DLNT, 73–76.
Bateman, Herbert W., ed. Four Views on the Warning Passages in Hebrews. Grand Rapids: Kregel, 2007.
Berkouwer, G. C. Faith and Perseverance. Translated by Robert D. Knudsen. Grand Rapids: Eerdmans, 1958.
Borchert, Gerald L. "Assurance." In BTDB, 40–41.
———. "Endurance." In BTDB, 203–204.
Carson, D. A. "Reflections on Christian Assurance." WTJ 54 (1992): 1–29.

Chung, M. "Assurance." In *EDT3*, 92.

Demarest, B. A. "Assurance." In *EDT1*, 91–92.

Dunnett, Walter M. "Perseverance." In *BTDB*, 600–602.

Elliott, M. W. "Assurance." In *NDBT*, 386–88.

Grudem, Wayne. "The Perseverance of the Saints: A Case Study From Heb. 6:4–6 and the Other Warning Passages of Hebrews." In *Still Sovereign*, edited by Tom Schreiner and Bruce Ware, 133–82. Grand Rapids: Baker, 2000.

Gundry, Stanley N., and J. Matthew Pinson, eds. *Four Views on Eternal Security.* Grand Rapids: Zondervan, 2002.

Gundry-Volf, J. M. "Apostasy, Falling Away, Perseverance." In *DPL*, 39–45.

Guthrie, William. *The Christian's Great Interest.* London: Banner of Truth, 1969. See esp. part 1, *The Trial of a Saving Interest in Christ* (first published as a separate book in 1658).

Hoekema, Anthony A. "The Perseverance of True Believers." In *Saved by Grace*, 234–56. Grand Rapids: Eerdmans; Exeter: Paternoster, 1989.

Johnson, D. H. "Assurance." In *DLNT*, 102–4.

Karlberg, Mark W. "Backsliding." In *BTDB*, 48.

Kearsley, R. "Perseverance." In *NDT1*, 506–7.

Marshall, I. Howard. *Kept by the Power of God: A Study of Perseverance and Falling Away.* 3rd ed. Milton Keynes: Paternoster, 2005.

McGowan, A. T. B. "Perseverance." In *NDT2*, 666–67.

McKnight, Scot. "The Warning Passages of Hebrews," *TrinJ* 13 (1992): 21–59.

Murray, John. "Perseverance." In *Redemption Accomplished and Applied*, 151–60. Grand Rapids: Eerdmans, 1955.

Ortlund, R. C., Jr. "Apostasy." In *NDBT*, 383–86.

Schreiner, Thomas R., and Ardel B. Caneday. *The Race Set Before Us: A Biblical Theology of Perseverance & Assurance.* Downers Grove, IL: InterVarsity Press, 2001.

Shank, Robert. *Life in the Son.* 2nd ed. Minneapolis: Bethany, 1989.

White, R. E. O. "Perseverance." In *EDT3*, 655–56.

## SCRIPTURE MEMORY PASSAGE

**John 10:27–28:** My sheep hear my voice, and I know them, and they follow me. I give them eternal life, and they will never perish, and no one will snatch them out of my hand.

## HYMN

**"Call Jehovah Thy Salvation"**

(Use tune of "Come, Thou Long Expected Jesus.")

Call Jehovah thy salvation, rest beneath th' Almighty's shade,
In his secret habitation dwell, and never be dismayed:
There no tumult shall alarm thee, thou shalt dread no hidden snare:
Guile nor violence can harm thee, in eternal safeguard there.

From the sword at noonday wasting, from the noisome pestilence,
In the depth of midnight blasting, God shall be thy sure defence:
He shall charge his angel legions watch and ward o'er thee to keep;
Though thou walk through hostile regions, though in desert wilds thou sleep.

*Since, with pure and firm affection thou on God*
   *hast set thy love,*
*With the wings of his protection he will shield*
   *thee from above:*

*Thou shalt call on him in trouble, he will*
   *hearken, he will save;*
*Here for grief reward thee double, crown with*
   *life beyond the grave.*

Author: James Montgomery, 1822

## CONTEMPORARY WORSHIP SONG

### "Yet Not I, but through Christ in Me"

*What gift of grace is Jesus, my redeemer!*
*There is no more for heaven now to give.*
*He is my joy, my righteousness, and freedom,*
*My steadfast love, my deep and boundless peace.*

*Refrain 1*
*To this I hold, my hope is only Jesus,*
*For my life is wholly bound to his.*
*Oh how strange and divine, I can sing: all is mine!*
*Yet not I, but through Christ in me.*

*The night is dark, but I am not forsaken,*
*For by my side, the Savior He will stay.*
*I labor on in weakness and rejoicing,*
*For in my need, His power is displayed.*

*Refrain 2*
*To this I hold, my Shepherd will defend me.*
*Through the deepest valley He will lead.*
*Oh the night has been won, and I shall overcome!*
*Yet not I, but through Christ in me.*

*No fate I dread, I know I am forgiven.*
*The future sure, the price it has been paid,*
*For Jesus bled and suffered for my pardon,*
*And He was raised to overthrow the grave.*

*Refrain 3*
*To this I hold, my sin has been defeated.*
*Jesus now and ever is my plea.*
*Oh the chains are released, I can sing: I am free!*
*Yet not I, but through Christ in me.*

*With every breath I long to follow Jesus,*
*For He has said that He will bring me home,*
*And day by day I know He will renew me,*
*Until I stand with joy before the throne.*

*Refrain 4*
*To this I hold, my hope is only Jesus.*
*All the glory evermore to Him.*
*When the race is complete, still my lips shall repeat:*
*Yet not I, but through Christ in me!*

*Tag*
*When the race is complete, still my lips shall repeat:*
*Yet not I, but through Christ in me!*
*Yet not I, but through Christ in me!*
*Yet not I, but through Christ in me!*

Words by Rich Thompson, Jonny
Robinson, and Michael Farran[36]

---

# CHAPTER 41

# Death and the Intermediate State

*What is the purpose of death in the Christian life?*
*What happens to our bodies and souls when we die?*

## EXPLANATION AND SCRIPTURAL BASIS

### A. Why Do Christians Die?

Our treatment of the application of redemption must include a consideration of death and the question of how Christians should view their own death and the death of others. We also must ask what happens to us between the time that we die and the time that Christ returns to give us new resurrection bodies.

### 1. Death Is Not a Punishment for Christians

Paul tells us clearly that there is "no condemnation for those who are in Christ Jesus" (Rom. 8:1). All the penalty for our sins has been paid. Therefore, even though we know that Christians die, we should not view the death of Christians as a punishment from God or in any way a result of a penalty due to us for our sins.[1] It is true that the penalty for sin is death, but that penalty no longer applies to us—not in terms of physical death and not in terms of spiritual death or separation from God. All of that has been paid for by Christ. Therefore, there must be another reason than punishment for our sins if we are to understand why Christians die.

### 2. Death Is the Final Outcome of Living in a Fallen World

In his great wisdom, God decided that he would not apply to us the benefits of Christ's redemptive work all at once. Rather, he has chosen to apply the benefits of salvation to us gradually over time (as we have seen in chapters 33–40). Similarly, he has not chosen to remove all evil from the world immediately but to wait until the

---

1. Even the death of some Corinthian Christians who had been abusing the Lord's Supper (1 Cor. 11:30) is viewed by Paul as a disciplining or chastening process, not as a result of condemnation: he says, "But when we are judged by the Lord, we are disciplined so that we may not be condemned along with the world" (1 Cor. 11:32). (In this discussion I am using the word *punishment* to mean retribution from God which is intended to do us harm, and *discipline* to mean hardship through which God intends to do us good.)

final judgment and the establishment of the new heaven and new earth (see chapters 56 and 57). In short, we still live in a fallen world and our experience of salvation is still incomplete.

The last aspect of the fallen world to be removed will be death. Paul says: "Then comes the end, when he delivers the kingdom to God the Father after destroying every rule and every authority and power. For he must reign until he has put all his enemies under his feet. *The last enemy to be destroyed is death*" (1 Cor. 15:24–26). When Christ returns,

then shall come to pass the saying that is written:

"Death is swallowed up in victory."
"O death, where is your victory?
    O death, where is your sting?" (1 Cor. 15:54–55)

But until that time, death remains a reality even in the lives of Christians. Although death does not come to us as a penalty for our individual sins (for that has been paid by Christ), it does come to us as a result of living in a fallen world, where the effects of sin have not all been removed. Related to the experience of death are other results of the fall that harm our physical bodies and signal the presence of death in the world—Christians as well as non-Christians experience aging, illnesses, injuries, and natural disasters (such as floods, violent storms, and earthquakes). Although God often answers prayers to deliver Christians (and also non-Christians) from some of these effects of the fall for a time (and thereby indicates the nature of his coming kingdom), Christians eventually experience all of these things to some measure, and until Christ returns, all of us will grow old and die. The "last enemy" has not yet been destroyed. And God has chosen to allow us to experience death before we gain all the benefits of salvation that have been earned for us.

### 3. God Uses the Experience of Death to Complete Our Sanctification

Throughout our Christian lives we know that we never have to pay any penalty for sin, for that has all been taken by Christ (Rom. 8:1). Therefore, when we do experience pain and suffering in this life, we should never think it is because God is *punishing* us (for our harm). Sometimes suffering is simply a result of living in a sinful, fallen world, and sometimes it is because God is *disciplining* us (for our good), but in all cases we are assured by Romans 8:28 that "for those who love God *all things work together for good*, for those who are called according to his purpose" (Rom. 8:28).

The positive purpose for God's discipline is clear in Hebrews 12, where we read: "The Lord disciplines the one he loves. . . . He disciplines us for our good, that we may share his holiness. For the moment all discipline seems painful rather than pleasant, but later it yields the peaceful fruit of righteousness to those who have been trained by it" (Heb. 12:6, 10–11).

Not all discipline is in order to correct us from sins that we have committed; it can also be allowed by God to strengthen us in order that we may gain greater ability to trust God and resist sin in the challenging path of obedience. We see this clearly in the life of Jesus, who, though he was without sin, "learned obedience *through what he suffered*" (Heb. 5:8).[2] He was made perfect "through suffering" (Heb. 2:10). Therefore, we should see all the hardship and suffering that comes to us in life as something that God brings to us *to do us good*, strengthening our trust in him and our obedience, and ultimately increasing our ability to glorify him.

Consequently, we should view the aging and weakness and sometimes sickness leading up to death as another kind of discipline that God allows us to go through in order that through this process our sanctification might be furthered and ultimately completed when we go to be in the Lord's presence. The challenge that Jesus gives to the church in Smyrna could really be given to every believer: "*Be faithful unto death, and I will give you the crown of life*" (Rev. 2:10). Paul says his goal in life is that he may become like Christ, "that I may know him and the power of his resurrection, and may share his sufferings, *becoming like him in his death*" (Phil. 3:10). Paul thought about the way Jesus died, and made it his goal to exemplify the same characteristics in his life when it came time for him to die—that in whatever circumstances he found himself, he, like Christ, would continue obeying God, trusting God, forgiving others, and caring for the needs of those around him, thus in every way bringing glory to God even in his death. Therefore, when in prison, without knowing whether he would die there or come out alive, he could still say, "it is my eager expectation and hope that I will not be at all ashamed, but that with full courage now as always *Christ will be honored* in my body, whether by life *or by death*" (Phil. 1:20).

Death is not in any way a punishment for sin but simply is something God brings us through in order to make us more like Christ. Understanding that fact should be a great encouragement to us. It should take away from us the fear of death that haunts the minds of unbelievers (cf. Heb. 2:15). Nevertheless, although God will bring good to us through the process of death, we must still remember that ultimately death is not natural; it is an enemy, something that Christ will finally destroy (1 Cor. 15:26).

### 4. Our Experience of Death Completes Our Union with Christ

Another reason why God allows us to experience death—rather than taking us immediately to heaven when we become Christians—is that through death we imitate Christ in what he did and thereby experience closer union with him. Paul can say that

---

2. For a discussion of how Jesus learned obedience through what he suffered, see chapter 26, p. 668.

we are fellow heirs with Christ "provided we *suffer with him* in order that we may also be glorified with him" (Rom. 8:17). Peter tells his readers not to be surprised at the fiery testing that comes on them, but he encourages them to "rejoice insofar as *you share Christ's sufferings*, that you may also rejoice and be glad when his glory is revealed" (1 Peter 4:13). As we noted above, such union with Christ in suffering includes union with him in death as well (see Phil. 3:10). Jesus is the "founder and perfecter of our faith" (Heb. 12:2), and we follow after him as we run the race of life. Peter writes, "Christ also suffered for you, leaving you an example, so that you might follow in his steps" (1 Peter 2:21).

## 5. Our Obedience to God Is More Important Than Preserving Our Own Lives

If God uses the experience of death to deepen our trust in him and to strengthen our obedience to him, then it is important that we remember that the world's goal of preserving one's physical life at all costs is not the highest goal for a Christian: obedience to God and faithfulness to him in every circumstance are far more important. This is why Paul could say, "I am ready not only to be imprisoned but even to die in Jerusalem for the name of the Lord Jesus" (Acts 21:13; cf. 25:11). He told the Ephesian elders, "I do not account my life of any value nor as precious to myself, if only I may finish my course and the ministry that I received from the Lord Jesus, to testify to the gospel of the grace of God" (Acts 20:24).

This conviction—that obedience to God is far more important than the preservation of life—gave Paul courage to go back into the city of Lystra after he had just been stoned and left for dead (Acts 14:20) and then to return there again shortly thereafter (Acts 14:21–22). He endured many sufferings and dangers (2 Cor. 11:23–27), often risking his life in order to obey Christ fully. Therefore, he could say at the end of his life, with a note of great triumph, "The time of my departure has come. *I have fought the good fight*, I have finished the race, I have kept the faith" (2 Tim. 4:6–7). This same conviction empowered Old Testament saints to accept martyrdom rather than sin: "Some were tortured, refusing to accept release, so that they might rise again to a better life" (more literally, "that they might obtain a better resurrection," Heb. 11:35, KJV, NKJV, NASB). This conviction also gave Peter and the other apostles courage, when facing the threat of death, to say, "We must obey God rather than men" (Acts 5:29). Certainly this was the point of Jesus' command to the church at Smyrna, "*Be faithful unto death*, and I will give you the crown of life" (Rev. 2:10). We also read that there will be rejoicing in heaven when the faithful saints have conquered the devil "by the blood of the Lamb and by the word of their testimony, for *they loved not their lives even unto death*" (Rev. 12:11).

The persuasion that we may honor the Lord even in our death, and that faithfulness to him is far more important than preserving our lives, has given courage and motivation to martyrs throughout the history of the church. When faced with a choice of sinfully preserving their lives or faithfully giving up their lives, they chose to give up their lives—"They loved not their lives even unto death" (Rev. 12:11). Even when there is little persecution and little likelihood of martyrdom, it would be good for us to fix this truth in our minds once for all, for if we are willing to give up even our lives for faithfulness to God, we shall find it much easier to give up everything else for the sake of Christ as well.

## B. How Should We Think of Our Own Death and the Death of Others?

### 1. Our Death

The New Testament encourages us to view our own death not with fear but with joy at the prospect of going to be with Christ. Paul says, "We would rather be away from the body and at home with the Lord" (2 Cor. 5:8). When he is in prison, not knowing whether he will be executed or released, he can say, "For to me to live is Christ, and *to die is gain*. If I am to live in the flesh, that means fruitful labor for me. Yet which I shall choose I cannot tell. I am hard pressed between the two. *My desire is to depart and be with Christ*, for that is far better" (Phil. 1:21–23). We also read John's word in Revelation, "And I heard a voice from heaven saying, 'Write this: Blessed are the dead who die in the Lord from now on.' 'Blessed indeed,' says the Spirit, 'that they may rest from their labors, for their deeds follow them!'" (Rev. 14:13).

Believers need not fear death therefore, for Scripture reassures us that not even death will "separate us from the love of God in Christ Jesus our Lord" (Rom. 8:38–39; cf. Ps. 23:4). In fact, Jesus died in order that he might "deliver all those who through fear of death were subject to lifelong slavery" (Heb. 2:15).[3] This verse reminds us that a clear testimony to our lack of fear of death will provide a strong witness for Christians in an age that tries to avoid talking about death and has no answer for it.

### 2. The Death of Christian Friends and Relatives

While we can look forward to our own death with a joyful expectation of being in Christ's presence, our attitude will be somewhat different when we experience the death of Christian friends and relatives. In these cases we will experience genuine sorrow—but mixed with joy that they have gone to be with the Lord.

It is not wrong to express real sorrow at the loss of fellowship with loved ones who have died and sorrow also for the suffering and hardship that they may have gone through prior to death. Sometimes Christians think it shows lack of faith to mourn deeply for a brother or sister Christian who has died. But Scripture does not support that view because when Stephen was stoned, we read that "Devout men buried Stephen *and made great lamentation over him*" (Acts 8:2). If there ever was certainty that someone went to be with the Lord, it occurred in the case of Stephen. As he died, he said, "Behold, I see

3. Berkhof is certainly correct to say that the burial of Jesus "did not merely serve to prove that Jesus was really dead, but also to remove the terrors of the grave for the redeemed and to sanctify the grave for them" (*Systematic Theology* [Grand Rapids: Eerdmans, 1941], 340).

the heavens opened, and the Son of Man standing at the right hand of God" (Acts 7:56). Then when he was dying, he prayed, "Lord Jesus, receive my spirit," and "Lord, do not hold this sin against them" (Acts 7:59–60). And this occurred in Jerusalem, with all the apostles still present, those apostles who had seen Jesus after he had been raised from the dead. There was no lack of faith on anyone's part that Stephen was in heaven experiencing great joy in the presence of the Lord. Yet in spite of this, "Devout men buried Stephen *and made great lamentation over him*" (Acts 8:2). Their sorrow showed the genuine grief that they felt at the loss of fellowship with someone whom they loved, and it was not wrong to express this sorrow—it was right. Even Jesus, at the tomb of Lazarus, "wept" (John 11:35), experiencing sorrow at the fact that Lazarus had died, that his sisters and others were experiencing such grief, and also, no doubt, that there was death in the world at all, for ultimately it is unnatural and (ultimately) ought not to exist in a world created by God. The very existence of death should trouble us deeply.

The Ephesian elders, whom Paul had taught personally for three years, expressed great sorrow in their last meeting with Paul: "And there was *much weeping* on the part of all . . . being sorrowful most of all because of the word he had spoken, that they would not see his face again" (Acts 20:37–38). And Paul, in the same letter in which he expressed such a desire to depart from this life and be with Christ, said that if Epaphroditus had died, Paul would have had *"sorrow upon sorrow"* (Phil. 2:27). Moreover, King David, the man after God's own heart, the man who in his psalms frequently spoke of living forever with God, nonetheless had great sorrow when he learned that Saul and Jonathan had died (2 Sam. 1:11–27). These many examples show that it is not wrong to feel and express deep sorrow at the death of loved ones.

Nevertheless, the sorrow that we feel is clearly mingled with hope and joy. Paul does not tell the Thessalonians that they should not grieve *at all* concerning their loved ones who have died, but he writes, "that you may not grieve *as others do* who have no hope" (1 Thess. 4:13)—they should not grieve in the same way, with the same bitter despair, that unbelievers have. But certainly they should grieve. He assures them that Christ "died for us so that whether we are awake or asleep we might live with him" (1 Thess. 5:10) and thereby encourages them that those who have died have gone to be with the Lord. That is why Scripture can say, *"Blessed are the dead who die in the Lord* from now on . . . that they may rest from their labors"* (Rev. 14:13). In fact, Scripture even tells us, "Precious in the sight of the LORD is the death of his saints" (Ps. 116:15).

Therefore, though we have genuine sorrow when Christian friends and relatives die, we also can say with Scripture, "O death, where is your victory? O death, where is your sting? . . . Thanks be to God, who gives us the victory through our Lord Jesus Christ" (1 Cor. 15:55–57). Though we mourn, our mourning should be mixed with worship of God and thanksgiving for the life of the loved one who has died. Worship is especially important at this time, as we see in the examples of David and of Job. When David's child died, he stopped praying for the child's health and worshiped God: "Then David arose from the earth and washed and anointed himself and changed his clothes. And he went into the house of the Lord *and worshiped*" (2 Sam. 12:20). Similarly, when Job heard of the death of his ten children, "Then Job arose and tore his robe and shaved his head and fell on the ground *and worshiped*. And he said, 'Naked I came from my mother's womb, and naked shall I return. The LORD gave, and the LORD has taken away; blessed be the name of the LORD'" (Job 1:20–21).

### 3. The Death of Unbelievers

When unbelievers die, the sorrow we feel is not mingled with the joy of assurance that they have gone to be with the Lord forever. This sorrow, especially regarding those we have been close to, is very deep and real. Paul himself, when thinking about some of his Jewish brothers who had rejected Christ, said, "I am speaking the truth in Christ—I am not lying; my conscience bears me witness in the Holy Spirit—that *I have great sorrow and unceasing anguish in my heart*. For I could wish that I myself were accursed and cut off from Christ for the sake of my brothers, my kinsmen according to the flesh" (Rom. 9:1–3).

Yet it also must be said that we often do not have absolute certainty that a person has persisted in refusal to trust in Christ all the way to the point of death. The knowledge of one's impending death often will bring about genuine heart searching on the part of the dying person, and sometimes words of Scripture or words of Christian testimony that have been heard long ago will be recalled and the person may come to genuine repentance and faith. Certainly, we do not have any assurance that this has happened unless there is explicit evidence for it, but it is also good to realize that in many cases we have only probable but not absolute knowledge that those whom we have known as unbelievers have persisted in their unbelief until the point of death. In some cases we simply do not know.

Nevertheless, after a non-Christian has died, it would be wrong to give any indication to others that we think that person has gone to heaven. This would simply be to give misleading information and false assurance and to diminish the urgency of the need for those who are still alive to trust in Christ. It is much better, as we have opportunity, to focus on the fact that the sorrow that we feel at the loss of someone whom we love causes us to reflect on our life and destiny as well. In fact, the times when we are able to talk as a friend to the loved ones of an unbeliever who has died are often times when the Lord will open up opportunities to talk about the gospel with those who are still living.

It is often very helpful in such circumstances to speak with genuine thankfulness about the good qualities that we have noticed and been encouraged by in the life of the person who has died.[4] A good example of that is seen in David's reaction when King Saul

---

4. It is right to thank God for the benefits of common grace in the lives of unbelievers; see the discussion of common grace in chapter 31.

died. Even though Saul had become an evil king and had pursued David and tried to kill him many times, once Saul had died, David spoke freely and publicly about the good things Saul had done:

> Your glory, O Israel, is slain on your high places! How the mighty have fallen! . . . Saul and Jonathan . . . they were swifter than eagles; they were stronger than lions. You daughters of Israel, weep over Saul, who clothed you luxuriously in scarlet, who put ornaments of gold on your apparel. How the mighty have fallen in the midst of battle! (2 Sam. 1:19–25)[5]

## C. What Happens When People Die?

### 1. The Souls of Believers Go Immediately into God's Presence

Death is a temporary cessation of bodily life and a separation of the soul from the body. Once a believer has died, though his or her physical body remains on the earth and is buried, at the moment of death the soul (or spirit) of that believer goes immediately into the presence of God with rejoicing. When Paul thinks about death he says, "We would rather be *away from the body and at home with the Lord*" (2 Cor. 5:8). To be away from the body is to be at home with the Lord. He also says that his desire is "to *depart and be with Christ*, for that is far better" (Phil. 1:23). Jesus said to the thief who was dying on the cross next to him, "*Today* you will be with me in paradise" (Luke 23:43).[6] The author of Hebrews says that when Christians come together to worship, they come not only into the presence of God in heaven but also into the presence of "the spirits of the righteous made perfect" (Heb. 12:23).[7] However, as we shall see in more detail in the next chapter, God will not leave our dead bodies in the earth forever, for when Christ returns the souls of believers will be reunited with their bodies, their bodies will be raised from the dead, and they will live with Christ eternally.

These passages also emphasize that we continue to be ourselves after we die. Jesus says to the thief, "You will be with me in Paradise." And it is Paul himself who wants to

---

5. Even this requires honesty and mature judgment, however, for if we are called upon to perform a funeral service for someone whose life has been widely known as evil and destructive, we do not want to give people the impression that what a person does in this life makes no difference or that we are ignorant of the noticeably bad qualities of such a person, or we will lose credibility with those who hear us. As an example of the inevitable reaction of people to the death of someone clearly evil, such as Adolf Hitler, note Prov. 11:10, "When the wicked perish there are shouts of gladness."

6. *Paradise* is simply another name for heaven; see chapter 27, pp. 734–35.

7. It must be said, however, that the fact that we go to be with Christ immediately when we die should not be taken as an encouragement to anyone to think that suicide would be right.

God says, "You shall not murder" (Ex. 20:13), and that means that we must not murder ourselves any more than we should murder others.

On the other hand, there are many faithful Christians who in wartime or shipwrecks or other trying circumstances have laid down their own lives for the sake of others, thus fulfilling Jesus' teaching, "Greater love has no one than this, that someone lay down his life for his friends" (John 15:13).

The larger principle is that as long as we remain in this life we are to be faithful to Christ in serving him and in prayer, for he calls us to be "faithful unto death" (Rev. 2:10). And though Paul, in thinking about his own personal desires, wanted to go to be with Christ, he realized that for the sake of the Philippians and for others that he ministered to, to stay alive would be "more necessary" on their behalf (Phil. 1:24).

"depart and be with Christ." In these and many other passages, the Bible disproves any theory of reincarnation—we remain ourselves forever, and we will never "come back" as some other person (or even as some kind of animal!).

**a. The Bible Does Not Teach the Doctrine of Purgatory.** The fact that the souls of believers go immediately into God's presence means that *there is no such thing as purgatory.* In Roman Catholic teaching, purgatory is the place where the souls of believers go to be further purified from sin until they are ready to be admitted into heaven. According to this view, the sufferings of purgatory are given to God in substitute for the punishment for sins that believers should have received in time but did not. Speaking of purgatory, the Catechism of the Catholic Church says,

> All who die in God's grace and friendship, but still imperfectly purified, are indeed assured of their eternal salvation; but after death they undergo purification, so as to achieve the holiness necessary to enter the joy of heaven.
>
> The Church gives the name Purgatory to this final purification of the elect, which is entirely different from the punishment of the damned.[8]

But this doctrine is not taught in Scripture and is, in fact, contrary to the verses quoted immediately above. The Roman Catholic Church has found support for this doctrine not in the pages of canonical Scripture, as defined in chapter 3 and as Protestants have accepted since the Reformation, but in the writings of the Apocrypha,[9] particularly in 2 Maccabees 12:42–45:

> [Judas Maccabeus, the leader of the Jewish forces] also took a collection, man by man, to the amount of 2,000 drachmas of silver, and sent it to Jerusalem to provide for a sin offering. In doing this he acted very well and honorably, taking into account the resurrection. For if he were not expecting that those who had fallen would rise again, it would have been superfluous and foolish *to pray for the dead.* But if he was looking to the splendid reward that is laid up for those who fall asleep in godliness, it was a holy and pious thought. Therefore *he made atonement for the dead, that they might be delivered from their sin.*

Here it is clear that prayer for the dead is approved, as well as making an offering to God to deliver the dead from their sin. But in response it must be said that this literature is not equal in authority to Scripture, so the passage should not be taken as an authoritative source of doctrine. Moreover, it contradicts the clear statements about departing and being with Christ quoted above, thereby opposing the clear teaching of New Testament

---

8. *Catechism of the Catholic Church* (New York: Doubleday, 1997), paragraphs 1030–31 (p. 291).

9. See chapter 3, pp. 44–47, for a discussion of the reasons why the Apocrypha should not be accepted as part of Scripture.

Scripture. Furthermore, when it talks about the offering of Judas making "atonement [Gk. *exilasmos* ('propitiation')] for the dead" it contradicts the explicit teaching of the New Testament that Christ alone made atonement for us. Finally, this passage in 2 Maccabees is difficult to square even with Roman Catholic teaching, because it teaches that soldiers who had died in the mortal sin of idolatry (which cannot be forgiven apart from repentance before death, according to Catholic teaching) should have prayers and sacrifices offered for them with the possibility that they will be delivered from their suffering.

Roman Catholic theology finds support for the doctrine of purgatory primarily in the passage from 2 Maccabees quoted above and in the teaching of the tradition of the church.[10] Other Scripture passages cited by Ott in support of the doctrine of purgatory are 2 Timothy 1:18; Matthew 5:26; 1 Corinthians 3:15; and Matthew 12:32.[11] Upon examination, these passages do not give convincing support to the idea of purgatory.

In 2 Timothy 1:18, Paul says, concerning Onesiphorus, "When he arrived in Rome he searched for me earnestly and found me—may the Lord grant him to find mercy from the Lord on that day!—and you well know all the service he rendered at Ephesus" (2 Tim. 1:17–18). The claim of those who find support for the doctrine of purgatory is that "Onesiphorus . . . apparently was no longer among the living at the time of the Second Epistle to Timothy."[12] This seems to be based on the fact that Paul refers not to Onesiphorus himself but "the household of Onesiphorus" (2 Tim. 1:16); however, that phrase does not prove that Onesiphorus had died but only that Paul was wishing blessings not only on him but on his entire household. This would not be unusual since Onesiphorus had served in Ephesus where Paul had worked for three years (2 Tim. 1:18; cf. 4:19). To build support for purgatory on the idea that Onesiphorus had already died is simply to build it on an assumption that cannot be supported with clear evidence. (It is not unusual for Paul to express a wish that some Christians would be blessed in the day of judgment; see 1 Thess. 5:23.)

In Matthew 12:32, Jesus says, "Whoever speaks against the Holy Spirit will not be forgiven, either in this age or in the age to come." Ott says that this sentence "leaves open the possibility that sins are forgiven not only in this world but in the world to come."[13] However, this is simply an error in reasoning: to say that something will not happen in the age to come does not imply that it might happen in the age to come![14] What is

10. Ludwig Ott, *Fundamentals of Catholic Dogma*, trans. Patrick Lynch (Rockford: Tan, 1960), 321–22, 482–85.

11. The *Catechism of the Catholic Church* similarly mentions Matt. 12:31 (I think they intended 12:32), 1 Cor. 3:15, and adds 1 Peter 1:7 (p. 291nn605–6). But in 1 Peter 1:7, Peter is not speaking about testing that will come in purgatory *after* people die, but is speaking about his readers' *present* suffering during this lifetime as something that shows that their faith is genuine like "gold that perishes though it is tested by fire."

12. Ibid., 321.
13. Ibid., 483.
14. This is a similar mistake to the one made by those who argue that, since Jesus says he will not blot someone's name out of the book of life (Rev. 3:5), it implies that he might blot the names of others out of the book of life (see chapter 40, pp. 985–86).

needed to prove the doctrine of purgatory is not a negative statement such as this but a positive statement that says that people suffer for the purpose of continuing purification after they die. But Scripture nowhere says this.

In 1 Corinthians 3:15 Paul says that on the day of judgment the work that everyone has done will be judged and tested by fire, and then he says, *"If anyone's work is burned up,* he will suffer loss, though he himself will be saved, but only as through fire." But this does not speak of a *person* being burned or suffering punishment but simply of *his work* as being tested by fire—that which is good will be like gold, silver, and precious stones that will last forever (v. 12). Moreover, Ott himself admits that this is something that occurs not during this age but during the day of "the general judgment,"[15] and this further indicates that it can hardly be used as a convincing argument for purgatory existing during this present age. Finally, in Matthew 5:26, after warning people to make friends quickly with their accusers while they are going to the court, lest the accuser hand them to the judge and the judge to the guard and they be put in prison, Jesus then says, "You will never get out until you have paid the last penny." Ott understands this as a parable teaching a "time-limited condition of punishment in the other world."[16] But surely there is no indication in context that this is a parable—Jesus is giving practical teaching about reconciliation of human conflicts and the avoidance of situations that naturally lead to anger and personal injury (see Matt. 5:21–26). Other passages of Scripture that have sometimes been referred to in support of the doctrine of purgatory[17] simply do not speak directly about this idea at all and can all easily be understood in terms of punishment and deliverance from distress in this life or in terms of a life of eternal blessing with God in heaven in the life to come.

An even more serious problem with this doctrine is that it teaches that we must add something to the redemptive work of Christ; thus his redemptive work for us was not enough to pay the penalty for all our sins. But this is certainly contrary to the teaching of Scripture.[18] Moreover, in a pastoral sense, the doctrine of purgatory robs believers of the great comfort that should be theirs in knowing that those who have died have immediately gone into the presence of the Lord and knowing that they also, when they die, will "depart and be with Christ, for that is far better" (Phil. 1:23).

**b. The Bible Does Not Teach the Doctrine of Soul Sleep.** The fact that souls of believers go immediately into God's presence also means that *the doctrine of soul sleep is incorrect.* This doctrine teaches that when believers die they go into a state of unconscious existence, and the next thing that they are conscious of will be when Christ returns and raises them to eternal life. This doctrine has been taught occasionally by

---

15. Ott, *Fundamentals of Catholic Dogma,* 483.

16. Ibid., 484.

17. Berkhof mentions that Roman Catholics have sometimes referred to Isa. 4:4; Mic. 7:8; Zech. 9:11; Mal. 3:2–3; and 1 Cor. 15:29.

18. See chapter 27, pp. 717–18, on the fact that Christ's death completely paid the penalty for all our sins.

one person or another in the history of the church, including some Anabaptists at the Reformation, some of the Irvingites in England in the nineteenth century, and Seventh-day Adventists today. One of John Calvin's first writings was a tract against this doctrine, a doctrine that has never found wide acceptance in the church.

Support for the doctrine of soul sleep has generally been found in the fact that Scripture several times speaks of the state of death as "sleep" or "falling asleep" (Matt. 9:24; 27:52; John 11:11; Acts 7:60; 13:36; 1 Cor. 15:6, 18, 20, 51; 1 Thess. 4:13; 5:10). Moreover, certain passages seem to teach that the dead do not have a conscious existence (see Pss. 6:5; 115:17 [but see v. 18!]; Eccl. 9:10; Isa. 38:19). But when Scripture represents death as sleep, sleep is simply a metaphorical expression used to indicate that death is only temporary for Christians, just as sleep is temporary. This is clearly seen, for example, when Jesus tells his disciples about the death of Lazarus. He says, "Our friend Lazarus has fallen asleep, but I go to awaken him" (John 11:11). We should notice that Jesus does not here say, "The soul of Lazarus is sleeping," nor, in fact, does any passage in Scripture say that the soul of a person is sleeping or unconscious (a statement that would be necessary to prove the doctrine of soul sleep). Rather, Jesus simply says that *Lazarus* has fallen asleep. Then John explains, "Now Jesus had spoken of his death, but they thought that he meant taking rest in sleep. Then Jesus told them plainly, 'Lazarus has died'" (John 11:13–14). The other passages that speak about people sleeping when they die are likewise to be interpreted as simply a metaphorical expression to teach that death is temporary.

As for the passages that indicate that the dead do not praise God or that there is a ceasing of conscious activity when people die, these are all to be understood from the perspective of life in this world. From our perspective it appears that once people die, they do not engage in these activities any longer. But Psalm 115 presents the full biblical perspective on this viewpoint. It says, "The dead do not praise the LORD, nor do any who go down into silence." But then it continues in the very next verse with a contrast indicating that those who believe in God will bless the LORD forever: "*But we will bless the* LORD *from this time forth and forevermore.* Praise the LORD!" (Ps. 115:17–18).

Finally, the passages quoted above demonstrating that the souls of believers go immediately into God's presence and enjoy fellowship with him there (2 Cor. 5:8; Phil. 1:23; Luke 23:43; Heb. 12:23) all indicate that there is conscious existence and fellowship with God immediately after death for the believer. Jesus did not say, "Today you will no longer have consciousness of anything that is going on," but "Today *you will be with me in paradise*" (Luke 23:43). Certainly the conception of Paradise understood at that time was not one of unconscious existence but one of great blessing and joy in the presence of God.[19] Paul did not say, "My desire is to depart and be unconscious for a long period

---

19. See the other uses of the word *Paradise* in 2 Cor. 12:3 and Rev. 2:7, where the word clearly refers to heaven itself where God is and lives and reigns; see also the discussion of this word in chapter 27, pp. 734–35.

of time," but rather "My desire is to depart *and be with Christ*" (Phil. 1:23)—and he certainly knew that Christ was not an unconscious, sleeping Savior, but one who was actively living and reigning in heaven. To be with Christ was to enjoy the blessing of fellowship in his presence, and that is why to depart and be with him was "far better" (Phil. 1:23). That is why he says, "We would rather be away from the body and at home with the Lord" (2 Cor. 5:8).

The fact that Hebrews 12:1 says, "We are surrounded by so great a cloud of witnesses," just after an entire chapter spent on the discussion of the faith of Old Testament saints who had died (Heb. 11) and the fact that the author encourages us to run the race of life with perseverance because we are surrounded by this great cloud of witnesses both suggest that those who have died and gone before have some awareness of what is going on in the earth. Scripture says very little about this, probably because it does not want us to pray to those who have died or to contact them in any way (note Saul's great sin in 1 Sam. 28:7–25). Nonetheless, Hebrews 12:1–2 does give us this slight hint, probably as an encouragement to us to continue also to be faithful to God as were those who have died and gone to heaven before us. Similarly, at the end of Hebrews 12, the author tells us that when we worship we come into the presence of God in heaven, and we come not to "the spirits of righteous people *who are sleeping in an unconscious state*" but "to innumerable angels in festal gathering, and to *the assembly of the firstborn who are enrolled in heaven*, and to God, the judge of all, and to *the spirits of the righteous made perfect*, and to Jesus, the mediator of a new covenant" (Heb. 12:22–24).[20]

Revelation 6:9–11 and 7:9–10 also clearly show the souls or spirits of those who have died and who have gone to heaven praying and worshiping, for they cry out with a loud voice, "O Sovereign Lord, holy and true, how long before you will judge and avenge our blood on those who dwell on the earth?" (Rev. 6:10), and they are seen "standing before the throne and before the Lamb, clothed in white robes, with palm branches in their hands, and crying out with a loud voice, 'Salvation belongs to our God who sits on the throne, and to the Lamb!'" (Rev. 7:9–10). All of these passages deny the doctrine of soul sleep, for they make it clear that the souls of believers experience conscious fellowship with God in heaven immediately upon death.

**c. Did Old Testament Believers Enter Immediately Into God's Presence?** Some have said that, although the souls of believers *since Christ's resurrection* go immediately into God's presence in heaven, the souls of believers who died *before Christ's resurrection* did not enjoy the blessings of heaven but went into a place of waiting for Christ's work of redemption to be complete. Sometimes this is called the *limbus patrum* or, simply, limbo.[21]

---

20. The phrase "the communion of saints" in the Apostles' Creed refers to the fact that we have in some sense a communion or fellowship with those who have died and gone before into heaven, an idea that is affirmed in Heb. 12:23. This does not imply that we can be aware of them but simply that when we worship we join in worship that is already going on in heaven

(see chapter 51, pp. 1238–41, on the fact that our worship now is also worship in heaven).

21. Strictly speaking, Roman Catholic theologians have held that there are two limbos, a place where unbaptized infants go when they die called *limbus infantum*, and a place where Old Testament believers went when they died called *limbus patrum*.

This view has been especially common in Roman Catholic theology, but it has also been held by some Lutherans. Some of the support for this doctrine comes from a particular view of the idea of Christ's descent into hell, which I discussed in an earlier chapter.[22]

Not many Scripture references talk about the state of Old Testament believers after they had died, but those that give us any indication of their state all point in the direction of immediate conscious enjoyment in the presence of God, not of a time of waiting away from God's presence. "Enoch walked with God, and he was not, for *God took him*" (Gen. 5:24; cf. Heb. 11:5). Elijah was not taken to a place on the border of hell, but he "went up by a whirlwind *into heaven*" (2 Kings 2:11; cf. Matt. 17:3, where Moses and Elijah appear, talking with Jesus). And David is confident that he will "*dwell in the house of the* LORD *forever*" (Ps. 23:6; cf. 16:10–11; 17:15; 115:18). Moreover, when Jesus answers the Sadducees, he reminds them that God says, "I am the God of Abraham, and the God of Isaac, and the God of Jacob" and then says, "He is not God of the dead, but of the living" (Matt. 22:32), thus implying that Abraham, Isaac, and Jacob *were living* even at that very moment and that God was their God. Moreover, in the story of the rich man and Lazarus, Jesus does not say that Lazarus is unconscious but reports Abraham as saying about Lazarus, "Now he is comforted here" (Luke 16:25). Abraham himself is portrayed as dwelling consciously in a place that is very desirable—that the rich man longed to go to—certainly not a place on the fringe of hell. It is important to notice that since this is before Christ's resurrection, Lazarus was in the same situation as the Old Testament saints.

Therefore, it seems likely that Old Testament believers also entered immediately into heaven and enjoyed a time of fellowship with God upon their death. However, it may well have been true that additional rich blessings and much greater rejoicing came to them when Christ returned to heaven at his ascension. But this does not mean that they were transported to heaven for the first time or that it was the first time they enjoyed the blessing of God's presence.

**d. Should We Pray for the Dead?** Finally, the fact that the souls of believers go immediately into God's presence means that *we should not pray for the dead.* Although this idea is taught in 2 Maccabees 12:42–45 (see above), it is taught nowhere in the Bible. Moreover, there is no indication that this was the practice of any Christians at the time of the New Testament, nor should it have been. Once *believers* die, they enter into God's presence and into a state of perfect happiness with him. What good would it do to pray for them anymore? Final heavenly reward will be based on deeds done in this life, as Scripture repeatedly testifies (1 Cor. 3:12–15; 2 Cor. 5:10, et al.).[23]

---

The Latin word *limbus* means "border"; these were thought to be places on the border of hell where people were excluded from the presence of God but also did not experience conscious suffering. There is no explicit support in Scripture for either doctrine.

22. For a discussion of the idea that Christ descended into hell when he died, see chapter 27, pp. 725–36.

23. See chapter 56, pp. 1408–10, on degrees of reward in heaven.

Further, the souls of perished *unbelievers* go to a place of punishment and eternal separation from God's presence. It would do no good to pray for them since their final destiny has been settled by their sin and rebellion against God in this life. To pray for the dead therefore is simply to pray for something that God has told us has already been decided.[24] Moreover, to teach that we should pray for the dead or to encourage others to do so would be to encourage false hope that the destinies of people might be changed after they die, something which Scripture nowhere encourages us to think. It may lead people to much useless anxiety and much time essentially wasted in prayers that will have absolutely no results, and will thereby divert attention from prayers that could be made for events for this life and could have great effect in advancing the work of the kingdom. We should spend time praying according to God's will.

## 2. The Souls of Unbelievers Go Immediately to Eternal Punishment

Scripture never encourages us to think that people will have a second chance to trust in Christ after death. In fact, the situation is quite the contrary. Jesus' story about the rich man and Lazarus gives no hope that people can cross from hell to heaven after they have died: though the rich man in hell called out, "Father Abraham, have mercy on me, and send Lazarus to dip the end of his finger in water and cool my tongue, for I am in anguish in this flame," Abraham replied to him, "Between us and you a great chasm has been fixed, in order that those who would pass from here to you may not be able, and *none may cross from there to us*" (Luke 16:24–26).

The book of Hebrews connects death with the consequence of judgment in close sequence: "just as it is appointed for man to die once, and after that comes judgment . . ." (Heb. 9:27). Moreover, Scripture never represents the final judgment as depending on anything done after we die but only on what has happened in this life (Matt. 25:31–46; Rom. 2:5–10; cf. 2 Cor. 5:10). Some have argued for a second chance to believe in the gospel on the basis of Christ's preaching to the spirits in prison in 1 Peter 3:18–20 and the preaching of the gospel "even to those who are dead" in 1 Peter 4:6, but those are inadequate interpretations of the verses in question and, on closer inspection, do not support such a view.[25]

---

24. Further indication that it is not right to pray for the dead is seen in the fact that David prayed intensely for his little son before that son died, but after he had died, David rose from prayer and washed and changed his clothes and "went into the house of the Lord and worshiped . . . and he ate" (2 Sam. 12:20; cf. v. 23). David realized that once the child had died his task of praying for him was done. When I speak of "praying for the dead" in this section, I mean praying that God would change their status or destiny. Of course there is nothing wrong with *thanking God* for the lives of people after they have died.

25. See the discussion of these verses in chapter 27, pp. 731–34; see also Wayne Grudem, *The First Epistle of Peter* (Leicester: Inter-Varsity Press; Grand Rapids: Eerdmans, 1988), 155–62, 170–72, 203–39.

We should also realize that the idea that there will be a second chance to accept Christ after death is based on the assumption that everyone deserves a chance to accept Christ and that eternal punishment only comes to those who consciously decide to reject him. But certainly that idea is not supported by Scripture: we all are sinners by nature and choice, and no one actually deserves any of God's grace or deserves any opportunity to hear the gospel of Christ—those come only because of God's unmerited favor. Condemnation comes not only because of a willful rejection of Christ but also because of the sins that we have committed and the rebellion against God that those sins represent (see John 3:18).

The idea that people have a second chance to accept Christ after death would also destroy most motivation for evangelism and missionary activity today. Furthermore, it is not consistent with the intense missionary zeal that was felt by the New Testament church as a whole, as exemplified in the missionary travels of the apostle Paul.

The fact that there is eternal conscious punishment for unbelievers after they die is certainly a difficult doctrine for us to contemplate. But the passages teaching it appear so clear that it seems that we must affirm it if we are to affirm what Scripture teaches. Jesus says that at the day of final judgment he will say to those at his left hand, "Depart from me, you cursed, into the *eternal fire* prepared for the devil and his angels," and he says that "these will go away into *eternal punishment*, but the righteous into eternal life" (Matt. 25:41, 46).[26]

These passages show that we cannot accept as faithful to Scripture the doctrine of *annihilationism*. This is a doctrine that says that unbelievers, either immediately upon death, or else after suffering for a period of time, will simply cease to exist—God will "annihilate" them and they will no longer be. Although the idea initially sounds attractive to us, and it avoids the emotional difficulty connected with affirming eternal conscious punishment for the wicked, such an idea is not explicitly affirmed in any passages of Scripture, and seems so clearly to be contradicted by those passages that connect the eternal blessing of the righteous with the eternal punishment of the wicked (Matt. 25:46) and that talk about punishment extending to the wicked day and night forever (Rev. 14:11; 20:10).[27]

Although unbelievers pass into a state of eternal punishment immediately upon death, their bodies will not be raised until the day of final judgment. On that day, their bodies will be raised and reunited with their souls, and they will stand before God's throne for final judgment to be pronounced upon them in the body (see Matt. 25:31–46; John 5:28–29; Acts 24:15; and Rev. 20:12, 15).[28]

---

26. See chapter 56, pp. 1404–18, for a discussion of the final judgment and the doctrine of hell.

27. See chapter 56, pp. 1415–18, for a more extended discussion of annihilationism.

28. See below, chapter 56, pp. 1404–5.

## QUESTIONS FOR PERSONAL APPLICATION

1. Have you thought very much about the possibility of your death? Has there been an element of fear connected with those thoughts? What, if anything, do you fear about death? Do you think that these fears have come from the influence of the world around you or from Scripture? How would the teachings of Scripture encourage you to deal with these fears?

2. Has this chapter changed your feelings about your death in any way? Can you honestly contemplate it now as something that will bring you nearer to Christ and increase your trust in God and faithfulness to him? How would you express your hopes regarding your death?

3. Do you think you would have the courage to refuse to sin even if it meant being thrown to the lions in a Roman coliseum, burned at the stake during the Reformation, or thrown in prison for years in some foreign country today? Do you think the Christian martyrs throughout history had thought that they would have enough courage when put to the test? What happened to them to equip them for this suffering (read 1 Cor. 10:13)? If you can obtain a copy, you may wish to read the account of the martyrdom of Polycarp, a stirring testimony of faith in God and of God's faithfulness in the second century AD.[29] Have you settled in your own mind that obedience to Christ is more important than preserving your life? What would make you hesitant to believe this or act on this conviction?

4. If you have experienced the death of a believer who was close to you, do you think that your reaction to that death was one of sorrow mingled with joy? How has this chapter influenced the way you feel about that situation, if at all?

5. Have you previously believed in the doctrine of purgatory? If you no longer believe in it now, can you describe the way the doctrine made you feel, and the way you now feel emotionally about the fact that that doctrine is not true and there is no such place as purgatory?

6. If death itself is viewed as part of the process of sanctification, then how should we view the process of growing older and weaker in this world? Is that the way the world views aging? What about you?

**Special Terms**

*annihilationism*

*communion of saints*

*death*

*limbo*

limbus patrum

*purgatory*

*soul sleep*

---

29. One version of *The Martyrdom of Polycarp* is available in *The Apostolic Fathers*, ed. Kirsopp Lake, 2 vols., Loeb Classical Library (Cambridge, MA: Harvard University Press, 1913), 307–45. It is also available in *The Ante-Nicene Fathers*, ed. A. Roberts and J. Donaldson, 10 vols. (repr., Grand Rapids: Eerdmans, 1979).

# BIBLIOGRAPHY

(For an explanation of this bibliography see the note on the bibliography to chapter 1, pp. 23–24. Complete bibliographical data may be found on pp. 1489–96.)

## SECTIONS IN EVANGELICAL SYSTEMATIC THEOLOGIES

**1. Anglican (Episcopalian)**
1882–92 . . . . . Litton, 543–78
1930 . . . . . . . . Thomas, 298–310, 508–21
2001 . . . . . . . . Packer, 247–49
2013 . . . . . . . . Bird, 309–25

**2. Arminian (Wesleyan or Methodist)**
1875–76 . . . . . Pope, 3:371–86
1892–94 . . . . . Miley, 2:430–39
1940 . . . . . . . . Wiley, 3:211–42
1983 . . . . . . . . Carter, 2:1109–13
1992 . . . . . . . . Oden, 3:369–96
2002 . . . . . . . . Cottrell, 202–14, 514–16

**3. Baptist**
1767 . . . . . . . . Gill, 2:179–211
1887 . . . . . . . . Boyce, 437–51
1907 . . . . . . . . Strong, 982–1003
1990–95 . . . . . Garrett, 2:727–50
2007 . . . . . . . . Akin, 902
2013 . . . . . . . . Erickson, 1070–86

**4. Dispensational**
1947 . . . . . . . . Chafer, 4:413–15
1949 . . . . . . . . Thiessen, 333–36
1986 . . . . . . . . Ryrie, 518–20
2002–2005 . . Geisler, 4:247–93, 361–89, 390–412, 690–91

2017 . . . . . . . . MacArthur and Mayhue, 835–42

**5. Lutheran**
1917–24 . . . . . Pieper, 3:507–15
1934 . . . . . . . . Mueller, 613–19

**6. Reformed (or Presbyterian)**
1679–85 . . . . . Turretin, *IET*, 1:322–29, 583, 2:257–61, 356–61, 3:105, 387, 561–74, 617–21
1724–58 . . . . . Edwards, 2:26–36
1871–73 . . . . . Hodge, 3:713–70
1878 . . . . . . . . Dabney, 817–29
1894 . . . . . . . . Shedd, 831–32, 842, 891, 831–62
1910 . . . . . . . . Vos, 2:16–19, 45, 61, 64, 86
1906–11 . . . . . Bavinck, *RD*, 4:589–627, 628–43
1937–66 . . . . . Murray, *CW*, 2:401–3; *CW*, 3:242–46
1938 . . . . . . . . Berkhof, 668–94
1998 . . . . . . . . Reymond, 439–40, 449, 1017–18, 1068–85
2008 . . . . . . . . Van Genderen and Velema, 826–37
2011 . . . . . . . . Horton, 906–15
2013 . . . . . . . . Frame, 858–59, 1076–77
2013 . . . . . . . . Culver, 1018–65
2016 . . . . . . . . Allen and Swain, 389–91
2017 . . . . . . . . Barrett, 736–39
2019 . . . . . . . . Letham, 619, 823–30, 888–97

*7. Renewal (or charismatic/Pentecostal)*

1988–92 . . . . . Williams, 3:400–401, 450

1993 . . . . . . . . Menzies and Horton, 243–44

1995 . . . . . . . . Horton, 606–14

2008 . . . . . . . . Duffield and Van Cleave, 523–28

## Sections in Representative Roman Catholic Systematic Theologies

*1. Roman Catholic: Traditional*

1955 . . . . . . . . Ott, 445–50, 473–76, 482–85

*2. Roman Catholic: Post–Vatican II*

1980 . . . . . . . . McBrien, 2:1135–47

2012 . . . . . . . . *CCC*, paragraphs 1030–32

## Other Works

Beckwith, Roger T. "Purgatory." In *NDT1*, 549–50.

Cooper, John W. *Body, Soul and Life Everlasting: Biblical Anthropology and the Monism-Dualism Debate.* Grand Rapids: Eerdmans, 1989, 81–103, 121–253.

Custance, Arthur C. *Journey Out of Time.* Brockville, ON: Doorway, 1981.

Davids, P. H. "Death." In *EDT3*, 233–34.

Donnelly, J. P. "Limbo." In *EDT3*, 495–96.

Elwell, Walter A. "Intermediate State." In *BTDB*, 375.

Feinberg, John S. "1 Peter 3:18–20, Ancient Mythology, and the Intermediate State." *WTJ* 48, no. 2 (Fall 1986): 303–36.

Ferguson, Paul. "Death, Mortality." In *BTDB*, 154–56.

———. "Second Death." In *BTDB*, 723.

Gomes, Alan W. *40 Questions about Heaven and Hell.* Grand Rapids: Kregel Academic, 2018.

Grudem, Wayne. "Christ Preaching Through Noah: 1 Peter 3:19–20 in the Light of Dominant Themes in Jewish Literature." In *The First Epistle of Peter*, 203–39. TNTC. Leicester: Inter-Varsity Press; Grand Rapids: Eerdmans, 1988.

Harris, Murray J. "Death." In *NDT2*, 243–44.

———. "Intermediate State." In *NDT1*, 339–40.

Hoekema, Anthony A. *The Bible and the Future.* Grand Rapids: Eerdmans, 1979, 79–108.

Johnston, P. S. "Death and Resurrection." In *NDBT*, 443–47.

Johnston, Philip S. *Shades of Sheol: Death and Afterlife in the Old Testament.* Leicester: Apollos, 2002.

Kreitzer, L. J. "Intermediate State." In *DPL*, 438–41.

Lane, A. N. S. "Purgatory." In *NDT2*, 718–19.

Morey, Robert A. *Death and the Afterlife.* Minneapolis: Bethany House, 1984.

Noble, T. A. "Intermediate State." In *NDT2*, 455–56.

Scott, J. J., Jr. "Life and Death." In *DPL*, 553–55.

Shogren, G. S. "Life and Death." In *DLNT*, 655–57.

Smith, S. M. "Intermediate State." In *EDT3*, 429–30.

Walls, Jerry L. *Heaven, Hell, and Purgatory: Rethinking the Things That Matter Most.* Grand Rapids: Brazos, 2015.

## SCRIPTURE MEMORY PASSAGE

**Philippians 1:20–24:** As it is my eager expectation and hope that I shall not be at all ashamed, but that with full courage now as always Christ will be honored in my body, whether by life or by death. For to me to live is Christ, and to die is gain. If it is to be life in the flesh, that means fruitful labor for me. Yet which I shall choose I cannot tell. I am hard pressed between the two. My desire is to depart and be with Christ, for that is far better. But to remain in the flesh is more necessary on your account.

# HYMN

## "My Jesus I Love Thee"

My Jesus, I love thee, I know thou art mine;
    For thee all the follies of sin I resign.
My gracious Redeemer, my Savior art thou;
    If ever I loved thee, my Jesus 'tis now.

I love thee because thou hast first loved me,
    And purchased my pardon on Calvary's tree.
I love thee for wearing the thorns on thy brow;
    If ever I loved thee, my Jesus, 'tis now.

I'll love thee in life, I will love thee in death;
    And praise thee as long as thou lendest
      me breath;
And say, when the death-dew lies cold on my brow:
    If ever I loved thee, my Jesus, 'tis now.

In mansions of glory and endless delight,
    I'll ever adore thee in heaven so bright;
I'll sing with the glittering crown on my brow:
    If ever I loved thee, my Jesus, 'tis now.

Author: William R. Featherstone, 1864

# CONTEMPORARY WORSHIP SONG

## "Cornerstone"

My hope is built on nothing less
Than Jesus' blood and righteousness.
I dare not trust the sweetest frame,
But wholly trust in Jesus' Name.

*Chorus*
Christ alone, cornerstone.
Weak made strong in the Savior's love.
Through the storm, He is Lord,
Lord of all.

When darkness seems to hide His face,
I rest on His unchanging grace.
In every high and stormy gale,
My anchor holds within the veil.
My anchor holds within the veil.

When He shall come with trumpet sound,
Oh, may I then in Him be found.
Dressed in His righteousness alone,
Faultless, stand before the throne.

Words by Edward Mote, Reuben Morgan,
Jonas Myrin, and Eric Liljero[30]

---

30. Copyright © 2012 Hillsong Music Publishing (APRA)
(adm. in the US and Canada at CapitolCMGPublishing.com).
All rights reserved. Used by permission.

# CHAPTER 42

# Glorification (Receiving a Resurrection Body)

*When will we receive resurrection bodies?*
*What will they be like?*

## EXPLANATION AND SCRIPTURAL BASIS

When Christ redeemed us, he did not just redeem our spirits (or souls)—he redeemed us as whole persons, and this includes the redemption of our bodies. Therefore, the application of Christ's work of redemption to us will not be complete until our bodies are entirely set free from the effects of the fall and brought to that state of perfection for which God created them. In fact, the redemption of our bodies will only occur when Christ returns and raises our bodies from the dead. But at this present time, Paul says that we wait for *"the redemption of our bodies"* and then adds, "for in this hope we were saved" (Rom. 8:23–24). The stage in the application of redemption when we receive resurrection bodies is called *glorification*. Referring to that future day, Paul says that believers will be *"glorified* with him" (Rom. 8:17). Moreover, when Paul traces the steps in the application of redemption, the last one he names is glorification: "Those whom he predestined he also called, and those whom he called he also justified, and those whom he justified he also *glorified"* (Rom. 8:30).

The day we are glorified will be a day of great victory because on that day the last enemy, death, will be destroyed, just as Scripture predicts: "For he must reign until he has put all his enemies under his feet. The last enemy to be destroyed is death" (1 Cor. 15:25–26). In the context of a discussion of the resurrection of our bodies when Christ returns, Paul says, "Then shall come to pass the saying that is written: 'Death is swallowed up in victory.' 'O death, where is your victory? O death, where is your sting?'" (1 Cor. 15:54–55). When our bodies are raised from the dead we will experience complete victory over the death that came as a result of the fall of Adam and Eve. Then our redemption will be complete.

We may therefore define *glorification* as follows: *Glorification is the final step in the application of redemption. It will happen when Christ returns, raises from the dead the bodies of all believers for all time who have died, reunites them with their souls, and changes the bodies of all believers who remain alive, thereby giving all believers at the same time perfect resurrection bodies like his own.*

## A. New Testament Evidence for Glorification

The primary New Testament passage on glorification or the resurrection of the body is 1 Corinthians 15:12–58. Paul says, "So also in Christ shall all be made alive. But each in his own order: Christ the firstfruits, then *at his coming* those who belong to Christ" (vv. 22–23).[1] Paul discusses the nature of the resurrection body in some detail in verses 35–50, which we will examine in section C below. He then concludes the passage by saying that not all Christians will die, but some who remain alive when Christ returns will simply have their bodies instantaneously changed into new, resurrection bodies that can never grow old or weak and can never die: "Behold! I tell you a mystery. We shall not all sleep, but *we shall all be changed*, in a moment, in the twinkling of an eye, at the last trumpet. For the trumpet will sound, and the dead will be raised imperishable, and we shall be changed" (1 Cor. 15:51–52).

Paul further explains in 1 Thessalonians that the souls of those who have died and gone to be with Christ will come back and be joined with their bodies on that day, for Christ will bring them with him: "For since we believe that Jesus died and rose again, even so, through Jesus, *God will bring with him those who have fallen asleep*" (1 Thess. 4:14). But here Paul affirms not only that God will bring with Christ those who have died; he also affirms that *"the dead in Christ will rise first"* (1 Thess. 4:16). So these believers who have died "in Christ" are also raised up to meet Christ (Paul says in v. 17, "We . . . will be caught up together with them in the clouds to meet the Lord in the air"). This only makes sense if it is the *souls* of believers who have gone into Christ's presence who return with him and if it is their *bodies* that are raised from the dead to be joined together with their souls and then to ascend to be with Christ.

In addition to these passages in 1 Corinthians 15 and 1 Thessalonians 4, several other New Testament passages affirm the reality of the doctrine of glorification. Jesus says, "An hour is coming when all who are in the tombs will hear his voice and come out, those who have done good *to the resurrection of life*, and those who have done evil to the resurrection of judgment" (John 5:28–29).[2] Jesus also says, "This is the will of him who sent me, that I should lose nothing of all that he has given me, but *raise it up on the last day*. For this is the will of my Father, that everyone who looks on the Son and believes in him should have eternal life, and *I will raise him up on the last day*" (John 6:39–40; cf. vv. 44, 54).

---

1. Murray J. Harris argues for the possibility of an alternative view, based on his understanding of 2 Cor. 5:1–10: that Christians receive their resurrection bodies immediately after they die. See Harris, *From Grave to Glory: Resurrection in the New Testament, Including a Response to Norman L. Geisler* (Grand Rapids: Zondervan, 1990), 207–10. But this view is exceptionally difficult to reconcile with 1 Cor. 15 and 1 Thess. 4; see the discussion in D. A. Carson, "Unity and Diversity in the New Testament: The Possibility of Systematic Theology," in *Scripture and Truth*, ed. Carson and John Woodbridge (Grand Rapids: Zondervan, 1983), 85–86.

2. Some evangelical Christians hold that believers and unbelievers will be resurrected at the same time (this is the position taken by amillennialists). Others (especially premillennialists) hold that the resurrection of believers occurs before the millennium and the resurrection of the unbelievers for judgment occurs 1,000 years later, after the millennium. See chapter 55 for a discussion of the issues involved, and of this particular verse.

Paul says, "He who raised Christ Jesus from the dead will also *give life to your mortal bodies* through his Spirit who dwells in you" (Rom. 8:11; cf. 2 Cor. 5:1–10). He realizes that Christians should live in eager expectation of Christ's return and of the change in our bodies to be like his perfect body. He says, "But our citizenship is in heaven, and from it we await a Savior, the Lord Jesus Christ, *who will transform our lowly body to be like his glorious body*, by the power that enables him even to subject all things to himself" (Phil. 3:20–21).

## B. Old Testament Support for Glorification

Sometimes people have claimed that the Old Testament has little if any evidence of hope in a future resurrection of the body, but there is in fact more Old Testament evidence for this than we might realize. First, even before Jesus was raised from the dead, the New Testament indicates that many Jewish people living at the time of Christ had some hope of a future bodily resurrection. When Jesus comes to the home of Lazarus after he had died and says to Martha, "Your brother will rise again," Martha responds, "I know that he will rise again *in the resurrection on the last day*" (John 11:23–24). Moreover, when Paul was on trial, he said to Felix that he had a "hope in God, which these men themselves [his Jewish accusers] accept, that *there will be a resurrection* of both the just and the unjust" (Acts 24:15).

As for the beliefs of those living in the time of the Old Testament, Hebrews 11 tells us that Abraham "was looking forward to the city that has foundations, whose designer and builder is God" (Heb. 11:10). We also read that many Old Testament saints "died in faith, not having received the things promised, but having seen them and greeted them from afar, and having acknowledged that they were strangers and exiles on the earth. . . . But as it is, *they desire a better country, that is, a heavenly one.* Therefore God is not ashamed to be called their God, for he has prepared for them a city" (Heb. 11:13–16). The author even says that Abraham "considered that God was able even to raise him from the dead" (Heb. 11:19).

When we look at the actual teachings of the Old Testament itself, there are indications that Old Testament authors had a strong expectation of the resurrection to come in the future. Job says: "For I know that my Redeemer lives, and at the last he will stand upon the earth. And after my skin has been thus destroyed, yet in my flesh I shall see God, whom I shall see for myself, and my eyes shall behold, and not another" (Job 19:25–27).[3]

---

3. Several words in this passage are difficult to interpret, and there is scholarly debate over the question of whether Job is looking forward to seeing God in this life (as he does in 42:5) or after his death (note that Job expects his Redeemer to stand upon the earth "in the end," and expects to see God "in my flesh" but this will be "after my skin has been destroyed"). For a summary of the exegetical issues and a persuasive defense of the view that Job is looking forward to a physical resurrection after he dies, see Francis L. Andersen, *Job*, TOTC (Leicester: Inter-Varsity Press, 1976), 193–94. The view that this passage looks forward to seeing God in this life only is largely based on some scholars' convictions that the idea of a future bodily resurrection was not found in Judaism until long after Job was written (but see Heb. 11:10, 19, commenting on Abraham's faith in the resurrection).

We read in Isaiah, "*Your dead shall live; their bodies shall rise*" (Isa. 26:19). Daniel has a very explicit prophecy that "*many of those who sleep in the dust of the earth shall awake, some to everlasting life, and some to shame and everlasting contempt*" (Dan. 12:2). (Cf. also Ezekiel's vision of the dry bones in Ezek. 37:1–14.)

Although Old Testament believers did not have as much detail about the nature of the resurrection or the way it would come about through the resurrection of the Messiah, and although they did not have as clear a basis for confidence in the resurrection as we do in the actual event of the bodily resurrection of Christ, which is a pattern for us, nonetheless there was certainly an *expectation* of a future day of bodily resurrection. People who for years had meditated on and believed these statements of Scripture (such as Martha in John 11:24) were prepared to receive the full-fledged New Testament teaching on the resurrection eagerly, for it simply provided more detail and more assurance for what they already had believed.

## C. What Will Our Resurrection Bodies Be Like?

If Christ will raise our bodies from the dead when he returns, and if our bodies will be like his resurrection body (1 Cor. 15:20, 23, 49; Phil. 3:21), then what will our resurrection bodies be like?

Using the example of sowing a seed and then watching it grow into something much more wonderful, Paul goes on to explain what our resurrection bodies will be like: "What is sown is perishable; what is raised is *imperishable*. It is sown in dishonor; it is raised *in glory*. It is sown in weakness; it is raised *in power*. It is sown a natural body; it is raised a *spiritual body*. . . . Just as we have borne the image of the man of dust, we shall also bear the image of the man of heaven" (1 Cor. 15:42–44, 49).

The fact that our new bodies will be "imperishable" means that they will not wear out or grow old or ever be subject to any kind of sickness or disease. They will be completely healthy and strong forever. Moreover, since the gradual process of aging is part of the process by which our bodies now are subject to "corruption," it is appropriate to think that our resurrection bodies will have no sign of aging but will have the characteristics of youthful but mature manhood or womanhood forever. There will be no evidence of disease or injury, for all will be made perfect.[4] Our resurrection bodies will show the fulfillment of God's perfect wisdom in creating us as human beings who are the pinnacle of his creation and the appropriate bearers of his likeness and image. In these resurrection bodies we will clearly see humanity as God intended it to be.

Paul also says our bodies will be raised "in glory (Gk. *doxa*)." When this term is contrasted with "dishonor," as it is here, there is a suggestion of the beauty or the attractiveness of appearance that our bodies will have. They will no longer be "dishonorable"

---

4. The fact that the scars of Jesus' nail prints remained on his hands is a special case to remind us of the price he paid for our redemption, and it should not be taken as an indication that any of our scars from physical injuries will remain; see chapter 28, p. 757.

or unattractive, but will look "glorious" in their beauty. Moreover, because the word "glory" is so frequently used in Scripture of the bright shining radiance that surrounds the presence of God himself, this term suggests that there will also be a kind of brightness or radiance surrounding our bodies that will be an appropriate outward evidence of the position of exaltation and rule over all creation that God has given to us. This is also suggested in Matthew 13:43, where Jesus says, "Then *the righteous will shine like the sun in the kingdom of their Father.*" Similarly, we read in Daniel's vision, "*Those who are wise shall shine like the brightness of the sky above*; and those who turn many to righteousness, like the stars forever and ever" (Dan. 12:3, in a passage talking about the final resurrection). Now both of these statements could be understood metaphorically, and in that case they would not indicate that an actual brightness or radiance will surround our resurrection bodies. But there is no reason in the context of either of them that would cause us to see them as metaphorical, and other pieces of evidence argue against doing so. The hints of the age to come that were seen in the shining of the glory of God from the face of Moses (Ex. 34:35), and in a much greater way, the bright light that shone from Jesus at the transfiguration (Matt. 17:2), together with the fact that we will bear the image of Christ and be like him (1 Cor. 15:49), combine to suggest that there will actually be a visible brightness or radiance that surrounds us when we are in our resurrection bodies.[5]

Our bodies will also be raised "in power (Gk. *dynamis*)" (1 Cor. 15:43). This is in contrast to the "weakness" that we see in our bodies now. Our resurrection bodies will not only be free from disease and aging, they will also be given fullness of strength and power—not infinite power like God, of course, and probably not what we would think of as "superhuman" power in the sense possessed by the "superheroes" in modern fictional writing, for example, but nonetheless full and complete human power and strength, the strength that God intended human beings to have in their bodies when he created them. It will therefore be strength that is sufficient to do all that we desire to do in conformity with the will of God.

Finally, Paul says that the body is raised a "spiritual body" (1 Cor. 15:44). In the Pauline Epistles, the word *spiritual* (Gk. *pneumatikos*) seldom means "nonphysical" but rather "consistent with the character and activity of the Holy Spirit" (see, for example, Rom. 1:11; 7:14; 1 Cor. 2:13, 15; 3:1; 14:37; Gal. 6:1 ["you who are spiritual"]; Eph. 5:19).[6] A clarifying paraphrase of this passage would be, "It is sown a *natural* body subject to the characteristics and desires of this age, and governed by its own sinful will, but it is raised a *spiritual* body, completely subject to the will of the Holy Spirit and

---

5. Jesus' body did not have a bright radiance surrounding it immediately after his resurrection, but when he returned to heaven and received from God the Father the glory that was rightfully his, then "his face was like the sun shining in full strength" (Rev. 1:16). Jesus at his transfiguration gave his disciples only a brief glimpse of the glory that was rightfully his and would be his again in heaven.

6. The RSV and NRSV translation, "It is sown a *physical* body, it is raised a *spiritual* body," is misleading; see the discussion in chapter 28, p. 753n3.

responsive to the Holy Spirit's guidance." Such a body is not at all "nonphysical," but it is *a physical body* raised to the degree of perfection for which God originally intended it.

In conclusion, when Christ returns he will give us new resurrection bodies to be like his resurrection body. "When he appears *we shall be like him*" (1 John 3:2; this statement is true not only in an ethical sense but also in terms of our physical bodies; cf. 1 Cor. 15:49; also Rom. 8:29).

In spite of this strong New Testament emphasis on the similarity between our bodies and Jesus' body after the resurrection, some have objected that we will not have physical bodies because Paul says, "*Flesh and blood cannot inherit the kingdom of God*, nor does the perishable inherit the imperishable" (1 Cor. 15:50). This is in the very section in which he has been discussing the resurrection of the dead. But it is surely a misunderstanding to say that this verse implies that we shall not have physical bodies. When Paul says, "flesh and blood cannot inherit the kingdom of God," what he means by "flesh and blood" is *our present human nature*, particularly our physical bodies, as they are now existing in the likeness of Adam after the fall—that is, subject to weakness, decay, and ultimate death. This is the point he has made in the previous four verses (1 Cor. 15:45–49), in which he has been contrasting Adam with Christ. He explains, "As was the man of dust, so also are those who are of the dust" (that is, we ourselves in this present age, 1 Cor. 15:48). Then he explains, "Just as we have borne the image of the man of dust, we shall also bear the image of the man of heaven" (1 Cor. 15:49). By "flesh and blood," Paul means "*flesh and blood in the present state of existence* with a body like Adam's after the fall, a body that is subject to decay and death." He does not mean that we shall exist in a nonphysical state, for the entire heaven and earth will be made new and renewed for us to live in (Rom. 8:18–25), and we ourselves "shall all be changed, in a moment, in the twinkling of an eye, at the last trumpet" (1 Cor. 15:51–52). We will not cease to exist in physical bodies, but we will be changed and have an imperishable body, "for this perishable body must put on the imperishable, and this mortal body must put on immortality" (1 Cor. 15:53).

Moreover, the repeated instances in which Jesus demonstrated to the disciples that he had a physical body that was able to be touched, that had flesh and bones (Luke 24:39), and that could eat food, show that Jesus' body, which is our pattern, was clearly a physical body that had been made perfect.[7]

What kind of continuity will there be between our present bodies and our future resurrection bodies? Will our bodies look exactly the same and have exactly the same characteristics? Will they be somewhat different? Or will they be almost entirely different? Will our resurrection bodies be made of the same molecules of which our earthly

---

7. See chapter 28, pp. 753–54, for a discussion of the nature of Christ's resurrection body.

bodies consist, will they be an entirely new creation from God, or will they be some combination of old and new?

Several passages indicate that Paul expected a considerable measure of continuity between our present earthly bodies and our future resurrection bodies. Paul said, "He who raised Christ Jesus from the dead will also give life to *your mortal bodies* through his Spirit who dwells in you" (Rom. 8:11). He said that Jesus "will transform *our lowly body* to be like his glorious body" (Phil. 3:21). And when Paul spoke about the nature of the resurrection body, he gave an example of a seed sown in the ground: "What you sow is not the body that is to be, but a bare kernel, perhaps of wheat or of some other grain. But God gives it a body as he has chosen, and to each kind of seed its own body" (1 Cor. 15:37–38). In this example, he draws on common human knowledge that there are differences between what is sown and what is raised (vv. 42–44), but there is also continuity—just as a seed grows into a larger plant, retaining the matter that was in it but taking other materials to itself from the ground as well, so we will have continuity and differences as well. On this analogy we can say that *whatever remains in the grave from our physical bodies* will be taken by God, transformed, and used to make a new resurrection body. But the details of how that will happen remain unclear since Scripture does not specify—we are to affirm this because Scripture teaches it, even if we cannot fully explain how it can happen.[8]

Another indication of significant continuity between our present bodies and the bodies that we will have is seen in the fact that those believers who remain alive on the day Christ returns will "be changed"—yet their bodies will not be replaced: "We shall not all sleep, but we shall all be *changed*, in a moment, in the twinkling of an eye, at the last trumpet. For the trumpet will sound, and the dead will be raised imperishable, and we shall be *changed*. For this perishable body must put on the imperishable, and this mortal body must put on immortality" (1 Cor. 15:51–53).

We must also clearly note that Christ's resurrection body, though it differed somewhat from the body he had before he died, so that the disciples did not immediately recognize him in every situation, was similar enough in appearance for the disciples to know who it was rather quickly. There were some instances when they did not immediately recognize him, but this may in part be accounted for by the fact that during his earthly life and ministry he had no doubt aged considerably, since he was "a man of sorrows and acquainted with grief" (Isa. 53:3). After his resurrection, Jesus would have been restored to full and perfect strength and youthfulness of appearance. Just as we sometimes do not immediately recognize a friend who has aged considerably since the last time we saw him or her, so the disciples may have had initial difficulty in

---

8. Someone may object that some bodies completely decay, are absorbed into plants, and then eventually into other bodies, so that nothing of the first body can be found. But in response we must simply say that God can keep track of enough of the elements from each body to form a "seed" from which to form a new body (see Gen. 50:25; Job 19:26; Ezek. 37:1–14; Heb. 11:22).

recognizing Christ because the opposite of aging had occurred.[9] On the other hand, significant continuity between Jesus' body before and after the resurrection is seen in the fact that even the nail prints in his hands and feet and the wound in his side remained in his resurrection body (John 20:20, 27).

Another piece of evidence indicating continuity between our earthly and heavenly bodies is the fact that apparently people will recognize and know one another in heaven. Jesus says that people will come from east and west and "recline at table with Abraham, Isaac, and Jacob in the kingdom of heaven" (Matt. 8:11). Moreover, Elijah, who had been taken up to heaven in his earthly body, was somehow recognizable to the disciples on the Mount of Transfiguration (Luke 9:30, 33)—of course, the disciples had not known Elijah or Moses in the flesh, but somehow these men retained their personal identities in such a way that the disciples believed that they were there and that they were just as real as Jesus was (see Luke 9:33). Finally, Matthew tells us that when Jesus died, "the tombs also were opened. And many *bodies* of the saints who had fallen asleep were raised, and coming out of the tombs after his resurrection they went into the holy city and appeared to many" (Matt. 27:52–53). The fact that these people's actual bodies were raised, as well as the fact that they appeared to many in Jerusalem, indicates again that there was significant continuity between their dead bodies that were in the graves and the bodies that were raised up. Since they came out of the tombs "after his resurrection," we may assume that these also were saints who had received resurrection bodies as a kind of fore-taste of the final day of glorification when Christ returns.[10] The fact that these people "appeared to many" suggests that they were recognizable—that people knew who they were. This evidence suggests significant continuity between the body that existed before the resurrection and the one that existed after it.

There is today some hesitancy on the part of many evangelicals to affirm clearly that there will be a "resurrection of the body," or at least that the raised body will be a material, physical body in some way continuous with the body that was placed in the grave. To some measure, this may be due to a sense of inability to understand how God could raise the same bodies from the grave, especially when some of those bodies have been dead for many centuries. Yet some of this hesitancy is probably also due to the continuing skepticism of unbelievers who challenge the Christian view with exactly the kind of problems just presented—does this not seem like a fantastic, unbelievable position? How could God bring about such a thing?

In both cases—whether the hesitancy comes from the honest questioning of the believer or from the hostile skepticism of the unbeliever—we should realize that our inability to understand or explain something should never be a reason for rejecting it if it is clearly taught in Scripture. The many passages cited above indicating that God

---

9. For a discussion on the failure of disciples to recognize Christ at once after his resurrection, see chapter 28, pp. 753–54.

10. See discussion of this passage in D. A. Carson, "Matthew," *EBC*, 8:581–82.

will raise *our mortal bodies from the grave*, just as he raised Jesus' body from the grave, indicate quite conclusively that there will be a definite continuity between our present bodies and the bodies we have in the resurrection. And if that is what Scripture teaches, then, even though we may not understand exactly *how* God will bring this about in every case, we should still believe it. The God who created the universe and created each one of us, who sovereignly rules over every bit of this creation at every moment, and who carries along all things by his word of power—this God can certainly keep track of the parts of our physical bodies that he wishes to preserve and use as the "seed" from which a new body will be made.

It is important to insist on the resurrection of a real, physical body, not only for the reasons above but also because this provides a clear affirmation of the goodness of God's physical creation. We will live in bodies that have all the excellent qualities God created us to have, and thereby we will forever be living proof of the wisdom of God in making a material creation that from the beginning was "very good" (Gen. 1:31). We will live as resurrected believers in those new bodies, and they will be suitable for inhabiting the "new heavens and a new earth in which righteousness dwells" (2 Peter 3:13).

## D. The Entire Creation Will Be Renewed as Well

When Adam sinned, God cursed the ground because of him (Gen. 3:17–19) so that it brought forth "thorns and thistles" and would only yield food for mankind by painful toil. But Paul says that *"the creation itself* will be set free from its bondage to corruption and obtain the freedom of the glory of the children of God" (Rom. 8:21). He explains that this will happen when we receive our resurrection bodies—in fact, he says that the creation is somehow longing for that day: "For the creation waits with eager longing for the revealing of the sons of God. . . . We know that the whole creation has been groaning together in the pains of childbirth until now. And not only the creation, but we ourselves, who have the firstfruits of the Spirit, groan inwardly as *we wait eagerly for* adoption as sons, *the redemption of our bodies*" (Rom. 8:19, 22–23). In this renewed creation, there will be no more thorns or thistles, no more floods or droughts, no more deserts or uninhabitable jungles, no more earthquakes or tornadoes, no more poisonous snakes or bees that sting or mushrooms that kill. There will be a productive earth, an earth that will blossom and produce food abundantly for our enjoyment. (See chapter 57 for further discussion of the renewed earth.)

## E. The Unbelieving Dead Will Be Raised for Judgment on the Day of Final Judgment

Although the emphasis of Scripture is on the fact that believers will experience a bodily resurrection, there are some passages that state that *unbelievers* will also be raised from the dead to face the final judgment. Jesus clearly teaches that "those who have done evil" will come forth "to *the resurrection of judgment*" (John 5:29); Paul also said that he believed "that there will be a resurrection of both the just *and the unjust*" (Acts 24:15; cf. Matt. 25:31–46; Dan. 12:2). (See chapter 56 for further discussion of the final judgment of unbelievers.)

## QUESTIONS FOR PERSONAL APPLICATION

1. Paul says that the expectation of a future bodily resurrection is the "hope" in which we were saved (Rom. 8:24). Is the hope of a future resurrection of your body one of the major things you look forward to in the future? If not, why not? What could increase your hope in the future resurrection of the body?

2. So strong was Paul's longing for the future day of resurrection, and so aware was he of the hardships that we still suffer in this life, that he could say, "If in Christ we have hope in this life only, we are of all people most to be pitied" (1 Cor. 15:19), and "If the dead are not raised, 'Let us eat and drink, for tomorrow we die'" (1 Cor. 15:32). Do you have a great longing for the future resurrection that gives you this kind of sentiment in your heart as well? If not, why do you not have the same perspective on the resurrection of the body that Paul did?

3. What do you think might occur in your life to give you a greater longing for the resurrection of your body? If you have a grandfather or grandmother or other older friend or relative who has died and gone to be with Christ, what do you think that person will look like on the day of resurrection? Can you imagine what it will be like meeting that person and becoming acquainted again? How will your relationship be different from what it was in this life?

**Special Terms**
*glorification*
*spiritual body*

## BIBLIOGRAPHY

(For an explanation of this bibliography see the note on the bibliography to chapter 1, pp. 23–24. Complete bibliographical data may be found on pp. 1489–96.)

### SECTIONS IN EVANGELICAL SYSTEMATIC THEOLOGIES

1. *Anglican (Episcopalian)*
   1882–92 . . . . . Litton, 585–91
   2001 . . . . . . . . Packer, 254–57

2013 . . . . . . . . Bird, 544–46

2. *Arminian (Wesleyan or Methodist)*
   1875–76 . . . . . Pope, 3:401–11
   1892–94 . . . . . Miley, 2:448–58
   1940 . . . . . . . . Wiley, 3:320–38
   1960 . . . . . . . . Purkiser, 561–67
   1983 . . . . . . . . Carter, 2:1116–18
   1992 . . . . . . . . Oden, 3:247–48
   2002 . . . . . . . . Cottrell, 571

### 3. Baptist
1767 . . . . . . . . Gill, 2:211–30
1887 . . . . . . . . Boyce, 454–61
1907 . . . . . . . . Strong, 1015–23
1990–95 . . . . . Garrett, 2:751–74
2007 . . . . . . . . Akin, 906
2013 . . . . . . . . Erickson, 924–29

### 4. Dispensational
1947 . . . . . . . . Chafer, 3:366–69
1949 . . . . . . . . Thiessen, 376–83
1986 . . . . . . . . Ryrie, 517–18
2002–2005 . . Geisler, 3:241–43; 4:262–72
2017 . . . . . . . . MacArthur and Mayhue,
          653–59, 842–44

### 5. Lutheran
1917–24 . . . . . Pieper, 3:534–39
1934 . . . . . . . . Mueller, 625–30

### 6. Reformed (or Presbyterian)
1559 . . . . . . . . Calvin, 2:987–1008 (3.25)
1679–85 . . . . . Turretin, *IET*, 3:617–32
1871–73 . . . . . Hodge, 3:771–89
1878 . . . . . . . . Dabney, 829–41
1894 . . . . . . . . Shedd, 863–66
1906–11 . . . . . Bavinck, *RD*, 4:693–98
1910 . . . . . . . . Vos, 4:5, 8, 23
1937–66 . . . . . Murray, *CW*, 2:403–13;
          *RAA*, 174–81
1938 . . . . . . . . Berkhof, 720–27
1998 . . . . . . . . Reymond, 795–801
2008 . . . . . . . . Van Genderen and Velema,
          240, 495, 578, 666, 865–69
2011 . . . . . . . . Horton, 915–18
2013 . . . . . . . . Frame, 998, 1009–13
2013 . . . . . . . . Culver, 764, 1062–65
2016 . . . . . . . . Allen and Swain, 389–91

2017 . . . . . . . . Barrett, 560
2019 . . . . . . . . Letham, 862–65

### 7. Renewal (or charismatic/Pentecostal)
1988–92 . . . . . Williams, 3:397–413
1993 . . . . . . . . Menzies and Horton, 154
1995 . . . . . . . . Horton, 597–606
2008 . . . . . . . . Duffield and Van Cleave,
          548–52

## SECTIONS IN REPRESENTATIVE ROMAN CATHOLIC SYSTEMATIC THEOLOGIES

### 1. Roman Catholic: Traditional
1955 . . . . . . . . Ott, 488–92

### 2. Roman Catholic: Post–Vatican II
1980 . . . . . . . . McBrien, 2:1147–50
2012 . . . . . . . . *CCC*, paragraphs 990, 996–97

## OTHER WORKS

Barber, Dan C., and Robert A. Peterson. *Life Everlasting: The Unfolding Story of Heaven*. Phillipsburg, NJ: P&R, 2012.

Gaffin, Richard B., Jr. "Glory." In *NDBT*, 507–11.

———. "Glory, Glorification." In *DPL*, 348–50.

———. *Resurrection and Redemption: A Study in Paul's Soteriology*. Formerly, *The Centrality of the Resurrection: A Study in Paul's Soteriology*. Phillipsburg, NJ: Presbyterian and Reformed, 1978.

Gomes, Alan W. *40 Questions about Heaven and Hell*. Grand Rapids: Kregel Academic, 2018.

Grider, J. K. "Glorification." In *EDT3*, 340–41.

Gundry, Robert N. *Soma in Biblical Theology*. Cambridge: Cambridge University Press, 1975.

Harris, Murray J. *From Grave to Glory: Resurrection in the New Testament, Including a Response to Norman L. Geisler*. Grand Rapids: Zondervan, 1990, 185–287.

———. *Raised Immortal: Resurrection and Immortality in the New Testament*. Grand Rapids: Eerdmans, 1983.

———. "Resurrection, General." In *NDT1*, 581–82.

Hoekema, Anthony A. "The Resurrection of the Body." In *The Bible and the Future*, 239–52. Grand Rapids: Eerdmans, 1979.

Huttar, David K. "Glorification." In *BTDB*, 287.

Lincoln, Andrew T. *Paradise Now and Not Yet: Studies in the Role of the Heavenly Dimension in Paul's Thought with Special Reference to His Eschatology*. Grand Rapids: Baker, 1991.

Murray, John. "Glorification." In *Redemption Accomplished and Applied*, 174–81. Grand Rapids: Eerdmans, 1955.

Ramm, Bernard. *Them He Glorified*. Grand Rapids: Eerdmans, 1963.

Schep, J. A. *The Nature of the Resurrection Body*. Grand Rapids: Eerdmans, 1964.

Stobart, A. J. "Resurrection, General." In *NDT2*, 769–70.

Turner, Nigel. "Glory and Glorification." In *Christian Words*, 185–89. Nashville: Nelson, 1982.

White, R. E. O. "Resurrection of the Dead." In *EDT3*, 745–47.

## SCRIPTURE MEMORY PASSAGE

**1 Corinthians 15:42–44:** So is it with the resurrection of the dead. What is sown is perishable; what is raised is imperishable. It is sown in dishonor; it is raised in glory. It is sown in weakness; it is raised in power. It is sown a natural body; it is raised a spiritual body. If there is a natural body, there is also a spiritual body.

## HYMN

**"Ten Thousand Times Ten Thousand"**

This hymn was written by Henry Alford, a New Testament professor at Cambridge University, England, and one of the greatest Greek scholars of the nineteenth century. The hymn pictures thousands of glorified believers streaming through the gates of heaven on the day of Christ's return, and ends with a prayer that Christ would come back quickly.

*Ten thousand times ten thousand in sparkling raiment bright,*
*The armies of the ransomed saints throng up the steeps of light:*
*'Tis finished, all is finished, their fight with death and sin:*
*Fling open wide the golden gates, and let the victors in.*

*What rush of alleluias fills all the earth and sky!*
*What ringing of a thousand harps bespeaks the triumph nigh!*
*O day, for which creation and all its tribes were made;*
*O joy, for all its former woes a thousand-fold repaid!*

*O then what raptured greetings on*
  *Canaan's happy shore;*
*What knitting severed friendships up*
  *where partings are no more!*
*Then eyes with joy shall sparkle, that*
  *brimmed with tears of late;*
*Orphans no longer fatherless, nor*
  *widows desolate.*

*Bring near thy great salvation, thou Lamb*
  *for sinners slain;*
*Fill up the roll of thine elect, then take*
  *thy pow'r, and reign:*
*Appear, desire of nations, thine exiles long*
  *for home;*
*Show in the heav'n thy promised sign;*
  *thou Prince and Saviour, come.*

Author: Henry Alford, 1867

## CONTEMPORARY WORSHIP SONG

### "My Redeemer Lives"

*For I know my redeemer lives,*
*And in the end He will stand on the earth.*
*For I know my redeemer lives,*
*And in the end He will reign on the earth.*

*Though my flesh it be destroyed,*
*Yet with my eyes I will see God.*

*For I know my redeemer lives,*
*And I will stand with Him on that day.*
*For I know my redeemer lives,*
*And I will stand with Him on that day.*

*Oh, my heart it yearns within me*
*For the day when Jesus returns.*
*Oh, my heart it yearns within me*
*For the day when Jesus shall reign.*

*Though my flesh it be destroyed,*
*Yet with my eyes I will see God.*

*For I know that my redeemer lives,*
*And I will stand with Him on that day.*
*For I know that my redeemer lives,*
*And I will stand with Him on that day.*

Words by John Willison[11]

---

# CHAPTER 43

# Union with Christ

*What does it mean to be "in Christ" or "united with Christ"?*

## EXPLANATION AND SCRIPTURAL BASIS

Although we have now completed our study of the steps in the application of redemption, one other subject is so frequently mentioned in Scripture and so wide-ranging in its application to our lives that it deserves a separate treatment here. That is the concept of union with Christ.[1] As we shall see below, *every aspect* of God's relationship to believers is in some way connected to our relationship with Christ. From God's counsels in eternity past before the world was created, to our fellowship with God in heaven in eternity future, and including every aspect of our relationship with God in this life—all has occurred in union with Christ. So in one sense the entire study of the application of redemption could be included in this subject. However, in this chapter we can simply summarize the incredible richness of the scriptural idea of union with Christ. John Murray says,

> Union with Christ has its source in the election of God the Father before the foundation of the world and has its fruition in the glorification of the sons of God. The perspective of God's people is not narrow; it is broad and it is long. It is not confined to space and time; it has the expanse of eternity. Its orbit has two foci, one the electing love of God the Father in the counsels of eternity; the other glorification with Christ in the manifestation of his glory. The former has no beginning, the latter has no end. . . . Why does the believer entertain the thought of God's determinate counsel with such joy? Why can he have patience in the perplexities and adversities of the present? Why can he have confident assurance with reference to the future and rejoice in hope of the glory of God? It is because he cannot think of past, present, or future apart from union with Christ.[2]

We may define *union with Christ* as follows: *Union with Christ is a phrase used to summarize several different relationships between believers and Christ, through which*

---

1. The material in this chapter is taken from an essay "Union with Christ" by Wayne Grudem, written for Tyndale House Publishers (Wheaton, IL) but never published. Used by permission.

2. John Murray, *Redemption Accomplished and Applied* (Grand Rapids: Eerdmans, 1955), 164.

*Christians receive every benefit of salvation. These relationships include the fact that we are in Christ, Christ is in us, we are like Christ, and we are with Christ.*

As this definition indicates, four different aspects of our union with Christ may be specified from the biblical material. We will look at each of these four in turn:

1. We are in Christ.
2. Christ is in us.
3. We are like Christ.
4. We are with Christ.[3]

## A. We Are in Christ

The phrase "in Christ" does not have one single sense but refers to a variety of relationships, as indicated below.

### 1. In God's Eternal Plan

Ephesians 1:4 tells us that, God *chose us in Christ* "before the foundation of the world." It was in Christ that we "obtained an inheritance, having been predestined . . . to the praise of his glory" (vv. 1:11–12). Later he "saved us and called us" because of "his own purpose" and because of the grace which he gave us "in Christ Jesus before the ages began" (2 Tim. 1:9).

Since we did not exist before the foundation of the world, these verses indicate that God, looking into the future and knowing that we would exist, *thought of us as* being in a special relationship with Christ. He did not first choose us and later decide to relate us to Christ. Rather, while choosing us, he at the same time thought about us as belonging to Christ in a special way, as being "in Christ." Therefore, he thought about us as eventually having the right to share in the blessings of Christ's work.

### 2. During Christ's Life on Earth

Throughout Christ's entire life on earth, from the time of his birth to the time of his ascension into heaven, God thought of us as being "in Christ." That is, whatever Christ did as our representative, God counted it as being something we did too. Of course, believers were not consciously present in Christ since most believers did not even exist yet when Christ was on earth. Nor were believers present in Christ in some mysterious, spiritual way (as if, for example, the souls of thousands of believers were somehow present in Christ's body during his earthly life). Rather, believers were present in Christ *only in God's thoughts.* God *thought of us* as being represented by Christ through his whole life.

---

3. Union with Christ is also sometimes referred to as the "mystical union" because we do not fully understand the workings of these relationships with Christ and because we know about them only through God's revelation in Scripture.

When Jesus had perfectly obeyed God for his whole life, God thought of us as having obeyed too. "By the one man's obedience the many will be made righteous" (Rom. 5:19). So Christ is our source of righteousness (1 Cor. 1:30; Phil. 3:9).

Because God thought of us as being "in" Christ, he also could think of our sins as belonging to Christ: "For our sake he made him to be sin who knew no sin" (2 Cor. 5:21), and "the Lord has laid on him the iniquity of us all" (Isa. 53:6). These were sins we had not yet committed, but God knew about them in advance and thought of them as belonging to Christ. Thus it was right that Christ should die for our sins. "He himself bore our sins in his body on the tree" (1 Peter 2:24; see also Rom. 4:25; 1 Cor. 15:3; Col. 2:14; Heb. 9:28).

But it was not just our sins that God thought of as belonging to Christ: it was we ourselves. When Christ died, God thought of us as (in some sense) having died. Our old self was *crucified with him* (Rom. 6:6). "I have been crucified with Christ" (Gal. 2:20). "One has died for all, therefore all have died" (2 Cor. 5:14; see also Rom. 6:4–5, 8; 7:4; Col. 1:22; 2:12, 20; 3:3; 2 Tim. 2:11).

In the same way, God thought of us as having been *buried* with Christ, *raised* with him, and *taken up to heaven* with him in glory. God "raised us up with him and seated us with him in the heavenly places in Christ Jesus" (Eph. 2:6; see also Rom. 6:4–11; 1 Cor. 15:22; Col. 2:12–13).

When Christ returned to heaven, therefore, all the blessings of salvation had been earned for us. God *thought of* these blessings as being rightfully ours, just as if we had earned them ourselves. Nevertheless, they were stored up for us in heaven—in God's mind, actually, and in Christ, our representative—waiting to be applied to us personally (1 Peter 1:3–5; Col. 3:3–4; Eph. 1:3).

### 3. During Our Lives Now

Once we have been born and exist as real people in the world, our union with Christ can no longer be something just in God's mind. We also must be brought into an actual relationship with Christ through which the benefits of salvation can be applied to our lives by the Holy Spirit. The richness of our present life in Christ can be viewed from four slightly different perspectives:

1. We have died and been raised with Christ.
2. We have new life in Christ.
3. All our actions can be done in Christ.
4. All Christians together are one body in Christ.

**a. Dying and Rising with Christ.** The death, burial, and resurrection of Jesus now have real effects in our lives. We have been "*buried with him* in baptism," and "*raised with him* through faith in the powerful working of God, who raised him from the dead"

(Col. 2:12). Here Paul's references to baptism and faith indicate that our dying and rising with Christ occur in this present life, at the time we become Christians.

Paul sees this present death and resurrection with Christ as a way of describing and explaining the change that the Holy Spirit brings about in our character and personality when we become Christians. It is as if the Holy Spirit reproduces Jesus' death and resurrection in our lives when we believe in Christ. We become so unresponsive to the pressures, demands, and attractions of our previous sinful way of life that Paul can say we are "dead" to these influences because we have died with Christ (Rom. 7:6; Gal. 2:20; 5:24; 6:14; Col. 2:20). On the other hand, we find ourselves wanting to serve God much more, and we are able to serve him with greater power and success, so much so that Paul says we are "alive" to God, because we have been raised up with Christ: "We were buried therefore with him by baptism into death, in order that, just as Christ was raised from the dead by the glory of the Father, we too might *walk in newness of life*" (Rom. 6:4). "So you also must consider yourselves dead to sin and *alive to God* in Christ Jesus" (Rom. 6:11; see also 1 Peter 1:3; 2:24). Because we died and rose with Christ, we have power to overcome personal sin more and more (Rom. 6:12–14, 19); we have been "filled in him" (Col. 2:10); in fact, we have become a "new creation" in him (2 Cor. 5:17, with vv. 14–15), and should therefore set our minds on things that are above, where Christ is (Col. 3:1–3).

**b. New Life in Christ.** These last verses suggest a second perspective on our being "in Christ." We can think not only in terms of Christ's *past* work of redemption but also in terms of his *present* life in heaven and his continuing possession of all the spiritual resources we need to live the Christian life. Since every spiritual blessing was earned by him and belongs to him, the New Testament can say that these blessings are "in him." Thus they are available only to those who are "in Christ," and if we are in Christ, these blessings are ours.

John writes, "God gave us eternal life, and this life is *in his Son*" (1 John 5:11), and Paul speaks of "the promise of the life that is *in Christ Jesus*" (2 Tim. 1:1). We read that "*in Christ*" are "faith and love" (1 Tim. 1:14; 2 Tim. 1:13), "grace" (2 Tim. 2:1), "salvation" (2 Tim. 2:10), "all the treasures of wisdom and knowledge" (Col. 2:3), and God's "riches in glory" (Phil. 4:19). Paul says that it is because of God's work that Christians "are in Christ Jesus, who became to us wisdom from God, righteousness and sanctification and redemption" (1 Cor. 1:30) and that "God . . . has blessed us *in Christ* with every spiritual blessing in the heavenly places" (Eph. 1:3).

In fact, every stage of the application of redemption is given to us because we are "in Christ." It is "in Christ" that we are *called* to salvation (1 Cor. 7:22), *regenerated* (Eph. 1:3; 2:10), and *justified* (Rom. 8:1; 2 Cor. 5:21; Gal. 2:17; Eph. 1:7; Phil. 3:9; Col. 1:14). "In Christ" we *die* (1 Thess. 4:16; Rev. 14:13) and "in him" our bodies *will be raised* up again (1 Cor. 15:22). These passages suggest that because our lives are inseparably connected to Christ himself, the Holy Spirit gives us all the blessings that Christ has earned.

**c. All Our Actions Can Be Done in Christ.** The foregoing changes within our individual lives are accompanied by a dramatic change in the realm in which we live. To become a Christian is to enter the newness of the age to come and to experience to some degree the new powers of the kingdom of God affecting every part of our lives. To be "in Christ" is to be in that new realm that Christ controls.

This means that every action in our lives can be done "in Christ," if it is done in the power of his kingdom and in a way that brings honor to him. Paul *speaks* the truth "in Christ" (Rom. 9:1; 2 Cor. 2:17; 12:19), *is proud* of his work "in Christ" (Rom. 15:17; 1 Cor. 15:31), reminds the Corinthians of his *ways* "in Christ" (1 Cor. 4:17), *hopes* "in the Lord Jesus" to send Timothy to Philippi (Phil. 2:19), *rejoices* greatly "in the Lord" (Phil. 4:10), and "in the Lord" *commands*, *asks*, and *urges* other Christians (1 Thess. 4:1; 2 Thess. 3:12; Philem. 8). He says, "I can *do all things* through him who strengthens me" (Phil. 4:13).

Paul also writes to believers about their actions "in Christ." He reminds the Corinthians, "In the Lord your *labor* is not in vain" (1 Cor. 15:58). It is "in the Lord" that children are to *obey* their parents (Eph. 6:1), wives are to *submit* to their husbands (Col. 3:18), and all believers are to *be strong* (Eph. 6:10), *be encouraged* (Phil. 2:1), *rejoice* (Phil. 3:1; 4:4), *agree* (Phil. 4:2), *stand firm* (Phil. 4:1; 1 Thess. 3:8), *live a godly life* (2 Tim. 3:12), and have *good behavior* (1 Peter 3:16). "In the Lord" they *work hard* (Rom. 16:12), *become confident* (Phil. 1:14), and *are approved* (Rom. 16:10). Paul's hope for Christians is that they *walk* the walk of the Christian life in Christ: "Therefore, as you received Christ Jesus the Lord, so walk in him, rooted and built up in him and established in the faith, just as you were taught, abounding in thanksgiving" (Col. 2:6–7). Then Paul will achieve his life's goal, to "present everyone *mature* in Christ" (Col. 1:28). John similarly encourages believers to "*abide* in him" (1 John 2:28; 3:6, 24), echoing Jesus' words, "Whoever abides in me and I in him, he it is that bears much fruit" (John 15:5).

**d. One Body in Christ.** We are not simply in Christ as isolated individual persons. Since Christ is the head of the body, which is the church (Eph. 5:23), all who are in union with Christ are also related to one another in his body. This joining together makes us "one body in Christ, and individually *members one of another*" (Rom. 12:5; 1 Cor. 10:17; 12:12–27). "If one member suffers, all suffer together; if one member is honored, all rejoice together" (1 Cor. 12:26). The ties of fellowship are so strong that Christians may only marry "in the Lord" (1 Cor. 7:39). In this body of Christ old hostilities disappear, sinful divisions among people are broken down, and worldly criteria of status no longer apply, for "there is neither Jew nor Greek, there is neither slave nor free, there is no male and female, for you are all one in Christ Jesus" (Gal. 3:28; cf. Eph. 2:13–22).

Because we are one body in Christ, entire churches can be "in Christ" (Gal. 1:22; 1 Thess. 2:14). And the church universal, the church made up of all true believers, is collectively united to Christ as a husband is united to his wife (Eph. 5:31–32; 1 Cor. 6:17). Christ's purpose is to perfect, cleanse, and purify the church so that it might more completely reflect what he is like and thereby bring glory to him (Eph. 5:25–27).

Yet another metaphor is used in 1 Peter 2:4–5, where believers, in coming to Christ, are said to be like living stones, built into a spiritual house (see also Eph. 2:20–22). Thus they are unified and forever dependent on one another, just as the stones of a building are united to each other and depend upon each other.

But the boldest analogy of all is used by Jesus, who prays for believers "*that they may all be one*, just as you, Father, are in me, and I in you, that they also may be in us" (John 17:21). Here Jesus prays that our unity would be like the perfect unity between the Father and the Son in the Trinity. This is a reminder to us that our unity should be eternal and perfectly harmonious (as God's unity is).

But this analogy with the members of the Trinity is very important for another reason: it warns us against thinking that union with Christ will ever swallow up our individual personalities. Even though the Father, Son, and Holy Spirit have perfect and eternal unity, they remain distinct persons. In the same way, even though we shall someday attain *perfect unity* with other believers and with Christ, we shall forever remain *distinct persons* with individual gifts, abilities, interests, responsibilities, circles of personal relationships, preferences, and desires.

## B. Christ Is in Us

Jesus spoke of a second kind of relationship when he said, "Whoever abides in me and *I in him*, he it is that bears much fruit" (John 15:5). It is not only true that we are in Christ; he is also in us, to give us power to live the Christian life. "I have been crucified with Christ. It is no longer I who live, but *Christ who lives in me*" (Gal. 2:20). The factor that determines whether someone is a Christian is whether Christ is in him (Rom. 8:10; 2 Cor. 13:5; Rev. 3:20). God's wise plan, hidden as a mystery for generations, was to save gentiles as well as Jews. Therefore, Paul can tell his gentile readers that God's mystery is "*Christ in you*, the hope of glory" (Col. 1:27).

It is important to maintain, on the basis of these verses, that there is a real personal dwelling of Christ in us, and that does not mean that we merely agree with Christ or that his ideas are in us. Rather, *he* is personally in us and remains in us through faith (Eph. 3:17; 2 Cor. 13:5).[4] To overlook this truth would be to neglect the great source of spiritual strength that we have within us (1 John 4:4). To remember it destroys our pride, gives us a constant feeling of deep dependence on Christ, and gives us great confidence, not in ourselves but in Christ working in us (Gal. 2:20; Rom. 15:18; Phil. 4:13).

This indwelling of Christ affects our response to those in need. Whatever we do to help a Christian brother or sister, we do to Christ (Matt. 25:40). Keeping Jesus' commandments is an indication that he is in us, and the Holy Spirit also bears witness to us that Christ is in us (1 John 3:24).

---

4. See chapter 26, pp. 684, 695–96, on the way in which Christ's divine nature is omnipresent but his human nature is not.

## C. WE ARE LIKE CHRIST

A third aspect of union with Christ is our *imitation of him.* "Be imitators of me, as I am of Christ," writes Paul (1 Cor. 11:1). John reminds us, "Whoever says he abides in him ought to walk in the same way in which he walked" (1 John 2:6). So union with Christ implies that we should imitate Christ. Our lives ought so to reflect what his life was like that we bring honor to him in everything we do (Phil. 1:20).

Thus the New Testament pictures the Christian life as one of striving to imitate Christ in all our actions. "Welcome one another *as Christ has welcomed you*" (Rom. 15:7). "Husbands, love your wives, *as Christ loved the church*" (Eph. 5:25). "*As the Lord has forgiven you*, so you also must forgive" (Col. 3:13). "He laid down his life for us, and we ought to lay down our lives for the brothers" (1 John 3:16). Throughout our lives, we are to run the race before us, "looking to Jesus, the founder and perfecter of our faith" (Heb. 12:2; see also Eph. 5:2; Phil. 2:5–11; 1 Thess. 1:6; 1 John 3:7; 4:17). By contrast, disobedience to Christ holds him in contempt (Heb. 6:6).

Our imitation of Christ is especially evident in suffering. Christians are called to take suffering patiently, "because Christ also suffered for you, leaving you an example, so that you might *follow in his steps*" (1 Peter 2:21). Paul's goal is to "share his [Christ's] sufferings, becoming *like him in his death*" (Phil. 3:10; see also 2 Cor. 1:5; 4:8–11; Heb. 12:3; 1 Peter 4:13).

Furthermore, our suffering is connected with sharing in Christ's glory when he returns: "We suffer with him in order that we may also be glorified with him" (Rom. 8:17). This is probably because it is through suffering and difficulty that God makes us more Christlike and causes us to grow to maturity in Christ (James 1:2–4; Heb. 5:8–9). Also, since Christ perfectly obeyed his Father even in the face of great suffering, so our obedience, trust, and patience in suffering more fully portray what Christ was like and so bring more honor to him. It gives us great comfort to know that we are only experiencing what he has already experienced and that he understands what we are going through and listens sympathetically to our prayers (Heb. 2:18; 4:15–16; 12:11). As the outcome of a life of obedience, we are able to share in Christ's glory: "The one who conquers, I will grant him to sit with me on my throne, as I also conquered and sat down with my Father on his throne" (Rev. 3:21).

Our imitation of Christ should not be thought of as a mere mimicking of Jesus' actions, however. The far deeper purpose is that in imitating him we are becoming more and more like him: *when we act like Christ, we become like Christ.* We grow up to maturity in Christ (Eph. 4:13, 15) as we are "being transformed into the same image from one degree of glory to another" (2 Cor. 3:18). The final result is that we shall become perfectly like Christ, for God has predestined us "to be conformed to the image of his Son" (Rom. 8:29; 1 Cor. 15:49), and "when he appears, *we shall be like him*" (1 John 3:2). When this happens, Christ will be fully glorified in us (2 Thess. 1:10–12; John 17:10).

Yet in all of this we never lose our individual personhood. We become perfectly *like*

Christ, but *we do not become Christ*, and we are not absorbed into Christ or lost forever as individuals. Rather, it is we as real individuals who shall still know as we are known (1 Cor. 13:12); it is we who shall see him as he is (1 John 3:2); it is we who shall worship him, see his face, have his name on our foreheads, and reign with him forever (Rev. 22:3–5).

Just as the Father, Son, and Holy Spirit are exactly like one another in character (John 14:7, 9) yet remain distinct persons, so too can we become more like Christ and remain distinct individuals with different gifts and functions (Eph. 4:15–16; 1 Cor. 12:4–27). In fact, the more like Christ we become, the more truly ourselves we become (Matt. 10:39; John 10:3; Rev. 2:17; Ps. 37:4). If we forget this, we will tend to neglect the diversity of gifts in the church and will want to make everyone like ourselves. We will also tend to deny any ultimate importance for ourselves as individuals. A proper biblical perspective will allow each believer to say not only, "We Christians are important to Christ," but also, "*I* am important to Christ: he knows my name, he calls me by name, he gives me a new name which is mine alone" (see John 10:3; Rev. 2:17).

## D. We Are with Christ

## 1. Personal Fellowship with Christ

Another aspect of union with Christ concerns our personal fellowship with him. It makes little difference whether we say that we are with Christ or that Christ is with us, for both phrases represent the same truth. Christ promised, "Where two or three are gathered in my name, there am I among them" (Matt. 18:20), and "I am *with you* always, to the end of the age" (Matt. 28:20). Once again, since Jesus' human body ascended to heaven (John 16:7; 17:11; Acts 1:9–11), these verses must speak of his divine nature being present with us. Yet it is still a personal presence in which we *work* together with Christ (2 Cor. 6:1), we *know* him (Phil. 3:8, 10), we are *comforted* by him (2 Thess. 2:16–17), we are *taught* by him (Matt. 11:29), and we live our whole lives *in his presence* (2 Cor. 2:10; 1 Tim. 5:21; 6:13–14; 2 Tim. 4:1). To become a Christian is to be "called into the *fellowship* of [God's] Son, Jesus Christ our Lord" (1 Cor. 1:9). Yet this fellowship can vary in intensity, since Paul's benediction on Christians, "The Lord be with you all" (2 Thess. 3:16; cf. 2 Tim. 4:22) can only express a hope for still closer fellowship with Christ and a deeper awareness of his presence.

Furthermore, in some sense yet imperceptible to us, when we come to worship, we now come into heaven itself, to "innumerable angels in festal gathering, and to the assembly of the firstborn who are enrolled in heaven, and to God, the judge of all, and to the spirits of the righteous made perfect, *and to Jesus*, the mediator of a new covenant" (Heb. 12:22–24). This participation in heavenly worship is what the Apostles' Creed calls the "communion of saints" and what a familiar hymn calls "mystic, sweet communion with those whose rest is won."[5] Hebrews 12 does not require that we have

---

5. This phrase is taken from the hymn, "The Church's One Foundation," written in 1866 by Samuel J. Stone.

a conscious awareness of being in the presence of this heavenly assembly, but it may indicate that those now in heaven witness our worship and rejoice in it, and it certainly implies that we can have a joyful awareness that our praise is being heard in God's temple in heaven.

In all our prayers now we are heard by Jesus and have fellowship with him (1 John 1:3), our great high priest, who has entered "into heaven itself, now to appear in the presence of God on our behalf" (Heb. 9:24; 4:16). Our fellowship with him will be greater yet when we die (2 Cor. 5:8; Phil. 1:23; 1 Thess. 5:10) and even greater still once Jesus returns (1 Thess. 4:17; 1 John 3:2). It gives us great joy to know that Christ actually desires to have us with him (John 17:24).

Our fellowship with Christ also brings us into fellowship with each other. John writes, "That which we have seen and heard we proclaim also to you, *so that you too may have fellowship with us*; and indeed our fellowship is with the Father and with his Son Jesus Christ" (1 John 1:3).

### 2. Union with the Father and with the Holy Spirit

This last verse suggests a final aspect of union with Christ. Because we are in union with Christ in these several relationships, we also are brought into union with the Father and with the Holy Spirit. We are *in the Father* (John 17:21; 1 Thess. 1:1; 2 Thess. 1:1; 1 John 2:24; 4:15–16; 5:20) and *in the Holy Spirit* (Rom. 8:9; 1 Cor. 3:16; 6:19; 2 Tim. 1:14). *The Father is in us* (John 14:23), and *the Holy Spirit is in us* (Rom. 8:9, 11). We are *like the Father* (Matt. 5:44–45, 48; Eph. 4:32; Col. 3:10; 1 Peter 1:15–16) and *like the Holy Spirit* (Rom. 8:4–6; Gal. 5:22–23; John 16:13). We have fellowship *with the Father* (1 John 1:3; Matt. 6:9; 2 Cor. 6:16–18) and *with the Holy Spirit* (Rom. 8:16; Acts 15:28; 2 Cor. 13:14; Eph. 4:30).

These additional relationships are not blurred into a distinctionless, mystical ecstasy, however. Both now and in eternity we relate to the Father in his distinct role as our heavenly Father, to the Son in his distinct role as our Savior and Lord, and to the Holy Spirit in his distinct role as the Spirit who empowers us, guides us, purifies us, and continually applies to us all the benefits of our salvation.

## QUESTIONS FOR PERSONAL APPLICATION

1. Before reading this chapter, had you thought of yourself as being united with Christ from the point of God's choosing you before the foundation of the world to the point of going to be with him in heaven forever? How does this idea change the way you think of yourself and your life? How does it affect the way you think of difficulties that you may be experiencing? In what ways can the ideas of having died with Christ and having been raised with him be an encouragement in your present efforts to overcome sin that remains in your life?

2. Have you previously thought of doing the actions that you do each day "in Christ" (see Phil. 4:13)? If you thought of doing the reading that you are presently doing "in Christ," how would it change your attitude or perspective? What difference would it make to think of doing your daily work "in Christ"? What about carrying on conversations with friends or family members? Or eating, or even sleeping?

3. How can the idea of union with Christ increase your love and fellowship for other Christians, both those in your church and those in other churches?

4. Do you have any awareness in your day-to-day life of Christ living in you (Gal. 2:20)? What would change in your life if you had a stronger awareness of Christ living in you throughout the day?

5. For one or two days, try reading some section of the gospels and asking how you might better imitate Christ in your life. What effect will the idea of following in Christ's steps (1 Peter 1:21) and walking as he walked (1 John 2:6) have in your life?

6. Can you name times in your life when you have sensed an especially close personal fellowship with Christ? What have those times been like? Can you think of anything that brought about that close fellowship with Christ? What can we do to increase the intensity of our daily fellowship with Christ?

7. In your personal experience, do you relate differently to God the Father, to Jesus Christ, and to the Holy Spirit? Can you describe those differences, if there are any?

### Special Terms

*being raised with Christ*
*communion of saints*
*dying with Christ*
*in Christ*
*mystical union*
*one body in Christ*
*union with Christ*

# BIBLIOGRAPHY

(For an explanation of this bibliography see the note on the bibliography to chapter 1, pp. 23–24. Complete bibliographical data may be found on pp. 1489–96.)

Note: This topic has not received explicit treatment in many systematic theologies, but the subjects mentioned in this chapter have been treated in a variety of ways under different topics.

## SECTIONS IN EVANGELICAL SYSTEMATIC THEOLOGIES

*1. Anglican (Episcopalian)*

1882–92 . . . . . Litton, 328–30
2013 . . . . . . . . Bird, 328
2013 . . . . . . . . Bray, 836–47

*2. Arminian (Wesleyan or Methodist)*

1992 . . . . . . . . Oden, 2:205–60

2002........Cottrell, 433, 542

**3. Baptist**
1907........Strong, 795–809
2007........Akin, 688–95
1990–95.....Garrett, 2:355–76
2013........Erickson, 876–83

**4. Dispensational**
1949........Thiessen, 278–82
2017........MacArthur and Mayhue, 602–9

**5. Lutheran**
(no explicit treatment)

**6. Reformed (or Presbyterian)**
1679–85.....Turretin, *IET*, 2:180–81, 3:105, 387, 561–74, 617–21
1878........Dabney, 612–17
1906–11.....Bavinck, *RD*, 4:248–52
1937–66.....Murray, *RAA*, 161–73
1938........Berkhof, 447–53
2011........Horton, 587–619
2013........Frame, 913–17, 940, 945, 969, 986–87, 991
2013........Culver, 615, 664–70, 735, 751
2016........Allen and Swain, 283–90, 352–62
2017........Barrett, 423–50
2019........Letham, 362, 597–616, 779–85

**7. Renewal (or charismatic/Pentecostal)**
1995........Horton, 392–93
2008........Duffield and Van Cleave, 274–79

## SECTIONS IN REPRESENTATIVE ROMAN CATHOLIC SYSTEMATIC THEOLOGIES

**1. Roman Catholic: Traditional**
1955........Ott (no explicit treatment)

**2. Roman Catholic: Post–Vatican II**
2012........*CCC*, paragraphs 772–73

## OTHER WORKS

Baker, J. P. "Union with Christ." In *NDT1*, 697–99.

Billings, J. Todd. *Calvin, Participation, and the Gift: The Activity of Believers in Union with Christ.* Oxford; New York: Oxford University Press, 2007.

———. *Union with Christ: Reframing Theology and Ministry for the Church.* Grand Rapids: Baker Academic, 2011.

Canlis, J. "Union with Christ." In *EDT3*, 908–9.

Demarest, Bruce. *The Cross and Salvation: The Doctrine of Salvation.* Wheaton, IL: Crossway, 2006, 38.

Gordon, Adoniram Judson. *In Christ; or the Believer's Union with His Lord.* 1872. Reprint, Grand Rapids: Baker, 1964.

Keathley, Kenneth. "The Work of God: Salvation." In *A Theology for the Church*, edited by Daniel L. Akin et al., 687–95. Nashville: B&H, 2007.

Letham, Robert. *Union with Christ: In Scripture, History, and Theology.* Phillipsburg, NJ: P&R, 2011.

Murray, John. "Union with Christ." In *Redemption Accomplished and Applied*, 161–73. Grand Rapids: Eerdmans, 1955.

Pierson, Arthur T. *In Christ Jesus: The Sphere of the Believer's Life.* New York; London: Funk & Wagnalls, 1898.

———. *Vital Union with Christ.* Grand Rapids: Zondervan, 1961.

Poythress, Vern. "Using Multiple Thematic Centers in Theological Synthesis: Holiness as a Test Case in Developing a Pauline Theology." Unpublished manuscript available from the Campus Bookstore, Westminster Theological Seminary, P.O. Box 27009, Philadelphia, PA 19118, or at https://www.wtsbooks.com.

Rightmire, R. David. "Union with Christ." In *BTDB*, 789–92.

Seifrid, M. A. "In Christ." In *DPL*, 433–36.

Smedes, Lewis B. *Union with Christ: A Biblical View of the New Life in Jesus Christ.* 2nd ed. Grand Rapids: Eerdmans, 1983.

Spence, A. J. "Union with Christ." In *NDT2*, 929–32.

Spurbeck, David K. *The Christian "In Christ": An Introduction to "In Christ" Truth; The Believer's Position and Possessions in Christ.* Forest Grove, OR: Know to Grow "In Christ," 1999.

Tamburello, Dennis E. *Union with Christ: John Calvin and the Mysticism of St. Bernard.* Louisville: Westminster John Knox, 1994.

Walvoord, J. F. "Identification with Christ." In *EDT1*, 542.

## SCRIPTURE MEMORY PASSAGE

**Galatians 2:20:** I have been crucified with Christ. It is no longer I who live, but Christ who lives in me. And the life I now live in the flesh I live by faith in the Son of God, who loved me and gave himself for me.

## HYMN

### "Jesus, Thou Joy of Loving Hearts"

This hymn has been attributed to Bernard of Clairvaux (1090–1153), a monk known for his love of God and deep piety. Other hymns attributed to him are "Jesus, the Very Thought of Thee" and "O Sacred Head Now Wounded." Though written eight hundred years ago, this hymn remains one of the most beautiful expressions of love for Christ in the history of the church.

Jesus, thou joy of loving hearts,
    Thou fount of life, thou light of men,
From the best bliss that earth imparts
    We turn unfilled to thee again.

Thy truth unchanged hath ever stood;
    Thou savest those that on thee call;
To them that seek thee thou art good,
    To them that find thee all in all.

We taste thee, O thou living bread,
    And long to feast upon thee still;
We drink of thee, the fountain-head,
    And thirst our souls from thee to fill.

Our restless spirits yearn for thee,
    Where'er our changeful lot is cast;
Glad when thy gracious smile we see,
    Blest when our faith can hold thee fast.

O Jesus, ever with us stay,
    Make all our moments calm and bright;
Chase the dark night of sin away,
    Shed o'er the world thy holy light.

Author: Bernard of Clairvaux, c. 1150

# CONTEMPORARY WORSHIP SONG

## "Glorious Day"

*I was buried beneath my shame.*
*Who could carry that kind of weight?*
*It was my tomb*
*'Til I met You.*
*I was breathing, but not alive.*
*All my failures I tried to hide.*
*It was my tomb*
*'Til I met You.*
*You called my name,*
*Then I ran out of that grave.*

### Chorus
*Out of the darkness*
*Into Your glorious day*
*You called my name,*
*And I ran out of that grave.*
*Out of the darkness*
*Into Your glorious day.*

*Now Your mercy has saved my soul.*
*Now Your freedom is all that I know.*
*The old made new.*
*Jesus, when I met You, whoa, what a day*
*When you called my name*
*And I ran out of that grave.*

### Bridge
*I needed rescue;*
*My sin was heavy,*
*But chains break at the weight of Your glory.*
*I needed shelter;*
*I was an orphan,*
*But You call me a citizen of Heaven.*
*When I was broken,*
*You were my healing;*
*Now Your love is the air that I'm breathing.*
*I have a future;*
*My eyes are open*
*'Cause when you called my name*
*I ran out of that grave.*

Words by Jason Ingram, Sean Curran,
Jonathan Smith, and Kristian Stanfill[6]

# PART 6

# The Doctrine of the Church

# CHAPTER 44

# The Church: Its Nature, Its Marks, and Its Purposes

*What is necessary to make a church?*
*How can we recognize a true church?*
*The purposes of the church.*

## EXPLANATION AND SCRIPTURAL BASIS

### A. THE NATURE OF THE CHURCH

### 1. Definition

There are at least two possible definitions of the church, and these two definitions differ over whether the people of God in the Old Testament should be considered part of the church. The definition that seems preferable to me is this: *the church is the community of all true believers for all time.* The other definition is this: the church is the community of all true believers since Pentecost. According to this second definition, the church does not include true believers during the time of the Old Testament.

There are several passages in Scripture that make me think it preferable to say that the church includes all true believers for all time. For example, Paul says, "Christ loved *the church* and gave himself up for her" (Eph. 5:25). Here the term *the church* is used to apply to all those whom Christ died to redeem, all those who arc saved by the death of Christ. But that must include all true believers for all time, both believers in the New Testament age and believers in the Old Testament age as well.[1] So great is God's plan for the church that he has exalted Christ to a position of highest authority for the sake of the church: "He put all things under his feet and gave him as head over all things *to the church*, which is his body, the fullness of him who fills all in all" (Eph. 1:22–23).

The author of Hebrews understands the present-day Christians who constitute the church on earth to be surrounded by a great "cloud of witnesses" (Heb. 12:1) that reaches back into the earliest eras of the Old Testament and includes Abel, Enoch, Noah, Abraham, Sarah, Gideon, Barak, Samson, Jephthah, David, Samuel, and the prophets (Heb. 11:4–32). All these "witnesses" surround the present-day people of God, and it

---

1. See section 5 below for a discussion of the dispensational view that the church and Israel must be thought of as distinct groups. In this book, I have taken a nondispensational position on that question, though it should be pointed out that many evangelicals who agree with much of the rest of this book will differ with me on this particular question.

seems only appropriate that they, together with the New Testament people of God, should be thought of as God's great spiritual "assembly" or "church."[2] Moreover, later in chapter 12 the author of Hebrews says that when New Testament Christians worship we come into the presence of "the *assembly* (or 'church,' Gk. *ekklēsia*) of the firstborn who are enrolled in heaven." This emphasis is not surprising in light of the fact that the New Testament authors see Jewish believers and Gentile believers alike to be now united in the church. Together they have been made "one" (Eph. 2:14), they are "one new man" (v. 15) and "fellow citizens" (v. 19), and "members of the household of God" (v. 19).

Therefore, even though there are certainly new privileges and new blessings that are given to the people of God in the New Testament, it seems appropriate to think of the church as constituting all the people of God for all time, both Old Testament believers and New Testament believers.[3] (For a discussion of the question of whether there remains a distinction between "the church" and "Israel" as two separate peoples of God; see section 5 below.)

On the other hand, there are good arguments for the view that the church did not begin until Pentecost. For example, most English Bible translations do not use the word *church* at all to refer to the "assemblies" of God's people in the Old Testament, even though the LXX uses *ekklēsia* more than seventy times to refer to an "assembly" of God's people. And it is significant that, beginning with Matthew 16:18 and 18:17 and then continuing in Acts and the Epistles, *ekklēsia* is applied to the people of God even when they are not assembled in public worship but simply exist in a certain place, such as "the church of God that is in Corinth" (1 Cor. 1:2). In addition, Jesus seemed to be speaking about future events when he said, "I will build my church" (Matt. 16:18). And Paul calls Christ the

---

2. The Greek word *ekklēsia*, translated "church" in the New Testament, simply means "assembly" (in the LXX it refers frequently to the assemblies of God's people).

3. Millard Erickson, *Christian Theology*, 3rd ed. (Grand Rapids: Baker, 2013), 1048, argues that the church does not start until Pentecost because Luke does not use the word *church* (*ekklēsia*) in his gospel but uses it twenty-four times in Acts. If the church existed before Pentecost, he reasons, why did Luke not speak of it before that time?

I would respond that the reason Luke did not use the word *church* to speak of the people of God during Jesus' earthly ministry is probably because there was no clearly defined or visible group to which it could refer during Jesus' earthly ministry. The true church *did* exist in the sense that it consisted of all true believers in Israel during that time, but this was such a small remnant of faithful Jews (such as Joseph and Mary, Zechariah and Elizabeth, Simeon, Anna, and others like them), that it was not an outwardly evident or well-defined group at all. Large segments of the Jewish population had strayed from God and had substituted other kinds of religious activities, such as legalism (the Pharisees), unbelieving "liberalism" (the Sadducees), speculative mysticism (those who wrote or believed apocalyptic

literature and followers of sects such as those in the Qumran community), crass materialism (the tax collectors and others for whom wealth was a false god), or political or military activism (the Zealots and others who sought salvation through political or military means). Though there were no doubt genuine believers among many or all of these groups, the nation as a whole did not constitute an assembly of people who worshiped God rightly.

Moreover, the idea of a people of God newly "called out" as an assembly to follow Christ first came to fruition on the day of Pentecost. Therefore, although the "church" in the sense of the group of all who truly believed in God did exist before the day of Pentecost, it came to much clearer visible expression on the day of Pentecost, and it is natural that Luke should begin to use the name "the church" at that point. Before that point the name "church" could not have referred to any clearly established entity apart from the nation of Israel as a whole (which contained many unbelievers); after Pentecost, however, it readily could be used to refer to those who willingly and visibly identified themselves with this new people of God.

We should also note that Jesus did use the word *church* (*ekklēsia*) twice in Matthew's gospel (16:18 and 18:17).

"cornerstone" of the church (Eph. 2:20), an image that suggests that the church did not begin until Christ laid the foundation by his life, death, and resurrection. Therefore, if others wish to define the church as "all true believers since Pentecost" (the second definition), I cannot raise a serious objection, and I do not think that very much is at stake so long as some kind of continuity with the people of the Old Testament is affirmed.

## 2. The Church Is Invisible yet Visible

In its true spiritual reality as the fellowship of all genuine believers, the church is invisible. This is because we cannot see the spiritual condition of people's hearts. We can see those who outwardly attend the church, and we can see outward evidences of inward spiritual change, but we cannot actually see into people's hearts and view their spiritual state—only God can do that. This is why Paul says, *"The Lord knows those who are his"* (2 Tim. 2:19). Even in our churches and neighborhoods, only God knows who are true believers with certainty and without error. In speaking of the church as invisible, the author of Hebrews speaks of the "assembly (or 'church,' Gk. *ekklēsia*) of the firstborn who are enrolled in heaven" (Heb. 12:23) and says that present-day Christians join with that assembly in worship.

We can give the following definition: *the invisible church is the church as God sees it.*

Both Martin Luther and John Calvin were eager to affirm this invisible aspect of the church over against the Roman Catholic teaching that the church was the one visible organization that had descended from the apostles in an unbroken line of succession (through the bishops of the church). The Roman Catholic Church had argued that only in the visible organization of the Roman Church could we find the one true church, the only true church. Even today such a view is held by the Roman Catholic Church. In the "Pastoral Statement for Catholics on Biblical Fundamentalism" issued March 25, 1987, the (United States) National Conference of Catholic Bishops Ad Hoc Committee on Biblical Fundamentalism criticized evangelical Christianity (which it called "biblical fundamentalism") primarily because it took people away from the one true church:

> The basic characteristic of biblical fundamentalism is that *it eliminates from Christianity the church as the Lord Jesus founded it.* . . . There is no mention of the historic, authoritative church in continuity with Peter and the other apostles. . . . A study of the New Testament . . . demonstrates the importance of belonging to the church started by Jesus Christ. Christ chose Peter and the other apostles as foundations of his church. . . . Peter and the other apostles have been succeeded by the bishop of Rome and the other bishops, and . . . the flock of Christ still has, under Christ, a universal shepherd.[4]

---

4. The full text of the Bishops' statement can be obtained from the National Catholic News Service, 1312 Massachusetts Avenue NW, Washington, DC, 20005. The text was published in "Pastoral Statement for Catholics on Biblical Fundamentalism," in *Origins* 17, no. 21, November 5, 1987, 376–77.

In response to that kind of teaching both Luther and Calvin disagreed. They said that the Roman Catholic Church had the outward form, the organization, but it was just a shell. Calvin argued that just as Caiaphas (the high priest at the time of Christ) was descended from Aaron but was no true priest, so the Roman Catholic bishops had "descended" from the apostles in a line of succession, but they were not true bishops in Christ's church. Because they had departed from the true preaching of the gospel, their visible organization was not the true church. Calvin said, "This pretense of succession is vain unless their descendants conserve safe and uncorrupted the truth of Christ which they have received at their fathers' hands, and abide in it. . . . See what value this succession has, unless it also include a true and uninterrupted emulation on the part of the successors!"[5]

On the other hand, the true church of Christ certainly has a visible aspect as well. We may use the following definition: *the visible church is the church as Christians on earth see it*. In this sense the visible church includes all who profess faith in Christ and give evidence of that faith in their lives.[6]

In this definition we do not say that the visible church is the church as any person in the world (such as an unbeliever or someone who held heretical teachings) might see it, but we mean to speak of the church as it is perceived by those who are genuine believers and have an understanding of the difference between believers and unbelievers.

When Paul writes epistles, he writes to the *visible* church in each community: "to the *church* of God that is in Corinth" (1 Cor. 1:2); "to the *church* of the Thessalonians" (1 Thess. 1:1); "to Philemon . . . and Apphia . . . and Archippus . . . and the *church* in your house" (Philem. 1–2). Paul certainly realized that there were unbelievers in some of those churches, some who had made a profession of faith that was not genuine, who appeared to be Christians but would eventually fall away. Yet neither Paul nor anyone else could tell with certainty who those people were. Paul simply wrote to the entire church that met together in any one place. In this sense, we could say today that the visible church is the group of people who come together each week to worship as a church and profess faith in Christ.

The visible church throughout the world will always include some unbelievers, and individual congregations will usually include some unbelievers, because we cannot see hearts as God sees them. Paul speaks of "Hymenaeus and Philetus, who have swerved from the truth" and who "are upsetting the faith of some" (2 Tim. 2:17–18). But he is confident that "The Lord knows those who are his" (2 Tim. 2:19). Paul says with sorrow, "Demas, in love with this present world, has deserted me and gone to Thessalonica" (2 Tim. 4:10).

---

5. John Calvin, *Institutes of the Christian Religion*, ed. John T. McNeill, trans. F. L. Battles, 2 vols., Library of Christian Classics (Philadelphia: Westminster, 1960), 4.2.2–3 (pp. 1043, 1045).

6. Both Calvin and Luther would add the third qualification that those who are considered part of the visible church must partake of the sacraments of baptism and the Lord's Supper. Others might consider this as a subcategory of the requirement that people give evidence of faith in their life.

Similarly, Paul warns the Ephesian elders that after his departure "fierce wolves will come in among you, not sparing the flock; and *from among your own selves* will arise men speaking twisted things, to draw away the disciples after them" (Acts 20:29–30). Jesus himself warned, "Beware of false prophets, *who come to you in sheep's clothing* but inwardly are ravenous wolves. You will recognize them by their fruits" (Matt. 7:15–16). Realizing this distinction between the church invisible and the church visible, Augustine said of the visible church, "Many sheep are without and many wolves are within."[7]

When we recognize that there are unbelievers in the visible church, there is a danger that we may become overly suspicious. We may begin to doubt the salvation of many true believers and thereby bring great confusion into the church. Calvin warned against this danger by saying that we must make a "charitable judgment" whereby we recognize as members of the church all who "by confession of faith, by example of life, and by partaking of the sacraments, profess the same God and Christ with us."[8] We should not try to exclude people from the fellowship of the church until they by public sin bring discipline upon themselves. On the other hand, of course, the church should not tolerate in its membership "public unbelievers" who by profession or life clearly proclaim themselves to be outside the true church.

### 3. The Church Is Local and Universal

In the New Testament the word "church" may be applied to a group of believers at any level, ranging from a very small group meeting in a private home all the way to the group of all true believers in the universal church. A "house church" is called a "church" in Romans 16:5 ("greet also *the church in their house*"), 1 Corinthians 16:19 ("Aquila and Prisca, together with *the church in their house*, send you hearty greetings in the Lord"). The church in an entire city is also called "a church" (1 Cor. 1:2; 2 Cor. 1:1; and 1 Thess. 1:1). The church in *an entire region* is referred to as a "church" in Acts 9:31: "So *the church throughout all Judea and Galilee and Samaria* had peace and was being built up."[9] Finally, the church throughout the entire world can be referred to as "the church." Paul says, "Christ loved *the church* and gave himself up for her" (Eph. 5:25) and says, "God has appointed *in the church* first apostles, second prophets, third teachers" (1 Cor. 12:28). In this latter verse the mention of "apostles," who were not given to any individual church, guarantees that the reference is to the church universal.

We may conclude that the group of God's people considered at any level from local to universal may rightly be called "a church." We should not make the mistake of saying

---

7. Quoted in Calvin, *Institutes*, 4.1.8 (p. 1022).

8. Calvin, *Institutes*, 4.1.8 (pp. 1022–23).

9. There is a textual variant among the Greek manuscripts of Acts 9:31, with some manuscripts having "the church" and some having "the churches." The singular reading "the church" is far preferable to the variant that has the plural. The singular reading is given an "A" probability (the highest degree of probability for a variant) in the United Bible Societies' (4th ed.) text. The singular is represented by many early and diverse texts while the plural reading is found in the Byzantine text tradition but in no texts before the fifth century AD. (In order for the grammar to be consistent, six words have to be changed in the Greek text; therefore the variant is an intentional alteration in one direction or the other.)

that only a church meeting in houses expresses the true nature of the church, or only a church considered at a city-wide level can rightly be called a church, or only the church universal can rightly be called by the name "church." Rather, the community of God's people considered at any level can be rightly called a church.

## 4. Metaphors for the Church

To help us understand the nature of the church, Scripture uses a wide range of metaphors and images to describe to us what the church is like.[10] There are several family images—for example, Paul views the church as (1) a *family* when he tells Timothy to act as if all the church members were members of a larger family: "Do not rebuke an older man but encourage him as you would a father, younger men as brothers, older women as mothers, younger women as sisters, in all purity" (1 Tim. 5:1–2). God is our heavenly Father (Eph. 3:14), and we are his sons and daughters, for God says to us, "I will be a father to you, and you shall be sons and daughters to me, says the Lord Almighty" (2 Cor. 6:18). We are therefore brothers and sisters with each other in God's family (Matt. 12:49–50; 1 John 3:14–18). A somewhat different family metaphor is seen when Paul refers to the church as (2) the *bride of Christ*. He says that the relationship between a husband and wife "refers to Christ and the church" (Eph. 5:32), and he says that he brought about the engagement between Christ and the church at Corinth and that it resembles an engagement between a bride and her husband-to-be: "I betrothed you to one husband, to present you as a pure virgin to Christ" (2 Cor. 11:2). Here Paul is looking forward to the time of Christ's return as the time when the church will be presented to him as his bride.

In other metaphors Scripture compares the church to (3) *branches on a vine* (John 15:5), (4) *an olive tree* (Rom. 11:17–24), (5) *a field of crops* (1 Cor. 3:6–9), (6) *a building* (1 Cor. 3:9), and (7) *a harvest* (Matt. 13:1–30; John 4:35). The church is also viewed as (8) *a new temple* not built with literal stones but built with Christian people who are "living stones" (1 Peter 2:5) built up on the "cornerstone" who is Christ Jesus (1 Peter 2:4–8). Yet the church is not only a new temple for worship of God; it is also (9) *a new group of priests*, a "holy priesthood" that can offer "spiritual sacrifices acceptable to God" (1 Peter 2:5). We are also viewed as (10) *God's house*: "We are his house" (Heb. 3:6), with Jesus Christ himself viewed as the "builder" of the house (Heb. 3:3). The church is also viewed as (11) "*a pillar* and *buttress of the truth*" (1 Tim. 3:15).

Finally, another familiar metaphor views the church as (12) *the body of Christ* (1 Cor. 12:12–27). We should recognize that Paul in fact uses two different metaphors of the human body when he speaks of the church. In one metaphor (12a), *the whole body* is taken as a metaphor for the church, because Paul speaks of the "ear" and the "eye" and

---

10. The list of metaphors given in this section is not intended to be exhaustive. For more discussion of metaphors for the church, see Edmund P. Clowney, "Interpreting the Biblical Models of the Church," in *Biblical Interpretation and the Church*, ed. by D. A. Carson (Nashville: Nelson, 1985), 64–109.

the "sense of smell" (1 Cor. 12:16–17), which of course are parts of a person's head. In this metaphor, Christ is *not* viewed as the head joined to the body, because the individual members are themselves the individual parts of the head. Christ is in this metaphor the Lord who is "outside" of that body that represents the church and is the one whom the church serves and worships.

But in Ephesians 1:22–23; 4:15–16, and in Colossians 2:19, Paul uses a different body metaphor to refer to the church. In these passages Paul says that Christ is the head and the church is like (12b) *the rest of the body, as distinguished from the head*: "We are to grow up in every way into him who is the head, into Christ, from whom the whole body, joined and held together by every joint with which it is equipped, when each part is working properly, makes the body grow so that it builds itself up in love" (Eph. 4:15–16).[11] We should not confuse these two metaphors in 1 Corinthians 12 and Ephesians 4, but keep them distinct.

The wide range of metaphors used for the church in the New Testament should remind us not to focus exclusively on any one. For example, while it is true that the church is the body of Christ, we must remember that this is only one metaphor among many. If we focus exclusively on that metaphor, we will be likely to forget that Christ is our Lord reigning in heaven as well as the one who dwells among us. Certainly we should not agree to the Roman Catholic view that the church is the "continuing incarnation" of the Son of God on earth today. The church is not the Son of God in the flesh, for Christ rose in his human body, he ascended in his human body into heaven, and he now reigns as the incarnate Christ in heaven, one who is clearly distinct from the church here on earth.

Each of the metaphors used for the church can help us to appreciate more of the richness of privilege that God has given us by incorporating us into the church. The fact that the church is like a family should increase our love and fellowship with one another. The thought that the church is like the bride of Christ should stimulate us to strive for greater purity, holiness, love for Christ, and submission to him. The image of the church as branches in a vine should cause us to rest in him more fully. The idea of an agricultural crop should encourage us to continue growing in the Christian life and obtaining for ourselves and others the proper spiritual nutrients to grow. The picture of the church as God's new temple should increase our awareness of God's very presence dwelling in our midst as we meet. The concept of the church as a priesthood should help us to see more clearly the delight God has in the sacrifices of praise and good deeds that we offer to him (see Heb. 13:15–16). The metaphor of the church as the body of Christ should increase our interdependence on one another and our appreciation of the diversity of

---

11. This second metaphor is not even a complete or "proper" metaphor, for bodily parts do not grow up into the head, but Paul is mixing the idea of Christ's headship (or authority), the idea of the church as a body, and the idea that we grow to maturity in Christ, and he combines them into one complex statement.

gifts within the body. Many other applications could be drawn from these and other metaphors for the church listed in Scripture.

## 5. The Church and Israel

Among evangelical Protestants there has been a difference of viewpoint on the question of the relationship between Israel and the church. This question was brought into prominence by those who hold to a "dispensational" system of theology. The most extensive systematic theology written by a dispensationalist, Lewis Sperry Chafer's *Systematic Theology*,[12] points out many distinctions between Israel and the church, and even between believing Israel in the Old Testament and the church in the New Testament.[13] Chafer argues that God has *two distinct plans* for the two different groups of people that he has redeemed: God's purposes and promises for *Israel* are for *earthly blessings*, and they will yet be fulfilled on this earth at some time in the future. On the other hand, God's purposes and promises for *the church* are for *heavenly blessings*, and those promises will be fulfilled in heaven. This distinction between the two different groups that God saves will especially be seen in the millennium, according to Chafer, for at that time Israel will reign on earth as God's people and enjoy the fulfillment of Old Testament promises, but the church will already have been taken up into heaven at the time of Christ's secret return for his saints ("the rapture"). On this view, the church did not begin until Pentecost (Acts 2). And it is not right to think of Old Testament believers together with New Testament believers as constituting one church.

While Chafer's position continues to have influence in some dispensational circles, and certainly in more popular preaching, a number of leaders among more recent dispensationalists have not followed Chafer in many of these points. Several dispensational theologians, such as Robert Saucy, Craig Blaising, and Darrell Bock, refer to themselves as "progressive dispensationalists,"[14] and they have gained a wide following. They *would not see the church as a parenthesis* in God's plan but as the first step toward the establishment of the kingdom of God. On a progressive dispensational view, *God does not have two separate purposes for Israel and the church*, but a single purpose—the establishment of the kingdom of God—in which Israel and the church will both share. Progressive

12. Lewis Sperry Chafer, *Systematic Theology* (1948; repr., Grand Rapids: Kregel, 1976). Although there are several other distinctive doctrines that usually characterize dispensationalists, the distinction between Israel and the church as two groups in God's overall plan is probably the most important. Other doctrines held by dispensationalists usually include a pretribulational rapture of the church into heaven (see chapter 54), a future literal fulfillment of Old Testament prophecies concerning Israel, the dividing of biblical history into seven periods or "dispensations" of God's ways of relating to his people, and understanding the church age as a parenthesis in God's plan for the ages, a parenthesis instituted when the Jews largely rejected Jesus as their Messiah. However, many present-day

dispensationalists would qualify or reject several of these other distinctives. Dispensationalism as a system began with the writings of J. N. Darby (1800–1882) in Great Britain, but was popularized in the USA through the Scofield Reference Bible.

13. Chafer, *Systematic Theology*, 4:45–53.

14. See Robert L. Saucy, *The Case for Progressive Dispensationalism* (Grand Rapids: Zondervan, 1993), and Darrell L. Bock and Craig A. Blaising, eds., *Progressive Dispensationalism* (Wheaton, IL: Victor, 1993). See also John S. Feinberg, ed., *Continuity and Discontinuity: Perspectives on the Relationship between the Old and New Testaments* (Wheaton, IL: Crossway, 1988).

dispensationalists would see *no distinction between Israel and the church in the future eternal state*, for all will be part of the one people of God. Moreover, they would hold that the church will reign with Christ in *glorified bodies on earth during the millennium* (see the discussion of the millennium in chapter 55).

However, there is still a difference between progressive dispensationalists and the rest of evangelicalism on one point: they would say that *the Old Testament prophecies concerning Israel will still be fulfilled in the millennium by ethnic Jewish people*, who will believe in Christ and live in the land of Israel as a "model nation" for all nations to see and learn from. Therefore, progressive dispensationalists would not say that the church is the "new Israel" or that all the Old Testament prophecies about Israel will be fulfilled in the church, for these prophecies will yet be fulfilled in ethnic Israel.

The position taken in this book differs quite a bit from Chafer's views on this issue and also differs somewhat with progressive dispensationalists. However, it must be said here that questions about the exact way in which biblical prophecies about the future will be fulfilled are, in the nature of the case, difficult to decide with certainty, and it is wise to have some tentativeness in our conclusions on these matters. With this in mind, the following may be said.

Both Protestant and Catholic theologians outside of the dispensational position have said that the church includes both Old Testament believers and New Testament believers in one church or one body of Christ. Yet even from the nondispensational view, a person may still hold that there will be a future large-scale conversion of the Jewish people, what Paul looks forward to as their "full inclusion" (Rom. 11:12; cf. 11:15, 23–24, 25–26, 28–31).[15] According to Paul, God still views the very Jews who have rejected the gospel of Christ as in some sense "beloved," for Paul says, "As regards the gospel, *they are enemies* for your sake. But as regards election, *they are beloved* for the sake of their forefathers" (Rom. 11:28). That is why Paul looks forward to their future large-scale conversion. Yet that conversion will only result in Jewish believers *becoming part of the one true church* of God—they will be "grafted back into their own olive tree" (Rom. 11:24). They will not constitute a different olive tree, a different group distinct from the church.

Many New Testament verses, particularly in Hebrews, James, and 1 Peter, understand the church as the "new Israel" or new "people of God." Hebrews 8 provides a strong argument for seeing the church as the recipient, and the fulfillment, of the Old Testament promises concerning Israel. In the context of speaking about the new covenant to which Christians belong, the author of Hebrews gives an extensive quotation from Jeremiah 31:31–34, in which he says, "The days are coming, declares the Lord, when I will establish a new *covenant with the house of Israel and with the house of*

---

15. See chapter 54, pp. 1351–52 and 1357–58, where I affirm the conviction that Rom. 9–11 teaches a future large-scale conversion of the Jewish people, even though I am not a dispensationalist in the commonly understood sense of that term.

*Judah.* . . . For this is the covenant that I will make with the house of Israel after those days, declares the Lord: I will put my laws into their minds, and write them on their hearts, and I will be their God, and they shall be my people" (Heb. 8:8–10). Here the author quotes the Lord's promise that he will make a new covenant *with the house of Israel* and *with the house of Judah*, and says that that is the new covenant that has now been made *with the church.* The new covenant that God predicted through Jeremiah is the covenant of which believers in the church are now members. It seems hard to avoid the conclusion that the author views the church as the true Israel of God in which the Old Testament promises to Israel find their fulfillment.

Similarly, James can write a general letter to many early Christian churches and say that he is writing "to the twelve tribes in the Dispersion" (James 1:1). Evidently he views New Testament Christians as the successors to and fulfillment of the twelve tribes of Israel.

Peter also speaks in the same way. From the first verse in which he calls his readers "exiles of the Dispersion" (1 Peter 1:1)[16] to the next-to-last verse in which he calls the city of Rome "Babylon" (1 Peter 5:13), Peter frequently speaks of New Testament Christians in terms of Old Testament imagery and promises given to the Jews. This theme comes to prominence in 1 Peter 2:4–10, where[17] Peter says that God has bestowed on the church almost all the blessings promised to Israel in the Old Testament. The dwelling place of God is no longer the Jerusalem temple, for Christians are the new "temple" of God (v. 5). The priesthood able to offer acceptable sacrifices to God is no longer descended from Aaron, for Christians are now the true "royal priesthood" with access before God's throne (vv. 4–5, 9). God's chosen people are no longer said to be those physically descended from Abraham, for Christians are now the true "chosen race" (v. 9). The nation blessed by God is no longer said to be the nation of Israel, for Christians are now God's true "holy nation" (v. 9). The people of Israel are no longer said to be the people of God, for Christians—both Jewish and gentile Christians—are now "God's people" who have "received mercy" (v. 10). Moreover, Peter takes these quotations from contexts in the Old Testament that repeatedly warn that God will reject his people who persist in rebellion against him and who reject the precious "cornerstone" (v. 6) that he has established. What further statement could be needed in order for us to say with assurance that the church has now become the true Israel of God and will receive all the blessings promised to Israel in the Old Testament?[18]

The same theme is seen in Paul's epistles. This present church age, which has brought

16. *Dispersion* was a term used to refer to the Jewish people scattered abroad from the land of Israel and living throughout the ancient Mediterranean world.

17. The remainder of this paragraph is largely taken from Grudem, *The First Epistle of Peter* (Leicester: Inter-Varsity Press; Grand Rapids: Eerdmans, 1988), 113.

18. A dispensationalist may grant at this point that the church has been the recipient of many *applications* of Old Testament prophecies concerning Israel but that the true *fulfillment* of these promises will yet come in the future for ethnic Israel. But with all these evident New Testament examples of clear application of these promises to the church, there does not seem to be any strong reason to deny that this really is the only fulfillment that God is going to give for these promises.

the salvation of many millions of Christians in the church, is not an interruption or a parenthesis in God's plan.[19] The church is a continuation of his plan expressed throughout the Old Testament to call a people to himself. Paul says, "For no one is a Jew who is merely one outwardly, nor is circumcision outward and physical. *But a Jew is one inwardly,* and circumcision is a matter of the heart, by the Spirit, not by the letter" (Rom. 2:28–29). Paul recognizes that though there is a literal or natural sense in which people who physically descended from Abraham are to be called Jews, there is also a deeper or spiritual sense in which a true "Jew" is one who is inwardly a believer and whose heart has been cleansed by God.

Paul says that Abraham is not only to be considered the father of the Jewish people in a physical sense. He is also in a deeper and more true sense *the father of all who believe* without being circumcised . . . the father of the circumcised who are not merely circumcised but who also walk in the footsteps of the faith that our father Abraham had before he was circumcised" (Rom. 4:11–12; cf. vv. 16, 18). Therefore, Paul can say, "Not all who are descended from Israel belong to Israel, and not all are children of Abraham because they are his offspring. . . . It is not the children of the flesh who are the children of God, but the children of the promise are counted as offspring" (Rom. 9:6–8). Paul here implies that *the true children of Abraham,* those who are in the most true sense "Israel," are not the nation of Israel by physical descent from Abraham but those who have believed in Christ. Those who truly believe in Christ are now the ones who have the privilege of being called "my people" by the Lord (Rom. 9:25, quoting Hos. 2:23); therefore, the church is now God's chosen people. This means that when the Jewish people according to physical descent are saved, they will be "grafted back *into their own olive tree*" (Rom. 11:24). Another passage indicating this is Galatians 3:29: "If you are Christ's, then *you are Abraham's offspring,* heirs according to promise." Similarly, Paul says that Christians are the true "circumcision" (Phil. 3:3).

Far from thinking of the church as a separate group from the Jewish people, Paul writes to gentile believers at Ephesus, telling them that they were formerly "alienated from the commonwealth of Israel and strangers to the covenants of promise" (Eph. 2:12) but now have been "brought near by the blood of Christ" (Eph. 2:13). And when the gentiles were brought into the church, Jews and gentiles were united into one new body. Paul says that God "*has made us both one* and has broken down in his flesh the dividing wall of hostility . . . that he might create in himself one new man in place of the two, so making peace, and might *reconcile us both to God in one body* through the cross" (Eph. 2:14–16). Therefore, Paul can say that gentiles are "*fellow citizens with the saints* and members of the household of God, built on the foundation of the apostles and prophets, Christ Jesus himself being the cornerstone" (Eph. 2:19–20). With his

---

19. Chafer's term is *intercalation,* meaning an insertion of a period of time into a previously planned schedule or calendar of events (Chafer, *Systematic Theology,* 4:41). Here Chafer says, "The present age of the church is an intercalation into the revealed calendar or program of God as that program was foreseen by the prophets of old."

extensive awareness of the Old Testament background to the New Testament church, Paul can still say that "the Gentiles are fellow heirs, members of the same body" (Eph. 3:6). The entire passage speaks strongly of the unity of Jewish and gentile believers in one body in Christ and gives no indication of any distinctive plan for Jewish people ever to be saved apart from inclusion in the one body of Christ, the church. The church incorporates into itself all the true people of God, and almost all of the titles used of God's people in the Old Testament are in one place or another applied to the church in the New Testament.

## 6. The Church and the Kingdom of God

What is the relationship between the church and the kingdom of God? The differences have been summarized well by George Ladd:

> The Kingdom is primarily the dynamic reign or kingly rule of God, and, derivatively, the sphere in which the rule is experienced. In biblical idiom, the Kingdom is not identified with its subjects. They are the people of God's rule who enter it, live under it, and are governed by it. The church is the community of the Kingdom but never the Kingdom itself. Jesus' disciples belong to the Kingdom as the Kingdom belongs to them; but they are not the Kingdom. The Kingdom is the rule of God; the church is a society of men.[20]

Ladd goes on to summarize five specific aspects of the relationship between the kingdom and the church: (1) The church is not the kingdom (for Jesus and the early Christians preached that the kingdom of God was near, not that the church was near, and preached the good news of the kingdom, not the good news of the church: Acts 8:12; 19:8; 20:25; 28:23, 31). (2) The kingdom creates the church (for as people enter into God's kingdom they become joined to the human fellowship of the church). (3) The church witnesses to the kingdom (for Jesus said, "this gospel of the kingdom will be proclaimed throughout the whole world," Matt. 24:14). (4) The church is the instrument of the kingdom (for the Holy Spirit, manifesting the power of the kingdom, works through the disciples to heal the sick and cast out demons, as he did in the ministry of Jesus: Matt. 10:8; Luke 10:17). (5) The church is the custodian of the kingdom (for the church has been given the keys of the kingdom of heaven: Matt. 16:19).[21]

Therefore, we should not identify the kingdom of God as the church (as in Roman Catholic theology), nor should we see the kingdom of God as entirely future, something distinct from the church age (as in older dispensational theology). Rather, we should recognize that there is a close connection between the kingdom of God and the church.

---

20. George Eldon Ladd, *Theology of the New Testament* (Grand Rapids: Eerdmans, 1974), 111.

21. These five points are summarized from Ladd, *Theology of the New Testament*, 111–19.

As the church proclaims the gospel of Christ, individual people are born again, and their hearts are changed. They begin to live increasingly in a Christlike way, showing that God's kingdom is advancing because he is increasingly reigning in their hearts and in their daily lives.

In the life of an individual, the future reign of God breaks into the present (it is "already" here: Matt. 12:28; Rom. 14:17; and "not yet" here fully: Matt. 25:34; 1 Cor. 6:9–10). Therefore, those who believe in Christ will begin to experience something of what God's final kingdom reign will be like: they will know some measure of victory over sin (Rom. 6:14; 14:17), over demonic opposition (Luke 10:17), and over disease (Luke 10:9). They will live in the power of the Holy Spirit (Matt. 12:28; Rom. 8:4–17; 14:17), who is the dynamic power of the coming kingdom. Eventually Jesus will return and his kingdom reign will extend over all creation (1 Cor. 15:24–28).

But then, *if the kingdom of God is advancing as it should*, these new believers will also begin to affect the people around them, including unbelievers, in whatever sphere of activity the new Christians find themselves. Soon marriages will be transformed, parent-child relationships will be restored, and entire communities will be changed. Through the influence and example of Christians, even non-Christians will tend to become more honest in their business transactions, and government officials will tend to become less corrupt and begin to work for the good of their people—that is, *if the kingdom of God is advancing as it should*, even non-Christians will be influenced by it. In fact, throughout the history of the church, Christians have been in the vanguard of establishing schools for the training of children and hospitals for caring for the sick. In these ways, the advance of the kingdom of God is seen both in the transformed lives of those who are born again and in the various benefits that non-Christians experience because of the influence of Christians around.

Sometimes critics will focus on the harmful things that Christian churches have done in past generations, such as the horrors of the Inquisition or the "wars of religion" in Europe in the sixteenth and seventeenth centuries. We must admit that people who professed to be Christians have made terribly harmful mistakes, and these do not represent the advance of the kingdom of God or the reign of God in people's hearts and lives.

On the other hand, historian Alvin Schmidt points out how the spread of Christianity and Christian influence on government was primarily responsible for many significant and beneficial changes in church history,[22] such as the outlawing of infanticide, child abandonment, and abortion in the Roman Empire (in AD 374);[23] the abolition of the brutal battles to the death in which thousands of gladiators had died

22. This paragraph is taken from Wayne Grudem, *Christian Ethics* (Wheaton, IL: Crossway, 2018), 475, and is reproduced here by permission of Crossway Books.

23. Alvin J. Schmidt, *How Christianity Changed the World*

(Grand Rapids: Zondervan, 2004; formerly published as *Under the Influence*, 2001), 51, 53, 59. See also D. James Kennedy and Jerry Newcombe, *What If Jesus Had Never Been Born?* (Nashville: Nelson, 1994).

(in 404);[24] the ending of the cruel punishment of branding the faces of criminals (in 315);[25] the institution of prison reforms, such as the segregating of male and female prisoners (by 361);[26] the discontinuation of the practice of human sacrifice among the Irish, the Prussians, and the Lithuanians, as well as among the Aztec and Mayan Indians;[27] the outlawing of pedophilia;[28] the granting of property rights and other protections to women;[29] the banning of polygamy (which is still practiced in some Muslim nations today);[30] the prohibition of the burning alive of widows in India (in 1829);[31] the end of the painful and crippling practice of binding young women's feet in China (in 1912);[32] persuading government officials to begin a system of public schools in Germany (in the sixteenth century);[33] and advancing the idea of compulsory education of all children in a number of European countries.[34]

During the history of the church, Christians have had a decisive influence in opposing and often abolishing slavery in the Roman Empire, Ireland, and most of Europe (though Schmidt frankly notes that a minority of "erring" Christian teachers have supported slavery in various centuries).[35] In England, William Wilberforce, a devout Christian, led the successful effort to abolish the slave trade and then slavery itself throughout the British Empire by 1840.[36]

## B. THE "MARKS" OF THE CHURCH (DISTINGUISHING CHARACTERISTICS)

### 1. There Are True Churches and False Churches

What makes a church a church? What is necessary to have a church? Might a group of people who claim to be Christians become so unlike what a church should be that they should no longer be called a church?

In the early centuries of the Christian church, there was little controversy about what was a true church. There was only one worldwide church, the "visible" church, and that was, of course, the true church. This church had bishops and local clergymen and church buildings that everyone could see. Any heretics who were found to be in serious doctrinal error were simply excluded from the church.

But at the Reformation a crucial question came up: How can we recognize a true church? Is the Roman Catholic Church a true church or not? In order to answer that question people had to decide what were the "marks" of a true church, the distinguishing characteristics that led us to recognize it as a true church.

24. Schmidt, *How Christianity Changed the World*, 63.
25. Ibid., 65.
26. Ibid.
27. Ibid., 65–66.
28. Ibid., 87–88.
29. Ibid., 111.
30. Ibid., 115.
31. Ibid., 116–17.
32. Ibid., 119.
33. Ibid., 179.
34. Ibid., 179–80. Although this is not a matter of merely influencing laws, Schmidt also points out the immense influence of Christians on higher education: By the year 1932 there were 182 colleges and universities in the United States, and of that number, 92 percent had been founded by Christian denominations (ibid., 190).
35. Ibid., 274–76.
36. Ibid., 276–78.

Scripture certainly speaks of false churches. Paul says of the pagan temples in Corinth, "What pagans sacrifice they offer to demons and not to God" (1 Cor. 10:20). He tells the Corinthians that "when you were pagans you were led astray to mute idols" (1 Cor. 12:2). These pagan temples were certainly false churches or false religious assemblies. Moreover, Scripture speaks of a religious assembly that is really a "synagogue of Satan" (Rev. 2:9; 3:9). Here the risen Lord Jesus seems to be referring to Jewish assemblies that claim to be Jews but were not true Jews who had saving faith. Their religious assembly was not an assembly of Christ's people but of those who still belonged to the kingdom of darkness, the kingdom of Satan. This also would certainly be a false church.

In large measure there was agreement between Luther and Calvin on the question of what constituted a true church. The Lutheran statement of faith, which is called the Augsburg Confession (1530), defined the church as "the congregation of saints in which the gospel is rightly taught and the Sacraments rightly administered" (Article 7).[37] Similarly, John Calvin said, "Wherever we see the Word of God purely preached and heard, and the sacraments administered according to Christ's institution, there, it is not to be doubted, a church of God exists."[38] Although Calvin spoke of the pure preaching of the Word whereas the Lutheran Confession spoke of the right preaching of the gospel, and although Calvin said that the Word must not only be preached but heard whereas the Augsburg Confession merely mentioned that it had to be rightly taught, their understanding of the distinguishing marks of a true church is quite similar.[39] In contrast to the view of Luther and Calvin regarding the marks of a church, the Roman Catholic position has been that *the visible church* that descended from Peter and the apostles *is the true church*.

It seems appropriate that we take Luther and Calvin's view on the marks of a true church as correct still today. Certainly if the Word of God is not being preached, but simply false doctrines or doctrines of men, then there is no true church. In some cases we might have difficulty determining just how much wrong doctrine can be tolerated before a church can no longer be considered a true church, but there are many clear cases where we can say that a true church does not exist. For example, the Church of Jesus Christ of Latter Day Saints (the Mormon Church) does not hold to any major Christian doctrines concerning salvation or the person of God or the person and work of Christ (see the additional note to chapter 14, p. 325). It is clearly a false church. Similarly, the Jehovah's Witnesses teach salvation by works, not by trusting in Jesus Christ alone. This is a fundamental doctrinal deviation because if people believe the teachings of the Jehovah's Witnesses, they simply will not be saved. So the Jehovah's Witnesses also must be considered a false church. When the preaching of a church conceals the gospel message of salvation by faith alone from its members, so that the gospel message is not

---

37. Quoted from Philip Schaff, *The Creeds of Christendom*, 3 vols. (1931; repr., Grand Rapids: Baker, 1983), 11–12.
38. Calvin, *Institutes*, 4.1.9 (p. 1023).

39. Later confessions sometimes added a third mark of the church (the right exercise of church discipline), but neither Luther nor Calvin listed this mark.

clearly proclaimed and has not been proclaimed for some time, the group meeting there is not a church.

The second mark of the church, the right administration of the sacraments (baptism and the Lord's Supper), was probably stated in opposition to the Roman Catholic view that saving grace came through the sacraments and thereby the sacraments were made "works" by which we earned merit for salvation. In this way, the Roman Catholic Church was insisting on payment rather than teaching faith as the means of obtaining salvation.

But another reason exists for including the sacraments as a mark of the church. Once an organization begins to practice baptism and the Lord's Supper, it is a continuing organization and is *attempting to function as a church*. (In modern American society, an organization that begins to meet for worship and prayer and Bible teachings on Sunday mornings also would clearly be attempting to function as a church.)

Baptism and the Lord's Supper also serve as "membership controls" for the church. Baptism is the means for admitting people into the church, and the Lord's Supper is the means for allowing people to give a sign of continuing in the membership of the church—the church signifies that it considers those who receive baptism and the Lord's Supper to be saved. Therefore, these activities indicate what a church thinks about salvation, and they are appropriately listed as a mark of the church today as well. By contrast, groups who do not administer baptism and the Lord's Supper signify that they are not intending to function as a church.[40] Someone may stand on a street corner with a small crowd and have true preaching and hearing of the Word, but the people there would not be a church. Even a neighborhood Bible study meeting in a home or a student group on a university campus can have the true teaching and hearing of the Word without becoming a church. But if a local Bible study began baptizing new converts and regularly participating in the Lord's Supper, and certainly if it also began to meet on Sunday mornings, these things would signify *an intention to function as a church*, and it would be difficult to say why it should not be considered a church in itself.

## 2. True and False Churches Today

In light of the question posed during the Reformation—whether the Roman Catholic Church was a true church—what about the Roman Catholic Church today? Is it a true church? Here it seems that we cannot simply make a decision regarding the Roman Catholic Church as a whole because it is far too diverse. To ask whether the Roman Catholic Church is a true church or a false church today is somewhat similar to asking whether Protestant churches are true or false today; there is great variety

---

40. The Salvation Army is an unusual case because it does not observe baptism or the Lord's Supper, yet it seems in every other way to be a true church. In this case the organization has substituted other means of signifying membership and continuing participation in the church, and these other means of signifying membership provide a substitute for baptism and the Lord's Supper in terms of "membership controls."

among them. Some Roman Catholic parishes certainly lack both marks: there is no pure preaching of the Word, and the gospel message of salvation by faith in Christ alone is not known or received by people in the parish. Participation in the sacraments is seen as a "work" that can earn merit with God. Such a group of people is not a true Christian church.

On the other hand, there are many Roman Catholic parishes in various parts of the world today where the local priest has a genuine saving knowledge of Christ and a vital personal relationship with Christ in prayer and Bible study. His homilies and private teaching of the Bible emphasize personal faith and the need for individual Bible reading and prayer. His teaching on the sacraments emphasizes their symbolic and commemorative aspects much more than it speaks of them as acts that merit some infusion of saving grace from God. In such a case, although we would have to say that we still have profound differences with Roman Catholic teaching on some doctrines,[41] it would seem that such a church would have a close enough approximation to the two marks of the church that it would be hard to deny that it is in fact a true church. It would seem to be a genuine congregation of believers in which the gospel is taught (though not purely) and the sacraments are administered more rightly than wrongly.

Are there false churches within Protestantism? If we again look at the two distinguishing marks of the church, in the judgment of this present writer it seems appropriate to say that many liberal Protestant churches are in fact false churches today.[42] Is the gospel of works-righteousness and unbelief in Scripture that these churches teach any more likely to save people than did Roman Catholic teaching at the time of the Reformation? And is not their administration of the sacraments without sound teaching to anyone who walks in the door likely to give as much false assurance to unregenerate sinners as did the Roman Catholic use of the sacraments at the time of the Reformation? When there is an assembly of people who take the name "Christian" but consistently teach that people cannot believe their Bibles—indeed a church whose pastor and congregation seldom read their Bibles or pray in any meaningful way, and do not believe or perhaps even understand the gospel of salvation by faith in Christ alone, then how can we say that this is a true church?[43]

---

41. Significant doctrinal differences would still include matters such as the authority of the pope and the church councils, the veneration of the Virgin Mary and her role in redemption, the doctrine of purgatory, and the extent of the biblical canon. See "Additional Note: Major Doctrinal Differences between Protestants and Roman Catholics," pp. 1080–89.

42. A similar conclusion was expressed by J. Gresham Machen as long ago as 1923: "The Church of Rome may represent a perversion of the Christian religion; but naturalistic liberalism is not Christianity at all" (*Christianity and Liberalism* [Grand Rapids: Eerdmans, 1923], 52).

43. In the next chapter I discuss the question of the purity of the church. Although Christians should not voluntarily associate with a false church, we must recognize that among true churches there are purer and less pure churches (see discussion in chapter 45, below). It is also important to note here that some liberal Protestant denominations today can have many false churches within the denomination (churches where the gospel is not preached or heard) and still have some local congregations that preach the gospel clearly and faithfully and are true churches.

## C. THE PURPOSES OF THE CHURCH

We can understand the purposes of the church in terms of ministry to God, ministry to believers, and ministry to the world.

### 1. Ministry to God: Worship

In relationship to God, the church's purpose is to worship him. Paul directed the church at Colossae to be "singing psalms and hymns and spiritual songs, with thankfulness in your hearts to God" (Col. 3:16). God has destined us and appointed us in Christ "to the praise of his glory" (Eph. 1:12). Worship in the church is not merely a preparation for something else: it is in itself fulfilling the major purpose of the church with reference to its Lord. That is why Paul can follow an exhortation that we are to be "making the best use of the time" with a command to be filled with the Spirit and then to be "singing and making melody to the Lord with your heart" (Eph. 5:16–19).

### 2. Ministry to Believers: Nurture

According to Scripture, the church has an obligation to nurture those who are already believers and build them up to maturity in the faith. Paul said that his goal was not simply to bring people to initial saving faith but to "present everyone *mature in Christ*" (Col. 1:28). And he told the church at Ephesus that God gave the church gifted persons "to equip the saints for the work of ministry, *for building up the body of Christ*, until we all attain to the unity of the faith and of the knowledge of the Son of God, to mature manhood, to the measure of the stature of the fullness of Christ" (Eph. 4:12–13). It is clearly contrary to the New Testament pattern to think that our *only* goal with people is to bring them to initial saving faith. Our goal as a church must be to present to God every Christian "mature in Christ" (Col. 1:28).

### 3. Ministry to the World: Evangelism and Mercy

Jesus told his disciples that they should "make disciples of all nations" (Matt. 28:19). This evangelistic work of declaring the gospel is the primary ministry that the church has toward the world. (I do not mean to say that evangelism is more important than worship or nurture, but only that it is our primary ministry towards the unbelieving world.) Yet accompanying the work of evangelism is also a ministry of mercy, a ministry that includes caring for the poor and needy in the name of the Lord. Although the emphasis of the New Testament is on giving material help to those who are part of the church (Acts 11:29; 2 Cor. 8:4; 1 John 3:17), there is still an affirmation that it is right to help unbelievers even if they do not respond with gratitude or acceptance of the gospel message. Jesus tells us, "Love your enemies, and do good, and lend, expecting nothing in return, and your reward will be great, and you will be sons of the Most High, for *he is kind to the ungrateful and the evil*. Be merciful, even as your Father is merciful" (Luke

6:35–36). The point of Jesus' explanation is that we are to imitate God in being kind to those who are being ungrateful and selfish as well. Moreover, we have the example of Jesus who did not attempt to heal only those who accepted him as Messiah. Rather, when great crowds came to him, "he laid his hands *on every one of them* and healed them" (Luke 4:40). This should give us encouragement to carry out deeds of kindness, and to pray for healing and other needs, in the lives of unbelievers as well as believers. Such ministries of mercy to the world may also include participation in civic activities or attempting to influence governmental policies to make them more consistent with biblical moral principles. In areas where there is systematic injustice manifested in the treatment of the poor and/or ethnic or religious minorities, the church should also pray and—as it has opportunity—speak against such injustice. All of these are ways the church can supplement its evangelistic ministry to the world and indeed adorn the gospel that it professes. But such ministries of mercy to the world should never become a substitute for genuine evangelism or for the other areas of ministry to God and to believers mentioned above.

## 4. Keeping These Purposes in Balance

Once we have listed these three purposes for the church someone might ask: Which is most important? Or someone else might ask: Might we neglect one of these three as less important than the others?

To that we must respond that all three purposes of the church are commanded by the Lord in Scripture; therefore, all three are important and cannot be neglected. In fact, a strong church will have effective ministries in all three of these areas. We should beware of any attempts to reduce the purpose of the church to only one of these three and to say that it should be our primary focus. In fact, such attempts to make one of these purposes primary will always result in some neglect of the other two. A church that emphasizes only worship will end up with inadequate Bible teaching of believers and its members will remain shallow in their understanding of Scripture and immature in their Christian lives. If it also begins to neglect evangelism, the church will cease to grow and influence others; it will become ingrown and eventually begin to wither.

A church that places the edification of believers as a purpose that takes precedence over the other two will tend to produce Christians who know much Bible doctrine but have spiritual dryness in their lives because they know little of the joy of worshiping God or telling others about Christ.

But a church that makes evangelism such a priority that it causes the other two purposes to be neglected will also end up with immature Christians who emphasize growth in numbers but have less and less genuine love for God expressed in their worship and less and less doctrinal maturity and personal holiness in their lives. All three purposes must be emphasized continually in a healthy church.

However, *individuals* are different from churches in placing a relative priority on one or another of these purposes of the church. Because we are like a body with diverse spiritual gifts and abilities, it is right for us to emphasize the fulfillment of the church's purpose that is most closely related to the gifts and interests God has given to us. There is certainly no obligation for every believer to attempt to give exactly one third of his or her time in the church to worship, one-third to nurturing other believers, and one-third to evangelism or deeds of mercy. Someone with the gift of evangelism should of course spend some time in worship and caring for other believers but may end up spending the vast majority of his or her time in evangelistic work. Someone who is a gifted worship leader may end up devoting 90 percent of his time in the church toward preparation for and leading of worship. This is only an appropriate response to the diversity of gifts that God has given us.

## 5. What about "Seeker-Sensitive" Churches?

With respect to the need to fulfill all three of these purposes of the church, I have some concerns about the "seeker-sensitive" church movement, particularly as represented by the worldwide influence of Willow Creek Community Church in South Barrington, Illinois. We must be thankful to God for the tens of thousands of people who have become Christians through the ministry of Willow Creek and its affiliates and for its leadership in understanding the thinking of contemporary non-Christians and for providing a pattern of innovation and excellence in presenting the gospel effectively today. However, I cannot agree with its practice of considering non-Christian visitors (or "seekers") as the primary audience to which Sunday morning church services are addressed. Yes, people who are already Christians are encouraged to attend Wednesday evening meetings to hear deeper and more extensive teaching aimed at those who are already Christians. But inevitably many more Christians come to the Sunday morning services than come to the Wednesday night teaching meeting.

The result is that Sunday morning services are addressed to (at most) the 10% of the audience that is non-Christian, and the remaining 90% of the audience that is Christian is left without substantial, in-depth Bible teaching month after month, year after year. Unless they seek out some other form of instruction, many remain frustrated, shallow, immature Christians. And the seeker-sensitive church is failing its responsibility to "present everyone *mature in Christ*" (Col. 1:28) on the Last Day. It has allowed one purpose of the church (evangelism) to crowd out another purpose of the church (nurturing believers to grow toward Christian maturity). A better approach would be to do what the best, most fruitful Bible-teaching churches have always done on Sundays: consider people who are already Christians and who want to mature in their faith to be the *primary audience* that is addressed on Sunday mornings and, at the same time, continue to welcome non-Christians, to be "sensitive" to their needs (and not needlessly offend them), and use a small portion of the Bible teaching time to speak directly to them.

G. A. Pritchard,[44] a scholar with expertise in the sociology of religion, devoted an entire year to an extensive sociological analysis of Willow Creek and expressed the following concern: "[Willow Creek's senior pastor Bill] Hybels's relevant teaching that God wants to meet individuals' needs and make them fulfilled unduly shapes his gospel message. The holiness of God and the convicting nature of God's moral law are obscured. . . . It is not that Hybels does not speak of God's holiness and the need to repent, it is merely that the message of God's transcendent holiness is flooded by the broader emphasis on God's immanent compassionate love."[45] Pritchard notes that the Willow Creek leadership has made some attempts to correct this imbalance in emphasis, but he does not see a lasting correction.[46] Significantly, Pritchard then adds, "Willow Creek is not alone in the problem I have depicted. The American evangelical church generally has lost a vision of the Lord's holiness."[47] Pritchard spends several pages detailing the harmful results of teaching that obscures God's holiness and our need for repentance and obedience.[48]

## 6. Conclusion about the Purposes of the Church

It is important for healthy churches to continue to give attention to all three purposes of the church and not to neglect any one of these three: worship of God, nurture of believers, and evangelism and mercy directed toward unbelievers.

## QUESTIONS FOR PERSONAL APPLICATION

1. When you think of the church as the invisible fellowship of all true believers throughout all time, how does it affect the way you think of yourself as an individual Christian? In the community in which you live, is there much visible unity among genuine believers (that is, is there much visible evidence of the true nature of the invisible church)? Does the New Testament say anything about the ideal size for an individual church?

2. Would you consider the church that you are now in to be a true church? Have you ever been a member of a church that you would think to be a false church? Do you think there is any harm done when evangelical Christians continue to give the impression that they think liberal Protestant churches are true Christian churches? Viewed from the perspective of the final

**Special Terms**

*body of Christ*
*church*
*ekklēsia*
*invisible church*
*marks of the church*
*seeker-sensitive*
*visible church*

---

44. This paragraph is taken from Grudem, *Christian Ethics* (Wheaton, IL: Crossway, 2018), 475. It is reproduced here by permission of Crossway Books.

45. Greg Pritchard, *Willow Creek Seeker Services: Evaluating a New Way of Doing Church* (Grand Rapids: Baker, 1996), 263.

(Pritchard's book was published several years ago, and I do not know if his analysis reflects current practice at Willow Creek.)

46. Ibid., 41–42.

47. Ibid., 271.

48. Ibid., 263–71.

judgment, what good and what harm might come from our failure to state that we think unbelieving churches are false churches?

3. Did any of the metaphors for the church give you a new appreciation for the church that you currently attend?

4. To which purpose of the church do you think you can most effectively contribute? Which purpose has God placed in your heart a strong desire to fulfill?

# BIBLIOGRAPHY

(For an explanation of this bibliography see the note on the bibliography to chapter 1, pp. 23–24. Complete bibliographical data may be found on pp. 1489–96.)

## SECTIONS IN EVANGELICAL SYSTEMATIC THEOLOGIES

### 1. Anglican (Episcopalian)
1882–92 . . . . . Litton, 363–86
1930 . . . . . . . . Thomas, 265–80
2001 . . . . . . . . Packer, 199–203
2013 . . . . . . . . Bird, 697–744
2013 . . . . . . . . Bray, 419, 582, 847–64

### 2. Arminian (Wesleyan or Methodist)
1875–76 . . . . . Pope, 3:259–87
1892–94 . . . . . Miley, 2:385–94
1940 . . . . . . . . Wiley, 3:103–17, 126–27
1960 . . . . . . . . Purkiser, 393–408
1983 . . . . . . . . Carter, 2:571–613
1992 . . . . . . . . Oden, 3:261–368
2002 . . . . . . . . Cottrell, 400–58

### 3. Baptist
1767 . . . . . . . . Gill, 2:558–74
1887 . . . . . . . . Boyce, 1:418–22
1907 . . . . . . . . Strong, 887–94
1976–83 . . . . . Henry, 4:524–92

1990–95 . . . . . Garrett, 2:499–526
2007 . . . . . . . . Akin, 768–816
2013 . . . . . . . . Erickson, 949–70

### 4. Dispensational
1947 . . . . . . . . Chafer, 4:30–153
1949 . . . . . . . . Thiessen, 305–13, 326–32
1986 . . . . . . . . Ryrie, 391–404, 435–36
2002–2005 . . Geisler, 4:17–103
2017 . . . . . . . . MacArthur and Mayhue, 739–52, 775–79

### 5. Lutheran
1917–24 . . . . . Pieper, 3:397–425
1934 . . . . . . . . Mueller, 541–56

### 6. Reformed (or Presbyterian)
1559 . . . . . . . . Calvin, 2:1009–52 (4.1–2)
1679–85 . . . . . Turretin, *IET*, 1:57, 90, 3:3–25, 32–41, 86–146, 210–22, 293–306, 337–54
1906–11 . . . . . Bavinck, *RD*, 4:273–325
1910 . . . . . . . . Vos, 3:134, 175, 181, 233
1937–66 . . . . . Murray, *CW*, 1:231–52; *CW*, 2:321–36
1938 . . . . . . . . Berkhof, 555–78
1998 . . . . . . . . Reymond, 805–61

2008 . . . . . . . . Van Genderen and Velema, 677–93

2011 . . . . . . . . Horton, 897–903

2013 . . . . . . . . Frame, 1017–28

2013 . . . . . . . . Culver, 799–878

2016 . . . . . . . . Allen and Swain, 311–338

2017 . . . . . . . . Barrett, 577–608

2019 . . . . . . . . Letham, 618–22, 790–96, 799

**7. *Renewal (or charismatic/Pentecostal)***

1988–92 . . . . . Williams, 3:15–157

1993 . . . . . . . . Menzies and Horton, 155–72

1995 . . . . . . . . Horton, 525–38

2008 . . . . . . . . Duffield and Van Cleave, 425–28, 436–70

## Sections in Representative Roman Catholic Systematic Theologies

**1. *Roman Catholic: Traditional***

1955 . . . . . . . . Ott, 270–324

**2. *Roman Catholic: Post–Vatican II***

1980 . . . . . . . . McBrien, 2:565–730

2012 . . . . . . . . *CCC*, paragraphs 748–80

## Other Works

Allison, Gregg. *Historical Theology: An Introduction to Christian Doctrine; A Companion to Wayne Grudem's* Systematic Theology. Grand Rapids: Zondervan, 2011, 565–87.

———. *Sojourners and Strangers: The Doctrine of the Church.* Wheaton, IL: Crossway, 2012, 44–53.

Banks, Robert J. *Paul's Idea of Community: Spirit and Culture in Early House Churches.* 3rd ed. Grand Rapids: Baker, 2020.

Bannerman, James. *The Church of Christ: A Treatise on the Nature, Powers, Ordinances, Discipline, and Government of the Christian Church.* Edinburgh; Carlisle, PA: Banner of Truth Trust, 2015.

Berkouwer, G. C. *The Church.* Translated by James E. Davidson. Grand Rapids: Eerdmans, 1976.

Bock, Darrell L., and Craig A. Blaising, eds. *Dispensationalism, Israel and the Church: The Search for Definition.* Grand Rapids: Zondervan, 1992.

———. *Progressive Dispensationalism.* Wheaton, IL: Victor, 1993.

Bradshaw, T. "Church." In *NDT2*, 180–84.

Bray, G. L. "Kingdom of God." In *NDT2*, 490–93.

Brand, Chad Owen, ed. *Perspectives on Israel and the Church: 4 Views.* Nashville: B&H, 2015.

Carson, D. A., ed. *Biblical Interpretation and the Church: Text and Context.* Exeter: Paternoster, 1984.

———. *The Church in the Bible and the World.* Grand Rapids: Baker, and Exeter: Paternoster, 1987.

Clowney, Edmund. "Church." In *NDT1*, 140–43.

———. *The Doctrine of the Church.* Philadelphia: Presbyterian and Reformed, 1969.

Dever, Mark. "The Church." In *A Theology for the Church*, edited by Daniel L. Akin et al., 766–95, 809–15, 838–40. Nashville: B&H, 2007.

Feinberg, John S., ed. *Continuity and Discontinuity: Perspectives on the Relationship between the Old and New Testaments.* Wheaton, IL: Crossway, 1988.

Gaffin, Richard B. "Kingdom of God." In *NDT1*, 367–69.

Gentry, Peter and Stephen J. Wellum. *Kingdom through Covenant: A Biblical-Theological Understanding of the Covenants.* 2nd ed. Wheaton, IL: Crossway, 2018.

Giles, K. N. "Church." In *DLNT*, 194–204.

Hoch, Carl B. *All Things New: The Significance of Newness for Biblical Theology.* Grand Rapids: Baker, 1995.

Kärkkäinen, V.-M. "Ecclesiology." In *GDT*, 251–62.

Ladd, George Eldon. "The Kingdom and the Church." In *A Theology of the New Testament.* Grand Rapids: Eerdmans, 1974, 105–19.

Marshall, I. H. "Church." In *DJG*, 122–25.

Martin, Ralph P. *The Family and the Fellowship: New Testament Images of the Church.* Grand Rapids: Eerdmans, 1979.

Metzger, P. L. "Church" In *EDT3*, 181–83.

O'Brien, P. T. "Church." In *DPL*, 123–31.

Omanson, R. L. "Church, The." In *EDT1*, 231–33.

Pate, C. Marvin. "Church, The." In *BTDB*, 95–98.

Poythress, Vern. *Understanding Dispensationalists.* Grand Rapids: Zondervan, 1987.

Saucy, Robert. *The Case for Progressive Dispensationalism.* Grand Rapids: Zondervan, 1993.

———. *The Church in God's Program.* Chicago: Moody Publishers, 1972.

Snyder, Howard A. *The Community of the King.* Downers Grove, IL: InterVarsity Press, 1977.

Tidball, D. J. "Church." In *NDBT*, 407–11.

VanGemeren, Willem. *The Progress of Redemption.* Grand Rapids: Zondervan, 1988.

Watson, David C. *I Believe in the Church.* Grand Rapids: Eerdmans, 1979.

Wellum, Stephen, and Brent Parker, eds. *Progressive Covenantalism: Charting a Course between Dispensational and Covenantal Theologies.* Nashville: B&H, 2016.

## SCRIPTURE MEMORY PASSAGE

**Ephesians 4:11–13:** And he gave the apostles, the prophets, the evangelists, the shepherds and teachers, to equip the saints for the work of ministry, for building up the body of Christ, until we all attain to the unity of the faith and of the knowledge of the Son of God, to mature manhood, to the measure of the stature of the fullness of Christ,

## HYMN

### "The Church's One Foundation"

*The church's one foundation is Jesus Christ her Lord;*
*  She is his new creation by water and the Word:*
*From heav'n he came and sought her to be his holy bride;*
*  With his own blood he bought her, and for her life he died.*

*Elect from ev'ry nation, yet one o'er all the earth,*
*  Her charter of salvation one Lord, one faith, one birth;*
*One holy name she blesses, partakes one holy food,*
*  And to one hope she presses, with ev'ry grace endued.*

*Though with a scornful wonder men see her sore oppressed,*
*  By schisms rent asunder, by heresies distressed,*
*Yet saints their watch are keeping, their cry goes up, "How long?"*
*  And soon the night of weeping shall be the morn of song.*

*The church shall never perish! Her dear Lord to defend,*
*  To guide, sustain and cherish, is with her to the end;*
*Though there be those that hate her, and false sons in her pale,*
*  Against or foe or traitor she ever shall prevail.*

*'Mid toil and tribulation, and tumult of her war,*
   *She waits the consummation of peace*
      *forevermore;*
*Til with the vision glorious her longing eyes*
   *are blest,*
   *And the great church victorious shall be the*
      *church at rest.*

*Yet she on earth hath union with God the Three*
   *in One,*
   *And mystic sweet communion with those*
      *whose rest is won:*
*O happy ones and holy! Lord, give us grace that we,*
   *Like them, the meek and lowly, on high may*
      *dwell with thee.*

Author: Samuel J. Stone, 1866

## CONTEMPORARY WORSHIP SONG

### "Build My Life"

*Worthy of every song we could ever sing,*
*Worthy of all the praise we could ever bring,*
*Worthy of every breath we could ever breathe,*
*We live for You.*

*Jesus, the name above every other name,*
*Jesus, the only one who could ever save,*
*Worthy of every breath we could ever breathe,*
*We live for You.*
*We live for You.*

*Chorus*
*Holy, there is no one like You.*
*There is none beside You.*
*Open up my eyes in wonder, and show me who*
   *You are,*
*And fill me with Your heart,*
*And lead me in Your love to those around me.*

*Bridge*
*I will build my life upon Your love—*
*It is a firm foundation.*
*I will put my trust in You alone,*
*And I will not be shaken.*

Words by Matt Redman, Karl Martin, Kirby
Kaple, Pat Barrett, and Brett Younker[49]

# CHAPTER 45

# The Purity and Unity of the Church

*What makes a church more or less pleasing to God?*
*What kinds of churches should we cooperate with or join?*

## EXPLANATION AND SCRIPTURAL BASIS

### A. More Pure and Less Pure Churches

In the previous chapter we saw that there are "true churches" and "false churches." In this chapter a further distinction must be made: among true churches, there are *more pure* and *less pure* churches.

This fact is evident from a brief comparison of Paul's epistles. When we look at Philippians or 1 Thessalonians, we find evidence of Paul's great joy in these churches and the relative absence of major doctrinal or moral problems (see Phil. 1:3–11; 4:10–16; 1 Thess. 1:2–10; 3:6–10; 2 Thess. 1:3–4; 2:13; cf. 2 Cor. 8:1–5). On the other hand, there were all sorts of serious doctrinal and moral problems in the churches of Galatia (Gal. 1:6–9; 3:1–5) and Corinth (1 Cor. 3:1–4; 4:18–21; 5:1–2, 6; 6:1–8; 11:17–22; 14:20–23; 15:12; 2 Cor. 1:23–2:11; 11:3–5, 12–15; 12:20–13:10). Other examples could be given, but it should be clear that among true churches there are *less pure* and *more pure* churches. This may be represented as in figure 45.1.

Among True Churches,
There Are Less Pure and More Pure Churches
Figure 45.1

### B. Definitions of Purity and Unity

We may define the purity of the church as follows: *the purity of the church is its degree of freedom from wrong doctrine and conduct, and its degree of conformity to God's revealed will for the church.*

As we shall see in the following discussion, it is right to pray and work for the greater purity of the church. But purity cannot be our only concern, or Christians would have a tendency to separate into tiny groups of very "pure" Christians and tend to exclude anyone who showed the slightest deviation in doctrine or conduct of life. Therefore the New Testament also speaks frequently about the need to strive for the *unity* of the visible church. This may be defined in the following way: *the unity of the church is its degree of freedom from divisions among true Christians.*

The definition specifies "true Christians" because, as we saw in the previous chapter, there are those who are Christian in name only, who have had no genuine experience of regeneration by the Holy Spirit. Nonetheless, many of these people take the name "Christian," and many churches that are filled with such unbelievers still call themselves Christian churches. We should not expect or work for organizational or functional unity that includes all of those people, and therefore there will never be unity with all churches that call themselves "Christian." But as we shall also see in the following discussion, the New Testament certainly encourages us to work for the unity of all true believers.

Therefore, this chapter, as a whole, will argue that we are obligated to work for *both the purity and the unity* of the visible church.

## C. Signs of a More Pure Church

Factors that make a church "more pure" include:

1. Biblical doctrine (or right preaching of the Word)
2. Proper use of the sacraments (or ordinances)
3. Right use of church discipline
4. Genuine worship
5. Effective prayer
6. Effective witness
7. Effective fellowship
8. Biblical church government
9. Spiritual power in ministry
10. Personal holiness of life among members
11. Care for the poor
12. Love for Christ

There may be other signs than these, but at least these can be mentioned as factors that increase a church's conformity to God's purposes. Of course, churches can be more pure in some areas and less pure in others—for example, a church may have excellent doctrine and sound preaching yet be a dismal failure in witness to others or in meaningful worship. Or a church may have a dynamic witness and very God-honoring times of worship but be weak in doctrinal understanding and Bible teaching.

Most churches will tend to think that the areas in which they are strong are the most important areas and the areas where they are weak are less important. But the New Testament encourages us to work for the purity of the church in all of these areas. Christ's goal for the church is *"that he might sanctify her*, having cleansed her by the washing of water with the word, *so that he might present the church to himself* in splendor, *without spot or wrinkle or any such thing*, that she might be holy and without blemish" (Eph. 5:26–27). Paul's ministry was one of "warning everyone and teaching everyone with all wisdom, that we may present everyone mature in Christ" (Col. 1:28). Moreover, Paul told Titus that elders must "be able to give instruction in sound doctrine and also to rebuke those who contradict it" (Titus 1:9), and he said that false teachers "must be silenced" (Titus 1:11). Jude urged Christians to "contend for the faith that was once for all delivered to the saints" (Jude 3). Proper use of the sacraments is commanded in 1 Corinthians 11:17–34, and right use of church discipline to protect the purity of the church is required in 1 Corinthians 5:6–7, 12–13.

The New Testament also mentions a number of other factors: we are to strive for spiritual worship (Eph. 5:18–20; Col. 3:16–17), effective witness (Matt. 28:19–20; John 13:34–35; Acts 2:44–47; 1 John 4:7), proper government of the church (1 Tim. 3:1–13), spiritual power in ministry (Acts 1:8; Rom. 1:16; 1 Cor. 4:20; 2 Cor. 10:3–4; Gal. 3:3–5; 2 Tim. 3:5; James 5:16), personal holiness (1 Thess. 4:3; Heb. 12:14), care for the poor (Acts 4:32–35; Rom. 15:26; Gal. 2:10), and love for Christ (1 Peter 1:8; Rev. 2:4). In fact, all Christians are to "strive to excel in *building up the church*" (1 Cor. 14:12), an exhortation that applies not only to an increase in the number of church members but also (and in fact primarily) to the building up or growth of the church toward Christian maturity. The force of all of these passages is to remind us that *we are to work for the purity of the visible church.*

Of course, if we are to work for the purity of the church, especially of the local church of which we are a part, we must recognize that this is a process and that any church of which we are a part will be somewhat impure in various areas. There were no perfect churches at the time of the New Testament, and there will be no perfect churches until Christ returns.[1] This means that Christians have no obligation to seek the *purest church* they can find and stay there, and then leave it if an even purer church comes to their attention. Rather, they should find a *true church* in which they can have effective ministry and in which they will experience Christian growth as well, and then they should stay and minister, continually working for the purity of that church. God will often bless their prayers and faithful witness, and the church will gradually grow in many areas of purity.

But we must realize that not all churches will respond well to influences that would bring them to greater purity. Sometimes, in spite of a few faithful Christians within a

---

1. This is recognized by the Westminster Confession of Faith: "The purest Churches under heaven are subject both to mixture and error" (25.5).

church, its dominant direction will be set by others who are determined to lead it on another course. Unless God graciously intervenes to bring reformation, some of these churches will become cults, and others will just die and close their doors. But more commonly these churches will simply drift into liberal Protestantism.

It is helpful at this point to remember that classical liberal Protestantism is humanistic, and its approaches are *primarily man-centered* rather than God-centered.[2] When a church begins to stray from faithfulness to Christ, this will be evident not only in the shift to impure doctrine (which can sometimes be concealed from church members by the use of evasive language) but also in the daily life of the church: its activities, its preaching, its counseling, and even the casual conversations among members will tend to become more and more man-centered and less and less God-centered. There will tend to be a repeated emphasis on the typical kinds of self-help advice given in popular journals and by secular psychologists. There will be a horizontal orientation as opposed to a vertical or God-centered orientation. There will be fewer and fewer extended times of prayer. There will be less and less emphasis on the direct application of Scripture to daily situations but greater emphasis on simply being a caring and sensitive person, on affirming others and acting in love toward them. The conversation and activities of the church will have very little genuine spiritual content—little emphasis on the need for daily prayer for individual concerns and for forgiveness of sins, little emphasis on daily personal reading of Scripture, and little emphasis on moment-by-moment trust in Christ and knowing the reality of his presence in our lives. Where there are admonitions to moral reformation, these will often be viewed as human deficiencies that people can correct by discipline and effort, and perhaps encouragement from others, but these moral aspects of life will not primarily be viewed as sin against a holy God, sin which can only effectively be overcome by the power of the Holy Spirit working within. When such humanistic emphases become dominant in a church, it has moved far toward the "less pure" end of the scale in many of the areas listed above, and it is moving in the direction of becoming a false church.

## D. NEW TESTAMENT TEACHING ON THE UNITY OF THE CHURCH

There is also a strong emphasis in the New Testament on the unity of the church. Jesus' goal is that "there will be *one flock, one shepherd*" (John 10:16), and he prays for all future believers "that they may all be one" (John 17:21). This unity will be a witness to unbelievers, for Jesus prays "that they may become *perfectly one, so that the world may know that you sent me* and loved them even as you loved me" (John 17:23).

Paul reminds the Corinthians that they are "called to be saints *together with all those who in every place call upon the name of our Lord Jesus Christ*, both their Lord and ours"

---

2. See the remarkably accurate analysis by J. Gresham Machen, *Christianity and Liberalism* (1923; repr., Grand Rapids: Eerdmans, 1968), esp. 64–68.

(1 Cor. 1:2). Then Paul writes to Corinth, "I appeal to you, brothers, by the name of our Lord Jesus Christ, that *all of you agree*, and that there be no divisions among you, but *that you be united* in the same mind and the same judgment" (1 Cor. 1:10; cf. v. 13).

He encourages the Philippians, "Complete my joy by being of the same mind, having the same love, *being in full accord and of one mind*" (Phil. 2:2). He tells the Ephesians that Christians are to be "eager to maintain the *unity* of the Spirit in the bond of peace" (Eph. 4:3) and that the Lord gives gifts to the church "for building up the body of Christ, *until we all attain to the unity of the faith and of the knowledge of the Son of God*, to mature manhood, to the measure of the stature of the fullness of Christ" (Eph. 4:12–13).

Paul can *command* the church to live in unity because there already is an *actual* spiritual unity in Christ which exists among genuine believers. He says, "There is one body and one Spirit—just as you were called to the one hope that belongs to your call—one Lord, one faith, one baptism, one God and Father of all, who is over all and through all and in all" (Eph. 4:4–6). And though the body of Christ consists of many members, those members are all *"one body"* (1 Cor. 10:17; 12:12–26).

Because they are jealous to protect this unity of the church, the New Testament writers give strong warnings against those who cause divisions: "I appeal to you, brothers, to watch out for those who cause divisions and create obstacles contrary to the doctrine that you have been taught; avoid them. For such persons do not serve our Lord Christ, but their own appetites" (Rom. 16:17–18). Paul opposed Peter to his face because he separated from gentile Christians and began eating only with Jewish Christians (Gal. 2:11–14). Those who promote "strife . . . dissensions, divisions . . . will not inherit the kingdom of God" (Gal. 5:20–21). And Jude warns that those who "cause divisions" are "worldly people, devoid of the Spirit" (Jude 19).

Consistent with this New Testament emphasis on the unity of believers is the fact that the direct commands to *separate* from other people are always commands to separate *from unbelievers*, not from Christians with whom one disagrees. When Paul says, "Therefore go out from their midst, and *be separate from them*" (2 Cor. 6:17), it is in support of his opening command of that section, "Do not be unequally yoked *with unbelievers*" (2 Cor. 6:14). And Paul tells Timothy that he is to "avoid such people" (2 Tim. 3:5), referring not to believers but to unbelievers, those who are "lovers of pleasure rather than lovers of God, having the appearance of godliness, but denying its power" (2 Tim. 3:4–5). He says that these people are "men corrupted in mind and disqualified regarding the faith" (2 Tim. 3:8). Of course, there is a kind of church discipline that requires separation from an individual who is causing trouble within the church (Matt. 18:17; 1 Cor. 5:11–13), and there may be other reasons for which Christians conclude that separation is required,[3] but it is important to note here, in discussing the unity of the church, that

---

3. See the discussion on reasons for separation in section F below, pp. 1079–80.

there are no direct New Testament commands to separate from Christians with whom one has doctrinal differences (unless those differences involve such serious heresy that the Christian faith itself is denied).[4]

These passages on church unity tell us that, in addition to working for the purity of the visible church, *we are also to work for the unity of the visible church*. Yet we must realize that such unity does not actually require one worldwide church government over all Christians. In fact, the unity of believers is often demonstrated quite effectively through voluntary cooperation and affiliation among Christian groups. Moreover, different types of ministries and different emphases in ministry may result in different organizations, all under the universal headship of Christ as Lord of the church. Therefore, the existence of different denominations, mission boards, Christian educational institutions, college ministries, and so forth is not necessarily a mark of disunity of the church (though in some cases it may be), for there may be a great deal of cooperation and frequent demonstrations of unity among such diverse bodies as these. (We should not allow the modern term *parachurch organization* to mislead us into thinking that organizations such as Christian mission agencies, colleges, publishing houses, and campus ministries are somehow "beside" and therefore "outside of" the church, whereas in reality they are simply different parts of the one universal church.) Moreover, many Christians argue that there *should not* be a worldwide government of the church because the New Testament pattern of church government never shows elders having authority over any more than their own local congregations (see chapter 47 below). In fact, even in the New Testament the apostles agreed that Paul should emphasize missionary work to the gentiles while Peter would emphasize missionary work to the Jews (Gal. 2:7), and Paul and Barnabas went their separate ways for a time because of a disagreement over whether they should take Mark with them (Acts 15:39–40), though certainly they had unity in every other way.[5]

## E. Brief History of Organizational Separation in the Church

There are sometimes reasons why the outward or visible unity of the church cannot be maintained. A brief survey of the history of organizational separation in the church may highlight some of these reasons,[6] and help explain where present-day denominational divisions came from.

During the first thousand years of the church, there was for the most part outward

4. Note that 2 John 10 forbids Christians to give a greeting to itinerant heretical teachers who were not proclaiming the true gospel at all; see discussion below.

5. Scripture hints that Paul was right and Barnabas wrong in this controversy, since it tells us that Paul and Silas left Antioch "having been commended by the brothers to the grace of the Lord" (Acts 15:40), whereas nothing similar is said about Barnabas. This incident is simply reported in Acts but is not strong evidence for the appropriateness of diversification

of ministry, since the report of a "sharp disagreement" (v. 39) between Paul and Barnabas indicates that we should not think of them as entirely free from fault.

6. From this point to the end of the chapter much of the material has been taken from the article, "Separation, Ecclesiastical" by Wayne Grudem, prepared for *The Tyndale Encyclopedia of Christian Knowledge* (Wheaton, IL: Tyndale, copyright 1971, but never published). Used by permission.

unity. There had been some minor divisions during controversies with groups like the Montanists (second century) and the Donatists (fourth century), and there was a minor separation by some Monophysite churches (fifth and sixth centuries), but the prevailing sentiment was one of strong opposition to division in the body of Christ. For example, Irenaeus, a second century bishop, said about those who cause divisions in the church, "No reformation able to be effected by them will be of great enough importance to compensate for the damage arising from their schism."[7]

The first major division in the church came in AD 1054 when the Eastern (now Orthodox) church separated from the Western (Roman Catholic) church. The reason was that the pope had changed a church creed simply on his own authority,[8] and the Eastern church protested that he had no right to do that.

The Reformation in the sixteenth century then separated the Western church into Roman Catholic and Protestant branches, yet there was often a strong reluctance to cause formal division. Martin Luther wanted to reform the church without dividing it, but he was excommunicated in 1521. The Anglican (Episcopalian) church did not separate from Rome, but was excommunicated in 1570; thus it can say, "We suffer schism, we did not cause it." On the other hand, many Protestants, especially among the Anabaptists, wanted to form churches of believers only and began as early as 1525 to form separate churches in Switzerland and then other parts of Europe.

In the centuries following the Reformation, Protestantism splintered into hundreds of smaller groups. Sometimes leaders of the new groups regretted such divisions: John Wesley, although he was the founder of Methodism, claimed that he lived and died a member of the Anglican church. It was often the case that matters of conscience or religious freedom forced the division, as with the Puritans and many Pietist groups. On the other hand, sometimes language differences among immigrant groups in America led to the founding of separate churches.

Have the reasons for separation into different organizations and denominations always been proper ones? Although there have almost always been strong theological differences in major church divisions, one fears that too often, especially in more recent history, the real motives for beginning or maintaining separation have been selfish ones. John Calvin may have been correct in saying, "Pride or self-glorification is the cause and starting point of all controversies, when each person, claiming for himself more than he is entitled to have, is eager to have others in his power."[9] Moreover, he says, "Ambition has been, and still is, the mother of all errors, of all disturbances and sects."[10]

---

7. Irenaeus, *Against Heresies* 4.33.7.

8. See the discussion of the *filioque* clause in chapter 14, pp. 289–90.

9. Calvin, *The First Epistle of Paul the Apostle to the Corinthians*, trans. John W. Fraser, ed. David W. Torrance and Thomas F. Torrance (Carlisle: Paternoster; Grand Rapids: Eerdmans, 1960), on 1 Cor. 4:6 (p. 90).

10. Calvin, *Commentaries on the Four Last Books of Moses Arranged in the Form of Harmony*, trans. Charles William Bingham, vol. 4 (Edinburgh: Calvin Translation Society, 1855), on Num. 12:1 (p. 42).

In the mid-twentieth century the ecumenical movement sought greater organizational unity among denominations, but without noteworthy success. It by no means received wholehearted approval or support from evangelicals. On the other hand, since the 1960s, the growth of the charismatic movement across almost all denominational lines, the rise of neighborhood Bible study and prayer groups, and a greatly diminished doctrinal awareness among laypeople have brought about a remarkable increase in actual unity of fellowship—even between Protestants and Catholics—at the local level.

## F. REASONS FOR SEPARATION

As we examine the motives people have had for church separation throughout history, and as we compare those motives with the New Testament requirements that we seek both the unity and the purity of the visible church, we can find *both right and wrong reasons for separation*. Wrong reasons would include such things as personal ambition and pride or differences on minor doctrines or practices (doctrinal or behavioral patterns that would not affect any other doctrine and that would not have a significant effect on the way one lives the Christian life).[11]

On the other hand, there are some situations where it seems necessary to separate from a church. For example, a church may so forsake the teachings of the Bible that it is no longer a place where those who believe its teachings will find salvation.[12] Remaining in such a church would seem to be giving endorsement to those teachings. But 2 John 10–11 forbids the receiving of false teachers in such a way as to appear to endorse their teaching: "If anyone comes to you and does not bring this teaching, do not receive him into your house or give him any greeting, for whoever greets him takes part in his wicked works." Such a visitor is teaching a serious heresy about the person of Christ, one that prevents people from having saving faith. (John is talking about anyone who "does not abide in the teaching of Christ" and "does not have God" [v. 9].) Moreover, this verse refers to false teachers, not to all individuals who hold false beliefs, because it speaks of someone who comes to you and "does not bring this teaching" (v. 10).

Another reason for separating from a church may be inferred from the command in 2 Corinthians 6:14 not to be yoked together with unbelievers. This would apply if the parent church became so dominated by those who gave no evidence of saving faith that such "yoking together" could not be avoided. In this passage the prohibition against being "yoked together" with unbelievers forbids not mere association or even acceptance of help (cf. Luke 9:50; 3 John 7) but rather *the giving up of control over one's activities and the loss of freedom to act in obedience to God*, for these restraints are what is implied in the metaphor of being "yoked" together.

In other situations, Christian believers may conclude that separation from a church

---

11. See chapter 1, p. 11, on the differences between major and minor doctrines.

12. After saying that "the purist Churches under heaven are subject both to mixture and error," the Westminster Confession of Faith adds, "and some have so degenerated, as to become no Churches of Christ, but synagogues of Satan" (25.5).

or denomination is not absolutely required but is the wisest decision because it seems that staying in the parent church would very likely result in more harm than good and more hindrances to ministry than helps. Expressions of the unity of the church can still be maintained through continued occasions of fellowship and cooperation with the previous church.

## ADDITIONAL NOTE: MAJOR DOCTRINAL DIFFERENCES BETWEEN PROTESTANTS AND ROMAN CATHOLICS

While Roman Catholics and evangelical Protestants would agree on many points of theology (such as the Trinity and the deity and humanity of Christ), we also respectfully disagree with our Catholic friends about some significant doctrines. I have listed thirteen of those differences here. In each topic, I first quote from specific paragraphs in the official *Catechism of the Catholic Church*.[13] Then I list a brief response from an evangelical Protestant standpoint and refer readers to a fuller treatment of that topic elsewhere in this book.

Some may object that they are faithful Catholics or that they know faithful Catholic friends who do not believe all of these doctrines that I have listed. That may well be true, for I suppose that every church—whether Protestant or Catholic—has some members who do not believe everything that the church officially teaches. But the *Catechism of the Catholic Church* contains the official teaching of the church. Pope John Paul II wrote about it in the introductory pages, "I declare it to be a sure norm for teaching the faith. . . . I ask all the Church's Pastors and the Christian faithful to receive this catechism. . . . This catechism is given to them that it may be a sure and authentic reference text for teaching catholic doctrine and particularly for preparing local catechisms."[14]

### A. The Bible

Here is a list of the thirteen doctrinal differences that seem to me to be most significant.

### 1. Infallible Authority of the Pope and the Church Magisterium[15]

**Catechism of the Catholic Church:** "The *Pope*, Bishop of Rome and Peter's successor, . . . by reason of his office as Vicar of Christ, and as pastor of the entire Church *has full, supreme, and universal power over the whole church*, a power which he can always exercise unhindered. . . . 'The *college or body of bishops* has no authority unless united with the Roman Pontiff, Peter's successor, as its head.' As such, this college has 'supreme

---

13. *Catechism of the Catholic Church*, 2nd ed. (New York: Doubleday, 1997).
14. *Catechism of the Catholic Church*, 5–6.

15. *Magisterium* means the Pope with the bishops speaking authoritatively.

and full authority over the universal Church; but this power cannot be exercised without the agreement of the Roman Pontiff" (882–83).[16]

"Thus, the pastoral duty of the Magisterium is aimed at seeing to it that the People of God abides in the truth that liberates. To fulfill this service, Christ endowed the Church's shepherds with the charism of *infallibility in matters of faith and morals*. The exercise of this charism takes several forms: '*The Roman Pontiff, head of the college of bishops, enjoys this infallibility in virtue of his office*, when, as supreme pastor and teacher of all the faithful—who confirms his brethren in the faith—he proclaims by a definitive act a doctrine pertaining to faith or morals'" (889–891).

**Protestant Response:** The apostles left the *writings* that they wrote or authorized (= the New Testament) to take their place as the highest earthly governing authority over the church. Therefore, the Bible, not any human person, has ultimate authority over the church.

> The *things I am writing to you* are a command of the Lord. (1 Cor. 14:37)

> The *Scripture* says. . . . "The laborer deserves his wages." (1 Tim. 5:18, quoting Luke 10:7 as "Scripture")

> The ignorant and unstable twist [Paul's writings] to their own destruction, as they do the other *Scriptures*. (2 Peter 3:16, referring to Paul's writings as "Scripture")

**See also:** chapters 3 (canon), 4 (authority of Scripture), and 8 (sufficiency of Scripture).

## 2. Tradition as an Authority Alongside Scripture

By *tradition*, I mean the authoritative teaching of the church through history.

**Catechism of the Catholic Church:** "In order that the full and living Gospel might always be preserved in the Church *the apostles left bishops as their successors*. They gave them 'their own position of teaching authority.' . . . Sacred Tradition and Sacred Scripture, then, are bound closely together. . . . As a result *the Church*, to whom the transmission and interpretation of Revelation is entrusted, '*does not derive her certainty about all revealed truths from the holy Scriptures alone. Both Scripture and Tradition must be accepted and honored with equal sentiments of devotion and reverence*'" (77–86).

**Protestant Response:** When the books of the New Testament were completed, the canon of Scripture was closed, and no later teachings have authority equal to the words of the Bible, which alone are the very words of God.

---

16. Italics have been inserted into the Catechism throughout this section in order to emphasize particular points.

Long ago, at many times and in many ways, God spoke to our fathers by the prophets, but *in these last days he has spoken to us by his Son*, whom he appointed the heir of all things, through whom also he created the world. (Heb.1:1–2)

You shall not add to the word that I command you, nor take from it, that you may keep the commandments of the LORD your God that I command you. (Deut. 4:2)

Everything that I command you, you shall be careful to do. You shall not add to it or take from it. (Deut. 12:32)

Every word of God proves true; he is a shield to those who take refuge in him. *Do not add to his words*, lest he rebuke you and you be found a liar. (Prov. 30:5–6)

Does this make any difference? Giving such authority to church tradition, and in actual practice often treating tradition as an equal authority to Scripture, opens the door for numerous doctrines to be taught that are contrary to the Bible. John Piper rightly notes that this wrongful emphasis on the authority of the Pope and tradition "has led many Roman Catholics away from a personal engagement with the Scriptures into a reliance on the church, even though the church is fallible. They ought to be relying on the Scriptures, the very word of God inspired and written."[17]

**See also:** chapters 3 (canon), 4 (authority of Scripture), and 8 (sufficiency of Scripture).

### 3. Seven Books of the Apocrypha as Part of the Bible

**Catechism of the Catholic Church:** "*The Old Testament*: Genesis, Exodus, Leviticus, Numbers, Deuteronomy, Joshua, Judges, Ruth, 1 and 2 Samuel, 1 and 2 Kings, 1 and 2 Chronicles, Ezra and Nehemiah, *Tobit, Judith*, Esther, *1 and 2 Maccabees*, Job, Psalms, Proverbs, Ecclesiastes, the Song of Songs, *Wisdom, Sirach (Ecclesiasticus)*, Isaiah, Jeremiah, Lamentations, *Baruch*, Ezekiel, Daniel, Hosea, Joel, Amos, Obadiah, Jonah, Micah, Nahum, Habakkuk, Zephaniah, Hagai, Zechariah and Malachi" (120).

"The Church accepts and venerates as inspired the 46 books of the Old Testament and the 27 books of the New" (138).

**Protestant Response:** There are only thirty-nine books in the Old Testament. The books of the Apocrypha are not the Word of God and should not be part of the Bible. The books of the Apocrypha were not considered part of Scripture by first century Jews, by Jesus, by the New Testament authors, or (officially) by the Roman Catholic church until 1546.

17. John Piper, "Can a Devout Roman Catholic Be Genuinely Born Again?," Desiring God, February 21, 2018, item 1, https://www.desiringgod.org/interviews/can-a-devout-roman-catholic-be-genuinely-born-again.

> You shall not add to the word that I command you, nor take from it, that you may keep the commandments of the LORD your God that I command you. (Deut. 4:2)

> Everything that I command you, you shall be careful to do. You shall not add to it or take from it. (Deut. 12:32)

> Every word of God proves true; he is a shield to those who take refuge in him. *Do not add to his words*, lest he rebuke you and you be found a liar. (Prov. 30:5–6)

**See also:** chapters 3 (canon), 4 (authority of Scripture), and 8 (sufficiency of Scripture).

## B. God, Prayer, and Worship
## 4. Prayer Should Be Made to Mary and to Other Saints

**Catechism of the Catholic Church:** "Beginning with Mary's unique cooperation with the working of the Holy Spirit, the Churches developed their *prayer to the holy Mother of God*, . . . In countless hymns and antiphons expressing this prayer, two movements usually alternate with one another: . . . the second *entrusts the supplications and praises of the children of God to the Mother of Jesus*, because she now knows the humanity which, in her, the Son of God espoused" (2675).

"Mary is the perfect *Orans* [one who prays], a figure of the Church. When we pray to her, we are adhering with her to the plan of the Father. . . . *We can pray with and to her. The prayer of the Church is sustained by the prayer of Mary* and united with it in hope" (2679).

**Protestant Response:** We should pray to God alone, through the one mediator, Jesus Christ, through whom all believers are now counted as priests and able to come into God's very presence in prayer. We are to honor Mary's memory for her faithful obedience to God as the mother of Jesus, but she is still a finite human being, even in heaven, and only an infinite God could listen to the prayers of millions of people all at one time.

> For there is one God, and there is *one mediator between God and men*, the man Christ Jesus. (1 Tim. 2:5)

> But you are a chosen race, a *royal priesthood*, a holy nation, a people for his own possession, that you may proclaim the excellencies of him who called you out of darkness into his marvelous light. (1 Peter 2:9)

This also has implications for people's personal spiritual lives. John Piper observes, "This elevation of Mary beyond anything in the Scriptures, based solely on church tradition, distances the people of God from the enjoyment of personal fellowship with Jesus and the kind of relationship and assurance they might otherwise enjoy with him."[18]

**See also:** chapter 18 (prayer).

## 5. "Veneration" of Mary

**Catechism of the Catholic Church:** "'The Church's devotion to the Blessed Virgin is intrinsic to Christian worship.' The Church rightly *honors* 'the Blessed Virgin with special devotion.* . . . This very special devotion . . . differs essentially from the adoration which is given to the Incarnate Word and equally to the Father and the Holy Spirit, and greatly fosters this adoration'" (971–972).

**Protestant Response:** We should honor the memory of Mary, but Roman Catholic veneration of Mary seems in fact to be a kind of worship of Mary. We should worship only God, not any created being.

My glory I will not give to another. (Isa. 48:11)

I, John, am the one who heard and saw these things. And when I heard and saw them, I fell down to worship at the feet of the angel who showed them to me, but he said to me, "*You must not do that!* I am a fellow servant with you and your brothers the prophets, and with those who keep the words of this book. *Worship God.* (Rev. 22:8–9)

**See also:** chapter 51 (worship).

## C. Christ's Redemptive Work
## 6. Mary as Co-Mediatrix with Christ

**Catechism of the Catholic Church:** "In a wholly singular way *she cooperated by her obedience, faith, hope, and burning charity in the Savior's work of restoring supernatural life to souls.* For this reason she is a mother to us in the order of grace.

"This motherhood of Mary in the order of grace continues uninterruptedly from the consent which she loyally gave at the Annunciation and which she sustained without wavering beneath the cross, until the eternal fulfillment of all the elect. Taken up to heaven she did not lay aside *this saving office* but *by her manifold intercession continues to bring us the gifts of eternal salvation.* . . . Therefore the Blessed Virgin is invoked in the Church under the titles of Advocate, Helper, Benefactress, and Mediatrix [*mediatrix* is the feminine of mediator]." (968–969).

**Protestant Response:** Salvation is earned for us by Christ alone, and the New Testament is saturated with praise to Christ alone, not to Mary, for our salvation.

---

18. Ibid., item 2.

> And being found in human form, he humbled himself by becoming obedient to the point of death, even death on a cross. Therefore God has highly exalted *him* and bestowed on *him* the name that is above every name, so that *at the name of Jesus every knee should bow*, in heaven and on earth and under the earth, *and every tongue confess that Jesus Christ is Lord, to the glory of God the Father*. (Phil. 2:8–11)

> For there is one God, and there is *one mediator* between God and men, *the man Christ Jesus*. (1 Tim. 2:5)

> Then I looked, and I heard around the throne and the living creatures and the elders the voice of many angels, numbering myriads of myriads and thousands of thousands, saying with a loud voice, *"Worthy is the Lamb who was slain, to receive power and wealth and wisdom and might and honor and glory and blessing!"* And I heard every creature in heaven and on earth and under the earth and in the sea, and all that is in them, saying, "To him who sits on the throne and to the Lamb be blessing and honor and glory and might forever and ever!" And the four living creatures said, "Amen!" and the elders fell down and worshiped. (Rev. 5:11–14)

**See also:** chapter 27 (atonement).

## D. SALVATION

### 7. Justification Is by Faith plus the Sacraments, Which Produces Moral Purity, and It Is Not Completed in This Life

**Catechism of the Catholic Church:** "The Church affirms that for believers *the sacraments of the New Covenant are necessary for salvation*" (1129).[19]

"*Justification is* not only the remission of sins, but *also the sanctification and renewal of the interior man*." (1989).

**Protestant Response:** Justification is by faith alone (this is the heart of the gospel). Justification is a legal declaration by God that we are counted not guilty but righteous in his sight. Justification does not produce moral purity in us (which is the work of sanctification).

> For by grace you have been saved through faith. And this is not your own doing; it is the gift of God, not a result of works, so that no one may boast. (Eph. 2:8–9)

---

19. The seven sacraments recognized by the Roman Catholic Church are listed in section 9 below.

Yet we know that a person is not justified by works of the law but through faith in Jesus Christ, so we also have believed in Christ Jesus, in order to be justified by faith in Christ and not by works of the law, because by works of the law no one will be justified. (Gal. 2:16)

**See also:** chapters 36 (justification) and 38 (sanctification).

## 8. Regeneration and Justification Come through Baptism

**Catechism of the Catholic Church:** "Through Baptism we are freed from sin and reborn as sons of God; we become members of Christ, are incorporated into the Church and made sharers in her mission" (1213).

"Children also have need of the new birth in Baptism to be freed from the power of darkness and brought into the realm of the freedom of the children of God" (1250).

"By Baptism *all sins* are forgiven, original sin and all personal sins, as well as all punishment for sin" (1263).

"Baptism not only purifies from all sins, but also makes the neophyte 'a new creature,' an adopted son of God, who has become a 'partaker of the divine nature,' member of Christ and co-heir with him, and a temple of the Holy Spirit" (1265).

**Protestant Response:** Baptism is only an outward physical symbol of an inward work of God, and, like all other outward "works," it does not save anyone.

Yet we know that *a person is not justified by works of the law but through faith in Jesus Christ*, so we also have believed in Christ Jesus, in order to be justified by faith in Christ and not by works of the law, because by works of the law no one will be justified. (Gal. 2:16)

Look: I, Paul, say to you that if you accept circumcision, Christ will be of no advantage to you. I testify again to every man who accepts circumcision that he is obligated to keep the whole law. You are severed from Christ, you who would be justified by the law; you have fallen away from grace. (Gal. 5:2–4)

A reliance on baptism for salvation does make a difference in people's lives. Piper observes, "The teaching of baptismal regeneration. . . . has produced, I would say, untold ill-founded confidence in the people of God who have little or no personal faith, or relationship with Christ, or love to Jesus. Yet, because of their baptism [they] believe they are heaven-bound."[20]

**See also:** chapter 49 (baptism).

20. Ibid., item 3

## 9. Saving Power of the Sacraments

**Catechism of the Catholic Church:** "There are seven sacraments in the Church: Baptism, Confirmation or Chrismation, Eucharist, Penance, Anointing of the Sick, Holy Orders, and Matrimony" (1113).

"Celebrated worthily in faith, *the sacraments confer the grace that they signify*. They are efficacious because in them Christ himself is at work: it is he who baptizes, he who acts in his sacraments in order to communicate the grace that each sacrament signifies" (1127).

"This is the meaning of the Church's affirmation that *the sacraments act ex opere operato* [that is, 'by the very fact that the action is performed'], i.e., by virtue of the saving work of Christ, accomplished once for all" (1128).

**Protestant Response:** No works (or sacraments) can earn us merit before God or contribute to our salvation.

> We know that *a person is not justified by works of the law but through faith in Jesus Christ*, so we also have believed in Christ Jesus, in order to be justified by faith in Christ and not by works of the law, because by works of the law no one will be justified. (Gal. 2:16)

> For by grace you have been saved through faith. And this is not your own doing; *it is the gift of God, not a result of works*, so that no one may boast. (Eph. 2:8–9)

The spiritual danger of the Roman Catholic position is that people will begin to put their trust more in the sacraments than directly in Christ himself, and that use of the sacraments will become a "work" that is performed in order to attempt to somehow earn us favor with God.

**See also:** chapter 48 (means of grace), 49 (baptism), and 50 (the Lord's Supper).

## 10. Purgatory as a Place of Suffering before Those Who Are Saved Can Enter Heaven

**Catechism of the Catholic Church:** "All who die in God's grace and friendship, but still imperfectly purified, are indeed assured of their eternal salvation; but *after death they undergo purification, so as to achieve the holiness necessary to enter the joy of heaven*" (1030).

"The Church gives the name *Purgatory* to this final purification of the elect, which is entirely different from the punishment of the damned. The Church formulated her doctrine of faith on Purgatory especially at the Councils of Florence and Trent" (1031).

**Protestant Response:** Believers who die go directly to heaven to be with Christ at once.

And as they were stoning Stephen, he called out, "Lord Jesus, receive my spirit." (Acts 7:59)

There is therefore now no condemnation for those who are in Christ Jesus. (Rom. 8:1)

And he said to him, "Truly, I say to you, *today* you will be with me in paradise." (Luke 23:43)

My desire is *to depart and be with Christ*, for that is far better. (Phil. 1:23)

I heard a voice from heaven saying, "Write this: Blessed are the dead who die in the Lord from now on." "Blessed indeed," says the Spirit, "that they may rest from their labors, for their deeds follow them!" (Rev. 14:13).

**See also:** chapter 41 (death and the intermediate state).

## 11. People Who Have Not Heard of Christ or Do Not Believe in Him Can Be Saved

**Catechism of the Catholic Church:** "Those who, through no fault of their own, *do not know the Gospel of Christ or his Church, but who nevertheless seek God with a sincere heart*, and, moved by grace, try in their actions to do his will as they know it through the dictates of their conscience—those too may achieve eternal salvation" (847; see 839–848).

**Protestant Response:** The Bible gives us no grounds for believing that people who have not trusted in Christ will be saved, nor does the Bible encourage us to believe this.

Jesus said to him, "I am the way, and the truth, and the life. *No one comes to the Father except through me.*" (John 14:6)

And there is salvation in no one else, for there is *no other name* under heaven given among men by which we must be saved. (Acts 4:12)

For "everyone who calls on the name of the Lord will be saved." But how are they to call on him in whom they have not believed? *And how are they to believe in him of whom they have never heard?* And how are they to hear without someone preaching? And how are they to preach unless they are sent?. . . . *So faith comes from hearing, and hearing through the word of Christ.* (Rom. 10:13–17)

**See also:** chapter 7 (necessity of Scripture).

## E. THE CHURCH

## 12. Roman Catholic Church as the One True Church

**Catechism of the Catholic Church:** : "*The sole Church of Christ* [is that] which our Savior, after his Resurrection, entrusted to Peter's pastoral care, commissioning him and the other apostles to extend and rule it. . . . This Church, constituted and organized as a society in the present world, subsists in (*subsistit in*) *the Catholic Church*, which is governed by the successor of Peter [that is, the Pope] and by the bishops in communion with him" (816; see 815–819, 837–838).

**Protestant Response:** The true church is wherever the gospel is truly preached and baptism and the Lord's Supper are rightly observed. The true successors of Peter are those who preach the same gospel that he preached.

> Christ is faithful over God's house as a son. And *we are his house*, if indeed we hold fast our confidence and our boasting in our hope. (Heb. 3:6)

> But even if we or an angel from heaven should preach to you a gospel contrary to the one we preached to you, let him be accursed. As we have said before, so now I say again: If anyone is preaching to you a gospel contrary to the one you received, let him be accursed. (Gal. 1:8–9)

**See also:** chapter 44 (the nature, marks, and purposes of the church)

## 13. Priesthood as a Necessary System for Dispensing Grace

**Catechism of the Catholic Church:** "The *ordained priesthood* guarantees that it really is Christ who acts in the sacraments through the Holy Spirit for the Church. The saving mission entrusted by the Father to his incarnate Son was *committed to the apostles and through them to their successors*: they receive the Spirit of Jesus to act in his name and in his person" (1120).

**Protestant Response:** All God's people are now a kingdom of priests, and all minister grace to one another through the gifts of the Holy Spirit.

> To each is given the manifestation of the Spirit for the common good. (1 Cor. 12:7)

> But you are a chosen race, *a royal priesthood*, a holy nation. (1 Peter 2:9)

> As each has received a gift, *use it to serve one another, as good stewards of God's varied grace.* (1 Peter 4:10)

**See also:** chapter 48 (means of grace) and 52 (gifts of the Holy Spirit).

# QUESTIONS FOR PERSONAL APPLICATION

1. In what areas is your church "purer"? In what areas do you think it is "less pure"?

2. On a scale of one to ten (one equals less pure; ten equals more pure), where would you rank your church in each of the categories that mark a purer church?

3. What do you think that you should be doing in order to work for greater purity in your church? Does the fact that you recognize a specific need in the church mean that God is calling you (rather than someone else) to meet that need?

4. Do you know of other churches in your area that you would consider purer than your own? What are the reasons that you might think it right to stay in your church even though it may not be the purest church you know of?

5. Are there marks of a purer church that evangelicals generally in this century have been negligent in emphasizing?

6. Since the first century, do you think that by and large the church has continued to increase in purity over time? Can you give specific reasons to support your answer?

7. In your lifetime, what encouraging signs do you see that the church is increasing in purity? What signs do you see that the church is increasing in unity?

8. In what ways do you think your church could grow in unity among its members?

9. In what ways could your church demonstrate greater unity with other true churches in the same geographical area? What do you think are the barriers to that unity (if any)? In what ways could that unity be expressed? What might be the benefits of such expressions of unity?

10. Are you in a church where you have wondered if God would have you leave and join another church? After reading this chapter, do you now think that you should stay in your present church or leave it? Has there been significant change for the better in your church in the last ten years? If you knew that the church were to remain substantially the same for the next ten years, would you decide to stay now or to leave it?

11. What are some ways in which the worldwide unity of true believers is already being expressed and demonstrated? What would the church around the world look like if there were much greater demonstration of the unity of the church? What would be the result in the world as a whole?

12. If a community already has several active and effective evangelical churches, is there any justification

## Special Terms

*Eastern church*
*purity of the church*
*separation*
*unity of the church*
*Western church*

for another evangelical denomination to attempt to plant its own church in that community?

13. Do you think it hinders evangelism and witness to society generally when the popular culture thinks of unbelieving or false churches and believing churches both as "Christians"? Can anything be done to change that impression?

14. What kinds of unity and cooperation can appropriately be demonstrated with believers within the Roman Catholic Church today? What are the limits to such cooperation?

# BIBLIOGRAPHY

(For an explanation of this bibliography see the note on the bibliography to chapter 1, pp. 23–24. Complete bibliographical data may be found on pp. 1489–96.)

## SECTIONS IN EVANGELICAL SYSTEMATIC THEOLOGIES

1. *Anglican (Episcopalian)*
   1882–92 . . . . . Litton, 380–86, 413–18
   2001 . . . . . . . . Packer, 204–6
   2013 . . . . . . . . Bird, 699–727
   2013 . . . . . . . . Bray, 847, 864

2. *Arminian (Wesleyan or Methodist)*
   1875–76 . . . . . Pope, 3:267–79
   1940 . . . . . . . . Wiley, 3:112–13
   1983 . . . . . . . . Carter, 2:594–95
   1992 . . . . . . . . Oden, 3: 297–368
   2002 . . . . . . . . Cottrell, 400–17

3. *Baptist*
   1990–95 . . . . . Garrett, 2:589–602, 659–88
   2007 . . . . . . . . Akin, 766–67
   2013 . . . . . . . . Erickson, 1008–15

4. *Dispensational*
   2002–2005 . . Geisler, 4:51–52
   2017 . . . . . . . . MacArthur and Mayhue, 795–97

5. *Lutheran*
   1917–24 . . . . . Pieper, 3:423–27
   1934 . . . . . . . . Mueller, 556–62

6. *Reformed (or Presbyterian)*
   1559 . . . . . . . . Calvin, 2:1011–53 (4.1–2)
   1679–85 . . . . . Turretin, *IET*, 3:27–29, 121–46, 235–45
   1894 . . . . . . . . Shedd, 809
   1906–11 . . . . . Bavinck, *RD*, 4:307–25
   1910 . . . . . . . . Vos, 3:177
   1887–1921 . . . Warfield, *SSW*, 1:299–307
   1937–66 . . . . . Murray, *CW*, 1:269–91; *CW*, 2:321–36
   1998 . . . . . . . . Reymond, 888–91
   2008 . . . . . . . . Van Genderen and Velema, 694–729
   2010 . . . . . . . . Allen and Swain, 311–38
   2011 . . . . . . . . Horton, 828–71

2013.........Frame, 498–501, 926, 1022–23

2013.........Culver, 879–88

2017.........Barrett, 586–608

2019.........Letham, 792–93, 810–11

### 7. *Renewal (or charismatic/Pentecostal)*

1988–92.....Williams, 3:25–35

1993.........Menzies and Horton, 162–63

1995.........Horton, 538–43

2008.........Duffield and Van Cleave, 445–49

## Sections in Representative Roman Catholic Systematic Theologies

### 1. *Roman Catholic: Traditional*

1955.........Ott, 290–309

### 2. *Roman Catholic: Post–Vatican II*

1980.........McBrien, 2:854–58

2012.........*CCC*, paragraphs 781–810

## Other Works

Allison, Gregg R. *Roman Catholic Theology and Practice: An Evangelical Assessment*. Wheaton, IL: Crossway, 2014.

———. *Sojourners and Strangers: The Doctrine of the Church*. Wheaton, IL: Crossway, 2012, 161–178.

Allison, Gregg R., and Chris Castaldo. *The Unfinished Reformation: What Unites and Divides Catholics and Protestants After 500 Years*. Grand Rapids: Zondervan, 2016.

Bromiley, G. W. "Unity." In *EDT*, 1127–28.

———. *The Unity and Disunity of the Church*. Grand Rapids: Eerdmans, 1963.

Burns, J. Patout. *Cyprian the Bishop*. London: Routledge, 2002.

Carson, Donald A. "Evangelicals, Ecumenism and the Church." In *Evangelical Affirmations*. Edited by Kenneth S. Kantzer and Carl F. H. Henry. Grand Rapids: Zondervan, 1990, 347–85.

Cleveland, Christena. *Disunity in Christ: Uncovering the Hidden Forces That Keep Us Apart*. Downers Grove, IL: InterVarsity Press, 2013.

Dever, Mark. "The Church." In *A Theology for the Church*, edited by Daniel L. Akin et al., 819–21. Nashville: B&H, 2007.

Frame, John M. *Evangelical Reunion: Denominations and the One Body of Christ*. Grand Rapids: Baker, 1991.

Gillies, Donald. *Unity in the Dark*. London: Banner of Truth Trust, 1964.

Goppelt, Leonhard. "The Purity and Unity of the Church: Heresy and the Sins of the Christians." In *Apostolic and Post-Apostolic Times*. Translated by Robert A. Guelich. Grand Rapids: Baker, 1980.

Kik, J. Marcellus. *Ecumenism and the Evangelical*. Philadelphia: Presbyterian & Reformed, 1958.

Lim, Paul Chang-Ha. *In Pursuit of Purity, Unity, and Liberty: Richard Baxter's Puritan Ecclesiology in Its Seventeenth-Century Context*. Leiden: Brill, 2004.

Murch, James DeForest. *Cooperation without Compromise*. Grand Rapids: Eerdmans, 1956.

Puritan and Reformed Studies Conference. *Approaches to Reformation of the Church*. London: *The Evangelical* magazine, 1965. Contains papers by D. W. Marshall, D. P. Kingdon, J. I. Packer, G. S. R. Cox, S. M. Houghton, and D. M. Lloyd-Jones.

Radmacher, Earl D. "The Interpretation and Application of Separation in 2 Corinthians 6:14–7:1." ThM thesis, Dallas Theological Seminary, 1959.

Reasoner, M. "Purity and Impurity." In *DPL*, 775–76.

Tinder, D. G. "Denominations." In *EDT3*, 239–40.

Weber, T. P. "Ecumenism." In *EDT3*, 261–63.

Whitlock, Luder G., Jr. *Divided We Fall: Overcoming a History of Christian Disunity*. Phillipsburg, NJ: P&R, 2017.

## SCRIPTURE MEMORY PASSAGE

**Ephesians 4:14–16:** So that we may no longer be children, tossed to and fro by the waves and carried about by every wind of doctrine, by human cunning, by craftiness in deceitful schemes. Rather, speaking the truth in love, we are to grow up in every way into him who is the head, into Christ, from whom the whole body, joined and held together by every joint with which it is equipped, when each part is working properly, makes the body grow so that it builds itself up in love.

## HYMN

**"Blest Be the Tie That Binds"**

This hymn speaks of the unity or the "tie" that binds the hearts of Christians together in love. It continues to speak of fellowship as like the fellowship of heaven: it is "like to that above." It also speaks of sharing in prayer and concern for each other and bearing of one another's burdens. The hymn goes on to speak of our hope that we will one day be united in "perfect love and friendship" for eternity in heaven.

Blest be the tie that binds
    Our hearts in Christian love:
The fellowship of kindred minds
    Is like to that above.

Before our Father's throne
    We pour our ardent prayers;
Our fears, our hopes, our aims, are one,
    Our comforts and our cares.

We share our mutual woes,
    Our mutual burdens bear,
And often for each other flows
    The sympathizing tear.

When we asunder part,
    It gives us inward pain;
But we shall still be joined in heart,
    And hope to meet again.

This glorious hope revives
    Our courage by the way,
While each in expectation lives,
    And longs to see the day.

From sorrow, toil and pain,
    And sin, we shall be free;
And perfect love and friendship reign
    Through all eternity.

Author: John Fawcett, 1782

# CONTEMPORARY WORSHIP SONG

## "Salvation Belongs To Our God"

*Salvation belongs to our God,*
*Who sits upon the throne,*
*And unto the Lamb.*
*Praise and glory wisdom and thanks,*
*Honor and power and strength—*

*Chorus*
*Be to our God forever and ever,*
*Be to our God forever and ever,*
*Be to our God forever and ever,*
*Amen.*

*And we the redeemed shall be strong*
*In purpose and unity,*
*Declaring aloud,*
*Praise and glory wisdom and thanks,*
*Honor and power and strength—*

Words by Adrian Howard and Pat Turner[21]

# CHAPTER 46

# The Power of the Church

*What kind of authority does the church have?*
*How should church discipline function?*

## EXPLANATION AND SCRIPTURAL BASIS

When we look at the powerful governments of the world and at business and educational organizations that have great influence, and then we consider our local churches, or even our denominational headquarters, the church may seem to us to be weak and ineffective. Moreover, when we recognize the rapid growth of evil that is seen daily in our society, we may wonder if the church has power to make any changes at all.

On the other hand, in some countries the officially recognized church has great influence on the conduct of national affairs. This was certainly true of the influence of the Roman Catholic Church in former times in some southern European and Latin American countries (and is still true today to some extent). It was true of the Church of England in previous centuries, and of John Calvin's church in Geneva, Switzerland, while he was alive, and of the church founded by the pilgrims in the Massachusetts Bay Colony in 1620. Situations like these where the church appears to have great influence cause us to ask whether Scripture places any limitations on the church's power.

We may define the power of the church as follows: *the power of the church is its God-given authority to carry on spiritual warfare, proclaim the gospel, and exercise church discipline.*

Although these three areas overlap and could be treated in any order, "spiritual warfare" will be treated first since it is the broadest category. This perspective on the church's power also reminds us that the power of the church, unlike the worldly influence exercised by human armies and governments, directly affects the spiritual realm.

### A. SPIRITUAL WARFARE

Paul reminds the Corinthians, "For though we walk in the flesh, we are not waging war according to the flesh. For *the weapons of our warfare are not of the flesh but have divine power to destroy strongholds*" (2 Cor. 10:3–4). These weapons, used against demonic forces that hinder the spread of the gospel and the progress of the church, include such things as prayer, worship, the authority to rebuke demonic forces, the words of Scripture, faith, and righteous conduct on the part of the members of the church.

(Paul gives further details about our spiritual conflict and the armor we wear for it in Eph. 6:10–18.)

When we consider this spiritual power in a broad sense, it certainly includes the power of the gospel to break through sin and hardened opposition and awaken faith in the hearts of unbelievers (see Rom. 10:17; James 1:18; 1 Peter 1:23). But this power also includes spiritual power that will render demonic opposition to the gospel ineffective. We see examples of this in Acts 13:8–11, where Paul pronounced judgment on Elymas the magician, who was opposing the preaching of the gospel, and in Acts 16:16–18, where Paul rebuked an evil spirit in the soothsaying girl who was annoying Paul while he proclaimed the gospel.[1] Such spiritual power to defeat evil opposition was seen frequently in the early church and was evident in instances such as the freeing of Peter from prison (Acts 12:1–17), and perhaps in the subsequent judgment on King Herod Agrippa I (Acts 12:20–24).[2]

Yet Paul realizes that he can use this spiritual power not only against those outside the church who oppose the gospel but also against those within the church who are active opponents of his apostolic ministry. He says about some arrogant troublemakers in the church, "I will come to you soon, if the Lord wills, and I will find out not the talk of these arrogant people but their power. For the kingdom of God does not consist in talk but in power" (1 Cor. 4:19–20). Such power was not to be trifled with, for it was the same power of the Holy Spirit that had brought death to Ananias and Sapphira (Acts 5:1–11) and blindness to Elymas (Acts 13:8–11). Paul did not wish to use this power in a judgmental capacity, but he was prepared to do so if necessary. Later he wrote again to the Corinthians that his actions when present would be as powerful as his letters when absent (2 Cor. 10:8–11), and he warned those who opposed his authority and had sinned publicly and not repented, "If I come again I will not spare them—since you seek proof that Christ is speaking in me. . . . For we also are weak in him, but in dealing with you we will live with him by the power of God" (2 Cor. 13:2–4). He then adds a final reminder of his reluctance to use this authority, telling them that he is writing before he comes "that when I come I may not have to be severe in my use of the authority that the Lord has given me for building up and not for tearing down" (2 Cor. 13:10).

Now we may question whether the church today has the same degree of spiritual power that the apostles Peter or Paul did. Certainly there is a distinction between the apostles and the other early Christians even in the book of Acts (note that immediately

---

1. Jesus often rebuked demonic spirits that created disturbances when he was ministering to people; see Mark 1:23–26; 5:1–13, et al.

2. The text does not specify that Herod's death was in any way connected to the "earnest prayer" (Acts 12:5) that was made for Peter by the church, but the fact that the narrative about Herod's death follows immediately upon the story of his killing James the brother of John with the sword and his putting Peter in prison certainly hints at the fact that God intended this as a judgment upon one of the primary enemies of the church, showing that no opposition could stand against the progress of the gospel. This understanding is also supported by the fact that the sentence immediately following the narrative of Herod's death is, "But the word of God increased and multiplied" (Acts 12:24).

after the death of Ananias and Sapphira "many signs and wonders" were done "by the hands of the apostles," but "none of the rest dared join them, but the people held them in high esteem," Acts 5:12–13). Moreover, Paul did not instruct any leaders of the church at Corinth, or even Timothy or Titus, to exercise that spiritual power at Corinth against his opponents. He spoke about the power which the Lord "has given *me*" (2 Cor. 13:10), not about the power which the Lord had given to the church or to Christians generally.

On the other hand, Paul did direct the Corinthian church to exercise church discipline in a case of incest in the church at Corinth, and to do it "when you are assembled in the name of the Lord Jesus and my spirit is present, with the power of our Lord Jesus" (1 Cor. 5:4). Moreover, the descriptions of spiritual warfare in Ephesians 6:10–18 and 2 Corinthians 10:3–4 seem applicable to Christians generally, and few today would deny that the church has authority to pray against and to speak with authority against demonic opposition to the work of the gospel.[3] So there would seem to be *some* significant degree of spiritual power against evil opposition that God is willing to grant to the church in every age (including the present one). Perhaps it is impossible to define more specifically the degree of spiritual power God will grant to the church in times of conflict against evil, but we do not need to know the details in advance; our calling is simply to be faithful to Scripture in praying and in exercising church discipline and then to leave the rest in God's hands, knowing that he will grant sufficient power to accomplish his purposes through the church.

## B. THE KEYS OF THE KINGDOM

The phrase "the keys of the kingdom" occurs only once in the Bible, in Matthew 16:19, where Jesus is speaking to Peter: "I will give you the keys of the kingdom of heaven, and whatever you bind on earth shall be bound in heaven, and whatever you loose on earth shall be loosed in heaven" (Matt. 16:19). What is the meaning of these "keys of the kingdom of heaven"?[4]

Elsewhere in the New Testament a key (whether literal or metaphorical) always implies *authority to open a door and give entrance to a place or realm.* Jesus says, "Woe to you lawyers! For you have taken away the key of knowledge. You did not enter yourselves, and you hindered those who were entering" (Luke 11:52). Moreover, Jesus says in Revelation 1:18, "I have the keys of Death and Hades," implying that he has the authority to grant entrance and exit from those realms (cf. Rev. 3:7; 9:1; 20:1 and the messianic prediction in Isa. 22:22).

The "keys of the kingdom of heaven" therefore represent at least the authority to

---

3. See chapter 20, pp. 541–66, on conflict with demonic forces in general, and pp. 542–43 on the question of "strategic level spiritual warfare."

4. The rest of this section discussing the keys of the

kingdom of heaven is adapted from the article, "Keys of the Kingdom" by Wayne Grudem, in *EDT*, 604–5, and is used here by permission.

preach the gospel of Christ (cf. Matt. 16:16) and thus to open the door of the kingdom of heaven and allow people to enter.

Peter first used this authority by preaching the gospel at Pentecost (Acts 2:14–42). But the other apostles also were given this authority in a primary sense (they wrote the gospel in permanent form in the New Testament). And all believers have this key in a secondary sense, for they can all share the gospel with others and thereby open the kingdom of heaven to those who will enter it.

But is there any other authority, in addition to this, that Jesus implies by the phrase "the keys of the kingdom of heaven"? There are two factors suggesting that the authority of the keys here also includes *the authority to exercise discipline within the church*: (1) The plural *keys* suggests authority over more than one door. Thus, more than simply entrance into the kingdom is implied; some authority *within* the kingdom is also suggested. (2) Jesus completes the promise about the keys with a statement about binding and loosing, which closely parallels another saying of his in Matthew 18, in which binding and loosing mean placing under church discipline and releasing from church discipline: "If he refuses to listen even to the church, let him be to you as a Gentile and a tax collector. Truly, I say to you, whatever you *bind* on earth shall be bound in heaven, and whatever you *loose* on earth shall be loosed in heaven" (Matt. 18:17–18). But if binding and loosing clearly refer to church discipline in Matthew 18, then it seems likely that they would also refer to church discipline in Matthew 16, where Jesus' words are very similar.[5]

This understanding of binding and loosing in terms of church discipline also fits the context of Matthew 16:19, for, on this understanding, after promising to build his church (v. 18), Jesus promises to give not only the authority to open the door of entrance into the kingdom but also some administrative authority to regulate the conduct of people once they are inside.[6] Therefore, it seems that "the keys of the kingdom of heaven" that Jesus promised to Peter in Matthew 16:19 included both (1) ability to admit people to the kingdom through preaching the gospel and (2) authority to exercise church discipline for those who do enter.

In Matthew 16:16–19, Jesus does not indicate whether the authority of the keys will later be given to others besides Peter. But certainly the authority to preach the gospel is

---

5. The statement in Matt. 16:19 uses singular pronouns for "whatever" and "you" (referring to Peter), while Matt. 18:18 uses plurals (referring to Christians generally), but the same Greek words are used for "bind" (*deō*) and "loose" (*luō*), and the grammatical construction (periphrastic future perfect) is the same.

6. Some have argued that binding and loosing do not refer to actions of church discipline but to an authority to make various rules for conduct, because in the rabbinic literature that comes from Jewish teachers around the time of Jesus the words *bind* and *loose* are sometimes used for forbidding and permitting various kinds of conduct. This interpretation does not

seem persuasive, however, because these rabbinic statements are a much more distant parallel than the statement of Jesus himself in Matt. 18:18, where church discipline is clearly in view. Moreover, it is difficult to know whether any of the rabbinic parallels predate the time of the New Testament, and the existing evidence is not sufficient to show that such words would have functioned as technical terms in the ordinary vocabulary of Jesus and his hearers—in fact, Matt. 18:18 shows that they did not function as technical terms to describe making new rules for human conduct because they were used rather to refer to church discipline in that verse.

given to others at a later time, and in Matthew 18:18 Jesus does state explicitly that the authority to exercise church discipline is given to the church generally whenever it meets and corporately carries out such discipline ("Tell it to the church," Matt. 18:17). Thus both aspects of the authority of the keys, though first given to Peter, were soon expanded to include the authority given to the other apostles and then to the church as a whole. *In preaching the gospel and in exercising discipline the church now exercises the authority of the keys of the kingdom.*

Yet the authority of the keys with respect to church discipline is not completely unlimited. It will only be effective against true sin (cf. Matt. 18:15), sin as defined by God's Word. The church does not have authority on its own to invent new standards about what is morally right and wrong, for the authority to define right and wrong belongs to God alone (see Rom. 1:32; 2:16; 3:4–8; 9:20; Ps. 119:89, 142, 160; Matt. 5:18). The church can only declare and teach what God has already commanded in his Word. Nor can the authority of the keys involve authority to forgive sins in any absolute sense, because in Scripture it is clear that that can only be done by God himself (Isa. 43:25; 55:7; Mark 2:7, 10; Ps. 103:3; 1 John 1:9).[7] Therefore the authority to carry out discipline in the church is an authority that must be carried out in accordance with the standards of Scripture.

Is it possible to be any more specific about the kind of spiritual authority that is involved in this use of the keys of the kingdom of heaven? Both Matthew 16:19 and 18:18 use an unusual Greek verbal construction (a periphrastic future perfect). It is explicitly translated by the NASB (and ESV mg.), "Whatever you shall bind on earth *shall have been bound* in heaven, and whatever you shall loose on earth *shall have been loosed* in heaven."[8] Several other examples of this construction show that it indicates not just a future action ("shall be bound"), for which a common Greek tense was available (future passive), but rather *an action that would be completed before some future point*, with effects that would continue to be felt.[9] Thus Jesus is teaching that church discipline will have heavenly sanction. But it is not as if the church must wait for God to endorse its actions after the actions have occurred. Whenever the church *enacts discipline*, it can be confident that God has already begun the process spiritually. Whenever it *releases from discipline*, forgives the sinner, and restores personal relationships, the church can be confident that God has already begun the restoration spiritually (cf. John 20:23). In this way Jesus promises that the spiritual relationship between God and the person subject to discipline will be immediately affected in ways consistent with the direction of the church's disciplinary action. Legitimate church discipline, therefore, involves the awesome certainty that corresponding heavenly discipline has already begun.

---

7. In John 20:23, the forgiveness of sins by the disciples is best understood as freeing from church discipline and restoring personal relationships in a sense similar to the "loosing" of Matt. 16:19 and 18:18.

8. See the grammatical discussion in D. A. Carson, "Matthew," *EBC*, 8:370–72.

9. See examples in Luke 12:52; Gen. 43:9; 44:32; Ex. 12:6; Sirach 7:25; Hermas, *Similitudes* 5.4.2; *Letter of Aristeas* 40.

Moreover, this teaching on the power of the keys has a significant application to individual Christians who begin to be subject to the discipline of a true church: Christians should submit to this discipline and not run from it because God himself has also put them under discipline for that sin.

## C. The Power of the Church and the Power of the State

The previous sections have discussed spiritual power and spiritual warfare to be exercised by the church. But should the church ever use physical force (weapons and armies, for example) to carry out its mission? The phrase commonly used to refer to the idea of physical, worldly warfare is "to take up the sword."

There are several indications in Scripture that the church must never take up the sword to carry out its purposes in the new covenant age. This was a dreadful mistake made in the Crusades, when church-sponsored armies marched across Europe and Asia to attempt to reclaim the land of Israel. In these cases the church was trying to use physical force to bring about its triumph over earthly territories. But Jesus said, "My kingdom is not of this world. If my kingdom were of this world, my servants would have been fighting" (John 18:36). The church has the power of the keys, which is spiritual power. It is to carry out spiritual battles using spiritual weapons but is not to use the power of the sword to accomplish its purposes. "The weapons of our warfare are not of the flesh" (2 Cor. 10:4).

Although the church should not use the sword (physical force and weapons) to attempt to advance the kingdom of God, defending a church's attendees against a possible mass murder attack by a terrorist or madman is another matter. In an age where such attacks have tragically occurred, some churches have established internal security officers for that defensive purpose. This seems to me to be a wise and appropriate decision, brought about by a newly dangerous situation.[10]

Certainly God does give *to civil government* the right to bear the sword, that is, to use force to restrain and punish evil in the world (Rom. 13:1–7). But there is no indication that the power of government is to be used to enforce adherence to Christianity upon any people.[11] Moreover, there are several indications that Jesus refused to use the power of physical force to compel people to accept the gospel. For example, when a Samaritan village would not receive Jesus, James and John asked, "Lord, do you want us to tell fire

---

10. Somewhat analogous protections for the safety of Christian believers may be seen in Jesus' direction to his disciples to carry a sword (used for self-defense in the ancient world) in Luke 22:36; the locked doors for the purpose of protecting the early disciples after Jesus' resurrection (John 20:19); and the apparently locked gate at Mary's house that required Peter to keep on knocking (Acts 12:12-16).

11. See my further discussion of the idea that the civil government should never try to compel people to follow any

particular religion in Wayne Grudem, *Politics according to the Bible* (Grand Rapids: Zondervan, 2010), 23–29. Edmund Clowney rightly observes, "We may not suppose that Christ denied to his apostles the right to bring in his kingdom with the sword, but conceded that right to Pilate" ("The Biblical Theology of the Church," in *The Church in the Bible and the World*, ed. D. A. Carson [Exeter: Paternoster; Grand Rapids: Baker, 1987], 33).

to come down from heaven and consume them?" (Luke 9:54). But Jesus "rebuked them" (v. 55) for even making that suggestion. Jesus came the first time to offer the gospel to all who would receive it, not to execute punishment on those who rejected it. This is why he could say, "For God did not send his Son into the world to condemn the world, but in order that the world might be saved through him" (John 3:17). He will one day come again in judgment, at the end of the church age, but during this age it is not the prerogative of the church to use physical force to carry out judgment.

Jesus clearly distinguished between the authority granted to the government and the authority that God exercises in our personal allegiance to him when he said, "Therefore render to Caesar the things that are Caesar's, and to God the things that are God's" (Matt. 22:21). And though Jesus recognized the authority of civil government, he refused to usurp that authority himself, telling someone, "Man, who made me a judge or arbitrator over you?" with respect to a matter of family inheritance (Luke 12:13–14).

A further reason why the government should not use force to require allegiance to Christianity is that in the new covenant, membership in the church and allegiance to Christ must be voluntary. As any parent who has raised children will attest, while parents can bring their children to church and teach them the Bible, not even parents can compel children to put their trust in Christ for salvation. That must be a personal decision and a voluntary one. And if parents cannot force their children to believe in Christ, surely it is futile for civil government to think it can do this. In fact, faith in Christ, to be truly held and practiced, cannot be compelled by force. If it is compelled, it changes its essential quality and is no longer a voluntary act of the individual, and cannot be true faith. From this it also follows that *the civil government should not enforce laws requiring or prohibiting kinds of church doctrine or abridging the people's freedom to worship as they choose.*

On the other hand, the church does not and should not rule over the state, as if it were some kind of higher authority over the state; it is not. Rather, the authority of the church and that of the state belong to distinct spheres (Matt. 22:21; John 18:36; 2 Cor. 10:3–4), and each should respect the authority God has given the other in its own sphere of operation.

These limitations on the activities of the church and the state are different from the practice of the Catholic Church through much of the Middle Ages, where it often had more power than the civil government. These principles also differ from the practice of the Church of England, which is subject to the authority of the Queen and Parliament in the appointment of bishops and any change in doctrinal standards. The failure to respect the distinct roles of church and state is seen in many Roman Catholic countries today, where the church still has strong influence on the government, and in the compulsory membership in state-sponsored Protestant churches of Northern Europe after the Reformation, a situation that caused many emigrants to flee to America for religious freedom.

However, it should be said that the degree of state-enforced religion in Protestant or Catholic countries is mild indeed compared to state-sponsored and state-enforced religion in most Muslim countries today, as well as in many Hindu and Buddhist countries. In fact, it is difficult to find genuine freedom of religion apart from the strong influence of healthy evangelical Christianity in any country around the world (except where various religions are so weak or so evenly balanced that no one religion has dominant political power). Whenever Christians are involved in the political realm, they ought clearly to affirm freedom of religion as a political policy that is nonnegotiable, and they should be willing to defend that freedom for religions other than their own as well. The Christian faith can stand on its own two feet and compete very well in the marketplace of ideas in any society and in any culture, provided it has the freedom to do so.

Finally, what has been said above should not be misunderstood as a prohibition against Christians attempting to bring positive moral influence on government and attempting to persuade governments to make laws consistent with biblical standards of morality.[12] It is right for Christians to attempt to persuade governments to make laws that protect families and private property and the lives of human beings—such as laws that both prohibit murder, theft, and the breaking of contracts (things that violate the Ten Commandments), as well as prohibit same-sex marriage, polygamy, incest, slander, drug abuse, abortion, and other things that are inconsistent with biblical standards of morality. These things are far different from requiring belief in certain types of church doctrine or theological conviction and from requiring that people attend certain kinds of church or worship services. The latter are clearly "religious" activities in the narrow sense in that they pertain to our relationship to God and our beliefs about him.[13] Governments should refrain from making laws about these things.

## D. Church Discipline

Since church discipline is one aspect of the use of the power of the church, it is appropriate here to give some discussion of the biblical principles relevant to the practice of church discipline.

### 1. The Purpose of Church Discipline.

#### a. Restoration and Reconciliation of the Believer Who Is Going Astray. Sin
hinders fellowship among believers and with God. In order for reconciliation to occur,

---

12. For a more extensive discussion of the view that there should be "significant Christian influence on government," see my discussion in *Politics according to the Bible*, 55–76.

13. The fact that Christians should try to influence government to make laws consistent with biblical standards is indicated by passages such as Matt. 6:10; 14:4; Acts 24:25; and 1 Tim. 2:1–4. We may hope that the moral standards of Scripture will also eventually gain general consent from most of the people of a given society, since those moral standards have also been inscribed on their hearts, which provides a witness in their consciences that these standards are correct (see

Rom. 2:14–15). It is also the case that God holds all societies and cultures responsible for obeying his moral standards, and often in the Old Testament God's prophets pronounced judgments upon not only the people of Israel but also upon immoral pagan societies, even though they did not have his written laws (see Deut. 9:5; Isa. 13–23; Ezek. 25–32; Dan. 4:27; Amos 1–2; Obadiah [written to Edom]; Jonah [prophesied to Nineveh]; Nahum [prophesied to Nineveh]; Hab. 2; Zeph. 2). In fact, civil governments are sent by God "to punish those who do evil and to praise those who do good" (1 Peter 2:14).

the sin must be dealt with. Therefore, the primary purpose of church discipline is to pursue the twofold goal of *restoration* (of the offender to right behavior) and *reconciliation* (between believers and with God).[14] Just as wise parents discipline their children (Prov. 13:24: "He who loves [his son] is diligent to discipline him"), and just as God our Father disciplines those whom he loves (Heb. 12:6; Rev. 3:19), so the church in its discipline is acting in love to bring back a brother or sister who has gone astray, reestablishing that person in right fellowship and rescuing him or her from destructive patterns of life. In Matthew 18:15, the hope is that discipline will stop at the first step, when someone goes alone: "If he listens to you, you have gained your brother." The phrase "you have gained your brother" implies that those carrying out discipline should keep the goal of personal reconciliation among Christians always in mind. Paul reminds us that we are to "restore" the sinning brother or sister "in a spirit of gentleness" (Gal. 6:1), and James encourages us to bring "back a sinner from his wandering" (James 5:20).

In fact, if church members were actively involved in giving private words of gentle admonition and in praying for one another when the first clear evidence of sinful conduct is seen, very little formal church discipline would have to be carried out because the process would begin and end with a conversation between two people that never becomes known to anyone else.

Even when the final step of "excommunication" (that is, putting someone out of the fellowship, or "communion," of the church) is taken, it is still with the hope that repentance will result. Paul delivered Hymenaeus and Alexander to Satan *"that they may learn not to blaspheme"* (1 Tim. 1:20), and the man living in incest at Corinth was to be delivered to Satan "that his spirit may be saved in the day of the Lord" (1 Cor. 5:5).[15]

If Christians who must take steps of church discipline will continue to remember this first purpose—the reconciliation of believers who are going astray with each other and with God, and their restoration to right patterns of life—then it will be much easier to continue to act in genuine love for the parties involved, and feelings of anger or desires for revenge on the part of those who have been hurt, which often lie near the surface, will much more easily be avoided.

**b. To Keep the Sin From Spreading to Others.** Although the primary goal of church discipline is restoration and reconciliation for the erring believer, in this present age reconciliation and restoration will not always come about. But whether restoration comes about or not, the church is told to carry out discipline because two other purposes are served as well.

---

14. In their excellent book on church discipline, *Church Discipline That Heals* (Downers Grove, IL: InterVarsity Press, 1985; originally published as *Healing the Wounded*), John White and Ken Blue note that a failure to keep reconciliation as the primary goal of church discipline has led to many abuses of the process in the history of the church (see esp. pp. 45–56). But they themselves say that "true reconciliation never takes place without change in the parties involved" (p. 46). Therefore I have combined reconciliation and restoration in this first section.

15. The unusual phrase "deliver to Satan" in these verses seems to mean "put out of the church" since that is clearly what Paul tells the Corinthians to do in 1 Cor. 5:2, 7, 13. Putting someone out of the church puts that person back into the kingdom of this sinful age, which is ruled by Satan.

One other purpose is that the sin will be kept from spreading to others. The author of Hebrews tells Christians to see to it that "no 'root of bitterness' springs up and causes trouble, and by it *many become defiled*" (Heb. 12:15). This means that if conflict between persons is not resolved quickly, the effects may spread to many others—something that sadly seems to be true in many cases of church division. Paul also says, "*A little leaven leavens the whole lump*," and tells the Corinthians to put out of the church a man living in incest (1 Cor. 5:2, 6–7), lest his sin affect the whole church. If that man were not disciplined, the effects of the sin would spread to many others who were aware of it and saw that the church paid little attention to it. This would cause many to think that perhaps that sin was not as bad as they had thought, and others might be tempted to commit similar or related sins. Moreover, if discipline against one specific offense is not carried out, then it will be much more difficult for the church to carry out discipline if a similar kind of sin is committed by someone else in the future.

Paul also told Timothy that elders who persist in sin are to be rebuked in the presence of all, "*so that the rest may stand in fear*" (1 Tim. 5:20)—that is, so that many others would realize that the sin will not be tolerated but will receive discipline both from the church and from God himself. In fact, Paul rebuked Peter publicly in order that others would not follow Peter's bad example of separating himself and eating only with Jewish believers (Gal. 2:11).

**c. To Protect the Purity of the Church and the Honor of Christ.** A third purpose of church discipline is that the purity of the church is to be protected, so that Christ will not be dishonored. Of course, no believer in this age has a completely pure heart, and we all have remaining sin in our lives. But when a church member continues to sin in a way that is outwardly evident to others, especially to unbelievers,[16] this clearly brings dishonor to Christ. It is similar to the situation of Jews who disobeyed God's law and led unbelievers to scoff and blaspheme God's name ("The name of God is blasphemed among the Gentiles because of you," Rom. 2:24).

This is why Paul is shocked that the Corinthians have not disciplined the man who continued in willful sin that was publicly known in the church ("And you are arrogant! Ought you not rather to mourn?" 1 Cor. 5:1–2). He is also greatly distressed to know that "brother goes to law against brother, and that before unbelievers" (1 Cor. 6:6). Rather than allowing such moral blemishes on the character of the church, Peter encourages believers to "be diligent to be found by [Christ] without spot or blemish, and at peace" (2 Peter 3:14). And our Lord Jesus wants to present to himself a church "without spot or wrinkle . . . holy and without blemish" (Eph. 5:27), for he is the head of the church, and its character reflects on his reputation. Even angels and demons look at the church and behold the wisdom of God expressed in it (Eph. 3:10); therefore (Eph. 4:1)

---

16. But also to angels (see Eph. 3:10; 1 Tim. 5:21).

Paul encourages Christians to be "eager to maintain the unity of the Spirit in the bond of peace" (Eph. 4:3).

This is a very serious matter. Since the Lord Jesus is jealous for his own honor, if the church does not exercise proper discipline, he will do it himself, as he did at Corinth, where the Lord's discipline resulted in sickness and death (1 Cor. 11:27–34), and as he warned he would do at Pergamum (Rev. 2:14–15) and Thyatira (Rev. 2:20). In these last two cases the Lord was displeased with the whole church for tolerating outward disobedience and not exercising discipline: "But I have this against you, that *you tolerate that woman Jezebel*, who calls herself a prophetess and is teaching and seducing my servants to practice sexual immorality and to eat food sacrificed to idols" (Rev. 2:20; cf. vv. 14–16).

The purposes of church discipline discussed above are well summarized in the Westminster Confession of Faith:

> Church censures are necessary, for the reclaiming and gaining of offending brethren, for deterring of others from the like offenses, for purging out of that leaven which might infect the whole lump, for vindicating the honor of Christ, and the holy profession of the gospel, and for preventing the wrath of God, which might justly fall upon the church, if they should suffer his covenant, and the seals thereof, to be profaned by notorious and obstinate offenders.

## 2. For What Sins Should Church Discipline Be Exercised?

On the one hand, Jesus' teaching in Matthew 18:15–20 tells us that if a situation involving personal sin against someone else cannot be resolved in a private or small group meeting, then the matter must be brought to the church:

> If your brother sins against you, go and tell him his fault, between you and him alone. If he listens to you, you have gained your brother. But if he does not listen, take one or two others along with you, that every charge may be established by the evidence of two or three witnesses. If he refuses to listen to them, tell it to the church. And if he refuses to listen even to the church, let him be to you as a Gentile and a tax collector. (Matt. 18:15–17)

In this case the matter has progressed from a private and informal situation to a public and much more formal process of discipline by the whole church.

On the other hand, the New Testament contains no explicit limitation on the kinds of sin that should be subject to church discipline. The examples of sins subject to church discipline in the New Testament are extremely diverse, and they include discipline for divisiveness (Rom. 16:17; Titus 3:10), incest (1 Cor. 5:1), laziness and refusing to work (2 Thess. 3:6–10), disobeying what Paul writes (2 Thess. 3:14–15), blasphemy (1 Tim. 1:20), and teaching heretical doctrine (2 John 10–11).

Nonetheless, a definite principle appears to be at work: all sins that were explicitly disciplined in the New Testament were *publicly known or outwardly evident sins*,[17] and many of them had continued over a period of time. The fact that the sins were publicly known meant that reproach was being brought on the church, Christ was being dishonored, and there was a real possibility that others would be encouraged to follow the wrongful patterns of life that were being publicly tolerated.

There is always the need, however, for mature judgment in the exercise of church discipline because there is lack of complete sanctification in all our lives. Furthermore, when we realize that someone is already aware of a sin and struggling to overcome it, a word of admonition may in fact do more harm than good. We should also remember that where there are issues of conduct on which Christians legitimately disagree, Paul encourages a wide degree of tolerance (Rom. 14:1–23).

### 3. How Should Church Discipline Be Carried Out?

**a. Knowledge of the Sin Should Be Disclosed Only to Those Who Need to Know.** This seems to be the purpose in Matthew 18:15–17 behind the gradual progression from a private meeting, to a meeting with two or three others, to telling the entire church. The fewer people who know about some sin, the better, because repentance is easier, fewer people are led astray, and less harm is done to the reputation of the person, the church, and Christ.[18] (However, see section c below on the requirement for public disclosure of the serious sins of a church leader.)

**b. Disciplinary Measures Should Increase in Strength until There Is a Solution.** Once again in Matthew 18 Jesus teaches us that we cannot stop simply with a private conversation if that has not brought satisfactory results. He requires that the wronged person first go alone, and then take one or two others (Matt. 18:15–16). Moreover, if a Christian thinks that he or she has wronged someone else (or even if that other person *thinks* that he or she has been wronged), Jesus requires that the person who has done the wrong (or is thought to have done the wrong) go to the person who considers himself the victim of wrongdoing (Matt. 5:23). This means that whether we have been wronged or others think they have been wronged, *it is always our responsibility* to take the initiative and go to the other person. Jesus does not allow us to wait for the other person to come to us.

---

17. One exception was the secret sin of Ananias and Sapphira in Acts 5:1–11. In this situation the Holy Spirit (vv. 3, 8) was so powerfully present that he brought about an event that anticipated the final judgment, which will happen when Christ returns and the secrets of all hearts will be disclosed. It is not surprising that "great fear came upon the whole church" (v. 11).

18. In the case of a pastoral staff member in a church who has been subject to church discipline, those who "need to know" would certainly include the search committee and elder board of another church that is considering hiring that staff member. (I am aware of at least two situations where a youth pastor was involved in sexual immorality with high school girls in church A, was discovered and dismissed, and then went to church B and repeated the same pattern of activity. But church B had hired him with no knowledge of his sinful conduct in church A, because the leaders in church A "wanted to give him a second chance," so they had kept the matter quiet when church B asked for a recommendation about him. As a result of their wrongful silence, several high school girls in church B suffered significant spiritual and emotional damage that in some cases lasted for decades.)

What about a meeting with the elders as an intermediate step before taking the matter to the whole church? After a private meeting and a small group meeting, Jesus does not specify that the elders or officers of the church are next to be consulted as a group, but certainly this intermediate step seems to be appropriate because Jesus may simply be summarizing the process without necessarily mentioning every possible step in it. In fact, there are several examples of small group admonition in the New Testament that are carried out by elders or other church officers (see 1 Thess. 5:12; 2 Tim. 4:2; Titus 1:13; 2:15; 3:10; James 5:19–20). Moreover, the principle of disclosing the sin only to those who need to know would certainly encourage this intermediate step as well.

Finally, if the situation cannot be resolved, Jesus says to "tell it to the church" (Matt. 18:17). In this case the church would be assembled to hear the facts of the case and to come to a decision. Since Jesus allows for the possibility that the person "refuses to listen even to the church" (v. 17), the church may have to meet once to decide what to say to the offender and then meet again to exclude that person from the fellowship of the church. (1 Cor. 5:4 also requires that the church be assembled for this final step in church discipline.)

Of course, the step in which the leaders "tell it to the church" does not have to be carried out at the main Sunday morning worship service, and is probably better suited to a church business meeting or a special meeting of members of the church. And in the case of a megachurch with thousands of people attending, it would probably be appropriate to carry out this action in the presence of some smaller subgroup within the larger church.

When Jesus gives these directions about church discipline, he reminds the church that his presence and power are behind the decisions made by the church: "Again I say to you, if two of you agree on earth about anything they ask, it will be done for them by my Father in heaven. For where two or three are gathered in my name, *there am I among them*" (Matt. 18:19–20). Jesus promises to be present in church gatherings generally— but specifically with respect to the church being gathered for discipline of an offending member. And Paul similarly tells the Corinthians to discipline the erring member when they are assembled "*with the power of our Lord Jesus*" (1 Cor. 5:4). This is not an activity to be taken lightly but is carried out in the presence of the Lord, with the spiritual component of it actually being carried out by the Lord.

If this ever must be done, the whole church will then know that the erring person is no longer considered a member of the church, and that person would not be allowed to take Communion since partaking in the Lord's Supper is a sign of partaking in the unity of the church ("Because there is one bread, we who are many are one body, *for we all partake of the one bread*," 1 Cor. 10:17).

Additional passages in the New Testament speak of avoiding fellowship with the excommunicated person. Paul tells the Corinthians, "I am writing to you *not to associate with anyone who bears the name of brother if he is guilty of sexual immorality or greed, or is an idolater, reviler, drunkard, or swindler—not even to eat with such a one" (1 Cor. 5:11). He tells the Thessalonians, "Now we command you, brothers, in the name of our Lord Jesus Christ, that you keep away from any brother who is walking in idleness and not in accord with the tradition that you received from us" (2 Thess. 3:6). Moreover, he says, "If anyone does not obey what we say in this letter, take note of that person, and have nothing to do with him, that he may be ashamed. Do not regard him as an enemy, but warn him as a brother" (2 Thess. 3:14–15). In addition, 2 John 10–11 prohibits greeting or welcoming into the house anyone who is promoting false teaching. These instructions are given apparently to prevent the church from giving to others the impression that it approves of the disobedience of the erring person.

**c. Discipline of Church Leaders.** In one passage Paul gives special directives concerning the discipline of church elders:

> Do not admit a charge *against an elder* except on the evidence of two or three witnesses. As for those who persist in sin, *rebuke them in the presence of all, so that the rest may stand in fear.* In the presence of God and of Christ Jesus and of the elect angels I charge you to keep these rules without prejudging, doing nothing from partiality. (1 Tim. 5:19–21)

Paul here gives a special caution to protect elders from individual attacks: even to *consider* ("admit a charge against") an accusation of wrongdoing against an elder should require the evidence of two or three witnesses. (Paul apparently expects church leaders to decide whether they need to hear from three witnesses or if two will be enough, according to their knowledge of the circumstances and the people involved.) "Those who persist in sin"[19] are to be rebuked "*in the presence of all*" (that is, all the members of the church). This is because the bad example of wrongful conduct by an elder will very likely have a widespread negative effect on others who see their lives. Then Paul reminds Timothy to do "nothing from partiality" in this situation, a very helpful warning, since Timothy was probably a close friend to many of the elders in the church at Ephesus.

Paul's command to rebuke a sinning elder publicly means that some statement of the nature of the offense must be made to the church ("*rebuke them* in the presence of all," v. 20).[20] On the other hand, not every detail of the sin has to be disclosed to the church. A helpful guideline is that the church should be told enough that (1) they will

---

19. This is apparently the sense of *tous harmartanontas* in 1 Tim. 5:20, since the present participle gives the sense of continuing in an action over a period of time.

20. When churches have to discipline a church leader, an easy mistake to make is failing to take Paul's command seriously, and thereby failing to give adequate disclosure to the church of the nature of the sin involved. If that happens, the congregation only hears that a leader was removed from office because of some sin (or maybe a general category of sin is mentioned). But this is not really an effective public rebuke. Because it is so vague, it will only result in confusion, speculation, and gossip. Moreover, serious divisions can arise in the church because in the absence of information some people will think the discipline process too harsh and others will think it too lenient, and the church will not be united in supporting the process.

understand how serious the offense was, (2) they will be able to understand and support the discipline process, and (3) they will not subsequently feel the sin was minimized or covered up if more details somehow leak out later.

Such a public disclosure of the sin of a leader will signal to the congregation that the leaders of the church will not hide such matters from them in the future. This will increase the confidence of the church in the integrity of the leadership board. It will also allow the sinning leader to begin the gradual process of rebuilding relationships and trust with the congregation, because he will not have to deal with people who have a hundred different speculations about what his sin was but with people who know the specific sin and can see the genuine repentance and change regarding that area of sin in his life.

What about the serious sins of people who are not church leaders? Scripture gives no command to disclose publicly the sins of people who are ordinary members but not recognized leaders in the church. Leaders, however, are treated differently because their lives are to be "above reproach" (1 Tim. 3:2), and their lives should be examples for other Christians to imitate (see 1 Tim. 4:12).[21]

**d. Other Aspects of Church Discipline.** Once discipline has occurred, as soon as there is repentance at any stage of the process, the Christians who have known about the discipline should welcome the repentant person back quickly into the fellowship of the church. Paul says, "You should rather turn to *forgive and comfort him,* or he may be overwhelmed by excessive sorrow. . . . I beg you to reaffirm your love for him" (2 Cor. 2:7–8; cf. 7:8–11). Once again, our purpose in church discipline should never be to punish out of a desire for vengeance but always to restore and heal.

The attitude with which discipline is carried out at any stage is also very important. It must be done with gentleness and humility and with a genuine appreciation for our own weakness and with a fear that we might fall into similar sins. "If anyone is caught in any transgression, you who are spiritual should restore him *in a spirit of gentleness. Keep watch on yourself, lest you too be tempted*" (Gal. 6:1).

It is unwise to set any timetable in advance, telling people how long the discipline process is expected to last. This is because it is impossible for us to predict how long it will be until the Holy Spirit brings about deep, genuine repentance and a change in the condition of the person's heart that led to the sin in the first place.

Finally, we should notice that immediately following the passage on church discipline in Matthew 18:15–20, Jesus emphasizes the need for personal forgiveness of those who sin against us (Matt. 18:21–35). We are to forgive even those who harm us "seventy-seven times" (v. 22), and Jesus tells us that our heavenly Father will punish us severely if we do not *forgive our brother from the heart* (v. 35). We should see the passage on church discipline and this passage as complementary, not contradictory. As individuals

---

21. I understand "above reproach" to mean that their lives are such that no charge of serious wrongdoing can be rightfully brought against them.

we must always forgive in our hearts and not bear grudges. Yet we can certainly forgive someone in our hearts and still seek church discipline for the good of the person who is committing a sin, for the good of the church, for the honor of Christ, and because God's Word commands it.

## QUESTIONS FOR PERSONAL APPLICATION

1. Have you previously thought of the church as rather weak or rather strong in its influence on the affairs of the world? How has your thinking changed as a result of this chapter? Do you now think there is any hope for transforming society apart from the strong redemptive influence of the church?

2. Have you previously thought of yourself as holding any of the "keys of the kingdom of heaven"? Do you in fact have some of those keys now? What are you doing with them?

3. In what ways could your church exercise its spiritual power against the forces of the enemy more effectively? In what ways could you use this power more effectively yourself?

4. What is the strongest enemy to the effective proclamation of the gospel in your community now? How might the power of the church be used against that enemy?

5. If you accept the principles that the church should not rule the state and the state should not rule over or restrict the freedom of the church, are these principles being played out effectively in your own country or local situation? What could be done to increase conformity to these principles? (Do you agree with these principles?)

6. Are you aware of situations where a gentle word of admonition has resulted in a positive change in your behavior or the behavior of another Christian? Are you aware of situations where church discipline has gone a step or two further than this and has resulted in restoration of the erring person? If you are aware of situations where the practice of church discipline has not brought a good result, what could have been done differently to bring about a better result?

7. If a church refuses to carry out church discipline at all for a number of years, even though there is an evident need for it, what will be the harmful results in the church? Are you aware of situations where those harmful results have occurred?

8. Have there been times when you wished that someone would have come to you earlier with a word of admonition or counsel concerning an area of sin that you were unaware of or that you were uncertain about? If so, why didn't that happen?

9. Are there now any relationships in your life where Matthew 5:23 and Matthew 18:15 combine to tell you that you have an obligation to go to another person and seek to make the situation right?

**Special Terms**

*binding and loosing*
*excommunication*
*keys of the kingdom*
*power of the church*
*to take up the sword*

# BIBLIOGRAPHY

(For an explanation of this bibliography see the note on the bibliography to chapter 1, pp. 23–24. Complete bibliographical data may be found on pp. 1489–96.)

## SECTIONS IN EVANGELICAL SYSTEMATIC THEOLOGIES

### 1. Anglican (Episcopalian)
1882–92 . . . . . Litton, 402–13, 418–27
1930 . . . . . . . . Thomas, 281–97, 434–46
2001 . . . . . . . . Packer, 220–22
2013 . . . . . . . . Bird, 699–712
2013 . . . . . . . . Bray, 847–64

### 2. Arminian (Wesleyan or Methodist)
1940 . . . . . . . . Wiley, 3:136–37
1992 . . . . . . . . Oden, 3:361–65
2002 . . . . . . . . Cottrell, 400–17

### 3. Baptist
1767 . . . . . . . . Gill, 2:607–20
1907 . . . . . . . . Strong, 924–26
1990–95 . . . . Garrett, 2:527–48, 689–710
2007 . . . . . . . . Akin, 805–9

### 4. Dispensational
1986 . . . . . . . . Ryrie, 433–35
2002–2005 . . Geisler, 3:281–82, 4:215–44
2017 . . . . . . . . MacArthur and Mayhue, 751–753, 792–93

### 5. Lutheran
1917–24 . . . . . Pieper, 1:530–31; 3:178–83, 416–20

### 6. Reformed (or Presbyterian)
1559 . . . . . . . . Calvin, 2:1149–1240 (4.8–12)
1679–85 . . . . . Turretin, *IET*, 3:166, 203, 223, 225, 258–68, 274–306, 316–36, 555
1724–58 . . . . . Edwards, 2:118–22
1878 . . . . . . . . Dabney, 873–87
1906–11 . . . . . Bavinck, *RD*, 4:389–440
1910 . . . . . . . . Vos, 3:177
1937–66 . . . . . Murray, *CW*, 1:253–59
1938 . . . . . . . . Berkhof, 593–603
1998 . . . . . . . . Reymond, 861–94
2008 . . . . . . . . Van Genderen and Velema, 745–52
2011 . . . . . . . . Horton, 892–903
2013 . . . . . . . . Frame, 1024–26
2013 . . . . . . . . Culver, 956–61
2016 . . . . . . . . Allen and Swain, 311–38
2017 . . . . . . . . Barrett, 586–608
2019 . . . . . . . . Letham, 603, 622

### 7. Renewal (or charismatic/Pentecostal)
1988–92 . . . . . Williams, 3:120–23, 265–85
1993 . . . . . . . . Menzies and Horton, 155–72
1995 . . . . . . . . Horton, 567–95
2008 . . . . . . . . Duffield and Van Cleave, 450–52

## SECTIONS IN REPRESENTATIVE ROMAN CATHOLIC SYSTEMATIC THEOLOGIES

### 1. Roman Catholic: Traditional
1955 . . . . . . . . Ott, 417–25

### 2. Roman Catholic: Post–Vatican II
1980 . . . . . . . . McBrien, 2:817–48
2012 . . . . . . . . *CCC*, paragraphs 811–870

### OTHER WORKS

Allison, Gregg. *Sojourners and Strangers: The Doctrine of the Church.* Wheaton, IL: Crossway, 2012, 179–204. Adams, Jay E. *Handbook of Church Discipline.* Grand Rapids: Zondervan, 1986.

Bauckham, Richard. *The Bible in Politics: How to Read the Bible Politically.* Louisville: Westminster John Knox, 1989.

Belleville, L. L. "Authority." In *DPL*, 54–59.

Carson, D. A. "Church, Authority in the." In *EDT3*, 183–85.

DeKoster, L. "Church Discipline." In *EDT3*, 185–86.

Dever, Mark. "The Church." In *A Theology for the Church*, edited by Daniel L. Akin et al., 805–9, 835–37. Nashville: B&H, 2007.

Eidsmoe, John. *God and Caesar: Christian Faith and Political Action.* Westchester, IL: Crossway, 1984.

Grudem, W. A. "Keys of the Kingdom." In *EDT3*, 464–65.

Hansen, G. W. "Authority." In *DLNT*, 105–10.

Johnson, K. Deede. "Political Theology." In *EDT3*, 672–76.

Kraft, Charles H. *I Give You Authority.* Grand Rapids: Chosen, 2000.

Laney, J. Carl. *A Guide to Church Discipline.* Minneapolis: Bethany, 1985.

Linder, R. D. "Church and State." In *EDT1*, 233–38.

Robertson, O. Palmer. "Reflections on New Testament Testimony Concerning Civil Disobedience." *JETS* 33, no. 3 (September 1990): 331–51.

Schaeffer, Francis. *A Christian Manifesto.* Westchester, IL: Crossway, 1981.

Schmidt, Thomas E. "Discipline." In *BTDB*, 177–80.

———. "Discipline." In *DLNT*, 304–6.

Stott, John R. W. *The Preacher's Portrait: Some New Testament Word Studies.* Grand Rapids: Eerdmans, 1961.

White, John, and Ken Blue. *Church Discipline That Heals: Putting Costly Love into Action.* (First published as *Healing the Wounded.*) Downers Grove, IL: InterVarsity Press, 1985.

## SCRIPTURE MEMORY PASSAGE

**2 Corinthians 10:3–4:** For though we walk in the flesh, we are not waging war according to the flesh. For the weapons of our warfare are not of the flesh but have divine power to destroy strongholds.

## HYMN

### "Onward Christian Soldiers"

This hymn does not talk about earthly warfare with swords and shields but with the spiritual warfare of prayer and praise, and the enemies are not earthly unbelievers but Satan and his demonic hosts: "Hell's foundations quiver at the shout of praise; Brothers, lift your voices, loud your anthems raise."

The hymn pictures the church moving as a worldwide army of God against the forces of Satan, and it proclaims the unity of the church as well: "We are not divided, all one body we, One in hope and doctrine, one in charity." It is a triumphant, joyful song of spiritual warfare by a church that will not be divided and will not be defeated.

*Onward, Christian soldiers, marching as to war,*
*With the cross of Jesus going on before:*
*Christ the royal Master leads against the foe;*
*Forward into battle, see his banners go.*

**Refrain**
*Onward, Christian soldiers, marching as to war,*
*With the cross of Jesus going on before.*

*At the sign of triumph Satan's host doth flee;*
*On then, Christian soldiers, on to victory:*
*Hell's foundations quiver at the shout of praise;*
*Brothers, lift your voices, loud your anthems raise.*

*Like a mighty army moves the church of God;*
*Brothers, we are treading where the saints*
*have trod;*

*We are not divided, all one body we,*
*One in hope and doctrine, one in charity.*

*Crowns and thrones may perish, kingdoms rise*
*and wane,*
*But the church of Jesus constant will remain;*
*Gates of hell can never 'gainst that church prevail;*
*We have Christ's own promise, and that*
*cannot fail.*

*Onward, then ye people, join our happy throng,*
*Blend with ours your voices in the triumph song;*
*Glory, laud, and honor unto Christ the King;*
*This through countless ages men and angels sing.*

Author: Sabine Baring-Gould, 1865

## CONTEMPORARY WORSHIP SONG

### "Hosanna (Praise Is Rising)"

*Praise is rising.*
*Eyes are turning to You.*
*We turn to You.*
*Hope is stirring.*
*Hearts are yearning for You.*
*We long for You.*

**Prechorus**
*'Cause when we see You*
*We find strength to face the day.*
*In Your presence*
*All our fears are washed away*
*(Washed away).*

**Chorus**
*Hosanna, hosanna,*
*You are the God who saves us,*
*Worthy of all our praises.*
*Hosanna, hosanna,*
*Come have Your way among us.*
*We welcome You here Lord Jesus.*

*Hear the sound of*
*Hearts returning to You.*
*We turn to You.*
*In Your Kingdom*
*Broken lives are made new.*
*You make us new.*

Words by Brenton Brown and Paul Baloche[22]

---

22. Copyright © 2006 Thankyou Music (PRS) (adm. worldwide at CapitolCMGPublishing.com excluding Europe which is adm. by Integrity Music, part of the David C Cook family. Songs@integritymusic.com) / Integrity's Hosanna! Music (ASCAP) (adm. at CapitolCMGPublishing.com). All rights reserved. Used by permission.

# CHAPTER 47

# Church Government

*How should a church be governed?*
*How should church officers be chosen?*
*Should women serve as pastors of churches?*

## EXPLANATION AND SCRIPTURAL BASIS

Churches today have many different forms of government. The Roman Catholic Church has a worldwide government under the authority of the Pope. Episcopalian churches have bishops with regional authority, and archbishops over them. Presbyterian churches grant regional authority to presbyteries and national authority to general assemblies. On the other hand, Baptist churches and many other independent churches have no formal governing authority beyond the local congregation, and affiliation with denominations is on a voluntary basis.

Within local churches, Baptists often have a single pastor with a board of deacons, but some have a board of elders as well. Presbyterians have a board of elders and Episcopalians have a vestry. Other churches simply have a church board.

Is there a New Testament pattern for church government? Is any one form of church government to be preferred over another? These are the questions addressed in this chapter.

However, at the outset it must be said that the form of church government is not a major doctrine like the Trinity, the deity of Christ, substitutionary atonement, or the authority of Scripture. Although I believe, after examining the New Testament evidence, that one particular form of church government is preferable to the others, nevertheless, each form has some weaknesses as well as strengths. And church history attests that several different forms of government have worked fairly well for several centuries. Moreover, while some aspects of church government seem to be reasonably clear from the New Testament, other matters (such as the way in which church officers should be chosen) are less clear, mainly because the New Testament evidence on them is not extensive, and thus our inferences from this evidence are less certain. It seems to me, then, that there ought to be room for evangelical Christians to differ amicably over this question, in the hope that further understanding may be gained. And it also seems that individual Christians—while they may have a preference for one system or another, and while they may wish at appropriate times to argue forcefully for one system over another—should nevertheless be willing to live and minister within any of several different Protestant systems of church government in which they may find themselves from time to time.

But I do not mean to say that this is an entirely unimportant matter. In this area as well as others, a church may be more or less pure. If there are clear New Testament patterns regarding some aspects of church government, then there will be negative consequences in our churches if we disregard them, even if we cannot foresee all of those consequences at the present time. Therefore, Christians are certainly free to speak and write on this subject in order to work for increased purity in the church.

In this chapter we will first survey the New Testament data concerning church officers, especially *apostle*, *elder*, and *deacon*. Then we will ask how church officers should be chosen. After that we will look at two controversial questions: Which form of church government—if any—is closest to the New Testament pattern? And may women serve as officers in the church?

## A. Church Officers

For purposes of this chapter, we will use the following definition: *a church officer is someone who has been publicly recognized as having the right and responsibility to perform certain functions for the benefit of the whole church.*

According to this definition, elders and deacons would be considered officers in a church, as would the pastor (if that is a distinct office). The church treasurer and church moderator would also be officers (these titles may vary from church to church). All of these people have had public recognition, usually at a service in which they are "installed" or "ordained" in an office. In fact, they *need* public recognition in order to fulfill their responsibilities: for example, it would not be appropriate for people to wonder from week to week who was to receive the offering and deposit it in the bank or for various people to argue that they had been gifted to take that responsibility in any particular week! The orderly functioning of the church requires that one person be recognized as having that responsibility. Similarly, the pastor who is responsible to do Bible teaching each Sunday morning must be recognized as having the right and responsibility to do that (at least, in most forms of church government). If this were not the case, then many people might prepare sermons and all claim the right to preach, or on some Sundays no one might prepare. Similarly, in order for people to follow the elders of the church and look to them for guidance, they must know who the elders are.

By contrast, many other people exercise gifts in the church, but we do not say they have an "office" because they do not need formal public recognition for their gifts to function. Those who have the gifts of "helps" (see 1 Cor. 12:28), especially strong faith, the ability to "distinguish between spirits" (1 Cor. 12:10), or exhorting or contributing (Rom. 12:8) do not need public recognition in order to function effectively in the church.

In the material that follows, we will see that the New Testament discusses one church office that was limited to the time when the early church was founded (the office of apostle) and two church offices that continue throughout the church age (the offices of elder and deacon).

## 1. Apostle

Earlier in this book we saw that the New Testament *apostles* had a unique kind of authority in the early church: authority to speak and write words which were "words of God" in an absolute sense. To disbelieve or disobey them was to disbelieve or disobey God. The apostles, therefore, had the authority to write words which became words of Scripture.[1] This fact in itself should suggest to us that there was something unique about the office of apostle, and that we would not expect it to continue today, for no one today can add words to the Bible and have them be counted as God's very words or as part of Scripture.[2]

In addition, the New Testament information on the qualifications of an apostle and the identity of the apostles also leads us to conclude that the office was unique and limited to the first century, and that we are to expect no more apostles today.[3] We will see this as we ask the following questions: What were the requirements for being an apostle? Who were the apostles? How many apostles were there? And are there apostles today?

At the outset it must be made clear that the answers to these questions depend on what one means by the word *apostle*. Today some people use the word *apostle* in a very broad sense, to refer to an effective church planter or a significant missionary pioneer ("William Carey was an apostle to India," for example). If we use the word *apostle* in this broad sense, everyone would agree that there are still apostles today—for there are certainly effective missionaries and church planters today. (However, the danger of using the word to apply to some people today is that it suggests a higher level of authority than is appropriate for church leaders today, as the following pages will indicate.)

The New Testament has three verses in which the word usually translated as *apostle* (Gk. *apostolos*) is used in a broad sense, not to refer to any specific church office and not to refer to effective missionaries or church planters but simply to mean "messenger." In Philippians 2:25, Paul calls Epaphroditus "your *messenger* [*apostolos*] and minister to my need"; in 2 Corinthians 8:23, Paul refers to those who accompanied the offering that he was taking to Jerusalem as "*messengers* [*apostoloi*] of the churches"; and in John 13:16, Jesus says, "Nor is *a* messenger [*apostolos*] greater than the one who sent him."

But there is another sense for the word *apostle*. Much more frequently in the New Testament the word refers to a special office, "*apostle of Jesus Christ*." In this narrow

---

1. See chapter 3, pp. 47–51, and chapter 4, pp. 65–66, for a discussion of the authority of the apostles.
2. See chapter 3, pp. 52–57, for a discussion of the closing of the New Testament canon.

3. The material from this point through p. 1122 has been taken from Wayne Grudem, *The Gift of Prophecy in the New Testament and Today* (Eastbourne, UK: Kingsway; Westchester, IL: Crossway, 1988), 269–76, and is used by permission.

sense of the term, there are no more apostles today, and we are to expect no more. This is because of what the New Testament says about the qualifications for being an apostle and about who the apostles were.

**a. Qualifications of an Apostle.** The two qualifications for being an apostle were (1) having seen Jesus after his resurrection with one's own eyes (thus, being an "eye-witness of the resurrection") and (2) having been specifically commissioned by Christ as his apostle.[4]

The fact that an apostle had to have seen the risen Lord with his own eyes is indicated by Acts 1:22, where Peter said that person to replace Judas "must become with us *a witness to his resurrection.*" Moreover, it was "to the apostles whom he had chosen" that "he presented himself alive to them after his suffering by many proofs, appearing to them during forty days" (Acts 1:2–3; cf. 4:33).

Paul makes much of the fact that he did meet this qualification even though it was in an unusual way (Christ appeared to him in a vision on the road to Damascus and appointed him as an apostle: Acts 9:5–6; 26:15–18). When he is defending his apostleship he says, "Am I not an apostle? *Have I not seen Jesus our Lord?*" (1 Cor. 9:1). And when recounting the people to whom Christ appeared after his resurrection, Paul says, "Then *he appeared to James*, then *to all the apostles.* Last of all, as to one untimely born, *he appeared also to me.* For I am the least of the apostles, unworthy to be called an apostle" (1 Cor. 15:7–9).

These verses combine to indicate that unless someone had seen Jesus after the resurrection with his own eyes, he could not be an apostle.

The second qualification, specific appointment by Christ as an apostle, is also evident from several verses. First, though the term *apostle* is not common in the gospels, the twelve disciples are called "apostles" specifically in a context where Jesus is commissioning them, "sending them out" to preach in his name:

> And he called to him his twelve disciples and gave them authority over unclean spirits, to cast them out, and to heal every disease and every affliction. The names of the twelve *apostles* are these. . . . *These twelve Jesus sent out*, instructing them, ". . . proclaim as you go, saying, 'The kingdom of heaven is at hand.'" (Matt. 10:1–7)

Similarly, Jesus commissions his apostles in a special sense to be his "witnesses . . . to the end of the earth" (Acts 1:8). And in choosing another apostle to replace Judas, the eleven apostles did not take the responsibility on themselves, but prayed and asked the ascended Christ to make the appointment: "'You, Lord, who know the hearts of all, *show which one of these two you have chosen* to take the place in this ministry and

---

4. These two qualifications are discussed in detail in the classic essay by J. B. Lightfoot, "The Name and Office of an Apostle," in his commentary, *The Epistle of St. Paul to the Galatians* (1865; repr., Grand Rapids: Zondervan, 1957), 92–101; see also K. H. Rengstorf, "*apostolos,*" *TDNT*, 1:398–447.

apostleship from which Judas turned aside. . . .' And they cast lots for them, and the lot fell on Matthias, and he was numbered with the eleven apostles" (Acts 1:24–26).

Paul himself insists that Christ personally appointed him as an apostle. He tells how, on the Damascus Road, Jesus told him that he was appointing him as an apostle to the Gentiles: "I have appeared to you for this purpose, to appoint you as a servant and witness . . . delivering you from your people and from the Gentiles—to whom I am sending you" (Acts 26:16–17). He later affirms that he was specifically appointed by Christ as an apostle (see Rom. 1:1; Gal. 1:1; 1 Tim. 1:12; 2:7; 2 Tim. 1:11).

**b. Who Were Apostles?** The initial group of apostles numbered twelve—the eleven original disciples who remained after Judas died, plus Matthias, who replaced Judas: "They cast lots for them, and the lot fell on Matthias, and *he was numbered with the eleven apostles*" (Acts 1:26). So important was this original group of twelve apostles, the "charter members" of the office of apostle, that we read that their names are inscribed on the foundations of the heavenly city, the New Jerusalem: "The wall of the city had twelve foundations, and on them were *the twelve names of the twelve apostles of the Lamb*" (Rev. 21:14).

We might at first think that such a group could never be expanded, that no one could be added to it. But then Paul clearly and repeatedly claims that he, also, is an apostle. And then Acts 14:14 calls both Barnabas and Paul apostles: "when *the apostles Barnabas and Paul* heard of it . . ." So with Paul and Barnabas there are fourteen "apostles of Jesus Christ."[5]

Then James the brother of Jesus (who was not one of the twelve original disciples) seems to be called an apostle in Galatians 1:19. Paul tells how, when he went to Jerusalem, "I saw none of *the other apostles* except James the Lord's brother."[6] Then in Galatians 2:9 James is classified with Peter and John as "pillars" of the Jerusalem church. And in Acts 15:13–21, James, along with Peter, exercises a significant leadership function in the Jerusalem Council, a function which would be appropriate to the office of apostle. Furthermore, when Paul is listing the resurrection appearances of Jesus he once again

---

5. If the apostles' writings were accepted as Scripture, someone may wonder why the extrabiblical document called *The Epistle of Barnabas* is not included in Scripture. The answer is that nearly unanimous scholarly opinion has concluded that it was not written by Barnabas but by some unknown Christian who probably lived in Alexandria between AD 70 and 100. The epistle claims that much of the Old Testament, including animal sacrifices, much of the Mosaic law, and the construction of a physical temple, were mistakes that were contrary to God's will (see *ODCC*, 134). (Text and translation are found in Kirsopp Lake, trans., *The Apostolic Fathers* [Cambridge, MA: Harvard University Press; London: Heinemann, 1970], 1:335–409.)

6. It is not absolutely necessary to translate the verse this way, including James among the apostles. (The NIV reads,

"I saw none of the other apostles—only James, the Lord's brother.") Yet the translation "except James the Lord's brother" seems clearly preferable, because (1) the Greek phrase is *ei mē*, which ordinarily means "except" (BDAG, 278, 6.i), and in the great majority of New Testament uses designates something that is part of the previous group but is "excepted" from it; and (2) in the context of Gal. 1:18, it would not make much sense for Paul to say that when he went to Jerusalem he saw Peter, and no other people except James—or Peter, and no other church leaders except James—for he stayed there "fifteen days" (Gal. 1:18). So he must mean he saw Peter, and *no other apostles* except James. But this classifies James with the apostles. See discussion in E. D. Burton, *The Epistle to the Galatians*, ICC (Edinburgh: T&T Clark, 1920), 60. (Burton says, "*ei mē* means here, as always before a noun, 'except'" [ibid.].)

readily classifies James with the apostles: "Then he appeared *to James*, then *to all the apostles*. Last of all, as to one untimely born, he appeared also to me. For I am the least of the apostles, unworthy to be called an apostle, because I persecuted the church of God" (1 Cor. 15:7–9).

Finally, the fact that James could write the New Testament epistle that bears his name would also be entirely consistent with his having the authority which belonged to the office of apostle, the authority to write words that were the words of God. All these considerations combine to indicate that James the Lord's brother was also commissioned by Christ as an apostle. That would bring the number to fifteen "apostles of Jesus Christ" (the twelve plus Paul, Barnabas, and James).

Were there more than these fifteen? There may possibly have been a few more, though we know little if anything about them, and it is not certain that there were any more. Others, of course, had seen Jesus after his resurrection ("Then he appeared to more than five hundred brothers at one time," 1 Cor. 15:6). From this large group it is possible that Christ appointed some others as apostles—but it is also very possible that he did not. The evidence is not sufficient to decide the issue.

Others have been suggested as apostles. Silas (Silvanus) and sometimes Timothy are mentioned because of 1 Thessalonians 2:6: "though *we* could have made demands *as apostles of Christ*." Does Paul include Silas and Timothy here, since the letter begins, "Paul, Silvanus, and Timothy" (1 Thess. 1:1)?

It is not likely that Paul is including Timothy in this statement for two reasons. (1) He says just four verses earlier, "We had already suffered and been shamefully treated at Philippi, as you know" (1 Thess. 2:2), but this refers to the beating and imprisonment which happened just to Paul and Silas, not to Timothy (Acts 16:19). So the *we* in verse 6 does not seem to include all of the people (Paul, Silvanus, Timothy) mentioned in the first verse. The letter in general is from Paul, Silas, and Timothy, but Paul knows that the readers will naturally understand the appropriate members of the *we* statements when he does not mean to include all three of them in certain sections of the letter. He does not specify "we—that is, Silas and I—had already suffered and been shamefully treated at Philippi, as you know" because the Thessalonians will know who the "we" are that he is talking about.

(2) This is also seen in 1 Thessalonians 3:1–2, where the *we* certainly cannot include Timothy: "Therefore when we could bear it no longer, we were willing to be left behind at Athens alone, and *we sent Timothy*, our brother and God's coworker in the gospel of Christ, to establish and exhort you in your faith" (1 Thess. 3:1–2). In this case, the *we* refers either to Paul and Silas or else just to Paul alone (see Acts 17:14–15; 18:5). Apparently Silas and Timothy had come to Paul in Athens "as soon as possible" (Acts 17:15)—though Luke does not mention their arrival in Athens—and Paul had sent them back to Thessalonica again to help the church there. Then he himself went to Corinth, and they later joined him there (Acts 18:5).

It is most likely that "*we* were willing to be left behind at Athens alone" (1 Thess. 3:1) refers to Paul alone, both because he picks up the argument again in verse 5 with the singular *I* ("When I could bear it no longer, I sent to learn about your faith," 1 Thess. 3:5) and because the point concerning extreme loneliness in Athens would not be made if Silas had stayed with him.[7] In fact, in the previous paragraph, Paul means *I*, for he says, "We wanted to come to you—I, Paul, again and again—but Satan hindered us" (1 Thess. 2:18). Apparently he is using *we* more frequently in this epistle as a courteous way of including Silas and Timothy, who had spent so much time in the Thessalonian church, in the letter to that church. But the Thessalonians would have had little doubt who was really in charge of this great mission to the gentiles and on whose apostolic authority the letter primarily (or exclusively) depended.

So it is just possible that Silas was himself an apostle and that 1 Thessalonians 2:6 hints at that. He was a leading member of the Jerusalem church (Acts 15:22) and could well have seen Jesus after his resurrection and then been appointed as an apostle. But we cannot be certain.

The situation with Timothy is different, however. Just as he is excluded from the *we* of 1 Thessalonians 2:2 (and 3:1–2), so he seems to be excluded from the *we* of 1 Thessalonians 2:6. Moreover, as a native of Lystra (Acts 16:1–3) who had learned of Christ from his grandmother and mother (2 Tim. 1:5), it seems impossible that he would have been in Jerusalem before Pentecost and would there have seen the risen Lord and come to believe in him and then suddenly have been appointed as an apostle. In addition, *Paul's pattern of address in his letters always jealously guards the title "apostle" for himself*, never allowing it to be applied to Timothy or others of his traveling companions (note 2 Cor. 1:1; Col. 1:1: "*Paul, an apostle* of Christ Jesus . . . *and Timothy our brother*"; and then Phil. 1:1: "*Paul and Timothy, servants* of Christ Jesus"). So Timothy, as important a role as he had, should not rightly be considered one of the apostles.

Some have claimed to find a woman apostle named Junia in Romans 16:7: "Greet Andronicus and Junia [or 'Junias'], my kinsmen and my fellow prisoners. They are *well known to the apostles* [or 'messengers'], and they were in Christ before me" (Rom. 16:7). In this translation, Andronicus and Junia are not apostles but are "well-known" to the apostles.

However, the NIV translation says, "Greet Andronicus and Junia, my fellow Jews who have been in prison with me. They are *outstanding among* [or 'are esteemed by'] *the apostles*, and they were in Christ before I was" (Rom. 16:7). If that is the correct translation, then Andronicus (a man) and Junia (a woman) were both outstanding apostles. (In both translations I have put in square brackets the alternative wording noted in the

---

7. See the discussion in Leon Morris, *The First and Second Epistles to the Thessalonians*, NIC (Grand Rapids: Eerdmans, 1959), 98–99. Morris says, "The practice in this epistle differs somewhat from that in the Pauline epistles generally. The plural is used throughout, whereas in most of his letters Paul prefers the singular" (98; cf. 46–47). Morris takes the plurals here to refer only to Paul.

footnotes.) The arguments about the proper translation of this verse are quite complex, but my conclusion is that the weight of evidence strongly favors the ESV translation, "well known to the apostles."[8]

This gives us a limited but somewhat imprecisely numbered group who had the office "apostles of Jesus Christ." There seem to have been at least fifteen, and perhaps even a few more who are not recorded in the New Testament.

Yet it seems quite certain that there were none appointed after Paul. When Paul lists the resurrection appearances of Christ, he emphasizes the unusual way in which Christ appeared to him, and connects that with the statement that this was the "last" appearance of all, and that he himself is indeed "the least of the apostles, unworthy to be called an apostle."

> He appeared to Cephas (Peter), then to the twelve. Then he appeared to more than five hundred brothers at one time, most of whom are still alive, though some have fallen asleep. Then he appeared to James, then to all the apostles. *Last of all*, as to one untimely born, *he appeared also to me*. For I am the least of the apostles, unworthy to be called an apostle. (1 Cor. 15:5–9)

**c. Summary.** The Greek word translated as *apostle* (Gk. *apostolos*) can be used in a broad or narrow sense. In a broad sense, it just means "messenger" or "pioneer missionary." But in a narrow sense, the most common sense in the New Testament, it refers to a specific office, "apostle of Jesus Christ." These apostles had unique authority to found and govern the early church, and they could speak and write words of God. Many of their written words became the New Testament Scriptures.

In order to qualify as an apostle, someone (1) had to have seen Christ with his own eyes after he rose from the dead and (2) had to have been specifically appointed by Christ as an apostle. There was a limited number of apostles, perhaps fifteen or a few more—the New Testament is not explicit on the number. The twelve original apostles (the eleven plus Matthias) were joined by Barnabas and Paul, very probably James, perhaps Silas, and maybe a few unnamed others. It seems that no apostles were appointed after Paul. Since no one today can meet the qualification of having seen the risen Christ with his own eyes, there are no apostles today.[9] In place of living apostles present in the

---

8. See the extensive discussion in Michael H. Burer and Daniel B. Wallace, "Was Junia Really an Apostle? A Re-examination of Rom. 16.7," *NTS* 47, no. 1 (January 2001): 76–91; and Michael Burer, "*EPISEMOI EN TOIS APOS-TOLOIS* in Rom 16:7 as 'Well Known to the Apostles': Further Defense and New Evidence" *JETS* 58, no. 4 (2015): 731–55. See also John Piper and Wayne Grudem, eds., *Recovering Biblical Manhood and Womanhood* (Wheaton, IL: Crossway, 1991), 79–81, 214, 221–22.

9. Someone may object that Christ could appear to someone today and appoint that person as an apostle. But the foundational nature of the office of apostle (Eph. 2:20; Rev. 21:14) and the fact that Paul views himself as the last one whom Christ appeared to and appointed as an apostle ("last of all, as to one untimely born," 1 Cor. 15:8), indicate that this will not happen. Moreover, God's purpose in the history of redemption seems to have been to give apostles only at the beginning of the church age (see Eph. 2:20).

church to teach and govern it, we have instead *the writings of the apostles* in the books of the New Testament. Those New Testament Scriptures fulfill for the church today the absolutely authoritative teaching and governing functions which were fulfilled by the apostles themselves during the early years of the church.

One objection to the idea that there are no longer apostles comes especially from people in the charismatic movement. The argument is that the "fivefold ministry" of Ephesians 4:11 should continue today. This verse says that when Christ ascended into heaven, "he gave the apostles, the prophets, the evangelists, the shepherds and teachers" (Eph. 4:11). Therefore, it is argued, the church today should have (1) apostles, (2) prophets, (3) evangelists, (4) pastors, and (5) teachers.

However, I am not persuaded that this is the correct interpretation. Ephesians 4:11 talks about a one-time event in the past when Christ ascended into heaven (vv. 8–10) and then at Pentecost poured out initial giftings on the church, giving the church apostles, prophets, evangelists, and pastor-teachers (or pastors and teachers). (Note the aorist *kai edōken*, "and he *gave*," which indicates a one-time completed event.) Whether or not Christ would *later* give *more* people for each of these offices *cannot be decided from this verse alone* but must be decided based on other New Testament teachings on the nature of these offices and whether they were expected to continue. In fact, we see that there were many prophets, evangelists, and pastor-teachers established by Christ throughout all of the early churches, but there was only one more apostle given after this initial time (Paul, "last of all," in unusual circumstances on the Damascus Road). Therefore, I do not think that Ephesians 4:11 is a persuasive argument for the existence of apostles today.

Though some may use the word *apostle* in English today to refer to very effective church planters or evangelists, doing so seems inappropriate and unhelpful, for it simply confuses people who read the New Testament and see the high authority that is attributed to the office of apostle there. It is noteworthy that no major leader in the history of the church—not Athanasius or Augustine, not Luther or Calvin, not Wesley or Whitefield—has taken to himself the title of apostle or let himself be called an apostle. If any in modern times want to take the title apostle, they immediately raise the suspicion that they may be motivated by inappropriate pride and desires for self-exaltation, along with excessive ambition and a desire for much more authority in the church than any one person should rightfully have.

### 2. Elder (Pastor/Overseer/Bishop)

**a. Plural Elders: The Pattern in All New Testament Churches.** The next church office to be considered is that of elder. Although some have argued that different forms of church government are evident in the New Testament,[10] a survey of the relevant texts

---

10. See, for example, Millard Erickson, *Christian Theology*, 3rd ed. (Grand Rapids: Baker, 2013), 1003.

shows the opposite to be true: there is quite a consistent pattern of *plural elders* as the main governing group in New Testament churches. For instance, in Acts 14:23 we read, "When they had appointed *elders*[11] for them in every church, with prayer and fasting they committed them to the Lord in whom they had believed." This is on Paul's first missionary journey, when he is returning through the cities of Lystra, Iconium, and Antioch. It indicates that Paul's normal procedure from the time of his first missionary journey was to establish a group of elders in each church shortly after the church began. We know that Paul also established elders in the church at Ephesus, for we read, "From Miletus he sent to Ephesus and called the *elders* of the church to come to him" (Acts 20:17). Moreover, Paul's apostolic assistants apparently were instructed to carry out a similar process, for Paul wrote to Titus, "This is why I left you in Crete, so that you might put what remained into order, and *appoint elders in every town* as I directed you" (Titus 1:5). Shortly after a church has been established, once again we see elders being established in office, in "every town" in which there was a church. And Paul reminded Timothy of the time "when the *council of elders* laid their hands on you" (1 Tim. 4:14).

James writes, "Is anyone among you sick? Let him call for the *elders* of the church, and let them pray over him, anointing him with oil in the name of the Lord" (James 5:14). This is a significant statement because the epistle of James is a general letter written to many churches, all the believers scattered abroad, whom James characterizes as "the twelve tribes in the Dispersion" (James 1:1). It indicates that James expected that there would be elders *in every New Testament church to which his general epistle went*—that is, in *all the churches in existence at that time.*

A similar conclusion can be drawn from 1 Peter. Peter writes, "So I exhort the *elders* among you . . . shepherd the flock of God that is among you." (1 Peter 5:1–2). First Peter is also a general epistle, written to dozens of churches scattered throughout four Roman provinces in Asia Minor (see 1 Peter 1:1; Bithynia and Pontus constituted one Roman province). Far from expecting different kinds of church government when he was writing (around AD 62, more than thirty years after Pentecost), Peter assumes that *all* these churches, whether founded by Paul or by others, whether predominantly gentile or predominantly Jewish or evenly divided in their make-up, would have elders leading them. Moreover, there were elders in the Jerusalem church (Acts 11:30; 15:2), and though the word *elders* is not used, there is a plurality of leaders in the congregation to which the epistle to the Hebrews is directed, for the author says, "Obey your leaders and submit to them, for they are keeping watch over your souls, as those who will have to give an account" (Heb. 13:17).

Two significant conclusions may be drawn from this survey of the New Testament evidence. First, no passage suggests that any church, no matter how small, had only one

---

11. The word translated "elder" in the New Testament is the Greek word *presbyteros*, which also was used in other contexts to mean simply an older person.

elder. The consistent New Testament pattern is a plurality of elders "in every church" (Acts 14:23) and "in every town" (Titus 1:5).[12] Second, we do not see a diversity of forms of government in the New Testament church but a unified and consistent pattern in which every church had elders governing it and keeping watch over it (Acts 20:28; Heb. 13:17; 1 Peter 5:2–3).

**b. Other Names for Elders: Pastors, Overseers, Bishops.** Elders are also called "pastors" or "bishops" or "overseers" in the New Testament. The least commonly used word (at least in the noun form) is *pastor* or shepherd (depending on which translation is used; Gk. *poimēn*). It may be surprising to us to find that this word, which has become so common in English, only occurs once in the New Testament when speaking about a church officer. In Ephesians 4:11, Paul writes, "And he gave the apostles, the prophets, the evangelists, the *shepherds* and teachers." The verse is probably better translated "shepherd-teachers" or "pastor-teachers" (one group) rather than "shepherds and teachers" (suggesting two groups) because of the Greek construction (though not every New Testament scholar agrees with that translation).[13] The connection with teaching suggests that these pastors were some (or perhaps all) of the elders who carried on the work of teaching, for one qualification for an elder is that he be "able to teach" (1 Tim. 3:2).

Although the noun for *shepherd* (or *pastor*; Gk. *poimēn*) is not used of church officers elsewhere in the New Testament,[14] the related verb which means "to act as a shepherd" or "to act as a pastor" (Gk. *poimainō*) is applied to elders in Paul's address to the Ephesian elders. He tells them "to *shepherd* the church of God" (Acts 20:28, using the verb *poimainō*), and in the same sentence he referred to God's people as "all the *flock*," using another related noun (Gk. *poimnion*) which means "a flock of sheep." So Paul directly charges these Ephesian elders to act as shepherds or "pastors."[15]

The same verb is used in 1 Peter 5:2 where Peter tells the elders to "*shepherd (poimainō)* the flock of God that is among you." Then two verses later Jesus is called the chief pastor or "chief shepherd" (Gk. *archipoimēn*, 1 Peter 5:4), implying quite clearly that Peter also viewed the elders as shepherds or "pastors" in the church. Therefore,

---

12. Some have suggested that perhaps there was one elder in every "house church" in a town, and that all of those elders from the different house churches together constituted the elders that Titus was to appoint in each town. If this was true, perhaps some support could be given for the idea of one pastor ("elder") over every church.

In response to this suggestion, we must note that this is a theory without any evidence to support it, for no verse in the New Testament hints at the idea that there was one elder in each "house church." In terms of supporting evidence, this suggestion stands in the same category as the statement, "Perhaps all the elders in Crete were blind in the left eye." Of course, scholars can say "perhaps" to any event for which there is no evidence, but such statements should carry no weight in our attempts to determine what pattern of church government actually existed in the first century.

13. The phrase "some pastors and teachers" has one definite article in front of two nouns joined by *kai* ("and"), a construction that always in Greek indicates that the two nouns are viewed by the writer as unified in some way. This construction often is used where two nouns refer to the same person or thing, but (especially with plural nouns) it is also used to speak of two different persons or groups viewed as a unity. In either case, the phrase ties together "pastors" and "teachers" more closely than any other titles.

14. It is used several times to speak of a "shepherd" who cares for his sheep, however.

15. The English word *pastor* is derived from a Latin term that means "one who cares for sheep," and the English word *pastor* earlier meant "shepherd" in the literal sense of one who took care of sheep (see *Oxford English Dictionary*, 2nd ed. [1989], s.v. "pastor," vol. P, 542).

although the Greek word representing the noun *pastor* (or *shepherd*) is only used once to refer to elders, the related verb is used twice in passages that explicitly identify the task of shepherding with the office of elder.

Another term used for elders in the New Testament is a Greek word *episkopos*, which is variously translated as "overseer" or "bishop," depending on the individual passage and the English translation. But this word also seems quite clearly to be another term for elders in New Testament usage. For example, when Paul has called to him the *elders* of the church at Ephesus (Acts 20:17), he says to them, "Pay careful attention to yourselves and to all the flock, in which the Holy Spirit has made you *overseers* (Gk. *episkopos*)" (Acts 20:28). Paul quite readily refers to these Ephesian elders as "overseers."

In 1 Timothy 3:1–2, Paul writes, "If anyone aspires to the office of *overseer*, he desires a noble task. Therefore an *overseer* must be above reproach." We must remember that Paul is writing to Timothy when Timothy is at Ephesus (see 1 Tim. 1:3, "remain at Ephesus"), and we already know from Acts 20 that there are *elders* at Ephesus (Acts 20:17–38). Furthermore, in 1 Timothy 5:17, we see that elders were ruling the church at Ephesus when Timothy was there, because it says, "Let the *elders who rule well* be considered worthy of double honor." Now the overseers in 1 Timothy 3:1–2 *also* are to rule over the church at Ephesus because one qualification is that "He must manage his own household well . . . for if someone does not know how to manage his own household, how will he care for God's church?" (1 Tim. 3:4–5). So here it also seems that *overseer* or *bishop* is simply another term for *elder* since these overseers fulfill the same function as elders quite clearly do elsewhere in this epistle and in Acts 20.

In Titus 1:5, Paul tells Titus to "appoint *elders* in every town" and gives some qualifications (v. 6). Then in the very next sentence (v. 7), he gives reasons for those qualifications, and he begins by saying, "For an *overseer*, as God's steward, must be above reproach." Here again he uses the word *overseer* to refer to the elders whom Titus was to appoint, giving another indication that the terms *elder* and *overseer* were interchangeable.

Finally, in Philippians 1:1, Paul writes "To all the saints in Christ Jesus who are at Philippi, with the *overseers* and deacons." Here it also seems appropriate to think that *overseers* is another name for *elders* because there certainly were elders at Philippi since it was Paul's practice to establish elders in every church (see Acts 14:23). And if there were elders ruling in the church at Philippi, it is unthinkable that Paul would write to the church and single out overseers and deacons—but not elders—if their offices were both different from that of the elders. Therefore, by "overseers and deacons" Paul must have meant the same thing as "elders and deacons."[16] Although in some parts of the church from the second century AD onward, the word *bishop* has been used to refer to a single

---

16. Even the Anglican scholar J. B. Lightfoot, says, "It is a fact now generally recognised by theologians of all shades of opinion, that in the language of the New Testament the same officer in the Church is called indifferently 'bishop' (*episkopos*) and 'elder' or 'presbyter' (*presbyteros*)" (*St. Paul's Epistle to the Philippians* [1868; repr., Grand Rapids: Zondervan, 1953], 95; on pp. 95–99 Lightfoot discusses the data to support this conclusion).

individual with authority over several churches, this was a later development of the term and is not found in the New Testament itself.

**c. The Functions of Elders.** One of the major roles of elders in the New Testament is to govern the New Testament churches. In 1 Timothy 5:17 we read, "Let the elders who *rule* well be considered worthy of double honor." Earlier in the same epistle Paul says that an overseer (or elder) "must manage his own household well, with all dignity keeping his children submissive, for if someone does not know how to manage his own household, how will he care for God's church?" (1 Tim. 3:4–5).

Peter also indicates a ruling function for elders when he exhorts them:

> Shepherd the flock of God that is among you, *exercising oversight*, not under compulsion, but willingly, as God would have you; not for shameful gain, but eagerly; not domineering over those in your charge, but being examples to the flock. And when the chief Shepherd appears, you will receive the unfading crown of glory. Likewise, you who are younger, be subject to the elders. (1 Peter 5:2–5)

The fact that they are to act as shepherds of the flock of God, and the fact that they are to exercise oversight but not to domineer (that is, not to rule harshly or oppressively) strongly suggest that elders have ruling or governing functions in the churches to which Peter is writing. This is consistent with his charge that especially those who are younger should "be subject to the elders" (v. 5).[17]

Although Hebrews 13:17 does not name elders, certainly there are some church officers with governing authority over the church, for the author says, "*Obey your leaders and submit to them*, for they are keeping watch over your souls, as those who will have to give an account." Since the New Testament gives no indication of any other officers in the church with this kind of authority, it is reasonable to conclude that the congregation is to submit to and obey its elders. (This conclusion is also consistent with the description of responsibilities Paul gives to the Ephesian elders in Acts 20:28.)

In addition to governing responsibility, elders also seem to have had some *teaching responsibilities* in the New Testament churches. In Ephesians 4:11, elders are referred to as "shepherd-teachers" (or, on an alternative translation, pastors who are viewed as quite closely united to teachers). And in 1 Timothy 3:2, an overseer (elder) must be "able to *teach*." Then in 1 Timothy 5:17, Paul says, "Let the elders who rule well be considered worthy of double honor, especially those who labor in *preaching and teaching*." Here Paul seems to imply that there is a special group of elders who "labor in preaching and teaching." This means at least that there are some among the elders who give more time to the activities of preaching and teaching, and may even mean that there are some who

---

17. For a defense of the view that church officers and not just older people are referred to in 1 Peter 5:5, see Grudem, *The* · *First Epistle of Peter* (Leicester: Inter-Varsity Press; Grand Rapids: Eerdmans, 1988), 192–93.

"labor" in the sense of earning their living from that preaching and teaching. The same conclusions can be drawn from Titus, where Paul says that an elder "must hold firm to the trustworthy word as taught, so that he may be *able to give instruction* in sound doctrine and also to rebuke those who contradict it" (Titus 1:9).[18]

Elders, then, had responsibility to rule and to teach in New Testament churches.

**d. Qualifications for Elders.** When Paul lists the qualifications for elders, he combines requirements concerning character traits and heart attitudes with requirements that cannot be fulfilled in a short time but will only become evident over a period of several years of faithful Christian living:

> Therefore an overseer must be above reproach, the husband of one wife, sober-minded, self-controlled, respectable, hospitable, able to teach, not a drunkard, not violent but gentle, not quarrelsome, not a lover of money. He must manage his own household well, with all dignity keeping his children submissive, for if someone does not know how to manage his own household, how will he care for God's church? He must not be a recent convert, or he may become puffed up with conceit and fall into the condemnation of the devil. Moreover, he must be well thought of by outsiders, so that he may not fall into disgrace, into a snare of the devil. (1 Tim. 3:2–7)

Similar but differently worded qualifications are found in Titus 1:6–9, where Paul says that Titus is to appoint elders in every town:

> If anyone is above reproach, the husband of one wife, and his children are believers and not open to the charge of debauchery or insubordination. For an overseer, as God's steward, must be above reproach. He must not be arrogant or quick-tempered or a drunkard or violent or greedy for gain, but hospitable, a lover of good, self-controlled, upright, holy, and disciplined. He must hold firm to the trustworthy word as taught, so that he may be able to give instruction in sound doctrine and also to rebuke those who contradict it. (Titus 1:6–9)

Those who are choosing elders in churches today would do well to look carefully at candidates in the light of these qualifications, and to look for these character traits and patterns of godly living rather than worldly achievement, fame, or success. Especially in churches in western industrial societies, there is sometimes a tendency to think that success in the world of business (or law, or medicine, or government) is an indication of suitability for the office of elder, but this is not the teaching of the New Testament.

---

18. Paul never says that all the elders are to be able to teach publicly or to preach sermons to the congregation, and it would be reasonable to think that an "apt teacher" could be someone who is able to explain God's Word privately. So perhaps not all elders are called to do public teaching—perhaps not all have gifts for teaching in that specific way. What is clear here is that Paul wants to guarantee that elders have a mature and sound understanding of Scripture and can explain it to others.

It reminds us that elders are to be "examples to the flock" in their daily lives, and that would certainly include their own personal relationships with God in Bible reading, prayer, and worship. Just as Paul could say, *"Be imitators of me,* as I am of Christ" (1 Cor. 11:1; cf. 2 Tim. 3:10–11), and just as he could command Timothy to *"set the believers an example* in speech, in conduct, in love, in faith, in purity" (1 Tim. 4:12), and just as he could tell Titus, "Show yourself in all respects to be a *model of good works,* and in your teaching show integrity, dignity, and sound speech that cannot be condemned" (Titus 2:7–8), so the pattern is to be continued in the lives of all church leaders today. It is not optional that their lives be examples for others to follow; it is a requirement.

**e. What Is the Meaning of "Husband of One Wife"?** The qualification *"the husband of one wife"* (1 Tim. 3:2; Titus 1:6) has been understood in different ways. Some people have thought that it excludes from the office of elder men who have been divorced and have then married someone else, since they have then been the husband of two wives. But this does not seem to be a correct understanding of these verses.

There are two alternative interpretations, both of which are more persuasive. The interpretation I favor is that Paul was prohibiting a polygamist (a man who *presently* has more than one wife) from being an elder. Several reasons support this view: (1) All the other qualifications listed by Paul refer to a man's *present status,* not his entire past life. For example, 1 Timothy 3:1–7 does not mean "one who has *never been* violent" but "one who is *not now* violent, but gentle." It does not mean "one who has *never been* a lover of money," but "one who is *not now* a lover of money." It does not mean "one who has been above reproach for his whole life," but "one who is now above reproach." If we made these qualifications apply to one's entire past life, then we would exclude from office almost everyone who became a Christian as an adult, for it is doubtful that any non-Christian could meet these qualifications.

(2) Paul could have said "having been married only once" if he had wanted to, but he did not.[19] (3) We should not prevent remarried widowers from being elders, but that would also be necessary if we take the phrase to mean "having been married only once." The qualifications for elders are all based on a man's moral and spiritual character, and there is nothing in Scripture to suggest that a man who remarried after his wife had died has lower moral or spiritual qualifications.[20] (4) Polygamy was possible in the first

---

19. The Greek expression for "having been married only once" would be *hapax gegamēmenos,* using the word "once" (*hapax*) plus a perfect participle, giving the sense, "having been married once and continuing in the state resulting from that marriage." (Such a construction is found, for example, in Heb. 10:2, and a similar construction is found in Heb. 9:26. Related expressions with aorist verbs are found in Heb. 6:4; 9:28; and Jude 3.) Another way Paul could have expressed the idea of having been married only once is using a perfect participle of *ginomai* to say "having been a husband of one wife" (*gegonōs mias gunaikos anēr*). This is, in fact, the force of the requirement for

widows in 1 Tim. 5:9, *"having been* the wife of one husband" (the force of the perfect participle *gegonuia* carries over from the previous phrase, and all the qualifications for enrolling widows in 1 Tim. 5:9–10 speak of past history in their lives). But in 1 Tim. 3:2 and Titus 1:6 the sense is different, because present tense forms of *eimi* ("to be") are used: (literally) "It is necessary for a bishop *to be* blameless, the husband of one wife."

20. Some interpreters in the early church did try to exclude remarried widowers from church office (see, for example, *Apostolic Constitutions* 2.2; 6.17 [third or fourth century AD], and *Apostolic Canons* 17 [fourth or fifth century AD]), but these

century. Although it was not common, polygamy was practiced, especially among the Jews. The Jewish historian Josephus says, "For it is an ancestral custom of ours to have several wives at the same time."[21] Rabbinic legislation also regulated inheritance customs and other aspects of polygamy.[22]

The second alternative interpretation is that the phrase "husband of one wife" refers to the quality of being a "one-woman man," that is, one who is faithful to his wife. It is possible to translate the Greek expression *mias gunaikos andra* as "a man of one woman," and one argument in support of this is the similar expression "the wife of one husband" (Greek *henos andros gunē*. "a one-man woman") in 1 Timothy 5:9.

My conclusion is that it is best to understand "the husband of one wife" to prohibit a polygamist from holding the office of elder. Another possibility is that the verse requires a man who is faithful to his wife. In either case, the verses say nothing that would automatically prohibit everyone who has been divorced and remarried or who has remarried after his first wife died from being considered for the office of elder.

**f. The Public Installation of Elders.** In connection with the discussion of elders, Paul says, "Do not be hasty in the laying on of hands" (1 Tim. 5:22). Although the context does not specify a process for selecting elders, the immediately preceding context (1 Tim. 5:17–21) deals entirely with elders, and laying on of hands would be an appropriate ceremony for setting someone apart to the office of elder (note the laying on of hands to ordain or establish people in certain offices or tasks in Acts 6:6; 13:3; 1 Tim. 4:14). Therefore, the setting apart of elders seems the most likely possibility for the action Paul has in mind. In this case he would be saying, "Do not be hasty in ordaining people as elders." This would be consistent with a process whereby deacons also are to be "tested first; then let them serve as deacons if they prove themselves blameless" (1 Tim. 3:10). Although Paul did ordain elders quite soon after the establishment of each church (Acts 14:23), here he cautions that such appointment should not be rushed, lest a mistake be made. And in the entire process, the church must be careful not to judge as the world judges, for "man looks on the outward appearance, but the LORD looks on the heart" (1 Sam. 16:7; cf. 2 Cor. 5:16). This necessity for evaluation of a person's spiritual condition was also evident when the apostles encouraged the church at Jerusalem to pick out "seven men of good repute, *full of the Spirit and of wisdom,* whom we will appoint to this duty" (Acts 6:3). Among those chosen was "Stephen, a man full of faith and of the Holy Spirit" (Acts 6:5).

---

statements reflect not a biblical perspective but a false asceticism which held that celibacy in general was superior to marriage. (These texts can be found in the *Ante-Nicene Fathers* series, 7:396, 457, and 501.) However, Chrysostom (d. AD 407) understood 1 Tim. 3:2 to prohibit polygamy, not second marriages after death or divorce (see his *Homilies* on 1 Tim. 3:2).

21. Josephus, *Antiquities* 17.14; in 17.19 he lists the nine women who were married to King Herod at the same time.

22. See Mishnah, *Yebamoth* 4:11; *Ketuboth* 10:1, 4, 5; *Sanhedrin* 2:4; *Kerithoth* 3:7; *Kiddushin* 2:7; *Bechoroth* 8:4. Other evidence on Jewish polygamy is found in Justin Martyr, *Dialogue with Trypho,* chapter 134. Evidence for polygamy among non-Jews is not as extensive but is indicated in Herodotus (d. 420 BC) 1.135; 4.155; 2 Macc. 4:30 (about 170 BC); Tertullian, *Apology* 46.

We should also note that the appointment of elders in Paul's early churches was accompanied by "prayer and fasting," perhaps in connection with the process of selection of the elders. (Note the example of Jesus who "went out to the mountain to pray, and all night he continued in prayer to God" before he chose his twelve disciples [Luke 6:12–13].)

**g. What about Timothy and Titus?** Finally, I should note that I have not discussed the office held by Timothy and Titus under the category of apostle or under the category of elder. This is because Timothy and Titus, together with some of Paul's other coworkers, are not apostles, but neither are they elders or deacons. They seem to fall in an unusual category that we might call "apostolic assistants," for they had some delegated authority from the apostles to supervise early churches while they were being established. Since there is today no living apostle to whom people like this would be accountable and from whom they would derive their authority, we should not expect to have any apostolic assistants like this in the church today either.

### 3. Deacon

The word *deacon* is a translation of the Greek word *diakonos*, which is the ordinary word for "servant" when it is used in contexts not dealing with church officers.

Deacons are mentioned clearly in Philippians 1:1: "To all the saints in Christ Jesus who are at Philippi, with the overseers and *deacons*." But there is no specification of their function, other than to indicate that they are different from the overseers (elders). Deacons are also mentioned in 1 Timothy 3:8–13 in a more extensive passage:

> Deacons likewise must be dignified, not double-tongued, not addicted to much wine, not greedy for dishonest gain. They must hold the mystery of the faith with a clear conscience. And let them also be tested first; then let them serve as deacons if they prove themselves blameless. Their wives likewise must be dignified, not slanderers, but sober-minded, faithful in all things. Let deacons each be the husband of one wife, managing their children and their own households well. For those who serve well as deacons gain a good standing for themselves and also great confidence in the faith that is in Christ Jesus. (1 Tim. 3:8–13)

The function of deacons is not spelled out here, but the qualifications for deacons suggest some functions. For instance, they seem to have had some responsibility in caring for the finances of the church, since they had to be people who were "not greedy for dishonest gain" (v. 8). They perhaps had some administrative responsibilities in other activities of the church as well because they were to manage their children and their households well (v. 12). They may also have ministered to the physical needs of those in the church or community who needed help (see discussion of Acts 6 below). Moreover, if verse 11 speaks of their wives (as in the ESV), then it would also be likely that they were involved in some house-to-house visitation and counseling, because the wives are to be "not slanderers." It would do no good for the church if the wives of deacons (who would no doubt also be involved in prayer and counseling along with the deacons) spread confidential matters around the church. But these are only suggestions of possible areas of responsibility hinted at in this passage.

The noun *deacon* is not itself used in Acts 6:1–6 but a related verb (Gk. *diakoneō* "to serve") is found in verse 2: "It is not right that we should give up preaching the word of God to *serve* tables." Here the apostles who ruled over the Jerusalem church found it necessary to delegate some administrative responsibilities to others. In this case, the responsibilities included the distribution of food to widows who were in need. It seems appropriate to think of these seven men as "deacons" even though the name *deacon* had perhaps not yet come to be applied to them as they began this responsibility, for they seem to be given tasks which fit well with the responsibilities of deacons hinted at in 1 Timothy 3:8–12.

There are other texts in which it is difficult to know whether the New Testament is speaking about a deacon as a special church officer or is simply using the word to refer to a "servant" in a general sense. This is the difficulty in Romans 16:1, where Phoebe is called a "servant" or a "deaconess" or "deacon" (this type of Greek noun has the same form in both masculine and feminine genders, so it is simply a question of which English word is most appropriate) of the church at Cenchreae. Because Paul's requirement for deacons was that they be "the husband of one wife" (1 Tim. 3:12), the translation "servant" seems preferable in Romans 16:1 (*diakonos* takes this sense in Rom. 13:4; 15:8; and 1 Cor. 3:5).[23] In general, the verses on deacons show that they had recognized offices to "serve" the church in various ways. Acts 6:1–6 suggests that they had some administrative responsibilities but were nevertheless subject to the authority of those who had rule over the entire church.

It is significant that nowhere in the New Testament do deacons have ruling authority over the church as the elders do, nor are deacons ever required to be able to teach Scripture or sound doctrine.

---

23. Some have argued that 1 Tim. 3:11, in translations such as the NIV, refers to women deacons: "In the same way, *the women* are to be worthy of respect, not malicious talkers but temperate and trustworthy in everything" (NIV). It is true that the Greek word *gunē* can mean either "woman" or "wife," depending on the context. However, if Timothy and the church at Ephesus knew that women could be deacons, it would seem very strange for Paul to have to add a separate verse that talked specifically about women deacons, and then specify nothing more about them than would have been required if the verse had not been there at all. Moreover, it would seem very odd for Paul to sandwich only one verse about women deacons in the middle of five verses (three preceding and two following) about men who are deacons. On the other hand, a verse referring to the wives of deacons in the middle of a list of qualifications for deacons would be very appropriate: Paul elsewhere includes family conduct as one aspect of the requirement for church office (1 Tim. 3:2, 4–5). It is true that Paul simply says "the wives" rather than "their wives," but Greek frequently omits possessive adjectives when the person named (brother, sister, father, mother, etc.) would have an obvious relationship to the person being discussed in the immediate context.

For two views of this verse, and two views on whether women should be deacons today, see Thomas R. Schreiner, "The Valuable Ministries of Women in the Context of Male Leadership: A Survey of Old and New Testament Examples and Teaching," in Piper and Grudem, *Recovering Biblical Manhood and Womanhood*, 213–14, 219–221, and 505n13; and, in the same volume, George W. Knight III, "The Family and the Church: How Should Biblical Manhood and Womanhood Work Out in Practice?," 353–54.

### 4. Other Offices?

In many churches today, there are other offices, such as treasurer, moderator (one responsible for chairing church business meetings), or trustees (in some forms of church government, these are people who have legal accountability for the property owned by the church). Moreover, churches with more than one paid staff member may have some staff members (such as music director, education director, youth worker, etc.) who are "publicly recognized as having the right and responsibility to perform certain functions in the church," and who thus fit our definition of church officer, and who may even be paid to perform such functions as a full-time occupation, but who may not be elders or deacons in the church.

There does not seem to be any reason to say that these should not be offices in the church as well, even though all of them could probably be put in the category of either elder or deacon (most of those mentioned above could be deacons with specific responsibilities, and the moderator could also be an elder who simply moderates church business meetings). Nevertheless, if these or other similar offices seem helpful for the functioning of the church, there seems to be no reason why they should not be established. Yet if they are established, it would be necessary to see that they not overshadow the importance of the offices specifically named in Scripture, and that they not have any authority that is not subject to the governing authority of those officers that are clearly named in Scripture. If significant influence or authority is gained by those who have offices not named in Scripture, then it is much less likely that people in the congregation or the office holders themselves will look to Scripture and find detailed descriptions of how they should act or how they should be chosen. This would tend to diminish the effective authority of Scripture to govern the church in the area of church leadership.

### B. How Should Church Officers Be Chosen?

In the history of the church there have been two major types of process for the selection of church officers: selection by a higher authority or selection by the local congregation. The Roman Catholic Church has its officers appointed by a higher authority: the Pope appoints cardinals and bishops, and the bishops appoint priests in local parishes. This is a "hierarchy," or system of government by a priesthood[24] that is distinct from the laypeople in the church. This system claims an unbroken line of descent from Christ and the apostles, and claims that the present priesthood stands as Christ's representatives in the church. Although the Church of England (the Episcopalian Church in the United States) does not submit to government by the Pope or have cardinals, it does have some similarities to the hierarchical system of the Roman Catholic Church, since it is governed by bishops and archbishops, and its clergy are thought of as priests. It also

---

24. The word *hierarchy* means "government by priests" and derives from the Greek words for "priest" (*hiereus*) and "rule" (*archē*).

claims direct succession from the apostles, and priests and bishops are appointed by a higher authority outside the local parish.[25]

In distinction from this system of appointment by higher authority, in most other Protestant groups church officers are chosen by the local church or by some group within the local church, even though the form of church government may vary in other significant ways (see below). Since this is an area in which there is no absolutely decisive biblical text, we ought to be patient with some diversity among evangelicals on this issue. However, there are several reasons why it seems most appropriate that church officers (such as elder and deacon, and certainly including the "pastor") should be chosen or at least affirmed or recognized in some way by the whole congregation.

(1) In the New Testament, there are several examples where church officers were apparently chosen by the whole congregation. In Acts 6:3, the apostles do not pick out the seven early deacons (if we see them as deacons), but they instead say to the whole church, *"Pick out from among you* seven men of good repute, full of the Spirit and of wisdom, whom we will appoint to this duty." The initial selection of these men was done by the whole congregation. When a replacement was chosen for Judas to be numbered among the apostles, *the whole congregation of 120 persons* (see Acts 1:15) made the initial selection of two, from whom the Lord indicated which one he would appoint: *"They* put forward two, Joseph called Barsabbas, who was also called Justus, and Matthias" (Acts 1:23). At the end of the Jerusalem council, the whole church had a part with the apostles and elders in choosing representatives to convey the decisions to the other churches, for the choosing and sending was done by "the apostles and the elders, *with the whole church*" (Acts 15:22; cf. "in assembly," v. 25). Moreover, when some of the churches sent an offering with Paul to be taken to the Jerusalem church, the churches also sent a representative to accompany Paul, one who, according to Paul, "has been appointed *by the churches* to travel with us as we carry out this act of grace" (2 Cor. 8:19).[26]

It may be objected that Paul and Barnabas *"appointed"* elders in every church (Acts 14:23), and Paul also told Titus to *"appoint* elders in every town" (Titus 1:5). Does this not seem more like the Roman Catholic or Anglican system than a system of congregational choice? Yet even those verses need not imply that the apostles alone made the selection but could certainly include congregational consultation and even consent before an official appointment or installation was made (as with the appointment in Acts 6:3, 6). The word translated *appointed* may also mean "installed."[27]

(2) Another reason for congregational participation in the selection of church officers is that in the New Testament generally, final governing authority seems to rest

---

25. The United Methodist Church in the United States also has appointment of local clergy by bishops and has some similarities to the Episcopal Church, from which it came.

26. Of course, this church representative *may* have been appointed only by officers within the church, but there is no statement to that effect: Paul just says that he had been "appointed by the churches" and certainly does not mention any higher authority outside the churches.

27. See the definitions for *cheirotoneō* In BDAG, 1083.

not with any group outside the church or any group within the church but with the church as a whole. The final step in church discipline before excommunication is to *"tell it to the church"* (Matt. 18:17). Excommunication, or the act of excluding someone from the fellowship of the church, is done when the *whole congregation* is "assembled" (1 Cor. 5:4) and is therefore apparently done by the entire congregation. One other consideration that is suggestive but not conclusive is the fact that the epistles that are written to churches are not sent to the elders or some other group of leaders within the churches but are written to entire churches, and the whole congregation is encouraged to read and expected to give heed to these epistles (Rom. 1:7; 1 Cor. 1:2; 2 Cor. 1:1; cf. 2 Cor. 1:13; Col. 4:16; 1 Tim. 4:13). This means that the apostles relate directly to the congregations, not to the congregations through the officers.

There are also some practical reasons that can be mentioned.

(3) If the entire congregation selects the officers of the church, there is more accountability to the congregation. Paul assumed some level of accountability when he provided for the fact that "two or three witnesses" could bring a charge of wrongdoing against an elder (1 Tim. 5:19). This accountability provides an additional safeguard against temptations to sin and excessive lust for power.[28]

(4) Historically, false doctrine often seems to be adopted by the theologians of the church first, by the pastors second, and by the informed laity, who are daily reading their Bibles and walking with the Lord, last. Therefore, if the leadership begins to stray in doctrine or in life, and there is no election by the congregation, then the church as a whole has no practical means of getting hold of the situation and turning it around. But if officers are elected by the church, then there is a system of accountability whereby even the governing authority of the church has some accountability to the church as a whole.

(5) Government works best when it has the consent of the people who are governed (cf., in the Old Testament, Ex. 4:29–31; 1 Sam. 7:5–6; 10:24; 2 Sam. 2:4; 1 Kings 1:39–40; and note the mistake of Rehoboam in 1 Kings 12:1, 15).

These factors combine to indicate that although Scripture does not explicitly command one specific system of choosing church officers, it would seem most wise to have a system whereby the entire church has a significant role in the selection and recognition of the officers of the church—perhaps through a congregational vote, or through some other process whereby congregational recognition is required before church officers can assume office.[29]

Can anything else be said about the process of selecting officers? Some additional congregational checks against excessive use of authority might be built into the selection process. There is room for wide variation here, but provisions such as election to limited

---

28. However, this situation also has a potential for abuse if a few influential members exert influence to keep the pastor from dealing with issues of sin in their own lives.

29. When I mention a congregational vote I do not mean to suggest the idea of a competitive election such as is found in secular politics. It may simply involve a requirement that the congregation vote to ratify candidates who have been nominated by a mature group within the church (such as the present elders), or, on the other hand, it may involve a church-wide election, or other processes may be used. Scripture is silent regarding the actual process; therefore, God has decided to leave the matter to the wisdom of each congregation in its own setting.

terms of office, a requirement for a mandatory year off (except for full-time pastoral staff members who are elders) every few years, a requirement for periodic reaffirmation of an elder's selection, and a provision in the nominating process whereby nominations can be made by the members of the congregation (even if most nominations come from the elders themselves) would all provide additional measures of accountability to the congregation without forfeiting any essential aspects of governing authority over the congregation once elders are elected.

These factors would also provide some arguments against a self-perpetuating group of elders that is not subject to election or periodic reconfirmation by the congregation, but once again it must be said that no specific directives are listed in Scripture and there is room for variation at this point.

## C. FORMS OF CHURCH GOVERNMENT

In discussing forms of church government there is some overlap with the previous section on the method of choosing church officers, for the selection of officers is one very important aspect of authority in the church. Different philosophies of church government will be reflected in different methods used for selecting officers of the church, as explained above.

This is evident in the fact that forms of church government can be broken down into three large categories, which we may call episcopalian, presbyterian, and congregational. The *episcopalian* forms have a government by a distinct category of church officers known as a priesthood, and final authority for decision making is found outside the local church.[30] The Episcopal Church system is the primary representative among Protestants of this form of government. The *presbyterian* forms have a government by elders, some of whom have authority not only over their local congregation but also, through the presbytery and the general assembly, over all the churches in a region and then in the denomination as a whole. The *congregational* forms of church government all have final governing authority resting with the local congregation, although various degrees of self-rule are given up through denominational affiliation, and the actual form of local church government may vary considerably. We will examine each of these forms of government in the following discussion.

## 1. Episcopalian

In the episcopalian system, an archbishop has authority over many bishops. They in turn have authority over a "diocese," which simply means the churches under the jurisdiction of a bishop. The officer in charge of a local parish is a rector (or sometimes a vicar, who is an "assistant" or one who substitutes for the rector). Archbishops, bishops,

---

30. The Roman Catholic Church also has government by a priesthood and is therefore "episcopalian" in form of government. Sometimes an episcopalian form of government is called a "hierarchical" government, especially when referring to the Roman Catholic Church.

and rectors are all "priests" since they have all at one time been ordained to the episcopalian priesthood (but in practice the rector is most often called the priest). However, Episcopalians understand the English word *priest* to be equivalent to the term *presbyter* (the Greek term for "elder"), while Roman Catholics understand the word *priest* differently, relating it to the Old Testament priesthood in its duty of offering sacrifices and representing the people to God and God to the people.

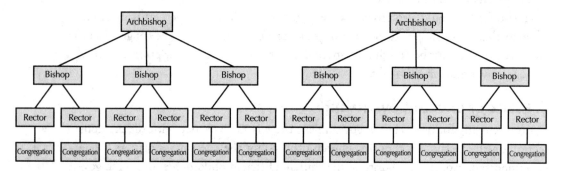

**Episcopalian Government**
*Figure 47.1*

The argument for the episcopalian system is not that it is found in the New Testament but that it is a natural outgrowth of the development of the church that began in the New Testament and that it is not forbidden by the New Testament. E. A. Litton writes, "No order of Diocesan Bishops appears in the New Testament," but he immediately adds:

> The evidence is in favour of the supposition that Episcopacy sprang from the Church itself, and by a natural process, and that it was sanctioned by Saint John, the last survivor of the Apostles. The Presbytery, when it assembled for consultation, would naturally elect a president to maintain order; first temporarily, but in time with permanent authority. . . . Thus it is probable that at an early period an informal episcopate had sprung up in each church. As the Apostles were one by one removed . . . the office would assume increased importance and become invested with greater powers.[31]

Moreover, since the office of bishop and the corresponding government structure found in the Episcopalian Church is both historical and beneficial, Litton argues that it should be preserved. Finally, the benefit of direct descent from the apostles is regarded as a strong reason in favor of the episcopalian system. Litton says, "The Apostles are the first link in the chain, and there is no reason why a succession, as regards to the external commission, should not proceed from age to age, the existing body of ministers handing down the official authority to their successors, and these latter in turn to theirs."[32]

But there are arguments that may be given on the other side of this question. (1) It is significant that the office of "bishop" is not a distinct office in the New Testament but is simply a synonym for the name "elder," as Litton himself agrees.[33] There is no *single* bishop in the New Testament, but bishops (or overseers) are always plural in number. This should not be seen merely as an incidental fact, for even among the apostles Jesus did not leave one with superior authority over the others, but he left a group of twelve who were equal in governing authority (and to whom others were later added, such as Paul). Though some apostles, such as Peter, James, and Paul, had prominence among the group, they did not have any greater authority than the others, and even Peter was rebuked by Paul in Antioch (Gal. 2:11).[34] This may well reflect the wisdom of Christ in guarding against the abuse of power that inevitably comes when any one human being has too much power without sufficient checks and balances from others. Just as Jesus left a plurality of apostles to have ultimate (human) authority in the early church, so the apostles always appointed a plurality of elders in every church, never leaving only one person with governing authority.

(2) The theory of a group of bishops established to replace the apostles is not taught in the New Testament, nor is there an implication of a need for *physical* continuity of ordination through the laying on of hands by those who have been ordained in an unbroken chain of succession from the apostles. For example, in Acts 13:3, it was not the Jerusalem apostles who ordained Paul and Barnabas but people in the church at Antioch who laid hands on them and sent them out. In fact, there is very little evidence that the apostles had any concern for a line of succession. Timothy apparently was ordained not simply by Paul but also by a "council of elders" (1 Tim. 4:14), though this may well have included Paul as well (see 2 Tim. 1:6). More importantly, ordaining is ultimately from the Lord himself (Acts 20:28; 1 Cor. 12:28; Eph. 4:11), and there is nothing in the nature of "ordaining" (when it is simply seen as public recognition of an office) that requires that it be done *only* by those previously ordained in *physical* descent from the apostles. If God has called an elder, he is to be recognized, and no concern about physical descent needs to be raised. In addition, if one is convinced that the local church should elect elders (see discussion above), then it would seem appropriate that the church that elected the elder—not an external bishop—should be the group to confer the outward recognition at election by installing the person in office or ordaining the pastor.[35]

---

32. Ibid., 390.

33. Ibid., 400.

34. Roman Catholics argue that Peter had greater authority than the other apostles from the beginning, but the New Testament evidence does not bear this out. (On the "power of the keys" in Matt. 16:19, see chapter 46, pp. 1097–1100.)

35. Episcopalians, who favor appointment of officers by a bishop, would of course not agree with the premise of this last consideration.

(3) While it may be argued that the development of an episcopalian system with single bishops in authority over several churches was a beneficial development in the early church, one may also argue that it was a deviation from New Testament standards and a result of human dissatisfaction with the system of elected local elders that had been established by the apostles and that had apparently worked very well from AD 33 to 100 throughout all of the New Testament church. But one's evaluation of the historical data will of course depend on one's evaluation of earlier arguments for and against an episcopalian system.

## 2. Presbyterian

In this system, each local church elects elders to a session (E in figure 47.2 stands for elder, and the dotted lines indicate that the whole congregation elects the elders). The pastor of the church will be one of the elders in the session, equal in authority to the other elders. This session has governing authority over the local church. However, the members of the session (the elders) are also members of a presbytery, which has authority over several churches in a region. This presbytery consists of some or all of the elders in the local churches over which it has authority. Moreover, some of the members of the presbytery are members of the "general assembly," which usually has authority over all the presbyterian churches in a nation or region.[36]

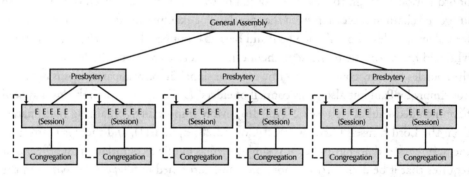

**Presbyterian Government**
*Figure 47.2*

The arguments in favor of this presbyterian system are (1) that those who have wisdom and gifts for eldership should be called on to use their wisdom to govern more than just one local church, and (2) a national (or even worldwide) government of the church shows the unity of the body of Christ. Moreover (3) such a system is able to prevent an

---

36. In the Christian Reformed Church, the form of government is similar to a presbyterian system, but the names of the governing bodies are different: the elders in a local church are called a *consistory* (instead of a session), the regional governing body is called a *classis* (instead of a *presbytery*), and the national governing assembly is called a *synod* (instead of a *general assembly*).

individual congregation from falling into doctrinal error much more effectively than any voluntary association of churches.[37]

The presbyterian system outlined above has many adherents among evangelical Christians today, and it certainly works effectively in many cases. However, some objections can be brought against this system: (1) Nowhere in Scripture do *elders* have regularly established authority over more than their own local church. The pattern is rather that elders are appointed in local churches and have authority over local churches. Against this claim the Jerusalem council in Acts 15 is often mentioned, but we should notice that this council was held in Jerusalem because of the presence of the apostles. Apparently the apostles and the elders in Jerusalem, with the representatives from Antioch (Acts 15:2), together sought God's wisdom on this matter. And there seems to have been some consultation with the whole church as well, for we read, at the conclusion of the discussion, "Then it seemed good to the apostles and the elders, *with the whole church*, to choose men from among them and send them to Antioch with Paul and Barnabas" (Acts 15:22). (If this narrative gives support to regional government by elders, it therefore also gives support to regional government by whole congregations!) This situation with the elders in Jerusalem is not a good pattern to defend a system whereby elders have authority over more than their local churches: the Jerusalem church did not send for all the elders in Judea, Samaria, and Galilee and call a meeting of "the Judean presbytery" or a "general assembly." Although the apostles in Jerusalem certainly had authority over all the churches, there is no indication that elders by themselves, even in the Jerusalem church, had any such authority. And certainly there is no New Testament pattern for elders exercising authority over any other than their own local churches.

On the other hand, advocates of a presbyterian system could answer that nowhere in the New Testament do we find an example of an independent church, because every church in the New Testament is subject to the worldwide governing authority of the apostles. Of course, a defender of independent churches might answer that we have no apostles today to exercise such authority. However, if we are looking to the New Testament for a pattern, the fact still remains that no independent churches are to be found there, and we would expect that *something* rather than *nothing* would replace a government by the apostles. This seems to me to indicate that some sort of denominational authority over local churches is still appropriate (though that will take different forms in different denominations).

(2) This system, in practice, results in much formal litigation, where doctrinal disputes are pursued year after year all the way to the level of the general assembly. One wonders if this should be characteristic of the church of Christ—perhaps so, but it seems

---

37. A fuller defense of the presbyterian system of church government is found in Louis Berkhof, *Systematic Theology* (Grand Rapids: Eerdmans, 1941), 581–92.

to the present author to be a system that encourages such litigation far more than is necessary or edifying for the body of Christ.

(3) The effective power in church government seems, in practice, to be too removed from the final control of the laypeople in the church. Although Berkhof, who defends this system of government, affirms quite clearly that "the power of the church resides *primarily* in the governing body of the local church,"[38] he also admits that "the more general the assembly, the more remote it is from the people."[39] Thus the system is very hard to turn around when it begins to go wrong since the laypersons who are not elders have no vote in the session or the presbytery or the general assembly, and the governing structure of the church is further removed from them than in other church government structures.

(4) Although in some cases it is true that a doctrinally sound denomination with a presbyterian system of government can keep a local church from going astray in its doctrine, in actuality very frequently the opposite has been true: the national leadership of a presbyterian-governed denomination has adopted false doctrine and has put great pressure on local churches to conform to it.

(5) Although the presbyterian system does represent in one form the national or even worldwide unity of Christ's church, such unity can certainly be shown in other ways than through this system of government. The churches with more purely congregational forms of government do have voluntary associations that manifest this unity. In fact, these associations involve *all* the people in the churches, not just the elders or the clergy, as in a presbyterian system. The national meeting of a Baptist denomination, for example, where large numbers of ministers and laypersons (who are delegates from their churches, not necessarily elders or deacons) join in fellowship, might be seen as a better demonstration of the unity of Christ's body than a presbyterian general assembly where only elders are present.

### 3. Congregational

**a. Single Elder (or Single Pastor).** We can now look at five varieties of congregational government for the church. The first one, which is common among Baptist churches in the United States, is the "single elder" form of government. In this kind of government the pastor is seen as the only elder in the church, and there is an elected board of deacons who serve under his authority and give support to him (D in figure 47.3 stands for deacon).

In this system, the congregation elects the pastor and the deacons. The amount of authority the pastor has varies greatly from church to church and generally will increase the longer a pastor remains in a church. The authority of the deacon board is often thought to be merely an advisory authority. In the way this system ordinarily functions, especially in smaller churches, many decisions must be brought before the congregation as a whole.

---

38. Ibid., 584.                                39. Ibid., 591.

**Single-Elder (Single-Pastor) Government**
*Figure 47.3*

The arguments in favor of this system are presented clearly in A. H. Strong's *Systematic Theology*, a text that was previously widely used in Baptist circles.[40] Strong gives the following arguments.

(1) The New Testament does not require a plurality of elders, but the pattern of plural elders seen in the New Testament was only due to the size of the churches at that time. He says,

> In certain of the New Testament churches there appears to have been a plurality of elders. . . . There is, however, no evidence that the number of elders was uniform, or that the plurality which frequently existed was due to any other cause than the size of the churches for which these elders cared. The New Testament example, while it permits the multiplication of assistant pastors according to need, does not require a plural eldership in every case.[41]

In this quotation Strong shows that he would regard additional pastors hired by a larger church to be elders as well, so that this system could be expanded beyond a single elder/pastor to include two or more elder/pastors. But the crucial distinction is that *the governing authority of the office of elder is possessed only by the professional pastor(s) of the church* and is not shared by laypersons in the church. And we must realize that in practice, the vast majority of churches that follow this pattern today are relatively small churches with only one pastor; therefore, in actuality, this usually becomes a single elder form of government.[42]

---

40. A. H. Strong, *Systematic Theology* (Valley Forge, PA: Judson, 1907), 914–17. Strong was President of Rochester Theological Seminary from 1872 to 1912.

41. Ibid., 915–16.

42. Another Baptist theologian, Millard Erickson, supports Strong's claim that the New Testament does not require plural elders in a church. He says that the New Testament examples of elders are "descriptive passages" that tell about a church order that already existed, but that "churches are not instructed to adopt a particular form of church order" (*Christian Theology*, 1003). Moreover, Erickson sees no one pattern of church government in the New Testament, but says, "There may well have been rather wide varieties of governmental arrangements. Each church adopted a pattern that fit its individual situation" (ibid.).

(2) Strong adds that "James was the pastor or president of the church at Jerusalem," and cites Acts 12:17; 21:18; and Galatians 2:12 to show that this leadership by James was a pattern that could then be imitated by other churches.

(3) Strong notes that some passages have "bishop" in the singular but "deacons" in the plural, hinting at something similar to this common Baptist form of government. If we translate the Greek word *episcopos* as "bishop" (instead of "overseer"), then a literal translation of the Greek text will show a singular definite article modifying "bishop" in two verses: "*The bishop* therefore must be without reproach" (1 Tim. 3:2, literal translation), and "*the bishop* must be blameless" (Titus 1:7, literal translation), but by contrast, we read, "*Deacons* likewise must be dignified" (1 Tim. 3:8).

(4) Finally, the "angel of the church" in Revelation 2:1, 8, 12, 18; 3:1, 7, 14, according to Strong, "is best interpreted as meaning the pastor of the church; and, if this be correct, it is clear that each church had, not many pastors, but one."[43]

(5) Another argument, not made by Strong, is found in literature on church growth. The argument is that churches need a strong single pastor in order to grow rapidly.[44]

Once again it must be said that this single elder form of government has worked successfully in many evangelical churches. However, there can be objections to the case presented by Strong and others.

(1) It seems inconsistent to argue that the New Testament falls short of giving a clear *command* that all churches should have a plurality of elders when the passages on qualifications of elders in 1 Timothy 3:1–7 and Titus 1:5–7 are used as scriptural *requirements* for church officers today. How can churches say that the *qualifications for elders* found in the New Testament Epistles and Acts are commanded for us today but the *system of plural elders* found in these very same New Testament books is not commanded but was required only in that time and in that society? Though it could be objected that these are commands written only to individual situations in Ephesus and Crete, much of the New Testament consists of apostolic commands written to individual churches (in Rome, Corinth, Philippi, Thessalonica, etc.) on how they should conduct themselves. Yet we do not say that, since they were written to local churches, we are free to disobey the instructions in these epistles. In fact, 1 Timothy and Titus give us a great deal of material on the conduct of local churches generally, material that all believing churches seek to follow.[45]

---

43. Strong, *Systematic Theology*, 916.

44. See, for example, C. Peter Wagner, *Leading Your Church to Growth* (Ventura, CA: Regal, 1984). He says, "The principal argument of this book is that if churches are going to maximize their growth potential they need pastors who are strong leaders. . . . Make no mistake about it: it is a rule" (73). The book is filled with anecdotes and pronouncements from church growth experts telling the reader that leadership by a strong single pastor is essential to significant church growth.

45. There are a very few (three or four) commands regarding physical actions that carry symbolic meaning that varies from culture, such as foot washing, a holy kiss, and head covering for women. We rightly obey these with different physical actions today. See discussion in Wayne Grudem, *Christian Ethics* (Wheaton, IL: Crossway, 2018), 1227–32.

Moreover, it seems to be quite unwise to ignore a clear New Testament pattern that existed throughout all the churches for which we have evidence at the time the New Testament was written. When the New Testament shows us that *no* church was seen to have a single elder ("in *every* church," Acts 14:23; "in every town," Titus 1:5; "let him call for the *elders*," James 5:14; "I exhort the *elders* among you," 1 Peter 5:1), then it seems unpersuasive to say that smaller churches would have only had one elder. Even when Paul had just founded churches on his first missionary journey, there were *elders* appointed "in every church" (Acts 14:23). And "every town" on the island of Crete was to have elders, no matter how large or small the church was.

In addition, there is an inconsistency in Strong's argument when he says that the large churches were those which had plural elders, for then he claims that "the angel of the church in Ephesus" (Rev. 2:1) was a single pastor, according to this common Baptist pattern. Yet the church at Ephesus at that time was exceptionally large: Paul, in founding that church, had spent three years there (Acts 20:31), during which time *"all the residents of Asia heard the word of the Lord,* both Jews and Greeks" (Acts 19:10). The population of Ephesus at that time was more than 250,000.[46]

We may ask, why should we follow Strong and adopt as the norm a pattern of church government which is *nowhere* found in the New Testament, and reject a pattern *everywhere* found in the New Testament?

(2) James may well have acted as moderator or presiding officer in the church in Jerusalem, for all churches will have some kind of designated leader like this in order to conduct meetings. But this does not imply that he was the "pastor" of the church in Jerusalem in a "single elder" sense. In fact, Acts 15:2 shows that there were *elders* (plural) in the church in Jerusalem, and James himself was probably numbered among the apostles (see Gal. 1:19) rather than the elders.

(3) In 1 Timothy 3:2 and Titus 1:7, the Greek definite article modifying "overseer" simply shows that Paul is speaking of general qualifications as they applied to any one example.[47] In fact, in both cases Strong cites we know there were *elders* (plural) in the churches involved: 1 Timothy 3:2 is written to Timothy at Ephesus, and Acts 20:17 shows us that there were "elders" in the church at Ephesus. And even in 1 Timothy, Paul writes, "Let the *elders* who rule well be considered worthy of double honor, especially those who labor in preaching and teaching" (1 Tim. 5:17). With regard to Titus 1:7 we need only look to verse 5, where Paul directs Titus explicitly to "appoint *elders* in every town."

---

46. Robert H. Mounce, *The Book of Revelation*, NIC (Grand Rapids: Eerdmans, 1977), 85.

47. In terms of Greek grammar, the use of the definite article here is best understood as a "generic" use, which is a use of the definite article that "distinguishes one class from another. . . . It categorizes rather than particularizes" (Daniel Wallace, *Greek Grammar beyond the Basics* [Grand Rapids: Zondervan, 1996], 227, and see 229 for the generic use of the definite article in 1 Tim. 3:2). Paul's use of the singular was natural after he said, "If *anyone* aspires to the office of overseer, he desires a noble task" (1 Tim. 3:1), or "If *anyone* is above reproach" (Titus 1:6).

The ESV gives a more appropriate translation for English readers, reflecting this generic use, at these two verses: "*an* overseer."

(4) The angels of the seven churches in Revelation 2–3 are unusual and rather weak evidence for single elders. "The angel of the church in Ephesus" (Rev. 2:1) can hardly mean that there was only one elder in that church, since we know there were "elders" there in this very large church (Acts 20:17). The word *angel* used in the address to the seven churches in Revelation 2–3 may simply designate a special messenger to each church, perhaps even the human messenger who would take what John wrote to each church,[48] or it may represent "the prevailing spirit of the church" rather than the ruling official of the congregation,[49] or it may even refer to an angel who was given special care over each congregation. Even if it did represent a presiding officer of some sort in each congregation, this "angel" is not shown to have any ruling authority or any functions equivalent to today's single pastor or to an elder in the New Testament churches. This passage does not furnish strong enough evidence to dislodge the clear data throughout the New Testament showing plural elders in every church, even in the church in Ephesus.

It is interesting that all of the New Testament passages cited by Strong (Acts 15, Jerusalem; 1 Tim. 3:2, Ephesus; Titus 1:7, Crete; Rev. 2–3, the seven churches, including Ephesus) speak of situations in which the New Testament points quite clearly to a plurality of elders in authority in the churches mentioned.

(5) The argument from church growth studies does not really prove that government led by a single pastor is necessary, for at least three reasons: (a) We should not reject a pattern supported in Scripture and adopt a different one just because people tell us that the different pattern seems to work well in producing large churches—our role here, as in all of life, should rather be to obey Scripture as closely as we can and expect God to bring appropriate blessing as he wills. (b) There are many large churches with government by plural elders (both Presbyterian churches and independent churches), so the argument from pragmatic considerations is not conclusive. (c) C. Peter Wagner admits that strong leaders can be found in various forms of church government,[50] and we must agree that a system of plural elders in which all have equal authority does not prevent one elder (such as the pastor) from functioning as a sort of "first among equals" and having a significant leadership role among those elders.

(6) A common practical problem with a "single elder" system is either an excessive concentration of power in one person or excessive demands laid upon him. In either case, the temptations to sin are very great, and a lessened degree of accountability makes yielding to temptation more likely. As was mentioned above, it was never the pattern in the New Testament, even with the apostles, to concentrate ruling power in the hands of any one person.

---

48. The word *angelos* ["angel"] in Rev. 2:1 et al. can mean not only "angel" but also just "messenger."

49. See Mounce, *The Book of Revelation*, 85.

50. Wagner says at one point that a pastor can be a strong leader within a variety of kinds of church government (*Leading Your Church to Growth*, 94–95). Therefore, it is not appropriate to take his study as an argument that solely supports a single elder form of government.

Here it should be noted that the "single elder" view of church government really has no more New Testament support than the "single bishop" (episcopalian) view. Both seem to be attempts to justify what has already happened in the history of the church, not conclusions that have grown out of an inductive examination of the New Testament.

(7) Finally, it should be noted that in actual practice the "single elder" system can change and *function* more like a "plural elders" government, only those who function as elders are instead called "deacons." This would happen if the deacons share the actual governing authority with the pastor, and the pastor and individual deacons all see themselves as accountable to the deacon board as a whole. The system then begins to look like figure 47.4.

**The Pastor and Deacons May Govern Together
and Thus Function like a Government of Plural Elders**
*Figure 47.4*

The problem with this arrangement is that it does not use biblical terminology to apply to the functions that people are carrying out, for deacons in the New Testament never had governing or teaching authority in the church. The result in such a situation is that people in the church (both the deacons and the other church members) will fail to read and apply scriptural passages on elders to those who are *in fact functioning as elders* in their church. Therefore, these passages lose the direct relevance that they should have in the church. In this case, however, the problem could be solved by changing the name "deacon" to "elder" and considering the pastor an elder along with the others.

**b. Plural Local Elders.** Is there any kind of church government that preserves the pattern of plural elders found in the New Testament and that avoids the expansion of elders' authority beyond the local congregation? Although such a system is not distinctive of any denomination today,[51] it is found in many individual congregations. Using the conclusions reached to this point on the New Testament data, I would suggest figure 47.5 as a possible pattern.

---

51. However, Pastor Ralph Perry pointed out to me that the Churches of Christ (noninstrumental) have practiced this pattern of church government for many years, as have many congregations of the Christian Church/Church of Christ (instrumental).

**Plural Local Elder Government**
*Figure 47.5*

Within such a system the elders govern the church and have authority to rule over it, authority that has been conferred by Christ himself, the head of the church, and by the Holy Spirit (Acts 20:28; Heb. 13:17). In this system of government, there is always more than one elder, a fact that distinguishes this form of government from the "single elder system" discussed above. In a contemporary congregation, the "pastor" (or "senior pastor") would be one among the elders in this system. He does not have authority over them, nor does he work for them as an employee. He has a somewhat distinct role in that he is engaged in the full-time work of "preaching and teaching" (1 Tim. 5:17) and derives part or all of his income from that work (1 Tim. 5:18). He also may frequently assume a leadership role (such as chairman) among the elders, which would fit with his leadership role among the congregation, but such a leadership role *among the elders* would not be necessary to the system. In addition, the pastor will ordinarily have considerable authority to make decisions and provide leadership in many areas of responsibility that have been delegated to him by the elder board as a whole. Such a system would allow a pastor to exercise strong leadership in the church while still having equal governing authority with the other elders.

The strength of this system of government is seen in the fact that the pastor does not have authority on his own over the congregation, but that authority belongs collectively to the entire group of elders (what may be called the elder board). Moreover, the pastor himself, like every other elder, is subject to the authority of the elder board as a whole. This can be a great benefit in keeping a pastor from making mistakes, supporting him in adversity, and protecting him from attacks and opposition.[52]

In such a system, are there limitations that should be placed on the authority of the elders? In the section above on the manner of choosing church officers, several reasons were given to have some limitations that would provide regular accountability

---

52. If the church has more than one pastor who is paid for his work, these other associate or assistant pastors may or may not be viewed as elders (depending on the qualifications of each staff member and the policies of the church), but in either case, it would be entirely consistent with this form of government to have those associate pastors accountable to the senior pastor alone in their day-to-day work, and he accountable to the elder board with respect to his supervision of their activity.

and put restrictions on the authority of the officers of a church.[53] Those arguments are also helpful here in indicating that, though elders have substantial governing authority over the church, *it should not be unlimited authority.* Examples of such limitations are (1) they may be elected rather than self-perpetuating, (2) they may have specific terms with a mandatory year off the board (except for the pastor, whose continuing leadership responsibilities require continuous participation as an elder), and (3) some large decisions may be required to be brought to the whole church for approval. Regarding this third point, congregational approval is already a biblical requirement for church discipline in Matthew 18:17 and for excommunication in 1 Corinthians 5:4. The principle of congregational election of elders would imply that the decision to call any pastor would also have to be approved by the congregation as a whole. Major new directions in the ministry of the church, which will require large-scale congregational support, may be brought to the church as a whole for approval. Finally, it would seem wise to require congregational approval on such large financial decisions as an annual budget, the decision to purchase property, or the decision to borrow money for the church (if that is ever done), simply because the church as a whole will be asked to give generously to pay for these commitments.[54]

In fact, the reasons for placing some limitations on the authority of church officers may appear so strong that they would lead us to think that all decisions and all governing authority should rest with the congregation as a whole. (Some churches have adopted a system of almost pure democracy in governing the church, whereby everything must come to the congregation as a whole for approval.) However, this conclusion ignores the abundant New Testament evidence about the clear ruling and governing authority given to elders in New Testament churches. Therefore, while it is important to have *some recognized limitations* on the authority of elders and to rest ultimate governing authority with the congregation as a whole, it still is necessary—if we are to remain faithful to the New Testament pattern—to have a strong level of authority vested in the elders themselves.

---

53. The arguments given above (pp. 921–22) for restrictions on the authority of church officers may be summarized as follows: (1) Church officers in the New Testament were apparently chosen by the whole congregation. (2) The final governing authority in New Testament churches seemed to rest with the whole church. (3) Accountability to the congregation provides a safeguard against temptations to sin. (4) Some degree of control by the entire congregation provides a safeguard against the leadership falling into doctrinal error. (5) Government works best with the consent of those governed. In addition to those, there is another reason for restricting the authority of church officers: (6) The doctrine of the clarity of Scripture (see chapter 6), and the doctrine of the priesthood of all believers (whereby the New Testament affirms that all Christians have access to God's throne in prayer and all share as members in a "royal priesthood" [1 Peter 2:9; cf. Heb. 10:19–25; 12:22–24])

combine to indicate that all Christians have some ability to interpret Scripture and some responsibility to seek God's wisdom in applying it to situations. All have access directly to God in order to seek to know his will. The New Testament allows for no special class of Christians who have greater access to God than others. Therefore, it is right to include all believers in some of the crucial decision-making processes of the church. "In an abundance of counselors there is safety" (Prov. 11:14).

54. It should be noted that a church government system with a self-perpetuating group of elders, rather than one elected by the congregation, would be very similar in function to this system, but would not be as extensive in the limitations put on the authority of the elders. Such a church may still think it wise to have some mechanism whereby the congregation could remove elders who strayed from faithfulness to Scripture in serious ways.

Should an associate pastor also be an elder? When this kind of "plural local elders" system functions in a large church, the elder board may decide that one of the associate pastors has the character traits and maturity that would qualify him to be an elder. I do not think, in principle, that there should be any objection to having a mature and wise associate pastor join the elder board. However, it does not seem wise for this to be a common practice because a large majority of the elder board should be persons *who are not associate pastors in the church*. This is because the associate pastors are subject to the senior pastor in all of their church work (he usually hires and fires them and sets their pay, and they report to him). Therefore, if several of the elders are associate pastors, the interpersonal dynamics involved will make it awkward for them to disagree with the senior pastor during the elder meetings, and the system will increasingly tend to function as a (somewhat disguised) form of "single pastor" government, not as a plural elder government.

Someone may object that in a large church only full-time staff members know enough about the life of the church to be effective elders, but this is not a persuasive objection. Government by boards who are not closely involved in the everyday activities of those whom they govern works well in many realms of human activity, such as college and seminary boards, local school boards, boards of directors of corporations, and even state and national governments. All of these governing bodies direct policies and give guidance to full-time administrators, and they are able to obtain detailed information about specific situations when the need arises. (I realize that all these systems *can* work poorly, but my point is simply that they can work very well when the right people are put in leadership positions.)

I have labeled this system one of "plural *local* elders" in order to distinguish it from a presbyterian system where elders, when gathered on the level of the presbytery or general assembly, have authority over more than their own local congregations. But in such a system of elected local elders, can there be any wider associations with churches beyond the local congregation? Yes, certainly. While churches with this system may choose to remain entirely independent, most will enter into voluntary associations with other churches of similar convictions in order to facilitate fellowship and the pooling of resources for mission activity (and perhaps for other things such as Christian camps, publications, theological education, etc.). However, the only authority these larger associations would have over the local congregation would be the authority to exclude an individual church from the association, not the authority to govern its individual affairs.

**c. Corporate Board.** The remaining three forms of congregational church government are not commonly used, but they are sometimes found in evangelical churches. The first one is patterned after the example of a modern corporation, where the board of directors hires an executive officer who then has authority to run the business as he sees fit. This form of government could also be called the "you-work-for-us" structure. It is depicted in figure 47.6.

**Corporate Board Model of Church Government**
*Figure 47.6*

In favor of this structure it might be argued that this system in fact works well in contemporary businesses. However, there is no New Testament precedent or support for such a form of church government. It is simply the result of trying to run the church like a modern business, and it sees the pastor not as a spiritual leader but merely as a paid employee.

Further objections to this structure are the fact that it deprives the pastor of sharing in the ruling authority that must be his if he is to carry out his eldership responsibilities effectively. Moreover, the members of the board are also members of the congregation over whom the pastor is supposed to have some authority, but that authority is seriously compromised if the leaders of the congregation are in fact his bosses.

**d. Pure Democracy.** This view, which takes congregational church government to its logical extreme, can be represented as in figure 47.7.

**Government by Pure Democracy**
*Figure 47.7*

In this system *everything* must come to the congregational meeting. The result is that decisions are often argued endlessly, and as the church grows, decision making reaches a point of near paralysis. While this structure does attempt to do justice to some of the passages cited above regarding the need for final governing authority to rest with the congregation as a whole, it is unfaithful to the New Testament pattern of recognized and designated elders who have actual authority to rule the church in most situations.

**e. "No Government but the Holy Spirit."** Some churches, particularly very new churches with more mystical or extremely pietistic tendencies, function with a church government that looks something like figure 47.8.

**No Government but the Holy Spirit**
*Figure 47.8*

In this case, the church would deny that any form of government is needed, it would depend on all the members of the congregation being sensitive to the leading of the Holy Spirit in their lives, and decisions would generally be made by consensus. This form of government never lasts very long. Not only is it unfaithful to the New Testament pattern of designated elders with governing authority in the church, but it is also subject to much abuse because subjective feelings rather than wisdom and reason prevail in the decision-making process.

### 4. Conclusions

It must be made clear, in concluding this discussion of church government, that the form of government adopted by a church is not a major point of doctrine. Christians have lived comfortably and ministered very effectively within several different kinds of systems, and there are many evangelicals within each of the systems mentioned. Moreover, a number of different types of church government systems seem to work *fairly well*. Where there are weaknesses that appear to be inherent in the governing structure, individuals within the system generally recognize those weaknesses and attempt to compensate for them in whatever ways the system will allow.

Nevertheless, a church can be *more pure* or *less pure* on this point, as in other areas. As we are persuaded by Scripture concerning various aspects of church government, then we should continue to pray and work for the greater purity of the visible church in this area as well.

### D. Should Women be Church Officers?

Most systematic theologies have not included a section on the question of whether women can be church officers because it has been assumed through the history of the church, with very few exceptions, that only men could be pastors or function as elders within a church.[55] But in recent years a major controversy has

---

55. See William Weinrich, "Women in the History of the Church: Learned and Holy, But Not Pastors," in Piper and Grudem, *Recovering Biblical Manhood and Womanhood*, 263–79. See also Ruth A. Tucker and Walter L. Liefeld, *Daughters of the Church: Women and Ministry from New Testament Times to the Present* (Grand Rapids: Zondervan, 1987).

arisen within the evangelical world: May women as well as men be pastors? May they share in all the offices of the church? I have treated this question much more extensively in a number of other books,[56] but a brief summary of the question can be given at this point.

We must affirm at the outset that the creation narrative in *Genesis 1:27 views men and women as equally created in the image of God.* "So God created man in his own image, in the image of God he created him; male and female he created them" (Gen. 1:27). The first page of the entire Bible affirms that men and women together are created in God's image, and therefore we have equal value to God, and this means that women should be seen by us as having absolutely equal value to men as persons and to the church. Moreover, Scripture assures men and women of equal access to all the blessings of salvation (see Acts 2:17–18; Gal. 3:28).[57] This is remarkably affirmed in the high dignity and respect that Jesus accorded to women in his earthly ministry.[58]

We must also admit that evangelical churches have often failed to recognize the full equality of men and women and thereby have failed to count women equal in value to men. The result has been a tragic failure to recognize that God often gives women equal or greater spiritual gifts than men, as well as a failure to encourage women to have full and free participation in the various ministries of the church and a failure to take full account of the wisdom that God has given to women with respect to important decisions in the life of the church. If the present controversy over women's roles in the church can result in the eradication of some of these past abuses, then the church as a whole will benefit greatly.

Yet the question remains, should women be pastors or elders in churches? (Or should they fill roles equivalent to that of an elder in churches that have alternative forms of government?) My conclusion on this issue is that the Bible does not permit women to function in the role of pastor or elder within a church. This has also been the conclusion of the vast majority of churches in various societies throughout history. The reasons that seem to me to be most persuasive in answering this question are the following.

---

56. See Piper and Grudem, eds., *Recovering Biblical Manhood and Womanhood*, and for a detailed analysis more than two decades later, see Wayne Grudem, *Evangelical Feminism and Biblical Truth: An Analysis of More Than 100 Disputed Questions* (Sisters, OR: Multnomah, 2004; repr., Wheaton, IL: Crossway, 2012). My 2004 book *Evangelical Feminism and Biblical Truth* (856 pages) was published in a condensed form as *Countering the Claims of Evangelical Feminism* (Colorado Springs: Multnomah, 2006; 320 pages). In addition, I claimed that all of the twenty-five main arguments used by evangelical feminists undermine the authority of Scripture and lead churches and denominations toward liberalism in another book, *Evangelical Feminism: A New Path to Liberalism?* (Wheaton, IL: Crossway, 2006). The position I have

taken in the following pages is consistent with the "Danvers Statement" issued in 1988 by the Council on Biblical Manhood and Womanhood, based in Louisville, Kentucky. The strongest arguments opposing my position and arguing in favor of an evangelical feminist position are found in *Discovering Biblical Equality: Complementarity without Hierarchy*, ed. Ronald Pierce and Rebecca Merrill Groothuis (Downers Grove, IL: InterVarsity Press, 2005).

57. See also Raymond C. Ortlund Jr., "Male-Female Equality and Male Headship: Gen. 1–3," in Piper and Grudem, *Recovering Biblical Manhood and Womanhood*, 95–112.

58. See James A. Borland, "Women in the Life and Teachings of Jesus," in Piper and Grudem, *Recovering Biblical Manhood and Womanhood*, 113–23.

## 1. 1 Timothy 2:11–15

The single passage in Scripture that addresses this question most directly is 1 Timothy 2:11–15:

> Let a woman learn quietly with all submissiveness. I do not permit a woman to teach or to exercise authority over a man; rather, she is to remain quiet. For Adam was formed first, then Eve; and Adam was not deceived, but the woman was deceived and became a transgressor. Yet she will be saved through childbearing—if they continue in faith and love and holiness, with self-control.

Here Paul is speaking about the church when it is assembled (see vv. 8–9). In such a setting, Paul says, "I do not permit a woman to *teach* or to *exercise authority* over a man" (v. 12). These are the functions that are carried out by the elders of the church, and especially by what we know as a pastor in contemporary church situations.[59] It is specifically these functions unique to elders that Paul prohibits for women in the church.[60]

**a. The Meaning of Verse 13.** Paul's first reason is the order of creation: "For Adam was formed first, then Eve." Paul does not use some local situation in Ephesus for a reason, such as saying, "For women aren't as well educated there in Ephesus," or "For you have some disruptive women teaching false doctrine there in Ephesus." No, he points back to the original time of creation, before there was any sin in the world, and sees that there was a purpose of God indicated in the order of creation: "For Adam was formed first, then Eve." Paul simply assumes that his readers will understand that when God created Adam first and then gave commands to him alone (Gen. 2:7, 15–17) and then later created Eve (Gen. 2:22), God was giving a leadership role to Adam.

People in the ancient world, where the first-born son had a leadership role in the family, would have understood this. But we do not need to assume that Paul was endorsing the entire system of "primogeniture," at least not in all its details. It is enough simply to say that people who were familiar with that system would have had no trouble understanding Paul's reasoning: the first-born male in any family is assumed to be the leader in that family in his generation, and Adam was the first-born in his generation, so he was the leader.

When Paul bases his argument on the order of creation of Adam and Eve, it indicates

---

59. See discussion on pp. 1126–27 above regarding the teaching and ruling functions of elders in a church.

60. For a more extensive treatment of this passage, see Douglas Moo, "What Does It Mean Not to Teach or Have Authority Over Men? 1 Tim. 2:11–15," in Piper and Grudem, *Recovering Biblical Manhood and Womanhood*, 179–93.

A recent, very extensive analysis of this passage is found in Andreas Köstenberger and Thomas Schreiner, ed., *Women in the Church: An Interpretation and Application of 1 Timothy*

2:9–15, 3rd ed. (Wheaton, IL: Crossway, 2016). A significant addition to the third edition of this book is Al Wolters's new and remarkably wide-ranging analysis of the verb *authenteō* ("to have authority") that, in my opinion, will remain the definitive treatment of that verb for many decades to come ("The Meaning of *Authenteō*," 65–115). The book also contains an extensive new survey of the history of translation of 1 Timothy 2:12: "New and Old Departures in the Translation of *Authentein* in 1 Timothy 2:12," by Denny Burk, 279–96.

that his command about women not teaching or having authority in the assembled congregation transcends cultures and societies. It applies to men and women as they were created by God at the beginning, and it is not due to any distortion brought on by sin or the fall. It applies, then, to all churches for all time, and it is a means by which the beauty of manhood and womanhood as God created them to be can be manifested in the life of the church.

**b. The Meaning of Verse 14.** As his second reason why Paul does not "permit a woman to teach or to exercise authority over a man," he says, "Adam was not deceived, but the woman was deceived and became a transgressor" (1 Tim. 2:14). We should not understand this to mean that Paul was punishing women for something that Eve did. The New Testament authors do not try to perpetuate the punishments of the curse in Genesis 3 but work to bring redemption and alleviate the punishments that came as a result of the fall. The goal of the gospel is redemption, not punishment.

There are two main interpretations of 1 Timothy 2:14. The first interpretation says that verse 14 refers to a *role reversal* in the fall. The idea is that Eve took the initiative and decided to eat the forbidden fruit on her own, but in doing this she took a leadership role that belonged to Adam.

The second major interpretation, and the one that I think best fits the wording of the verse, is that Paul is saying something about the nature of men and women as God created them. This is by far the most common viewpoint in the history of interpretation of this passage. While some authors have wrongly understood this text to be teaching the intellectual inferiority of women, that misunderstanding is certainly not necessary to the passage, nor am I aware of any modern author who holds that view today.

Rather, this interpretation says that while God made men and women (in general) with equal intellectual abilities, there are still differences in preferences and inclinations, and those differences are consistent or "congruent" with God's purposes in entrusting leadership in the church to men. Paul is saying, therefore, that women should not teach or have authority over men in the congregation of God's people for two reasons: (1) God gave Adam a leadership role when he created him first and Eve second (v. 13), and (2) God gave men, in general, a disposition that is better suited to teaching and governing in the church, a disposition that inclines more to rational, logical analysis of doctrine and a desire to protect the doctrinal purity of the church, and God gave women, in general, a disposition that inclines more toward a relational, nurturing emphasis that places a higher value on unity and community in the church (v. 14). Both emphases are needed, of course, and both men and women have some measure of both tendencies. But Paul understands the kinder, gentler, more relational nature of women (in general) as something that made Eve less inclined to oppose the deceptive serpent and more inclined to accept his words as something helpful and true.

**c. The Meaning of Verse 15.** Paul's concluding sentence in this section is, "Yet she will be saved through childbearing—if they continue in faith and love and holiness, with self-control" (1 Tim. 2:15). The general force of the sentence is clear, although people differ about the details. Paul has just finished saying that "the woman was deceived and became a transgressor." In this final comment his purpose is to assure readers that Eve's sin was not the final word regarding women! Though Eve sinned, salvation is now possible through Christ.

The phrase "through childbearing" is probably best understood as *an example* of being obedient to God's calling on one's life. Women are not to teach or govern the church, but God has given them a special responsibility, the awesome responsibility of bearing and raising children. Paul understands that not all women will be able to have children (for the Old Testament and life experience both testify to that fact), and he also gives a long section on widows in 1 Timothy 5:3–16, so he knows there are many women in the church at Ephesus who do not have husbands. But Paul is speaking of "childbearing" as a representative example of how a woman should be obedient to God's calling on her life and fulfill the role or roles God has called her to do, whether that includes bearing and raising of children, or showing "hospitality" (1 Tim. 5:10), or caring for the afflicted (5:10), or managing their households (5:14), or ministering through "supplications and prayers" (5:5), or training younger women (Titus 2:4–5), or any mixture of these or other callings. Paul takes "childbearing" as one obvious and representative example of a woman's distinctive role and calling from God.

What does it mean then to say that "she will be saved through childbearing"? It surely does not mean that a woman is justified or forgiven of her sins because of childbearing or fulfilling other tasks to which God calls her, for Paul clearly teaches that salvation in this sense is a "gift of God, not a result of works, so that no one would boast" (Eph. 2:8–9) and it comes "through faith" (Eph. 2:8).

But Paul can use *salvation* and related terms in another sense, to refer to the Christian life from initial conversion until our death, a life in which we live in increasing obedience to God and see more and more good works as a consequence and as an evidence of the change that God has brought about in our lives. So Paul means that a woman will be "saved"—she will continue to work out the results of her salvation—"through childbearing," that is, through obedience to God in the various tasks and roles that he calls her to rather than attempting to teach or govern the church, which is a role God has not called women to.

**d. However, the Bible Encourages Other Kinds of Teaching and Speaking by Women.**

**(1) Acts 18:26: Explaining the Bible in informal settings.**[61] In discussing 1 Timothy 2:12, it is important to read it in the light of other passages that view some kinds of teaching by women in a positive way. For example, we read in Acts 18:26 concerning

---

61. From here to the end of this chapter, much of the material is adapted from Wayne Grudem, *Evangelical Feminism and Biblical Truth*, 62–101, and is used with permission of the publisher.

Apollos: "He began to speak boldly in the synagogue, but when Priscilla and Aquila heard him, *they* took him and *explained to him* the way of God more accurately" (Acts 18:26). The word translated "explained" (Greek *ektithēmi*) is plural and it indicates *both* Aquila and Priscilla were involved in explaining the way of God more fully to Apollos.

This incident is viewed with approval in the book of Acts, for there is no indication that anything was wrong with this conduct as it fits the ongoing narrative of the spread of the gospel to many gentile cities. Therefore, *this passage gives warrant for women and men to talk together about the meaning of biblical passages and to "teach" one another in such settings.* A parallel example in modern church life would be a home Bible study where both men and women contribute to the discussion of the meaning and application of Scripture. In such discussions, everyone is able to "teach" everyone else in some sense, for such discussions of the meaning of the Word of God are not the authoritative teaching that would be done by a pastor or elder to an assembled congregation, as in 1 Timothy 2.

Another modern parallel to the private conversation between Priscilla and Aquila and Apollos would be *the writing of books on the Bible and theology by women.* When I read a Bible commentary written by a woman, for example, it is as if the author were talking privately to me, explaining her interpretation of the Bible, much as Priscilla talked to Apollos in Acts 18:26. Reading a book by a woman author is much like having a private conversation with a woman author. The woman author does not have teaching authority over an assembled congregation or a group of men.

**(2) 1 Corinthians 11:4–5: Praying and prophesying in the assembled congregation.** Another example of an activity in the church that Scripture approves is *praying aloud before the assembled congregation,* because Paul says, "Every man who prays or prophesies with his head covered dishonors his head, but every wife who *prays or prophesies* with her head uncovered dishonors her head—it is the same as if her head were shaven" (1 Cor. 11:4–5). Paul implies that it would be normal and natural in the church at Corinth for women to pray and to prophesy aloud. If it were wrong for women to pray or prophesy in the church service, Paul would not have said they should have their heads covered when they do so!

This passage also implies that giving prophecies aloud in the assembled congregation is appropriate for women. As I explain more fully in chapter 53, giving a prophecy is simply reporting something that God has spontaneously brought to mind.[62] Prophecy is always listed as a separate gift from teaching in the New Testament, and prophecy is always to be subject to the teaching and governing authority of the elders and is to be tested for its conformity to Scripture (see 1 Cor. 14:29; 1 Thess. 5:20–21). In churches that believe this gift is still valid for today, giving prophecies is another appropriate activity for women.

---

62. See below, pp. 1293–1313. See also Grudem, *The Gift of Prophecy in the New Testament and Today.*

**(3) Titus 2:3–5: Women teaching women.** Paul encourages another kind of teaching activity by women when he says, "Older women . . . are to teach what is good, and so *train the young women* to love their husbands and children, to be self-controlled, pure, working at home, kind, and submissive to their own husbands, that the word of God may not be reviled" (Titus 2:3–5). All kinds of Bible teaching ministries from women to other women are encouraged by this passage. Organizations such as Bible Study Fellowship have outstanding ministries in training women in the knowledge of the Word of God, and in the United States at least, some excellent women Bible teachers will speak to conferences of several thousand at one time. These are valuable ministries that should be encouraged. They are not the kind of teaching or having authority over men that Paul prohibits in 1 Timothy 2.

**(4) John 4:28–30 and Matthew 28:5–10: Evangelism.** Evangelism of all kinds is another activity not restricted to men alone but open to men and women alike. For example, the woman at the well in Samaria went and told her village about Jesus:

> So the woman left her water jar and went away into town and said to the people, "Come, see a man who told me all that I ever did. Can this be the Christ?" They went out of the town and were coming to him. (John 4:28–30)

In addition, the women at the tomb became the first eyewitnesses of the resurrection, and Jesus sent them to tell his disciples about the resurrection (Matt. 28:5–10). These passages suggest that it would be appropriate for women to do evangelism in any setting, whether privately or in large groups. In speaking to non-Christians, they are not having the kind of teaching or governing authority over the church that Paul prohibits in 1 Timothy 2 because the unbelievers who hear the gospel message are not a congregation of assembled believers.

The history of missions has many stories of courageous women who went by themselves to proclaim the gospel to unreached people. For example, Wycliffe Bible translator Joanne Shetler tells a beautiful story of her work with the Balango people in the Philippines, and her interaction with a man in the village (her "daddy") who had adopted her into his family and who was reading pages of the New Testament for her as she produced it:

> I continued translating in Timothy with my daddy. And we came to a verse where Paul says to Timothy, "I don't allow women to teach men." My daddy didn't bat an eyelash. But that afternoon, after we'd finished work, he said to me, "Now what is that we're going to study on Sunday?" I thought he was just curious. I didn't know what was on his mind since fathers don't report to their children. So I told him. Sunday morning came, and before I could stand up to start, he stood up and said, "My daughter here knows more about this than I do, but we found in the Bible that

women aren't supposed to teach men. So I guess I have to be the one!" And that was the end of my career, and the beginning of their teaching.[63]

It was a beautiful picture of a key turning point in the transition from an informal group of new Christians to an established congregation with indigenous male leadership naturally taking charge.

Situations similar to this have probably occurred hundreds of times throughout the history of the church, and no doubt God gives much grace as new Christians seek to be faithful to his Word, even when it might be difficult to say exactly what point a transition should occur without being present in the actual situation. The important point is that the transition does occur, and male leadership is established in the church.

**(5) Other kinds of speaking in the assembled church.** Churches should encourage women in several other kinds of speaking in church, such as giving a personal testimony of God's work in a woman's own life or in the lives of others, reading Scripture, singing a solo or singing in a group, acting as part of a dramatic presentation—whatever goes on in the assembled church other than what is explicitly prohibited by Scripture (Bible teaching and governing over the congregation of God's people).

### e. Objections related to 1 Timothy 2:12

Several objections have been brought against the view that 1 Timothy 2:12 prohibits women from teaching the assembled church or governing the church as an elder.[64]

**(1) Objection: Paul says this only because women were teaching false doctrine in Ephesus.** It has been argued that this passage applies only to the specific situation that Paul is addressing, probably one where women were teaching heretical doctrine within the church at Ephesus. But this objection is not persuasive, since there is no clear statement in 1 Timothy that says that women were actually *teaching* false doctrines (1 Tim. 5:13 talks about women who are gossiping, but does not mention false doctrine). In addition, the only false teachers named in Ephesus are men, not women (see 1 Tim. 1:20; 2 Tim. 2:17–18; also note that Paul tells the elders at Ephesus "from among your own selves will arise *men* [plural of Greek *anēr*, "man"] speaking twisted things," Acts 20:30).

Moreover, Paul does not simply tell certain women who are teaching false doctrine to be silent, but he says, "I do not permit a woman to teach or to exercise authority over a man." And finally, the *reason* Paul gives for this prohibition is not the one proposed in this objection, but a far different one: the situation of Adam and Eve before the fall, and before there was any sin in the world (see v. 13), and the way in which a reversal in male and female roles occurred at the time of the fall (see v. 14). These reasons are not

---

63. Joanne Shetler, "Faithful in Obedience," lecture, Urbana Student Missions Conference, 1984. Audio file available from https://urbana.org/urbana-84.

64. For more extensive statements of these objections see the books marked "Favors women as pastors" in the bibliography at the end of this chapter, especially the books by Mickelsen, Spencer, Bilezikian, and Pierce and Groothuis. I have given a much fuller analysis of these and other objections in Grudem, *Evangelical Feminism and Biblical Truth*, especially chapters 7, 8, and 9.

limited to one situation in the church at Ephesus, but have application to manhood and womanhood generally.

**(2) Objection: Paul says this because the women in Ephesus weren't well educated.** Another objection is to say that Paul gave this prohibition because women were not well educated in the first century and therefore were not qualified for teaching or governing roles in the church. But Paul does not give lack of education as a reason for saying that women cannot "teach or . . . exercise authority over a man" but rather points back to creation (vv. 13–14). It is precarious to base an argument on a reason Paul did *not* give instead of the reason he *did* give.

In addition, this objection misunderstands the actual facts of the ancient church and the ancient world. Formal training in Scripture was not required for church leadership in the New Testament church because several of the apostles did not have formal biblical training (see Acts 4:13). On the other hand, the skills of basic literacy and therefore the ability to read and study Scripture were available to men and women alike (note Acts 18:26; Rom. 16:1; 1 Tim. 2:11; Titus 2:3–4). There were many well-educated women in the ancient world and particularly in a cultural center such as Ephesus.[65]

In *Women and Men in Ministry: A Complementary Perspective*,[66] Clinton Arnold and Robert Saucy report further evidence of the significant educational achievements of women in ancient Ephesus:

> In a very important recent study, Paul Trebilco has accumulated and presented the inscriptional evidence attesting to the role of women in civic positions in western Asia Minor. . . . [67] It is frequently assumed in some of the literature that women in Ephesus (and in Asia Minor and the entire Roman world, for that matter) lacked education and the opportunity for an education. This has been drastically overstated. . . .
>
> There is now inscriptional evidence that women served in some of the cities in a position that would be a close functional equivalent of our "superintendent of schools," that is, in the capacity of a gymnasiarch (*gymnasiarchos*). The "gymnasium" was the center for education in a Greek city. . . . The "gymnasiarch" had oversight of the intellectual training of the citizens and for the general management of the facility. Inscriptions dating from the first to the third centuries attest to fifty women who served as gymnasiarchs in twenty-three cities of Asia Minor and the coastal islands. This suggests that women not only had access to education, but also that in many places they were leading the educational system.[68]

65. See Piper and Grudem, eds., *Recovering Biblical Manhood and Womanhood*, 82.

66. Robert L. Saucy and Judith K. TenElshof, eds., *Women and Men in Ministry: A Complementary Perspective* (Chicago: Moody Publishers, 2001).

67. Arnold and Saucy at this point referred to Paul Trebilco, *Jewish Communities in Asia Minor*, SNTSMS 69 (Cam-

bridge: Cambridge University Press, 1991), especially chapter 2, "The Prominence of Women in Asia Minor," 104–26. (Information taken from Arnold and Saucy, 366n4.)

68. Clinton Arnold and Robert Saucy, "The Ephesian Background of Paul's Teaching on Women's Ministry," in Saucy and TenElshof, *Women and Men in Ministry*, 281–83.

Finally, Paul was writing to Ephesus (1 Tim. 1:3), which was the home church of Priscilla and Aquila (see Acts 18:18–19, 21). It was in this very church at Ephesus that Priscilla knew Scripture well enough to help instruct Apollos in AD 51 (Acts 18:26). Then she had probably learned from Paul himself for another three years while he stayed at Ephesus teaching "the whole counsel of God" (Acts 20:27; cf. v. 31; also 1 Cor. 16:19). In fact, Paul himself had lived in Priscilla and Aquila's home during his time at Ephesus (Acts 18:2–3)! No doubt many other women in Ephesus had followed her example and also had learned from Paul. Although they later went to Rome, we find Aquila and Priscilla back in Ephesus at the end of Paul's life (2 Tim. 4:19), about AD 67. Therefore, it is likely that they were in Ephesus in AD 65, about the time Paul wrote 1 Timothy (about *fourteen years after Priscilla had helped instruct Apollos*). Yet Paul does not allow even well-educated Priscilla or any other well-educated women at Ephesus to teach men in the public assembly of the church. The reason was not lack of education, but the order of creation which God established between men and women.

**(3) Objection: This verse does not prohibit women from having authority but from "domineering" or misusing authority.** Those who make this objection claim that Paul did not intend to say that a woman should not "exercise authority over a man" (understanding "exercise authority" as a valued, positive function in the church), but rather his meaning was that a woman should not "domineer" or "misuse authority" over a man (understanding the Greek verb *authenteō* to refer to a harmful, destructive abuse of authority). (A related objection claims other meanings for the verb *authenteō*, such as, "I do not permit a woman to murder a man," or "instigate violence against a man.")

Elsewhere I have analyzed in some detail such claims for a negative meaning for *authenteō*,[69] with the conclusion that they simply lack any support from valid evidence from ancient Greek literature. The substantial evidence that we have regarding the meaning of this word is that it has a positive meaning that is appropriately rendered in English by "exercise authority" to "have authority."

In addition, this objection does not make sense in the context of 1 Timothy 2. If this verb meant that Paul was prohibiting teaching "in a domineering way," then why did he not prohibit men as well as women from doing this?

**(4) Objection: This verse only says that a woman should not "assume authority" (NIV 2011) over a man.** In 1 Timothy 2:12 the 2011 edition of the NIV Bible adopted a novel translation that gave the egalitarian side of this issue everything they have wanted for years in a Bible translation. It reads, "I do not permit a woman to teach or to *assume authority* over a man." If churches adopt this translation, the debate over women's roles in the church will be over, because women pastors and elders can just say,

---

69. See Grudem, *Evangelical Feminism and Biblical Truth*, 304–22. An even more comprehensive and more recent analysis of *authenteō* is the remarkably wide-ranging and erudite article by Al Wolters, "The Meaning of *Authenteō*," in Köstenberger and Schreiner, *Women in the Church*, 3rd ed., 65–115. In my opinion, this study by Wolters will remain the definitive treatment of that verb for many decades to come.

"I'm not *assuming* authority on my own initiative; it was given to me by the other pastors and elders." Therefore, any woman could be a pastor or elder so long as she does not take it upon herself to "assume authority."[70]

The problem with this translation is the lack of valid evidence from the ancient world that *authenteō* could ever take a negative or pejorative meaning with the sense of "wrongly take authority upon oneself," which is the sense that many readers will give it. The same or similar objections that I raised in the previous section to the meaning "domineer," or other pejorative meanings, also apply here. This meaning is contrary to the substantial evidence in the book by Köstenberger and Schreiner (*Women in the Church*, 3rd ed.),[71] and it fails to explain why Paul would only prohibit women from wrongly assuming authority rather than prohibiting both men and women from doing this.

**(5) Objection: This verse only prohibits a wife from having authority over her husband in the church.** Because the Greek word that is translated as "woman" (Greek *gunē*) can also mean "wife," depending on the context, some have argued that 1 Timothy 2:12 actually means "I do not permit a woman to teach or to exercise authority over her husband." However, this objection is not convincing, because when we look at passages where *gunē* means "wife," there are always decisive clues that require that meaning in those other contexts, and in every case it is clear that those contexts are discussing marriage. Here are some examples:

> Romans 7:2: "A *married* (*hupandros*) woman"
> 1 Corinthians 7:2: "Each man should have his *own* (*heautou*) wife and each woman her *own* (*idion*) husband"
> 1 Corinthians 7:12: "If any brother *has* (*echei*) a wife" (and the entire context of 1 Cor. 7 is a discussion about marriage)
> 1 Corinthians 7:39: "A wife is bound to *her* (*autēs*) husband as long as he lives"
> Ephesians 5:22: "Wives submit to your *own* (*idiois*) husbands"

By contrast, 1 Timothy 2:11–15 has no such indicators in the words or the context to show that Paul is speaking about marriage. Paul does not say, "to teach or have authority over her own husband," which he could have done. In addition, it is unlikely that Paul would give strict instructions about family life in the middle of the context devoted to a discussion of officers for the entire church (chapters 1–3). And it is highly unlikely that Paul would only require *married* men to refrain from "anger or quarreling" (1 Tim. 2:8)

---

70. This paragraph is adapted from Wayne Grudem, *Evangelical Feminism: A New Path to Liberalism?* (Wheaton, IL: Crossway, 2006), 260, and is used with permission of the publisher. (The paragraph was originally written about the TNIV 2005 translation.)

71. See especially the critique of the 2011 NIV translation by Denny Burk, "New and Old Departures in the Translation of *authenteō* in 1 Timothy 2:12," in Köstenberger and Schreiner, *Women in the Church*, 3rd ed., 286–96.

or only require *married* women to dress "in respectable apparel, with modesty and self-control" (v. 9), which means that in this very context the word *gunē* clearly means "woman," not "wife."

**(6) Objection: This is a temporary command because Paul uses a present tense verb.** People who support this objection claim that we should understand 1 Timothy 2:12 to mean, "I am *not now permitting* a woman to teach or to exercise authority over a man" (this view assumes it was a temporary command for this situation only).

But this argument simply misunderstands how Paul often uses present tense verbs to give instructions that apply permanently to all Christians. There are numerous examples, such as Romans 12:1, "I appeal (*parakalō*, present indicative) to you therefore, brothers, by the mercies of God, to present your bodies as a living sacrifice, holy and acceptable to God," or 1 Timothy 2:1, "I urge (*parakalō*, present indicative) that supplications, prayers, intercessions, and thanksgivings be made for all people." (This does not mean, "I temporarily urge that you pray.") These and many similar verses give instructions that apply to all Christians just as much today as they did when Paul wrote them. The process that is advocated in this objection would lead to the nullification of many New Testament instructions for Christians.

**(7) Objection: This verse only prohibits one activity ("authoritative teaching," as an elder), not two activities (teaching or having authority). Therefore a woman can preach sermons to a church as long as she is not an elder.** Craig Blomberg has argued that "I do not permit a woman to teach or to exercise authority over a man" (1 Tim. 2:12) means that "the only thing Paul is prohibiting women from doing in that verse is occupying the office of overseer or elder."[72] He argues this because teaching and having authority over the church are the two responsibilities unique to the office of elder, and because

> Philip Payne has demonstrated that the conjunction *oude* ("nor") that connects the two key verbs in verse 12 regularly joins together expressions that in some sense are mutually defining. In formal terminology this is called a "hendiadys" (from Greek words that mean "one through two"). In other words, Paul is not forbidding two separate actions here; rather the two verbs together define one specific function or role.[73]

72. Craig Blomberg, "Women in Ministry: A Complementarian Perspective," in *Two Views on Women in Ministry*, ed. James Beck (Grand Rapids: Zondervan, 2005), 169. Based on Blomberg's argument, Kathy Keller adopts the same position (Kathy Keller, *Jesus, Justice, and Gender Roles: A Case for Gender Roles in Ministry* [Grand Rapids: Zondervan, 2012], 18–22).

73. Ibid. The endnote points to an unpublished paper by Philip Payne, read at the Evangelical Theological Society in November 1986. However, Payne published an article on the same topic in 2008: Philip Payne, "1 Tim 2.12 and the Use of *oude* to Combine Two Elements to Express a Single Idea," in *New Testament Studies* 54, no. 2 (2008): 235–53. For example, he claims there is a single idea represented in Rom. 11:21: "if God did not spare the natural branches, *neither* (*oude*) will he spare you" (238). But these are clearly two distinct—though related—ideas (as are his other examples), so Payne's article is not persuasive.

Beginning in 2009, Philip Payne and Andreas Köstenberger each published articles in an extensive back-and-forth discussion over *oude* in 1 Timothy 2:12. In my judgment, Köstenberger has decisively won the argument in his chapter 3 of *Women in the Church*, 117–63, especially 145–52. He gives

Blomberg attempts to demonstrate that Paul "regularly" used two verbs joined by the conjunction *oude* to describe one function by listing ten other examples in 1 Timothy 2. But when we actually look up these ten examples, not one of them uses this conjunction (Gk. *oude*)![74] If Paul had written, "I do not permit a woman to teach *and* to exercise authority over a man," it would provide the parallel that Blomberg is searching for. But that is exactly what Paul did not write. Blomberg's explanation is not faithful to the meaning of the words in the text.

**(8) Objection: A woman can teach and have authority over men if she does so under the authority of the pastor or if the elders give her permission.** This objection may sound appealing at first because it recognizes the leadership role of pastor and male elders. But when we consider the objection more carefully, it is establishing a dangerous precedent. In essence, it is saying that the (male) pastor and (male) elders have the ability to give a woman permission to disobey a direct command of Scripture.

The question here is, what does the Bible say? It does not merely say, "Preserve *some kind of male authority* in the congregation." It does not say, "A woman may not teach men unless she is under the authority of the elders." Rather, it says, "I do not permit a woman to teach or to exercise authority over a man" (1 Tim. 2:12).

Can a pastor or the elders of a church give a woman permission to disobey this statement of Scripture? Certainly not! Can a woman do what the Bible says *not* to do and excuse it by saying "I'm under the authority of the elders"? Would we say that the elders of a church could tell people "under their authority" that they have permission to

---

bibliographical information about the previous articles written by him and by Payne (119–20). He concludes that Payne "presents a novel view insufficiently grounded in previous grammatical and lexicographical work" (120).

Köstenberger's critique of Payne makes this crucial distinction: "There is ... a difference between a single idea that *encompasses* two elements joined by *oude* (that is, an idea that is larger than either of the two elements) and a single idea that *combines* two elements joined by *oude* (that is, an idea that is more limited than either of the two elements) to the extent that they all but lose their distinctness" (147). His point is that Payne erroneously uses examples of the first type to argue that 1 Tim. 2:12 fits the second type.

74. Here are Blomberg's examples: "While not always employing formal hendiadys and while using conjunctions other than *oude*, Paul seems to have a propensity to use pairs of largely synonymous words to say just about everything important twice (or, occasionally, four times)! Thus we find in verse 1 'petitions, prayers, intercession and thanksgiving'; in verse 2a, 'kings and all those in authority'; in verse 2b, 'peaceful and quiet,' and 'godliness and holiness'; in verse 3, 'good and acceptable' (KJV; TNIV, 'pleases God'); in verse 4, 'to be saved and to come to a knowledge of the truth'; in verse 7a, 'a herald and an apostle'; in verse 7b, 'I'm telling the truth, I am not lying'; in verse 8, 'without anger or disputing'; in verse 9, 'decency and propriety'; and in verse 11, 'quietness and full

submission.' With this many examples of the pattern, we might well expect to find a similar pair in verse 12" (169). This collection of ten examples looks impressive—until we look them up. Then we discover that not one of these examples is really similar to verse 12 because not one of them uses the conjunction *oude* that Paul uses to say, "I do not permit a woman to teach or (Gk. *oude*) to exercise authority over a man" (of Blomberg's ten examples, eight use *kai*, "and," and two have no conjunction).

In fact, *oude* has exactly the opposite meaning from *kai*. While *kai* means "and," *oude* means, "and not." In English, it would be the difference between "I did not eat bacon and eggs" and "I did not eat bacon and I did not eat eggs." In the first sentence, I might have eaten bacon alone or eggs alone. But in the second sentence, I did not either one. Blomberg's examples are similar to the first sentence, but 1 Timothy 2:12 is similar to the second sentence.

It is true that "hendiadys" is a recognized category in Greek grammar, but to be fair to the readers, Blomberg should have explained that it is only a recognized category with the conjunction *kai*, "and" (see BDF, §442 [16], p. 228), but 1 Tim. 2:12 does not use that conjunction, so 1 Tim. 2:12 cannot legitimately be considered a hendiadys according to any recognized principle of Greek grammar. Blomberg's entire argument is based on these alleged parallel examples, none of which are actually parallel.

disobey *other* passages of Scripture? Such a process would enable pastors to nullify many of the teachings of the New Testament.

**(9) Objection: Paul was moving in a "trajectory" toward full equality of roles for women.** This objection claims that if we study the ancient cultural setting in which the Bible was written, we will find that the apostle Paul had a much higher view of the value of women than the culture in which he lived. Paul's writings and teachings lead to an improvement in the status of women compared to their status in the non-Christian culture. Today we can follow the trajectory that moves from (a) the low status of women in ancient culture to (b) the improved status of women in Paul's writings, and when we follow the direction in which Paul was moving, we can today promote (c) the full equality of women and men, with all church offices open to women as well as men. This was the goal that Paul was moving toward, but he didn't reach that goal during his lifetime. Those who make this objection sometimes note a similar argument about slavery: we can trace a trajectory moving from (a) the low status of slaves in the ancient world to (b) an improvement in the status of slaves in the writings of Paul and then to (c) advocating the complete abolition of slavery today.

The problem with this objection is that it effectively nullifies the teachings of the New Testament as a moral standard for Christians to follow today. In place of the writings of the New Testament, it means that Christians would be subject to the multiple conflicting estimates of numerous scholarly "experts" telling us their best guesses about exactly where a trajectory would lead. This means that the teachings of the New Testament are no longer our final authority. Our authority would now become *our ideas of the direction the New Testament was heading* but never quite reached. This view abandons the crucial Reformation doctrine of *sola Scriptura*, or "the Bible alone," as our ultimate authority for doctrine and life.

Furthermore, the Christian leaders who opposed slavery in Britain and the United States in the 1800s did not use this kind of trajectory argument but assumed the abiding moral authority of what is taught in the Bible itself, and they argued against slavery on that basis. And they won the argument.[75]

**(10) Most of these alternative views of 1 Timothy 2:12 have arisen since 1966.** As far as I can determine, most of the previous eight objections to saying that 1 Timothy 2:12 prohibits women from teaching or having authority over men today have arisen, in the published academic literature, since 1966.[76] This does not automatically mean that these

---

75. For further discussion of the teachings of the Bible regarding slavery, see Grudem, *Evangelical Feminism and Biblical Truth*, 340–45, 354–55, 613–16.

76. I am speaking of arguments in published commentaries and other mainstream academic literature. Some groups such as the Quakers and some holiness and Pentecostal denominations have historically ordained women as well as men (or have allowed whole-church Bible teaching by women).

The argument that the church today should not "play first century," and therefore should not seek to follow the practices of the first century church as found in the New Testament, was first expressed by Krister Stendahl, *The Bible and the Role of Women: A Case Study in Hermeneutics*, trans. Emilie T. Sanders (Philadelphia: Fortress, 1966; first Swedish edition, 1958). (Therefore technically some of this argument was first published in 1958, but it did not receive widespread attention objections are incorrect, but it does cast some doubt on them. If any of these interpretations are correct, why did no one think of them for so many centuries? And why did they arise soon after secular feminism gained widespread influence in society in the 1960s?

## 2. 1 Corinthians 14:33–36

In a passage similar to 1 Timothy 2:12, Paul writes to the church at Corinth:

> As in all the churches of the saints, the women should keep silent in the churches. For they are not permitted to speak, but should be in submission, as the Law also says. If there is anything they desire to learn, let them ask their husbands at home. For it is shameful for a woman to speak in church. Or was it from you that the word of God came? Or are you the only ones it has reached? (1 Cor. 14:33b–36)

In this section Paul cannot be prohibiting all public speech by women in the church, for he clearly allows them to pray and prophesy in church in 1 Corinthians 11:5. Therefore, it is best to understand this passage as referring to speech that is in the category being discussed in the immediate context, namely, the spoken evaluation and judging of prophecies in the congregation (see v. 29: "Let two or three prophets speak, and *let the others weigh what is said*"). While Paul allows women to speak and give prophecies in the church meeting, he does not allow them to speak up and give evaluations or critiques of the prophecies that have been given, for this would be a ruling or governing function with respect to the whole church.[77] This understanding of the passage depends on our view of the gift of prophecy in the New Testament age, namely, that prophecy involves not authoritative Bible teaching and not speaking words of God that are equal to Scripture but rather reporting something which God spontaneously brings to mind.[78] In this way, Paul's teachings are quite consistent in 1 Corinthians 14 and 1 Timothy 2: in both cases he is concerned to preserve male leadership in the teaching and governing of the church.[79]

---

until its translation into English in 1966.) At the time of the publication of the English translation in 1966, Stendhal was Dean of Harvard Divinity School.

77. For a fuller discussion of this question, see D. A. Carson, "'Silent in the Churches': On the Role of Women in 1 Cor. 14:33b–36," in *Recovering Biblical Manhood and Womanhood*, 140–53. See also Grudem, *The Gift of Prophecy in the New Testament and Today*, 217–24; also Wayne Grudem, "Prophecy—Yes, but Teaching—No: Paul's Consistent Advocacy of Women's Participation without Governing Authority," *JETS* 30, no. 1 (March 1987): 11–23.

78. This view of the gift of prophecy is explained more fully in chapter 53, pp. 1293–1313.

79. One recent evangelical objection to this conclusion on 1 Cor. 14:33–36 is simply to say that these verses were not written by Paul and do not belong in the text of 1 Corinthians,

and are therefore not to be considered authoritative Scripture for us today; see Gordon Fee, *The First Epistle to the Corinthians*, NICNT (Grand Rapids: Eerdmans, 1987), 699–708. Fee's basic argument is that it is impossible to reconcile this passage with 1 Cor. 11:5, where Paul clearly allows women to speak in the church. (He also places much weight on the fact that vv. 34–35 are moved to the end of 1 Cor. 14 in some ancient manuscripts.) But Fee does not give adequate consideration to the view represented here, namely, that Paul is simply prohibiting women from the authoritative task of judging prophecies in the assembled church. Fee's position is surprising in light of the fact that no ancient manuscript of 1 Corinthians omits these verses. (The few manuscripts that place this section at the end of chapter 14 are far less reliable manuscripts that have frequent variations elsewhere in 1 Corinthians as well.)

### 3. 1 Timothy 3:1–7 and Titus 1:5–9

Both 1 Timothy 3:1–7 and Titus 1:5–9 assume that elders are going to be men. An elder (or bishop/overseer) must be "the husband of one wife" (1 Tim. 3:2; also Titus 1:6) and "must manage his own household well, with all dignity keeping his children submissive" (1 Tim. 3:4). Some may object that these were directions given only for the cultural situation in the ancient world, where women were not well educated, but the same response that was given above concerning 1 Timothy 2 would apply in this case as well.

## 4. The Relationship between the Family and the Church

The New Testament makes frequent connections between the life of the family and the life of the church. Paul says, "If someone does not know how to manage his own household, how will he care for God's church?" (1 Tim. 3:5). He says to Timothy, "Do not rebuke an older man but encourage him as you would a *father*, younger men as *brothers*, older women as *mothers*, younger women as *sisters*, in all purity" (1 Tim. 5:1–2). Several other passages could be cited, but the close relationship between the family and the church should be clear.

Because of this connection, it is inevitable that leadership patterns in the family will reflect leadership patterns in the church, and vice versa. It is very appropriate that, as godly men fulfill their leadership responsibilities in the family, they should also fulfill leadership responsibilities in the church. Conversely, if patterns of female leadership are established in the church, it will inevitably bring pressures toward greater female leadership and toward abdication of male leadership within the family.[80]

## 5. The Example of the Apostles

While the apostles are not the same as elders in local churches, it is still important to realize that Jesus established a pattern of male leadership in the church when he appointed twelve men (not six men and six women) as apostles. It is simply not true that women have equal access to all offices in the church, for Jesus, the head of the church, is a man. And the twelve apostles, who will sit on twelve thrones judging the twelve tribes of Israel (see Matt. 19:28), and whose names are written forever on the foundations of the heavenly city (Rev. 21:14), are all men. Therefore, *there will be no eternal modeling of equal roles for men and women at all levels of authority in the church*. Rather, there is a pattern of male leadership in the highest governing roles of the church, a pattern that will be evident to all believers for all eternity.

One objection brought against this argument is the claim that the culture at that time would not have allowed Jesus to choose six men and six women as apostles, or six

---

80. For further discussion of this point, see Vern Poythress, "The Church as Family: Why Male Leadership in the Family Requires Male Leadership in the Church," in *Recovering Biblical Manhood and Womanhood*, 233–47.

husband-wife teams as apostles, and this is the reason he did not do so. But such an objection impugns Jesus' integrity and courage. Jesus was not afraid to break social customs when a moral principle was at stake: he criticized the Pharisees publicly, healed on the Sabbath, cleansed the temple, spoke with a Samaritan woman, ate with tax collectors and sinners, and ate with unwashed hands.[81] If Jesus had wanted to establish a principle of equal access to church leadership by both men and women, he certainly could have done so in the appointment of his apostles, and he would have done so, in spite of cultural opposition, if it had been the pattern he wanted to establish in his church. But he did not.[82]

Another objection to this argument is to say that, if this is true, then only Jews can be leaders in our churches, since all twelve apostles were Jewish as well. But this objection is not persuasive because it fails to recognize that the church was entirely Jewish at its beginning. This was because it was God's plan to bring salvation through the Jews, and this led to twelve Jewish apostles. Yet within the pages of the New Testament, we see that the church soon expanded to include gentiles (Matt. 28:19; Eph. 2:16), and gentiles soon became elders and leaders in the New Testament church. A gentile (Luke) wrote two books of the New Testament (Luke and Acts), and several gentiles such as Titus and Epaphroditus were Paul's apostolic assistants and coworkers. In fact, God had progressively revealed from the time of Abraham (Gen. 12:3; 17:5) that it was his plan eventually to include countless gentiles among his people.

So the Jewishness of the early apostles is not like their maleness. The church began as entirely Jewish, but soon became Jewish and gentile as well. But the church did not begin all male, and only later include females as well. *Christ's followers were male and female from the beginning*, and both men and women were present at the beginning of the church at Pentecost. So this objection is not persuasive either.

## 6. The History of Male Teaching and Leadership Throughout the Whole Bible

Sometimes opponents of the view presented here have said it is based only on one text, 1 Timothy 2. Several of the foregoing sections have demonstrated that this is not the case, but there is one further argument that can be made: throughout the history of the entire Bible, from Genesis to Revelation, there is a consistent pattern of male leadership among God's people. Though there are occasional examples of women having leadership in government positions such as queen (Athaliah did reign as sole monarch in 2 Kings 11:1–20, but she is hardly an example to imitate) or judge (note Deborah in Judg. 4–5), and though there were occasionally women such as Deborah and Huldah who were prophetesses (see Judg. 4–5; 2 Kings 22:14–20), we should note that these are

---

81. This argument and the following one are taken from James Borland, "Women in the Life and Teachings of Jesus," in Piper and Grudem, *Recovering Biblical Manhood and Womanhood*, 120–22.

82. Regarding "Junia" or "Junias" in Rom. 16:7, see p. 1120.

rare exceptions in unusual circumstances. They occur in the midst of an overwhelming pattern of male leadership in teaching and governance, and as such, they hardly serve as patterns for New Testament church office.[83] Moreover, *there is not one example in the entire Bible of a woman doing the kind of congregational Bible teaching that is expected of pastors/elders in the New Testament church.* In the Old Testament it was the priests who had teaching responsibilities for the people, and the priesthood was exclusively male; moreover, even the women prophets Deborah and Huldah prophesied only privately, not publicly to a congregation of people.[84]

## 7. The History of the Church

As was mentioned above, the overwhelming pattern through the entire history of the church has been that the office of pastor/elder (or its equivalent) has been reserved for men. Although this does not demonstrate conclusively that such a position is correct, it should give us reason to reflect very seriously on the question before we rush ahead and declare that almost the entire church throughout its history has been wrong on this issue.[85]

## 8. Objections against the Entire Complementarian Position

Numerous objections have been brought against the position outlined here, only a few of which can be treated at this point.[86] It is objected that (1) *ministry should be determined by gifts, not by gender.* But in response, it must be said that spiritual gifts have to be used within the guidelines given in Scripture. The Holy Spirit who empowers spiritual gifts is also the Holy Spirit who inspired the Bible, and he does not want us to use his gifts in disobedience to his words.

---

83. For further discussion of these narrative examples, see Thomas R. Schreiner, "The Valuable Ministries of Women in the Context of Male Leadership: A Survey of Old and New Testament Examples and Teaching," in Piper and Grudem, *Recovering Biblical Manhood and Womanhood*, 209–24. With reference to Deborah in particular, we must realize that the historical events narrated in the entire book of Judges require great care in interpretation before we can assume that they should be taken as models for us to imitate. And Deborah was different from other (male) prophets in that she did not prophesy in public, only in private (Jud. 4:5; Huldah does the same in 2 Kings 22:14–20). There is no record anywhere of Deborah teaching an assembled group of God's people. She delivered a prophecy from the Lord to Barak, a man (Judg. 4:6–10); and then encouraged him to lead the people of Israel in battle. Although God did bring blessing through her, it is interesting that there is no explicit affirmation of the fact that the Lord raised her up—making her unlike the other major judges such as Othniel (3:9), Ehud (3:15), Gideon (6:14), Jephthah (11:29), and Samson (13:25; 14:6), for whom there is explicit statement of their calling from God.

84. See the previous footnote. Regarding the fact that women could prophesy in New Testament congregations, see the discussion under section 2 above (p. 1164).

85. See n56 above. A number of recent books have highlighted the neglected contributions that women have made to the church throughout its history; see especially Tucker and Liefeld, *Daughters of the Church*, a book that is a treasure-house of information and provides extensive additional bibliography. But none of these studies overthrows the clear conclusion that the great majority of the church throughout its history has not accepted women as pastors.

86. For further discussion of these and many other objections, see Grudem, *Evangelical Feminism and Biblical Truth*, especially chapters 9, 10, and 11; see also *Recovering Biblical Manhood and Womanhood*, esp. 60–92. Fuller statements of the objections listed here can be found in the books marked "Favors women as pastors" in the bibliography at the end of this chapter, esp. the volumes by Mickelsen, Spencer, and Bilezikian.

Another objection is to say that (2) *if God has genuinely called a woman to be a pastor, she should not be prevented from acting as one.* The response to this objection is similar to the one given above: an individual claim to have experienced a call from God must always be tested by subjecting it to the words of God in Scripture. If the Bible teaches that God wills for men alone to bear the primary teaching and governing responsibilities of the pastorate, then by implication the Bible also teaches that God does not call women to be pastors. However, we should add that often what a woman discerns as a divine call to the pastorate may be indeed a call to full-time Christian ministry, not to be a pastor/elder in a church. In fact, many opportunities for full-time occupational ministry exist, within the local church and elsewhere, apart from being a teaching pastor or an elder—for example, church staff positions in counseling, women's ministries, Christian education, and children's ministries, as well as ministries of music and worship, campus student ministries, evangelistic ministries, ministries to the poor, and administrative responsibilities that do not involve functioning in the elder's role of government over the entire church.[87] This list could be expanded,[88] but the point is that we should not make restrictions where Scripture itself does not place restrictions. Instead, we should allow and encourage full and free participation by women as well as men in all of these other areas.

Some object that (3) *the New Testament emphasis is on servant leadership,* and therefore we should not be so concerned about authority, since that is more a pagan than a Christian concern. But this objection makes a false distinction between servanthood and authority. Certainly Jesus himself is the model of a servant leader, but Jesus also has authority—great authority! He is the Lord of our lives and the Lord of the church. By analogy, elders ought to follow Jesus' example of servant leadership (see 1 Peter 5:1–5) but that does not mean that they should neglect to govern with authority when the Bible itself gives them this responsibility (see 1 Tim. 5:17; Heb. 13:17; 1 Peter 5:5).[89]

Another objection says that, (4) *just as we no longer require head coverings for women (as in 1 Corinthians 11:5–6), so we should no longer prohibit women from teaching men in the church.* The answer to this objection is that each practice must be evaluated and must stand or fall on its own merits. The most likely meaning of a woman wearing a head covering in first-century Corinth was to indicate that she was married.[90] But no such meaning would be understood from a woman's head covering today. The modern equivalent would be wearing a wedding ring. We no longer require head covering today because in ancient Corinth it was a physical object that was a symbol of a deeper reality. We do not disobey 1 Corinthians 11:5–6 today, but we obey it by encouraging women to wear whatever symbolizes being married in their own culture.

---

87. For further discussion, see *Recovering Biblical Manhood and Womanhood,* 54–59.

88. See my section entitled "But What *Should* Women Do in the Church?," in *Evangelical Feminism and Biblical Truth,* 84–101.

89. See also the discussion of the authority of elders on pp. 1145–47, above.

90. See the literary and archaeological evidence for this in Grudem, *Evangelical Feminism and Biblical Truth,* 334–36.

But prohibiting women from teaching or having authority over men is not a mere physical symbol, a culturally variable object that is used to symbolize a deeper reality. The activities of teaching and having governing authority are the reality itself, not something merely symbolic.

Sometimes people object that (5) *just as the church finally realized that slavery was wrong, so the church today should recognize that male leadership is wrong,* and is an outdated cultural tradition that should be discarded. But this objection fails to realize the difference between the temporary cultural institution of slavery, which God certainly did not establish at creation, and the existence of a difference in male-female roles in marriage (and, by implication, in relationships within the church), which God established at creation. The seeds for the destruction of slavery were sown in the New Testament (see Philem. 16; Eph. 6:9; Col. 4:1; 1 Tim. 6:1–2), but no seeds for the destruction of marriage, or the destruction of male-female differences as created, are sown in the Bible. Moreover, the objection can be turned around: it is likely that a closer parallel to the Christian defenders of slavery in the nineteenth century is found in evangelical feminists who today use arguments from the Bible to justify conformity to some extremely strong pressures in contemporary society (in favor of slavery then, and women being pastors now).

Sometimes it is objected that (6) *it is inconsistent to allow women to vote in churches that have congregational government, but not to serve as elders.* But the authority of the church as a whole is not the same as the authority given to specific individuals within the church. When we say that the congregation as a whole has authority, we do not mean that each man and each woman in the congregation has the authority to speak or act for the congregation. Therefore, gender, as a part of individual personhood, is not significantly in view in corporate congregational decisions.

Another way of putting this is to say that the only question we are asking in this section is whether women can be officers within the church, and specifically whether they can be elders within the church. In any congregational system where the elders are elected by the congregation, it is evident to everyone in the church that the elders have a kind of delegated authority which other members of the congregation do not have—even though the other members of the congregation have voted for these people in the first place. It is the same in all systems of government where officials are elected: once the President of the United States or the mayor of a city is elected, that person has a delegated authority over the people who elected him or her and it is an authority that is greater than the authority of any individual person who voted.[91]

Finally, some people have raised the objection that (7) *experience shows that many women have been blessed by God in their Bible teaching ministries, and this blessing shows that God approves of their ministries.* In reply, of course there will be some good results

---

91. See above, pp. 1132–35, for arguments in favor of participation by the entire congregation in some decision making in the church, and especially in the selection of officers in the church.

when a woman prays, trusts God, and teaches God's Word because God's Word has power and because God in his grace often blesses us in spite of our mistakes. But that does not make the mistakes right, and God may withdraw his protection and blessing at any time. God is a God of grace and there are many times when he blesses his people even when they disobey him (as he did frequently, for example, in the life of Samson; see Judges, chapters 13–16).

(8) Following this discussion of all these objections, it is appropriate to end on a more positive note. Everyone reading this paragraph should recognize that God has given much insight and wisdom to women as well as to men, and that any church leaders who neglect to draw on the wisdom that women have are really acting foolishly. Therefore, any group of elders or other male leaders who make decisions affecting the entire church should frequently have procedures within the church whereby the wisdom and insight of other members of the church, especially the wisdom and insight of women as well as men, can be drawn upon as an aid in making decisions.

## 9. What about Other Offices within the Church?

The entire discussion above has focused on the question of whether women should function as pastors or elders within the church. But what about other offices?

The biblical teaching regarding the office of *deacon* is much less extensive than that regarding the office of elder,[92] and what is involved in the office of deacon varies considerably from church to church. If deacons are actually functioning as elders and have the highest governing authority within a local church, then the arguments given above against women being elders would apply directly to this situation, and it would follow that Scripture does not permit women to be deacons in this sense. On the other hand, if deacons simply have delegated administrative responsibility for certain aspects of the ministry of the church, then there seems to be no good reason to prevent women from functioning as deacons. Regarding the question of women as deacons in 1 Timothy 3:8–13, it does not seem to me that this passage allows women to be deacons *in the way deacons were understood in Timothy's situation in Ephesus*, but there is a significant difference of viewpoint among evangelicals over the understanding of this passage,[93] and it is much less clear to us exactly what deacons did at that time than it is clear what elders did.[94]

With regard to other offices, such as treasurer, for example, or other staff positions such as youth minister or counseling director or children's minister, and so forth, the only question to be asked is whether these offices include the ruling and teaching functions reserved for elders in the New Testament. If not, then *all of these offices would be open to women as well as to men*, for we must be careful not to prohibit what the New Testament does not prohibit.

---

92. See above, pp. 1130–31, on the office of deacon.
93. See n23 above for information.
94. Note that Acts 6:3 also requires that only men (Gk.

*anēr*) be selected as the first deacons (if we understand that passage to be speaking of the office of deacon).

# QUESTIONS FOR PERSONAL APPLICATION

1. No matter what kind of church government structure you currently find yourself in, are there ways in which you could be more encouraging and supportive to the current leaders in your church?

2. If you are currently an officer in your church, or if you someday would like to be one, is your pattern of life such that you would like to see it imitated by others in the church? If you have had a part in the process of selecting church leaders, have you tended to emphasize the character traits and spiritual qualifications talked about in Scripture, or have you emphasized other qualifications that the world would look for in selecting its leaders?

3. Do you think that the current governing structure of your church works quite well? How could it be improved, without changing the basic philosophy of church government to which it is committed? Whether or not your church has officers who are called "elders," who are the people who carry out the functions of elders in your church? Do you know if your own pastor would like to see some modifications in the government of your church, to enable him to carry out his task more effectively?

4. Before reading this chapter, what was your view on the question of women serving as teaching pastors or elders in a church? How has this chapter changed your view, if at all? Why do you think people's emotions are often very strong concerning this issue? Can you explain how you personally feel (emotionally) about the teaching presented in this chapter? Does it seem right to you, or not?

## Special Terms

*apostle*
*bishop*
*classis*
*congregational government*
*consistory*
*deacon*
*diocese*
*elder*
*episcopalian government*
*general assembly*
*hierarchical government*
*local elders*
*officer*
*overseer*
*pastor*
*presbyterian government*
*presbytery*
*priest*
*rector*
*session*
*synod*
*vicar*

# BIBLIOGRAPHY

(For an explanation of this bibliography see the note on the bibliography to chapter 1, pp. 23–24. Complete bibliographical data may be found on pp. 1489–96.)

## SECTIONS IN EVANGELICAL SYSTEMATIC THEOLOGIES

*1. Anglican (Episcopalian)*
    1882–92 . . . . . Litton, 384–418

1930........Thomas, 313–18, 429–33,
              452–58
2001........Packer, 207–08
2013........Bird, 629–31
2013........Bray, 764–77

**2. Arminian (Wesleyan or Methodist)**
1875–76.....Pope, 3:335–59
1892–94.....Miley, 2:415–19
1940........Wiley, 3:117–37
1983........Carter, 2:619–20
1992........Oden, 3:354–60
2002........Cottrell, 418–442

**3. Baptist**
1767........Gill, 2:574–607
1907........Strong, 894–929
1990–95.....Garrett, 2:639–58
2007........Akin, 798–805
2013........Erickson, 989–1015

**4. Dispensational**
1947........Chafer, 4:150–53
1949........Thiessen, 314–318
1986........Ryrie, 403–20
2002–2005..Geisler, 4:104–45
2017........MacArthur and Mayhue,
              753–75

**5. Lutheran**
1917–24.....Pieper, 3:427–38, 439–72
1934........Mueller, 563–84

**6. Reformed (or Presbyterian)**
1559........Calvin, 2:1053–1228
              (4.3–11)
1679–85.....Turretin, *IET*, 3:146–54,
              223–34, 243

1906–11........Bavinck, *RD*, 4:326–88
1910.........Vos, 3:175
1937–66.....Murray, *CW*, 1:260–68; *CW*,
              2:336–65
1938........Berkhof, 579–92
1998........Reymond, 895–910
2008........Van Genderen and Velema,
              730–44
2011........Horton, 874–892
2013........Frame, 1026–28, 1040–43
2013........Culver, 941–55
2016........Allen and Swain, 311–38
2017........Barrett, 133
2019........Letham, 796–812

**7. Renewal (or charismatic/Pentecostal)**
1988–92.....Williams, 3:177–220
1993........Menzies and Horton, 173–88
1995........Horton, 545–52
2008........Duffield and Van Cleave,
              429–35

## SECTIONS IN REPRESENTATIVE ROMAN CATHOLIC SYSTEMATIC THEOLOGIES

**1. Roman Catholic: Traditional**
1955........Ott, 276–90, 450–60

**2. Roman Catholic: Post–Vatican II**
2012........*CCC*, paragraphs 871–945

## OTHER WORKS

Akin, Daniel L. "Deacon, Deaconess." In *BTDB*,
    149–50.
———. "Overseer." In *BTDB*, 586–87.
Allison, Gregg. *Historical Theology: An Introduction
    to Christian Doctrine; A Companion to Wayne
    Grudem's* Systematic Theology. Grand Rapids:
    Zondervan, 2011, 588–610.
———. *Sojourners and Strangers: The Doctrine of the
    Church.* Wheaton, IL: Crossway, 2012, 205–320.

Avis, P. D. L. "Church Government." In *NDT2*, 186–89.

Babbage, S. B. "Church Officers." In *EDT3*, 188–89. (Contains a list of various titles for church officers used in different denominations today, with definitions.)

Bannerman, James. *The Church of Christ*. 2 vols. 1869. Reprint, London: Banner of Truth, 1960.

Bartlett, Andrew. *Men and Women in Christ: Fresh Light from the Biblical Texts*. London: Inter-Varsity Press, 2019.

Baxter, Richard. *The Reformed Pastor*. Reprint, Carlisle, PA: Banner of Truth, 1979.

Bilezikian, Gilbert. *Beyond Sex Roles*. 3rd ed. Grand Rapids: Baker, 2006. (Favors women as pastors.)

Brand, Chad Owen, and R. Stanton Norman, eds. *Perspectives on Church Government: Five Views of Church Polity*. Nashville: B&H, 2004.

Burge, G. M. "Deacon, Deaconess." In *EDT3*, 230.

Carson, D. A. "Church, Authority in." In *EDT3*, 183–85.

Clark, Stephen B. *Man and Women in Christ*. Ann Arbor, MI: Servant, 1980. (Opposes women as pastors.)

Clowney, Edmund. *Called to the Ministry*. Chicago: InterVarsity Press, 1964.

———. "Presbyterianism." In *EDT1*, 530–31.

Cowan, Steven B., and Paul E. Engle, eds. *Who Runs the Church? Four Views on Church Government*. Grand Rapids: Zondervan, 2004.

Dever, Mark. "The Church." In *A Theology for the Church*, ed. Daniel L. Akin et al., 795–805, 832–35. Nashville: B&H, 2007.

Foh, Susan. *Women and the Word of God: A Response to Biblical Feminism*. Philadelphia: Presbyterian and Reformed, 1980. (Opposes women as pastors.)

Fung, Ronald Y. K. "Ministry in the New Testament." In *The Church in the Bible and the World*, edited by D. A. Carson. Exeter: Paternoster; Grand Rapids: Baker, 1987.

Grudem, Wayne. *Evangelical Feminism and Biblical Truth*. Wheaton, IL: Crossway, 2012. (Opposes women as pastors.)

Gundry, Patricia. *Neither Slave nor Free: Helping Women Answer the Call to Church Leadership*. San Francisco: Harper and Row, 1987. (Favors women as pastors.)

———. *Women Be Free! The Clear Message of Scripture*. Grand Rapids: Zondervan, 1988. (Favors women as pastors.)

Gundry, Stanley N., and James R. Beck, eds. *Two Views on Women in Ministry*. Rev. ed. Grand Rapids: Zondervan, 2005.

Harrison, E. F. "Apostle, Apostleship." In *EDT3*, 72–74.

Hildebrand, David. "Leadership." In *BTDB*, 473–77.

Hodge, Charles. *Discussions in Church Polity*. New York: Scribner's, 1878.

Hort, F. J. A. *The Christian Ecclesia*. London: Macmillan, 1898.

House, H. Wayne. *The Role of Women in Ministry Today*. Nashville: Nelson, 1990. (Opposes women as pastors.)

Hurley, James B. *Man and Woman in Biblical Perspective*. Leicester: Inter-Varsity Press; Grand Rapids: Zondervan, 1981. (Opposes women as pastors.)

Kärkkäinen, V.-M. "Ecclesiology." In *GDT*, 251–62.

Keener, C. "Woman and Man." In *DLNT*, 1205–15. (Favors women as pastors.)

Kirby, G. W. "Congregationalism." In *EDT1*, 159–61.

Knight, George W., III. *The Role Relationship of Men and Women*. Rev. ed. Chicago: Moody Publishers, 1985. (Opposes women as pastors.)

Köstenberger, Andreas, and Thomas Schreiner. *Women in the Church: An Interpretation and Application of 1 Timothy 2:9-15*. 3rd ed. Wheaton, IL: Crossway, 2016. (Opposes women as pastors.)

Kroeger, C. C. "Women In the Early Church." In *DLNT*, 1215–22. (Favors women as pastors.)

Kroeger, Richard and Catherine. *I Suffer Not a Woman*. Grand Rapids: Baker, 1992. (Favors women as pastors.)

Liefeld, W. L. "Ministry." In *EDT3*, 550–51.

Lim, P. C. H. and A. J. Martin. "Reformed Tradition." In *EDT3*, 732–34.

Macleod, D. "Church Government." In *NDT*, 143–46.

Marshall, I. Howard. "Apostle." In *EDT*, 40.

Mickelsen, Alvera, ed. *Women, Authority, and the Bible*. Downers Grove, IL: InterVarsity Press, 1986. (A collection of essays by several authors, most of whom favor women as pastors.)

Morris, L. "Church Government." In *EDT1*, 238–41.

———. *Ministers of God*. London: Inter-Varsity Press, 1964.

Ortlund, R. C., Jr. "Man and Woman." In *NDBT*, 650–54.

Piper, John, and Wayne Grudem, eds. *Recovering Biblical Manhood and Womanhood: A Response to Evangelical Feminism*. Wheaton, IL: Crossway, 1991. (A collection of twenty-eight essays by twenty-two authors; opposes women as pastors.)

Richards, Lawrence O. *A Theology of Church Leadership*. Grand Rapids: Zondervan, 1980.

Rightmire, R. David. "Apostle." In *BTDB*, 33–35.

Saucy, Robert L. "Authority in the Church." In *Walvoord: A Tribute*, edited by Donald K. Campbell, 219–37. Chicago: Moody Publishers, 1982. (An extensive argument in favor of congregational government.)

———. *The Church in God's Program*. Chicago: Moody Publishers, 1972.

Spencer, Aida Besancon. *Beyond the Curse: Women Called to Ministry*. Nashville: Nelson, 1985. (Favors women as pastors.)

Stott, John R. W. *The Preacher's Portrait*. Grand Rapids: Eerdmans, 1961.

Strauch, Alexander. *Biblical Eldership: An Urgent Call to Restore Biblical Church Leadership*. Littleton, CO: Lewis and Roth, 1986.

Tiller, J. "Ministry." In *EDT1*, 430–33.

Toon, Peter. "Bishop." In *EDT3*, 134–35.

———. "Ministry, Minister." In *BTDB*, 530–31.

Tucker, Ruth A., and Walter L. Liefeld. *Daughters of the Church: Women and Ministry from New Testament Times to the Present*. Grand Rapids: Zondervan, 1987. (Favors women as pastors.)

Van Dam, Cornelis. "Elder." In *BTDB*, 197–99.

Wallace, R. S. "Elder." In *EDT3*, 266–67.

## SCRIPTURE MEMORY PASSAGE

**1 Peter 5:1–4:** So I exhort the elders among you, as a fellow elder and a witness of the sufferings of Christ, as well as a partaker in the glory that is going to be revealed: shepherd the flock of God that is among you, exercising oversight, not under compulsion, but willingly, as God would have you; not for shameful gain, but eagerly; not domineering over those in your charge, but being examples to the flock. And when the chief Shepherd appears, you will receive the unfading crown of glory.

## HYMN

### "Glorious Things of Thee Are Spoken"

There are not many hymns—if any—written about church government! I have put here a hymn which thanks God for the blessings of being a member of God's people in general, and therefore a citizen of the heavenly Mount Zion, the heavenly city where God's people dwell. But in the hymn the author also uses Old Testament imagery from the journey of God's people through the wilderness ("see the cloud and fire appear," v. 3), and the entire hymn can also be seen as one of thanks to God for the blessing of dwelling (spiritually) within the walls of the church today.

The author, John Newton, is also the author of the well-known hymn "Amazing Grace."

*Glorious things of thee are spoken, Zion, city of
    our God;*
    *He whose Word cannot be broken formed thee
        for his own abode:*
*On the Rock of Ages founded, what can shake thy
    sure repose?*
    *With salvation's walls surrounded, thou
        may'st smile at all thy foes.*

*See, the streams of living waters, springing from
    eternal love,*
    *Well supply thy sons and daughters, and all
        fear of want remove:*
*Who can faint, while such a river ever flows their
    thirst t'assuage?*
    *Grace which, like the Lord, the giver, never
        fails from age to age.*

*Round each habitation hov'ring, see the cloud
    and fire appear*
    *For a glory and cov'ring, showing that the
        Lord is near:*
*Thus deriving from their banner light by night
    and shade by day,*
    *Safe they feed upon the manna which he gives
        them when they pray.*

*Savior, if of Zion's city I, through grace, a member am,*
    *Let the world deride or pity, I will glory in
        thy name:*
*Fading is the worldling's pleasure, all his boasted
    pomp and show;*
    *Solid joys and lasting treasure none but Zion's
        children know.*

Author: John Newton, 1779

## CONTEMPORARY WORSHIP SONG

### "Come People of the Risen King"

*Come, people of the Risen King,*
*Who delight to bring Him praise;*
*Come all and tune your hearts to sing*
*To the Morning Star of grace.*
*From the shifting shadows of the earth*
*We will lift our eyes to Him,*
*Where steady arms of mercy reach*
*To gather children in.*

*Chorus*
*Rejoice, Rejoice! Let every tongue rejoice!*
*One heart, one voice; O Church of Christ, rejoice!*

*Come, those whose joy is morning sun,*
*And those weeping through the night;*
*Come, those who tell of battles won,*

*And those struggling in the fight.*
*For His perfect love will never change,*
*And His mercies never cease,*
*But follow us through all our days*
*With the certain hope of peace.*

*Come, young and old from every land—*
*Men and women of the faith;*
*Come, those with full or empty hands—*
*Find the riches of His grace.*
*Over all the world, His people sing—*
*Shore to shore we hear them call*
*The Truth that cries through every age:*
*"Our God is all in all."*

Words by Kristyn Lennox Getty, Stuart
Townend, and Keith Getty[95]

## CHAPTER 48

# Means of Grace within the Church

*What are the different activities within the life of the church that God uses to bring blessing to us?*
*What do we miss if we neglect involvement in a local church?*

## EXPLANATION AND SCRIPTURAL BASIS

### A. How Many Means of Grace Are Available to Us?

All of the blessings we experience in this life are ultimately undeserved—they are all of *grace*. In fact, for Peter, the entire Christian life is lived by grace (1 Peter 5:12).

But are there any special *means* that God uses to give additional grace to us? Specifically, *within the fellowship of the church* are there certain means—that is, certain activities, ceremonies, or functions—that God uses to give more grace to us? Another way of formulating that question is to ask whether there are certain *means* through which the Holy Spirit works to convey blessings into the life of the believer. Of course, personal prayer, worship, and Bible study, and personal faith, are all means through which God works to bring grace to us as individual Christians. But in this chapter we are dealing with the doctrine of the church, and we are asking specifically *within the fellowship of the church* what the means of grace are that God uses to bring blessing to us.

We may define the means of grace as follows: *the means of grace are any activities within the fellowship of the church that God uses to give more grace to Christians.*

In the history of the discussion of "means of grace within the church," some theologians have restricted them to three: the preaching of the Word and the two sacraments, baptism and the Lord's Supper.[1]

---

1. This is the position of Louis Berkhof, *Systematic Theology* (Grand Rapids: Eerdmans, 1941), 604–6. He calls these three means "objective channels which Christ has instituted in the church" (604–5), but the significant criterion in Berkhof's thinking appears to be the fact that these three are the special functions administered by the ordained clergy. Berkhof calls these "the *official* means of the church of Jesus Christ" (605) and later says, "As the *official* means of grace placed at the disposal of the Church, both the Word and the sacraments *can* only be administered by the lawful and properly qualified officers of the Church" (610). In this way, he clearly restricts the "means of grace" to those means administered by the ordained clergy. Although those who follow Berkhof on this point could argue that this procedure is wise and serves the interest of maintaining good order in the church, we may ask whether in fact this restriction carries overtones of the view of the Roman Catholic Church that there is a special "priesthood" of ordained people within the church who have a special authority or ability to

1176

But is it wise to make such a short list of "means of grace"? If we wish to list and discuss all the means of receiving the Holy Spirit's blessing that come to believers specifically through the fellowship of the church, then it does not seem wise to limit the "means of grace" to three activities whose administration is restricted to the ordained clergy or officers of the church. There is wisdom, for example, in Charles Hodge's view that prayer is a fourth means of grace.[2]

But should we limit our discussion of the means of grace to these four activities only? It would seem more helpful to list all of the *many varied activities* within the church that God has given as special ways of receiving his "grace" day by day and week by week. Such a list may become quite long and, depending on how it is organized, may include various numbers of elements. The following list may not be exhaustive, but it does include most of the means of grace that believers have access to within the fellowship of the church:

1. Teaching of the Word
2. Baptism
3. The Lord's Supper
4. Prayer for one another
5. Worship
6. Church discipline
7. Giving
8. Spiritual gifts
9. Fellowship
10. Evangelism
11. Personal ministry to individuals

All these are available to believers *within* the church. The Holy Spirit works through all of them to bring various kinds of blessing to individuals. Therefore, departing from the much shorter lists usually given in systematic theologies, I have decided to call all of these "means of grace" within the church.

The Roman Catholic Church has traditionally believed that God's "grace" comes to people only through the official ministry of the church, particularly through the priests of the church. Therefore, when it specifies the means of grace (what it calls the "sacraments") that are available to people within the church, it has in view activities that are supervised and/or performed by only the priests of the church. The seven "sacraments" in Roman Catholic teaching are the following:

---

extend God's grace to people in the church. (See chapter 49, p. 1195, for a discussion of the use of the two terms *sacraments* and *ordinances* to refer to baptism and the Lord's Supper.)

2. Hodge, *Systematic Theology*, 3 vols. (1871–73; repr., Grand Rapids: Eerdmans, 1970), 3:692–709.

1. Baptism
2. Confirmation
3. Eucharist (the Lord's Supper as experienced in the Mass)
4. Penance
5. Anointing of the sick (the anointing with oil that is most commonly administered to a dying person, sometimes called "extreme unction")
6. Holy orders (ordination to the priesthood or diaconate)
7. Matrimony[3]

There is not only a difference in the lists given by Catholics and Protestants; there is also a difference in fundamental meaning. Catholics view these as "means of salvation" that make people more fit to receive justification from God.[4] But on a Protestant view, the means of grace are simply means of additional blessing within the Christian life, and do not add to our fitness to receive justification from God. Catholics teach that the means of grace impart grace whether or not there is subjective faith on the part of the minister or the recipient,[5] while Protestants hold that God only imparts grace when there is faith on the part of the persons receiving these means. And while the Roman Catholic Church firmly restricts the administration of the sacraments to the clergy, our list of means of grace includes many activities that are carried out by all believers.

## B. Discussion of Specific Means

## 1. Teaching of the Word

Even before people become Christians, the Word of God as preached and taught brings God's grace to them in that it is the instrument God uses to impart spiritual life to them and bring them to salvation. Paul says that the gospel is the "power of God for salvation" (Rom. 1:16) and that the preaching of Christ is "the power of God and the wisdom of God" (1 Cor. 1:24). God caused us to be born again or "brought . . . forth by the word of truth" (James 1:18). Peter says, "You have been born again, not of perishable seed but of imperishable, through the living and abiding word of God" (1 Peter 1:23). It is the written Word of God, the Bible, that is "able to make you wise for salvation through faith in Christ Jesus" (2 Tim. 3:15).[6]

Moreover, once we have become Christians, Paul reminds us that it is the Word of God that is "able to build you up" (Acts 20:32). The Word is necessary for spiritual nourishment and for maintaining spiritual life because we do not live on bread alone

---

3. This list is found in *Catechism of the Catholic Church* (New York: Doubleday, 1997), paragraph 1113.

4. See chapter 36, pp. 890–92, on the Roman Catholic view of justification. The *Catechism of the Catholic Church* affirms that "for believers the sacraments of the New Covenant are *necessary for salvation*" (paragraph 1129, italics in original).

5. See chapter 49, p. 1202, on the Roman Catholic view that the sacraments work *ex opere operato*.

6. See chapter 33 for a fuller discussion of the gospel call.

but on "every word that comes from the mouth of God" (Matt. 4:4). Moses speaks of the absolute necessity of the written Word of God when he tells the people, "It is no empty word for you, but your very life, and by this word you shall live long in the land that you are going over the Jordan to possess" (Deut. 32:47).

It is the Word of God that convicts us of sin and turns us to righteousness, for it is profitable "for teaching, for reproof, for correction, and for training in righteousness" (2 Tim. 3:16). It gives direction and guidance as a "lamp" to our feet and a "light" to our path (Ps. 119:105). In the midst of an ungodly culture, Scripture gives wisdom and guidance like "a lamp shining in a dark place" (2 Peter 1:19). Moreover, it is active in giving wisdom to all, even "making wise the simple" (Ps. 19:7). It gives hope to those who are in despair, because Paul says that it was written "that through endurance and through the encouragement of the Scriptures we might *have hope*" (Rom. 15:4).

The Word of God is not weak or powerless in accomplishing these goals, for it speaks to us with the power of God and accomplishes God's purposes. The Lord says,

> For as the rain and the snow come down from heaven
>    and do not return there but water the earth,
> making it bring forth and sprout,
>    giving seed to the sower and bread to the eater,
> so shall my word be that goes out from my mouth;
>    it shall not return to me empty,
> but it shall accomplish that which I purpose,
>    and shall succeed in the thing for which I sent it. (Isa. 55:10–11)

God's Word is not weak but has his divine power accompanying it: "Is not my word *like fire*, declares the LORD, and *like a hammer* that breaks the rock in pieces?" (Jer. 23:29). It is so sharp and powerful that it is the "*sword* of the Spirit" (Eph. 6:17), and it is so effective in speaking to people's needs that the author of Hebrews says, "the word of God is living and active, sharper than any *two-edged sword*, piercing to the division of soul and of spirit, of joints and of marrow, and discerning the thoughts and intentions of the heart" (Heb. 4:12).

Therefore, the actual words of the Bible are far more powerful and far more effective in changing people's minds and hearts than any merely human words spoken by a pastor or Bible teacher in the (admittedly important) tasks of explaining and applying and summarizing what the Bible says. The superior power of the very words of God in Scripture provides the reason why, in the long run, the most effective preachers are those who repeatedly bring their hearers back to the very words of the biblical text about which they are speaking that day, so that they hear the very words of Scripture with their ears again and again and read the very words of Scripture with their eyes again and again.

So closely are the growth and strength of the church linked to the reign of the Word of God in people's lives that more than once the book of Acts can describe the growth of the church as the growth of the Word of God: "*The word of God continued to increase, and the number of the disciples multiplied greatly in Jerusalem*" (Acts 6:7); "*The word of God increased and multiplied*" (Acts 12:24); "*The word of the Lord was spreading throughout the whole region*" (Acts 13:49).

So important is the Bible as the primary means of grace that God gives to his people that Charles Hodge reminds us that throughout history true Christianity has flourished "just in proportion to the degree in which the Bible is known, and its truths are diffused among the people." Moreover, he notes that there are no evidences of salvation or sanctification to be found where the Word of God is not known. "The nations where the Bible is unknown sit in darkness."[7]

It is appropriate that we list the teaching of the Word as the first and most important means of grace within the church. But we should add that such teaching includes not only officially recognized teaching by ordained clergy in the church, but also all the teaching that occurs in Bible studies, Sunday School classes, the reading of Christian books on Scripture, and even in personal Bible study.

## 2. Baptism

Since Jesus commanded his church to baptize (Matt. 28:19), we would expect that there would be a measure of blessing connected with baptism because all obedience to God by Christians brings God's favor with it. This obedience is specifically a public act of confessing Jesus as Savior, an act which in itself brings joy and blessing to a believer. Moreover, it is a sign of the believer's death and resurrection with Christ (see Rom. 6:2–5; Col. 2:12), and it seems fitting that the Holy Spirit would work through such a sign to increase our faith, to increase our experiential realization of death to the power and love of sin in our lives, and to increase our experience of the power of new resurrection life in Christ that we have as believers. Since baptism is a physical symbol of the death and resurrection of Christ and our participation in them, it should also give additional assurance of union with Christ to all believers who are present. Finally, since water baptism is an outward symbol of inward spiritual baptism by the Holy Spirit, we may expect that the Holy Spirit will ordinarily work alongside the baptism, giving to believers an increasing realization of the benefits of the spiritual baptism to which it points.

When baptism very closely accompanies someone's initial profession of faith and is in fact the outward form that profession of faith takes, there is certainly a connection between baptism and receiving the gift of the Holy Spirit, for Peter says to his hearers at Pentecost, "Repent and be baptized every one of you in the name of Jesus Christ for the forgiveness of your sins, and you will receive the gift of the Holy Spirit" (Acts 2:38). Moreover, Paul says that believers have "been buried with him in baptism, in which

---

7. Hodge, *Systematic Theology*, 3:468–69.

you were also raised with him through faith in the powerful working of God, who raised him from the dead" (Col. 2:12). The statement that this happens "*through faith in the powerful working of God*" reminds us that there is no magical property in the act of baptism that causes a spiritual result to come about, yet the verse also indicates that when faith accompanies baptism, there is genuine spiritual work in the life of the person being baptized. As we would expect, sometimes great spiritual joy follows upon baptism—a great joy in the Lord and in the salvation that baptism so vividly pictures (see Acts 8:39; 16:34).

Although we must avoid the Roman Catholic teaching that grace is imparted even *apart from* the faith of the person being baptized, we must not react so strongly to this error that we say that no spiritual benefit at all comes from baptism, that the Holy Spirit *does not* work through it, and that it is *merely symbolic*. Where there is genuine faith on the part of the person being baptized, and where the faith of the church that watches the baptism is stirred up and encouraged by this ceremony, then the Holy Spirit certainly does work through baptism, and baptism becomes a "means of grace" through which the Holy Spirit brings blessing to the person being baptized and to the church as well. (Baptism will be more fully discussed in chapter 49.)

## 3. The Lord's Supper

In addition to baptism, the other ordinance or ceremony that Jesus commanded the church to carry out is participation in the Lord's Supper. Although this subject will be discussed more thoroughly in chapter 50, it is appropriate to note here that participation in the Lord's Supper is also very clearly a means of grace that the Holy Spirit uses to bring blessing to the church. The Lord's Supper is not simply an ordinary meal among human beings—it is a fellowship with Christ, in his presence and at his table.

Once again, we must avoid the idea that any automatic or magical benefit comes from sharing in the Lord's Supper, whether a person participates in faith or not.[8] But when a person participates in faith, renewing and strengthening his or her trust in Christ for salvation, and believing that the Holy Spirit will bring spiritual blessing through such participation, then certainly additional blessing may be expected. We must be careful here, as with baptism, to avoid the mistake of overreacting to Roman Catholic teaching and maintaining that the Lord's Supper is *merely symbolic* and not a means of grace. Paul says, "The cup of blessing that we bless, is it not a *participation* (Gk. *koinōnia*, "sharing," "fellowship") in the blood of Christ? The bread that we break, is it not a *participation* [*koinōnia*] in the body of Christ?" (1 Cor. 10:16). Because there is such a sharing in the body and blood of Christ (apparently meaning a sharing in the benefits of Christ's body and blood given for us), the unity of believers is beautifully exhibited at the time of the

---

8. This view that there is blessing that comes automatically from participation in the Lord's Supper is the Roman Catholic doctrine of *ex opere operato* ("by the work performed"), which is discussed in chapter 50, pp. 1223–27; see also p. 1202.

Lord's Supper: "Because there is one bread, we who are many are one body, for we all partake of the one bread" (1 Cor. 10:17). And since we are participants at "the table of the Lord" (1 Cor. 10:21), Paul warns the Corinthians that they cannot participate in the Lord's table and also participate in idol worship: "You cannot partake in the table of the Lord and the table of demons" (1 Cor. 10:21). There is a spiritual union among believers and with the Lord that is strengthened and solidified at the Lord's Supper, and it is not to be taken lightly.

This is why the Corinthians were experiencing judgment for their abuse of the Lord's Supper ("For anyone who eats and drinks without discerning the body eats and drinks judgment on himself. That is why many of you are weak and ill, and some have died," 1 Cor. 11:29–30). But if Paul says there will be judgment for *wrong* participation in the Lord's Supper, then certainly we should expect *blessing* for right participation in the Lord's Supper. When we obey Jesus' command, "Take, eat" (Matt. 26:26), and go through the physical activity of eating and drinking at the Lord's table, our physical action *pictures* a corresponding spiritual nourishment, a nourishment of our souls that will occur when we participate in obedience and faith. Jesus says, "For my flesh is true food, and my blood is true drink. Whoever feeds on my flesh and drinks my blood abides in me, and I in him" (John 6:55–56; cf. vv. 52–54, 57–58; also vv. 27, 33–35, 48–51).

As with baptism, therefore, we should expect that the Lord would give spiritual blessing as we participate in the Lord's Supper in faith and in obedience to the directions laid down in Scripture, and in this way it is a "means of grace" which the Holy Spirit uses to convey blessing to us.

## 4. Prayer

We have already studied prayer in chapter 18, so we need only note here that corporate prayer within the church as it assembles, and prayer by church members for one another, are powerful means that the Holy Spirit uses daily to bring blessing to Christians within the church. Certainly we are to *pray together* as well as individually, following the example of the early church. When they heard the threats of the Jewish leaders, "they lifted their voices *together* to God" in prayer (Acts 4:24–30), "and when they had prayed, the place in which they were gathered together was shaken, and they were all filled with the Holy Spirit and continued to speak the word of God with boldness" (Acts 4:31; cf. 2:42). When Peter was put in prison, "earnest prayer for him was made to God by the church" (Acts 12:5).

If prayer from the church is not simply the mouthing of words without heartfelt intention but is the genuine expression of our hearts and the reflection of sincere faith, then we should expect that the Holy Spirit will bring a great blessing through it. Certainly when prayer is done "in the Spirit" (Eph. 6:18; cf. Jude 20: "praying in the Holy Spirit"), it involves fellowship with the Holy Spirit and therefore a ministry of the Holy Spirit to the people praying. And the author of Hebrews reminds us that as we "draw near" to God in prayer before the throne of grace, we do so "that we may receive mercy and find grace to help in time of need" (Heb. 4:16).

The more the genuine fellowship of a church increases, the more there ought to be continual prayer for one another within the church, and the more genuine spiritual blessing from the Holy Spirit may be expected to flow through the church.

## 5. Worship

Genuine worship is worship "in spirit" (John 4:23–24; Phil. 3:3), which probably means worship that is in the spiritual realm of activity (not merely the outward physical action of attendance at a worship service or singing of songs).[9] When we enter that spiritual realm of activity and minister to the Lord in worship, God also ministers to us. So, for example, in the church at Antioch, *"while they were worshiping the Lord* and fasting, the Holy Spirit said, 'Set apart for me Barnabas and Saul for the work to which I have called them'" (Acts 13:2). This parallels the experience of the people of Israel in the Old Testament who knew the presence of God when they engaged in genuine worship:

> *When the song was raised,* with trumpets and cymbals and other musical instruments, *in praise to the* LORD, "For he is good, for his steadfast love endures forever," the house, the house of the LORD was filled with a cloud, so that the priests could not stand to minister because of the cloud, for *the glory of the* LORD *filled the house of God.* (2 Chron. 5:13–14)

When God's people worshiped, he came in a very visible way in the cloud of glory to dwell in their midst. Similarly in the New Testament, James promises, "Draw near to God, and *he will draw near to you*" (James 4:8). In fact, as God's people worshiped, he delivered them from their enemies (2 Chron. 20:18–23) or at other times gave them true spiritual insight into the nature of events around them ("Until I went into the sanctuary of God; then I discerned their end," Ps. 73:17).

If worship is genuinely an experience of drawing near to God, coming into his presence, and giving him the praise he deserves, then we certainly ought to count it one of the primary "means of grace" available to the church. Through genuine congregational worship God will very often bring great blessing, both individually and corporately, to his people.

## 6. Church Discipline

Because church discipline is a means by which the purity of the church is advanced and holiness of life is encouraged, we certainly should count it as a "means of grace" as

---

9. See the discussion of worship "in spirit" in chapter 51, p. 1244. (The whole of chapter 51 discusses worship in general.)

well. However, blessing is not automatically given: when the church disciplines, no spiritual good comes to the wrongdoer unless the Holy Spirit convicts him or her of sin and brings about a "godly grief" that "produces a repentance that leads to salvation without regret" (2 Cor. 7:10), and no spiritual good comes to the church unless the Holy Spirit is active in the other members' lives when they become aware of the process. This is why the church is to carry out discipline with the knowledge that it is done in the presence of the Lord (1 Cor. 5:4; cf. 4:19–20), and with the assurance that it has heavenly sanction connected with it (Matt. 16:19; 18:18–20).[10]

It would be very healthy for the church to begin to think of church discipline not as an onerous burden placed upon it by the Lord but as a genuine "means of grace" by which great blessing can come to the church—in reconciling believers to one another and to God, in restoring the erring brother or sister to walk in obedience, in warning all to "stand in fear" (1 Tim. 5:20), in increasing moral purity in the church, and in protecting and advancing Christ's honor. Though sorrow and pain are often connected with church discipline, when it is rightly done with faith that the Lord is working through it, the sorrow will ultimately lead to "salvation without regret" (2 Cor. 7:10). When carried out in this way, church discipline should certainly be seen as a means of grace by which the Holy Spirit will bring blessing to his church.[11]

## 7. Giving

Giving is ordinarily done through the church as it receives and distributes gifts to the various ministries and needs cared for by the church. Once again, there is no automatic or mechanical bestowing of benefits on those who give. Simon the sorcerer was strongly rebuked for thinking that he "could obtain the gift of God with money" (Acts 8:20). But if giving is done in faith, out of commitment to Christ and love for his people, then certainly there will be great blessing in it. It is most pleasing to God when gifts of money are accompanied by an intensification of the giver's personal commitment to God, as was the case among the Macedonians who "*gave themselves* first to the Lord and then by the will of God to us" (2 Cor. 8:5), and then gave to help the poor Christians in Jerusalem. When giving is carried out joyfully, "not reluctantly or under compulsion," there is the great reward of God's favor with it, "for God loves a cheerful giver" (2 Cor. 9:7).

Paul views the giving of money to the Lord's work as spiritual sowing that will lead to a harvest: "Whoever sows sparingly will also reap sparingly, and whoever sows bountifully will also reap bountifully" (2 Cor. 9:6). And Paul expects that as the Corinthians give rightly God will bless them: "God is able to make *all grace abound to you*, so that having all sufficiency in all things at all times, you may abound in every good work" (2 Cor. 9:8). He tells them, "*You will be enriched in every way to be generous in every way,*

---

10. See discussion of the "power of the keys" in chapter 46, pp. 1097–1110.

11. See chapter 46, pp. 1102–10, for a fuller discussion of church discipline.

which through us will produce thanksgiving to God" (2 Cor. 9:11). Therefore, giving blesses the *recipient* in that his or her needs are met, and faith and thanksgiving for God's provision are increased; it blesses the *giver* because "God loves a cheerful giver" and will grant an abundant spiritual harvest, and brings blessing to *all who know about it* since it produces a harvest of "many thanksgivings to God" (2 Cor. 9:12). Rather than seeing giving as an unpleasant obligation, we would do well to view it as a rich means of grace within the church and to expect that through it the Holy Spirit will bring blessing.

## 8. Spiritual Gifts

Peter views spiritual gifts as channels through which God's grace comes to the church because he says, "As each has received a gift, use it to serve one another, *as good stewards of God's varied grace*" (1 Peter 4:10). When gifts are used for one another in the church, God's grace is thereby dispensed to those for whom God intended it. Great blessing will come to the church through proper use of spiritual gifts, as the church follows Paul's command to use the gifts to "strive to excel in building up the church" (1 Cor. 14:12; cf. Eph. 4:11–16).

If we listed all the spiritual gifts as separate means of grace, our list of the means of grace would be much longer than eleven items. But even if we contain them all in this one category, we should recognize that the different spiritual gifts in the church are all means by which the Holy Spirit brings blessing through individual Christians. This should remind us of the abundant favor that God has given us as undeserving sinners and should also make us realize that many different Christians with diverse gifts can be the channels through which grace comes to us. In fact, in Peter's exhortation to use spiritual gifts as stewards of "God's *varied* grace" (1 Peter 4:10), the word translated "varied" (Gk. *poikilos*) means "having many facets or aspects; richly varied; having great diversity." Moreover, we should remember that these gifts are distributed not only to clergy or a limited number of Christians, but to all believers who have the Holy Spirit within them (1 Cor. 12:7, 11; 1 Peter 4:10).[12]

## 9. Fellowship

We should not neglect ordinary Christian fellowship as a valuable means of grace within the church. The early church "devoted themselves to the apostles' teaching *and the fellowship,* to the breaking of bread and the prayers" (Acts 2:42). The author of Hebrews reminds believers, "Let us consider how to stir up one another to love and good works, *not neglecting to meet together,* as is the habit of some, but encouraging one another, and all the more as you see the Day drawing near" (Heb. 10:24–25). In the fellowship of believers, ordinary friendship and affection for one another will grow, and Jesus' injunction that we "love one another" (John 15:12) will be fulfilled. Moreover,

---

12. See chapters 52 and 53 for a discussion of spiritual gifts.

as believers care for one another, they will "bear one another's burdens, and so fulfill the law of Christ" (Gal. 6:2).

An emphasis on the fellowship of believers with one another as a means of grace would also help to overcome an excessive focus on the ordained clergy as the primary dispensers of grace within the church, particularly when the whole church is assembled. It would also be healthy for Christians to recognize that a measure of God's grace is experienced when Christians talk together and eat together, when they have times of work and play together, enjoying one another's fellowship. "And day by day, attending the temple together and breaking bread in their homes, they received their food with glad and generous hearts, praising God and having favor with all the people" (Acts 2:46–47).

## 10. Evangelism

In Acts, there is a frequent connection between proclaiming the gospel (even in the face of opposition) and being filled with the Holy Spirit (see Acts 2:4 with vv. 14–36; 4:8, 31; 9:17 with v. 20; 13:9, 52). Evangelism is a means of grace, then, not only in the sense that it ministers saving grace to the unsaved but also because those who evangelize experience more of the Holy Spirit's presence and blessing in their lives. Sometimes evangelism is carried out by individuals, but at other times it is a corporate activity of the church (as in evangelistic campaigns). Even individual evangelism often involves other church members who will welcome an unbelieving visitor and give attention to his or her needs. So evangelism is rightly considered a means of grace in the church.

## 11. Personal Ministry to Individuals

Along with the previous ten "means of grace" within the church, it is appropriate to list one more specific means that the Holy Spirit very frequently uses to bring blessing to individual Christians. This means of grace operates when one or more Christians within the church take time to minister, in various ways, to very specific needs of another individual in the church.

Sometimes this ministry takes the form of *words of encouragement or exhortation or wise counsel*. We are to be "teaching and admonishing one another in all wisdom" (Col. 3:16) and to speak words that "give grace to those who hear" (Eph. 4:29). We are to attempt to bring back "a sinner from his wandering" (James 5:20) and to "consider how to stir up one another to love and good works" and to be "encouraging one another" (Heb. 10:24–25). At other times such ministry involves *giving to assist the material needs of a brother or sister*: James rebukes those who merely say, "Go in peace, be warmed and filled," without "giving them the things needed for the body" (James 2:16). John warns us, "If anyone has the world's goods and sees his brother in need, yet closes his heart against him, how does God's love abide in him?" (1 John 3:17). Therefore, the early church gave readily to the needs of poor Christians, so that "there was not a needy person among them" (Acts 4:34). And Paul said that the leaders of the church in Jerusalem "asked us to remember the poor, the very thing I was eager to do" (Gal. 2:10).

Another form this interpersonal ministry may take is the *anointing with oil* in conjunction with prayer for a sick person. Jesus' disciples "anointed with oil many who were sick and healed them" (Mark 6:13). Similarly, James says that a sick person should "call for the elders of the church, and let them pray over him, anointing him with oil in the name of the Lord" (James 5:14). In these cases the oil seems to have been a physical symbol of the healing power of the Holy Spirit coming to the sick person.

Finally, one more means of exercising personal ministry to individuals in the New Testament is the use of physical touch, particularly the *laying on of hands* in connection with prayer for someone in need. A survey of the New Testament may surprise many modern Christians (as it did to me) when they see how frequently the laying on of hands and other kinds of physical touch are seen to function as a "means of grace" in the ministry of Jesus and the early church.

It seems that the laying on of hands was by far the most common method that Jesus used to pray for people. When crowds came bringing people "with various diseases" to him, "*he laid his hands on every one of them* and healed them" (Luke 4:40). Other passages specifically describe Jesus' placing his hands on people to heal them (Matt. 8:3; Mark 1:41; 6:5; 8:23–25; Luke 5:13; 13:13). But more significant than these individual passages is the fact that people who came to Jesus for healing would come specifically asking him to lay his hands on a sick person: "*Come and lay your hand on her*, and she will live" (Matt. 9:18), or "*Come and lay your hands on her*, so that she may be made well and live" (Mark 5:23; cf. 7:32). The fact that people came with this request suggests that the laying on of hands was commonly recognized as the method Jesus usually used to heal people. In imitation of Jesus' method of healing, when the father of Publius was sick, "Paul visited him and prayed, and *putting his hands on him*, healed him" (Acts 28:8).[13]

In other cases people sought more generally to touch Jesus or asked that he would touch them in order to be healed. "Some people brought to him a blind man and begged him to *touch* him" (Mark 8:22). Similarly, people "brought to him all who were sick and implored him that they might only touch the fringe of his garment. And as many as touched it were made well" (Matt. 14:35–36). This was because the power of the Holy Spirit was conveyed through Jesus' physical touch and that the power of the Holy Spirit came forth and healed people. "All the crowd sought to *touch* him, for power came out from him and healed them all" (Luke 6:19; cf. Matt. 9:20–22, 25; 20:34; Mark 1:31; 5:41; 9:27; Luke 7:14; 8:54; 22:51).

However, it was not simply to heal that Jesus and the early church laid on hands or

---

13. Although the longer ending of Mark is doubtful as part of Scripture (see chapter 17, p. 481), Mark 16:18 certainly does represent at least one stream of early tradition within the church as well: it says that those who believe in Jesus "will lay their hands on the sick, and they will recover."

touched people. When children came to Jesus, "he took them in his arms and blessed them, laying his hands on them" (Mark 10:16; cf. Matt. 19:13–15; Luke 18:15).

When Jesus so frequently touched people to bring healing or otherwise to bring blessing to them, it is not surprising that people would mention the miracles done by his hands: "How are such mighty works (Gk. *dynamis,* "miracle") done *by his hands?*" (Mark 6:2).[14] Similarly, when Paul and Barnabas were on their first missionary journey, the Lord "bore witness to the word of his grace, granting signs and wonders to be done *by their hands*" (Acts 14:3).[15] In the same way, "God was doing extraordinary miracles by the *hands* of Paul" (Acts 19:11).[16] Since there was, as with the other means of grace, no automatic or magical power inherent in the hands of the early Christians but healing and other kinds of blessing only came as God himself was pleased to work through the laying on of hands, it is not surprising that the early church prayed specifically that God would stretch forth *his hand* to heal. They prayed, "Now, Lord, look upon their threats and grant to your servants to continue to speak your word with all boldness, *while you stretch out your hand to heal*" (Acts 4:29–30). They realized that while they stretched forth their hands to touch those who were sick, it would not be effective at all unless God's own mighty hand of power was working through their hands.

At other times the laying on of hands was done for some other purpose. Apparently it was done in connection with asking God to empower or equip people for some service or ministry. When the first deacons were appointed, the church brought them before the apostles, "and they prayed and *laid their hands on them*" (Acts 6:6). Similarly, when the church at Antioch sent out Paul and Barnabas, "Then after fasting and praying *they laid their hands on them* and sent them off" (Acts 13:3).

When the gospel came to a new group of people, those who proclaimed the gospel would sometimes lay hands on the new believers in order that they might receive the new covenant power of the Holy Spirit. At Samaria, the apostles "laid their hands on them and they received the Holy Spirit" (Acts 8:17). Ananias laid his hands on Saul in order that he might regain his sight and "be filled with the Holy Spirit" (Acts 9:17). When Paul "laid his hands on" the disciples at Ephesus who had just come to believe in Jesus, "the Holy Spirit came on them" (Acts 19:6).

---

14. Because the gospels so frequently emphasize the fact that Jesus laid hands on people or touched them with his hands, this expression should not be understood to be merely a metaphor meaning "how are such mighty works done by *him?*" It is better understood to be a reference to the specific way in which Jesus' hands were the means by which his miracles were frequently done.

Unfortunately, in this verse and several others mentioning miracles done by people's *hands,* the NIV has decided that a strictly literal translation is not important and has given the English reader no mention of hands. For example, it simply translates Mark 6:2, "What are these remarkable miracles he is performing?" (Mark 6:2 NIV). But the Greek text specifically says that miracles are done *"through his hands"* (*dia tōn cheirōn autou*). In the following section I have pointed out only some of the places where the NIV fails to translate the Greek word *cheir* ("hand"), but it is present in the Greek text in all the verses I quote, and readers who do not find it in their NIV translations should consult another translation, such as the ESV or NASB, that has a more literal translation policy.

15. The NIV simply translates, "enabling *them* to do miraculous signs and wonders" (see previous footnote).

16. The NIV simply says, "God did extraordinary miracles *through Paul*" (see previous two footnotes).

In other cases the laying on of hands resulted in the impartation of some spiritual gift. In the incident just mentioned, the disciples at Ephesus "began speaking in tongues and prophesying" (Acts 19:6) after Paul laid his hands on them. Moreover, he reminds Timothy, "Do not neglect the gift you have, which was given you by prophecy when the council of elders laid their hands on you" (1 Tim. 4:14). Paul may have been referring to the same event or a different one when he said later, "I remind you to fan into flame the *gift* of God, which is in you *through the laying on of my hands*" (2 Tim. 1:6). (In 1 Timothy 5:22, the statement "Do not be hasty in the laying on of hands" refers to the ordination of elders; see chapter 47, p. 1129.)

If people in the early church were frequently praying for one another's needs, and if they imitated the example of Jesus and his disciples in the laying on of hands to pray for people for healing, bringing blessing, receiving the Holy Spirit at the time of conversion, receiving spiritual gifts, or empowering for ministry, then we would expect that instruction given to new Christians would have included the teaching that prayer for individual needs would ordinarily be accompanied by the placing of a hand or hands upon the person who was being prayed for. If this were so, then it would not be surprising that "the laying on of hands" would be classified as an "elementary" doctrine, something that belongs to the "foundation" of Christian instruction—which is in fact what we find in Hebrews 6:1–2: "not laying again a *foundation* of repentance from dead works and of faith toward God, and of instruction about washings, *the laying on of hands*, the resurrection of the dead, and eternal judgment." Although some have understood this to refer more narrowly to the laying on of hands that accompanies installation in some specific church office, that is only one small aspect of the pattern of situations in which laying on of hands is found in the New Testament. It seems much better to understand this phrase in Hebrews 6:2 to refer to elementary instruction about how to pray for others in various situations of need so that young Christians would immediately be able to begin ministering to others as well.

It seems appropriate, then, to count the laying on of hands as one other dimension of the rich diversity of "means of grace" that God has placed within the church to bring blessing to his people.

## 12. Should Footwashing Be Practiced As a Means of Grace within the Church?

From time to time some Christian groups have practiced a ceremony of washing one another's feet at a public meeting of the church. They have based this practice on Jesus' command, "If I then, your Lord and Teacher, have washed your feet, *you also ought to wash one another's feet*" (John 13:14). Those who advocate footwashing consider it a ceremony that Jesus commanded, similar to the ceremonies of baptism and the Lord's Supper.

However, there are several reasons why we should not think that in John 13:14 Jesus was establishing another ceremony for the church in addition to baptism and the Lord's Supper. (1) Baptism and the Lord's Supper explicitly symbolize the greatest event in the history of redemption, Christ's death and resurrection for us, but footwashing symbolizes no such redemptive-historical event. (2) Baptism and the Lord's Supper were clearly *symbolic* actions, but when Jesus washed the disciples' feet it was clearly *functional*, not merely symbolic, in that it met an ordinary human need of the day (dirty feet). (3) Baptism and the Lord's Supper are appropriate symbols of beginning and continuing in the Christian life,[17] but no such symbolism attaches to footwashing. (4) To make footwashing an ordinance like baptism and the Lord's Supper reduces it to a symbol—and if it is a symbol, then Jesus' words command us only to perform a symbol, and the real force of Jesus' command (to act in humility and love) is lost. (5) Whereas the Epistles give evidence that baptism and the Lord's Supper were continuing ordinances observed by the New Testament churches, there is no evidence that the apostles or the early church observed footwashing as an ordinance. (6) There is a simple and straightforward explanation for Jesus' command: he is telling his disciples to take lowly tasks in serving one another. But if this is what the text means (and the vast majority of the church through history has understood it this way), then we need not look for an additional meaning (that Jesus is also instituting a new ceremony). By contrast, the New Testament texts about baptism and the Lord's Supper cannot be understood to command something *other* than a ceremony. Therefore, while all Christians would profit from pondering the application of Jesus' statement about footwashing to their present patterns of life, none should think that Jesus is encouraging them to practice a ceremony of footwashing.

## C. Conclusions

At the end of this discussion of the means of grace within the church, we should realize first of all that when any of these are carried out in faith and obedience, we should eagerly expect and look for evidence that the Holy Spirit is actually ministering to people at the same time as these actions are being done. We as Christians ought not to neglect to "meet together" (Heb. 10:25), but ought to look forward eagerly to any assembly of believers in which any of these means would occur, expecting that God will bring blessing from each of these means!

On the other hand, we must realize that all of these means of grace occur within the fellowship of the church. Those who neglect the fellowship of the church willfully cut themselves off from all of these means of grace and thereby cut themselves off from most of the ordinary means that the Holy Spirit uses to bring blessing to his people.

These means of grace ought to give us great appreciation for the amazing privilege of being members of the body of Christ, the church.

---

17. See chapter 49, pp. 1197–99, on the symbolism of baptism, and chapter 50, pp. 1221–23, on the symbolism of the Lord's Supper.

# QUESTIONS FOR PERSONAL APPLICATION

1. Before reading this chapter, did you think that it made very much difference if a Christian continued to be active in the fellowship of the church or not? How has this chapter changed your perspective on that question, if at all?

2. Which of the means of grace mentioned in this chapter has been most helpful to you in your Christian life?

3. Which of the means of grace mentioned in this chapter do you think you appreciated least before reading the chapter? How has your appreciation for that means of grace increased? How do you think this will affect your actions from now on?

4. As you look over the list of means of grace, are there some areas in which people are not actually experiencing "grace" or blessing in your church? What could be done to increase the effectiveness of these weak areas as means of grace in the life of your church?

5. Which of the means of grace are actually least helpful in your life? Are there some that have become rather mechanical and that you are performing only as an outward or physical activity without any real participation in your heart? What could you do to increase the effectiveness of those means in your life?

6. As you look over the list of the means of grace again, name one or more in which you could begin to help the church be more effective in bringing blessing to its people.

## Special Terms

*Eucharist*
*extreme unction*
*holy orders*
*laying on of hands*
*means of grace*
*sacrament*

# BIBLIOGRAPHY

(For an explanation of this bibliography see the note on the bibliography to chapter 1, pp. 23–24. Complete bibliographical data may be found on pp. 1489–96.)

## SECTIONS IN EVANGELICAL SYSTEMATIC THEOLOGIES

### 1. *Anglican (Episcopalian)*
1882–92 . . . . . Litton, 428–59
1930 . . . . . . . . Thomas, 313–38, 343–70, 447–51
2001 . . . . . . . . Packer, 207–8

2013 . . . . . . . . Bird, 735–44
2013 . . . . . . . . Bray, 480

### 2. *Arminian (Wesleyan or Methodist)*
1875–76 . . . . . Pope, 3:294–310, 335–59
1892–94 . . . . . Miley, 2:392–94
1940 . . . . . . . . Wiley, 3:150–60
1960 . . . . . . . . Purkiser, 409–27
1983 . . . . . . . . Carter, 2:615
1992 . . . . . . . . Oden, 3:261–96
2002 . . . . . . . . Cottrell, 306–17

**3. Baptist**

1767 . . . . . . . . Gill, 2:621, 660–82
1990–95 . . . . . Garrett, 2:527–48
2007 . . . . . . . . Akin, 809–16
2013 . . . . . . . . Erickson, 930–46

**4. Dispensational**

1949 . . . . . . . . Thiessen, 296–304
1986 . . . . . . . . Ryrie, 421, 427
2017 . . . . . . . . MacArthur and Mayhue, 780–95

**5. Lutheran**

1917–24 . . . . . Pieper, 3:104–215, 439–72
1934 . . . . . . . . Mueller, 441–69

**6. Reformed (or Presbyterian)**

1559 . . . . . . . . Calvin, 2:1276–1302, 1448–84 (4.14, 19)
1679–85 . . . . . Turretin, *IET*, 3:337–560
1871–73 . . . . . Hodge, 3:466–526
1878 . . . . . . . . Dabney, 726–57
1894 . . . . . . . . Shedd, 2809–30
1906–11 . . . . . Bavinck, *RD*, 4:441–60, 461–95, 496–539, 540–85
1910 . . . . . . . . Vos, 3:17–18
1937–66 . . . . . Murray, *CW*, 2:366–69
1938 . . . . . . . . Berkhof, 604–21
1998 . . . . . . . . Reymond, 911–78
2008 . . . . . . . . Van Genderen and Velema, 753–818
2011 . . . . . . . . Horton, 751–87
2013 . . . . . . . . Frame, 647–49, 1023–24, 1047–57, 1060–69
2016 . . . . . . . . Allen and Swain, 27–28
2017 . . . . . . . . Barrett, 562
2019 . . . . . . . . Letham, 616–18, 634–47, 751–68

**7. Renewal (or charismatic/Pentecostal)**

1988–92 . . . . . Williams, 2:287–94, 3:159–63
1993 . . . . . . . . Menzies and Horton, 163–72
1995 . . . . . . . . Horton, 552–56
2008 . . . . . . . . Duffield and Van Cleave, 436–41

## SECTIONS IN REPRESENTATIVE ROMAN CATHOLIC SYSTEMATIC THEOLOGIES

**1. Roman Catholic: Traditional**

1955 . . . . . . . . Ott, 325–472

**2. Roman Catholic: Post–Vatican II**

1980 . . . . . . . . McBrien, 2:731–49, 775–816
2012 . . . . . . . . *CCC*, paragraphs 1420–1690

## OTHER WORKS

Allison, Gregg. *Sojourners and Strangers: The Doctrine of the Church.* Wheaton, IL: Crossway, 2012, 413–66.
Bartos, E. "Fellowship." In *NDT2*, 335–36.
Blackaby, Henry T. *A God Centered Church: Experiencing God Together.* Nashville: B&H, 2007.
Bridges, Jerry. *True Community: The Biblical Practice of Koinonia.* Colorado Springs: NavPress, 2012.
Casurella, A. "Fellowship." In *DLNT*, 373–74.
Dever, Mark. "The Church." In *A Theology for the Church*, edited by Daniel L. Akin et al., 774–75. Nashville: B&H, 2007.
Hellerman, Joseph H. *When the Church Was a Family: Recapturing Jesus' Vision For Authentic Christian Community.* Nashville: B&H Academic, 2009.
House, H. Wayne. *Charts of Christian Theology and Doctrine.* Grand Rapids: Zondervan, 1992, 101.
Hughes, P. E. "Grace, Means of." In *EDT3*, 358.
Martens, E. A. "Community." In *GDT*, 189–91.
McRay, J. R. "Fellowship." In *EDT3*, 312.
Milne, Bruce. *We Belong Together: The Meaning of Fellowship.* Downers Grove, IL: InterVarsity Press, 1978.
O'Brien, P. T. "Fellowship, Communion, Sharing." In *DPL*, 293–95.
Strukova, J. "Community." In *EDT3*, 199–200.
Toon, Peter. "Fellowship." In *BTDB*, 255–56.

## SCRIPTURE MEMORY PASSAGE

**Acts 2:41–42:** So those who received his word were baptized, and there were added that day about three thousand souls. And they devoted themselves to the apostles' teaching and the fellowship, to the breaking of bread and the prayers.

## HYMN

**"I Love Thy Kingdom, Lord"**

This hymn expresses joy at the privilege of being in the church. In fact, the author exclaims, "Beyond my highest joy I prize her heavenly ways, her sweet communion, solemn vows, her hymns of love and praise." Here he is meditating on some of the means of grace within the church ("her heavenly ways"), particularly the fellowship or communion that comes within the church, the vows to God that are made there, and the hymns that are sung within it. Moreover, using the figure of Mount Zion to refer to the church, he says that "to Zion shall be given the brightest glories earth can yield, and brighter bliss of heaven." When we sing this, we can think of all the rich blessings that the Holy Spirit bestows on the church through the many means of grace.

The author of this hymn, Timothy Dwight, was President of Yale University from 1795 to 1817, during which time he reformed the administration and the curriculum and tripled the enrollment. He also was professor of divinity, and under his preaching a revival broke out in 1802, in which a third of the students were converted.

*I love thy kingdom, Lord, the house of thine abode,*
*The church our blest Redeemer saved with his own precious blood.*

*I love thy church, O God: her walls before thee stand,*
*Dear as the apple of thine eye, and graven on thy hand.*

*For her my tears shall fall, for her my prayers ascend;*
*To her my cares and toils be giv'n, till toils and cares shall end.*

*Beyond my highest joy I prize her heav'nly ways,*
*Her sweet communion, solemn vows, her hymns of love and praise.*

*Jesus, thou Friend divine, our Savior and our King,*
*Thy hand from ev'ry snare and foe shall great deliv'rance bring.*

*Sure as thy truth shall last, to Zion shall be giv'n*
*The brightest glories earth can yield, and brighter bliss of heav'n.*
Author: Timothy Dwight, 1800

# CONTEMPORARY WORSHIP SONG

## "We Will Dance"

*Sing a song of celebration,*
*Lift up a shout of praise,*
*For the Bridegroom will come,*
*The glorious one,*
*And oh we will look on His face.*
*We'll go to a much better place.*

*And dance with all your might.*
*Lift up your hands and clap for joy.*
*The time's drawing near*
*When He will appear,*
*And oh we will stand by His side,*
*A strong pure spotless bride.*

*Oh, we will dance on the streets that are golden,*
*The glorious bride and the great Son of Man.*
*Let every tongue and tribe and nation*
*Rejoice in the song of the Lamb.*

*Yes—spoken*

*Oh, sing a song of celebration,*
*Lift up a shout of praise,*
*For the Bridegroom will come,*
*The glorious one,*
*And oh we will look on His face.*
*We'll go to a much better place.*

*And dance with all your might.*
*Lift up your hands and clap for joy.*
*The time's drawing near*
*When He will appear,*
*And oh we will stand by His side,*
*A strong pure and spotless bride.*

*We will dance on the streets that are golden,*
*The glorious bride and the great Son of Man.*
*Let every tongue and tribe and nation*
*Rejoice in the song of the Lamb.*

Words by David Ruis[18]

---

18. © 1993 Mercy/Vineyard Publishing (ASCAP) admin. in North America by Music Services o/b/o Vineyard Music USA.

# CHAPTER 49

# Baptism

*Who should be baptized?*
*How should it be done?*
*What does it mean?*

## EXPLANATION AND SCRIPTURAL BASIS

In this chapter and the next we treat baptism and the Lord's Supper, two ceremonies that Jesus commanded his church to perform. But before we begin consideration of either one of them we must note that there is disagreement among Protestants even over the general term that should be applied to them. Because the Roman Catholic Church calls these two ceremonies "sacraments," and because the Catholic Church teaches that these sacraments *in themselves* actually *convey grace* to people (without requiring faith from the persons participating in them), some Protestants (especially Baptists) have refused to refer to baptism and the Lord's Supper as "sacraments." They have preferred the word *ordinances* instead. This is thought to be an appropriate term because baptism and the Lord's Supper were "ordained" by Christ.[1] On the other hand, other Protestants such as those in the Anglican, Lutheran, and Reformed traditions, have been willing to use the word *sacraments* to refer to baptism and the Lord's Supper, without thereby endorsing the Roman Catholic position.

It does not seem that any significant point is at issue here in the question of whether to call baptism and the Lord's Supper "ordinances" or "sacraments." Since Protestants who use both words explain clearly what they mean by them, the argument is not really over doctrine but over the meaning of an English word. If we are willing to explain clearly what we mean, it does not seem to make any difference whether we use the word *sacrament* or not.[2] In this text, when referring to baptism and the Lord's Supper in Protestant teaching, I will use *ordinances* and *sacraments* interchangeably and regard them as synonymous.

Before beginning our discussion of baptism, we must recognize that there has been

---

1. A. H. Strong says, "No ordinance is a sacrament in the Romanist sense of conferring grace" (*Systematic Theology* [Valley Forge, PA: Judson, 1907], 930). He also says, "The Romanist regards the ordinances as actually conferring grace and producing holiness" (ibid.).

2. The *American Heritage Dictionary* (Boston: Houghton

Mifflin, 1981) allows a range of meanings, defining a sacrament as a rite considered as "a testament to inner grace *or* a channel that mediates grace" (p. 1141). Even the most conscientious Baptist would not object to calling baptism "a testament to inner grace" while Catholics would not object to calling baptism "a channel that mediates grace."

historically, and is today, a strong difference of viewpoint among evangelical Christians regarding this subject. The position advocated in this book is that baptism is not a "major" doctrine that should be the basis of division among genuine Christians,[3] but it is nonetheless a matter of importance for ordinary church life, and it is appropriate that we give it full consideration.

The position advocated in this chapter is "Baptistic"—namely, that *baptism is appropriately administered only to those who give a believable profession of faith in Jesus Christ.*[4] (This position is also called a "believer's baptism" position.)[5] During the discussion, we shall interact particularly with the paedobaptist ("infant baptist") position as advocated by Louis Berkhof in his *Systematic Theology*, since this is a careful and responsible representation of the paedobaptist position in a widely used systematic theology text.

## A. THE MODE AND MEANING OF BAPTISM

The practice of baptism in the New Testament was carried out in one way: the person being baptized was *immersed* or put completely under the water and then brought back up again. Baptism *by immersion* is therefore the "mode" of baptism or the way in which baptism was carried out in the New Testament. This is evident for the following reasons.

(1) The Greek word *baptizō* means "to plunge, dip, immerse" something in water. This is the commonly recognized and standard meaning of the term in ancient Greek literature both inside and outside of the Bible.[6]

(2) The sense "immerse" is appropriate and probably required for the word in several New Testament passages. In Mark 1:5, people were baptized by John "*in* the river Jordan" (the Greek text has *en*, "in," and not "beside" or "by" or "near" the river).[7] Mark

---

3. See chapter 1, p. 11, for a discussion of major and minor doctrines. Not all Christians agree with my view that this is a minor doctrine. Many Christians in previous generations were persecuted and even put to death because they differed with the official state church and its practice of infant baptism. For them, the issue was not merely a ceremony: it was the right to have a believers' church, one that did not automatically include all the people born in a geographical region. Viewed in this light, the controversy over baptism involves a larger difference over the nature of the church: Does one become part of the church by birth into a believing family, or by voluntary profession of faith?

4. I have given a detailed personal account of how I came to believe the Bible, and how I came to hold to believer's baptism in my essay, "A Baptist Because of the Bible," in *Why I Am a Baptist*, ed. Tom J. Nettles and Russell Moore (Nashville: B&H, 2001), 201–8.

5. Yet another term used, though less commonly, is *credobaptist*, which is based on the Latin word *credo*, meaning "believe, trust."

6. So *LSJ*, 305: "plunge"; passive, "to be drowned." Similarly, BDAG, 164: "In Greek literature generally to put or go underwater in a variety of senses.... In our literature only in ritual or ceremonial sense." Also Albrecht Oepke, "*baptō, baptizō,*

etc.," in *TDNT*, 1:530: "to immerse ... to sink the ship"; passive, "to sink ... to suffer shipwreck, to drown (the sense of 'to bathe' or 'to wash' is only occasionally found in Hellenism ... the idea of going under or perishing is nearer the general usage)." Strong, *Systematic Theology*, 933–35, gives much additional evidence to this effect.

Berkhof, *Systematic Theology*, 630, objects and gives some counterexamples, but his evidence is unconvincing because he indiscriminately mixes examples of *baptizō* with a related but different word, *baptō*. (Passages that speak of "bathing" or washing [in the Septuagint, Judith 12:7, for example, and in the New Testament, Mark 7:4] would most likely involve covering one's body [or hands, in Mark 7:4] completely with water.)

If any New Testament author had wanted to indicate that people were sprinkled with water, a perfectly good Greek word meaning "to sprinkle" was available: *rhantizō* is used in this sense in Heb. 9:13, 19, 21; 10:22; see BAGD, 734.

7. Berkhof asks, "Was John the Baptist capable of the enormous task of immersing the multitudes that flocked unto him at the river Jordan...?" (*Systematic Theology*, 630). Certainly over a period of several days he would have been capable of immersing many hundreds of people, but it is also possible that his disciples (Matt. 9:14, et al.) assisted him with some of the baptisms.

also tells us that when Jesus had been baptized "he came up *out of the water*" (Mark 1:10). The Greek text specifies that he came "out of" (*ek*) the water, not that he came away from it (this would be expressed by Gk. *apo*). The fact that John and Jesus went into the river and came up out of it strongly suggests immersion, since sprinkling or pouring of water could much more readily have been done standing beside the river, particularly because multitudes of people were coming for baptism. John's gospel tells us, further, that John the Baptist "was baptizing at Aenon near Salim, because water was plentiful there" (John 3:23). Again, it would not take a "plentiful" amount of water to baptize people by sprinkling, but it would need to be plentiful to baptize by immersion.

When Philip had shared the gospel with the Ethiopian eunuch, "as they were going along the road they came to some water, and the eunuch said, 'See, here is water! What prevents me from being baptized?'" (Acts 8:36). Apparently neither of them thought that sprinkling or pouring a handful of water from the container of drinking water that would have been carried in the chariot was enough to constitute baptism. Rather, they waited until there was a body of water near the road. Then "he commanded the chariot to stop, and they both went *down into the water*, Philip and the eunuch, and he baptized him. And when they came *up out of the water*, the Spirit of the Lord carried Philip away, and the eunuch saw him no more, and went on his way rejoicing" (Acts 8:38–39). As in the case of Jesus, this baptism occurred when Philip and the eunuch went *down into* a body of water, and after the baptism they came *up out of* that body of water. Once again baptism by immersion is the only satisfactory explanation of this narrative.[8]

(3) The symbolism of union with Christ in his death, burial, and resurrection seems to require baptism by immersion. Paul says, "Do you not know that all of us who have been baptized into Christ Jesus were baptized into his death? We were buried therefore with him by baptism into death, in order that, just as Christ was raised from the dead by the glory of the Father, we too might walk in newness of life" (Rom. 6:3–4). Similarly, Paul tells the Colossians that they have "been *buried with him in baptism*, in which you were also *raised with him* through faith in the powerful working of God, who raised him from the dead" (Col. 2:12).

Now this truth is clearly symbolized in baptism by immersion. When the candidate for baptism goes down into the water, it is a picture of going down into the grave and being buried. Coming up out of the water is then a picture of being raised with Christ to walk in newness of life. Baptism thus very clearly pictures death to one's old way of life and rising to a new kind of life in Christ. But baptism by sprinkling or pouring simply misses this symbolism.

---

8. Berkhof (*Systematic Theology*, 630–31) objects that in Acts 8:38 the Greek word *eis* can mean "to" and not necessarily "into." It is true that the word can take either meaning, but we must also note v. 39, where *ek* certainly means "out of," not "away from," which would be expressed by *apo*. And the going down and coming up (*katabainō* and *anabainō*) are not going down from the chariot and going back up into the chariot but are specifically said to be going down *into the water* and coming up *out of the water*.

In fact, the waters of baptism have an even richer symbolism than simply the symbolism of the grave. The waters also remind us of the waters of God's judgment that came upon unbelievers at the time of the flood (Gen. 7:6–24) or the drowning of the Egyptians in the exodus (Ex. 14:26–29). Similarly, when Jonah was thrown into the deep (Jonah 1:7–16), he was thrown down to the place of death because of God's judgment on his disobedience—even though he was miraculously rescued and thus became a sign of the resurrection. Therefore, those who go down into the waters of baptism really are going down into the waters of judgment and death, death that they deserve from God for their sins. When they come back up out of the waters of baptism it shows that they have come safely through God's judgment only because of the merits of Jesus Christ, with whom they are united in his death and resurrection. This is why Peter can say in 1 Peter 3:21 that baptism "corresponds to" the saving of Noah and his family from the waters of judgment in the flood.

Sometimes it is objected that the essential thing symbolized in baptism is not death and resurrection with Christ but purification and cleansing from sins. Certainly it is true that water is an evident symbol of washing and cleansing, and the waters of baptism do symbolize washing and purification from sins as well as death and resurrection with Christ. Titus 3:5 speaks of "the washing of regeneration," and even though the word *baptism* is not used in this text, it is certainly true that there is a cleansing from sin that occurs at the time of conversion. Ananias told Saul, "Rise and be baptized and *wash away your sins*, calling on his name" (Acts 22:16).

But to say that washing away of sins is the only thing (or even the most essential thing) pictured in baptism does not faithfully represent New Testament teaching. Both washing and death and resurrection with Christ are symbolized in baptism, but Romans 6:1–11 and Colossians 2:11–12 place a clear emphasis on dying and rising with Christ. Even the washing is much more effectively symbolized by immersion than by sprinkling or pouring, and death and resurrection with Christ are symbolized only by immersion, not at all by sprinkling or pouring.

What then is the positive meaning of baptism? In all the discussion over the mode of baptism and the disputes over its meaning, it is easy for Christians to lose sight of the significance and beauty of baptism and to disregard the tremendous blessing that accompanies this ceremony. Passing through the waters of judgment safely, dying and rising with Christ, and having our sins washed away—these are amazing truths of momentous and eternal proportion and ought to be an occasion for giving great glory and praise to God. If churches would teach these truths more clearly, baptisms would be the occasion of much more blessing in the church.

## B. THE SUBJECTS OF BAPTISM

The pattern revealed at several places in the New Testament is that only those who give a believable profession of faith should be baptized. This view is often called "believer's baptism," since it holds that only those who have themselves believed in Christ (or, more precisely, those who have given reasonable evidence of believing in Christ) should be baptized. This is because baptism, which is a *symbol of beginning the Christian life*, should only be given to those who have *in fact* begun the Christian life.

### 1. The Argument From the New Testament Narrative Passages on Baptism

The narrative examples of those who were baptized suggest that baptism was administered only to those who gave a believable profession of faith. After Peter's sermon at Pentecost we read, *"Those who received his word* were baptized"* (Acts 2:41). The text specifies that baptism was administered to those who "received his word" and therefore trusted in Christ for salvation.[9] Similarly, when Philip preached the gospel in Samaria, we read, *"When they believed* Philip as he preached good news about the kingdom of God and the name of Jesus Christ, *they were baptized*, both men and women"* (Acts 8:12). Likewise, when Peter preached to the gentiles in Cornelius' household, he allowed baptism for those who had *heard* the Word and *received the Holy Spirit*—that is, for those who had given persuasive evidence of an internal work of regeneration. While Peter was preaching, "the Holy Spirit fell on all who heard the word," and Peter and his companions "were hearing them speaking in tongues and extolling God" (Acts 10:44–46). Peter's response was that baptism is appropriate for those who have received the regenerating work of the Holy Spirit: "Can anyone withhold water for baptizing these people, *who have received the Holy Spirit* just as we have?" Then Peter "commanded them to be baptized in the name of Jesus Christ" (Acts 10:47–48). The point of these three passages is that baptism is appropriately given to those who have received the gospel and trusted in Christ for salvation. There are other texts that indicate this as well—Acts 16:14–15 (Lydia and her household, after "the Lord opened her heart" to believe); Acts 16:32–33 (the family of the Philippian jailer, after Paul preached "the word of the Lord to him and to all who were in his house"); and 1 Corinthians 1:16 (the household of Stephanas)—but these will be discussed more fully below when we look at the question of "household baptisms."

### 2. The Argument From the Meaning of Baptism

In addition to these indications from New Testament narratives that baptism always followed upon saving faith, there is a second consideration that argues for believer's baptism: the outward symbol of *beginning* the Christian life should only be given to those who *show evidence* of having begun the Christian life. The New Testament authors wrote as though they clearly assumed that everyone who was baptized had also

---

9. Berkhof cautions against making too much of the silence of Scripture regarding infant baptism. Commenting on the fact that in some cases whole households were baptized, he says, "If there were infants, it is morally certain that they were baptized along with the parents" (634). But this is not what Acts 2:41 says: it specifies that *"those who received his word* were baptized," not those who did not receive his word but were infants belonging to the households of those who received his word.

personally trusted in Christ and experienced salvation. For example, Paul says, "As many of you as were baptized into Christ have put on Christ" (Gal. 3:27). Paul here assumes that baptism is the outward sign of inward regeneration. This simply would not have been true of infants—Paul could not have said, "As many *infants* as have been baptized into Christ have put on Christ," for infants have not yet come to saving faith or given any evidence of regeneration.[10]

Paul speaks the same way in Romans 6:3–4: "Do you not know that *all of us who have been baptized into Christ Jesus* were baptized into his death? We were buried therefore with him by baptism into death." Could Paul have said this of infants?[11] Could he have said that "all infants who have been baptized into Christ Jesus were baptized into his death" and "were buried therefore with him by baptism into death"? But if Paul could not have said those things about infants, then those who advocate infant baptism must say that baptism means something *different* for infants than what Paul says it means for "all of us who have been baptized into Christ Jesus." Those who argue for infant baptism at this point resort to what seems to the present author to be vague language about infants being adopted "into the covenant" or "into the covenant community," but the New Testament does not speak that way about baptism. Rather, it says that all of those who have been baptized have been buried with Christ, have been raised with him, and have put on Christ.

A similar argument can be made from Colossians 2:12: "having been *buried with him in baptism, in which you were also raised with him* through faith in the powerful working of God, who raised him from the dead." But it could not be said of infants that they were buried with Christ or were raised with him through faith, since they were not yet old enough to exercise faith for themselves.

## 3. Alternative 1: The Roman Catholic View

The Roman Catholic Church teaches that baptism should be administered to infants.[12] The reason for this is that the Catholic Church believes that baptism is *necessary* for salvation, and that the act of baptism itself *causes regeneration*. Therefore, in this view, baptism is a *means* whereby the church bestows saving grace on people. And if it is this kind of a channel of saving grace, it should be given to all people.

The Catechism of the Catholic Church says,

> The Lord himself affirms that Baptism is necessary for salvation [the footnote at this point refers to John 3:5].[13]

---

10. This is not to argue that *no* infants can be regenerated (see above, chapter 24, pp. 629–31) but simply that Paul could have no theological basis for saying that *all* infants who have been baptized have begun the Christian life. He is talking in Gal. 3:27 of "as many of you as were baptized into Christ."

11. See section 3 below for a response to the Roman Catholic view that baptism causes regeneration.

12. The act of baptizing an infant, including giving a name to the infant at that time, is sometimes called "christening," especially in Roman Catholic and Episcopalian churches.

13. *Catechism of the Catholic Church* (New York: Doubleday, 1997), paragraph 1257. I discuss John 3:5 below.

By Baptism *all sins* are forgiven, original sin and all personal sins, as well as all punishment for sin.[14]

Baptism not only purifies from all sins, but also makes the neophyte "a new creature," an adopted son of God, who has become a "partaker of the divine nature," member of Christ and co-heir with him, and a temple of the Holy Spirit. . . . The Most Holy Trinity gives the baptized sanctifying grace, the grace of *justification*.[15]

The Church and the parents would deny a child the priceless grace of becoming a child of God were they not to confer Baptism shortly after birth.[16]

Ludwig Ott, in his *Fundamentals of Catholic Dogma*, gives the following explanations:[17]

Baptism is that Sacrament in which man being washed with water in the name of the Three Divine Persons is spiritually reborn. (p. 350; Ott gives John 3:5; Titus 3:5; and Eph. 5:26 in support of this statement)

Baptism, provided that the proper dispositions (Faith and sorrow for sin) are present, effects: a) the eradication of sins, both original sin and, in the case of adults, also personal, mortal or venial sins; b) inner sanctification by the infusion of sanctifying grace. (p. 354)

Even if it be unworthily received, valid Baptism imprints on the soul of the recipient an indelible spiritual mark, the Baptismal Character. . . . The baptized person is incorporated, by the Baptismal Character, into the Mystical Body of Christ. (p. 355)

Ott goes on to explain that baptism is necessary for salvation: "Baptism by water . . . is, since the promulgation of the Gospel, necessary for all men without exception for salvation" (p. 356).[18]

Though infants cannot exercise saving faith themselves, the Roman Catholic Church teaches that the baptism of infants is valid: "Faith, as it is not the effective cause of justification . . . need not be present. The faith which infants lack is . . . replaced by the faith of the Church" (p. 359).

---

14. *CCC*, paragraph 1263, italics in original.
15. *CCC*, paragraphs 1265–66, italics in original.
16. *CCC*, paragraph 1250.
17. Ott, *Fundamentals of Catholic Dogma*, trans. Patrick Lynch, ed. James Bastible, 4th ed. (Rockford, IL: Tan, 1960). The following in-text citations refer to Ott's text.

18. In extreme cases Ott and the teaching of the Catholic Church allow for baptism of desire (for one who sincerely longs to be baptized but cannot be) or baptism by blood (in martyrdom).

Essential to understanding the Roman Catholic view of baptism is the realization that Catholics hold that the sacraments work even apart from the faith of the people participating in the sacrament. And if this is so, then it follows that baptism would confer grace on infants who do not have the ability to exercise faith. Several statements in Ott's book make this clear:

> The Catholic Church teaches that the Sacraments have an objective efficacy, that is, an efficacy independent of the subjective disposition of the recipient or of the minister. . . . The Sacraments confer grace immediately, that is, without the mediation of Fiducial faith. (pp. 328–29)

> The Sacraments of the New Covenant contain the grace which they signify, and bestow it on those who do not hinder it. (p. 328)

> The Sacraments work *ex opere operato*. . . . That is, the Sacraments operate by the power of the completed sacramental rite. (p. 329)[19]

> The formula *"ex opere operato"* asserts, negatively, that the sacramental grace is not conferred by reason of the subjective activity of the recipient, and positively, that the sacramental grace is caused by the validly operated sacramental sign. (p. 330)

However, Ott is careful to explain that the Catholic teaching must not be interpreted "in the sense of mechanical or magical efficacy" (p. 330). He says,

> On the contrary, in the case of the adult recipient faith is expressly demanded . . . nevertheless the subjective disposition of the recipient is not the cause of grace; it is merely an indispensable precondition of the communication of grace. . . . The measure of the grace effected *ex opere operato* even depends on the grade of the subjective disposition. (p. 330)

In giving a response to this Roman Catholic teaching, we should remember that the Reformation centered upon this issue. Martin Luther's great concern was to teach that salvation depends on faith alone, not on faith *plus works*. But if baptism and participating in the other sacraments are *necessary for salvation* because they are *necessary* for receiving saving grace, then salvation really is based on faith plus works. In contrast to this, the clear New Testament message is that justification is by faith *alone*. "By grace you have been saved *through faith*. And this is not your own doing; it is the gift of God, *not a*

---

19. The phrase *ex opere operato* represents an essential part of Roman Catholic teaching on the sacraments. This Latin phrase literally means "by work performed," and it means that the sacraments work in virtue of the actual activity done, and that the power of the sacraments does not depend on any subjective attitude of faith in the people participating in them.

*result of works*, so that no one may boast" (Eph. 2:8–9). Moreover, "the *free gift* of God is eternal life in Christ Jesus our Lord" (Rom. 6:23).

The Roman Catholic argument that baptism is necessary for salvation is similar to the argument of Paul's opponents in Galatia who said that circumcision was necessary for salvation. Paul's response is that those who require circumcision are preaching "a different gospel" (Gal. 1:6). He says that "all who rely on works of the law are under a curse" (Gal. 3:10), and he speaks severely to those who attempt to add any form of obedience as a requirement for justification: "You are severed from Christ, you who would be justified by the law; you have fallen away from grace" (Gal. 5:4). Therefore, we must conclude that no *work* is necessary for salvation. And therefore *baptism* is not necessary for salvation.

But what about John 3:5, "Unless one is *born of water* and the Spirit, he cannot enter the kingdom of God"? Although some have understood this as a reference to baptism, it is better understood against the background of the promise of the new covenant in Ezekiel 36:

> *I will sprinkle clean water on you*, and you shall be clean from all your uncleannesses, and from all your idols I will cleanse you. And I will give you a new heart, and a new spirit I will put within you. And I will remove the heart of stone from your flesh and give you a heart of flesh. And I will put my Spirit within you, and cause you to walk in my statutes and be careful to obey my rules. (Ezek. 36:25–27)

Ezekiel here speaks of a "spiritual" washing that will come in the days of the new covenant when God puts his Spirit within his people. In the light of this, to be born of water and the Spirit is a "spiritual" washing that occurs when we are born again, just as we receive a spiritual, not a physical, "new heart" at that time as well.

Similarly, Titus 3:5 specifies not water baptism but "the washing of regeneration," explicitly stating that it is a *spiritual* giving of new life. Water baptism is simply not mentioned in this passage. A spiritual rather than literal washing is also referred to in Ephesians 5:26, where Paul says that Christ gave himself up for the church "that he might sanctify her, having cleansed her by the washing of water with the word." It is the Word of God that does the washing referred to here, not physical water.

As for the Roman Catholic view that baptism conveys grace apart from the subjective disposition of the recipient or the minister (a position that is consistent with baptizing infants, who do not exercise faith for themselves), we must recognize that no New Testament examples exist to prove this view, nor is there New Testament testimony to indicate this. Rather, the narrative accounts of those who were baptized indicate that *they had first come to saving faith* (see above). And when there are doctrinal statements about baptism they also indicate the need of saving faith. When Paul says, "having been buried with him in baptism, in which you were also raised with him," he immediately specifies "*through faith* in the powerful working of God, who raised him from the dead" (Col. 2:12).

Finally, what about 1 Peter 3:21, where Peter says, "*Baptism . . . now saves you*"? Does this not give clear support to the Roman Catholic view that baptism itself brings saving grace to the recipient?[20] No, for when Peter uses this phrase he continues in the same sentence to explain exactly what he means by it. He says that baptism saves you "*not as a removal of dirt from the body*" (that is, not as an outward, physical act which washes dirt from the body—that is not the part which saves you) "*but as an appeal to God for a good conscience*" (that is, as an inward, spiritual transaction between God and the individual, a transaction symbolized by the outward ceremony of baptism). We could paraphrase Peter's statement by saying, "Baptism now saves you—not the *outward* physical ceremony of baptism but the *inward* spiritual reality that baptism represents." In this way, Peter guards against any view of baptism that would attribute automatic saving power to the physical ceremony itself.

Peter's phrase "an appeal to God for a good conscience" is another way of saying "a request for forgiveness of sins and a new heart." When God gives a sinner a "good conscience," that person has the assurance that every sin has been forgiven and that he or she stands in a right relationship with God (Heb. 9:14 and 10:22 speak this way about the cleansing of one's conscience through Christ). To be baptized rightly is to make such an "appeal" to God: it is to say, in effect, "Please, God, as I enter this baptism which will cleanse my body outwardly I am asking you to cleanse my heart inwardly, forgive my sins, and make me right before you." Understood in this way, baptism is an appropriate symbol for the beginning of the Christian life.[21]

So 1 Peter 3:21 certainly does not teach that baptism saves people automatically or confers grace *ex opere operato*. It does not even teach that the act of baptism itself has saving power but rather that salvation comes about through the inward exercise of faith that is represented by baptism (cf. Col. 2:12). In fact, Protestants who advocate believer's baptism might well see in 1 Peter 3:21 some support for their position: baptism, it might

---

20. The next three paragraphs are adapted from Wayne Grudem, *The First Epistle of Peter*, TNTC (Leicester: Inter-Varsity Press; Grand Rapids: Eerdmans, 1988), 163–65. They are used by permission.

21. Some have argued that *pledge* is a better word than *appeal* in this verse. Thus, the NIV translates, "the *pledge* of a good conscience towards God." The data from other examples of the word are slim with regard to both meanings, and no conclusions can be drawn from an examination of other uses of the word alone (see discussion in Grudem, *1 Peter*, 164).

But much more significant is the fact that the translation "pledge" introduces a theological problem. If baptism is a "*pledge* to God" to maintain a good conscience (or a pledge to live an obedient life, which flows from a good conscience),

then the emphasis is no longer on dependence on God to give salvation, but is rather on dependence on one's effort or strength of resolve. And since this phrase in 1 Peter 3:21 is so clearly connected with the beginning of the Christian life and identified as the feature of baptism that "saves you," the translation "pledge" seems to be inconsistent with the New Testament teaching on salvation by faith alone; it would be the only place where a promise to be righteous is said to be the thing that "saves you." And since the lexical data are inconclusive for both senses (while suggesting that both senses are apparently possible), it is better to adopt the translation "appeal" as a sense much more in accord with the doctrinal teaching of the rest of the New Testament.

be argued, is appropriately administered to anyone who is old enough personally to make "an appeal to God for a good conscience."[22]

In conclusion, the Roman Catholic teachings on baptism—that baptism is necessary for salvation, that the act of baptism in itself confers saving grace, and that baptism is therefore appropriately administered to infants—are not persuasive in the light of the New Testament.

### 4. Alternative 2: The Protestant Paedobaptist View

In contrast both to the Baptist position defended in the earlier part of this chapter and to the Roman Catholic view just discussed, another important view is that baptism is rightly administered to *all infant children of believing parents*. This is a common view in many Protestant groups (especially Lutheran, Episcopalian, Methodist, Presbyterian, and Reformed churches). This view is sometimes known as the covenant argument for paedobaptism. It is called a "covenant" argument because it depends on seeing infants born to believers as part of the "covenant community" of God's people. The word "paedobaptism" means the practice of baptizing infants (the prefix *paedo-* means "child" and is derived from the Greek word *pais*, "child").[23] I will be interacting primarily with the arguments put forth by Louis Berkhof, who explains clearly and defends well the paedobaptist position.

The argument that infants of believers should be baptized depends primarily on the following three points.

**a. Infants Were Circumcised in the Old Covenant.** In the Old Testament, circumcision was the outward *sign* of entrance into the covenant community or the community of God's people. Circumcision was administered to all Israelite children (that is, male children) when they were eight days old.

**b. Baptism Is Parallel to Circumcision.** In the New Testament, the outward sign of entrance into the "covenant community" is baptism. Therefore, baptism is the New Testament counterpart to circumcision. It follows that baptism should be administered to all infant children of believing parents. To deny them this benefit is to deprive them of a privilege and benefit that is rightfully theirs—the *sign* of belonging to the community of God's people, the "covenant community." The parallel between circumcision and baptism is seen quite clearly in Colossians 2: "In him also *you were circumcised* with a circumcision made without hands, by putting off the body of the flesh, by the circumcision of Christ, *having been buried with him in baptism*, in which you were also

---

22. Col. 2:12 can be used in the same manner: Paul says that in baptism Christians were "raised with [Christ] *through faith* in the powerful working of God, who raised him from the dead." This presupposes that those who were baptized were exercising faith when they were baptized—that is, that they were old enough to believe.

23. Roman Catholics are also paedobaptists, but their supporting arguments are different, as explained above (they teach that baptism causes regeneration). In the material that follows, I will be comparing a Protestant defense of *paedobaptism* with a Protestant defense of *believer's baptism*. Therefore, I will use the term *paedobaptist* to refer to Protestant paedobaptists who hold to a covenant paedobaptist position.

raised with him through faith in the powerful working of God, who raised him from the dead" (Col. 2:11–12). Here it is said that Paul makes an explicit connection between circumcision and baptism.

**c. Household Baptisms.** Further support for the practice of baptizing infants is found in the "household baptisms" reported in Acts and the Epistles, particularly the baptism of the household of Lydia (Acts 16:15), the family of the Philippian jailer (Acts 16:33), and the household of Stephanas (1 Cor. 1:16). It is also claimed that Acts 2:39, which declares that the promised blessing of the gospel is "to you and to your children," supports this practice.

In response to these arguments for paedobaptism, the following points may be made.

(1) It is certainly true that baptism and circumcision are in many ways similar, but we must not forget that what they symbolize is also different in some important ways. The old covenant had a *physical, external means of entrance* into the "covenant community." One became a Jew by being born of Jewish parents. Therefore all Jewish males were circumcised. Circumcision was not restricted to people who had true inward spiritual life but rather was given to *all who lived among the people of Israel*. God said,

> Every male among you shall be circumcised. . . . He who is eight days old among you shall be circumcised. Every male throughout your generations, whether born in your house or bought with your money from any foreigner who is not of your offspring, both *he who is born in your house and he who is bought with your money*, shall surely be circumcised. (Gen. 17:10–13)

It was not only the physical descendants of the people of Israel who were circumcised, but also those *servants* who were purchased by them and lived among them. The presence or absence of inward spiritual life made no difference whatsoever in the question of whether one was circumcised. So "Abraham took Ishmael his son *and all those born in his house or bought with his money*, every male among the men of Abraham's house, and he circumcised the flesh of their foreskins that very day, as God had said to him" (Gen. 17:23; cf. Josh. 5:4).

We should realize that circumcision was given to every male living among the people of Israel even though *true circumcision* is something inward and spiritual: "Circumcision is a matter of the heart, by the Spirit, not by the letter" (Rom. 2:29). Moreover, Paul in the New Testament explicitly states that "not all who are descended from Israel belong to Israel" (Rom. 9:6). But even though there was at the time of the Old Testament (and more fully in the time of the New Testament) a realization of the inward spiritual reality that circumcision was intended to represent, there was *no attempt* to restrict circumcision only to those whose hearts were *actually circumcised spiritually* and who had genuine saving faith. Even among the adult males, circumcision was applied to everyone, not just those who gave evidence of inward faith.

(2) We now join God's people by faith, not by physical birth. Under the new covenant the situation is very different. The New Testament does not talk about a "covenant community" made up of believers *and* their unbelieving children and relatives and servants who happen to live among them. (In fact, in the discussion of baptism, the phrase "covenant community" as used by paedobaptists often tends to function as a broad and vague term that blurs the differences between the Old Testament and the New Testament on this matter.) In the New Testament church, the only question that matters is whether one has saving faith and has been spiritually incorporated into the body of Christ, the true church. The only "covenant community" discussed is *the church,* the fellowship of the redeemed.

But how does one become a member of the church? The means of entrance into the church is *voluntary, spiritual, and internal.* One becomes a member of the true church by being *born again* and by having *saving faith,* not by physical birth. It comes about not by an external act but by internal faith in one's heart. It is certainly true that baptism is the sign of entrance into the church, but this means that it should only be given to those who *give evidence* of membership in the church, only to those who profess faith in Christ.[24]

(3) We should not be surprised that there was a change from the way the covenant community was entered in the Old Testament (physical birth) to the way the church is entered in the New Testament (spiritual birth). There are many analogous changes between the old and new covenants in other areas as well. (a) While the Israelites fed on physical manna in the wilderness, New Testament believers feed on Jesus Christ, the true bread that comes down from heaven (John 6:48–51). (b) The Israelites drank physical water that gushed from the rock in the wilderness, but those who believe in Christ drink of the living water of eternal life that he gives (John 4:10–14). (c) The old covenant had a physical temple to which Israel came for worship, but in the new covenant believers are built into a spiritual temple (1 Peter 2:5). (d) Old covenant believers offered physical sacrifices of animals and crops upon an altar, but New Testament believers offer "spiritual sacrifices acceptable to God through Jesus Christ" (1 Peter 2:5; cf. Heb. 13:15–16). (e) Old covenant believers received from God the physical land of Israel which he had promised to them, but New Testament believers receive "a better country, that is, a heavenly one" (Heb. 11:16). (f) In the same way, in the old covenant those who were the physical seed or descendants of Abraham were members of the people of Israel, but in the New Testament those who are the spiritual "seed" or descendants of Abraham by faith are members of the church (Gal. 3:29; cf. Rom. 4:11–12).

---

24. At this point an advocate of paedobaptism may ask whether we should not have an idea of a "covenant community" in the New Testament church which is broader than the church and includes unbelieving children who belong to church families. But the New Testament speaks of no such community, nor does it give indication that unbelieving children of believing parents are members of the new covenant. And it certainly does not speak of baptism as a sign of entrance into such a broader group. Baptism symbolizes new birth and entrance into the church.

In all these contrasts we see the truth of the distinction that Paul emphasizes between the old covenant and the new covenant. The physical elements and activities of the old covenant were only "a shadow of the things to come," but the true reality, the "substance," is found in the new covenant relationship which we have in Christ (Col. 2:17). Therefore, it is consistent with this change of systems that infant (male) children would automatically be circumcised in the old covenant since their *physical descent and physical presence* in the community of Jewish people meant that they were members of that community in which faith was not an entrance requirement. But in the new covenant it is appropriate that infants *not* be baptized and that baptism only be given to those who give evidence of genuine saving faith, because membership in the church is based on an internal spiritual reality, not on physical descent.

(4) The examples of household baptisms in the New Testament are really not decisive for one position or another. When we look at the actual examples more closely, we see that in a number of them there are indications of saving faith on the part of all of those baptized. For example, it is true that the family of the Philippian jailer was baptized (Acts 16:33), but it is also true that Paul and Silas "spoke the word of the Lord to him and *to all who were in his house*" (Acts 16:32). If the Word of the Lord was spoken to all in the house, there is an assumption that all were old enough to understand the word and believe it. Moreover, after the family had been baptized, we read that the Philippian jailer "*rejoiced along with his entire household* that he had believed in God" (Acts 16:34). So we have not only a household baptism but also a household reception of the Word of God and a household rejoicing in faith in God. These facts suggest quite strongly that the entire household had individually come to faith in Christ.[25]

With regard to the fact that Paul baptized "the household of Stephanas" (1 Cor. 1:16), we must also note that Paul says at the end of 1 Corinthians "that the household of Stephanas were the first converts in Achaia, and that they have devoted themselves to the service of the saints" (1 Cor. 16:15). So they were not only baptized; they were also converted and had worked at serving other believers. Once again the example of *household baptism* gives indication of *household faith*.

In fact, there are other instances where baptism is not mentioned but where we see explicit testimony to the fact that an entire household had come to faith. After Jesus healed the official's son, we read that the father "himself believed, *and all his household*" (John 4:53). Similarly, when Paul preached at Corinth, "Crispus, the ruler of the synagogue, *believed* in the Lord, *together with his entire household*" (Acts 18:8).

This means that of all the examples of "household baptisms" in the New Testament, the only one that does not have some indication of household faith as well is Acts

---

25. The idea that everyone in the Philippian jailer's household had individually and personally come to faith in Christ is explicitly affirmed by the alternative translation, "having believed in God with his whole household" (NASB; similarly, NIV, CSB, NET, NLT, KJV, NKJV). These alternative translations are also entirely legitimate renderings of the Greek grammar and syntax, and a decision between the two alternatives is not easy.

16:14–15, speaking of Lydia: "The Lord opened her heart to pay attention to what was said by Paul. . . . she was baptized, and her household as well." The text simply does not contain any information about whether there were infants in her household or not. It is ambiguous and certainly not weighty evidence for infant baptism. It must be considered inconclusive in itself.

With regard to Peter's statement at Pentecost that "the promise is for you and for your children," we should note that the sentence continues as follows: "For the promise is for you and for your children and for all who are far off, *everyone whom the Lord our God calls to himself*" (Acts 2:39). Moreover, the same paragraph specifies not that believers and unbelieving children were baptized but that "*those who received his word were baptized, and there were added that day about three thousand souls*" (Acts 2:41).

(5) A further argument in objection to the paedobaptist position can be made when we ask the simple question, "What does baptism *do*?" In other words, we might ask, "What does it actually accomplish? What benefit does it bring?"

Roman Catholics have a clear answer to this question: Baptism *causes* regeneration. And Baptists have a clear answer: Baptism *symbolizes* the fact that inward regeneration has occurred. But paedobaptists cannot adopt either of these answers. They do not want to say that baptism causes regeneration, nor are they able to say (with respect to infants) that it symbolizes a regeneration that has already occurred.[26] The only alternative seems to be to say that it symbolizes a regeneration that will occur in the future, when the infant is old enough to come to saving faith. But even that is not quite accurate because it is not certain that the infant will be regenerated in the future—some infants who are baptized never come to saving faith later. So the most accurate paedobaptist explanation of what baptism symbolizes is that it symbolizes *probable future regeneration*.[27] It does not cause regeneration, nor does it symbolize actual regeneration; therefore, it must be understood as symbolizing probable regeneration at some time in the future.

But at this point it seems apparent that the paedobaptist understanding of baptism is quite different from that of the New Testament. The New Testament never views baptism as something that symbolizes a probable future regeneration. The New Testament authors do not say, "Can anyone withhold water for baptizing those who will probably someday be saved?" (cf. Acts 10:47), or "As many of you as were baptized into Christ will probably someday put on Christ" (cf. Gal. 3:27), or "Do you not know that all of us who have been baptized into Christ Jesus will probably someday be baptized into his death?" (cf. Rom. 6:3). This is simply not the way the New Testament speaks of baptism. Baptism in the New Testament is a sign of being born again, being cleansed from sin,

---

26. However, some Protestant paedobaptists will *presume* that regeneration has occurred (and the evidence will be seen later). Others, including many Episcopalians and Lutherans, would say that regeneration occurs at the time of baptism, or even that baptism is the means by which God imparts regeneration (a view known as baptismal regeneration).

27. This is not a quotation from any specific paedobaptist writer but is my own conclusion from the logic of the paedobaptist position, which would seem to require this understanding of what paedobaptism signifies with respect to regeneration.

and beginning the Christian life. It seems fitting to reserve this sign for those who give evidence that that is actually true in their lives.

One other perspective on the symbolism of baptism is given by Michael Green.[28] He says,

> Infant baptism stresses the objectivity of the gospel. It points to the solid achievement of Christ crucified and risen, whether or not we respond to it. . . . Not that we gain anything from it unless we repent and believe. But it is the standing demonstration that our salvation does not depend on our own very fallible faith; it depends on what God has done for us.[29]

He goes on to say:

> Infant baptism stresses the initiative of God in salvation. . . . Should it be attached primarily to man's response, or to God's initiative? That is the heart of the question. . . . For the Baptist, baptism primarily bears witness to what *we do* in responding to the grace of God. For the paedobaptist, it primarily bears witness to what *God has done* to make it all possible.[30]

But several points can be noted in response to Green. (a) His analysis at this point overlooks the fact that baptism does not *only* symbolize Christ's death and resurrection; as we have seen in the foregoing analysis of New Testament texts, it *also* symbolizes the application of redemption to us, as a result of our response of faith. Baptism pictures the fact that we have been united with Christ in his death and resurrection, and the washing with water symbolizes that we have been cleansed from our sins. In saying that the paedobaptist stresses God's initiative and the Baptist stresses man's response, Green has presented the reader with two incorrect alternatives from which to choose, because baptism pictures both of these and more. Baptism pictures (i) Christ's redemptive work, (ii) my response in faith (as I come to be baptized), and (iii) God's application of the benefits of redemption to my life. Believer's baptism pictures all three aspects (not just my faith, as Green suggests), but according to Green's view paedobaptism pictures only the first one. It is not a question of which is "primary"; it is a question of which view of baptism includes all that baptism stands for.

(b) When Green says that our salvation does not depend on our faith but on God's work, the expression "depend on" is capable of various interpretations. If "depend on" means "what we rely on," then of course both sides would agree that we rely on Christ's

---

28. Michael Green, *Baptism: Its Purpose, Practice, and Power* (London: Hodder and Stoughton; Downers Grove, IL: InterVarsity Press, 1987). This book contains an excellent statement of a paedobaptist position and also contains much helpful

analysis of the biblical teaching about baptism which both sides could endorse.

29. Ibid., 76.

30. Ibid., 76–77.

work, not on our faith. If "depend on" means that faith does not have any merit in itself whereby we can earn favor with God, then also both sides would agree. But if "depend on" means it makes no difference to our salvation whether we believe or not, then neither side would agree: Green himself says in the previous sentence that baptism does us no good unless we repent and believe. Therefore, if baptism in any way represents the application of redemption to a person's life, then it is not enough to practice a form of baptism that *only* pictures Christ's death and resurrection; we should *also* picture our response in faith and the subsequent application of redemption to us. By contrast, on Green's view, there is a real danger of portraying a view (which Green would disagree with) that people will have salvation applied to them by God whether they believe or not.

(6) Finally, those who advocate believer's baptism often express concern about the practical consequences of paedobaptism. They argue that the practice of paedobaptism in actual church life frequently leads persons baptized in infancy to presume that they have been regenerated, and thereby they fail to feel the urgency of their need to come to personal faith in Christ. Over a period of years, this tendency is likely to result in more and more *unconverted* members of the "covenant community"—members who are not truly members of Christ's church. Of course, this would not make a paedobaptist church a false church, but it would make it a less pure church, and one that will frequently be fighting tendencies toward liberal doctrine or other kinds of unbelief that are brought in by the unregenerate sector of the membership.

## C. THE EFFECT OF BAPTISM

We have argued above that baptism symbolizes regeneration or spiritual rebirth. But does it only symbolize? Or is there some way in which it is also a "means of grace," that is, a means that the Holy Spirit uses to bring blessing to people? We have already discussed this question in the previous chapter,[31] so here it only is necessary to say that when baptism is properly carried out, of course it brings some spiritual benefit to believers. There is the blessing of God's favor that comes with all obedience, as well as the joy that comes through public profession of one's faith, and the reassurance of having a clear physical picture of dying and rising with Christ and of washing away sins. Certainly the Lord gave us baptism to strengthen and encourage our faith—and it should do so for everyone who is baptized and for every believer who witnesses a baptism.

## D. THE NECESSITY OF BAPTISM

While we recognize that Jesus commanded baptism (Matt. 28:19), as did the apostles (Acts 2:38), we should not say that baptism is *necessary* for salvation.[32] This question

---

31. See chapter 48, pp. 1180–81.

32. At this point I am differing not only with Roman Catholic teaching, but also with the teaching of several Protestant denominations that teach that, in some sense, baptism is necessary for salvation. Although there are different nuances in their teaching, such a position is held by many Episcopalians, many Lutherans, and by the Churches of Christ.

was discussed to some extent above under the response to the Roman Catholic view of baptism. To say that baptism or any other action is *necessary* for salvation is to say that we are not justified by faith alone but by faith plus a certain "work," the work of baptism. The apostle Paul would have opposed the idea that baptism is necessary for salvation just as strongly as he opposed the similar idea that circumcision was necessary for salvation (see Gal. 5:1–12).

Those who argue that baptism is necessary for salvation often point to Mark 16:16: "*Whoever believes and is baptized will be saved*, but whoever does not believe will be condemned." But the very evident answer to this is simply to say that the verse says nothing about those who *believe* and *are not baptized*. The verse is simply talking about general cases without making a pedantic qualification for the unusual case of someone who believes and is not baptized. But certainly the verse should not be pressed into service and made to speak of something it is not talking about.[33]

More to the point is Jesus' statement to the dying thief on the cross, "Today you will be with me in paradise" (Luke 23:43). The thief could not be baptized before he died on the cross, but he was certainly saved that day. Moreover, the force of this point cannot be evaded by arguing that the thief was saved under the old covenant (under which baptism was not necessary to salvation), because the new covenant took effect at the death of Jesus (see Heb. 9:17), and Jesus died *before* either of the two thieves who were crucified with him (see John 19:32–33).

Another reason why baptism is not necessary for salvation is that our justification from sins takes place at the point of saving faith, not at the point of water baptism, which usually occurs later.[34] But if a person is already justified and has sins forgiven eternally at the point of saving faith, then baptism is not necessary for forgiveness of sins or for the bestowal of new spiritual life.[35]

Baptism, then, is not necessary for salvation. But it is necessary if we are to be obedient to Christ, for he commanded baptism for all who believe in him.

## E. The Age for Baptism

Those who are convinced by the arguments for believer's baptism must then begin to ask, "How old should children be before they are baptized?"

The most direct answer is that they should be old enough to give a *believable* profession of faith. It is impossible to set a precise age that will apply to every child, but when parents see convincing evidence of genuine spiritual life and some degree of

---

33. Moreover, it is doubtful whether this verse should be used in support of a theological position at all, since there are many ancient manuscripts that do not have this verse (or Mark 16:9–20), and it seems most likely that this verse was not in the gospel as Mark originally wrote it. (See discussion of Mark 16:9–20 in chapter 17, p. 481.)

34. See discussion of justification in chapter 36, pp. 884–908.

35. See chapter 34, pp. 850–56, for a discussion of regeneration.

understanding regarding the meaning of trusting in Christ, then baptism is appropriate. Of course, this will require careful administration by the church, as well as a good explanation by parents in their homes. The exact age for baptism will vary from child to child, and somewhat from church to church as well.[36]

## F. REMAINING QUESTIONS

## 1. Do Churches Need to Be Divided Over Baptism?

In spite of many years of division over this question among Protestants, is there a way in which Christians who differ on baptism can demonstrate greater unity of fellowship? And is there a way that progress can be made in bringing the church closer to unity on this question?

Much progress in this regard has already been made. Christians who differ over baptism already demonstrate their unity in Christ through individual fellowship, Bible studies and prayer groups in their communities, occasional joint worship services, cooperation in city and regional evangelistic campaigns, joint support of many mission agencies and other parachurch groups, joint sponsorship of youth activities, pastors' fellowship groups, and so forth. Although baptism remains a difference, that difference does not generally lead to harmful divisions. In fact, most Christians seem to realize that baptism is not a major doctrine of the faith.[37]

A very few denominations have decided that they would allow both views of baptism to be taught and practiced within their denominations. The Evangelical Free Church of America (EFCA) does this, for example, as a result of a "compromise" reached in 1950 when the denomination was formed from two different groups that had different views on baptism. The EFCA allows ordination for pastors who hold to believer's baptism and for pastors who hold to infant baptism. And they allow into membership those who had

---

36. I participated in baptizing my three children at a time when each was between seven and ten years old and showed a fair degree of understanding of the gospel together with genuine evidence of faith in Christ. In all three cases, I think they could have been baptized somewhat earlier, but we delayed out of deference to the ordinary pattern followed by the churches we were in, whereby children under seven were not usually baptized. (Among Baptists in the United Kingdom, it is customary to wait until children are somewhat older than this, however.)

37. I realize that some readers will object to this sentence and will say that baptism is *very important* because of what the differing positions represent: differing views of the nature of the church. Many Baptists would argue that *practicing* infant baptism is inherently inconsistent with the idea of a church made up of believers only, and many paedobaptists would argue that *not practicing* infant baptism is inherently inconsistent with the idea of a covenant community that includes the children of believers.

I would encourage those who reason this way to consider how much they hold in common with evangelical believers on the other side of this issue—not necessarily with those far from them on other matters as well, but especially with those on the other side who agree with them on most other aspects of the Christian life. Many Baptists *do* encourage and demonstrate a valued place for their children within their churches, and many paedobaptists *do* pray for the salvation of their *baptized* children with the same fervency with which Baptist parents pray for the salvation of their *unbaptized* children. Regarding church membership, evangelical paedobaptists *do* require a believable profession of faith before children can become full members of the church (their term is "communicant members"; that is, those who take Communion). They also require a believable profession of faith before any adults are allowed to join the church.

When these procedures are functioning well, both Baptists and paedobaptists use very similar procedures as they seek to have a church membership consisting of believers only, and both love and teach and pray for their children as most precious members of the larger church family who they hope will someday become true members of the body of Christ.

been baptized as infants in a Christian church, without requiring them to be baptized as believers before joining the church. If some parents want to have their infant child baptized and the local pastor does not hold to infant baptism, the local church invites some other Evangelical Free Church pastor who holds to infant baptism to come and baptize the infant.

Although the Evangelical Free Church continues as a strong, healthy denomination today, there remain some difficulties inherent in this position. One is that there can be a tendency to minimize the importance of baptism: since members disagree on this topic, it is easier not to talk about it much or emphasize its importance.

But the most serious difficulty arises when people begin to think about what such a "compromise position" implies about the views of baptism held by the people who go along with this compromise. For people who hold to infant baptism, they have to be able to say that it is acceptable for believing parents not to baptize their infant children. But according to a paedobaptist view, this seems close to saying that it is acceptable for these parents to disobey a teaching of Scripture regarding the responsibility of parents to baptize their children. How can they really say this?

On the other side, those who hold to believer's baptism (as I do) would have to be willing to admit into church membership people who have been baptized as infants, and who did not make a personal profession of faith at the time they were baptized. But from a believer's baptism position, genuine baptism has to follow a personal profession of faith. So how can believer's baptism advocates in good conscience say that infant baptism is also a valid form of baptism? That contradicts what they believe about the essential nature of baptism—that it is an outward sign of an inward spiritual change, so that the apostle Paul could say, "As many of you as were baptized into Christ have put on Christ" (Gal. 3:27).

For someone who holds to believer's baptism, admitting to church membership someone who has not been baptized upon profession of faith, and telling the person that he or she never has to be baptized as a believer, is really giving up one's view on the proper nature of baptism. It is saying that infant baptism really is valid baptism! But then how could anyone who holds to this position tell anyone who had been baptized as an infant that he or she still needed to be baptized as a believer? This difficulty makes me think that some kind of "compromise" position on baptism is not very likely to be adopted by denominational groups in the future.

However, we should still be thankful that believers who differ on the issue of baptism can have wonderful fellowship with one another across denominational lines and can have respect for each other's sincerely held views.

## 2. Who Can Baptize?

Finally, we may ask, "Who can perform the ceremony of baptism? Can only ordained clergy perform this ceremony?"

We should recognize here that Scripture simply does not specify any restrictions on who can perform the ceremony of baptism. Those churches that have a special priesthood through which certain actions (and blessings) come (such as Roman Catholics and, to some extent, Anglicans) will wish to insist that only properly ordained clergy should baptize in ordinary circumstances (though exceptions could be made in unusual circumstances). But if we truly believe in the priesthood of all believers (see 1 Peter 2:4–10), then there seems to be no need *in principle* to restrict the right to perform baptism only to ordained clergy.

However, another consideration arises: Since baptism is the sign of entrance into the body of Christ, the church (cf. 1 Cor. 12:13 on inward spiritual baptism), then it seems appropriate that it be done *within the fellowship of the church* wherever possible, so that the church as a whole can rejoice with the person being baptized and so that the faith of all believers in that church might be built up.[38] Moreover, since baptism is a sign of beginning the Christian life and therefore of beginning life in the true church as well, it is fitting that the local church be assembled to give testimony to this fact and to give visible welcome to the baptized person. Also, in order that the people being baptized have a right understanding of what actually is happening, it is right for the church to safeguard the practice of baptism and keep it from abuse. Finally, if baptism is the sign of entering the fellowship of the visible church, then it seems appropriate that some officially designated representative or representatives of the church be selected to administer it. For these reasons it is usually the ordained clergy who baptize, but there seems to be no reason why the church from time to time, and where it deems it appropriate, might not call on other church officers or mature believers to baptize new converts. For example, someone effective in evangelism in a local church may be an appropriately designated person to baptize people who have come to Christ through the practice of that person's evangelistic ministry. (Note in Acts 8:12 that Philip preached the gospel in Samaria and then apparently baptized those who came to faith in Christ.)

## QUESTIONS FOR PERSONAL APPLICATION

1. Have you been baptized? When? If you were baptized as a believer, what was the effect of the baptism on your Christian life (if any)? If you were baptized as an infant, what effect did the knowledge of your baptism have in your own thinking when you eventually learned that you had been baptized as an infant?
2. What aspects of the meaning of baptism have you come to appreciate more as a result of reading this chapter (if any)? What aspects of the meaning of baptism would you like to see taught more clearly in your church?

---

38. The fact that baptism is an outward sign of *entrance* into the church, the body of Christ, would also make it appropriate to require baptism before someone is counted as a member of a local church.

3. When baptisms occur in your church, are they a time of rejoicing and praise to God? What do you think is happening to the person being baptized at that moment (if anything)? What do you think should be happening?

4. Have you modified your view on the question of infant baptism versus believer's baptism as a result of reading this chapter? In what way?

5. What practical suggestions can you make for helping to overcome the differences among Christians on the question of baptism?

6. How can baptism be an effective help to evangelism in your church? Have you seen it function in this way?

**Special Terms**

*believable profession of faith*
*believers' baptism*
*covenant community*
ex opere operato
*immersion*
*paedobaptism*

# BIBLIOGRAPHY

(For an explanation of this bibliography see the note on the bibliography to chapter 1, pp. 23–24. Complete bibliographical data may be found on pp. 1489–96.)

## SECTIONS IN EVANGELICAL SYSTEMATIC THEOLOGIES

1. *Anglican (Episcopalian)*
   1882–92 . . . . . Litton, 459–74
   1930 . . . . . . . . Thomas, 371–87, 521–22
   2001 . . . . . . . . Packer, 212–16
   2013 . . . . . . . . Bird, 740, 755, 761–71
   2013 . . . . . . . . Bray, 410–21, 422–23,
       597–99, 586–87, 598–99

2. *Arminian (Wesleyan or Methodist)*
   1875–76 . . . . . Pope, 3:310–24
   1892–94 . . . . . Miley, 2:395–410
   1940 . . . . . . . . Wiley, 3:161–89
   1960 . . . . . . . . Purkiser, 409–11
   1983 . . . . . . . . Carter, 2:616
   1992 . . . . . . . . Oden, 3:274–277

   2002 . . . . . . . . Cottrell, 360–374

3. *Baptist*
   1767 . . . . . . . . Gill, 4:621–47
   1907 . . . . . . . . Strong, 931–59
   1990–95 . . . . . Garrett, 2:549–88
   2007 . . . . . . . . Akin, 785–89
   2013 . . . . . . . . Erickson, 1016–32

4. *Dispensational*
   1947 . . . . . . . . Chafer, 7:32–43
   1949 . . . . . . . . Thiessen, 319–22
   1986 . . . . . . . . Ryrie, 421–25
   2002–2005 . . Geisler, 4:150–51, 154–55,
       162–71
   2017 . . . . . . . . MacArthur and Mayhue,
       782–86

5. *Lutheran*
   1917–24 . . . . . Pieper, 7:253–89
   1934 . . . . . . . . Mueller, 486–505

## 6. Reformed (or Presbyterian)

1559 . . . . . . . . Calvin, 2:1303–58 (4.15–16)

1679–85 . . . . . Turretin, *IET*, 2:584, 3:23–25, 339, 359, 367–420, 499

1871–73 . . . . . Hodge, 3:526–611

1878 . . . . . . . . Dabney, 758–99

1887–1921 . . . Warfield, *SWW*, 1:325–31

1894 . . . . . . . . Shedd, 816–24

1906–11 . . . . . Bavinck, *RD*, 4:496–539

1910 . . . . . . . . Vos, 4:19, 31, 44–45, 50, 136

1937–66 . . . . . Murray, *CW*, 2:370–75

1938 . . . . . . . . Berkhof, 622–43

1998 . . . . . . . . Reymond, 923–54

2008 . . . . . . . . Van Genderen and Velema, 787–801

2010 . . . . . . . . Allen and Swain, 339–62

2011 . . . . . . . . Horton, 788–98

2013 . . . . . . . . Frame, 648–49, 1060–66

2013 . . . . . . . . Culver, 976–90

2017 . . . . . . . . Barrett, 609–42

2019 . . . . . . . . Letham, 665–67, 705–22

## 7. Renewal (or charismatic/Pentecostal)

1988–92 . . . . . Williams, 2:278–87, 3:136–39, 221–41

1993 . . . . . . . . Menzies and Horton, 111–15

1995 . . . . . . . . Horton, 558–62

2008 . . . . . . . . Duffield and Van Cleave, 442–43

## SECTIONS IN REPRESENTATIVE ROMAN CATHOLIC SYSTEMATIC THEOLOGIES

### 1. Roman Catholic: Traditional

1955 . . . . . . . . . Ott, 350–61

### 2. Roman Catholic: Post–Vatican II

1980 . . . . . . . . McBrien, 1:248–52; 2:349–54

2012 . . . . . . . . *CCC*, paragraphs 1213–84

## OTHER WORKS

Allison, Gregg. *Historical Theology: An Introduction to Christian Doctrine; A Companion to Wayne Grudem's* Systematic Theology. Grand Rapids: Zondervan, 2011, 611–34.

———. *Sojourners and Strangers: The Doctrine of the Church.* Wheaton, IL: Crossway, 2012, 321–64.

Beasley-Murray, G. R. "Baptism." In *DPL*, 60–66.

———. *Baptism in the New Testament.* Grand Rapids: Eerdmans, 1962.

———. and R. F. G. Burnish. "Baptism." In *EDT1*, 69–73.

Berkouwer, G. C. *The Sacraments.* Translated by Hugo Bekker. Grand Rapids: Eerdmans, 1969.

Bridge, Donald, and David Phypers. *The Water That Divides.* Downers Grove, IL: InterVarsity Press, 1977.

Bromiley, G. W. "Baptism." In *EDT3*, 107–8.

———. "Baptism, Believers'." In *EDT3*, 108–9.

———. "Baptism, Infant." In *EDT3*, 109–10.

———. "Baptism, Lay." In *EDT3*, 110–11.

———. *The Baptism of Infants.* London: Vine, 1955.

———. *Children of Promise.* Grand Rapids: Eerdmans, 1979.

Brown, R. "Baptist Theology." In *EDT1*, 75–76.

Cottrell, Jack. *Baptism: A Biblical Study.* Joplin, MO: College Press, 1989. (Written from a Churches of Christ perspective, understanding baptism as necessary for salvation.)

Dever, Mark. "The Church." In *A Theology for the Church*, edited by Daniel L. Akin et al., 785–89. Nashville: B&H, 2007.

Dockery, D. S. "Baptism." In *DJG*, 55–58.

Engle, Paul E., and John H. Armstrong, eds. *Understanding Four Views on Baptism.* Grand Rapids: Zondervan, 2007.

Estep, William. *The Anabaptist Story.* Grand Rapids: Eerdmans, 1975.

Fape, M. O. "Baptism." In *NDBT*, 395–97.

Green, Michael. *Baptism: Its Purpose, Practice, and Power.* London: Hodder and Stoughton; Downers Grove, IL: InterVarsity Press, 1987.

Jewett, Paul K. *Infant Baptism and the Covenant of Grace.* Grand Rapids: Eerdmans, 1978.

Kevan, E. F. "Baptist Tradition, The." In *EDT3*, 114–15.

Kingdon, David. *Children of Abraham: A Reformed Baptist View of Baptism, the Covenant, and Children*. Haywards Heath, UK: Carey, 1973.

Lane, A. N. S. "Baptism in Water." In *GDT*, 97–101.

Marcel, Pierre Ch. *The Biblical Doctrine of Infant Baptism*. Translated by Philip E. Hughes. London: Clarke, 1953.

Murray, John. *Christian Baptism*. Philadelphia: Presbyterian and Reformed, 1970.

Rayburn, R. S. "Baptism, Modes of." In *EDT3*, 111.

Schreiner, Thomas R., Shawn D. Wright, eds. *Believer's Baptism: Sign of the New Covenant in Christ*. Nashville: B&H Academic, 2006.

Wainwright, G. "Baptism, Baptismal Rites." In *DLNT*, 112–25.

Watson, T. E. *Baptism Not for Infants*. Worthing, UK: Henry E. Walter, 1962.

White, R. E. O. "Baptize, Baptism." In *BTDB*, 50–53.

## SCRIPTURE MEMORY PASSAGE

**Romans 6:3–4:** Do you not know that all of us who have been baptized into Christ Jesus were baptized into his death? We were buried therefore with him by baptism into death, in order that, just as Christ was raised from the dead by the glory of the Father, we too might walk in newness of life.

## HYMN

### "Up from the Grave He Arose"

There are few familiar hymns written specifically to be used during a baptismal service. It would be helpful for the church if more were written.

This hymn is appropriate for the topic of baptism, because it speaks triumphantly of Christ's resurrection. When we sing it, we should realize that Jesus not only triumphed over death and the grave for himself, but also for all of us who believe in him. This fact is vividly symbolized in the ceremony of baptism.

Alternative hymn: Most paedobaptist hymnals contain hymns to be sung at the baptism of infants, but I did not find any that were widely familiar.

*Low in the grave he lay—Jesus, my Savior,*
*Waiting the coming day—Jesus, my Lord.*

*Refrain*
*Up from the grave he arose,*
*With a mighty triumph o'er his foes.*
*He arose a Victor from the dark domain,*
*And he lives forever with his saints to reign.*
*He arose! He arose! Hallelujah! Christ arose!*

*Vainly they watch his bed—Jesus, my Savior;*
*Vainly they seal the dead—Jesus, my Lord.*

*Death cannot keep his prey—Jesus, my Savior;*
*He tore the bars away—Jesus, my Lord.*

Author: Robert Lowrey, 1874.

# CONTEMPORARY WORSHIP SONG

## "Christ Is Enough"

*Christ is my reward*
*And all of my devotion.*
*Now there's nothing in this world*
*That could ever satisfy.*
*Through every trial*
*My soul will sing,*
*No turning back;*
*I've been set free.*

### Chorus
*Christ is enough for me.*
*Christ is enough for me.*
*Everything I need is in You,*
*Everything I need.*

*Christ my all in all,*
*The joy of my salvation,*
*And this hope will never fail.*
*Heaven is our home.*
*Through every storm*
*My soul will sing,*
*Jesus is here,*
*To God be the glory.*

### Bridge
*I have decided to follow Jesus.*
*No turning back,*
*No turning back.*
*I have decided to follow Jesus.*
*No turning back,*
*No turning back.*
*The cross before me,*
*The world behind me.*
*No turning back,*
*No turning back.*
*The cross before me,*
*The world behind me.*
*No turning back,*
*No turning back.*

Words by Reuben Morgen and Jonas Myrin[39]

# CHAPTER 50

# The Lord's Supper

*What is the meaning of the Lord's Supper? How should it be observed?*

## EXPLANATION AND SCRIPTURAL BASIS

The Lord Jesus instituted two ordinances (or sacraments) to be observed by the church. The previous chapter discussed *baptism*, an ordinance that is only observed once by each person as a sign of the beginning of his or her Christian life. This chapter discusses *the Lord's Supper*, an ordinance that is to be observed repeatedly throughout our Christian lives as a sign of continuing in fellowship with Christ.

### A. BACKGROUND IN THE HISTORY OF REDEMPTION

Jesus instituted the Lord's Supper in the following way:

> Now as they were eating, Jesus took bread, and after blessing it broke it and gave it to the disciples, and said, "Take, eat; this is my body." And he took a cup, and when he had given thanks he gave it to them, saying, "Drink of it, all of you, for this is my blood of the covenant, which is poured out for many for the forgiveness of sins. I tell you I will not drink again of this fruit of the vine until that day when I drink it new with you in my Father's kingdom." (Matt. 26:26–29)

Paul adds the following sentences from the tradition he received (1 Cor. 11:23): "This cup is the new covenant in my blood. Do this, as often as you drink it, in remembrance of me" (1 Cor. 11:25).

Is there a background to this ceremony in the Old Testament? It seems that there is, for there were instances of eating and drinking in the presence of God in the old covenant as well. For example, when the people of Israel were camped before Mount Sinai, just after God had given the Ten Commandments, God called the leaders of Israel up to the mountain to meet with him: "Then Moses and Aaron, Nadab, and Abihu, and seventy of the elders of Israel went up, and they saw the God of Israel. . . . *They beheld God, and ate and drank*" (Ex. 24:9–11). Moreover, every year the people of Israel were to tithe (give one-tenth of) all their crops. Then the law of Moses specified,

> Before the LORD your God, in the place that he will choose, to make his name dwell there, you shall eat the tithe of your grain, of your wine, and of your oil, and

the firstborn of your herd and flock, that you may learn to fear the LORD your God always. . . . You shall eat there before the LORD your God and rejoice, you and your household. (Deut. 14:23, 26)

But even earlier than that, God had put Adam and Eve in the garden of Eden and given them all of its abundance to eat (except the fruit of the tree of the knowledge of good and evil). Since there was no sin in that situation, and since God had created them for fellowship with himself and to glorify himself, every meal that Adam and Eve ate would have been a meal of feasting in the presence of the Lord.

When this fellowship in God's presence was later broken by sin, God still allowed some meals (such as the tithe of fruits mentioned above) that the people would eat in his presence. These meals were a partial restoration of the fellowship with God that Adam and Eve enjoyed before the fall, even though it was marred by sin. But the fellowship of eating in the presence of the Lord that we find in the Lord's Supper is far better. The Old Testament sacrificial meals continually pointed to the fact that sins were not yet paid for, because the sacrifices in them were repeated year after year, and because they looked forward to the Messiah who was to come and take away sin (see Heb. 10:1–4). The Lord's Supper, however, reminds us that Jesus' payment for our sins has already been accomplished, so we now eat in the Lord's presence with great rejoicing.

Yet even the Lord's Supper looks forward to a more wonderful fellowship meal in God's presence in the future when the fellowship of Eden will be restored. Then there will be even greater joy because those who eat in God's presence will be forgiven sinners now confirmed in righteousness, never able to sin again. That future time of great rejoicing and eating in the presence of God is hinted at by Jesus when he says, "I tell you I will not drink again of this fruit of the vine *until that day when I drink it new with you* in my Father's kingdom" (Matt. 26:29). We are told more explicitly in Revelation about the marriage supper of the Lamb: "The angel said to me, 'Write this: Blessed are those who are invited to the marriage supper of the Lamb'" (Rev. 19:9). This will be a time of great rejoicing in the presence of the Lord, as well as a time of reverence and awe before him.

From Genesis to Revelation, God's aim has been to bring his people into fellowship with himself, and one of the great joys of experiencing that fellowship is the fact that we can eat and drink in the presence of the Lord. It would be healthy for the church today to recapture a more vivid sense of God's presence at the table of the Lord.

## B. The Meaning of the Lord's Supper

The meaning of the Lord's Supper is complex, rich, and full. There are several things symbolized and affirmed in the Lord's Supper.[1]

---

1. These seven points are adapted and reworded from Louis Berkhof, *Systematic Theology* (Grand Rapids: Eerdmans, 1941), 650–51.

## 1. Christ's Death

When we participate in the Lord's supper, we symbolize the death of Christ because our actions give a picture of his death for us. When the bread is broken, it symbolizes the breaking of Christ's body, and when the cup is poured out, it symbolizes the pouring out of Christ's blood for us. This is why participating in the Lord's Supper is also a proclamation: "For as often as you eat this bread and drink the cup, *you proclaim the Lord's death* until he comes" (1 Cor. 11:26).

## 2. Our Participation in the Benefits of Christ's Death

Jesus commanded his disciples, "Take, eat; this is my body" (Matt. 26:26). As we individually reach out and take the cup for ourselves, each one of us is by that action proclaiming, "I am taking the benefits of Christ's death to myself." When we do this, we give a symbol of the fact that we participate in or share in the benefits earned for us by the death of Jesus.

## 3. Spiritual Nourishment

Just as ordinary food nourishes our physical bodies, so the bread and wine of the Lord's Supper nourish us. But they also picture the fact that there is spiritual nourishment and refreshment that Christ is giving to our souls—indeed, the ceremony that Jesus instituted is in its very nature designed to teach us this. Jesus said,

> Unless you eat the flesh of the Son of Man and drink his blood, you have no life in you. Whoever feeds on my flesh and drinks my blood has eternal life, and I will raise him up on the last day. For my flesh is true food, and my blood is true drink. Whoever feeds on my flesh and drinks my blood abides in me, and I in him. As the living Father sent me, and I live because of the Father, so whoever feeds on me, he also will live because of me. (John 6:53–57)

Certainly Jesus is not speaking of a *literal* eating of his flesh and blood. Instead, then he must have in mind a *spiritual* participation in the benefits of the redemption he earns. This spiritual nourishment, so necessary for our souls, is both symbolized and experienced in our participation in the Lord's Supper.

## 4. The Unity of Believers

When Christians participate in the Lord's Supper together, they also give a clear sign of their unity with one another. In fact, Paul says, "Because there is one bread, we who are many are one body, for we all partake of the one bread" (1 Cor. 10:17).

When we put these four things together, we begin to realize some of the rich meaning of the Lord's Supper: when I participate, I come into the presence of Christ, I remember that he died for me, I participate in the benefits of his death, I receive spiritual nourishment, and I am united with all other believers who participate in this Supper. What great cause for thanksgiving and joy is to be found in this Supper of the Lord!

But in addition to these truths visibly portrayed by the Lord's Supper, the fact that Christ has instituted this ceremony for us means that by it he is also promising or affirming certain things to us as well. When we participate in the Lord's Supper, we should be reminded again and again of the following affirmations that Christ is making to us.

### 5. Christ Affirms His Love for Me

The fact that I am able to participate in the Lord's Supper—indeed, that Jesus *invites me* to come—is a vivid reminder and visual reassurance that Jesus Christ loves *me*, individually and personally. When I come to take of the Lord's Supper, I thereby find reassurance again and again of Christ's personal love for me.

### 6. Christ Affirms That All the Blessings of Salvation Are Reserved for Me

When I come at Christ's invitation to the Lord's Supper, the fact that he has invited me into his presence assures me that he has abundant blessings for me. In this Supper, what I am eating and drinking is a foretaste of the great banquet table of the King. I come to his table as a member of his *eternal* family. When the Lord welcomes me to this table, he assures me that he will welcome me to all the other blessings of earth and heaven as well, especially to the great marriage supper of the Lamb, at which a place has been reserved for me.

### 7. I Affirm My Faith in Christ

Finally, as I take the bread and cup, by my actions I am proclaiming, "I need you and trust you, Lord Jesus, to forgive my sins and give life and health to my soul, for only by your broken body and shed blood can I be saved." In fact, as I partake in the breaking of the bread when I eat it and the pouring out of the cup when I drink from it, I proclaim again and again that *my sins* were part of the cause of Jesus' suffering and death. In this way, sorrow, joy, thanksgiving, and deep love for Christ are richly intermingled in the beauty of the Lord's Supper.

## C. How Is Christ Present in the Lord's Supper?

### 1. The Roman Catholic View: Transubstantiation

According to the teaching of the Roman Catholic Church, the bread and wine *actually become* the body and blood of Christ. This happens at the moment the priest says, "This is my body" during the celebration of the Mass. At the same time as the priest says this, the bread is raised up (elevated) and adored. This action of elevating the bread and pronouncing it to be Christ's body can only be performed by a priest.

When this happens, according to Roman Catholic teaching, grace is imparted to those present *ex opere operato*, that is, "by the work performed,"[2] but the amount of grace dispensed is in proportion to the subjective disposition of the recipient of grace.[3]

The *Catechism of the Catholic Church* teaches the following:

> In the most blessed sacrament of the Eucharist[4] "the body and blood, together with the soul and divinity, of our Lord Jesus Christ and, therefore, *the whole Christ is truly, really, and substantially* contained."[5]

> It is by the conversion of the bread and wine into Christ's body and blood that Christ becomes present in this sacrament. . . . By the consecration of the bread and wine there takes place a change of the whole substance of the bread into the substance of the body of Christ our Lord and of the whole substance of the wine into the substance of his blood. This change the holy Catholic Church has fittingly and properly called transubstantiation.[6]

> That in this sacrament are the true Body of Christ and his true Blood is something that "cannot be apprehended by the senses," says St. Thomas, "but *only by faith*, which relies on divine authority.[7]

> Only validly ordained priests can preside at the Eucharist and consecrate the bread and the wine so that they become the Body and Blood of the Lord.[8]

In Catholic teaching, because the elements of bread and wine literally become the body and blood of Christ, the church for many centuries did not allow the laypeople to drink from the cup of the Lord's Supper (for fear that the blood of Christ would be spilled) but only to eat the bread. However, since the Vatican II council (1962–65), administration of both the bread and the wine to laypersons has been allowed, but it is not always practiced. The Catechism of the Catholic Church says, "Since Christ is sacramentally present under each of the species, Communion under the species of bread alone makes it possible to receive all the fruit of Eucharistic grace. . . . But 'the sign of

---

2. See discussion of the term *ex opere operato* in relationship to baptism in chapter 49 above, pp. 1202–5.

3. Ludwig Ott, *Fundamentals of Catholic Dogma*, says, "Since the measure of the grace conferred *ex opere operato* is in proportion to the subjective disposition of the recipient, the reception of Holy Communion should be preceded by a good preparation, and an appropriate thanksgiving should follow it. . . . An unworthy Communion is a sacrilege" (399).

4. The word *eucharist* simply means the Lord's Supper. (It is derived from the Greek word *eucharistia*, "giving of thanks." The related verb *eucharisteō*, "to give thanks," is found in the biblical records of the Last Supper in Matt. 26:27; Mark 14:23;

Luke 22:19; and 1 Cor. 11:24: "when he had *given thanks*.") The term *eucharist* is often used by Roman Catholics and frequently by Episcopalians as well. Among many Protestant churches the term *Communion* is commonly used to refer to the Lord's Supper.

5. *Catechism of the Catholic Church* (New York: Doubleday, 1995), para. 1374, italics in original (quoting from the Council of Trent).

6. Ibid., paragraphs 1375–76.

7. Ibid., paragraph 1381, italics in original.

8. Ibid., paragraph 1411.

community is more complete when given under both kinds, since in that form the sign of the Eucharistic meal appears more clearly.'"[9]

With respect to the actual sacrifice of Christ in the Mass, the Catechism says,

> As often as a sacrifice of the Cross . . . is celebrated on the altar, the work of our redemption is carried out. . . . The Eucharist is also a sacrifice. . . . This sacrifice is truly propitiatory.[10]

> As sacrifice, the Eucharist is also offered in reparation for the sins of the living and the dead.[11]

In a similar way, Ott's textbook says,

> The Holy Mass is a true and proper Sacrifice. . . .
> In the Sacrifice of the Mass and in the Sacrifice of the Cross the Sacrificial Gift and the Primary Sacrificing Priest are identical; only the nature and mode of the offering are different. . . . According to the Thomistic view, *in every Mass Christ also performs an actual immediate sacrificial activity* which, however, must not be conceived as a totality of many successive acts but as one single uninterrupted sacrificial act of the Transfigured Christ.
> *As a propitiatory sacrifice . . . the Sacrifice of the Mass effects the remission of sins and the punishment for sins*; as a sacrifice of appeal . . . it brings about the conferring of supernatural and natural gifts. The Eucharistic Sacrifice of propitiation can, as the Council of Trent expressly asserted, be offered, not merely for the living, but also for the poor souls in Purgatory.[12]

In response to this Roman Catholic teaching on the Lord's Supper, it must be said that it first fails to give sufficient weight to the symbolic character of Jesus' statements when he declared, "This is my body," and "This is my blood." Jesus spoke in symbolic ways many times when speaking of himself. He said, for example, "*I am the true vine*" (John 15:1), or "*I am the door*. If anyone enters by me, he will be saved" (John 10:9), or "I am the bread that came down from heaven" (John 6:41). In a similar way, when Jesus says, "This is my body," he means it in a symbolic way, not in an actual, literal, physical way. In fact, as he was sitting with his disciples holding the bread, the bread was in his hand, but it was distinct from his body, and that was, of course, evident to the disciples. None of the disciples present would have thought that the loaf of bread that Jesus held in his hand when he said "this is my body" was actually his physical body, for they could

---

9. Ibid., paragraph 1390.
10. Ibid., paragraphs 1364–67.
11. Ibid., paragraph 1414.
12. Ott, *Fundamentals of Catholic Dogma*, 402, 412–13.

see his body before their eyes. They would have naturally understood Jesus' statement in a symbolic way. Similarly, when Jesus said, "*This cup* that is poured out for you *is the new covenant* in my blood" (Luke 22:20), he certainly did not mean that the cup was actually the new covenant, but that the cup *represented* the new covenant.

Moreover, the Roman Catholic view fails to recognize the clear New Testament teaching on the *finality* and *completeness* of Christ's sacrifice once for all time for our sins: the book of Hebrews emphasizes this many times, as when it says, "*Nor was it to offer himself repeatedly,* as the high priest enters the holy places every year with blood not his own, for then he would have had to suffer repeatedly since the foundation of the world. But as it is, he has appeared *once* for all at the end of the ages to put away sin by the sacrifice of himself. . . . Christ, having been offered *once* to bear the sins of many, will appear a second time" (Heb. 9:25–28). To say that Christ's sacrifice continues or is repeated in the Mass has been, since the Reformation, one of the most objectionable Roman Catholic doctrines from the standpoint of Protestants. When we realize that Christ's sacrifice for our sins is finished and completed ("*It is finished,*" John 19:30; cf. Heb. 1:3), it gives us great assurance that our sins are all paid for, and there remains no sacrifice yet to be paid. But the idea of a continuation of Christ's sacrifice every time the Mass is celebrated destroys our assurance that the payment has been made by Christ and accepted by God the Father and that "no condemnation" (Rom. 8:1) remains for us.

For Protestants the idea that the Mass is in any sense a repetition of the death of Christ seems to mark a return to the repeated sacrifices of the old covenant, which were "a reminder of sins every year" (Heb. 10:3). Instead of the assurance of complete forgiveness of sins through the once for all sacrifice of Christ (Heb. 10:12), the idea that the Mass is a repeated sacrifice gives a constant reminder of sins and remaining guilt to be atoned for week after week.[13]

With regard to the teaching that only priests can officiate at the Lord's Supper, the New Testament gives no instructions that place restrictions on the people who can preside at Communion. And since Scripture places no such restrictions on us, it would not seem to be justified to say that only priests can dispense the elements of the Lord's Supper. Moreover, since the New Testament teaches that all believers are priests and members of a "royal priesthood" (1 Peter 2:9; cf. Heb. 4:16; 10:19–22), we should not specify a certain class of people who have the rights of priests, as in the old covenant, but we should emphasize that all believers share the great spiritual privilege of coming near to God.

Finally, any continuation of the restriction that will not allow laypersons to drink of the cup of the Lord's Supper would be arguing from caution and tradition to justify

---

13. This is why many Protestants have felt that they could readily partake of the Lord's Supper in any other Protestant church, even in high church Anglican services that in form appear quite similar to Roman Catholic services, but could not in good conscience participate in a Roman Catholic mass, because of the Roman Catholic teaching on the nature of the Mass itself.

disobedience to Jesus' direct commands, not only the command to his disciples where he said, "Drink of it, *all of you*" (Matt. 26:27), but also the direction Paul recorded, in which Jesus said, "Do this, as often as *you drink it*, in remembrance of me" (1 Cor. 11:25).

## 2. The Lutheran View: "In, With, and Under"

Martin Luther rejected the Roman Catholic view of the Lord's Supper, yet he insisted that the phrase "This is my body" had to be taken in some sense as a literal statement. He concluded not that the bread actually *becomes* the physical body of Christ but that the physical body of Christ *is present* "in, with, and under" the bread of the Lord's Supper. The example sometimes given is to say that Christ's body is present in the bread as water is present in a sponge—the water is not the sponge but is present wherever the sponge is present, that is, "in, with, and under" the sponge. Other examples given are that of magnetism in a magnet or a soul in the body.

The Lutheran understanding of the Lord's Supper can be found in the textbook of Francis Pieper, *Christian Dogmatics*.[14] He quotes Luther's Small Catechism: "What is the Sacrament of the Altar? It is the true body and blood of our Lord Jesus Christ, under the bread and wine, for us Christians to eat and to drink, instituted by Christ Himself."[15] Similarly, the Augsburg Confession says, "Of the Supper of the Lord they teach that the Body and Blood of Christ are truly present, and are distributed to those who eat in the Supper of the Lord."[16]

However, in order to affirm this doctrine, Luther had to answer an important question: How can Christ's physical body, or more generally Christ's human nature, be everywhere present? Is it not true that Jesus in his human nature ascended into heaven and remains there until his return? Did he not say that he was leaving the earth and would no longer be in the world but was going to the Father (John 16:28; 17:11)? In answer to this problem Luther taught the *ubiquity* of Christ's human nature after his ascension—that is, that Christ's human nature was present everywhere ("ubiquitous"). But theologians ever since Luther's time have suspected that he taught the ubiquity of Christ's human nature not because it is found anywhere in Scripture but because he needed it to explain how his view of Christ's presence in the Lord's supper could be true.

In response to the Lutheran view, it can be said that it too fails to realize that Jesus is speaking of a *spiritual* reality but using *physical* objects to teach us when he says, "This is my body." We should take this no more literally than we take the corresponding sentence, "*This cup* that is poured out for you *is the new covenant* in my blood" (Luke 22:20). In fact, Luther does not really do justice to Jesus' words in a literal sense at all. Berkhof rightly objects that Luther really makes the words of Jesus mean, "This accompanies

---

14. Pieper, *Christian Dogmatics*, 4 vols. (St. Louis: Concordia, 1950–57).

15. Ibid., 296.

16. Ibid. Augsburg Confession, article 10. Mueller says Lutherans reject the term *consubstantiation* to describe their views (528).

my body."[17] In this matter it would help to read again John 6:27–59, where the context shows that Jesus is talking in literal, physical terms about bread, but he is continually explaining it in terms of spiritual reality.

### 3. The Rest of Protestantism: A Symbolic and Spiritual Presence of Christ

In distinction from Martin Luther, John Calvin and other Reformers argued that the bread and wine of the Lord's Supper did not change into the body and blood of Christ, nor did they somehow contain the body and blood of Christ. Rather, the bread and wine *symbolized* the body and blood of Christ, and they gave a visible sign of the fact that Christ himself was truly present.[18] Calvin said,

> By the showing of the symbol the thing itself is also shown. For unless a man means to call God a deceiver, he would never dare assert that an empty symbol is set forth by him. . . . And the godly ought by all means to keep this rule: whenever they see symbols appointed by the Lord, to think and be persuaded that the truth of the thing signified is surely present there. For why would the Lord put in your hand the symbol of his body, except to assure you of a true participation in it?[19]

Yet Calvin was careful to differ both with Roman Catholic teaching (which said that the bread became Christ's body) and with Lutheran teaching (which said that the bread contained Christ's body). "But we must establish such a presence of Christ in the Supper as may neither fasten him to the element of bread, nor enclose him in bread, nor circumscribe him in any way (all which things, it is clear, detract from his heavenly glory)."[20]

Today most Protestants would say, in addition to the fact that the bread and wine symbolize the body and blood of Christ, that Christ is also *spiritually present* in a special way as we partake of the bread and wine. Indeed, Jesus promised to be present whenever believers worship: "Where two or three are gathered in my name, there am I among them" (Matt. 18:20).[21] And if he is especially present when Christians gather to worship, then we would expect that he will be present in a special way in the Lord's Supper:[22] We

---

17. Berkhof, *Systematic Theology*, 653.

18. There was some difference between Calvin and another Swiss Reformer, Ulrich Zwingli (1484–1531) on the nature of the presence of Christ in the Lord's supper, both agreeing that Christ was present in a symbolic way, but Zwingli being much more hesitant about affirming a real spiritual presence of Christ and, instead, emphasizing that the Lord's supper commemorates and calls us to meditate on Christ's sacrifice. However, the actual teaching of Zwingli in this regard is a matter of some difference among historians.

19. John Calvin, *Institutes of the Christian Religion*, ed. John T. McNeill, trans. F. L. Battles, 2 vols., Library of Christian Classics (Philadelphia: Westminster, 1960), 4.17.10 (p. 1371).

20. Calvin, *Institutes*, 4.17.19 (p. 1381).

21. It is true that this sentence is spoken in a context that applies specifically to church discipline (vv. 15–19), but it is a statement of a general truth used here to support a specific application, and there is no good reason to restrict its application to occasions of church discipline. It tells us that Jesus is always present when believers gather in his name.

22. Sometimes Protestants have become so concerned to deny the Roman Catholic view of the "real presence" of Christ in the elements that they have wrongly denied even any spiritual presence. Millard Erickson notes the humorous situation that results: "Out of a zeal to avoid the conception that Jesus is present in some sort of magical way, certain Baptists among others have sometimes gone to such extremes as to give the impression

meet him at *his* table, to which he comes to give himself to us. As we receive the elements of bread and wine in the presence of Christ, so we partake of him and all his benefits. We "feed upon him in our hearts" with thanksgiving. Indeed, even a child who knows Christ will understand this without being told and will expect to receive a special blessing from the Lord during this ceremony, because the meaning of it is so inherent in the very actions of eating and drinking. Yet we must not say that Christ is present apart from our personal faith but only meets and blesses us there in accordance with our faith in him.

In what way is Christ present then? Certainly there is a symbolic presence of Christ, but it is also a genuine spiritual presence and there is genuine spiritual blessing in this ceremony.

## D. WHO SHOULD PARTICIPATE IN THE LORD'S SUPPER?

Despite differences over some aspects of the Lord's Supper, most Protestants would agree, first, that *only those who believe in Christ* should participate in it because it is a sign of being a Christian and continuing in the Christian life.[23] Paul warns that those who eat and drink unworthily face serious consequences: "For anyone who eats and drinks without discerning the body eats and drinks judgment on himself. That is why many of you are weak and ill, and some have died" (1 Cor. 11:29–30).

Second, many Protestants would argue from the meaning of baptism and the meaning of the Lord's Supper that, ordinarily, *only those who have been baptized* should participate in the Lord's Supper. This is because baptism is so clearly a symbol of *beginning* the Christian life, while the Lord's Supper is clearly a symbol of *continuing* the Christian life. Therefore, if someone is taking the Lord's Supper and thereby giving public proclamation that he or she is continuing in the Christian life, then that person should be asked, "Wouldn't it be good to be baptized now and thereby give a symbol that you are beginning the Christian life?"

But others, including the present author, would object to a policy saying that only baptized people could participate in the Lord's supper. This is because a different problem arises if someone who is a genuine believer, but not yet baptized, is *not* allowed to participate in the Lord's Supper when Christians get together. In that case the person's nonparticipation symbolizes that he or she is *not* a member of the body of Christ which is coming together to observe the Lord's Supper in a unified fellowship (see 1 Cor. 10:17: "Because there is one bread, we who are many are one body, for we all partake of the one bread"). Therefore, churches may think it best to allow nonbaptized believers to participate in the Lord's Supper but to urge them to be baptized as soon as possible. For if they are willing to participate in one outward symbol of being a Christian, there

---

that the one place where Jesus most assuredly is not to be found is the Lord's supper. This is what one Baptist leader termed 'the doctrine of the real absence' of Jesus Christ" (*Christian Theology*, 1123).

23. However, some in the Church of England and elsewhere have recently begun to allow young children to participate in the Lord's Supper, reasoning that if they have been given the sign of baptism it is wrong to deny them the sign of the Supper.

seems no reason why they should not be willing to participate in the other, a symbol that appropriately comes first.

Of course, the problems that arise in both situations (when unbaptized believers take Communion and when they do not) can all be avoided if new Christians are regularly baptized shortly after coming to faith. And, whichever position a church takes on the question of whether unbaptized believers should take Communion, in the teaching ministry of the church, it would seem wise to teach that the ideal situation is for new believers first to be baptized and then to partake of the Lord's Supper.

The third qualification for participation is *self-examination*:

> Whoever, therefore, eats the bread or drinks the cup of the Lord in an unworthy manner will be guilty concerning the body and blood of the Lord. *Let a person examine himself, then, and so eat of the bread and drink of the cup.* For anyone who eats and drinks without discerning the body eats and drinks judgment on himself. (1 Cor. 11:27–29)

In the context of 1 Corinthians 11, Paul is rebuking the Corinthians for their selfish and inconsiderate conduct when they come together as a church: "When you come together, it is not the Lord's supper that you eat. For in eating, each one goes ahead with his own meal. One goes hungry, another gets drunk" (1 Cor. 11:20–21). This helps us understand what Paul means when he talks about those who eat and drink "without discerning the body" (1 Cor. 11:29). The problem at Corinth was *not* a failure to understand that the bread and cup represented the body and blood of the Lord— they certainly knew that. The problem rather was their selfish, inconsiderate conduct toward each other while they were at the Lord's table. They were not understanding or "discerning" the true nature of the church *as one body*. This interpretation of "without discerning the body" is supported by Paul's mention of the church as the body of Christ just a bit earlier, in 1 Corinthians 10:17: "Because there is one bread, we who are many *are one* body, for we all partake of the one bread."[24] So the phrase "not discerning the *body*" means "not understanding the unity and interdependence of people in the church, which is the body of Christ." It means not taking thought for our brothers and sisters when we come to the *Lord's* Supper, at which we ought to reflect his character.[25]

What does it mean, then, to eat or drink "in an unworthy manner" (1 Cor. 11:27)? We might at first think the words apply rather narrowly and pertain only to the way we

---

24. Moreover, from this very brief mention of the idea of one body we may rightly suppose that it was not a new idea, but that Paul had taught them this idea while staying in Corinth for two years when he founded the church there.

25. Two other reasons for this interpretation are (1) Paul only says "not discerning the body," and he does not say "not discerning the body and blood of the Lord," which he more

likely would have done if he had meant "not understanding that the bread and cup represent the body and blood of the Lord." (2) In addition, Paul says, "Let a person examine *himself*" (and this would no doubt include examining his relationships with others in the church), but Paul does not say, "Let him see if he understands what the bread and wine stand for."

conduct ourselves when we actually eat and drink the bread and wine. But when Paul explains that unworthy participation involves "not discerning the body," he indicates that we are to take thought for all of our relationships within the body of Christ: Are we acting in ways that vividly portray not the unity of the one bread and one body but disunity? Are we conducting ourselves in ways that proclaim not the self-giving sacrifice of our Lord but enmity and selfishness? In a broad sense, then, "Let a man examine himself" means that we ought to ask whether our relationships in the body of Christ are in fact reflecting the character of the Lord whom we meet there and whom we represent.

In this connection, Jesus' teaching about coming to worship in general should also be mentioned: "So if you are offering your gift at the altar and there remember that your brother has something against you, leave your gift there before the altar and go. First be reconciled to your brother, and then come and offer your gift" (Matt. 5:23–24). Jesus here tells us that whenever we come to worship we should be sure that our relationships with others are right, and if they are not, we should act quickly to make them right and then come to worship God. This admonition ought to be especially true when we come to the Lord's Supper.

Of course, no pastor or church leader will know whether people are examining themselves or not (except in cases where clearly offensive or sinful conduct becomes evident to others). For the most part, the church must depend on the pastors and teachers to explain clearly the meaning of the Lord's Supper and to warn of the dangers of participating unworthily. Then people will have the responsibility to examine their own lives in accordance with what Paul says. Indeed, Paul does not say that the pastors should examine everyone else's lives, but encourages individual self-examination instead: "Let a person examine himself" (1 Cor. 11:28).[26]

## E. OTHER QUESTIONS

Who should administer the Lord's Supper? Scripture gives no explicit teaching on this question, so we are left simply to decide what is wise and appropriate for the benefit of the believers in the church. In order to guard against abuse of the Lord's Supper, a responsible leader ought to be in charge of administering it, but it does not seem that Scripture requires that only ordained clergy or selected church officers could do this. In ordinary situations, of course, the pastor or other leader who ordinarily officiates at the worship services of the church would appropriately officiate at Communion as well. But beyond this, there would seem to be no reason why only officers or only leaders or only men should distribute the elements. Would it not speak much more clearly of our

---

26. In cases of church discipline or in cases where outward behavior gives clear evidence that a person is straying from Christ, the leaders of the church may wish to give a strong and clear verbal warning against participation in the Lord's Supper, so that the erring brother or sister does not eat and drink judgment upon himself or herself. But these cases should be rare, and we must also avoid the mistake of some churches that have been so strict in administration of the Lord's Supper that many true believers have been kept away and thus the unity of the true body of Christ has not been represented, nor have believers had access to the spiritual blessings that should rightly be theirs in Christ in participating in this ordinance and thereby obeying their Lord.

unity and spiritual equality in Christ if both men and women, for example, assisted in distributing the elements of the Lord's Supper?[27]

How often should the Lord's Supper be celebrated? Scripture does not tell us. Jesus simply said, "As often as you eat this bread and drink the cup" (1 Cor. 11:26). Paul's directive here regarding worship services would also be appropriate to consider: "Let all things be done for building up" (1 Cor. 14:26). In actuality it has been the practice of most of the church throughout its history to celebrate the Lord's Supper every week when believers gather. However, in many Protestant groups since the Reformation, there has been a less frequent celebration of the Lord's Supper—sometimes once a month or twice a month or, in many Reformed churches, only four times a year. If the Lord's Supper is planned and explained and carried out in such a way that it is a time of self-examination, confession, and thanksgiving and praise, then it does not seem that celebrating it once a week would be too often, however, and it certainly could be observed that frequently "for building up."

## QUESTIONS FOR PERSONAL APPLICATION

1. What things symbolized by the Lord's Supper have received new emphasis in your thinking as a result of reading this chapter? Do you feel more eager to participate in the Lord's Supper now than before you read the chapter? Why?
2. In what ways (if any) will you approach the Lord's Supper differently now? Which of the things symbolized in the Lord's Supper is most encouraging to your Christian life right now?
3. Which view of the nature of Christ's presence in the Lord's Supper have you been taught in your church previously? What is your view now?
4. Are there any broken personal relationships that you need to make right before you come to the Lord's Supper again?
5. Are there areas in which your church needs to do more teaching about the nature of the Lord's Supper? What are they?

**Special Terms**
*Communion*
*consubstantiation*
*Eucharist*
*not discerning the body*
*spiritual presence*
*symbolic presence*
*transubstantiation*
*ubiquity of Christ's human nature*

---

27. Of course, where distribution of the Lord's Supper is thought to be a priestly function (as in Anglican churches), churches may decide that another approach to this question is more consistent with their teachings. Moreover, in a church where only the leading officers of the church have assisted in serving Communion for many years, the church may decide that allowing anyone else to participate in distributing the elements would be symbolizing the participation of those people in the leadership and governing of the church, and they may wish to delay making a change at least until some clear teaching could be given. Other churches may feel that the leadership function of the church is so clearly tied up with the distribution of the elements that they would wish to continue with that restriction on their practice.

# BIBLIOGRAPHY

(For an explanation of this bibliography see the note on the bibliography to chapter 1, pp. 23–24. Complete bibliographical data may be found on pp. 1489–96.)

## SECTIONS IN EVANGELICAL SYSTEMATIC THEOLOGIES

### 1. *Anglican (Episcopalian)*
1882–92 ..... Litton, 472–542
2001 ......... Packer, 217–19
2013 ......... Bird, 757–806
2013 ......... Bray, 453–63

### 2. *Arminian (Wesleyan or Methodist)*
1875–76 ..... Pope, 3:325–34
1892–94 ..... Miley, 2:411–14
1940 ......... Wiley, 3:189–208
1960 ......... Purkiser, 411–15
1983 ......... Carter, 2:616–19
1992 ......... Oden, 3:274–77
2002 ......... Cottrell, 449–50

### 3. *Baptist*
1767 ......... Gill, 2:647–60
1907 ......... Strong, 959–80
1990–95 ..... Garrett, 2:659–88
2007 ......... Akin, 789–91
2013 ......... Erickson, 1033–51

### 4. *Dispensational*
1947 ......... Chafer, 7:229
1949 ......... Thiessen, 322–25
1986 ......... Ryrie, 425–26
2002–2005 .. Geisler, 4:171–85
2017 ......... MacArthur and Mayhue, 786–89

### 5. *Lutheran*
1917–24 ..... Pieper, 3:290–96
1934 ......... Mueller, 506–40

### 6. *Reformed (or Presbyterian)*
1559 ......... Calvin, 2:1359–1448 (4.27–28)
1679–11 ..... Turretin, *IET*, 2:323, 413, 3:293, 303–5, 339–40, 371–74, 376–78, 421–519
1724–58 ..... Edwards, 1:431–532
1871–73 ..... Hodge, 3:611–92
1878 ......... Dabney, 800–817
1887–1921 ... Warfield, *SSW*, 1:332–38
1894 ......... Shedd, 810–16
1906–11 ..... Bavinck, *RD*, 4:540–85
1910 ......... Vos, 3:66, 107, 234
1937–66 ..... Murray, *CW*, 2:376–84; *CW*, 3:275–88
1938 ......... Berkhof, 644–58
1998 ......... Reymond, 955–66
2008 ......... Van Genderen and Velema, 802–18
2011 ......... Horton, 798–827
2013 ......... Frame, 892–93, 1061, 1066–69
2013 ......... Culver, 991–1006
2016 ......... Allen and Swain, 339–62
2017 ......... Barrett, 643–74
2019 ......... Letham, 751–68

### 7. *Renewal (or charismatic/Pentecostal)*
1988–92 ..... Williams, 3:241–63
1993 ......... Menzies and Horton, 115–20
1995 ......... Horton, 562–65
2008 ......... Duffield and Van Cleave, 443–44

## SECTIONS IN REPRESENTATIVE ROMAN CATHOLIC SYSTEMATIC THEOLOGIES

### 1. Roman Catholic: Traditional

1955 . . . . . . . . Ott, 370–416

### 2. Roman Catholic: Post–Vatican II

1980 . . . . . . . . McBrien, 2:757–68; 1:552–56

2012 . . . . . . . . CCC, paragraphs 1322–1419

## OTHER WORKS

Allison, Gregg. *Historical Theology: An Introduction to Christian Doctrine; A Companion to Wayne Grudem's* Systematic Theology. Grand Rapids: Zondervan, 2011, 635–58.

———. *Sojourners and Strangers: The Doctrine of the Church.* Wheaton, IL: Crossway, 2012, 365–412.

Beckwith, Roger T. "Eucharist." In *EDT1*, 236–38.

Berkouwer, G. C. *The Sacraments.* Translated by Hugo Bekker. Grand Rapids: Eerdmans, 1969.

Bridge, D., and D. Phypers. *Communion: The Meal That Unites?* London: Hodder and Stoughton, 1981.

Dever, Mark. "The Church." In *A Theology for the Church*, edited by Daniel L. Akin et al., 789–91. Nashville: B&H, 2007.

Engle, Paul E., and John H. Armstrong, eds. *Understanding Four Views on the Lord's Supper.* Grand Rapids: Zondervan, 2007.

Forrester, D. B. "Eucharist." In *NDT2*. 305–8.

Marshall, I. Howard. *Last Supper and Lord's Supper.* Grand Rapids: Eerdmans, 1980.

———. "Lord's Supper." In *DPL*, 569–75.

Osterhaven, M. E. "Lord's Supper, Views of." In *EDT3*, 504–6.

Schreiner, Thomas R., and Matthew R. Crawford. *The Lord's Supper: Remembering and Proclaiming Christ until He Comes.* Nashville: B&H Academic, 2010.

Smith, G. T. "Lord's Supper." In *GDT*, 505–9.

Stein, R. H. "Lord's Supper." In *DJG*, 444–50.

Toon, Peter. "Lord's Supper, The." In *BTDB*, 491–94.

Wainwright, G. "Lord's Supper, Love Feast." In *DLNT*, 686–94.

Wallace, R. S. "Lord's Supper." In *EDT3*, 502–4.

# SCRIPTURE MEMORY PASSAGE

**1 Corinthians 11:23–26:** For I received from the Lord what I also delivered to you, that the Lord Jesus on the night when he was betrayed took bread, and when he had given thanks, he broke it, and said, "This is my body, which is for you. Do this in remembrance of me." In the same way also he took the cup, after supper, saying, "This cup is the new covenant in my blood. Do this, as often as you drink it, in remembrance of me." For as often as you eat this bread and drink the cup, you proclaim the Lord's death until he comes.

# HYMN

### "Here, O My Lord, I See Thee Face to Face"

This beautiful hymn is not frequently sung, but it speaks so directly to Jesus himself and speaks so clearly of the spiritual reality that we need to remember in the Lord's supper that it is one of the greatest hymns ever written regarding this doctrine. It conveys an attitude of reverence in the Lord's presence, joy in salvation, and genuine repentance for sin as well. The sweet beauty of spirit that Horatius Bonar exemplified in this hymn is matched by very few hymns in the history of the church.

Tune: "Spirit of God, Descend Upon My Heart"

*Here, O my Lord, I see thee face to face;*
*    Here would I touch and handle things unseen,*
*Here grasp with firmer hand th' eternal grace,*
*    And all my weariness upon thee lean.*

*Here would I feed upon the bread of God,*
*    Here drink with thee the royal wine*
*        of heaven;*
*Here would I lay aside each earthly load,*
*    Here taste afresh the calm of sin forgiven.*

*This is the hour of banquet and of song;*
*    This is the heav'nly table spread for me:*

*Here let me feast, and, feasting, still prolong*
*    The brief, bright hour of fellowship with thee.*

*I have no help but thine, nor do I need*
*    Another arm save thine to lean upon:*
*It is enough, my Lord, enough indeed;*
*    My strength is in thy might, thy might alone.*

*Mine is the sin, but thine the righteousness;*
*    Mine is the guilt, but thine the cleansing blood;*
*Here is my robe, my refuge, and my peace,*
*    Thy blood, thy righteousness, O Lord my God.*

Author: Horatius Bonar, 1855

# CONTEMPORARY WORSHIP SONG

### "How Deep The Father's Love For Us"

*How deep the Father's love for us,*
*How vast beyond all measure,*
*That He should give His only Son*
*To make a wretch His treasure.*
*How great the pain of searing loss—*
*The Father turns His face away,*
*As wounds which mar the Chosen One*
*Bring many sons to glory.*

*Behold the man upon a cross,*
*My sin upon His shoulders;*
*Ashamed I hear my mocking voice*
*Call out among the scoffers.*
*It was my sin that held Him there*

*Until it was accomplished;*
*His dying breath has brought me life—*
*I know that it is finished.*

*I will not boast in anything,*
*No gifts no pow'r no wisdom;*
*But I will boast in Jesus Christ,*
*His death and resurrection.*
*Why should I gain from His reward?*
*I cannot give an answer;*
*But this I know with all my heart—*
*His wounds have paid my ransom.*

Words by Stuart Townend[28]

# CHAPTER 51

# Worship

*How can our worship fulfill its great purpose in the New Testament age?*
*What does it mean to worship "in spirit and in truth"?*

## EXPLANATION AND SCRIPTURAL BASIS

The term *worship* is sometimes applied to all of a Christian's life, and it is rightly said that everything in our life should be an act of worship, and everything the church does should be considered worship, for everything we do should glorify God. However, in this chapter I am not using the word in that broad sense. Rather, I am using *worship* in a more specific sense to refer to the music and words that Christians direct to God in praise, together with the heart attitudes that accompany that praise, especially when Christians assemble together. (The term *worship* is used in this narrower sense several places in Scripture, such as Ps. 95:6; Matt. 2:11; 28:9; Acts 13:2; Rev. 4:10.) Since the chapters in this part of the book deal with the doctrine of the church, it is appropriate in this chapter to focus attention on the worship activities of the assembled church.

### A. Definition and Purpose of Worship

*Worship is the activity of glorifying God in his presence with our voices and hearts.*

In this definition we note that worship is an act of glorifying God. Yet all aspects of our lives are supposed to glorify God, so this definition specifies that worship is something we do especially when we come into God's presence, when we are conscious of adoring him in our hearts, and when we praise him with our voices and speak about him so others may hear. Paul encourages the Christians in Colossae, "Let the word of Christ dwell in you richly, *teaching and admonishing one another* in all wisdom, *singing psalms and hymns and spiritual songs, with thankfulness in your hearts to God*" (Col. 3:16).

The idea of the people of God coming together to worship him in an assembly has a rich background in the Old Testament. Edmund Clowney briefly traces the way this developed in several stages:

> God had demanded of Pharaoh, "Let my people go, *so that they may worship me* in the desert" (Ex. 7:16b).... God brings them out that he might bring them in, into his assembly, to the great company of those who stand before his face.... *God's assembly at Sinai is therefore the immediate goal of the exodus. God brings his people into his presence that they might hear his voice and worship him.*

But Clowney explains that the worshiping assembly at Mount Sinai could not remain in session before God forever. Therefore, God established other festivals in which the whole nation would assemble before him three times a year. He says that "Israelites are a nation formed for worship, called to assemble in the courts of the Lord, and to praise together the name of the Most High."[1]

Yet Clowney points out that rather than worshiping God in a unified, holy assembly, the people turned aside to serving idols, and rather than assembling the people to worship before him, "in judgment God scattered the people in exile."[2]

But God promised that his purposes for his people would yet be fulfilled, that there would someday be a great assembly not just of Israel but of all nations before his throne (Isa. 2:2–4; 25:6–8; 49:22; 66:18–21; cf. Jer. 48:47; 49:6, 39). Clowney notes that the fulfillment of that promise began only when Jesus started to build his church:

> Pentecost was the time of the firstfruits, the beginning of the great harvest of redemption. Peter preached the fulfillment of the prophecy of Joel. The Spirit had been poured out, *the worship of the new age had been ushered in. The church, the assembly for worship, was praising God.* . . . Now the ingathering had begun.
>
> The gospel call is a call to worship, to turn from sin and call upon the name of the Lord. . . . The picture of the church as a worshiping assembly is nowhere more powerfully presented than by the author of the Epistle to the Hebrews (12:18–29). . . . In our worship in Christ's church we approach the throne of God the judge of all. *We enter the festival assembly of the saints and the angels.* We gather in spirit with the spirits of just men made perfect. We enter the assembly of glory through Christ our mediator, and the blood of his atoning death. . . .
>
> *Reverent corporate worship*, then, is not optional for the church of God. . . . Rather, it *brings to expression the very being of the church*. It manifests on earth the reality of the heavenly assembly.[3]

Worship is therefore a *direct* expression of our ultimate purpose for living, "to glorify God and fully to enjoy him forever."[4] God speaks of his "sons" and "daughters" as "everyone who is called by my name, whom I created *for my glory*, whom I formed and made" (Isa. 43:6–7). And Paul uses similar language when he says that "we who were the first to hope in Christ might be *to the praise of his glory*" (Eph. 1:12). Scripture is clear here and in many other passages that God created us to glorify him.[5]

---

1. Edmund Clowney, "The Biblical Theology of the Church" in *The Church in the Bible and the World*, ed. D. A. Carson (Exeter: Paternoster; Grand Rapids: Baker, 1987), 17–19 (italics mine).

2. Ibid.

3. Ibid., 20–22.

4. This familiar phrase has been widely used in Christian teachings. It is found in the *Westminster Larger Catechism*, "Question 1: *What is the chief and highest end of man?* Answer: Man's chief and highest end is to glorify God, and fully to enjoy him forever."

5. See the additional discussion in chapter 21, pp. 565–67, on the fact that God created us for his own glory.

When we reflect on the purpose of worship it also reminds us that *God is worthy of worship and we are not*. Even the apostle John had to be told that he should not worship any creature, not even a powerful angel in heaven. When he "fell down to worship" at the feet of the angel who showed him marvelous visions in heaven, the angel said to him, "You must not do that! . . . Worship God" (Rev. 22:8–9).

This is because God is jealous for his honor and he rightly seeks his honor. He says, "I the LORD your God am a jealous God" (Ex. 20:5), and "My glory I will not give to another" (Isa. 48:11). Something within us should tremble and rejoice at this fact. We should tremble with fear lest we rob God's glory from him. And we should rejoice that it is *right* that God seek his honor and be jealous for his honor, for he, infinitely more than anything he has made, is *worthy* of honor. The twenty-four elders in heaven feel this reverence and joy, for they fall down before God's throne and cast their crowns before him singing, "Worthy are you, our Lord and God, to receive glory and honor and power, for you created all things, and by your will they existed and were created" (Rev. 4:11). When we feel the absolute *rightness* of this deep within ourselves, we then have the appropriate heart attitude for genuine worship.

Because God is worthy of worship and seeks to be worshiped, everything in our worship services should be designed and carried out not to call attention to ourselves or bring glory to ourselves but to call attention to God and to cause people to think about him. It would be appropriate for us frequently to reevaluate the various elements in our Sunday services—the preaching, public prayer, leading of worship, special music, celebration of the Lord's Supper, and even the announcements and the offering. Are they really bringing glory to God in the way they are done? Few things destroy an atmosphere of worship more quickly than a soloist or choir who enjoy drawing attention to themselves or a preacher who parades his intelligence in his speaking. "God opposes the proud but gives grace to the humble" (1 Peter 5:5). Peter says that spiritual gifts are to be used in such a way that "in everything *God may be glorified* through Jesus Christ" (1 Peter 4:11).

## B. The Results of Genuine Worship

When we worship God in the sense described above, truly giving him glory in our hearts and with our voices, several things happen as a result.

## 1. We Delight in God

God created us not only to glorify him but also to enjoy him and delight in his excellence.[6] We probably experience delight in God more fully in worship than in any other activity in this life. David confesses that the "one thing" that he will seek for above all else is "that I may dwell in the house of the LORD all the days of my life, to gaze upon the beauty of the LORD and to inquire in his temple" (Ps. 27:4). He also says, "*In your*

---

6. See the excellent discussion of living all of life by delighting in God in John Piper, *Desiring God* (Portland: Multnomah, 1986); also his analysis of God's delight in himself and what reflects his excellence, in John Piper, *The Pleasures of God* (Portland: Multnomah, 1991).

*presence there is fullness of joy*; at your right hand are pleasures forevermore" (Ps. 16:11). Similarly, Asaph knows that God alone is the fulfillment of all his hopes and desires: *"Whom have I in heaven but you? And there is nothing on earth that I desire besides you"* (Ps. 73:25). And the sons of Korah say:

> How lovely is your dwelling place,
>> O Lord of hosts!
> My soul longs, yes, faints
>> for the courts of the LORD;
> My heart and flesh sing for joy
>> to the living God ...
> Blessed are those who dwell in your house,
>> ever singing your praise! ...
> For a day in your courts is better
>> than a thousand elsewhere. (Ps. 84:1–2, 4, 10)

The early church knew such joy in worship, for "day by day, attending the temple together and breaking bread in their homes, they received their food with glad and generous hearts, *praising God* and having favor with all the people" (Acts 2:46–47). In fact, immediately after Jesus' ascension into heaven, the disciples "returned to Jerusalem with great joy, *and were continually in the temple blessing God"* (Luke 24:52–53).

Of course, such activity of continual praise cannot last forever in this age, for living in a fallen world requires that we give time to many other responsibilities as well. But extended praise does give us a foretaste of the atmosphere of heaven, where the four living creatures "never cease to say, 'Holy, holy, holy, is the Lord God Almighty, who was and is and is to come!'" (Rev. 4:8), and the other heavenly creatures and the redeemed who have died join in that heavenly worship and extol "the Lamb who was slain" (Rev. 5:12).

## 2. God Delights in Us

What does God do when we worship him? The amazing truth of Scripture is that as the creation glorifies God, he also takes delight in it. When God first made the universe, he looked on all of it with delight, and saw that "it was very good" (Gen. 1:31). God takes special delight in human beings whom he has created and redeemed. Isaiah reminded the people of the Lord,

> You shall be a crown of beauty in the hand of the LORD ...
> you shall be called My Delight Is in Her ...
> for the LORD delights in you ...
> as the bridegroom rejoices over the bride,
>> so shall your God rejoice over you. (Isa. 62:3–5)

Zephaniah echoes the same theme when he says,

> The LORD your God is in your midst,
>     a mighty one who will save;
> he will rejoice over you with gladness;
>     he will quiet you by his love;
> he will exult over you with loud singing. (Zeph. 3:17)

This truth should bring great encouragement to us, for as we love God and praise him we realize that we are bringing joy and delight to his heart. And the deepest joy of love is the joy of bringing delight to the heart of the one you love.

### 3. We Draw Near to God: The Amazing Unseen Reality of New Covenant Worship

In the old covenant believers could only draw near to God in a limited way through the temple ceremonies; indeed, most of the people of Israel could not enter into the temple itself but had to remain in the courtyard. Even the priests could only go into the outer court of the temple, the "Holy Place," when it was their appointed duty. But into the inner room of the temple, the "Most Holy Place," no one could go except the high priest, and he only once a year (Heb. 9:1–7).

Now, under the new covenant, believers have the amazing privilege of being able to enter directly into the "Most Holy Place" in heaven when they worship. "We have confidence to enter the holy places by the blood of Jesus" (Heb. 10:19).[7] Since we have that confidence to enter into the very presence of God, the author of Hebrews encourages us, "*Let us draw near* with a true heart in full assurance of faith" (Heb. 10:22). Worship in the New Testament church is not simply practice for some later heavenly experience of genuine worship, nor is it simply pretending, or going through some outward activities. It is *genuine worship* in the presence of God himself, and when we worship, we stand before his throne.

This reality is expressed more fully by the author of Hebrews in chapter 12, when he tells Christians that they have not come to a place like the earthly Mount Sinai where the people of Israel received the Ten Commandments from God, but they have come to something far better, the heavenly Jerusalem:

> For *you have not come* to what may be touched, a blazing fire and darkness and gloom and a tempest and the sound of a trumpet and a voice whose words made the hearers beg that no further messages be spoken to them. . . . *But you have come to*

---

7. The ESV is correct here in speaking about "holy places" because the plural *tōn hagiōn* is used elsewhere in Hebrews to refer to the holy place and the most holy place together as "the holy places" (Heb. 8:2; 9:8, 25; 13:11). (The NASB renders these plurals as singulars, an uncommon departure from its ordinary tendency to translate more literally.)

*Mount Zion and to the city of the living God*, the heavenly Jerusalem, and to innumerable angels in festal gathering, and to the assembly of the firstborn who are enrolled in heaven, and to God, the judge of all, and to the spirits of the righteous made perfect, and to Jesus, the mediator of a new covenant, and to the sprinkled blood that speaks a better word than the blood of Abel. (Heb. 12:18–24)

This is the reality of new covenant worship: it actually *is* worship in the presence of God, though we do not now see him with our physical eyes, nor do we see the angels gathered around his throne or the spirits of believers who have gone before and are now worshiping in God's presence. But it is all there, and it is all real, more real and more permanent than the physical creation that we see around us, which will someday be destroyed in the final judgment. And if we believe Scripture to be true, then we must also believe it to be actually true that *we ourselves* come to that place and join *our* voices with those already worshiping in heaven whenever we come to God in worship. Our only appropriate response is this: "Let us offer to God acceptable worship, with reverence and awe, for our God is a consuming fire" (Heb. 12:28–29).

## 4. God Draws Near to Us

James tells us, "Draw near to God, and he will draw near to you" (James 4:8). This has been the pattern of God's dealings with his people throughout the Bible, and we should be confident that it will be true also today.

In the Old Testament, when God's people began to praise him at the dedication of the temple, he descended and made himself known in their midst:

*When the song was raised*, with trumpets and cymbals and other musical instruments, in praise to the Lord, "For he is good, for his steadfast love endures forever," the house, *the house of the* Lord, *was filled with a cloud*, so that the priests could not stand to minister because of the cloud, *for the glory of the* Lord *filled the house of God*. (2 Chron. 5:13–14)

Though this only speaks of one specific incident, it does not seem wrong to suppose that God will also make his presence known at other times among his people, whenever he is pleased with the praise they offer (even if he does not come in the form of a visible cloud). David says, "Yet you are holy, enthroned on the praises of Israel" (Ps. 22:3).

## 5. God Ministers to Us

Although the primary purpose of worship is to glorify God, the Scriptures teach that in worship something also happens to us: we ourselves are built up or edified. To some extent this happens, of course, when we learn from the Bible teachings that are given or the words of encouragement that others speak to us—Paul says, "Let all things be done for building up" (1 Cor. 14:26), and that we are to be "teaching and admonishing one another in all wisdom" (Col. 3:16) and "addressing one another in psalms and hymns and spiritual songs" (Eph. 5:19; cf. Heb. 10:24–25).

But in addition to the edification that comes from growth in understanding the Bible and hearing words of encouragement from others, there is another kind of edification that occurs in worship: when we worship God, he meets with us and directly ministers to us, strengthening our faith, intensifying our awareness of his presence, and granting refreshment to our spirits. Peter says that as Christians are continually coming to Christ (in worship and prayer and faith), they are then "*being built up* as a spiritual house for a holy priesthood, to offer up spiritual sacrifices acceptable to God through Jesus Christ" (1 Peter 2:5 NASB). When we come to worship, we come into God's presence in a special way, and we may expect that he will meet us there and minister to us: as we "draw near to the throne of grace" we will "receive mercy and find grace to help in time of need" (Heb. 4:16).[8] During genuine worship we will often experience an intensification of the sanctifying work of the Holy Spirit, who is at work continually changing us into the likeness of Christ "from one degree of glory to another" (2 Cor. 3:18).[9]

## 6. The Lord's Enemies Flee

When the people of Israel began to worship, God at times would fight for them against their enemies. For example, when the Moabites, Edomites, and Syrians came against Judah, King Jehoshaphat sent out the choir praising God in front of the army: "He appointed those who were to sing to the LORD and praise him in holy attire, as they went *before the army*. . . . And *when they began to sing and praise*, the LORD set an ambush against the men of Ammon, Moab, and Mount Seir, who had come against Judah, so that they were routed" (2 Chron. 20:21–22). Similarly, when God's people offer him worship today, we may expect that the Lord will battle against demonic forces that oppose the gospel and cause them to flee.

## 7. Unbelievers Know They Are in God's Presence

Though Scripture does not emphasize evangelism as a primary purpose when the church meets for worship, Paul does tell the Corinthians to take thought for unbelievers and outsiders who come to their services, to be sure that the Christians speak in understandable ways (see 1 Cor. 14:23). He also tells them that if the gift of prophecy is functioning properly, unbelievers will from time to time have the secrets of their heart

---

8. See also Ps. 34:4–5, 8; 37:4.

9. Somehow, the more we see of God the more we become like him. That is evident especially when we enter the age to come, for John says, "When he appears we shall be like him, *because we shall see him as he is*" (1 John 3:2). But it is also true to some degree in this life, as we run the race that is set before us, "looking to Jesus, the founder and perfecter of our faith" (Heb.

12:2). At times the presence of the Lord and the accompanying working of the Holy Spirit in our hearts will be so evident that we will recognize that God is doing something within us—as the disciples certainly did when Jesus walked with them on the Emmaus road, for later they said, "Did not our hearts burn within us while he talked with us on the road, while he opened to us the Scriptures?" (Luke 24:32).

disclosed, and they will fall on their face and *"worship God and declare that God is really among you"* (1 Cor. 14:25; cf. Acts 2:11). But evangelism is not seen as a primary purpose when the church assembles for worship, and it would therefore not be right to have the only weekly gathering of believers designed primarily with an evangelistic purpose. Paul's concern is rather that visitors understand what is going on (and not think that Christians are "out of your minds," 1 Cor. 14:23), and that they recognize that "God is really among you" (1 Cor. 14:25).

## C. The Eternal Value of Worship

Because worship glorifies God and fulfills the purpose for which God created us, it is an activity of eternal significance and great value. When Paul cautions the Ephesians not to waste their time but to use it well, he puts it in the context of living as those who are wise: "Look carefully then how you walk, not as unwise but as wise, *making the best use of the time*, because the days are evil" (Eph. 5:15–16).

Paul then explains what it is to be wise and to make the most of the time:

> Therefore do not be foolish, but understand what the will of the Lord is. And do not get drunk with wine, for that is debauchery, but be filled with the Spirit, addressing one another in psalms and hymns and spiritual songs, *singing and making melody to the Lord with your heart*, giving thanks always and for everything to God the Father in the name of our Lord Jesus Christ. (Eph. 5:17–20)

Therefore, in the context of using time wisely and making the most of the time, Paul includes both singing of spiritual psalms to one another and singing to the Lord with our hearts.

This means that *worship is doing the will of God*. Worship is the result of understanding "what the will of the Lord is." It is "making the best use of the time." Moreover, because God is eternal and omniscient, the praise that we give him will never fade from his consciousness but will continue to bring delight to his heart for all eternity (cf. Jude 25: "To the only God, our Savior, through Jesus Christ our Lord, be glory, majesty, dominion, and authority, before all time and now *and forever*").

The fact that worship is an activity of great significance and eternal value is also evident in the fact that it is regularly carried on by those who are already in heaven (cf. Rev. 4:8–11; 5:11–14).

## D. How Can We Enter into Genuine Worship?
## 1. True Worship Happens in the Invisible Spiritual Realm

Ultimately, worship is a spiritual activity and must be empowered by the Holy Spirit working within us. This means that we must pray that the Holy Spirit will enable us to worship rightly.

The fact that genuine worship is to be carried on in the unseen, spiritual realm is evident in Jesus' words: "The hour is coming, and is now here, when the true worshipers will worship the Father *in spirit and truth,* for the Father is seeking such people to worship him. God is spirit, and those who worship him must worship in spirit and truth" (John 4:23–24). To worship "in spirit and truth" is best understood to mean not "in the Holy Spirit" but rather "*in the spiritual realm, in the realm of spiritual activity.*"[10] This means that true worship involves not only our physical bodies but also our spirits, the immaterial aspect of our existence that primarily acts in the unseen realm. Mary knew she was worshiping in that way, for she exclaimed, "*My soul* magnifies the Lord, and *my spirit* rejoices in God my Savior" (Luke 1:46–47).

We should realize also that God continually "is seeking" (John 4:23) those who will worship him in the spiritual realm and therefore those whose spirit as well as body and mind is worshiping God. Such worship is not optional because those who worship God "*must* worship in spirit and truth" (v. 24). Unless our spirits are worshiping God we are not truly worshiping him.

### 2. We Truly Worship When We See Who God Is and Respond to Him

An attitude of worship comes upon us when we begin to see God as he is and then respond to his presence. Even in heaven the seraphim who behold God's glory cry out, "Holy, holy, holy is the LORD of hosts; the whole earth is full of his glory!" (Isa. 6:3). When the disciples saw Jesus walking on the water and then saw the wind cease when he got into the boat, "those in the boat *worshiped him,* saying, 'Truly you are the Son of God'" (Matt. 14:33). The author of Hebrews knows that when we come into the presence of God (Heb. 12:18–24), the proper response is to "offer to God acceptable worship, with reverence and awe, for our God is a consuming fire" (Heb. 12:28–29). Therefore, genuine worship is not something that is self-generated or that can be worked up within ourselves. It must rather be the outpouring of our hearts *in response* to a realization of who God is.

### 3. Factors That Contribute to Genuine and Effective Worship

It is appropriate to ask whether there is much genuine, deep, heartfelt worship in our churches. And if genuine worship is lacking in our churches, we should ask how we can bring ourselves to experience much more of the depth and richness of worship, which

---

10. This is because (1) the discussion that Jesus is having with the woman at the well in this context is a discussion about the *location* of worship (see vv. 20–21)—should it be in Samaria or in Jerusalem? Jesus' answer would fit this inquiry much better if he were speaking about the spiritual realm in which we worship, as opposed to the physical location of Jerusalem or Samaria. (2) In the Greek text the word *en* ("in") of the phrase "in spirit and truth" corresponds to the same word (*en*) used in v. 21 to speak of (literally) "in this mountain" and "in Jerusalem." Once again the contrast is in terms of location "in" which one is to worship. (3) The word *truth* refers to a quality of worship, not to a person. The parallel would be more understandable if "in spirit" likewise referred not to a person but to some quality of the worship, such as the realm in which it is to be done.

is the natural response of the believing heart to a clear awareness of God's presence and character.[11]

Is there anything else we can do to make worship more effective? We must remember that worship is a spiritual matter (John 4:21–24), and the primary solutions will therefore be spiritual ones.

**a. Prayer.** It is important to have prayer in preparation for worship, especially on the part of those in leadership, asking that God will bless the worship times and make himself known to us. "Draw near to God, and he will draw near to you" (James 4:8).

**b. Teaching.** Most congregations would benefit from teaching about the spiritual nature of worship and the New Testament understanding of worship in God's presence (see John 4:23–24; Heb. 12:22–24; James 4:8).

**c. Personal Reconciliation.** Christians should be encouraged to make right any broken interpersonal relationships. Paul says that men are to lift holy hands "without anger or quarreling" (1 Tim. 2:8), and Jesus reminds us that we are first to "be reconciled" to our brother and then come before God's altar and offer a gift (Matt. 5:24). In fact, John says that anyone who says, "I love God" but hates his brother "is a liar" (1 John 4:20). Husbands particularly need to make sure they are living "in an understanding way" with their wives and honoring them in order that their prayers "may not be hindered" (1 Peter 3:7). And the entire church is responsible to watch "that no 'root of bitterness' springs up and causes trouble, and by it many become defiled" (Heb. 12:15)—an indication that sin and broken relationships among a few can spread to many and result in the withholding of God's blessing from the whole congregation.

**d. Pursuing Personal Holiness.** If we want to truly draw near to God in worship, it is important to strive for personal holiness. The author of Hebrews reminds believers to strive for "the holiness without which no one will see the Lord" (Heb. 12:14), and Jesus says that it is the "pure in heart" who shall "see God" (Matt. 5:8)—a promise that is fulfilled partially in this life and completely in the age to come. Specifically in connection with prayer, John says, "If our heart does not condemn us, we have confidence before God" (1 John 3:21), but this principle certainly applies to worship as well, as we have boldness to come into God's presence to offer him praise. James indicates a similar concern when, immediately after saying, "Draw near to God and he will draw near to you," he adds, "*Cleanse* your hands, you sinners, and *purify* your hearts, you double-minded" (James 4:8).[12]

**e. A Physical Setting Conducive to Worship.** The physical setting of worship services does matter, for there are indications that Jesus thought that the atmosphere

---

11. Of course, God's character can be revealed not only through the preaching of the Word but also through the words of the hymns that are sung, through prayer, and through the reading of Bible passages even without comment.

12. Other Scripture passages indicate a connection between personal holiness and worship of God. See Prov. 15:8: "The sacrifice of the wicked is an abomination to the LORD, but the prayer of the upright is acceptable to him." See also Prov. 15:29; 28:9; also Ps. 34:15–18; 66:18.

of worship was very important. He "entered the temple and drove out all who sold and bought in the temple, and he overturned the tables of the money-changers and the seats of those who sold pigeons." In explanation of this action, Jesus insisted that the temple was to be a house of prayer, for he said, "It is written, 'My house shall be called a house of prayer,' but you make it a den of robbers" (Matt. 21:12–13). He also told believers, "When you pray, *go into your room and shut the door* and pray to your Father who is in secret" (Matt. 6:6), not only because in our rooms we will not be seen by others and will not pray so as to receive glory from others but also because the knowledge that others are watching us in our prayers so easily distracts our attention so that then we pray in part to be heard by others or at least so as not to offend them. This does not mean that corporate worship and prayer are forbidden (for both are very evident in both the Old Testament and New Testament), but it is to say that we should choose a *setting* for prayer or for worship that avoids distractions as much as possible. This is consistent with the fact that worship is to be done in an orderly way, for "God is not a God of confusion but of peace" (1 Cor. 14:33; cf. v. 40). The atmosphere and mood of worship are important because we are to "offer to God acceptable worship, with reverence and awe" (Heb. 12:28). This means that it is appropriate to come together as a church in a setting that is conducive to worship, one that is ordinarily private and free from distractions, giving opportunity to focus attention on the Lord.[13]

**f. Wise Allocation of Time.** In addition, it is important to allow enough time for the various aspects of corporate worship. Genuine prayer can certainly take time (see Luke 6:12; 22:39–46; Acts 12:12; 13:2). Solid Bible teaching can often take a long time as well (Matt. 15:32; Acts 20:7–11). Moreover, genuine, heartfelt worship and praise will also take quite a bit of time if it is to be effective.

This is true in part because different aspects of a worship service require different attitudes and states of mind. Listening to Bible teaching requires attentiveness to the text and the teacher. Praise requires joy and a focus on the Lord and his excellence. Prayers of petition require a focus on needs and a deep concern for others. Times when offerings are given require a focus on sacrificing ourselves to the Lord as well as giving to him from our means and trusting him to provide for our needs. The Lord's Supper requires a time of reflection, self-examination, and perhaps repentance, along with thanksgiving. But we cannot have all of these attitudes at once, for we are finite. Different attitudes of

---

13. The practical considerations discussed in this section can be applied to many different forms of worship, but I have not discussed the actual forms that worship will take. Those will vary widely, from the extensive structured liturgies of Episcopalian services to the unstructured spontaneity of charismatic services. Since Scripture does not prescribe any one form, the major principle to use is Paul's directive, "Let all things be done for building up" (1 Cor. 14:26). Evangelicals need to be cautious, however, that they do not too quickly dismiss unfamiliar forms of worship: people in liturgical churches should realize that spontaneity can be managed in an orderly way, and people in charismatic groups should realize that edification and genuine worship can occur within a detailed structure. (Regarding the unison reading of a liturgy, if Christians can worship and pray by *singing* words in unison, there is nothing to prevent them from genuinely worshiping and praying by *reading* words aloud in unison!) Yet any one form that is used excessively can become a meaningless routine for most participants.

mind require time to attain and dwell in. For that reason it is impossible to fulfill all the tasks necessary for an assembled congregation simply in one hour on Sunday morning, and it is harmful even to try. Those who do try to do everything crowd too much into a brief time and fail to do anything well.[14] If congregations are to fulfill the various purposes for which God wants them to assemble together, and especially to have extended times of reverent worship, they will probably need to find creative solutions that enable them to meet for longer periods of time and omit or reschedule some activities that have become habitual or traditional on Sunday mornings but are really not necessary.

## 4. Worship Music: Some Personal Observations

In the following section, I have included some arguments from Scripture and also some personal observations and preferences based on my experiences. I realize that some readers may have different opinions, but I hope that, in general, churches will find these observations helpful.

a. "Look at Me!" Vs. "Look at God!" The first consideration when thinking about worship music is the heart attitude of the worship leader (and the same questions should be asked of any others in the worship band or choir). Is the worship leader's main goal to get people to think, "He (or she) is an excellent musician and put on an excellent musical performance," or is the main goal to get people to think, "He (or she) led me into the presence of God, and I truly worshiped God." The first answer produces a "performance mentality" where the musicians seek to show off their musical abilities, and if people clap at the end, they will be mainly clapping for the musicians. The second answer leads to a "worship atmosphere" where people often sense the powerful presence of the Holy Spirit, where the time of singing sometimes will end with reverent silence, and if people do clap at the end, they will be clapping for God, as in Psalm 47:1: "Clap your hands, all peoples! Shout to God with loud songs of joy!"

Avoiding a "performance mentality" is admittedly difficult, perhaps especially so for highly trained musicians who have been receiving acclamation for years for their outstanding musical performances. But it is certainly possible through prayer and through recognizing that "God opposes the proud but gives grace to the humble" (James 4:6; 1 Peter 5:5).[15]

---

14. Unfortunately, pastors who try to officiate at a service into which too many activities are crowded begin to resemble the master of ceremonies at a three-ring circus who shouts, "Look here! Look there!" at one act after another. In a similar way the pastor exhorts, "Praise God! Be generous! Think about Scripture! Pray! Shake hands with your neighbor! Say hello to your friends! Examine yourselves! Repent of your sins! Sing to the Lord! Amen? Amen!" In a situation like this people's emotions are jerked back and forth so quickly that they are unable to respond as whole persons, and the result is that they withdraw emotionally and do not respond from the heart. They will leave the service feeling frustrated and disappointed because the need of their hearts to experience genuine worship, prayer, and learning from Scripture has not been satisfied.

For most human beings, focused attention is slowly attained and easily lost.

15. In some churches with large auditoriums, an enlarged picture of the pastor is projected on one or more large screens during the sermon. I think this is a good idea because the pastor's facial expressions and body language are important factors in the communicative process. But (and here I'm giving only my personal opinion) I would be more hesitant to project pictures

Because of these same considerations, my personal preference (others may differ) is for a worship leader to speak to the congregation between songs rarely, and then very briefly, and sometimes not at all. At the end of a wonderful worship song, I am often thinking about God and his presence in the room, and then if the worship leader starts talking, this breaks my concentration, and I have to start thinking about the worship leader and what he or she is saying.

**b. Volume.** Many years ago, my wife, Margaret, and I were part of an exciting new church where God was evidently at work, many people were being saved, and the church was bursting with hundreds of people in their twenties and thirties. We especially loved the times of worship with new contemporary worship songs. But one Sunday a friend from another state visited our church. After the service, he said, "The drums were so loud that I guess you don't want anyone over forty years old coming to your church." (He himself was a mature, wise pastor of a large, influential church.) I didn't understand what he meant, because we loved the music in that church, but now at age seventy-one I clearly understand. After age forty or so, many people's ears become more sensitive to loud noises, and for some it becomes physically painful to sit in a church with a loud worship band. (This is true for many but not all people after age forty or fifty.)

I am now aware, through many personal conversations, that there are several churches in our area with good Bible teaching but with music so loud that many of our friends won't consider attending, or they will show up thirty minutes late so that they miss the worship time but hear the sermon. In either case, they are prevented from participating in the corporate worship life of that church. Commenting in *Christianity Today* on the same problem, Canadian professor John G. Stackhouse Jr. wrote, "I find almost every worship band in every church I visit to be too loud—not just a little bit loud, but uncomfortably, even painfully, loud."[16]

The situation has some parallels with the church at Corinth, where some people were enjoying speaking in tongues during the worship service but other people could not understand what they were saying. Paul rebuked them: "You may be giving thanks well enough, but the other person is not being built up" (1 Cor. 14:17). The Corinthian tongue-speakers were genuinely worshiping and giving thanks to God, but when there was no interpretation of the tongues, they were leaving others out and not acting in love. Reflecting a similar concern, my comments to the worship leader in a high music-volume church would be to paraphrase Paul's statement in 1 Corinthians 14:17: "You may be praising God well enough, but your music is so loud that many other people are not allowed to worship with you."

---

of the worship band on the same jumbo screens, because it may tend to make the congregation focus attention on the musicians rather than on God and may make it more difficult for the musicians to resist a "performance mentality." These challenges are minimized if only the words of the worship songs are projected on the large screens.

16. John G. Stackhouse Jr., "Memo to Worship Bands: Five Sound Reasons to Lower the Volume," *Christianity Today*, February 2009, 50.

Of course, there is a place for Christian bands to give loud concerts aimed at (for example) people under thirty. This may be for an evangelistic purpose, or it may simply be a special concert for people to enjoy listening to. But the Sunday morning worship service, where the whole church should be worshiping together, is not the place for such a concert.

**c. Are People Mostly Singing or Mostly Listening?** Corporate worship should be a time when the vast majority of people in the congregation actually sing songs of worship and praise to God. A *worship leader* should *lead* people to worship, not simply worship God by himself or with the band while everybody else watches.

Paul was writing to *the entire church* in Colossae when he said they should be "singing psalms and hymns and spiritual songs, with thankfulness in your hearts to God" (Col. 3:16). This was not just a command for a few Christians with unusual skill in playing instruments or singing, but it was for everyone. But I have visited churches I could see hardly anyone singing but almost everyone standing listening with mouths closed. In such a case, the worship band was not *leading* congregational worship but was replacing congregational worship with a mini concert.

In a related verse, Paul writes to the Christians in Ephesus, "Be filled with the Spirit, *addressing one another* in psalms and hymns and spiritual songs, singing and making melody to the Lord with your heart" (Eph. 5:18). In this verse Paul specifies that the songs in our worship times can be addressed both to "one another" and also to "the Lord." One implication of Paul's encouragement to be "addressing one another" in our songs is that a congregation should be able to hear itself singing. When a worship band is so loud that people in the congregation cannot hear themselves or others singing, the people can hardly be said to be "addressing one another in psalms and hymns and spiritual songs."

On the other hand, sometimes a worship leader will silence all the instruments and lead the entire congregation in *a cappella* singing. I find these times especially meaningful, as I hear the entire congregation "addressing one another" and "making melody to the Lord" in songs of worship.

**d. Are the Songs Easily Singable?** Many of the most popular hymns that have endured in the church through centuries have melody lines that are relatively easy to remember and easy to sing, even without musical instruments. (Think of "Amazing Grace," "When I Survey the Wondrous Cross," or "Great Is Thy Faithfulness.") Some contemporary worship music shares that characteristic: once you learn the songs, they are easy to sing.

But other songs used in modern worship have strange melody lines that are hard to learn and hard to remember. Some have pauses that need to be filled in by musical instruments, with the result that people cannot easily sing them by themselves or in small groups. And on Sunday mornings, few people will sing along with songs that are not easy to sing.

**e. Do Most of the People Know Most of the Songs?** There is certainly a place for teaching a congregation new songs ("Oh sing to the Lord a new song," Ps. 96:1; see also Ps. 33:3; 40:3; 98:1; Rev. 5:9; 14:3). But the vast majority of songs in any worship service should be ones that people already know because people worship best with songs they know.

Twice a year at Phoenix Seminary (where I teach) we have a special evening chapel service for the whole seminary community, and every time we do this, we invite a worship leader from one of the more than 100 churches that send students to our seminary. These different worship leaders nearly always do a good job of leading such a diverse group in worship because they stick to familiar worship songs that almost everyone already knows. But occasionally a worship leader will try to teach us a new song that he himself has recently composed. It never works well. This is because people cannot worship very effectively while they are trying to learn a song they have never heard before—their minds are concentrating on trying to learn the melody and the words, and not very much of their attention is focused on coming into the presence of God.

**f. Older Hymns Vs. Contemporary Worship Songs.** I am thankful to God for the proliferation of many thousands of new worship songs in recent decades. I find many of them conducive to deep, heartfelt worship, both in the assembly of the church and in private times of praise at home or in my car.

However, I am surprised to find that some churches now sing *only* songs written in the last twenty or thirty years (or less). The church of Christ has a rich history of hymns that have endured through the centuries and have effectively expressed people's faith and love for God. It is true that in previous generations churches have regularly adopted new songs and hymns, but they have not entirely discarded the older ones.

I have carried around a favorite hymn book for about forty years,[17] and when I went through the index recently I found that I knew 324 of the 538 hymns in that book. I would feel a great loss if I attended a church where none of those familiar hymns were ever sung. While I appreciate many contemporary worship songs, I also love to sing songs like "Jesus, Thou Joy of Loving Hearts," originally written (in Latin) by Bernard of Clairvaux, who lived 1091–1153. If this song has ministered to people's hearts for over 800 years, that is a good argument for continuing its use from time to time. What about "Be Thou My Vision" (from an Irish hymn, eighth century AD), "All Creatures of Our God and King" (Francis of Assisi, lived 1182–1226), or "A Mighty Fortress Is Our God," written by Martin Luther (lived 1483–1546)? More recently composed but still nearly 300 years old are hymns by Isaac Watts (lived 1674–1748), such as "When I Survey the Wondrous Cross."

Future generations will continue to reap spiritual blessings from the richness of these

---

17. *Great Hymns of the Faith*, ed. John W Peterson (Grand Rapids: Zondervan, 1968). I have also frequently used the Trinity Hymnal (Philadelphia: Orthodox Presbyterian Church, 1961).

older hymns if churches today continue to use them in worship, along with contemporary worship music as well. But a word of caution—worship leaders who incorporate some older hymns as well as newer worship songs should realize that, for people who have sung these hymns for decades, they are truly the music of their hearts, music with which they have long familiarity. Therefore any efforts at "improving" the words or the music should be done minimally, if at all, and only when really necessary, not just for novelty, because this would then be asking people to learn a (partially) new song (see section e above). Just as an older generation can learn new worship songs, so a younger generation can certainly learn some of the older hymns of the church.

**g. The Theological Content of Worship Songs.** It is important, as a first priority, that the words of all the songs used in worship faithfully represent the teachings of Scripture. Paul tells Titus, "*Teach* what accords with sound doctrine" (Titus 2:1), and that also applies to worship songs because the songs sung by a church have a teaching function—and that teaching needs to be theologically sound.

Over time, the songs should also encompass the wide range of topics taught by the Bible. The well-used hymnal that I mentioned in the previous section has a "Topical Index" with 101 categories of theological and practical topics that are addressed by these hymns. I do not know if a compilation of modern worship songs would have such a diverse range of topics. Whatever songs are used in worship in a church, it would be beneficial to the entire church if, over the course of months and years, the songs as a whole imitated the content of the teaching of the apostle Paul, who proclaimed "the whole counsel of God" (Acts 20:27).

## QUESTIONS FOR PERSONAL APPLICATION

1. Do you experience genuine, fulfilling worship in your church each Sunday? How much time is specifically allotted to worship (narrowly defined)—that is, to times of praise and thanksgiving to God? Would you like the time to be longer? What aspects of the worship time do you find most meaningful? Which aspects are least meaningful? How could your church take steps to strengthen and deepen its experience of worship (if that is needed)?

2. Have you ever felt a strong sense of the presence of God in corporate worship? When was this? Can you describe it? Do you know what factors contributed to this sense?

3. During times of worship, can you describe the emotions that are most prominent in your consciousness? Is this experience similar to other experiences in daily life, or are these feelings unique to times of worship? Have you ever sensed that God is ministering to you while you are worshiping him? What made you aware of that?

4. Do you think there is enough genuine worship in a typical week in your life? If not, what are the hindrances to such worship?

5. How do you feel about the fact that God is jealous for his own honor and seeks his honor? Can you think of anything in the universe that would be more right than for God to seek his own honor? Can you think of anything other than worship of God that would make you feel more deeply that you are doing the thing for which you were created?

**Special Terms**
*worship*

# BIBLIOGRAPHY

(For an explanation of this bibliography see the note on the bibliography to chapter 1, pp. 23–24. Complete bibliographical data may be found on pp. 1489–96.)

## Sections in Evangelical Systematic Theologies

### 1. Anglican (Episcopalian)
2001........Packer, 98–101
2013........Bird, 755–56

### 2. Arminian (Wesleyan or Methodist)
1875–76.....Pope, 3:287–94
1940........Wiley, 3:138–50
1960........Purkiser, 415–20
1983........Carter, 2:614–15
1992........Oden, 3:468
2002........Cottrell, 444–52

### 3. Baptist
1767........Gill, 2:341–52, 558, 682–729
1990–95.....Garrett, 2:639–58
2007........Akin, 925

### 4. Dispensational
1986........Ryrie, 428–30
2017........MacArthur and Mayhue, 790–92

### 5. Lutheran
(no explicit treatment)

### 6. Reformed (or Presbyterian)
1679–85.....Turretin, *IET*, 1:25, 51, 2:33–34, 38–66, 183–184, 3:124–27
1724–58.....Edwards, 2:913–18
1894........Shedd, 52, 264, 269–70
1937–66.....Murray, *CW*, 1:165–68
1998........Reymond, 868–77
2008........Van Genderen and Velema, 761, 815
2011........Horton, 278
2013........Frame, 1037–39
2013........Culver, 731, 915–16, 919, 962–71, 994–95
2016........Allen and Swain, 341–43
2017........Barrett, 59–60, 586
2019........Letham, 83–86

### 7. Renewal (or charismatic/Pentecostal)
1988–92.....Williams, 3:85–109
1993........Menzies and Horton, 119, 181
1995........Horton, 544, 586–87
2008........Duffield and Van Cleave, 439–40

## SECTIONS IN REPRESENTATIVE ROMAN CATHOLIC SYSTEMATIC THEOLOGIES

### 1. Roman Catholic: Traditional

1955 . . . . . . . . Ott (no explicit treatment)

### 2. Roman Catholic: Post–Vatican II

2012 . . . . . . . . *CCC*, paragraphs 939, 1123

## OTHER WORKS

Allen, Ronald, and Gordon Borror. *Worship: Rediscovering the Missing Jewel.* Portland, OR: Multnomah, 1982.

Allison, Gregg. *Historical Theology: An Introduction to Christian Doctrine; A Companion to Wayne Grudem's* Systematic Theology. Grand Rapids: Zondervan, 2011, 659–682.

———. *Sojourners and Strangers: The Doctrine of the Church.* Wheaton, IL: Crossway, 2012, 424–433.

Carson, Herbert M. *Hallelujah! Christian Worship.* Welwyn, UK: Evangelical, 1980.

Engle, Paul E. *Discovering the Fullness of Worship.* Philadelphia: Great Commission, 1978.

Farris, S. C. "Worship." In *DJG*, 891–94.

Frame, John M. *Contemporary Worship Music: A Biblical Defense.* Phillipsburg, NJ: P&R. 1997.

———. *Worship in Spirit and Truth.* Phillipsburg, NJ: P&R, 1996.

Harrison, E. F. "Worship." In *EDT1*, 1192–93.

Hill, Andrew E. *Enter His Courts with Praise: Old Testament Worship for the New Testament Church.* Grand Rapids: Baker, 1996.

———. "Worship." In *BTDB*, 837–45.

Humphrey, Edith McEwan. *Grand Entrance: Worship on Earth As in Heaven.* Grand Rapids: Brazos, 2011.

Kauflin, Bob. *True Worshipers: Seeking What Matters to God.* Wheaton, IL: Crossway, 2015.

———. *Worship Matters: Leading Others to Encounter the Greatness of God.* Wheaton, IL: Crossway, 2008.

Kraeuter, Tom. *Keys to Becoming an Effective Worship Leader.* Lynnwood, WA: Emerald Books; Hillsboro, MO: Training Resources, 2011.

Manson, P. D. "Worship." In *EDT1*, 730–32.

Martin, Ralph P. "Worship." In *DPL*, 982–91.

———. "Worship and Liturgy." In *DLNT*, 1224–38.

———. *Worship in the Early Church.* Westwood, NJ: Revell, 1964.

———. *The Worship of God.* Grand Rapids: Eerdmans, 1982.

Moule, C. F. D. *Worship in the New Testament.* Richmond, VA: John Knox, 1961.

Peterson, D. G. "Worship." In *NDBT*, 855–63.

Peterson, David. *Engaging with God: A Biblical Theology of Worship.* Leicester: Inter-Varsity Press; Grand Rapids: Eerdmans, 1992.

Pierce, Timothy M. *Enthroned on Our Praise: An Old Testament Theology of Worship.* Nashville: B&H Academic, 2008.

Pinson, J. Matthew, ed. *Perspectives on Christian Worship: 5 Views.* Nashville: B&H Academic, 2009.

Rayburn, Robert G. *O Come, Let Us Worship.* Grand Rapids: Baker, 1980.

Ross, Allen P. *Recalling the Hope of Glory: Biblical Worship from the Garden to the New Creation.* Grand Rapids: Kregel, 2006.

Stamm, M. W., and C. M. Hawn. "Liturgy, Worship." In *GDT*, 492–500.

Taylor, Jack R. *The Hallelujah Factor.* Nashville: Broadman, 1983.

Truscott, J. A. "Worship." In *NDT2*, 973–75.

Wainwright, Geoffrey. *Doxology: The Praise of God in Worship, Doctrine, and Life.* New York: Oxford University Press, 1980.

Webber, Robert E. *Worship Old and New.* Grand Rapids: Zondervan, 1982.

Webber, Robert, ed. *The Complete Library of Christian Worship.* 8 vols. Nashville: Star Song, 1993–94.

Wimber, John, ed. *Thoughts on Worship.* Anaheim, CA: Vineyard Music Group, 1996.

Witvliet, J. D. "Worship." In *EDT3*, 952–55.

## SCRIPTURE MEMORY PASSAGE

**Revelation 4:11:**
*Worthy are you, our Lord and God,*
*    to receive glory and honor and power,*
*for you created all things,*
*    and by your will they existed and were*
*    created.*

## HYMN

**"Thou Art Worthy"**

*Thou art worthy, thou art worthy, thou art*
*    worthy, O Lord.*
*To receive glory, glory and honor, glory and honor*
*    and power.*
*For thou hast created, hast all things created,*
*    thou hast created all things;*

*And for thy pleasure, they are created, thou art*
*    worthy, O Lord.*

Author: Pauline Michael Mills
(from Rev. 4:11). Copyright © Fred Bock
Music, 1963, 1975. Used by permission.

## CONTEMPORARY WORSHIP SONG

**"All Glory"**

*Holy, holy, You are God Almighty,*
*And You reign victorious over all the earth.*
*Holy, holy, You are God Almighty.*
*Yes, You reign victorious over all the earth.*

*Chorus*
*Let Your Kingdom come, let Your will be done*
*Here on Earth as it is in Heaven,*
*And to Your renown, hear our hearts cry out,*
*Singing, "Holy is the Lord!"*

*God of glory, see Your victory story*
*In the lives of those who gather at the cross.*
*Rock of ages, be adorned with praises*
*As Your people raise their voice in thanks and love.*

*Bridge*
*All glory, all honor,*
*All wisdom, strength, and power,*
*All glory, all honor,*
*Are Yours alone forever.*

Words by Andi Rozier[18]

---

18. © HBC Worship Music (ASCAP) / All Essential
Music (ASCAP) / (admin at EssentialMusicPublishing.com
[3]). All rights reserved. Used by permission.

# CHAPTER 52

# Gifts of the Holy Spirit: (1) General Questions

*What are spiritual gifts?*
*How many are there?*
*Have some gifts ceased?*
*Seeking and using spiritual gifts.*

## EXPLANATION AND SCRIPTURAL BASIS

### A. QUESTIONS REGARDING SPIRITUAL GIFTS IN GENERAL

In previous generations, systematic theologies did not have chapters on spiritual gifts, for there were few questions regarding the nature and use of spiritual gifts in the church. But the twentieth century has seen a remarkable increase in interest in spiritual gifts, primarily because of the influence of the Pentecostal and charismatic movements within the church. In this chapter we will first look at some general questions regarding spiritual gifts, then examine the specific question of whether some (miraculous) gifts have ceased. In the next chapter we shall analyze the New Testament teaching about particular gifts.

Before beginning the discussion, however, we may define spiritual gifts as follows: *a spiritual gift is any ability that is empowered by the Holy Spirit and used in any ministry of the church.* This broad definition includes both gifts that are related to natural abilities (such as teaching, showing mercy, or administration) and gifts that seem to be more "miraculous" and less related to natural abilities (such as prophecy, healing, or distinguishing between spirits). The reason is that when Paul lists spiritual gifts (Rom. 12:6–8; 1 Cor. 12:8–10, 28; Eph. 4:11), he includes both kinds of gifts. Yet not every natural ability that people have is included here because Paul is clear that all spiritual gifts must be empowered "by one and the same Spirit" (1 Cor. 12:11), that they are given "for the common good" (1 Cor. 12:7), and that they are all to be used for "building up" (1 Cor. 14:26) the church.[1]

---

1. When seemingly natural gifts (such as teaching, helps, administration, or musical gifts) are empowered by the Holy Spirit, they will generally show increased effectiveness and power in their use. Paul says the Corinthians were "enriched" in all their speech and knowledge as spiritual gifts came to them (1 Cor. 1:5–7). Any pastor who has preached for a time knows the difference between preaching in his "natural" ability and preaching the same sermon under the anointing or empowering of the Holy Spirit.

## 1. Spiritual Gifts in the History of Redemption

Certainly the Holy Spirit was at work in the Old Testament, bringing people to faith and working in remarkable ways in a few individuals such as Moses or Samuel, David or Elijah. But in general there was *less powerful* activity of the Holy Spirit in the lives of most believers. Effective evangelism of the nations was very uncommon, casting out of demons[2] was unknown, miraculous healing was uncommon (though it did happen, especially in the ministries of Elijah and Elisha), prophecy was restricted to a few prophets or small bands of prophets, and "resurrection power" over sin in the sense of Romans 6:1–14 and Philippians 3:10 was rarely experienced.

But at several points the Old Testament looks forward to a time when there would be a greater empowering of the Holy Spirit that would reach to all of God's people. Moses said, "Would that all the LORD's people were prophets, that the LORD would put his Spirit on them!" (Num. 11:29). And the Lord prophesied through Joel:

> And it shall come to pass afterward,
>> that I will pour out my Spirit on all flesh;
> your sons and your daughters shall prophesy,
>> your old men shall dream dreams,
>> and your young men shall see visions.
> Even on the male and female servants
>> in those days I will pour out my Spirit. (Joel 2:28–29)

John the Baptist heightens people's expectations of the fulfillment of Joel's prophecy when he announces that someone is coming after him who "will baptize you with the Holy Spirit and fire" (Matt. 3:11; cf. Mark 1:8; Luke 3:16; John 1:33; Acts 1:5).

When Jesus begins his ministry, he comes bringing the fullness and power of the Holy Spirit in his person. Luke writes, "And Jesus returned *in the power of the Spirit* to Galilee" (Luke 4:14). The result is that he teaches with great power (Luke 4:15–22), and he heals and casts out demons from all who are oppressed (Luke 4:31–41). Clearly, Jesus has come in the *greater new covenant power of the Holy Spirit*, and he has come to *conquer* Satan's kingdom.

In fact, he says that the power of the Holy Spirit at work in him enabling him to cast out demons is an indication that the kingdom of God has come in power: "If it is by the Spirit of God that I cast out demons, then the kingdom of God has come upon you" (Matt. 12:28). Looking back on Jesus' life and ministry, John tells us, "The reason the Son of God appeared was to destroy the works of the devil" (1 John 3:8).

---

2. The only thing that comes close to casting out of demons in the Old Testament is the fact that when David played the lyre for King Saul, "Saul was refreshed and was well, and the harmful spirit departed from him" (1 Sam. 16:23), but David had to do this "whenever the harmful spirit from God was upon Saul" (ibid.), indicating that there was no permanent relief from the demonic oppression that Saul experienced.

But this new covenant power of the Holy Spirit is not limited to the ministry of Jesus alone. He sent his disciples out, saying, "The kingdom of heaven is at hand," and told them, "Heal the sick, raise the dead, cleanse lepers, cast out demons" (Matt. 10:7–8). Nevertheless, at this point such new covenant power of the Holy Spirit is not yet distributed to all who believed in Jesus or followed him but only to his twelve disciples or to the seventy disciples (Luke 10:1–12).

The pouring out of the Holy Spirit in new covenant fullness and power in the church occurred at Pentecost. Before Jesus ascended into heaven he commanded his apostles "not to depart from Jerusalem, but to wait for the promise of the Father," and the content of that promise was that "you will be baptized with the Holy Spirit not many days from now" (Acts 1:4–5). He promised them, *"You will receive power when the Holy Spirit has come upon you"* (Acts 1:8). When the Spirit was poured out on the church at Pentecost, Peter recognized that Joel's prophecy was being fulfilled, for he said, "This is what was uttered through the prophet Joel" (Acts 2:16). Then he quoted Joel's prophecy (vv. 17–21). Peter recognized *that the new covenant empowering of the Holy Spirit had come to God's people* and that the new covenant age had begun as a direct result of the activity of Jesus in heaven, for Peter said, "This Jesus God raised up, and of that we all are witnesses. Being therefore exalted at the right hand of God, and having received from the Father the promise of the Holy Spirit, he has poured out this that you yourselves are seeing and hearing" (Acts 2:32–33).

Against the background of Jesus' ministry and the earlier ministry of the disciples with Jesus, the disciples present at Pentecost would rightly have expected that powerful evangelistic preaching, deliverance from demonic oppression, physical healing, and perhaps also prophecy, dreams, and visions would all begin and continue among those who believe in Christ, and that these things would be *characteristic* of the new covenant age that began at Pentecost. A further characteristic of this outpouring of the Holy Spirit was a widespread distribution of spiritual gifts to all people—sons and daughters, young men and old men, menservants and maidservants, in the words of Joel—*all* received a new covenant empowering of the Holy Spirit, and it would also be expected that all would receive gifts of the Holy Spirit then as well.[3] In fact, that is what happened in the early church (see 1 Cor. 12–14; Gal. 3:5; James 5:14–15). As B. B. Warfield said, "We are justified in considering it characteristic of the Apostolic churches that such miraculous gifts should be displayed in them. The exception would be, not a church with, but a church without, such gifts. . . . *The Apostolic Church was characteristically a miracle-working church.*"[4] (This is true regardless of what view one takes about the continuation of miraculous gifts after the time of the apostles.)

---

3. See chapter 39, pp. 945–53, on the question of baptism in the Holy Spirit.

4. B. B. Warfield, *Counterfeit Miracles* (1918; repr., Edinburgh: Banner of Truth, 1972), 5.

## 2. The Purpose of Spiritual Gifts in the New Testament Age

Spiritual gifts are given *to equip the church to carry out its ministry until Christ returns.* Paul tells the Corinthians, "*You are not lacking in any gift, as you wait for the revealing of our Lord Jesus Christ*" (1 Cor. 1:7). Here he connects the possession of spiritual gifts and their situation in the history of redemption (waiting for Christ's return), suggesting that gifts are given to the church for the period between Christ's ascension and his return. Similarly, Paul looks forward to the time of Christ's return and says, "When the perfect comes, the partial will pass away" (1 Cor. 13:10), indicating also that these "partial" gifts (mentioned in vv. 8–9) will be in operation until Christ returns, when they will be superseded by something far greater.[5] Indeed, the pouring out of the Holy Spirit in "power" at Pentecost (Acts 1:8) was to equip the church to preach the gospel (Acts 1:8)—something that will continue until Christ returns. And Paul reminds believers that in their use of spiritual gifts they are to "strive to excel in *building up* the church" (1 Cor. 14:12). Finally, in writing to the Ephesians, Paul specifies that when Christ ascended into heaven he gave gifts "to *equip* the saints for the work of ministry, for building up the body of Christ" (Eph. 4:12). All of these purposes will remain valid until Christ returns.

But spiritual gifts not only equip the church for the time until Christ returns, they also *give a foretaste of the age to come.* Paul reminds the Corinthians that they were "enriched" in all their speech and all their knowledge, and the result of this enriching was that they were "not lacking in any gift" (1 Cor. 1:5, 7). Of course, this *enrichment* in their speech and knowledge did not give them the perfect speech or the perfect knowledge that would be theirs in heaven, but it gave them a foretaste or down payment of that heavenly perfection. Similarly, Paul reminds the Corinthians that spiritual gifts are "partial" but when the "perfect" way of knowing comes at the Lord's return, then these gifts will pass away (1 Cor. 13:10). Just as the Holy Spirit himself is in this age a "down payment" (2 Cor. 1:22 NASB mg.; cf. 2 Cor. 5:5; Eph. 1:14) of the fuller work of the Holy Spirit within us in the age to come, so the gifts the Holy Spirit gives us are *partial foretastes* of the fuller working of the Holy Spirit that will be ours in the age to come.

In this way, gifts of insight and discernment prefigure the much greater discernment we will have when Christ returns. Gifts of knowledge and wisdom prefigure the much greater wisdom that will be ours when we "know as we are known" (cf. 1 Cor. 13:12). Gifts of healing give a foretaste of the perfect health that will be ours when Christ grants to us resurrection bodies. Similar parallels could be found with all the New Testament gifts. Even the diversity of gifts should lead to greater unity and interdependence in the church (see 1 Cor. 12:12–13, 24–25; Eph. 4:13), and this diversity in unity will itself be a foretaste of the unity that believers will have in heaven.

---

5. This interpretation of 1 Cor. 13:10 is defended at greater length in section B below.

## 3. How Many Gifts Are There?

The New Testament Epistles list specific spiritual gifts in different passages. Consider the table below.

What is obvious is that these lists are all quite different. No one list has all these gifts, and no gift except prophecy is mentioned on all the lists (prophecy is certainly included in the "whoever speaks" of 1 Peter 4:11).[6]

These facts indicate that Paul was not attempting to construct exhaustive lists of gifts when he specified the ones he did. Although there is sometimes an indication of order (he puts apostles first, prophets second, and teachers third, but tongues last in 1 Cor. 12:28), it seems that in general Paul was almost randomly listing a series of different examples of gifts as they came to mind.

| 1 Corinthians 12:28 | 1 Corinthians 12:8–10 | Ephesians 4:11[7] | Romans 12:6–8 | 1 Peter 4:11 |
|---|---|---|---|---|
| 1. apostle[8] | 9. word of wisdom | (1) apostle | (2) prophecy | Whoever speaks (covering several gifts) |
| 2. prophet | 10. word of knowledge | (2) prophet | 16. serving | |
| 3. teacher | 11. faith | 14. evangelist | (3) teaching | Whoever renders service (covering several gifts) |
| 4. miracles | (5) gifts of healing | 15. pastor-teacher | 17. encouraging | |
| 5. kinds of healings | (4) miracles | | 18. contributing | |
| 6. helps | (2) prophecy | | 19. leadership | |
| 7. administration | 12. distinguishing between spirits | | 20. mercy | |
| 8. tongues | (8) tongues | | | |
| | 13. interpretation of tongues | | | |

Moreover, there is some degree of overlap among the gifts listed at various places. No doubt the gift of administration (*kybernēsis*, 1 Cor. 12:28) is similar to the gift of leadership (*ho proistamenos*, Rom. 12:8), and both terms could probably be applied to many who have the office of pastor-teacher (Eph. 4:11). Moreover, in some cases Paul

---

6. In the first edition of this book, I considered 1 Cor. 7:7 to be another very brief list of spiritual gifts, including only the two gifts of marriage and celibacy. In a context of speaking of marriage and celibacy, Paul says, "Each has his own *gift* from God, one of one kind and one of another." Therefore, I counted marriage and celibacy as spiritual gifts. But I now think that analysis was incorrect because in 1 Cor. 7:7 Paul is speaking about everyone in the church, all the married people and all the single people, and he is not using the Greek term *charisma* to refer to an ability that is empowered by the Holy Spirit and used in the ministry of the church. Rather, he is using the word in a more general sense to refer to something freely given to us from God. The word *charisma* is used in this more general sense in Romans 5:15; 6:23; 2 Corinthians 1:11 (where it is represented by the word "blessing").

7. This list gives four kinds of persons in terms of offices or functions, not, strictly speaking, four gifts. For three of the functions on the list, the corresponding gifts would be prophecy, evangelism, and teaching.

8. Strictly speaking, to be an apostle is an office, not a gift (see chapter 47, pp. 1116–22, on the office of apostle).

lists an activity and in other cases lists the related noun that describes the person (such as "prophecy" in Rom. 12:6 and 1 Cor. 12:10 but as "prophet" in 1 Cor. 12:28 and Eph. 4:11).[9]

Another reason for thinking that Paul could have made much longer lists if he had wanted to is the fact that some of the gifts listed will have many different expressions as they are found in different people. Certainly the gift of serving (Rom. 12:6) or helps (1 Cor. 12:28) will take many different forms in different situations and among different people. Some may serve or help by giving wise counsel, others by cooking meals, others by caring for children or befriending an older person, others by giving specialized legal or medical or financial advice when needed within the church. These gifts differ greatly. Among those who possess the gift of evangelism, some will be good at personal evangelism within a neighborhood, others at evangelism through writing of tracts and Christian literature, and others at evangelism through large campaigns and public meetings. Still others will be good at evangelism through radio and television, and others through blogs or emails or Facebook. Not all of these evangelistic gifts are the same, even though they fall under the broad category of evangelism. The same could be said about gifts of teaching or administration.[10] All of this simply means that no two people's gifts are exactly alike.

How many different gifts are there then? It simply depends on how specific we wish to be. We can make a very short list of only two gifts as Peter does in 1 Peter 4:11: "whoever *speaks*" and "whoever *serves*." In this list of only two items Peter includes all the gifts mentioned in any other list because all of them fit in one of these two categories. On the other hand, we could take the Old Testament offices of prophet, priest, and king

---

9. Something can be said at this point about the relationship between gifts and offices in the church. As we look at these lists, it is evident that in some cases Paul names the specific gift (such as gifts of healing or administration or tongues), and in other cases he names the *persons* who have those gifts (such as apostles, prophets, or evangelists). Some lists name only the gifts (such as 1 Cor. 12:8–10), while other lists name only the people who possess those gifts (such as Eph. 4:11 and 1 Peter 4:11). And some lists are mixed, naming some gifts and some persons who have the gifts (such as Rom. 12:6–8 and 1 Cor. 12:28).

In addition to that, another distinction should be made: In cases where Paul names *persons*, he sometimes gives a name that refers to an officially recognized *office* in the church (such as "apostles" or "pastor-teachers"). We would expect that such people would begin to function in those offices after they had received formal recognition by the church as a whole (this would be called "ordination" or "installation in office" for the office of pastor [or elder] for example). But in other cases, though the person is named, it is not necessary to think there was any official recognition or establishment in office in front of the entire church. This would be the case, for example, for "the one who encourages" and "the one who contributes" and

"the one who does acts of mercy" in Rom. 12:6–8. Similarly, the New Testament does not clearly indicate that prophets or evangelists were established in any formally recognized offices in the early church, and the word *prophet* probably just refers to one who prophesied regularly and with evident blessing in the church. *Evangelist* could similarly refer to those who regularly functioned effectively in the work of evangelism, and *teachers* could include both those who had formally recognized teaching functions in the church, perhaps in connection with the office of elder, and those who had teaching functions in less formal capacities in the church but regularly taught with effectiveness in informal or smaller group settings.

For convenience, we will continue to refer to these lists as lists of "spiritual gifts," although, to be more precise, we should realize that they include both spiritual gifts and persons who exercise those gifts. Since both the gifts and the persons are given to the church by Jesus Christ, it is appropriate that both are named in various parts of these lists.

10. See the excellent discussion in John R. W. Stott, *Baptism and Fullness: The Work of the Holy Spirit Today* (Downers Grove, IL: InterVarsity Press, 1964), 88–89.

and have a list of three kinds of gifts: *prophetic* gifts (in this broad sense) would include anything that involves teaching, encouraging, exhorting, or rebuking others; *priestly* gifts would include anything that involves showing mercy and care for those in need or involve interceding before God (such as praying in tongues); and *kingly* gifts would involve anything having to do with administration or government or order in the church.

Other classifications of gifts are gifts of *knowledge* (such as distinguishing between spirits, word of wisdom, and word of knowledge), gifts of *power* (such as healing, miracles, and faith), and gifts of *speech* (tongues, interpretation, and prophecy).[11] Then again we could make a much longer list, such as the list of twenty gifts enumerated above. But even that list does not include all the possible gifts (no list includes a gift of intercessory prayer, for instance, which may be related to a gift of faith but is not the same as a gift of faith; no musical gifts are included on any list either; neither is any gift of casting out demons, even though Paul must have known that some Christians were more effective in that area than others). If we wished to divide up *different kinds* of service or administration or evangelism or teaching, then we could quite easily have a list that included fifty or even a hundred items.[12]

The point of all of this is simply to say that God gives the church an amazing variety of spiritual gifts, and they are all tokens of his varied grace. In fact, Peter says as much: "As each has received a gift, use it to serve one another, as good stewards of God's *varied grace*" (1 Peter 4:10; the word *varied* is *poikilos*, which means "having many facets or aspects; having rich diversity").

The practical outcome of this discussion is that we should be willing to recognize and appreciate people who have gifts that differ from ours and whose gifts may differ from our expectations of what certain gifts should look like. Moreover, a healthy church will have a great diversity of gifts, and this diversity should not lead to fragmentation but to greater unity among believers in the church. Paul's whole point in the analogy of the body with many members (1 Cor. 12:12–26) is to say that God has put us in the body with these differences *so that we might depend on each other.* "The eye cannot say to the hand, 'I have no need of you,' nor again the head to the feet, 'I have no need of you.' On the contrary, the parts of the body that seem to be weaker are indispensable" (1 Cor. 12:21–22; cf. vv. 4–6). It runs counter to the world's way of thinking to say that we will enjoy greater unity when we join closely together with those who are different from us, but that is precisely the point that Paul makes in 1 Corinthians 12, demonstrating the glory of God's wisdom in not allowing anyone to have all the necessary gifts for the church but requiring us to depend upon each other for the proper functioning of the church.

---

11. This classification is from Dennis and Rita Bennett, *The Holy Spirit and You* (Plainfield, NJ: Logos International, 1971), 83. The Bennetts' actual categorization is gifts of revelation, gifts of power, and inspirational or fellowship gifts, and they list them in reverse order to what I have given here.

12. This variety of ways of classifying gifts allows us to say that many types of classification are possible for teaching purposes, but we should beware of any claim that a certain way of classifying or listing gifts is the only valid one, for Scripture does not limit us to any one scheme of classification.

## 4. Gifts May Vary in Strength

Paul says that if we have the gift of prophecy, we should use it "*in proportion to our faith*" (Rom. 12:6), indicating that the gift can be more or less strongly developed in different individuals or in the same individual over different points in time. This is why Paul can remind Timothy, "Do not neglect the gift you have" (1 Tim. 4:14), and can say, "I remind you to *fan into flame* the gift of God, which is in you" (2 Tim. 1:6). It was possible for Timothy to allow his gift to weaken, apparently through infrequent use, and Paul reminds him to stir it up by using it and thereby strengthening it. This should not be surprising, for we realize that many gifts increase in strength and effectiveness as they are used, whether evangelism, teaching, encouraging, administration, or faith. Apollos had a strong gift of preaching and teaching, for we read that he was "mighty (or "powerful," Gk. *dynatos*) in the Scriptures" (Acts 18:24 NASB). And Paul apparently had a frequently used and very effective gift of speaking in tongues because he says, "I thank God that I speak in tongues more than all of you" (1 Cor. 14:18).[13]

All of these texts indicate that *spiritual gifts may vary in strength*. If we think of any gift, whether teaching or evangelism on the one hand or prophecy or healing on the other, we should realize that within any congregation there will likely be people who are very effective in the use of that gift (perhaps through long use and experience), others who are moderately strong in that gift, and others who probably have the gift but are just beginning to use it. This variation in strength in spiritual gifts depends on a combination of divine and human influence. The divine influence is the sovereign working of the Holy Spirit as he "apportions to each one individually as he wills" (1 Cor. 12:11). The human influence comes from experience, training, wisdom, and natural ability in the use of that gift. It is usually not possible to know in what proportion the divine and human influences combine at any one time, nor is it really necessary to know, for even the abilities we think to be "natural" are from God (1 Cor. 4:7) and under his sovereign control (see chapter 16 on God's providence and human responsibility).

But this leads to an interesting question: How strong does an ability have to be before it can be called a spiritual gift? How much teaching ability does someone need before he or she could be said to have a gift of teaching, for example? Or how effective in evangelism would someone need to be before we would recognize a gift of evangelism? Or how frequently would someone have to see prayers for healing answered before he or she could be said to have a gift of healing?

Scripture does not directly answer this question, but the fact that Paul speaks of these gifts as useful for the building up of the church (1 Cor. 14:12) and the fact that Peter likewise says that each person who has received a gift should remember to employ it "to serve one another" (1 Peter 4:10) suggest that both Paul and Peter thought of gifts

---

13. See also 1 Cor. 13:1–3 where Paul gives examples of some gifts developed to the highest imaginable degree, examples which he uses to show that even such gifts without love would bring no benefit.

as abilities that were *strong enough to function for the benefit of the church*, whether for the assembled congregation (as in prophecy or teaching) or for individuals at various times in the congregation (as helps or encouragement).

Probably no definite line can be drawn in this matter, but Paul does remind us that *not all have every gift or any one gift*. He is quite clear in this in a set of questions that expect the answer no at each point: "Are all apostles? Are all prophets? Are all teachers? Do all work miracles? Do all possess gifts of healing? Do all speak with tongues? Do all interpret?" (1 Cor. 12:29–30). The Greek text (with the particle *mē* before each question) clearly expects the answer no to every question. Therefore, not all are teachers, for example, nor do all possess gifts of healing, nor do all speak in tongues.

But even though not all have the gift of teaching, it is true that all people "teach" *in some sense* of the word *teach*. Even people who would never dream of teaching a Sunday school class will read Bible stories to their children and explain the meaning to them— indeed, Moses commanded the Israelites to do this very thing with their children (Deut. 6:7), explaining God's words to them as they sat in their house or walked on the road. So we must say on the one hand that not everyone has the *gift* of teaching. But on the other hand we must say that there is *some general ability* related to the gift of teaching that all Christians have. Another way of saying this would be to say that there is no spiritual gift that all believers have, yet there is some general ability similar to every gift that all Christians have.

We can see this with a number of gifts. Not all Christians have a gift of evangelism, but all Christians have the ability to share the gospel with their neighbors. Not all Christians have gifts of healing (in fact, as we shall see below, some people say that no one today has genuine gifts of healing); nevertheless, every Christian can and does pray for God to heal friends or relatives who are ill. Not every Christian has the gift of faith, but every believer has some degree of faith, and we would expect it to be growing in the life of an ordinary Christian.

We can even say that other gifts, such as prophecy and speaking in tongues, not only vary in strength among those who have the gift but also find a counterpart in some general abilities that are found in the life of every Christian. For example, if we understand prophecy (according to the definition given in chapter 53)[14] to be "reporting something that God spontaneously brings to mind," then it is true that not everyone experiences this as a gift, for not everyone experiences God spontaneously bringing things to mind with such clarity and force that he or she feels free to speak about them among an assembled group of Christians. But probably every believer has at one time or another had a sense that God was bringing to mind the need to pray for a distant friend or to write or phone a word of encouragement to someone distant, and later has

---

14. See chapter 53, pp. 1293–1313, for a definition of the gift of prophecy in the church.

found that that was exactly the thing that was needed at the moment. Few would deny that God sovereignly brought that need to mind in a spontaneous way, and though this would not be called a gift of prophecy, it is a general ability to receive special direction or guidance from God that is similar to what happens in the gift of prophecy, although it is functioning at a weaker level.

We can even consider the gift of speaking in tongues from this perspective. If we think of speaking in tongues as prayer in syllables not understood by the speaker (see 1 Cor. 14:2, 14),[15] then it is true that not every Christian has the gift of speaking in tongues (and once again it must be said that some Christians would argue that no one has that gift today, since the age of the apostles has ended). But we must recognize that every Christian has times of prayer in which his or her prayer is expressed not only in intelligible words and syllables but also in terms of sighs, groans, or weeping that is understood and heard by the Lord and that expresses needs and concerns of our hearts that we cannot fully put into words (cf. Rom. 8:26–27). Once again we should not call this a gift of speaking in tongues, but it does seem to be a general ability in our Christian lives that is somewhat related to the gift of speaking in tongues, in that it gives expression to prayer in syllables that we do not fully understand, but that the Holy Spirit nonetheless makes into effective prayer that is heard by God.

The point of this whole discussion is simply to say that spiritual gifts are not as mysterious and "other worldly" as people sometimes make them out to be. Many of them are only intensifications or highly developed instances of phenomena that most Christians experience. The other important point to be drawn from this discussion is that even though we have been given gifts by God, we are still responsible to use them effectively, and to seek to grow in their use that the church may receive more benefit from the gifts of which God has allowed us to be stewards.

Finally, the fact that gifts may vary in strength allows us to recognize that a certain person's gift (such as teaching or administration, for example) may not be strong enough to function for the benefit of the entire church in a large church where many people already have that gift developed to a very high degree. But that same person, moving to a younger, smaller church where few have gifts of teaching or administration, may find that his or her gifts are very much in demand and able to function for the benefit of the entire congregation. (In this sense, something that is only considered a general ability in one setting might rightly be considered a spiritual gift in another setting.)

## 5. Do Christians Possess Gifts Temporarily or Permanently?

In most cases, it seems that the New Testament pictures a *permanent* possession of spiritual gifts. The analogy of the parts of the body in 1 Corinthians 12:12–26 fits

---

15. See also the discussion of the gift of speaking in tongues in chapter 53, pp. 1321–32.

this, in that the eye does not become a hand, nor does the ear become a foot, but various parts exist in the body permanently.[16] Moreover, Paul says that some people have titles that describe a continuing function. Some people can be called "prophets" or "teachers" (1 Cor. 12:29) or "evangelists" (Eph. 4:11). We would expect that those people have a permanent possession of the gifts of prophecy, teaching, and evangelism, unless some unusual circumstance would come along that would take that gift away. Similarly, Paul talks in terms of possessing spiritual gifts when he says, "And if I *have* prophetic powers" (1 Cor. 13:2). And when Paul requires that there be an interpreter present for anyone to speak in tongues (1 Cor. 14:28), he assumes that the church will know whether someone who has the gift of interpretation is present, which implies that that gift would be possessed by someone over time. When he says, "If anyone thinks that he is a prophet" (1 Cor. 14:37), he realizes that some at Corinth will have functioned with the gift of prophecy frequently enough to think of themselves as "prophets." All of these verses point in the direction of a permanent, or at least abiding and continuing, possession of spiritual gifts.

Indeed, in Romans 12, Paul begins his sentence, *"Having gifts* that differ according to the grace given to us" (Rom. 12:6). And he tells Timothy, "Do not neglect the gift *that is in you*" (1 Tim. 4:14, literal translation), again indicating that Timothy had had that gift over a period of time. In general the New Testament indicates that people have spiritual gifts given to them, and once they have them, they are usually able to continue to use them over the course of their Christian life.

However, some important qualifications must be made, because there are some senses in which gifts are *not permanent*. Some gifts, though perhaps exercised fairly frequently, still cannot be exercised at will. Effectiveness in the gift of healing, for example, depends on God's sovereign will in answering prayer for healing. Similarly, prophecy depends on the giving of a spontaneous "revelation" (1 Cor. 14:30) from God and simply cannot be exercised at will. The same could even be said about the gift of evangelism: it is ultimately the work of the Holy Spirit to bring regeneration and enable someone to believe, so the evangelist may pray and preach, but only God can give the harvest of souls.

In other cases, some particular gift may be given for a unique need or event. Though it is not, strictly speaking, a spiritual gift in the New Testament sense, the return of Samson's strength one last time at the end of his life (Judg. 16:28) was given temporarily for one final moment in his life. And in the New Testament, the remarkable revelation of heaven Stephen had when he, "full of the Holy Spirit, gazed into heaven and saw the glory of God, and Jesus standing at the right hand of God" (Acts 7:55) was a manifestation of the Spirit given to him only for that specific moment.

Another sense in which a gift may be nonpermanent is if a person neglects his or

---

16. We should not press the metaphor of the body too far, of course, for people *do* receive other gifts, and Paul even encourages people to seek additional spiritual gifts (1 Cor. 14:1). But the metaphor does suggest *some* degree of stability or permanence in the possession of gifts.

her gift and perhaps grieves the Holy Spirit or falls into serious doctrinal or moral error (as Samson did in the Old Testament, for example). In such a case the gift may be withdrawn. Certainly Paul warned Timothy, "Do not neglect the gift you have" (1 Tim. 4:14), and we may perhaps also learn from the parable of the talents, in which Jesus says that "to everyone who has will more be given, and he will have an abundance. But from the one who has not, even what he has will be taken away" (Matt. 25:29).[17]

Moreover, we must remember that *the Holy Spirit is still sovereign in distributing gifts*: he "apportions to each one individually *as he wills*" (1 Cor. 12:11). The word here translated "apportions" is a present participle, which indicates continuing activity over time, and we could paraphrase, "The Holy Spirit *is always continuing to distribute or apportion gifts* to each person individually just as he wills to do." This means that, although it is *ordinarily* the custom of the Holy Spirit to continue to empower the same gift or gifts in people over time, nonetheless, there is a continual willing and deciding of the Holy Spirit to do this or not, and he may for his own reasons withdraw a gift for a time or cause it to be much stronger or much weaker than it was.

Finally, 1 Corinthians 13:8–13 (to be discussed below) indicates that the present spiritual gifts which we have are only for this age and will be superseded by something far greater. In that sense no gift is "permanent" since every gift will be rendered useless at the time of the Lord's return.

Within this discussion of whether spiritual gifts are temporary or permanent, sometimes Romans 11:29 is mentioned: "For the gifts and the calling of God are irrevocable." It does not seem to be appropriate to use the verse in the context of this discussion, however, for in this case Paul is talking about the status of the Jewish people, including their calling as God's people and the gifts or blessings bestowed on them as a result of that status. Here Paul is arguing that God still has a purpose for his people Israel, but the question of gifts of the Holy Spirit in the sense of 1 Corinthians 12–14 is not in view at all in Romans 11:29. And certainly, in any case, this sentence would not be true as a totally unrestricted statement concerning spiritual gifts, for it is evident that through misuse, neglect, or grieving of the Holy Spirit, people can have their gifts diminished or removed by God's sovereign choice.

## 6. Are Gifts Miraculous or Nonmiraculous?

The answer to this question really depends on the definition of the word *miracle*. If we define *miracle* as "a direct activity of God in the world," then all the spiritual gifts are miraculous because they are all empowered by the Holy Spirit (1 Cor. 12:11; cf. vv. 4–6). But in that sense *everything* that happens in the world might be said to be miraculous because all of it is brought about by God's providential work in creation (see Eph. 1:11;

---

17. Although the primary point of this parable has to do with rewards at the final judgment, it nonetheless encourages faithfulness in stewardship with what one has been given, and it is not unreasonable to expect that God would act toward us in that way, at least in principle, in this life as well.

Dan. 4:35; Matt. 5:45).[18] Therefore, the word *miracle* loses its usefulness because it is difficult for us to find something that happens in the world that is *not* miraculous in this sense.

It is better to define *miracle* in a narrower sense, as we did in chapter 17, above: "A miracle is a less common activity of God in which he arouses people's awe and wonder and bears witness to himself."[19] In terms of this definition, only some gifts are miraculous—namely, those gifts that people think to be miraculous because they are amazed at the activity of God operating in them. Certainly this category would include prophecy (note the amazement of the unbeliever in 1 Cor. 14:24–25), healing (similarly, note the response of people in Acts 3:10 et al.), casting out of demons (see Acts 19:11–13, 17), and speaking in tongues when it is an actual foreign language and understood by others (see the description of Pentecost in Acts 2:7). Probably other remarkable phenomena would be included in the gift of miracles (1 Cor. 12:10) as well.

On the other hand, in this definition, some gifts would be thought of as nonmiraculous. Gifts of serving, teaching, encouraging, contributing, and doing acts of mercy (in Rom. 12:7–8) would fall in this category, as would the gifts of those who act as helpers and administrators (1 Cor. 12:28). But it is still the same Holy Spirit who gives them and works through them.

The point of this analysis is to caution us against making a supernatural/natural distinction in our minds whereby we think that some gifts are supernatural and some gifts are simply natural. The Bible makes no such distinction, and the danger of doing this is that we may tend to think that some gifts (which we think to be supernatural) are more important or more clearly from the Lord, and we may tend to devalue or deemphasize the gifts which we think to be natural. If we do this we will fail to see God's hand in the working of all the gifts and fail to thank him for all of them.

On the other hand, the misleading supernatural/natural distinction could also cause us to be very suspicious about those which we think to be supernatural, or it could lead us to think that they are very unlikely to happen. In that case, we would tend to emphasize the gifts we thought to be natural and have a very low degree of expectation or faith regarding anything which we thought to be supernatural.

In contrast to this perspective, Scripture says that "all" the gifts are worked in us by the same Holy Spirit, the same Lord, and the same God (1 Cor. 12:4–6). The worldview of Scripture is one of continuity and continual interaction between the *visible world* that we can see and touch and the *invisible world* that Scripture tells us is there and is real. God works in both, and we do ourselves and the church a great disservice by separating these aspects of creation into supernatural and natural categories.

Finally, should we seek the more unusual or miraculous gifts, or should we seek the

---

18. See the discussion of various definitions for the word *miracle* in chapter 17, pp. 470–73.

19. See chapter 17, p. 470.

more ordinary gifts? Once again, Scripture does not make this kind of distinction when it tells us what kind of gifts to seek. Paul says to the Corinthians, "Since you are eager for manifestations of the Spirit, *strive to excel in building up the church*" (1 Cor. 14:12). This means that we should learn which gifts are most needed in the church we attend or the community where we live, and then pray that God would give those gifts to ourselves or to others. Whether those gifts are thought to be miraculous or nonmiraculous really is not the important point at all.[20]

## 7. Discovering and Seeking Spiritual Gifts

Paul seems to assume that believers will know what their spiritual gifts are. He simply tells those in the church at Rome to use their gifts in various ways: "If prophecy, in proportion to our faith . . . the one who contributes, in generosity; the one who leads, with zeal; the one who does acts of mercy, with cheerfulness" (Rom. 12:6–8). Similarly, Peter simply tells his readers how to use their gifts, but he does not say anything about discovering what they are: "*As each has received a gift*, use it to serve one another, as good stewards of God's varied grace" (1 Peter 4:10).

But what if many members in a church do not know what spiritual gift or gifts God has given to them? In such a case, the leaders of the church need to ask whether they are providing sufficient opportunities for varieties of gifts to be used.[21] Though the lists of gifts given in the New Testament are not exhaustive, they certainly provide a good starting point for churches to ask whether at least there is opportunity for *these gifts* to be used. If God has placed people with certain gifts in a church where these gifts are not encouraged or perhaps not allowed to be used, they will feel frustrated and unfulfilled in their Christian ministries and will perhaps move to another church where their gifts can function for the benefit of the church.

In the case of individuals who do not know what their gifts are, they can begin by asking what the needs and opportunities for ministry are in their church. Specifically, they can ask what gifts are most needed for the building up of the church at that point. In addition, each individual believer who does not know what his or her gifts are should do some self-examination. What interests and desires and abilities does he or she have? Can others give advice or encouragement pointing in the direction of specific gifts? Moreover, has there been blessing in the past in ministering in a particular kind of service? In all of this, the person seeking to discover his or her gifts should pray and ask God for wisdom, confident that it will be given according to his promise, "If any of you lacks wisdom, let him ask God, who gives generously to all without reproach, and it will be given him. But let him ask in faith, with no doubting" (James 1:5–6). Sometimes

---

20. See chapter 17, pp. 486–88, for a discussion of the objection that it is wrong to seek miraculous gifts or miracles today.
21. A very helpful book giving practical guidance about developing the use of spiritual gifts in a church is Sam Storms, *Practicing the Power: Welcoming the Gifts of the Holy Spirit in Your Life* (Grand Rapids: Zondervan, 2017).

God will grant this wisdom in terms of more accurate insight into one's abilities. At other times it may come through advice from others or through seeing increased blessing in one area of ministry. And Paul indicates that in some cases there may be prophecy that gives indication of a specific gift, for he says to Timothy, *"Do not neglect the gift you have, which was given you by prophecy* when the council of elders laid their hands on you" (1 Tim. 4:14).

Finally, the person wondering what his or her spiritual gifts are should simply begin to try ministering in various areas and see where God brings blessing. Teaching a Sunday school class or home Bible study is an excellent way to begin using the gift of teaching. Every community has opportunities for greater use of the gift of evangelism. People who think they may have a gift of healing could ask their elders for opportunities to accompany them when they go to pray for the sick. People who think they may have a gift of faith or a gift of intercessory prayer could begin to ask some Christian friends for specific needs about which to pray. In all of this, churches can give encouragement and opportunities for people to try using various gifts and can also give teaching and practical training in the proper methods of using various gifts. In addition, churches should continually be praying that God would allow people to find what their gifts are and then to be able to use them. In all of this the goal is that the body of Christ in each location grow up to maturity, until "the whole body, joined and held together by every joint with which it is equipped, *when each part is working properly*, makes the body grow so that it builds itself up in love" (Eph. 4:16).

Beyond the question of discovering what gifts one has is the question of seeking additional spiritual gifts. Paul commands Christians, *"Earnestly desire the higher gifts"* (1 Cor. 12:31), and says later, "Pursue love, and *earnestly desire the spiritual gifts*, especially that you may prophesy" (1 Cor. 14:1). In this context, Paul defines what he means by "higher gifts" or "greater gifts" because in 1 Corinthians 14:5 he repeats the word he used in 12:31 for "higher" (Gk. *meizōn*) when he says, "The one who prophesies is *greater* than the one who speaks in tongues, unless someone interprets, *so that the church may be built up*" (1 Cor. 14:5). Here the "greater" gifts are those that most build up the church. This is consistent with Paul's statement a few verses later, when he says, "since you are eager for manifestations of the Spirit, strive to excel in building up the church" (1 Cor. 14:12). The *higher gifts* are *those that build up the church more and bring more benefit to others.*

But how do we seek more spiritual gifts? First, we should *ask God for them.* Paul says directly that "one who speaks in a tongue *should pray that he may interpret*" (1 Cor. 14:13; cf. James 1:5, where James tells people that they should ask God for wisdom). Next, people who seek additional spiritual gifts should *have right motives.* If spiritual gifts are sought only so that the person may be more prominent or have more influence or power, this certainly is wrong in God's eyes. This was the motivation of Simon the Sorcerer in Acts 8:19, when he said, "Give me this power also, so that anyone on whom

I lay my hands may receive the Holy Spirit" (see Peter's rebuke in vv. 21–22). Similarly, Ananias and Sapphira sought glory for themselves when they purported to be giving the entire proceeds of the sale of their land to the church, but it was not true, and both lost their lives (Acts 5:1–11). It is a fearful thing to want spiritual gifts or prominence in the church only for our glory, not for God's glory or to help others. Therefore, those who seek spiritual gifts must first ask if they are seeking them out of love for others and a concern to be able to minister to their needs because those who have great spiritual gifts but "have not love" are "nothing" in God's sight (cf. 1 Cor. 13:1–3). This is why Paul says, "*Pursue love*," and only after that adds, "and earnestly desire the spiritual gifts" (1 Cor. 14:1). He repeats the same theme again when he says, "Since you are eager for manifestations of the Spirit, *strive to excel in building up the church*" (1 Cor. 14:12). Every person asking God for an additional spiritual gift should search his or her heart frequently, asking why this particular gift is desired. Is it really out of a love for others and a desire to build up the church and to see God glorified?

After that, it is appropriate to *seek opportunities to try the gift*, just as in the case of a person trying to discover his or her gift, as explained above. Small group Bible studies or prayer meetings in homes often provide a good setting in which people can try gifts of teaching or intercessory prayer or encouragement or prophecy or healing, for example.

Finally, those who are seeking additional spiritual gifts should *continue to use the gifts they now have* and should *be content* if God chooses not to give them more. The master approved of the servant whose mina had "made ten minas more," but he condemned the one who hid his mina in a handkerchief and did nothing with it (Luke 19:16–17, 20–23)—certainly showing us that we have responsibility to *use* and *attempt to increase* whatever talents or abilities God has given to us as his stewards.

To balance this emphasis on seeking and growing in spiritual gifts, we must also remember that Paul clearly says that spiritual gifts are apportioned to each person individually by the Holy Spirit "*as he wills*" (1 Cor. 12:11) and that "God arranged the members in the body, each one of them, *as he chose*" (1 Cor. 12:18). He says that God has put various gifts in the church and not all are apostles or prophets or teachers (1 Cor. 12:28–30). In this way he reminds the Corinthians that ultimately the distribution of gifts is a matter of God's sovereign will, and it is for the good of the church and for our good that none of us have all of the gifts, and that we will need to depend continually on others who have gifts differing from ours. These considerations should make us content if God chooses not to give us the other gifts that we seek.

## 8. Gifts Are Tools for Ministry and Are Not Necessarily Related to Christian Maturity

We must recognize that spiritual gifts are given to *every* believer (1 Cor. 12:7, 11; 1 Peter 4:10). Even immature Christians receive spiritual gifts from the Lord—this was certainly evident in the Corinthian church, which had an abundance of spiritual gifts (1 Cor. 1:7), but was still very immature in many areas of doctrine and conduct. Paul says, "But I, brothers, could not address you as spiritual people, but as people of the flesh, as infants in Christ" (1 Cor. 3:1). So spiritual gifts are not necessarily a sign of spiritual maturity. It is possible to have remarkable spiritual gifts in one area or another but still be quite immature in doctrinal understanding or in Christian conduct, as was the case at Corinth. Or someone could be a gifted Bible teacher and yet lack spiritual maturity in certain areas of his life. Indeed, on occasion even *unbelievers* are able to prophesy and cast out demons and do miracles, for Jesus says that at the last day many will say to him, "Lord, Lord, did we not prophesy in your name, and cast out demons in your name, and do many mighty works in your name?" But Jesus will declare to them, "I *never* knew you; depart from me, you workers of lawlessness" (Matt. 7:22–23). It is not that Jesus knew them once and later did not know them; he says, "I never knew you." They were never Christians, yet they performed many remarkable works. So *we must not evaluate spiritual maturity on the basis of spiritual gifting.* Maturity comes through a close walk with Jesus, and results in obedience to his commands in everyday life: "Whoever says he abides in him ought to walk in the same way in which he walked" (1 John 2:6).

Why then does the Holy Spirit give us spiritual gifts? They are given for the work of ministry and are *simply tools* to be used for that end. They should never be a source of personal pride on the part of those who possess them, nor should they be thought of as a mark of maturity. We should strive simply to excel in loving others, caring for their needs, building up the church, and living a life of conformity to the pattern of Christ's life. If we do that, and if God chooses to give us spiritual gifts that equip us for those tasks, then we should thank him for that and pray that he would keep us from pride over gifts that have been freely and graciously given and that we did not earn.

## B. Have Some Gifts Ceased? The Cessationist Debate

Within the evangelical world today there are differing positions over the question, "Are all the gifts mentioned in the New Testament valid for use in the church today?" Some would say yes.[22] Others would say no and would argue that some of the more miraculous gifts (such as prophecy, tongues plus interpretation, and perhaps healing and casting out of demons) were given only during the time of the apostles, as "signs" to authenticate the apostles during the early preaching of the gospel. They state that these gifts are no longer needed as signs today and that the gifts ceased at the end of the apostolic age, probably at the end of the first century or beginning of the second century AD.

We should also realize that there is a large "middle" group with respect to this question, a group of "mainstream evangelicals" who are neither charismatics or Pentecostals

---

22. Many who say yes, such as the present author, would add the qualification that "apostle" is an office, not a gift, and that the office of apostle does not continue today (see chapter 47, pp. 1121–22, for this argument).

nor "cessationists"[23] but are simply undecided. Many of them would consider themselves to be "open but cautious" regarding the possibility of miraculous gifts today.[24]

Although some aspects of this question were discussed in chapter 17 on miracles, there are additional considerations that can be addressed here, specifically related to the topic of spiritual gifts.[25]

## 1. Does 1 Corinthians 13:8–13 Tell Us When Miraculous Gifts Will Cease?

Paul says,

> Love never ends. As for prophecies, they will pass away; as for tongues, they will cease; as for knowledge, it will pass away. For we know in part and we prophesy in part, but *when the perfect comes, the partial will pass away.* When I was a child, I spoke like a child, I thought like a child, I reasoned like a child. When I became a man, I gave up childish ways. For now we see in a mirror dimly, but then face to face. Now I know in part; then I shall know fully, even as I have been fully known. So now faith, hope, and love abide, these three; but the greatest of these is love. (1 Cor. 13:8–13)

This passage is important to the discussion because in it Paul mentions the gift of prophecy as something that functions "in part" (Gk. *ek merous*, "partial") and then says that what is "partial" (Gk. *ek merous*) will "pass away" (1 Cor. 13:10). He even says when this will happen: "when the perfect comes." But when is that? And even if we can determine when it is, does that mean that Paul had in mind something that would answer this "cessation" question for the church today? Can the gift of prophecy in this passage be representative of miraculous gifts in general in the church age?

a. **The Purpose of 1 Corinthians 13:8–13.** Paul interrupts his discussion of spiritual gifts with chapter 13 of 1 Corinthians, in which he intends to put the entire discussion of gifts in proper perspective. It is not enough simply to "seek the greater gifts" (12:31, NASB, NIV). One must also "pursue love" (14:1), thus coupling proper goals with proper motives. Without love, the gifts are without value (13:1–3). In fact, Paul argues, love is superior to all the gifts; therefore, it is more important to act in love than to have any of the gifts.

In order to show the superiority of love, Paul argues that it lasts forever, whereas the gifts are all temporary (13:8). Verses 9–12 further explain why the gifts are temporary.

---

23. *Cessationist* refers to someone who thinks that certain miraculous spiritual gifts *ceased* long ago when the apostles died and Scripture was complete. By contrast, a *continuationist* would say that miraculous gifts continue today.

24. The category "open but cautious" is one of the views defended in the book *Are Miraculous Gifts for Today? Four Views*, ed. Wayne Grudem (Grand Rapids: Zondervan, 1996). That position was defended by Robert Saucy.

25. The discussion in the remainder of this section on the cessationist debate is adapted from Wayne Grudem, *The Gift of Prophecy in the New Testament and Today* (Eastbourne: Kingsway; Westchester, IL: Crossway, 1988), 227–52, and is used by permission.

Our present knowledge and prophesying are partial and imperfect (v. 9), but someday something perfect will come to replace them (v. 10). This is explained by the analogy of a child who gives up childish thought and speech for the thought and speech of an adult (v. 11). Paul then elaborates further on verses 9–10 by explaining that our present perception and knowledge are indirect and imperfect, but someday they will be direct and perfect (v. 12).

In this argument Paul connects the function of prophecy with the time of its cessation. It fills a certain need now, but it does so only imperfectly. When "the perfect" comes, that function will be better fulfilled by something else, and prophecy will cease because it will be made obsolete or useless (this is the probable nuance of the Greek term used here, *katargeō*, "pass away" in vv. 8, 10). So the overall function of 1 Corinthians 13:8–13 is to show that love is superior to gifts like prophecy because those gifts will pass away but love will not pass away.

**b. 1 Corinthians 13:10: The Cessation of Prophecy When Christ Returns.** Paul writes in verse 10, "*When the perfect comes*, the partial will pass away." The phrase "the partial" (Gk. *ek merous*, "partial, imperfect") refers most clearly to knowing and prophesying, the two activities that are said to be done "partially, imperfectly" in verse 9 (also using in both cases the same Greek phrase, *ek merous*). To bring out this connection, we could translate,

> Love never ends. As for prophecies, they will pass away; as for tongues, they will cease; as for knowledge, it will *pass away*. For we know *in part* and we prophesy *in part*, but when the perfect comes, the *"in part"* [ESV, "the partial"] will *pass away*. (1 Cor. 13:8–10)

Thus the strong links between the statements are made clear by the repetition of two key terms, *pass away* and *partial*.

No doubt Paul also intended tongues to be included in the sense of verse 9 as among those activities that are "partial" but omitted overly pedantic repetition for stylistic reasons. Yet tongues must be understood as part of the sense of verse 9, for verse 9 is the reason for verse 8, as the word *for* (Gk. *gar*) shows. Thus verse 9 must give the reason why tongues, as well as knowledge and prophecy, will cease. In fact, the repeated "if . . . if . . . if" in verse 8 suggests that Paul could have listed more gifts here (wisdom, healing, interpretation?) if he had wished.

So 1 Corinthians 13:10 could be paraphrased, "When the perfect is come, *prophecy and tongues and other imperfect gifts* will pass away." The only remaining problem is to determine what time is meant by the word *when*. Several factors argue that the time of the Lord's return is what Paul has in mind.

(1) First, the meaning of verse 12 seems to require that verse 10 is talking about the time of the Lord's return. The word *then* (Gk. *tote*) in verse 12 refers to the time "when

the perfect comes" in verse 10. This is evident from looking at verse 12: "For now we see in a mirror dimly, but then face to face. Now I know in part; *then* I shall know fully, even as I have been fully known."

When shall we see "face to face"? When shall we know "even as we have been fully known"? These events can only happen when the Lord returns.

The phrase "see face to face" is several times used in the Old Testament to refer to seeing God personally[26]—not fully or exhaustively, for no finite creature can ever do that, but personally and truly nonetheless. So when Paul says, "but then face to face," he clearly means, "but then *we shall see God* face to face." Indeed, that will be the greatest blessing of heaven and our greatest joy for all eternity (Rev. 22:4: "They will see his face").

The second half of verse 12 says, "Now I know in part; then I shall know fully, even as I have been fully known." The second and third word for "know"—the one used for "then I shall *know* fully, even as I have been fully *known*"—is a somewhat stronger word for knowing (Gk. *epiginōskō*), but it certainly does not imply infinite knowledge or omniscience. Paul does not expect to know all things, and he does not say, "Then I shall know all things," which would have been easy to say in Greek.[27] Rather, he means that when the Lord returns, Paul expects to be freed from the misconceptions and inabilities to understand (especially to understand God and his work) that are part of this present life. His knowledge will resemble God's present knowledge of him because it will contain no false impressions and will not be limited to what is able to be perceived in this age. But such knowledge will only occur when the Lord returns.

Now what is the word *then* in verse 12 referring to? Paul says, "For now we see in a mirror dimly, but *then* we shall see face to face. Now I know in part; but *then* I shall know even as I have been known" (author's translation). The word *then* has to refer back to something in the previous verses that he has been explaining. We look first to verse 11, but we see that nothing in verse 11 can be a future time Paul refers to as "then": "When I was a child, I spoke like a child, I thought like a child, I reasoned like a child; when I became a man, I gave up childish ways." All of this refers to the past, not the future. It speaks of past events in Paul's life by way of providing a natural human illustration of what he has said in verse 10. But nothing in the verse speaks of a future time when something *will* happen.

So we look back to verse 10: "When the perfect comes, the partial will pass away." Here is a statement about the future. At some point in the future, Paul says that "the perfect" *will* come, and "the partial" *will* pass away, *will* be "made useless." When will

---

26. See, for example, Gen. 32:30 and Judg. 6:22 (exactly the same Greek wording as 1 Cor. 13:12); Deut. 5:4; 34:10; Ezek. 20:35 (very similar wording); Ex. 33:11 (the same concept and the same wording as some of the preceding passages in Hebrew but different wording in the Septuagint).

27. Greek *epignōsomai ta panta* would say, "I shall know all things."

this happen? This is what is explained by verse 12. *Then*, at the time the perfect comes, we shall see "face to face" and know "even as we are known."

This means that the time when "the perfect" comes must be the time of Christ's return.[28] Therefore, we can paraphrase verse 10: "But *when Christ returns*, the partial will pass away."[29] Or to use our conclusion above that "the partial" included prophecy and tongues, we can paraphrase, "But *when Christ returns, prophecy and tongues (and other partial gifts) will pass away*." Thus we have in 1 Corinthians 13:10 a definite statement about the time of the cessation of imperfect gifts like prophecy: they will "be made useless" or "pass away" *when Christ returns*. And this would imply that they will continue to exist and be useful for the church, throughout the church age, including today, and right up to the day when Christ returns.

(2) Another reason why the time when "the perfect" comes is the time when Christ returns is also evident from the purpose of the passage: Paul is attempting to emphasize the greatness of love, and in so doing he wants to establish that "Love never ends" (1 Cor. 13:8). To prove his point he argues that it will last beyond the time when the Lord returns, unlike present spiritual gifts. This makes a convincing argument: love is so fundamental to God's plans for the universe that it will last beyond the transition from this age to the age to come at Christ's return—it will continue for eternity.

(3) A third reason why this passage refers to the time of the Lord's return can be found in a more general statement from Paul about the purpose of spiritual gifts in the New Testament age. In 1 Corinthians 1:7 Paul ties the possession of spiritual gifts (Gk. *charismata*) to the activity of waiting for the Lord's return: "You are not lacking in any gift, as you wait for the revealing of our Lord Jesus Christ."

This suggests that Paul saw the gifts as a temporary provision made to equip believers for ministry *until the Lord returns*. So this verse provides a close parallel to the thought of 1 Corinthians 13:8–13, where prophecy and knowledge (and no doubt tongues) are seen, similarly, as useful until Christ's return but unnecessary beyond that time.

1 Corinthians 13:10, therefore, refers to the time of Christ's return and says that these spiritual gifts will last among believers until that time. This means that we have a clear biblical statement that Paul expected these gifts to continue through the entire church age and to function for the benefit of the church until the Lord returns.

---

28. I have stated it this way because, more precisely, "the perfect" in 1 Cor. 13:10 is not Christ himself but is the kind of knowledge that is so superior to present knowledge and prophecy that it makes these two obsolete. For when this "perfect" comes, it renders the partial (imperfect) useless. But only the kind of knowledge Paul expected in the final consummation of all things could be so qualitatively different from present knowledge that it could provide this kind of contrast and be called "the perfect" as opposed to "the partial."

29. D. A. Carson, *Showing the Spirit: A Theological Exposition of 1 Corinthians 12–14* (Grand Rapids: Baker, 1987),

70–72, gives several similar reasons why the time "when the perfect comes" must be the time of Christ's return (with references to other views, and to the relevant literature).

Among "cessationists" (those who hold that gifts such as prophecy have "ceased" and are not valid for today), some, but not all, agree that the time "when the perfect comes" must be the time of Christ's return. See John F. MacArthur Jr., *The Charismatics: A Doctrinal Perspective* (Grand Rapids: Zondervan, 1978), 165–66; and Richard B. Gaffin, *Perspectives on Pentecost* (Phillipsburg, NJ: Presbyterian and Reformed, 1979), 109.

**c. Objections.** Various objections to this conclusion have been raised, usually by those who hold that these gifts have ceased in the church and should no longer be used.

**1. This passage does not specify when the gifts will cease.** The first objection to our conclusion above comes from Richard Gaffin's thoughtful study *Perspectives on Pentecost*. While Gaffin agrees that "when the perfect comes" refers to the time of Christ's return, he does not think that this verse specifies the time of the cessation of certain gifts. He thinks, rather, that Paul is just viewing "the entire period until Christ's return, without regard to whether or not discontinuities may intervene during the course of this period."[30]

In fact, Gaffin argues, Paul's overall purpose is to emphasize the enduring qualities of faith, hope, and love, especially love, and not to specify the time in which certain gifts will cease. Gaffin says,

> Paul is not intending to specify the time when any particular mode will cease. What he does affirm is the termination of the believer's present, fragmentary knowledge ... when "the perfect" comes. The time of the cessation of prophecy and tongues is an open question so far as this passage is concerned and will have to be decided on the basis of other passages and considerations.[31]

He also says that, in addition to prophecy, tongues, and knowledge, Paul might just as well have added "inscripturation" too—and if he had done this, the list would then have included an element that ceased long before Christ's return. (Inscripturation is the process of writing Scripture.) So, Gaffin concludes, it might be true of some of the others in the list as well.

In response to this objection it must be said that it does not do justice to the actual words of the text. Evangelicals have rightly insisted (and I know that Gaffin agrees with this) that passages of Scripture are true not only in the main point of each passage but also in the minor details that are affirmed as well. The main point of the passage may well be that love lasts forever, but another point, and certainly an important one as well, is that verse 10 affirms not just that these imperfect gifts will cease *sometime*, but that they will cease "*when* the perfect comes." Paul specifies a certain time: "*When the perfect comes*, the imperfect will pass away." But Gaffin seems to claim that Paul is not actually saying this. Yet the force of the words cannot be avoided by affirming that the overall theme of the larger context is something else.

---

30. Gaffin, *Perspectives on Pentecost*, 109–10. Thomas Schreiner takes the same position as Gaffin on this question. He says, "Though 1 Corinthians 13:8–12 tells us the gifts will end when Christ returns, it doesn't require that all the gifts last until Jesus returns" (Thomas Schreiner, *Spiritual Gifts: What They Are and Why They Matter* [Nashville: B&H, 2018], 156).

It is not clear to me how the first and second halves of this sentence fit together. It seems to me to be saying (1) the gifts will end when Christ returns, and (2) some gifts may end before Christ returns.

31. Ibid., 111.

In addition, Gaffin's suggestion does not seem to fit with the logic of the passage. Paul's argument is that it is specifically the coming of "the perfect," which does away with prophecy, tongues, and knowledge, because then there is a new far-superior way of learning and knowing things "even as I have been known." But *until* that time, the new and superior way of knowing has not come, and therefore these imperfect gifts are still valid and useful. Finally, it is precarious to put much weight on something we think Paul might have said but in fact did not say. To say that Paul might have included "inscripturation" in this list means that Paul might have written, "When Christ returns, inscripturation will cease." But I cannot believe at all that Paul could have written such a statement, for it would have been false—indeed, a "false prophecy" in the words of Scripture. For "inscripturation" ceased long before Christ's second coming. It ceased when the book of Revelation was written by the apostle John.[32]

So Gaffin's objections do not seem to overturn our conclusions on 1 Corinthians 13:10. If "the perfect" refers to the time of Christ's return, then Paul says that gifts such as prophecy and tongues will cease at that time, and implies therefore that they continue through the church age.

**2. "When the perfect comes" in 1 Corinthians 13:10 refers to a time earlier than the time of the Lord's return.** Those who make this second objection argue that "when the perfect comes" means one of several different things, such as "when the church is mature" or "when Scripture is complete" or "when the gentiles are included in the church." Probably the most careful statement of this view is found in the book by Robert L. Reymond, *What about Continuing Revelations and Miracles in the Presbyterian*

---

32. R. Fowler White, however, argued that Gaffin's viewpoint on 1 Corinthians 13:10 was correct and mine was incorrect in "Richard Gaffin and Wayne Grudem on 1 Cor. 13:10: A Comparison of the Cessationist and Noncessationist Argumentation," JETS 35, no. 2 (June 1992): 173–81. White's argument is that Gaffin correctly understands Paul to be comparing the *state of knowledge* we have during this age with the state of knowledge we will have after Christ's return, but Grudem incorrectly thinks Paul is comparing the *means of acquiring knowledge* now (spiritual gifts) with the means of acquiring knowledge after Christ returns. The reason White gives is that the expression *ek merous* ("in part, partial") clearly refers to the state of knowledge before Christ returns in verse 12, and so it must refer to the state of knowledge in verses 9 and 10 as well. He says, "Finally, and most importantly, since the prepositional phrase *ek merous* describes the present state of knowledge in v. 12 we should interpret its function in vv. 9–10 in a similar fashion" (178). Therefore the dominant theme of verses 9–12 "is the knowledge that the gifts convey, not the gifts that convey the knowledge" (179). He criticizes me because, he says, Grudem "interprets the function of *ek merous* in vv. 9–10 and v. 12 in an inconsistent fashion—as a description of gifts in the former but as a description of knowledge in the latter—and thereby obscures the unity of Paul's argument" (179).

Remarkably, White fails even to mention a third possibility, which is the position I actually hold. That is the view that the partial nature of *gifts* in this present age ("we prophesy in part," v. 9) results in partial *knowledge* in this present age ("Now I know in part; then I shall know fully," v. 12). Therefore, it is Paul himself who uses the phrase *ek merous* ("in part, partial") to refer both to the means of acquiring knowledge and to the knowledge that results from those means. I was not "inconsistent" (as White claims, p. 179) in understanding this prepositional phrase as applying both to the gift and to the knowledge that results from that gift, for I was being faithful to the meaning of the passage itself. White's argument is based on the strange (and unproven) assumption that if an author uses a prepositional phrase to modify item XYZ in one place, then he can only use it to modify item XYZ in other places. But language does not work that way.

Therefore, the point still remains that Paul is not merely talking about different states of knowledge, but he is clearly talking about the time when miraculous gifts will cease in 1 Corinthians 13:10. And his meaning is, "When Christ returns, prophecy (and other miraculous but only partially effective gifts) will cease."

*Church Today?*,[33] but another clear statement of a similar position is found in Walter Chantry's book, *Signs of the Apostles*.[34]

Chantry's argument depends on the fact that elsewhere in 1 Corinthians the word here translated "perfect" (Gk. *teleios*) is used to refer to human maturity (1 Cor. 14:20, "in your thinking be mature") or to maturity in the Christian life (as in 1 Cor. 2:6). Yet here again we must note that a word does not have to be used to refer to the same thing every time it is used in Scripture—in some cases *teleios* may refer to "mature" or "perfect" manhood, in other cases some other kind of "completeness" or "perfection." The word *teleios* is used in Hebrews 9:11, for example, to refer to the "more perfect tent"—yet we would not therefore conclude that "perfect" in 1 Corinthians 13:10 must refer to a perfect tent. The precise referent of the word must be determined by the individual context, and there, as we have seen, the context indicates that "when the perfect comes" refers to the time of Christ's return.

Reymond's argument is somewhat different. He reasons as follows:

a.  "The imperfect" things mentioned in verses 9–10—prophecy, tongues, and knowledge—are incomplete means of revelation, "all relating to God's making his will known to his church."

b.  "The perfect" in this context must refer to something in the same category as the "imperfect" things.

c.  Therefore, "the perfect" in this context must refer to a means of revelation, but a completed one. And this completed means of God's making his will known to his church is Scripture.

d.  Conclusion: "When the perfect comes" refers to the time when the canon of Scripture will be complete.[35]

Reymond notes that he is not saying that "the perfect" refers exactly to the canon of Scripture but rather to "the completed revelatory process" that resulted in Scripture. And in response to the objection that "then we shall see face to face" in verse 12 refers to seeing God face to face, he answers that it may not mean this but may simply mean seeing "plainly" as opposed to "obscurely."[36]

In response, it may be said that this argument, while careful and consistent in itself, still depends on one prior assumption that is really the point at issue in this whole discussion: the authority of New Testament prophecy and related gifts. Once Reymond

33. Robert L. Reymond, *What About Continuing Revelations and Miracles in the Presbyterian Church Today?* (Phillipsburg, NJ: Presbyterian and Reformed, 1977), 32–34. Kenneth L. Gentry Jr., *The Charismatic Gift of Prophecy: A Reformed Analysis* (Memphis: Whitefield Seminary Press, 1986), 31–33, lists both this view and the view of Gaffin (see objection 1 above) as acceptable options. See also the entries under Robert

Thomas, Victor Budgen, and Thomas Edgar in the bibliography to chapter 53, pp. 1137–39.

34. Walter J. Chantry, *Signs of the Apostles*, 2nd ed. (Edinburgh: Banner of Truth, 1976), 50–52.

35. Reymond, *What About Continuing Revelations and Miracles*, 34.

36. Ibid., 32.

assumes that prophecy (and tongues and the kind of "knowledge" mentioned here) are Scripture-quality revelation, the whole argument falls into place. The argument could be recast as follows:

a. Prophecy and tongues are Scripture-quality revelation.
b. Therefore, this whole passage is about Scripture-quality revelation.
c. Therefore, "the perfect" refers to the perfection or completion of Scripture-quality revelation, or the completion of Scripture.

In such an argument the initial assumption determines the conclusion. However, before this assumption can be made, it needs to be demonstrated from an inductive analysis of the New Testament texts on prophecy.[37] Yet, to my knowledge, no such inductive demonstration of the Scripture-quality authority of New Testament congregational prophecy has been made.

Moreover, there are some other factors in the text of 1 Corinthians 13:8–13 that are hard to reconcile with Reymond's position. The regular Old Testament usage of seeing "face to face" as an expression not just for seeing clearly but for *personally* seeing God (see above) remains unexplained. And the fact that Paul includes himself in the expressions "Then *we* shall see face to face" and "Then I shall know fully, even as I have been fully known" make it difficult to view these as references to the time of the completion of Scripture. Does Paul really think that when the other apostles finally finish their contributions to the New Testament, he will suddenly gain such a remarkable change in his knowledge that he will know as he has been known, and he will go from seeing in a mirror dimly to seeing face to face?

In addition to the views of Reymond and Chantry, there have been other attempts to see "when the perfect comes" as some time before Christ's return, but we will not treat them in detail here. Such views all break down at verse 12, where Paul implies that believers will see God "face to face" "when the perfect comes." This cannot be said about the time suggested in any of these other proposals.

The proposal about the completion of the canon of New Testament Scripture (the group of writings that came to be included in the New Testament) also fails to fit Paul's purpose in the context. If we take AD 90 as the approximate date of the writing of Revelation, the last New Testament book written, then the end of the writing of Scripture came about thirty-five years after Paul wrote 1 Corinthians (about AD 55). But would it be persuasive to argue as follows: "We can be sure that love will *never* end, for we know that it will last more than thirty-five years"? This would hardly be a convincing argument. The context requires rather that Paul be contrasting this age with the age to come, and

---

37. See chapter 53, pp. 1293–1313, for a fuller discussion of the gift of prophecy; also Grudem, *The Gift of Prophecy in the New Testament and Today*.

saying that love will endure into eternity.[38] In fact, we see a similar procedure elsewhere in 1 Corinthians. When Paul wants to demonstrate the eternal value of something, he does this by arguing that it will last beyond the day of the Lord's return (cf, 1 Cor. 3:13–15; 15:51–58). By contrast, prophecy and other gifts will not last beyond that day.

Finally, these proposals fail to find any support in the immediate context. Whereas Christ's return is clearly implied in verse 12, no verse in this section mentions anything about the completion of Scripture or a collection of the books of the New Testament or the inclusion of the gentiles in the church or the "maturity" of the church (whatever that means—is the church really mature even today?). All of these suggestions bring in new elements not found in the context to replace the one element—Christ's return—which clearly is right there in the context already. In fact, Richard Gaffin, who holds that the gift of prophecy is not valid for today, nevertheless says that the "perfect" in verse 10 and the "then" in verse 12 "no doubt refer to the time of Christ's return. The view that they describe the point at which the New Testament canon is completed cannot be made credible exegetically."[39]

D. Martyn Lloyd-Jones observes that the view that makes "when the perfect comes" equal the time of the completion of the New Testament encounters another difficulty:

> It means that you and I, who have the Scriptures open before us, know much more than the apostle Paul of God's truth. . . . It means that we are altogether superior . . . even to the apostles themselves, including the apostle Paul! It means that we are now in a position in which . . . "we know, even as also we are known" by God. . . . Indeed, there is only one word to describe such a view, it is nonsense.[40]

And John Calvin, referring to 1 Corinthians 13:8–13, says, "It is stupid of people to make the whole of this discussion apply to the intervening time."[41]

## 2. Would the Continuation of Prophecy Today Challenge the Sufficiency of Scripture?

**a. The Authority of the Gift of Prophecy.** Those who take a cessationist view argue that once the last New Testament book was written (probably the book of Revelation around AD 90), there were to be no more "words of God" spoken or written in the church. This is especially relevant for the gift of prophecy, according to the cessationist

---

38. Some argue that faith and hope will not endure in heaven, so 1 Cor. 13:13 only means that faith and hope last until, not beyond, Christ's return. However, if faith is dependence on God and trust in him, and if hope is a confident expectation of future blessings to be received from God, then there is no reason to think that we will cease to have faith and hope in heaven. (See Carson's good discussion of faith, hope, and love as "eternally permanent virtues" in *Showing the Spirit*, 74–75.)

39. Gaffin, *Perspectives*, 109; cf. Max Turner, "Spiritual Gifts Then and Now," *Vox Evangelica* 15 (1985): 38.
40. D. Martyn Lloyd-Jones, *Prove All Things*, ed. Christopher Catherwood (Eastbourne, UK: Kingsway, 1985), 32–33.
41. John Calvin, *The First Epistle of Paul the Apostle to the Corinthians*, trans. J. W. Fraser, ed. D. W. Torrance and T. F. Torrance (Grand Rapids: Eerdmans, 1960), 281 (on 1 Cor. 13:10).

position, because from that point on *Scripture* was the complete and sufficient source of God's words for his people. To add any more words from continuing prophetic utterances would be, in effect, either to add to Scripture or to compete with Scripture. In both cases, the sufficiency of Scripture itself would be challenged, and, in practice, its unique authority in our lives compromised.

Now *if* New Testament congregational prophecy was like Old Testament prophecy and New Testament apostolic words in its authority, then this cessationist objection would indeed be true. *If* prophets today, for example, spoke words that we knew were the very words of God, then these words *would be* equal to Scripture in authority, and we *would be* obligated to write them down and add them to our Bibles whenever we heard them. But if we are convinced that God stopped causing Scripture to be written when the book of Revelation was completed, then we have to say that *this* kind of speech, uttering the very words of God, cannot happen today. And any claims to have "new" Scripture, "new" words of God, must be rejected as false.

This question is very important because the claim that New Testament congregational prophecy had authority equal to Scripture is the basis of many cessationist arguments. Yet it must be noted that continuationists (or noncessationists) do not seem to view prophecy that way. George Mallone writes, "To my knowledge no noncessationist in the mainstream of Christianity claims that revelation today is equal with Scripture."[42] Perhaps it would be good for those arguing against continuing prophecy today to give a more sympathetic hearing to the most responsible charismatic writers, simply for the purpose of being able to respond to something that charismatics *actually believe* (even if not always expressed in theologically precise form), instead of responding to something that cessationists *say* that charismatics believe or say that charismatics should believe.

Furthermore, aside from the question of current practice or belief, I have argued extensively elsewhere that ordinary congregational prophecy in New Testament churches did *not* have the authority of Scripture.[43] It was not spoken in words that were the very words of God but rather in merely human words. And because it has this lesser authority, there is no reason to think that it will not continue in the church until Christ returns. It does not threaten or compete with Scripture in authority but is subject to Scripture, as well as to the mature judgment of the congregation.

**b. The Question of Guidance.** Another objection is sometimes raised at this point. Some will argue that even if those who use the gift of prophecy today *say* that it does not equal Scripture in authority, *in fact* it functions in their lives to compete with or even

---

42. George Mallone, *Those Controversial Gifts* (Downers Grove, IL: InterVarsity Press, 1983), 21.

43. For further discussion of the authority of the gift of prophecy, see chapter 53, pp. 1293–1313. See also Wayne Grudem, *The Gift of Prophecy in 1 Corinthians* (Lanham, MD: University Press of America, 1982); Grudem, *The Gift*

*of Prophecy in the New Testament and Today*; D. A. Carson, *Showing the Spirit: A Theological Exposition of 1 Corinthians 12–14*, 91–100; Graham Houston, *Prophecy: A Gift For Today?* (Downers Grove, IL: InterVarsity Press, 1989). (Alternative views are noted in the discussion in chapter 53; see esp. the book by Richard Gaffin, *Perspectives on Pentecost*.)

replace Scripture in giving guidance concerning God's will. Thus prophecy today, it is said, challenges the doctrine of the sufficiency of Scripture for guidance in our lives.[44]

Here it must be admitted that many mistakes have been made in the history of the church. John MacArthur points to the way in which the idea of further revelations has given rise to many heretical movements in the church.[45]

But here the question must be: Are abuses *necessary* to the functioning of the gift of prophecy? If we are to argue that mistakes and abuses of a gift make the gift itself invalid, then we would have to reject Bible teaching (for many Bible teachers have taught error and started cults) and church administration as well (for many church leaders have led people astray), and so forth. The *abuse* of a gift does not mean that we must prohibit the *proper use* of the gift, unless it can be shown that there cannot be proper use—that *all* use has to be abuse.[46]

Moreover, specifically with respect to guidance, it is good to note how cautious many in the charismatic movement are about the use of prophecy to give specific guidance. Several quotations will illustrate this point.

Michael Harper (Church of England):

> Prophecies which tell other people what they are to do—are to be regarded with great suspicion.[47]

Dennis and Rita Bennett (American Episcopalians):

> We should also be careful of personal, directive prophecy, especially outside the ministry of a mature and submitted man of God. Unrestrained "personal prophecy"

---

44. I have written more extensively about the question of guidance elsewhere. See Wayne Grudem, *Christian Ethics* (Wheaton, IL: Crossway, 2018), chapter 6, 148–88 ("How to Know God's Will"), and (the same material published as a short book) Wayne Grudem, *What the Bible Says about How to Know God's Will* (Wheaton, IL: Crossway, 2020).

45. MacArthur, *The Charismatics: A Doctrinal Perspective*, chapters 2–6; see esp. pp. 27ff. MacArthur has expanded his criticisms in an updated edition, *Charismatic Chaos* (Grand Rapids: Zondervan, 1992), 47–84. A thoughtful and extensive critique of MacArthur is found in Rich Nathan, *A Response to Charismatic Chaos* (Anaheim, CA: Association of Vineyard Churches, 1993). MacArthur's latest critique of the charismatic movement is *Strange Fire: The Danger of Offending the Holy Spirit with Counterfeit Worship* (Nashville: Nelson, 2013).

46. Some may object that prophecy has more potential for abuse than other gifts because the idea that God can reveal things to people today (in prophecies) inevitably leads to competition with the authority of Scripture. In response, three points can be made: (1) Teaching on the fallible nature of all contemporary prophecies has not been as extensive as needed to prevent abuse, especially at the popular level, among groups that allow prophecy today. Therefore, there has been more misuse of prophecy than there should have been. Even where strong cautions have been proclaimed, there has seldom been an explanation of how prophecy can be from God but still not equal to God's words in authority—that is, very few Pentecostal or charismatic writers have explained prophecy as a *human* report of something that God has spontaneously brought to mind (the view which I defend in chapter 53, pp. 1293–1313). (However, see the helpful cautions from several charismatic writers in the following paragraphs in the text above.) (2) It is simply not true that teaching a congregation that prophecy must always be *subject* to Scripture inevitably leads people to exalt prophecies *above* Scripture. This will happen where such teaching is neglected, not where it is propagated. (3) If the Bible indeed teaches that prophecy can be expected to continue today in a form that does not challenge scriptural authority, then we are not free to reject it because we recognize a potential for abuse. (Other gifts have potential for abuse in other areas.) Rather, we should encourage the gift and do our best to guard against abuse.

47. Michael Harper, *Prophecy: A Gift for the Body of Christ* (Plainhill, NJ: Logos, 1964), 26.

did much to undermine the movement of the Holy Spirit which began at the turn of the century.... Christians are certainly given words for one another "in the Lord" ... and such words can be most refreshing and helpful, but there must be a witness of the Spirit on the part of the person receiving the words, and extreme caution should be used in receiving any alleged directive or predictive prophecy. Never undertake any project simply because you were told to by presumed prophetic utterance or interpretation of tongues, or by a presumed word of wisdom, or knowledge. Never do something just because a friend comes to you and says: "The Lord told me to tell you to do thus and thus." If the Lord has instructions for you, He will give you a witness in your own heart, in which case the words coming from a friend ... will be a confirmation to what God *has already been* showing you. Your guidance must also agree with Scripture.[48]

Donald Gee (Assemblies of God):

[There are] grave problems raised by the habit of giving and receiving personal "messages" of guidance through the gifts of the Spirit.... The Bible gives a place for such direction from the Holy Spirit.... But it must be kept in proportion. An examination of the Scriptures will show us that as a matter of fact the early Christians did *not* continually receive such voices from heaven. In most cases they made their decisions by the use of what we often call "sanctified common-sense" and lived quite normal lives. Many of our errors where spiritual gifts are concerned arise when we want the extraordinary and exceptional to be made the frequent and habitual. Let all who develop excessive desire for "messages" through the gifts take warning from the wreckage of past generations as well as of contemporaries.... The Holy Scriptures are a lamp unto our feet and a light unto our path.[49]

On the other hand, even among very Reformed cessationists, there is a willingness to admit some kind of continuing "illumination" by the Holy Spirit in believers' lives. For example, Richard Gaffin says,

Often, too, what is seen as prophecy is actually a spontaneous, Spirit-worked application of Scripture, a more or less sudden grasp of the bearing that biblical teaching has on a particular situation or problem. All Christians need to be open to these more spontaneous workings of the Spirit.[50]

---

48. Dennis and Rita Bennett, *The Holy Spirit and You*, 107.

49. Donald Gee, *Spiritual Gifts in the Work of Ministry Today* (Springfield, MO: Gospel, 1963), 51–52.

50. Gaffin, *Perspectives*, 120.

And Robert Reymond defines *illumination* as "the Holy Spirit's enabling of Christians generally to understand, to recall to mind, and to apply the Scriptures they have studied."[51]

But if these writers will allow for the present activity of the Holy Spirit enabling Christians to "understand" or "recall to mind" or "apply" or "grasp" the teachings of Scripture, then there does not seem to be such a great difference in principle between what they are *saying* and what many in the charismatic movement are *doing* (even though there will probably be some remaining differences over the precise way guidance functions—yet this is not so much a difference about prophecy as about guidance generally, and particularly the way guidance from Scripture relates to guidance from advice, counsel, conscience, circumstances, sermons, etc.). The larger point is that what Gaffin and Reymond here call "illumination," the New Testament seems to call a "revelation," and what they would call a spoken report of such illumination, the New Testament seems to call a "prophecy."

So I wonder if there may be room for more joint theological reflection in this area. Charismatics need to realize that cessationists are skeptical about the scope and frequency of such "illumination," whether it is right to call it New Testament prophecy, whether it really does have value for the church, and whether it should be sought after. And cessationists need to realize that their highly developed and carefully formulated doctrine of the sufficiency of Scripture in guidance is not usually shared or even understood by much of evangelicalism, including those in the charismatic movement. Nevertheless, perhaps the Reformed idea of "illumination" allows for what is happening in prophecy today and may provide a way of understanding it that is not seen as challenging the sufficiency of Scripture.

What shall we conclude then about the relationship between the gift of prophecy and the sufficiency of Scripture? We must say that we appreciate the desire of the cessationists to protect the uniqueness of Scripture and not to allow anything to compete with the authority of Scripture in our lives. We also must be thankful for the desire of cessationists that Christians understand and follow sound principles of guidance in their daily lives and not get off into an area of excessive subjectivism that does not have the controls of Scripture attached to it. On the other hand, there is certainly a danger that comes with the cessationist viewpoint if it is wrong here. It is the very real danger of opposing something that God is doing in the church today and failing to give him glory for that work. God is jealous for his works and seeks glory from them for himself, and we must continually pray not only that he would keep us from endorsing error but also that he would keep us from opposing something that is genuinely from him.

---

51. Reymond, *What About Continuing Revelations and Miracles*, 28–29.

### 3. Were Miraculous Gifts Limited to the Apostles and Their Companions?

Another cessationist argument is that miraculous gifts were limited to the apostles and their close companions. Since I have discussed this argument at length in chapter 17, I will not repeat the discussion here.[52]

### 4. Did Miraculous Gifts Only Accompany the Giving of New Scripture?

Another objection is to say that miraculous gifts accompanied the giving of Scripture and served to authenticate the giving of new Scripture, but since there is no new Scripture given today, we should expect no new miracles today.

But in response to that it must be said that this is not the only purpose for miraculous gifts. As we noted in chapter 17, miracles have several other purposes in Scripture: (1) they authenticate the gospel message throughout the church age; (2) they give help to those in need and thereby demonstrate God's mercy and love; (3) they equip people for ministry; and (4) they glorify God.[53]

We should also note that not all miracles accompany the giving of additional Scripture. For example, the ministries of Elijah and Elisha were marked by several miracles in the Old Testament, but they wrote no books or sections of the Bible. In fact, Jack Deere points out that Jeremiah (ministered 626 BC to sometime after 586 BC) claims that miracles have occurred throughout the entire history of Israel since the exodus: "You have shown signs and wonders in the land of Egypt, *and to this day* in Israel and among all mankind, and have made a name for yourself, as at this day" (Jer. 32:20).[54]

In the New Testament, there were many occurrences of miracles that were not accompanied by the giving of Scripture. Both Stephen and Philip in the book of Acts worked miracles but wrote no Scripture. There were prophets who wrote no Scripture in Caesarea (Acts 21:4), Tyre (Acts 21:9–11), Rome (Rom. 12:6), Thessalonica (1 Thess. 5:20–21), Ephesus (Eph. 4:11), and the communities to which 1 John was written (1 John 4:1–6). There were apparently many miracles in the churches of Galatia (Gal. 3:5), but these churches did not produce any books of Scripture. Many miraculous things were occurring at Corinth (1 Cor. 12:8–10), but Paul denies that any Scripture has come forth from the Corinthian church (1 Cor. 14:36).[55] And James expects that healing will occur at the hands of the elders in all the churches to which he writes (see James 5:14–16), but certainly not all of these churches were producing Scripture.

---

52. See chapter 17, pp. 484–85, for a discussion of the question of whether miraculous gifts were limited to the apostles and their close companions.

53. See chapter 17, pp. 475–77, for a discussion of these purposes for miracles.

54. See Jack Deere's extensive evaluation of evidence that

God worked miracles throughout the entire time of biblical history in Jack Deere, *Surprised by the Power of the Spirit* (Grand Rapids: Zondervan, 1993), 253–66. He discusses Jeremiah 32:20 on p. 254.

55. See chapter 53, p. 1299, for a discussion of 1 Cor. 14:36.

## 5. Is It a Historical Fact That Miraculous Gifts Ceased Early in the History of the Church?

Some cessationists have argued that miraculous gifts in fact ceased when the apostles died because the purpose of miracles was to give authentication to the apostles. For this reason, it is argued, there should be no miraculous gifts today. B. B. Warfield argued this extensively in his book *Counterfeit Miracles.*[56]

In response, it must be said first that the premise just stated is very doubtful on historical grounds. There is increasing historical evidence[57] that miraculous gifts were occurring throughout the history of the church in greater or lesser degree, even when exaggerated or evidently spurious claims are discounted. Healings and other kinds of miraculous answers to prayer are often recorded. There were also people claiming to be prophets throughout the history of the early church—the problem was that too often they misunderstood their gift, or others misunderstood it, so that their utterances were (mistakenly) treated like actual words of God. Sometimes they would be tolerated, and sometimes they were too much of a threat to the established leadership of the churches and they would begin splinter groups—tragically, no longer under the restraining and evaluating authority of the established churches. Then, too, others may have had "revelations" given to them that they then did not express or that they included without comment in a prayer or in a sermon or word of exhortation or in the writing of a hymn or some devotional literature.[58]

---

56. It should be noted that Warfield's argument, though frequently quoted, is really a historical survey, not an analysis of biblical texts. Moreover, Warfield's purpose was not to refute any use of spiritual gifts among Christians like those in the charismatic movement today, whose doctrine (on all matters other than spiritual gifts) and whose church affiliation put them in the mainstream of evangelical Protestantism. Warfield rather was refuting the spurious claims to miracles which had come from some branches of Roman Catholicism at various periods in the history of the church, and from various heretical sects (Warfield includes discussion of the followers of Edward Irving [1792–1834], who strayed into eccentric teachings and was excommunicated from the Church of Scotland in 1833). It is open to question whether modern-day cessationists are right to claim Warfield's support when opposing something which is far different in doctrine and life from that which Warfield himself opposed.

57. Warfield's position has come in for criticism from several evangelical studies; see Max Turner, "Spiritual Gifts Then and Now," *Vox Evangelica* 15 (1985): 41–43, with notes to other literature; Donald Bridge, *Signs and Wonders Today* (Leicester: Inter-Varsity Press, 1985), 166–77; and Ronald A. Kydd, *Charismatic Gifts in the Early Church* (Peabody, MA: Hendrickson, 1984). Significant evidence of miraculous gifts in early church history is found in Eusebius A. Stephanou, "The Charismata in the Early Church Fathers," *The Greek Orthodox Theological Review* 21, no. 2 (Summer 1976): 125–46.

A broad-ranging but popularly written study of the history of miraculous gifts in the church is found in Paul Thigpen, "Did the Power of the Spirit Ever Leave the Church?" *Charisma* 18, no. 2 (September 1992): 20–28. Most recently, see Jon Ruthven, *On the Cessation of the Charismata: The Protestant Polemic on Post-Biblical Miracles* (Sheffield: Sheffield University Academic Press, 1993); this is a revision and expansion of the author's PhD dissertation responding to the arguments of cessationists from Warfield to the present.

The argument from church history can be turned the other way by an analysis of events from about 1970 to the present. Church growth analysts tell us that Pentecostal and charismatic churches, which encourage miraculous gifts, are experiencing growth unprecedented in the history of the church. Fuller Seminary professor C. Peter Wagner says, "While back in 1945 Pentecostals/charismatics could count only sixteen million members worldwide, by 1975 they had grown to ninety-six million and then ten years later in 1985 they numbered an astounding 247 million. I am not aware of any non-political, non-militaristic voluntary association which has grown at that rate in all of human history" ("Exploring the Supernatural Dimensions of Church Growth," *Global Church Growth*, October–December 1988, 3). (By way of comparison, if the world population was 5 billion in 1985, then 247 million constituted 5 percent of the population of the world.)

58. We must realize that unless people understand prophecy as the fallible report of something that God spontaneously

When Paul said, "When the perfect comes, the partial will pass away" (1 Cor. 13:10), he was not saying anything about the relative *frequency* of miraculous gifts in the history of the church. That would be subject to much variation depending on the spiritual maturity and vitality of the church in various periods, the degree to which these gifts were sought as a blessing or rejected as a heresy, the frequency with which the meetings of Christians normally made provision for the exercise of these gifts, the degree to which the nature of these gifts was correctly understood, and, over all of this, the Holy Spirit's sovereign work in distributing gifts to the church.

What Paul is speaking about, however, is the total and final abolition of these gifts that is to be brought about by divine initiative at the return of Christ. And he is saying that he thinks that until the return of Christ these gifts will at least to some extent remain available for use, and the Holy Spirit will continue to distribute these gifts to people. Calvin notes the abundance of spiritual gifts in Paul's day and then comments (on 1 Cor. 14:32): "Today we see our own slender resources, our poverty in fact; but this is undoubtedly the punishment we deserve, as the reward for our ingratitude. For God's riches are not exhausted, nor has His liberality grown less; but we are not worthy of His largess, or capable of receiving all that He generously gives."[59]

## 6. Are Miraculous Gifts Today the Same As the Miraculous Gifts in Scripture?

Yet another objection to the continuation of miracles today is to say that the alleged miracles today are not like the miracles in Scripture because they are far weaker and often are only partially effective. In response we must ask whether it really matters whether the miracles today are exactly as powerful as those that occurred at the time of the New Testament. For one thing, we have very little information about the kind of miracles done by ordinary Christians in various congregations, such as the Christians at Corinth and in the churches in Galatia. Moreover, although remarkable miracles done by Jesus are recorded in the gospels, when Jesus healed "every disease and every afflic-tion" (Matt. 9:35), this must have included many with less serious diseases. We must also ask what the expected benefit is for the objection that miracles today are not as power-ful as those in Scripture. If today only three hundred are converted at an evangelistic

---

brings to mind, it will be very difficult for the church to encour-age or even tolerate it. If prophecy is indeed based on something God suddenly brings to mind, it would eventually be very easy for Christian prophets, whether for good or ill motives, to begin to claim not only that they had received a "revelation" from God or Christ but also that they spoke with a divine authority like that of Scripture. This apparently happened, at least in Mon-tanism (second century AD) and probably in many other cases as well. Of course, if these prophets began to promote heretical ideas, the reaction of the rest of the church would eventually be to drive them out altogether: someone who claims absolute

divine authority would eventually be accepted or rejected; he could not be merely tolerated.

But along with this rejection of prophets who misunder-stood their status, there was perhaps also a rejection of the gift of prophecy altogether, so that a failure on the part of the church to understand the nature of the gift of prophecy might have been the cause of a fairly complete suppression of at least the public expression of the gift of prophecy in the church.

59. Calvin, *The First Epistle of Paul the Apostle to the Cor-inthians*, 305.

meeting instead of the three thousand converted on the day of Pentecost (Acts 2:41), shall we say that the speaker does not really have the gift of evangelism, since the gift did not operate as powerfully as it did with the apostles? Or if only 30 percent of the people we pray for regarding physical illness are fully healed instead of 100 percent in the life of Jesus or of the apostles, shall we say this is not the New Testament gift of healing?[60] We must remember that gifts can vary in strength, and no gift is perfect in this age. But does that mean that we should stop using these gifts altogether or oppose them where we see them functioning with some degree of effectiveness? Shall we not praise God if 300 are converted rather than three thousand or if 30 percent are healed rather than 100 percent of those for whom we pray? Is not the work of the Lord being done? If the quantity is not as great as in New Testament times, then we may ask the Lord for more grace or mercy, but it does not seem appropriate to give up on the use of these gifts or to oppose those who do use them.

### 7. Is It Dangerous for a Church to Allow for the Possibility of Miraculous Gifts Today?

A final objection from the cessationist position is to say that a church that emphasizes the use of miraculous gifts is in danger of becoming imbalanced and will likely neglect other important things such as evangelism, sound doctrine, and moral purity of life.

To say that the use of miraculous gifts is "dangerous" is not by itself an adequate criticism because some things that are right are dangerous, at least in some sense. Missionary work is dangerous. Driving a car is dangerous. If we define dangerous to mean "something might go wrong," then we can criticize anything that anybody might do as "dangerous," and this just becomes an all-purpose criticism when there is no specific abuse to point to. A better approach with respect to spiritual gifts is to ask, "Are they being used in accordance with Scripture?" and "Are adequate steps being taken to guard against the dangers of abuse?"

---

60. The figure of 30 percent is simply an example for illustrative purposes, but it is close to two recent tabulations concerning people who received prayer for healing. One tabulation is found in David C. Lewis, *Healing: Fiction, Fantasy, or Fact?* (London: Hodder and Stoughton, 1989), an academic investigation of 1,890 people who attended one of John Wimber's conferences in Harrogate, England, in 1986. The author is a social anthropologist who prepared a detailed questionnaire that people filled out during the conference, and then followed up some randomly selected cases several months later. Of 862 cases of prayer for physical healing, 32 percent (or 279) reported a "great deal" of healing or "total healing." Another 26 percent (or 222) reported a "fair amount" of healing. The remaining 42 percent (or 366) reported "little" or "no healing" (pp. 21–22). Many case studies are reported in detail, in several instances with medical reports quoted at length. All the physical problems prayed for are listed in a detailed appendix (pp. 276–83). (These physical problems are distinguished from prayer for spiritual problems such as inner healing and deliverance, which are tabulated separately by Lewis.) The other tabulation is found in John Wimber with Kevin Springer, *Power Healing* (San Francisco: Harper and Row, 1987), 188, who says that, of people who received extended prayer for healing at his church, "During 1986 thirty-two percent of all people prayed for were completely healed, while overall eighty-six percent showed evidence of some significant healing." (D. A. Carson, *How Long, O Lord?* [Grand Rapids: Baker, 1990], 124, says, "Wimber is quite candid: he estimates that his 'success rate' is about 2 percent," but Carson gives no documentation for this statement, and it is apparently incorrect in light of what Wimber has actually written.)

Of course it is true that churches can become imbalanced, and some in fact have done so. But not all will, nor do they have to do so. Furthermore, since this argument is one based on actual results in the life of a church, it is also appropriate to ask: Which churches in the world today have the most effective evangelism? Which have the most sacrificial giving among their members? Which in fact have the most emphasis on purity of life? Which have the deepest love for the Lord and for his Word? It seems to me that it is difficult to answer these questions clearly, but I do not think that we can fairly say that those churches in the charismatic and Pentecostal movements *by and large* are *weaker* in these areas than other evangelical churches. In fact, in some cases they may be stronger in these areas. The point is simply that any argument that says that churches emphasizing miraculous gifts *will* become imbalanced is simply not proven in actual practice.

The most extreme critic of modern charismatic and Pentecostal Christians is probably John MacArthur. In the introduction to his book *Strange Fire*, MacArthur says,

> The Charismatic Movement. . . . is the fastest-growing religious movement in the world. Charismatics now number more than half a billion worldwide. Yet the gospel that is driving those surging numbers is not the true gospel, and the spirit behind them is not the Holy Spirit. What we are seeing is *in reality* the explosive growth of a false church as dangerous as any cult or heresy that has ever assaulted Christianity. The Charismatic Movement was a farce and a scam from the outset; it has not changed into something good.[61]

MacArthur then proceeds to report dozens of examples of unbiblical teachings, immoral behavior, and bizarre abuses of the use of spiritual gifts that he has found from various parts of the world. I have no objection to having someone point out these wrongful teachings and actions, and for that we should be thankful to MacArthur.

However, most charismatics and Pentecostals reading MacArthur's book will not recognize their own churches or movements in these pages. For the most part, MacArthur is describing events on the far fringes of the charismatic movement, yet on this basis he mistakenly characterizes the entire movement as "a false church" that preaches a gospel that is "not the true gospel." In a critical review of MacArthur's book, Craig Keener, professor of New Testament at Asbury Theological Seminary, writes as someone who has had the experience of "thirty-eight years as a charismatic," and he says, "Reading MacArthur's astonishingly broadbrushed condemnation of all charismatic experience was so over-the-top that I would have been tempted to find it entertaining were it not for the tragic likelihood that some readers will accept it uncritically. . . . He practices

---

61. John MacArthur, *Strange Fire: The Danger of Offending the Holy Spirit with Counterfeit Worship* (Nashville: Nelson, 2013), xvii.

guilt-by-association in such an indiscriminate way, and sometimes with such limited research, that some will be tempted to charge him with slandering fellow believers."[62]

Rather than condemning all for the mistakes of a few, it seems to me preferable to evaluate a movement according to the teachings and practices of its best representatives, not its worst and most poorly trained.

### 8. A Final Note: Cessationists and Charismatics Need Each Other

Finally, it can be argued that those in the charismatic and Pentecostal camps and those in the cessationist camp (primarily Reformed and dispensational Christians) really need each other, and they would do well to appreciate each other more. The former tend to have more practical experience in the use of spiritual gifts and in vitality in worship that cessationists could benefit from, if they were willing to learn. On the other hand, Reformed and dispensational groups have traditionally been very strong in understanding of Christian doctrine and in deep and accurate understanding of the teachings of Scripture. Charismatic and Pentecostal groups could learn much from them if they would be willing to do so. But it certainly is not helpful to the church as a whole for both sides to think they can learn nothing from the other or that they can gain no benefit from fellowship with each other.

## QUESTIONS FOR PERSONAL APPLICATION

1. Before reading this chapter, what spiritual gift or gifts did you think you had? Has your understanding of your spiritual gift(s) changed after studying this chapter? In what way?

2. Explain how each of the spiritual gifts that you understand yourself to have is greater than what would have been known to most old covenant believers. Explain how each gift is a foretaste of some knowledge or ability you will have after Christ returns.

3. What can you do to stir up or strengthen those spiritual gifts in you that need strengthening? Are there gifts that you have been given but have neglected? Why do you think you have neglected them? What could be done to stir up or rekindle them in you?

4. As you think about your church, which spiritual gifts do you think are most effectively functioning at the present time? Which are most needed in your church? Is there anything you can do to help meet those needs?

---

62. Craig Keener, "John MacArthur's Strange Fire, Reviewed by Craig S. Keener," *Pneuma Review*, November 15, 2013. http://pneumareview.com/john-macarthurs-strange-fire-reviewed-by-craig-s-keener/. Other critiques of MacArthur's book include Robert Graves, ed., *Strangers to Fire: When Tradition Trumps Scripture* (Tulsa, OK: Harrison House, 2014); and Michael Brown, *Authentic Fire: A Response to John MacArthur's Strange Fire* (Lake Mary, FL: Creation House, 2015).

5. What do you think could be done to help churches avoid having controversies, and even divisions, over the question of spiritual gifts? Are there tensions in your church with regard to these questions today? If so, what can you do to help alleviate these tensions?

6. Do you think that some spiritual gifts mentioned in the New Testament ceased early in the history of the church and are no longer valid for today? Has your opinion on this question changed as a result of reading this chapter?

7. In your viewpoint, would a church be healthier and more unified if it concentrated on a few gifts and used them carefully and well or if it encouraged a multiplicity of different gifts and allowed them to be used at many different times by many different people? If you answered with the latter option, what things might your church do to include a greater diversity and distribution in the use of spiritual gifts? What are some of the dangers that might accompany such widespread use, and how can they be guarded against?

> **Special Terms**
>
> *See the list at the end of the next chapter.*

## BIBLIOGRAPHY

See the list at the end of the next chapter.

## SCRIPTURE MEMORY PASSAGE

**1 Peter 4:10–11:** As each has received a gift, use it to serve one another, as good stewards of God's varied grace: whoever speaks, as one who speaks oracles of God; whoever serves, as one who serves by the strength that God supplies—in order that in everything God may be glorified through Jesus Christ. To him belong glory and dominion forever and ever. Amen.

## HYMN

### "Come, Thou Almighty King"

This is a Trinitarian hymn in which the first verse is addressed to God the Father, the second to God the Son, and the third to God the Holy Spirit. The third verse is a request that the Holy Spirit would come and rule in our hearts, be ever-present among us, and dwell among us as the "Spirit of power." The final verse is a hymn of praise to God "the great One in Three." In the midst of a long discussion on spiritual gifts, it is good to refocus our attention on God himself, who is the giver of all good gifts, and whose glory is the goal of the use of every gift.

*Come, thou almighty King, Help us thy name
    to sing,
Help us to praise:
Father, all glorious, O'er all victorious,
Come, and reign over us, Ancient of Days.*

*Come, thou incarnate Word, Gird on thy mighty
    sword,
Our prayer attend:
Come, and thy people bless, And give thy Word
    success;
Spirit of holiness, on us descend.*

*Come, holy Comforter, Thy sacred witness bear
In this glad hour:
Thou who almighty art, Now rule in every heart,
And ne'er from us depart, Spirit of pow'r.*

*To the great One in Three, Eternal praises be,
Hence evermore.
His sovereign majesty May we in glory see,
And to eternity love and adore.*

Author: Anonymous, 1757

## CONTEMPORARY WORSHIP SONG

### "When You Move"

*Father, come reveal the love
That You've freely given us,
Poured from Calvary like a flood.
We look to You.
Spirit, move and shine Your light,
Change our hearts and fill our minds
With the radiance of Christ.
We look to You, we look to You.*

*Father, You know all our needs
Long before we even speak,
But Your heart is what we seek.
We look to You.
Jesus, come and build Your church,
Let Your gospel fill the earth
Till the day that You return.
We look to You, we look to You.*

Words by Steve Cook and Vikki Cook[63]

### Chorus
*For when You move, our lives are changed.
We know a taste of heaven here.
We're crying out for more of You.
Lord, come and move.*

# CHAPTER 53

# Gifts of the Holy Spirit: (2) Specific Gifts

*How should we understand and use specific spiritual gifts?*

## EXPLANATION AND SCRIPTURAL BASIS

In this chapter we will build on the general discussion about spiritual gifts in the previous chapter and examine several specific gifts in more detail. We will not consider every gift mentioned in the New Testament, but will focus on several gifts that are not well understood or whose use has aroused some controversy today. Therefore, we will not examine gifts whose meaning and use are self-evident from the term involved (such as serving, encouraging, contributing, showing leadership, or showing mercy) but will rather concentrate on those in the following list, primarily taken from 1 Corinthians 12:28 and 12:8–10:

1. prophecy
2. teaching
3. miracles
4. healing
5. tongues and interpretation
6. word of wisdom/word of knowledge
7. distinguishing between spirits

### A. Prophecy

Although several definitions have been given for the gift of prophecy, a fresh examination of the New Testament teaching on this gift will show that it should be defined not as "predicting the future," nor as "proclaiming a word from the Lord," nor as "powerful preaching"—but rather as *telling something that God has spontaneously brought to mind.* The first four points in the following material support this conclusion; the remaining points deal with other considerations regarding this gift.[1]

---

1. For a more extensive development of all of the following points about the gift of prophecy, see Wayne Grudem, *The Gift* *of Prophecy in 1 Corinthians* (Lanham, MD: University Press of America, 1982); and Grudem, *The Gift of Prophecy in the New*

## 1. The New Testament Counterparts to Old Testament Prophets Are New Testament Apostles

Old Testament prophets had an amazing responsibility—they were able to speak and write words that had absolute divine authority.[2] They could say, "Thus says the Lord," and the words that followed were the very words of God. The Old Testament prophets wrote their words as God's words in Scripture for all time (see Num. 22:38; Deut. 18:18–20; Jer. 1:9; Ezek. 2:7, et al.). Therefore, to disbelieve or disobey a prophet's words was to disbelieve or disobey God (see Deut. 18:19; 1 Sam. 8:7; 1 Kings 20:36; and many other passages).

In the New Testament there were also people who spoke and wrote God's very words and had them recorded in Scripture, but we may be surprised to find that Jesus no longer calls them prophets but uses a new term, *apostles*. The apostles are the New Testament counterpart to the Old Testament prophets (see 1 Cor. 2:13; 2 Cor. 13:3; Gal. 1:8–9, 11–12; 1 Thess. 2:13; 4:8, 15; 2 Peter 3:2). It is the apostles, not the prophets, who have authority to write the words of New Testament Scripture.

When the apostles want to establish their unique authority, they never appeal to the title "prophet" but rather call themselves "apostles." For example, "Paul, called by the will of God to be an apostle of Christ Jesus" (1 Cor. 1:1; see also Rom. 1:1; 1 Cor. 9:1–2; 2 Cor. 1:1; 11:12–13; 12:11–12; Gal. 1:1; Eph. 1:1; 1 Peter 1:1; 2 Peter 1:1; 3:2, et al.).

## 2. The Meaning of the Word *Prophet* in the Time of the New Testament

Why did Jesus choose the new term *apostle* to designate those who had the authority to write Scripture? It was probably because the Greek word *prophētēs* ("prophet") at the time of the New Testament had a very broad range of meanings. It generally did not have the sense "one who speaks God's very words" but rather "one who speaks on the

*Testament and Today* (Eastbourne, UK: Kingsway; Westchester, IL: Crossway, 1988). (The first book is more technical, with much more interaction with the scholarly literature.)

Much of the following material on prophecy is adapted from my article, "Why Christians Can Still Prophesy," in *CT*, September 16, 1988, 29–35, and is used by permission; see also my articles, "What Should Be the Relationship between Prophet and Pastor?," in *Equipping the Saints* (Fall 1990): 7–9, 21–22; and "Does God Still Give Revelation Today?," in *Charisma* (September 1992): 38–42.

Several writers have differed with my understanding of the gift of prophecy. For alternative views to the position presented in this chapter, see Richard Gaffin, *Perspectives on Pentecost* (Phillipsburg, NJ: Presbyterian and Reformed, 1979) (Gaffin is primarily responding to an unpublished version of my 1982 book), and the bibliography entries at the end of the chapter under Victor Budgen, F. David Farnell, Kenneth L. Gentry Jr., Robert Saucy, Robert L. Thomas, and R. Fowler White. On the other hand, the studies listed in the bibliography by D. A.

Carson, Graham Houston, Charles Hummel, and M. M. B. Turner, along with several book reviews, have expressed substantial agreement with the position I advocated in my 1982 and 1988 books.

2. This is a generalization that clearly applies to the Old Testament prophets who wrote books of Scripture and other major prophetic figures such as Elijah and Elisha. However, Iain Duguid has recently argued—persuasively, it seems to me—that the Old Testament contains examples both of what he calls capital-*P* Prophecy (speaking God's very words) and small-*p* prophecy (including "a broader range of Spirit-inspired activities, including preaching, teaching, leading in worship, and recording history"). See Iain Duguid, "What Kind of Prophecy Continues? Defining the Differences between Continuationism and Cessationism," in *Redeeming the Life of the Mind: Essays in Honor of Vern Poythress*, ed. John Frame, Wayne Grudem, and John Hughes (Wheaton, IL: Crossway, 2017), 112–28; quote from p. 121.

basis of some external influence" (often a spiritual influence of some kind). Titus 1:12 uses the word in this sense, where Paul quotes the pagan Greek poet Epimenides: "One of the Cretans, a *prophet* of their own, said, 'Cretans are always liars, evil beasts, lazy gluttons.'" The soldiers who mock Jesus also seem to use the word *prophesy* in this way, when they blindfold Jesus and cruelly demand, "Prophesy! Who is it that struck you?" (Luke 22:64). They do not mean, "Speak words of absolute divine authority," but "Tell us something that has been revealed to you" (cf. John 4:19).

Many writings outside the Bible use the word *prophet* (Gk. *prophētēs*) in this way without signifying any divine authority in the words of one called a prophet. In fact, by the time of the New Testament the term *prophet* in everyday use often simply meant "one who has supernatural knowledge" or "one who predicts the future"—or even just "spokesman" (without any connotations of divine authority). Several examples near the time of the New Testament are given in Helmut Krämer's article in *Theological Dictionary of the New Testament*:[3]

> A philosopher is called "a *prophet* of immortal nature" (Dio Chrysostom, AD 40–120)
> A teacher (Diogenes) wants to be "a *prophet* of truth and candor" (Lucian of Samosata, AD 120–180)
> Those who advocate Epicurean philosophy are called "*prophets* of Epicurus" (Plutarch, AD 50–120)
> Written history is called "the *prophetess* of truth" (Diodorus Siculus, wrote c. 60–30 BC)
> A "specialist" in botany is called a "*prophet*" (Dioscurides of Cilicia, first century AD)
> A "quack" in medicine is called a "*prophet*" (Galen of Pergamum, AD 129–99)

Krämer concludes that the Greek word for "prophet" (*prophētēs*) "simply expresses the formal function of declaring, proclaiming, making known." Yet because "every prophet declares something which is not his own," the Greek word for "herald" (*kēryx*) "is the closest synonym."[4]

Just as an apostle could sometimes be called a "teacher" (which Paul calls himself in 1 Timothy 2:7) along with other teachers in the churches, and just as an apostle could sometimes be called an "elder" (Peter calls himself a "fellow elder" in 1 Peter 5:1) along with other elders in the churches, so too the apostles could sometimes be called "prophets" or give a "prophecy," though there were other prophets in the churches as well (so the book of Revelation, written by John, is called a "prophecy" in Rev. 1:3; 22:7), but there were also many other prophets in the churches. However, the apostles were not often called "teachers" or "elders" or "prophets."

The important point is that, in first century Greek, the terms *prophet* and *prophecy* did not imply divine authority for their speech or writing. Much more commonly, the

---

3. The following examples are taken from *TDNT*, 6:794.    4. Ibid., 795.

words *prophet* and *prophecy* were used of ordinary Christians who spoke not with absolute divine authority but simply to report something that God had laid on their hearts
or brought to their minds. There are many indications in the New Testament that this
ordinary gift of prophecy had authority less than that of the Bible, and even less than
that of recognized Bible teaching in the early church.

### 3. Indications That Prophets Did Not Speak with Authority Equal to the Words of Scripture

a. **Acts 21:4.** In Acts 21:4, we read of the disciples at Tyre: "Through the Spirit they
were telling Paul not to go on to Jerusalem." Although the word *prophecy* is not in this
verse, it seems to be a reference to prophecy directed towards Paul, but Paul disobeyed
it! He never would have done this if this prophecy contained God's very words and had
authority equal to Scripture.[5]

b. **Acts 21:10–11.** Then in Acts 21:10–11, Agabus prophesied that the Jews at
Jerusalem would "bind" Paul and "deliver him into the hands of the Gentiles," a prediction that was nearly correct but not quite: the Romans, not the Jews, bound Paul (v. 33;
also 22:29),[6] and the Jews, rather than delivering him voluntarily, tried to kill him, and
he had to be rescued by force (v. 32).[7] The prediction was not far off, but it had inaccuracies in detail that would have called into question the validity of any Old Testament
prophet. However, this text could be perfectly well explained by supposing that Agabus
had had a vision of Paul as a prisoner of the Romans in Jerusalem, surrounded by an
angry mob of Jews. His interpretation of such a "vision" or "revelation" from the Holy
Spirit would be that the Jews had bound Paul and handed him over to the Romans, and
that is what Agabus would (somewhat erroneously) prophesy. This is exactly the kind
of fallible prophecy that would fit the definition of New Testament congregational
prophecy proposed above—reporting in one's own words something that God has
spontaneously brought to mind.

One objection to this view is to say that Agabus' prophecy was in fact fulfilled, and
that Paul even reports that in Acts 28:17: "I was delivered as a prisoner from Jerusalem
into the hands of the Romans."[8]

---

5. In a very gracious and thoughtful book, my long-time
friend Thomas Schreiner explains Paul's disobedience to the
prophecies given in Tyre by saying that the prophets had a revelation of Paul suffering in Jerusalem and drew their own inferences (that Paul shouldn't go to Jerusalem). But Schreiner says
"the inference drawn from the prophecy was not part of the
prophecy itself" (*Spiritual Gifts: What They Are and Why They
Matter* [Nashville: B&H, 2018], 117). My response would be
to say that it was the warning itself that was the content of the
prophecy, for it was "through the Spirit" that "they were telling
Paul not to go on to Jerusalem" (Acts 21:4). But Paul disobeyed.

6. In both verses Luke uses the same Greek verb (*deō*) that
Agabus had used to predict that the Jews would bind Paul.

7. The verb that Agabus used (*paradidōmi*, "to deliver,
hand over") requires the sense of voluntarily, consciously, deliberately giving over or handing over something to someone else.
That is the sense it has in all 119 other instances of the word in
the New Testament. But that sense is not true with respect to
the treatment of Paul by the Jews: they did not voluntarily hand
Paul over to the Romans!

8. This is the view of Gaffin, *Perspectives*, 65–66, and F.
David Farnell, "The Gift of Prophecy in the Old and New Testaments," *BibSac* 149, no. 596 (October–December 1992): 395,
both of whom refer to Acts 28:17 for support.

But the verse itself will not support that interpretation. The Greek text of Acts 28:17 explicitly refers to Paul's transfer *out of* (Gk. *ex*) Jerusalem as *a prisoner*.[9] Paul's statement describes his transfer out of the Jewish judicial system (the Jews were seeking to bring him again to be examined by the Sanhedrin in Acts 23:15, 20) and *into* the Roman judicial system at Caesarea (Acts 23:23–35). Paul correctly says in Acts 28:18 that the same Romans into whose hands he had been delivered as a prisoner (v. 17) were the ones who (Gk. *hoitines*, v. 18), "when they had examined me . . . wished to set me at liberty, because there was no reason for the death penalty in my case" (Acts 28:18; cf. 23:29; also 25:11, 18–19; 26:31–32). Then Paul adds that when the Jews objected, he was compelled "to appeal to Caesar" (Acts 28:19; cf. 25:11). This *whole section of narrative in Acts 28:17–19* refers to Paul's transfer out of Jerusalem to Caesarea in Acts 23:12–35 and explains to the Jews in Rome why Paul is in Roman custody. This narrative does not refer to Acts 21:27–36 and the mob scene near the Jerusalem temple at all. So this objection is not persuasive. The verse does not point to a fulfillment of either half of Agabus' prophecy: it does not mention any binding by the Jews, nor does it mention that the Jews handed Paul over to the Romans. In fact, in the scene it refers to (Acts 23:12–35), once again Paul had just been taken from the Jews "by force" (Acts 23:10), and, far from seeking to hand him over to the Romans, they were waiting in an ambush to kill him (Acts 23:13–15).

Another objection to my understanding of Acts 21:10–11 is to say that the Jews did not really have to bind Paul and deliver him into the hands of the gentiles for the prophecy of Agabus to be true because the Jews were *responsible* for these activities even if they did not carry them out. Robert Thomas says, "It is common to speak of the responsible party or parties as performing an act even though he or they may not have been the immediate agent(s)."[10] Thomas cites similar examples from Acts 2:23 (where Peter says that the Jews crucified Christ, whereas the Romans actually did it) and John 19:1 (we read that Pilate scourged Jesus, whereas his soldiers no doubt carried out the action). Thomas concludes, "The Jews were the ones who put Paul in chains just as Agabus predicted."[11]

In response, I agree that Scripture can speak of someone as doing an act that is carried out by that person's agent. But *in every case* the person who is said to do the action both *wills* the act to be done and *gives directions* to others to do it. Pilate directed

---

9. The NIV translation, "I was arrested *in* Jerusalem and handed over to the Romans," completely misses the idea (which the Greek text requires) of being delivered *out of* (*ex*) Jerusalem, and it removes the idea that he was delivered as a prisoner (Gk. *desmios*), adding rather the idea that he was arrested in Jerusalem, an event that is not mentioned here in the Greek text.

Thomas Schreiner argues that Paul, in Acts 28:17, uses language that shows that he thought the prophecy of Agabus was fulfilled when he was arrested in the temple area in Acts 21:27–36 (*Spiritual Gifts*, 113–14). But Schreiner gives no explanation for the key phrase "from Jerusalem" in Acts 28:17, which decisively indicates that Paul is referring to his transfer *out of* Jerusalem in Acts 23.

10. Robert L. Thomas, "Prophecy Rediscovered? A Review of The Gift of Prophecy in the New Testament and Today," *BibSac* 149, no. 593 (January–March 1992): 91. The same argument is made by Kenneth L. Gentry Jr., *The Charismatic Gift of Prophecy: A Reformed Response to Wayne Grudem*, 2nd ed. (Memphis: Footstool, 1989), 43.

11. Thomas, "Prophecy Rediscovered?," 91.

his soldiers to scourge Jesus. The Jews actively demanded that the Romans would crucify Christ. By contrast, in the situation of Paul's capture in Jerusalem, there is no such parallel. The Jews did not order him to be bound but the Roman tribune did it: "Then the tribune came up and arrested him and ordered him to be bound with two chains" (Acts 21:33). And in fact the parallel form of speech is found here because although the tribune *ordered* Paul to be bound, later we read that "the tribune also was afraid, for he realized that Paul was a Roman citizen and that *he had bound him*" (Acts 22:29). So this narrative does speak of the binding as done either by the responsible agent or by the people who carried it out, but in both cases these are Romans, not Jews. In summary, this objection says that the Jews put Paul in chains. But Acts says twice that the Romans bound him. This objection says that the Jews turned Paul over to the gentiles. But Acts says that they violently refused to turn him over, so that he had to be taken from them by force. The objection does not fit the words of the text.[12]

**c. 1 Thessalonians 5:19–21.** Paul tells the Thessalonians, "Do not quench the Spirit. Do not despise prophecies, but test everything; hold fast what is good" (1 Thess. 5:19–21). If the Thessalonians had thought that prophecy equaled God's Word in authority, he would never have had to tell the Thessalonians not to despise it—they "received" and "accepted" God's Word "with the joy of the Holy Spirit" (1 Thess. 1:6; 2:13; cf. 4:15). But when Paul tells them to "test everything" it must include at least the prophecies he mentioned in the previous phrase. He implies that prophecies contain some things that are good and some things that are not good when he encourages them to "hold fast *what is good*." This is something that could never have been said of the words of an Old Testament prophet or the authoritative teachings of a New Testament apostle. Therefore, prophecies that were given by ordinary Christians in the church at Thessalonica did not have the authority of God's very words. These prophecies must have been ordinary human words reporting something that God had brought to mind.

It is significant that Paul tells the Thessalonians to test the prophecies, not the prophets. "Do not despise *prophecies*, but test everything; hold fast what is good" (1 Thess. 5:20–21). It is the "prophecies" (plural of Gk. *prophēteia*, "prophecy") that are not to be despised but are to be tested.[13] It is the "good" content in prophecies that they are to "hold fast."

**d. 1 Corinthians 14:29–38.** More extensive evidence on New Testament prophecy is found in 1 Corinthians 14. When Paul says, "Let two or three prophets speak, and *let the others weigh what is said*" (1 Cor. 14:29), he suggests that they should listen carefully

---

12. See below, p. 1304, on the question of Agabus' introductory phrase, "Thus says the Holy Spirit."

13. Schreiner, *Spiritual Gifts*, 110, seems to agree that the *prophecies* are being tested, but then he says this is to determine whether the prophet was a true prophet or false prophet.

However, nothing in these verses gives any hint of a process of judging whether the speakers were true prophets or false prophets. These verses simply speak of evaluating each individual prophecy that was spoken.

and sift the good from the bad, accepting some and rejecting the rest (for this is the implication of the Greek word *diakrinō*, here translated "weigh what is said").[14] We cannot imagine that an Old Testament prophet like Isaiah would have said, "Listen to what I say and weigh what is said—sort the good from the bad, what you accept from what you should not accept"! If prophecy had absolute divine authority, it would be sin to do this. But here Paul commands that it be done, suggesting that New Testament prophecy did not have the authority of God's very words.[15]

In 1 Corinthians 14:30–31, Paul allows one prophet to interrupt another one: "If a revelation is made to another sitting there, let the first be silent. For you can all prophesy one by one." Again, if prophets had been speaking God's very words, equal in value to Scripture, it is hard to imagine that Paul would say they should be interrupted and not be allowed to finish their message. But that is what Paul commands.

Paul suggests that no one at Corinth, a church that had much prophecy, was able to speak God's very words. He says in 1 Corinthians 14:36, "Or was it from you that the word of God came? Or are you the only ones it has reached?" Paul expects the answer "no" to both questions. But this means that "the word of God" did not come from the church at Corinth even though there were many people giving prophecies (as Paul's instructions in chapters 12–14 indicate).

Then in verses 37 and 38, he claims authority far greater than any prophet or any potential prophet at Corinth: "If anyone thinks that he is a prophet, or spiritual, he should acknowledge that the things I am writing to you are a command of the Lord. If anyone does not recognize this, he is not recognized." Paul would not allow the possibility that any prophet at Corinth could speak with authority equal to his authority as an apostle. This implies an assumption that no prophets at Corinth were speaking the very words of God.

All of these passages indicate that the idea that prophets spoke "words of the Lord" when the apostles were not present in the early churches is simply incorrect.

**e. Apostolic Preparations for Their Absence.** In addition to the verses we have considered so far, one other type of evidence suggests that New Testament congregational prophets spoke with less authority than New Testament apostles or Scripture: the problem of successors to the apostles is solved not by encouraging Christians to

---

14. If Paul had meant the congregation was to judge whether the speaker was a true prophet or a false prophet, the appropriate Greek verb would have been *krinō*, "to judge." But the verb used here, *diakrinō*, suggests rather "to differentiate by separating, separate, arrange" (BDAG, 231), a sense more appropriate to sifting and evaluating each part of each *prophecy* (as in 1 Thess. 5:19–21) rather than judging each prophet.

In addition, when the New Testament authors warn about the dangers of false prophets, they never mention evaluating whether a prophecy is true or false. Rather, they mention

doctrinal tests (as in 1 John 4:1–6; 2 John 7–9) and testing the fruit of their actions (Matt. 7:15–20; 24:11, 24).

15. Paul's instructions are different from those in the early Christian document known as the *Didache*, which tells people, "Do not test or examine any prophet who is speaking in a spirit [or 'in the Spirit']" (chapter 11). But the *Didache* says several things that are contrary to New Testament doctrine (see Grudem, *The Gift of Prophecy in the New Testament and Today*, 106–8; also pp. 55–56, above).

listen to the *prophets* (even though there were prophets around) but by pointing to the *Scriptures*.[16]

So Paul, at the end of his life, emphasizes "rightly handling the word of truth" (2 Tim. 2:15), and the "God-breathed" character of "Scripture" for "teaching, for reproof, for correction, and for training in righteousness" (2 Tim. 3:16). Jude urges his readers to "contend for the faith that was once for all delivered to the saints" (Jude 3). Peter, at the end of his life, encourages his readers to "pay attention" to Scripture, which is like "a lamp shining in a dark place" (2 Peter 1:19–20), and reminds them of the teaching of the apostle Paul "in all his letters" (2 Peter 3:16). In no case do we read exhortations to "give heed to the prophets in your churches" or to "obey the words of the Lord through your prophets." Yet there certainly were prophets prophesying in many local congregations after the death of the apostles. It seems that they did not have authority equal to the apostles, and the authors of Scripture knew that. The conclusion is that prophecies today are not "the words of God" either.

**f. Objection: Ephesians 2:20 Shows That Prophets Were Foundational in the New Testament Church.** Paul writes about prophets in Ephesians as follows: "So then you are no longer strangers and aliens, but you are fellow citizens with the saints and members of the household of God, built on the foundation of *the apostles and prophets*, Christ Jesus himself being the cornerstone" (Eph. 2:19–20).

A frequent objection to my view (that prophets in New Testament churches did not speak the very words of God) is based on Ephesians 2:20: if the entire church throughout the world ("the household of God") is built on the foundation of the apostles and prophets, then it seems evident that these "prophets," like the apostles, spoke the very words of God—words that were equal to Scripture in their authority. And therefore, it is argued, since no more words are now being added to Scripture, the gift of prophecy has now ceased.[17]

In response, I agree that the kind of "prophets" mentioned in Ephesians 2:20 ceased in the first century. The "foundation" for the church throughout the world was laid once for all in the first century and will not be laid again. But the question is whether this verse describes *all who had the gift of prophecy* in the New Testament churches. I see no convincing evidence that it describes all who prophesied in the early church. Rather, the context clearly indicates a very limited group of such prophets.[18] In fact, just a few verses later, Paul gives us more information about these apostles and prophets:

---

16. I have taken this idea from Roy Clements, *Word and Spirit: The Bible and the Gift of Prophecy Today* (Leicester: UCCF Booklets, 1986), 24; cf. D. A. Carson, *Showing the Spirit* (Grand Rapids: Baker, 1987), 96.

17. Ephesians 2:20 is the primary argument that Thomas Schreiner uses to argue that the gift of prophecy no longer exists today, because the foundation of the church was laid long ago, once for all time; see Thomas Schreiner, *Spiritual Gifts: What They Are and Why They Matter* (Nashville: B&H, 2018), 107–10, 157–60. His entire argument assumes but does not argue for

or provide evidence for the idea that the "prophets" mentioned in Ephesians 2:20 refers to *all the prophets in all the New Testament churches* at that time rather than a small group of prophets closely tied to the apostles. My argument in this chapter is that many New Testament passages indicate that the many ordinary prophets in all the New Testament churches were significantly different from the foundational prophets, who were closely associated with the apostles.

18. I had earlier argued that, in Eph. 2:20, Paul could be speaking of one group (the apostle-prophets) instead of two

When you read this, you can perceive my insight into the *mystery* of Christ, which was not made known to the sons of men in other generations as it has now been revealed to *his holy apostles and prophets* by the Spirit. This *mystery* is that the Gentiles are fellow heirs, members of the same body, and partakers of the promise in Christ Jesus through the gospel. (Eph. 3:4–6)

In Paul's writings, a "mystery" (Gk. *mystērion*) is often a truth that was only faintly revealed in the Old Testament but now has been clearly revealed in the New Testament age. And in Ephesians 3:6 the specific "mystery" that Paul is talking about is the fact that God wants to include gentiles (!) as well as Jews among God's people and that these gentiles will have equal standing with Jews before God (they will be "fellow heirs" and "members of the same body" with the Jewish believers in Christ). Paul says that the understanding of this mystery was revealed to "his holy apostles and prophets by the Spirit."

Therefore, the "prophets" that Paul is talking about in Ephesians 2:20 and 3:5 are a very limited, very specific group: they were (a) part of the very foundation of the church, (b) closely connected with the apostles, and (c) recipients of the new revelation from God that the gentiles were equal members with Jews in the church.

But surely that group does not include all the Christians with the gift of prophecy in all the New Testament churches at that time. The Ephesian Christians to whom Paul was writing were not pictured by Paul as part of the "foundation" because he says they were "built on" the foundation—they were part of the (metaphorical) building that was continually being built up after the foundation had been laid.

The same can be said for all the "sons" and "daughters" and "male servants and female servants" who prophesied in fulfillment of Peter's sermon at Pentecost (Acts 2:17–18), the prophets in Jerusalem (Acts 11:27), the prophets at Antioch (Acts 13:1), the brand-new believers who suddenly "began speaking in tongues and prophesying" in Ephesus (Acts 19:6), the Christians with the gift of prophecy in Tyre (Acts 21:4), Phillip's four daughters who prophesied in Caesarea (Acts 21:9), people with the gift of prophecy in Rome (Rom. 12:6), the men and women who were prophesying during the church services in Corinth (1 Cor. 11:4–5), the Christians in Corinth who were given a gift of prophecy after they followed Paul's encouragement to "earnestly desire to prophesy" (1 Cor. 14:39), and the ordinary Christians who had a gift of prophecy in the churches of Ephesus (Eph. 4:11) and Thessalonica (1 Thess. 5:20).[19]

---

groups (apostles and prophets) because the Greek text contains a grammatical construction that allows for (does not require, but allows for) the translation, "built on the foundation of the apostles who are also prophets" (Grudem, *The Gift of Prophecy in the New Testament and Today*, 46–47; 329–46). But I realize that a number of interpreters have disagreed with me on this point and so I have not made it any part of my argument above

regarding the meaning of Eph. 2:20 and 3:5, but I have assumed that *two separate groups* (apostles and prophets) are intended.

19. Sam Storms rightly asks, "Are we really prepared to say that the apostle urged every Christian in every local congregation to earnestly desire that he or she might be the recipient of inspired and authoritative revelation that would serve to lay the foundation for the body of Christ throughout all ages? I'm

Surely not all of these prophets were laying again and again the "foundation" of the church, and receiving again and again the revelation about the gentiles being included with Jews in the church (about which Paul had already written), but they were part of the (metaphorical) church building that was being *built on* the foundation. And for these ordinary Christian prophets in churches throughout the New Testament world, the passages I have discussed in the previous sections indicate again and again their prophecies were ordinary human words (not God's words) in which they were reporting things that God spontaneously brought to mind.

This is certainly a different situation from the Old Testament, where there were individual prophets or small groups of prophets from time to time in Israel, but there is no indication that there were prophets in every village and every city. But now in the New Testament our impression (from multiple verses) is that there were people with the gift of prophecy in every church. This is another argument showing that these ordinary prophets in the churches were not speaking the words of God. Or are we prepared to say that thousands of "prophets" in hundreds of churches throughout the Mediterranean world were actually speaking the very words of God? Were God's people to be expected to go around to the many hundreds or even thousands of churches in the first century world, collect the prophecies given week after week, write them down, and produce hundreds of volumes of "words of the Lord" that they were to obey like Scripture? In fact, we have no record of anything like this happening, nor do we have any record anywhere in the New Testament of churches recording or preserving these prophecies as if they were "words of the Lord" that were foundational for the entire church throughout the world. Rather, they preserve and obey the writings and teachings of the apostles, not of the prophets.[20]

Who then were the small group of "prophets" in Ephesians 2:20 and 3:5 who were part of the foundation of the church? There are two possibilities. The first possibility, and the one on which I have based my argument above, is that they were a small group of individuals who were not actually apostles but who were *closely connected to the apostles*, and who played a foundational role in the beginning of the church. Perhaps this group even included some of the authors of New Testament books who were not themselves apostles, such as Mark, Luke, Jude, and the (unknown) author of Hebrews.

The second possibility, which I have advocated elsewhere in writing (though it is not at all important to my understanding of the gift of prophecy), is that the expression "the

---

not" (Sam Storms, "Revelatory Gifts of the Spirit and the Sufficiency of Scripture: Are They Compatible?," in *Scripture and the People of God: Essays in Honor of Wayne Grudem*, ed. John DelHousaye, John Hughes, and Jeff Purswell [Wheaton, IL: Crossway, 2018], 89).

20. Thomas Schreiner responds to this kind of argument by saying that there were also many prophets in the Old Testament whose words were not recorded yet "everything they prophesied was true!" (*Spiritual Gifts*, 111). My reply is that

it is unclear what kind of "prophesying" was occurring with these bands of Old Testament prophets (see Iain Duguid's article, "What Kind of Prophecy Continues?," mentioned in n2). But in any case they are far different from hundreds or even thousands of prophets who (on Schreiner's view) laid the very foundation of the New Testament church, but none of whose foundational words for the worldwide church were ever recorded.

apostles and prophets" is referring to one group of people, "the apostle-prophets," or, in other words, the apostles functioning in the role of prophets (just as apostles can elsewhere be referred to as teachers or elders or preachers). The grammatical construction in Ephesians 2:20 is the same as the construction in Ephesians 4:11, which speaks about "the shepherds and teachers," which some commentators understand to be one group, the shepherd-teachers.[21] I have not based my understanding of Ephesians 2:20 on that second possibility.

## 4. How Should We Speak about the Authority of Prophecy Today?

My conclusion is that prophecies in the church today should be considered merely human words, not God's words, and not equal to God's words in authority. But does this conclusion conflict with current charismatic teaching or practice? I think it conflicts with much charismatic practice but not with most charismatic teaching.

Most charismatic teachers today would agree that contemporary prophecy is not equal to Scripture in authority. Though some will speak of prophecy as being the "word of God" for today, there is almost uniform testimony from all sections of the charismatic movement that prophecy is imperfect and impure and will contain elements that are not to be obeyed or trusted. For example, Bruce Yocum, the author of a widely used charismatic book on prophecy, writes, "Prophecy can be impure—our own thoughts or ideas can get mixed into the message we receive—whether we receive the words directly or only receive a sense of the message."[22]

But it must be said that in actual practice much confusion results from the habit of prefacing prophecies with the common Old Testament phrase, "Thus says the Lord" (a phrase nowhere spoken in the New Testament by any prophets in New Testament churches). This habit is unfortunate because it gives the impression that the words that follow are God's very words, whereas the New Testament does not justify that position,

---

21. My friend Dan Wallace, whose knowledge of Greek I greatly respect, incorrectly says that my view of the grammar of Eph. 2:20 is "essential to [Grudem's] view of NT prophecy" (Daniel Wallace, *Greek Grammar Beyond the Basics* [Grand Rapids: Zondervan, 1996], 284). But as I point out above, it is not essential at all, for whether someone understands one group (apostle-prophets) or two groups (apostles and prophets), the context shows this to be a limited group, and it is not speaking about ordinary Christians who had the gift of prophecy in the New Testament churches.

Wallace also says that "the apostles and prophets" in Eph. 2:20 should not be understood as one group because the Granville Sharp rule about the Greek construction article-noun-*kai*-noun only applies to singular nouns, not plurals as in Eph. 2:20. However, it seems to me that sometimes this construction can use plural nouns to refer to the same group of people (though at other times it refers to different groups). See, for example, this construction with plural nouns in John 20:29; Rom. 16:7;

2 Cor. 12:21; Phil. 3:3; Eph. 1:1; 4:11; Col. 1:2; and so forth, each of which includes a plural noun in a similar construction used to refer to one group. (Wallace puts these in different special categories.) For further discussion see Grudem, *The Gift of Prophecy in the New Testament and Today*, 345–46; see also the discussion between Stanley Porter and Dan Wallace about the applicability of the rule to plural nouns as part of their dialogue in Stanley Porter, review of *Granville Sharp's Canon and Its Kin: Semantics and Significance* by Daniel B. Wallace, *JETS* 53, no. 4 (2010): 828–32; Daniel Wallace, "Sharp's Rule Revisited: A Response to Stanley Porter," *JETS* 56, no. 1 (2013): 79–91; Porter, "Granville Sharp's Rule: A Response to Dan Wallace, or Why a Critical Book Review Should Be Left Alone," *JETS* 56, no. 1 (2013): 93–100; and Wallace, "Granville Sharp's Rule: A Rejoinder To Stan Porter," *JETS* 56, no. 1 (2013): 100–6.

22. See Yocum, *Prophecy* (Ann Arbor, MI: Word of Life, 1976), 79.

and when pressed, most responsible charismatic spokesmen would not want to claim it for every part of their prophecies anyway. So there would be much gain and no loss if that introductory phrase were dropped.

Now it is true that Agabus uses a similar phrase ("Thus says the Holy Spirit") in Acts 21:11, but the same words (Gk. *tade legei*) are used by Christian writers just after the time of the New Testament to introduce very general paraphrases or greatly expanded interpretations of what is being reported (so Ignatius, *Epistle to the Philadelphians* 7:1–2 [about AD 108] and *Epistle of Barnabas* 6:8; 9:2, 5 [AD 70–100]). The phrase can apparently mean, "This is generally (or approximately) what the Holy Spirit is saying to us."

If someone really does think God is bringing something to mind that should be reported in the congregation, there is nothing wrong with saying, "*I think* the Lord is putting on my mind that . . ." or "*It seems to me that* the Lord is showing us . . ." or some similar expression. Of course that does not sound as authoritative as "Thus says the Lord," but if the message is really from God, the Holy Spirit will cause it to speak with great power to the hearts of those who need to hear.

## 5. Do Christians Receive "Impressions" Today?

As I indicated above, Thomas Schreiner has argued that the gift of prophecy does not continue today because he thinks that New Testament prophets spoke the very words of God and were foundational to the New Testament church. What then does he say about people who claim to be receiving prophecies today? Here is his explanation:

> It is better to characterize what is happening today as the sharing of *impressions* rather than prophecy. God may impress something on a person's heart and mind, and he may use such impressions to help others in their spiritual walk. . . . What some people call prophecies are actually impressions, where someone senses that God is leading them to speak to someone or to make some kind of statement about a situation. . . . Impressions may be a mixture of truth and error. . . . The difference between cessationists and continuationists is in some way insignificant at the practical level when it comes to prophecy, for what continuationists call prophecy, cessationists call impressions. As a cessationist, I affirm that God may speak to his people through impressions.[23]

I was thankful to read this statement because it provides a basis for charismatic and noncharismatic Christians together to do kingdom work, pray, worship, and have conversations about what God is doing in their lives. Still, the labels we use have significance. Schreiner says that impressions "can't be of great importance because Scripture doesn't address them."[24] But Paul says, "Earnestly desire the spiritual gifts, especially that you may prophesy" (1 Cor. 14:1), which makes prophecy very important.

---

23. Schreiner, *Spiritual Gifts*, 118–19.     24. Ibid., 120.

In addition, it does seem to me a bit strange to say that God gives impressions today but that Scripture says nothing about them, while God does not give prophecies today but Scripture says quite a lot about them. I think the continuationist position has a better match between experience and Scripture when we say God *does* give prophecies today *and* Scripture says quite a lot about them. If God planned that Christians would have experiences of direct personal guidance and encouragement throughout the church age, is it not likely that he would also give instructions about these experiences in Scripture?

I also find it interesting that Tom Schreiner also says, "If the prophecies of New Testament prophets could be mixed with error, then I would have no quarrel with New Testament prophets existing today."[25] From this, it seems that our positions may not be very far apart.

## 6. A Spontaneous "Revelation" Made Prophecy Different From Other Gifts

If prophecy does not contain God's very words, then what is it? In what sense is it from God?

Paul indicates that God could bring something spontaneously to mind so that the person prophesying would report it in his or her own words. Paul calls this a *revelation*: "If a revelation is made to another sitting there, let the first be silent. For you can all prophesy one by one, so that all may learn and all be encouraged" (1 Cor. 14:30–31). Here he uses the words "a *revelation is made*" (using the Gk. verb *apokalyptō*) in a broader sense than the technical way theologians have used it to speak of the words of Scripture—but the New Testament elsewhere uses the terms *reveal* (Gk. *apokalyptō*) and *revelation* (Gk. *apokalypsis*) in this broader sense of communication from God that does not result in written Scripture or words equal to written Scripture in authority (see Phil. 3:15: "if in anything you think otherwise, God will *reveal* that also to you"; see also Rom. 1:18; Eph. 1:17; Matt. 11:27).

Paul is simply referring to something that God may suddenly bring to mind or something that God may impress on someone's consciousness in such a way that the person has a sense that it is from God. It may be that the thought brought to mind is surprisingly distinct from the person's own train of thought, that it is accompanied by a sense of vividness or urgency or persistence, or that in some other way it gives the person a rather clear sense that it is from the Lord.[26]

Figure 53.1 illustrates the idea of a revelation from God that is reported in the prophet's own (merely human) words.

---

25. Ibid., 159.

26. Although I argued above that the *authority* of prophecy in the New Testament church is far different from the authority of Old Testament canonical prophecy, this does not mean that everything about New Testament prophecy has to be different.

With respect to *the form in which the revelation comes* to the prophet, there may be not only words or ideas that come to mind, but also mental pictures (or "visions," Acts 2:17) and dreams (Acts 2:17) as well.

**Prophecy Occurs When a Revelation from God
Is Reported in the Prophet's Own (Merely Human) Words**
*Figure 53.1*

Thus, if a stranger comes in and all prophesy, "the secrets of his heart are disclosed, and so, falling on his face, he will worship God and declare that God is really among you" (1 Cor. 14:25). I have heard a report of this happening in a clearly noncharismatic Baptist church in America. A missionary speaker paused in the middle of his message and said something like this: "I didn't plan to say this, but it seems the Lord is indicating that someone in this church has just walked out on his wife and family. If that is so, let me tell you that God wants you to return to them and learn to follow God's pattern for family life." The missionary did not know it, but in the unlit balcony sat a man who had entered the church moments before for the first time in his life. The description fit him exactly, and he made himself known, acknowledged his sin, and began to seek after God.

In this way, prophecy serves as a "sign" for believers (1 Cor. 14:22)—it is a clear demonstration that God is definitely at work in their midst, a "sign" of God's hand of blessing on the congregation. And since it will work for the conversion of unbelievers as well, Paul encourages this gift to be used when "outsiders or unbelievers enter" (1 Cor. 14:23).

Many Christians in all periods of the church have experienced or heard of similar events—for example, an unplanned but urgent request may have been given to pray for certain missionaries in Nigeria. Then much later those who prayed discovered that just at that time the missionaries had been in an auto accident or at a point of intense spiritual conflict and had needed those prayers. Paul would call the sense or intuition of those things a "revelation," and the report to the assembled church of that prompting from God would be called a "prophecy." It may have elements of the speaker's understanding or interpretation in it and it certainly needs evaluation and testing, yet it has a valuable function in the church nonetheless.[27]

---

27. We must caution people, however, that the mere fact of a "revelation" that seems supernatural (and that even may contain some surprisingly accurate information) does not guarantee that a message is a true prophecy from God, for false

## 7. God Communicates Personally and Individually with His People throughout Biblical History

In the previous section I argued that a "prophecy" had to be based on something that God had revealed (or brought to mind). But advocates of the cessationist view of spiritual gifts (see chapter 52), object that, if God reveals something to an individual, *that must be a Scripture-quality revelation containing God's very words*, and that is not possible because the canon of Scripture is closed (see chapter 3). Therefore, they argue, the gift of prophecy does not continue today.

I realize that this is the heart of the cessationist argument.[28] In response, I would say, first, that I do not think there is any passage of Scripture, or any combination of passages, that should lead us to think that God does not communicate directly with his people throughout all of history in individual, personal ways that occur *in addition to* his communication in and through the written words of Scripture.

If we look at the whole scope of biblical history, we see that from beginning to end God has a *personal relationship* with his people, a relationship in which he communicates directly and personally with them, and this communication is never limited to the words that he gave to all of his people in "the book of the covenant" or the writings of the canon of Scripture. God had a personal relationship and direct interpersonal communication with Adam and Eve, Cain and Abel, Enoch (who walked with God, Gen. 5:24), Noah, Abraham, Isaac, Jacob, Moses, David, Solomon, and many other Old Testament prophets and kings.

In the person of Jesus, God the Son communicated individually and personally with many people while he was on earth. After the resurrection, the Lord Jesus or the Holy Spirit interacted personally with Paul not only on the Damascus road (Acts 9:4–6) but also in directing his second missionary journey (16:6–7), encouraging him in Corinth (18:9–10), confirming his decision to go to Jerusalem (19:21), showing him what would happen in Jerusalem (20:23), encouraging him in prison in Jerusalem (23:11), assuring him that he would arrive safely in Rome (this time by an angel, 27:23–24), telling him

---

prophets can "prophesy" under demonic influence. (See chapter 20, pp. 537–38, on the fact that demons can know about hidden activities or private conversations in our thoughts, even though they cannot know the future or read our thoughts.)

John warns that "many false prophets have gone out into the world" (1 John 4:1), and he gives tests of true doctrine to discern them (vv. 1–6), and says "The world listens to them" (v. 5). Other marks of false prophets can be found in 2 John 7–9 (denying the incarnation and not abiding in the doctrine of Christ); Matt. 7:15–20 ("You will recognize them by their fruits," v. 16); Matt. 24:11 (leading many astray); and Matt. 24:24 (showing signs and wonders for the purpose of leading astray the elect). On the other hand, 1 Cor. 12:3 seems to tell us that we should not think that genuine Christians will be false

prophets, speaking by the power of demons (see the discussion of 1 Cor. 12:3 on p. 1077), and 1 John 4:4 reassures Christians that "he who is in you is greater than he who is in the world."

28. For example, this is one of the main arguments of O. Palmer Robertson in his book, *The Final Word: A Biblical Response to the Case for Tongues and Prophecy Today* (Edinburgh: Banner of Truth, 1993). He argues that New Testament prophecy must have the same authority as Old Testament prophecy on pages 11, 88, 105, 106, 121, 122, and elsewhere. I will respond to that position over the next several pages. I have also posted a more detailed response to Robertson's book at my own website: http://www.waynegrudem.com/wp -content/uploads/2012/04/Robertson-O-Palmer-response -by-WG.pdf.

he would not heal his thorn in the flesh (2 Cor. 12:9), directing him to go to Jerusalem (Gal. 2:2), and standing by him at his trial in Rome (2 Tim. 4:17).

This was the case not only with Paul but also with others, for God gave direct guidance for Philip (Acts 8:26, 29), Ananias (9:10–16), Cornelius (10:3–6), Peter (10:13–20; 12:7–8), the church at Antioch (13:2), and the church in Jerusalem (15:28).

In addition, the New Testament promises that each individual believer will have a personal relationship with the Father, Son, and Holy Spirit:

> If anyone loves me, he will keep my word, and my Father will love him, and we will come to him and *make our home with him*. (John 14:23)

> For all who are *led by the Spirit of God* are sons of God. (Rom. 8:14; the present indicative Greek verb *agontai* views this "leading" as an ongoing process)

> But I say, *walk by the Spirit*, and you will not gratify the desires of the flesh. . . . But if you are *led by the Spirit* you are not under the law. (Gal. 5:16, 18; the present indicative Greek verb *agesthe* views this as an ongoing activity)

> [I pray] that the God of our Lord Jesus Christ, the Father of glory, may give you the Spirit of wisdom and of revelation *in the knowledge of him*. (Eph. 1:17)

> [I desire] that I may *know him* and the power of his resurrection, and may share his sufferings, becoming like him in his death. (Phil. 3:10)

> Let those of us who are mature think this way, and if in anything you think otherwise, *God will reveal that also to you*. (Phil. 3:15)

> Behold, I stand at the door and knock. If anyone hears my voice and opens the door, I will come in to him *and eat with him*, and he with me. (Rev. 3:20)

Now someone may argue that many of these examples are special cases that do not establish a pattern for ordinary Christians today. But my counterargument is this: look at the overall pattern of Scripture.

From beginning to end the Bible tells us of a God who relates *individually and personally* to his people. And now the cessationist view tells us, contrary to the experience of God's people throughout all of the Bible, that God seldom or never communicates personally and individually with his people except through the written words in the canon of Scripture.

So the cessationist view is asking us to believe (1) that throughout the Bible God communicated to his people both through written Scripture (as much as they had at any point) and through direct personal fellowship and interaction with people and (2) that God now communicates *only* through the written words of the canon and no longer through direct personal fellowship and interaction with people. This is quite strange in light of the fact that the new covenant, in which we now live, is seen to be better in every way (see 2 Cor. 3; Heb. 8–9). But how can it be better if we have lost many of the elements of personal relationship with God and personal communication from him that characterized all the periods of history that the Bible talks about? Where is *anything* in the Bible that would lead us to believe that?

I realize, of course, that the canon of Scripture is closed (see chapter 3), and no more writings are to be added to the Bible. But that is not the question. The question is: What about communication from God to specific individuals *that is not part of the canon*? If the Bible is the "book of the covenant" that stipulates the terms of the relationship between God as King and us as his covenant people, then are we to say that *the King can never communicate with his people in any additional ways besides the covenant document*? Can a God who loves his people never communicate with them directly and personally?

Evangelical theologian Carl F. H. Henry rightly commented as follows: "Any statement of evangelical experience that does not include the possibility both of communion with God and the communication of the particularized divine will to the surrendered life seems to me artificially restrictive."[29]

Surely the vast majority of Christians throughout all history have known and experienced the guidance of the Holy Spirit in making decisions, especially while they were praying and reading the words of Scripture, and they have known that this guidance included not only the directions, commands, and principles of Scripture, but also subjective perceptions of God's will, as well as thoughts or specific memories that the Lord brings to mind.

## 8. The Difference between Prophecy and Teaching

As far as we can tell, all New Testament "prophecy" (Gk. *prophēteia*), every activity of prophesying (Gk. *prophēteuō*), and every message from a "prophet" (Gk. *prophētēs*) in New Testament churches was based on this kind of spontaneous prompting from the Holy Spirit (1 Cor. 14:30; cf. Acts 11:28; 21:4, 10–11; and note the ideas of prophecy represented in Luke 7:39; 22:63–64; John 4:19; 11:51). Unless a person receives a spontaneous "revelation" from God, there is no prophecy.

By contrast, no human speaking in New Testament churches that is called a "teaching" (Gk. *didaskalia*) or done by a "teacher" (Gk. *didaskalos*) or described by the verb "teach" (Gk. *didaskō*) is ever said to be based on a "revelation." Rather, "teaching" is often an explanation or application of Scripture (Acts 15:35; 18:11, 24–28; Rom. 2:21;

---

29. Carl F. H. Henry, *Confessions of a Theologian* (Waco, TX: Word, 1986), 53.

15:4; Col. 3:16; Heb. 5:12) or a repetition and explanation of apostolic instructions (Rom. 16:17; 2 Tim. 2:2; 3:10, et al.). It is what we would call "Bible teaching" or "preaching" today.

So prophecy has less authority than "teaching," and prophecies in the church are always to be subject to the authoritative teaching of Scripture. Timothy was not told to *prophesy* Paul's instructions in the church; he was to *teach* them (1 Tim. 4:11; 6:2). Paul did not *prophesy* his lifestyle in Christ in every church; he *taught* it (1 Cor. 4:17). The Thessalonians were not told to hold firm to the traditions that were "prophesied" to them but to the traditions that they were "taught" by Paul (2 Thess. 2:15). Contrary to some views, teachers, not prophets, gave leadership and direction to the early churches.

Among the elders, therefore, were "those who labor in preaching and teaching" (1 Tim. 5:17) and an elder was to be "able to teach" (1 Tim. 3:2; cf. Titus 1:9)—but nothing is said about any elders whose work was prophesying, nor is it ever said that an elder has to be "able to prophesy" or that elders should be "holding firm to sound prophecies." In his leadership function Timothy was to take heed to himself and to his "teaching" (1 Tim. 4:16), but he is never told to take heed to his prophesying. James warned that those who teach, not those who prophesy, will be judged with greater strictness (James 3:1).

The task of interpreting and applying Scripture, then, is called "teaching" in the New Testament. Although a few people have claimed that the prophets in New Testament churches gave "charismatically inspired" interpretations of Old Testament Scripture, that claim has hardly been persuasive, primarily because it is hard to find in the New Testament any convincing examples where the "prophet" (Gk. *prophētēs*) word group is used to refer to someone engaged in this kind of activity.

So the distinction is quite clear: if a message is the result of conscious reflection on the text of Scripture, containing interpretation of the text and application to life, then it is (in New Testament terms) a teaching. But if a message is the report of something God brings suddenly to mind, then it is a prophecy. And of course, even prepared teachings can be interrupted by unplanned additional material that the Bible teacher suddenly felt God was bringing to his mind—in that case, it would be a "teaching" with an element of prophecy mixed in.

## 9. Objection: This Makes Prophecy "Too Subjective"

At this point some have objected that waiting for such "promptings" from God is "just too subjective" a process. But in response, it may be said that, for the health of the church, it is often the people who make this objection who need this subjective process most in their Christian lives! This gift requires waiting on the Lord, listening for him, hearing his prompting in our hearts. For Christians who are evangelical, doctrinally sound, intellectual, and "objective," probably what is needed most is the strong balancing influence of a more vital "subjective" relationship with the Lord in everyday life.

And these people are also those who have the least likelihood of being led into error, for they already place great emphasis on solid grounding in the Word of God.

Yet there is an opposite danger of excessive reliance on subjective impressions for guidance, and that must be clearly guarded against. People who continually seek subjective "messages" from God to guide their lives must be cautioned that subjective personal guidance is not a primary function of New Testament prophecy. They need to place much more emphasis on Scripture and seeking God's sure wisdom written there.

Many charismatic writers would agree with this caution, as the following quotation from British charismatic pastor Donald Bridge indicates:

> The illuminist constantly finds that "God tells him" to do things. . . . Illuminists are often very sincere, very dedicated, and possessed of a commitment to obey God that shames more cautious Christians. Nevertheless they are treading a dangerous path. Their ancestors have trodden it before, and always with disastrous results in the long run. Inner feelings and special promptings are by their very nature subjective. The Bible provides our objective guide.[30]

## 10. Prophecies Could Include Any Edifying Content

The examples of prophecies in the New Testament mentioned above show that the idea of prophecy as only "predicting the future" is certainly wrong. There were some predictions (Acts 11:28; 21:11), but there was also the disclosure of sins (1 Cor. 14:25). In fact, anything that edified could have been included, for Paul says, "The one who prophesies speaks to people *for their upbuilding and encouragement and consolation*" (1 Cor. 14:3). Another indication of the value of prophecy was that it could speak to the needs of people's hearts in a spontaneous, direct way.

## 11. Many People in the Congregation Can Prophesy

Another great benefit of prophecy is that it provides opportunity for participation by everyone in the congregation, not just those who are skilled speakers or who have gifts of teaching. Paul says that he wants "all" the Corinthians to prophesy (1 Cor. 14:5), and he says, "You can all prophesy one by one, so that all may learn and all be encouraged" (1 Cor. 14:31).[31] This does not mean that every believer will actually be able to prophesy, for Paul says, "Not all are prophets, are they?" (1 Cor. 12:29, author's translation). But it does mean that anyone who receives a "revelation" from God has permission to prophesy (within Paul's guidelines), and it suggests that many will.[32] Because of this, greater

---

30. Bridge, *Signs and Wonders Today* (Leicester: Inter-Varsity Press, 1985), 183.

31. Here Paul's meaning is that all who receive a revelation in the sense just mentioned in v. 29 will be able to take turns and prophesy one at a time. He does not mean that every single Christian at Corinth had the gift of prophecy.

32. In a large church, only few would be able to speak when the whole church assembled, for Paul says, "Let two or three prophets speak" (1 Cor. 14:29). But many more would find opportunities to prophesy in smaller gatherings in homes.

openness to the gift of prophecy could help overcome the situation where many who attend our churches are merely spectators and not participants. Perhaps we are contributing to the problem of "spectator Christianity" by quenching the work of the Spirit in this area.

## 12. We Should "Earnestly Desire" Prophecy

Paul valued this gift so highly that he told the Corinthians, "Pursue love, and earnestly desire the spiritual gifts, *especially that you may prophesy*" (1 Cor. 14:1). Then at the end of his discussion of spiritual gifts he said again, "So, my brothers, *earnestly desire to prophesy*" (1 Cor. 14:39). And he said, "The one who prophesies builds up the church" (1 Cor. 14:4).

If Paul was eager for the gift of prophecy to function at Corinth, troubled as the church was by immaturity, selfishness, divisions, and other problems, then should we not also actively seek this valuable gift in our congregations today? We evangelicals who profess to believe and obey all that Scripture says, should we not also believe and obey this? And might a greater openness to the gift of prophecy perhaps help to correct a dangerous imbalance in church life, an imbalance that comes because we are too exclusively intellectual, objective, and narrowly doctrinal?

## 13. Encouraging and Regulating Prophecy in the Local Church

Finally, if a church begins to encourage the use of prophecy where it has not been used before, what should it do? How can it encourage this gift without falling into abuse?

For all Christians, and especially for pastors and others who have teaching responsibilities in the church, several steps would be both appropriate and pastorally wise: (1) Pray seriously for the Lord's wisdom on how and when to approach this subject in the church. (2) There should be teaching on this subject in the regular Bible teaching times the church already provides. (3) The church should be patient and proceed slowly—church leaders should not be "domineering" (or "pushy") (1 Peter 5:3), and a patient approach will avoid frightening people away or alienating them unnecessarily. (4) The church should recognize and encourage the gift of prophecy in ways it has already been functioning in the church—at church prayer meetings, for example, when someone has felt unusually "led" by the Holy Spirit to pray for something, when it has seemed that the Holy Spirit was bringing to mind a hymn or Scripture passage, or when giving a common sense of the tone or the specific focus of a time of group worship or prayer. Even Christians in churches not open to the gift of prophecy can at least be sensitive to promptings from the Holy Spirit regarding what to pray for in church prayer meetings and can then express those promptings in the form of a prayer (what might be called a "prophetic prayer") to the Lord.

(5) If the first four steps have been followed, and if the congregation and its leadership will accept it, some opportunities for the gift of prophecy to be used might be

made in the less formal worship services of the church or in smaller home groups. If this is allowed, those who prophesy should be kept within scriptural guidelines (1 Cor. 14:29–36), should genuinely seek the edification of the church and not their own prestige (1 Cor. 14:12, 26), and should not dominate the meeting or be overly dramatic or emotional in their speech (and thus attract attention to themselves rather than to the Lord). Prophecies should certainly be evaluated according to the teachings of Scripture (1 Cor. 14:29–36; 1 Thess. 5:19–21).

(6) If the gift of prophecy begins to be used in a church, the church should place even more emphasis on the vastly superior value of Scripture as the source to which Christians can always go to hear the voice of the living God. Prophecy is a valuable gift, as are many other gifts, but it is in Scripture that God and only God speaks to us his very words, even today, and throughout our lives. Rather than hoping at every worship service that the highlight would be some word of prophecy, those who use the gift of prophecy need to be reminded that we should find our focus of joy, our expectation, and our delight in God himself as he speaks to us through the Bible. There we have a treasure of infinite worth: the actual words of our Creator speaking to us in language we can understand. And rather than seeking frequent guidance through prophecy, we should emphasize that it is in Scripture that we are to find guidance for our lives. In Scripture is our source of direction, our focus when seeking God's will, our sufficient and completely reliable standard. It is of God's words in Scripture that we can with confidence say, "Your word is a lamp to my feet and a light to my path" (Ps. 119:105).

## B. TEACHING

The gift of teaching in the New Testament is *the ability to explain Scripture and apply it to people's lives.* This is evident from a number of passages. In Acts 15:35, Paul and Barnabas and "many others" are in Antioch "*teaching* and preaching the word of the Lord." At Corinth, Paul stayed one and a half years "*teaching* the word of God among them" (Acts 18:11). And the readers of the epistle to the Hebrews, though they ought to have been teachers, needed rather to have someone to teach them again "the basic principles of the oracles of God" (Heb. 5:12). Paul tells the Romans that the words of the Old Testament Scriptures "were written for our instruction (or "teaching," Gk. *didaskalia*)" (Rom. 15:4), and he writes to Timothy that "all Scripture" is "profitable for teaching [*didaskalia*]" (2 Tim. 3:16).

Of course, if "teaching" in the early church was so often based on Old Testament Scripture, it is not surprising that it could also be based on something equal to Scripture in authority, namely, a received body of apostolic instructions. So Timothy was to take the teaching he had received from Paul and commit it to faithful men who would be able to "teach others also" (2 Tim. 2:2). And the Thessalonians were to "stand firm and hold to the traditions" they were "taught" by Paul (2 Thess. 2:15). Far from being based on a spontaneous revelation that came during the worship service of the church (as prophecy was), this kind of "teaching" was the repetition and explanation of authentic apostolic teaching. To teach contrary to Paul's instructions was to teach different or heretical doctrine (*heterodidaskaleō*) and to fail to give heed to "the sound words of our Lord Jesus Christ and the *teaching* that accords with godliness" (1 Tim. 6:3). In fact, Paul said that Timothy was to remind the Corinthians of Paul's ways "as I *teach* them everywhere in every church" (1 Cor. 4:17). Similarly, Timothy was to "command and teach" (1 Tim. 4:11) and to "teach and urge" (1 Tim. 6:2) Paul's instructions to the Ephesian church. Thus it was not prophecy but teaching which in a primary sense (from the apostles) first provided the doctrinal and ethical norms by which the church was regulated. And as those who learned from the apostles also taught, their teaching guided and directed the local churches.[33]

So teaching in terms of the New Testament Epistles consisted of repeating and explaining the words of Scripture (or the equally authoritative teachings of Jesus and of the apostles) and applying them to the hearers. In the New Testament Epistles, "teaching" is something very much like what is described by our phrase "Bible teaching" today.

## C. MIRACLES

Just after apostles, prophets, and teachers, Paul says "then miracles" (1 Cor. 12:28). Although many of the miracles seen in the New Testament were specifically miracles of healing, Paul here lists healing as a separate gift. Therefore, in this context he must have something other than physical healing in view.

We should realize that the English word *miracles* may not give a very close approximation to what Paul intended, since the Greek word is simply the plural form of the word *dynamis*, "power."[34] This means that the term may refer to any kind of activity where God's mighty power is evident. It may include answers to prayer for deliverance from physical danger (as in the deliverance of the apostles from prison in Acts 5:19–20 or 12:6–11), powerful works of judgment on the enemies of the gospel or those who require discipline within the church (see Acts 5:1–11; 13:9–12), or miraculous deliverance from injury (as with Paul and the viper in Acts 28:3–6). But such acts of spiritual power may also include power to triumph over demonic opposition (as in Acts 16:18; cf. Luke 10:17).

Since Paul does not define *miracles* any more specifically than this, we can say that the gift of miracles may include the working of divine power in deliverance from danger, in intervention to meet special needs in the physical world (as in the case of Elijah in 1 Kings 17:1–16), in judgment on those who irrationally and violently oppose the gospel message, in vanquishing the demonic forces that wage war against the church, and in any other way in which God's power is manifested in an evident way to further God's

---

33. See also the discussion in section A.8 above, pp. 1309–10, on the differences between prophecy and teaching.

34. The NIV translates this word "miraculous powers" at

1 Cor. 12:10, and the NASB mg. translates "works of power" in both places.

purposes in a situation. All of these would be works of "power" in which the church would be helped and God's glory would be made evident. (See also the discussion of miracles in chapter 17.)

## D. Healing

### 1. Introduction: Sickness and Health in the History of Redemption

We must realize at the outset that physical sickness came as a result of the fall of Adam. Illness and disease are simply part of the outworking of the curse after the fall, and they will eventually lead toward physical death. However, Christ redeemed us from that curse when he died on the cross: "Surely he has borne our griefs and carried our sorrows . . . and with his wounds we are healed" (Isa. 53:4–5). This passage refers to both physical and spiritual healing that Christ purchased for us, for Peter quotes it to refer to our salvation: "He himself *bore our sins* in his body on the tree, that we might die to sin and live to righteousness. *By his wounds you have been healed*" (1 Peter 2:24). But Matthew quotes the same passage from Isaiah with reference to the physical healings Jesus performed: "He cast out the spirits with a word and *healed all who were sick*. This was to fulfill what was spoken by the prophet Isaiah: '*He took our illnesses* and bore our diseases'" (Matt. 8:16–17).

All Christians would probably agree that in the atonement Christ has purchased for us not only complete freedom from sin but also complete freedom from physical weakness and infirmity in his work of redemption (see chapter 42 on glorification). And all Christians would also no doubt agree that our full and complete possession of all the benefits that Christ earned for us will not come until Christ returns: it is only "at his coming" (1 Cor. 15:23) that we receive our perfect resurrection bodies. So it is with physical healing and redemption from the physical sickness that came as a result of the curse in Genesis 3; our complete possession of redemption from physical illness will not be ours until Christ returns and we receive resurrection bodies.[35]

But the question that confronts us with respect to the gift of healing is whether God may from time to time grant us a foretaste or a down payment of the physical healing which he will grant us fully in the future.[36] The healing miracles of Jesus certainly demonstrate that at times God is willing to grant a partial foretaste of the perfect health that will be ours for eternity. And the ministry of healing seen in the lives of the apostles and others in the early church also indicates that this was part of the ministry of the new covenant age. As such, it fits the larger pattern of blessings in the new covenant, many or

---

35. When people say that complete healing is "in the atonement," the statement is true in an ultimate sense, but it really does not tell us anything about when we will receive "complete healing" (or any part of it).

36. For two very helpful treatments of this question, and of the gift of healing in general, see John Wimber with Kevin Springer, *Power Healing* (San Francisco: Harper and Row,

1987), and Ken Blue, *Authority to Heal* (Downers Grove, IL: InterVarsity Press, 1987). See also the excellent discussion in Jack Deere, *Surprised by the Power of the Holy Spirit* (Grand Rapids: Zondervan, 1993). Several scholarly defenses of a ministry of healing today are found in Gary Greig and Kevin Springer, eds., *The Kingdom and the Power* (Ventura, CA: Gospel Light, 1993).

all of which give partial foretastes of the blessings that will be ours when Christ returns. We "already" possess some of the blessings of the kingdom, but those blessings are "not yet" fully ours.

### 2. The Purposes of Healing

As with other spiritual gifts, healing has several purposes. Certainly it functions as a "sign" to authenticate the gospel message and show that the kingdom of God has come. Then also healing brings comfort and health to those who are ill and thereby demonstrates God's attribute of mercy toward those in distress. Third, healing equips people for service, as physical impediments to ministry are removed. Fourth, healing provides opportunity for God to be glorified as people see physical evidence of his goodness, love, power, wisdom, and presence.

### 3. What about the Use of Medicine?

What is the relationship between prayer for healing and the use of medicine and the skill of a physician? Certainly we should use medicine if it is available because God has also created substances in the earth that can be made into medicine with healing properties. Medicines thus should be considered part of the whole creation that God considered "very good" (Gen. 1:31). We should willingly use medicine with thankfulness to the Lord, for "the earth is the LORD's and the fullness thereof" (Ps. 24:1). In fact, when medicine is available, and we refuse to use it (in cases where it would put ourselves or others in danger), then it seems that we are wrongly "forcing a test" on the Lord our God (cf. Luke 4:12): this is similar to the case of Satan tempting Jesus to jump from the temple rather than walking down the steps. Where ordinary means of getting down from the temple (the steps) are available, it is "forcing a test" on God to jump and thereby demand that he perform a miracle at that exact moment. To refuse to use effective medicine, insisting that God perform a miracle of healing instead of healing through the medicine, is very similar to this.

Of course, it is wrong to rely on doctors or medicine *instead* of relying on the Lord, a mistake tragically made by King Asa: "In the thirty-ninth year of his reign Asa was diseased in his feet, and his disease became severe. Yet even in his disease *he did not seek the LORD, but sought help from physicians*. And Asa slept with his fathers, dying in the forty-first year of his reign" (2 Chron. 16:12–13).

But if medicine is used in connection with prayer, then we should expect God to bless and often multiply the effectiveness of the medicine.[37] Even when Isaiah had received from the Lord a promise of healing for King Hezekiah, he told Hezekiah's servants to bring a cake of figs and apply it (as a medical remedy) to a boil that Hezekiah suffered

---

37. Note Paul's recommendation of a use of wine for health purposes in 1 Tim. 5:23: "No longer drink only water, but use a little wine for the sake of your stomach and your frequent ailments."

from: "Isaiah said, 'Bring a cake of figs. And let them take and lay it on the boil, that he may recover'" (2 Kings 20:7).

However, sometimes there is no appropriate medicine available, or the medicine does not work. Certainly we must remember that God can heal where doctors and medicine cannot heal (and it may amaze us to realize how frequently doctors cannot heal, even in the most medically advanced countries). Moreover, there may be many times when an illness is not putting us or others in immediate danger, and we decide to ask God to heal our sickness without the use of medicine, simply because we wish for another opportunity to exercise our faith and give him glory, and perhaps because we wish to avoid spending the time or money to use medical means, or we wish to avoid the side-effects that some medicines have. In all of these cases, it is simply a matter of personal choice and would not seem to be "forcing a test" on God. (However, a decision not to use medicine in these cases should be a personal choice and not one that is forced on others.)

We see Jesus healing explicitly where medical means have failed, when "a woman who had had a discharge of blood for twelve years, and though she had spent all her living on physicians, she *could not be healed by anyone*" then "came up behind him and touched the fringe of his garment, and immediately her discharge of blood ceased" (Luke 8:43–44). There were no doubt many people beyond the help of physicians who came whenever Jesus was teaching and healing, yet we read that "*all* those who had *any* who were sick with various diseases brought them to him, and he laid his hands on *every one of them* and healed them" (Luke 4:40). There was no disease that Jesus was unable to heal.

## 4. Does the New Testament Show Common Methods Used in Healing?

The methods used by Jesus and the disciples to bring healing varied from case to case, but most frequently they included laying on of hands.[38] In the verse just quoted, Jesus no doubt could have spoken a powerful word of command and healed everyone in the large crowd instantly, but instead "*he laid his hands on every one of them* and healed them" (Luke 4:40). Laying on of hands seems to have been the primary means Jesus used to heal because when people came and asked him for healing they did not simply ask for prayer but said, for example, "come and lay your hand on her, and she will live" (Matt. 9:18).[39]

Another physical symbol of the Holy Spirit's power coming for healing was anointing with oil. Jesus' disciples "*anointed with oil* many who were sick and healed them" (Mark 6:13). And James tells the elders of the church to anoint the sick person with oil when they pray: "Is anyone among you sick? Let him call for the elders of the church, and let them pray over him, *anointing him with oil* in the name of the Lord. And the

---

38. See the discussion of laying on of hands in chapter 48, pp. 1187–89.

39. See also Luke 5:13; 13:13; Acts 28:8; also Mark 6:2, and several other verses in the gospels that mention laying on of hands. Jesus did not always heal in this way, however.

prayer of faith will save the one who is sick, and the Lord will raise him up. And if he has committed sins, he will be forgiven" (James 5:14–15).[40]

The New Testament often emphasizes the role of faith in the healing process—sometimes the faith of the sick person (Luke 8:48; 17:19), but at other times the faith of others who bring the sick person for healing. In James 5:15 it is the elders who pray, and James says it is "the prayer of faith" that saves the sick person—this then must be the faith of the elders praying,[41] not the faith of the one who is sick. When the four men let down a paralytic through a hole in the roof where Jesus was preaching, we read, "And when Jesus saw *their* faith . . ." (Mark 2:5). At other times Jesus mentions the faith of the Canaanite woman regarding the healing of her daughter (Matt. 15:28), or of the centurion for the healing of his servant (Matt. 8:10, 13).[42]

## 5. How Then Should We Pray for Healing?

How then should we pray regarding physical illness? Certainly it is right to ask God for healing, for Jesus tells us to pray, "Deliver us from evil" (Matt. 6:13), and the apostle John writes to Gaius, "I pray that all may go well with you and *that you may be in good health*" (3 John 2). Moreover, Jesus frequently healed *all* who were brought to him, and he never sent people away, telling them it would be good for them to remain ill for a longer time! In addition to this, whenever we take any kind of medicine or seek any medical help for an illness, *by those actions we admit that we think it to be God's will that we seek to be well*. If we thought that God wanted us to continue in our illness, we would never seek medical means for healing! So when we pray it seems right that our first assumption, unless we have specific reason to think otherwise, should be that God would be pleased to heal the person we are praying for—as far as we can tell from Scripture, this is God's revealed will.[43]

Ken Blue has a helpful observation here. He argues that if we want to understand God's attitude toward physical healing we should look at Jesus' life and ministry. Blue says, "If Jesus truly reveals the character of God to us, then we may cease speculating

40. The anointing with oil in James 5:14 should be understood as a symbol of the power of the Holy Spirit, not simply as medicinal, because oil would not be appropriate as a medicine for all diseases. Moreover, if its use were just medicinal, it is hard to see why only the elders should apply it. Oil is frequently a symbol of the Holy Spirit in the Old Testament (see Ex. 29:7; 1 Sam. 16:13; cf. Ps. 45:7), and this seems to be the case here as well. (See the thorough discussion in Douglas Moo, *The Letter of James*, TNTC [Leicester: Inter-Varsity Press; Downers Grove, IL: InterVarsity Press, 1985], 177–81.)

41. We may wonder why it is the elders who are called to come and pray for healing in James 5:14–15. Although James does not give a reason, it may be because they had responsibilities for pastoral care, maturity and wisdom in dealing with the possible sin involved (see vv. 15–16), and a measure of spiritual authority that accompanied their office. They would certainly

be able to bring others with gifts of healing if they wished. Moreover, James broadens his directions to include all Christians in v. 16: "Therefore confess your sins to one another and *pray for one another, that you may be healed.*" By saying this, James encourages all Christians to follow the example of the elders in this passage and pray for healing for those who are sick.

42. By contrast, we can note that when the disciples could not cast out a demon, Jesus says it was "because of your little faith" (Matt. 17:20).

43. See discussion in chapter 13, pp. 254–57, on the secret and revealed will of God. Of course we realize that God's *secret* will, unknown to us in any specifics, is that not all will be healed, just as it is his secret will that not all will be saved. But in both situations we should pray for what we see in Scripture to be God's revealed will: to save sinners and to heal those who are ill.

about and arguing over God's will in sickness and healing. Jesus healed people because he loved them. Very simply, he had compassion for them; he was on their side; he wanted to solve their problems."[44] This is a strong argument, especially when coupled with the realization that Jesus came to inaugurate the presence of the kingdom of God among us and to show us what the kingdom of God would be like.

How then should we pray? Certainly it is right to ask God for healing, and we should go to him with the simple *request* that he give physical healing in time of need. James warns us that simple unbelief can lead to prayerlessness and failure to receive answers from God: "You do not have, because you do not ask" (James 4:2). But when we pray for healing we should remember that we must pray for God to be glorified in the situation, whether he chooses to heal or not. And we also ought to pray out of the same compassion of heart that Jesus felt for those whom he healed. When we pray this way, God will sometimes—and perhaps often—grant answers to our prayers.

Someone may object at this point that, from a pastoral standpoint, much harm is done when people are encouraged to believe that a miracle of healing will occur and then nothing happens—disappointment with the church and anger at God may result. Those who pray for people to be healed today need to hear this objection and use wisdom in what they tell people who are ill.

But we also need to realize that there is more than one kind of mistake to make: (1) *Not praying for healing at all* is not a correct solution, for it involves disobedience to James 5. (2) Telling people that *God seldom heals today* and that they should expect nothing to happen is not a correct solution either, for it does not provide an atmosphere conducive to faith and is inconsistent with the pattern we see in the ministry of Jesus and the early church in the New Testament. (3) Telling people that *God always heals today* if we have enough faith is a cruel teaching not supported by Scripture (see section 6 below).

The pastorally wise solution, it seems, lies between (2) and (3) above. We can tell people that God frequently heals today (if we believe that is true), and that it is very possible that they will be healed,[45] but that we are still living in an age when the kingdom of God is "already" here but "not yet" fully here. Therefore, Christians in this life will experience healing (and many other answers to prayer), but they will also experience continuing illness and eventual death. In each individual case it is God's sovereign wisdom that decides the outcome, and *our role is simply to ask him* and wait for him to answer (whether "yes" or "no" or "keep praying and wait").

---

44. Blue, *Authority to Heal*, 72, 78.

45. Sometimes God may grant a strong subjective assurance of faith, something like what James calls "the prayer of faith" (James 5:15), and Heb. 11:1 calls "the assurance of things hoped for," and Mark 11:24 calls believing "that you have received it." In those cases the person praying may feel confidence to say that it is probable or even very likely that someone will be healed. But I do not think that God gives anyone warrant to promise or "guarantee" healing in this age, for his written Word makes no such guarantee, and our subjective sense of his will is always subject to some degree of uncertainty and some measure of error in this life.

Those with "gifts of healings" (a literal translation of the plurals in 1 Cor. 12:9, 28) will be those people who find that their prayers for healing are answered more frequently and more thoroughly than others. When that becomes evident, a church would be wise to encourage them in this ministry and give them more opportunities to pray for others who are ill. We should also realize that gifts of healing could include ministry not only in terms of physical healing but also in terms of emotional healing. And it may at times include the ability to set people free from demonic attack, for this is also called "healing" sometimes in Scripture (see Luke 6:18; Acts 10:38). Perhaps the gifts of being able to pray effectively in different kinds of situations and for different kinds of needs are what Paul referred to when he used the plural expression, *"gifts of healings."*

### 6. What If God Does Not Heal?

Nonetheless, we must realize that not all prayers for healing will be answered in this age. Sometimes God will not grant the special "faith" (James 5:15) that healing will occur, and at times God will choose not to heal because of his own sovereign purposes. In these cases we must remember that Romans 8:28 is still true: though we experience the "sufferings of this present time," and though we "groan inwardly as we wait eagerly for . . . the redemption of our bodies" (Rom. 8:18, 23), nonetheless, "we know that for those who love God all things work together for good, for those who are called according to his purpose" (Rom. 8:28). This includes working in our circumstances of suffering and illness as well.

Whatever Paul's thorn in the flesh was (and centuries of work by Bible-believing interpreters have failed to turn up a definitive answer), Paul realized that God allowed it to remain with him "to keep me from becoming conceited" (2 Cor. 12:7), that is, to keep Paul humble before the Lord.[46] So the Lord told him, "My grace is sufficient for you, for my power is made perfect in weakness" (2 Cor. 12:9). There are indications in the early church that even in the presence of the apostles not all people were healed. Paul recognized that "our outer self is wasting away" (2 Cor. 4:16), and sometimes disease and illness will not be healed. When Epaphroditus came to visit Paul, he had an illness that brought him "near to death" (Phil. 2:27). Paul indicates in the narrative of Philippians 2 that it appeared as though Epaphroditus was going to die—that God did not heal him immediately when he became ill. But eventually God did heal (Phil. 2:27) in answer to prayer. Paul told Timothy that he should drink a little wine "for the sake of your stomach and your frequent ailments" (1 Tim. 5:23). He said, "I left Trophimus, *who was ill*, at Miletus" (2 Tim. 4:20). And both Peter (1 Peter 1:6–7; 4:19) and James (James

---

46. After some study of the "thorn in the flesh" passage in 2 Cor. 12:7, my own conclusion at this point is that there is not enough information in the text to decide what Paul's thorn in the flesh was. There are reasons that can be given in support of all three main possibilities: (1) a physical ailment of some kind; (2) a demon that was harassing him; or (3) Jewish persecutors. The fact that we are unable to decide conclusively has some benefits, however. It means that we can apply this text to all of these kinds of situations in our own lives, when the Lord in his sovereign wisdom decides not to remove them from us.

1:2–4) have words of encouragement and counsel for those who are suffering trials of various kinds:[47]

> Count it all joy, my brothers, when you meet trials of various kinds, for you know that the testing of your faith produces steadfastness. And let steadfastness have its full effect, that you may be perfect and complete, lacking in nothing. (James 1:2–4)

When God chooses not to heal, even though we ask him for it, then it is right that we "give thanks in all circumstances" (1 Thess. 5:18) and realize that God can use sickness to draw us closer to himself and to increase in us obedience to his will. So the psalmist can say, "*It is good for me that I was afflicted,* that I might learn your statutes" (Ps. 119:71), and, "Before I was afflicted I went astray, but now I keep your word" (Ps. 119:67).

Therefore God can bring increased sanctification to us through illness and suffering—just as he can bring sanctification and growth in faith through miraculous healing. But the emphasis of the New Testament, both in Jesus' ministry and in the ministry of the disciples in Acts, seems to be one that encourages us in most cases eagerly and earnestly to seek God for healing, and then to continue to trust him to bring good out of the situation, whether he grants the physical healing or not. The point is that in everything God should receive glory and our joy and trust in him should increase.

## E. Tongues and Interpretation

It should be said at the outset that the Greek word *glōssa*, translated "tongue," is used not only to mean the physical tongue in a person's mouth but also to mean "language." In the New Testament passages where speaking in tongues is discussed, the meaning "languages" is certainly in view. It is unfortunate, therefore, that English translations have continued to use the phrase "speaking in tongues," which is an expression not otherwise used in ordinary English and which gives the impression of a strange experience, something completely foreign to ordinary human life. But if English translations were to use the expression "speaking in languages," it would not seem nearly as strange and would give the reader a sense much closer to what first century Greek speaking readers

---

47. Some have attempted to establish a difference between sickness and other kinds of suffering and to say that the passages in Scripture that tell Christians they should expect to suffer have to do with *other* kinds of suffering, such as persecution, but do not include physical sickness.

This argument seems unconvincing to me for two reasons: first, Scripture talks about "trials of *various kinds*" (James 1:2; also 1 Peter 1:6), and the intention of the authors in both cases seems to be to speak of *all* the kinds of trials that we experience in this life, including physical illness and affliction. Did James and Peter *not* want Christians who were ill to apply those passages to their own situations? This is hardly likely. (These are both general epistles written to thousands of Christians.)

Second, unless the Lord returns, we will all know the progressive aging and deterioration of our physical bodies, and eventually we will die. Paul says, "Our outer self is wasting away" (2 Cor. 4:16). Almost inevitably this aging process includes various kinds of physical ailments.

It seems best to conclude that the sufferings which God allows us to experience from time to time in this life may at times include physical illness, which God in his sovereign wisdom decides not to heal. There may in fact be many cases when, for various reasons, we do not feel freedom to ask in faith for God to heal. Yet even in these cases the heart of faith will take God's Word as true and believe that this also has come into our lives "for good" (Rom. 8:28), and that God will bring good to us from it.

would have heard in the phrase when they read it in Acts or 1 Corinthians. However, because current usage of the phrase "speaking in tongues" is so widely established, we will continue to use it in this discussion.[48]

## 1. Tongues in the History of Redemption

In the Bible, the phenomenon of speaking in tongues is unique to the new covenant age. Before Adam and Eve fell into sin, there was no need to speak in other languages because they spoke the *same language* and were *united in service of God* and in fellowship with him. After the fall people spoke the *same language* but eventually became *united in opposition to God*, and "the wickedness of man was great in the earth" and "every intention of the thoughts of his heart was only evil continually" (Gen. 6:5). This unified language used in rebellion against God culminated in the building of the tower of Babel at a time when "the whole earth had one language and the same words" (Gen. 11:1). In order to stop this united rebellion against him, God at Babel "confused the language of all the earth" and scattered people abroad over the face of the earth (Gen. 11:9).

In the New Testament, at Pentecost, the disciples in Jerusalem "began to speak in other tongues [or languages] as the Spirit gave them utterance" (Acts 2:4). (This verse shows that the miracle was one of speaking, not of hearing. The disciples "began to *speak* in other tongues [or languages].") Jewish visitors from various nations all heard in their own languages a proclamation of "the mighty works of God" (Acts 2:11). This was a remarkable symbol of the fact that the gospel message was about to go forth to all the nations of the world. Such a symbolic action would have been inappropriate in the Old Testament, for there the evangelistic message was one of inviting people from other nations *to come and join themselves to the Jewish people* and become Jews, and thereby worship God. But here the message is about *to go to each nation* in its own language, encouraging people in every place to turn to Christ and be saved. [49]

Moreover, within the context of the worship service of the church, speaking in tongues plus interpretation gives further indication of a promise that one day the differences in languages that originated at Babel will be overcome. If this gift is operating in a church, no matter what language a word of prayer or praise is given in, once there is an interpretation, everyone can understand it. This is, of course, a two-step process that is "partial," as are all gifts in this age (1 Cor. 13:10), but it is still an improvement on the situation from Babel to Pentecost when there was no provision to enable people to understand a message in a language they did not know.

Now if we look ahead to the age to come, we see that once again unity of language

---

48. The most comprehensive and, I think, biblically balanced continuationist book about speaking in tongues is now Sam Storms, *The Language of Heaven: Crucial Questions about Speaking in Tongues* (Lake Mary, FL: Charisma House, 2019).

49. The speaking in tongues at Pentecost was unusual in that it was accompanied by "divided tongues as of fire" that "rested on each one of them" (Acts 2:3). Since fire in Scripture is often a symbol of God's purifying judgment, the presence of fire here may be a symbol of the fact that God was purifying language for use in his service.

will apparently be restored, but this time everyone will once again speak the *same language in service of God*, and in praise to him. "For at that time I will change the speech of the peoples to a pure speech, that all of them may call upon the name of the LORD and serve him with one accord" (Zeph. 3:9; cf. 1 Cor. 13:8: "As for tongues, they will cease").

Finally, prayer in tongues in a private setting is another form of prayer to God. Paul says, "If I pray in a tongue, *my spirit prays* but my mind is unfruitful" (1 Cor. 14:14). In the overall context of the history of redemption, this also may be seen as one more partial solution to the results of the fall, whereby we were cut off from fellowship with God. Of course, this does not mean that people's spirits can *only* have fellowship with God when they speak in tongues—for Paul affirms that he prays and sings both in tongues and in his own language (1 Cor. 14:15). However, Paul does see prayer in tongues as an additional means of fellowship directly with God in prayer and worship. Once again, this aspect of the gift of speaking in tongues was not operative, so far as we know, before the new covenant age.

## 2. What Is Speaking in Tongues?

We may define this gift as follows: *speaking in tongues is prayer or praise spoken in syllables not understood by the speaker.*

**a. Words of Prayer or Praise Spoken to God.** This definition indicates that speaking in tongues is primarily speech directed toward God (that is, prayer or praise). It is unlike the gift of prophecy, which frequently consists of messages directed *from* God toward people in the church. Paul says, "One who speaks in a tongue speaks not to men but *to God*" (1 Cor. 14:2), and if there is no interpreter present at the church service, Paul says that someone who has a gift of speaking in tongues should "keep silent in church and speak to himself and *to God*" (1 Cor. 14:28).

What kind of speech is this that is directed toward God? Paul says, "If I *pray* in a tongue, *my spirit prays* but my mind is unfruitful" (1 Cor. 14:14; cf. vv. 14–17, where Paul categorizes speech in tongues as praying and giving thanks, and v. 28). Therefore speaking in tongues apparently is prayer or praise directed to God, and it comes from the "spirit" of the person who is speaking. This is not inconsistent with the narrative in Acts 2 because the crowd said, "We hear them telling in our own tongues the mighty works of God" (Acts 2:11), a description that certainly could mean that the disciples were all glorifying God and proclaiming his mighty works in worship, and the crowd began to listen to this as it occurred in various languages.[50]

I do not want to rule out the possibility that speaking in tongues could sometimes include speech directed to people, not to God, because it is just possible that Paul's

---

50. In Acts 10:46 the people at Cornelius' household began "speaking in tongues and extolling God." Again, this either means that the speech consisted of praise to God or was very closely connected with it—grammatically one cannot tell from the text itself.

statement in 1 Corinthians 14:2 is not intended to cover every instance. In any case, the main point of the verse is that only God can *understand* uninterpreted tongues, not that God is the only one to whom speech in tongues can be addressed. In fact, speech to other people might be what is happening in Acts 2. Nevertheless, the evidence that we do have in 1 Corinthians 14 indicates speech directed toward God, and it seems safe to say that that is generally what speaking in tongues will be.

**b. Not Understood by the Speaker.** Paul says that "one who speaks in a tongue speaks not to men but to God; *for no one understands him*, but he utters mysteries in the Spirit" (1 Cor. 14:2). Similarly, he says that if there is speaking in tongues without interpretation no meaning will be communicated: "I will be a foreigner to the speaker and the speaker a foreigner to me" (1 Cor. 14:11). Moreover, the entire paragraph of 1 Corinthians 14:13–19 assumes that speech in tongues in the congregation, when it is not accompanied by interpretation, is *not understood* by those who hear:

> Therefore, one who speaks in a tongue should pray that he may interpret. For if I pray in a tongue, my spirit prays but my mind is unfruitful. What am I to do? I will pray with my spirit, but I will pray with my mind also; I will sing praise with my spirit, but I will sing with my mind also. Otherwise, if you give thanks with your spirit, how can anyone in the position of an outsider say "Amen" to your thanksgiving when he does not know what you are saying? For you may be giving thanks well enough, but the other person is not being built up. I thank God that I speak in tongues more than all of you. Nevertheless, in church I would rather speak five words with my mind *in order to instruct others*, than ten thousand words in a tongue.

**c. Sometimes Known Languages, Sometimes Not.** At Pentecost, speech in tongues was in *known languages* that were understood by those who heard: "each one was hearing them speak *in his own language*" (Acts 2:6). But once again the speech was not understood by the speakers, for what caused the amazement was that Galileans were speaking all these different languages (v. 7). It seems, therefore, that *at times* speaking in tongues may involve speech in actual human languages, sometimes even languages that are understood by some of those who hear. But at other times—and Paul assumes that this will ordinarily be the case—the speech will be in a language that "no one understands" (1 Cor. 14:2).

Some have objected that speaking in tongues must always consist of speech in *known* human languages, since that is what happened at Pentecost. But the fact that speaking in tongues occurred in known human languages *once* in Scripture does not require that it *always* happen with known languages, especially when another description of speaking in tongues (1 Cor. 14) indicates exactly the opposite.

Paul does not say that foreign visitors to Corinth will understand the speaker, but he says that when someone speaks in tongues "*no one*" will understand and the outsider will not know what the person is saying (1 Cor. 14:2, 16).[51] In fact, Paul explicitly says that quite the opposite of the phenomenon at Pentecost will happen in the ordinary conduct of church life: if "all speak in tongues" and "outsiders or unbelievers enter," far from understanding the message, they will say "that you are out of your minds" (1 Cor. 14:23).

Moreover, we must realize that 1 Corinthians 14 is Paul's general instruction based on a wide experience of tongues-speaking in many different churches, whereas Acts 2 simply describes one unique event at a significant turning point in the history of redemption (Acts 2 is historical narrative while 1 Cor. 14 is doctrinal instruction). Therefore, it would seem appropriate to take 1 Corinthians 14 as the passage that most closely describes the ordinary experience of New Testament churches and to take Paul's instructions there as the standard by which God intends churches to regulate the use of this gift. In addition, at Pentecost this speaking in tongues had another characteristic that was not shared by any later speech in tongues: there were tongues of fire appearing over the heads of those who spoke (Acts 2:3). But this is not a paradigm for all later experiences of speaking in tongues, not even for those found later in Acts.

Are tongues known human languages then? Sometimes this gift may result in speaking in a known human language that the speaker has not learned, but more often it seems that it will involve speech in a language that no one understands, whether that be a human language or not.[52]

**d. Prayer with the Spirit, Not with the Mind.** Paul says, "If I pray in a tongue, *my spirit prays* but my *mind is unfruitful*. What am I to do? I will pray with my spirit, but I will pray with my mind also; I will sing praise with my spirit, but I will sing with my mind also" (1 Cor. 14:14–15). Paul is not talking about the Holy Spirit praying through us. The contrast between "my spirit" and "my mind" in verse 14 indicates that it is Paul's human spirit that he is talking about, the nonmaterial aspect of his being. As he uses this gift, his spirit speaks directly to God, even though his mind does not have to formulate

---

51. Robertson and Plummer note that 1 Cor. 14:18, "I thank God that I speak in tongues more than all of you," is "strong evidence that Tongues are not foreign languages" (A. Robertson and A. Plummer, *A Critical and Exegetical Commentary on the First Epistle of St. Paul to the Corinthians*, ICC [Edinburgh: T&T Clark, 1914], 314). If they were known foreign languages that foreigners could understand, as at Pentecost, why would Paul speak more than all the Corinthians in private, where no one would understand, rather than in church where foreign visitors could understand?

52. Paul does say, "If I speak in the tongues of men *and of angels*" (1 Cor. 13:1), suggesting that he sees the possibility that speaking in tongues may include more than merely human speech. Whether he thinks this is only a hypothetical possibility or a real one is difficult to say, but we certainly cannot rule out the idea that angelic languages would be involved with this speech as well.

Some have objected that since *glōssa* elsewhere in Greek (outside the New Testament) refers to *known* human languages,

it must refer to known languages in the New Testament as well. But this objection is not convincing, since there was no other word in Greek better suited to refer to this phenomenon, even if it involved talking to God in languages that were not human languages or not fully developed languages of any sort, so long as some content or information was conveyed by the speech.

I am not here arguing that speaking in tongues in Acts 2 was a different phenomenon from the speaking in tongues that Paul discusses in 1 Cor. 14. I am simply saying that the phrase "speaking in tongues" in Acts 2 and 1 Cor. 14 refers to speech in syllables not understood by the speaker but understood by God, to whom this speech is directed. In Acts 2 this happened to be speech in known human languages that had not been learned by the speakers, whereas in 1 Cor. 14 the speech may have been in unknown human languages, or in angelic languages, or in some specialized kind of language given by the Holy Spirit to various speakers individually. The expression is broad enough to include a wide variety of phenomena.

words and sentences and decide what to pray for.[53] Paul sees this kind of prayer as an activity that occurs in the spiritual realm, whereby our spirits speak directly to God, but our minds are somehow bypassed and do not understand what we are praying.

We may wonder why God would give the church a gift that operates in the unseen, spiritual realm and that is not understood by our minds. One reason may be to keep us humble, helping prevent intellectual pride. Another reason may be to remind us that God is greater than our understanding and that he works in ways that transcend our understanding. Finally, it is characteristic of much that God does in the new covenant age that it is done in the unseen, spiritual realm: regeneration, genuine prayer, worship "in spirit and in truth," the spiritual blessings that come through the Lord's Supper, spiritual warfare, laying up treasures in heaven, setting our minds on things above, where Christ is—all these and many more elements of the Christian life involve activities that occur in the unseen, spiritual realm, activities that we do not see or fully understand. In that light, speaking in tongues is simply another activity that occurs in the unseen spiritual realm, an activity we believe is effective because Scripture tells us it is, not because we can comprehend it with our minds (cf. 1 Cor. 14:5).

**e. Not Ecstatic but Self-Controlled.** The New English Bible (1970) translated the phrase "speaking in tongues" as "ecstatic speech," thus giving further support to the idea that those who speak in tongues lose awareness of their surroundings or lose self-control or are forced to speak against their will. Moreover, some of the extreme elements in the Pentecostal movement have allowed frenzied and disorderly conduct at worship services, and this has, in the minds of some, perpetuated the notion that speaking in tongues is a kind of ecstatic[54] speech.

But this is not the picture given in the New Testament. Even when the Holy Spirit came with overwhelming power at Pentecost, the disciples were able to stop speaking in tongues so that Peter could give his sermon to the assembled crowd. More explicitly, Paul says, "If any speak in a tongue, let there be *only two or at most three, and each in turn*, and let someone interpret. But if there is no one to interpret, let each of them keep silent in church and speak to himself and to God" (1 Cor. 14:27–28). Here Paul requires that those who speak in tongues take turns, and he limits the number to three, indicating clearly that those who spoke in tongues were aware of what was going on around them

---

53. The phrase "praying in the Holy Spirit" in Jude 20 is not the same expression since it is specifically the "Holy Spirit" who is designated. Jude is simply saying that Christians should pray in conformity to the character and leading of the Holy Spirit, and that may certainly include prayer in tongues, but it would include any other kind of prayer in an understandable language as well. Similarly, "praying at all times *in the Spirit*, with all prayer and supplication" (Eph. 6:18) is specifically a statement that claims to cover all prayer that is made at all times. It refers to prayer in conformity to the character of the Holy Spirit and sensitive to the leading of the Holy Spirit, but

it should not be restricted to speaking in tongues. Once again, it may include speaking in tongues, but should include all other types of prayer as well. (See the discussion of activities done "in the Holy Spirit" in chapter 30, pp. 795–96.)

54. The word *ecstatic* when used to describe speech activity means either "a state of emotion so intense that one is carried beyond rational thought and self-control" or "the trance, frenzy, or rapture associated with mystic or prophetic exaltation" (*American Heritage Dictionary*, 4th ed. [Boston: Houghton Mifflin, 2006], s.v. ecstatic [p. 567]).

and were able to control themselves so as to speak only when it was their turn, when no one else was speaking. If there was no one to interpret, they were easily able to keep silent and not speak. All of these factors indicate a high degree of self-control and give no support to the idea that Paul thought of tongues as ecstatic speech of some kind.[55]

**f. 1 Corinthians 14:20–25: Tongues and Prophecy as Signs of God's Attitude.** In 1 Corinthians 14:20–25 Paul says that if believers speak in tongues without interpretation in church, they will be acting and thinking like "children" (1 Cor. 14:20). He first quotes a prophecy of judgment from Isaiah 28:11–12: "In the Law it is written, 'By people of strange tongues and by the lips of foreigners will I speak to this people, and even then they will not listen to me, says the Lord'" (1 Cor. 14:21).

In the context of Isaiah 28, God is warning the rebellious people of Israel that the next words they heard from him would be words of foreigners that they could not understand—the Assyrian army would come on them as agents of God's judgment. Now Paul is about to take this as a general principle—when God speaks to people in language they cannot understand, it is quite evidently a sign of God's judgment.

Paul rightly applies that to the situation of speaking in tongues without interpretation in the church service. He calls it a sign (that is, a sign of judgment) on unbelievers: "Thus *tongues are a sign* not for believers but *for unbelievers*, while prophecy is a sign not for unbelievers but for believers. If, therefore, the whole church comes together and all speak in tongues, and outsiders or unbelievers enter, will they not say that you are out of your minds?" (1 Cor. 14:22–23). Here Paul uses the word *sign* to mean "sign of God's attitude" (whether positive or negative). Tongues that are not understood by outsiders are certainly a *negative* sign—a sign of judgment. Therefore, Paul cautions the Corinthians not to give such a sign to outsiders who come in. He tells them if an outsider comes in and hears only unintelligible speech, he will certainly not be saved but will conclude that the Corinthians are out of their minds, and the uninterpreted tongues will, in this case, function as a sign of God's judgment.

By contrast, Paul says that prophecy is a sign of God's attitude as well, but here it is a *positive* sign of God's blessing. This is why he can say that prophecy is a sign "for believers" (v. 22). And this is why he concludes his section by saying, "If all prophesy, and an unbeliever or outsider enters, he is convicted by all, he is called to account by all, the secrets of his heart are disclosed, and so, falling on his face, he will worship God and declare that God is really among you" (vv. 24–25). When this happens, believers will certainly realize that God is active among them to bring blessing, and prophecy will regularly function as a sign *for believers* of God's positive attitude for them.[56]

---

55. Therefore, it is unfortunate that Thomas Schreiner only lists two alternatives for the nature of speaking in tongues: it is either human languages or else "ecstatic speech" (*Spiritual Gifts*, 123–46), which is, at best, a mildly pejorative label. By contrast, I and all continuationist writers known to me understand tongues to be *nonecstatic* speech in syllables the speaker does not understand.

56. For further discussion of this passage, see Wayne Grudem, "1 Corinthians 14:20–25: Prophecy and Tongues as Signs of God's Attitude," *WTJ* 41, no. 2 (Spring 1979): 381–96.

**g. Tongues without Interpretation.** If no one known to have the gift of interpretation is present in the assembly, Paul gives a different guideline: "But if there is no one to interpret, let each of them keep silent in church and speak to himself and to God" (1 Cor. 14:27–28). In other words, speaking in tongues should be in private. No speech in tongues without interpretation should be given in the church service.[57]

Paul speaks of praying in tongues and singing in tongues when he says, "I will *pray with my spirit*, but I will pray with my mind also; I will *sing praise with my spirit*, but I will sing with my mind also" (1 Cor. 14:15). This gives further confirmation to the definition given above in which we viewed tongues as something primarily directed toward God in prayer and praise. It also gives legitimacy to the practice of singing in tongues, whether publicly or privately. Yet the same rules apply for singing as for speaking: if there is no interpreter, it should only be done in private.[58]

Nevertheless, however much Paul warns against using tongues without interpretation *in church*, he certainly views it positively and encourages it in *private*. He says, "The one who speaks in a tongue *builds up himself*, but the one who prophesies builds up the church" (1 Cor. 14:4). What is his conclusion? It is not (as some would argue) that Christians should decide not to use the gift or decide that it has no value when used privately. Rather, he says, "What am I to do? I will pray with my spirit, but I will pray with my mind also" (v. 15). And he says, "I thank God that I speak in tongues more than all of you" (v. 18), and "Now *I want you all to speak in tongues*, but even more to prophesy" (v. 5), and "Earnestly desire to prophesy, and do not forbid speaking in tongues" (v. 39). If our previous understanding of tongues as prayer or praise to God is correct, then we would certainly expect that edification would follow, even though the speaker's mind does not understand what is being said, and his or her spirit is communicating directly with God. Just as prayer and worship in general build us up as we engage in them, so this kind of prayer and worship builds us up too, according to Paul.

**h. Tongues with Interpretation: Building Up the Church.** Paul says, "The one who prophesies is greater than the one who speaks in tongues, *unless someone interprets*,

---

57. It is troubling that, in some churches today where speaking in tongues is allowed, those who do *not* give a message publicly (perhaps because it is not the appropriate time in the service or perhaps because they do not know if someone will interpret) will still sometimes speak in tongues not "silently" but so that four or five people nearby can hear their speech in tongues. This is simply *disobedience* to Paul's directive, and is not acting in love toward others in the church. Paul says to "keep *silent* in church" if one is not giving a public message in tongues. (Many who have spoken in tongues today say that it can easily be done in an inaudible whisper, so that no one else will hear, and Paul's directions will be obeyed.)

58. Many churches today, however, practice what is sometimes called "singing in the Spirit," in which many or all the congregation will simultaneously sing in tongues, individually improvising their melodies around a certain dominant musical chord. While many people will testify that there is beauty and spiritual power in such occurrences, once again we must object that it is directly contrary to Paul's instructions in 1 Cor. 14:27–28, where those who speak in tongues are to take turns, and there are to be at most three in a worship service, and interpretation is to follow. Though this practice may sound beautiful to those who are familiar with it, and though God may at times graciously use it as a means of winning an unbeliever, Paul explicitly says that the expected result generally will be that unbelievers will say "that you are out of your minds" (1 Cor. 14:23). An alternative to this practice, and one that would both be consistent with Scripture and follow the path of love toward outsiders, would be for everyone to sing in this way, not in tongues, but in an understandable language (whether English or whatever language is commonly understood in the area where the church assembles).

so that the church may be built up" (1 Cor. 14:5). Once a message in tongues is interpreted, all can understand. In that case, Paul says that the message in tongues is *as valuable* to the church as prophecy.

It is important to note here that *Paul does not say that prophecy and tongues have the same function* (for other passages indicate that prophecy is communication from God toward humans, while tongues is generally communication from humans to God). But Paul clearly says they have equal value in edifying the church. We may define the gift of interpretation as *reporting to the church the general meaning of something spoken in tongues.*

**i. Not All Speak in Tongues.** Just as not all Christians are apostles, not all are prophets or teachers, and not all possess gifts of healing, so also not all speak with tongues. Paul clearly implies this when he asks a series of questions, all of which expect the answer "no," and includes the question "Do all speak with tongues?" (1 Cor. 12:30). The implied answer is no.[59]

Some have argued that Paul here only means that not all speak with tongues *publicly*, and perhaps he would have admitted that all can speak in tongues privately. But this distinction seems foreign to the context and unconvincing. He does not specify that not all speak with tongues *publicly* or *in church*, but he simply says that not all speak with tongues. His next question is, "Do all interpret?" (v. 30). His previous two questions were, "Do all work miracles? Do all possess gifts of healing?" (vv. 29–30). Would we wish to make the same arguments about these gifts—that not all interpret tongues *publicly*, but that all Christians are able to do it *privately*? Or that not all work miracles publicly, but that all are able to work miracles privately? Such a distinction seems unwarranted by the context in every case.

In actuality, the desire to say that every Christian can speak in tongues (even though Paul says that not all speak in tongues) is probably motivated in most cases by a prior doctrinal understanding that views baptism in the Holy Spirit as an experience subsequent to conversion[60] and sees speaking in tongues as an initial "sign" of receiving this baptism in the Holy Spirit.[61] But there are serious questions that remain about this doctrinal position (as explained in chapter 39). It seems better to take 1 Corinthians 12:30 to mean just what it says: not all speak in tongues. The gift of tongues—just like every other gift—is not given by the Holy Spirit to every Christian who seeks it. He "apportions to each one individually as he wills" (1 Cor. 12:11).

However, Scripture does not indicate that only a few will receive the gift of speaking in tongues, and since it is a gift Paul views as edifying and useful in prayer and worship (on a personal level even if not in church), it would not be surprising if the Holy Spirit gave a very widespread distribution of this gift, and many Christians in fact received it.[62]

---

59. The Greek particle *mē*, which precedes this question, expects the answer "no" from the reader. The NASB captures this sense: "All do not speak with tongues, do they?"

60. See chapter 39 about baptism in the Holy Spirit.

61. This is still the official doctrinal position of the Assemblies of God, for example.

62. Mark 16:17 is sometimes used to claim that all Christians can speak in tongues: "And these signs will accompany

**j. What about the Danger of Demonic Counterfeit?** At times Christians have been afraid to speak in tongues, wondering if speaking something they do not understand might involve them in speaking blasphemy against God or speaking something that is prompted by a demon rather than by the Holy Spirit.

First, it must be said that this is not Paul's concern, even in the city of Corinth where many had come from pagan temple worship, and where Paul had clearly said that "what pagans sacrifice they offer to demons and not to God" (1 Cor. 10:20). Nonetheless, Paul says, "I want you all to speak in tongues" (1 Cor. 14:5). He gives no warning that they should beware of demonic counterfeit or even think that this would be a possibility when they use this gift.

The theological reason underlying Paul's encouragement at that point is the fact that the Holy Spirit is working powerfully within the lives of believers. Paul says, "I want you to understand that no one speaking in the Spirit of God ever says 'Jesus is accursed!' and no one can say 'Jesus is Lord' except in the Holy Spirit" (1 Cor. 12:3). Here Paul reassures the Corinthians that if they are speaking by the power of the Holy Spirit working within them, they will not say, "Jesus is accursed!"[63] Coming as it does at the beginning of a discussion of spiritual gifts, 1 Corinthians 12:3 is intended to function as reassurance to the Corinthians who may have suspected some Christians who came from backgrounds of demon worship in the temples at Corinth. Might this demonic influence still affect their use of a spiritual gift? Paul lays down the ground rule that those who genuinely profess faith that "Jesus is Lord" are doing so by the Holy Spirit working within and that no one speaking by the power of the Holy Spirit will ever speak blasphemy or curses against Jesus.[64] This fear, then, is not one that Paul seemed troubled by. He simply encouraged believers to pray in tongues and said that if they did so they would be edifying themselves.[65]

---

those who believe: in my name they will cast out demons; they will speak in new tongues." But in response to this verse it must be noted (1) that the verse probably was not originally part of Mark's gospel, since many early and very reliable manuscripts do not include Mark 16:9–20, and its doubtful status means that it is a precarious basis upon which to build doctrine (see discussion in chapter 17, p. 481); (2) that even if it is not part of Scripture, it does of course bear witness to a very early tradition in the history of the church, but even in this case, it does not affirm that all believers will speak with tongues: the immediately following phrase says, "They will pick up serpents" (v. 18), something that no responsible interpreter would say should be true of every Christian; and (3) that no connection is made between speaking in tongues and baptism in the Holy Spirit in this passage.

63. It might be objected at this point that speaking in tongues is not speech empowered by the Holy Spirit but is speech that comes from the speaker's own human spirit. But Paul clearly views all these spiritual gifts as generally *empowered* by the Holy Spirit, even the ones in which human personality comes fully into play. This would be true of teachers and helpers and administrators, as well as those who speak with tongues. In each of these cases the active agent in performing the activity is the Christian who has the particular gift and uses it, but all these are nonetheless empowered by the Holy Spirit in their functioning, and that would be true of the gift of tongues as well.

64. Also relevant at this point is John's reassurance to his readers, in the context of demonic spirits that had gone out into the world: "He who is in you is greater than he who is in the world" (1 John 4:4).

65. Some popular books have given anecdotal accounts of Christians who say they spoke in tongues for a time and then found that there was a demon within them who was empowering this speech, and the demon was cast out. (See, for example, C. Fred Dickason, *Demon Possession and the Christian* [Westchester, IL: Crossway, 1987], 126–27; 188–91; 193–97.) But this is just another example of a case where experience is to be subject to Scripture and tested by Scripture, and the teaching of Scripture should not be subject to experience. We must be

**k. Is Romans 8:26–27 Related to Speaking in Tongues?** Paul writes in Romans 8:26–27: "Likewise the Spirit helps us in our weakness. For we do not know what to pray for as we ought, but the Spirit himself intercedes for us with groanings too deep for words. And he who searches hearts knows what is the mind of the Spirit, because the Spirit intercedes for the saints according to the will of God." Paul does not mention speaking in tongues explicitly here, and the statement is a general one concerning the life of all Christians, so it does not seem correct to say that Paul here is referring to speaking in tongues. He is referring to a more general experience that occurs in the prayer life of every Christian.

But what exactly is he talking about? Some have thought that he is referring to an intercessory activity completely imperceptible to us, in which the Holy Spirit intercedes for us by making sighs and groans to the Father. On this view, such intercessory work of the Spirit goes on continually, but we have no idea that it is happening (except for the fact that Scripture tells us this). In this way it would be similar to the intercessory work of Christ mentioned in Romans 8:34 and Hebrews 7:25.

But this does not appear to be a satisfactory explanation of the passage, for several reasons: (1) It would not seem probable that Paul would say that the intercessory work of the Holy Spirit, who is the infinite, omnipotent, omniscient God, would be carried out in "wordless *groans*" (literal translation of *stenagmois alalētois* in Rom. 8:26), especially when we realize that *groans* refers to the intense sighs of fatigue that are appropriate to weary, burdened creatures in a fallen world.[66] (2) Within the larger context the groanings in view seem to be those due to the burden of living in this present evil age,

---

careful that we not let such reports of experiences cause us to adopt a different position than Scripture itself on this issue. Specifically, if 1 Cor. 12–14 views tongues as a good gift from the Holy Spirit that is valuable for edification and for the good of the church, and if Paul can say, "I want you all to speak in tongues" (1 Cor. 14:5), then interpretations of contemporary experiences that, in effect, say, "I want you all to be afraid of tongues," go contrary to the emphasis of the New Testament. (Note Dickason's quotation of Kurt Koch: "Seeking this gift for ourselves can be a very dangerous experience" [p. 127].) This is just not the perspective Paul has in the New Testament.

I realize that Dickason has a cessationist view with respect to speaking in tongues today (see p. 189: "I told her I doubted that there were any genuine tongues from God today in the New Testament sense"). Therefore, from his perspective, he is not making Scripture subject to experience, but sees these experiences as confirming his understanding of Scripture. (I have discussed the cessationist position in chapter 52, pp. 1271–90.)

There is the possibility of demonic counterfeit of every gift *in the lives of unbelievers* (see Matt. 7:22; also chapter 17, pp. 485–86, on false miracles). Therefore, the fact that there is some kind of "speaking in tongues" in pagan religions should not surprise us or cause us to think that all speaking in tongues is false. But *in the lives of believers*, especially when there is positive fruit in their lives and from their gifts, 1 Cor. 12:3,

1 John 4:4, Luke 11:11–13, and Matt. 7:16–20 tell us that these are not counterfeit gifts but real gifts from God. We must remember that Satan and demons do not do good; they do evil; and they do not bring blessing; they bring destruction.

(Neil T. Anderson, in *The Bondage Breaker* [Eugene, OR: Harvest House, 1990], 159–60, relates a story of a man who was apparently a Christian and who had a counterfeit gift of tongues. But Anderson notes that the gift was conferred on the man "by false teachers" [p. 159] and that this "gift" brought obviously destructive consequences in the man's life. These factors, and not just the words of a demon as the only evidence, gave clear indication of the counterfeit nature of that supposed "gift." Unlike Dickason, Anderson affirms that he is not opposed to speaking in tongues; see p. 160.)

An alternative explanation for the stories given by Dickason is to say that the demons who *said* they were "tongues spirits," and that they came in when some charismatics laid hands on the Christian in question, were lying. Satan "is a liar and the father of lies" (John 8:44), and he would love to have Christians afraid of as many of the Holy Spirit's gifts as possible.

66. The word *groan* (*stenagmos*) is elsewhere used in the New Testament only at Acts 7:34, of the groanings of Israel under oppression in Egypt. But the related verb *stenazō* is used several times, always of finite creatures groaning under the burden of this fallen creation. In the immediately previous context *stenazō* refers to our groaning because our redemption is

particularly the groans associated with our suffering in this age (see vv. 17, 18, 23). (3) The verb *helps* in Romans 8:26 ("The Spirit *helps* us in our weakness") does not refer to something the Holy Spirit does *apart from us and on our behalf* but rather something the Holy Spirit does *in cooperation with us.* The verb Paul uses here (*synantilambanomai*) is also used in Luke 10:40, where Martha wants Jesus to tell Mary "to *help* me"—certainly she does not want Mary to do the food preparation *instead* of her but rather to come and take part *with* her in doing it.[67] Therefore, Paul is not talking about something the Holy Spirit does completely apart from our participation but something the Holy Spirit does in cooperation with our activity.

These reasons combine to indicate that Paul is not talking about a work of the Holy Spirit done apart from us and unknown by us but about the inarticulate sighs and groans that we utter in prayer, which the Holy Spirit then makes into effective intercession before the throne of God. We could paraphrase, "The Holy Spirit assists our prayers when he intercedes (for us) by taking our wordless groans and making them into effective prayer."[68]

What is the relationship between this and speaking in tongues? There is some similarity because it is effective prayer which *we pray* even though we do not understand fully what we are praying. But there are some differences in that the sighs or groans that we utter in prayer very often relate to situations or hardships that we are very conscious of in our minds as we pray, so we know what we are praying about. But Paul says that we do not know how to pray for these situations as we ought to pray. Therefore, the Holy Spirit helps us and intercedes in these situations "according to the will of God" (Rom. 8:27). There is no explicit mention of our spirit praying (though that may indeed be true as well), nor is there mention of our mind being unfruitful or lacking understanding (though that may at times be at least partially true). Nor do these sighs or groans come forth in "other tongues" or "other languages." So there are several differences, even though Romans 8:26–27 talks about intercession that we make in sounds that are not fully understood by us, and therefore it is a phenomenon that has some similarities to speaking in tongues.

## F. Word of Wisdom and Word of Knowledge

Paul writes, "For to one is given the *word of wisdom* through the Spirit, and to another the *word of knowledge* according to the same Spirit" (1 Cor. 12:8 NASB; ESV

---

incomplete (Rom. 8:23; a related compound word is used in v. 22 of the creation itself). The verb is also used of finite creatures groaning under the burden of this creation in Mark 7:34 (Jesus as a man); 2 Cor. 5:2, 4 (believers who have a corruptible, earthly body); Heb. 13:17 (church leaders who may be tempted to groan under the burden of church leadership); and James 5:9 (a warning for Christians not to grumble or groan against one another). Though the verb was once used of Jesus who groaned while under the limitations of this human existence, it does not seem an appropriate term to use of the activity of the Holy

Spirit, who would not experience a similar weakness because he never took on human nature.

67. Though the word is not elsewhere used in the New Testament, its sense is also transparent from the *syn* ("with") prefix that Paul attaches to a very common word for "help."

68. An alternative view is found in the helpful discussion by Douglas Moo, *The Epistle to the Romans*, NIC (Grand Rapids: Eerdmans, 1996), 522–27, who understands the groans to be not ours but the Holy Spirit's.

has "the utterance of wisdom" and "the utterance of knowledge"). At the beginning of this discussion it must be understood that these two gifts are mentioned nowhere else in Scripture,[69] and no other early Christian literature outside the Bible has been found to use these phrases of any spiritual gift either. This means that the *only* information we have about these gifts is contained in this verse: we have the words used to describe these two gifts, and we have the context in which the phrases occur. No interpreter anywhere has any more information than this to work with. This warns us that our conclusions will probably be somewhat tentative in any case.

The major alternatives for understanding these gifts are two: (1) These gifts are commonly thought to be the ability to receive a special revelation from the Holy Spirit and on that basis to speak words that give wisdom in a situation or give specific knowledge of a situation in the life of someone present in a congregation. In this interpretation these gifts would be more "miraculous," in that they would call forth wonder and amazement from the people present since they would not be based on information ordinarily available to the person using the gift.

(2) The other interpretation of these gifts would see them as more "nonmiraculous" or ordinary: the "word of wisdom" simply means the ability to speak a wise word in various situations, and "word of knowledge" is the ability to speak with knowledge about a situation. In both cases the knowledge and wisdom would not be based on a special revelation spontaneously given by the Holy Spirit but would be based on wisdom acquired in the ordinary course of life, the knowledge and wisdom that would be characteristic of Bible teachers or elders and other mature Christians in a church, for example. These would be empowered by the Holy Spirit and thereby made effective when they were spoken. Examples of "words of wisdom" in this sense would be found in Acts 6:1–6 (the appointment of the first "deacons," or assistants to the apostles); Acts 6:10 (Stephen's wisdom in proclaiming the gospel); Acts 15:19–29 (the decision of the Jerusalem council); and even in King Solomon's statement, "Divide the living child in two, and give half to the one and half to the other" (1 Kings 3:25; see also 1 Cor. 6:5–6).

In favor of the first interpretation, it might be argued that all the other seven gifts listed in 1 Corinthians 12:8–10 are in the "miraculous" category, and therefore these two gifts should be understood that way as well.

However, there are some weighty considerations against this view: (1) The words Paul uses for "word" (*logos*), "wisdom" (*sophia*), and "knowledge" (*gnōsis*) are not specialized or technical terms. They are extremely common words in the Greek New Testament. They are simply the ordinary words frequently used for "word" and "wisdom" and "knowledge." Moreover, they are not ordinarily used to denote miraculous events (as are the words *revelation* and *prophecy,* for example), but are simply the words used for human

---

69. At least no other place in Scripture calls something a "word of wisdom" or "word of knowledge" or uses those phrases in any other way.

knowledge and wisdom. So from the meanings of the words themselves, no indication of a miraculous gift seems to be given.

(2) Probably the most decisive consideration is the fact that the New Testament already has a term to describe the action of receiving a special revelation from the Holy Spirit and reporting it in the congregation—this is what Paul calls "prophecy." Since he discusses prophecy at some length, describing it and regulating it, we can know fairly clearly what prophecy was. But to say that these other gifts functioned in exactly the same way (perhaps differing only in content) does not seem justified by anything in the text other than a preconceived notion of what these gifts should be.[70]

Therefore, it would seem preferable to understand these in a "nonmiraculous" way, simply as the ability to speak with wisdom or with knowledge in various situations. What many people today call "word of wisdom" and "word of knowledge" in charismatic circles, it would seem better simply to refer to as "prophecy."[71]

## G. DISTINGUISHING BETWEEN SPIRITS AND SPIRITUAL WARFARE

The gift of distinguishing between spirits is another gift that is mentioned only once in the New Testament (in the list at 1 Cor. 12:10), but the nature of this gift connects it with a number of other passages that describe the spiritual warfare that occurs between Christians and demonic spirits. We may define the gift of distinguishing between spirits as follows: *distinguishing between spirits is a special ability to recognize the influence of the Holy Spirit or of demonic spirits in a person.*

In the perspective of the history of redemption, this gift also gives a foretaste of the age to come, foreshadowing the ability to recognize Satan and his influence that will be made perfect for us in heaven when everything that is covered or hidden will be revealed and brought to the light (Matt. 10:26; cf. Rev. 20:11–15). This ability is probably also stronger than that possessed by most or all believers in the Old Testament, where mentions of demonic activity are infrequent, and where demonic attacks against God's people most often were embodied in military attacks by unbelieving nations against the people of Israel or in overt temptations to go and serve pagan deities. Demonic activity was therefore perceived primarily through observation of outward physical events and circumstances in which Satan's purpose was carried out and could be clearly seen.

This New Testament gift of distinguishing between spirits involves the ability to distinguish the presence of evil spirits from the presence of the work of the Holy Spirit in a person's life. Paul knows that the Corinthians previously were "led astray to mute

---

70. In fact, everything that modern Pentecostal and charismatic Christians call "words of knowledge" and "words of wisdom" would fit exactly into the definition of prophecy as given by Paul, and would fit well under the general umbrella of prophecy. This would have the distinct advantage of making the use of this gift subject to Paul's rules for understanding and regulating prophecy in the church.

71. For further discussion of these gifts, see Wayne Grudem, "What is the Real Meaning of a 'Word of Wisdom' and a 'Word of Knowledge'?," in *Ministries Today* (January–February 1993): 60–65.

idols" (1 Cor. 12:2), and John similarly realizes that there is a need for Christians to "test the spirits to see whether they are from God, for many false prophets have gone out into the world" (1 John 4:1).

Beyond this, it is also possible that the gift would involve distinguishing between various *types* of evil spirits, such as a spirit of infirmity (Luke 13:11), a spirit of divination (Acts 16:16), a dumb and deaf spirit (Mark 9:25, 29), and a spirit of error (1 John 4:6). From a lexical and grammatical standpoint there is nothing that would prevent us from understanding the gift of "distinguishing between spirits" to include this kind of ability as well.[72]

Of course, to some degree the presence of demonic activity is outwardly evident, sometimes from the blurting out of blatantly false doctrinal statements (see 1 Cor. 12:2–3; 1 John 4:1–6), and sometimes from violent and bizarre physical actions, especially in the face of Christian preaching (see Mark 1:24; 9:20; Matt. 8:29; etc.). Satan's influence is characteristically destructive, and the person influenced by a demon will have a destructive influence on the church and others around him or her and a self-destructive influence that harms the life of the troubled individual himself or herself.

But in addition to these outward indications of demonic influence, there is probably also a more subjective perception that occurs at the spiritual and emotional level, whereby the presence of demonic activity is distinguished. When this is more highly developed and is able to function for the benefit of the church as a whole, then Paul would no doubt call it a gift of distinguishing between spirits.[73]

In connection with the gift of distinguishing between spirits, the discussion of spiritual warfare given above in chapter 20 (on Satan and demons) is also relevant.

## QUESTIONS FOR PERSONAL APPLICATION

1. Have you ever experienced a gift of prophecy as defined in this chapter? What have you called it? Has this gift (or something like it) functioned in your church? If so, what have been the benefits—and dangers? If not, do you think this gift might be of help to your church? (Why or why not?)

**Special Terms**

(This list applies to chapters 52 and 53.)

*apostle*
*cessationist*
*distinguishing between spirits*
*gifts of the Holy Spirit*
*healing*
*interpretation of tongues*
*miracles*
*miraculous gifts*
*nonmiraculous gifts*
*office*
*prophecy*
*speaking in tongues*
*teaching*
*word of knowledge*
*word of wisdom*

---

72. For a very extensive linguistic and grammatical analysis of this phrase, see Wayne Grudem, "A Response to Gerhard Dautzenberg on 1 Cor. 12:10," in *Biblische Zeitschrift* 22, no. 2 (1978): 253–70.

73. Of course, no gift is perfect in any Christian in this age (1 Cor. 13:9–10), and we should not expect that this gift would be perfect, or that those who have it would never make mistakes. See chapter 52, pp. 1262–64, on the fact that spiritual gifts vary in strength.

2. Does the gift of teaching function effectively in your church? Who uses this gift in addition to the pastor or elders? Do you think your church adequately appreciates sound Bible teaching? In what areas (if any) do you think your church needs to grow in its knowledge and love of the teachings of Scripture?

3. Of the other gifts discussed in this chapter, have you ever used any of them yourself? Are there any which you think your church needs but does not have at this time? What do you think would be best for you to do in response to this need?

# BIBLIOGRAPHY

(For an explanation of this bibliography see the note on the bibliography to chapter 1, pp. 23–24. Complete bibliographical data may be found on pp. 1489–96. Note: Very few systematic theologies have sections on spiritual gifts, but a few that do are listed below. This bibliography applies to chapters 52 and 53.)

## SECTIONS IN EVANGELICAL SYSTEMATIC THEOLOGIES

1. *Anglican (Episcopalian)*
   2001 . . . . . . . . Packer, 226–28
   2013 . . . . . . . . Bird, 629–31
   2013 . . . . . . . . Bray, 836–88

2. *Arminian (Wesleyan or Methodist)*
   1983 . . . . . . . . Carter, 1:449–57
   1992 . . . . . . . . Oden, 3:177–204
   2002 . . . . . . . . Cottrell, 289, 296, 300, 454

3. *Baptist*
   1990–95 . . . . . Garrett, 215–40
   2007 . . . . . . . . Akin, 675–78
   2013 . . . . . . . . Erickson, 798–804

4. *Dispensational*
   1947 . . . . . . . . Chafer, 7:215–20

   1986 . . . . . . . . Ryrie, 367–74
   2002–2005 . . Geisler, 4:187–214
   2017 . . . . . . . . MacArthur and Mayhue, 379–87, 390–92, 800–18

5. *Lutheran*
   (no explicit treatment)

6. *Reformed (or Presbyterian)*
   1894 . . . . . . . . Shedd, 269
   1906–11 . . . . . Bavinck, *RD*, 3:499–505, 4:299–300
   1998 . . . . . . . . Reymond, 57
   2008 . . . . . . . . Van Genderen and Velema, 640, 702–5, 708, 738
   2011 . . . . . . . . Horton, 884–86
   2013 . . . . . . . . Frame, 542–57, 927–32
   2013 . . . . . . . . Culver, 208, 889–90, 994–95
   2017 . . . . . . . . Barrett, 399–400

7. *Renewal (or charismatic/Pentecostal)*
   1988–92 . . . . . Williams, 2:209–36, 243–63, 323–409, 3:159–77
   1993 . . . . . . . . Menzies and Horton, 133–144, 189–208
   1995 . . . . . . . . Horton, 457–524
   2008 . . . . . . . . Duffield and Van Cleave, 330–64

## SECTIONS IN REPRESENTATIVE ROMAN CATHOLIC SYSTEMATIC THEOLOGIES

### 1. Roman Catholic: Traditional

1955 . . . . . . . . Ott (no explicit treatment)

### 2. Roman Catholic: Post-Vatican II

1980 . . . . . . . . McBrien, 2:1086–88

2012 . . . . . . . . *CCC*, paragraphs 1830–32

## OTHER WORKS

Allison, Gregg. *Sojourners and Strangers: The Doctrine of the Church*. Wheaton, IL: Crossway, 2012, 413–466.

Baker, J. P. "Gifts of the Spirit." In *NDT1*, 269–71.

Bennett, Dennis and Rita. *The Holy Spirit and You*. Plainfield, NJ: Logos, 1971. (Charismatic.)

Berding, Kenneth. *What Are Spiritual Gifts? Rethinking the Conventional View*. Grand Rapids: Kregel, 2007.

Blomberg, Craig L. "Holy Spirit, Gifts of." In *BTDB*, 348–51.

Blue, Ken. *Authority to Heal*. Downers Grove, IL: InterVarsity Press, 1987.

Bridge, Donald. *Signs and Wonders Today*. Leicester: Inter-Varsity Press, 1985. (Charismatic.)

———, and David Phypers. *Spiritual Gifts and the Church*. Downers Grove, IL: InterVarsity Press, 1973. (Charismatic.)

Budgen, Victor. *The Charismatics and the Word of God*. Phillipsburg, NJ: Presbyterian and Reformed, 1985. (Cessationist.)

Carson, D. A. *Showing the Spirit: A Theological Exposition of 1 Corinthians 12–14*. Grand Rapids: Baker, 1987.

Chantry, Walter J. *Signs of the Apostles*. 2nd ed. Edinburgh and Carlisle, PA: Banner of Truth, 1976. (Cessationist.)

Davids, P. H. "Healing, Illness." In *DLNT*, 436–39.

———. "Tongues." In *DLNT*, 1177–79.

Deere, Jack. *Surprised by the Power of the Spirit: A Former Dallas Seminary Professor Discovers That God Still Speaks and Heals Today*. Grand Rapids: Zondervan, 1993. (This is the most balanced and persuasive argument I have ever read against the cessationist position. A revised edition titled *Why I Am Still Surprised by the Power of the Spirit* is due to be released in April 2020.)

Edgar, Thomas. "The Cessation of the Sign Gifts." *BibSac* 145, no. 180 (October–December 1988): 371–86. (Cessationist.)

Ellis, E. E. "Prophecy, Theology of." In *NDT1*, 537–38.

Farnell, F. David. "The Current Debate about New Testament Prophecy." *BibSac* 149, no. 595 (July–September 1992): 277–303.

———. "Does the New Testament Teach Two Prophetic Gifts?" *BibSac* 150 (January–March 1993): 62–88.

———. "Fallible New Testament Prophecy/Prophets? A Critique of Wayne Grudem's Hypothesis." *The Master's Seminary Journal* 2, no. 2 (Fall 1991): 157–80.

———. "The Gift of Prophecy in the Old and New Testaments." *BibSac* 149, no. 596 (October–December 1992): 387–410.

———. "When Will the Gift of Prophecy Cease?" *BibSac* 150 (April–June 1993): 171–202.

Fee, G. D. "Gifts of the Spirit." In *DPL*, 339–47.

Gaffin, Richard B. *Perspectives on Pentecost: Studies in New Testament Teaching on the Gifts of the Holy Spirit*. Phillipsburg, NJ: Presbyterian and Reformed, 1979. (Cessationist.)

Gee, Donald. *Concerning Spiritual Gifts*. Rev. ed. Springfield, MO: Gospel, 1972. (Traditional Pentecostal.)

———. *Spiritual Gifts in the Work of Ministry Today*. Springfield, MO: Gospel, 1963. (Traditional Pentecostal.)

Gentry, Kenneth L., Jr. *The Charismatic Gift of Prophecy: A Reformed Response to Wayne Grudem*. 2nd ed. Memphis: Footstool, 1989. (Cessationist.)

Green, Michael. *I Believe in the Holy Spirit*. London: Hodder and Stoughton; Grand Rapids: Eerdmans, 1975.

Greig, Gary, and Kevin Springer, eds. *The Kingdom and the Power: Are Healing and the Spiritual Gifts Used by Jesus and the Early Church Meant for the Church Today?* Ventura, CA: Regal, 1993.

Gromacki, Robert G. *The Modern Tongues Movement.* Rev. ed. Phillipsburg, NJ: Presbyterian and Reformed, 1972. (Cessationist.)

Grudem, Wayne. "Does God Still Give Revelation Today?" *Charisma,* September 1992, 38–42.

———. *The Gift of Prophecy in 1 Corinthians.* Lanham, MD: University Press of America, 1982.

———. *The Gift of Prophecy in the New Testament and Today.* Westchester, IL: Crossway, 1988.

———. *Power and Truth: A Response to the Critiques of Vineyard Teaching and Practice by D. A. Carson, James Montgomery Boice, and John H. Armstrong in Power Religion.* Anaheim, CA: Association of Vineyard Churches, 1993.

———. "What Is the Real Meaning of a 'Word of Wisdom' and a 'Word of Knowledge'?" *Ministries Today,* January–February 1993, 60–65.

———. "What Should Be the Relationship between Prophet and Pastor?" *Equipping the Saints,* Fall 1990, 7–9, 21–22.

Hayford, Jack W. *The Beauty of Spiritual Language.* Dallas: Word, 1992.

Horton, Michael Scott, ed. *Power Religion: The Selling Out of the Evangelical Church?* Chicago: Moody Publishers, 1992.

House, H. Wayne. "Tongues and the Mystery Religions of Corinth." *Bibliotheca Sacra* 140, no. 558 (April 1983): 134–50.

Houston, Graham. *Prophecy: A Gift For Today?* Leicester: Inter-Varsity Press; Downers Grove, IL: InterVarsity Press, 1989.

Hummel, Charles E. *Fire in the Fireplace: Charismatic Renewal in the Nineties.* Downers Grove, IL: InterVarsity Press, 1993.

Lewis, David. *Healing: Fiction, Fantasy, or Fact?* London: Hodder and Stoughton, 1989.

MacArthur, John F., Jr. *Charismatic Chaos.* Grand Rapids: Zondervan, 1992. (Cessationist.)

———. *The Charismatics: A Doctrinal Perspective.* Grand Rapids: Zondervan, 1978. (Cessationist.)

Mallone, George. *Those Controversial Gifts.* Downers Grove, IL: InterVarsity Press, 1983.

Moo, Douglas. "Divine Healing in the Health and Wealth Gospel." *TrinJ* 9, No. 2 (Fall 1988): 191–209.

Moreland, J. P., and James Adams. *Recover the Christian Mind, Renovate the Soul, Restore the Spirit's Power.* Grand Rapids: Zondervan, 2007.

Moseley, C. A. E. "Healing." In *NDT2,* 389–91.

Nathan, Richard. *A Response to* Charismatic Chaos. Anaheim, CA: Association of Vineyard Churches, 1993. (An extensive response to John MacArthur's 1992 book.)

Osborne, Grant. "Tongues, Speaking in." In *EDT3,* 885–88.

Poythress, Vern. "Linguistic and Sociological Analyses of Modern Tongues-Speaking: Their Contributions and Limitations." In *WTJ* 42 (1979): 367–98.

Pytches, David. *Spiritual Gifts in the Local Church.* Originally published as *Come, Holy Spirit.* Minneapolis: Bethany, 1985. (Charismatic.)

Rainey, D. L. "Gifts of the Spirit." In *NDT2,* 362–63.

Reymond, Robert L. *What about Continuing Revelations and Miracles in the Presbyterian Church Today?* Phillipsburg, NJ: Presbyterian and Reformed, 1977. (Cessationist.)

Robeck, C. M., Jr. "Charismatic Movements." In *GDT,* 145–54.

Robertson, O. Palmer. *The Final Word.* Edinburgh and Carlisle, PA: Banner of Truth, 1993. (Cessationist.)

Ruthven, Jon. *On the Cessation of the Charismata: The Protestant Polemic on Post-Biblical Miracles.* Sheffield: Sheffield Academic Press, 1993. (Charismatic; a revision and expansion of the author's PhD dissertation, in which he responds to the arguments of cessationists from Warfield to the present.)

Smail, T. A. "Charismatic Movement / Theology." In *NDT2,* 161–62.

Saucy, Robert. "Prophecy Today? An Initial Response." *Sundoulos* (Spring 1990): 1–5. (Cessationist.)

Schatzmann, Siegfried. *A Pauline Theology of Charismata.* Peabody, MA: Hendrickson, 1987.

Schreiner, Thomas. *Spiritual Gifts: What They Are and Why They Matter.* Nashville: B&H, 2018.

Solomon, R. "Healing and Deliverance." In *GDT,* 361–68.

Stephanou, Eusebius A. "The Charismata in the

Early Church Fathers," *The Greek Orthodox Theological Review* 21, no. 2 (Summer 1976): 125–46.

Storms, C. Samuel. *Healing and Holiness: A Biblical Response to the Faith-Healing Phenomenon.* Phillipsburg, NJ: Presbyterian and Reformed, 1990.

Storms, C. Samuel. *Practicing the Power: Welcoming the Gifts of the Holy Spirit in Your Life.* Grand Rapids: Zondervan, 2017.

Thomas, Robert L. "Prophecy Rediscovered? A Review of *The Gift of Prophecy in the New Testament and Today.*" *BibSac* 149, no. 593 (January–March 1992): 83–96. (Cessationist.)

Thompson, J. G. S. S., and Walter A. Elwell. "Spiritual Gifts." In *EDT3*, 832–35.

Turner, M. "Spiritual Gifts." In *NDBT*, 789–96.

Turner, Max. "Spiritual Gifts Then and Now." *Vox Evangelica* 15 (1985): 7–64.

———. *The Holy Spirit and Spiritual Gifts, Then and Now.* Carlisle: Paternoster, 1996.

Vondey, W. "Glossolalia." In *GDT*, 343–45.

Warfield, Benjamin B. *Counterfeit Miracles.* 1918. Reprint, London: Banner of Truth, 1972.

White, John. *When the Spirit Comes with Power.* Downers Grove, IL: InterVarsity Press, 1988.

White, R. Fowler. "Gaffin and Grudem on Ephesians 2:20: In Defense of Gaffin's Cessationist Exegesis." *WTJ* 54 (Fall 1993): 303–20. (Cessationist.)

———. "Richard Gaffin and Wayne Grudem on 1 Corinthians 13:10: A Comparison of Cessationist and Noncessationist Argumentation." *JETS* 35, no. 2 (June 1992): 173–82. (Cessationist.)

Wilkinson, J. "Healing." In *NDT1*, 287–88.

Wilson, Andrew. *Spirit and Sacrament: An Invitation to Eucharismatic Worship.* Grand Rapids: Zondervan, 2019.

Wimber, John, with Kevin Springer. *Power Evangelism.* San Francisco: Harper and Row, 1986.

———. *Power Healing.* San Francisco: Harper and Row, 1987.

Yarnell, Malcolm B. "The Person and Work of the Holy Spirit." In *A Theology for the Church*, edited by Daniel L. Akin et al., 673–76. Nashville: B&H, 2007.

## SCRIPTURE MEMORY PASSAGE

**1 Corinthians 12:7–11:** To each is given the manifestation of the Spirit for the common good. For to one is given through the Spirit the utterance of wisdom, and to another the utterance of knowledge according to the same Spirit, to another faith by the same Spirit, to another gifts of healing by the one Spirit, to another the working of miracles, to another prophecy, to another the ability to distinguish between spirits, to another various kinds of tongues, to another the interpretation of tongues. All these are empowered by one and the same Spirit, who apportions to each one individually as he wills.

## HYMN

**"Come, O Come, Thou Quickening Spirit"**

(A possible alternative tune is the tune for "Guide Me, O Thou Great Jehovah.")

*Come, O come, thou quick'ning Spirit, God from all eternity!*
*May thy power never fail us; dwell within us constantly.*
*Then shall truth and life and light banish all the gloom of night.*

*Grant our hearts in fullest measure wisdom, counsel, purity,*
*That we ever may be seeking only that which pleaseth thee.*
*Let thy knowledge spread and grow, working error's overthrow.*

*Show us, Lord, the path of blessing; when we trespass on our way,*
*Cast, O Lord, our sins behind thee and be with us day by day.*
*Should we stray, O Lord, recall; work repentance when we fall.*

*Holy Spirit, strong and mighty, thou who makest all things new,*
*Make thy work within us perfect and the evil foe subdue.*
*Grant us weapons for the strife and with vict'ry crown our life.*

Author: Heinrich Held, 1664

# CONTEMPORARY WORSHIP MUSIC

### "Come Holy Spirit"

*Come, Holy Spirit,*
*Come, Holy Spirit,*
*Come to this place.*

*We will embrace your presence.*

*Come soften our hearts,*
*Come soften our hearts,*
*That we may obey.*
*Teach us your way.*
*Come lead us.*

*Come, Holy Spirit,*
*Come, Holy Spirit.*

Words by Mark Foreman[74]

---

# PART 7

# The Doctrine of the Future

# CHAPTER 54

# The Return of Christ: When and How?

*When and how will Christ return?*
*Could he come back at any hour?*

## EXPLANATION AND SCRIPTURAL BASIS

As we begin the final unit of this book, we turn to consider events that will happen in the future. The study of future events is often called "eschatology," from the Greek word *eschatos*, which means "last." The study of eschatology, then, is the study of "the last things."

Unbelievers can make reasonable predictions about future events based on patterns of past occurrences, but in the nature of human experience it is clear that human beings of themselves cannot *know* the future. Therefore, unbelievers can have no certain knowledge of any future event. But Christians who believe the Bible are in a different situation. Although we cannot know everything about the future, God knows everything about the future, and he has in Scripture told us about the major events yet to come in the history of the universe. About these events occurring we can have absolute confidence because God is never wrong and never lies.

Regarding our personal future as individuals, we have already discussed the teaching of Scripture in chapter 41 (on death and the intermediate state) and chapter 42 (on glorification). The study of these future events that will happen to individuals is sometimes called "personal eschatology." But the Bible also talks about certain major events that will affect the entire universe. Specifically, it tells us about the second coming of Christ, the millennium, the final judgment, eternal punishment for unbelievers and eternal reward for believers, and life with God in the new heaven and new earth. The study of these events is sometimes called "general eschatology." In this chapter we will study the question of the return of Christ, or his "second coming." Subsequent chapters will deal with the remaining topics in a study of the last things.

There have been many debates—often heated ones—in the history of the church over questions regarding the future. In this chapter we will begin with aspects of Christ's second coming with which all evangelicals agree and then, at the end, move to one matter of disagreement: whether Christ could return at any time. Then in the next chapter we will discuss the question of the millennium, a topic that has long been a source of disagreement among Christians.

## A. THERE WILL BE A SUDDEN, PERSONAL, VISIBLE, BODILY RETURN OF CHRIST

Jesus often spoke about his return. "You also must be ready, for the Son of Man is coming at an hour you do not expect" (Matt. 24:44). He said, "*I will come again* and will take you to myself, that where I am you may be also" (John 14:3). Immediately after Jesus had ascended into heaven, two angels said to the disciples, "This Jesus, who was taken up from you into heaven, *will come* in the same way as you saw him go into heaven" (Acts 1:11). Paul taught, "*The Lord himself will descend from heaven* with a cry of command, with the voice of an archangel, and with the sound of the trumpet of God" (1 Thess. 4:16). The author of Hebrews wrote that Christ "*will appear a second time*, not to deal with sin but to save those who are eagerly waiting for him" (Heb. 9:28). James wrote, "the coming[1] of the Lord is at hand" (James 5:8). Peter said, "The day of the Lord will come like a thief" (2 Peter 3:10). John wrote, "When he appears we shall be like him, because we shall see him as he is" (1 John 3:2). And the book of Revelation has frequent references to Christ's return, ending with Jesus' promise, "Surely *I am coming soon*," and John's response, "Amen. Come, Lord Jesus!" (Rev. 22:20).

This theme is frequently mentioned throughout the New Testament. It is the dominant hope of the New Testament church. These verses predict a sudden return of Christ that will be dramatic and visible ("He is coming with the clouds, and every eye will see him," Rev. 1:7). The passages are far too explicit to allow the idea (once popular in liberal Protestant circles) that Christ will not return himself but that the spirit of Christ, meaning an acceptance of his teaching and an imitation of his lifestyle of love, would increasingly return to the earth. It is not his teachings or his style of conduct, but "the Lord himself" who will descend from heaven (1 Thess. 4:16). It is Jesus himself "who was taken up from you into heaven" who "will come *in the same way* as you saw him go into heaven" (Acts 1:11). His appearing will not be a mere spiritual coming to dwell within people's hearts but will be a *personal* and *bodily* return "in the same way as you saw him go into heaven."

## B. WE SHOULD EAGERLY LONG FOR CHRIST'S RETURN

John's response at the end of Revelation should characterize Christians' hearts in all ages: "Amen. Come, Lord Jesus!" (Rev. 22:20). True Christianity trains us "to live self-controlled, upright, and godly lives in the present age, *waiting for our blessed hope, the appearing of the glory of our great God and Savior Jesus Christ*" (Titus 2:12–13).[2] Paul

---

1. The term *parousia* is used in theology to mean "second coming" (of Christ). This term comes from the Greek word for "coming" (*parousia*) which is used to refer to Christ's second coming in James 5:8 and several other New Testament passages.

Because *parousia* is not a commonly used term in ordinary English, I have not used it in this book.

2. The word translated "awaiting" here (*prosdechomai*) has a nuance of earnest or eager expectation: it is used of Joseph of

says, "Our citizenship is in heaven, and from it we *await a Savior*, the Lord Jesus Christ" (Phil. 3:20).[3] The term *Maranatha* in some translations of 1 Corinthians 16:22 (KJV; NASB) similarly means, "Our Lord, come!" (1 Cor. 16:22 ESV).

Do Christians in fact eagerly long for Christ's return? The more Christians are caught up in enjoying the good things of this life, and the more they neglect genuine Christian fellowship and their personal relationship with Christ, the less they will long for his return. On the other hand, many Christians who are experiencing suffering or persecution or who are elderly and infirm, as well as those whose daily walk with Christ is vital and deep, will have a more intense longing for his return. To some extent, the degree to which we actually long for Christ's return is a measure of the spiritual condition of our lives at the moment. It also gives some measure of the degree to which we see the world as it really is, as God sees it, in bondage to sin and rebellion against God, and in the power of the evil one (1 John 5:19).

But does this mean that we should not undertake long-term projects? If a scientist who is a Christian eagerly longs for Christ's return, then should he or she begin a ten-year research project? Or should a Christian begin a three-year course in a theological seminary or a Bible college? What if Christ were to return the day before graduation from that institution, before there was any chance to give a significant amount of one's time to actual ministry?

Certainly we should commit ourselves to long-term activities. It is precisely for this reason that Jesus does not allow us to know the actual time of his return (see below): he wants us to be engaged in obedience to him, no matter what our walk of life, up until the very moment of his return. To "be ready" for Christ's return (Matt. 24:44) is to be faithfully obeying him in the present, actively engaged in whatever work he has called us to. In the nature of the situation, since we do not know when he will return, on that day there will no doubt be some missionaries just departing for the mission field, who will never reach their destination. There will be some students in their last year of seminary education who will never use their training to pastor a church. There will be some researchers handing in their doctoral dissertations on that day, the fruit of years of research that will never be published and never have an influence on the world. But to all of those people who are Christians, Jesus will say, "Well done, good and faithful servant. You have been faithful over a little; I will set you over much. Enter into the joy of your master" (Matt. 25:21).

## C. We Do Not Know When Christ Will Return

Several passages indicate that we do not, and cannot, know the time when Christ will return. "The Son of Man is coming *at an hour you do not expect*" (Matt. 24:44).

---

Arimathea, who was "looking for the kingdom of God" (Mark 15:43; Luke 23:51) and of righteous Simeon who was "waiting for the consolation of Israel" (Luke 2:25).

3. The word here translated "await" is *apekdechomai*, "await eagerly" (note its use in this sense in Rom. 8:19, 23; 1 Cor. 1:7; Gal. 5:5).

"Watch therefore, for *you know neither the day nor the hour*" (Matt. 25:13). Moreover, Jesus said, "But concerning that day or that hour, no one knows, not even the angels in heaven, nor the Son, but only the Father. Be on guard, keep awake. For *you do not know* when the time will come" (Mark 13:32–33).

It is simply an evasion of the force of those passages to say that we cannot know the day or the hour but that we can know the month or the year. The fact remains that Jesus is coming "at an hour you do not expect" (Matt. 24:44; also Luke 12:40). (In these verses the word *hour* [*hōra*] is best understood in a more general sense, to refer to the time when something will take place, not necessarily a sixty-minute period of time.)[4] The point of these passages is that Jesus is telling us that we *cannot* know when he is coming back. Since he will come at an unexpected time, we should be ready at all times for him to return.

The practical result of this is that anyone who claims to know specifically when Jesus is coming back is automatically to be considered wrong. The Jehovah's Witnesses have made many predictions of specific dates for Christ's return, and all of them have turned out to be wrong.[5] But others in the history of the church have made such predictions as well, sometimes claiming new insight into biblical prophecies, and sometimes claiming to have received personal revelations from Jesus himself indicating the time of his return. It is unfortunate that many people have been deceived by these claims because if people are convinced that Christ will return (for example) within a month, they will begin to withdraw from all long-term commitments. They may take their children out of school, sell their houses, quit their jobs, and give up work on any long-term projects whether in the church or elsewhere. They may initially have an increased zeal for evangelism and prayer, but the unreasonable nature of their behavior will offset any evangelistic impact they may have. Moreover, they are simply *disobeying* the teaching of Scripture that the date of Christ's return cannot be known, which means that even their prayer and fellowship with God will be hindered. Anyone who claims to know the date on which Christ will return—from whatever source—should be rejected as incorrect.[6]

---

4. BDAG, 1103, meaning 3.

5. Their attempt to save face by claiming that Jesus actually did return on October 1, 1914, in an invisible way, is incorrect because it denies the visible, bodily nature of Christ's return that is so clearly specified in several passages quoted above.

6. Even in the "enlightened" twentieth century, such alarms can be persuasive to many people. In the summer of 1988 a former rocket scientist with impressive academic credentials circulated a booklet claiming that Jesus would return on September 12, 1988, and tens of thousands of copies of the book found their way around the United States and to various parts of the world. I was surprised to find that some otherwise sober Christian friends had read it and were alarmed, and to hear that some Christians in our community had pulled their

children out of school in order to be together as a family when Christ came back. When the prediction failed, the author, Edgar Whisenant, revised his prediction, saying his calculations were one year off and Christ would return instead on September 1, 1989 (or one day earlier or later), or, if not then, on Rosh Hashanah 1990 or 1991 or 1992, or, at the latest, September 15–17, 1993. Of course, those predictions also failed. But many lives were disrupted and many people had false expectations aroused and then dashed by the publication of this booklet and its sequel. See Edgar Whisenant, *88 Reasons Why the Rapture Will Be in 1988* (Nashville: World Bible Society, 1988); and Edgar Whisenant and Greg Brewer, *The Final Shout: Rapture Report 1989* (Nashville: World Bible Society, 1989).

## D. All Evangelicals Agree on the Final Results of Christ's Return

No matter what their differences on the details, all Christians who take the Bible as their final authority agree that the final and ultimate result of Christ's return will be the judgment of unbelievers and the final reward of believers, and believers will live with Christ in a new heaven and a new earth for all eternity. God the Father, Son, and Holy Spirit will reign and will be worshiped in a never-ending kingdom with no more sin or sorrow or suffering. We will discuss these details more fully in the following chapters.

## E. There Is Disagreement over the Details of Future Events

Nevertheless, Christians differ over specific details leading up to and immediately following Christ's return. Specifically, they differ over the nature of the millennium and the relationship of Christ's return to the millennium, the sequence of Christ's return and the great tribulation period that will come to the earth, and the question of the salvation of the Jewish people (and the relationship between Jews who are saved and the church).

Before we examine some of those questions in more detail, it is important to affirm the genuine evangelical standing of those who have differing positions on these questions. Evangelicals who hold to these various positions all agree that Scripture is inerrant, and they have a commitment to believe *whatever* is taught by Scripture. Their differences concern the interpretation of various passages relating to these events, but their differences on these matters should be seen as matters of secondary importance, not as differences over primary doctrinal matters.

Nevertheless, it is worth our time to study these questions in more detail, both because we may gain further insight into the nature of the events that God has planned and promised for us and because there is still hope that greater unity will come about in the church when we agree to examine these issues again in more detail and to engage in discussion about them.

## F. Could Christ Come Back at Any Time?

One of the significant areas of disagreement is over the question of whether Christ could return at any time. On the one hand, there are many passages encouraging us to be ready because Christ will return at an hour we do not expect. On the other hand, there are several passages that speak of certain events that will happen before Christ returns. There have been different ways of resolving the apparent tension between these two sets of passages, with some Christians concluding that Christ could still return *at any time*, and others concluding that he could not return *for at least a generation*, since it would take that long to fulfill some of the predicted events that must occur before his return.

### 1. Verses Predicting a Sudden and Unexpected Coming of Christ

In order to feel the cumulative force of the numerous passages that predict that Christ could come very soon, it is helpful simply to list them here in order:

*Therefore, stay awake*, for you do not know on what day your Lord is coming. But know this, that if the master of the house had known in what part of the night the thief was coming, he would have stayed awake and would not have let his house be broken into. Therefore *you also must be ready*, for the Son of Man is coming *at an hour you do not expect*. (Matt. 24:42–44; cf. vv. 36–39)

The master of that servant *will come on a day when he does not expect him* and at an hour he does not know. (Matt. 24:50)

*Watch therefore*, for you know neither the day nor the hour. (Matt. 25:13)

But *concerning that day or that hour, no one knows*, not even the angels in heaven, nor the Son, but only the Father. *Be on guard, keep awake*. For you do not know when the time will come. (Mark 13:32–33)

It is like a man going on a journey, when he leaves home and puts his servants in charge, each with his work, and commands the doorkeeper to stay awake. *Therefore stay awake—for you do not know when the master of the house will come*, in the evening, or at midnight, or when the rooster crows, or in the morning—lest he come suddenly and find you asleep. And what I say to you I say to all: *Stay awake*." (Mark 13:34–37)

You also must be ready, for the Son of Man is coming at an hour you do not expect. (Luke 12:40)

Our Lord, come! (1 Cor. 16:22)

For our citizenship is in heaven, from which also *we eagerly wait for a Savior*, the Lord Jesus Christ. (Phil. 3:20 NASB)

For you yourselves are fully aware that *the day of the Lord will come like a thief in the night*. (1 Thess. 5:2)

Training us to . . . live self-controlled, upright, and godly lives in the present age, *waiting for our blessed hope*, the appearing of the glory of our great God and Savior Jesus Christ. (Titus 2:12–13)

Encouraging one another, and all the more *as you see the Day drawing near*. (Heb. 10:25)

Be patient, therefore, brothers, until the coming of the Lord. . . . Establish your hearts, for *the coming of the Lord is at hand.* . . . *Behold, the Judge is standing at the door.* (James 5:7–9)

The end of all things is at hand. (1 Peter 4:7)

But *the day of the Lord will come like a thief,* and then the heavens will pass away with a roar, and the heavenly bodies will be burned up and dissolved, and the earth and the works that are done on it will be exposed. (2 Peter 3:10)

The time is near. (Rev. 1:3)

Behold, *I am coming soon.* (Rev. 22:7)

Behold, *I am coming soon,* bringing my recompense with me, to repay each one for what he has done. (Rev. 22:12)

He who testifies to these things says, *"Surely I am coming soon."* Amen. *Come, Lord Jesus!* (Rev. 22:20)

What shall we say to these passages? If there were no passages in the New Testament about signs that would precede Christ's return, we would probably conclude from the passages just quoted that Jesus could come at any moment. In this sense, we can say that Christ's return is *imminent.*[7] It would seem to blunt the force of the commands to *be ready* and to *watch* if there was a reason to think that Christ would not come soon.

Before we look at passages on signs that precede Christ's coming, another problem must be considered at this point. Were Jesus and the New Testament authors wrong in their expectation that he would return soon? Did they not think and even teach that the second coming of Christ would be in just a few years? In fact, a very prominent view among liberal New Testament scholars has been that Jesus mistakenly taught that he would return soon.

But none of the texts just quoted require this interpretation. The texts that say to be ready do not say how long we will have to wait, nor do the texts that say that Jesus is

---

7. In this chapter, it must be made clear that I am *not* using *imminent* as a technical term for a pretribulational rapture position (explained below) but simply to mean that Christ could return at any day or any hour.

Furthermore, I am not using the word *imminent* to mean that Christ *certainly will* come soon (for then the verses teaching imminence would have been untrue when they were written). I am using the word *imminent* to mean that Christ *could* come and *might* come at any time and that we are to be prepared for him to come at any day. (Others define *imminent* more broadly, taking it to mean that Christ could come in any generation. I am not using the term in that way in this chapter.)

coming at a time we do not expect. As for the texts that say Jesus is coming "soon," we must realize that biblical prophets often speak in terms of "prophetic foreshortening," which sees future events but does not see the intervening time before those events occur.

George Ladd says,

> The prophets were little interested in chronology, and the future was always viewed as imminent . . . the Old Testament prophets blended the near and the distant perspectives so as to form a single canvas. Biblical prophecy is not primarily three-dimensional but two; it has height and breadth but is little concerned about depth, i.e., the chronology of future events . . . the distant is viewed through the transparency of the immediate. It is true that the early church lived in expectancy of the return of the Lord, and it is the nature of biblical prophecy to make it possible for every generation to live in expectancy of the end.[8]

Peter also reminds us that the Lord has a different perspective on time than we do, so that "soon" with him may not be what we expect: "But do not overlook this one fact, beloved, that with the Lord one day is as a thousand years, and a thousand years as one day. The Lord is not slow to fulfill his promise as some count slowness" (2 Peter 3:8–9).

## 2. Verses that Say Several Signs Must Precede Christ's Return

The other set of texts to be considered tells of several signs that Scripture says will precede the time of Christ's return. In fact, Berkhof says, "According to Scripture several important events must occur before the return of the Lord, and therefore it cannot be called imminent."[9] It will be helpful to list those passages that most directly refer to signs that must occur before Christ's return.

### a. The Preaching of the Gospel to All Nations.

> And this gospel of the kingdom will be proclaimed throughout the *whole world as a testimony to all nations*, and then the end will come. (Matt. 24:14; cf. Mark 13:10)

### b. The Great Tribulation.

> And when you hear of wars and rumors of wars, do not be alarmed. This must take place, but the end is not yet. For nation will rise against nation, and kingdom against kingdom. There will be *earthquakes* in various places; there will be *famines*.

---

8. George Eldon Ladd, *A Commentary on the Revelation of John* (Grand Rapids: Eerdmans, 1972), 22.

9. Louis Berkhof, *Systematic Theology* (Grand Rapids: Eerdmans, 1941), 696. He lists several events, such as the preaching of the gospel to all nations, the conversion of the fullness of Israel, the great tribulation, the revelation of the antichrist, and a remarkable conjunction of many ominous signs and wonders (wars, famines, earthquakes, false prophets doing miracles, and fearful signs in the sun, moon, and stars), all of which he discusses on pp. 697–703.

*These are but the beginning of the birth pains.* (Mark 13:7–8; cf. Matt. 24:15–22; Luke 21:20–24)

For in those days there will be such tribulation as has not been from the beginning of the creation that God created until now, and never will be. And if the Lord had not cut short the days, no human being would be saved. But for the sake of the elect, whom he chose, he shortened the days. (Mark 13:19–20)

### c. False Prophets Working Signs and Wonders.

For false christs and false prophets will arise and perform signs and wonders, to lead astray, if possible, the elect. (Mark 13:22; cf. Matt. 24:23–24)

### d. Signs in the Heavens.

But in those days, after that tribulation, the sun will be darkened, and the moon will not give its light, and the stars will be falling from heaven, and the powers in the heavens will be shaken. And then they will see the Son of Man coming in clouds with great power and glory. (Mark 13:24–26; cf. Matt. 24:29–30; Luke 21:25–27)

**e. The Appearance of the Man of Lawlessness (or the "Antichrist").** Paul writes to the Thessalonians that Christ will not come unless the man of sin is first revealed, and then the Lord Jesus will destroy him at his coming. This "man of sin" is sometimes identified with the beast in Revelation 13 and is sometimes called the antichrist, the final and worst of the series of "antichrists" mentioned in 1 John 2:18. Paul writes,

Now concerning the coming of our Lord Jesus Christ . . *that day will not come, unless the rebellion comes first, and the man of lawlessness is revealed*, the son of destruction, who opposes and exalts himself against every so-called god or object of worship, *so that he takes his seat in the temple of God, proclaiming himself to be God. . . .* And you know what is restraining him now so that he may be revealed in his time. For the mystery of lawlessness is already at work. Only he who now restrains it will do so until he is out of the way. *And then the lawless one will be revealed, whom the Lord Jesus will kill with the breath of his mouth and bring to nothing by the appearance of his coming.* The coming of the lawless one is by the activity of Satan with *all power and false signs and wonders, and with all wicked deception for those who are perishing*, because they refused to love the truth and so be saved. (2 Thess. 2:1–10)

**f. The Salvation of "all Israel."** Paul talks about the fact that many Jews have not trusted in Christ, but he says that sometime in the future a large number would be saved:

Now if their trespass means riches for the world, and if their failure means riches for the Gentiles, how much more will their *full inclusion* mean! (Rom. 11:12)[10]

Lest you be wise in your own sight, I do not want you to be unaware of this mystery, brothers: a partial hardening has come upon Israel, until the fullness of the Gentiles has come in. *And in this way all Israel will be saved.* (Rom. 11:25–26)

**g. Conclusions from These Signs That Precede Christ's Return.** The impact of these passages seems so clear that, as was mentioned above, many Christians have felt that Christ simply cannot return at any moment.[11] As we look over the list of signs[12] given above, it would not seem to take much argument to demonstrate that most of these events, or perhaps all of them, *have not yet occurred.* Or at least that is what appears to be the case on a first reading of these passages.

### 3. Possible Resolutions of These Two Sets of Verses

How can we reconcile the passages that seem to warn us to be ready because Christ could suddenly return with passages that indicate that several important and visible events must take place before Christ can return? Several solutions have been proposed.

**a. "Any Time" Return Is Impossible.** One solution is to say that *Christ could not come at any time.* This position is taken by Louis Berkhof, in the sentence quoted above at the beginning of section 2. Just how long it would be before Christ returns depends on each person's estimate of how long it will take some of the signs to be fulfilled, such as the preaching of the gospel to all nations, the coming of the great tribulation, and the ingathering of the full number of the Jews who will be saved.

The difficulty with this view is twofold. First, it really seems to nullify the force of the warnings of Jesus that we should watch and be ready because he is returning at an hour we do not expect. What force is there in a warning to be ready for Christ to come at an unexpected time when we know that this coming *cannot* occur for many years? The sense of urgent expectancy of Christ's return is greatly diminished or denied altogether in this position, and that result seems quite contrary to Jesus' intention in giving these warnings.

Second, this position seems to use these signs in a way quite opposite from the way

---

10. The Greek word translated "full inclusion" here is *plērōma*, "fullness." This future full inclusion of Israel among God's people is sometimes also called the "fullness" of Israel.

11. Louis Berkhof also mentions Matt. 25:19, in which the master returned "after a long time," and Matt. 25:5, which speaks of the delay of the bridegroom's return (*Systematic Theology*, 697). But both passages are vague as to the exact length of time, and both would be consistent even with a delay of ten or twenty years after Jesus returned to heaven.

12. I have not listed "wars and rumors of wars" and "famines and earthquakes in various places" (Matt. 24:6–7) as signs that must precede Christ's return, because they have been present throughout history, and because they are not given by Jesus as signs that immediately precede his return but as events that come before those signs, as "the beginning of the birth pains" (Matt. 24:8). Nevertheless, an intensification of these things may well indicate the beginning of the last days, with other signs soon to follow.

Jesus intended them to be used. The signs are given so that, when we see them, they will *intensify our expectation* of Christ's return. Jesus said, "Now *when these things begin to take place, straighten up and raise your heads, because your redemption is drawing near*" (Luke 21:28). And the warnings are also given to keep believers from going astray and following false messiahs: "See that no one leads you astray. Many will come in my name, saying, 'I am he!' and they will lead many astray. . . . And then if anyone says to you, 'Look, here is the Christ!' or 'Look, there he is!' do not believe it" (Mark 13:5–6, 21). So the signs are given to keep Christians from being surprised by these remarkable events, to assure them that God knows them all in advance, and to keep them from following after alleged messiahs who do not come in the dramatic, visible, world-conquering way in which Jesus will come. *But the signs are never given to make us think, "Jesus couldn't come for a few years."* Jesus did not say anything like, "When you do not see these signs, you will know that I will *not* return very soon." There is no indication that Jesus gave these signs in order to provide Christians with a reason *not to be ready* for his return or in order to encourage them *not to expect* that he could come at any time! To use the signs that will precede Christ's return in this way (as Berkhof does, for example), is to use them in a way that Jesus never intended. Therefore it does not seem convincing to say that Christ could not come at any time.

**b. "Any Time" Return Is Possible.** The other major solution to this problem is to say that *Christ indeed could come at any time* and to reconcile the two sets of passages in various ways.

**1. Because there will be two different returns.** One way to reconcile them is to say that *the New Testament talks about two distinct returns of Christ,* or two second comings of Christ,[13] that is, a *secret* coming at which Christ takes Christians out of the world (a coming "for his saints"), and then, after seven years of tribulation have occurred on the earth, a visible, *public,* triumphant coming (a coming "with his saints") in which Christ comes to reign over the earth. During the seven-year interval all the signs that have not yet been fulfilled (the great tribulation, the false prophets with signs and wonders, the antichrist, the salvation of Israel, and the signs in the heavens) will be fulfilled, so that there is no tension at all between waiting for a coming that could occur "at any moment" and realizing that a later coming will be preceded by many signs.[14]

The problem with this solution is that it is hard to derive two separate comings of Christ from the passages that predict his return. However, we will not discuss this matter here, but will treat it in the next chapter, when considering the pretribulational

---

13. Those who hold to this view object to the characterizing of it as two second comings and prefer to speak of two aspects of the same second coming, but since these two comings are separated by an interval of at least seven years, it does not seem inaccurate to characterize the view as holding to two second comings.

14. This view is the pretribulational view, often referred to as the pretribulational rapture view, since those who hold this view often refer to Christ's first, secret return to take Christians out of the world as the *"rapture"* (from Lat. *rapio,* "to seize, snatch, carry away"). This view is discussed in chapter 55, pp. 1372–74 and 1394–99.

premillennial view of Christ's return.[15] It should also be noted that this solution is historically quite recent, for it was unknown in the history of the church before it was proposed in the last century by John Nelson Darby (1800–82). This should alert us to the fact that this solution is not the only possible one to the tension presented by the passages quoted above.

2. **Because all the signs have already happened.** Another solution is to say that *all the signs have been fulfilled, and therefore Christ in fact could return at any moment.* On this view, one could look for possible fulfillments of these signs in the events of the early church, even in the first century. In some sense, it might be said, the gospel was indeed preached to all nations, false prophets arose and opposed the gospel, there was great tribulation in the persecution the church suffered at the hands of some of the Roman emperors, the man of lawlessness was in fact the emperor Nero, and the full number of the Jewish people who are to be saved has gradually come about through the history of the church, since Paul even gives himself as one example of the beginning of this ingathering of the Jewish people (Rom. 11:1). We will discuss in more detail in the following section the view that the signs preceding Christ's return *might* have already been fulfilled,[16] but here we can simply note that many people have not found convincing any view saying that they *have* happened because these signs seem to them to point to much larger events than those that occurred in the first century.

3. **Because it is unlikely but possible that the signs have already happened.** There is still another way of resolving these two sets of passages. That is to say that it is *unlikely but possible that the signs have already been fulfilled*, and therefore we simply cannot know with certainty at any point in history whether all the signs have been fulfilled or not.

This position is an attractive one because it takes seriously the primary purpose for the signs, the primary purpose for the warnings, and the fact that we are not to know when Christ will return. With regard to the signs, their primary purpose is to intensify our expectation of Christ's return. Therefore, whenever we see indications of things that resemble these signs, our expectation of Christ's return will be aroused and intensified. With regard to the warnings to be ready, advocates of this position would say that Christ *could* return at any time (since we cannot be certain that the signs have not been fulfilled), and so we must be ready, even though it is *unlikely* that Christ will return at once (because it seems that there are several signs yet to be fulfilled). Finally, this position agrees that we cannot know when Christ will return and that he is coming at an hour we do not expect.

But is it possible that these signs have been fulfilled? We can examine them one at a time. In each case our conclusion will be that it is *unlikely but possible that the sign has been fulfilled already.*

---

15. See chapter 55, pp. 1372–74, for an analysis of the pretribulational premillennial view of Christ's return.

16. See pp. 1355–59 for a discussion of the view that it is *unlikely* but possible that all the signs preceding Christ's return have already been fulfilled.

## 4. It Is Unlikely but Possible That the Signs Have Been Fulfilled

(In the following paragraphs I will repeat the categories of signs that must precede Christ's return but not the relevant Bible passages because I have already quoted them in section 2 above.)

**a. The Preaching of the Gospel to All Nations.** Has the gospel been preached to all nations? Probably not, since there are many language groups and tribes that have still never heard the gospel. It is unlikely, therefore, that this sign has been fulfilled. However, Paul does speak in Colossians about the worldwide spread of the gospel. He speaks of "the gospel which has come to you, as indeed *in the whole world* it is bearing fruit and increasing" (Col. 1:5–6). He also speaks of "the gospel that you heard, *which has been proclaimed in all creation under heaven*, and of which I, Paul, became a minister" (Col. 1:23). In these verses he does not mean that every creature alive has heard the proclamation of the gospel but that the proclamation has gone forth to the whole world and that, in a representative sense at least, the gospel has been preached to the whole world or to all nations.[17] Therefore, it is unlikely—but still possible—that this sign was initially fulfilled in the first century, and it has been fulfilled in a greater sense many times since then. (I do not think there is any nation on earth today where there are no Christians at all.)

**b. Great Tribulation.** Once again, it seems likely that the language of Scripture indicates a period of suffering coming to the earth that is far greater than anything that has yet been experienced. But it must be realized that many interpreters throughout history have understood Jesus' warnings about great tribulation to refer to the Roman siege of Jerusalem in the Jewish War of AD 66–70.[18] The suffering during that war was indeed terrible and could be what was described by Jesus in predicting this tribulation. In fact, since the first century, there have been many periods of violent and intense persecution of Christians, and even in our lifetimes much of it has occurred over large portions of the globe, with Christians being horribly persecuted in the former Soviet Union, in communist China, in North Korea, and in Muslim countries. It would be difficult to convince some Christians today, who have undergone decades of persecution for their faith and have known that persecution to affect thousands of other Christians throughout large segments of the world, that such a great tribulation has certainly not yet occurred. They have longed and prayed for years for Christ to come and rescue them from the tribulation that they are enduring.

---

17. R. T. France, *The Gospel according to Matthew*, TNTC (Leicester: Inter-Varsity Press, Grand Rapids: Eerdmans, 1985), 339, says of Jesus' statement that "this gospel of the kingdom will be proclaimed throughout the whole world as a testimony to all nations, and then the end will come" (Matt. 24:14) the following words: "The *world* is *oikoumenē*, lit. 'the inhabited area', a standard term originally for the Greek world (as opposed to barbarians), then for the Roman Empire, and subsequently for the whole of the then known world; it is thus not so much a geographical term that must include every area and community now known to be on earth, but rather an indication of the universal offer of the gospel *to all nations*, i.e., outside the confines of the Jewish community.... In one sense Paul could claim long before AD 70 to have 'fully preached the gospel' in a large area of Asia and Europe (Rom. 15:19) and at many times since then similar claims could have been made with reference to an area far wider than the *oikoumenē* known in Jesus' time."

18. See description of these events in France, *Matthew*, 340–41, with reference to the description of the horrors of this Roman conquest found in Josephus, *Jewish War* 5.512–18.

Therefore, though we may think that Jesus' words indicate the likelihood of a yet greater persecution coming in the future, it is difficult to be certain of this. It seems appropriate to conclude that it is *unlikely but possible* that the prediction of a great tribulation has already been fulfilled or is being fulfilled in various parts of the world at this very moment.

**c. False Christs and False Prophets.** With regard to the false christs and false prophets who will work signs and wonders, any missionary who has worked among people where witchcraft and demonic activity are rampant will readily testify that seemingly miraculous "signs and wonders" have been worked frequently by demonic powers in opposition to the spread of the gospel. Certainly demonic miracles and false signs have been done for centuries, at least since the time that the magicians in Pharaoh's court produced false signs in opposition to Moses' miracles (Ex. 7:11; 8:7; cf. the activity of Simon the Sorcerer in Acts 8:9–11). Whatever the specific form it takes, such working of deceptive miracles is always accompanied by false religions, leading many people astray (leaders of such groups could be called false christs and false prophets). The apostle John actually wrote, "Children, it is the last hour, and as you have heard that antichrist is coming, so now *many antichrists have come*" (1 John 2:18). While it seems likely that Jesus' words predict a far greater manifestation of this kind of activity in the time just prior to his return, it is difficult to be certain that this will be so. It is best to conclude that it is unlikely but still possible that this sign has been fulfilled already.

**d. Powerful Signs in the Heavens.** This sign is the only one that does not fit into the "unlikely but possible" category. The occurrence of such powerful signs in the heavens almost certainly has not yet occurred. Of course, there have been eclipses of the sun and moon, and comets have appeared, since the world began. But Jesus speaks of something far greater: "*The sun will be darkened*, and *the moon will not give its light*, and *the stars will fall from heaven*, and *the powers of the heavens will be shaken*" (Matt. 24:29).

However, there have been some attempts to explain this as symbolic language. For example, R. T. France attempts to explain "The sun will be darkened, and the moon will not give its light, and the stars will fall from heaven" (Matt. 24:29) as symbolic language that refers to the destruction of Jerusalem and God's judgment on it.[19] But the argument is not persuasive. He must base this claim on the assertion that Isaiah 13:10 (from which Jesus' words in Matt. 24:29 seem to be drawn) is also merely symbolic language to refer to the fall of Babylon: "For the stars of the heavens and their constellations will not give their light; the sun will be dark at its rising, and the moon will not shed its light" (Isa. 13:10). But this need not be understood as merely a symbol of God's judgment. It is more likely that both Isaiah 13:10 and Matthew 24:29 speak of a yet future literal falling of the stars and blackening of the sun and moon, something that would be a suitable prelude to the shaking of the earth and heaven and the cosmic destruction that will come

---

19. France, *Matthew*, 343–44.

after the return of Christ (see the next verse, Isa. 13:11, which speaks of punishing "the world"; see also Heb. 1:10–12; 12:27; 2 Peter 3:10–11).

Moreover, it is significant that this description of cosmic events in Matthew 24:29 is followed in the rest of the sentence with the description of "the Son of Man *coming on the clouds of heaven* with power and great glory" (v. 30). France must take this, not as a description of Christ's literal return, but as a description of the destruction of the Jewish Temple in Jerusalem in AD 70, a highly unlikely explanation.[20] Given these facts, it is not persuasive to say that the descriptions of the falling of the stars from heaven and the darkening of the sun and moon are merely symbolic language. It is better to regard them *as literal signs* that will occur just before Christ's return, and as such, they fall in a different category from the other signs, since it seems certain that they have not yet occurred. Nonetheless, they could occur very quickly—within the space of a few minutes or at most an hour or two—to be followed immediately by Christ's return. These particular signs are not the type that would lead us to deny that Christ could return at any time.

**e. The Appearance of the Man of Lawlessness (or the "Antichrist").** Many attempts have been made throughout history to identify the man of lawlessness (the "antichrist") with historical figures who had great authority and brought havoc and devastation among people on the earth. The ancient Roman emperors Nero and Domitian, both of whom severely persecuted Christians, were thought by many to be the antichrist. (Many Roman emperors, including these two, claimed deity for themselves and demanded to be worshiped.) In more recent times Adolf Hitler was commonly thought to be the antichrist, as was Joseph Stalin. On the other hand, many Protestants since the Reformation, especially those who were persecuted by the Catholic Church, have thought that one or another of the popes was the antichrist.

But all of these identifications have proved false,[21] and it is likely that a yet worse "man of lawlessness" will arise on the world scene and bring unparalleled suffering and persecution, only to be destroyed by Jesus when he comes again. But the evil perpetrated by many of these other rulers has been so great that, at least while they were in power, it would have been difficult to be certain that the "man of lawlessness" mentioned in 2 Thessalonians 2 has not yet appeared.[22] Once again, it is unlikely but possible that this sign has already been fulfilled.

**f. The Salvation of "All Israel."** With regard to the salvation of "all Israel" (Rom. 11:26), Romans 9–11 most likely indicates that there will be a yet future massive

---

20. France says that Matt. 24:30 speaks of "coming to God to receive vindication and authority" and therefore indicates not Christ's return in the flesh, but the vindication of his authority "over the Jewish establishment which has rejected him" when the temple is destroyed in AD 70 (ibid., 344).

21. However, John says, "as you have heard that antichrist is coming, so now many antichrists have come" (1 John 2:18), and he speaks of "the spirit of the antichrist," which, he says,

"is in the world already" (1 John 4:3). Therefore, even if these previous persecutors of the church were not *the* antichrist, many of them were precursors of the final antichrist.

22. It might be argued that Paul did not want the Thessalonian church to expect that Christ could return at any time since he writes them "not to be quickly shaken in mind or alarmed, either by a spirit or a spoken word, or a letter seeming to be from us, to the effect that the day of the Lord has come" (2 Thess.

ingathering of the Jewish people as they turn to accept Jesus as their Messiah. But it is not certain that Romans 9–11 predicts this, and many have argued that no further ingathering of the Jewish people will occur beyond the kind that we have already seen as many thousands of Jewish people have trusted in Jesus as their Messiah throughout the history of the church. One argument in support of this view is that Paul gives himself as a primary example of this ingathering (Rom. 11:1–2). Therefore, once again, it is unlikely but possible that this sign has already been fulfilled.

**g. Conclusion.** Except for the spectacular signs in the heavens, it is unlikely but possible that all of these signs have already been fulfilled. Moreover, the only sign that seems certainly not to have occurred, the darkening of the sun and moon and the falling of the stars, could occur within the space of a few minutes, and therefore it seems appropriate to say that Christ could now return at any hour of the day or night. It is therefore unlikely—but certainly possible—that Christ could return *at any time.*

But does this position do justice to the warnings that we should be ready and that Christ is coming at a time we do not expect? Is it possible to *be ready* for something that we think *unlikely* to happen in the near future? Certainly it is. Everyone who wears a seatbelt when driving, or purchases auto insurance, gets ready for an event he or she thinks to be unlikely.[23] In a similar way it seems possible to take seriously the warnings that Jesus could come when we are not expecting him and nonetheless to say that the signs preceding his coming will *probably* yet occur in the future.

This position has positive spiritual benefits as we seek to live the Christian life in the midst of a rapidly changing world. In the ebb and flow of world history, we see from time to time events that *could be* the final fulfillment of some of these signs. They happen, and then they fade away. During the blackest days of World War II, it seemed to many people that Hitler was likely the antichrist. During times of persecution against

---

2:2). He then goes on to say, "Let no one deceive you in any way. For that day will not come, unless the rebellion comes first, and the man of lawlessness is revealed" (2 Thess. 2:3). Someone might ask whether Paul is not reasoning as follows: you know that the man of lawlessness has not yet appeared; therefore, you know that Christ has not yet come. And Christ will not come until this man of lawlessness appears on the scene.

But it must be noted that Paul does not tell the Thessalonians that Christ could not come at any time. He does not tell them that they should fail to be ready or fail to expect Christ's return. He simply tells them that Christ's return *has not already occurred*, which is something far different. And the reason he gives is not only the fact that the man of lawlessness must first appear but also that Christ, when he returns, will defeat this man of lawlessness and destroy him: "And then the lawless one will be revealed, *whom the Lord Jesus will kill with the breath of his mouth and bring to nothing by the appearance of his coming*" (2 Thess. 2:8). It is not just that they have not seen the man of lawlessness—they have not seen him appear *and be destroyed by Jesus at his coming.* The conclusion is that Christ has not

come, because he has not come destroying this man of lawlessness. Yet he certainly could have come at any time, even in the context of 2 Thessalonians, and immediately destroyed the currently reigning Roman emperor (for Roman emperors regularly claimed to be God and to be worthy of worship, and John himself said that "many antichrists have come," 1 John 2:18).

23. I thank God that I have driven for fifty-five years without a major auto accident, and I pray and expect that I will not have one, but I still buckle my seatbelt every time I get in the car. I prepare for an event that I think to be unlikely, but nonetheless possible. Similarly, I *think* that many of the signs will have yet greater fulfillment, and that it is unlikely that Jesus will return within the next few days or weeks. In fact, I am working on the second edition of this book, which will not be published for many more months, on the assumption that Jesus will not have returned by then. Nonetheless, I seek to frequently examine my heart and my life to see if there is anything of which I would be ashamed when Jesus returns because I want to be ready for him to return at any moment, even at a moment I do not expect.

the church, it can seem more likely that Christians are in the middle of the great tribulation. When we hear of earthquakes and famines and wars, it makes us wonder if the coming of Christ might be near. Then these events fade into the background and world leaders pass off the scene, and the tide of events leading to the end of the age seems to have receded for a time. Then once again a new wave of events will break on the world scene, and once again our expectation of Christ's return is increased.

With each successive "wave" of events, *we do not know* which one will be the last. And this is good because God does not intend us to know. He simply wants us to continue to long for Christ's return and to expect that it could occur at any time. It is spiritually unhealthy for us to say that we know that these signs *have not* occurred, and it seems to stretch the bounds of credible interpretation to say that we know that these signs have occurred. But it seems to fit exactly in the middle of the New Testament approach toward Christ's return to say that *we do not know* with certainty if these events have occurred. Responsible exegesis, an expectation of Christ's sudden return, and a measure of humility in our understanding are all three preserved in this position.

Then if Christ does return suddenly, we will not be tempted to object (even mentally), saying that one or another sign has not yet occurred! We will simply be ready to welcome him when he appears. If there is great suffering yet to come, and if we begin to see intense opposition to the gospel, a large revival among the Jewish people, remarkable progress in the preaching of the gospel through the world, and even spectacular signs in the heavens, then we will not be dismayed or lose heart because we will remember Jesus' words, "When these things begin to take place, straighten up and raise your heads, because your redemption is drawing near" (Luke 21:28).

## G. HAS CHRIST ALREADY RETURNED? THE PRETERIST VIEW

An entirely different view has gained some followers in recent years. This is the "preterist" view, which says that Christ returned in AD 70 when the Jerusalem temple was destroyed.

### 1. The Preterist Argument

The arguments in favor of preterism are as follows.[24]

(1) Jesus predicts in Matthew 24:34 that he will return during the lifetime of "this generation."

> Immediately after the tribulation of those days the sun will be darkened, and the moon will not give its light, and the stars will fall from heaven, and the powers of the heavens will be shaken. Then will appear in heaven the sign of the Son of Man, and then all the tribes of the earth will mourn, and *they will see the Son of Man coming*

---

24. For a brief summary of preterist arguments, see John Noë, *Dead in Their Tracks: Stopping the Liberal/Skeptic Attack on the Bible* (Bradford, PA: International Preterist Association, 2001).

*on the clouds of heaven with power and great glory.* And he will send out his angels with a loud trumpet call, and they will gather his elect from the four winds, from one end of heaven to the other. "From the fig tree learn its lesson: as soon as its branch becomes tender and puts out its leaves, you know that summer is near. So also, when you see all these things, you know that he is near, at the very gates. Truly, I say to you, *this generation will not pass away until all these things take place.*" (Matt. 24:29–34; other events are predicted earlier in Matt. 24, including the great tribulation and the preaching of the gospel to all nations)

(2) The only legitimate understanding of "this generation" in Matthew 24:34 is that it means the people who were alive when Jesus said these things.[25]

(3) Therefore, in order for Jesus' words to be true, he must have come back during the lifetime of the people who heard him in Matthew 24. Noē writes, "This is the Preterist position. . . . All eschatological events came to pass within the lifetime of Jesus' contemporaries—i.e., within 'this generation'. . . . This includes our Lord's time-restricted return."[26]

(4) Jesus did come back, but he did so invisibly when Roman armies destroyed the Jewish temple in Jerusalem in AD 70. This event fulfilled Jesus' predictions of his return to earth and other end-time predictions. Although Jesus did not return to earth visibly in his resurrection body, *he returned invisibly* by bringing judgment on the Jewish temple and with it the Jewish religious system. Therefore, we should not expect any future second coming of Christ to earth.

According to the preterist view, the prediction of Christ "coming on the clouds of heaven" (Matt. 24:30) does not mean a literal, physical return of Christ but is "a common metaphor borrowed from Old Testament portrayals of God descending from heaven and coming in power and glory to execute judgment on a people or nation."[27] Noē gives several verses to support the idea that that "coming on the clouds of heaven" is a common metaphor for God coming in judgment (Isa. 19:1; Jer. 4:13; Ezek. 30:3; Ps. 68:4; 104:3–4; also Ezek. 30:18; Ps. 18:9–12; 2 Sam. 22:10–12; Nah. 1:3; Joel 2:1–2; Zeph. 1:14–15).

Noē also writes, "Jesus did return, bodily and literally, just *as* and *when* He said He would. He no longer is departed. He is here with us!"[28] He also summarizes his view as saying "that all Bible prophecy has been fulfilled and Jesus has returned [past tense]."[29] Later, in promoting what he sees as a worldview advantage to preterism, he says, "Your motivation is going to be quite different if you believe Jesus has already returned *as* and *when* He said He would, and that He has consummated his kingdom and expects you to reign with him on earth, here and now (Rev. 5:9–10)."[30]

25. See Noē, publishers preface to *Dead in Their Tracks*; see also 22, 60, 65.
26. Noē, *Dead in Their Tracks*, 23.
27. Ibid., 43.
28. Ibid., 60. He does not explain just how this invisible return could be a "bodily" return.
29. Ibid., 25.
30. Ibid., 73.

## 2. Response to Preterism

(1) There are other legitimate understandings of "this generation" in Matthew 24:34: (a) "This generation" could mean "the generation that sees the signs of Christ's return," such as the great tribulation and the stars falling from heaven (Matt. 24:21, 29). (b) "This generation" could mean "this type of person," as in Mark 8:38, "whoever is ashamed of me and of my words in *this adulterous and sinful generation*, of him will the Son of Man also be ashamed when he comes in the glory of his Father with the holy angels." (Mark 8:38; cf. Luke 16:8).[31] (c) It is not decisive to argue that "this generation" refers to people presently alive in all its other occurrences in the New Testament, because it is necessary to decide from the context what the word *this* refers to in each individual context, and in Matthew 24 these other meanings are certainly possible.

In addition, there is still another possible explanation of Matthew 24:34: (d) Even if "this generation" is understood to mean the people alive at the time Jesus was speaking, the phrase "all these things" in Matthew 24:34 does not necessarily include the return of Christ. This is because "all these things" in the immediately preceding verse means the sufferings and disruptions mentioned in verses 4–28 that must take place *before* Christ will return: "So also, when you see *all these things*, you know that he is near, at the very gates. (Matt. 24:33). In that verse, "all these things" warn people to *be ready* for Christ's return, and therefore the phrase cannot include Christ's return.

(2) It is not true that God "coming on the clouds of heaven" is a "common metaphor" for God coming *invisibly in judgment* in the Old Testament. Noē claims this is evident from eleven Old Testament verses, but only one of those verses actually speaks of God coming "on the clouds" to execute judgment: "Behold, the LORD is *riding on a swift cloud* and comes to Egypt; and the idols of Egypt will tremble at his presence, and the heart of the Egyptians will melt within them" (Isa. 19:1). Even in that verse, it is more likely that this speaks of a *literal, visible appearance* of a cloud that surrounded God's presence because that was the way God appeared in the pillar of cloud that protected the Israelites from the Egyptians in the exodus (Exod. 14:19), in the cloud that went before them in the wilderness (Exod. 13:21–22), in the cloud that descended on Mount Sinai (Exod. 19:9), in the cloud that descended on the tent when God came to speak to Moses (Exod. 33:9), in the cloud that filled the temple built by Solomon (1 Kings 8:10–11), and in the cloud that surrounded Jesus on the Mount of Transfiguration (Matt. 17:5). These are not examples of God coming invisibly in judgment, for in these cases God was coming with a visible cloud to bring *blessing* to his people.[32]

---

31. Other examples of Greek *genea* meaning "type of person" are found in Ps. 14:5 ("God is with the generation of the righteous") and 24:6 ("such is the generation of those who seek him").

32. With regard to the other ten verses that Noē mentions, some do not even say that God is coming "on the clouds" (Jer. 4:13; Ezek. 30:3, 18; 38:9, 16; Nah. 1:3; Joel 2:1–2; Zeph. 1:14–15), and others are in contexts where the focus is not on God coming in judgment but on God coming to save his people (Pss. 18: 9–12; 68:4 [NIV]; 2 Sam. 22:10–12).

(3) The claim of preterists that Christ's second coming occurred when he returned invisibly in judgment in the destruction of the Jerusalem temple in AD 70 denies the evident meaning of numerous New Testament verses that predict events that clearly did not take place in AD 70 and have not yet taken place, such as the following:

> Immediately after the tribulation of those days *the sun will be darkened, and the moon will not give its light, and the stars will fall from heaven*, and the powers of the heavens will be shaken. (Matt. 24:29)

> Then will appear in heaven the sign of the Son of Man, and then *all the tribes of the earth will mourn*, and *they will see the Son of Man* coming on the clouds of heaven with power and great glory. (Matt. 24:30)

> He will send out his angels with a loud trumpet call, and they will gather his elect from the four winds, from one end of heaven to the other. (Matt. 24:31)

> Then they will see the Son of Man coming in a cloud with power and great glory. (Luke 21:27)

> If I go and prepare a place for you, I will come again and will take you to myself, that where I am you may be also. (John 14:3).

> Men of Galilee, why do you stand looking into heaven? This Jesus, who was taken up from you into heaven, will come in the same way as you saw him go into heaven. (Acts 1:11)

> For the Lord himself will descend from heaven with a cry of command, with the voice of an archangel, and with the sound of the trumpet of God. And the dead in Christ will rise first. Then we who are alive, who are left, will be caught up together with them in the clouds to meet the Lord in the air, and so we will always be with the Lord. (1 Thess. 4:16–17)

> Among them are Hymenaeus and Philetus, who have swerved from the truth, saying that the resurrection has already happened. (2 Tim. 2:17–18; this is similar to the preterist claim that all the end-times events have already occurred)

> But the day of the Lord will come like a thief, and then the heavens will pass away with a roar, and the heavenly bodies will be burned up and dissolved, and the earth and the works that are done on it will be exposed. (2 Peter 3:10)

> Beloved, we are God's children now, and what we will be has not yet appeared; but we know that when he appears we shall be like him, because we shall see him as he is. (1 John 3:2)

> Behold, he is coming with the clouds, and every eye will see him, even those who pierced him, and all tribes of the earth will wail on account of him. Even so. Amen. (Rev. 1:7).

It is somewhat ironic that the clear force of so many texts that speak of a highly visible and even audible return of Christ to earth can be denied by a book that claims to rely on "the plain meaning of clear and emphatic statements," and "the plain sense of . . . normal, commonly used and understood words," and "the plain, literal meaning" of words and statements.[33]

(4) The preterist claim that Christ has already returned invisibly is remarkably similar to the claims of an "invisible return" that Jesus warned against: "So, if they say to you, 'Look, he is in the wilderness,' do not go out. If they say, 'Look, he is in the inner rooms,' do not believe it. For as the lightning comes from the east and shines as far as the west, so will be the coming of the Son of Man" (Matt. 24:26–27; the imagery of lightning shows that Christ's return will be something that everyone can see).

(5) The claim that Christ has already returned contradicts some of the historic creeds of the Christian church, such as the Apostles Creed, which puts Christ's second coming in the future when it says, "He ascended into heaven; and sitteth at the right hand of God the Father Almighty; from thence *he shall come* to judge the quick and the dead." The Nicene Creed (325/381 AD) similarly says, "and sitteth on the right hand of the Father; and *he shall come again, with glory, to judge both the quick and the dead*; whose kingdom shall have no end."[34] The Westminster Confession of Faith says, "and there sitteth at the right hand of his Father, making intercession, *and shall return, to judge men and angels, at the end of the world*" (8:4).

(6) Doctrinal error sometimes comes into the church from groups that latch onto one verse that is difficult to understand in the Bible, claim that their interpretation is the only legitimate one, and then use that interpretation to deny the plain force of many other passages of Scripture. This is done by the Mormons with their emphasis on the puzzling "baptism on behalf of the dead" passage in 1 Corinthians 15:29, and it is done by preterists in their insistence that their understanding of Matthew 24:34 is the "only possible solution" to that passage.[35]

(7) Because of points (3), (4), and (5) above, I do not think that the "full preterist"

---

33. Noë, *Dead in Their Tracks*, 10, 15, 56.

34. Writing in a "publisher's response" to John Noë's book, Edward E. Stevens admits the "lack of recognition [of preterism] by the early church," but he then asks the reader to conclude that "a mistake has to be charged to . . . the uninspired church fathers" (Stevens, publishers response to *Dead in Their Tracks*, 66).

35. Noë, publishers preface to *Dead in Their Tracks*; see also 22, 60, 65.

position (that claims that Christ has already returned and there is no future second coming to wait for) should be considered to be a legitimate evangelical position or should be given any opportunity to promote its viewpoints within evangelical circles.

### 3. "Partial Preterism" Is Something Entirely Different

A number of evangelical interpreters have argued that *some* of the end-times events that Jesus predicted in Matthew 24 were fulfilled (at least partially, with possible greater fulfillment yet to come) in the destruction of Jerusalem in AD 70. They definitely would not say that the return of Christ happened then, but perhaps the great tribulation, the preaching of the gospel to all nations, and the rise of false christs and false prophets have already occurred. In fact, I argued earlier in this chapter that I think it unlikely but still possible that some of these things have already happened.

But I think it is more confusing than helpful to call this "partial preterism," and thereby to lend an air of legitimacy to the full preterism that I have been discussing and that I believe to be outside the bounds of Christian orthodoxy.

## QUESTIONS FOR PERSONAL APPLICATION

1. Before reading this chapter, did you think that Christ could return at any hour? How did that affect your Christian life? Now what do you think? If your viewpoint has changed, what effect do you think it will have on your life?

2. Why do you think Jesus decided to leave the world for a time and then return, rather than staying on earth after his resurrection and preaching the gospel throughout the world himself?

3. Do you now eagerly long for Christ's return? Have you had a greater longing for it in the past? If you do not have a very strong yearning for Christ's return, what factors in your life do you think contribute to that lack of longing?

4. Have you ever decided not to undertake a long-term project because you thought Christ's return was near? Do you have any hesitancy now about long-term projects because of that reason? If so, do you think that hesitancy has any negative consequences on your life?

5. Are you ready for Christ to return today? If you knew he were going to return within twenty-four hours, what situations or relationships would you want to straighten out before he returned? Do you think that the command to "be ready" means that you should attempt to straighten out those things now, even if you think it unlikely that he would return today?

**Special Terms**

*eschatology*
*general eschatology*
*imminent*
maranatha
parousia
*personal eschatology*
*preterism*
*second coming of Christ*

# BIBLIOGRAPHY

(For an explanation of this bibliography see the note on the bibliography to chapter 1, pp. 23–24. Complete bibliographical data may be found on pp. 1489–96.)

## SECTIONS IN EVANGELICAL SYSTEMATIC THEOLOGIES

### 1. Anglican (Episcopalian)
1882–92 . . . . . Litton, 579–81
1930 . . . . . . . . Thomas, 87–88, 525
2001 . . . . . . . . Packer, 250–53
2013 . . . . . . . . Bird, 258–73
2013 . . . . . . . . Bray, 542–53

### 2. Arminian (Wesleyan or Methodist)
1875–76 . . . . . Pope, 3:387–401
1892–94 . . . . . Miley, 2:440–47
1940 . . . . . . . . Wiley, 3:243–81
1960 . . . . . . . . Purkiser, 537–50
1983 . . . . . . . . Carter, 2:113–16
1992 . . . . . . . . Oden, 3:409–21
2002 . . . . . . . . Cottrell, 525–51

### 3. Baptist
1767 . . . . . . . . Gill, 2:230–43
1887 . . . . . . . . Boyce, 451–61
1907 . . . . . . . . Strong, 1003–15
1990–95 . . . . . Garrett, 775–89
2007 . . . . . . . . Akin, 902–08
2013 . . . . . . . . Erickson, 1087–95, 1104

### 4. Dispensational
1947 . . . . . . . . Chafer, 4:255–63; 5:280–314
1949 . . . . . . . . Thiessen, 337–50
1986 . . . . . . . . Ryrie, 273–74, 463
2002–2005 . . Geisler, 4:413–58, 597–661

2017 . . . . . . . . MacArthur and Mayhue, 850–84

### 5. Lutheran
1917–24 . . . . . Pieper, 3:515–34
1934 . . . . . . . . Mueller, 619–25

### 6. Reformed (or Presbyterian)
1679–85 . . . . . Turretin, *IET*, 3:561–637
1871–73 . . . . . Hodge, 3:790–836
1887–1921 . . . Warfield, *SSW*, 1:348–64
1894 . . . . . . . . Shedd, 863–66
1906–11 . . . . . Bavinck, *RD*, 4:644–63, 686–90
1937–66 . . . . . Murray, *CW*, 1: 86–95; *CW*, 2:387–410
1938 . . . . . . . . Berkhof, 695–707
1998 . . . . . . . . Reymond, 979–1066
2008 . . . . . . . . Van Genderen and Velema, 838–64
2011 . . . . . . . . Horton, 919–56
2013 . . . . . . . . Frame, 1075, 1086, 1089, 1093–96
2013 . . . . . . . . Culver, 1111–28
2016 . . . . . . . . Allen and Swain, 389–91
2017 . . . . . . . . Barrett, 721–56
2019 . . . . . . . . Letham, 817–841, 854–60

### 7. Renewal (or charismatic/Pentecostal)
1988–92 . . . . . Williams, 3:297–396
1993 . . . . . . . . Menzies and Horton, 213–26
1995 . . . . . . . . Horton, 614–34
2008 . . . . . . . . Duffield and Van Cleave, 529–44

## SECTIONS IN REPRESENTATIVE ROMAN CATHOLIC SYSTEMATIC THEOLOGIES

### 1. Roman Catholic: Traditional
1955 . . . . . . . . Ott, 485–88

**2. *Roman Catholic: Post–Vatican II***

1980 . . . . . . . . McBrien, 2:1101–6

2012 . . . . . . . . *CCC*, paragraphs 522–24, 550, 1040

## OTHER WORKS

Allison, Gregg. *Historical Theology: An Introduction to Christian Doctrine; A Companion to Wayne Grudem's* Systematic Theology. Grand Rapids: Zondervan, 2011, 683–701.

Archer, Gleason, Paul Feinberg, Douglas Moo, and Richard Reiter. *The Rapture: Pre-, Mid-, or Post-Tribulational?* Grand Rapids: Zondervan, 1984.

Bauckham, Richard J. "Apocalyptic." In *NDT1*, 33–35.

Beale, G. K. "Eschatology." In *DLNT*, 330–45.

Beechick, Allen. *The Pre-Tribulation Rapture.* Denver: Accent, 1980.

Berkouwer, G. C. *The Return of Christ.* Translated by James Van Oosterom. Edited by Marlin J. Van Elderen. Grand Rapids: Eerdmans, 1972.

Brower, K. E. "Eschatology." In *NDBT*, 459–64.

Clouse, F. G. "Rapture of the Church." In *EDT3*, 719–21.

Dumbrell, William J. *The Search for Order: Biblical Eschatology in Focus.* Grand Rapids: Baker, 1992.

Erickson, Millard. *Contemporary Options in Eschatology.* Grand Rapids: Baker, 1977.

Gundry, R. H. *The Church and the Tribulation.* Grand Rapids: Zondervan, 1973.

Gundry, Stanley N., and Alan Hultberg, eds. *Three Views on the Rapture: Pretribulation, Prewrath, or Posttribulation.* 2nd ed. Grand Rapids: Zondervan, 2010.

Hoekema, Anthony A. *The Bible and the Future.* Grand Rapids: Eerdmans, 1979, 109–238.

Kreitzer, L. J. "Apocalyptic, Apocalypticism." In *DLNT*, 55–68.

———. "Parousia." In *DLNT*, 856–75.

Ladd, George Eldon. *The Blessed Hope.* Grand Rapids: Eerdmans, 1956.

Lightner, Robert P. *The Last Days Handbook: A Comprehensive Guide to Understanding the Different Views of Prophecy; Who Believes What about Prophecy and Why.* Nashville: Nelson, 1990.

Moore, Russell D. "Personal and Cosmic Eschatology." In *A Theology for the Church*, edited by Daniel L. Akin et al., 901–6. Nashville: B&H, 2007.

Morris, Leon L. "Second Coming of Christ." In *BTDB*, 719–23.

Noble, T. A. "Eschatology." In *NDT2*, 296–99.

Porter, S. E. "Tribulation, Messianic Woes." In *DLNT*, 1179–82.

Rosenthal, Marvin. *The Pre-Wrath Rapture of the Church.* Nashville: Nelson, 1990.

Sizer, S. "Apocalyptic." In *NDT2*, 46–48.

Travis, S. H. "Eschatology." In *NDT1*, 228–31.

VanGemeren, Willem. *The Progress of Redemption.* Grand Rapids: Zondervan, 1988.

Van Kampen, Robert. *The Sign.* Wheaton, IL: Crossway, 1992.

Vos, Geerhardus. *The Pauline Eschatology.* Grand Rapids: Eerdmans, 1961.

Walvoord, John F. *The Blessed Hope and the Tribulation.* Grand Rapids: Zondervan, 1976.

———. *The Return of the Lord.* Grand Rapids: Zondervan, 1981.

# SCRIPTURE MEMORY PASSAGE

**1 Thessalonians 4:15–18:** For this we declare to you by a word from the Lord, that we who are alive, who are left until the coming of the Lord, will not precede those who have fallen asleep. For the Lord himself will descend from heaven with a cry of command, with the voice of an archangel, and with the sound of the trumpet of God. And the dead in Christ will rise first. Then we who are alive, who are left, will be caught up together with them in the clouds to meet the Lord in the air, and so we will always be with the Lord. Therefore encourage one another with these words.

# HYMN

### "Lo! He Comes, With Clouds Descending"

This song vividly pictures the event of Christ's return, with millions of believers coming with him and many more on earth welcoming him as he comes. The "clouds" with which Christ comes, mentioned in the first line of the hymn, are the clouds of God's glory. The hymn does not hesitate (in v. 3) to portray brilliantly the shaking of the heavens and the earth and the fact that unbelievers will be called to judgment. It ends with a dramatic stanza directly addressing Jesus himself, asking him to come quickly and reign. (Use tune known as "Sicilian Mariners.")

*Lo! He comes, with clouds descending, once for*
*favored sinners slain;*
*Thousand thousand saints attending swell the*
*triumph of his train:*
*Alleluia! Alleluia! God appears on earth to reign.*

*Ev'ry eye shall now behold him, robed in dreadful*
*majesty;*
*Those who set at naught and sold him,*
*pierced, and nailed him to the tree,*
*Deeply wailing, deeply wailing, shall the true*
*Messiah see.*

*Ev'ry island, sea, and mountain, heav'n and earth,*
*shall flee away;*
*All who hate him must, confounded, hear the*
*trump proclaim the Day;*

*Come to judgment! Come to judgment! Come to*
*judgment, come away!*

*Now redemption, long expected, see in solemn*
*pomp appear!*
*All his saints, by man rejected, now shall meet*
*him in the air:*
*Alleluia! Alleluia! See the Day of God appear!*

*Yea, amen! Let all adore thee, high on thine*
*eternal throne;*
*Savior, take the pow'r and glory, claim the*
*kingdom for thine own:*
*O come quickly; O come quickly; alleluia! Come,*
*Lord, come.*

Authors: Charles Wesley, 1758 (stanzas 1, 2, 5)
and John Cennick, 1752 (stanzas 3, 4)

Alternative hymn: "Rejoice, All Ye Believers"

# CONTEMPORARY WORSHIP SONG

### "This We Know"

*You are who You say You are.*
*You'll do what You say You'll do.*
*You'll be who You've always been to us,*
*Jesus.*

*Our hope is in You alone.*
*Our strength in Your mighty name.*
*Our peace in the darkest day remains,*
*Jesus.*

*Chorus*
*This we know:*
*We will see the enemy run.*
*This we know:*
*We will see the victory come.*
*We hold on to every promise You ever made.*
*Jesus, You are unfailing.*

*Our guide through the wilderness.*
*Our joy in the heaviness.*
*Our way when it seems there is no way,*
*Jesus.*

*Bridge*
*We trust You.*
*We trust You.*
*Your ways are higher than our own.*

Words by Kristian Stanfill and Jason Ingram[36]

---

## CHAPTER 55

# The Millennium

*What is the millennium?*
*When does it occur?*
*Will Christians go through the Great Tribulation?*

## EXPLANATION AND SCRIPTURAL BASIS

The word *millennium* means "one thousand years" (from Lat. *millennium*, "thousand years"). The term comes from Revelation 20:4–5, where it says that certain people "came to life and reigned with Christ *for a thousand years*. The rest of the dead did not come to life until *the thousand years* were ended." Just prior to this statement, we read that an angel came down from heaven and seized the devil "and bound him for *a thousand years*, and threw him into the pit, and shut it and sealed it over him, so that he might not deceive the nations any longer, until *the thousand years* were ended" (Rev. 20:2–3).

Throughout the history of the church there have been three major views on the time and nature of this "millennium."

### A. EXPLANATION OF THE THREE MAJOR VIEWS

### 1. Amillennialism

We begin with the simplest view, amillennialism. It can be pictured as in figure 55.1.

**Amillennialism**
*Figure 55.1*

According to this position the passage in Revelation 20:1–10 describes *the present church age*. This is an age in which Satan's influence over the nations has been greatly reduced so that the gospel can be preached to the whole world. Those who are said to be reigning with Christ for the thousand years are Christians who have died and are already reigning with Christ in heaven. Christ's reign in the millennium, according to this view, is not a bodily reign here on earth but rather the heavenly reign he spoke of when he said, "All authority in heaven and on earth has been given to me" (Matt. 28:18).

This view is called "amillennial" because it maintains that there is *no future millennium yet to come.* Since amillennialists believe that Revelation 20 is now being fulfilled in the church age, they hold that the "millennium" described there is currently happening. The exact duration of the church age cannot be known, and the expression "thousand years" is simply a figure of speech for a long period of time in which God's perfect purposes will be accomplished.

According to this position, the present church age will continue until the time of Christ's return (see figure 55.1). When Christ returns, there will be a resurrection of both believers and unbelievers. The bodies of believers will rise to be reunited with their spirits and enter into full enjoyment of heaven forever. Unbelievers will be raised to face the final judgment and eternal condemnation. Believers will also stand before the judgment seat of Christ (2 Cor. 5:10), but this judgment will only determine degrees of reward in heaven, for only unbelievers will be condemned eternally. At this time also the new heavens and new earth will begin. Immediately after the final judgment, the eternal state will commence and continue forever.

This scheme is quite simple because all of the end time events happen at once, immediately after Christ's return. Some amillennialists say that Christ could return at any time, while others (such as Berkhof) argue that certain signs have yet to be fulfilled.

## 2. Postmillennialism

The prefix *post-* means "after." According to this view, Christ will return *after* the millennium. The postmillennial view may be represented as in figure 55.2.

POSTMILLENNIALISM
Christ comes after
the Millennium

Christ

Church Age >> Millennium

Eternal State

Resurrection of believers
Resurrection of unbelievers
Judgment
New heaven, new earth

**Postmillennialism**
*Figure 55.2*

According to this view, the progress of the gospel and the growth of the church will gradually increase, so that a larger and larger proportion of the world's population will be Christians. As a result, there will be significant Christian influences on society, society will function more and more according to God's standards, and gradually a "millennial age" of peace and righteousness will occur on the earth. This "millennium" will last for a long period of time (not necessarily a literal one thousand years), and finally, *at the end of this period, Christ will return to earth*, believers and unbelievers will be raised, the final judgment will occur, and there will be a new heaven and new earth. We will then enter into the eternal state.

The primary characteristic of postmillennialism is that it is very optimistic about the power of the gospel to change lives and bring about much good in the world. Belief in postmillennialism tends to increase in times when the church is experiencing great revival, when there is an absence of war and international conflict, and when it appears that great progress is being made in overcoming the evil and suffering in the world. But postmillennialism in its most responsible form is not based simply on the observation of events in the world around us but on arguments from various Scripture passages, which will be examined below.

### 3. Premillennialism

**a. Classic or Historic Premillennialism.** The prefix *pre-* means "before," and the "premillennial" position says that Christ will come back *before* the millennium.[1] This viewpoint has a long history from the earliest centuries onward. It may be represented as in figure 55.3.

CLASSICAL PREMILLENNIALISM
Christ comes before the Millennium

"Catching up" of believers to be with Christ
— IMMEDIATE —

Christ

| Church Age | T | Bel / Christ / Bel | Millennium | Eternal State |

Resurrection of believers
(Renewed earth)*

Resurrection of unbelievers
Judgment
(Renewed earth)*

\* Classical Premillennialists differ over whether the renewed earth will begin in the millennium or the eternal state.

**Classic or Historic Premillennialism**
*Figure 55.3*

---

1. Another name sometimes used to refer to premillennialism is *chiliasm*, from the Greek word *chilioi*, "a thousand." This term is more often found in older literature and is rarely used today.

According to this viewpoint, the present church age will continue until, as it nears the end, a time of great tribulation and suffering comes on the earth (T in the figure above stands for tribulation).[2] *After* that time of tribulation *at the end of the church age, Christ will return to earth to establish a millennial kingdom.* When he comes back, believers who have died will be raised from the dead, their bodies will be reunited with their spirits, and *these believers will reign with Christ on earth for one thousand years.* (Some premillennialists take this to be a literal one thousand years, and others understand it to be a symbolic expression for a long period of time.) During this time, Christ will be physically present on the earth in his resurrected body and will reign as King over the earth. The *believers* who have been raised from the dead, along with those who are still alive on earth when Christ returns, will receive glorified resurrection bodies that will never die, and in these resurrection bodies they will live on the earth and reign with Christ. Of the *unbelievers* who remain on earth, many (but not all) will turn to Christ and be saved. Jesus will reign in perfect righteousness, and there will be peace throughout the earth. Many premillennialists hold that the earth will be renewed, and we will in fact see the new heavens and new earth at this time (but it is not essential to premillennialism to hold to this, for one could be a premillennialist and hold that the new heavens and new earth will not occur until after the final judgment). At the beginning of this time Satan will be bound and cast into the bottomless pit so that he will have no influence on the earth during the millennium (Rev. 20:1–3).

According to this premillennial viewpoint, at the end of the thousand years Satan will be loosed from the bottomless pit and will join forces with many unbelievers who have submitted outwardly to Christ's reign but have inwardly been seething in rebellion against him. Satan will gather these rebellious people for battle against Christ, but they will be decisively defeated. Christ will then raise from the dead all the unbelievers who have died throughout history, and they will stand before him for final judgment. After the final judgment has occurred, believers will enter into the eternal state.

It seems that premillennialism has tended to increase in popularity as the church has experienced persecution and as suffering and evil have increased in the earth. But, as in the case of postmillennialism, the arguments for the premillennial position are not based on an observation of current events but on specific passages of Scripture, especially (but not exclusively) Revelation 20:1–10.

### b. Pretribulational Premillennialism (or Dispensational Premillennialism).
Another variety of premillennialism gained widespread popularity in the nineteenth and twentieth centuries, particularly in the United Kingdom and the United States. According to this position, Christ will return not only before the millennium (Christ's return is *pre*millennial), but also it will occur *before* the great tribulation (Christ's return

---

2. An alternative type of premillennialism holds that Christ will come back *before* the period of great tribulation begins on earth. We shall examine that alternative form of premillennialism below.

is *pre*tribulational). This position is similar to the classical premillennial position mentioned above but with one important difference: it will add another return of Christ before his return to reign on earth in the millennium. This return is thought to be a secret return of Christ to take believers out of the world.[3] The pretribulational premillennial view may be represented as in figure 55.4.

**Pretribulational Premillennialism**
*Figure 55.4*

According to this view, this present church age will continue until, *suddenly, unexpectedly, and secretly, Christ will return part way to earth and then will call believers to himself*: "The dead in Christ will rise first. Then we who are alive, who are left, will be caught up together with them in the clouds to meet the Lord in the air" (1 Thess. 4:16–17). *Christ will then return to heaven with the believers who have been removed from the earth.* When that happens, there will be *a great tribulation on the earth* for a period of seven years.[4]

This *pretribulation* premillennial view explains that during this seven-year period of tribulation, many of the signs that were predicted to precede Christ's return will be fulfilled.[5] The great ingathering of the fullness of the Jewish people will occur, as they trust Christ as their Messiah. In the midst of great suffering there will also be much effective evangelism, especially carried out by the new Jewish Christians. *At the end of the tribulation, Christ will then come back with his saints to reign on the earth for one thousand years.* After this millennial period there will be a rebellion, resulting in the

---

3. Sometimes this secret coming of Christ for believers is called the "rapture," from the Latin word *rapio*, meaning "seize, snatch, carry away."

4. Some interpreters hold to a variation of this view, such that Christ comes back in the middle of the tribulation and rescues believers. After that, there will be three-and-one-half additional years of tribulation on the earth. This is called the "midtribulation rapture" view. For further discussion of this view, see Gleason Archer, "The Case for the Mid-Seventieth-Week Rapture Position" in Gleason Archer, Paul Feinberg, Douglas Moo, and Richard Reiter, *The Rapture: Pre-, Mid-, or Post-Tribulational?* (Grand Rapids: Zondervan, 1984), 113–45.

5. See chapter 54, pp. 1350–52, for a discussion of the signs that will precede Christ's return.

final defeat of Satan and his forces, and then will come the resurrection of unbelievers, the last judgment, and the beginning of the eternal state.

One further characteristic of pretribulational premillennialism should be mentioned: this view is found almost exclusively among dispensationalists who wish to maintain a clear distinction between the church and Israel. This pretribulational viewpoint allows the distinction to be maintained, since the church is taken out of the world before the widespread conversion of the Jewish people. These Jewish people therefore remain a distinct group from the church. Another characteristic of pretribulational premillennialism is its insistence on interpreting biblical prophecies "literally where possible." This especially applies to prophecies in the Old Testament concerning Israel. Those who hold this view argue that those prophecies of God's future blessing to Israel will yet be fulfilled among the Jewish people themselves; they are not to be "spiritualized" by finding their fulfillment in the church. Finally, one attractive feature about pretribulational premillennialism is that it allows people to insist that Christ's return could occur "at any moment" and therefore does justice to the full force of the passages that encourage us to be ready for Christ's return, while it still allows for a very literal fulfillment of the signs preceding Christ's return, since it says these will come to pass in the tribulation.

Before examining the arguments for these three (or four) positions, it is important to realize that the interpretation of the details of prophetic passages regarding future events is often a complex and difficult task involving many variable factors. Therefore, the degree of certainty that attaches to our conclusions in this area will be less than with many other doctrines. Even though I will argue for one position (classical premillennialism), I also think it important for evangelicals to recognize that this area of study is complex and to extend a large measure of grace to others who hold different views regarding the millennium and the tribulation period.

## B. A Consideration of the Arguments for Amillennialism

In favor of the amillennial view, the following arguments are advanced.[6]

1. When we look through the whole of the Bible, amillennialists will say, *only one passage* (Rev. 20:1–6) appears to teach a future earthly millennial rule of Christ, and that passage is itself obscure. It is unwise to base such a major doctrine on one passage of uncertain and widely disputed interpretation.

But how do amillennialists understand Revelation 20:1–6? The amillennial interpretation sees this passage as referring to the present church age. The passage reads as follows:

---

6. For a recent and very extensive argument in support of an amillennial viewpoint, see Sam Storms, *Kingdom Come: The Amillennial Alternative* (Ross-Shire, Scotland: Mentor, 2013).

> Then I saw an angel coming down from heaven, holding in his hand the key to the bottomless pit and a great chain. And he seized the dragon, that ancient serpent, who is the devil and Satan, and bound him for a thousand years, and threw him into the pit, and shut it and sealed it over him, so that he might not deceive the nations any longer, until the thousand years were ended. After that he must be released for a little while.
>
> Then I saw thrones, and seated on them were those to whom the authority to judge was committed. Also I saw the souls of those who had been beheaded for the testimony of Jesus and for the word of God, and those who had not worshiped the beast or its image and had not received its mark on their foreheads or their hands. They came to life and reigned with Christ for a thousand years. The rest of the dead did not come to life until the thousand years were ended. This is the first resurrection. Blessed and holy is the one who shares in the first resurrection! Over such the second death has no power, but they will be priests of God and of Christ, and they will reign with him for a thousand years.

According to an amillennial interpretation[7] the binding of Satan in verses 1–2 is the binding that occurred during Jesus' earthly ministry. He spoke of binding the strong man in order that he may plunder his house (Matt. 12:29) and said that the Spirit of God was at that time present in power to triumph over demonic forces: "If it is by the Spirit of God that I cast out demons, then the kingdom of God has come upon you" (Matt. 12:28). Similarly, with respect to the breaking of Satan's power, Jesus said during his ministry, "I saw Satan fall like lightning from heaven" (Luke 10:18).

The amillennialist argues that this binding of Satan in Revelation 20:1–3 is for a specific purpose: *that he might not deceive the nations any longer* (v. 3). This is exactly what happened when Jesus came and the gospel began to be proclaimed not simply to Jews but, after Pentecost, to all the nations of the world. In fact, the worldwide missionary activity of the church, as well as the presence of the church in most or all of the nations of the world, shows that the power Satan had in the Old Testament to "deceive the nations" and keep them in darkness has been broken.

On the amillennialist view the scene described in verse 4 occurs in heaven. John said, "I saw the *souls* of those who had been beheaded for the testimony of Jesus. . . . They came to life and reigned with Christ for a thousand years" (v. 4). Since John sees "souls" and not physical bodies, it is argued, this scene must be occurring in heaven. When the text says that "they came to life," it does not mean that they received a bodily resurrection. It possibly means simply that "they lived," since the aorist verb *ezēsan* can readily

---

7. I am largely following the excellent and widely-recognized discussion of Anthony A. Hoekema, "Amillennialism," in *The Meaning of the Millennium: Four Views*, ed. Robert G. Clouse (Downers Grove, IL: InterVarsity Press, 1977), 155–87. I will also interact with some of the arguments put forth by Sam Storms, *Kingdom Come*.

be interpreted to be a statement of an event that occurred over a long period of time. (The verb for "they reigned" is also an aorist indicative and refers to an occurrence over a thousand years, so the verb for "they lived" should have a similar meaning.) On the other hand, some amillennial interpreters will take the verb *ezēsan* to mean "they came to life" in the sense of coming into heavenly existence in the presence of Christ and beginning to reign with him from heaven.

According to this view, the phrase "first resurrection" (v. 5) refers to going to heaven to be with the Lord in the intermediate state (see chapter 41). This is not a *bodily* resurrection but living spiritually in the presence of God in heaven. (Another amillennial view of "first resurrection" is that it refers to the resurrection of Christ, and to believers' participation in Christ's resurrection through union with Christ.)

The overall structure of the book of Revelation is also seen to favor the amillennial view. On this view, Revelation consists of "seven sections which run parallel to each other, each of which depicts the church and the world from the time of Christ's first coming to the time of his second."[8] But the seventh parallel section is Revelation 20–22, which means that Revelation 20 must also be describing the present church age in which we live.[9]

2. A second argument often proposed in favor of amillennialism is the fact that Scripture teaches only *one resurrection*, when both believers and unbelievers will be raised, not two resurrections (a resurrection of believers before the millennium begins and a resurrection of unbelievers to judgment after the end of the millennium). This is an important argument because the premillennial view requires two separate resurrections, separated by a thousand years.

Evidence in favor of only one resurrection is found in at least three passages. Jesus says, "*An hour is coming when all who are in the tombs will hear his voice and come out,* those who have done good to the resurrection of life, and those who have done evil to the resurrection of judgment" (John 5:28–29). Here Jesus speaks of a single "hour" when both believing and unbelieving dead will come forth from the tombs. Similarly, when Paul is on trial before Felix he explains that he has a hope in God that his Jewish opponents also accept "that *there will be a resurrection of both the just and the unjust*" (Acts 24:15). Once again, he speaks of a single resurrection of both believers and unbelievers. Finally, we read in Daniel: "Many of those who sleep in the dust of the earth shall awake, some to everlasting life, and some to shame and everlasting contempt" (Dan. 12:2).

3. *The idea of glorified believers and sinners living on earth together is too difficult to accept.* Berkhof says, "It is impossible to understand how a part of the old earth and of sinful humanity can exist alongside a part of the new earth and of a humanity that is

---

8. Hoekema, "Amillennialism," in Clouse, *Meaning of the Millennium*, 156–57.

9. Storms also adopts this view of the structure of Revelation; see *Kingdom Come*, 387–406, 427–28.

glorified. How can perfect saints in glorified bodies have communion with sinners in the flesh? How can glorified sinners live in this sin-laden atmosphere and amid scenes of death and decay?"[10]

4. *If Christ comes in glory to reign on the earth, then how could people still persist in sin?* Once Jesus is actually present in his resurrection body and reigning as King over the earth, does it not seem highly unlikely that people would still reject him and that evil and rebellion would grow on the earth until eventually Satan could gather the nations for battle against Christ?[11]

5. There seems to be no convincing *purpose* for such a millennium. Once the church age has ended and Christ has returned, then what is the reason for delaying the start of the eternal state?

6. In conclusion, amillennialists say that Scripture seems to indicate that *all the major events yet to come* before the eternal state will occur at once. Christ will return, there will be one resurrection of believers and unbelievers, the final judgment will take place, and a new heaven and new earth will be established. Then we will enter immediately into the eternal state, with no future millennium.[12]

At this point we can respond briefly to these amillennialist arguments, though on some points a fuller answer will be developed in the arguments for premillennialism.

1. In response to the objection that only one passage teaches a future earthly millennium, several comments can be made:

a. The Bible only needs to say something once in order for it to be true and something that we must believe. The story of the confusion of languages at the tower of Babel, for example, is only taught in Genesis 11:1–9, yet we believe it to be true because Scripture teaches it. Similarly, even if only one passage taught a future millennial reign of Christ, we still should believe it.

Moreover, it is not surprising that this doctrine should be clearly taught in the book of Revelation. There was somewhat of a similar situation at the end of the Old Testament era. The entire Old Testament has no explicit teaching to the effect that the Messiah would come twice, once as a suffering Messiah who would die and rise again, earning our salvation, and then later as a conquering King to rule over the earth. The first and second comings of Christ may be hinted at in the Old Testament prophets, but they are nowhere explicitly taught because God did not deem it necessary to reveal that amount

---

10. Louis Berkhof, *Systematic Theology* (Grand Rapids: Eerdmans, 1941), 715.

11. This argument is especially developed in Arthur H. Lewis, *The Dark Side of the Millennium* (Grand Rapids: Baker, 1980).

12. Since they believe that Rev. 20:1–6 applies to the present age, amillennialists sometimes say, "Premillennialists are *waiting* for the millennium, postmillennialists are *working* for it, but we are *enjoying* it."

It should be noted that some amillennialists dislike the term *amillennial* because it implies they do not believe in any millennium at all, whereas it is more accurate to say that they do not believe in a *future* millennium. They prefer a more positive term such as "realized millennialism," which allows them more easily to point out that they do believe in the millennial reign of Christ taught in Rev. 20:1–6; however, they believe the passage speaks of the present church age. (See Jay Adams, *The Time Is at Hand* [Phillipsburg, NJ: Presbyterian and Reformed, 1970], 7–11.)

of detail about his plan of redemption before it happened. Similarly, in several of the Old and New Testament books leading up to the time of the writing of Revelation, there are *hints* of a future earthly millennium prior to the eternal state, but the explicit teaching about it was left until John wrote Revelation. Since Revelation is the New Testament book that most explicitly teaches about things yet future, it is appropriate that this more explicit revelation of the future millennium would be put at this point in the Bible.

b. In response to the allegation that the passage that teaches a millennium is obscure, premillennialists respond that they do not find it obscure at all. They argue that one advantage of the premillennial position is that it understands Revelation 20:1–6 in a straightforward sense: the text says that Satan will be bound and cast into the bottomless pit for a thousand years, and the premillennialist says a time is coming when Satan will be bound and cast into a bottomless pit for a thousand years. The text speaks of a thousand-year reign of Christ, and the premillennialist expects a future thousand-year reign of Christ on earth. It speaks of those raised in the "first resurrection," and the premillennialist says that there will be a first resurrection of believers who are "blessed and holy" (Rev. 20:6) and a second resurrection at the end of the thousand years for "the rest of the dead" (v. 5). According to premillennialists, "obscurity" only enters the passage when an interpreter tries to find in it something other than such a straightforward interpretation.

c. Finally, many premillennialists argue that several other passages, especially in the Old Testament, require us to believe in a future period that is far greater than the present age but that still falls short of the eternal state (see Ps. 72:8–14; Isa. 11:2–9; 65:20; Zech. 14:6–21; 1 Cor. 15:24; Rev. 2:27; 12:5; 19:15).[13] These passages, they say, portray a period that looks very much like the millennium as they understand it.

d. With respect to the interpretation of Revelation 20:1–6 as given by amillennialists, several difficulties arise. Although Matthew 12:28–29 and Luke 10:18 do speak of a "binding" of Satan during Jesus' earthly ministry, the binding of Satan described in Revelation 20 seems to be much more extensive than that. The passage does not simply say that Satan is bound at this time, but speaks of "the bottomless pit" and says that the angel that came down from heaven "*threw him into the pit*, and *shut it* and *sealed it over him*, so that he might not deceive the nations any longer, until the thousand years were ended" (Rev. 20:2–3). More than a mere binding or restriction of activity is in view here. The imagery of throwing Satan into a pit and shutting it and sealing it over him gives *a picture of total removal from influence on the earth*. This is true even though the verse uses images of physical realities (such as key and a chain and a cover for a pit) to speak of invisible spiritual realities.[14] To say that Satan is now in a bottomless pit that is shut

---

13. See below, pp. 1390–94, for a discussion of these passages.

14. Sam Storms, as an amillennialist, argues that it is wrong for a premillennial interpreter to insist that the binding of Satan in Revelation 20 "must be interpreted in a literal, spatial way" (*Kingdom Come*, 442). But I am not arguing that these verses speak of a literal, physical key and chain and door to a pit, but that the total picture given by these symbolic elements is one of complete removal of Satan's influence from the earth.

and sealed over simply does not fit the present world situation during the church age, in which Satan's activity is still very strong, in which he "prowls around like a roaring lion, seeking someone to devour" (1 Peter 5:8), in which he can fill someone's heart "to lie to the Holy Spirit" (Acts 5:3), and in which "what pagans sacrifice they offer to demons and not to God" (1 Cor. 10:20).

Moreover, even after the binding of Satan during Jesus' ministry, it remains true that "the god of this world has blinded the minds of the unbelievers, to keep them from seeing the light of the gospel of the glory of Christ" (2 Cor. 4:4). This is why Christians still must contend not "against flesh and blood, but against the rulers, against the authorities, against the cosmic powers over this present darkness, against the spiritual forces of evil in the heavenly places" (Eph. 6:12). This is because even during the church age, although the gospel is able to come with triumph and break down the forces of demonic opposition to the spread of the kingdom of God, Satan's influence has not fully been removed from the world: "The spirit of the antichrist . . . is in the world already" (1 John 4:3), and, in fact, "We know that we are from God, and *the whole world lies in the power of the evil one*" (1 John 5:19). This repeated theme in the New Testament, the theme of Satan's continual activity on earth throughout the church age, makes it extremely difficult to think that Satan has been thrown into the bottomless pit, which has been shut and sealed over for a thousand years. That imagery can only speak of the total removal of Satan's active influence from the earth.

But what can be said with respect to the fact that amillennialists say that the binding and imprisonment of Satan in Revelation 20 is said to be "that he might not *deceive the nations any longer*" (v. 3)? Does that not simply mean that the gospel can now be preached effectively among the nations?[15] While the phrase might mean that, it seems more consistent with the use of the word *deceived* (Gk. *planaō*), especially in Revelation, to say that this is a *deception that is now going on during the entire church age* and that ends only when the millennium begins. Satan is called "the deceiver of the whole world" (Rev. 12:9), and the sorcery of Babylon is said to have "deceived" "all nations" before its judgment comes (Rev. 18:23).[16] Therefore, it seems more appropriate to say that Satan is *now* still deceiving the nations, but at the beginning of the millennium this deceptive influence will be removed. There was an even *greater* deception before Christ came, but there is still significant deception that remains today. There is no great difficulty with saying that God partially removes Satan's ability to deceive the world during the church age and then completely removes it during the millennium.

15. Writing from an amillennial perspective, Sam Storms advocates an alternative interpretation, namely, that this binding of Satan in Revelation 20 means that "Satan will never be permitted to incite and organize the unbelieving nations of the world in a final, catastrophic assault against the church, until such time as God in his providence so determines" (*Kingdom Come*, 440). This is a much narrower scope for such binding, but my arguments showing that Revelation 20 pictures a much more extensive binding of Satan are still applicable as an answer to this position as well.

16. Both of these passages use the same term *planaō*. The same verb is used in Matthew 24:4, 5, 11, 24 to speak of Jesus' warnings that many will be deceived or led astray by false christs and false prophets.

The fact that John saw "souls" in his vision does not require that the scene be set in heaven. Since these souls are persons who then "came to life" in "the first resurrection," we should see these as *people* who obtained resurrection bodies and who began to reign on the earth. Moreover, Revelation 20:1 indicates that the scene is focused on events on the earth, for it says, "Then I saw an angel *coming down from heaven.*" But if the angel came down from heaven, then he carries out his activity on the earth, and the entire scene is set on the earth.

Moreover, amillennialist interpretations of the phrase "first resurrection" are unconvincing. Elsewhere, the word *resurrection* (Gk. *anastasis*) never means "going to heaven" or "going into the presence of God in the intermediate state" but rather signifies a *bodily* resurrection. This is the sense in which first-century readers would have understood the word. The other amillennialist view, which understands "the first resurrection" to be Christ's resurrection (and our union with him) does not seem likely because those who "came to life" are the ones who had been "beheaded for the testimony of Jesus" (v. 4), which suggests a bodily resurrection after death.[17]

What about the argument that the *structure* of Revelation, with seven parallel sections, shows that Revelation 20 is the seventh description of the present church age? We can readily admit that Revelation has such a skillfully constructed seven-fold structure, but that does not require that the seventh section must speak of the *same events* as the previous six sections. Hoekema himself, in arguing for an amillennial position, admits that "though these seven sections are parallel to each other, they also reveal a certain amount of eschatological progress. The last section, for example, takes us further into the future than the other sections."[18] If the wording of Revelation 20 shows that it speaks about a millennial age that had not been mentioned in the previous six sections, then we simply must understand it as a culminating section that reveals much more about future events than we learned in chapters 1–19. In fact, chapters 21 and 22 clearly do that already.

2. Does Scripture teach only *one* resurrection, so that believers and unbelievers will be raised at the same time? It is hard to accept this when we realize that Revelation 20 explicitly speaks about "the *first* resurrection," thus implying that there will be a second resurrection as well. Speaking of those who came to life and reigned with Christ a thousand years, we read, "This is the first resurrection. Blessed and holy is the one who shares in the first resurrection! Over such the second death has no power" (vv. 5–6).

17. Other reasons to reject this interpretation are (1) "The rest of the dead" are said to "come to life" after the thousand years are ended (v. 5)—a reference to the bodily resurrection of unbelievers—but this implies that the phrase "came to life" refers to bodily resurrection in both cases, not just to spiritual union with Christ in his resurrection; and (2) when the text says, "This is the first resurrection" (v. 5), the most evident antecedent in context is the coming to life of believers in v. 4, but no mention of Christ's resurrection occurs in the context.

18. Hoekema, "Amillennialism," in Clouse, *Meaning of the Millennium*, 158.

The passage distinguishes those who share in this first resurrection and are blessed from others who do not share in it. They are "the rest of the dead" and the implication is that "the second death" (that is, facing final judgment and being condemned to eternal punishment away from the presence of God) does have power over them, and they will experience it. But if this passage clearly teaches a first resurrection and that the rest of the dead will come to life at the end of a thousand years, then there is clear teaching on two separate resurrections here in Revelation 20.

As for the other passages that amillennialists claim to support the view that there is only one resurrection, it must be said that those passages do not exclude the idea of two resurrections, but they simply do not specify whether or not the resurrection of believers and unbelievers will be separated in time. In fact, Jesus' statement in John 5 does hint at the possibility of two resurrections. He says that those who are in the tombs will come forth, "those who have done good *to the resurrection of life*, and those who have done evil *to the resurrection of judgment*" (John 5:28–29). In this way Jesus in fact speaks of two different resurrections.[19]

As for Daniel 12:2, it simply says that those who sleep in the dust of the earth shall awake, "some to everlasting life, and some to shame and everlasting contempt," but it does not specify whether this will happen simultaneously or at different times. It simply says that both types of people will be raised. The same is true of Acts 24:15, where Paul says there will be "a resurrection of both the just and the unjust." This affirms that both types of people will be raised from the dead, but it does not exclude the possibility that this would happen at different times. All of these verses, in the absence of Revelation 20:5–6, might or might not be speaking of a single future time of resurrection. But with the explicit teaching of Revelation 20:5–6 about two resurrections, these verses must be understood to refer to the future certainty of a resurrection for each type of person, without specifying that those resurrections will be separated in time.

3. The idea of glorified believers and sinners living on earth together during the millennium does sound strange to us now, but it is certainly not impossible for God to bring this about. We must realize that Jesus lived on the earth with a glorified body for

---

19. The fact that Jesus says in this context, "*An hour* is coming when all who are in the tombs will hear his voice" does not require that both resurrections happen at the same time, for the word *hour* elsewhere in John's gospel can refer to a long period of time; just three verses previously, Jesus said, "Truly, truly, I say to you, *an hour* is coming, and is now here, when the dead will hear the voice of the Son of God, and those who hear will live" (John 5:25). Here the "hour" refers to the entire church age when those who are spiritually dead hear Jesus' voice and come to life. John can also use the word *hour* (Gk. *hōra*) to speak of the time when true worshipers worship the Father in spirit and in truth (John 4:21, 23), or when intense persecution will come on the disciples (John 16:2). These examples also speak of long periods of time, even entire ages.

A similar way of speaking is possible in English: I can tell a class of sixty students, "Don't be discouraged—*graduation day is coming* for every one of you." But I know that some will graduate this year, some will graduate next year, and some will graduate two or three years later. I can still speak of "graduation day" rather than "graduation days" because it is clear that I am speaking about the kind of day it is, not about the time it will occur or whether it will be one day or several that are of the same type.

forty days after his resurrection, and apparently there were many other people who lived with glorified bodies on earth during that time as well (Matt. 27:53).[20] It will indeed be a kind of world situation that is far different and far more God-glorifying than the world is now, but it does not seem that we are justified in asserting that God could not or would not bring about such a state of affairs. Certainly he *could* do it, and several passages seem to indicate that he has a good purpose and intention of doing it as well.

4. It is certainly not impossible that evil and secret rebellion could persist on the earth in spite of the bodily presence of Christ reigning as King. We must remember that Judas lived with Jesus on the closest terms for three years and still betrayed him. Moreover, many of the Pharisees *saw* Jesus' miracles, and even saw him raising people from the dead, and they still did not believe. In fact, even when the disciples were in the presence of the glorified Lord Jesus, we read that "some doubted" (Matt. 28:17). Such persistent unbelief in the very presence of Christ is hard to understand, but we must remember that Satan himself fell from an exalted position in the presence of God in heaven.

When the amillennialists object that people could not persist in sin in the presence of Christ's bodily reign on the earth, their position simply fails to realize the deep-seated and highly irrational nature of sin. It also fails fully to reckon with the fact that even "massive proof" and "undeniable evidence" cannot compel genuine conversion. Genuine repentance and faith is brought about by the enabling and persuasive work of the Holy Spirit in people's hearts. Such is the irrational nature of sin that those who are "dead in trespasses and sins" will often persist in rebellion and unbelief even in the face of overwhelming evidence to the contrary.[21]

This is not to say that no one will be converted to Christ during the millennium. No doubt millions of people will become Christians during that time, and the influence of the reign of Christ will permeate into every aspect of every society in the world. Yet at the same time it is not at all difficult to understand how evil and rebellion will grow simultaneously.

5. God may have several purposes in mind for a future millennium, not all of which may now be clear to us. But certainly such a millennium would show *the outworking of God's good purposes in the structures of society*, especially the structures of the family and civil government. During the church age, the good purposes of God are primarily seen in individual lives and the blessings that come to those who believe in Christ. To some extent now (and to a greater extent in times of revival) this affects civil government and educational institutions and corporations and to a larger extent it affects the family. But in none of these structures are God's good purposes manifested to the extent they could

---

20. See chapter 42, p. 1025, on Matt. 27:52–53.

21. A somewhat similar example is the fact that many people today refuse to believe that there is a God who created the universe, in spite of the incredible complexity of every living being, and in spite of what is for all practical purposes the mathematical impossibility that the entire universe could have come about by chance.

be, showing God's great wisdom and goodness not only in his plans for individuals but also for societal structures. In the millennium the beauty of God's wisdom will show forth to his glory from all of these societal structures.

Moreover, the millennium will further vindicate God's righteousness. The fact that some continue in sin and unbelief will show that "sin—rebellion against God—is not due to an evil society or to a bad environment. It is due to the sinfulness of the hearts of men. Thus the justice of God will be fully vindicated in the day of final judgment."[22] With Satan bound for a thousand years, the fact that sin can persist will also show that the ultimate blame for sin is not demonic influence in people's lives but deep-rooted sinfulness in people's hearts.

Third, the entire scope of the Bible reveals to us that it is God's good pleasure to unfold his purposes and reveal more and more of his glory *gradually* over time. From the calling of Abraham to the birth of Isaac, the sojourn in Egypt and the exodus, the establishment of the people in the promised land, the Davidic kingdom and the divided monarchy, the exile and return with the rebuilding of the temple, the preservation of a faithful remnant, and finally the coming of Jesus in the flesh, God's purposes were increasingly seen to be glorious and wonderful. Even in Jesus' life the progressive revealing of his glory took thirty-three years, culminating in the last three years of his life. Then in Jesus' death, resurrection, and ascension into heaven, the completion of our redemption was accomplished. Yet the spread of the church throughout all nations has now occupied nearly 2,000 years, and we do not know how long it is to continue. All this is to say that God's way is not to bring to realization all of his good purposes at once, but to unfold them gradually over time. This is so even in the individual lives of Christians, who grow daily in grace and in fellowship with God and in likeness to Christ. Therefore, it would not be surprising if, before the eternal state, God instituted one final step in the progressive unfolding of the history of redemption. It would serve to increase his glory as men and angels look on in amazement at the wonder of God's wisdom and plan.

6. Finally, a major objection to amillennialism must continue to be the fact that it can propose no really satisfying explanation of Revelation 20.[23]

## C. A CONSIDERATION OF ARGUMENTS FOR POSTMILLENNIALISM

The arguments in favor of postmillennialism are as follows.

1. The Great Commission leads us to expect that the gospel will go forth in power and eventually result in a largely Christian world: Jesus explicitly said, "*All authority in heaven and on earth* has been given to me. Go therefore and make disciples of all nations,

---

22. George Ladd, "Historic Premillennialism," in *The Meaning of the Millennium: Four Views*, 40.

23. Some other interpretations of Rev. 20 have been proposed by amillennialists, but they all have the disadvantage of having to labor under the burden of explaining away what seems to be a straightforward understanding of the text because they are convinced that the rest of Scripture does not teach a future earthly millennium. But if the rest of Scripture does not deny it (and in some places hints at it), and if this text does teach it, then it would seem much more appropriate to accept it.

baptizing them in the name of the Father and of the Son and of the Holy Spirit, teaching them to observe all that I have commanded you. And behold, I am with you always, to the end of the age" (Matt. 28:18–20). Since Christ has all authority in heaven and on earth, and since he promises to be with us in the fulfillment of this commission, we would expect that it would transpire without hindrance and eventually triumph in the whole world.

2. Parables of the gradual growth of the kingdom indicate that it eventually will fill the earth with its influence. Here postmillennialists point to the following: "He put another parable before them, saying, 'The kingdom of heaven is like a grain of mustard seed that a man took and sowed in his field. It is the smallest of all seeds, but when it has grown it is larger than all the garden plants and becomes a tree, so that the birds of the air come and make nests in its branches'" (Matt. 13:31–32). We can also note the following verse: "He told them another parable. 'The kingdom of heaven is like leaven that a woman took and hid in three measures of flour, till it was all leavened'" (Matt. 13:33). According to postmillennialists both of these parables indicate that the kingdom will grow in influence until it permeates and in some measure transforms the entire world.

3. Postmillennialists will also argue that the world is becoming more Christian. The church is growing and spreading throughout the world, and even when it is persecuted and oppressed it grows remarkably by the power of God.[24]

At this point we must make a very significant distinction, however. The "millennium" that postmillennialists hold to is *very different* from the "millennium" the premillennialists talk about. In a sense, they are not even discussing the same topic. While *pre*millennialists talk about a renewed earth with Jesus Christ physically present and reigning as King, together with glorified believers in resurrection bodies, *post*millennialists are simply talking about an earth with many, many Christians influencing society. They do not envisage a millennium consisting of a renewed earth or glorified saints or Christ present in bodily form to reign (for they think that these things will only occur after Christ returns to inaugurate the eternal state).[25] Therefore, the entire discussion of the millennium is more than simply a discussion of the sequence of events surrounding it. It also involves a significant difference over the nature of this period of time.

In fact, though I am not aware if anyone has done this, it would not be impossible for someone to be a postmillennialist and a premillennialist at the same time, with two different senses of the term *millennium*. Someone could conceivably be a postmillennialist

---

24. The postmillennialist A. H. Strong argues that Rev. 20:4–10 "does not describe the events commonly called the second advent and resurrection, but rather describes the great spiritual changes in the later history of the church, which are typical of, and preliminary to, the second advent and resurrection." He sees Rev. 20, therefore, simply as a prediction of "the latter days of the church militant" and a time when "under the special influence of the Holy Ghost" the church shall "to an extent unknown before, triumph over the powers of evil, both within and without" (A. H. Strong, *Systematic Theology* [Valley Forge, PA: Judson, 1907], 1013).

25. Similarly, when amillennialists talk about presently "enjoying" the millennium, which they understand on the basis of Rev. 20 to refer to the church age, they are also talking about a very different kind of "millennium" than would be envisaged by either postmillennialists or premillennialists.

and think that the gospel will grow in influence until the world is largely Christian, and that then Christ will return and set up a literal earthly reign, raising believers from the dead to reign with him in glorified bodies. Or, on the other hand, a very optimistic premillennialist could conceivably adopt many of the postmillennialist teachings about the increasingly Christian nature of this present age.[26]

In response to the postmillennialist arguments, the following points may be made:

1. The Great Commission does indeed speak of the authority that is given into Christ's hand, but that does not necessarily imply that Christ will use that authority to bring about the conversion of the majority of the population of the world. To say that Christ's authority is great is simply another way of saying that God's power is infinite, which no one will deny. But the question is the extent to which Christ will *use* his power to bring about the numerical growth of the church. We may *assume* that he will use it to a very full extent and will bring about worldwide Christianization, but such an assumption is merely that—an assumption. It is not based on any specific evidence in the Great Commission or in other texts that talk about Christ's authority and power in this present age.[27]

2. The parables of the mustard seed and the leaven do tell us that the kingdom of God will gradually grow from something very small to something very large, but they do not tell us the *extent* to which the kingdom will grow. For example, the parable of the mustard seed does not tell us that the tree grew so that it spread throughout the whole earth. And the parable of the leaven simply talks about gradual growth that permeates society (as the church has already done), but it says nothing about the degree or effect that that influence has (it does not tell us, for example, whether in the end 5 percent of the loaf was leaven and 95 percent bread dough, or 20 percent leaven and 80 percent bread, or 60 percent leaven and 40 percent bread, and so forth). It is simply pressing the parable beyond its intended purpose to attempt to make it say more than that the kingdom will grow gradually and eventually have an influence on every society in which it is planted.

3. In response to the argument that the world is becoming more Christian, it must be said that the world is also becoming more evil. No student of history or modern society will argue that mankind has made much progress through the centuries in overcoming the depth of perversity and the extent of immorality that remain in people's hearts. Indeed, modernization in western societies in the twentieth century has often been accompanied not by moral improvement but by an unprecedented level of drug abuse,

---

26. This is not to say that such a position would be free of internal tensions and difficulties (especially the difficulty of explaining how evil could diminish when Christ was absent from the earth but grow into widespread rebellion when he is physically present and reigning), but it is to say that there would be no absolute inconsistency within this position.

27. In 1 Cor. 15:25 Paul says, "For he must reign until he has put all his enemies under his feet," but the immediate context (vv. 24, 26) talks about destroying his enemies (including death in v. 26), not about converting people and bringing them into the church.

marital infidelity, pornography, homosexuality, rebellion against authority, superstition (in astrology and fortune-telling, for example), materialism, greed, theft, and falsehood in speech. Even among professing Christians there is repeated evidence of dismaying imperfection in the Christian life, especially in the realms of personal morality and depth of intimacy with God. In places where Bible-believing Christians comprise large segments of the population, still nothing like an earthly millennial kingdom occurs.[28] It is true that the growth of the church as a percentage of world population has been remarkable in recent decades,[29] and we should be greatly encouraged by this. It is possible that we will someday see a far greater influence of genuine Christianity upon many societies, and if that occurred, it would make the postmillennial position seem more plausible. But such events could also be understood within a premillennial or amillennial framework, so the final decision regarding these competing positions must still be made by interpreting the relevant biblical texts.

4. Finally, we should note that there are several New Testament passages that seem to give explicit denial to the postmillennial position. Jesus said, "Enter by the narrow gate. For the gate is wide and the way is easy that leads to destruction, and those who enter by it are many. For the gate is narrow and the way is hard that leads to life, and *those who find it are few*" (Matt. 7:13–14). Rather than teaching that a majority of the world will become Christians, Jesus seems here to be saying that those who are saved will be "few" in contrast to the "many" who travel toward eternal destruction. Similarly, Jesus asks, "*When the Son of Man comes, will he find faith on earth?*" (Luke 18:8), a question that suggests that the earth will not be filled with those who believe but rather will be dominated by those who do not have faith.

Contrary to the view that the world will get better and better as the influence of the church grows, Paul predicts that before Christ returns "the *rebellion*" will come and "the *man of lawlessness*" will be revealed, "the son of destruction" who "takes his seat in the temple of God, proclaiming himself to be God" (2 Thess. 2:3–4).[30]

---

28. One interesting example in the United States is the state of Texas. Statistics indicate that over 50 percent of the people of Texas belong to Southern Baptist churches, a denomination that preaches a genuine gospel of salvation by faith alone, and the need for each individual personally to be born again. This in itself is a wonderful fact for which we should be thankful to God, but no one living in Texas today would seriously claim to be living already in the millennium (at least in the way postmillennialists understand it). If we add to the Southern Baptists all the other Bible-believing Christians in the state, far more than half of the state's population consists of born-again Christians. But if a population of 50 percent Christians cannot bring us anywhere near to an earthly millennium, then what percentage of the world would have to become Christian before the postmillennialist's hope would be realized? And where is there evidence throughout history that we are making significant progress toward the realization of such a millennium?

29. "Between 1950 and 1992, Bible believing Christians went from just 3% of the world population to 10% of the world population. This is a jump from 80 million to 540 million" (Rick Wood, "Christianity: Waning or Growing?," in *Mission Frontiers Bulletin*, Pasadena, CA, January–February, 1993, 25). This journal publishes similar statistics from different countries in almost every issue, leading one to conclude that the growth of the church since 1950 is so remarkable as to be without precedent in the history of the world.

30. Some postmillennialists believe that there will be a final rebellion before Christ's return. These verses would not constitute an objection to their position, but the following verses indicating the dominant non-Christian pattern of world affairs just prior to Christ's return would still weigh against such a postmillennial view because they picture a world decisively different from the millennium of peace and righteousness brought about by the spread of the gospel in a postmillennial system.

When writing to Timothy about the last days, Paul says,

> *In the last days* there will come times of difficulty. For people will be lovers of self, lovers of money, proud, arrogant, abusive, disobedient to their parents, ungrateful, unholy, heartless, unappeasable, slanderous, without self-control, brutal, not loving good, treacherous, reckless, swollen with conceit, lovers of pleasure rather than lovers of God, having the appearance of godliness, but denying its power. (2 Tim. 3:1–5)

He says further,

> All who desire to live a godly life in Christ Jesus will be persecuted, while evil people and impostors will go on from bad to worse, deceiving and being deceived. . . . The time is coming when people will not endure sound teaching, but having itching ears they will accumulate for themselves teachers to suit their own passions, and will turn away from listening to the truth and wander off into myths. (2 Tim. 3:12–13; 4:3–4)

Finally, and perhaps most conclusively, Matthew 24:15–31 speaks of a great tribulation that will precede the time of Christ's return:

> For then there will be great tribulation, such as has not been from the beginning of the world until now, no, and never will be. And if those days had not been cut short, no human being would be saved. But for the sake of the elect those days will be cut short. . . . Immediately after the tribulation of those days the sun will be darkened, and the moon will not give its light, and the stars will fall from heaven, and the powers of the heavens will be shaken. Then will appear in heaven the sign of the Son of Man, and then all the tribes of the earth will mourn, and they will see the Son of Man coming on the clouds of heaven with power and great glory. (Matt. 24:21–30)

This passage pictures not a Christianized world but a world of great suffering and evil, a great tribulation that exceeds all previous periods of suffering on the earth. It does not say that the great majority of the world will welcome Christ when he comes. But when the sign of the Son of man appears in heaven, "then all the tribes of the earth will mourn" (Matt. 24:30).

Since Matthew 24 is such a difficult passage from the postmillennialist perspective, there have been several attempts to explain it not as a prediction of events that will occur just prior to Christ's second coming but as something that was mainly fulfilled in the destruction of Jerusalem in AD 70.

To sustain this interpretation, postmillennialists make most of the elements of

Matthew 24:29–31 symbolic:[31] the sun and moon being darkened, the stars falling from heaven, and the powers of the heavens being shaken are not to be understood as literal events but as imagery for God's coming in judgment. Similar imagery for judgment is said to be found in Ezekiel 32:7; Joel 2:10; and Amos 8:9—but these passages simply speak of judgments of darkness, and do not mention the stars falling from heaven or the powers of the heavens being shaken. R. T. France also mentions Isaiah 13:10 and 34:4, which do talk about the sun and moon being darkened and the host of heaven falling, but it is far from certain that France is correct in claiming that those passages are merely symbolic—they are set in contexts in which they could easily be understood as literal predictions of the cosmic changes preceding the final judgment. So it is far from obvious that these passages are merely apocalyptic imagery for judgment on Jerusalem.[32]

Moreover, the interpretation that sees these as merely symbolic statements grows more difficult as the statement of Jesus continues, for he does not only talk about signs in the sun, moon, and stars, but he says immediately after that, "*then* will appear in heaven the sign of the Son of Man . . and *they will see the Son of Man coming on the clouds of heaven with power and great glory*" (Matt. 24:30). Consistent with his previous symbolic interpretation of this passage, France says that "all the tribes of the earth" refers merely to the Jews, that is, "all the tribes (families) of the land,"[33] that is, the land of Israel. And he says that the reference to the Son of Man coming on the clouds of heaven with power and great glory does not refer to Christ's return but to his coming *to the Father in heaven* "to receive vindication and authority."[34] France quotes with approval the statement of G. B. Caird, who says that "the coming of the Son of Man in the clouds of heaven was never conceived as a primitive form of space travel, but as a symbol for a mighty reversal of fortunes within history and at the national level."[35] Then the sending out of Christ's angels with a loud trumpet call to gather his elect from one end of heaven to the other is understood to refer to messengers who preach the gospel throughout the earth. The gathering of the elect then is gathering them into the church by the preaching of the gospel.

However, on this interpretation France cannot satisfactorily account for the fact that Jesus says that all the tribes of the earth "*will see* the Son of Man coming on the clouds

---

31. Here I am following the interpretation of R. T. France, *The Gospel according to Matthew*, TNTC (Leicester: Inter-Varsity Press, Grand Rapids: Eerdmans, 1985), 343–46.

32. Another argument in favor of the postmillennial view may be taken from the statement "this generation will not pass away until all these things take place" in Matt. 24:34. A postmillennialist can take "this generation" in a perfectly natural sense to refer to the people who heard Jesus as he spoke, and thus support is given to the view that all the events of vv. 29–31 (or even vv. 5–31) occurred by AD 70. But such an interpretation is not necessary to Matt. 24:34 because "this generation" could be understood to refer to the generation that sees "all

these things" (v. 33) take place, whenever that may be. (The "fig tree" in v. 32 should not be understood as a prophetic symbol for a particular time in history—such as the rebirth of Israel as a nation—because Jesus uses it simply as an illustration from nature: when the fig tree puts forth leaves, you know that summer will come soon; similarly, when these signs [vv. 5–31] occur, you know that the Son of man will return soon.)

33. France, *Matthew*, 345.

34. Ibid., 344.

35. Ibid., 344, quoting G. B. Caird, *Jesus and the Jewish Nation* (London: Athlone, 1965), 20.

of heaven with power and great glory" (Matt. 24:30). This is not an invisible heavenly transaction in which Christ receives authority from God the Father, but it is his return with power and great glory which is here predicted. Those who preach the gospel are never elsewhere called angels who give a loud trumpet call, and the preaching of the gospel is not elsewhere called the gathering of "his elect from the four winds, from one end of heaven to the other" (Matt. 24:31). Moreover, when Jesus elsewhere speaks of his coming on the clouds, he speaks not of a coming *to God the Father* in heaven, but a coming *to people on earth*: "Behold, he is coming with the clouds, and every eye will see him, even those who pierced him, and all tribes of the earth will wail on account of him" (Rev. 1:7). And when Christ returns, Paul says that we who are alive "will be caught up together with them *in the clouds* to meet the Lord in the air" (1 Thess. 4:17). When Christ comes on the clouds of glory with great power and authority, he comes to reign over the earth, and this is the sense of Matthew 24:30–31. (France does not comment on the fact that Jesus says the tribes of the earth who mourn *"will see* the Son of Man coming on the clouds of heaven" [v. 30]. The fact that these tribes will see Jesus coming makes it difficult to understand any symbolic or invisible heavenly interpretation here.) Moreover, the piling up of factors that we know from other texts to be connected with Christ's return (cosmic signs, Christ's coming with power, the loud trumpet call, the angels gathering the elect) provides a cumulative case for believing that Christ's *second* coming, not just a symbolic representation of his receiving authority, is in view here. And if Matthew 24 talks about Christ's second coming, then it talks about his coming just *after* a period of great tribulation, not after a millennium of peace and righteousness has been established on the earth.[36]

Finally, all of the passages indicating that Christ could return soon and that we must be ready for him to return at any time[37] must be considered a significant argument against postmillennialism as well. For if Christ could return at any time, and we are to be ready for his return, then the long period required for the establishment of the millennium on earth before Christ returns simply cannot be thought a persuasive theory. The essential element of the postmillennial view—the idea of a gradual, long-term increase in Christian influence on the earth before Christ returns—seems to make it impossible to hold a postmillennial view and also hold that Christ could return at any time.

## D. A Consideration of the Arguments for Premillennialism

The position advocated in this book is historic premillennialism. The arguments against the premillennial position have essentially been presented in the arguments for amillennialism and postmillennialism and will therefore not be repeated again here in a separate section, but incidental objections to these arguments will be considered along the way.

---

36. It is true that some postmillennialists hold that there will be a time of rebellion at the end of the millennium, just before Christ returns. But a period of rebellion against a dominant millennial kingdom of righteousness and peace is not the same as a tribulation period in which evil is dominant and Christians experience great persecution.

37. See chapter 54, pp. 1347–49, on the passages teaching Christ's imminent return.

## 1. Several Old Testament Passages Seem to Fit Neither in the Present Age nor in the Eternal State

These passages indicate some future stage in the history of redemption that is far greater than the present church age but that still does not see the removal of all sin and rebellion and death from the earth.

Speaking of Jerusalem at some time in the future, Isaiah says:

> No more shall there be in it
>   an infant who lives but a few days,
>   or an old man who does not fill out his days,
> for the young man shall die a hundred years old,
>   and the sinner a hundred years old shall be accursed. (Isa. 65:20)

Here we read that there will be no more infants who die in infancy, and no more old men who die prematurely, something far different from this present age. But death and sin will still be present, for the child who is one hundred years old shall die, and the sinner who is one hundred years old "shall be accursed." The larger context of this passage may mingle elements of the millennium and the eternal state (cf. vv. 17, 25), but it is in the nature of Old Testament prophecy not to distinguish among events in the future, just as these prophecies do not distinguish between the first and second comings of Christ. Therefore, in the larger context there may be mixed elements, but the point remains that this single element (the infants and old men who live long, the child dying one hundred years old, and the sinner being accursed) indicates a specific time in the future that is different from the present age.

Isaiah seems to predict a millennial kingdom in another place when he says,

> The wolf shall dwell with the lamb,
>   and the leopard shall lie down with the young goat,
> and the calf and the lion and the fattened calf together;
>   and a little child shall lead them.
> The cow and the bear shall graze;
>   their young shall lie down together;
>   and the lion shall eat straw like the ox.
> The nursing child shall play over the hole of the cobra,
>   and the weaned child shall put his hand on the adder's den.
> They shall not hurt or destroy
>   in all my holy mountain;
> for the earth shall be full of the knowledge of the LORD
>   as the waters cover the sea. (Isa. 11:6–9)

This passage clearly speaks of a momentous renewal of nature that takes us far beyond the present age, a time in which "the earth shall be full of the knowledge of the LORD as the waters cover the sea" (v. 9). Yet in the very next verse Isaiah says,

> *In that day* the root of Jesse, who shall stand as a signal for the peoples—*of him shall the nations inquire*, and his resting place shall be glorious.
> *In that day* the Lord will extend his hand yet a second time to recover the remnant that remains of his people, from Assyria, from Egypt, from Pathros, from Cush. (Isa. 11:10–11)

Here some are still seeking the Messiah and apparently coming to salvation, and here also the Lord is still gathering the remnant of his people from various nations of the earth. It does not seem, therefore, that the eternal state has begun, yet the reversal of nature far exceeds anything that will happen in this present age. Does this not indicate a future millennial kingdom?

Psalm 72 seems to go beyond a description of Solomon's reign and to predict the glories of the reign of the Messiah over the entire earth:

> May he have dominion from sea to sea,
>     and from the River to the ends of the earth!
> May desert tribes bow down before him,
>     and his enemies lick the dust!
> May the kings of Tarshish and of the coastlands render him tribute;
>     may the kings of Sheba and Seba bring gifts!
> May all kings fall down before him,
>     all nations serve him!
> For he delivers the needy when he calls,
>     the poor and him who has no helper.
> He has pity on the weak and the needy,
>     and saves the lives of the needy.
> From oppression and violence he redeems their life,
>     and precious is their blood in his sight. (Ps. 72:8–14)

This passage certainly speaks of a messianic rule far more extensive than that experienced by David or Solomon because this Messiah's kingdom extends "to the ends of the earth," and "all nations serve him" (vv. 8, 11; note that the psalm also says: "May they fear you while the sun endures, and as long as the moon, throughout all generations!" v. 5). This will be a reign in righteousness, in justice—but it certainly will not be the eternal state. There are still "the needy" and "the poor and him who has no helper";

there are still people who need to be rescued "from oppression and violence" (vv. 12–14). There will still be enemies who "will lick the dust" under the reign of this righteous King (v. 9). All of this speaks of an age far different from the present age but short of the eternal state in which there is no more sin or suffering.

Zechariah also prophesies a coming age in which there is great transformation in the earth, in which the Lord is King over all the earth, and in which there is still rebellion and sin, suffering, and death:

> Then the LORD my God will come, and all the holy ones with him. On that day there shall be no light, cold, or frost. And there shall be a unique day, which is known to the LORD, neither day nor night, but at evening time there shall be light.
>
> On that day living waters shall flow out from Jerusalem, half of them to the eastern sea and half of them to the western sea. It shall continue in summer as in winter.
>
> And the LORD will be king over all the earth. On that day the LORD will be one and his name one. . . .
>
> And this shall be the plague with which the LORD will strike all the peoples that wage war against Jerusalem: their flesh will rot while they are still standing on their feet, their eyes will rot in their sockets, and their tongues will rot in their mouths. . . .
>
> And the wealth of all the surrounding nations shall be collected, gold, silver, and garments in great abundance. . . .
>
> Then everyone who survives of all the nations that have come against Jerusalem shall go up year after year to worship the King, the LORD of hosts, and to keep the Feast of Booths. And if any of the families of the earth do not go up to Jerusalem to worship the King, the LORD of hosts, there will be no rain on them. (Zech. 14:5–17)

Here again the description does not fit the present age, for the Lord is King over all the earth in this situation. But it does not fit the eternal state either because of the disobedience and rebellion against the Lord that is clearly present. One might object that this is a typical Old Testament prophecy in which distinct future events are conflated and not distinguished in the prophet's vision, though they may be separated by long ages when they actually occur. However, it is difficult to make such a distinction in this passage because it is specifically rebellion against the Lord who is King over all the earth that is punished by these plagues and lack of rain.[38]

2. There are also New Testament passages other than Revelation 20 that suggest a future millennium. When the risen Lord Jesus speaks to the church at Thyatira, he says, *"The one who conquers and who keeps my works until the end, to him I will give authority*

---

38. The passage still describes blessings in terms of old covenant sacrifices and mentions the feast of booths, an old covenant festival. This was the terminology and description available to the people of that day, but the New Testament can allow for greater (spiritual) fulfillment of a number of these items.

*over the nations*, and *he will rule them with a rod of iron*, as when earthen pots are broken in pieces, even as I myself have received authority from my Father" (Rev. 2:26–27). The imagery used (ruling with a rod of iron; shattering earthen pots) implies a rule of force over rebellious people. But when will believers who conquer over evil participate in this rule? The idea fits well into a future millennial kingdom when glorified saints rule with Christ on the earth, but it does not fit well at any time in the present age or in the eternal state. (The idea of ruling the nations "with a rod of iron" is also found in Rev. 12:5–6 and 19:15.)

When Paul talks about the resurrection, he says that each person will receive a resurrection body in his own order: "Christ the firstfruits, *then* [*epeita*] at his coming those who belong to Christ. *Then* [*eita*] comes the end, when he delivers the kingdom to God the Father after destroying every rule and every authority and power. For he must reign until he has put all his enemies under his feet" (1 Cor. 15:23–25). The two words translated "then" in this passage (*epeita* and *eita*) both take the sense "after that," not the sense "at that same time." Therefore the passage gives some support to the idea that, just as there is an interval of time between Christ's resurrection and his second coming when we receive a resurrection body (v. 23), so there is an interval of time between Christ's second coming and "the end" (v. 24), when Christ delivers the kingdom to God after having reigned for a time and put all his enemies under his feet.[39]

3. With the background of a number of other passages that hint at or clearly suggest a future time far greater than the present age but short of the eternal state, it is appropriate then to look at Revelation 20 once again. Several statements here are best understood as referring to a future earthly reign of Christ prior to the future judgment.

a. The binding and imprisonment of Satan in the bottomless pit (vv. 2–3) imply a far greater restriction of his activity than anything we know in this present age (see discussion above, under amillennialism).

b. The statement that those who were faithful "came to life" (v. 4) is best taken as referring to a bodily resurrection, for the next verse says, "This is the first resurrection." The verb *ezēsan*, "came to life," is the same verb and the same form of the verb used in Revelation 2:8, where Jesus identifies himself as the one "who died and *came to life*," here obviously referring to his resurrection.[40]

c. On a premillennial interpretation, the reigning with Christ (in Rev. 20:4) is something that is still future, not something that is occurring now (as amillennialists claim). This is consistent with the rest of the New Testament, where we are frequently told that

---

39. The Greek word *eita* does mean "after that" (see Mark 4:17, 28; 1 Cor. 15:5, 7; 1 Tim. 2:13). It does not always indicate temporal sequence, because it can also introduce the next item or argument in a logical progression, but in narrating historical occurrences it indicates something that happens after something else (see BDAG, 295; also LSJ, 498: "used to denote the sequence of one act or state upon another . . . *then, next*").

40. I understand the aorist indicative *ezēsan* in both cases as an inceptive aorist, marking the beginning of an action.

believers will reign with Christ and be given authority by him to reign over the earth (see Luke 19:17, 19; 1 Cor. 6:3; Rev. 2:26–27; 3:21). But nowhere does Scripture say that believers *in the intermediate state* (between their death and Christ's return) are reigning with Christ or sharing in rule with him. In fact, Revelation earlier pictures saints in heaven before Christ's return *waiting* under the altar and crying out to the Lord to begin to judge evildoers on the earth (Rev. 6:9–10). Nowhere is it said that Christians who have died are already reigning with Christ.

Those who come to life and reign with Christ in Revelation 20 include people "*who had not worshiped the beast or its image and had not received its mark on their foreheads or their hands*" (Rev. 20:4). This is a reference to those who did not yield to the persecution by the beast spoken of in Revelation 13:1–18. But if the severity of persecution described in Revelation 13 leads us to conclude that at the present time the beast *has not yet come* on the world scene but is yet future, then the persecution by this beast is still future as well. And *if this persecution is still future, then the scene in Revelation 20* where those "who had not worshiped the beast . . . and had not received its mark on their foreheads or their hands" (Rev. 20:4) *is still future as well*. This means that Revelation 20:1–6 does not describe the present church age but is best understood to refer to a future millennial reign of Christ.

These considerations combine to make a case in favor of premillennialism. If we are convinced of this position, it really is an incidental question whether the thousand-year period is thought to be a literal thousand years or simply a long period of time of indeterminate duration. And though we may not have much clarity on all the details of the nature of the millennium, we can be reasonably certain that there will be a future earthly reign of Christ that will be markedly different from this present age.

## E. The Time of the Great Tribulation

For those who are persuaded by the arguments in favor of premillennialism, one further question must be decided: Will Christ return before or after the "great tribulation"?

The expression "great tribulation" itself comes from Matthew 24:21 (and parallels), where Jesus says, "For then there will be *great tribulation*, such as has not been from the beginning of the world until now, no, and never will be." Historic premillennialism believes that Christ will return *after* that tribulation, for the passage continues, "Immediately after the tribulation of those days the sun will be darkened. . . . Then will appear in heaven the sign of the Son of Man, and then all the tribes of the earth will mourn, and they will see the Son of Man coming on the clouds of heaven with power and great glory" (Matt. 24:29–30). But, as explained above, in the nineteenth and twentieth centuries a variety of premillennialism that holds to a pretribulational coming of Christ became popular. This is often called a "*pretribulation rapture*" view, because it holds that Christ will return (secretly) *before* that time of tribulation, and when he returns the church will be "raptured" or snatched up into heaven to be with him.

The arguments for such a pretribulation rapture are as follows.[41]

1. The entire period of the tribulation will be a time of the outpouring of God's wrath on all the earth. Therefore it would not be appropriate for Christians to be on the earth at that time.

2. Jesus promises in Revelation 3:10, *"I will keep you from the hour of trial that is coming on the whole world, to try those who dwell on the earth."* This passage indicates that the church will be taken out of the world before that hour of trial comes.

3. If Christ returns *after* the tribulation and defeats all his enemies (the *post*tribulation view), then where will the unbelievers come from who are necessary to populate the millennial kingdom? The pretribulation position, however, envisages thousands of Jewish believers who have become Christians during the tribulation and who will go into the millennial kingdom in nonglorified bodies.

4. This view makes it possible to believe that Christ could come at any moment (his coming before the tribulation) and yet that many signs must be fulfilled before he comes (his coming after the tribulation, when the signs will be fulfilled).

Although it is not specifically an argument in favor of a pretribulation position, it must also be noted that pretribulationists then view the teaching about the tribulation in Matthew 24 and the warnings and encouragements given to believers in that situation as applying to Jewish believers during the tribulation, and not to the church generally.[42]

In response to these arguments, the following points may be made.

1. It is inconsistent with the New Testament descriptions of the tribulation to say that *all* the suffering that occurs during that time is specifically the result of the wrath of God. Much of the suffering is due to the fact that "lawlessness will be increased" (Matt. 24:12) and the fact that persecution of the church and opposition from Satan greatly increases during this period. Of course all Christians (whether gentile or Jewish believers) will avoid the wrath of God at all times, but this does not mean they will avoid all suffering, even in times of intense hardship.

2. The fact that Jesus tells faithful believers in the church in Philadelphia (Rev. 3:10) that he will keep them from the hour of trial that is coming on the whole world is not strong enough evidence to say that the entire church will be taken out of the world before the tribulation. First, this statement is made to one specific church (Philadelphia) and should not be applied to the whole church at some future point in history. Moreover, "the hour of trial that is coming on the whole world" need not refer to the time of the great tribulation; it more likely refers to a time of great suffering and persecution that

---

41. Much of the argumentation for the pretribulation rapture position is taken from the very thorough essay by Paul D. Feinberg, "The Case for Pretribulation Rapture Position," in *The Rapture: Pre-, Mid-, or Post-Tribulational?*, 45–86.

42. Feinberg gives an additional argument on the differences between the passages he sees as describing the rapture (before the tribulation) and the passages he sees as describing the second coming (after the tribulation). However, most of these differences are not insurmountable contradictions but only cases where an event is mentioned in one passage and not in another (a point well made by Douglas Moo in his "Response," 99–101).

would come upon the entire Roman Empire or the entire inhabited world. Finally, the promise that the church in Philadelphia will be *guarded* does not imply that they will be taken out of the world but simply that they will be kept faithful and will be guarded from being harmed by that period of suffering and testing.

3. It is no argument for the pretribulation view to say that there must be some people in nonglorified bodies who will enter the millennium because (on a posttribulational view) when Christ comes at the end of the tribulation he will *defeat* all the forces arrayed against him, but that does not mean he will kill or annihilate all of them. Many will simply surrender without trusting Christ and will thus enter the millennium as unbelievers. And during the entire period of the millennium no doubt many will be converted to Christ and become believers as well.

4. The pretribulational view is not the only one consistent with the ideas that Christ could come back at any time and that there are signs that precede his return. The position presented in the previous chapter—that it is unlikely but possible that the signs have been fulfilled—is also consistent with these ideas.[43]

But it must be said that behind this argument of pretribulationists is probably a more fundamental concern: the desire to preserve a distinction between *the church* (which they think will be taken up into heaven to be with Christ) and *Israel* (which they think will constitute the people of God on earth during the tribulation and then during the millennial kingdom). But, as we noted in an earlier chapter,[44] the New Testament does not support a distinction of this kind between Israel and the church. Hence it does not imply a need to see a distinction between these groups at the time of the tribulation and the millennium.

There is a variation of the pretribulation rapture position that is known as the *midtribulation rapture* view. It is defended by Gleason Archer in his essay, "The Case for the Mid-Seventieth-Week Rapture Position."[45] He sees the tribulation as separated into two halves. The first three and a half years are characterized by the wrath of man, and the church is present at that time. The second three and a half years are characterized by the wrath of God, and during that time the church is absent from the earth. The primary argument from Scripture to support a midtribulational rapture is the fact that in Daniel 7:25; 9:27; and 12:7 and 11, as well as in Revelation 12:14, the seven days or times indicated are cut in half, mentioning the interval of three and a half times or three and a half days in a symbolic week, thus indicating a period of three and a half years, after which God's people will be rescued from tribulation. Another argument in favor of this position is that it gives a heightened sense of expectancy of Christ's return, since three and a half years is a shorter period of time than seven years.

---

43. See chapter 54, pp. 1355–59.

44. See chapter 44, pp. 1054–58, on the question of a distinction between Israel and the church.

45. In *The Rapture*, 113–45.

However, though the passages in Daniel do speak of an *interruption* of the seventieth week which Daniel predicts for the future, they do not give any clear indication that mid-way through the week believers will be removed from the earth.[46] It is also hard to see that the expectation of a three-and-a-half-year tribulation provides a much greater sense of imminence than does the expectation of a seven-year tribulation.

Finally, some objections to the *pre*tribulational rapture position can be stated in the form of arguments in favor of the *post*tribulational rapture view (the historic premillennial view that Christ will return after a period of tribulation on the earth):

1. The New Testament nowhere clearly says that the church will be taken out of the world before the tribulation. If this significant event were to happen, we might at least expect that explicit teaching to that effect would be found in the New Testament. Certainly Jesus tells us that he will come again and take us to be with himself (John 14:3). Paul tells us that we shall be caught up in the clouds to meet the Lord in the air (1 Thess. 4:17) and that we shall be changed in the twinkling of an eye and receive resurrection bodies (1 Cor. 15:51–52). But each of these passages has been understood by believers throughout history as speaking not of a *secret* rapture of the church before the tribulation but of a very visible *public* rapture (or "taking up") of the church to be with Christ just a few moments prior to his coming to earth *with them* to reign during the millennial kingdom (or, on the amillennial view, during the eternal state).[47]

Moreover, it is very difficult to understand 1 Thessalonians 4:17, the only passage that explicitly speaks of the fact that the church will be "caught up" (or "raptured"), to speak of the idea of a secret coming. It says, "The Lord himself will descend from heaven *with a cry of command, with the voice of an archangel, and with the sound of the trumpet of God*" (1 Thess. 4:16). Of these words Leon Morris rightly says, "It may be that from this he intends us to understand that the rapture will take place secretly, and that no one except the saints themselves will know what is going on. But one would hardly gather this from his words. It is difficult to see how he could more plainly describe something that is open and public."[48]

The doctrine of a pretribulation rapture is an inference from several passages, all of which are disputed. Moreover, even if one believes this doctrine to be in Scripture, it is taught with such little clarity that it was not discovered until the nineteenth century. This does not make it seem likely.

---

46. See Paul D. Feinberg, "Response," in *The Rapture*, 147–50.

47. When Paul says that "we who are alive, who are left, will be caught up together with them in the clouds to *meet* the Lord in the air" (1 Thess. 4:17), he uses the Greek word *apantēsis*, for "meet," which is used in Greek literature outside the Bible to speak of citizens going out of a city to meet an arriving magistrate, then to return to the city with him. "The word *apantēsis* is to be understood as a technical term for a civic custom of antiquity whereby a public welcome was accorded by a city to important visitors" (Erik Peterson, *"apantēsis," TDNT*, 1:380). Moulton and Milligan say, "The word seems to have been a kind of technical term for the official welcome of a newly arrived dignitary—a usage which accords excellently with its New Testament usage" (MM, 53).

48. Morris, *The First and Second Epistles to the Thessalonians*, NIC (Grand Rapids: Eerdmans, 1959), 145.

2. The tribulation is quite clearly linked with the Lord's return in some passages. First, the loud trumpet call to gather the elect in Matthew 24:31, the sound of the trumpet of God in 1 Thessalonians 4:16, and the last trumpet at which our bodies are changed in 1 Corinthians 15:51–52, all seem to be the same trumpet—the last trumpet that is blown just before the millennium. If it is indeed the "last trumpet" (1 Cor. 15:52), then it is hard to see how another loud trumpet call (Matt. 24:31) could follow it seven years later.

In addition, Matthew 24 is very difficult to understand as referring not to the church but to Jewish people who would be saved during the tribulation. Jesus is addressing *his disciples* (Matt. 24:1–4) and warning them of persecution and suffering to come. He tells them of the great tribulation to come, and then says that "immediately after the tribulation of those days" cosmic signs will appear and "then all the tribes of the earth will mourn, and they will see the Son of Man coming on the clouds of heaven with power and great glory" (Matt. 24:30). But is it likely that Jesus, in saying all these things *to his disciples,* intended his words to apply not to the church but only to a future earthly kingdom of Jewish people who would be converted during the tribulation? How could the disciples have known that he had such a meaning in mind? Nor does it seem likely that the disciples are here as representatives of a future Jewish kingdom and not as representatives of the church, with whose founding they were so integrally connected as to be its foundation (Eph. 2:20).

3. Finally, the New Testament does not seem to justify the idea of two separate returns of Christ (once *for* his church before the tribulation and then seven years later *with* his church to bring judgment on unbelievers). Once again, no such view is explicitly taught in any passage, but it is simply an inference drawn from differences between various passages that describe Christ's return from different perspectives. But it is not at all difficult to see these passages as referring to a single event occurring at one time.[49]

It seems best to conclude, with the great majority of the church throughout history, that the church will go through the time of tribulation predicted by Jesus. We would probably not have chosen this path for ourselves, but the decision was not ours to make. And if God wills that any of us now alive remain on earth until the time of this great tribulation, then we should heed Peter's words, "If you are insulted for the name of Christ, you are blessed, because the Spirit of glory and of God rests upon you" (1 Peter 4:14), and "Christ also suffered for you, leaving you an example, so that you might follow in his steps" (1 Peter 2:21). This idea that Christians should be prepared to endure suffering is also seen in Paul's words that we are fellow heirs with Christ, "provided we suffer with him in order that we may also be glorified with him" (Rom. 8:17). And we may remember that from the time of Noah to the time of the martyrdom of the early apostles, it has frequently been God's way to bring his people through suffering to

---

49. See n37 above; the primary passages are given on
pp. 1347–49.

glory, for thus he did even with his own Son. "For it was fitting that he, for whom and by whom all things exist, in bringing many sons to glory, should make the founder of their salvation perfect through suffering" (Heb. 2:10). It is from the Savior who himself has suffered more than any of his children will ever suffer that we have the admonition, "Do not fear what you are about to suffer. . . . Be faithful unto death, and I will give you the crown of life" (Rev. 2:10).

## QUESTIONS FOR PERSONAL APPLICATION

1. Before reading this chapter, did you have any conviction about whether Christ's return would be amillennial, postmillennial, or premillennial? And whether it would be posttribulational or pretribulational? If so, how has your view now changed, if at all?

2. Explain how your present view of the millennium affects your Christian life today. Similarly, explain how your view of the tribulation affects your present Christian life.

3. What do you think it will feel like to be living on earth with a glorified body, and with Jesus Christ as King over the whole world? Can you describe in any detail some of the attitudes and emotional responses you will have toward various situations in such a kingdom? Do you really look forward to such a kingdom? (Your answers will differ somewhat depending on whether you expect a glorified body during the millennium or not until the eternal state.)

4. What might be both the positive and the negative results of a pretribulation rapture position in the everyday lives and attitudes of Christians? Similarly, what might be the positive and negative results of a posttribulation rapture position?

### Special Terms

*amillennialism*
*dispensational premillennialism*
*great tribulation*
*historic premillennialism*
*midtribulation rapture*
*millennium*
*postmillennialism*
*posttribulational premillennialism*
*posttribulation rapture*
*premillennialism*
*pretribulational premillennialism*
*pretribulation rapture*
*rapture*

## BIBLIOGRAPHY

(For an explanation of this bibliography see the note on the bibliography to chapter 1, pp. 23–24. Complete bibliographical data may be found on pp. 1489–96.)

### SECTIONS IN EVANGELICAL SYSTEMATIC THEOLOGIES

*1. Anglican (Episcopalian)*
    1882–92 . . . . . Litton, 581–85

2001 . . . . . . . . . . . Packer, 250–53
2013 . . . . . . . . Bird, 274–300
2013 . . . . . . . . Bray, 542–53

**2. Arminian (Wesleyan or Methodist)**
1940 . . . . . . . . Wiley, 3:280–319
1983 . . . . . . . . Carter, 2:1118–27
1992 . . . . . . . . Oden, 3:421–30
2002 . . . . . . . . Cottrell, 477–503

**3. Baptist**
1767 . . . . . . . . Gill, 2:268–302
1907 . . . . . . . . Strong, 1010–15
1990–95 . . . . . Garrett, 2:821–46
2007 . . . . . . . . Akin, 908–12
2013 . . . . . . . . Erickson, 1105–23

**4. Dispensational**
1947 . . . . . . . . Chafer, 4:264–78; 5:315–58
1949 . . . . . . . . Thiessen, 351–75, 391–95
1986 . . . . . . . . Ryrie, 439–52, 461–511
2002–2005 . . Geisler, 4:547–96
2017 . . . . . . . . MacArthur and Mayhue, 884–913

**5. Lutheran**
1934 . . . . . . . . Mueller, 621–25

**6. Reformed (or Presbyterian)**
1679–85 . . . . . Turretin, *IET*, 3:574–82
1724–58 . . . . . Edwards, 2:278–313
1871–73 . . . . . Hodge, 3:861–68
1894 . . . . . . . . Shedd, 863–66
1887–1921 . . . Warfield, *BD*, 643–64
1906–11 . . . . . Bavinck, *RD*, 4:655–63, 664–90
1938 . . . . . . . . Berkhof, 695–707
1998 . . . . . . . . Reymond 979–1066

2008 . . . . . . . . . . . Van Genderen and Velema, 838–64
2011 . . . . . . . . Horton, 920–56
2013 . . . . . . . . Frame, 1086–96
2013 . . . . . . . . Culver, 1138–52
2016 . . . . . . . . Allen and Swain, 389–91
2017 . . . . . . . . Barrett, 721–56
2019 . . . . . . . . Letham, 842–54

**7. Renewal (or charismatic/Pentecostal)**
1988–92 . . . . . Williams, 3:421–44
1993 . . . . . . . . Menzies and Horton, 227–40
1995 . . . . . . . . Horton, 629–34
2008 . . . . . . . . Duffield and Van Cleave, 553–56

## SECTIONS IN REPRESENTATIVE ROMAN CATHOLIC SYSTEMATIC THEOLOGIES
**1. Roman Catholic: Traditional**
1955 . . . . . . . . Ott (no explicit treatment)

**2. Roman Catholic: Post–Vatican II**
2012 . . . . . . . . *CCC*, paragraphs 675–77

## OTHER WORKS
Adams, Jay. *The Time Is at Hand*. Phillipsburg, NJ: Presbyterian and Reformed, 1970. (Amillennial.)
Allis, O. T. *Prophecy and the Church*. Philadelphia: Presbyterian and Reformed, 1945. (Amillennial.)
Allison, Gregg. *Historical Theology: An Introduction to Christian Doctrine; A Companion to Wayne Grudem's* Systematic Theology. Grand Rapids: Zondervan, 2011, 683–701.
Archer, Gleason, Paul Feinberg, Douglas Moo, and Richard Reiter. *The Rapture: Pre-, Mid-, or Post-Tribulational?* Grand Rapids: Zondervan, 1984. (Contains well-argued essays representing the three different positions.)
Bauckham, R. J. "Millennium." In *NDT2*, 471–73.
Beechick, Allen. *The Pre-Tribulation Rapture*. Denver: Accent, 1980.

Berkouwer, G. C. *The Return of Christ*. Translated by James Van Oosterom. Edited by Marlin J. Van Elderen. Grand Rapids: Eerdmans, 1972.

Boettner, Loraine. *The Millennium*. Philadelphia: Presbyterian and Reformed, 1957. (Postmillennial.)

Clouse, F. G. "Rapture of the Church." In *EDT3*, 719–21.

Clouse, Robert G., ed. *The Meaning of the Millennium: Four Views*. Downers Grove, IL: InterVarsity Press, 1977. (The chapters by Ladd and Hoekema are excellent statements of the classical premillennial and amillennial positions.)

Davis, John Jefferson. *Christ's Victorious Kingdom*. Grand Rapids: Baker, 1986. (This is an excellent argument for the postmillennial position.)

Dodd, B. J. "Millennium." In *DLNT*, 738–41.

Erickson, Millard. *Contemporary Options in Eschatology*. Grand Rapids: Baker, 1977.

Feinberg, Charles L. *Millennialism: The Two Major Views*. Chicago: Moody Publishers, 1980. (Pretribulational premillennial.)

Fruchtenbaum, Arnold G. *Israelology: The Missing Link in Systematic Theology*. Tustin, CA: Ariel Ministries, 1993. (Pretribulational premillennial.)

Grier, W. J. *The Momentous Event*. London: Banner of Truth, 1970.

Gundry, R. H. *The Church and the Tribulation*. Grand Rapids: Zondervan, 1973. (Posttribulational premillennial.)

Gundry, Stanley N., and Darrell L. Bock, eds. *Three Views on the Millennium and Beyond*. Grand Rapids: Zondervan, 1999.

Hendriksen, William. *More Than Conquerors: An Interpretation of the Book of Revelation*. London: Tyndale Press, 1962. (Amillennial.)

Hoekema, Anthony A. *The Bible and the Future*. Grand Rapids: Eerdmans, 1979, 109–238. (Amillennial.)

Kik, J. Marcellus. *An Eschatology of Victory*. Nutley, NJ: Presbyterian and Reformed, 1974. (Postmillennial.)

Kromminga, D. H. *The Millennium in the Church: Studies in the History of Christian Chiliasm*. Grand Rapids: Eerdmans, 1945. (Classic or posttribulational premillennial.)

Ladd, George Eldon. *The Blessed Hope*. Grand Rapids: Eerdmans, 1956. (Classic or posttribulational premillennial.)

Lightner, Robert P. *The Last Days Handbook: A Comprehensive Guide to Understanding the Different Views of Prophecy, Who Believes What about Prophecy and Why*. Nashville: Nelson, 1990.

McClain, Alva J. *The Greatness of the Kingdom*. Grand Rapids: Zondervan, 1959. (Pretribulational premillennial.)

Moore, Russell D. "Personal and Cosmic Eschatology." In *A Theology for the Church*, edited by Daniel L. Akin et al., 908–912. Nashville: B&H, 2007.

Murray, Iain. *The Puritan Hope*. London: Banner of Truth, 1971. (Postmillennial.)

Noble, T. A. "Eschatology." In *NDT2*, 296–99.

Pentecost, J. Dwight. *Things to Come*. Findlay, OH: Dunham, 1958. (Pretribulational premillennial.)

Poythress, Vern. *Understanding Dispensationalists*. Grand Rapids: Zondervan, 1987. (Amillennial.)

Travis, S. H. "Eschatology." In *NDT1*, 228–31.

Vos, Geerhardus. *The Pauline Eschatology*. Grand Rapids: Eerdmans, 1961. (Amillennial.)

Walvoord, John F. *The Blessed Hope and the Tribulation*. Grand Rapids: Zondervan, 1976. (Pretribulational premillennial.)

———. *The Millennial Kingdom*. Findlay, OH: Dunham, 1959. (Pretribulational premillennial.)

## SCRIPTURE MEMORY PASSAGE

**Revelation 20:4–6:** Then I saw thrones, and seated on them were those to whom the authority to judge was committed. Also I saw the souls of those who had been beheaded for the testimony of Jesus and for the word of God, and those who had not worshiped the beast or its image and had not received its mark on their foreheads or their hands. They came to life and reigned with Christ for a thousand years. The rest of the dead did not come to life until the thousand years were ended. This is the first resurrection. Blessed and holy is the one who shares in the first resurrection! Over such the second death has no power, but they will be priests of God and of Christ, and they will reign with him for a thousand years.

## HYMN

### "Jesus Shall Reign Where'er the Sun"

This hymn by Isaac Watts beautifully describes the reign of Christ over the whole earth. Whether our personal convictions on the millennium lead us to understand this hymn as referring to the millennium or to the eternal state, in either case it gives an excellent picture of the kingdom for which our hearts long and the blessings that will come when Jesus is King over the earth.

Jesus shall reign where'er the sun
   Does his successive journeys run;
His kingdom stretch from shore to shore,
   Til moons shall wax and wane no more.

To him shall endless prayer be made,
   And praises throng to crown his head;
His name, like sweet perfume, shall rise
   With every morning sacrifice.

People and realms of every tongue
   Dwell on his love with sweetest song;

And infant voices shall proclaim
   Their early blessings on his name.

Blessings abound where'er he reigns;
   The pris'ner leaps to loose his chains,
The weary find eternal rest,
   And all the sons of want are blest.

Let every creature rise and bring
   Peculiar honors to our King,
Angels descend with songs again,
   And earth repeat the loud amen.

Author: Isaac Watts, 1719

## CONTEMPORARY WORSHIP SONG

### "Revelation Song"

Worthy is the Lamb who was slain,
Holy, holy is He.
Sing a new song to Him who sits on
Heaven's mercy seat.

**Chorus**
Holy, holy, holy
Is the Lord God Almighty,
Who was and is and is to come.
With all creation I sing,
Praise to the King of kings;
You are my everything,
And I will adore You.

*Clothed in rainbows of living color,*
*Flashes of lightning, rolls of thunder.*
*Blessing and honor, strength and glory*
*And power be to You the only wise King.*

*Filled with wonder, awestruck wonder,*
*At the mention of Your name.*
*Jesus, Your name is power, breath, and living water,*
*Such a marvelous mystery.*

Words by Jennie Lee Riddle[50]

# CHAPTER 56

# The Final Judgment and Eternal Punishment

*Who will be judged?*
*What is hell?*

## EXPLANATION AND SCRIPTURAL BASIS

### A. The Fact of Final Judgment

### 1. Scriptural Evidence for a Final Judgment

Scripture frequently affirms the fact that there will be a great final judgment of believers and unbelievers. They will stand before the judgment seat of Christ in resurrected bodies and hear his proclamation of their eternal destiny.

The final judgment is vividly portrayed in John's vision in Revelation:

> Then I saw a great white throne and him who was seated on it. From his presence earth and sky fled away, and no place was found for them. And I saw the dead, great and small, standing before the throne, and books were opened. Then another book was opened, which is the book of life. And the dead were judged by what was written in the books, according to what they had done. And the sea gave up the dead who were in it, Death and Hades gave up the dead who were in them, and they were judged, each one of them, according to what they had done. Then Death and Hades were thrown into the lake of fire. This is the second death, the lake of fire. And if anyone's name was not found written in the book of life, he was thrown into the lake of fire. (Rev. 20:11–15)

Many other passages teach this final judgment. Paul tells the Greek philosophers in Athens that God "now . . . commands all people everywhere to repent, because *he has fixed a day on which he will judge the world in righteousness* by a man whom he has appointed; and of this he has given assurance to all by raising him from the dead" (Acts 17:30–31).[1] Similarly, Paul talks about "the day of wrath when God's righteous

---

1. It is interesting that Paul proclaimed eternal judgment to unbelieving gentiles who had little if any knowledge of the teachings of the Old Testament. Paul also argued about "future judgment" (Acts 24:25) before another unbeliever, the Roman governor Felix. In both cases Paul apparently realized that the brute fact that a day of accountability before God was coming

judgment will be revealed" (Rom. 2:5). Other passages speak clearly of a coming day of judgment (see Matt. 10:15; 11:22, 24; 12:36; 25:31–46; 1 Cor. 4:5; Heb. 6:2; 2 Peter 2:4; Jude 6, et al.).

This final judgment is the culmination of many precursors in which God rewarded righteousness or punished unrighteousness throughout history. While he brought blessing and deliverance from danger to those who were faithful to him, including Abel, Noah, Abraham, Isaac, Jacob, Joseph, Moses, David, and the faithful among the people of Israel, he also from time to time brought judgment on those who persisted in disobedience and unbelief: his judgments included the flood, the dispersion of the people from the tower of Babel, the judgments on Sodom and Gomorrah, and continuing judgments throughout history, both on individuals (Rom. 1:18–32) and on nations (Isa. 13–23, et al.) who persisted in sin. Moreover, in the unseen spiritual realm he brought judgment on angels who sinned (2 Peter 2:4). Peter reminds us that God's judgments have been carried out periodically and with certainty, and this reminds us that a final judgment is yet coming, for "the Lord knows how to rescue the godly from trials, and to keep the unrighteousness under punishment until the day of judgment, and especially those who indulge in the lust of defiling passion and despise authority" (2 Peter 2:9–10).

## 2. Will There Be More Than One Judgment?

According to a dispensational view, there is more than one judgment to come. For example, dispensationalists would not see the final judgment in Matthew 25:31–46:

> When the Son of Man comes in his glory, and all the angels with him, then he will sit on his glorious throne. *Before him will be gathered all the nations*, and he will separate people one from another as a shepherd separates the sheep from the goats. And he will place the sheep on his right, but the goats on the left. Then the King will say to those on his right, "Come, you who are blessed by my Father, inherit the kingdom prepared for you from the foundation of the world. For I was hungry and you gave me food. . . . As you did it to one of the least of these my brothers, you did it to me." Then he will say to those on his left, "Depart from me, you cursed, into the eternal fire prepared for the devil and his angels. For I was hungry and you gave me no food. . . . As you did not do it to one of the least of these, you did not do it to me." And these will go away into eternal punishment, but the righteous into eternal life.

From a dispensational perspective, this passage does not refer to final judgment (the "great white throne judgment" spoken of in Rev. 20:11–15), but rather to a judgment that comes after the tribulation and before the beginning of the millennium. They say

---

to all men would give to his hearers a sobering realization that their eternal destiny was at stake as they listened to him preach about Jesus.

that this will be a "*judgment of the nations*" in which the nations are judged according to how they have treated the Jewish people during the tribulation. Those who have treated the Jews well and are willing to submit to Christ will enter into the millennium, and those who have not will be refused entrance.

Thus, in a dispensationalist view there are different judgments: (a) a "judgment of the nations" (Matt. 25:31–46) to determine who enters the millennium; (b) a "judgment of believers' works" (sometimes called the *bēma* judgment after the Greek word for "judgment seat" in 2 Cor. 5:10) in which Christians will receive degrees of reward; and (c) a "great white throne judgment" at the end of the millennium (Rev. 20:11–15) to declare eternal punishments for unbelievers.[2]

The view taken in this book is that these three passages all speak of the same final judgment, not of three separate judgments. With regard to Matthew 25:31–46 in particular, it is unlikely that the dispensational view is correct: there is no mention of entering into the millennium in this passage. Moreover, the judgments pronounced speak not of entrance into the millennial kingdom on earth or exclusion from that kingdom but of eternal destinies of people: "Inherit the kingdom prepared for you from the foundation of the world. . . . Depart from me, you cursed, into the eternal fire prepared for the devil and his angels. . . . And these will go away into *eternal punishment*, but the righteous into *eternal life*" (vv. 34, 41, 46). Finally, it would be inconsistent with God's ways throughout Scripture to deal with people's *eternal* destiny on the basis of what nation they belong to, for unbelieving nations have believers within them, and nations that exhibit more conformity to God's revealed will still have many wicked within them. And "God shows no partiality" (Rom. 2:11). Though indeed "all the nations" are gathered before Christ's throne in this scene (Matt. 25:32), the picture of judgment is one of judgment on individuals (sheep are separated from goats, and those individuals who treated Christ's brothers kindly are welcomed into the kingdom while those who rejected them are rejected, vv. 35–40, 42–45).

## B. The Time of Final Judgment

The final judgment will occur after the millennium and the rebellion that occurs at the end of it. John pictures the millennial kingdom and the removal of Satan from influence on the earth in Revelation 20:1–6 (see the discussion in the previous two chapters) and then says that "when the thousand years are ended, Satan will be released from his prison and will come out to deceive the nations . . . to gather them for battle" (Rev. 20:7–8). After God decisively defeats this final rebellion (Rev. 20:9–10), John tells us that judgment will follow: "Then I saw a great white throne and him who is seated on it" (v. 11).

---

2. See Lewis Sperry Chafer, *Systematic Theology* (1948; repr., Grand Rapids: Kregel, 1976), 7:213–17, who includes other judgments as well.

## C. The Nature of the Final Judgment

### 1. Jesus Christ Will Be the Judge

Paul speaks of "Christ Jesus, who is to judge the living and the dead" (2 Tim. 4:1). Peter says that Jesus Christ "is the one appointed by God to be the judge of the living and the dead" (Acts 10:42; compare 17:31; Matt. 25:31–33). This right to act as judge over the whole universe is something that the Father has given to the Son: "The Father . . . has given him authority to execute judgment, because he is the Son of Man" (John 5:26–27).

### 2. Unbelievers Will Be Judged

It is clear that all unbelievers will stand before Christ for judgment, for this judgment includes "the dead, great and small" (Rev. 20:12), and "on the day of wrath when God's righteous judgment will be revealed," Paul says, "he will render to each one according to his works . . . for those who are self-seeking and do not obey the truth, but obey unrighteousness, there will be wrath and fury" (Rom. 2:5–8).[3]

This judgment of unbelievers will include *degrees of punishment*, for we read that the dead were judged "according to what they had done" (Rev. 20:12, 13), and this judgment according to what people had done must therefore involve an evaluation of the works that people have done.[4] Similarly, Jesus says, "That servant who knew his master's will but did not get ready or act according to his will, will receive a severe beating. But the one who did not know, and did what deserved a beating, will receive a light beating" (Luke 12:47–48). When Jesus says to the cities of Chorazin and Bethsaida, "It will be *more bearable* on the day of judgment for Tyre and Sidon than for you" (Matt. 11:22; cf. v. 24), or when he says that the scribes "will receive the *greater condemnation*" (Luke 20:47), he implies that there will be degrees of punishment on the last day.

In fact, every wrong deed done will be remembered and taken account of in the punishment that is meted out on that day because "on the day of judgment people will give account for every careless word they speak" (Matt. 12:36). Every word spoken, every deed done will be brought to light and receive judgment: "For God will bring every deed into judgment, with every secret thing, whether good or evil" (Eccl. 12:14).

As these verses indicate, on the day of judgment the secrets of people's hearts will be revealed and made public. Paul speaks of the day when "God judges the secrets of men by Christ Jesus" (Rom. 2:16; compare Luke 8:17). "Nothing is covered up that will not

---

3. This passage does not mean that we can be justified on the basis of good works, but that good works provide evidence that a person has been justified by faith and has experienced a changed life as a result of the internal work of the Holy Spirit that occurs in connection with saving faith (see chapters 33–38 regarding the complex set of events involved in "becoming a Christian").

4. The fact that there will be degrees of punishment for unbelievers according to their works does not mean that

unbelievers can ever do enough good to merit God's approval or earn salvation, for salvation only comes as a free gift to those who trust in Christ: "Whoever believes in him is not condemned, but whoever does not believe is condemned already, because he has not believed in the name of the only Son of God" (John 3:18).

For a discussion of the fact that there will be no "second chance" for people to accept Christ after they die, see chapter 41, pp. 1012–13.

be revealed, or hidden that will not be known. Therefore *whatever you have said in the dark shall be heard in the light, and what you have whispered in private rooms shall be proclaimed on the housetops*" (Luke 12:2–3).

## 3. Believers Will Be Judged

In writing to Christians Paul says, "*We will all stand before the judgment seat of God.* . . . Each of us will give an account of himself to God" (Rom. 14:10, 12). He also tells the Corinthians, "For *we must all appear before the judgment seat of Christ, so that each one may receive what is due for what he has done in the body,* whether good or evil" (2 Cor. 5:10; cf. Rom. 2:6–11; Rev. 20:12, 15). In addition, the picture of the final judgment in Matthew 25:31–46 includes Christ separating the sheep from the goats, and rewarding those who receive his blessing.

It is important to realize that this judgment of believers will be a judgment to evaluate and bestow various degrees of reward (see below), but the fact that they will face such a judgment should never cause believers to fear that they will be eternally condemned or shamed. Jesus says, "Whoever hears my word and believes him who sent me has eternal life. *He does not come into judgment,* but has passed from death to life" (John 5:24). Here *judgment* must be understood in the sense of eternal condemnation and death since it is contrasted with passing from death into life. At the day of final judgment more than at any other time, it is of utmost importance that "there is therefore now *no condemnation for those who are in Christ Jesus*" (Rom. 8:1). Thus the day of judgment can be portrayed as one in which believers are rewarded and unbelievers are punished: "The nations raged, but your wrath came, and the time for the dead to be judged, *and for rewarding your servants*, the prophets and saints, and those who fear your name, both small and great, and for destroying the destroyers of the earth" (Rev. 11:18).

Will all the secret words and deeds of believers, and all their sins, also be revealed on that last day? We might at first think so because Paul says that when the Lord comes he will "*bring to light the things now hidden in darkness* and will disclose the purposes of the heart. Then each one will receive his commendation from God" (1 Cor. 4:5; cf. Col. 3:25). However, this is a context that talks about "commendation," or praise (*epainos*), that comes from God, so it may not refer to sins. Other verses suggest that God will never again call our sins to remembrance: "You will cast all our sins into the depths of the sea" (Mic. 7:19); "as far as the east is from the west, so far does he remove our transgressions from us" (Ps. 103:12); "*I will not remember your sins*" (Isa. 43:25); "*I will remember their sins no more*" (Heb. 8:12; compare 10:17). Both Peter and Paul assure us, "Whoever believes in him *will not be put to shame*" (Rom. 9:33; 1 Peter 2:6).

Scripture also teaches that there will be *degrees of reward for believers*. Paul encourages the Corinthians to be careful how they build the church on the foundation that has already been laid—Jesus Christ.

Now if anyone builds on the foundation with gold, silver, precious stones, wood, hay, straw—each one's work will become manifest, for the Day will disclose it, because it will be revealed by fire, and the fire will test what sort of work each one has done. *If the work that anyone has built on the foundation survives, he will receive a reward.* If anyone's work is burned up, he will suffer loss, though he himself will be saved, but only as through fire. (1 Cor. 3:12–15)

Paul similarly says of Christians that "we must all appear before the judgment seat of Christ, so that each one may receive *what is due for what he has done in the body*, whether good or evil" (2 Cor. 5:10), again implying degrees of reward for what we have done in this life. Likewise, in the parable of the minas, the one who made ten minas more was told, "You shall have authority over ten cities," and the one whose mina had made five minas more was told, "You are to be over five cities" (Luke 19:17, 19). Many other passages likewise teach or imply degrees of reward for believers at the final judgment (see also Dan. 12:2; Matt. 6:10, 20–21; 19:21; Luke 6:22–23; 12:18–21, 32, 42–48; 14:13–14; 1 Cor. 3:8; 9:18; 13:3; 15:19, 29–32, 58; Gal. 6:9–10; Eph. 6:7–8; Phil. 4:17; Col. 3:23–24; 1 Tim. 6:18; Heb. 10:34, 35; 11:10, 14–16, 26, 35; 1 Peter 1:4; 2 John 8; Rev. 11:18; 22:12; cf. also Matt. 5:46; 6:2–6, 16–18, 24; Luke 6:35).

But we must guard against misunderstanding here: Even though there will be degrees of reward in heaven, the joy of each person will be full and complete for eternity. If we ask how this can be when there are different degrees of reward, it simply shows that our perception of happiness is based on the assumption that happiness depends on what we possess or the status or power that we have, especially in comparison to others who have more. In actuality, however, our true happiness consists in delighting in God and rejoicing in the status and recognition that he has given us. The foolishness of thinking that only those who have been highly rewarded and given great status will be fully happy in heaven is seen when we realize that no matter how great a reward we are given, there will always be those with greater rewards, or who have higher status and authority, including the apostles, the heavenly creatures, and Jesus Christ and God himself. Therefore, if highest status were essential for people to be fully happy, no one but God would be fully happy in heaven, which is certainly an incorrect idea. Moreover, those with greater reward and honor in heaven, those nearest the throne of God, delight not in their status but only in the privilege of falling down before God's throne to worship him (see Rev. 4:10–11).

It would be morally and spiritually beneficial for us to have a greater consciousness of this clear New Testament teaching on degrees of heavenly reward. Rather than making us competitive with one another, it would cause us to help and encourage one another that we all may increase our heavenly reward, for God has an infinite capacity to bring blessing to us all, and we are all members of one another (cf. 1 Cor. 12:26–27). We would more eagerly heed the admonition of the author of Hebrews, "*Let us consider how to stir up one another to love and good works*, not neglecting to meet together, as is the habit of some, but *encouraging one another*, and all the more as you see the Day drawing near" (Heb. 10:24–25). Moreover, in our lives a heartfelt seeking of future heavenly reward would motivate us to work wholeheartedly for the Lord at whatever task he calls us to, whether great or small, paid or unpaid. It would also make us long for his approval rather than for wealth or success. It would motivate us to work at building up the church on the one foundation, Jesus Christ (1 Cor. 3:10–15).

## 4. Angels Will Be Judged

Peter says that the rebellious angels have been committed to pits of nether gloom "to be kept until the judgment" (2 Peter 2:4), and Jude says that rebellious angels have been kept by God "until the judgment of the great day" (Jude 6). This means that at least the *rebellious* angels (that is, the demons) will be subject to judgment on that last day as well.

Scripture does not clearly indicate whether righteous angels will undergo some kind of evaluation of their service as well, but it is possible that they are included in Paul's statement "Do you not know that *we are to judge angels*?" (1 Cor. 6:3). It is probable that this includes righteous angels because there is no indication in the context that Paul is speaking of demons (fallen angels), and the word *angel* without further qualification in the New Testament would normally be understood to refer to righteous angels. But the text is not explicit enough to give us certainty.

## 5. We Will Help in the Work of Judgment

It is a rather amazing aspect of New Testament teaching that we (believers) will take part in the process of judgment. Paul says: "Do you not know that *the saints will judge the world*? And if the world is to be judged by you, are you incompetent to try trivial cases? Do you not know that *we are to judge angels*? How much more, then, matters pertaining to this life?" (1 Cor. 6:2–3).

It might be argued that this simply means we will be watching the declaration of judgment by Christ and approving it, but this does not seem to fit the context well, for here Paul is encouraging the Corinthians to settle legal disputes among themselves rather than taking them to court before unbelievers. In this very context he says, "Can it be that there is no one among you wise enough to settle a dispute between the brothers, but brother goes to law against brother, and that before unbelievers?" (1 Cor. 6:5–6). This kind of judgment certainly involves careful evaluation and wise discernment. And this implies that such careful evaluation and discernment will be exercised by us in judging angels and in judging the world on the day of final judgment.

This is similar to the teaching of Revelation 20, where John says that he saw thrones, and "seated on them were *those to whom the authority to judge was committed*" (Rev. 20:4). Although the text does not explain the identity of those seated on the thrones, the fact that they are mentioned in the plural indicates that Christ does not reserve every aspect of the process of judging for himself alone. Indeed, he tells his twelve disciples that they will "sit on twelve thrones, *judging* the twelve tribes of Israel" (Matt. 19:28; compare Luke 22:30). This accords with the fact that throughout the history of redemption God has from time to time given the right to exercise judgment into the hands of human authorities, whether Moses and the elders who assisted him, the judges of Israel whom God raised up during the period of the judges, the wise kings such as David and Solomon, the civil government of many nations (see Rom. 13:1–7; 1 Peter 2:13–14), or those who have authority to rule and govern within the church and to oversee the exercise of church discipline.

## D. Necessity of Final Judgment

Since when believers die they pass immediately into the presence of God, and when unbelievers die they pass into a state of separation from God and the endurance of punishment,[5] we may wonder why God has a time of final judgment established at all. Berkhof wisely points out that the final judgment is not for the purpose of letting God find out the condition of our hearts or the pattern of conduct of our lives, for he already knows that in every detail. Berkhof rather says of the final judgment:

> It will serve the purpose rather of displaying before all rational creatures the declarative glory of God in a formal, forensic act, which magnifies on the one hand His holiness and righteousness, and on the other hand, His grace and mercy. Moreover, it should be borne in mind that the judgment at the last day will differ from that of the death of each individual in more than one respect. It will not be secret, but public; it will not pertain to the soul only, but also to the body; it will not have reference to a single individual, but to all men.[6]

## E. Justice of God in the Final Judgment

Scripture clearly affirms that God will be entirely just in his judgment and that no one will be able to complain against him on that day. God is the one who "judges impartially according to each one's deeds" (1 Peter 1:17), and "God shows no partiality" (Rom. 2:11; cf. Col. 3:25). For this reason, on the last day "every mouth" will be "stopped," and the whole world will be "held accountable to God" (Rom. 3:19), with no one being able to complain that God has treated him or her unfairly. In fact, one of the great blessings of the final judgment will be that saints and angels will see demonstrated in millions of

---

5. See chapter 41, pp. 1005–13, for evidence supporting the idea that believers go immediately into God's presence when they die, and unbelievers go immediately to a place of punishment separated from God. (See also Luke 16:24–26; Heb. 9:27.)

6. Louis Berkhof, *Systematic Theology* (Grand Rapids: Eerdmans, 1941), 731.

lives the absolutely pure justice of God, and this will be a source of praise to him for all eternity. At the time of God's judgment on wicked Babylon, there will be great praise in heaven, for John says, "I heard what seemed to be the loud voice of a great multitude in heaven, crying out, '*Hallelujah*! Salvation and glory and power belong to our God, for *his judgments are true and just*'" (Rev. 19:1–2).

## F. Moral Application of the Final Judgment

The doctrine of final judgment has several positive moral influences in our lives.

### 1. The Doctrine of Final Judgment Satisfies Our Inward Sense of a Need for Justice in the World

The fact that there will be a final judgment assures us that ultimately God's universe is *fair*, for God is in control, and he keeps accurate records and renders just judgment. When Paul tells slaves to be submissive to their masters, he reassures them, "For the wrongdoer will be paid back for the wrong he has done, and there is no partiality" (Col. 3:25). When the picture of a final judgment mentions the fact that "books were opened" (Rev. 20:12; cf. Mal. 3:16), it reminds us (whether the books are literal or symbolic) that a permanent and accurate record of all our deeds has been kept by God, and ultimately all accounts will be settled and all will be made right.

### 2. The Doctrine of Final Judgment Enables Us to Forgive Others Freely

We realize that it is not up to us to take revenge on others who have wronged us, or even to want to do so, because God has reserved that right for himself. "Beloved, never avenge yourselves, but leave it to the wrath of God, for it is written, '*Vengeance is mine, I will repay, says the Lord*'" (Rom. 12:19). In this way whenever we have been wronged, we can give into God's hands any desire to harm or pay back the person who has wronged us, knowing that every wrong in the universe will ultimately be paid for—either it will turn out to have been paid for by Christ when he died on the cross (if the wrongdoer becomes a Christian), or it will be paid for at the final judgment (for those who do not trust in Christ for salvation). But in either case we can give the situation into God's hands, and then pray that the wrongdoer will trust Christ for salvation and thereby receive forgiveness of his or her sins. This thought should keep us from harboring bitterness or resentment in our hearts for injustices we have suffered that have not been made right: God is just, and we can leave these situations in his hands, knowing that he will someday right all wrongs and give absolutely fair rewards and punishments. In this way we are following in the example of Christ, who "when he was reviled, he did not revile in return; when he suffered, he did not threaten, but *continued entrusting himself to him who judges justly*" (1 Peter 2:23). He also prayed, "Father, forgive them, for they know not what they do" (Luke 23:34; cf. Acts 7:60, where Stephen followed Jesus' example in praying for those who put him to death).

### 3. The Doctrine of the Final Judgment Provides a Motive for Righteous Living

For believers, the final judgment is an incentive to faithfulness and good works, not as a means of earning forgiveness of sins, but as a means of gaining greater eternal reward.[7] This is a healthy and good motive for us—Jesus tells us, "Lay up for yourselves treasures in heaven" (Matt. 6:20)—though it runs counter to the popular views of our secular culture, a culture that does not really believe in heaven or eternal rewards at all.

For unbelievers, the doctrine of final judgment still provides some moral restraint on their lives. If in a society there is a widespread general acknowledgment that all will someday give account to the Creator of the universe for their lives, some "fear of God" will characterize many people's lives. By contrast, those who have no deep consciousness of final judgment give themselves up to greater and greater evil, demonstrating that "there is *no fear of God* before their eyes" (Rom. 3:18). Those who deny the final judgment, Peter says, will be "scoffers" who "will come in the last days with scoffing, *following their own sinful desires*. They will say, 'Where is the promise of his coming?'" (2 Peter 3:3–4). He also declares that evildoers who "are surprised when you do not join them in the same flood of debauchery" and who "malign you" will nonetheless "give account to him who is ready to judge the living and the dead" (1 Peter 4:4–5). An awareness of final judgment is both a comfort to believers and a warning to unbelievers not to continue in their evil ways.

### 4. The Doctrine of Final Judgment Provides a Great Motive for Evangelism

The decisions made by people in this life will affect their destiny for all eternity, and it is right that our hearts feel and our mouths echo the sentiment of the appeal of God through Ezekiel, "*Turn back, turn back from your evil ways, for why will you die, O house of Israel?*" (Ezek. 33:11). In fact, Peter indicates that the delay of the Lord's return is due to the fact that God "is patient toward you, not wishing that any should perish, but that all should reach repentance" (2 Peter 3:9).

### G. HELL

It is appropriate to discuss the doctrine of hell in connection with the doctrine of final judgment. We may define hell as follows: *hell is a place of eternal conscious punishment for the wicked.* Scripture teaches in several passages that there is such a place. At the end of the parable of the talents, the master says, "Cast the worthless servant into the outer darkness. In that place there will be weeping and gnashing of teeth" (Matt. 25:30). This is one among several indications that there will be consciousness of punishment after the final judgment. Similarly, at the judgment the king will say to some, "Depart from me, you cursed, into *the eternal fire* prepared for the devil and his angels" (Matt.

---

7. The idea of working for greater heavenly reward is a frequent theme in the New Testament; see the verses listed on p. 1409 above.

25:41), and Jesus says that those thus condemned "will go away into *eternal punishment*, but the righteous into eternal life" (Matt. 25:46).[8] In this text, the parallel between "eternal life" and "eternal punishment" indicates that both states will be without end.[9]

Jesus refers to hell as "the unquenchable fire" (Mark 9:43) and says that hell is a place "where their worm does not die and the fire is not quenched" (Mark 9:48).[10] The story of the rich man and Lazarus also indicates a horrible consciousness of punishment: "The rich man also died and was buried, and in Hades, being in torment, he lifted up his eyes and saw Abraham far off and Lazarus at his side. And he called out, 'Father Abraham, have mercy on me, and send Lazarus to dip the end of his finger in water and cool my tongue, for I am in anguish in this flame'" (Luke 16:22–24). He then begs Abraham to send Lazarus to his father's house, "for I have five brothers—so that he may warn them, lest they also come into *this place of torment*" (Luke 16:28).

When we turn to Revelation, the descriptions of this eternal punishment are also explicit:

> If anyone worships the beast and its image and receives a mark on his forehead or on his hand, he also will drink the wine of God's wrath, poured full strength into the cup of his anger, and he will be tormented with fire and sulfur in the presence of the holy angels and in the presence of the Lamb. *And the smoke of their torment goes up forever and ever, and they have no rest, day or night*, these worshipers of the beast and its image, and whoever receives the mark of its name. (Rev. 14:9–11)

This passage very clearly affirms the idea of eternal conscious punishment of unbelievers.

With respect to the judgment on the wicked city of Babylon, a large multitude in heaven cries, "Hallelujah! *The smoke from her goes up forever and ever*" (Rev. 19:3). After the final rebellion of Satan is crushed, we read, "The devil who had deceived them was thrown into the lake of fire and sulfur where the beast and the false prophet were, and *they will be tormented day and night forever and ever*" (Rev. 20:10). This passage is also significant in connection with Matthew 25:41, in which unbelievers are sent "into the eternal fire prepared for the devil and his angels." These verses should make us realize the immensity of the evil that is found in sin and rebellion against God and the magnitude of the holiness and the justice of God that calls forth this kind of punishment.

The idea that there will be *eternal* conscious punishment of unbelievers has been denied recently even by some evangelical theologians.[11] It has previously been denied by

---

8. The word translated "punishment" here is *kolasis*, which is used elsewhere of great physical suffering or torture that was endured by persecuted Christians (*Martyrdom of Polycarp* 2.4; cf. Ignatius, *To the Romans* 5.3). At other times it simply refers to divine punishment in general, without specification of the nature of that punishment (cf. BDAG, 555).

9. These texts and others which are quoted in the following

paragraphs clearly indicate that the Bible does not teach *universalism* (the doctrine that all people will ultimately be saved).

10. Cf. Isa. 66:24, speaking of those who have rebelled against God: "For their worm shall not die, their fire shall not be quenched."

11. See Philip E. Hughes, *The True Image: The Origin and Destiny of Man in Christ* (Grand Rapids: Eerdmans, 1989),

the Seventh Day Adventist Church and by various individuals throughout church history. Those who deny eternal conscious punishment often advocate *"annihilationism,"* a teaching that, after the wicked have suffered the penalty of God's wrath for a time, God will "annihilate" them so that they no longer exist.[12] Many who believe in annihilationism also hold to the reality of final judgment and punishment for sin, but they argue that after sinners have suffered for a certain period of time, bearing the wrath of God against their sin, they will finally cease to exist. The punishment will therefore be "conscious" but it will not be "eternal."[13]

Arguments advanced in favor of annihilationism are (1) the biblical references to the *destruction* of the wicked, which, some say, implies that they will no longer exist after they are destroyed (Phil. 3:19; 1 Thess. 5:3; 2 Thess. 1:9; 2 Peter 3:7, et al.); (2) the apparent inconsistency of eternal conscious punishment with the *love of God*; (3) the apparent injustice involved in the *disproportion* between sins committed in time and punishment that is eternal; and (4) the fact that the *continuing presence of evil creatures in God's universe* will eternally mar the perfection of a universe that God created to reflect his glory.

In response, (1) it must be said that the passages which speak of *destruction* (such as Phil. 3:19; 1 Thess. 5:3; 2 Thess. 1:9; 2 Peter 3:7) do not necessarily imply the cessation of existence, for in these passages the terms used for "destruction" can simply be ways of referring to the harmful and destructive effects of final judgment on unbelievers, and they do not necessarily imply a ceasing to exist or some kind of annihilation.[14]

(2) With respect to the argument from the love of God, the same difficulty in reconciling God's love with eternal punishment would seem to be present in reconciling God's love with the idea of divine punishment at all, and, conversely, if (as Scripture abundantly testifies) it is consistent for God to punish the wicked for a certain length of time after the last judgment, then there seems to be no necessary reason why it would be inconsistent of God to inflict the same punishment for an unending period of time.

This kind of reasoning may lead some people to adopt another kind of

---

405–407; David L. Edwards and John R. W. Stott, *Essentials: A Liberal-Evangelical Dialogue* (London: Hodder and Stoughton, 1988), 275–76; Clark Pinnock, "The Destruction of the Finally Impenitent," *CThRev* 4 (Spring 1990): 243–59.

12. A variation of the view that God will eventually annihilate unbelievers (annihilationism proper) is the view called *"conditional immortality,"* the idea that God has created people so that they only have immortality (the power to live forever) if they accept Christ as Savior. Those who do not become Christians, then, do not have the gift of immortal life and at death or at the time of final judgment they simply cease to exist. This view is very close to that of annihilationism, and I have not discussed it separately in this chapter. (Some versions of conditional immortality deny conscious punishment altogether, even for a brief time.)

13. I argued briefly against annihilationism earlier (see chapter 41, p. 1013).

14. In Phil. 3:19 and 2 Peter 3:7, the term for "destruction" is *apōleia*, which is the same word used by the disciples in Matt. 26:8 to speak of the "waste" (in their view) of the ointment that had just been poured on Jesus' head. Now the ointment did not cease to exist; it was very evident on Jesus' head. But it had been "destroyed" in the sense that it was no longer able to be used on someone else, or sold. In 1 Thess. 5:3 and 2 Thess. 1:9 another word, *olethros*, is used of the destruction of the wicked, but again this word does not imply that something will cease to exist, for it is used in 1 Cor. 5:5 of delivering a man to Satan (putting him out of the church) for the *destruction* of the flesh—but certainly his flesh did not cease to exist when he was put out of the church, even though he may have suffered in his body (this would be true whether we take "flesh" to mean his physical body or his sinful nature).

annihilationism, one in which there is no conscious suffering at all, not even for a brief time, and the only punishment is that unbelievers cease to exist after they die. But, in response, it may be wondered whether this kind of immediate annihilation can really be called a punishment, since there would be no consciousness of pain. In fact, the guarantee that there would be a cessation of existence would seem to many people, especially those who are suffering and in difficulty in this life, to be in some ways a desirable alternative. And if there was no punishment of unbelievers at all, even people like Hitler and Stalin would have nothing coming to them, and there would be no ultimate justice in the universe. Then people would have great incentive to be as wicked as possible in this life.

(3) The argument that *eternal* punishment is unfair (because there is a disproportion between temporary sin and eternal punishment) wrongly assumes that we know the extent of the evil done when sinners rebel against God. David Kingdon observes that "sin against the Creator is heinous to a degree utterly beyond our sin-warped imaginations' [ability] to conceive of. . . . Who would have the temerity to suggest to God what the punishment . . . should be?"[15] He also responds to this objection by suggesting that unbelievers in hell may go on sinning, receiving punishment for their sin, and never repenting, and notes that Revelation 22:11 points in this direction: "Let the evildoer still do evil, and the filthy still be filthy."[16]

At this point, moreover, an argument based on God's justice may be brought against annihilationism. Does the short time of punishment envisaged by the annihilationist actually *pay* for all of the unbeliever's sin and satisfy God's justice? If it does not, then God's justice has not been satisfied and the unbeliever should not be annihilated. But if it does, then the unbeliever should be allowed to go to heaven, and he or she should not be annihilated. In either case, annihilationism is not necessary or right.

(4) Regarding the fourth argument, while evil *that remains unpunished* does detract from God's glory in the universe, we also must realize that when God *punishes* evil and *triumphs* over it, the glory of his justice, righteousness, and power to triumph over all opposition will be seen (see Rom. 9:17, 22–24). The depth of the riches of God's mercy will also then be revealed, for all redeemed sinners will recognize that they too deserve such punishment from God and have avoided it only by God's grace through Jesus Christ (cf. Rom. 9:23–24).

Yet after all this has been said, we have to admit that the ultimate resolution of the depths of this question lies far beyond our ability to understand, and it remains hidden in the counsels of God. Were it not for the scriptural passages cited above that so clearly affirm eternal conscious punishment, annihilationism might seem to us to be an attractive option. Though annihilationism can be countered by theological arguments, it is

---

15. David Kingdon, "Annihilationism: Gain or Loss?,"    16. Ibid., 9–10.
unpublished paper obtained from the author, March 1992, 9.

ultimately the clarity and forcefulness of the passages themselves that convince us that annihilationism is incorrect and that Scripture does indeed teach the eternal conscious punishment of the wicked.

Because the doctrine of eternal conscious punishment is so foreign to the thought patterns of our culture and, on a deeper level, to our instinctive and God-given sense of love and desire for redemption for every human being created in God's image, this doctrine is emotionally one of the most difficult doctrines for Christians to affirm today. It also tends to be one of the first doctrines given up by people who are moving away from a commitment to the Bible as absolutely truthful in all that it affirms. Among liberal theologians who do not accept the absolute truthfulness of the Bible, there is probably no one today who believes in the doctrine of eternal conscious punishment.

What then are we to think of this doctrine? It is hard—and it should be hard—for us to think of this doctrine today. If our hearts are never moved with deep sorrow when we contemplate this doctrine, then there is a serious deficiency in our spiritual and emotional sensibilities. When Paul thinks of the lostness of his kinsmen the Jews, he says, "I have *great sorrow* and *unceasing anguish* in my heart" (Rom. 9:2). This is consistent with what God tells us of his own sorrow at the death of the wicked: "As I live, declares the Lord God, *I have no pleasure in the death of the wicked*, but that the wicked turn from his way and live; turn back, turn back from your evil ways, for why will you die, O house of Israel?" (Ezek. 33:11). And Jesus' agony is evident as he cries out, "O Jerusalem, Jerusalem, the city that kills the prophets and stones those who are sent to it! How often would I have gathered your children together as a hen gathers her brood under her wings, and you were not willing! See, your house is left to you desolate" (Matt. 23:37–38; cf. Luke 19:41–42).

The reason it is hard for us to think of the doctrine of hell is because God has put in our hearts a portion of his love for people created in his image, even his love for sinners who rebel against him. As long as we are in this life, and as long as we see and think about others who need to hear the gospel and trust in Christ for salvation, it should cause us great distress and agony of spirit to think about eternal punishment. Yet we must also realize that whatever God in his wisdom has ordained and taught in Scripture is *right*. Therefore, we must be careful that we do not hate this doctrine or rebel against it, but rather we should seek, insofar as we are able, to come to the point where we acknowledge that eternal punishment is good and right, because in God there is no unrighteousness at all.

It may help us to realize that if God were not to execute eternal punishment, then, apparently, his justice would not be satisfied and his glory would not be furthered in the way he deems wise. And it will perhaps also help us to realize that from the perspective of the world to come there is a much greater recognition of the necessity and rightness of eternal punishment. Martyred believers in heaven are heard by John to cry out, "O sovereign Lord, holy and true, how long before you will judge and avenge our blood on those who dwell on the earth?" (Rev. 6:10). Moreover, at the final destruction of Babylon, the loud voice of a great multitude in heaven cries out with praise to God for the rightness of his judgment as they finally see the heinous nature of evil for what it really is: "Hallelujah! Salvation and glory and power belong to our God, for his judgments are true and just; for he has judged the great prostitute who corrupted the earth with her immorality, and has avenged on her the blood of his servants. . . . Hallelujah! The smoke from her goes up forever and ever" (Rev. 19:1–3). As soon as this happened, "the twenty-four elders and the four living creatures fell down and worshiped God who was seated on the throne, saying, 'Amen. Hallelujah!'" (Rev. 19:4). We cannot say that this great multitude of the redeemed and the living creatures in heaven have wrong moral judgment when they praise God for executing justice on evil, for they are all free from sin and their moral judgments are pleasing to God.

In this present age, however, we should only approach such a celebration of the justice of God in the punishment of evil when we meditate on the eternal punishment given to Satan and his demons. When we think of them we do not instinctively love them, though they too were created by God. But now they are fully devoted to evil and beyond the potential of redemption. So we cannot long for their salvation as we long for the redemption of all humanity. We must believe that eternal punishment is true and just, yet we should also long that even those people who most severely persecute the church should come to faith in Christ and thus escape eternal condemnation.

## QUESTIONS FOR PERSONAL APPLICATION

1. Have you thought before that there will be a final judgment for believers? How do you think of it now? How does the awareness of the fact that we will all stand before the judgment seat of Christ affect your life today? What do you think it will feel like to have all your words and deeds made public on that last day? Is there an element of fear as you contemplate that day? If so, meditate on 1 John 4:16–18:

   > So we have come to know and to believe the love that God has for us. God is love, and whoever abides in love abides in God, and God abides in him. By this is love perfected with us, so *that we may have confidence for the day of judgment*, because as he is so also are we in this world. *There is no fear in love, but perfect love casts out fear.* For fear has to do with punishment, and whoever fears has not been perfected in love.

2. Have you previously thought very much about laying up treasures in heaven or about earning greater heavenly reward? If you really believe this doctrine, what kind of effect do you think it should have on your life?

3. How do you think it will feel to participate with Christ in the judging of angels, and indeed in the judging of the whole world (see 1 Cor. 6:2–3)? What does the fact that God allows us to participate in this final judgment say about our creation in the image of God and his purposes for us in the universe? How does that make you feel about yourself and your eternal relationship to God?

4. Think of some of your Christian friends in your church. How do you think you will feel when you watch them stand before Christ at the final judgment? How will they feel about you at that time? Does the contemplation of this future judgment affect the way you think of your fellowship with each other as brothers and sisters in Christ today?

5. Are you glad that there will be a final judgment of both believers and unbelievers? Does it make you feel a sense of God's justice, or do you sense some unfairness and injustice in the whole idea?

6. Are you convinced that Scripture teaches that there will be eternal conscious punishment of the wicked? When you think of that idea in relationship to Satan and demons, do you feel that it is right?

7. Is there anyone who has wronged you in the past and whom you have had difficulty forgiving? Does the doctrine of final judgment help you to be more able to forgive that person?

## Special Terms

*annihilationism*
*conditional immortality*
*eternal conscious punishment*
*final judgment*
*great white throne judgment*
*hell*
*judgment of the nations*
*universalism*

# BIBLIOGRAPHY

(For explanation of this bibliography see note at bibliography to chapter 1, pp. 23–24. Complete bibliographical data may be found on pp. 1489–96.)

## SECTIONS IN EVANGELICAL SYSTEMATIC THEOLOGIES

1. *Anglican (Episcopalian)*
   1882–92 . . . . . Litton, 591–600
   1930 . . . . . . . . Thomas, 525–26
   2001 . . . . . . . . Packer, 258–63
   2013 . . . . . . . . Bird, 326–40
   2013 . . . . . . . . Bray, 542–53

2. *Arminian (Wesleyan or Methodist)*
   1875–76 . . . . . Pope, 3:401–47
   1892–94 . . . . . Miley, 2:458–71
   1940 . . . . . . . . Wiley, 3:338–75
   1960 . . . . . . . . Purkiser, 567–74
   1983 . . . . . . . . Carter, 2:1105–9, 1127–30,
   1133–36
   1992 . . . . . . . . Oden, 3:430–41
   2002 . . . . . . . . Cottrell, 552–60, 588–602

3. *Baptist*
   1767 . . . . . . . . Gill, 2:302–29
   1887 . . . . . . . . Boyce, 461–71, 477–93

## SECTIONS IN REPRESENTATIVE ROMAN CATHOLIC SYSTEMATIC THEOLOGIES

## OTHER WORKS

Alcorn, Randy C., *The Law of Rewards*. Wheaton, IL: Tyndale House Publishers, 2003.

Allison, Gregg. *Historical Theology: An Introduction to Christian Doctrine; A Companion to Wayne Grudem's* Systematic Theology. Grand Rapids: Zondervan, 2011, 702–22.

Beckwith, R. T. "Purgatory." In *NDT1*, 549–50.

Benware, Paul N. *The Believer's Payday: Why Standing before Christ Should Be Our Greatest Moment*. Chattanooga, TN: AMG, 2002.

Blamires, Harry. *Knowing the Truth about Heaven and Hell*. Knowing the Truth Series, edited by J. I. Packer and Peter Kreeft. Ann Arbor: Servant, 1988.

Boa, Kenneth, and Robert M. Bowman. *Sense and Nonsense about Heaven and Hell*. Grand Rapids: Zondervan, 2007.

Bock, Darrell L. "Crown." In *BTDB*, 137–38.

Boettner, L. "Purgatory." In *EDT3*, 710–11.

Bradshaw, T. "Judgment of God." In *NDT2*, 477–79.

Buis, Harry. *The Doctrine of Eternal Punishment*. Philadelphia: Presbyterian and Reformed, 1957.

Cameron, Nigel M. de S., ed. *Universalism and the Doctrine of Hell*. Carlisle: Paternoster; Grand Rapids: Baker, 1992.

Cleveland, H. Z. "Reward." In *EDT1*, 951–52.

Crockett, William V., Z. J. Hayes, Clark H. Pinnock, and John F. Walvoord. *Four Views on Hell*. Grand Rapids: Zondervan, 1992.

Date, Christopher M., Gregory G. Stump, and Joshua W. Anderson, eds. *Rethinking Hell: Readings in Evangelical Conditionalism*. Eugene, OR: Cascade, 2014.

Davids, P. H. "Crown." In *EDT*, 310–11.

Dillow, Joseph C. *Final Destiny: The Future Reign of the Servant Kings*. 4th ed. Monument, CO: Grace Theology, 2018.

Donnelly, J. P. "Limbo." In EDT3, 496–97.

Fudge, Edward. *The Fire That Consumes: A Biblical and Historical Study of Final Punishment*. Houston: Providential, 1982.

Fudge, Edward, and Robert A. Peterson. *Two Views of Hell: A Biblical & Theological Dialogue*. Downers Grove, IL: InterVarsity Press, 2000.

Fuller, R. M. "Rewards." In *DLNT*, 1038–41.

Gerig, Wesley L. "Reward." In *BTDB*, 685–87.

Gerstner, John H. *Repent or Perish*. Ligonier, PA: Soli Deo Gloria, 1990.

Gundry, Stanley N., and Alan P. Stanley, eds. *Four Views on the Role of Works at the Final Judgment*. Grand Rapids: Zondervan, 2013.

Gundry, Stanley N., and William V. Crockett, eds. *Four Views on Hell*. Grand Rapids: Zondervan, 1996.

Helm, Paul. "Universalism and the Threat of Hell." *TrinJ* 4, No. 1 (Spring 1983): 35–43.

Hoekema, Anthony A. *The Bible and the Future*. Grand Rapids: Eerdmans, 1979, 253–73.

Hoehner, H. W. "Reward." In *NDBT*, 738–40.

Hubbard, D. A. "Last Judgment, The." In *EDT3*, 476–77.

Johnston, P. S. "Hell." In *NDBT*, 542–44.

Keller, Timothy, Christopher W. Morgan, and Robert A. Peterson. *Is Hell for Real or Does Everyone Go to Heaven?* Grand Rapids: Zondervan, 2011.

Lane, A. N. S. "Purgatory." In *NDT2*, 718–19.

Lunde, J. "Heaven and Hell." In *DJG*, 307–12.

Martin, James P. *The Last Judgment*. Grand Rapids: Eerdmans, 1983.

Milne, Bruce. *The Message of Heaven and Hell: Grace and Destiny*. Downers Grove, IL: InterVarsity Press, 2002.

Moore, Russell D. "Personal and Cosmic Eschatology." In *A Theology for the Church*, edited by Daniel L. Akin et al., 897–901. Nashville: B&H, 2007.

Morgan, Christopher W., and Robert A. Peterson, eds. *Hell under Fire: Modern Scholarship Reinvents Eternal Punishment*. Grand Rapids: Zondervan, 2004.

Morris, L. "Eternal Punishment." In *EDT3*, 281–82.

———. "Judgment." In *BTDB*, 436–37.

——— "Judgment, Day of." In *BTDB*, 437–39.

——— "Judgment Seat of Christ." In *BTDB*, 439–40.

Motyer, J. A. "Judgment." In *NDBT*, 612–15.

O'Donovan, O. M. T., and R. J. Song. "Punishment." In *NDT2*, 717–18.

Packer, J. I. "Evangelicals and the Way of Salvation: New Challenges to the Gospel—Universalism and Justification by Faith." In *Evangelical Affirmations*, edited by Kenneth S. Kantzer and Carl F. H. Henry, 107–36. Grand Rapids: Zondervan, 1990.

Peterson, Robert A. "Eternal Punishment." In *BTDB*, 212–13.

Phillips, Timothy R. "Hell." In *BTDB*, 338–40.

———. "Lake of Fire." In *BTDB*, 460.

Powys, David J. *'Hell': A Hard Look at a Hard Question: The Fate of the Unrighteous in New Testament Thought*. Carlisle: Paternoster, 1998.

Reid, D. G. "Heaven." In *GDT*, 368–72.

Seifrid, M. A. "Judgment." In *DLNT*, 621–25.

Shedd, William G. T. *The Doctrine of Endless Punishment*. Edinburgh: Banner of Truth Trust, 1986.

Shogren, G. S. "Hell, Abyss, Eternal Punishment." In *DLNT*, 459–62.

Tiessen, T. L. "Hell." In *GDT*, 372–76.

Travis, S. H. "Judgment." In *DJG*, 408–11.

———."Judgment." In *DPL*, 516–17.

———. "Judgment of God." In *NDT1*, 358.

Walls, Jerry L. *Heaven, Hell, and Purgatory: Rethinking the Things That Matter Most*. Grand Rapids: Brazos, 2015.

## SCRIPTURE MEMORY PASSAGE

**Revelation 20:11–13:** Then I saw a great white throne and him who was seated on it. From his presence earth and sky fled away, and no place was found for them. And I saw the dead, great and small, standing before the throne, and books were opened. Then another book was opened, which is the book of life. And the dead were judged by what was written in the books, according to what they had done. And the sea gave up the dead who were in it, Death and Hades gave up the dead who were in them, and they were judged, each one of them, according to what they had done.

## HYMN

### "O Quickly Come, Dread Judge of All"

(The tune is the familiar tune for "Eternal Father, Strong to Save")

*O quickly come, dread judge of all; for, awful*
*though thine advent be,*
*All shadows from the truth will fall, and*
*falsehood die, in sight of thee:*
*O quickly come; for doubt and fear like clouds*
*dissolve when thou art near.*

*O quickly come, great king of all; reign all around*
*us, and within;*
*Let sin no more our souls enthrall, let pain and*
*sorrow die with sin:*
*O quickly come; for thou alone canst make thy*
*scattered people one.*

*O quickly come, true life of all; for death is*
*mighty all around;*
*On ev'ry home his shadows fall, on ev'ry heart his*
*mark is found:*
*O quickly come; for grief and pain can never*
*cloud thy glorious reign.*

*O quickly come, sure light of all; for gloomy night*
*broods o'er our way;*
*And weakly souls begin to fall with weary*
*watching for the day:*
*O quickly come; for round thy throne no eye is*
*blind, no night is known.*

Author: Lawrence Tuttiett, 1854

## ALTERNATE HYMN

### "Great God, What Do I See and Hear!"

A tone of gloom and judgment pervades both these hymns, yet this alternate also contains a strong focus on the soul's preparing to meet Christ and a sense of joyful anticipation.

*Great God, what do I see and hear! The end of*
*things created!*

*The Judge of mankind doth appear, on clouds of*
*glory seated!*

*The trumpet sounds; the graves restore the dead*
    *which they contained before:*
*Prepare, my soul, to meet him.*

*The dead in Christ shall first arise, at the last*
    *trumpet's sounding,*
*Caught up to meet him in the skies, with joy their*
    *Lord surrounding;*
*No gloomy fears their souls dismay; his presence*
    *sheds eternal day*
*On those prepared to meet him.*

*But sinners, filled with guilty fears, behold his*
    *wrath prevailing;*

*For they shall rise, and find their tears and sighs*
    *are unavailing:*
*The day of grace is past and gone; trembling they*
    *stand before the throne,*
*All unprepared to meet him.*

*Great God, what do I see and hear! The end of*
    *things created!*
*The Judge of mankind doth appear, on clouds of*
    *glory seated!*
*Beneath his cross I view the day when heav'n and*
    *earth shall pass away,*
*And thus prepare to meet him.*

Author: First stanza, Anonymous, 1802;
Stanzas 2–4, William B. Collyer, 1812;
Alternate rendering, Thomas Cotterill, 1820

## CONTEMPORARY WORSHIP SONG

### "He Will Hold Me Fast"

*When I fear my faith will fail,*
*Christ will hold me fast;*
*When the tempter would prevail,*
*He will hold me fast.*
*I could never keep my hold,*
*Through life's fearful path,*
*For my love is often cold,*
*He must hold me fast.*

***Chorus***
*He will hold me fast,*
*He will hold me fast;*
*For my Savior loves me so,*
*He will hold me fast.*

*Those He saves are His delight,*
*Christ will hold me fast;*

*Precious in His holy sight,*
*He will hold me fast.*
*He'll not let my soul be lost,*
*His Promises shall last;*
*Bought by Him at such a cost,*
*He will hold me fast.*

*For my life He bled and died,*
*Christ will hold me fast;*
*Justice has been satisfied,*
*He will hold me fast.*
*Raised with Him to endless life,*
*He will hold me fast;*
*Till our faith is turned to sight,*
*When He comes at last.*

Words by Matthew Merker and Ada Habershon[17]

---

17. © 2016 Getty Music Publishing/Matthew Merker
Music (both admin. by Music Services). All rights reserved. BMI.

CHAPTER 57

# The New Heavens
# and New Earth

*What is heaven?*
*Is it a place?*
*How will the earth be renewed?*
*What will it be like to live in the new heavens and new earth?*

## EXPLANATION AND SCRIPTURAL BASIS

### A. We Will Live Eternally with God in New Heavens and a New Earth

After the final judgment, believers will enter into the full enjoyment of life in the presence of God forever. Jesus will say to us, "Come, you who are blessed by my Father, inherit the kingdom prepared for you from the foundation of the world" (Matt. 25:34). We will enter a kingdom where "no longer will there be anything accursed, but the throne of God and of the Lamb will be in it, and his servants will worship him" (Rev. 22:3).

When referring to this place, Christians often talk about living with God "in heaven" forever. But in fact the biblical teaching is richer than that: it tells us that there will be new heavens *and a new earth*—an entirely renewed creation—and we will live with God there.

The Lord promises through Isaiah, "For behold, I create *new heavens and a new earth*, and the former things shall not be remembered" (Isa. 65:17), and speaks of "the new heavens and the new earth that I make" (Isa. 66:22). Peter says, "According to his promise we are waiting for *new heavens and a new earth* in which righteousness dwells" (2 Peter 3:13). In John's vision of events to follow the final judgment, he says, "Then I saw a *new heaven and a new earth*, for the first heaven and the first earth had passed away" (Rev. 21:1). He goes on to tell us that there will also be a new kind of unification of heaven and earth, for he sees the holy city, the "new Jerusalem," coming "down out of heaven from God" (Rev. 21:2), and hears a voice proclaiming that "the dwelling place of God is with man. He will dwell with them, and they will be his people, and God himself will be with them as their God" (v. 3). So there will be a joining of heaven and earth in this new creation, and there we will live in the presence of God.

## 1. What Is Heaven?

During this present age, the place where God dwells is frequently called "heaven" in Scripture. The Lord says, "Heaven is my throne" (Isa. 66:1), and Jesus teaches us to pray, "Our Father in *heaven*" (Matt. 6:9). Jesus now "*has gone into heaven*, and is at the right hand of God" (1 Peter 3:22). In fact, heaven may be defined as follows: *heaven is the place where God most fully makes known his presence to bless.*

We discussed earlier how God is present everywhere[1] but how he especially manifests his presence to bless in certain places. The greatest manifestation of God's presence to bless is seen in heaven, where he makes his glory known, and where angels, other heavenly creatures, and redeemed saints all worship him.

## 2. Heaven Is a Place, Not Just a State of Mind

But someone may wonder how heaven can be joined together with earth. Clearly the earth is a *place* that exists at a certain location in our space-time universe, but can heaven also be thought of as a *place* that can be joined to the earth?

Outside of the evangelical world the idea of heaven as a place is often denied, chiefly because its existence can only be known from the testimony of Scripture. Recently even some evangelical scholars have been hesitant to affirm the fact that heaven is a place.[2] Should the fact that we *only* know about heaven from the Bible and cannot give any empirical evidence for it be a reason not to believe that heaven is a real place?

The New Testament teaches the idea of a location for heaven in several different ways and quite clearly. When Jesus ascended into heaven, the fact that he went to a *place* seems to be the entire point of the narrative, and the point that Jesus intended his disciples to understand by the way in which he gradually ascended even while speaking to them: "As they were looking on, he was lifted up, and a cloud took him out of their sight" (Acts 1:9; cf. Luke 24:51: "While he blessed them, he parted from them"). The angels exclaimed, "This Jesus, who was taken up from you *into heaven*, will come in the same way as you saw him go into heaven" (Acts 1:11). It is hard to imagine how the fact of Jesus' ascension to a *place* could be taught more clearly.

A similar conclusion can be drawn from the story of Stephen's death. Just before he was stoned, he, "full of the Holy Spirit, *gazed into heaven* and saw the glory of God, and Jesus standing at the right hand of God. And he said, 'Behold, I see the heavens

---

1. See chapter 11, pp. 206–11, on the omnipresence of God.

2. Millard Erickson, *Christian Theology*, 3rd ed. (Grand Rapids: Baker, 2013), 1232, says, "While heaven is both a place and a state, it is primarily a state," a statement that is difficult to understand. Something either is a place or it is not a place; it is not somewhat a place but "primarily a state." Even stronger is Donald Guthrie, who says of the New Testament, "We shall not expect, however, to find a description of a place, so much as the presence of a person" (Guthrie, *New Testament Theology* [Leicester: Inter-Varsity Press; Downers Grove, IL: InterVarsity Press, 1981], 875), and "Paul does not think of heaven as a place, but thinks of it in terms of the presence of God" (880). But does such a distinction make any sense? If a person is *present*, then by definition there is a *place*, because to be "present" means to be "located in this place."

opened, and the Son of Man standing at the right hand of God'" (Acts 7:55–56). He did not see mere symbols of a state of existence. It seems rather that his eyes were opened to see a spiritual dimension of reality that God has hidden from us in this present age, a dimension that nonetheless really does exist in our space/time universe, and within which Jesus now lives in his physical resurrection body, waiting even now for the time when he will return to earth.[3] Moreover, the fact that we will have resurrection bodies like Christ's resurrection body indicates that heaven will be a place, for in such physical bodies (made perfect, never to become weak or die again),[4] we will inhabit a specific place at a specific time, just as Jesus now does in his resurrection body.

The idea of heaven as a place is also the easiest sense in which to understand Jesus' promise, "I go to prepare a *place* [Gk. *topos*, 'place'] for you" (John 14:2). He speaks quite clearly of going from his existence in this world back to the Father, and then returning again: "If I go and prepare a *place* for you, I will come again and will take you to myself, that *where I am* you may be also" (John 14:3).

These texts lead us to conclude that heaven is even now a place—though one whose location is now unknown to us and whose existence is now unable to be perceived by our natural senses. It is this place of God's dwelling that will be somehow made new at the time of the final judgment and will be joined to a renewed earth.

## 3. The Physical Creation Will Be Renewed and We Will Continue to Exist and Act in It

In addition to a renewed heaven, God will make a "new earth" (2 Peter 3:13; Rev. 21:1). Several passages indicate that the physical creation will be renewed in a significant way. "The creation waits with eager longing for the revealing of the sons of God. For the creation was subjected to futility, not willingly, but because of him who subjected it, in hope that *the creation itself will be set free from its bondage to corruption and obtain the freedom of the glory of the children of God*" (Rom. 8:19–21).

But will earth simply be renewed, or will it be completely destroyed and replaced by another earth, newly created by God? Some passages appear to speak of an entire new creation. The author of Hebrews (quoting Ps. 102) tells us of the heavens and earth, "They will perish, but you remain; they will all wear out like a garment, like a robe you will roll them up, like a garment they will be changed" (Heb. 1:11–12). Later he tells us that God has promised, "Yet once more I will shake not only the earth but also the heavens," a shaking so severe as to involve "the removal of things that are shaken . . . in order that the things that cannot be shaken may remain" (Heb. 12:26–27). Peter says, "The day of the Lord will come like a thief, and then *the heavens will pass away with a roar*, and the heavenly bodies will be burned up and dissolved, and *the earth and the works that are*

---

3. See the discussion of Christ's resurrection body and his ascension in chapter 28, pp. 752–62.

4. See chapter 42, pp. 1021–26, on the nature of our resurrection bodies.

*done on it will be exposed*" (2 Peter 3:10). A similar picture is found in Revelation, where John says, "From his presence earth and sky fled away, and no place was found for them" (Rev. 20:11). Moreover, John says, "Then I saw a new heaven and a new earth, for the first heaven and the first earth had passed away, and the sea was no more" (Rev. 21:1).

Within the Protestant world, there has been disagreement as to whether the earth is to be destroyed completely and replaced or just changed and renewed. Berkhof says that Lutheran scholars have emphasized the fact that it will be an entirely new creation, while Reformed scholars have tended to emphasize those verses that say simply that this present creation will be renewed.[5] The Reformed position seems preferable here, for it is difficult to think that God would entirely annihilate his original creation, thereby seeming to give the devil the last word and scrapping the creation that was originally "very good" (Gen. 1:31). The passages above that speak of shaking and removing the earth and of the first earth passing away may simply refer to its existence in its present form, not its very existence itself.

### 4. Our Resurrection Bodies Will Be Part of the Renewed Creation

In the new heavens and new earth, there will be a place and activities for our resurrection bodies, which will never grow old or become weak or ill. A strong consideration in favor of this viewpoint is the fact that God made the original physical creation "very good" (Gen. 1:31). There is therefore nothing inherently sinful or evil or "unspiritual" about the physical world that God made or the creatures that he put in it, or about the physical bodies that he gave us at creation. Though all these things have been marred and distorted by sin, God will not completely destroy the physical world (which would be an acknowledgement that sin had frustrated and defeated God's purposes), but rather he will perfect the entire creation and bring it into harmony with the purposes for which he originally created it. Therefore, we can expect that in the new heavens and new earth there will be a fully perfect earth that is once again "very good." And we can expect that we will have physical bodies that will once again be "very good" in God's sight and that will function to fulfill the purposes for which he originally placed man on the earth.

When the author of Hebrews says that we do "not yet" see everything in subjection to man (Heb. 2:8), he implies that eventually all things will eventually be subject to us, under the kingship of the man Christ Jesus (note v. 9: "But we see . . . Jesus, crowned with glory and honor"). This will fulfill God's original plan to have everything in the world subject to the human beings that he had made.[6] In this sense, then, we will "inherit the earth" (Matt. 5:5) and reign over it as God originally intended.

For that reason, it should not strike us as surprising to find that some of the descriptions of life in heaven include features that are very much part of the physical or material

---

5. Louis Berkhof, *Systematic Theology* (Grand Rapids: Eerdmans, 1941), 737.

6. See pp. 573–75 and 1022 on God's original purpose to have man rule over all creation.

creation that God has made. We shall *eat and drink* at "the marriage supper of the Lamb" (Rev. 19:9). Jesus will once again *drink wine* with his disciples in the heavenly kingdom (Luke 22:18).[7] The "*river* of the water of life" will flow "from the throne of God and of the Lamb through the middle of the *street of the city*" (Rev. 22:1). The *tree of life* will bear "twelve kinds of fruit, yielding its fruit each month" (Rev. 22:2). There is no strong reason to say these expressions are merely symbolic, without any literal reference. Are symbolic banquets and symbolic wine and symbolic rivers and trees somehow superior to real banquets and real wine and real rivers and trees in God's eternal plan? These things are just some of the excellent features of the perfection and final goodness of the physical creation that God has made.

Of course, there are symbolic descriptions in the book of Revelation, and it is inevitable that at some points we will be unable to decide whether something is to be taken symbolically or literally. But it does not seem difficult to think that the description of the heavenly city with gates and a wall and foundations is a description of something that is literal and real, "the holy city Jerusalem coming down out of heaven from God, having the glory of God, its radiance like a most rare jewel" (Rev. 21:10–11). "The street of the city was pure gold, like transparent glass. . . . The kings of the earth will bring their glory into it, and its gates will never be shut by day—and there will be no night there. They will bring into it the glory and the honor of the nations" (Rev. 21:21–26).

While we may have some uncertainty about the understanding of certain details, it does not seem inconsistent with this picture to say that we will literally eat and drink in the new heavens and new earth, and carry on other physical activities as well. Since music certainly is prominent in the descriptions of heaven in Revelation, it is likely that both musical and artistic activities will be performed to the glory of God. Once we abandon the unbiblical notion of a merely spiritual (nonphysical) existence in the new heaven and new earth and begin to reflect on the concrete physicality of our existence in the age to come, then it will seem very likely that we will work at a remarkably wide range of investigation and development of the creation by technological, creative, and inventive means, thus exhibiting more of our excellent creation in the image of God, and thus discovering and enjoying more of the excellence of the creation over which God has given us dominion, and which he wants us to enjoy, with thanksgiving to him, forever.[8]

Moreover, since God is infinite and we can never exhaust his greatness (Ps. 145:3), and since we are finite creatures who will never equal God's knowledge or be omniscient,[9]

---

7. I'm unsure of this, but it is possible we will even eat meat, and not just vegetables, in the age to come, because Jesus ate fish after his resurrection (Luke 24:42–43).

8. Randy Alcorn explores thoughtfully and creatively a vast range of wonderful activities, especially physical activities in which we might be able to participate in the new heaven and new earth, as we interact with a renewed but still very physical creation; see Alcorn, *Heaven* (Wheaton, IL: Tyndale House, 2004).

9. Note that 1 Cor. 13:12 does not say that we will be omniscient or know everything (Paul could have said we will know all things, *ta panta*, if he had wished to do so) but, rightly translated, simply says that we will know in a fuller or more intensive way, "even as we have been known," that is, without any error or misconceptions in our knowledge.

we may expect that for all eternity we will be able to go on learning more about God and about his relationship to his creation. In this way we will continue the process of learning that was begun in this life, in which a life "fully pleasing to him" is one that includes continually "increasing in the knowledge of God" (Col. 1:10).

## 5. The New Creation Will Not Be "Timeless" but Will Include an Unending Succession of Moments

Although an old hymn speaks of the time "when the trumpet of the Lord shall sound and time shall be no more," Scripture does not give support to that idea. Certainly the heavenly city that receives its light from the glory of God (Rev. 21:23) will never experience darkness or night: "There will be no night there" (Rev. 21:25). But this does not mean that heaven will be a place where time is unknown or where things cannot be done one after another. Indeed, all the pictures of heavenly worship in the book of Revelation include words that are spoken one after another in coherent sentences and actions (such as falling down before God's throne and casting crowns before his throne) that involve a sequence of events. When we read that "the kings of the earth . . . will bring into it the glory and the honor of the nations" (Rev. 21:24–26), we see another activity that involves a sequence of events, one happening after another. And certainly that is the clear implication of the fact that the tree of life has twelve kinds of fruit, "yielding its fruit *each month*" (Rev. 22:2).[10]

Since we are finite creatures, we might also expect that we will always live in a succession of moments. Just as we will never attain to God's omniscience or omnipresence, so we shall never attain to God's eternity in the sense of seeing all time equally vividly and not living in a succession of moments or being limited by time. As finite creatures, we will rather live in a succession of moments that will never end.

## B. THE DOCTRINE OF THE NEW CREATION PROVIDES A GREAT MOTIVATION FOR STORING UP TREASURES IN HEAVEN RATHER THAN ON EARTH

When we consider the fact that this present creation is a temporary one and that our life in the new creation will last for eternity, we have a strong motivation for godly living and for living in such a way as to store up treasures in heaven. In reflecting on the fact that heaven and earth will be destroyed, Peter says the following:

> Since all these things are thus to be dissolved, what sort of people ought you to be in lives of holiness and godliness, waiting for and hastening the coming of the day of God, because of which the heavens will be set on fire and dissolved, and the heavenly bodies will melt as they burn! But according to his promise we are waiting for new heavens and a new earth in which righteousness dwells. (2 Peter 3:11–13)

---

10. On the KJV translation of Rev. 10:6, see chapter 11, p. 206n25.

And Jesus very explicitly tells us:

> Do not lay up for yourselves treasures on earth, where moth and rust destroy and where thieves break in and steal, but *lay up for yourselves treasures in heaven*, where neither moth nor rust destroys and where thieves do not break in and steal. For where your treasure is, there your heart will be also. (Matt. 6:19–21)[11]

## C. The New Creation Will Be a Place of Great Beauty and Abundance and Joy in the Presence of God

Amid all the questions that we naturally have concerning the new heavens and new earth, we must not lose sight of the fact that Scripture consistently portrays this new creation as a place of great beauty and joy. In the description of heaven in Revelation 21 and 22, this theme is repeatedly affirmed. It is a "holy city" (21:2), a place "prepared as a bride adorned for her husband" (21:2). In that place "death shall be no more, neither shall there be mourning, nor crying, nor pain anymore" (21:4). There we can drink "from the spring of the water of life without payment" (21:6). It is a city that has "the glory of God, its radiance like a most rare jewel, like a jasper, clear as crystal" (21:11). It is a city of immense size, whether the measurements be understood as literal or symbolic. Its length measures "12,000 stadia" (21:16), or about 1,400 miles (2,250 kilometers), and "its length and breadth *and height* are equal" (21:16). Parts of the city are constructed of immense precious jewels of various colors (21:18–21). It will be free from all evil, for "nothing unclean will ever enter it, nor anyone who does what is detestable or false, but only those who are written in the Lamb's book of life" (21:27). In that city we shall also have positions of rule over God's entire creation, for "they will reign forever and ever" (22:5).

But more important than all the physical beauty of the heavenly city, more important than the fellowship we will enjoy eternally with all God's people from all nations and all periods in history, more important than our freedom from pain and sorrow and physical suffering, and more important than reigning over God's kingdom—more important by far than any of these will be the fact that we will be in the presence of God and enjoying unhindered fellowship with him. "Behold, *the dwelling place of God is with man*. He will dwell with them, and they will be his people, and *God himself will be with them as their God*. He will wipe away every tear from their eyes" (21:3–4).

In the Old Testament, when the glory of God filled the temple, the priests were unable to stand and minister (2 Chron. 5:14). In the New Testament, when the glory of God surrounded the shepherds in the field outside Bethlehem, "they were filled with great fear" (Luke 2:9). But here in the heavenly city we will be able to endure the power

---

11. See the discussion of degrees of heavenly reward in chapter 56, pp. 1408–10.

and holiness of the presence of God's glory, for we will live *continually* in the atmosphere of the glory of God. "And the city has no need of sun or moon to shine on it, *for the glory of God gives it light, and its lamp is the Lamb*" (21:23). This will be the fulfillment of God's purpose to call us "to his own glory and excellence" (2 Peter 1:3); then we shall dwell continually in *"the presence of his glory with great joy"* (Jude 1:24; cf. Rom. 3:23; 8:18; 9:23; 1 Cor. 15:43; 2 Cor. 3:18; 4:17; Col. 3:4; 1 Thess. 2:12; Heb. 2:10; 1 Peter 5:1, 4, 10).

In that city we shall live in the presence of God, for "the throne of God and of the Lamb will be in it, and his servants will worship him" (22:3). From time to time here on earth we experience the joy of genuine worship of God, and we realize that it is our highest joy to be giving him glory. But in that city this joy will be multiplied many times over, and we will know the fulfillment of that for which we were created. Our greatest joy will be in seeing the Lord himself and in being with him forever.

When John speaks of the blessings of the heavenly city, the culmination of those blessings comes in the short statement, *"They will see his face,* and *his name will be on their foreheads"* (Rev. 22:4). When we look into the face of our Lord and he looks back at us with infinite love, he will see "his name" on our foreheads—in John's vision, this represents a proclamation to all that we are filled with his character, that we are conformed to the image of his Son. We will see in the face of God that he remembers and understands all the trials and hardships that we have endured for his sake on earth, and we will realize that he knows and values all the service that we have carried out in his name. "Well done, good and faithful servant. You have been faithful over a little; I will set you over much. Enter into the joy of your master" (Matt. 25:21).

We will also see in God's face the fulfillment of everything that we know to be good and right and desirable in the universe. We will experience the fulfillment of all the longing we have ever had to know perfect love, peace, and joy and to know truth and justice, holiness and wisdom, goodness and power, and glory and beauty. As we gaze into the face of our Lord, we will know more fully than ever before that *"in your presence there is fullness of joy, at your right hand are pleasures forevermore"* (Ps. 16:11). Then will be fulfilled the longing of our hearts with which we have cried out in the past, "One thing have I asked of the Lord, that will I seek after: that I may dwell in the house of the Lord all the days of my life, *to gaze upon the beauty of the Lord* and to inquire in his temple" (Ps. 27:4).

When we finally see the Lord face to face, our hearts will want nothing else. *"Whom have I in heaven but you?* And there is nothing on earth that I desire besides you. . . . God is the strength of my heart and my portion forever" (Ps. 73:25–26). Then with joy our hearts and voices will join with the redeemed from all ages and with the mighty armies of heaven singing, "Holy, holy, holy, is the Lord God Almighty, who was and is and is to come!" (Rev. 4:8).

## QUESTIONS FOR PERSONAL APPLICATION

1. In your Christian life to this point, have you spent much time thinking about life in the new heavens and new earth? Do you think there is a very strong longing for this in your heart? If it has not been strong, why do you think this has been the case?

2. In what ways has this chapter made you more excited about entering the heavenly city? What positive effects on your Christian life do you think would come about because of a stronger longing for the life to come?

3. Are you convinced that the new creation is a place where we will exist with physical bodies that are made perfect? If so, are you encouraged or discouraged by this idea? Why? Why do you think it is necessary to insist that heaven is an actual place even today?

4. What are some ways in which you already have stored up treasure in heaven rather than on earth? Are there more ways you could do that in your own life now? Do you think you will?

5. Sometimes people have thought that they would be bored in the life to come. Do you feel that way? What is a good answer to the objection that the eternal state will be boring?

6. Can you describe at all what you think you will feel like when you finally stand in the presence of God and see him face-to-face?

**Special Terms**

*heaven*

*new heavens and new earth*

## BIBLIOGRAPHY

(For explanation of this bibliography see note at bibliography to chapter 1, pp. 23–24. Complete bibliographical data may be found on pp. 1489–96.)

### SECTIONS IN EVANGELICAL SYSTEMATIC THEOLOGIES

*1. Anglican (Episcopalian)*

1882–92 . . . . . Litton, 600–605
2001 . . . . . . . . . Packer, 264–67
2013 . . . . . . . . Bird, 326–40
2013 . . . . . . . . Bray, 542–553

*2. Arminian (Wesleyan or Methodist)*

1875–76 . . . . . Pope, 3:447–54
1892–94 . . . . . Miley, 2:472–75
1940 . . . . . . . . . Wiley, 3:375–93
1960 . . . . . . . . Purkiser, 574–77
1983 . . . . . . . . . Carter, 2:1130–33, 1136–40
1992 . . . . . . . . . Oden, 3:441–68
2002 . . . . . . . . Cottrell, 573–87

*3. Baptist*

1767 . . . . . . . . Gill, 2:258–68, 329–40
1887 . . . . . . . . Boyce, 471–77

1907.........Strong, 1029–33
1976–83.....Henry, 4:593–614
1990–95.....Garrett, 2:889–904
2007.........Akin, 901–16
2013.........Erickson, 1124–33

**4. Dispensational**
1947.........Chafer, 4:433–39; 5:365–76
1949.........Thiessen, 397–99
2002–2005..Geisler, 4:294–326
2017.........MacArthur and Mayhue, 848–850

**5. Lutheran**
1917–24.....Pieper, 3:550–55
1934.........Mueller, 639–44

**6. Reformed (or Presbyterian)**
1724–58.....Edwards, 2:617–41
1871–73.....Hodge, 3:855–61
1878.........Dabney, 849–52
1894.........Shedd, 882–83
1906–11.....Bavinck, *RD*, 2:443–472, 4:716–20, 727–30
1910.........Vos, 3:173, 231–32
1938.........Berkhof, 736–38
1998.........Reymond, 979–1066
2008.........Van Genderen and Velema, 878–86
2010.........Allen and Swain, 389–91
2011.........Horton, 973–90
2013.........Frame, 39–40, 191, 1075–81
2013.........Culver, 1096–1110
2017.........Barrett, 721–56
2019.........Letham, 899–907

**7. Renewal (or charismatic/Pentecostal)**
1988–92.....Williams, 3:479–508

1993.........Menzies and Horton, 253–62
1995.........Horton, 635–637
2008.........Duffield and Van Cleave, 560–64

## SECTIONS IN REPRESENTATIVE ROMAN CATHOLIC SYSTEMATIC THEOLOGIES

**1. Roman Catholic: Traditional**
1955.........Ott, 476–79

**2. Roman Catholic: Post–Vatican II**
1980.........McBrien, 2:1141–42, 1155–56
2012.........*CCC*, paragraphs 1042–48

## OTHER WORKS

Alcorn, Randy C. *Heaven*. Wheaton, IL: Tyndale, 2004.

Allison, Gregg. *Historical Theology: An Introduction to Christian Doctrine; A Companion to Wayne Grudem's* Systematic Theology. Grand Rapids: Zondervan, 2011, 723–33.

Barber, Dan C., and Robert A. Peterson. *Life Everlasting: The Unfolding Story of Heaven.* Phillipsburg, NJ: P&R, 2012.

Blamires, Harry. *Knowing the Truth about Heaven and Hell.* Knowing the Truth, ed. J. I. Packer and Peter Kreeft. Ann Arbor: Servant, 1988.

Boa, Kenneth, and Robert M. Bowman. *Sense and Nonsense about Heaven and Hell.* Grand Rapids: Zondervan, 2007.

Carson, D. A. "Jerusalem, New" In *EDT3*, 442.

deSilva, D. A. "Heaven, New Heavens." In *DLNT*, 439–43.

Gilmore, John. *Probing Heaven: Key Questions on the Hereafter.* Grand Rapids: Baker, 1989.

Gomes, Alan W. *40 Questions about Heaven and Hell.* Grand Rapids: Kregel Academic, 2018.

Gouvea, F. Q. "New Heavens and New Earth." In *EDT3*, 589.

Grider, J. K. "Heaven." In *EDT3*, 370–71.

Hoekema, Anthony A. "The New Earth." In *The Bible and the Future*. Grand Rapids: Eerdmans, 1979, 274–87.

Johnston, P. S. "Heaven." In *NDBT*, 540–42.

Lincoln, Andrew T. *Paradise Now and Not Yet: Studies in the Role of the Heavenly Dimension in Paul's Thought with Special Reference to His Eschatology.* Society for New Testament Studies Monograph Series. London; New York: Cambridge, 1981.

Lunde, J. "Heaven and Hell." In *DJG*, 307–12.

MacArthur, John. *The Glory of Heaven: The Truth about Heaven, Angels, and Eternal Life.* 2nd ed. Wheaton, IL: Crossway, 2013.

Maile, J. F. "Heaven, Heavenlies, Paradise." In *DPL*, 381–83.

Meadors, Gary T. "New Heavens and a New Earth." In *BTDB*, 563–65.

———. "New Jerusalem." In *BTDB*, 564–65.

Middleton, J. Richard. *A New Heaven and a New Earth: Reclaiming Biblical Eschatology.* Grand Rapids: Baker, 2014.

Milne, Bruce. *The Message of Heaven and Hell: Grace and Destiny.* Downers Grove, IL: InterVarsity Press, 2002.

Moore, Russell D. "Personal and Cosmic Eschatology." In *A Theology for the Church*, edited by Daniel L. Akin et al., 901–2. Nashville: B&H, 2007.

Mullen, Bradford A. "Heaven, Heavens, Heavenlies." In *BTDB*, 332–35.

Murray, John. "Glorification." In *Redemption Accomplished and Applied*, 174–81. Grand Rapids: Eerdmans, 1955.

Reid, D. G. "Heaven." In *GDT*, 368–72.

Smith, S. M. "Intermediate State." In *EDT3*, 429–30.

Smith, Wilbur M. *The Biblical Doctrine of Heaven.* Chicago: Moody Publishers, 1968.

## SCRIPTURE MEMORY PASSAGE

**Revelation 21:3–4:** And I heard a loud voice from the throne saying, "Behold, the dwelling place of God is with man. He will dwell with them, and they will be his people, and God himself will be with them as their God. He will wipe away every tear from their eyes, and death shall be no more, neither shall there be mourning, nor crying, nor pain anymore, for the former things have passed away."

## HYMN

**"The Sands of Time Are Sinking"**

This is one of the most beautiful hymns ever written in any language. It expresses so clearly the fact that the beauty of heaven is the glory of God, and the great beauty of God's glory is the Lamb who died for us and now reigns.

*The sands of time are sinking, the dawn of heaven breaks,*
*The summer morn I've sighed for, the fair sweet morn awakes;*
*Dark, dark hath been the midnight, but dayspring is at hand,*
*And glory, glory dwelleth in Emmanuel's land.*

*The king there in his beauty without a veil is seen;*
*It were a well-spent journey though sev'n deaths lay between:*
*The Lamb with his fair army doth on Mount Zion stand,*
*And glory, glory dwelleth in Emmanuel's land.*

*O Christ, he is the fountain, the deep sweet well*
    *of love!*
    *The streams on earth I've tasted, more deep*
    *I'll drink above:*
*There to an ocean fullness his mercy doth expand,*
    *And glory, glory dwelleth in*
    *Emmanuel's land.*

*The bride eyes not her garment, but her dear*
    *bridegroom's face;*
    *I will not gaze at glory, but on my King*
    *of grace;*
*Not at the crown he giveth, but on his*
    *pierced hand:*
    *The lamb is all the glory of Emmanuel's land.*

Author: Anne R. Cousin, 1857

## CONTEMPORARY WORSHIP SONG

### "We Will Feast in the House of Zion"

*Chorus*
*We will feast in the house of Zion.*
*We will sing with our hearts restored.*
*He has done great things, we will say together.*
*We will feast and weep no more.*

*We will not be burned by the fire.*
*He is the LORD our God.*
*We are not consumed, by the flood,*
*Upheld, protected, gathered up.*

*In the dark of night, before the dawn,*
*My soul, be not afraid,*
*For the promised morning, oh how long?*
*Oh God of Jacob, be my strength.*

*Every vow we've broken and betrayed,*
*You are the Faithful one,*
*And from the garden to the grave,*
*Bind us together, bring shalom.*

Words by Sandra McCracken and Joshua Moore[12]

---

# APPENDIX 1

# Historic Confessions of Faith

This appendix reprints several of the most significant confessions of faith from various periods in the history of the church. From the ancient church I have included the four great ecumenical confessions: the Apostles' Creed (third–fourth centuries AD), the Nicene Creed (AD 325/381), the Athanasian Creed (late fourth–early fifth century AD), and the Chalcedonian Creed (AD 451). From the Protestant churches since the Reformation I have included four other confessions: the Thirty-Nine Articles (1571) [Church of England; also Methodist]; the Westminster Confession of Faith (1643–1646) [British Reformed and Presbyterian]; the New Hampshire Baptist Confession (1833); and the Baptist Faith and Message (1925/1963/2000) [Southern Baptist]. Finally, I have also included the Chicago Statement on Biblical Inerrancy (1978) because it was the product of a conference representing a broad variety of evangelical traditions and because it has gained widespread acceptance as a valuable doctrinal standard concerning an issue of recent and current controversy in the church.

Because of space limitations, I was able to include only one of the very long confessions of faith that came out of the Reformation, and I chose the Westminster Confession of Faith, which represents a doctrinal position very close to the position of this book. This meant that I did not have space to include either of the two great Lutheran confessions, the Augsburg Confession (1530) or the Formula of Concord (1576).[1]

Students who take the time to read these creeds thoughtfully will find that they provide excellent summaries of the doctrinal teachings of Scripture.

Following is a list of creeds found in this appendix:

---

1. These Lutheran confessions may conveniently be found in Philip Schaff, *The Creeds of Christendom*, 3 vols. (1931; repr., Grand Rapids: Baker, 1983), 3:3–73, 93–180.

## THE APOSTLES' CREED (THIRD–FOURTH CENTURY AD)

I believe in God the Father Almighty; Maker of heaven and earth.

And in Jesus Christ his only Son our Lord; who was conceived by the Holy Spirit,[2] born of the virgin Mary; suffered under Pontius Pilate, was crucified, dead and buried;[3] the third day he rose from the dead; he ascended into heaven; and sitteth at the right hand of God the Father Almighty; from thence he shall come to judge the quick and the dead.

I believe in the Holy Spirit; the holy catholic Church; the communion of saints; the forgiveness of sins; the resurrection of the body; and the life everlasting. Amen.

## THE NICENE CREED (AD 325; REVISED AT CONSTANTINOPLE AD 381)

I believe in one God the Father Almighty; Maker of heaven and earth, and of all things visible and invisible.

And in one Lord Jesus Christ, the only-begotten Son of God, begotten of the Father before all worlds, God of God, Light of Light, very God of very God, begotten, not made, being of one substance with the Father; by whom all things were made; who, for us men and for our salvation, came down from heaven, and was incarnate by the Holy Spirit of the Virgin Mary, and was made man; and was crucified also for us under Pontius Pilate; he suffered and was buried; and the third day he rose again, according to the Scriptures; and ascended into heaven, and sitteth on the right hand of the Father; and he shall come again, with glory, to judge both the quick and the dead; whose kingdom shall have no end.

And in the Holy Spirit, the Lord and Giver of Life; who proceedeth from the Father and the Son;[4] who with the Father and the Son together is worshiped and glorified; who

---

2. I have used the modern translation "Holy Spirit" instead of the archaic name "Holy Ghost" throughout the ancient creeds. (But I have not made such a change in the Westminster Confession, which is still used today in its original wording and which sometimes uses "Holy Ghost.")

3. I have not included the phrase, "he descended into hell," because it is not attested in the earliest versions of the Apostles' Creed, and because of the doctrinal difficulties associated with it (see further discussion in chapter 27, pp. 725–36).

4. The phrase "and the Son" was added after the Council of Constantinople in 381 but is commonly included in the text of the Nicene Creed as used by Protestant and Roman Catholic churches today. The phrase is not included in the text used by Orthodox churches. (See discussion in chapter 14, pp. 289–90.) The phrase "God of God" was not in the version of 381 but was in the version of 325 and is commonly included today.

spake by the Prophets. And one Holy Catholic and Apostolic Church. I acknowledge one Baptism for the remission of sins; and I look for the resurrection of the dead, and the life of the world to come. Amen.

## THE CHALCEDONIAN CREED (AD 451)

We, then, following the holy Fathers, all with one consent, teach men to confess one and the same Son, our Lord Jesus Christ, the same perfect in Godhead and also perfect in manhood; truly God and truly man, of a reasonable soul and body; consubstantial with the Father according to the Godhead, and consubstantial with us according to the Manhood; in all things like unto us, without sin; begotten before all ages of the Father according to the Godhead, and in these latter days, for us and for our salvation, born of the Virgin Mary, the Mother of God, according to the Manhood; one and the same Christ, Son, Lord, Only-begotten, to be acknowledged in two natures, inconfusedly, unchangeably, indivisibly, inseparably; the distinction of natures being by no means taken away by the union, but rather the property of each nature being preserved, and concurring in one Person and one Subsistence, not parted or divided into two persons, but one and the same Son, and only begotten, God the Word, the Lord Jesus Christ, as the prophets from the beginning have declared concerning him, and the Lord Jesus Christ himself has taught us, and the Creed of the holy Fathers has handed down to us.

## THE ATHANASIAN CREED (FOURTH–FIFTH CENTURIES AD)

1. Whosoever will be saved: before all things it is necessary that he hold the Catholic Faith:
2. Which Faith except every one do keep whole and undefiled: without doubt he shall perish everlastingly.
3. And the Catholic Faith is this: That we worship one God in Trinity, and Trinity in Unity;
4. Neither confounding the Persons: nor dividing the Substance.
5. For there is one Person of the Father: another of the Son: and another of the Holy Spirit.
6. But the Godhead of the Father, of the Son, and of the Holy Spirit, is all one: the Glory equal, the Majesty coeternal.
7. Such as the Father is: such is the Son: and such is the Holy Spirit.
8. The Father uncreated: the Son uncreated: and the Holy Spirit uncreated.
9. The Father incomprehensible: the Son incomprehensible: and the Holy Spirit incomprehensible.
10. The Father eternal: the Son eternal: and the Holy Spirit eternal.
11. And yet they are not three eternals: but one eternal.

12. And also there are not three uncreated: nor three incomprehensibles, but one uncreated: and one incomprehensible.

13. So likewise the Father is Almighty: the Son Almighty: and the Holy Spirit Almighty.

14. And yet they are not three Almighties: but one Almighty.

15. So the Father is God: the Son is God: and the Holy Spirit is God.

16. And yet they are not three Gods: but one God.

17. So likewise the Father is Lord: the Son Lord: and the Holy Spirit Lord.

18. And yet not three Lords: but one Lord.

19. For like as we are compelled by the Christian verity: to acknowledge every Person by himself to be God and Lord:

20. So are we forbidden by the Catholic Religion: to say, There be three Gods, or three Lords.

21. The Father is made of none: neither created, nor begotten.

22. The Son is of the Father alone: not made, nor created: but begotten.

23. The Holy Spirit is of the Father and of the Son: neither made, nor created, nor begotten: but proceeding.

24. So there is one Father, not three Fathers: one Son, not three Sons: one Holy Spirit, not three Holy Spirits.

25. And in this Trinity none is afore, or after another: none is greater, or less than another.

26. But the whole three Persons are coeternal, and coequal.

27. So that in all things, as aforesaid: the Unity in Trinity, and the Trinity in Unity, is to be worshipped.

28. He therefore that will be saved, must thus think of the Trinity.

29. Furthermore it is necessary to everlasting salvation: that he also believe rightly the Incarnation of our Lord Jesus Christ.

30. For the right Faith is, that we believe and confess: that our Lord Jesus Christ, the Son of God, is God and Man;

31. God, of the Substance of the Father; begotten before the worlds: and Man, of the Substance of his Mother, born in the world.

32. Perfect God: and perfect Man, of a reasonable soul and human flesh subsisting.

33. Equal to the Father, as touching his Godhead: and inferior to the Father as touching his Manhood.

34. Who although he be God and Man; yet he is not two, but one Christ.

35. One; not by conversion of the Godhead into flesh: but by taking of the Manhood into God.

36. One altogether; not by confusion of Substance: but by unity of Person.

37. For as the reasonable soul and flesh is one man; so God and Man is one Christ;

38. Who suffered for our salvation: descended into hell: rose again the third day from the dead.

39. He ascended into heaven, he sitteth on the right hand of the Father God Almighty.
40. From whence he shall come to judge the quick and the dead.
41. At whose coming all men shall rise again with their bodies;
42. And shall give account for their own works.
43. And they that have done good shall go into life everlasting: and they that have done evil, into everlasting fire.
44. This is the Catholic Faith: which except a man believe faithfully, he can not be saved.

# ARTICLES OF RELIGION (THIRTY-NINE ARTICLES) (1571: CHURCH OF ENGLAND)

## I. OF FAITH IN THE HOLY TRINITY.

There is but one living and true God, everlasting, without body, parts, or passions; of infinite power, wisdom, and goodness; the Maker, and Preserver of all things both visible and invisible. And in unity of this Godhead there be three Persons, of one substance, power, and eternity: the Father, the Son, and the Holy Spirit.

## II. OF THE WORD OR SON OF GOD, WHICH WAS MADE VERY MAN.

The Son, which is the Word of the Father, begotten from everlasting of the Father, the very and eternal God, and of one substance with the Father, took Man's nature in the womb of the blessed Virgin, of her substance: so that two whole and perfect Natures, that is to say, the Godhead and Manhood, were joined together in one Person, never to be divided, whereof is one Christ, very God, and very Man; who truly suffered, was crucified, dead and buried, to reconcile his Father to us, and to be a sacrifice, not only for original guilt, but also for actual sins of men.

## III. OF THE GOING DOWN OF CHRIST INTO HELL.

As Christ died for us, and was buried, so also is it to be believed, that he went down into Hell.

## IV. OF THE RESURRECTION OF CHRIST.

Christ did truly rise again from death, and took again his body, with flesh, bones, and all things appertaining to the perfection of Man's nature; wherewith he ascended into Heaven, and there sitteth, until he return to judge all Men at the last day.

## V. OF THE HOLY SPIRIT.

The Holy Spirit, proceeding from the Father and the Son, is of one substance, majesty, and glory, with the Father and the Son, very and eternal God.

## VI. OF THE SUFFICIENCY OF THE HOLY SCRIPTURES FOR SALVATION.

Holy Scripture containeth all things necessary to salvation: so that whatsoever is not read therein, nor may be proved thereby, is not to be required of any man, that it should be believed as an article of the Faith, or be thought requisite or necessary to salvation. In the name of the Holy Scripture we do understand those canonical Books of the Old and New Testament, of whose authority was never any doubt in the Church.

## OF THE NAMES AND NUMBER OF THE CANONICAL BOOKS.

| | |
|---|---|
| Genesis, | The First Book of Chronicles, |
| Exodus, | The Second Book of Chronicles, |
| Leviticus, | The First Book of Esdras, |
| Numbers, | The Second Book of Esdras, |
| Deuteronomy, | The Book of Esther, |
| Joshua, | The Book of Job, |
| Judges, | The Psalms, |
| Ruth, | The Proverbs, |
| The First Book of Samuel, | Ecclesiastes or Preacher, |
| The Second Book of Samuel, | Cantica, or Song of Solomon, |
| The First Book of Kings, | Four Prophets the greater, |
| The Second Book of Kings, | Twelve Prophets the less. |

And the other Books the Church doth read for example of life and instruction of manners; but yet doth it not apply to them to establish any doctrine: such are these following:

| | |
|---|---|
| The Third Book of Esdras, | Baruch the Prophet, |
| The Fourth Book of Esdras, | The Song of the Three Children, |
| The Book of Tobias, | The Story of Susanna, |
| The Book of Judith, | Of Bel and the Dragon, |
| The rest of the Book of Esther, | The Prayer of Manasses, |
| The Book of Wisdom, | The First Book of Maccabees, |
| Jesus the Son of Sirach, | The Second Book of Maccabees. |

All the Books of the New Testament, as they are commonly received, we do receive, and account them Canonical.

## VII. OF THE OLD TESTAMENT.

The Old Testament is not contrary to the New: for both in the Old and New Testament everlasting life is offered to mankind by Christ, who is the only Mediator between God and Man, being both God and Man. Wherefore they are not to be heard, which feign that the old Fathers did look only for transitory promises. Although the Law given from God by Moses, as touching Ceremonies and Rites, do not bind Christian men, nor the Civil precepts thereof ought of necessity to be received in any commonwealth; yet notwithstanding, no Christian man whatsoever is free from the obedience of the Commandments which are called Moral.

## VIII. Of the Creeds.

The Nicene Creed, and that which is commonly called the Apostles' Creed, ought thoroughly to be received and believed: for they may be proved by most certain warrants of Holy Scripture.

## IX. Of Original or Birth-Sin.

Original Sin standeth not in the following of Adam, (as the Pelagians do vainly talk;) but it is the fault and corruption to the Nature of every man, that naturally is ingendered of the offspring of Adam; whereby man is very far gone from original righteousness, and is of his own nature inclined to evil, so that the flesh lusteth always contrary to the spirit; and therefore in every person born into this world, it deserveth God's wrath and damnation. And this infection of nature doth remain, yea in them that are regenerated; whereby the lust of the flesh, called in the Greek *phronēma sarkos* (which some do expound the wisdom, some sensuality, some of the affection, some of the desire, of the flesh), is not subject to the Law of God. And although there is no condemnation for them that believe and are baptized; yet the Apostle doth confess, that concupiscence and lust hath of itself the nature of sin.

## X. Of Free-Will.

The condition of Man after the fall of Adam is such, that he cannot turn and prepare himself, by his own natural strength and good works, to faith, and calling upon God. Wherefore we have no power to do good works pleasant and acceptable to God, without the grace of God by Christ preventing us, that we may have a good will, and working with us, when we have that good will.

## XI. Of the Justification of Man.

We are accounted righteous before God, only for the merit of our Lord and Saviour Jesus Christ by Faith, and not for our own works or deservings. Wherefore, that we are justified by Faith only, is a most wholesome Doctrine, and very full of comfort, as more largely is expressed in the Homily of Justification.

## XII. Of Good Works.

Albeit that Good Works, which are the fruits of Faith, and follow after Justification, cannot put away our sins, and endure the severity of God's judgment; yet are they pleasing and acceptable to God in Christ, and do spring out necessarily of a true and lively faith; insomuch that by them a lively Faith may be as evidently known as a tree discerned by the fruit.

## XIII. Of Works Before Justification.

Works done before the grace of Christ, and the Inspiration of his Spirit, are not pleasant to God, forasmuch as they spring not of faith in Jesus Christ; neither do they make men meet to receive grace, or (as the School-authors say) deserve grace of congruity: yea rather, for that they are not done as God hath willed and commanded them to be done, we doubt not but they have the nature of sin.

## XIV. Of Works of Supererogation.

Voluntary Works besides, over and above, God's Commandments, which they call Works of Supererogation, cannot be taught without arrogancy and impiety: for by them men do declare, that they do not only render unto God as much as they are bound to do, but that they do more for his sake, than of bounden duty is required: whereas Christ saith plainly, When ye have done all that are commanded to you, say, We are unprofitable servants.

## XV. Of Christ Alone without Sin.

Christ in the truth of our nature was made like unto us in all things, sin only except, from which he was clearly void, both in his flesh, and in his spirit. He came to be the Lamb without spot, who, by sacrifice of himself once made, should take away the sins of the world; and sin, (as Saint John saith) was not in him. But all we the rest, although baptized, and born again in Christ, yet offend in many things; and if we say we have no sin, we deceive ourselves, and the truth is not in us.

## XVI. Of Sin after Baptism.

Not every deadly sin willingly committed after Baptism is sin against the Holy Spirit, and unpardonable. Wherefore the grant of repentance is not to be denied to such as fall into sin after Baptism. After we have received the Holy Spirit, we may depart from grace given, and fall into sin, and by the grace of God we may arise again, and amend our lives. And therefore they are to be condemned, which say, they can no more sin as long as they live here, or deny the place of forgiveness to such as truly repent.

## XVII. Of Predestination and Election.

Predestination to Life is the everlasting purpose of God, whereby (before the foundations of the world were laid) he hath constantly decreed by his counsel secret to us, to deliver from curse and damnation those whom he hath chosen in Christ out of mankind, and to bring them by Christ to everlasting salvation, as vessels made to honour.

Wherefore, they which be endued with so excellent a benefit of God, be called according to God's purpose by his Spirit working in due season: they through Grace obey the calling: they be justified freely: they be made sons of God by adoption: they be made like the image of his only-begotten Son Jesus Christ: they walk religiously in good works, and at length, by God's mercy, they attain to everlasting felicity.

As the godly consideration of Predestination, and our Election in Christ, is full of sweet, pleasant, and unspeakable comfort to godly persons, and such as feel in themselves the working of the Spirit of Christ, mortifying the works of the flesh, and their earthly members, and drawing up their mind to high and heavenly things, as well because it doth greatly establish and confirm their faith of eternal Salvation to be enjoyed through Christ, as because it doth fervently kindle their love towards God: So, for curious and carnal persons, lacking the Spirit of Christ, to have continually before their eyes the sentence of God's Predestination, is a most dangerous downfall, whereby the Devil doth thrust them either into desperation, or into wretchlessness of most unclean living, no less perilous than desperation.

Furthermore, we must receive God's promises in such wise, as they be generally set forth to us in Holy Scripture: and, in our doings, that Will of God is to be followed, which we have expressly declared unto us in the Word of God.

### XVIII. Of Obtaining Eternal Salvation Only by the Name of Christ.

They also are to be had accursed that presume to say, That every man shall be saved by the Law or Sect which he professeth, so that he be diligent to frame his life according to that Law, and the light of Nature. For Holy Scripture doth set out unto us only the Name of Jesus Christ, whereby men must be saved.

### XIX. Of the Church.

The visible Church of Christ is a congregation of faithful men, in the which the pure Word of God is preached, and the Sacraments be duly ministered according to Christ's ordinance, in all those things that of necessity are requisite to the same.

As the Church of Jerusalem, Alexandria, and Antioch, have erred; so also the Church of Rome hath erred, not only their living and manner of Ceremonies, but also in matters of Faith.

### XX. Of the Authority of the Church.

The Church hath power to decree Rites or Ceremonies, and authority in Controversies of Faith: and yet it is not lawful for the Church to ordain any thing that is contrary to God's Word written, neither may it so expound one place of Scripture, that it be repugnant to another. Wherefore, although the Church be a witness and a keeper of Holy Writ, yet, as it ought not to decree any thing against the same, so besides the same ought it not to enforce any thing to be believed for necessity of Salvation.

## XXI. Of the Authority of General Councils.

General Councils may not be gathered together without the commandment and will of Princes. And when they be gathered together (foreasmuch as they be an assembly of men, whereof all be not governed with the Spirit and Word of God) they may err, and sometimes have erred, even in things pertaining unto God. Wherefore, things ordained by them as necessary to salvation have neither strength nor authority, unless it may be declared that they be taken out of holy Scripture.

## XXII. Of Purgatory.

The Romish Doctrine concerning Purgatory, Pardons, Worshipping and Adoration, as well of Images as of Relics, and also Invocation of Saints, is a fond thing, vainly invented, and grounded upon no warranty of Scripture, but rather repugnant to the Word of God.

## XXIII. Of Ministering in the Congregation.

It is not lawful for any man to take upon him the office of public preaching, or ministering the Sacraments in the Congregation, before he be lawfully called, and sent to execute the same. And those we ought to judge lawfully called and sent, which be chosen and called to this work by men who have public authority given unto them in the Congregation, to call and send Ministers into the Lord's vineyard.

## XXIV. Of Speaking in the Congregation in Such a Tongue As the People Understandeth.

It is a thing plainly repugnant to the Word of God, and the custom of the Primitive Church, to have public Prayer in the Church, or to minister the Sacraments in a tongue not understanded of the people.

## XXV. Of the Sacraments.

Sacraments ordained of Christ be not only badges or tokens of Christian men's profession, but rather they be certain sure witnesses, and effectual signs of grace, and God's good will toward us, by the which he doth work invisibly in us, and doth not only quicken, but also strengthen and confirm our Faith in him.

There are two Sacraments ordained of Christ our Lord in the Gospel, that is to say, Baptism, and the Supper of the Lord.

Those five commonly called Sacraments, that is to say, Confirmation, Penance, Orders, Matrimony, and Extreme Unction, are not to be counted for Sacraments of the Gospel, being such as have grown partly of the corrupt following of the Apostles, partly are states of life allowed in the Scriptures; but yet have not like nature of Sacraments with Baptism, and the Lord's Supper, for that they have not any visible sign or ceremony ordained of God.

The Sacraments were not ordained of Christ to be gazed upon, or to be carried about, but that we should duly use them. And in such only as worthily receive the same, they have a wholesome effect or operation: but they that receive them unworthily, purchase to themselves damnation, as Saint Paul saith.

## XXVI. OF THE UNWORTHINESS OF THE MINISTERS, WHICH HINDERS NOT THE EFFECT OF THE SACRAMENT.

Although in the visible Church the evil be ever mingled with the good, and sometimes the evil have chief authority in the Ministration of the Word and Sacraments, yet forasmuch as they do not the same in their own name, but in Christ's, and do minister by his commission and authority, we may use their Ministry, both in hearing the Word of God, and in receiving the Sacraments. Neither is the effect of Christ's ordinance taken away by their wickedness, nor the grace of God's gifts diminished from such as by faith, and rightly, do receive the Sacraments ministered unto them; which be effectual, because of Christ's institution and promise, although they be ministered by evil men.

Nevertheless, it appertaineth to the discipline of the Church, that inquiry be made of evil Ministers, and that they be accused by those that have knowledge of their offences; and finally, being found guilty, by just judgment be deposed.

## XXVII. OF BAPTISM.

Baptism is not only a sign of profession, and mark of difference, whereby Christian men are discerned from others that be not christened, but it is also a sign of Regeneration or New-Birth, whereby, as by an instrument, they that receive Baptism rightly are grafted into the Church; the promises of forgiveness of sin, and of our adoption to be the sons of God by the Holy Spirit, are visibly signed and sealed; Faith is confirmed, and Grace increased by virtue of prayer unto God. The Baptism of young Children is in any wise to be retained in the Church, as most agreeable with the institution of Christ.

## XXVIII. OF THE LORD'S SUPPER.

The Supper of the Lord is not only a sign of the love that Christians ought to have among themselves one to another; but rather it is a Sacrament of our Redemption by Christ's death: insomuch that to such as rightly, worthily, and with faith, receive the same, the Bread which we break is a partaking of the Body of Christ; and likewise the Cup of Blessing is a partaking of the Blood of Christ.

Transubstantiation (or the change of the substance of Bread and Wine) in the Supper of the Lord, cannot be proved by Holy Writ; but is repugnant to the plain words of Scripture, overthroweth the nature of a Sacrament, and hath given occasion to many superstitions.

The Body of Christ is given, taken, and eaten, in the Supper, only after an heavenly and spiritual manner. And the mean whereby the Body of Christ is received and eaten in the Supper, is Faith.

The Sacrament of the Lord's Supper was not by Christ's ordinance reserved, carried about, lifted up, or worshipped.

## XXIX. Of the Wicked, Which Eat Not the Body of Christ in the Use of the Lord's Supper.

The Wicked, and such as be void of a lively faith, although they do carnally and visibly press with their teeth (as Saint Augustine saith) the Sacrament of the Body and Blood of Christ; yet in no wise are they partakers of Christ: but rather, to their condemnation, do eat and drink the sign or Sacrament of so great a thing.

## XXX. Of Both Kinds.

The Cup of the Lord is not to be denied to the Lay-people: for both the parts of the Lord's Sacrament, by Christ's ordinance and commandment, ought to be ministered to all Christian men alike.

## XXXI. Of the One Oblation of Christ Finished Upon the Cross.

The Offering of Christ once made is that perfect redemption, propitiation, and satisfaction, for all the sins of the whole world, both original and actual; and there is none other satisfaction for sin, but that alone. Wherefore the sacrifices of Masses, in the which it was commonly said that the Priest did offer Christ for the quick and the dead, to have remission of pain or guilt, were blasphemous fables, and dangerous deceits.

## XXXII. Of the Marriage of Priests.

Bishops, Priests, and Deacons, are not commanded by God's Law, either to vow the estate of single life, or to abstain from marriage: therefore it is lawful for them, as for all other Christian men, to marry at their own discretion, as they shall judge the same to serve better to godliness.

## XXXIII. Of Excommunicate Persons, How They Are to be Avoided.

That person which by open denunciation of the Church is rightly cut off from the unity of the Church, and excommunicated, ought to be taken of the whole multitude of the faithful, as a Heathen and Publican, until he be openly reconciled by penance, and received into the Church by a judge that hath authority thereunto.

## XXXIV. Of the Traditions of the Church.

It is not necessary that Traditions and Ceremonies be in all places one, or utterly like; for at all times they have been divers, and may be changed according to the diversities of countries, times, and men's manners, so that nothing be ordained against God's Word. Whosoever through his private judgment, willingly and purposely, doth openly break the Traditions and Ceremonies of the Church, which be not repugnant to the Word of God, and be ordained and approved by common authority, ought to be rebuked openly, (that others may fear to do the like) as he that offendeth against the common order of the Church, and hurteth the authority of the Magistrate, and woundeth the consciences of the weak brethren.

Every particular or national Church hath authority to ordain, change, and abolish, Ceremonies or Rites of the Church ordained only by man's authority, so that all things be done to edifying.

## XXXV. Of the Homilies.

The Second Book of Homilies, the several titles whereof we have joined under this Article, doth contain a godly and wholesome Doctrine, and necessary for these times, as doth the former Book of Homilies, which were set forth in the time of Edward the Sixth; and therefore we judge them to be read in Churches by the Ministers, diligently and distinctly, that they may be understanded of the people.

### Of The Names of the Homilies

1. Of the right Use of the Church.
2. Against Peril of Idolatry.
3. Of the repairing and keeping clean of Churches.
4. Of good Works: first of Fasting.
5. Against Gluttony and Drunkenness.
6. Against Excess of Apparel.
7. Of Prayer.
8. Of the Place and Time of Prayer.
9. That Common Prayers and Sacraments ought to be ministered in a known tongue.
10. Of the reverend Estimation of God's Word.
11. Of Alms-doing.
12. Of the Nativity of Christ.
13. Of the Passion of Christ.
14. Of the Resurrection of Christ.
15. Of the worthy receiving of the Sacrament of the Body and Blood of Christ.
16. Of the Gifts of the Holy Spirit.
17. For the Rogation-days.
18. Of the State of Matrimony.
19. Of Repentance.
20. Against Idleness.
21. Against Rebellion.

## XXXVI. Of Consecration of Bishops and Ministers.

The Book of Consecration of Archbishops and Bishops, and Ordering of Priests and Deacons, lately set forth in the time of Edward the Sixth, and confirmed at the same time by authority of Parliament, doth contain all things necessary to such Consecration and Ordering: neither hath it any thing that of itself is superstitious and ungodly. And therefore whosoever are consecrated or ordered according to the Rites of that Book, since the second year of the forenamed King Edward unto this time, or hereafter shall be consecrated or ordered according to the same Rites; we decree all such to be rightly, orderly, and lawfully consecrated and ordered.

## XXXVII. Of the Civil Magistrates.

The Queen's Majesty hath the chief power in this Realm of England, and other her Dominions, unto whom the chief Government of all Estates of this Realm, whether they be Ecclesiastical or Civil, in all causes doth appertain, and is not, nor ought to be, subject to any foreign Jurisdiction.

Where we attribute to the Queen's Majesty the chief government, by which Titles we understand the minds of some slanderous folks to be offended; we give not to our Princes the ministering either of God's Word, or of the Sacraments, the which thing the Injunctions also lately set forth by Elizabeth our Queen do most plainly testify; but that only prerogative, which we see to have been given always to all godly Princes in holy Scriptures by God himself; that is, that they should rule all estates and degrees committed to their charge by God, whether they be Ecclesiastical or Temporal, and restrain with the civil sword the stubborn and evil-doers.

The Bishop of Rome hath no jurisdiction in this Realm of England.

The Laws of the Realm may punish Christian men with death, for heinous and grievous offences.

It is lawful for Christian men, at the commandment of the Magistrate, to wear weapons, and serve in the wars.

## XXXVIII. Of Christian Men's Goods, Which Are Not Common.

The Riches and Goods of Christians are not common, as touching the right, title, and possession of the same; as certain Anabaptists do falsely boast. Notwithstanding, every man ought, of such things as he possesseth, liberally to give alms to the poor, according to his ability.

## XXXIX. Of a Christian Man's Oath.

As we confess that vain and rash Swearing is forbidden Christian men by our Lord Jesus Christ, and James his Apostle, so we judge, that Christian Religion doth not prohibit, but that a man may swear when the Magistrate requireth, in a cause of faith and charity, so it be done according to the Prophet's teaching, in justice, judgment, and truth.

# WESTMINSTER CONFESSION OF FAITH (1643–46) [TEXT OF AMERICAN VERSION]

## CHAPTER 1: OF THE HOLY SCRIPTURE

1. Although the light of nature, and the works of creation and providence do so far manifest the goodness, wisdom, and power of God, as to leave men unexcusable; yet are they not sufficient to give that knowledge of God, and of his will, which is necessary unto salvation. Therefore it pleased the Lord, at sundry times, and in divers manners, to reveal himself, and to declare that his will unto his church; and afterwards, for the better preserving and propagating of the truth, and for the more sure establishment and comfort of the church against the corruption of the flesh, and the malice of Satan and of the world, to commit the same wholly unto writing: which maketh the holy Scripture to be most necessary; those former ways of God's revealing his will unto his people being now ceased.

2. Under the name of holy Scripture, or the Word of God written, are now contained all the books of the Old and New Testaments, which are these:

### Old Testament

| | | | |
|---|---|---|---|
| Genesis | 1 Kings | Ecclesiastes | Obadiah |
| Exodus | 2 Kings | Song of Songs | Jonah |
| Leviticus | 1 Chronicles | Isaiah | Micah |
| Numbers | 2 Chronicles | Jeremiah | Nahum |
| Deuteronomy | Ezra | Lamentations | Habakkuk |
| Joshua | Nehemiah | Ezekiel | Zephaniah |
| Judges | Esther | Daniel | Haggai |
| Ruth | Job | Hosea | Zechariah |
| 1 Samuel | Psalms | Joel | Malachi |
| 2 Samuel | Proverbs | Amos | |

### New Testament

| | | | |
|---|---|---|---|
| Matthew | 2 Corinthians | 1 Timothy | 2 Peter |
| Mark | Galatians | 2 Timothy | 1 John |
| Luke | Ephesians | Titus | 2 John |
| John | Philippians | Philemon | 3 John |
| Acts | Colossians | Hebrews | Jude |
| Romans | 1 Thessalonians | James | Revelation |
| 1 Corinthians | 2 Thessalonians | 1 Peter | |

All which are given by inspiration of God to be the rule of faith and life.

3. The books commonly called Apocrypha, not being of divine inspiration, are no part of the canon of the Scripture, and therefore are of no authority in the

church of God, nor to be any otherwise approved, or made use of, than other human writings.

4. The authority of the holy Scripture, for which it ought to be believed, and obeyed, dependeth not upon the testimony of any man, or church; but wholly upon God (who is truth itself) the author thereof: and therefore it is to be received, because it is the Word of God.

5. We may be moved and induced by the testimony of the church to an high and reverent esteem of the holy Scripture. And the heavenliness of the matter, the efficacy of the doctrine, the majesty of the style, the consent of all the parts, the scope of the whole (which is, to give all glory to God), the full discovery it makes of the only way of man's salvation, the many other incomparable excellencies, and the entire perfection thereof, are arguments whereby it doth abundantly evidence itself to be the Word of God: yet notwithstanding, our full persuasion and assurance of the infallible truth and divine authority thereof, is from the inward work of the Holy Spirit bearing witness by and with the Word in our hearts.

6. The whole counsel of God concerning all things necessary for his own glory, man's salvation, faith and life, is either expressly set down in Scripture, or by good and necessary consequence may be deduced from Scripture: unto which nothing at any time is to be added, whether by new revelations of the Spirit, or traditions of men. Nevertheless, we acknowledge the inward illumination of the Spirit of God to be necessary for the saving understanding of such things as are revealed in the Word: and that there are some circumstances concerning the worship of God, and government of the church, common to human actions and societies, which are to be ordered by the light of nature, and Christian prudence, according to the general rules of the Word, which are always to be observed.

7. All things in Scripture are not alike plain in themselves, nor alike clear unto all: yet those things which are necessary to be known, believed, and observed for salvation, are so clearly propounded, and opened in some place of Scripture or other, that not only the learned, but the unlearned, in a due use of the ordinary means, may attain unto a sufficient understanding of them.

8. The Old Testament in Hebrew (which was the native language of the people of God of old), and the New Testament in Greek (which, at the time of the writing of it, was most generally known to the nations), being immediately inspired by God, and, by his singular care and providence, kept pure in all ages, are therefore authentical; so as, in all controversies of religion, the church is finally to appeal unto them. But, because these original tongues are not known to all the people of God, who have right unto, and interest in the Scriptures, and are commanded, in the fear of God, to read and search them, therefore they are to be translated into the vulgar language of every nation unto which they come, that, the Word of God dwelling plentifully in all, they may worship him in an acceptable manner; and, through patience and comfort of the Scriptures, may have hope.

9. The infallible rule of interpretation of Scripture is the Scripture itself: and therefore, when there is a question about the true and full sense of any Scripture (which is not manifold, but one), it must be searched and known by other places that speak more clearly.

10. The supreme judge by which all controversies of religion are to be determined, and all decrees of councils, opinions of ancient writers, doctrines of men, and private spirits, are to be examined, and in whose sentence we are to rest, can be no other but the Holy Spirit speaking in the Scripture.

## Chapter 2: Of God, and of the Holy Trinity

1. There is but one only, living, and true God, who is infinite in being and perfection, a most pure spirit, invisible, without body, parts, or passions; immutable, immense, eternal, incomprehensible, almighty, most wise, most holy, most free, most absolute; working all things according to the counsel of his own immutable and most righteous will, for his own glory; most loving, gracious, merciful, long-suffering, abundant in goodness and truth, forgiving iniquity, transgression, and sin; the rewarder of them that diligently seek him; and withal, most just, and terrible in his judgments, hating all sin, and who will by no means clear the guilty.

2. God hath all life, glory, goodness, blessedness, in and of himself; and is alone in and unto himself all-sufficient, not standing in need of any creatures which he hath made, nor deriving any glory from them, but only manifesting his own glory in, by, unto, and upon them. He is the alone fountain of all being, of whom, through whom, and to whom are all things; and hath most sovereign dominion over them, to do by them, for them, or upon them whatsoever himself pleaseth. In his sight all things are open and manifest, his knowledge is infinite, infallible, and independent upon the creature, so as nothing is to him contingent, or uncertain. He is most holy in all his counsels, in all his works, and in all his commands. To him is due from angels and men, and every other creature, whatsoever worship, service, or obedience he is pleased to require of them.

3. In the unity of the Godhead there be three persons, of one substance, power, and eternity: God the Father, God the Son, and God the Holy Ghost: the Father is of none, neither begotten, nor proceeding; the Son is eternally begotten of the Father; the Holy Ghost eternally proceeding from the Father and the Son.

## Chapter 3: Of God's Eternal Decree

1. God, from all eternity, did, by the most wise and holy counsel of his own will, freely, and unchangeably ordain whatsoever comes to pass: yet so, as thereby neither is God the author of sin, nor is violence offered to the will of the creatures; nor is the liberty or contingency of second causes taken away, but rather established.

2. Although God knows whatsoever may or can come to pass upon all supposed conditions, yet hath he not decreed anything because he foresaw it as future, or as that which would come to pass upon such conditions.

3. By the decree of God, for the manifestation of his glory, some men and angels are predestinated unto everlasting life; and others foreordained to everlasting death.

4. These angels and men, thus predestinated, and foreordained, are particularly and unchangeably designed, and their number so certain and definite, that it cannot be either increased or diminished.

5. Those of mankind that are predestinated unto life, God, before the foundation of the world was laid, according to his eternal and immutable purpose, and the secret counsel and good pleasure of his will, hath chosen, in Christ, unto everlasting glory, out of his mere free grace and love, without any foresight of faith, or good works, or perseverance in either of them, or any other thing in the creature, as conditions, or causes moving him thereunto; and all to the praise of his glorious grace.

6. As God hath appointed the elect unto glory, so hath he, by the eternal and most free purpose of his will, foreordained all the means thereunto. Wherefore, they who are elected, being fallen in Adam, are redeemed by Christ, are effectually called unto faith in Christ by his Spirit working in due season, are justified, adopted, sanctified, and kept by his power, through faith, unto salvation. Neither are any other redeemed by Christ, effectually called, justified, adopted, sanctified, and saved, but the elect only.

7. The rest of mankind God was pleased, according to the unsearchable counsel of his own will, whereby he extendeth or withholdeth mercy, as he pleaseth, for the glory of his sovereign power over his creatures, to pass by; and to ordain them to dishonor and wrath for their sin, to the praise of his glorious justice.

8. The doctrine of this high mystery of predestination is to be handled with special prudence and care, that men, attending the will of God revealed in his Word, and yielding obedience thereunto, may, from the certainty of their effectual vocation, be assured of their eternal election. So shall this doctrine afford matter of praise, reverence, and admiration of God; and of humility, diligence, and abundant consolation to all that sincerely obey the gospel.

## CHAPTER 4: OF CREATION

1. It pleased God the Father, Son, and Holy Ghost, for the manifestation of the glory of his eternal power, wisdom, and goodness, in the beginning, to create, or make of nothing, the world, and all things therein whether visible or invisible, in the space of six days; and all very good.

2. After God had made all other creatures, he created man, male and female, with reasonable and immortal souls, endued with knowledge, righteousness, and true holiness, after his own image; having the law of God written in their hearts, and power to fulfil it: and yet under a possibility of transgressing, being left to the liberty of their own will, which was subject unto change. Beside this law written in their hearts, they received a command, not to eat of the tree of the knowledge of good and evil; which while they kept, they were happy in their communion with God, and had dominion over the creatures.

## CHAPTER 5: OF PROVIDENCE

1. God the great Creator of all things doth uphold, direct, dispose, and govern all creatures, actions, and things, from the greatest even to the least, by his most wise and holy providence, according to his infallible foreknowledge, and the free and immutable counsel of his own will, to the praise of the glory of his wisdom, power, justice, goodness, and mercy.

2. Although, in relation to the foreknowledge and decree of God, the first Cause, all things come to pass immutably, and infallibly; yet, by the same providence, he ordereth them to fall out, according to the nature of second causes, either necessarily, freely, or contingently.

3. God, in his ordinary providence, maketh use of means, yet is free to work without, above, and against them, at his pleasure.

4. The almighty power, unsearchable wisdom, and infinite goodness of God so far manifest themselves in his providence, that it extendeth itself even to the first fall, and all other sins of angels and men; and that not by a bare permission, but such as hath joined with it a most wise and powerful bounding, and otherwise ordering, and governing of them, in a manifold dispensation, to his own holy ends; yet so, as the sinfulness thereof proceedeth only from the creature, and not from God, who, being most holy and righteous, neither is nor can be the author or approver of sin.

5. The most wise, righteous, and gracious God doth oftentimes leave, for a season, his own children to manifold temptations, and the corruption of their own hearts, to chastise them for their former sins, or to discover unto them the hidden strength of corruption and deceitfulness of their hearts, that they may be humbled; and, to raise them to a more close and constant dependence for their support upon himself, and to make them more watchful against all future occasions of sin, and for sundry other just and holy ends.

6. As for those wicked and ungodly men whom God, as a righteous Judge, for former sins, doth blind and harden, from them he not only withholdeth his grace whereby they might have been enlightened in their understandings, and wrought upon in their hearts; but sometimes also withdraweth the gifts which they had, and exposeth them to such objects as their corruption makes occasions of sin; and, withal, gives them over to their own lusts, the temptations of the world, and the power of Satan, whereby it comes to pass that they harden themselves, even under those means which God useth for the softening of others.

7. As the providence of God doth, in general, reach to all creatures; so, after a most special manner, it taketh care of his church, and disposeth all things to the good thereof.

## CHAPTER 6: OF THE FALL OF MAN, OF SIN, AND OF THE PUNISHMENT THEREOF

1. Our first parents, being seduced by the subtlety and temptation of Satan, sinned, in eating the forbidden fruit. This their sin, God was pleased, according to his wise and holy counsel, to permit, having purposed to order it to his own glory.

2. By this sin they fell from their original righteousness and communion with God, and so became dead in sin, and wholly defiled in all the parts and faculties of soul and body.

3. They being the root of all mankind, the guilt of this sin was imputed; and the same death in sin, and corrupted nature, conveyed to all their posterity descending from them by ordinary generation.

4. From this original corruption, whereby we are utterly indisposed, disabled, and made opposite to all good, and wholly inclined to all evil, do proceed all actual transgressions.

5. This corruption of nature, during this life, doth remain in those that are regenerated; and although it be, through Christ, pardoned, and mortified; yet both itself, and all the motions thereof, are truly and properly sin.

6. Every sin, both original and actual, being a transgression of the righteous law of God, and contrary thereunto, doth, in its own nature, bring guilt upon the sinner, whereby he is bound over to the wrath of God, and curse of the law, and so made subject to death, with all miseries spiritual, temporal, and eternal.

## Chapter 7: Of God's Covenant with Man

1. The distance between God and the creature is so great, that although reasonable creatures do owe obedience unto him as their Creator, yet they could never have any fruition of him as their blessedness and reward, but by some voluntary condescension on God's part, which he hath been pleased to express by way of covenant.

2. The first covenant made with man was a covenant of works, wherein life was promised to Adam; and in him to his posterity, upon condition of perfect and personal obedience.

3. Man, by his fall, having made himself incapable of life by that covenant, the Lord was pleased to make a second, commonly called the covenant of grace; wherein he freely offereth unto sinners life and salvation by Jesus Christ; requiring of them faith in him, that they may be saved, and promising to give unto all those that are ordained unto eternal life his Holy Spirit, to make them willing, and able to believe.

4. This covenant of grace is frequently set forth in Scripture by the name of a testament, in reference to the death of Jesus Christ the Testator, and to the everlasting inheritance, with all things belonging to it, therein bequeathed.

5. This covenant was differently administered in the time of the law, and in the time of the gospel: under the law, it was administered by promises, prophecies, sacrifices, circumcision, the paschal lamb, and other types and ordinances delivered to the people of the Jews, all foresignifying Christ to come; which were, for that time, sufficient and efficacious, through the operation of the Spirit, to instruct and build up the elect in faith in the promised Messiah, by whom they had full remission of sins, and eternal salvation; and is called the Old Testament.

6. Under the gospel, when Christ, the substance, was exhibited, the ordinances in which this covenant is dispensed are the preaching of the Word, and the administration of the sacraments of Baptism and the Lord's Supper: which, though fewer in number, and administered with more simplicity, and less outward glory, yet, in them, it is held forth in more fullness, evidence and spiritual efficacy, to all nations, both Jews and Gentiles; and is called the New Testament. There are not therefore two covenants of grace, differing in substance, but one and the same, under various dispensations.

## Chapter 8: Of Christ the Mediator

1. It pleased God, in his eternal purpose, to choose and ordain the Lord Jesus, his only begotten Son, to be the Mediator between God and man, the Prophet, Priest, and King, the Head and Savior of his church, the Heir of all things, and Judge of the world: unto whom he did from all eternity give a people, to be his seed, and to be by him in time redeemed, called, justified, sanctified, and glorified.

2. The Son of God, the second person in the Trinity, being very and eternal God, of one substance and equal with the Father, did, when the fullness of time was come, take upon him man's nature, with all the essential properties, and common infirmities thereof, yet without sin; being conceived by the power of the Holy Ghost, in the womb of the virgin Mary, of her substance. So that two whole, perfect, and distinct natures, the Godhead and the manhood, were inseparably joined together in one person, without conversion, composition, or confusion. Which person is very God, and very man, yet one Christ, the only Mediator between God and man.

3. The Lord Jesus, in his human nature thus united to the divine, was sanctified, and anointed with the Holy Spirit, above measure, having in him all the treasures of wisdom and knowledge; in whom it pleased the Father that all fullness should dwell; to the end that, being holy, harmless, undefiled, and full of grace and truth, he might be thoroughly furnished to execute the office of a mediator, and surety. Which office he took not unto himself, but was thereunto called by his Father, who put all power and judgment into his hand, and gave him commandment to execute the same.

4. This office the Lord Jesus did most willingly undertake; which that he might discharge, he was made under the law, and did perfectly fulfil it; endured most grievous torments immediately in his soul, and most painful sufferings in his body; was crucified, and died, was buried, and remained under the power of death, yet saw no corruption. On the third day he arose from the dead, with the same body in which he suffered, with which also he ascended into heaven, and there sitteth at the right hand of his Father, making intercession, and shall return, to judge men and angels, at the end of the world.

5. The Lord Jesus, by his perfect obedience, and sacrifice of himself, which he, through the eternal Spirit, once offered up unto God, hath fully satisfied the justice of his Father; and purchased, not only reconciliation, but an everlasting inheritance in the kingdom of heaven, for all those whom the Father hath given unto him.

6. Although the work of redemption was not actually wrought by Christ till after his incarnation, yet the virtue, efficacy, and benefits thereof were communicated unto the elect, in all ages successively from the beginning of the world, in and by those promises, types, and sacrifices, wherein he was revealed, and signified to be the seed of the woman which should bruise the serpent's head; and the Lamb slain from the beginning of the world; being yesterday and today the same, and forever.

7. Christ, in the work of mediation, acts according to both natures, by each nature doing that which is proper to itself; yet, by reason of the unity of the person, that which is proper to one nature is sometimes in Scripture attributed to the person denominated by the other nature.

8. To all those for whom Christ hath purchased redemption, he doth certainly and effectually apply and communicate the same; making intercession for them, and revealing unto them, in and by the Word, the mysteries of salvation; effectually persuading them by his Spirit to believe and obey, and governing their hearts by his Word and Spirit; overcoming all their enemies by his almighty power and wisdom, in such manner, and ways, as are most consonant to his wonderful and unsearchable dispensation.

## Chapter 9: Of Free Will

1. God hath endued the will of man with that natural liberty, that it is neither forced, nor, by any absolute necessity of nature, determined to good, or evil.

2. Man, in his state of innocency, had freedom, and power to will and to do that which was good and well pleasing to God; but yet, mutably, so that he might fall from it.

3. Man, by his fall into a state of sin, hath wholly lost all ability of will to any spiritual good accompanying salvation: so as, a natural man, being altogether averse from that good, and dead in sin, is not able, by his own strength, to convert himself, or to prepare himself thereunto.

4. When God converts a sinner, and translates him into the state of grace, he freeth him from his natural bondage under sin; and, by his grace alone, enables him freely to will and to do that which is spiritually good; yet so, as that by reason of his remaining corruption, he doth not perfectly, nor only, will that which is good, but doth also will that which is evil.

5. The will of man is made perfectly and immutably free to good alone, in the state of glory only.

## Chapter 10: Of Effectual Calling

1. All those whom God hath predestinated unto life, and those only, he is pleased, in his appointed and accepted time, effectually to call, by his Word and Spirit, out of that state of sin and death, in which they are by nature, to grace and salvation, by Jesus Christ; enlightening their minds spiritually and savingly to understand the things of God, taking away their heart of stone, and giving unto them a heart of flesh; renewing

their wills, and, by his almighty power, determining them to that which is good, and effectually drawing them to Jesus Christ: yet so, as they come most freely, being made willing by his grace.

2. This effectual call is of God's free and special grace alone, not from anything at all foreseen in man, who is altogether passive therein, until, being quickened and renewed by the Holy Spirit, he is thereby enabled to answer this call, and to embrace the grace offered and conveyed in it.

3. Elect infants, dying in infancy, are regenerated, and saved by Christ, through the Spirit, who worketh when, and where, and how he pleaseth: so also are all other elect persons who are incapable of being outwardly called by the ministry of the Word.

4. Others, not elected, although they may be called by the ministry of the Word, and may have some common operations of the Spirit, yet they never truly come unto Christ, and therefore cannot be saved: much less can men, not professing the Christian religion, be saved in any other way whatsoever, be they never so diligent to frame their lives according to the light of nature, and the laws of that religion they do profess. And, to assert and maintain that they may, is very pernicious, and to be detested.

## CHAPTER 11: OF JUSTIFICATION

1. Those whom God effectually calleth, he also freely justifieth: not by infusing righteousness into them, but by pardoning their sins, and by accounting and accepting their persons as righteous; not for anything wrought in them, or done by them, but for Christ's sake alone; nor by imputing faith itself, the act of believing, or any other evangelical obedience to them, as their righteousness; but by imputing the obedience and satisfaction of Christ unto them, they receiving and resting on him and his righteousness, by faith; which faith they have not of themselves, it is the gift of God.

2. Faith, thus receiving and resting on Christ and his righteousness, is the alone instrument of justification: yet is it not alone in the person justified, but is ever accompanied with all other saving graces, and is no dead faith, but worketh by love.

3. Christ, by his obedience and death, did fully discharge the debt of all those that are thus justified, and did make a proper, real, and full satisfaction to his Father's justice in their behalf. Yet, inasmuch as he was given by the Father for them; and his obedience and satisfaction accepted in their stead; and both, freely, not for anything in them; their justification is only of free grace; that both the exact justice and rich grace of God might be glorified in the justification of sinners.

4. God did, from all eternity, decree to justify all the elect, and Christ did, in the fullness of time, die for their sins, and rise again for their justification: nevertheless, they are not justified, until the Holy Spirit doth, in due time, actually apply Christ unto them.

5. God doth continue to forgive the sins of those that are justified; and, although they can never fall from the state of justification, yet they may, by their sins, fall under God's fatherly displeasure, and not have the light of his countenance restored unto them,

until they humble themselves, confess their sins, beg pardon, and renew their faith and repentance.

6. The justification of believers under the Old Testament was, in all these respects, one and the same with the justification of believers under the New Testament.

## CHAPTER 12: OF ADOPTION

1. All those that are justified, God vouchsafeth, in and for his only Son Jesus Christ, to make partakers of the grace of adoption, by which they are taken into the number, and enjoy the liberties and privileges of the children of God, have his name put upon them, receive the spirit of adoption, have access to the throne of grace with boldness, are enabled to cry, Abba, Father, are pitied, protected, provided for, and chastened by him, as by a Father: yet never cast off, but sealed to the day of redemption; and inherit the promises, as heirs of everlasting salvation.

## CHAPTER 13: OF SANCTIFICATION

1. They, who are once effectually called, and regenerated, having a new heart, and a new spirit created in them, are further sanctified, really and personally, through the virtue of Christ's death and resurrection, by his Word and Spirit dwelling in them: the dominion of the whole body of sin is destroyed, and the several lusts thereof are more and more weakened and mortified; and they more and more quickened and strengthened in all saving graces, to the practice of true holiness, without which no man shall see the Lord.

2. This sanctification is throughout, in the whole man; yet imperfect in this life, there abiding still some remnants of corruption in every part; whence ariseth a continual and irreconcilable war, the flesh lusting against the Spirit, and the Spirit against the flesh.

3. In which war, although the remaining corruption, for a time, may much prevail; yet, through the continual supply of strength from the sanctifying Spirit of Christ, the regenerate part doth overcome; and so, the saints grow in grace, perfecting holiness in the fear of God.

## CHAPTER 14: OF SAVING FAITH

1. The grace of faith, whereby the elect are enabled to believe to the saving of their souls, is the work of the Spirit of Christ in their hearts, and is ordinarily wrought by the ministry of the Word, by which also, and by the administration of the sacraments, and prayer, it is increased and strengthened.

2. By this faith, a Christian believeth to be true whatsoever is revealed in the Word, for the authority of God himself speaking therein; and acteth differently upon that which each particular passage thereof containeth; yielding obedience to the commands, trembling at the threatenings, and embracing the promises of God for this life, and that which is to come. But the principal acts of saving faith are accepting, receiving, and

resting upon Christ alone for justification, sanctification, and eternal life, by virtue of the covenant of grace.

3. This faith is different in degrees, weak or strong; may be often and many ways assailed, and weakened, but gets the victory: growing up in many to the attainment of a full assurance, through Christ, who is both the author and finisher of our faith.

## Chapter 15: Of Repentance Unto Life

1. Repentance unto life is an evangelical grace, the doctrine whereof is to be preached by every minister of the gospel, as well as that of faith in Christ.

2. By it, a sinner, out of the sight and sense not only of the danger, but also of the filthiness and odiousness of his sins, as contrary to the holy nature, and righteous law of God; and upon the apprehension of his mercy in Christ to such as are penitent, so grieves for, and hates his sins, as to turn from them all unto God, purposing and endeavoring to walk with him in all the ways of his commandments.

3. Although repentance be not to be rested in, as any satisfaction for sin, or any cause of the pardon thereof, which is the act of God's free grace in Christ; yet it is of such necessity to all sinners, that none may expect pardon without it.

4. As there is no sin so small, but it deserves damnation; so there is no sin so great, that it can bring damnation upon those who truly repent.

5. Men ought not to content themselves with a general repentance, but it is every man's duty to endeavor to repent of his particular sins, particularly.

6. As every man is bound to make private confession of his sins to God, praying for the pardon thereof; upon which, and the forsaking of them, he shall find mercy; so, he that scandalizeth his brother, or the church of Christ, ought to be willing, by a private or public confession, and sorrow for his sin, to declare his repentance to those that are offended, who are thereupon to be reconciled to him, and in love to receive him.

## Chapter 16: Of Good Works

1. Good works are only such as God hath commanded in his holy Word, and not such as, without the warrant thereof, are devised by men, out of blind zeal, or upon any pretense of good intention.

2. These good works, done in obedience to God's commandments, are the fruits and evidences of a true and lively faith: and by them believers manifest their thankfulness, strengthen their assurance, edify their brethren, adorn the profession of the gospel, stop the mouths of the adversaries, and glorify God, whose workmanship they are, created in Christ Jesus thereunto, that, having their fruit unto holiness, they may have the end, eternal life.

3. Their ability to do good works is not at all of themselves, but wholly from the Spirit of Christ. And that they may be enabled thereunto, beside the graces they have already received, there is required an actual influence of the same Holy Spirit, to work

in them to will, and to do, of his good pleasure: yet are they not hereupon to grow negligent, as if they were not bound to perform any duty unless upon a special motion of the Spirit; but they ought to be diligent in stirring up the grace of God that is in them.

4. They who, in their obedience, attain to the greatest height which is possible in this life, are so far from being able to supererogate, and to do more than God requires, as that they fall short of much which in duty they are bound to do.

5. We cannot by our best works merit pardon of sin, or eternal life at the hand of God, by reason of the great disproportion that is between them and the glory to come; and the infinite distance that is between us and God, whom, by them, we can neither profit, nor satisfy for the debt of our former sins, but when we have done all we can, we have done but our duty, and are unprofitable servants: and because, as they are good, they proceed from his Spirit; and as they are wrought by us, they are defiled, and mixed with so much weakness and imperfection, that they cannot endure the severity of God's judgment.

6. Notwithstanding, the persons of believers being accepted through Christ, their good works also are accepted in him; not as though they were in this life wholly unblamable and unreprovable in God's sight; but that he, looking upon them in his Son, is pleased to accept and reward that which is sincere, although accompanied with many weaknesses and imperfections.

7. Works done by unregenerate men, although for the matter of them they may be things which God commands; and of good use both to themselves and others: yet, because they proceed not from an heart purified by faith; nor are done in a right manner, according to the Word; nor to a right end, the glory of God, they are therefore sinful, and cannot please God, or make a man meet to receive grace from God: and yet, their neglect of them is more sinful and displeasing unto God.

## CHAPTER 17: OF THE PERSEVERANCE OF THE SAINTS

1. They, whom God hath accepted in his Beloved, effectually called, and sanctified by his Spirit, can neither totally nor finally fall away from the state of grace, but shall certainly persevere therein to the end, and be eternally saved.

2. This perseverance of the saints depends not upon their own free will, but upon the immutability of the decree of election, flowing from the free and unchangeable love of God the Father; upon the efficacy of the merit and intercession of Jesus Christ, the abiding of the Spirit, and of the seed of God within them, and the nature of the covenant of grace: from all which ariseth also the certainty and infallibility thereof.

3. Nevertheless, they may, through the temptations of Satan and of the world, the prevalency of corruption remaining in them, and the neglect of the means of their preservation, fall into grievous sins; and, for a time, continue therein: whereby they incur God's displeasure, and grieve his Holy Spirit, come to be deprived of some measure of their graces and comforts, have their hearts hardened, and their consciences wounded; hurt and scandalize others, and bring temporal judgments upon themselves.

## CHAPTER 18: OF ASSURANCE OF GRACE AND SALVATION

1. Although hypocrites and other unregenerate men may vainly deceive themselves with false hopes and carnal presumptions of being in the favor of God, and estate of salvation (which hope of theirs shall perish): yet such as truly believe in the Lord Jesus, and love him in sincerity, endeavoring to walk in all good conscience before him, may, in this life, be certainly assured that they are in the state of grace, and may rejoice in the hope of the glory of God, which hope shall never make them ashamed.

2. This certainty is not a bare conjectural and probable persuasion grounded upon a fallible hope; but an infallible assurance of faith founded upon the divine truth of the promises of salvation, the inward evidence of those graces unto which these promises are made, the testimony of the Spirit of adoption witnessing with our spirits that we are the children of God, which Spirit is the earnest of our inheritance, whereby we are sealed to the day of redemption.

3. This infallible assurance doth not so belong to the essence of faith, but that a true believer may wait long, and conflict with many difficulties before he be partaker of it: yet, being enabled by the Spirit to know the things which are freely given him of God, he may, without extraordinary revelation, in the right use of ordinary means, attain thereunto. And therefore it is the duty of everyone to give all diligence to make his calling and election sure, that thereby his heart may be enlarged in peace and joy in the Holy Ghost, in love and thankfulness to God, and in strength and cheerfulness in the duties of obedience, the proper fruits of this assurance; so far is it from inclining men to looseness.

4. True believers may have the assurance of their salvation divers ways shaken, diminished, and intermitted; as, by negligence in preserving of it, by falling into some special sin which woundeth the conscience and grieveth the Spirit; by some sudden or vehement temptation, by God's withdrawing the light of his countenance, and suffering even such as fear him to walk in darkness and to have no light: yet are they never utterly destitute of that seed of God, and life of faith, that love of Christ and the brethren, that sincerity of heart, and conscience of duty, out of which, by the operation of the Spirit, this assurance may, in due time, be revived; and by the which, in the meantime, they are supported from utter despair.

## CHAPTER 19: OF THE LAW OF GOD

1. God gave to Adam a law, as a covenant of works, by which he bound him and all his posterity to personal, entire, exact, and perpetual obedience, promised life upon the fulfilling, and threatened death upon the breach of it, and endued him with power and ability to keep it.

2. This law, after his fall, continued to be a perfect rule of righteousness; and, as such, was delivered by God upon Mount Sinai, in ten commandments, and written in two tables: the four first commandments containing our duty towards God; and the other six, our duty to man.

3. Beside this law, commonly called moral, God was pleased to give to the people of Israel, as a church under age, ceremonial laws, containing several typical ordinances, partly of worship, prefiguring Christ, his graces, actions, sufferings, and benefits; and partly, holding forth divers instructions of moral duties. All which ceremonial laws are now abrogated, under the New Testament.

4. To them also, as a body politic, he gave sundry judicial laws, which expired together with the state of that people; not obliging any other now, further than the general equity thereof may require.

5. The moral law doth forever bind all, as well justified persons as others, to the obedience thereof; and that, not only in regard of the matter contained in it, but also in respect of the authority of God the Creator, who gave it. Neither doth Christ, in the gospel, any way dissolve, but much strengthen this obligation.

6. Although true believers be not under the law, as a covenant of works, to be thereby justified, or condemned; yet is it of great use to them, as well as to others; in that, as a rule of life informing them of the will of God, and their duty, it directs and binds them to walk accordingly; discovering also the sinful pollutions of their nature, hearts, and lives; so as, examining themselves thereby, they may come to further conviction of, humiliation for, and hatred against sin, together with a clearer sight of the need they have of Christ, and the perfection of his obedience. It is likewise of use to the regenerate, to restrain their corruptions, in that it forbids sin: and the threatenings of it serve to show what even their sins deserve; and what afflictions, in this life, they may expect for them, although freed from the curse thereof threatened in the law. The promises of it, in like manner, show them God's approbation of obedience, and what blessings they may expect upon the performance thereof: although not as due to them by the law as a covenant of works. So as, a man's doing good, and refraining from evil, because the law encourageth to the one, and deterreth from the other, is no evidence of his being under the law; and, not under grace.

7. Neither are the forementioned uses of the law contrary to the grace of the gospel, but do sweetly comply with it; the Spirit of Christ subduing and enabling the will of man to do that freely, and cheerfully, which the will of God, revealed in the law, requireth to be done.

## CHAPTER 20: OF CHRISTIAN LIBERTY, AND LIBERTY OF CONSCIENCE

1. The liberty which Christ hath purchased for believers under the gospel consists in their freedom from the guilt of sin, the condemning wrath of God, the curse of the moral law; and, in their being delivered from this present evil world, bondage to Satan, and dominion of sin; from the evil of afflictions, the sting of death, the victory of the grave, and everlasting damnation; as also, in their free access to God, and their yielding obedience unto him, not out of slavish fear, but a childlike love and willing mind. All which were common also to believers under the law. But, under the New Testament, the liberty of Christians is further enlarged, in their freedom from the yoke of the ceremonial law, to which the Jewish church was subjected; and in greater boldness of

access to the throne of grace, and in fuller communications of the free Spirit of God, than believers under the law did ordinarily partake of.

2. God alone is Lord of the conscience, and hath left it free from the doctrines and commandments of men, which are, in anything, contrary to his Word; or beside it, if matters of faith, or worship. So that, to believe such doctrines, or to obey such commands, out of conscience, is to betray true liberty of conscience: and the requiring of an implicit faith, and an absolute and blind obedience, is to destroy liberty of conscience, and reason also.

3. They who, upon pretense of Christian liberty, do practice any sin, or cherish any lust, do thereby destroy the end of Christian liberty, which is, that being delivered out of the hands of our enemies, we might serve the Lord without fear, in holiness and righteousness before him, all the days of our life.

4. And because the powers which God hath ordained, and the liberty which Christ hath purchased, are not intended by God to destroy, but mutually to uphold and preserve one another, they who, upon pretense of Christian liberty, shall oppose any lawful power, or the lawful exercise of it, whether it be civil or ecclesiastical, resist the ordinance of God. And, for their publishing of such opinions, or maintaining of such practices, as are contrary to the light of nature, or to the known principles of Christianity (whether concerning faith, worship, or conversation), or to the power of godliness; or, such erroneous opinions or practices, as either in their own nature, or in the manner of publishing or maintaining them, are destructive to the external peace and order which Christ hath established in the church, they may lawfully be called to account, and proceeded against, by the censures of the church.

## CHAPTER 21: OF RELIGIOUS WORSHIP, AND THE SABBATH-DAY

1. The light of nature showeth that there is a God, who hath lordship and sovereignty over all, is good, and doth good unto all, and is therefore to be feared, loved, praised, called upon, trusted in, and served, with all the heart, and with all the soul, and with all the might. But the acceptable way of worshiping the true God is instituted by himself, and so limited by his own revealed will, that he may not be worshiped according to the imaginations and devices of men, or the suggestions of Satan, under any visible representation, or any other way not prescribed in the holy Scripture.

2. Religious worship is to be given to God, the Father, Son, and Holy Ghost; and to him alone; not to angels, saints, or any other creature: and, since the fall, not without a Mediator; nor in the mediation of any other but of Christ alone.

3. Prayer, with thanksgiving, being one special part of religious worship, is by God required of all men: and, that it may be accepted, it is to be made in the name of the Son, by the help of his Spirit, according to his will, with understanding, reverence, humility, fervency, faith, love, and perseverance; and, if vocal, in a known tongue.

4. Prayer is to be made for things lawful; and for all sorts of men living, or that shall live hereafter: but not for the dead, nor for those of whom it may be known that they have sinned the sin unto death.

5. The reading of the Scriptures with godly fear, the sound preaching and conscionable hearing of the Word, in obedience unto God, with understanding, faith, and reverence, singing of psalms with grace in the heart; as also, the due administration and worthy receiving of the sacraments instituted by Christ, are all parts of the ordinary religious worship of God: beside religious oaths, vows, solemn fastings, and thanksgivings upon special occasions, which are, in their several times and seasons, to be used in an holy and religious manner.

6. Neither prayer, nor any other part of religious worship, is now, under the gospel, either tied unto, or made more acceptable by any place in which it is performed, or towards which it is directed: but God is to be worshiped everywhere, in spirit and truth; as, in private families daily, and in secret, each one by himself; so, more solemnly in the public assemblies, which are not carelessly or wilfully to be neglected, or forsaken, when God, by his Word or providence, calleth thereunto.

7. As it is the law of nature, that, in general, a due proportion of time be set apart for the worship of God; so, in his Word, by a positive, moral, and perpetual commandment binding all men in all ages, he hath particularly appointed one day in seven, for a sabbath, to be kept holy unto him: which, from the beginning of the world to the resurrection of Christ, was the last day of the week; and, from the resurrection of Christ, was changed into the first day of the week, which, in Scripture, is called the Lord's day, and is to be continued to the end of the world, as the Christian sabbath.

8. This sabbath is then kept holy unto the Lord, when men, after a due preparing of their hearts, and ordering of their common affairs beforehand, do not only observe an holy rest, all the day, from their own works, words, and thoughts about their worldly employments and recreations, but also are taken up, the whole time, in the public and private exercises of his worship, and in the duties of necessity and mercy.

## Chapter 22: Of Lawful Oaths and Vows

1. A lawful oath is a part of religious worship, wherein, upon just occasion, the person swearing solemnly calleth God to witness what he asserteth, or promiseth, and to judge him according to the truth or falsehood of what he sweareth.

2. The name of God only is that by which men ought to swear, and therein it is to be used with all holy fear and reverence. Therefore, to swear vainly, or rashly, by that glorious and dreadful Name; or, to swear at all by any other thing, is sinful, and to be abhorred. Yet, as in matters of weight and moment, an oath is warranted by the Word of God, under the New Testament as well as under the Old; so a lawful oath, being imposed by lawful authority, in such matters, ought to be taken.

3. Whosoever taketh an oath ought duly to consider the weightiness of so solemn an act, and therein to avouch nothing but what he is fully persuaded is the truth: neither may any man bind himself by oath to anything but what is good and just, and what he believeth so to be, and what he is able and resolved to perform.

4. An oath is to be taken in the plain and common sense of the words, without equivocation, or mental reservation. It cannot oblige to sin; but in anything not sinful, being taken, it binds to performance, although to a man's own hurt. Nor is it to be violated, although made to heretics, or infidels.

5. A vow is of the like nature with a promissory oath, and ought to be made with the like religious care, and to be performed with the like faithfulness.

6. It is not to be made to any creature, but to God alone: and, that it may be accepted, it is to be made voluntarily, out of faith, and conscience of duty, in way of thankfulness for mercy received, or for the obtaining of what we want, whereby we more strictly bind ourselves to necessary duties; or, to other things, so far and so long as they may fitly conduce thereunto.

7. No man may vow to do anything forbidden in the Word of God, or what would hinder any duty therein commanded, or which is not in his own power, and for the performance whereof he hath no promise of ability from God. In which respects, popish monastical vows of perpetual single life, professed poverty, and regular obedience, are so far from being degrees of higher perfection, that they are superstitious and sinful snares, in which no Christian may entangle himself.

## Chapter 23: Of the Civil Magistrate

1. God, the supreme Lord and King of all the world, hath ordained civil magistrates, to be, under him, over the people, for his own glory, and the public good: and, to this end, hath armed them with the power of the sword, for the defense and encouragement of them that are good, and for the punishment of evil doers.

2. It is lawful for Christians to accept and execute the office of a magistrate, when called thereunto: in the managing whereof, as they ought especially to maintain piety, justice, and peace, according to the wholesome laws of each commonwealth; so, for that end, they may lawfully, now under the New Testament, wage war, upon just and necessary occasion.

3. Civil magistrates may not assume to themselves the administration of the Word and sacraments; or the power of the keys of the kingdom of heaven; or, in the least, interfere in matters of faith. Yet, as nursing fathers, it is the duty of civil magistrates to protect the church of our common Lord, without giving the preference to any denomination of Christians above the rest, in such a manner that all ecclesiastical persons whatever shall enjoy the full, free, and unquestioned liberty of discharging every part of their sacred functions, without violence or danger. And, as Jesus Christ hath appointed a regular government and discipline in his church, no law of any commonwealth should interfere with, let, or hinder, the due exercise thereof, among the voluntary members of any denomination of Christians, according to their own profession and belief. It is the duty of civil magistrates to protect the person and good name of all their people, in such an effectual manner as that no person be suffered, either upon pretense of religion or of infidelity, to offer any

indignity, violence, abuse, or injury to any other person whatsoever: and to take order, that all religious and ecclesiastical assemblies be held without molestation or disturbance.

4. It is the duty of people to pray for magistrates, to honor their persons, to pay them tribute or other dues, to obey their lawful commands, and to be subject to their authority, for conscience' sake. Infidelity, or difference in religion, doth not make void the magistrates' just and legal authority, nor free the people from their due obedience to them: from which ecclesiastical persons are not exempted, much less hath the pope any power and jurisdiction over them in their dominions, or over any of their people; and, least of all, to deprive them of their dominions, or lives, if he shall judge them to be heretics, or upon any other pretense whatsoever.

## CHAPTER 24: OF MARRIAGE AND DIVORCE

1. Marriage is to be between one man and one woman: neither is it lawful for any man to have more than one wife, nor for any woman to have more than one husband, at the same time.

2. Marriage was ordained for the mutual help of husband and wife, for the increase of mankind with legitimate issue, and of the church with an holy seed; and for preventing of uncleanness.

3. It is lawful for all sorts of people to marry, who are able with judgment to give their consent. Yet it is the duty of Christians to marry only in the Lord. And therefore such as profess the true reformed religion should not marry with infidels, papists, or other idolaters: neither should such as are godly be unequally yoked, by marrying with such as are notoriously wicked in their life, or maintain damnable heresies.

4. Marriage ought not to be within the degrees of consanguinity or affinity forbidden by the Word. Nor can such incestuous marriages ever be made lawful by any law of man or consent of parties, so as those persons may live together as man and wife.

5. Adultery or fornication committed after a contract, being detected before marriage, giveth just occasion to the innocent party to dissolve that contract. In the case of adultery after marriage, it is lawful for the innocent party to sue out a divorce: and, after the divorce, to marry another, as if the offending party were dead.

6. Although the corruption of man be such as is apt to study arguments unduly to put asunder those whom God hath joined together in marriage: yet, nothing but adultery, or such wilful desertion as can no way be remedied by the church, or civil magistrate, is cause sufficient of dissolving the bond of marriage: wherein, a public and orderly course of proceeding is to be observed; and the persons concerned in it not left to their own wills, and discretion, in their own case.

## CHAPTER 25: OF THE CHURCH

1. The catholic or universal church, which is invisible, consists of the whole number of the elect, that have been, are, or shall be gathered into one, under Christ the head thereof; and is the spouse, the body, the fullness of him that filleth all in all.

2. The visible church, which is also catholic or universal under the gospel (not confined to one nation, as before under the law), consists of all those throughout the world that profess the true religion; and of their children: and is the kingdom of the Lord Jesus Christ, the house and family of God, out of which there is no ordinary possibility of salvation.

3. Unto this catholic visible church Christ hath given the ministry, oracles, and ordinances of God, for the gathering and perfecting of the saints, in this life, to the end of the world: and doth, by his own presence and Spirit, according to his promise, make them effectual thereunto.

4. This catholic church hath been sometimes more, sometimes less visible. And particular churches, which are members thereof, are more or less pure, according as the doctrine of the gospel is taught and embraced, ordinances administered, and public worship performed more or less purely in them.

5. The purest churches under heaven are subject both to mixture and error; and some have so degenerated, as to become no churches of Christ, but synagogues of Satan. Nevertheless, there shall be always a church on earth, to worship God according to his will.

6. There is no other head of the church but the Lord Jesus Christ. Nor can the pope of Rome, in any sense, be head thereof.

## Chapter 26: Of Communion of Saints

1. All saints, that are united to Jesus Christ their head, by his Spirit, and by faith, have fellowship with him in his graces, sufferings, death, resurrection, and glory: and, being united to one another in love, they have communion in each other's gifts and graces, and are obliged to the performance of such duties, public and private, as do conduce to their mutual good, both in the inward and outward man.

2. Saints by profession are bound to maintain an holy fellowship and communion in the worship of God, and in performing such other spiritual services as tend to their mutual edification; as also in relieving each other in outward things, according to their several abilities and necessities. Which communion, as God offereth opportunity, is to be extended unto all those who, in every place, call upon the name of the Lord Jesus.

3. This communion which the saints have with Christ, doth not make them in any wise partakers of the substance of his Godhead; or to be equal with Christ in any respect: either of which to affirm is impious and blasphemous. Nor doth their communion one with another, as saints, take away, or infringe the title or propriety which each man hath in his goods and possessions.

## Chapter 27: Of the Sacraments

1. Sacraments are holy signs and seals of the covenant of grace, immediately instituted by God, to represent Christ, and his benefits; and to confirm our interest in him:

as also, to put a visible difference between those that belong unto the church, and the rest of the world; and solemnly to engage them to the service of God in Christ, according to his Word.

2. There is, in every sacrament, a spiritual relation, or sacramental union, between the sign and the thing signified: whence it comes to pass, that the names and effects of the one are attributed to the other.

3. The grace which is exhibited in or by the sacraments rightly used, is not conferred by any power in them; neither doth the efficacy of a sacrament depend upon the piety or intention of him that doth administer it: but upon the work of the Spirit, and the word of institution, which contains, together with a precept authorizing the use thereof, a promise of benefit to worthy receivers.

4. There be only two sacraments ordained by Christ our Lord in the gospel; that is to say, Baptism, and the Supper of the Lord: neither of which may be dispensed by any, but by a minister of the Word lawfully ordained.

5. The sacraments of the Old Testament, in regard of the spiritual things thereby signified and exhibited, were, for substance, the same with those of the New.

## CHAPTER 28: OF BAPTISM

1. Baptism is a sacrament of the New Testament, ordained by Jesus Christ, not only for the solemn admission of the party baptized into the visible church; but also, to be unto him a sign and seal of the covenant of grace, of his ingrafting into Christ, of regeneration, of remission of sins, and of his giving up unto God, through Jesus Christ, to walk in newness of life. Which sacrament is, by Christ's own appointment, to be continued in his church until the end of the world.

2. The outward element to be used in this sacrament is water, wherewith the party is to be baptized, in the name of the Father, and of the Son, and of the Holy Ghost, by a minister of the gospel, lawfully called thereunto.

3. Dipping of the person into the water is not necessary; but Baptism is rightly administered by pouring, or sprinkling water upon the person.

4. Not only those that do actually profess faith in and obedience unto Christ, but also the infants of one, or both, believing parents, are to be baptized.

5. Although it be a great sin to contemn or neglect this ordinance, yet grace and salvation are not so inseparably annexed unto it, as that no person can be regenerated, or saved, without it; or, that all that are baptized are undoubtedly regenerated.

6. The efficacy of Baptism is not tied to that moment of time wherein it is administered; yet, notwithstanding, by the right use of this ordinance, the grace promised is not only offered, but really exhibited, and conferred, by the Holy Ghost, to such (whether of age or infants) as that grace belongeth unto, according to the counsel of God's own will, in his appointed time.

7. The sacrament of Baptism is but once to be administered unto any person.

## CHAPTER 29: OF THE LORD'S SUPPER

1. Our Lord Jesus, in the night wherein he was betrayed, instituted the sacrament of his body and blood, called the Lord's Supper, to be observed in his church, unto the end of the world, for the perpetual remembrance of the sacrifice of himself in his death; the sealing all benefits thereof unto true believers, their spiritual nourishment and growth in him, their further engagement in and to all duties which they owe unto him; and, to be a bond and pledge of their communion with him, and with each other, as members of his mystical body.

2. In this sacrament, Christ is not offered up to his Father; nor any real sacrifice made at all, for remission of sins of the quick or dead; but only a commemoration of that one offering up of himself, by himself, upon the cross, once for all: and a spiritual oblation of all possible praise unto God, for the same: so that the popish sacrifice of the mass (as they call it) is most abominably injurious to Christ's one, only sacrifice, the alone propitiation for all the sins of his elect.

3. The Lord Jesus hath, in this ordinance, appointed his ministers to declare his word of institution to the people; to pray, and bless the elements of bread and wine, and thereby to set them apart from a common to an holy use; and to take and break the bread, to take the cup, and (they communicating also themselves) to give both to the communicants; but to none who are not then present in the congregation.

4. Private masses, or receiving this sacrament by a priest, or any other, alone; as likewise, the denial of the cup to the people, worshiping the elements, the lifting them up, or carrying them about, for adoration, and the reserving them for any pretended religious use; are all contrary to the nature of this sacrament, and to the institution of Christ.

5. The outward elements in this sacrament, duly set apart to the uses ordained by Christ, have such relation to him crucified, as that, truly, yet sacramentally only, they are sometimes called by the name of the things they represent, to wit, the body and blood of Christ; albeit, in substance and nature, they still remain truly and only bread and wine, as they were before.

6. That doctrine which maintains a change of the substance of bread and wine, into the substance of Christ's body and blood (commonly called transubstantiation) by consecration of a priest, or by any other way, is repugnant, not to Scripture alone, but even to common sense, and reason; overthroweth the nature of the sacrament, and hath been, and is, the cause of manifold superstitions; yea, of gross idolatries.

7. Worthy receivers, outwardly partaking of the visible elements, in this sacrament, do then also, inwardly by faith, really and indeed, yet not carnally and corporally but spiritually, receive, and feed upon, Christ crucified, and all benefits of his death: the body and blood of Christ being then, not corporally or carnally, in, with, or under the bread and wine; yet, as really, but spiritually, present to the faith of believers in that ordinance, as the elements themselves are to their outward senses.

8. Although ignorant and wicked men receive the outward elements in this sacrament; yet, they receive not the thing signified thereby; but, by their unworthy coming thereunto,

are guilty of the body and blood of the Lord, to their own damnation. Wherefore, all ignorant and ungodly persons, as they are unfit to enjoy communion with him, so are they unworthy of the Lord's table; and cannot, without great sin against Christ, while they remain such, partake of these holy mysteries, or be admitted thereunto.

## CHAPTER 30: OF CHURCH CENSURES

1. The Lord Jesus, as king and head of his church, hath therein appointed a government, in the hand of church officers, distinct from the civil magistrate.

2. To these officers the keys of the kingdom of heaven are committed; by virtue whereof, they have power, respectively, to retain, and remit sins; to shut that kingdom against the impenitent, both by the Word, and censures; and to open it unto penitent sinners, by the ministry of the gospel; and by absolution from censures, as occasion shall require.

3. Church censures are necessary, for the reclaiming and gaining of offending brethren, for deterring of others from the like offenses, for purging out of that leaven which might infect the whole lump, for vindicating the honor of Christ, and the holy profession of the gospel, and for preventing the wrath of God, which might justly fall upon the church, if they should suffer his covenant, and the seals thereof, to be profaned by notorious and obstinate offenders.

4. For the better attaining of these ends, the officers of the church are to proceed by admonition; suspension from the sacrament of the Lord's Supper for a season; and by excommunication from the church; according to the nature of the crime, and demerit of the person.

## CHAPTER 31: OF SYNODS AND COUNCILS

1. For the better government, and further edification of the church, there ought to be such assemblies as are commonly called synods or councils: and it belongeth to the overseers and other rulers of the particular churches, by virtue of their office, and the power which Christ hath given them for edification and not for destruction, to appoint such assemblies; and to convene together in them, as often as they shall judge it expedient for the good of the church.

2. It belongeth to synods and councils, ministerially to determine controversies of faith, and cases of conscience; to set down rules and directions for the better ordering of the public worship of God, and government of his church; to receive complaints in cases of maladministration, and authoritatively to determine the same: which decrees and determinations, if consonant to the Word of God, are to be received with reverence and submission; not only for their agreement with the Word, but also for the power whereby they are made, as being an ordinance of God appointed thereunto in his Word.

3. All synods or councils, since the apostles' times, whether general or particular, may err; and many have erred. Therefore they are not to be made the rule of faith, or practice; but to be used as a help in both.

4. Synods and councils are to handle, or conclude nothing, but that which is ecclesiastical: and are not to intermeddle with civil affairs which concern the commonwealth, unless by way of humble petition in cases extraordinary; or, by way of advice, for satisfaction of conscience, if they be thereunto required by the civil magistrate.

## Chapter 32: Of the State of Men After Death, and of the Resurrection of the Dead

1. The bodies of men, after death, return to dust, and see corruption: but their souls, which neither die nor sleep, having an immortal subsistence, immediately return to God who gave them: the souls of the righteous, being then made perfect in holiness, are received into the highest heavens, where they behold the face of God, in light and glory, waiting for the full redemption of their bodies. And the souls of the wicked are cast into hell, where they remain in torments and utter darkness, reserved to the judgment of the great day. Beside these two places, for souls separated from their bodies, the Scripture acknowledgeth none.

2. At the last day, such as are found alive shall not die, but be changed: and all the dead shall be raised up, with the selfsame bodies, and none other (although with different qualities), which shall be united again to their souls forever.

3. The bodies of the unjust shall, by the power of Christ, be raised to dishonor: the bodies of the just, by his Spirit, unto honor; and be made conformable to his own glorious body.

## Chapter 33: Of the Last Judgment

1. God hath appointed a day, wherein he will judge the world, in righteousness, by Jesus Christ, to whom all power and judgment is given of the Father. In which day, not only the apostate angels shall be judged, but likewise all persons that have lived upon earth shall appear before the tribunal of Christ, to give an account of their thoughts, words, and deeds; and to receive according to what they have done in the body, whether good or evil.

2. The end of God's appointing this day is for the manifestation of the glory of his mercy, in the eternal salvation of the elect; and of his justice, in the damnation of the reprobate, who are wicked and disobedient. For then shall the righteous go into everlasting life, and receive that fullness of joy and refreshing, which shall come from the presence of the Lord; but the wicked who know not God, and obey not the gospel of Jesus Christ, shall be cast into eternal torments, and be punished with everlasting destruction from the presence of the Lord, and from the glory of his power.

3. As Christ would have us to be certainly persuaded that there shall be a day of judgment, both to deter all men from sin; and for the greater consolation of the godly in their adversity: so will he have that day unknown to men, that they may shake off all carnal security, and be always watchful, because they know not at what hour the Lord will come; and may be ever prepared to say, Come Lord Jesus, come quickly, Amen.

# THE NEW HAMPSHIRE BAPTIST CONFESSION (1833)

## DECLARATION OF FAITH

### I. Of the Scriptures.

We believe that the Holy Bible was written by men divinely inspired, and is a perfect treasure of heavenly instruction; that it has God for its author, salvation for its end, and truth without any mixture of error for its matter; that it reveals the principles by which God will judge us; and therefore is, and shall remain to the end of the world, the true center of Christian union, and the supreme standard by which all human conduct, creeds, and opinions should be tried.

### II. Of the True God.

We believe that there is one, and only one, living and true God, an infinite, intelligent Spirit, whose name is JEHOVAH, the Maker and Supreme Ruler of heaven and earth; inexpressibly glorious in holiness, and worthy of all possible honor, confidence, and love; that in the unity of the Godhead there are three persons, the Father, the Son and the Holy Spirit; equal in every divine perfection, and executing distinct and harmonious offices in the great work of redemption.

### III. Of the Fall of Man.

We believe that man was created in holiness, under the law of his Maker; but by voluntary transgression fell from that holy and happy state; in consequence of which all mankind are now sinners, not by constraint, but choice; being by nature utterly void of that holiness required by the law of God, positively inclined to evil; and therefore under just condemnation to eternal ruin, without defense or excuse.

### IV. Of the Way of Salvation.

We believe that the salvation of sinners is wholly of grace, through the mediatorial offices of the Son of God; who by the appointment of the Father, freely took upon him our nature, yet without sin; honored the divine law by his personal obedience, and by his death made a full atonement for our sins; that having risen from the dead, he is now enthroned in heaven; and uniting in his wonderful person the tenderest sympathies with divine perfections, he is every way qualified to be a suitable, a compassionate, and all-sufficient Saviour.

### V. Of Justification.

We believe that the great gospel blessing which Christ secures to such as believe in him is Justification; that Justification includes the pardon of sin, and the promise of eternal life on principles of righteousness; that it is bestowed, not in consideration of any works of righteousness which we have done, but solely through faith in the Redeemer's blood; by virtue of which faith his perfect righteousness is freely imputed to us of God; that it brings us into a state of most blessed peace and favor with God, and secures every other blessing needful for time and eternity.

## VI. Of the Freeness of Salvation.

We believe that the blessings of salvation are made free to all by the gospel; that it is the immediate duty of all to accept them by a cordial, penitent, and obedient faith; and that nothing prevents the salvation of the greatest sinner on earth but his own inherent depravity and voluntary rejection of the gospel; which rejection involves him in an aggravated condemnation.

## VII. Of Grace in Regeneration.

We believe that, in order to be saved, sinners must be regenerated, or born again; that regeneration consists in giving a holy disposition to the mind; that it is effected in a manner above our comprehension by the power of the Holy Spirit, in connection with divine truth, so as to secure our voluntary obedience to the gospel; and that its proper evidence appears in the holy fruits of repentance, and faith, and newness of life.

## VIII. Of Repentance and Faith.

We believe that Repentance and Faith are sacred duties, and also inseparable graces, wrought in our souls by the regenerating Spirit of God; whereby being deeply convinced of our guilt, danger, and helplessness, and of the way of salvation by Christ, we turn to God with unfeigned contrition, confession, and supplication for mercy; at the same time heartily receiving the Lord Jesus Christ as our Prophet, Priest, and King, and relying on him as the only and all-sufficient Saviour.

## IX. Of God's Purpose of Grace.

We believe that Election is the eternal purpose of God, according to which he graciously regenerates, sanctifies, and saves sinners; that being perfectly consistent with the free agency of man, it comprehends all the means in connection with the end; that it is a most glorious display of God's sovereign goodness, being infinitely free, wise, holy, and unchangeable; that it utterly excludes boasting, and promotes humility, love, prayer, praise, trust in God, and active imitation of his free mercy; that it encourages the use of means in the highest degree; that it may be ascertained by its effects in all who truly believe the gospel; that it is the foundation of Christian assurance; and that to ascertain it with regard to ourselves demands and deserves the utmost diligence.

## X. Of Sanctification.

We believe that Sanctification is the process by which, according to the will of God, we are made partakers of his holiness; that it is a progressive work; that it is begun in regeneration; and that it is carried on in the hearts of believers by the presence and power of the Holy Spirit, the Sealer and Comforter, in the continual use of the appointed means—especially the Word of God, self-examination, self-denial, watchfulness, and prayer.

### XI. Of the Preservation of Saints.

We believe that such only are real believers as endure unto the end; that their persevering attachment to Christ is the grand mark which distinguishes them from superficial professors; that a special Providence watches over their welfare; and they are kept by the power of God through faith unto salvation.

### XII. Of the Harmony of the Law and the Gospel.

We believe that the Law of God is the eternal and unchangeable rule of his moral government; that it is holy, just, and good; and that the inability which the Scriptures ascribe to fallen men to fulfill its precepts arises entirely from their love of sin; to deliver them from which, and to restore them through a Mediator to unfeigned obedience to the holy Law, is one great end of the Gospel, and of the means of grace connected with the establishment of the visible Church.

### XIII. Of a Gospel Church.

We believe that a visible Church of Christ is a congregation of baptized believers, associated by covenant in the faith and fellowship of the gospel; observing the ordinances of Christ; governed by his laws, and exercising the gifts, rights, and privileges invested in them by his Word; that its only scriptural offices are Bishops, or Pastors, and Deacons, whose qualifications, claims, and duties are defined in the Epistles to Timothy and Titus.

### XIV. Of Baptism and the Lord's Supper.

We believe that Christian Baptism is the immersion in water of a believer, into the name of the Father, and Son, and Holy Spirit; to show forth, in a solemn and beautiful emblem, our faith in the crucified, buried, and risen Savior, with its effect in our death to sin and resurrection to a new life; that it is prerequisite to the privileges of a Church relation; and to the Lord's Supper, in which the members of the Church, by the sacred use of bread and wine, are to commemorate together the dying love of Christ; preceeded always by solemn self-examination.

### XV. Of the Christian Sabbath.

We believe that the first day of the week is the Lord's Day or Christian Sabbath; and is to be kept sacred to religious purposes, by abstaining from all secular labor and sinful recreations; by the devout observance of all the means of grace, both private and public; and by preparation for that rest that remaineth for the people of God.

## XVI. Of Civil Government.

We believe that civil government is of divine appointment, for the interests and good order of human society; and that magistrates are to be prayed for, conscientiously honored and obeyed; except only things opposed to the will of our Lord Jesus Christ, who is the only Lord of the conscience, and the Prince of the kings of the earth.

## XVII. Of the Righteous and the Wicked.

We believe that there is a radical and essential difference between the righteous and the wicked; that such only as through faith are justified in the name of the Lord Jesus, and sanctified by the Spirit of our God, are truly righteous in his esteem; while all such as continue in impenitence and unbelief are in his sight wicked, and under the curse; and this distinction holds among men both in and after death.

## XVIII. Of the World to Come.

We believe that the end of the world is approaching; that at the last day Christ will descend from heaven and raise the dead from the grave to final retribution; that a solemn separation will then take place; that the wicked will be adjudged to endless punishment, and the righteous to endless joy; and that this judgment will fix forever the final state of men in heaven or hell, on principles of righteousness.

# THE BAPTIST FAITH AND MESSAGE SOUTHERN BAPTIST CONVENTION (1925, REVISED 1963, 2000)

## I. THE SCRIPTURES

The Holy Bible was written by men divinely inspired and is God's revelation of Himself to man. It is a perfect treasure of divine instruction. It has God for its author, salvation for its end, and truth, without any mixture of error, for its matter. Therefore, all Scripture is totally true and trustworthy. It reveals the principles by which God judges us, and therefore is, and will remain to the end of the world, the true center of Christian union, and the supreme standard by which all human conduct, creeds, and religious opinions should be tried. All Scripture is a testimony to Christ, who is Himself the focus of divine revelation.

## II. GOD

There is one and only one living and true God. He is an intelligent, spiritual, and personal Being, the Creator, Redeemer, Preserver, and Ruler of the universe. God is infinite in holiness and all other perfections. God is all powerful and all knowing; and His perfect knowledge extends to all things, past, present, and future, including the future decisions of His free creatures. To Him we owe the highest love, reverence, and obedience. The eternal triune God reveals Himself to us as Father, Son, and

Holy Spirit, with distinct personal attributes, but without division of nature, essence, or being.

**A. God the Father** God as Father reigns with providential care over His universe, His creatures, and the flow of the stream of human history according to the purposes of His grace. He is all powerful, all knowing, all loving, and all wise. God is Father in truth to those who become children of God through faith in Jesus Christ. He is fatherly in His attitude toward all men.

**B. God the Son** Christ is the eternal Son of God. In His incarnation as Jesus Christ He was conceived of the Holy Spirit and born of the virgin Mary. Jesus perfectly revealed and did the will of God, taking upon Himself human nature with its demands and necessities and identifying Himself completely with mankind yet without sin. He honored the divine law by His personal obedience, and in His substitutionary death on the cross He made provision for the redemption of men from sin. He was raised from the dead with a glorified body and appeared to His disciples as the person who was with them before His crucifixion. He ascended into heaven and is now exalted at the right hand of God where He is the One Mediator, fully God, fully man, in whose Person is effected the reconciliation between God and man. He will return in power and glory to judge the world and to consummate His redemptive mission. He now dwells in all believers as the living and ever present Lord.

**C. God the Holy Spirit** The Holy Spirit is the Spirit of God, fully divine. He inspired holy men of old to write the Scriptures. Through illumination He enables men to understand truth. He exalts Christ. He convicts men of sin, of righteousness, and of judgment. He calls men to the Saviour, and effects regeneration. At the moment of regeneration He baptizes every believer into the Body of Christ. He cultivates Christian character, comforts believers, and bestows the spiritual gifts by which they serve God through His church. He seals the believer unto the day of final redemption. His presence in the Christian is the guarantee that God will bring the believer into the fullness of the stature of Christ. He enlightens and empowers the believer and the church in worship, evangelism, and service.

## III. Man

Man is the special creation of God, made in His own image. He created them male and female as the crowning work of His creation. The gift of gender is thus part of the goodness of God's creation. In the beginning man was innocent of sin and was endowed by his Creator with freedom of choice. By his free choice man sinned against God and brought sin into the human race. Through the temptation of Satan man transgressed the command of God, and fell from his original innocence whereby his posterity inherit a nature and an environment inclined toward sin. Therefore, as soon as they are capable of moral action, they become transgressors and are under condemnation. Only the grace of God can bring man into His holy fellowship and enable man to fulfill the creative purpose of God. The sacredness of human personality is evident in that God created man in His own image, and in that Christ died for man; therefore, every person of every race possesses full dignity and is worthy of respect and Christian love.

## IV. SALVATION

Salvation involves the redemption of the whole man, and is offered freely to all who accept Jesus Christ as Lord and Saviour, who by His own blood obtained eternal redemption for the believer. In its broadest sense salvation includes regeneration, justification, sanctification, and glorification. There is no salvation apart from personal faith in Jesus Christ as Lord.

A. Regeneration, or the new birth, is a work of God's grace whereby believers become new creatures in Christ Jesus. It is a change of heart wrought by the Holy Spirit through conviction of sin, to which the sinner responds in repentance toward God and faith in the Lord Jesus Christ. Repentance and faith are inseparable experiences of grace.

Repentance is a genuine turning from sin toward God. Faith is the acceptance of Jesus Christ and commitment of the entire personality to Him as Lord and Saviour.

B. Justification is God's gracious and full acquittal upon principles of His righteousness of all sinners who repent and believe in Christ. Justification brings the believer unto a relationship of peace and favor with God.

C. Sanctification is the experience, beginning in regeneration, by which the believer is set apart to God's purposes, and is enabled to progress toward moral and spiritual maturity through the presence and power of the Holy Spirit dwelling in him. Growth in grace should continue throughout the regenerate person's life.

D. Glorification is the culmination of salvation and is the final blessed and abiding state of the redeemed.

## V. GOD'S PURPOSE OF GRACE

Election is the gracious purpose of God, according to which He regenerates, justifies, sanctifies, and glorifies sinners. It is consistent with the free agency of man, and comprehends all the means in connection with the end. It is the glorious display of God's sovereign goodness, and is infinitely wise, holy, and unchangeable. It excludes boasting and promotes humility.

All true believers endure to the end. Those whom God has accepted in Christ, and sanctified by His Spirit, will never fall away from the state of grace, but shall persevere to the end. Believers may fall into sin through neglect and temptation, whereby they grieve the Spirit, impair their graces and comforts, and bring reproach on the cause of Christ and temporal judgments on themselves; yet they shall be kept by the power of God through faith unto salvation.

## VI. The Church

A New Testament church of the Lord Jesus Christ is an autonomous local congregation of baptized believers, associated by covenant in the faith and fellowship of the gospel; observing the two ordinances of Christ, governed by His laws, exercising the gifts, rights, and privileges invested in them by His Word, and seeking to extend the gospel to the ends of the earth. Each congregation operates under the Lordship of Christ through democratic processes. In such a congregation each member is responsible and accountable to Christ as Lord. Its scriptural officers are pastors and deacons. While both men and women are gifted for service in the church, the office of pastor is limited to men as qualified by Scripture.

The New Testament speaks also of the church as the Body of Christ which includes all of the redeemed of all the ages, believers from every tribe, and tongue, and people, and nation.

## VII. Baptism and the Lord's Supper

Christian baptism is the immersion of a believer in water in the name of the Father, the Son, and the Holy Spirit. It is an act of obedience symbolizing the believer's faith in a crucified, buried, and risen Saviour, the believer's death to sin, the burial of the old life, and the resurrection to walk in newness of life in Christ Jesus. It is a testimony to his faith in the final resurrection of the dead. Being a church ordinance, it is prerequisite to the privileges of church membership and to the Lord's Supper.

The Lord's Supper is a symbolic act of obedience whereby members of the church, through partaking of the bread and the fruit of the vine, memorialize the death of the Redeemer and anticipate His second coming.

## VIII. The Lord's Day

The first day of the week is the Lord's Day. It is a Christian institution for regular observance. It commemorates the resurrection of Christ from the dead and should include exercises of worship and spiritual devotion, both public and private. Activities on the Lord's Day should be commensurate with the Christian's conscience under the Lordship of Jesus Christ.

## IX. The Kingdom

The Kingdom of God includes both His general sovereignty over the universe and His particular kingship over men who willfully acknowledge Him as King. Particularly the Kingdom is the realm of salvation into which men enter by trustful, childlike commitment to Jesus Christ. Christians ought to pray and to labor that the Kingdom may come and God's will be done on earth. The full consummation of the Kingdom awaits the return of Jesus Christ and the end of this age.

## X. Last Things

God, in His own time and in His own way, will bring the world to its appropriate end. According to His promise, Jesus Christ will return personally and visibly in glory to the earth; the dead will be raised; and Christ will judge all men in righteousness. The unrighteous will be consigned to Hell, the place of everlasting punishment. The righteous in their resurrected and glorified bodies will receive their reward and will dwell forever in Heaven with the Lord.

## XI. Evangelism and Missions

It is the duty and privilege of every follower of Christ and of every church of the Lord Jesus Christ to endeavor to make disciples of all nations. The new birth of man's spirit by God's Holy Spirit means the birth of love for others. Missionary effort on the part of all rests thus upon a spiritual necessity of the regenerate life, and is expressly and repeatedly commanded in the teachings of Christ. The Lord Jesus Christ has commanded the preaching of the gospel to all nations. It is the duty of every child of God to seek constantly to win the lost to Christ by verbal witness undergirded by a Christian lifestyle, and by other methods in harmony with the gospel of Christ.

## XII. Education

Christianity is the faith of enlightenment and intelligence. In Jesus Christ abide all the treasures of wisdom and knowledge. All sound learning is, therefore, a part of our Christian heritage. The new birth opens all human faculties and creates a thirst for knowledge. Moreover, the cause of education in the Kingdom of Christ is co-ordinate with the causes of missions and general benevolence, and should receive along with these the liberal support of the churches. An adequate system of Christian education is necessary to a complete spiritual program for Christ's people.

In Christian education there should be a proper balance between academic freedom and academic responsibility. Freedom in any orderly relationship of human life is always limited and never absolute. The freedom of a teacher in a Christian school, college, or seminary is limited by the pre-eminence of Jesus Christ, by the authoritative nature of the Scriptures, and by the distinct purpose for which the school exists.

## XIII. Stewardship

God is the source of all blessings, temporal and spiritual; all that we have and are we owe to Him. Christians have a spiritual debtorship to the whole world, a holy trusteeship in the gospel, and a binding stewardship in their possessions. They are therefore under obligation to serve Him with their time, talents, and material possessions; and should recognize all these as entrusted to them to use for the glory of God and for helping others. According to the Scriptures, Christians should contribute of their means cheerfully, regularly, systematically, proportionately, and liberally for the advancement of the Redeemer's cause on earth.

## XIV. COOPERATION

Christ's people should, as occasion requires, organize such associations and conventions as may best secure cooperation for the great objects of the Kingdom of God. Such organizations have no authority over one another or over the churches. They are voluntary and advisory bodies designed to elicit, combine, and direct the energies of our people in the most effective manner. Members of New Testament churches should cooperate with one another in carrying forward the missionary, educational, and benevolent ministries for the extension of Christ's Kingdom. Christian unity in the New Testament sense is spiritual harmony and voluntary cooperation for common ends by various groups of Christ's people. Cooperation is desirable between the various Christian denominations, when the end to be attained is itself justified, and when such cooperation involves no violation of conscience or compromise of loyalty to Christ and His Word as revealed in the New Testament.

## XV. THE CHRISTIAN AND THE SOCIAL ORDER

All Christians are under obligation to seek to make the will of Christ supreme in our own lives and in human society. Means and methods used for the improvement of society and the establishment of righteousness among men can be truly and permanently helpful only when they are rooted in the regeneration of the individual by the saving grace of God in Jesus Christ. In the spirit of Christ, Christians should oppose racism, every form of greed, selfishness, and vice, and all forms of sexual immorality, including adultery, homosexuality, and pornography. We should work to provide for the orphaned, the needy, the abused, the aged, the helpless, and the sick. We should speak on behalf of the unborn and contend for the sanctity of all human life from conception to natural death. Every Christian should seek to bring industry, government, and society as a whole under the sway of the principles of righteousness, truth, and brotherly love. In order to promote these ends Christians should be ready to work with all men of good will in any good cause, always being careful to act in the spirit of love without compromising their loyalty to Christ and His truth.

## XVI. PEACE AND WAR

It is the duty of Christians to seek peace with all men on principles of righteousness. In accordance with the spirit and teachings of Christ they should do all in their power to put an end to war.

The true remedy for the war spirit is the gospel of our Lord. The supreme need of the world is the acceptance of His teachings in all the affairs of men and nations, and the practical application of His law of love. Christian people throughout the world should pray for the reign of the Prince of Peace.

## XVII. Religious Liberty

God alone is Lord of the conscience, and He has left it free from the doctrines and commandments of men which are contrary to His Word or not contained in it. Church and state should be separate. The state owes to every church protection and full freedom in the pursuit of its spiritual ends. In providing for such freedom no ecclesiastical group or denomination should be favored by the state more than others. Civil government being ordained of God, it is the duty of Christians to render loyal obedience thereto in all things not contrary to the revealed will of God. The church should not resort to the civil power to carry on its work. The gospel of Christ contemplates spiritual means alone for the pursuit of its ends. The state has no right to impose penalties for religious opinions of any kind. The state has no right to impose taxes for the support of any form of religion. A free church in a free state is the Christian ideal, and this implies the right of free and unhindered access to God on the part of all men, and the right to form and propagate opinions in the sphere of religion without interference by the civil power.

## XVIII. The Family

God has ordained the family as the foundational institution of human society. It is composed of persons related to one another by marriage, blood, or adoption.

Marriage is the uniting of one man and one woman in covenant commitment for a lifetime. It is God's unique gift to reveal the union between Christ and His church and to provide for the man and the woman in marriage the framework for intimate companionship, the channel of sexual expression according to biblical standards, and the means for procreation of the human race.

The husband and wife are of equal worth before God, since both are created in God's image. The marriage relationship models the way God relates to His people. A husband is to love his wife as Christ loved the church. He has the God-given responsibility to provide for, to protect, and to lead his family. A wife is to submit herself graciously to the servant leadership of her husband even as the church willingly submits to the headship of Christ. She, being in the image of God as is her husband and thus equal to him, has the God-given responsibility to respect her husband and to serve as his helper in managing the household and nurturing the next generation.

Children, from the moment of conception, are a blessing and heritage from the Lord. Parents are to demonstrate to their children God's pattern for marriage. Parents are to teach their children spiritual and moral values and to lead them, through consistent lifestyle example and loving discipline, to make choices based on biblical truth. Children are to honor and obey their parents.

# THE CHICAGO STATEMENT ON BIBLICAL INERRANCY (1978)

## PREFACE

The authority of Scripture is a key issue for the Christian Church in this and every age. Those who profess faith in Jesus Christ as Lord and Savior are called to show the reality of their discipleship by humbly and faithfully obeying God's written Word. To stray from Scripture in faith or conduct is disloyalty to our Master. Recognition of the total truth and trustworthiness of Holy Scripture is essential to a full grasp and adequate confession of its authority.

The following Statement affirms this inerrancy of Scripture afresh, making clear our understanding of it and warning against its denial. We are persuaded that to deny it is to set aside the witness of Jesus Christ and of Holy Spirit and to refuse that submission to the claims of God's own word which marks true Christian faith. We see it as our timely duty to make this affirmation in the face of current lapses from the truth of inerrancy among our fellow Christians and misunderstanding of this doctrine in the world at large.

This Statement consists of three parts: a Summary Statement, Articles of Affirmation and Denial, and an accompanying Exposition. It has been prepared in the course of a three-day consultation in Chicago. Those who have signed the Summary Statement and the Articles wish to affirm their own conviction as to the inerrancy of Scripture and to encourage and challenge one another and all Christians to growing appreciation and understanding of this doctrine. We acknowledge the limitations of a document prepared in a brief, intensive conference and do not propose that this Statement be given creedal weight. Yet we rejoice in the deepening of our own convictions through our discussions together, and we pray that the Statement we have signed may be used to the glory of our God toward a new reformation of the Church in its faith, life, and mission.

We offer this Statement in a spirit, not of contention, but of humility and love, which we purpose by God's grace to maintain in any future dialogue arising out of what we have said. We gladly acknowledge that many who deny the inerrancy of Scripture do not display the consequences of this denial in the rest of their belief and behavior, and we are conscious that we who confess this doctrine often deny it in life by failing to bring our thoughts and deeds, our traditions and habits, into true subjection to the divine Word.

We invite responses to this statement from any who see reason to amend its affirmations about Scripture by the light of Scripture itself, under whose infallible authority we stand as we speak. We claim no personal infallibility for the witness we bear, and for any help which enables us to strengthen this testimony to God's Word we shall be grateful.

## A SHORT STATEMENT

1. God, who is Himself Truth and speaks truth only, has inspired Holy Scripture in order thereby to reveal Himself to lost mankind through Jesus Christ as Creator and Lord, Redeemer and Judge. Holy Scripture is God's witness to Himself.

2. Holy Scripture, being God's own Word, written by men prepared and super-intended by His Spirit, is of infallible divine authority in all matters upon which it touches: it is to be believed, as God's instruction, in all that it affirms; obeyed, as God's command, in all that it requires; embraced, as God's pledge, in all that it promises.

3. The Holy Spirit, Scripture's divine Author, both authenticates it to us by His inward witness and opens our minds to understand its meaning.

4. Being wholly and verbally God-given, Scripture is without error or fault in all its teaching, no less in what it states about God's acts in creation, about the events of world history, and about its own literary origins under God, than in its witness to God's saving grace in individual lives.

5. The authority of Scripture is inescapably impaired if this total divine inerrancy is in any way limited or disregarded, or made relative to a view of truth contrary to the Bible's own; and such lapses bring serious loss to both the individual and the Church.

## ARTICLES OF AFFIRMATION AND DENIAL
### Article I
We affirm that the Holy Scriptures are to be received as the authoritative Word of God.

We deny that the Scriptures receive their authority from the Church, tradition, or any other human source.

### Article II
We affirm that the Scriptures are the supreme written norm by which God binds the conscience, and that the authority of the Church is subordinate to that of Scripture.

We deny that Church creeds, councils, or declarations have authority greater than or equal to the authority of the Bible.

### Article III
We affirm that the written Word in its entirety is revelation given by God.

We deny that the Bible is merely a witness to revelation, or only becomes revelation in encounter, or depends on the responses of men for its validity.

### Article IV
We affirm that God who made mankind in His image has used language as a means of revelation.

We deny that human language is so limited by our creatureliness that it is rendered inadequate as a vehicle for divine revelation. We further deny that the corruption of human culture and language through sin has thwarted God's work of inspiration.

### Article V
We affirm that God's revelation in the Holy Scriptures was progressive.

We deny that later revelation, which may fulfill earlier revelation, ever corrects or contradicts it. We further deny that any normative revelation has been given since the completion of the New Testament writings.

## Article VI

We affirm that the whole of Scripture and all its parts, down to the very words of the original, were given by divine inspiration.

We deny that the inspiration of Scripture can rightly be affirmed of the whole without the parts, or of some parts but not the whole.

## Article VII

We affirm that inspiration was the work in which God by His Spirit, through human writers, gave us His Word. The origin of Scripture is divine. The mode of divine inspiration remains largely a mystery to us.

We deny that inspiration can be reduced to human insight, or to heightened states of consciousness of any kind.

## Article VIII

We affirm that God in His work of inspiration utilized the distinctive personalities and literary styles of the writers whom He had chosen and prepared.

We deny that God, in causing these writers to use the very words that He chose, overrode their personalities.

## Article IX

We affirm that inspiration, though not conferring omniscience, guaranteed true and trustworthy utterance on all matters of which the Bible authors were moved to speak and write.

We deny that the finitude or fallenness of these writers, by necessity or otherwise, introduced distortion or falsehood into God's Word.

## Article X

We affirm that inspiration, strictly speaking, applies to the autographic text of Scripture, which in the providence of God can be ascertained from available manuscripts with great accuracy. We further affirm that copies and translations of Scripture are the Word of God to the extent that they faithfully represent the original.

We deny that any essential element of the Christian faith is affected by the absence of the autographs. We further deny that this absence renders the assertion of Biblical inerrancy invalid or irrelevant.

## Article XI

We affirm that Scripture, having been given by divine inspiration, is infallible, so that, far from misleading us, it is true and reliable in all matters it addresses.

We deny that it is possible for the Bible to be at the same time infallible and errant in its assertions. Infallibility and inerrancy may be distinguished, but not separated.

## Article XII

We affirm that Scripture in its entirety is inerrant, being free from all falsehood, fraud, or deceit.

We deny that Biblical infallibility and inerrancy are limited to spiritual, religious or redemptive themes, exclusive of assertions in the fields of history and science. We further deny that scientific hypotheses about earth history may properly be used to overturn the teaching of Scripture on creation and the flood.

## Article XIII

We affirm the propriety of using inerrancy as a theological term with reference to the complete truthfulness of Scripture.

We deny that it is proper to evaluate Scripture according to standards of truth and error that are alien to its usage or purpose. We further deny that inerrancy is negated by Biblical phenomena such as a lack of modern technical precision, irregularities of grammar or spelling, observational descriptions of nature, the reporting of falsehoods, the use of hyperbole and round numbers, the topical arrangement of material, variant selections of material in parallel accounts, or the use of free citations.

## Article XIV

We affirm the unity and internal consistency of Scripture.

We deny that alleged errors and discrepancies that have not yet been resolved vitiate the truth of claims of the Bible.

## Article XV

We affirm that the doctrine of inerrancy is grounded in the teaching of the Bible about inspiration.

We deny that Jesus' teaching about Scripture may be dismissed by appeals to accommodation or to any natural limitation of His humanity.

## Article XVI

We affirm that the doctrine of inerrancy has been integral to the Church's faith throughout its history.

We deny that inerrancy is a doctrine invented by Scholastic Protestantism, or is a reactionary position postulated in response to negative higher criticism.

## Article XVII

We affirm that the Holy Spirit bears witness to the Scriptures, assuring believers of the truthfulness of God's written Word.

We deny that this witness of the Holy Spirit operates in isolation from or against Scripture.

## Article XVIII

We affirm that the text of Scripture is to be interpreted by grammatico-historical exegesis, taking account of its literary forms and devices, and that Scripture is to interpret Scripture.

We deny the legitimacy of any treatment of the text or quest for sources lying behind it that leads to relativizing, dehistoricizing, or discounting its teaching, or rejecting its claims to authorship.

## Article XIX

We affirm that a confession of the full authority, infallibility, and inerrancy of Scripture is vital to a sound understanding of the whole of the Christian faith. We further affirm that such confession should lead to increasing conformity to the image of Christ.

We deny that such confession is necessary for salvation. However, we further deny that inerrancy can be rejected without grave consequences, both to the individual and to the Church.

# APPENDIX 2

# Annotated Bibliography of Evangelical Systematic Theologies

T his bibliography lists most of the major evangelical systematic theologies available in English and a few shorter guides to Christian doctrine. With the exception of the two Roman Catholic theologies (by McBrien and Ott), which are included because I have cross-referenced them at the end of each chapter, all of the authors on this list fall generally within a "conservative evangelical" theological position.[1]

In the appendix following this bibliography I have added a master list of the fifty-one Protestant and three Roman Catholic theologies which I cross-referenced at the end of each chapter.

---

Akin, Daniel L., ed. *A Theology for the Church*. Nashville: B&H, 2007.

    Akin is the widely respected president of Southeastern Baptist Theological Seminary in Wake Forest, North Carolina. He edited this collection of fifteen essays on the major doctrines of the Christian faith and their importance for life, all written by contemporary Baptist scholars.

Allen, Michael, and Scott R. Swain. *Christian Dogmatics: Reformed Theology for the Church Catholic*. Grand Rapids, Baker: 2016.

    A compilation of sixteen essays on major Christian doctrines, written by twelve contemporary Reformed scholars.

Allison, Greg R. *50 Core Truths of the Christian Faith: A Guide to Understanding and Teaching Theology*. Grand Rapids: Baker, 2018.

Arminius, James. *The Writings of James Arminius*. 3 vols. Vols. 1 and 2, translated by James Nichols. Vol. 3, translated by W. R. Bagnell. Grand Rapids: Baker, 1956.

    Arminius (1560–1609) was a Reformed pastor in Amsterdam and later professor of theology at the University of Leyden. His disagreement with some of the central tenets of Calvinism led to a great controversy in the Netherlands that continued long after his death. His ideas became the foundation of a system of thought now known as Arminianism,

---

1. A very helpful and more broadly based annotated bibliography, including notes on works from several prominent liberal scholars, may be found in John Jefferson Davis, *Theology Primer* (Grand Rapids: Baker, 1981), 74–79; see also his "Brief Guide to Modern Theologians" on pp. 39–55. In addition, valuable brief notes on dozens of important theologians from all theological traditions may be found in Millard Erickson, *Concise Dictionary of Christian Theology* (Grand Rapids: Baker, 1986).

which continues today in conservative Wesleyan and Methodist churches and in many other Protestant groups. This collection of writings, assembled after his death, is not strictly organized as a systematic theology, but it does contain discussions of most important theological topics.

Barrett, Matthew. *Reformation Theology: A Systematic Summary*. Wheaton, IL: Crossway, 2017.

This volume contains twenty essays by various authors, with an emphasis on the main doctrines taught by the Protestant Reformers in the Reformation of the sixteenth century.

Bavinck, Herman. *Reformed Dogmatics*. Edited by John Bolt. Translated by John Vriend. 4 vols. Grand Rapids: Baker, 2008.

Bavinck (1854–1921) was a Dutch theologian and one of this century's most brilliant spokesmen for a Reformed theological position.

Berkhof, Louis. *Introduction to Systematic Theology*. Grand Rapids: Eerdmans, 1932. Reprint, Grand Rapids: Baker, 1979.

———. *Systematic Theology*. 4th ed. Grand Rapids: Eerdmans, 1939.

The standard Reformed textbook for systematic theology by a former president of Calvin Seminary in Grand Rapids, Michigan. This book is a great treasure-house of information and analysis and is probably the most useful one-volume systematic theology available from any theological perspective. Berkhof lived from 1873 to 1957.

Berkouwer, G. C. *Studies in Dogmatics*. 14 vols. (1952–76).

———. *The Church*. Translated by James E. Davidson. Grand Rapids: Eerdmans, 1976.

———. *Divine Election*. Translated by Hugo Bekker. Grand Rapids: Eerdmans, 1960.

———. *Faith and Justification*. Translated by Lewis B. Smedes. Grand Rapids: Eerdmans, 1954.

———. *Faith and Perseverance*. Translated by Robert D. Knudsen. Grand Rapids: Eerdmans, 1958.

———. *Faith and Sanctification*. Translated by John Vriend. Grand Rapids: Eerdmans, 1952.

———. *General Revelation*. [No translator named.] Grand Rapids: Eerdmans, 1955.

———. *Man: The Image of God*. Translated by Dirk W. Jellma. Grand Rapids: Eerdmans, 1962.

———. *Holy Scripture*. Translated and edited by Jack B. Rogers. Grand Rapids: Eerdmans, 1975.

———. *The Person of Christ*. Translated by John Vriend. Grand Rapids: Eerdmans, 1954.

———. *The Providence of God*. Translated by Louis B. Smedes. Grand Rapids: Eerdmans, 1952.

———. *The Return of Christ*. Translated by James Van Oosterom. Edited by Marlin J. Van Elderen. Grand Rapids: Eerdmans, 1972.

———. *The Sacraments*. Translated by Hugo Bekker. Grand Rapids: Eerdmans, 1969.

———. *Sin*. Translated by Philip C. Holtrop. Grand Rapids: Eerdmans, 1971.

———. *The Work of Christ*. Translated by Cornelius Lambregtse. Grand Rapids: Eerdmans, 1965.

Major contemporary studies by a Reformed theologian who was professor of systematic theology at the Free University of Amsterdam.

Bird, Michael F. *Evangelical Theology: A Biblical and Systematic Introduction*. Grand Rapids: Zondervan, 2013.

A very readable systematic theology structured around the message of the gospel, written by a New Testament scholar who is academic dean at Ridley College in Melbourne, Australia.

Bloesch, Donald G. *Essentials of Evangelical Theology*. 2 vols. New York: Harper and Row, 1978–79.

A work by a contemporary theologian who is in the Reformed tradition broadly but much less clear on the doctrines of election and the authority of Scripture, for example, than other writers classified as "Reformed" in this bibliography. (More recently, Bloesch has begun to publish a multivolume systematic theology.)

Boice, James Montgomery. *Foundations of the Christian Faith*. Revised one-volume edition. Downers Grove, IL: InterVarsity Press, 1986.

A recent Reformed guide to systematic theology written by the theologian-pastor of Tenth Presbyterian Church, Philadelphia. This work is written in a popular, readable style, with helpful application of doctrines to life. It was previously published in four separate volumes: *The Sovereign God* (1978), *God the Redeemer* (1978), *Awakening to God* (1979), and *God and History* (1981).

Boyce, James Pettigru. *Abstract of Systematic Theology*. 1887. Reprint, Christian Gospel Foundation, n.d.

A Baptist systematic theology that is also Reformed in doctrinal orientation by a former president and professor of systematic theology in the Southern Baptist Seminary, Louisville, Kentucky. Boyce lived from 1827 to 1888.

Bray, Gerald. *God Has Spoken: A History of Christian Theology*. Wheaton, IL: Crossway, 2014.

Bray is a remarkably erudite Anglican scholar who says his aim in this book is "to make the history of Christian theology comprehensible to nonspecialists while at the same time providing a useful resource for those who want to take the subject further" (22). Bray is now retired, but he taught for many years at Beeson Divinity School in Birmingham, Alabama.

Buswell, James Oliver, Jr. *A Systematic Theology of the Christian Religion.* 2 vols. Grand Rapids: Zondervan, 1962–63.

A Reformed systematic theology by the former dean of the graduate faculty at Covenant College and Seminary in St. Louis, Missouri.

Calvin, John. *Institutes of the Christian Religion.* 2 vols. Edited by John T. McNeill. Translated and indexed by Ford Lewis Battles. The Library of Christian Classics, vols. 20–21. Philadelphia: Westminster, 1960. Translated from the 1559 text and collated with earlier versions.

This is the best available English translation of Calvin's systematic exposition of the Christian faith. Calvin (1509–64) was a French reformer who became the greatest theologian of the Reformation and, according to many estimates, the greatest theologian in the history of the church. Reformed in doctrinal perspective.

Carter, Charles W., ed. *A Contemporary Wesleyan Theology: Biblical, Systematic, and Practical.* 2 vols. Grand Rapids: Francis Asbury Press (Zondervan), 1983.

This is a collection of twenty-four essays on major doctrinal themes by several scholars representing a wide range of conservative Wesleyan denominations and institutions. The set also includes some essays on practical theology and ethics. Charles Carter, who contributed four of the chapters, is professor of religion and missions at Marion College, Marion, Indiana. The advisory committee for the volumes includes representatives of United Methodist, Free Methodist, Church of the Nazarene, Missionary Church, Salvation Army, Wesleyan Church, and other groups.

Chafer, Lewis Sperry. *Systematic Theology.* 7 vols. plus index vol. Dallas: Dallas Seminary Press, 1947–48.

———. *Systematic Theology.* Abridged ed. 2 vols. Edited by John F. Walvoord, Donald K. Campbell, and Roy B. Zuck. Wheaton, IL: Victor, 1988.

Chafer (1871–1952) was the first president of Dallas Theological Seminary. The seven-volume

edition is the most extensive dispensational systematic theology ever written. The two volume edition is a condensation of the earlier work.

Challies, Tim, and Josh Byers. *A Visual Theology Guide to the Bible: Seeing and Knowing God's Word.* Grand Rapids: Zondervan, 2019.

Cottrell, Jack. *The Faith Once for All: Bible Doctrine for Today.* Joplin, MO: College Press, 2002.

Culver, Robert Duncan. *Systematic Theology: Biblical and Historical.* 2005. Reprint, Geanies House, UK: Mentor, 2008.

Culver taught at Greece Theological Seminary, Wheaton College and Graduate School, and Trinity Evangelical Divinity School. This lengthy volume contains significant emphasis on the biblical basis for Christian doctrines.

Dabney, Robert L. *Discussions: Evangelical and Theological.* 1980. Reprint, London: Banner of Truth, 1967.

———. *Systematic Theology.* Edinburgh: Banner of Truth, 1985. Reprint of 1878 edition.

A Southern Presbyterian who represented a strongly Reformed position, Dabney (1820–98) was professor of theology at Union Seminary in Virginia. He was also chaplain and later chief of staff for General Stonewall Jackson during the American Civil War.

Dorman, Taylor A. *A Faith for All Seasons.* Nashville: B&H, 2001.

Driscoll, Mark, and Gerry Breshears. *Doctrine: What Christians Should Believe.* Wheaton, IL: Crossway, 2010.

Duffield, Guy P., and Nathaniel M. Van Cleave. *Foundations of Pentecostal Theology.* Lake Mary, FL: Creation House, 2008.

An extensive treatment of Christian doctrine, written by two veteran Pentecostal pastor-teachers, with extensive discussion of "baptism with the Holy Spirit," various spiritual gifts, and much material on divine healing.

Enns, Paul P. *The Moody Handbook of Theology.* Chicago: Moody Publishers, 2008.

Erickson, Millard. *Christian Theology.* 3rd ed. Grand Rapids: Baker, 2013.

A clear and very thorough recent textbook in systematic theology from a moderately Reformed and Baptist perspective. Erickson is distinguished professor of theology at Western Seminary in Portland, Oregon. He previously was Academic Dean at Bethel Theological Seminary in St. Paul, Minnesota, and later at Southwestern Baptist Seminary in Ft. Worth, Texas, and at Baylor University. This book includes interaction with all the major trends in contemporary nonevangelical theology, as well as helpful material for personal application.

Finney, Charles G. *Finney's Lectures on Systematic Theology*. Edited by J. H. Fairchild. 1878. Reprint, Grand Rapids: Eerdmans, 1953.

> Finney (1792–1875) was a revivalist and president of Oberlin College 1851–66. Not representative of any one theological position, but he articulated some strong Arminian arguments. Emphasis on personal holiness and perfectionism. Not really a complete systematic theology because many topics are not covered.

Frame, John. *Systematic Theology: An Introduction to Christian Belief*. Phillipsburg, NJ: P&R, 2013.

> This excellent volume is a wonderfully clear, refreshingly insightful, and profoundly biblical treatment of systematic theology, written by the now-retired professor of systematic theology at Reformed Theological Seminary in Orlando, Florida, who previously had taught at Westminster Seminary California and Westminster Theological Seminary in Philadelphia.

Garret, James Leo. *Systematic Theology: Biblical, Historical, Evangelical*. 2 vols. Grand Rapids: Eerdmans, 1990, 1995.

> Garret was a professor of theology at Southwestern Baptist Theological Seminary. He is Baptistic and evangelical in his convictions, yet he gives much more space to representing different positions clearly than to arguing for his position. With 1,530 total pages, these volumes are an amazingly rich resource for historical, bibliographical, and biblical data on each doctrine treated.

Geisler, Norman. *Systematic Theology*. 4 vols. Minneapolis: Bethany House, 2002.

> Geisler, who died in July 2019, was a prolific author of works on theology, apologetics, and ethics, and a strong defender of biblical inerrancy.

Gill, John. *Complete Body of Doctrinal and Practical Divinity*. 2 vols. Grand Rapids: Baker, 1978. First published as *A Body of Doctrinal Divinity* (1767) and *A Body of Practical Divinity* (1770).

> Gill (1697–1771) was a highly influential Baptist pastor, a prolific writer, and a respected theologian in eighteenth-century England. He was also Reformed (or Calvinistic) in his view of God's sovereignty.

His book, *The Cause of God and Truth* (1735–38; reprint, Grand Rapids: Baker, 1981) is one of the most thorough defenses of Calvinistic theology ever written.

Harle, Wilfried. *Outline of Christian Doctrine: An Evangelical Dogmatics*. Edited by Nicholas Sagovsky. Translated by Ruth Yule. Grand Rapids: Eerdmans, 2015.

Henry, Carl F. H. *God, Revelation, and Authority*. 6 vols. Waco, TX: Word, 1976–83.

> A major work containing detailed interaction with hundreds of other scholarly positions. Henry, who died in 2003, was a leading evangelical theologian with great strengths especially in the areas of apologetics and philosophical theology.

Heppe, Heinrich. *Reformed Dogmatics: Set Out and Illustrated From the Sources*. Revised and edited by Ernst Bizer. Translated by G. T. Thompson. First published 1861. English translation first published 1950. Reprint, Grand Rapids: Baker, 1978.

> Heppe (1820–79) was a German scholar who collected and quoted extensively from many earlier Reformed theologians. Because the quotations are arranged according to the topics of systematic theology, this book is a valuable sourcebook.

Hodge, Charles. *Systematic Theology*. 3 vols. 1871–73. Reprint, Grand Rapids: Eerdmans, 1970.

> A major Reformed systematic theology that is still widely used today. Hodge (1797–1878) was professor of systematic theology at Princeton Theological Seminary.

Horton, Michael. *The Christian Faith: A Systematic Theology for Pilgrims on the Way*. Grand Rapids: Zondervan, 2011.

> Horton is a prolific author and a professor of systematic theology and apologetics at Westminster Seminary California. This is a clear statement of contemporary Reformed theology.

Horton, Stanley. *Systematic Theology*. Revised ed. Springfield, MO: Gospel, 1994.

> This is a collection of eighteen essays on major Christian doctrines, written by twenty different Pentecostal authors.

Kelly, Douglas F. *Systematic Theology*. Vols. 1 and 2. Fearn, Ross-Shire: Christian Focus, 2008, 2014.

> These first two volumes of a projected series show a broad command of both biblical literature and historical theology. Kelly is professor of systematic theology at Reformed Theological Seminary in Charlotte, North Carolina.

Lewis, Gordon R., and Bruce Demarest. *Integrative Theology*. 3 vols. Grand Rapids: Zondervan, 1987–94.

Lewis and Demarest are both professors of systematic theology at Denver Seminary in Colorado (a Conservative Baptist seminary). This is an excellent contemporary work that integrates historical, biblical, apologetic, and practical material with systematic theology.

Litton, Edward Arthur. *Introduction to Dogmatic Theology*. New ed., edited by Philip E. Hughes. First published 1882–92. Reprint, London: James Clarke, 1960.

A standard Anglican (or Episcopalian) systematic theology by an evangelical British theologian of the nineteenth century. Litton lived from 1813 to 1897.

MacArthur, John, and Richard Mayhue. *Biblical Doctrine: A Systematic Summary of Biblical Truth*. Wheaton, IL: Crossway, 2017.

MacArthur is the president and Mayhue the former vice president of the Master's Seminary in Sun Valley, California, where MacArthur also carries on a worldwide ministry of Bible exposition as the pastor-teacher of Grace Community Church. Clearly written and biblically based, with frequent application to life. MacArthur and Mayhue defend biblical inerrancy, believer's baptism, a Reformed view of salvation, and a cessationst view regarding spiritual gifts.

McBrien, Richard P. *Catholicism*. 2 vols. Minneapolis: Winston, 1980.

A responsible and extensive explanation of Catholic teachings as they have been affected by the period since Vatican II. Contains bibliographies with each chapter.

Menzies, William W., and Stanley M. Horton. *Bible Doctrines: A Pentecostal Perspective*. Springfield, MO: Gospel, 1993.

This is a brief, popular overview of the standard doctrinal categories covered in most systematic theology texts, but with additional chapters on "The Baptism in the Holy Ghost," speaking in tongues, and healing. Menzies was president of Asia Pacific Theological Seminary in the Philippines, and Horton was a professor of Bible and theology at the Assemblies Of God Theological Seminary in Springfield, Missouri.

Miley, John. *Systematic Theology*. 2 vols. Library of Biblical and Theological Literature, vols. 5–6. New York: Eaton and Mains, 1892–94. Reprint, Peabody, MA: Hendrikson, 1989.

This is probably the most scholarly and extensive Arminian systematic theology ever written. Miley was a professor at Drew Theological Seminary, Madison, New Jersey.

Miller, Perry, ed. *The Works of Jonathan Edwards*. New Haven, CT: Yale University Press, 1957–.

A twenty-five-volume set of Edwards's works has been published by Yale University Press (1957–2006). Edwards (1703–58) was a pastor in Northampton, Massachusetts, and for one month before his death from a smallpox injection, president of Princeton. Some consider him the greatest American philosopher-theologian. He did not write an entire systematic theology, but his works contain writings on most theological topics. He is strongly Reformed in outlook, and combines profound thought with warm-hearted devotion to Christ.

Milne, Bruce. *Know the Truth*. 3rd ed. Nottingham: InterVarsity Press, 2009.

A thoughtful, clearly written evangelical guide to Christian doctrine which has found wide use among students. Milne lectured in biblical and historical theology at Spurgeon's College, London.

Mueller, John Theodore. *Christian Dogmatics*. St. Louis: Concordia, 1934.

A condensation and translation of Francis Pieper's *Christliche Dogmatik* (Christian Dogmatics) by a professor of systematic theology at Concordia Seminary in St. Louis, a Missouri Synod Lutheran seminary. An excellent statement of conservative Lutheran theology.

Mullins, Edgar Young. *The Christian Religion in Its Doctrinal Expression*. Philadelphia: Judson Press, 1917.

An evangelical systematic theology by a former president of the Southern Baptist Seminary in Louisville, Kentucky. Mullins lived from 1860 to 1928.

Murray, John. *Collected Writings of John Murray*. 4 vols. Carlisle, PA: Banner of Truth, 1976–82.

———. *The Imputation of Adam's Sin*. Grand Rapids: Eerdmans, 1959. Reprint, Nutley, NJ: Presbyterian and Reformed, 1977.

———. *Principles of Conduct*. Grand Rapids: Eerdmans, 1957.

———. *Redemption Accomplished and Applied*. Grand Rapids: Eerdmans, 1955.

Murray (1898–1975) was professor of systematic theology at Westminster Theological Seminary in Philadelphia and one of the most articulate modern defenders of Reformed theology.

Oden, Thomas C. *Classic Christianity: A Systematic Theology*. New York: HarperOne, 2009.

   This volume is a condensation of Oden's three-volume *Systematic Theology*, which was published in 1987, 1989, and 1992. Oden is a Methodist theologian who moved from his previous liberal theological convictions to a conservative evangelical position. He interacts extensively with theologians from the early history of the church.

Olson, Arnold T. *This We Believe: The Background and Exposition of the Doctrinal Statement of The Evangelical Free Church of America*. Minneapolis: Free Church Publications, 1961.

   A guide to Christian doctrine based on the widely used statement of faith of the Evangelical Free Church of America. Olson was the first president of the Evangelical Free Church.

Ott, Ludwig. *Fundamentals of Catholic Dogma*. Edited by James Canon Bastible. Translated by Patrick Lynch. St Louis: Herder, 1955. First published in German in 1952.

   A standard textbook of traditional Roman Catholic theology.

Packer, J. I. *Concise Theology: A Guide to Historic Christian Beliefs*. Wheaton, IL: Tyndale, 1993.

   This readable volume lives up to its name because Packer, an Anglican with strong Reformed convictions, is a master of saying much in a few words. He is a professor of theology at Regent College in Vancouver, British Columbia, and one of the most widely respected evangelical theologians today.

Pieper, Francis. *Christian Dogmatics*. 4 vols. First published in German, 1917–24. Translated by Theodore Engelder et al. St. Louis: Concordia, 1950–57.

   This is standard systematic theology of conservative Lutheranism. Pieper (1852–1931) was a Missouri Synod theologian and professor and president of Concordia Seminary in St. Louis.

Pope, William Burt. *A Compendium of Christian Theology*. 2nd ed. 3 vols. New York: Phillips and Hunt, n.d.

   This work, first published in 1875–76, is one of the greatest systematic theologies written from a Wesleyan or Arminian perspective.

Purkiser, W. T., ed. *Exploring our Christian Faith*. Kansas City, MO: Beacon Hill, 1960.

   A more popular Arminian systematic theology with contributions from several authors.

Reymond, Robert. *A New Systematic Theology of the Christian Faith*. Nashville: Nelson, 1998.

   Raymond, who died in 2013, was professor of systematic theology at Knox Theological Seminary in Fort Lauderdale, Florida, and prior to that he taught at Covenant Theological Seminary in St. Louis for many years. He was an ordained minister in the Presbyterian Church in America. This volume clearly advocates Reformed theological distinctives with a strong emphasis on scriptural grounding for each doctrine.

Ryrie, Charles. *Basic Theology*. Wheaton, IL: Victor, 1986.

   A very clearly written introduction to systematic theology from a dispensationalist perspective, by a former professor of systematic theology at Dallas Theological Seminary.

Roman Catholic Church. *Catechism of the Catholic Church*. 2nd ed. New York: Double Day, 2003.

Scholes, Alan Kent. *Enjoying God: An Introduction to Christian Theology*. Orlando: Campus Crusade for Christ, 2010.

Shedd, William G. T. *Dogmatic Theology*. 3rd ed. Edited by Alan W. Gomes. Phillipsburg, NJ: P&R, 2003.

   Shedd was professor of systematic theology at Union Theological Seminary in New York City, 1874–1890. He was a staunch defender of Reformed theology in this classic text. Alan Gomes has combined the previous three volume set into one volume and has provided organization and section headings that make the work much more accessible to the ordinary reader.

Strong, Augustus H. *Systematic Theology*. Valley Forge, PA: Judson, 1907.

   Strong (1836–1921) was president and professor of theology at Rochester Theological Seminary and, from 1905 to 1910, was the first president of the Northern Baptist Convention. This text was widely used in Baptist circles for most of the twentieth century, until it was largely replaced by Millard Erickson's *Christian Theology* (1983–85).

Thiessen, Henry Clarence. *Introductory Lectures in Systematic Theology*. Revised by Vernon D. Doerksen. 1949. Reprint, Grand Rapids: Eerdmans, 1977.

   An evangelical systematic theology textbook by a former chairman of the faculty of the graduate school at Wheaton College. Thiessen is Baptistic and Dispensational in theological perspective.

Thomas, W. H. Griffith. *The Principles of Theology: An Introduction to the Thirty-Nine Articles*. 5th ed. 1930. London: Church Book Room, 1956.

Although this book is structured around the Anglican Thirty-Nine Articles, it functions well as a thoughtful introductory text in Christian doctrine even for those outside the Anglican tradition. It has been widely used in British evangelical circles for many years. Thomas (1861–1924) was principal of Wycliffe Hall, Oxford and then professor of Old Testament at Wycliffe College, Toronto. He also played a role in founding Dallas Seminary just before his death.

Thornwell, James Henley. *The Collected Writings of James Henley Thornwell*. 4 vols. Edited by John B. Adger. New York: Carter, 1871–73. Reprint, Edinburgh; Carlisle, PA: Banner of Truth, 1974.

Thornwell (1812–62) was a Reformed theologian who was professor of theology in the Presbyterian Theological Seminary at Columbia, South Carolina.

Turretin, Francis. *Institutes of Elenctic Theology*. 3 vols. Translated by George Musgrave Giger. Edited by James T. Dennison Jr. Phillipsburg, NJ: Presbyterian and Reformed, 1992–97.

Turretin (1623–87) taught theology for over thirty years at the Academy in Geneva. His work, written in Latin, is said to be one of the fullest expressions of Calvinistic theology ever published. It was reprinted (in Latin) in 1847 and widely used as a theological textbook for American Presbyterians, most notably by Charles Hodge at Princeton. George Giger translated Turretin's *Institutes* in the mid-nineteenth century, but the translation lay unpublished for over a century. James Dennison of Westminster Theological Seminary has done extensive editorial work to make this great theology text finally available to English readers.

Van Til, Cornelius. *In Defense of the Faith*. Vol. 5, *An Introduction to Systematic Theology*. N.p.: Presbyterian and Reformed, 1976.

This volume contains Van Til's discussions of the nature of systematic theology, of revelation, and of the doctrine of God. Van Til was a Reformed theologian and philosopher who taught at Westminster Theological Seminary in Philadelphia and is best known for his "presuppositional" system of apologetics.

Van Genderen and W. H. Velema. *Concise Reformed Dogmatics*. Translated by Gerrit Bilkes and Ed M. van der Maas. Phillipsburg, NJ: P&R, 2008.

First published in Dutch in 1992, this book was originally written by two professors at the Theological University of the Christian Reformed Churches in the Netherlands, and it represents contemporary Dutch Reformed theology.

Vos, Geerhardus J. *Reformed Dogmatics*. Translated by Richard B Gaffin Jr. 5 vols. Bellingham, WA: Lexham, 2013–2016.

Vos was professor of biblical theology at Princeton Seminary from 1892–1932. These volumes, published posthumously, were written originally in Dutch.

Warfield, Benjamin B. *Biblical and Theological Studies*. Philadelphia: Presbyterian and Reformed, 1976.

———. *Christology and Criticism*. London and New York: Oxford University Press, 1929.

———. *The Inspiration and Authority of the Bible*. Edited by Samuel G. Craig. Introduction by Cornelius Van Til. Philadelphia: Presbyterian and Reformed, 1967.

———. *The Lord of Glory*. New York: American Tract Society, 1907.

———. *Perfectionism*. Philadelphia: Presbyterian and Reformed, 1958.

A condensation of Warfield's earlier two-volume work on perfectionism published by Oxford University Press, omitting extensive interaction with particular German theologians.

———. *The Person and Work of Christ*. Philadelphia: Presbyterian and Reformed, 1950.

Contains reprints of two articles from *ST*, 5 from *BD*, 6 from *CC*, and one other article.

———. *The Plan of Salvation*. Rev. ed. Grand Rapids: Eerdmans, 1942.

———. *Selected Shorter Writings of Benjamin B. Warfield*. 2 vols. Nuttley, NJ: Presbyterian and Reformed, 1970–73.

———. *Studies in Theology*. New York: Oxford University Press, 1932.

Warfield (1851–1921) was a Reformed theologian who taught New Testament and then systematic theology at Princeton Theological Seminary from 1887–1921. In the estimate of many people, he was one of the greatest American theologians.

Watson, Richard. *Theological Institutes*. 2 vols. New York: G. Lane and P. Sandford, 1843. First published 1823.

This is the earliest systematic theology by a Methodist. Watson (1781–1833) was Arminian in theological perspective.

Wiley, H. Orton. *Christian Theology*. Three vols. Kansas City, MO: Nazarene, 1940–43.

A recent Arminian systematic theology by a respected theologian in the Church of the Nazarene.

Probably the best Arminian systematic theology published in the twentieth century, but it does not match Miley in scholarly depth.

Williams, J. Rodman. *Renewal Theology: Systematic Theology From a Charismatic Perspective*. 3 vols. Grand Rapids: Zondervan, 1988–92.

Williams is a charismatic scholar who died in 2008. He taught at Regent University (formerly CBN University) in Virginia Beach, Virginia. This clearly written theology interacts extensively with the biblical text and with other literature. It is the first published from an explicitly charismatic perspective.

# Master List of Systematic Theologies Indexed at the End of Each Chapter

Full bibliographical data for these works may be found in the bibliography in appendix 2. If one of these works is not listed at the end of a chapter, it means that I was unable to find a treatment of that chapter's topic in that specific work.

## SECTIONS IN EVANGELICAL SYSTEMATIC THEOLOGIES

1. *Anglican (Episcopalian)*
   1882–92 . . . . . Litton
   1930 . . . . . . . . Thomas
   2001 . . . . . . . . Packer
   2013 . . . . . . . . Bird
   2013 . . . . . . . . Bray

2. *Arminian (Wesleyan or Methodist)*
   1875–76 . . . . . Pope
   1892–94 . . . . . Miley
   1940 . . . . . . . . Wiley
   1960 . . . . . . . . Purkiser
   1983 . . . . . . . . Carter
   1983 . . . . . . . . Cottrell
   1992 . . . . . . . . Oden
   2002 . . . . . . . . Cottrell

3. *Baptist*
   1767 . . . . . . . . Gill

   1887 . . . . . . . . Boyce
   1907 . . . . . . . . Strong
   1976–83 . . . . . Henry
   1983–85 . . . . . Erickson
   1987–94 . . . . . Lewis and Demarest
   1990–95 . . . . . Garrett
   2007 . . . . . . . . Akin
   2013 . . . . . . . . Erickson

4. *Dispensational*
   1947 . . . . . . . . Chafer
   1949 . . . . . . . . Thiessen
   1986 . . . . . . . . Ryrie
   2002–2005 . . Geisler
   2017 . . . . . . . . MacArthur and Mayhue

5. *Lutheran*
   1917–24 . . . . . Pieper
   1934 . . . . . . . . Mueller

6. *Reformed (or Presbyterian)*
   1559 . . . . . . . . Calvin
   1724–58 . . . . . Edwards
   1871–73 . . . . . Hodge
   1878 . . . . . . . . Dabney
   1910 . . . . . . . . Vos
   1887–1921 . . . Warfield
   1894 . . . . . . . . Shedd
   1906–11 . . . . . Bavinck
   1937–66 . . . . . Murray
   1938 . . . . . . . . Berkhof
   1992–97 . . . . . Turretin
   1998 . . . . . . . . Reymond

2008 . . . . . . . . Van Genderen and Velema
2011 . . . . . . . . Horton
2013 . . . . . . . . Culver
2013 . . . . . . . . Frame
2016 . . . . . . . . Allen and Swain
2017 . . . . . . . . Barrett
2019 . . . . . . . . Letham

7. *Renewal (or charismatic/Pentecostal)*
   1988–92 . . . . . Williams
   1993 . . . . . . . . Menzies and Horton
   1995 . . . . . . . . Horton
   2008 . . . . . . . . Duffield and Van Cleave

## SECTIONS IN REPRESENTATIVE ROMAN CATHOLIC SYSTEMATIC THEOLOGIES

1. *Roman Catholic: Traditional*
   1955 . . . . . . . . Ott

2. *Roman Catholic: Post–Vatican II*
   1980 . . . . . . . . McBrien
   2012 . . . . . . . . *CCC*

# Glossary

*By Jeff Purswell*
*Revised by Brett Gray*

*(Numbers in parentheses at the end of each entry refer to chapters and sections in this book.)*

**absolute authority:** The highest authority in one's life; an authority that cannot be disproved by appeal to any higher authority. (4A.4)

**accommodation:** The theory that the biblical writers at times incidentally affirmed falsehoods believed by the people of their time so as not to obscure the larger points they were trying to make. (5B.4)

**active obedience:** A term referring to Christ's perfect obedience to God during his earthly life that earned the righteousness that God credits to those who place their faith in Christ. (27C.1)

**adoption:** An act of God whereby he makes us members of his family. (37A)

**adoptionism:** The false teaching that Jesus lived as an ordinary man until his baptism, at which time God "adopted" him as his "Son" and conferred on him supernatural powers; this teaching thus denies Jesus' preexistence and divine nature. (14C.2.c)

**age of accountability:** The term used by some theologians to indicate a point in a person's life before which (according to their view) he is not held responsible for sin and is not counted guilty before God. (24D.3)

**amillennialism:** The view that there will be no literal thousand-year bodily reign of Christ on earth prior to the final judgment and the eternal state; on this view, scriptural references to the millennium in Revelation 20 actually describe the present church age. (55A.1)

**angel:** A created, spiritual being with moral judgment and high intelligence, but without a physical body. (19A)

**Angel of the Lord:** A form that God took on at various times in Scripture in order to appear to human beings. (19A.11)

**annihilationism:** The teaching that after death unbelievers suffer the penalty of God's wrath for a time, and then are "annihilated," or destroyed, so that they no longer exist. Some forms of this teaching hold that annihilation occurs immediately upon death. (41C.2)

**anthropomorphic language:** Language that speaks of God in human terms. (11A.2)

**antichrist:** The "man of lawlessness" who will appear prior to the second coming of Christ and will cause great suffering and persecution, only to be destroyed by Jesus. The term is also used to describe other figures who embody such an opposition to Christ and are precursors of the final antichrist. (54F.3.e)

**Apocrypha:** The collection of books included in the canon of Scripture by the Roman Catholic Church but not included in the canon by Protestants (from the Greek word *apocrypha*, "things that are hidden"). (3A)

**Apollinarianism:** The fourth-century heresy which held that Christ had a human body but not a human mind or spirit, and that the mind and spirit of Christ were from the divine nature of the Son of God. (26C.1.a)

**apologetics:** The discipline that seeks to provide a defense of the truthfulness of the Christian faith for the purpose of convincing unbelievers. (1A.1)

**apostle:** A recognized office of the early church. Apostles are in several ways the New Testament counterpart to the Old Testament prophet and as such had the authority to write words of Scripture. (47A.1)

**archangel:** An angel with authority over other angels. (19A.4)

**Arianism:** The erroneous doctrine that denies the full deity of Jesus Christ and the Holy Spirit. (14C.2.a)

**Arminianism:** A theological tradition that seeks to preserve the free choices of human beings and denies God's providential control over the details of all events. (16G)

**ascension:** The rising of Jesus from the earth into heaven forty days after his resurrection. (28B.1)

**asceticism:** An approach to living that renounces the comforts of the material world. (15D)

**aseity:** Another name for the attribute of God's independence or self-existence. (11B.1)

**assurance of salvation:** The internal sense we may have based upon certain evidences in our lives that we are truly "born again" and will persevere as Christians until the end of our lives. (40D)

**atemporal eternity:** The idea that God has eternally existed without time in his own being. (11B.3)

**atonement:** The work Christ did in his life and death to earn our salvation. (27)

**attributes of being:** Aspects of God's character that describe his essential mode of existence. (12A)

**attributes of purpose:** Aspects of God's character that pertain to making and carrying out decisions. (13D)

**authority of Scripture:** The idea that all the words in Scripture are God's in such a way that to disbelieve or disobey any word of Scripture is to disbelieve or disobey God. (4)

**autograph:** The original copy of a biblical document (from *auto-*, "self," and *graph*, "writing"). (5B.3)

**baptism by the Holy Spirit:** A rendering of a phrase also translated "baptism in/with the

Holy Spirit." The translation of the Greek preposition *en* with the word "by" can seem to indicate that the Holy Spirit is the agent doing the baptizing, but the phrase more accurately refers to the Spirit as the element "in" which (or "with" which) believers are "baptized" at conversion. (39B)

**baptism in/with the Holy Spirit:** A phrase the New Testament authors use to speak of coming into the new covenant power of the Holy Spirit. This would include the impartation of new spiritual life (in regeneration), cleansing from sin, a break with the power and love of sin, and empowering for ministry. (39B)

**beatific vision:** The true and real, though not exhaustive, seeing of God that will occur in heaven (lit., "the vision that makes blessed or happy"). (12A.2)

**beauty:** That attribute of God whereby he is the sum of all desirable qualities. (13E.19)

**being filled with the Holy Spirit:** See "filled with the Holy Spirit."

**being raised with Christ:** See "raised with Christ."

**belief:** In contemporary culture this term usually refers to the acceptance of the truth of something, such as facts about Christ, with no necessary element of personal commitment or dependence involved. In the New Testament this term often involves this sense of commitment (cf. John 3:16; see also "faith"). (35A.1–3)

**believable profession of faith:** A central component of the "baptistic" view of baptism, which holds that only those who have given reasonable evidence of believing in Christ should be baptized. (49B)

**believers' baptism:** The view that baptism is appropriately administered only to those who give a believable profession of faith in Jesus Christ. (49B)

**biblical theology:** The study of the teaching of the individual authors and sections of the Bible and of the place of each teaching in the historical development of the Bible. (1A.1)

**"binding and loosing":** Words of Jesus that refer to the actions of placing under and releasing from church discipline (Matt. 18:17–18; 16:19). (46B)

**bishop:** Translation of the Greek *episkopos*, a term used interchangeably with "pastor," "overseer," and "elder" to refer to the main governing office of a local church in the New Testament. The term also refers to a priest who has authority over a group of churches in an episcopalian form of church government. (47A.2.b; 47C.1)

**blameless:** Morally perfect in God's sight, a characteristic of those who follow God's word completely (Ps. 119:1). (8A)

**blasphemy against the Holy Spirit:** The unusually malicious, willful rejection and slander against the Holy Spirit's work attesting to Christ, and attributing that work to Satan (also see "unpardonable sin"). (24D.6)

**blessedness:** The doctrine that God delights fully in himself and in all that reflects his character. (13E.18)

**blood of Christ:** A phrase referring to Christ's death in its saving aspects, since the blood he shed on the cross was the clear outward evidence that his life blood was poured out when he died a sacrificial death to pay for our redemption. (27C.2.c.3)

**body of Christ:** A scriptural metaphor for the church. This metaphor is used in two different ways, one to stress the interdependence of the members of the body, and one to stress Christ's headship of the church. (44A.4)

**born again:** A scriptural term (John 3:3–8) referring to God's work of regeneration by which he imparts new spiritual life to us. (34A)

**born of the Spirit:** Another term for "regeneration" that indicates the special role played by the Holy Spirit in imparting new spiritual life to us. (34A)

**born of water:** A phrase used by Jesus in John 3:5 that refers to the spiritual cleansing from sin that accompanies God's work of regeneration (cf. Ezek. 36:25–26). (34C)

**Calvinism:** A theological tradition named after the sixteenth-century French reformer John Calvin (1509–64) that emphasizes the sovereignty of God in all things, man's inability to do spiritual good before God, and the glory of God as the highest end of all that occurs. (16)

**canon:** The list of all the books that belong in the Bible (from the Greek *kanōn*, "reed; measuring rod; standard of measure"). (3)

**canonical:** A term describing preserved writings that are deemed to have divine authorship and therefore which are to be included in the canon of Scripture as God's authoritative words in written form. (3)

**certain knowledge:** Knowledge that is established beyond doubt or question. Because God knows all the facts of the universe and never lies, the only absolutely certain knowledge we can have is found in God's words in Scripture. (3C)

**cessationist:** Someone who thinks that certain miraculous spiritual gifts ceased when the apostles died and Scripture was complete. (17D.2; 52B)

**Chalcedonian definition:** The statement produced by the Council of Chalcedon in AD 451 that has been regarded by most branches of Christianity as the orthodox definition of the biblical teaching on the person of Christ. (26C.2)

**charismatic:** A term referring to any groups or people that trace their historical origin to the charismatic renewal movement of the 1960s and 1970s. Such groups seek to practice all the spiritual gifts mentioned in the New Testament but, unlike many Pentecostal denominations, allow differing viewpoints on whether baptism in the Holy Spirit is subsequent to conversion and whether tongues is a sign of baptism in the Holy Spirit. (39)

**cherubim:** A class of created spiritual beings who, among other things, guarded the entrance to the garden of Eden. (19A.3.a)

**Christian ethics:** Any study that answers the question, "What does God require us to do and what attitudes does he require us to have today?" with regard to any given situation. (1A.4)

**church:** The community of all true believers for all time. (44A.1)

**circular argument:** An argument that seeks to prove its conclusion by appealing to a claim that depends on the truth of the conclusion. (4A.5)

**clarity of Scripture:** The idea that the Bible is written in such a way that its teachings are able to be understood by all who will read it seeking God's help and being willing to follow it. (6B)

**classis:** The term for a regional governing body within the Christian Reformed Church (similar to a presbytery in a presbyterian system). (47C.2)

**common grace:** The grace of God by which he gives people innumerable blessings that are not part of salvation. (31A)

**communicable attributes:** Aspects of God's character that he shares or "communicates" with us. (11A.1)

**communication of attributes:** A term referring to the giving of certain attributes from Jesus' divine nature to his human nature (and vice versa) that resulted from the uniting of the two natures in one person, each nature retaining its respective unique properties. (26C.3.e)

**communion:** A term commonly used to refer to the Lord's Supper. (50C.1)

**communion of saints:** A term in the Apostles' Creed referring to the fellowship that believers on earth have with believers in heaven by virtue of a common worship. (41C.1.b)

**compatibilism:** Another term for the Reformed view of providence. The term indicates that absolute divine sovereignty is compatible with human significance and real human choices. (16A)

**complementarian:** The view that men and women are equal in value before God but that some governing and teaching roles in the church are reserved for men. (Preface, 2; 47D)

**concordist theory:** Another term for the day-age theory of creation, so named because it seeks agreement or "concord" between the Bible and scientific conclusions about the age of the earth. (15E.4.a.1)

**concurrence:** An aspect of God's providence whereby he cooperates with created things in every action, directing their distinctive properties to cause them to act as they do. (16B)

**conditional immortality:** The teaching that God has created people so that they only have immortality (the power to live forever) if they accept Christ as Savior. Under this view, those who do not become Christians will simply cease to exist at death or at the time of the final judgment. (56G)

**congregational government:** The form of church government in which final governing authority rests with the local congregation. (47C)

**consequent absolute necessity:** The view that the atonement was not absolutely necessary, but, as a "consequence" of God's decision to save some human beings, the atonement was absolutely necessary. (27B)

**consistory:** The term for a local board of elders in the Christian Reformed Church (similar to a "session" in a presbyterian system). (47C.2)

**contradiction:** A set of two statements, one of which denies the other. (1E.3)

**conversion:** Our willing response to the gospel call, in which we sincerely repent of sins and place our trust in Christ for salvation. (35)

**cosmological argument:** An argument for the existence of God based on the observation that, since every known thing in the universe has a cause, the universe itself must also have a cause, which can only be God. (9C)

**covenant:** An unchangeable, divinely imposed legal agreement between God and man that stipulates the conditions of their relationship. (25)

**covenant community:** The community of God's people. Protestant proponents of infant baptism view baptism as a sign of entrance into the "covenant community" of God's people. (49B.4)

**covenant of grace:** The legal agreement between God and man, established by God after the fall of Adam, whereby man could be saved. Although the specific provisions of this covenant varied at different times during redemptive history, the essential condition of requiring faith in Christ the redeemer remained the same. (25C)

**covenant of redemption:** The agreement between the members of the Trinity in which each agreed to fulfill his respective role to accomplish the salvation of human beings. (25B)

**covenant of works:** The legal agreement between God and Adam and Eve in the garden of Eden whereby participation in the blessings of the covenant depended on the obedience, or "works," of Adam and Eve. (25A)

**covenantal nomism:** A belief that the Jewish people at the time of Christ considered themselves to be God's people not because they obeyed the Mosaic laws but because of God's election and grace. Therefore, they obeyed the Mosaic laws out of gratitude to God not to become the people of God ("to get in") but rather to show that they were the people of God ("to stay in"). (36G.1.e)

**creation** *ex nihilo*: The doctrine that God created the entire universe out of nothing. The universe was originally very good; and he created it to glorify himself. (15)

**creationism:** The view that God creates a new soul for each person and sends it to that person's body sometime between conception and birth. (23F)

**Darwinian evolution:** The general theory of evolution (see also "macroevolution") named after Charles Darwin, the British naturalist who expounded this theory in 1859 in his *Origin of Species by Means of Natural Selection.* (15E.2.c.1)

**day-age theory:** An "old earth" theory of creation that views the days of Genesis 1 as extremely long "ages" of time. (15E.4.a.1)

**deacon:** A translation of the Greek *diakonos* ("servant"). In certain contexts the term refers to a church officer whose responsibilities involve various forms of service, including financial oversight, administrative responsibilities, and caring for the physical needs of the congregation. (47A.3)

**death:** The termination of life brought about by the entrance of sin into the world. (For the Christian, death brings us into the presence of God because of Christ's payment of the penalty for our sins.) (41A)

**decrees of God:** The eternal plans of God whereby, before the creation of the world, he determined to bring about everything that happens. (2B.1; 16D)

**deism:** The view that God created the universe but is not now directly involved in the creation. (15B)

**demonized:** To be under demonic influence (Greek *daimonizomai*). The term often suggests more extreme cases of demonic influence. (20D.3)

**demon possession:** A misleading phrase found in some English translations of the Bible that seems to suggest that a person's will is completely dominated by a demon. The Greek term *daimonizomai* is better translated "under demonic influence," which could range from mild to strong influence or attack. (20D.3)

**demons:** Evil angels who sinned against God and who now continually work evil in the world. (20)

**depravity:** Another term for "inherited corruption." (24C.2.a)

**determinism:** The idea that acts, events, and decisions are the inevitable results of some condition or decision prior to them that is independent of the human will. (32C.2.d)

**dichotomy:** The view that man is made up of two parts, body and soul/spirit. (23A)

**dictation:** The idea that God expressly spoke every word of Scripture to the human authors. (4A.6)

**difference in role:** The idea that men and women have been given by God different primary functions in the family and the church. (22C)

**diocese:** In an episcopalian system of church government, the churches under the jurisdiction of a bishop. (47C.1)

**dispensationalism:** A theological system that began in the nineteenth century with the writings of J. N. Darby. Among the general doctrines of this system are the distinction between Israel and the church as two groups in God's overall plan, the pretribulational rapture of the church, a future literal fulfillment of Old Testament prophecies concerning Israel, and the dividing of biblical history into seven periods, or "dispensations," of God's ways of relating to his people. (55A.3.b)

**dispensational premillennialism:** Another term for pretribulational premillennialism. The term *dispensational* is used because most proponents of this view wish to maintain a clear distinction between the church and Israel, with whom God deals under different arrangements, or "dispensations." (55A.3.b)

**distinguishing between spirits:** A special ability to recognize the influence of the Holy Spirit or of demonic spirits in a person. (20D.4; 53G)

**distortion of roles:** The idea that in the punishments God gave to Adam and Eve after their sin, he did not introduce new roles or functions but simply introduced pain and distortion into the functions they previously had. (22C.2.h)

**docetism:** The heretical teaching that Jesus was not really a man but only seemed to be one (from the Greek verb *dokeō*, "to seem, to appear to be"). (26A.5)

**doctrine:** What the whole Bible teaches us today about some particular topic. (1A.4)

**dogma:** Another term for "doctrine." The word is often used to refer more specifically to doctrines that have official church endorsement. (1A.4)

**dogmatic theology:** Another term for "systematic theology." (1A.4)

**dualism:** The idea that both God and the material universe have eternally existed side by side as two ultimate forces in the universe. It implies that there is an eternal conflict between God and the evil aspects of the material universe. (15B; 24B)

**dying with Christ:** A phrase that describes a person's break with his old way of life by virtue of his being united with Christ through faith. (43A.3.a)

**Eastern church:** A major segment of the church, now known as the Orthodox church, that separated from the Western (Roman Catholic) church in AD 1054. (45E)

**economic subordination:** The teaching that certain members of the Trinity have roles or functions that are subject to the control or authority of other members. (14D.2)

**effective calling:** An act of God the Father, speaking through the human proclamation of the gospel, in which he summons people to himself in such a way that they respond in saving faith. (33A)

**egalitarian:** The view that all functions and roles in the church are open to men and women alike. (Preface, 2; 47D)

*ekklēsia*: A Greek term translated "church" in the New Testament. The word literally means "assembly" and in the Bible indicates the assembly or congregation of the people of God. (44A.1)

**elder:** The main governing group in a church in the New Testament (Greek *presbyteros*). (47A.2.a)

**election:** An act of God before creation in which he chooses some people to be saved, not on account of any foreseen merit in them, but only because of his sovereign good pleasure. (32)

**empowerment for service:** A primary aspect of the work of the Holy Spirit to bring evidence of God's presence and to bless. (30A.2)

**episcopalian government:** A hierarchical form of church government in which bishops have governing authority over groups of churches (from the Greek *episkopos*, "overseer," "bishop"). (47C.1)

**equality in personhood:** The idea that men and women are created equally in God's image and therefore are equally important to God and equally valuable to him. (22B)

**eschatology:** The study of "the last things," or future events (from the Greek *eschatos*, "last"). (54)

**eternal begetting of the Son:** See "eternal generation of the Son."

**eternal generation of the Son:** Within the Trinity, the Son is eternally "from" the Father, in some sense. However, it does not mean that the Son was created by the Father. (14C.1.2.a)

**eternal conscious punishment:** A description of the nature of punishment in hell, which will be unending and of which the unbeliever will be fully aware. (56G)

**eternal security:** Another term for "perseverance of the saints." However, this term can be misunderstood to mean that all who have once made a profession of faith are "eternally secure" in their salvation when they may not have been genuinely converted at all. (40D.3)

**eternity:** When used of God, the doctrine that God has no beginning, end, or succession of moments in his own being, and he sees all time equally vividly, yet God sees events in time and acts in time. (11B.3)

**ethics:** See "Christian ethics."

**Eucharist:** Another term for the Lord's Supper (from the Greek *eucharistia*, "giving of thanks"). (50C.1)

**Eutychianism:** Another term for monophysitism, named after the fifth-century monk Eutyches. (26C.1.c)

**evangelism:** The proclamation of the gospel to unbelievers (from the Greek *euangelizō*, "to announce good news"). (44C.3; also 48B.10)

**exaltation of Christ:** One of the two "states" of Christ, the other being humiliation. The state of exaltation includes four aspects of his work: his resurrection, ascension into heaven, session at the right hand of God, and return in glory and power. (28C)

**example theory:** The view that in the atonement Christ did not bear the just penalty of God for our sins but that he simply provided us with an example of how we should trust and obey God perfectly, even if this leads to death. (27C.2.d.3)

**excommunication:** The final step of church discipline in which a person is put out of the fellowship, or "communion," of the church. (46D.1.a)

**exegesis:** The process of interpreting a text of Scripture. (6D)

*ex nihilo:* A Latin phrase meaning "out of nothing," referring to God's creation of the universe without the use of any previously existing materials. (15A.1)

*ex opere operato:* A Latin phrase meaning "by the work performed." In Roman Catholic teaching the phrase is used to indicate that the sacraments, such as baptism, work in virtue of the actual activity done independent of the subjective attitude of faith in the participants. (50B.3)

**exorcism:** The action of driving out an evil spirit by a spoken command. (20D.6)

**external calling:** The general gospel invitation offered to all people that comes through human proclamation of the gospel. Also referred to as "general calling" or "the gospel call," this call can be rejected by people. (33A)

**extreme unction:** One of the seven sacraments in Roman Catholic teaching, the anointing with oil that is administered to a dying person (also known as "last rites"). (48A)

**faith:** Trust or dependence on God based on the fact that we take him at his word and believe what he has said. (See also "saving faith.") (18C.2; also 35A.3)

**faith and practice:** A term used by some people who, denying the inerrancy of the Bible, claim that the Bible's purpose is only to tell us about these two subjects. (5B.1)

**faithfulness:** The doctrine that God will always do what he has said and fulfill what he has promised. (12B.5)

**fasting:** The discipline of abstaining for a time from all or certain foods. In the Bible, fasting often accompanies prayer for the purpose of intensive intercession, repentance, worship, or the seeking of guidance. (18C.12)

**fatalism:** A system in which human choices and human decisions make no real difference because things will turn out as they have been previously ordained. This is in contrast to the doctrine of election, in which people make real choices that have real consequences and for which they will be held accountable. (32C.1)

**filioque:** Latin for "and from the Son," a term referring to a clause inserted into the Nicene Creed to indicate that the Holy Spirit proceeds not from the Father only but also from the Son. The controversy that arose over this doctrinal point contributed to the split between the Eastern and Western churches in AD 1054. (14C.2.d)

**filled with the Holy Spirit:** An event subsequent to conversion in which a believer experiences a fresh infilling with the Holy Spirit that may result in a variety of consequences, including greater love for God, greater victory over sin, greater power for ministry, and sometimes the receiving of new spiritual gifts. (39D.2.c)

**final judgment:** The last and ultimate proclamation by Jesus Christ of the eternal destinies of all people which will take place after the millennium and the rebellion that occurs at the end of it. (56A.1)

**firstfruits:** The first portion of a ripening harvest (Greek *aparchē*). In describing Christ in his resurrection as the "firstfruits" (1 Cor. 15:20), the Bible indicates that our resurrection bodies will be like his when God raises us from the dead. (28A.4.c)

**flood geology:** The view that attributes the present geological status of the earth to the tremendous natural forces caused by the flood of Genesis 6–9. (15E.4.b.2)

**foreknowledge:** Relating to the doctrine of election, the personal, relational knowledge by which God thought of certain people in a saving relationship to himself before creation. This is to be distinguished from the mere knowledge of facts about a person. (32C.2.a)

**forensic:** A term that means "having to do with legal proceedings." This term is used to describe justification as being a legal declaration by God that in itself does not change our internal nature or character. (36A)

**free choices:** Choices made according to our free will (see "free will"). (16B.9)

**Free Grace theology:** The belief that "justification by faith alone" implies that saving faith does not require repentance from sin (because, for most advocates of this view, repentance is understood as an initial change of mind rather than an inward resolve to turn from sin), that good works do not necessarily result from saving faith, and that good works should not ordinarily be used as a basis for giving someone an assurance of salvation. (35C, 40.D.4)

**free will:** (a) with respect to God: All things that God decided to will but had no necessity to will according to his nature. (13D.14.b)

(b) with respect to man: The ability to make willing choices that have real effects (however, other people define this in other ways, including the ability to make choices that are not determined by God). (16B.9)

**freedom:** That attribute of God whereby he does whatever he pleases. (13D.15)

**freedom of inclination:** Human beings are free in the sense that we choose to do what we are most inclined to do; that is, what we most want to do. (16.B.9; 32.D.1)

**freedom of voluntary choice:** See "freedom of inclination."

**gap theory:** The idea that between Genesis 1:1 and 1:2 is a gap of millions of years during which God judged an earlier creation, making it "without form and void" and necessitating a second creation depicted in Genesis 1:3–2:3. (15E.2.d)

**general assembly:** In a presbyterian form of church government, the term for the national (or regional) governing body. (47C.2)

**general eschatology:** The study of future events that will affect the entire universe, such as the second coming of Christ, the millennium, and the final judgment. (54)

**general redemption:** Another term for "unlimited atonement." (27D)

**general revelation:** The knowledge of God's existence, character, and moral law that comes through creation to all humanity. (7E)

**gifts of the Holy Spirit:** All abilities that are empowered by the Holy Spirit and used in any ministry of the church. (52A)

**glorification:** The final step in the application of redemption. It will happen when Christ returns and raises from the dead the bodies of all believers for all time who have died, and reunites them with their souls, and changes the bodies of all believers who remain alive, thereby giving all believers at the same time perfect resurrection bodies like his own. (42)

**glory:** The created brightness that surrounds God's revelation of himself. In another sense of the term, it refers to God's honor. (13E.20)

**God:** In the New Testament, a translation of the Greek word *theos*, which is usually, but not always, used to refer to God the Father. (26B.1.a)

**God-breathed:** A translation of the Greek *theopneustos* (sometimes translated "inspired by God"), which the Bible (2 Tim. 3:16) uses metaphorically to describe the words of Scripture as being spoken by God. (4A)

**goodness:** The doctrine that God is the final standard of good, and that all that God is and does is worthy of approval. (12C.6)

**gospel call:** The general gospel invitation to all people that comes through human proclamation of the gospel. Also referred to as "external calling." (33A)

**government:** An aspect of God's providence that indicates that God has a purpose in all that he does in the world and providentially governs or directs all things in order that they accomplish his purposes. (16C)

**governmental theory:** The theory that Christ's death was not a payment for our sins but God's demonstration of the fact that, since he is the moral governor of the universe, some kind of penalty must be paid whenever his laws are broken. (27C.2.e.4)

**grace:** God's goodness toward those who deserve only punishment. (12C.8)

**Great Commission:** The final commands of Jesus to the disciples, recorded in Matthew 28:18–20. (1C.1)

**great tribulation:** An expression from Matthew 24:21 referring to a period of great hardship and suffering prior to the return of Christ. (54F.3.b; 55E)

**great white throne judgment:** Another term for the final judgment spoken of in Revelation 20:11–15. (56A.2)

**healing:** A gift of the Holy Spirit that functions to bring a restoration to health as a foretaste of the complete freedom from physical weakness and infirmity that Christ purchased for us by his death and resurrection. (53D)

**heaven:** The place where God most fully makes known his presence to bless. It is in heaven where God most fully reveals his glory, and where angels, other heavenly creatures, and redeemed saints all worship him. (57A.1)

**hell:** A place of eternal conscious punishment for the wicked. (56G)

**hermeneutics:** The study of correct methods of interpreting texts. (6D)

**hierarchical government:** Another term for an episcopalian form of church government in which final decision-making authority lies outside the local church. (47C).

**historical theology:** The historical study of how Christians in different periods have understood various theological topics. (1A.1)

**historic premillennialism:** The view that Christ will return to the earth after a period of great tribulation and then establish a millennial kingdom. At this time believers who have died will be raised from the dead and believers who are alive will receive glorified resurrection bodies, and both will reign with Christ on earth for a thousand years. (55A.3.a)

**history of redemption:** The series of events throughout history by which God acted to bring about the salvation of his people. (3B)

**holiness:** The doctrine that God is separated from sin and devoted to seeking his own honor. (12C.9)

**holy orders:** One of the seven sacraments in Roman Catholic teaching, the ordination to the priesthood or diaconate. (48A)

**Holy Spirit:** One of the three persons of the Trinity whose work it is to manifest the active presence of God in the world, and especially in the church. (30)

***homoiousios:*** A Greek word meaning "of a similar nature," used by Arius in the fourth century to affirm that Christ was a supernatural heavenly being but to deny that he was of the *same* nature as God the Father. (14C.2.a)

***homoousios:*** A Greek word, meaning "of the same nature," which was included in the Nicene Creed to teach that Christ was of the exact same nature as God the Father and therefore was fully divine as well as fully human. (14C.2.a)

***homo sapiens:*** The scientific designation for an early form of man (lit., "wise man"), believed by many to have lived sometime between 300,000 BC and 40,000 BC (15E.3.b)

**humiliation of Christ:** One of the two "states" of Christ, the other being exaltation. The state of humiliation includes four aspects of his work: his incarnation, suffering, death, and burial. (28C)

**hypostatic union:** The union of Christ's human and divine natures in one person (from the Greek *hypostasis*, "being"). (26C.2)

**ICBI:** International Council on Biblical Inerrancy. This organization drafted the "Chicago Statement on Biblical Inerrancy" in 1978 that affirmed the inerrancy of Scripture and defined what most evangelicals understand by the term *inerrancy*. (5B.2; Appendix 1)

**ideal time theory:** Another name for "mature creationism." (15E.4.b. (1))

**image of God:** The nature of man such that he is like God and represents God. (21C.1)

**imago Dei:** A Latin phrase meaning "image of God." (21C.1)

**immanent:** Existing or remaining in. The term is used in theology to speak of God's involvement in creation. (15B)

**immersion:** The mode of baptism in the New Testament in which the person is put completely under the water and then brought back up again. (49A)

**imminent:** A term referring to the fact that Christ could return and might return at any time, and that we are to be prepared for him to come at any day. (54F.1)

**immutability:** Another term for God's unchangeableness. (11B.2)

**impassibility:** The belief that God is incapable of suffering harm in the sense that his being cannot be changed or harmed by anything outside of himself. (11B.2.c)

**impeccability:** The doctrine that Christ was not able to sin. (26A.4)

**impute:** To think of as belonging to someone, and therefore to cause it to belong to that person. God "thinks of" Adam's sin as belonging to us, and it therefore belongs to us, and in justification he thinks of Christ's righteousness as belonging to us and so relates to us on this basis. (24C.1; 36C)

**incarnation:** The act of God the Son whereby he took to himself a human nature. (26B)

**"in Christ":** A term referring to a variety of relationships between believers and Christ through which Christians receive the benefits of salvation. (43A)

**incommunicable attributes:** Aspects of God's character that God does not share with us. (11A.1)

**incomprehensible:** Not able to be fully understood. As this applies to God, it means that God cannot be understood fully or exhaustively, although we can know true things about God. (10B)

**incorruptible:** The nature of our future resurrection bodies, which will be like Christ's resurrection body and therefore will not wear out, grow old, or be subject to any kind of sickness or disease. (28A.4.c)

**independence:** The doctrine that God does not need us or the rest of creation for anything, yet we and the rest of creation can glorify him and bring him joy. (11B.1)

**inerrancy:** The idea that Scripture in the original manuscripts does not affirm anything that is contrary to fact. (5A)

**infallibility:** The idea that Scripture is not able to lead us astray in matters of faith and practice. (5B.1)

**infant baptism:** See "paedobaptism."

**infinite:** When used of God, a term referring to the fact that he is not subject to any of the limitations of humanity or of creation in general. (11B.2.e)

**infinity with respect to space:** Another term for God's omnipresence. (11B.4)

**infinity with respect to time:** Another term for God's eternity. (11B.3)

**infused righteousness:** Righteousness that God actually puts into us and that changes us internally. The Roman Catholic Church understands justification to involve such an infusion, which differs from Protestantism's view that justification is a legal declaration by God. (36C)

**inherited corruption:** The sinful nature, or the tendency to sin, which all people inherit because of Adam's sin (often referred to as "original pollution"). This idea entails that (1) in our natures we totally lack spiritual good before God; and (2) in our actions we are totally unable to do spiritual good before God. (24C.2)

**inherited guilt:** The idea that God counts all people guilty because of Adam's sin (often referred to as "original guilt"). (24C.1)

**inherited sin:** The guilt and the tendency to sin that all people inherit because of Adam's sin (often referred to as "original sin"). (24C)

**"in Jesus' name":** A term referring to prayer made on Jesus' authorization and consistent with his character. (18B.3)

**inner sense of God:** An instinctive awareness of God's existence that every human being has. (9A)

**inspiration:** A term referring to the fact that the words of Scripture are spoken by God. Because of the weak sense of this word in ordinary usage, this text prefers the term *God-breathed* to indicate that the words of Scripture are spoken by God. (4A.1)

**intelligent design:** The view that God directly created the world and its many life forms, which stands against the view that new species came about through an evolutionary process of random mutation. (15E.2.b)

**intercession:** Jesus' ongoing act of standing in God's presence and making petitions before him on our behalf as our great high priest. (29B.3) The term is also used to refer to prayers of request for ourselves or others. (18)

**intermediate state:** The condition or mode of being of a person between the time of one's death and the time that Christ returns to give believers new resurrection bodies. (41C)

**internal calling:** Another term for "effective calling." (33A)

**interpretation of tongues:** The gift of the Holy Spirit by which the general meaning of something spoken in tongues is reported to the church. (53E.2.e)

**"in the Holy Spirit":** The state of consciously dwelling in an atmosphere of God's manifested presence. (30E)

**invisibility:** The doctrine that God's total essence, all of his spiritual being, will never be able to be seen by us, yet God still shows himself to us partially in this age and more fully in the age to come through visible, created things. (12A.2)

**invisible church:** The church as God sees it. (44A.2)

**"in, with, and under"**: A phrase descriptive of the Lutheran view of the Lord's Supper that holds, in contrast to the idea that the bread actually becomes the physical body of Christ, that the physical body of Christ is present "in, with, and under" the bread of the Lord's Supper. (50C.2)

**irresistible grace**: A term that refers to the fact that God effectively calls people and also gives them regeneration, both of which guarantee that we will respond in saving faith. This term is subject to misunderstanding since it *seems* to imply that people do not make a voluntary, willing choice in responding to the gospel. (34A)

**jealousy**: The doctrine that God continually seeks to protect his own honor. (12C.12)

**judgment**: See "final judgment."

**judgment of the nations**: In the dispensational premillennial view, a judgment that will come between the tribulation and the beginning of the millennium, during which time nations are judged according to how they have treated the Jewish people during the tribulation. (56A.2)

**justice**: Another term for God's righteousness. (12C.11)

**justification**: An instantaneous legal act of God in which he (1) thinks of our sins as forgiven and Christ's righteousness as belonging to us, and (2) declares us to be righteous in his sight. (36)

**kenosis theory**: The theory that Christ gave up some of his divine attributes while he was on earth as a man (from the Greek verb *kenoō*, which means "to empty"). (26B.3)

**"keys of the kingdom"**: A phrase used by Jesus in Matthew 16:19 referring to the authority to preach the gospel and to exercise discipline within the church. (46B)

**king**: One of the three offices fulfilled by Christ in which he rules over the church and the universe. (29)

**knowable**: A term referring to the fact that we can know true things about God, and that we can know God himself and not simply facts about him. (9A)

**knowledge**: The doctrine that God fully knows himself and all things actual and possible in one simple and eternal act. (12B.3)

**laying on of hands**: A practice that often accompanied prayer in the New Testament as a means of personal ministry to individuals. (48B.11)

**liberalism**: The belief that the Bible is composed of merely human words reporting various people's religious experiences and ideas, but the Bible is not also the words of God. Therefore, theology consists of doctrines made by human beings, not truths revealed by God. (4.E, 4. Additional Note, 6.D.1)

**libertarian free will**: The viewpoint that man has the ability, all things being just what they are, to choose differently. According to this view, God might know human choices before they occur, but he does not determine them.) (16.B.9; 32.D.1)

**likeness**: A term referring to something that is similar but not identical to the thing it represents, such as man's being made after God's "likeness" (Gen. 1:26, translating Hebrew *demût*). (21C.1)

**limbo:** See "*limbus patrum.*"

**limbus patrum:** *Limbus* means "border" in Latin, and *patrum* means "of the fathers." According to Roman Catholic doctrine, *limbus patrum* refers to places on the border of hell where Old Testament believers were excluded from the presence of God but also did not experience conscious suffering. (Sometimes this is merely called limbo.) (41C.1.c)

**limited atonement:** The Reformed view that Christ's death actually paid for the sins of those whom he knew would ultimately be saved. A preferable term for this view is "particular redemption" in that the power of the atonement is not limited, but rather it is fully effective for particular people. (27D.1)

**literary framework theory:** An "old earth" theory of creation that views the six days of Genesis 1, not as a chronological sequence of events, but as a literary "framework" that the author uses to teach about God's creative activity. (15E.4.a.2)

**living creatures:** A class of created spiritual beings with appearances like a lion, an ox, a man, and an eagle who are said to worship around the throne of God. (19A.3.c)

**local elders:** A type of church government in which elders are selected from the local congregation to govern the church, and in which the senior pastor is ordinarily one of these elders. (47C.3.b)

**logos:** The Greek term for "word" by which the apostle John refers to Jesus in John 1:1. As applied to Jesus, the term implies both the Old Testament concept of the powerful, creative word of God and the Greek idea of the organizing and unifying principle of the universe. (26B.1.c)

**Lord:** In the New Testament, a translation of the Greek word *kyrios* that is usually, but not always, used to refer to Christ. In the Greek translation of the Old Testament, this word is used to translate the Hebrew *yhwh*, the personal name of the omnipotent God. (26B.1.b)

**Lord's Supper:** One of the two ordinances that Jesus commanded his church to observe. This is an ordinance to be observed repeatedly throughout our Christian lives as a sign of continuing in fellowship with Christ. (50)

**love:** When used of God, the doctrine that God eternally gives of himself to others. (12C.7)

**macroevolution:** The "general theory of evolution," or the view that all organisms emerged from nonliving substance. (15E.2.c.1)

**major doctrine:** A doctrine that has a significant impact on our thinking about other doctrines, or that has a significant impact on how we live the Christian life. (1C.2)

**manifestation of God's active presence:** A description of the work of the Holy Spirit, the member of the Trinity whom Scripture most often represents as being present to do God's work in the world. (30)

**maranatha:** An Aramaic term used in 1 Corinthians 16:22, meaning "Our Lord, come," expressing eager longing for Christ's return. (54B)

**marks of the church:** The distinguishing characteristics of a true church. In Protestant tradition, these have usually been recognized as the right preaching of the Word of God and the right administration of the sacraments (baptism and the Lord's Supper). (44B.1)

**materialism:** The view that the material universe is all that exists. (15B)

**mature creationism:** A "young earth" theory of creation which holds that the original creation had an "appearance of age" from the very beginning. Also called the "ideal time" theory, in that the appearance of age does not in fact indicate any actual time. (15E.4.b.1)

**means of grace:** Any activities within the fellowship of the church that God uses to give more grace to Christians. (48A)

**mediator:** The role that Jesus plays in coming between God and us, enabling us to come into the presence of God. (18B.2)

**mental attributes:** Aspects of God's character that describe the nature of his knowing and reasoning. (12B)

**mercy:** God's goodness toward those in misery and distress. (12C.8)

**methodological naturalism:** the belief that to qualify as scientific, a theory must explain all phenomena by reference to purely physical or material causes or processes. (15E.1.m)

**Michael:** An archangel who appears as a leader in the angelic army. (19A.4)

**micro-evolution:** The view that small developments occur within one species without creating new species. (15E.2.c.1)

**middle knowledge:** An Arminian view of God's foreknowledge which teaches that, because God knows what every creature would do in any given set of circumstances, he therefore foreknows everything that happens in the world by bringing about the situations in which all creatures act. (16H.5.a)

**midtribulation rapture:** A variation of the pretribulational premillennial view in which Christ returns in the middle of the seven year tribulation to rescue believers, and then again after the tribulation to reign on earth for 1,000 years. (55A.1.3.b)

**mighty work:** A biblical term for miracles (translating the Hebrew *gebûrāh* and the Greek *dynamis*), indicating an act displaying great or divine power. (17A)

**millennium:** A term that refers to the period of 1,000 years mentioned in Revelation 20:4–5 as the time of the reign of Christ and believers over the earth (from Latin *millennium*, "thousand years"). (55)

**minor doctrine:** A doctrine that has very little impact on how we think about other doctrines, and that has very little impact on how we live the Christian life. (1C.2.c)

**miracle:** A less common kind of God's activity in which he arouses people's awe and wonder and bears witness to himself. (17A)

**miraculous gifts:** Gifts given by the Holy Spirit that are less common, and that arouse people's awe and wonder and bear witness to God. (52A.6)

**modalism:** The heretical teaching that holds that God is not really three distinct persons, but only one person who appears to people in different "modes" at different times. (14C.1)

**modalistic monarchianism:** Another term for modalism. (14C.1)

**Molinism:** The viewpoint that the future choices of people are not *directly* determined by God, but God knows them anyway, because he knows *how each free creature would* *respond* in any set of circumstances that might occur, and then he creates a world in which those circumstances will occur. (16.G.5.a.3)

**monism:** The view that man is only one element, and that his body is the person. (23A)

**monogenēs:** A Greek word that means "only begotten." It is used to describe the relationship of the Son to the Father in John 1:14; 3:16, 18, and 1 John 4:9. However, in an alternative view, many scholars and Bible translations understand the term to mean "unique, only." (14D.2)

**monophysitism:** The fifth-century heresy which held that Christ had only one nature, that being a mixture of divine and human natures (from the Greek *monos*, "one," and *physis*, "nature"). (26C.1.c)

**monothelite view:** The position that Jesus had only one will, a view that was rejected as heretical in the seventh century. (26C.3.a)

**moral argument:** An argument for the existence of God which reasons that there must be a God who is the source of man's sense of right and wrong. (9C)

**moral attributes:** Aspects of God's character that describe his moral or ethical nature. (12C)

**moral influence theory:** The theory that Christ's death was not a payment for sins, but simply a demonstration of how much God loved human beings by identifying with their sufferings, even to the point of death. This becomes, then, an example designed to draw from us a grateful response. (27C.2.e.2)

**mortal sin:** In Roman Catholic teaching, a sin that causes spiritual death. (24D.4.b)

**mutual submission:** A phrase that proponents of egalitarianism use to describe the type of relationship they believe should exist between husband and wife, in which each is subject to the other in the same way. In this understanding of "mutual submission," it undermines the unique authority that the Bible gives to the husband in the marriage relationship. (22C.3)

**mystical union:** A term referring to the union between the believer and Christ, the workings of which are not fully understood and are known only through God's revelation in Scripture. (43)

**names of God:** Various descriptions of God's character that are found in Scripture. (11A.2)

**natural law:** Relative to the discussion on miracles, any of the "laws of nature" or inherent qualities of the natural order that are viewed by some people as operating independently of God. (17A)

**natural revelation:** The way in which God has revealed himself to humanity through the natural world that he created, apart from his revelation in Scripture. (7A.1)

**natural selection:** The idea, assumed in evolutionary theory, that living organisms that are most fitted to their environment survive and multiply while others perish (also called "survival of the fittest"). (15E.2.c.1)

**necessary will:** Those things that God must will according to his own nature. (13D.14.b)

**necessity of Scripture:** The idea that the Bible is necessary for knowing the gospel, for maintaining spiritual life, and for knowing God's will, but is not necessary for knowing that God exists or for knowing something about God's character and moral laws. (7)

**neo-catastrophism:** Another term for the flood geology view of the geological status of the earth. (15E.4.b.2)

**neo-orthodoxy:** A twentieth-century theological movement represented by the teachings of Karl Barth. Instead of the orthodox position that all the words of Scripture were spoken by God, Barth taught that the words of Scripture become God's words to us as we encounter them. (4A.2)

**Nestorianism:** A fifth-century heresy that taught that there were two separate persons in Christ, a human person and a divine person. (26C.1.b)

**new covenant:** The administration of the covenant of grace established after the death and resurrection of Christ, a covenant in which Christ's atoning death covers all of the believer's sins and the Holy Spirit empowers the believer to fulfill the righteous demands of the law. (25C.2)

**new covenant experience of the Holy Spirit:** The more powerful work of the Holy Spirit in people's lives that began at Pentecost for the disciples and now happens at conversion for believers. (39B)

**new heavens and new earth:** A description of the entirely renewed creation in which believers will dwell after the final judgment. (57A)

**new perspective on Paul:** The belief that justification does not mean that God declares us to be forgiven of sins and legally righteous before him, but instead means that God declares us to be members of his covenant community (God's people). It denies the idea that Christ's righteousness is imputed to the believer's account and says that the gospel is not primarily about being saved, but is rather about declaring the Lordship of Christ (36G.1.a–d)

**New Testament theology:** The study of the teaching of the individual authors and sections of the New Testament, and of the place of each teaching in the historical development of the New Testament. (1A.1)

**nonmiraculous gifts:** Gifts given by the Holy Spirit that are more common and appear to be more ordinary, such as serving, teaching, encouraging, and doing acts of mercy. (52A.6)

**"not discerning the body":** A phrase used in 1 Corinthians 11:29 of the Corinthians' abuse of the Lord's Supper. In their selfish, inconsiderate conduct toward each other during the Lord's Supper, they were not understanding the unity and interdependence of people in the church, which is the body of Christ. (50D)

**office:** A publicly recognized position of one having the right and responsibility to perform certain functions for the benefit of the whole church. (47A)

**officer:** Someone who has been recognized as having the right and responsibility to perform certain functions for the benefit of the whole church. (47A)

**old covenant:** A term referring specifically to the Mosaic covenant established at Mount

Sinai, which was an administration of detailed written laws given for a time to restrain the sins of the people and to be a custodian to point people to Christ. (25C.2)

**old covenant experience of the Holy Spirit:** The less powerful and less extensive work of the Holy Spirit that characterized the old covenant before the day of Pentecost. (39B)

**"old earth" theory:** A theory of creation that views the earth as very old, perhaps as old as 4.5 billion years. (15E.3)

**Old Testament theology:** The study of the teaching of the individual authors and sections of the Old Testament, and of the place of each teaching in the historical development of the Old Testament. (1A.1)

**omnipotence:** The doctrine that God is able to do all his holy will (from Latin *omni*, "all," and *potens*, "powerful"). (13D.16)

**omnipresence:** The doctrine that God does not have size or spatial dimensions and is present at every point of space with his whole being, yet God acts differently in different places. (11B.4)

**omniscience:** The doctrine that God fully knows himself and all things actual and possible in one simple and eternal act. (12B.3)

**one body in Christ:** The understanding that all Christians are individually related to each other, since in Christ we are one spiritual body, of whom Christ is the head. (43A.3.d)

**one simple and eternal act:** A term referring to an aspect of God's knowledge whereby he is always fully aware of everything and his knowledge never changes or grows. (12B.3)

**only begotten:** A translation of the Greek word *monogenēs*, which refers to Christ in five NT verses (John 3:16 et al.). It does not mean that the Son was created, but that the Son is in some sense eternally "from" the Father, yet he is also fully divine and equal to the Father in every attribute. (14.D.2-3)

**ontological argument:** An argument for the existence of God that begins with the idea of God as the greatest of beings that can be imagined. As such, the characteristic of existence must belong to such a being, since it is greater to exist than not to exist. (9C)

**ontological equality:** A phrase that describes the members of the Trinity as eternally equal in being or existence. (14D.2)

**open theism:** The belief that God is incapable of knowing any future free choices by human beings because the future has not yet occurred, and therefore it is not knowable.

**order:** Another term for God's peace. (12B.3)

**order of salvation:** A theological term referring to a list of the events in which God applies salvation to us in the specific order in which they are believed to occur in our lives (sometimes referred to by the Latin phrase *ordo salutis*). (32)

**ordinance:** A term commonly used by Baptists to refer to baptism and the Lord's Supper; other Protestants such as those in Lutheran, Reformed, and Anglican churches have preferred the word "sacrament" for these ceremonies. (See also "sacrament.") (49)

**ordinary means:** The ordinary resources that people can use to help them understand Scripture. These include a Bible translation in one's own language, Bible teachers, commentaries, the history of interpretation, fellowship with others, concordances, dictionaries, and historical background information. (6B.3)

**original guilt:** Another term for "inherited guilt." (24C.1)

**original pollution:** Another term for our inherited sinful nature (see "inherited corruption"). (24C.2)

**original sin:** The traditional term for the doctrine referred to in this text as "inherited sin." (24C)

**overseer:** A translation of the Greek *episkopos*, a term used interchangeably with "overseer," "pastor," and "elder" to refer to the main governing office of a local church in the New Testament. (47A.2.b)

**paedobaptism:** The practice of baptizing infants (the prefix *paido-* is derived from the Greek *pais*, "child"). (49B.4)

**pantheism:** The idea that the whole universe is God or part of God. (15B)

**paradox:** A seemingly contradictory statement that may nonetheless be true; an apparent but not real contradiction. (1D.3)

**parousia:** The second coming of Christ (from the Greek *parousia*, "coming"). (54A)

**particular redemption:** Another, more preferable term for the Reformed doctrine of "limited atonement." (27D.1)

**passive obedience:** A term referring to Christ's sufferings for us in which he took the penalty due for our sins and as a result died for our sins. (27C.2)

**pastor:** A term used interchangeably with "elder," "overseer," and "bishop" to refer to the main governing office of a local church in the New Testament. Translating the Greek *poimēn*, the term identifies the shepherding task with the office of elder. (47A.2.b)

**patience:** God's goodness in withholding of punishment toward those who sin over a period of time. (12C.8)

**peace:** The doctrine that God is separate from all confusion and disorder in his being and in his actions, yet he is continually active in innumerable well-ordered, fully controlled, simultaneous actions. (12C.10)

**Pelagius:** A fifth-century monk who taught (Pelagianism) that man has the ability to obey God's commands and can take the first and most important steps toward salvation on his own. (24D.2)

**penal substitution:** The view that Christ in his death bore the just penalty of God for our sins as a substitute for us. (27C.2.c.4)

**Pentecost:** A Jewish feast during which, following the ascension of Jesus, the Holy Spirit was poured out in new covenant fullness and power on the disciples. This day marked the point of transition between the old covenant work and ministry of the Holy Spirit and the new covenant work and ministry of the Holy Spirit. (39B)

**Pentecostal:** Any denomination or group that traces its historical origin to the Pentecostal revival that began in the United States in 1901 and that holds to the doctrinal positions (a) that baptism in the Holy Spirit is ordinarily an event subsequent to conversion,

(b) that baptism in the Holy Spirit is made evident by the sign of speaking in tongues, and (c) that all the spiritual gifts mentioned in the New Testament are to be sought and used today. (39)

**perfection:** The doctrine that God completely possesses all excellent qualities and lacks no part of any qualities that would be desirable for him. (13E.17)

**perfectionism:** The view that sinless perfection, or freedom from conscious sin, is possible in this life for the Christian. (38B.4)

**perseverance of the saints:** The doctrine that all those who are truly "born again" will be kept by God's power and will persevere as Christians until the end of their lives, and that only those who persevere until the end have been truly "born again." (40)

**personal address:** A form of God's word in which he speaks directly to people on earth. (2B.2)

**personal eschatology:** The study of future events that will happen to individuals, such as death, the intermediate state, and glorification. (54)

**perspicuity:** An older term for the clarity of Scripture. (6B)

**philosophical theology:** The study of theological topics that primarily employs the tools and methods of philosophical reasoning and what can be known about God from observing the universe. (1A.1)

**pictorial-day theory:** Another term for the literary framework view of Genesis 1. (15E.4.a.2)

**plenary inspiration:** The idea that all the words of Scripture are God's words, *plenary* meaning "full." (4A.1)

**postmillennialism:** The view that Christ will return to the earth after the millennium. In this view, the millennium is an age of peace and righteousness on the earth, brought about by the progress of the gospel and the growth of the church. (55A.2)

**posttribulational premillennialism:** Another term for historic premillennialism (or "classic premillennialism"). This is distinguished from other premillennial views by the idea that Christ will return after the great tribulation. (55A.3.a)

**posttribulational rapture:** The "taking up" of believers after the great tribulation to be with Christ just a few moments prior to his coming to earth with them to reign during the millennial kingdom (or, on the amillennial view, during the eternal state). (55E)

**power:** Another term for God's omnipotence. (13D.16)

**power of the church:** The church's God-given authority to carry on spiritual warfare, proclaim the gospel, and exercise church discipline. (46)

**prayer:** Personal communication with God. (18)

**predestination:** Another term for "election"; in Reformed theology generally, this is a broader term that includes not only election (for believers), but also reprobation (for nonbelievers). (32)

**premillennialism:** A term that includes a variety of views having in common the belief that Christ will return to the earth before the millennium. (55A.3)

**preterism:** The belief that Christ returned spiritually in AD 70 when the Jewish temple was destroyed, and that therefore we should not expect any additional future return of Christ. (54G.1)

**presbyterian government:** A form of church government in which elders govern their respective local churches, and some elders, through a presbytery and general assembly, govern churches in a region and the denomination as a whole. (47C.2)

**presbytery:** A group of elders drawn from several churches in a region and having governing authority over those churches. (See also "classis.") (47C.2)

**preservation:** An aspect of God's providence whereby he keeps all created things existing and maintaining the properties with which he created them. (16A)

**presupposition:** An assumption that forms the beginning point of any study. (1B)

**pretribulational premillennialism:** The view that Christ will return secretly before the great tribulation to call believers to himself, and then again after the tribulation to reign on earth for 1,000 years. (55A.3.b)

**pretribulational rapture:** The "taking up" of believers into heaven secretly during Christ's first return prior to the great tribulation. (55E)

**priest:** A person appointed by God in the Old Testament to offer sacrifices, prayers, and praises to God on behalf of the people. This office was fulfilled by Christ, who has become the great high priest for all believers. The term can also refer to a category of church officers in both Roman Catholic and Anglican churches, though they each attach different meanings to the word "priest." (29; 47C)

**primary cause:** The divine, invisible, directing cause of everything that happens. (16B.4)

**primogeniture:** The Old Testament practice in which the firstborn in any generation in a human family has leadership in the family for that generation. (22C.2.a)

**principalities and powers:** Other names for demonic powers in some verses of the Bible.

**progressive covenantalism:** The belief that there are five covenants described in Scripture—with creation (and renewed with Noah), Abraham, Israel, and David, which are all ultimately fulfilled in Christ. Each covenant is both conditional and unconditional. (25D)

**progressive creationism:** An "old earth" theory which holds that God created new types of plant and animal creatures at several different points of time in the earth's history, and between those points, plant and animal life developed more diversity on its own. (15)

**prophecy** (as a spiritual gift in the New Testament): The New Testament gift of the Holy Spirit that involves telling something that God has spontaneously brought to mind. (53A)

**prophet:** One of the offices fulfilled by Christ, the office by which he most fully reveals God to us and speaks to us the words of God. (29A)

**propitiation:** A sacrifice that bears God's wrath to the end and in so doing changes God's wrath toward us into favor. (27C.2.b.4)

**providence:** The doctrine that God is continually involved with all created things in such a way that he (1) keeps them existing and maintaining the properties with which he created them; (2) cooperates with created things in every action, directing their distinctive properties to cause them to act as they do; and (3) directs them to fulfill his purposes. (16)

**purgatory:** In Roman Catholic doctrine, the place where the souls of believers go to be further purified from sin until they are ready to be admitted into heaven. (41C.1.a)

**purity of the church:** The church's degree of freedom from wrong doctrine and conduct, and its degree of conformity to God's revealed will for the church. (45B)

**raised in glory:** A phrase describing our future resurrection bodies, which will exhibit a beauty and radiance appropriate to the position of exaltation and rule over creation that God will give us after the manner of Christ. (28A.4.c; also 42C)

**raised in power:** A phrase describing our future resurrection bodies, which will exhibit the fullness of strength and power that God intended human beings to have in their bodies when he created them. (28A.2; also 42C)

**raised with Christ:** A phrase that describes the aspect of union with Christ by which a person receives new spiritual life and a change in his character and personality after coming to faith. (43A.3.a)

**random mutation:** The view that various life forms resulted from an evolutionary process in which random differences occurred when cells reproduced themselves. (15E.2.b)

**ransom to Satan theory:** The view that in the atonement Christ paid a ransom to Satan to redeem us out of his kingdom. (27C.2.e.1)

**rapture:** The "taking up" or snatching up (from Latin *rapio*, "seize, snatch, carry away") of believers to be with Christ when he returns to the earth. (55A.3.b; also 55E)

**reasonable self-determination:** The understanding of human freedom proposed by Augustine that says that people make decisions that seem most reasonable to them at the time, and that these decisions really do determine what will happen. (This definition does not use the word "free" with respect to human choices.) (12B.3.f)

**reconciliation:** The removal of enmity and the restoration of fellowship between two parties. (27C.2.d.3)

**rector:** The officer in charge of a local parish in an episcopalian system of church government. (47C.1)

**redemption:** Christ's saving work viewed as an act of "buying back" sinners out of their bondage to sin and to Satan through the payment of a ransom (though the analogy should not be pressed to specify anyone to whom a ransom was paid). (27C.2.d.4)

**Reformed:** Another term for the theological tradition known as Calvinism. (16)

**regeneration:** A secret act of God in which he imparts new spiritual life to us; sometimes called "being born again." (34)

**repentance:** A heartfelt sorrow for sin, a renouncing of it, and a sincere commitment to forsake it and walk in obedience to Christ. (35B)

**reprobation:** The sovereign decision of God before creation to pass over some persons, in sorrow deciding not to save them, and to punish them for their sins and thereby to manifest his justice. (32E)

**resurrection:** A rising from the dead into a new kind of life not subject to sickness, aging, deterioration, or death. (28A)

**revealed will:** God's declared will concerning what we should do or what God commands us to do. (13D.14.b.2)

**righteousness:** The doctrine that God always acts in accordance with what is right and that he is himself the final standard of what is right. (12C.11)

**Sabellianism:** Another name for modalism, a term derived from the third-century teacher Sabellius, who propagated this doctrine. (14C.1)

**sacrament:** In Protestant teaching, a ceremony or rite that the church observes as a sign of God's grace and as one means by which those who are already justified receive God's continuing grace in their lives. The two Protestant sacraments are baptism and the Lord's Supper. In Roman Catholic teaching, there are seven sacraments, and they are understood as a necessary means of conveying saving grace. (See also "ordinance.") (48A; 49)

**sacrifice:** Christ's death on the cross viewed from the standpoint that he paid the penalty that we deserved. (27C.2.d.1)

**sanctification:** A progressive work of God and man that makes us more and more free from sin and more like Christ in our actual lives. (38)

**Satan:** The personal name of the head of the demons. (20B)

**saving faith:** Trust in Jesus Christ as a living person for forgiveness of sins and for eternal life with God. (35A.3)

**Scripture:** The writings (Greek *graphē*, rendered in Latin by *scriptura*) of the Old and New Testaments, which have historically been recognized as God's words in written form. Another term for the Bible. (4A)

**secondary cause:** The properties and actions of created things that bring about events in the world. (16B.4)

**second coming of Christ:** The sudden, personal, visible, bodily return of Christ from heaven to earth. (54A)

**secret will:** God's hidden decrees by which he governs the universe and determines everything that will happen. (13D.14.b.2)

**seeker-sensitive:** A church that makes non-Christian visitors the primary audience for the Sunday morning worship service. (44C.5)

**self-attesting:** The self-authenticating nature of the Bible by which it convinces us that its words are God's words. (4A.4)

**self-existence:** Another term for God's independence. (11B.1)

**separation:** With reference to the church, the act of formal division of one group from another on the basis of doctrinal differences, matters of conscience, or practical considerations. Such separation can take more severe forms, such as the refusal to cooperate or the avoidance of personal fellowship. (45E-F)

**seraphim:** A class of created spiritual beings that are said to continually worship God. (19A.3.b)

**session:** The "sitting down" of Christ at God's right hand after his ascension, indicating that his work of redemption was complete and that he received authority over the universe. The term can also refer to the group of elders with governing authority over a local church in a presbyterian form of church government (28B.3; 47C.2)

**sign:** A biblical term for miracles (translating the Hebrew *'ôth* and the Greek *sēmeion*), specifically meaning something that points to or indicates something else, especially God's activity and power. (17A)

**"signs of an apostle":** A phrase used by the apostle Paul in 2 Corinthians 12:12 that refers to those various things that distinguished him as a true apostle from others who were false apostles. Some who deny the continuation of miracles today use this phrase to contend that miracles were uniquely the signs that distinguished apostles from ordinary Christians. (17D.2)

**simplicity:** Another term for the unity of God. (11B.5)

**sin:** Any failure to conform to the moral law of God in act, attitude, or nature. (24A)

**sinless perfection:** The state of being totally free from sin; some hold that such a state is possible in this life. (See also "perfectionism.") (38B.4)

**Son of God:** A title often used of Jesus to designate him as the heavenly, eternal Son who is equal in nature to God himself. (26B.1.c)

**Son of Man:** The term by which Jesus referred to himself most often, which had an Old Testament background, especially in the heavenly figure who was given eternal rule over the world in the vision in Daniel 7:13. (26B.1.c)

**sons of God:** Another name for angels (Job 1:6; 2:1). (19A.2)

**soul:** The immaterial part of man; used interchangeably with "spirit." (23B.1)

**soul sleep:** The doctrine that believers go into a state of unconscious existence when they die, and that they return to consciousness when Christ returns and raises them to eternal life. (41C.1.b)

**sovereignty:** God's exercise of power over his creation. (13D.16)

**speaking in tongues:** Prayer or praise spoken in syllables not understood by the speaker. (53E.2)

**special grace:** The grace of God that brings people to salvation; also known as "saving grace." (31A)

**special revelation:** God's words addressed to specific people, including the words of the Bible. This is to be distinguished from general revelation, which is given to all people generally. (7E)

**spirit:** The immaterial part of man, a term used interchangeably with "soul." (23B.1)

**spiritual body:** The type of body we will receive at our future resurrection, which will not be "immaterial" but rather suited to and responsive to the guidance of the Holy Spirit. (28A.2; 42C)

**spirituality:** The doctrine that God exists as a being that is not made of any matter, has no parts or dimensions, is unable to be perceived by our bodily senses, and is more excellent than any other kind of existence. (12A.1)

**spiritual presence:** A phrase descriptive of the Reformed view of the Lord's Supper that regards Christ as spiritually present in a special way as we partake of the bread and wine. (50C.3)

**states of Jesus Christ:** The different relationships Jesus had to God's law, to the possession of authority, and to receiving honor for himself, during the various stages in his work. The two states of Jesus Christ are humiliation and exaltation. (28C)

**subordinationism:** The heretical teaching that the Son was inferior or "subordinate" in being to God the Father. (14C.2.b)

**sufficiency of Scripture:** The idea that Scripture contained all the words of God he intended his people to have at each stage of redemptive history, and that it now contains all the words of God we need for salvation, for trusting him perfectly, and for obeying him perfectly. (8A)

**summary attributes:** God's attributes of perfection, blessedness, beauty, and glory, which are called "summary" attributes in this book because they have to do with looking at and evaluating all the other attributes of God considered together as a whole.

**symbolic presence:** The common Protestant view that the bread and wine of the Lord's Supper symbolize the body and blood of Christ, rather than change into or somehow contain the body and blood of Christ. (50C.3)

**synod:** A national governing assembly of a denomination (sometimes called a general assembly). (47C.2)

**systematic theology:** Any study that answers the question, "What does the whole Bible teach us today?" about any given topic. (1A)

**teaching:** In the New Testament, the ability to explain Scripture and apply it to people's lives. (53B)

**teleological argument:** An argument for the existence of God which reasons that, since the universe exhibits evidence of order and design, there must be an intelligent and purposeful God who created it to function in this way. (9C)

**temporary blessings:** Influences of the Holy Spirit and the church that make unbelievers look or sound like genuine believers when in fact they are not. (40C)

**textual variants:** Occurrences of different words in different ancient copies of the same verse of Scripture. (5B.3)

**theistic evolution:** The theory that God used the process of evolution to bring about all of the life forms on earth. (15E.2.b)

**theophany:** An "appearance of God" in which he takes on a visible form to show himself to people. (12A.2)

**total depravity:** The traditional term for the doctrine referred to in this text as "total inability." (24C.2.a)

**total inability:** Man's total lack of spiritual good and inability to do good before God (often referred to as "total depravity"). (24C.2.a)

**traducianism:** The view that the soul of a child is inherited from the baby's mother and father at the time of conception. (23F).

**transcendent:** The term used to describe God as being greater than the creation and independent of it. (15B)

**transitional types:** Fossils showing some characteristics of one animal and some of the next developmental type, which, if found, would provide evidence for evolutionary theory by filling in the gaps between distinct kinds of animals. (15E.2.c)

**transubstantiation:** The Roman Catholic teaching that the bread and wine of the Lord's Supper (often referred to as "the eucharist") actually become the body and blood of Christ. (50C.1)

**trichotomy:** The view that man is made up of three parts: body, soul, and spirit. (23C)

**Trinity:** The doctrine that God eternally exists as three persons—Father, Son, and Holy Spirit—and each person is fully God, and there is one God. (14)

**tritheism:** The belief that there are three gods. (14C.3)

**trust:** An aspect of biblical faith or belief in which we not only know and agree with facts about Jesus, but also place personal trust in him as a living person. (35A.3)

**truthfulness:** The doctrine that God is the true God and that all his knowledge and words are both true and the final standard of truth. (12B.5)

**twenty-four-hour day theory:** The view that the six "days" of creation in Genesis 1 are to be understood as literal twenty-four-hour days. (15E.3.e)

**two-class Christianity:** A view of the church that divides it into two categories of believers, such as ordinary believers versus "sanctified" believers, or ordinary believers versus Spirit-baptized believers. (39D.1)

**ubiquity of Christ's human nature:** The teaching, put forth by Martin Luther in support of his view of the Lord's Supper, that Christ's human nature was present everywhere ("ubiquitous") after his ascension. (50C.2)

**unchangeableness:** The doctrine that God is unchanging in his being, perfections, purposes, and promises, yet he does act and feel emotions, and he acts and feels differently in response to different situations. (11B.2)

**union with Christ:** A phrase that summarizes several different relationships between believers and Christ, through which Christians receive every benefit of salvation. These relationships include the fact that we are in Christ, Christ is in us, we are like Christ, and we are with Christ. (43)

**unity:** The doctrine that God is not divided into parts, yet we see different attributes of God emphasized at different times. (11B.5)

**unity of the church:** The church's degree of freedom from divisions among true Christians. (45B)

**universalism:** The doctrine that all people will ultimately be saved. (56G)

**unlimited atonement:** The view that Christ's death actually paid for the sins of all people who ever lived. (27D)

**unpardonable sin:** The unusually malicious, willful rejection and slander against the Holy Spirit's work attesting to Christ, and attributing that work to Satan. (24D.6)

**valid proofs:** Arguments for the existence of God that are based on facts and that correctly reason to a true conclusion. No such proofs, however, are able to compel agreement from everyone who considers them. (9C)

**venial sin:** In Roman Catholic teaching, a sin that can be forgiven, although perhaps after punishments in this life or in purgatory. (24D.4.b)

**veracity:** Another term for God's truthfulness. (12B.5)

**vicar:** In an episcopalian system of church government, a church officer in charge of a local parish and acting in place of a rector. (47C.1)

**vicarious atonement:** The work Christ did to earn our salvation by standing in our place in his life and death. (27C.2.c.4)

**virgin birth:** The biblical teaching that Jesus was conceived in the womb of his mother Mary by a miraculous work of the Holy Spirit and without a human father. (26A.1)

**visible church:** The church as Christians on earth see it. Because only God sees our hearts, the visible church will always include some unbelievers. (44A.2)

**voluntary choices:** Choices that are made in accord with our desires, with no awareness of restraints on our will or compulsion against our will. (16H.3)

**waiting on the Lord:** A posture of the heart during prayer in which we wait quietly before God for some sense of guidance in our prayer, and also for an assurance of God's presence and of his answer to our prayer. (18C.9)

**watchers:** Another name for angels (Dan. 4:13, 17, 23). (19A.2)

**Western church:** A term referring to the Roman Catholic Church, from which the Eastern (Orthodox) church separated in AD 1054. Later, the Western church split into Protestant and Roman Catholic branches. (45E)

**will:** The attribute of God whereby he approves and determines to bring about every action necessary for the existence and activity of himself and all creation. (13D.14)

**willing choices:** Choices that are made in accord with our desires, with no awareness of restraints on our will. (16B.9).

**wisdom:** The doctrine that God always chooses the best goals and the best means to those goals. (12B.4)

**wonder:** A biblical word for miracles (translating the Hebrew *môpēth* and the Greek *teras*), specifically referring to an event that causes people to be amazed or astonished. (17A)

**Word of God:** A phrase that refers to several different things in the Bible, including the Son of God, the decrees of God, God's words of personal address, God's words spoken through human lips, and God's words in written form, the Bible. It is this last form of the Word of God that is the focus of systematic theology, since it is the form that is available for study, for public inspection, for repeated examination, and as a basis for mutual discussion. (2)

**word of knowledge:** The ability to speak with knowledge about a situation. (53F)

**word of wisdom:** The ability to speak a wise word in various situations. (53F)

**worship:** The activity of glorifying God in his presence with our voices and hearts. (51A)

**wrath:** As an attribute of God, the doctrine that God intensely hates all sin. (12C.13)

**"young earth" theory:** A theory of creation that views the earth as relatively young, perhaps as young as 10,000 to 20,000 years old. (15E.3)

# Hymn and Contemporary Worship Song Index

# Scripture Index

## 1 CORINTHIANS

# Subject Index

# Author Index